THE OXFORD ANTHOLOGY
OF ENGLISH LITERATURE

Volume I

General Editors: Frank Kermode and John Hollander

VOLUME II

1800 to the Present

Romantic Poetry and Prose
HAROLD BLOOM AND LIONEL TRILLING
Yale University   Columbia University

Victorian Prose and Poetry
LIONEL TRILLING AND HAROLD BLOOM

Modern British Literature
FRANK KERMODE AND JOHN HOLLANDER

The Oxford Anthology of English Literature

VOLUME I

The Middle Ages through the Eighteenth Century

Medieval English Literature
J. B. TRAPP
Warburg Institute

The Literature of Renaissance England
JOHN HOLLANDER AND FRANK KERMODE
Hunter College   University College London

The Restoration and the Eighteenth Century
MARTIN PRICE
Yale University

NEW YORK
OXFORD UNIVERSITY PRESS
LONDON   TORONTO   1973

Selections from the following works were made possible by the kind permission of their respective publishers and representatives:

Medieval

An Anthology of Old English Poetry, translated by Charles W. Kennedy, copyright © 1960 by Oxford University Press, Inc.; reprinted by permission.
Beowulf: The Oldest English Epic, translated by Charles W. Kennedy, copyright 1940 by Oxford University Press, Inc.; renewed 1968 by Charles W. Kennedy; reprinted by permission.
Sir Gawain and the Green Knight, translated by Brian Stone, copyright © 1959, 1964, 1973 by Brian Stone; reprinted by permission of Penguin Books Ltd.
The Oxford Book of Ballads, edited by James Kinsley, copyright © 1969 by Oxford University Press; reprinted by permission of The Clarendon Press, Oxford.
The Romance of the Rose, translated by F. S. Ellis, reprinted by permission of J. M. Dent & Sons Ltd.

Eighteenth Century

"Jubilate Agno," by Christopher Smart, is reprinted by permission of Rupert Hart-Davis Ltd.

Printed in the United States of America

General Editors' Preface

The purpose of the Oxford Anthology is to provide students with a selective canon of the entire range of English Literature from the beginnings to recent times, with introductory matter and authoritative annotation. Its method is historical, in the broadest sense, and its arrangement, commentary, and notes, both analytic and contextual, have benefited not only from the teaching experience of the several editors, but from a study of the virtues and shortcomings of comparable works. A primary aim has been to avoid the insulation of any one section from the influence of others, and more positively, to allow both student and instructor to come to terms with the manner in which English literature has generated its own history. This aim has been accomplished in several ways.

First, a reorganization of chronological phases has allowed the Tudor and Stuart periods to be unified under the broad heading of the English Renaissance, with two editors collaborating over the whole extended period. Similarly, the nineteenth century has two editors, one for the poetry of the whole period, and one for the prose. This arrangement seemed appropriate in every way, especially since neither of these scholars could be called a narrow specialist in "Romantic" or "Victorian," as these terms are used in semester- or course-labels.

Every contributing editor has worked and taught in at least one period or field outside the one for which he is, in this anthology, principally responsible, and none has ever allowed specialization to reduce his broader commitment to humane studies more largely considered. Thus we were able to plan a work which called for an unusual degree of cross reference and collaboration. During a crucial phase in the preparation of the text, the editors held daily discussions of their work for a period of months. By selection, allusion, comparison, by direction and indirection, we contrived to preserve continuity between epochs, and to illuminate its character. At the same time, the close co-operation of the various editors has precluded the possibility of common surrender to any single dominating literary theory; and the teacher need have no fear that he must prepare to do battle with some critical Hydra showing a head on every page.

The method of selecting text was consistent with these principles. In the eighteenth- and nineteenth-century sections it was our general policy to exclude the novel, for obvious reasons of length; but in the twentieth, where short fiction becomes more prominent and more central, we have included entire works of fiction, or clearly defined parts of them—for example, *Heart of Darkness*, "The Dead," the "Nausicaa" episode of *Ulysses*, and *St. Mawr*. On the other hand we were persuaded, after much reflection, that a different principle must apply in the cases of Spenser and Milton, where we waived the requirement of completeness. To have given the whole of one book—say, the First of *The Faerie Queene*—would have been a solution as easy as it is, no doubt, defensible; but it is asking a great deal of students to see that portion of the poem as an epitome of the rest, which is often so delightfully different; and we decided that we must provide selections from the whole poem, with linking commentary. We did the same for *Paradise Lost* though without abandoning the practice of providing complete texts when this was both possible and desirable; for example, *Comus* is reprinted entire, and so is a lesser-known but still very important masque, Jonson's *Pleasure Reconciled to Virtue*, which is interesting not only in relation to *Comus* but as an illustration of the part poetry can play in political spectacle and—more generally—in the focusing of the moral vision. Minor texts have been chosen for their exemplary force and their beauty, as well as to embody thematic concerns. If the teacher wishes, he or she may work, both within and across periods, with recurrent patterns as large as the conception of the Earthly Paradise, or with sub-genres as small but as fascinating as the Mad Song. It will also be evident from certain patterns of selection—*The Tempest* as the Shakesperean play, the very large amount of Blake, the emphasis given to D. H. Lawrence's poems as well as his fiction—that a genuinely modern taste, rather than an eager modishness, has helped to shape our presentation of the historical canon. It is also hoped that the unusually generous sampling of material in certain sections—notably the Renaissance, eighteenth century, and the Romantics—will allow the teacher to use secondary or minor works, if he so chooses, to highlight these newer concerns or to fill in contextual background.

As for the annotations, the editors have never been afraid to be lively or even speculative. They have consistently tried to avoid usurping the teacher's role, as providing standard or definitive readings might do. On the other hand, the commentary goes beyond merely providing a lowest common denominator of information by suggesting interpretive directions and levels along which the teacher is free to move or not; and of course he always has the freedom to disagree. The editors have been neither prudish nor portentous in their tone, nor have they sought—in the interests of some superficial consistency, but with leaden effect—to efface their personal styles.

Texts have all been based on the best modern editions, which happen quite often to be published by the Oxford University Press. Spelling and punctuation have been modernized throughout, save in three instances: portions of the medieval period, and the texts of Spenser and Blake, two poets whose spelling and punctuation are so far from idiosyncrasies to be silently normalized that they constitute attempts to refashion poetic language. In the medieval section, modern verse translations of *Beowulf* (by C. W. Kennedy) and of *Gawain* (by Brian Stone) have been adopted. Glossaries of literary and historical terms in all periods have been provided, sometimes keyed to the annotations, sometimes supplementing the larger headnotes. These, it will be noticed, seek to illuminate the immediate contexts of the literature of a period rather than to provide a dense précis of its social, political, and economic history. Similarly, the reading lists at the end of each volume are not exhaustive bibliographies; in the happy instance where a teacher finds an extensive bibliography advisable, he or she will want to supply one.

A word about the pictures. They are not to be thought of simply as illustrations, and certainly not as mere decorations, but rather as part of the anthologized material, like the musical examples and the special sections (such as the one on Ovidian mythology in the Renaissance and on the Urban Scene in the eighteenth century). Throughout, the reader is introduced to the relations between poem as speaking picture, and picture as mute poem. Aside from contextual and anecdotal illustration, of which there is indeed a good deal, the pictorial examples allow teachers, or students on their own, to explore some of the interrelations of texts and the visual arts in all periods, whether exemplified in Renaissance emblems or in contemporary illustrations of Victorian poems.

Finally, an inevitable inadequate word of acknowledgment. To the English Department of Dartmouth College the editors are deeply indebted for having so generously and hospitably provided a place in which to work together for a sustained period. The staff of the Dartmouth College Library was extraordinarily helpful and attentive.

All of the editors would like to extend a note of gratitude to the many academics throughout the United States who willingly made suggestions as to what should be included as well as excluded. A special note of thanks to Jim Cox of Dartmouth College and Paul Dolan of the State University of New York at Stony Brook for their challenging and always helpful comments.

And finally to the entire staff of the New York branch of the Oxford University Press who have done more than could be humanly expected in connection with the planning and execution of this book. We would especially like to thank our editor John Wright, as well as Leona Capeless and her staff, Mary Ellen Evans, Patricia Cristol, Joyce Berry, Deborah Zwecher, and Jean Shapiro. An unusual but very deserved note of thanks to the Production people, especially Gerard S. Case and Leslie Phillips and to the designer, Frederick Schneider, whose excellent work speaks for itself.

Frank Kermode
John Hollander

New York
September 1972

BRITISH ISLES

N

Atlantic
Ocean

North Sea

SCOTLAND

Clyde
Glasgow Edinburgh

Belfast

LAKE
DISTRICT

YORKSHIRE

Irish Sea   Blackpool   York Hull
                        Leeds
            Liverpool   Manchester
                        Sheffield

IRELAND

Shannon

Dublin

Trent
MERCIA

Nottingham   Norwich

WALES

Birmingham   EAST
                ANGLIA

Avon

ENGLAND

Severn   Oxford

Thames   London
Bristol
Southampton   KENT

WESSEX

English Channel

FRANCE

Miles

0   50   100   150

Contents

* An asterisk indicates that a work does not appear in its entirety.

SEVENTEENTH-CENTURY LYRIC MODES, 1099

The Development of Prose

THE RESTORATION
AND THE EIGHTEENTH CENTURY, 1549

Eighteenth Century

THE MOCK FORM, 1837

THE URBAN SCENE, 2017

Later Eighteenth Century

THE GARDEN AND THE WILD, 2165

SENSE AND SENSIBILITY, 2286

Medieval English Literature

Medieval English Literature

HISTORICAL BACKGROUND

Britain's first experience of a literate civilization came in 55 B.C., when Julius Caesar's military expedition from across the Channel initiated the Romanization of this part of the known world. Settled by Celtic tribes from Gaul in the fifth century B.C., Britain had hitherto been, for Rome, the remotest of countries, known only from traders' reports and garbled accounts. Caesar's two brief forays in successive years established Roman dominion and opened up the island. "Corn, cattle, gold, silver and iron; also hides, slaves and clever hunting dogs" were the British commodities that could help to maintain the Roman standard of living, while in return British chieftains received food, drink, furniture, and household equipment of a luxury never before available to them.

For nearly a century Britain remained a trading outpost of the Roman Empire. Not until after 43 A.D., under the Emperor Claudius, did the island come fully under Roman political and military domination. Even then, remoter areas in Scotland retained independence, and Ireland, never conquered by Rome, was free to continue its Celtic tradition.

Roman conquest meant that Roman civic organization created an urban civilization on the Roman model within the conglomeration of small local Celtic tribal units. The Romans encouraged the chiefs and leading families to adopt their way of life and to have their sons educated in the Roman manner. Walled towns were laid out in the Roman style, some at the old tribal centers, some outside the walls of Roman fortresses, some as settlements of discharged veterans. In the countryside, villas replaced older farm complexes and served as rural centers.

Roman civilization in Britain managed to weather the first raids of Saxon pirates in the late third century, but once the Roman forces were withdrawn (c. 410) it soon collapsed under the impact of much larger armed migration. During the first half of the fifth century the Angles, Saxons, and Jutes descended on the country in great numbers from northern Germany and Jutland or the Jutish Peninsula. The initial wave of this migration is dated 449 by many Anglo-Saxon writers, on the basis of a statement by the Venerable Bede (c. 673–735), the first historian of the English church and people. According to Bede, the Britain of his time comprised four nations—English, British (Welsh), Picts, and Scots—each having its own language yet united in the study of God's truth by the fifth—Latin. When the English invasion began, the Picts inhabited the northernmost parts of the island, the modern Scotland, the Scots (confusingly) occupied Ireland, and the Britons held possession of all the island of Britain to the south of the Firth of Forth. The invaders, according to race, settled in the South-East (the Jutes, in Kent and on the Isle of Wight); in Essex (north of Kent: "East Saxony"), Sussex (south of Kent: "South Saxony," and Wessex (South-West as far as Gloucestershire and Devon, "West Saxony"); and in the North-East (East Anglia), North (Northumbria) and North-West (Mercia), these last three being occupied by the Angles.

While Bede's division corresponds too closely to the political divisions of his day to be entirely reliable, it is a useful guide. It is valuable particularly as suggesting the disunity within unity of these pagan Germanic invaders, a disunity reflected in the cultural differences that continued throughout the Anglo-Saxon and Middle English periods. It is important to remember that despite centralizing influences English provincial cultures remained vigorous. Canterbury, in Kent, the town from which Roman Christianity spread from the sixth century, is today the primatial Anglican see of England and was throughout the Middle Ages a notable literary and artistic center, besides being later a place of pilgrimage. Winchester, the chief town of the Anglo-Saxon kingdom of Wessex, was highly influential in both the visual and the verbal arts during the later Anglo-Saxon period, as well as being a city where Norman kings held court. Superb manuscripts were produced in later medieval East Anglia, and manuscript writing and illumination and wood and stone carving, as well as literary studies, flourished in late seventh- and early eighth-century Northumbria. Later, in the fourteenth century, poems in the West Midland dialect and plays in the Northern sustained the standard of provincial culture in regions remote (by medieval reckoning) from the capital. A pilgrim to Canterbury took four days to cover the sixty miles from London; the West Midland area where *Sir Gawain and the Green Knight* was written was more than twice as far from the metropolis.

In the fifth century this flourishing England provincial and metropolitan culture was of course far in the future. The invaders were a hardy, warlike race, their characteristics still resembling those of the Germans as described by Tacitus (see Headnote to *Beowulf*, below). An index of their success is the degree to which the Celtic languages were supplanted: only a very few words of Celtic origin survived to find their way into later medieval and modern English. The English drove the Britons from their land and brought much more of the land under the plow; basically, however, like Tacitus's Germans, they were not prone to group themselves into large social organisms—let alone urban societies—or to maintain the quite elaborate communications system between groups that would have been possible if they had taken over existing towns with their connecting Roman roads.

A centralized urban society developed only very slowly among the small, oligarchic, local units of the various English kingdoms. For long, chieftains and petty kings moved with their courts from one royal estate to the other, expecting and receiving generous hospitality. Their counselors, chosen by them and not elected by any democratic process, served one month in three and retired to their estates for the other two. Gradually, more permanent establishments evolved, kingdoms grew in size and strength, and learning and the arts of peace began to flourish. The kingdoms of Northumbria, Mercia, and Wessex rose to a dominant position in the seventh, eighth, and ninth-tenth centuries respectively.

During the eighth century the nascent civilization of the English was already menaced by the Norwegian sea-raiders, who sacked the Northumbrian monastery of Lindisfarne in 793. The Danes made great inroads into England during the next two hundred years. In 870 they came down by land to attack the southwestern kingdom of Wessex; when later defeated by King Alfred the Great they retired, to be confined by treaty to the territory in the North and East Midlands known as the Danelaw. A century and a half later, a Danish king, Canute, succeeded to the throne of Wessex and ruled a great part of England.

Throughout the Anglo-Saxon period and for centuries thereafter, the Church remained the most powerful force in the written culture of the English nation. Since St. Augustine's mission from Rome had landed in Canterbury in 597, the English church had flourished, although the Roman Christianity represented by Augustine had been in doctrinal conflict with Celtic Christianity, which had earlier evangelized the North and the South-West. The two were notably at loggerheads about the date of Easter, and their differences were not settled until the Synod held at Whitby Abbey in Northumbria in 664, when Canterbury won the day. Later during the same century, Englishmen began to evangelize heathen Germany, and finally in the eighth brought that entire territory to Christianity.

The importance of the Church and of its monastic, predominantly Latin, culture for the cultural life of Anglo-Saxon England can hardly be overemphasized. In the development of a beautiful script for the writing of texts, in the decoration and illumination of manuscripts, as well as in scholarship and the arts of architecture and sculpture, Church patronage was paramount. This was especially so of monastic patronage: a monastic community was a small town in itself, in this respect a kind of equivalent of the country villa of Roman times, with a community existing on the fruit of its own toil and on charitable benefactions.

THE NORMAN CONQUEST AND LATER

The men who followed Duke William of Normandy to England in 1066, to assert his right to the West-Saxon throne, were the descendants of Scandinavians who had landed on the north coast of France a century and a half before. Nominally subjects of the French king and speaking the French language, the Normans comprised virtually an independent state, with territorial ambitions and a Viking joy in war. During the same century in which they conquered England they founded states in South Italy and Sicily.

These invaders, like the Romans before them, were a compact, efficient army, many of them mercenaries, rather than half a nation on the move like the Angles, Saxons, and Jutes. Immediately on landing, William won the decisive Battle of Hastings, to become—by right of conquest as well as by family—King of England and Duke of Normandy. For four hundred years, until the end of the Hundred Years' War between England and France (1453), this dual kingdom was the most powerful state in Europe. Its territories on the French side of the Channel were greatly extended by William the Conqueror's successors. The kings of England gave at least as much of their time and attention to their French dominions as to their English, held their court at least as often in France as in England, and regularly engaged in military operations on French soil.

The Normans brought to England their northern dialect of the French language, and their social and political dominance imposed this dialect on the almost exclusively Germanic (with borrowings from Latin) language of the conquered English as the norm of educated and aristocratic communication. Latin remained the language of learning, and Old English continued to be spoken and written; but the machinery of government and the law functioned in French. Throughout the Middle Ages, French taste in literature and the arts prevailed, especially in southern English noble and royal circles. The language that grew up in this situation was an amalgam known as Middle English: its syntax and grammar largely remained English while its vocabulary was greatly augmented by French.

Before the coming of the Normans the English had created a society remarkable for a degree of civilization that had continued to flourish in spite of Danish invasions. After the Danish wars of the ninth century the Kingdom of Wessex had established a military and cultural ascendancy over the whole country, but the kingdoms of Mercia and Northumbria, as well as the Norse kingdom of York, survived in a shadow form in 1066. Despite the ascendancy of Wessex, and the existence of a consistent and workable system of law, local government, and taxation throughout the land, England before the Norman Conquest was by no means a close-knit unity. The Frenchmen, as the conquered called the conquerors, imposed themselves on England, driving the older English aristocracy from the court and to a lower position in society in general, and creating one kingdom from many.

William the Conqueror's method of asserting his power (binding on the whole realm) was orderly, simple, autocratic—and novel to the English. Every inch of the land was declared to be the king's; retaining great estates for himself, he distributed the remainder among his followers, who held it as his tenants only in return for the performance of exactly defined services. Within this feudal system the Norman barons were free to govern and exploit their lands as they wished. They were encouraged to build strongholds, and William himself saw to it that a castle, with a constable (a noble vassal of the king), was erected in every county town and at strategic points throughout the country. These great stone fortresses, on ground naturally or artificially elevated, with moats around them and stockades for an outer defense, became the symbol of Norman power. The English had never seen anything like them.

William also took care to know, by means of a systematic enquiry made in the 1080's and recorded in Doomsday Book, the feudal obligation of each of his vassals. He also took care to strengthen the towns already established during the Anglo-Saxon period, as centers of trade, justice, and administration in peace, and defense in war. Ports such as Southampton on the south coast and London on the navigable River Thames gradually came into greater prominence because of their advantages in these respects. London, already a major town in Roman days, had become by the beginning of the thirteenth century a community strong and rich enough to turn the scale in a dispute—according as it supported the barons against the king (as in 1215 against King John) or vice versa. It was by far the largest, wealthiest, and most powerful town in England, and the administrative and cultural hub of the country as well.

By the fourteenth century the English kingdom—in the British Isles and in France—was at the height of its political strength and economic prosperity. The power of Edward III (d. 1377), the military exploits of his eldest son the Black Prince, and the political and cultural influence of his fourth son, John of Gaunt, are among the outstanding features of English life at the time. Even though social unrest and political strife were prevalent during the reign of Richard II (deposed 1399), these did not destroy the social and economic conditions in which literature and the arts could flourish.

Though the power and influence of the King of England tended to concentrate itself in the south, both because of its proximity to the French territories of the king and because of the metropolis of London and the ports of the south coast, mercantile centers in the provinces also came to prosper. The Yorkshire farms and towns in the north grew rich on the production of wool, and the eastern and western counties, on weaving and the export trade. The rising well-to-do bourgeois society of London and of these provincial towns began to exert an influence on taste. The most obvious example in literature is the fourteenth-century mystery play in the north and the Midlands. The exactions of great landowners in pursuit of more profitable means of farming became a staple source of the literature of social complaint.

One of the most distinctive features of the later Middle Ages in England and in Europe was the change that came about in institutions of education. The first universities were founded in Europe during the twelfth century. Their curricula included civil and canon (ecclesiastical) law, the Latin classics, the newly revived Aristotelian philosophy, especially logic (in Latin translation), mathematics, and medicine. Until the late twelfth century an English boy acquired his education either in a school— perhaps attached to a cathedral but in any case licensed by the bishop of the diocese, or in a royal or noble household whose life he shared, or an abbey or monastery, where he was trained by the monks. Little care was taken for the education of girls. The late twelfth century saw the beginnings of the University of Oxford (its constituent colleges were not founded until later); and Cambridge was founded during the early thirteenth century. These two remained the only English universities for more than five hundred years.

After elementary schooling in cathedral, court, or abbey, a boy would enter university at the age of about fourteen, and spend seven years or so equipping himself for a career in the church or the administration of the realm. From the last years of the thirteenth century onward, he had another choice. During the reign of Edward I (1272–1307) the laws of England became the object of serious study and definition and at about the same time the "common" or civil lawyers began to group themselves into societies known as Inns of Court. In these "Inns" the senior members lived, studied, and taught; and there a boy could be sent as an alternative to university or for post-university education.

In the thousand years between the coming of the Anglo-Saxons in the fifth century and the waning of the Middle Ages in the fifteenth, England had advanced from a land conquered and sparsely populated by a alien race to a civilization in full flower. From a country divided among many petty rulers, she had become one powerful kingdom, commercially prosperous, with a unified legal system and the beginnings of parliamentary government by two houses, Lords and Commons. At various times architecture, sculpture, painting, and the minor arts had all been brought to a point where they excelled what the rest of Europe had to offer. By the end of the fifteenth century, however, she was beginning to lag behind in the arts and in scholarship. Italy, in particular, was now the leader: when Gothic was still the style of England, Italian Renaissance painters, sculptors, and architects were producing the masterpieces that set the standard for the next three hundred years. In learning, too, England was retardataire. But vernacular literature, both popular and courtly, was still her great glory, and she had already produced, in Geoffrey Chaucer, a great European poet who united both French and English traditions, as well as other English masters working in a poetic that was the lineal descendant of Old English verse techniques.

ANGLO-SAXON (OLD ENGLISH) LITERATURE

It is no accident that the entire Old English section of this anthology is in verse. All cultures find their first verbal artistic expression in rhythmic utterance, the organization into less free, more formal repetitive patterns of the basic prosodic structures of language. These patterns are first used in ritual, that is to say, in the oral realization of a solemn or joyful effect, involving the raising and fulfilling of an exalted expectation, sometimes with the aid of music, sometimes without. This often occurs at a pre-literate stage, since poetry depends less than prose on the written word. Nevertheless, all poems seek and some are felt to have—or else they would never be written down at all—a validity beyond the single performance, as well as a dimension and an influence that go beyond the merely verbal and either imitate or command some basic and universal pattern or harmony.

While any artistic utterance seeks the condition of permanence, oral poetry always retains something of the occasional quality of performance. Chief among the accidents of time as they affect the transmission of literature, especially medieval literature, is the point in its development at which a text was committed to writing. Sometimes the act of writing down crystallized and solidified the text; sometimes it allowed it an existence of continued change as spoken art—as in the popular ballads. To a certain extent this is true of all literature: the form in which we read a modern poem or novel is the form in which the author was finally obliged to give it to the publisher—which may or may not be "final." Its transmission, even in a literate society that produces multiple copies of books by mechanical means—Western society as it has been since the invention of printing—is not entirely straightforward. Still, modern texts are comparatively stable and the range of variant conditions remains relatively narrow, growing narrower the nearer we approach our own times.

Of many of the poems that make up the first part of this anthology, we can say little with certainty about date of composition or authorship. We have more information about the poets and other authors of the later Middle Ages, but never as much as we should like—and it is surprising how frequently we are unable to give even the name of an author to some of the most remarkable works of the fourteenth century.

To go back to the time when the earliest poetry of the English people is thought to have been composed, we must pick an arbitrary date, say about 500 A.D., when the migration of the Germanic tribes was more or less complete. The written records we possess from that time amount only to a handful of inscriptions, serving a no longer definable magical function, expressed in pagan characters known as runes. Runes continue to appear on Christian monuments, such as the Ruthwell Cross (Fig. 23), on which a portion of the poem *The Dream of the Rood* is carved, and on such objects as the Franks Casket (Fig. 22); yet with very few exceptions they are not used in the transcription of any extant manuscript texts. The vernacular manuscripts originating in the seventh century used an alphabet based on the Latin script of the Irish missionaries to England, with a few extra characters for Anglo-Saxon sounds having no equivalent in Latin (Fig. 4).

By the seventh century the physical means for recording texts and enough trained scribes to write them were in existence, particularly in Northumbria. The Lindisfarne Gospels (Fig. 5), now in the British Museum, are only one witness to the skill and sophistication exercised at the end of the seventh century and the beginning of the eighth. On the other hand, the manuscripts in which Old English poetry is preserved are almost all unique, and almost none of them were written until the end of the tenth century. Scribal effort, in other words, had been expended on the new learning in the new language of culture—Latin—rather than on what we now think of as the earliest monuments of our literature, the heroic poetry of the Anglo-Saxon people. This means that many poems, in the form in which we have them, were not written down until perhaps two and one-half centuries after their composition. On the other hand, certain works, such as *The Battle of Maldon,* which commemorates a historical event of 991, must have been copied into a manuscript almost as soon as composed. Most scholars think that earlier manuscripts of the earlier poems must have existed, and that they were probably transcribed in various dialects rather than only in the literary West Saxon in which the tenth-century versions are expressed. We cannot be sure, but it seems likely that *Beowulf,* for example, was given a form approximating that which we know, by a singer or singers at some time during the eighth century. The poet was probably binding together materials from an earlier time and adding to them. During the Anglo-Saxon period, however, it looks as though the transcription of works which were predominantly secular, or only indirectly didactic—especially those based on pagan materials and pagan codes of value and behavior—must have taken a very secondary place to the writing of sacred works.

Throughout the Middle Ages, in all Europe, the Bible was by far the most frequently copied text, either in itself or in the many liturgical books for which it formed the basis. Without the Christian missionaries from Ireland and Rome, the impulse toward a written culture in England would have come far later; yet the culture that the missionaries brought with them and in which they educated their converts was primarily a sacred one, Latin not English, learned rather than popular. Those who came under its influence were more likely to busy themselves with Latin verse and prose (especially Christian) than with the vernacular. Since Latin was the common language of learned Europe, Englishmen could make a European reputation in that language: St. Aldhelm of Malmesbury (640–709), in Wessex; the Venerable Bede (c.653–735) scholar, grammarian, poet, encyclopedist, Scripture commentator, hagiographer, and historian, monk of Jarrow in Northumbria; and Alcuin of York (735–804) did exactly that. After a distinguished career in his native York, Alcuin spent most of the last twenty years of his life as principal educator to the Emperor Charlemagne and the Frankish court.

By translation from the Latin, too, the most beneficial works of the new faith could be made available—the Bible itself, the *Pastoral Care* and the *Dialogues* of St. Gregory the Great, the *Consolation of Philosophy* of Boethius (a pagan philosopher, d. c.524, then thought to be Christian). This was the ambition of King Alfred, in Wessex during the later ninth century; and though there is evidence that he was an admirer of *Beowulf,* there is stronger evidence that he was more an admirer of piety and learning, which he wished to see flourish in a kingdom at peace and secure from the attacks of Scandinavian marauders.

The further development of the Alfredian program during the late tenth- and early eleventh-century movement which goes under the name of the Benedictine Revival is associated especially with the name of St. Dunstan, Archbishop of Canterbury from 959 to 988, whose program of monastic reform brought education, learning, and the arts into still closer contact than ever before in England. In its beginnings the Benedictine Revival was primarily Latin in character, but in its wake was produced some of the greatest vernacular work of the entire medieval period, in both the visual and the verbal arts. The inspiration is classical and Mediterranean, the finished product characteristically English. With a writer such as Ælfric (955–1020), it is no longer a matter of saving oneself for Latin or of producing a stiff rendering of Latin into Old English, but rather of a highly conscious, fully mastered rhetorical art in Old English prose. So too, in the manuscript illumination of the century preceding the Norman Conquest: in the Benedictional of St. Æthelwold, St. Dunstan's collaborator (Fig. 6), a Mediterranean model has been assimilated into a style recognizably national and entirely independent and self-assured. A later example still, with influences from Byzantium, is seen in Fig. 7, from the St. Albans Psalter of the first quarter of the twelfth century.

The Benedictine Revival was the summing up and crowning of a process that had begun in the sixth century and had produced a large body of English prose by the time of the Norman Conquest in 1066. Much of this prose consists of sermons or of works of devotion or morality, private and public. Some is legal and administrative, some annalistic, like the sometimes lively (and often dull) narrative of the *Anglo-Saxon Chronicle*. Some pieces, like the translations of the Greek romance of *Apollonius of Tyre* and of the *Marvels of the East*, seem to exist for the sake of the tale alone. Most of it would have been intended for reading aloud, since only a small proportion of the population could read and write; and some of the sermons, in particular, must have been delivered with a sense of performance almost as great as that of poetry. But it is unlikely that such prose was intended to be memorized to the same extent as verse, even in an age when men's verbal memories were more exercised and more tenacious than they are today. It is recorded of King Alfred that as a boy he received a coveted book of poetry as a reward for memorizing its entire contents after having them read to him.

By comparison with the mass of prose writings, the amount of Old English verse that survives is small. Some of it is religious: *The Dream of the Rood*, brief and highly wrought, is perhaps its high point. Much consists of what is loosely described as heroic: that is to say, it takes as its basic assumptions the older Germanic pagan insistence on the virtues of courage in battle and endurance in the face of all the ills that beset a man as he passes from youth to old age. Its greatest monument is *Beowulf*, its most perfect epitome *The Battle of Maldon*—a late, fully crystallized statement of the heroic ideal which is also a memorial for an aged English leader against the Danes.

Though it is probable that poetry, the older literary form, took second place in the monastic scriptoria to English and Latin prose, the poetic gift was always held in high esteem among the English. The singer of tales, the *scop*, with a repertoire part memorized and part improvised, and accompanying his verses on the harp, was an important member of a noble household. He could expect his stock-in-trade to command a receptive audience, his listeners themselves versed in, and hence appreciative of, his poetic skills. Performances by such trained and (so to speak) professional minstrels, as well as by the guests themselves in turn, were an important feature of any feast.

While we have the names of many scholars and prose writers of the Anglo-Saxon period, and even considerable biographical information about a good number, we can name only three poets, all of them Christian and active in a monastic ambience. Cædmon is one, Aldhelm another; six lines of vernacular poetry survive from one, none at all from the second. Of the third, Cynewulf, we know little, except that he has left us about twenty-six hundred lines of verse, including a long poem, *Elene* (on St. Helena and the finding of the True Cross). More survives from what is known as the school of Cynewulf, all of it seemingly written by ecclesiastics during the late eighth and early ninth centuries. Its subject matter is religious—saints' lives, Gospel stories, and Christian allegory. Works such as *The Phoenix*, adapted from pseudo-Lactantius (see the section The Other World: Paradise), and *The Dream of the Rood*, the latter chiefly because of resemblance to *Elene* in subject, are often called Cynewulfian. Though the *Dream* has a depth and richness and is of a quality that sets it above the other work of Cynewulf and his "school," there are enough resemblances between the two in style and diction to make the comparison useful.

The remainder of the Old English poetic corpus is anonymous and untitled. In a very few cases, such as the Riddles, to have given a title would have been to destroy the point of the game, which was to describe a familiar object in language as figurative and impenetrable as possible, provoking admiration for poetic skill in the making and surprised pleasure at the solution. This delight in figurative diction is one of the chief characteristics of Old English poetry—as indeed of medieval literature in general. For the medieval poet, richness and difficulty of language were not to be avoided, but rather to be cultivated. Rhetoric and ornament were not the terms of abuse that they have become in modern times. Old English poetry, naturally, does not bear the strong impress of Latin rhetorical theory and practice that marks later English medieval verse and prose. But it loves ornament, repeated in patterns—just as Anglo-Saxon art did (Figs. 5–6, 21). It preserves a careful balance between what is strange and what is familiar and it orders its rhythms and effects according to metrical and structural principles that are strict in operation. Particularly in a heroic epic like *Beowulf*, but also in shorter elegiac poems, it achieves an effect of carefully contrived and ordered ceremonial performance. Like oral poetry in general, it is essentially an art of preservation rather than of innovation, using and re-using traditional materials. The hearer or reader is made to feel that he is on familiar ground as he recognizes the highly conventional—the word is again not one of abuse in medieval times—figurative vocabulary, with its formulaic repetitions and fossilized poetic terms, and the poet's use of one incident to convey the parallel implications of another.

One of the chief marks distinguishing the literature of medieval and Renaissance Europe from that of our day is its profound belief in the didactic and exemplary value of the verbal work of art. *Beowulf* is a poem of praise punctuated, in a manner typical of Old English poetry, by passages of Christian and pagan moralizing. In one sense it can be very loosely called an allegory of the perpetual struggle of light against dark, good against evil. Over and above the pleasure it was undoubtedly expected to give its audience, the weight of the poem is thrown into the attempt to move and persuade this audience that Beowulf's example is one that it would be admirable to follow if one wished for fame in this generation and the generations to come.

MIDDLE ENGLISH LITERATURE

This belief survives the changes in both the language itself and the forms of English literature as they develop during the centuries succeeding the Norman Conquest. If anything, it becomes stronger, as influences from other literatures, especially French, begin to assert themselves. The language of English poetry and prose becomes more recognizably our own. Both are refined and augmented by contact with and imitation of the French language and the new narrative and lyrical poetic that came into being in France during the twelfth century. Latin culture continues to play a large part in the formation of English literature, but for at least four centuries France becomes the dominant outside influence. Its power is greater for the fact that for so much of the time England was first of all a province of the Dukes of Normandy and later the ruler of large tracts of France. The influence of France on England was often direct, but often, and in some respects more significantly, it was indirect, acting as the intermediary between English and Latin or Italian literature. Frequently, instead of going to originals for translation or adaptation, an English writer went to a French version.

From the century or so after the Norman Conquest we now possess comparatively little literature in English. The works written at the beginning of what historians call the Middle English period—from a little before 1200 to the end of the fifteenth century—suggest, however, that the tradition of vernacular writing was continuous and that there was constant interaction between Latin, French, and English. English prose works of religious instruction have a continuous tradition from Anglo-Saxon times to the end of the Middle Ages—the late twelfth-century *Ancrene Riwle* (a manual for women religious recluses) is an early example of devout impulse and sophisticated performance. In secular literature the Latin and French form of verse debate is naturalized in the lively late-twelfth-century rhyming poem *The Owl and the Nightingale*, in which the two birds put the case respectively for the solemn and the joyous ways of life. Layamon, at about the same time, is the first writer to give substance in English to what becomes one of the most potent myths of the English Middle Ages and Renaissance: the legendary history of King Arthur and his ancestor Brutus, eponymous founder of Britain, and descendant of Aeneas, the Trojan hero and founder of Rome. Layamon writes in an alliterative measure that is the intermediary between Old English poetic and the verse of the alliterative revival in the West and North-West Midlands in the fourteenth century (Langland and the *Gawain*-Poet).

During the twelfth century the English poet and the English writer of devotional prose, in particular, came to have at their disposal, either directly or through French, a much larger range of classical literature and literary theory—and, increasingly, of medieval adaptations of them—than ever before. Their enlarged education gave them access to the sources of knowledge contained in the liberal arts—the *trivium* (grammar, rhetoric, and logic) and the *quadrivium* (astronomy, arithmetic, geometry, and music)— as well as to the poets and rhetoricians of Rome. The development of the Latin liturgy and of the literature of devotion and religious instruction, in both verse and prose, enormously enlarged their sacred range.

France provided a recognized classification of the materials of secular story. The "matter of France," less important for England, yielded the stories of Charlemagne, Roncevaux, Roland, and the rest; the "matter of Britain" (i.e. Brittany) comprised the Arthurian legend and the so-called Breton lays, of which Chaucer's *Franklin's Tale* is an adaptation; and the "matter of Rome," including the Troy story (Rome being a Trojan foundation), the story of Thebes, and the stories of Alexander the Great, was the largest in scope and most influential of all. While many of these stories, especially those of the "matter of Rome," were available in Latin, it was their French versions that made them the narrators' basic material, the inexhaustible well from which they could draw. It was never thought to be the poet's task to make it new: these stories were worth the telling again and again. They are the tales that displace the Germanic heroic legends.

The romances—ancestors of the novel—that are made from them differ from the oral epic poetry which they supplant almost as much in the manner of their telling as in their matter. They reflect a different society from the earlier Germanic variety, and a new valuation of social activity. Bravery in battle becomes less an end in itself, less the prime opportunity to win reputation, so that it occupies relatively less space in the social experience and consequently in literature. As the institution of chivalry comes into being, warlike courage begins to function, still importantly but less prominently, as part of a larger and more sophisticated pattern of social activity. The virtues of chivalry were in part an elaboration and refinement of the older pagan heroic ideals of the conduct befitting a man of good birth. Courage and generosity, the keeping of an oath remained, as they still remain, part of the groundwork of virtuous behavior, but they were incorporated in a system of values radically transformed by Christian ethics and a philosophy of love. True courtesy, honor, the practice of the ideal of knighthood, implied the exercise in their various aspects of the "cardinal" virtues of prudence, fortitude, temperance, and justice, controlled and enriched by the "theological"—faith, hope, and charity. All these words and concepts had a much wider and less institutionalized application than they do today; they embraced such other virtues as generosity, honor, good temper, friendliness, truth, and their various manifestations. In the world of the romances and, at a lower pitch, in the real world, fame and life everlasting were to be won by the practice of these virtues in the service of the Christian faith and of both a heavenly lady—the Virgin Mary—and an earthly.

The matter of Britain, especially, and the matter of Rome are deployed to tell stories of true lovers, to explore the nature of their thoughts and actions, in a context of martial adventure and fairy magic, and often at great length. The nature of love itself, religious and profane, becomes a subject for exploration by philosophers and poets, who picked up some of what had been written about its theory and practice by Plato and by the Latin and Arabic authors through whom Plato became known to the Middle Ages; and by the love poets of ancient Rome, especially Ovid. In philosophy, the investigation is carried on most remarkably during the twelfth century by the school of Chartres in the north; in poetry by the Provençal poets of the south, who shape the new genre of love lyric. The first of these secular poets of France known to us by name is William, Duke of Aquitaine (1071–1127), who already had behind him a tradition of classical and medieval love poetry in Latin and Arabic-Spanish for which there are no more than one or two parallels in the earlier Germanic languages. The troubadour poets, in their exploration of love's nature and transforming power and of the anguish of love-longing, evolve the notion of fin' amors: gracious love, noble and ennobling, love-worship, for which nineteenth-century scholars coined the term "courtly love." Nothing illustrates better the change from an old Germanic to a typical European medieval society than this complex of ideas in which women, love, and praise of women occupy a dominant position.

The same change in values is apparent in the songs that deal less with love as a state of being than with imagined love-encounters: the alba—the song of lovers' prearranged secret meeting by night and their despairing parting at dawn, and the pastourelle—the song of lovers' chance meeting by day and what comes of it, as well as in the other varieties of love lyric. The lyrical stanzaic form in which many of these songs are expressed had already been developed in Latin religious poetry of the ninth century. Rhyme, too, is first to be found in Latin poetry and is transferred from that to the vernacular. Throughout the early development of medieval lyric poetry there is constant interplay between Latin and vernacular, sacred and secular. Religious poetry, in particular, exploits the notion of figura, either in its narrower typological sense or in the broader and universal, in which Eve or the Maiden in the Moor can stand for all women, all humanity.

Some of the developing poetic genres reflect the growing taste, in a society where women were assuming a considerable role, for what much later came to be called polite literature. The *carole* is one example: a dance-song in which the leader sang the verse and the rest of the dancers, men and women, the refrain. It was a graceful musical diversion for a festival, a winter evening, or a summer afternoon; and typical of its age in that it was inseparable from its musical accompaniment. The *fabliau* is another example, wittier, more polished than the popular prose "merry tale." The longer comic beast fable or poem—the ironic, satiric counterpart of the chivalric romance, as in the cycle of stories concerned with Reynard the Fox—is a third. More important, often longer still, and most characteristic is the allegorical poem, such as the *Romance of the Rose,* exploring the nature of love and of many other philosophical matters, by means of a story whose characters are personifications of the qualities of a lover and his mistress, of Nature herself, of Fortune, and of the other abstractions which preside over a systematic view of human life.

At the same time as these French poetic forms and modes of thought were passing into currency in England, a huge body of prose was being produced, particularly in the field of moral instruction and exhortation—treatises, sermons, meditations. A vast increase in these works came with the thirteenth-century rise of the friars, the Mendicant Orders, vowed to poverty. Prayer, penance, and (for the Dominicans) the preaching of God's word was their major obligation; and the volume of their (and others') sermons continues to expand throughout the Middle Ages.

Another form that seems to have developed earlier in France than in England was the religious drama, which emerged into vigorous life in northern provincial centers of England—York, Wakefield, Coventry and Chester—in the fourteenth century. The drama was the vehicle of bourgeois piety and religious instruction in a half-secular context. It displayed the whole scheme of salvation, from the Creation and the Fall of Man to the Resurrection and the Harrowing of Hell, its production being under the control of the tradesmen's guilds and the solemnity of its message tempered with the beginnings of dramatic comedy. Later still, dramatized moral instruction was presented in morality plays.

When French literary genres passed into English they underwent changes of various kinds. Romances, for example, tended to be shorn of their speculative and spiritualized dimensions, and the Arthurian stories of *Sir Gawain and the Green Knight* or Malory's *Morte Darthur* are more down-to-earth than their French counterparts.

Some fourteenth-century English works have no French equivalent. One is *Piers Plowman,* which preserves the older English verse technique of the alliterative long line and conducts its investigation of the nature of goodness and of the ordering of a truly Christian society in such a way as to leave no room for doubt in the reader's mind that this is what the poem is really about. We can be sure of this, as we cannot be quite sure what the author of *Sir Gawain and the Green Knight* intended us to take from his poem.

Even taking into account exceptions like *Piers Plowman* and allowing for the changes wrought by English variations on originally French forms and themes, English medieval literature is strongly tinctured with French. It is the measure of Chaucer's greatness that he has assimilated the French tradition and made it his own. His shorter lyrics can deal with the values of "courtly love" seriously or satirically; his *Troilus and Criseyde,* the greatest romance in our language, investigates the experience of love in depth and at length; his *Book of the Duchess, Parliament of Fowls,* and *House of Fame* show his self-assurance in handling the allegorical vision; his Franklin's Tale is a perfectly balanced work of art in its transformation of the fairy "matter of Britain" into an exploration of love and its obligations; his Miller's Tale is a perfectly judged *fabliau;* his Pardoner's Tale and Nun's Priest's Tale are literary transformations of sermons, exactly adjusted to the characters of their tellers. The Nun's Priest's Tale holds in equilibrium the animal-story-for-moral-instruction of the *Bestiary,* the sermon, and the rhetorical mode, in a magnificently managed parody of genres and of manner.

At the other end of the scale of sophistication are some of the short lyrics of moral and religious instruction. These, and their less direct and simple companions in the lyric genre, emphasize the fact that by far the largest part of what was written during the Middle Ages was intended for instruction, direct or indirect. This is true of all medieval fiction—or at least of most of it:

> St. Paul saith that all that written is
> To our doctrine it is ywrit, iwis . . .

If a fourteenth-century Englishman had been asked to defend himself against the old Platonic or the Christian-ascetic charge leveled at the artist—that he made fictions that were lies—he might have replied (as one in fact did) that St. Paul did not mean that everything that is written for our "doctrine" (teaching) is or need be true. He meant that, if we take it aright, everything that is written can give us useful instruction. If what we feign in our fictions has some signification and is not merely empty, then it is not a lie but indeed a figure of the truth.

The same Englishman would not have doubted that if his treatise or his fiction was to be fully effective it ought to be constructed with true rhetorical decorum, employing the tropes—the figures of thought and of speech inherited by medieval authors from the classics—to bring home story and lesson with all its force. He would have been especially concerned that his language should be rich and strong enough to support the weight of the doctrine and the richness of the effect that he wished it to carry. It would never have occurred to him to speak of "mere rhetoric" or "mere ornament." Only the greatest poet of the English Middle Ages, Chaucer himself, can afford to demonstrate his independence of a tradition he respects.

The generations following Chaucer's saw an increasing concern with richness of diction and—at its best as in the work of the "Scottish Chaucerians"—an exuberance of rhetoric that were to help the English language toward its triumph in the sixteenth century. Didactic and exemplary verse and prose flourished as perhaps never before during the reign of the pious Henry VI (1422–61). In the turbulent period of the Wars of the Roses (1455–85), when the throne of England was being battled for—the twilight of the Middle Ages—two literary figures stand out: the reprobate knight, Sir Thomas Malory, author of the *Morte Darthur,* and the thriving bourgeois, William Caxton.

Caxton not only brought printing to England but moreover was Malory's first printer. Both were deeply concerned with the values of an aristocratic, chivalric social system that was already in decline. For a hundred years the English archer had displaced the mounted knight as the architect of England's military strength. The commercial and professional men of the cities were thrusting themselves forward to form the beginnings of the English urban middle class, while the smaller landowners were also rising in power and wealth. Malory chose to write of the legendary, knightly King Arthur and his followers, providing the last medieval expression of the myth that was to serve the Tudor dynasty (1485–1603, founded by Henry VII) so well and to reach its finest expression in Edmund Spenser's *Faerie Queene*. Caxton, too, concerned himself with chivalric codes and practices, but still more with the provision of entertaining and edifying literature in a strengthened, refined, and uniform English. The printing press made more copies of a given work available to more people than had ever before been possible: a whole culture changed with the end of the era of the hand-produced book. The process by which the writer's audience became a reading, rather than a read-to, public had begun.

VERSIFICATION

The reader coming to Old and Middle English poetry for the first time will find a great deal that is unfamiliar and disconcerting in its verse techniques. He has been led, by his reading in the verse of the sixteenth to the twentieth century, to expect that poetry will be written in a regular series of lines, rhyming or not rhyming, with regularly alternating stresses and a strict attention to form. Modern free-verse techniques will have done something to prepare him for what he will find in this selection from poets who wrote before Chaucer, and from two of Chaucer's contemporaries; yet the close-knit accentual patterns of Old English verse are much firmer and stricter in their requirements than the modifications of such patterns that have been used by modern poets.

The Old English poets built their poems of single-line units of accentual verse, each single line divided at its center by a pause or caesura. Rhyme, either to link two half-lines or to hold together single lines in couplets, stanzaic forms, or verse paragraphs, is almost unknown among them. Instead of rhyme they developed alliteration—that is, the choice of words beginning with the same sound.

A song I sing   of sorrow unceasing

is a translation of one typical line in an Old English poem. Such a line contains four main stresses, two on either side of the caesura, here marked by a space. The line is welded into a unit by the fact that both stressed words of the first half begin with the same sound as the first stress of the second half. Further, the same sound is picked up again in the second element of the second stressed word of the second half-line.

This is only one of the line patterns used by Old English poets. The poet had the further option that any vowel could alliterate with any other vowel. But he was strictly limited as to the number of the patterns of half-line that he could employ, by the number of unstressed syllables that he was allowed and by the patterns in which they might be placed, and by other prescriptions.

The metrical effect of Old English poetry is of a disciplined series of dignified (though not slow-moving), single utterances in a regular and very marked rhythm, taut and carefully timed. Heightened and pointed by being sung or chanted to the accompaniment of a harp, Old English verse must have achieved in recitation—for it was predominantly oral in character, like most vernacular poetry written throughout the Middle Ages—a tone equal to that of the best of its kind.

After the Norman Conquest, French literary models came to supplant the older English tradition of unrhymed alliterative verse. The chief differences between the two were that French verse employed rhyme, and later stanza form, and was written in a pattern of metrical feet—that is, with alternating stressed and unstressed syllables. But the older tradition was not immediately and entirely supplanted by the new. What happened was that its patterns of alliteration became looser and more permissive of extra syllables and more accents to the line. Rhyme is still not employed, though some poets combine the rhymed and the alliterative techniques and there is still a strongly marked caesura in the middle of each line. To either side of the break there are deviations and license. Often, the line consists of the basic four stresses, but as often it has five or six or even more. The alliteration may be the bare minimum—one stress in each half-line; or it may run through almost every stress in the line. There are no norms for the number of unstressed syllables, so that short lines like

> And had leave to lie   all their life after

may occur next to lines like

> To each a tale that they told   their tongue was tempered to lie.

The effect of control that a poet such as Langland can give the alliterative measure is exceptional—and even Langland slips into formlessness from time to time. When Langland came to use the alliterative meter it was already out of fashion: it was his achievement to give it new life. The same may be said of the poet of *Sir Gawain and the Green Knight*, also writing in a center of provincial culture remote from the capital and, as far as can be told, making a conscious effort to revive the form. In his other poems the *Gawain* poet uses rhyme; and even in *Sir Gawain* he organizes the poem into unrhymed blocks, each of them marked off and in a sense summed up by the "bob" (a two- or three-syllable half-line) rhyming with one of the rhymes of the four-line "wheel" that follows it. So he gives an impression of a tighter and more organized form to his poem, especially since these little comments form a kind of synopsis-commentary to the whole. Rhetorically as well as metrically he holds his poem together in the large unit, however free his treatment of the single alliterating line.

Both before and after Chaucer there is much rhymed verse in Middle English in which the meter is irregular and shambling and seemingly constructed after no metrical principle except a rough approximation to an uneven rhythm. But there is a good deal of sophistication in stanzaic form; and even a poem that appears to be largely imitating the rhythms of common speech (such as the *Second Shepherd's Play*), keeps a firm and regular stanza. But one cannot have the same expectation of disciplined variety in regularity that is to become the norm in the sixteenth century, nor the feeling of deliberate and rhetorically controlled irregularity that one has from John Skelton—as will be illustrated later in this volume.

When one comes to Chaucer's verse, however, the situation changes. There were, in his day, poets who could handle with entire competence the meters and stanzaic forms of the French tradition, even the very forms and meters that Chaucer uses. But none have his variety, whether in the octosyllabic couplets (already naturalized in English) that he adopted from his French models; or the lyric forms also taken over from French; or the various stanzaic patterns, especially the rhyme royal (iambic pentameters, rhyming *ababbcc* in a seven-line stanza) of *Troilus and Criseyde* and the *Parliament of Fowls*. Chaucer's greatest achievement was with a verse form that he may have introduced into England and certainly naturalized there—the heroic couplet in which most of the *Canterbury Tales* are written. To state that this basic unit consists of ten- or eleven-syllable iambic pentameters rhyming in twos

> In Flaundres whilom was a compaignye
> Of yonge folk that haunteden folye . . .

gives no notion of the variations, the force, and the richness Chaucer imparts to it. He is able to give an effect of even greater metrical fluidity and variety than if he were using a stanzaic form, maintaining the metrical units of line and couplet while building the large unit of sentence and paragraph from it, playing off sentence structure against the rhythm of the verse. The rhythms of speech provide a constant counterpoint to the accentuation of the meter, the verse running in the smooth, rising rhythm of the iambic pentameter, always varied, never monotonous. It is incomparable poetry for reading aloud.

Old English Poetry

Cædmon's Hymn

Cædmon, a layman to whom the gift of poetry came late in life, was received into the abbey of Whitby in Northumbria, where he composed a great deal of religious verse. The nine lines given below are all of what survives that can reasonably be attributed to him.

All that we know of Cædmon's life, we know from the greatest English scholar of the next generation, the Venerable Bede, monk of Jarrow (c. 673–735), who tells his story in *The Ecclesiastical History of the English People* (completed in 731). When St. Hilda ruled Whitby Abbey (which she had founded)—between 658 and 680—there was brought to her one day a layman who was employed on the abbey's estates. The night before, at a feast, he had seen that his turn to sing to the harp and entertain the others was approaching and, as he always did from bashfulness, he had escaped and taken himself off to tend the farm animals. His bed was in their quarters and, as he lay asleep there, he dreamed that someone came to him, commanding: "Cædmon, sing me something." Cædmon excused himself, saying "I cannot sing; and it was for just this reason that I left the feast when I saw that my turn was coming." His visitor was not to be put off and ordered him to sing "the beginning of created things," which he did. On waking, he remembered what he had composed and could—we must suppose—recite it to the Abbess or dictate it to a scribe.

Cædmon's new gift never deserted him, Bede tells us, but it remained an oral one and could be devoted to sacred subjects only—a kind of metrical prayer. He never learned to read, his method being to make, very rapidly, a verse paraphrase of the sacred writings that were read to him. Bede gives a long list of his writings, but we cannot certainly identify any of them with surviving Old English works and have to be content with this, his first brief effort.

Old English verse is nowadays printed in lines composed of two half-lines, the caesura being indicated by an extra space between the halves; with modern punctuation and in a modern English alphabet. Three Old English letters are used: æ (aesc, pronounced ash), which is either a short sound (a) or a long (open e long); þ (thorn) and ð (eth), which are both pronounced *th*.

This is not the way that Old English poetry was written down in manuscripts. There it appears as if it were continuous prose, without caesura markings; without line divisions; without punctuation, except the period; and with some other no-longer-used letter forms (long ſ, for example, for *s*; ƿ (wynn) for *w*; ꞃ for *r*); and with scribal contractions (e.g. ⁊ for *ond* [and]). A few lines from the manuscript of *Beowulf* are shown in Figure 4.

Cædmon's Hymn is here given in a West Saxon version, with a literal prose translation.

Cædmon's Hymn

Nu sculon° herigean   heofonrices weard,°
metodes meahte   and his modgeþanc,°
weorc wuldorfæder,   swa he wundra° gehwæs,
ece drihten,   or onstealde.
He ærest sceop°   eorðan° bearnum°
heofon to hrofe,   halig scyppend;
þa middangeard°   moncynnes weard,
ece drihten,   æfter teode
firum foldan,   frea° ælmihtig.
658–680

Now must we praise   of heaven's kingdom the Keeper
Of the Lord the power   and his Wisdom
The work of the Glory-Father,   as he of marvels each,
The eternal Lord,   the beginning established.
He first created   of earth for the sons
Heaven as a roof,   the holy Creator.
Then the middle-enclosure   of mankind the Protector
The eternal Lord,   thereafter made
For men, earth   the Lord almighty.

Beowulf

The finest surviving long poem in Old English has come down to us in a single manuscript, now MS. Cotton Vitellius A.XV in the British Museum, transcribed in the West Saxon dialect at the end of the tenth century, at least two centuries after its composition. We still do not know the name of its author, and it was not given the title *Beowulf* until 1805 and not printed until 1815.

We need not be surprised at this. Almost all Old English poetry is untitled and anonymous: we know the names of only two poets whose work survives—Cædmon and Cynewulf, and of Cædmon's poetry we possess only the few lines presented at the head of the present selection. Almost all Old English poems survive in a single manuscript, often in a copy that includes other texts composed at an earlier or a later date. Most of these manuscripts were written down in the West Saxon dialect at about the end of the tenth century, when the full force of the monastic revival had made itself felt and the literary culture of England had reached its high point.

It is not clear just how far the fact that most of the Old English poetry we possess was transcribed about this time and in this dialect reflects a conscious program aimed at preserving, in a written "literary standard" language, what was thought to be best.

---

sculon the modern "shall," in its old meaning "must"
weard mod. "ward," "guard(ian)"
modgeþanc compound noun: heart, mind plus thought, intention
wundra mod. "wonders" (poss. case)
sceop lit. shaped

eorðan the reading of later manuscripts; earlier have *ielda*, of men
bearnum See Scots *bairns*, children (poss. case).
middangeard the dwelling in the middle—between heaven above and hell below—therefore the earth. *Geard* is modern "yard."
frea chief, leader

20

We know that *Beowulf* was admired in the ninth century, by King Alfred among others, and that poets then used it to strengthen their own work. The author of *The Battle of Maldon*, at the end of the tenth century, borrowed from *Beowulf*, and an anonymous sermon-writer used the description of Grendel's mere.

Nor is it clear how much Old English poetry, for want of such copying down, has been lost. It is generally assumed that a great deal has perished without trace, leaving a remainder of a scant 30,000 lines—about the length of some single poems of a few centuries later. There must have been other manuscripts of many, if not all, of the poems, often earlier and in other dialects.

We possess *Beowulf* only because the unique manuscript survived the fire of 1731, which destroyed or damaged much of the remarkable library of Sir Robert Cotton (1571–1631), in which the *Beowulf* manuscript then was. But the scorching that it then received caused its edges to crumble, so that some of the text was already lost when the Icelandic scholar G. J. Thorkelin came to make the transcriptions which were completed in 1787. All modern editions of the poem use Thorkelin's transcripts to reconstruct, as far as possible, the words and letters that are missing from the manuscript as it is today. The text is divided into forty-three fitts or sections, with line-endings and, less frequently, half-line endings, indicated by punctuation. The arrangement of the text as verse is the work of modern editors.

Scholars agree that the Cotton manuscript of *Beowulf* does not represent the first occasion on which the poem was written down. Its reputation suggests that there must have been earlier manuscripts, perhaps transcribed in West Mercia, the modern West Midlands, or further north, in Northumbria, where the poem may well have been composed. We do not know the date of the first of these, though archaic verbal forms suggest that a written version existed by the middle of the eighth century.

No evidence so far, however, is conclusive for date and place of composition. Some have put the composition earlier than the eighth century, but most agree that the Christian coloring of the diction and of some of the subject matter of the poem reflects an audience and a poet to whom Christianity and the usages of the church have been familiar long and thoroughly enough for the one to use and the other to catch allusions to the Bible and Christian literature—to Cain, to the giants, to the Devil as the "old enemy" or the "enemy of mankind." This can hardly have been before the eighth century. By 664, the date of the Synod of Whitby, at which important differences between the Celtic church and the Roman church in England were settled, Christianity was the dominant religion in the country—but thirty years later bishops still found it necessary to prescribe penance for those who sacrificed to devils (i.e. the Germanic pagan gods). Moreover, the poem can hardly be earlier than the work of the Northumbrian poet Cædmon, which must have been dictated between 658 and 680 and which established many of the modes of Christian heroic poetry. It may be of a specific poem by Cædmon that the *Beowulf* poet is thinking when he makes Hrothgar's *scop* or minstrel sing of the Creation of the World. Some scholars feel that *Beowulf* would fit best the Christian culture of Northumbria at this time, the golden age of the Venerable Bede (c. 673–735), one of the greatest European scholars of the early Middle Ages. This was the civilization that produced the superb Lindisfarne Gospels, now in the British Museum (Fig. 5), and the Northumbrian crosses of Ruthwell (Fig. 23) and Bewcastle. Such monuments are Christian in a sense in which *Beowulf* is not: a fairer comparison with the poem is the whalebone box in the British Museum known as the Franks Casket—a more provincial work, on which scenes from Germanic legend mingle with Christian scenes: the Germanic smith of the gods, Weland, and the Adoration of the Magi side by side (Fig. 22).

Other scholars, now in the majority, argue for a West Mercian origin for the poem, which may imply a date sometime in the eighth century. Strong support for West Mercia as *Beowulf*'s place of composition comes from the supposition that the poem was written for the court of Offa the Great, king of Mercia from 757 to 796. This Offa's ancestor, Offa the Angle, is especially praised by the *Beowulf* poet in an episode whose structural function seems to be to commend Queen Hygd, Hygelac's consort, by comparing her with the cruel queen of the earlier Offa.

Beowulf, the longest surviving Old English poem, is a somber masterpiece, the first great English work in the oral, primary epic mode. English as it is in language, and written in English as it must have been, it makes mention only twice, or perhaps three times, of an Englishman. It must have been written when English and Scandinavian events were of enough mutual interest for an English audience to grasp their implications, perhaps a time when the Germanic tribes still retained a consciousness of common origins and history. Scholars agree that, as far as can be told from other evidence, including the archaeological, the *Beowulf* poet has got his Swedish history—for example—right. English-Scandinavian relations must still have been close in the eighth century: we find at Sutton Hoo, dating from about 670, a mixture of English and Scandinavian cultures in both the manner of the burial and the goods in the burial mounds.

The hero of the poem is a Geat, a prominent member of a tribe known by that name from only a few other sources, but said by the poet to be ancient and powerful. Earlier scholarship identified the Geats with the Jutes (whose name in Old English was Eotan), who came either from Jutland or from the country east of the Lower Rhine. Modern opinion more strongly favors their being the Gautar, who seem to have lived in what is now southern Sweden. It is also possible that they are the Getae, believed in late classical and medieval times to inhabit southern Scandinavia, a land as remote and forbidding as Scythia, thought to have been their original home. These Getae, founding fathers of the Germanic nations as legend made them out, would be a fitting people to be the heroes of a poem set in a remote and indefinite Germanic heroic past. (See map, Fig. 2.)

Identification cannot be pressed too far nor historical consistency demanded in a poem which relies so much on indirectness and allusion, on the atmosphere of far away and long ago, shaded, deliberately darkened, and misty—a time when men still fought the evil creatures of the dark which they believed to threaten and beset them hard. An English poet is writing about the common heroic past of the Germanic race: the tribes who take part in the action are out there somewhere, distant in time and space. This is an essential assumption of the poet's art.

Nevertheless, a kind of historical and geographical frame for *Beowulf* clearly exists. The Danes, neighbors of the Geats, inhabit the island which is now Zealand: that is historical fact. The Geats come to their aid, led by Beowulf, from what is now southeast Sweden. North of the Geats are the Swedes and other tribes—again historical fact. South of the Danes, on the European mainland, are the Heathobards, sworn enemies, while farther to the west, at the extreme edge of the Merovingian domain, in Frisia, are the Hetware, the Atuarii, raided by Hygelac the Geat, who finds defeat and death among them.

This raid is the one piece of hard history in *Beowulf*. According to Frankish historians such as Gregory of Tours (c. 540–594), one Chlochilaicus was killed on such a raid in about 520. But the mode of the poem is such that this may mean that all Hygelac's doings—even much of the poem's action—have a historical basis, or it may not: we cannot tell. We can safely say that Grendel and his dam are fabulous monsters of the night—and so is the dragon, though sober historical sources record a dragon in England as late as the end of the eighth century, and men went on believing in the physical existence of such creatures for many centuries after. The supernatural elements might belong to almost any age. The incidents of the digressions, elliptically and allusively told, clearly cannot all be referred to the same limited portion of time. If we ask the date of the events of *Beowulf*, rather than the date at which the poem was composed, the best answer is that some belong to the early sixth century and others are probably older, while others again are fabulous. To expect a more exact answer is as pointless as to try to fix the direction and distance of Beowulf's swimming match with Breca, or how many suits of armor Beowulf actually carried as he swam home after the fatal conclusion of Hygelac's raid. We are dealing with a poem, not a piece of history.

Nevertheless, the poem embodies and takes as the basis of its characters' actions a social system and a set of behavioral assumptions which were common to the Germanic peoples of history. These were set out in their earliest, simplest, and most clearly recorded form by the first-century Roman historian Tacitus, in his *Germania*. These Germans, Tacitus says, are a warrior race, fierce and cruel, setting courage above all the other virtues, finding their deepest shame in cowardice, ready to use any end to gain the victory: "To retreat, provided that you return to the attack, is thought to be cunning, not cowardly." They choose their leaders for courage and demand that they continue to set a courageous example. They have a profound belief in Fate and in casting lots to foresee the future. Their warlike character is seen in the fact that all come to their assemblies and transact their business fully armed—and a young men enters manhood when he is publicly equipped (after due proof of valor), with spear and shield. Young and old group themselves round the chief as his retinue, the companions or *comitatus*. Their numbers and their bravery lend him power. He holds their allegiance by courage and generosity: his keenest disgrace is to be outdone by retainer or enemy. The companions, having sworn him allegiance, must not fall short: they must die on the battlefield rather than leave it—especially once the chieftain is killed (cf. the praise of Wiglaf in *Beowulf* and the close of *The Battle of Maldon*). "The chieftain battles for victory, the companions fight for their chief," Tacitus goes on. If the young men find no fighting at home, they seek it abroad, for they have no taste for peace. They are grasping and demanding, which encourages war and plunder to maintain the supply of what they value—horses, arms and armor, jewelry, collars. They live not in cities, but in scattered houses, each house a community. Monogamous, reverencing their women for the gift of holiness and prophecy they find in them, the men bring the dowry. Women bring men weapons, and their exchange of gifts symbolizes the holiest of bonds, the sharing of burdens. Germanic reverence for women is mirrored in their recognition of an especially close tie between a man and his sister's son—a tie as close as that between father and son.

Everyone is bound to continue the feuds and the friendships of his father and his family. Feuds are often concluded by payment of tribute, and even murder can be paid for, in money and goods (*wergild*), so that—for a time—the dishonor is wiped out.

The Germans love to feast and entertain, holding it sinful to turn a man from the door. If a host cannot continue to give the visitor the hospitality he deserves, he sends him on to another. Drinking bouts of a day and a night are commonplace and the quarrels they engender are settled by blows. Banquets have peaceful, ceremonial functions, too: they are the setting to discuss truces, form marriage alliances, make new chiefs, decide for peace or war. Feasts are chosen as a time for making such decisions because the heart is then open and exalted. At these feasts a sort of "juice extracted from barley or grain" washes down plain food: there is no excess in their eating. Their addiction to gambling may lead them to gamble away their freedom; if this happens, they go uncomplainingly into slavery, as a point of "honor." Slaves are agricultural serfs rather than household or body servants, and even when freed seldom rise to positions of influence. Usury is unknown. The land is tilled communally and shares in it are allotted according to rank.

Death is attended by no pomp, though their great men are cremated, after the pagan usage, on a pyre on which arms and armor, and sometimes also horses, are placed. Over the body is raised a barrow, a high mound of earth. Excessive mourning is frowned on: women are permitted to express their grief, but men hide it in their hearts.

Physically, these men are hardy, tough and trained, savage and vigorous, placing their trust in courage, the one thing they see as sure, though like all that is mortal, it is subject to fortune and chance. Some are hardy, sea-going people, their ships, oar-propelled, having a prow at each end for easier putting into land. Some tribes wear the images of boars for protection (Fig. 20).

Tacitus is writing of the Germanic tribes of the end of the first century A.D., three hundred and fifty years before some of them migrated to England, nearly five hundred before Pope Gregory the Great sent St. Augustine of Canterbury to bring Roman Christianity to the country, nearly six hundred before it can be said that England was Christian, and perhaps a little more before *Beowulf* was written down. Nevertheless, Tacitus tells us much about the world of *Beowulf* and of heroic poetry in general. His picture of warrior societies close-knit in small units by the ties of blood and of mutual duty between lord and retainer, finding in the ethos of the *comitatus* the most effective of social bonds and in courage the only possible stance in response to the harsh and inescapable decrees of fate and the duties of life—this picture is closely relevant to the poem. The virtues of such a society, like its vices, are fierce and combative. There is dignity, but it is martial dignity: renown can be won in battle and nowhere else. Age is more poignant in that it lessens appetite for battle and chances of success in it. Ancestry counts for much, for this is an aristocratic society, but each generation must confirm by its own courage the family's title to consideration.

This was the society to which Roman Christianity came with the arrival of St. Augustine in England in 597. The progress of the new religion was sporadic. Areas like Essex were notably slow to accept conversion, and there especially pagan practices and much of the pagan flavor of everyday life must have long remained. *Beowulf*, at least in the form in which we have it, reflects the usages of a pagan society of an indeterminate period before the Christian conversion and perhaps a time near the migration of the Angles, Saxons, and Jutes to England about the middle of the fifth century, with later accretions. The poet, almost certainly a Christian, is perhaps, like a less sophisticated Virgil, recalling to his people a past which is heroic but legendary, indeterminate, undifferentiated, and therefore ever present.

The poet's allusive, apparently unstructured technique—regular in oral poetry—

seems to expect an audience conversant with its own legendary past, with details of this and other stories. He is touching on the known to awaken resonances which will enhance what he is saying. The digressions concerning the feud between Danes and Heathobards, the Fight at Finnsburg, Hygelac's fatal expedition against the Frisians and the Hetware, the story of Sigemund and the dragon, in addition to the story of Offa and his cruel queen—are all intended not to stop the march of the narrative but to reinforce its episodic, disjointed progress. The poet counts on his audience to apply the associations of these to the other events of the poem. All tragic in their outcome, they prepare the hearers, singly and cumulatively, for the tragic outcome, in human terms, of *Beowulf*. The allusions are planted with skill to bring home the transitoriness of human glory and human life, the forward seeping of the menacing dark. At the height of exultation, the poet will slip in the hint of deadliness that lurks in all actions—often in an understatement that strikes us as flat or banal, but achieves its strong effect from the narrowness of its ironic range. Hrothgar's high hall, Heorot, glitters with gold—but its future destruction in the Heathobard feud is foretold within the first hundred lines of the poem and recalled seven hundred lines later. Hrothgar's brother, Hrothulf, who will be the betrayer of his blood, breaker of loyalty, instigator of civil war in Denmark, usurper, sits enthroned in Heorot with Hrothgar—but an allusion to his future treachery will be taken up later by Queen Wealhtheow's poignant expression of trust and confidence in her brother-in-law. These are two of the lesser digressions. The greater episodes operate in the same way. Hygelac's piracy is frequently referred to after its first mention about a third of the way through the poem.

On that first occasion, a pang of mortality strikes Beowulf as he looks at the splendid neck-ring he has been given by Hrothgar as part of his reward for victory over Grendel. It reminds him of the magic necklace of the fire dwarfs which Hygelac took with him on his last raid. Later, just before Beowulf's own fatal last encounter with the dragon, his own behavior at the time of the raid is recounted—his superhuman feat of swimming back with thirty suits of armor, his punctilious refusal of the throne, his protection of Hygelac's widowed queen and of the rightful heir, the young Heardred, as well as his own final ascent of the throne when Heardred had been killed in fighting against the Swedes. He has fulfilled all that a hero should do—and the audience is intended to have in mind at this moment that heroic as he has been, magnanimous and good, especially by contrast with Hrothulf's behavior in a similar situation, he has now grown old and his end is near. Nor is it only his destruction that the audience is aware to be looming, but the annihilation of the whole Geatish race at the hands of the Swedes, once Beowulf, the protector hero of the Geats, has been taken from them. The poet manages to deal even-handed justice to Beowulf the hero and Beowulf the mortal, exalting him only to deepen the tragedy.

So, too, he throws into relief by example and counter-example the qualities of spirit and action in which the heroic society found its fulfillment, the duties that it enjoined upon its members. The lay that the *scop* (bard) sings in Heorot of the Fight at Finnsburg and the story of the strife between Danes and Heathobards mirror the overriding necessity for vengeance to be taken by a member of the *comitatus* for the killing of the lord—a necessity that justifies dissemblance and treachery, as it overrides any attempt to compose the feud. The power of social obligation is too strong for single human instance: strife and violence, restrained for a time by material or spiritual generosity, hasten the death which is every man's lot. The details of these two stories parallel each other, foreshadowing the strife between Geats and Swedes with its fatal outcome.

These digressions, by which the poet binds his poem together, throwing the reference forward and backward, seem to modern taste to slow the pace. Meditative, moralizing passages from the poet himself, or from such characters as Hrothgar, also deepen the elegiac tone. The language—formalized, traditional, often arranged in elaborately parallel double statement—and the steady dignity of the style keep the movement of the poem deliberate and exalted. To this effect the mode of performance—chanting aloud to the accompaniment of a stringed instrument—must have greatly contributed.

The poetic vocabulary of *Beowulf* is remarkable for the large number of words it contains of the same or very similar meaning—words for "warrior," for example— which could be brought into play according to the demands of expressing a precise meaning or to the more mechanical needs of rhythm and alliteration. Compound nouns and adjectives are also plentiful and are found, like many of the simple words, only in poetry, the more exalted medium than prose: rain-hard, shower-hard, enmity-hard, fire-hard, iron-hard; ring-bestower, battle-flasher (for sword) are examples. They are one way in which the poet sustains the promise of a performance arresting and rich made with the opening word of his poem: "Hwæt!", "Lo!", the formulaic call to silence and attention. Still more characteristic and important are the condensed metaphors (Old English is not rich in the conventional metaphor or simile and has no equivalent of the extended Homeric simile) known as *kennings* (an Old Norse word).

The stateliness of the language, its tonal resources—we must always imagine it as it would have sounded—enhance and justify the slowness of the action and drive home the realization that *Beowulf* is essentially a poem of praise, elegiac only because its hero is human. Its mode is the superlative. Essentially it is a poem in praise of earthly life and the glory that a man may win in it by courage, and magnanimity—*lof* (reputation) is one of its key words—even as he realizes that life is short, passing, and often bitter.

There is no trace of any confidence in a greater triumph, in a life after death, such as raises even the simplest narratives of the passions of saints to a kind of epic level and is characteristic of the literature of Christian heroism. Nevertheless, scholarly opinion agrees to call *Beowulf* a Christian poem in that it was written by a Christian and many parts of it would be intelligible only to a Christian audience— particularly its Christian moralizing and many of its allusions. But given the relatively short time that had elapsed since Christianity had come to Britain, and given the firm structure of social institutions and ethical and religious assumptions already existing, we could hardly expect that a heroic poem of such a time would be permeated with the spirit of the New Testament. *Beowulf* is not a poem of Grace, but of the Law: its morality is nearer that of the Old Testament, partly perhaps because of direct influence, partly owing to a joint participation in the epic genre. All the biblical references that it contains are to the Old Testament. It is the power and glory of God the Creator that move the poet and his characters to joy in the Creation or to at least sporadic recognition of his will as equivalent to Fate, just as they are moved to fear of judgment, to certainty that the souls of giants and monsters, Grendel and his dam, will fall to Hell and the Devil while those of believers will go to God. The bloodthirsty monster Grendel is made the descendant of Cain, the first murderer, and the sword which Beowulf catches up to kill Grendel's mother has its blade decorated with the destruction of the Old Testament giants by the Flood. None of these allusions, nor even the moralizing sermon of Hrothgar, give us any reason to suppose that the poet thought of Beowulf as passing to immortality in a Christian Heaven.

Beowulf is a tragedy, as it must be: a gigantic elegy for its hero in which the moments of glory serve only to emphasize the completeness and inevitability of his end. In its broadest dimension, it is a tragedy of the human predicament: more narrowly, of the warrior's situation. A Germanic hero's fulfillment is not reached in victory alone, but in unflinching courage in all circumstances, most of all when the odds—adversaries, conditions, age, and the rest—are stacked against him and he must die. A glorious death is the only fitting close to a glorious life. We are meant to feel the contrast between Hrothgar, a good king, generous and firm, but now old and lacking the true heroic spirit which would send him out to battle with this enemy of his land (at the beginning of the poem), and Beowulf, Hrothgar's rescuer, who dies in his moment of triumph over the enemy of his people, at the poem's end. The hero knows that his fate has long been decided and he knows it at every moment of his life, with every successive battle. He can only trust, as encounter follows encounter, that his doom is not yet written and that therefore his courage will suffice for one more occasion. These occasions, with the shadow of the human condition lengthening as the hero passes from fierce and aggressive youth to fierce and unyielding old age, are the stuff of the poem.

The poet who produced *Beowulf* and the audience which heard it recited were aristocratic and of considerable literary and artistic cultivation. Of their standard of material culture, the frequent reference to splendor of ornament is witness enough, even if we did not have from the poem's period the masterpieces of Northumbrian stone sculpture and manuscript illumination (Figs. 23, 5), the earlier jewelry and other objects from Sutton Hoo (Figs. 9, 11, 13–17, 19), and the richly decorated metal work of other centers (Figs. 18, 21). We can get some idea, too, of what the musical instrument ment to which the poem was later recited probably looked like—from manuscripts (Fig. 10) and from the present reconstruction of the Sutton Hoo instrument (Fig. 11). Some notion of the arms and armor of the period 650–1050 can be got from surviving fragments and from manuscripts (Figs. 8, 9, 18–21).

Of the level of literary culture little need be added to what has already been said in the General Introduction. Poet and audience may well have known Virgil's *Aeneid* and there are many allusions which would be lost on those unfamiliar with the writings of the Fathers of the Church and the Bible itself. The audience that enjoyed *Beowulf* must have had a considerable body of heroic verse to compare with it, as well as a body of other verse of great skill in the handling of feeling and incident, of the formal, exalted, "distanced" language and the narrow though varied metrical range which are the media of Old English poetry.

The translation used here is by Charles W. Kennedy, and appears below as it was first published in 1940, with the exception of the numbering of lines. The line numbers are not those of the original poem but serve merely as a guide.

I. The Danes (Scyldings; East-, South-, Spear-Danes; Honor-, Victor-Scyldings; Ingwines)

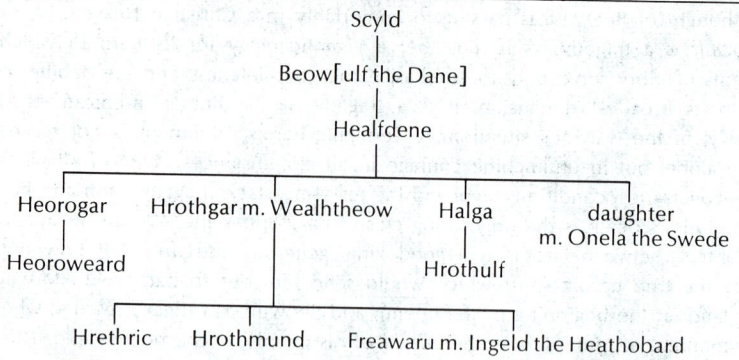

```
                          Scyld
                            |
                    Beow[ulf the Dane]
                            |
                        Healfdene
          ┌──────────┬─────────────┬──────────────┐
      Heorogar   Hrothgar m. Wealhtheow   Halga      daughter
          |                              |        m. Onela the Swede
    Heoroweard                       Hrothulf
          ┌──────────┬──────────────┐
      Hrethric   Hrothmund   Freawaru m. Ingeld the Heathobard
```

II. The Geats (Weders, Sea-Geats; Hrethlings)

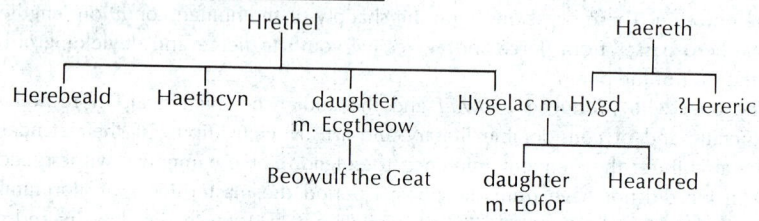

```
                    Hrethel                        Haereth
        ┌──────────┬──────────┬───────────┐    ┌───────────┐
    Herebeald   Haethcyn   daughter    Hygelac m. Hygd    ?Hereric
                         m. Ecgtheow
                            |
                    Beowulf the Geat      daughter    Heardred
                                         m. Eofor
```

III. The Half-Danes and The Frisians

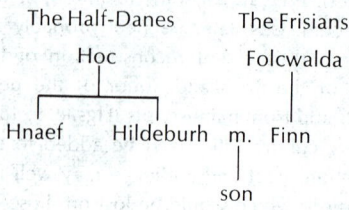

```
        The Half-Danes      The Frisians
            Hoc             Folcwalda
        ┌─────────┐             |
    Hnaef    Hildeburh  m.  Finn
                         |
                        son
```

IV. The Heathobards

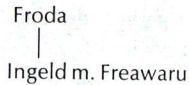

```
            Froda
              |
        Ingeld m. Freawaru
```

V. The Swedes (Scylfings; Battle-Scylfings)

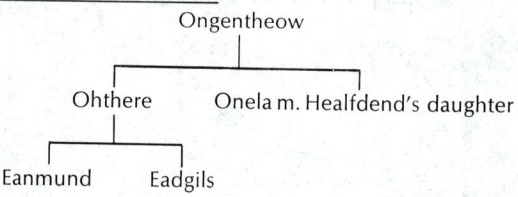

```
                Ongentheow
        ┌───────────┬─────────────┐
    Ohthere    Onela m. Healfdend's daughter
    ┌─────────┐
Eanmund    Eadgils
```

Beowulf

[The Danish Court and the Raids of Grendel]

Lo! we have listened to many a lay
Of the Spear-Danes'° fame, their splendor of old,
Their mighty princes, and martial deeds!
Many a mead-hall° Scyld,° son of Sceaf,
Snatched from the forces of savage foes.
From a friendless foundling, feeble and wretched,
He grew to a terror as time brought change.
He throve under heaven in power and pride
Till alien peoples beyond the ocean
10   Paid toll and tribute. A good king he!

    To him thereafter an heir was born,
A son of his house, whom God had given
As stay to the people; God saw the distress
The leaderless nation had long endured.
The Giver of glory, the Lord of life,
Showered fame on the son of Scyld;
His name was honored, Beowulf° known,
To the farthest dwellings in Danish lands.
So must a young man strive for good
20   With gracious gifts from his father's store,
That in later seasons, if war shall scourge,
A willing people may serve him well.°
'Tis by earning honor a man must rise
In every state. Then his hour struck,
And Scyld passed on to the peace of God.

    As their leader had bidden, whose word was law
In the Scylding° realm which he long had ruled,
His loving comrades carried him down
To the shore of ocean; a ring-prowed ship,°
30   Straining at anchor and sheeted with ice,

Spear-Danes The Danes are given various epithets in the course of the poem—perhaps partly to help out alliteration, partly as an aid to characterization—e.g. Bright-, Half-, Ring-, Spear-, North-, East-, South- and West-Danes. **mead-hall** rather "mead-bench," i.e. he conquered other tribes and took away the symbol of the independence of the chief, the high bench in the hall from which he dispensed gifts and justice
Scyld The arrival and departure of the mysterious Scyld, eponymous hero of the Danes (Scyldings: men of the shield, sons of Scyld), form a prologue to the poem, and Scyld's life is perhaps intended to be a parallel to the career of Beowulf in capsule form. Scyld is well known in Scandinavian tradition: the poet's account of how he came, young, weak, and friendless to the coast of Denmark and founded a mighty dynasty is, however, unique and makes Scyld into a figure frequent in folktale: the apparently poor foundling, whose royalty is revealed by his later deeds (cf. Theseus and Arthur). The poet is also planting at the beginning a sense of the dignity and antiquity of the Danish race, drawing out, by suggestion, its genealogies and at the same time implying that this great and ancient people, in all its strength and power, will be found to be helpless against the attacks of the monster Grendel, against whom only the greater hero from outside, Beowulf, can deliver Hrothgar and his Danes. Beowulf's stature is thus magnified. **Beowulf** not Beowulf the Geat, who is the hero of the poem, but a Danish king whom most now agree to call Beow or Beo, the Dane, grandfather of Hrothgar
So . . . well (ll. 19-22) the first of the poet's moralizing comments, pauses in the motion of the poem, statements of the heroic virtues which its action exemplifies
Scylding Danish
ring-prowed ship It is not quite certain what "ring-prowed" means. Ships were broad, with a tall prow and stern, and of shallow draft, so that they could easily be beached and dragged up on land (Fig. 12).

Rode in the harbor, a prince's pride.
Therein they laid him, their well-loved lord,
Their ring-bestower, in the ship's embrace,°
The mighty prince at the foot of the mast
Amid much treasure and many a gem
From far-off lands. No lordlier ship
Have I ever heard of, with weapons heaped,
With battle-armor, with bills and byrnies.°
On the ruler's breast lay a royal treasure
40 As the ship put out on the unknown deep.
With no less adornment they dressed him round,
Or gift of treasure, than once they gave
Who launched him first on the lonely sea
While still but a child. A golden standard
They raised above him, high over head,
Let the wave take him on trackless seas.
Mournful their mood and heavy their hearts;
Nor wise man nor warrior knows for a truth
Unto what haven that cargo came.
50   Then Beowulf ruled o'er the Scylding realm,
Beloved and famous, for many a year—
The prince, his father, had passed away—
Till, firm in wisdom and fierce in war,
The mighty Healfdene held the reign,
Ruled, while he lived, the lordly Scyldings.
Four sons and daughters were seed of his line,
Heorogar and Hrothgar, leaders of hosts,
And Halga, the good. I have also heard
A daughter was Onela's consort° and queen,
60 The fair bed-mate of the Battle-Scylfing.
      To Hrothgar was granted glory in war,
Success in battle; retainers bold
Obeyed him gladly; his band increased
To a mighty host. Then his mind was moved
To have men fashion a high-built hall,
A mightier mead-hall than man had known,
Wherein to portion to old and young
All goodly treasure that God had given,
Save only the folk-land,° and lives of men.°

---

ship's embrace The sea burial of Scyld reflects earlier pagan Scandinavian practice, but by the time *Beowulf* was written ship burials on land, with the dead chieftain surrounded by rich possessions and a barrow, or burial-mound, heaped above, were common.
bills and byrnies swords and coats of ring-mail
Onela's consort The text being defective at this point we can only conjecture that Onela the Swede is referred to, and we are not given the name of Healfdene's daughter, Onela's wife.

Onela was son of Ongentheow (ll. 2750 ff.), His nephews Eadgils and Eanmund rebelled against him (ll. 2466 ff.) and took refuge at the Geatish court. Onela pursued them there and killed the young Geatish king Heardred. Eanmund was also killed. Later, Beowulf helps Eadgils in a punitive expedition against Onela, who is slain (ll. 2261 ff.).
folk-land public common land, which Germanic law gave by inalienable right to be held by the community at large for grazing
men i.e. men's bodies; the reference is unclear

70 His word was published to many a people
  Far and wide o'er the ways of earth
  To rear a folk-stead richly adorned;
  The task was speeded, the time soon came
  That the famous mead-hall was finished and done.
  To distant nations its name was known,
  The Hall of the Hart;° and the king kept well
  His pledge and promise to deal out gifts,
  Rings at the banquet. The great hall rose
  High and horn-gabled,° holding its place
80 Till the battle-surge of consuming flame
  Should swallow it up; the hour was near
  That the deadly hate of a daughter's husband
  Should kindle to fury and savage feud.°

   Then an evil spirit who dwelt in the darkness
  Endured it ill that he heard each day
  The din of revelry ring through the hall,
  The sound of the harp, and the scop's° sweet song.
  A skillful bard sang the ancient story
  Of man's creation;° how the Maker wrought
90 The shining earth with its circling waters;
  In splendor established the sun and moon
  As lights to illumine the land of men;
  Fairly adorning the fields of earth
  With leaves and branches; creating life
  In every creature that breathes and moves.
  So the lordly warriors lived in gladness,
  At ease and happy, till a fiend from hell
  Began a series of savage crimes.
  They called him Grendel, a demon grim
100 Haunting the fen-lands, holding the moors,
  Ranging the wastes, where the wretched wight
  Made his lair with the monster kin;
  He bore the curse of the seed of Cain°
  Whereby God punished the grievous guilt
  Of Abel's murder. Nor ever had Cain

Hart Heorot, probably situated near modern Lejre, on the north coast of Zealand, not far from Roskilde, the ancient seat of Danish kingship. The royalty of the hall is emphasized by its name, Hart or Stag, a symbol of kingship—see the stag on the Sutton Hoo scepter (Fig. 17).
horn-gabled rather "wide-gabled"
consuming flame . . . feud (ll. 80–83) Heorot stood until it was burned to the ground, probably during an attack by Ingeld, king of the Heathobards, on Hrothgar, which the poet later describes (ll. 1893 ff). The poet is using his characteristic device of "tragic anticipation" for an audience already familiar with the story: the contrast is made between the present mag-

nificence of Hrothgar's mead-hall and its later fate.
scop's the singer of tales, the bard chanting stories in verse at the feast to the sound of the harp
creation i.e. all created good (cf. "Cædmon's Hymn"), and man, sinless and perfect.
seed of Cain The first murderer—Genesis 4:8 ff. The giant race before Noah's flood (Genesis 6:4) is taken by the Biblical commentators, from very early times, to be not merely strong but also cruel and cunning—cf. Genesis 6:5: "And God saw that the wickedness of man was great in the earth." The giants were thought to spring from the union of the descendants of Cain the wrongdoer with the descendants of the righteous Seth.

Cause to boast of that deed of blood;
God banished him far from the fields of men;
Of his blood was begotten an evil brood,
Marauding monsters and menacing trolls,
110   Goblins and giants who battled with God
A long time. Grimly He gave them reward!
     Then at the nightfall the fiend drew near
Where the timbered mead-hall towered on high,
To spy how the Danes fared after the feast.
Within the wine-hall he found the warriors
Fast in slumber,° forgetting grief,
Forgetting the woe of the world of men.
Grim and greedy the gruesome monster,
Fierce and furious, launched attack,
120   Slew thirty spearmen asleep in the hall,
Sped away gloating, gripping the spoil,
Dragging the dead men home to his den.
Then in the dawn with the coming of daybreak
The war-might of Grendel was widely known.
Mirth was stilled by the sound of weeping;
The wail of the mourner awoke with day.
And the peerless hero, the honored prince,
Weighed down with woe and heavy of heart,
Sat sorely grieving for slaughtered thanes,
130   As they traced the track of the cursed monster.
From that day onward the deadly feud
Was a long-enduring and loathsome strife.
     Not longer was it than one night later
The fiend returning renewed attack
With heart firm-fixed in the hateful war,
Feeling no rue for the grievous wrong.
'Twas easy thereafter to mark the men
Who sought their slumber elsewhere afar,
Found beds in the bowers,° since Grendel's hate
140   Was so baldly blazoned in baleful signs.
He held himself at a safer distance
Who escaped the clutch of the demon's claw.
So Grendel raided and ravaged the realm,
One against all, in an evil war
Till the best of buildings was empty and still.
'Twas a weary while! Twelve winters' time
The lord of the Scyldings had suffered woe,
Sore affliction and deep distress.

---

slumber The mead-hall was the place of honor and of communal living for the lord's close companions, the *comitatus*, who also slept there. This was a mark of the lord's generous hospitality and of the companions' acceptance of their honorable vassalage.
bowers the small separate rooms elsewhere in the building complex rather than the central hall

And the malice of Grendel, in mournful lays,
150   Was widely sung by the sons of men,
The hateful feud that he fought with Hrothgar—
Year after year of struggle and strife,
An endless scourging, a scorning of peace
With any man of the Danish might.
No strength could move him to stay his hand,
Or pay for his murders;° the wise knew well
They could hope for no halting of savage assault.
Like a dark death-shadow° the ravaging demon,
Night-long prowling the misty moors,
160   Ensnared the warriors, wary or weak.
No man can say how these shades of hell
Come and go on their grisly rounds.
     With many an outrage, many a crime,
The fierce lone-goer, the foe of man,
Stained the seats of the high-built house,
Haunting the hall in the hateful dark.
But throne or treasure he might not touch,
Finding no favor or grace with God.°
Great was the grief of the Scylding leader,
170   His spirit shaken, while many a lord
Gathered in council considering long
In what way brave men best could struggle
Against these terrors of sudden attack.
From time to time in their heathen temples
Paying homage they offered prayer
That the Slayer of souls° would send them succor
From all the torment that troubled the folk.
Such was the fashion and such the faith
Of their heathen hearts that they looked to hell,
180   Not knowing the Maker, the mighty Judge,
Nor how to worship the Wielder of glory,
The Lord of heaven, the God of hosts.
Woe unto him who in fierce affliction
Shall plunge his soul in the fiery pit
With no hope of mercy or healing change;
But well with the soul that at death seeks God,
And finds his peace in his Father's bosom.
     The son of Healfdene° was heavy-hearted,
Sorrowfully brooding in sore distress,

---

pay . . . murders i.e. pay *wergild*, lit., "man-money," the money payment which Germanic law prescribed for a killer to buy peace from the dead man's family; payable only for the life of a free man, it varied according to the social status of the victim
death-shadow The word is used elsewhere of Satan, but Grendel throughout preys on bodies,

not, like the Devil (l. 176), on souls.
Finding . . . God The sense is difficult, but seems to apply to Grendel and mean that, since he does not obey the laws of God or of man he cannot share in either human or divine gifts.
Slayer of souls the Devil. The Danes are here pointedly thought of as pagan idolaters.
son of Healfdene Hrothgar

190 Finding no help in a hopeless strife;
Too bitter the struggle that stunned the people,
The long oppression, loathsome and grim.

[*The Coming of Beowulf*]
Then tales of the terrible deeds of Grendel
Reached Hygelac's thane° in his home with the Geats;
Of living strong men he was the strongest,
Fearless and gallant and great of heart.°
He gave command for a goodly vessel
Fitted and furnished; he fain would sail
Over the swan-road to seek the king
200 Who suffered so sorely for need of men.
And his bold retainers found little to blame
In his daring venture, dear though he was;
They viewed the omens, and urged him on.
Brave was the band he had gathered about him,
Fourteen stalwarts seasoned and bold,
Seeking the shore where the ship lay waiting,
A sea-skilled mariner sighting the landmarks.
Came the hour of boarding; the boat was riding
The waves of the harbor under the hill.
210 The eager mariners mounted the prow;
Billows were breaking, sea against sand.
In the ship's hold snugly they stowed their trappings,
Gleaming armor and battle-gear;
Launched the vessel, the well-braced bark,
Seaward bound on a joyous journey.
Over breaking billows, with bellying sail
And foamy beak, like a flying bird
The ship sped on, till the next day's sun
Showed sea-cliffs shining, towering hills
220 And stretching headlands. The sea was crossed,
The voyage ended, the vessel moored.
And the Weder° people waded ashore
With clatter of trappings and coats of mail;
Gave thanks to God that His grace had granted
Sea-paths safe for their ocean-journey.
       Then the Scylding coast-guard watched from the sea-cliff
Warriors bearing their shining shields,
Their gleaming war-gear, ashore from the ship.
His mind was puzzled, he wondered much
230 What men they were. On his good horse mounted,

Hygelac's thane Beowulf the Geat, hero of the poem. The word "thane," originally meaning "servant," by this time meant "a royal vassal of some consequence." Beowulf was bound to Hygelac by his obligation both as a companion and as an especially close kinsman. He was Hygelac's sister's son and would therefore be regarded as in a special relationship with his uncle.
Of living . . . heart For the poet, Beowulf's heroic magnanimity is sufficient reason for his going to Hrothgar's help.
Weder Weder-Geats or "Storm-loving" Geats—Beowulf's people

Hrothgar's thane made haste to the beach,
Boldly brandished his mighty spear
With manful challenge: 'What men are you,
Carrying weapons and clad in steel,
Who thus come driving across the deep
On the ocean-lanes in your lofty ship?
Long have I served as the Scylding outpost,
Held watch and ward at the ocean's edge
Lest foreign foemen with hostile fleet
240   Should come to harry our Danish home,
And never more openly sailed to these shores
Men without password, or leave to land.
I have never laid eyes upon earl on earth
More stalwart and sturdy than one of your troop,
A hero in armor; no hall-thane° he
Tricked out with weapons, unless looks belie him,
And noble bearing. But now I must know
Your birth and breeding, nor may you come
In cunning stealth upon Danish soil.
250   You distant-dwellers, you far sea-farers,
Hearken, and ponder words that are plain:
'Tis best you hasten to have me know
Who your kindred and whence you come.'
       The lord of the seamen gave swift reply,
The prince of the Weders unlocked his word-hoard:
'We are sprung of a strain of the Geatish stock,
Hygelac's comrades and hearth-companions.°
My father was famous in many a folk-land,
A leader noble, Ecgtheow° his name!
260   Many a winter went over his head
Before death took him from home and tribe;
Well nigh every wise man remembers him well
Far and wide on the ways of earth.
With loyal purpose we seek your lord,
The prince of your people, great Healfdene's son.
Be kindly of counsel; weighty the cause
That leads us to visit the lord of the Danes;
Nor need it be secret, as far as I know!
You know if it's true, as we've heard it told,
270   That among the Scyldings some secret scather,
Some stealthy demon in dead of night,
With grisly horror and fiendish hate
Is spreading unheard-of havoc and death.
Mayhap I can counsel the good, old king
What way he can master the merciless fiend,

---

no hall-thane i.e. not merely splendid-looking on ceremonial occasions, but tough and powerful in battle

hearth-companions the *heorthwerod*, the close companions of the lord
Ecgtheow Nothing is known of Beowulf's father.

If his coil of evil is ever to end
And feverish care grow cooler and fade—
Or else ever after his doom shall be
Distress and sorrow while still there stands
280   This best of halls on its lofty height.'
     Then from the saddle the coast-guard spoke,
The fearless sentry: 'A seasoned° warrior
Must know the difference between words and deeds,
If his wits are with him. I take your word
That your band is loyal° to the lord of the Scyldings.
Now go your way with your weapons and armor,
And I will guide you; I'll give command
That my good retainers may guard your ship,
Your fresh-tarred floater, from every foe,
290   And hold it safe in its sandy berth,
Till the curving prow once again shall carry
The loved man home to the land of the Geat.
To hero so gallant shall surely be granted
To come from the swordplay sound and safe.'
     Then the Geats marched on; behind at her mooring,
Fastened at anchor, their broad-beamed boat
Safely rode on her swinging cable.
Boar-heads° glittered on glistening helmets
Above their cheek-guards, gleaming with gold;
300   Bright and fire-hardened the boar held watch
Over the column of marching men.
Onward they hurried in eager haste
Till their eyes caught sight of the high-built hall,
Splendid with gold, the seat of the king,
Most stately of structures under the sun;
Its light shone out over many a land.
The coast-guard showed them the shining hall,
The home of heroes; made plain the path;
Turned his horse; gave tongue to words:
310   'It is time to leave you! The mighty Lord
In His mercy shield you and hold you safe
In your bold adventure. I'll back to the sea
And hold my watch against hostile horde.'

    [*Beowulf's Welcome at Hrothgar's Court*]
The street had paving of colored stone;
The path was plain to the marching men.
Bright were their byrnies, hard and hand-linked;
In their shining armor the chain-mail sang

---

seasoned *scearp*, more likely "acute, keen-witted." The sentry is courteously apologizing for his challenge.
loyal friendly
Boar-heads images of boars placed on Germanic helmets as a protection to the wearers in the material sense—giving extra protection against a blow at the head or upper part of the face—and to invoke the strength and cunning of the boar for the wearer

As the troop in their war-gear tramped to the hall.
The sea-weary sailors set down their shields,
320 Their wide, bright bucklers along the wall,
And sank to the bench. Their byrnies rang.
Their stout spears stood in a stack together
Shod with iron and shaped of ash.
'Twas a well-armed troop! Then a stately warrior°
Questioned the strangers about their kin:
'Whence come you bearing your burnished shields,
Your steel-gray harness and visored helms,
Your heap of spears? I am Hrothgar's herald,
His servant-thane. I have never seen strangers,
330 So great a number, of nobler mien.
Not exiles,° I ween, but high-minded° heroes
In greatness of heart have you sought out Hrothgar.'
Then bold under helmet the hero made answer,
The lord of the Weders, manful of mood,°
Mighty of heart: 'We are Hygelac's men,
His board-companions; Beowulf is my name.
I will state my mission to Healfdene's son,
The noble leader, your lordly prince,
If he will grant approach to his gracious presence.'
340 And Wulfgar answered, the Wendel° prince,
Renowned for merit° in many a land,
For war-might and wisdom: 'I will learn the wish
Of the Scylding leader, the lord of the Danes,
Our honored ruler and giver of rings,
Concerning your mission, and soon report
The answer our leader thinks good to give.'
        He swiftly strode to where Hrothgar sat
Old and gray with his earls about him;
Crossed the floor and stood face to face
350 With the Danish king; he knew courtly custom.°
Wulfgar saluted his lord and friend:°
'Men from afar have fared to our land
Over ocean's margin—men of the Geats,
Their leader called Beowulf—seeking a boon,
The holding of parley, my prince, with thee.
O gracious Hrothgar, refuse not the favor!

stately warrior a proud-hearted and haughty—rather than stately—warrior, who is later named as Wulfgar
exiles i.e. you do not come seeking a new lord and protector because you have lost or been dismissed by your old one; cf. "The Wanderer" below
high-minded brave
mood mind, heart
Wulfgar . . . Wendel perhaps a Vandal, but more likely a man from Vendel in Sweden or Vendill in Jutland, Denmark (where the Vandals may have left pockets of settlement); he is a foreign prince serving Hrothgar—like Beowulf, and recognizing the likeness—from heroic magnanimity and love of adventure, not from necessity
merit courage
courtly custom the usage of the *comitatus*
friend This emphasizes the close but not carefully defined nature of the relationship. The obligations of allegiance and friendship are the ties that bind lord and man together, not, as in the later feudal system, a more exactly set-out complex of legal obligation.

In their splendid war-gear they merit well
The esteem of earls;° he's a stalwart leader
Who led this troop to the land of the Danes.'
360   Hrothgar spoke, the lord of the Scyldings:
'Their leader I knew when he still was a lad.
His father was Ecgtheow; Hrethel° the Geat
Gave him° in wedlock his only daughter.
Now is their son come, keen for adventure,
Finding his way to a faithful friend.
Sea-faring men who have voyaged to Geatland
With gifts of treasure° as token of peace,
Say that his hand-grip has thirty men's strength.
God, in His mercy, has sent him to save us—
370 So springs my hope—from Grendel's assaults.
For his gallant courage I'll load him with gifts!
Make haste now, marshal the men to the hall,
And give them welcome to Danish ground.'
      Then to the door went the well-known warrior,°
Spoke from the threshold welcoming words:
'The Danish leader, my lord, declares
That he knows your kinship; right welcome you come,
You stout sea-rovers, to Danish soil.
Enter now, in your shining armor
380 And vizored helmets, to Hrothgar's hall.
But leave your shields and the shafts of slaughter
To wait the issue and weighing of words.'
      Then the bold one rose with his band around him,
A splendid massing of mighty thanes;
A few stood guard as the Geat gave bidding
Over the weapons stacked by the wall.
They followed in haste on the heels of their leader
Under Heorot's roof. Full ready and bold
The helmeted warrior strode to the hearth;°
390 Beowulf spoke; his byrny glittered,
His war-net woven by cunning of smith:
'Hail! King Hrothgar! I am Hygelac's thane,
Hygelac's kinsman. Many a deed
Of honor and daring I've done in my youth.
This business of Grendel was brought to my ears
On my native soil. The sea-farers say
This best of buildings, this boasted hall,
Stands dark and deserted when sun is set,

---

earls originally men of the higher class of
society; later use, in poetry, gives it the sense
of "warriors"
Hrethel king of the Geats, father of Hygelac,
grandfather of Beowulf
him Ecgtheow, Beowulf's father
gifts of treasure The giving of gifts to followers

and to equals was the obligation and the pleasure of Germanic chieftains, see Tacitus, *Germania*, 15.
warrior Wulfgar
strode . . . hearth rather "took up his stand
inside the hall"

When darkening shadows gather with dusk.
400   The best of my people, prudent and brave,
Urged me, King Hrothgar, to seek you out;
They had in remembrance my courage and might.
Many had seen me come safe from the conflict,
Bloody from battle; five foes I bound
Of the giant kindred, and crushed their clan.
Hard-driven in danger and darkness of night
I slew the nicors° that swam the sea,
Avenged the woe they had caused the Weders,
And ended their evil—they needed the lesson!
410   And now with Grendel, the fearful fiend,
Single-handed I'll settle the strife!
Prince of the Danes, protector of Scyldings,
Lord of nations, and leader of men,
I beg one favor—refuse me not,
Since I come thus faring from far-off lands—
That I may alone with my loyal earls,
With this hardy company, cleanse Hart-Hall.
I have heard that the demon in proud disdain
Spurns all weapons; and I too scorn—
420   May Hygelac's heart have joy of the deed—
To bear my sword, or sheltering shield,
Or yellow buckler, to battle the fiend.
With hand-grip only I'll grapple with Grendel;
Foe against foe I'll fight to the death,
And the one who is taken must trust to God's grace!
The demon, I doubt not, is minded to feast
In the hall unaffrighted, as often before,
On the force of the Hrethmen,° the folk of the Geats.
No need then to bury the body he mangles!
430   If death shall call me, he'll carry away
My gory flesh to his fen-retreat
To gorge at leisure and gulp me down,
Soiling the marshes with stains of blood.
There'll be little need longer to care for my body!
If the battle slays me, to Hygelac send
This best of corselets that covers my breast,
Heirloom of Hrethel, and Wayland's work,°
Finest of byrnies. Fate goes as Fate must!'
      Hrothgar spoke, the lord of the Scyldings:
440   'Deed of daring and dream of honor
Bring you, friend Beowulf, knowing our need!
Your father once fought the greatest of feuds,

---

nicors water monsters
Hrethmen Perhaps a name for the Geats; it may not be a proper name at all but a compound noun meaning "glorious warriors."
Wayland's work i.e. a mail-shirt which is both ancient and excellent. Wayland or Weland, the cunning smith of the gods in Germanic legend, was a magician in his own right; see "Deor's Lament" below.

Laid Heatholaf° low, of the Wylfing line;°
And the folk of the Weders refused him shelter
For fear of revenge.° Then he fled to the South-Danes,
The Honor-Scyldings beyond the sea.
I was then first governing Danish ground,
As a young lad ruling the spacious realm,
The home-land of warriors. Heorogar° was dead,
450   The son of Healfdene no longer living,
My older brother, and better than I!
Thereafter by payment composing the feud,
O'er the water's ridge I sent to the Wylfing
Ancient treasure; he° swore me oaths!
It is sorrow sore to recite to another
The wrongs that Grendel has wrought in the hall,
His savage hatred and sudden assaults.
My war-troop is weakened, my hall-band is wasted;
Fate swept them away into Grendel's grip.
460   But God may easily bring to an end
The ruinous deeds of the ravaging foe.
Full often my warriors over their ale-cups
Boldly boasted,° when drunk with beer,
They would bide in the beer-hall the coming of battle,
The fury of Grendel, with flashing swords.
Then in the dawn, when the daylight strengthened,
The hall stood reddened and reeking with gore,
Bench-boards wet with the blood of battle;
And I had the fewer of faithful fighters,
470   Beloved retainers, whom Death had taken.
Sit now at the banquet, unbend your mood,
Speak of great deeds as your heart may spur you!'
    Then in the beer-hall were benches made ready
For the Geatish heroes. Noble of heart,
Proud and stalwart, they sat them down
And a beer-thane° served them; bore in his hands
The patterned ale-cup, pouring the mead,°
While the scop's sweet singing was heard in the hall.
There was joy of heroes, a host at ease,
480   A welcome meeting of Weder and Dane.

Heatholaf not otherwise known
Wylfing line lit. "Wolves' sons"—Germanic tribe which lived on the southern shores of the Baltic
revenge i.e. Ecgtheow could not pay the necessary *wergild*, so that Heatholaf's people would have the obligation to take revenge; fear of this caused the Geats to refuse Beowulf's father leave to stay with them.
Heorogar Danish king, elder brother of Hrothgar
he Ecgtheow; Hrothgar had composed the feud by sending ancient prized treasure to the Wylfings, and Ecgtheow presumably swore an oath of friendship and good conduct.
boasted formal boasting, especially of future exploits, protestations of what would be done; a prominent feature of Germanic warriors' feasting
beer-thane the cup-bearer, the butler of later chivalric society—an important person in the household of the chieftain
mead a drink made from fermented honey; but the Old English word used here means literally "sweet drink," which may be beer

[*Unferth Taunts Beowulf*]
Then out spoke Unferth,° Ecglaf's son,
Who sat at the feet of the Scylding lord,
Picking a quarrel—for Beowulf's quest,
His bold sea-voyaging, irked him sore;
He bore it ill that any man other
In all the earth should ever achieve
More fame under heaven than he himself:
'Are you the Beowulf that strove with Breca°
In a swimming match in the open sea,
490　Both of you wantonly tempting the waves,
Risking your lives on the lonely deep
For a silly boast? No man could dissuade you,
Nor friend nor foe, from the foolhardy venture
Of ocean-swimming; with outstretched arms
You clasped the sea-stream, measured her streets,
With plowing shoulders parted the waves.
The sea-flood boiled with its wintry surges,
Seven nights you toiled in the tossing sea;
His strength was the greater, his swimming the stronger!
500　The waves upbore you at break of day
To the stretching beach of the Battle-Ræmas;°
And Breca departed, beloved of his people,
To the land of the Brondings, the beauteous home,
The stronghold fair, where he governed the folk,
The city and treasure; Beanstan's son°
Made good his boast to the full against you!
Therefore, I ween, worse fate shall befall,
Stout as you are in the struggle of war,
In deeds of battle, if you dare to abide
510　Encounter with Grendel at coming of night.'
　　　Beowulf spoke, the son of Ecgtheow:
'My good friend Unferth, addled with beer
Much have you made of the deeds of Breca!
I count it true that I had more courage,
More strength in swimming than any other man.
In our youth we boasted—we were both of us boys—
We would risk our lives in the raging sea.
And we made it good! We gripped in our hands
Naked swords, as we swam in the waves,
520　Guarding us well from the whales' assault.
In the breaking seas he could not outstrip me,

Unferth Hrothgar's courtier, a type of the "wicked counsellor," sets out to mock Beowulf, but is put down by the hero. His name means "Peace-spoiler" and he here tries to cast doubt on Beowulf's ability to deal with Grendel. **Breca** Tales of swimming matches and other such trials of strength occur in later Germanic literature: they usually involve endurance rather than speed. Breca's name may mean "rush, storm": he is known from other Germanic myths. His people, the Brondings, are not. **Battle-Ræmas** Heatho-Ræmas, a tribe living in Norway, north of modern Oslo **Beanstan's son** Breca

Nor would I leave him. For five nights long
Side by side we strove in the waters
Till racing combers wrenched us apart,
Freezing squalls, and the falling night,
And a bitter north wind's icy blast.
Rough were the waves; the wrath of the sea-fish
Was fiercely roused; but my firm-linked byrny,
The gold-adorned corselet that covered my breast,
530   Gave firm defense from the clutching foe.
Down to the bottom a savage sea-beast
Fiercely dragged me and held me fast
In a deadly grip; none the less it was granted me
To pierce the monster with point of steel.
Death swept it away with the swing of my sword.
    The grisly sea-beasts again and again
Beset me sore; but I served them home
With my faithful blade as was well-befitting.
They failed of their pleasure to feast their fill
540   Crowding round my corpse on the ocean-bottom!
Bloody with wounds, at the break of day,
They lay on the sea-beach slain with the sword.
No more would they cumber the mariner's course
On the ocean deep. From the east came the sun,
Bright beacon of God, and the seas subsided;
I beheld the headlands, the windy walls.
Fate often delivers an undoomed earl°
If his spirit be gallant! And so I was granted
To slay with the sword-edge nine of the nicors.
550   I have never heard tell of more terrible strife
Under dome of heaven in darkness of night,
Nor of man harder pressed on the paths of ocean.
But I freed my life from the grip of the foe
Though spent with the struggle. The billows bore me,
The swirling currents and surging seas,
To the land of the Finns.° And little I've heard
Of any such valiant adventures from you!
Neither Breca nor you in the press of battle
Ever showed such daring with dripping swords—
560   Though I boast not of it! But you stained your blade
With blood of your brothers,° your closest of kin;

Fate . . . undoomed earl i.e. a warrior not singled out for death by Fate. Fortune favors the
brave, but only as Fate preordains: Fate is inescapable. This concept permeates the entire poem.
It is typically pagan Germanic and especially
typical of Old English poetry.
land of the Finns often identified with Finn-
marken, in northern Norway, but probably the
territory of the Lapps (frequently called Finns
in Old English poetry) in southwest Sweden
you stained . . . brothers Beowulf turns Un-

ferth's taunts in a devastating way: if this
Danish spokesman is a boaster and a fratricide,
Grendel has nothing to fear from the people he
represents. Unferth might have retorted that his
fratricide was the result of the *comitatus* system,
where a brother serving one lord might have to
fulfill his obligation to that lord by killing a
brother serving another. But the blood-tie was
always very strong—and the poet leaves Beowulf in possession of the field.

And for that you'll endure damnation in hell,
Sharp° as you are! I say for a truth,
Son of Ecglaf, never had Grendel
Wrought such havoc and woe in the hall,
That horrid demon so harried your king,
If your heart were as brave as you'd have men think!
But Grendel has found that he never need fear
Revenge from your people, or valiant attack
570   From the Victor-Scyldings; he takes his toll,
Sparing none of the Danish stock.
He slays and slaughters and works his will
Fearing no hurt at the hands of the Danes!
But soon will I show him the stuff of the Geats,
Their courage in battle and strength in the strife;
Then let him who may go bold to the mead-hall
When the next day dawns on the dwellings of men,
And the sun in splendor shines warm from the south.'
Glad of heart was the giver of treasure,
580   Hoary-headed and hardy in war;
The lordly leader had hope of help
As he listened to Beowulf's bold resolve.
          There was revel of heroes and high carouse,
Their speech was happy; and Hrothgar's queen,
Of gentle manners, in jewelled splendor
Gave courtly greeting° to all the guests.
The high-born lady first bore the beaker
To the Danish leader, lord of the land,
Bade him be blithe at the drinking of beer;
590   Beloved of his people, the peerless king
Joined in the feasting, had joy of the cup.
Then to all alike went the Helming° lady
Bearing the beaker to old and young,
Till the jewelled queen with courtly grace
Paused before Beowulf, proffered the mead.
She greeted the Geat and to God gave thanks,
Wise of word, that her wish was granted;
At last she could look to a hero for help,
Comfort in evil. He took the cup,
600   The hardy warrior, at Wealhtheow's hand
And, eager for battle, uttered his boast;
Beowulf spoke, the son of Ecgtheow:
'I had firm resolve when I set to sea
With my band of earls in my ocean-ship,
Fully to work the will of your people

---

sharp keen-witted
courtly greeting The Queen's social graces are
emphasized: she knows what is due to each
person according to his rank and attainments.

Helming the ruling family of the Wylfings—of
which Helm was the founder—to which Hrothgar's queen, Wealhtheow, belongs

Or fall in the struggle slain by the foe.
I shall either perform deeds fitting an earl
Or meet in this mead-hall the coming of death!'
Then the woman was pleased with the words he uttered,
610   The Geat-lord's boast; the gold-decked queen
Went in state to sit by her lord.

[*Beowulf Slays Grendel*]
In the hall as of old were brave words spoken,
There was noise of revel; happy the host
Till the son of Healfdene would go to his rest.
He knew that the monster would meet in the hall
Relentless struggle when light of the sun
Was dusky with gloom of the gathering night,
And shadow-shapes crept in the covering dark,
Dim under heaven. The host arose.
620   Hrothgar graciously greeted his guest,
Gave rule of the wine-hall, and wished him well,
Praised the warrior in parting words:
'Never to any man, early or late,
Since first I could brandish buckler and sword,
Have I trusted this ale-hall save only to you!
Be mindful of glory, show forth your strength,
Keep watch against foe! No wish of your heart
Shall go unfulfilled if you live through the fight.'
Then Hrothgar withdrew with his host of retainers,
630   The prince of the Scyldings, seeking his queen,
The bed of his consort. The King of Glory
Had stablished a hall-watch, a guard against Grendel,
Dutifully serving the Danish lord,
The land defending from loathsome fiend.
The Geatish hero put all his hope
In his fearless might and the mercy of God!
He stripped from his shoulders the byrny of steel,
Doffed helmet from head; into hand of thane
Gave inlaid° iron, the best of blades;
640   Bade him keep well the weapons of war.
Beowulf uttered a gallant boast,
The stalwart Geat, ere he sought his bed:
'I count myself nowise weaker in war
Or grapple of battle than Grendel himself.
Therefore I scorn to slay him with sword,
Deal deadly wound, as I well might do!
Nothing he knows of a noble fighting,
Of thrusting and hewing and hacking of shield,
Fierce as he is in the fury of war.

inlaid "engraved," "patterned"; the reference
is not necessarily to the blade, but may be to
hilt or pommel

650 In the shades of darkness we'll spurn the sword
If he dares without weapon to do or to die.
And God in His wisdom shall glory assign,
The ruling Lord, as He deems it right.'
Then the bold in battle bowed down to his rest,
Cheek pressed pillow; the peerless thanes
Were stretched in slumber around their lord.
Not one had hope of return to his home,
To the stronghold or land where he lived as a boy.
For they knew how death had befallen the Danes,
660 How many were slain as they slept in the wine-hall.
But the wise Lord wove them fortune in war,
Gave strong support to the Weder people;
They slew their foe by the single strength
Of a hero's courage. The truth is clear,
God rules forever the race of men.
  Then through the shades of enshrouding night
The fiend came stealing; the archers slept
Whose duty was holding the horn-decked hall—
Though one was watching—full well they knew
670 No evil demon could drag them down
To shades under ground if God were not willing.°
But the hero watched awaiting the foe,
Abiding in anger the issue of war.
  From the stretching moors, from the misty hollows,
Grendel came creeping, accursed of God,
A murderous ravager minded to snare
Spoil of heroes in high-built hall.
Under clouded heavens he held his way
Till there rose before him the high-roofed house,
680 Wine-hall of warriors gleaming with gold.
Nor was it the first of his fierce assaults
On the home of Hrothgar; but never before
Had he found worse fate or hardier hall-thanes!
Storming the building he burst the portal,
Though fastened of iron, with fiendish strength;
Forced open the entrance in savage fury
And rushed in rage o'er the shining floor.
A baleful glare from his eyes was gleaming
Most like to a flame. He found in the hall
690 Many a warrior sealed in slumber,
A host of kinsmen. His heart rejoiced;
The savage monster was minded to sever
Lives from bodies ere break of day,
To feast his fill of the flesh of men.
But he was not fated to glut his greed

God . . . willing Here it is God, not Fate, who
has pre-decided the issue.

With more of mankind when the night was ended!
   The hardy kinsman of Hygelac waited
To see how the monster would make his attack.
The demon delayed not, but quickly clutched
700 A sleeping thane in his swift assault,
Tore him in pieces, bit through the bones,
Gulped the blood, and gobbled the flesh,
Greedily gorged on the lifeless corpse,
The hands and the feet. Then the fiend stepped nearer,
Sprang on the Sea-Geat lying outstretched,
Clasping him close with his monstrous claw.
But Beowulf grappled and gripped him hard,
Struggled up on his elbow; the shepherd of sins
Soon found that never before had he felt
710 In any man other in all the earth
A mightier hand-grip; his mood was humbled,
His courage fled; but he found no escape!
He was fain to be gone; he would flee to the darkness,
The fellowship of devils. Far different his fate
From that which befell him in former days!
The hardy hero, Hygelac's kinsman,
Remembered the boast he had made at the banquet;
He sprang to his feet, clutched Grendel fast,
Though fingers were cracking, the fiend pulling free.
720 The earl pressed after; the monster was minded
To win his freedom and flee to the fens.
He knew that his fingers were fast in the grip
Of a savage foe. Sorry the venture,
The raid that the ravager made on the hall.
   There was din in Heorot. For all the Danes,
The city-dwellers, the stalwart Scyldings,
That was a bitter spilling of beer!°
The walls resounded, the fight was fierce,
Savage the strife as the warriors struggled.
730 The wonder was that the lofty wine-hall
Withstood the struggle, nor crashed to earth,
The house so fair; it was firmly fastened
Within and without with iron bands
Cunningly smithied; though men have said
That many a mead-bench gleaming with gold
Sprang from its sill as the warriors strove.
The Scylding wise men had never weened
That any ravage could wreck the building,
Firmly fashioned and finished with bone,
740 Or any cunning° compass its fall,

---

bitter . . . beer the characteristic Old English
grimly allusive poetic understatement: i.e. that
was no feast, such as the hall had been built
for

cunning skill

Till the time when the swelter and surge of fire
Should swallow it up in a swirl of flame.
    Continuous tumult filled the hall;
A terror fell on the Danish folk
As they heard through the wall the horrible wailing,
The groans of Grendel, the foe of God
Howling his hideous hymn of pain,
The hell-thane shrieking in sore defeat.
He was fast in the grip of the man who was greatest
750 Of mortal men in the strength of his might,
Who would never rest while the wretch was living,
Counting his life-days a menace to man.
    Many an earl of Beowulf brandished
His ancient iron° to guard his lord,
To shelter safely the peerless prince.
They had no knowledge, those daring thanes,
When they drew their weapons to hack and hew,
To thrust to the heart, that the sharpest sword,
The choicest iron in all the world,
760 Could work no harm to the hideous foe.
On every sword he had laid a spell,
On every blade; but a bitter death
Was to be his fate; far was the journey
The monster made to the home of fiends.
    Then he who had wrought such wrong to men,
With grim delight as he warred with God,
Soon found that his strength was feeble and failing
In the crushing hold of Hygelac's thane.
Each loathed the other while life should last!
770 There Grendel suffered a grievous hurt,
A wound in the shoulder, gaping and wide;
Sinews snapped and bone-joints broke,
And Beowulf gained the glory of battle.
Grendel, fated, fled to the fens,
To his joyless dwelling, sick unto death.
He knew in his heart that his hours were numbered,
His days at an end. For all the Danes
Their wish was fulfilled in the fall of Grendel.
The stranger from far, the stalwart and strong,
780 Had purged of evil the hall of Hrothgar,
And cleansed of crime; the heart of the hero
Joyed in the deed his daring had done.
The lord of the Geats made good to the East-Danes
The boast he had uttered; he ended their ill,
And all the sorrow they suffered long
And needs must suffer—a foul offense.

---

ancient iron a sword, sometimes with a name, which was of especially good quality and strength and would be handed down as a prized heirloom from generation to generation

The token was clear when the bold in battle
Laid down the shoulder and dripping claw—
Grendel's arm—in the gabled hall!

[*The Joy of the Danes and the Lay of Sigemund*]

790 When morning came, as they tell the tale,
Many a warrior hastened to hall,
Folk-leaders faring from far and near
Over wide-running ways, to gaze at the wonder,
The trail of the demon. Nor seemed his death
A matter of sorrow to any man
Who viewed the tracks of the vanquished monster
As he slunk weary-hearted away from the hall,
Doomed and defeated and marking his flight
With bloody prints to the nicors' pool.
800 The crimson currents bubbled and heaved
In eddying reaches reddened with gore;
The surges boiled with the fiery blood.
But the monster had sunk from the sight of men.
In that fenny covert the cursed fiend
Not long thereafter laid down his life,
His heathen spirit; and hell received him.
Then all the comrades, the old and young,
The brave of heart, in a blithesome band
Came riding their horses home from the mere.°
810 Beowulf's prowess was praised in song;
And many men stated that south or north,
Over all the world, or between the seas,
Or under the heaven, no hero was greater,
More worthy of rule. But no whit they slighted
The gracious Hrothgar, their good old king.
Time and again they galloped their horses,
Racing their roans° where the roads seemed fairest;
Time and again a gleeman° chanted,
A minstrel mindful of saga and lay.
820 He wove his words in a winsome° pattern,
Hymning the burden of Beowulf's feat,
Clothing the story in skillful verse.
All tales he had ever heard told he sang of Sigemund's° glory,
Deeds of the Wælsing° forgotten, his weary roving and wars,

---

mere pond, lake
roans horses of mixed color
gleeman *scop*, bard
winsome pleasing, beautiful
Sigemund Germanic hero, son of Wæls, well known from the Old Norse *Volsungasaga* and the German *Nibelungenlied*. The Old Norse tradition makes him father of Fitela. Here he slays the dragon who guards the treasure: in the other two versions his son Sigurd or Siegfried does so. The story is meant to set up resonances

—of Sigurd-Siegfried-Sigemund's dragon-slaying, taking away of the treasure, of the curse that was on the treasure, and of his tragic fate— which the audience will apply to Beowulf. The parallel with Beowulf's past and future life, the proleptic reference to his death in battle with the dragon and the melancholy sense that even the greatest and bravest of heroes must grow old and meet death, would all be present in the minds of the listeners.
Wælsing son of Wæls, Sigemund-Sigurd

Feuds and fighting unknown to men, save Fitela° only,
Tales told by uncle to nephew when the two were companions,
What time they were bosom-comrades in battle and bitter strife.
Many of monster blood these two had slain with the sword-edge;
Great glory Sigemund gained that lingered long after death,
830 *When he daringly slew the dragon that guarded the hoard of gold.*
Under the ancient rock the warrior ventured alone,
No Fitela fighting beside him; but still it befell
That his firm steel pierced the worm,° the point stood fast in the wall;
The dragon had died the death! And the hero's daring
Had won the treasure to have and to hold as his heart might wish.
Then the Wælsing loaded his sea-boat, laid in the breast of the ship
Wondrous and shining treasure; the worm dissolved in the heat.
Sigemund was strongest of men in his deeds of daring,
Warrior's shield and defender, most famous in days of old
840 *After Heremod's° might diminished, his valor and vigor in war,*
Betrayed in the land of the Jutes to the hands of his foemen, and slain.
Too long the surges of sorrow swept over his soul; in the end
His life was a lingering woe to people and princes.
In former days his fate was mourned by many a warrior
Who had trusted his lord for protection from terror and woe,
Had hoped that the prince would prosper, wielding his father's wealth,
Ruling the tribe and the treasure, the Scylding city and home.
Hygelac's kinsman had favor and friendship of all mankind,
But the stain of sin sank deep into Heremod's heart.
850   Time and again on their galloping steeds
Over yellow roads they measured the mile-paths;
Morning sun mounted the shining sky
And many a hero strode to the hall,
Stout of heart, to behold the wonder.
The worthy ruler, the warder of treasure,
Set out from the bowers with stately train;
The queen with her maidens paced over the mead-path.°
        Then spoke Hrothgar; hasting to hall
He stood at the steps, stared up at the roof
860 High and gold-gleaming; saw Grendel's hand:
'Thanks be to God for this glorious sight!
I have suffered much evil, much outrage from Grendel,
But the God of glory works wonder on wonder.
I had no hope of a haven from sorrow
While this best of houses stood badged with blood,
A woe far-reaching for all the wise

Fitela nephew and son of Sigurd, by his sister Signy, who had seduced her brother in disguise in order to bear a true Volsung son who could revenge the wrongs done to her and to her family
worm dragon; the word once meant reptile, serpent, of any kind

Heremod See ll. 1596 ff. The intention is to contrast the savagery and tyranny of this king, his early goodness and later evil-doing and failure, with Beowulf, who has already been exalted by the comparison with Sigemund-Sigurd.
paced . . . mead-path i.e. walked from their apartments to the mead-hall

Who weened that they never could hold the hall
Against the assaults of devils and demons.
But now with God's help this hero has compassed
870   A deed our cunning could no way contrive.
Surely that woman may say with truth,
Who bore this son, if she still be living,
Our ancient God showed favor and grace
On her bringing-forth! O best of men,
I will keep you, Beowulf, close to my heart
In firm affection; as son to father
Hold fast henceforth to this foster-kinship.°
You shall know not want of treasure or wealth
Or goodly gift that your wish may crave,
880   While I have power. For poorer deeds
I have granted guerdon,° and graced with honor
Weaker warriors, feebler in fight.
You have done such deeds that your fame shall flourish
Through all the ages! God grant you still
All goodly grace as He gave before.'
    Beowulf spoke, the son of Ecgtheow:
'By the favor of God we won the fight,
Did the deed of valor, and boldly dared
The might of the monster. I would you could see
890   The fiend himself lying dead before you!
I thought to grip him in stubborn grasp
And bind him down on the bed of death,
There to lie straining in struggle for life,
While I gripped him fast lest he vanish away.
But I might not hold him or hinder his going
For God did not grant it, my fingers failed.
Too savage the strain of his fiendish strength!
To save his life he left shoulder and claw,
The arm of the monster, to mark his track.
900   But he bought no comfort; no whit thereby
Shall the wretched ravager racked with sin,
The loathsome spoiler, prolong his life.
A deep wound holds him in deadly grip,
In baleful bondage; and black with crime
The demon shall wait for the day of doom
When the God of glory shall give decree.'
    Then slower of speech was the son of Ecglaf,°
More wary of boasting of warlike deeds,
While the nobles gazed at the grisly claw,
910   The fiend's hand fastened by hero's might
On the lofty roof. Most like to steel

---

foster-kinship tie regarded as equivalent to the
bond of blood
guerdon reward

then slower . . . Ecglaf Unferth, now discomfited and unable to taunt Beowulf at all

Were the hardened nails, the heathen's hand-spurs,
Horrible, monstrous; and many men said
No tempered sword, no excellent iron,
Could have harmed the monster or hacked away
The demon's battle-claw dripping with blood.

[*The Feast and the Lay of Finnsburg*]
In joyful haste was Heorot decked
And a willing host of women and men
Gaily dressed and adorned the guest-hall.
920 Splendid hangings with sheen of gold
Shone on the walls, a glorious sight
To eyes that delight to behold such wonders.
The shining building was wholly shattered
Though braced and fastened with iron bands;
Hinges were riven; the roof alone
Remained unharmed when the horrid monster,
Foul with evil, slunk off in flight,
Hopeless of life. It is hard to flee
The touch of death, let him try who will;
930 Necessity urges the sons of men,
The dwellers on earth, to their destined place
Where the body, bound in its narrow bed,
After the feasting is fast in slumber.
Soon was the time when the son of Healfdene
Went to the wine-hall; he fain would join
With happy heart in the joy of feasting.
I never have heard of a mightier muster
Of proud retainers around their prince.
All at ease they bent to the benches,
940 Had joy of the banquet; their kinsmen bold,
Hrothgar and Hrothulf,° happy of heart,
In the high-built hall drank many a mead-cup.
The hall of Hrothgar was filled with friends;
No treachery yet had troubled the Scyldings.
Upon Beowulf, then, as a token of triumph,
Hrothgar bestowed a standard of gold,
A banner embroidered, a byrny and helm.
In sight of many, a costly sword
Before the hero was borne on high;
950 Beowulf drank of many a bowl.
No need for shame in the sight of heroes
For gifts so gracious! I never have heard
Of many men dealing in friendlier fashion,
To others on ale-bench, richer rewards,
Four such treasures fretted with gold!

Hrothulf Danish prince, nephew of Hrothgar,
son of his brother Halga. Hrothulf seems to have
usurped the throne after Hrothgar's death.

On the crest of the helmet a crowning wreath,
Woven of wire-work,° warded the head
Lest tempered swordblade, sharp from the file,
Deal deadly wound when the shielded warrior
960   Went forth to battle against the foe.
Eight horses also with plated headstalls
The lord of heroes bade lead into hall;
On one was a saddle skillfully fashioned
And set with jewels, the battle-seat
Of the king himself, when the son of Healfdene
Would fain take part in the play of swords;
Never in fray had his valor failed,
His kingly courage, when corpses were falling.
And the prince of the Ingwines° gave all these gifts
970   To the hand of Beowulf, horses and armor;
Bade him enjoy them! With generous heart
The noble leader, the lord of heroes,
Rewarded the struggle with steeds and with treasure,
So that none can belittle, and none can blame,
Who tells the tale as it truly happened.
    Then on the ale-bench to each of the earls
Who embarked with Beowulf, sailing the sea-paths,
The lord of princes dealt ancient heirlooms,
Gift of treasure, and guerdon of gold
980   To requite his slaughter whom Grendel slew,
As he would have slain others, but all-wise God
And the hero's courage had conquered Fate.
The Lord ruled over the lives of men
As He rules them still. Therefore understanding
And a prudent spirit are surely best!
He must suffer much of both weal and woe
Who dwells here long in these days of strife.
    Then song and revelry rose in the hall;
Before Healfdene's leader the harp was struck
990   And hall-joy wakened; the song was sung,
Hrothgar's gleeman rehearsed the lay
Of the sons of Finn when the terror befell them:

Hnæf° of the Scyldings, the Half-Dane, fell in the Frisian slaughter;
Nor had Hildeburh cause to acclaim the faith of the Jutish folk,

crowning . . . wire-work rather, as on the
Sutton Hoo helmet, which is Swedish work, a
metal ridge adorned with wire-work running
from the top of the head to the nose (Fig. 19)
Ingwines lit. "friends of Ing," i.e. Danes
Hnæf Hnæf, king of the Danes, who had succeeded his father, King Hoc, had gone with his
retainers on a visit to his sister Hildeburh and
her husband Finn, king of the Frisians (or Jutes)
at their home, Finnsburg. During the festivities,
Jutish treachery—according to the poet—provoked a fight in which Hnæf and his sister's son,
his closest kinsman, though half Jute, were

killed. They were cremated on the same pyre
and a truce was made. Hengest, the new Danish
king, stayed the winter with Finn, meditating
revenge for the death of Hnæf. Two Danish
warriors then provoked another battle, in which
Finn was killed. The Danes returned home, taking plunder and Hildeburh with them.
    The *scop*'s version, since he is a Dane singing
to his fellow Danes, lays the blame for the
initial bloodshed on the Jutes. He tells it as a
piece of old Danish lore, a story that would be
familiar to his hearers, in an oblique and
highly allusive manner, designed to set up reso-

Blameless, bereft of her brothers in battle, and stripped of her sons
Who fell overcome by their fate and wounded with spears!
Not for nothing Hoc's daughter bewailed death's bitter decree,
In the dawn under morning skies, when she saw the slaughter of kinsmen
In the place where her days had been filled with the fairest delights
  of the world.
1000 *Finn's thanes were slain in the fight, save only a few;*
Nor could he do battle with Hengest or harry his shattered host;
And the Frisians made terms with the Danes, a truce, a hall for their dwelling,
A throne, and a sharing of rights with the sons of the Jutes,
And that Finn, the son of Folcwalda, each day would honor the Danes,
The host of Hengest, with gifts, with rings and guerdon of gold,
Such portion of plated treasure as he dealt to the Frisian folk
When he gladdened their hearts in the hall. So both were bound by the truce.°
And Finn swore Hengest with oaths that were forceful and firm
He would rightfully rule his remnant, follow his council's decree,
1010 *And that no man should break the truce, or breach it by word or by will,*
Nor the lordless in malice lament they were fated to follow
The man who had murdered their liege; and, if ever a Frisian
Fanned the feud with insolent speech, the sword should avenge° it.

  Then a funeral pyre° was prepared, and gold was drawn from the hoard,
The best of the Scylding leaders° was laid on the bier;
In the burning pile was a gleaming of blood-stained byrnies,
The gilded swine° and the boar-helm hard from the hammer,
Many a warrior fated with wounds and fallen in battle.
And Hildeburh bade that her son be laid on the bier of Hnæf,
1020 *His body consumed in the surging flame at his uncle's shoulder.*
Beside it the lady lamented, singing her mournful dirge.°
The hero was placed on the pyre;° the greatest of funeral flames
Rolled with a roar to the skies at the burial barrow.
Heads melted and gashes gaped, the mortal wounds of the body,
Blood poured out in the flames; the fire, most greedy of spirits,
Swallowed up all whom battle had taken of both their peoples.
Their glory was gone! The warriors went to their homes,
Bereft of their friends, returning to Friesland,° to city and strong-hold.
  Then Hengest abode with Finn all the slaughter-stained winter,
1030 *But his heart longed ever for home, though he could not launch on the sea*

---

nances in the minds of his hearers. We should
know far less of the background if we did not
have the story in the much more straightforward
narrative of the independent fragment known
as the Fight at Finnsburg.

Some think that the allusiveness is carried
still further and that the Finnsburg lay is a kind
of forecast of the treachery by which Hrothulf,
Hrothgar's nephew, usurped the Danish throne
from the rightful heirs, Hrothgar's sons, after
the death of the old king.

truce This involved Hengest's taking service
with the man who had killed his lord—a crime
against the Germanic code and only to be

justified because it served the final end of
revenge.
avenge i.e. settle the dispute
pyre According to the older pagan custom the
dead man's precious possessions were burned
with him.
best . . . leaders i.e. Hnæf
swine boar-image on the helmet
dirge This was the pagan custom; cf. the woman
at Beowulf's funeral, below; and Tacitus, *Germania,* 27.
hero . . . pyre probably a reference to Hildeburh's son
Friesland i.e. Frisian or Jutish country

His ring-stemmed ship, for the billows boiled wtih the storm,
Strove with the wind, and the winter locked ocean in bonds of ice;
Till a new Spring shone once more on the dwellings of men,
The sunny and shining days which ever observe their season.
The winter was banished afar, and fair the bosom of earth.
Then the exile longed to be gone, the guest from his dwelling,
But his thoughts were more on revenge than on voyaging over the wave,
Plotting assault on the Jutes, renewal of war with the sword.
So he spurned not° the naked hint when Hunlafing laid in his lap
1040   The battle-flasher, the best of blades, well known to the Jutes!
In his own home death by the sword befell Finn, the fierce-hearted,
When Guthlaf and Oslaf° requited the grim attack,
The woe encountered beyond the sea, the sorrow they suffered,
Nor could bridle the restive spirits within their breasts!
        Then the hall was reddened with blood and bodies of foemen,
Finn killed in the midst of his men, and the fair queen taken.
The Scylding warriors bore to their ships all treasure and wealth,
Such store as they found in the home of Finn of jewels and gems.
And the noble queen they carried across the sea-paths,
1050   Brought her back to the Danes, to her own dear people.
So the song was sung, the lay recited,
The sound of revelry rose in the hall.
Stewards poured wine from wondrous vessels;
And Wealhtheow, wearing a golden crown,
Came forth in state where the two were sitting,
Courteous comrades, uncle and nephew,
Each true to the other in ties of peace.°
Unferth, the orator,° sat at the feet
Of the lord of the Scyldings; and both showed trust
1060   In his noble mind, though he had no mercy
On kinsmen in swordplay; the Scylding queen spoke:
'My sovereign lord, dispenser of treasure,
Drink now of this flagon, have joy of the feast!
Speak to the Geats, O gold-friend of men,
In winning words as is well-befitting;
Be kind to the Geat-men and mindful of gifts
From the gold you have garnered from near and far.°
You have taken as son, so many have told me,
This hardy hero. Heorot is cleansed,
1070   The gleaming gift-hall. Rejoice while you may

So . . . not This passage can be interpreted in several ways. As translated it seems to mean that the son of Hunlaf the Dane, who had taken part in the Danish-Frisian feud, placed a naked sword in Hengest's lap, as a token of allegiance and a reminder that the deaths of Hnæf and of Hunlaf in the fight at Finnsburg are still unavenged. The action is also a pledge that the son of Hunlaf will take part in the revenge, when it is taken. "Battle-flasher" may be the name of a special sword or a *kenning* (condensed metaphor) for any sword.

Guthlaf . . . Oslaf These two Danish warriors, brothers of Hunlaf, seem to have begun the second fight at Finnsburg.

peace perhaps a reference by ironic contrast to the usurpation and strife after Hrothgar's death

orator spokesman, counsellor, again represented as sitting in the place of honor

Be kind . . . far an incitement to generosity: the best sense that can be made of this obscure and difficult passage; the text may be corrupt

In lavish bounty, and leave to your kin
People and kingdom when time shall come,
Your destined hour, to look on death.
I know the heart of my gracious Hrothulf,
That he'll safely shelter and shield our sons
When you leave this world, if he still is living.
I know he will favor with gracious gifts
These boys of ours, if he bears in mind
The many honors and marks of love
1080　We bestowed upon him while he still was a boy.'
　　　She turned to the bench where her boys were sitting,
Hrethric and Hrothmund,° the sons of heroes,
The youth together; there the good man sat,
Beowulf of the Geats, beside the two brothers.
Then the cup was offered with gracious greeting,
And seemly presents of spiraled gold,
A corselet, and rings, and the goodliest collar°
Of all that ever were known on earth.
1090　In the hoarding of heroes beneath the sky
I have never heard tell of a worthier treasure
Since Hama bore off to the shining city
The Brosings' jewel,° setting and gems,
Fled from Eormanric's cruel craft
And sought the grace of eternal glory.
Hygelac,° the Geat, grandson of Swerting
Wore the ring in the last of his raids,
Guarding the spoil under banner in battle,
Defending the treasure. Overtaken by Fate,
In the flush of pride he fought with the Frisians
1100　And met disaster. The mighty prince
Carried the ring o'er the cup of the waves,
The precious jewel, and sank under shield.
Then his body fell into Frankish hands,
His woven corselet and jewelled collar,
And weaker warriors plundered the dead
After the carnage and welter of war.
The field of battle was covered with corpses
Of Geats who had fallen, slain by the sword.
　　　The sound of revelry rose in the hall;
1110　Wealhtheow spoke to the warrior host:
'Take, dear Beowulf, collar and corselet,
Wear these treasures with right good will!

Hrethric and Hrothmund sons of Hrothgar and
Wealhtheow
collar torc, neck-ring, of gold
Brosings' jewel This was a necklace, which
had, according to Old Norse legend, been made
for the goddess Freyja, wife of Odin and
goddess of love, fecundity, and death, by the
Brisingas. The legend of how Hama, apparently,
stole the necklace from Eormanric, king of the
Ostrogoths—the historical Eormanric died about
375—is not otherwise known. In Norse legend
Freyja loses the necklace through the treachery
of Loki.
Hygelac cf. ll. 194 ff. and ll. 2222 ff., 2742 ff.

Thrive and prosper and prove your might!
Befriend my boys with your kindly counsel;
I will remember and I will repay.
You have earned the undying honor of heroes
In regions reaching as far and wide
As the windy walls that the sea encircles.
May Fate show favor while life shall last!
1120   I wish you wealth to your heart's content;
In your days of glory be good to my sons!
Here each hero is true to other,
Gentle of spirit, loyal to lord,
Friendly thanes and a folk united,
Wine-cheered warriors who do my will.'

[*The Troll-Wife° Avenges Grendel*]
Then she went to her seat. At the fairest of feasts
Men drank of the wine-cup, knowing not Fate,
Nor the fearful doom that befell the earls
When darkness gathered, and gracious Hrothgar
1130   Sought his dwelling and sank to rest.
A host of heroes guarded the hall
As they oft had done in the days of old.
They stripped the benches and spread the floor
With beds and bolsters. But one of the beer-thanes
Bowed to his hall-rest doomed to death.
They set at their heads their shining shields,
Their battle-bucklers; and there on the bench
Above each hero his towering helmet,
His spear and corselet hung close at hand.
1140   It was ever their wont to be ready for war
At home or in field, as it ever befell
That their lord had need. 'Twas a noble race!
    Then they sank to slumber. But one paid dear
For his evening rest, as had often happened
When Grendel haunted the lordly hall
And wrought such ruin, till his end was come,
Death for his sins; it was easily seen,
Though the monster was slain, an avenger survived
Prolonging the feud, though the fiend had perished.
1150   The mother of Grendel, a monstrous hag,
Brooded over her misery, doomed to dwell
In evil waters and icy streams
From ancient ages when Cain had killed
His only brother, his father's son.
Banished and branded with marks of murder
Cain fled far from the joys of men,
Haunting the barrens, begetting a brood

Troll-Wife i.e. woman evil-spirit

Of grisly monsters; and Grendel was one,
The fiendish ogre who found in the hall
1160   A hero on watch, and awaiting the fray.
The monster grappled; the Geat took thought
Of the strength of his might, that marvelous gift
Which the Lord had given; in God he trusted
For help and succor and strong support,
Whereby he humbled the fiend from hell,
Destroyed the demon; and Grendel fled,
Harrowed in heart and hateful to man,
Deprived of joy, to the place of death.
But rabid and raging his mother resolved
1170   On a dreadful revenge for the death of her son!
       She stole to the hall where the Danes were sleeping,
And horror fell on the host of earls
When the dam of Grendel burst in the door.
But the terror was less as the war-craft is weaker,
A woman's strength, than the might of a man
When the hilted sword, well shaped by the hammer,
The blood-stained iron of tempered edge,
Hews the boar from the foeman's helmet.
Then in the hall was the hard-edged blade,
1180   The stout steel, brandished above the benches;
Seizing their shields men stayed not for helmet
Or ample byrny, when fear befell.
As soon as discovered, the hag was in haste
To fly to the open, to flee for her life.
One of the warriors she swiftly seized,
Clutched him fast and made off to the fens.
He was of heroes the dearest to Hrothgar,
The best of comrades between two seas;
The warrior brave, the stout-hearted spearman,
1190   She slew in his sleep. Nor was Beowulf there;
But after the banquet another abode
Had been assigned to the glorious Geat.
There was tumult in Heorot. She tore from its place
The blood-stained claw. Care was renewed!
It was no good bargain when both in turn
Must pay the price with the lives of friends!
       Then the white-haired warrior, the aged king,
Was numb with sorrow, knowing his thane
No longer was living, his dearest man dead.
1200   Beowulf, the brave, was speedily summoned,
Brought to the bower; the noble prince
Came with his comrades at dawn of day
Where the wise king awaited if God would award
Some happier turn in these tidings of woe.
The hero came tramping into the hall

With his chosen band—the boards resounded—
Greeted the leader, the Ingwine lord,
And asked if the night had been peaceful and pleasant.
    Hrothgar spoke, the lord of the Scyldings:
1210 'Ask not of pleasure; pain is renewed
For the Danish people. Æschere° is dead!
Dead is Yrmenlaf's elder brother!
He was my comrade, closest of counsellors,
My shoulder-companion as side by side
We fought for our lives in the welter of war,
In the shock of battle when boar-helms crashed.
As an earl should be, a prince without peer,
Such was Æschere, slain in the hall
By the wandering demon! I know not whither
1220 She fled to shelter, proud of her spoil,
Gorged to the full. She avenged the feud
Wherein yesternight you grappled with Grendel
And savagely slew him because so long
He had hunted and harried the men of my folk.
He fell in the battle and paid with his life.
But now another fierce ravager rises
Avenging her kinsman, and carries it far,
As it seems to many a saddened thane
Who grieves in his heart for his treasure-giver.
1230 This woe weighs heavy! The hand lies still
That once was lavish of all delights.
    Oft in the hall I have heard my people,
Comrades and counsellors, telling a tale
Of evil spirits their eyes have sighted,
Two mighty marauders who haunt the moors.
One shape, as clearly as men could see,
Seemed woman's likeness, and one seemed man,
An outcast wretch of another world,
And huger far than a human form.
1240 Grendel my countrymen called him, not knowing
What monster-brood spawned him, what sire begot.
Wild and lonely the land they live in,
Wind-swept ridges and wolf-retreats,
Dread tracts of fen where the falling torrent
Downward dips into gloom and shadow
Under the dusk of the darkening cliff.
Not far in miles lies the lonely mere
Where trees firm-rooted and hung with frost
Overshroud the wave with shadowing gloom.
1250 And there a portent appears each night,
A flame in the water; no man so wise

Æschere not otherwise known

Who knows the bound of its bottomless depth.
The heather-stepper, the horned stag,
The antlered hart hard driven by hounds,
Invading that forest in flight from afar
Will turn at bay and die on the brink
Ere ever he'll plunge in that haunted pool.
'Tis an eerie spot!° Its tossing spray
Mounts dark to heaven when high winds stir
1260   The driving storm, and the sky is murky,
And with foul weather the heavens weep.
On your arm only rests all our hope!
Not yet have you tempted those terrible reaches
The region that shelters that sinful wight.
Go if you dare! I will give requital
With ancient treasure and twisted gold,
As I formerly gave in guerdon of battle,
If out of that combat you come alive.'
        Beowulf spoke, the son of Ecgtheow:
1270   'Sorrow not, brave one! Better for man
To avenge a friend than much to mourn.
All men must die; let him who may
Win glory ere death. That guerdon is best
For a noble man when his name survives him.
Then let us rise up, O ward of the realm,
And haste us forth to behold the track
Of Grendel's dam. And I give you pledge
She shall not in safety escape to cover,
To earthy cavern, or forest fastness,
1280   Or gulf of ocean, go where she may.
This day with patience endure the burden
Of every woe, as I know you will.'
Up sprang the ancient, gave thanks to God
For the heartening words the hero had spoken.

[*Beowulf Slays the Troll-Wife*]
Quickly a horse was bridled for Hrothgar,
A mettlesome charger with braided mane;
In royal splendor the king rode forth
Mid the trampling tread of a troop of shieldmen.
The tracks lay clear where the fiend had fared
1290   Over plain and bottom and woodland path,
Through murky moorland making her way
With the lifeless body, the best of thanes
Who of old with Hrothgar had guarded the hall.

eerie spot lit. "that is no pleasant spot." There are general resemblances to the visit to the underworld in the sixth book of Virgil's *Aeneid* and to the apocryphal *Vision of St. Paul*, but there are many features here for which the poet seems to have drawn on a typically North-ern winter scene. There are also parallels with the Old Norse saga of Grettir. Later, an English sermon, perhaps of the ninth or earlier tenth century, draws on this passage in *Beowulf* for a description of an icy Hell.

By a narrow path the king pressed on
Through rocky upland and rugged ravine,
A lonely journey, past looming headlands,
The lair of monster and lurking troll.
Tried retainers, a trusty few,
Advanced with Hrothgar to view the ground.
1300   Sudden they came on a dismal covert
Of trees that hung over hoary stone,
Over churning water and blood-stained wave.
Then for the Danes was the woe the deeper,
The sorrow sharper for Scylding earls,
When they first caught sight, on the rocky sea-cliff,
Of slaughtered Æschere's severed head.
The water boiled in a bloody swirling
With seething gore as the spearmen gazed.
The trumpet sounded a martial strain;
1310   The shield-troop halted. Their eyes beheld
The swimming forms of strange sea-dragons,
Dim serpent shapes in the watery depths,
Sea-beasts sunning on headland slopes;
Snakelike monsters that oft at sunrise
On evil errands scour the sea.
Startled by tumult and trumpet's blare,
Enraged and savage, they swam away;
But one the lord of the Geats brought low,
Stripped of his sea-strength, despoiled of life,
1320   As the bitter bow-bolt pierced his heart.
His watery-speed grew slower, and ceased,
And he floated, caught in the clutch of death.
Then they hauled him in with sharp-hooked boar-spears,
By sheer strength grappled and dragged him ashore,
A wondrous wave-beast; and all the array
Gathered to gaze at the grisly guest.
    Beowulf donned his armor for battle,
Heeded not danger; the hand-braided byrny,
Broad of shoulder and richly bedecked,°
1330   Must stand the ordeal of the watery depths.
Well could that corselet defend the frame
Lest hostile thrust should pierce to the heart.
Or blows of battle beat down the life.
A gleaming helmet guarded his head
As he planned his plunge to the depths of the pool
Through the heaving waters—a helm adorned
With lavish inlay and lordly chains,
Ancient work of the weapon-smith
Skillfully fashioned, beset with the boar,

richly bedecked "Strongly made" is more accurate.

1340   That no blade of battle might bite it through.
        Not the least or the worst of his war-equipment
        Was the sword° the herald of Hrothgar° loaned
        In his hour of need—Hrunting° its name—
        An ancient heirloom, trusty and tried;
        Its blade was iron, with etched design,
        Tempered in blood of many a battle.
        Never in fight had it failed the hand
        That drew it daring the perils of war,
        The rush of the foe. Not the first time then
1350   That its edge must venture on valiant deeds.
        But Ecglaf's stalwart son was unmindful
        Of words he had spoken while heated with wine,
        When he loaned the blade to a better swordsman.
        He himself dared not hazard his life
        In deeds of note in the watery depths;
        And thereby he forfeited honor and fame.
        Not so with that other undaunted spirit
        After he donned his armor for battle.
        Beowulf spoke, the son of Ecgtheow:
1360   'O gracious ruler, gold-giver to men,
        As I now set forth to attempt this feat,
        Great son of Healfdene, hold well in mind
        The solemn pledge we plighted of old,
        That if doing your service I meet my death
        You will mark my fall with a father's love.
        Protect my kinsmen, my trusty comrades,
        If battle take me. And all the treasure
        You have heaped on me bestow upon Hygelac,
        Hrothgar beloved! The lord of the Geats,
1370   The son of Hrethel, shall see the proof,
        Shall know as he gazes on jewels and gold,
        That I found an unsparing dispenser of bounty,
        And joyed, while I lived, in his generous gifts.
        Give back to Unferth the ancient blade,
        The sword-edge splendid with curving scrolls,
        For either with Hrunting I'll reap rich harvest
        Of glorious deeds, or death shall take me.'
                After these words the prince of the Weders
        Awaited no answer, but turned to the task,
1380   Straightway plunged in the swirling pool.
        Nigh unto a day he endured the depths
        Ere he first had view of the vast sea-bottom.
        Soon she found, who had haunted the flood,
        A ravening hag, for a hundred half-years,

sword The text calls it "gleaming with venom   herald of Hrothgar Unferth
twigs," which may mean that the blade had a   Hrunting perhaps meaning Thruster
serpentine pattern.

Greedy and grim, that a man was groping
In daring search through the sea-troll's home.
Swift she grappled and grasped the warrior
With horrid grip, but could work no harm,
No hurt to his body; the ring-locked byrny
1390   Cloaked his life from her clutching claw;
Nor could she tear through the tempered mail
With her savage fingers. The she-wolf bore
The ring-prince down through the watery depths
To her den at the bottom; nor could Beowulf draw
His blade for battle, though brave his mood.
Many a sea-beast, strange sea-monsters,
Tasked him hard° with their menacing tusks,
Broke his byrny and smote him sore.
            Then he found himself in a fearsome hall
1400   Where water came not to work him hurt,
But the flood was stayed by the sheltering roof.
There in the glow of firelight gleaming
The hero had view of the huge sea-troll.
He swung his war-sword with all his strength,
Withheld not the blow, and the savage blade
Sang on her head its hymn of hate.
But the bold one found that the battle-flasher
Would bite no longer, nor harm her life.
The sword-edge failed at his sorest need.
1410   Often of old with ease it had suffered
The clash of battle, cleaving the helm,
The fated warrior's woven mail.
That time was first for the treasured blade
That its glory failed in the press of the fray.
But fixed of purpose and firm of mood
Hygelac's earl was mindful of honor;
In wrath, undaunted, he dashed to earth
The jewelled sword with its scrolled design,
The blade of steel; staked all on strength,
1420   On the might of his hand, as a man must do
Who thinks to win in the welter of battle
Enduring glory; he fears not death.
The Geat-prince joyed in the straining struggle,
Stalwart-hearted and stirred to wrath,
Gripped the shoulder of Grendel's dam
And headlong hurled the hag to the ground.
But she quickly clutched him and drew him close,
Countered the onset with savage claw.
The warrior staggered, for all his strength,
1430   Dismayed and shaken and borne to earth.

Tasked him hard i.e. tore at him

She knelt upon him and drew her dagger,
With broad bright blade, to avenge her son,
Her only issue. But the corselet's steel
Shielded his breast and sheltered his life
Withstanding entrance of point and edge.
    Then the prince of the Geats would have gone his journey,
The son of Ecgtheow, under the ground;
But his sturdy breast-net, his battle-corselet,
Gave him succor, and holy God,
1440   The Lord all-wise, awarded the mastery;
Heaven's Ruler gave right decree.
    Swift the hero sprang to his feet;
Saw 'mid the war-gear a stately sword,
An ancient war-brand of biting edge,
Choicest of weapons worthy and strong,
The work of giants,° a warrior's joy,
So heavy no hand but his own could hold it,
Bear to battle or wield in war.
Then the Scylding warrior, savage and grim,
1450   Seized the ring-hilt and swung the sword,
Struck with fury, despairing of life,
Thrust at the throat, broke through the bone-rings;
The stout blade stabbed through her fated flesh.
She sank in death; the sword was bloody;
The hero joyed in the work of his hand.
The gleaming radiance shimmered and shone
As the candle of heaven shines clear from the sky.
Wrathful and resolute Hygelac's thane
Surveyed the span of the spacious hall;
1460   Grimly gripping the hilted sword
With upraised weapon he turned to the wall.
The blade had failed not the battle-prince;
A full requital he firmly planned
For all the injury Grendel had done
In numberless raids on the Danish race,
When he slew the hearth-companions of Hrothgar,
Devoured fifteen of the Danish folk
Clasped in slumber, and carried away
As many more spearmen, a hideous spoil.
1470   All this the stout-heart had stern requited;
And there before him bereft of life
He saw the broken body of Grendel
Stilled in battle, and stretched in death,
As the struggle in Heorot smote him down.
The corpse sprang wide as he struck the blow,
The hard sword-stroke that severed the head.
    Then the tried retainers, who there with Hrothgar

work of giants i.e. huge, old, and powerful

Watched the face of the foaming pool,
Saw that the churning reaches were reddened,
1480   The eddying surges stained with blood.
And the gray, old spearmen spoke of the hero,
Having no hope he would ever return
Crowned with triumph and cheered with spoil.
Many were sure that the savage sea-wolf
Had slain their leader. At last came noon.
The stalwart Scyldings forsook the headland;
Their proud gold-giver departed home.
But the Geats sat grieving and sick in spirit,
Stared at the water with longing eyes,
1490   Having no hope they would ever behold
Their gracious leader and lord again.
    Then the great sword, eaten with blood of battle,
Began to soften and waste away
In iron icicles, wonder of wonders,
Melting away most like to ice
When the Father looses the fetters of frost,
Slackens the bondage that binds the wave,
Strong in power of times and seasons;
He is true God! Of the goodly treasures
1500   From the sea-cave Beowulf took but two,
The monster's head and the precious hilt
Blazing with gems; but the blade had melted,
The sword dissolved, in the deadly heat,
The venomous blood of the fallen fiend.

    [*Beowulf Returns to Heorot*]
Then he who had compassed the fall of his foes
Came swimming up through the swirling surge.
Cleansed were the currents, the boundless abyss,
Where the evil monster had died the death
And looked her last on this fleeting world.
1510   With sturdy strokes the lord of the seamen
To land came swimming, rejoiced in his spoil,
Had joy of the burden he brought from the depths.
And his mighty thanes came forward to meet him,
Gave thanks to God they were granted to see
Their well-loved leader both sound and safe.
From the stalwart hero his helmet and byrny
Were quickly loosened; the lake lay still,
Its motionless reaches reddened with blood.
Fain of heart men fared o'er the footpaths,
1520   Measured the ways and the well-known roads.
From the sea-cliff's brim the warriors bore
The head of Grendel, with heavy toil;
Four of the stoutest, with all their strength,

Could hardly carry on swaying spear
Grendel's head to the gold-decked hall.
Swift they strode, the daring and dauntless,
Fourteen Geats, to the Hall of the Hart;
And proud in the midst of his marching men
Their leader measured the path to the mead-hall.
1530 The hero entered, the hardy in battle,
The great in glory, to greet the king;
And Grendel's head by the hair was carried
Across the floor where the feasters drank—
A terrible sight for lord and for lady—
A gruesome vision whereon men gazed!
　　　Beowulf spoke, the son of Ecgtheow:
'O son of Healfdene, lord of the Scyldings!
This sea-spoil wondrous, whereon you stare,
We joyously bring you in token of triumph!
1540 Barely with life surviving the battle,
The war under water, I wrought the deed
Weary and spent; and death had been swift
Had God not granted His sheltering strength.
My strong-edged Hrunting, stoutest of blades,
Availed me nothing. But God revealed—
Often His arm has aided the friendless—
The fairest of weapons hanging on wall,
An ancient broadsword; I seized the blade,
Slew in the struggle, as fortune availed,
1550 The cavern-warders. But the war-brand old,
The battle-blade with its scrolled design,
Dissolved in the gush of the venomous gore;
The hilt alone I brought from the battle.
The record of ruin, and slaughter of Danes,
These wrongs I avenged, as was fitting and right.
Now I can promise you, prince of the Scyldings,
Henceforth in Heorot rest without rue
For you and your nobles; nor need you dread
Slaughter of follower, stalwart or stripling,°
1560 Or death of earl, as of old you did.'
Into the hand of the aged leader,
The gray-haired hero, he gave the hilt,
The work of giants, the wonder of gold.
At the death of the demons the Danish lord
Took in his keeping the cunning craft,
The wondrous marvel, of mighty smiths;
When the world was freed of the ravaging fiend,
The foe of God, and his fearful dam

stalwart or stripling i.e. member of the *duguth*,
the tried and seasoned warriors; or the *geogoth*,
the young retainers

Marked with murder and badged° with blood,
1570   The bound hilt passed to the best of kings
Who ever held sceptre beside two seas,
And dealt out treasure in Danish land!
  Hrothgar spoke, beholding the hilt,
The ancient relic whereon was etched
An olden record of struggle and strife,
The flood that ravaged the giant race,°
The rushing deluge of ruin and death.
That evil kindred were alien to God,
But the Ruler avenged with the wrath of the deep!
1580   On the hilt-guards, likewise, of gleaming gold
Was rightly carven in cunning runes,
Set forth and blazoned, for whom that blade,
With spiral tooling and twisted hilt,
That fairest of swords, was fashioned and smithied.
Then out spoke Hrothgar, Healfdene's son,
And all the retainers were silent and still:
'Well may he say, whose judgment is just,
Recalling to memory men of the past,
That this earl was born of a better stock!
1590   Your fame, friend Beowulf, is blazoned abroad
Over all wide ways, and to every people.
In manful fashion have you showed your strength,
Your might and wisdom. My word I will keep,
The plighted friendship we formerly pledged.
Long shall you stand as a stay to your people,
A help to heroes, as Heremod° was not
To the Honor-Scyldings, to Ecgwela's° sons!
Not joy to kindred, but carnage and death,
He wrought as he ruled o'er the race of the Danes.
1600   In savage anger he slew his comrades,
His table-companions, till, lawless and lone,
An odious outcast, he fled from men.
Though God had graced him with gifts of strength,
Over all men exalting him, still in his breast
A bloodthirsty spirit was rooted and strong.
He dealt not rings to the Danes for glory;
His lot was eternal torment of woe,
And lasting affliction. Learn from his fate!
Strive for virtue! I speak for your good;
1610   In the wisdom of age I have told the tale.
  'Tis a wondrous marvel how mighty God°

badged marked, distinguished by
The flood . . . race Noah's flood, which over-
whelmed the wicked race of giants
Heremod see above, ll. 841 ff. His name means
"Warlike disposition." King of the Danes before
Scyld, he seems to have given promise of being
a splendid king, but he turned out to be cruel,
avaricious, and oppressive.

Ecgwela's a Danish king, otherwise unknown:
his name means "Sword-wealth"
'Tis . . . God Hrothgar seizes the occasion to
moralize the encounter—cf. the earlier Heremod
digression above—in terms of spiritual attack
and defense, the transitoriness of human life
and happiness.

In gracious spirit bestows on men
The gift of wisdom, and goodly lands,
And princely power! He rules over all!
He suffers a man of lordly line
To set his heart on his own desires,
Awards him fullness of worldly joy,
A fair home-land, and the sway of cities,
The wide dominion of many a realm,
1620   An ample kingdom, till, cursed with folly,
The thoughts of his heart take no heed of his end.
He lives in luxury, knowing not want,
Knowing no shadow of sickness or age;
No haunting sorrow darkens his spirit,
No hatred or discord deepens to war;
The world is sweet, to his every desire,
And evil assails not—until in his heart
Pride overpowering gathers and grows!
The warder slumbers, the guard of his spirit;
1630   Too sound is that sleep, too sluggish the weight
Of worldly affairs, too pressing the Foe,
The Archer who looses the arrows of sin.
        Then is his heart pierced, under his helm,
His soul in his bosom, with bitter dart.
He has no defense for the fierce assaults
Of the loathsome Fiend. What he long has cherished
Seems all too little! In anger and greed
He gives no guerdon of plated rings.
Since God has granted him glory and wealth
1640   He forgets the future, unmindful of Fate.
But it comes to pass in the day appointed
His feeble body withers and fails;
Death descends, and another seizes
His hoarded riches and rashly spends
The princely treasure, imprudent of heart.
Beloved Beowulf, best of warriors,
Avoid such evil and seek the good,
The heavenly wisdom. Beware of pride!
Now for a time you shall feel the fullness
1650   And know the glory of strength, but soon
Sickness or sword shall strip you of might,
Or clutch of fire, or clasp of flood,
Or flight of arrow, or bite of blade,
Or relentless age; or the light of the eye
Shall darken and dim, and death on a sudden,
O lordly ruler, shall lay you low.
        A hundred half-years I've been head of the Ring-Danes,
Defending the folk against many a tribe
With spear-point and sword in the surges of battle
1660   Till not one was hostile 'neath heaven's expanse.

But a loathsome change swept over the land,
Grief after gladness, when Grendel came,
That evil invader, that ancient foe!
Great sorrow of soul from his malice I suffered;
But thanks be to God who has spared me to see
His bloody head at the battle's end!
Join now in the banquet; have joy of the feast,
O mighty in battle! And the morrow shall bring
Exchange of treasure in ample store.'

1670   Happy of heart the Geat leader hastened,
Took seat at the board as the good king bade.
Once more, as of old, brave heroes made merry
And tumult of revelry rose in the hall.
    Then dark over men the night shadows deepened;
The host all arose, for Hrothgar was minded,
The gray, old Scylding, to go to his rest.
On Beowulf too, after labor of battle,
Came limitless longing and craving for sleep.
A hall-thane graciously guided the hero,

1680 Weary and worn, to the place prepared,
Serving his wishes and every want
As befitted a mariner come from afar.
The stout-hearted warrior sank to his rest;
The lofty building, splendid and spacious,
Towered above him. His sleep was sound
Till the black-coated raven, blithesome of spirit,
Hailed the coming of Heaven's bliss.°

[*The Parting of Beowulf and Hrothgar*]
Then over the shadows uprose the sun.
The Geats were in haste, and eager of heart

1690 To depart to their people. Beowulf longed
To embark in his boat, to set sail for his home.
The hero tendered the good sword Hrunting
To the son of Ecglaf,° bidding him bear
The lovely blade; gave thanks for the loan,
Called it a faithful friend in the fray,
Bitter in battle. The greathearted hero
Spoke no word in blame of the blade!
Arrayed in war-gear, and ready for sea,
The warriors bestirred them; and, dear to the Danes,

700 Beowulf sought the high seat of the king.
The gallant in war gave greeting to Hrothgar;
Beowulf spoke, the son of Ecgtheow:
'It is time at last to tell of our longing!
Our homes are far, and our hearts are fain
To seek again Hygelac over the sea.

Heaven's bliss i.e. the sun   **son of Ecglaf** Unferth

You have welcomed us royally, harbored us well
As a man could wish; if I ever can win
Your affection more fully, O leader of heroes,
Swift shall you find me to serve you again!
1710   If ever I learn, o'er the levels of ocean,
That neighboring nations beset you sore,
As in former days when foemen oppressed,
With thanes by the thousand I will hasten to help.
For I know that Hygelac, lord of the Geats,
Prince of the people, though young in years,
Will favor and further by word and deed
That my arm may aid you, and do you honor,
With stout ash-spear and succor of strength
In the press of need. And if princely Hrethric°
1720   Shall purpose to come to the court of the Geats,
He will find there a legion of loyal friends.
That man fares best to a foreign country
Who himself is stalwart and stout of heart.'
    Hrothgar addressed him, uttered his answer:
'Truly, these words has the Lord of wisdom
Set in your heart, for I never have harkened
To speech so sage from a man so young.
You have strength, and prudence, and wisdom of word!
I count it true if it come to pass
1730   That point of spear in the press of battle,
Or deadly sickness, or stroke of sword,
Shall slay your leader, the son of Hrethel,
The prince of your people, and you still live,
The Sea-Geats could have no happier choice
If you would be willing to rule the realm,
As king to hold guard o'er the hoard and the heroes.
The longer I know you, the better I like you,°
Beloved Beowulf! You have brought it to pass
That between our peoples a lasting peace
1740   Shall bind the Geats to the Danish-born;
And strife shall vanish, and war shall cease,
And former feuds, while I rule this realm.
And many a man, in the sharing of treasure,
Shall greet another with goodly gifts
O'er the gannet's° bath. And the ring-stemmed ship
Shall bear over ocean bountiful riches
In pledge of friendship. Our peoples, I know,
Shall be firm united toward foe and friend,
Faultless in all things, in fashion of old.'
1750   Then the son of Healfdene, shelter of earls,
Bestowed twelve gifts on the hero in hall,

Hrethric eldest son of Hrothgar   heart pleases me more the more I see of it . . ."
The longer . . . you lit. "The temper of your   **gannet's** sea-bird's

Bade him in safety with bounty of treasure
Seek his dear people, and soon return.
The peerless leader, the Scylding lord,
Kissed the good thane and clasped to his bosom
While tears welled fast from the old man's eyes.
Both chances he weighed in his wise, old heart,
But greatly doubted if ever again
They should meet at council or drinking of mead.
1760 Nor could Hrothgar master—so dear was the man—
His swelling sorrow; a yearning love
For the dauntless hero, deep in his heart,
Burned through his blood. Beowulf, the brave,
Prizing his treasure and proud of the gold,
Turned away, treading the grassy plain.
The ring-stemmed sea-goer, riding at anchor,
Awaited her lord. There was loud acclaim
Of Hrothgar's gifts, as they went their way.
He was a king without failing or fault,
1770 Till old age, master of all mankind,
Stripped him of power and pride of strength.

[Beowulf Returns to Geatland]

Then down to the sea came the band of the brave,
The host of young heroes in harness of war,
In their woven mail; and the coast-warden viewed
The heroes' return, as he heeded their coming!
No uncivil greeting he gave from the sea-cliff
As they strode to ship in their glistening steel;
But rode toward them and called their return
A welcome sight for their Weder kin
1780 There on the sand the ring-stemmed ship,
The broad-bosomed bark, was loaded with war-gear,
With horses and treasure; the mast towered high
Over the riches of Hrothgar's hoard.
A battle-sword Beowulf gave to the boatwarden
Hilted with gold; and thereafter in hall
He had the more honor because of the heirloom,
The shining treasure. The ship was launched.
Cleaving the combers of open sea
They dropped the shoreline of Denmark astern.
1790 A stretching sea-cloth, a bellying sail,
Was bent on the mast; there was groaning of timbers;
A gale was blowing; the boat drove on.
The foamy-necked plunger plowed through the billows,
The ring-stemmed ship through the breaking seas,
Till at last they sighted the sea-cliffs of Geatland,
The well-known headlands; and, whipped by the wind,
The boat drove shoreward and beached on the sand.
Straightway the harbor-watch strode to the seashore;

Long had he watched for the well-loved men,
1800 Scanning the ocean with eager eyes!
The broad-bosomed boat he bound to the shingle
With anchor ropes, lest the rip of the tide
Should wrench from its mooring the comely craft.

From the good ship Beowulf bade them bear
The precious jewels and plated gold,
The princely treasure.° Not long was the path
That led to where Hygelac, son of Hrethel,
The giver of treasure, abode in his home
Hard by the sea-wall, hedged by his thanes.
1810 Spacious the castle, splendid the king
On his high hall-seat; youthful was Hygd,°
Wise and well-born—though winters but few
Hæreth's daughter had dwelt at court.
She was noble of spirit, not sparing in gifts
Of princely treasure to the people of the Geats.

Of the pride of Thryth,° and her crimes, the fair folk-queen was free;
Thryth, of whose liegemen none dared by day, save only her lord,
Lift up his eyes to her face, lest his fate be a mortal bondage,
Seizure and fetters and sword, a blow of the patterned blade
1820 *Declaring his doom, and proclaiming the coming of death.*
That is no way of a queen, nor custom of lovely lady,
Though peerless her beauty and proud, that a weaver of peace°
Should send a dear man to his death for a feigned affront.
But the kinsman of Hemming° at last made an end of her evil.
For men at the drinking of mead tell tale of a change,
How she wrought less ruin and wrong when, given in marriage
Gleaming with jewels and gold, to the high-born hero and young,
Over the fallow° flood she sailed, at her father's bidding
Seeking the land of Offa, and there while she lived,
1830 *Famed for goodness, fulfilled her fate on the throne.*
She held high love for her lord, the leader of heroes,
The best, I have heard, of mankind or the children of men

treasure A gift to Beowulf would have at least to be formally offered to his lord, who could remit it to him.
Hygd Hygelac's queen, a young woman, daughter of Hæreth, is suddenly introduced into the narrative. She may have married Beowulf after Hygelac's death. Later, she offers the Geat throne to Beowulf in place of her young son Heardred.
Thryth "Strength." Some investigators take the name to be Modthryth. Thryth seems to be a version of the cruel queen who puts to death all except one who look at her. She is the equivalent of Brunhild in another Germanic romance, the *Nibelungenlied.* The male exception, in such tales, is sometimes the father of the cruel woman, or the hero who conquers her (for another, in the case of Brunhild). The digression is probably meant to throw Hygd's virtues into high relief by comparison with Thryth's evil nature.

weaver of peace a woman, one of whose functions it would be to heal differences—or, more specifically, a king's daughter given in marriage to seal a peace or alliance
kinsman of Hemming King Offa, husband of Thryth. According to an Anglian legend, he was the ancestor of another ruler, named Offa: the king of Mercia, one of the Anglo-Saxon kingdoms. Nothing more is known of his kinsman, Hemming. The use of Thryth to praise Hygd *per contrariam* modulates into a praise by direct comparison with Offa, with Hygd. A version of the legend of Offa and Thryth (the Constance legend), with the cruelties reversed, is later told by Chaucer's Man of Law. Offa and his kinsmen are the only Englishmen mentioned in the poem.
fallow gray-brown

Between the two seas; for Offa, the stalwart, was honored
For his gifts and his greatness in war. With wisdom he governed;
And from him Eomær descended, Hemming's kinsman, grandson of Garmund,°
Stalwart and strong in war, and the helper of heroes.

Then the hero strode with his stalwart band
Across the stretches of sandy beach,
The wide sea-shingle. The world-candle shone,
1840 The hot sun hasting on high from the south.
Marching together they made their way
To where in his stronghold the stout young king,
Ongentheow's slayer,° protector of earls,
Dispensed his treasure. Soon Hygelac heard
Of the landing of Beowulf, bulwark of men,
That his shoulder-companion had come to his court
Sound and safe from the strife of battle.
The hall was prepared, as the prince gave bidding,
Places made ready for much travelled men.
1850 And he who came safe from the surges of battle
Sat by the side of the king himself,
Kinsman by kinsman; in courtly speech
His liege lord greeted the loyal thane
With hearty welcome. And Hæreth's daughter
Passed through the hall-building pouring the mead,
With courtesy greeting the gathered host,
Bearing the cup to the hands of the heroes.
In friendly fashion in high-built hall
Hygelac questioned his comrade and thane;
1860 For an eager longing burned in his breast
To hear from the Sea-Geats the tale of their travels.
'How did you fare in your far sea-roving,
Beloved Beowulf, in your swift resolve
To sail to the conflict, the combat in Heorot,
Across the salt waves? Did you soften at all
The sorrows of Hrothgar, the weight of his woe?
Deeply I brooded with burden of care
For I had no faith in this far sea-venture
For one so beloved. Long I implored
1870 That you go not against the murderous monster,
But let the South Danes settle the feud
Themselves with Grendel. To God be thanks
That my eyes behold you unharmed and unhurt.'
Beowulf spoke, the son of Ecgtheow:
'My dear lord Hygelac, many have heard°

Eomær . . . Garmund Little or nothing is known of these two.
Ongentheow's slayer Hygelac did not kill Ongentheow with his own hands, though he led the Geats in their attack on Ongentheow's people,
the Scylfings. The full story is told below (ll. 2749 ff.).
many . . . heard lit. "from many it is not concealed"

Of that famous grapple 'twixt Grendel and me,
The bitter struggle and strife in the hall
Where he formerly wrought such ruin and wrong,
Such lasting sorrow for Scylding men!
1880　All that I avenged! Not any on earth
Who longest lives of that loathsome brood,
No kin of Grendel cloaked in his crime,
Has cause to boast of that battle by night!
First, in that country, I fared to the hall
With greeting for Hrothgar; Healfdene's kinsman
Learned all my purpose, assigned me a place
Beside his own son. 'Twas a happy host!
I never have seen under span of heaven
More mirth of heroes sitting at mead!
1890　The peerless queen, the peace-pledge° of peoples,
Passed on her round through the princely hall;
There was spurring of revels, dispensing of rings,
Ere the noble woman went to her seat.
　　　At times in the host the daughter of Hrothgar
Offered the beaker to earls in turn;
Freawaru men called her, the feasters in hall,
As she held out to heroes the well-wrought cup.
Youthful and gleaming with jewels of gold
To the fair son of Froda° the maiden is plighted.
1900　For the Scylding leader, the lord of the land,
Deems it wise counsel, accounting it gain,
To settle by marriage the murderous feud,
The bloody slaughter! But seldom for long
Does the spear go ungrasped when a prince has perished,
Though the bride in her beauty be peerless and proud!
Ill may it please the Heathobard prince
And all his thanes, when he leads his lady
Into the hall, that a Danish noble
Should be welcomed there by the Heathobard host.
1910　For on him shall flash their forefathers' heirlooms,°
Hard-edged, ring-hilted, the Heathobards' hoard
When of old they had war-might, nor wasted in battle
Their lives and the lives of their well-loved thanes.
　　　Then an aged spearman° shall speak at the beer-feast,
The treasure beholding with sorrow of heart,
Remembering sadly the slaughter of men,

---

peace-pledge i.e. her marriage had been part of a peace settlement between nations
son of Froda Froda was king of the Heathobards, an unidentified Germanic tribe. Freawaru, Hrothgar's daughter, had been betrothed to Ingeld, Froda's son, in pledge of peace between the Danes and the Heathobards. The poet's purpose in putting the story of the Danish-Heathobard feud into the mouth of Beowulf is much debated: it may be intended as a sort of prophecy or as a display of political wisdom on the part of the Geat, who can see the dangers of Hrothgar's attempt to settle the feud by marriage.
heirlooms Armor and ornaments that had been Heathobard property before they were captured by the Danes; they will remind the Heathobards of vengeance untaken.
spearman a Heathobard

Grimly goading the young hero's spirit,
Spurring to battle, speaking this word:
"Do you see, my lord, the sword of your father,
1920   The blade he bore to the last of his fights,
The pride of his heart as, under his helmet,
The Scyldings slew him, the savage Danes,
When Withergyld° fell, and after the slaughter,
The fall of heroes, they held the field?
And now a son of those bloody butchers,
Proud in his trappings, tramps into hall
And boasts of the killing, clothed with the treasure
That is yours by your birthright to have and to hold?"
      Over and over the old man will urge him,
1930   With cutting reminders recalling the past
Till it comes at last that the lady's thane,°
For the deeds of his father, shall forfeit his life
In a bloody slaughter, slain by the sword,
While the slayer goes scatheless knowing the land.
On both sides then shall sword-oaths be broken
When hate boils up within Ingeld's heart,
And his love of his lady grows cooler and lessens
Because of his troubles. I count not true
Heathobard faith, nor their part in the peace,
1940   Nor their friendship firm to the Danish folk.
      I must now speak on, dispenser of treasure,
Further of Grendel, till fully you know
How we fared in that fierce and furious fight!
When the jewel of heaven had journeyed o'er earth,
The wrathful demon, the deadly foe,
Stole through the darkness spying us out
Where still unharmed we guarded the gold-hall.
But doom in battle and bitter death
Were Handscio's° fate! He was first to perish
1950   Though girded with weapon and famous in war.
Grendel murdered him, mangled his body,
Bolted the dear man's bloody corpse.
No sooner for that would the slaughterous spirit,
Bloody of tooth and brooding on evil,
Turn empty-handed away from the hall!
The mighty monster made trial of my strength
Clutching me close with his ready claw.
Wide and wondrous his huge pouch° hung
Cunningly fastened, and fashioned with skill
1960   From skin of dragon by devil's craft.
Therein the monster was minded to thrust me

Withergyld a Heathobard warrior
lady's thane a Dane attendant on Freawaru
Handscio's a Geat warrior companion of
Beowulf's

pouch lit. "glove"; a huge glove is carried by
trolls in Old Norse stories

Sinless and blameless, and many beside.
But it might not be, when I rose in wrath,
And fronted the hell-fiend face to face.
Too long is the tale how I took requital
On the cursed foe for his every crime,
But the deeds I did were a lasting honor,
Beloved prince, to your people's name.
He fled away, and a fleeting while
1970   Possessed his life and the world's delights;
But he left in Heorot his severed hand,
A bloody reminder to mark his track.
Humbled in spirit and wretched in heart
Down he sank to the depths of the pool.
     When the morrow fell, and we feasted together,
The Scylding ruler rewarded me well
For the bloody strife, in guerdon bestowing
Goodly treasure of beaten gold.
There was song and revel. The aged Scylding
1980   From well-stored mind spoke much of the past.
A warrior sang to the strains of the glee-wood,°
Sometimes melodies mirthful and joyous,
Sometimes lays that were tragic and true.
And the great-hearted ruler at times would tell
A tale of wonder in fitting words.
Heavy with years the white-haired warrior
Grieved for his youth and the strength that was gone;
And his heart was moved by the weight of his winters
And many a memory out of the past.
1990   All the long day we made merry together
Till another night came to the children of men,
And quickly the mother of Grendel was minded
To wreak her vengeance; raging with grief
She came to the hall where the hate of the Weders
Had slain her son. But the hideous hag
Avenged his killing; with furious clutch
She seized a warrior—the soul of Æschere,
Wise and aged, went forth from the flesh!
Not at all could the Danes, when the morrow dawned,
2000   Set brand° to his body or burn on the bale°
Their well-loved comrade. With fiendish clasp
She carried his corpse through the fall of the force.°
That was to Hrothgar, prince of the people,
Sorest of sorrows that ever befell!
For your sake the sad-hearted hero° implored me
To prove my valor and, venturing life,°

glee-wood harp
brand i.e. firebrand
bale funeral pyre
force waterfall, cascade

hero Hrothgar
venturing life lit. "by your life," perhaps "for your sake"

To win renown in the watery depths.
He promised reward. Full well is it known
How I humbled the horrible guard of the gulf.
2010 Hand to hand for a space we struggled
Till the swirling eddies were stained with blood;
With cleaving sword-edge I severed the head
Of Grendel's hag in that hall of strife.
Not easily thence did I issue alive,
But my death was not fated; not yet was I doomed!
    Then the son of Healfdene, the shelter of earls,
Gave many a treasure to mark the deed.
The good king governed with courtly custom;
In no least way did I lose reward,
2020 The meed° of my might; but he gave me treasure,
Healfdene's son, to my heart's desire.
These riches I bring you, ruler of heroes,
And warmly tender with right good will.
Save for you, King Hygelac, few are my kinsmen,
Few are the favors but come from you.'
    Then he bade men bring the boar-crested headpiece,
The towering helmet, and steel-gray sark,°
The splendid war-sword, and spoke this word:
'The good king Hrothgar gave me this gift,
2030 This battle-armor, and first to you
Bade tell the tale of his friendly favor.
He said King Heorogar,° lord of the Scyldings,
Long had worn it, but had no wish
To leave the mail to his manful son,
The dauntless Heoroweard, dear though he was!
Well may you wear it! Have joy of it all.'
As I've heard the tale, he followed the trappings
With four bay° horses, matched and swift,
Graciously granting possession of both,
2040 The steeds and the wealth. 'Tis the way of a kinsman,
Not weaving in secret the wiles of malice
Nor plotting the fall of a faithful friend.
To his kinsman Hygelac, hardy in war,
The heart of the nephew was trusty and true;
Dear to each was the other's good!
To Hygd, as I've heard, he presented three horses
Gaily saddled, slender and sleek,
And the gleaming necklace Wealhtheow gave,
A peerless gift from a prince's daughter.
2050 With the gracious guerdon, the goodly jewel,
Her breast thereafter was well bedecked.

meed reward
sark shirt of mail

Heorogar Hrothgar's brother and predecessor
as king of the Danes
bay lit. "apple-fallow"—bright brown

So the son of Ecgtheow bore himself bravely,
Known for his courage and courteous deeds,
Strove after honor, slew not his comrades
In drunken brawling; nor brutal his mood.
But the bountiful gifts which the Lord God gave him
He held with a power supreme among men.
He had long been scorned,° when the sons of the Geats
Accounted him worthless; the Weder lord
2060   Held him not high among heroes in hall.
Laggard they deemed him, slothful° and slack.
But time brought solace for all his ills!
    Then the battle-bold king, the bulwark of heroes,
Bade bring a battle-sword banded with gold,
The heirloom° of Hrethel; no sharper steel,
No lovelier treasure, belonged to the Geats.
He laid the war-blade on Beowulf's lap,
Gave him a hall and a stately seat
And hides° seven thousand. Inherited lands
2070   Both held by birth-fee, home and estate.°
But one held rule o'er the spacious realm,
And higher therein his order and rank.

    [The Fire-Dragon and the Treasure]
It later befell in the years that followed
After Hygelac sank in the surges of war,
And the sword slew Heardred° under his shield
When the Battle-Scylfings, those bitter fighters,
Invaded the land of the victor-folk
Overwhelming Hereric's nephew in war,
That the kingdom came into Beowulf's hand.
2080   For fifty winters he governed it well,
Aged and wise with the wisdom of years,
Till a fire-drake° flying in darkness of night
Began to ravage and work his will.
On the upland heath he guarded a hoard,
A stone barrow lofty. Under it lay
A path concealed from the sight of men.
There a thief broke in on the heathen treasure,
Laid hand on a flagon all fretted with gold,

---

scorned We have no other information on Beowulf's younger, feebler days. The scorned weakling who grows into a mighty hero is a frequent figure in folktales.
slothful weak
heirloom i.e. inherited by Hrothgar from his father
hides a huge tract of land. A hide was basically the area of land required for the subsistence of one free peasant family and its dependents, or, alternatively, as much land as could be worked by one plow in one year. Thus the size varies with the peasant's standard of living in different

parts of the country from 40 to 120 acres. The gift to Beowulf is a princely one.
Inherited . . . estate Both Hygelac and Beowulf had inherited land, a house, and the estate that went with it.
Heardred The story is told more fully below. Heardred, Hygelac's son, succeeded his father as king, but was killed by the Swedes (Battle-Scylfings) on his own territory. Hereric was probably his maternal uncle, Hygd's brother.
fire-drake a fiery dragon, such as the *Anglo-Saxon Chronicle* records as having been seen in the late 8th century.

As the dragon discovered, though cozened in sleep
2090 By the pilferer's cunning. The people soon found
That the mood of the dragon was roused to wrath!°
      Not at all with intent, of his own free will,
Did he ravish the hoard, who committed the wrong;
But in dire distress the thrall° of a thane,
A guilty fugitive fleeing the lash,
Forced his way in. There a horror befell him!
Yet the wretched exile escaped from the dragon,
Swift in retreat when the terror arose.
A flagon he took. There, many such treasures
2100 Lay heaped in that earth-hall where the owner of old
Had carefully hidden the precious hoard,
The countless wealth of a princely clan.
Death came upon them in days gone by
And he who lived longest, the last of his line,
Guarding the treasure and grieving for friend,
Deemed it his lot that a little while only
He too might hold that ancient hoard.
A barrow new-built near the ocean billows
Stood cunningly° fashioned beneath the cliff;
2110 Into the barrow the ring-warden bore
The princely treasure, the precious trove
Of golden wealth, and these words he spoke:
'Keep thou, O Earth, what men could not keep—
This costly treasure—it came from thee!
Baleful slaughter has swept away,
Death in battle, the last of my blood;
They have lived their lives; they have left the mead-hall.
Now I have no one to wield the sword,
No one to polish the plated cup,
2120 The precious flagon—the host is fled.
The hard-forged helmet fretted with gold
Shall be stripped of its inlay; the burnishers sleep
Whose charge was to brighten the battle-masks.
Likewise the corselet that countered in war
'Mid clashing of bucklers the bite of the sword—
Corselet and warrior decay into dust;
Mailed coat and hero are moveless and still.
No mirth of gleewood, no music of harp,
No good hawk swinging in flight through the hall;
2130 No swift steed stamps in the castle yard;
Death has ravished an ancient race.'
So sad of mood he bemoaned his sorrow,

There . . . wrath (ll. 2087–91) The manuscript is badly damaged at this point; so it is possible only to guess at the precise meaning of the text.

thrall a slave escaping from his master
cunningly lit. "made difficult of access"

Lonely and sole survivor of all,
Restless by day and wretched by night
Till the clutch of death caught at his heart.
Then the goodly treasure was found unguarded
By the venomous dragon enveloped in flame,
The old naked night-foe flying in darkness,
Haunting the barrows; a bane that brings
2140   A fearful dread to the dwellers of earth.
His wont is to hunt out a hoard under ground
And guard heathen gold, growing old with the years.
But no whit for that is his fortune more fair!
     For three hundred winters this waster of peoples
Held the huge treasure-hall under the earth
Till the robber aroused him to anger and rage,
Stole the rich beaker and bore to his master,
Imploring his lord for a compact of peace.
So the hoard was robbed and its riches plundered;
2150   To the wretch was granted the boon that he begged;
And his liege-lord first had view of the treasure,
The ancient work of the men of old.
Then the worm awakened and war was kindled,
The rush of the monster along the rock,
When the fierce one found the tracks of the foe;
He had stepped too close in his stealthy cunning
To the dragon's head. But a man undoomed
May endure with ease disaster and woe
If he has His favor who wields the world.
2160   Swiftly the fire-drake sought through the plain
The man who wrought him this wrong in his sleep.
Inflamed and savage he circled the mound,
But the waste was deserted—no man was in sight.
The worm's mood was kindled to battle and war;
Time and again he returned to the barrow
Seeking the treasure-cup. Soon he was sure
That a man had plundered the precious gold.
Enraged and restless the hoard-warden waited
The gloom of evening. The guard of the mound
2170   Was swollen with anger; the fierce one resolved
To requite with fire the theft of the cup.
Then the day was sped as the worm desired;
Lurking no longer within his wall
He sallied forth surrounded with fire,
Encircled with flame. For the folk of the land
The beginning was dread as the ending was grievous
That came so quickly upon their lord.
     Then the baleful stranger belched fire and flame,
Burned the bright dwellings—the glow of the blaze
2180   Filled hearts with horror. The hostile flier

Was minded to leave there nothing alive.
From near and from far the war of the dragon,
The might of the monster, was widely revealed
So that all could see how the ravaging scather
Hated and humbled the Geatish folk.
Then he hastened back ere the break of dawn
To his secret den and the spoil of gold.
He had compassed the land with a flame of fire,
A blaze of burning; he trusted the wall,
2190   The sheltering mound, and the strength of his might—
But his trust betrayed him! The terrible news
Was brought to Beowulf, told for a truth,
That his home was consumed in the surges of fire,
The goodly dwelling and throne of the Geats.
The heart of the hero was heavy with anguish,
The greatest of sorrows; in his wisdom he weened
He had grievously angered the Lord Everlasting,
Blamefully broken the ancient law.
Dark thoughts stirred in his surging bosom,
2200   Welled in his breast, as was not his wont.
The flame of the dragon had levelled the fortress,
The people's stronghold washed by the wave.
But the king of warriors, prince of the Weders,
Exacted an ample revenge for it all.
The lord of warriors and leader of earls
Bade work him of iron a wondrous shield,
Knowing full well that wood could not serve him
Nor linden defend him against the flame.
The stalwart hero was doomed to suffer
2210   The destined end of his days on earth;
Likewise the worm, though for many a winter
He had held his watch o'er the wealth of the hoard.
The ring-prince scorned to assault the dragon
With a mighty army, or host of men.
He feared not the combat, nor counted of worth
The might of the worm, his courage and craft,
Since often aforetime, beset in the fray,
He had safely issued from many an onset,
Many a combat and, crowned with success,
2220   Purged of evil the hall of Hrothgar
And crushed out Grendel's loathsome kin.
     Nor was that the least of his grim engagements
When Hygelac fell, great Hrethel's son;
When the lord of the people, the prince of the Geats,
Died of his wounds in the welter of battle,
Perished in Friesland, smitten with swords.
Thence Beowulf came by his strength in swimming;
Thirty sets of armor he bore on his back

As he hasted to ocean. The Hetware° men
2230 Had no cause to boast of their prowess in battle
When they gathered against him with linden shields.
But few of them ever escaped his assault
Or came back alive to the homes they had left;
So the son of Ecgtheow swam the sea-stretches,
Lonely and sad, to the land of his skin.
Hygd then tendered him kingdom and treasure,
Wealth of riches and royal throne,
For she had no hope with Hygelac dead
That her son could defend the seat of his fathers
2240 From foreign foemen. But even in need,
No whit the more could they move the hero
To be Heardred's liege,° or lord of the land.
But he fostered Heardred with friendly counsel,
With honor and favor among the folk,
Till he came of age and governed the Geats.
Then the sons of Ohthere° fleeing in exile
Sought out Heardred over the sea.
They had risen against the lord of the Scylfings,
Best of the sea-kings, bestower of rings,
2250 An illustrious prince in the land of the Swedes.
So Heardred fell. For harboring exiles
The son of Hygelac died by the sword.
Ongentheow's son,° after Heardred was slain,
Returned to his home, and Beowulf held
The princely power and governed the Geats.
He was a good king, grimly requiting
In later days the death of his prince.
Crossing the sea with a swarming host
He befriended Eadgils,° Ohthere's son,
2260 In his woe and affliction, with weapons and men;
He took revenge in a savage assault,
And slew the king. So Ecgtheow's son
Had come in safety through all his battles,
His bitter struggles and savage strife,
To the day when he fought with the deadly worm.
With eleven comrades, kindled to rage
The Geat lord went to gaze on the dragon.
Full well he knew how the feud arose,
The fearful affliction; for into his hold

Hetware men i.e. the Atuarii
Heardred's liege Beowulf, though free to do so, refused to usurp the Geatish throne which rightfully belonged to Hygelac's son Heardred. Instead, he acted as the young king's counsellor and protector.
sons of Ohthere the Swedes Eanmund and Eadgils, driven into exile by their uncle Onela, who had usurped the throne of Ohthere and made himself king of the Scylfings (Swedes). Hear-dred took them into the protection of the Geat court and was attacked by Onela for this act of hospitality, and killed, along with Eanmund. Beowulf then ruled the kingdom, and acted as Eadgils's protector.
Ongentheow's son Onela
befriended Eadgils Beowulf helped Eadgils to get back the Swedish throne from Onela. It is not clear whether it is Eadgils or Beowulf who kills Onela.

2270   From hand of finder the flagon had come.
The thirteenth man in the hurrying throng
Was the sorrowful captive who caused the feud.
With woeful spirit and all unwilling
Needs must he guide them, for he only knew
Where the earth-hall stood near the breaking billows
Filled with jewels and beaten gold.
The monstrous warden, waiting for battle,
Watched and guarded the hoarded wealth.
No easy bargain for any of men
2280   To seize that treasure! The stalwart king,
Gold-friend of Geats, took seat on the headland,
Hailed his comrades and wished them well.
Sad was his spirit, restless and ready,
And the march of Fate immeasurably near;
Fate that would strike, seek his soul's treasure,
And deal asunder the spirit and flesh.
Not long was his life encased in the body!
        Beowulf spoke, the son of Ecgtheow:
'Many an ordeal I endured in youth,
2290   And many a battle. I remember it all.
I was seven winters old when the prince of the people,
The lord of the treasure-hoard, Hrethel the king,
From the hand of my father had me and held me,
Recalling our kinship with treasure and feast.
As long as he lived I was no less beloved,
As thane in his hall, than the sons of his house,
Herebeald and Hæthcyn and Hygelac, my lord.
For the eldest brother the bed of death
Was foully fashioned by brother's deed
2300   When Hæthcyn let fly a bolt from his horn-bow.°
Missed the mark, and murdered his lord;
Brother slew brother with bloody shaft—
A tragic deed and beyond atonement,
A foul offense to sicken the heart!
Yet none the less was the lot of the prince
To lay down his soul and his life, unavenged.°
        Even so sad and sorrowful is it,
And bitter to bear, to an old man's heart,
Seeing his young son swing on the gallows.°
2310   He wails his dirge and his wild lament
While his son hangs high, a spoil to the raven;
His aged heart can contrive no help.
Each dawn brings grief for the son that is gone

---

horn-bow Either a bow tipped with a horn or curved like a horn; the bow was not a common Anglo-Saxon weapon.
unavenged The crime could not be wiped out by *wergild* or by vengeance since it was unwit-ting and the king was father of both parties.
gallows Similarly, since no *wergild* or vengeance could be exacted for an executed criminal, his father could only mourn.

And his heart has no hope of another heir,
Seeing the one has gone to his grave.
In the house of his son he gazes in sorrow
On wine-hall deserted and swept by the wind,
Empty of joy. The horsemen and heroes
Sleep in the grave. No sound of the harp,
2320 No welcoming revels as often of old!
He goes to his bed with his burden of grief;
To his spirit it seems that dwelling and land
Are empty and lonely, lacking his son.
    So the helm of the Weders° yearned after Herebeald
And welling sadness surged in his heart.
He could not avenge the feud on the slayer
Nor punish the prince for the loathsome deed,
Though he loved him no longer, nor held him dear.
Because of this sorrow that sore befell
2330 He left life's joys for the heavenly light,
Granting his sons, as a good man will,
Cities and land, when he went from the world.
    Then across the wide water was conflict and war,
A striving and struggle of Swedes and Geats,
A bitter hatred, when Hrethel died.
Ongentheow's sons° were dauntless and daring,
Cared not for keeping of peace overseas;
But often around Hreosnabeorh° slaughtered and slew.
My kinsmen avenged the feud and the evil,
2340 As many have heard, though one of the Weders
Paid with his life—a bargain full bitter!
Hæthcyn's° fate was to fall in the fight.
It is often recounted, a kinsman with sword-edge
Avenged in the morning the murderer's deed
When Ongentheow met Eofor. Helm split asunder;
The aged Scylfing° sank down to his death.
The hand that felled him remembered the feud
And drew not back from the deadly blow.
    For all the rich gifts that Hygelac gave me
2350 I repaid him in battle with shining sword,
As chance was given. He granted me land,
A gracious dwelling and goodly estate.
Nor needed he seek of the Gifths,° or the Spear-Danes,
Or in Swedish land, a lesser in war

helm . . . Weders protector (helmet) of the
Geats, i.e. Hrethel
Ongentheow's sons Onela and Ohthere, of the
Swedish royal family
Hreosnabeorh a hill in Geat territory
Hæthcyn a prince of the Geats, second son of
Hrethel, who had accidentally killed his elder
brother Herebeald with an arrow and there-
fore succeeded his father on the throne. Hæth-
cyn was killed by Ongentheow, the Swedish

king (see below) in battle at Ravenswood and
was succeeded by Hygelac. Eofor avenged
Hæthcyn's death by killing Ongentheow.
aged Scylfing Ongentheow
Gifths an East Germanic tribe, the Gepidae,
having affinities with the Goths. They originally
lived near the delta of the Vistula, but moved
in the third century down to Hungary. Here
they still seem to be thought of as a Baltic
people.

To fight for pay; in the press of battle
I was always before him alone in the van.
So shall I bear me while life-days last,
While the sword holds out that has served me well
Early and late since I slew Dæghrefn,°
2360   The Frankish hero, before the host.
He brought no spoil from the field of battle,
No corselet of mail to the Frisian king.
Not by the sword the warden of standards,
The stalwart warrior, fell in the fight.
My battle-grip shattered the bones of his body
And silenced the heart-beat. But now with the sword,
With hand and hard blade, I must fight for the treasure.'

[*Beowulf and Wiglaf Slay the Dragon*]
For the last time Beowulf uttered his boast:
'I came in safety through many a conflict
2370   In the days of my youth; and now even yet,
Old as I am, I will fight this feud,
Do manful deeds, if the dire destroyer
Will come from his cavern to meet my sword.'
The king for the last time greeted his comrades,
Bold helmet-bearers and faithful friends:
'I would bear no sword nor weapon to battle
With the evil worm, if I knew how else
I could close with the fiend, as I grappled with Grendel.
From the worm I look for a welling of fire,
2380   A belching of venom, and therefore I bear
Shield and byrny. Not one foot's space
Will I flee from the monster, the ward of the mound.
It shall fare with us both in the fight at the wall
As Fate shall allot, the lord of mankind.
Though bold in spirit, I make no boast
As I go to fight with the flying serpent.
Clad in your corselets and trappings of war,
By the side of the barrow abide you to see
Which of us twain may best after battle
2390   Survive his wounds. Not yours the adventure,
Nor the mission of any, save mine alone,
To measure his strength with the monstrous dragon
And play the part of a valiant earl.
By deeds of daring I'll gain the gold
Or death in battle shall break your lord.'
Then the stalwart rose with his shield upon him,
Bold under helmet, bearing his sark
Under the stone-cliff; he trusted the strength

Dæghrefn a Frankish (Huga) warrior, standard
bearer, and perhaps slayer of Hygelac on his
last expedition; killed by Beowulf at that time

Of his single might. Not so does a coward!
2400 He who survived through many a struggle,
Many a combat and crashing of troops,
Saw where a stone-arch stood by the wall
And a gushing stream broke out from the barrow.
Hot with fire was the flow of its surge,
Nor could any abide near the hoard unburned,
Nor endure its depths, for the flame of the dragon.
Then the lord of the Geats in the grip of his fury
Gave shout of defiance; the strong-heart stormed.
His voice rang out with the rage of battle,
2410 Resounding under the hoary stone.
Hate was aroused; the hoard-warden knew
'Twas the voice of a man. No more was there time
To sue for peace; the breath of the serpent,
A blast of venom, burst from the rock.
The ground resounded; the lord of the Geats
Under the barrow swung up his shield
To face the dragon; the coiling foe
Was gathered to strike in the deadly strife.
The stalwart hero had drawn his sword,
2420 His ancient heirloom of tempered edge;
In the heart of each was fear of the other!
The shelter of kinsmen stood stout of heart
Under towering shield as the great worm coiled;
Clad in his war-gear he waited the rush.
In twisting folds the flame-breathing dragon
Sped to its fate. The shield of the prince
For a lesser while guarded his life and his body
Than heart had hoped. For the first time then
It was not his portion to prosper in war;
2430 Fate did not grant him glory in battle!
Then lifted his arm the lord of the Geats
And smote the worm with his ancient sword
But the brown° edge failed as it fell on bone,
And cut less deep than the king had need
In his sore distress. Savage in mood
The ward of the barrow countered the blow
With a blast of fire; wide sprang the flame.
The ruler of Geats had no reason to boast;
His unsheathed iron, his excellent sword,
2440 Had weakened as it should not, had failed in the fight.
It was no easy journey for Ecgtheow's son
To leave this world and against his will
Find elsewhere a dwelling! So every man shall
In the end give over this fleeting life.
     Not long was the lull. Swiftly the battlers

brown lit. "bright," "shining"

Renewed their grapple. The guard of the hoard
Grew fiercer in fury. His venomous breath
Beat in his breast. Enveloped in flame
The folk-leader suffered a sore distress.
2450   No succoring band of shoulder-companions,
No sons of warriors aided him then
By valor in battle. They fled to the forest
To save their lives; but a sorrowful spirit
Welled in the breast of one of the band.
The call of kinship can never be stilled
In the heart of a man who is trusty and true.
　　　　His name was Wiglaf,° Weohstan's° son,
A prince of the Scylfings, a peerless thane,
Ælfhere's° kinsman; he saw his king
2460   Under his helmet smitten with heat.
He thought of the gifts which his lord had given,
The wealth and the land of the Wægmunding line
And all the folk-rights his father had owned;
Nor could he hold back, but snatched up his buckler,
His linden shield and his ancient sword,
Heirloom of Eanmund, Ohthere's son,
Whom Weohstan slew with the sword in battle,
Wretched and friendless and far from home.
The brown-hued° helmet he bore to his kinsmen,
2470   The ancient blade and the byrny of rings.
These Onela° gave him—his nephew's arms—
Nor called for vengeance, nor fought the feud,
Though Weohstan had slaughtered his brother's son.°
He° held the treasures for many half-years,
The byrny and sword, till his son was of age
For manful deeds, as his father before him.
Among the Geats he gave him of war-gear
Countless numbers of every kind;
Then, full of winters, he left the world,
2480   Gave over this life. And Wiglaf, the lad,

Wiglaf The passage seems at first contradictory about the origins of Wiglaf in that he is said to be both Swede (Scylfing) and Geat (the Wægmundings were the Geat family to which Beowulf belonged). But the poet may mean that the young Wiglaf is of Swedish royal blood and now under the protection of Beowulf, as one of his household. This system of putting children, sometimes as young as seven years old, to be brought up in another family was common among Germanic peoples.
Weohstan's Wiglaf's father, a Swede, may also have changed his allegiance and become a vassal of Beowulf's. Previously, he had taken part in Swedish King Onela's attack on Heardred, king of the Geats, and himself killed Eanmund, whom Heardred was protecting, receiving Eanmund's sword and armor as the spoils of war. Wiglaf had inherited Eanmund's sword from

his father and was now using it against the dragon.
Ælfhere not otherwise known
brown-hued lit. "shining bright"
Onela All the spoils of war belonged by right to the lord, who apportioned them among his followers.
Nor called . . . brother's son The remark has nothing to do with *wergild*: in the heroic age the normal thing would have been for Eanmund's killing to be avenged in blood by his uncle Onela, but Eanmund, having fought against his uncle, has forfeited this family right and Onela is, on the contrary, grateful to Weohstan for killing his kinsman, so that he rewards Weohstan instead of demanding retribution from him.
he Weohstan

Was to face with his lord the first of his battles,
The hazard of war. But his heart did not fail
Nor the blade of his kinsman weaken in war,
As the worm soon found when they met in the fight!
    Wiglaf spoke in sorrow of soul,
With bitter reproach rebuking his comrades:°
'I remember the time, as we drank in the mead-hall,
When we swore to our lord who bestowed these rings
That we would repay for the war-gear and armor,

2490 The hard swords and helmets, if need like this
Should ever befall him. He chose us out
From all the host for this high adventure,
Deemed us worthy of glorious deeds,
Gave me these treasures, regarded us all
As high-hearted bearers of helmet and spear—
Though our lord himself, the shield of his people,
Thought single-handed to finish this feat,
Since of mortal men his measure was most
Of feats of daring and deeds of fame.

2500 Now is the day that our lord has need
Of the strength and courage of stalwart men.
Let us haste to succor his sore distress
In the horrible heat and the merciless flame.
God knows I had rather the fire should enfold
My body and limbs with my gold-friend and lord.
Shameful it seems that we carry our shields
Back to our homes ere we harry the foe
And ward the life of the Weder king.
Full well I know it is not his due

2510 That he alone, of the host of the Geats,
Should suffer affliction and fall in the fight.
One helmet and sword, one byrny and shield,
Shall serve for us both in the storm of strife.'
Then Wiglaf dashed through the deadly reek
In his battle-helmet to help his lord.
Brief were his words: 'Beloved Beowulf,
Summon your strength, remember the vow
You made of old in the years of youth
Not to allow your glory to lessen

2520 As long as you lived. With resolute heart,
And dauntless daring, defend your life
With all your force. I fight at your side!'
    Once again the worm, when the words were spoken,
The hideous foe in a horror of flame,
Rushed in rage at the hated men.
Wiglaf's buckler was burned to the boss

comrades a typical *comitatus* speech

In the billows of fire; his byrny of mail
Gave the young hero no help or defense.
But he stoutly pressed on under shield of his kinsman
2530 When his own was consumed in the scorching flame.
Then the king once more was mindful of glory,
Swung his great sword-blade with all his might
And drove it home on the dragon's head.
But Nægling° broke, it failed in the battle,
The blade of Beowulf, ancient and gray.
It was not his lot that edges of iron
Could help him in battle; his hand was too strong,
Overtaxed, I am told, every blade with its blow.
Though he bore a wondrous hard weapon to war,
2540 No whit the better was he thereby!
　　　A third time then the terrible scather,
The monstrous dragon inflamed with the feud,
Rushed on the king when the opening offered,
Fierce and flaming; fastened its fangs
In Beowulf's throat; he was bloodied with gore;
His life-blood streamed from the welling wound.
　　　As they tell the tale, in the king's sore need
His shoulder-companion showed forth his valor,
His craft° and courage, and native strength.
2550 To the head of the dragon he paid no heed,
Though his hand was burned as he helped his king.
A little lower the stalwart struck
At the evil beast, and his blade drove home
Plated° and gleaming. The fire began
To lessen and wane. The king of the Weders
Summoned his wits; he drew the dagger
He wore on his corselet, cutting and keen,
And slit asunder the worm with the blow.
So they felled the foe and wrought their revenge;
2560 The kinsmen together had killed the dragon.
So a man should be when the need is bitter!
That was the last fight Beowulf fought;
That was the end of his work in the world.

　　　[*Beowulf's Death*]
The wound which the dragon had dealt him began
To swell and burn; and soon he could feel
The baneful venom inflaming his breast.
The wise, old warrior sank down by the wall
And stared at the work of the giants of old,°
The arches of stone and the standing columns
2570 Upholding the ancient earth-hall within.

Nægling Beowulf's sword
craft skill in battle
plated or ornamented

work . . . old ancient buildings, usually taken
to be Roman ruins

His loyal thane, the kindest of comrades,
Saw Beowulf bloody and broken in war;
In his hands bore water and bathed his leader,
And loosened the helm from his dear lord's head.
    Beowulf spoke, though his hurt was sore,
The wounds of battle grievous and grim.
Full well he weened that his life was ended,
And all the joy of his years on earth;
That his days were done, and Death most near:
2580 'My armor and sword I would leave to my son
Had Fate but granted, born of my body,
An heir to follow me after I'm gone.
For fifty winters I've ruled this realm,
And never a lord of a neighboring land
Dared strike with terror or seek with sword.
In my life I abode by the lot assigned,
Kept well what was mine, courted no quarrels,
Swore no false oaths. And now for all this
Though my hurt is grievous, my heart is glad.
2590 When life leaves body, the Lord of mankind
Cannot lay to my charge the killing of kinsmen!
Go quickly, dear Wiglaf, to gaze on the gold
Beneath the hoar stone. The dragon lies still
In the slumber of death, despoiled of his hoard.
Make haste that my eyes may behold the treasure,
The gleaming jewels, the goodly store,
And, glad of the gold, more peacefully leave
The life and the realm I have ruled so long.'
    Then Weohstan's son, as they tell the tale,
2600 Clad in his corselet and trappings of war,
Hearkened at once to his wounded lord.
Under roof of the barrow he broke his way.
Proud in triumph he stood by the seat,
Saw glittering jewels and gold on the ground,
The den of the dragon, the old dawn-flier,
And all the wonders along the walls.
Great bowls and flagons of bygone men
Lay all unburnished and barren of gems,
Many a helmet ancient and rusted,
2610 Many an arm-ring cunningly wrought.
Treasure and gold, though hid in the ground,
Override man's wishes, hide them who will!
High o'er the hoard he beheld a banner,°
Greatest of wonders, woven° with skill,
All wrought of gold; its radiance lighted
The vasty ground and the glittering gems.

---

banner The word may mean a standard, not a   woven "Worked" is more accurate.
flag.

But no sign of the worm! The sword-edge had slain him.
As I've heard the tale, the hero unaided
Rifled those riches of giants of old,
2620 The hoard in the barrow, and heaped in his arms
Beakers and platters, picked what he would
And took the banner, the brightest of signs.
The ancient sword with its edge of iron
Had slain the worm who watched o'er the wealth,
In the midnight flaming, with menace of fire
Protecting the treasure for many a year
Till he died the death. Then Wiglaf departed
In haste returning enriched with spoil.
He feared, and wondered if still he would find
2630 The lord of the Weders alive on the plain,
Broken and weary and smitten with wounds.
With his freight of treasure he found the prince,
His dear lord, bloody and nigh unto death.
With water he bathed him till words broke forth
From the hoard of his heart and, aged and sad,
Beowulf spoke, as he gazed on the gold:
'For this goodly treasure whereon I gaze
I give my thanks to the Lord of all,
To the Prince of glory, Eternal God,
2640 Who granted me grace to gain for my people
Such dower of riches before my death.
I gave my life for this golden hoard.
Heed well the wants, the need of my people;
My hour is come, and my end is near.
Bid warriors build, when they burn my body,
A stately barrow on the headland's height.
It shall be for remembrance among my people
As it towers high on the Cape of the Whale,°
And sailors shall know it as Beowulf's Barrow,
2650 Sea-faring mariners driving their ships
Through fogs of ocean from far countries.'
Then the great-hearted king unclasped from his throat
A collar of gold, and gave to his thane;
Gave the young hero his gold-decked helmet,
His ring and his byrny, and wished him well.
'You are the last of the Wægmunding line.
All my kinsmen, earls in their glory,
Fate has sent to their final doom,
And I must follow.' These words were the last
2660 The old king spoke ere the pyre received him,

Cape of the Whale Hrones-næs, a headland on the coast of Geatland. The almost literal parallel with the make-up and position of the funeral pyre here with that of Achilles and Patroclus in the *Odyssey* (XXIV. 80 ff.) has often been noticed. Earlier, cremation of Germanic chieftains was less elaborate; see Tacitus, *Germania*, 27.

The leaping flames of the funeral blaze,
And his breath went forth from his bosom, his soul
Went forth from the flesh, to the joys of the just.
    Then bitter it was for Beowulf's thane
To behold his loved one lying on earth
Suffering sore at the end of life.
The monster that slew him, the dreadful dragon,
Likewise lay broken and brought to his death.
The worm no longer could rule the hoard,
2670 But the hard, sharp sword, the work of the hammer,
Had laid him low; and the winged dragon
Lay stretched near the barrow, broken and still.
No more in the midnight he soared in air,
Disclosing his presence, and proud of his gold;
For he sank to earth by the sword of the king.
But few of mankind, if the tales be true,
Has it prospered much, though mighty in war
And daring in deed, to encounter the breath
Of the venomous worm or plunder his wealth
2680 When the ward of the barrow held watch o'er the mound.
Beowulf bartered his life for the treasure;
Both foes had finished this fleeting life.
    Not long was it then till the laggards in battle
Came forth from the forest, ten craven in fight,
Who had dared not face the attack of the foe
In their lord's great need. The shirkers in shame
Came wearing their bucklers and trappings of war
Where the old man lay. They looked upon Wiglaf.
Weary he sat by the side of his leader
2690 Attempting with water to waken his lord.
It availed him little; the wish was vain!
He could not stay his soul upon earth,
Nor one whit alter the will of God.
The Lord ruled over the lives of men
As He rules them still. With a stern rebuke
He reproached the cowards whose courage had failed.
Wiglaf addressed them, Weohstan's son;
Gazed sad of heart on the hateful men:
'Lo! he may say who would speak the truth
2700 That the lord who gave you these goodly rings,
This warlike armor wherein you stand—
When oft on the ale-bench he dealt to his hall-men
Helmet and byrny, endowing his thanes
With the fairest he found from near or from far—
That he grievously wasted these trappings of war
When battle befell him. The king of the folk
Had no need to boast of his friends in the fight.
But the God of victory granted him strength

To avenge himself with the edge of the sword
2710 When he needed valor. Of little avail
The help I brought in the bitter battle!
Yet still I strove, though beyond my strength,
To aid my kinsman. And ever the weaker
The savage foe when I struck with my sword;
Ever the weaker the welling flame!
Too few defenders surrounded our ruler
When the hour of evil and terror befell.
Now granting of treasure and giving of swords,
Inherited land-right and joy of the home,
2720 Shall cease from your kindred. And each of your clan
Shall fail of his birthright when men from afar
Hear tell of your flight and your dastardly deed.
Death is better for every earl
Than life besmirched with the brand of shame!'

[*The Messenger Foretells the Doom of the Geats*]
Then Wiglaf bade tell the tidings of battle
Up over the cliff in the camp of the host
Where the linden-bearers° all morning long
Sat wretched in spirit, and ready for both,
The return, or the death, of their dear-loved lord.
2730 Not long did he hide, who rode up the headland,
The news of their sorrow, but spoke before all:
'Our leader lies low, the lord of the Weders,
The king of the Geats, on the couch of death.
He sleeps his last sleep by the deeds of the worm.
The dreadful dragon is stretched beside him
Slain with dagger-wounds. Not by the sword
Could he quell the monster or lay him low.
And Wiglaf is sitting, Weohstan's son,
Bent over Beowulf, living by dead.
2740 Death watch he keeps in sorrow of spirit
Over the bodies of friend and foe.

Now comes peril of war when this news is rumored abroad,
The fall of our king known afar among Frisians and Franks!
For a fierce feud rose with the Franks when Hygelac's warlike host
Invaded the Frisian fields, and the Hetware vanquished the Geats,
Overcame with the weight of their hordes, and Hygelac fell in the fray;
It was not his lot to live on dispensing the spoils of war.
And never since then of the Franks had we favor or friend.
And I harbor no hope of peace or faith from the Swedish folk,
2750 *For well is it known of men that Ongentheow° slew with the sword*
Hæthcyn, the son of Hrethel, near Ravenswood, in the fight

linden-bearers shield-bearers, warriors
Ongentheow See ll. 2342 ff. for the battle at
Ravenswood.

When the Swedish people in pride swept down on the Geats.°
And Ohthere's aged father,° old and a terror in battle,
Made onslaught, killing their king, and rescued his queen,°
Ohthere's mother and Onela's, aged, bereft of her gold.
He followed the flying foe till, lordless and lorn,
They barely escaped into Ravenswood. There he beset them,
A wretched remnant of war, and weary with wounds.
And all the long hours of the night he thundered his threats
2760   That some on the morrow he would slay with the edge of the sword,
And some should swing on the gallows for food for the fowls!°
But hope returned with the dawn to the heavy-hearted
When they heard the sound of the trumpets and Hygelac's horn,
As the good king came with his troops marching up on their track.
        Then was a gory meeting of Swedes and Geats;
On all sides carnage and slaughter, savage and grim,
As the struggling foemen grappled and swayed in the fight.
And the old earl Ongentheow, crestfallen and cowed,
Fled with his men to a fastness, withdrew to the hills.
2770   He had tasted Hygelac's strength, the skill of the hero in war,
And he had no hope to resist or strive with the sea-men,
To save his hoard from their hands, or his children, or wife.
So the old king fled to his fortress; but over the plain
Hygelac's banners swept on in pursuit of the Swedes,
Stormed to the stronghold's defenses, and old Ongentheow°
Was brought to bay with the sword, and subject to Eofor's will!
Wulf, son of Wonred, in wrath then struck with his sword,
And the blood in streams burst forth from under the old man's hair.
Yet the aged Scylfing was all undaunted and answered the stroke
2780   With a bitter exchange in the battle; and Wonred's brave son
Could not requite the blow, for the hero had cleft his helmet,
And, covered with blood, he was forced to bow; he fell to the earth.
But his death was not doomed, and he rallied, though the wound was deep.
Then Hygelac's hardy thane,° when his brother lay low,
Struck with his ancient blade, a sturdy sword of the giants,
Cut through the shield-wall, cleaving the helmet. The king,
The folk-defender, sank down. He was hurt unto death.
Then were many that bound Wulf's wounds when the fight was won,
When the Geats held the ground of battle; as booty of war
2790   Eofor stripped Ongentheow of iron byrny and helm,
Of sword-blade hilted and hard, and bore unto Hygelac

Swedish . . . Geats The Swedes had perhaps first provoked a battle—now the Geats had made an expedition in revenge.
father Ongentheow
queen The Geats, under their king, Hæthcyn, are at first successful and capture Ongentheow's queen. Then Ongentheow rescues her and kills Hæthcyn, after which he drives the Geatish forces into Ravenswood. Then Hygelac, Hæthcyn's brother and successor, arrives with reinforcements, and Ongentheow in his turn is

driven to take refuge and is killed. The next stages in the Geat-Swedish war have already been told at ll. 2464 ff. and 2246 ff.
fowls carrion birds
Ongentheow Ongentheow first fells, but does not kill, Wulf, one of the sons of Wonred, who has wounded him. Wonred's other son, Eofor, then kills Ongentheow and strips him of his armor and ornaments.
thane Eofor

The old man's trappings of war. And Hygelac took the treasures,
Promising fair rewards, and this he fulfilled.
The son of Hrethel, the king of the Geats, when he came to his home,
Repaid with princely treasure the prowess of Eofor and Wulf;
Gave each an hundred thousand° of land and linked rings,
And none could belittle or blame. They had won the honor in war.
He gave to Eofor also the hand of his only daughter
To be a pledge of good will, and the pride of his home.

2800   This is the fighting and this the feud,
The bitter hatred, that breeds the dread
Lest the Swedish people should swarm against us°
Learning our lord lies lifeless and still.
His was the hand that defended the hoard,
Heroes, and realm against ravaging foe,
By noble counsel and dauntless deed.
Let us go quickly to look on the king
Who brought us treasure, and bear his corpse
To the funeral pyre. The precious hoard
2810   Shall burn with the hero. There lies the heap
Of untold treasure so grimly gained,
Jewels and gems he bought with his blood
At the end of life. All these at the last
The flames shall veil and the brands devour.
No man for remembrance shall take from the treasure,
Nor beauteous maiden adorn her breast
With gleaming jewel; bereft of gold
And tragic-hearted many shall tread
A foreign soil, now their lord has ceased
2820   From laughter and revel and rapture of joy.
Many a spear in the cold of morning
Shall be borne in hand uplifted on high.
No sound of harp shall waken the warrior,
But the dusky raven despoiling the dead
Shall clamor and cry and call to the eagle
What fare he found at the carrion-feast
The while with the wolf he worried the corpses.'°
    So the stalwart hero had told his tidings,
His fateful message; nor spoke amiss
2830   As to truth or telling. The host arose;
On their woeful way to the Eagles' Ness°
They went with tears to behold the wonder.

hundred thousand If this meant 100,000 hides or measures of land (see above), it would equal the size of Geatland itself: probably the meaning is "the value of 100,000 (coins) in land and gold."
Lest . . . us The point of the Ravenswood story: the messenger fears that, once the death of Beowulf becomes known, the Swedes will renew their attacks on the Geats, now without their protector.
eagle . . . corpses See "The Wanderer" (ll. 74–75).
Eagles' Ness Earna-næs, perhaps modern Swedish Ornäs—the promontory near the scene of Beowulf's battle with the dragon

They found the friend, who had dealt them treasure
In former days, on the bed of death,
Stretched out lifeless upon the sand.
The last of the good king's days was gone;
Wondrous the death of the Weder prince!
They had sighted first, where it lay outstretched,
The monstrous wonder, the loathsome worm,
2840 The horrible fire-drake, hideous-hued,
Scorched with the flame. The spread of its length
Was fifty foot-measures! Oft in the night
It sported in air, then sinking to earth
Returned to its den. Now moveless in death
It had seen the last of its earthly lair.
Beside the dragon were bowls and beakers,
Platters lying, and precious swords
Eaten with rust, where the hoard had rested
A thousand winters in the womb of earth.
2850 That boundless treasure of bygone men,
The golden dower, was girt with a spell
So that never a man might ravage the ring-hall
Save as God himself, the Giver of victory—
He is the Shelter and Shield of men—
Might allow such man as seemed to Him meet,
Might grant whom He would, to gather the treasure.
      His way of life, who had wickedly hoarded
The wealth of treasure beneath the wall,
Had an evil end, as was widely seen.
2860 Many the dragon had sent to death,
But in fearful fashion the feud was avenged!
'Tis a wondrous thing when a warlike earl
Comes to the close of his destined days,
When he may no longer among his kinsmen
Feast in the mead-hall. So Beowulf fared
When he sought the dragon in deadly battle!
Himself he knew not what fate was in store
Nor the coming end of his earthly life.
The lordly princes who placed the treasure
2870 Had cursed it deep to the day of doom,
That the man who plundered and gathered the gold
Might pay for the evil imprisoned in hell,
Shackled in torment and punished with pain,
Except the invader should first be favored
With the loving grace of the Lord of all!
      Then spoke Wiglaf, Weohstan's son:
'Often for one man many must sorrow
As has now befallen the folk of the Geats.
We could not persuade the king by our counsel,
2880 Our well-loved leader, to shun assault

On the dreadful dragon guarding the gold;
To let him lie where he long had lurked
In his secret lair till the world shall end.
But Beowulf, dauntless, pressed to his doom.
The hoard was uncovered; heavy the cost;
Too strong the fate that constrained the king!
I entered the barrow, beholding the hoard
And all the treasure throughout the hall;
In fearful fashion the way was opened,
2890   An entrance under the wall of earth.
Of the hoarded treasure I heaped in my arms
A weighty burden, and bore to my king.
He yet was living; his wits were clear.
Much the old man said in his sorrow;
Sent you greeting, and bade you build
In the place of burning a lofty barrow,
Proud and peerless, to mark his deeds;
For he was of all men the worthiest warrior
In all the earth, while he still might rule
2900   And wield the wealth of his lordly land.
Let us haste once more to behold the treasure,
The gleaming wonders beneath the wall.
I will show the way that you all may see
And closely scan the rings and the gold.
Let the bier be ready, the pyre prepared,
When we come again to carry our lord,
Our leader beloved, where long he shall lie
In the kindly care of the Lord of all.'

[*Beowulf's Funeral*]
Then the son of Weohstan, stalwart in war,
2910   Bade send command to the heads of homes
To bring from afar the wood for the burning
Where the good king lay: 'Now gleed° shall devour,
As dark flame waxes, the warrior prince
Who has often withstood the shower of steel
When the storm of arrows, sped from the string,
Broke over shield, and shaft did service,
With feather-fittings guiding the barb.'
Then the wise son of Weohstan chose from the host
Seven thanes of the king, the best of the band;
2920   Eight heroes together they hied to the barrow
In under the roof of the fearful foe;
One of the warriors leading the way
Bore in his hand a burning brand.
They cast no lots who should loot the treasure

gleed fire

When they saw unguarded the gold in the hall
Lying there useless; little they scrupled
As quickly they plundered the precious store.
Over the sea-cliff into the ocean
They tumbled the dragon, the deadly worm,

2930 Let the sea-tide swallow the guarder of gold.
Then a wagon was loaded with well-wrought treasure,
A countless number of every kind;
And the aged warrior, the white-haired king,
Was borne on high to the Cape of the Whale.

The Geat folk fashioned a peerless pyre
Hung round with helmets and battle-boards,°
With gleaming byrnies as Beowulf bade.
In sorrow of soul they laid on the pyre
Their mighty leader, their well-loved lord.

2940 The warriors kindled the bale° on the barrow,
Wakened the greatest of funeral fires.
Dark o'er the blaze the wood-smoke mounted;
The winds were still, and the sound of weeping
Rose with the roar of the surging flame
Till the heat of the fire had broken the body.
With hearts that were heavy they chanted their sorrow,
Singing a dirge for the death of their lord;
And an aged woman with upbound locks
Lamented for Beowulf, wailing in woe.°

2950 Over and over she uttered her dread
Of sorrow to come, of bloodshed and slaughter,
Terror of battle, and bondage, and shame.
The smoke of the bale-fire rose to sky!

The men of the Weder folk fashioned a mound
Broad and high on the brow of the cliff,
Seen from afar by seafaring men.
Ten days they worked on the warrior's barrow
Inclosing the ash of the funeral flame
With a wall as worthy as wisdom could shape.

2960 They bore to the barrow the rings and the gems,
The wealth of the hoard the heroes had plundered.
The olden treasure they gave to the earth,
The gold to the ground, where it still remains
As useless to men as it was of yore.
Then round the mound rode the brave in battle,°
The sons of warriors, twelve in a band,
Bemoaning their sorrow and mourning their king.

---

battle-boards i.e. shields
bale pyre, bonfire
And . . . woe (ll. 2948–49) The manuscript
is damaged at this point, but the word "Geatish"
has been deciphered as describing the woman.

Some take this to mean that Beowulf had
married Hygelac's widow, Hygd.
round . . . battle See the account in the sixth-
century Gothic historian Jordanes of the funeral
of Attila the Hun; and Virgil's *Aeneid* XI.182–
212.

They sang their dirge and spoke of the hero
Vaunting his valor and venturous deeds.
2970 So is it proper a man should praise
His friendly lord with a loving heart,
When his soul must forth from the fleeting flesh.
So the folk of the Geats, the friends of his hearth,
Bemoaned the fall of their mighty lord;
Said he was kindest of worldly kings,
Mildest, most gentle, most eager for fame.

8th century   1815

Deor's Lament

This poem and "The Wanderer," which follows it here, are preserved in the Exeter Book, a manuscript collection of Anglo-Saxon poetry transcribed at the end of the tenth century and given to the chapter of Exeter Cathedral, in Devon, by its Archbishop, Leofric, in the middle of the eleventh. The book is still kept in the chapter library at Exeter. None of the poems in it has a title: the titles by which the poems are now known have all been supplied by modern editors.

Nothing is known of the bard who names himself *Deor* (Brave or Excellent) in line 35. We do not know, either, when he wrote his poem. It cannot (by reason of the references to Theodoric the Ostrogoth) be earlier than the sixth century in origin; it may belong to the eighth; and there is evidence that it existed in King Alfred's time (reigned 871–99). Perhaps the most likely date is the late ninth century.

The mood of "Deor's Lament" is elegiac, and its genre that of the *consolatio*, the topics of which go back at least as far as Homer. The Roman poets use them often— Horace, for example:

> Dead too is the sire of Pelops, the guest of the gods
> And Tithonus, carried off into air,
> And Minos, party to Jove's secrets. Now Tartarus
> Keeps Panthous' son . . .

All these great men had to die: their greatness could not save them from the greatest misfortune of all. We who remain must take what consolation we can from the realization that our lot is common to all. What must happen must happen. We can hope for better in this life than its misfortunes, but the ways of the gods are inscrutable.

When Christian writers took over the topics of the *consolatio*, they could add a dimension: God's ways were mysterious, but there was the promise of eternal life, vindication, and happiness for the good man. But though "Deor's Lament" is a poem written by a Christian, it can hardly be called a Christian poem: hope is for the passing of sorrow in this world, not in the world to come. The quality of that hope can be read as stoical resignation toward, or as heroic defiance of, the lot of Deor. The refrain which drives home the moral and separates the single *exempla* of misfortune one from another can be read in either sense. In the conventional consolatory mode, the poem proceeds by these *exempla* of misfortune, its structure a set of such units, its movement punctuated by the refrain. In this it is unusual, almost unique in Anglo-

Saxon poetry: only one other poem, and that a late one, uses a stanza division, and only one other any kind of refrain.

Though the poet is using a genre that was popular in the Latin poetry of the early Middle Ages, his *exempla* are all drawn from Germanic legend. His characters would be well known to his audience. Weland, Beadohild, and Mæthhild are entirely mythological; Theodoric and Eormanric were historical characters around whom legend grew. But though all but Mæthhild are familiar figures, no coherent or convincing explanation of their presence together in the poem has yet been offered.

The translations of this poem and the three that follow ("The Wanderer," *The Battle of Maldon,* and *The Dream of the Rood*) are those of C. W. Kennedy, published in his *An Anthology of Old English Poetry,* 1960. The lines have been numbered here merely as a guide.

Deor's° Lament

Weland° knew fully° affliction and woe,
Hero unflinching enduring distress;
Had for companionship heart-break and longing,
Wintry exile and anguish of soul,
When Nithhad bound him, the better man,
Grimly constrained him with sinewy bonds.°

That evil ended.° So also may this!

 Nor was brother's death to Beadohild
A sorrow as deep as her own sad plight,
10 When she knew the weight of the child in her womb,
But little could know what her lot might be.

That evil ended.° So also may this!

 Many have heard of the rape of Hild,°
Of her father's affection and infinite love,
Whose nights were sleepless with sorrow and grief.

That evil ended. So also may this!

Deor's This poet is mentioned nowhere else and nothing is known of him beyond the poem's implication that he was an exile; the name is probably a persona adopted by the poet.
Weland or Wayland or Welund, whose name means "maker" or "workman," the smith of Germanic legend, a supernatural being corresponding to the Vulcan of classical mythology. He had been captured by Nithhad, set to work, and hamstrung to prevent his escape. But he managed to escape, after all, killing the two sons of Nithhad and raping his daughter Beadohild. Weland is shown on the whalebone reliefs of the Franks Casket (Northumbria, *c.* 700) in the British Museum (Fig. 22).
fully a fill-in for two words in the Old English for which no one has yet suggested a suitable translation

sinewy bonds bonds imposed by cutting the sinews
That . . . ended Weland got away (by flying, in one form of the story).
That . . . ended (l. 12) As a result of the rape, Beadohild bore the hero Widia; the poet considers that to be the mother of a hero is sufficient compensation for her.
Hild Beadohild. This translation takes this and the obscure next two lines to be a restatement of Beadohild's plight as it affected her father. The reference may rather be to an unidentified Hild or Mæthhild and an unidentified Geat, her lover, so that **affection . . . love** should be rendered "passion," and **sorrow and grief** as "bitter love."

For thirty winters   Theodoric° held,
As many have known,   the Mæring's stronghold.

That evil ended.   So also may this!

20   We have heard of Eormanric's°   wolf-like ways,
Widely ruling   the realm of the Goths;°
Grim was his menace,   and many a man,
Weighted with sorrow   and presage of woe,
Wished that the end   of his kingdom were come.

That evil ended.   So also may this!

He who knows sorrow,   despoiled of joys,
Sits heavy of mood;   to his heart it seemeth
His measure of misery   meeteth no end.
Yet well may he think   how oft in this world
30   The wise Lord varies   His ways to men,
Granting wealth and honor   to many an eorl,°
To others awarding   a burden of woe.

And so I can sing   of my own sad plight
Who long stood high   as the Heodenings'° bard,
Deor my name,   dear to my lord.
Mild was my service   for many a winter,
Kindly my king   till Heorrenda° came
Skillful in song   and usurping the land-right°
Which once my gracious lord   granted to me.

40   That evil ended.   So also may this!

Late 9th century

The Wanderer

"The Wanderer," anonymous, untitled, and elegiac, is preserved in the Exeter Book along with the group of poems usually known as the *Elegies:* "The Ruin," "The Seafarer," "The Husband's Message," and "The Wife's Lament." All deal with exile, solitariness, separation, loss—generally the loss of fellow warriors and protectors. Anglo-Saxon literature has little to say about the pangs of lovers, almost nothing that can be called love-poetry.

Theodoric probably Theodoric the Great, 454–526, king of the Ostrogoths, lord of Italy, who murdered Odoacer, the barbarian mercenary who had made himself Emperor of the West in 493; the reference is not clear. Others have suggested that Theodoric the Frank (Wolfdietrich), who also suffered exile and defeat, may be meant. The Mæring (l. 18) may be Theodoric.
Eormanric's the historical Eormanric, or Ermanric, king of the Ostrogoths, who died about 375, having made himself ruler from the Baltic to the Black Sea; later legend made him a cruel tyrant.

Goths the Ostrogoths, who originated in southern Russia and held Italy during the late fifth and early sixth century
eorl The word means either a nobleman, man of the upper class (as it does here), or a warrior: by this time its use was largely confined to poetry.
Heodenings' ruling family, descended from Heoden
Heorrenda Nothing is known of this bard, either.
land-right estate granted to Deor as a reward for his poetry

No trace of love between man and woman is found in "The Wanderer," the finest of the elegiac lyrics. Its poignancy, its desolate chill, the atmosphere of physical and mental suffering it conveys, spring from the loss of the lord, protector of and provider for his household, from the loss of companions-at-arms, of the joys of feasting, drinking, of song and story and boast in the mead-hall, from the transitoriness of what is glorious and desirable in this world. The lord's death is the greatest of tragedies: it casts a man, old and unprotected when he most needs protection, on a hostile world, where all is perpetual winter.

The poem is a difficult one. Its language presents many problems, and the exact connotations that the poet intends us to catch are elusive. In genre it is an elegiac *consolatio*, written by a Christian poet who had some familiarity with Latin literature, as well as being steeped in the traditions of the Anglo-Saxon poetic craft. For some, the poem is an allegory: the exile it portrays is the spiritual exile from God of the Christian, while he is still in the world—so that the exile's journey is a kind of *Pilgrim's Progress*, by sea and not by land, the sea being the chosen road of the early Germanic peoples. The difficulty about this view is that such a specifically Christian allegory is not found elsewhere in Anglo-Saxon poetry, except in the set forms of the *Bestiary* or *The Phoenix*, both of which are, significantly, translations. The poem is perhaps best read as a moralization on the theme of the vanity of worldly things and worldly joy.

The Wanderer's opening statement of his faith that, after all the weariness and bitter cold of his life on earth, he will at last find comfort (ll. 1–7), is taken up again to round off the poem (ll. 103 ff.). Between, he tells of the tribulations of the man who must seek a new lord and new comrades, and the desolation he endures when, frozen and weary upon a freezing sea, he falls asleep, to dream of the warmth and happiness of companionship and feasting, only to wake and find it all a dream (ll. 8–53). Then, in the second section of the poem, he turns to meditate on his experience, to apply its lessons. Some have assumed that this second part of the poem is spoken by a third person, the sage who (l. 103) takes up the argument after the poet has provided the framework (ll. 6–7 and other occasional remarks) and the Wanderer has made his catalogue of wretchedness.

Of the poet who wrote "The Wanderer" we know nothing, not even an approximate date of birth or death. The most likely date of composition is the early tenth century.

The Wanderer°

Oft to the Wanderer,   weary of exile,
Cometh God's pity,   compassionate love,
Though woefully toiling   on wintry seas
With churning oar   in the icy wave,
Homeless and helpless   he fled from Fate.°
Thus saith the Wanderer   mindful of misery,
Grievous disasters,   and death° of kin:

Wanderer "Wanderer" is the translator's choice for words that literally would be "man alone" (l. 1) and "earth-walker" (l. 6).
Fate The translation of *wyrd* as "Fate" deserves comment because of basic etymologic differences. "Fate" is from a Latin root connected with speaking: that which has been decreed by the gods; *wyrd* is connected with the word for "become," and so literally means "what comes to pass" in the broadest context or, applied to men or to a single man, "the human lot," the state of change to which all are subject except God and the angels.
death by violence

'Oft when the day broke,   oft at the dawning,
Lonely and wretched   I wailed my woe.
10   No man is living,   no comrade left,
To whom I dare fully   unlock my heart.
I have learned truly   the mark of a man
Is keeping his counsel°   and locking his lips,
Let him think what he will!   For, woe of heart
Withstandeth not Fate;   a failing° spirit
Earneth no help.   Men eager for honor
Bury their sorrow   deep in the breast.
   'So have I also,   often in wretchedness
Fettered my feelings,   far from my kin,
20   Homeless and hapless,   since days of old,
When the dark earth   covered my dear lord's face,
And I sailed away   with sorrowful heart,
Over wintry seas,   seeking a gold-lord,°
If far or near   lived one to befriend me
With gift in the mead-hall   and comfort for grief.
   'Who bears it, knows   what a bitter companion,
Shoulder to shoulder,   sorrow can be,
When friends are no more.   His fortune is exile,
Not gifts of fine gold;   a heart that is frozen,
30   Earth's winsomeness dead.   And he dreams of the hall-men,
The dealing of treasure,   the days of his youth,
When his lord bade welcome   to wassail and feast.
But gone is that gladness,   and never again
Shall come the loved counsel   of comrade and king.
   'Even in slumber   his sorrow assaileth,
and, dreaming he claspeth   his dear lord again,
Head on knee, hand on knee,   loyally laying,
Pledging his liege°   as in days long past.
Then from his slumber   he starts lonely-hearted,
40   Beholding gray stretches   of tossing sea,
Sea-birds bathing,   with wings outspread,
While hailstorms darken,   and driving snow.
Bitterer then   is the bane of his wretchedness,
The longing for loved one: his grief is renewed.
The forms of his kinsmen   take shape in the silence;
In rapture he greets them;   in gladness he scans
Old comrades remembered.   But they melt into air
With no word of greeting   to gladden his heart.
Then again surges   his sorrow upon him;
50   And grimly he spurs   his weary soul

keeping . . . counsel According to Tacitus, in
his *Germania*, the Germanic peoples held that
"a woman may decently express her grief in
public; a man should nurse his in his heart."
failing Another translation is "fierce," to make
a contrasting pair—i.e. neither sorrow nor anger
will avail—rather than a repetitive pair.
gold-lord a generous giver of gold and gifts,
who would take him into his household
Head . . . liege kneeling before the lord and
making his profession of allegiance

Once more to the toil   of the tossing sea.
  'No wonder° therefore,   in all the world,
If a shadow darkens   upon my spirit
When I reflect   on the fates of men—
How one by one   proud warriors vanish
From the halls that knew them,   and day by day
All this earth ages   and droops unto death.
No man may know wisdom   till many a winter
Has been his portion.   A wise man is patient,
60   Not swift to anger,   nor hasty of speech,
Neither too weak,°   nor too reckless, in war,
Neither fearful nor fain,°   nor too wishful of wealth,
Nor too eager in vow°—   ere he know the event.
A brave man must bide   when he speaketh his boast
Until he know surely   the goal of his spirit.
  'A wise man will ponder   how dread is that doom
When all this world's wealth   shall be scattered and waste
As now, over all,   through the regions of earth,
Walls stand rime-covered   and swept by the winds.
70   The battlements crumble,   the wine-halls decay;
Joyless and silent   the heroes are sleeping
Where the proud host fell   by the wall they defended.
Some battle launched   on their long, last journey;
One a bird° bore   o'er the billowing sea
One the gray wolf° slew;   one a grieving eorl°
Sadly gave   to the grave's embrace.
The Warden of men   hath wasted this world
Till the sound of music   and revel is stilled,
And these giant-built structures°   stand empty of life.
80   'He who shall muse   on these mouldering ruins,
And deeply ponder   this darkling life,
Must brood on old legends   of battle and bloodshed,
And heavy the mood   that troubles his heart:
'Where now is the warrior?°   Where is the war horse?
Bestowal of treasure,   and sharing of feast?
Alas! the bright ale-cup,   the byrny-clad warrior,
The prince in his splendor°   —those days are long sped
In the night of the past,   as if they never had been!'

No wonder Some scholars see a break here, with a second speaker, not the Wanderer but the sage or wise man of l. 103, taking up the tale. A case can be made for this reading of the poem, but it is not necessary to make the division.
weak unreliable
fain probably fawning, servile
vow boastful promise
bird No completely convincing explanation has yet been offered of the bird; perhaps it is the eagle or the raven, feeding on corpses, a common occurrence in the battle scenes of Anglo-Saxon literature.

wolf perhaps, again, feeding on the dead in battle
eorl warrior
giant-built structures usually taken to be Roman ruins, buildings of the great men of far-off times
Where . . . warrior This brief *ubi sunt* lament, a further variation on the theme of transitoriness, on which the poem turns, is an echo of Latin homiletic and other works, applied to the things that the warrior prizes most.
splendor i.e. as the center of the heroic community

And now remains only,   for warriors' memorial,
90   A wall wondrous high   with serpent shapes° carved.
Storms of ash-spears°   have smitten the eorls,
Carnage of weapon,   and conquering Fate.
   'Storms now batter   these ramparts of stone;
Blowing snow   and the blast of winter
Enfold the earth;   night-shadows fall
Darkly lowering,   from the north driving
Raging hail   in wrath upon men.
Wretchedness fills   the realm of earth,
And Fate's decrees   transform the world.
100   Here wealth is fleeting,   friends are fleeting,
Man is fleeting,   maid is fleeting;
All the foundation of earth   shall fail!'
   Thus spake the sage   in solitude pondering.
Good man is he   who guardeth his faith.
He must never too quickly   unburden his breast
Of its sorrow, but eagerly   strive for redress;
And happy the man   who seeketh for mercy
From his heavenly Father,   our Fortress° and Strength.

? 10th century

The Battle of Maldon

This poem must have been written not long after the battle itself, which took place in 991. In this year, the terse prose narrative of the *Anglo-Saxon Chronicle* tells us, the Danes descended on the southeast coast of England. They came "with ninety-three ships to Folkestone, plundered the neighborhood and sailed on to Sandwich, whence they went to Ipswich, overran the whole countryside, and then proceeded to Maldon. Ealdorman Byrhtnoth came against them with the *fyrd* (the home levies) and fought them, but they killed the Ealdorman there and had possession of the battlefield . . ." Another version gives the information that "in this year it was decided for the first time to pay tribute to the Danes, because of the great terror they spread along the coast." This first time the amount was 10,000 pounds in gold and silver, but it was more later.

The annalists' bare little paragraphs set down the dismal facts, telling us nothing about the Battle of Maldon itself and next to nothing about the English leader, Byrhtnoth, except that he was a great nobleman. Nothing is said of how his noble qualities showed in the battle. Humiliation fills the scene, obliterating or crowding out everything else.

There had been for some years past plenty to be ashamed of. Scandinavian raiders had first attacked England in the late eighth century, and the contest between them

serpent shapes No architecture survives which would answer to this description; the nearest approaches are in Celtic minor art, the interlace patterns of Anglo-Saxon cross-shafts, metal work such as the Sutton Hoo buckle, or the Fetter-Lane sword pommel, all of which are on a much smaller scale.

ash-spears *æsc*, from the wood of which the shaft was made, one of the two normal names for a spear
Fortress See Proverbs 18:10, Psalms 17:2 for the notion of God as a fortress; Luther's *feste Burg* is a later example.

and the English had not finally been settled in England's favor until the early years of the tenth century, in spite of King Alfred's considerable victories. Since the Battle of Brunanburh in 937, there had been peace. Within a couple of years of the accession of King Ethelred II, the Unready (noble-counsel-no-counsel would be a way to render the Anglo-Saxon pun in his name and nickname), who reigned ignominiously from 978 to 1016, Danish raiders had begun again to harry the English coasts. They continued to do so throughout Ethelred's reign: countermeasures were sporadic, ill-organized, and unsuccessful. Treachery and betrayal were common among the nobility who ought to have been leading the resistance, and the payments by which the raiders were bought off became, later in Ethelred's reign, an annual and growing imposition (the tax was known as Danegeld). At Ethelred's death in 1016, a Dane, Canute, was finally crowned king of England.

Histories of Ethelred's reign chronicle warfare, misery, and defeat. Beside their grim story and spare language, the poem's depictions of Byrhtnoth's heroic qualities in stately and formal diction stand in marked contrast. The tale of his final battle emphasizes both the courage of other resistances and the cowardice of capitulations.

The poet's hero, Byrhtnoth, was at this time a man well over sixty, white-haired but still strikingly handsome, of giant height and strength. From a family of great land-owners near Cambridge, he had himself been made (in 956) *ealdorman* ("earl" would be a good modern equivalent) of the East Saxons (Essex), that is to say, a kind of sub-king, the king's deputy in all the functions of government. He was a man of great power in his district, high in the king's favor, a great respecter and patron of monastic foundations, as well as a great scourge of the Danes. Byrhtnoth's legend was still alive in the twelfth century, when most others had been forgotten. The poet's celebration of the Christian Earl's fruitless courage against the pagan raiders, glorifying the heroic ideal, with contempt—not less strongly felt for being formally expressed—for cowardice and breaking of allegiance, must have contributed substantially to the legend.

The poem, as we have it, lacks a beginning and an end; both were already missing when the poem perished in the fire of 1731 that damaged the manuscript of *Beowulf*. We have the text only from a transcript which had fortunately been made. It is probable that the fragment preserved is, in fact, almost the whole of the work and that the poet intended to plunge us immediately into the middle of the action—bringing us, as in so much oral poetry, quickly to the heart of its significance. We, like the original audience, are expected to know something of the events previous to the mutual and ceremonial tauntings of the two sides that precede the battle itself.

The Danish raiders had sailed up the estuary of the River Blackwater and established a base on Northey Island from which they could set out, by land or sea, in search of fresh plunder. The arm of the river that lay between them and the mainland was good protection from attack by land, but it had the disadvantage of being navigable only in a narrow channel at its center, so that ships could not be used to help them make raids further inland. Their only way across was by a ford, the *brycg*, with a causeway at water level, and this *brycg* was also the only means by which the English force could arrive at a hand-to-hand battle with the Vikings. At the landward end of the causeway the English force was stationed. In this position of stalemate, one side had to give, if there was to be any contest. Since it was essential to the English that the issue be decided, Byrhtnoth withdrew, placing his men to best tactical advantage at the head of a slope—and lost the battle (see map, Fig. 3).

Byrhtnoth had had little choice, but we should not assume that tactical considerations alone determined his action in allowing the raiders to cross. There is a strong element of heroic pride in his action, and the *Maldon* poet emphasizes this dimension. The word that he uses to characterize it—*ofermod*—is generally translated "rashness," but it more likely means "magnanimity," noble warrior's pride, scorning expediency, relying on fate and force of arms to settle the matter. The poem is, indeed, from first to last a presentation, the most richly compact and striking in Anglo-Saxon literature, of the heroic ideal of the Germanic peoples and its implications: the acceptance by the lesser nobility of the obligation of service to the lord, whose responsibility it was to provide the materials of combat, generous gifts of clothing, ornament and property, entertainment and protection, in return for unflinching service in peace and war. In this code, defeat was shame, even though it had involved no drawing back: cowardice, consequently, was an abomination. It is perfectly summed up in the words of Byrhtwold at the end of the poem:

> Heart must be braver, courage the bolder,
> Mood the stouter, as our strength grows less.

The poet's theme turns on this narrow Germanic convention of honor and loyalty. The heroic dimension to what was essentially a local battle, between marauding and experienced pirates and a largely untrained local force led by the small aristocratic retinue of the Ealdorman, is imparted by a rigorous restraint in language and in incident. Concentration and severity are the keynotes of the style, and a deliberate avoidance of richness in vocabulary and rhetoric. The battle resolves itself into a series of formal exchanges of insults, followed by descriptions of single combat. Nowhere in the whole corpus of Anglo-Saxon poetry is there such a complete and satisfying artistic success.

The Battle of Maldon

                        . . . . was broken.
He° bade a warrior°   abandon his horse°
And hurry forward   to join the fighters,
Take thought to his hands   and a stout heart.
Then Offa's kinsman°   knew that the eorl°
Would never suffer   weakness or fear;
And he let from hand   his beloved hawk
Fly to the forest,   and made haste to the front;
By which one could know   the lad would never

He Byrhtnoth
a warrior Offa's kinsman, see below
abandon . . . horse Cavalry was not much used in battle by the English at this period: the horses, having served for travel and transport, would be turned off for the duration of the fighting, partly to get them out of the way, partly as a deterrent from flight. On the terrain over which the Battle of Maldon was fought, horses would have been especially useless. The contest was one of bow, arrow, throwing-spear, and later, a hand-to-hand affair with sword, thrusting-spear, and axe (Figs. 8, 18, 21).

Byrhtnoth is the last to dismount, having used his horse to make his battle dispositions.
Offa's kinsman Offa was one of Byrhtnoth's chief followers, but we do not know the name of his young kinsman, who is made to realize that the serious business of battle is afoot.
eorl In this poem the word means "noble warrior" when used of Byrhtnoth's followers; as applied to Byrhtnoth himself it carries the additional meaning of a nobleman of the highest class, an *Ealdorman*, as he is called in other sources.

10 Weaken in war   when he seized a sword.
    Eadric° also   stood by his lord,
His prince, in the battle;   forward he bore
His spear to the fight;   he had firm resolve
While he could hold   in hard hand-grip
Broad sword and buckler;   he made good his boast
That he would battle   beside his lord.
    Byrhtnoth began   to hearten his fighters;
He rode and gave counsel,   instructing the men
How they should stand   and defend the spot.°
20 He bade that they hold   their bucklers aright
Firm in their hands,   and be not afraid.
When he had fairly   mustered the folk
He lighted down   where it liked him well,°
Where he knew his retainers°   were truest and best.
    Then stood on the strand   and boldly shouted
The Viking herald,   boastfully° hurled
To the eorl on the shore   the shipmen's message:
'These dauntless seamen   have sent me to you,
Bade me say   you must quickly send
30 Riches for ransom;°   better for you
That you buy off with tribute   a battle of spears
Than that we should wage   hard war against you.
Nor need we waste strength   if you will consent;
But we for the gold   will confirm a peace.
If you will agree,   who are greatest here,
To ransom your people   and promise to pay
On their own terms   unto the shipmen
Gold for goodwill,   and have peace at our hands,
We with the treasure   will take to our ships,
40 Put to sea,   and observe the peace.'
    Byrhtnoth addressed him;   brandished° his shield;
Shook pliant ash-spear;   speaking with words
Enraged and resolute,   gave him answer:
'Hear you, sea-rover,   what my people say?
The tribute they'll send you   is tribute of spears,
Ancient sword-edge   and poisoned point,
Weapons availing you   little in war!
Pirate messenger,   publish this answer,
Proclaim to your people   tidings more grim:
50 Here stands no ignoble   eorl with his army
Guarding my lord Æthelred's°   country and coast,

Eadric another of Byrhtnoth's followers
the spot They had been drawn up at the head of a slope, in a position of advantage.
liked him well seemed good to him
retainers the *heorthwerod* or *comitatus*, the picked men of Byrhtnoth's own household, who need no instructions from Byrhtnoth, unlike the *fyrd*, the troops levied locally

boastfully rather "threateningly"
ransom i.e. to buy peace
brandished The Anglo-Saxon word more likely means "raised," to call for silence while formal reply is made.
Æthelred's King Ethelred II, the Unready

His land and his folk.   The heathen shall fall
In the clash of battle.   Too shameful it seems
That you with our tribute   should take to your ships
Unfought, when thus far   you've invaded our land.
You shall not so easily   take our treasure,
But sword-edge and spear-point   first shall decide,
The grim play of battle,   ere tribute is granted.'
   Then he bade bear buckler,   warriors advance
60 And form their ranks   on the river's edge;
Not yet, for the tide,   could either attack.
The flood-tide was flowing   after the ebb,
And the currents locked.°   Too long it seemed
Till men to battle   might bear their spears.
Near Panta River°   in proud array
Stood the East Saxon host°   and the Viking horde;
Nor could either army   do harm to the other
Except who through arrow-flight   found his death.
   Then the flood-tide ebbed;   the raiders stood ready,
70 The pirate army   eager for war.
The lord commanded   a war-hardened man
To defend the ford,   Wulfstan° his name,
Brave among kinsmen,   Ceola's son.
He wounded with weapon°   the foremost man
Who first there fiercely   set foot on the ford.
At Wulfstan's shoulder   stood fearless fighters,
Ælfere and Maccus,   a mighty pair.
Never would such   take flight at the ford!
But they bravely defended   against the foe
80 What time they were able   to wield their weapons.
   When the pirates perceived   and clearly saw
That they had been met   by bitter bridge-wardens,
The Viking shipmen   began to dissemble,
Asked for permission   to make approach,
To fare over ford   and take their troops.
It was then the eorl   disdainfully granted
Too much ground   to the hostile host.
Across cold° water   Byrhthelm's° son
Shouted reply,   and the shipmen hearkened:
90 'Now way is made open,   come quickly to us,
Warriors to the onset;   God only knows
Who shall hold sway   on the field of slaughter.'
   The war-wolves advanced,   heeded not water,
West across Panta;   the Viking host

---

locked i.e. the tide came up the estuary to
meet the current of the river
Panta River the Blackwater River
East Saxon host the men of Essex
Wulfstan A relative of Byrhtnoth's, a local man;
nothing more is known of him or his companions.

weapon lit. spear; etymologically, Frankish
spear, barbed and long-headed
cold dire, baleful
Byrhthelm's Byrhtnoth's father, not otherwise
known

Over shining water   carried their shields.
Among his warriors   Byrhtnoth stood bold
Against the grim foe;   bade form with shields
The war-hedge° for battle,   hold firm the folk
Against the foemen.   Then fighting was near,
100   Honor in battle.   The hour was come
Doomed men must fall.   A din arose.
Raven and eagle   were eager for carnage;
There was uproar on earth.   Men let from their hands
File-hard° darts   and sharp spears fly.
Bows were busy,   shield stopped point,
Bitter was the battle-rush.   Warriors fell
In both the armies.   Young men lay dead.
Wulfmær was wounded;   Byrhtnoth's kin,
His sister's son,°   was savagely butchered
110   Choosing the slaughter-bed,   slain with the sword.
   Then to the seamen   requital was made.
I have heard that Eadweard°   slew one with sword,
Withheld not the blow;   the fated fighter
Fell at his feet.   And for that the prince
Thanked his retainer   when later was time.
So resisted   the stout of heart,
Young men in battle;   boldly strove
Who first with spear,   warrior with weapon,
Could visit death   on life that was doomed.
120   There was slaughter on earth;   steadfast they stood,
And Byrhtnoth heartened them,   bidding each man
Take thought to the war   who would win° from the Danes.
   The battle-hard brandished   his weapon for war,
His shield for defense,   and stormed at the foe;
Even so bold   went eorl against churl.°
Both purposed evil,   each for the other.
Then the shipman cast   a southern spear°
And the lord of warriors   suffered a wound.
He thrust° with his shield   so the shaft was shattered,
130   The lance was broken,   the parts fell back.
The prince was angered;   he stung with his spear
The arrogant Viking   who gave him the wound.
He fought with skill   driving his dart

war-hedge a close defensive formation, a wall of shields (l. 236), the front rank with shields overlapping in front of their bodies, the rank behind holding shields above their heads to protect both themselves and the front rank
File-hard The file was used to test the temper of the blade.
Wulfmær . . . sister's son The bond between a man and his sister's son was especially close in Germanic society. See *Beowulf* ll. 194 ff.
Eadweard may or may not be the same as the Eadweard the Long, of l. 267.
win i.e. win glory

eorl . . . churl a poetic formula: noble against base
southern spear A spear made in a country south of the Viking lands, for example in England or France; such weapons seem to have been highly prized.
thrust Byrhtnoth swept the spear aside with his shield, from the point where it had struck him, and broke it into pieces. He could have done this only to the light throwing-spear; the thrusting-spear had a deep socket to prevent its being hacked or splintered with sword or shield.

Through the pirate's throat;   he thrust with hand
So he touched the life   of the savage foe.
Then most quickly   he cast another
And the byrny° burst.   He was wounded in breast
Through his woven mail,   and the poisoned point
Bit at his heart.   The eorl was the blither;
140   The proud man laughed,   gave thanks to God
For that day's work   which the Lord had granted.
    But one of the shipmen   hurled from his hand
A flying spear;   and the speeding dart
Pierced through Æthelred's   princely thane.°
A stripling lad   stood at his shoulder,
A boy in the battle,   who bravely drew
The bloody spear   from the warrior's side,
Wulmær the youthful,   Wulfstan's son.
Back he hurled   the battle-hard dart;
150   The point pierced in   and he sank to earth
Whose hand had given   the grievous hurt.
    Then a pirate warrior   went to the eorl;
Soon would he seize   his jewels and gems,
His armor of rings,   and his well-wrought sword.
But Byrhtnoth snatched   his sword from the sheath,
Broad and brown-edged,°   and struck at his byrny.
Too speedily one   of the shipmen hindered,
Striking aside   the arm of the eorl;
And the gold-hilted sword   fell to the ground,
160   Nor might he hold longer   the hard blade,
Or wield his weapon.   Once more he spoke;
The aged ruler   rallied his men,
Bade them go forward   and bear them well.
No more could he stand   firm on his feet,
But he looked to heaven. . . .
    'I give Thee thanks,   O God of men,
For all the joys   I have had on earth.
O Lord of mercy,   I have most need
That now Thou wilt grant me   good to my soul,
170   That my spirit may come   into Thy kingdom,
O Prince of angels,   departing in peace
Into Thy power.   To Thee I pray
No fiend of hell   may have hold upon me.'
Then the heathen scoundrels   hacked him down
And both the fighters   who stood at his side.
Ælfnoth and Wulmær   both were fallen;
They laid down their lives   beside their lord.

---

byrny shirt of ring-mail
thane The word originally meant "servant," but
as the dignity of the king advanced with the
passing of time, so the dignity of his servants
went up. A king's thane was a considerable
person, a great nobleman.
brown-edged shining, bright-edged

Then fled from the battle   who feared to be there:
The sons of Odda   were first in flight,
180 Godric from battle,   leaving his lord
Who had given him many   a goodly steed;
He leaped on the horse   that belonged to his leader,
Rode in the trappings   that were not his right,
And his brothers with him   both galloped off.
Godrinc° and Godwig   recked not of war,
But turned from the fighting,   took to the wood,
Fled to the fastness,   and saved their lives;
And more of men   than was any way right
If they had remembered   the many gifts
190 Their lord had given them   to their good.
As Offa once said,   at an earlier time
In the meeting-place   when he held assembly,
That many were there   making brave boasts°
Who would never hold out   in the hour of need.
Then was fallen   the lord of the folk,
Æthelred's eorl;   and his hearth-companions
All beheld   that their lord lay dead.
    Forward they pressed,   the proud retainers,
Fiercely charged   those fearless thanes.
200 Each of them wished   one thing of two:
To avenge his leader   or lose his life.
Ælfric's° son   spurred them to battle,
A warrior young;   in words that were bold
Ælfwine spoke,   undaunted of spirit:
    'Take thought of the times   when we talked at mead,
Seated on benches   making our boasts,
Warriors in hall,   concerning hard battle.
Now comes the test   who truly is bold!
I purpose to prove   my lineage to all men:
210 That in Mercia° I come   of a mighty clan;
Ealhelm° the name   of my aged father,°
A powerful ealdorman   wealthy and wise.
None shall reproach me   among that people
That I was willing   to slink from the strife,
Hastening home   when my lord lies dead,
Slain in the battle.   Of all disasters

Godrinc The name may be, rather, Godrine or Godwine.
boasts Formal boasting of deeds to be done, rather than of past achievements, was characteristic of Germanic social custom, especially at feasts (see l. 285 below).
Ælfric's probably the Ælfric who became ealdorman of Mercia in 983 and was banished in 986. This is perhaps the reason why his son Ælfwine does not boast of him as he does of his grandfather. Ælfwine was with Byrhtnoth because of his father's banishment: he needs the protection of another lord.

Mercia the Midland territory originally occupied by the Mierce, "boundary people." The kingdom of Mercia rose to great power in the eighth century, being supreme over England south of the Humber, but declined in the ninth and became partially subject to the Danes, from whom it was liberated later in the same century. **Ealhelm** ealdorman of Mercia (c. 940–c. 951) frequently mentioned in records of the period **aged father** The word so translated more likely means "grandfather."

That to me   is the greatest of griefs,
For he was my kinsman;   he was my lord.'
Then he dashed forward,   took thought of the feud;
220 One of the shipmen   he stabbed with spear
Among the folk,   and he fell to earth
Slain with weapon.   He encouraged his comrades,
Friends and companions   to press to the front.
    Offa spoke   and brandished his ash-spear:
'Now hast thou, Ælfwine,   heartened us all
In the hour of need.   Now our lord lies dead,
Our eorl on earth,   there is need that we all,
Each of us here   embolden the others,
Warriors to combat,   while hand may bear
230 Good sword and spear,   and hold hard blade.
This sneaking Godric,   Odda's son,
Has betrayed us all;   for when he rode off
Sitting on horse,   on our lord's proud steed,
Many men weened   that it was our lord.
On the field of fate now   the folk is divided,
The shield-hedge is shattered;   cursed be his deed
That he caused so many   to flee from the fight.'
    Leofsunu spoke,   lifted his buckler,
His board° for protection,   making his boast:
240 'I promise you here   I will never turn hence
Or flee one foot,   but I'll fight in the front,
In the bitter strife,   and avenge my lord.
Steadfast warriors   by the River Stour°
Shall never have need   of words to reproach me,
Now my lord is fallen,   that lordless I fled,
Turned back from the battle   and went to my home;
But weapon shall take me,   sword-edge and spear.'
Then in rage   he rushed to the fighting
Despising to flee.
                    Dunnere shook spear,
250 The aged churl,°   called out to them all,
Bidding take vengeance   for Byrhtnoth's fall:
'He may not weaken   who thinks to avenge
His lord on this folk,   nor fear for his life.'
Then they rushed forward,   recked not of life,
Household-retainers   fierce in the fight,
Bitter spear-bearers   beseeching God
They might work revenge   for their friendly lord
In death and destruction   upon the foe.
    Then a hostage° began   to give them help,

---

board shield
Stour a river near by in Essex, near which
Leofsunu lived
churl yeoman, free commoner. The word here
does not, as it does in l. 125, imply baseness, but
merely non-noble birth.

hostage A noble hostage, living in the household of a nobleman, would receive the privileges
of other members of the household and accept
their obligations, such as that of serving the lord
in battle.

260 Of Northumbrian° race   and hardy kin,
A son of Ecglaf,   Æscferth his name.
He wavered not   in the midst of the war-play
But forward pressed   to the arrow-flight,
Now shooting on shield,   now piercing a shipman,
But oft and often   dealing a wound,
While he could wield   his weapon in war.
   In front line still   stood Eadweard the Long,
Skillful and eager;   he spoke his boast:
That he would not flee   foot-measure of ground
270 Nor turn from the battle   where his better lay dead.
He shattered the shield-wall   and fought with the Danes.
Upon the shipmen   he stoutly avenged
His gracious lord   ere he sank in the slaughter.
So did Ætheric,   excellent comrade,
Sibyrht's brother;   he boldly strove
Eager and ready;   and many another
Stood their ground   and shattered the shields.
Bucklers broke,   and byrnies sang
A song of terror.   Then Offa smote
280 One of the shipmen   and laid him low;
But Gadd's kinsman also   fell in the fight.
Quickly in battle   was Offa cut down.
But he had performed   what he promised his lord,
When he made his boast   to his bracelet-bestower,°
That both unharmed   they would ride to the borough,°
Back to their homes,   or fall in the fight
And perish of wounds   in the place of slaughter.
Thane-like° he lay   beside his lord.
   Then was breaking of bucklers,   shipmen advanced
290 Bold to the battle;   sharp spears pierced
Life-house of doomed men.   Wistan hastened,
Thurstan's son,   and strove with the Danes.
Three he slew   in the stress of battle
Ere Wigelm's son   was slain in the war.
The strife was stern,   warriors were steadfast,
Bold in battle;   fighters fell
Weary with wounds.   Death covered earth.
Oswold and Ealdwald   all the while,
Both the brothers,   marshalled their men;
300 Bade friend and kinsman   endure in combat
And never weaken,   but wield the sword.
   Byrhtwold encouraged them,   brandishing buckler,

Northumbrian The kingdom of Northumbria extended to the Lowlands of Scotland north from the River Humber; its time of greatest glory was the seventh and eighth centuries. The Danes had begun to settle there in the ninth century. It is not clear why a Northumbrian hostage was with Byrhtnoth's forces.

bracelet-bestower lord, giver of gifts borough Fortified town, administrative center, where the lord lived and dispensed justice; or the meaning may simply be "manorhouse." Thane-like i.e. having fulfilled his obligation of service

Aged companion shaking ash-spear;
Stout were the words he spoke to his men:
 'Heart must be braver,° courage the bolder,
Mood the stouter as our strength grows less!
Here on the ground my good lord lies
Gory with wounds. Always will he regret it
Who now from this battle thinks to turn back.
I am old in years; I will never yield,
But here at the last beside my lord,
By the leader I love I think to lie.'
 And Godric to battle heartened them all;
Æthelgar's son hurled many a spear
At the Viking horde. First in the front
He hacked and hewed till he fell in the slaughter.
He was not the Godric who fled from the fight.°. . .

310 (line marker)

? End of 10th century

The Dream of the Rood

The Dream of the Rood was written, probably at the end of the seventh century, in Northumbria, the northernmost of the Anglo-Saxon kingdoms, by a poet whose name we do not know. We have the text from the collection of Anglo-Saxon poetry and sermons known as the Vercelli Book, written down in the second half of the tenth century and preserved for centuries in the cathedral library at Vercelli, in north Italy. Certain passages are carved, in runic script, on the sculptured stone cross at Ruthwell in Dumfriesshire, Scotland, probably erected in the early eighth century, the golden age of Northumbria (Fig. 23).

The poem, standing out from the rest of Anglo-Saxon poetry in its graphic intensity, its richly visual quality, and its firmly integrated structure, seems to owe little to any known particular source. There are analogies with and reminiscences of Latin hymns, but they are not many or important. Though the biblical narrative of Christ's Passion naturally stands behind it, the poem's imaginative achievement is far beyond that of the common Anglo-Saxon poetic form of biblical paraphrase. It is built with great skill round the co-existence in the Passion of the human suffering and divine triumph of Christ. Giving the Cross (the Rood) a share in each, and using its degradation and glorification as a figure of Christ on Golgotha, the poet is probably echoing the doctrinal disputes of his day.

In the prelude, he describes how the glorious Cross, glittering with gold and gems (compare the late fourth-century mosaic picture in Sta. Pudenziana at Rome of the jeweled Cross), changes its appearance to the Cross unadorned and bloodied by Christ's Passion, and then becomes again the figure of his triumph. Then, when the Cross itself, by the rhetorical device known as *prosopopeia*, is made to speak, it is

---

Heart . . . braver the perfect statement of the heroic code of battle, "Heart" being "warrior's pride"

He . . . fight ironic, rhetorical understatement, not naïveté. Great shame was attached to leaving a battlefield alive if one's lord had been killed —cf. Tacitus, *Germania*, 6.

transformed into a figure of Christ's suffering, its own tortures detailed: as it is hewn from the forest and dragged to become a gallows for criminals, sadly bends to receive Christ, feels his wounds and his agony with him, is itself cut down and buried. Then, in a parallel to the resurrection of Christ, it is discovered, adorned and worshiped, triumphant in the triumph of Christ as he harrows Hell, breaking down the gates and elevating the just to heaven (Fig. 7). Similarly, Christ the divine warrior, hastening boldly and willingly to mount the Cross, confident in divine victory but suffering for a time in his human nature, rises triumphant at his Resurrection and comes again to triumph over Hell and the Devil. The figure of Christ as warrior-hero voluntarily accepting the contest with the forces of evil is an example of both the Anglo-Saxon convention of restating a Christian subject in terms of its own heroic code and the borrowing of a notion of Christ as warrior-contestant that goes back to Greek patristic sources. (A visual expression can be seen in the figure of the imperial, victorious Christ in the Chapel of the Palace of the Archbishop at Ravenna.)

Throughout the poem, the paradoxes of the Passion, its extremes of suffering and glory, of darkness and light, alternate with each other, and culminate in the final triumphant image.

The Dream of the Rood

Lo! I will tell   the dearest° of dreams
That I dreamed in the midnight   when mortal men
Were sunk in slumber.   Me-seemed I saw
A wondrous Tree   towering in air,
Most shining of crosses   compassed with light.
Brightly that beacon   was gilded with gold;
Jewels adorned it   fair at the foot,
Five on the shoulder-beam,°   blazing in splendor.
Through all creation   the angels of God
10   Beheld it shining—   no cross of shame!
Holy spirits   gazed on its gleaming,
Men upon earth   and all this great creation.
   Wondrous that Tree,   that Token of triumph,°
And I a transgressor   soiled with my sins!
I gazed on the Rood   arrayed in glory,
Shining in beauty   and gilded with gold,
The Cross of the Saviour   beset with gems.
But through the gold-work   outgleamed a token
Of the ancient evil   of sinful men
20   Where the Rood on its right side°   once sweat blood.
Saddened and rueful,   smitten with terror

dearest most splendid
Five . . . shoulder-beam i.e. either on the cross-beam or at the intersection of the beams, symbolizing the five wounds of Christ
triumph The Cross is often called the Tree of Triumph in Latin hymns.

right side In art the wound in Christ's side is usually shown (especially before the later seventeenth century, but often later as well) on the right of his body.

At the wondrous Vision,   I saw the Cross
Swiftly varying   vesture and hue,
Now wet and stained   with the Blood outwelling,
Now fairly jeweled   with gold and gems.
     Then, as I lay there,   long I gazed
In rue and sadness   on my Saviour's Tree,
Till I heard in dream   how the Cross addressed me,
30 Of all woods worthiest,   speaking these words:
     'Long years ago   (well yet I remember)
They hewed me down   on the edge of the holt,°
Severed my trunk;   strong foemen took me,
For a spectacle wrought me,   a gallows for rogues.
High on their shoulders   they bore me to hilltop,°
Fastened me firmly,   an army of foes!
     'Then I saw the King   of all mankind
In brave mood hasting   to mount upon me.
Refuse I dared not,   nor bow nor break,
40 Though I felt earth's confines   shudder in fear;
All foes I might fell,   yet still I stood fast.
     'Then the young Warrior,°   God, the All-Wielder,
Put off His raiment,   steadfast and strong;
With lordly mood   in the sight of many
He mounted the Cross   to redeem mankind.
When the Hero clasped me   I trembled in terror,
But I dared not bow me   nor bend to earth;
I must needs stand fast.   Upraised as the Rood
I held the High King,   the Lord of heaven.
50 I dared not bow!   With black nails driven
Those sinners pierced me;   the prints are clear,
The open wounds.   I dared injure none.
They mocked us both.   I was wet with blood
From the Hero's side   when He sent forth His spirit.
     'Many a bale°   I bore on that hillside
Seeing the Lord   in agony outstretched.
Black darkness° covered   with clouds God's body,
That radiant splendor.   Shadow went forth
Wan° under heaven;   all creation wept°
60 Bewailing the King's death.   Christ was on the Cross.
     'Then many° came quickly,   faring from far,
Hurrying to the Prince.   I beheld it all.
Sorely smitten with sorrow   in meekness I bowed

holt forest
hilltop i.e. of Calvary
Warrior The Old English word is parallel to
Greek *athlētēs*.
bale torment
darkness the eclipse at the Crucifixion, as Christ
died; see Matthew 27:45; Luke 23:44–5
Wan dark
creation wept See the Norse story of the lament
of all nature, save only one giantess, for the
death of Baldr, the young and beautiful. Christ
was thought to be thirty, or thirty-three, years
old at the Crucifixion, and to have been surpassingly handsome.
many presumably Joseph of Arimathea and
Nicodemus—see John 19:38–39; perhaps with
the three Maries and St. John, who were already
present—John 19:25–27. In medieval art, all
are sometimes shown as taking part in the Dep-
osition.

To the hands of men.   From His heavy and bitter pain
They lifted Almighty God.   Those warriors left me
Standing bespattered with blood;   I was wounded with spears.
Limb-weary they laid Him down;   they stood at His head,
Looked on the Lord of heaven   as He lay there at rest
From His bitter ordeal all forspent.°   In sight of His slayer°
70 They made Him a sepulcher   carved from the shining stone;
Therein laid the Lord of triumph.   At evening tide
Sadly they sang their dirges   and wearily turned away
From their lordly Prince;   there He lay all still and alone.
  'There at our station   a long time we° stood
Sorrowfully weeping   after the wailing of men
Had died away.   The corpse grew cold,
The fair life-dwelling.   Down to earth
Men hacked and felled us,   a grievous fate!
They dug a pit   and buried us deep.°
80 But there God's friends   and followers° found me
And graced me with treasure   of silver and gold.
  'Now may you learn,   O man beloved,
The bitter sorrows   that I have borne,
The work of caitiffs.°   But the time is come
That men upon earth   and through all creation
Show me honor   and bow to this sign.
On me a while   God's Son once suffered;
Now I tower under heaven   in glory attired
With healing for all   that hold me in awe.°
90 Of old I was once   the most woeful of tortures,
Most hateful to all men,   till I opened for them
The true Way of Life.   Lo! the Lord of glory,
The Warden of heaven,   above all wood
Has glorified me   as Almighty God
Has honored His Mother,   even Mary herself,
Over all womankind   in the eyes of men.
  'Now I give you bidding,   O man beloved,
Reveal this Vision   to the sons of men,
And clearly tell   of the Tree of glory
100 Whereon God suffered   for man's many sins
And the evil that Adam   once wrought of old.
  'Death He suffered,   but our Saviour rose
By virtue of His great might   as a help to men.
He ascended to heaven.   But hither again
He shall come unto earth   to seek mankind,

forspent utterly wearied
slayer i.e. the Cross
we the Cross of Christ and the crosses on which
the two thieves had been crucified
buried us deep i.e. in shame for what had
passed
God's . . . followers St. Helena, the mother of
the Emperor Constantine, was said by 4th-cen-
tury writers to have discovered the True Cross
at Jerusalem on her visit there in 326. Other
accounts, including Old English, speak of her
adornment of it.
caitiffs villains, evil-doers
Now . . . awe The mosaic cross in the apse of
Sta. Pudenziana at Rome towers from earth to
heaven—see Headnote; such a cross would be
always before the eyes of the faithful at worship,
and promise salvation.

The Lord Himself on the Day of Doom,°
Almighty God with His angel hosts.
And then will He judge, Who has power of judgment,
To each man according as here on earth
110 In this fleeting life he shall win reward.
 'Nor there may any be free from fear
Hearing the words which the Wielder shall utter.
He shall ask before many: Where is the man
Who would taste bitter death as He did on the Tree?
And all shall be fearful and few shall know
What to say unto Christ. But none at His Coming
Shall need to fear if he bears in his breast
This best of symbols; and every soul
From the ways of earth through the Cross shall come
120 To heavenly glory, who would dwell with God.'
 Then with ardent spirit and earnest zeal,
Companionless, lonely, I prayed to the Cross.
My soul was fain of death. I had endured
Many an hour of longing. It is my life's hope
That I may turn to this Token of triumph,
I above all men, and revere it well.
 This is my heart's desire, and all my hope
Waits on the Cross. In this world now
I have few powerful friends; they have fared hence
130 Away from these earthly gauds seeking the King of glory,
Dwelling now with the High Father in heaven above,
Abiding in rapture. Each day I dream
Of the hour when the Cross of my Lord, whereof here on earth
I once had vision, from this fleeting life may fetch me
And bring me where is great gladness and heavenly bliss,
Where the people of God are planted and stablished for ever
In joy everlasting. There may it lodge me
Where I may abide in glory knowing bliss with the saints.
 May the Lord be gracious who on earth of old
140 Once suffered on the Cross for the sins of men.
He redeemed us, endowed us with life and a heavenly home.
Therein was hope renewed with blessing and bliss
For those who endured the burning.° In that great deed
God's Son was triumphant, possessing power and strength!
Almighty, Sole-Ruling He came to the kingdom of God
Bringing a host of souls to angelic bliss,
To join the saints who abode in the splendor of glory,
When the Lord, Almighty God, came again to His throne.

Late 7th century

Day of Doom Day of Judgment (Fig. 50)
those . . . burning This is a reference to the
Harrowing of Hell, when Christ, the King of
Glory, descended after his death to break down
the gates of Hell, and bring out of it the souls
of those (including Adam and Eve, the patriarchs and prophets) who have awaited this
manifestation of his victory and his mercy. The
chief biblical basis for the Descent into Hell is
Matthew 27:52 ff.

GEOFFREY CHAUCER

c. 1343–1400

Geoffrey Chaucer was born into a well-to-do bourgeois family, in London, about 1343. Of his life he himself tells us almost nothing in his poetry, but from the documents, by which it has been possible to piece together the career of moderately distinguished public service which he made for himself, we know a good many details.

His family name goes back to the thirteenth century in the London area, and the Chaucers were already prosperous members of the rising commercial class in the days of Geoffrey's grandfather. Chaucer's father, a wine merchant, was a member of the growing number of men in the commercial centers of England, especially in London, who were beginning to exert a powerful effect on the structure of English society. They were commoners who were advancing in wealth, office-holding, and social prestige to a position above the ordinary, but were excluded from the aristocracy by birth, and from the country gentry by their city occupations. They were somewhere in between: the beginnings of the English middle class.

There was no place in their thinking—or in Chaucer's—for the leveling doctrines of John Ball, the fourteenth-century social agitator: ". . . matters cannot go well in England and never will until all things be in common, and there shall be neither serfs nor gentlemen, but we shall all be equal. . . ." A father from Chaucer's stratum of society would wish to advance his son's interests. He would send him first to school and then either to the University (which would often mean that the son was intended for the priesthood, the third order of English society); or he would place him in a noble household, where he might have the chance to continue his education in a less formal and devout way. In his early teens, Geoffrey Chaucer was made a page in the household of one of England's most considerable noblemen, Prince Lionel, third son of King Edward III, and later Duke of Clarence. The connections he made there must have served him well in later life and we know that his talents kept him in association with members of the aristocracy. His first great patron was John of Gaunt, fifth son of the king and the most powerful noble in England, who may also have been his friend. From the successive kings, Edward III, Richard II, and Henry IV, Chaucer received offices, grants of money, and other privileges for his services in various capacities. He married well; his wife Philippa was a member of the households of both Queen Philippa and of the third wife of John of Gaunt, and was probably the daughter of a knight. A Thomas Chaucer, probably their son, rose to public prominence and Alice Chaucer, possibly their granddaughter, married into the aristocracy not once but twice. From this tangle of connections, it emerges that the family was steadily rising in its social position.

Geoffrey Chaucer was the chief agent in this rise. The fact that his family had money and had been able to give him certain advantages obviously helped greatly, but his abilities also kept him on the road to advancement. In 1359 he went on one of Edward III's many expeditions against the French, was taken prisoner, and ransomed the following year; he then probably spent some time in study of the law, was made "valet" to the King in 1367 (an honor, not a servant's position), went on diplomatic missions to France several times, to Flanders in 1377 and to Italy in 1372–73 and 1378. In 1374 he was given a rent-free London house and made Controller of the Customs and Subsidies on Wool, Skins, and Hides for the Port of London. This was a lucrative office, for the wool trade was England's most important at the time. Other Customs appointments followed, but in 1386 Chaucer seems to have fallen on less good times and gone to live in Kent—perhaps only at Greenwich, now a suburb of London, a little way down the river. He had meantime become a public man of modest importance, being Justice of the Peace for Kent in 1385 and Knight of the Shire (representative in parliament) for Kent in 1386. After a short time in apparently rather straitened circumstances, he received in 1389 the office of Clerk of the King's Works, which put him in charge of the buildings and their repair at ten of the royal residences, of preparing places for tournaments, and of the walls, ditches, and sewers along a stretch of the Thames. There were later appointments, grants of wine, of money, and of privileges. In 1399, he rented a house in London again, near Westminster Abbey. He died the following year.

These bare facts about Chaucer's career indicate that he was given considerable responsibilities and, presumably, that he discharged them well. But they are the record, in the main, of a public servant's career, not a poet's. This is hardly surprising, since official documents are not the most obvious place to look for critical remarks on poetry, but it is significant because it indicates that the professional man-of-letters has not yet begun to emerge. The functioning of such a person depended upon the growth of a much larger reading public (even in 1533, Sir Thomas More estimated that fewer than four people in ten in England could read), the establishment of a system of printing and publishing, and an enlarged demand for dramatic performance. On the other hand, Chaucer provides a pattern of the writer which will serve for England for two centuries after his lifetime: the poet, whether a cleric or not, who holds ecclesiastical or secular office as a means to gain the leisure to write. A further— and often the most important—source of livelihood would be the dedication of poems to rich or noble patrons, and we know that Chaucer did just that with his first major poem, The Book of the Duchess, written in 1369–70 to commemorate the death of Blanche, Duchess of Lancaster, wife of John of Gaunt.

This position of the writer in his society is also a European one, especially in France and Italy. The new status that poets were now claiming is reflected in the ceremony— which Chaucer and all Europe knew about—performed on the Capitol at Rome in 1341, when Francesco Petrarca ("Francis Petrarch, the laureate poet," as Chaucer calls him) had himself formally crowned as a poet with a laurel garland. Petrarch thought he was reviving an ancient Roman custom, admirable because ancient and Roman and therefore pointing the way to the resuscitation of Roman virtue and glory. He also made a speech on the occasion, proclaiming the nobility and dignity of poetry and therefore of the poet, who was necessary to society because he could confer immortality on others as well as upon himself by his verses, and because beneath what seemed poetic fancies and dreams there lurked profound truth. The poet, indeed, was a moral philosopher, as Petrarch held: what he wrote would tend toward the inculcation of virtue in all its aspects.

Petrarch's Coronation Oration has been called "the first manifesto of the Renaissance," and the influence of the concept of the poet that it embodies is clear through to Sir Philip Sidney and even to the last English Renaissance poet, John Milton. But it has, in its serious statement of the poet's role, relevance to Chaucer, the first English poet to write in a manner that is as self-aware as it is self-assured and controlled. Petrarch's example as a poet meant much, consciously and unconsciously, to Chaucer. The first translation of a Petrarch sonnet into English (see below) is embedded in Chaucer's Troilus and Criseyde, and there are other indications in his work of his admiration for his Italian mentor. This is not to say that Chaucer would agree with all Petrarch's solemn claims: he was too much the satirist for that. Nor would he hold Petrarch's beliefs about the moral value of poetry as simply and directly as did Petrarch. His poetic method of slipping into and out of one of his characters—especially in *The Canterbury Tales*—often makes it difficult to hold in the mind exactly where he himself stands. We must balance his statement in the Retraction of the *Tales*, where he specifically disowns all in his work which tends toward the encouragement of sin, against the superb, controlled irony of the Clerk's Tale of patient Griselda; she endures in resignation and obedience to her husband all the trials he puts upon her, even to having her children taken from her and given up for dead, and to being put away by him. For Petrarch, this story was an exhortation to the Christian to be as steadfast for God as Griselda had been for her husband under her tribulations. Chaucer, by his very inclusion of the tale in his dramatic framework, has already lowered the story's tone and mode. But, fully in control of his manipulation, he raises the tone of the story again by giving it to the unworldly, idealist Clerk (see the General Prologue, ll. 287 ff.), who reiterates Petrarch's point and then goes on to concede that such absolute patience is a thing of the past and we must now do the best we can with what we have. Chaucer himself adds his ironic comment: a man should not try his wife's patience as hard as that "in trust to finde / Grisildis, for in certein he shall faile."

The Clerk's Tale operates at several levels: for the Clerk it is a moral tale, of trials and their endurance, turned so that it is also a hit at the Wife of Bath and her termagant ways, but it is capped by Chaucer's final encouragement—ironical, too—to sturdy wives to stand no nonsense from husbands. We must here, as always, make up our own minds as to how far we can identify anything that Chaucer says in *The Canterbury Tales* with Chaucer's own views, and judge for ourselves the extent of his irony and detachment. His intention is basically serious, even in the comic tales, but this is not to say that his poems are all moral allegories, lessons as directly applied as Petrarch would apply the Clerk's Tale.

Of the great Italians besides Petrarch, Chaucer was most indebted to Boccaccio and to Dante, but it is now becoming clear that much, though not all, of the influence on him that was formerly thought to be directly from the Italian, came via the French. This is natural: English culture for nearly three centuries before Chaucer and for nearly a century after him, relied heavily on France as a model. For a good part of those centuries, the two countries were, if not one kingdom, at least intimately connected in friendship or enmity. French was still the language of the English court, and in the manners and courtesies of polite society, especially in literature and in music, French practice was still the norm for imitation and modification.

Chaucer's youth, passed in a court milieu where such matters would be taken for granted, must have exposed him to French models, but in attempting to say just what these were and when and how he read and used them, we come up against one of our major difficulties with the poet: we simply do not know, except by inference, when exactly he wrote most of his works, major and minor. In general, his translations and direct imitations are reckoned to be early—the part of the incomplete English translation of the *Roman de la Rose* which is thought to be his, and some short poems, are given to the 1360's. The *Roman de la Rose* was a vast French poem of the thirteenth century, its first half a dream exploration of the process of falling in love according to the approved courtly canons, which had made of human love a deeply refining and ennobling influence on the spirit. This part was the work of Guillaume de Lorris (see below, The Other World: Paradise). To this was added, by Jean de Meun, an immense encyclopedic continuation, dealing with matters such as love, women, nobility, society and its foundations, the clergy, providence, fortune, the nature of dreams, sorcery, and the physical sciences. Chaucer frequently drew on these materials.

The Book of the Duchess (which can be dated exactly to 1369–70), uses a traditional English octosyllabic meter but often borrows directly from Jean Froissart, the French historian and poet who was Chaucer's almost exact contemporary, and from the French poet and musician Guillaume de Machaut (c. 1300–1377). It is an elegy and a dream vision at once. Sleepless, as the dreamer in such visions so often pictures himself, he reads and re-tells Ovid's story of Ceix and Alcyone from the Metamorphoses (the legend of how the kingfisher came into being), falls asleep, and dreams of a May morning encounter in the forest with a Man in Black, who tells his sorrow. Such dream visions were a highly fashionable literary form at the time. They allowed the poet to distance his illusion from his reader; they prepared the reader for the unrealities he might encounter, notably the personification of abstract qualities used to explore the nature of an experience or emotion; and they vouched, in one sense, for the validity of the vision. (See below, the Nun's Priest's Tale.)

The Book of the Duchess is an exquisitely turned evocation of grief at the death of Blanche "who every day hir beauté newed," already an assured and skillful poem combining French material with the literature of the ancient world. Of the classical writers who must have formed a part of Chaucer's education, by far the most important for him was Ovid, as both the poet of love and the poet of mythology, even the ancient poet most resembling him in temperament, with his characteristic blend of tenderness and satire, his love of a story. On no other classical author does Chaucer draw so heavily for material and for suggestions. He knew his Virgil, too, especially the Aeneid, but the Eclogues and the Georgics as well. Lucan and Statius (see below, the epilogue to Troilus and Criseyde), who were much admired in the Middle Ages, he knew and used also, but it seems probable that much of his knowledge of the Roman poets came from French translations and adaptations.

In the 1370's or early 1380's, again using a French version to help him, Chaucer translated the Latin work which influenced him most profoundly. This was the Consolation of Philosophy of Boethius, the Roman statesman, philosopher, and polymath put to death by the Emperor Theodoric in 524 A.D. Boethius wrote influential works on music, on geometry, on arithmetic—which became standard textbooks in medieval education for three of the four subjects of the quadrivium (see Glossary)—and on the philosophy of Aristotle. But his chief work, for the Middle Ages and for Chaucer, was the Consolation, a work of Stoic doctrine, teaching detachment from the troubles and difficulties of daily life and the patient bearing of adversity, which had the greater reputation because it was thought that Boethius was a Christian. Cast in the form of a vision, in alternate verse and prose, it tells how Boethius, in prison, was visited by the Lady Philosophy, who showed him how the afflictions of life—from which one must not try simply to escape—were transitory and could be borne once one had determined to put one's trust in absolute good and not allow oneself to come under the domination of Fortune, worldly good. Evil itself, Philosophy taught, could have no existence, since it has no part in absolute good: the evil of the world is therefore illusory. (See below, the Nun's Priest's Tale, ll. 472 ff.). The use Chaucer made of the Consolation to construct the philosophical framework for his Troilus and Criseyde makes it clear that Boethius's thought had for him the status of philosophic explanation as well as a guide to conduct and consolation in adversity.

At some time before he translated Boethius, Chaucer had tried his hand at a poem which one can already call typically Chaucerian, but which remains fragmentary: *The House of Fame*. The work owes much to many writers—Macrobius on dreams (see below, the Nun's Priest's Tale, II. 353 ff.), Ovid and Virgil—but especially to Dante. It contains some of the best and most moving lines that Chaucer ever wrote and it has many echoes of Dante, transformed by the lively Chaucerian technique. Indeed, it has elements of burlesque Dante; and it may well be that Chaucer left it off because he did not feel himself equal to the *tour de force* he was attempting. Later, using Dante's words in the conclusion to *Troilus and Criseyde*, he was to show that he could intermittently rise, in all seriousness, to something like Dante's grave exaltation. But he could not keep it up.

Though it is true that Chaucer often used Italian literature, through French versions, it was only during the 1370's that it came to be a major influence on his poetry. Certainly his interest must have derived in part from his visits to Italy. The Italian author who most influenced him was Giovanni Boccaccio (1313–75), best known among his contemporaries for his Latin collections of exemplary lives, *The Falls of Princes* and *Of Famous Ladies*, but also a poet and prose writer of genius in Italian. To Boccaccio, directly or indirectly, Chaucer is indebted for a long passage in *The Parliament of Fowls*. This extended poem is a debate about the nature of love (a *demande d'amours*) in dream allegory form, as argued by birds with the intervention of Dame Nature, on St. Valentine's day. More importantly, Boccaccio provided the plot for one of the greatest love poems in the language, Chaucer's Troy-romance, *Troilus and Criseyde*, which is based, perhaps via the French *Roman de Troyle*, on Boccaccio's *Il Filostrato*. Chaucer never acknowledges this; indeed he never anywhere acknowledges that he has taken anything from Boccaccio, though the debt is enormous. But his poem is far more than Boccaccio, good as Boccaccio's story is. Chaucer transformed it into a more profound work—partly because of the Boethian philosophic character which he gave it, partly because of the depth and subtlety of his insight, and partly because of the unforgettable trio of characters he created from the much more conventional figures of Boccaccio's poem: Pandarus, Troilus, and Criseyde. Like *The Parliament of Fowls* the poem is also an exploration of the nature of earthly love, but played out this time by human actors, not personified abstractions or birds. Troilus has put himself on the wheel of Fortune through love of Criseyde and, through her fickleness, he comes to see the falseness of earthly love: this is his final vision. We, however, cannot forget the glory and the sweetness that have gone before—and Chaucer does not mean us to.

THE CANTERBURY TALES

There is no way of avoiding the feeling that all that has gone before in Chaucer's poetic career merely leads up to *The Canterbury Tales*. Chronologically, the *Tales* are his final achievement, though it looks as if he had long before worked out drafts of some of the stories which he proposed to use (the "tragedies" of the Monk's Tale, the Second Nun's Tale of St. Cecilia, an early version of the Knight's Tale—for the plot of which he was again indebted to Boccaccio). In terms of artistry the *Tales* represent the peak of his gigantic and varied talent, his fullest and most mature production. Chaucer seems to have given to this great poem the major part of his poetic time for the last fifteen or so years of his life. The only interruptions seem to have been his *Treatise on the Astrolabe* and, quite early in the period, a somewhat half-hearted attempt, in *The Legend of Good Women,* at a poem on the Ovidian model concerning women who were martyrs to their faithful love.

The *Tales* are certainly the expression of Chaucer's fully matured genius; yet even if he had never written them he would have done enough to make it clear that he has no superior as an English poet except Shakespeare. He dwarfs his contemporaries —and the poets of the next hundred and fifty years—in the same way as Shakespeare dwarfs his. The isolation of Chaucer's performance, indeed, makes it all the more astonishing. Nothing in the tradition of English poetry prepares us for him, and it appears, though he obviously knew a good deal of what had been written in English before and around him, that he did not find it very helpful. He acknowledges a debt to his older London contemporary, John Gower, "moral Gower"—or rather he dispatches his *Troilus and Criseyde,* perhaps ironically, to Gower for "correction." But he does not seem, anywhere, really to owe anything to any other writer in English—and the kind of poem that he can produce is entirely beyond the reach of any other writer of the time, let alone of the careful, often charming, but pedestrian Gower. It is easy to exaggerate the picture either way and to see—for example, in his mockery of the jog-trot of English romances in his own virtuoso piece, the Tale of Sir Thopas—more knowledge of English poetry than in fact he possessed. Throughout his life his models seem to have been French. His genius was to transform those models and naturalize them in English as thoroughly as he did—verse forms, meters, literary modes and all—to absorb influences from a number of literatures and make himself the first English poet fit to stand with the best that the rest of Europe could produce.

There were many respects in which he shared European preoccupations, one of the most important being the conscious artistry of his verse. As with any great poet, this is partly a matter for which instinct must account. But it is also partly a matter of self-awareness in the handling of subject and verse, so as to produce the maximum effect of "sentence and solas": profit and delight. One means of doing this was to imitate the ancient poets, to show oneself truly worthy to be in their company, inheritor of their poetic. This is one of the things that Petrarch was asserting in his Coronation Oration: Chaucer proclaims it in the epilogue to *Troilus and Criseyde,* with his humble recommendation of the book to the great classical poets. They represent the solid block of tradition behind any true poet. Remembrance of the past, constant remaking of its great stories—stories of Troy, Alexander, Rome, Thebes, Britain—was the essential task of the poet—and this, not any slavish desire for simple support, is the reason for the stress constantly laid on the necessity for authority and example in medieval literature—"auctoritee" and "ensaumple": "And if that olde bokes weren aweye, / Yloren were of remembrance the keye."

Chaucer's sense of the imperfections of his language and his treatment of the stories is not a modesty topos (see Glossary), still less mock modesty: it is the index of a deep concern for literary art: "The lyf so short, the craft so long to lerne," as he says in *The Parliament of Fowls.* Similarly, his conscious parodies of rhetoric (see Glossary) and rhetoricians are the index of his concern for the effects and effectiveness of language. Even when they mock, they mock something which is conceded to be necessary: "The dayes honour and the hevenes ye, / The nyghtes foo. . . ." Chaucer means us to recognize these rhetorical *traductiones* ("conceits"), piled up in *frequentatio* (repetition of the same structure) and with *polysyndeton* (use of the same syntactical scheme). The joke that he then springs on us, "al this clepe I the sonne," is a kind of double-take: he pretends to be amazed that he has been writing rhetoric all the time, mocking himself too for seeing that he is doing so. So too in the famous lament for "black Friday" in the Nun's Priest's Tale, where Chaucer, in the character of the Nun's Priest, is parodying a famous rhetorical set piece without implying that all such set pieces are pompous and useless. Chaucer is a profoundly rhetorical poet, with an explicit concern for his craft. Some of his uses of it are self-mocking, but for every one of these we can discover a hundred where the ordinary devices recommended by the rhetoricians—for beginning an argument, inventing arguments or incidents, varying a theme, making it both effective and pleasant—are being deployed. It is important to remember that rhetoric, for Chaucer, meant effective writing, not bombast, and that when he called a fellow poet "rhetor," it was a compliment.

The question of Chaucer's rhetoric—now taking the word in its widest sense—is much complicated in *The Canterbury Tales* by the dramatic illusion of the tellers within a framework of tales, the double fiction being simultaneously maintained.  There was nothing new in the notion of framing a set of stories by putting them into the mouths of different tellers, and collections of such stories were composed from the fifth century A.D. onward. They were common enough in later medieval times. Boccaccio had arranged the hundred tales of his *Decameron* among ten men and women who had left the city for fear of the plague. Each told a tale on ten successive days. Boccaccio's fellow countryman Giovanni Sercambi, probably about 1374, also put together a set of such tales, told by one narrator on a journey and sometimes varied to fit the locality the travelers had reached at a given stage of their journey. We do not know whether Chaucer knew either Boccaccio's or Sercambi's collection—though he certainly knew an analogous use of the framing device by Gower in his *Confessio Amantis* (The Lover's Confession). His exploitation of the device is a brilliant variation on other uses: unlike Boccaccio, he fits tale to teller; unlike Sercambi and Gower, he provides more than one narrator. It is possible that Chaucer's pilgrim-framework was the result of what he could see himself at any moment, especially from his house at Greenwich, where he was living when he began the *Tales* in earnest—a party of pilgrims on the road to the shrine of St. Thomas Becket at Canterbury, England's most famous and most frequented place of pilgrimage, within easy reach of London. Such pilgrimages were well known, even notorious, for the convoys in which they were made, and the diversions and tale-telling that went on by the way. (Fig. 35)

As he tells us, through the Host in the Prologue, Chaucer had originally planned some one hundred and twenty tales, two for each pilgrim on the way to Canterbury and two more for the way back. Like many ambitious plans, this was severely curtailed in the execution. Before his death at age fifty-seven—which was considered advanced in Chaucer's day—he had completed only twenty-two, had left two more uncompleted, and had done a certain amount of shuffling of tales from those for whom they were originally intended. The result, especially after the addition of the links between tales, with the backchat between pilgrims, the tensions, anger, insults, alliances, and friendships these reveal between teller and teller, tale and tale, is the richest and most complex collection of its kind in any language.

The cheerful, lively General Prologue, with its descriptions of all the pilgrims and the relationships that exist between them before the beginning of the pilgrimage, is followed by the grave, chivalric tale of the Knight—a story of Athens long ago, and the knightly contest of Palemon and Arcite for the love of Emily, a tale perfectly proportioned to its teller. So too, is the Miller's *fabliau* (see Headnote and Glossary) about a stupid carpenter cuckolded by his dapper young lodger, told with force and gusto and rousing the anger of the Reeve, himself a carpenter by trade and resenting the implication that one of his fellow workmen should be treated in this way. The Reeve's turn comes immediately, and he takes advantage of it to tell another *fabliau* about a miller who is outwitted by two students whom he has tried to cheat. Not only do they get back their bread which the miller has stolen, but they manage to lay both his wife and daughter. Later, the Friar and the Summoner also quarrel and each tells a tale against the profession of the other. These are single examples of pairing, but there is one instance where something more seems to have been intended. This occurs in the group of tales known as the Marriage Group: the Wife of Bath, with her militant feminism and aggression and her curious tale of faery love and "maistry," begins it. Then, in the usual order of the *Tales,* we have the disagreement between Summoner and Friar and their opposing tales—and then, to counter the Wife and to calm the atmosphere, the gentle, cool, placid tale of the Clerk, about the patient Griselda and obedience in marriage—followed, to keep the tone from staying too cool, by Chaucer's ironic *envoi* (see Glossary). There follows the Merchant's Tale about the old man, January, who married a young wife, May, and was cuckolded for it—another *fabliau* of cleverness and quick-thinking, its pace much quicker than the Clerk's. Finally comes the moving, sober, simple tale of the Franklin. Since we do not know the exact order of tales that Chaucer had in mind, we cannot be sure that his intention was that these particular tales should function as a close-knit group or should run through the series as a kind of counterpoint, or thematic unifier.

The problem about discovering thematic unity in *The Canterbury Tales* is that we cannot be sure that this was what Chaucer meant us to find. The headlinks give us some clues, but the unfinished state of the work makes it impossible to know whether the sequence is due to chance or design. In the manuscripts the tales are grouped into a number of blocks or fragments, but the order of these is far from invariable. The General Prologue and the tales of the Knight, Miller, Reeve, and Cook (unfinished) are always a beginning; the Parson's Tale and the Retraction always come last. Within that framework, order varies. Here the General Prologue and the tales of the Miller, Nun's Priest, Pardoner, Wife of Bath, and Franklin are presented; this corresponds with the grouping of some manuscripts. It presents the general introduction, followed by two comic tales, one a *fabliau,* one a burlesque beast fable with a final serious "morality." Then comes the self-portrait of the much-married Wife of Bath, and her tale; and the deeply serious and affecting tale of the Franklin; with the dark moral apologue of the Pardoner, preceded by the teller's devastating self-portrait, for a finale.

Of all Chaucer's works, *The Canterbury Tales* has always been the most popular. We can only guess at when exactly most of the tales were composed, for neither Chaucer nor his scribes give us any help. The more than eighty manuscripts, mostly of the fifteenth century, and Caxton's two editions of about 1478 and 1484, besides many other early printings, are indications of how well the poet's successors thought of his great poem.

CHAUCER'S ENGLISH

Chaucer gave both prestige and currency to the English spoken in London at his time, but this was not the only dialect of the language in which works of literature were composed during the fourteenth century. In particular, the regional dialects of the West and North of England and the North-West Midland of the time had a literature of their own, in a language which would often have been next to unintelligible to a Southern reader. This literature is often of great stature—Langland's *Piers Plowman* was originally written in the dialect of the West; the works of the *Gawain*-poet were written in North-West Midland. In the fourteenth and fifteenth centuries, too, the cycles of mystery plays were composed in the Northern dialect (Chaucer makes one of the students speak it in the Reeve's Tale). The comic scenes in *The Second Shepherds' Play* use the difference to set the affected Southern speech of the character Mak against the plain, blunt Northern outspokenness of the shepherds. The difficulty that one part of the country had in understanding another was still present in Caxton's day (see below, his Preface to the *Aeneid*). These two fifteenth-century examples of dialect difference indicate the continuance of the problem: despite Chaucer, London English was not established as the English norm overnight—and considerable dialect differences remain, even today. (The longer Middle English texts in this volume which are not written in the London dialect have been modernized or translated.)

Chaucer, along with John Gower and other London authors of the fourteenth century, took the English of London just at a time when it was beginning to assert itself as the major dialect and carried it farther along the road. Their use of it represents the true beginning of modern standard English. Hitherto, French had been the language of cultured entertainment, and Latin the language of scholarly instruction—and up to a point remained so until the sixteenth century. Gower, in fact, wrote in French and Latin as well as in English. The fifteenth and sixteenth centuries see a conscious effort on the part of poets, prose writers, and their printers alike to bring English to a level of richness and expressive subtlety where it can compete with both French and Latin on equal terms (see Caxton's Prefaces below).

The London English that Chaucer used was a composite, made up of the dialects of the neighboring counties, chiefly of the East Midlands, but with some South-Eastern (Kentish) features and a few South-Western. It is so much the ancestor of modern English that there is comparatively little in vocabulary, syntax, and grammar that is not easily recognizable to a modern reader. The elaborate system of inflections which had characterized Old English and earlier Middle English was being leveled, and unstressed final -e was becoming a silent letter. Most of Chaucer's vocabulary is still recognizable, even though the spelling often differs considerably from the modern: *dayeseye* for "daisy," for example; or *defaute*, a French spelling for "default." Spelling is not uniform, and the same word may be spelled in different ways: thus, *mone, moone,* for "moon." About a third of Chaucer's vocabulary is French. There are differences in sense between Chaucer's vocabulary and ours: *parcel*, for example, for "part"; *chalange* for "claim"; *lust* for "pleasure." "*Him thoughte,*" "*me thoughte*" do not mean "he (or I) thought" but "it seemed to him/me."

The best way to understand Chaucer is to read him aloud. Though we cannot hope to recover the exact manner in which his language was spoken, we can achieve a reasonably good notion of it. Reading aloud minimizes the difficulties of understanding Chaucer, which lie in the different meanings of much of his vocabulary and the subtlety of his poetry, rather than in his grammar or syntax. The merest skeleton of these two is therefore given below, but the pronunciation is dealt with rather more fully.

PRONUNCIATION

The chief points to note about Chaucerian pronunciation are:

Vowels

Stressed short vowels are pronounced as in Modern English, with the exception of *a*, which is open, i.e. a "rounder" sound than in modern "man," as in Modern French *patte*, and *u* (often spelled *o* as in *love*), which has only the sound of modern *put*. A vowel is always short when it is followed by two consonants. Otherwise, it may be short or long: modern pronunciation is a good guide.

Long vowels are pronounced as they are in modern Italian or French. A long vowel can be recognized as long if it is doubled in spelling (*maad, reed, wood*); or if it occurs in a stressed position at the end of a word (*he, mo, wisly*). *A, e, o* are long if followed by a single consonant plus *-e* (*made, rede, wode*).

a as in Modern English "father": *fader, maad.*

e as in Modern English "air": *ese, heed;* or as in Modern French "été": *nede, theef.*

> (A practical guide here is modern spelling: Chaucer's words with the open sound as in modern "air" tend to be spelled today with *ea: ease; head;* those with the close sound to be spelled with *ee* or *ie: need, thief.* In the early stages of familiarizing oneself with Chaucerian pronounciation, it may be best to ignore the distinction and use only the pronunciation as in "air.")

i(y) as in Modern English "machine": *sire, slyde.*

o as in Modern English "note": *oo, stoon;* or as in Modern French "chose": *do, good.*

> (Modern English sometimes spells the open sound *oa: boat;* and the closed *oo.* Again, the best advice to the beginner is to ignore the distinction and use only the pronunciation as in *boat.*)

u generally spelled *ou, ow* as in Modern English "rude": *luce.* (In words of French origin, such as *aventure,* the French pronunciation of *u* is kept.)

Diphthongs combine the two elements, as given above:

ai (ay), ei (ey) are midway between Modern English "play" and "aisle": *fair, way, veines, wey.*

au (aw) as in Modern English "house": *baume, bawd.* (In words of French origin, such as *daunce,* it is pronounced as in *haunt.*)

eu (ew) as in Modern English "few": *newe, knew;* or as in Modern English "lewd": *fewe, lewed.*

Unstressed vowels (chiefly final *-e*).

> as in Modern English "about."

By Chaucer's time, final unstressed *-e* was probably not sounded in everyday speech, but in verse it is sounded or not, according to the demands of the meter. It is usually elided, i.e. merged into the following word, if that word begins with a vowel. It is usually sounded before the caesura or at the end of a line.

Consonants

All consonants are pronounced, except the initial *h-* in some words of French origin: *honour.* Both elements of initial *gn, kn, wr* are pronounced *g-naw, g-not, k-nyt, k-now, w-rap, w-recche.* Similarly both elements of *lk, lf, lm: folk, half, palmer.* The combination *gh* is pronounced gutturally like German *-ch.*

GRAMMAR

The features of Chaucerian grammar on which the modern reader needs most guidance are:

Nouns and adjectives. Almost all older case-endings have disappeared, and those that remain are similar to those surviving in Modern English. The plural of most nouns ends in *-es* or *-s;* with an occasional *-en* plural (*eyen,* or *yën* for "eyes") and an occasional uninflected plural (*pound, yeer*). The possessive case ends in *-es* or *-s.* Adjectives add *-e* to their final consonant in certain circumstances.

Pronouns. Both *thou* and *you* are used, *you* sometimes to signify respectful or formal use of language. The third person singular uses *his* for the possessive of *it;* and the plural uses *hem, here, hir*(e) for the objective and possessive of they.

Adverbs are formed from adjectives by adding *-e,* or *-lich*(e), *-ly.*

Verbs. Infinitives end in *-e* or *-en.*

   Present participles usually end in *-ing*(e), *-yng*(e), with an occasional *-and.*

   Past participles end in *-en* or *-e* and often begin with *y-.* Chaucer uses several different forms: *sworn, swore, ysworn, yswore, comen.*

   Present indicative ends in *-e, -est, -eth* for the first three persons of the singular, and all these endings may be contracted after a final vowel or final *-d* or *-t. Lith, lieth, lyeth,* and *last, laste, lasteth* may all be found. All persons of the plural end in *-e*(n).

   Past definite. The plural usually ends in *-e* or *-en. Goon* (go) has two forms for the past: *yede* and *wente.*

SYNTAX

Chaucer's syntax is often oral syntax, sometimes tortuous and inverted, full of omissions and with occasional superfluous words and constructions, but not difficult. One major point to note is that in Chaucer, as in Middle English in general, negatives do not cancel each other out as they do in Modern English. They intensify, so that "That nevere . . . / Ne sholde upon him take no maistrie" is a strong negative. Another important point is the frequent use of impersonal constructions: *him list* for "it pleased him," *me thoughte* for "it seemed to me." Another is the frequent use of auxiliary verbs: *gan* is used to form a simple past tense: *gan slyde* means "did slide," or "slid," and it may be used also to express a sense of beginning. *Do* is used in the sense of "make"—*do me lyve*: "make me live"; *go* in the sense of "let us"—*go we soupe*: "let us have supper."

   The text is based on that of W. W. Skeat, first published in 1894–97, with readings introduced from other sources. For the General Prologue, the helpful text of Phyllis M. Hodgson, 1969, has been much drawn upon. As an aid to the reader, an e which has now become silent has been printed e where the meter requires it to be pronounced as a syllable; an acute accent indicates an e pronounced like modern French é; and accentuation which differs from Modern English is marked thus: *àppearence.*

   It is hoped that this will encourage the reader to recite Chaucer's verse aloud, following the indications for pronunciation given above. This was the way in which many of Chaucer's contemporaries would have made their acquaintance with his works, for they were composed with recitation in mind (Fig. 24).

The Canterbury Tales

General Prologue

With the General Prologue, as with all Chaucer's works, the difficulty is to know art from nature, and to see how Chaucer, from the mass of conventions in which he worked, achieved an utterly unconventional and original masterpiece, the first and the greatest of its kind in our literature. We cannot say what gave him the idea of building his great poem out of a slice of society which is typical but not entirely representative. We do not know whether he began with the notion of a set of tales told by pilgrims, or whether he had written a number of stories before deciding to link them together in this way. We do not know whether the General Prologue, as we have it, is a final version or only the draft for one: we can only say that it was probably written in the 1380's.

The Prologue opens with a rhetorical passage which at once poses a problem. It is a hymn to the regenerative power of the sun and to the rise of the sap in nature, the rebirth of the dead year that sends men and women to seek spiritual regeneration at a place of pilgrimage and physical and mental recreation during the journey. It is often praised as a miracle of naturalistic description: this *is* how it happens. Yet it is thoroughly conventional in two ways. First, a hymn to Spring was a recognized literary commonplace, especially for beginning a poem. Second, it is not, as is so often claimed, utterly lifelike: for example, March is not a dry month in England and the description of it as such is part of a literary convention that, far from being English, goes back to classical literature. Yet the life and vigor are undoubtedly there, in this perfectly wrought, eighteen-line verse paragraph, the striking beginning recommended by rhetorical theory which at once engages the reader and then modulates gently into the lower rhetorical mode of the portraits that are to follow.

The portraits themselves are as difficult to characterize as the opening passage. They are types, without doubt, and intended in their total to represent contemporary English society, with the exception of the higher nobility, who would go on pilgrimage with their own train and not in a company. If we were dealing with an attempt at naturalistic description, we should expect to find more than one representative of each profession or each rank. Yet the characters are so individual that they seem to ride out of the pages. Are we to conclude that they are portraits drawn from life? So many exact details are given for so many of them that Chaucer must, at the very least, be making some reference to existing persons, the point of which is now lost to us but would have been understood by his listeners or his readers. It may be that there is more to it than that: the Host has been identified with an actual innkeeper, and people living in Chaucer's day have been found whose characters would certainly fit the characters that Chaucer gives in the Prologue. He may have taken hints from contemporary men and women who were known to him personally or by repute to diversify the types he was drawing.

Once more our difficulty is to know what is convention and what is not. The tender and delicate portrait of the Prioress, for example, plays with the tension between the heavenly love to which she is vowed and the earthly love which shows in her love of small, delicate, pretty things, and on the ambiguities of applying a single language to both. She is described in terms that fit a heroine of romance—some of her features are a direct imitation of the features of Leisure/Idleness in the *Roman de la*

Rose, and the description of her table manners is derived from the same text. The ambiguities of her character are typical human ambiguities. Her own gentleness is matched by the gentleness of the portrait: the satire is light, controlled, unwounding. She is individual and type in one, lovingly and gently yet satirically placed in relation to the other ecclesiastics of the pilgrimage. Later, Chaucer will intensify the portrait by means of her pitiful tale of the murdered little boy, Hugh of Lincoln, just as he will poke gentle fun at the young, modest, learned Clerk—the type of the earnest young scholar—in his tale. Here the irony and satiric method are quiet, caressing, indirect. For the "noble ecclesiast" who is the Pardoner, or the worldly Monk and begging Friar, much harsher ironic treatment is reserved. As types, they are set against what a religious man ought to be; as characters they are set against what the other religious characters in the Prologue actually are. We are intended to see both how they fall short of what should be—that is, of their profession—and of the example they might take from the pious, decent Parson.

In the Parson and the Plowman, his brother, Chaucer has taken stock types from another sort of literature. In the contemporary prose and poetry of social complaint and criticism, the Plowman in particular figures as critic and as the example of the true laborer, against whose simple piety, scrupulousness in performing his allotted task, poverty, and oppressed condition may be measured the surface devotion, cynicism, neglect of duty, money-grubbing, and love of power of those who profess to be his betters. The same holds true, to a lesser extent, of the country priest—whom Chaucer significantly makes the Plowman's brother.

In presenting his characters Chaucer—like a modern author drawing on present-day psychology—frequently uses the psychological theory of his time, which gave the planets in a man's horoscope at birth, and their positions at different times during his life, an influence on the kind of man he was. Similarly, the bodily fluids, or humors, of which he was composed—blood, phlegm, choler (bile), and melancholy (black bile)—with their "qualities" of hot, cold, dry, and moist, according to their mixture in him, would determine character and behavior. One could, too, according to the theory of the time, read the signs of character in the face (physiognomy, physiognomics) or the outward bodily characteristics (see Fig. 37). The Wife of Bath's horoscope would predispose her to the lasciviousness she glories in. The description of the Miller's physical traits can be interpreted to mean that he is bold, angry, shameless, and talkative. The Summoner's appearance is both the result and the expression of his lecherous temperament. The Pardoner's spiritual degeneracy is partly due to his physical state: he is a eunuch born. The Franklin's love of rich food and wine and hospitality might be deduced from the combination of humors which make up his temperament: blood predominates, so that he is red-faced, outgoing, confident, generous, quick to anger.

Yet to say this about the kind of detail from all sources that Chaucer uses for his descriptions of the pilgrims is not to arrive at the heart of his mystery. It is merely an indication of how incomparably rich were the materials on which he was able to draw and how remarkably he handles them. The poet William Blake has the last word: "Of Chaucer's characters . . . some of the names or titles are altered by time, but the characters themselves remain forever unaltered."

General Prologue

Here biginneth the Book of the Tales of Caunterbury.

Whan that Aprille° with hise shourès˃ sote˃   *showers / sweet*
The droghte of March hath percèd˃ to the rote,   *pierced*
And bathèd every vèyne° in swich licour
Of which vertu engendrèd is the flour;
Whan Zephirus° eek˃ with his sweetè breeth˃   *also / breath*
Inspirèd hath in every holt˃ and heeth˃   *wood/ field*
The tendre croppès,˃ and the yongè sonne°   *shoots*
Hath in the Ram his halfè cours yronne,˃   *run*
And smalè fowlès˃ maken melodye   *birds*
10 That slepen al the night with open iye°
(So priketh hem˃ Nature in hir corages)˃:   *them / their hearts*
Thanne longen˃ folk to goon˃ on pilgrimages,   *long / go*
And palmeres° for to seken straungè strondes,˃   *foreign shores*
To fernè halwès, couthe in sondry londes;°
And specially from every shirès ende
Of Engèlond to Caunterbury° they wende,˃   *go*
The holy blisful˃ martir for to seeke,   *blessed*
That hem hath holpen˃ whan that they were seke.˃   *helped / sick*
Bifel˃ that in that seson˃ on a day,   *It happened / season*
20 In Southwerk° at the Tabard as I lay
Redy to wenden˃ on my pilgrimage
To Caunterbury with ful devout corage,   *go*
At nyght was come into that hostelrye˃   *inn*
Wel nine and twenty in a companye,
Of sondry folk, by aventure˃ yfalle   *chance*
In felawship,˃ and pilgrimes were they alle   *companionship*
That toward Caunterbury wolden˃ ryde.   *wished to*
The chambres˃ and the stables weren wyde,   *bedrooms*
And wel we weren esèd attè beste. °
30 And shortly, whan the sonnè was to reste,
So hadde I spoken with hem everichon˃   *every one*
That I was of hir felawship˃ anon,˃   *company / at once*
And madè forward˃ erly for to ryse,   *agreement*

Aprille the traditional Spring opening. Zephirus, Nature, and the zodiacal dating are part of the stock of the medieval poet.
veyne vein (of plants), sap vessel; thus, "And bathèd every vein in such a liquid, by the power of which the flower is begotten"
Zephirus the West wind
yonge sonne young, because just passed out of the first zodiacal sign (Fig. 37) of the solar year, Aries, the Ram, which in Chaucer's time was thought to govern March 12 to April 11
open iye i.e. do not sleep at all in Spring
palmeres originally, pilgrims who carried a palm leaf to show that they had been to the Holy Land; later applied to all pilgrims

To ferne . . . londes to far-off shrines, famous ones, in various countries
Caunterbury the most popular medieval place of pilgrimage in England because of the tomb there of St. Thomas Becket, murdered in the Cathedral in 1170 and canonized 1174
Southwerk Southwark, then a suburb of London on the south bank of the Thames, stood at the beginning of the road to Dover and Canterbury. The Tabard, now destroyed, was a famous inn. Its sign would have shown the short, sleeveless surcoat worn by knights and heralds, called a tabard.
And wel . . . beste and we were made comfortable in the best manner

To take oure wey theras⁷ I yow devyse.⁷   *where / tell*
   But natheles,⁷ whil I have tyme and space,°   *nevertheless*
Er⁷ that I ferther in this talė pace⁷,   *before / pass*
Me thynketh it acordaunt to resoùn°
To tellė yow al the condicioùn°
Of ech of hem,⁷ so as it semėd me,   *them*
40 And whiche⁷ they weren, and of what degree,⁷   *who / status*
And eek in what array° that they were inne;
And at a knyght then wol I first biginne.

KNYGHT

A knyght ther was, and that a worthy⁷ man,   *distinguished*
That fro the tymė that he first bigan
To riden out, he lovėd chivalrie,
Trouthe and honoùr, fredom and curteisie.°
Ful worthy⁷ was he in his lordės werre,⁷   *brave / war*
And therto hadde he riden, no man ferre,⁷   *further*
As wel in Cristendom as in hethenesse,⁷   *pagan lands*
50 And evere honoured for his worthynesse.
At Alisaundre° he was whan it was wonne.
Ful oftė tyme he hadde the bord bigonne°
Aboven allė nacions in Pruce;
In Lettow hadde he reysėd,⁷ and in Ruce,   *campaigned*
No Cristen man so ofte of his degree.
In Gernade at the seege eek hadde he be
Of Algezir, and riden in Belmarye.
At Lyeys was he, and at Satalye,
Whan they were wonne; and in the Gretė See°
60 At many a noble armee⁷ hadde he be.   *invading force*
At mortal batailles° hadde he been fiftene,
And foughten for oure feith at Tramissene°
In lystės° thriės, and ay⁷ slayn his foo.⁷   *always / enemy*
This ilkė⁷ worthy knyght hadde been also   *same*
Somtymė⁷ with the lord of Palatye   *formerly*
Agayn⁷ another hethen in Turkye.   *against*

tyme and space an oral formula; the words carry less than their full value: "while I can" **resoùn** perhaps French *raison*, right; or Latin *ratio*, rhetorical order; or reason
condicioùn whole state of being, inner and outer
array dress or order
Trouthe . . . curteisie knightly virtues; see Chaucer's *balade*, "Truth," below. *Trouthe* here is integrity; *fredom* is liberality, material and spiritual; *curteisie* is well-bred behavior.
Alisaundre The Knight had fought against all three of the great enemies of 14th-century Christendom: the Saracens in the Middle East (Christians captured Alexandria in Egypt, 1365 (Fig. 36); Attalia (Sattalye) in Turkey, 1361; Ayas (Lyes in Armenia, 1367); some-

times in alliance with the pagan "Lord of Palatye," the Turkish sultan, against other infidels—a not infrequent Christian-heathen alliance; the Moors in Spain and North Africa (Granada, Algeciras, Ben-Marin, 1344 and after); the barbarians of Lithuania (Lettow; to 1385), and the Tartars of Russia.
bord bigonne taken the head of the table at a banquet; perhaps of the Teutonic Order of Knights in (East) Prussia
Gretė See Mediterranean
batailles tournaments between champions fought to the death, for a decision between armies
Tramissene Tlemçen, Algeria, then a Berber stronghold
lystes space enclosed by barriers for tournaments or jousts (Fig. 48)

NO CONTRADICTORY STATEMENTS

And everemore° he hadde a sovereyn prys,°   *always / reputation*
And though that he were worthy, he was wys,°   *prudent*
And of his port° as meeke as is a mayde.   *behavior*
₇₀ He nevere yet no vilainye ne sayde
In al his lyf unto no maner wight.°   *Not sarcastic*
He was a verray,° parfit,° gentil knyght!   *Modest*   *true / perfect*
But for to tellen yow of his array,°   *equipage*
His hors° were godė, but he was nat gay.°   *gaudy*
Of fustian he werėd a gypoun°
Al bismoterėd° with his habergeoun,   *rust-stained*
For he was late° ycome from his viage,°   *just / expedition*
And wentė for to doon his pilgrimage.

SQUIER° *Son*

With hym ther was his sone, a young squièr,
₈₀ A lovyere, and a lusty° bachelèr,   *lively*
With lokkės crulle,° as they were layd in presse.°   *curled / crimped*
Of twenty yeer of age he was, I gesse.
Of his statùre he was of evene° lengthe,   *moderate*
And wonderly deliver,° and greet of strengthe.   *agile*
And he hadde been somtyme in chyvachie°
In Flaundres, in Artoys, and Picardye,
And born hym° weel, as of so litel space,°   *carried himself*
In hope to stonden° in his lady grace.   *stand well*
Embroudėd° was he, as it were a mede°   *embroidered / meadow*
₉₀ Al ful of fresshė flowrės, whyte and reede.°
Syngyng he was, or floytinge° al the day.
He was as fressh as is the month of May.
Short was his gowne, with slevės longe and wyde.
Wel coude he sitte on hors and fairė ryde.
He coudė songės make, and wel endite,°   *write poetry*
Juste° and eek daunce, and weel portraye° and write.   *joust / draw*
So hoote he lovėde, that by nightertale
He slepte namore than dooth a nightingale.
Curteis he was, lowly, and servysable,
₁₀₀ And carf biforn his fader at the table.°

He nevere . . . wight Middle English uses an accumulation of negatives to strengthen, not cancel each other out; thus, "He never yet, in all his life, said anything base to anyone of any kind."

hors horses; an uninflected plural

gypoun jupon, the close-fitting tunic worn under a coat of mail (*habergeoun*). His was of a thick, coarse cloth (*fustian*).

squier properly speaking not yet a knight but one who served a knight. Later he is called *bacheler*, a young knight who has not yet set up his own banner and is still in the service of a senior knight.

chyvachie cavalry campaigns, perhaps the single one of 1383 during the Hundred Years' War between England and France

as of . . . space considering the short time he had campaigned

whyte and reede stock phrase: "of all colors"

floytinge whistling or playing the flute or pipe

So hoote . . . table (ll. 97–100) "So hotly did he love, that at night-time he slept no more than a nightingale. He was courtly of behavior, modest and ready to serve; and he carved in front of his father at the table." To carve the roast, so that his lord was fittingly served, was a frequently mentioned duty of a squire.

YEMAN°

A yeman hadde he, and servaùnts namo˃   *no more*
At that tyme, for him liste˃ ridè so;   *it pleased*
And he was clad in cote and hood of grene.°
A sheef of pecok arwès, bright and kene,
Under his belt he bar˃ ful thriftily,˃   *carried / handily*
(Wel coude he dresse˃ his takel˃ yemanly: *see to / gear*
His arwes droupèd noght with fetherès lowe°)
And in his hand he baar˃ a myghty bowe.°   *bore*
A not-heed° hadde he, with a brown visage.˃   *face*
110 Of wodècraft˃ wel coude he al the usage.   *woodmanship*
Upon his arm he bar a gay bracer,°
And by his syde, a swerd and a bokeler,°
And on that other syde, a gay daggere,
Harneisèd˃ wel, and sharp as point of spere;   *mounted*
A Cristofre° on his brest, of silver shene;˃   *shining*
An horn he bar,˃ the bawdrik° was of grene.   *bore*
A forster˃ was he soothly,˃ as I gesse. ~Forester~   *forester / truly*

PRIORESSE° *Table manners / what's her Attitude towards people*
Ther was also a nonne,˃ a prioresse, *her tale is About*   *nun*
That of hir smiling was ful simple and coy.° *Murder + gore*
120 Hire gretteste ooth˃ was but 'by Saint Loy.'°   *greatest oath*
And she was clepèd˃ Madame Eglentyne.°   *called*
Ful wel she song the service divine,
Entunèd˃ in hir nose ful semèly.˃ *Laughter at NUN* *intoned / becomingly*
And Frensh she spak ful faire and fetisly,˃   *prettily*
After the scole˃ of Stratford-attè-Bowe,°   *style*
For Frensh of Paris was to hir unknowe.
At metè˃ wel ytaught was she withalle:˃   *meal-time / moreover*
She leet˃ no morsel from hir lippès falle,   *let*
Ne wette hir fingrès in hir saucè depe;
130 Wel coude she carie a morsel, and wel kepe˃   *take care*
That no drope ne fille˃ upon hir brist.˃   *fell / breast*
In curteisie was set ful muchel hir list.° *polite behavior*

Yeman a yeoman or free man, a commoner
attending the knight as his only other servant.
A knight was obliged to have a retinue, to uphold his dignity. This knight makes do with
squire and yeoman.
he . . . grene The yeoman was dressed in the
huntsman's Lincoln green, and had a sheaf of
arrows with peacock feathers tucked into his
belt.
lowe Peacock feathers tended to disturb the
flight of the arrow, but the yeoman can counteract this.
bowe the long-bow was 6 feet tall
not-heed close-cropped head
bracer guard on the left forearm, to prevent
friction from the bow-string
swerd . . . bokeler sword and small round
shield

Cristofre medal of St. Christopher, patron of
travelers
bawdrik baldric, strap worn round the waist
or diagonally across the body
Prioresse mother superior of a nunnery
simple and coy sincere and demure; monastic
rule enjoined that laughter should be controlled, unaffected, and silent. *Simple and coy*
is a stock phrase in medieval literature when
a lover is praising his mistress.
Loy St. Eligius (Eloi), patron of goldsmiths and
carters
Eglentyne sweetbriar
Stratford-atte-Bowe anglicized French, learned
at the Benedictine nunnery of St. Leonard's,
Kent
In . . . list her pleasure was strongly fixed on
polite behavior

Hir overlippe wypéd she so clene
That in hir coppe° ther was no ferthyng° sene   cup / morsel
Of grece,° whan she dronken hadde hir draughte.   grease
Ful semély after hir mete she raughte.°
And sikerly, she was of greet desport,°
And ful plesaùnt, and amyable of port,°   bearing
And peyned hire to countrefeté cheere
140 Of court, and to been estatlich of manere,
And to ben holden digne of reverence.°
But for to speken of hire conscience,
She was so charitable and so pitous,°   full of pity
She woldé wepe, if that she sawe a mous
Caught in a trappe, if it were deed° or bledde.°   dead / bleeding
Of° smalé houndés hadde she that she fedde   some
With rosted flesh,° or milk and wastel breed.°   meat
But sore wepte she, if any of hem were deed,
Or if men smoot° it with a yerdé° smerte.°   struck / stick / hard
150 And al was conscience° and tendre herte.   soft feelings
Ful semély hir wimpel pinchéd was,°
Hir nose tretys,° hir eyen greye as glas,°   well-made
Hir mouth ful smal, and therto° softe and reed.°   also / red
But sikerly° she hadde a fair forheed—   certainly
It was almoost a spanné brood,° I trowe;°   believe
For, hardily,° she was nat undergrowe.   assuredly
Ful fetis° was hir cloke, as I was war.°   well-made / aware
Of smal coral,° aboute hire arm she bar
A paire of bedés,° gauded al with grene,
160 And theron heng° a brooch of gold ful shene,°   hung / bright
On which ther was first write a crownéd A,°
And after, *Amor vincit omnia.*°

3
NONNE AND III PREESTES

Another nonné with hir haddé she
That was hir chapéleyne,° and preestés thre.°   chaplain

MONK

A monk ther was, a fair° for the maistrie,°		*fine one*
An outridere,° that lovede venerie,°		
A manly man, to been an abbot able.		
Ful many a deyntee° hors hadde he in stable,		*fine*
And whan he rood,° men myghte his brydel heere		*rode*
170 Gynglen° in a whistlynge wynd als cleere,		*jingle*
And eek° as loude, as dooth the chapel belle		*also*
Ther as° this lord was kepere° of the celle.		*where*
The reule° of Saint Maure° or of Saint Beneit,		*rule*
Bycause that it was old, and somdel streit°—		*somewhat strict*
This ilke° monk leet olde thynges pace,°		*same*
And heeld after the newe world the space.°		*meanwhile*
He yaf nat of° that text a pulled° hen		*gave not for / plucked*
That seith° that hunters beth° nat holy men,°		*says / are*
Ne that a monk, whan he is recchelees,°		*negligent*
180 Is likned til° a fissh that is waterlees.°		*like to a*
This is to seyn,° a monk out of his cloystre—		*say*
But thilke° text heeld he nat worth an oystre		*that very*
And I seyde his opinioun was good.		
What° sholde he studie, and make hymselven wood,°		*why / mad*
Upon a book in cloystre alwey to poure,°		
Or swynken° with his handes, and laboure,		*toil*
As Austyn° bit?° How shal the world be served?		*bids*
Lat Austyn have his swink to him reserved!		
Therfore, he was a pricasour° aright:		*hard rider*
190 Grehoundes° he hadde as swift as fowel° in flight;		*greyhounds / bird*
Of priking° and of hunting for the hare		
Was al his lust;° for no cost wolde he spare.		*pleasure*
I seigh° his sleves purfiled° at the hond		*saw / trimmed*
With grys,° and that the fyneste of a lond;		*gray fur*
And for to festne° his hood under his chyn,		*fasten*
He hadde of gold wroght° a ful curious° pyn;		*made / elaborate*
A love-knotte° in the gretter° ende ther was.		*larger*
His heed was balled,° that shoon as any glas,		*bald*
And eek his face, as it hadde been anoint.		
200 He was a lord ful fat, and in good poynt;°		
Hise eyen stepe,° and rollynge in his heed,		*prominent*

for the maistrie surpassing all others
outridere a monk who rides out to supervise the monastery's property outside its immediate limits
venerie hunting, but also sexual pursuit
kepere supervisor of an outlying house or dependent community
Saint Maure (Maurus) credited with introducing the monastic *Rule* of St. Benedict (Beneit) to France
pace go their way
That . . . holy men St. Jerome (*c.* 342–420) and St. Augustine (354–430) condemn hunting.
waterlees Wyclif, Gower, and Langland use the comparison.

poure pore. The Benedictines were great supporters of study.
Austyn St. Augustine, on whose writings the Augustinian rule was based, believed in monastic labor.
Lat . . . reserved! Let Augustine have the toil (that he talks so much about) kept for himself alone!
priking literally, following the tracks of. *Prick* is the footprint or track of the hare; or the verb may simply here mean *riding*, as Spenser thought.
love-knotte strands of gold tied to signify the affection of lovers
in good poynt in good condition, plump

Eyes rolled + glittered [handwritten]

That stemèd as a forneys of a leed;°

His bootès souple,° his hors in greet estat.°   *supple / array*

Now certeinly he was a fair prelat.°   *not pale + tormented* [handwritten]

He was nat pale, as a-forpynèd goost.°   *like fat swans* [handwritten]   *pined-away ghost*

A fat swan loved he best of any roost,

His palfrey° was as brown as is a berye.   *brown horse* [handwritten]   *saddle horse*

all date [handwritten, red]

FRERE°

wanton + merry [handwritten]

A frere ther was, a wantown° and a merye,

A limitour,° a ful solempnè° man.   *imposing*

210 In alle the ordrès foure° is noon that can°   *knows*

So muche of daliaùnce° and fair langàge.   *flirtation*

He haddè maad ful many a mariàge

Of yongè wommen at his ownè cost.

Unto his ordre he was a noble post.°   *support*

And wel biloved and famulier° was he   *intimate*

With frankeleyns° overal° in his contree,°   *LADIES MAN* [handwritten]   *throughout / district*

And with worthy wommen of the toun—

For he had power of confessioùn,

As seyde hymself, more than a curàt,°   *parish priest*

220 For of° his ordre he was licenciat.°   *by*

IRONIC APPROVAL [handwritten]   *bigger the gift the > the Absolution* [handwritten]

Ful swetèly herde he confessioùn,°

And plesaunt was his absolucioùn.

He was an esy° man to yeve° penaunce   *indulgent / give*

Ther as° he wiste° to have a good pitaunce.   *where / expected*

For unto a poure° ordre for to yive   *poor*

Is signè that a man is wel yshrive;°   *absolved*

For if he yaf,° he dorstè° make avaunt°   *gave / dared / boast*

He wistè° that a man was repentaùnt;   *knew*

For many a man so hard is of his herte,

230 He may nat wepe, althogh hym sorè smerte.°

Therfore, in stede of wepynge and preyères,°   *prayers*

Men moot yeve silver to the pourè freres.   *gave little things to girls + wives* [handwritten]

His tipet° was ay farsèd° ful of knyves

And pynnès, for to yeven fairè wyves.°   *always stuffed*   *women*

And certeinly, he haddè a mery note;

That . . . leed that glowed like a furnace under a cauldron

prelat a churchman of the upper ranks, who has received preferment

Frere Chaucer's portrait is composed of the regular accusations against the friars, the mendicant (begging) religious orders founded during the spiritual revival of the 13th century. Vowed to poverty and to preaching, they had multiplied and become rich by Chaucer's time.

wantown Ranges in meaning from "playful" to "lascivious."

limitour religious field-worker (begging, hearing confessions, burying, preaching) within the district (*limitatio*) assigned to his convent

ordres foure Dominicans, Franciscans, Carmelites, Augustinians

frankeleyns See l. 333.

licenciat licensed by the church to hear confessions

confessioùn The sinner who comes to confession must satisfy the confessor that he is contrite before being granted absolution. He must then perform an act of mortification imposed by the confessor, to express remorse and good intentions. This friar would impose a light penance on those able to give pious donations ("pitaunce") to his order: to be ready to part with money was to him a sure sign of repentance.

hym sore smerte he is greatly pained

tipet the long narrow piece of cloth, part of hood or sleeve, which could be used as pocket

Wel coude he singe, and pleyen on a rote;°
Of yeddinges he bar utterly the pris.°
His nekke whit was as the flour-de-lys.°
Therto,ʳ he strong was as a champioùn.°   *moreover*
240 He knew the tavernes wel in every toun,   *every / innkeeper*
And everichʳ hostilerʳ and tappestere
Bet than a lazar or a beggestere;°
For unto swich a worthy man as he
Acorded nat, as by his facultee,°   *sick*
To have with sikeʳ lazars aqueyntaùnce.   *good / get one anywhere*
It is nat honeste,ʳ it may nat avaunce,ʳ
For to deelen with no swich poraille,°
But al with riche, and sellers of vitaille.ʳ   *food and drink*
And overal ther asʳ profit sholde arise,   *wherever*
250 Curteisʳ he was, and lowelyʳ of servyse.   *courteous / humble*
Ther nas no man nowher so vertuous.ʳ   *capable*
He was the beste beggere in his hous;ʳ   *friary*
And yaf a certeyn ferme for the graunt°
Noon of his bretheren cam ther in his haunt.
For thogh a widweʳ hadde noght a sho,ʳ   *widow / shoe*
So plesaunt was his 'In principio,'°
Yet wolde he have a ferthyngʳ er he wente.   *farthing*
His purchas was wel bettre than his rente.°
And rage he coude, as it were right a whelp.°
260 In love-dayes° ther coude he muchelʳ help,   *much*
For ther he was nat lyk a cloisterer°
With a thredbare cope,ʳ as is a poure scoler,ʳ   *cape / scholar*
But he was lyk a maister,° or a Pope.
Of double worsted° was his semicope,°
That rounded as a belle out of the presse.ʳ   *mould*
Somwhat he lipsed,ʳ for his wantownesse,ʳ   *lisped / affectation*
To make his English sweete upon his tonge;
And in his harping, whan that he hadde songe,ʳ   *sung*
Hise eyen twynkled in his heed aryght,ʳ   *truly*

---

rote stringed instrument
Of . . . pris for ballads, he took the prize entirely
flour-de-lys lily; more often used of a woman
champioùn literally, a knight specially chosen to fight in a tournament to the death
tappestere . . . beggestere tapster, better than a leper or a beggar. The ending -ere is normally feminine, but a tapster can be either male or female: barman or barmaid.
as . . . facultee in view of his profession
poraille poor people, whom a friar was bound by his vows to comfort and succor. The Franciscan rule was based on the Gospel injunction "Sell all thou hast and give to the poor."
And yaf . . . graunt He paid a certain sum for the monopoly of practicing in his district. This line and the next do not occur in all manuscripts and the accusation of "farming" is not supported by the historical facts.

'In principio' the opening words of St. John's gospel: "In the beginning [was the word . . .]"; constantly quoted by the friars to justify their preaching and also used by them as a salutation
purchas . . . rente His pickings on the side were better than the income he was authorized to collect.
And rage . . . whelp and he knew how to frolic like a puppy
love-dayes days set aside for amicable settlement of legal disputes by arbitration out of court. Clergy were forbidden to take part, except on behalf of the poor.
cloisterer a member of a religious order confined to the monastery
maister master, university graduate or teacher
double worsted expensive, heavy woolen cloth
semicope short (half-length) cloak

270 As doon° the sterrės° in the frosty nyght.   *do / stars*
•   This worthy limitour was cleped° Huberd.   *called*

     ♦ •MARCHANT

     A marchant was ther, with a forkėd berd,°   *beard*
     In mottėlee,° and hye on horse he sat,
     Upon his heed a Flaundrish° bėvere hat;°   *Flemish*
     His bootės claspėd faire° and fetisly,°   *neatly / elegantly*
     His resòns° he spak ful solempnėly,°   *sayings / pompously*
     Souninge° alway th'encrees of his winning.   *publishing*
     He wolde the see were kept for any thyng°
     Bitwixė Middelburgh° and Orėwelle.
280 Wel coude he in eschaungė sheeldės° selle.
     This worthy man ful wel his wit bisette:°   *ingenuity employed*
     Ther wistė° no wight that he was in dette,   *knew*
     So estatly° was he of his governaunce,°   *impressive / conduct*
     With his bargàynes,° and with his chevisaunce.°   *bargaining / loans*
     Forsothe,° he was a worthy man withalle;   *In truth*
     But sooth to seyn, I noot how men hym calle.°

     CLERK° OF OXENFORD

     A clerk ther was of Oxenford also,
     That unto logik° haddė longe ygo.
     As leenė was his hors as is a rake,
290 And he nas nat° right fat I undertake,   *was not*
     But lookėd holwe,° and therto sobrely.°   *hollow / grave*
     Ful thredbare was his overeste° courtepy,°   *outermost*
     For he haddė geten° hym yet no benefice,°   *gotten / church living*
     Ne was so worldly for to have office.°
     For hym was lever° have at his beddes heed,   *more pleasing*
     Twenty bookės, clad in blak or reed,
     Of Aristotle° and his philosophie,
     Than robės riche, or fithele,° or gay sautrie.°   *fiddle*
     But al be° that he was a philosòphre,   *although*
300 Yet haddė he but litel gold° in cofre.°   *coffer*
     But al that he mighte of his freendės hente,°   *get*

---

mottelee parti-colored cloth
bevere hat an expensive fur hat
He wolde . . . thyng he wished the sea policed,
at all costs
Middelburgh Middelburg, in Holland, almost opposite Orwell, in Suffolk; both were important ports for the import and export of wool and cloth, the basis of English trade with Flanders at the time.
sheeldes écus (French coins). The Merchant was a successful illegal speculator in enemy currency.
But sooth . . . calle but, to tell the truth, I don't know what he was called
Clerk literally, cleric, advanced student (at Oxford). A clerk professed his intention of entering the priesthood before going to university. He might remain there in minor orders all his life, going no farther up the ladder in the

church, and seeking no post outside. Many university scholars were clerks and the word gained the connotation of "learned man."
logik the art of reasoning and argument. The Clerk is long past the elementary stage of his education, and is an accomplished logician.
courtepy short jacket
office a secular, administrative post such as many clerics took to make their living
Aristotle The rediscovered Aristotle, in Latin translation, formed the basis of the university curriculum.
sautrie psaltery, a stringed instrument, played with the hand
But . . . gold "Philosophy" could also mean "alchemy"; so the Clerk did not have the philosopher's stone to turn base metal into gold.

On bookės and on lernynge he it spente, *moral vrtve*
And bisily gan for the soulės preye°
Of hem that yaf⌐ hym wherwith to scoleye.⌐ *gave / study*
Of studie took he most cure⌐ and most heede. *care*
Noght o⌐ word spak he more than was neede, *one*
And that was seyd in forme and reverence,°
And short, and quyk,⌐ and ful of hy sentence.° *lively*
Souninge in⌐ moral vertu was his speche, *tending towards*
310 And gladly wolde he lerne and gladly teche.

SERGEANT OF LAWE° *Also JUDGE*
A sergeant of the lawe, war⌐ and wys,⌐ *cautious / prudent*
That often haddė been at the Parvys° *wary tense*
Ther was also, ful riche of excellence.
Discreet he was, and of greet reverence°—
He semėd swich, his wordes weren so wise. *"seemed to be wise"*
Justice he was ful often in assise° *Fees-determined his work*
By patente,° and by pleyn commissioùn.°
For his science,⌐ and for his heigh renoun, *knowledge*
Of fees and robės hadde he many oon. *seemed to be busy*
320 So greet a purchasour⌐ was nowher noon: *property speculator*
Al was fee simple° to hym in effect;⌐ *virtually*
His purchasing mighte nat been infect.⌐ *proved invalid*
Nowher so bisy a man as he ther nas,⌐ *was not*
And yet he semėd bisier than he was. *learned in Statutes*
In termės hadde he caas and doomės alle
That from the tyme of Kyng William° were yfalle.⌐ *had occurred*
Therto, he coude endite⌐ and make a thing,⌐ *compose / deed*
Ther coudė no wight pinche⌐ at his writyng; *complain*
And every statut coude he pleyn⌐ by rote. *complete*
330 He rood but hoomly,⌐ in a medlee⌐ cote *unpretentiously / parti-colored*
Girt with a ceint⌐ of silk, with barrės⌐ smale. *belt / stripes*
Of his array telle I no lenger tale.

FRANKELEYN° *Free man*
A frankéleyn was in his companye,
Whit was his beerd, as is the dayėsye.⌐ *White beard* *daisy*
Of his complexioùn he was sangwyn.° *ruddy*

gan . . . preye prayed. The Middle English *gan* and *can* are often used to form a simple past tense.
reverence in due form, with decorum and respect
sentence Latin: *sententia* (moral) significance; weighty, memorable saying
Sergeant of Lawe a lawyer of high rank and competence, who could also act as judge
Parvys area in front of a church, where lawyers and their clients met
of greet reverence highly respected
assise judicial sessions held periodically throughout England
patente "open [letter]": the royal letter of appointment, to be displayed to all

pleyn commissioùn full commission, full authority to adjudicate
fee simple i.e. land owned outright, with no legal complications
termes . . . William Either he had memorized all the cases and decisions since the reign of William the Conqueror (1066–87) or he had the legal yearbooks from that time to his.
Frankeleyn originally "free (*franc*) man." Many rose to be wealthy landowners equivalent to the gentry, and important figures in their district.
sangwyn sanguine; his constitution or temperament (*complexioùn*) dominated by the humor of blood

Wel loved he by the morwe° a sop in wyn;°   *in the morning*
To liven in delit° was evere his wone,°   *habit*
For he was Epicurus° ownė sone,
That heeld opinioùn that pleyn° delit   *full*
340 Was verraily° felicitee parfit.   *truly*
An housholdere, and that a greet, was he;
Saint Julian° he was in his contree.°   *district*
His breed, his ale, was alweys after oon;°
A bettre envynėd° man was nowher noon;
Withoutė bakė mete was never his hous
Of fish and flesh, and that so plentevous,°   *plentiful*
It snewėd° in his hous of mete° and drynke,   *snowed / food*
Of allė deyntees° that men coudė thynke.   *dainties*
After° the sondry sesons of the yeer,   *according to*
350 So chaunged he his mete and his soper.°   *supper*
Ful many a fat partrich hadde he in muwe,°   *coop*
And many a breem and many a luce in stewe.°   *unless*
Wo was his cook but if° his sauce were   *unless*
Poynaunt° and sharp, and redy al his geere.   *piquant*
His table dormant in his halle° alway
Stood redy covered° al the longė day.°   *set*
At sessioùns ther was he lord and sire;°
Ful ofte tyme he was knyght of the shire.°
An anlas,° and a gipser° al of silk   *dagger / purse*
360 Heeng° at his girdel,° whit as mornė milk.   *hung / belt*
A shirreve° hadde he been, and a countour.°
Was nowher swich a worthy vavasour.°

HABERDASSHERE,° CARPENTER, WEBBE, DYERE, TAPICER
An haberdasshere and a carpenter
A webbe,° a dyere and a tapycer,°—   *weaver / tapestry-maker*
And they were clothed alle in o lyveree°
Of a solempne° and a greet fraternitee.   *dignified*
Ful fresh and newe hir geere apikėd° was;   *adorned*

sop in wyn piece of fine toasted bread, soaked in spiced wine
delit sensuous pleasure
Epicurus (342–270 B.C.) Greek philosopher, for whom absence of pain because of virtuous living was the supreme good. The popular form of his doctrine is that pleasure itself is the true end of life.
Saint Julian patron saint of hospitality
after oon of one standard
envyned stocked with wine
breem . . . stewe and many a carp and pike in his fishpond
halle the main living room
Stood . . . day Medieval tables were usually on trestles, set up as required and then taken down. The Franklin's was permanently established and permanently loaded.
At . . . sire He took the chair at the (quarterly) sessions of the justices of the peace.

knyght of the shire county member of parliament, not necessarily a dubbed knight; Chaucer was himself such a representative, for the county of Kent in 1386
shirreve sheriff; next to the lord-lieutenant, the most important administrative officer of the county, whose revenue he had to collect and take to the exchequer.
countour "auditor," "accountant"; also "special pleader"—a county official
vavasour a member of the landed gentry, below the aristocracy
Haberdasshere dealer in needles, tapes, buttons; or in hats. Chaucer never wrote tales for any of the characters listed here.
lyveree livery; the (uniform) clothes of their guild, a group of tradesmen with common commercial interests and social and religious observances

Hir knivės were ychaped⟩ noght with bras   *mounted*
But al with silver; wroght ful clene and weel
370 Hire girdles and hir pouches everydeel.⟩   *in every part*
Wel semėd ech of hem a fair burgeys⟩   *burgher*
To sitten in a yeldhalle,⟩ on a deÿs.⟩   *guildhall / dais*
Everich,⟩ for the wisdom that he can,   *each*
Was shaply⟩ for to been an alderman.°   *fit*
For catel⟩ haddė they ynogh and rente,⟩   *property / income*
And eek hir wyvės wolde it wel assente;
And ellės certeyn werė they to blame.
It is ful fair to been yclept 'Madame',
And goon to vigiliės° al bifore,
380 And have a mantel royalliche ybore.

COOK

A cook they haddė with hem for the nones°
To boille the chikens with the marybones,⟩   *marrowbones*
And poudrė-marchant° tart, and galyngale.°
Wel coude he knowe⟩ a draughte of Londoun ale.   *recognize*
He coude roste and sethe,⟩ and broille and frye,   *boil*
Maken mortreux,⟩ and wel bake a pye.⟩   *thick soups / meat-pie*
But greet harm was it, as it thoughtė⟩ me,   *seemed to*
That on his shine⟩ a mormal° haddė he.   *shin*
For blankmanger,° that made he with the beste.

SHIPMAN

390 A shipman was ther, wonynge⟩ fer by⟩ weste;   *living / in the*
For aught I woot,⟩ he was of Dertėmouthe.°   *know*
He rood upon a rouncy,° as he couthe,⟩   *as best he could*
In a gowne of falding⟩ to the knee.   *coarse wool*
A daggere hangynge on a laas⟩ haddė he   *strap*
Aboute his nekke, under his arm adoun.
The hote somer haddė mad his hewe⟩ al brown.   *color*
And certeinly he was a good felawe.
Ful many a draughte of wyn had he ydrawe°
Fro Burdeux-ward,° whil that the chapman sleep.⟩   *merchant slept*
400 Of nycė⟩ conscience took he no keep.⟩   *fastidious / heed*
If that he faught, and haddė the hyer⟩ hond,   *upper*
By water he sente hem hoom to every lond.

---

alderman leading member of town council
vigilies vigils; eves of saints' days; ceremonies on the evenings before guild festivals, in which the aldermen's wives would take the head of the procession
for the nones oral formula, without much meaning: "then"
poudre-marchant sharp spicy flavoring in powder form
galyngale a preparation of sweet spices
mormal ulcer associated with dirty living (in all senses)

blankmanger chopped creamed chicken, flavored with sugar and spice
Dertemouthe Dartmouth; a port in Devon, on the southwest coast of England, still used as a naval base
rouncy a cob or short-legged horse
ydrawe drawn, i.e. dishonestly
Burdeux-ward from Bordeaux, the great wine-shipping port on the west coast of France
By water . . . lond i.e. he threw his captives overboard

But of his craft,ˀ to rekene wel his tydes,	*calling*
His stremės,ˀ and his daungers hym bisides,°	*currents*
His herberwe,ˀ and his moone,° his lodemenage,°	*haven*
Ther nas noon swich from Hull° to Cartage.°	
Hardy he was and wys to undertake.	
With many a tempest hadde his berd been shake.	
He knew wel alle the havenes,ˀ as they were,	*harbors*

410

Fro Gootlond to the Cape of Fynystere,°	
And every cryke ˀ in Britaigne° and in Spayne.	*inlet*
His barge yclepėd was the Maudelayne.°	

DOCTOUR OF PHISIK

With us ther was a doctour of phisik.ˀ	*medicine*
In al this world ne was ther noon hym lik,	
To speke of phisik and of surgerye.	
For he was grounded in astronomye,° ASTRONOMY	
He kepteˀ his paciènt a ful greet deel	*treated*
In hourės,° by his magyk natureel.°	
Wel coude he fortunen the ascendent°	

420

Of hise ymagės for his paciėnt.	
He knew the cause of everich maladye,	
Were it of hoot, or coold, or moyste, or drye, HUMORS	
And where they engendred, and of what humour.°	
He was a verray, parfit° practisour.ˀ	*practitioner*
The cause yknowe,ˀ and of his harm the roote,	*known*
Anon he yaf the sikė man his boote.ˀ	*remedy*
Ful redy hadde he hise apothecaries	
To sende hym droggėsˀ and his letuaries,°	*drugs*

hym bisides all around him
moone i.e. phases of the moon
lodemenage navigation, pilotage
Hull port in Yorkshire, on the northeast coast of England
Cartage Cartagena, on the Mediterranean coast of Spain
Gootlond . . . Fynystere Gotland (island in the Baltic Sea) to Cape Finisterre, the westernmost point of Spain
Britaigne Brittany. The piling up of these names marks out the regular English sea-trade area: their cumulative meaning is "everywhere on the sea."
Maudelayne Magdalene, a popular name for a ship
astronomye astrology (see Glossary and Fig. 37); the movements of the planets insofar as they were thought to affect the constitutions of men
hourės the astrologically favorable or unfavorable planetary (not clock) times for treatment of disease, governed by the conjunctions of the planets in zodiacal or other houses
natureel "Natural" magic was the harnessing of the natural and supernatural forces of created things to produce a desired result; as opposed to "black" magic, which involved the invocation of evil spirits.
fortunen the ascendent The ascendant was any

one of the 360° of the zodiac rising above the horizon at a given moment. The doctor knew how to calculate the best time to make the talismanic images concentrating the forces which would help his patient recover. A degree of the zodiac favorable to a given disease in given circumstances and governing a given part of the body had to be ascendant and the planetary conjunctions in it also auspicious.
hoot . . . humour. All matter was held to contain the four primary contrasting qualities, hot and cold, moist and dry, in varying proportions, and the physician's aim was to keep them in harmonious and healthy balance in the patient's body. Man's constitution was composed of the four humors or vital fluids (the doctrine goes back to ancient Greek medicine): blood (hot and moist); phlegm (cold and moist); black bile (melancholy: cold and dry); yellow bile (choler: hot and dry). Their proportions, determined by the planetary conjunctions at a man's birth, in turn determined his temperament. Disturbance of their proportions caused disease: an excess of one humor or one quality had to be reduced by a medicine which would apply its contrary.
verray, parfit true and consummate
letuaries electuaries; medicinal pastes or preserves

For ech of hem made other for to wynne°—
430 Hir frendshipe nas nat newe to bigynne.
Wel knew he the olde Esculapius,°
And Deïscorides, and eek Rufus,
Olde Ypocras, Haly, and Galien,
Serapion, Razis, and Avicen,
Averrois, Damascien, and Constantyn,
Bernard, and Gatesden, and Gilbertyn.
Of his diete mesurable° was he,   *moderate*
For it was of no superfluitee,
But of greet norissing,° and digestible.   *nourishment*
440 His studie was but litel on the Bible.
In sangwin and in pers° he clad was al,
Lyned with taffata and with sendal;°   *silk*
And yet he was but esy of dispence;°   *expenditure*
He kepte that he wan° in pestilence.   *gained*
For° gold in phisik is a cordial,   *because*
Therfore he lovede gold in special.

          THE WYF OF BATHE

A good-wyf° was ther, of biside° Bathe,
But she was somdel° deef and that was scathe.°   *somewhat / a pity*
Of clooth-makyng she hadde swich an haunt,°   *practice*
450 She passed° hem of Ypres and of Gaunt.°   *surpassed*
In al the parisshe wif ne was ther noon
That to the offring bifore hire sholde goon;°
And if ther dide, certeyn so wrooth° was she   *angry*
That she was out of alle charitee.
Hir coverchiefs° ful fyne were of ground;°   *head-drapery / in texture*
I dorste° swere they weyeden° ten pound   *dare / weighed*

made other . . . wynne gave the other an
opportunity of profit
Esculapius This catalogue of medical authorities, perhaps drawn from a medieval encyclopedia, is not chronological. Aesculapius, the mythical founder of medicine, had treatises attributed
to him in the Middle Ages, but is probably
here only for the authority of his name. He
was supposedly the son of Apollo, god of
healing, and was already worshiped in Greece
in the 6th century B.C. Dioscorides and Rufus
of Ephesus were Greeks who flourished in the
1st and 2nd century A.D. and wrote on pharmacy and on anatomy respectively. Ypocras is
the Greek, Hippocrates of Cos, 5th century
B.C., the first scientific writer on medicine;
Haly may be either of two famous 10th-century
Arab doctors who played a large part in trans-
mitting Greek medicine to the West. Galen, most
influential of all, was court physician under
Marcus Aurelius (2nd century A.D.) and wrote
in Greek on many other topics besides medicine.
Serapion is a name owned by a Greek (2nd
century B.C.), a Damascus Christian (9th century), and an Arab (11th or 12th). Rhazes,
also alchemist and philosopher, lived in Baghdad

(9th to 10th century) and wrote a medical
encyclopedia. Avicenna, the 11th-century Arab,
and Averroes, the 12th-century Spanish Arab,
were both famous philosophers who wrote on
medicine. John of Damascus is a shadowy figure,
perhaps of the 9th century. Constantine the
African brought Arabic medicine to Salerno,
a famous Italian medical school, in the 11th
century. Bernard Gordon and John of Gaddesden
were 14th-century authorities; Gilbertus Angli-
cus, 13th.
sangwin . . . pers scarlet and in Persian blue
(a bluish gray)
cordial Potable (drinking) gold was sometimes
used in medicine—perhaps for the heart (cordial)—but the joke here is at the doctor's expense.
good-wyf woman of some means and standing
biside just outside; the center of Bath's textile
industry was the parish of St. Michael's without
the North Gate
Ypres . . . Gaunt Flemish towns, famous for
fine cloth; or hem of may refer to natives of
these towns working in England.
to the offring . . . goon should make her
offering in church before her

That on a Sonday were upon hir heed.
Hir hosen weren of fyn scarlet reed,
Ful streite yteyd,˘ and shoes ful moiste˘ and newe.　　　*tightly laced / soft*
460　Bold was hir face, and fair and reed of hewe.
She was a worthy womman al hir lyve.
Housbondes at chirchė dore she haddė fyve,°
Withouten other companye in youthe—
But therof nedeth nat to speke as nowthe.˘　　　*just now*
And thriės˘ hadde she been at Jerusalem;°　　　*three times*
She haddė passed many a straungė˘ strem;　　　*foreign*
At Rome she haddė been, and at Boloigne,
In Galice at Seint Jame, and at Coloigne;°
She coudė˘ much of wandrynge° by the weye—　　　*knew*
470　Gat-tothėd° was she, soothly˘ for to seye.　　　*truly*
Upon an amblere° esily° she sat,
Ywimpled° wel, and on hir heed an hat
As brood as is a bokėler or a targe;°
A foot-mantel˘ aboute hir hipės large,　　　*riding-skirt*
And on hir feet a paire of sporės˘ sharpe.　　　*spurs*
In felawschip wel coudė she laughe and carpe.˘　　　*talk*
Of˘ remedies° of love she knew per chaunce,　　　*about*
For she coude of that art the oldė daunce.°

PERSOUN OF A TOUN

A good man was ther of religioùn,
480　And was a pourė persoun˘ of a toun,　　　*parson*
But riche he was of holy thoght and werk.
He was also a lernėd man, a clerk.°
That Cristės gospel trewėly˘ wolde preche;　　　*faithfully*
Hise parisshens˘ devoutly wolde he teche.　　　*parishioners*
Benigne he was, and wonder˘ diligent,　　　*marvelously*
And in adversitee ful paciėnt.
And swich˘ he was yprevėd˘ oftė sithes.˘　　　*such / proved / times*
Ful looth were hym to cursen for hise tithes,°
But rather wolde he yeven,˘ out of doute,°　　　*give*
490　Unto his pourė parisshens aboute

Housbondes . . . fyve See John 4:18 and the Wife's Prologue below; *at church dore* refers to the fact that medieval marriages were performed outside the church door; nuptial mass was then celebrated within.
Jerusalem The greatest of all pilgrimages would take a full year.
Rome . . . Cologne These are the chief European centers of pilgrimage: Rome; Galicia, in northwest Spain, which has the shrine of St. James the Greater at Compostela; Cologne, which has the tomb of the Three Kings; and Boulogne with its famous image of the Virgin.
She . . . wandrynge She left no pilgrimage undone, but she also strayed from the path of virtue
Gat-tothed Teeth set wide apart, according to medieval physiognomics, betokened a traveling woman—in both senses.

amblere comfortable horse, pacing, not trotting
esily comfortably, perhaps astride
Ywimpled The wimple covered head, sides of face and neck: it was by this time rather old-fashioned for a laywoman; see l. 151.
bokeler . . . targe small round shields
remedies an allusion to Ovid, the Roman poet (1st century A.D.), writer of *The Remedies of Love* and other lovers' manuals of the Middle Ages; but probably also meaning that she was expert in love potions
the olde daunce a literal translation of the French phrase; so, "All the old routine"
clerk learned man. See l. 287.
looth . . . tithes He was unwilling to excommunicate (*cursen*) anyone for non-payment of tithes.
out of doute without doubt, surely

Of his offring,° and eek of his substaunce.⁾ *property*
He coude in litel thyng have suffisaunce.⁾ *enough*
Wyd was his parisshe, and houses fer asonder,
But he ne leftė⁾ nat, for reyn ne thonder, *neglected*
In siknesse nor in meschief,⁾ to visìte *misfortune*
The ferrestė⁾ in his parisshe, muche and lite,° *farthest*
Upon his feet, and in his hand a staf.
This noble ensample⁾ to his sheep° he yaf, *example*
That first he wroghte,⁾ and afterward he taughte. *did*
500 Out of the gospel° he tho⁾ wordės caughte,⁾ *those / took*
And this figùre he added eek therto,
That if gold rustė, what shal iren do?
For if a preest be foul, on whom we truste,
No wonder is a lewėd⁾ man to ruste.⁾ *simple*
And shame it is, if a preest take keep,⁾ *heed*
A shiten⁾ shepherde and a clenė sheep. *filthy*
Wel oghte a preest ensample for to yive,
By his clennesse, how that his sheep sholde live.
He settė nat his benefice to hyre°
510 And leet⁾ his sheep encombred in the myre *left*
And ran to Londoun, unto Saint Poules,°
To seken hym a chaunterie° for soules,
Or with a bretherhed° to been withholde;⁾ *supported*
But dwelte at hoom, and keptė wel his folde,
So that the wolf ne made it nat miscarie.
He was a shepherde, and no mercenarie,
And though he holy were, and vertuous,
He was to synful men nat despitous,⁾ *contemptuous*
Ne of his spechė daungerous⁾ ne digne,⁾ *disdainful / superior*
520 But in his teching discreet and benygne.
To drawen folk to hevene by fairnesse,
By good ensample, was his bisynesse:
But⁾ it were⁾ any persone obstinat, *if / there were*
What so he were, of heigh or lowe estat,
Hym wolde he snybben⁾ sharply for the nonys.⁾ *rebuke / at any time*
A bettrė preest I trowe⁾ that nowher noon ys. *believe*
He waited⁾ after no pompe and reverence,⁾ *looked for / deference*
Ne makėd hym a spicėd conscience.°
But Cristės loore⁾ and hise apostles twelve *teaching*
530 He taughte, but first he folwed it himselve.

---

offring Whatever the people gave at mass was the property of the parish priest.
muche and lite great and small
sheep See John 10:1–14 for the parable of the Good Shepherd.
gospel Matthew 5:19(?)
benefice to hyre It was common practice to hire a substitute priest at a small wage and, pocketing the difference, take other employment as well.
Saint Poules St. Paul's Cathedral, London

chaunterie endowment providing for perpetual masses for the soul of the donor and his nominees
bretherhed Guilds (see l. 366) often had their own chaplain.
Ne . . . conscience either "did not cultivate a too-scrupulous conscience" or "did not pretend to a heightened sense of right and wrong"
apostles twelve [the teaching of] his twelve apostles [also]

PLOWMAN

With hym ther was a plowman, was his brother,	
That hadde yladᐞ of dongᐞ ful many a fother.ᐞ	carried / dung / load
A trewė swinkerᐞ and a good was he,	toiler
Lyvynge in peesᐞ and parfit charitee.	peace
God loved he best with al his holėᐞ herte	whole
At allė tymės, thogh hym gamed or smerte,°	
And thanne his neighėbore right as himselve.°	
He woldė thresshe, and therto dykeᐞ and delve,	dig ditches
For Cristės sake, for every pourė wight,	
540 Withouten hire,ᐞ if it lay in his might.ᐞ	wages / power
Hise tithės payėd he ful faire and wel,	
Bothe of his propreᐞ swinkᐞ and his catel.ᐞ	own / work / possessions
In a tabardᐞ he rood upon a mere.°	smock
Ther was also a reve and a millere,	
A somnour, and a pardoner also,	
A maunciple,ᐞ and myself—ther were namo.ᐞ	steward / no more

MILLER

The miller was a stout carl° for the nones.	
Ful big he was of brawn,ᐞ and eek of bones.	muscle
That provėd wel,ᐞ for overalᐞ ther he cam,	was clear / wherever
550 At wrastling he wolde have alwey the ram.°	
He was short-sholdred,ᐞ brood,ᐞ a thikkė knarre.°	stocky / broad
Ther was no dore that he ne wolde heve ofᐞ harre,ᐞ	lift off / hinges
Or breke it at a renningᐞ with his heed.ᐞ	running / head
His berd as any sowe or fox was reed,°	
And therto brood, as though it were a spade.	
Upon the cop° right of his nose he hade	
A werte,ᐞ and theron stood a tuft of herys,ᐞ	wart / hairs
Reed as the bristlės of a sowės erys.ᐞ	ears
Hise nosėthirlėsᐞ blakė were and wyde.	nostrils
560 A swerd and a bokeler barᐞ he by his syde.	bore
His mouth as greet was as a greet forneys.ᐞ	oven
He was a janglere,ᐞ and a goliardeys,°	noisy babbler
And that was moost of sinne and harlotries.°	
Wel coude he stelen corn, and tollen thries;°	

---

thogh . . . smerte whether it made him happy or afflicted him
God . . . himselve (ll. 535–37) See Matthew 22:37–39: "Thou shalt love the lord thy God . . . Thou shalt love thy neighbor as thyself."
mere: a lower-class mount
carl fellow, usually of the lower class
ram the usual prize at a wrestling match
knarre a knot in wood: so a tough, knotty man; physiognomically, an angry lecherous bully
reed A red beard or head was not to be trusted, according to physiognomic theory. Judas, the arch-traitor, was said to have had red hair; see also Reynard the Fox.

cop bridge, top, or tip
goliardeys from goliards, the student and clerical authors of satirical Latin verse in the 12th and 13th centuries, who called their leader and patron, a mythical figure, Golias. Their writings were often scurrilous, and goliardeys here has come to mean a teller of dirty jokes.
harlotries i.e. obscenities. Harlot was not applied only to women in the Middle Ages.
tollen . . . thries take his toll three times, instead of once. The Miller's payment was a percentage of what he ground.

And yet he hadde a thombe of gold,° pardee.   *by heaven*
A whit cote and a blew hood wered° he.   *wore*
A baggepipe wel coude he blowe and sowne,°   *sound*
And therwithal° he broghte us out of towne.   *therewith*

MAUNCIPLE

A gentil maunciple° was ther of a Temple,°
570   Of which achatours° mighte take exemple   *buyers*
For to be wise° in bying of vitaille;°   *thrifty / victuals*
For whether that he payde, or took by taille,°
Algate° he wayted° so in his achat°   *always / watched / buying*
That he was ay biforn,° and in good staat.°   *ahead / financial position*
Now is nat that of God a ful fair grace
That swich a lewed° mannes wit shal pace°   *unlearned / surpass*
The wisdom of an heep of lerned men?
Of maistres° hadde he mo than thries ten   *masters*
That weren of lawe expert and curious,°   *subtle*
580   Of whiche ther weren a doseyne° in that hous   *dozen*
Worthy to been stiwardes of rente° and lond   *income*
Of any lord that is in Engelond,
To make hym lyve by his propre good;°
In honour dettelees, but° he were wood,°   *unless / mad*
Or lyve as scarsly° as hym list° desire;   *frugally / it pleases*
And able for to helpen al a shire
In any cas° that mighte falle or happe;   *event*
And yet this manciple sette hir aller cappe.°

REVE°

The reve was a sclendre° colerik° man.   *slim*
590   His berd was shave as ny° as ever he can;   *close*
His heer° was by his eres° round yshorn;   *hair / ears*
His top was dokked° lyk a preest biforn.
Ful longe were his legges, and ful lene,
Ylyk° a staf, ther was no calf ysene.°   *like / visible*
Wel coude he kepe a gerner° and a bynne;   *granary*
Ther was noon auditour coude of hym wynne.°   *get the better of*
Wel wiste° he by the droghte and by the reyn°   *knew in advance / rain*
The yeldynge of his seed and of his greyn.°   *grain*

---

thombe of gold See the proverb: "An honest miller has a golden thumb"; i.e. there are no honest millers.
maunciple steward at one of the Inns of Court (societies of lawyers in London) or at a college
Temple an Inn of Court, perhaps specifically the Middle or Inner Temple, whose quarters in London had formerly been occupied by the Knights Templars
by taille by tally, on credit. Credit was recorded by cutting (Fr. *tailler*) notches on a stick.
To . . . good keep him from bankruptcy by making him live without borrowing
sette . . . cappe made fools of them all

Reve Usually a man of lowly origin, elected by his fellow peasants for a term as a foreman on the manor. He looked after fields and woods, saw that work was done, collected dues, and gave annual account of all. On larger estates he would be subordinate to a bailiff, who in turn was subordinate to a steward.
colerik having an excess of the humor choler (see l. 422) making him suspicious, prone to anger. Physiognomically, he is avaricious and lustful.
dokked cropped; a sign of low social status in a layman. Clergy wore their hair cut short or tonsured as a token of humility.

His lordės sheep, his neet,⸗ his dayerye,⸗ — *cattle / dairy*
600 His swyn, his hors, his stoor,⸗ and his pultrye — *produce*
Was hoolly⸗ in this revės governyng, — *wholly*
And by his covenant yaf the rekenyng,°
Sin⸗ that his lord was twenty yeer of age. — *since*
Ther coude no man bringe hym in arrerage.°
Ther nas baillif, ne herde,° nor other hyne,°
That he ne knew his sleighte and his covyne.°
They were adrad⸗ of hym as of the deeth.° — *afraid*
His wonyng⸗ was ful faire upon an heeth;⸗ — *house / common*
With grenė treës shadwed was his place.
610 He coudė bettre than his lord purchace:⸗ — *buy*
Ful riche he was astorėd prively.⸗ — *stocked stealthily*
His lord wel coude he plesen subtilly,
To yeve and lene⸗ hym of his ownė good,⸗ — *lend / property*
And have a thank, and yet a cote° and hood.
In youthe he haddė lerned a good mister:⸗ — *trade*
He was a wel good wrighte,⸗ a carpenter. — *craftsman*
This revė sat upon a ful good stot,°
That was al pomely⸗ grey, and hightė⸗ Scot. — *dapple / was named*
A long surcote of pers upon he hade,°
620 And by his syde he bar⸗ a rusty blade. — *bore*
Of Northfolk° was this reve of which I telle,
Biside a toun men clepen Baldėswelle.⸗ — *Bawdswell*
Tukkėd⸗ he was, as is a frere, aboute. — *hitched up*
And ever he rood the hindreste⸗ of oure route.⸗ — *hindmost / group*

SOMNOUR°
A somnour was ther with us in that place,
That haddė a fyr-reed⸗ cherubinnės° face, — *fiery red*
For sawcėfleem⸗ he was, with eyėn narwe. — *pimply*
As hoot he was, and lecherous as a sparwe,°
With scallėd⸗ browės blake and pilėd° berd — *scabby*
630 Of his visagė children were aferd.⸗ — *afraid*
Ther nas quiksilver, litarge, ne brimstoon,
Boras, ceruce, ne oille of tartre noon,°

And by . . . rekenyng according to his covenant [he] gave his account
arrerage find him in arrears, short on his accounts
herde herd, shepherd
hyne hind, farm laborer
sleighte . . . covyne cunning, quickness and
guile, fraud
the deeth most frequently the plague, the most
feared of epidemics. The Black Death (1348–49,
1360, 1379) was strong in men's memories.
cote Clothing was sometimes given as part of
wages, sometimes as a bonus.
stot a favorite Norfolk breed of horse
A . . . hade He had on a long overcoat of
Persian blue.
Northfolk Norfolk
Somnour A summoner bore the citation to a
person, clergy or lay, required to appear in an

ecclesiastical court, for offenses against canon
law and morals; and had to make sure that he
obeyed. By Chaucer's time, summoner was a
byword for corruption.
cherubinnes Cherubim were fiery red (Ezekiel
1:13); physiognomically, the summoner is a
drunken lecher.
As hoot . . . sparwe As hot and lecherous as
a sparrow. This bird was a byword for those
qualities; see Skelton, *Philip Sparrow* below.
piled straggling or falling out in patches
quiksilver . . . noon The medieval name for
the summoner's skin disease was *alopecia*,
thought to be sexual in origin; the remedies—
mercury, peroxide of lead, sulphur, borax, white-
lead ointment, oil of tartar—suggest that he may
have been syphilitic.

Ne oynément that woldé clensé and byte,
That hym myghté helpen of his whelkés° white,   *pimples*
Nor of the knobbés sittinge on his chekes.
Wel loved he garleek, oynons, and eek lekes,°
And for to drinken strong wyn, reed as blood.
Thanne wolde he speke and crie as he were wood.°
And whan that he wel dronken hadde the wyn,   *mad*
640   Than wolde he speké no word but Latyn.
A fewé termés hadde he, two or three,
That he had lernéd out of som decree—
No wonder is, he herde it al the day;
And eek ye knowen wel that how a jay°   *jackdaw*
Can clepen° 'Watte'° as wel as kan the Pope.   *say*
But whoso coude in other thyng hym grope,°   *question*
Thanne hadde he spent al his philosophìe;°   *learning*
Ay° 'Questio quid iuris,'° wolde he crie.   *always*
He was a gentil harlot° and a kinde;
650   A bettre felawe sholdé men noght fynde:
He woldé suffre° for a quart of wyn   *permit*
A good felawe to have his concubyn
A twelf monthe, and excuse hym atté fulle.°
Ful privély a fynch eek coude he pulle.°
And if he fond owher° a good felawe,   *found anywhere*
He woldé techen hym to have noon awe,°   *fear*
In swich° cas, of the erchédekenés curs,°   *such*
But if° a mannés soule were in his purs;   *unless*
For in his purs he sholde ypunisshed be.
660   'Purs is the erchédekenés Helle,'° seyde he.
But wel I woot he lyéd right indede;
Of cursing° oghte ech gilty man him drede,   *excommunication*
For curs wol slee° right as assoilling° saveth,   *kill / absolution*
And also war hym of a *Significavit.*°
In daunger° hadde he at his owene gise°   *in his power / at will*
The yongé girlés° of the diocise,
And knew hir conseil,° and was al hir reed.°   *secrets / advisor*
A gerland hadde he set upon his heed
As greet as it were for an alé-stake.°
670   A bokéleer hadde he maad hym of a cake.°   *loaf of bread*

---

garleek . . . lekes pimple-inducing foods, with bad moral connotations (Numbers 11:5)
Watte common name for tame, "talking" jackdaw
'Questio . . . iuris' "I ask, what is the law [on this matter]": a legal catchphrase, common in the ecclesiastical courts.
harlot rascal. See l. 563.
atte fulle i.e. completely. Sexual offenses were dealt with by the ecclesiastical courts, and the Summoner had no authority to use his discretion.
fynche . . . pulle "pluck a pigeon": have sex with a woman

erchedekenes curs excommunication by the archdeacon
Purs . . . Helle i.e. a man is punished only in his purse
And also . . . Significavit And also beware of a writ for imprisonment. The church courts could not imprison: for this they had to call in the civil authorities. *Significavit* was the first word of the writ which did this.
girles perhaps in its other meaning of "young people" of both sexes
ale-stake a pole, with a "bush" of green leaves on it to symbolize refreshment, marked an alehouse (Fig. 39)

PARDONER°
With hym ther was a gentil pardoner
Of Rouncivale,° his freend and his compeer,>   companion
That streight was comen fro the court of Rome.
Ful loude he song 'Com hider, love, to me!'°   sang
This somnour bar to hym a stif> burdoun;°   strong
Was nevere tromp> of half so greet a soun.   trumpet
This pardoner hadde heer as yelow as wex,
But smothe it heng, as dooth a strike of flex;>   hank of flax
By ounces,> henge hise lokkes that he hadde,   thin strands
680   And therwith he hise shuldres overspradde;>   overspread
But thinne it lay, by colpons,> oon and oon.   in "rats'-tails"
But hood, for jolitee, ywered> he noon,   wore
For it was trussed up in his walet.>   pack
Hym thoughte he rood al of the newe jet;>   fashion
Dischevelee,> save his cappe, he rood al bare.   with hair loose
Swiche glaringe° eyen hadde he as an hare.
A vernicle° hadde he sowed upon his cappe.
His walet lay biforn hym in his lappe,
Bretful> of pardoun, come from Rome al hoot.>   brimful / hot
690   A voys he hadde as smal as hath a goot.>   goat
No berd hadde he, ne nevere sholde have;
As smothe it was as it were late yshave,
I trowe he were a geldyng or a mare.
But of his craft, fro Berwyk into Ware,°
Ne was ther swich another pardoner.
For in his male> he hadde a pilwe-beer,>   pack / pillow-case
Which that he seyde was Oure Lady veyl.
He seyde he hadde a gobet of the seyl>   piece / sail
That Seint Peter hadde, whan that he wente
700   Upon the see, til Jesu Crist hym hente.°
He hadde a croys of latoun,° ful of stones,
And in a glas he hadde pigges bones.
But with thise relikes, whan that he fond>   found
A poure persoun> dwellynge upon lond,>   parson / up country
Upon a day he gat> hym more moneye   got
Than that the persoun gat in monthes tweye.

Pardoner A seller of "pardons," indulgences, papal bulls allowing some remittance of penance in return for money. Later, such bulls came to be regarded as giving some exemption from Purgatory and, by the simple, as guaranteeing forgiveness of sins. Unscrupulous salesmen used them to gain money for the church, specific institutions in it—and themselves.
Rouncivale St. Mary Roncevall, near Charing Cross in London, an English branch of an important Spanish religious house
'Com . . . me!' presumably a popular song
burdoun either burden, i.e. refrain, or accompaniment
glaringe staring, bulging
vernicle Pilgrims to Rome bought a small replica

of the handkerchief (in St. Peter's) with which St. Veronica was said to have wiped away the sweat from Christ's face on the road to Calvary, on which occasion the likeness of his features had been miraculously transferred to the handkerchief.
Berwyk . . . Ware the length of England (Berwick on Tweed in Northumberland to Ware in Hertfordshire, near London)
That . . . hente either before Christ took Peter as a disciple; or when he tried to walk on the waters (Matthew 14:28–31)
croys of latoun cross made of a brassy base metal, to be passed off as gold (as the pig's bones were to be passed off as saints' relics)

And thus, with feynéd⁷ flatery and japes,⁷   *false / tricks*
He made the persoun and the peple his apes.⁷   *dupes*
But trewély to tellen atté laste,
710 He was in chirche a noble ecclesiaste;
Wel coude he rede a lessoun or a storie,⁷   *sacred narrative*
But alderbest⁷ he song an offertorie;   *best of all*
For wel he wisté, whan that song was songe,
He mosté⁷ preche and wel affile⁷ his tonge   *must / sharpen*
To wynné silver, as he ful wel coude;
Therfore he song so meriely and loude.

Now have I told you shortly⁷in a clause⁷   *briefly / short space*
Th'estat, th'array, the nombre, and eek the cause
Why that assembled was this companye
720 In Southwerk, at this gentil hostelrye
That highte the Tabard, fasté⁷ by the Belle.°   *close*
But now is tymé to yow for to telle
How that we baren⁷ us that ilké⁷ nyght,   *behaved / same*
Whan we were in that hostelrie alight;
And after wol I telle of oure viage,⁷   *journey*
And al the remenaunt⁷ of oure pilgrimage.   *remainder*
But first I pray yow, of youre curteisye,
That ye n'arette⁷ it nat my vileinye,⁷   *attribute / ill-breeding*
Thogh that I pleynly speke in this matere,
730 To tellé yow hir wordés and hir cheere,⁷   *behavior*
Ne thogh I speke hir wordés proprely.⁷   *exactly*
For this ye knowen also⁷ wel as I,   *as*
Whoso shal tellé a tale after a man,
He moot reherce⁷ as ny⁷ as evere he kan   *must repeat / near*
Everich a word, if it be in his charge,⁷   *power*
Al⁷ speke he never so rudéliche⁷ or large,⁷   *although / coarsely / broadly*
Or ellis⁷ he moot⁷ telle his tale untrewe,   *else / must*
Or feyné⁷ thyng, or fyndé wordés newe.   *falsify*
He may nat spare, althogh he were his brother;
740 He moot as wel seye o word as another.
Crist spak hymself ful brode⁷ in holy writ,   *plainly*
And wel ye woot no vileynye is it.
Eek Plato seïth, whoso can hym rede,
'The wordés mote be cosin to the dede.'°
Also I prey yow to foryeve it me,
Al⁷ have I nat set folk in hir degree   *although*
Heere in this tale, as that they sholdé stonde.
My wit is short, ye may wel understonde.
Greet cheré made oure host° us everichon,
750 And to the soper sette he us anon.

Belle another pilgrim inn. See l. 20.
Plato . . . dede' in Plato's *Timaeus*, which
Chaucer might have read in Latin translation,
though he probably found it in Boethius
host Harry Bailly, the landlord of the Tabard

He servèd us with vitaille° at the beste. — *victuals*
Strong was the wyn, and wel to drynke us leste.° — *it pleased*

A semely man oure hostè was withalle
For to han been a marchal° in an halle.
A largè° man he was, with eyen stepe°— — *broad / prominent*
A fairer burgeys° was ther noon in Chepe°— — *burgher*
Boold of his speche, and wys, and wel ytaught,
And of manhod hym lakkedè right naught.°
Eek therto he was right a mery° man,— — *pleasant*
760 And after soper pleyen° he bigan, — *to jest*
And spak of mirthe, amongès othere thynges—
Whan that we haddè maad oure rekeninges°—
And seydè thus: 'Now, lordinges,° trewèly, — *ladies and gentlemen*
Ye been to me right welcome, hertèly.° — *sincerely*
For by my trouthe, if that I shal nat lye,
I saugh nat this yeer so mery a compaunye
At onès in this herberwe° as is now. — *inn*
Fayn° wolde I doon yow mirthè, wiste° I how. — *willingly / knew*
And of a mirthe I am right now bithoght,
770 To doon yow ese,° and it shal costè noght. — *pleasure*
Ye goon to Caunterbury—God yow speede!
The blisful martir quitè° yow youre mede!° — *pay / reward*
And wel I woot, as ye goon by the weye,
Ye shapen° yow to talen° and to pleye; — *intend / tell tales*
For trewèly, confort ne myrthe is noon
To ridè by the weye doumb as the stoon.° — *stone*
And therfore wol I maken yow disport,
As I seydè erst,° and doon yow som confort. — *before*
And if yow liketh alle, by oon assent,
780 For to stonden at° my jugèment, — *abide by*
And for to werken° as I shal yow seye, — *do*
Tomorwe, whan ye riden by the weye,
Now, by my fader° soulè that is deed, — *father's*
But if° ye be merye, I wol yève yow myn heed.° — *unless / head*
Hold up youre hond, withouten morè speche.'
Oure counseil was nat longè for to seche.° — *seek*
Us thoughte it was noght worth to make it wys,°
And graunted hym, withouten moore avys,° — *deliberation*
And bad hym seye his verdit as hym leste.
790 'Lordinges,' quod he, 'now herkneth for the beste;
But taak it nought, I prey yow, in desdeyn.° — *disdain*
This is the poynt, to speken short and pleyn,
That ech of yow, to shortè° with oure weye — *shorten*

---

marchal master of ceremonies in a [lord's] hall
Chepe Cheapside, in the City of London, the
commercial center
naught unlike the Pardoner

Whan . . . rekeninges after we had paid our
bills
Us . . . wys it seemed to us not worthwhile to
make a business of it

In this viage, shal tellé talés tweye°
To Caunterbury-ward, I mene it so,
And homward, he shal tellen othere two,
Of aventures that whilomʾ han bifalle.   *once upon a time*
And which of yow that bereth hym best of alle,
That is to seyn, that telleth in this cas
800   Tales of best sentènceʾ and moost solas,ʾ   *profit / delight*
Shal have a soper at oure aller cost°
Heere in this place, sitting by this post,ʾ   *inn sign*
Whan that we come agayn fro Caunterbury.
And for to maké yow the moré mery,
I wol myselven goodlyʾ with yow ryde,   *willingly*
Right at myn owene cost, and be youre gyde.
And whoso wole my jugément withseyeʾ   *contradict*
Shal paye al that we spenden by the weye.
And if ye vouchèsauf that it be so,
810   Tel me anon, withouten wordès mo,ʾ   *more*
And I wol erly shapéʾ me therfore.'   *prepare*
     This thyng was graunted, and ouré othes swore
With ful glad herte, and preydenʾ hym also   *begged*
That he wolde vouchèsauf for to do so,
And that he woldé been oure governour,
And of oure talés juge and reportour,ʾ   *bringer of verdict*
And sette a soper, at a certeyn pris,ʾ   *price*
And we wolʾ reuléd been at his devys   *will*
In heigh and lowe;ʾ and thus by oon assent   *completely*
820   We been acorded to his jugément.
And therupon the wyn was fetʾ anon;   *fetched*
We dronken, and to resté wente echonʾ   *everyone*
Withouten any lenger taryinge.ʾ   *delay*
     Amorwe,ʾ whan that day gan° for to springe,   *in the morning*
Up roos oure hoost and was oure aller cok,°
And gadredeʾ us togidre,ʾ alle in a flok,   *gathered / together*
And forth we riden,ʾ a litel moore than pas,ʾ   *rode / walking pace*
Unto the Watering of Saint Thomas.°
And there oure hoost bigan his hors areste,ʾ   *stopped*
830   And seyde: 'Lordynges, herkneth, if yow leste!ʾ   *it please*
Ye woot youre forward, and I it yow recorde.°
If even-song and morwe-song accorde,ʾ   *morning-song agree*
Lat se now who shal tellé the firste tale.
As evere motéʾ I drynké wyn or ale,   *may*
Whoso be rebel to my jugément
Shal paye for al that by the wey is spent.

ech . . . tweye Less than a quarter of this num-   Watering . . . Thomas   watering-place   for
ber of tales was written.   horses, two miles on the way
at . . . cost at the cost of us all   Ye . . . recorde you know your agreement, and
gan an auxiliary, to make simple past tense   I recall it to you
oure aller cok the rooster who woke us all

Now draweth cut,° er that we ferrer twinne;⸫   *travel farther*
He which that hath the shorteste shal biginne.
Sire Knyght,' quod he, 'my mayster and my lord,
840 Now draweth cut, for that is myn accord.⸫   *agreement*
Cometh neer,' quod he, 'my lady Prioresse.
And ye, sire Clerk, lat be youre shamefastnesse,⸫   *modesty*
Ne studieth noght. Ley hond to, euery man.'
   Anon to drawen every wight bigan,
And shortly, for to tellen as it was,
Were it by aventure,⸫ or sort,⸫ or cas,⸫   *luck / fate / chance*
The sothe⸫ is this, the cut fil⸫ to the knyght,   *truth / fell*
Of which ful blithe and glad was every wyght,
And telle he moste⸫ his tale, as was resoùn,⸫   *must / right*
850 By forward and by composicioùn,⸫   *compact*
As ye han herd. What nedeth wordès mo?
And whan this goode man saugh that it was so,
As he that wys was and obedient
To kepe his forward by his free assent,
He seyde, 'Syn I shal biginne the game,
What, welcome be the cut, a⸫ Goddès name!   *in*
Now lat us ryde, and herkneth what I seye.'
   And with that word we ryden forth oure weye,
And he bigan with right a mery cheere⸫   *face*
860 His tale anon, and seyde in this manere.°
      Here endeth the prolog of this book
    c. 1385–1400   1478

The Miller's Prologue and Tale

Chaucer has skillfully planted in the General Prologue a notion of what sort of tale we can expect from the bag-piping Miller. His drunken thrusting forward of himself to tell the next tale as soon as the grave, sober Knight has done with his is another pointer. The Reeve, slender, choleric man that he is—timid and prone to ineffectual anger on account of his constitution and his advanced age—also senses what is up: this is going to be a tale of old age, youth, carpentry, and cuckoldry, and, as an elderly carpenter and perhaps a cuckold himself, he bursts into fury. But the great, thick Miller coarsely puts the poor man aside and begins.

What we get is one of Chaucer's several *fabliaux*: a dirty story told with wit and point. The *fabliau* developed in France in the thirteenth century—though such verse tales exist in both Latin and the vernacular from an earlier period—and was hardly used there after the early fourteenth. French *fabliaux* are realistic, short, plain in style, and rapid in narration, but they are a skillful and courtly and not a popular or folk literary form. Rather, they are an aristocratic mocking of the antics of the lower classes: amoral, not pornographic. Chaucer's are among the few written in English, another example of his ability to take a convention and work in it to masterly effect.

---

cut lot. Straws of different lengths would be used.   may heere"—which will remind us that Chau-
in this manere Some manuscripts read "as ye   cer's poetry was intended for reading aloud.

This is the literary mode in which Chaucer is working in such tales as the Miller's, the Reeve's, and the Merchant's—and to some extent in the Wife of Bath's Prologue. What we have holds the two requirements of the *fabliau* genre perfectly in balance: the dirty story which we might expect from the Miller, and the aristocratically brutal and polished tone. Chaucer has woven together what were probably two disparate narratives (one German, the other Italian in origin); both arrive at their climax at the same moment in one of the great comic scenes of English literature.

Prologue

Here folwen the wordes bitwene the Host and the Millere

Whan that the Knight had thus his tale ytold,
In al the routė> nas ther yong ne old — *group*
That he ne seyde it was a noble storie,
And worthy for to drawen> to memorie; — *recall*
And namėly> the gentils° everichoon. — *especially*
Our Hoste lough> and swoor, 'So moot I goon, — *laughed*
This gooth aright; unbokeled is the male;°
Lat see now who shal telle another tale:
For trewėly, the game is wel bigonne.
Now telleth ye, sir Monk, if that ye conne,> — *can*
Somwhat, to quytė> with the Knightės tale.' — *requite*
The Miller, that fordronken° was al pale,
So that unnethe> upon his hors he sat, — *with difficulty*
He nolde avalen> neither hood ne hat, — *would not take off*
Ne abydė no man for his curteisie,
But in Pilàtės vois° he gan to crye,
And swoor by armės and by blood and bones,°
'I can> a noble talė for the nones, — *know*
With which I wol now quyte the Knightės tale.'
Our Hostė saugh> that he was dronke of ale, — *saw*
And seyde: 'Abydė, Robin, my leve> brother, — *dear*
Som bettrė man shal telle us first another:
Abyde, and lat us werken thriftily.'> — *sensibly*
'By Goddes soul,' quod he, 'that wol nat I;
For I wol speke, or ellės go my wey.'
Our Hoste answerde: 'Tel on, a devel wey!°
Thou art a fool, thy wit is overcome.'
'Now herkneth,' quod the Miller, 'alle and some>! — *one*

gentils the better born among the pilgrims, to whom a chivalrous tale would most appeal
'So moot . . . male' as I may walk (i.e. continue able to walk), this is going well; the pack is unstrapped
fordronken completely drunk; or, reading "for dronken": because of being drunk
Pilates vois a high, harsh voice, like that used for Pontius Pilate in the mystery plays
by armes . . . bones i.e. by Christ's arms, blood, and bones. See the Pardoner's Tale, l. 188.
devel wey i.e. in the Devil's name; originally a strengthening of "away," the parts divided as in "unto the gardinward," l. 464.

But first I make a protestacioùn°

30 That I am dronke, I knowe it by my soun;>   *how I sound*

And therfore, if that I misspeke or seye,

Wyte> it the ale of Southwerk, I yow preye;   *blame it on*

For I wol telle a legende° and a lyf

Bothe of a carpenter, and of his wyf,

How that a clerk hath set the wrightès cappe.'°

    The Reve answerde and seydè, 'Stint> thy clappe,>   *stop / babble*

Lat be thy lewèd> dronken harlotrye.°   *ignorant*

It is a sinne and eek> a greet folye   *also*

To apeiren> any man, or him diffame,   *injure*

40 And eek to bringen wyvès in swich fame.>   *reputation*

Thou mayst ynogh of othere thingès seyn.'

    This dronken Miller spak ful sone ageyn,

And seydè, 'Levè> brother Osèwold,   *dear*

Who hath no wyf, he is no cokewold.°

But I sey nat therfore that thou art oon;

Ther been ful godè wyvès many oon,>   *a one*

And ever a thousand gode ayeyns oon badde,

That knowestow wel thyself, but if> thou madde.>   *unless / are mad*

Why artow angry with my talè now?

50 I have a wyf, pardee, as well as thou,

Yet nolde> I, for the oxen in my plough,   *would not*

Taken upon me more than ynough,

As demen of myself that I were oon;°

I wol belevè wel that I am noon.

An housbond shal> nat been inquisitif   *must*

Of Goddès privetee,> nor of his wyf.   *secrets*

So> he may findè Goddès foyson> there,   *provided / plenty*

Of the remenant nedeth nat enquere.>'   *enquire*

    What sholde I morè seyn, but this Millere

60 He nolde his wordès for no man forbere,

But tolde his cherlès> tale in his manere;   *lout's*

M'athinketh that I shal reherce it here.°

And therfore every gentil wight I preye,

For Goddès love, demeth nat that I seye

Of evel entente, but that> I moot> reherce   *because / must*

Hir talès allè, be they bettre or werse,

Or ellès falsen som of my matere.

And therfore, whoso list it nat yhere,>   *to listen*

Turne over the leef, and chese> another tale;   *choose*

70 For he shal finde ynowè,> grete and smale,   *plenty*

---

protestacioun formal, public avowal
legende usually a holy story, a saint's life
clerk . . . cappe scholar made a fool of the workman
harlotrye obscenity, low conduct of all kinds

Who . . . cokewold Only the man who has no wife cannot be a cuckold.
As . . . oon to think that I myself were one, i.e. a cuckold
M'athinketh . . . here I regret that I must tell it here

Of storial° thing that toucheth gentillesse,
And eek moralitee and holinesse;
Blameth nat me if that ye chese amis.
The Miller is a cherl, ye knowe wel this;
So was the Reve, and otherė many mo,
And harlotrye they tolden bothė two.
Avyseth⁊ yow and putte me out of blame;   *consider*
And eek men shal nat make ernèst of game.°

Here endeth the prologe

Tale

Here biginneth the Millere his Tale

Whylom⁊ ther was dwellinge at Oxenford   *once*
80   A richė gnof,⁊ that gestès heeld to bord,°   *boor*
And of his craft he was a carpenter.
With him ther was dwellinge a poore scoler,
Had lernėd art, but al his fantasye°
Was turnėd for to lerne astrologye,
And coude a certeyn of conclusioùns°
To demen by interrogacioùns,
If that men axėd⁊ him in certein houres,   *asked*
Whan that men sholde have droghte or ellès shoures,
Or if men axėd him what sholde bifalle
90   Of every thing; I may nat rekene hem alle.
        This clerk was clepėd⁊ hendė° Nicholas.   *called*
Of dernė love he coude and of solas;°
And therto he was sleigh⁊ and ful privee,⁊   *sly / secretive*
And lyk a mayden mekė for to see.
A chambre hadde he in that hostelrye
Allone, withouten any companye,
Ful fetisly ydight⁊ with herbès swote;⁊   *adorned / sweet*
And he himself as swete as is the rote⁊   *root*
Of licorys, or any cetewale.°

---

storial literally, historical; thus, not a made-up story but something refined, moral, exemplary, based on what really happened, told for pleasure and instruction
And eek . . . game and also one must not make serious tales of jokes
bord literally, table. The carpenter took in boarders, some of them students.
fantasye originally the mental process of sense perception: so, all his intellectual effort, with overtones of disapproval. This poor scholar had passed through the trivium and gone on to the quadrivium (see Glossary).
coude . . . conclusiouns i.e. and knew a cer-

tain number of conclusions or propositions, the use of which would allow him to determine astrologically the answers to such questions as "At this or that time, shall we have drought or rain?"
hende agreeable, handsome
Of derne . . . solas He knew all about love-in-secret and what pleasure was. That is, he knew all the refinements of concealment, to protect the lady's reputation (and his own), and the whole range of meaning of solace (comfort from the lady in and out of bed).
cetewale setwall, zedoary, an aromatic Eastern root. Licorice root was proverbially sweet.

100 His *Almageste*° and bokės grete and smale,
His astrelabie,° longinge for˃ his art,˃   *belonging to / craft*
His augrim stonės° layen faire apart,
On shelvės couchėd,˃ at his beddes heed: *laid*
His presse ycovered with a falding reed.°
And al above ther lay a gay sautrye,°
On which he made a-nightės melodye
So swetėly that al the chambre rong;˃   *rang*
And *Angelus ad virginem*° he song;
And after that he song the *Kingės Note;*°
110 Ful often blessėd was his mery throte.
And thus this swetė clerk his tymė spente
After his freendės finding and his rente.°
 This carpenter had wedded newe˃ a wyf   *recently*
Which that he lovede morė than his lyf;
Of eightėtenė yeer she was of age.
Jalous he was, and heeld hir narwe˃ in cage,   *closely*
For she was wilde and yong, and he was old,°
And demed himself ben lyk a cokėwold.°
He knew nat Catoun,° for his wit was rude,
120 That bad man sholdė wedde his similitude.°
Men sholdė wedden after˃ hir estaat,˃   *according to / condition*
For youthe and elde˃ is often at debaat.   *age*
But sith that he was fallen in the snare,
He moste endure, as other folk, his care.
 Fair was this yongė wyf, and therwithal
As any wesele hir body gent and smal.°
A ceynt she werede barrėd al of silk,°
A barmclooth˃ eek as whyt as mornė milk   *apron*
Upon hir lendės,˃ ful of many a gore.˃   *loins / pleat*
130 Whyt was hir smok,˃ and brouded˃ al bifore   *undergarment / embroidered*
And eek bihinde, on hir coler˃ aboute,   *collar*
Of˃ col-blak silk, withinne and eek withoute.   *with*
The tapės˃ of hir whytė voluper˃   *ribbons / cap*

Almageste the astronomical treatise of Claudius Ptolemy, the Greek astronomer and geographer; see the Wife of Bath's Prologue, l. 188
atrelabie astrolabe; an astronomical instrument for taking observations of the sun, moon, and planets, measuring heights and distances, determining latitudes and longitudes, and preparing horoscopes
augrim stones stones or counters for use on an abacus
his presse . . . reed his large, shelved, doorless cupboard curtained off with coarse woolen cloth ("falding") of red
sautrye psaltery; a stringed instrument played with the hand
Angelus ad virginem "The Angel to the Virgin," the first words of a famous hymn on the Annunciation
Kinges Note "The King's Tune" has not been identified. Nicholas could sing sacred or secular

songs to order and be thanked for either—his gay voice ("throte") was often blessed by his listeners.
After . . . rente He lived on what his friends provided for him and his own income.
For . . . old See Chaucer's Merchant's Tale, his "courtly" treatment of the old husband-young wife theme.
And . . . cokėwold and thought himself likely to be a cuckold
Catoun Dionysius Cato, 4th-century author of verses of moral instruction, the *Distichs*, a popular medieval schoolbook
bad . . . similitude a bad man should marry someone like him. This particular proverb occurs in a supplement to the *Distichs*.
As . . . smal her body graceful and slim as a weasel's
A . . . silk She wore a belt, with cross-stripes, of silk.

Were of the same suyte° of hir coler;　　　　　　　　*headband broad*
Hir filet brood⁊ of silk, and set ful hye;　　　　*certainly / wanton*
And sikerly⁊ she hadde a likerous⁊ yë.
Ful smale ypullèd° were hir browès two,
And tho were bent, and blake as any sloo.
She was ful more blisful on to see
140　Than is the newè perèjonette° tree;
And softer than the wolle⁊ is of a wether.°　　　　*wool*
And by hir girdel⁊ heeng⁊ a purs of lether　　　　*belt / hung*
Tasseld with silk, and perlèd with latoun.°
In al this world, to seken up and doun,
There nis no man so wys, that coudè thenche⁊　　　*imagine*
So gay a popelote,⁊ or swich⁊ a wenche.　　　　　*poppet / such*
Ful brighter was the shyning of hir hewe
Than in the Towr the noble° yforgèd newe.
But of hir song, it was as loude and yerne⁊　　　　*lively*
150　As any swalwè sittinge on a berne.⁊　　　　　　*barn*
Therto she coudè skippe and makè game,
As any kide or calf folwinge his dame.⁊　　　　　*mother*
Hir mouth was swete as bragot or the meeth,°　　　*heather*
Or hord of apples leyd in hay or heeth.⁊　　　　　*skittish / lively*
Winsinge⁊ she was, as is a joly⁊ colt,　　　　　　*straight / arrow*
Long as a mast, and upright⁊ as a bolt.⁊
A brooch she baar upon hir lowe coler,
As brood as is the bos⁊ of a bocler.⁊　　　　　　*boss / round shield*
Hir shoes were lacèd on hir leggès hye;
160　She was a prymèrole,° a piggès-nye°
For any lord to leggen⁊ in his bedde,°　　　　　　*lay*
Or yet for any good yeman to wedde.
　　Now sire, and eft⁊ sire, so bifel the cas,　　　*again*
That on a day this hendè Nicholas
Fil⁊ with this yongè wyf to rage⁊ and pleye,　　　*happened / sport*
Whyl that hir housbond was at Osèneye,°
As clerkès ben ful subtile⁊ and ful queynte;⁊　　*clever / inventive*
And privèly he caughte hir by the queynte,°
And seyde, 'Ywis,⁊ but if⁊ ich⁊ have my wille,　　*surely / unless / I*
170　For dernè love of thee, lemman, I spille.'°
And heeld⁊ hir hardè by the haunchè-bones,　　　*held*

---

suyte literally, suit, following; i.e. the ribbons
of her cap matched her collar
smale ypulled plucked to a narrow line
perejonette early-ripe pear, in bloom. Its fruit
was also delicate and sweet.
wether strictly, a castrated ram; here used simply
for sheep
perled . . . latoun spangled with brass. Latoun
was a base brassy metal, imitation gold; see
the General Prologue, l. 701.
Towr . . . noble The Tower of London held
the principal mint of the kingdom at the time.
The noble, also called an angel, was a gold
coin worth two-thirds of a pound.
bragot . . . meeth Bragget, honey and ale fer-

mented together; meeth is mead, also a fermented honey drink.
prymerole a primrose, a cowslip
pigges-nye pig's eye, a charming little eye; so,
a doll
lord . . . wedde The lord need not marry her,
but the yeoman would have to be honorable.
Oseneye Osney, now a suburb of Oxford, then
some distance from the city, site of Osney
abbey, for which the carpenter did work
queynte pudendum. See the Wife of Bath's Prologue, l. 338, and Fig. 39
For derne . . . spille for my hidden love of
you, darling, I'm dying

And seydė, 'Lemman, love me al at ones,⸌   *on the spot*
Or I wol dyen, also⸌ God me save!⸌   *so*
And she sprong as a colt doth in the trave,°
And with hir heed she wryėd⸌ faste awey,   *twisted*
And seyde, 'I wol nat kisse thee, by my fey,⸌   *faith*
Why, lat be,' quod she, 'lat be, Nicholas,
Or I wol crye out "Harrow"° and "allas!"
Do wey your handės for your curteisye!'
180   This Nicholas gan mercy for to crye,
And spak so faire, and profred hir so faste,°
That she hir love him grauntèd attė laste,
And swoor hir ooth, by Seint Thomas° of Kent,
That she wol been at his comandėment,
Whan that she may hir leyser° wel espye.
'Myn housbond is so ful of jalousye,
That but ye waytė⸌ wel and been privee,⸌   *watch / discreet*
I woot right wel I nam⸌ but deed,' quod she.   *am not*
'Ye mostė been ful derne, as in this cas.'
190   'Nay therof care⸌ thee noght,' quod Nicholas,
'A clerk had litherly biset his whyle,°   *worry*
But if he coude a carpenter bigyle.'
And thus they been acorded and ysworn
To wayte⸌ a tyme, as I have told biforn.
Whan Nicholas had doon thus everydeel,
And thakkėd⸌ hir aboute the lendes⸌ weel,   *patted / loins*
He kist hir swete, and taketh his sautrye,
And pleyeth faste, and maketh melodye.
Than fil⸌ it thus, that to the parish chirche,   *happened*
200   Cristės ownė werkės for to wirche,⸌   *do*
This godė wyf wente on an haliday;°
Hir forheed shoon as bright as any day,
So was it wasshen whan she leet⸌ hir werk.   *gave over*
     Now was ther of that chirche a parish clerk,
The which that was ycleped⸌ Absolon.°   *called*
Crul⸌ was his heer, and as the gold it shoon,   *curled*
And strouted as a fannė large and brode.°
Ful streight and even lay his joly shode,°
His rode⸌ was reed, his eyen greye as goos;⸌   *complexion / goose-feather*

---

sprong . . . trave shied as a colt does in the
trave—i.e. in the frame used to keep restive
horses still while being shod
'Harrow' French *haro:* a cry of distress; see
ll. 404, 717.
profred . . . faste offered himself so often
Thomas St. Thomas Becket, the premier saint
of England; see General Prologue, l. 16; and
below, l. 353.
leyser time to spare, opportunity
A clerk . . . whyle A clerk would have made
poor use of his time.
haliday holy day, saint's day or feast day

Absolon For the name and the emphasis on the
beauty of the hair, see Chaucer's *balade*, "Hide
Absolon," and, for the original Absalom, II
Samuel 14:26: " . . . he weighed the hair of
his head at two hundred shekels, after the king's
weight." Absalom is a traditional type of masculine beauty.
And strouted . . . brode and spread out wide
and broad like a winnowing fan; i.e. a flat
shovel or wide-mouthed basket for separating
grain from chaff by throwing it in the air
Ful . . . shode The beautiful parting of his
hair was very straight and exact.

210 With Powlès window corven on his shoes,°   *stockings / elegantly*
    In hoses⌐ rede he wentè fetisly.⌐
    Yclad he was ful smal° and proprèly,
    Al in a kirtel⌐ of a light wachet;°   *tunic*
    Ful faire and thikkè been the poyntès° set.
    And therupon he hadde a gay surplys°
    As whyt as is the blosme upon the rys.⌐   *bough*
    A mery child he was, so God me save,
    Wel coude he laten blood and clippe and shave,°
    And make a chartre of lond or acquitaunce.°
220 In twenty manere⌐ coude he trippe and daunce   *ways*
    After the scole of Oxenfordè tho,°
    And with his leggès casten⌐ to and fro,   *fling*
    And pleyen songès on a small rubìble;°
    Therto he song somtyme a loud quinible;°
    And as wel coude he pleye on his giterne.°
    In al the toun nas brewhous ne taverne
    That he ne visited with his solas,⌐   *gaiety*
    Ther any gaylard tappesterè° was.
    But sooth to seyn, he was somdel squaymous⌐   *squeamish*
230 Of farting, and of spechè daungerous.⌐   *disdainful*
        This Absolon, that joly⌐ was and gay,   *frisky*
    Gooth with a sencer⌐ on the haliday,   *censer*
    Sensinge the wyvès of the parish faste;
    And many a lovely look on hem he caste,
    And namely⌐ on this carpenterès wyf.   *especially*
    To loke on hir him thoughte a mery lyf,
    She was so propre and swete and likerous.°
    I dar wel seyn, if she had been a mous,
    And he a cat, he wolde hir hente⌐ anon.   *pounce on*
240   This parish clerk, this joly Absolon,
    Hath in his hertè swich a love-longinge,°
    That of no wyf ne took he noon offringe—
    For curteisye, he seyde, he woldè⌐ noon.   *wished for*
    The moone, whan it was night, ful brightè shoon,⌐ *shone*
    And Absolon his giterne hath ytake,
    For paramours,° he thoghtè for to wake.⌐   *revel*

With . . . shoos Windowed shoes were shoes with uppers cut and latticed so as to resemble windows. *Powles*, St. Paul's Cathedral in London, is Chaucer's invention in the context.
smal neatly, with close-fitting clothes
wachet a light blue, sky-color
poyntes tagged laces to fasten the tunic, hold up the hose, and otherwise perform the function of buttons
surplys overgarment, loose robe
Wel . . . shave He knew well how to let blood, cut hair and shave: i.e. he was a skillful barber-surgeon; this knowledge would be part of a learned man's equipment.
And . . . acquitaunce He was a good convey-ancer also, who could draw up a title to land or a legal release.
After . . . tho It is not clear whether Oxford then, or at any time, had a great reputation for, or special style of, dancing.
rubible a two-stringed musical instrument played with a bow; a kind of fiddle
quinible the highest pitch of the voice
giterne a kind of guitar
gaylard tappestere lively, gay barmaid. Tappestere, the ending suggests, is probably feminine here.
propre . . . likerous handsome and sweet and toothsome
love-longinge lovesickness, lover's melancholy
paramours being in love

And forth he gooth, jolif and amorous,
Til he cam to the carpenteres hous
A litel after cokkes hadde ycrowe;
250   And dressed him up by a shot windòwe°
That was upon the carpenteres wal.
He singeth in his vois gentil and smal,°
'Now, derè lady, if thy willè be,
I preyè yow that ye wol rewe⌐ on me,'   *pity*
Ful wel acordaunt to his giterninge.°
This carpenter awook, and herde him singe,
And spak unto his wyf, and seyde anon,
'What! Alison! heerestow nat Absolon
That chaunteth thus under our bourès⌐ wal?'   *bedroom*
260   And she answerde hir housbond therwithal,
'Yis, God wot, John, I here it everydel.'⌐   *all*
    This passeth forth: what wol ye bet than wel?°
Fro day to day this joly Absolon
So woweth⌐ hir, that him is wo bigon.   *woos*
He waketh⌐ al the night and al the day;   *stays awake*
He kembed⌐ hise lokkès brode,⌐ and mad him gay;   *combed / spreading*
He woweth⌐ hir by menès and brocage,°   *woos*
And swoor he woldè been hir ownè page;⌐   *servant*
He singeth, brokkinge⌐ as a nightingale;   *trilling*
270   He sente hir pimènt,° meeth, and spycèd ale,
And wafres,⌐ pyping hote out of the glede;⌐   *wafers / coals*
And for she was of towne,⌐ he profrèd mede;⌐   *townswoman / bribery*
For som folk wol ben wonnen for richesse,
And som for strokes,⌐ and som for gentillesse.   *blows*
    Somtyme, to shewe his lightnesse and maistrye,°
He pleyeth Heròdès on a scaffold hye.°
But what availleth him as in this cas?
She loveth so this hendè Nicholas,
That Absolon may blowe the bukkès horn;°
280   He ne hadde for his labour but a scorn;
And thus she maketh Absolon hir ape,°
And al his ernest turneth til a jape.⌐   *joke*
Ful sooth is this provèrbe, it is no lye,
Men seyn right thus, 'Alwey the nyè slye
Maketh the ferrè levè to be looth.'°

And . . . windòwe He placed himself by a casement. A shot-window was a window opening on hinges, like a shutter.
smal fine and delicate
Ful . . . giterninge in excellent accord with his guitar-playing
what wol . . . wel would you have things go better than well?
menes and brocage intermediaries and go-betweens
pimènt wine sweetened with honey and mixed with spices

lightnesse . . . maistrye quickness and mastery, virtuosity
pleyeth . . . hye Takes the part of Herod in a nativity play, on a high platform stage; this would imply a change of character, for Herod is usually shown as a blustering bully.
blowe . . . horn blow the buck's horn, i.e. get nowhere
she . . . ape she makes light of, makes a fool of Absolon
'Alwey . . . looth' "Always the clever man who is close at hand makes the distant, dear one unloved."

For though that Absolon be woodᐳ or wrooth,ᐳ   *mad / enraged*
Bycausė that he fer was from hir sighte,
This nyėᐳ Nicholas stood in his lighte.   *nearby*
    Now bere thee wel,° thou hendė Nicholas!
290   For Absolon may waille and singe 'Allas!'
And so bifel it on a Saterday,
This carpenter was goon tilᐳ Osėnay;   *to*
And hendė Nicholas and Alisoun
Acordėd been to this conclusioun,
That Nicholas shal shapenᐳ him a wyleᐳ   *fix up / trick*
This selyᐳ jalous housbond to bigyle;   *poor innocent*
And if so be the gamė wente aright,
She sholdė slepen in his arm al night;
For this was his desyr and hirᐳ also.   *hers*
300   And right anon, withouten wordės mo,
This Nicholas no lenger woldė tarie,
But doth ful softe unto his chambre carie
Bothe meteᐳ and drinkė for a day or tweye;   *food*
And to hir housbonde bad hir for to seye,
If that he axėdᐳ after Nicholas,   *asked*
She sholdė seye she nistėᐳ where he was: *did not know*
Of al that day she saugh him nat with yë;
She trowėdᐳ that he was in maladye,   *believed*
For, for no cry, hir maydė coude him calle;
310   He nolde answère, for nothing that mighte falle.
    This passeth forth al thilkėᐳ Saterday,   *that*
That Nicholas stille° in his chambre lay,
And eetᐳ and sleep,ᐳ or didė what him leste,ᐳ   *ate / slept / pleased*
Til Sonday, that the sonnė gooth to reste.
    This sely carpenter hath greet mervayle
Of Nicholas, or what thing mighte him ayle,
And seyde, 'I am adrad,ᐳ by Saint Thomas,   *afraid*
It stondeth nat aright with Nicholas.
God shildėᐳ that he deydėᐳ sodeynly!   *avert / is dead*
320   This world is now ful tikel,ᐳ sikerly;ᐳ   *unstable / certainly*
I saughᐳ today a corsᐳ yborn to chirche   *saw / corpse*
That now, on Monday last, I saugh him wirche.ᐳ   *at work*
    Go up,' quod he unto his knaveᐳ anoon,   *boy*
'Clepeᐳ at his dore, or knokkė with a stoon,ᐳ   *call / stone*
Loke how it is, and tel me boldėly.'
    This knavė gooth him up ful sturdily,
And at the chambre dore, whyl that he stood,
He cryde and knokkėd as that he were wood:ᐳ   *mad*
'What how! what do ye, maister Nicholay?
330   How may ye slepen al the longė day?'
    But al for noght, he herdė nat a word;

bere thee wel conduct yourself well   **stille** all the time

An hole he fond, ful lowe upon a bord,
Ther as the cat was wont in for to crepe;
And at that hole he lookèd in ful depe,
And at the laste he hadde of him a sighte.
This Nicholas sat gaping ever uprighte,
As he had kykèd° on the newè mone.°
Adown he gooth, and tolde his maister sone˃   *at once*
In what array˃ he saugh this ilkè˃ man.   *condition / same*
340   This carpenter to blessen him˃ bigan,   *cross himself*
And seyde, 'Help us, Sainte Fridèswyde!°
A man woot litel what him shal bityde.
This man is fallè, with his astromye,°
In som woodnesse˃ or in som agonye;   *insanity*
I thoghte ay wel how that it sholdè be!°
Men sholdè˃ nat knowe of Goddès privetee.˃   *must / secrets*
Ye,˃ blessèd be alwey a lewèd˃ man,   *yes / ignorant*
That noght but oonly his bilevè can!˃   *creed knows*
So ferde˃ another clerk with astromye;   *fared*
350   He walkèd in the feeldès for to prye˃   *look*
Upon the sterrès,˃ what ther sholde bifalle,   *stars*
Til he was in a marlè-pit° yfalle;
He saugh nat that. But yet, by Saint Thomas,
Me reweth sore˃ of hendè Nicholas.   *I greatly pity*
He shal be rated of ˃ his studying,   *scolded for*
If that I may, by Jesus, hevenè king!
Get me a staf, that I may underspore,°
Whyl that thou, Robin, hevest˃ up the dore.   *lift*
He shal˃ out of his studying, as I gesse.'   *must*
360   And to the chambre dore he gan him dresse.˃   *address himself*
His knavè was a strong carl˃ for the nones,°   *tough*
And by the haspe he haf˃ it up atones;˃   *heaved / at once*
Into the floor the dorè fil anon.
This Nicholas sat ay as stille as stoon,°
And ever gaped upward into the air.
This carpentèr wende˃ he were in despair,°   *thought*
And hentè˃ him by the sholdres mightily,   *seized*
And shook him harde, and crydè spitously,˃   *vehemently*

---

kyked Scots "keeked," i.e. looked, peeped. Many of Chaucer's words stay in use longer in the North of England and in Scotland than in the South.
newe mone i.e. as if he had gone mad
Frideswyde St. Frideswide, an Anglo-Saxon saint, d. 735, patron saint of the city and University of Oxford
astromye Like Nowelis for Noah's, this mispronunciation is meant to emphasize the carpenter's lack of education; see l. 349.
I thoghte . . . be I knew all along that it would be like this
marle-pit pit from which marl, a clayey soil used as a fertilizer, is dug. The story of the

astronomer Thales, to whom this accident happened, first occurs in Plato, and there are medieval versions.
underspore pry up; they are going to lift the door off its hinges
for the nones oral formula, with little meaning here
stille as stoon silent and still. "Still" keeps some of its older meaning in this proverbial comparison.
despair the condition of the sinner who falls into inactive melancholy because he believes that his sins are too great for God's mercy to forgive

'What! Nicholay! what, how! what! loke adown!
370 Awake, and thenk on Cristès passioùn;
I crouchè thee from elvès and fro wightes!'°
Therwith the night-spel seyde he anon rightes°
On fourè halvès˒ of the hous aboute,   *sides*
And on the threshfold˒ of the dore withoute: *threshold*
'Jesu Crist, and seynt Benedight,°
Blesse this hous from every wikkèd wight,
For nightès verye,° the white Pater-noster!°
Where wentèstow,˒ Seynte Petres soster?'°   *did you go*
    And attè laste this hendè Nicholas
380 Gan for to sykè˒ sore, and seyde, 'Allas!   *sigh*
Shal al the world be lost eftsonès˒ now?'   *again*
    This carpenter answerdè, 'What seystow?
What! thenk on God, as we don, men that swinke.'˒   *toil*
    This Nicholas answerdè, 'Fecche me drinke;
And after wol I speke in privetee
Of certeyn thing that toucheth me and thee;
I wol telle it non other man, certeyn.'
    This carpenter goth doun, and comth ageyn,
And broghte of mighty ale a largè quart;
390 And whan that ech of hem had dronke his part,
This Nicholas his dorè fastè shette,˒   *shut*
And doun the carpenter by him he sette.
    He seydè, 'John, myn hostè lief˒ and dere,   *beloved*
Thou shalt upon thy trouthè˒ swere me here,   *oath*
That to no wight thou shalt this conseil wreye;˒   *secret betray*
For it is Cristès conseil that I seye,
And if thou telle it man,˒ thou are forlore;˒   *anyone / lost*
For this vengaùnce thou shalt han˒ therfore,   *have*
That if thou wreyè me, thou shalt be wood!'°
400 'Nay, Crist forbede it, for His holy blood!'
Quod tho this sely man, 'I nam no labbe,
Ne, though I seye, I nam nat lief to gabbe.°
Sey what thou wolt, I shal it never telle
To child ne wyf, by Him that harwed Helle!'°

I crouche . . . wightes I cross you; i.e. defend
you (with the sign of the cross) from supernatural beings and wicked creatures of all kinds.
Elves are not necessarily small in Chaucer's
English.
Therwith . . . rightes Then he said the night-
charm at once. This was a formula to protect the
house from evil influence while the occupants
were asleep. Children's blessings, such as: "Matthew, Mark, Luke, and John / Bless the bed
that I lie on," belong to this family.
Benedight St. Benedict, founder of Western
monasticism
For . . . verye This may mean: against the
evil spirits of night. The reading, nerye for verye
can be made to give the sense: save [us] from
the [perils of the] night.

white Pater-noster the white Lord's Prayer, most
likely the prayer said against the powers of
darkness on going to bed
Seynte Petres soster uncertain significance
if . . . wood if you betray me, you will go
mad
Ne . . . gabbe I am no blabberer nor, though
I say it myself, do I like to gossip.
by . . . Helle through Christ who harrowed
Hell. The harrowing of Hell (Fig. 7), the descent of Christ to bring the just out of Limbo,
got its English name from the outcry (harrow,
see l. 178 above) of the devils as their doors
were beaten down and they were defeated. It
was an episode in several cycles of mystery
plays.

'Now John,' quod Nicholas, 'I wol nat lye;
I have yfounde in myn astrologye,
As I have lokėd in the moonė bright,°
That now, a Monday next, at quarter-night,°
Shal falle a rayn and that so wilde and wood,⟩   *fierce*
410   That half so greet was never Noës° flood.
This world,' he seyde, 'in lasse⟩ than in an hour   *less*
Shal al be dreynt,⟩ so hidous is the shour;   *drowned*
Thus shal mankyndė drenche⟩ and lese⟩ hir lyf.'   *drown / lose*
   This carpenter answerde, 'Allas, my wyf!
And shal she drenche? Allas! myn Alisoun!'
For sorwe of this he fil almòst adoun,°
And seyde, 'Is ther no remedie in this cas?'
   'Why, yis, for⟩ Gode,' quod hendė Nicholas,   *before*
'If thou wolt werken after lore and reed;°
420   Thou mayst nat werken after thyn owene heed.⟩   *head*
For thus seith Salomon, that was ful trewe,⟩   *wise*
"Werk al by conseil, and thou shalt nat rewe."°
And if thou werken wolt by good conseil,
I undertake, withouten mast and seyl,⟩   *sail*
Yet shal I saven hir and thee and me.
Hastow nat herd how savėd was Noė,
Whan that our Lord had warned him biforn
That al the world with water sholde be lorn?'⟩   *lost*
   'Yis,' quod this carpenter, 'ful yore⟩ ago.'   *long*
430   'Hastow nat herd,' quod Nicholas, 'also
The sorwe⟩ of Noė with his felawshipe,⟩   *difficulty / company*
Er that he mightė gete his wyf to shipe?'°
Him had be lever,⟩ I dar wel undertake,   *rather*
At thilkė tyme, than alle hise wetherės blake,°
That she hadde had a ship hirself allone.
And therfore, wostou⟩ what is best to done?   *do you know*
This asketh⟩ haste, and of an hastif⟩ thing   *requires / urgent*
Men may nat preche or maken tarying.
   Anon go gete us faste into this in⟩   *lodging*
440   A kneding trogh, or elles a kimelin,°
For ech of us, but loke that they be large,⟩   *broad-bottomed*
In which we mowė⟩ swimme⟩ as in a barge,   *may float*
And han therinne vitaillė suffisànt⟩   *provisions sufficient*

---

moone bright On the importance of the moon in prognostication, see Franklin's Tale, l. 421.
quarter-night If this is the end of the first quarter of the night, i.e. about 9 p.m., the time-scheme of the story would be wrong; perhaps therefore, at the beginning of the last quarter, about 3 a.m.
Noės Noah's; *Noë* is the usual Latin form.
For sorwe . . . adoun for sorrow at this he almost fell down
If . . . reed if you will act according to learning and counsel

"Werk . . . rewe" do nothing without advice; and when thou hast once done, repent not (Ecclesiasticus 32:19, then attributed to Solomon)
Er . . . shipe Noah's difficulties in getting his wife on to the Ark provided the comic relief in the mystery plays on the Flood.
wetheres blake black rams (or wethers; see above, l. 141); i.e. his most highly prized sheep
A kneding trogh . . . kimelin a dough-trough or else a brewing vat

But for a day; fy on the remenant!°
The water shal aslake˃ and goon away   *diminish*
Aboutè pryme° upon the nextè day.
But Robin may nat wite˃ of this, thy knave,   *know*
Ne eek thy maydè Gille I may nat save;
Axè nat why, for though thou askè me,
450   I wol nat tellen Goddès privetee.
Suffiseth thee, but if˃ thy wittès madde,˃   *unless / are crazy*
To han˃ as greet a grace˃ as Noë hadde.   *have / favor*
Thy wyf shal I wel saven, out of doute.
Go now thy wey, and speed thee heeraboute.
   'But whan thou hast, for hir and thee and me,
Ygeten us thise kneding-tubbès three,
Than shaltow hange hem in the roof ful hye,
That no man of our purveyaùncè° spye.
And whan thou thus hast doon as I have seyd,
460   And hast our vitaille faire in hem ylayd,
And eek an ax, to smyte the corde atwo˃   *in two*
When that the water comth, that we may go,
And broke an hole an heigh,˃ upon the gable,   *up high*
Unto the gardinward,° over the stable,
That we may frely passen forth our way
Whan that the gretè showr is goon away
Than shaltow swimme as myrie,˃ I undertake,   *carefree*
As doth the whytè doke˃ after hir drake.   *duck*
Than wol I clepe,˃ "How! Alison! how! John!   *call*
470   Be myrie, for the flood wol passe anon."˃   *soon*
And thou wolt seyn, "Hayl, maister Nicholay!
Good morwe, I se thee wel, for it is day."
And than shul we be lordès al our lyf
Of al the world, as Noë and his wyf.
   But of o thyng I warnè thee ful right,
Be wel avysèd,˃ on that ilkè night   *careful*
That we ben entred into shippès bord,
That noon of us ne spekè nat a word,
Ne clepe, ne crye, but been in his prayere;
480   For it is Goddès ownè hestè dere.˃   *commandment precious*
   Thy wyf and thou mote hangè fer atwinne,˃   *far apart*
For that bitwixè yow shal be no sinne°
No more in looking than ther shal in dede;
This ordinance is seyd, go, God thee spede!
Tomorwe at night, whan men ben alle aslepe,
Into our kneding-tubbès wol we crepe,
And sitten ther, abyding Goddès grace.

fy . . . remenant no bother about the rest
Aboutè pryme First thing in the morning; prime
was the first of the canonical divisions of the
day, 6 a.m. to 9 a.m.
purveyaùnce advance preparations

Unto the gardinward looking toward the garden
For . . . sinne at this second flood you must be
as entirely pure as Noah, without even a venial
sin on your conscience

Go now thy wey, I have no lenger space°   *time*
To make of this no lenger sermoning.
490 Men seyn thus, "Send the wyse, and sey nothing";°
Thou art so wys, it nedeth thee nat teche;
Go, save our lyf, and that I thee biseche.'
    This sely carpenter goth forth his wey.
Ful ofte he seith 'Allas' and 'Weylawey,'
And to his wyf he tolde his privetee;
And she was war,° and knew it bet° than he,   *forewarned / better*
What al this queynte cast° was for to seye. °   *subtle plan / meant*
But nathelees she ferde° as she wolde deye,   *acted*
And seyde, 'Allas! go forth thy wey anon,
500 Help us to scape,° or we ben lost echon;°   *escape / each one*
I am thy trewe verray° wedded wyf;   *faithful true*
Go, dere spouse, and help to save our lyf.'
    Lo! which a greet thyng is affeccioun!°
Men may dye of imaginacioun,
So depe° may impressioun be take.   *deeply*
This sely carpenter biginneth quake;
Him thinketh verraily° that he may see   *truly*
Noës flood come walwing° as the see   *rolling*
To drenchen° Alisoun, his hony dere.   *drown*
510 He wepeth, weyleth, maketh sory chere,
He syketh° with ful many a sory swogh.°   *sighs / groan*
He gooth and geteth him a kneding-trogh,
And after that a tubbe and a kimelin,
And prively he sente hem to his in,°   *house*
And heng° hem in the roof in privetee.   *hung*
His owne hand he made laddres three,
To climben by the ronges° and the stalkes°   *rungs / uprights*
Unto the tubbes hanginge in the balkes,°   *rafters*
And hem vitailled,° bothe trogh and tubbe,   *victualed*
520 With breed and chese, and good ale in a jubbe,°   *jug*
Suffysinge right ynogh° as for a day.   *in plenty*
But er that he had maad al this array,°   *arrangement*
He sente his knave, and eek his wenche° also,   *maidservant*
Upon his nede° to London for to go.
And on the Monday, whan it drow to° night,   *approached*
He shette° his dore withoute candel-light,   *shut*
And dressed° al thing as it sholde be.   *arranged*
And shortly, up they clomben° alle three;   *climbed*
They sitten stille wel a furlong-way.°
530 'Now, Pater-noster, clom!'° seyde Nicholay,
And 'Clom,' quod John, and 'Clom,' seyde Alisoun.

"Send . . . nothing" proverbial: a word to the wise is enough
affeccioun the faculty of the soul concerned with emotion, desire, will; here emotional excitement or disturbance

Upon his nede for something he wanted; on an errand
furlong-way a short time—the time it takes to walk a furlong (1/8 mile)
Pater . . . clom Our Father, hush!

This carpenter seyde his devocioùn,
And stille he sit,° and biddeth° his preyere,   *sits / prays*
Awaytinge on the reyn, if he it here.°   *might hear*
   The dedè sleep, for wery bisinesse,
Fil° on this carpenter right, as I gesse,   *descended*
Aboutè corfew tyme,° or litel more;
For travail° of his goost° he groneth sore,   *affliction / spirit*
And eft° he routeth,° for his heed mislay.°   *then / snores*
Doun of the laddrè stalketh° Nicholay,   *climbs stealthily*
And Alisoun, ful softe adoun she spedde;
Withouten wordès mo, they goon to bedde
Theras° the carpenter is wont to lye.   *where*
Ther was the revel and the melodye;
And thus lyth° Alison and Nicholas,   *lie*
In bisinesse of mirthe and of solas,°   *pleasure*
Til that the belle of Laudès° gan to ringe,
And frerès in the chauncel° gonnè singe.   *chancel*
   This parish clerk, this amorous Absolon,
That is for love alwey so wo bigon,
Upon the Monday was at Osèneye
With companye, him to disporte and pleye,
And axèd upon cas° a cloisterer°   *by chance*
Ful privèly after John the carpenter;
And he drough° him apart out of the chirche,   *drew*
And seyde, 'I noot,° I saugh him here nat wirche°   *don't know / work*
Sin Saterday; I trow that he be went
For timber, ther our abbot hath him sent;
For he is wont for timber for to go,
And dwellen at the grange° a day or two;
Or ellès he is at his hous, certeyn;
Wher that he be, I can nat sothly° seyn.'   *truly*
   This Absolon ful joly° was and light,°   *frisky / gay*
And thoghtè, 'Now is tymè wake° al night;   *to wake*
For sikirly I saugh him nat stiringe
Aboute his dore sin day bigan to springe.
So moot° I thryve, I shal, at cokkès crowe,°   *may*
Ful privèly knokken at his windowe
That stant° ful lowe upon his bourès° wal.   *stands / bedroom*
To Alison now wol I tellen al
My love-longing, for yet I shal nat misse
That at the lestè wey° I shal hir kisse.   *at least*

540

550

560

570

<hr>

corfew tyme about dusk, when the town gates would be shut; perhaps 8 p.m.
his heed mislay his head lay awry
Laudes lauds; the first office (church service) of the day, usually between 3 and 4 a.m., before day actually broke
cloisterer a member of a religious order living in a convent or monastery; here an Augustinian canon of Osney Abbey

grange barn or granary; but here an outlying farm belonging to the Abbey
at cokkes crowe a vague indication of time. First cockcrow was not long after midnight; second about 3 a.m., about the time of lauds. So the time scheme works—just about lauds, when Nicholas and Alison were finishing their bouts, Absolon arrives.

Som maner confort shal I have, parfay,˃   *in faith*
My mouth hath icchėd° al this longė day;
That is a signe of kissing attė leste.
Al night me mette˃ eek, I was at a feste.   *dreamed*
Therfor I wol gon slepe an houre or tweye,
And al the night than wol I wake and pleye.'
   Whan that the firstė cok hath crowe, anon
580 Up rist˃ this joly lover Absolon,   *rises*
And him arrayeth gay, at point devys.°
But first he cheweth greyn° and lycorys,
To smellen swete, er he had kembed˃ his heer.   *combed*
Under his tonge a trewe love° he beer,˃   *bore*
For therby wende he to ben gracïoùs.
He rometh˃ to the carpenterės hous,   *walks*
And stille he stant under the shot windowe;
Unto his brest it raughte,˃ it was so lowe;   *reached*
And softe he cogheth with a semisoun˃—   *low voice*
590 'What do ye, hony-comb, swete Alisoun?
My fairė brid,° my swetė cinamome,
Awaketh, lemman˃ myn, and speketh to me!   *darling*
Wel litel thenken ye upon my wo,
That for your love I swetė˃ ther˃ I go.   *sweat / wherever*
No wonder is thogh that I swelte˃ and swete;   *swelter*
I moorne˃ as doth a lamb after the tete.˃   *long / teat*
Ywis,˃ lemman, I have swich love-longinge,   *indeed*
That lyk a turtel° trewe is my moorninge;
I may nat ete na morė than a mayde.'
600 'Go fro the window, Jakkė fool,' she sayde,
'As help me God, it wol nat be "Com ba˃ me,"   *kiss*
I love another, and elles I were to blame,
Wel bet˃ than thee, by Jesu, Absolon!   *better*
Go forth thy wey, or I wol caste a ston,
And lat me slepe, a twenty devel wey!'°
   'Allas,' quod Absolon, 'and weylawey!
That trewė love was ever so yvel biset!˃   *hardly used*
Than kissė me, sin it may be no bet,
For Jesus love and for the love of me.'
610   'Wiltow˃ than go thy wey therwith?' quod she.   *will you*
'Ye, certės, lemman,' quod this Absolon.
'Thanne make thee redy,' quod she, 'I come anon.'
And unto Nicholas she seydė stille,˃   *quietly*
'Now hust,˃ and thou shalt laughen al thy fille.'   *hush*
   This Absolon doun sette him on his knees,

My . . . icched Divination from involuntary movements was widely practiced in ancient times and in the Middle Ages.
at point devys very neatly and elegantly; to perfection
greyn grain of Paris or Paradise, a seed used as spice; like licorice, a sweetener of the breath

trewe love probably a four-leafed sprig of herb-paris, with a flower or berry in the middle, and looking like a true-love knot
brid bird, most likely; or perhaps bride
turtel turtledove, proverbially true to its mate, and pining away at its absence or death
a . . . wey for twenty devils' sake

And seyde, 'I am a lord at alle degrees;°
For after this I hope ther cometh more!
Lemman, thy grace, and swetė brid,⸃ thyn ore⸃!'   *bird / favor*
   The window she undoth, and that in haste,
620 'Have do,' quod she, 'com of, and speed thee faste,
Lest that our neighėborės thee espye.'
   This Absolon gan wype his mouth ful drye;
Derk was the night as pich, or as the cole,
And at the window out she putte hir hole,
And Absolon, him fil no bet ne wers,°
But with his mouth he kiste hir naked ers⸃   *ass*
Ful savourly,⸃ er he was war of this.   *with great relish*
   Abak he sterte,⸃ and thoghte it was amis,   *jumped*
For wel he wiste a womman hath no berd;⸃   *beard*
630 He felte a thing al rough and long yherd,⸃   *haired*
And seydė, 'Fy! allas! what have I do?'
   'Teehee!' quod she, and clapte the window to;
And Absolon goth forth a sory pas.°
   'A berd, a berd!' quod hendė Nicholas,
'By Goddės corpus,⸃ this goth faire and weel!'   *body*
   This sely⸃ Absolon herde every deel,   *poor*
And on his lippe he gan for anger byte;
And to himself he seyde, 'I shal thee quyte⸃!'   *pay back*
   Who rubbeth now, who froteth⸃ now his lippes   *scrubs*
640 With dust, with sond,⸃ with straw, with clooth, with chippes,   *sand*
But Absolon, that seith ful ofte, 'Allas!
My soule bitake I unto Sathanas,
But me wer lever than al this town,' quod he,
'Of this despyt awroken for to be!°
Allas!' quod he, 'allas! I ne hadde ybleynt!'⸃   *turned away*
His hotė⸃ love was cold and al yqueynt;⸃   *hot / quenched*
For fro that tyme that he had kiste hir ers,
Of paramours he settė nat a kers,°
For he was helėd of his maladye;
650 Ful oftė paramours he gan deffye,⸃   *give up*
And weep⸃ as dooth a child that is ybete.   *wept*
A softė paas° he wente over⸃ the strete   *across*
Until⸃ a smith men clepėd Daun Gerveys,°   *to*
That in his forgė smithėd plough harneys;⸃   *equipment*
He sharpeth shaar° and culter bisily.
This Absolon knokketh al esily,⸃   *quietly*

---

at alle degrees in all ways, completely
him . . . wers it happened to him neither better nor worse: i.e. it happened just like this
sory pas at a sad pace; walking dejectedly
My soule . . . be (ll. 642–44) I would give my soul to Satan. That is, I'll be damned, if I wouldn't rather have my revenge than be the owner of this whole town.
Of . . . kers On love of women he set no

value at all; *kers* is cress, a worthless piece of vegetation.
softe paas quiet walk, quietly
Daun Gerveys Master Gervase (*Daun* is short for *dominus*, master). It is still before daybreak, but many would already be at work; and smiths were notorious early workers.
shaar plowshare, the blade that turns the turf over on its side; *culter*, coulter, the tip on the share which cuts the turf vertically

And seyde, 'Undo, Gerveys, and that anon.'
  'What, who artow?' 'It am I, Absolon.'
'What, Absolon! for Cristès swetè tree,   *cross*
660 Why rysè ye so rathe, ey, Benedicite!   *early / bless me*
What ayleth yow? som gay gerl, God it woot,
Hath broght yow thus upon the viritoot;°
By Seÿnt Note,° ye woot wel what I mene.'
  This Absolon ne roghtè nat a bene   *cared / bean*
Of al his pley, no word agayn he yaf;   *returned*
He haddè morè tow on his distàf°
Than Gerveys knew, and seydè, 'Freend so dere,
That hotè culter in the chimenee here,   *fireplace*
As lene° it me, I have therwith to done,
670 And I wol bringe it thee agayn ful sone.'
  Gerveys answerde, 'Certès, were it gold,
Or in a pokè nobles alle untold,°
Thou sholdest have, as I am trewè smith;
Ey, Cristès foo!° what wol ye do therwith?'
  'Therof,' quod Absolon, 'be as be may;
I shal wel telle it thee tomorwe day'—
And caughte the culter by the coldè stele.   *handle*
Ful softe out at the dore he gan to stele,
And wente unto the carpenterès wal.
680 He cogheth first, and knokketh therwithal
Upon the windowe, right as he dide er.   *before*
  This Alison answerde, 'Who is ther
That knokketh so? I warante° it a theef.'
  'Why, nay,' quod he, 'God woot, my swetè leef,   *dear*
I am thyn Absolon, my derèling!
Of gold,' quod he, 'I have thee broght a ring;
My moder yaf it me, so God me save,   *mother*
Ful fyn it is, and therto wel ygrave;   *engraved*
This wol I gevè thee, if thou me kisse!'   *give*
690 This Nicholas was risen for to pisse,
And thoghte he wolde amenden al the jape,   *better / jest*
He sholdè kisse his ers er that he scape.
And up the windowe didè he hastily,   *put*
And out his ers he putteth privèly
Over the buttok, to the haunchè-bon;
And therwith spak this clerk, this Absolon,
'Spek, swetè brid, I noot nat wher thou art.' *bird / don't know*
  This Nicholas anon leet flee a fart,   *let fly*
As greet as it had been a thonder-dent,   *thunder-clap*

---

viritoot meaning unknown; perhaps, on the prowl
Seynt Note Neot, a 9th-century Saxon saint
He . . . distaf proverbial phrase: he had more flax to spin into linen thread; i.e. he had plenty of other things to think of

As lene please lend
Or . . . untold or gold coins all uncounted in a bag; for *nobles*, see l. 148
Cristes foo by Christ's foe, i.e. the Devil; or short for "by Christ's foot"; cf. l. 17
warante guarantee or wager

700 That with the strook he was almost yblent;˃ *blinded*
And he was redy with his iren hoot,˃ *hot*
And Nicholas amidde˃ the ers he smoot.˃ *in the middle of / smote*
Of gooth the skin an handė-brede˃ aboute, *hand's breadth*
The hotė culter brendė so his toute,˃ *rump*
And for the smert he wendė for˃ to dye. *expected*
As he were wood,˃ for wo he gan to crye: *crazy*
'Help! water! water! help, for Goddės herte!'
This carpenter out of his slomber sterte,
And herde oon cryen 'Water' as he were wood,
710 And thoghte, 'Allas! now comth Nowelis° flood!'
He sit him up withouten wordes mo,
And with his ax he smoot the corde atwo,
And down goth al; he fond neither to selle,
Ne breed ne ale, til he cam to the celle
Upon the floor;° and ther aswowne˃ he lay. *unconscious*
Up sterte˃ hir Alison, and Nicholay, *jumped*
And cryden 'Out' and 'Harrow' in the strete.
The neighėborės, bothė smale and grete,
In ronnen,˃ for to gauren˃ on this man, *ran / gape*
720 That yet aswowne he lay, bothe pale and wan;
For with the fal he brosten˃ hadde his arm; *broken*
But stonde he moste˃ unto his owne harm. *must*
For whan he spak, he was anon bore doun˃ *overcome*
With˃ hendė Nicholas and Alisoun. *by*
They tolden every man that he was wood,
He was agast so of 'Nowelis flood'
Thurgh fantasye,˃ that of his vanitee˃ *imagination / folly*
He hadde yboght him kneding-tubbės three,
And hadde hem hangėd in the roof above;
730 And that he preyėd hem, for Goddės love,
To sitten in the roof, par companye.°
The folk gan laughen at his fantasye;
Into the roof they kyken˃ and they gape, *peer*
And turnėd al his harm unto a jape.
For what so that this carpenter answerde,
It was for noght, no man his reson˃ herde; *argument*
With othės grete he was so sworn adoun,˃ *sworn under*
That he was holden˃ wood in al the toun; *held*
For every clerk anon right˃ heeld˃ with other. *at once / sided*
740 They seyde, 'The man is wood, my leve brother'; *fuss*
And every wight gan laughen of this stryf.˃

Nowelis Noah's; like astromye, l. 343, this is a mispronunciation of the carpenter's, confusing Noah with Nowel, Christmas
he . . . floor He found no opportunity to sell bread or ale until he reached the floorboards; i.e. he went down with a great rush. "Celle" and "floor" seem to mean the same thing; or

"celle" is the floor, and "floor" the ground beneath it. Perhaps "celle" means the house's main room, above which the carpenter had been suspended.
par companye for company's sake; to keep him company

Thus swyvéd⁊ was the carpenterès wyf,   *screwed*
For al his keping⁊ and his jalousye;   *guarding*
And Absolon hath kist hir nether yë;⁊   *lower eye*
And Nicholas is scalded in the toute.
This tale is doon, and God save al the route!⁊   *company*

Here endeth the Millere his tale.

The Nun's Priest's Prologue and Tale

The Nun's Priest is one of the characters in the *Tales* of whom we know least: in the General Prologue he is one of three priests, given a bare mention after the Prioress. But only one Nun's Priest tells a tale; and our only description of him comes from the Host, who calls him brawny and a "tread-fowl" (Fig. 28).

His tale, which may have been written at any time after 1381 (there is a reference in it to the Peasants' Revolt of that year), is based on an animal fable which Chaucer probably found in one of the popular collections of stories concerning Reynard the Fox and his tricks which had begun to be built into beast epics in the twelfth century. The idea of presenting a story in which beasts act as human beings—and so giving some sort of moral lesson from a world thus turned upside down—goes back as far as Greek literature, and is associated with the name of Aesop, in the sixth century B.C. In these fables the fox is always the embodiment of deceit.

Preachers naturally found such stories useful in sermons. These would open with a text from the Bible or other sacred work, out of which flowed the *exordium*, the arresting beginning, and next the illustrative *exemplum*. Then came the application of its story (the *moralitee*) to the moral lives of the audience, and finally the *peroration*, the finale, with its exhortation to a better life. This is the classic model for an oration and the rhetorical principle on which a medieval sermon was built. The Nun's Priest's Tale is, in the mouth of its teller, such a sermon, in perfectly conventional form, with the lesson firmly stated at the end: don't trust flatterers.

The Nun's Priest's Tale is, however, far more than sermon or moral lesson: it is yet another illustration of that quality which makes Chaucer one of the greatest poets in the language: his ability to work within a convention and transform it. Here he has taken two conventions—the theory and practice of rhetoric and the beast fable—and put this superbly witty and lively comedy into the mouth of a nobody, an ordinary priest. Moreover, he seems to have intended it to follow immediately upon the tale told by a somebody: the sleek, huntsman Monk, whose pedestrian, lifeless series of "tragedies" make a dramatic contrast with the lively, witty, erudite tale of the Nun's Priest.

The Nun's Priest's Tale too is peopled with its great men—but they are barnyard animals. Chaunticleer displays vast learning on dreams—at least that is what he would wish us to think—claiming for himself, noblest of birds, the privilege of visions that, in the technical language of dream classification at the time, are truly prophetic. These are not the foolish, invalid dreams that come from physical causes such as his wife, with her lesser nature, thinks that his dream of the fox has been. They do not, he claims, result from something he has eaten or because of some excess of one or other humor (or bodily fluid): that sort of dream is for lesser mortals. But Chaunticleer is not quite on top of his subject: the joke is, in fact, that he has not perceived the true relation between what happens of necessity and what happens through free will. Someone so noble cannot quite be bound by his dream: he flies down and is lost.

The comedy of knowledge is seen also in Pertelote, but her learning though correct and full according to the medical theory of the day, is practical and down-to-earth. She is the complete feminine materialist, downright and doubly annoying to a masculine mind such as Chaunticleer's, which thinks it sees more deeply into the true nature of things.

Chaunticleer's vainglorious learning and Pertelote's sympathetic wisdom are subtly deployed to keep the story slow and even-paced in its first part; all the bustle and action are at the end. This skillful rhetorical design in Chaucer's hands contrasts with the continuous parody of rhetorical inflation that goes on throughout the poem, especially in Chaunticleer's speeches and finally in the stream of *exempla* which flows from the climactic moment of the poem. Constantly, as the poem goes on, the simplest matters are treated in a highly ornamental manner. Long illustrative stories are introduced. *Sententiae* are bandied about. Chaucer's parody of rhetoric is presented with the maximum rhetorical sophistication and force, in the first true mock-heroic masterpiece in English.

The question has often been asked whether there is not a great deal more to this story of a cock and a hen than meets the eye. The Nun's Priest's words, "Saint Paul saith that al that writen is / To oure doctrine it is ywrit, ywis," state one of the most consistently held notions about literature during the entire Middle Ages. Should we then see in the poem an indirect meaning or application other than the warning against flatterers issued by the teller of the tale? It has been read as a much more sophisticated allegory of the friars (the fox), the secular clergy, i.e. parish priests, and other ecclesiastics not bound by a rule (Chaunticleer), and the Church (the widow); or as the Christian (Chaunticleer) carried off by the Devil or seduced by the heretic (the fox), as in the *Bestiary*. The first of these readings develops from the application of methods of interpreting the Bible that were not widely used in England in Chaucer's day, and suffers from inconsistencies. The second, simpler explanation has more to recommend it—but everyone must make up his own mind about these explanations and the view of medieval literature that they imply.

Two other Reynard and Chaunticleer stories are added here. The selections from the *Bestiary* show another mode of moralizing the animal kingdom, which is a great deal more literal and crude than Chaucer's. The selection from Caxton shows how far the notion of the fox as a deceitful animal was turned to the specific purposes of satire against the clergy (Fig. 34).

The Prologue

The prologue of the Nonne Preestes Tale

'Ho!' quod the Knight, 'good sir, namore of this,
That ye han seyd is right ynough, ywis,
And mochel° more; for litel hevinesse°   *much / sadness*
Is right ynough to mochel° folk, I gesse.   *many*

I seye for me, it is a greet disese˃ — *distress*
Wheras men han ben in greet welthe and ese,˃ — *comfort*
To heren of hir sodeyn˃ fall, allas! — *sudden*
And the contrarie is joie and greet solas,˃ — *relief*
As whan a man hath been in poore estaat,°
10   And clymbeth up, and wexeth˃ fortunat, — *grows*
And ther abydeth in prosperitee,
Swich thing is gladsom, as it thinketh me,
And of swich thing were goodly for to telle.'
'Ye,' quod our hoste, 'by Seint Poulès° belle,
Ye seye right sooth; this monk, he clappeth˃ loude, — *prattles*
He spak how 'Fortune covered with a cloude'
I noot˃ never what, and als˃ of a 'Tragedie' — *know not / also*
Right now ye herde, and pardè!° no remedie
It is for to biwaillè,˃ ne compleyne — *bewail*
20   That that is doon; and als it is a peyne,
As ye han seyd,˃ to here˃ of hevinesse. — *said / hear*
Sir Monk, namore of this, so God yow blesse!
Your tale anoyeth˃ al this companye; — *displeases*
Swich talking is nat worth a boterflye;
For therin is ther no desport˃ ne game.˃ — *recreation / pleasure*
Wherfor, sir Monk, or Dan° Piers by your name,
I preye yow hertèly, telle us somwhat elles,˃ — *else*
For sikerly,˃ nere° clinking of your belles, — *certainly*
That on your brydel hange on every syde,
30   By heven˃ king, that for us allè dyde,˃ — *Heaven's / died*
I sholde er this han fallen doun for slepe,
Although the slough˃ had never been so depe; — *mire*
Than had your talè al be told in vayn.
For certeinly, as that thisè clerkès˃ seyn, — *learned men*
'Wheras˃ a man may have noon audience, — *when*
Noght helpeth it to tellen his sentence.'˃ — *matter, wisdom*
And wel I woot the substance is in me,°
If any thing shal wel reported be.
Sir, sey˃ somwhat of hunting, I yow preye.' — *say*
40   'Nay,' quod this monk, 'I have no lust˃ to pleye;˃ — *pleasure / jest*
Now let another telle, as I have told.'
Than spak our host, with rudè speche and bold,
And seyde unto the Nonnès Preest anon,˃ — *at once*
'Com neer,˃ thou preest, com hider,˃ thou Sir John,° — *closer / hither*
Tel us swich thing as may our hertès glade,˃ — *gladden*
Be blythè, though thou ryde upon a jade.˃ — *wretched horse*

---

estaat state, status. The image does not necessarily involve Fortune's wheel (see below and
Fig. 41) but may do so.
Seint Poules St. Paul's Cathedral, the chief
church of London
parde i.e. *par dieu*, by God
Dan Dan = *dominus*, master; a title of respect,
especially for a religious and/or learned man
nere were it not for
wel . . . me i.e. and I know very well I have
the capacity to understand; or: I know very well
I understand the meat of the matter
Sir John the regular nickname for a priest

What though thyn hors be bothė foule˃ and lene,˃   *dirty / lean*
If he wol serve thee, rekkė˃ nat a bene;˃   *care / bean*
Look that thyn herte be mery evermo.'
50 'Yis, sir,' quod he, 'yis, host, so mote I go,
But˃ I be mery, ywis,˃ I wol be blamed.'   *unless / indeed*
And right anon his tale he hath attamed,˃   *broached*
And thus he seyde unto us everichon,
This swetė preest, this goodly man, Sir John.

      Explicit°

[handwritten: Parody of rhetoric + flattery turning a man's head. moral tale. Animals are people]

The Tale

   Here biginneth the Nonne Preestes Tale of the Cok
   and Hen, Chauntėcleer and Pertėlote.

A povre˃ widwe, somdel stape˃ in age,   *poor / advanced*
Was whylom˃ dwelling in a narwe˃ cotage,   *formerly / little*
Bisyde a grovė, stonding in a dale.˃   *valley*
This widwė, of which I telle yow my tale,
Sin thilkė˃ day that she was last a wyf,   *since the same*
60 In paciėnce laddė˃ a ful simple lyf,   *led*
For litel was hir catel° and hir rente;˃   *income*
By housbondrye,˃ of such as God hir sente,   *economy*
She fond° hirself, and eek˃ hir doghtren˃ two.   *also / daughters*
Three largė sowės hadde she, and namo,˃   *no more*
Three kyn,˃ and eek a sheep that hightė˃ Malle.   *cows / was called*
Ful sooty was hir bour, and eek hir halle,°
In which she eet˃ ful many a sclendre˃ meel.   *ate / frugal*
Of poynaunt sauce hir neded never a deel.°
No deyntee morsel passėd thurgh hir throte;
70 Hir dyete was accordant˃ to hir cote.˃   *according / cottage*
Repleccioùn˃ ne made hir never syk;˃   *over-eating / sick*
Attempree˃ dyete was al hir phisyk,˃   *temperate / medicine*
And exercyse, and hertės suffisaunce.˃   *heart's contentment*
The goutė lette˃ hir nothing for to daunce,   *hindered*
Napoplexye shentė˃ nat hir heed;   *injured*
No wyn˃ ne drank she, neither whyt ne reed;   *wine*
Hir bord˃ was servėd most with whyt and blak,   *table*
Milk and brown breed,˃ in which she fond no lak,˃   *bread / defect*

Explicit Literally, it is finished.
catel chattels, property
fond found, provided for: see Miller's Tale, l.
112
bour . . . halle The widow's house probably
had only one room serving as living room and
bedroom for the widow, her daughters, and
assorted livestock. Chaucer describes the little

cottage in terms of a grand house, in which the
hall was the large room where household and
guests assembled for food and entertainment;
the bower, originally the private apartments,
by Chaucer's time was a usual term for bedroom.
Of poynaunt . . . deel she did not need even
a touch of piquant sauce to provoke an appetite

Seynd° bacoun, and somtyme an ey⁀ or tweye,	*egg*
80 For she was, as it were, a maner deye.°	
A yerd⁀ she hadde, enclosèd al aboute	*yard*
With stikkès, and a dryè dich⁀ withoute,	*ditch*
In which she hadde a cok,⁀ hight⁀ Chauntècleer,°	*rooster / called*
In al the land, of crowing, nas⁀ his peer.⁀	*was not / equal*
His vois was merier⁀ than the mery orgon⁀	*gayer / organ*
On messè-dayes⁀ that in the chirchè gon;°	*mass-days*
Wel sikerer⁀ was his crowing in his logge,⁀	*surer / lodge*
Than is a clokke, or an abbèy orlogge.°	
By nature knew he ech ascencioùn	
90 Of equinoxial° in thilkè toun;	
For whan degrees fiftenè were ascended,	
Thanne crew he, that it mightè nat ben amended.⁀	*bettered*
His comb was redder than the fyn coral,	
And batailed,⁀ as it were a castel wal.	*battlemented*
His bile⁀ was blak, and as the jeet⁀ it shoon;	*bill / jet*
Lyk asur° were his leggès, and his toon;⁀	*toes*
His naylès⁀ whytter than the lilie flour,	*claws*
And lyk the burnèd⁀ gold was his coloùr.	*burnished*
This gentil⁀ cok hadde in his governaùnce	*noble*
100 Sevene hennès, for to doon al his plesaùnce,⁀	*pleasure*
Whiche were his sustres⁀ and his paramoùrs,	*sisters*
And wonder lyk⁀ to him, as of coloùrs.	*amazingly like*
Of whiche the faireste hewèd⁀ on hir throte⁀	*colored / throat*
Was cleped⁀ faire damoyselè° Pertèlote.	*called*
Curteis° she was, discreet, and debonaire,	
And compaignable, and bar⁀ hirself so faire,	*bore*
Sin thilkè day that she was seven night old,	
That trewèly⁀ she hath the herte in hold⁀	*firmly / keeping*
Of Chauntècleer, loken⁀ in every lith;⁀	*locked / limb*
110 He loved hir so, that wel was him therwith.°	
But such a joye was it to here⁀ hem singe,	*hear*
Whan that the brightè sonnè gan to springe,⁀	*rise*
In swete accord, 'My lief is faren in londe.'°	
For thilkè tyme, as I have understonde,⁀	*heard*
Bestès and briddès⁀ coudè speke and singe.	*birds*
And so befel,⁀ that in a dawèninge,⁀	*it happened / dawn*

Seynd singed, i.e. broiled; or perhaps fat, as in French *saindoux*, lard
maner deye a kind of dairywoman
Chauntecleer the usual name for the cock in the Reynard story, from his clear singing voice
gon The verb is plural, because "orgon" was frequently plural, on the analogy of Latin *organa*, literally a set of pipes.
orlogge the great public clock, often giving astronomical information as well as time
equinoxial The equinoxial circle or celestial equator, thought to make a complete rotation round the earth every natural (24-hour) day, at

the rate of 15° per hour. So Chaunticleer crowed every hour, on the hour.
asur lapis lazuli; bright blue
damoysele Literally, young (unmarried) woman, especially of good family. The word signals Chaucer's description of the hen-heroine, called Pinte in other Reynard stories, in terms of the lady in a poem of courtly love.
Curteis full of courtly qualities, refined in manners
wel . . . therwith all was well with him for it; he was perfectly happy
'My . . . londe' My dear one has gone away; a popular song of the time. See below, p. 417.

As Chauntėcleer among his wyvės alle
Sat on his perchė, that was in the halle,
And next him sat this fairė Pertėlote,
120 This Chauntėcleer gan gronen> in his throte,
As man that in his dreem is drecchėd> sore.
And whan that Pertėlote thus herde him rore,>
She was agast,> and seyde, 'O hertė dere,
What eyleth> yow, to grone in this manere?
Ye been a verray> sleper, fy for shame!'
And he answerde and seydė thus, 'Madame,
I pray yow, that ye take it nat agrief:°
By God, me mette> I was in swich meschief>
Right now, that yet myn herte is sore afright.>
130 Now God,' quod he, 'my swevene recche aright,°
And keep my body out of foul prisoun!
Me mette,> how that I romėd> up and down
Withinne our yerde, wheras> I sawe a beste,
Was lyk an hound, and wolde han maad areste
Upon my body, and wolde han had me deed.°
His colour was bitwixe yellow and reed;
And tippėd was his tail, and bothe his eres,>
With blak, unlyk the remnant> of his heres;>
His snowtė smal,> with glowinge eyen tweye.>
140 Yet of his look for fere almost I deye;>
This causėd me my groning, doutėles.'
    'Avoy!'> quod she, 'fy on yow, hertėles!>
Allas!' quod she, 'for, by that God above,
Now han ye lost myn herte and al my love;
I can nat love a coward, by my faith.
For certės,> what so any womman seith,
We alle desyren, if it mightė be,
To han housbondės° hardy,> wyse, and free,>
And secree,> and no nigard, ne no fool,
150 Ne him that is agast> of every tool,>
Ne noon avauntour,° by that God above!
How dorste> ye seyn> for shame unto your love,
That any thing mightė make yow aferd?>
Have ye no mannės herte, and han a berd?>
Allas! and conne> ye been agast of swevenis?>
Nothing, God wot, but vanitee,> in sweven is.
Swevenes° engendren> of repleccioùns,>

(did) groan
afflicted
roar
afraid
ails
fine

I dreamed / trouble
frightened

dreamed / walked
where

ears
rest / hairs
narrow / two
die

fie / coward

indeed

brave / generous
discreet
afraid / weapon

dare / say
afraid
beard
can / dreams
emptiness
grow / over-eating

take . . . agrief don't take my groaning amiss
my . . . aright interpret my dream well, i.e.
make it be a dream that presages good fortune
wolde . . . deed (ll. 134–35) wanted (i.e.
tried) to make seizure of my body and kill me.
There is a tinge of legal process about "areste."
housbondes Pertelote describes the sort of husband she approves of in terms of the male
ideal of courtly love.

avauntour either a boaster in general, or merely
one who boasts of success in love, a crime against
the code
Swevenes Learned argument now ensues about
the nature, cause, and meaning of Chaunticleer's
dream. Pertelote, down-to-earth, wise in practical things, attributes it to indigestion or to a
possibly consequent overplus of one of the
humors: Chaunticleer has been on the wrong

And ofte of fume,° and of complecciouns,°
Whan humours been to habundant° in a wight.
¹⁶⁰ Certes this dreem, which ye han met tonight,˃   *dreamed last night*
Cometh of the grete superfluitee
Of youre rede colera,° pardee,
Which causeth folk to dreden in here dremes
Of arwes,˃ and of fyr with rede lemes,˃   *arrows / flames*
Of grete bestes, that they wol hem byte,
Of contek,˃ and of whelpes grete and lyte;°   *strife*
Right as the humour of malencolye°
Causeth ful many a man, in sleep, to crye,
For fere of blake beres,˃ or boles˃ blake,   *bears / bulls*
¹⁷⁰ Or elles, blake develes wole hem take.
Of othere humours coude I telle also,
That warken many a man in sleep ful wo;
But I wol passe as lightly˃ as I can.   *rapidly*
    Lo Catoun,° which that was so wys a man,
Seyde he nat thus, ne do no fors° of dremes?
Now, sire,' quod she, 'whan we flee˃ fro the bemes,˃   *fly / rafters*
For Goddes love, as tak som laxatyf;
Up˃ peril of my soule, and of my lyf,   *upon*
I counseille yow the beste, I wol nat lye,
¹⁸⁰ That bothe of colere and of malencolye
Ye purge yow; and for˃ ye shul nat tarie,   *so that*
Though in this toun is noon apothecarie,
I shal myself to herbes techen˃ yow,   *direct*
That shul ben for your hele,˃ and for your prow;˃   *health / advantage*
And in our yerd tho˃ herbes shal I finde,   *these*
The whiche han of hir propretee, by kinde,˃   *nature*
To purgen yow binethe, and eek above.°
Forget not this, for Goddes owene love!

---

diet. He needs only digestives followed by laxatives. There is danger, but to health only, not to life, and not from some exterior disaster. The dream is a natural dream, rising from his bodily state, not a dream sent from above, or below, to prophesy or deceive; not even a dream rising from a disturbance of the mind or emotions. "Peck it up, there's nothing wrong with you," the verse runs rapidly on. Pertelote's rhetoric is plain and to the point: she is for experience, not authority.

fume exhalation: either the vapor rising to the mind from the decoction or digestion of food and drink in the stomach, hastening the process begun by fermentation in wine or beer; or stomach gas, indigestion; or the vapor rising from one of the four humors, not counteracted by its opposite humors and so disturbing the psychosomatic balance

complecciouns i.e. the individual combinations of bodily fluids or humors (General Prologue, l. 423), of which behavior, temperament, and outward appearance were both the signs and the result

habundant a learned spelling; it was wrongly thought that the word abundant was connected with Latin *habere*, to have

superfluitee . . . colera An excess of the humor of red choler, bile (hot and dry) mixed with blood (hot and moist). Medieval medical authorities such as Arnold of Villanova (13th century) agree with Pertelote's categories of things appearing in the dreams of men so afflicted (see the Wife of Bath's Prologue, l. 587). Choler was the humor of anger, hence the dreams of strife and aggression.

whelpes . . . lyte dogs, big and little

malencolye melancholy, black bile, thought to be secreted in the liver, causing a man to dream fearfully of black, sad, and menacing things

Catoun Dionysius Cato; cf. the Miller's Tale, l. 119

ne . . . fors Attach no importance, take no notice. "Cato's" advice is a Stoic philosopher's. Pertelote quotes only this single elementary authority by name.

To purgen . . . above purging both downward (laxative, aperient) and upward (emetic or snuff-like) to bring your humors into balance; or merely, to clear your stomach and your head

Ye been ful colerik of compleccioùn.
190   Warė' the sonne in his ascencioùn
Ne fynde yow nat repleet' of humours hote;°
And if it do, I dar wel leye' a grote,°
That ye shul have a fevere terciane,°
Or an agù,' that may be youre bane.'
A day or two ye shul have digestyves °
Of wormės, er ye take your laxatyves,°
Of lauriol, centaure, and fumétere,
Or ellės of ellebor, that groweth there,
Of catapuce, or of gaytrės beryis,
200   Of erbe yvė, growing in our yerd, ther mery is;°
Pekke hem up right as they growe, and ete hem in.
Be mery, housbond, for your fader kin!'
Dredeth no dreem; I can say yow namore.'
    'Madame,' quod he, 'graunt mercy' of your lore.'
But nathėlees, as touching daun Catoun,°
That hath of wisdom such a greet renoun,
Though that he bad no dremės for to drede,
By God, men may in oldė bokės rede
Of many a man, more of auctoritee
210   Than ever Catoun was, so mote I thee,'
That al the rèvers seyn of his sentence,'
And han wel founden by experience,
That dremės ben significacioùns,
As wel of joye as tribulacioùns
That folk enduren in this lyf present.
Ther nedeth make of this noon argument;
The verray' prevė' sheweth it in dede.
    Oon of the gretteste auctour° that men rede
Seith thus, that whylom' two felawės wente
220   On pilgrimage, in a ful good entente;
And happėd so, thay come into a toun,
Wheras ther was swich congregacioun
Of peple, and eek so streit of herbergage,°
That they ne founde as muche as o cotage,

beware lest
over-full
wager

ague / death

father's lineage

thank you / teaching

thrive
opinion

actual / experience

formerly

humours hote Hot humors (choler and blood) would be super-heated by the sun, especially when it was high in the heavens, so that further imbalance would be caused in a man in whom they were already in dangerous disproportion.
grote an English silver coin, worth only a small sum
terciane a tertian ague or fever, in which the paroxysm recurred on alternate days. Pertelote's diagnosis is medically impeccable.
digestyves Gentler in action than harsh laxatives, they absorb or dissipate bile, whether red or black. In the Middle Ages worms were used in human medicine.
laxatyves Pertelote offers a depth-charge rather than a purge, acting both upward and downward. Laureole causes vomiting, centaury purges the

bowels, fumitory the urine; hellebore purges choler downward, catapuce is a general cathartic, and so are gaiter-berries and bitter herb-ivy.
ther mery is where it is agreeable, pleasant
Catoun Chaunticleer despises Pertelote and Master Cato, her one elementary authority, and his rhetoric is grave and stately.
Oon . . . auctour Either the greatest author, or one of the greatest; probably Cicero, one of the great ancient authorities on such matters, who tells the story which follows in his *Of Divination*. Valerius Maximus (see the Wife of Bath's Prologue, l. 648) also has it; Chaucer may have got it from another medieval source.
So . . . herbergage such a shortage of lodgings

In which they bothe mighte ylogged> be.   *lodged*
Wherfor thay mosten,> of necessitee,   *must*
As for that night, departen> compaignye;   *part*
And ech of hem goth to his hostelrye,
And took his logging as it wolde falle.>   *happen*
230   That oon of hem was logged in a stalle,
Fer> in a yerd, with oxen of the plough;   *isolated*
That other man was logged wel ynough,
As was his aventure,> or his fortune,   *luck*
That us governeth alle as in commune.°

And so bifel, that, longe er it were day,
This man mette> in his bed, theras he lay,   *dreamed*
How that his felawe gan upon him calle,
And seyde, "Allas! for in an oxes stalle
This night I shal be mordred> ther I lye.   *murdered*
240   Now help me, dere brother, er I dye;
In alle haste com to me," he sayde.
This man out of his sleep for fere abrayde;>   *leapt*
But whan that he was wakned of his sleep,
He turned him, and took of this no keep;>   *notice*
Him thoughte his dreem nas but a vanitee.
Thus twyes in his sleping dremed he.
And atte thridde tyme yet his felawe
Cam, as him thoughte, and seide, "I am now slawe;>   *slain*
Bihold my blody woundes, depe and wyde!
250   Arys> up erly in the morwe tyde,>   *rise / morning*
And at the west gate of the toun," quod he,
"A carte ful of donge> ther shaltow see,   *dung*
In which my body is hid ful prively;
Do> thilke carte aresten> boldely.   *have / stopped*
My gold caused my mordre, sooth to sayn";
And tolde him every poynt how he was slayn,
With a ful pitous> face, pale of hewe.   *pitiful*
And truste wel, his dreem he fond> ful trewe;   *found*
For on the morwe,> as sone as it was day,   *morning*
260   To his felawes in> he took the way;   *lodging*
And whan that he cam to this oxes stalle,
After his felawe he bigan to calle.
The hostiler> answered him anon,   *innkeeper*
And seyde, "Sire, your felawe is agon,>   *gone*
As sone as day he wente out of the toun."
This man gan fallen in suspecioun,
Remembring on his dremes that he mette,>   *dreamed*
And forth he goth, no lenger wolde he lette,>   *stay*
Unto the west gate of the toun, and fond
270   A dong carte, as it were to donge> lond,   *manure*

That . . . commune that has power over each
and every one of us

That was arrayèd° in the samè wyse   *ordered*
As he han herd the dedè° man devyse;°   *dead / describe*
And with an hardy herte he gan to crye
Vengeaunce and justice of this felonye:—
"My felawe mordrèd is this same night,
And in this carte he lyth° gapinge upright.°   *lies / on his back*
I crye out on the ministres,°" quod he,   *governors*
"That sholden kepe and reulen this citee;
Harrow!° allas! her lyth° my felawe slayn!"   *help / lies*
280 What sholde I more unto this talè sayn?
The peple out sterte,° and caste the cart to grounde,   *rushed out*
And in the middel of the dong they founde
The dedè man, that mordred was al newe.°   *recently*
    O blisful° God, that art so just and trewe!   *blessed*
Lo, how that thou biwreyest° mordre alway!   *uncover*
Mordre wol out, that see we day by day.
Mordre is so wlatsom° and abhominable°   *loathsome*
To God, that is so just and resonable,
That he ne wol nat suffre it helèd° be;   *hidden*
290 Though it abyde a yeer, or two, or three,
Mordre wol out, this my conclusioun.
And right anoon, ministrès of that toun
Han hent° the carter, and so sore him pyned,°   *taken / tortured*
And eek the hostiler so sore engyned,°   *racked*
That thay biknewe° hir wikkednesse anoon,   *confessed*
And were anhangèd° by the nekkè-boon.   *hanged*
    Here may men seen that dremès been to drede.°   *be feared*
And certès, in the samè book° I rede,°   *read*
Right in the nexte chapìtre after this,
300 (I gabbè° nat, so have I joye or blis,)   *babble*
Two men that wolde han passèd over see,
For certeyn cause, into a fer° contree,   *far*
If that the wind ne hadde been contrarie,
That made hem in a citee for to tarie,
That stood ful mery° upon an haven° syde.   *pleasant / harbor*
But on a day, agayn° the eventyde,   *toward*
The wind gan chaunge, and blew right as hem leste.°   *in good spirits*
Jolif° and glad they wente unto hir reste,   *intended*
And casten° hem ful erly for to saille;   *one / happened*
310 But to that oo° man fil° a greet mervaille.
That oon of hem, in sleping as he lay,
Him mette a wonder dreem, agayn the day;°
Him thoughte a man stood by his beddès syde,

---

abhominable The spelling is due to the belief
that the word meant inhuman (Latin *ab:* non +
homo: a man).
same book See l. 218: Cicero, and the other
authorities; all have this story, but not in the
next chapter.

The . . . leste the wind did change and blew
just as they wanted
Him . . . day he dreamed a very strange
dream, just before day. Such waking dreams
were often thought of as having special importance as prophecies.

And him comaunded, that he sholde abyde,° — *stay*
And seyde him thus, "If thou to-morwe wende,° — *go*
Thou shalt be dreynt;° my tale is at an ende." — *drowned*
He wook, and tolde his felawe what he mette,° — *dreamed*
And preydė him his viage° for to lette;° — *voyage / stop*
As for that day, he preydė him to abyde.
His felawė, that lay by his beddės syde,
Gan for to laughe, and scornėd him ful faste.
"No dreem," quod he, "may so myn herte agaste,° — *frighten*
That I wol lettė° for to do my thinges.° — *delay / business*
I settė not a straw by thy dreminges,
For swevenes been but vanitees and japes.
Men dreme alday° of owlės or of apes,° — *constantly*
And eke of many a masė° therwithal; — *bewilderment*
Men dreme of thing that nevere was ne shal.° — *shall be*
But sith I see that thou wolt heer abyde,
And thus forsleuthen wilfully thy tyde,° — *makes me sorry*
God wot it reweth me;° and have good day."
And thus he took his leve, and wente his way.
But er that he hadde halfe his cours ysayled,
Noot I nat why, ne what mischaunce it ayled,
But casuelly the shippės botmė rente,°
And ship and man under the water wente
In sighte of otherė shippės it byside,
That with hem saylėd at the samė tyde.
And therfor, fairė Pertėlote so dere,
By swiche ensamples° oldė maistow° lere,° — *may you / learn*
That no man sholdė been to recchėlees° — *regardless*
Of dremės, for I sey thee, doutėless,
That many a dreem ful sore is for to drede.
    Lo, in the lyf of Saint Kenelm,° I rede,
That was Kenulphus sone, the noble king
Of Mercenrike,° how Kenelm mette a thing; — *Mercia*
A lyte° er he was mordrėd, on a day, — *little*
His mordrė in his avisioùn° he say.° — *dream / saw*
His norice° him expounėd every del° — *nurse / part*
His sweven, and bad him for to kepe him° wel — *himself*
For° traisoun; but he nas but seven yeer old, — *for fear of*
And therfore litel talė hath he told°

320 (marginal line number)
330 (marginal line number)
340 (marginal line number)
350 (marginal line number)

---

owles . . . apes foolish, absurd things
And thus . . . tyde either: And thus you deliberately miss your chance (or: the tide) for pure idleness; or: And thus you deliberately and idly waste your time
Noot I . . . rente I do not know why, nor what misfortune befell it, but by some accident the ship's bottom split
ensamples *exempla*, examples; the more ancient, the more effective as illustrations
Kenelm The last two dreams that Chaunticleer has told from Cicero are not fully prophetic,

nor of the best and most trustworthy sort. He therefore gives examples of true visions, experienced by men who are more his equals. St. Kenelm became king of Mercia at the age of 7, in 821. His high-born innocence was allowed a dream of himself sitting high in a splendid tree, which one of his best friends cut down, whereupon his soul flew to heaven in the form of a bird. This was a true prophecy of his murder on the orders of his aunt.
litel . . . told he took little account

Of any dreem, so holy was his herte.
By God, I haddė lever than my sherte
That ye had rad his legende, as have I.°
Dame Pertėlote, I sey yow trewėly,
Macrobeus, that writ the *Avisioùn*°
In Affrike of the worthy Cipioùn,
Affermeth⸍ dremes, and seïth that they been   *confirms*
360   Warning of thingės that men after seen.
And forthermore, I pray yow loketh wel
In the Olde Testament, of Danièl,°
If he held⸍ dremės any vanitee.   *considered*
Reed eek of Joseph,° and ther shul ye see
Wher⸍ dremės ben somtyme⸍ (I sey nat alle)   *whether / sometimes*
Warning of thingės that shul after falle.
Loke of Egipt the king, daun⸍ Pharäo,°   *Lord*
His bakere and his botėler⸍ also,   *butler*
Wher they ne feltė noon effect in dremes.
370   Whoso wol seken actes of sondry remes,⸍   *realms*
May rede of dremės many a wonder thing.
Lo Cresus,° which that was of Lydė king,
Mette he nat that he sat upon a tree,
Which signified he sholde anhangėd⸍ be?   *hanged*
Lo heer Andromacha,° Ectorės wyf,
That day that Ector sholdė lese⸍ his lyf,   *lose*
She dremėd on the samė night biforn,
How that the lyf of Ector sholde be lorn,⸍   *lost*
If thilkė day he wente into bataille;
380   She warnėd him, but it mighte nat availle;
He wentė for to fightė nathelees,

I . . . have I I had rather than my shirt; i.e.
I'd give my shirt if you had read his life
(legend: a saint's life), as I have
Avisioun The *Somnium Scipionis*, the *Dream
of Scipio*, or *Avisioun* of *Cipioun* forms part
of Cicero's *On the State* (*De Republica*), which
was unknown to the Middle Ages. What they
had was the long commentary on the *Dream*
(*avisioun* or *visio* was the technical term for a
true, prophetic vision experienced by a notable
historical person), by Macrobius, written about
400, which was the source of much of the information available to the Middle Ages on the
nature of dreams. The story is told of how
Scipio Africanus Minor, in Africa, was taken,
in his dream, by his grandfather Scipio, the
conqueror of Hannibal, up to heaven through
the spheres of the universe, and shown a vision
of his future as final conqueror of Carthage,
as well as how insignificant is worldly glory
when compared with strictly virtuous conduct,
mortal with immortal. (Cf. the *envoi* to Chaucer's *Troilus and Criseyde*, below.) Macrobius
discusses the nature of dreams and, at greater
length, the nature of virtue: medieval science
and literature used the discussion of dreams a
great deal; medieval moral theology used the
discussion of the virtues at least as much.

Daniel The Bible, more authoritative still, is
now added to the authority of the classics,
with a general reference to the prophetic visions described in Daniel 5 ff.
Joseph Genesis 37:5ff.: Joseph's dream of his
brothers' sheaves bowing down to him, signifying his future exaltation
Pharäo Genesis 40–41: Joseph's exposition of
the dreams of Pharaoh's imprisoned butler and
baker, signifying that the first would be restored to favor and the second executed; and
of Pharaoh's dream of the seven fat and the
seven lean cows, signifying years of plenty and
of famine in Egypt.
Cresus Croesus, king of Lydia. Chaucer's version differs from others current: he refers to
it more than once.
Andromacha Andromache, Hector's wife; her
dream is not in Homer or any ancient "authority" for the Trojan War: it occurs in Dares
Phrygian, a late Latin author whom the Middle Ages believed to be more reliable than
Homer in Trojan matters and on whom the medieval Troy romances which Chaucer knew are
partly based. Andromache's dream also occurs
in these romances.

But he was slayn anoon˃ of Achilles.   *at once*
But thilkė tale is al too long to telle,
And eek it is ny day, I may nat dwelle.
Shortly I seye, as for conclusioùn,
That I shal han of this avisioùn°
Adversitee; and I seye forthermore,
That I ne telle of laxatyves no store,°
For they ben venimous,˃ I woot it wel;   *poisonous*
390 I hem defye, I love hem never a del.˃   *bit*
  Now let us speke of mirthe, and stinte˃ al this;   *cease*
Madàmė Pertèlote, so have I blis,°
Of o thing God hath sent me largė grace;
For whan I see the beautee of your face,
Ye ben so scarlet reed˃ about your yën,˃   *red / eyes*
It maketh al my dredė for to dyen;˃   *die (down)*
For, also siker as In principio,
Mulier est hominis confusio;°
Madàme, the sentence˃ of this Latin is—   *meaning*
400 Womman is mannės joye and al his blis.
For wan I fele anight your softė syde,
Albeit that I may nat on you ryde,
For that our perche is maad so narwe, alas!
I am so ful of joye and of solas˃   *delight*
That I defye bothė sweven and dreem.'°
And with that word he fley˃ down fro the beem,   *flew*
For it was day, and eek his hennės alle;
And with a 'Chuk' he gan hem for to calle,
For he had foundė a corn, lay˃ in the yerd.   *that lay*
410 Royal he was, he was namore aferd;˃   *afraid*
He fetherėd Pertèlote twenty tyme,
And trad as oftė, er that it was pryme.°
He loketh as it were a grim leoùn;
And on his toos he rometh up and doun,
Him deynėd˃ not to sette his foot to grounde.   *he deigned*
He chukketh, whan he hath a corn yfounde,
And to him rennen˃ thanne his wyvės alle.   *run*
Thus royal, as a prince is in his halle,
Leve I this Chauntėcleer in his pastùre;
420 And after wol I tell his adventùre.
  Whan that the month in which the world bigan,

Shortly . . . avisioun Chaunticleer insists again that his was a truly prophetic dream: Briefly I say, in conclusion, that I shall have ill-fortune from this divinely-inspired vision.
ne . . . store I set no store whatever by laxatives. The several negatives intensify.
so . . . blis as I hope to go to heaven
For also . . . confusio For, as sure as "In the beginning," woman is the ruination of man. *In principio*, the first words of St. John's Gospel,

were thought to possess a special truth. See General Prologue, l. 256.
sweven and dreem A distinction between true visions and mere insignificant dreams may be intended, but Chaucer's usage is not consistent or definite enough to be sure.
He fethered . . . pryme He embraced Pertelote twenty times and screwed her as often, before prime. Prime is the time—see the Miller's Tale, l. 446 above—between 6 a.m. and 9 a.m.

That highté March, whan God first makéd man,°
Was complet, and ypassed were also,
Sin March bigan, thritty dayes and two,°
Bifel that Chauntécleer, in al his pryde,
His seven wyvés walking by his syde,
Caste up his eyen to the brighté sonne,
That in the signe of Taurus hadde yronne
Twenty degrees and oon, and somwhat more;
430 And knew by kynde,ᐳ and by noon other lore,   *nature*
That it was pryme, and crew with blisful stevene.ᐳ   *voice*
'The sonne,' he sayde 'is clomben ᐳ up on hevene   *has climbed*
Fourty degrees and oon, and more, ywis.ᐳ   *indeed*
Madamé Pertélote, my worldés blis,
Herkneth thise blisful briddésᐳ how they singe,   *birds*
And see the fresshé flourés how they springe;
Ful is myn herte of revel and solas.'
But sodeinly him fil ᐳ a sorweful cas;ᐳ   *befell / chance*
For ever the latter ende of joye is wo.
440 God woot that worldly joye is sone ago;
And if a rethor° coudé faire endyte,ᐳ   *write*
He in a cronique saufly ᐳ mighte it wryte,   *chronicle safely*
As for a sovereyn notabilitee.°
Now every wys man, lat him herkne me;
This storie is alsoᐳ trewe, I undertake,   *as*
As is the book of Launcelot de Lake,°
That wommen holde in ful gret reverence.
Now wol I torne agayn to my sentence.ᐳ   *purport*

A col-fox,° ful of sly iniquitee,
450 That in the grove hadde wonédᐳ yerés three,   *lived*
By heigh imaginacioùn forncast,°
The samé night thurghout the heggés brastᐳ   *hedges burst*
Into the yerd, ther Chauntécleer the faire
Was wont, and eek his wyvés, to repaire;
And in a bed of wortésᐳ stille he lay,   *vegetables*

---

whan . . . man The common opinion was that
the Creation took place at the spring equinox.
thritty . . . two This may be elaborate rhetorical parody. It is not certain whether we
are intended to read April 3 or May 3. May 3
would be appropriate, since it is an unlucky
"Egyptian" day (two or three days each month
were marked as "evil" or "Egyptian" because
of God's plagues on Egypt)—see the Franklin's Tale, l. 198. Chaucer also uses this day in
his Knight's Tale, and in Troilus and Criseyde.
On that day the sun would have passed through
about 20° of Taurus, the Bull, the second zodiacal sign. It would be 40° high in the sky, from
the horizon, at about 9 a.m.
rethor Rhetorician, i.e. polished writer; Chaucer
(or the Nun's Priest) is making a tacit and insincere apology for lack of polish in writing;
reinforcing, perhaps, the effect of the elaborate
dating and timing just past.

sovereyn notabilitee something worthy of the
most careful note—an important *sententia*
Launcelot de Lake The false lover of Queen
Guinevere in the popular Arthurian romances
(Dante put him into *Inferno*). The Nun's Priest
is bringing home his little lesson to the ladies,
for whose reading the stories of Lancelot were
intended; to them these romances seemed true
as well as beautiful. The Priest is also having a
little private joke at the ladies' expense.
col-fox a fox with much black fur, or with black
markings
forncast Predestined by divine planning. The
Nun's Priest shifts to an attempt to reach a more
exalted plane: he feels it necessary to argue the
matter of whether Chaunticleer's fate was predestined or not; and he becomes the counter-
weight to Chaunticleer's valuation of his dream.

Til it was passèd undern° of the day,
Wayting⸵ his tyme⸵ on Chauntėcleer to falle,   *watching / opportunity*
As gladly doon thise homicydes alle,
That in awayt liggen to mordre men.°
460   O false mordrer, lurking in thy den!
O newė Scariot,° newė Genilon!°
False dissimilour,⸵ O Greek Sinon,°   *dissembler*
That broghtest Troye al outrely⸵ to sorwe!   *completely*
O Chauntėcleer, acursėd be that morwe,
That thou into that yerd flough⸵ fro the bemes!   *flew*
Thou were ful wel ywarnėd by thy dremes,
That thilkė day was perilous to thee.
But what that God forwoot mot⸵ nedes be,   *foreknows must*
After⸵ the opinioùn of certeyn clerkis.°   *according to*
470   Witnesse on him, that any perfit⸵ clerk is,   *perfect*
That in scole is gret altercacioùn
In this matere, and greet disputisoùn,°
And hath ben of an hundred thousand men.
But I ne can not bulte⸵ it to the bren,⸵   *sift / bran*
As can the holy doctour Augustyn,
Or Boece, or the bishop Bradwardyn,
Whether that Goddės worthy forwiting⸵   *noble foreknowledge*
Streyneth⸵ me nedely⸵ for to doon a thing,   *constrains / necessarily*
('Nedely' clepe I simple necessitee);
480   Or ellės, if free choys be graunted me
To do that samė thing, or do it noght,
Though God forwoot⸵ it, er that it was wroght;   *foreknew*
Or if his witing⸵ streyneth nevere a del   *knowledge*
But by necessitee condicionel.°
I wol not han to do of swich matere;

---

undern literally, the intervening or middle period, of morning or afternoon; here mid-morning
As gladly . . . men as all such murderers usually (or: willingly) do, that lie in ambush to murder men
Scariot The Nun's Priest shifts into top preaching gear, and Chaucer into another mock-heroic mode, with a list of traitors and deceivers, beginning with the worst, Judas Iscariot, betrayer of Christ.
Genilon Ganelon, the traitor who caused the defeat of Charlemagne and the death of Roland in the medieval French epic *The Song of Roland*
Sinon the Greek decoy, who persuaded the Trojans to drag the Wooden Horse into Troy
After . . . clerkis The matter of free-will and predestination, of how much freedom of choice a man can have, given an all-knowing Creator, had been much discussed by Christian philosophers, especially by St. Augustine in his early 5th-century controversy with Pelagius. Augustine takes the side of predestination. Boethius (Boece) the early 6th-century Roman philosopher, whose *Consolation of Philosophy* Chaucer translated, evolved a solution (see below). Thomas Brad-
wardine, Archbishop of Canterbury, d. 1349, came in on the side of Augustine in his *On the Cause of God,* during a renewal of the controversy in the 14th century. The Nun's Priest says modestly that he cannot completely sift out the flour from the husks (bran) and decide who is right and who wrong.
Witnesse . . . disputisoùn (ll. 466–68). Any fully educated man can bear witness that in the schools (i.e. philosophical faculties of the universities) there is great argument and dispute on the matter.
condicionel Boethius's solution to the question was to divide necessity, predestination, and God's foreknowledge into two categories, simple and conditional. Strictly speaking, God foreknows everything, so that man has no full and true freedom of choice, but only a limited degree. Men are mortal and must die, by simple necessity. Man has no voice in the matter. But he is not constrained by necessity to walk, though if he does so, he does so necessarily. His necessary walking is conditional on his free choice whether to walk or stay still. See Boethius, *On the Consolation of Philosophy,* Bk. 5.

My tale is of a cok, as ye may here,
That took his counseil of his wyf, with sorwe,°   *dreamed*
To walken in the yerd upon that morwe   *advice*
That he had met˃ the dreem, that I yow tolde.
490   Wommennės counseils˃ been ful oftė colde;°
Wommennės counseil broghte us first to wo,
And made Adam fro Paradys to go,   *content*
Ther as he was ful mery,˃ and wel at ese.   *know not*
But for I noot,˃ to whom it mighte displese,
If I counseil of wommen woldė blame,
Passe over, for I seyde it in my game.˃   *jest*
Rede auctours, wher they trete of swich matere,
And what thay seyn of wommen ye may here.
Thise been the cokkės wordės, and nat myne;   *discover*
500   I can noon harm of no womman divyne.˃   *dust*
   Faire in the sond,˃ to bathe hir merily,
Lyth Pertelote, and alle hir sustrės by,
Agayn˃ the sonne; and Chauntėcleer so free˃   *in / noble*
Song merier than the mermayde in the see;
For *Phisiologus*° seith sikerly,˃   *certainly*
How that they singen wel and merily.
And so bifel that, as he caste his yë,
Among the wortės, on a boterflye,˃   *butterfly*
He was war of this fox that lay ful lowe.
510   Nothing ne liste him thannė for to crowe,°   *leapt*
But cryde anon, 'Cok, cok,' and up he sterte,˃   *frightened*
As man that was affrayėd˃ in his herte.
For naturelly a beest desyreth flee
Fro his contrarie,° if he may it see,   *before*
Though he never erst˃ had seyn it with his yë.
   This Chauntėcleer, whan he gan him espye,
He wolde han fled, but that the fox anon
Seyde, 'Gentil sire, allas! wher wol ye gon?
Be ye affrayed of me that am your freend?
520   Now certės, I were worsė than a feend,   *intended*
If I to yow wold˃ harm or vileinye.   *secrets*
I am nat come your counseil˃ for t'espye;
But trewėly, the cause of my cominge
Was only for to herkne how that ye singe.   *voice*
For trewėly ye have as mery a stevene˃
As any aungel hath, that is in hevene;

with sorwe sad to say
colde chilly, comfortless
Phisiologus A book, not a man: the *Bestiary.*
First written in Greek in Alexandria, 2nd century A.D., it was translated into Latin in the 4th or 5th, and attributed to one Theobaldus. Later, it was translated into the medieval European languages. It consisted of descriptions of real and fabulous creatures, with moralizations (see below). The Mermaids or Sirens, who lure sailors to destruction with the sweetness of their song, represented destructive worldly and fleshly delights.
Nothing . . . crowe he had no desire at all to crow, then
contrarie opposite, natural enemy; every creature was supposed to have an opposite to whom it felt antipathy by nature

Therwith ye han in musik more felinge
Than hadde Boece,° or any that can singe.
My lord your fader (God his soulé blesse!)

530 And eek your moder, of hir gentilesse,˃   *courtesy*
Han in myn hous ybeen, to my gret ese;
And certés, sire, ful fayn˃ wolde I yow plese.   *gladly*
But for men speke of singing, I wol saye,
So mote I broukė wel° myn eyen tweye,
Save yow, I herdė never man so singe,
As dide your fader in the morweninge;
Certes, it was of˃ herte, al that he song.˃   *from the / sang*
And for to make his voys the moré strong,
He wolde so peyne him, that with bothe his yën

540 He moste winke,° so loudė he wolde cryen,
And stonden on his tiptoon therwithal,
And strecchė forth his nekkė long and smal.
And eek he was of swich discrecioùn,
That ther nas no man in no regioùn
That him in song or wisdom mightė passe.
I have wel rad in *Daun Burnel the Asse,*°
Among his vers, how that ther was a cok,
For that a preestés sone yaf him a knok
Upon his leg, whyl he was yong and nyce,˃   *foolish*

550 He made him for to lese˃ his benefyce.°   *lose*
But certeyn, ther nis no comparisoùn
Bitwix the wisdom and discrecioùn
Of yourė fader, and of his subtiltee.
Now singeth, sire, for seïnte˃ charitee,   *sainted*
Let see, conne˃ ye your fader countrefete˃?'   *can / imitate*
This Chauntėcleer his wingės gan to bete,
As man that coude his tresoun˃ nat espye,   *deceit*
So was he ravisshed with his flaterye.

Allas! ye lordės, many a fals flatour˃   *flatterer*
560 Is in your courtes, and many a losengeour,˃   *fawner*
That plesen yow wel moré, by my feith,
Than he that soothfastnesse˃ unto yow seith.   *truth*
Redeth Ecclesiaste° of flaterye;
Beth war, ye lordės, of hir trecherye.
  This Chauntėcleer stood hye upon his toos,
Strecching his nekke, and heeld his eyen cloos,

Therwith . . . Boece Boethius's *On Music* was a standard medieval textbook.
So . . . broukė wel as I may properly enjoy the use of
He wolde . . . winke he would take such pains that he had to close both his eyes
Daun . . . Asse Master Burnellus, the hero of *The Mirror of Fools,* a satirical poem by Nigel Wireker (12th century); a donkey dissatisfied with the length of his tail, he roamed the world looking for a longer one

For that . . . benefyce (ll. 548–50) Because a priest's son gave him a blow on his leg, when he was young and foolish, the cock caused him to lose his benefice by refusing to crow at the proper time and wake the young man on the morning he was to be ordained, so that he was late and missed his chance.
Ecclesiaste Ecclesiasticus 12:10–11, 16: Never trust thine enemy . . . take good heed and beware of him . . .

And gan to crowe loude for the nones;°
And Daun Russel° the fox sterte up at ones,
And by the gargat hente⸃ Chauntecleer,   *throat grabbed*
570   And on his bak toward the wode him beer,⸃   *bore*
For yet ne was ther no man that him sewed.⸃   *pursued*
O destinee, that mayst nat been eschewed!⸃   *escaped*
Allas, that Chauntecleer fleigh⸃ fro the bemes!   *flew*
Allas, his wyf ne roghte nat° of dremes!
And on a Friday° fil al this meschaunce.
O Venus, that art goddesse of plesaunce,
Sin that thy servant was this Chauntecleer,
And in thy service dide al his power,
More for delyt, than world to multiplye,°
580   Why woldestow suffre him on thy day° to dye?
O Gaufred,° dere mayster soverayn,
That, whan thy worthy King Richard was slayn
With shot,° compleynedest his deth so sore,
Why ne hadde I now thy sentence⸃ and thy lore,⸃   *wisdom / learning*
The Friday for to chide, as diden ye?
(For on a Friday soothly slayn was he.)
Than wolde I shewe yow how that I coude pleyne⸃   *lament*
For Chauntecleres drede, and for his peyne.
    Certes, swich cry ne lamentacioun
590   Was never of ladies maad, whan Ilioun⸃   *Troy*
Was wonne, and Pirrus with his streite swerd,°
Whan he hadde hent King Priam by the berd,
And slayn him (as saith us *Eneydos*),°
As maden alle the hennes in the clos,⸃   *enclosure*
Whan they had seyn⸃ of Chauntecleer the sighte.   *seen*
But sovereynly⸃ Dame Pertelote shrighte,⸃   *royally / shrieked*
Ful louder than dide Hasdrubales° wyf,
Whan that hir housbond hadde lost his lyf,
And that the Romayns hadde brend⸃ Cartage;   *burned*
600   She was so ful of torment and of rage,⸃   *violent grief*
That wilfully into the fyr she sterte,
And brende hirselven with a stedfast herte.

for the nones on this occasion
Daun Russel Master Red
roghte nat cared not for, took no account of
Friday traditionally an unlucky day of the week
—and an "Egyptian" day (May 3) as well; see
l. 424
More . . . multiplye more for the pleasure than
to increase the population
thy day Friday is the day of the planet and
goddess Venus; French *vendredi*, Italian *venerdi*.
Gaufred Geoffrey of Vinsauf, a 12th-century
rhetorician, whose treatise on Latin poetics,
Poetria Nova, published soon after the death of
Richard I, Coeur-de-Lion, contained, as a model
of a lament, verses on the death of that king.
Friday is a day of mischance, especially because
Richard was killed on it, and its very existence

is lamented and scolded. Chaucer, and the Nun's
Priest, are again professing weakness as rhetoricians.
shot a missile, actually an arrow
Pirrus . . . swerd Pyrrhus, with his naked
(Latin: *stricta*) sword. Pyrrhus was the Greek
who killed King Priam of Troy when the Greeks
sacked the city.
as . . . Eneydos As Virgil's *Aeneid* tells us
(II.550–53). Chaucer may have taken his references to Troy, Carthage, and Rome from Geoffrey's treatise cited above.
Hasdrubales See the Franklin's Tale, ll. 691 ff;
this Hasdrubal was not Hannibal's brother, but
the King of Carthage who committed suicide
when his city was burned by the Romans in 146
B.C.

O woful hennės, right so cryden ye,
As, whan that Nero° brendė the citee
Of Romė, cryden senatourės wyves,
For that hir housbondes losten alle hir lyves;
Withouten gilt this Nero hath hem slayn.
Now wol I tornė to my tale agayn.
   This sely˃ widwe, and eek hir doghtres two,   *poor*
610 Herden thise hennės crye and maken wo,
And out at dorės sterten˃ they anoon,   *rushed*
And syen˃ the fox toward the grovė goon,   *saw*
And bar upon his bak the cok away;
And cryden, 'Out! Harrow!˃ and weylaway!   *help*
Ha, ha, the fox!' and after him they ran,
And eek with stavės many another man;
Ran Colle° our dogge, and Talbot, and Gerland,°
And Malkin,° with a distaf in hir hand;
Ran cow and calf, and eek the verray hogges
620 So were they fered˃ for berking of the dogges   *afraid*
And shouting of the men and wimmen eke,
They ronnė˃ so, hem thoughte hir hertė brekc.˃ *ran / would burst*
They yellėden as feendės˃ doon in helle;   *devils*
The dokės˃ cryden as men wolde hem quelle;˃ *ducks / kill*
The gees for ferė flowen˃ over the trees;   *flew*
Out of the hyvė cam the swarm of bees;
So hidous was the noyse, a! Benedicitė!
Certės,˃ he Jakkė Straw,° and his meynee,˃ *surely / company*
Ne madė never shoutės half so shrille,
630 Whan that they wolden any Fleming kille,
As thilkė day was maad upon the fox.
Of bras thay broghten bemės,˃ and of box,˃ *trumpets / boxwood*
Of horn, of boon,˃ in whiche they blewe and pouped,˃ *bone / tooted*
And therwithal thay shrykėd˃ and they houped;˃ *shrieked / whooped*
It semėd as that heven sholdė falle.
Now, godė men, I pray yow herkneth alle!
   Lo, how fortune turneth˃ sodeinly   *overturns*
The hope and prydė eek of hir enemy!
This cok, that lay upon the foxes bak,
640 In al his drede, unto the fox he spak,
And seydė, 'Sire, if that I were as ye,

Nero Nero, wishing to re-enact the burning of Troy, set fire to Rome in 64 A.D. and enjoyed the laments that he heard from the dying and the survivors of all classes. He had previously put to death many innocent patricians.
Colle a common dog's name
Talbot, and Gerland two other dogs, or perhaps two men
Malkin traditional name for a maidservant
Jakke Straw One of the leaders of the Peasants'

Revolt of 1381. Foreigners working and trading in London were commonly held to be doing native Englishmen out of their jobs and were therefore attacked. The Flemings were mainly cloth-workers (see the General Prologue, l. 450), and many were killed "with the usual row"—as a contemporary chronicler puts it. "Meynee" often has the sense of rabble. The Nun's Priest is bringing the noise and strife of his story close home to his hearers.

Yet sholde I seyn (as wis God helpė me°):
"Turneth agayn, ye proudė cherlės alle!
A verray pestilence upon yow falle!
Now am I come unto this wodės syde,
Maugree your heed,° the cok shal heer abyde;
I wol him ete, in feith, and that anon."'
The fox answerde, 'In feith, it shal be don;'
And as he spak that word, al sodeinly
650   This cok brak from his mouth deliverly,   *nimbly*
And heighe upon a tree he fleigh anon.
And whan the fox saugh that he was ygon,
'Allas!' quod he, 'O Chauntėcleer, allas!
I have to yow,' quod he, 'ydoon trespas,
Inasmuche as I makėd yow aferd,
When I yow hente, and broghte out of the yerd;
But, sire, I dide it in no wikke entente;   *evil*
Com doun, and I shal telle yow what I mente.
I shal seye sooth to yow, God help me so.'
660   'Nay than,' quod he, 'I shrewe us bothė two,   *curse*
And first I shrewe myself, bothe blood and bones,
If thou bigylė me ofter than ones.
Thou shalt namore, thurgh thy flaterye,
Do me to singe and winkė with myn yë.   *cause*
For he that winketh, whan he sholdė see,
Al wilfully, God lat him never thee!'   *thrive*
'Nay,' quod the fox, 'but God yeve him meschaunce,
That is so undiscreet of governaunce,   *self-control*
That jangleth whan he sholdė holde his pees.'   *babbles*
670   Lo, swich it is for to be recchėlees,   *reckless*
And necligent, and truste on flaterye.
But ye that holden this tale a folye,
As of a fox, or of a cok and hen,
Taketh the moralitee,° good men.
For Saint Paul° seith, that al that writen is,
To our doctryne it is ywrite, ywis.
Taketh the fruyt, and lat the chaf be stille.
Now, godė God, if that it be thy wille,
As seith my Lord,° so make us alle good men;
680   And bringe us to his heighė blisse. Amen.
     Here is ended the Nonne Preestes Tale.

---

as wis . . . me as surely as God may help me.
Maugree your heed in spite of your head; for
anything you can do about it
moralitee Morality, lesson. The Nun's Priest
winds up in a little confusion, but makes his
point: this tale has a lesson for us all.

Saint Paul Romans 15:4: "For whatsoever
things were written aforetime were written for
our learning that we through patience and comfort of the scriptures might have hope." The
Nun's Priest stops to drive home the moral lesson, turning his story into a sermon.
Lord i.e. Christ

Two Cock-and-Fox Stories

Here are two stories, one heavily moralizing the habits of the cock and the fox, one telling the story of Chaunticleer and Reynard as part of a long series of the fox's tricks and adventures.

The first, from the *Bestiary* (*Physiologus,* see l. 505n above), paints the kind of *moralitee* that the Nun's Priest would expect his hearers to have at the back of their minds. Such *exempla,* illustrative stories, were much used by preachers. Our text is a free modern version of a fifteenth-century Latin translation.

The second is from Caxton's translation from the Dutch in his *Reynard the Fox,* printed in 1481, which goes back ultimately to the French *Roman de Renart* (late twelfth century). There are more than forty such tales in Caxton's book. Caxton still moralizes the story, but he gives it none of Chaucer's wit and spirit; his public wanted stories and stories alone. The fox as a sham cleric was a regular feature of Reynard literature.

The text, based on the edition of 1481, is modernized in spelling and punctuation.

From The Bestiary—

Of the Fox

The nature or characteristic of the fox is as follows. The fox is an animal with a heart full of tricks and deceptions; for when it wishes to catch rooks and crows it stretches itself out on the ground and closes its eyes as if it had been lying dead for many days. The rooks and crows, greedy to dine off the corpse, come and begin to tear at it. Then the fox, quickly jumping up, seizes them and gobbles them up.

Morality In the fox we see the Devil, full of guile, who deceives sinners as the fox deceives birds like rooks and crows. The Devil cannot deceive good, honest, and holy men because they are clothed in the righteousness of virtue. . . .

Of the Cock

The nature or characteristic of the cock is that the more the night approaches, the louder it crows; and when day approaches, it sings more often.

Morality We should imitate its character, and the nearer the night approaches with its perils and doubts and with the Devil at hand, we should sing loudly and devoutly, asking the aid of God to defend us from all perils; and when the dawn is near, we should pray to God as often as we can. . . .

Another characteristic of the cock is that when it wishes to crow, it strikes itself with its wings three times beforehand.

Morality This shows that a man ought to beat himself on the breast for the blame of his sins and offenses before praying, so that he can sing better and more righteously his praises of God. . . .

From William Caxton's The History of Reynard the Fox

How the Cock Complained on Reynard

Chanticleer came forth and smote piteously his hands and his feathers; and on each side of the bier went twain sorrowful hens. That one was called Cantart and that other good hen, Crayant; they were two the fairest hens that were between

Holland[1] and Ardennes. These hens bare each of them a burning taper which was long and strait.[2] These two hens were Coppen's sisters, and they cried so piteously, 'Alas and weleaway!'[3] for the death of their dear sister Coppen. Two young hens bare the bier, which cackled so heavily[4] and wept so loud for the death of Coppen their mother, that it was far heard. Thus came they together before the King.

And Chanticleer then said, 'Merciful lord, my lord the King, please it you to hear our complaint and abhor the great scathe[5] that Reynard hath done to me and my children that here stand. It was so that in the beginning of April, when the weather is fair, as that I was hardy[6] and proud because of the great lineage that I am come of, and also had.[7] For I had eight fair sons and seven fair daughters which my wife had hatched, and they were all strong and fat and went in a yard which was walled round about, in which was a shed wherein were six great dogs which had totore[8] and plucked many a beast's skin in such wise as my children were not afraid. On whom Reynard the Thief had great envy because they were so secure that he could none get of them. How well oft-times hath this fell[9] thief gone round about this wall and hath laid for us in such wise that the dogs have been set on him and have hunted him away. And once they leapt on him upon the bank, and that cost him somewhat for his theft. I saw that his skin smoked.[10] Nevertheless, he went his way.[11] God amend it![12]

'Thus were we quit of Reynard a long while. At last came he in likeness of an hermit,[13] and brought to me a letter for to read, sealed with the King's seal, in which stood written that the King had made peace over all in his realm, and that all manner beasts and fowls should do none harm nor scathe to one another. Yet said he to me more, that he was a cloisterer or a closed recluse[14] become, and that he would receive great penance for his sins. He showed me his slavin and pilch and an hair shirt thereunder;[15] and then said he, "Sir Chanticleer, after this time be no more afraid of me nor take no heed, for I

1. The northern coastal country, not the United Netherlands now called Holland, and the Ardennes, in the southern Netherlands; thus, from north to south, anywhere.
2. Slender.
3. Happiness is gone, alas!
4. Sorrowfully.
5. Harm.
6. Bold.
7. The great lineage that I am sprung from and that is sprung from me.
8. Torn to pieces.
9. Fierce.
10. I saw the dust rise from his skin.
11. He got away.
12. God see that things go better next time.
13. In the guise of a hermit.
14. Both words mean a member of a monastic order, prevented by religious vows from leaving the monastery or receiving visitors, except by special dispensation.
15. A slavin was a pilgrim's mantle; a pilch, originally an outer garment of dressed skin with the hair still on it, but later merely of leather or coarse wool. The hair shirt, which was woven of animal hair, was worn next to the skin by penitents and religious to mortify the flesh. There is a sort of joke here at Chanticleer's gullibility: Reynard's innermost shirt would naturally be of hair.

now will eat no more flesh.[16] I am forthon so old that I would fain remember my soul.[17] I will now go forth, for I have yet to say my sext, none, and mine evensong.[18] To God, I betake[19] you." Then went Reynard thence, saying his Credo;[20] and laid him under an hawthorn.

'Then I was glad and merry, and also took no heed, and went to my children and clucked them together, and went without the wall for to walk, whereof is much harm come to us. For Reynard lay under a bush and came creeping between us and the gate, so that he caught one of my children and laid him in his male.[21] Whereof we have great harm; for since he hath tasted of him there might never hunter nor hound save nor keep him from us. He hath waited by night and day in such wise that he hath stolen so many of my children that of fifteen I have but four; in such wise hath this thief forslongen[22] them. And yet yesterday was Coppen my daughter, that here lieth upon the bier, with the hounds rescued. This complain I to you, gracious King; have pity on my great and unreasonable damage and loss of my fair children!'
1481

The Wife of Bath's Prologue and Tale

The Wife of Bath's horoscope, as she herself states it in her Prologue, gives astrological clues to her character that would have been recognized by Chaucer's contemporaries. Her zodiacal sign is Taurus, one of the "mansions" of the planet Venus, the love star. Taurus was just rising above the horizon when the Wife was born but, most unfortunately, Mars, the warlike planet, was in conjunction with Venus at the same time. The sign just rising above the eastern horizon, the ascendant, was held to govern a nativity; and if only Venus had been alone in Taurus, the Wife would have been everything that was gentle, playful, loving, slim, and beautiful. But the effect of Mars turned gentleness to fierceness, play to aggression, love to insatiability, and slim, blonde beauty to heavier, fleshier, darker charms. The Wife is thus still an attractive woman, but more of a handful (Fig. 29).

All this we should have been led to expect, too, from her description in the General Prologue—her proud behavior, her confident skill in her trade, her roving eye—all add to and help to round out the picture into what has always been rightly thought one of Chaucer's most lifelike characters. But she also, like the Prioress, has a literary prototype in the *Roman de la Rose:* the Duenna, protectress, imparter of the secrets of catching men, and ironic commentator.

16. That is, I will make the religious observance of fasting by eating no meat.
17. Moreover, so old that I wish to be mindful of my soul.
18. The meeting must have taken place in the forenoon, since the canonical hours mentioned begin at noon. The recitation of the Divine Office, as contained in the Breviary, was (and is) obligatory for anyone in major orders in the Catholic Church. The office of sext was recited at the sixth hour (noon) after prime (the first hour, 6 a.m.); nones at the ninth (3 p.m.) and evensong (vespers) shortly before sunset.
19. Commend.
20. Creed, from the opening words *Credo in unum Deum* ("I believe in God"), the confession of faith; part of the mass. Reynard repeats it as an act of pretended devotion.
21. Bag.
22. Swallowed down.

It is characteristic of the Wife that, when her turn comes to tell a tale, she prefaces it with a great comic account of her life and marryings, dealing first with the question of whether her own successive experiences of marriage can be justified from Scripture —and in the eyes of the church and of society. Her experience falls foul of the authority of St. Jerome (c. 342–420), the most famous and influential representative of the tradition which, beginning in the unquestioning acceptance of male superiority in pre-classical societies, passes into Greek and Roman thought as explicit anti-feminism. *The Golden Book of Marriage* is attributed to Theophrastus (c. 372–287 B.C.), the pupil of Aristotle, but we know of it only from its use by later Christian writers, who drew on it for ammunition. They also drew—and so perhaps did Chaucer—on the savage sixth satire of the Roman poet Juvenal (c. 60–140 A.D.) directed against women. But it was the Fathers of the Christian Church, especially St. Jerome, who saw in the biblical account of Eden and its loss the first example of man brought to destruction by woman. Justification of their attitude was found in the pagan philosophy in which they had been educated, and the dispraise of women became the subject of works designed to encourage male and female chastity. The Fathers' great Christian weapon was St. Paul's First Epistle to the Corinthians, chapter 7, which figures largely in the Wife's Prologue. St. Jerome's tract, *Adversus Jovinianum* (Against Jovinian), written about A.D. 400, is the most comprehensive and influential statement of the anti-feminist case. Jovinian, a monk, had ventured to suggest that fasting and chastity were not necessarily higher states than reasonable indulgence in food, drink, and sex. Jerome refuted him with authorities, eloquence, and abuse. Jerome's tract was, however, only the beginning of a long tradition of Christian anti-feminist literature which Chaucer uses in the Wife's Prologue.

In presenting all this, Chaucer is operating in his accustomed mode of transformation. The Wife, we feel, has made out her case for successive remarriages with the brand of defiance that is conscious of running counter to social and religious pressures, hinting that part of her excuse must be that she is Venerian by temperament. Then, as the anti-feminist stories begin to flow and she warms to the description of her fifth husband, Jankin, and his little ways, her stature as Chaucer's character grows. Our sympathy for her as a representative of slandered womanhood increases. In the end, she stands unharmed by the whole tide of it. She is life itself, ready for another husband, or whatever the future has in store.

The tale that Chaucer gives her to tell is a version of the ancient and widely diffused folk-tale of the Loathly Lady: the repulsive hag, whom a vow or an obligation forces a young man to accept as his wife. The lady has received her ill-favored shape by enchantment and must keep it until true courtesy frees her from it; in some versions she has assumed it as a matter of choice. In each case, the true perceptions and the courtesy of the man who has somehow, wittingly or unwittingly, put himself in her power are tested. He has to show either that he is not led astray by outward unattractiveness, or that his obligation of noble behavior toward women is fulfilled, before the happy ending to the tale can ensue.

At least one other version of the story was current in Chaucer's day. This was the tale of Florent in the first book of John Gower's *Confessio Amantis* (Lover's Confession). It is also probable that more versions of it were available, such as those in the ballad *The Marriage of Sir Gawain* and the poem *The Wedding of Sir Gawain and Dame Ragnell*. The versions involving Sir Gawain turn on his knightly perfection. In accepting the loathly bride, he demonstrates his true nobility, holding to the obligation that courtesy has conferred on him. "He wolde algate his trowthe holde"—he wanted in all ways to keep faith—as the ballad puts it.

None of these versions, including Chaucer's, is derived from the other, yet all are clearly interrelated, in spite of minor differences. Chaucer's tale, in the Wife's mouth, becomes an *exemplum* of her view of what the marital situation should be, and what it is unlikely to be in male-dominated society without active intervention by women themselves. As the Wife tells it, the story illustrates the validity of the admission she has exhorted from her husband in her Prologue: "Myn owene trewe wyf, / Do as thee lust the terme of al thy lyf." The hero of the story, instead of being King Arthur, or Gawain, the flower of courtesy, is a rogue, who has to solve a riddle in order to exculpate himself from a rape. Having put himself into the Loathly Lady's power, in order to answer the Queen's riddle, he must acknowledge the superiority of the woman. To the Wife this is all quite plain and as it should be; there is no suggestion, as there is in the Gawain poems, that sovereignty is yielded out of *gentilesse*, in accordance with the subtler modes of another female retort to male domination: the code of courtly love (see Glossary). The terms of the choice offered the knight have been slanted by Chaucer to fit the wife's character; they emphasize the nature of the submission that any man—even in an illustrative fiction—must make if he comes within her orbit. This knight is not offered the plain choice between beauty and ugliness: he must choose rather between a mate who is ugly but faithful and one who is beautiful and unfaithful. Things turn out fairly well for him in the end: he yields his authority to her, but his wife is both beautiful and obedient. She is the correlative of the discussion of *gentilesse*. In the overriding fiction of the *Tales*, however, the Wife has the last word, in her final prayer for young, vigorous husbands—and for mastery over them. Her Prologue and this final prayer for men apt to be mastered bracket her tale and give it its predominant tinge, so well suited to the teller, of feminine militancy in the face of male provocation. The final prayer lowers the level on which the nature of nobility is so high-mindedly discussed in the tale—but this does not mean that Chaucer does not intend the discussion to be taken seriously.

At the end of the Wife of Bath's Tale, there is added, by the editor, an example of another use than Chaucer's of one of the Wife's fifth husband's favorite stories (Prologue, ll. 763–70). It is a modern English translation of a fifteenth-century story from the *Gesta Romanorum* (Deeds of the Romans), with its moralization given in a summary form. The *Gesta Romanorum* is a collection of tales, perhaps composed in Franciscan circles, for use by preachers and others. It may be of English origin and was probably first put together about 1300.

This particular short tale is chosen as an illustration of how, given the firm intention of moralizing in a certain direction, any story can be turned into an allegory. The corollary of this is that we cannot say of any allegorical interpretation that it is impossible: someone, at some time, may have used it. Medieval allegory did not, of course, always function in such a crude and *ad hoc* fashion: it drew on a long and rich tradition of the allegorization of Scripture. But if we wish to see allegorical meanings in the *Tales*, we must carefully distinguish between the possible and the likely and bear in mind the complication of the fictional mode of the *Tales*, placed as they are in the mouths of so many different tellers.

Prologue

The Prologe of the Wyves Tale of Bathe

Experience, though noon auctoritee°
Were in this world, is right ynough for me
To speke of wo that is in mariàge;
For, lordinges,° sith I twelve yeer was of age,   *ladies and gentlemen*
Thonkèd be God that is eterne on lyve,°   *alive*
Housbondes at chirchèdore° I have had fyve;
(For I so oftè have ywedded be);
And alle were worthy men in hir degree.°   *rank*
But me was told certeyn, nat longe agon° is,   *ago*
10 That sith° that Crist ne wente nevèr but onis°   *since / once*
To wedding, in the Cane° of Galilee,
That by the same ensample° taughte he me   *example*
That I ne sholdè wedded be but ones.
Herkne eek,° lo! which° a sharp word for the nones°   *also / what*
Besyde a welle° Jesus, God and man,   *well*
Spak in repreve° of the Samaritan:°   *reproof*
'Thou hast yhad fyve housbondès,' quod he,
'And thilke° man, the which that hath now thee,   *the same*
Is noght thyn housbond;' thus seyde he certeyn.
20 What that he mente therby, I can nat seyn;
But that I axe,° why that the fifthe man   *ask*
Was noon housbond to the Samaritan?
How manye mighte she have in mariàge?
Yet herde I never tellen in myn age
Upon this nombre diffinicioùn;°
Men may devyne° and glosen° up and doun.   *guess / interpret*
But wel I woot expres,° withoutè lye,   *know expressly*
God bad us for to wexe° and multiplye;
That gentil° text can I wel understonde.   *noble*
30 Eek wel I woot he seÿde, myn housbonde
Sholde lete° fader and moder, and take me;°   *leave*
But of no nombre mencion made he,
Of bigamye or of octogamye;°

12

Chided her 3 husbands

Cuckholded 1853

Experience . . . auctoritee The Wife begins by making her position clear. A good plain woman, she sets herself against contemporary respect for learning. She will use no book-learning, no citations of authorities, to make her case. In the event she quotes much of it, though she finally answers it by an act of violence.
chirchedore See the General Prologue, l. 460; the wedding ceremony was performed outside the church door, in public, after which nuptial mass was celebrated within the church.
Cane Cana, in Galilee, where the miracle of water into wine was performed (John 2:1ff.). The question of whether a woman could marry more than once was much discussed.
for the nones for the nonce, on the occasion, to the purpose—but a conventional formula, with little meaning

Samaritan John 4:16 ff. Jesus's retort to the Samaritan woman at the well was that she had had five husbands, but that her sixth man was not her husband. The passage was often cited in such discussions. The Wife adapts it slightly to her own case: she has had five husbands—but not yet six.
diffinicioun definition, but also carrying the sense of finite number, limit; neither five nor any other number has been laid down
wexe increase; Genesis 1:28: "Be fruitful and multiply and replenish the earth."
Sholde . . . take me Matthew 19:5
octogamye Chaucer took the word from St. Jerome. Here, bigamy and octogamy mean two and eight successive, not simultaneous, marriages.

Why sholde men speke of it vileinye?   *evil*
  Lo, here the wyse king, dan° Salomon;
I trowe he hadde wyves mo than oon.
As wolde God it leveful were to me
To be refresshed half so ofte as he!°
Which yifte° of God hadde he for alle his wyvis!
40 No man hath swich,˃ that in this world alyve is.   *such*
God woot, this noble king, as to my wit,˃   *knowledge*
The firste night had many a mery fit˃   *bout*
With ech of hem, so wel was him on lyve!°
Blessed be God that I have wedded fyve
Of whiche I have pyked out the beste,°
Both of here nether˃ purs and of here cheste.˃   *lower / coffer*
Diverse scoles maken parfyt clerkes:˃   *perfect learned men*
And diverse practyk° in many sondry werkes
Maketh the werkman parfit sikerly;˃   *surely*
50 Of five husbondes scoleying˃ am I.   *schooling*
Welcome the sixte, whan that ever he shal.°
Forsothe,˃ I wol nat kepe me chaste in al;   *in truth*
Whan myn housbond is fro the world ygon,
Som Cristen man shal wedde me anon;
For thanne, th'Apostle° seith, that I am free
To wedde, a Goddes half, wher it lyketh˃ me.   *it pleases*
He seith that to be wedded is no sinne;
Bet˃ is to be wedded than to brinne.˃   *better / burn*
What rekketh me,˃ thogh folk seye vileinye   *do I care*
60 Of shrewed˃ Lamech° and his bigamye?   *cursed*
I woot˃ wel Abraham was an holy man,   *know*
And Jacob eek, as ferforth as I can;°
And ech of hem hadde wyves mo than two;
And many another holy man also.
  When saugh˃ ye ever, in any maner age,   *saw*
That hye God defended˃ mariage   *forbade*
By expres word? I pray you, telleth me;
Or wher comanded he virginitee?
I woot as wel as ye, it is no drede,˃   *doubt*

---

dan Latin, *dominus,* master: Lord Solomon; he had 700 wives, besides 300 concubines (I Kings 11:3)
As wolde . . . he (ll. 37–38) Would to God it were permitted to me to take recreation half as often as he!
Which yifte what a gift
so wel . . . lyve such a happy life he led
beste I have picked out the best both in their balls and their bank balance; or perhaps: I have drawn out all their substance from either of these places
practyk practice, practical work
whan . . . shal whenever he shall turn up
th'Apostle St. Paul: I Corinthians 7:39 ("The

wife is bound by the law as long as her husband liveth; but if her husband be dead, she is at liberty to be married to whom she will; only in the Lord"); **Bet is . . . brinne** I Corinthians 7:8–9 ("I say therefore to the unmarried and widows . . . if they cannot contain, let them marry: for it is better to marry than to burn").
Lamech Genesis 4:19–24; great-great-grandson of Cain. Lamech was a murderer and the first man to divide one flesh between two wives. The Wife is careful of the example of this villain; she prefers to invoke the example of the virtuous patriarchs Abraham and Jacob, both polygamists, but not—at least—murderers.
ferforth . . . can as far as I know

70 Th'Apostel,° whan he speketh of maydenhede;ˀ   *virginity*
He seyde, that precept therof hadde he noon.
Men may conseille a womman to been oon,ˀ   *single*
But conseilling is no comandèment;
He putte it in our owene jugèment.
For haddè God comanded maydenhede,
Thanne hadde he dampnèdˀ wedding with the dede;°   *condemned*
And certès,ˀ if ther were no seed ysowe,°   *certainly*
Virginitee, wherof than sholde it growe?
Paul dorstè nat comanden attèˀ leste   *at the*
80 A thing of which his maister yafˀ noon heste.ˀ   *gave / command*
The dart° is set up for virginitee;
Cacche who so may, who rennethˀ best lat see.   *runs*
    But this word is nat take of° every wight,
But therˀ as God listˀ give it of his might.   *where / it pleases*
I woot wel, that th'Apostel was a mayde;ˀ   *virgin*
But natheless, thogh that he wroot and sayde,°
He woldeˀ that every wight were swichˀ as he,°   *wished / such*
Al nis but conseil to virginitee;
And for to been a wyf, he yaf me leve
90 Of indulgence;° so it is no repreveˀ   *reproof*
To weddè me,° if that my makèˀ dye—   *mate*
Withoute excepcioùn of bigamye°—
Al were it good no womman for to touche°
(He mente as in his bed or in his couche,
For peril is bothe fyrˀ and towˀ t'assemble—   *fire / flax*
Ye knowe what this ensample may resemble°).
This is al and som,° he heeld virginitee
More parfit than wedding in frelètee.°   *call (it) / unless*
Freletee clepeˀ I, but ifˀ that he and she
100 Wolde leden al hir lyf in chastitee.
    I grauntè it wel, I havè noon envye,
Thogh maydenhedè prèferre bigamye;ˀ   *surpass remarriage*
Hem lykethˀ to be clene in body and goost,ˀ   *pleases / spirit*
Of myn estaatˀ I nil nat make no boost.   *condition*

th'Apostel St. Paul: I Corinthians 7:25 ("Now concerning virgins, I have no commandment of the Lord"). The recommendation of virginity and the institution of monasticism rest on the tradition of the church, not on Scripture—but the church holds that its tradition is of equal authority.
with . . . dede when he did (the other); at the same time
if ther . . . ysowe if no seed were sown; the argument is used by St. Jerome
dart spear, apparently as a prize in a race, perhaps "set up" for the winner to take (*cacche*) at the finish line. Chaucer is translating St. Jerome, and perhaps making a sexual pun.
take of received, understood by
wroot and sayde wrote and said. This sort of meaningless doublet, perhaps the survival of an oral formula, is a favorite with Chaucer's successors.
He . . . he I Corinthians 7:7 ("For I would that all men were even as myself [i.e. chaste]")
indulgence I Corinthians 7:6 ("I speak this by [your] permission [indulgence], not of commandment")
wedde me marry me. The verb is still reflexive; I Corinthians 7:39 again.
Withoute . . . bigamye so that no exception can be taken to my second marriage
touche I Corinthians 7:1
Ye . . . resemble you know what this figure means
al and som the sum total of it
in freletee for the frailty of our humanity

For wel ye knowe, a lord in his houshold,
He hath nat every vessel al of gold;
Somme been of tree,> and doon hir lord servyse.   *wood*
God clepeth> folk to him in sondry wyse,   *calls*
And everich hath of God a propre yifte,°
110   Som> this, som that—as him lyketh shifte.>   *one / command*
    Virginitee is greet perfeccioùn,
And continence eek with devocioùn.
But Crist, that of perfeccioùn is welle,>   *fountain-head*
Bad nat every wight he sholde go selle
All that he hadde, and give it to the pore,
And in swich wyse folwe him and his fore.°
He spak to hem that wolde live parfitly;>   *perfectly*
And lordinges, by your leve, that am nat I.
I wol bistowe the flour of al myn age
120   In the actès and in fruit of marïage.
    Telle me also, to what conclusioùn>   *end*
Were membres maad> of generacioùn,   *made*
And of so parfit wis a wright ywroght?°
Trusteth right wel, they wer nat maad for noght.
Glose> whoso wole, and seye bothe up and doun,   *comment*
That they were makèd for purgacioùn>   *purging*
Of urine, and our bothè thingès smale>   *narrow*
Were eek to knowe a femele from a male,
And for noon other causè: sey ye no?
130   The experience woot wel it is noght so.
So that the clerkès be nat with me wrothe,
I sey this, that they makèd been for bothe,
This is to seye, for office,° and for ese
Of engendrure, ther> we nat God displese.   *procreation where*
Why sholde men ellès in hir bokès sette,
That man shal yeldè> to his wyf hir dette?   *pay*
Now wherwith sholde he make his payèment,
If he ne used his sely° instrument?
Than were they maad, upon> a creätùre,   *in*
140   To purge uryne, and eek for engendrùre.
    But I seye noght that every wight is holde,>   *bound*
That hath swich harneys> as I to yow tolde,   *tackle*
To goon and usen hem in engendrùre;
Than sholde men take of chastiteè no cure.>   *care*
Crist was a mayde,> and shapen as a man,   *virgin*
And many a saint, sith that the world bigan:
Yet lived they ever in parfit chastitee.

<hr/>

propre yifte a gift of his own; his individual bent: I Corinthians 7:7
fore track, footsteps. Matthew 19:21 is the source for ll. 114–16.
And of . . . ywroght One reading would give here: And for what purpose was a creature made. The sense of the reading adopted—and

so perfectly wise a Maker made—translates St. Jerome.
office might mean urinating, but more frequently means excretion; the sense here is more general: for natural functions
sely little, innocent

I nil envyė no virginitee;
Lat hem be breed⟩ of purėd⟩ whetė seed, *bread / refined*
150 And lat us wyvės hoten⟩ barly breed; *be called*
And yet with barly breed, Mark° tellė can,
Our Lord Jesu refresshėd many a man.
In swich estaat as God hath clepėd° us
I wol persèvere, I nam nat precious.⟩ *choosy*
In wyfhode⟩ I wol use myn instrument *wifehood*
As frely⟩ as my Maker hath it sent. *liberally*
If I be daungerous,° God yeve⟩ me sorwe! *give*
Myn housbond shal it have bothe eve and morwe,⟩ *morning*
Whan that him list⟩ com forth and paye his dette. *it pleases him*
160 An housbonde I wol have, I nil nat° lette,
Which shal be bothe my dettour⟩ and my thral,⟩ *debtor / slave*
And have his tribulatioùn withal°
Upon his flessh, whyl that I am his wyf.
I have the power duringe al my lyf
Upon his propre⟩ body, and noght he.° *own*
Right thus the Apostel tolde° it unto me;
And bad our housbondes for to love us weel.
Al this sentence⟩ me lyketh every deel.⟩ *matter / every part*
Up sterte⟩ the Pardoner, and that anon,⟩ *started / at once*
170 'Now dame,' quod⟩ he, 'by God and by Saint John, *said*
Ye been a noble prechour in this cas!
I was aboute to wedde a wyf; allas!
What⟩ sholde I bye it on my flesh so dere? *why*
Yet hadde I lever⟩ wedde no wyf to-yere!'° *rather*
 'Abyde!' quod she, 'my tale is nat bigonne;
Nay, thou shalt drinken of another tonne⟩ *barrel*
Er that I go, shal savoure⟩ wors than ale. *taste*
And whan that I have told thee forth my tale
Of tribulacioùn in marïage,
180 Of which I am expert in al myn age,
This to seyn, myself have been the whippe;
Than maystow chese⟩ whether thou wolt sippe *choose*
Of thilkė tonne⟩ that I shal abroche.⟩ *barrel / broach*
Bewar of it, er thou too ny⟩ approache; *near*
For I shal telle ensamples mo than ten.
Whoso that nil⟩ be war by otherė men, *will not*
By him shul otherė men corrected be.
The samė wordės wryteth Ptholomee;°

Mark miracle of the loaves and fishes, when about 5000 were fed with five loaves. Mark (8:5) does not say that they were barley-loaves; John (6:9) does.
cleped called; see I Corinthians 7:20
daungerous careful, difficult of access
nil nat will not; double negative, intensifying
withal moreover; see I Corinthians 7:28
I have . . . he I Corinthians 7:4

tolde Ephesians 5:25
to-yere literally, this year, but meaning next year, sometime, never
Ptholomee Claudius Ptolemy, the most influential ancient astronomer, an Alexandrian Greek of the 2nd century A.D. whose chief work is the *Almagest*. This proverb does not appear in it, but is included in a collection of sayings attributed to him in the Middle Ages.

Rede in his *Almageste*, and take it there.'
190 'Dame, I wolde praye yow, if your wil it were,'
Seyde this Pardoner, 'as ye bigan,
Telle forth your talė, spareth for no man,
And teche us yongė men of your praktike.'   *practice*
 'Gladly,' quod she, 'sith it may yow lyke.'   *please*
But yet I praye to al this companye,
If that I speke after my fantasye,°
As taketh not agrief' of that I seye;   *offense*
For myn ententė nis but for to pleye.'   *divert*
 Now sires, now wol I tellė forth my tale.
200 As ever mote I drinken wyn or ale,
I shal seye sooth, tho' housbondes that I hadde,   *those*
As three of hem were gode' and two were badde.   *good*
The threė men were gode, and riche, and olde;
Unnethė' mightė they the statut' holde   *scarcely / covenant*
In which that they were bounden unto me.
Ye woot' wel what I mene of this, pardee!   *know*
As help me God, I laughė whan I thinke
How pitously anight I made hem swinke;'   *toil*
And by my fey,' I tolde of it no stoor.°   *faith*
210 They had me yeven hir' gold and hir tresoor;   *given their*
Me neded nat do lenger' diligence   *longer*
To winne hir love, or doon hem reverence.
They lovėd me so wel by God above,
That I ne tolde no dayntee of hir love!°
A wys womman wol sette hir ever in oon:°
To gete hir lovė, theras' she hath noon.   *where*
But sith I hadde hem hoolly' in myn hond,   *completely*
And sith they hadde me yeven' all hir lond,   *given*
What' sholde I taken heed hem for to plese,   *why*
220 But it were for my profit and myn ese?
I sette hem so a-werkė,' by my fey,   *to work*
That many a night they songen' weilawey!'   *sang / alas*
The bacoun was nat fet' for hem, I trowe,   *fetched*
That som men han in Essex at Dunmowe.°
I governed hem so wel, after' my lawe,   *according to*
That ech of hem ful blisful' was and fawe'   *happy / glad*
To bringė me gaye thingės fro the fayre.
They were ful glad whan I spak to hem fayre;
For God it woot, I chidde' hem spitously.'   *chided / unmercifully*
230 Now herkneth, how I bar me° proprely,

---

fantasye strictly, a specific faculty of the mind, imagination; thus, "as I feel like"

I . . . stoor I did not take much account of it; or perhaps: I gained no money by it (since I'd already got it from them)

That I . . . love i.e. I needed to take no special pains to get their love

A wys . . . in oon a sensible woman will set herself one object

Dunmowe At this town and elsewhere a flitch or side of bacon was offered to any couple who could prove they had not quarreled or regretted their marriage during the year just past.

bar me behaved myself

Ye wysė wyvės, that can understonde.
Thus shulde ye speke and bere hem wrong on honde;°
For half so boldėly can ther no man
Swere and lyen° as a womman can.   *lie*
I sey nat this by° wyves that ben wyse,°   *about / careful*
But if° it be whan they hem misavyse.°   *unless / go wrong*
A wys wyf, if that she can hir good,°
Shal beren him on hond the cow is wood,°
And takė witnesse of hir owene mayde
240   Of hir assent;° but herkneth how I sayde.
      "Sir olde kaynard,° is this thyn array°°   *dotard*
Why is my neighėborės wyf so gay?
She is honoùred over al ther° she goth;°   *wherever / goes*
I sitte at hoom, I have no thrifty cloth.°   *good clothes*
What dostow° at my neighėborės hous?   *do you*
Is she so fair? artow so amorous?
What rowne° ye with our mayde? Benedicitė!°   *whisper*
Sir oldė lechour, lat thy japes° be!   *tricks*
And if I have a gossib° or a freend,   *confidant*
250   Withouten gilt, thou chydest as a feend,°   *fiend*
If that I walke or pleye unto his hous!
Thou comest hoom as dronken as a mous,
And prechest on thy bench, with yvel preef!°
Thou seist to me, it is a greet meschief°   *misfortune*
To wedde a poorė womman, for costage;°   *because of expense*
And if that she be riche, of heigh parage,°   *descent*
Than seistow° that it is a tormentrye   *you say*
To suffre hir pryde and hir malėncolye.°
And if that she be fair, thou verray knave,
260   Thou seyst that every holour° wol hir have;   *adulterer*
She may no whyle in chastitee abyde,
That is assaillėd upon ech a side.
      Thou seyst, som folk desyre us for richesse,
Somme for our shap, and somme for our fairnesse;
And som, for she can outher° singe or daunce,   *either*
And som, for gentillesse° and daliaunce;°   *kindness / favor*
Som, for hir handės and hir armės smale;°   *slender*
Thus goth al to the devel by° thy tale.   *according to*
Thou seyst, men may nat kepe° a castel wal;   *hold*
270   It may so longe assailled been overal.°   *everywhere*
      And if that she be foul, thou seïst that she

bere . . . on honde pretend that they have insulted you
wys . . . good clever wife, if she knows what's
good for her
Shal . . . wood Shall make him believe the
chough is mad. Cf. Chaucer's Manciple's Tale:
an anti-feminist *exemplum.* The chough or
jackdaw, a talking bird. tells a husband that his
wife has been unfaithful. She has been, but

she persuades him that the bird is crazy and
he wrings its neck.
And take . . . assent and she will call her own
maid, who sides with her, to witness
array way of going on
Benedicite bless me
yvel preef bad luck to you
malencolye melancholy, excess of black bile;
thus, indifference

Coveiteth° every man that she may se;   *longs for*
For as a spaynel° she wol on him lepe,   *spaniel*
Til that she findé som man hir to chepe;°   *buy*
Ne noon so grey goos goth ther in the lake,
As, seïstow, that wol been withoute make.°   *mate*
And seÿst, it is an hard thing for to welde°   *control*
A thing that no man wol, his thankés,° helde.°   *willingly / hold*
Thus seïstow, lorel,° whan thow goost to bedde;   *wretch*
280 And that no wys° man nedeth for to wedde,   *prudent*
Ne no man that entendeth° unto hevene.   *hopes for*
With wildé thonder-dint° and firy levene°   *thunderbolt / lightning*
Mote thy welkéd nekké be to-broke!°   *leaking*

Thow seÿst that dropping° houses, and eek smoke,   *leaking*
And chyding wyves, maken men to flee
Out of hir owene hous; a! Benedicité!
What eyleth° swich an old man for to chyde?   *ails*
Thow seyst, we wyvés wol our vyces hyde
Til we be fast,° and than we wol hem shewe;
290 Wel may that be a proverbe of a shrewe!°   *scoundrel*
Thou seïst, that oxen, asses, hors,° and houndes,
They been assayéd at diversé stoundes;°   *times*
Bacins, lavours,° er that men hem bye,   *washbasins*
Sponés and stoles,° and al swich housbondrye,°   *stools / household goods*
And so been° pottés, clothés, and array;°   *are / ornaments*
But folk of wyvés maken noon assay
Til they be wedded; oldé dotard shrewe!
And than, seïstow, we wol oure vices shewe.
Thou seïst also, that it displeseth me
300 But if that thou wolt preysé my beautee.
And but thou poure alwey° upon my face,   *gaze*
And clepé° me 'Faire dame' in every place;   *call*
And but thou make a feste° on thilké° day   *feast / the same*
That I was born, and make me fresh and gay,
And but thou do to my norìce° honoùr,   *nurse*
And to my chamberere° withinne my bour,°   *chambermaid / room*
And to my fadres° folk and his allyes;°   *father's / relatives*
Thus seïstow, olde barel ful of lyes!
And yet of our apprentice Janekyn,
310 For his crisp heer,° shyninge as gold so fyn,   *curly hair*
And for he squiereth me bothe up and doun,
Yet hastow caught a fals suspecioun;
I wol° hym noght, thogh thou were deed° tomorwe.   *want / dead*

Mote . . . to-broke may your withered neck be
broken; to- intensifies
fast firmly tied, married
hors Horses. The complaint that one can have
a good look at a horse one is buying, but not
at a prospective wife, goes back as far as the
Roman poet Horace (65–8 B.C.). Sir Thomas

More's solution may be found in *Utopia*, Bk. ii.
Chaucer here, as he has done earlier, and as he
goes on doing, is borrowing from Theophrastus,
The Golden Book of Marriage, quoted by St.
Jerome, perhaps, through a French reworking
—in this case Eustache Deschamps' *Mirror of
Marriage*.

But tel me this, why hydėstow, with sorwe,°
The keyės of thy cheste awey fro me?
It is my good⁷ as wel as thyn, pardee.   *property*
What wenestow⁷ make an idiot of our dame?   *think you to*
Now by that lord, that called is Saint Jame,°
Thou shalt not bothė, thogh that thou were wood,⁷   *angry*
320 Be maister of my body and of my good;
That oon thou shalt forgo, maugree thyne yën;°
What nedeth thee of me to enquere⁷ or spyën?   *enquire*
I trowė, thou woldst loke⁷ me in thy chiste!⁷   *lock / money-chest*
Thou sholdest seye, 'Wyf, go wher thee liste,⁷   *it pleases*
Tak your disport, I wol nat leve⁷ no talis;   *believe*
I knowe yow for a trewė wyf, dame Alis.'
We love no man that taketh keep⁷ or charge⁷   *heed / notice*
Wher that we goon, we wol⁷ ben at our large.⁷   *want / liberty*
Of allė men yblessed moot he be,
330 The wyse astrologien° Dan Ptholome,
That seith this proverbe in his *Almageste,*
'Of allė men his wisdom is the hyeste,
That rekketh⁷ never who hath the world in honde.'   *cares*
By this proverbė thou shalt understonde,
Have thou ynogh,° what thar⁷ thee recche⁷ or care   *need / trouble*
How merily⁷ that othere folkės fare?   *happily*
For certeyn, oldė dotard, by your leve,
Ye shul have queyntė° right ynough⁷ at eve.   *plenty*
He is to greet a nigard that wol werne⁷   *refuse*
340 A man to lighte his candle at his lanterne;
He shal have never the lassė⁷ light, pardee;   *less*
Have thou ynough, thee thar nat pleynė thee.
    Thou seÿst also, that if we make us gay
With clothing and with precïous array,
That it is peril of our chastitee;
And yet, with sorwe, thou most enforcė⁷ thee,   *reinforce*
And seye thise wordės in the Apostle's name,
'In habit,⁷ maad with chastitee and shame,   *clothes*
Ye wommen shul⁷ apparaille yow,' quod he,°   *must*
350 'And noght in tressėd heer and gay perree,
As perlės, ne with gold, ne clothės riche;'
After thy text, ne after thy rubriche°

with sorwe literally, with sorrow; thus, damn it
Jame St. James (the Great), patron saint of
Spain; see the General Prologue, l. 468. The
Wife had made the pilgrimage to Santiago de
Compostela.
maugree . . . yën despite (Fr. malgré) your
eyes; i.e. damn your eyes
astrologien The line between astrologers and
astronomers is hard to draw in the Middle Ages,
but Ptolemy was by all counts an astronomer.
For his aphorism, see l. 188n above; its sense
is: he is the wisest of men who does not care
if others have much wealth.

Have . . . ynogh if you have enough
queynte pudendum. It would not be in the
Wife's nature to use a polite expression, but the
form she uses may be a kind of genteelism, a
variant spelling of *cuinte;* see her use of *quoniam, bele chose, chambre of Venus* below.
he I Timothy 2:9 ("modest apparel, with
shamefastness and sobriety; not with braided
hair or gold or pearls, or costly array");
"perree" (Fr. *pierrerie*) is jewelry
rubriche the opening words or headings in a
manuscript, written in red to give the reader an
orientation; thus, direction

I wol nat wirche as muchel' as a gnat.°   *much*
Thou seydest this, that I was lyk a cat;°
For whoso wolde senge' a cattes skin,   *singe*
Thanne wolde the cat wel dwellen in his in;'   *house*
And if the cattes skin be slyk and gay,
She wol nat dwelle in house half a day,
But forth she wole, er' any day be dawed,'   *before / dawned*
360   To shewe hir skin, and goon a-caterwawed;'   *caterwauling*
This is to seye, if I be gay, sir shrewe,
I wol renne' out, my borel' for to shewe.   *run / clothes*
   Sire olde fool, what eyleth' thee to spyën?   *ails*
Thogh thou preye Argus,° with his hundred yën,
To be my warde-cors,' as he can' best,   *bodyguard / knows how*
In feith, he shal nat kepe me but me lest;'   *unless it pleases me*
Yet coude I make his berd,° so moot I thee.'   *thrive*
   Thou seydest eek, that ther ben thinges three,
The whiche thinges troublen al this erthe,
370   And that no wight ne may endure the ferthe;'   *fourth*
O leve' sir shrewe, Jesu shorte' thy lyf!   *dear / shorten*
Yet prechestow, and seyst, an hateful wyf
Yrekened' is for oon of thise meschances.'   *reckoned / misfortunes*
Been ther none othere maner resemblances
That ye may lykne your paràbles to,°
But if a sely wyf be oon' of tho'?   *one / them*
   Thou lykenest eek wommanes love to helle,
To bareyne' land, ther' water may not dwelle.   *barren / where*
Thou lyknest it also to wilde fyr;°
380   The more it brenneth,' the more it hath desyr   *burns*
To consume every thing that brent' wol be.   *burned*
Thou seyst, that right' as wormes° shende' a tree,   *just / destroy*
Right so a wyf destroyeth hir housbonde;
This knowe they that been to wyves bonde."'   *bound*
   Lordinges, right thus, as ye have understonde,
Bar I stifly myne olde housbondes on honde,°
That thus they seyden in hir dronkenesse;
And al was fals, but that I took witnesse
On Janekin and on my nece also.
390   O Lord, the peyne I dide hem and the wo,
Ful giltelees,' by Goddes swete pyne!°   *innocent / sufferings*
For as an hors I coude byte and whyne.°

I . . . gnat i.e. I don't care a fly for them
cat a singed cat dwells at home (a proverb)
Argus Argus, unsleeping because of his hundred
eyes, was set by Juno to watch Io, whom
Jupiter was currently involved with; but Mercury
charmed him asleep and killed him. Do what
you like in the way of watching, says the Wife,
it will do you no good.
make his berd outwit him
Been . . . to i.e. are there no other similarities

you can apply your moral tales to rather than
to a poor, innocent woman?
wilde fyr Wild fire was a naphtha preparation
that was especially fierce and difficult to put out.
wormes grubs, crawling creatures of all kinds
Bar . . . honde I pressed my pretense on my
old husbands
byte and whyne bite when in a bad temper and
whinny when in a good

I coudė pleyne,° thogh I were in the gilt,°   *complain / wrong*
Or ellės oftentyme hadde I ben spilt.°   *ruined*
Whoso that first to millė comth, first grint;°   *grinds*
I pleynėd first, so was our werre ystint.°   *ceased*
They were ful glad to excusen hem ful blyve°   *quickly*
Of thing of which they never agilte hir lyve.°

    Of wenches wolde I beren him on honde,
400 Whan that for syk unnethės° mighte he stonde.   *sickness scarcely*
Yet tikled it his hertė, for that he
Wende° that I hadde of him so greet chiertee.°   *thought / love*
I swoor that al my walkinge out by nighte
Was for to espyė wenches that he dighte;°   *laid*
Under that colour° hadde I many a mirthe.   *pretense*
For al swich wit is yeven° us in our birthe;   *given*
Deceitė, weping, spinning God hath yive
To wommen kindėly,° whyl° they may live.   *by nature / as long as*
And thus of o thing I avauntė me,°   *boast*
410 Atte ende I hadde the bettre in ech degree,
By sleighte,° or force, or by som maner thing,   *cleverness*
As by continuel murmur° or grucching;°   *complaint / grumbling*
Namely° abeddė hadden they meschaunce,   *especially*
Ther wolde I chyde and do hem no plesaunce;°   *pleasure*
I wolde no lenger in the bed abyde,
If that I feltė his arm over my syde,
Til he had maad his raunson° unto me;   *payment*
Than wolde I suffre him do his nycetee.°   *folly*
And therfore every man this tale I telle,
420 Winne whoso° may, for al is for to selle.   *whoever*
With empty hand men may none hawkės lure;
For winning° wolde I al his lust endure,   *profit*
And makė me a feynėd appetyt;
And yet in bacon° hadde I never delyt;
That made me that ever I wolde hem chyde.
For thogh the Pope had seten° hem biside,   *sat*
I wolde nat spare hem at hir owene bord.°   *table*
For by my trouthe, I quitte° hem word for word.   *requited*
As help me verray God omnipotent,
430 Thogh I right now sholde make my testament,
I ne owe hem nat a word that it nis quit.
I broghte it so aboutė by my wit,
That they moste yeve it up, as for the beste;°
Or ellės hadde we never been in reste.
For thogh he lokėd as a wood leoùn,°   *raging lion*
Yet sholde he faille of his conclusioùn.°   *purpose*

Of thing . . . lyve of something of which they were never guilty in their lives
bacon old, dried, tough, pig's meat; cf. Lechery in *Dr. Faustus*, scene VI, ll. 151–52: "I am she who likes an inch of raw mutton better than an ell of dried stockfish."
as . . . beste and make the best of it

Thanne wolde I seyė, "Godė lief,° tak keep°   *dear one / note*
How mekely loketh Wilkin ourė sheep;°
Com neer, my spouse, lat mė ba° thy cheke!   *kiss*
440 Ye sholdė been al pacïent and meke,
And han a swetė spycėd° conscience,   *delicate*
Sith ye so preche of Jobės pacience.
Suffreth alwey, sin ye so wel can preche;
And but° ye do, certein we shal yow teche   *unless*
That it is fair° to have a wyf in pees.   *good*
Oon of us two moste bowen, douteless;
And sith a man is more resonable°
Than womman is, ye moste been suffrable.°   *long-suffering*
What ayleth yow to grucchė° thus and grone?   *grumble*
450 Is it for ye wolde have my queynte allone?
Why taak it al, lo, have it everydeel;°   *all*
Peter!° I shrewe° yow but° ye love it weel!   *curse / unless*
For if I woldė selle my belė chose,°   *fair thing*
I coudė walke as fresh° as is a rose;   *sweet*
But I wol kepe it for your owene tooth.°   *enjoyment*
Ye be to blame, by God, I sey yow sooth."
 Swiche maner wordės haddė we on honde.°
Now wol I speken of my fourthe housbonde.
 My fourthė housbonde was a revelour,
460 This is to seyn, he haddė a paramour;°   *mistress*
And I was yong and ful of ragerye,°   *passion*
Stiborn° and strong, and joly as a pye.°   *vigorous / magpie*
Wel coude I dauncė to an harpe smale,°
And singe, ywis,° as any nightingale,   *indeed*
Whan I had dronke a draughte of swetė wyn.
Metellius,° the foulė cherl, the swyn,
That with a staf birafte° his wyf hir lyf,   *bereft*
For° she drank wyn, thogh° I hadde been his wyf,   *because / if*
He sholdė nat han daunted me fro drinke;
470 And, after wyn, on Venus moste° I thinke: *most*
For al so siker° as cold engendreth hayl,   *sure*
A likerous mouth moste han a likerous tayl.°
In womman vinolent° is no defence:
This knowen lechours by experience.
 But, Lord Crist! whan that it remembreth° me

How . . . sheep i.e. you, old lamb, how patient you look
And . . . resonable Men were held to be more rational, more capable of intellectual operations, than women.
Peter by St. Peter
Swiche . . . honde this was the kind of words we dealt in
smale perhaps, gracefully; or an adjective going with "harp," in reference to its thin, elegant, graceful sound
Metellius For this anti-husband story, the Wife reaches into another bin of *exempla* much used in the Middle Ages—the handbook, by Valerius Maximus (1st century A.D.), of Greek and Roman history.
A likerous . . . tayl A gluttonous mouth means a lecherous tail. Gluttony and lechery go together in the moral treatises of the time, and sin in Eden is often shown as a combination of the two in 14th-century art.
vinolent full of wine
whan . . . me impersonal construction: when I look back and recollect it all

Upon my youthe, and on my jolitee,
It tikleth me aboute myn herte rote.°   *heart's root*
Unto this day it dooth myn herte bote°   *good*
That I have had my world as in my tyme.
480   But age, allas! that al wol envenyme,°   *poison*
Hath me biraft° my beautee and my pith;°   *deprived / strength*
Lat go, farewel, the Devil go therwith!
The flour is goon, ther is namore to telle,
The bren,° as I best can,° now moste I selle;   *bran*
But yet to be right mery wol I fonde.°   *try*
Now wol I tellen of my fourthe housbonde.

      I seye, I hadde in herte greet despyt°   *contempt*
That he of any other had delyt.
But he was quit,° by God and by Saint Joce!°   *repaid*
490   I made him of the same wode a croce;°
Nat of my body in no foul manere,
But certeinly, I made folk swich chere,   *from in his own fat*
That in his owene grece° I made him frye   *fat*
For angre, and for verray jalousye.
By God, in erthe I was his purgatorie,°
For which I hope his soule be in glorie.
For God it woot, he sat ful ofte and song°   *sang*
Whan that his shoo ful bitterly him wrong.°
Ther was no wight, save God and he, that wiste,°   *knew*
500   In many wyse, how sore I him twiste.°   *wrung*
He deyde° whan I cam fro Jerusalem,   *died*
And lyth ygrave° under the rode-beem,°   *buried*
Al° is his tombe noght so curious°   *although / splendid*
As was the sepulcre of him, Darius,°
Which that Appelles wroghte subtilly;°   *skillfully*
It nis but waste to burie him preciously.°   *expensively*
Lat him fare wel,° God yeve° his soule reste,   *go in peace / give*
He is now in the grave and in his cheste.°   *coffin*
      Now of my fifthe housbond wol I telle.
510   God lete his soule never come in helle!
And yet was he to me the moste shrewe;°   *vicious*
That fele I on my ribbes al by rewe,°
And ever shal, unto myn ending day.

can as best I can—but still with a hint of the old meaning of "can": I know best how it is done
Joce a Breton saint; Chaucer found a knight with the same name in the French of Jean de Meun (d. 1305)
I . . . croce I made him a staff (crutch, not cross) of the same wood [to beat him with]; cf. l. 493: I made him fry in his own fat
I . . . purgatorie Matrimony as purgatory on earth was a frequent concept in medieval literature; the consolation for its pains was that, unlike heaven and hell, it did not retain people forever.

Whan . . . wrong when his shoe pinched him most painfully; the figure, in relation to marriage, goes back to St. Jerome, at least
rode-beem a beam across a church at the chancel-area, separating nave from choir, with the crucifix (rood) mounted on its middle
Darius king of the Persians (d. 330 B.C.), defeated by Alexander the Great, whose court painter was Apelles. Medieval versions of the story of Alexander make him magnanimously order from Apelles splendid tombs of marble, gold, and silver for Darius and his queen.
by rewe in a row, each one

But in our bed he was so fresh⟩ and gay,   *lively*
And therwithal so wel coude he me glose,⟩   *B∫ATHER*   *flatter*
Whan that he wolde han⟩ my belė chose,   *have*
That thogh he hadde me bet⟩ on every boon,⟩   *beaten / bone*
He coudė winnen agayn my love anoon.⟩   *at once*
I trowe I loved him bestė, for that he
520 Was of his lovė daungerous⟩ to me.   *sparing*
We wommen han, if that I shal nat lye,
In this matere a queyntė fantasye;⟩   *fancy*
Wayte what° thing we may nat lightly have,
Therafter wol we crye al day and crave.
Forbede us thing, and that desyren we;
Prees⟩ on us faste,⟩ and thannė wol we flee.   *press / hard*
With daunger° outė⟩ we al our chaffàre;⟩   *display / wares*
Greet prees⟩ at market maketh derė ware,⟩   *crowd / goods*
And too greet cheep⟩ is holdė at litel prys;⟩   *bargain / value*
530 This knoweth every wommàn that is wys.
   My fifthė housbonde, God his soule blesse!
Which that I took for love and no richesse,
He somtyme⟩ was a clerk° of Oxenford,   *formerly*
And had left scole, and wente at hoom to bord⟩   *as boarder*
With my gossib,° dwellinge in oure toun,
God have hir soule! hir name was Alisoun.
She knew myn herte and eek my privetee⟩   *secrets*
Bet⟩ than our parisshe preest, so moot I thee!⟩   *better / thrive*
To hir biwreyėd⟩ I my conseil⟩ al.   *disclosed / secrets*
540 For had myn housbonde pissėd on a wall,
Or doon a thing that sholde han cost his lyf,
To hir, and to another worthy wyf,
And to my nece,° which that I lovėd weel,
I wolde han told his conseil every deel.⟩   *part*
And so I dide ful often, God it woot,⟩   *knows*
That made his face ful often reed⟩ and hoot⟩   *red / hot*
For verray shame, and blamed himself for he
Had told to me so greet a privetee.
   And so bifel that onės, in a Lente,⟩   *Lent*
550 (So often tymes I to my gossib wente,
For ever yet I lovede to be gay,
And for to walke, in March, Averille, and May,
Fro hous to hous, to herė sondry talės),
That Jankin clerk, and my gossib Dame Alis,
And I myself, into the feldės wente.
Myn housbond was at London al that Lente;
I hadde the bettre leyser⟩ for to pleye,°   *opportunity*

Wayte what whatever
daunger care, parsimony; caution
clerk See the General Prologue, l. 287.
gossib literally, God-relation: God-child, God-

parent: thus, anyone to whom one is especially close
nece niece or cousin
pleye She should have passed Lent in religious observances.

And for to see, and eek for to be seye⸢   *seen*
Of lusty⸢ folk; what wiste I wher my grace   *lively*
560 Was shapen for to be, or in what place?°
Therefore I made my visitaciòuns,
To vigilies° and to processiòuns,
To preching eek and to thise pilgrimàges,
To pleyes of miracles° and mariàges,
And wered upon my gayè scarlet gytes.°
Thise wormès, ne thise mothès, ne thise mites,
Upon my peril,° frete⸢ hem never a deel;⸢   *ate / part*
And wostow⸢ why? for they were used weel.⸢   *know you / much*
     Now wol I tellen forth what happèd me.
570 I seye, that in the feeldès walked we,
Til trewèly we hadde swich daliànce,⸢   *pleasure*
This clerk and I, that of my purveyànce°
I spak to him, and seyde him, how that he,
If I were widwe, sholdè weddè me.
For certeinly, I sey for no bobance,⸢   *without boasting*
Yet was I never withouten purveyànce⸢   *prospect*
Of mariage, nof⸢ otherè thingès eek.   *nor of*
I holde a mouses herte⸢ nat worth a leek,°   *life*
That hath but oon hol for to sterte⸢ to,   *escape*
580 And if that faillè, thanne is al ydo.°
     I bar him on honde,⸢ he hadde enchanted⸢ me;   *pretended / bewitched*
My damè⸢ taughtè me that soutiltee.⸢   *mother / trick*
And eek I seyde, I mette⸢ of him al night;   *dreamed*
He wolde han slayn me as I lay up-right,⸢   *on my back*
And al my bed was ful of verray⸢ blood,   *real*
But yet I hope that he shal do me good;
For blood bitokeneth gold,° as me was taught.
And al was fals, I dremed of it right naught,⸢   *nothing*
But as I folwèd ay⸢ my damès lore,⸢   *always / teaching*
590 As wel of this as of other thingès more.
     But now sir, lat me see, what I shal seyn?
Aha! by God, I have my tale ageyn.
     Whan that my fourthè housbond was on bere,⸢   *bier*
I weep algate,⸢ and madè sory chere,⸢   *anyway / behavior*
As wyvès moten,⸢ for it is usàge,⸢   *must / custom*
And with my coverchief covered my visàge;

---

what . . . place I didn't know where my good
luck was ordained to be; or: how could I know
where my favor was destined to be bestowed
vigilies feasts or festivals on the eves of saints'
days
miracles plays based on the historical books of
the Bible and on legends of the saints
And . . . gytes and wore upon [me] my bright
scarlet gowns
peril an oath: upon peril of my soul; damn me!
purveyance providing for my future (so that
I wouldn't ever be without a husband—but

you can't sleep with me until I'm a widow and
we can be married)
leek The accumulation of little worthless things
is meant to emphasize her own provident
vigor, with a probable pun on *hole*. The mouse
with only one place to go was proverbial.
thanne . . . al ydo then it is all up
blood . . . gold This was regular doctrine in
the medieval books on the interpretation of
dreams: one red thing (blood) betokens another
(red gold); cf. the Nun's Priest's Tale.

But for that I was purveyed of° a make,°   *provided with / mate*
I weep° but smal, and that I undertake.   *wept*
   To chirchė was myn housbond born amorwe°   *carried in the morning*
600 With° neighėbores, that for him maden sorwe;   *by*
And Jankin, ourė clerk, was oon of tho.
As help me God, whan that I saugh° him go   *saw*
After the bere, me thoughte he hadde a paire
Of leggės and of feet so clene° and faire,°   *neat / handsome*
That al myn herte I yaf unto° his hold.°   *into / keeping*
He was, I trowe, a twenty winter old,
And I was fourty, if I shal seye sooth;
But yet I hadde alwey a coltės tooth.°
Gat-tothed° I was, and that bicam° me weel;   *suited*
610 I hadde the prente° of Seÿnt Venus' seel.°   *imprint / seal*
As help me God, I was a lusty° oon,   *good-looking*
And faire and riche, and yong, and wel bigoon;°   *fortunate*
And trewėly, as myne housbondes tolde me,
I had the bestė quoniam° mighte be.
For certės, I am al Venerien
In felinge,° and myn herte is Marcien.°   *feelings*
Venus me yaf my lust, my likerousnesse,°   *lecherousnesse*
And Mars yaf me my sturdy hardinesse.°   *boldness*
Myn ascendent was Taur,° and Mars therinne.
620 Allas! allas! that ever love was sinne!
I folwed ay myn inclinacioùn°   *bent*
By vertu of my constellacioùn;
That madė me I coudė noght withdrawe
My chambre of Venus from a good felawe.
Yet have I Martės mark upon my face,°
And also in another privee° place.   *secret*
For, God so wis° be my savacioùn,°   *surely / salvation*
I ne loved never by no discrecioùn,
But ever folwedė myn appetyt;
630 Al were he short or long, or blak or whyt,
I took no kepe,° so that he lyked° me,   *heed / pleased*

---

coltes tooth a young appetite
Gat-tothed See the General Prologue, l. 470.
quoniam Latin: whereas, whatever; another of
the Wife's coy words for pudendum
Venerien . . . Marcien influenced by the planets
Venus and Mars; thus, lustful and bold
Taur The Wife's ascendant (the sign of the
zodiac just rising in the east at her birth) was
Taurus, the Bull: therefore, she would be industrious, energetic, prudent, a money-maker,
one who usually comes out on top; florid, bold-
eyed, wide-mouthed, short-legged, big-but-
tocked; gossipy, given to love affairs. Venus in
her mansion of Taurus makes people cheerful,
with good figures, attractive, lovable, passionate
and voluptuous, lovers of fine clothes: there is,
essentially, no evil in them. Mars, masculine,
baleful, and angry, in conjunction (*constellacioùn*) with Venus in Taurus counteracts these

good influences and has made the Wife into
the holy terror that she is. She cannot keep her
chamber of Venus from a good man. Between
them, then, Taurus and Mars take away or
change for the worse her most agreeable characteristics.
Yet . . . face Every person was thought to have
placed on him, at conception or birth, a (birth)
mark representing the ascendant sign and dominant star of the moment, by which his fortunes
were ruled. They would appear on that part
of the body ruled by a particular sign or
planet. The Wife's sign, as she was born in
Taurus, should be on the neck; she has also
the "print of Saint Venus's seal," l. 610, a
red mark, probably, on the thigh; and Mars's
mark, a scar on the face and on the thigh or
groin ("another privee place").

(handwritten at top: Does him act these who are Scholars who Grant meet River + think they — ?? ette)

	How pore⟩ he was, ne eek of what degree.	*poor*
	What sholde I seye, but, at the monthès ende,	
	This joly⟩ clerk Jankin, that was so hende,⟩	*handsome / pleasant*
	Hath weddèd me with greet solempnitee,⟩	*ceremony*
	And to him yaf I al the lond⟩ and fee⟩	*property / money*
	That ever was me yeven therbifore;	
	But afterward repented me ful sore.	
	He noldè suffre⟩ nothing of my list.⟩	*allow / pleasure*
640	By God, he smoot me onès⟩ on the list,°	*once*
	For that I rente⟩ out of his book a leef,	*tore*
	That of the strook myn erè wex⟩ al deef.⟩	*became / deaf*
	Stiborn⟩ I was as is a leonesse,	*fierce*
	And of my tonge a verray jangleresse,⟩	*babbler*
	And walke I wolde, as I had doon biforn,⟩	*before*
	From hous to hous, although he had it sworn.⟩	*forbidden*
	For which he oftentymès woldè preche,	
	And me of oldè Romayn gestès° teche,	
	How he, Simplicius Gallus,° lefte his wyf,	
650	And hir forsook for terme⟩ of al his lyf,	*duration*
	Noght but for open-heeded⟩ he hir say⟩	*hatless / saw*
	Lokinge out at his dore⟩ upon a day.⟩	*door / one day*
	Another Romayn° tolde he me by name,	
	That, for⟩ his wyf was at a somerès⟩ game	*because / summer's*
	Withoute his witing,⟩ he forsook hir eke.	*knowledge*
	And than wolde he upon⟩ his Bible seke⟩	*in / seek*
	That ilkè⟩ proverbe of Ecclesiaste,°	*same*
	Wher he comandeth and forbedeth faste,⟩	*absolutely*
	Man shal nat suffre⟩ his wyf go roule⟩ aboute;	*allow / gad*
660	Than wolde he seye right thus, withouten doute,	
	"Whoso that buildeth his hous al of salwes,⟩	*willow-twigs*
	And priketh⟩ his blindè hors over the falwes,⟩	*rides / plowed ground*
	And suffreth his wyf to go seken halwès,⟩	*shrines*
	Is worthy to been hangèd on the galwès⟩!"	*gallows*
	But al for noght, I settè noght an hawe°	
	Of his proverbès nof⟩ his oldè sawe,⟩	*nor of / sayings*
	Ne I wolde nat of him corrected be.	
	I hate him that my vices telleth me,	
	And so do mo,⟩ God woot! of us than I.	*more*
670	This made him with me wood⟩ al outrely;⟩	*furious / completely*
	I noldè noght forbere⟩ him in no cas.	*endure*

(handwritten margin note near line 640: because he was deaf he struck her)

---

list i.e. cheek. To rhyme two words that look the same but have different meanings was thought good, as in French *rime riche*.
gestes Latin: (*res*) *gestae*, things done; the regular medieval word for stories of feats of arms
Gallus This story is from Valerius Maximus; see l. 466 above.
Romayn P. Sempronius Sophus, from the same chapter in Valerius

Ecclesiaste Ecclesiasticus 25:25: "Give . . . neither a wicked woman liberty to gad abroad." The clerk is threatening the Wife with authorities from the two most powerful sources known to the Middle Ages—the classics and the Bible. They are not just moral tales: all carry the specific threat of divorce.
I . . . hawe I give not a hawthorn berry

pokes fun at those who cite scholarly works + think they know all—

Now wol I seye yow sooth, by Seint Thomas,°
Why that I rente out of his book a leef,
For which he smoot me so that I was deef.
  He hadde a book that gladly, night and day,
For his desport� he woldė rede alway.⸥   *recreation / always*
He clepėd⸥ it Valerie° and Theofraste,°   *called*
At whichė book he lough⸥ alwey ful faste.⸥   *laughed / much*
And eek ther was somtyme⸥ a clerk⸥ at Rome,   *once / scholar*

680   A cardinal, that hightė⸥ Saint Jerome,   *was called*
That made a book agayn Jovinian;°   *against*
In whichė book eek ther was Tertulan,°
Crisippus,° Trotula,° and Helowys,°
That was abbessė nat fer⸥ fro Parys;   *far*
And eek the Parables of Salomon,°
Ovydes Art,° and bokės many on,
And allė thise wer bounden in o volume.
And every night and day was his custume,⸥   *custom*
Whan he had leyser⸥ and vacacioùn⸥   *lesiure / free time*

690   From other worldly occupacioùn,
To reden on this book of wikked wyves.⸥   *women*
He knew of hem mo legendės and lyves
Than been of godė wyvės in the Bible.
For trusteth wel, it is an impossible⸥   *impossibility*
That any clerk wol spekė good of wyves,
But if⸥ it be of holy seintės lyves,   *unless*
Ne of noon other womman never the mo.°
Who peyntedė the leoun, tel me who?°
By God, if wommen haddė writen stories,

700   As clerkės han withinne hir oratories,⸥   *cells*
They wolde han writen of men more wikkednesse

Seint Thomas St. Thomas Becket of Canterbury, the premier saint of England; see General Prologue, l. 16
Valerie The clerk had a manuscript, perhaps specially written for him, containing a number of related texts teaching him the ways and wiles of women. Valerie is not Valerius Maximus, but the *Letter of Valerius to Rufinus About Not Marrying* by Walter Map (12th century).
Theofraste Theophrastus' work *On Marriage*, mentioned and used by St. Jerome; see l. 291n
Jovinian For the Jovinian-Jerome controversy see the Headnote. The Wife uses St. Jerome freely, against his sense, for her defense of herself; and, in his sense, for her and Jankin's examples of unchastity. Cf. Dorigen, in the Franklin's Tale, ll. 659 ff.
Tertulan Tertullian (*c.* 160–*c.* 220), Father of the Church, who wrote *An Exhortation to Chastity, On Having Only One Husband,* and *On Modesty*
Crisippus perhaps the Stoic philosopher
Trotula probably never existed; she was thought to have been the author of books on gynecology and pediatrics, as well as on cosmetics, and to have been active in the famous medical center Salerno, in southern Italy, during the 11th century
Helowys Héloïse (d. 1164), the secret wife of Peter Abélard, the great Parisian philosopher who was castrated by Héloïse's uncle, Fulbert, for seducing her. She became a nun, and was later prioress of Argenteuil, near Paris. The correspondence of Héloïse and Abélard has been preserved: it was famous in the Middle Ages.
Parables of Salomon the Proverbs of Solomon—not merely the biblical book Proverbs, but a compendium from all those biblical books of which Solomon was, or was thought to be, the author, including Ecclesiasticus and Wisdom
Ovydes Art the *Ars Amatoria* (Art of Love) by the Roman poet Ovid (43 B.C.–c.18 A.D.), the lover's textbook, for his time, the Middle Ages, and the Renaissance
Ne . . . mo a heavy negative line: and nothing at all of any other woman
Who . . . who In one of the Aesopic fables a lion, seeing a picture of a lion being killed by a man, points out that all depends on the point of view; a lion would paint a man being killed by a lion.

Than all the mark of Adam° may redresse.
The children of Mercurie and of Venus°   *occupations / opposed*
Been in hir wirking⁊ ful contrarious;⁊
Mercurie loveth wisdom and science,⁊   *knowledge*
And Venus loveth ryot⁊ and dispence.⁊   *debauchery / expenditure*
And, for hir diverse disposicioùn,
Ech falleth in otherès exaltacioùn;°
And thus, God woot! Mercury is desolat
710   In Pisces, wher Venus is exaltat;
And Venus falleth ther Mercurie is reysed;⁊   *exalted*
Therfore no womman of no clerk is preysed.
The clerk, whan he is old, and may noght do
Of Venus werkès worth his oldè sho,°
Than sit⁊ he doun, and writ⁊ in his dotàge   *sits / writes*
That wommen can nat kepe hir mariàge!⁊   *marriage-vows*
But now to purpos,⁊ why I toldè thee   *point*
That I was beten for a book, pardee.
Upon a night Jankin, that was our syre,⁊   *lord*
720   Redde on his book, as he sat by the fyre,
Of Eva° first, that, for hir wikkednesse,
Was al mankindè broght to wrecchednesse,⁊   *destruction*
For which that Jesu Crist himself was slayn,
That boghte⁊ us with his hertès blood agayn.   *redeemed*
Lo, here expres⁊ of womman may ye finde,   *made clear*
That womman was the los⁊ of al mankinde.   *destruction*
Tho⁊ redde he me how Sampson° loste his heres,⁊   *then / hair*
Slepinge, his lemman kitte⁊ hem with hir sheres;   *lover cut*
Thurgh whichè tresoun⁊ loste he bothe his yën.⁊   *betrayal / eyes*
730   Tho⁊ redde he me, if that I shal nat lyen,   *then*
Of Hercules and of his Dianyre,°
That causèd him to sette himself afyre.
Nothing forgat he the penaùnce and wo
That Socrates had with hise wyvès two;°

mark of Adam the image of Adam: men; cf. the Franklin's Tale, l. 172
The children . . . Venus I.e. those born under the influence of each. It is not clear whether Chaucer means that the operations of the planets are different or that the occupations of those born under them differ. Mercury was the planetary god of knowledge and eloquence; his children are scholars, painters, sculptors, skilled metalworkers and so on. Venus was the planetary goddess of love and lovers; her children are courtiers, weavers, and dyers. But Chaucer may simply mean clerks (Mercury) and women (Venus).
exaltacioun The zodiacal sign in which a planet's influence is greatest: it is at the same time the dejection of another planet whose nature is contrary. Venus (female: pleasure) is in exaltation (*exaltat*) in Pisces, the fishes; Mercury (male: wisdom) is therefore in dejection (*desolat*) in the same sign.
of . . . sho a clerk is not worth his own old shoe in the occupations of Venus

Eva the primal female sinner. This spelling of her name is frequently used because, backward, it spells **Ave**, the salutation to Mary at the Annunciation, the beginning of our salvation. Most of the examples which follow are common knowledge, or come from St. Jerome's *Against Jovinian*, Walter Map (l. 677n), or the *Romance of the Rose*.
Sampson the story of Samson and Delilah, Judges 16
Dianyre Deianeira caused the death of her unfaithful husband Hercules, by giving him the shirt of the centaur Nessus, previously killed by Hercules for trying to rape her. The shirt had been poisoned by Nessus' blood and gave Hercules such burning pain that he preferred to build a funeral pyre and die in its flames.
wo . . . two The Athenian philosopher was famous for his patience and had, according to Jerome and others, two wives, of whom Xantippe, the second, tormented him continually.

How Xantippe caste pisse upon his heed;›   *head*
This sely› man sat stille, as he were deed;   *poor*
He wyped his heed, namore dorste› he seyn   *dared*
But 'Er that thonder stinte,› comth of a reyn.'›   *ceases / rain*
Of Phasipha,° that was the quene of Crete—
740   For shrewèdnesse,› him thoughte the talè swete—   *nastiness*
Fy! spek› namore—it is a grisly thing—   *speak*
Of hir horrìble lust and hir lyking.›   *pleasure*
Of Clitèmistra,° for hir lecherye,
That falsly made hir housbond for to dye,
He redde it with ful good devocioùn.
He tolde me eek for what occasioùn
Amphiorax° at Thebès loste his lyf;
Myn housbond hadde a legende of his wyf,
Eriphilem, that for an ouche of gold
750   Hath prively› unto the Grekès told   *secretly*
Wher that hir housbonde hidde him in a place,
For which he hadde at Thebès sory grace.›   *sad treatment*
Of Livia° tolde he me, and of Lucye,°
They bothè made hir housbondes for to dye;
That oon for love, that other was for hate;
Livia hir housbond, on an even› late,   *evening*
Empoysoned hath, for that she was his fo.
Lucya, likerous,› loved hir housbond so,   *lecherous*
That, for› he sholde alwey upon hir thinke,   *so*
760   She yaf him swich a maner lovè drinke,
That he was deed,› er it were by the morwe;›   *dead / morning*
And thus algatès› housbondès han sorwe.   *all ways*
Than tolde he me, how oon Latumius°
Compleynèd to his felawe› Arrius,   *companion*
That in his gardin growèd swich› a tree,   *such*
On which, he seyde, how that his wyvès three
Hangèd hemself for hertè despitoùs.°
"O leve› brother," quod› this Arrius,   *dear / said*
"Yif me a plante› of thilkè blissed tree,   *cutting*
770   And in my gardin planted shal it be!"
Of latter date, of wyvès hath he red,
That somme han slayn hir housbondes in hir bed,
And lete› hir lechour dighte› hir al the night   *let / lay*

Phasipha Pasiphaë, queen of Minos of Crete, fell in love with a bull and bore by him the Minotaur, half-man, half-bull.
Clitemistra Clytemnestra, Agamemnon's queen; she and her lover, Aegisthus, killed her husband on his return to Greece after the Trojan War.
Amphiorax Amphiareus, in hiding so as not to go to the siege of Thebes, was betrayed by his wife, Eriphyle, for a necklace (*ouche*) of gold and diamonds, and had to go on the expedition, where he knew himself fated to die. He was swallowed up in an earthquake at Thebes.

Livia Wife of Drusus, son of the Roman Emperor Tiberius. She poisoned her husband at the prompting of her lover Sejanus (23 A.D.).
Lucye Lucilia, wife of the Roman poet Lucretius (1st century B.C.), gave her husband a love-potion to keep him true to her. It killed him quickly: see Tennyson's *Lucretius*.
Latumius The story is told by Walter Map (l. 677n), who gives the name as Pacuvius; and it is in the *Gesta Romanorum* (see below) with a moralization. It comes, ultimately, from Cicero's *De Oratore*.
for . . . despitoùs for the malice of their hearts

Whyl that the corps⸱ lay in the floor upright.⸱ *corpse / on its back*
And somme han drivė⸱ naylės° in hir brayn *driven*
Whyl that they slepte, and thus they han hem slayn.
Somme han hem yevė⸱ poysoun in hir drinke. *given*
He spak more harm than hertė may bithinke.⸱ *imagine*
And therwithal, he knew of mo⸱ proverbes *more*
780   Than in this world ther growen gras or herbes.
"Bet⸱ is," quod he, "thyn habitacioùn *better*
Be with a leoun or a foul dragoùn,°
Than with a womman usinge⸱ for to chyde. *accustomed*
Bet is," quod he, "hye⸱ in the roof abyde° *high*
Than with an angry wyf doun in the hous;
They been so wikkėd and contrarious;⸱ *contrary*
They haten⸱ that hir housbondes loveth ay." *hate*
He seyde, "A womman cast⸱ hir shame away, *casts*
Whan she cast of⸱ hir smok";° and forthermo, *off*
790   "A fair womman, but⸱ she be chaast also, *unless*
Is lyk a gold ring in a sowės nose."°
Who woldė wenen,⸱ or who wolde suppose *imagine*
The wo that in myn hertė was, and pyne⸱? *torment*
    And whan I saugh⸱ he woldė never fyne⸱ *saw / finish*
To reden on this cursėd book al night,
Al sodeynly three levės have I plight⸱ *plucked*
Out of his book, right as he radde,⸱ and eke, *read*
I with my fist so took him on the cheke,
That in our fyr he fil⸱ bakward adoun.⸱ *fell / down*
800   And he up stirte⸱ as dooth a wood⸱ leoùn, *jumped / raging*
And with his fist he smoot⸱ me on the heed,⸱ *struck / head*
That in the floor I lay as I were deed.
And when he saugh how stillė that I lay,
He was agast,⸱ and wolde han fled his way, *afraid*
Til attė laste out of my swogh⸱ I breyde:⸱ *swoon / burst*
"O! hastow slayn me, falsė theef?" I seyde,
"And for my land thus hastow mordred⸱ me? *murdered*
Er I be deed, yet wol I kissė thee."
    And neer⸱ he cam, and knelėd faire adoun, *closer*
810   And seydė, "Derė suster° Alisoun,
As help me God, I shal thee never smyte;
That I have doon, it is thyself to wyte.⸱ *blame*
Foryeve it me, and that I thee biseke."⸱ *beg*
And yet eftsones⸱ I hit him on the cheke, *again*
And seydė, "Theef, thus muchel⸱ am I wreke;⸱ *much / revenged*
Now wol I dye, I may no lenger⸱ speke." *longer*

nayles Joel killed the tyrant Sisera thus (Judges 4:21).
Bet . . . dragoùn Ecclesiasticus 25:16
Bet . . . abyde Proverbs 21:9
A . . . smok from *Against Jovinian;* Jerome took it from the Greek historian Herodotus (died *c.* 425 B.C.)
A fair . . . nose See Proverbs 11:22: "As a jewel of gold in a swine's snout, so is a fair woman who is without discretion."
suster term of affection

But atte laste, with muchel care° and wo,   *trouble*
We fille acorded,° by us selven two.   *fell agreed*
He yaf me al the brydel° in myn hond   *bridle*
820   To han the governance of hous and lond,
And of his tonge° and of his hond also;   *tongue*
And made him brenne his book anon right tho.°
And whan that I hadde geten° unto me,   *gotten*
By maistrie,° al the soveraynetee,°   *mastering / sovereignty*
And that he seyde, "Myn owene trewe wyf,
Do as thee lust° the terme° of al thy lyf,   *pleases / duration*
Keep thyn honour, and keep eek myn estaat"°—   *possessions*
After that day we hadden never debaat.
God help me so, I was to him as kinde
830   As any wyf from Denmark unto Inde,°   *India*
And also trewe, and so was he to me.
I prey to God that sit° in magestee,   *sits*
So blesse his soule, for His mercy dere!
Now wol I seye my tale, if ye wol here.'°   *hear*

Biholde the wordes bitween the Somonour and the Frere
The Frere lough,° whan he hadde herd al this,   *laughed*
'Now, dame,' quod he, 'so have I joye or blis,
This is a long preamble of a tale!'
And whan the Somnour herde the Frere gale,°   *exclaim*
'Lo!' quod the Somnour, 'Goddes armes two!
840   A frere wol entremette him evermo.°
Lo, gode men, a flye and eek a frere
Wol falle in every dish and eek matere.°
What spekestow of preambulacioùn?
What! amble, or trotte, or pees,° or go sit doun;
Thou lettest° our disport° in this manere.'   *hinderest / enjoyment*
    'Ye, woltow so, sir Somnour?' quod the Frere,
'Now, by my feith, I shal, er that I go,
Telle of a Somnour swich a tale or two,
That alle the folk shal laughen in this place.'
850   'Now elles,° Frere, I bishrewe° thy face,'   *curse*
Quod this Somnoùr, 'and I bishrewe me,
But if I telle tales two or thre
Of freres er I come to Sidingborne,°
That I shal make thyn herte for to morne;
For wel I woot thy pacience is goon.'
    Our Hoste cryde 'Pees! and that anoon!'
And seyde, 'Lat the womman telle hir tale

And made . . . tho and I made him burn his book on the spot
A frere . . . evermo a friar will always be meddling
a flye . . . matere a proverb
pees be still; some prefer the reading "pisse"

Now elles now otherwise; i.e. now unless
Sidingborne Sittingbourne, in Kent, about 40 miles from London, more than two-thirds of the way to Canterbury. The pilgrim-journey to Canterbury usually took three days and part of a fourth.

Ye fare as folk that dronken been of ale.
Do, dame, tel forth your tale, and that is best.'

860   'Al redy, sir,' quod she, 'right as yow lest,>   *it pleases*
If I have licence of this worthy Frere.'
   'Yis, dame,' quod he, 'tel forth, and I wol here.'

Here endeth the Wyf of Bathe hir Prologe.

Tale

Here biginneth the Tale of the Wyf of Bathe

In tholdė dayės of the king Arthoùr,
Of which that Britons> speken greet honoùr,   *Bretons*
All was this land fulfild of fayėrye.°
The elf-queen, with hir joly companye,
Daunced ful ofte in many a grenė mede;>   *meadow*
This was the olde opinion, as I rede.
I speke of manye hundred yeres ago;

870 But now can no man see none elvės mo.
For now the gretė charitee and prayeres
Of limitours° and othere holy freres,
As thikke as motės in the sonnė-beem,
That serchen every lond and every streem,
Blessinge hallės, chambres, kichenes, boures,
Citees, burghės,° castels, hyė toures,
Thropės, bernės, shipnės, dayėryes,°
This maketh that ther been no fayėryes.
For ther as wont to walken was an elf,

880 Ther walketh now the limitour himself
In undermelės° and in morweninges,>   *mornings*
And seÿth his matins and his holy thinges
As he goth in his limitacioùn.°
Wommen may go saufly> up and doun,   *safely*
In every bush, or under every tree;
Ther is noon other incubus but he,
And he ne wol doon hem but dishonoùr.°
   And so bifel it, that this King Arthoùr
Hadde in his hous a lusty bacheler,

All . . . fayerye i.e. this land was teeming with supernatural creatures
limitours friars licensed to beg and hear confessions within a certain district; cf. the General Prologue, l. 209
burghes literally, boroughs; i.e. towns
Thropes . . . dayeryes thorps (i.e. villages), barns, stables, dairies
undermeles The word could mean mid-mornings or mid-afternoons: here it seems to be the latter.

And . . . limitacioùn And says his morning prayers and his holy office as he goes about his district. All clergy were bound to repeat the office at the required hours; friars were allowed to do so as they walked or rode.
Ther . . . dishonour There is no other incubus now but the friar—and he only dishonors them (without making them conceive). An incubus was an evil spirit (or fallen angel) who got children on women.

890 That on a day cam rydinge fro river;°   *it chanced*
    And happèd> that, allone as she was born,
    He saugh a maydè walkinge him biforn,
    Of whichè mayde anon, maugree hir heed,°
    By verray force he rafte> hir maydenheed;   *took*
    For which oppressioùn> was swich clamoùr   *rape*
    And swich pursute> unto the King Arthoùr,   *appeal*
    That dampnèd was this knight for to be deed°
    By cours of lawe, and sholde han lost his heed
    Paraventure,> swich was the statut> tho;   *perhaps / law*
900 But that the quene and othere ladies mo
    So longè preyèden the king of grace,
    Til he his lyf him graunted in the place,
    And yaf him to the quene al at hir wille,
    To chesè,> whether she wolde him save or spille.°   *choose*
        The quene thanketh the king with al hir might,
    And after this thus spak she to the knight,
    Whan that she saugh hir tyme,> upon a day: *opportunity*
    'Thou standest yet,' quod she, 'in swich array,>   *state*
    That of thy lyf yet hastow no suretee.>   *certainty*
910 I grante thee lyf, if thou canst tellen me
    What thing is it that wommen most desyren?
    Be war, and keep thy nekkè-boon> from yren.>   *neck-bone / iron*
    And if thou canst nat tellen it anon,
    Yet wol I yeve> thee levè for to gon   *give*
    A twelf-month and a day, to seche> and lere>   *seek / learn*
    An answere suffisànt in this matere.
    And suretee> wol I han, er that thou pace,>   *pledge / go*
    Thy body for to yelden in this place.'
        Wo was this knight and sorwefully he syketh;>   *sighs*
920 But what! he may nat do al as him lyketh.
    And at the laste, he chees> him for to wende,   *chose*
    And come agayn, right at the yerès ende,
    With swich answere as God wolde him purveye;>   *provide*
    And taketh his leve, and wendeth forth his weye.
        He seketh every hous and every place,
    Wheras he hopeth for to findè grace,
    To lernè, what thing wommen loven most;
    But he ne coude arryven in no cost,>   *region*
    Wheras he mightè finde in this matere
930 Two creätùrès àccordinge in fere.°
        Somme seydè,> wommen loven best richesse,   *said*
    Somme seydè, honour, somme seyde, jolynesse;°
    Somme, riche array, somme seyden, lust> abedde,   *pleasure*

---

fro river i.e. from hawking for wild-fowl by the river-side
maugree hir heed literally, in spite of her head; thus, despite anything she could do

That . . . deed that this knight was condemned to death
save or spille spare or put to death
accordinge in fere agreeing together
jolynesse good looks, happiness

SCOTLAND

········ Danish and Norse occupied territory north of this line.

NORTHUMBRIA

N

IRELAND

ISLE OF MAN

KINGDOM OF YORK • York

WIRRAL

Chester •

Lincoln •

WALES

ENGLISH MERCIA

EAST ANGLIA

• Coventry

• Cambridge

MALVERN HILLS

Oxford •

Maldon •

London •

KENT

Winchester •

CANTERBURY •

WESSEX

Southampton •

Hastings •

ISLE OF WIGHT

Miles

0   50   100

A. Karl

1. Medieval England.

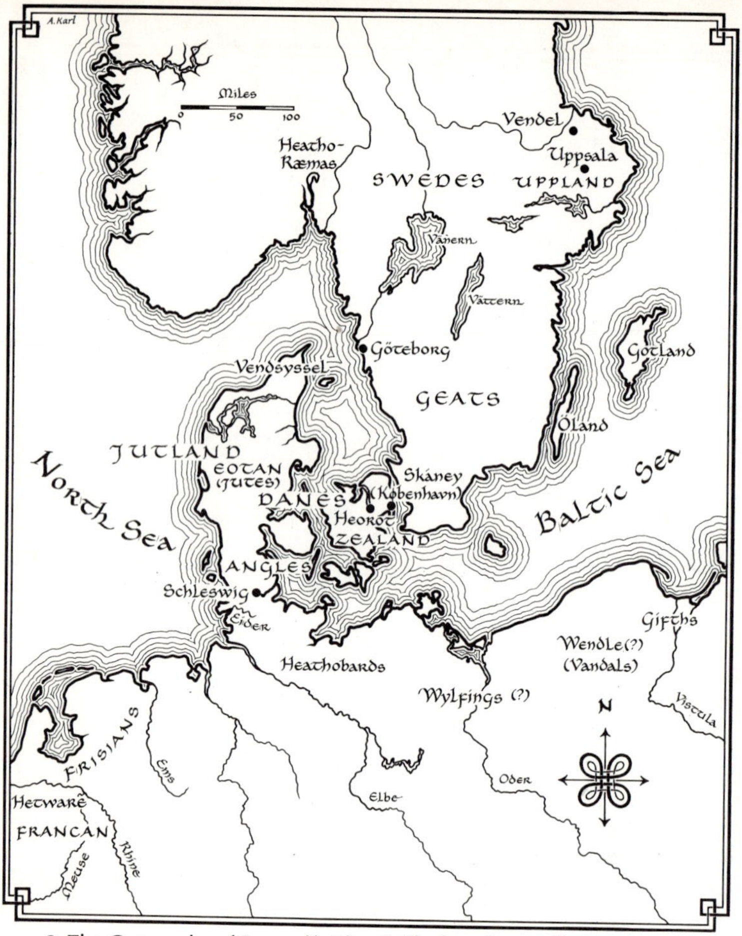

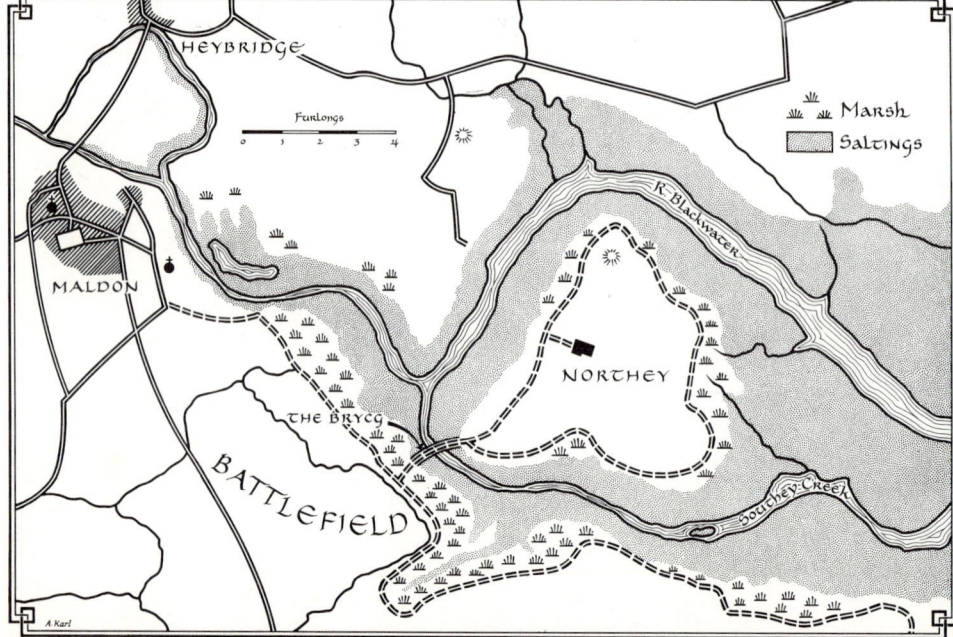

2. The Geography of Beowulf. After F. Klaeber, *Beowulf*.

3. The Site of the Battle of Maldon. From E. V. Gordon, ed., *The Battle of Maldon*.

4. *Beowulf*, ll. 444-64, the manuscript, c. 1000. *British Museum*, MS Cotton Vitellius A. XV, fol. 140r.

5. Cruciform Carpet-page, with interlace ornament, from Lindisfarne Gospels. Northumbria, c. 700. *British Museum*, MS Cotton Nero D. IV, fol. 26v.

6. The Annunciation, from the Benedictional of St. Æthelwold, Bishop of Winchester 975-80. Winchester, c. 975. *British Museum*, MS Add. 49598, fol. 5v.

7. The Harrowing of Hell, from an English Psalter. First quarter of twelfth century. Hildesheim, *St. Godehard*, p. 49.

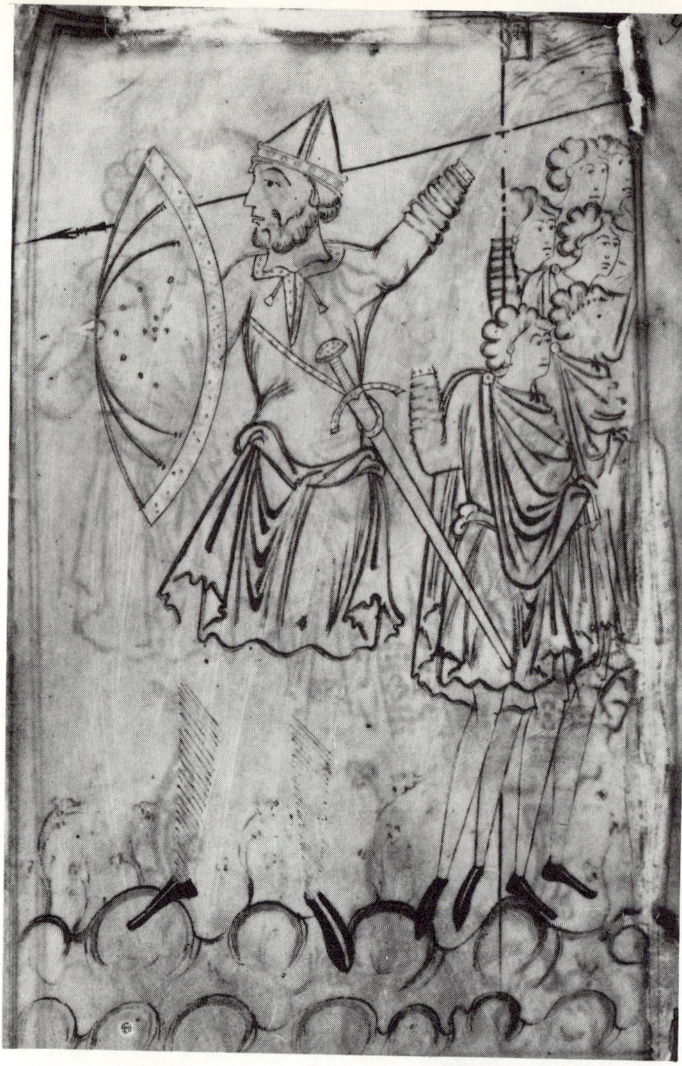

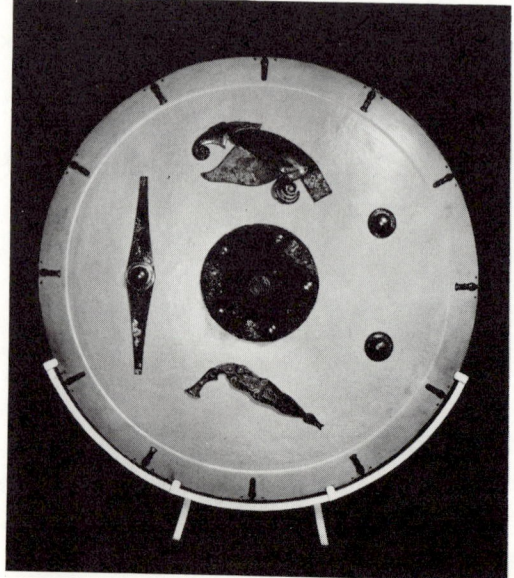

8. Goliath threatening David, from a Winchester Psalter. English, c. 1050. *British Museum*, MS Cotton Tiberius C. VI, fol. 9r.

9. Sutton Hoo: Shield (front view, reconstruction). ?First half of the seventh century. *British Museum*.

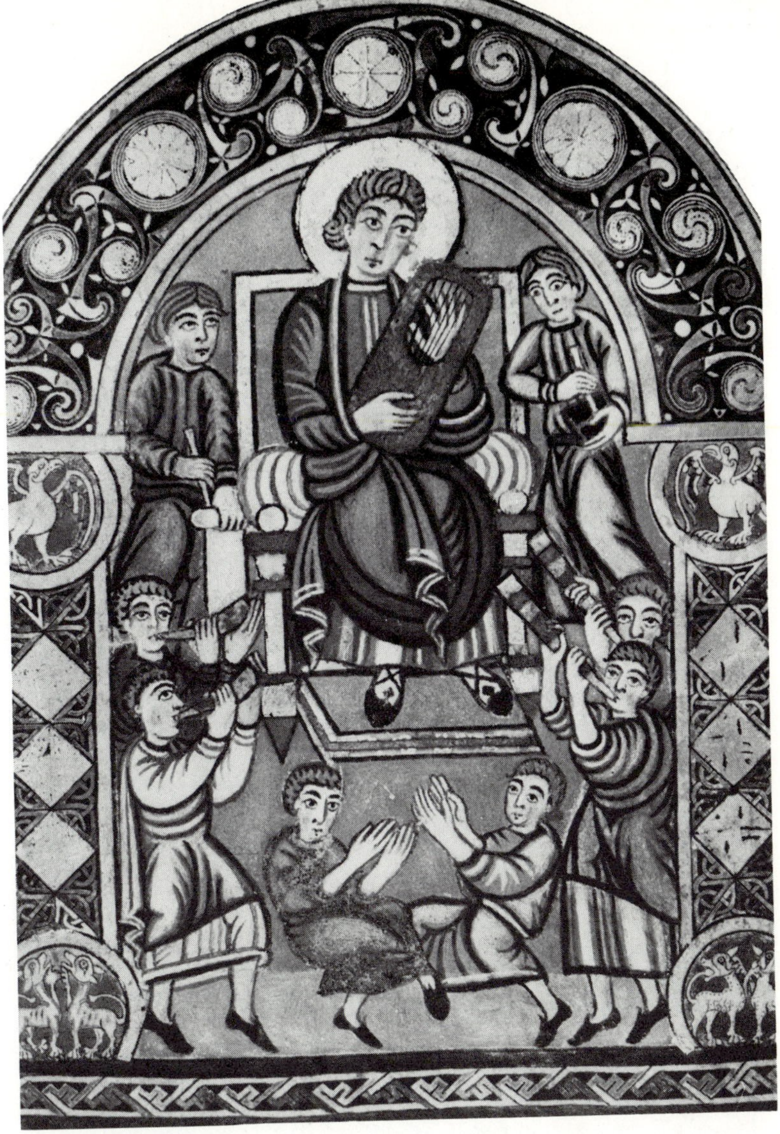

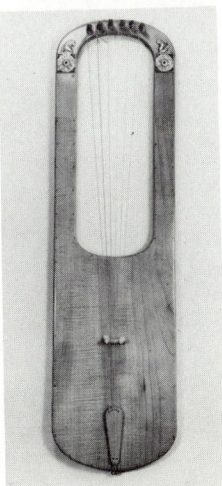

10. David as Musician, from a Canterbury Psalter. English, c. 750. *British Museum*, MS Cotton Vespasian A. I, fol. 30v.

11. Sutton Hoo: the Harp as at present reconstructed. ?First half of seventh century. *British Museum*.

12. The Oseberg Ship. Viking luxury ship, not a warship. From a barrow in Norway, c. 800. Oslo, *Universitetets Oldsaksamling.*

13. Sutton Hoo: Purse-lid of gold, enamel, glass, and garnet. ?English, first half of seventh century, *British Museum.*

14. Sutton Hoo: the great gold Belt Buckle, with ornament of interlaced snakes and animals. English, first half of seventh century. *British Museum.*

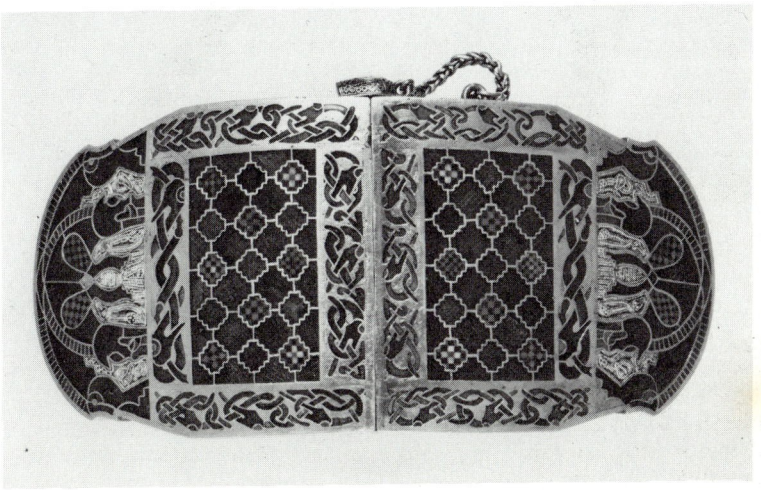

15. Sutton Hoo: Shoulder Clasps, one of a pair, of gold, garnet, and enamel. ?English, first half of seventh century. *British Museum.*

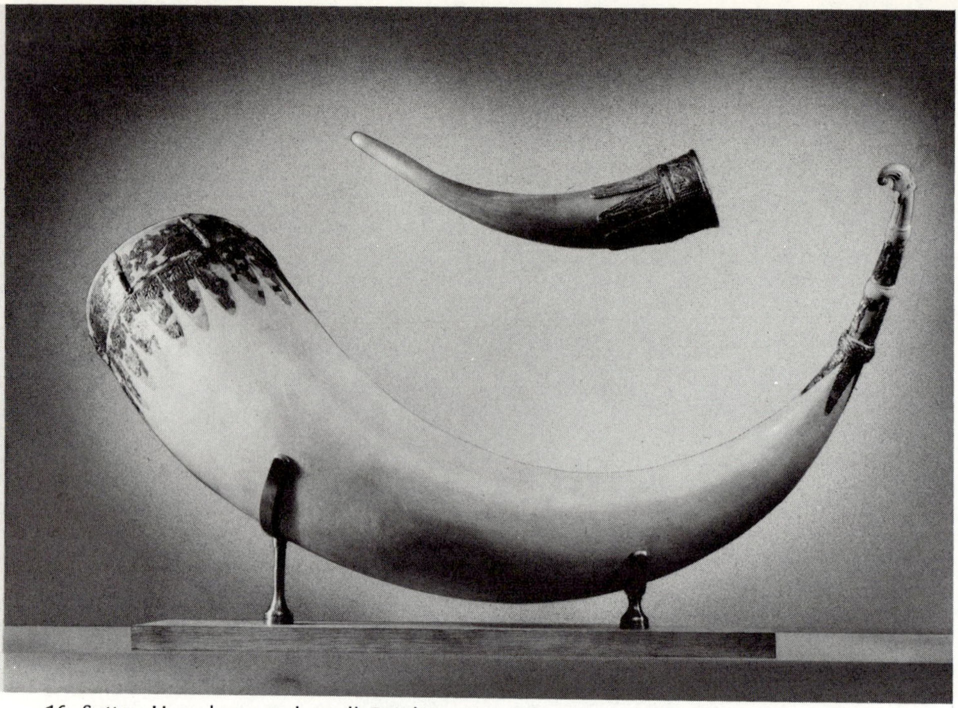

16. Sutton Hoo: large and small Drinking Horns. ?Early seventh century. There were seven in all: two large ones, of aurochs horn, had a capacity of six imperial quarts, a greatest diameter of 7.2", and circumference of 41½" along the outer curve; the small horns were cow horns. *British Museum.*

17. Sutton Hoo: Stag, height about 4" from the head of the Scepter. ?First half of seventh century. *British Museum.*

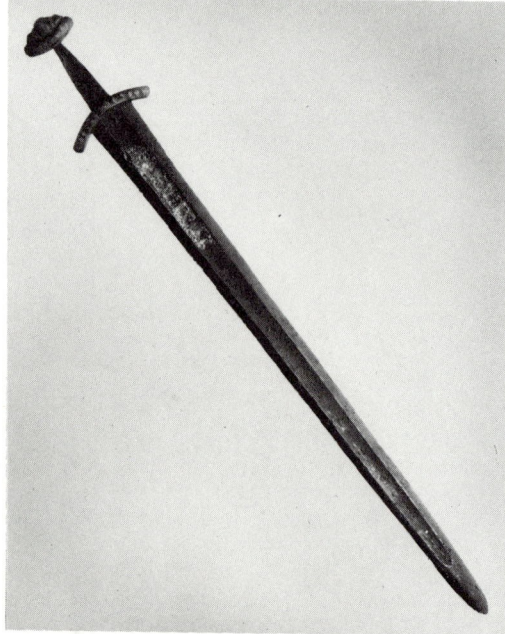

18. Sword with inlaid decoration. English, ninth or tenth century. *British Museum.*

19. Sutton Hoo: the Helmet. Swedish work, early sixth century. *British Museum*.

20. Boar Crest, from Benty Grange Helmet. English, seventh century. Sheffield, *City Museum*.

21. The Fetter Lane Sword Pommel, with snake design. English, ninth century. *British Museum*.

22. The Franks Casket (front) of whale-bone ivory, is carved in relief. North-umbrian workmanship, early eighth century. *Left:* a scene from the story of Weland; *Right:* the Adoration of the Magi; both surrounded by a runic inscription in the Northumbrian dialect of Old English. *British Museum.*

23. Christ and Mary Magdalene, stone relief from the Ruthwell Cross, Ruth-well, Dumfriesshire. (The runes of the *Dream of the Rood* are not shown.) Northumbrian, ?early eighth century.

24. Chaucer reading his poem *Troilus and Criseyde* at court. English, c. 1410. Cambridge, *Corpus Christi College*, MS 61, fol. lv.

25. Richard II, with Saints Edmund, Edward the Confessor, and John the Baptist, adoring the Virgin and Child (Wilton Diptych). English, c. 1395-1405. London, *The National Gallery*.

26. *Upper left:* Geoffrey Chaucer, from the Ellesmere MS of the *Canterbury Tales*. English c. 1410. His clothes and the pen case hung around his neck identify him as a man of letters. San Marino, California, *Henry E. Huntington Library*, MS 26. c.9, fol. 159v.
27. *Upper right:* The Miller, fol. 34v. 28. *Lower left:* The Nun's Priest, fol. 185.
29. *Lower right:* The Wife of Bath, fol. 72.

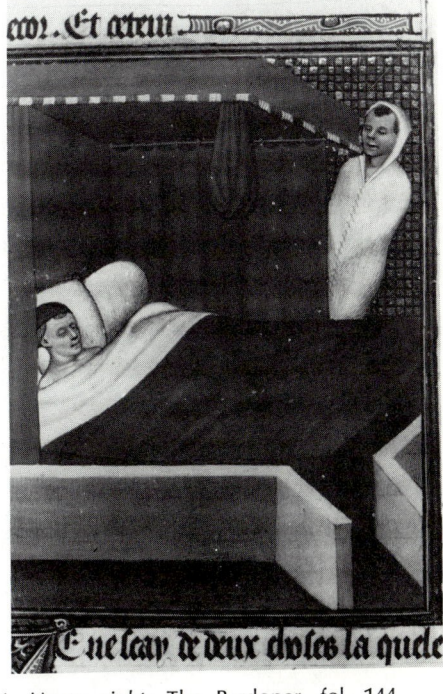

30. *Upper left:* The Franklin, fol. 129v.   31. *Upper right:* The Pardoner, fol. 144.
32. *Lower left:* Friar confessing a nun, from Luttrell Psalter. English, c. 1340. *British Museum*, MS Add. 42130, fol. 74.   33. *Lower right:* The Drowned Man warns Simonides in a dream not to sail, from Boccaccio, *De casibus virorum illustrium*. French, 1409-14. Paris, *Bibliothèque de l'Arsenal*, MS 5193, fol. 76v.

34. Reynard as a bishop, preaching to the birds; and Reynard escaping with a goose, chased by the farmer's wife, from the Smithfield Decretals. English, c. 1340. *British Museum*, MS Royal 10.E.IV, fol. 49v.

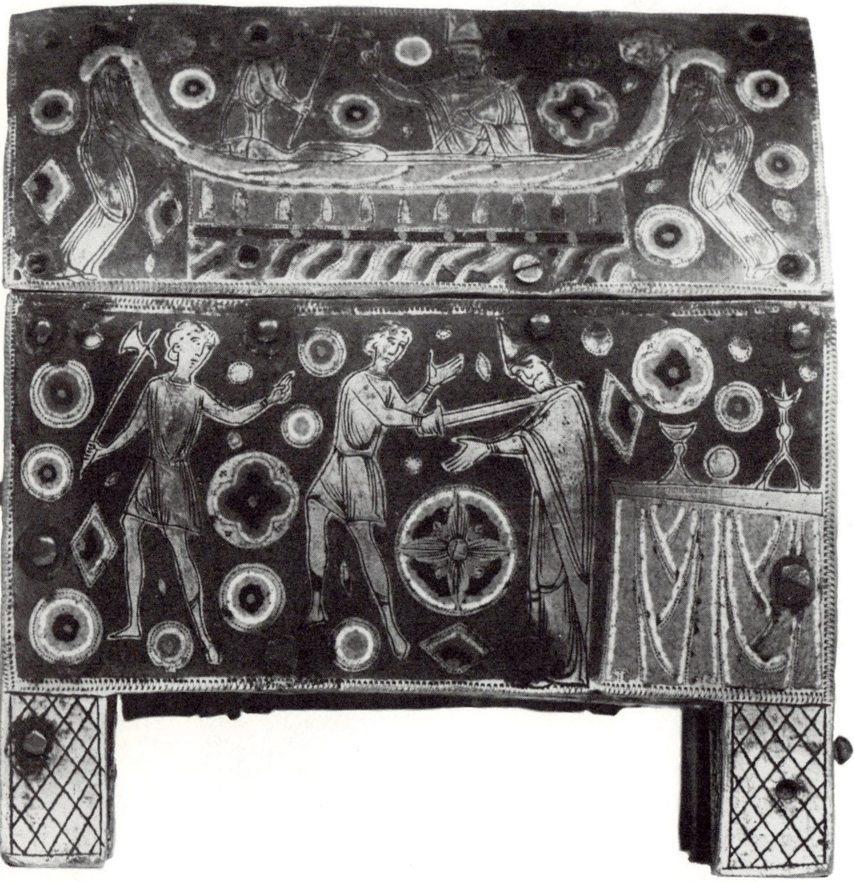

35. St. Thomas Becket taking ship from England (*above*) and his martyrdom in Canterbury Cathedral (*below*), on a Limoges enamel *châsse* (case for relics, etc.). French, thirteenth century. *British Museum*.

36. The Capture of Alexandria, in which the Knight took part. French, fourteenth century. Paris, *Bibliothèque Nationale*, MS franç. 1584, fol. 309.

37. Zodiac Man and Vein Man, with the Qualities. By the Brothers Limbourg; from the *Très Riches Heures du duc de Berry*. Franco-Flemish, before 1416. Chantilly, *Musée Condé*, MS 65 (1284), fol. 14v. *Photo Giraudon.*

An important part of the physician's skill was to know the correct time of year, month, or day in which treatment, especially by bloodletting, would be feasible and effective by virtue of a favorable relation between macrocosm and microcosm: planets, zodiacal signs, qualities, humors, sex, and parts of the body. The zodiacal sign of the Ram governs the head, so that a time when the sun was in the Ram would be favorable for treating that part. Taurus governed the neck, Gemini the shoulders and arms, and so on. In this miniature, the "qualities," hot, cold, moist, and dry, which are combined in the "humors," blood, phlegm, choler, and melancholy, are associated with zodiacal signs and with male and female sexes in the corners, which are the cardinal points of the compass.

38. The Buying of the Poison and the Deaths of the "Rioters," from Chaucer's Pardoner's Tale. English wood-relief, c. 1400. London, private collection.

39. Lechery. English, mid-fourteenth century. The man's gesture (which is also that of Nicholas of Chaucer's Miller's Tale) is obviously associated with lechery, as is the tavern before which the couple stand, with its ale-bush. *British Museum*, Taymouth Hours, fol. 177.

40. Swearing and Gambling: "rioters" tear Christ's body apart. Broughton, Bucks., wall-painting in St. Lawrence Church. English c. 1430. *Royal Commission on Historical Monuments, Crown Copyright.*

41. Philosophy and Blind Fortune with her Wheel, from **Boethius**, *De Consolatione Philosophiae* (trans. Jean de Meun). French, c. 1450-60. *British Museum*, MS Add. 10341, fol. 31v.

42. Sir Gawain visited by the Lady of the Castle. English, c. 1400. *British Museum*, MS Cotton Nero A.X., art. 3, fol. 125r.

43. A New Year feast in the court of Jean duc de Berry, with the sun in his chariot in the zodiacal signs of Capricorn and Aquarius (January), and a tournament in the background. By the Brothers Limbourg; from the *Très Riches Heures du duc de Berry*, Chantilly, *Musée Condé*, MS 65 (1284), fol. 1v. *Giraudon*.

44. A Castle, with the vintage being gathered, and the sun in the signs of Virgo and Libra (September). Begun by the Brothers Limbourg before 1416, and completed by Jean Colombe c. 1485; from the *Très Riches Heures du duc de Berry*, Chantilly, *Musée Condé*, MS 65 (1284), fol. 9v. *Giraudon*.

45. A Boar Hunt, with the sun in Sagittarius and Capricorn (December). By the Brothers Limbourg; from the *Très Riches Heures du duc de Berry*, Chantilly, *Musée Condé*, MS 65 (1284), fol. 12v. *Giraudon.*

46. King Arthur, from the Berry tapestry of the Nine Worthies. French, late fourteenth century. *New York, the Cloisters, Metropolitan Museum of Art.*

47. The Round Table. From *Lancelot,* Rouen, Dupré, 1488.

In cefte partie
nous dist thif
tour que appes
ce que la nuit
du tournoieut
fu passee et que ce vint a len
de main matin le roy artus fe
leua chauffa et vestir et lors quil

fu appareillie il oy la messe pze
mier ouvit Car il en estoit
coustumier Et pour ce le tenoi
ent tous ceuls qui le connuoif
soient a moult preudome Tan
tost que la messe fu ditte et que
tous ses barons furet assemble
ou en partie il leur commenca

48. A Joust before King Arthur. By the so-called Master of Edward IV, from a Flemish manuscript of (?) Hélie de Borron, *Guiron le courtois, c.* 1480-1500. Oxford, *Bodleian Library*, MS Douce 383, fol. 16r.

49. The Annunciation to the Shepherds. By
the Brothers Limbourg. *Très Riches Heures du
duc de Berry*, Chantilly, *Musée Condé*, MS 65
(1284), fol. 48r. *Giraudon.*

50. The Last Judgment. By the Brothers Limbourg; from *Très Riches Heures du duc de
Berry*, Chantilly, *Musée Condé*, MS 65 (1284),
fol. 34r. *Giraudon.*

51. Everyman seeking Profit. By Peter Bruegel the Elder (1525/30–1569), Flemish, about 1558. Later than the play of *Everyman* and illustrating a Flemish proverb, this nevertheless depicts what the play warns against.

52. Death in True Piety, from *Ars Moriendi,* Netherlandish block-book, 1466. The soul of the penitent received into Heaven by the mediation of Christ, with Mary, John, and Mary Magdalene below the Cross. The confessor places a candle in the dying man's hand, while the frustrated devils exclaim in fury and despair.

53. The Miracles of the Cherry Tree and the Corn-field. See "Cherry-Tree Carol." The cornfield be-low is a reference to a miracle that enabled Joseph, Mary, and the Christ Child to escape their pursuers on the Flight into Egypt. By Jean Colombe c. 1485; from the Très Riches Heures *du duc de Berry*, Chantilly, *Musée Condé*, MS 65 (1284), fol. 57r. *Giraudon*.

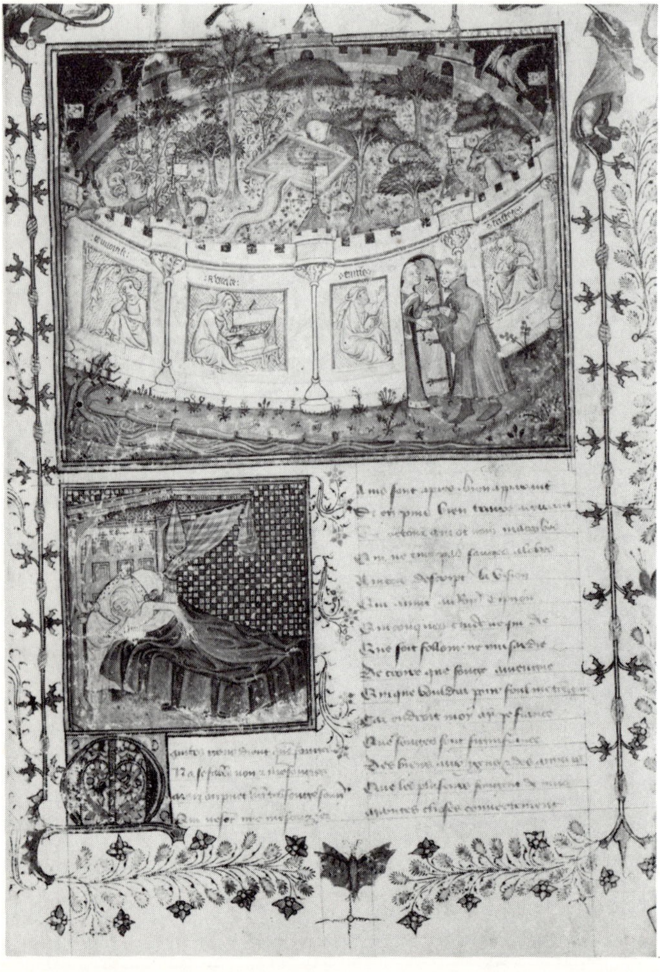

54. The Garden of the *Romance of the Rose.* French, 15th century. The Dreamer asleep (be-low) and the Lover admitted by Idleness into the Garden (above); Covetousness, Avarice, Envy, Sorrow, on the walls; Danger (Stand-offishness) with a club inside; Narcissus at the fountain in the center. *British Museum,* MS Egerton 1069, fol. 1r.

55. *Mappa mundi* (mappemonde), from Jean Mansel, *La Fleur des histoires*. Flemish, c. 1455. Brussels, *Bibliothèque Royale*, MS 9231, fol. 281v.

Other maps are much more detailed. This is more schematic and decorative than utilitarian: it shows earth surrounded by the other elements (water, air, and fire) in concentric circles, and the starry heaven outside them. As usual, the East is at the top with the phoenix in the woods of Paradise, Noah's Ark on Mt. Ararat, and the sons of Noah (from whom post-diluvial man is sprung) on the three then-known continents: Sem on Asia, Ham (Cham) on Africa, and Japhet on Europe.

56. Paradise. By the Brothers Limbourg; from the *Très Riches Heures du duc de Berry*, Chantilly, *Musée Condé*, MS 65 (1284), fol. 25v. *Giraudon.*

Paradise, high in the mountains, walled with the Fountain of Life at the center; Eve tempted by the Serpent "with a lady visage"; Eve tempting Adam; Adam pointing to Eve as the source of the trouble as God rebukes them; the Expulsion by the fiery angel.

And ofté tyme to be widwe and wedde.
Somme seydé, that our hertés been most esed,
Whan that we been yflatered and yplesed.
He gooth ful ny the sothe,⸲ I wol nat lye;   *truth*
A man shal winne us best with flaterye;
And with attendance, and with bisinesse,⸲   *assiduity*
940 Been we ylyméd,⸲ bothé more and lesse.   *ensnared*
   And sommé seyn, how that we loven best
For to be free, and do right as us lest,⸲   *it pleases*
And that no man repreve⸲ us of our vyce,   *reprove*
But seye that we be wyse, and no thing nyce.⸲   *silly*
For trewély, ther is noon of us alle,
If any wight wol clawe us on the galle,⸲   *sore place*
That we nil kiké,⸲ for⸲ he seith us sooth;   *kick / since*
Assay, and he shal finde it that so dooth.
For be we never so vicioùs withinne,
950 We wol⸲ been holden⸲ wyse, and clene of sinne.   *want / thought*
   And sommé seyn, that greet delyt han we
For to ben holden stable and eek secree,°
And in o purpos stedefastly to dwelle,
And nat biwreyé⸲ thing that men us telle.   *disclose*
But that tale is nat worth a raké-stele;⸲   *rake-handle*
Pardee, we wommen conné nothing hele;⸲   *hide*
Witnesse on Myda;° wol ye here the tale?
   Ovyde, amongés othercé thingés smale,
Seyde, Myda hadde, under his longé heres,
960 Growinge upon his heed two asses eres,
The which vycé⸲ he hidde, as he best mighte,   *defect*
Ful subtilly⸲ from every mannés sighte,   *cleverly*
That, save his wyf, ther wiste of it namo.⸲   *no more*
He loved hir most, and trusted hir also;
He preyéde hir, that to no creätùre
She sholdé tellen of his disfigùre.⸲   *disfigurement*
   She swoor him 'nay, for al this world to winne,
She noldé do that vileinye or sinne,
To make hir housbond han so foul a name;
970 She nolde nat telle it for hir owene shame.'
But nathélees, hir thoughté⸲ that she dyde,⸲   *it seemed / was dying*
That she so longé sholde a conseil⸲ hyde;   *secret*
Hir thoughte it swal⸲ so sore aboute hir herte,   *swelled*
That nedély som word hir moste asterte;°
And sith she dorste telle it to no man,
Doun to a mareys fasté⸲ by she ran;   *marsh close*
Til she came there, hir herté was afyre,

For . . . secree to be thought stable and discreet
Myda See Ovid, *Metamorphoses* XI. 174–93.
Midas, King of Phrygia, had been given asses'
ears by Apollo because he thought the music
of Pan's pipes superior to that of the god's
lyre. In Ovid's story, he was actually betrayed
by his barber.
nedely . . . asterte necessarily some word must
escape her

And, as a bitore bombleth in the myre,°

She leyde hir mouth unto the water doun:

980 'Biwreye me nat, thou water, with thy soun,'   *betray / sound*

Quod she, 'to thee I telle it, and namo;'   *no other*

Myn housbond hath longe asses erès two!

Now is myn herte all hool, now is it oute;   *whole*

I mighte no lenger kepe it, out of doute.'

Heer may ye se, thogh we a tyme abyde,

Yet out it moot, we can no conseil hyde;   *must*

The remenant of the tale if ye wol here,

Redeth Ovyde, and ther ye may it lere.'   *learn*

    This knight, of which my tale is specially,

990 Whan that he saugh he mighte nat come therby,   *saw*

This is to seye, what wommen loven moost,

Withinne his brest ful sorweful was the goost;'   *spirit*

But hoom he gooth, he mightè nat sojourne.'   *stay*

The day was come, that hoomward moste he tourne,   *must*

And in his wey it happèd him to ryde,

In al this care, under a forest syde,   *by*

Wheras he saugh upon a daunce go

Of ladies foure and twenty, and yet mo;

Toward the whichè daunce he drow ful yerne,°

1000 In hopè that som wisdom sholde he lerne.

But certeinly, er he came fully there,

Vanisshed was this daunce, he nistè where.   *knew not*

No creatùrè saugh he that bar lyf,   *bore*

Save on the grene he saugh sittinge a wyf;'   *woman*

A fouler wight ther may no man devyse.'   *creature / imagine*

Agayn the knight this oldè wyf gan ryse,   *before*

And seyde, 'Sir knight, heer-forth ne lyth no wey.'   *lies / road*

Tel me, what that ye seken, by your fey?'   *faith*

Paraventure it may the bettre be;

1010 Thise oldè folk can muchel thing,' quod she.   *know much*

    'My levè mooder,' quod this knight, certeyn,   *dear mother*

'I nam but deed, but if that I can seyn   *am*

What thing it is that wommen most desyre;

Coude ye me wisse, I wolde wel quyte your hyre.'°

    'Plighte me thy trouthe, heer in myn hand,' quod she,

'The nextè thing that I requerè thee,   *ask*

Thou shalt it do, if it lye in thy might;

And I wol telle it yow er it be night.'

'Have heer my trouthè,' quod the knight, 'I grante.'

1020   'Thannè,' quod she, 'I dar me wel avante,'   *boast*

Thy lyf is sauf, for I wol stonde therby,   *safe*

---

bitore . . . myre A bittern makes a booming sound in the mud. The bittern, a kind of small heron, was thought to make its characteristic bellowing cry by plunging its beak into the mud.

drow . . . yerne approached very eagerly
Coude . . . hyre if you could make me know, I would pay you a good reward for it

Upon my lyf, the queen wol seye as I.
Lat see which is the proudeste of hem alle,
That wereth on a coverchief or a calle,°
That dar seye nay, of that I shal thee teche;
Lat us go forth withouten lenger speche.'
Tho rounèd she a pistel in his ere,°
And bad him to be glad, and have no fere.
    Whan they be comen to the court, this knight
1030 Seyde, 'He had holde his day, as he hadde hight,⸃   *promised*
And redy was his answere,' as he sayde.
Ful many a noble wyf, and many a mayde,
And many a widwe, for that they ben wyse,
The quene hirself sittinge as a justyse,
Assembled been, his answere for to here;
And afterward this knight was bode⸃ appere.   *bidden*
    To every wight commanded was silènce,
And that the knight sholde telle in audience,°
What thing that worldly wommen loven best.
1040 This knight ne stood nat stille⸃ as doth a best,⸃   *silent / beast*
But to his questioùn anon answerde
With manly voys, that al the court it herde:
    'My ligè⸃ lady, generally,' quod he,   *liege*
'Wommen desyren to have sovereyntee⸃   *dominion*
As wel over hir housbond as hir love,
And for to been in maistrie him above;
This is your moste desyr, thogh ye me kille,
Doth as yow list, I am heer at your wille.'°
    In al the court ne was ther wyf ne mayde,
1050 Ne widwe, that contraried⸃ that he sayde,   *contradicted*
But seyden, 'He was worthy han⸃ his lyf.'   *to keep*
    And with that word up stirte⸃ the oldè wyf,   *started*
Which that the knight saugh sittinge in the grene:
'Mercy,' quod she, 'my sovereyn lady quene!
Er that your court departè, do me right.
I taughtè this answère unto the knight;
For which he plightè me his trouthè there,
The firstè thing I wolde of him requere,
He wolde it do, if it lay in his might.
1060 Bifore the court than preye I thee, sir knight,'
Quod she, 'that thou me take unto thy wyf;
For wel thou wost⸃ that I have kept⸃ thy lyf.   *knowest / saved*
If I sey fals, sey nay, upon thy fey!'
    This knight answerde, 'Allas! and weylawey!

That . . . calle that wears upon her head-
covering or caul; the caul was a close-fitting
netted cap or headdress
Tho rouned . . . ere then she whispered a short
lesson (epistle) in his ear

in audience in formal hearing
thogh . . . wille even if you kill me (for saying it), do as pleases you, I am at your
disposal here

I woot right wel that swich was my biheste.˃   *promise*
For Goddès love, as chees˃ a newe requeste;   *choose*
Tak al my good, and lat my body go.'
　'Nay than,' quod she, 'I shrewe˃ us bothè two!   *curse*
For thogh that I be foul, and old, and pore,
1070　I nolde for al the metal, ne for ore,
That under erthe is grave,˃ or lyth˃ above,   *buried / lies*
But if thy wyf I were, and eek thy love.'
　'My love?' quod he; 'nay, my dampnacioùn!˃   *damnation*
Allas! that any of my nacioùn°
Sholde ever so foulè disparàgèd˃ be!'   *disgraced*
But al for noght, the ende is this, that he
Constreynèd˃ was, he nedès moste hir wedde;   *forced*
And taketh his olde wyf, and gooth to bedde.
　Now wolden som men seye, paraventùre,
1080　That, for my necligence, I do no cure°
To tellen yow the joye and al th'array°
That at the festè was that ilkè day.
To whichè thing shortly answere I shal;
I seye, ther nas no joye ne feste at al,
Ther nas but hevinesse and muchè sorwe;
For privèly he wedded hir on a morwe,˃   *morning*
And al day after hidde him as an oule;
So wo was him, his wyf lookèd so foule.
　Greet was the wo the knight hadde in his thoght,
1090　Whan he was with his wyf abedde ybroght;
He walweth,˃ and he turneth to and fro.   *tosses*
His oldè wyf lay smylinge evermo,
And seyde, 'O derè housbond, Benedicitè!˃   *bless me*
Fareth˃ every knight thus with his wyf as ye?   *behaves*
Is this the lawe of King Arthùrès hous?
Is every knight of his so dangerous?˃   *unapproachable*
I am your owenè love and eek your wyf;
I am she, which that savèd hath your lyf;
And certès, yet dide I yow never unright;
1100　Why fare ye thus with me this firstè night?
Ye faren lyk a man had lost his wit;
What is my gilt? for Goddes love, tel me it,
And it shal been amended, if I may.'
　'Amended?' quod this knight, 'allas! nay, nay!
It wol nat been amended never mo!
Thou art so loothly,˃ and so old also,   *hateful*
And therto comen of so lowe a kinde,˃   *nature*
That litel wonder is, thogh I walwe and winde.˃   *toss and turn*
So woldè God myn hertè woldè breste!'˃   *break*

nacioùn birth; i.e. family   th'array the arrangements, special preparations
for . . . cure because of my negligence, I do
not take the trouble

1110   'Is this,' quod she, 'the cause of your unreste?'
'Ye, certainly,' quod he, 'no wonder is.'
'Now, sire,' quod she, 'I coude amende al this,
If that me liste, er it were dayės three,
So wel ye mightė bere yow° unto me.
But for ye speken of swich gentillesse°
As is descended out of old richesse,
That therfore sholden ye be gentil men,
Swich arrogàncė is nat worth an hen.
Loke who that is most vertuous alway,

1120   Privee and apert,° and most entendeth ay°
To do the gentil dedės that he can,
And tak him for the grettest⟩ gentil man.   *greatest*
Crist wol,⟩ we clayme of him our gentillesse,   *wishes that*
Nat of our eldrės for hir old richesse.°
For thogh they yeve us al hir heritage,
For which we clayme to been of heigh parage,⟩   *descent*
Yet may they nat biquethė, for nothing,
To noon of us hir vertuous living,
That made hem gentil men ycallėd be;

1130   And bad us folwen hem in swich degree.°
    Wel can the wysė poete of Florènce,
That hightė⟩ Dant,° speken in this sentènce;⟩   *is called / wisdom*
Lo in swich maner rym is Dantės tale:
"Ful seldė⟩ up ryseth by his branches smale   *seldom*
Prowesse⟩ of man, for God, of his goodnesse,   *excellence*
Wol that of him we clayme our gentillesse";
For of our eldrės may we nothing clayme
But temporel thing, that man may hurte and mayme.
    Eek every wight wot this as wel as I,

1140   If gentillesse were planted naturelly
Unto a certeyn linage, doun the lyne,
Privee ne apert, than wolde they never fyne⟩   *cease*
To doon of gentillesse the faire offyce;⟩   *function*
They mightė do no vileinye or vyce.°
    Tak fyr,⟩ and ber⟩ it in the derkeste hous   *fire / bear*
Bitwix this and the mount of Caucasus,°
And lat men shette⟩ the dorės and go thenne;⟩   *shut / thence*
Yet wol the fyr as fairė lye° and brenne,⟩   *burn*
As twenty thousand men mighte it biholde;

bere yow behave
gentillesse gentleness, noble kindness; see Chaucer's poem below
Privee and apert in private and in public
entendeth ay always sets himself
Nat . . . richesse not from our ancestors, because of their ancient wealth
And . . . degree and they commanded us to follow them to that state
Dant Dante. The quotation is from his *Purgatorio* VII.121 ff. and emphasizes that gentillesse is not the inevitable result of noble blood and "old richesse."
If gentillesse . . . vyce (ll. 1140–44) If gentillesse were naturally implanted in a family and merely transmitted from father to son, then none of that family could ever do evil.
Caucasus i.e. to the furthest, coldest, and darkest of places
lye blaze; i.e. it is the nature of fire to be bright and warm, whether we are looking at it or not

His office naturel° ay wol it holde,
Up˃ peril of my lyf, til that it dye. — *upon*
Heer may ye see wel, how that genterye°
Is nat annexėd˃ to possessioùn,° — *tied*
Sith folk ne doon hir operacioùn
Alwey, as dooth the fyr, lo! in his kinde.˃ — *nature*
For, God it woot, men may wel often finde
A lordės sone˃ do shame and vileinye; — *son*
And he that wol han prys of his gentrye°
For he was boren˃ of a gentil hous, — *born*
And hadde hise eldrės noble and vertuous,
And nil himselven do no gentil dedis,
Ne folwe his gentil auncestre that deed˃ is, — *dead*
He nis nat gentil, be he duk or erl;
For vileyns sinful dedės make a cherl.
For gentillessė nis but renomee˃ — *renown*
Of thyne auncestres, for hir heigh bountee,°
Which is a strangė˃ thing to thy persone. — *foreign*
Thy gentillessė cometh fro God allone;
Than comth our verray gentillesse of grace,
It was nothing biquethe us with our place.
Thenketh how noble, as seith Valerius,°
Was thilkė Tullius Hostilius,°
That out of povert˃ roos to heigh noblesse. — *poverty*
Redeth Senek,° and redeth eek Boëce,°
Ther shul ye seen expres that it no drede˃ is, — *doubt*
That he is gentil that doth gentil dedis;
And therfore, leve˃ housbònd, I thus conclude, — *dear*
Al˃ were it that myne auncestres were rude,˃ — *although / lowly*
Yet may the hyė God, and so hope I,
Grantė me grace to liven vertuously.
Thanne am I gentil, whan that I biginne
To liven vertuously and weyvė˃ sinne. — *leave off*
And theras ye of povert me repreve,
The hyė God, on whom that we bileve,
In wilful˃ povert chees˃ to live his lyf. — *voluntary / chose*
And certės every man, mayden, or wyf,
May understonde that Jesus, Hevenė king,
Ne wolde nat chese a vicioùs living.
Glad povert is an honest˃ thing, certèyn; — *honorable*
This wol Senek and otherė clerkės seyn.

office naturel the function which belongs to it by nature
genterye noble conduct, gentilesse
possessioun worldly riches, hereditary wealth
he . . . gentrye he that wants to have reputation on account of gentle birth
For . . . bountee what you claim as your nobility is only due to your ancestors, because of their great goodness
Valerius Valerius Maximus, 1st century A.D. Roman author of a book of *exempla* for rhetoricians
Tullius Hostilius Tullus Hostilius, the third king of Rome, 673–642 B.C., who began life as a shepherd, according to the story, and is used by Valerius as an example of rags-to-riches
Senek Lucius Annaeus Seneca, *c.*5 B.C.–65 A.D., Roman Stoic philosopher and dramatist; see his *Moral Epistles* 44
Boëce Boethius

Whoso that halt him payd of° his poverte,
I holde him riche, al hadde he nat a sherte.⸃   *shirt*
He that coveyteth is a povrė wight,°
For he wolde han that is nat in his might.
But he that noght hath, ne covèyteth have,
Is riche, although ye holde him but a knave.
   Verray⸃ povert, it singeth proprely;⸃   *true / appropriately*
Juvenal seith of povert merily:
"The povrė man, whan he goth by the weye,
1200 Bifore the thevės he may singe and pleye."°
Povert is hateful good, and, as I gesse,
A ful greet bringer out of bisiness;°
A greet amender eek of sapience⸃   *wisdom*
To him that taketh it in pacience.
Povert is this, although it seme elenge:⸃   *hard to bear*
Possessioùn, that no wight wol chalenge.⸃   *claim*
Povert ful oftė, whan a man is lowe,
Maketh° his God and eek himself to knowe.
Povert a spectacle⸃ is, as thinketh me,   *eyeglass*
1210 Thurgh which he may his verray frendės see.
And therfore, sire, sin that I noght⸃ yow greve,   *ought not*
Of my povert namore ye me repreve.⸃   *reproach*
   Now, sire, of eldė⸃ ye prevė me;   *old age*
And certės, sire, thogh noon auctoritee
Were in no book, ye gentils of honour
Seyn that men sholde an old wight doon favour,
And clepe him fader,⸃ for your gentillesse;   *father*
And auctours⸃ shal I finden, as I gesse.   *authorities*
   Now ther ye seye, that I am foul and old,
1220 Than drede you noght to been a cokėwold;⸃   *cuckold*
For filthe and eldė, also moot I thee,°
Been gretė wardeyns⸃ upon chastitee.   *guardians*
But nathelees, sin I knowe your delyt,
I shal fulfille your worldly appetyt.
   Chese now,' quod she, 'oon of thise thingės tweye,
To han me foul and old til that I deye,
And be to yow a trewė humble wyf,
And never yow displese in al my lyf,
Or ellės ye wol han me yong and fair,
1230 And take your aventure⸃ of the repair°   *chance*
That shal be to your hous, bycause of me,
Or in som other placė, may wel be.
Now chese yourselven, whether⸃ that yow lyketh.'   *which*

Whoso . . . of whoever is contented with
He . . . wight he that covets more money is a
poor person, i.e. the true pauper
Juvenal . . . pleye Juvenal, *Satire* X. 22
bisinesse Preoccupations. Most of these definitions are taken ultimately from the favorite
medieval moral text, *Hadrian and Epictetus*,
an apocryphal dialogue between the Emperor
and the Philosopher. Chaucer probably got
them from the 13th-century encyclopedist
Vincent of Beauvais.
Maketh makes him
also . . . thee as I may thrive
repair frequenting, resort

This knight avyseth him° and soré syketh,°   *considers / sighs*
But atté laste he seyde in this manere,
'My lady and my love, and wyf so dere,
I put me in your wysé governance;
Cheseth° yourself, which may be most plesance,°   *choose / pleasure*
And most honour to yow and me also.
1240   I do no fors the whether° of the two;
For as yow lyketh,° it suffiseth° me.'   *it pleases / satisfies*
    'Thanne have I gete° of yow maistrye,' quod she,   *got*
'Sin I may chese, and governe as me lest?'°   *pleases*
    'Ye, certés, wyf,' quod he, 'I holde it best.'
    'Kis me,' quod she, 'we be no lenger wrothe;
For, by my trouthe, I wol be to yow bothe,
This is to seyn, ye, bothé fair and good.
I prey to God that I mot sterven wood,°
But° I to yow be also° good and trewe   *unless / as*
1250   As ever was wyf, sin that the world was newe.
And, but I be to morn° as fair to sene   *tomorrow morning*
As any lady, emperyce, or quene,
That is bitwixe the est and eke the west,
Doth with my lyf and deeth right as yow lest.
Cast up the curtin, loke how that it is.'
    And whan the knight saugh verraily al this,
That she so fair was, and so yong therto,
For joye he hente° hir in his armés two,   *took*
His herté bathéd in a bath of blisse;
1260   A thousand tyme arewe° he gan hir kisse.   *in succession*
And she obeyéd him in every thing
That mighté doon him plesance° or lyking.°   *happiness / pleasure*
    And thus they live, unto hir lyvés ende,
In parfit° joye; and Jesu Crist us sende   *perfect*
Housbondes meké, yonge, and fresshe abedde,
And grace t'overbyde° hem that we wedde.   *outlast*
And eek I preyé Jesu shorte° hir lyves   *shorten*
That wol nat be govérnéd by hir wyves;
And olde and angry nigardes of dispence,°   *paying*
1270   God sende hem soné° verray° pestilence.   *at once / true*

    Here endeth the Wyves Tale of Bathe

From Gesta Romanorum

    Of Hanging

Valerius tells us that a man named Paletinus one day burst into a flood of
tears; and, calling his son and his neighbours around him, said, 'Alas! alas! I
have now growing in my garden a fatal tree, on which my first poor wife hung
herself, then my second, and after that my third. Have I not therefore cause

I . . . whether I do not care which   mot . . . wood may die crazy for the wretchedness I exhibit?' 'Truly,' said one who was called Arrius, 'I marvel that you should weep at such an unusual instance of good fortune! Give me, I pray you, two or three sprigs of that gentle tree, which I will divide with my neighbours, and thereby afford every man an opportunity of indulging the laudable wishes of his spouse.' Paletinus complied with his friend's request; and ever after found this remarkable tree the most productive part of his estate.

Application

My beloved, the tree is the cross of Christ. The man's three wives are, pride, lusts of the heart, and lusts of the eyes, which ought to be thus suspended and destroyed. He who solicited a part of the tree is any good Christian.

The Franklin's Prologue and Tale

The Franklin's Tale is about *gentilesse,* true nobility and virtue (see Chaucer's short poem of that title). It explores the relation between *trouthe,* or integrity, the central notion of the short "balade of good counsel" and the keeping of an oath, which is part of *gentilesse;* and demonstrates how *fredom,* or generosity, if exercised by all those involved in a situation, will bring it to good issue. Perhaps Chaucer means to suggest, in the Franklin's preoccupation with the idea, a sense of the social position he occupies as a member of the rising country gentry, aspiring to the aristocracy.

According to the Franklin, his tale is an old "Breton lay," a literary genre first popularized in twelfth-century France as a short narrative romance in verse, usually on a theme of love, promises, and magical occurrences. Though many of the motifs of the tale occur in extant lays, the exact source of Chaucer's tale has not been discovered—and even the exact placing of the scene in a locality in Brittany paradoxically tells against it. There are extant fourteenth-century English poems of the "lay" type, but the form was at that date somewhat old-fashioned. Chaucer may be giving us some suggestion of the kind of man the Franklin was by putting into his mouth an out-of-date form set in the long ago.

The plot of the tale is probably taken either from Boccaccio's *Il Filocolo* or from his *Decameron* (it appears in both works); but the germ of the story goes back very much farther in time and can be found in a widely diffused Eastern folk-tale in which a woman's unconsidered promise to a second lover puts her in the same embarrassing position as Dorigen. Her first lover advises her to keep her promise, and her second then releases her from it. The question is asked, as it is in Boccaccio, which of the three showed the greatest generosity.

Chaucer's treatment of the story, with the mass of astrological and magical detail laid onto, but never obscuring, the delicate articulation of its central moral content, is not the statement of a question about love (*questione d'amore*). It is an exploration of the basis of marriage, refining some of the questions that have already been raised by the Wife of Bath, the Clerk, and the Merchant. Dorigen, opting for love in marriage of the most idealistic kind, is brought to realize that virtue is not single and cannot be exercised in isolation, so that virtues may come into conflict with each other as well as with vices.

Prologue

The Prologe of the Frankeleyns Tale

Thise oldė gentil Britons in hir dayes
Of diverse adventùrės maden layes,
Rymeyėd in hir firstė Briton tonge;°
Which layės with hir instruments they songe,
Or ellės redden˃ hem for hir pleasunce;˃   *read / pleasure*
And oon of hem have I in remembraùnce,
Which I shal seyn with good wil as I can.

    But, sirės, bycause I am a burel˃ man,   *plain*
At my biginning first I yow biseche
10 Have me excusėd of my rudė speche;°
I lernėd never rethoryk, certeyn;
Thing that I speke, it moot˃ be bare and pleyn.   *must*
I sleep never on the mount of Pernaso,°
Ne lernėd Marcus Tullius Cithero.°
Coloùrs ne knowe I none, withouten drede,°
But swiche˃ coloùrs as growen in the mede˃,   *such / meadow*
Or ellės swiche as men dye or peynte.
Coloùrs of rethoryk ben me to queynte;˃   *ingenious*
My spirit feeleth noght of swich matere
20 But if yow list,˃ my talė shul ye here.   *it pleases*

Thise . . . tonge (ll. 1–3) These noble old Bretons, in their own day, made lays about various happenings, written in rhyme in their earliest Breton language.
rude speche This is the conventional Chaucerian disclaimer, in an age where ornateness and enrichment of the language was highly thought of, whether the poet speaks in his own person or through the mouth of one of his characters. The Franklin speaks as a good plain man, who never knew rhetoric. As so often in Chaucer, the character is here made to protest his unfitness as an orator by using the exact form in which a skilled orator would do the same thing: *diminution* of oneself, to begin; then varying of the theme (ll. 10–19); with elegant circumlocution in the oblique references to poetry; and a play on the word *color* (ornament of style / natural color / artificial color), a figure of speech known as *adnomination*.

The Franklin uses a slightly stiff and elaborate rhetoric for his higher-flown moments, but in general his narrative is direct.
Pernaso Parnassus, the double-peaked mountain in Phocis, Greece; sacred to Apollo, god of music and poetry; to his servants the nine Muses, daughters of Memory and guardians of poetry, music, dance, and learning; and to Dionysus (Bacchus), god of wine and song. Chaucer took the bit about sleeping on Parnassus (and the exact form of the word) from the Roman satirist Persius (34–62 A.D.): it was a very popular quotation.
Cithero Marcus Tullius Cicero (106–43 B.C.), the Roman statesman and writer, the best-known and most used of all classical rhetoricians in the Middle Ages. So, says the Franklin, I am eloquent in neither poetry nor prose.
withouten drede conventional oral formula: "without fear," hence, "certainly"

Tale

In Armorik,° that callèd is Britayne,
Ther was a knight that loved and dide his payne°
To serve a lady in his bestè wyse;˃   *manner*
And many a labour, many a greet empryse˃   *enterprise*
He for his lady wroghte,˃ er she were wonne.   *did*
For she was oon the faireste° under sonne,
And eek˃ therto come of so heigh kinrede,˃   *also / ancestry*
That wel unnethès dorste˃ this knight, for drede,   *hardly dared*
Telle hir his wo, his peyne, and his distresse.
30 But attè laste, she, for his worthinesse,
And namely˃ for his meke obeÿsaùnce,˃   *especially / obedience*
Hath swich a pitee caught of his penaùnce,
That privèly˃ she fil of his accord   *secretly*
To take him for hir housbonde and hir lord,
Of swich lordshipe as men han over hir wyves.
And for to lede the more in blisse hir lyves,
Of his free will he swoor hir as a knight,
That never in al his lyf he, day ne night,
Ne sholde upon him takè no maistrye°
40 Agayn hir wil, ne kythe˃ hir jalousye,   *show*
But hir obeye, and folwe hir will in all
As any lovere to his lady shall;
Save that the name of soveraynètee,
That wolde he have for shame of his degree.°
    She thankèd him, and with ful greet humblesse˃   *meekness*
She seyde: 'Sire, sith˃ of your gentillesse°   *since*
Ye profre˃ me to have so large˃ a reyne,   *offer / loose*
Ne woldè never God bitwixe us tweyne,
As in my gilt,˃ were outher˃ werre or stryf.   *responsibility / either*
50 Sir, I wol be your humble trewè wyf,
Have heer my trouthe, til that myn hertè breste.˃   *break*
Thus been they bothe in quiete and in reste.
    For o thing, sirès, saufly˃ dar I seye,˃   *confidently / say*
That frendès everich˃ other moot˃ obeye,   *each / must*
If they wol longè holden˃ companye.   *keep*
Love wol nat ben constreynèd by maistrye;

Armorik Armorica (*Ar vor*, land by the sea) was the old name for Brittany, before, so the legend goes, it was named Little Britain "beyond the sea," to emphasize its links with Greater Britain. Chaucer uses this bit of recondite, ancient information to enhance the "once upon a time" atmosphere of the Franklin's romance of magic and true nobility.
payne The hero's pains, service, and undertakings for the lady; the woe, pain and distress he suffers in silence because he loves her; and his entire submission, mark him as the courtly lover.

oon the faireste either "one of the most beautiful" or "the most beautiful"
no maistrye i.e. his love would tame his natural masculine desire for domination, mastery
Save . . . degree only that he wished to have the title of ruler, so as not to bring shame on his status (as a husband); love might make them equal, but the ordinary and courtly appearances must be kept up
gentillesse magnanimous behavior becoming a man of true nobility in birth and feeling; it is self, not birth, that is important

Whan maistrie comth, the god of love anon
Beteth⸥ hise winges, and farewel! he is gon!   *beats*
Love is a thing as any spirit free;
60 Wommen of kinde⸥ desiren libertee,   *nature*
And nat to ben constreynėd as a thral;⸥   *slave*
And so don men, if I soth⸥ seyen shal.⸥   *truth / must*
Loke who that is most pacient in love,
He is at his avantage al above.
Pacience is an heigh vertù, certeyn,
For it venquisseth, as thise clerkės seyn,°
Thingės that rigour sholdė never atteyne.
For every word men may nat chyde or pleyne.
Lerneth to suffre, or elles, so moot I goon,
70 Ye shul it lerne, wherso ye wole or noon.°
For in this world, certein, ther no wight is,
That he ne dooth or seith somtyme amis.
Irė, siknesse, or constellacioùn,°
Wyn,⸥ wo, or chaunginge of complexioùn⸥   *wine / constitution*
Causeth ful ofte to doon amis or speken.
On every wrong a man may nat be wreken.⸥   *revenged*
After⸥ the tymė,⸥ moste be temperaunce   *according to / occasion*
To every wight that can on⸥ governaunce.   *is wise in*
And therfore hath this wysė worthy knight,
80 To live in esė, suffrance⸥ hir bihight,⸥   *permission / promised*
And she to him ful wisly⸥ gan to⸥ swere   *firmly / did*
That never sholde ther be defaute° in here.⸥   *her*
    Heer may men seen an humble wys accord;
Thus hath she take hir servant and hir lord,°
Servant in love, and lord in mariàge;
Than was he bothe in lordship and servage;
Servage? nay, but in lordshipe above,
Sith he hath bothe his lady and his love;
His lady, certės,⸥ and his wyf also,   *indeed*
90 The which that⸥ lawe of love acordeth⸥ to.   *who / agrees*
And whan he was in this prosperitee,⸥   *happiness*
Hoom with his wyf he gooth to his contree,
Nat fer fro Penmark,° ther his dwelling was,
Wheras he liveth in blisse and in solas.⸥   *comfort*
    Who coudė telle, but⸥ he had wedded be,   *unless*

Pacience . . . seyn a glance at the Clerk's Tale of the patient Griselda, with overtones from the Bible (Proverbs 16:32; James 1:4), and at such collections of moral precepts for schools as the *Distichs of Cato* (see the Miller's Tale, l. 119)
Lerneth . . . noon learn to bear things, or else, as true as I walk, you will have to learn it, whether you want to or not
constellacioun the combination of the planets, at any given time, was thought to influence every aspect of earthly life
defaute anything lacking

servant . . . lord The knight's love is better than love within the courtly conventions, for he has the best of both worlds, his mistress also being his wife.
Penmark Penmarc'h just south of Brest, in Brittany; its headland, like much of the coast of Brittany, has a rocky shore, with a chain of granite rocks out to sea. Chaucer may have seen the place or heard it described, since the rocks of Brittany were proverbial, and lay on a much-used trade route.

The joye, the ese, and the prosperitee
That is bitwixe an housbonde and his wyf?
A yeer and more lasted his blisful lyf,
Til that the knight of which I speke of thus,
100 That of Kayrrud° was cleped⁷ Arveragus,°   *called*
Shoop⁷ him to goon, and dwelle a yeer or tweyne⁷   *arranged / two*
In Engelond, that cleped was eek⁷ Briteyne,°   *also*
To seeke in armes worship and honour;
For al his lust⁷ he sette in swich labour;   *pleasure*
And dwelled ther two yeer, the book seith thus.
    Now wol I stinte⁷ of this Arveragus,   *cease*
And speken I wole of Dorigene° his wyf,
That loveth hir housbonde as hir hertes lyf.
For his absence wepeth she and syketh,⁷   *sighs*
110 As doon thise noble wyves° whan hem lyketh.⁷   *it pleases*
She moorneth,⁷ waketh, waileth, fasteth, pleyneth;⁷ *mourns / complains*
Desyr of his presence hir so distreyneth,⁷   *constrains*
That al this wyde world she sette⁷ at noght.   *valued*
Hir frendes, whiche that knewe hir hevy thoght,
Conforten hir in al that ever they may;
They prechen hir, they telle hir night and day,
That causelees she sleeth⁷ hirself, allas!   *is killing*
And every confort possible in this cas
They doon to hir with al hir bisinesse,⁷   *diligence*
120 Al for to make hir leve hir hevinesse.
    By proces,⁷ as ye knowen everichoon,⁷   *gradually / everyone*
Men may so longe graven⁷ in a stoon,°   *engrave*
Til som figure therinne emprented⁷ be.   *imprinted*
So longe han they conforted hir, til she
Receyved hath, by hope and by resoun,⁷   *reason*
The emprenting of hir consolacioun,
Thurgh which hir grete sorwe gan aswage;⁷   *diminish*
She may nat alwey duren⁷ in swich rage.⁷   *endure / great grief sorrow*
    And eek Arveragus, in al this care,⁷
130 Hath sent hir lettres hoom of his welfare,
And that he wol come hastily⁷ agayn;   *soon*
Or elles hadde this sorwe hir herte slayn.
    Hir freendes sawe hir sorwe gan to slake,⁷   *slacken*
And preyede hir on knees, for Goddes sake,

Kayrrud A Celtic name, *kaer* is a fortified place; *rud* may mean red. The name does not occur near Penmarc'h.
Arveragus Latinized form of a Celtic name; Chaucer may have taken it from Geoffrey of Monmouth's 12th-century chronicle (*Historia Regum Britanniae*), where the name of Aurelius also occurs. Some scholars have suggested that Chaucer found the idea for this tale in the chronicle, but the evidence is inconclusive.
Briteyne See l. 21.
Dorigene a Breton name

For . . . wyves The Squire had already told a story involving a wife's grief at separation, reinforcing some remarks in the tale of his father, the Knight.
graven . . . stoon Chaucer refines the image which he probably found in Boccaccio. Constant dripping wears away a stone, as Boccaccio says, but in this courtly context the patience and delicacy needed by the gem-engraver are paralleled by the same qualities in Dorigen's friends when they try to console her. This is the atmosphere of the poem.

To come and romen⸱ hir in companye,   *go about*
Awey to dryve hir derkė fantasye.⸱   *gloomy imaginings*
And finally, she grauntėd that requeste;
For wel she saugh⸱ that it was for the beste.   *saw*
 Now stood hir castel fastė by the see,
140 And often with hir freendės walketh she
Hir to disporte upon the bank on heigh,
Wheras she many a ship and bargė seigh.⸱   *saw*
Seilinge⸱ hir cours, wheras hem listė⸱ go;   *sailing / it pleased*
But than was that a parcel⸱ of hir wo.   *part*
For to hirself ful ofte 'Allas!' seith she,
'Is ther no ship, of so manye as I see,
Wol bringen hom my lord? than were myn herte
Al warisshed⸱ of his bittre peynės smerte.⸱'   *cured / sharp*
 Another tyme ther wolde she sitte and thinke,
150 And caste hir eyen dounward fro the brinke.
But whan she saugh the grisly rokkės blake,°
For verray fere so wolde hir hertė quake,
That on hir feet she mighte hir noght sustene.⸱   *sustain*
Than wolde she sitte adoun upon the grene,
And pitously⸱ into the see biholde,   *pitifully*
And seyn⸱ right thus, with sorweful sykės⸱ colde: *say / sighs*
'Eternė God, that thurgh thy purveyaùnce⸱   *foreknowledge*
Ledest the world by certein governaùnce,
In ydel,⸱ as men seyn, ye nothing make;   *vain*
160 But, Lord, thise grisly feendly⸱ rokkės blake,   *hostile*
That semen rather a foul confusioùn
Of werk than any fair creacioùn
Of swich a parfit wys God and a stable,⸱   *sure*
Why han ye wroght this werk unresonable?
For by this werk, south, north, ne west, ne eest,
Ther nis yfostrėd⸱ man, ne brid,⸱ ne beest;   *helped / bird*
It dooth no good, to my wit,⸱ but anoyeth.⸱   *knowledge / harms*
See ye nat, Lord, how mankinde it destroyeth?
An hundred thousand bodies of mankinde
170 Han rokkės slayn, al be they nat in minde,⸱   *remembered*
Which mankinde is so fair part of thy werk
That thou it madest lyk to thyn owene merk.°
Than semėd it ye hadde a greet chiertee⸱   *love*
Toward mankinde; but how than may it be
That ye swiche menės⸱ make, it to destroyen,   *means*

rokkes blake Black rocks; Dorigen's meditation, in her sorrow at being parted from Arveragus, with its accumulation of evil and hellishness as she looks at the rocks, is on the theme of how a good Creator could bring himself to create sorrow, evil, and misshapenness. He must have known what He was about, since He has "purveyaunce" (l. 157): foreknowledge, providence. Boethius (born *c.*480 A.D.) explains this in *The Consolation of Philosophy*. The godhead, perfect and single, is outside all His creation, though it is He who keeps all creation in being. Everything, even the causes of things, have true existence only within God's mind and as far as they are part of the plan of the universe which is in His mind and is called Providence. See Romans 8:28ff.
merk Likeness, image (Genesis 1:27: "So God created man in his own image"). *Merk* originally meant the image or likeness on a coin.

Which menės do no good, but ever anoyen?° *hurt*
I woot wel clerkes wol seÿn, as hem leste,° *it pleases*
By arguments,° that al is for the beste,
Though I ne can the causes nat yknowe.
180 But thilkė God, that madė wind to blowe,
As kepe my lord!° this my conclusioùn;
To clerkės lete° I al disputisoùn.° *leave / dispute*
But woldė God that alle thise rokkės blake
Were sonken° into Hellė for his sake! *sunken*
Thise rokkės sleen myn hertė for the fere.° *fear*
Thus wolde she seyn, with many a pitous tere.

Hir freendės sawe that it was no disport° *pleasure*
To romen° by the see, but disconfòrt; *walk*
And shopen° for to pleyen° somwher elles. *arranged / amuse themselves*
190 They leden hir by riverės and by wellės,° *pools*
And eek in otherė places delitables;° *pleasant*
They dauncen, and they pleyen at ches and tables.°

So on a° day, right in the morwė° tyde, *one / morning*
Unto a gardin that was ther bisyde,
In which that they had maad hir ordinaùnce° *orders*
Of vitaille° and of other purveyaùnce,° *food / prearrangements*
They goon and pleye hem al the longė day.
And this was on the sixtė morwe of May,°
Which May had peynted with his softė shoures
200 This gardin° ful of levės and of floures;
And craft of mannės hand so curiously° *ingeniously*
Arrayėd° hadde this gardin, trewėly, *laid out*
That never was ther gardin of swich prys,° *excellence*
But if° it were the verray Paradys. *unless*
The odour of flourės and the fresshė sighte
Wolde han maad any hertė for to lighte° *lighten*
That ever was born, but if too gret siknesse,
Or too gret sorwe helde it in distresse;
So ful it was of beautee with plesaunce.
210 At after diner gonnė° they to daunce, *began*
And singe also, save Dorigen allone,
Which made alwey hir còmpleint and hir mone;° *moan*

---

arguments Arguments, causes, conclusions are all terms in Scholastic logic: a mild bit of sarcasm by Dorigen on "explainers."
But . . . lord but may that same God as made winds blow, preserve my master
ches . . . tables chess and backgammon; the latter a board game, played by two opponents with dice and "men"
sixte . . . May The sixth morning of May. Two or three days in each month were marked as "evil" or "Egyptian" (because of God's plagues on Egypt) days in medieval calendars. May 6 is sometimes one. On such a day it was thought especially dangerous to fall ill or begin any-

thing in which one hoped to be successful. See Nun's Priest's Tale, l. 424.
gardin The garden setting is meant to recall, with a hint of coming disaster, the exemplar of all gardens, the Garden of Eden, where Adam and Eve, our first parents, were said to have spent only one brief hour, before the first sin and their expulsion (Fig. 56). Medieval literature teems with descriptions of such lovely spots (*loci amoeni*), especially in a love context: they give solace for pain physical, mental, and spiritual. Chaucer's description may have been borrowed from the French of Guillaume de Machaut (*c.* 1300–1377); it balances the description of the rocks, above.

For she ne saugh him on the dauncė go,
That was hir housbonde and hir love also.
But nathélees she moste a tyme abyde,
And with good hopė lete hir sorwe slyde.
    Upon this daunce, amongės othere men,
Dauncėd a squyer° biforen Dorigen,
That fressher⸗ was and jolyer of array,   *handsomer*
220 As to my doom,⸗ than is the monthe of May.°   *judgment*
He singeth, daunceth, passinge⸗ any man   *surpassing*
That is, or was, sith⸗ that the world bigan.   *since*
Therwith he was, if men sholde him discryve,⸗   *describe*
Oon of the bestė faringe⸗ man on lyve;   *most handsome*
Yong, strong, right vertuous,⸗ and riche and wys,   *accomplished*
And wel biloved, and holden in gret prys.⸗   *esteem*
And shortly, if the sothe⸗ I tellen shal,   *truth*
Unwiting⸗ of this Dorigen at al,   *unknown*
This lusty squyer, servant to Venus,°
230 Which that yclepėd⸗ was Aurelius,   *called*
Had loved hir best of any creatùre
Two yeer and more, as was his aventùre,⸗   *fortune*
But never dorste he telle hir his grevaùnce;⸗   *distress*
Withouten coppe he drank al his penaùnce.°
He was despeyrėd, nothing dorste he seye,
Save in his songės somwhat wolde he wreye⸗   *disemble*
His wo, as in a general compleyning;
He seyde he loved, and was biloved nothing.
Of swich materė made he manye layes,
240 Songės, compleintės, roundels, virėlayes,°
How that he dorstė nat his sorwe telle,
But languissheth, as a Furie° dooth in Helle;
And die he moste, he seyde, as dide Ekko°
For Narcisus, that dorste nat telle hir wo.
In other manere than ye here⸗ me seye,   *hear*
Ne dorste he nat to hir his wo biwreye;⸗   *reveal*
Save that, paràventure,⸗ somtyme at daunces,   *by chance*
Ther yongė folk kepen hir observaùnces,

---

squyer The squire has a Romano-British name (Aurelius) to suggest the long ago; and may be intended to recall Chaucer's Squire.
That fressher . . . May conventional description of a young man; in medieval calendars May is sometimes shown as a brightly dressed squire on horseback
Venus goddess of love
Withouten . . . penaunce perhaps "without measure he took his medicine" (*coppe*-cup); or "under difficulties"; or "he drank his penance eagerly"; i.e. scooping it up with his hands instead of using a cup—a reference to the contraries of love
layes . . . virelayes All these are varieties of the short lyrical love-song, of which the complaint could also deal with religious love. Lays

and songs are general terms, meaning the same thing in this context: "lay" is not used in the technical sense of l. 2. The complaint bewails lack of success in love; see Chaucer's satirical *Complaint to His Purse* below. It was a French genre, like the roundel (rondeau) and virelay (see Glossary).
Furie The three Furies were daughters of Pluto, king of the underworld, who pursued evil-doers: always in pain themselves (*languissheth*), because in hell; see Skelton, *Philip Sparrow*, l. 74, below.
Ekko The nymph Echo loved Narcissus, who preferred his own reflected self to her. She took to the woods and pined away for grief, until there was nothing left of her but her voice (Fig. 54).

It may wel be he lokėd on hir face
In swich a wyse, as man that asketh grace;
But nothing wistė˃ she of his entente.   *knew*
Nathėlees, it happėd, er˃ they thennės wente,   *before*
Bycausė that he was hir neighėbour,
And was a man of worship and honour,
And hadde yknowen him of tymė yore,°
They fillė in˃ speche; and forth more and more   *fell into*
Unto his purpose drough˃ Aurelius,   *moved*
And whan he saugh his tyme, he seydė thus:
    'Madame,' quod he, 'by God that this world made,
So˃ that I wiste it mightė your hertė glade,˃   *if / delight*
I wolde, that day that your Arveragus
Wente over the see, that I, Aurelius,
Had went ther˃ never I sholde have come agayn;   *gone where*
For wel I woot˃ my service is in vayn.   *know*
My guerdon˃ is but bresting˃ of myn herte;   *reward / breaking*
Madame, reweth˃ upon my peynės smerte;˃   *have pity / sharp*
For with a word ye may me sleen˃ or save,   *slay*
Heer at your feet God wolde that I were grave!˃   *buried*
I ne have as now no leyser˃ more to seye;   *leisure*
Have mercy, swete, or ye wol do˃ me deye˃!'   *make / die*
    She gan to loke upon Aurelius:
'Is this your wil,' quod she, 'and sey ye thus?
Never erst,˃ quod she, 'ne wiste I what ye mente.   *before*
But now, Aurelie, I knowe your entente,
By thilkė God that yaf˃ me soule and lyf,   *gave*
Ne shal I never been untrewė wyf
In word ne werk,˃ as far as I have wit: *deed*
I wol ben his to whom that I am knit;
Tak this for fynal answer as of me.'
But after that in pley˃ thus seydė she: *jest*
    'Aurelie,' quod she, 'by heighė God above,
Yet wolde I grauntė yow to been your love,
Sin I yow see so pitously complayne;
Loke what day that, endėlong˃ Britayne,   *all along*
Ye remove alle the rokkės, stoon by stoon,°
That they ne lettė˃ ship ne boot˃ to goon: *hinder / boat*
I seye, whan ye han maad the coost˃ so clene   *coast*
Of rokkės, that ther nis no stoon ysene,
Than wol I love yow best of any man,
Have heer my trouthe,˃ in al that ever I can.'   *word*
    'Is ther non other grace in yow?' quod he.
'No, by that Lord,' quod she, 'that makėd me!

And hadde . . . yore and she had known him
for some time past
stoon by stoon Every one. Dorigen's condition
is an extravagant parody (to emphasize her love
for Arveragus) of the tasks that heroines of the
romance would lay on their lovers; but with the
connotation "sooner shall you move these rocks
than me."

For wel I woot that it shal never bityde.˒   *happen*
Lat swiche foliès out of your hertè slyde.
What deyntee˒ sholde a man han in his lyf   *pleasure*
For to go love another mannès wyf,
That hath hir body whan so that him lyketh?˒
    Aurelius ful oftè sorè syketh;˒   *sighs*
Wo was Aureliè, whan that he this herde,
300 And with a sorweful herte he thus answerde:
    'Madame,' quod he, 'this were an inpossìble!˒   *impossibility*
Than moot I dye of sodein˒ deth horrìble.'   *sudden*
And with that word he turnèd him anoon.˒   *at once*
Tho come hir othere freendès many oon,
And in the aleyes romeden˒ up and doun,   *paths walked*
And nothing wiste of this conclusioùn,
But sodeinly bigonnè revel˒ newe   *began diversion*
Til that the brightè sonnè loste his hewe;˒   *color*
For th'orisonte˒ hath reft˒ the sonne his light;   *the horizon / taken*
310 (This is as muche to seye as it was night).
And hoom they goon in joye and in solas,
Save only wrecche Aurelius, allas!
He to his hous is goon with sorweful herte;
He seeth he may nat fro his deeth asterte.˒   *escape*
Him semèd that he felte his hertè colde;
Up to the hevene his handès he gan holde,
And on his knowès˒ bare he sette˒ him doun,   *knees / put*
And in his raving˒ seyde his orisoùn.˒   *delirium / prayer*
For verray wo out of his wit˒ he breyde.˒   *mind / went*
320 He nistè˒ what he spak, but thus he seyde;   *knew not*
With pitous˒ herte his pleynt hath he bigonne   *sad*
Unto the goddes, and first unto the sonne:
    He seyde, 'Appollo,° god and governour
Of every plauntè, herbè, tree and flour,
That yevest,˒ after thy declinacioùn,°   *gives*
To ech of hem his tyme and his sesoùn,
As thyn herberwè˒ chaungeth lowe or hye;   *position*
Lord Phebus, cast thy merciable˒ yë   *merciful*
On wrecche Aurelie, which that am but lorn.˒   *lost*
330 Lo, lord! my lady hath my deeth ysworn
Withoutè gilt,° but thy benignitee
Upon my dedly˒ herte have som pitee!   *doomed*
For wel I woot,˒ lord Phebus, if yow lest,   *know*
Ye may me helpen, save my lady, best.°
Now voucheth sauf˒ that I may yow devyse˒   *grant / show*
How that I may been holpe˒ and in what wyse.   *helped*

Appollo Apollo (Phoebus), god of light, the sun
after thy declinacioùn according to your celestial latitude or seasonal position in the sky;
herberwe (1. 327) is literally lodging

Withoute gilt i.e. when I am innocent
Ye may . . . best you can be my best helper
of anyone, except my lady

Your blisful suster, Lucina° the shene,°   *shining*
That of the see is chief goddesse and quene,
Though Neptunus° have deitee in the see,
340 Yet emperesse aboven him is she:
Ye knowen wel, lord, that right as hir desyr
Is to be quiked° and lightned of your fyr,°   *enlivened / fire*
For which she folweth yow ful bisily,°   *assiduously*
Right so the see desyreth naturelly
To folwen hir, as she that is goddesse
Bothe in the see and riveres more and lesse.
Wherfore, lord Phebus, this is my requeste—
Do this miracle, or do myn hertè breste—
That now, next at this opposicioùn,°
350 Which in the signe shal be of the Leoùn,°
As preyeth hir so greet a flood to bringe,
That fyve fadme° at the leeste it overspringe°   *fathoms / rise above*
The hyeste rokke in Armorik Briteyne;
And lat this flood endurè yerès tweyne;
Than certès to my lady may I seye:
"Holdeth° your heste,° the rokkès been aweye."   *keep / promise*
Lord Phebus, dooth this miracle for me;
Preye hir she go no faster cours than ye;°
I seye, preyeth your suster that she go
360 No faster cours than ye thise yerès two.
Than shal she been evene attè fulle alway,
And spring-flood° lastè bothè night and day.   *spring-tide*
And, but° she vouchèsauf° in swiche manere   *unless / grant*
To grauntè me my sovereyn lady dere,
Prey hir to sinken every rok adoun
Into hir owene derkè regioùn
Under the ground, ther Pluto° dwelleth inne,
Or nevermo shal I my lady winne.
Thy temple in Delphos° wol I barefoot seke;
370 Lord Phebus, see the terès on my cheke,
And of my peyne have som compassioùn.'
And with that word in swowne° he fil adoun,   *swoon*

Lucina I.e. the triple goddess of the universe, manifesting herself as Luna (the moon) in the skies; Diana on earth; Proserpina (Hecate) in the underworld. He means the moon, who governs the tides of the sea and depends upon the sun for her light. The sun is to use his influence with the moon to bring a lasting spring tide, and cover the rocks. Lucina was that manifestation of the goddess who presided over childbirth. **Neptunus** Neptune, god of the sea **opposicioun** i.e. 180° apart, at full moon, when the influence of sun and moon reinforce each other to bring about the spring tides, and the water is higher than normal at both rise and ebb **Leoun** The sun's power is greatest when it is in the zodiacal sign of Leo, the Lion, because that is its own mansion or house. But the sun was, on May 6, in Taurus, the Bull; and Aurelius is ready to wait until July for his miracle, which will be most effective because the sun will be in Leo and the moon in opposition in Aquarius, the Water-carrier, an appropriate sign for a flood. **Lord . . . ye** The sun is being asked to slow the moon's pace (28-day orbit) to his own (1-year orbit) for two years, so that their oppositions will continue and the tide remain at flood all that time. **Pluto** god of the underworld, husband of Proserpina-Luna **Delphos** Delphi, in a valley of Mt. Parnassus, the chief shrine of Apollo and the seat of the most famous ancient oracle; Aurelius vows to make a barefoot pilgrimage there.

And longe tyme he lay forth˃ in a traunce.   *continually*
His brother, which that knew of his penaunce,˃   *pain*
Up caughte him and to bedde he hath him broght.
Dispeyrèd˃ in this torment and this thoght   *despairing*
Lete˃ I this woful creätùrè lye;   *let*
Chese he, for me, whether he wol live or dye.°
　　Arveragus, with hele˃ and greet honour,   *prosperity*
380　As he that was of chivalrye the flour,
Is comen hoom, and othere worthy men.
O blisful artow˃ now, thou Dorigen,   *art thou*
That hast thy lusty housbonde in thyne armes,
The fresshè knight, the worthy man of armes,
That loveth thee, as his owene hertès lyf.
Nothing list him to been imaginatyf˃   *suspicious*
If any wight had spoke, whyl he was oute,˃   *abroad*
To hire of love; he hadde of it no doute.
He noght entendeth˃ to no swich matere,   *attends*
390　But daunceth, justeth,˃ maketh hir good chere;   *jousts*
And thus in joye and blisse I lete hem dwelle,
And of the syke˃ Aurelius wol I telle.   *sick*
　　In langour and in torment furious
Two yeer and more lay wrecche Aurelius,
Er any foot he mighte on erthè goon;
Ne confort in this tymè hadde he noon,
Save of his brother, which that was a clerk;˃   *learned man*
He knew of al this wo and al this werk.
For to non other creätùre certeyn
400　Of this matère he dorstè no word seyn.
Under his brest he bar it more secree˃   *secret*
Than ever dide Pamphilus° for Galathee.
His brest was hool,˃ withoutè for to sene,   *whole*
But in his herte ay˃ was the arwe˃ kene.   *ever / arrow*
And wel ye knowe that of a sursanure°
In surgerye is perilous the cure,
But˃ men mighte touche the arwe, or come therby.   *unless*
His brother weep and waylèd prively,
Til attè laste him fil in remembraunce,
410　That whyl he was at Orliens° in Fraunce,
As yongè clerkès, that been likerous˃   *eager*

Chese . . . dye let him choose, as far I am
concerned, whether he live or die
Pamphilus One of the catalogue of famous and
unfortunate lovers. The name is a corruption of
Polyphemus, the Sicilian Cyclops who loved and
was rejected by the nymph Galatea. Pamphilus
himself is the timid hero of the medieval Latin
comic poem *Pamphilus de Amore*, who cannot
make his girl without personal instruction from
Venus and the help of a madam.
sursanure a wound healed only on the outside,
with the cause of the wound (arrow) sealed
inside and causing suppuration. Chaucer has

enlarged a hint from *Pamphilus de Amore.*
Orliens The schools of Orleans, in France, had
been famous since perhaps the 6th century; the
University was founded in the early 13th century. Its reputation for learning, especially in
the law, fostered the legend that some had
acquired magical knowledge by deep study
there. The equation, learned men/philosophers =
magicians/alchemists, was easily made in the
Middle Ages and later—see l. 853. With Orleans
and its magicians, compare Oxford and Roger
("Friar") Bacon, or Wittenberg and Dr.
Faustus.

To reden artès that been curious,°
Seken in every halke and every herne
Particuler sciènces for to lerne,°
He him remembred that, upon a day,
At Orliens in studie a book he say⸾   *saw*
Of magik naturel,° which his felawe,⸾   *companion*
That was that tyme a bacheler of lawe,
Al⸾ were he ther to lerne another craft,⸾   *although / profession*
420 Had privèly° upon his desk ylaft;
Which book spak muchel⸾ of the operaciòuns,°   *much*
Touchinge the eighte and twenty mansiòuns
That longen to the mone, and swich folye,
As in our dayès is nat worth a flye;
For holy chirchès° feith in our bileve⸾   *belief*
Ne suffreth noon illusion us to greve.⸾   *harm*
And whan this book was in his remembràunce,
Anon for joye his hertè gan to daunce,
And to himself he seydè privèly:⸾   *privately*
430 'My brother shal be warisshed⸾ hastily;   *cured*
For I am siker⸾ that ther be sciènces,   *sure*
By whichè men make diverse apparènces
Swiche as thise subtile tregetourès° pleye.
For ofte at festès have I wel herd seye,
That tregetours, withinne an hallè large,
Have maad come in a water and a barge,
And in the hallè rowen up and doun.
Somtyme hath semèd come a grim leòun;⸾   *lion*
And somtyme flourès springe as in a mede;
440 Somtyme a vyne, and grapès whyte and rede;
Somtyme a castel, al of lym and stoon;
And whan hem lykèd, voyded⸾ it anoon.   *emptied*
Thus semèd it to every mannès sighte.
    Now than conclude I thus, that if I mighte
At Orliens som old felawe yfinde,⸾   *find*
That hadde this monès mansiòns in minde,
Or other magik naturel above,⸾   *in addition*
He sholde wel make my brother han his love.

artes . . . curious books of instruction that are recondite, or: arts that are occult
Seken . . . lerne seek, in every hiding-place and corner to learn out-of-the-way knowledge
magik naturel See General Prologue, l. 418.
privèly i.e. he had left it hidden, so that he would not be known to have it
operaciòuns Magical workings concerning the 28 mansions of the moon, one for each day of the lunar month (see Astrology in the Glossary). Moreover, as the nearest planet to earth the moon is the most powerful planetary influence to be manipulated; as possessing the shortest orbit it is the trickiest to manipulate; as the planet of darkness the most obvious for magic.

The position of the moon was vital for any astrological purpose.
chirches The church naturally condemned any attempt to alter the course of a nature preordained and created by God, who was the only truth. The truth of astrology could never be more than apparent. Magical operations were permitted, as long as they were natural and not black, but they could only be rational, scientific demonstrations of God's wonders and purposes, not imitations or disturbances of them.
tregetoures Conjurors, illusionists; also used for jugglers, sleight-of-hand entertainers. The brother is unknowingly insulting the noble craft of true magicians, who claim to work on a larger scale.

For with an apparènce a clerk may make
450   To mannès sighte, that alle the rokkès blake
Of Britaigne weren yvoyded° everichon,   *swept away*
And shippès by the brinkè comen and gon,
And in swich forme endure a day or two;
Than were my brother warisshed° of his wo.   *cured*
Than moste she nedès holden hir biheste,
Or ellès he shal shame hir atte leste.'
    What° sholde I make a lenger tale of this?   *why*
Unto his brotherès bed he comen is,
And swich confort he yaf him for to gon
460   To Orliens, that he up stirte° anon,   *jumped*
And on his wey forthward thanne is he fare,°   *gone*
In hope for to ben lissèd° of his care.   *cured*
    Whan they were come almost to that citee,
But if° it were a two furlong° or three,   *all but*
A yong clerk rominge by himself they mette,
Which that in Latin thriftily° hem grette,   *well*
And after that he seyde a wonder thing:
'I knowe,' quod he, 'the cause of your coming';
And er they ferther any foté° wente,   *foot*
470   He tolde hem al that was in hir entente.
    This Briton° clerk him askéd of felawes   *Breton*
The whiche that he had knowe in oldè dawes;°   *days*
And he answerde him that they dede were,
For which he weep ful oftè many a tere.
    Doun of his hors Aurelius lighte° anon,   *alighted*
And forth with this magicien is he gon
Hoom to his hous, and made hem wel at ese.
Hem lakkèd no vitaìlle that mighte hem plese;
So wel arrayéd hous as there was oon
480   Aurelius in his lyf saugh never noon.°
    He shewed him, er he wentè to sopeer,°   *supper*
Forestès, parkès ful of wildè deer;
Ther saugh he hertès° with hir hornès hye,   *harts*
The gretteste that ever werè seyn with yë.
He saugh of hem an hondred slayn with houndes,
And somme with arwes blede of bittre woundes.°
He saugh, whan voided° were thise wildè deer,   *gone*
Thise fauconers° upon a fair river,°   *falconers / river bank*
That with hir hawkès han the heron slayn.
490   Tho saugh he knightès jousting in a playn;
And after this, he dide him swich plesaunce,
That he him shewed his lady on a daunce
On which himself he dauncéd, as him thoughte.°   *it seemed*

---

furlong one-eighth mile
never noon intensifying double negative: Aurelius never saw such a well-ordered (or: well-
supplied) house in his life as that one

He sough . . . woundes he saw a hundred of
them killed (after hunting) with dogs; and
some bleeding with painful arrow-wounds

And whan this maister, that this magik wroughte,˃   *did*
Saugh it was tyme, he clapte his handès two,
And farewel! al our revel° was ago.˃   *gone*
And yet remoeved they never out of the hous,
Whyl they saugh al this sightè merveillous,
But in his studie, theras his bookès be,
500   They seten stille, and no wight but they three.
    To him this maister callèd his squyèr,
And seyde him thus: 'Is redy our sopèr?
Almost an houre it is, I undertake,˃   *swear*
Sith I yow bad our soper for to make,
Whan that thise worthy men wenten with me
Into my studie, theras my bookès be.'
    'Sire,' quod this squyer, 'whan it lyketh˃ yow,   *pleases*
It is al redy, though ye wol˃ right now.'   *want it*
'Go we than soupe,' quod he, 'as for the beste;°   *must*
510   This amorous folk somtyme mote˃ han reste.'   *discussion*
    At after-soper fille they in tretee,˃   *master's reward*
What sommè sholde this maistres guerdon˃ be,
To remoeven alle the rokkès of Britayne,
And eek from Gerounde° to the mouth of Sayne.   *difficult*
    He made it straunge,˃ and swoor, so God him save,
Lasse than a thousand pound he wolde nat have,
Ne gladly for that somme he wolde nat goon.
    Aurelius, with blisful herte anoon,
Answerdè thus, 'Fy on a thousand pound!
520   This wydè world, which that men seye is round,°
I wolde it yeve, if I were lord of it.   *complete*
This bargayn is ful drive,˃ for we ben knit.   *word of honor*
Ye shal be payèd trewely, by my trouthe!˃   *laziness*
But loketh now, for no necligence or slouthe,˃   *delay*
Ye tarie˃ us heer no lenger than to-morwe.'   *as pledge*
'Nay,' quod this clerk, 'have heer my feith to borwe.˃
    To bedde is goon Aurelius whan him leste,
And wel ny al that night he hadde his reste;
What for his labour and his hope of blisse,
530   His woful herte of penaunce hadde a lisse.˃   *relief*
    Upon the morwe, whan that it was day,
To Britaigne tokè they the rightè˃ way,   *direct*
Aurelius, and this magicien bisyde,
And been descended ther˃ they wolde abyde;   *where*
And this was, as the bokès me remembre,˃   *tell*
The coldè frosty seson of Decembre.

---

revel See Prospero, in *The Tempest* IV.i; overall, Chaucer and Shakespeare often say much
the same thing about the ennobling power of
love.
Go . . . beste let us go sup, said he, it is the
best thing

Gerounde the river Gironde, as far south of
Penmarc'h as the river Seine is north
world . . . round See *Rosemounde* below and
see Fig. 55.

Phebus wex old, and hewėd lyk latoùn,
That in his hotė declinatioùn
Shoon as the burnėd gold with stremės brighte;°
540 But now in Capricorn adoun he lighte,˃   *alighted*
Wheras he shoon ful pale, I dar wel seyn.˃   *say*
The bittre frostės, with the sleet and reyn,
Destroyėd hath the grene in every yerd.˃   *yard*
Janus sit by the fyr, with double berd,°
And drinketh of his bugle-horn the wyn.
Biforn him stant brawn° of the tuskėd swyn,
And 'Nowel'° cryeth every lusty˃ man.   *jocund*
    Aurelius, in al that ever he can,
Doth to his maister chere˃ and reverence,˃   *entertainment / respect*
550 And preyeth him to doon his diligence
To bringen him out of his peynės smerte,
Or with a swerd that he wolde slitte his herte.
    This subtil˃ clerk swich routhe˃ had of this man,   *skilled / pity*
That night and day he spedde˃ him that˃ he can,   *hastened / as much as*
To wayte˃ a tyme˃ of his conclusioùn;°   *watch / opportunity*
This is to seye, to make illusioùn,
By swich an apparènce of jogelrye˃—   *conjuring*
I ne can˃ no termės of astrologye—   *know*
That she and every wight sholde wene˃ and seye,˃   *think / say*
560 That of Britaigne the rokkės were aweye,
Or ellės they were sonken under grounde.
So attė laste he hath his tyme yfounde
To maken his japès and his wrecchednesse°
Of swich a supersticious cursednesse.
His tables Toletanès° forth he broght,

Phebus . . . brighte (ll. 537–39) The sun
grew old and latten-colored, he who in his hot
position shone, with bright beams, like burnished gold. (For latten, and the same base
metal-gold comparison, see the General Prologue,
l. 701.) The sun has declined from its highest
latitude in Cancer (summer solstice) to its
lowest in Capricorn (Figs. 43, 45, winter
solstice—December 12 in the 14th century). So
Aurelius has had to wait even longer for the
miracle he wanted (l. 350).
Janus . . . berd Janus sits by the fire, with
his double face (literally, "beard"). Janus, the
Roman god of comings-in and goings-out, had
two faces, one looking forward, the other back.
He gave his name to the month of January and
represents the turn of the year.
brawn boar's flesh; a boar was a traditional,
prized Christmas dish
'Nowel' A greeting for Christmas, the great
feast, lasting from Christmas Day to Twelfth
Night. "Nowel" = Latin: *natalis*, birthday. The
cry ends this gay, homely little interlude and
we return to serious, high-flown magical endeavor.
conclusioun object and end of his "operation"
japes . . . wrecchednesse tricks and wickednesses, so diabolically cursed

Toletanes I.e. of Toledo, in Spain; astronomical
tables, for calculating the positions of the
heavenly bodies; also called Alfonsine tables,
having been made by order of Alfonso X of
Castile about 1272. The magician was up-to-
date: these were the most accurate available.
The pile-up of technical terms reinforces the
impression of competence and we are expected
to be bullied into respect by its mysteries.
Collect years show the amount of a planet's
motion over more than 20 years; *expans* years
over a period of anything less than that. *Rotes*
are tables for making astrological propositions;
geres are paraphernalia; *centre* is part of
an astrolabe; *argument* is an astronomical
mathematical quantity from which another
may be deduced. *Proportioneels conveniens* are
fitting proportionals, to find planetary movements during part of a year. The eighth sphere
was the sphere of the fixed stars. The magician
allows for its slow rotation. *Alnath* was in the
eighth sphere, at the beginning of the constellation Aries, below the stable Aries in the
ninth sphere—the sign of the zodiac—so that
the two were out of kilter. The mass of astrological terms goes on—Alnath was also the first
mansion of the moon; *face* and *terme* (l. 580)
seem to be divisions of the zodiacal sign.

Ful wel corrected, ne ther lakkèd noght,
Neither his collect ne his expans yeres,
Ne his rotès, ne his othere geres,
As been his centres and his arguments,
570 And his proporcionels convenients
For his equaciòns in every thing.
And, by his eightè spere in his wirking,
He knew ful wel how fer Alnath was shove
Fro the heed of thilkè fixe Aries above
That in the ninthè speere considered is;
Ful subtilly⁊ he calculèd⁊ al this.   *skillfully / calculated*
    Whan he had founde his firstè mansioùn,
He knew the remenant⁊ by proporcioùn;⁊   *rest / adjustment*
And knew the arysing of his monè⁊ weel,   *moon*
580 And in whos face, and terme, and every deel;
And knew ful weel the monès mansioùn
Acordaunt⁊ to his operacioùn,   *answering*
And knew also his othere observaùnces⁊   *rites*
For swiche illusiouns and swiche meschaunces⁊   *evil doings*
As hethen folk usèd in thilkè dayes;
For which no lenger⁊ makèd he delayes,   *longer*
But thurgh his magik, for a wyke or tweye,
It semed that alle the rokkès were aweye.
    Aurelius, which that yet despeirèd⁊ is   *desperate*
590 Wher⁊ he shal han his love or fare amis,   *whether*
Awaiteth night and day on this miracle;
And whan he knew that ther was noon obstàcle,
That voided were thise rokkès everichon,
Doun to his maistres feet he fil anon,
And seyde, 'I woful wrecche, Aurelius,
Thankè yow, lord, and lady myn Venus,
That me han holpen⁊ fro my carès colde':   *helped*
And to the temple his wey forth hath he holde,⁊   *taken*
Wheras he knew he sholde his lady see.
600 And whan he saugh his tyme, anon right⁊ he,   *at once*
With dredful⁊ herte and with ful humble chere,⁊ *fearful / appearance*
Salewèd⁊ hath his sovereyn lady dere: *saluted*
'My rightè lady,' quod this woful man,
'Whom I most drede and love as I best can,
And lothest⁊ were of al this world displese,   *most reluctant*
Nere it° that I for yow have swich disese,⁊   *pain*
That I moste dyen⁊ heer at your foot anon,   *die*
Noght wolde I telle how me is wo bigon;
But certès outher⁊ moste I dye or pleyne;   *either*
610 Ye slee me giltèlees for verray peyne.
But of my deeth, thogh that ye have no routhe,⁊   *pity*

Nere it were it not

Avyseth° yow, er that ye breke your trouthe. *consider*
Repenteth yow, for thilkė God above,
Er ye me sleen° bycause that I yow love. *slay*
For, madame, wel ye woot° what ye han hight;° *know / promised*
Nat that I chalange° any thing of right *claim*
Of yow my sovereyn lady, but your grace;
But in a gardin yond, at swich a place,
Ye woot right wel what ye bihighten° me; *promised*
620 And in myn hand your trouthė plighten° ye *word gave*
To love me best. God woot, ye seydė so,
Al be that I unworthy be therto.
Madame, I speke it for the honour of yow,
More than to save myn hertės lyf right now:
I have do so as ye comanded me;
And if ye vouchėsauf,° ye may go see. *grant*
Doth as yow list, have your biheste° in minde, *promise*
For quik° or deed, right ther ye shul me finde; *living*
In yow lyth al, to do° me live or deye— *make*
630 But wel I woot the rokkės been aweye!'
 He taketh his leve, and she astonied° stood, *stunned*
In al hir facė nas a drope of blood;
She wendė° never han come in swich a trappe: *expected*
'Allas!' quod she, 'that ever this sholde happe!° *chance*
For wende I never, by possibilitee,
That swich a monstre° or merveille mighte be!
It is agayns the process of natùre':
And hoom she gooth a sorweful creäture.
For verray fere unnethė° may she go, *scarcely*
640 She wepeth, wailleth, all a day or two,
And swowneth,° that it routhė° was to see; *swoons / pity*
But why it was, to no wight toldė she;
For out of toune was goon Arveragus.
But to hirself she spak, and seydė thus,
With facė pale and with ful sorweful chere,
In hir compleynt,° as ye shul after here.
 'Allas,' quod she, 'on thee, Fortune,° I pleyne,
That unwar° wrappėd hast me in thy cheyne; *unawares*
Fro which, t'escape, woot I no socoùr° *help*
650 Save only deeth or ellės dishonoùr;
Oon of thise two bihoveth° me to chese.° *it is necessary /choose*
But nathėlees, yet have I lever° to lese° *rather / lose*
My lyf than of my body have a shame,
Or knowe myselven fals,° or lese my name,° *false / reputation*
And with my deth I may be quit,° ywis. *freed*

---

monstre unnatural thing
compleynt see l. 239 above
Fortune The Roman goddess, taken over by
the Middle Ages to help explain the existence
of wrong and injustice in the world; blind and
capricious, she offers and takes away her gifts
of exterior goods and is not to be trusted
(Fig. 41).

Hath ther nat many a noble wyf, er this,
And many a mayde yslayn hirself, allas!
Rather than with hir body doon trespas?
  Yis, certès, lo, thise stories° beren witnesse;
660 Whan thretty tyraunts,° ful of cursednesse,
Had slayn Phidoun in Athenes, attè feste,˃   *at the feast*
They comanded his doghtrès for t'areste,
And bringen hem biforn hem in despyt˃   *contempt*
Al naked, to fulfille hir foul delyt,˃   *pleasure*
And in hir fadrès˃ blood they made hem daunce   *fathers'*
Upon the pavement. God yeve hem mischaunce!
For which thise woful maydens, ful of drede,
Rather than they wolde lese hir maydenhede,
They privèly˃ ben stirt˃ into a welle,   *stealthily / leaped*
670 And dreynte˃ hemselven, as the bokès telle.   *drowned*
  They of Messenè° lete enquere˃ and seke   *caused to enquire*
Of Lacedomie fifty maydens eke,
On whiche they wolden doon hir lecherye;
But was ther noon of al that companye
That she nas slayn, and with a good entente
Chees˃ rather for to dyè than assente   *chose*
To be oppressèd˃ of hir maydenhede.   *raped*
Why sholde I thanne to dyè been in drede?
  Lo, eek, the tiraunt Aristoclides
680 That loved a mayden, heet˃ Stimphalides,   *called*
Whan that hir fader slayn was on a night,
Unto Dianès temple goth she right,˃   *straight*
And hente˃ the image in hir handès two,   *took*
Fro which imagè wolde she never go.
No wight ne mighte hir handes of it arace,˃   *tear*
Til she was slayn right in the selvè˃ place.   *same*
Now sith that maydens hadden swich despyt˃   *scorn*

stories All these *exempla* of maids, wives, and widows come from the most famous anti-feminist work of the Middle Ages, St. Jerome's late 4th-century treatise *Against Jovinian* (see the Wife of Bath's Prologue, l. 679). Chaucer makes the Franklin use this text as a counterblast to the Wife, who tears from it anything that will support her case for generation; Dorigen is more scrupulous and uses only Jerome's own stories in praise of womanly virtue. Chaucer follows Jerome very closely, but Jerome's versions are often garbled.
tyraunts The Thirty Tyrants began a reign of of terror in Athens when they seized power at the end of the Peloponnesian War (404 B.C.). Pheidon was one of them. The long list that now follows isolates, as *exempla* do, a single trait or incident; these are not intended to be a comment on the character of Aurelius or to cast him in the role of a monster who combines the worst features of all these would-be rapists. It is a list of women who had kept faith.
Messene The men of Messene attempted to rape fifty Spartan virgins; Aristoclides killed

Stymphalis for refusing to sleep with him; Hasdrubal's wife (see the Nun's Priest's Tale, l. 591) joined her husband in death when Carthage was taken; Lucretia killed herself after her rape by Tarquinius Sextus; Miletus was sacked by the Gauls; Abradates' wife Panthea killed herself on his corpse; Demotion's daughter died rather than marry another after her fiancé's death; Scedasus' two daughters killed themselves after being raped by two Spartans—and so on, through Nicanor, Nicerates, Alcibiades: Alcestis, who accepted death in place of her husband; Penelope, the wife of Odysseus, who kept herself by tricks from the suitors who laid siege to her in her husband's absence; Laodameia, who joined her husband Protesilaus in the shades when he was killed by Hector at Troy; Portia, wife of Brutus, the conspirator; Artemisia, who built the mausoleum at Halicarnassus for her husband and was honored throughout barbarian lands for it; Teuta, queen of Illyria; Bilia, who was a martyr for her husband; Rhodogone and Valeria, who both refused a second marriage.

To been defouled with mannės foul delyt,
Wel oghte a wyf rather hirselven slee⸲   *slay*
690   Than be defoulėd, as it thinketh⸲ me.   *seems*
     What shal I seyn of Hasdrubalės wyf,
That at Cartage birafte⸲ hirself hir lyf⸲   *took*
For whan she saugh that Romayns wan⸲ the toun,   *won*
She took hir children alle, and skipte⸲ adoun   *jumped*
Into the fyr, and chees rather to dye
Than any Romayn dide hir vileinye.
     Hath nat Lucresse yslayn hirself, allas!
At Romė, whannė she oppressėd was
Of Tarquin, for hir thoughte it was a shame
700   To liven whan she haddė lost hir name?
     The sevene maydens of Milesie also
Han slayn hemself, for verray drede and wo,
Rather than folk of Gaule hem sholde oppresse.
Mo than a thousand stories, as I gesse,
Coude I now telle as touchinge this matere.
     Whan Habradate was slayn, his wyf so dere
Hirselven slow,⸲ and leet hir blood to glyde⸲   *slew / flow*
In Habradatės woundės depe and wyde,
And seyde, "My body, at the leestė way,
710   Ther shal no wight defoulen, if I may."⸲   *can help it*
     What sholde I mo ensamples heerof sayn,
Sith that so manye han hemselven slayn
Wel rather than they wolde defoulėd be?
I wol conclude, that it is bet⸲ for me   *better*
To sleen myself, than been defoulėd thus.
I wol be trewe unto Arveragus,
Or rather sleen myself in som manere,
As dide Democionės doghter dere,⸲   *dear*
Bycause that she wolde nat defoulėd be.
720   O Cedasus! it is ful greet pitee,
To reden how thy doghtren deyde,⸲ allas!   *daughters died*
That slowe hemselven for swich maner cas.⸲   *happening*
     As greet a pitee was it, or wel more,
The Theban mayden, that for Nichanore
Hirselven slow,⸲ right for swich maner wo.   *slew*
     Another Theban mayden dide right so;
For oon of Macedoine hadde hir oppressed,
She with hir deeth hir maydenhede redressed.
     What shal I seye of Niceratės wyf,
730   That for swich cas birafte hirself hir lyf?
     How trewe eek was to Alcebiades
His love, that rather for to dyen chees⸲   *chose*
Than for to suffre his body unburied be!
Lo which⸲ a wyf was Alcestė,' quod she.   *what*
     'What seith Omer of gode⸲ Penalopee?   *good*

Al Grecé knoweth of hir chastitee.
Pardee, of Laodomya is writen thus,
That whan at Troye was slayn Protheselaus,
No lenger wolde she live after his day.
740   The same of noble Porcia telle I may;
Withouté Brutus coudé she nat live,
To whom she hadde al hool⟩ hir herté yive.   *completely*
The parfit⟩ wyfhod of Arthemesye   *perfect*
Honouréd is thurgh al the Barbarye.
O Teuta, queen! thy wyfly chastitee
To allé wyvés may a mirour be.
The samé thing I seye of Bilia,
Of Rodogone, and eek Valeria.'
Thus pleynéd Dorigene a day or tweye,
750   Purposinge⟩ ever that she woldé deye.   *intending*
But nathélees, upon the thriddé⟩ night,   *third*
Hom⟩ cam Arveragus, this worthy knight,   *home*
And askéd hir, why that she weep so sore?
And shé gan wepen ever lenger the more.°
'Allas!' quod she, 'that ever was I born!
Thus have I seyd,' quod she, 'thus have I sworn'—
And told him al as ye han herd bifore;
It nedeth nat reherce⟩ it yow namore.   *tell*
This housbond with glad chere,⟩ in freendly wyse,   *look*
760   Answerde and seyde as I shal yow devyse.⟩   *tell*
'Is ther oght ellés,⟩ Dorigen, but this?'   *else*
'Nay, nay,' quod she 'God help me so, as wys
This is to muche, and it were Goddés wille.'°
'Ye, wyf,' quod he, 'lat slepen that is stille;
It may be wel, paràventure,⟩ yet to-day.   *perhaps*
Ye shul your trouthé holden, by my fay!⟩   *faith*
For God so wisly have mercy on me,°
I hadde wel lever ystikéd⟩ for to be,   *rather stabbed*
For verray love which that I to yow have,
770   But if ye sholde your trouthé kepe and save.
Trouthe is the hyesté⟩ thing that man may kepe.'   *highest*
But with that word he brast⟩ anon to wepe,   *burst*
And seyde, 'I yow forbede, up⟩ peyne of deeth,⟩   *on / death*
That never, whyl thee lasteth lyf ne breeth,
To no wight tel thou of this aventùre⟩—   *happening*
As I may best, I wol my wo endure—
Ne make no contenance⟩ of hevinesse,⟩   *appearance / sadness*
That folk of yow may demen harm⟩ or gesse.'   *suspect evil*
And forth he clepéd⟩ a squyer and a mayde: *called*

And she . . . more and she wept more and
more, the longer she went on
God help . . . wille God help me, this is too
much, even if it is God's will

For God . . . me as surely as God will have
mercy on me

780 'Goth forth anon with Dorigen,' he sayde,
     'And bringeth hir to swich a place anon.'
     They take hir leve, and on hir wey they gon;
     But they ne wiste why she thider wente.
     He nolde no wight tellen his entente.
        Paràventure an heep⸢ of yow, ywis,⸣   *lot / indeed*
     Wold holden him a lewed⸣ man in this,   *stupid*
     That he wol putte his wyf in jupartye;⸣   *jeopardy*
     Herkneth the tale, er ye upon hir crye.
     She may have bettre fortune than yow semeth;
790 And whan that ye han herd the tale, demeth.⸣   *judge*
        This squyer, which that highte Aurelius,
     On Dorigen that was so amorous,⸣   *in love*
     Of aventure⸣ happed hir to mete   *chance*
     Amidde the toun, right in the quikkest⸣ strete,   *busiest*
     As she was boun⸣ to goon the wey forthright⸣   *ready / direct*
     Toward the gardin theras she had hight.⸣   *promised*
     And he was to the gardinward° also;
     For wel he spyed, whan she wolde go
     Out of hir hous to any maner⸣ place.   *kind of*
800 But thus they mette, of aventure or grace;°
     And he saleweth⸣ hir with glad entente,⸣   *salutes / mind*
     And asked of hir whiderward⸣ she wente?   *whither*
        And she answerde, half as she were mad,
     'Unto the gardin, as myn housbond bad,
     My trouthe for to holde, allas! allas!'
        Aurelius gan wondren on this cas,⸣   *chance*
     And in his herte had greet compassioùn
     Of hir and of hir lamentacioùn,
     And of Arveragus, the worthy knight,
810 That bad hir holden al that she had hight,
     So looth⸣ him was his wyf sholde breke hir trouthe;   *hateful to*
     And in his herte he caughte of this greet routhe,⸣   *compassion*
     Consideringe the beste on every syde,
     That fro his lust yet were him lever abyde⸣   *rather abstain*
     Than doon so heigh a cherlish⸣ wrecchednesse   *mean*
     Agayns franchyse⸣ and allé gentillesse;⸣   *generosity / courtesy*
     For which in fewe wordes seyde he thus:
        'Madame, seyth⸣ to your lord Arveragus,   *say*
820 That sith I see his grete gentillesse
     To yow, and eek I see wel your distresse,
     That him were lever han shame (and that were routhe)
     Than ye to me sholde breke thus your trouthe,
     I have wel lever ever to suffre wo°

---

gardinward toward the garden
of . . . grace by chance or (God's) grace—a
favorite conventional formula, meaning: however
it happened

I have . . . wo I had much rather suffer unhappiness forever

Than I departe> the love bitwix yow two.   *part*
I yow relessė,> madame, into your hond   *release*
Quit,> every surement> and every bond,°   *paid / security*
That ye han maad to me as heerbiforn,>   *heretofore*
Sith thilkė tymė which that ye were born.
My trouthe I plighte, I shal yow never repreve>   *reproach*
830 Of no biheste.> And here I take my leve,   *promise*
As of the treweste and the bestė wyf
That ever yet I knew in al my lyf.
But every wyf be war of hir biheste,
On Dorigene remembreth attė leste.
Thus can a squyer doon a gentil> dede,   *noble*
As well as can a knight, withouten drede.'
    She thonketh him upon hir knees al bare,
And hoom unto hir housbond is she fare,>   *gone*
And tolde him al as ye han herd me sayd.>   *say*
840 And be ye siker,> he was so weel apayd,   *sure*
That it were inpossìble me to wryte.
    What sholde I lenger> of this cas endyte?>   *longer / write*
Arveragus and Dorigene his wyf
In sovereyn> blissė leden forth hir lyf.   *supreme*
Never eft ne was ther angre hem bitwene;
He cherisseth hir as though she were a quene;
And she was to him trewe for evermore.
Of thise two folk ye gete of me namore.
    Aurelius, that his cost hath al forlorn,>   *lost*
850 Curseth the tyme that ever he was born:
'Allas,' quod he, 'allas! that I bihighte>   *promised*
Of purėd> gold a thousand pound of wighte>   *refined / weight*
Unto this philosòphre°! how shal I do?
I see namore but that I am fordo.>   *undone*
Myn heritagė moot> I nedės selle,   *must*
And been a begger. Heer may I nat dwelle,
And shamen al my kinrede in this place,
But> I of him may getė bettre grace.   *unless*
But nathėlees, I wol of him assaye,>   *attempt*
860 At certeyn dayės, yeer by yeer, to paye,
And thankė him of his grete curteisye;
My trouthė wol I kepe, I wol nat lye.'
    With hertė soor> he gooth unto his cofre,>   *sore / coffer*
And broghtė gold unto this philosòphre,
The value of fyve hundred pound, I gesse,
And him bisecheth,> of his gentillesse,   *begs*
To grauntė him dayės of the remenaunt,°

I yow . . . bond legal language: a solemn,
formal renunciation, in contractual terms; with
puns on the meanings of the words in the terminology of courtly love

philosòphre wise man; often a magician/alche-
mist (see l. 410)
dayes . . . remenaunt time to pay the rest

And seydė, 'Maister, I dar wel make avaunt,˃   *boast*
I faillėd never of my trouthe as yit;˃   *so far*
870 For sikerly˃ my dettė shal be quit˃   *certainly / paid*
Towardės yow, however that I fare
To goon abeggėd˃ in my kirtle˃ bare.   *begging / tunic*
But woldė ye vouchesauf, upon seurtee,˃   *surety*
Two yeer or three for to respyten˃ me,   *give respite*
Than were I wel. For ellės moot I selle
Myn heritage; ther is namore to telle.'
This philosòphre sobrely˃ answerde,   *gravely*
And seyde thus, whan he thisė wordės herde:
'Have I nat holden covenant unto thee?'
880 'Yes, certės, wel and trewėly,' quod he.
'Hastow nat had thy lady as thee lyketh?'
'No, no,' quod he, and sorwefully he syketh.˃   *sighs*
'What was the causė? tel me if thou can.'
Aurelius his tale anon bigan,
And tolde him al, as ye han herd bifore;
It nedeth nat to yow reherce˃ it more.   *tell*
He seide, 'Arveragus, of gentillesse,
Had lever dye in sorwe and in distresse
Than that his wyf were of hir trouthė fals.'
890 The sorwe of Dorigen he tolde him als,˃   *also*
How looth hir was to been a wikked wyf,
And that she lever had lost that day hir lyf,
And that hir trouthe she swoor,˃ thurgh innocence.   *swore*
'She never erst herde speke of apparènce;°
That made me han˃ of hir so greet pitee.   *have*
And right as frely˃ as he sente hir me,   *generously*
As frely sente I hir to him ageyn.
This al and som,° ther is namore to seyn.'
This philosòphre answerde, 'Levė brother,
900 Everich of yow dide gentilly til˃ other.   *nobly to*
Thou art a squyer, and he is a knight;
But God forbedė, for his blisful might,
But if a clerk coude doon a gentil dede
As wel as any of yow, it is no drede!°
Sire, I relessė thee thy thousand pound,
As thou right now were cropen out of the ground,°
Ne never er˃ now ne haddest knowen me.   *before*
For sire, I wol nat take a peny of thee
For al my craft,˃ ne noght for my travaille.˃   *work / trouble*
910 Thou hast ypayėd wel for my vitaille.
It is ynogh, and farewel, have good day.'

'She . . . apparence she never before had heard
so much as talk of illusions (such as Aurelius
had had conjured up)
al and som i.e. everything
But God . . . drede (ll. 902–4) but God forbid, in his blessed power, that a learned man
can't do a courteous deed—there's no doubt (he
can)
As thou . . . ground as if you'd just come out
of a hole in the ground

And took his hors, and forth he gooth his way.
Lordinges, this question wolde I aske now,
Which was the mostė free,⸵ as thinketh yow⸵   *generous*
Now telleth me, er that ye ferther wende.
I can⸵ namore, my tale is at an ende.   *can say*

Here is ended the Frankeleyns Tale

The Pardoner's Prologue and Tale

Chaucer's portrait of the Pardoner in the General Prologue has prepared us for his Tale, but not fully for either the open cynicism of his behavior or the dark power of his story. His Prologue here, with its direct self-revelation—a technique that Chaucer does not often employ in the *Tales*—is followed by the long, indirect comment of his tale, an impressive demonstration of his abilities to preach upon his favorite theme: "Love of money is the root of evil." In the Epilogue the virtuoso feels that he ought to improve the occasion by attempting to do a little business.

From the General Prologue it is clear that this ecclesiastical fund-raiser is a rogue and a cheat, with his fake relics and pious threats, though Chaucer concedes his ability as a performer in church—an ability to be borne out by his tale. We need no more than Chaucer's description to let us know this; in the General Prologue, he seems to have reserved his most direct picture of villainy for the last, his portrait of the Pardoner. The Pardoner is a born eunuch, whom medieval character psychology made out much worse than a man who had merely been castrated. Eunuchs were, according to the doctrine, always evil-natured, foolish, lustful, and presumptuous, but those who had been born so were much worse; they could be recognized from their lack of beard, long scrawny necks and thin bodies, high voices, and prominent, rolling, lecherous eyes—physical defects indicating defects of character. Inclined to lechery, but unable to fulfill their desires, they are reduced, like the Pardoner in his Prologue, to boasting of them; he openly confesses he is a "ful vicious man" (Fig. 31).

The audience would have been familiar with the activities of this man, both from literature (the figure of Hypocrisy in the *Roman de la Rose* is strongly similar) and from life. Pardoners were already a source of some embarrassment to the Church, which licensed them to sell "pardons" to raise money for church purposes. Unscrupulous pardoners claimed more for their wares than they were authorized to do, and ordinary people believed them. What they were licensed to sell was partial remission of penance for sin, granted by papal authority through a "bull" or written proclamation—that is to say, a man could show his remorse for sin by a charitable contribution instead of by performing some act commanded by his confessor. Gradually, the notion grew up—encouraged by such corrupt practitioners as Chaucer's Pardoner—that exemption from purgatory (the place or state of expiation before admission to heaven) could be so purchased. A pardon was never intended by the Church to grant forgiveness of sins, but ignorant people could be made to believe that it did.

A pardoner was officially appointed and could operate only with the permission of the bishop, who could also license him to preach—a source of much dispute with the friars, who earned part of their livelihood from the same source. In practice, he would often display and sell relics—bodily parts of Christ or the saints or objects associated with them—which were venerated and thought by the simple to give the entree to heaven.

The Pardoner's demonstration of his powers as a preacher is one of the most economical and powerful of *The Canterbury Tales*. It is cast in the form of a set sermon on the desire for money as the root of all evil, opening with a denunciation of the sins of the tavern—drunkenness, gluttony, lechery, blasphemy, and gambling, with the implication that one sin leads to another, that all are related—but reserving his main theme, or *exemplum*, until the audience has been thoroughly drawn into the story (Fig. 38).

The story itself, like many tales that found their way to Europe in the Middle Ages, is Eastern in origin and known in many versions, medieval and modern: it is used by Kipling in his *The King's Ankus*. The irony of it is centered on the fact that three hardened sinners, who have never given a Christian thought to Death, set out in anger and drunkenness to find this murdering creature and kill him. Their ignorance of what they do and what they seek is continually played on; they cannot realize that they are attempting the thing that only Christ and belief in Christ can do, give victory over death and the grave.

The wordes of the Host to the Phisicien and the Pardoner

Oure Hostè gan to swere⸴ as he were wood;⸴	*did swear / mad*
'Harrow!°' quod he, 'by naylès and by blood!°	
This was a fals cherl and a fals justise.°	
As shamful deeth as hertè may devyse	
Come to thise juges and hir advocats!	
Algate⸴ this sely° mayde is slayn, allas!	*anyway*
Allas! to derè boghtè she beautee!	
Wherfore I seye al day,⸴ as men may see	*always*
That yiftès of Fortùne or of Natùre°	
Ben cause of deeth to many a creätùre.	
Hire beautee was hire deth, I dar wel sayn.	
Allas! so pitously as she was slayn!	
Of bothè yiftès that I speke⸴ of now	*spoke*
Men han ful oftè morè harm than prow.⸴	*profit*
But trewèly, myn owene maister dere,	
This is a pitous talè for to heere.	
But nathèlees, passe over, is no fors.⸴	*it is no matter*

10

Harrow help!; here an expression only of astonishment; see the Miller's Tale, l. 178, and the Nun's Priest's Tale, l. 614
by nayles . . . blood By the nails that held Christ on the cross, and by His blood; or, by God's fingernails; but see l. 365. The Pardoner's Tale will later reprove such oaths.
This . . . justise The Host is referring to the Physician's Tale, which has just been told, of Appius and Virginia. Appius Claudius, the Roman magistrate, wanted the beautiful maiden

Virginia as his mistress, and, in a trumped-up law-suit, adjudged her to be the slave of an unscrupulous dependent of his (*cherl*: plebeian, low-born man). Virginia's father killed her on the spot, to preserve her chastity.
sely defenseless, innocent
yiftes . . . Natùre the gifts of Nature are usually youth, beauty, and so on; the gifts of Fortune are wealth and high rank. The distinction is a frequent topos in medieval and Renaissance literature.

I pray to God, so save thy gentil cors,⸣   *body*
And eek thyne urinals and thy jordanes,°

20   Thyn ypocras,° and eek thy galianes,°
And every boist⸣ ful of thy letuarie;°   *box*
God blesse hem, and oure lady Seïnte Marie!
So mot I theen,⸣ thou art a propre man,   *as I may thrive*
And lyk a prelat,° by Saïnt Ronyan!°
Seyde I nat wel? I can nat speke in terme;⸣   *technically*
But wel I woot⸣ thou doost⸣ myn herte to erme,°   *know / make*
That I almost have caught a cardinacle.°
By corpus bonès!° but⸣ I have triacle,°   *unless*
Or elles a draughte of moiste and corny° ale,

30   Or but I here anon⸣ a mery tale,   *quickly*
Myn herte is lost for pitee of this mayde.
Thou bel amy,° thou Pardoner,' he seyde,
'Telle us som myrthe or japès° right anon.'
    'It shal be doon,' quod he, 'by Saint Ronyon!
But first,' quod he, 'heere at this alèstake°
I wol bothe drinke, and eten of a cake.'
    But right anon thise gentils gonne to crye,
'Nay, lat hym telle us of no ribaudye!⸣   *ribaldry*
Telle us som moral thing, that we may lere⸣   *learn*

40   Som wit,° and thannè wol we gladly here.'
    'I graunte, ywis,⸣ quod he, 'but I mot thinke   *certainly*
Upon som honest⸣ thing while that I drinke.'   *a respectable*

---

urinals . . . jordanes Urinals are glass phials used for collecting urine; jordans are here probably round-bellied glass vessels used when urine was to be diagnosed. Or, jordan may here mean chamber-pot: the Host, in his pride at being able to "speak good," may be either mixing up his terms a bit, or he may be mocking the Physician as a looker into urine-pots.
ypocras corruption of the name of Hippocrates, the founder of Greek medicine. It was red wine mixed with spices and sugar, strained through a cloth, and taken as a pleasant drink after food and as a kind of tonic.
galianes either "medicines" or, perhaps, Galen's works; possibly a blunder of the Host's, but certainly connected with the great Greco-Roman doctor Galen (2nd century A.D.), whose name was usually spelled Galien in the Middle Ages
letuarie electuary: medicine in the form of conserve or paste, to be mixed with syrup or other liquid
prelat church dignitary

Ronyan either St. Ronan or St. Ninian; or there may be a pun on runnion (sexual organ)
erme grieve
cardinacle a confusion between cardiacle (the reading of some manuscripts), i.e. cardiac spasm or pain, and cardinal
By . . . bones a blasphemous oath, an illiterate conflation of God's bones! and Corpus Dei! (God's body!)
triacle the best restorative medicine: *theriakon* was originally a remedy for snake-bite and other poisons, and contained the flesh of the snake that had bit one
moiste and corny fresh, new, and malty
bel amy fair friend
som . . . japes something diverting or some jokes
alestake the pole sticking out at an angle from an alehouse wall, with a green bush or garland on it as a sign that refreshment is available (Fig. 39); *cake:* piece of bread
wit knowledge; something that will improve us mentally and morally

Here folweth The Prologe of the Pardoners Tale

Radix malorum est Cupiditas: Ad Thimotheum, sexto.°

'Lordings,' quod he, 'in chirchès' whan I preche,
           ladies and gentlemen / churches
I peynè me' to han an hauteyn° speche,   *take pains*
And ringe it out as round as gooth a belle,
For I can al by rotè' that I telle.   *know all by heart*
My theme° is alwey oon,' and ever was—   *one*
Radix malorum est Cupiditas.
   First I pronouncè whennès' that I come,   *whence*
50 And than my bullès° shewe I, alle and somme.'   *one and all*
Our ligè lordès seel° on my patente,°
That shewe I first, my body to warente,°
That no man be so bold, ne preest ne clerk,°
Me to destourbe' of Cristès holy werk;   *hinder*
And after that than telle I forth my tales:°
Bullès of popès and of cardinales,
Of patriarkes, and bishoppès I shewe;
And in Latyn I speke a wordès fewe,
To saffron' with my predicacioùn,'   *color / preaching*
60 And for to stire' men to devocioùn.   *incite*
Than shewe I forth my longè cristal stones,°
Ycrammèd ful of cloutès' and of bones;   *rags*
Reliks° been they, as wenen' they, echoon.'   *think / each one*
Than have I in latoùn° a sholder-boon
Which that was of an holy Jewès° shepe.
"Good men," seye I, "Tak of my wordès kepe;'   *heed*
If that this boon' be wasshe in any welle,°   *bone*
If cow, or calf, or sheep, or oxè swelle
That any worm hath ete, or worm ystonge,°

Radix . . . sexto "The love of money is the root of evil" (I Timothy 6:10)
hauteyn loud; the word has overtones of exaltation, pride
theme Text. The medieval preacher regularly announced his text, made a sort of introduction (pro-theme), then an exposition or dilatation; followed by an *exemplum* or story which would illustrate the theme; next came an application or peroration, in which the lesson was drawn; and then a closing formula. Not all sermons were arranged to such an exact scheme, and these parts tend to run into each other, but most are built around theme, exposition, *exemplum*, and application. The Pardoner's Tale is more directly a sermon than the Nun's Priest's, but both are in the genre.
bulles papal mandates, permitting the sale of indulgences and setting out their benefits; and perhaps also his bishop's confirmations, which he would carry as his credentials
lordes seel i.e. the pope's or bishop's seal on his official license

patente document open for inspection by anyone
warente warrant; to protect against violence from other clergy or their hirelings who might try to stop him by violence
preest ne clerk no member of the clergy whatever
And . . . tales and after that I carry on with my stories
stones glass jars or encasings
Reliks Trade in false relics was both frequent and a regular object of satire.
latoun Base brassy metal; see the General Prologue, l. 701. The sheep's shoulder-blade was mounted in this imitation gold.
Jewes one of the Old Testament patriarchs, who were pastoralists
welle well, pool, or spring
That . . . ystonge That has eaten any worm or any snake has bitten. Diseases of cattle were thought to come from eating worms; see Milton's *Lycidas*, l. 46. Worm in the second half of the clause probably has its older meaning of serpent.

70 Tak water of that welle, and wash his tonge,	
And it is hool anon;° and forthermore,	*sound at once*
Of pokkès° and of scabbe, and every sore	*pox*
Shal every sheep be hool, that of this welle	
Drinketh a draughte. Tak kepe eek° what I telle,	*notice also*
If that the good-man,° that the bestès oweth,°	*beasts owns*
Wol every wike,° er that the cok him croweth,°	*week*
Fastinge, drinken of this welle a draughte,	
As thilkè° holy Jewe our eldrès taughte,	*the same*
His bestès and his stoor° shal multiplye.	
80 And, sirs, also it heleth° jalousye;	*heals*
For, though a man be falle in jalous rage,	
Let maken with this water his potage,°	*soup*
And never shal he more his wyf mistriste,°	*mistrust*
Though he the sooth° of hir defautè wiste;°	*truth / infidelity knew*
Al had she° taken preestès two or three.	*even though she had*
Heer is a miteyn° eek,° that ye may see.	*also*
He that his hond wol° putte in this miteyn,	*will*
He shal have multiplying of his greyn,°	*grain*
Whan he hath sowen, be it whete° or otes,°	*wheat / oats*
90 So that° he offrè pens, or ellès grotes.°	*as long as*
Good men and wommen, o° thing warne I yow,	*one*
If any wight° be in this chirchè now,	*person*
That hath doon sinnè horrible, that he	
Dar nat,° for shame, of it yshriven be,°	*dare not*
Or any womman, be she yong or old,	
That hath ymaad hir housbond cokèwold,°	*cuckold*
Swich folk shul have no powèr ne no grace	
To offren° to my reliks in this place.	
And whoso findeth him out of swich° blame,	*such*
100 He wol com up and offre in Goddes name,	
And I assoille° him by the auctoritee°	*absolve / authority*
Which that by bulle ygraunted was to me."	
By this gaude° have I wonnè, yeer by yeer,	*trick*
An hundred mark° sith° I was Pardoner.	*since*
I stondè lyk a clerk in my pulpet,	
And whan the lewèd peple is doun yset,°	
I prechè, so as ye han herd bifore,	
And telle an hundred falsè japès° more.	*deceptions*
Than peyne I me° to strecchè forth the nekke,	*take pains*

good-man worthy man, man of substance
er . . . croweth before cock-crow
stoor property, produce, what he has stored in his barns
miteyn a sower's glove
pens . . . grotes pennies or else groats, i.e. silver coins worth four pennies
yshriven be confess it, be shriven of it
Swich . . . offren such people shall not have the power nor the favor to make offerings in reverence to my relics; unconfessed persons can-

not receive the sacraments, or worship at my shrine
mark The mark was worth 13s. 4d., two-thirds of a pound; 100 marks was a large sum, about five times Chaucer's salary from the king; and ten times a schoolmaster's salary.
whan . . . yset when the congregation has sat down; *lewèd:* simple, lay, uneducated. *Yset* may imply that medieval churches had seats for the congregation; but they may well have either brought their own or sat on the floor.

110 And est and west upon the peple I bekke,˃   *nod my head*
    As doth a dowve˃ sitting on a berne.˃   *dove / barn*
    Myn hondes and my tonge goon so yerne.˃   *eagerly*
    That it is joye to see my bisinesse.˃   *activity*
    Of avaryce and of swich cursednesse
    Is al my preching, for to make hem free˃   *open-handed*
    To yeve her pens,˃ and namely˃ unto me.   *money / especially*
    For my entente is nat but˃ for to winne,˃   *only / gain*
    And nothing for correccioun of sinne.
    I rekke˃ never, whan that they ben beried,˃   *care / buried*
120 Though that her soules goon a blakeberied!°
    For certes, many a predicacioun
    Comth oftetyme of yvel entencioun;°
    Som for plesaunce˃ of folk and flaterye,   *pleasure*
    To been avaunced˃ by ipocrisye,   *promoted*
    And som for veyne glorie,˃ and som for hate.   *vainglory*
    For, whan I dar non otherweyes debate,°   .
    Than wol I stinge him with my tonge smerte˃   *sharply*
    In preching, so that he shal nat asterte˃   *escape*
    To been defamed falsly, if that he
130 Hath trespased° to my brethren or to me.   *actual*
    For, though I telle noght his propre˃ name,
    Men shal wel knowe that it is the same
    By signes and by othere circumstances.
    Thus quyte˃ I folk that doon us displesances;˃   *repay / annoyances*
    Thus spitte I out my venim under hewe˃   *color*
    Of holynesse, to seme holy and trewe.
    But shortly myn entente I wol devyse;˃   *describe*
    I preche of nothing but for coveityse.°
    Therfor my theme is yet, and ever was—
140   *Radix malorum est cupiditas.*
    Thus can I preche agayn that same vyce
    Which that I use, and that is avaryce.
    But, though myself be gilty in that sinne,
    Yet can I maken other folk to twinne˃   *separate*
    From avaryce, and sore to repente.
    But that is nat my principal entente.
    I preche nothing˃ but for coveityse;   *not at all*
    Of this matere it oughte ynogh suffyse.°
    Than telle I hem ensamples° many oon
150 Of olde stories, longe tyme agoon:
    For lewed˃ peple loven tales olde;   *simple*

---

goon a-blakeberied go blackberrying, wander anywhere, to Hell, for all I care
many . . . entencioun good preaching often comes from bad intention; i.e. even my badness can be turned to good by Christ; see ll. 173–74
whan . . . debate when I dare attack in no other way

trespased sinned against, injured
I . . . coveityse I preach about nothing except for covetousness
Of . . . suffyse that's enough of that
ensamples *exempla*

Swich thingès can they wel reporte˃ and holde.˃   *repeat / remember*
What˃ trowè˃ ye, the whylès I may preche,   *believe*
And winnè gold and silver for˃ I teche,   *because*
That I wol live in povert wilfully?°
Nay, nay, I thoghte˃ it never trewèly!   *intended*
For I wol preche and begge in sondry londes;
I wol not do no labour with myn hondes,
Ne makè baskettes,° and live therby,
160   Because I wol nat beggen ydelly.°
I wol non of the apostles counterfete;°
I wol have money, wollè,˃ chese,˃ and whete,˃   *wool / cheese / wheat*
Al were it yeven of the povrest page,°
Or of the povrest widwe in a village,
Al sholde hir children stervè° for famyne.
Nay! I wol drinke licour of the vyne,
And have a joly wenche in every toun.
But herkneth,˃ lordings, in conclusioùn;   *listen*
Your lyking˃ is that I shal telle a tale.   *pleasure*
170   Now have I dronke a draughte of corny ale;
By God, I hope I shal yow telle a thing
That shal, by resoun, been at˃ your lyking.   *to*
For, though myself be a ful vicious man,
A moral talè° yet I yow telle can,
Which I am wont to prechè, for to winne.˃   *gain*
Now holde your pees, my tale I wol beginne.'

The Tale

In Flaundres whylom˃ was a companye   *once upon a time*
Of yongè folk, that haunteden˃ folye,   *practiced*
As ryot, hasard, stewès,° and tavernes,
180   Wheras, with harpès, lutès, and giternes,°
They daunce and pleye at dees˃ bothe day and night,   *dice*
And ete also and drinken over hir might,˃   *capacity*
Thurgh which they doon the devel sacrifyse
Within that develes temple, in cursed wyse
By superfluitee˃ abhominàble;°   *overindulgence*

wilfully gladly, voluntarily. Glad Poverty, to be content with what one has, is the reply to Fortune.
make baskettes St. Paul the Hermit is said to have made his living thus.
Because . . . ydelly I will not be a beggar in idleness, or without making money—a hit, like the preceding few lines, at the friars, the preaching orders who were his rivals in supporting themselves by charitable contributions.
counterfete imitate; i.e. by giving up all to follow Christ, which was the precept on which the Franciscan Order was founded
Al . . . page although it were given by the poorest servant-lad
Al . . . sterve even though her children should die (of famine)
For . . . tale See ll. 121–22.
ryot . . . stewes riotous living, gambling, brothels
giternes kind of guitar
abhominable thus spelled because supposed to mean inhuman

Hir othès⸾ been so grete and so dampnàble,⸾   *oaths / damnable*
That it is grisly for to here hem swere;
Our blissed Lordès body they to-tere,°
Hem thoughtè Jewès rente⸾ him noght ynough;   *tore*
190 And ech of hem at otherès sinnè lough.⸾   *laughed*
And right anon than comen tombesterès°
Fetys⸾ and smale,⸾ and yongè fruytesterès,   *well-made / slim*
Singers with harpès, baudès, wafererès,
Whiche been the verray⸾ develès officerès   *true*
To kindle and blowe the fyr of lecherye,
That is annexèd unto glotonye;°
The Holy Writ° take I to my witnesse,
That luxurie⸾ is in wyn and dronkenesse.   *lechery*
   Lo, how that dronken Loth,° unkindely,⸾   *unnaturally*
200 Lay by his doghtrès two, unwitingly;
So dronke he was, he nistè⸾ what he wroghte.   *did not know*
   Heròdès, whoso wel the stories soghte,°
Whan he of wyn was replet at his feste,⸾   *feast*
Right at his owenè table he yaf⸾ his heste⸾   *gave / command*
To sleen⸾ the Baptist John ful giltèlees.⸾   *slay / innocent*
   Senek° seith eek⸾ a good word doutèlees;   *also*
He seith, he can no differencè finde
Bitwix a man that is out of his minde
And a man which that is dronkèlewe,⸾   *drunk*
210 But that woodnesse, yfallen in a shrewe,°
Persevereth lenger than doth dronkenesse.
O glotonyè, ful of cursednesse,⸾   *evil*
O causè first° of our confusioùn,⸾   *downfall*
O original of our dampnacioùn,⸾   *damnation*
Til Crist had boght⸾ us with his blood agayn!   *redeemed*
Lo, how derè,⸾ shortly for to sayn,   *dearly*
Aboght⸾ was thilkè⸾ cursed vileinye;   *paid for / same*
Corrupt⸾ was al this world for glotonye!   *corrupted*
   Adam our fader,⸾ and his wyf also,   *father*
220 Fro Paradys to labour and to wo
Were driven for that vyce, it is no drede;⸾   *doubt*
For whyl that Adam fasted, as I rede,°
He was in Paradys; and whan that he

---

to-tere tear to pieces, by oaths referring to God or Christ's body and limbs (Fig. 40).
tombesteres Dancing girls; *fruytesteres,* fruit sellers; and *wafereres,* cake vendors. But the *tombesteres* may be male tumblers and the *wafereres* male pastry cooks, confectioners; the *baudes*—prostitutes—too can be male or female.
annexed . . . glotonye That is a near neighbor to gluttony. From the first sin in Eden, which combined them, lechery and gluttony are close cousins, not to be separated, as Chaucer says in the Parson's Tale. (See Fig. 39.)
Holy Writ Ephesians 5:18

Loth Lot, who slept with his daughters while drunk (Genesis 19:32 ff.)
Heròdes . . . soghte Herod, whoever looks up the stories properly (see Mark 6:17–29 and Matthew 14:1–11)
Senek Lucius Annaeus Seneca (*c.*4 B.C.–*c.*65 A.D.), Roman Stoic philosopher and dramatist, in his *Moral Letters,* 83:18
But . . . shrewe except that madness, come upon a wicked man
cause first i.e. by Eve's eating the forbidden fruit and giving it to Adam
rede in St. Jerome's *Against Jovinian,* for which see the Wife of Bath's Prologue, l. 681

Eet° of the fruyt defended° on the tree,   *ate / forbidden*
Anon° he was outcast to wo and peyne.
O glotonye, on thee wel oghte us pleyne!°   *cry out*
O, wiste a man° how many maladyes   *if only one knew*
Folwen of èxcesse and of glotonyes,
He woldè been the morè mesuràble°   *moderate*
230   Of his dietè, sittinge at his table.
Allas! the shortè throte, the tendrè mouth,°
Maketh that, Est and West, and North and South,
In erthe, in eir,° in water men to swinke°   *air / toil*
To gete a glotoun deyntee° mete and drinke!   *delicious*
Of this matere, o Paul,° wel canstow trete,°   *can you write*
'Mete unto wombe, and wombe eek unto mete,
Shal God destroyen bothe,' as Paulus seith.
Allas! a foul thing is it, by my feith,
To seye° this word, and fouler is the dede,   *say*
240   Whan man so drinketh of the whyte and rede,°
That of his throte he maketh his privee,°   *privy*
Thurgh thilkè cursèd superfluitee.°   *excess*
    The apostel° weping seith ful pitously,°   *sadly*
'Ther walken many of whiche yow told have I,
I seye it now weping with pitous voys,
That they been enemys of Cristès croys,
Of whiche the ende is deeth, wombe° is her god.'   *stomach*
O wombe! O bely! O stinking cod,°
Fulfild° of donge° and of corrupcioùn!   *filled full / dung*
250   At either ende of thee foul is the soun.°   *sound*
How greet labour and cost is thee to finde!°   *provide for*
Thise cokès,° how they stampe,° and streyne, and grinde,   *pound*
And turnen substaunce into accident,°
To fulfille al thy likerous° talent!
Out of the hardè bonès knokkè they
The mary,° for they castè noght awey   *marrow*
That may go thurgh the golet° softe and swote;°   *gullet / sweetly*

Anon It was a frequent opinion that Adam and Eve spent only one hour together in Paradise.
shorte . . . mouth little throat and soft mouth; or: the brief pleasure of swallowing—a paraphrase of a passage in St. Jerome's *Against Jovinian*
Paul I Corinthians 6:13 ("Meats for the belly and the belly for meats; but God shall destroy them both")
whyte and rede both kinds of wine
apostel St. Paul, Philippians 3:18 ("For many walk, of whom I have told you often, and now tell you even weeping, that they are the enemies of the cross of Christ: whose end is destruction, whose God is their belly")
cod Bag; more frequently used of the scrotum. The discourse on gluttony is from Pope Innocent III's (1160–1216) *De Contemptu Mundi* (On Despising the World), a tract against earthly pleasures.

cokes The passage on the cooks is a close paraphrase of Innocent III.
substaunce . . . accident This philosophic pun is also in Innocent III. In Aristotelian (and so in Scholastic) philosophy, substance is the permanent, inherent, and essential; accident is the changeable and outward, which can be changed without affecting the substance. In ordinary usage, substance is material; in this case, food. So the cooks change substance (the meat, etc.) into its attributes of flavor, taste, smell, etc., the essential into the non-essential. Chaucer may be glancing at the controversies of his day between the opposing philosophic schools of Realists and Nominalists; or at the alchemists, whose aim was to find a way of changing substance.
likerous greedy, fond of choice food; **talent** [evil] inclination, desire, appetite

Of spicerye,ˀ of leef, and bark, and roteˀ	*spices / root*
Shal been his sauce ymakėd, by delytˀ	*through pleasure*
260 To make him yet a newer appetyt.	
But certės, he that haunteth swich delycesˀ	*pleasures*
Is deed,ˀ whyl that he liveth in thoˀ vyces.°	*dead / those*
A lecherous thing is wyn, and dronkėnesse°	
Is ful of stryvingˀ and of wrecchednesse.ˀ	*quarreling / evil*
O dronkė man, disfigured is thy face,	
Sour is thy breeth, foul artowˀ to embrace,	*are you*
And thurgh thy dronkė nose semeth the sounˀ	*sound*
As though thou seydest ayˀ 'Sampsoun, Sampsoun';	*always*
And yet, God wot,ˀ Sampsoun drank never no wyn.°	*knows*
270 Thou fallest, as it were a stikėd swyn;ˀ	*stuck pig*
Thy tonge is lost, and al thyn honest cure;°	
For dronkenesse is verray sepultureˀ	*true burial*
Of mannės wit and his discrecioùn.	
In whom that drinke hath dominacioùn,	
He can no conseil° kepe, it is no drede.ˀ	*doubt*
Now kepe yow fro the whytė and fro the rede,	
And namelyˀ fro the whytė wyn of Lepe,°	*especially*
That is to selleˀ in Fish-strete or in Chepe.°	*for sale*
This wyn of Spaynė crepeth subtilly°	
280 In otherė wynės, growing fastėˀ by,	*close*
Of which ther ryseth swich fumositee,°	
That whan a man hath dronken draughtės three,	
And wenethˀ that he be at hoom in Chepe,	*believes*
He is in Spaynė, right at the toune of Lepe,	
Nat at the Rochel, ne at Burdeux toun;	
And thannė wol he seye, 'Sampsoun, Sampsoun.'	
But herkneth, lordings, o word, I yow praye,	
That alle the sovereyn actės,ˀ dar I seye,	*supreme deeds*
Of victories in the Oldė Testament,	
290 Thurgh verray God, that is omnipotent,	
Were doon in abstinence and in preyère;	
Lokethˀ the Bible, and ther ye may it lere.ˀ	*look at / learn*
Loke, Attila,° the gretė conquerour,	
Deyde in his sleep, with shame and dishonoùr,	

But . . . vyces I Timothy 5:6 ("But she that liveth in pleasure is dead while she liveth"). Quotations from St. Paul, often also used by St. Jerome and Innocent III, are continually interwoven.
dronkenesse Proverbs 20:1 ("Wine is a mocker, strong drink is raging")
Sampsoun . . . wyn Judges 13:4,7; Samson's mother is commanded to drink no wine, and told that her son will be a Nazarite, a sect denying itself wine and strong drink.
cure care for decent behavior, self-respect
conseil secrets, discretion
Lepe a town near Cadiz, Spain, famous for strong wines

Chepe Fish Street and either Eastcheap, near it, or Cheapside; all streets in the City of London, the commercial center
This . . . subtilly a joke about either the mixing of stronger, cheaper Spanish wines with the finer French wines exported from Bordeaux and La Rochelle; or simply selling Spanish wines as French
fumositee See the Nun's Priest's Tale, l. 158.
Attila leader of the Huns—invaders of Italy in the 5th century—who died drunk, of a burst blood vessel, on the last of his many wedding nights

Bledinge ay⁾ at his nose in dronkénesse;   *continually*
A capitayn shoulde live in sobrenesse.
And over⁾ al this, avyseth⁾ yow right wel   *above / consider*
What was comaunded unto Lamuel°—
Nat Samuel, but Lamuel, seye I—
300   Redeth the Bible, and finde it expresly
Of wyn-yeving⁾ to hem that han justyse.°   *wine-serving*
Namore of this, for it may wel suffyse.
    And now that I have spoke of glotonye,
Now wol I yow defenden hasardrye.⁾   *forbid gambling*
Hasard is verray moder⁾ of lesinges,⁾   *mother / lies*
And of deceite, and cursed forsweringes,°
Blasphemé of Crist, manslaughtre, and wast⁾ also   *waste*
Of catel° and of tyme; and forthermo,
It is repreve⁾ and contrarie of honoùr   *reproach*
310   For to ben holde a commune hasardoùr.⁾   *gambler*
And ever the hyër he is of estaat,⁾   *status*
The more is he holden desolaat.⁾   *abandoned*
If that a prince useth hasardrye,
In allé governaunce and policye
He is, as by commune opinioùn,
Yholde⁾ the lasse in reputacioùn.   *considered*
    Stilbon,° that was a wys⁾ embassadoùr,   *prudent*
Was sent to Corinthe, in ful greet honoùr,
Fro Lacidomie,⁾ to make hir alliaùnce.   *Sparta*
320   And whan he cam, him happedé, par chaunce,°
That alle the grettest that were of that lond,
Pleyinge atté hasard° he hem fond.
For which, as sone as it mighté be,
He stal him⁾ hoom agayn to his contree,   *stole away*
And seyde, 'Ther wol I nat lesé⁾ my name;   *lose*
Ne I wol nat take on me so greet defame,⁾   *dishonor*
Yow for to allye unto none hasardoùrs.
Sendeth otheré wyse embassadoùrs;
For, by my trouthe, me were lever⁾ dye,   *I had rather*
330   Than I yow sholde to hasardoùrs allye.
For ye that been so glorious in honoùrs
Shul nat allyen yow with hasardoùrs
As by my will, ne as by my tretee.'⁾   *treaty*
This wyse philosòphre thus seyde he.
    Loke eek⁾ that, to the king Demetrius°   *also*

Lamuel Proverbs 31:4–5; Lemuel's mother told
him: "It is not for kings to drink wine . . . nor
for princes strong drink."
han justyse have judicial power
forsweringes Perjury; the passage is imitated
from the Latin *Policraticus*, a mirror for princes
by John of Salisbury (*c.*1115–80).
catel chattels, possessions, material wealth
Stilbon This story is also in John of Salisbury,
where the ambassador's name is Chilon. Stilbon

was a name for the planet Mercury.
him . . . chaunce it happened to him, by
chance
hasard here, dice
Demetrius Probably Demetrius Nicator, king of
the Parthians, an Asian people; his story is also
in the *Policraticus.* Chaucer may have confused
him with another Demetrius, and got the name
Stilbon above, from a passage in Seneca, where
the two are mentioned together.

The king of Parthès, as the book seith us,
Sente him a paire of dees⸳ of gold in scorn,   *dice*
For he hadde usèd hasard therbiforn;
For which he heeld his glorie or his renoùn
340   At no value or reputacioùn.
Lordès may finden other maner pley⸳   *kind of pastime*
Honeste ynough to dryve the day awey.⸳   *pass the time*
      Now wol I speke of othès⸳ false and grete   *oaths*
A word or two, as oldè bokès trete.
Gret swering is a thing abhominàble,
And false swering is yet more reprevàble.⸳   *reprehensible*
The heighè God forbad swering at al,
Witnesse on Mathew;° but in special
Of swering seith the holy Jeremye,°
350   'Thou shalt seye sooth thyn othès, and nat lye,
And swere in dome, and eek in rightwisnesse';
But ydel swering is a cursèdnesse.
Bihold and see, that in the firstè table°
Of heighè Goddès hestès⸳ honurable,   *commandments*
How that the seconde heste of Him is this—
'Tak nat my name in ydel or amis.'
Lo, rather⸳ he forbedeth swich swering   *sooner*
Than homicyde or many a cursed thing;
I seye that, as by ordre, thus it stondeth;
360   This knoweth that His hestès understondeth,°
How that the second° heste of God is that.
And forther-over,⸳ I wol thee telle al plat,⸳   *moreover / flat*
That vengeance shal nat parten⸳ from his hous,   *depart*
That of his othes⸳ is too outrageous.°   *oaths*
'By Goddès precious herte, and by his nayles,°
And by the blode of Crist that is in Hayles,°
Seven is my chaunce,⸳ and thyn is cink⸳ and treye;⸳   *throw / five / three*
By Goddès armès, if thou falsly pleye,
This dagger shal thurghout thyn herte go'—
370   This fruyt cometh of the bicchèd bonès° two,
Forswering,⸳ irè, falsnesse, homicyde.   *perjury*
Now, for the love of Crist that for us dyde,
Leveth your othès, bothè grete and smale;
But, sirs, now wol I tellè forth my tale.
      Thise ryotourès⸳ three, of whiche I telle,   *revelers*

Mathew Matthew 5:34 ("But I say unto you, swear not at all")
Jeremye Jeremiah 4:2 ("And thou shalt swear: [As] the Lord liveth, in truth, in judgment (*dome*) and in righteousness")
table of the Law, the Ten Commandments, written on two tablets of stone; the first tablet contained the first four, concerning duty toward God
This . . . understondeth this he knows who

understandeth his (God's) commandments
second according to the Vulgate; in the English Bible, the third Commandment
outrageous See Ecclesiaticus 23:12.
nayles See above, l. 2; nails of the Cross, often shown with Christ's pierced heart.
Hayles Hailes, an abbey in Gloucestershire, supposed to possess a phial of Christ's blood
bicched bones bitched, or damned, dice

Longe erst er⸜ prymé° rong of any belle,   *before*
Were set hem in a taverne for to drinke;
And as they satte, they herde a bellé clinke
Biforn a cors,⸜ was caried to his grave;   *corpse*
380 That oon of hem gan callen° to his knave,⸜   *servant*
'Go bet,'° quod he, 'and axé redily,⸜   *ask promptly*
What cors is this that passeth heer forby;⸜   *nearby*
And look⸜ that thou reporte his namé wel.'   *be sure*
        'Sir,' quod this boy, 'it nedeth never-a-del.°
It was me told, er ye cam heer, two houres;
He was, pardee,° an old felawe⸜ of youres;   *companion*
And sodeynly he was yslayn tonight,⸜   *last night*
For-dronké,° as he sat on his bench upright;
Ther cam a privee⸜ theef, men clepeth⸜ Deeth,   *secret / call*
390 That in this contree al the peple sleeth,⸜   *slays*
And with his spere° he smoot his herte atwo,⸜   *in two*
And wente his wey withouten wordés mo.
He hath a thousand slayn this pestilence:⸜   *during this plague*
And, maister, er ye come in his presence,
Me thinketh that it weré necessarie
For to be war⸜ of swich an adversarie: *be careful*
Beth redy for to meete him evermore.
Thus taughté me my dame,⸜ I sey namore.'   *mother*
'By sainté Marie,' seyde this taverner,⸜   *innkeeper*
400 'The child seith sooth, for he hath slayn this yeer,
Henne⸜ over a myle, within a greet village,   *hence*
Both man and womman, child and hyne,⸜ and page   *farm-laborer*
I trowe⸜ his habitacioùn be there;   *believe*
To been avyséd⸜ greet wisdom it were,   *forewarned*
Er that he dide a man a dishonoùr.'
'Ye, Goddés armés,' quod this ryotour,
'Is it swich peril with him for to meete?
I shal him seke by wey and eek by streete,°
I make avow to Goddés digné⸜ bones!   *worshipful*
410 Herkneth, felawes, we three been al ones;⸜   *of one mind*
Lat ech of us holde up his hond til⸜ other,   *to the*
And ech of us bicomen otherés brother,
And we wol sleen⸜ this falsé traytour Deeth;   *slay*
He shal be slayn, which that so many sleeth,
By Goddés dignitee,⸜ er it be night.'   *reverence*
        Togidres han thise three her trouthés plight,°

---

pryme some time between 6 a.m. and 9 a.m.; or just after sunrise; see the Miller's Tale, l. 446, and the Nun's Priest's Tale, ll. 412, 431
gan callen did call
bet better, i.e. as fast as you can
it . . . never-a-del it isn't the least bit necessary
pardee indeed (literally, *par Dieu*, by God)
For-dronke blind drunk
spere Death's dart
by wey . . . streete by path and paced road; by highway and byway; everywhere
her . . . plight pledged their words, swearing to be as brothers by blood

To live and dyen ech of hem for other,
As though he were his owene yborenᐳ brother.   *born*
And up they sterteᐳ al dronken, in this rage,   *leapt*
420   And forth they goon towardes that village,
Of which the taverner had spoke biforn,
And many a grislyᐳ ooth than han they sworn,   *terrible*
And Cristes blessed body° they to-renteᐳ—   *tore apart*
'Deeth shal be deed,ᐳ if that they may him hente.ᐳ   *dead / catch*
    Whan they han goon nat fully half a myle,
Right as they wolde han trodenᐳ over a style,   *stepped*
An old man° and a povreᐳ with hem mette.   *poor*
This olde man ful mekely hem grette,ᐳ   *greeted*
And seyde thus, 'Now, lordes, God yow see!ᐳ   *protect*
430   The proudest of thise ryotoures three
Answerde agayn, 'What! carl,ᐳ with sory grace,°   *churl*
Why artowᐳ al forwrappedᐳ save thy faceᐳ   *are you / completely swathed*
Why livestow so longe in so greet age?ᐳ
    This olde man gan loke in his visage,
And seyde thus, 'Forᐳ I ne can nat finde   *because*
A man, though that I walked into Inde,°
Neither in citee nor in no village,
That wolde chaunge his youthe for myn age;
And therfore mootᐳ I han myn age stille,ᐳ   *must / always*
440   As longe time as it is Goddes wille.
    Ne deeth, allas! ne wol nat han my lyf;
Thus walke I, lyk a restelees caityf,ᐳ   *captive*
And on the ground, which is my modresᐳ gate,   *mother's*
I knokke with my staf, bothe erly and late,
And seye, "Leveᐳ moder, leet me in!   *dear*
Lo, how I vanish, flesh, and blood, and skin!
Allas! whan shul my bones been at reste?
Moder, with yow wolde I chaungeᐳ my cheste,   *exchange*
That in my chambre longe tyme hath be,
450   Ye! for an heyre clowt to wrappe me!"°
But yet to me she wol nat do that grace,
For which ful pale and welkedᐳ is my face.   *withered*
    But, sirs, to yow it is no curteisye
To speken to an old man vileinye,ᐳ   *roughness*
Butᐳ he trespasse in worde, or elles in dede.   *unless*
In Holy Writ ye may yourself wel rede,°

---

body See Fig. 40.
old man seemingly Chaucer's invention. In the
Italian version there is a hermit, fleeing from
Death as the riotors go to meet him.
with . . . grace with wretched looks; or, an
imprecation: Devil take it
Inde India, an image of remoteness, the Far
East. Chaucer makes his old man a version of
the legendary Wandering Jew, Ahasuerus, who
was condemned to walk the earth eternally for

having refused a resting place to Christ on the
road to Calvary. To find death would be for him
a release.
Moder . . . me (ll. 448–50) Mother, I should
like to exchange with you my chest [earthly pos-
sessions], which has long been in my bedroom,
even for a hair-cloth to wrap myself in; i.e. he
asks Earth to take him, in a common shroud
rede Leviticus 19:32: "Thou shalt rise up before the hoary head."

"Agayns° an old man, hoor° upon his heed,   *before / white*
Ye sholde aryse"; wherfor I yeve° yow reed,°   *give / advice*
Ne dooth unto an old man noon harm now,
460 Namorė than ye wolde men dide to yow
In agė, if that ye so longe abyde;
And God be with yow, wher ye go or ryde.°
I moot go thider as I have to° go.'   *where I must*
      'Nay, oldė cherl, by God, thou shalt nat so,'
Seydė this other hasardour anon;
'Thou partest nat so lightly,° by Saint John!   *easily*
Thou spak right now of thilkė traitour Deeth,
That in this contree alle our frendės sleeth.
Have heer my trouthe,° as thou art his aspye,°   *word / spy*
470 Tel wher he is, or thou shalt it abye,°   *pay for it*
By God, and by the holy sacrament!°
For soothly thou art oon of his assent,°
To sleen us yongė folk, thou falsė theef!'
      'Now, sirs,' quod he, 'if that yow be so leef°   *wishful*
To findė Deeth, turne up this crookėd wey,
For in that grove I laft° him, by my fey,°   *left / faith*
Under a tree, and ther he wol abyde;
Nat for your boost° he wol him nothing hyde.   *boasting*
See ye that ook?° Right ther ye shul him finde.   *oak*
480 God savė yow, that boghte agayn° mankinde,   *redeemed*
And yow amende!'° Thus seydė this oldė man.
And everich° of thise ryotourės ran,   *each*
Til he cam to that tree, and ther they founde
Of florins° fyne of goldė ycoynėd rounde
Wel ny an eightė busshels, as hem thoughte.
No lenger thanne after Deeth they soughte,
But ech of hem so glad was of that sighte,
For that the florins been so faire and brighte,
That doun they sette hem by this precious hord.
490 The worste of hem he spake the firstė word.
      'Brethren,' quod he, 'tak kepė what I seye;
My wit is greet, though that I bourde° and pleye.   *jest*
This tresor hath Fortune unto us yiven,°   *given*
In mirthe and jolitee our lyf to liven,
And lightly° as it comth, so wol we spende.   *easily*
Ey! Goddės precious dignitee!° who wende°   *reverence / expected*
To-day, that we sholde han so fair a grace?
But mighte this gold be cariėd fro this place
Hoom to myn hous, or ellės unto youres—
500 For wel ye woot that al this gold is oures—

wher . . . ryde whether you walk or ride; an   And . . . amende bring you to better state
oral formula: whatever you do   florins originally coined in Florence. In Chaucer's
sacrament Eucharist   time the English florin, worth 6s. 8d. (one-
oon . . . assent one of those who accept him;   third of a pound), was relatively new.
one of his following

Than were we in heigh felicitee.
But trewely, by daye it may nat be;
Men wolde seyn that we were theves stronge,°   *violent*
And for our owene tresor doon us honge.°   *have us hanged*
This tresor moste ycaried be by nighte
As wysly° and as slyly as it mighte.   *carefully*
Wherfore I rede° that cut° among us alle   *advise*
Be drawe, and lat se wher the cut wol falle;
And he that hath the cut with herte blythe

510 Shal renne° to the toune, and that ful swythe,°   *run / quickly*
And bringe us breed and wyn ful prively.°   *secretly*
And two of us shul kepen° subtilly   *guard*
This tresor wel; and, if he wol nat tarie,
Whan it is night, we wol this tresor carie
By oon assent,° wheras us thinketh best.'   *agreement*
That oon of hem the cut broughte in his fest,°   *closed fist*
And bad hem drawe, and loke wher it wol falle;
And it fil° on the yongeste of hem alle;   *fell*
And forth toward the toun he wente anon.

520 And also° sone as that he was gon,   *as*
That oon of hem spak thus unto that other,
'Thou knowest wel thou art my sworne brother,
Thy profit wol I telle thee anon.
Thou woost wel that our felawe is agon;°   *gone*
And heer is gold, and that ful greet plentee,
That shal departed° been among us three.   *divided*
But natheles, if I can shape° it so   *arrange*
That it departed were among us two,
Hadde I nat doon a freendes torn° to thee?'   *turn*

530 That other answerde, 'I noot° how that may be;   *do not know*
He woot how that the gold is with us tweye,
What shal we doon, what shal we to him seye?'
'Shal it be conseil?° seyde the firste shrewe,°   *secret / villain*
'And I shal tellen thee, in wordes fewe,
What we shal doon, and bringe it wel aboute.'
'I graunte,' quod that other, 'out of doute,
That, by my trouthe, I wol thee nat biwreye.'°   *expose*
'Now,' quod the firste, 'thou woost wel we be tweye,°   *two*
And two of us shul strenger° be than oon.   *must stronger*

540 Look whan that he is set,° and right anoon   *seated*
Arys,° as though thou woldest with him pleye;   *get up*
And I shal ryve° him thurgh the sydes tweye   *pierce*
Whyl that thou strogelest with him as in game,
And with thy dagger look thou do the same;
And than shal al this gold departed be,
My dere freend, bitwixen me and thee;

cut lot; see the General Prologue, l. 837. They
draw lots to see who will go to town.

Than may we bothe our lustès° al fulfille,   *desires*
And pleye at dees° right at our owene wille.'   *dice*
And thus acorded° been thise shrewès tweye   *agreed*
550 To sleen° the thridde, as ye han herd me seye.   *slay*
　　　This yongest, which that wente unto the toun,
Ful ofte in herte he rolleth up and doun
The beautee of thise florins newe and brighte.
'O Lord!' quod he, 'if so were that I mighte
Have al this tresor to myself allone,
Ther is no man that liveth under the trone°   *throne*
Of God, that sholdè live so mery as I!'
And attè laste the Feend,° our enemy,   *devil*
Putte in his thought that he shold poyson beye,°   *buy*
560 With which he mightè sleen his felawes tweye;
For why the Feend fond him in swich lyvinge,°
That he had levè° him to sorwe bringe,   *leave*
For this was outrèly° his fulle entente   *utterly*
To sleen hem bothe, and never to repente.
And forth he gooth, no lenger wolde he tarie,
Into the toun, unto a pothecarie,°   *apothecary*
And preyèd him, that he him woldè selle
Som poyson, that he mighte his rattès quelle;°   *kill*
And eek ther was a polcat° in his hawe,°   *polecat / yard*
570 That, as he seyde, his capouns hadde yslawe,°   *slain*
And fayn° he woldè wreke° him, if he mighte,   *gladly / revenge*
On vermin,° that destroyèd° him by nighte.   *ruined*
　　　The pothecarie answerde, 'And thou shalt have
A thing that, also° God my soulè save,   *as*
In al this world ther nis no creätùre,
That ete or dronke hath of this confitùre°   *mixture*
Noght but the mountance° of a corn° of whete,   *amount / grain*
That he ne shal his lyf anon forlete;°   *lose*
Ye, sterve° he shal, and that in lassè whyle   *die*
580 Than thou wolt goon a paas° nat but a myle;   *at walking pace*
This poyson is so strong and violent.'
　　　This cursed man hath in his hond yhent°   *taken*
This poyson in a box, and sith° he ran   *then*
Into the nextè strete, unto a man,
And borwed of him largè botels three;
And in the two his poyson pourèd he;
The thridde he keptè clenè for his drinke.
For al the night he shoop° him for to swinke°   *intended / toil*
In caryinge of the gold out of that place.
590 And whan this ryotour, with sory grace,
Had filled with wyn his gretè botels three,

For why . . . lyvinge because the Devil found　　the Devil can only act with His permission.
him in such a state of life that he had leave　　**vermin** any reptile or marauding animal
to bring him to grief. Since God foreordains all,

To his felawes agayn repaireth he.
    What nedeth it to sermone of it more?
For right as they had cast° his deeth bifore,   *plotted*
Right so they han him slayn, and that anon.
And whan that this was doon, thus spak that oon,
'Now lat us sitte and drinke, and make us merie,
And afterward we wol his body berie.'°   *bury*
And with that word it happèd him, par cas,°   *by chance*
600   To take the botel ther° the poyson was,   *where*
And drank, and yaf his felawe drinke also,
For which anon they storven° bothè two.   *died*
    But, certès, I suppose that Avicen°
Wroot never in no canon, ne in no fen,
Mo wonder signès° of empoisoning
Than hadde thise wrecchès two, er° hir ending.   *before*
Thus ended been thise homicydès two,
And eek the false empoysoner also.

        O cursed sinnè,° ful of cursednesse!
610   O traytours homicyde, o wikkednesse!
O glotonye, luxurie,° and hasardrye!   *lechery*
Thou blasphemoùr of Crist with vileinye
And othès° grete, of usage° and of pryde!   *oaths / habit*
Allas! mankinde, how may it bityde,°   *happen*
That to thy creatoùr which that thee wroghte,°   *made*
And with his precious hertè-blood thee boghte,°   *redeemed*
Thou art so fals and so unkinde,° allas!°   *unnatural*
        Now, goode men, God forgeve yow your trespas,
And ware° yow fro the sinne of avaryce.   *guard*
620   Myn holy pardoun may yow alle waryce,°   *preserve*
So that ye offre nobles° or sterlinges,°
Or ellès silver brochès, sponès, ringes.
Boweth your heed° under this holy bulle!   *head*
Cometh up, ye wyves, offreth of your wolle!°   *wool*
Your name I entre heer in my rolle anon;
Into the blisse of hevene shul ye gon;
I yow assoilè,° by myn heigh power,   *absolve*
Yow that wol offre, as clene and eek as cleer
As ye were born and, lo, sirs, thus I preche.
630   And Jesu Crist, that is our soulès leche,°   *physician*

Avicen Avicenna (d. 1037), the Arab philosopher and physician, whose *Canon of Med-*
icine, divided into fens or sections, was a
standard textbook and included a section on
poisons. Cf. the General Prologue, l. 434.
wonder signes extraordinary symptoms
sinne The Pardoner turns to the application of
his *exemplum* and to his *peroration:* exclamation
upon the horror of sin, followed by invitation
to repent—on the Pardoner's terms.
Allas! mankinde . . . allas (ll. 614–17) an

imitation of the Reproach of Christ, part of
the Office for the fourth Sunday in Lent and
often made into English lyric verse; Christ addresses man from the Cross: "Man, full dearly
I have thee bought / How is it that thou lov'st
me not? . . ."
nobles gold, valuable coins; see the Miller's
Tale, l. 148
sterlinges silver pennies, less valuable, 80 to
the noble

So graunté yow his pardon to receyve;
For that is best; I wol yow nat deceyve.
  But sirs, o word forgat I in my tale,
I have relikes and pardon in my male,˃   *bag*
As faire as any man in Engèlond,
Whiche were me yeven by the popès hond.
If any of yow wol, of devocioùn,
Offren, and han myn absolucioùn,
Cometh forth anon, and kneleth heer adoun,
640   And mekèly receyveth my pardoùn:
Or ellès, taketh pardon as ye wende,˃   *go*
Al newe and fresh, at every tounès ende,
So that ye offren alwey newe and newe˃   *again and again*
Nobles and pens, which that be gode and trewe.°
It is an honour˃ to everich that is heer,   *good thing*
That ye mowe have a suffisant˃ pardoneer   *competent*
T'assoillé yow, in contree as ye ryde,
For aventurès˃ which that may bityde.   *chances*
Peràventure˃ ther may falle oon or two   *perhaps*
650   Doun of his hors, and breke his nekke atwo.
Look which a seuretee˃ is it to yow alle   *safeguard*
That I am in your felaweship yfalle,
That may assoille yow, bothè more and lasse,°
Whan that the soule shal fro the body passe.
I redè˃ that our hoste heer shal biginne,   *counsel*
For he is most envolupèd˃ in sinne.   *wrapped*
Com forth, sir Hoste, and offre first anon,
And thou shalt kisse the reliks everichon,
Ye, for a grote! unbokel˃ anon thy purs.'   *unbuckle*

660   'Nay, nay,' quod he, 'than have˃ I Cristès curs!   *would have*
Lat be,' quod he, 'it shal nat be, so theech!˃   *may I thrive*
Thou woldest make me kissè thyn old breech,˃   *breeches*
And swere it were a relik of a saint,
Thogh it were with thy fundement depeint!˃   *stained*
But by the croys which that Saint Eleynè° fond,
I wolde I hadde thy coillons˃ in myn hond   *testicles*
In stede of relikes or of seintuarie;˃   *reliquary*
Lat cutte hem of, I wol thee helpe hem carie;
Thay shul be shrynèd in an hoggès tord.'˃   *turd*
670   This pardoner answerdè nat a word;
So wrooth he was, no word ne wolde he seye.
  'Now,' quod our Host, 'I wol no lenger pleye
With thee, ne with noon other angry man.'

Nobles . . . trewe Nobles and pennies, good and not forgeries. The debasement of currency, by forgery and otherwise, was a continual problem.

more and lasse great and small; everybody
Eleyne St. Helena, mother of the Emperor Constantine the Great, and said to have discovered the true Cross

But right anon the worthy Knight bigan,
Whan that he saugh that al the peple lough,°   *laughed*
'Namore of this, for it is right ynough;
Sir Pardoner, be glad and mery of chere;
And ye, sir Host, that been to me so dere,
I prey yow that ye kisse the Pardoner.°
680 And Pardoner, I prey thee, drawe thee neer,
And, as we diden, lat us laughe and pleye.'
Anon they kiste, and riden forth hir weye.

Here is ended the Pardoners Tale

Retraction

Heere taketh the makere of this book his leve

Now preye I to hem alle that herkne[1] this litel tretys[2] or rede, that if ther be any thyng in it that liketh[3] hem, that therof they thanken oure Lord Jhesu Crist, of whom procedeth al wit[4] and al goodnesse. And if ther be any thyng that displese hem, I preye hem also that they arrette it to the defaute of myn unkonnynge,[5] and nat to my wyl, that wolde ful fayn have seyd bettre if I hadde had konnynge. For oure book[6] seith, 'Al that is writen is writen for oure doctrine,'[7] and that is myn entente. Wherfore I biseke[8] yow mekely, for the mercy of God, that ye preye for me that Crist have mercy on me and foryeve me my giltes; and namely[9] of my translacions and enditynges[10] of worldly vanitees, the whiche I revoke in my retracciouns: as is the book of Troilus;[11] the book also of Fame;[12] the book of the xxv. Ladies;[13] the book of the Duchesse; the book of Seint Valentynes day of the Parlement of Briddes;[14] the tales of Caunterbury, thilke that sownen into[15] synne; the book of the Leoun;[16] and many another book, if they were in my remembrance, and many

kisse the Pardoner Kissing between men, especially as a sign of peace-making, was normal. The Knight and the Host use the familiar "thou" when addressing the Pardoner, but the more formal "you" with each other.

1. Hear, listen to.
2. Treatise.
3. Pleases.
4. Knowledge.
5. Ascribe it to my defect of lack of skill.
6. The Bible.
7. Romans 15:4; see the Nun's Priest's Tale, l. 675.
8. Beseech.
9. Especially.
10. Verses.
11. *Troilus and Criseyde.*
12. *The House of Fame.*
13. *The Legend of Good Women.*
14. Birds, i.e. *The Parliament of Fowls.*
15. Tend toward.
16. This has not survived and we do not know what it was.

a song and many a leccherous lay; that Crist for his grete mercy foryeve me the synne. But of the translacion of Boece de Consolacione,[17] and othere bookes of legendes of saintes, and omelies,[18] and moralitee, and devocioun, that thanke I oure Lord Jhesu Crist and his blisful [19] Mooder, and alle the saintes of hevene, bisekynge hem that they from hennes forth [20] unto my lyves ende sende me grace to biwayle my giltes, and to studie to the salvacioun of my soule, and graunte me grace of verray penitence, confessioun and satisfaccioun to doon in this present lyf, thurgh the benigne grace of hym that is kyng of kynges and preest over alle preestes, that boghte [21] us with the precious blood of his herte; so that I may been oon of hem at the day of doom [22] that shulle be saved. *Qui cum patre et Spiritu Sancto vivit et regnat Deus per omnia secula.*[23] Amen.

> *Heere is ended the book of the tales of Caunterbury, compiled by Geffrey Chaucer, of whos soule Jhesu Crist have mercy. Amen.*

c. 1400

Shorter Poems

In many ways the handful of short poems that Chaucer wrote are the best introduction to his genius and to some of the basic concepts of his world of thought. The metric and the verse forms of all of the short poems are borrowed from French, the concepts that they play with are ultimately French; yet each is individually Chaucerian, with his characteristic witty turn. The first two here given, "Gentilesse" and "Truth," are *balades* on the French model, rhyming stanzas with refrain, seriously exploring the moral virtues of their titles. The roundel from *The Parliament of Fowls* is a "straight" performance, and so is Troilus's song, translated from a sonnet by Petrarch into the French *rime royal* of the long poem from which it is taken. The *balade* from *The Legend of Good Women* is a serious, rhetorical amassing of examples of true ladies, but "To Rosemounde" is a parody of the courtly love lyric, and "The Complaint to His Purse" a turning upside-down of all the values of the courtly code of love, expressed in the strictest and most exact form of the love complaint. "To Adam" is a biting comment on the fallibility of scribes, written as if it were one of those rhyming tags by which manuscript copyists congratulate themselves on the completion of their task.

17. Boethius, *De Consolatione Philosophiae* (Of the Consolation of Philosophy).
18. Homilies.
19. Blessed.
20. Henceforth.
21. Bought, redeemed.
22. Judgment.
23. "Who, with the Father and the Holy Ghost, lives and reigns, God in all eternity"; a doxology, or praise to God, at completion of a prayer or intercession.

Gentilesse°

The firstè stok,° fader⸦ of gentilesse—	*father*
What man that claymeth gentil for to be	
Must followe his trace, and alle his wittès° dresse	
Vertu to sewe,⸦ and vyces for to flee.	*follow*
For unto vertu longeth dignitèe,⸦	*belongs rank*
And noght the revers, saufly dar⸦ I deme,⸦	*safely dare / judge*
Al were he mytre, croune, or diademe.°	

This firstè stok was ful of rightwisnesse,⸦	*righteousness*
Trewe of his word, sobre, pitous,⸦ and free,⸦	*merciful / generous*
10 Clene of his gost,⸦ and lovèd besinesse,⸦	*pure in spirit / industry*
Ageinst the vyce of slouthe,⸦ in honestee;⸦	*sloth / righteousness*
And, but⸦ his heir love vertu, as dide he,	*unless*
He is noght gentil, thogh he richè seme,°	
Al were he mytre, croune, or diademe.	

Vyce may wel be heir to old richesse;	
But ther may no man, as men may wel see,	
Bequethe his heir his vertuous noblesse	
That is appropred⸦ unto no degree,	*assigned solely*
But to the firstè fader in magestee,	
20 That maketh him his heyre that can him queme,⸦	*please*
Al were he mytre, croune, or diademe.	

c. 1385

Truth

Flee fro the prees⸦ and dwell with soothfastnesse;⸦	*throng / truth*
Suffice unto thy good, though it be smal;	
For hord⸦ hath hate, and climbing tikelnesse,⸦	*hoarding / insecurity*
Prees hath envye, and welè blent overal;°	
Savour no more than thee behovè shal.°	
Wirche⸦ wel thyself, that other folk canst rede;⸦	*act / advise*
And Trouthè shal delivere, it is no drede.°	

Tempest thee not al crokèd to redresse,°	
In trust of hir that turneth as a bal°—	

Gentilesse Four important discussions of the sources and nature of *gentilesse* are Boethius, *De Consolatione Philosophiae* III, prose 6 and meter 6; Dante, *Convivio*, tract. 4; the *Roman de la Rose*, ll. 18607–896; and Chaucer's Wife of Bath's Tale, ll. 1109–64.
stok Literally, trunk, stem (of a tree); thus, founder of a family or line of descent. The reference is probably to Christ, the perfection of humanity and the New Adam, i.e. the repairer of the perfect condition of humanity possessed by Adam before the Fall.
Must . . . wittes he must follow in his footsteps and dispose all his wits, i.e. the five senses of sight, hearing, smell, taste, touch
Al . . . diademe even if he should wear miter, crown, or diadem—i.e. should be a prince of the church, a king, or a nobleman
thogh . . . seme though he is outwardly rich
Prees . . . overal the crowd is full of striving, and prosperity blinds one completely
Savour . . . shal taste no more than you ought
And . . . drede And truth shall make you free, there is no fear; see the words of Christ to his disciples, John 8:32: "And ye shall know the truth and the truth shall make you free."
Tempest . . . redresse do not harass yourself to set right all that is not straight
hir . . . bal Fortune, unstable and continually turning. She is sometimes, a little later, shown as sitting on a ball which is balanced on a knife edge.

10　For grete rest stant⸴ in litel bisinesse;⸴ *stands / agitation*
　　And elk be ware to sporne ayen an al;°
　　Strive not as doth the crokké with the wal.°
　　　Daunté⸴ thyself, that dauntest otheres dede;⸴ *govern / deed*
　　And Trouthé shal delivere, it is no drede.

　　That thee is sent, receive in buxumnesse;⸴ *with good grace*
　　The wrestling for this worlde asketh⸴ a fal: *asks for*
　　Here is none home, here nis but wildernesse:
　　　Forth, pilgrim,° forth! Forth, beest,° out of thy stal!⸴ *stall*
　　Know thy countree,⸴ look up,° thank God of⸴ al. *(heavenly) homeland / for*
20　Hold the high way and let thy gost⸴ thee lede; *spirit*
　　And Trouthé shal delivere, it is no drede.

　　　Envoy

　　Therfore, thou Vache,° leve thyn olde wrecchednesse⸴ *evil condition*
　　Unto the world; leve⸴ now to be thrall.⸴ *cease / slave*
　　Crye Him mercy° that of His heigh goodnesse
　　Made thee of nought, and in especial
　　Draw unto him, and praye in general,
　　　For thee and eek for othere, hevenlich meede.⸴ *reward*
　　And Trouthé shal delivere, it is no drede.
　　　c. 1390

Roundel° *from* The Parliament of Fowls

680　Now welcome, somer, with thy sunné softe,⸴ *warm*
　　That hast this wintres wedres overshake⸴ *storms shaken off*
　　And driven away the longé nightés blake!

　　Saint Valentin,° that art ful hy on-lofte,⸴ *aloft*
　　Thus singen smalé fowlés⸴ for thy sake: *birds*
　　　'Now welcome, somer, with thy sunné softe,
　　　That hast this wintres wedres overshake!'

　　Wel han they causé for to gladden ofte,°
　　Sith⸴ ech of hem recovered hath his make;⸴ *since / mate*
690　Ful blissful mowe⸴ they singé when they wake: *may*
　　　'Now welcome, somer, with thy sunné softe,

al awl; i.e. be careful not to kick against the pricks (Acts 9:5)
Strive . . . wal Do not contend, or you will be broken, like an earthenware pot against a wall. See the Aesopic fable of the metal and earthen pots.
pilgrim Life as a pilgrimage was an especially popular image in the Middle Ages.
beest Animals, not having reason, could not be expected to behave reasonably, i.e. virtuously. A man who does not behave reasonably reduces himself to the condition of an animal. Chaucer now begins to play with this notion.
look up A quadruped's head hung down, which was held to be a sign of its lack of rationality. If it were rational, it would look up.
Vache you cow (Fr. *vache*), i.e. beast; probably with a pun on the name of Sir Philip de la Vache
Crye . . . mercy Beg mercy of Him; or: thank Him, who fashioned you from nothing
Roundel a short poem, also called a triolet—developed in France—in which the first lines recur as a refrain; see the Franklin's Tale, l. 240
Saint Valentin The traditional association of St. Valentine with courtship has no foundation except that his day, February 14, was a Roman fertility festival at the beginning of spring.
Wel . . . ofte they have good reason to rejoice often

That hast this wintres wedres overshake
And driven away the longe nightes blake!'
1382–83

From Troilus and Criseyde

Book I

CANTUS TROILI°

400 'If no love is,° O God, what fele I so?	*there is*
And if love is, what thing and whiche is he?	
If love be good, from whennes° comth my wo?	*whence*
If it be wikke,° a wonder thinketh me,°	*bad*
When every torment and adversitee	
That cometh of him, may to me savory° thinke;	*pleasant*
For ay° thurst I, the more that I it drinke.	*ever*
And if that at myn owene lust° I brenne,°	*pleasure / burn*
Fro whennes cometh my wailing and my pleynte?°	*complaint*
If harme agree me,° wher-to pleyne I thenne?	
410 I noot,° ne why unwery that I faynte.	*do not know*
O quike° deeth, o swete harm° so queynte,	*living / curious*
How may of thee in me swich quantitee,°	
But if that I consente that it be?	
And if that I consente, I wrongfully	
Compleyne, y-wis;° thus possed° to and fro,	*certainly*
Al sterelees° withinne a boot am I	
Amid the see,° bytwixen° windes two,	*sea / between*
That in contrarie stonden° evermo.	*opposition stand*
Allas! what is this wonder° maladye?	*strange*
420 For hete° of cold, for cold of hete, I dye.'	*heat*
c. 1385	

Cantus Troili the song of Troilus, now fallen in love with Criseyde, a translation from the Italian of Petrarch's Sonnet LXXXVIII to Laura, "S'amor non è," "amplified" to three *Troilus*-stanzas. It is the first English work based on any of Petrarch's Italian poetry, complete with mistranslations.
a wonder . . . me it seems to me very strange (a marvel)
If . . . me if hurt gives me pleasure
quike . . . harm rhetorical use of contradic-

tory terms (oxymoron), especially common in Petrarch and in ancient, medieval, and Renaissance love poetry
How may . . . quantitee How can there be such a quantity of you [the contrasts of love] in me, unless I consent to it?
possed pushed; thus, tossed
sterelees i.e. completely rudderless in a boat. The image of the sea-tossed lover is a favorite one in classical and Petrarchan poetry.

Balade *from* The Legend of Good Women°

Hide, Absolon,° thy giltĕˀ tresses clere;ˀ	*golden / shining*
250 Ester, lay thou thy meekness al adoun;° | |
Hide, Jonathas,° al thy frendly manère; | |
    Penalopee° and Marcia Catoùn,° | |
    Make of your wifhood no comparisoùn; | |
      Hide ye your beautés, Isoude° and Eleyne:° | |
      My lady comth, that al this may disteine.ˀ | *outshine* |

Thy fairĕ body let it not appere,	
    Lavine;° and thou, Lucresse° of Romĕ toun, | |
And Polixene,° that boughtenˀ love so dere,ˀ | *bought / dearly* |
    And Cleopatre,° with al thy passioùn, | |
260 Hide ye your troutheˀ of love and your renoùn; | *fidelity* |
      And thou, Tisbé,° that hastˀ for love swichˀ peine: | *had / such* |
      My lady comth, that al this may disteine. | |

Hero,° Dido,° Laodamia,° alle y-fere,ˀ	*together*
    And Phillis,° hanging for thy Demophoun,° | |
And Canacee,° espiĕdˀ by thy chere,ˀ | *found out / appearance* |
    Ysiphilee,° betraisĕd withˀ Jasoùn, | *betrayed by* |
      Make of your troutheˀ neither bostˀ ne soun;ˀ | *fidelity / boast / vaunt* |
      Nor Ypermestre° or Adriane,° ye tweine:ˀ | *two* |
      My lady comth, that al this may disteine. | |

c. 1385

The Legend . . . Women For a discussion of this poem, see the Headnote to Chaucer. Though *The Legend* is the first English poem in heroic couplets, this lyric in *balade* form occurs in it.
Absolon Absalom, famed for the beauty of his hair; see the Miller's Tale, l. 128
Ester . . . adoun Esther, resign your title to graciousness. Esther was the beautiful Jewish maiden whom King Ahasuerus chose as his queen instead of Queen Vashti.
Jonathas Jonathan, David's friend, the pattern of "friendliness"
Penalopee Penelope, the patient and loyal wife of Ulysses
Marcia Catoun daughter of Cato of Utica, who refused to remarry
Isoude Isolde, who gave up husband and life for love of Tristram
Eleyne Helen, wife of Menelaus, who ran off with Paris and provoked the Trojan War
Lavine Lavinia, wife of Aeneas
Lucresse Lucretia, who killed herself after her rape by Tarquin

Polixene Polyxena, who stayed with her father Priam and was killed with him
Cleopatra, Cleopatra, mistress of Julius Caesar and Mark Antony, who killed herself at Antony's death
Tisbé Thisbe, who killed herself because she thought her lover Pyramus dead
Hero Hero of Sestos, loved by Leander
Dido Dido of Carthage, lover of Aeneas
Laodamia Laodameia, wife of Protesilaus, who accompanied him to the shades
Phillis Phyllis, who hanged herself when her lover Demophon abandoned her
Canacee committed suicide when her incest with her brother Macaraeus was discovered
Ysiphilee Hypsipyle, pregnant and abandoned by Jason, leader of the Argonauts
Ypermestre Hypermnestra, who refused to murder her husband
Adriane Ariadne, abandoned wife of Theseus. Both she and Hypermnestra had abandoned their fathers for love.

To Rosemounde°

Madame, ye ben of al beautè shryne
As fer as cercled is the mappèmounde,°
For as the cristal° glorious ye shyne,
And likè ruby ben your chekès rounde.
Therwith ye ben so mery and so jocoùnde°
That at a revel whan that I see you daunce,
It is an oynèment> unto my wounde,   *ointment*
Thogh ye to me ne do no daliaùnce.°

For thogh I wepe of terès> ful a tyne,>   *tears / vat*
10 Yet may that wo myn hertè nat confounde;
Your semy voys, that ye so smal out-twyne,°
Maketh my thoght in joy and blis habounde.°
So curteisly° I go, with lovè bounde,
That to myself I sey, in my penaùnce,°
'Suffyseth me to love you, Rosemounde,
Thogh ye to me ne do no daliaùnce.'

Nas never pyk walwed in galauntyne°
As I in love am walwed and ywounde,>   *wound about*
For which ful ofte I of myself divyne>   *discover*
20 That I am trewè Tristam° the secoùnde.
My love may not refreydè nor affounde;°
I brenne> ay in an amorous plesaùnce.>   *burn / pleasure*
Do what you lyst,> I wil your thral> be founde, *(it) pleases you / slave*
Thogh ye to me ne do no daliaùnce.

c. 1385?

The Complaint° of Chaucer to His Purse

To you, my purse, and to non other wight>   *creature*
Compleyne I, for ye be my lady dere!
I am so sory,> now that ye be light,   *sad*

To Rosemounde This *balade* is a virtuoso parody of the love lyric in which the lady is the subject of extravagant comparisons. The movement of the verse is perfectly under control, and rhyme and rhetoric are also handled masterfully, so that absurdity is allowed to creep in only at intervals: the vat of tears and the fish swimming in sauce.
mappemounde map of the world, see Fig. 55; you are the shrine of all the beauty that is within the circle of the whole world
cristal Jewel imagery is usual in such contexts and is much used by Chaucer's imitators.
jocounde gay and elegant
ye . . . daliaunce you do not give me any kindness; *daliaunce:* consenting, encouraging behavior from the lady to the lover
Your . . . out-twyne your little voice, which you so delicately spin out
habounde to be abundant; the word was thought

to be connected with Latin *habere*, to have
curteisly courteously, like a true lover
penaunce sad state, because my love is not returned
pyk . . . galauntyne pike, smothered in galantine. It was usual to serve pike covered with this pickle sauce made of bread, vinegar, and cinnamon.
Tristam Tristram, the lover of Isolde, type of the true and constant in love
refreyde . . . affounde be cooled again and chilled
Complaint In conventional three-stanza *balade* form, with an envoi addressing it to a royal or noble patron, in the hope of reward; see the Franklin's Tale, l. 240. Chaucer's witty request is imitated from the French. It was successful, since a few days after his accession in 1399 Henry IV renewed and augmented the pension granted to the poet by Richard II in 1394.

That certès,⟩ but⟩ ye make me hevy chere,   *certainly / unless*
Me were as leef be leyd upon my bere;°
For which unto your mercy thus I crye:
Beth hevy again, or ellès mot⟩ I dye!   *must*

Now voucheth⟩ sauf this day, or⟩ it be night,   *grant / before*
That I of yow the blisful soun⟩ may here,   *blessed sound*
10 Or see your colour, lik the sonnè bright,
That of yelownesse hadde never pere.⟩   *equal*
Ye be my lif, ye be myn hertès stere,⟩   *steersman*
Quene of comfòrt and of good companye:
Beeth hevy ageyne, or ellès mot I dye!

Now purse, that been to me my livès lyght
And saviour, as doun in this world here,
Out of this tounè helpe me thurgh your might,
Syn⟩ that ye wol nat ben my tresorere;⟩   *since / treasurer*
For I am shave⟩ as nye⟩ as any frere.°   *shaven / close*
20 But yet I pray unto your curtesie:
Beth hevy agen,⟩ or ellès mot I dye!   *again*

     Envoy [to Henry IV]

O conquerour of Brutès Albyon,°
Which that by line⟩ and free eleccioùn⟩   *lineage / choice*
Been verray⟩ king, this song to you I sende;   *true*
And ye, that mowèn⟩ alle oure harmes amende,   *may*
Have minde⟩ upon my supplicacioùn!   *remember*
1399

To Adam, His Scribe

Adam scrivein,⟩ if ever it thee bifalle   *scribe*
Boèce° or *Troilus*° for to writen newe,
Under thy long lokkes thou most⟩ have the scalle⟩   *may you / scab*
  But after my making thou write more trewe!°
  So ofte a-daye⟩ I mot⟩ thy werk renewe,   *each day / must*
    It to correcte and eek⟩ to rubbe and scrape;   *also*
    And al is through thy negligence and rape.⟩   *haste*
  c. 1390

Me . . . bere I'd just as soon be dead
For . . . frere A friar's head was tonsured, i.e. shaven.
O . . . Albyon The legend was that Brutus, great-grandson of Aeneas, founder of Rome, brought Trojans to Britain (Albion) and founded New Troy (London) as his capital.

Boèce Chaucer's translation of Boethius, *De Consolatione Philosophiae*
Troilus *Troilus and Criseyde*
But . . . trewe unless you copy accurately [according to] what I have composed

SIR GAWAIN AND THE GREEN KNIGHT
c. 1380–1400

Of the author of *Sir Gawain and the Green Knight*, the finest of medieval English romances, nothing is known for certain. From this poem we can tell that he was a great literary artist working in a provincial center located in the northwest Midland area, perhaps in Lancashire, Staffordshire, or Cheshire, at least 150 miles distant from London. We can also say that he wrote toward the end of the century, so that he was more or less Chaucer's contemporary.

His poem exists in one manuscript (Fig. 42); it was not printed until 1839. The manuscript contains two other poems in the same unrhymed alliterative meter, though not divided into stanzas like *Sir Gawain*. They are: *Patience*, the Biblical story of Jonah, to illustrate the virtue of patience, and *Purity*, the stories of the Flood, of Sodom and Gomorrah, and of Belshazzar, to illustrate God's vengeance on impurity. It also contains a third poem, *Pearl*, a dream allegory which is an elegy for the poet's two-year-old daughter culminating in a vision of the Heavenly Jerusalem. This poem also uses the alliterative technique, but subordinates it to a pattern of four-stressed rhyming lines in twelve-line stanzas, elaborately linked together. All these poems, as well as a fifth, the legend of St. Erkenwald, Bishop of London, known from another manuscript, are probably by the same poet. It is not easy to be sure of this, however. Though all the poems are in the same dialect and are often remarkably like one another, the techniques of alliterative poetry, with its firm conventions of phrase, rhythm, and set piece, make it difficult to distinguish between imitation of one poet by another and variations by the same. If the author of *Sir Gawain* wrote all five, he was a great poet in range, power, subtlety, invention, and individuality. If he wrote *Sir Gawain* alone he was, with Chaucer and Langland, still one of the three finest English poets of his century.

Langland and the *Gawain* poet were products of a provincial, not a London culture of which little is known beyond the poems produced there by these authors. Their alliterative meter was unfashionable in London by the time they were writing, though perhaps the stanzaic arrangement of *Sir Gawain*, varying the long lines with the rhyming "bob and wheel" (see Glossary), might have been regarded as less monotonous than Langland's poetic. Also, the directness and sting of Langland's satire may not have been acceptable to the court and the wider reading public of the metropolis. Although the numerous manuscripts show that Langland was widely read, the fact that most of them were made in the area of his presumed origin is significant. Of the *Gawain* poet, we possess one manuscript only, in a provincial dialect that would have seemed difficult, barbarous, and nearly unintelligible to a London reader.

Whatever contemporary metropolitan London thought of *Sir Gawain* and whatever its difficulties, and ours, with the language, there can be no doubt of its stature. Its basic structure is taut and simple, its narrative subtle, its vocabulary rich. A knight, challenged by a supernatural adversary, is required first to show courage in the face of such a being, further courage in accepting his challenge; and then honor, constancy, and "truth" in the fulfillment of that obligation, meeting on his way to do so temptations of all kinds. This plot the poet may have found in a French romance or a Celtic story, which has not survived. Elements of the plot may go back much farther: the beheading of the Green Knight is often said to be a rationalization of a primitive fertility rite, the winter sacrifice to assure the return of spring. It is a very long way from this to the poem as we have it, and the beheading game is to be found in Irish sources of some centuries earlier than *Sir Gawain* as well as in French Arthurian romances, where fulfillment of the obligation sometimes leads to the lifting of an enchantment. There may be an echo of this last in the reference to Morgan le Fay at the end of the poem.

None of these echoes will account for the unique poem of *Sir Gawain and the Green Knight.* The close-knit and economically told story is ornamented with blazing set pieces, such as the description of Arthur's Christmas feast, of Sir Gawain's arming for his journey, the account of the castle, miraculously appearing in the wilderness when Sir Gawain three times crosses himself, and the full treatment of the hunts. Yet each of these digressions is carefully placed and has its function in the story: Arthur's Christmas court is soon contrasted with the dreariness of the next winter, when the knight must set out. (It is characteristic of romance that narrative time tends to be compressed into a rapid series of significant events, the intervening long spaces being passed over in a few lines.) The splendid arming of Sir Gawain, stressing the physical danger of his quest, is meant to make us aware that less tangible dangers are lurking for him. The castle, appearing at his prayer, is to be his first moral testing ground. The three hunts, of two noble, dangerous animals and a base one, elaborately balanced against Gawain's temptations and the return he must make to the lord of the castle, are still in the mind as Sir Gawain stands his three blows.

Despite the supernatural Green Knight, the miraculous appearance of the castle, and the reference to the sorceress Morgan le Fay, the *Gawain* poet has reduced the element of the marvelous in his romance. We are already on the way to Malory with the strong sense of reality and the actual that takes over as soon as the Green Knight has galloped out of the hall at Arthur's court with his head in his hand. The poet has been careful to set his poem in the long-ago, but once the action gets under way we perceive that this is the story of a man whose power of moral recognition and right action is put to the test. It is a man of the greatest virtue who is being tested—the best knight of Arthur's court, itself the mirror of all virtue. (The poet takes the older view, since by his time it was generally Sir Lancelot who set the pattern.) He is being tried in a way that all of us can recognize and apply to ourselves.

As in Chaucer's Franklin's Tale, or as in his Clerk's Tale of the patient Griselda, the audience is being invited to consider the rival claims of two powerful obligations. In the Franklin's Tale, the dilemma is whether to keep the marriage vow of fidelity or the conditional promise; in the Clerk's it is how far one must honor the oath of obedience in marriage. The *Gawain* poet's exploration is no less noble than Chaucer's. Once out of Arthur's court, Gawain becomes a man like ourselves. Meeting his obligation will not be pleasant for him, but he must set off, through the cold of winter, from the Christmas warmth of Arthur's Camelot to the bleak cold of North Wales in December: a real place, not the shadowy country of the earlier romances. Coming to the castle, he is flattered by the warmth and the welcome he finds there, lulled after the chilly journey, reassured that he is near his goal. Once there, he is tested once more, before he is fully prepared, and fails the final test not only by accepting, but also by concealing his acceptance of, the magic girdle which is to save his life. His trials come in layers, too. When the castle's lady presses herself on him, he must decide among courtesy toward her, his obligation as a knight, and courtesy toward his host, equally his obligation. Morality is always a matter of choice between overlaps, not opposites.

Whether the poet intended us to see in Sir Gawain's deceitful conduct the beginning of self-knowledge is not clear. The poem is probably less a conscious attempt to cut the Arthurian heroes down to size than it is a Christian exploration, in the form of a romance, of "the cycle of social living, alienation, self-discovery, desolation, recovery and restoration" (J. A. Burrow). Its exemplary value, the questions constantly before the reader: how to recognize temptation and how to steer the right moral course, must have given the poem its power over medieval audiences and is still its attraction. Arm, protect himself as he will, among his fellows at court, with the pentangle, with "powerful," talismanic gems, with the magic belt, Gawain has still to face the cycle of experience. He does not come home to journey's end and rest, but back to society, wearing the badge that will remind him of his condition, and seeing others wear it too, in token that humility, true penitence, and trust in God's grace are man's only possible rejoinder to his sinful condition.

The translation, which attempts to keep the meter and alliteration of the original, is by Brian Stone, published in 1959 and fully revised in 1972. It is based on the text of Sir Israel Gollancz (1940), with readings adopted from that of J. R. R. Tolkien and E. V. Gordon (2nd ed., 1967). Annotation is by the present editor.

Sir Gawain and the Green Knight°

Fitt° 1

I

The siege and the assault being ceased at Troy,°
The battlements broken down and burnt to brands and ashes,
The treacherous trickster° whose treasons there flourished
Was famed for his falsehood, the foulest on earth.
Aeneas the noble and his knightly kin
Then conquered kingdoms, and kept in their hand
Wellnigh all the wealth of the western lands.
Royal Romulus° to Rome first turned,
Set up the city in splendid pomp,
10 Then named her with his own name, which now she still has:
Ticius° founded Tuscany, townships raising,
Longbeard° in Lombardy lifted up homes,

Sir . . . Knight The manuscript of the poem is untitled. The numbering of parts and stanzas is also modern.
Fitt the Old and Middle English word for a section or canto of a poem
Troy Medieval belief was that western European civilization began after the destruction of Troy by the Greeks, after which the Trojan Aeneas eventually reached Italy. The descendants of Aeneas made themselves masters of the rest of the European continent.
trickster Probably Aeneas himself, or perhaps Antenor. Both, according to medieval tradition, were traitors who plotted to hand over Troy to

the Greeks if they could not get away by other means. Antenor, the legendary founder of Padua, is the less likely candidate, since he is not necessary for the little genealogy by which we are here being taken to the founder of Britain. The "treachery" of both is meant to set off the "truth" of Gawain.
Romulus the legendary founder of Rome, therefore given Trojan ancestry
Ticius perhaps Tuscus, legendary founder of Tuscany; or Tirius, his father
Longbeard *Langaberde:* Langobardus, legendary ancestor of the Lombards, and allegedly Aeneas's descendant

And far over the French flood Felix Brutus°
On many spacious slopes set Britain with joy
      And grace;
    Where war and feud and wonder
    Have ruled the realm a space,
    And after, bliss and blunder
    By turns have run their race.

      II

20 And when this Britain was built by this brave noble,
Here bold men bred, in battle exulting,
Stirrers of trouble in turbulent times.
Here many a marvel, more than in other lands,
Has befallen by fortune since that far time.
But of all who abode here of Britain's kings,
Arthur° was highest in honour, as I have heard;
So I intend to tell you of a true wonder,
Which many folk mention as a manifest marvel,
A happening eminent among Arthur's adventures.
30 Listen to my lay but a little while.
Straightway shall I speak it, in city as I heard it,°
      With tongue;
    As scribes have set it duly
    In the lore of the land so long,
    With letters linking° truly
    In story bold and strong.

      III

This king lay at Camelot° one Christmastide°
With many mighty lords, manly liegemen,
Members rightly reckoned of the Round Table,°
40 In splendid celebration, seemly and carefree.
There tussling in tournament time and again
Jousted in jollity these gentle knights,
Then in court carnival sang catches and danced;°
For fifteen days the feasting there was full in like measure

Felix Brutus grandson or great-grandson of Aeneas, and founder of Britain. *Felix* ("happy") may reflect the *sele* ("fortunate"), used of him in other sources—and *felix* was a conventional adjective for founders.
Arthur a Welsh form of the Latin Artorius; in contrast to most names in Middle English Arthurian romance, which reach it through Old French (see Fig. 46)
heard it an appeal to an older, probably nonexistent authority, a regular medieval way of placing author and reader on the same footing
letters linking i.e. by the alliterative technique; but the meaning may also be "embodied in truthful words"
Camelot King Arthur's capital, identified by Malory as Winchester, but placed by others in

Wales or in the southwestern (Celtic) parts of England
Christmastide One of the great religious feasts and occasions for chivalric gatherings: festivities lasted until Twelfth Night, the eve of Epiphany (January 6). Arthur was said to hold court and wear his crown five times a year: at Easter, Ascension Day, Pentecost, All Saints, and Christmas (see Malory, *Morte Darthur*, below).
Round Table part of Queen Guinevere's dowry to King Arthur, made for King Uther by the wonder-worker Merlin; a "holy table" for 150 knights, preventing dispute about whose was the more honorable place (see Fig. 47)
sang . . . danced performed "caroles," or dances accompanied by song

With all the meat and merry-making men could devise,
Gladly ringing glee, glorious to hear,
A noble din by day, dancing at night!
All was happiness in the height in halls and chambers
For lords and their ladies, delectable joy.
50 With all delights on earth they housed there together,
Saving Christ's self, the most celebrated knights,
The loveliest ladies to live in all time,
And the comeliest king ever to keep court.
For this fine fellowship was in its fair prime
          Far famed,
      Stood well in heaven's will,
      Its high-souled king acclaimed:
      So hardy a host on hill
      Could not with ease be named.

            IV
60 The year being so young that yester-even saw its birth,
That day double on the dais were the diners served.
Mass sung and service ended, straight from the chapel
The King and his company came into hall.
Called on with cries from clergy and laity,
Noël° was newly announced, named time and again.
Then lords and ladies leaped forth, largesse distributing,
Offered New Year gifts° in high voices, handed them out,
Bustling and bantering about these offerings.
Ladies laughed full loudly, though losing their wealth,
70 And he that won was not woeful, you may well believe.
All this merriment they made until meal time.
Then in progress to their places they passed after washing,
In authorized order, the high-ranking first;°
With glorious Guinevere,° gay in the midst,
On the princely platform with its precious hangings
Of splendid silk at the sides, a state° over her
Of rich tapestry of Toulouse° and Turkestan°
Brilliantly embroidered with the best gems
Of warranted worth that wealth at any time
80   Could buy.
      Fairest of form was this queen,
      Glinting and grey° of eye;
      No man could say he had seen
      A lovelier, but with a lie.

Noël Latin *natalis*, birthday
New Year gifts the regular medieval custom
first at the kind of table the poet knew, at
which guests were seated in order of rank, not
the Round Table (see Figs. 43, 47)
Guinevere Arthur's queen

state canopy
Toulouse *tolouse*, a rich fabric, perhaps from
Toulouse in France
Turkestan *tars*, rich and costly Eastern stuff
grey the regular color for a medieval heroine's
eyes

V

But Arthur would not eat until all were served.
He was charming and cheerful, child-like and gay,
And loving active life, little did he favour
Lying down for long or lolling on a seat,
So robust his young blood and his beating brain.
90   Still, he was stirred now by something else:
His noble announcement that he never would eat
On such a fair feast-day till informed in full
Of some unusual adventure,° as yet untold,
Of some momentous marvel that he might believe,
About ancestors, or arms, or other high theme;
Or till a stranger should seek out a strong knight of his,
To join with him in jousting, in jeopardy to lay
Life against life, each allowing the other
The favour of Fortune, the fairer lot.
100 Such was the King's custom when he kept court,
At every fine feast among his free° retinue
      In hall.
   So he throve amid the throng,
   A ruler royal and tall,
   Still standing staunch and strong,
   And young like the year withal.

VI

Erect stood the strong king, stately of mien,
Trifling time with talk before the topmost table.°
Good Gawain° was placed at Guinevere's side,
110 And Agravain° of the Hard Hand sat on the other side,
Both the King's sister's sons, staunchest of knights.
Above, Bishop Baldwin began the board,°
And Ywain, Urien's son,° ate next to him.
These were disposed on the dais and with dignity served,
And many mighty men next, marshalled at side tables.
Then the first course came in with such cracking of trumpets,
(Whence bright bedecked blazons° in banners hung)
Such din of drumming and a deal of fine piping,
Such wild warbles whelming and echoing

adventure a custom of Arthur's often mentioned in French romances. The adventure (chance encounter, French *aventure*) might happen to one of the company then and there, or merely be reported by someone present.
free *fre*, noble
topmost table Arthur would face down the hall, from the middle of the long side of the high table on the dais, the most honored guests to either side of him. The side tables (l. 115) were on the floor of the hall, along the walls, at right angles to the high table. The guests sat on benches or forms.

Gawain Gawain is usually presented, in early Arthurian romance, as the greatest of Arthur's knights for his courtesy and war-like prowess. Later, his status is reduced. He was Arthur's nephew and his estates were in Scotland.
Agravain Gawain's brother
Baldwin . . . board The bishop, Arthur's adviser, sat in the place of honor at his right hand.
Ywain, . . . son. Ywain and Urien may have been historical Welsh kings. Ywain was also Arthur's nephew and one of his best knights.
blazons coats of arms

120 That hearts were uplifted high at the strains.
 Then delicacies and dainties were delivered to the guests,
 Fresh food in foison,° such freight of full dishes
 That space was scarce at the social tables
 For the several soups set before them in silver
        On the cloth.
        Each feaster made free with the fare,
        Took lightly and nothing loth;
        Twelve plates were for every pair,
        Good beer and bright wine both.

        VII
130 Of their meal I shall mention no more just now,
 For it is evident to all that ample was served;
 Now another noise,° quite new, neared suddenly,
 Likely to allow the liege lord to eat;
 For barely had the blast of trump abated one minute
 And the first course in the court been courteously served,
 When there heaved in at the hall door an awesome fellow
 Who in height outstripped all earthly men.
 From throat to thigh he was so thickset and square,
 His loins and limbs were so long and so great,
140 That he was half a giant on earth, I believe;
 Yet mainly and most of all a man he seemed,
 And the handsomest of horsemen, though huge, at that;
 For though at back and at breast his body was broad,
 His hips and haunches were elegant and small,
 And perfectly proportioned were all parts of the man,
        As seen.
        Men gaped at the hue of him
        Ingrained in garb and mien,
        A fellow fiercely grim,
150   And all a glittering green.

        VIII
 And garments of green girt the fellow about—
 A two-third-length tunic, tight at the waist,
 A comely cloak on top, accomplished with lining
 Of the finest fur to be found, made of one piece,
 Marvellous fur-trimmed material, with matching hood
 Lying back from his locks and laid on his shoulders;
 Fitly held-up hose, in hue the same green,
 That was caught at the calf, with clinking spurs beneath
 Of bright gold on bases of embroidered silk,
160 But no iron shoe armoured that horseman's feet.

foison plenty
noise The "adventure" was arriving which had   to take place before Arthur would consent to
                                                    eat.

And verily his vesture was all vivid green,
So were the bars on his belt and the brilliants set
In ravishing array on the rich accoutrements
About himself and his saddle on silken work.
It would be tedious to tell a tithe of the trifles
Embossed and embroidered, such as birds and flies,°
In gay green gauds,° with gold everywhere.
The breast-hangings of the horse, its haughty crupper,°
The enamelled knobs and nails on its bridle,
170   And the stirrups that he stood on, were all stained with the same;
So were the splendid saddle-skirts and bows
That ever glimmered and glinted with their green stones.
The steed that he spurred on was similar in hue
      To the sight,
   Green and huge of grain,
   Mettlesome in might
   And brusque with bit and rein—
   A steed to serve that knight!

      IX
Yes, garbed all in green was the gallant rider,
180   And the hair of his head was the same hue as his horse,
And floated finely like a fan round his shoulders;
And a great bushy beard on his breast flowing down,
With the heavy hair hanging from his head,
Was shorn below the shoulder, sheared right round,
So that half his arms were under the encircling hair,
Covered as by a king's cape, that closes at the neck.
The mane of that mighty horse, much like the beard,
Well crisped and combed, was copiously plaited
With twists of twining gold, twinkling in the green,
190   First a green gossamer, a golden one next.
His flowing tail and forelock followed suit,
And both were bound with bands of bright green,
Ornamented to the end with exquisite stones,
While a thong running through them threaded on high
Many bright golden bells, burnished and ringing.
Such a horse, such a horseman, in the whole wide world
Was never seen or observed by those assembled before,
      Not one.
   Lightning-like he seemed
200   And swift to strike and stun.
   His dreadful blows, men deemed,
   Once dealt, meant death was done.

flies butterflies
gauds ornaments
crupper harness strap passing under the horse's
tail, or saddle skirts. The harness and trappings of a knight's horse were often very elaborate.

X

Yet hauberk° and helmet had he none,
Nor plastron° nor plate-armour proper to combat,
Nor shield for shoving, nor sharp spear for lunging;
But he held a holly° cluster in one hand, holly
That is greenest when groves are gaunt and bare,
And an axe in his other hand, huge and monstrous,
A hideous helmet-smasher for anyone to tell of;
210   The head of that axe was an ell-rod long.
Of green hammered gold and steel was the socket,
And the blade was burnished bright, with a broad edge,
Acutely honed for cutting, as keenest razors are.
The grim man gripped it by its great strong handle,
Which was wound with iron all the way to the end,
And graven in green with graceful designs.
A cord curved round it, was caught at the head,
Then hitched to the haft at intervals in loops,
With costly tassels attached thereto in plenty
220   On bosses of bright green embroidered richly.
In he rode, and up the hall, this man,
Driving towards the high dais, dreading no danger.
He gave no one a greeting, but glared over all.
His opening utterance was, 'Who and where
Is the governor of this gathering? Gladly would I
Behold him with my eyes and have speech with him.'
        He frowned;
        Took note of every knight
        As he ramped and rode around;
230   Then stopped to study who might
        Be the noble most renowned.

XI

The assembled folk stared, long scanning the fellow,
For all men marvelled what it might mean
That a horseman and his horse should have such a colour
As to grow green as grass, and greener yet, it seemed,
More gaudily° glowing than green enamel on gold.
Those standing studied him and sidled towards him
With all the world's wonder as to what he would do.
For astonishing sights they had seen, but such a one never;
240   Therefore a phantom from Fairyland the folk there deemed him.
So even the doughty were daunted and dared not reply,
All sitting stock-still, astounded by his voice.

hauberk coat of chain-mail armor
plastron armor for upper breast and neck
holly evergreen cluster from that shrub, perhaps
to signify the knight's immortality, or merely
to match his color. Holly is the symbol of
Christmas and of the immortal Christ, the red
berry symbolizing his blood.
gaudily beautifully

Throughout the high hall was a hush like death;
Suddenly as if all had slipped into sleep, their voices were
      At rest;
    Hushed not wholly for fear,
    But some at honour's behest;
    But let him whom all revere
    Greet that gruesome guest.

XII

250   For Arthur sensed an exploit before the high dais,
And accorded him courteous greeting, no craven he,
Saying to him, 'Sir knight, you are certainly welcome.
I am head of this house: Arthur is my name.
Please deign to dismount and dwell with us
Till you impart your purpose, at a proper time.'
'May He that sits in heaven help me,' said the knight,
'But my intention was not to tarry in this turreted hall.
But as your reputation, royal sir, is raised up so high,
And your castle and cavaliers are accounted the best,
260   The mightiest of mail-clad men in mounted fighting,
The most warlike, the worthiest the world has bred,
Most valiant to vie with in virile contests,
And as chivalry is shown here, so I am assured,
At this time, I tell you, that has attracted me here.
By this branch that I bear, you may be certain
That I proceed in peace, no peril seeking;
For had I fared forth in fighting gear,
My hauberk and helmet, both at home now,
My shield and sharp spear, all shining bright,
270   And other weapons to wield, I would have brought;
However, as I wish for no war here, I wear soft clothes.
But if you are as bold as brave men affirm,
You will gladly grant me the good sport I demand
      By right.'
    Then Arthur answer gave:
    'If you, most noble knight,
    Unarmoured combat crave,
    We'll fail you not in fight.'

XIII

'No, it is not combat I crave, for come to that,
280   On this bench only beardless boys are sitting.
If I were hasped in armour on a high steed,
No man among you could match me, your might being meagre.
So I crave in this court a Christmas game,
For it is Yuletide and New Year, and young men abound here.
If any in this household is so hardy in spirit,

Of such mettlesome mind and so madly rash
As to strike a strong blow in return for another,
I shall offer to him this fine axe freely;
This axe, which is heavy enough, to handle as he please.
290   And I shall bide the first blow, as bare as I sit here.
If some intrepid man is tempted to try what I suggest,
Let him leap towards me and lay hold of this weapon,
Acquiring clear possession of it, no claim from me ensuing.
Then shall I stand up to his stroke, quite still on this floor—
So long as I shall have leave to launch a return blow
      Unchecked.
        Yet he shall have a year
        And a day's reprieve,° I direct.
        Now hasten and let me hear
300   Who answers, to what effect.'

     XIV

If he had astonished them at the start, yet stiller now
Were the henchmen in hall, both high and low.
The rider wrenched himself round in his saddle
And rolled his red eyes about roughly and strangely,
Bending° his brows, bristling and bright, on all,
His beard swaying as he strained to see who would rise.
When none came to accord with him, he coughed aloud,
Then pulled himself up proudly, and spoke as follows:
'What, is this Arthur's house, the honour of which
310   Is bruited abroad so abundantly?
Has your pride disappeared? Your prowess gone?
Your victories, your valour, your vaunts, where are they?
The revel and renown of the Round Table
Is now overwhelmed by a word from one man's voice,
For all flinch for fear from a fight not begun!'
Upon this, he laughed so loudly that the lord grieved.
His fair features filled with blood
      For shame.
        He raged as roaring gale;
320   His followers felt the same.
        The King, not one to quail,
        To that cavalier then came.

     XV

'By heaven,' then said Arthur, 'What you ask is foolish,
But as you firmly seek folly, find it you shall.
No good man here is aghast at your great words.
Hand me your axe now, for heaven's sake,
And I shall bestow the boon you bid us give.'

year . . . reprieve the usual term for a legal   **Bending** directing
contract

He sprang towards him swiftly, seized it from his hand,
And fiercely the other fellow footed the floor.°
330   Now Arthur had his axe, and holding it by the haft
Swung it about sternly, as if to strike with it.
The strong man stood before him, stretched to his full height,
Higher than any in the hall by a head and more.
Stern of face he stood there, stroking his beard,
Turning down his tunic in a tranquil manner,
Less unmanned and dismayed by the mighty strokes
Than if a banqueter at the bench° had brought him a drink
    Of wine.
        Then Gawain at Guinevere's side
340   Bowed and spoke his design:
        'Before all, King, confide
        This fight to me. May it be mine.'

        XVI
'If you would, worthy lord,' said Gawain to the king,
'Bid me stir from this seat and stand beside you,
Allowing me without lèse-majesty° to leave the table,
And if my liege lady were not displeased thereby,
I should come there to counsel you before this court of nobles.
For it appears unmeet to me, as manners go,
When your hall hears uttered such a haughty request,
350   Though you gladly agree, for you to grant it yourself,
When on the benches about you many such bold men sit,
Under heaven, I hold, the highest-mettled,
There being no braver knights when battle is joined.
I am the weakest, the most wanting in wisdom, I know,
And my life, if lost, would be least missed, truly.
Only through your being my uncle, am I to be valued;
No bounty but your blood in my body do I know.°
And since this affair is too foolish to fall to you,
And I first asked it of you, make it over to me;
360   And if I fail to speak fittingly, let this full court judge
        Without blame.'
        Then wisely they whispered of it,
        And after, all said the same:
        That the crowned king should be quit,°
        And Gawain given the game.

        XVII
Then the King commanded the courtly knight to rise.
He directly uprose, approached courteously,

---

footed the floor jumped off his horse
banqueter . . . bench a man at his seat
lèse-majesty French *lèse-majesté*, offense against
the dignity of a ruler, severe discourtesy

No bounty . . . know i.e. the only good in my
body comes from your blood
quit excused from the contest

Knelt low to his liege lord, laid hold of the weapon;
And he graciously let him have it, lifted up his hand
370 And gave him God's blessing, gladly urging him
To be strong in spirit and stout of sinew.
'Cousin, take care,' said the King, 'To chop once,°
And if you strike with success, certainly I think
You will take the return blow without trouble in time.'
Gripping the great axe, Gawain goes to the man
Who awaits him unwavering, not quailing at all.
Then said to Sir Gawain the stout knight in green,
'Let us affirm our pact freshly, before going farther.
I beg you, bold sir, to be so good
380 As to tell me your true name, as I trust you to.'
'In good faith,' said the good knight, 'Gawain is my name,
And whatever happens after, I offer you this blow,
And in twelve months' time I shall take the return blow
With whatever weapon you wish, and with no one else
            Shall I strive.'
        The other with pledge replied,
        'I'm the merriest man alive
        It's a blow from you I must bide,
        Sir Gawain, so may I thrive.'

                XVIII
390 'By God,' said the Green Knight, 'Sir Gawain, I rejoice
That I shall have from your hand what I have asked for here.
And you have gladly gone over, in good discourse,
The covenant I requested of the King in full,
Except that you shall assent, swearing in truth,
To seek me yourself, in such place as you think
To find me under the firmament, and fetch your payment
For what you deal me today before this dignified gathering.'
'How shall I hunt for you? How find your home?'
Said Gawain, 'By God that made me, I go in ignorance;
400 Nor, knight, do I know your name or your court.
But instruct me truly thereof, and tell me your name,
And I shall wear out my wits to find my way there;
Here is my oath on it, in absolute honour!'
'That is enough this New Year,° no more is needed,'
Said the gallant in green to Gawain the courteous,
'To tell you the truth, when I have taken the blow
After you have duly dealt it, I shall directly inform you
About my house and my home and my own name.
Then you may keep your covenant, and call on me,
410 And if I waft you no words, then well may you prosper,

----

take . . . once take care that you give one
stroke only   **New Year** a time associated with friendship
and piety

Stay long in your own land and look for no further
    Trial.
     Now grip your weapon grim;
     Let us see your fighting style.'
     'Gladly,' said Gawain to him,
     Stroking the steel the while.

       XIX

On the ground the Green Knight graciously stood,
With head slightly slanting to expose the flesh.
His long and lovely locks he laid over his crown,
420   Baring the naked neck for the business now due.
Gawain gripped his axe and gathered it on high,
Advanced the left foot before him on the ground,
And slashed swiftly down on the exposed part,
So that the sharp blade sheared through, shattering the bones,
Sank deep in the sleek flesh, split it in two,
And the scintillating steel struck the ground.
The fair head fell from the neck, struck the floor,
And people spurned it as it rolled around.
Blood spurted from the body, bright against the green.
430   Yet the fellow did not fall, nor falter one whit,
But stoutly sprang forward on legs still sturdy,
Roughly reached out among the ranks of nobles,
Seized his splendid head and straightway lifted it.
Then he strode to his steed, snatched the bridle,
Stepped into the stirrup and swung aloft,
Holding his head in his hand by the hair.
He settled himself in the saddle as steadily
As if nothing had happened to him, though he had
      No head.
440   He twisted his trunk about,
     That gruesome body that bled;
     He caused much dread and doubt
     By the time his say was said.

       XX

For he held the head in his hand upright,
Pointed the face at the fairest in fame° on the dais;
And it lifted its eyelids and looked glaringly,
And menacingly said with its mouth as you may now hear:
'Be prepared to perform what you promised, Gawain;
Seek faithfully till you find me, my fine fellow,
450   According to your oath in this hall in these knights' hearing.
Go to the Green Chapel without gainsaying to get
Such a stroke as you have struck. Strictly you deserve

fairest in fame noblest; those at the high table

That due redemption on the day of New Year.
As the Knight of the Green Chapel I am known to many;
Therefore if you ask for me, I shall be found.
So come, or else be called coward accordingly!'
Then he savagely swerved, sawing at the reins,
Rushed out at the hall door, his head in his hand,
And the flint-struck fire flew up from the hooves.
460 What place he departed to no person there knew,
Nor could any account be given of the country he had come from.
       What then?
   At the Green Knight Gawain and King
   Grinned and laughed again;
   But plainly approved the thing
   As a marvel in the world of men.

       XXI
Though honoured King Arthur was at heart astounded,
He let no sign of it be seen, but said clearly
To the comely queen in courtly speech,
470 'Do not be dismayed, dear lady, today:
Such cleverness° comes well at Christmastide,
Like the playing of interludes,° laughter and song,
As lords and ladies delight in courtly carols.
However, I am now able to eat the repast,
Having seen, I must say, a sight to wonder at.'
He glanced at Sir Gawain, and gracefully said,
'Now sir, hang up your axe: you have hewn enough.'
And on the backcloth above the dais it was boldly hung
Where all men might mark it and marvel at it
480 And with truthful testimony tell the wonder of it.
Then to the table the two went together,
The King and the constant knight, and keen° men served them
Double portions of each dainty with all due dignity,
All manner of meat,° and minstrelsy too.
Daylong they delighted till darkness came
       To their shores.
   Now Gawain give a thought,
   Lest peril make you pause
   In seeking out the sport
490   That you have claimed as yours.

---

cleverness or: curious deeds   keen quick
interludes pageants, short humorous plays, at   meat food
entertainments or between the acts of sacred
dramas

Fitt 2

XXII

Such earnest° of noble action° had Arthur at New Year,
For he was avid to hear exploits vaunted.
Though starved of such speeches when seated at first,
Now had they high matter indeed, their hands full° of it.
Gawain was glad to begin the games in hall,
But though the end be heavy, have no wonder,
For if men are spritely in spirit after strong drink,
Soon the year slides past, never the same twice;
There is no foretelling its fulfilment from the start.
500   Yes, this Yuletide passed and the year following;
Season after season in succession went by.
After Christmas comes the crabbed Lenten time,
Which forces on the flesh fish and food yet plainer.
Then weather° more vernal wars with the wintry world,
The cold ebbs and declines, the clouds lift,
In shining flowers the rain sheds warmth
And falls upon the fair plain, where flowers appear;
The grassy lawns and groves alike are garbed in green;
Birds prepare to build, and brightly sing
510   The solace of the ensuing summer that soothes hill
            And dell.
        By hedgerows rank and rich
        The blossoms bloom and swell,
        And sounds of sweetest pitch
        From lovely woodlands well.

XXIII

Then comes the season of summer with soft winds,
When Zephyrus° himself breathes on seeds and herbs.
In paradise is the plant that springs in the open
When the dripping dew drops from its leaves,
520   And it bears the blissful gleam of the bright sun.
Then Harvest comes hurrying, urging it on,
Warning it because of winter to wax ripe soon;
He drives the dust to rise with the drought he brings,
Forcing it to fly up from the face of the earth.
Wrathful winds in raging skies wrestle with the sun;
Leaves are lashed loose from the trees and lie on the ground
And the grass becomes grey which was green before.
What rose from root at first now ripens and rots;

---

earnest pledge
action MS. "adventures," meaning chance encounters
Now . . . full literally: Now they were fully
provided with stern deeds (to talk of), whole
fistfuls of them

weather famous passage of welcome to spring,
preparing for change in the action of the poem
and echoing Gawain's lack of care—as yet—for
the debt he will have to pay when the year
sinks again
Zephyrus the west wind

So the year in passing yields its many yesterdays,
530 And winter returns, as the way of the world is,
       I swear;
         So came the Michaelmas° moon,
         With winter threatening there,
         And Gawain considered soon
         The fell way he must fare.

         XXIV
       Yet he stayed in hall with Arthur till All Saints Day,°
       When Arthur provided plentifully, especially for Gawain,
       A rich feast and high revelry at the Round Table.
       The gallant lords and gay ladies grieved for Gawain,
540 Anxious on his account; but all the same
       They mentioned only matters of mirthful import,
       Joylessly joking for that gentle knight's sake.
       For after dinner with drooping heart he addressed his uncle
       And spoke plainly of his departure, putting it thus:
       'Now, liege lord of my life, I beg my leave of you.
       You know the kind of covenant it is: I care little
       To tell over the trials of it, trifling as they are,
       But I am bound to bear the blow and must be gone tomorrow
       To seek the gallant in green, as God sees fit to guide me.'
550 Then the most courtly in that company came together,
       Ywain and Eric and others in troops,
       Sir Dodinal the Fierce, the Duke of Clarence,
       Lancelot and Lionel and Lucan the Good,
       Sir Bors and Sir Bedivere, both strong men,
       And many admired knights, with Mador of the Gate.°
       All the company of the court came near to the King
       With carking° care in their hearts, to counsel the knight.
       Much searing sorrow was suffered in the hall
       That such a gallant man as Gawain should go in quest
560 To suffer a savage blow, and his sword no more
                 Should bear.
             Said Gawain, gay of cheer,
             'Whether fate be foul or fair,
             Why falter I or fear?
             What should man do but dare?'

Michaelmas Feast of St. Michael, September 29
All Saints Day November 1, one of the great
religious festivals. See l. 37n above.
Eric . . . Gate (ll. 551–55) i.e. the flower of
the court. Eric was famous in French romances;
Sir Dodinal was a great hunter in the wild; the
Duke of Clarence, one of whose adventures
parallels Gawain's, was Arthur's nephew; Lancelot was, in the later Arthurian tradition, one of
Arthur's greatest knights and Queen Guinevere's
lover; Lionel was Lancelot's cousin; Lucan was
the royal butler, an important official (see
Malory, *Morte Darthur,* below) and one of the
last survivors of the knights at Arthur's death;
Bors was probably Lionel's brother; Bedivere
was one of the earliest of Arthur's knights, and
in Malory is Arthur's last companion; Mador was
the keeper of the castle gate.
carking oppressive

XXV

He dwelt there all that day, and at dawn on the morrow
Asked for his armour. Every item was brought.
First a crimson carpet was cast over the floor
And the great pile of gilded war-gear glittered upon it.
570 The strong man stepped on it, took the steel in hand.
The doublet he dressed in was dear Turkestan stuff.
Then came the courtly cape, cut with skill,
Finely lined with fur, and fastened close.
Then they set the steel shoes on the strong man's feet,
Lapped his legs in steel with lovely greaves,°
Complete with knee-pieces, polished bright
And connecting at the knee with gold-knobbed hinges.
Then came the cuisses,° which cunningly enclosed
His thighs thick of thew,° and which thongs secured.
580 Next the hauberk, interlinked with argent° steel rings
Which rested on rich material, wrapped the warrior round.
He had polished armour on arms and elbows,
Glinting and gay, and gloves of metal,
And all the goodly gear to give help whatever
     Betide;
   With surcoat richly wrought,
   Gold spurs attached in pride,
   A silken sword-belt athwart,
   And steadfast blade at his side.

XXVI

590 When he was hasped in armour his harness° was noble;
The least lace or loop was lustrous with gold.
So, harnessed as he was, he heard his mass
As it was offered at the high altar in worship.
Then he came to the King and his court-fellows,
Took leave with loving courtesy of lord and lady,
Who commended him to Christ and kissed him farewell.
By now Gringolet° had been got ready, and girt with a saddle
That gleamed most gaily with many golden fringes,
Everywhere nailed newly for this noble occasion.
600 The bridle was embossed and bound with bright gold;
So were the furnishings° of the fore-harness° and the fine skirts.
The crupper and the caparison° accorded with the saddle-bows,
And all was arrayed on red with nails of richest gold,
Which glittered and glanced like gleams of the sun.

---

greaves armor for the leg, from ankle to knee
cuisses armor for the thigh
thew muscle
argent silvery
harness man's armor
Gringolet the name of Gawain's horse, most

likely via 12th-century French, but possibly Welsh in origin, meaning "white-hard"
furnishings ornaments
fore-harness armor for the horse's fore-parts
caparison rich ornamental cloth covering for a horse

Then his casque,° equipped with clasps of great strength
And padded inside, he seized and swiftly kissed;
It towered high on his head and was hasped at the back,
With a brilliant silk band over the burnished neck-guard,
Embroidered and bossed° with the best gems
610 On broad silken borders, with birds about the seams,
Such as parrots painted with periwinkles° between,
And turtles° and true-love-knots° traced as thickly
As if many beauties in a bower° had been busy seven winters
          Thereabout.
     The circlet on his head
     Was prized more precious no doubt,
     And perfectly diamonded,
     Threw a gleaming lustre out.

        XXVII
Then they showed him the shield of shining gules,°
620 With the Pentangle° in pure gold depicted thereon.
He brandished it by the baldric,° and about his neck
He slung it in a seemly way, and it suited him well.
And I intend to tell you, though I tarry therefore,
Why the Pentangle is proper to this prince of knights.
It is a symbol which Solomon conceived once
To betoken holy truth, by its intrinsic right,
For it is a figure which has five points,
And each line overlaps and is locked with another;
And it is endless everywhere, and the English call it,
630 In all the land, I hear, the Endless Knot.°
Therefore it goes with Sir Gawain and his gleaming armour,
For, ever faithful in five things, each in fivefold manner,°
Gawain was reputed good and, like gold well refined,
He was devoid of all villainy, every virtue displaying
          In the field.
     Thus this Pentangle new

casque helmet
bossed studded
parrots . . . periwinkles The silk would have
something of the appearance of border decoration in contemporary manuscripts.
turtles turtledoves—emphasizing Gawain's true
and faithful courtesy and knighthood in love as
in war
true-love-knots two bands with a knot in the
center to symbolize union
bower ladies' quarters
gules the heraldic name for red; Gawain's arms
are usually green and gold
Pentangle Not elsewhere part of Gawain's coat
of arms, it was a five-pointed star, which
could be drawn without taking pen from paper,
symbol of safety and perfection, and came to
be known as Solomon's sign. It is related to the
similar hexagram of two interlocking triangles,
the "Star of David." The pentangle/pentagram

was also used as a magic sign, to give power
over spirits; it is sometimes associated with
the five letters of the name of Jesus or with his
five wounds.
baldric a belt, often richly embroidered, worn
diagonally across the body to support sword,
bugle, or other such article
Endless Knot i.e. because its interlacing lines
are joined and continuous
five . . . manner These five times five are each
a side of the pentangle: the five wits, i.e. senses
—sight, hearing, touch, taste, smell; the five
fingers; the five wounds of Christ on the cross—
two hands, two feet, and side; the five joys of
the Virgin, the joyful mysteries of the rosary—
Annunciation, Nativity, Resurrection, Ascension,
and Assumption; and the five social virtues. The
five wits and especially the five wounds and five
joys were frequently the subject of religious
meditation and religious lyrics.

He carried on coat and shield,
As a man of troth most true
And knightly name annealed.

XXVIII

640 First he was found faultless in his five wits.
Next, his five fingers never failed the knight,
And all his trust on earth was in the five wounds
Which came to Christ on the Cross, as the Creed tells.
And whenever the bold man was busy on the battlefield,
Through all other things he thought on this,
That his prowess all depended on the five pure Joys
That the holy Queen of Heaven had of her Child.
Accordingly the courteous knight had that queen's image°
Etched on the inside of his armoured shield,
650 So that when he beheld her, his heart did not fail.
The fifth five I find the famous man practised
Were—Liberality and Lovingkindness leading the rest;
Then his Continence and Courtesy,° which were never corrupted;
And Piety, the surpassing virtue. These pure five
Were more firmly fixed on that fine man
Than on any other, and every multiple,
Each interlocking° with another, had no end,
Being fixed to five points which never failed,°
Never assembling on one side, nor sundering either,
660 With no end at any angle; nor can I find
Where the design started or proceeded to its end.
Thus on his shining shield this knot was shaped
Royally in red gold upon red gules.
That is the pure Pentangle, so people who are wise
        are taught.
        Now Gawain was ready and gay;
        His spear he promptly caught
        And gave them all good day
        For ever, as he thought.

XXIX

670 He struck the steed with his spurs and sprang on his way
So forcefully that the fire flew up from the flinty stones.
All who saw that seemly sight were sick at heart,
And all said to each other softly, in the same breath,

---

image Arthur was said to have had the Virgin's picture on his armor and shield, and to draw strength from the sight. Gawain's spotless piety and courage are emphasized by the transfer of the image.
Liberality . . . Courtesy Gawain's knightly virtues do not here include the one that he displays most in the poem: truth to one's word. Liberality and loving-kindness—beneficence and broth-

erly love—are courtly virtues; so is continence, or sinlessness; all together go to make up courtesy, truly chivalrous behavior.
interlocking i.e. as in the pentangle; each virtue reinforcing and feeding into the others
five points . . . failed Five was thought the first perfect number, the union of male three and female two.

In care for that comely knight, 'By Christ, it is evil
That yon lord should be lost, who lives so nobly!
To find his fellow on earth, in faith, is not easy.
It would have been wiser to have worked more warily,
And to have dubbed the dear man a duke of the realm.
A magnificent master of men he might have been,
680   And so had a happier fate than to be utterly destroyed,
Beheaded by an unearthly being out of arrogance.
Who supposed the Prince would approve such counsel
As is giddily given in Christmas games by knights?'
Many were the watery tears that whelmed from weeping eyes,
When on quest that worthy knight went from the court
      That day.
    He faltered not nor feared,
    But quickly went his way;
    His road was rough and weird,
690   Or so the stories say.

      xxx
Now the gallant Sir Gawain in God's name goes
Riding through the realm of Britain,° no rapture in his mind.
Often the long night he lay alone and companionless,
And did not find in front of him food of his choice;
He had no comrade but his courser in the country woods and hills,
No traveller to talk to on the track but God,
Till he was nearly nigh to Northern Wales.°
The isles of Anglesey he kept always on his left,
And fared across the fords by the foreshore
700   Over at Holy Head to the other side
Into the wilderness of Wirral,° where few dwelled
To whom God or good-hearted man gave his love.
And always as he went, he asked whomever he met
If they knew or had knowledge of a knight in green,
Or could guide him to the ground where a green chapel stood.
And there was none but said him nay, for never in their lives
Had they set eyes on someone of such a hue
      As green.
    His way was wild and strange
710   By dreary hill and dean.°
    His mood would many times change
    Before that fane° was seen.

Britain MS. *Logres,* Arthur's kingdom; England south of the Humber
Northern Wales Gawain came from Camelot in southern England north through Logres almost up to the north coast of Wales, and then cut east, keeping Anglesey on his left. The poet seems to expect that people will know the route, which probably then led across the River Dee between Chester and the estuary. The modern Holyhead in Anglesey cannot be the Holyhead of the poem.
Wirral the Wilderness of Wirral in Cheshire, a forested area, noted in the 14th century for criminals and outlaws
dean valley
fane church

XXXI

He rode far from his friends, a forsaken man,
Scaling many cliffs in country unknown.
At every bank or beach where the brave man crossed water,
He found a foe in front of him, except by a freak of chance,
And so foul and fierce a one that he was forced to fight.
So many marvels° did the man meet in the mountains,
It would be too tedious to tell a tenth of them.
720   He had death-struggles with dragons, did battle with wolves,
Warred with wild men who dwelt among the crags,
Battled with bulls and bears and boars at other times,
And ogres that panted after him on the high fells.
Had he not been doughty in endurance and dutiful to God,
Doubtless he would have been done to death time and again.
Yet the warring little worried him; worse was the winter,
When the cold clear water cascaded from the clouds
And froze before it could fall to the fallow° earth.
Half-slain by the sleet, he slept in his armour
730   Night after night among the naked rocks,
Where the cold streams splashed from the steep crests
Or hung high over his head in hard icicles.
So in peril and pain, in parlous plight,
This knight covered the country till Christmas Eve
      Alone;
      And he that eventide
      To Mary made his moan,
      And begged her be his guide
      Till some shelter should be shown.

XXXII

740   Merrily in the morning by a mountain he rode
Into a wondrously wild wooded cleft,
With high hills on each side overpeering a forest
Of huge hoary oaks, a hundred together.
The hazel and the hawthorn were intertwined
With rough ragged moss trailing everywhere,
And on the bleak branches birds in misery
Piteously piped away, pinched with cold.
The gallant knight on Gringolet galloped under them
Through many a swamp and marsh, a man all alone,
750   Fearing lest he should fail, through adverse fortune,
To see the service of him who that same night
Was born of a bright maiden to banish our strife.
And so sighing he said, 'I beseech thee, Lord
And thee Mary, mildest mother so dear,

marvels like any hero of romance, riding out in   **fallow** dun-colored, untilled
search of adventure

That in some haven with due honour I may hear Mass
And Matins tomorrow morning: meekly I ask it,
And promptly thereto I pray my Pater and Ave
      And Creed.'°
    He crossed himself and cried
760   For his sins, and said, 'Christ speed
    My cause, his cross my guide!'°
    So prayed he, spurring his steed.

      XXXIII
Thrice the sign of the Saviour° on himself he had made,
When in the wood he was aware of a dwelling with a moat
On a promontory above a plateau, penned in by the boughs
And tremendous trunks of trees, and trenched° about;
The comeliest castle that ever a knight owned,
It was pitched on a plain, with a park all round,
Impregnably palisaded with pointed stakes,
770 And containing many trees in its two-mile circumference.
The courteous knight contemplated the castle from one side
As it shimmered and shone through the shining oaks.
Then humbly he took off his helmet and offered thanks
To Jesus and Saint Julian,° gentle patrons both,
Who had given him grace and gratified his wish.
'Now grant it be good lodging!' the gallant knight said.
Then he goaded Gringolet with his golden heels,
And mostly by chance emerged on the main highway,
Which brought the brave man to the bridge's end
780   With one cast.
    The drawbridge vertical,
    The gates shut firm and fast,
    The well-provided wall—
    It blenched at never a blast.

      XXXIV
The knight, still on his steed, stayed on the bank
Of the deep double ditch that drove round the place.°
The wall went into the water wonderfully deep,
And then to a huge height upwards it reared
In hard hewn stone, up to the cornice;
790 Built under the battlements in the best style, courses jutted°
And turrets protruded between,° constructed
With loopholes in plenty with locking shutters.

Pater . . . Creed the Lord's Prayer, the Hail
Mary, and the Creed
Christ . . . guide common formula of prayer
sign of the Saviour i.e., he crossed himself
trenched moated
Saint Julian patron saint of travelers
place a castle of the elaborate, pinnacled, chim-

neyed, later 14th-century type, on the way to
being more a place to live in than a stronghold
(Fig. 44)
jutted continuous horizontal bands of stone projected from the wall below the battlements, to
discourage scalers
between at intervals

No better barbican° had ever been beheld by that knight.
And inside he could see a splendid high hall
With towers and turrets on top, all tipped with crenellations,°
And pretty pinnacles placed along its length,
With carved copes,° cunningly worked.
Many chalk-white chimneys the chevalier saw
On the tops of towers twinkling whitely,
So many painted pinnacles sprinkled everywhere,
Congregated in clusters among the crenellations,
That it appeared like a prospect of paper patterning.
To the gallant knight on Gringolet it seemed good enough
If he could ever gain entrance to the inner court,
And harbour in that house while Holy Day lasted,
   Well cheered.
    He hailed, and at a height
    A civil porter appeared,
    Who welcomed the wandering knight,
    And his inquiry heard.

   XXXV
'Good sir,' said Gawain, 'will you give my message
To the high lord of this house, that I ask for lodging?'
'Yes, by Saint Peter,'° replied the porter, 'and I think
You may lodge here as long as you like, sir knight.'
Then away he went eagerly, and swiftly returned
With a host of well-wishers to welcome the knight.
They let down the drawbridge and in a dignified way
Came out and did honour to him, kneeling
Courteously on the cold ground to accord him worthy welcome.
They prayed him to pass the portcullis, now pulled up high,
And he readily bid them rise and rode over the bridge.
Servants held his saddle while he stepped down,
And his steed was stabled by sturdy men in plenty.
Strong knights and squires descended then
To bring the bold warrior blithely into hall.
When he took off his helmet, many hurried forward
To receive it and to serve this stately man,
And his bright sword and buckler° were both taken as well.
Then graciously he greeted each gallant knight,
And many proud men pressed forward to pay their respects.
Garbed in his fine garments, he was guided to the hall,
Where a fine fire was burning fiercely on the hearth.
Then the prince of those people appeared from his chamber
To meet in mannerly style the man in his hall.
'You are welcome to dwell here as you wish,' he said,

800

810

820

830

---

barbican outer fortification of a castle
crenellations battlements
copes ornamental tops

Saint Peter One porter swears by another, the
castle porter by the porter of heaven.
buckler shield

'Treat everything as your own, and have what you please
         In this place.'
      'I yield my best thanks yet:
      May Christ make good your grace!'
840   Said Gawain and, gladly met,
      They clasped in close embrace.

XXXVI

Gawain gazed at the gallant who had greeted him well
And it seemed to him the stronghold possessed a brave lord,
A powerful man in his prime, of stupendous size.
Broad and bright was his beard, all beaver-hued;
Strong and sturdy he stood on his stalwart legs;
His face was fierce as fire, free° was his speech,
And he seemed in good sooth a suitable man
To be prince of a people with companions of mettle.
850 This prince led him to an apartment and expressly commanded
That a man be commissioned to minister to Gawain;
And at his bidding a band of men bent to serve
Brought him to a beautiful room where the bedding was noble.
The bed-curtains, of brilliant silk with bright gold hems,
Had skilfully-sewn coverlets with comely facings,
And the fairest fur on the fringes was worked.
With ruddy gold rings on the cords ran the curtains;
Toulouse and Turkestan tapestries on the wall
And fine carpets underfoot, on the floor, were fittingly matched.
860 There amid merry talk the man was disrobed,
And stripped of his battle-sark° and his splendid clothes.
Retainers readily brought him rich robes
Of the choicest kind to choose from and change into.
In a trice when he took one, and was attired in it,
And it sat on him in style, with spreading skirts,
It certainly seemed to those assembled as if spring
In all its hues were evident before them;
His lithe limbs below the garment were gleaming with beauty.
Jesus never made, so men judged, more gentle and handsome
870   A knight:
      From wherever in the world he were,
      At sight it seemed he might
      Be a prince without a peer
      In field where fell men fight.

XXXVII

At the chimneyed hearth where charcoal burned, a chair was placed
For Sir Gawain in gracious style, gorgeously decked
With cushions on quilted work, both cunningly wrought;

---

free noble   **battle-sark** shirt of mail

And then on that man a magnificent mantle was thrown,
A gleaming garment gorgeously embroidered,
880 Fairly lined with fur, the finest skins
Of ermine on earth, and his hood of the same.
In that splendid seat he sat in dignity,
And warmth came to him at once, bringing well-being.
In a trice on fine trestles a table was put up,°
Then covered with a cloth shining clean and white,
And set with silver spoons, salt-cellars and overlays.
The worthy knight washed willingly, and went to his meat.
In seemly enough style servants brought him
Several fine soups, seasoned lavishly,
890 Twice-fold, as is fitting, and fish of all kinds—
Some baked in bread, some browned on coals,
Some seethed,° some stewed and savoured with spice,
But always subtly sauced, and so the man liked it.
The gentle knight generously judged it a feast,
And often said so, while the servers spurred him on thus
     As he ate:
     'This present penance° do:
     It soon shall be offset.'
     The knight rejoiced anew,
900   For the wine his spirits whet.

     XXXVIII
Then in seemly style they searchingly inquired,
Putting to the prince private questions,
So that he courteously conceded he came of that court
Where high-souled Arthur held sway alone,
Ruler most royal of the Round Table;
And that Sir Gawain himself now sat in the house,
Having come that Christmas, by course of fortune.
Loudly laughed the lord when he learned what knight
He had in his house; such happiness it brought
910 That all the men within the moat made merry,
And promptly appeared in the presence of Gawain,
To whose person are proper all prowess and worth,
And pure and perfect manners, and praises unceasing.
His reputation rates first in the ranks of men.
Each knight neared his neighbour and softly said,
'Now we shall see displayed the seemliest manners
And the faultless figures of virtuous discourse.
Without asking we may hear how to hold conversation
Since we have seized upon this scion of good breeding.

In . . . up Tables were put up and taken down
as required in the Middle Ages. See Chaucer,
the General Prologue, l. 355.
seethed boiled

penance On the eve of Christmas, Gawain is
technically abstaining—i.e. eating no meat—but
he is being given a feast of fish. Still, they tell
him, he will do better on Christmas Day.

920 God has given us of his grace good measure,
In granting us such a guest as Gawain is,
When, contented at Christ's birth, the courtiers shall sit
And sing.
This noble knight will prove
What manners the mighty bring;
His converse of courtly love
Shall spur our studying.'

XXXIX

When the fine man had finished his food and risen,
It was nigh and near to the night's mid-hour.
930 Priests to their prayers paced their way
And rang the bells royally, as rightly they should,
To honour that high feast with evensong.
The lord inclines to prayer, the lady too;
Into her private pew she prettily walks;
Gawain advances gaily and goes there quickly,
But the lord gripped his gown and guided him to his seat,
Acknowledged him by name and benevolently said
In the whole world he was the most welcome of men.
Gawain spoke his gratitude, they gravely embraced,
940 And sat in serious mood the whole service through.
Then the lady had a longing to look on the knight;
With her bevy of beauties she abandoned her pew.
Most beautiful of body and bright of complexion,
Most winsome in ways of all women alive,
She seemed to Sir Gawain, excelling Guinevere.
To squire that splendid dame, he strode through the chancel.
Another lady led her by the left hand,
A matron, much older, past middle age,
Who was highly honoured by an escort of squires.
950 Most unlike to look on those ladies were,
For if the one was winsome, then withered was the other.
Hues rich and rubious° were arrayed on the one,
Rough wrinkles on the other rutted the cheeks.
Kerchiefed with clear pearls clustering was the one,
Her breast and bright throat bare to the sight,
Shining like sheen of snow shed on the hills;
The other was swathed with a wimple° wound to the throat
And choking her swarthy chin in chalk-white veils.
On her forehead were folded enveloping silks,
960 Trellised about with trefoils and tiny rings.
Nothing was bare on that beldame but the black brows,
The two eyes, protruding nose and stark lips,
And those were a sorry sight and exceedingly bleary:

rubious ruby-red   wimple cloth covering the neck, sides of the
                                               head, and forehead

A grand lady, God knows, of greatness in the world
        Well tried!
    Her body was stumpy and squat,
    Her buttocks bulging and wide;
    More pleasure a man could plot
    With the sweet one at her side.

      XL

970 When Gawain had gazed on that gracious-looking creature
He gained leave of the lord to go along with the ladies.
He saluted the senior, sweeping a low bow,
But briefly embraced the beautiful one,
Kissing her in courtly style and complimenting her.
They craved his acquaintance and he quickly requested
To be their faithful follower, if they would so favour him.
They took him between them, and talking, they led him
To a high room. By the hearth they asked first
For spices, which unstintingly men sped to bring,
980 And always with heart-warming, heady wine.
In lovingkindness the lord leaped up repeatedly
And many times reminded them that mirth should flow;
Elaborately lifted up his hood, looped it on a spear,
And offered it as a mark of honour to whoever should prove able
To make the most mirth that merry Yuletide.
'And I shall essay, I swear, to strive with the best
Before this garment goes from me, by my good friends' help.'
So with his mirth the mighty lord made things merry
To gladden Sir Gawain with games in hall
990   That night;
    Until, the time being spent,
    The lord demanded light.
    Gawain took his leave and went
    To rest in rare delight.

      XLI

On that morning when men call to mind the birth
Of our dear Lord born to die for our destiny,
Joy waxes in dwellings the world over for His sake:
And so it befell there on the feast day with fine fare.
Both at main meals and minor repasts strong men served
1000 Rare dishes with fine dressings to the dais company.
Highest, in the place of honour, the ancient crone sat,
And the lord, so I believe, politely next.
Together sat Gawain and the gay lady
In mid-table, where the meal was mannerly served first;
And after throughout the hall, as was held best,
Each gallant by degree was graciously served.
There was meat and merry-making and much delight,

To such an extent that it would try me to tell of it,
Even if perhaps I made the effort to describe it.
1010 But yet I know the knight and the nobly pretty one
Found such solace and satisfaction seated together,
In the discreet confidences of their courtly dalliance,
Their irreproachably pure and polished repartee,
That with princes' sport their play of wit surpassingly
      Compares.
    Pipes and side-drums sound,
    Trumpets entune their airs;
    Each soul its solace found,
    And the two were enthralled with theirs.

     XLII
1020 That day they made much merriment, and on the morrow again,
And thickly the joys thronged on the third day after;
But gentle was the jubilation on St. John's Day,°
The final one for feasting, so the folk there thought.
As there were guests geared to go in the grey dawn
They watched the night out with wine in wonderful style,
Leaping night-long in their lordly dances.
At last when it was late those who lived far off,
Each one, bid farewell before wending their ways.
Gawain also said good-bye, but the good host grasped him,
Led him to the hearth of his own chamber,
And held him back hard, heartily thanking him
For the fine favour he had manifested to him
1030 In honouring his house that high feast-tide,
Brightening his abode with his brilliant company:
'As long as I live, sir, I believe I shall thrive
Now Gawain has been my guest at God's own feast.'
'Great thanks, sir,' said Gawain, 'In good faith, yours,
All yours is the honour, may the High King requite it!
I stand at your service, knight, to satisfy your will
1040 As good use engages me, in great things and small,
      By right.'
    The lord then bid his best
    Longer to delay the knight,
    But Gawain, replying, pressed
    His departure in all despite.

     XLIII
Then with courteous inquiry the castellan° asked
What fierce exploit had sent him forth, at that festive season,
From the King's court at Camelot, so quickly and alone,
Before the holy time was over in the homes of men.

St. John's Day feast of John the Evangelist,   **castellan** keeper of the castle
December 27

1050   'You may in truth well demand,' admitted the knight.
     'A high and urgent errand hastened me from thence,
     For I myself am summoned to seek out a place
     To find which I know not where in the world to look.
     For all the land in Logres°—may our Lord help me!
     I would not fail to find it on the feast of New Year.
     So this is my suit, sir, which I beseech of you here,
     That you tell me in truth if tale ever reached you
     Of the Green Chapel, or what ground or glebe° it stands on,
     Or of the knight who holds it, whose hue is green.
1060   For at that place I am pledged, by the pact between us,
     To meet that man, if I remain alive.
     From now until the New Year is not a great time,
     And if God will grant it me, more gladly would I see him
     Than gain any good possession, by God's son!
     I must wend my way, with your good will, therefore;
     I am reduced to three days in which to do my business,
     And I think it fitter to fall dead than fail in my errand.'
     Then the lord said laughingly, 'You may linger a while,
     For I shall tell you where your tryst is by your term's end.
1070   Give yourself no more grief for the Green Chapel's whereabouts,
     For you may lie back in your bed, brave man, at ease
     Till full morning on the First, and then fare forth
     To the meeting-place at mid-morning to manage how you may
             Out there.
          Leave not till New Year's Day,
          Then get up and go with cheer;
          You shall be shown the way;
          It is hardly two miles from here.'

       XLIV
     Then Gawain was glad and gleefully exclaimed,
1080   'Now above all, most heartily do I offer you thanks!
     For my goal is now gained, and by grace of yours
     I shall dwell here and do what you deem good for me.'
     So the lord seized Sir Gawain, seated him beside himself,
     And to enliven their delight, he had the ladies fetched,
     And much gentle merriment they long made together.
     The lord, as one like to take leave of his senses
     And not aware of what he was doing, spoke warmly and merrily.
     Then he spoke to Sir Gawain, saying out loud,
     'You have determined to do the deed I ask:
1090   Will you hold to your undertaking here and now?'
     'Yes, sir, in good sooth,' said the true knight,
     'While I stay in your stronghold, I shall stand at your command.'
     'Since you have spurred,' the lord said, 'from afar,

    Logres Britain south of the Humber   **glebe** field

Then watched awake° with me, you are not well supplied
With either sustenance or sleep, for certain, I know;
So you shall lie long in your room, late and at ease
Tomorrow till the time of mass, and then take your meal
When you will, with my wife beside you
To comfort you with her company till I come back to court.
1100   You stay,
    And I shall get up at dawn.
    I will to the hunt away.'
    When Gawain's agreement was sworn
    He bowed, as brave knights may.

        XLV
'Moreover,' said the man, 'Let us make a bargain
That whatever I win in the woods be yours,
And any achievement you chance on here, you exchange for it.
Sweet sir, truly swear to such a bartering,
Whether fair fortune or foul befall from it.'
1110 'By God,' said the good Gawain, 'I agree to that,
And I am happy that you have an eye to sport.'
Then the prince of that people said, 'What pledge of wine
Is brought to seal the bargain?' And they burst out laughing.
They took drink and toyed in trifling talk,
These lords and ladies, as long as they liked,
And then with French refinement and many fair words
They stood, softly speaking, to say good-night,
Kissing as they parted company in courtly style.
With lithe liege servants in plenty and lambent torches,
1120 Each brave man was brought to his bed at last,
        Full soft.
    Before they fared to bed
    They rehearsed their bargain oft.
    That people's prince, men said,
    Could fly his wit aloft.

    Fitt 3
        XLVI
In the faint light before dawn folk were stirring;
Guests who had to go gave orders to their grooms,
Who busied themselves briskly with the beasts, saddling,
Trimming their tackle and tying on their luggage.
1130 Arrayed for riding in the richest style,
Guests leaped on their mounts lightly, laid hold of their bridles,
And each rider rode out on his own chosen way.
The beloved lord of the land was not the last up,

watched awake reveled

Being arrayed for riding with his retinue in force.
He ate a sop° hastily when he had heard mass,
And hurried with horn to the hunting field;
Before the sun's first rays fell on the earth,
On their high steeds were he and his knights.
Then these cunning hunters came to couple° their hounds,
1140   Cast open the kennel° doors and called them out,
And blew on their bugles three bold notes.°
The hounds broke out barking, baying fiercely,
And when they went chasing, they were whipped back.
There were a hundred choice huntsmen there, whose fame
      Resounds.
    To their stations keepers strode;
    Huntsmen unleashed hounds:
    The forest overflowed
    With the strident bugle sounds.

      XLVII
1150   At the first cry wild creatures quivered with dread.
The deer in distraction darted down to the dales
Or up to the high ground, but eagerly they were
Driven back by the beaters, who bellowed lustily.
They let the harts with high-branching heads have their freedom,
And the brave bucks, too, with their broad antlers,
For the noble prince had expressly prohibited
Meddling with male deer in the months of close season.°
But the hinds were held back with a 'Hey' and a 'Whoa!'
And does driven with much din to the deep valleys.
1160   Lo! the arrows' slanting flight as they were loosed!
A shaft flew forth at every forest turning,
The broad head biting on the brown flank.
They screamed as the blood streamed out, sank dead on the sward,
Always harried by hounds hard on their heels,
And the hurrying hunters' high horn notes.
Like the rending of ramped° hills roared the din.
If one of the wild beasts slipped away from the archers
It was dragged down and met death at the dog-bases
After being hunted from the high ground and harried to the water,
1170   So skilled were the hunt-servants at stations lower down,
So gigantic the greyhounds that grabbed them in a flash,
Seizing them savagely, as swift, I swear,
      As sight.

---

sop bread dipped in spiced wine; see Chaucer, the General Prologue, l. 336
couple put leashes on
kennel The hounds would have been in one large kennel.
notes The hunting horn had only one note, so that differentiation was by long and short. The names of the calls were mote, trut, trororout, trorororout.
close season Winter, September to June, was the closed season for male deer; only females were hunted during winter.
ramped sloping

The lord, in humour high
Would spur, then stop and alight.
In bliss the day went by
Till dark drew on, and night.

XLVIII

Thus by the forest borders the brave lord sported,
And the good man Gawain, on his gay bed lying,
1180 Lay hidden till the light of day gleamed on the walls.
Covered with fair canopy, the curtains closed,
And as in slumber he slept on, there slipped into his mind
A slight, suspicious sound, and the door stealthily opened.
He raised up his head out of the bedclothes,
Caught up the corner of the curtain a little
And watched warily towards it, to see what it was.
It was the lady, loveliest to look upon,
Who secretly and silently secured the door,
Then bore towards his bed: the brave knight, embarrassed,
1190 Lay flat with fine adroitness and feigned sleep.
Silently she stepped on, stole to his bed,
Caught up the curtain, crept within,
And seated herself softly on the side of the bed.
There she watched a long while, waiting for him to wake.
Slyly close this long while lay the knight,
Considering in his soul this circumstance,
Its sense and likely sequel, for it seemed marvellous.
'Still, it would be more circumspect,' he said to himself,
'To speak and discover her desire in due course.'
1200 So he stirred and stretched himself, twisting towards her,
Opened his eyes and acted as if astounded;
And, to seem the safer by such service, crossed himself
        In dread.
        With chin and cheek so fair,
        White ranged with rosy red,
        With laughing lips, and air
        Of love, she lightly said:

XLIX

'Good morning, Sir Gawain,' the gay one murmured,
'How unsafely you sleep, that one may slip in here!
1210 Now you are taken in a trice. Unless a truce come between us,
I shall bind you to your bed—of that be sure.'
The lady uttered laughingly those playful words.
'Good morning, gay lady,' Gawain blithely greeted her.
'Do with me as you will: that well pleases me.
For I surrender speedily and sue for grace,
Which, to my mind, since I must, is much the best course.'
And thus he repaid her with repartee and ready laughter.
'But if, lovely lady, your leave were forthcoming,

And you were pleased to free your prisoner and pray him to rise,
1220 I would abandon my bed for a better habiliment,
And have more happiness in our honey talk.'
'Nay, verily, fine sir,' urged the voice of that sweet one,
'You shall not budge from your bed. I have a better idea.
I shall hold you fast here on this other side as well
And so chat on with the chevalier my chains have caught.
For I know well, my knight, that your name is Sir Gawain,
Whom all the world worships, wherever he ride;
For lords and their ladies, and all living folk,
Hold your honour in high esteem, and your courtesy.
1230 And now—here you are truly, and we are utterly alone;
My lord and his liege man are a long way off;
Others still bide in their beds, my bower-maidens too;
Shut fast and firmly with a fine hasp is the door;
And since I have in this house him who pleases all,
As long as my time lasts I shall lingering in talk take
    My fill.
    My young body is yours,
    Do with it what you will;
    My strong necessities force
1240   Me to be your servant still.'°

    L

'In good truth,' said Gawain, 'that is a gain indeed,
Though I am hardly the hero of whom you speak.
To be held in such honour as you here suggest,
I am altogether unworthy, I own it freely.
By God, I should be glad if you granted it right,
For me to essay by speech or some other service,
To pleasure such a perfect lady—pure joy it would be.'
'In good truth, Sir Gawain,' the gay lady replied,
'If I slighted or set at naught your spotless fame
1250 And your all-pleasing prowess, it would show poor breeding.
But there is no lack of ladies who would love, noble one,
To hold you in their arms, as I have you here,
And linger in the luxury of your delightful discourse,
Which would perfectly pleasure them and appease their woes,—
Rather than have riches or the red gold they own.
But as I love that Lord, the Celestial Ruler,
I have wholly in my hand what all desire
    Through his grace.'
    Not loth was she to allure,
1260   This lady fair of face;
    But the knight with speeches pure
    Answered in each case.

My young . . . still (ll. 1237–40) This seems like a direct assault for the first temptation of Gawain, engineered at least—see below—by a sorceress.

LI

'Madam,' said the merry man, 'May Mary requite you!
For in good faith I have found in you free-hearted generosity.
Certain men for their deeds receive esteem from others,
But for myself, I do not deserve the respect they show me;
Your honourable mind makes you utter only what is good.'
'Now by Mary,' said the noble lady, 'Not so it seems to me,
For were I worth the whole of womankind,
1270 And all the wealth in the world were in my hand,
And if bargaining I were to be bid to bring myself a lord,
With your noble qualities, knight, made known to me now,
Your good looks, gracious manner, and great courtesy,
All of which I had heard of before, but here prove true,
No lord that is living could be allowed to excel you.'
'Indeed, dear lady, you did better,' said the knight,
'But I am proud of the precious price you put on me,
And solemnly as your servant say you are my sovereign.
May Christ requite it you: I have become your knight.'
1280 Then of many matters they talked till mid-morning and after,
And all the time she behaved as if she adored him;
But Sir Gawain was on guard in a gracious manner.
Though she was the winsomest woman the warrior had known,
He was less love-laden because of the loss he must
        Now face—
    His destruction by the stroke,
    For come it must was the case.
    The lady of leaving then spoke;
    He assented with speedy grace.

LII

1290 Then she gave him good-bye, glinting with laughter,
And standing up, astounded him with these strong words:
'May He who prospers every speech for this pleasure reward you!
I cannot bring myself to believe that you could be Gawain.'
'How so?' said the knight, speaking urgently,
For he feared he had failed to observe the forms of courtesy.
But the beauteous one blessed him and brought out this argument:
'Such a great man as Gawain is granted to be,
The very vessel of virtue and fine courtesy,
Could scarcely have stayed such a sojourn with a lady
300 Without craving a kiss out of courtesy,
Touched by some trifling hint at the tail-end of a speech.'
'So be it, as you say,' then said Gawain,
'I shall kiss at your command, as becomes a knight
Who fears to offend you; no further plea is needed.'
Whereupon she approached him, and penned him in her arms,
Leaned over him lovingly and gave the lord a kiss.
Then they commended each other to Christ in comely style,

And without more words she went out by the door.
He made ready to rise with rapid haste,
1310 Summoned his servant, selected his garb,
And walked down, when he was dressed, debonairly° to mass.
Then he went to the well-served meal which awaited him.
And made merry sport till the moon rose
      At night.
    Never was baron bold
    So taken by ladies bright,
    The young one and the old:
    They throve all three in delight.

      LIII
And still at his sport spurred the castellan,
1320 Hunting the barren hinds in holt° and on heath.
So many had he slain, by the setting of the sun,
Of does and other deer, that it was downright wonderful.
Then at the finish the folk flocked in eagerly,
And quickly collected the killed deer in a heap.
Those highest in rank came up with hosts of attendants,
Picked out what appeared to be the plumpest beasts
And, according to custom, had them cut open with finesse.
Some who ceremoniously assessed° them there
Found two fingers' breadth of fat on the worst.
1330 Then they slit open the slot, seized the first stomach,°
Scraped it with a keen knife and tied up the tripes.
Next they hacked off all the legs, the hide was stripped,
The belly broken open and the bowels removed
Carefully, lest they loosen the ligature of the knot.
Then they gripped the gullet, disengaged deftly
The wezand° from the windpipe and whipped out the guts.
Then their sharp knives shore through the shoulder-bones,
Which they slid out of a small hole, leaving the sides° intact.
Then they cleft the chest clean through, cutting it in two.
1340 Then again at the gullet a man began to work
And straight away rived it, right to the fork,
Flicked out the shoulder-fillets, and faithfully then
He rapidly ripped free the rib-fillets.
Similarly, as is seemly, the spine was cleared
All the way to the haunch, which hung from it;
And they heaved up the whole haunch and hewed it off;
And that is called, according to its kind, the numbles,°
    I find.

debonairly elegantly
holt wood
assessed i.e. to see how good and thick the flesh was. The chief of the hunt cut a slit down the breast, or brisket. Hunting was a highly formalized, aristocratic pastime, with an elaborate language and etiquette.

slit . . . stomach slit open the hollow at the base of the throat; and seized the gullet
wezand esophagus
sides skin of the sides
numbles offal from back and loins

At the thigh-forks then they strain
1350 And free the folds behind,
Hurrying to hack all in twain,
The backbone to unbind.

LIV

Then they hewed off the head and also the neck,
And after sundered the sides swiftly from the chine,
And into the foliage they flung the fee of the raven.°
Then each fellow, for his fee,° as it fell to him to have,
Skewered through the stout flanks beside the ribs,
And then by the hocks of the haunches they hung up their booty.
On one of the finest fells° they fed their hounds,
1360 And let them have the lights,° the liver and the tripes,
With bread well imbrued with blood mixed with them.
Boldly they blew the kill amid the baying of hounds.
Then off they went homewards, holding their meat,
Stalwartly sounding many stout horn-calls.
As dark was descending, they were drawing near
To the comely castle where quietly our knight stayed.
        Fires roared,
        And blithely hearts were beating
        As into hall came the lord.
1370   When Gawain gave him greeting,
        Joy abounded at the board.

LV

Then the master commanded everyone to meet in the hall,
Called the ladies to come down with their company of maidens.
Before all the folk on the floor, he bid men
Fetch the venison and place it before him.
Then gaily and in good humour to Gawain he called,
Told over the tally of the sturdy beasts,
And showed him the fine fat flesh flayed from the ribs.
'How does the sport please you? Do you praise me for it?
1380 Am I thoroughly thanked for thriving as a huntsman?'
'Certainly,' said the other, 'Such splendid spoils
Have I not seen for seven years in the season of winter.'
'And I give you all, Gawain,' said the good man then,
'For according to our covenant you may claim it as your own.'
'Certes, that is so, and I say the same to you,'
Said Gawain, 'For my true gains in this great house,
I am not loth to allow, must belong to you.'

---

fee . . . raven bit of gristle flung into a tree
for the crows and ravens gathered around the
hunt
fellow . . . fee The portions of the carcasses

were assigned to members of the hunt in strict
order.
fells skins
lights lungs

And he put his arms round his handsome neck, hugging him,
And kissed him in the comeliest way he could think of.
1390 'Accept my takings, sir, for I received no more;
Gladly would I grant them, however great they were.'
'And therefore I thank you,' the thane said, 'Good!
Yours may be the better gift, if you would break° it to me
Where your wisdom won you wealth of that kind.'
'No such clause in our contract! Request nothing else!'
Said the other, 'You have your due: ask more,
                        None should.'
                    They laughed in blithe assent
                    With worthy words and good;
1400   Then to supper they swiftly went,
                    To fresh delicious food.

        LVI
And sitting afterwards by the hearth of an audience chamber,
Where retainers repeatedly brought them rare wines,
In their jolly jesting they jointly agreed
On a settlement similar to the preceding one;
To exchange the chance achievements of the morrow,
No matter how novel they were, at night when they met.
They accorded on this compact, the whole court observing,
And the bumper was brought forth in banter to seal it.
1410 And at last they lovingly took leave of each other,
Each man hastening thereafter to his bed.
The cock having crowed and called only thrice,°
The lord leaped from bed, and his liege men too,
So that mass and a meal were meetly dealt with,
And by first light the folk to the forest were bound
                    For the chase.
                    Proudly the hunt with horns
                    Soon drove through a desert place:
                    Uncoupled through the thorns°
1420   The great hounds pressed apace.

        LVII
By a quagmire they quickly scented quarry and gave tongue,
And the chief huntsman urged on the first hounds up,
Spurring them on with a splendid spate of words.°
The hounds, hearing it, hurried there at once,
Fell on the trail furiously, forty together,
And made such echoing uproar, all howling at once,
That the rocky banks round about rang with the din.

---

break disclose
cock . . . thrice Third cock-crow was just before dawn.

thorns looking for boars, which lurk in such
difficult places
spate . . . words Hounds needed more encouragement to tackle boars. See Fig. 45.

Hunters inspirited them with sound of speech and horn.
Then together in a group, across the ground they surged
1430 At speed between a pool and a spiteful crag.
On a stony knoll by a steep cliff at the side of a bog,
Where rugged rocks had roughly tumbled down,
They careered on the quest, the cry following;
They surrounded the crag and the rocky knoll as well,
Certain their prey skulked inside their ring,
For the baying of the bloodhounds meant the beast was there.
Then they beat upon the bushes and bade him come out,
And he swung out savagely aslant the line of men,
A baneful boar of unbelievable size,
1440 A solitary long since sundered from the herd,
Being old and brawny, the biggest of them all,
And grim and ghastly when he grunted: great was the grief
When he thrust through the hounds, hurling three to earth,
And sped on scot-free, swift and unscathed.
They hallooed, yelled, 'Look out!' cried 'Hey, we have him!'
And blew horns boldly, to bring the bloodhounds together;
Many were the merry cries from men and dogs
As they hurried clamouring after their quarry to kill him on
          The track.
1450   Many times he turns at bay
          And tears the dogs which attack.
          He hurts the hounds, and they
          Moan in a piteous pack.

          LVIII
Then men shoved forward, shaped to shoot at him,
Loosed arrows at him, hitting him often,
But the points, for all their power, could not pierce his flanks,
Nor would the barbs bite on his bristling brow.°
Though the smooth-shaven shaft shattered in pieces,
Wherever it hit, the head rebounded.
1460 But when the boar was battered by blows unceasing,
Goaded and driven demented, he dashed at the men,
Striking them savagely as he assailed them in rushes,
So that some lacking stomach stood back in fear.
But the lord on a lithe horse lunged after him,
Blew on his bugle like a bold knight in battle,
Rallied the hounds as he rode through the rank thickets,
Pursuing this savage boar till the sun set.
And so they disported themselves this day
While our lovable lord lay in his bed.
1470 At home the gracious Gawain in gorgeous clothes
          Reclined:

brow The bristles grow thicker here on a boar
in winter.

The gay one did not forget
To come with welcome kind,
And early him beset
To make him change his mind.

LIX

She came to the curtain and cast her eye
On Sir Gawain, who at once gave her gracious welcome,
And she answered him eagerly, with ardent words,
Sat at his side softly, and with a spurt of laughter
1480 And a loving look, delivered these words:
'It seems to me strange, if, sir, you are Gawain,
A person so powerfully disposed to good,
Yet nevertheless know nothing of noble conventions,
And when made aware of them, wave them away!
Quickly you have cast off what I schooled you in yesterday
By the truest of all tokens of talk I know of.'
'What?' said the wondering knight, 'I am not aware of one.
But if it be true what you tell, I am entirely to blame.'
'I counselled you then about kissing,' the comely one said;
1490 'When a favour is conferred, it must be forthwith accepted:
That is becoming for a courtly knight who keeps the rules.'
'Sweet one, unsay that speech,' said the brave man,
'For I dared not do that lest I be denied.
If I were forward and were refused, the fault would be mine.'
'But none,' said the noblewoman, 'could deny you, by my faith!
You are strong enough to constrain with your strength if you wish,
If any were so ill-bred as to offer you resistance.'
'Yes, good guidance you give me, by God,' replied Gawain,
'But threateners are ill thought of and do not thrive in my country,
1500 Nor do gifts thrive when given without good will.
I am here at your behest, to offer a kiss to when you like;
You may do it whenever you deem fit, or desist,
      In this place.'
    The beautiful lady bent
    And fairly kissed his face;
    Much speech the two then spent
    On love, its grief and grace.

LX

'I would know of you, knight,' the noble lady said,
'If it did not anger you, what argument you use,
1510 Being so hale and hearty as you are at this time,
So generous a gentleman as you are justly famed to be;
Since the choicest thing in chivalry, the chief thing praised,
Is the loyal sport of love, the very lore of arms?°

lore of arms the "learning" of the knightly
profession

For the tale of the contentions of true knights
Is told by the title and text of their feats,
How lords for their true loves put their lives at hazard,
Endured dreadful trials for their dear loves' sakes,
And with valour avenged and made void their woes,
Bringing home abundant bliss by their virtues.
1520   You are the gentlest and most just of your generation;
Everywhere your honour and high fame are known;
Yet I have sat at your side two separate times here
Without hearing you utter in any way
A single syllable of the saga of love.
Being so polished and punctilious a pledge-fulfiller,°
You ought to be eager to lay open to a young thing
Your discoveries in the craft of courtly love.
What! Are you ignorant, with all your renown?
Or do you deem me too dull to drink in your dalliance?
1530   For shame!
        I sit here unchaperoned, and stay
        To acquire some courtly game;
        So while my lord is away,
        Teach me your true wit's fame.'

        LXI
'In good faith,' said Gawain, 'may God requite you!
It gives me great happiness, and is good sport to me,
That so fine a fair one as you should find her way here
And take pains with so poor a man, make pastime with her knight,
With any kind of clemency—it comforts me greatly.
1540   But for me to take on the travail of interpreting true love
And construing the subjects of the stories of arms
To you who, I hold, have more skill
In that art, by half, than a hundred of such
As I am or ever shall be on the earth I inhabit,
Would in faith be a manifold folly, noble lady.
To please you I would press with all the power in my soul,
For I am highly beholden to you, and evermore shall be
True servant to your bounteous self, so save me God!'
So that stately lady tempted him and tried him with questions
1550   To win him to wickedness, whatever else she thought.°
But he defended himself so firmly that no fault appeared,
Nor was there any evil apparent on either side,
              But bliss;
        For long they laughed and played
        Till she gave him a gracious kiss.

pledge-fulfiller The chief virtue that Gawain displays throughout the poem. The lady's exposition
of a knight's social obligations takes in almost
all the qualities he would be expected to display.

whatever . . . thought There was some ulterior
motive in the temptations, beyond simple gratification of desire.

A fond farewell she bade,
And went her way on this.

LXII

Sir Gawain bestirred himself and went to mass:
Then dinner was dressed and with due honour served.
All day long the lord and the ladies disported,
But the castellan coursed across the country time and again,
Hunted his hapless boar as it hurtled over the hills,
Then bit the backs of his best hounds asunder
Standing at bay, till the bowmen obliged him to break free
Out into the open for all he could do,
So fast the arrows flew when the folk there concentrated.
Even the strongest he sometimes made start back,
But in time he became so tired he could tear away no more,
And with the speed he still possessed, he spurted to a hole
On a rise by a rock with a running stream beside.
He got the bank at his back, and began to abrade the ground.
The froth was foaming foully at his mouth,
And he whetted his white tusks; a weary time it was
For the bold men about, who were bound to harass him
From a distance, for none dared to draw near him
      For dread.
    He had hurt so many men
    That it entered no one's head
    To be torn by his tusks again,
    And he raging and seeing red.

LXIII

Till the castellan came himself, encouraging his horse,
And saw the boar at bay with his band of men around.
He alighted in lively fashion, left his coursers,
Drew and brandished his bright sword and boldly strode forward,
Striding at speed through the stream to where the savage beast was.
The wild thing was aware of the weapon and its wielder,
And so bridled° with its bristles in a burst of fierce snorts
That all were anxious for the lord, lest he have the worst of it.
Straight away the savage brute sprang at the man,
And baron and boar were both in a heap
In the swirling water: the worst went to the beast,
For the man had marked him well at the moment of impact,
Had put the point precisely at the pit° of his chest,
And drove it in to the hilt, so that the heart was shattered,
And the spent beast sank snarling and was swept downstream,
    Teeth bare.
    A hundred hounds and more

1560

1570

1580

1590

bridled made his bristles stand on end   **pit** in the "slot"; see above, l. 1330

Attack and seize and tear;
Men tug him to the shore
1600 And the dogs destroy him there.

LXIV

Bugles blew the triumph, horns blared loud.
There was hallooing in high pride by all present;
Braches° bayed at the beast, as bidden by their masters,
The chief huntsmen in charge of that chase so hard.
Then one who was wise in wood-crafts°
Started in style to slash open the boar.
First he hewed off the head° and hoisted it on high,
Then rent him roughly along the ridge of his back,
Brought out the bowels and broiled them on coals
1610 For blending with bread as the braches' reward.°
Then he broke out the brawn° from the bright broad flanks,
Took out the offal,° as is fit,
Attached the two halves entirely together,
And on a strong stake stoutly hung them.
Then home they hurried with the huge beast,
With the boar's head borne before the baron himself,
Who had destroyed him in the stream by the strength of his arm,
    Above all:
    It seemed to him an age
1620 Till he greeted Gawain in hall.
    To reap his rightful wage
    The latter came at his call.

LXV

The lord exclaimed loudly, laughing merrily
When he saw Sir Gawain, and spoke joyously.
The sweet ladies were sent for, and the servants assembled.
Then he showed them the shields, and surely described
The large size and length, and the malignity
Of the fierce boar's fighting when he fled in the woods;
So that Gawain congratulated him on his great deed,
1630 Commended it as a merit he had manifested well.
For a beast with so much brawn, the bold man said,
A boar of such breadth, he had not before seen.
When they handled the huge head the upright man praised it,
Expressed horror thereat for the ear of the lord.
'Now Gawain,' said the good man, 'this game is your own
By our contracted treaty, in truth, you know.'
'It is so,' said the knight, 'and as certainly

Braches small hounds, rather like beagles
wood-crafts woodmanship, including all kinds of hunting
hewed . . . head Both to bleed the carcass as soon as possible, and in triumph; a boar was the traditional noble Christmas dish, and the head was carried into hall with ceremony.
reward the technical hunting term
brawn boar's flesh
offal edible entrails

I shall give you all my gains as guerdon,° in faith.'
He clasped the castellan's neck and kissed him kindly,
1640 And then served him a second time in the same style.
'In all our transactions since I came to sojourn,' asserted Gawain,
'Up to tonight, as of now, there's nothing that
      I owe.'
      'By Saint Giles,'° the castellan quipped,
      'You're the finest fellow I know:
      Your wealth will have us whipped
      If your trade continues so!'

      LXVI
Then the trestles and tables were trimly set out,
Complete with cloths, and clearly flaming cressets°
1650 And waxen torches were placed in the wall-brackets
By retainers, who then tended the entire hall-gathering.
Much gladness and glee then gushed forth there
By the fire on the floor: and in multifarious ways
They sang noble songs at supper and afterwards,
A concert of Christmas carols and new dance-songs,°
With the most mannerly mirth a man could tell of,
And our courteous knight kept constant company with the lady.
In a bewitchingly well-mannered way she made up to him,
Secretly soliciting the stalwart knight
1660 So that he was astounded, and upset in himself.
But his upbringing forbade him to rebuff her utterly,
So he behaved towards her honourably, whatever aspersions might
      Be cast.
      They revelled in the hall
      As long as their pleasure might last,
      And then at the castellan's call
      To the chamber hearth they passed.

      LXVII
There they drank and discoursed and decided to enjoy
Similar solace and sport on New Year's Eve.
1670 But the princely knight asked permission to depart in the morning,
For his appointed time was approaching, and perforce he must go.
But the lord would not let him and implored him to linger,
Saying, 'I swear to you, as a staunch true knight,
You shall gain the Green Chapel to give your dues,
My lord, in the light of New Year, long before sunrise.
Therefore remain in your room and rest in comfort,
While I fare hunting in the forest; in fulfilment of our oath

---

guerdon reward
Saint Giles a 7th-century hermit, whose only companion was a stag, which led a huntsman-king to the saint. The association makes St.

Giles a fitting patron for the knight of the castle.
cressets torches
carols . . . songs literally, conducts and carols: Christmas part-songs and dance-songs

Exchanging what we achieve when the chase is over.
For twice I have tested you, and twice found you true.
1680   Now "Third time, throw best!" Think of that tomorrow!
Let us make merry while we may, set our minds on joy,
For hard fate can hit man whenever it likes.'
This was graciously granted and Gawain stayed.
Blithely drink was brought, then to bed with lights
          They pressed.
     All night Sir Gawain sleeps
     Softly and still at rest;
     But the lord his custom keeps
     And is early up and dressed.

          LXVIII
1690   After mass, he and his men made a small meal.°
Merry was the morning; he demanded his horse.
The men were ready mounted before the main gate,
A host of knightly horsemen to follow after him.
Wonderfully fair was the forest-land, for the frost remained,
And the rising sun shone ruddily on the ragged clouds,
In its beauty brushing their blackness off the heavens.
The huntsmen unleashed the hounds by a holt-side,°
And the rocks and surrounding bushes rang with their horn-calls.
Some found and followed the fox's° tracks,
1700   And wove various ways in their wily fashion.
A small hound cried the scent, the senior huntsman called
His fellow foxhounds to him and, feverishly sniffing,
The rout of dogs rushed forward on the right path.
The fox hurried fast, for they found him soon
And, seeing him distinctly, pursued him at speed,
Unmistakably giving tongue with tumultuous din.
Deviously in difficult country he doubled on his tracks,
Swerved and wheeled away, often waited listening,
Till at last by a little ditch he leaped a quickset hedge,
1710   And stole out stealthily at the side of a valley,
Considering his stratagem had given the slip to the hounds.
But he stumbled on a tracking-dogs' tryst-place unawares,
And there in a cleft three hounds threatened him at once,
          All grey.
     He swiftly started back
     And, full of deep dismay,
     He dashed on a different track;
     To the woods he went away.

small meal a bite
holt-side wood-side
fox's Descriptions of medieval set fox-hunts are
rare; Chaucer's Nun's Priest's Tale is an example in another genre.

LXIX

Then came the lively delight of listening to the hounds
1720 When they had all met in a muster, mingling together,
For, catching sight of him, they cried such curses on him
That the clustering cliffs seemed to be crashing down.
Here he was hallooed when the hunters met him,
There savagely snarled at by intercepting hounds;
Then he was called thief and threatened often;
With the tracking dogs on his tail, no tarrying was possible.
When out in the open he was often run at,
So he often swerved in again, that artful Reynard.
Yes, he led the lord and his liegemen a dance
1730 In this manner among the mountains till mid-afternoon,
While harmoniously at home the honoured knight slept
Between the comely curtains in the cold morning.
But the lady's longing to woo would not let her sleep,
Now would she impair the purpose pitched in her heart,
But rose up rapidly and ran to him
In a ravishing robe that reached to the ground,
Trimmed with finest fur from pure pelts,
Not coifed as to custom,° but with costly jewels
Strung in scores on her splendid hairnet.
1740 Her fine-featured face and fair throat were unveiled,
Her breast was bare and her back as well.
She came in by the chamber door and closed it after her,
Cast open a casement and called on the knight,
And briskly thus rebuked him with bountiful words
       Of good cheer.
    'Ah sir! What, sound asleep?
    The morning's crisp and clear.'
    He had been drowsing deep,
    But now he had to hear.

LXX

1750 The noble sighed ceaselessly in unsettled slumber
As threatening thoughts thronged in the dawn light
About destiny, which the day after would deal him his fate
At the Green Chapel where Gawain was to greet his man,
And be bound to bear his buffet unresisting.
But having recovered consciousness in comely fashion,
He heaved himself out of dreams and answered hurriedly.
The lovely lady advanced, laughing adorably,
Swooped over his splendid face and sweetly kissed him.
He welcomed her worthily with noble cheer
1760 And, gazing on her gay and glorious attire,

coifed . . . custom For this third, subtler, and
more important temptation, she has prepared
more fully and less modestly.

Her features so faultless and fine of complexion,
He felt a flush of rapture suffuse his heart.
Sweet and genial smiling slid them into joy
Till bliss burst forth between them, beaming gay
      And bright;
    With joy the two contended
    In talk of true delight,
    And peril would have impended
    Had Mary not minded her knight.

LXXI

1770 For that peerless princess pressed him so hotly,
So invited him to the very verge, that he felt forced
Either to allow her love or blackguardly rebuff her.
He was concerned for his courtesy, lest he be called caitiff,
But more especially for his evil plight if he should plunge into sin,
And dishonour the owner of the house treacherously.
'God shield me! That shall not happen, for sure,' said the knight.
So with laughing love-talk he deflected gently
The downright° declarations that dropped from her lips.
Said the beauty to the bold man, 'Blame will be yours
1780 If you love not the living body lying close to you
More than all wooers in the world who are wounded in heart;
Unless you have a lover more beloved, who delights you more,
A maiden to whom you are committed, so immutably bound
That you do not seek to sever from her—which I see is so.
Tell me the truth of it, I entreat you now;
By all the loves there are, do not hide the truth
      With guile.'
    Then gently, 'By Saint John,'°
    Said the knight with a smile,
    'I owe my oath to none,
    Nor wish to yet a while.'

LXXII

'Those words,' said the fair woman, 'are the worst there could be,
But I am truly answered, to my utter anguish.
Give me now a gracious kiss, and I shall go from here
As a maid that loves much, mourning on this earth.'
Then, sighing, she stooped, and seemlily kissed him,
And, severing herself from him, stood up and said,
'At this adieu, my dear one, do me this pleasure:
Give me something as gift, your glove° if no more,
1800 To mitigate my mourning when I remember you.'
'Now certainly, for your sake,' said the knight,
'I wish I had here the handsomest thing I own,

downright literally, loving
Saint John the oath by the "beloved disciple,"
whose feast day was December 27—appropriate

to the time, the situation, and the character of
Gawain
glove a frequent love token

For you have deserved, forsooth, superabundantly
And rightfully, a richer reward than I could give.
But as tokens of true love, trifles mean little.
It is not to your honour to have at this time
A mere glove as Gawain's gift to treasure.
For I am here on an errand in unknown regions,
And have no bondsmen, no baggages with dear-bought things in them.
1810   This afflicts me now, fair lady, for your sake.
Man must do as he must; neither lament it
            Nor repine.'
        'No, highly honoured one,'
        Replied that lady fine,
        'Though gift you give me none,
        You must have something of mine.'

        LXXIII
She proffered him a rich ring wrought in red gold,
With a sparkling stone set conspicuously in it,
Which beamed as brilliantly as the bright sun;
1820   You may well believe its worth was wonderfully great.
But the courteous man declined it and quickly said,
'Before God, gracious lady, no giving just now!
Not having anything to offer, I shall accept nothing.'
She offered it him urgently and he refused again,
Fast affirming his refusal on his faith as a knight.
Put out by this repulse, she presently said,
'If you reject my ring as too rich in value,
Doubtless you would be less deeply indebted to me
If I gave you my girdle,° a less gainful gift.'
1830   She swiftly slipped off the cincture° of her gown
Which went round her waist under the wonderful mantle,
A girdle of green silk with a golden hem,
Embroidered only at the edges, with hand-stitched ornament.
And she pleaded with the prince in a pleasant manner
To take it notwithstanding its trifling worth;
But he told her that he could touch no treasure at all,
Not gold nor any gift, till God gave him grace
To pursue to success the search he was bound on.
'And therefore I beg you not to be displeased:
1840   Press no more your purpose, for I promise it never
            Can be.
        I owe you a hundredfold
        For grace you have granted me;
        And ever through hot and cold
        I shall stay your devotee.'

girdle belt, which turns out to have magical   cincture French *ceinture*, belt
properties (ll. 1851 ff.), as elsewhere in the
romances

LXXIV

'Do you say "no" to this silk?' then said the beauty;
'Because it is simple in itself? And so it seems.
Lo! It is little indeed, and so less worth your esteem.
But one who was aware of the worth twined in it
1850 Would appraise its properties as more precious perhaps,
For the man that binds his body with this belt of green,
As long as he laps it closely about him,
No hero under heaven can hack him to pieces,
For he cannot be killed by any cunning on earth.'
Then the prince pondered, and it appeared to him
A precious gem to protect him in the peril appointed him
When he gained the Green Chapel to be given checkmate:°
It would be a splendid stratagem to escape being slain.
Then he allowed her to solicit him and let her speak.
1860 She pressed the belt upon him with potent words
And having got his agreement, she gave it him gladly,
Beseeching him for her sake to conceal it always,
And hide it from her husband with all diligence.
That never should another know of it, the noble swore
         Outright.
     Then often his thanks gave he
     With all his heart and might,
     And thrice by then had she
     Kissed the constant knight.

LXXV

1870 Then with a word of farewell she went away
For she could not force further satisfaction from him.
Directly she withdrew, Sir Gawain dressed himself,
Rose and arrayed himself in rich garments,
But laid aside the love-lace the lady had given him,
Secreted it carefully where he could discover it later.
Then he went his way at once to the chapel,
Privily° approached a priest and prayed him there
To listen to his life's sins and enlighten him
On how he might have salvation in the hereafter.
1880 Then, confessing his faults, he fairly shrove himself,°
Begging mercy for both major and minor sins.
He asked the holy man for absolution
And was absolved with certainty and sent out so pure
That Doomsday° could have been declared the day after.
Then he made merrier among the noble ladies,
With comely carolling and all kinds of pleasure,

---

checkmate to get the final blow; see l. 2195
Privily secretly, discreetly
shrove himself But he keeps the belt; the poet seems not to regard this as major or minor sin, since Gawain confesses and receives absolution.

Doomsday the Day of General Judgment. Gawain has been made so clean of sin as to be ready for heaven tomorrow, should tomorrow be Judgment Day.

Than ever he had done, with ecstasy, till came
  Dark night.
    Such honour he did to all,
1890   They said, 'Never has this knight
    Since coming into hall
    Expressed such pure delight.'

LXXVI

Now long may he linger there, love sheltering him!
The prince was still on the plain, pleasuring in the chase,
Having finished off the fox he had followed so far.
As he leaped over a hedge looking out for the quarry,
Where he heard the hounds that were harrying the fox,
Reynard came running through a rough thicket
With the pack all pell-mell, panting at his heels.
1900 The lord, aware of the wild beast, waited craftily,
Then drew his dazzling sword and drove at the fox.
The beast baulked at the blade to break° sideways,
But a dog bounded at him before he could,
And right in front of the horse's feet they fell on him,
All worrying their wily prey with a wild uproar.
The lord quickly alighted and lifted him up,
Wrenched him beyond reach of the ravening fangs,
Held him high over his head and hallooed lustily,
While the angry hounds in hordes bayed at him.
1910 Thither hurried the huntsmen with horns in plenty,
Sounding the rally° splendidly till they saw their lord.
When the company of his court had come up to the kill,
All who bore bugles blew at once,
And the others without horns hallooed loudly.
The requiem that was raised for Reynard's soul
And the commotion made it the merriest meet ever,
    Men said.
    The hounds must have their fee:
    They pat them on the head,
1920   Then hold the fox; and he
    Is reft of his skin of red.

LXXVII

Then they set off for home, it being almost night,
Blowing their big horns bravely as they went.
At last the lord alighted at his beloved castle
And found upon the floor a fire, and beside it
The good Sir Gawain in a glad humour
By reason of the rich friendship he had reaped from the ladies.
He wore a turquoise tunic° extending to the ground;

break turn away   **tunic** robe. Blue was the color of fidelity.
rally recall

His softly-furred surcoat suited him well,
1930 And his hood of the same hue hung from his shoulder.
All trimmed with ermine were hood and surcoat.
Meeting the master in the middle of the floor,
Gawain went forward gladly and greeted him thus:
'Forthwith, I shall be the first to fulfil the contract
We settled so suitably without sparing the wine.'
Then he clasped the castellan and kissed him thrice
As sweetly and steadily as a strong knight could.
'By Christ!' quoth the other, 'You will carve yourself a fortune
By traffic in this trade when the terms suit you!'
1940 'Do not chop logic about the exchange,' chipped in Gawain,
'As I have properly paid over the profit I made.'
'Marry,' said the other man, 'Mine is inferior,
For I have hunted all day and have only taken
This ill-favoured fox's skin,° may the Fiend take it!
And that is a poor price to pay for such precious things
As you have pressed upon me here, three pure kisses
          So good.'
      'Enough!' acknowledged Gawain,
      'I thank you, by the Rood.'°
1950   And how the fox was slain
      The lord told him as they stood.

      LXXVIII
With mirth and minstrelsy, and meals when they liked,
They made as merry then as ever men could;
With the laughter of ladies and delightful jesting,
Gawain and his good host were very gay together,
Save when excess or sottishness seemed likely.
Master and men made many a witty sally,
Until presently, at the appointed parting-time,
The brave men were bidden to bed at last.
1960 Then of his host the hero humbly took leave,
The first to bid farewell, fairly thanking him:
'May the High King° requite you for your courtesy at this feast,
And the wonderful week of my dwelling here!
I would offer to be one of your own men if you liked,
But that I must move on tomorrow, as you know,
If you will give me the guide you granted me,
To show me the Green Chapel where my share of doom
Will be dealt on New Year's Day, as God deems for me.'
'With all my heart!' said the host, 'In good faith,
1970 All that I ever promised you, I shall perform.'
He assigned him a servant to set him on his way,

---

fox's skin Even this, the worst gift on the third
day, is also the nearest yet to a fair exchange.

Rood cross
High King Christ

And lead him in the hills without any delay,
Faring through forest and thicket by the most straightforward route
      They might.
    With every honour due
    Gawain then thanked the knight,
    And having bid him adieu,
    Took leave of the ladies bright.

LXXIX

So he spoke to them sadly, sorrowing as he kissed,°
1980 And urged on them heartily his endless thanks,
And they gave to Sir Gawain words of grace in return,
Commending him to Christ with cries of chill sadness.
Then from the whole household he honourably took his leave,
Making all the men that he met amends
For their several services and solicitous care,
For they had been busily attendant, bustling about him;
And every soul was as sad to say farewell
As if they had always had the hero in their house.
Then the lords led him with lights to his chamber,
1990 And blithely brought him to bed to rest.
If he slept—I dare not assert it—less soundly than usual,
There was much on his mind for the morrow, if he meant to give
      It thought.
    Let him lie there still,
    He almost has what he sought;
    So tarry a while until
    The process I report.

Fitt 4

LXXX

Now the New Year neared, the night passed,
Daylight fought darkness as the Deity ordained.
2000 But wild was the weather the world awoke to;
Bitterly the clouds cast down cold on the earth,
Inflicting on the flesh flails from the north.
Bleakly the snow blustered, and beasts were frozen;
The whistling wind wailed from the heights,
Driving great drifts deep in the dales.
Keenly the lord listened as he lay in his bed;
Though his lids were closed, he was sleeping little.
Every cock that crew recalled to him his tryst.
Before the day had dawned, he had dressed himself,°

---

sorrowing . . . kissed Elaborate leavetaking   **dressed himself** literally, risen from bed
would be thought necessary in courtesy.

2010 For the light from a lamp illuminated his chamber.
He summoned his servant, who swiftly answered,
Commanded that his mail-coat and mount's saddle be brought.
The man fared forth and fetched him his armour,
And set Sir Gawain's array in splendid style.
First he clad him in his clothes to counter the cold,
Then in his other armour which had been well kept;
His breast- and belly-armour had been burnished bright,
And the rusty rings of his rich mail-coat rolled clean,°
And all being as fresh as at first, he was fain to give thanks
2020   Indeed.
     Each wiped and polished piece
     He donned with due heed.
     The gayest from here to Greece,
     The strong man sent for his steed.

     LXXXI
While he was putting on apparel of the most princely kind—
His surcoat, with its symbol of spotless deeds
Environed on velvet with virtuous° gems,
Was embellished° and bound with embroidered seams,
And finely fur-lined with the fairest skins—
2030 He did not leave the lace belt, the lady's gift:
For his own good, Gawain did not forget that!
When he had strapped the sword on his swelling hips,
The knight lapped his loins with his love-token° twice,
Quickly wrapped it with relish round his waist.
The green silken girdle suited the gallant well,
Backed by the royal red cloth that richly showed.
But Gawain wore the girdle not for its great value,
Nor through pride in the pendants, in spite of their polish,
Nor for the gleaming gold which glinted on the ends,
2040 But to save himself when of necessity he must
Stand an evil stroke, not resisting it with knife
        Or sword.
     When ready and robed aright,
     Out came the comely lord;
     To the men of name and might
     His thanks in plenty poured.

     LXXXII
Then was Gringolet got ready, that great huge horse.
Having been assiduously° stabled in seemly quarters,
The fiery steed was fit and fretting for a gallop.

---

rolled clean in sand
virtuous powerful. Gems were believed to possess protective, talismanic qualities.
embellished embroidered

love-token He wears it outside his surcoat, not
expecting to see his host again.
assiduously literally, to his liking

2050 Sir Gawain stepped to him and, inspecting his coat,
Said earnestly to himself, asserting with truth,
'Here in this castle is a company whose conduct is honourable.
The man who maintains them, may he have joy!
The delightful lady, love befall her while she lives!
Thus for charity they cherish a chance guest
Honourably and open-handedly; may He on high,
The King of Heaven, requite you and your company too!
And if I could live any longer in lands on earth,
Some rich recompense, if I could, I should readily give you.'
2060 Then he stepped into the stirrup and swung aloft.
His man showed him° his shield; on his shoulder he put it,
And gave the spur to Gringolet with his gold-spiked heels.
The horse sprang forward from the paving, pausing no more
     To prance.
    His man was mounted and fit,
    Laden with spear and lance.
    'This castle to Christ I commit:
    May He its fortune enhance!'

     LXXXIII
The drawbridge was let down and the broad double gates
2070 Were unbarred and borne open on both sides.
Passing over the planks, the prince blessed himself
And praised the kneeling porter, who proffered him 'Good day,'
Praying God to grant that Gawain would be saved.
And Gawain went on his way with the one man
To put him on the right path for that perilous place
Where the sad assault must be received by him.
By bluffs where boughs were bare they passed,
Climbed by cliffs where the cold clung:
Under the high clouds, ugly mists
2080 Merged damply with the moors and melted on the mountains;
Each hill had a hat, a huge mantle of mist.
Brooks burst forth above them, boiling over their banks
And showering down sharply in shimmering cascades.
Wonderfully wild was their way through the woods;
Till soon the sun in the sway of that season
     Brought day.
    They were on a lofty hill
    Where snow beside them lay,
    When the servant stopped still
2090   And told his master to stay.

     LXXXIV
'For I have guided you to this ground, Sir Gawain, at this time,
And now you are not far from the noted place

His . . . him or: the guide produced

Which you have searched for and sought with such special zeal.
But I must say to you, forsooth, since I know you,
And you are a lord whom I love with no little regard,
Take my governance as guide, and it shall go better for you.
For the place is perilous that you are pressing towards.
In that wilderness dwells the worst man in the world,
For he is valiant and fierce and fond of fighting,
2100　And mightier than any man that may be on earth,
And his body is bigger than the best four
In Arthur's house, or Hector,° or any other.
At the Green Chapel he gains his great adventures.
No man passes that place, however proud in arms,
Without being dealt a death-blow by his dreadful hand.
For he is an immoderate man, to mercy a stranger;
For whether churl or chaplain by the chapel rides,
Monk or mass-priest or man of other kind,
He thinks it as convenient to kill him as keep alive himself.°
2110　Therefore I say, as certainly as you sit in your saddle,
If you come there you'll be killed, I caution you, knight,
Take my troth for it, though you had twenty lives
　　　And more.
　　　He has lived here since long ago
　　　And filled the field with gore.
　　　You cannot counter his blow,
　　　It strikes so sudden and sore.

　　　LXXXV
'Therefore, good Sir Gawain, leave the grim man alone!
Ride by another route, to some region remote!
2120　Go in the name of God, and Christ grace your fortune!
And I shall go home again and undertake
To swear solemnly by God and his saints as well
(By my halidom,° so help me God, and every other oath)
Stoutly to keep your secret, not saying to a soul
That ever you tried to turn tail from any man I knew.'
'Great thanks,' replied Gawain, somewhat galled, and said,
'It is worthy of you to wish for my well-being, man,
And I believe you would loyally lock it in your heart.
But however quiet you kept it, if I quit this place,
2130　Fled from the fellow in the fashion you propose,
I should become a cowardly knight with no excuse whatever.
For I will go to the Green Chapel, to get what Fate sends,
And have whatever words I wish with that worthy,
Whether weal or woe is what Fate
　　　Demands.

Hector the Trojan hero, or Sir Ector, one of King Arthur's best knights
convenient . . . himself He is not bound by the laws of true chivalry, which would respect the clergy and disdain to kill a base-born churl.
halidom holy thing, e.g., a relic, on which an oath could be taken

Fierce though that fellow be,
Clutching his club° where he stands,
Our Lord can certainly see
That his own are in safe hands.'

LXXXVI

2140 'By Mary!' said the other man, 'If you mean what you say,
You are determined to take all your trouble on yourself.
If you wish to lose your life, I'll no longer hinder you.
Here's your lance for your hand, your helmet for your head.
Ride down this rough track round yonder cliff
Till you arrive in a rugged ravine at the bottom,
Then look about on the flat, on your left hand,
And you will view there in the vale that very chapel,
And the grim gallant who guards it always.
Now, noble Gawain, good-bye in God's name.
2150 For all the gold on God's earth I would not go with you,
Nor foot it an inch further through this forest as your fellow.'
Whereupon he wrenched at his reins, that rider in the woods,
Hit the horse with his heels as hard as he could,
Sent him leaping along, and left the knight there
     Alone.
    'By God!' said Gawain, 'I swear
    I will not weep or groan:
    Being given to God's good care,
    My trust in Him shall be shown.'

LXXXVII

2160 Then he gave the spur to Gringolet and galloped down the path,
Thrust through a thicket there by a bank,
And rode down the rough slope right into the ravine.
Then he searched about, but it seemed savage and wild,
And no sign did he see of any sort of building;
But on both sides banks, beetling and steep,
And great crooked crags, cruelly jagged;
The bristling barbs of rock seemed to brush the sky.
Then he held in his horse, halted there,
Scanned on every side in search of the chapel.
2170 He saw no such thing anywhere, which seemed remarkable,
Save, hard by in the open, a hillock of sorts,
A smooth-surfaced barrow° on a slope beside a stream
Which flowed forth fast there in its course,
Foaming and frothing as if feverishly boiling.
The knight, urging his horse, pressed onwards to the mound,
Dismounted manfully and made fast to a lime-tree

---

club the sort of weapon one would expect from
a giant in the wilderness. It has never been
specified what weapon Gawain is to get his blow

from. In l. 384 the Green Knight was offered
a choice of weapons.
barrow artificial mound

The reins, hooking them round a rough branch;
Then he went to the barrow, which he walked round, inspecting,
Wondering what in the world it might be.
2180 It had a hole in each end and on either side,
And was overgrown with grass in great patches.
All hollow it was within, only an old cavern
Or the crevice of an ancient crag: he could not explain it
           Aright.
      'O God, is the Chapel Green
        This mound?' said the noble knight.
      'At such might Satan be seen
        Saying matins at midnight.'

      LXXXVIII
'Now certainly the place is deserted,' said Gawain,
2190 'It is a hideous oratory, all overgrown,
And well graced for the gallant garbed in green
To deal out his devotions in the Devil's fashion.
Now I feel in my five wits, it is the Fiend himself
That has tricked me into this tryst, to destroy me here.
This is a chapel of mischance—checkmate° to it!
It is the most evil holy place I ever entered.'
With his high helmet on his head, and holding his lance,
He roamed up to the roof of that rough dwelling.
Then from that height he heard, from a hard rock
2200 On the bank beyond the brook, a barbarous noise.
What! It clattered amid the cliffs fit to cleave them apart,
As if a great scythe were being ground on a grindstone there.
What! It whirred and it whetted, like water in a mill.
What! It made a rushing, ringing din, rueful to hear.
'By God!' then said Gawain, 'that is going on,
I suppose, as a salute to myself, to greet me
           Hard by.
      God's will be warranted:
        "Alas!" is a craven cry.
2210   No din shall make me dread
        Although today I die.'

      LXXXIX
Then the courteous knight called out clamorously,
'Who holds sway here and has an assignation with me?
For the good knight Gawain is on the ground here.
If anyone there wants anything, wend your way hither fast,
And further your needs either now, or not at all.'
'Bide there!' said one on the bank above his head,
'And you shall swiftly receive what I once swore to give you.'

checkmate destruction; see l. 1857

Yet for a time he continued his tumult of scraping,
2220   Turning away as he whetted, before he would descend.
Then he thrust himself round a thick crag through a hole,
Whirling round a wedge of rock with a frightful weapon,
A Danish axe° duly honed for dealing the blow,
With a broad biting edge, bow-bent along the handle,
Ground on a grindstone, a great four-foot blade—
No less, by that love-lace° gleaming so brightly!
And the gallant in green was garbed as at first,
His looks and limbs the same, his locks and beard;
Save that steadily on his feet he strode on the ground,
2230   Setting the handle to the stony earth and stalking beside it.
He would not wade through the water when he came to it,
But vaulted over on his axe, then with huge strides
Advanced violently and fiercely along the field's width
            On the snow.
        Sir Gawain went to greet
        The knight, not bowing low.
        The man said, 'Sir so sweet,
        Your honour the trysts you owe.'°

            XC
'Gawain,' said the Green Knight, 'may God guard you!
2240   You are welcome to my dwelling, I warrant you,
And you have timed your travel here as a true man ought.
You know plainly the pact we pledged between us:
This time a twelvemonth ago you took your portion,
And now at this New Year I should nimbly requite you.
And we are on our own here in this valley
With no seconds to sunder us, spar as we will.
Take your helmet off your head, and have your payment here.
And offer no more argument or action than I did
When you whipped off my head with one stroke.'
2250   'No,' said Gawain, 'by God who gave me a soul,
The grievous gash to come I grudge you not at all;
Strike but the one stroke and I shall stand still
And offer you no hindrance; you may act freely,
            I swear.'
        Head bent,° Sir Gawain bowed,
        And showed the bright flesh bare.
        He behaved as if uncowed,
        Being loth to display his care.

Danish axe the sort of ferocious, long-bladed axe originally used by the Viking pirates, without a spike on the back. At King Arthur's court the Green Knight had carried a *guisarme*, spiked and richly ornamented, a much more knightly weapon.

love-lace The original reads simply "thong." **trysts you owe** The stress is on Gawain's keeping of his oath. **Head bent** The words pick up the description of the Green Knight awaiting the stroke at Arthur's court.

XCI

Then the gallant in green quickly got ready,
2260 Heaved his horrid weapon on high to hit Gawain,
With all the brute force in his body bearing it aloft,
Swinging savagely enough to strike him dead.
Had it driven down as direly as he aimed,
The daring dauntless man would have died from the blow.
But Gawain glanced up at the grim axe beside him
As it came shooting through the shivering air to shatter him,
And his shoulders shrank slightly from the sharp edge.
The other suddenly stayed the descending axe,
And then reproved the prince with many proud words:
2270 'You are not Gawain,' said the gallant, 'whose greatness is such
That by hill or hollow no army ever frightened him;
For now you flinch for fear before you feel harm.
I never did know that knight to be a coward.
I neither flinched nor fled when you let fly your blow,
Nor offered any quibble in the house of King Arthur.
My head flew to my feet, but flee I did not.
Yet you quail cravenly though unscathed so far.
So I am bound to be called the better man
        Therefore.'
2280   Said Gawain, 'Not again
        Shall I flinch as I did before;
        But if my head pitch to the plain,
        It's off for evermore.'

XCII

'But be brisk, man, by your faith, and bring me to the point;
Deal me my destiny and do it out of hand,
For I shall stand your stroke, not starting at all
Till your axe has hit me. Here is my oath on it.'
'Have at you then!' said the other, heaving up his axe,
Behaving as angrily as if he were mad.
2290 He menaced him mightily, but made no contact,°
Smartly withholding his hand without hurting him.
Gawain waited unswerving, with not a wavering limb,
But stood still as a stone or the stump of a tree
Gripping the rocky ground with a hundred grappling roots.
Then again the Green Knight began to gird:°
'So now you have a whole heart I must hit you.
May the high knighthood which Arthur conferred
Preserve you and save your neck, if so it avail you!'
Then said Gawain, storming with sudden rage,
2300 'Thrash on, you thrustful fellow, you threaten too much.

made . . . contact possible manuscript reading: gird mock
ryve, i.e. "cleave"; thus, "did not cut through
the man"; or: *ryne*, "touch"

It seems your spirit is struck with self-dread.'
'Forsooth,' the other said, 'you speak so fiercely
I will no longer lengthen matters by delaying your business,
    I vow.'
      He stood astride to smite,
      Lips pouting, puckered brow.
      No wonder he lacked delight
      Who expected no help now.

    XCIII

Up went the axe at once and hurtled down straight
2310   At the naked neck with its knife-like edge.
Though it swung down savagely, slight was the wound,
A mere snick on the side, so that the skin was broken.
Through the fair fat to the flesh fell the blade,
And over his shoulders the shimmering blood shot to the ground.
When Sir Gawain saw his gore glinting on the snow,
He leapt feet close together a spear's length away,
Hurriedly heaved his helmet on to his head,
And shrugging his shoulders, shot his shield to the front,
Swung out his bright sword and said fiercely,
2320   (For never had the knight since being nursed by his mother
Been so buoyantly happy, so blithe in this world)
'Cease your blows, sir, strike me no more.
I have sustained a stroke here unresistingly,
And if you offer any more I shall earnestly reply,
Resisting, rest assured, with the most rancorous
      Despite.
      The single stroke is wrought
      To which we pledged our plight
      In high King Arthur's court:
2330   Enough now, therefore, knight!'

    XCIV

The bold man stood back and bent over his axe,
Putting the haft to earth, and leaning on the head.
He gazed at Sir Gawain on the ground before him,
Considering the spirited and stout way he stood,
Audacious in arms; his heart warmed to him.
Then he gave utterance gladly in his great voice,
With resounding speech saying to the knight,
'Bold man, do not be so bloodily resolute.
No one here has offered you evil discourteously,
2340   Contrary to the covenant made at the King's court.
I promised a stroke, which you received: consider yourself paid.
I cancel all other obligations of whatever kind.
If I had been more active, perhaps I could
Have made you suffer by striking a savager stroke.

First in foolery I made a feint at striking,
Not rending you with a riving cut—and right I was,
On account of the first night's covenant we accorded;
For you truthfully kept your trust in troth with me,
Giving me your gains, as a good man should.
2350   The further feinted blow was for the following day,
When you kissed my comely wife, and the kisses came to me:
For those two things, harmlessly I thrust twice at you
       Feinted blows.
      Truth for truth's the word;
      No need for dread, God knows.
      From your failure at the third
      The tap you took arose.

    XCV

'For that braided belt you wear belongs to me.
I am well aware that my own wife gave it you.
2360   Your conduct and your kissings are completely known to me,
And the wooing by my wife—my work set it on.
I instructed her to try you, and you truly seem
To be the most perfect paladin ever to pace the earth.
As the pearl to the white pea in precious worth,
So in good faith is Gawain to other gay knights.
But here your faith failed you, you flagged somewhat, sir,
Yet it was not for a well-wrought thing, nor for wooing either,
But for love of your life, which is less blameworthy.'
The other strong man stood considering this a while,
2370   So filled with fury that his flesh trembled,
And the blood from his breast burst forth in his face
As he shrank for shame at what the chevalier spoke of.
The first words the fair knight could frame were:
'Curses on both cowardice and covetousness!°
Their vice and villainy are virtue's undoing.'
Then he took the knot, with a twist twitched it loose,
And fiercely flung the fair girdle to the knight.
'Lo! There is the false thing, foul fortune befall it!
I was craven about our encounter, and cowardice taught me
2380   To accord with covetousness and corrupt my nature
And the liberality and loyalty belonging to chivalry.
Now I am faulty and false and found fearful always.
In the train of treachery and untruth go woe
       And shame.
      I acknowledge, knight, how ill
      I behaved, and take the blame.
      Award what penance you will:
      Henceforth I'll shun ill-fame.'

covetousness more than desire for wealth and
possessions: entanglement in the values of this
world

XCVI

Then the other lord laughed and politely said,
'In my view you have made amends for your misdemeanour;
You have confessed your faults fully with fair acknowledgement,
And plainly done penance at the point of my axe.
You are absolved of your sin and as stainless now
As if you had never fallen in fault since first you were born.
As for the gold-hemmed girdle, I give it you, sir,
Seeing it is as green as my gown. Sir Gawain, you may
Think about this trial when you throng in company
With paragons of princes, for it is a perfect token,
At knightly gatherings, of the great adventure at the Green Chapel.
You shall come back to my castle this cold New Year.
To revel away the rest of this rich feast
          We shall go.
     Thus urging him, the lord
     Said, 'You and my wife, I know
     We shall bring to clear accord,
     Though she was your fierce foe.'

XCVII

'No, forsooth,' said the knight, seizing his helmet,
And doffing it with dignity as he delivered his thanks,
'My stay has sufficed me.° Still, luck go with you!
May He who bestows all good, honour you with it!
And commend me to the courteous lady, your comely wife;
Indeed, my due regards to both dear ladies,
Who with their wanton wiles have thus waylaid their knight.
But it is no marvel for a foolish man to be maddened thus
And saddled with sorrow by the sleights of women.°
For here on earth was Adam taken in by one,
And Solomon by many such, and Samson likewise;
Delilah dealt him his doom; and David, later still,
Was blinded by Bathsheba, and badly suffered for it.
Since these were troubled by their tricks, it would be true joy
To love them but not believe° them, if a lord could,
For these were the finest of former times, most favoured by fortune
Of all under the heavenly kingdom whose hearts were
          Abused;
     These four all fell to schemes
     Of women whom they used.
     If I am snared, it seems
     I ought to be excused.°

2390
2400
2410
2420

My stay . . . me I have been long enough
away from Arthur's court
sleights of women The stock anti-feminist *ex-*
empla of the Old Testament: Adam and Eve
(Genesis 3); Solomon and his 700 wives and
300 concubines (I Kings 11:3); Samson and
Delilah (Judges 16); David and Bathsheba, wife
of Uriah (II Samuel 11:2–4). See Chaucer's
Wife of Bath's Prologue. They seem to come in

oddly, but the point is merely that these were
all women who had made men swerve from the
path of (knightly) virtue.
believe i.e. put full trust in
If . . . excused Gawain seems now to be excusing himself on the ground that if such great
men were deceived by women, it is no wonder
if it happens to him.

XCVIII

'But your girdle,' said Gawain, 'God requite you for it!
Not for the glorious gold shall I gladly wear it,
Nor for the stuff nor the silk for the swaying pendants,
Nor for its worth, fine workmanship or wonderful honour;
But as a sign of my sin I shall see it often,
Remembering with remorse, when I am mounted in glory,
The fault and faintheartedness of the perverse flesh,
How it tends to attract tarnishing sin.
So when pride° shall prick me for my prowess in arms,
One look at this love-lace will make lowly my heart.
But one demand I make of you, may it not incommode you:
Since you are master of the demesne I have remained in a while,
Make known, by your knighthood—and now may He above,
Who sits on high and holds up heaven, requite you!—
How you pronounce your true name; and no more requests.'
'Truly,' the other told him, 'I shall tell you my title.
Bertilak of the High Desert° I am called here in this land.
Through the might of Morgan the Fay,° who remains in my house
Through the wiles of her witchcraft, a lore well learned,—
Many of the magical arts of Merlin° she acquired,
For she lavished fervent love long ago
On that susceptible sage: certainly your knights know
          Of their fame.
        So "Morgan the Goddess"
        She accordingly became;
        The proudest she can oppress
        And to her purpose tame—

XCIX

'She sent me forth in this form to your famous hall
To put to the proof the great pride of the house,
The reputation for high renown of the Round Table;
She bewitched me in this weird way to bewilder your wits,
And to grieve Guinevere and goad her to death
With ghastly fear of that ghost's ghoulish speaking
With his head in his hand before the high table.
That is the aged beldame who is at home:
She is indeed your own aunt, Arthur's half-sister,
Daughter of the Duchess of Tintagel° who in due course,

2430 (line 2430)
2440 (line 2440)
2450 (line 2450)
2460 (line 2460)

---

pride mother of the deadly sins, which a knight, especially, must avoid
Bertilak The name Bertilak is Celtic. High Desert *(Haut-desert)* probably refers to his castle.
Morgan le Fay sorceress half-sister of King Arthur, who imprisoned his knights, first called "goddess" (l. 2452) by the 12th-century Gerald of Wales. She was said to have told Arthur of Lancelot's adultery with Guinevere; and Guinevere is said to have revealed her intrigue with

another knight—hence their enmity (l. 2460).
Merlin the wizard of Arthur's court, who fell in love with Morgan and taught her his magic
Duchess of Tintagel See Malory, *Morte Darthur,* below. The story is first told by Geoffrey of Monmouth (12th century). Igraine, Duchess of Tintagel, conceived Arthur by King Uther Pendragon, who deceived her in the likeness of her husband; after her husband's death she married Uther.

By Uther, was mother of Arthur, who now holds sway.
Therefore I beg you, bold sir, come back to your aunt,
Make merry in my house, for my men love you,
And by my faith, brave sir, I bear you as much good will
2470   As I grant any man under God, for your great honesty.'
But Gawain firmly refused with a final negative.
They clasped and kissed, commending each other
To the Prince of Paradise,° and parted on the cold ground
        Right there.
        Gawain on steed serene
        Spurred to court with courage fair,
        And the gallant garbed in green
        To wherever he would elsewhere.

        c
Now Gawain goes riding on Gringolet
2480   In lonely lands, his life saved by grace.
Often he stayed at a house, and often in the open,
And often overcame hazards in the valleys,
Which at this time I do not intend to tell you about.
The hurt he had had in his neck was healed,
And the glittering girdle that girt him round
Obliquely, like a baldric, was bound by his side
And laced under the left arm with a lasting knot,
In token that he was taken in a tarnishing sin;
And so he came to court, quite unscathed.
2490   When the great became aware of Gawain's arrival,
There was general jubilation at the joyful news.
The King kissed the knight, and the Queen likewise,
And so did many a staunch noble who sought to salute him.
They all asked him about his expedition,
And he truthfully told them of his tribulations—
What chanced at the chapel, the good cheer of the knight,
The lady's love-making, and lastly, the girdle.
He displayed the scar of the snick° on his neck
Where the bold man's blow had hit, his bad faith to
2500   Proclaim;
        He groaned at his disgrace,
        Unfolding his ill-fame,
        And blood suffused his face
        When he showed his mark of shame.

        CI
'Look, my lord,' said Gawain, the lace in his hand.
'This belt confirms the blame I bear on my neck,
My bane and debasement, the burden I bear

Prince of Paradise Christ   **snick** nick

For being caught by cowardice and covetousness.
This is the figure of the faithlessness found in me,
2510 Which I must needs wear while I live.
For man can conceal sin but not dissever from it,
So when it is once fixed, it will never be worked loose.'
First the king, then all the court, comforted the knight,
And all the lords and ladies belonging to the Table
Laughed at it loudly, and concluded amiably
That each brave man of the brotherhood should bear a baldric,°
A band, obliquely about him, of bright green,
Of the same hue as Sir Gawain's and for his sake wear it.
So it ranked as renown to the Round Table,
2520 And an everlasting honour to him who had it,
As is rendered in Romance's rarest book.
Thus in the days of Arthur this exploit was achieved,
To which the books of Brutus° bear witness;
After the bold baron, Brutus, came here,
The siege and the assault being ceased at Troy
     Before.
     Such exploits, I'll be sworn,
     Have happened here of yore.
     Now Christ with his crown of thorn
2530   Bring us his bliss evermore! AMEN.
     HONY SOYT QUI MAL PENCE

c. 1380–1400

THE VISION OF PIERS PLOWMAN

It is surprising how little we know about when, where, and by whom *The Vision of Will Concerning Piers Plowman* was written. The poem was widely known and read, for it exists in a large number of manuscripts of the fourteenth and fifteenth centuries, was printed several times in the sixteenth, and was used, known, and referred to by sixteenth-century poets such as Skelton, by the religious Reformers a little later, and by others. But the few clues that we have to the identity of its author amount to little. He names himself several times as Will; he seems to have come from the West of England and to have been brought up in the area of the Malvern Hills, in Worcestershire, the scene of his vision. Many of the manuscripts of his book were copied there and thereabouts, and the long alliterative line that he uses for his meter survived, or was revived, with more strength in the West than elsewhere during the fourteenth century. The poet certainly spent some time in London.

The name of William Langland, traditionally associated with the poem, must serve

---

baldric This has been thought to mean, in conjunction with the motto of the Order of the Garter—*Hony soyt qui mal pence*—placed at the end of the poem by the scribe, that the poem commemorates the founding of the Garter by Edward III about 1347. But the colors are wrong: the garter was dark blue. A later Gawain romance makes the lace white and sees in it the origin of the collar worn by Knights of the Bath. The association looks like an afterthought, not intended by the *Gawain* poet, despite his concern with chivalric values.
books of Brutus i.e. any chronicle or romance of the "matter of Britain"

until scholarship finds a better. Even so, we are not much ahead, since we know nothing of William Langland either, and may be giving this name to at least two separate poets. *Piers Plowman* exists in three versions, called by scholars A, B, and C, all composed between about 1360 and about 1385. A, the earliest and shortest (about 2500 lines), opens with an allegorical vision of the corruption of society and the attempt to purify it through Piers the Plowman. Piers personifies the ordinary man, seeking goodness through humility, honest endeavor, and obedience to the law of God. This section is followed by another, much shorter: *The Vita de Dowel, Dobet and Dobest* (The Life of Do Well, Do Better, and Do Best), in which another vision is presented. In his quest for the good Christian life and for the rational and intellectual foundations of faith, the poet asks information from Thought (intellectual activity), Wit (rational understanding resulting from thought), Study (Wit's wife: formal, disciplined reading and thought), and others. The search is inconclusive.

The B text, of about fifteen years later, is a radical revision and expansion of A. Adding further books, or passus (Latin *passus*, a step or stage), this version almost trebles the length of the whole. The search for Do Well is expanded, leading to Do Better (the life of Christ) and then to Do Best (the life of the church), each of them embodied in Piers.

The C text is a revised version of B, about ten years later, of much the same length, with some major cuts and additions.

Scholars are divided as to whether these three versions are the work of one man, or more. Though many now believe that one man was the author, this is not certain and the situation is baffling. It is less easy to explain the correspondences between the versions if more than one poet had been at work than it is to explain the differences if we accept A, B, and C as the work of a single poet rewriting his poem, keeping his theme intact, developing parts of it, and cutting out others, in response to changes in opinion and interest, and to contemporary events and pressures. It is hard to imagine a reviser, C, entering so thoroughly into the highly individual, vivid, and complicated style and personality of the original poet, B, and rising, in his additions, to the power and intensity of the earlier version. Nevertheless, the poetic quality of C is sometimes weaker, so that it may be the work of a later reviser rather than the poet of the B text's final revision, made toward the end of his life.

"Langland," then, is a fiction, but a convenient one. His long dream-allegory poem describes those ingredients of the social and religious condition of England in his day which he wishes to see reformed. The form in which it is cast allows the poet to pass easily from one mode of existence to another, from the description and out-spoken criticism of current religious and social practices to the introduction of allegori-cal personages such as Holy Church, Lady Meed, Conscience, Kind Wit, and the rest. As in a dream, the real fits perfectly well with the abstract or symbolic; and the dream may help us to see the essential truth behind the apparent, the spiritual implication of the actual. Neither cancels out the other: they are coordinates.

This is not to say that the poem always has the fourfold significance that in the medieval period was drawn out of the text of the Bible—that it can everywhere be read for its literal meaning, its allegorical significance, its application to Christ and the church, and its application to divine love. The poem always functions on at least two levels, however—literal and figural—and sometimes on more; and it transposes easily from one to another.

So, this first and most important principle underlying the procedures of *Piers*

Plowman—its allegorical nature—gives it its unity, which is thematic rather than narrative. Transitions are often bewilderingly rapid. The story line is constantly being interrupted, or apparently interrupted, so that the larger figural significance can be emphasized, and the position of a given event in the scheme of salvation pointed out. Langland's poem exists not as a story, but as an exploration of Christian truth and its implications for someone who wishes to follow it. It is, like the *Divine Comedy* of Dante, basically an account of how the soul might get to God, its final resting place, in spite of difficulties and detours.

In genre, *Piers Plowman* is difficult to characterize. It uses the techniques of the dream allegory, but for religious purposes, to examine the nature of heavenly love and virtue, not of earthly love between the sexes. Unlike some dream-allegory poems of its time, it nevertheless remains in the world: there is no journey up to heaven or to a *figura* of the Earthly Paradise. *Piers Plowman* is also frequently cast in the stock medieval form, descended from the classical, of debate or dialogue, in which the nature of a given thing is established by question and answer, or statement and counter-statement. It is a satire on, or a complaint against, the abuses of the world, especially against the love of money. It is often like a commentary on biblical texts and on the precepts of Christianity; or like a huge sermon or series of sermons, packed with *exempla* and exhortation.

This sounds like confusion—and it is true that the poem is difficult to read and to hold together. Yet it is strongly and carefully structured, beginning with an examination of the necessity to seek salvation, and the difficulties of the search, passing to the problems posed in attempting to act rightly, then to the vision of God's love and mercy and finally to the role of God's church in the salvation of the individual. *Piers Plowman* is learned, didactic, and above all a religious work, resembling no other of its time and place, using poetry rather than prayer as a means of seeking understanding, ceaselessly stalking this elusive subject. Its message is the message of God, not of art.

Characteristically, Langland chose not to use the fashionable rhyming verse which the Londoner Chaucer (his only superior as a poet in the century) employed. To the polish, precision, firm rapidity, and sophistication of this French technique Langland prefers the loose, long, easy-paced, swinging, older English alliterative line, based on the four-stress accentual measure, the meter of the *Gawain* poet also. But where the *Gawain* poet gives an effect of jeweled richness and ornament, reinforced by his elaborate digressions and descriptions, Langland is unique in the sheer size of his vision, in his expressive force and energy, the tautness he often achieves, the way in which he can use alliteration to establish and reinforce patterns of sense as well as patterns of sound.

Langland's vision of what the world might be did not leave room for much sympathy for the world as it was, corrupted by the love of money and by vice of all sorts pretending to be virtue, especially among the clergy. But his concern for the poor, the oppressed, and the wretched is passionate and tender. The figures of the simple, uninstructed Dreamer—a man like ourselves, or of Piers the Plowman—who also takes on the dimensions of Adam, Moses, Christ, St. Peter, the good Pope, and the true Christian—allow him the opportunity of pointing the contrast between true goodness and simplicity and the polluted values of all those whose professions are not matched by their practice. As the Plowman—who does not appear until well on in the poem— he is in the line of rustic social, and later religious, critics which stretches back to classical times and beyond.

Given this and given the passion and point of Langland's denunciations, it is not surprising that the first echoes of his influence come from the Peasants' Revolt of 1381, when phrases from *Piers Plowman* are found being used in a revolutionary context. The poem continued to be thought of as an armory of anti-clerical phrases and sentiments throughout the fifteenth century. Imitations of this dimension were written—and ascribed to Chaucer, whose satirical methods are much more controlled, refined, and oblique. The influence of Langland and of these imitations is still strong in the polemical literature of the English Reformation.

Langland himself would have been aghast at this. As his first printer put it in 1550, he had "godly, learnedly and wittily rebuked" all vice, but his vision of goodness was always a vision of what might come to pass within the Catholic Church and her institutions, not outside it. It was the passion and energy of his renunciation of abuses in society, of which the spiritual leaders ought to be the clergy, his contention that the corruption of the best is the worst kind of corruption, that laid him open to this use.

The text here used is a modernization, by the editor, of the B text as given in W. W. Skeat's edition (Oxford 1886; reprinted, with additional bibliography, 1954). An attempt has been made to keep the rhythm and alliteration of the original, and some archaic words have been retained where either sense or alliteration seemed to demand this.

The Vision of Piers Plowman

[In the Prologue and Passus I, Piers himself makes no appearance. In them, and as far as Passus VIII, the poet is concerned with St. Paul's "first man . . . of the earth, earthy," with the primary, major occupations in which men engage, by which ordinary society exists. The Dreamer's vision of the field full of folk going about its sinful, anarchic, money-making business without thought of the tower of Truth above or the dungeon of Error below, is a picture of the society which must be changed, church and state alike. The fable of the rats and mice, and of belling the cat, is a parody of the confusion and self-seeking of current politics.

The Prologue describes the state of society as it is. In Passus I, Langland goes on to show how it is that all this may be redeemed and brought to order, if only man will be conscious of Truth, i.e. if he will accept the law of God, which is the truth, and the law of love that are given to him. These laws he must obey faithfully, i.e. display his own truth, as all orders of society ought to do, in imitation of the angels. The church will be man's safeguard, and the means of mediating God's love to the people.]

> From *The Prologue*
> In a summer season, when soft was the sun°
> I shaped me into shrouds as though I were a shepherd,
> In habit like a hermit, unholy of works,°
> Went wide in this world, wonders to hear.

In . . . sun the spring opening, conventional for dream allegory, preparing the readers for the type of fiction, peopled with personifications, that they will meet, the poet acting as "presenter," through the dream
I . . . works i.e. I put myself into rough (or: long) clothes, like a shepherd, as if I were a

hermit, evil in my doings. Langland is severe on "feigned contemplatives," living as hermits to avoid working for a living. He may also be showing himself aware that his own life as a poet looks an idle one, bringing himself down, like Chaucer, to the reader with a mock-modest formula.

But on a May morning, on Malvern Hills,°
There befell me a ferly, of fairy methought.°
I was wearily wandered out, and went me to rest
Under a broad bank by a brook's side,
And as I lay and leaned° and looked into the waters,   *reclined*
10   I slumbered° into sleep, it sounded so merry.   *dozed*
        Then did I meet° a marvellous sweven,°   *dream / dream*
That I was in a wilderness, wist° I never where;   *knew*
As I looked into the east,° high into the sun,
I saw a tower on a toft,° triely° made;   *hill / excellently*
A deep dale beneath, a dungeon° therein,
With deep ditches and dark and dreadful to see.
A fair field full of folk found I there between,
Of all manner of men, the mean° and the rich,   *poor*
Working and wandering as the world demands.
20   Some put themselves to the plough and played full seldom:
In setting° and sowing sweated full hard   *planting*
To win what wasters° with gluttony destroy.
And some put themselves in pride, apparelled themselves like that,
In countenance of clothing came disguised.°
    In prayers and in penance put themselves many,
All for love of Our Lord lived full strictly,
In hope for to have heaven-kingdom's bliss;
Like anchorites and hermits who hold to their cells°
And covet not in country to cairen° about,   *wander*
30   For no lickerish° living their licham° to please.   *fancy / body*
    And some chose chaffer; they achieved the better°—
Or so it seems to our sight, that such men thrive.
And some mirths to make, as minstrels know how,
And get gold with their glee°—guiltless, I believe—   *singing*
But japers° and janglers,° Judas's children,   *jokers / blabbers*
Feign them fantasies and make fools of themselves
And have their wit at will to work if they wished;°
What Paul° preaches of them, I will not prove it here:
Qui loquitur turpiloquium is Lucifer's hind.°
40   Bidders° and beggars fast about went   *beggars*
With their bellies and their bags of bread full crammed,
Faited° for their food, fought at the alehouse:
In gluttony, God knows, they go to bed,

Malvern Hills the poet's native spot, in Worcestershire, about 130 miles northwest of London. The area was noted for its religious houses, at one of which Langland may have gone to school.
a ferly . . . methought i.e. a marvel, which seemed to me supernatural
east i.e. in God's direction
dungeon literally, a keep or central stronghold-tower, i.e. prison
win . . . wasters i.e. provider and conspicuous consumer
In countenance . . . disguised i.e. came got up in pompous clothes

hold . . . cells i.e. they kept their vows—a crucial issue for Langland
some . . . better some chose trade and succeeded better
Feign . . . wished (ll. 36–37) pretend that they have visions and that they are feebleminded —and yet they have their wits at their command and could work if they wished
Paul See II Thessalonians 3:10: "If any would not work, neither should he eat."
Qui . . . hind The man who speaks slander is the servant of the Devil
Faited i.e. begged fraudulently

And rise with ribaldry, those robber knaves.
Sleep and sorry sloth pursue them always.
    Pilgrims and palmers° plighted them together
To seek St. James° and saints in Rome.
They went forth in their way with many wise tales—
And had leave to lie all their lives thereafter.
50   I saw some that said they had sought saints:
For every tale that they told, their tongues were tempered to lie
More than to say sooth, it seemed by their speech.
    Hermits in a heap, with hooked staves
Went to Walsingham° and their wenches after them:
Great lubbers and long that loth were to swink,⸽   *toil*
Clothed themselves in copes to be known from the others,°
And shaped themselves hermits, their ease to have.
    I found there friars, all the four orders,°
Preaching to the people for profit of themselves,
60   Glossing° the Gospel as seemed good to them,
For covetousness of copes construing it as they wished.
Many of these Master Friars° may clothe themselves at pleasure,
For their money and their merchandise march together.°
For since Charity has been chapman and the chief to shrive lords,°
Many ferlies⸽ have fallen in a few years.   *marvels*
Unless Holy Church and they hold better together,
The most mischief on mould⸽ is mounting well⸽ fast.   *earth / very*
    There preached a Pardoner° as if he were a priest,
Brought forth a bull,° with bishop's seals,
70   And said that himself might absolve them all,°
Of falsehood in fasting, of vows broken.
Simple men believed him well and liked his words,
Came up and kneeled to kiss his bulls.
He banged⸽ them with his brevet° and blinded their eyes,   *tapped*
And raked in with his ragman° rings and brooches.
Thus they give their gold to gluttons to keep,
And lend⸽ it to losels⸽ that lechery practice.   *give / rogues*
Were the bishop blessed and worth both his ears,
His seal should not be sent to deceive the people.

palmers originally pilgrims who had been at Jerusalem; but by now pilgrims of any sort
St. James the shrine of St. James of Compostela, in Galicia, northwestern Spain
Walsingham the shrine of Our Lady of Walsingham, in Norfolk, next in prestige to Canterbury as a place of pilgrimage in England
Clothed . . . others i.e. put on religious clothing, to mark themselves out from other people
orders Dominicans, Franciscans, Augustinians, Carmelites
Glossing interpreting, a regular accusation against the friars
Master Friars those who have completed their religious training
money . . . together their avarice and their trade (in confessions) go hand in hand

Charity . . . lords Charity has bought and sold like a merchant and been confessor-in-chief to noblemen. The friars' ideal had been poverty and charity, but they had become wealthy. Most of the important men of the time had friars for confessors.
Pardoner See Chaucer, the General Prologue, ll. 671 ff.—also for satiric method. He could give, by papal permission, indulgences in exchange for money given to charity.
bull papal edict proclaiming the indulgence which the Pardoner was selling
absolve . . . all He claimed this falsely. All he was empowered to do was remit penance; he could not absolve men from sin.
brevet letter of authority
ragman roll of parchment

80   But it is not by the bishop that the boy preaches,°
For the parish priest and the pardoner part⁼ the silver,   *share*
Which the poor people of the parish ought to have, if it were not done.
Parsons and parish priests complained to the bishop
That their parishes were poor since the time of plague,°
So as to have a licence and a leave at London to live
And sing there for simony,° for silver is sweet.
    Bishops and bachelors, both masters and doctors°
That have cure° under Christ and, in token, tonsure,°
A sign that they should shrive⁼ their parishioners,   *confess*
90   Preach to them and pray for them, and feed the poor—
They lie in London, in Lent and else.°
Some serve the King and his silver tell,⁼   *account for*
In Exchequer and Chancery, challenge his debts
From wards and wardmoots, waifs and strays.°
And some serve,° as servants, lords and ladies
And in the stead of stewards, sit and judge.
Their mass and their matins and many of their hours°
Are done undevoutly. Dread is, at the last,
Lest Christ in consistory° curse full many.
100   I perceived the power,° that Peter had, to keep
To bind and to unbind, as the book⁼ tells   *Bible*
How he placed it with love, as Our Lord commanded,
To four virtues, the best of all virtues
That cardinals be called, and closing the gates
To where Christ is in His Kingdom—to close and to shut,
And to open it to them and Heaven's bliss show.
But of the cardinals at court,° that caught that name,
And power presumed in themselves a Pope to make,
Who has that power that Peter had—impugn I wish not.
110   Since to love and learning the election belongs,
Therefore I can—but cannot—of Curia say more.°

by . . . preaches for the benefit of the bishop that the rogue preaches; i.e. the bishop does not receive the money to apply to charity, as he should
plague especially the Black Death of 1348–49 and the other outbreaks of the 1360's and 1370's, causing famine and depopulation in rural areas
licence . . . simony Be given leave to be an absentee rector and hold, more than one office by acting as chantry or guild priest in London. A chantry was an endowment to pay for masses for the repose of specified souls. Simony is the buying and selling of spiritual things, so named from Simon Magus, who wished to buy spiritual power from the Apostles (Acts 8:18–24).
masters . . . doctors graduates (in theology)
cure care of souls
tonsure shaving of the head, to indicate religious profession
lie . . . else stay in London during Lent (when, especially, they should be in their parishes) and at other times
In . . . strays (ll. 93–94) In the courts of Exchequer and Chancery (two of the law-courts of the time, with specific jurisdiction) claim

the debts owed the king from the wards (districts of the city) at the ward-meetings, and the waifs (property without an owner) and strayed cattle (which both became royal property); i.e. the priests acted as legal officials. Cf. Chaucer's commendation of the Clerk, General Prologue, l. 294.
some serve Serving priests, attached to a household, with secular functions, were often complained of.
hours A priest was obliged to say his office (from his breviary) at the canonical hours.
consistory church council or assembly of prelates—here, the Day of Judgment
power St. Peter gave the power of the keys (Matthew 16:19) to the four cardinal virtues—prudence, temperance, fortitude, and justice. The word "cardinal" is derived from the Latin *cardo*, a hinge. These virtues ought to be the spiritual hinges of Christendom: instead the hinges are the corrupt cardinals of the church.
court the Curia, the papal court at Rome
Since . . . more I have more to say about them, but cannot say it, out of reverence

Then came there a King,° Knights leading him,
Might of the Commons made him to reign:
And then came Kind Wit° and clerks he made
For to counsel the King and the Commons keep safe.
The King, and the Knights and clergy both,
Cast⁾ that the Commons must needs find⁾ their selves.   *decreed / provide for*
The Commons contrived, by Kind Wit, crafts:
And for the profit of all people, ploughmen° ordained
120 To till and to travail, as true life demands.
The King and the Commons—Kind Wit made a third—
Shaped law and loyalty, each knew rights and duty.°

Then ran out a rout° of rats, all at once,
And little mice with them, more than a thousand,
And came to a council for their common profit.
For a cat from a court came when he pleased
150 And leaped on them lightly⁾ and latched on them at will,   *quickly*
And played with them perilously and pushed them about.
'For doubt of diverse dreads, we dare not look about.
And if we grudge⁾ about his games, he'll give us all grief,   *complain*
Scratch us and claw us and in his clutches hold
So that we loathe life before he lets us go.
Could we with any wit his will withstand
We might be lofty lords and live at our ease.'
A rat of renown, most reasonable⁾ of tongue   *eloquent*
Said as a sovereign⁾ help, for his part: *most excellent*
160 'I have seen sirs⁾,' said he, 'in the City of London°   *men*
Bear bighes⁾ full bright about their necks   *necklaces*
And others collars° of crafty⁾ work; uncoupled they go   *skillful*
Both in warren and waste,° wherever they wish;
And at other times they are elsewhere, as I hear tell.
Were there a bell on their bighe, by Jesus, it seems to me,
Men could know where they went and run from them!
And right thus,' said the rat, 'reason counsels me

King Langland now begins an exposition of how a country ought to be governed, with the king, aided by his knights, depending for his power on the Commons, and all estates knit in a harmonious whole.
Kind Wit natural intelligence, understanding, by which learned men give the king advice and so preserve his subjects from oppression by him
ploughmen i.e. all rustic laborers
duty Langland here, in the short passage omitted, develops the theme of the King and his Commons and their roles in government.
rout Crowd. Langland now passes suddenly into a fable, in which the story of belling the cat is applied to the political situation of his time. The tale occurs in collections of animal stories from the 12th century onward. Langland may be making specific reference here to the Parliaments of 1376 and 1377, when the Commons were attempting to assert their rights. The cat

would then be old Edward III, the kitten the young Richard II, who succeeded him at the age of ten in 1377. Richard's youth and his succession to a strong ruler like Edward III gave much concern to Parliament, and a council was established. The rats are the burgesses and important members of Parliament, the mice the lower order of such men. They are anxious to control the king, though without a king's authority they would live in anarchy. Langland's theme is always the interdependence of all orders under a ruler within a hierarchy (in church and state), every member conscientiously performing his allotted function.
City of London the business and legal center
collars chains of office, worn round the neck
uncoupled . . . waste they go unimpeded wherever they wish; "warren" is literally an enclosed space for breeding game; "waste" is common, unused land

To buy a bell of brass or of bright silver,
And attach it to a collar, for our common profit,
170   And knot it on the cat's neck. Then may we hear
Whether he is riding or resting, or running to play.
And if it please him to play, then out we may peep
And appear in his presence, as long as he is so inclined;
And if he's feeling warlike, be wary and shun his way.'
 All the rout of rats assented to this scheme.
But, though the bell was bought, and fastened to the bighe
There was no rat in all the rout, for all the realm of France,
That dared bind the bell about the cat's neck,
Nor hang it about the cat's halse,° to win all England;   *neck*
180   And they held themselves unhardy° and their counsel feeble *cowardly*
And felt all their labour lost and all their long planning.
 A mouse,° that knew much good counsel, as it seemed,
Stepped out boldly and stood before them all,
And to the rout of rats rehearsed° these words: *spoke*
'Though we killed the cat, there would come another,
To scratch us and all our kind, even if we crept under benches.
Therefore I counsel all the commons to let the cat be;
And let us be not so bold as to show him the bell.
For I heard my sire say, seven years past,
190   "Where the cat is a kitten, the court is unwell."°
That Holy Writ witnesses, whoever wishes to read it:
  Ve terre ubi puer rex est etc.°
For no rank may have rest there, for rats by night.
While he is catching coneys° he covets not our corpses, *rabbits*
But is full fed with "venison":° let us not defame him.
For better is a little loss than a long sorrow:
Confusion among us all, though we lose a shrew.°
For many men's malt we mice could destroy—
And also the rout of rats could rend men's clothes—
Were it not for the cat in the court, who can jump on you:
200   For if you rats had your way, you could not rule yourselves.
 'I say for my part,' said the mouse, 'I see so much consequence,
The cat or the kitten shall never, by my counsel, be grieved;
(No carping about the collar: it cost me nothing—
But even if it had cost me chattels, confess it I would not°);
But suffer them as they wish to do—as they please—
Coupled or uncoupled, to catch what they can.
Therefore every wise wight° I warn; wit well your own!'° *creature*

mouse perhaps one Peter de la Mare, who in 1377 proposed a council to advise the young King Richard II

Where . . . unwell i.e. be careful, because a new, young king may not know how to handle things and control his nobles, who will oppress the Commons

Ve . . . etc. Woe to the land where the king is a child (adaptation of Ecclesiastes 10:16)

venison rabbit meat

better . . . shrew we would do better to lose one or two of ourselves, perhaps a worthless one of us, than mourn a great slaughter by provoking him

No . . . not I don't want to talk about the collar—I didn't contribute to the cost and even if I had I wouldn't tell you

wit . . . own know your own; i.e. look to your own affairs

What this meteles> means, you men that are merry   *dream*
Devine, for I dare not, by dear God in Heaven!
210   Yet hove> there a hundred in hoves° of silk   *waited*
Serjeants° they seemed that served at the bar
Pleaded for pence and impounded the law°
And not for love of Our Lord unloosed their lips once.
You might better measure mist on Malvern Hills
Than get a mumble from their mouths, unless money were showed.
Barons and burgesses and bondmen also
I saw in this assembly as you shall hear afterwards.
Bakers and brewers and butchers many,
Wool-websters° and weavers of linen,
220   Tailors and tinkers, and tollers° in markets,
Masons and miners and many other crafts,
Of all kinds of living labourers leaped forth some,
Such as ditchers and delvers> that do their deeds ill,   *diggers*
And drive on the long day with 'Dieu vous save, Dame Emme!'°
Cooks and their knaves> cried 'Hot pies, hot!   *kitchen-boys*
Good gris° and geese! Go dine, go!'
Taverners to them told the same story:
'White wine of Alsace and red wine of Gascony,
Of the Rhine and of La Rochelle, the roast to digest.'
230   All this saw I asleep and seven sithes> more.   *times*

Passus I

What this mountain means, and the murky dale
And the field full of folk, I shall you fairly show.
A lady lovely of lere,> in linen clothed   *face*
Came down from a castle and called me fair,
Said, 'Son, do you sleep? Do you see these people
How busy they are about the maze?
The most part of these people that pass on this earth,
Have they worship in this world,° they wish for no better,
Of another heaven than here they hold no account.'
10   I was afraid of her face, though she was fair,
And said 'Mercy, Madam, what is the meaning of this?'
'The tower on the toft,' said she, 'Truth is therein.
And would have you work as His word teaches;
For He is the Father of Faith and formed you all
With both fell> and face and gave you five wits,°   *skin*
To worship Him with them while you are here.
And for this He hight> the earth to help you, each one   *ordered*

hoves lawyers' hoods
Serjeants sergeants-at-law, eminent pleaders; see
Chaucer, General Prologue, ll. 311 ff.
Pleaded . . . law made pleas in court for
money and made the law their property
Wool-websters wool-weavers (women); cf.
Chaucer's *webbe*, weaver, General Prologue,
l. 364

tollers collectors of tolls or dues from stall-
holders
Dieu . . . Emme "God save you, Dame Em-
ma!", either a line from a song or a greeting in
hope of a tip
gris little (sucking) pigs
worship . . . world earthly honor and success
five wits five senses—sight, smell, hearing,
touch, taste

Of wool, of linen, of livelihood at need
In measurable⌐ manner to make yourself at ease.   *temperate*
20   And commanded, of His courtesy, in common three things°
None are needed but they, and name them I will—
And reckon them by reason⌐—repeat you them after me?   *in order*
The first is clothing, to save you from chill
And meat at meal-time, for misease⌐ of yourself   *against discomfort*
And drink when you are dry—but take nothing beyond reason
Lest you worth⌐ the worse when you must work.   *become*
    For Lot° while he lived through his liking of drink,
Did with his daughters what pleased the Devil
Delighted in drink as the Devil wanted—
30   And Lechery latched⌐ him and he lay by them both.   *caught*
And all he wited⌐ wine that wicked deed.   *accused*
    Inebriamus eum vino, dormiamus cum eo,
        Ut servare possemus de Patre nostro semen.°
Through wine and through women there Lot was encumbered
And there begot in gluttony girls that were churls.°
Therefore dread delectable drink and you shall do the better.
Measure⌐ is medicine, though you much yearn—   *moderation*
It is not all good to the ghost⌐ that the gut asks   *spirit*
Nor a living for your licham⌐ that lief⌐ is to your soul.   *body / dear*
Believe not your licham, for a liar teaches him
Which is the wretched world that wishes to betray you.
40   For the Fiend and your flesh° pursue you together:
This and that pursue your soul; and say this in your heart,°
And so that you shall be wary, I wiss⌐ you the best.'   *tell*
'Madam, merci,⌐ I said, 'Your words please me well.   *thank you*
But the wealth of this world,° that men hold so fast
Tell me to whom, Madam, that treasure belongs?'
'Go to the Gospel,' said she, 'see what God said Himself
Though the people apposed Him of a penny in the Temple:°
Whether they should with it honour King Caesar.
And God asked of them of whom spoke the lettering
50   And the image, too, that stood thereon.
"Caesar's," they said; "Each of us sees well."
"*Reddite Caesari*," said God, "that *Caesari* belongs,

---

three things i.e. those necessary to sustain life;
cf. Ecclesiasticus 29:31: "The chief thing for
life is water and bread and clothing and an
house to cover shame"
Lot Lot and Noah were the two great biblical
exempla of drunkenness, and Lot also of the
closely related sin of lechery, on account of
his incest. He is regularly used in sermon literature as a caution against drunkenness and its
consequences; cf. Chaucer's Pardoner's Tale,
l. 199. Lot's story is told in Genesis 19:30–38.
Inebriamus . . . semen Genesis 19:32: "Come,
let us make our father drink wine and we will
lie with him, that we may preserve seed of
our father"—the text of Langland's "sermon"
girls . . . churls i.e. children that were base-

born. *Girl* at this time can mean male or female;
here it refers to Lot's two sons, Moab and
Ammon.
world . . . flesh The World, the Flesh, and the
Devil are the enemies of the soul.
say . . . heart perhaps: suggest evil to your
heart
wealth . . . world The rest of this *passus*
examines the theme of the right use of worldly
wealth and goods.
apposed . . . Temple When the people questioned him about a penny in the temple; see
Matthew 22:16–22. Christ the Teacher is placed
in direct opposition to the world, the liar who
is the teacher of the *licham* (l. 37).

Et quae sunt Dei, Deo;° or else you do ill."
For rightfully Reason° ought to rule you completely,
And Kind Wit° be warden your wealth to ward,⸜   *guard*
And tutor⸜ of your treasure, and take⸜ it you at need,   *custodian / bring*
For husbandry° and he hold together.'
Then I frained⸜ her fairly, by Him that her made,   *asked*
'That dungeon in the dale, that dreadful is of sight,
60   What may it be meaning, Madam, I beseech you?'
        'That is the Castle of Care, whoever comes into it
May ban⸜ that he born was in body or in soul.   *curse*
There wons⸜ a wight⸜ that Wrong is called,   *lives / creature*
Father of Falsehood—and founded it himself.
Adam and Eve he egged on° to ill
Counselled Cain° to kill his brother;
Judas he japed with Jewish silver°
Who after on an alder° hanged himself then.
He is letter of love,° and he lies to them all,
70   Those who trust in his treasure, he soonest betrays.'
        Then had I wonder in my wit what woman she was
That such wise words of Holy Writ showed
And asked her by the High Name,° ere she thence went
What she was witterly⸜ that wissed⸜ me so fair?   *in fact / instructed*
        'Holy Church° I am,' said she, 'You ought to know me.
I undertook⸜ you first and taught you faith   *received*
And you brought me borrows,⸜ my bidding to fulfill   *pledges*
And to love me loyally while your life endures.'
        Then I kneeled on my knees and cried to her for grace
80   And prayed her pitifully to pray for my sins;
And also ken me kindly° in Christ to believe
That I might work his will that wrought⸜ me a man.   *made*
'Teach⸜ me to no treasure, but tell me this ilk⸜   *direct / same*
How I may save my soul,° you that sacred are held.'
        'When all treasures are tried,' said she, 'Truth° is the best;
I do it on *Deus caritas* to deem the sooth.°
It is as dear-worth⸜ a drury⸜ as dear God himself.   *valuable / love gift*

Reddite . . . Deo Again the theme of the discourse is emphasized by being quoted verbatim in Latin: "Render therefore unto Caesar the things which are Caesar's and unto God the things which are God's" (Matthew 22:21).
Reason the mind's reflective faculty
Kind Wit natural wisdom or intelligence, the gift of God, with a natural tendency toward good
husbandry i.e. wise use of worldy goods
Adam . . . on Wrong, the Devil, was the Serpent in Eden that tempted Adam & Eve (Genesis 3:1 ff.) to sin the first sin of all, which embraces all the others.
Cain the first murderer (Genesis 4:8)
Jewish silver the thirty pieces of silver for which Judas betrayed Christ (Matthew 26:15)—the prime example of wrong use of money

alder Judas was supposed to have hanged himself on an alder tree.
letter of love hinderer of love; i.e. hostile to Christ
High Name the name of God
Holy Church Christ's representative on earth, who received the Dreamer at baptism, when he promised by proxy to keep her commandments
ken . . . kindly teach me naturally, instinctively
save . . . soul i.e. store up treasure in heaven, not on earth
Truth i.e. the law of God and the Christian's obedience to that law
I . . . sooth I base myself on "God is love" (i.e. on the text from I John 4:8), so that I may judge truly; again the announcement of the text that will govern the proposition to be explored—God is Truth and God is Love

Whoever is true in his tongue and tells nothing else°
And does the works that go with it and wills no-one ill,
90 He is a god by the Gospel, aground and aloft
And alike to Our Lord, by St. Luke's words.°
The clerks that know this should ken it about°
For Christian and unchristian claim truth each of them.
    Kings and knights should keep it by reason°
Ride and rap˃ down in realms about˃   *strike / around*
And take˃ transgressors and tie them fast,   *capture*
Till Truth has determined their trespass to the end.°
And that is the profession apertly that appends to knights,°
Not to fast only one Friday in five-score˃ winters;   *a hundred*
100 But to hold˃ with him and with her that wish for all truth   *stay*
And never leave them, for love nor for latching˃ on silver. *seizing*
    For David in his day dubbed knights°
And made them swear on their swords to serve Truth ever:
And whoever passes that point is apostate to the order.°
    But Christ, King of Kings, knighted ten:°
Cherubin and seraphim, seven such and one other,
And gave them might in his majesty—the merrier they seemed—
And over his mean meyny,° made them archangels
Taught them by the Trinity, truth to know,
110 And to be buxom˃ at his bidding: he bade them nought else.   *obedient*
    Lucifer° with legions, learned it in heaven
But because he broke buxomness, his bliss did he tine˃   *lose*
And fell from that fellowship, in a fiend's likeness
Into a deep, dark hell, to dwell there forever;
And more thousands with him, than man knows to number
Leaped out with Lucifer, in loathly form,
For they believed on him that lied in this manner:
    Ponam pedem in aquilone, et similis ero altissimo.°

    And all that hoped it might be so, no heaven might hold them
But they fell out in fiends' likeness, nine days° together,

---

nothing else i.e. speaks only truth
St. Luke's words The texts Langland is alluding to are probably Luke 16:10, the parable of the steward, and Luke 8:21: "My mother and my brethren are these which hear the word of God and do it."
clerks . . . about learned men that know this should make it widely known
by reason according to reason
determined . . . end made a full and final examination of their sin
profession . . . knights and that is clearly the vow (and its execution) that belongs to knights
David . . . knights The knights that David made may be the Levites, whom he appointed to keep the Ark of the Covenant (I Chronicles 15).
whoever . . . order He who transgresses that canon has become a deserter from the order. Langland has been talking about the evil of the neglect of spiritual duties by earthly knights —but those described in the next lines are much

worse, because they were once the best and fell from pride.
knighted ten i.e. the ten orders of angels, as they were before Lucifer and his angels fell; cherubim, seraphim, and thrones (the three highest); dominions, virtues, powers; and principalities, archangels, and angels. Lucifer's angels, the tenth order, are the representatives of the first act of disobedience, prior to and worse than man's, irredeemable.
mean meyny lower orders
Lucifer The only injunction laid upon angels and men is obedience to God's commands. This is what Lucifer breaks.
Ponam . . . altissimo "I will set my foot in the north and I will be like the most high" (cf. Isaiah 14:13–14). Lucifer usually is placed in the north—by Milton among others—and Hell in Germanic mythology is placed in that region also.
nine days the usual interval; cf. Milton, *Paradise Lost* VI.871

120   Till God, of His goodness, did stop and stint⸴   *pause*
And made heavens to stay firm and to stand still.⸴   *silent*
    When these wicked ones went, wonderwise they fell,
Some in air, some on earth,° and some in Hell-deep;
But Lucifer lowest lies of them all:
For pride that he put out,⸴ his pain has no end   *showed*
And all that work with wrong, wend⸴ they must   *go*
After their death-day and dwell with that shrew.⸴   *wicked one*
But those that work well, as Holy Writ tells,
And end—as I ere⸴ said—in Truth that is best,   *before*
130   May be sure that their souls shall wend to Heaven,
Where Truth is in Trinity and enthrones them all.
Therefore I say, as I said before, by sight⸴ of these texts,   *witness*
When all treasures are tried, Truth is the best.
Learn⸴ it to these lewd⸴ men, for lettered men it know: *teach / simple*
That Truth is treasure, the triest⸴ on earth.'   *finest*
    'Yet have I no kind knowledge,' said I; 'yet must you ken me better,°
By what craft in my corpse° it commences, and where.'
    'You dotard daff⸴,' said she, 'dull are your wits;   *idiot*
Too little Latin you learned, lad, in your youth:
    Heu michi, quod sterilem duxi vitam iuvenilem!°

140   It is kind knowledge,' said she, 'that kens in your heart
For to love your Lord liever⸴ than yourself;   *more dearly*
No deadly sin to do, die though you should;
This I trow⸴ be truth. Who can teach you better,   *believe*
Look you suffer him to say,° and sithen⸴ learn it after.   *then*
    For thus witnesses His Word, work you thereafter;
For Truth tells that love is treacle° of Heaven
There may no sin be on him seen that uses that spice.⸴   *medicine*
And all His works he wrought, with love as him list,⸴   *it pleased*
And learned it Moses as the lievest thing° and most like heaven;
150   And also the plant of peace, most precious of virtues.
    For Heaven might not hold it, it was so heavy in itself,
Till it had of the earth, eaten its fill.
    And when it had of this fold,⸴ flesh and blood taken,   *earth*
There was never leaf upon linden° lighter thereafter

---

when . . . earth I.e. they became the evil spirits of earth and air as well as the devils of hell. This explanation lasts until at least the 17th century.
have I . . . better I have no natural way of knowing . . . you must teach me better. He cannot understand by his natural faculties and needs the teaching of the church to set him right.
craft . . . corpse power in my body; i.e. what is its origin in me
Heu . . . iuvenilem "Ah me, how useless a life I led when I was young." The source has not been identified.
suffer . . . say allow to speak
treacle the finest and most effective medicine, originally a remedy for snakebite, compounded from vipers' flesh

lievest thing dearest thing. Love is gradually modulating into the person of Christ in this section. The reference to Moses is to the Tables of the Law, the Ten Commandments, the first four concerned with the love of God and the second six with the love of one's neighbor, on which hang "all the Law and the Prophets."
leaf upon linden proverbial expression for lightness. Once Love has become incarnate in Christ upon earth (the sprig of the tree of Jesse) it becomes paradoxically light, where in heaven it had been too heavy to be held there. Love holds in itself the contraries of overwhelming weight and force, so that none can resist it, and unbelievable quickness and fineness, so that it can creep in anywhere.

And portative˃ and piercing as the point of a needle,   *rapid*
So that no armour might let˃ it, and no high walls.   *stop*
    Therefore is love the leader, of the Lord's folk of Heaven,
And a mean;˃ as the Mayor is between the King and the Commons,   *mediator*
Right so is Love a leader and the Law shapes.°

160 Upon man for his misdeeds, the amercement˃ he taxes.˃   *fine / exacts*
And for to know it kindly, it commences by might°
And in the heart is its head and its high source.
    For from kind knowing in heart, there a might˃ begins.°   *power*
And that falls˃ to the Father, that formed us all;   *belongs*
Looked on us with love and let His Son die
Meekly for our misdeeds, to amend us all.
And yet wished He them no woe, that wrought˃ Him that torment,   *made*
But meekly by mouth mercy he besought
To have pity on that people that pained˃ Him to death.   *tortured*

170 Here might you see examples—in Himself one
That He was mightful and meek and mercy did grant
To them that hanged him on high and his heart holed.˃   *pierced*
    Therefore I rede˃ you richly, have ruth˃ of the poor;   *counsel / pity*
Though you be mighty to moot,° be meek in your works.
For by the same measures that you mete,˃ amiss or otherwise,   *deal out*
You shall be weighed therewith, when you wend hence:
    Eadem mensura qua mensi fueritis, remecietur vobis.°

    For though you be true of your tongue and truly win,˃   *honestly gain*
And as chaste as a child, that in church weeps,
Unless you love loyally and lend˃ to the poor   *give*
180 Such goods as God sends you goodly divide,
You have no more merit, in mass or in hours,°
Than Malkin from her maidenhead which no man desires.°
    For James the Gentle judged in his books
That faith without the feat,° is right nothing worth
And as dead as a door-tree,° unless the deeds follow:
    Fides sine operibus mortua est, etc.

    Therefore chastity without charity will be chained in Hell:
It is as lewd˃ as a lamp that no light is in.   *worthless*
    Many chaplains are chaste, but charity is absent;
Are no men more avaricious than they, when they are advanced;°

love . . . shapes In the supernatural world Love dictates all that God does and softens his justice. To men on earth the love that he showed in the Incarnation does the same.
for . . . might Love can be recognized naturally (by instinct), for it begins as a strong impulse.
for . . . begins for from natural understanding in the heart, there begins this impulse
mighty . . . moot powerful in the law courts
Eadem . . . vobis Cf. Luke 6:38; "With the same measure that ye mete withal, it shall be measured to you again." Cf. Matthew 7:2.
hours the canonical hours

Than . . . desires Than Maudie from her maidenhead, which nobody wants to take; i.e. you can be as good as you like, but unless you are active in good works, in charity, it will help you nothing. Malkin is sometimes used of a whore; here she seems to be an unattractive old thing, but chaste.
faith . . . feat See James 2:26: "Faith without works is dead." The Latin is quoted two lines on.
door-tree door-post. Some manuscripts read door-nail.
when . . . advanced when given preferment, promoted in the church

190 Unkind to their kin and to all Christians,
Chew up their charity and chide for more.°
Such chastity without charity will be chained in Hell!
    Many curates² keep themselves clean in their flesh: *priests*
They are encumbered with covetousness, they cannot put it from them,
So hard has avarice hasped² them together.   *clamped*
And that is no truth of the Trinity, but treachery of Hell,
And a lesson to lewd men, the later to dole out.°
    Therefore these words be written in the Gospel:
Date et dabitur vobis:° for I dole² you all.   *give to*
200 And that is the lack of love and lets out my grace,
To comfort the care-full, encumbered with sin.
    Love is leech² of life, and next Our Lord's self;   *healer*
And also the graith gate² that goes to Heaven.   *narrow way*
Therefore I say, as I said ere through the texts:
When all treasures be tried, Truth is the best.
    Now I have told you what truth is, than which no treasure is better,
I may no longer linger with you: now Our Lord look to you.'
c. 1377

DRAMA

MYSTERY PLAYS (MIRACLES)

When a medieval author speaks of a comedy or tragedy he does not mean a play: he usually means a poem intended to edify and instruct, which ends happily or unhappily. The poem may be a sophisticated presentation of character and motive, often through dialogue (like Chaucer's *Troilus and Criseyde*); or it may be cast in the form of dialogue or debate (*The Owl and the Nightingale*).

The Middle Ages knew nothing of Greek drama. Medieval authors treated the Roman tragedies of Seneca as storehouses of useful knowledge, moral and philological; and though the tenth-century German nun Hrotsvitha wrote Christian Latin comedies in purified imitation of Terence, Roman writers of comedy were thought of in the same way as Seneca. A different kind of Latin text was the starting point for medieval drama: the Latin of the mass, with its daily re-enactment of the Passion of Christ, essentially dramatic in its performance and designed to keep remembrance of the Passion, its antecedents and its implications, before the eyes and minds of the people. Other services of the church also played their part, but the decisive factor was the elaborate ceremonies developed for the great festivals, such as Easter and Christmas. The dramatic element is present in the mass not only as spoken dialogue and ceremonial interchange between celebrant and acolytes, but as sung dialogue. In antiphonal singing, two halves of the choir deliver alternate versicles and responsories. One of the texts (or "tropes") of these antiphons for the Easter mass is an adaptation of the exchange between the three Marys and the angel at the empty tomb of the risen

---

Chew . . . more get through what they are given and scream for more
a lesson . . . out an indication to wicked men that they should be slow in giving

Date . . . vobis Luke 6:38: "Give and it shall be given unto you."

Christ (Matthew 28:1–7 and Mark 16:1–7), known (from its opening phrase) as the *Quem quaeritis* ("Whom do you seek?").

One voice, or set of voices, representing the angel, sang: "Whom seek ye in the sepulchre, ye followers of Christ?" and was answered: "Jesus of Nazareth, the crucified, O heavenly ones." The angelic voices then sang: "He is not here; He is risen as He foretold; go and tell how He is risen from the tomb."

Many of the steps by which this reverent rudimentary form of dramatic representation within the church, with its sung dialogue in Latin, developed into the vernacular spoken play performed in the city, on non-consecrated ground, are still not clear. Secular forms of popular and courtly entertainment—dancing, games, festivals, and perhaps folk ritual, with the "acts" of professional minstrels, dancers, jugglers and acrobats, singly or in roving bands—must have made their contribution, but we cannot say exactly how they did so or what that contribution was. The purpose of medieval drama, however, always remained sacred: drama was the "quick [i.e. living] book" in which the ordinary Christian might read the mysteries of his faith (hence the name "mystery" by which the plays came to be known). They reinforce the message of sermons and other forms of religious instruction by presenting in dramatic form the biblical story of mankind, from Creation and Fall to Redemption and Judgment.

Though in England their performance was generally the prerogative of associations of pious laymen, the plays were devised and probably written by clergy. The clergy retained at least a guiding hand on the cycles. The English vernacular play, in nine- or ten-line stanzes, loose in rhythm and in a prosody sometimes reminiscent of such poems as *Sir Gawain and the Green Knight,* is a relatively late development. There was already vernacular drama in France in the twelfth century, but the earliest extant English plays date from the fourteenth century, and the texts we possess usually belong to the fifteenth or sixteenth. During the lifetime of the biblical drama cycles in England, between the fourteenth and the seventeenth centuries, more than a hundred towns performed single plays or consecutive cycles of from five to forty-eight separate plays. While these towns were chiefly in the North of England—York and Wakefield are the most famous—or the Midlands (Coventry, in Warwickshire), plays were performed in London, and there is a surviving late cycle in Cornish, a Celtic language spoken in the extreme South-West. The demise of the form was hastened by a policy of systematic suppression during the sixteenth century, especially during the reign of Elizabeth I.

Generally speaking, the actual performance of the plays was in the hands of the trade guilds, which came into prominence during the fourteenth century. These were associations of laymen who followed the same craft, often with a priest or priests attached to them as chaplains. They regulated trade and also performed the functions of religious confraternities—that is, brotherhoods associated with a particular church and under the patronage of a particular saint, meeting on religious festivals for liturgical celebration and social functions, and dispensing charity. Their members were often substantial citizens, the leaders of the new mercantile classes; and from their ranks civic officials were chosen. These guilds were responsible for the entire business of staging the plays, each guild choosing a play whose subject matter fitted with the craft it represented. Thus at Chester the Water-Drawers of the river Dee took the play of Noah. Parts were regularly taken in successive years by the same actors, sometimes especially imported from other towns.

The cycles were played from dawn to dusk, in the open, at set points in the city, on "pageants" (*paginae*), wagons that consisted of roofed platforms on wheels and were moved from point to point, so that the audience could see the successive stages of the cycle while remaining in one place—or on fixed stages. At York forty-eight pageants were presented at twelve points in the city. These "pageants" and stages must have been of fair size. Two levels were sometimes created by the use of a balcony or of the ground in front of the stage. Scenery was scanty and not very realistic, though the late property lists surviving are often quite long, and include such items as "Hell-Mouth." Some ingenuity was employed in staging—such as the special waist-high wall round "Paradise," to allow Adam and Eve to be seen and heard without showing their nakedness; yet much in the way of stage setting must have been supplied by the players' words themselves—as in *The Second Shepherds' Play*, where one of the shepherds remarks that he will "abide on a balk, or sit on a stone." Costumes, in the style of the time, were often elaborate, and stage wardrobes were maintained: wigs, robes, a close-fitting skin for the Serpent in Eden, and skin-tight white leather suits for the naked Adam and Eve were a few of the items.

The staging of these plays at the feast of Whitsun (Pentecost) was natural. Corpus Christi, a few days after Whitsun, was an even more favored day. It was the commemoration of the institution of the Eucharist at the Last Supper, and its observance as a high festival had recently been commanded by papal decree: from the early fourteenth century onward it was kept throughout England. Since it fell in early June, one could hope for good weather for the outdoor performances, for a sunny holy-day to watch the tidings of joy that the plays conveyed: the redemption of mankind from death and damnation, from the consequence of Adam's sin in Paradise (Fig. 57). The cycles of plays end triumphantly, showing the history of mankind as a progress toward salvation.

This is what even the short cycles present: the fulfillment of the Old Testament, its culmination in the New. They emphasize the typological dimension, in which Old Testament events are seen as fulfilled in those of the New. The sacrifice of Abraham, for example, is a prefiguration of the Crucifixion; while the brazen serpent set up by Moses to expel serpents, prefigures Christ hung on a cross to expel the serpents of sin.

The inclusiveness of the biblical drama of salvation allowed plenty of scope for its presentation. Incidents from outside the canonical books of the Bible, and from independent invention, were added to the plays. (The sheep-stealing scenes of *The Second Shepherds' Play* are an example of comic elaboration from outside the source texts.) The most important sources for these incidents were the apocryphal Gospels, written in perhaps the second or third century and for the Middle Ages having an authority as great as that of the genuine New Testament books. These were full of homely and miraculous detail about the lives of the Virgin and of Christ— the legend told in "The Cherry-tree Carol," for example, or the story of how Christ broke down the gates of Hell, in the Harrowing of Hell (Figs. 53 and 7).

Within such a large repertoire of play and incident, there was much room for improvisation. Conventions of acting and presentation grew up: a loud, high voice for Pontius Pilate; the portrayal of Herod as a cruel, ranting tyrant; the brutality of Christ's torturers and their carrying off by devils. The domestic difficulties of Noah and the drinking scene between his wife and her cronies in the Chester play are also variations on a well-used theme. All these examples of comic elaboration, often seemingly introduced for their own sake, and certainly serving as comic relief—contribute to the larger design of the plays and their dramatic culmination in the Redemption.

The author of *The Second Shepherds' Play* is anonymous. Usually referred to as the Wakefield Master, after the prosperous market town in Yorkshire where his plays were performed, and almost certainly a cleric, he seems to have written between 1400 and 1450. His pageants form a group in the Towneley manuscript, probably a "register" of the Wakefield plays, and so called after the family that formerly owned it.

The main comic incident by which the Angel's Annunciation to the Shepherds (Fig. 49) is fleshed out into the full-length Wakefield *Second Shepherds' Play* comes from an old folk-tale. Its skillful handling, by which the swaddled sheep is made the figure of the Christ Child in the manger, is the responsibility of the Wakefield Master. The rustic comedy, complete with the complaints of laboring men against the landlords and employers, wretched food and clothing, and troublesome wife and family, moves gently into the promise of spiritual plenty. In the same way, the swaddled sheep in the cradle, horned like the Devil, is balanced by the Christ Child of the touching and tender finale. Mak the sheep-stealer's deceitful wife Gill, grumbling at her lot and groaning in pretended post-natal anguish, is set against the apotheosis of motherhood, the Virgin Mary. The shepherds' song and the "song" of Gill, Mak, and the sheep are ironically described in the same technical terms as the Angel's glorious hymn. The shepherds' mercy to Mak finds its counterpart in the promised mercy of the Child to the Shepherds.

Mak is a comic character in his own right, the trickster of earlier folk-tradition, but also something more: a more rounded comic character than anything previously found in an English play. Not even his antics, all the same, can bring us—nor were they intended to bring the audience—to prefer them to the tenderness and sweetness of the journey to Bethlehem and the scene of adoration there.

MORALITY PLAYS

In the mystery plays, the divine and the human speak to each other quite naturally across a small stage, making clear the relevance of natural and supernatural, actual and historical, events to each other. The other medieval dramatic mode of bringing this lesson home to men was the morality play, which began to develop at about the same time and was sometimes also played under the auspices of the guilds. The morality, however, was a single play, not a cycle. It too, appears to begin in northern English cities. But where the mystery play dramatized biblical events in order to show their relevance to everyday life, the morality, in a more directly didactic way, dramatized the conflict between good and evil, the struggle between opposing qualities, between virtue and vice, which Christianity teaches is always in progress within the soul of the individual Christian. In the morality play this contest was presented through personification allegory, the virtues and vices contending for the soul of man. Such battles of personifications of virtues and vices appear for the first time in a Latin poem by Prudentius, about A.D. 400, the *Psychomachia,* where the conflict is shown in the form of a series of armed contests between a given virtue and its opposite vice (Patience vs. Anger, Pride vs. Humility). There the form is narrative, not dramatic.

By the later Middle Ages both personification allegory and the moral theology of vices and virtues had developed to a much more sophisticated state. In particular an elaborate series of subdivisions of virtues and vices had been evolved and carefully connected with the observances and customs of the church, especially with the theory and practice of penance—that is, with the formal recognition and confession of sin by the sinner, to the priest, followed by his absolution, on condition of his performing certain penances or undergoing discipline. One of the shaping themes of *Everyman,* for example, is the necessity of penitence for sin before death and the full participation in the church's observances concerning it.

Like the mystery play, the morality has much in common with didactic literature—the literature of moral instruction such as the sermon, the religious lyric and the book of devotion. The *Ars Moriendi* (Art of Dying Well) is one devotional work which has been shown to have a relation to *Everyman:* it too depicts a man, on the point of death, deserted by all the gifts of Fortune and Nature—wealth, friends, strength, senses—and with no support but his trust in the mercy of God and in the virtues of faith, hope, and charity. It is these which, by God's grace, will save his soul from damnation.

Not all the moralities are as somber and unrelieved as *Everyman,* which is perhaps the most famous of them. The morality *Mankind,* of about 1475, has some lighter elements, including comic characters such as Mischief, Naught, and New Guise; and a late example, John Skelton's *Magnificence,* of about 1515/16, is also satiric and comic as well as moral.

Everyman may be a translation of a Dutch play on the same theme, *Elckerlijk,* but some scholars maintain that the Dutch play is a translation of the English. It is certain that they are closely related. The English play seems to have been written about 1485, by an anonymous author, but was not published until 1528 or 1529. It is not entirely typical of the English morality—as we have seen—in its uniformly dark tone, with little humor and little satire. Nor is it a play about the battle for man's soul between opposites: it works by showing Everyman stripped of the worldly gifts on which he had thought himself able to rely, concentrating on the increasing isolation of a man on the point of death, until he descends alone into the grave, with only Good Deeds to stand between him and Judgment (see Fig. 52).

The central story, of a man forsaken by all his friends but one, who pleads for him before the king, is Eastern in origin and had found its way into Western collections of fables and moral tales by the twelfth century. The turn given it by the author of *Everyman* toward a moral allegory of preparation for death is typical of the later Middle Ages. He uses it for a dramatic exposition which is at the same time a statement of the universal human predicament and an exposition of the doctrine of the church. We do not know the hour when Death will summon us. We cannot deny the summons and must be always prepared, not relying on any worldly gifts, but on our good deeds, being penitent for the evil we have done. It is not that Everyman has been wholly evil: the message is not that the gifts of fortune which he has enjoyed are wrong in themselves, but that excessive attachment to such temporal gifts as wealth and friends is as wrong as excessive trust in gifts of nature such as strength and beauty. None of these will see Everyman through to salvation by themselves—wealth, friends, even family, if they are not recognized as transitory goods, will lead a man to damnation. Knowledge—i.e. self-knowledge through all the five senses, which leads to a clear vision of oneself as sinful and in need of God's mercy, and so to acknowledgment of sin and contrition—will be the first sign that he recognizes the true way to heaven, and Knowledge will ensure that Good Deeds will be able to stand by him.

The Wakefield Second Shepherds' Play°

(Secunda Pastorum)

FIRST SHEPHERD (COLL)	GILL, *his wife*
SECOND SHEPHERD (GIB)	ANGEL
THIRD SHEPHERD (DAW)	MARY
MAK	CHRIST-CHILD

[*Enter* FIRST SHEPHERD]

FIRST SHEPHERD   Lord! What these weathers are cold, and I am ill happed.°
I am near-hand⸵ dold,° so long have I napped.   *almost*
My legs they fold,⸵ my fingers are chapped;   *fail*
It is not as I would, for I am all lapped⸵   *enfolded*
    In sorrow.
In storms and tempest,
Now in the east, now in the west,
Woe is him has never rest
    Midday nor morrow!⸵   *morning*

10   But we sely husbands⸵ that walk on the moor,   *poor husbandmen*
In faith, we are near-hands out of the door;°
No wonder, as it stands, if we be poor,
For the tilth⸵ of our lands lies fallow⸵ as the floor,   *arable / unseeded*
    As ye ken.⸵   *know*
We are so hammed,
For-taxed and rammed,
We are made hand-tamed
    With these gentlery men.°

Thus they reave⸵ us our rest. Our Lady them wary!⸵   *rob of / curse*
20 These men that are lord-fast,° they cause the plough tarry.
That men say is for the best we find it contrary.
Thus are husbands oppressed, in point to miscarry,
    On live.°
Thus hold they us under;
Thus they bring us in blunder.⸵   *misfortune*
It were great wonder
    And⸵ ever should we thrive.   *if*

This text is based on that of A. W. Pollard, *The Towneley Plays* (1897), but very freely treated. Spelling has been modernized and normalized, except where this would impair rhyme or meter, and modern punctuation has been used. The stage directions in the manuscript have been translated from the original Latin, and those added by the present editor have been placed within brackets.

What . . . happed How cold this weather is and I am poorly clad.
dold dulled; numb in body and brain
we . . . door we are nearly homeless
hammed . . . men crippled, over-taxed, and crushed, we are brought to submission by these gentry; the peasant's lot, as the landlords and the government become more exacting and powerful
lord-fast bound to a lord
in point . . . live in danger of destruction during our lives

For may he get a painted° sleeve, or a brooch, now-a-days,

Woe to him that him grieves,› or once gainsays;   *complains*

30   Dare no man him repreve, what mastery he mays°

And yet may no man leve› one word that he says,   *believe*

    No letter.

He can make purveyance,°

With boast and bragance;›   *bragging*

And all is through maintenance°

    Of men that are greater.

There shall come a swain as proud as a po;°

He must borrow my wain,› my plough also.   *wagon*

Then I am full fain› to grant ere he go.   *glad*

40   Thus live we in pain, anger, and woe

    By night and day.

He must have if he langed,›   *wished*

If I should forgang it;°

I were better be hanged

    Than once say him nay.

It does me good, as I walk thus by mine own,

Of this world for to talk in manner of moan.

To my sheep will I stalk and hearken anon;

There abide on a balk,° or sit on a stone,

50   Full soon.

For I trow,› pardee,›   *think / by God*

True men if they be,

We get more company

    Ere it be noon.

      [*Enter* SECOND SHEPHERD]

SECOND SHEPHERD   Bensté° and Dominus! What may this bemean?›   *mean*

Why, fares this world thus? Oft have we not seen.°

Lord, these weathers are spitous,› and the winds full keen,   *cruel*

And the frosts so hideous, they water mine een:›   *eyes*

    No lie.

60   Now in dry, now in wet,

Now in snow, now in sleet,

When my shoon› freeze to my feet,   *shoes*

    It is not all easy.

---

painted i.e. embroidered with a badge; like the brooch, a sign on the "maintained" man (l. 35) of the delegated authority of his lord. Mak later pretends to be such a man.
Dare . . . mays no man dare oppose him, such power has he
purveyance the preferential right of purchasing provisions and so forth at a price fixed by the buyer
maintenance keeping of retainers, "maintained" men

po Latin *pavo:* peacock
If . . . it even though I have to go without
balk strip of pasture dividing two ploughed parts of common land, where shepherds grazed sheep; or perhaps simply a ridge
Bensté *Benedicite:* Bless me; *Dominus:* Good Lord
Oft . . . seen We have not often seen the like of this.

But as far as I ken, or yet as I go,
We sely wedmen dree mickle woe;°   *always*
We have sorrow then and then;> it falls oft so.
Silly Capell° our hen, both to and fro
    She cackles;
But begin she to croak,
70 To groan or to cluck,
Woe is him our cock,°
    For he is in the shackles.

These men that are wed have not all their will.
When they are full hard bestead,> they sigh full still.>   *pressed / always*
God wot> they are led full hard and full ill;   *knows*
In bower nor in bed they say naught theretill.>   *thereto*
    This tide>   *time*
My part have I fun,>   *found*
I know my lesson.
80 Woe is him that is bun,>   *bound*
    For he must abide.>   *endure*

But now late in our lives—a marvel to me,
That I think my heart rives> such wonders to see,   *breaks*
What that destiny drives, it should so be°—
Some men will have two wives, and some men three
    In store.
Some are woe that has any;°
But so far can> I,   *know*
Woe is him that has many,
90   For he feels sore.>   *pain*

But, young men, of wooing, for God that you bought,>   *redeemed*
Be well ware> of wedding, and think in your thought,   *very wary*
'Had I wist'> is a thing that serves of naught.   *known*
Mickle still> mourning has wedding home brought,   *much constant*
    And griefs,
With many a sharp shower;°
For thou mayst catch in an hour
That shall sow thee full sour°
    As long as thou lives.

100 For, as ever read I 'pistle,° I have one to> my fere,>   *as / mate*
Sharp as a thistle, as rough as a brere,>   *briar*

But . . . woe But as far as I know or as far as I can go, we poor married men suffer much woe.
Capell regular name for a hen; capple: bird's crest
Woe . . . cock Bad luck for our rooster: the Shepherd is comparing the husband's lot in marriage to the rooster's bondage to the hen: conventional medieval antifeminism.

What . . . be Whatever Destiny sets in motion must happen.
Some are . . . any For some it is (enough) unhappiness to have one wife.
shower pain or fight
sow . . . sour pain you very sorely
as . . . 'pistle as I hope to go on reading the Epistle; i.e. he seems to imagine himself minor clergy

She is browed like a bristle, with a sour-loten cheer;°
Had she once wet her whistle, she could sing full clear
    Her paternoster.
She is great as a whale;
She has a gallon of gall;
By Him that died for us all,
    I would I had run to° I had lost her!   *till*

FIRST SHEPHERD God, look over the raw!° Full deafly ye stand.
110 SECOND SHEPHERD Yea, the devil in thy maw—so tariand!°
Sawst thou awre° of Daw?°   *anywhere*
FIRST SHEPHERD   Yea, on a lea-land°   *pasture*
Heard I him blaw.° He comes here at hand,
    Not far. Stand still.
SECOND SHEPHERD Why?
FIRST SHEPHERD For he comes, hope° I.   *expect*
SECOND SHEPHERD He will make° us both a lie   *tell*
    But if° we beware.   *unless*

    [*Enter* THIRD SHEPHERD]

THIRD SHEPHERD Christ's cross me speed,° and Saint Nicholas!° *prosper*
Thereof had I need; it is worse than it was.
120 Whoso could, take heed and let the world pass;
    It is ever in dread° and brickle° as glass,   *doubt / brittle*
      And slithes.°   *slips away*
This world fore° never so,   *fared*
With marvels mo° and mo,   *more*
Now in weal, now in woe,
    And all things writhes.°   *change*

Was never sin° Noah's flood° such floods seen,   *since*
Winds and rains so rude,° and storms so keen;   *rough*
Some stammered, some stood in doubt, as I ween.°
130 Now God turn all to good! I say as I mean,
    For ponder:°   *consider*
These floods so they drown,
Both in fields and in town,
    And bear all down,
      And that is a wonder.

She . . . cheer She has bristling brows, with a sour-looking face.
raw i.e. row, possibly meaning hedgerow (sense obscure)
Yea . . . tariand Yes, indeed; may the Devil be in your guts for dawdling so long.
Daw perhaps a diminutive of David; or, more likely, "stupid, foolish rustic"
blaw blow, i.e. sound his horn
Nicholas It is close to the first Christmas. St. Nicholas's feast day was December 6. He was also the patron of children, and is therefore invoked by the youngest shepherd.
Noah's flood A further reminder of Christmas since Noah was the Old Testament "type" of Christ. His deliverance from the flood was likened to our deliverance from sin.
Some . . . ween Some [men at Noah's Flood] staggered and were afraid, I understand.

We that walk in the nights our cattle° to keep,   *property*
We see sudden sights when other men sleep.
Yet methink my heart lights; I see shrews peep.°   *rogues looking*
Ye are two ill wights! I will give my sheep
140   A turn.°
But full ill have I meant;°
As I walk on this bent°   *field*
I may lightly° repent,   *quickly*
    My toes if I spurn.°   *stub*

      [*To the other two*]
Ah, sir, God you save, and master mine!
A drink fain would I have, and somewhat to dine.
    FIRST SHEPHERD   Christ's curse, my knave, thou art a lither hine!°
    SECOND SHEPHERD   What! the boy list° rave! Abide unto syne°   *likes to*
    We have made it.°
150 Ill thrift on thy pate!
Though the shrew came late,
Yet is he in state°
    To dine—if he had it.   *ready*

    THIRD SHEPHERD   Such servants as I, that sweats and swinks,°   *toil*
Eat our bread full dry, and that me forthinks.°   *displeases*
We are oft wet and weary when master men winks;°   *sleep*
Yet come full late both dinners and drinks.
    But nately°   *thoroughly*
Both our dame and our sire,
160 When we have run in the mire,
They can nip° at our hire,°   *cut / wages*
    And pay us full lately.

But hear my troth, master, for the fare that ye make,
I shall do thereafter, work as I take
I shall do a little, sir, and among ever lake,°
For yet lay my supper never on my stomach
    In fields.
Whereto should I threap?°   *haggle*
With my staff can I leap;°   *escape*
170 And men say 'Light cheap
    Litherly foryields.'°

    FIRST SHEPHERD   Thou were an ill lad, to ride on wooing
With a man that had but little of spending.°

Ye are . . . turn You are two worthless creatures! I will go and look at my sheep.
But . . . meant I have done much evil. (These lines do not make easy sense.)
Christ's . . . hine Christ's curse on you, boy, you are a worthless farmhand.
Abide . . . syne wait until later
We . . . it i.e. we've already eaten dinner
But hear . . . lake (ll. 163–65) But listen to my pledge, master. In return for the food you give, I shall do according to that—work as I am paid. I shall work a bit, sir, and enjoy myself between times.
Litherly foryields proverbial: a cheap bargain gives a poor return
Thou . . . spending You would be a bad one to be taken wooing by a man who hadn't much to spend.

SECOND SHEPHERD   Peace, boy! I bade; no more jangling,
Or I shall make thee full rad, by the Heaven's King,
  With thy gawds.°
Where are our sheep, boy? We scorn.°
 THIRD SHEPHERD   Sir, this same day at morn
I them left in the corn,
180 When they rang lauds.°

They have pasture good; they cannot go wrong.
 FIRST SHEPHERD   That is right. By the rood,˃ these nights are long! *cross*
Yet I would, ere we yode˃ one gave us a song.   *went*
 SECOND SHEPHERD   So I thought as I stood, to mirth us among.°
 THIRD SHEPHERD   I grant.
 FIRST SHEPHERD   Let me sing the tenory.
 SECOND SHEPHERD   And I the treble so high.
 THIRD SHEPHERD   Then the mean falls to me.°
  Let see how ye chant.

 Enter MAK, *with a cloak over his tunic.*°

190 MAK   Now, Lord, for thy names seven, that made both moon and starns
Well more than I can neven, thy will, Lord, of me tharns.
I am all uneven; that moves oft my harns.°
Now would God I were in heaven, for there weep no barns˃ *children*
  So still.˃   *continually*
 FIRST SHEPHERD   Who is that pipes so poor?°
 MAK   Would God ye wist˃ how I fore!˃   *knew / fared*
Lo, a man that walks on the moor,
  And has not all his will!

 SECOND SHEPHERD   Mak, where hast thou gane?˃ Tell us tiding.˃ *gone / news*
200 THIRD SHEPHERD   Is he come? Then ilkane˃ take heed to *everyone*
  his thing.˃   *possessions*
  [*Takes the cloak from him.*]
 MAK   What! Ich° be a yeoman, I tell you, of the king;
The self and the same, sond˃ from a great lording,˃ *messenger / lord*
  And sich.˃   *suchlike*
Fie on you! Go thence!
Out of my presence!
I must have reverence.
  Why, who be ich?

no . . . gawds perhaps: no more arguing, or I'll make you (stop) very quickly, by God, for all your tricks
We scorn sense obscure; perhaps: we scorn you
rang lauds i.e. rang the bells for the first church office of the day, before dawn
to . . . among to give us pleasure in the meantime
mean . . . me the middle part is mine. In medieval three-part harmony the tenor was the bass part, "holding" the melody.
Enter . . . tunic Mak is elaborately dressed and speaks with a superior, urban, southern English accent. He is playing the role of "maintained man" or yeoman, lording it over the rustics.
Lord . . . harns (ll. 190–93) Lord, for Thy seven names, Thou who madest both moon and stars (and) far more than I can name, Thy will is wanting in regard to me. I am all at sixes and sevens—and it often disturbs my mind. God's seven names are a Hebrew tradition.
pipes so poor i.e. cries so sadly
Ich the Southern form of I

FIRST SHEPHERD   Why make ye it so quaint?° Mak, ye do wrong,ʾ   *wrong*
SECOND SHEPHERD   But Mak, list ye saint? I trow for that you lang.°
THIRD SHEPHERD   I trow the shrewʾ can paint!ʾ The devil   *rascal / deceive*
    might him hang!
MAK   Ich shall make complaint, and make you all to thwang,°
    At a word,
And tell evenʾ how ye doth.ʾ   *just / do*
FIRST SHEPHERD   But, Mak, is that sooth?
Now take out that southern tooth,°
    And set in a turd.°

SECOND SHEPHERD   Mak, the devil in your ee!ʾ A stroke   *eye*
    would I leneʾ you.   *give*
THIRD SHEPHERD   Mak, know ye not me? By God, I could teenʾ you.   *hurt*
MAK   God lookʾ you all three! Methought I had seen you.   *save*
Ye are a fair company.
FIRST SHEPHERD   Can ye now mean you?°
SECOND SHEPHERD   Shrew, peep!°
Thus late as thou goes,
What will men suppose?ʾ   *suspect*
And thou hast an ill noiseʾ   *reputation*
    Ofʾ stealing of sheep.   *for*

MAK   And I am true as steel, all men wate,ʾ   *know*
But a sickness I feel that holds me full hote;ʾ   *feverish*
My belly fares not well, it is out of estate.ʾ   *condition*
THIRD SHEPHERD   Seldom lies the devil dead by the gate.°
MAK   Therefore
Full sore am I and ill;
If I stand stone still,
I eat not a needle°
    This month and more.

FIRST SHEPHERD   How fares thy wife? By my hood, how fares sho?ʾ   *she*
MAK   Lies waltering,ʾ by the rood, by the fire, lo!   *sprawling*
And a house full of brood.ʾ She drinks well, too;   *children*
Ill speed other good that she will do!°
    But sho
Eats as fast as she can;
And ilkʾ year that comes to man   *each*
She brings forth a lakanʾ—   *baby*
    And some years two.

210
220
230
240

Why . . . quaint Why are you so high and mighty?
Mak . . . lang Mak, do you want to seem a saint? I think you do long for it.
make . . . thwang have you all flogged
take . . . tooth give up that southern accent
set . . . turd stop your mouth with shit; the insult enhances the rustic-urban contrast
Can . . . you Can you remember now?
Shrew, peep "Rogue, looking about!" or "Rogue, look out!"

Seldom . . . gate Seldom does the Devil lie dead by the road ("gate" is a northern form); i.e. the Devil is always prowling about.
If . . . needle May I be turned to stone if I ate the smallest bit.
Ill speed . . . do Bad luck to the other good that she can do; i.e. if that is the only good thing she can do, let her not do anything else like it.

But were I now more gracious° and richer by far,   *wealthy*
I were eaten out of house and of harbar.°   *home*
Yet is she a foul dowse° if ye come near;
There is none that trows° nor knows a war°   *thinks of / worse*
    Than ken° I.   *know*
Now will ye see what I proffer?
250 To give all in my coffer
Tomorn at next to offer
    Her head-masspenny.°

    SECOND SHEPHERD   I wot so forwaked° is none in this shire.
I would sleep, if I taked less to my hire.°
    THIRD SHEPHERD   I am cold and naked, and would have a fire.
    FIRST SHEPHERD   I am weary, forraked,° and run in the mire.
    Wake, thou!
    SECOND SHEPHERD   Nay, I will lie down by,
For I must sleep, truly.
260   THIRD SHEPHERD   As good a man's son was I
    As any of you.

But, Mak, come hither! Between shalt thou lie down.
    MAK   Then might I let you, bedene, of that ye would rown,°
    No dread.
From my top to my toe,
Manus tuas commendo,
Pontio Pilato,
    Christ's cross me speed!°

       Then he gets up, while the other shepherds are asleep, and says:

Now were time° for a man that lacks what he would   *chance*
270 To stalk privily than° unto a fold,   *then*
And neemly° to work than, and be not too bold,   *nimbly*
For he might abuy° the bargain, if it were told,   *purchase dearly*
    At the ending.
Now were time for to reel,°   *move quickly*
But he needs good counsel
That fain would fare weel,°   *well*
    And has but little spending.

But about you a circill° as round as a moon,   *magic circle*
To° I have done that I will, till that it be noon,   *till*
280 That ye lie stone still to that I have done,
And I shall say theretill° of good words a fone°   *as well / few*
    On height

---

dowse French *douce:* sweetheart
Tomorn . . . masspenny (to be able) to offer,
tomorrow morning at the latest, a penny to the
priest to sing mass for her departed soul
I . . . forwaked I know that so worn out with
being awake

if . . . hire even if I were to get less wages
forraked worn out with walking
might . . . rown I might hinder you, certainly,
from whispering together what you want.
Manus . . . speed Thy hands I commend to
Pontius Pilate, Christ's cross prosper me: a blasphemous parody of Luke 23:46

Over your heads my hand I lift:
'Out go your eyen, fordo your sight!'°
But yet I must make better shift
　　And it be right.°

Lord, whatʾ they sleep hard! That may ye all hear.　　　　*how*
Was I never a shephard, but now will I lereʾ　　　　　*learn*
If the flock be scared, yet shall I nip nere.°
290　How! Draw hitherward! Now mends our cheer
　　From sorrow.
A fat sheep, I dare say;
A good fleece, dare I lay!ʾ　　　　　　　　　　　*bet*
Eft-whitʾ when I may,　　　　　　　　　　　*pay back*
　　But this will I borrow.

　　　[MAK *carries the sheep to his house*]

How, Gill, art thou in? Get us some light.
　　WIFE　Who makes such din this time of the night?
I am setʾ for to spin; I hope not I might　　　　　*sitting*
Rise a penny to win.° I shrewʾ them on height!　　　*curse*
300　So fares
A housewife that has been
To be raised thus between;
Here may no note be seen,
　　For such small chares.°
　　MAK　Good wife, open the hek!ʾ Seest thou not what I bring?　*inner door*
　　WIFE　I may tholeʾ thee draw the snek.ʾ Ah, come in, my　*let / latch*
　　　　sweeting!
　　MAK　Yea, thou tharʾ not reckʾ of my long standing.　*need / mind*
　　WIFE　By thy naked neck art thou like for to hing.ʾ　*hang*
　　MAK　Do way:ʾ　　　　　　　　　　　　　*get away*
310　I am worthy my meat,ʾ　　　　　　　　　*worth my keep*
For in a straitʾ can I get　　　　　　　　　　*tight spot*
More than they that swinkʾ and sweat　　　　　　*toil*
　　All the long day.

Thus it fell to my lot, Gill, I had such grace.
　　WIFE　It were a foul blot to be hanged for the case.
　　MAK　I have scaped,ʾ Gillot, often as hard a glase.ʾ　*escaped / blow*
　　WIFE　But so long goes the pot to the water, men say,
　　　At last
Comes it home broken.°

Out . . . sight Your power of sight is lost. Mak is the wicked black magician, a clear villain. He has just previously recited the "white" night spell (cf. Chaucer, the Miller's Tale, l. 379) to keep them all from harm.
But yet . . . right But still I must do better before it will come right.
nip nere probably: grab a sheep more closely, tightly

I hope . . . win I don't think I could get up, even to gain a penny.
So fares . . . chares (ll. 300–304) So does it fare with anyone who has been a housewife, to be got up thus all the time. There is no work to show here, because of such little chores.
But . . . broken Proverbial.

320   MAK   Well know I the token,°°   *portent*
But let it never be spoken;
    But come and help fast.

I would he were flain;° I lis° well eat.   *skinned / want*
This twelvemonth was I not so fain of one sheep's meat.
    WIFE   Come they ere he be slain, and hear the sheep bleat—
    MAK   Then might I be ta'en! That were a cold sweat!
      Go spar°   *fasten*
The gate-door.°   *outer door*
    WIFE   Yes, Mak,
For and° they come at thy back—   *if*
330   MAK   Then might I buy, for all the pack,
    The devil of the war.°

    WIFE   A good bourd° have I spied, since thou can° none.   *trick / know*
Here shall we him hide to that they be gone
In my cradle. Abide, let me alone,
And I shall lie beside in childbed, and groan.
    MAK   Thou red:°   *get ready*
And I shall say thou was light°   *delivered*
Of a knave° child this night.   *boy*
    WIFE   Now well is day bright,
340   That ever I was bred.°

This is a good guise° and a fair cast;°   *way / idea*
Yet a woman's advise helps at the last!
I wot° never who spies.° Again go thou fast.   *know / is looking*
    MAK   But° I come ere they rise, else blows a cold blast!   *unless*
    I will go sleep.

        [MAK *returns to the shepherds*]

Yet sleeps all this meney°   *company*
And I shall go stalk privily,
As it never had been I
    That carried their sheep.

350   FIRST SHEPHERD   *Resurrex a mortruus!*° Have hold my hand.
Judas carnas dominus!° I may not well stand;
My foot sleeps, by Jesus; and I walter fastand.°   *sprawl fasting*
I thought that we laid us full near England.
    SECOND SHEPHERD   Ah, yea.
Lord, what° I have slept weel.°   *how / well*
As fresh as an eel,

Then might . . . war Perhaps: Then might I
have, from the whole pack of them, the devil of
the worse of it—i.e. the devil of a bad time.
Now . . . bred Now happy be the day that I
was born.
Resurrex . . . mortruus The bad Latin: "I have
risen from the dead"—i.e. I've been dead
asleep—is also a blasphemous reference to
Christ's resurrection.
Judas . . . dominus worse Latin, presumably
meaning "Judas incarnate Lord"

As light I me feel
    As leaf on a tree.

THIRD SHEPHERD   Bensté° be herein! So my body quakes,
My heart is out of skin, whatso˃ it makes.˃   *whatever / causes*
Who makes all this din? So my brows blakes.°
To the door will I win. Hark, fellows,˃ wakes!   *comrades*
    We were four:
See ye awre of Mak now?°
FIRST SHEPHERD   We were up ere thou.
SECOND SHEPHERD   Man, I give God a vow,
    Yet yede he nawre.°

THIRD SHEPHERD   Methought he was lapped˃ in a wolf's skin.   *wrapped*
FIRST SHEPHERD   So are many happed now, namely, within.°
THIRD SHEPHERD   When we had long napped, methought with a gin˃   *snare*
A fat sheep he trapped; but he made no din.
SECOND SHEPHERD   Be still!
Thy dream makes thee wood.˃   *mad*
It is but phantom, by the rood.
FIRST SHEPHERD   Now God turn all to good,
    If it be his will!

SECOND SHEPHERD   Rise, Mak! For shame! Thou liest right lang.
MAK   Now Christ's holy name be us amang!
What is this? For Saint Jame, I may not well gang!˃   *walk*
I trow I be the same. Ah! my neck has lain wrang˃   *crooked*
    Enough.   [*They help* MAK *up*]
Mickle˃ thank! Since yester-even,   *much*
Now, by Saint Stephen,
I was flayed with a sweven:
    My heart out of slough.°

I thought Gill began to croak and travail˃ full sad,˃   *labor / hard*
Well night at the first cock, of a young lad
For to mend˃ our flock. Then be I never glad;   *increase*
I have tow on my rock° more than ever I had.
    Ah, my head!
A house full of young tharms!˃   *bellies*
The devil knock out their harns!˃   *brains*
Woe is him has many barns!˃   *children*
    And thereto little bread!

I must go home, by your leave, to Gill, as I thought.˃   *intended*
I pray you look˃ my sleeve that I steal nought;   *examine*

Bensté See l. 54n.
brows blakes brows darken; i.e. sight is dim,
he is struggling to consciousness
See . . . now Can you see Mak anywhere now?
Yet . . . nawre He's gone nowhere yet.
So are many . . . within Many are wrapped so
now, especially within; cf. Matthew 7:15: "inwardly they are ravening wolves."

flayed . . . slough Literally, I was skinned by
a dream (so that) my heart was outside my
skin; i.e. I was so terrified that my heart seemed
exposed.
tow on my rock flax on my distaff; i.e. trouble
enough already

I am loath you to grieve or from you take aught.

    THIRD SHEPHERD Go forth; ill might thou chieve!˃ Now would   *prosper*

        I we sought,°

400   This morn,

That we had all our store.

    FIRST SHEPHERD But I will go before;

Let us meet.

    SECOND SHEPHERD Whore?˃   *where*

    THIRD SHEPHERD At the crooked thorn.

    [MAK's *house*]

    MAK Undo this door! Who is here? How long shall I stand?

    WIFE Who makes such a bere?˃ Now walk in the wenyand!°   *din*

    MAK Ah, Gill, what cheer? It is I, Mak, your husband.

    WIFE Then may we see here the devil in a band,°

      Sir Guile!

Lo, he comes with a lote˃   *noise*

410 As he were holden in˃ the throat.   *held by*

I may not sit at my note˃   *work*

    A hand-long˃ while.   *short*

    MAK Will ye hear what fare˃ she makes to get her a glose?˃   *fuss / excuse*

And does naught but lakes,˃ and claws her toes?   *play*

    WIFE Why, who wanders? Who wakes? Who comes? Who goes?

Who brews? Who bakes? What makes me thus hose?˃   *hoarse*

    And than,

It is ruth˃ to behold,   *a pity*

Now in hot, now in cold,

420 Full woeful is the household

    That wants˃ a woman.   *lacks*

But what end has thou made with the herds,˃ Mak?   *shepherds*

    MAK The last word that they said, when I turned my back,

They would look that they had their sheep, all the pack.

I hope˃ they will not be well paid˃ when they their sheep lack,   *expect / pleased*

    Pardie!˃   *by God*

But how-so˃ the game goes,   *however*

To me they will suppose,˃   *suspect*

And make a foul noise,

430   And cry out upon me.

But thou must do as thou hight.˃   *promised*

    WIFE   I accord me theretill;°

I shall swaddle him right in my cradle.

If it were a greater sleight, yet could I help till.°

I will lie down straight.˃ Come, hap˃ me.   *at once / cover*

Now . . . sought now I want us to search

Now . . . wenyand May you go in the waning
moon—a time of ill omen.

devil in a band the devil in a noose, bound

I . . . theretill I agree to that

If . . . till Even if the trick were more difficult,
I could still help with it.

MAK   I will.
  WIFE   Behind!
Come Coll and his marrow°   *mate*
They will nip us full narrow.
  MAK   But I may cry 'Out, harrow!'°   *help*
    The sheep if they find.

440
  WIFE   Hearken ay when they call; they will come anon.
Come and make ready all, and sing by thine own;
Sing lullay° thou shall, for I must groan,
And cry out by the wall on Mary and John,°
    For sore.°   *pain*
Sing lullay on fast
When thou hears at the last;
And but° I play a false cast,°   *unless / trick*
    Trust me no more.

    [*At the crooked hawthorn*]

  THIRD SHEPHERD   Ah, Coll, good morn! Why sleepst thou not?
450
  FIRST SHEPHERD   Alas, that ever was I born! We have a foul blot.
A fat wether° have we lorn.°   *ram / lost*
  THIRD SHEPHERD   Marry, God's forbot!°   *God forbid*
  SECOND SHEPHERD   Who should do us that scorn?° That were a   *injury*
    foul spot.°   *insult*
  FIRST SHEPHERD   Some shrew.
I have sought with my dogs
All Horbury shrogs,°
And of fifteen hogs
    Found I but one ewe.°

  THIRD SHEPHERD   Now trow° me if ye will; by Saint Thomas of   *believe*
    Kent,°
Either Mak or Gill was at that assent.°   *conspiracy*
460
  FIRST SHEPHERD   Peace, man, be still!° I saw when he went.   *silent*
Thou slanders him ill. Thou ought to repent,
    Good speed.°   *instantly*
  SECOND SHEPHERD   Now as ever might I thee,°   *thrive*
If I should even here dee,°   *die*
I would say it were he
    That did that same deed.

  THIRD SHEPHERD   Go we thither, I rede,° and run on our feet. *advise*
I shall never eat bread the sooth to I weet.°   *until I know*
  FIRST SHEPHERD   No drink in my head, with him till I meet.

---

lullay perhaps, lullaby, a foreshadowing of the Nativity
Mary and John the Virgin and St. John, Christ's beloved disciple—powerful helpers of man
Horbury shrogs Horbury thickets. Horbury is a town near Wakefield, where this play was performed.
of fifteen . . . ewe with fifteen young sheep I found only the ewe; i.e. the ram was gone
Saint . . . Kent St. Thomas (Becket) of Canterbury

470   SECOND SHEPHERD I will rest in no stead⸧ till that I him greet,   *place*
    My brother!
  One I will hight:°
  Till I see him in sight
  Shall I never sleep one night
    There⸧ I do another.   *where*

    [MAK's *house*. GILL *groans and* MAK *sings a lullaby*]

    THIRD SHEPHERD Will ye hear how they hack?° Our sire list⸧   *wants to*
    croon.
    FIRST SHEPHERD Heard I never none crack⸧ so clear out of tune!   *sing*
  Call on him.
    SECOND SHEPHERD Mak! Undo your door soon.⸧   *at once*
    MAK Who is it that spake, as⸧ it were noon,   *as if*
480   On loft?⸧   *aloud*
  Who is that, I say?
    THIRD SHEPHERD Good fellows, were it day°—
    MAK As far as ye may,
    Good,⸧ speak soft   *good men*

  Over a sick woman's head, that is at malease;
  I had liefer be dead ere she had any disease.°
    WIFE Go to another stead! I may not well wheeze.⸧   *breathe*
  Each foot that ye tread goes thorough my nese,⸧   *nose*
    So high!⸧   *loudly*
490   FIRST SHEPHERD Tell us, Mak, if ye may,
  How fare ye, I say?
    MAK But are ye in this town today?°
  Now how fare ye?

  Ye have run in the mire, and are wet yet.
  I shall make you a fire, if ye will sit.
  A nurse would I hire. Think ye on that.°
  Well quit is my hire—my dream, this is it—
    A season.°   *children*
  I have barns,⸧ if ye knew,   *more / enough*
500 Well mo⸧ than enew.⸧
  But we must drink as we brew,
    And that is but reason.⸧   *right*

  I would ye dined ere ye yode.⸧ Methinks that ye sweat.   *went*
    SECOND SHEPHERD Nay, neither mends our mood, drink nor meat.

One . . . hight One thing I'll promise.
hack sing contrapuntally
were it day if only it were day
Over . . . disease Standing over a sick woman who is not well; I had rather be dead than that she should suffer distress.
But . . . today i.e. fancy seeing you here. Townsman Mak is again in opposition to the rustics.

Think . . . that The reading is difficult and "that" is an emendation; perhaps: Think about it; or, reading "yet": Do you still remember (my dream)?
Well . . . season My wages are fully paid for the time being: this is my dream (of Gill having another child, ll. 348 ff.).

MAK   Why, sir, ails you aught but good?

THIRD SHEPHERD   Yea, our sheep that we get°   *tend*
Are stolen as they yode. Our loss is great.

MAK   Sirs, drink!
Had I been thore,°   *there*
Some should have bought it° full sore.   *paid for*

FIRST SHEPHERD   Marry, some men trow° that ye wore;°   *believe / were*
510   And that us forthinks.°   *troubles*

SECOND SHEPHERD   Mak, some men trows that it should be ye.

THIRD SHEPHERD   Either ye or your spouse. So say we.

MAK   Now, if ye have suspouse° to Gill or to me,   *suspicion*
Come and rip° our house, and then ye may see   *ransack*
    Who had her;
If I any sheep fot,°   *fetched*
Any cow or stott.°   *heifer*
And Gill, my wife, rose not
520   Here since she laid her.

As I am true and leal,° to God here I pray   *honest*
That this be the first meal that I shall eat this day.

FIRST SHEPHERD   Mak, as have I sele, advise thee, I say:
He learned timely to steal that could not say nay.°

WIFE   I swelt!°   *am dying*
Out, thieves, from my wones!°   *house*
Ye come to rob us, for the nones.°

MAK   Hear ye not how she groans?
    Your hearts should melt.

530   WIFE   Out, thieves, from my barn!° Nigh° him not thore!°   *come near / there*
MAK   Wist ye how she had farn,° your hearts would be sore.   *fared*
Ye do wrong, I you warn, that thus come before
To a woman that has farne.° But I say no more.

WIFE   Ah, my middle!
I pray to God so mild,
If ever I you beguiled,
That I eat° this child   *may eat*
    That lies in this cradle.

MAK   Peace, woman, for God's pain, and cry not so!
540   Thou spills° thy brain, and makes me full woe.   *spoil, injure*

SECOND SHEPHERD   I trow our sheep be slain. What find ye two?

THIRD SHEPHERD   All work we in vain; as well may we go.
    But, hatters,°
I can find no flesh,
Hard nor nesh,°   *soft*

Mak . . . nay Now Mak, as I hope to be
blessed, think it over, I say: he learned to steal
young who could not say no.
Ye come . . . nones You come on purpose to
rob us.

barn bairn, child
farne farrowed, pigged
hatters Obscure; perhaps "Damn it!"

Salt nor fresh,
    Butᐟ two tomeᐟ platters.   *only / empty*

Quick cattle but this, tame nor wild,
None, as have I bliss, as loud as he smiled.°

550   WIFE   No, so God me bliss,ᐟ and give me joy of my child!   *bless*
    FIRST SHEPHERD We have markedᐟ amiss; I hold us beguiled.   *aimed*
    SECOND SHEPHERD Sir, done.ᐟ   *completely*
Sir, Our Lady him save!
Is your child a knave?ᐟ   *boy*
    MAK   Any lord might him have,
    This child to his son.

When he wakens he kips,° that joy is to see.
    THIRD SHEPHERD In good time to his hips, and in sely.°
Who were his gossips,ᐟ so soon ready?°   *godparents*
    MAK   So fair fall their lips!
560   FIRST SHEPHERD   Hark now, a le!ᐟ   *lie*
    MAK   So God them thank,
Parkin and Gibbon Waller, I say,
And gentle John Horn,° in good fay,ᐟ   *faith*
He made all the garrayᐟ   *commotion*
    With his great shank.ᐟ   *long legs*

    SECOND SHEPHERD Mak, friends will we be, for we are all one.ᐟ   *agreed*
    MAK   We! Now I hold for me,° for amends get I none.
Farewell, all three! All glad were ye gone!°
    THIRD SHEPHERD Fair words may there be, but love there is none
570   This year.
      [*Shepherds go out*]
    FIRST SHEPHERD Gave ye the child anything?
    SECOND SHEPHERD I trow, not one farthing!
    THIRD SHEPHERD Fast againᐟ will I fling;   *back*
    Abide ye me there.

     [*Shepherds re-enter*]

Mak, take it to no grief,ᐟ if I come to thy barn.   *amiss*
    MAK Nay, thou does me great repreef;ᐟ and foul has thou   *shame*
    farn.ᐟ   *done*
    THIRD SHEPHERD The child will it not grief, that little day-starn.°
    Mak, with your leef,ᐟ let me give your barn   *leave*
    But sixpence.
580   MAK Nay, do way! He sleeps.
    THIRD SHEPHERD Methinks he peeps.

Quick . . . smiled No livestock, tame or wild, as I hope to be saved, smelled as high as this baby.
kips Obscure; perhaps kicks, or keeps, i.e. behaves
In good . . . sely May he have a good and happy future.

Who . . . ready A child was often baptized on the day it was born.
Parkin . . . Horn other shepherds
I . . . me I must look after myself.
All glad . . . gone Good luck to you as you go.
day-starn day-star, morning star, a preparation for Christ, the true day-star

MAK   When he wakens he weeps;
  I pray you go hence.

THIRD SHEPHERD   Give me leave him to kiss, and lift up the clout.° *cloth*
What the devil is this? He has a long snout!
FIRST SHEPHERD   He is marked amiss. We wate ill about.
SECOND SHEPHERD   Ill-spun weft, ywis,° ay° comes foul   *indeed / always*
  out.°
    Aye, so!°
He is like to our sheep!
590
THIRD SHEPHERD   How, Gib! May I peep?
FIRST SHEPHERD   I trow, kind will creep
  Where it may not go!°

SECOND SHEPHERD   This was a quaint gawd and a fair cast!°
It was a high fraud!
THIRD SHEPHERD   Yea, sirs, was't.
Let burn this bawd, and bind her fast.
Ah, false scaud,° hang at the last,   *scold*
  So shall thou.
Will ye see how they swaddle
His four feet in the middle?°
600
Saw I never in a cradle
  A horned lad°ere now.

MAK   Peace, bid I! What! Let be your fare!°   *carrying-on*
I am he that him gat,° and yond woman him bare.   *begot*
FIRST SHEPHERD   What devil shall he hatt?° Mak?   *be called*
  Lo, God, Mak's heir!
SECOND SHEPHERD   Let be all that. Now God give him care,
  I say.
WIFE   A pretty child is he
As sits on a woman's knee;
A dilly-downe,° pardie,   *darling*
610
  To gar° a man laugh.   *make*

THIRD SHEPHERD   I know him by the ear-mark; that is a good token.
MAK   I tell you, sirs, hark! His nose was broken;
  Sithen° told me a clerk that he was forspoken.°   *later / bewitched*
FIRST SHEPHERD   This is a false wark; I would fain be wroken.°   *revenged*
  Get weapon!
WIFE   He was taken with° an elf,   *by*
I saw it myself;

He is . . . out He is misshapen. It is wrong of
us to go on looking about. We are wasting our
time. A badly spun thread makes a bad piece
of cloth.
Aye, so! a double-take
kind . . . go Nature will creep in where it cannot walk: i.e. it will show itself in one way or
another. Cf. *Everyman*, l. 316.

quaint . . . cast a clever dodge and a good
trick
His . . . middle The sheep has been thoroughly
swaddled.
horned lad i.e. this is no baby, it's a monster,
the Devil

When the clock struck twelve
　　Was he forshapen.>　　　　　　　　　　　　　*transformed*

620　SECOND SHEPHERD　Ye two are well feft, same in a stead.°
　　THIRD SHEPHERD　Sin they maintain their theft, let do them to dead!°
　　MAK　If I trespass eft,> gird> off my head!　　　*sin again / strike*
With you will I be left.°
　　FIRST SHEPHERD　Sirs, do my rede:>　　　　　　*advice*
　　For this trespass
We will neither ban> nor flyte>　　　　　　　　*curse / scold*
Fight nor chide,
But have done as tite>　　　　　　　　　*as soon as we can*
　　And cast> him in canvas.　　　　　　　　　*toss*

　　[*They toss* MAK *in a blanket and go*]

　　FIRST SHEPHERD　Lord, what> I am sore; in point for to brist>　*how / burst*
630 In faith, I may no more; therefore will I rist.>　　　*rest*
　　SECOND SHEPHERD　As a sheep of seven score° he weighed in my fist.
For to sleep aywhore> methinks that I list.>　　*anywhere / please*
　　THIRD SHEPHERD　Now I pray you,
Lie down on this green.
　　FIRST SHEPHERD　On these thieves yet I mene.>　　*think*
　　THIRD SHEPHERD　Whereto should ye teen>　　*be troubled*
　　　So, as I say you? [*They sleep*]

　　An ANGEL *sings 'Gloria in excelsis'; then let him say:*°

　　ANGEL　Rise, herd-men hend!> For now is he born　*gentle*
That shall take from the fiend that Adam had lorn:°
640 That warlock° to shend> this night is he born;　　*destroy*
God is made your friend now at this morn,
　　He behests.>　　　　　　　　　　　*promises*
At Bedlem> go see,　　　　　　　　　*Bethlehem*
　　There> lies that free>　　　　*where / noble one*
In a crib full poorly
　　Between two beasts.

　　FIRST SHEPHERD　This was a quaint steven° that ever yet I heard.
It is a marvel to neven,> thus to be scared.　　*tell*
　　SECOND SHEPHERD　Of God's son of heaven he spake upward.>　*on high*
650 All the wood in a levin> methought that he gard　*lightning*
　　Appear.°

THIRD SHEPHERD   He spake of a barn>   *child*
In Bedlem, I you warn.>   *tell*
   FIRST SHEPHERD   That betokens yond starn.>   *yonder star*
   Let us seek him there.

   SECOND SHEPHERD   Say, what was his song? Heard ye not how he cracked it,
Three breves to a long?°
   THIRD SHEPHERD   Yea, marry, he hacked it;°
Was no crotchet wrong, nor nothing that lacked it.
660   FIRST SHEPHERD   For to sing us among, right as he knacked° it,
    I can.>   *know how*
   SECOND SHEPHERD   Let see how ye croon.
Can ye bark at the moon?°
   THIRD SHEPHERD   Hold your tongues, have done!
   FIRST SHEPHERD   Hark after, than!

   SECOND SHEPHERD   To Bedlem he bade that we should gang;>   *go*
I am ful rad> that we tarry too lang.   *afraid*
   THIRD SHEPHERD   Be merry and not sad; of mirth is our sang;>   *song*
Everlasting glad> to meed> may we fang>   *joy / reward / get*
   Without noise.
670   FIRST SHEPHERD   Hie we thither forthy>   *therefore*
If> we be wet and weary,   *though*
To that child and that lady.
   We have it not to lose.°

   SECOND SHEPHERD   We find by the prophecy—let be your din—
Of David and Isay—and mo then I min°—
They prophesied by clergy> that in a virgin   *learning*
Should He light> and lie, to sloken> our sin   *alight / slacken*
   And slake> it,   *relieve*
Our kind> from woe.   *race*
680 For Isay° said so:
'Ecce virgo
   Concipiet' a child that is naked.

   THIRD SHEPHERD   Full glad may we be, and> we abide that day   *if*
That lovely to see, that all mights may.°
Lord, well were me, for once and for ay,
Might I kneel on my knee some word for to say
   To that Child.
But the angel said,
In a crib was He laid;
690 He was poorly arrayed,
   Both mean> and mild.   *lowly*

cracked . . . **long** sang it loudly, three short
notes to a long, in perfect rhythm
hacked it improvised a contrapuntal part
knacked sang skilfully
Can . . . moon In trying to imitate the Angel,
you are like a dog barking at the moon.
We . . . lose We must not omit to do it.
Of David . . . min David and Isaiah and more

than I remember; two of the prophets of Christ,
a procession of whom comprises the cast in an
early form of drama, the *Ordo prophetarum*
Isay Isaiah 7:14: "Behold a Virgin shall conceive and bear a child." This was regularly
included in the Christmas tropes.
That . . . may to see that beautiful one who is
almighty

FIRST SHEPHERD   Patriarchs that has been, and prophets beforn,
They desired to have seen this Child that is born.
They are gone full clean;° that have they lorn.°   *utterly / missed*
We shall see Him, I ween,° ere it be morn,   *think*
    To° token.   *as*
When I see Him and feel,
Then wot° I full weel   *know*
It is true as steel
700   That prophets have spoken:

To so poor as we are that He would appear,
First find, and declare by His messenger.°
SECOND SHEPHERD   Go we now, let us fare; the place is us near.
THIRD SHEPHERD   I am ready and yare;° go we in fere°   *prepared / together*
    To that bright.°   *lovely one*
Lord, if thy will be—
We are lewd° all three—   *simple*
Grant us some kind of glee°   *happiness*
    To comfort Thy wight.°   *creatures*

    [*They enter the stable*]

700   FIRST SHEPHERD   Hail, comely and clean!° Hail, young Child!   *pure*
Hail, Maker, as I mean, of° a maiden so mild!   *come from*
Thou has waried, I ween, the warlock so wild;°
The false guiler of teen,° now goes he beguiled.
    Lo, he merry is!
Lo, he laughs, my sweeting!
A well fair meeting!
I have holden° my heting.°   *kept / promise*
    Have a bob° of cherries!°   *bunch*

SECOND SHEPHERD   Hail, sovereign Saviour, for Thou has us sought!
710 Hail, freely food° and flower, that all things has wrought!   *noble child*
Hail, full of favour, that made all of naught!
Hail! I kneel and I cower.° A bird have I brought   *crouch*
    To my barn.°   *baby*
Hail, little tiny mop!°   *doll*
Of our creed° Thou art crop.°   *faith / head*
I would drink of Thy cop,°
    Little day-starn.

THIRD SHEPHERD   Hail, darling dear, full of Godhead!
I pray Thee be near when that I have need.
730 Hail! Sweet is Thy cheer!° My heart would bleed   *face*
To see Thee sit here in so poor weed,°   *clothes*
    With no pennies.

First . . . messenger first to find us and then to
make it known through this messenger
Thou . . . wild I believe that thou hast cursed
the Devil so fierce.

false . . . teen the false, tormenting deceiver
cherries fruit not in season, to suggest the miracle of Christ's birth
cop cup; a rustic prophecy of the Eucharist

Hail! Put forth Thy dall!>   *fist*
I bring Thee but a ball:
Have and play Thee withal,
    And go to the tennis.°

    MARY   The Father of Heaven, God omnipotent,
That set> all in seven> his Son has He sent.   *created / seven days*
My name couthe He neven and light ere He went.
740   I conceived Him full even, through might, as He meant;°
    And now is He born.
He> keep you from woe!   *may he*
I shall pray Him so.
Tell it forth as ye go,
    And min on> this morn.   *remember*

    FIRST SHEPHERD   Farewell, Lady, so fair to behold,
With Thy child on Thy knee!
    SECOND SHEPHERD   But he lies full cold.
Lord, well is me. Now we go, thou behold.
    THIRD SHEPHERD   Forsooth, already it seems to be told
750   Full oft.
    FIRST SHEPHERD   What grace we have fun!>   *received*
    SECOND SHEPHERD   Come forth; now are we won!>   *redeemed*
    THIRD SHEPHERD   To sing are we bun.>   *bound*
    Let take on loft!°
c. 1400–1450

Everyman°

MESSENGER	KNOWLEDGE
GOD	CONFESSION
DEATH	BEAUTY
EVERYMAN	STRENGTH
FELLOWSHIP	DISCRETION
KINDRED	FIVE WITS
COUSIN	ANGEL
GOODS	DOCTOR
GOOD DEEDS	

Here beginneth a treatise how the High Father of Heaven sendeth Death to summon every creature to come and give account of their lives in this world, and is in manner of a moral play.

tennis Royal tennis was already a popular game at the end of the 14th century.
My name . . . meant (ll. 739–40) My name did He name and He alighted in me before He went. I conceived Him through God's might, just as His purpose was.
Let . . . loft Let us strike up.

This text is based on the first printed version by John Skot, of about 1528–29, as edited by W. W. Greg (Louvain, 1904). There is no manuscript. The text has been very freely treated, spelling has been modernized, except where this would interfere with rhyme or meter, and modern punctuation has been used. Some stage directions have been added and are set off in brackets.

MESSENGER   I pray you all give your audience,°   *hearing*
And hear this matter with reverence,
By figure° a moral play:
The *Summoning of Everyman* called it is,
That of our lives and ending shows
How transitory we be all day.°   *every day*
This matter is wondrous precious,
But the intent of it is more gracious,°
And sweet to bear away.
10   The story saith: Man, in the beginning,
Look well, and take good heed to the ending,°
Be you never so gay!
Ye think sin in the beginning full sweet,
Which in the end causeth the soul to weep,
When the body lieth in clay.
Here shall you see how Fellowship and Jollity,
Both Strength, Pleasure, and Beauty,°
Will fade from thee as flower in May.
For ye shall hear how our Heaven-King
20   Calleth Everyman to a general reckoning.
Give audience, and hear what he doth say.   [*Exit*]

GOD° *speaketh:*

GOD   I perceive, here in my majesty,
How that all creatures be to me unkind,°
Living without dread in worldly prosperity.
Of ghostly° sight the people be so blind,°   *spiritual*
Drowned in sin, they know me not for their God;
In worldly riches is all their mind,°   *intention*
They fear not of my righteousness the sharp rod;
My law° that I showed, when I for them died
30   They forget clean, and shedding of my blood red;
I hanged between two,° it cannot be denied;
To get them life I suffered° to be dead;   *consented*
I healed their feet,° with thorns hurt was my head.
I could do no more than I did, truly;
And now I see the people do clean forsake me.
They use the seven deadly sins damnàble;

matter . . . figure Matter and form (figure)
are Aristotelian principles taken over by medieval science and philosophy; form shapes and
directs matter. The matter here is the story
and the moral doctrine; figure, the shape in
which it is presented, i.e. visually and dramatically.
the intent . . . gracious the purport, the comfort we can take from it, are more holy and
good
take . . . ending proverbial saying; Ecclesiasticus 7:36: "Remember the end, and thou shalt
never do amiss"
Strength . . . Beauty exterior, social gifts and

goods, from Nature or Fortune, not constant and
eternal
God the Trinity, especially the Son, probably
speaking from a position raised above the stage,
as in mystery plays
unkind unnatural and ungrateful
people . . . blind Compare Ephesians 4:18;
the blindness of sin was a commonplace.
law i.e. the law of love, the Gospel
hanged . . . two I was crucified between two
thieves
healed . . . feet an allusion to Christ's washing
the disciples' feet, symbolizing his power to
heal mankind in spirit

As pride, covetise,° wrath, and lechery,°   *avarice*
Now in the world be made commendàble;
And thus they leave of angels the heavenly company.
40 Every man liveth so after his own pleasure,
And yet of their life they be nothing sure.°
I see the more that I them forbear
The worse they be from year to year;
And that liveth appaireth° fast.   *degenerates*
Therefore I will, in all the haste,
Have a reckoning of every man's person;
For, and° I leave the people thus alone   *if*
In their life and wicked tempests,°   *turmoil*
Verily they will become much worse than beasts;
50 For now one would by envy another up eat;°
Charity° they all do clean forget.
I hoped well that every man
In my glory should make his mansion,
And thereto I had them all elect;°   *chosen*
But now I see, like traitors deject,°   *degraded*
They thank me not for the pleasure that I to them meant,°   *intended*
Nor yet for their being that I them have lent.°   *given*
I proffered the people great multitude of mercy,
And few there be that asketh it heartily;°   *sincerely*
60 They be so cumbered with° worldly riches,   *involved in*
That needs on them I must do justice,
On every man living, without fear.
Where art thou, Death, thou mighty messenger?

[*Enter* DEATH]

DEATH   Almighty God, I am here at your will,
Your commandment to fulfil.
GOD   Go thou to Everyman,°
And show him, in my name,
A pilgrimage° he must on him take,
Which he in no wise may escape;
70 And that he bring with him a sure reckoning
Without delay or any tarrying.
DEATH   Lord, I will in the world go run overall,°   *everywhere*
And cruelly out search both great and small.   [*Exit* GOD]
Every man will I beset° that liveth beastly°   *attack / bestially*
Out of God's laws, and dreadeth not folly.

pride . . . lechery Four of the seven deadly sins, the others being envy, gluttony, and sloth. They represent the World, the Flesh, and the Devil and often attend the personifications of these.
And . . . sure and yet they are in no way secure in their lives
envy . . . eat Envy is often represented as biting, but usually as eating her own entrails; see Galatians 5:15.

Charity love of God, love of one's neighbor, and love of oneself
Everyman mankind, personified here for the first time in the play. The Messenger has been talking, we feel, in general terms, but now the matter comes home to us more strongly.
pilgrimage Life as a pilgrimage is an especially common image in the later Middle Ages.

He that loveth riches I will strike with my dart,

His sight to blind, and from heaven to depart°—   *separate*

Except that alms be his good friend°—

In hell for to dwell, world without end.

80   Lo, yonder I see Everyman walking;

Full little he thinketh on my coming;

His mind is on fleshly lusts and his treasure;°

And great pain it shall cause him to endure

Before the Lord, Heaven-King.   [*Enter* EVERYMAN]

Everyman, stand still! Whither art thou going

Thus gaily? Hast thou thy Maker forgeet?°   *forgotten*

    EVERYMAN   Why askest thou?

Wouldst thou weet?°   *know*

    DEATH   Yea, sir; I will show you:

90   In great haste I am sent to thee

From God, out of his Majesty.

    EVERYMAN   What, sent to me?

    DEATH   Yea, certainly.

Though thou have forgot him here,

He thinketh on thee in the heavenly sphere,

As, ere we depart, thou shalt know.

    EVERYMAN   What desireth God of me?

    DEATH   That shall I show thee:

A reckoning he will needs have

100   Without any longer respite.

    EVERYMAN   To give a reckoning longer leisure I crave;

This blind° matter troubleth my wit.°   *difficult / intellect*

    DEATH   On thee thou must take a long journey;

Therefore thy book of count° with thee thou bring;   *accounts*

For turn again° thou cannot by no way.   *return*

And look thou be sure of thy reckoning,

For before God thou shalt answer, and show

Thy many bad deeds, and good but a few,

How thou hast spent thy life, and in what wise,

110   Before the Chief Lord of Paradise.

Have ado that we were in that way,°

For weet° thou well, thou shalt make none attornay.°   *know*

    EVERYMAN   Full unready I am such reckoning to give.

I know thee not. What messenger art thou?

    DEATH   I am Death, that no man dreadeth.°

For every man I 'rest,° and no man spareth;   *arrest*

For it is God's commandment°

Except . . . friend unless the alms he has given in life stand him in good stead—the restricted meaning of charity

lusts . . . treasure pleasures of the flesh (lechery, gluttony, sloth) and the world (avarice); but Death will give Everyman some leisure to repent

Have . . . way let us set about making that journey

thou . . . attornay you can give no one power of attorney; i.e. send no substitute

that . . . dreadeth that fears no man. One of the regular properties of death in sermon literature: he neither spares nor fears rich or poor, he cares for no bribe, he gives no respite

God's commandment from Eden: Genesis 3:19

That all to me should be obedient.

EVERYMAN   O Death! thou comest when I had thee least in mind!°
120   In thy power it lieth me to save,
Yet of my good⁊ will I give thee, if thou will be kind.   *goods*
Yea, a thousand pound shalt thou have,
And⁊ defer this matter till another day.   *if you*

DEATH   Everyman, it may not be, by no way!
I set⁊ not by gold, silver, nor riches,   *set store*
Nor by pope, emperor, king, duke, nor princes.
For, and⁊ I would receive⁊ gifts great,   *if / accept*
All the world I might get;
But my custom is clean contrary.
130   I give thee no respite. Come hence, and not tarry.

EVERYMAN   Alas! shall I have no longer respite?
I may say Death giveth no warning.
To think on thee, it maketh my heart sick,
For all unready is my book of reckoning.
But twelve year and I might have abiding,
My counting-book I would make so clear,°
That my reckoning I should not need to fear.
Wherefore, Death, I pray thee, for God's mercy,
Spare me till I be provided of remedy.

140   DEATH   Thee availeth not to cry, weep, and pray;
But haste thee lightly⁊ that thou were gone that journay,   *quickly*
And prove⁊ thy friends if thou can.   *test*
For weet thou well the tide abideth no man;°
And in the world each living creature
For Adam's sin must die of nature.°

EVERYMAN   Death, if I should this pilgrimage take,
And my reckoning surely make,
Show me, for saint⁊ charity,   *holy*
Should I not come again shortly?

150   DEATH   No, Everyman; and⁊ thou be once there,   *if*
Thou mayst never more come here,
Trust me verily.

EVERYMAN   O gracious⁊ God, in the high seat celestial,   *merciful*
Have mercy on me in this most need!
Shall I have no company from this vale terrestrial
Of mine acquaintance that way me to lead?°

DEATH   Yea, if any be so hardy,
That would go with thee and bear thee company.
Hie⁊ thee that thou were gone to God's magnificence,   *hasten*
160   Thy reckoning to give before his presence.

Death . . . mind See Matthew 24:50–51.
But . . . clear if I could have a deferment for
only twelve years, I would make my account-
book so clear of debt
tide . . . man time waits for no man: proverbial
of nature in the course of nature; St. Paul, Ro-

mans 5:12: "as by one man sin entered into the
world, and death by sin; and so death passed
upon all men"
Shall . . . lead May I have no one of my
acquaintance as company to lead the way from
this terrestrial valley? Now the solitariness of
Death begins to be emphasized.

What! weenest° thou thy life is given thee,   *suppose*
And thy worldly goods also?
    EVERYMAN   I had weened so, verily.
    DEATH   Nay, nay; it was but lent thee;
For, as soon as thou art go°   *gone*
Another a while shall have it, and then go therefro°   *from it*
Even as thou hast done.
Everyman, thou art mad! Thou hast thy wits five,°
And here on earth will not amend thy life;
170 For suddenly I do come.
    EVERYMAN   O wretched caitiff!° whither shall I flee,
That I might 'scape this endless sorrow?
Now, gentle° Death, spare me till tomorrow,   *noble*
That I may amend me
With good advisement.°   *consideration*
    DEATH   Nay, thereto I will not consent,
Nor no man will I respite,
But to the heart suddenly I shall smite
Without any advisement.°   *warning*
180 And now out of thy sight I will me hie;
See thou make thee ready shortly,
For thou mayst say this is the day
That no man living may 'scape away.   [*Exit* DEATH]
    EVERYMAN [*alone*] Alas! I may well weep with sighs deep.
Now have I no manner of company
To help me in my journey and me to keep;°   *guard*
And also my writing° is full unready.   *account book*
How shall I do now for to excuse me?
I would to God I had never be gete!°   *been begotten*
190 To my soul a full great profit° it had be;   *benefit*
For now I fear pains huge and great.
The time passeth; Lord, help, that all wrought.°   *made*
For though I mourn, it availeth nought.
The day passeth, and is almost ago;°   *gone*
I wot° not well what for to do.   *know*
To whom were I best my complaint to make?
What and° I to Fellowship thereof spake,   *if*
And showed him of this sudden chance,
For in him is all mine affiance?°   *trust*
200 We have in the world so many a day
Been good friends in sport and play.
I see him yonder, certainly.
I trust that he will bear me company;
Therefore to him will I speak to ease my sorrow.
Well met, good Fellowship, and good morrow!

---

wits five Personified later on, they are the agents   **wretched caitiff** captive wretch
of perception: sight, smell, hearing, taste, and
touch.

FELLOWSHIP *speaketh:*

FELLOWSHIP   Everyman, good morrow, by this day!°
Sir, why lookest thou so piteously?
If any thing be amiss, I pray thee me say,
That I may help to remedy.
210   EVERYMAN   Yea, good Fellowship, yea,
I am in great jeopardy.
FELLOWSHIP   My true friend, show to me your mind;
I will not forsake thee to thy life's end
In the way of good company.°
EVERYMAN   That was well spoken, and lovingly.
FELLOWSHIP   Sir, I must needs know your heaviness;>   *sorrow*
I have pity to see you in any distress;
If any have you wronged, ye shall revenged be,
Though I on the ground be slain for thee,
220   Though that I know before that I should die.
EVERYMAN   Verily, Fellowship, gramercy.>   *thank you*
FELLOWSHIP   Tush! by thy thanks I set not a stree>   *straw*
Show me your grief,> and say no more.   *trouble*
EVERYMAN   If I my heart should to you break,>   *disclose*
And then you to turn your mind from me,
And would not me comfort when ye hear me speak,
Then should I ten times sorrier be.
FELLOWSHIP   Sir, I say as I will do indeed.
EVERYMAN   Then be you a good friend at need;°
230   I have found you true herebefore.
FELLOWSHIP   And so ye shall evermore;
For, in faith, and thou go to hell,
I will not forsake thee by the way!
EVERYMAN   Ye speak like a good friend; I believe you well.
I shall deserve> it, and> I may.   *repay / if*
FELLOWSHIP   I speak of no deserving, by this day!
For he that will say and nothing do
Is not worthy with good company to go;
Therefore show me the grief of your mind,
240   As to your friend most loving and kind.
EVERYMAN   I shall show you how it is:
Commanded I am to go a journay,
A long way, hard and dangerous,
And give a strait count> without delay,   *strict account*
Before the high judge, Adonai.°
Wherefore, I pray you, bear me company,
As ye have promised, in this journay.

good . . . day A hearty good day to you!   Then . . . need proverbial
This sets the tone of Fellowship's empty prom-   Adonai Master, Lord; Hebrew name for God,
ises.   substitute for the unutterable name of Jehovah;
good company pleasure and diversion; but   in Christian liturgy, Christ
Everyman mistakes the sense of "good"

FELLOWSHIP   That is matter indeed. Promise is duty;°
But, and I should take such a voyage on me,
250   I know it well, it should be to my pain.
Also it makes me afeard,° certain.   *afraid*
But let us take counsel here as well as we can,
For your words would fear° a strong man.   *frighten*
        EVERYMAN   Why, ye said if I had need,
Ye would me never forsake, quick ne° dead,   *living nor*
Though it were to hell, truly.
        FELLOWSHIP   So I said, certainly,
But such pleasures° be set aside, the sooth° to say.   *jokes / truth*
And also, if we took such a journey,
260   When should we come again?
        EVERYMAN   Nay, never again till the day of doom.°   *Judgment*
        FELLOWSHIP   In faith, then will not I come there!
Who hath you these tidings brought?
        EVERYMAN   Indeed, Death was with me here.
        FELLOWSHIP   Now, by God that all hath bought,°   *redeemed*
If Death were the messenger,
For no man that is living today
I will not go that loath° journay—   *hateful*
Not for the father that begat me!
270   EVERYMAN   Ye promised otherwise, pardie.°   *by God*
        FELLOWSHIP   I wot well I said so, truly;
And yet if thou wilt eat, and drink, and make good cheer,
Or haunt to women the lusty company,°
I would not forsake you while the day is clear,
Trust me verily!
        EVERYMAN   Yea, thereto ye would be ready;
To go to mirth,° solace,° and play,   *gaiety / pleasure*
Your mind will sooner apply°   *attend*
Than to bear me company in my long journey.
280   FELLOWSHIP   Now, in good faith, I will not that way.
But and thou wilt murder, or any man kill,
In that I will help thee with a good will.
        EVERYMAN   O, that is a simple° advice indeed!   *stupid*
Gentle° fellow, help me in my necessity;   *dear*
We have loved long, and now I need;°   *am in need*
And now, gentle Fellowship, remember me.
        FELLOWSHIP   Whether ye have loved me or no,
By Saint John, I will not with thee go.
        EVERYMAN   Yet, I pray thee, take the labour, and do so much for me
290   To bring° me forward, for saint° charity,   *escort / holy*
And comfort me till I come without the town.
        FELLOWSHIP   Nay, and thou would give me a new gown,°

Promise . . . duty proverbial; cf. l. 821
haunt . . . company frequent the pleasant company of women

and . . . gown Even if you give me a new
gown. A man's salary often included a regular
payment in kind.

I will not a foot with thee go;
But, and thou had tarried, I would not have left thee so.
And, as now, God speed thee in thy journey,
For from thee I will depart as fast as I may.
    EVERYMAN   Whither away, Fellowship? Will you forsake me?
    FELLOWSHIP   Yea, by my fay,ᐧ to God I betakeᐧ thee.   *faith / commend*
    EVERYMAN   Farewell, good Fellowship! For thee my heart is sore;
300 Adieu for ever! I shall see thee no more.
    FELLOWSHIP   In faith, Everyman, farewell now at the end!
For you I will remember that parting is mourning.°

    [*Exit* FELLOWSHIP]

    EVERYMAN   Alack! shall we thus departᐧ indeed   *part*
(Ah, Lady, help!) without any more comfort?
Lo, Fellowship forsaketh me in my most need.
For help in this world whither shall I resort?
Fellowship herebefore with me would merry make,
And now little sorrow for me doth he take.
It is said, 'In prosperity men friends may find,
310 Which in adversity be full unkind.'°
Now whither for succour shall I flee,
Sithᐧ that Fellowship hath forsaken me?   *since*
To my kinsmen I will, truly,
Praying them to help me in my necessity;
I believe that they will do so,
For kind will creep where it may not go.°
I will go 'say,ᐧ for yonder I see them,   *assay, try*
Whereᐧ be ye now my friends and kinsmen.   *whether*

    [*Enter* KINDRED *and* COUSIN]

    KINDRED   Here be we now, at your commandment.
320 Cousin, I pray you show us your intent
In any wise, and not spare.°
    COUSIN   Yea, Everyman, and to us declare
If ye be disposed to go anywhither,ᐧ   *anywhere*
For, weet you well, we will live and die togither.
    KINDRED   In wealth and woe we will with you hold,ᐧ   *stay*
For over his kin a man may be bold.°
    EVERYMAN   Gramercy,ᐧ my friends and kinsmen kind.   *thank you*
Now shall I show you the grief of my mind.
I was commanded by a messenger
330 That is a high king's chief officer;
He bade me go a pilgrimage, to my pain,

---

parting . . . mourning proverbial
In . . . unkind again proverbial
kind . . . go Kinship will crawl where it cannot walk; i.e. relatives will always do what
they can. Cf. *The Second Shepherds' Play,* ll.
280–81.

In . . . spare in every way, and don't hold
back. The relatives are more ingratiating than
Fellowship.
over . . . bold a man may ask much of his
family

And I know well I shall never come again;
Also I must give a reckoning strait,°   *strict*
For I have a great enemy that hath me in wait,°
Which intendeth me for to hinder.
    KINDRED   What account is that which ye must render?
That would I know.
    EVERYMAN   Of all my works I must show
How I have lived, and my days spent;
340 Also of ill deeds that I have used°   *practiced*
In my time, sith life was me lent;
And of all virtues that I have refused.
Therefore I pray you go thither with me,
To help to make mine account, for saint charity.
    COUSIN   What, to go thither? Is that the matter?°   *what's doing*
Nay, Everyman, I had liefer fast bread and water°
All this five year and more.
    EVERYMAN   Alas, that ever I was bore!°   *born*
For now shall I never be merry
350 If that you forsake me.
    KINDRED   Ah, sir, what ye be a merry man!°
Take good heart to you, and make no moan.
But one thing I warn you, by Saint Anne,
As for me, ye shall go alone.
    EVERYMAN   My Cousin, will you not with me go?
    COUSIN   No, by our Lady! I have the cramp in my toe.
Trust not to me; for, so God me speed,°   *prosper*
I will deceive° you in your most need.   *fail*
    KINDRED   It availeth not us to 'tice.°
360 Ye shall have my maid with all my heart;
She loveth to go to feasts, there to be nice,°   *gay*
And to dance, and abroad to start;°
I will give her leave to help you in that journey,
If that you and she may agree.
    EVERYMAN   Now show me the very effect° of your mind.   *intention*
Will you go with me, or abide behind?
    KINDRED   Abide behind? Yea, that will I, and° I may!   *if*
Therefore farewell till another day.   [*Exit* KINDRED]
    EVERYMAN   How should I be merry or glad?
370 For fair promises men to me make,
But when I have most need, they me forsake.
I am deceived; that maketh me sad.
    COUSIN   Cousin Everyman, farewell now,
For verily I will not go with you;

I . . . **wait** I have a powerful enemy who is
lying in wait for me; i.e. the Devil, who watches
and tempts until the last moment, to see if he
can get a man's soul.
I . . . **water** I had rather fast on bread and
water

ye . . . man what a joker you are
It . . . 'tice There's no point in your trying to
entice us.
start gad about

Also of mine own life an unready reckoning
I have to account; therefore I make tarrying.
Now God keep thee, for now I go.   [*Exit* COUSIN]
    EVERYMAN   Ah, Jesus, is all come hereto?°   *to this*
Lo, fair words maketh fools fain;°
380   They promise, and nothing will do, certain.°   *certainly*
My kinsmen promised me faithfully
For to abide with me steadfastly,
And now fast away do they flee:
Even so Fellowship promised me.
What friend were best me of to provide?°
I lose my time here longer to abide.
Yet in my mind a thing there is:
All my life I have loved riches;
If that my Good° now help me might,   *possessions*
390   He would make my heart full light.
I will speak to him in this distress.
Where art thou, my Goods and riches?
    GOODS [*within*]   Who calleth me? Everyman? What, hast thou haste?
I lie here in corners, trussed and piled so high,
And in chests I am locked so fast,
Also sacked in bags. Thou mayst see with thine eye.
I cannot stir; in packs low I lie.
What would ye have? Lightly° me say.   *quickly*
    EVERYMAN   Come hither, Goods, in all the haste thou may.
400   For of counsel I must desire thee.°

    [*Enter* GOODS]

    GOODS   Sir, and° ye in the world have sorrow or adversity,   *if*
That can I help you to remedy shortly.
    EVERYMAN   It is another disease° that grieveth me;   *distress*
In° this world it is not, I tell thee so.   *of*
I am sent for, another way to go,
To give a strait count general°
Before the highest Jupiter° of all;
And all my life I have had joy and pleasure in thee;
Therefore I pray thee go with me,
410   For, peradventure, thou mayst before God Almighty
My reckoning help to clean and purify:
For it is said ever among,°
That money maketh all right that is wrong.
    GOODS   Nay, Everyman; I sing another song,
I follow no man in such voyages;
For, and I went with thee,

fair . . . fain fine words make fools glad
(proverbial)
What . . . provide What friend it would be
best to provide myself with?
For . . . thee For I must beg your advice.

count general general account, balance
highest Jupiter i.e. Almighty God
For . . . among for it is always said everywhere

Thou shouldst fare much the worse for me;
For because on me thou did set thy mind,
Thy reckoning I have made blotted and blind,°   *illegible*
420   That thine account thou cannot make truly;°   *correctly*
And that hast thou for the love of me.
     EVERYMAN   That would grieve me full sore,
When I should come to that fearful answer.°
Up, let us go thither together.
     GOODS   Nay, not so! I am too brittle, I may not endure;
I will follow no man one foot, be ye sure.
     EVERYMAN   Alas, I have thee loved, and had great pleasure
All my life-days in goods and treasure.
     GOODS   That is to thy damnation, without lesing!°   *lie*
430   For my love is contrary to the love everlasting.
But if thou had me loved moderately during,°   *meanwhile*
As° to the poor to give part of me,   *so as*
Then shouldst thou not in this dolour° be,   *distress*
Nor in this great sorrow and care.
     EVERYMAN   Lo, now was I deceived ere I was ware,°   *aware*
And all I may wite° misspending of time.   *blame*
     GOODS   What, weenest° thou that I am thine?   *suppose*
     EVERYMAN   I had weened so.
     GOODS   Nay, Everyman, I say no.
440   As for a while I was lent thee,
A season° thou hast had me in prosperity.   *time*
My condition° is man's soul to kill;   *nature*
If I save one, a thousand I do spill;°   *ruin*
Weenest thou that I will follow thee
From this world? Nay, verily.
     EVERYMAN   I had weened otherwise.
     GOODS   Therefore to thy soul Good is a thief;
For when thou art dead, this is my guise°—   *practice*
Another to deceive in the same wise
450   As I have done thee, and all to his soul's reprief.°   *harm*
     EVERYMAN   O false Good, cursed thou be!
Thou traitor to God, that hast deceived me
And caught me in thy snare.
     GOODS   Marry, thou brought thyself in care,°   *sorrow*
Whereof I am glad.
I must needs laugh, I cannot be sad.
     EVERYMAN   Ah, Good, thou hast had long my heartly° love;   *sincere*
I gave thee that which should be the Lord's above.°
But wilt thou not go with me indeed?
460   I pray thee truth to say.
     GOODS   No, so God me speed!
Therefore farewell, and have good day.   [*Exit* GOODS]

When . . . answer when I must come to that   **I gave . . . above** the definition of deadly sin
terrible account; i.e. when I am judged by God

EVERYMAN   O, to whom shall I make my moan
For to go with me in that heavy° journay?   *sad*
First Fellowship said he would with me gone;°   *go*
His words were very pleasant and gay,
But afterward he left me alone.
Then spake I to my kinsmen, all in despair,°
And also they gave me words fair,
470   They lacked no fair speaking,
But all forsook me in the ending.
Then went I to my Goods, that I loved best,
In hope to have comfort, but there had I least;
For my Goods sharply did me tell
That he bringeth many into hell.
Then of myself I was ashamed,
And so I am worthy to be blamed;
Thus may I well myself hate.
Of whom shall I now counsel take?
480   I think that I shall never speed°   *prosper*
Till that I go to my Good Deed.
But, alas, she is so weak
That she can neither go° nor speak.   *walk*
Yet will I venture on her now.
My Good Deeds,° where be you?

[GOOD DEEDS *speaks from the ground*]

GOOD DEEDS   Here I lie, cold in the ground.
Thy sins hath me sore bound,
That I cannot stere.°   *stir*
EVERYMAN   O Good Deeds! I stand in fear;
490   I must you pray of counsel,
For help now should come right well.°
GOOD DEEDS   Everyman, I have understanding
That ye be summoned account to make
Before Messias, of Jerusalem King;°
And you do by me,° that journey with you will I take.
EVERYMAN   Therefore I come to you my moan to make;
I pray you that ye will go with me.
GOOD DEEDS   I would full fain,° but I cannot stand, verily.   *gladly*
EVERYMAN   Why, is there anything on you fall?°   *fallen*
500   GOOD DEEDS   Yea, sir, I may thank you of all;
If ye had perfectly cheered° me,   *fully encouraged*
Your book of count full ready had be.
Look, the books of your works and deeds eke;°   *also*
Ah, see how they lie under the feet,

---

despair the most dangerous spiritual condition,
the sin against the Holy Ghost: lack of trust in
God's promised and infinite mercy
Good Deeds Good Deeds lies helpless; Everyman's virtuous actions are nullified by his sins.

help . . . well help now would be very wel-
come
Messias . . . King Christ
And . . . me if you do as I advise

To your soul's heaviness.˃   *sorrow*
    EVERYMAN   Our Lord Jesus help me!
For one letter here I cannot see.
    GOOD DEEDS   There is a blind reckoning in time of distress!°
    EVERYMAN   Good Deeds, I pray you, help me in this need,
510 Or else I am for ever damned indeed;
Therefore help me to make reckoning
Before the Redeemer of all thing,
That King is, and was, and ever shall.
    GOOD DEEDS   Everyman, I am sorry of your fall,
And fain would I help you, and˃ I were able.   *if*
    EVERYMAN   Good Deeds, your counsel I pray you give me.
    GOOD DEEDS   That shall I do verily;
Though that on my feet I may not go,
I have a sister that shall with you also,
520 Called Knowledge,° which shall with you abide,
To help you to make that dreadful reckoning.

      [*Enter* KNOWLEDGE]

    KNOWLEDGE   Everyman, I will go with thee, and be thy guide
In thy most need to go by thy side.
    EVERYMAN   In good condition I am now in every thing,
And am wholly content with this good thing;
Thanked be God my Creator.
    GOOD DEEDS   And when she hath brought thee there,
Where thou shalt heal thee of thy smart,˃   *pain*
Then go you with your reckoning and your Good Deeds together
530 For to make you joyful at heart
Before the blessed Trinity.
    EVERMAN   My Good Deeds, gramercy!
I am well content, certainly,
With your words sweet.
    KNOWLEDGE   Now go we together lovingly
To Confession,° that cleansing river.
    EVERYMAN   For joy I weep; I would we were there!
But, I pray you, give me cognition˃   *knowledge*
Where dwelleth that holy man, Confession.
540   KNOWLEDGE   In the house of salvation;°
We shall find him in that place,
That shall us comfort, by God's grace.

    [KNOWLEDGE *conducts* EVERYMAN *to* CONFESSION]

Lo, this is Confession. Kneel down and ask mercy,
For he is in good conceit˃ with God almighty.   *esteem*

There . . . distress There is an illegible account in the hour of need; i.e. the sinful man finds that he cannot see the accounts.
Knowledge acknowledgment of sin, the first step to contrition; the recognition that God is merciful as well as just

Confession i.e. the personification of auricular confession, Shrift (l. 552), second of the four parts of the sacrament of penance, the others being contrition, true sorrow for sin (l. 549), absolution (ll. 568 ff.), and satisfaction (l. 707)
house of salvation church

EVERYMAN [*Kneeling*]   O glorious fountain,° that all uncleanness
      doth clarify,›   *purify*
Wash from me the spots of vice unclean,
That on me no sin may be seen.
I come, with Knowledge, for my redemption,
Redempt with hearty and full contrition;°
550 For I am commanded a pilgrimage to take,
And great accounts before God to make.
Now, I pray you, Shrift,› mother of salvation.   *Confession*
Help my Good Deeds for my piteous exclamation.°
    CONFESSION   I know your sorrow° well, Everyman.
Because with Knowledge ye come to me,
I will you comfort as well as I can,
And a precious jewel I will give thee,
Called Penance, voider› of adversity;   *expeller*
Therewith shall your body chastised be,
560 With abstinence, and perseverance in God's service.
Here shall you receive that scourge° of me.
Which is penance strong› that ye must endure   *harsh*
To remember thy Saviour was scourged for thee
With sharp scourges, and suffered it patiently;
So must thou ere thou 'scape› that painful pilgrimage.°   *end*
Knowledge, keep› him in this voyage,   *look after*
And by that time Good Deeds will be with thee.
But in any wise be siker› of mercy,   *sure*
For your time draweth fast. And ye will saved be,
570 Ask God mercy, and He will grant, truly.
When with the scourge of penance man doth him bind,› *himself beat*
The oil of forgiveness° then shall he find.   [*Exit* CONFESSION]
    EVERYMAN   Thanked be God for his gracious work!
For now I will my penance begin;
This hath rejoiced and lighted my heart,°
Though the knots be painful and hard within.°
    KNOWLEDGE   Everyman, look your penance that ye fulfil,
What pain that ever it to you be;
And Knowledge shall give you counsel at will
580 How your account ye shall make clearly.

---

fountain See Zechariah 13:1.
Redempt . . . contrition redeemed with sincere
and complete contrition, distinguished from
attrition, insincere or incomplete sorrow for sin
for . . . exclamation in answer to my pathetic
cry
sorrow sorrow for sin, but the actual words of
absolution are not spoken: this is a stage performance
scourge Scourging or beating as satisfaction for
sin might be performed by oneself or by the
priest. It had become a more frequent form of
satisfaction in the 14th century and remained
common in the 15th and 16th.
So . . . pilgrimage Everyman has confessed

his sins, with sincere contrition, and received
absolution, so that God's mercy will save him
from eternal punishment. But he has not yet
made full satisfaction, i.e. suffered punishment
on earth (the scourging prescribed is only
partial satisfaction) or after death in the purifying but not eternal fire of Purgatory (l. 618).
Only then will he attain the true end of life's
pilgrimage, eternal bliss.
oil of forgiveness the holy oil of Extreme Unction, the sacrament administered to the dying
lighted my heart His heart is illumined by grace,
and he can bear the scourge.
Though . . . within though the knots of the
scourge be painful and hard to my soul within

[EVERYMAN *kneels*]

EVERYMAN   O eternal God,° O heavenly figure,
O way of righteousness, O goodly vision,
Which descended down in⸀ a Virgin pure   *into*
Because he would every man redeem,
Which Adam forfeited by his disobedience.
O blessed Godhead, elect and high Divine,⸀   *divinity*
Forgive me my grievous offence:
Here I cry thee mercy in this presence.°
O ghostly⸀ Treasure, O Ransomer and Redeemer,   *spiritual*
590   Of all the world Hope and Conduiter⸀   *guide*
Mirror of joy, Foundator of mercy,
Which enlumineth⸀ heaven and earth thereby,   *lights up*
Hear my clamorous complaint,⸀ though it late be.   *lament*
Receive my prayers, of thy benignity.
Though I be a sinner most abhominable,
Yet let my name be written in Moses' table.°
O Mary, pray to the Maker of all thing,
Me for to help at my ending;
And save me from the power of my enemy,°
600   For Death assaileth me strongly.
And, Lady, that I may by means of thy prayer°
Of your Son's glory to be partner,
By the means of his Passion I it crave;
I beseech you, help my soul to save.   [*He rises*]
Knowledge, give me the scourge of penance;
My flesh therewith shall give acquittance.°
I will now begin, if God give me grace.
    KNOWLEDGE   Everyman, God give you time and space.⸀   *opportunity*
Thus I bequeath you in⸀ the hands of our Saviour,   *to*
610   Now may you make your reckoning sure.
    EVERYMAN   In the name of the Holy Trinity,
My body sore⸀ punished shall be.   [*Scourges himself*]   *harshly*
Take this, body, for the sin of the flesh!
Also⸀ thou delightest to go gay and fresh,°   *because*
And in the way of damnation thou did me bring,
Therefore suffer now strokes of punishing.
Now of penance I will wade the water clear,
To save me from Purgatory,° that sharp fire.

O . . . God Everyman's exclamations resemble the prayers recommended to the dying.
presence in the presence of Knowledge and
Confession
Moses' table The two tables of the Law were
thought of by medieval theologians as prefiguring the sacraments of Baptism and Penance.
Everyman, now a penitent, asks to escape damnation by having his name inscribed on the table
of penance.
enemy the Devil

And . . . **prayer** He asks the Virgin for intercession: And Lady, I beg that, through your
prayer, I may be partaker of your Son's glory,
by His Passion.
acquittance satisfaction, requital
gay and fresh well clothed and scented
Purgatory Those dying in God's grace must be
purified in the fire of Purgatory from their
venial sins, and suffer punishment still due for
forgiven mortal sins, before admission to the
Beatific Vision.

[GOOD DEEDS *rises from the ground*]

GOOD DEEDS   I thank God, now I can walk and go,°
620 And am delivered of my sickness and woe.
Therefore with Everyman I will go, and not spare;
His good works I will help him to declare.
    KNOWLEDGE   Now, Everyman, be merry and glad!
Your Good Deeds cometh now, ye may⁾ not be sad.   *must*
Now is your Good Deeds whole and sound,
Going⁾ upright upon the ground.   *walking*
    EVERYMAN   My heart is light, and shall be evermore.
Now will I smite faster than I did before.
    GOOD DEEDS   Everyman, pilgrim, my special friend,
630 Blessed be thou without end.
For thee is preparate⁾ the eternal glory.   *prepared*
Ye have me made whole and sound,
Therefore I will bide by thee in every stound.⁾   *trouble*
    EVERYMAN   Welcome, my Good Deeds; now I hear thy voice,
I weep for very sweetness of love.
    KNOWLEDGE   Be no more sad, but ever rejoice;
God seeth thy living⁾ in his throne above.   *way of life*
Put on this garment° to thy behove⁾   *advantage*
Which is wet with your tears,
640 Or else before God you may it miss,
    When you to your journey's end come shall.
    EVERYMAN   Gentle Knowledge, what do ye it call?
    KNOWLEDGE   It is the garment of sorrow;
From pain it will you borrow;⁾   *redeem*
Contrition it is
That getteth forgiveness;
It pleaseth God passing⁾ well.   *exceedingly*
    GOOD DEEDS   Everyman, will you wear it for your heal?°

[EVERYMAN *puts on the garment of contrition*]

    EVERYMAN   Now blessed be Jesu, Mary's Son,
650 For now have I on true contrition.
And let us go now without tarrying;
Good Deeds, have we clear our reckoning?
    GOOD DEEDS   Yea, indeed I have it here.
    EVERYMAN   Then I trust we need not fear.
Now, friends, let us not part in twain.
    KNOWLEDGE   Nay, Everyman, that will we not, certain.
    GOOD DEEDS   Yet must thou lead with thee
Three persons of great might.

---

now . . . go Good Deeds has been powerless
up to now because, until mortal sins are confessed and absolved, good deeds have no merit.
garment the clothing of contrition; perhaps the
white sheet worn by public penitents. It would
either hide his gay clothes or cover his naked
body; and would suggest the shroud he will
shortly wear.
heal health, salvation

EVERYMAN   Who should they be?
660 GOOD DEEDS   Discretion and Strength they hight,°   *are called*
And thy Beauty may not abide behind.
KNOWLEDGE   Also ye must call to mind
Your Five Wits° as for your counsellors.
GOOD DEEDS   You must have them ready at all hours.
EVERYMAN   How shall I get them hither?
KNOWLEDGE   You must call them all together,
And they will hear you incontinent.°   *immediately*
EVERYMAN   My friends, come hither and be present;
Discretion, Strength, my Five Wits, and Beauty.

[*Enter* DISCRETION, STRENGTH, FIVE WITS, *and* BEAUTY]

670 BEAUTY   Here at your will we be all ready.
What will ye that we should do?
GOOD DEEDS   That ye would with Everyman go,
And help him in his pilgrimage.
Advise you,° will ye with him or not in that voyage?   *consider*
STRENGTH   We will bring him all thither,
To his help and comfort, ye may believe me.
DISCRETION   So will we go with him all together.
EVERYMAN   Almighty God loved° may thou be!   *praised*
I give thee laud° that I have hither brought   *praise*
680 Strength, Discretion, Beauty, and Five Wits. Lack I nought;
And my Good Deeds, with Knowledge clear,
All be in company at my will here.°
I desire no more to° my business.   *for*
STRENGTH   And I, Strength, will by you stand in distress,
Though thou would in battle fight on the ground.
FIVE WITS   And though it were through the world round,
We will not depart for sweet nor sour.°
BEAUTY   No more will° I, unto° death's hour,   *wish / until*
Whatsoever thereof befall.
690 DISCRETION   Everyman, advise you first of all;
Go with a good advisement and deliberation.
We all give you virtuous monition°   *powerful forewarning*
That all shall be well.
EVERYMAN   My friends, hearken what I will tell:
I pray God reward you in his heavenly sphere.
Now hearken, all that be here,
For I will make my testament°
Here before you all present:
In alms half my good I will give with my hands twain

Five Wits The five senses and the gifts of Nature,
along with Discretion, which allows him to use
them as a rational creature, are now mobilized.
All . . . here are all together here at my command
for . . . sour in happiness nor adversity

testament disposal of spiritual and earthly possessions. A will always began with the disposal
of the soul to God and made provision for charitable gifts as well as apportioning property to
heirs.

700 In the way of charity, with good intent,
And the other half stillˣ shall remain   *which still*
In queath° to be returned thereˣ it ought to be.   *where*
This I do in despiteˣ of the fiend of hell,   *contempt*
To go quit out of his peril
Ever after and this day.°
      KNOWLEDGE Everyman, hearken what I say;
Go to Priesthood,° I you advise,
And receive of him in any wiseˣ   *without fail*
The holy sacrament and ointment together;
710 Then shortly see ye turn again hither;
We will all abide you here.
      FIVE WITS Yea, Everyman, hieˣ you that ye ready were.   *hasten*
There is no emperor, king, duke, nor baron,
That of God hath commission°
As hath the least priest in the world being;ˣ   *alive*
For of the blessed sacraments pure and benign
He beareth the keys, and thereof hath the cureˣ   *charge*
For man's redemption—it is ever sure—
Which God for our soul's medicine
720 Gave us out of his heart with great pineˣ   *suffering*
Here in this transitory life, for thee and me.
The blessed sacraments seven° there be:
Baptism, confirmation, with priesthood good,
And the sacrament of God's precious flesh and blood,
Marriage, the holy extreme unction, and penance.
These seven be good to have in remembrance,
Graciousˣ sacraments of high divinity.   *full of grace*
      EVERYMAN Fainˣ would I receive that Holy Bodyˣ   *gladly / Eucharist*
And meekly to my ghostlyˣ father I will go.   *spiritual*
730   FIVE WITS Everyman, that is the best that ye can do.
God will you to salvation bring,
For priesthood exceedeth all other thing;
To us Holy Scripture they do teach,
And convertethˣ man from sin, heaven to reach;   *turn away*
God hath to them more power given,
Than to any angel that is in heaven.
With five words° he may consecrate
God's body in flesh and blood to make,
And handleth his Maker between his hands.

In queath as a bequest; strictly, the restitution of improperly acquired property
To . . . day to pass free out of his power to harm, today and forever
Priesthood i.e. someone who has received the sacrament of Holy Orders; a priest who alone can give the sinner Everyman, now in a state of grace, Communion and Extreme Unction (l. 709)
There . . . commission All civil authority was derived from God; but a priest's authority, being spiritual, not temporal, was held to be superior.
blessed . . . seven Catholic doctrine counts seven sacraments: Baptism, Confirmation, Eucharist, Penance, Extreme Unction (now called the Anointing of the Sick), Matrimony, and Holy Orders. In the text Holy Orders is placed third, to stress the importance of the priesthood.
five words the consecration of the host, as used by the priest at Mass: "*Corpus Domini nostri Jesu Christi*" (the body of our Lord Jesus Christ)

740   The priest bindeth and unbindeth all bands,°
        Both in earth and in heaven.
        Thou ministers⁾ all the sacraments seven;   *administer*
        Though we kissed thy feet, thou were worthy;°
        Thou art surgeon that cureth sin deadly:
        No remedy we find under God
        But all only priesthood.°
        Everyman, God gave priests that dignity,
        And setteth them in his stead among us to be;
        Thus be they above angels in degree.⁾   *rank*

        [*Exit* EVERYMAN]

750   KNOWLEDGE   If priests be good,° it is so, surely.
        But when Jesus hanged on the cross with great smart,⁾   *suffering*
        There he gave out of his blessèd heart
        The same sacrament in great torment:
        He sold them not to us, that Lord omnipotent.
        Therefore Saint Peter the Apostle doth say°
        That Jesu's curse hath all they
        Which God their Saviour do buy or sell,
        Or they for any, money do take or tell.°
        Sinful priests giveth the sinners example bad;
760   Their children sitteth by other men's fires,° I have heard;
        And some haunteth women's company
        With unclean life, as⁾ lusts of lechery.   *such as*
        These be with sin made blind.
            FIVE WITS   I trust to God no such may we find.
        Therefore let us priesthood honour,
        And follow their doctrine for our souls' succour.
        We be their sheep, and they shepherds be
        By whom we all be kept in surety.
        Peace,⁾ for yonder I see Everyman come,   *quiet*
770   Which hath made true satisfaction.
            GOOD DEEDS   Methink it is he indeed.

        [*Re-enter* EVERYMAN]

        EVERYMAN   Now Jesu be your alder speed.°
        I have received the sacrament for my redemption,
        And then mine extreme unction:

bindeth . . . bands the power of binding and loosing, Matthew 16:19, 18:18; the priest, heir of the Apostles, can retain or remit sins
Though . . . worthy i.e. you would be worthy to have your feet kissed
But . . . priesthood except priesthood alone
If . . . good then they are above the angels. The attack on sinful priests is frequent in English literature from at least Chaucer onwards. This one may draw its doctrine of good priests' being above the angels from Thomas à Kempis, the presumed author of the 15th-century de-

votional work *The Imitation of Christ.*
Peter . . . say Acts 8:18–20. The reference is to the sin of simony, the buying and selling of spiritual things, so named from Simon Magus, who was cursed by St. Peter for wishing to buy the gifts of the Holy Ghost.
Or . . . tell or who, for any sacrament, accept or count out money
Their . . . fires i.e. they farm out their bastards upon their parishioners; or, they have committed adultery with their parishioners' wives
Jesu . . . speed Jesus prosper you all

Blessed be all they that counselled me to take it!
And now, friends, let us go without longer respite;
I thank God that ye have tarried so long.
Now set each of you on this rood° your hand,
And shortly⌐ follow me.   *quickly*
780 I go before, there⌐ I would be;   *where*
God be our guide.
    STRENGTH   Everyman, we will not from you go,
Till ye have done this voyage long.
    DISCRETION   I, Discretion, will bide by you also.
    KNOWLEDGE   And though this pilgrimage be never so strong,⌐   *hard*
I will never part you fro.⌐   *from*
    STRENGTH   Everyman, I will be as sure by thee
As ever I did by Judas Maccabee.°

    [*They go together to the grave*]

    EVERYMAN   Alas! I am so faint I may not stand,
My limbs under me doth fold.
790 Friends, let us not turn again to this land,
Not for all the world's gold;
For into this cave must I creep,
And turn⌐ to earth, and there to sleep.   *return*
    BEAUTY   What, into this grave? Alas!°
    EVERYMAN   Yea, there shall you consume,⌐ more and less.⌐   *decay / utterly*
    BEAUTY   And what, should I smother here?
    EVERYMAN   Yea, by my faith, and never more appear.
In this world live no more we shall,
But in heaven before the highest Lord of all.
800   BEAUTY   I cross out all this;° adieu, by Saint John!
I take my tap in my lap° and am gone.
    EVERYMAN   What, Beauty, whither will ye?
    BEAUTY   Peace! I am deaf. I look not behind me,
Not and⌐ thou would give me all the gold in thy chest.   [*Exit* BEAUTY]   *if*
    EVERYMAN   Alas, whereto may I trust?
Beauty goeth fast away from me;
She promised with me to live and die.
    STRENGTH   Everyman, I will thee also forsake and deny.
Thy game liketh⌐ me not at all.   *pleases*
810   EVERYMAN   Why then, ye will forsake me all!
Sweet Strength, tarry a little space!⌐   *while*
    STRENGTH   Nay, sir, by the rood of grace!
I will hie me from thee fast,
Though thou weep till thy heart to-brast.⌐   *break in pieces*

---

rood cross, i.e. as placed in the hands of the
dying
Judas Maccabee Judas Maccabaeus, one of the
Nine Worthies (see Glossary) and leader of
the Jews in their revolt against Syria; see I
Maccabees 3:4: "In his acts he was like a lion
and like a lion's whelp roaring for his prey."
Alas The gifts of Nature, reason (Discretion),

and the senses desert him now, in that order,
and he goes alone to the grave, except for Good
Works.
I . . . this I cancel all this
tap . . . lap Tape, i.e. I tuck my skirts up and
secure them; or tap, the tow on a distaff; or one
may read "cap." The reading is difficult, the
sense plain: "I'm off!"

EVERYMAN   Ye would ever bide by me, ye said.

STRENGTH   Yea,° I have you far enough conveyed.°   *true / escorted*
Ye be old enough, I understand,
Your pilgrimage to take on° hand.   *in*
I repent me that I hither came.

820   EVERYMAN   Strength, you to displease I am to blame;°
Yet promise is debt, this ye well wot.°   *know*

STRENGTH   In faith, I care not.
Thou art but a fool to complain;
You spend your speech and waste your brain.
Go, thrust thee into the ground.   [*Exit* STRENGTH]

EVERYMAN   I had weened° surer I should you have found.   *expected*
He that trusteth in his Strength
She him deceiveth at the length.
Both Strength and Beauty forsaketh me;
830   Yet they promised me fair and lovingly.

DISCRETION   Everyman, I will after Strength be gone;
As for me, I will leave you alone.

EVERYMAN   Why, Discretion, will ye forsake me?

DISCRETION   Yea, in faith, I will go from thee,
For when Strength goeth before
I follow after evermore.

EVERYMAN   Yet, I pray thee, for the love of the Trinity,
Look in my grave once piteously.

DISCRETION   Nay, so nigh will I not come.
840   Farewell, every one!   [*Exit* DISCRETION]

EVERYMAN   O all thing faileth, save God alone—
Beauty, Strength, and Discretion;
For when Death bloweth his blast,
They all run from me full fast.

FIVE WITS   Everyman, my leave now of thee I take;
I will follow the other, for here I thee forsake.

EVERYMAN   Alas, then may I wail and weep,
For I took you for my best friend.

FIVE WITS   I will no longer thee keep;°   *guard*
850   Now farewell, and there an end.   [*Exit* FIVE WITS]

EVERYMAN   O Jesu, help! All hath forsaken me!

GOOD DEEDS   Nay, Everyman; I will bide with thee,
I will not forsake thee indeed;
Thou shalt find me a good friend at need.

EVERYMAN   Gramercy, Good Deeds! Now may I true friends see.
They have forsaken me, every one;
I loved them better than my Good Deeds alone.
Knowledge, will ye forsake me also?

KNOWLEDGE   Yea, Everyman, when ye to Death shall go;
860   But not yet, for no manner of danger.

Strength . . . blame Strength, I am to blame
for displeasing you.

EVERYMAN   Gramercy, Knowledge, with all my heart.

KNOWLEDGE   Nay, yet I will not from hence depart

Till I see where ye shall become.°

EVERYMAN   Methink, alas, that I must be gone

To make my reckoning and my debts pay,

For I see my time is nigh spent away.

Take example, all ye that this do hear or see,

How they that I loved best do forsake me,

Except my Good Deeds that bideth truly.

870   GOOD DEEDS   All earthly things is but vanity:°

Beauty, Strength, and Discretion do man forsake,

Foolish friends and kinsmen, that fair spake—

All fleeth save Good Deeds, and that am I.

EVERYMAN   Have mercy on me, God most mighty;

And stand by me, thou Mother and Maid, holy Mary.

GOOD DEEDS   Fear not: I will speak for thee.

EVERYMAN   Here I cry God mercy.

GOOD DEEDS   Short our end, and minish our pain.°

Let us go and never come again.

880   EVERYMAN   Into thy hands, Lord, my soul I commend.

Receive it, Lord, that it be not lost.

As thou me boughtest, so me defend,

And save me from the fiend's boast,

That I may appear with that blessed host

That shall be saved at the day of doom.°

In manus tuas—of mights most

For ever—*commendo spiritum meum.*°

[EVERYMAN *and* GOOD DEEDS *descend into the grave*]

KNOWLEDGE   Now hath he suffered that we all shall endure;

The Good Deeds shall make all sure.

890   Now hath he made ending.

Methinketh that I hear angels sing,

And make great joy and melody

Where Everyman's soul received shall be.

ANGEL [*within*]   Come, excellent elect° spouse to Jesu!

Hereabove thou shalt go

Because of thy singular virtue.

Now the soul is taken the body fro,°   *from*

Thy reckoning is crystal clear.

Now shalt thou into the heavenly sphere,°

---

where . . . become what shall become of you
All . . . vanity Ecclesiastes 12:8
Short . . . pain Shorten our time of dying and
diminish our pain.
day of doom General Judgment. All men come
twice to judgment, according to Catholic doctrine, once at death and once on Doomsday, at
the end of the world (Fig. 50).
In manus . . . meum "Into thy hands, most

mighty and everlasting One, I commend my
spirit"; the words, spoken by Christ just before
his death (Luke 23:46), are recommended for
repetition by the dying in *Ars Moriendi* (The
Art of Dying Well) (Fig. 52).
elect chosen; the soul as the bride of Christ is
a common late-medieval image
heavenly sphere the highest of all the spheres,
the changeless Empyrean

900   Unto the which all ye shall come
      That liveth well before the day of doom.

      [*Exit* KNOWLEDGE. *Enter* DOCTOR.°]

      DOCTOR   This memorial° men may have in mind;   *reminder*
      Ye hearers, take it of worth,° old and young,
      And forsake Pride, for he deceiveth you in the end,
      And remember Beauty, Five Wits, Strength, and Discretion,
      They all at the last do Everyman forsake,
      Save his Good Deeds there doth he take.
      But beware, for and° they be small   *if*
      Before God, he hath no help at all.
910   None excuse may be there for Everyman.
      Alas, how shall he do then?
      For, after death, amends may no man make,
      For then mercy and pity doth him forsake.
      If his reckoning be not clear when he doth come,
      God will say, *Ite, maledicti, in ignem aeternum.*°
      And he that hath his account whole and sound,
      High in heaven he shall be crowned;
      Unto which place God bring us all thither,
      That we may live body and soul together.
920   Thereto help the Trinity!
      Amen, say ye, for saint charity.

          THUS ENDETH THIS MORAL PLAY OF EVERYMAN.
      c. 1485   1528–29

MIDDLE ENGLISH LYRICS

Anyone coming to Middle English lyric poetry with Ruskin's definition in his mind
("lyric poetry is the expression by the poet of his own feelings") will be disconcerted,
for neither in the shorter religious verse which goes by that name, nor in the love
poetry and other secular verse, is there any indication of an emotion which is other
than widely felt and general. The imagery is not individual, but conventional; and the
themes are conventional also. The poems have little metrical subtlety or range and
many of them have little music of their own, though the secular lyrics were set to
music very often, and the religious occasionally. For both types, musical settings were
more common in the fifteenth century than earlier, while some early lyrics were set
in the sixteenth century. One that we know was given music early is "Summer Is
Ycumen In," perhaps the work of a monk of Reading Abbey about 1240, though the
tune we have for it may be as late as 1310. In the manuscript, an alternative set of
pious words is provided, in Latin—which may indicate that the church was not happy
with the prevalence of secular song among its clergy. We know that a bishop of

---

Doctor A learned theologian provides the Epilogue, in a short sermon, pointing the moral.
take . . . worth take heed
Ite . . . aeternum "Depart, ye cursèd, into everlasting fire" (Matthew 25:41). Everyman has had his judgment at death, but this quotation emphasizes his function as Mankind by invoking the General Judgment.

Ossory, in the fourteenth century, collected about sixty Latin texts in the *Red Book of Ossory* to go with popular airs of the day—taking the Devil's best tunes from him. Among the secular airs so used was that of "The Maid of the Moor."

Many of the lyrics that we have are translations from French or Latin. Almost all are anonymous. If we except the lyric poems on French models of Chaucer and his followers, we can find few short poems of the thirteenth, fourteenth, and fifteenth centuries to which we can put an author's name.

They are also extremely difficult to date accurately. We can sometimes say that, in the form in which we have them, they are "early" or "late," but this is not very definite and we cannot tell how they looked and sounded in their original form. Often an early poem has been re-worked by a later poet or altered, perhaps inadvertently, by a later copyist.

The poems given here aim to provide a sample of variety, but by no means exhaust it. Of the secular lyrics, there are imitations of the French *reverdie* or spring song, and versions of the love complaint which are so simple and direct that they seem to come from another world than Chaucer's poems in the same genre. Their very lack of sophistication is the quality that appeals to us today. The two riddling poems are examples of a popular genre, which goes back to Anglo-Saxon and Latin poetry of the early Middle Ages, and here uses sexual puns and symbolism. "The Agincourt Carol" is a kind of parody of a solemn, religious thanksgiving, or of a sacred carol celebrating the victory of Christ's birth, the refrain being part of the Mass and associated especially with Christmas. The drinking song "Bring Us in Good Ale" is a hearty form that has something in common with Latin drinking poetry of the twelfth century. Precise relations are much more difficult to establish.

These poems are in the main a bare announcement of experience: they do not dwell on it or explore its nature. They are simple, but not sensuous and passionate, they do not individualize. Above all they do not seek for conceit or surprise and originality, and they have little self-regard. But they somehow convey the impression of freshness in the renewal of spring, or new love; or of gaiety and pleasure.

The religious lyrics, likewise, do not seek to startle with originality of emotion or description, or to particularize the character of the feelings they deal with. With some exceptions, they use the same genres and verse forms as the secular poetry of their day. (Until the fifteenth century the *balade* remained almost entirely a secular form in England, whereas it was used for religious subjects in France; the complaint, or *planctus*, originally sacred, was used for both sacred and secular lament.) Almost all the English religious lyrics, with the fifteenth century providing more exceptions than earlier times, are meditations, or didactic pieces based on meditations. Their themes are death and the last things, Christ's passion, centered on the figure of the crucified Savior, divine love, divine mercy, the Virgin and her joys and sorrows. Beside these things, the question of who wrote the poems is irrelevant: it is the common religious experience that counts to the medieval author and his audience. The medieval author in this instance seems very often to have been a friar, using the religious poem as a means of bringing home the central Christian truths. Such an author frequently uses conventions that are not immediately apparent to us. Chief among these is typology (see Glossary)—to which the mystery plays owe so much. The simile in "I Sing of a Maiden," for example, which likens Christ entering the womb of Mary to "dew in Aprill / That falleth on the grass," reads as charmingly naïve. One's first reaction would be that dew as a symbol for grace is striking and might well be ancient—which is correct. But the image has a more precise reference, being an adaptation of the typological interpretation of Gideon's fleece (Judges 6:37-40). For a sign that he would save Israel, God impregnated with dew the fleece that Gideon had laid out, and then, to confirm his promise, kept the fleece dry while the dew fell on the ground. So now, for a sign that he will save mankind, God impregnates the Virgin. Similarly, the gay little carol "Adam Lay Ybounden" is a statement of the doctrine of the fortunate fall: we must be grateful to Adam, for he has made it necessary for God to show us what true womanhood is, in the Virgin, mother of Christ.

The carols are a slightly different case, in that they all seem to have been composed for singing, rather than as meditations. They are more public celebrations than private and intimate poems, in a relatively simple but highly rhythmical form, often in quatrains, with a chorus. Like ballads, they give the sense of being compendious, of compressing much narrative into little space. They are associated with Christmas—cf. "The Cherry-tree Carol" in Popular Ballads below. The two last carols given here, however, are untypical in that neither is concerned with joy and with Christmas, one being cast in the form of a *chanson d'aventure*, a form of love poetry in which the poem is represented as overheard conversation. It has the macaronic refrain used by Dunbar in his "Lament for the Makers," taken from the Office of the Dead, and it is rather a hybrid, combining the love poem's form with sacred content, and also having something of the nature of a meditation on death (again like Dunbar's poem)—a kind of *ubi sunt* motif, lamenting the passing of all things earthly: Where are they now? The "Corpus Christi Carol" is one of those poems that appeals as a poem, however uncertain one is about its precise meaning and application. Clearly it has reference to the Eucharist, the body of Christ, the sacrament of the altar which is the remembrance of the Sacrifice. Its other resonances just as clearly have relations with the symbolism of legends of the Grail, but the poem remains mysterious.

The basis of most of the texts—and many of the titles—of the poems in this section is Celia and Kenneth Sisam (eds.), *The Oxford Book of Medieval English Verse.*

Spring

Lenten is come with love to towne,°
With blosmen˃ and with briddės˃ rowne,˃   *blossom / birds' voices*
    That al this blissė bringeth:
Dayėsèyės˃ in the dales,   *daisies*
Notės swete of nightėgales—
    Ech fowl˃ song singeth.   *bird*
The threstelcok him threteth o,°
Away is herė˃ winter wo,˃   *their / sorrow*
    When wodėrovė˃ springeth.   *woodruff*
10 Thes fowlės singeth ferly fele,˃   *wonderfully many*

Lenten . . . towne Lent, i.e. Spring, has come joyously to the dwellings of men, i.e. to the world.   **The threstelcok . . . o** the cock-thrush trills (or: chides) continually

And wliteth on here winné wele,°
 That al the wodé ringeth.   *forest*

The rosé raileth hiré rode,   *displays / redness*
The levés on the lighté wode   *bright wood*
 Waxen al with wille.   *grow / joyously*
The mooné mandeth hiré blee,°
The lilie is lofsom to see,   *beautiful*
 The fenil and the fille.   *fennel / thyme*
Wowés thesé wildé drakés;   *woo*
20 Milés murgeth heré makés,°
As strem that striketh stille.°
Mody meneth, so doth mo—
Ich'ot ich am one of tho
 For love that likés ille.°

The mooné mandeth hiré light;
So doth the seemly sunné bright,   *beautiful*
 When briddés singeth breme.   *birds / gloriously*
Dewés donketh the downes;   *moisten*
Deerés with here derné rownes,
30 Domés for to deme;°
Wormés woweth under cloude;   *earth*
Wimmen waxeth wonder proude—   *excited*
 So wel it wil hem seme.°
If me shal wanté wille of on,
This winné wele I wil forgon,
 And wight in wode be fleme.°
 c. 1330

Now Springs the Spray

Now springés the spray,°
 All for love ich am so seek   *sick*
That slepen I ne may.   *sleep / can*

As I me rode this endré day
 O my playinge,°

And . . . wele perhaps: and whistle of their wealth in joys
mandeth . . . blee casts her radiance
murgeth . . . makes gladden their mates; the meaning of "Miles" is unknown
strem . . . stille stream that flows softly
Mody . . . ille (ll. 22–24) The passionate man makes moan—and so do others. I know I am one of those that love has made unhappy (ill-pleased). *Mody* is Old English *mōdig:* proud, angry.
Deeres . . . deme (ll. 29–30) animals with their silent (secret) voices through which they speak to one another (literally, make statements)

So . . . seme It will seem to them so good.
If . . . fleme If I must go without my will of (i.e. not sleep with) one of them, I want to forego this joyous wealth (of spring) and at once become an outlaw (a creature exiled in the woods).
Now . . . spray Now that the twig is in leaf. This poem is an adaptation of a French *chanson d'aventure*, though the English version does not let the teller win the maiden, as the French does.
As . . . playinge as I was riding the other day, for my diversion

Seigh⁀ ich where a litel may⁀   *saw / maid*
    Bigan to singe:
    'The clot him clinge!
    Wai is him i love-longinge
10   Shal libben ay!'°
      Now springės, *etc.*

Soon ich herde that mirie note
    Thider I drough;
I fonde hire in an erber swote°
    Under a bough,
    With joy enough.⁀   *much*
      Soon⁀ I asked: 'Thou mirie⁀ may,   *at once / happy*
      Why singest thou ay?'⁀   *all the time*
      Now springės, *etc.*

20   Then answėrde that maiden swote⁀   *sweet*
    Mid⁀ wordės few: *with*
'My lemmàn me haves bihote
    Of lovė trewe:°
    He chaunges anew.
    If I may, it shal him rew,°
    By this day!'
      Now springės, *etc.*
      c. 1300

Sumer Is Ycumen In°

Sing, cuccu, nu! Sing, cuccu!
Sing, cuccu! Sing, cuccu, nu!
Sumer is ycumen⁀ in,   *has come*
    Ludė⁀ sing, cuccu!   *loudly*
Groweth seed and bloweth med⁀   *blossoms meadow*
And springth the wodė nu.⁀   *wood now*

    Sing, cuccu!
Awė⁀ bleeteth after lamb,   *ewe*
    Lowth after calvė cu,⁀   *calf cow*
10   Bulloc sterteth,⁀ buckė verteth.°   *leaps*
    Meriė sing, cuccu!
    Cuccu, cuccu,

The clot . . . ay (ll. 8–10) May the clod (earth, grave) waste him away! Wretched is he who, in lovesickness, must live forever.
Soon . . . swote As soon as I heard that charming song, I went there; I found her in a delightful arbor
My . . . trewe My lover has vowed me his true love.
If . . . rew If I can (manage it), he shall be sorry.

Sumer . . . In A straightforward song of welcome to the new season, a *reverdie* or spring song, without a trace of moralization or of love-longing, it is in the form of a *rota* or round, in which the voices repeat one another in succession, pausing and beginning in turn.
verteth either "jumps, twists," from Latin *vertere*, to turn, or "breaks wind, farts"; probably the former

Wel singès thu,^{>} cuccu;   *thou*
Ne swink^{>} thu never nu!   *don't stop*
c. 1240

Alison

Betwenė^{>} March and Avėril,   *during*
When spray^{>} biginneth to springe,^{>}   *twig / shoot*
The litel fowl^{>} hath hirė wil^{>}   *bird / takes pleasure*
   On hirė lud^{>} to singe.   *in her language*
Ich libbe^{>} in love-longinge   *I live*
For semlokest^{>} of allė thinge;^{>}   *loveliest / creatures*
Heo may^{>} me blissė bringe—   *she can*
   Ich am in hire bandòun.^{>}   *power*
      An hendy hap ich habbe yhent;°
      Ich'ot^{>} from hevene it is me sent;   *I know*
      From allė^{>} wimmen my love is lent,^{>}   *all other / departed*
      And light^{>} on Alysoun.   *fallen*

On hew hire her is fair ynough,°
   Hire browė^{>} browne, hire eyė blake;^{>}   *eyebrows / dark*
With lofsom chere heo on me lough,°
   With middel smal and wel ymake.°
Bute^{>} heo me willė to hire take   *unless*
For to been hire owėn make,^{>}   *mate*
   Longe to liven ich'ille^{>} forsake,   *I will*
      And feyė^{>} fallen adown.   *doomed to die*
      An hendy hap, *etc.*

Nightės when I wende and wake—
   Forthy myn wongės waxeth won:°
Levedy,^{>} al for thinė sake   *lady*
   Longing is ylent me on.^{>}   *come on me*
In world n'is^{>} non so witer mon^{>}   *is not / wise man*
   That al hire bounté tellė con:°
Hire swire^{>} is whiter than the swan,   *neck*
   And fairest may^{>} in town.   *maid*
      An hendy hap, *etc.*

Ich am for wowing al forwake,°
   Wery so water in wore,
Lest any revė me my make
   Ich habbe yyernéd yore.

10
20
30

An . . . yhent a happy lot I have received
On . . . ynough in color her hair is entirely
beautiful
With . . . lough with lovable looks she smiled
on me
With . . . ymake with a slender and well-made
waist

Nightes . . . won at nights I toss and am restless, so that my cheeks turn pale
That . . . con that he knows enough to describe all her worth
Ich . . . forwake through my wooing I am worn
out from lying awake

Betere is tholién whilé sore
Than mournen evermore.°
Gainest under gore,°
   Herkné to my roun.ˀ   *words*
     An hendy hap, *etc.*
   c. 1330

Separated Lovers

My lefeˀ is farenˀ in londe;°   *dear / gone*
   Allas! why is she so?
And I am so sore in bondeˀ   *cruelly confined*
   I may not come her to.
She hath my hert in hold°
   Wherever she ride or go,°
With trew love a thousandfold.

14th century

Western Wind

Westron wind,° when will thou blow?
   The small° rain down canˀ rain: *does*
Christ, if my love were in my arms
   And I in my bed again!

early 16th century

He Is Far

Were it undo that is ydo,ˀ   *done*
I wold be war.°

I loved a childˀ of this contree,   *young man*
And so I wendeˀ he had do me;   *thought*
Now myself the sootheˀ I see,   *truth*
   That he is far.

He saide to me he wolde be trewe
And chaunge me for no other newe;ˀ   *new love*
Now I sikeˀ and am pale of hewe,ˀ   *sigh / colour*
10   For he is far.

Wery . . . evermore (ll. 32–36) As tired as
water in a (?) turbulent pool. I have been long
anxious lest anyone take my girl (mate) away
from me. It is better to endure pain for a time
than to mourn forever.
Gainest . . . gore most beautiful beneath clothing; i.e. alive
in londe up-country, away. This is presumably
the song sung by Pertelote and Chauntecleer in

Chaucer's Nun's Priest's Tale, l. 113; see above.
She . . . hold she holds my heart captive
wherever she is
ride or go literally, ride or walk, but a formula,
not to be translated at the full value of the
words
Westron wind Zephyrus, the spring wind
small thin, biting
I . . . war I would be (more) careful

He saide his sawes> he wold fulfille;   *promises*
Therfore I let him have al his wille.
Now I sike and mournė stille,°
   For he is far.

14th century

I Have a Young Sister°

I have a yong suster>   *sister*
   Far beyonden see,>   *over the sea*
Many be the drouries>   *gifts*
   That she sentė me.

She sentė me the cherrye
   Withouten any stone;
And so she did the dove
   Withouten any bone.

She sentė me the brere>   *briar*
10   Withouten any rind;>   *bark*
She bad me love my lemman>   *lover*
   Withoutė longing.°

How shuld any cherrye
   Be withoutė stone?
And how shuld any dove
   Be withoutė bone?

How shuld any brere
   Been withoutė rind?
How shuld I love myn lemman
20   Withoutė longing?

When the cherrye was a flowr
   Then had it no stone.
When the dovė was an ey>   *egg*
   Then had it no bone.

When the brerė was onbred>   *unbred*
   Then had it no rind.
When the maiden hath that> she loveth   *what*
   She is without longing.

15th century

The Maid of the Moor°

Maiden in the mor lay,⁾   *lived*
  In the mor lay,
Sevenightė fulle,⁾   *a week fully*
Sevenightė fulle,
Maiden in the mor lay,
  In the mor lay,
Sevenightė fulle and a day.

Wellᵖ was hirė mete;⁾   *good / food*
  What was hirė mete?
The primėroleᵖ and the——   *primrose*
The primėrole and the——
Well was hirė mete;
  What was hirė mete?
The primėrole and the violete.

Well was hirė dring;⁾   *drink*
  What was hirė dring?
The cheldėᵖ water of the——   *cold*
The cheldė water of the——
Well was hirė dring;
  What was hirė dring?
The cheldė water of the wellė-spring.⁾   *spring*

Well was hirė bowr;⁾   *chamber*
  What was hirė bowr?
The redė rose and the——
The redė rose and the——
Well was hirė bowr;
  What was hirė bowr?
The redė rose and the lilie-flowr.

14th century

The Maid . . . Moor Until quite recently, this little poem existed peacefully as a secular piece of popular origin and obscure meaning, riddling perhaps, but artless, of wide and immediate appeal. Then it was suggested that, beneath its secular surface, there lay a spiritual, allegorical meaning. The moor, for example, might symbolize the waste world before the coming of Christ, so that "welle-spring" could be the fountain of God's grace, and the maiden the Virgin Mary. The articulation of the poem, read in this sense, is far from perfect—and we have no evidence that it was ever so read, though a sacred interpretation or use of it, in whole or in part, might well have occurred to contemporary readers of a pious turn of mind or a religious profession. (Cf. the interpretation of the tale from the *Gesta Romanorum* following Chaucer's Wife of Bath's Tale above.) Those who wished to retain the secular interpretation pointed out that, in the *Red Book of Ossory*, pious Latin words had been provided to replace—as it seemed—the English, something that would hardly have been thought worthwhile if the poem had been regarded as religious in the first place. A new counter to this argument has now been provided. It seems as though what the bishop of Ossory was doing was not replacing secular words, but merely using secular tunes—among them that to which "The Maid of the Moor" was rendered—for sacred purposes, just as, at the end of the last century, the tune of "Clementine" was used for solemn songs. A case has now been made for explicating this lyric in terms of the medieval legend of the penitence of St. Mary Magdalene in the wilderness (moor) —though the Magdalene's maiden status is more than questionable. Those who prefer a secular interpretation have the tone of the poem in their favor: few, if any, short religious poems read like this one.

The Agincourt Carol°

Deo gracias, Anglia,
Redde pro victoria.°

Our King went forth to Normandy
With grace and might of chivalry;°
Ther⁾ God for him wrought mervelusly;⁾   *where / wonderfully*
Wherfore England may call and cry
    'Deo gracias.'

He sette a sege,⁾ the sooth⁾ for to say,   *laid siege / truth*
To Harfleur town with royal aray;
10 That town he won and made afray⁾   *attack*
That Fraunce shal rewe⁾ til Domèsday:°   *regret*
    Deo gracias.

Then went our King with alle his host
Thorough Fraunce, for all the Frenshè boast;
He spared no drede of lest ne most°
Til he come⁾ to Agincourt coast:⁾   *came / district*
    Deo gracias.

Then, forsooth, that knight comely
In Agincourt feeld he fought manly.⁾   *manfully*
20 Thorough grace of God most mighty
He had both the feeld and the victory:
    Deo gracias.

There dukes and erles,⁾ lord and baròne   *earls*
Were take and slain, and that wel sone;⁾   *very quickly*
And sume were ledde into Lundòne
With joy and merth and gret renone:⁾   *pomp*
    Deo gracias.

Now gracious God He save our King,
His peple, and alle his wel-willing;⁾   *well-wishers*
30 Yef⁾ him good life and good ending,   *give*
That we with merth mowe savely⁾ sing   *may confidently*
    'Deo gracias.'
1415

The Agincourt Carol Henry V's victory at
Agincourt on October 25, 1415, must indeed
have seemed something to be grateful to God
for. After taking Harfleur he was in difficulties
and the French could have starved him into
submission. They chose to fight, with a force
many times Henry's. Unusual quantities of rain
had made the ground a morass: the French
chose to use armored knights on horseback. The
English archers, unarmored and on foot, shot
and cut them down, losing only 100 killed plus
13 men-at-arms. The French lost 5000 nobles
killed and 1000 taken prisoner. There is a
legend that Henry, returning to England, was
greeted by crowds who shouted his praises for
the victory: he stopped them, saying that thanks
for it were owed solely to God.
Deo . . . victoria England, give thanks to God
for victory; see the Headnote and also "Adam
Lay Ybounden" below
With . . . chivalry with God on his side and
strength of knights
Domesday the Day of (general) Judgment, the
end of the world (Fig. 50)
He . . . most he neither spared nor feared the
least nor the greatest

Bring Us In Good Ale°

Bring us in good ale, and bring us in good ale!
For our blessed Lady's sake, bring us in good ale!

Bring us in no brown bread, for that is made of bran.°
Nor bring us in no white bread, for therein is no game,⌐   *pleasure*
    But bring us in good ale!

Bring us in no beef, for there is many bones,
But bring us in good ale, for that goth down at ones,⌐   *once*
    And bring us in good ale!

Bring us in no bacon, for that is passing⌐ fat,   *very*
10 But bring us in good ale, and give us enough of that,
    And bring us in good ale!

Bring us in no mutton, for that is often lean,
Nor bring us in no tripes, for they be seldom clean,
    But bring us in good ale!

Bring us in no eggs, for there are many shells,
But bring us in good ale, and give us nothing else,
    And bring us in good ale!

Bring us in no butter, for therein are many hores,⌐   *hairs*
Nor bring us in no pigs' flesh, for that will make us boars,
20   But bring us in good ale!

Bring us in no capons' flesh, for that is often dear,
Nor bring us in no ducks' flesh, for they slobber in the mere,
    But bring us in good ale!

    15th century

I Have Set My Heart So High

I have set my hert so hye,
    Me liketh no love that lowere is;°
And alle the paines that I may drye,⌐   *endure*
    Me think it do me good, ywis.°

For on that Lorde that loved us alle
    So hertély⌐ have I set my thought,   *devotedly*
It is my joye on Him to calle:
    For love me hath in balés brought,°
    Me think it do me good, ywis.
    c. 1380

Bring . . . Ale both a carol and a drinking
song, defining by negatives
bran powdered wheat husk
Me . . . lowere is that no love inferior to this
satisfies me

Me . . . ywis it seems to me that they do me
good, indeed
For . . . brought since love has brought me to
torments

All Too Late°

When mine eynen⁾ misteth   *eyes*
And mine eren sisseth⁾   *ears sing*
And my nose coldeth
And my tunge foldeth⁾   *tongue fails*
And my rude⁾ slaketh   *ruddiness*
And mine lippes blaketh°
And my mouth grenneth⁾   *gapes*
And my spotel renneth⁾   *spittle runs*
And myn her riseth⁾   *hair stands on end*
10 And myn herte griseth⁾   *heart quakes*
And mine handen bivieth⁾   *hands tremble*
And mine feet stivieth⁾—   *stiffen*
Al too late, al too late,
Whenne the bere⁾ is at the gate!   *bier*
Thenne I shal flit⁾   *must go*
From bedde to flore,
From flore to here,°
From here to bere,
From bere to pit,⁾   *grave*
20 And the pit fordit.⁾   *will be closed*
Thenne lith myn hous uppe myn nese;
Of al this world ne give ich a pese!°

c. 1275

Divine Love°

Christ made to man a fair presènt,
His bloody body with love ybrent;⁾   *afire*
That blisful body His lif hath lent⁾   *given*
For love of man whom sinne hath blent.⁾   *blinded*
O love, love, what hast thou ment?
Me thinketh⁾ that love to wrathe is went.⁾   *it seems / turned*
Thy lovèliche⁾ handes love hath to-rent,⁾   *lovely / torn to pieces*
And thy lithe⁾ armes wel streite ytent;°   *gentle*
Thy brest is bare, thy body is bent,
10 For wrong hath wonne and right is shent.⁾   *destroyed*

Thy mildè⁾ bones love hath to-drawe,⁾   *gentle / dragged apart*
Thy nailes, thy feet been al to-gnawe.⁾   *consumed*

All Too Late Such catalogues of the signs of
death are found in late classical and medieval
Latin (one is ascribed to St. Jerome) and other
European languages, including Old English. Cf.
Falstaff's death, in Shakespeare's *Henry V.* Here
the signs are turned into a little *contemptus
mundi* poem.
my rude . . . blaketh my complexion fades and
my lips grow pale

here shroud of hair-cloth; common and rough,
with a hint of torment to come
Thenne . . . pese When my house (i.e. the
grave) presses upon my face (literally, nose), I
shall not give a pea for this world.
Divine Love This poem takes the form of a
meditation on the Passion, the Five Wounds,
and the Love of Christ.
wel . . . ytent very cruelly pulled apart

The Lord of love love hath now slawe°—
When love is strong, love hath no lawe.

His herte is rent, His body is bent,
    Upon the roodė-tree;⟩   *cross-tree*
Wrong is went,⟩ the Devil is shent,⟩   *departed / destroyed*
    Christ, thorugh⟩ the might of thee.   *through*

For thee that herte is laid⟩ to wedde.   *pledged*
20 Swich was the love that herte us kedde,⟩   *showed*
That hertė brast,⟩ that hertė bledde,   *burst*
That hertė-blood oure soulės fedde.

That herte He yaf⟩ for treuthe° of love;   *gave*
Therfore in Him one⟩ is trewe love.   *alone*
For love of thee that herte is yove;⟩   *given*
Keep thou that herte, and thou art above.⟩ *victorious*

Love, love, wher shalt thou wone?⟩   *live*
Thy woning-sted is thee binome.°
For Christės herte, that was thyn home;
30 He is ded, now hast thou none.

Love, love, why dost thou so?
Love, thou brekest myn herte a-two.

Love hath shewed his gretė might,
For love hath made of day the night;
Love hath slawe the King of right,
And love hath ended the strongė fight.

So muchel love was nevere non;°
That witeth⟩ ful wel Marìe and John,°   *know*
And also witeth they everichon⟩   *all those*
40 That love with Him hath made at on.⟩ *brought together*

Love maketh, Christ, thyn hertė myn:⟩   *mine*
So maketh love myn hertė thyn.
Thenne shal my love be trewe and fyn,
And love in love shal makė fyn.⟩   *an end*

c. 1375

I Sing of a Maiden

I sing of a maiden
    That is makėles;⟩   *matchless*
King of alle kingės

Lord . . . slawe love has now slain the King of Love
treuthe a pun on "truth"; faith, pledge, truth
Thy . . . binome Thy dwelling-place (i.e. Christ) is taken from thee.
So . . . non There was never such great love;

John 15:13: "Greater love hath no man than this . . ."
Marie and John Christ's mother and (by tradition) the beloved disciple, to whom Christ entrusted his mother at the foot of the Cross (John 19:26) (Fig. 52).

To her son she ches.°   *chose*
He cam also stille°   *as silently*
  Ther° His moder° was,   *where / mother*
As dew in Aprille
  That falleth on the gras.
He cam also stille
10   To His moderes bowr,°
As dew in Aprille
  That falleth on the flowr.
He cam also stille
  Ther His moder lay,
As dew in Aprille
  That falleth on the spray.
Moder and maiden
  Was never none but she;
Wel may swich° a lady   *such*
20   Godės moder be.

15th century?

Adam Lay Ybounden°

Adam lay ybounden,°   *bound*
  Bounden in a bond;
Four thousand winter°
  Thought° him not to long;   *seemed to*
And al was for an appel,°
  An appel that he took,
As clerkės° finden writen   *learned men*
  In her° book.   *their*

Ne hadde the appel takė° been,   *taken*
10   The appel takė been,
Ne hadde never our Lady
  A° been hevenė-queen.°   *have*
Blessėd be the time
  That appel takė was!
Therfore we moun° singen   *may*
  'Deo Gracias!'°

15th century

bowr bower, room; thus, womb
Adam Lay Ybounden This famous carol on the Annunciation, in honor of the Virgin, carries the notion of Adam's fall (Fig. 56) as *felix culpa* ("happy fault") back one generation, from Christ, the Redeemer of the fault, to his Mother, who conceived him without sin and was crowned by him Queen of Heaven.
Four . . . winter Adam's bondage in Limbo, expiating his great sin by exclusion from the full beatific vision, was often so computed. Enduring without complaint for that time, he was liberated by Christ in the Harrowing of Hell. (Fig. 7)
appel The forbidden fruit was identified as an apple by the 4th century A.D., because of the useful pun *malum*/evil: *malum*/apple. The Vulgate has *pomum*: fruit.
hevene-queen Queen of Heaven. The coronation of the Virgin was becoming more and more popular at this time in literature and art.
Deo Gracias "Thanks be to God": liturgical formula used in the mass after the Epistle and the last Gospel, in which the good tidings of salvation are given to the people

Corpus Christi Carol°

Lully, lulley; lully, lulley;
The fawcon> hath born my mak> away.   *falcon / mate*

He bare him up, he bare him down;
He bare him into an orchard brown.

In that orchard there was an hall,
That was hangèd with purpel and pall.°

And in that hall there was a bed;°
It was hangèd with gold so red.

10   And in that bed there lieth a knight,°
His woundès bleeding day and night.

By that bedes side there kneeleth a may,°
And she weepeth both night and day.

And by that bedes side there standeth a ston,°
'Corpus Christi'° writen theron.

15th century

POPULAR BALLADS

Ballads are short, anonymous, narrative poems, preserved by oral transmission and sung, often with accompaniment and dance, before gatherings of people. They exist in all nations. Some ballad themes and stories pass freely from one culture to another and from language to language over many centuries, their words and characters altered to fit the new context. Some are passed on with very little change. Their subject is usually tragic, death by accident or by treachery in love or in war, often with supernatural accompaniments, being the most frequent. Motif and incident may be taken from a folklore tradition stretching back many centuries, or from a comparatively recent historical occurrence. Since ballads were passed on by word of mouth, they exist in many versions even within one language and are sung to more than one tune. But since ballad meter is so simple, a single tune will do duty for many

Corpus Christi Carol There is much dispute over the interpretation of this carol. Some think it refers to the stealing away of Henry VIII's affections from his first wife, Catherine of Aragon, by his second, Anne Boleyn, whose badge was a white falcon—but then why should the falcon bear her Henry to the place where the abandoned first wife is weeping before the sacrament (ll. 11–12)? Others make it refer to the Grail, the paten of the Last Supper, said to have been brought by Joseph of Arimathea to Avalon, Isle of Apples (Glastonbury, in Somerset, ll. 3–4), so that the hall would be the Castle of the Keeper of the Grail, the wounded knight of l. 9. Or it may be that the poem is "about" the Eucharist, and the orchard is the church, the hall the aumbry or cupboard in which the body of Christ lies, and the "may" or maiden the Virgin Mary. The poem may be even more closely connected with the sacrifice of Christ in that the "hall" may be an Easter sepulcher, in which the Eucharist was laid on Good Friday to be raised again on Easter Day. Whatever the precise nature of the symbolic meaning, the poem succeeds superbly as poem and mystery. Cf. the ballad "The Three Ravens."
purpel and pall rich purple fabric
bed either the couch of the wounded Keeper of the Grail or the altar of the mass, on which the body of Christ is offered in re-enactment of his sacrifice
knight either the Keeper of the Grail, or Christ, present in the eucharist
may either the maid who serves the Grail, or the Virgin Mary
ston the stone may be the paten of the eucharist, a symbol of the stone at the entrance to Christ's sepulcher
Corpus Christi "Body of Christ"

ballads. (We have a more sophisticated parallel in the case of hymns, where the rhythm is also simple: the same words are sung to many tunes, and the same tune is used for many hymns.) Basically, ballad meter is the Western norm for the simple melodic phrase, four primary beats to the line. The lines are usually arranged in quatrains, i.e. groups of four lines.

The simplicity of ballad form implies a simplicity of language and of syntax, as well as an economy of expression. Few ballads are longer than a page or two of print, and those that exceed this limit are generally historical narratives with a simple story-line. Since they were intended to be understood by an audience that would hear them only once and since they were performed by a single singer, they could not make use of the sophisticated imagery and complicated sentence structure of the written lyric. The ballads operate with "and" clauses, not "though" or "if" clauses, with successive statements, not with statement followed by qualifications. Their imagery, even where it seems not fully articulate and is difficult to interpret fully, is simple and direct.

The popular ballad is essentially a primitive art form, composed and transmitted in a society such as that of the Scottish Border counties between the later Middle Ages and the early nineteenth century. These societies are made up of small, self-contained local units, relatively unmixed and homogeneous; their outlook is limited to their own locality and their own past; and they value ballad-makers both as story-tellers and as news-vendors. Naturally, the demands of this audience influenced ballad composers, and its criticisms of a performance influenced the singers. Earlier theories of the origin of the popular ballad gave the audience a much greater role than this and saw the ballads as the corporate poetic expression of the folk, the cooperative productions of a whole community, related to the chorus songs and dances which accompany primitive work and play. This idea is not now widely accepted: it originated in late eighteenth-century Germany at a time when the ballads were beginning to be collected, studied, and imitated.

Modern study has shown the importance of the bard, the singer of tales, in primitive societies and the privileged position he often occupies in them, even where he has some other trade or duty. Each performance that he gives of a ballad, old or new, is a unit in itself and may include variations. He is the chief, but not the only, hander-on of the ballads to other executants. The handing-on may be lateral, across a society or societies; or vertical and chronological, through successive generations in the same community or family. These considerations explain both the existence of many variants of a single ballad and the often surprising consistency in those variants. As in all orally transmitted literature, differences between variants may be the result of conscious manipulation to fit the ballad to new circumstances or a different audience—of children, perhaps, rather than adults (as in some of the versions of "Lord Randal"), or an audience drawn from another community on whom the allusions would be lost, or which is more sophisticated in its tastes. Or they may be accidental, the result of over- or under-sophistication in the transmitter, of failure of understanding or memory, or even of simple mishearing.

A good number of the ballads that we now possess were not written down until the eighteenth century or even later, and when they were recorded in this way, they were recorded in a composite of the forms in which they were then being recited. In consequence, it is not possible to decide, of many of them, what the original version would have looked liked, or when it was composed. All we can say is that most were composed at some time between 1200 and 1700, though some are later than that. The earliest references in other literature to ballads belong to the later fourteenth century: Langland, in *Piers Plowman,* has a slighting remark about the Robin Hood ballads. Of some, we have sixteenth-century versions; others, such as "The Carpenter's Wife" ("The Demon Lover") we know from mid-seventeenth-century printed broadsides; others again, like "The Three Ravens," are found in early seventeenth-century printed collections; yet others in manuscript poetical miscellanies of the same century. Of some, such as "Sir Patrick Spence," we have no version before the eighteenth century, or the mid-nineteenth ("The Unquiet Grave"), so that we cannot be quite sure that we are not dealing with a modern poem masquerading as an old ballad.

That we know them at all is due to eighteenth-century antiquarian scholarship, with its interest in origins and in the romantic past of one's own people. It is also due to the rise, during the eighteenth and nineteenth centuries, of the primitive and "natural" as a valued literary mode. Sir Philip Sidney, in the *Defence of Poesie* (1595), felt it necessary to apologize for his barbarousness in finding himself moved by the ballad of "Chevy Chase." Joseph Addison, in 1711, finds ballad verse despicably simple, but the sentiment moving because genuine and unaffected. As the eighteenth century goes on, the distinction between natural and artificial poetry is more and more used to favor the natural. The publication, in 1765, of Bishop Thomas Percy's *Reliques of Ancient English Poetry,* its texts largely drawn from a manuscript of about 1650, marks the beginning of modern ballad study and ballad collection. Percy's example inspired others, in Germany as well as in England (the communal theory of ballad composition mentioned above was developed by German scholars on the basis of their reading of Percy's collection). But the most important result of his publication was the new impetus it gave to ballad collecting in the North, notably to Sir Walter Scott, whose *Minstrelsy of the Scottish Border,* published in 1802–3, incorporated the results of ten years' work taking down ballads from the lips of the ballad singers themselves. Like all his contemporaries, Scott emended and improved these versions: his aim was to construct one coherent poem from the variants.

In this he was moved by practical considerations as well as by his interest in the ballads as records of older beliefs and superstitions and of past events—as can be seen from the use he made of their material and their prosody in his own poems. It was Scott who set the pattern for the nineteenth-century ballad of romantic chivalry and love.

By the time Scott published his *Minstrelsy* the ballad had already been accepted in England and Germany as a new literary model for the short poem of tragic love, of rustic life, of childhood, or of any combination of these, together with the poem of "faerie" and the supernatural. The simplicity of language and prosody could reflect the directness and purity of the emotions involved, whether war-like, loving, gentle or pathetic; or it could reflect the directness of the relationship between the natural and the supernatural worlds. The *Lyrical Ballads* of Wordsworth and Coleridge share an influence from this direction with the poems based on ballad meter written by such poets as Thomas Chatterton, William Blake, and Robert Burns. The literary ballad further evolved in the nineteenth century in the hands of writers as different as Thomas Moore, Dante Gabriel Rossetti, and Algernon Charles Swinburne. Later still, the ballad influences the poetry of Rudyard Kipling, A. E. Housman, and W. B. Yeats.

Most of the texts selected here are tragic in tone. Many give the feeling of suspension between natural and supernatural, and the sensation that one has been plunged, without preparation, into the middle of the action, which are hallmarks of the ballad. In many, the quality of dramatic performance that also goes with ballads is to be seen. (It has been said that reading a ballad is like going to the theater when the play has already reached its fifth act.) A tune is given for most, since the ballad can barely be said to exist without its tune, which shapes and controls it in important ways. The tune also enhances the impression of performance, of a single act performed with variations, which is essential to our understanding of this form of poetry. The same effect of performance, almost of rite, is aided, in many of the ballads, by the repeated refrain or burden. In some ballads this consists of nonsense, incantatory words or syllables.

The first ballad below, "The Cherry-tree Carol," has a biblical theme, handled with great tenderness and delicacy. It might equally well have been put among the religious lyrics above, but is included here because of its meter and as a specimen of the overtly sacred ballad. The next five are "faerie" ballads, involving supernatural beings and feats, forfeits, riddles, changings of shape, the returning dead, with overtones of tragic love. Only the first of them—and the ballad of Thomas the Rhymer, for which see The Other World section below—suggest that an encounter with the supernatural can breed anything but ill. The next two ("Lord Randal" and "The Three Ravens") are also grim in tone, with echoes of violence and perhaps of Border feuds. The single Robin Hood ballad gives an adequate impression of the not very high poetic quality, the simplicity, and low intensity of this large class. The final ballad, "Sir Patrick Spence," is possibly based on historical incidents.

The standard collection of ballads is still F. J. Child's monumental five-volume *The English and Scottish Ballads* (1882–98), now supplemented by B. H. Bronson's four volumes of *The Traditional Tunes of the Child Ballads* (1959–70). Child succeeded in assembling all the significant versions of each ballad then known: references to his numberings are given in the footnotes. The versions and tunes used here are, with modifications, those of *The Oxford Book of Ballads* (ed. J. Kinsley, 1969). Some spellings and capitalization have been normalized, but Northern forms have been retained where they occur.

The Cherry-tree Carol°

Joseph was an old man,
    And an old man was he,
When he wedded Mary
    In the land of Galilee.

Joseph and Mary walked
    Through an orchard good,
Where was cherries and berries
    So red as any blood.

Joseph and Mary walked
10   Through an orchard green,
Where was berries and cherries
    As thick as might be seen.

O then bespoke° Mary   *spoke*
    So meek and so mild:°
'Pluck me one cherry, Joseph,
    For I am with child.'

O then bespoke Joseph
    With words most unkind:
'Let him pluck thee a cherry
20   That brought° thee with child.'   *got*

O then bespoke the Babe
    Within his Mother's womb:
'Bow down then the tallest tree
    For my Mother to have some.'

Then bowed down the highest tree
    Unto his Mother's hand;
Then she cried, 'See, Joseph,
    I have cherries at command.'

O then bespake Joseph:
30   'I have done Mary wrong;

The Cherry-tree Carol Child, no. 54. Air: William Sandys, *Christmas Carols . . . .*, 1833. This carol in ballad meter, of uncertain date, is a version of one of the miracles (Fig. 53) told in the apocryphal *Gospel of Pseudo-Matthew*, chapter 20, perhaps 2nd or 3rd century A.D., which is chiefly concerned with the infancy of Christ. There were several such apocryphal Gospels, popularly believed during the Middle Ages to be as authentic and authoritative as the canonical ones. They have much influence on literature and art. In the mystery plays, Joseph's suspicions of Mary are treated as comedy, but in lyrics of that period they are not. **So . . . mild** alliterative oral formula: Mary's usual attributes

But cheer up, my dearest,
   And be not cast down.'

Then Mary plucked a cherry
   As red as the blood,°
Then Mary went home
   With her heavy load.

Then Mary took her Babe°
   And sat him on her knee,
Saying, 'My dear Son, tell me
40   What this world will be.'

'O I shall be as dead, Mother,
   As the stones in the wall;
O the stones in the streets, Mother,
   Shall mourn for me all.

Upon Easter-day, Mother,
   My uprising shall be;
O the sun and the moon,° Mother,
   Shall both rise with me.'

The Wee Wee Man°

As I was walking all alane
   Between a water and a wa';°   *wall*
And there I spied a wee wee man
   And he was the least° that ere I saw.   *smallest*

blood The mood changes. The blood-red cherry symbolizes the blood of Christ, the Passion for which he was born, and the Redemption.
Babe The ballad narrative compresses the time scheme, and the poem gathers speed as it approaches the climax of Christ's death and resurrection.

sun . . . moon Isaiah 30:26
The Wee Wee Man Child, no. 38. Air: J. Johnson, *The Scots Musical Museum* (1787 f.). A "faerie" ballad, first collected in the 18th century, with similarities to "Thomas the Rhymer" (see below).

His legs were scarce a shathmont's° length
　　And thick and thimber⁾ was his thigh,　　　　　　　　　　*heavy*
Between his brows there was a span°
　　And between his shoulders there was three.

He took up a meikle⁾ stane　　　　　　　　　　　　　　　　*big*
10　　And he flang 't as far as I could see;
Tho I had been as Wallace wight°
　　I couldna liften⁾ it to my knee.　　　　　　　　　　*have lifted*

'O wee wee man but thou be strong,
　　O tell me whare thy dwelling be';
'My dwelling's down at yon bonny bower
　　O will you go with me and see?'

On we lap⁾ and awa we rade⁾　　　　　　　　　　　*leapt / rode*
　　Till we came to yon bonny green;°
We lighted⁾ down for to bait° our horse　　　　　　*dismounted*
20　　And out there came a lady fine;

Four and twenty at her back
　　And they were a'⁾ clad out in green;　　　　　　　*all*
Tho the King of Scotland had been there
　　The warst o' them might hae⁾ been his Queen.　　*have*

On we lap and awa we rade
　　Till we cam to yon bonny ha'⁾　　　　　　　　　　*hall*
Whare the roof was o' the beaten gold
　　And the floor was o' the cristal a'.⁾　　　　　　*all*

When we came to the stair foot
30　　Ladies were dancing jimp⁾ and sma',⁾　　　*graceful / slender*
But in the twinkling of an eye
　　My wee wee man was clean awa'.

The Two Magicians°

The lady stands in her bower⁾ door　　　　　　　　　*boudoir*
　　As straight as willow wand;⁾　　　　　　　　　　　*twig*
The blacksmith° stood a little foreby⁾　　　　　　*aside*
　　Wi' hammer in his hand.

shathmont's a measurement, about 6 inches, from the tip of the outstretched thumb across the palm of the hand
span the extended hand, from outstretched thumb to outstretched little finger, about 9 inches
as Wallace wight as strong as Sir William Wallace (*c.* 1207–1305), the Scottish national hero, outlaw, and rebel against the English
green fairy place and fairy color
bait feed and rest a horse
The Two Magicians Child, no. 44. There are two texts, one Scottish, the version above, and one weaker English. The ballad exists in many other European languages, particularly French. This transformation contest is cousin to the riddling-contest ballad. Two opponents match transformations, or question and answer, in order to gain or avoid gaining a mate, who may also be the opponent in the contest. The changing of shape to win or avoid something has parallels in all mythologies.
blacksmith a trade renowned in folklore for lechery, potency, and lack of attractiveness

'Weel may ye dress ye, lady fair,
    Into your robes o' red;
Before the morn at this same time
    I'll gain your maidenhead.'

'Awa', awa', ye coal-black smith,
10   Would ye do me the wrang
To think to gain my maidenhead
    That I hae° kept sae° lang?'   *have / so*

Then she has hadden° up her hand   *held*
    And she sware by the mold:°   *earth*
'I wu'dna° be a blacksmith's wife   *would not*
    For the full° o' a chest o' gold.   *whole*

I'd rather I were dead and gone
    And my body laid in grave,
Ere a rusty stock° o' coal-black smith
20   My maidenhead should have.'

But he has hadden up his hand
    And he sware by the mass;
'I'll cause ye be my light leman°   *wanton lover*
    For the hauf° o' that and less.'   *half*

      'O bide,° lady, bide,
          And aye° he bade her bide: *always*
      The rusty smith your leman shall be
          For a'° your muckle° pride.'   *all / great*

Then she became a turtle dove
30   To fly up in the air,
And he became another dove
    And they flew pair and pair.°
      'O bide, lady, bide, &c.'

She turned hersell° into an eel   *herself*
    To swim into yon burn,°   *brook*
And he became a speckled trout
    To gie the eel a turn.
      'O bide, lady, bide, &c.'

Then she became a duck, a duck,
40   To puddle in a peel,°   *pool*
And he became a rose-kaim'd° drake   *red-combed*
    To gie the duck a dreel.°   *doing over*
      'O bide, lady, bide, &c.'

---

rusty stock i.e. churlish, stupid oaf; or "rusty"   **O bide** . . . The burden, or refrain, appears
may be literally rust-smeared   every sixth stanza: "Stay, lady, stay."
                                               pair and pair together, two by two

She turned hersell into a hare
  To rinˀ upon yon hill,   *run*
And he became a gudeˀ greyhound   *good*
  And boldly he did fill.°
    'O bide, lady, bide, &c.'

Then she became a gay grey mare
50   And stood in yonder slack,ˀ   *hollow*
And he became a gilt saddle
  And sat upon her back.
    Was she wae,° he held her sae,
      And stillˀ he bade her bide: *always*
    The rusty smith her leman was
    For a' her muckle pride.

Then she became a het girdleˀ   *hot griddle*
  And he became a cake,
And a' the ways she turned hersell
60   The blacksmith was her make.°
    Was she wae, &c.

She turned hersell into a ship
  To sail out owerˀ the flood,   *over*
He ca'd a nail intill her tail°
  And syneˀ the ship she stood.   *then*
    Was she wae, &c.

Then she became a silken plaidˀ   *coverlet*
  And stretched upon a bed,
And he became a green° covering
70   And gained her maidenhead.
    Was she wae, &c.

---

fill fulfil, perform
Was she wae Woe was her; she was woeful.
Holding fast, no matter what the transformations,
was the way to win such a contest.

make mate or match; the pun is probably intended
He . . . tail he called (i.e. drove) a nail into her stern
green the color of nature and love

The Carpenter's Wife°
[The Demon Lover]

'O whare hae⁾ ya been, my dearest dear,   *where have*
   These seven lang years and more?'
'O I am come to seek my former vows
   That ye promised me before.'

'Awa wi'⁾ your former vows,' she says,   *away with*
   'Or else ye will breed strife:
Awa wi' your former vows,' she says,
   'For I'm become a wife.

I am married to a ship-carpenter,
10   A ship-carpenter he's bound;⁾   *engaged*
I wadna° he kend⁾ my mind this nicht⁾   *knew / night*
   For twice five hundred pound.'

'I have seven ships upon the sea
   Laden with the finest gold,
And mariners to wait us upon;
   All these you may behold.

And I have shoes for my love's feet
   Beaten of the purest gold,
And lined wi' the velvet soft
20   To keep my love's feet from the cold.'

She has put her foot on gude⁾ ship-board,   *good*
   And on shipboard she's gane,⁾   *gone*
And the veil that hung oure⁾ her face   *over*
   Was a' wi' gowd begane.⁾   *gold overlaid*

'O how do you love the ship,' he said,
   'Or how do you love the sea?
And how do you love the bold mariners
   That wait upon thee and me?'

The Carpenter's Wife Child, no. 243. Air: William Motherwell, *Minstrelsy, Ancient and Modern* (1827). Also called "The House Carpenter." Over 145 versions have been collected. First known in English Restoration broadsides, one version is entitled: "A warning for married women, being an example of Mrs. Jane Reynolds (a West-country woman), born near Plymouth, who, having plighted her troth to a seaman, was afterwards married to a carpenter, and at last carried away by a spirit, the manner how shall presently be recited. To a West-country tune called 'The Fair Maid of Bristol,' 'Bateman' or 'John Tone'." **wadna** would not wish

'O I do love the ship,' she said,
30   'And I do love the sea;
But woe be to the dim mariners
    That nowhere I can see!'

She had na° sailed a league, a league,   *not*
    A league but barely twa,°   *two*
Till she did mind on° the husband she left   *remember*
    And her wee young son alsua.°   *also*

'O haud° your tongue, my dearest dear,   *hold*
    Let all your follies abee;°   *abide*
I'll show whare° the white lilies grow   *where*
40   On the banks of Italie.'°

She had na sailed a league, a league,
    A league but barely three,
Till grim, grim grew his countenance
    And gurly° grew the sea.   *stormy*

'O haud your tongue, my dearest dear,
    Let all your follies abee;
I'll show whare the white lilies grow
    In the bottom of the sea.'

He's tane° her by the milk-white hand   *taken*
50   And he's thrown her in the main;
And full five and twenty hundred ships
    Perished all on the coast of Spain.

The Wife of Usher's Well°

There lived a wife° at Usher's Well   *woman*
    And a wealthy wife was she;
She had three stout and stalwart sons
    And sent them o'er the sea.

They hadna° been a week from her,   *had not*
    A week but barely ane,°   *one*

Italie i.e. a fair country, far away
The Wife . . . Well Child, no. 79; Air: Scott,

Minstrelsy; a widespread ballad and tune in
the modern Appalachians

Whan word came to the carline wife°
    That her three sons were gane.>   *lost*

They hadna been a week from her,
10   A week but barely three,
Whan word came to the carline wife
    That her sons she'd never see.

'I wish the wind may never cease,
    Nor fishes° in the flood,
Till my three sons come hame to me
    In earthly flesh and blood.'

It fell about the Martinmas°
    Whan nights are lang and mirk,>   *dark*
The carline wife's three sons came hame
20   And their hats were of the birk.>   *birch*

It neither grew in syke> nor ditch   *stream*
    Nor yet in ony sheugh,°
But at the gates o' Paradise
    That birk grew fair eneugh.>   *very*

'Blow up the fire, my maidens,
    Bring water from the well;
For all my house shall feast this night
    Since my three sons are well.'

And she has made to them a bed,
30   She's made it large and wide,
And she's ta'en her mantle her about,
    Sat down at the bed-side.

Up then crew° the red, red cock
    And up and crew the grey;
The eldest to the youngest said,
    ' 'Tis time we were away.'

The cock he hadna crawed but once
    And clapp'd his wings at a'
Whan the youngest to the eldest said,
40   'Brother, we must awa'.

The cock doth craw, the day doth daw,>   *dawn*
    The channering worm doth chide;°
Gin> we be mist out of our place   *if*
    A sair pain we maun bide.°

carline wife old woman, witch
fishes perhaps a corrupt reading
Martinmas Feast of St. Martin, November 11,
not long after All Hallows Eve; the beginning
of winter, a dark, bloody time, when cattle and
hogs were slaughtered for winter food

sheugh trench, ditch, or furrow; thus, ground
crew The dead could not be abroad after first
cockcrow.
The . . . chide the grumbling worm chides
us; i.e. calls us back to the grave
A . . . bide a harsh torture we must endure

Fare ye weel, my mother dear;
  Fareweel to barn and byre,°
And fare ye weel, the bonny lass
  That kindles my mother's fire.'

cow-barn

The Unquiet Grave°

The wind doth blow today, my love,
  And a few small drops of rain;
I never had but one true-love,
  In cold grave she was lain.

I'll do as much for my true-love
  As any young man may:
I'll sit and mourn all at her grave
  For a twelvemonth and a day.

The twelvemonth and a day being up
10   The dead began to speak:
'Oh who sits weeping on my grave°
  And will not let me sleep?'

' 'Tis I, my love, sits on your grave
  And will not let you sleep;
For I crave one kiss of your clay-cold lips
  And that is all I seek.'

'You crave one kiss of my clay-cold lips,
  But my breath smells earthy strong;
If you have one kiss of my clay-cold lips
20   Your time will not be long.

'Tis down in yonder garden green,
  Love, where we used to walk,
The finest flower that ere was seen
  Is withered to a stalk.

The Unquiet Grave Child, no. 78. Air: C. J. Sharp, *English Folk-Songs* . . . (1907). First published, 1868. The lateness of this ballad may be suspicious: it was current in oral tradition in Sussex in the mid-19th century. Its first lines are similar to a 15th-century carol, to which it may be related; and it exists in well over 40 versions.
Oh . . . grave It is both an Oriental and a Western superstition that after a certain time mourning disturbs the dead, and brings them out to claim the disturber.

The stalk is withered dry, my love,
  So will our hearts decay;
So make yourself content, my love,
  Till God calls you away.'

Lord Randal°

'O where ha' you been, Lord Randal my son?
And where ha' you been, my handsome young man?'
'I ha' been at the greenwood; mother, make my bed soon,
For I'm wearied wi' hunting and fain wad˃ lie down.'

gladly would

'An' wha˃ met ye there, Lord Randal my son?
An' wha met you there, my handsome young man?'
'O I met wi' my true-love; mother, make my bed soon,
For I'm wearied wi' huntin' an' fain wad lie down.'

who

'And what did she give you, Lord Randal my son?
And what did she give you, my handsome young man?'
'Eels fried in a pan; mother, make my bed soon,
For I'm wearied wi' huntin' and fain wad lie down.'

'And wha gat your leavins,˃ Lord Randal my son?
And wha gat your leavins, my handsome young man?'
'My hawks and my hounds; mother, make my bed soon,
For I'm wearied wi' hunting and fain wad lie down.'

leavings

'And what becam of them, Lord Randal my son?
And what becam of them, my handsome young man?'

Lord Randal Child, no. 12. Air: J. Johnson, *Scots Musical Museum* (1787 f.). This famous ballad has analogues in both Italian and German, which survive in forms older than the English. The young man is sometimes poisoned by his false true love and sometimes by his wicked step-mother, as in the popular fairy-tales. There may be a connection with Ranulf, Earl of Chester (d. 1232), whose heir's wife was supposed to have poisoned her husband. The English version cannot be traced back farther than the late 18th century; the Italian is at least a century older. The form of this ballad varies less than most in its various versions; each stanza is divided equally between question and answer, with the second line of the answer used as a refrain.

'They stretched their legs out an' died; mother, make my bed soon,
20   For I'm wearied wi' huntin' and fain wad lie down.'

'O I fear you are poisoned, Lord Randal my son,°
I fear you are poisoned, my handsome young man.'
'O yes, I am poisoned; mother, make my bed soon,
For I'm sick at the heart and fain wad lie down.'

'What d'ye leave to your mother, Lord Randal my son?
What d'ye leave to your mother, my handsome young man?'
'Four and twenty milk kye;° mother, make my bed soon,   *cows*
For I'm sick at the heart and fain wad lie down.'

'What d'ye leave to your sister, Lord Randal my son?
30   What d'ye leave to your sister, my handsome young man?'
'My gold and my silver; mother, make my bed soon,
For I'm sick at the heart an' fain wad lie down.'

'What d'ye leave to your brother, Lord Randal my son?
What d'ye leave to your brother, my handsome young man?'
'My houses and my lands; mother, make my bed soon,
For I'm sick at the heart and fain wad lie down.'

'What d'ye leave to your true-love, Lord Randal my son?
What d'ye leave to your true-love, my handsome young man?'
'I leave her hell and fire; mother, make my bed soon,
40   For I'm sick at the heart and fain wad lie down.'

The Three Ravens°

There were three ravens sat on a tree,
  Down a downe, hay down, hay downe,
There were three ravens sat on a tree,
  With a downe;

I . . . son The poem, beginning its second half, darkens, and the refrain changes from an expression of listlessness to a fear of coming death. The Three Ravens Child, no. 26. Air: Thomas Ravenscroft, *Melismata* . . . (1611). In this form, or as the grimmer "Twa Carbies" (Two Crows), very well known and widespread. It is also one of the earliest ballads we have, and this version may be the elaboration of an early popular poem by the addition of material similar to the "Corpus Christi Carol" (see above). Rhythm and refrain also suggest a carol or dance song.

There were three ravens sat on a tree,
They were as blacke as they might be,
   With a downe derrie, derrie, derrie, downe, downe.

The one of them said to his make,°   *mate*
Where shall we our breakfast take?

10   Downe in yonder greenè field
There lies a knight slain under his shield.

His hounds they lie downe at his feete,
So well they can° their master keepe.   *do*

His hawkes they flie so eagerly°   *fiercely*
There's no fowle° dare him come nie.°   *bird / near*

Downe there comes a fallow doe°
As great with yong° as she might goe.   *young*

She lift up his bloody hed
And kist his wounds that were so red.

20   She got him up upon her back
And carried him to earthen lake.°

She buried him before the prime,°
She was dead her selfe ere even-song° time.

God send every gentleman
Such hawkes, such hounds, and such a leman.°   *lover*

The Birth of Robin Hood°

O Willie's large o' limb and lith°   *joint*
    And come o'° high degree,   *of*
And he is gane° to Earl Richard°   *gone*
    To serve for meat° and fee.   *food*

Earl Richard had but ae° daughter   *one*
    Fair as a lily flower;

doe The fallow deer was yellowish-brown in color and smaller than the red deer. Like the white doe of other ballads and of folklore, perhaps this creature is the knight's lover changed into a doe. Or she may be the Christian soul come for Christ, her bridegroom; or the knight may be the wounded Keeper of the Grail, the Maimed King of the Grail legend. There is surely some allusion to the daily sacrifice of Christ in the Mass.
earthen lake pit, cavity in the earth; i.e. grave
prime the first liturgical hour (6 a.m.), or any time between that and 9 a.m. (great prime)
even-song vespers, the evening office (6 p.m.), or dusk
The Birth . . . Hood Text after Robert Jamie-

son, *Popular Ballads and Songs from Tradition* (1806). One of many Robin Hood ballads, some of them very long and the nearest approach in ballad form to the long, heroic, folk tale in verse produced by "singers of tales," composers of oral epics. The earliest mentions of Robin Hood are in the ballads: Sloth, in *Piers Plowman*, says he knows "rhymes of Robin Hood and Randolf, Earl of Chester." Others are certainly of the 15th century. The stories of his activities are a form of indirect complaint and social criticism.
Earl Richard Robin's birth, of a yeoman and a noblewoman, accounts for his possessing all the best qualities of each class.

And they made up their love-contract
   Like proper paramour.°

It fell upon a simmer's nicht⸴   *summer's night*
10   Whan the leaves were fair and green,
That Willie met his gay ladie
   Intil⸴ the wood alane.⸴   *within / alone*

'O narrow is my gown, Willie,
   That wont to be sae⸴ wide;   *so*
And gane is a'⸴ my fair colour   *all*
   That wont⸴ to be my pride.   *used*

But gin⸴ my father should get word   *if*
   What's past between us twa,⸴   *two*
Before that he should eat or drink
20   He'd hang you o'er that wa'.⸴   *wall*

But ye'll come to my bower,⸴ Willie,   *room*
   Just as the sun gaes down;
And keep me in your arms twa
   And latna⸴ me fa'⸴ down.'   *let not /fall*

O whan the sun was now gane down
   He's doen him⸴ till her bower;   *taken himself*
And there by the lee⸴ licht o' the moon   *pale*
   Her window she lookit o'er.

Intill a robe o' red scarlet
30   She lap,⸴ fearless o' harm;   *hurried*
And Willie was large o' lith and limb
   And keppit⸴ her in his arm.   *held*

And they've gane to the gude⸴ greenwood;   *good*
   And ere the night was deen⸴   *done*
She's born to him a bonny young son
   Amang the leaves sae green.

Whan night was gane and day was come
   And the sun began to peep,
Up and raise the Earl Richard
40   Out o' his drowsy sleep.

He's ca'd⸴ upon his merry young men   *called*
   By ane,⸴ by twa, and by three: *by ones*
'O what's come⸴ o' my daughter dear,   *become*
   That she's nae come to me?

I dreamt a dreary⸴ dream last night—   *terrible*
   God grant it come to gude—

Like . . . paramour in accord with the canons
of true courteous love

I dreamt I saw my daughter dear
    Drown in the saut⁾ sea flood.

          salt

But gin my daughter be dead or sick,
    Or yet be stown awa,⁾
I make a vow, and I'll keep it true,
    I'll hang ye ane and a'.'

          stolen away

They sought her back, they sought her fore,
    They sought her up and down;
They got her in the gude greenwood
    Nursing her bonny young son.

He took the bonny boy in his arms
    And kist him tenderlie;
Says, 'Though I would your father hang,
    Your mother's dear to me.'

He kist him o'er and o'er again:
    'My grandson I thee claim;
And Robin Hood in gude greenwood,
    And that shall be your name.'

And mony ane sings o' grass, o' grass,
    And mony ane sings o' corn,
And mony ane sings o' Robin Hood
    Kens⁾ little whare he was born.

          knows

It wasna⁾ in the ha',⁾ the ha'
    Nor in the painted bower,
But it was in the gude greenwood
    Amang the lily flower.

          was not / hall

Sir Patrick Spence°

The king sits in Dunferline° toune,°
   Drinking the blude-reid° wine:
'O quhar° will I get a guid° sailor,
   To sail this schip of mine?'

Up and spak an eldern° knicht,
   Sat at the king's richt° knee
'Sir Patrick Spence is the best sailor,
   That sails upon the see.'

The king has written a braid° letter,
10   And signed it wi' his hand;
And sent it to Sir Patrick Spence,
   Was walking on the sand.

The first line that Sir Patrick red,
   A loud lauch° lauched he:
The next line that Sir Patrick red,
   The teir° blinded his e'e.°

'O quha° is this has don this deid,°
   This ill deid don to me;
To send me out this time o' the yeir,°
20   To sail upon the see?

Mak haste, mak haste, my mirry men all,
   Our guid schip sails the morne.'
'O say na sae,° my master deir,°
   For I feir° a deadlie storme.

Late, late yestreen° I saw the new moone
   Wi' the auld° moone in hir arme;°
And I feir, I feir, my deir master,
   That we will com to harme.'

town
blood-red
where / good

old
right

laugh

tear / eye

who / deed

year

not so / dear
fear

last evening
old

Sir Patrick Spence Child, no. 58. Air: Child, 1882. This famous and popular ballad (cf. the first line of Coleridge, "Dejection: An Ode") may be an 18th-century fabrication. It is not known earlier than Bishop Thomas Percy's *Reliques* (1765). Possibly, a historical event lies somewhere in the background: either the drowning of many Scots nobles in 1281, on their return voyage from escorting the Scottish king's daughter, Margaret, and her new husband, Eric of Norway, to their new house; or the death at sea of Margaret's daughter, the Maid of Norway, when she was being fetched home to be married, a few years later. But no Sir Patrick Spence is connected with either voyage.
Dunferline Dunfermline, royal borough north of the Firth of Forth, on the west coast of Scotland. The kings of Scotland formerly lived there.
braid broad, open; patent, a commission for all to see
Late . . . arme the waning moon: an evil portent

O our Scots nobles wer> richt laith — *loath*
To weet> their cork-heil'd schoone;° — *wet*
Bot lang owre a'> the play wer played, — *ere all*
Thair hats they swam aboone.°

O lang, lang may thair ladies sit
Wi' thair fans into their hand,
Or eir> they se Sir Patrick Spence — *before*
Com sailing to the land.

O lang, lang may the ladies stand
Wi' thair gold kems> in their hair, — *combs*
Waiting for thair ain> deir lords, — *own*
For they'll se thame> na mair.> — *them / more*

Half owre,> haf owre to Aberdour,° — *half-way over*
It's fiftie fadom° deip:> — *deep*
And thair lies guid Sir Patrick Spence,
Wi' the Scots lords at his feit.> — *feet*

SIR THOMAS MALORY

c. 1410–1471

What we know of Sir Thomas Malory the man, we know in essentials from his book—or books: that he was a knight, that he finished the work that we call *Morte Darthur* in prison in the ninth year of the reign of Edward IV, i.e. between March 1469 and March 1470. The details—where he was born and when, why and for how long he was in prison, when he began his career as a writer, when he died—have all to be established from other documents. We must infer that these relate to Malory the author; we cannot be certain. They add up to a character which, it seems to many, does not fit the man who wrote the first—and only—English version of the Arthurian chivalric stories which is both comprehensive in scope and great as literature.

Assuming that the knight of the documents and the knight-author of the book are the same, we can say that he was born in the early years of the fifteenth century, had estates in Warwickshire, served with the Earl of Warwick, and was Member of Parliament for Warwickshire, all before 1445. In 1443 he fell foul of the law and from 1450 onward he was either in prison or on the run from the authorities for escaping from custody (by swimming a moat), ambush with intent to murder, breaking into a man's house and raping his wife (this may mean, as it may in the case of Chaucer, that he merely carried her off against her will), cattle raiding, extortion, breaking into an abbey, assaulting the abbot and stealing property, jail-breaking with violence. Malory pleaded not guilty to them all, but we cannot know the exact truth either of the charges or the plea. The royal pardon he received in 1456 is no guarantee

schoone shoes; elegant shoes, not clogs, but pantofles
aboone either: they were floating head downward; or: their hats were floating on the surface
Aberdour on the north shore of the Firth of Forth, below Dunfermline
fadom fathoms, 6 feet each

of his innocence, especially as he was shortly afterward imprisoned again, remaining in jail for most of the next five or six years. The interval between this and his next imprisonment he seems to have passed in campaigning, first for the Yorkists and then for the Lancastrians. Some of this pattern of violence, crime, and shifting loyalties is probably the effect of the disturbed times of the Wars of the Roses (see Glossary) in which he had to survive. Some of his exploits may be less serious than the formal accusations make them appear. Nevertheless, the impression remains of an adventurous and unscrupulous opportunist nobleman, rash and sudden, who may have owed his neck to his knighthood and to the fact that he never, as far as we know, murdered anyone. He may well have died still a prisoner.

In 1468 Malory had been excluded from the amnesties granted to the Lancastrians by the Yorkist King Edward IV. It seems likely that he wrote most of his over twelve hundred large pages (in the modern edition) in prison, for there is a reference to his being a prisoner quite early on in the manuscript, and this would mean that he either composed or translated quickly, to finish it in a little over two years at most, or that he had begun it earlier.

Malory's romance is a glorification of chivalric values and of King Arthur, the British king, at one and the same time. We do not know what he himself called his book. The only manuscript, discovered in 1934, lacks its beginning and its end and is not Malory's autograph. In 1485, William Caxton, using another manuscript, edited the text rather freely, cutting some passages, rewriting others in what he thought a more suitable style, and adding chapter headings. Caxton gave it no title—many fifteenth-century printed books lack a title at their beginning—but he gave it a preface and a colophon (inscription at the end) in which he called it "the book of King Arthur and of his noble knights of the Round Table" and "this noble and joyous book entitled Le Morte Darthur." *Morte Darthur* it has remained. There is at present much dispute as to how far the effect of Caxton's editing was to make one book out of what Malory intended to be several, and how far the aims of author and publisher diverged from each other in other respects. It may be that Malory intended that any one of his major episodes could be read singly, but this would not mean that he did not intend the reader to begin at the first and read his way through to the end. There are repetitions and there are confusing inconsistencies in the chronological scheme, so that we are often in doubt about the time-relation of one event or stage in the story to another, but the episodes are related, not independent. The narrative often advances in parallels and overlaps, but it advances.

It may also be true that Caxton saw the chivalry of the *Morte Darthur* as more of a moral force, inciting men to practice its virtue and expect honor for them, than Malory, for whom the example of Arthur and his knights was something more political and practical, an example of a firmly ordered, well-ruled commonwealth under a strong king.

This practical intention behind the work goes well with the way he handles his story. He was, in the main, translating and adapting from the immensely long French cycles of Arthurian romance, which were built around an elaborate religious and doctrinal framework, glorifying the Holy Grail as the object of the knightly quest. These "French books," as Malory calls them, had spiritualized the earlier Lancelot-Grail stories by opposing to the earthly chivalry of the Round Table the perfections of divine love, as symbolized in the Grail, and of contempt for the world. Malory drops the French theology. For him the Round Table is something good in itself, not something less good in contrast to a divine ideal. Its shortcomings are human. In the end, being of the mortal world, it fails: Arthur, the image of the good king and of order, is killed by the forces of evil and disorder. But Arthur, in his own person or that of a later English king, will come again. The knights fail in oath and loyalty one by one—as in Lancelot's adultery with Guinevere and in his too-late arrival to help Arthur in the final battle. The moral dimensions of Malory's story are those of Sir Kay's claiming the throne in the first selection below; or poor Sir Bedivere, in the second, torn between his love for King Arthur, the loyalty he owes him, and his wish to have Arthur's rich sword Excalibur for himself. All of these things are culpable, and all are, in the end, condemned by Malory, but with no suggestion that all such worldly failings merely show the worthlessness of the world.

He also frequently tones down the magical and supernatural elements: the Lady of the Lake, instead of walking on the water without getting her feet wet, very sensibly uses a boat. Malory's attitude, even in chivalric adventure, is down-to-earth: at one famous point he makes it clear that Queen Guinevere knew that the search for Lancelot would be a costly matter and sent the knights who were to find him their expenses in advance. Malory's knights are not like the knights of romance satirized in the seventeenth century by Samuel Butler in *Hudibras*:

> Unless they grazed, there's not one word
> Of their provision on record,
> Which made some confidently write,
> They had no stomachs but to fight.

One must not, all the same, assume that Malory did not mean them to be exemplary or that he was not fired by the notion of knight-errantry, originally developed in France in the twelfth century. His deliberate rejection of the fairy-tale element in the French romances of Arthur and his knights makes him give the tales a greater reality and importance as *exempla*. The courteous and gentle knight will, he says, find favor in every place. He must never fight for fighting's sake; simply to show his strength like this is to be a bully. Sir Lancelot is described as the pattern (in earlier versions it had been Sir Gawain). In Malory, Lancelot is the most courteous, the truest of friends and of lovers among sinful men, the kindest man who ever gave a blow with his sword, the handsomest, the humblest and gentlest in company with men and women, the fiercest to his deadly enemy. King Arthur, too, is the true embodiment of heroic knighthood, the conqueror, the ruler of the Roman Empire, the ideal ruler: strong, wise, prudent, humane, generous, courteous.

Malory is recommending the example of Arthur to the English king, as well as recommending the example of Arthur's knights to English nobility. It is even possible that he was at times comparing the deeds of Arthur to those of Henry V, establishing a succession of greatness and asserting by implication England's succession to the position of Rome and the leadership of the world. The claim is already present in earlier versions of the Arthurian story and was to be made explicitly by the Tudor monarchs.

The historical Arthur may have been a British king who resisted the Anglo-Saxon invasions of the sixth century. Tradition made of him the ruler of all Europe, the English equivalent of Charlemagne, to whom the sovereignty of the Roman Empire had been transferred. Geoffrey of Monmouth gathered up these traditions in his *History of the Kings of Britain* (c. 1136), adding some of his own, so that the picture of Arthur and his court as a model of knightly society (Figs. 46–48) together with the plot of the Arthurian romances, was established. Later Arthurian romances depend upon Geoffrey, but their refinement into courtly stories, exalting the love of man for woman to the plane of the spiritual and establishing the ideal of knighthood as the perform- ance of great deeds for its sake, was the work of French authors, such as Chrétien de Troyes, under the influence of the Provençal poets. Malory did not use these earlier French versions for his adaptation-translation. By his time, the Arthurian legends had been embodied in long prose cycles, and he had also at his disposal an English allitera- tive poem called *Morte Arthure.*

His technique was always, it seems, to "reduce," and this is generally taken to mean that he selected and compressed as well as translated. He keeps the order of the French "novels," with occasional additions and variations, but often destroys, perhaps deliberately, the elaborate system of cross-links and interconnections in the story. He cuts down the minor characters and subtleties of motive, and puts his story into an English which Caxton must have approved, composed of "the common terms that be daily used," fluent and quick, with a touch of archaic quality about it, straightforward but sensitive, balanced but not artificial, simple but not bare and low, almost spoken English, but rising—as in the famous passage on the death of Arthur —to a rich movement which is assured, majestic, and masterly.

Morte Darthur

The selections given below are two of the best known in Malory's book: how Arthur became king by pulling out the sword from the stone and how he met his death. Both display Malory's superb narrative skill and the care and composure of his literary idiom.

His tale begins with the King of all England, Uther Pendragon, lusting after Igraine, the wife of his enemy the Duke of Cornwall, lord of the castle of Tintagel. Igraine refuses to sleep with the king, and she and her husband abruptly terminate the visit they have been making to Uther, whereupon he renews war with them. For love of Igraine, Uther falls sick and the magician Merlin is called in, to bring it about that Uther, taking the form of the Duke of Cornwall, shall gain entrance to the castle of Tintagel and to Igraine, just at the moment when her true husband is being killed. Shortly after, Igraine and Uther are married. The story of Uther and Igraine comes in the first place from the *History of the Kings of Britain* by Geoffrey of Monmouth (1100?–1154).

One of the ways in which Malory's story is affected by the times in which he lived is the tinge of reminiscence, perhaps unconscious, of the conditions and events of the Wars of the Roses. In the first selection, for example, there is a possible allusion to Henry VI at the first battle of St. Albans. Moreover, the way in which Malory constantly makes the North the enemy, apparently has a special weakness for Wales, and makes the king's strength center on London and its vicinity, may carry a sug- gestion of the Yorkists as the enemy and the Lancastrians as the party in the right.

As the title of his book indicates, Malory must have regarded the death of Arthur as the climactic moment of his story. He rises to the occasion in recounting, as Tennyson was to do four centuries later, the final passing of the British king into his long sleep, half Christian death, half fairy slumber, from which he may come again, if the need is great enough, to the salvation of his old kingdom: the "once and future king."

Arthur, laying siege to Sir Lancelot's castle, has made him yield up Arthur's queen, Guinevere, whose lover Lancelot has been; and Lancelot has left England for France. Sir Gawain, Arthur's nephew, who has quarreled with Lancelot, persuades Arthur that Lancelot has not been punished enough and Arthur raises an army to besiege Lancelot in France. During Arthur's absence his bastard son Sir Mordred seizes the kingdom, and Arthur, hearing the news, hastily brings his army back. As they land at Dover, Mordred attacks and Gawain is killed, repentant at having involved Arthur in his fruitless expedition, and calling on Lancelot to honor his oath of allegiance and come to the help of the king. He does not do so, and those who had supported him previously in England enlist with Mordred.

The final battle approaches and Arthur dreams (on Trinity Sunday) that he sits high on his throne, which is tied to a wheel (the Wheel of Fortune; Fig 41) above a turbulent black pool full of serpents and monsters, into which he is thrown as the wheel turns. In a second dream he sees Sir Gawain, and the ladies on behalf of whom he had fought. Gawain warns him that if, he gives battle next day, he will be killed. He must make a truce with Mordred for a month, so that Lancelot can reach him with help. Arthur agrees, and a tournament is arranged in which Arthur, Mordred, and fourteen knights from either side will participate. But Arthur has commanded that, if sword be drawn on either side, the tournament shall become a battle. When a knight, stung by an adder, draws his sword and kills it, battle commences, though Arthur fears his fate.

The first selection is modernized in spelling and punctuation after Caxton's printing of 1485, since the Winchester manuscript is defective at the beginning. It is from Bk. I, *Merlin*, Chaps. 3–6: "Of the birth of King Arthur and of his nurture, and of the death of King Uther Pendragon, and how Arthur was chosen king and of the wonders and marvels of a sword taken out of a stone by the said Arthur." The second selection is modernized in spelling and freely treated, after E. Vinaver's second edition of the Winchester manuscript, with some readings from Caxton's printing and some editorial expansions introduced. It is from Bk. XXI, *The Day of Destiny*, Chaps. 4–7.

From Morte Darthur

[The Birth of Arthur and the Sword in the Stone]

Then Queen Igraine waxed [1] daily greater and greater.[2] So it befell after, within half a year, as King Uther lay by his queen, he asked her by the faith she ought [3] to him whose was the child within her body. Then was she sore abashed [4] to give answer.

1. Grew.
2. More and more pregnant.
3. Owed.
4. Ashamed.

'Dismay you not,' said the King, 'but tell me the truth, and I shall love you the better, by the faith of my body!'

'Sire,' said she, 'I shall tell you the truth. The same night that my lord was dead, the hour of his death, as his knights record, there came into my castle of Tintagel [5] a man like my lord in speech and in countenance, and two knights with him in likeness of his two knights Brastias and Jordanus, and so I went unto bed with him as I ought to do with my lord; and the same night, as I shall answer unto God, this child was begotten upon me.'

'That is truth,' said the King, 'as ye say, for it was I myself that came in the likeness. And therefore, dismay you not, for I am father to the child,' and there he told her all the cause [6] how it was by Merlin's counsel. Then the Queen made great joy when she knew who was the father of her child.

Soon came Merlin unto the King and said, 'Sir, ye must purvey [7] you for the nourishing [8] of your child.'

'As thou wilt,' said the King, 'be it.'

'Well,' said Merlin, 'I know a lord of yours in this land that is a passing true man and a faithful, and he shall have the nourishing of your child; and his name is Sir Ector [9] and he is a lord of fair livelihood [10] in many parts in England and Wales. And this lord, Sir Ector, let him be sent for for to come and speak with you, and desire him yourself, as he loveth you, that he will put his own child to nourishing to another woman and that his wife nourish yours. And when the child is born let it be delivered to me at yonder privy postern [11] unchristened.' [12]

So like as Merlin devised, [13] it was done. And when Sir Ector was come he made fiaunce [14] to the King for to nourish the child like as the King desired; and there the King granted Sir Ector great rewards. Then when the lady was delivered the King commanded two knights and two ladies to take the child, bound in a cloth of gold, 'and that ye deliver him to what [15] poor man ye meet at the postern gate of the castle.' So the child was delivered unto Merlin, and so he bare it forth unto Sir Ector and made an holy man to christen him and named him Arthur. And so Sir Ector's wife nourished him with her own pap. [16]

Then within two years King Uther fell sick of a great malady. And in the meanwhile his enemies usurped upon him and did a great battle upon his men and slew many of his people.

'Sir,' said Merlin, 'ye may not lie so as ye do, for ye must to the field, though ye ride on an horse-litter. For ye shall never have the better of your

5. On the north coast of Cornwall. There is still a ruined 12th-century castle there, high on the cliffs overlooking the sea.
6. Affair.
7. Provide, arrange for.
8. Nursing, upbringing.
9. Sir Ector de Maris, brother of Sir Lancelot.
10. Estates, possessions.
11. Secret, secluded side-door.
12. In peril of its soul. A child in the Middle Ages was often christened on the same day that it was born.
13. Arranged, set out.
14. Promise.
15. That.
16. Breast.

enemies but if [17] your person be there, and then shall ye have the victory.'

So it was done as Merlin had devised, and they carried the King forth in an horse-litter with a great host toward his enemies, and at Saint Albans [18] there met with the King a great host of the North.[19] And that day Sir Ulfius [20] and Sir Brastias did great deeds of arms, and King Uther's men overcame the northern battle [21] and slew many people and put the remnant to flight; and then the King returned unto London and made great joy of his victory.

And then he fell passing sore [22] sick, so that three days and three nights he was speechless; wherefore all the barons made great sorrow and asked Merlin what counsel were best.

'There nis [23] none other remedy,' said Merlin, 'but God will have His will. But look ye all barons be before King Uther to-morrow, and God and I shall make him to speak.'

So on the morning all the barons, with Merlin, came tofore [24] the King. Then Merlin said aloud unto King Uther: "Sire, shall your son Arthur be King after your days, of this realm with all the appurtenance?' [25]

Then Uther Pendragon turned him and said in hearing of them all, 'I give him God's blessing and mine, and bid him pray for my soul, and righteously and worshipfully [26] that he claim the crown, upon forfeiture of my blessing,' and therewith he yielded up the ghost.

And then was he interred as belonged to a king, wherefore the Queen, fair Igraine, made great sorrow and all the barons.

Then stood the realm in great jeopardy long while, for every lord that was mighty of men [27] made him strong,[28] and many weened [29] to have been king. Then Merlin went to the Archbishop of Canterbury and counselled him for to send for all the lords of the realm and all the gentlemen of arms, that they should to London come by Christmas upon pain of cursing,[30] and for this cause, that Jesus, that was born on that night, that He would of His great mercy show some miracle, as He was come to be King of mankind, for to show some miracle who should be rightly king of this realm. So the Archbishop, by the advice of Merlin, sent for all the lords and gentlemen of arms,

17. Unless.
18. In Hertfordshire. Perhaps a reminiscence of the first Battle of St. Albans, May 22, 1455, the first battle of the Wars of the Roses, when the sick King Henry VI was carried onto the battlefield and then defeated and captured by the Northern armies under the Duke of York.
19. The North in Malory is always enemy territory, as it was to the Lancastrian party, which found much support in the South, the West, and in Wales at the time of the Wars of the Roses.
20. The retainer of Uther Pendragon who had counseled calling in Merlin to work out a way for Uther to sleep with Igraine.
21. Army.
22. Extremely severely.
23. Is not.
24. Before.
25. Property rights, privileges belonging to an estate.
26. Honorably.
27. Having a large following.
28. Strengthened himself.
29. Expected.
30. Excommunication.

that they should come by Christmas even unto London; and many of them made themselves clean of their life,[31] that their prayer might be the more acceptable unto God.

So, in the greatest church of London—whether it were Paul's [32] or not the French book [33] maketh no mention—all the estates were long ere [34] day in the church for to pray. And when matins [35] and the first mass was done there was seen in the churchyard against [36] the high altar a great stone four square, like unto a marble stone, and in midst thereof was like an anvil of steel a foot on high,[37] and therein stuck a fair sword, naked, by the point, and letters there were written in gold about the sword that said thus: 'WHOSO PULLETH OUT THIS SWORD OF THIS STONE AND ANVIL IS RIGHTLY BORN KING OF ALL ENGLAND.' [38] Then the people marvelled and told it to the Archbishop.

'I command,' said the Archbishop, 'that ye keep yourselves within your church and pray unto God still; [39] that no man touch the sword till the high mass be all done.'

So when all masses were done all the lords went to behold the stone and the sword. And when they saw the scripture [40] some essayed, such as would have been king, but none might stir the sword nor move it.

'He is not here,' said the Archbishop, 'that shall achieve [41] the sword, but doubt not God will make him known. But this is my counsel,' said the Archbishop, 'that we let purvey [42] ten knights, men of good fame, they to keep this sword.'

So it was ordained, and then there was made a cry [43] that every man should essay [44] that would for to win the sword. And upon New Year's Day [45] the barons let make a joust and a tournament,[46] that all knights that would joust or tourney there might play. And all this was ordained for to keep the lords together and the commons, for the Archbishop trusted that God would make him known that should win the sword.

31. I.e. made confession.
32. St. Paul's Cathedral.
33. The *Suite de Merlin*, Malory's source for this section of his work; or, more generally, the French cycle of Arthurian romance on which he drew.
34. Before.
35. Morning prayers.
36. Opposite the spot where the high altar stood within the church.
37. In height.
38. The French version makes him the king of all the land, chosen by Jesus Christ.
39. Continually.
40. Inscription.
41. Obtain.
42. Appoint, choose.
43. Public announcement.
44. Try.
45. The turn of the year: part of the festivities during the great religious feast of Christmas.
46. By Malory's time a joust and a tournament were indistinguishable from one another. Twelfth-century tournaments were pitched battles between two sides of knights; the joust was originally a combat between two single knights. With the development of the theory and practice of chivalry, both were combined in one festival, lasting some days and including entertainments and dancing. Ladies looked on, and blunted or fragile weapons were used. (Fig. 50)

So upon New Year's Day, when the service was done, the barons rode unto the field, some to joust and some to tourney. And so it happened that Sir Ector, that had great livelihood about London, rode unto the joust, and with him rode Sir Kay, his son, and young Arthur, that was his nourished brother; [47] and Sir Kay was made knight at All Hallowmass [48] afore. So as they rode to the joust-ward Sir Kay had lost his sword, for he had left it at his father's lodging, and so he prayed young Arthur for to ride for his sword.

'I will well,' [49] said Arthur, and rode fast after the sword.

And when he came home, the lady and all were out to see the jousting. Then was Arthur wroth and said to himself, 'I will ride to the churchyard and take the sword with me that sticketh in the stone, for my brother Sir Kay shall not be without a sword this day.' So when he came to the churchyard, Sir Arthur alight and tied his horse to the stile, and so he went to the tent and found no knights there, for they were at the jousting. And so he handled the sword by the handle, and lightly and fiercely pulled it out of the stone, and took his horse and rode his way until he came to his brother Sir Kay and delivered him the sword. And as soon as Sir Kay saw the sword he wist [50] well it was the sword of the stone, and so he rode to his father Sir Ector and said, "Sire, lo here is the sword of the stone, wherefore I must be king of this land.'

When Sir Ector beheld the sword he returned again and came to the church, and there they alighted all three and went into the church and anon [51] he made Sir Kay to swear upon a book how he came to that sword.

'Sir,' said Sir Kay, 'by my brother Arthur, for he brought it to me.'

'How got ye this sword?' said Sir Ector to Arthur.

'Sir, I will tell you. When I came home for my brother's sword I found nobody at home to deliver me his sword. And so I thought my brother Sir Kay should not be swordless, and so I came hither eagerly and pulled it out of the stone without any pain.'

'Found ye any knights about this sword?' said Sir Ector.

'Nay,' [52] said Arthur.

'Now,' said Sir Ector to Arthur, 'I understand ye must be king of this land.'

'Wherefore I?' said Arthur, 'and for what cause?'

'Sire,' said Sir Ector, 'for God will have it so; for there should never man have drawn out this sword but he that shall be rightfully king of this land. Now let me see whether ye can put the sword there as it was and pull it out again.'

'That is no maistry,' [53] said Arthur, and so he put it in the stone. Therwithal [54] Sir Ector essayed to pull out the sword and failed.

---

47. Foster-brother, *frère-de-lait*.
48. All Saints Day, November 1, a major religious festival, hence suitable for assemblies of knights and receiving of knighthood.
49. I will, with pleasure.
50. Knew.
51. At once.
52. No, indeed.
53. Mastery, deed of prowess.
54. Thereupon.

'Now essay,' said Sir Ector unto Sir Kay. And anon he pulled at the sword with all his might, but it would not be.

'Now shall ye essay,' said Sir Ector to Arthur.

'I will well,' said Arthur, and pulled it out easily.

And therwithal Sir Ector kneeled down to the earth, and Sir Kay.

'Alas!' said Arthur, 'my own dear father and brother, why kneel ye to me?'

'Nay, nay, my lord Arthur, it is not so. I was never your father nor of your blood, but I wot [55] well ye are of an higher blood than I weened ye were.' And then Sir Ector told him all how he was betaken [56] him for to nourish him and by whose commandment, and by Merlin's deliverance.[57]

1468?–70   1485

[The Death of Arthur]

'Now tide me [1] death, tide me life,' said the King, 'now I see him yonder alone, he shall never escape my hands! For at a better avail [2] shall I never have him.'

'God speed [3] you well!' said Sir Bedivere.

Then the King got his spear in both his hands, and ran toward Sir Mordred, crying and saying, 'Traitor, now is thy death-day come!'

And when Sir Mordred saw King Arthur he ran unto him with his sword drawn in his hand, and there King Arthur smote Sir Mordred under the shield with a foin [4] of his spear, throughout the body more than a fathom.[5] And when Sir Mordred felt that he had his death's wound, he thrust himself with the might that he had up to the burr [6] of King Arthur's spear, and right so he smote his father, King Arthur, with his sword held in both his hands, upon the side of the head, that the sword pierced the helmet and the tay [7] of the brain. And therewith Mordred dashed down stark dead to the earth.

And noble King Arthur fell in a swoon to the earth, and there he swooned oftentimes, and Sir Lucan the Butler [8] and Sir Bedivere the Bold ofttimes hove him up. And so weakly betwixt them they led him to a little chapel not far from the sea, and when the King was there, him thought him [9] reasonably eased.

Then heard they people cry in the field.

'Now go thou, Sir Lucan,' said the King, 'and do me to wit [10] what betokens that noise in the field.'

55. Know.
56. Entrusted to.
57. Handing over.
1. Betide, befall.
2. Advantage.
3. Prosper.
4. Thrust.
5. Six feet.
6. Hand-guard.
7. Outer membrane.
8. Originally the knight who had charge of the wine for the king's table.
9. He seemed to himself.
10. Cause me to know.

So Sir Lucan departed, for he was grievously wounded in many places; and so as he yode [11] he saw and hearkened [12] by the moonlight how that pillours [13] and robbers were come into the field to pill and to rob many a full noble knight of brooches and bees [14] and of many a good ring and many a rich jewel. And who that were not dead all out [15] there they slew them for their harness [16] and their riches.

When Sir Lucan understood this work, he came to the King as soon as he might, and told him all that he had heard and seen.

'Therefore, by my rede,' [17] said Sir Lucan, 'it is best that we bring you to some town.'

'I would it were so,' said the King, 'but I may not stand, my head works [18] so . . . Ah, Sir Lancelot!' said King Arthur, 'this day have I sore missed thee! And alas, that ever I was against thee! For now have I my death, whereof Sir Gawain me warned in my dream.'

Then Sir Lucan took up the King the one part [19] and Sir Bedivere the other part, and in the lifting up the King swooned, and in the lifting Sir Lucan fell in a swoon, that part of his guts fell out of his body, and therewith the noble knight's heart burst. And when the King awoke he beheld Sir Lucan, how he lay foaming at the mouth and part of his guts lay at his feet.

'Alas,' said the King, 'this is to me a full heavy [20] sight, to see this noble duke so die for my sake, for he would have helped me, that had more need of help than I! Alas, that he would not complain him, for [21] his heart was so set to help me. Now Jesus have mercy upon his soul!'

Then Sir Bedivere wept for the death of his brother.

'Now leave this mourning and weeping, gentle [22] knight,' said the King, 'for all this will not avail me. For wit [23] thou well, and [24] I might live myself, the death of Sir Lucan would grieve me evermore. But my time passeth on fast,' said the King. 'Therefore,' said King Arthur unto Sir Bedivere, 'take thou here Excalibur,[25] my good sword, and go with it to yonder water's side; and when thou comest there, I charge thee throw my sword in that water, and come again and tell me what thou there seest.'

'My lord,' said Sir Bedivere, 'your commandment shall be done, and lightly [26] bring you word again.'

11. Went, walked.
12. Noticed.
13. Plunderers.
14. Neck chains, bracelets.
15. Completely.
16. Armor.
17. According to my advice.
18. Aches, hurts.
19. On one side.
20. Sad.
21. Because.
22. Noble, good.
23. Know.
24. If.
25. "Cut-steel"; the name was revealed to Arthur by the Lady of the Lake after she had given it to him.
26. Quickly.

So Sir Bedivere departed. And by the way he beheld that noble sword, and the pommel [27] and the haft was all precious stones. And then he said to himself: 'If I throw this rich sword in the water, thereof shall never come good, but harm and loss.' And then Sir Bedivere hid Excalibur under a tree, and so as soon as he might he came again unto the King and said he had been at the water and had thrown the sword into the water.

'What saw thou there?' said the King.

'Sir,' he said, 'I saw nothing but waves and winds.'

'That is untruly said of thee,' said the King. 'And therefore go thou lightly again and do my commandment; as thou art to me leve [28] and dear, spare not, but throw it in.'

Then Sir Bedivere returned again and took the sword in his hand; and yet him thought [29] sin and shame to throw away that noble sword. And so eft [30] he hid the sword and returned again and told the King that he had been at the water and done his commandment.

'What sawest thou there?' said the King.

'Sir,' he said, 'I saw nothing but waters wap [31] and waves wan.' [32]

'Ah, traitor unto me and untrue,' said King Arthur, 'now hast thou betrayed me twice! Who would ween that thou hast been to me so leve and dear, and also named so noble a knight, that thou wouldst betray me for the riches of this sword? But now go again lightly; for thy long tarrying putteth me in great jeopardy of my life, for I have taken cold. And but if thou do now as I bid thee, if ever I may see thee, I shall slay thee [with] my own hands, for thou wouldst for my rich sword see me dead.'

Then Sir Bedivere departed and went to the sword and lightly took it up, and so he went unto the water's side. And there he bound the girdle [33] about the hilt, and threw the sword as far into the water as he might. And there came an arm and a hand above the water, and took it and clutched it, and shook it thrice and brandished [it] and then vanished with the sword into the water.

So Sir Bedivere came again to the King and told him what he saw.

'Alas,' said the King, 'help me hence, for I dread me I have tarried over long.'

Then Sir Bedivere took the King upon his back and so went with him to the water's side. And when they were there, even fast [34] by the bank hove [35] a little barge [36] with many fair ladies in it, and among them all was a queen and all they had black hoods. And all they wept and shrieked when they saw King Arthur.

'Now put me into that barge,' said the King.

27. The knob at the top of the hilt (haft).
28. Beloved.
29. It seemed.
30. Again.
31. Presumably, lapping.
32. Presumably, darkening.
33. Belt of the sword.
34. Close.
35. Was waiting.
36. Flat-bottomed boat.

And so he did softly, and there received him three ladies with great mourning. And so they sat them down, and in one of their laps King Arthur laid his head. And then the queen said:

'Ah my dear brother! Why have ye tarried so long from me? Alas, this wound on your head hath caught overmuch cold!'

And anon [37] they rowed fromward [38] the land, and Sir Bedivere beheld all the ladies go fromward him. Then Sir Bedivere cried and said: 'Ah, my lord Arthur, what shall become of me, now ye go from me and leave me here alone among my enemies?'

'Comfort thyself,' said the King, 'and do as well as thou mayest, for in me is no trust for to trust in. For I must into the vale of Avylyon [39] to heal me of my grievous wound. And if thou hear nevermore of me, pray for my soul!'

But ever the queen and ladies wept and shrieked, that it was pity to hear. And as soon as Sir Bedivere had lost the sight of the barge he wept and wailed, and so took [to] the forest and went all that night.

And in the morning he was aware, betwixt two holts hoar,[40] of a chapel and a hermitage.[41] Then was Sir Bedivere fain,[42] and thither he went, and when he came into the chapel he saw where lay a hermit grovelling on all fours, fast there by a tomb [43] was newly graven.[44] When the hermit saw Sir Bedivere he knew him well, for he was but little tofore [45] Bishop [46] of Canterbury that Sir Mordred fleamed.[47]

'Sir,' said Sir Bedivere, 'what man is there here interred that ye pray so fast [48] for?'

'Fair son,' said the hermit, 'I wot [49] not verily but by deeming.[50] But this same night, at midnight, there came a number of ladies and brought here a dead corpse and prayed me to inter him. And here they offered a hundred tapers,[51] and they gave me a thousand besants.' [52]

'Alas!' said Sir Bedivere, 'that was my lord King Arthur, which lyeth here graven [53] in this chapel.'

37. At once.
38. Away from.
39. Avalon, the valley, sometimes identified with Glastonbury in Somerset, where Joseph of Arimathea is supposed to have brought the Holy Grail; and sometimes with the other world, the Earthly Paradise.
40. Bare woods.
41. The cell of a hermit, i.e. an ascetic religious living alone.
42. Glad.
43. I.e. grave.
44. Dug.
45. Before.
46. Archbishop.
47. Put to flight. The Archbishop had remonstrated with and excommunicated the usurper Mordred and Mordred had tried to kill him. The Archbishop fled, according to Malory, to Glastonbury, where Sir Bedivere finds him, guarding Arthur's tomb. The placing of Arthur's tomb at Glastonbury derives from Gerald of Wales (Giraldus Cambrensis, 1146?–1220?), who states that the tomb was found there in 1189.
48. Hard and frequently.
49. Know.
50. By guesswork.
51. Wax candles.
52. Bezant, gold coin first struck at Byzantium.
53. Buried.

Then Sir Bedivere swooned, and when he awoke he prayed the hermit that he might abide with him still,[54] there to live with fasting and prayers: 'For from hence will I never go,' said Sir Bedivere, 'by my will, but all the days of my life here to pray for my lord Arthur.' . . .

Thus of Arthur I find no more written in books that been authorised,[55] nor more of the very certainty of his death heard I never read, but thus was he led away in a ship wherein were three queens; that one was King Arthur's sister, Queen Morgan le Fay,[56] the other [57] was the Queen of North Wales,[58] and the third was the Queen of the Waste Lands.[59] Also there was Dame Nynyve,[60] the chief Lady of the Lake, which had wedded Sir Pelleas,[61] the good knight; and this lady had done much for King Arthur. (And this Dame Nynyve would never suffer Sir Pelleas to be in no place where he should be in danger of his life, and so he lived unto the uttermost of his days with her in great rest.)

Now more of the death of King Arthur could I never find, but that these ladies brought him to his grave, and such one was interred there which the hermit bare witness that sometime [62] was Bishop of Canterbury. . . .

Yet some men say in many parts of England that King Arthur is not dead, but had by the will of our Lord Jesus into another place; and men say that he shall come again, and he shall win the Holy Cross.[63] Yet I will not say that it shall be so, but rather I would say: here in this world he changed his life. And many men say that there is written upon the tomb this:

HIC IACET ARTHURUS

REX QUONDAM REXQUE FUTURUS.[64]

And thus leave I here Sir Bedivere with the hermit that dwelled that time in a chapel beside Glastonbury,[65] and there was his hermitage. And so they lived in prayers and fasting and great abstinence.

And when Queen Guinevere [66] understood that King Arthur was dead and all the noble knights, Sir Mordred and all the remnant, then she stole away with five ladies with her, and so she went to Amesbury.[67] And there she let

54. Always.

55. Perhaps: written or reliable.

56. Arthur's sorceress sister and opponent, who had imprisoned his knights, and tried to kill him.

57. Second.

58. Northgalys, i.e. North Wales; this queen was also a sorceress.

59. This queen was the aunt of Sir Perceval, one of the three knights admitted to the presence of the Holy Grail.

60. Vivian, the Lady of the Lake, who gave Excalibur to Arthur and befriended him in danger.

61. The lover, the dolorous knight, one of the knights in attendance on Guinevere, and her defender in battle.

62. Formerly.

63. I.e. shall liberate the Holy Land from the Turks.

64. "Here lies Arthur, the once and future king": i.e. who was once king and will come to be king again.

65. See note 47.

66. Arthur's Queen, Lancelot's mistress.

67. In Wiltshire, north of Glastonbury, where Lancelot arrives too late to see her before her death. He lives in holiness for the short remainder of his life.

make [68] herself a nun, and wore white clothes and black; and great penance she took upon her, as ever did sinful woman in this land. And never creature could make her merry, but ever she lived in fasting, prayers, and alms-doing, that all manner of people marvelled how virtuously she was changed.
1468?–70   1485

WILLIAM CAXTON
1415(-24)–1491

William Caxton, businessman and England's first printer, was born in Kent at some time between 1415 and 1424. After schooling, he was apprenticed to a member of the Mercers' Company, which dealt in cloth and silks and was one of the oldest and richest guilds of the City of London. Much of their trade abroad was with the Low Countries and, after Caxton had served his apprenticeship, some time in the 1440's he made Bruges the center of his activities. These included the selling of the manuscripts that were then produced in large numbers in Flanders. Having prospered and having become a bookseller on the side, he saw the opportunity in the English market offered by the new invention of printing. In 1469, he set himself to translate Raoul Lefèvre's French version of the *History of Troy,* continued the translation under the patronage of Margaret of Burgundy (sister of the English King Edward IV), and went to Cologne, the nearest town where printing was carried on, to learn the craft. Leaving Cologne late in 1472, he returned to Belgium, set up his press at Bruges, and issued the first book printed in English, his translation of Lefèvre, in 1473 or 1474. Before transferring his press to London in 1476, he had printed six books, four of them in French.

Like any printer, Caxton did a great deal of bread-and-butter work—official documents, school-books—in the next fifteen years. But he had always aimed at a noble and wealthy audience, and the bulk of his production consists of his own translations from French, Flemish, and Latin; of English poetry, especially Gower, Chaucer, and Chaucer's followers; and of works in English prose, such as Chaucer's translation of Boethius and Sir Thomas Malory's *Morte Darthur.* Caxton's aim was here not merely to make money: he set himself continually to raise the style of English language and literature as well as the style of English life itself, especially by the importation of French and Burgundian culture. The English authors whom he chose to print were those who had called in the help of Latin or French to enrich and refine their style and language. In his own translations he attempted to transfer some of the polish of the originals to the English tongue. But he was as much concerned to import into England some of the civilized spiritual and chivalric values of the late medieval Burgundian court, under whose patronage he had begun his literary career. He was always deeply concerned with the exemplary value of the works he printed, though sometimes, as in his translation of *The History of Reynard the Fox* (see above), the concern is allowed to slip a little and pleasure in the tale as tale takes over.

Caxton's deep involvement with the texts he prints comes out clearly in his habit of adding prologue and epilogue to almost all of them. In the Proem (preface) to his second edition of Chaucer's *Canterbury Tales* of 1484, he tells how, after he had printed the first edition (about 1478), he learned that his "copy" had been unsatis-

68. Had herself made.

factory and undertook another edition for the sake of an author whom he admired. His praise of literature and the written word at the beginning of the preface is a topos (see Glossary) of the emerging Renaissance, and so is his praise of Chaucer as laureate poet and philosopher; yet both represent a firm conviction. Chaucer's role as a refiner, embellisher, and rhetorician is given significant praise: Caxton's lament for the roughness and variety of English as against the smoothness, richness, and uniformity of Latin and French is, again, not merely a modesty topos, but a matter of real concern. Chaucer, too, is a poet from whom one may learn wisdom, and not an entertainer only. Caxton echoes Chaucer's own Retraction at the end of *The Canterbury Tales,* but it is not an empty echo.

In the second of the two prefaces here printed, that to his prose version of the *Aeneid,* Caxton justifies his own rhetorical practice in terms of his function and his audience, showing himself, in a famous passage, clearly aware of the influence toward uniformity and improvement of language that his principles and practice might have.

Both selections are modernizations, by the present editor, based on *The Prologues and Epilogues of William Caxton,* ed. W. J. B. Crotch (Early English Text Society, 1928).

The Proem to the Canterbury Tales

Great thanks, laud and honour ought to be given unto the clerks,[1] poets and historiographers that have written many noble books of wisdom of the lives, passions and miracles of holy saints, of histories, of noble and famous acts and feats; [2] and of the chronicles sith [3] the beginning of the creation of the world unto this present time, by which we be daily informed and have knowledge of many things; of whom we should not have known, if they had not left to us their monuments written.[4] Among whom and in especial tofore [5] all other we ought to give a singular [6] laud unto that noble and great philosopher [7] Geoffrey Chaucer, the which for his ornate [8] writing in our tongue may well have the name of a laureate [9] poet. For tofore that he by his labour embellished, ornated and made fair our English, in this realm was had rude [10] speech and incongru-

1. Learned men.
2. Deeds of arms.
3. Since. Medieval world chronicles always began with the Creation and the events of the Pentateuch, especially Genesis.
4. Caxton takes up the topos of the power of the written word, and the immortalizing function of the writer, a favorite idea among Roman authors and now being vigorously taken up by the emerging Renaissance.
5. Before.
6. Special.
7. Poets were held to be moral philosophers, hiding their lesson under the cloud of their story.
8. Polished and rich, a term of praise during the 15th century especially, when writers were trying to polish and enrich their rough vernacular and make it as fine and enduring a language as the Latin they wished to replace.
9. Distinguished. Petrarch (1304–74) had given the word new currency and poetry a boost by having himself laureated in Rome in 1341. Laureate here means "worthy of laureation," i.e. of formal recognition of excellence.
10. Rough, unpolished.

ous,[11] as yet it appeareth by old books, which at this day ought not to have place ne be compared among ne to his beauteous volumes [12] and ornate writings, of whom he made many books and treatises of many a noble history as well in metre as in rhyme and prose, and them so craftily [13] made, that he comprehended his matter in short, quick [14] and high [15] sentences,[16] eschewing prolixity, casting away the chaff of superfluity, and showing the picked grain of sentence,[17] uttered by crafty and sugared [18] eloquence. Of whom, among all other of his books, I purpose to print by the grace of God the book of the Tales of Canterbury, in which I find many a noble history of every estate and degree; first rehearsing the conditions [19] and the array [20] of each of them as properly [21] as possible is to be said; and after, their Tales, which be of noblesse,[22] wisdom, gentilesse,[23] mirth [24] and also of very [25] holiness and virtue, wherein he finisheth this said book; which book I have diligently overseen and duly examined to the end that it be made according unto his own making. For I find many of the said books, which writers have abridged it and many things left out; and in some places have set certain verses that he never made [26] ne set in his book. Of which books so incorrect was one brought to me six years past, which I supposed had been very true and correct; and according to the same I did imprint [27] a certain number of them, which anon were sold to many and divers gentlemen, of whom one gentleman came to me and said that this book was not according in many places unto the book that Geoffrey Chaucer had made. To whom I answered that I had made it according to my copy, and by me was nothing added ne diminished.[28] Then he said he knew a book which his father had, and much loved, that was very true and according unto his own first book [29] by him made; and said more, if I would print it again, he would get me the same book for a copy,[30] howbeit [31] he wist [32] well that his father

11. Of all kinds and dialects; lacking both the uniformity and decorum that an educated single-speech standard, on the model of Latin, would confer.
12. Nor be put on a level with either his splendid volumes.
13. Skillfully.
14. Lively.
15. Exalted.
16. Statements, or perhaps approximating the modern sentences.
17. Sententia, didactic import, moral lesson.
18. Sweet, without any derogatory associations.
19. Social status, a paraphrase of Chaucer's General Prologue.
20. Dress.
21. Exactly, fittingly.
22. Noble, virtuous behavior.
23. "Courtesy," refinement.
24. Fun.
25. True.
26. The manuscripts and early editions of Chaucer, including Caxton's, contain tales and other verse by disciples and other poets.
27. Had printed. Caxton's first edition of *The Canterbury Tales* was published in 1478, the first printed English "classic."
28. Taken out, subtracted.
29. Chaucer's own fair manuscript copy. This is not likely and, in any case, it would have been written by a scribe.
30. "Copy" to print from.
31. Although.
32. Knew.

would not gladly part from it. To whom I said, in case that he could get me such a book true and correct, yet I would once endeavour me to print it again, for to satisfy the author, whereas tofore by ignorance I erred in hurting and defaming [33] his book in divers places, in setting in some things that he never said nor made and leaving out many things that he made which be requisite to be set in it. And thus we fell at accord.[34] And he full gentilly [35] got of his father the said book, and delivered it to me, by which I have corrected my book, as hereafter all along by the aid of Almyghty God shall follow, whom I humbly beseech to give me grace and aid to achieve and accomplish, to his laud, honour, and glory; and that all ye that shall in this book read or hear, will of your charity among your deeds of mercy,[36] remember the soul of the said Geoffrey Chaucer, first author and maker of this book. And also that all we that shall see and read therein, may so take and understand the good and virtuous Tales,[37] that it may so profit unto the health of our souls that after this short and transitory life we may come to everlasting life in heaven. Amen.

1484

From The Preface to the Aeneid

. . . And when I had advised me [1] in this said book I deliberated and concluded [2] to translate it, in to English, and forthwith took a pen and ink and wrote a leaf or twain, which I oversaw [3] again to correct it. And when I saw the fair and strange [4] terms therein, I doubted that it should not please some gentlemen which late blamed me, saying that in my translations I had over curious [5] terms, which could not be understood of common people, and desired me to use old and homely terms in my translations. And fain [6] would I satisfy every man, and so to do took an old book and read therein and certainly the English was so rude and broad that I could not well understand it. And also my lord Abbot of Westmynster did do show to me late certain evidences [7] written in old English, for to reduce it into our English now used. And certainly it was written in such wise that it was more like to Dutch [8] than English. I could not reduce ne [9] bring it to be understood. And certainly our language now used varieth far from that which was used and spoken when I was born.

33. Harming.
34. Agreement.
35. Kindly.
36. The conventional formula at the close of a book: Caxton echoes Chaucer's Retraction.
37. Again echoing the Retraction: literature tends toward good.

1. Looked carefully through.
2. Decided.
3. Looked over, checked.
4. Foreign, difficult.
5. Far-fetched, artificial.
6. Gladly.
7. Documents.
8. Middle Dutch, the dialect of Caxton's day in the Netherlands.
9. Nor.

For we Englishmen be born under the domination of the moon,[10] which is never steadfast, but ever wavering, waxing one season and waneth and discreaseth another season. And that common English that is spoken in one shire varieth from another, insomuch that in my days [it] happened that certain merchants were in a ship in Tamyse [11] for to have sailed over the sea into Zealand,[12] and for lack of wind they tarried at the foreland, and went to land for to refresh them. And one of them, named Sheffelde, a mercer,[13] came into a house [14] and asked for meat,[15] and specially he asked after eggs. And the good-wife [16] answered that she could speak no French. And the merchant was angry, for he also could speak no French, but would have had eggs; and she understood him not. And then at last another said that he would have eyren.[17] Then the good-wife said that she understood him well. Lo, what should a man in these days now write, eggs or eyren? Certainly, it is hard to please every man, because of diversity and change of language. For in these days every man, that is in any reputation in his country, will utter his communication and matters in such manners and terms, that few men shall understand them. And some honest and great clerks [18] have been with me and desired me to write the most curious terms that I could find. And thus, between plain, rude [19] and curious I stand abashed; [20] but in my judgment the common terms, that be daily used, be lighter [21] to be understood than the old and ancient English. And forasmuch as this present book is not for a rude, uplandish [22] man to labour therein, ne read it, but only for a clerk and a noble gentleman that feeleth and understandeth in feats of arms,[23] in love, and in noble chivalry. Therefore, in a mean [24] between both, I have reduced and translated this said book into our English, not over rude ne curious but in such terms as shall be understood by God's grace, according to my copy. And if any man will intermit [25] in reading of it and findeth such terms that he cannot understand, let him go read and learn Virgil or the Epistles of Ovid, and there he shall see and understand

10. The moon, the quickest in motion of the planets, with its 28-day cycle of waxing and waning, was a byword for inconstancy. All things below the moon were considered transitory and subject to change.
11. Thames.
12. Province of the Netherlands, a regular trading area, especially for cloth, with England.
13. A dealer, often very wealthy, in wool and cloth; and possibly, like Caxton, a member of the guild or company of Mercers in the City of London.
14. Inn.
15. Food.
16. Hostess.
17. *Eyren* is the older Southern English plural form of *eye*, egg; *egg* was a Northern form, influenced by Norse, now on the point of ousting the other form throughout the country.
18. Learned men.
19. Rustic, rough.
20. Confused.
21. Easier.
22. Up-country, rustic.
23. Warlike deeds and tournaments. Caxton published *The Book of the Order of Chivalry* in 1484; and *The Book of Feats of Arms and of Chivalry* in 1489 or 1490. He is important for his part in the importing of Burgundian chivalric ideas and practices into England.
24. Middle.
25. Engage.

lightly all, if he have a good reader and informer.[26] For this book is not for every rude and uncunning [27] man to see, but to clerks and very [28] gentlemen that understand gentleness [29] and science.[30]

Thence I pray all them that shall read in this little treatise, to hold me for excused for the translating of it. For I acknowledge myself ignorant of cunning [31] to emprise [32] on me so high and noble a work.

1490

WILLIAM DUNBAR
c.1460–c.1520?

William Dunbar was born in Scotland, perhaps of noble parents, about 1460, perhaps attended the University of St. Andrews, and perhaps became a Franciscan friar. By 1500 he was in the service of James IV of Scotland, the first great Scottish patron of arts and letters. He died at an unknown date as a beneficed clergyman.

Dunbar's career follows the pattern of the court poet (or "makar," as he was called in Scotland). Unlike Chaucer, Dunbar was a cleric as well as a courtier and diplomat. (A good comparison would be Petrarch in Italy.) He moved in the atmosphere of a highly civilized and learned royal circle, receptive of the new learning, much under French influence, both directly and through England. Chaucer, whom he calls "reverend" (not "holy" but "to be revered") and "rose of rethoris" ("orators"), was his poetic master, along with John Gower and John Lydgate. He used the metrical and poetic forms that they had used, and he developed from them his elaborate, jeweled, Latinate, "aureate" language.

Dunbar's poetry—allegorical as in *The Golden Targe*, satirical as in *The Two Married Women and the Widow*, or elegaic as in the *Lament for the Makers*—is technically controlled and masterly, full of variety, rapid, exuberant, parodistic, wildly and often scabrously witty, as well as, when necessary, formally reverent or deeply moving.

26. Guide.
27. Unschooled, not knowledgeable.
28. True.
29. Noble, courteous behavior of all kinds.
30. Knowledge. The knowledge one would be expected to gain from the *Aeneid* would not be acquaintance with the story and characters, but with the moral lessons it carried. In Italy the poem was still in Caxton's day being presented as an allegory of human life, and continued to be so thought of throughout the Renaissance.
31. Knowledge, skill.
32. Enterprise, undertake.

Lament for the Makers°

I that in heill° was and gladness   *health*
Am trublit° now with great sickness   *afflicted*
And feblit° with infirmitie.   *enfeebled*
    Timor Mortis conturbat me.°

Our plesance° here is all vain glory,   *pleasure*
This fals world is but transitory,
The flesh is bruckle,° the Feynd is slee.°   *frail / wily*
    Timor Mortis conturbat me.

The state of man does change and vary,
10 Now sound, now sick, now blyth, now sary,°   *sad*
Now dansand° merry, now like to die.   *dancing*
    Timor Mortis conturbat me.

No state in erd° here standis sicker;   *earth*
As with the wynd wavis the wicker°
So wavis this world's vanitie.
    Timor Mortis conturbat me.

Unto the death° gois all estatis,   *to death*
Princis, prelatis,° and potestatis,°   *prelates / potentates*
Baith° rich and poor of all degree.   *both*
20   *Timor Mortis conturbat me.*

He takis the knichtis° in to field°   *knights / in battle*
Enarmit° under helm and scheild;   *fully armed*
Victor he is at all mellie.°
    Timor Mortis conturbat me.

That strong unmerciful tyrand°   *tyrant*
Takis, on the motheris breast sowkand,°   *sucking*
The babe full of benignitie.°   *innocence*
    Timor Mortis conturbat me.

He takis the campion° in the stour,°   *champion / conflict*
30 The captain closit° in the tour,°   *enclosed / tower*
The lady in bour° full of bewtie.   *bower*
    Timor Mortis conturbat me.

He sparis no lord for his piscence,°   *power*
Na clerk° for his intelligence;   *scholar*
His awful straik° may no man flee.   *terrible stroke*
    Timor Mortis conturbat me.

Lament for the Makers The title is traditional, not Dunbar's. Early printed versions end "Quod [said] Dunbar when he was sick." An *ubi sunt* poem, a dance of death, a statement of poetic indebtedness, this is a good example of the mixing of genres which makes Dunbar's poetry so difficult to categorize. *Makers,* or "makaris," means poets; etymologically the words are the same, "poet" coming from the Greek *poiein,* to make.
Timor . . . me "The fear of death confounds me." The refrain, from the Office of the Dead, had been used by Lydgate and others in the 15th century.
wicker strictly willow twig, so any living branch easily stirred by the wind
mellie French *mêlée*

Art magicianis° and astrologgis,⸜   *astrologers*
Rethoris, logicianis, and theologgis,°
Them helpis no conclusionis slee.°
40   *Timor Mortis conturbat me.*

In medecine the most practicianis,
Leechis, surrigianis,⸜ and physicianis,   *doctors, surgeons*
Themself from Death may not supplee.⸜   *beg off*
      Timor Mortis conturbat me.

I see that makaris⸜ amang the laif⸜   *poets / rest*
Playis here their pageant,° syne⸜ gois to graif;⸜   *soon / grief*
Sparit⸜ is nocht⸜ their facultie.°   *spared / not*
      Timor Mortis conturbat me.

He has done petuously⸜ devour   *frighteningly*
50   The noble Chaucer, of makaris flour,
The Monk of Bury,° and Gower,° all three.
      Timor Mortis conturbat me.

The good Sir Hew° of Eglintoun,
And eik Heriot, and Wintoun,
He has tane⸜ out of this cuntrie.⸜   *taken / country*
      Timor Mortis conturbat me.

That scorpion fell⸜ has done infeck⸜   *terrible / infected*
Maister John Clerk, and James Affleck,
Fra ballat⸜-making and tragedie.   *poem*
60   *Timor Mortis conturbat me.*

Holland and Barbour he has berevit;⸜   *bereft*
Alas! that he not with us levit⸜   *left*
Sir Mungo Lockart of the Lee.
      Timor Mortis conturbat me.

Clerk of Tranent eik⸜ he has tane,   *also*
That made the Anteris⸜ of Gawaine;   *adventures*
Sir Gilbert Hay endit has he.
      Timor Mortis conturbat me.

He has Blind Harry and Sandy Traill
70   Slain with his schour⸜ of mortal⸜ hail,   *shower / deadly*

art magicianis masters of the magical art
Rethoris . . . theologgis masters of eloquence,
logicians, theologians
conclusionis slee I.e. clever judgments. Conclusion is the technical term in logic for a proposition deduced by reasoning from two previous propositions, the last of the three propositions in a syllogism, what follows from the two premises. Dunbar uses it to mean a formal judgment or opinion arrived at by the academically correct deployment of acumen and learning.
pageant unsubstantial play of life on earth
facultie profession
Monk of Bury John Lydgate (*c.* 1370–*c.* 1449), prolific poet and monk of Bury St. Edmunds, one of Dunbar's acknowledged masters

Gower John Gower (1325?–1408), Chaucer's older London fellow poet and master, author of the *Confessio Amantis*. Gower, Chaucer, and Lydgate are regarded by the later 15th- and early 16th-century poets as the founders of their craft and models for imitation.
Sir Hew These Scottish poets are not equally well known. Sir Hugh (the title Sir, though here indicating knighthood, at least as often simply means a priest) Eglinton is not known as a poet; Heryot, Clerk, and Affleck (Auchinleck) are unknown; Andrew of Wyntoun wrote a chronicle of Scotland; John Barbour (d. 1395) is the author of the poem *Bruce*. The names are a roll call, not necessarily more.

Quhilk⸜ Patrick Johnstoun might nocht flee.   *which*
    Timor Mortis conturbat me.

He has reft⸜ Merseir his endite,⸜   *bereft / poetry*
That did in luvè⸜ so lively write,   *love*
So short, so quick, of sentence° hie.
    Timor Mortis conturbat me.

He has tane Rowll of Aberdene,
And gentill Rowll of Corstorphine;
Two better fallowis⸜ did no man see.   *companions*
80   *Timor Mortis conturbat me.*

In Dunfermline he has done roune⸜   *talked*
With Maister Robert Henrysoun;°
Sir John the Ross enbrast⸜ has he.   *embraced*
    Timor Mortis conturbat me.

And he has now tane, last of aw,⸜   *all*
Good gentil Stobo and Quintin Shaw,
Of quhom all wichtis hes pitie.°
    Timor Mortis conturbat me.

Good Maister Walter Kennedy
90 In point of Death lies verily;
Great ruth⸜ it were that so shuld be.   *pity*
    Timor Mortis conturbat me.

Sen he has all my brether tane,°
He will nocht let me live alane;⸜   *alone*
Of force⸜ I man⸜ his next prey be.   *necessarily / must*
    Timor Mortis conturbat me.

Since for the Death remeid⸜ is none,   *remedy*
Best is that we for Death dispone,
After our death that live may we.
100   *Timor Mortis conturbat me.*
    c. 1508

JOHN SKELTON
1460(-64?)–1529

Not much is known of Skelton's early life. About 1488 he received the "degree" of laureate (a graduate qualification in poetry and rhetoric) from Oxford. This, and two other such degrees from the universities of Cambridge and Louvain a few years

---

sentence Latin, *sententia*, i.e. morally profitable matter, knowledge: "So brief, so lively, of great pith."
Robert Henrysoun Henryson (1429–1508), schoolmaster of Dunfermline, the best Scottish poet, after Dunbar, of the century, author of

fables (e.g. *The Uponlandis Mous and the Burges Mous*) and *The Testament of Cresseid*
Of . . . pitie whom all men regret
Sen . . . tane since he has all my brethren taken

later, would have formally established his fitness to practice Latin poetry, for the eternal glory of himself and those he wrote about. He had become a professional man of letters, in the style of Petrarch, who had set the fashion for Renaissance Europe by being laureated at Rome in 1341. Most such men supported themselves by going into the service of their ruler or the church: Skelton did both. He was tutor to the young prince who became Henry VIII, rector of Diss in Norfolk, and finally royal orator and cleric-courtier for the rest of his life.

Skelton was a translator (of historian Diodorus Siculus), a moralist and satirist, admired by his contemporaries for his learning, his ornate style, inventiveness, vigor, quickness, and pith. Knowing the works of Chaucer and of Langland well, he was sure of his own place in the English poetic tradition, and his responsibilities to the enrichment of the English language, as his *Garland of Laurel* makes clear.

Some of his satires use the dream-allegory form; some, like *Colin Clout* (Skelton also looks forward to Spenser), are much more rapid and direct statements of the complaints of ordinary Christians about their material and spiritual life. Here, and in *Speak, Parrot,* he is flaying his age and his church, but he is no Protestant reformer. *Magnificence,* an interlude or morality play, is also a "complaint" about the follies of the court and a mirror for princes: the magnanimous man, the prince, must display the virtue of fortitude against all branches of temptation.

These "satires" are often harsh, but they all have flashes of Skelton's quick, gay, inventive wit: his great poetic merits are his speed and metrical skill. In them and in other earlier poems he often uses the verse form (Troilus stanza; rime royal) and rhetoric of Chaucer's successors, reinforced by the long-lined alliterative tradition (of Langland as well as the Chaucerians). His best verse uses the "Skeltonic" meter—the rapid, two- or three-stressed lines, held together by single-rhyme patterns of up to fourteen lines. The stresses are often emphasized by alliteration, which may also hold together blocks of two or three lines, the helter-skelter controlled by Skelton's standard couplet or triplet, which gives a breathing space in the verbal and rhyming virtuosity.

Skelton is both an obviously difficult and a disarmingly simple poet. *The Tunning of Elinor Rumming* is a riot of words and rhymes, tossed off, almost, as the old bags toss off their ale. *Philip Sparrow* is perfectly and subtly structured: a mock-childish, mock-religious, mock-heroic poem built around the Office of the Dead. It looks forward to Alexander Pope's *Rape of the Lock* and Thomas Gray's *Ode on the Death of a Favourite Cat* as well as back to Catullus. The tone is of neither ridicule nor cosmic pathos; the seeming artlessness is poised between the observed innocence of the girl mourning the death of her pet sparrow (without knowing the connotations of lechery attached to the bird) and the conscious, aureate rhetoric which she is made to use as she invents a burial service and laments that her simple reading in romances and "historious tales" is not the right preparation to commemorate him suitably. In this early work, as always, Skelton shows himself inventive master both of the "high" style and of the simple. The two are most clearly differentiated in the long, ornate, *Garland of Laurel,* an elaborate, artificial, dream allegory, with its seven lyrics, building their praise of court ladies around simple, gentle rhyme, rhythm and refrain.

From Colin Clout°

. . . And if ye stand in doubt
Who brought this rhyme about,
My name is Colin Clout.
50   I purpose to shake out
All my cunning° bag,   *learned*
Like a clerkly° hag.°   *erudite*
For though my rhyme be ragged,°
Tattered and jagged,
Rudely rain-beaten,
Rusty and moth-eaten,
If ye take well therewith,
It hath in it some pith.
For, as far as I can see,
60   It is wrong with each degree:°   *class*
For the temporalitie°
Accuseth the spiritualitie;
The spiritual again
Doth grudge and complain
Upon the temporal men:
Thus each of other blother°   *gabble*
The one against the other:
Alas, they make me shudder!
For in hudder-mudder°   *secrecy*
70   The Church is put in fault;
The prelates° be so haute,°   *haughty*
They say, and look so high,
As though they would fly
Above the starry sky.

Lay men say indeed
How they take no heed
Their silly sheep° to feed,
But pluck away and pull
The fleeces of their wool
80   Unneth° they leave a lock   *scarcely*
Of wool among their flock! . . .
c. 1523

Colin Clout The double name is Skelton's invention, later taken up by Spenser. Compare
the earlier Piers Plowman, Jack Upland, the
critics of their society: plain-spoken countrymen.
Colin, a shepherd (see French poetry of the
15th and 16th centuries); Clout, either clod,
rustic, or (patched) cloak or cloth. Colin Clout
is either a shepherd or an itinerant academic,
deeply concerned about the state of his church
and about following the precepts and example
of Christ.

hag applied to man or woman
ragged like my cloak; I am no fine orator—conventional modesty
temporalitie temporal men, laymen; as opposed
to the spirituality, the clergy, whose jurisdictions
and exactions were coming under attack, especially in matters of worldly wealth
prelates senior clergy, who have received preferment in the church
silly sheep poor, innocent flock

Philip Sparrow

Philip Sparrow is a mock elegy, like the Roman poet Catullus' (84–54 B.C.) elegy on Lesbia's sparrow. Jane Scroop, a young friend of Skelton's, mourns the killing by a cat of her beloved pet sparrow, Philip. Rhetorically, the poem is a re-working of the Office of the Dead, during which Jane officiates, inviting us and all bird-kind to share her grief, and begging for a suitable epitaph. This structural wit is complicated and reinforced by Jane's professions of modesty as she deploys her own elaborate rhetoric.

From Philip Sparrow

Pla ce bo,°
Who is there? Who?
Di le xi.°
Dame Margery?°
Fa, re, my, my.°
Wherefore and why, why?
For the soul of Philip° Sparrow,
That was late slain at Carrow,
Among the Nunnès Black,
10 For that sweet soulès sake
And for all sparrows' souls
Set in our bead-rolls,°
Pater noster qui,°
With an Ave Mari,°
And with the corner of a Creed,°
The more shall be your meed.°   *reward*
    When° I remember again
How my Philip was slain,
Never half the pain
20 Was between you twain,
Pyramus and Thisbe,°
As then befell to me.

Placebo the first word of the opening antiphon (psalm verse recited as a prelude and as a conclusion), and the title of the first section of the vespers of the Office of the Dead, Psalm 114:9 (Vulgate numbering used): "I will please [the Lord in the land of the living.]" Key words and phrases from the Office are used in the order in which they occur in the liturgy, their sense matching what Jane is saying at the time.
Dilexi the first word of the opening psalm of the Office, Psalm 114:1: "I have loved, [because the Lord will hear the voice of my prayer]"
Margery A Margery was superior at Carrow Abbey, the Benedictine convent (Black Nuns) near Norwich—see l. 8—where Jane Scroop was probably educated.
Fa . . . my the musical notes of the ending of the *Placebo*

Philip Philip, Phip, or Pip was a favorite name for a pet sparrow, in imitation of its chirping
bead-rolls the lists of persons for whom religious were bound to say prayers (*bedes*)
Pater noster qui "Our Father, who [art in heaven]"; the beginning of the Lord's Prayer
Ave Mari "Hail Mary, [full of grace]"; the angelic salutation to the Virgin, repeated as an act of devotion
Creed recited as an act of devotion. These three are the prayers that will be daily said for the soul of Philip Sparrow.
When Jane is beginning to use rhetorical devices —*demonstratio, exclamatio,* and *digressio*—to express her grief; and Skelton begins his variations on the monorhyme.
Pyramus . . . Thisbe young lovers, each of whom killed himself for grief in the belief that the other had been killed

I wept and I wailed,
The tearès down hailed,
But nothing it availed
To call Philip again,
Whom Gib,° our cat, hath slain.
　Gib, I say, our cat
Worried her⌐ on that　　　　　　　　　　*choked herself*
30 Which I loved best.
It cannot be expressed,
My sorrowful heaviness,
But all without redress;
For within that stound,⌐　　　　　　　　　*moment*
Half slumbering in a sound,⌐　　　　　　　*swoon*
I fell down to the ground.
　Unneth⌐ I cast mine eyes　　　　　　　　*scarcely*
Toward the cloudy skies;
But when I did behold
40 My sparrow dead and cold,
No creature but that would
Have ruèd⌐ upon me,　　　　　　　　　　*had pity*
To behold and see°
What heaviness did me pang:
Wherewith my hands I wrang,⌐　　　　　　*wrung*
That my sinews cracked
As though I had been racked,°
So pained and so strained⌐　　　　　　　 *tortured*
That no life well nigh remained.
　I sighed and I sobbed,
50 For that I was robbed
Of my sparrow's life.
O maiden, widow, and wife,°
Of what estate ye be,
Of high or low degree,
Great sorrow then ye might see,
And learn to weep at me!
Such painès⌐ did me fret⌐　　　　　　　　*tortures / torment*
That mine heart did beat,
My visage pale and dead,
60 Wan⌐ and blue as lead;°　　　　　　　　　*livid*
The pangs of hateful death
Well nigh had stopped my breath.
　Heu, heu, me,°

Gib short for Gilbert, the commonest medieval name for a cat
behold . . . see a popular rhetorical amplifying doublet in 15th-century English
racked tortured by being fastened to the rack and stretched
O maiden . . . wife perhaps a reminiscence of the Middle English laments of the Virgin Mary
Wan . . . lead like *black and blo* (l. 75): livid, lead-colored (with grief at or association with death)
Heu . . . me "Woe is me, [that my sojourning is prolonged]!"—opening of the second antiphon, Psalm 119:5

That I am woe for thee!
Ad Dominum cum tribularer, clamavi.°
Of God nothing else crave I
But Philip's soul to keep
From the marish⟩ deep   *marsh*
70 Of Acherontes'° well,⟩   *pool*
That is a flood⟩ of Hell;   *river*
And from the great Pluto,°
The prince of endless woe;
And from foul Alecto°
With visage black and blo;
And from Medusa,° that mare,⟩   *witch*
That like a fiend doth stare;
And from Megera's edders,
For ruffling of Philip's feders,⟩   *feathers*
80 And from her fiery sparklings
For burning of his wings;
And from the smokes sour
Of Proserpina's bower;°
And from the dennes⟩ dark   *dens*
Where Cerberus° doth bark,
Whom Theseus° did affray,⟩   *frighten*
Whom Hercules° did outray,⟩   *overcome*
As famous poets say;
From that hell-hound
90 That lieth in chaines bound
With ghastly heades three,
To Jupiter° pray we
That Philip preserved may be!
Amen, say ye with me!
   Do mi nus,°
Help now, sweet Jesus!
Levavi oculos meos in montes.°

Ad . . . clamavi "In trouble I cried to the Lord: [and he heard me"]—opening of the second vesper psalm, Psalm 119:1
Acherontes' Acheron was a bitter river that ran through the marshes of Hell, over which the souls of the dead were conveyed. Jane begins to pray that Philip's soul will be delivered also from the pagan Hades and its baleful guardians.
Pluto god of death, inexorable ruler of the underworld, father of the three Eumenides (Furies), who sat by his throne and hunted down wrongdoers on behalf of the gods
Alecto Alecto and Megaera (l. 78) were Eumenides; "edders" are adders, the snakes which these ladies had instead of hair.
Medusa One of the three snaky-locked Gorgons, whose look could kill or turn to stone; Medusa was killed by Perseus.
Proserpina's bower the underworld, to which Proserpina, daughter of Ceres, had been carried off by Pluto as his wife. She presided over the deaths of men.

Cerberus three-headed dog who guarded the entrance to the underworld
Theseus King of Athens. He went down into the underworld with his friend Pirithous to carry off Proserpina, but they were caught and Theseus was tied to the stone on which he was resting. Hercules tore him free, but so roughly that his skin was left behind.
Hercules The "whom" of this line may refer to Theseus, whom Hercules brought out of hell; or Cerberus, whom Hercules overcame and bound when he went down to the underworld to bring back Alcestis.
Jupiter king of the gods. The piled-up classical images are suddenly now confronted again with the Office of the Dead.
Dominus "The Lord [is thy keeper from all evil]"—the opening of the third antiphon, Psalm 120:7
Levavi . . . montes "I have lifted up my eyes to the mountains"—opening of the third vesper psalm, Psalm 120:1

Would God I had Zenophontes,°
Or Socrates the wise,
100 To show me their devise⸠   *advice*
Moderately to take
This sorrow that I make
For Philip Sparrow's sake!
So fervently I shake,
I feel my body quake;
So urgently I am brought
Into careful⸠ thought.   *sad*
Like Andromach,° Hector's wife,
Was weary of her life,
110 When she had lost her joy,
Noble Hector of Troy;
In like manner also
Increaseth my deadly woe,
For my sparrow is go.⸠   *gone*
    It was so pretty a fool;
It would sit on a stool,
And learned after my school,
For to keep his cut,°
With, 'Philip, keep your cut!'
120 It had a velvet cap,°
And would sit upon my lap
And seek after small worms
And sometime white bread-crumbs;
And many times and oft
Between my brestės soft°
It would lie and rest—
It was proper and prest.⸠   *active*
    Sometimes he would gasp⸠   *gape*
When he saw a wasp;
130 A fly or a gnat,
He would fly at that;
And prettily he would pant
When he saw an ant;
Lord, how he would pry⸠   *search*
After the butterfly!
Lord, how he would hop
After the gressop!⸠   *grasshopper*
And when I said, 'Phip! Phip!'

Zenophontes Xenophon, *c.* 430–*c.* 355 B.C., a
non-philosopher, but admirer and biographer of
Socrates, many of whose sayings and actions he
preserved
Andromach Andromache, the "type" of wifely
devotion (to Hector, the Trojan hero, whose
death she mourned in a famous lament)
keep his cut i.e. behave with propriety; cf.

Sir Philip Sidney, *Astrophel and Stella*, Sonnet
LXXXIII
velvet cap the brown-feathered top of the
sparrow's head
Between . . . soft See Catullus II.1–2: "Sparrow, you my girl's delight / With whom she
toys there in her lap / And gives you finger-tips
to bite . . .". Sparrows were associated with
lechery.

Then he would leap and skip,
140 And take me by the lip.
Alas, it will me slo°   *slay*
That Philip is gone me fro!°   *from*
  Si in i qui ta tes.°
Alas, I was evil at ease!
De pro fun dis cla ma vi,°
When I saw my sparrow die! . . .
c. 1505–7   *c.* 1545

From The Tunning of Elinor Rumming°

  . . . Then Margery Milk-Duck
Her kirtle° she did uptuck
420 An inch above her knee,
Her legs that ye might see;
But they were sturdy and stubbed,°   *thick*
Mighty pestles and clubbed;
As fair and as white
As the foot of a kite.°
She was somewhat foul,
Crook-nebbed° like an owl;
And yet she brought her fees:
A cantel° of Essex cheese,°   *cut*
430 Was well° a foot thick,   *fully*
Full of maggots quick;°   *live*
It was huge and great,
And mighty strong meat°   *food*
For the devil to eat.
It was tart and pungete!°   *sharp*

  Another sort° of sluts: *company*
Some brought walnuts,
Some apples, some pears,
Some brought their clipping shears,
440 Some brought this and that,
Some brought I wot n'er° what,   *know not*
Some brought their husband's hat,
Some puddings and links,°   *sausage links*
Some tripes that stinks.

Si iniquitates "If thou, Lord, wilt mark iniquities: [Lord who shall stand it]"—the fourth
antiphon, Psalm 128:3
De . . . clamavi "Out of the depths I have
cried [to thee, O Lord]"—opening of the fourth
vesper psalm, Psalm 128:1
The Tunning . . . Rumming *tunning* is pouring
ale into barrels; here, "brewing"; Elinor Rumming was an actual Surrey ale-wife, in trouble
for selling dear and short measure in 1525.
kirtle skirt or outer petticoat
As fair . . . kite "as yellow as a kite's foot"
was a proverbial comparison
Crook-nebbed crooked-beaked, crooked-nosed
Essex cheese Essex ewe's milk cheeses were
famous for their size and tendency to mag-
gotiness. The dirty ladies will bring anything
to pay for their invitation and their drinks.

But of all this throng
One came them among,
(She seemed half a leech°),   *doctor*
And began to preach
Of the Tuesday in the week
450 When the mare doth kick,
Of the virtue of an unset leek,°
Of her husband's breek;°   *breeches*
With the feathers of a quail
She could to Bordeaux sail;
And with good ale-barm°   *ale-froth*
She could make a charm
To help withal° a stitch: *moreover*
She seemed to be a witch. . . .
1517?   *c.* 1521

The Garland of Laurel

The Garland of Laurel is a poetic, dream-allegory discussion of the function of the poet and the nature and dignity of his calling, between Queen Fame and Dame Pallas (reputation and learning). The upshot is that Skelton is received into the company of his great English predecessors (see Chaucer's envoi to *Troilus and Criseyde* below), who present him to Occupation (assiduity). Occupation takes him to the Countess of Surrey and her ladies, as they weave his poet's garland for him from the evergreen bay tree around which the Muses dance. Skelton, in gratitude, confers immortality on each lady in turn, by means of a lyric in style answering to her nature and condition.

From The Garland of Laurel

To Mistress Margery Wentworth

906 With margerain° gentle,
     The flower of goodlihead,°   *goodness*
     Embroidered the mantle
     Is of your maidenhead.°

910 Plainly (I cannot glose°),   *flatter*
     Ye be, as I divine,
     The pretty primrose,°
     The goodly columbine.°

leek the unset (young, untransplanted) leek was thought to be better medicinally than the set (transplanted and fully grown)
margerain Marjoram gentle, the best sort, symbolizes high-born excellence (*gentilesse*). A warmer and comforter in scent and taste, it is like Margery in name and qualities.

maidenhead the maidenly qualities which clothe you
primrose the first flower of spring, exemplifying Margery's fresh, clear, young beauty
columbine again a flower image, with a hint of the innocence and faithfulness of the dove (*columba*)

With margerain gentle,
   The flower of goodlihead,
Embroiderèd the mantle
   Is of your maidenhead.

Benign, courteous, and meek,
   With wordès well devised,
920   In you, who list⸴ to seek,   *pleases*
   Be virtues well comprised.

With margerain gentle,
   The flower of goodlihead,
Embroiderèd the mantle
   Is of your maidenhead.

To Mistress Margaret Hussey

1004   Merry Margaret,
   As midsummer flower:
   Gentle as falcon°
   Or hawk of the tower.°
   With solace and gladness,
   Much mirth and no madness,
1010   All good and no badness,
   So joyously,
   So maidenly,
   So womanly
   Her demeaning⸴   *behavior*
   In every thing—
   Far, far passing
   That I can endite,⸴   *write*
   Or suffice⸴ to write   *am fit*
   Of Merry Margaret,
1020   As midsummer flower,
   Gentle as falcon,
   Or hawk of the tower;
   As patient and still
   And as full of good will,
   As fair Isaphill.°
   Coliander,°
   Sweet pomander,°
   Good Cassander;°

falcon noble hunting bird. The emphasis is throughout on Margaret's good breeding and refinement (*gentle*), with a pun on *falcon-gentle,* the female and young of the goshawk.
hawk of the tower high-flying hawk that towers high in the air to swoop on the prey: again an image of lightness, beauty, and nobility
Isaphill Hypsipyle, legendary Queen of Lemnos, the perfection of womanly beauty and devotion to father and children; her story is told by Boccaccio in his *Of Famous Women,* Chap. 15
Coliander Coriander was a sweet, aromatic, comforting herb.
pomander ball of aromatics, carried or worn as a preservative against bad air and disease
Cassander Cassandra, the Trojan prophetess of doom, who had (the story is again in Boccaccio, Chap. 33) suffered for but adhered to her prophecies of Helen's coming and Troy's destruction: an *exemplum* of constancy

Steadfast of thought,
1030   Well made, well wrought;
Far may be sought,
Erst that⸲ ye can find,   *before*
So courteous, so kind,
As merry Margaret,
This midsummer flower:
Gentle as falcon
Or hawk of the tower.
c. 1495   1523

THE OTHER WORLD: PARADISE

In the beginning, when God had created all things, he made man lord of them all, and planted a garden eastward in Eden where man and woman could live in peace and joy. By disobedience and the Fall, they exchanged their happiness for misery (Fig. 56)—and their fault condemned us all to our condition.

This great myth of a Paradise lost to us was fact for the Middle Ages, firmly based on the biblical account. Was there a way to that happy garden state, so remote from us in time and place? Could we hope to reach it, in body or in soul?

For the church, there was one true answer. The only way a man could escape the misery of his life on earth was by living a truly virtuous life within the church, trusting that after death his soul would be numbered among the blessed. He must hope that the grace of God and the sacrifice of Christ would save him from passing out of the temporary torment of this world into the eternal torment of Hell. Then his soul might travel up to heaven through the concentric spheres of the universe (Fig. 55); despise the world, and see God face to face.

But the hope of even temporarily enjoying a place of rest and freedom from all things unpleasant while still in this life never quite died. Nor did the hope of coming, far off in the east on the mountain tops, upon the Garden of Eden itself. Columbus, when he discovered America, thought he must be near it; Marco Polo, journeying to China, felt he might find it somewhere out there. So "Sir John Mandeville," describing Paradise, has to say that he has never actually been there and must rely on hearsay. But the implication is that he believed in the possibility of someday traveling far enough—and his account has reminiscences of genuine descriptions of Eastern countries in the general area where he would look for it.

If Paradise were found, what would it be like? The word itself already gives a clue. It is known to derive from a Persian word meaning a walled park or pleasure ground and it passed into Greek in that sense. Its use in the Bible is decisive for its meaning throughout the Middle Ages; but the biblical description in Genesis 2 has much in common with Greek and Roman accounts of the conditions prevailing in Elysium, the abode of the blessed after death. All descriptions of Paradise, the *locus amoenus* (delightful place), and its literary-garden imitations, share certain features. They are secluded, shut off by a wall, often far-off in the East; inaccessible, because of being on a mountain top; they enjoy a perpetual sunny season which combines spring, summer, and autumn, with flowers and fruits always flourishing, evergreen trees, fountains, rivers, riches, jewels, perpetual abundance; the exclusion of all that is harmful in thought, word, or deed. All the features of "soft" primitivism are there, and they add up to a place of utter freedom from care.

These features are often elaborated or treated symbolically. The four rivers of the account in Genesis, for example, may be made to symbolize the four cardinal virtues—prudence, temperance, fortitude, and justice—and the whole turned into an allegory of man's soul. Or, at the other end of the scale, as in *The Land of Cokaygne*, they may merely signify fat plenty: oil, wine, milk, and honey, or sweet, soothing medicaments.

The selections given below are, first, the biblical text from Genesis on which all the later accounts are built; then two descriptions, from four centuries apart, where there is an allegorical tinge, sacred and implicit in the Old English ninth-century poem on the *Phoenix*, secular and explicit in the description of the garden from the thirteenth-century *Roman de la Rose*. Then comes a satirical, popular version, the fourteenth-century poem *Land of Cokaygne*, in which the description is stood on its head; then another, popular account of a journey from this world to Elfland-Paradise, in the ballad of "Thomas the Rhymer"; then "Mandeville's" description of what Paradise actually looked like. Finally, there come the spiritual Paradises in the conclusions of the greatest medieval English poem, Geoffrey Chaucer's *Troilus and Criseyde*, and of the greatest poem of the whole European Middle Ages, Dante's *Divine Comedy*.

The ninth-century Old English *Phoenix*, from which our selection is taken, is based on a fourth-century Latin poem attributed to Lactantius (c. 270–340 A.D.), as much pagan as Christian in character. This happy land is a welcome relief from the glowering winter landscapes of most Old English poetry. The second half of the poem makes it an allegory of the perfection from which man has fallen and to which he will be restored by the phoenix, the symbol of a loving Christ.

The Paradise garden of *The Romance of the Rose* (Fig. 54) is the work of the first of its two authors, Guillaume de Lorris (fl. c. 1225–40). It is part of the dream-allegory vision which, by using the personified qualities of the true courtly lover, and their opposites, sets out the process by which noble and refined human love, free of all taint of lowness, can come to man and woman and be maintained. The garden wall excludes all base impediments to love: inside, all is pleasure, except for the threat of the God of Love's five discouraging arrows, which will, however, be used only in extreme cases. Cupid, the pagan god, and Narcissus, the pagan exemplar of self-love, accord quite naturally with the abstractions.

The Paradise of *The Land of Cokaygne*, written about 1315, is a down-to-earth reversal of such sentiments. It is part of a genre of fable that goes back to the Greek satirist Lucian of Samosata (b. 125? A.D.) and forward to the folk-ballad "The Big Rock-Candy Mountain." There is nothing refined and spiritual in this poor-man's satirical, anti-clerical presentation of the Paradise enjoyed by the monks who live on the fat of the land in jeweled luxury, without serfdom or toil, passing their time in eating, drinking, flying about, and tumbling the nuns. There is pleasure for them even in their religious observances.

The Paradise journey of Thomas the Rhymer is made to a far-off place: an elfin, sinister land, not a divine one, with echoes of sin and judgment, transformations of the Virgin Mary, of the waters of Paradise, of the prohibition on Adam and Eve (and of Proserpina, whose tasting of food in Hades condemned her to stay there half the year). Thomas seems to owe his return from the strange journey and his gift of prophecy to his refusal to accept the Queen of Elfland's gift.

"Mandeville's" Paradise has all the usual features in a much more recognizable form. His enormously popular book, first written in French, possibly at Liège in Belgium about 1357, was rapidly translated into other languages. Nobody knows who "Mandeville" was: the name is a fabrication. His book is one long traveler's tale, an account of the Holy Land and of the Marvels of the East as far as Cathay. It has elements of the hero's travels in chivalric romance, as well as of a popular encyclopedia, and it is full of "new things and new tidings" lifted and embroidered from genuine itineraries and from learned works.

The earthly Paradise one might reach, in dream or in fact, during one's lifetime: the celestial could be attained only when one had put off the encumbrances of the body and flown, in a vision or as a disembodied soul, up beyond the changeable spheres of the planets, to the eternal rest and harmony of heaven. The last two selections concern two different versions of this soul-journey, the literary source of which is Macrobius (see Chaucer's Nun's Priest's Tale, l. 353). In the first, Chaucer is bidding good-bye to his book, the story of the true love of Troilus for the false Criseyde, and telling how Troilus, having lost his love, who was his world, seeks death in battle to rid himself of a pointless life. Only when he is dead can he be carried up to a realization of the pettiness of earth and the joys of life after death. As a pagan he cannot enjoy the true love which Chaucer recommends to young lovers who are Christian—but he goes as far as he can.

The closing words of the final canto of Dante's *Paradiso* are the supreme medieval statement of the beatific vision, when Dante's dream-journey to heaven with Beatrice culminates in his realization of the nature of divine love. They have long passed the virtues of the active life on earth. Faith, hope, and charity have strengthened Dante until, finally reaching the abode of rest and stillness where God is, his will and divine love come together in the Paradise of the mind.

Genesis, 2:8–22 (Authorized Version)

8 And the Lord God planted a garden eastward in Eden; and there he put the man whom he had formed.

9 And out of the ground made the Lord God to grow every tree that is pleasant to the sight, and good for food; the tree of life also in the midst of the garden, and the tree of knowledge of good and evil.

10 And a river went out of Eden to water the garden; and from thence it was parted, and became into four heads.

11 The name of the first is Pison: that is it which compasseth the whole land of Havilah, where there is gold;

12 and the gold of that land is good: there is bdellium and the onyx stone.

13 And the name of the second river is Gihon: the same is it that compasseth the whole land of Ethiopia.

14 And the name of the third river is Hiddekel: that is it which goeth toward the east of Assyria. And the fourth river is Euphrates.

15 And the Lord God took the man, and put him into the garden of Eden to dress it and to keep it.

16 And the Lord God commanded the man, saying, Of every tree of the garden thou mayest freely eat:

17 but of the tree of the knowledge of good and evil, thou shalt not eat of it: for in the day that thou eatest thereof thou shalt surely die.

18 And the LORD God said, It is not good that the man should be alone; I will make him a help meet for him.

19 And out of the ground the LORD God formed every beast of the field, and every fowl of the air; and brought them unto Adam to see what he would call them: and whatsoever Adam called every living creature, that was the name thereof.

20 And Adam gave names to all cattle, and to the fowl of the air, and to every beast of the field; but for Adam there was not found a help meet for him.

21 And the LORD God caused a deep sleep to fall upon Adam, and he slept: and he took one of his ribs, and closed up the flesh instead thereof;

22 and the rib, which the LORD God had taken from man, made he a woman, and brought her unto the man.

1611

From The Phoenix°

Lo! I have learned of the loveliest of lands
Far to the eastward, famous among men.
But few ever fare to that far-off realm
10 Set apart from the sinful by the power of God. . . .
 The plain is winsome, the woods are green,
Widespread under heaven. No rain or snow,
Or breath of frost or blast of fire,
Or freezing hail or fall of rime,
Or blaze of sun or bitter-long cold,
Or scorching summer or winter storm
Work harm a whit, but the plain endures
Sound and unscathed. The lovely land
Is rich with blossoms. No mountains rise,
20 No lofty hills, as here with us;
No high rock-cliffs, no dales or hollows,
No mountain gorges, no caves or crags,
Naught rough or rugged; but the pleasant plain
Basks under heaven laden with bloom.
 Twelve cubits° higher is that lovely land,
As learned writers in their books relate,
Than any of these hills that here in splendour
Tower on high under heavenly stars.
Serene that country sunny groves gleaming;
30 Winsome the woodlands; fruits never fail
Or shining blossoms. As God gave bidding
The groves stand for ever growing and green.

Phoenix The translation is by Charles W. Kennedy, in his *An Anthology of Old English Poetry*, New York, 1960.   **cubits** The cubit was either 18 or 21 inches.

Winter and summer   the woods alike
Are hung with blossoms;   under heaven no leaf
Withers, no fire   shall waste the plain
To the end of the world.   As the waters of old,
The sea-floods, covered   the compass of earth
And the pleasant plain   stood all uninjured,
By the grace of God   unhurt and unharmed,
40 So shall it flourish   till the fire of Judgment
When graves shall open,   the dwellings of death.
    Naught hostile lodges   in all that land,
No pain or weeping   or sign of sorrow,
No age or anguish   or narrow death;
No ending of life   or coming of evil,
No feud or vengeance   or fret of care;
No lack of wealth   or pressure of want,
No sorrow or sleeping   or sore disease.
No winter storm   or change of weather
50 Fierce under heaven,   or bitter frost
With wintry icicles   smites any man there.
No hail or hoar-frost   descends to earth,
No windy cloud;   no water falls
Driven by storm.   But running streams
And welling waters   wondrously spring
Overflowing earth   from fountains fair.
    From the midst of the wood   a winsome water
Each month breaks out   from the turf of earth,
Cold as the sea-stream,   coursing sweetly
60 Through all the grove. . . .
    In that woodland dwelleth,   most wondrous fair
And strong of wing,   a fowl° called Phoenix;°   *bird*
There dauntless-hearted   he has his home,
His lonely lodging.   In that lovely land
Death shall never   do him a hurt,
80 Or work him harm   while the world standeth.
    Each day he observes   the sun's bright journey
Greeting God's candle,   the gleaming gem,
Eagerly watching   till over the ocean
The fairest of orbs   shines forth from the East,
God's bright token   glowing in splendour,
The ancient hand-work   of the Father of all.
The stars are hid   in the western wave,
Dimmed at dawn,   and the dusky night
Steals darkly away;   then, strong of wing
90 And proud of pinion,   the bird looks out

Phoenix Symbol of rebirth, a legendary, unique Egyptian bird associated with the sun. When, after many thousand years, it felt death approaching, it flew to Heliopolis, placed itself in a nest of spices on the altar of the sun and was burned to ashes, from which a new phoenix then rose. In the *Bestiary* (see Chaucer's Nun's Priest's Tale, l. 505) the phoenix signifies Christ and his resurrection, or the resurrection of mankind.

Over the ocean   under the sky,
Eagerly waiting   when up from the East
Heaven's gleam comes gliding   over the wide water.
   Then the fair bird,   changeless in beauty,
Frequents at the fountain   the welling streams;
Twelve times the blessed one   bathes in the burn⌐   *brook*
Ere the bright beacon comes,   the candle of heaven;
And even as often   at every bath
Tastes the pleasant water   of brimcold° wells.
100   Thereafter the proud one   after his water-play
Takes his flight   to a lofty tree
Whence most easily   o'er the eastern ways
He beholds the course   of the heavenly taper
Brightly shining   over the tossing sea,
A blaze of light.   The land is made beautiful,
The world made fair,   when the famous gem
O'er the ocean-stretches   illumines the earth
All the world over,   noblest of orbs.
   When the sun climbs high   over the salt streams
110 The grey° bird wings   from his woodland tree
And, swift of pinion,   soars to the sky
Singing and caroling   to meet the sun. . . .

?9th century

From Guillaume de Lorris: The Romance of the Rose°

Short space my feet had traversed ere⌐   *before*
A garden spied I, great and fair,
The which a castled wall hemmed round,
140 And pictured thereupon I found
Full many a figure rich and bright
Of colour, and how each one hight⌐   *was called*
Clear writ beneath it; now will I
To you declare from memory
The semblance and the name of each,
And somewhat of their natures teach.

     HATE
   Amidmost stood Hell's daughter, Hate,
Malignant, base, and desolate
Of countenance; prime mover she

---

brimcold i.e. cool and brimming full
grey The phoenix is usually said to be brilliantly colored. Milton's picture of Satan sitting like an evil cormorant on the tree in the midst of Eden may be a deliberate evocation of the contrary of the good phoenix sitting on its palm-tree.

The Romance of the Rose Though Chaucer translated this part of the *Roman de la Rose*, and the translation here, by F. S. Ellis, makes it into a Pre-Raphaelite poem, Ellis's version is used as being more easily understandable.

150   Of quarrel, strife, and jealousy.
Her very being, as meseemed,
With black and treacherous poison teemed
Of evil passion, while her dark
And frowning visage bore the mark
Of frenzied madness. Heavenward rose,
As if in scorn, her camusʾ nose,   *snub*
And round her head, as if with will
To make her foulness fouler still,
A filthy cloutʾ had she enwrapped.   *cloth*

.   .   .

ELD

To Sorrow next was pictured Eld:ʾ   *old age*
Time's hand all care for food had quelled
Within her, and a foot was she
350   Less than in youth she wonedʾ to be,   *used*
Bowed down by toil and drearihead.ʾ   *dreariness*
Her beauty, years long past, had fled,
And foul of face was she become.
And though old Time had left her some
Sparse, straggling locks, her head was white
As though 'twere floured: the loss were light
If that poor body, worn and waste,
The doubtful woe of death should taste;
For shrivelled were her limbs, and dry.
360   Faded her once bright lustrous eye;
Wrinkled the cheeks once soft and smooth;
And those once pink-shell ears, forsooth,
Now pendent hung; her pearl-like teeth,
Alas! had long since left their sheath,
And barely could she walk as much
As fathomsʾ four without her crutch.   *six feet*

.   .   .

[The poet sees a gate in the wall.]

Full many a time with sounding blow
I struck the door, and, head bent low,
Stood hearkening who might make reply.
The hornbeam wicketʾ presently   *small gate*
Was opened by a dame of air
Most gracious, and of beauty rare:
Her flesh as tender chicken's was;
Her blond locks bright as bowl of brass;
Radiant her brow; of arching due
540   Her eyebrows; and well spaced the two;
Neither too small, nor yet too great
Her nose, but straight and delicate.
No falcon, I would boldly swear,

Hath eyes that could with hers compare.
Her breath was sweet as breeze, thyme-fed;
Her cheeks, commingled white and red;
Her mouth a rosebud, and her chin
Well rounded, with sweet cleft therein.
Her tower-like neck, of measure meet,⸳   *fitting*
550 The purest lily well might beat
For fairness, free of spot or wem.⸳   *blemish*
'Twixt this and far Jerusalem
I trow⸳ were found none other such,   *believe*
So fair to sight, so soft to touch.
Her bosom would outshine the snow
New-fallen, ere it soil⸳ doth show;   *dirt*
And all her body formed and knit
So well, as nought might equal it.
Much doubt I, if since Time had birth,
560 A fairer dame hath trod dull earth. . . .

[Idleness/Leisure welcomes him and tells him what the garden
is and to whom it belongs.]

No more I spake, but thanked kind fate,
When Idleness the garden gate
Threw open wide, and unafraid
To that sweet spot quick entry made.
Then burst on my astonished eyes
650 A dream—an Earthly Paradise:
And suddenly my soul seemed riven
From earth, to dwell in highest heaven;
Yet doubt I much if heaven can give
A place where I so soon would live
As this sweet garden, sacred haunt
Of birds whose soft melodious chaunt
Ravished mine ears; the nightingales
Here sang, and there the green wood-wales;⸳   *orioles*
The bullfinch piped beneath, above,
660 I heard the crooning turtle-dove,
Near by, the sweet-voiced tiny wren,
While high in air, beyond my ken,
The skylark soared; the titmouse shrilled
The fauvette's⸳ gentle treble trilled.   *warbler's*
The merle⸳ and mavis⸳ seemed to shake   *blackbird / song thrush*
The leaves in cadence, while each brake
With small fowl⸳ rang, as they would try   *birds*
Their throats in choral rivalry.
'Twould seem as all and each of these
670 Sweet birds sang joyance to the breeze,
And then, their hearts disburdened, flew
To keep some loving rendezvous.

·   ·   ·

[Idleness/Leisure having let the poet in, he wanders through the garden until he comes to the owner, Mirth, and his company, who are dancing to a tune and a song by Gladness. Courtesy comes to him, to ask him to join the dance. Then he sees the God of Love, with his companion Sweet Looking, who carries the quivers with the god's arrows of gold, whose wounds make happy and successful love: Beauty, Simplicity, Franchise (Generosity), Companionship, Fair Seeming; and his other arrows, symbolizing obstacles to love: Pride, Villainy (Base Behavior), Shame, Despair, and Fickleness. The god has, as his special companions, ladies called Beauty, Richesse (Wealth), Largesse (Gift-Giving), and Franchise. The poet now finally accepts Courtesy's invitation to join the dance.]

And next stood gracious Courtesy,
Who ne'er midst men can fail to be
Welcome: strangers to her are pride
And folly. Straightway to her side
She summoned me with kindly call
To join the gladsome dance withal.
Frank-eyed she was, and no deal⸵ shy   *part*
1280 Or timid, but most graciously
Spake forth to me in friendly wise,
With pleasant words and quaint⸵ replies,   *ingenious*
Wherein one found no poison lurk.
Her form was nature's perfect work,
And e'en as stars like candles mean
Beside the moon's bright rays are seen,
So her companions showed beside
Her dazzling beauty's winsome pride.
Than this fair damsel who shall find
1290 A nobler face or gentler mind,
Or one who would more worship gain
Should she as Queen or Empress reign?

    Beside her stood a valiant knight,
Who knew to choose his words aright
Whene'er he spake; well loved seemed he
Of her who bare him company.
Well skilled in feats of arms, his grace
Showed forth alike in form and face.

    Then, Idleness came near to me,
1300 Whose hand I took most willingly
To join the dance. Erewhile⸵ I've said   *before*
How fraught with grace and goodlihead
She was, and she 'twas raised the pin
That kept the wicket, and within
The close⸵ through her I entrance gained,   *enclosure*
My trembling heart set free and fained.⸵   *gladdened*

            ·   ·   ·

[After the dance, the poet wanders through the garden, in
some alarm because the God of Love is pursuing him with his bow.]

No thought had I to stay or rest,
But roved north, south, and east and west,
Desiring leisurely to view
The close, and all that 'longed⟩ thereto.   *belonged*

    I noted that from side to side
The garden was nigh broad as wide,
And every angle duly squared.
1380 The careful planter had not spared
To set of every kind of tree
That beareth fruit some two or three,
Or more perchance, except some few
Of evil sort. Among them grew
Pomegranates filled with seeds and thick
Of skin, most wholesome for the sick;
Strange nut trees, which in season bore
Rich fragrant nutmegs, good for store,
And nowise cursed with nauseous taste
1390 But savouring well. Near by were placed
Almonds and gillyflower cloves,
Brought hither from hot Ind's⟩ far groves,   *India's*
Dates, figs, and liquorice which deals
Contentment while misease it heals. . . .
Moreover in this garden rare
Grew many a tree familiar,
As cherry, pear and knotted quince,
'Neath which a tender tooth will wince,
Brown medlars, plums both black and white,
Apples and chestnuts, peaches bright. . . .
And all around this pleasant close
1410 Holly, and laurel, and holm° arose
With yew and hornbeam, fit I trow
For flitting shaft, and speeding bow;
The cypress sad, and pines that sigh
To soft south breezes mournfully,
Beech, loved of squirrels, olive dark,
And graceful birch with silvery bark;
The shimmering aspen, maple tall,
And lofty ash that topped the wall. . . .
But this I say, such skilful art
Had planned the trees that each apart
Six fathoms stood, yet like a net
The interlacing branches met,
Through which no scorching rays could pass

holm holly-oaks, evergreen oaks

To sear the sward, and thus the grass
Kept ever tender, fresh and green,
1430   Beneath their cool and friendly screen.

Roebuck and deer strayed up and down
The mead, and troops of squirrels brown
The tree-boles scoured, while coniesʾ grey   *rabbits*
Shot merrily in jocund play
Around their burrows on the fresh
And fragrant greensward, void of mesh.°

Within the glades sprang fountains clear:
No frog or newt e'er came anearʾ   *near*
Their waters, but 'neath cooling shade
1440   They gently sourded.ʾ Mirth had made   *flowed*
Therefrom small channelled brooks to fling
Their waves with pleasant murmuring
In tiny tides. Bright green and lush,
Around these sparkling streams, did push
The sweetest grass. There might one lie
Beside one's love, luxuriously
As though 'twere bed of down. The earth,
Made pregnant by the streams, gave birth
To thymy herbage and gay flowers,
1450   And when drear winter frowns and lowersʾ   *scowls*
In spots less genial, ever here
Things bud and burgeonʾ through the year.   *sprout*

.   .   .

[The poet comes finally to the Fountain of Narcissus, who scorned the love
of Echo. She pined away and Narcissus was punished by being made to fall
in love with his own reflection.]

1595   Without the door
Of paradise the blest, I ween
No sight more beauteous may be seen
Than this bright well. The gushing source
Springs ever fresh and sweet. . . .
Fast in the fountain's pavement shone
1610   Two sparkling spheres of crystal stone,
Whereon my gaze with wonder fell:
And, when the tale thereof I tell,
Your ears will tingle as I trow,
And pleasure unto marvel grow.
When that the sun, which searcheth all
The things that live on earth, lets fall
His rays within this fount we see
An hundred colours gorgeously

mesh i.e. clear of rabbit-net or snare

Shine forth within the water bright,
1620 Vermilion, azure, silvery white,
And richest gold. Such virtuous power
These crystals have that every flower
And tree within this pleasaunce seen,
Reflection finds in their sweet sheen. . . .
    By reason of the seed there sown,
This Fountain is to all men known
As that of Love: thereof is told
The tale full oft in many an old
Romance and song, but ne'er before
1670 Hath any man so fully or
So truly set all forth as now
'Tis writ within this book I trow.

[Moving on, the poet finds the rose which is the object of his search, but before he can pluck it from behind its protecting hedge, the God of Love shoots him with all his golden arrows. He then anoints the poet's wounds and the poet acknowledges himself forever love's devotee.]
1225–40

The Land of Cokaygne°

Far in the sea, to the west of Spain,°
Is a country called Cokaygne.°
There's no land not anywhere,
In goods or riches to compare.
Though Paradise be merry and bright
Cokaygne is of far fairer sight.
In Paradise's happy bowers,
They've only grass and trees and flowers,
Though they've joy and pleasure great,
10   There they've only fruit to eat;
There's no boudoir, hall nor bench
And water only, thirst to quench.
And there are no men there but two:
Elijah° and Enoch° also:
Miserably must they roam,
When they live there all alone.
In Cokaygne there's meat and drink,

Land of Cokaygne This paraphrase by the present editor, in doggerel no worse than that of the original, has been made on the basis of the text in R. H. Robbins, *Historical Poems of the 15th and 16th Centuries* (1959).
Far . . . Spain a reminiscence of the Fortunate Islands of the ancients, and a reversal in position of Paradise, usually placed in the East
Cokaygne The origin of the name is obscure,
but it has something to do with cakes and cookery.
Elijah the prophet, taken up to heaven by fiery chariot in a whirlwind (II Kings 2:11)
Enoch the righteous man, carried off by God (Genesis 5:24; Hebrews 11:5), who lived in heaven and—the story was—learned its secrets. He and Elijah were, according to the Bible, the only mortal men taken into Paradise.

Without trouble, fuss and swink.°
The food is fine, the drink is clear
20   At noon, at snack-time, at supper.
In truth—I say so without fear—
There's no land on earth its peer,
Nor under heaven a land—I hiss
To you—where there's such joy and bliss.

There are many sweetest sights,
All is day, there are no nights;
There's no quarrelling or strife
Nor is there death, but lasting life;
There's no lack of food or cloth
30   There's no man nor woman wroth.
There's no serpent, wolf or fox
Horse or hack or cow or ox
There's no sheep, or swine, or goat
No, nor filth there—God takes note—
Nor breeding stable, no, nor stud
The land is full of all things good.
There's no fly, no flea, no louse
In clothes, in town, in bed, in house;
There's no thunder, sleet or hail;
40   Nor any filthy worm, or snail;
Nor any storm, or rain, or wind;
Nor is there man or woman blind
But all is play and joy and glee
Happy he that there may be.

There are rivers broad and fine
Of oil and honey, milk and wine;
Water serves there for no thing
But looking at or washing in.
There are fruits of many sorts,
50   Endless pleasures, joys and sports.

There appears a fine abbèy
Of white monks and, also, of grey.°
There are bowers and there are halls,
All of pasties° are the walls,
Of rich food, of fish and meat
Which are delectable to eat.
Cakes of flour are the shingles all
Of church and cloister, bower and hall.
The roofing-pins are fat puddings—
60   Rich food for princes and for kings—

swink toil
white . . . grey white friars (Carmelites) and
gray (Franciscans)

pasties meat pies

All he wants a man may eat
As of right and without threat.
All is common to young and old,
To brave and tough, to meek and bold.
There's a cloister, fine and light,
Broad and long, a splendid sight:
The pillars of that cloister all
Are fashioned out of pure crystàl,
Have their base and capital
70   Of jasper green and red coràl.
In the meadow is a tree
Most delicious to see:
The root is ginger and galingale,°
The shoots are all of cetewale°
And three maces are the flower;
Cinnamon bark makes sweet odour,
Cloves are its fruit, of spicy taste—
And cubebs° never go to waste.
There are roses, red in hue
80   And lilies lovely, just for you,
Never withering, day or night;
Sure this is the sweetest sight.
Four springs gush out from this abbèy
Of treacle and of halewey,°
Of balm° and also of spiced wine
Flowing freely, always fine;
And of those streams the èntire bed
Is precious stones and gold so red.
There are sapphires and uniunes
90   Carbuncles and astiunes
Emerald, ligure and prasine
Beryl, onyx, topazine
Amethyst and chrysolite
Chalcedòny, hepatite.°

There are so many birds they jostle:
Thrush and nightingale and throstle,°
Golden orioles, chalènders,°
And many others, of all genders,
Who never cease, by day or night,
100   Singing sweetly with all their might.
Another thing—I must tell it—
Geese, ready roasted on a spit.

galingale i.e. spice
cetewale zedoary, fragrant herb
cubebs spicy seeds
treacle . . . halewey Sweet, healing medicines, potions or lotions. Treacle was originally theriake, remedy for snakebite.
balm fragrant, healing medicine

sapphires . . . hepatite The rich gems are in imitation of the Heavenly Jerusalem. Uniunes are large pearls, carbuncles are garnets, astiunes are star sapphires, prasines are chrysopase, topazine is topaz, hepatite is bloodstone.
throstle song-thrush
chalènders larks

Fly to that abbey—God hear me talk—
And 'Geese, all hot, all hot,' they squawk.
They bring of garlic great supply
The best prepared that man may spy.
The larks, so tasty to every youth,
Flutter gently to man's mouth,
Cooked in a stew, upon the stove,
110   Flavoured with cinnamon and clove.
To drink there's need of no permission:
Just take your fill: no intermission.

And when the monks arrive at mass
All the windows, that are of glass,
Turn at once into crystal bright
So that the monks may have more light.
When the masses have been said
And the mass-books put to bed,
The crystal turns again to glass—
120   Back to the state it formerly was.

All the young monks every day
After food go off to play:
There's no hawk or bird, so high
Or swiftly flying through the sky,
As the monks in merry mood
Swooping on wings of sleeves and hood.

When the abbot sees them fly
Then with joy he winks his eye
But even so, and he's not wrong,
130   He calls them back to even-song.
But the monks will not come home.
They fly on: in a flock they roam.

When the abbot still can't spy
That his monks will back home fly
He takes a maiden, from a mass
And turning upward her white ass
He rattles the drum with his right hand
To make his monks come back to land.

When his monks that fine sight see
140   Back to the maid they quickly flee
And gather about her, with one mind,
To get a smack at her white behind.
And so they quietly, after the session,
Go off home in a procession
And from their food they do not shrink,
As long as they're given enough to drink.

Another abbey lies nearby:
It is a fine great nunnery,
Beside a stream of sweetest milk,
150   Where there's also plenty of silk.
When the summer's day is hot
The young nuns get themselves a boat
And launch it out and make it shudder
So fast they handle oars and rudder.
When they are safely behind the bluff
And hidden, they quickly strip to the buff.
They slip down into the waters brimming
And happily pass their time in swimming.
When the young monks cast their eye
160   On this, they get up fast and fly
And reach the nuns' pool at the run.
Then each and every monk takes one
And quickly carries off his prey
As far as his fine and great abbèy
And teaches the nuns an orison°
With jigging up and jigging down.

The monk who'd be a stallion good
And knows how to arrange his hood
He shall have, without refusal
170   Twelve wives a year (the number's usual),
As of right, not special grace,
So as to give him his solace.
And the monk of all that nation,
Who orders best his recreation
It's hoped that he, by help of God,
Will soon be chosen new abbòt.

Whoever wants to reach that land
Must do great penance at command:
In a pig-pen seven long years
180   He must wade, up to his ears
In muck—perhaps just up to the chin
Will do—on the way that land to win.

Gentlemen good and gentlemen gay
May you never go from this world away
Until you see and grab your chance,
Perform completely this penance
So that you may that land see plain
And nevermore come back again.
Let's pray God that so it be
190   Amen, for holy Charity.

c. 1315

orison prayer

Thomas the Rhymer°

True Thomas lay on Huntly bank,
   A ferlie⁷ he spied wi' his e'e;⁷   *marvel / eye*
And there he saw a lady bright
   Come riding down by the Eildon Tree.°

Her shirt° was o' the grass-green silk,
   Her mantle o' the velvet fyne;
At ilka tett⁷ of her horse's mane   *every braid*
   Hung fifty siller⁷ bells and nine.   *silver*

10 True Thomas, he pull'd off his cap
   And louted⁷ low down to his knee: *bowed*
'All hail, thou mighty Queen of Heaven!°
   For thy peer on earth I never did see.'

'O no, O no, Thomas,' she said,
   'That name does not belong to me;
I am but the Queen of fair Elfland
   That am hither come to visit thee.

Harp and carp,⁷ Thomas,' she said,   *sing*
   'Harp and carp along wi' me,
And if ye dare to kiss my lips,
20   Sure of your bodie I will be.'

'Betide me weal,⁷ betide me woe,   *happiness*
   That weird⁷ shall never daunton⁷ me.'   *fate / daunt*
Syne⁷ he has kissed her rosy lips   *at once*
   All underneath the Eildon Tree.

'Now ye maun⁷ go wi' me,' she said,   *must*
   'True Thomas, ye maun go wi' me;
And ye maun serve me seven years
   Thro' weal or woe, as may chance to be.'

Thomas the Rhymer Child, no. 37. Air: Blaikie
ms. (National Library of Scotland, ms. 1578).
Thomas Rymour, Thomas the Rhymer (i.e.
Minstrel), Thomas of Erceldoune, True Thomas,
is spoken of as a poet during the 14th century
and in the 15th acquired a reputation as a
seer, a kind of Scots Merlin, which lasted until the
19th. He seems to have been a historical person
of the late 13th century. A 15th-century romance of Thomas of Erceldoune exists, relating
his gift of prophecy to his visit to the Queen
of Elfland. It and the ballad are other-world
journeys, with features that go back to the
earliest of such tales, to other romances such as
Ogier the Dane, to Merlin stories, to St. Patrick's
Purgatory, and the like.
Eildon Tree Also in the romance; the Eildon
Hills are near Melrose, in Berwickshire, Scotland. Woods and trees are the natural habitat
of fairies and supernatural beings.
shirt i.e. skirt
Heaven i.e. the Virgin Mary

She mounted on her milk-white steed,
30   She's ta'en True Thomas up behind;
And aye° whene'er her bridle rung   *always*
    The steed flew swifter than the wind.

O they rade° on, and farther on—   *rode*
    The steed gaed° swifter than the wind—   *went*
Until they reached a desert wide
    And living land was left behind.

'Light° down, light down now, True Thomas,   *dismount*
    And lean your head upon my knee;
Abide and rest a little space
40   And I will show you ferlies° three.   *wonders*

O see ye not yon narrow road°
    So thick beset with thorns and briars?
That is the path of righteousness,
    Though after it but few enquires.

And see ye not that braid,° braid road   *broad*
    That lies across that lily leven?°   *lovely plain*
That is the path of wickedness,
    Though some call it the road to heaven.

And see not ye that bonny° road   *fine*
50   That winds about the fernly brae?°   *hillside*
That is the road to fair Elfland,
    Where thou and I this night maun gae.°   *go*

But Thomas, ye maun hold your tongue
    Whatever ye may hear or see,
For if you speak word in Elflyn land
    Ye'll ne'er get back° to your ain° countrie.'   *own*

O they rade on, and farther on,
    And they waded through rivers aboon° the knee,   *above*
And they saw neither sun nor moon
60   But they heard the roaring of the sea.

It was mirk,° mirk night and there was nae stern° light   *dark / star*
    And they waded through red blude° to the knee;   *blood*
For a'° the blude that's shed on earth   *all*
    Rins° through the springs o' that countrie.   *runs*

Syne° they came on to a garden green°   *then*
    And she pu'd° an apple frae a tree: *plucked*

road Thus begins the supernatural knowledge which Thomas acquires and which allows him to prophesy truly on his return to earth.
Ye'll . . . back But he does get back; in the romance, the Queen sends him back after three years to avoid his being captured by the Devil.
garden green Paradise; the Queen repeats Eve's gift of the apple to Adam, but the fairy gift gives him the gift of true speech and prophecy, rather than causes him harm or permanent residence in the lower world. Perhaps this is because of his rather churlish, but independent, reply in the next stanza.

'Take this for thy wages, True Thomas,
   It will give thee the tongue that can never lee.'   *lie*

'My tongue is mine ain,' True Thomas said,   *own*
70   'A gudely gift ye wad gie' to me;   *give*
I neither dought' to buy nor sell   *dare*
   At fair or tryst' where I may be;   *market*

I dought neither speak to prince or peer
   Nor ask of grace from fair ladye.'
'Now hold thy peace, the lady said,
   For as I say, so must it be.'

He has gotten a coat of the even' cloth   *smooth*
   And a pair of shoes of velvet green;°
And till seven years were gane and past
80   True Thomas on earth was never seen.

From Mandeville's Travels°

. . . Of Paradise [1] ne can [2] I not speak properly, for I was not there. It is far beyond, and that forethinketh [3] me, and also I was not worthy. But as I have heard say of wise men beyond,[4] I shall tell you with good will. Paradise Terrestre, as wise men say, is the highest place of earth that is in all the world, and it is so high that it toucheth nigh to the circle of the moon,[5] there as the moon maketh her turn. For she [6] is so high that the Flood of Noah ne might not come to her that would have covered all the earth of the world all about and above and beneath, save Paradise only alone. And this Paradise is enclosed all about with a wall, and men wit [7] not whereof it is, for the walls be covered all over with moss, as it seemeth. And it seemeth not that the wall is stone of nature nor of no other thing that the wall is. And that wall stretcheth from the south to the north, and it hath not but [8] one entry that is closed with fire burning,[9] so that no man that is mortal ne dare not enter.

green fairy, forest color
1. "Mandeville" gives a color of truth-telling to his tale: *properly* means "in my own person."
2. Double negative intensifies.
3. Grieves.
4. In addition.
5. In the so-called Ptolemaic universe, with the earth at the center and the planets arranged in concentric spheres outward, the lowest sphere was that of the moon, the quickest in orbit and the most changeable. All below the sphere of the moon was subject to mutability. Paradise is far to the East, at the edge of the world, where the moon dips below it.
6. I.e. Paradise.
7. Do not know of what material.
8. Only.
9. Genesis 3:24. God placed fiery cherubims and a flaming sword at the gates of Eden after the expulsion of Adam and Eve. "Mandeville's" account is based ultimately on Genesis.
Mandeville's Travels The text used is a modernization by M. C. Seymour, *Mandeville's Travels.*

And in the most high place of Paradise, even in the middle place, is a well [10] that casteth out the four floods that run by diverse lands; [11] of the which the first is cleped [12] Pison or Ganges, that is all one, and it runneth throughout Ind [13] or Havilah,[14] in the which river be many precious stones and much lignum aloes [15] and much gravel of gold. And that other river is cleped Nile or Gihon, that goeth by Ethiopia and after by Egypt. And that other is cleped Tigris, that runneth by Assyria and by Armenia the Great. And that other is cleped Euphrates, that runneth also by Media and by Armenia and by Persia. And men there beyond say that all the sweet waters of the world above and beneath take their beginning of that well of Paradise, and out of that well all waters come and go.

The first river is cleped Pison, that is to say in their language 'assembly,' for many rivers meet them there and go into that river. And some men clepe it Ganges, for a king that was in Ind that hight [16] Gangeres and that it ran throughout his land. And that water is in some [17] place clear and in some place troubled, in some place hot and in some place cold.

The second river is cleped Nile or Gihon, for it is always troubled and Gihon in the language of Ethiopia is to say 'troubled' and in the language of Egypt also.

The third river that is cleped Tigris is as much for to say as 'fast running,'— for he runneth more fast than any of the other, and also there is a beast that is cleped tiger that is fast running.

The fourth river is cleped Euphrates, that is to say 'well bearing,' for there grow many goods upon that river, as corns, fruits, and other goods [18] enough plenty.

And ye shall understand that no man that is mortal ne may not approach [19] to that Paradise. For by land no man may go for wild beasts that be in the deserts and for the high mountains and great huge rocks that no man may pass by for the dark places that be there and that many. And by the rivers may no man go, for the water runneth so rudely [20] and so sharply because that it cometh down so outrageously [21] from the high places above that it runneth in so great waves that no ship may not row nor sail against it. And the water roareth so and maketh so huge noise and so great tempest that no man may hear other in the ship, though he cried with all the craft [22] that he could in the

10. Spring that gives rise to the four rivers (floods).
11. Genesis 2:10–14, where the rivers are named. "Mandeville" does not, as many medieval writers do, allegorize the rivers into the cardinal virtues. Where he can, he identifies them with real rivers and gives a derivation of their names.
12. Called.
13. Literally, India; but often the Far East in general.
14. "Sandy," i.e. Arabia.
15. Aromatic wood, used in pharmacy, thought to be carried down by the Nile.
16. Was called.
17. One . . . another.
18. Good things.
19. Men still hoped to discover Paradise as late as the 16th century. Marco Polo carried a copy of "Mandeville."
20. Roughly and quickly.
21. Excessively. These details may derive from a genuine account of the cataracts of the Nile.
22. Power.

highest [23] voice that he might. Many great lords have assayed with great will many times for to pass by those rivers toward Paradise with full great companies, but they might not speed [24] in their voyage. And many died for weariness of rowing against those strong waves. And many of them became blind and many deaf for the noise of the water. And some were perished and lost within the waves. So that no mortal man may approach to that place without special grace of God, so that of that place I can say you no more. And therefore I shall hold me still [25] and return to that that I have seen.

c. 1375

From Geoffrey Chaucer: Troilus and Criseyde

From Book 5: The Finale°

Go, litel book, go litel myn tragedie,
Ther�︣ God thy maker yet er that he° dye,   *where*
So sendė might to make° in som comedie!
But litel book, ne making thou n'envye,°
1790 But subgit⁆ be to allė poesye;   *subject*
And kis the steppes, wheras thou seëst pace⁆   *pass*
Virgile, Ovyde, Omer, Lucan, and Stace.

And for⁆ ther is so greet diversitee   *since*
In English and in wryting of our tonge,
So preye⁆ I God that noon miswrytė thee,   *pray*
Ne thee mismetre for defaute of tonge.°
And red⁆ wherso thou be, or ellės songe,   *read*
That thou be understonde⁆ I God beseche!   *understood*
But yet to purpos of my rather speche.°

1800 The wrathe, as I began yow for to seye,
Of Troïlus, the Grekes boughten dere;⁆   *paid for dearly*
For thousandės his hondės⁆ maden deye,⁆   *hands / die*
As he that was withouten any pere,⁆   *equal*
Save Ector,° in his tyme, as I can here.°
But weylaway, save only Goddės wille!°
Dispitously him slough the fiers Achille.°

23. Loudest.
24. Succeed.
25. Silent.

Finale Chaucer slips in and out of this *envoi* or conclusion, in which he gathers up and seals his story, claims kinship with the poetic masters of past and present, and sums up the "morality" to which his whole poem has been leading. Like Troilus, he surveys his doings in the world below the spheres: imperfect as they are, his tenderness cannot quite condemn them.
he i.e. Chaucer, the "maker" of this book
make match with, not turn into; the pun is intended
n'envye Do not be envious, take your place below the Roman and Greek poets Virgil, Ovid, Homer, Lucan (author of the *Pharsalia*, 39–65

A.D.) and Statius (author of the *Thebaid*, *Achilleid*, and *Silvae*, 61–96 A.D.). The reputation of the last two was higher in the Middle Ages than it is today.
defaute of tonge Chaucer recognizes the effect of dialect and linguistic change.
But . . . speche Back to the purport of my earlier words—i.e. back to my story of Troilus.
Ector Hector, the Trojan champion
as I can here as I understand
But . . . wille alas for everything, unless God wills it
Achille Achilles, the Greek hero: without mercy, the fierce Achilles slew him.

And whan that he was slayn in this manere,
His lightė goost ful blisfully is went
Up to the holownesseˀ of the eighth spere.°   *concavity*
1810   In convers letingeˀ every element;   *leaving behind*
And ther he saughˀ with ful avysément,ˀ   *saw / in full view*
The erratik sterrės, herkeninge armonyeˀ   *hearing harmony*
With sownėsˀ fulle of hevenishˀ melodye.   *sounds / heavenly*

And down from thenėsˀ faste he gan avyseˀ   *thence / did consider*
This litel spot of erthe, that with the seeˀ   *sea*
Enbracėd° is, and fully gan despyse
This wrecched world, and held alˀ vanitee   *everything*
Toˀ rèspect of the pleynˀ felicitee   *in / absolute*
That is in hevene above; and at the laste,
1820   Therˀ he was slayn, his loking doun he caste;   *to where*

And in himself he loughˀ right at the wo   *laughed*
Of hem that wepten for his deeth so faste;
And dampnėdˀ al our werkˀ that folweth so   *damned / doings*
The blindė lust,ˀ the which that may notˀ laste,   *pleasure / cannot*
And sholden al our herte on hevene caste.°
And forth he wentė, shortly for to telle,
Therˀ as Mercùrie° sortedˀ him to dwelle.   *where / allotted*

Swich fynˀ hath, lo, this Troïlus for love,   *ending*
Swich fyn hath al his gretė worthinesse;ˀ   *valiance*
1830   Swich fyn hath his estat reäl above,°
Swich fyn his lust,ˀ swich fyn hath his noblesse;ˀ   *pleasure / nobility*
Swich fyn hath falsė worldės brotelnesse.ˀ   *brittleness*
And thus bigan his lovinge of Criseyde,
As I have told, and in this wyseˀ he deyde.ˀ   *manner / died*

O yongė fresshė folkės, he or she,
In which that love up groweth with your age,
Repeyrethˀ hoom from worldly vanitee,°   *return*
And of your herte up casteth the visage
To thilkėˀ God that after his image   *that same*
1840   Yow made, and thinketh al nisˀ but a fayreˀ   *is nothing / show*
This world, that passeth sone as flourės fayre.

And loveth him, the which that right for love
Upon a cros, our soules for to beye,ˀ   *redeem*
First starf,ˀ and roos,ˀ and sit in hevene above;   *died / ascended*
For he nil falsen no wight,ˀ dar I seye,   *will deceive no-one*
That wol his herte al hoollyˀ on him leye.ˀ   *wholly / set*

spere Troilus' insubstantial soul travels joyfully
from the earth up through the concentric spheres
of the planets (erratic, i.e. moving, stars),
until he can hear the perfect music they
make as they pass on their courses. Sitting in
heaven, leaving behind all the elements of which
matter is composed (air, fire, earth, and water),
he can see the true nature of things.
Enbraced i.e. encircled; see Fig. 55

And . . . caste i.e. when we ought to set our
whole heart on heaven
Mercurie Mercury, messenger of the gods, who
led souls where they were to live henceforth
estat . . . above i.e. exalted, royal condition
Repeyreth . . . vanitee The repudiation of
earthly love for heavenly was a literary convention, but one that was also deeply felt.

And sin⸵ he best to love is, and most meke,   *since*
What nedeth feynéd⸵ lovės for to seke?   *false*

1850 Lo here, of payens corsėd⸵ oldė rytes,   *pagans cursed*
Lo here, what alle hir⸵ goddės may availle;   *their*
Lo here, these wrecched worldės appetytes;
Lo here, the fyn⸵ and guerdon⸵ for travaille⸵   *end / reward / toil*
Of Jove, Appollo, of Mars,° of swich rascaille!⸵   *riff-raff*
Lo here, the forme of oldė clerkės⸵ speche   *learned men*
In poetrye, if ye hir bokės seche.

O moral Gower,° this book I directe
To thee, and to thee, philosophical Strode,°
To vouchensauf, ther nede is, to corecte,
Of your benignitees and zelės gode.
1860 And to that sothfast⸵ Crist, that starf on rode,⸵   *true / cross*
With al myn herte of mercy ever I preye;
And to the Lord right thus I speke and seye:

Thou oon, and two, and three,° eterne on lyve,⸵   *eternally living*
That regnest ay in three and two and oon,
Uncircumscript, and al mayst circumscryve,⸵   *embrace*
Us from visìble and invisìble foon⸵   *foes*
Defende: and to thy mercy, everychoon,⸵   *everyone*
So make us, Jesus, for thy gracė, digne,⸵   *worthy*
For love of mayde and moder⸵ thyn benigne! Amen.   *mother*

    Explicit Liber Troili et Criseydis.°
1380–86

From Dante: The Divine Comedy: Paradise [1]

. . . As is he who dreaming sees, and after the dream the passion remains imprinted, and the rest returns not to the mind, such am I; for my vision almost wholly fails, while the sweetness that was born of it yet distils within my heart. Thus the snow is by the sun unsealed; thus on the wind, in the light leaves, was lost the saying of the Sibyl.[2]

O Supreme Light, that so high upliftest Thyself from mortal conceptions, re-lend a little to my mind of what Thou didst appear, and make my tongue so powerful that it may be able to leave one single spark of Thy glory for the

Jove . . . Mars Jupiter, ruler of the gods; Apollo, god of the sun, of music and poetry; Mars, god of war
Gower John Gower (1325?–1408), Chaucer's senior and—in a sense—poetic master, author of the *Confessio Amantis* (Lover's Confession)

Strode probably the Oxford philosopher Ralph Strode
three an adaptation of Dante, *Paradiso* XIV. 28–30
Explicit . . . Criseydis Here ends the book of Troilus and Criseyde.

1. Canto xxxiii, ll. 58–145. The translation is by Charles Eliot Norton.
2. The Cumaean Sibyl wrote her prophecies on leaves which the wind scattered at the opening of her cave.

future people; for, by returning somewhat to my memory and by sounding a little in these verses, more of Thy victory shall be conceived.

I think that by the keenness of the living ray which I endured, I should have been bewildered if my eyes had been averted from it. And it comes to my mind that for this reason I was the more hardy to sustain so much, that I joined my look unto the Infinite Goodness.

O abundant Grace, whereby I presumed to fix my eyes through the Eternal Light so far that there I consumed my sight!

In its depth I saw that whatsoever is dispersed through the universe is there included, bound with love in one volume; substance and accidents and their modes, fused together, as it were, in such wise, that that of which I speak is one simple Light. The universal form of this knot [3] I believe that I saw, because in saying this I feel that I more at large rejoice. One instant only is greater oblivion for me than five and twenty centuries to the emprise which made Neptune wonder at the shadow of Argo.[4]

Thus my mind, wholly rapt, was gazing fixed, motionless, and intent, and ever with gazing grew enkindled. In that Light one becomes such that it is impossible he should ever consent to turn himself from it for other sight; because the Good which is the object of the will is all collected in it, and outside of it that is defective which is perfect there.

Now will my speech be shorter, even in respect to that which I remember, than an infant's who still bathes his tongue at the breast. Not because more than one simple semblance was in the Living Light wherein I was gazing, which is always such as it was before; but through my sight, which was growing strong in me as I looked, one sole appearance, as I myself changed, was altering itself to me.

Within the profound and clear subsistence of the lofty Light appeared to me three circles of three colours and of one dimension; and one appeared reflected by the other, as Iris by Iris,[5] and the third appeared fire which from the one and from the other is equally breathed forth.

O how short is the telling, and how feeble toward my conception! and this toward what I saw is such that it suffices not to call it little.

O Light Eternal, that sole dwellest in Thyself, sole understandest Thyself, and, by Thyself understood and understanding, lovest and smilest on Thyself! That circle, which, thus conceived, appeared in Thee as a reflected light, being somewhile regarded by my eyes, seemed to me depicted within itself, of its own very colour, by our effigy, wherefore my sight was wholly set upon it. As is the geometer [6] who wholly applies himself to measure the circle, and finds

---

3. The unity of all being and all modes of being in the Creator, bound as leaves in a book, or as in an inextricable knot, by his power.

4. The shadow of Argo, ship of Jason and his Argonauts, seeking the Golden Fleece, and the first ship ever to sail, astonished Neptune, god of the sea, as it sailed over him. This happened 2500 years ago. Dante's vision was so splendid that the minute which elapsed after it had faded seemed like 2500 years.

5. Iris is the rainbow. The rainbows reflected in and begotten of each other represent the Trinity.

6. An impossibility topos. The geometrician cannot find the principle on which the circle can be measured, and Dante cannot find the measure of God, who is immeasurable, or tell the immensity of his infinite vision in the finite medium of words, however infinite his will.

not by thinking that principle of which he is in need, such was I at that new sight. I wished to see how the image accorded with the circle, and how it has its place therein; but my own wings were not for this, had it not been that my mind was smitten by a flash in which its wish came.

To my high fantasy here power failed; but now my desire and my will, like a wheel which evenly is moved, the Love was turning which moves the Sun and the other stars.

1318?–21

The Renaissance

The Renaissance

RENAISSANCE AND RENASCENCES

As a historical term, the "Renaissance" can mean a good many things, most of them having to do with what was happening to Europe half a millennium ago. Used purely to refer to a rebirth of interest in, and knowledge of, some of the ideas and discursive forms of classical antiquity which had been lost for a thousand years, it could, of course, be pushed back even farther. Some scholars have found in the design of some of the great Gothic architecture of the twelfth century the operation of principles of proportion and numerical order which we usually associate with the kind of neo-classical architecture called "humanist." An economic historian might be far more excited about what was happening to the production of woolen cloth in the fourteenth century than about some of the changes two centuries later in the ritualized behavior —religious, political, and linguistic—of the people who used and were enriched by that cloth.

The invention (1454) of movable-block printing (for texts, as distinguished from carved woodcuts for pictures, which had come earlier) and the discovery (1492) of the New World across the western oceans were both crucial events in the history of the shaking-loose of European culture from the political and conceptual structures in which it had lived for so long. And yet, artists and thinkers in fourteenth- and early fifteenth-century Italy were taking leaps of the eye, hand, and mind which would remain unexcelled in other realms of human activity for nearly a hundred years. The relation between discovery and invention is always a complex one, rather like a matter of deciding on the precedence of chicken over egg: the discovery of certain properties of the ground lens leads to the invention of a telescope which leads to the discovery of Jupiter's moons, but the chain has no beginning and never ends. It is even harder to trace the links between the social and technological events during the period from 1450 to 1650, say, and the aspects of the human imagination which, if they are being born again, are appearing in a new form. Wherever one tries to pin down the life-span of the period—in Italy, earlier; in Northern Europe, later—whether in painting, sculpture, and architecture, or in music, or in the technologies of exploration and economic expansion, it will begin and end differently. But there is a trace of common self-awareness in the name itself, for the general rebirth which, by consensus, all historians of all fields continue, when talking generally, to use.

The word "Renaissance" was probably employed in this context for the first time by Giorgio Vasari (1511–74), the Italian painter and architect who is today best known for his *Lives of the Most Excellent Painters, Sculptors and Architects* (1568), in a passage in which he was arguing for the modern view, which was not necessarily that of the early Renaissance, that an artist is not a mere handicraftsman, but a learned and imaginative figure—a "creator" in our sense, rather than a "maker." The community of artists could feel this sense of itself, and its recent history (Vasari saw the predecessor of the painting of his age in Giotto, as the Elizabethan writers in England would, as we shall see, look back to Chaucer). A general sense, of newness and freshness, all over Europe and in every sphere of activity, however, is the literary dream of the nineteenth century. The unique problem of England's Renaissance with respect to the Continent is a result of her twofold alienation from sources of influence during the fifteenth century: she was Northern and she was insular. England had no "quattrocento" like Italy's, and no local traditions in the arts like those of the very great painters of Flanders in the fifteenth century, or like the Flemish musicians who were so to influence the Italian Renaissance composers. John Dunstable, who died in 1453, was the last English practitioner of the arts to have much of an impact on the Continent for more than a century and a half. Scotland, which in the fifteenth century had a much more exciting literary culture than England, maintained very close ties with France—Mary, Queen of Scots (1542–87) was half-French, and married to the Dauphin of France—and in a particular way was thereby less insular. Scotland's intellectual traditions, as manifested, for example, in its approach to the Reformation, and in its subsequent educational system, were quite different from England's.

The literary and intellectual culture of England, during a period which overlapped only at the beginning what is called the Renaissance in Italy, was a complex product of the energies and talents of individual men and of the institutions, conventions, and styles which were open to them as instruments for those energies. To try to understand Shakespeare's genius as a function of a historical moment seems hopeless; to try to understand why, from 1590 to around 1610, the genius of a middle-class, self-educated man from Warwickshire might have flowered in the theater, to such a degree that some of the greatest wisdom of his age might be embodied in popular plays, is not. More than in any other period in recent history, the sixteenth and seventeenth centuries represent the use of what would look to us like imprisoning conventions—linguistic and intellectual patterns—in order to escape from other conventions which had preceded their use, and for so long a time that they resembled Nature, that they were all there was. The radical, humanistic notion of *originality* involved going back to true sources, to origins (today we would call this being "derivative," but our view reflects an intervening cultural phase of Romantic elevation of the notion of the self). In contemplating this long historical moment, then, we must try to understand the ways in which these new conventions—of everything from verse forms and rhyme schemes to ways of making sense out of something shown one—are used and transformed by major talents, and are beautifully exemplified by minor ones. (It is always instructive to learn how something which one truly admires in a great writer is merely a phrase, a turn, a strategy, an element of style, which he shares with even his tedious contemporaries, and that what we have admired is simply what defines our distance from his historical period.) All these conventions would themselves have arisen by adaptation or outright borrowing of ancient, or contemporary European, ones. It may seem strange that in the evolution of a great literary culture an important part might be played by the struggle, not totally successful, of a courtier and diplomat to translate and paraphrase some Italian love poems written two hundred years before. But Sir Thomas Wyatt's getting Petrarch's *Rime* (or sonnets) into English was just the kind of act which, unlike the action of vast, impersonal forces massively taking place over decades, has observable, and traceable, consequences for the individual human imagination.

By the English Renaissance, historians of literature and culture mean the period from about 1509 to 1660, the reign of the Tudor Henry VIII and his children and the first two Stuarts, and the revolutionary government of the Commonwealth which was brought about by troubles boiling up in the reigns of the Stuarts. Culturally speaking, there is a great deal of continuity in English life after the restoration of Charles II to the throne until the end of the century, though the lives and careers of individual writers and thinkers stretch across its chronological boundaries. Literary history is always concerned with self-consciousness, or at least with self-awareness; what an age thinks of itself defines it as an age, and the Restoration, with its Frenchified court fashions, its irreversibly altered Parliament, its Royal Society, and its integration of the lives of Court and Town (London) is really a part of the Europe of the Enlightenment. But there are other continuities, like the one between the convictions of the earliest Tudor humanists, Bacon's visions of the Institution of Reason in the middle of that period, and Milton's final and total presentation of the humanist program in the broadest sense. (This might be called attempting to transform the future of man by refocusing the light of his past.) It is such traditions, too, which help to shape this century and a half of both evolution and violent change.

HUMANISM

One of the important things to remember about the sixteenth century in England is that the New Learning, the interest in and access to classical culture, did not become fully associated with courtly life and patronage until late in the period of Elizabeth's reign. In Italy there were not only many local princes and wealthy families, as in Florence, or corporate municipalities, like Venice, but also the princes of the church in Rome to encourage the arts of splendor and, for a long while, of enlightenment. In England there was a court intent on its international and religious politics, for some time involved in a kind of cold war with Spain; and although it did support some humanistic scholarship, it was unable to bring together the arts and learning in anything like European fashion until the last years of Elizabeth's reign. The great Italian families had subsidized scholarship as well as pageantry; in England the early classical learning was the work and dream of the universities and of schoolmasters.

The rise of humanism can itself certainly be pushed back farther into history. Petrarch's Laureate Oration in 1341 was a dramatic instance in the career of that great precursor not only of Renaissance lyric poetry and its personal muses but also of classical scholarship. (Petrarch himself discovered texts of Cicero and Quintilian, the Roman rhetorician who became so important for the shape of written style later on.) But when the Dutch scholar Desiderius Erasmus (1466–1536), as he called himself—in a made-up Greek-Latin name both halves of which meant "lovable"—came to England, first to Oxford and then, later, to Cambridge in 1509, the new approach to classical learning that had emerged in Europe was only beginning to take hold. The use of Cicero's Latin rather than that of the medieval church, the study of Greek and even of Hebrew, the publication, editing, commentary upon, and appreciation of texts by classical authors became part of a vast institution for shifting the grounds of authority in human affairs. In the intellectual sphere this consisted of a turning from the rigid logical and rhetorical systems of scholasticism (see Glossary), in their day instruments of light, but by the fifteenth century more like walls. The use of classical models for prose style and for kinds of verse was far more than merely a stylistic change. They were assertions of the learned mind's unchallengeable right to make its own contract with classical learning, unmediated by the systems of medieval scholasticism.

THE REFORMATION

If some humanist scholars like Erasmus and, in England, Sir Thomas More, could remain in the church, there were others who could not. All across sixteenth-century Europe, we can observe a parallel to the humanist program in the various movements to substitute for the authority of the Roman Catholic Church a previously unthinkable notion of Christianity, of civilization, as something not necessarily embodied therein. In 1517, Martin Luther tacked his ninety-five theses to the door of his church in Wittenberg. In 1532, John Calvin's *Institutes of the Christian Religion* was published in Switzerland. In 1535, Henry VIII was able to designate himself the Supreme Head of the Church of England. In 1558, the Scottish reformer John Knox returned to his native country from Geneva, and the Calvinist character of the church in Scotland was firmly established; in the North, the Highlanders remained Roman Catholic, but elsewhere the "kirk" (as it is called in Scots) was Presbyterian. The Church of England itself, it must be remembered, was still by no means truly reformed. By confiscating the wealth of the monasteries Henry VIII dotted the English countryside with ruins, but it was only at the end of his reign that he began to build upon them, and over the bones of men like Sir Thomas More, who, as Lord Chancellor, refused to acknowledge, in place of the papal authority, a king who had broken with it over a divorce refused. In 1539 the Great Bible was in use in churches, but it was not until the brief reign of his son Edward VI (from 1547 to 1553) that the famous English Prayer Book, over which so much fighting would be done in less than a hundred years, was made available for a purely English liturgy. The Book of Common Prayer was published in 1549; four years later the Articles of Faith made the English church a Protestant one beyond doubt. Mass had become a communion service, and worship and Scripture had been brought over into the vernacular.

Thomas Cranmer, the Archbishop of Canterbury under whom all this was happening, and who had allowed the burning of various sorts of deviationists—too papal in outlook, or too Protestant—was himself one of the victims of the next monarch's reign. Mary Tudor, Henry's daughter by Catharine of Aragon and wife of Philip II, was Roman Catholic, and until her sister Elizabeth's accession in 1558, a compensatory reaction raged. Catholicism and the influence of Spanish power were two fears that plagued England until the succeeding reign of James. Despite its own mode of reformation, the English church still thought of itself as Catholic, and it was groups of reformers within it, whom we loosely designate as Puritan, who sought continuously to make it less so. They ranged from those who wanted to do away with bishops altogether, to those who merely wanted to stem the drift toward re-alliance with Rome which seemed to them to be a natural movement toward decay. Some of the more extreme of them fled en masse to Holland, which, since it had became independent of Spain, was a haven for religious refugees of all sorts. Others stayed behind, suffering various changes of fortune in the early decades of the seventeenth century. In general, it should be remembered that the English church was seeking throughout this period to maintain a kind of balance between two strong forces, Rome and the more thoroughgoing consequences of Geneva, home of Calvinism.

In 1603, James VI of Scotland became king of England (he was the great-grandson of Henry VII's daughter, Margaret). He had already planted some of the seeds of later discontent by introducing (in 1600) bishops into Scotland, much to the hatred of the Presbyterians there. Almost forty years later, his son Charles allowed his Puritan-persecuting Archbishop of Canterbury, William Laud, to try again to Anglicize the Scottish church, and precipitated the fighting known as the "Bishops' War" (1639). Charles's attempts to raise more money for its continuance led to the calling of the Long Parliament, which eventually beheaded both Archbishop Laud (1645) and the King (1649). Throughout the reigns of the first two Stuarts, the dangers of Rome and Spain were not a matter of universal national consciousness as they had been under Elizabeth, but when the Catholicism of Charles I's French wife, Henrietta Maria, helped to jeopardize national trust in him as Defender of the (English) Faith, Puritan factions in Parliament and Presbyterian ones in Scotland and England united for a while in maintaining the course and safety of the Reformation. For an absolutely committed mid-seventeenth-century Protestant like John Milton, the Reformation continued through the course of the Commonweath, and through the eventual conflicts between the powerful, official Presbyterian party (which had become for him the abrogator of freedom) and the more liberal congregationalist faction called the Independents. The Reformation must be seen as an institutional process which, after it had succeeded in establishing Protestant churches, continued, like a kind of permanent revolution, to unfold in the individual positions and visions of particular religious thinkers. Its primary movement, from the time of its beginning in the sixteenth century, was toward the *internalization* of institutions: individual conscience, rather than the structure of a church hierarchy to mediate between God and Man; an identification of Christ as the Light of the World with an inner light within men, and so forth. It was a process which continued later in the seventeenth and eighteenth centuries, in such manifestations as millenarian sects, the Quakers, and, later on, in the religious revival among a rising middle class, which eventually gave rise to Methodism within the Church of England itself.

It should also be briefly observed that the Roman church's own reaction to the rise of Protestantism, the Counter Reformation as it is called, produced a new approach to what Protestantism had isolated from other parts of life as *religion* (rather than the totality of spiritual life in its infusion of the material life, which marked the organic quality of medieval Christianity). The Council of Trent, which met sporadically between 1545 and 1563 to reformulate the doctrine of the Roman church, initiated this trend toward reform of some of the material abuses attacked by the early Protestants, as well as toward new modes of religiousness, including missionary work and more practical popular religious instruction—the Jesuits were instrumental in this. But English hopes that the Council would see the way to some kind of *via media* (or "middle way"), not unlike Richard Hooker's "Anglicanism," were disappointed, and in the end the Council sharpened the differences between the Roman and the Reformed churches. There was an English interest (because a Protestant one) in the Thirty Years' War in Germany (ended 1648), and at times an almost paranoid fear of the Jesuits; aside from these the Counter Reformation remained a curiosity of Continental faith.

A NEW IMAGE OF THE WORLD

Another revision of authority previously vested in an older order occurred in connection with the mixture of invention and discovery mentioned earlier. The explorations of the New World for purposes of economic development and, particularly in England's case, the undermining of Spanish colonial power in the West Indies by naval strength brought with them one kind of opening up. Another was in the exploration of the conceptual new world of the cosmos. The Ptolemaic cosmology which had prevailed since classic times was being gradually undermined, during the sixteenth and seventeenth centuries, by new discoveries which could not be accommodated to it as they previously had been (see Glossary: Astronomy and Astrology). Without cataloguing the scientific developments of the period under discussion, we may observe in one sequence of revisions of the older world picture some of the sorts of change which might affect the life of the mind for all men of thought. The Ptolemaic model of the universe corresponded to observed phenomena by positing transparent spheres of huge magnitude, moving concentrically about the earth, each carrying a heavenly body, or, the last but outside one, all the fixed stars which do not move in relation to each other. Circles and spheres were traditional symbols of perfection, and in order to maintain both the idea of a perfectly constructed universe and the actuality of what happened in the sky night after night, astronomers since classical times had been forced to adapt and change the model slightly; for example, they built so-called "epicycles," or circular reroutings, onto the circular path of the planets. But the basic idea of planned and patterned circularity was there. In the year of his death, the Polish astronomer Nicolaus Copernicus (1473–1543) published his treatise *On the Revolution of the Spheres,* which put the sun, not the earth, at the center of the model, but left the notion of circular paths of motion about it. This meant asserting that what "really" happened in the sky was not what "apparently" happened, but that a picture of reality with concentric circles on it, no matter how disturbing in its decentralization of the earth—and, by implication, of humanity—in the divine scheme, could still look orderly.

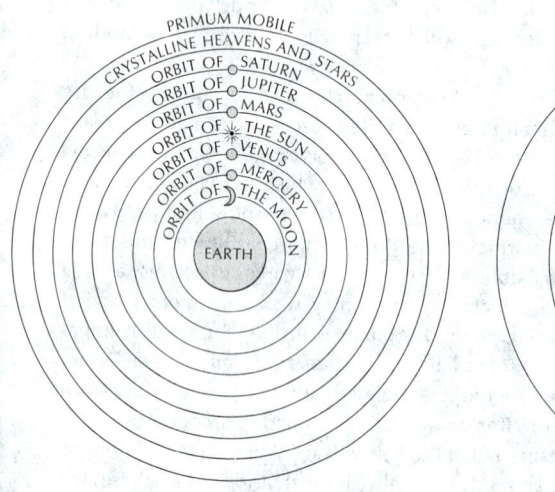

The Ptolemaic World-System

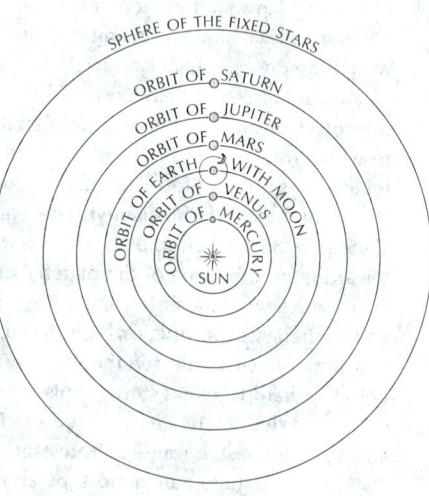

Copernican World System, 1543

Johannes Kepler (1571–1630) wrecked that order when he formulated his laws of planetary motion, published in 1609: the planets, he showed, moved in elliptical orbits, not circular ones, with the sun at one of the foci of the ellipse. But he showed a kind of beautiful regularity in their motion which to us, today, looks as mysteriously contrived as any nest of circles. The planets move more quickly when nearer the sun, more slowly when far away; but these changes in speed are so orderly that the planets, as he put it, sweep out "equal areas in equal times." That means merely this: if we take two points on the elliptical path that are, say, one planetary month apart, and then take two more at the other end of the orbit, at the "fast end" they will be farther apart than at the distant one. Now, if we draw lines from those points toward the sun, at one of the foci of the ellipse, we will get two pie-shaped wedges, one long and thinnish, the other shorter and fatter. But their areas will always be equal. Moreover, Kepler showed, the square of its periodic time at any point around its ellipse will be proportional to the cube of its mean distance from the sun.

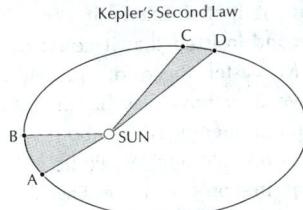

Kepler's Second Law

If the time taken to travel A-B and C-D is the same, then the two shaded bits, different in shape, will always be equal in area.

These are elegances of order which it takes a bit more than simple arithmetic to comprehend as orderly at all. But one more shift or dislocation of the idea of orderliness occurs during the seventeenth century which we might glance at. For Kepler, these were "laws," but if one could not show *why* they were true, then, no matter how carefully formulated, they might recede into the status of phenomena again. This is what finally happened. Galileo Galilei (1564–1642) discovered that the earth's gravitational pull on all objects could be mathematically described as an accelerating force (this is aside from the astronomical observations for which he was so famous—his perfecting of the refracting telescope led him to conclude that the moon shone by reflected light, that Jupiter had four satellites, that the Milky Way was the massed effect of countless stars, etc.). Sir Isaac Newton (1642–1727) would finally take a huge conceptual leap, and argue that the gravity which Galileo had described was *not* just a local peculiarity of the surface of the earth, but applied as a force acting between any two or more bodies, anywhere. Kepler's Second Law, then, could be shown to be an effect which would have to be true, given the gravitational situation of the sun and the planet in question. With such a notion, any connection between simple observation of what were called the "appearances," obvious to any reasonable man, and the proper explanation or mathematical model, was gone. By the end of the English Renaissance, science (or "natural philosophy" as it was called) had become a special sort of explanation, given in totally different sorts of language from moral, or metaphysical, or even psychological accounts.

Cosmology, banishing the older astrology, was, of course, not the only kind of

revision of the older picture of the world. Alchemy, with its highly symbolic interpretation of the realities behind natural processes, gave way to chemistry, whose
concerns had been mostly a by-product of the true, religious alchemical quest. The
inner structure of the human totality, with its humors and spirits which reflected in
their composition the basic, four-part grouping of elements in the universe, gave way
to specific biological answers to clearly defined questions. The whole program sketched
out in Francis Bacon's dream of methods for reaching truth (see Headnote to Bacon)
began to be, with the establishment of the Royal Society in 1660, an actuality.

THE INSTRUMENT OF PROSE

Just as the new science would need mathematical languages in which to express
complicated relationships, the far more general problem of human discourse required
a new sort of language as well. The humanist program had started with Latin, and the
Classics generally; it soon moved to a rebuilding of the vernacular. There are really
two phases to this development in the sixteenth century: the first established the
authority of antiquity, the second insisted that it could be fulfilled in the vernacular.
Schoolmasters like Richard Mulcaster (head of the Merchant Taylors' School and
teacher of Spenser) might have their boys play ball in Latin, and by the 1590's there
were still debates going on among literary critics about whether English poetry should
be written in classical meters or not, although Sir Philip Sidney had argued persuasively
in his *Defence of Poesie* that the only way for English poets to be truly like the
classical ones they so admired was by being themselves. The modes of eloquence
were, of course, prose and verse. It is hard for a twentieth-century reader, with his
built-in notion that prose is plain, universal, and ordinary and that verse is special,
ornate, and idiosyncratic, to understand how this was not true, really, until the end of
the seventeenth century. An ordinarily competent sonnet, for example, written as a
dedicatory poem to some friend's book on anything from logic to gardening, would
be truly anonymous in character—unless a considerable poet with a marked style
were to put it to such a purpose, those verses would constitute the equivalent of a
formal, common prose in our day and before. Any literate person might have learned
in school to compose verses in Latin and, later on, in Greek. To do so in English was
no indication of special poetic gifts.

The prose styles of the sixteenth and seventeenth centuries were in a state of
flux just because of the phases of the humanist learning mentioned above. The first
style taught for English prose was modeled on Cicero—elaborate, balanced, ornate,
with many dependent clauses and rounded periods. In one of its more affected and
personal styles, it developed into the so-called Euphuistic prose (see Headnote to
John Lyly) of the last decades of the sixteenth century. But in sermons, treatises, tracts,
and even translations of foreign authors, the so-called Senecan prose favored by Bacon,
a livelier, jumpier style involving short sentences and sudden turns and variations of
pace, began to replace it. The spoken language could not enter the written one to
shape and extend its resources as easily as one might think. There was no prose fiction
in our sense of the word, and even a picaresque romance of great brilliance and
linguistic power like Thomas Nashe's *The Unfortunate Traveller* (1594) is written in a
prose more highly patterned than most contemporary verse today. It is, indeed,
through the verse and occasional prose of the theater on the one hand, and in certain
kinds of song texts which contain more of the music of speech than they allow for

the addition of melody on the other, that the spoken word begins to inform the written one.

TRANSLATIONS; THE EXAMPLE OF MONTAIGNE

One of the ways in which the resources of the language could be augmented was a natural concomitant of decreasing insularity through translation of the classical and contemporary European authors who both might and might not be read in the original. The English Bible was a matter of necessity to the reform not only of liturgy but of the relation of even the simplest of men to God's word. Translations of secular authors served two purposes: in the case of, say, Sir Thomas North's very important translation of Plutarch's *Parallel Lives* (1579) from the Greek, to which fewer people would have access than to Latin. The fragments of the *Aeneid* done into verse by the Earl of Surrey (1517–47) were more than merely toying with a new verse form (the blank verse which he borrowed from the Italian), but a kind of act of commitment to a literary tradition that he and the other earlier Tudor writers were trying to join. Getting the great works of other languages into English meant also creating a canon, a basic body of almost *scriptural* secular works, which would have the same power and general reference as biblical texts. Arthur Golding's Ovid of 1567 (see *The Renaissance Ovid*) and George Chapman's Homer (*Iliad*, 1611; *Odyssey*, 1616) were verse translations of the first importance. But perhaps the most important piece of Elizabethan translation as far as the subsequent history of English prose was concerned, was the version by the linguistic scholar John Florio (c. 1553–1625) of the *Essays* of Montaigne.

Michel Eyquem de Montaigne (1533–92) was a scholar, lawyer, and skeptical philosopher who retired to his tower near Bordeaux to meditate and put together those commonplace books or scraps of quotations with an added commentary which eventually outgrew the quotations, and became his meditational trials, or essays into thought. His is the final blow struck against dogmatism, and he is the predecessor, writing from his book-lined study, not only of French philosophers of subsequent centuries but, in Florio's translation, of many English writers as well. Bacon knew him, and so did Burton, Shakespeare, Donne, Ralegh, Ben Jonson, and many others. His vision of the contemplative life, vastly different from that of medieval Christianity, saw a new kind of relation between man's mind and the thoughts of others, and he defined solitude in a new way:

> A man that is able may have wives, children, goods, and chiefly health, but not so tie himself unto them that his felicity depend on them. We should reserve a storehouse for ourselves, what need soever chance, altogether ours and wholly free, wherein we may hoard up and establish true liberty and principal retreat and solitariness, wherein we must go alone to ourselves to take our ordinary entertainment, and so privately that no acquaintance or communication of any strange thing may therein find place; there to discourse, to meditate and laugh, as without wife, without children and goods, without train or servants, that if by any occasion they be lost it seem not strange to us to pass it over. We have a mind moving and turning in itself; it may keep itself company; it hath wherewith to offend and defend, wherewith to receive and wherewith to give. . . . [*Of Solitude*]

This "storehouse" (*arrière-boutique*—"back of the shop," Montaigne calls it) becomes for humanist meditative writers more than merely a locale, a room, a place, but rather a whole region of the mind, a condition of relation to thought and nature. But perhaps one of the most famous and resonant examples of Montaigne's concept of what was in his phrase "the human condition" and its dignity is to be found in his famous essay "Of Cannibals," in which he broods over the meaning of civilization itself. In 1562 at Rouen he had met some natives of the New World, and in his essay of about 1580 he describes the condition of some of these inhabitants of the tropical Americas, and goes on to remark that "there is nothing in that nation that is either barbarous or savage, unless men call that barbarism which is not common to them." The whole following passage is of great interest and merit:

> As indeed we have no other aim of truth and reason than the example and *Idea* of the opinions and customs of the country we live in. There is ever perfect religion, perfect policy,[1] perfect and complete use of all things. They are even savage, as we call those fruits wild which nature of herself and of her ordinary progress hath produced; whereas indeed they are those which ourselves have altered by our artificial devices and diverted from their common order, we should rather term savage. In those are the true and most profitable virtues and natural properties most lively and vigourous, which in these we have bastardised, applying them to the pleasure of our corrupted taste. And if, notwithstanding, in diverse fruits of those countries that were never tilled we shall find that in respect of ours they are most excellent and as delicate unto our taste, there is no reason art should gain the point of honour of our great and puissant[2] mother nature. We have so much by our inventions surcharged the beauties and riches of her works that we have altogether overchoked her. Yet, wherever her purity shineth she makes our vain and frivolous enterprises wonderfully ashamed.

> Ivies spring better of their own accord,
> Unhaunted plots much fairer trees afford.
> Birds by no art much sweeter notes record.
> Propertius[3] I *Elegies* ii 10.

> All our endeavour or wit cannot so much as reach to represent the nest of the least birdlet, its contexture,[4] beauty, profit and use, no nor the web of a silly[5] spider. *All things*, saith *Plato, are produced either by nature, by fortune, or by art: the greatest and fairest by one or other of the two first, the least and imperfect by the last.* Those nations seem, therefore, so barbarous unto me, because they have received very little fashion from human wit and are yet near their original naturality. The laws of nature do yet command them, which are but little bastardised by ours; and that with such purity as I am sometimes grieved the knowledge of it came no sooner to light, at what time there were men that better than we could have judged of it. I am sorry Lycurgus[6] and Plato had it not, for meseemeth that what in those nations we see by experience doth not only exceed all the pictures wherewith licentious Poesy had proudly embellished the golden age, and all her quaint inventions to feign a happy condition of man, but also the conception and desire of Philosophy. They could not imagine a genuity[7] so pure and simple as we see it by experience, nor ever believe our society might be maintained with so little art and human combination. It is a nation, would I answer *Plato*, that hath no kind of traffic, no knowledge of Letters, no intelligence of numbers, no name of

1. Government.
2. Capable.
3. Sextus Propertius, Roman elegiac poet (*c.* 54 B.C.–*c.* 2 B.C.).
4. Structure.
5. Simple.
6. As framer of the constitution of Sparta; Plato, as propounder of a Utopian republic (in *Laws* X).
7. Nature.

magistrate nor of politic superiority; no use of service, of riches or of poverty; no contracts, no successions, no partitions, no occupation but idleness; no respect of kindred but common, no apparel but natural, no manuring [8] of lands, no use of wine, corn, or metal. The very words that import lying, falsehood, treason, dissimulations, covetousness, envy, detraction, and pardon, were never heard of amongst them. How dissonant would he find his imaginary commonwealth from this perfection! [9]

COMMONPLACES

Montaigne's meditative prose was a great instrument for both the transmission of knowledge and the discovery of the self. It arose from commentary on texts of other authors, and it should be observed that this process of taking off from a text, obviously basic to scriptural commentaries and those of classical scholars, and the fundamental method of homiletic prose, the sermons of both Anglican and Puritan divines throughout this period, was an intellectual operation of a much more general character. In a way, there remained an unbroken tradition going back to medieval times of beginning all exposition with a text from tradition; if there was not a particular passage from biblical or classical sources, there might be one of a number of received ideas, set themes or topics, the response to which on the part of the writer would generate copy (from copia or "plenty"). Thus, the notion of the "theatrum mundi," that "all the world's a stage" was one topic; the concept of the locus amoenus or "lovely place," the garden associated with pastoral ideal realms, Eden, and various classical gardens was another. And in a peculiar way, the presence of classical mythology, whether embodied in particular formulations or quotations from Ovid or Virgil, or passed through a filter of received tradition and interpretive commentary (see The Renaissance Ovid) was always available. It is only the philosophical tradition of the seventeenth century which begins, as a counterpart to the raising of scientific questions based only on observed phenomena, to produce discourse based only upon the topic questions posed by self-awareness. Montaigne had, while still surrounded by his books, allowed their light to strike a spark of questioning ("Who am I? What do I know? What is what I know good for?") in him. His French follower, René Descartes (1596–1650), would carry this even farther by wondering what, if anything, it was possible to be absolutely certain of. Thomas Hobbes (1588–1679), although his view of the lives of Montaigne's noble savages was vastly different, also stems from him in a different way. (See the Glossary: Rhetoric.)

LANGUAGE AND THE THEATER

The theater in the sixteenth century blended a native, vernacular popular tradition with a learned one. Latin plays based on the tragedies of Seneca were written and acted in schools; it was not until an English drama with recognizable links to that classical tradition developed that any truly public theater was able to emerge. In 1561, an English blank-verse tragedy called Gorboduc, by Thomas Norton and Thomas Sackville, was played first at the Inner Temple and then before the Queen, as a kind

---

8. Cultivation.
9. The foregoing passage seems to be imitated in Shakepeare's *The Tempest*, II.i.54 ff. It is interesting that Florio's Protestant reticence leads him not to translate the quotation which follows: "Men sprung from the Gods" (from Seneca's *Epistles* XC).

of warning to her to beget an heir, so that the English throne would be safe from the disasters of division portrayed in the play. The Inns of Court—the Middle Temple, Inner Temple, Gray's Inn, and Lincoln's Inn—were the London law schools whose students and fellows contributed so much to the intellectual and cultural life of the city of London. The two universities were producing students who, after classical studies and training in rhetoric, might often read law before going into government service. Younger sons of noble families and older ones of the merchant classes and yeomanry shared a background in classical learning and a sense of sophistication that made the dining halls of the Inns of Court a breeding ground for the theater that would later come outdoors. An outdoor theater was built in London in 1576, and from then until 1642, in the more generally public theaters built south of the Thames, and in the more private coteries of the Inns of Court, a great theatrical tradition arose and flourished. Traveling companies of actors, writing and producing their own plays, attached to the household of some nobleman for protection against ordinances hostile to strolling players, moved about the country; but the theaters bred their own companies and audiences with their own expectations and, consequently, styles produced to meet them. There were also intimate, learned court plays which, in the early years of James's reign, developed into the court masque, a unique and totally unreconstructable lost theatrical realm. During this period of almost seventy years, the English stage developed a complex literary and political history of its own, and at this point it will only be remarked again how that history was the function of contributions as various as those of song-and-dance clowns on the one hand, and learned poets like Christopher Marlowe, who brought to blank-verse tragedy a kind of poetic style nurtured on nondramatic (epic and elegiac) classical verse in English, on the other. The stage remained, despite the Puritan attacks upon it, a public institution which attracted the interests and energies of men as diverse as the highly learned, ideologically neoclassical Ben Jonson and the prosaic, popularly entertaining Thomas Dekker (c. 1570–c. 1641), who attacked Jonson (his erstwhile collaborator) in a broad satiric onslaught. It reflected the rest of the literary culture of the nation which surrounded it in all of its phases (the Jacobean tragedies of John Webster and Cyril Tourneur will be recognized even by the beginning student of the period as having more to do with the world of John Donne's later poems and sermons, and with Burton's *Anatomy of Melancholy*, than with the literary conventions of the 1590's). When the theaters finally closed, by order of the Puritan Parliament in 1642, a whole chapter in the development of English imaginative language came to an end.

THE FORMS OF VERSE

In some periods of change, the question of forms of activity can seem to matter more than content. In the practical history of the Reformation in England, the form of a prayer book could be defended with force of arms; in the literary history of the 1580's and 90's, arguments about verse forms could conceal debates about larger issues. One such argument was about how literally classical English verse should be. Upholders of quantitative scansion tried to establish Latin and Greek traditions in the actual structure of English poetry; their opponents maintained that analogues of classical forms were the only appropriate ones. But the two sides agreed that there were ways of working from classical models of form, as well as of reference and allusion. The case of the English heroic couplet is a good instance of this. During the later decades of the sixteenth century, the rhymed pairs of iambic pentameter lines in English served various purposes: closing scenes in blank-verse drama, closing the English form of the sonnet, translating (as with Marlowe's *Hero and Leander*) classical heroic verse, which in Greek or Latin was in unrhymed hexameters. After Wyatt and Surrey the so-called "fourteener,"

A line that rumbles on like this for just a bit too long

when used in couplets, had a classical ring to it, for it was "long" like the hexameter. Golding's Ovid (see *The Renaissance Ovid*) is in this meter. But the pentameter couplet began to eclipse the longer ones, both for translating and, even more important, *standing for*, heroic verse. Then, too, there were the forms of epigram and satire. In classical verse, these are written in unrhymed "elegiac" couplets, a longer hexameter followed by a shorter pentameter. The English heroic couplet served for this as well. By the beginning of the seventeenth century the form was doing both jobs—so much so, that Ben Jonson, careful neoclassicist that he was, indented the second line of his couplets when used in epigrams, to stand for the classical couplets, but had them printed flush left when they stood for heroic hexameters. By the mid-century, the heroic couplets were so entrenched as the verse mode of both heroic and elegiac that Milton had to apologize, in a second printing, for the blank verse which he had used for the epic meter of *Paradise Lost*.

The later sixteenth century and the early seventeenth century saw a proliferation of lyric forms for verse, and with them, an ever varying set of relations between what the forms stood for, or suggested, about the poet's intention, and what the forms did in the way of affecting the language of the poem. Sir Philip Sidney's great experiments in the songs from the *Arcadia* developed in two directions the possibilities of using the formal structures of verse to control tone of voice and the structure of poetic discourse. One of these moved toward a patterning of surface, a decorative draping of grammatical parallelisms and mirrorings over the basic shape of a line. The other involved the opposition between line structure, its fixed number of stressed and unstressed syllables, and the ways in which the sound of a speaking voice would push against those patterns. From one of these directions the Spenserian diction branches off; from the other, the sonnets of Shakespeare and the lyrics of Donne. It should be remembered that there was, up through the turn of the seventeenth century, a strong general sense of formal discovery and invention, and that between the pre-1590's verse of the kind which C. S. Lewis has called "drab" and the carefully controlled and measured "plain style" of some of Ben Jonson's verse and that of his followers, there are not only a few decades of literary development, but changing assumptions about the relation of imagery, density of thought, and allusion to the verse forms in which they were set out.

While the Elizabethan literary debates frequently centered on the ways in which style should mirror intention, Jacobean and Caroline poets moved in one of three directions. Either they helped to make a tradition of the strong lines of John Donne—the so-called Metaphysical school, or they took the course that ran, through what Alexander Pope would call in the next century "Denham's strength and Waller's sweetness"—the contrived elegance in the way in which tone of voice is submerged in the formality of verse, and the tact with which imagery is introduced and led away from in poetry of statement or praise—to the Augustan style of John Dryden. There was also a third tradition (and it must be understood that individual poets often drew upon more than one stream) which had a curious fate—Spenser's followers in the early seventeenth century, Michael Drayton, William Browne, Giles and Phineas Fletcher, all interested in extended mythological poems, found themselves running against a tide. They were more admired in the nineteenth century than in our day, which is still influenced by the reinterpretation of the seventeenth century brought about by the influence of T. S. Eliot in his poetry and criticism. The only poem attributed to John Donne in Palgrave's *Golden Treasury of Songs and Lyrics,* a major Victorian anthology, is not by Donne at all. The minor Spenserians, poets of great skill and more than charm, will one day again be read with interest.

Some of the literary history of the last forty years may lead the beginning student of seventeenth-century poetry to believe that "lines" meant factions. This was not true, although occasionally the rhetoric of criticism might make it seem so. The cavalier poets, for example, while united in their loyalty to the king and the church, differed widely in how much Donne's wit and energy (Thomas Carew, for example, pledges himself to these), and how much Jonson's elegance and firm tactfulness characterized their verse. The Spenserian tradition ends up in Milton, a very great poet of the Puritan faction, and perhaps rightly so, Spenser's vision being radical and Protestant. But Andrew Marvell, a major talent and a devoted political servant of the Commonwealth, extends the styles of cavalier verse in developing his own. Many of the seventeenth-century lyric poets were clergymen, and the student cannot help but notice how many poets in the line of Donne were, like him, in holy orders; when they were, they were Anglican and, when the fighting started, Royalist.

THE CIVIL WAR

The Revolution was the second major center of upheaval in the period we have been calling the English Renaissance, the first being the turbulent fluctuations of Catholic and Anglican power in the mid-sixteenth century and the ensuing uneasiness about Rome and Spain which lasted well into Elizabeth's reign. Even after the defeat of the Armada (1588), the Elizabethan court was marked by uncertainty, rapid changes in the wind of favor, and the lack of norms of approach to preferment and finding appropriate governmental posts; thus a well-connected and useful man like Francis Bacon could get nowhere in the court of Elizabeth, and it was only with the accession of James that, particularly for men of letters, there was more of an official openness.

James's tutor, as a boy, had been the Great Scotch humanist George Buchanan (another of whose pupils, earlier on, had been Montaigne). James, however, did not respond with any sympathy to the teachings of his former tutor's tract *De Jure Regni* (On the Law of the Realm), in which the rule of kings is subjected to popular will and welfare. Instead, he formulated a doctrine of the divine right of kings. Intellectual, learned, and contentious, James was impractically given to the elevation of his favorites; men like Robert Carr (who became involved in a major scandal when he arranged for the murder of Sir Thomas Overbury), and, after him, the Duke of Buckingham, whom James ennobled as he did many others, engendered some mistrust.

The court of his son Charles was marked by a certain royal grandeur without the intellectual cast of his father's: Charles was a great patron of painters (Van Dyck and Rubens) and a collector of pictures—many of which Cromwell subsequently sold; and he preferred the pure spectacle and stage effects of Inigo Jones, the great stage designer, in his masques, or court entertainments, to the allegorical visions of Ben Jonson for which that spectacle had been originally employed. Despite his almost spiritual sense of the condition of kingship, he agreed, three years after ascending the throne in 1628, to Parliament's Petition of Right, in order to secure its vote on funds he needed. The Petition, although aimed at specific grievances such as the king's ability to declare martial law, and certain taxing privileges, in fact established the supremacy of parliamentary law over regal power. Charles largely ignored its provisions, and from 1629 until 1640 he ruled without calling any Parliament at all. A war with France made him unpopular, as did an attempt to extend to inland counties with no use for ships a tax known as *ship-money* (traditionally a levy only on certain port cities to help finance the royal support of shipping). But Charles needed money, and called what turned out to be a short, querulous session of Parliament lasting for three weeks in 1640. Several months later the so-called Long Parliament, under whom Charles was eventually beheaded, was called into session.

The Long Parliament drafted a Grand Remonstrance against Charles, in his absence, in 1641; his attempt, early in 1642, to arrest five members of Parliament brought on war that year. After four years of fighting, Charles surrendered, was imprisoned, escaped and was recaptured, and finally, after trial at Westminster as "the tyrant, traitor and murderer, Charles Stuart," was executed in 1649. The parliamentary government which succeeded him had split into two factions, a Presbyterian one and an Independent one, under Oliver Cromwell (1599–1658). For a while Parliament had been dominated by the first, while Cromwell had control of the army; but fearful that the Presbyterian faction might finally return power to the crown, Cromwell took virtual control of the nation. An Instrument of Government in 1653 named him Lord Protector and formally established a Commonwealth.

During all this, Royalist refugees, aristocratic and clerical, and those who were neither but were ideologically committed to established power, like Thomas Hobbes, had fled to France, and a circle of English émigrés remained there for various lengths of time. Charles II, who had himself crowned in 1651 in Scotland, attempted to lead an attacking force into England that year, was defeated, and joined the rest of the exiles in France after a dramatic forty days of escape through England. Following nine years of exile, the wave of political confusion after Cromwell's death and during the tenure of Richard Cromwell, his son, allowed Charles to return to England. He landed at Dover on May 29, 1660, his thirtieth birthday.

The continuities of English town and country life had been far less disturbed by the events of the past two decades—the closing of the theaters being a notable exception —than had institutions of power and patronage. Strongly Anglican clergyman and fellows of Oxford and Cambridge colleges had lost their posts. But largely, the Restoration signaled the donning of new styles, new fashions or, as the fashionably French word went, "modes." The tight lacing of Elizabethan corsets had given way, after lasting through the Jacobean reign, to a loosening of line of dress and of hair; this had been associated with Cavalier rather than with "Roundhead" or Puritan factions in the time of the Civil War, and came back to Restoration fashion with a vengeance. But traces of the world view which such styles of costume reflect are evident in the literature, primarily in the poetry, of the 1630's and after; for the imagination, outward styles can be seen as the objectification of states of mind. The peculiar paradoxes of English cultural styles during this whole period—particularly with respect to Continental ones—remain fascinating. King's College Chapel, in Cambridge, finished in 1539, remains a triumph of late English gothic architecture; when it was dedicated, the high-

Renaissance triumph of St. Peter's in Rome was already under construction. The peculiar blending of the gothic and the baroque temperaments which we find in John Donne, those strange remnants of medievalism in Shakespeare, are reflected in the seventeenth-century façade of the chapel of Peterhouse, Cambridge, whose gothic arched long window is surmounted, on the outside, by a typically seventeenth-century baroque broken pediment. These co-existing and contrasting strands of tradition, the pulls and tensions of orthodoxy and Protestantism, royalism and republicanism, insularlity and cosmopolitanism, make for a complex and often slightly awkward picture. But perhaps by virtue of this very awkwardness, this being out of phase with so many normative developments of European cultural history, the magnificent aspects of the earliest humanist programs continued to flower and bear fruit in a visionary mid-century literature well after it should have. The massive geniuses of Shakespeare, Spenser, and Milton, concentrated in this brief time, are enough for any culture's life history.

THE RENAISSANCE OVID

Along with Virgil and eventually, through him, Homer, the greatest repository of narrative aside from the Bible upon which Renaissance poetry depended was Ovid's *Metamorphoses*. The Roman poet's epic of transformations ("Change is my subject," he starts out) was not merely a brilliant collection of much of the classical mythology which involved changes of state of being—people into animals, plants, rocks, and fountains, even stars. It provided a kind of form or template for poetic realization of a whole world view. In the sixteenth and seventeenth centuries, that view still embraced a vision of cosmic order reflected in smaller orders and structures; of the signatures of a transcendent world being legible in the appearances of the immediate one; of theories of the relation of eternal patterns to changeable substances; of the objectification of human feelings and thoughts in ways more fluid than those provided by surviving medieval personifications and allegories. Ovid's book was not merely a handbook of stories, for his own sensuous, artful, witty, and often very dramatic poetic style provided many rhetorical and figurative models for English poets of the Tudor and Stuart eras.

Modern readers think of ancient myths primarily as stories. Some more sophisticated readers, particularly those with some experience of modern anthropology or with the history of science, will understand them as early kinds of explanations about natural phenomena and processes. For poetry, however, the importance of mythology has always resided in the relation of stories to the meanings that were to be extracted from them by imaginative readings. The notion of a "moralized" story goes back to early Greek philosophical commentators on Homer, and, in a sense, the whole allegorical tradition can be said to stem from ways of reading traditional stories. With Ovid, this process began with the tedious homily and sometimes farfetched moralizings of the fourteenth-century French *Ovide Moralisé*, but Renaissance writers and painters began building up a massive body of Ovidian interpretation. These readings of the classical stories occurred in special handbooks of mythology and in poems, plays, and masques which derived from them, and continued the interpretation further. This is not to speak of paintings and prints, which from this point of view are silent texts, what Ben Jonson called "a mute poesy."

Arthur Golding (1536?–1605?) published in 1567 his great translation of the *Metamorphoses* in rhyming fourteener couplets, which was known by Shakespeare and his contemporaries along with the Latin original; and although its own virtues are those of capturing some of Ovid's poetic art to a remarkable degree, it makes a bow toward interpretation in an appended "Epistle" which Golding wrote in the manner of some earlier mythographers. Two passages from Golding's version appear below. The first is Ovid's description of the Golden Age, one of the four phases, as originally given by the Greek poet Hesiod, of human history, and an important parallel to the Judaeo-Christian story of the Fall from Paradise. The Golden Age, presided over by Saturn before any of the final structures of Olympian gods, men, animals, underworld, and so forth had arisen, was followed by a declining series of silver, bronze, and iron epochs, the last of which all human history seems to have occupied. It is a concept central to English Renaissance notions of pleasure and virtue, and Ovid's vision of it influences countless verbal and visual pictures of lovely places, from Eden through the backgrounds for pastoral poetry to imagined worlds in which there is no gap between what is good, what gives pleasure, and what is for both of those reasons beautiful.

519

The other passage from Golding's Ovid is a small part of the well-known story of the sculptor Pygmalion and his statue, with which he falls in love. Ovid tells it in his famous tenth book, of which Golding says in his "Epistle":

> The tenth book chiefly doth contain one kind of argument
> Reproving most prodigious lusts of such as have been bent
> To incest most unnatural . . . Moreover, it doth show
> That beauty (will they, nill they) aye doth men in danger throw,
> And that it is a foolishness to strive against the thing
> Which God before determineth to pass in time to bring.
> And last of all, Adonis' death doth show that manhood strives
> Against forewarning, though men see the peril of their lives.

(Had Shakespeare believed this last to be a good reading, he could have written no poem on it.) The Pygmalion story is cited by Ovid as part of the legendary material surrounding the background of the Venus story, for the eventual child of the union of Pygmalion and his quickened creation was named Paphos, and Paphos became the poetic name for Cyprus, the island of the goddess's birth. The tale is best known to modern readers through George Bernard Shaw's play, which ingeniously transforms substance into language, converting the sculptural act into the skill of a professor of linguistics in making a cockney street-girl talk like a lady of high degree, and the enlivening of the statue into her spiritual awakening to a sense of her own freedom. Golding's version of Ovid is followed by two brief commentaries, and finally by a longer passage from the great translation of George Sandys in 1626, with a full and detailed commentary added in 1632. The various mythographers move from the crudest readings, which try to account for the myth on the basis of distorted fact or else to glue a moral onto it, to far more imaginative and symbolic views. Caxton's early reading is of the first type; aimed primarily at artists is that of the Dutch poet, painter, and writer on art Carel van Mander, who commented on the meanings in Ovid as part of an artist's handbook (Het Schilderbouck) in 1604. A German emblem book from the late sixteenth century shows a picture of the sculptor and his statue with a motto stating that the best marriages are made in heaven ("Der best heürath kompt den gott schüpt").

Also given are two different examples of the ways in which Ovidian materials, known through their interpreted versions, work their way into minor literary forms. Aside from the massive use of mythography by Spenser and Milton, who not only drew upon Renaissance writers on myth in many languages but also derived further mythologies of their own from them, Ovidian story could be used anecdotally, as in the concluding section of a poem from Tottel's Miscellany of 1557, and as part of an erotic epyllion by John Marston, The Metamorphoses of Pygmalion's Image (see Headnote to Hero and Leander), although, in this instance, a not very good one.

A mid-seventeenth-century critical work devoted to the continuing life of ancient myth in its contemporary interpretation was Henry Reynolds's Mythomystes (1632), "wherein a short survey is taken of the nature and value of true poesy, and depth of the ancients above our modern poets." A passage from it concludes this section. Reynolds was arguing for the poetic importance of mythological themes at a time when a fashionable poet could speak of "the goodly exiled train / Of gods and goddesses" and of "The silenced tales of the Metamorphoses" as having lost imaginative relevance, at least to erotic poetry.

Throughout all these mythographic ingenuities, distortions, and homilies lay such

Renaissance convictions as the one that held classical mythology to be at worst a distorted, slightly crippled but reconstructible model of biblical truth. The act of reconstruction could itself be thought of as one of the nobler activities of the mind or, at very least, as exemplifying that twofold source of pleasure and profit which poetry and art were felt to be:

> If poets then with leesings° and with fables shadowed° so
> The certain truth, what letteth° us to pluck these visors fro
> Their doings, and to bring again the darkened truth to light,
> That all men may behold thereof the clearness shining bright?
> The readers therefore earnestly admonished are to be
> To seek a further meaning than the letter gives to see.
> The travail tane in that behalf although it have some pain,
> Yet makes it double recompense with pleasure and with gain. . . .
> (Golding, "Epistle" XV. 537–44)

From Arthur Golding's Ovid's Metamorphoses

[The Golden Age°]

> Then sprang up first the golden age, which of itself maintained
> The truth and right of everything, unforced and unconstrained.
> There was no fear of punishment, there was no threatening law
> In brazen tables nailèd up to keep the folk in awe.
> There was no man would crouch or creep to Judge, with cap in hand:
> They livèd safe without a Judge in every realm and land.
> The lofty pine tree was not hewn from mountains where it stood,
> In seeking strange and foreign lands, to rove upon the flood.°
> Men knew no other countries yet than where themselves did keep;
> There was no town enclosèd yet, with walls and ditches deep.
> No horn nor trumpet was in use, no sword or helmet worn:
> The world was such that soldiers' help might easily be forborn.
> The fertile earth as yet was free, untouched of spade or plough,
> And yet it yielded of itself of every thing enough.
> And men themselves, contented well with plain and simple food,
> That on the earth of nature's gift, without their travail stood,
> Did live by raspis,° hips and haws,° by cornels,° plums and cherries,
> By sloes and apples, nuts and pears, and loathsome bramble berries,
> And by the acorns dropped on ground from Jove's broad tree in field.
> The springtime lasted all the year, and Zephyr with his mild
> And gentle blast did cherish things that grew of own accord,

110 and 120 are line numbers.

leesings lies
fables shadowed "Shadow" means "image," and the stories are thought of as being "imaged" or conceived so as to be pregnant with meanings.
letteth prevents

The Golden Age from I. 89–150
rove upon the flood that is, as the mast of a ship—the point being that there was no technology, no rearrangement of the natural into the artificial, nor was there need of it
raspis berries
hips and haws rose hips and hawthorne berries
cornels cherries

The ground untilled, all kinds of fruit did plenteously afford.
No muck nor tillage was disposed on lean and barren land,
To make the crops of better head, and ranker for to stand.
Then streams ran milk, then streams ran wine, and yellow honey flowed
From each green tree whereon the rays of fiery Phoebus glowed.

1567

[Pygmalion's Statue Comes to Life°]

As soon as he came home,° straightway Pygmalion did repair
Unto the image of his wench, and leaning on the bed
Did kiss her. In her body straight a warmness seemed to spread;
He put his mouth again to hers, and on her breast did lay
His hand. The ivory waxèd° soft, and putting quite away
All hardness, yielded underneath his fingers, as we see
310 A piece of wax made soft against the sun, or drawn to be
In divers shapes by chafing it between one's hands, and so
To serve to uses. He amazed stood wavering to and fro
Tween joy and fear to be beguiled again he burnt in love,
Again with feeling he began his wishèd hope to prove.
He felt it very flesh indeed. By laying on his thumb,
He felt her pulse's beating. Then he stood no longer dumb
But thankèd Venus with his heart, and at the length he laid
His mouth to hers, who was as then become a perfect maid.
She felt the kiss and blushed thereat, and lifting fearfully
320 Her eyelids up, her lover and the light at once did spy.

1567

From William Caxton's Ovid, His Book of Metamorphose

This is to say that some great lord might have a maid or a servant in his house,
which[1] was poor, naked and coude[2] no good; but[3] she was gentle and of fair
form; but she was dry and lean as an image. This rich man that saw the fair
clothed, nourished and taught her so much, that she was well endoctrined.[4]
And that it pleased him to espouse her and take her to[5] his wife, of whom
he had after a fair son, prudent, wise and of great renomee.[6]

1480

Pygmalion's . . . Life from X. 243–97
came home from a festival of Venus, at which

he had prayed for his beautiful statue of a girl
to come to life
waxèd grew

1. Who.
2. Knew.
3. Except that.

4. Educated.
5. For.
6. Renown.

From Carel van Mander's Painter's Manual

Pygmalion in love with his own handiwork is to be compared with those who, too much in love with their own good works, trust in themselves, wherein no life is to be found, until they emerge from themselves, and turn toward the true *Venus*, which is to be explained as true love of God and of one's neighbour, through which the virtues become alive and fruitful.

1604

From George Sandys's Ovid's Metamorphosis°

Pygmalion seeing these to spend their times
So beast-like, frighted with the many crimes
That rule in women, chose a single life,
And long forbore the pleasure of a wife.
Meanwhile, in ivory with happy art
A statue carves, so graceful in each part
120 As women never equalled it, and stands
Affected to the fabric of his hands.
It seemed a virgin, full of living flame,
That would have moved if not withheld by shame.
Such art his art concealed, which he admires,
And from it draws imaginary fires;
Then often feels it with his hands, to try
If 'twere a body, or cold ivory.
Nor could resolve: who, kissing, thought it kissed;
Oft courts, embraces, wrings it by the wrist,
130 The flesh impressing (his conceit was such)
And fears to hurt it with too rude a touch.
Now flatters her, now sparkling stones presents
And orient pearl (love's witching instruments),
Soft-singing birds, each several-coloured flower,
First lilies, painted balls, and tears that pour
From weeping trees.° Rich robes her person deck;
Her fingers, rings; reflecting gems, her neck;
Pendants her ears; glittering zone,° her breast.
In all, showed well, but showed, when naked, best.
140 Now lays he her upon a gorgeous bed,
With carpets of Sidonian purple spread,
Now calls her wife. Her head a pillow pressed,
Of plumy down, as if of sense possessed.
Now came the day of *Venus'* festival,

Ovid's Metamorphosis George Sandys (1578–1644) was famous for his work as a colonial administrator in the first Virginia colony, and the earlier books of his translation may have been the first literary poetry (balladry aside) produced in the English colonies in America. His translation, it will be noticed, makes fre-quent use of a dramatic shift of verb tense in the narration; it was also highly influential in in the history of the heroic couplet in English verse.
tears . . . trees amber
glittering zone sparkling band

Through wealthy *Cyprus* solemnized by all.
White heifers decked with golden horns° by strokes
Of axes fall; ascending incense smokes.
He, with his gift, before the altar stands:
'You Gods, if all we crave be in your hands,
150   Give me the wife I wish, one like—' he said,
But durst not say, 'Give me my ivory maid.'°
The golden *Venus*, present at her feast,
Conceives his wish, and friendly signs expressed;
The fire thrice blazing, thrice in flames aspires.
To his admired image he retires,
Lies down beside her, raised her with his arm,
Then kissed her tempting lips, and found them warm.
That lesson oft repeats, her bosom oft
With amorous touches feels, and felt it soft.
160   The ivory dimpled with his fingers lacks
Accustomed hardness; as Hymettian wax°
Relents with heat, which chafing thumbs reduce
To pliant forms, by handling framed for use.
Amazed with doubtful joy and hope that reels,
Again the lover, what he wishes, feels.
The veins beneath his thumbs impression beat:
A perfect virgin, full of juice and heat.
The Cyprian prince with joy expressing words
To pleasure-giving *Venus* thanks affords.
170   His lips to hers he joins, which seem to melt;
The blushing virgin now his kisses felt,
And fearfully erecting her fair eyes,
Together with the light, her lover spies.
Venus the marriage blessed which she had made.

                                        1626

[Commentary]

Pygmalion . . . deterred by . . . the many vices which reigned in women, resolved to live a single life; who, carving the image of a virgin in ivory surpassing the perfection of nature, fell in love with his own workmanship. Nor is it extraordinary for excellent artisans to admire their own skill, which adds to industry as industry to perfection. And perhaps the life which was given it by the Goddess was no other than the grace and beauty of the figure which Apelles,[1] in his pictures, called the *Venus*, which made it live in the estimation of those times and the admiration of posterity, as his son by her might be taken for the honour acquired by his admirable art, the Grecian and the Roman statues, after so many hundreds of years, affording as long a life to the fame of the artificer.

golden horns gilded, for the festival
ivory maid Sandys later calls her Eburnia, "ivory."
Hymettian wax from a mountain in Attica famed for its honey

1. Fabled painter of antiquity.

But taken historically, this statue may be some virgin on whom Pygmalion was enamoured, who long as obdurate as the matter whereof she was made, was mollified [2] at length by his obsequiousness, the ivory expressing the beauty of her body, and her blushes the modesty of her mind. . . . Blushing is a resort of the blood to the face, which in the passion of shame labours most in that part, and is seen in the breast as it ascendeth, but most apparent in those that are young, in regard of their greater heat and tender complexions. Which proceeds not from an infirmity of the mind, but the novelty of the thing, nor can be either put on or restrained: the ensign [3] of native modesty and the colour of virtue. A beautiful and modest wife is therefore here said to be given him by the Goddess in reward of his devotion, as the greatest temporal happiness.

Neither may Pygmalion's being in love with an image be altogether fictitious: since both Pliny and Lucian make mention of a youth of no ignoble family (his name suppressed for the foulness of the fact) who grew so desperately enamoured on that celebrated statue of naked Venus carved in Parian marble by Praxiteles, and enshrined in her temple at Knidos, that all the day long he would gaze thereon, moving his lips as if he sued for acceptance, sigh, change colour, and expressing all the distemperatures of a lover, offering at her altar whatsoever his means would afford. And so far his fury increased, that hiding himself one evening in the temple, and being locked in by the sexton, he ran to the statue, embraced it strictly [4] in his arms, warming the cold marble with his burning kisses, and so contaminated it with his lust,[5] that the stains ever after remained as a monument of his impiety. Who either struck with the horror of the deed, or that it was not in nature to satisfy his desires, threw himself from a rock and so perished. Beautiful women, though metamorphosized into stone, would not want [6] their lovers.

1632

From Tottel's Miscellany

[The Tale of Pygmalion
with Conclusion upon the Beauty of His Love]

Twixt nature and Pygmalion there might appear great strife,
So seemly was this image wrought, it lacked nothing but life.
His curious eye beheld his own devisèd work,
And, gazing oft thereon, he found much venom there to lurk;
For all the featured shape so did his fancy move,
That with his idol whom he made Pygmalion fell in love.
To whom he honour gave, and decked with garlands sweet,

20

---

2. Literally, "softened"; usually used figuratively to apply to the emotions, obdurate reserve or "hard-heartedness" being, as it were, melted; notice how Sandys uses in his explication the very image of melting drawn from the myth.
3. Emblem, insignia; but here, more like a flag, in the modern sense.
4. Tightly.
5. He ejaculated on it.
6. Lack.

And did adorn with jewels rich, as is for lovers meet.
   Sometimes on it he swooned, sometime in rage would cry:
It was a wonder to behold how fancy bleared his eye.
   Since that this image dumb inflamed so wise a man,
30 My dear, alas, since I you love, what wonder is it then?
   In whom hath nature set the glory of her name,
And brake her mould in great dispraise your like she could not frame.

1557

From John Marston's The Metamorphosis of Pygmalion's Image

'O gracious Gods, take compassion,
140 Instill into her some celestial fire
That she may equalise affection
And have a mutual love, and love's desire.
   Thou knowest the force of love: then pity me,
   Compassionate° my true love's ardency.'

Thus having said, he riseth from the floor
As if his soul divinèd him good fortune,
Hoping his prayers to pity moved some power;
For all his thoughts did all good luck importune,
   And therefore straight he strips him naked quite,
150   That in the bed he might have more delight.

Then thus, 'Sweet sheets,' he says, 'which now do cover
The idol of my soul, the fairest one
That ever loved, or had an amorous lover,
Earth's only model of perfection,
   Sweet happy sheets, deign for to take me in,
   That I my hopes and longing thoughts may win.

With that his nimble limbs do kiss the sheets,
And now he bows him for to lay him down,
And now each part, with her fair parts do meet,
160 Now doth he hope for to enjoy love's crown:
   Now do they dally, kiss, embrace together,
   Like Leda's twins at sight of fairest weather.°

Yet all's conceit—but shadow of that bliss
Which now my Muse strives sweetly to display
In this my wondrous metamorphosis.

Compassionate sympathize with
Like . . . weather Leda was raped by Zeus in the form of a swan; she produced two eggs, from which emerged Castor and Pollux, and Helen. Helen and her half-sister Clytemnestra (the offspring of Leda and her husband Tyndareus, king of Sparta) are central to the stories of the Trojan War and the House of Atreus; the brothers, known as the Dioscuri, became the constellation of Gemini, the twins, which when visible ahead in a storm, was an omen of good weather to come, according to Horace in one of his poems.

Deign to believe me, now I sadly say:
  The stony substance of his Image feature
  Was straight transformed into a living creature.

For when his hands her fair-formed limbs had felt,
170   And that his arms her naked waist embraced,
  Each part like wax before the sun did melt,
  And now, O now, he finds how he is graced
    By his own work. Tut! Women will relent
  When as they find such moving blandishment.

1598

From Henry Reynolds's Mythomystes [1]

. . . who can make that rape of Proserpine—whom her mother Ceres (that under the species of corn might include as well the whole genus of the vegetable nature [2]) sought so long for in the earth—to mean other than the putrefaction and succeeding generation of the seeds we commit to Pluto, or the earth, whom they make the god of wealth, calling him also *Dis quasi dives* (the same in Latin that *Pluto* is in Greek), rich or wealthy, because all things have their original [3] from the earth, and return to the earth again? Or what can Jupiter's blasting of his beloved Semele, after his having deflowered her, and the wrapping of his son he got on her (Bacchus or wine) in his thigh after his production, mean other than the necessity of the air's heat to his birth in generation, and (after a violent pressure and dilaceration [4] of his mother the grape) the like close imprisoning of him also, in a fit vessel, till he gain his full maturity and come to be fit aliment? . . . the adultery of Mars and Venus, by which the chemists [5] will have meant the inseparability of those two metals that carry their names (witness that exuberance of Venus, or copper, which we call Vitriol, [6] that is seldom or never found without some mixture more or less of Mars, or iron, in it, as her husband Vulcan, or material fire, finds and shows the practitioners in chemistry). And . . . Hebe's stumbling and falling with the nectar-bowl in her hand, and thereby discovering her hidden parts to the gods as she served them at their board, meaning the nakedness of the trees and plants in autumn, when all their leaves are fallen from them by the downfall or departure of the spring, which their Hebe (or goddess of youth, as the ancients called her, because the spring renews and makes young all things) means.

1633

1. This strange treatise of mystical, neoplatonist interpretation, based heavily on the thought of Pico della Mirandola (1463–94), contains strong arguments for mythopoetic treatments of the old stories, in many ways opposed to the spirit of its age (except for Milton). It is a good example of how the Greek myths had penetrated alchemical thinking, and of the later sort of general, rather than specifically moral, interpretation.
2. Vegetable kingdom.
3. Origin.
4. Tearing apart.
5. The alchemists, whose own conceptual language was full of sexual metaphors, and whose very names for metals and minerals and processes were mythological.
6. Copper sulphate.

THE ENGLISH BIBLE

The men who translated the Bible into English had to face the problem of all translators, in its most concentrated form. Their version had to be faithful to a divinely inspired, incorruptible original, preserved by the authority of the church.

The first real biblical translation, made in Alexandria about the third century B.C., was the Greek Old Testament, known as the Septuagint (Greek: seventy, because completed by, the story goes, seventy-two translators in seventy-two days), which became the Old Testament of the Greek-speaking world. From this version of the original Hebrew and from the original Greek of the New Testament were made the Old Latin translations. These were superseded, from the fifth century A.D. onward, by the Vulgate (Latin: made public or common), prepared by St. Jerome, between 383 and 405. Jerome used the Greek and Hebrew to check his Latin. His Vulgate became and remained the Bible of the West: on it the medieval church based itself. Even its mistranslations became hallowed by use and tradition.

Bible translation in England begins in the late seventh century, when Cædmon, a monk of Whitby (see Vol. I), is said to have made a metrical paraphrase of parts of Scripture. Other Old English paraphrases exist, dating from the ninth century onward (Genesis, Exodus, and Daniel), and there is much poetry on biblical themes, such as Cynewulf's *Christ*. There is a metrical paraphrase of the story of Judith and Holofernes (tenth century) and, in the eleventh, Ælfric's paraphrase of the Heptateuch (the first seven books of the Bible). The Psalter, used in public worship and private devotion, was given Old English glosses in the ninth century and fully translated in the tenth. There is a metrical version of the late thirteenth and two prose renderings of the fourteenth, one by Richard Rolle, the hermit and mystic.

Of the New Testament, partial prose and verse translations were made during the fourteenth century, but none of these—nor any of those that had gone before— were intended to give the very words of Scripture to ordinary people. The notion of translating the whole Bible into English belongs to John Wyclif (c. 1330-84), the famous Oxford theologian and religious reformer, to whom the law of faith and morals was the Bible, rather than the authority of a pope and church whose example had been weakened by dissension and corruption. To obey the Bible's precepts meant that the words of the Bible must be available to all men. This was to become the characteristic Protestant position.

Though Wyclif probably did not translate himself, his ideas fired his followers to produce two English translations of the entire Bible. The first, made during Wyclif's lifetime, probably between 1380 and 1384, was literal; the second (of the 1390's), more free, in a vigorous native English. It is not the work of a "simple creature" as its Prologue says, but fully answers the translator's aim "to translate as clearly as he could to the sentence" (that is, according to the sense). There must have been "many good fellows [companions] and cunning [knowledgeable] at the correcting of the translation."

"A translator hath great need," says the author of the Prologue (probably John Purvey), "to study well the sense both before and after, and then also he hath need to live a clean life and be full devout in prayers, and have not his wit occupied about worldly things, that the Holy Spirit, author of all wisdom, knowledge and truth, dress him for his work and suffer him not to err."

The translation of the Bible was associated, in the official mind, with the more inflammatory social precepts and practices of the Lollards, as Wyclif's followers were called. In 1408, translation of the Scriptures into English, or even reading such translations, without the permission of the church authorities, was forbidden. (This was the prohibition which must have hindered William Caxton from printing the Bible in English, as he had done for so many other books.)

With the Renaissance, there came a renewed interest in the text of the Scriptures. Erasmus published an edition of the Greek New Testament in 1516, with his own new Latin translation; and the renewed study of Greek and Hebrew gave scholars a deeper insight into the meaning of the Bible. With the Reformation, a new interest in having the Bible in the vernacular was added: in 1522, Martin Luther published his translation into German. Luther's example inspired William Tyndale (c. 1494–1536), an exile in Germany for his Protestant opinions. In 1526, complete printed copies of the New Testament in English were smuggled into England. This translation by Tyndale, printed in Germany, had a profound influence on all subsequent Protestant versions. Its circulation was still illegal, since it had been made without sanction of the authorities and contained unacceptable turns of phrase (often adopted by translators today): "washing" for "baptism," "love" for "charity," "congregation" for "church," "elder" for "priest"—simple words, from which the filth of centuries of corrupt practice and insincerity and institutionalism—as Tyndale saw it—had been cleansed.

Tyndale was burned for his beliefs and his practice of them, with the approval of Henry VIII. Henry later sanctioned the use of the Bible prepared by Miles Coverdale (1488–1569), published abroad in 1535; and of another version in 1537. Both are greatly indebted to Tyndale's New Testament (revised 1534) and to his partial translations, published and unpublished, of the Old. Work on the Great Bible, Coverdale's revision of the 1537 version, began in 1538, on the King's command to provide "one book of the whole Bible of the largest volume in England"; and to "expressly provoke, stir and exhort every person to read the same, as that which is the very lively word of God, that every Christian person is bound to embrace, believe and follow, if he look to be saved."

This was the Bible that was prescribed for use in churches until the end of the reign of Edward VI. During that reign other translations were made, including an experimental partial Gospel translation by Sir John Cheke, who was attempting to replace the Greek words of the original by exact native English copies: "crossed" for "crucified," "mooned" for "lunatic." In 1557, when the Catholic Queen Mary was on the throne, a group of Puritan exiles began an independent version (the Geneva Bible), which they finally dedicated in 1560 to Queen Elizabeth, the Protestant sovereign who was to build up again "the ruins of God's house" in England, and war against the Roman church, the "Whore of Babylon." The Geneva translation, though the most accurate so far, was not acceptable to the leaders of the church in England, who set about revising the Great Bible to produce the Bishops' Bible (1568–69), which became the official Bible of the Elizabethan church.

The Roman church's reply was the translation prepared from the Latin Vulgate— not from the Hebrew and Greek, as were the Protestant versions, following the dictates of the New Learning. It was the work of English Catholic exiles, but chiefly of Gregory Martin, during Elizabeth's reign. Known now as the Douay-Rheims version (1582–1610), it aimed to counter the "false translations" of the Protestants, corrupting, "adding, detracting, altering, transposing, pointing and [using] all other guileful means: specially where it serveth for the advantage of their private opinions."

After Elizabeth's death in 1603, King James I and his bishops decreed "that a translation be made of the whole Bible, as consonant as can be to the original Hebrew and Greek," for exclusive use in the English church. Six panels of translators, forty-seven scholars in all, divided the work, which was published in 1611 as

> The Holy Bible, Conteyning the Old Testament and the New: Newly Translated out of the Originall tongues, with the former Translations diligently compared and revised, by his Majesties speciall commandement. Appointed to be read in Churches.

This is the Authorized Version. The translators disclaim any intention of making a new translation; their purpose was to revise old ones. (How true this is can be seen from the way in which they echo Tyndale's translation throughout.) They were not puffed up with their own knowledge; they "prayed to the Lord, the Father of our Lord," to the effect that St. Augustine did: " 'O let thy Scriptures be my pure delight; let me not be deceived in them, neither let me deceive by them.' " They set themselves to translate the Hebrew of the Old Testament and the Greek of the New—thus going back to the original texts and avoiding, as had Tyndale, the suspicion of "Popery." But they use "charity" and "church" and "priest." They give alternative translations in the margins when they are in doubt. They make deliberate use of the richness of English in synonyms:

> we have not tied ourselves to an uniformity of phrasing, or to an identity of words . . . For is the Kingdom of God become words and syllables? Why should we be in bondage to them, if we may be free? . . . We have on the one side avoided the scrupulosity of the Puritans, who leave the old Ecclesiastical words . . . as when they put *washing* for *baptism,* and *congregation* instead of *church;* as also on the other side we have shunned the obscurity of the Papists, in their *azymes,*[1] *tunike, rational, holocausts,*[2] *prepuce,*[3] *pasche*[4] and a number of such like, whereof their late translation [the Douay-Rheims] is full, and that of purpose to darken the sense, that since they must needs translate the Bible, yet by the language thereof it may be kept from being understood. But we desire that the Scripture may speak like itself, as in the language of Canaan,[5] that it may be understood even of the very vulgar.[6]

The Authorized Version sums up in itself all the aspects of English Bible translation: its strong conservatism and traditionalism; its determination to present the very words of Scripture in a form as simple and as near the language in which they were originally written, so that their sanctity, not any hallowing and mystery conferred on them by the church, will carry them direct to the minds and souls of the readers.

The particular passage, I Corinthians 13, chosen to display these various versions is not only a magnificent and widely quoted one, but its most famous image has suffered a curious fate, in the Authorized Version, because of changes in meaning since the seventeenth century. Verse 12 represents, in the Greek, the state of mediation of reality that the earthly life entails; in an image from Plato, St. Paul says that it is like the difference between seeing in a mirror and seeing what the mirror reflects. "Glass" no longer means mirror primarily, particularly with an article; the words "dark" and

1. Passover cakes, unleavened bread.
2. Burnt offerings.
3. Foreskin.
4. Easter.
5. Hebrew (Isaiah 19:18), the language common to more lands than Israel.
6. True common people, ordinary folk.

"obscure" have switched some of their tones of meaning (Spenser talks of his allegory as a "darke conceit," meaning a puzzling or difficult one). Modern students tend to read verse 12 as if it meant: "Now we see things as if through smoked or dark glasses; then, they will be removed"—a good image of mediation (suggesting having to stare at solar eclipses through dark glasses, etc.) but not St. Paul's. (See John Donne's sermon on this text, below.)

J. B. Trapp prepared the Headnote to this section and I Corinthians 13; John Hollander edited The Psalms in English Verse.

From The Second Wycliffite Version

If I speke with tungis of men and of aungels, and I have not charite, I am maad as bras sownynge, or a cymbal tynklynge.² And if I have prophecie, and knowe alle mysteries, and al kunnynge, and if I have al feith, so that I meve hillis fro her place, and I have not charite, I am nought. ³ And if I departe alle my goodis in to the metis of pore men, and if I bitake my bodi, so that I brenne, and if I have not charite, it profitith to me no thing. ⁴ Charite is pacient, it is benygne; charite envyeth not, it doith not wickidli, it is not blowun, ⁵ it is not coveytouse, it sekith not tho thingis that ben hise owne, it is not stirid to wrathe, it thenkith not yvel, ⁶ it joyeth not on wickidnesse, but it joyeth togidere to treuthe; ⁷ it suffrith alle thingis, it bileveth alle thingis, it hopith alle thingis, it susteyneth alle thingis. Charite fallith nevere doun, ⁸ whether prophecies schulen be voided, ethir langagis schulen ceesse, ethir science schal be distried. ⁹ For a parti we knowun, and a parti we prophecien; ¹⁰ but whanne that schal come that is parfit, that thing that is of parti schal be avoidid. 'Whanne I was a litil child, I spak as a litil child, I undurstood as a litil child, I thoughte as a litil child; but whanne I was maad a man, I avoidide tho thingis that weren of a litil child. ¹² And we seen now bi a myrour in derknesse, but thanne face to face; now I knowe of parti, but thanne I schal knowe, as I am knowun. ¹³ And now dwellen feith, hope, and charite, these thre; but the most of these is charite.'

c. 1395

From Tyndale's Translation

Though I spake with the tonges of men and angels, and yet had no love, I were even as soundynge brasse: or as a tynklynge cymball. ² And though I coulde prophesy, and understode all secretes, and all knowledge: yee, yf I had all fayth, so that I coulde move mountayns oute of ther places, and yet had no love, I were nothinge. ³ And though I bestowed all my gooddes to fede the poore, and though I gave my body even that I burned, and yet had no love, it profeteth me nothinge.

⁴ Love suffreth longe and is corteous. Love envieth not. Love doth not frowardly, swelleth not, ⁵ dealeth not dishonestly, seketh not her awne, is not provoked to anger, thinketh not evyll, ⁶ rejoyseth not in iniquite: but rejoyseth in the trueth, ⁷ suffreth all thinges, beleveth all thinges, hopeth all thinges, endureth in all thinges. ⁸ Though that prophesyinge fayle, other tonges shall cease, or knowledge vanysshe awaye, yet love falleth never awaye.

⁹ For oure knowledge is unparfect and oure prophesyinge is unperfect. ¹⁰ But when that which is parfect, is come, then that which is unparfect, shall be done awaye. ¹¹ When I was a chylde, I spake as a chylde, I understode as a chylde, I ymagened as a chylde. But assone as I was a man, I put away chyldeshnes. ¹² Now we se in a glasse, even in a darke speakynge: but then shall we se face to face. Now I knowe unparfectly: but then shall I knowe even as I am knowen. ¹³ Now abydeth fayth, hope, and love, even these thre: but the chefe of these is love.

1525; revised 1535

From The Great Bible

Though I spake with the tonges of men and of angels, and have no love, I am even as sounding brasse, or as a tynklinge cymball. ² And though I coulde prophesy, and understode all secretes, and all knowledge: yee yf I have all fayth, so that I can move mountayns oute of their places, and yet have no love, I am nothynge. ³ And though I bestowe all my goodes to fede the poore, and though I geve my body even that I burned, and yet have no love, it profyteth me nothynge.

⁴ Love suffreth longe, and is curteous. Love envyeth not. Love doth not frowardly, swelleth not, ⁵ dealeth not dishonestly, seketh not her awne, is not provoked to anger, thynketh no evyll, ⁶ rejoyseth not in iniquyte: but rejoyseth in the trueth, ⁷ suffreth all thynges, beleveth all thynges, hopeth all thynges, endureth all thynges. ⁸ Though that prophesyinges fayle, other tonges cease, or knowledge vanysshe awaye, yet love falleth never awaye.

⁹ For oure knowledge is unperfect, and oure prophesyinge is unperfect. ¹⁰ But when that whych is perfect, is come, then that whych is unperfect, shall be done awaye. ¹¹ When I was a chylde, I spake as a chylde, I understode as a chylde, I ymagined as a chylde. But assone as I was a man, I put awaye chyldeshnes. ¹² Nowe we se in a glasse, even in a darcke speakyng: but then shall we se face to face. Nowe I knowe unperfectly: but then shall I knowe even as I am knowen. ¹³ Nowe abydeth fayth, hope, and love, even these thre: but the chefe of these is love.

1539, revised 1540

From The Geneva Bible

Thogh I speake with the tongues of men and Angels, and have not love, I am as sounding brasse, or a tinkling cymbal. ² And thogh I had the gift of prophecie, and knewe all secretes and all knowledge, yea, if I had all faith, so that I colde remove mountaines and had not love, I were nothing. ³ And thogh I fede the poore with all my goods, and thogh I give my bodie, that I be burned, and have not love, it profiteth me nothing. ⁴ Love suffreth long: it is bountiful: love envieth not: love doeth not boast it self: it is not puffed up: ⁵ It disdaineth not: it seketh not her owne things: it is not provoked to anger: it thinketh not evil: ⁶ It rejoyceth not in iniquitie, but rejoyceth in the trueth. ⁷ It suffreth all things:

it beleveth all things: it hopeth all things: it endureth all things. [8] Love doeth never fall away, thogh that prophecyings be abolished, or the tongues cease or knowledge vanish away. [9] For we knowe in parte, and we prophecie in parte. [10] But when that which is perfite, is come, then that which is in parte, shalbe abolished. [11] When I was a childe, I spake as a childe, I understode as a childe, I thoght as a childe: but when I became a man, I put away childish things. [12] For now we se through a glasse darkely: but then shal we se face to face. Now I know in parte: but then shal I knowe even as I am knowen. [13] And now abideth faith, hope and love, even these thre: but the chiefest of these is love.

1560, revised 1602

From The Bishops' Bible

Though I speake with the tongues of men, and of Angels, and have not charitie, I am as sounding brasse, or as a tinckling cymbal. [2] And though I have prophecie, and understand all secrets, and all knowledge: yea, if I have all faith, so that I can remoove mountaines, and have not charitie, I am nothing. [3] And though I bestow all my goods to feed the poore, and though I give my body that I should be burned, and have not charitie, it profiteth me nothing. [4] Charitie suffereth long, and is courteous: Charitie envieth not, charity doth not frowardly, swelleth not, [5] Dealeth not dishonestly, seeketh not her owne, is not bitter, thinketh not evill, [6] Rejoyceth not in iniquitie, but rejoyceth in the trueth: [7] Suffreth all things, beleeveth all things, hopeth all things, endureth all things. [8] Though that prophecyings faile, either tongues cease, or knowledge vanish away, yet charitie falleth never away. [9] For our knowledge is unperfect, and our prophecying is unperfect: [10] But when that which is perfect is come, then that which is unperfect shalbe done away. [11] When I was a childe, I spake as a childe, I understood as a childe, I imagined as a childe: but assoone as I was a man, I put away childishnesse. [12] Now wee see in a glasse, even in a darke speaking: but then shall we see face to face. Now I know unperfectly: but then shall I know, even as I am knowen. [13] Now abideth faith, hope, and charitie, these three: but the chiefe of these is charitie.

1568, revised 1602

From The Douay-Rheims Version

If I speake with the tonges of men and of Angels, and have not charitie: I am become as sounding brasse, or a tinkling cymbal. [2] And if I should have prophecie, and knew al mysteries, and al knowledge, and if I should have al faith so that I could remove mountaines, and have not charitie, I am nothing. [3] And if I should distribute al my goods to be meate for the poore, and if I should deliver my body so that I burne, and have not charitie, it doth profit me nothing.

[4] Charitie is patient, is benigne: Charitie envieth not, dealeth not perversly: is not puffed up, [5] is not ambitious, seeketh not her owne, is not provoked to anger, thinketh not evil: [6] rejoyceth not upon iniquitie, but rejoyceth with the

truth: [7] suffereth al things, beleeveth al things, hopeth al things, beareth al things. [8] Charitie never falleth away: whether prophecies shal be made voide, or tonges shal cease, or knowledge shal be destroied. [9] For in part we know, and in part we prophecie. [10] But when that shal come that is perfect, that shal be made voide that is in part. [11] When I was a litle one, I spake as a litle one, I understood as a litle one, I thought as a litle one. But when I was made a man, I did away the things that belonged to a litle one. [12] We see now by a glasse in a darke sort: but then face to face. Now I know in part: but then I shal know as also I am knowen. [13] And now there remaine, faith, hope, charitie, these three, but the greater of these is charitie.

1582

From The King James Authorized Version

Though I speak with the tongues of men and of angels, and have not charity, I am become as sounding brass, or a tinkling cymbal. [2] And though I have the gift of prophecy, and understand all mysteries, and all knowledge; and though I have all faith, so that I could remove mountains, and have no charity, I am nothing. [3] And though I bestow all my goods to feed the poor, and though I give my body to be burned, and have not charity, it profiteth me nothing. [4] Charity suffereth long, and is kind; charity envieth not; charity vaunteth not itself, is not puffed up, [5] doth not behave itself unseemly, seeketh not her own, is not easily provoked, thinketh no evil; [6] rejoiceth not in iniquity, but rejoiceth in the truth; [7] beareth all things, believeth all things, hopeth all things, endureth all things. [8] Charity never faileth: but whether there be prophecies, they shall fail; whether there be tongues, they shall cease; whether there be knowledge, it shall vanish away. [9] For we know in part, and we prophesy in part. [10] But when that which is perfect is come, then that which is in part shall be done away. [11] When I was a child, I spake as a child, I understood as a child, I thought as a child: but when I became a man, I put away childish things. [12] For now we see through a glass, darkly; but then face to face: now I know in part; but then shall I know even as also I am known. [13] And now abideth faith, hope, charity, these three; but the greatest of these is charity.

1611, in edition of 1873

The Psalms in English Verse

Of central importance to the Reformation's concern both with liturgical reconstruction and the unmediated availability of vernacular Scripture were the metrical versions of the Psalter. Martin Luther had versified the Psalms, and paraphrased them in verse chorales, to which he had also written melodies, in order that the entire congregation in church might sing in their own language, rather than passively partaking in a dispensed Latin incantation. The French poet Clément Marot had versified the Psalms in the 1530's; in Geneva, the congregational singing of the Psalms in verse was established early (although in 1559, when introduced into an English church, the practice was still thought a novelty). Then, too, sophisticated biblical scholarship wanted to make clear that the Psalms in the original Hebrew were poetry, not prose; that David the musician-shepherd-king had composed sacred verse, and that this should be demonstrated in translation. In addition, the purely private practice among poets (Sir Thomas Wyatt and the Earl of Surrey are examples) of versifying the Psalms was a kind of penitential exercise.

In 1562 Thomas Sternhold, John Hopkins, and others completed a version of the Psalms in what is still called "common meter"—the familiar ballad stanza rhymed *abcd*, in four-beat lines alternating with three-beat ones (also used, in more learnedly literary poetry, as "fourteeners"). From their first publication until 1640, some 280 editions of the Sternhold-Hopkins renderings appeared. Rival translations were constantly being attempted, and the Scottish church had its own. A great tradition of psalm paraphrase grew up, in which a free adaptation of a psalm text became a literary form of its own, as well as a hymn for eventual musical setting and liturgical use. Often poets of the first rank attempted paraphrases, both in Latin and English verse, as exercises at once stylistic and spiritual, and it is interesting to observe the way in which changing poetic conventions affect the way in which the poetry of the Bible is rendered, often at three or four removes, linguistically.

The Psalm 137 (136 in the Vulgate) is a powerful and moving chant of protest, containing an extremely compelling and popular image. It is the refusal of a captive people to sing their native songs for the amusement or even the serious delectation of their conquerors; hanging the harp on the trees is a gesture of that refusal, standing for locking away all one's gifts and talents and skills, to live only the saddest and simplest of lives under one's captors. The versions presented below reflect changes in formal style and structure, and in the organization of imagery, over the course of more than a century. The King James Version of Psalm 137 is given complete; thereafter, the section comprising verses 1 through 6 will be given from various translations and paraphrases. In the case of Campion, Bacon, Crashaw, Carew, and Denham, the relevant Headnotes should be consulted. This text appealed to a great many poets who paraphrased it alone, not as part of a group of versions of the Psalms; the subject of song (poetry, creative power) refused, abandoned, or lost must have had great personal appeal.

From The King James Authorized Version

1 By the rivers of Babylon, there we sat down, yea, we wept, when we remembered Zion.

2 We hanged our harps upon the willows in the midst thereof.

3 For there they that carried us away captive required of us a song; and they that wasted us required of us mirth, saying, Sing us one of the songs of Zion.

4 How shall we sing the Lord's song in a strange land?

5 If I forget thee, O Jerusalem, let my right hand forget her cunning.

6 If I do not remember thee, let my tongue cleave to the roof of my mouth; if I prefer not Jerusalem above my chief joy.

7 Remember, O Lord, the children of Edom in the day of Jerusalem; who said Rase it, rase it, even to the foundation thereof.

8 O daughter of Babylon, who art to be destroyed; happy *shall he be,* that rewardeth thee as thou hast served us.

9 Happy *shall he be,* that taketh and dasheth thy little ones against the stones.

1611

From The Second Wycliffite Version

The Hundred and six and thirtieth Salm

On the floodis of Babiloyne there we saten,
and wepten; while we bithoughten on Syon.
In salwes° in the myddil thereof, we hangiden
up our orguns.° For thei that ledden us
prisoners, axiden us there the wordis of songis.
And their that ledden awei us seiden: Synge
ye to us an ympne° of the songis of Syon. Hou
schule we singe a songe of the Lord, in an
alien lond? If I forgete thee, Jerusalem,
my right hond be gouun to forgeting. Mi
tunge cleve to my chekis, if I bithenke not
on thee.

c. 1390

From The Geneva Bible

By the rivers of Babel we sate, and there we wept, when we remembered Zion.
We hanged our harps upon the willows in the middes thereof.
When they that led us captives required of us songs and mirth, when we had
    hanged up our harps, saying Sing us one of the songs of Zion.
How shall we sing, said we, a song of the Lord in a strange land.
If I forget thee, O Jerusalem, may my right hand forget to play.

1560

From The Douay-Rheims Version

Upon the rivers of Babylon, there we sat and wept: when we remembered Sion.
On the willows in the midst thereof we hung up our instruments.
For there they that led us into captivity required of us the words of songs.
And they that carried us away, said: Sing ye to us a hymn of the songs of Sion.
How shall we sing the song of the Lord in a strange land?
If I forget thee, O Jerusalem, may my right hand be forgotten.

salwes sallows, willows   **ympne** hymn
orguns instruments

Let my tongue cleave to my jaws if I do not remember thee:
If I make not Jerusalem the beginning of my joy.
                    1582–1610

By Thomas Sternhold and John Hopkins

Whenas we sat in Babylon,
    the rivers round about,
And in remembrance of Ziòn
    the tears for grief burst out.
We hanged our harps and instruments°
    the willow trees upon,
For in that place men for their use
    had planted many one.

Then they to whom we prisoners were
    said to us tauntingly:
Now let us hear your Hebrew songs
    and pleasant melody.
Alas, said we, who can once frame
    his sorrowful heart to sing
The praises of our loving God,
    thus under the strange king.

But yet if I Jerusalem
    out of my heart let slide,
Then let my fingers quite forget
    the warbling harp to guide;
And let my tongue within my mouth
    be tied for ever fast,
If that I joy before I see
    thy full deliverance past.
                    1562

By The Countess of Pembroke°

Nigh seated where the river flows
    That watereth Babel's thankful plain,
Which then our tears in pearlèd rows
    Did help to water with their rain,
The thought of Zion bred such woes

harps and instruments this not for poetic elaboration, but out of uncertainty about how to translate the Vulgate *organum* (the Hebrew, *kinnor*, means "harp")
The Countess of Pembroke Sir Philip Sidney's sister wrote this paraphrase entitled "*Super Flumina*" (the opening words of the Latin translation: *Super flumina Babylonis*). It was part of a number she did to complete Sidney's own paraphrase of half the Psalter. Based on French paraphrases, their version embraces an amazing array of verse forms and brings to the rendering of the text all of those arts of language which Sidney so loved. This text is from a manuscript copied by Sir John Davies.

That, though our harps we did retain,
Yet useless and untouchèd there
On willows only hanged they were.

Now while our harps were hangèd so,
    The men whose captives there we lay
Did on our griefs insulting go,
    And more to grieve us thus did say:
You that of music make such show,
    Come sing us now a Zion lay.
––O no, we have nor voice nor hand
For such a song, in such a land.

Though far I lie, sweet Zion hill,
    In foreign soil exiled from thee,
Yet let my hand forget his skill
    If ever thou forgotten be;
Yea, let my tongue fast gluèd still
    Unto my roof lie mute in me,
If thy neglect within me spring,
Or ought I do but Salem sing.
c. 1590?

By Thomas Campion°

As by the streams of Babylon
Far from our native soil we sat,
Sweet Zion, thee we thought upon,
And every thought a tear begat.

Aloft the trees that spring up there
Our silent harps we pensive hung.°
Said they that captived us: 'Let's hear
Some song which you in Zion sung.'

Is then the song of our God fit
To be profaned in foreign land?
O Salem, thee when I forget,
Forget his skill may my right hand.

Fast to the roof may cleave my tongue
If mindless I of thee be found,
Or if, when all my joys are sung,
Jerusalem be not the ground.°
            c. 1614

Thomas Campion from his undated *Two Books of Airs*
pensive hung calling attention, delicately, to the etymological connection, in Latin, of these two words (*pendere*, to hang)

ground A personally meaningful musical pun: "ground" means the bass part, and the repeated melody or harmonic structure presented there, over which "divisions" or improvised melodic material will be composed or played.

By Francis Bacon°

When as we sat all sad and desolate,
  By Babylon upon the river's side,
Eased from the tasks which in our captive state
  We were enforcèd daily to abide,
      Our harps we had brought with us to the field,
      Some solace to our heavy souls to yield.

But soon we found we failed of our account,
  For when our minds some freedom did obtain,
Straightways the memory of Zion Mount
  Did cause afresh our wounds to bleed again;
      So that with present griefs, and future fears,
      Our eyes burst forth into a stream of tears.

As for our harps, since sorrow struck them dumb,
  We hanged them on the willow-trees were near;
Yet did our cruel masters to us come,
  Asking of us some Hebrew songs to hear:
      Taunting us rather in our misery,
      Than much delighting in our melody.

Alas (said we) who can once force or frame
  His grievèd and oppressèd heart to sing
The praises of Jehovah's glorious name,
  In banishment, under a foreign king?
      In Zion is his seat and dwelling place,
      Thence doth he shew the brightness of his face.

Hierusalem, where God his throne hath set,
  Shall any hour absent thee from my mind?
Then let my right hand quite her skill forget,
  Then let my voice and words no passage find;
      Nay, if I do not thee prefer in all,
      That in the compass of my thoughts can fall.
  1624   1624–25

By Richard Crashaw°

On the proud banks of great Euphrates' flood
  There we sat, and there we wept:
Our harps that now no music understood

Francis Bacon Bacon did a whole set of paraphrases while "in a fit of sickness" in 1624; it
was common for writers to translate the penitential Psalms, at least, under such circumstances. Bacon uses a variety of meters; these
rime royal stanzas must have had a plaintive
connotation for him.

Richard Crashaw from *Steps to the Temple*
(1646). The baroque poet's emblematic energy
animates the harps, dramatizes the rhetoric,
and concentrates with extreme detail on the
treatment of verse 6.

Nodding on the willows slept,
    While unhappy, captived we,
    Lovely Zion, thought on thee.

They, they that snatched us from our country's breast
  Would have a song carved to their ears
In Hebrew numbers then (O cruel jest!)
  When harps and hearts were drowned in tears:
    Come, they cried, come sing and play
    One of Zion's songs today.

Sing? Play? to whom (ah!) shall we sing or play,
  If not, Jerusalem, to thee?
Ah thee, Jerusalem! ah, sooner may
  This hand forget the mastery
    Of music's dainty touch, than I
    The music of thy memory.

Which when I lose, O may at once my tongue
  Lose this same busy, speaking art,
Unperched, her vocal arteries unstrung,
  No more acquainted with my heart,
    On my dry palate's roof to rest,
    A withered leaf, an idle guest.
               1646

By Thomas Carew°

Sitting by the streams that glide
  Down by Babel's towering wall,
With our tears we filled the tide
  Whilst our mindful thoughts recall
  Thee, O Zion, and thy fall.

Our neglected harps unstrung,
  Not acquainted with the hand
Of the skillful tuner, hung
  On the willow trees that stand
  Planted in the neighbour land.

Yet the spiteful foe commands
  Songs of mirth, and bids us lay
To dumb harps, our captive hands
  And (to scoff our sorrows) say:
  'Sing us some sweet Hebrew lay.'

But say we, our holy strain
  Is too pure for heathen land,

Thomas Carew first published from manuscript in 1655. The harps are here "neglected"—a far cry from the door-slamming gesture of the Hebrew text.

Nor may we God's Hymnés profane,
  Or move either voice or hand
  To delight a savage band.

Holy Salem, if thy love
  Fall from my forgetful heart,
May the skill by which I move
  Strings of music, tuned with art,
  From my withered hand depart!

May my speechless tongue give sound
  To no accents, but remain
To my prison roof fast bound,
  In my sad soul entertain
  Mirth, till thou rejoice again!
                    1655

By Sir John Denham°

When on Euphrates' banks we sate,
Deploring Zion's dolefull state,
Our harps to which we lately sang,
Mute as ourselves, on willows hang.

Our sadness thus our spoiler jeers:
'Change into mirth your sighs and tears,
And give us with your hands and tongues
One of your pleasant Hebrew songs.'

Oh! how can we our airs compose
And sing of God amongst his foes!
When I forget his sacred hill,
May my right hand forget her skill!

When I shall thy remembrance leave,
My tongue to her dry roof shall cleave;
All other joys I shall contemn,
Calling to mind Jerusalem.
before 1668   1714

By Nahum Tate and Nicholas Brady°

When we, our weary limbs to rest,
  Sat down by proud Euphrates' stream,
We wept, with doleful thoughts oppressed,

Sir John Denham Famous during the later 17th and the 18th century for his stylistic elegance and power, Denham here neatly but unsubtly blares out all the undertones which make the original so poignant ("Mute as ourselves").

Nahum Tate and Nicholas Brady The complete Tate-Brady version was designed to supplant Sternhold and Hopkins for liturgical use, and to appeal to Restoration taste.

And Zion was our mournful theme.
Our harps, that when with joy we sung
Were wont their tuneful parts to bear,
With silent strings, neglected, hung
On willow trees that withered° there.

Meanwhile our foes, who all conspired
To triumph in our slavish wrongs,
Music and mirth of us required:
'Come sing us one of Zion's songs.'
How shall we tune our voice to sing?
Or touch our harps with skillful hands?
Shall hymns of joy to God our King
Be sung by slaves in foreign lands?

O Salem, once our happy seat!
When I of thee forgetful prove,
Let then my trembling hand forget
The speaking strings with art to move!
If I to mention thee forbear,
Eternal silence seize my tongue,
Or if I sing one cheerful air
Till thy deliverance is my song.

1696

THE NEW WORLD

For the Renaissance mind, the end of the fifteenth century witnessed the dawn of the New World as well as the intellectual reawakening of the Ancient one. The exploration and colonization of the Western hemisphere and of parts of the Orient (the two "Indies," East and West) were initiated by the Spanish and Portuguese voyagers, and the British were in fact rather slow to develop and dispatch expeditionary fleets. The Venetian John Cabot, sailing under the English flag, attained the Labrador coast on a voyage that started from Bristol years after Columbus set out from Lisbon, but it was not until the second half of the sixteenth century that such expeditions as those of Sir Francis Drake (1540?–96), Sir John Hawkins (1532–95), Sir Martin Frobisher (1532?–94), and Sir Humphrey Gilbert (1509–38), planner of a Northeast Passage to the Orient, would be launched. Circumnavigations and exploratory routes followed for their own sake gave way to naval expeditions and the near-piracy committed against Spanish shipping in the West Indies by Drake, and subsequently to early colonizations, such as Sir Richard Grenville's attempt in Virginia in 1585, and Sir Walter Ralegh's in Guiana ten years later.

Accounts of all these voyages were published and republished during the course of the century. The body of Renaissance travel writing reveals a domestication of fable into fact, an encompassing of the marvelous by the truthful that is far in advance of

---

withered This word has cropped up before in these versions; here, the willows may have withered partially in the sentimental rhetoric of the adaptation, partially because of an unstated half-pun on "withies" (= "willows").

contemporary scientific description in many other areas. An important prototype for English travel literature was the *De Orbe Novo* (Of the New World) of Peter Martyr of Anghiera (*fl.* 1510), of which the first part was published in 1511. In 1555 Richard Eden (1521–76) translated the whole work as *The Decades of the New World or West India*, making available in English a systematic account of the voyages of Columbus and his followers. Such records are of particular interest to literary history because of the mythological contexts in which the natural history of the New World was interpreted. The more speculative accounts considered the relation between the primitive and the civilized, and emerged with a complex set of attitudes conditioned by the romanticizing of rustic simplicity in pastoral literature, the myth of the Golden Age, and so forth. These accounts fed back into formal literature in a variety of ways, ranging from the elaborate meditations of Montaigne's essay "Of Cannibals" (see the Introduction to the Renaissance) to some of the backgrounds for Shakespeare's *The Tempest.*

A clergyman named Richard Hakluyt (1553–1616), made aware of the poor reputation of English maritime enterprise while attached to the embassy in Paris, attempted to improve that reputation by collecting and publishing reports of English voyages. In 1589 he brought out his *Principal Navigations, Voyages and Discoveries of the English Nation* (greatly augmented in three volumes in 1598–1600). Accounts of the expeditions of the Cabots, Hawkins, Frobisher, Drake, Gilbert, Ralegh, and others were systematically gathered together, and Hakluyt's work was continued by Samuel Purchas (1575–1626) in several books, including *Hakluytus Posthumus or Purchas His Pilgrims* (1625).

The excerpts given below commence with some passages from Eden's *Decades*, including as a postscript a remarkable disquisition on the varied skin colors of aboriginal races which interprets the diversification, without any racial or colonial condescension, as part of the providential decoration and beautification of created nature. Following these are two longer passages. The first is from Thomas Hariot's *Brief and True Report of the New-found Land of Virginia* (1588) from Hakluyt's 1600 edition; Hariot was a mathematician and astronomer of great gifts, a friend of Marlowe, Ralegh, and Drake among others, who accompanied Grenville on the 1585 Virginia adventure. The last selection is from Hakluyt's reprinting of Sir Francis Drake's account of his landing in what is today called Drake's Bay, just north of San Francisco, in the course of his 1577–80 circumnavigation of the globe. Sailing in his flagship *Pelican* (later renamed *The Golden Hind*), he passed through the Strait of Magellan, sailed up the coast of South America, attacking Spanish shipping all the way, and finally, in an attempt to discover a passage into the Atlantic, went as far north as latitude 48, almost as far as Vancouver. Stopping on the way back at Drake's Bay, he named the whole California coast New Albion and claimed it in the Queen's name. His discussion of the Indians' responses to the landing is quite different from Hariot's, being both colder and less discerning.

From The Decades of the New World or West India

[The Golden World] [1]

The inhabitants of these Islands have been ever so used to live at liberty, in play and pastime, that they can hardly away with the yoke of servitude, which they attempt to shake off by all means they may. And surely if they had received our religion, I would think their life most happy of all men, if they might therewith enjoy their ancient liberty. . . . Among these simple souls, a few clothes serve the naked; weights and measures are not needful to such as can [2] not skill of craft and deceit, and have not the use of pestiferous money . . . they seem to live in that golden world of which the old writers speak so much, wherein men lived simply and innocently without enforcement of laws, without quarrelling, judges and libels, content only to satisfy nature, without further vexation for knowledge of things to come.

[During his exploration of Cuba, Columbus is at one point [3] extremely moved by the directness and simplicity of the aborigines and wonders "if that land were not heaven, which brought forth such a kind of man?" The argument continues:]

For it is certain that among them the land is as common as the sun and water, and that Mine and Thine (the seeds of all mischief) have no place with them. They are content with so little, that in so large a country they have rather superfluity than scarceness, so that (as we have said before) they seem to live in the golden world without toil, living in open gardens, not entrenched with ditches, divided with hedges, or defended with walls. They deal truly with one another without laws, without books and without judges. They take him for an evil and mischievous man, which taketh pleasure in doing hurt to another. . . .

[Of the Color of the Indians]

One of the marvellous things that God useth in the composition of man is colour, which doubtless can not be considered without great admiration in beholding one to be white, and another black, being colours utterly contrary. Some likewise to be yellow, which is between black and white, and other of other colours, as it were of divers liveries.[4] And as these colours are to be marvelled at, even so is it to be considered how they differ from another as it were by degrees, forasmuch as some men are white after divers sorts of whiteness, yellow after divers manners of yellow, and black after divers sorts of blackness; and how from white they go to yellow by discolouring to brown and red, and to black by ash colour, and murrey [5] somewhat lighter than black; and tawny like unto the West Indians which are altogether in general either purple or tawny like unto sod quinces, or of the colour of chestnuts or olives— which colour is to them natural and not by their going naked, as many have thought, albeit their nakedness have somewhat helped them thereunto. There-

---

1. From the First Decade, Book II.
2. Know.
3. From the First Decade, Book III.
4. Official uniforms.
5. Mulberry-colored.

fore in like manner and with such diversity as men are commonly white in
Europe and black in Africa, even with like variety are they tawny in these
Indies, with divers degrees diversely inclining more or less to black or white.
No less marvel is it to consider that men are white in Seville, and black at the
cape of Buena Speranza, and of chestnut colour at the river of Plata, being all
in equal degrees from the equinoctial line. Likewise that the men of Africa and
Asia that live under the burnt line (called *Zona Torrida*) [6] are black, and not
they that live beneath or on this side the same line as in Mexico, Yucatan,
Quauhtema, Lian, Nicaragua, Panama, Santo Domingo, Paria, Cape, Saint
Augustine, Lima, Quito and the other lands of Peru which touch in the same
equinoctial. . . . It may seem that such variety of colours proceedeth of man,
and not of the earth, which may well be although we be all born of Adam
and Eve, and know not the cause why God hath ordained it, otherwise than
to consider that his divine majesty hath done this as infinite other to declare
his omnipotence and wisdom in such diversity of colours as appear not only in
the nature of man, but the like also in beasts, birds and flowers, where diverse
and contrary colours are seen in one little feather, or the leaves growing out
of one little stalk. Another thing is also to be noted as touching these Indians,
and this is that their hair is not curled as is the Moors' and Ethiopians' that
inhabit the same clime; neither are they bald except very seldom, and that but
little. All which things may give further occasion to philosophers to search the
secrets of nature and complexions of men with the novelties of the new
world. . . .

1555

From A Brief and True Report

[A Renaissance Traveler Describes the Religion of Indians in Virginia]
In respect of us they are a people poor, and for want of skill and judgment
in the knowledge and use of our things, do esteem our trifles before things of
greater value. Notwithstanding, in their proper manner (considering the want
of such means as we have), they seem very ingenious. For although they have
no such tools, nor any such crafts, sciences, and arts as we, yet in those things
they do, they show excellency of wit.[1] And by how much they upon due consideration shall find our manner of knowledges and crafts to exceed theirs in
perfection, and speed for doing or execution, by so much the more is it probable
that they should desire our friendship and love, and have the greater respect
for pleasing and obeying us. Whereby may be hoped, if means of good government be used, that they may in short time be brought to civility and the
embracing of true religion.

Some religion they have already, which although it be far from the truth, yet
being as it is, there is hope it may be the easier and sooner reformed.

They believe that there are many gods, which they call *Mantoac*, but of

---

6. The torrid zone is the region of the earth's surface lying between the tropics of Capricorn
and Cancer.

1. Intelligence.

different sorts and degrees, one only chief and great god, which hath been from all eternity. Who, as they affirm, when he purposed to make the world, made first other gods of a principal order to be as means and instruments to be used in the creation and government to follow, and after the sun, moon, and stars as petty gods, and the instruments of the other order more principal. First, they say, were made waters, out of which by the gods was made all diversity of creatures that are visible or invisible.

For mankind, they say a woman was made first which, by the working of one of the gods, conceived and brought forth children. And in such sort, they say, they had their beginning. But how many years or ages have passed since, they say they can make no relation, having no letters nor other such means as we to keep records of the particularities of times past, but only tradition from father to son.

They think that all the gods are of human shape, and therefore, they represent them by images in the forms of men, which they call *Kewasowok* (one alone is called *Kewas*). These they place in houses appropriate or temples, which they call *Machicomuck*, where they worship, pray, sing, and make many times offering unto them. In some *Machicomuck*, we have seen but one *Kewas*, in some two, and in other some three. The common sort think them to be also gods.

They believe also the immortality of the soul that, after this life as soon as the soul is departed from the body, according to the works it hath done, it is either carried to heaven, the habitat of gods, there to enjoy perpetual bliss and happiness, or else to a great pit or hole which they think to be in the furthest parts of their part of the world toward the sunset, there to burn continually. The place they call *Popogusso*.

For the confirmation of this opinion, they told me two stories of two men that had been lately dead and revived again. The one happened, but a few years before our coming into the country, of a wicked man, which having been dead and buried, the next day the earth of the grave being seen to move, was taken up again, who made declaration where his soul had been. That is to say, very near entering into *Popogusso*, had not one of the gods saved him, and gave him leave to return again and teach his friends what they should do to avoid that terrible place of torment. The other happened in the same year we were there, but in a town that was sixty miles from us, and it was told me for strange news, that one being dead, buried, and taken up again as the first, showed that although his body had lain dead in the grave, yet his soul was alive and had travelled far in a long broad way, on both sides whereof grew most delicate and pleasant trees, bearing more rare and excellent fruits, than ever he had seen before or was able to express, and at length came to most brave and fair houses, near which he met his father that had been dead before, who gave him great charge to go back again and show his friends what good they were to do to enjoy the pleasures of that place, which when he had done he should after come again.

What subtlety soever be in the *Wiroances* [2] and priests, this opinion worked so much in many of the common and simple sort of people, that it maketh them have great respect to their governors, and also great care what they do,

2. Wiroances, chieftains.

to avoid torment after death, and to enjoy bliss, although notwithstanding there is punishment ordained for malefactors, as stealers, whoremongers, and other sort of wicked-doers, some punished with death, some with forfeitures, some with beating, according to the greatness of the facts.

And this is the sum of their religion, which I learned by having special familiarity with some of their priests. Wherein they were not so sure grounded, nor gave such credit to their traditions and stories, but through conversing with us they were brought into great doubts of their own, and no small admiration of ours, with earnest desire in many, to learn more than we had means for want of perfect utterance in their language to express.

Most things they saw with us, as mathematical instruments, sea compasses, the virtue of the lodestone in drawing iron, a perspective glass [3] whereby was showed many strange sights, burning glasses, wild fireworks, guns, hooks, writing and reading, spring-clocks that seem to go of themselves, and many other things that we had were so strange unto them, and so far exceeded their capacities to comprehend the reason and means how they should be made and done, that they thought they were rather the works of gods than of men, or at the leastwise, they had been given and taught us by the gods. Which made many of them have such opinion of us, as that if they knew not the truth of God and religion already, it was rather to be had from us whom God so specially loved, than from a people that were so simple as they found themselves to be in comparison of us. Whereupon greater credit was given unto that we spoke of, concerning such matters.

Many times and in every town where I came, according as I was able, I made declaration of the contents of the Bible, that therein was set forth the true and only God, and his mighty works, that therein was contained the true doctrine of salvation through Christ, with many particulars of miracles and chief points of religion, as I was able then to utter, and thought fit for the time. And although I told them the book materially and of itself was not of any such virtue, as I thought they did conceive, but only the doctrine therein contained, yet would many be glad to touch it, to embrace it, to kiss it, to hold it to their breasts and heads, and stroke over all their body with it, to show their hungry desire of that knowledge which was spoken of. [4]

1600

From Drake's Account

[Sir Francis Drake Lands Near What Is Now San Francisco]

In this bay we anchored the seventeenth of June, and the people of the country, having their houses close by the water's side, showed themselves unto us, and sent a present to our general.

When they came unto us, they greatly wondered at the things which we

3. An early telescope Hariot had developed; the "strange sights" included magnification, image-inversion, etc. "Burning glasses," however, were concave mirrors used to concentrate solar heat.

4. This misinterpretation of the Indians' totemic attachment to the book itself is ironically generous; it represents what a Christian humanist who believed in natural reason would want to be true.

brought, but our general, according to his natural and accustomed humanity, courteously entreated them, and liberally bestowed on them necessary things to cover their nakedness, whereupon they supposed us to be gods, and would not be persuaded to the contrary. The presents which they sent unto our general were feathers and cawls of network.

Their houses are digged round about with earth, and have from the uttermost brims of the circle clifts [1] of wood set upon them, joining close together at the top like a spire steeple, which by reason of that closeness are very warm.

Their bed is the ground with rushes strawed on it, and, lying about the house, they have the fire in the middest.[2] The men go naked, the women take bulrushes and kemb [3] them after the manner of hemp, and thereof make their loose garments, which being knit about their middles hang down about their hips, having also about their shoulders a skin of deer, with the hair upon it. These women are very obedient and serviceable [4] to their husbands.

After they were departed from us, they came and visited us the second time, and brought with them feathers and bags of tobacco for presents. And when they came to the top of the hill, at the bottom whereof we had pitched our tents, they stayed themselves, where one appointed for speaker wearied himself with making a long oration, which done, they left their bows upon the hill and came down with their presents.

In the meantime the women remaining on the hill tormented themselves lamentably, tearing their flesh from their cheeks, whereby we perceived that they were about [5] a sacrifice. In the meantime our general, with his company, went to prayer and to reading of the Scriptures, at which exercise they were attentive and seemed greatly to be affected with it. But when they were come unto us they restored again unto us those things which before we had bestowed upon them.

The news of our being there being spread through the country, the people that inhabited round about came down, and amongst them the king himself, a man of a goodly stature and comely personage,[6] with many other tall and warlike men, before whose coming were sent two ambassadors to our general to signify that their king was coming, in doing of which message their speech was continued about half an hour. This ended, they by signs requested our general to send something by their hand to their king, as a token that his coming might be in peace. Wherein our general having satisfied them, they returned with glad tidings to their king, who marched to us with a princely majesty, the people crying continually after their manner, and, as they drew near unto us, so did they strive to behave themselves in their actions with comeliness.

In the forefront was a man of a goodly personage, who bare the sceptre or mace before the king, whereupon hanged two crowns, a less and a bigger, with three chains of a marvellous length. The crowns were made of knitwork wrought

1. Stakes (because cleft from branches): clearly, a tepee is being described.
2. Midst.
3. Comb.
4. Prepared to serve.
5. Engaged in.
6. Appearance.

artificially with feathers of divers colours. The chains were made of a bony substance, and few be the persons among them that are admitted to wear them, and of that number also the persons are stinted, as some ten, some twelve, etc. Next unto him which bare the sceptre was the king himself, with his guard about his person, clad with cony [7] skins and other skins. After them followed the naked common sort of people, every one having his face painted, some with white, some with black, and other colours, and having in their hands one thing or other for a present, not so much as their children but they also brought their presents.

In the meantime, our general gathered his men together, and marched within his fenced place, making against their approaching a very warlike show. They being trooped together in their order, and a general salutation being made, there was presently a general silence. Then he that bare the sceptre before the king, being informed by another whom they assigned to that office, with a manly and lofty voice proclaimed that which the other spake to him in secret, continuing half an hour, which ended and a general amen, as it were, given, the king, with the whole number of men and women (the children excepted), came down without any weapon, who descending to the foot of the hill set themselves in order.

In coming towards our bulwarks and tents, the sceptre-bearer began a song, observing his measures in a dance, and that with a stately countenance, whom the king with his guard, and every degree of persons following, did in like manner sing and dance, saving only the women, which danced and kept silence. The general permitted them to enter within our bulwark, where they continued their song and dance a reasonable time. When they had satisfied themselves, they made signs to our general to sit down, to whom the king and divers others made several orations, or rather supplication, that he would take their province and kingdom into his hand and become their king, making signs that they would resign unto him their right and title of the whole land and become his subjects. In which to persuade us the better, the king and the rest with one consent and with great reverence, joyfully singing a song, did set the crown upon his head, enriched his neck with all their chains, and offered unto him many other things, honouring him by the name of *Hioh*, adding thereunto, as it seemed, a sign of triumph, which thing our general thought not meet to reject, because he knew not what honour and profit it might be to our country. Wherefore in the name and to the use of her Majesty he took the sceptre, crown, and dignity of the said country in his hands, wishing that the riches and treasure thereof might so conveniently be transported to the enriching of her kingdom at home as it aboundeth in the same.

The common sort of the people, leaving the king and his guard with our general, scattered themselves together with their sacrifices among our people, taking a diligent view of every person; and such as pleased their fancy (which were the youngest) they, enclosing them about, offered their sacrifices unto them with lamentable weeping, scratching, and tearing the flesh from their faces with their nails, whereof issued abundance of blood. But we used signs to them of disliking this, and stayed their hands from force, and directed them

7. Rabbit.

upwards to the living God, whom only they ought to worship. They showed unto us their wounds, and craved help of them at our hands, whereupon we gave them lotions, plasters, and ointments agreeing to the state of their griefs, beseeching God to cure their diseases. Every third day they brought their sacrifices unto us, until they understood our meaning, that we had no pleasure in them. Yet they could not be long absent from us, but daily frequented our company to the hour of our departure, which departure seemed so grievous unto them that their joy was turned into sorrow. They entreated us that being absent we would remember them, and by stealth provided a sacrifice, which we misliked.[8]

Our necessary business being ended, our general with his company travelled up into the country to their villages, where we found herds of deer by a thousand in a company, being most large and fat of body.

1600

THE ENGLISH HUMANISTS

The authors in this brief selection would not have called themselves humanists or used the word humanism to describe their activities. The Italian scholars of a generation earlier, who coined the word humanist, meant by it a teacher of the *studia humanitatis,* that is to say, of the language, literature, and antiquities of ancient Rome and later of Greece. For them, though they despised "monkish" stupidity, narrow pedantry, and restricted, technical learning, the word had none of the secular connotations—implying an emphasis on profane, human values rather than on divine—which it began to acquire in the nineteenth century. Their chief concern was with sound and wholesome doctrine —religious, philosophical, and moral—so eloquently expressed that men would be persuaded to accept it and put its precepts into action. The sixteenth-century Englishmen who occupied themselves with the study of classical literature, science, and philosophy had all consciously set themselves to improve the quality of life in their country by this means.

When John Colet (1466?–1519), Dean of St. Paul's and son of a former Lord Mayor of London, decided in about 1508 to use his large private fortune for the foundation of a school in which 153 boys should receive a free education, he wrote into the statutes of the school a kind of manifesto of what an elementary education should consist of. His statutes were copied by other foundations in England during the century: they set the tone of learned piety (*pietas letterata*)—to use the Protestant term—which is characteristic of the country and the century. The boys are to be taught the Christian faith and "good literature." They are to read only "good authors, such as have the very [i.e. true] Roman eloquence, joined with wisdom," and their curriculum is to set aside the "barbarousness and corruption" of medieval authors ("ignorant, blind fools," Colet calls them), with their adulterated Latin, "which may rather be called blotterature than literature." The ultimate end of their schooling is to "increase . . . good Christian life and manners" in the children.

Colet's language reflects the strength and impatience of his temper: his statutes mirror his fervor for the morally good life and his zeal for the ancient tongues as they had been spoken and written in ancient Rome itself, before the Dark Ages began with

8. Disliked.

its sack by the barbarians. The educational methods of his younger friend Thomas More were less formal, more private, and perhaps more subtle. More's "school" was his household, where every younger member, boy or girl, mastered Latin and Greek, so that Erasmus and others held it up as a model to the rest of Europe. Colet's aim, and his mode of putting it into operation, were more practical and more immediately productive: More's are at least as significant and, ultimately, effective. His unspoken intentions are in part embodied in his *Utopia*.

Both More and Colet lived through an age which seemed to be, as Erasmus put it, a golden one for the arts and letters—the early years of the young King Henry VIII's reign. Colet did not live to see what would have seemed to him, as it did to More, the disaster of England's severance, in religion, from the Church of Rome. Both had written the most significant part of their output in the international language of Latin; both were well known, Colet less than More, to learned circles in Europe. Both had been much influenced by European scholars and philosophers, Italian, French, and Netherlandish.

A consciousness of European contexts runs through the implicit and explicit patriotism which is a feature of the life and work of both Colet and More. They were, on the other hand, less concerned with the status of their own language. More, under the pressure of time and circumstance in later life, wrote his works of religious controversy, which had a specifically English reference, in English, but neither More nor Colet makes a deliberate, conscious effort to strengthen and improve the language part of their program.

The rise of English as a general, even as a learned, means of communication goes back to the fourteenth century, and the effort to strengthen and adorn it is constant among the poets and prose writers of the fifteenth. Translation had played a large part in this, as a practice by which one could expect to improve both the matter and the manner of vernacular writing. It continued to do so in the sixteenth century, growing more and more an accepted mode as the century went on.

Sir Thomas More's contemporary, Sir Thomas Elyot, is typical of the early phase of English "vernacular humanism." Like More, he was a lawyer—a member of the profession that the Italian professional humanist held in contempt for money-grubbing and bad Latin. He is the first of the English humanists to set down an extended program, in his case largely borrowed from Italian sources, for the training of English youth to serve the commonwealth. He also sets himself to enrich the English language by introducing Latin vocabulary and Greek syntax, seeking semantic wealth and pithy brevity to help him get his program across. Later in the century, the fondness for the learned word, to the exclusion rather than the augmentation of the English, was to result in the vogue for "inkhorn" terms, Latinized forms fetched out of the bottom of scholarly inkwells to increase the eloquence and expressiveness of the English language. It was this kind of thing that later provoked Sir John Cheke to the protest of his prefatory letter to Sir Thomas Hoby's translation of Castiglione's *Il Cortegiano*:

> I am of this opinion, that our own tongue should be written clean and pure, unmixed and unmangled with borrowing of other tongues, wherein if we take not heed betimes, ever borrowing and never repaying, she shall be fain to keep her house as bankrupt. . . .

Cheke had his own excesses in his search for a plain English for Englishmen to write. In his translation of the Gospel according to St. Matthew, he makes an attempt to produce a native English equivalent for the words he is translating, which will also cut away the Catholic associations of the usual words. So he replaces the Greek-derived "apostle" by its etymological equivalent, "frosent," i.e. from + sent; and "lunatic" by "mooned." The experiment is bizarre, but it reflects the concern that Cheke and his fellow scholars felt for their language and its role in the intellectual and religious life of the nation.

In other areas, too, English had been steadily gaining ground: by Cheke's day it was already the accepted language for professional writing, in legal and in scientific treatises for example. In 1582 Richard Mulcaster, speaking from the most conservative of professions, as headmaster of the same St. Paul's School that Colet had founded, can say: "I love Rome, but London better, I favour Italy, but England more, I honour the Latin, but I worship the English." Mulcaster was recognizing a *fait accompli* at the same time as he was framing a manifesto. By this time, the translators had done their work thoroughly and the patriots, like Roger Ascham, had also done their best to naturalize Latin rhetoric and make it speak with an English tongue.

In Ascham, concern for the language takes the form of a careful imitation of Ciceronian prose as the model for Latin composition—which was a Renaissance commonplace—and the attempt to apply the firm structural principles of Ciceronian rhetoric to the writing of English as well. Other experiments, such as the imitation of classical meters and the discarding of rhyme in English verse, did not meet with much success.

Ascham's enthusiasm for ancient Italy and Greece was not accompanied by a delight in modern Italy: in life and in doctrine she was an example to be avoided. For Ascham's friend Sir Thomas Hoby, Italian example, as represented in the finest of all the Renaissance "courtesy books," the works that set out the requirements of life in a truly civilized society, was above all an example to be followed. His translation of Castiglione's *Il Cortegiano* is a spirited achievement, far surpassing Elyot's earlier imitation of another Italian courtesy book in the sophistication of its doctrine and the elegance of its presentation.

The achievement of these men, their teachers and pupils, is to have brought English finally to the point where it could rival any of the languages of Europe as a literary medium. It was never the function of humanism to dwell in the past: the lessons which the humanists asked the classical past to give them in language and in wisdom were lessons which they hoped could be applied toward the perfection of the present. They sought to know Latin and Greek as the means both of bridging the gap between their own times and the glories of the past and of claiming kinship with it. The empire of England was rising to the point where it felt that it could challenge comparison with its ancestor, the Roman empire, in all the arts of peace and war.

The Headnote, text, and glosses for this section were prepared by J. B. Trapp.

SIR THOMAS MORE
1478?–1535

Thomas More, knighted by Henry VIII in 1521, was executed by Henry's order in 1535 and canonized four hundred years after his death. The son of a prominent lawyer who became a judge, he spent his early years in the household of Cardinal Morton, from whom he may have got some of his information about Richard III. After continuing his education at Oxford University he studied at the Inns of Court, where he completed his legal training, meanwhile living, without taking vows, among the Carthusian monks in London. His object was to test his religious vocation: and he characteristically chose the most austere of the orders with which to live. Finally opting for the law rather than the church, he rose rapidly in his profession, as a public man—Member of Parliament, an Under-Sheriff of the City of London (legal adviser to the Mayor and other officers)—and a favored counselor of Henry VIII. He went on several occasions as ambassador to Flanders and to France, became a member of the King's Council (1517), Under-Treasurer of England (1521), Speaker of the House of Commons (1523), and finally Lord Chancellor, the highest secular office in the kingdom, in 1529. In 1532 he resigned this office. More had always opposed the King's divorce from Catharine of Aragon, but his resignation was on the issue of Henry's claim, as a temporal ruler, to be Supreme Head of the Church. Two years of poverty and ill-health followed before More's arrest in 1534 and committal to the Tower. On July 1, 1535 he was tried and convicted of treason on perjured evidence; he was beheaded on July 6.

More was the friend and often the benefactor of most of the leading scholars in the England of his day, as well as being the most famous Englishman—the King and perhaps Cardinal Wolsey excepted—on the continent of Europe. His fame abroad he owed chiefly to his *Utopia,* written in Latin, partly during his embassy to Flanders in 1516 and partly on his return to London, and published at Louvain in 1516. Desiderius Erasmus, the great Dutch humanist scholar, with whom More had become friendly during his first visit to England in 1499, saw it through the press. Erasmus is partly responsible for More's European reputation, having attended to the publication of most of his Latin works—few of them published in More's native country in their author's lifetime—and made him known to correspondents. His pen-pictures of the man and the academy he had made of his home in London, where as much care was taken for the education of daughters as for that of his son and the other male members of the household, reflect the serenity and happiness, the rational, learned, but not solemn calm, that he and others found there, just as they found in the person of More himself a model and a stay.

Thomas More's first literary works were probably some English poems, followed by Latin epigrams, and, with Erasmus, translations of Lucian's Greek into Latin. His *Life of John Picus, Earl of Mirandula,* translated about 1505–10 for the instruction of a nun, tells us, by implication, much about the formation of More's character: his austerity, the evenness of his temper, his wit, his detachment, and his love of piety and learning.

For some years after this translation, More seems to have written little, presumably because of the demands of his career and of the four children born between about 1505 and 1509 to him and his first wife. (His second marriage, to a lady neither young nor beautiful, as he uncharitably put it, was contracted within a month of the early death of his first wife, probably about 1511. There were no more children.) But in 1515 More found himself on an embassy to Flanders with a little time on his hands. The result was *Utopia.* In its second book, written after his return to London, More debates the classic dilemma of the humanist scholar: whether, in occupying oneself in public affairs and the service of one's king, one is making better use of oneself and one's talents than in the pursuit of philosophic wisdom. It was the decision that More was himself faced with at just this time. Having married and acquired a family and having ruled out a monastic calling, he could not hope to lead the life of a detached scholar. But he could, as his experience so far had shown, make a lucrative career in the law. Like most of his fellow humanists, who both wrote and spoke the international language of Latin, he was in demand for embassies abroad as well as counsel at home. Should he serve his king or not? By 1517 he had decided and had entered Henry's service: twenty years later, on the point of execution, he was to protest that he had kept the oath he had taken to the King, dying "the King's good servant, but God's first."

The *Utopia* was followed by a historical masterpiece: the *History of Richard III*, which exists in two versions, Latin and English, and was probably written about 1517–18. There were also more Latin verses.

After 1520 More wrote little that was not official business or religious controversy, except for the devotional works, in English, that were probably produced almost entirely during the last year or two of his life. His career as a religious controversialist begins explicitly in the service of Henry VIII, whose reply to the tract by Martin Luther on the *Babylonian Captivity of the Church*—the reply that earned Henry the papal title of Defender of the Faith—was edited by More. Luther retorted and More replied, pseudonymously, in his Latin *Responsio ad Lutherum* (1523). Five years later, at the request of the Church in England, More again embarked on works of religious controversy, this time in English: he was licensed by the Bishop of London to read the Lutheran and other heretical books that were now being imported into England, and to refute their errors. The refutation runs to half a dozen books in six years, amounting to over three-quarters of a million words. Later still, in the little time that remained to him, he wrote his *Dialogue of Comfort in Tribulation,* in English, a debate between a pious old Hungarian nobleman and his nephew on how they are to behave in the face of the conquering and cruel Turk. The work clearly concerns More's own case, the theme being the proper conduct of a pious Catholic in the face of a tyrannical ruler. This book, and the *Treatise on the Passion,* a meditation begun in English and completed in Latin, are, with the exception of letters to his family and friends, the last works that More wrote.

Most of what More produced, in English or in Latin, was published in his lifetime, the most notable exceptions being the *Dialogue of Comfort* and the *Treatise on the Passion,* as well as the *History of Richard III.* All these were included in the edition of his collected English *Works,* brought out in London during the reign of Queen Mary, in 1557. Editions of his Latin works appeared in 1563, 1565 (the first complete edition, published at Louvain), 1566, and 1689, this last including the Latin biography by Thomas Stapleton, written in 1588.

We possess several sixteenth-century biographies of More in English, the shortest and in many ways the best being that of his son-in-law, William Roper, probably written in the 1550's, but not published until 1626. Roper's account of More's death is given below. The fullest is by Nicholas Harpsfield, written in 1558, first published in full in 1932.

Utopia

The book which made More famous immediately after it was published in 1516 came out in five more editions before 1520. It was translated into German in 1524, but did not appear in English until 1551, when Ralph Robinson made the version from which the following extracts are taken.

The first book of *Utopia* was written second, on More's return to England from his embassy, in the time he could snatch from the demands of a busy family and professional life. Its object is to point the contrast between a rationally ordered state, such as the far-off island commonwealth of the Utopians described in the second book, and the Europe of More's day, where all, from kings downward, are bent on self-aggrandizement and self-enrichment. Kings manipulate alliances, war with each other for territory, extort money from their subjects. Their subjects, in turn, oppress others of their subjects.

More's account of the exactions of the great landlords given in the *Utopia* takes us over some of the same grievances as the *Second Shepherds' Play* and *Piers Plowman*. Wealthy English landowners, dispossessing small farmers of their land so as to increase the pasture for sheep, create unemployment. The unemployed turn to beggary and theft as alternatives to starvation, and English justice, instead of using a system of forced labor as a means of punishment, adopts the foolish deterrent of hanging thieves, which does not, in fact, reduce their number. The sheep are the culprits: it is they that should be punished.

It is important to realize that in this account of the evils of his day as well as in the description of Utopia itself, More is no radical reformer, looking to see a system swept away and a bright new one put in its place. His view of society is of an ordered hierarchy and just keeping of degree, from the divinely invested, God-fearing king downward. It was to the keeping of that social order in its best and fairest form that More devoted himself both in theory and in practice and it is to full participation in that form that he invites the scholar and philosopher in the first book of his *Utopia*.

Like the first book, the second is put into the mouth of a chance-met traveler, Raphael Hythlodaeus, whose name is derived from Greek, like most of the names in the *Utopia*, and means "babbler." It describes the island state that this traveler found during the voyages that he made after he had parted company with his commander, Amerigo Vespucci, from whose accounts of Indian customs in his *New World* and *Four Voyages* some of the details of Utopian social organization and practices seem to have been taken. Hythlodaeus tells of a society where all is ordered according to the dictates of reason and of nature, where people do not say one thing and do another. It is therefore No-place (Greek *ou-*, not, *topos*, place) and the narrative throughout is conditioned by the favorite late medieval and Renaissance mode of defining by negatives in its exploration of the paradox of the irrational behavior of man, the rational, social animal. If the reasoned usages of *Utopia* sometimes strike us as too severe, we must remember that More is always saying "This happens nowhere."

This is the overriding condition of his "poetry," as his Protestant religious enemies were to call it. The *Utopia* is not, like Plato's *Republic* or *Laws*, to whose ideas and ultimately to whose literary form it owes so much, a serious account of an ideal or even a possible commonwealth. Its title, which may be the work of Erasmus rather than More, proclaims it *A little book, truly golden, not less useful than entertaining*, and it aims, in what was More's favorite mode, to use irony, wit, and satire as a means of making men see what is good and true. In form and in spirit it is much closer to Lucian of Samosata, the Greek satirist of the second century A.D., one of More's favorite authors, than it is to Plato. Lucian's dialogues aim to be entertaining as well as to explore a serious topic in an interesting way. More and Erasmus translated some of them together in 1505, and among those translated by More was the *Menippus*, which may well have given him the idea for *Utopia*. It opens with a serious discussion among friends and continues with a traveler's tale of a fabulous place (in this case Hell), the lessons of which are applied to the questions raised in the preliminary discussion.

More's serious wit never obscures the implied comparison between the virtuous pagans of Utopia with the professed Christians of Europe, who fall so short of standards of reasonable conduct, either pagan or Christian. Utopia demands that all its citizens participate for a set time in the agriculture which supplies the necessities of an unpretentious life from the labor of a six-hour day. Its social organization is patriarchal, in family units, with slaves for menial duties. All property is held in common and the Utopians are indifferent to money, gold, silver, and precious stones. All the activities of the citizens are carefully supervised, including travel, marriage, the care of the sick, the elimination of the old and infirm. The Utopians hate war, but if they cannot avoid it they try to minimize its harm to the state by shortening it by every means available, including treachery, and by hiring mercenaries to fight it for them. They are not afraid to do what is morally reprehensible in order to secure a greater good. In peace they keep faith, both public and private, and therefore have no need of laws and lawyers. They love knowledge and wisdom, they pursue happiness in "good and decent" pleasure, they worship a single god, and they believe in the immortality of the soul and the happiness of the life after death. They observe the greatest solemnity in the practice of their religion and are convinced of its truth, but they would abandon it for one that could be proved better.

In all this, More is saying, the Utopians are right and we in Christian Europe wrong. Utopia is nowhere: we can only wish that it were here, now, in our part of the world.

Utopia

From *Book I*

[Utopian Communism]

That is it which I meant (quoth he) when I said philosophy had no place among kings.

Indeed (quoth I) this school philosophy [1] hath not, which thinketh all things meet for every place. But there is another philosophy more civil,[2] which knoweth, as ye would say, her own stage, and thereafter ordering and behaving herself in the play that she hath in hand, playeth her part accordingly with comeliness, uttering nothing out of due order and fashion. And this is the philosophy that you must use. Or else whiles a comedy of Plautus [3] is playing, and the vile bondmen [4] scoffing and trifling among themselves, if you should suddenly come upon the stage in a philosopher's apparel, and rehearse out of Octavia [5] the place wherein Seneca disputeth with Nero: had it not been better

1. Academic. This is a reference to the medieval system of scholasticism, regarded as purely speculative and useless.
2. Relating to society; practical.
3. Roman writer of comedies, 254–184 B.C.
4. Slaves, who were characters in the play.
5. Lucius Annaeus Seneca, Roman Stoic philosopher and playwright, c. 5 B.C.–65 A.D., did not write the play *Octavia*, a historical drama. The dispute of Seneca and Nero in the second act concerns the royal and civic virtues that More deals with here. Seneca has been extolling retirement and withdrawal, but then turns to engagement as the better course.

for you to have played the dumb person,[6] than by rehearsing that, which served neither for the time nor place, to have made such a tragical comedy or gillimaufry?[7] For by bringing in other stuff that nothing appertaineth to the present matter, you must needs mar and pervert the play that is in hand, though the stuff that you bring be much better. What part soever you have taken upon you, play that as well as you can and make the best of it: and do not therefore disturb and bring out of order the whole matter, because that another, which is merrier, and better, cometh to your remembrance. So the case standeth in a commonwealth, and so it is in the consultations of kings and princes. If evil opinions and naughty[8] persuasions cannot be utterly and quite plucked out of their hearts, if you cannot, even as you would, remedy vices, which use and custom hath confirmed: yet for this cause you must not leave and forsake the commonwealth: you must not forsake the ship[9] in a tempest, because you cannot rule and keep down the winds. No, nor you must not labour to drive into their heads new and strange informations, which you know well shall be nothing regarded with them that be of clean contrary minds. But you must with a crafty wile and a subtle train[10] study and endeavour yourself, as much as in you lieth, to handle the matter wittily[11] and handsomely[12] for the purpose, and that which you cannot turn to good, so to order it that it be not very bad. For it is not possible for all things to be well, unless all men were good. Which I think will not be yet this good many years.

By this means (quoth he) nothing else will be brought to pass, but whiles that I go about to remedy the madness of others, I should be even as mad as they. For if I would speak things that be true I must needs speak such things; but as for to speak[13] false things, whether that be a philosopher's part or no; I cannot tell, truly it is not my part. Howbeit this communication of mine, though peradventure it may seem unpleasant to them, yet can I not see why it should seem strange, or foolishly newfangled. If so be that I should speak those things that Plato feigneth in his weal public:[14] or that the Utopians do in theirs, these things though they were (as they be indeed) better, yet they might seem spoken out of place. Forasmuch as here amongst us, every man hath his possessions several[15] to himself, and there all things be common. But what was in my communication contained, that might not, and ought not in any place to be spoken? Saving that to them which have thoroughly decreed and determined with themselves to roam headlong the contrary way, it connot be acceptable and pleasant, because it calleth them back, and showeth them the jeopardies. Verily if all things that evil and vicious manners have caused to

6. A regular role, the "thinking" part, in Greek and Roman drama.
7. Originally a dish made up of odds and ends of food, hodge-podge.
8. Wicked.
9. The ship of state is a regular metaphor, from Plato's *Republic* onward.
10. Device, strategy.
11. Wisely.
12. Suitably. This is the principle of "accommodation"—regular advice to civil philosophers not to insist on strict and pure virtue, but to bring princes to see what they must do by less direct means.
13. That is, as for speaking.
14. That is, commonwealth, i.e. Plato's *Republic,* the classic account of an ideal state.
15. Separate.

seem inconvenient and nought[16] should be refused, as things unmeet and reproachful, then we must among Christian people wink at[17] the most part of
all those things, which Christ taught us,[18] and so strictly forbade them to be
winked at, that those things also which he whispered in the ears of his disciples,
he commanded to be proclaimed in open houses.[19] And yet the most part of
them is more dissident from the manners of the world nowadays, than my
communication was. But preachers, sly and wily men, following your counsel
(as I suppose) because they saw men evil willing[20] to frame their manners
to Christ's rule, they have wrested[21] and perverted his doctrine, and like a rule
of lead[22] have applied it to men's manners: that by some means at the least-
ways, they might agree together. Whereby I cannot see what good they have
done: but that men may more sickerly[23] be evil. And I truly should prevail
even as much in king's councils. For either I must say otherways than they say,
and then I were as good to say nothing, or else I must say the same that they
say, and (as Mitio saith in Terence[24]) help to further their madness. For that
crafty wile, and subtle train of yours, I cannot perceive to what purpose it
serveth, wherewith you would have me to study and endeavour myself, if all
things cannot be made good, yet to handle them wittily and handsomely for
the purpose, that as far forth as is possible they may not be very evil. For
there is no place to dissemble in, nor to wink in. Naughty counsels must be
openly allowed and very pestilent decrees must be approved. He shall be
counted worse than a spy, yea almost as evil as a traitor, that with a faint heart
doth praise evil and noisome decrees. Moreover a man can have no occasion to
do good, chancing into the company of them which will sooner make nought a
good man, than be made good themselves: through whose evil company he shall
be marred, or else if he remain good and innocent, yet the wickedness and
foolishness of others shall be imputed to him, and laid in his neck.[25] So that
it is impossible with that crafty wile and subtle train to turn anything to better.
Wherefore Plato[26] by a goodly similitude[27] declareth, why wise men refrain
to meddle in the commonwealth. For when they see the people swarm into
the streets, and daily wet to the skin with rain, and yet cannot persuade them
to go out of the rain and to take their houses, knowing well, that if they should

16. Worthless, wrong.
17. Close their eyes to.
18. Erasmus and others at this time were of the opinion that communism was according to
Christ's intention: it was Aristotle who said that a commonwealth in which things are common cannot flourish.
19. Matthew 10:27: "What ye hear in the ear, that preach ye upon the housetops." Cf.
Luke 12:3.
20. That is, of ill will.
21. Twisted.
22. The lead rule, or Lesbian rule, was a flexible measuring stick used by ancient Greek
architects, so called because it could be bent to fit curved Lesbian mouldings. It was proverbial for the adaptation or accommodation of law to morals.
23. Surely, certainly.
24. Roman writer of comedies, d. 159 B.C. Mitio is a character in his play *Adelphi* (The
Brothers).
25. That is, laid to his charge.
26. In the *Republic* 496.
27. That is, image.

go out to them, they should nothing prevail, nor win aught by it, but be wet also in the rain, they do keep themselves within their houses, being content that they be safe themselves, seeing they cannot remedy the folly of the people. Howbeit doubtless, Master More (to speak truly as my mind giveth me) [28] wheresoever possessions be private, where money beareth all the stroke,[29] it is hard and almost impossible that there the weal public may justly be governed, and prosperously flourish. Unless you think thus: that justice is there executed, where all things come into the hands of evil men; or that prosperity there flourisheth, where all is divided among a few; which few nevertheless do not lead their lives very wealthily, and the residue live miserably, wretchedly and beggarly.[30] Wherefore when I consider with myself and weigh in my mind the wise and godly ordinances of the Utopians, among whom with very few laws all things be so well and wealthily ordered, that virtue is had in price [31] and estimation, and yet, all things being there common, every man hath abundance of everything. Again on the other part,[32] when I compare with them so many nations ever making new laws, yet none of them all well and sufficiently furnished with laws; where every man calleth that he hath gotten, his own proper [33] and private goods; where so many new laws daily made be not sufficient for every man to enjoy, defend, and know from another man's that which he calleth his own; which thing the infinite controversies in the law, that daily rise never to be ended, plainly declare to be true. These things (I say) when I consider with myself, I hold well with Plato,[34] and do nothing marvel, that he would make no laws for them, that refused those laws, whereby all men should have and enjoy equal portions of wealths and commodities. For the wise man did easily foresee, that this is the one and only way to the wealth of a commonalty,[35] if equality of all things should be brought in and established. Which I think is not possible to be observed, where every man's goods be proper and peculiar [36] to himself. For where every man under certain titles and pretences draweth and plucketh to himself as much as he can, and so a few divide among themselves all the riches that there is, be there never so much abundance and store, there to the residue is left lack and poverty. And for the most part it chanceth, that this latter sort is more worthy to enjoy that state of wealth, than the other be: because the rich men be covetous, crafty and unprofitable.[37] On the other part the poor be lowly, simple, and by their daily labour more profitable to the commonwealth than to themselves. Thus I do fully persuade myself, that no equal and just distribution of things can be

---

28. As my feelings incline me.
29. That is, has the greatest influence.
30. Amerigo Vespucci had reported of the Indians that one of their happinesses was to have no private property, and no king or other ruler.
31. In high value.
32. That is, hand.
33. That is, individual.
34. The story is in Diogenes Laertius, *On the Lives of the Philosophers* (3rd century A.D.). Plato refused to go and govern the new city of the Arcadians and Thebans when he heard that property would not be held in common there.
35. Commonwealth.
36. Private.
37. Harmful.

made, nor that perfect wealth shall ever be among men, unless this propriety[38] be exiled and banished. But so long as it shall continue, so long shall remain among the most and best part of men the heavy and inevitable burden of poverty and wretchedness. Which, as I grant that it may be somewhat eased, so I utterly deny that it can wholly be taken away. For if there were a statute made, that no man should possess above a certain measure of ground,[39] and that no man should have in his stock above a prescript and appointed[40] sum of money: if it were by certain laws decreed, that neither the king should be of too great power, neither the people too proud and wealthy, and that offices should not be obtained by inordinate suit,[41] or by bribes and gifts: that they should neither be bought nor sold, nor that it should be needful for the officers, to be at any cost or charge in their offices: for so occasion is given to the officers by fraud and ravin[42] to gather up their money again,[43] and by reason of gifts and bribes the offices be given to rich men, which should rather have been executed of wise men: by such laws I say, like as sick bodies that be desperate and past cure, be wont with continual good cherishing to be kept and botched[44] up for a time: so these evils also might be lightened and mitigated. But that they may be perfectly cured, and brought to a good and upright state, it is not to be hoped for, whiles every man is master of his own to himself. Yea, and whiles you go about to do your cure of one part, you shall make bigger the sore of another part, so the help of one causeth another's harm: forasmuch as nothing can be given to any man unless that be taken from another.[45]

But I am of a contrary opinion (quoth I) for methinketh[46] that men shall never there live wealthily,[47] where all things be common. For how can there be abundance of goods, or of anything, where every man withdraweth his hand from labour? Whom the regard of his own gains driveth not to work, and the hope that he hath in other men's travails maketh him slothful. Then when they be pricked with poverty, and yet no man can by any law or right defend that for his own, which he hath gotten with the labour of his own hands, shall not there of necessity be continual sedition and bloodshed? Specially the authority and reverence of magistrates being taken away, which, what place it may have with such men among whom is no difference, I cannot devise. . . .

From *Book II*
[Utopian Contempt for Gold]

For it must needs be, that how far a thing is dissonant and disagreeing from the guise and trade[1] of the hearers, so far shall it be out of their belief. Howbeit, a wise and indifferent esteemer[2] of things will not greatly marvel per-

38. Private property, ownership.
39. Later legislation proposed just this in England (1548).
40. Prescribed and laid down.
41. Over-pressing solicitation.
42. Plunder, spoils.
43. Recoup themselves.
44. Patched.
45. Proverbial saying, from classical times onward.
46. It seems to me.
47. In plenty.

1. Manners and ways.
2. Impartial judge.

chance, seeing all their other laws and customs do so much differ from ours, if the use also of gold and silver among them be applied,[3] rather to their own fashions than to ours. I mean in that they occupy[4] not money themselves, but keep it for that chance, which as it may happen, so it may be that it shall never come to pass. In the meantime gold and silver, whereof money is made, they do so use,[5] as none of them doth more esteem it, than the very nature of the thing deserveth. And then who doth not plainly see how far it is under iron: as without the which men can no better live than without fire and water.[6] Whereas to gold and silver nature hath given no use, that we may not well lack:[7] if that the folly of men had not set it in higher estimation for the rareness sake. But of the contrary part, nature as a most tender and loving mother, hath placed the best and most necessary things open abroad: as the air, the water and the earth itself. And hath removed and hid farthest from us vain and unprofitable things. Therefore if these metals among them should be fast locked up in some tower, it might be suspected, that the prince and the council (as the people is ever foolishly imagining) intended by some subtlety[8] to deceive the commons, and to take same profit of it to themselves. Furthermore if they should make thereof plate and such other finely and cunningly[9] wrought stuff: if at any time they should have occasion to break it, and melt it again, and therewith to pay their soldiers' wages, they see and perceive very well, that men would be loath to part from those things, that they once began to have pleasure and delight in. To remedy all this they have found out a means, which, as it is agreeable to all their other laws and customs, so it is from ours, where gold is so much set by and so diligently kept, very far discrepant and repugnant: and therefore incredible, but only to them that be wise. For whereas they eat and drink in earthen and glass vessels, which indeed be curiously and properly[10] made, and yet be of very small value: of gold and silver they make commonly chamber pots, and other like vessels,[11] that serve for most vile uses, not only in their common halls, but in every man's private house. Furthermore of the same metals they make great chains, with fetters, and gyves[12] wherein they tie their bondmen.[13] Finally whosoever for any offence be infamed,[14] by their ears hang rings of gold, upon their fingers they wear rings of gold, and about their necks chains of gold, and in conclusion their heads be tied about with gold. Thus by all means that may be they procure to have gold and silver among them in reproach and infamy. And therefore these metals, which other nations do as grievously and sorrowfully forgo, as in a manner from their own lives: if they

3. Adapted.
4. Employ.
5. Vespucci reported that the Indians despised gold, silver, and gems.
6. See Ecclesiasticus 39:26: "The principal things for the whole use of life are water, fire, iron . . .". The argument is that the test of how natural a thing is, is how useful it is.
7. Endure the absence of.
8. Trick.
9. Cleverly.
10. Ingeniously and handsomely.
11. This is a regular praise of primitive peoples in the Renaissance: they are "natural" men and use only "natural," things, not what is more valuable than is necessary.
12. Shackles.
13. Slaves.
14. That is, disgraced.

should altogether at once be taken from the Utopians, no man there would think that he had lost the worth of one farthing. They gather also pearls by the seaside, and diamonds and carbuncles [15] upon certain rocks, and yet they seek not for them: but by chance finding them, they cut and polish them. And therewith they deck their young infants. Which like as in the first years of their childhood, they make much and be fond [16] and proud of such ornaments, so when they be a little more grown in years and discretion, perceiving that none but children do wear such toys and trifles: they lay them away even of their own shamefacedness, without any bidding of their parents: even as our children, when they wax [17] big, do cast away nuts, brooches, and puppets.[18] Therefore these laws and customs, which be so far different from all other nations, how divers fantasies also and minds [19] they do cause, did I never so plainly perceive, as in the ambassadors of the Anemolians.[20]

These ambassadors came to Amaurote [21] whiles I was there. And because they came to entreat [22] of great and weighty matters, those three citizens [23] apiece out of every city were come thither before them. But all the ambassadors of the next countries, which had been there before, and knew the fashions and manners of the Utopians, among whom they perceived no honour given to sumptuous and costly apparel, silks to be contemned, gold also to be infamed [24] and reproachful, were wont to come thither in very homely and simple apparel. But the Anemolians, because they dwell far thence and had very little acquaintance with them, hearing that they were all apparelled alike, and that very rudely and homely: thinking them not to have the things which they did not wear: being therefore more proud, than wise: determined in the gorgeousness of their apparel to represent very [25] gods, and with the bright shining and glistering of their gay clothing to dazzle the eyes of the silly poor Utopians. So there came in three ambassadors with one hundred servants all apparelled in changeable [26] colours: the most of them in silks: the ambassadors themselves (for at home in their own country they were noblemen) in cloth of gold, with great chains of gold, with gold hanging at their ears, with gold rings upon their fingers, with brooches and aglets [27] of gold upon their caps, which glistered full of pearls and precious stones: to be short, trimmed and adorned with all those things, which among the Utopians were either the punishment of bondmen, or the reproach of infamed persons, or else trifles for young children to play withal. Therefore it would have done a man good at his heart to have seen how proudly they displayed their peacock's feathers, how much they made

15. Rubies.
16. Foolish about.
17. Grow.
18. Dolls.
19. Intentions.
20. The name is derived from *anemos*, the Greek word for wind; thus, Windbags.
21. From Greek, "dark, dim": i.e. Shadow City, Ghost City, the capital of Utopia.
22. Negotiate.
23. The three wise men sent annually from every city to a parliament in the capital.
24. Despised.
25. True.
26. Either particolored or "shot-silk."
27. Small pendants.

of their painted [28] sheaths, and how loftily they set forth and advanced themselves, when they compared their gallant [29] apparel with the poor raiment of the Utopians. For all the people were swarmed forth into the streets. And on the other side it was no less pleasure to consider how much they were deceived, and how far they missed of their purpose, being contrariwise taken than they thought they should have been. For to the eyes of all the Utopians, except very few, which had been in other countries for some reasonable cause, all that gorgeousness of apparel seemed shameful and reproachful. Insomuch that they most reverently saluted the vilest and most abject of them for lords: passing over the ambassadors themselves without any honour: judging them by their wearing of golden chains to be bondmen. Yea you should have seen children also, that had cast away their pearls and precious stones, when they saw the like sticking upon the ambassadors' caps, dig and push their mothers under the sides, saying thus to them: 'Look, mother, how great a lubber [30] doth yet wear pearls and precious stones, as though he were a little child still.' But the mother, yea, and that also in good earnest: 'Peace, son,' saith she: 'I think he be some of the ambassadors' fools.' Some found fault at their golden chains, as to no use nor purpose, being so small and weak, that a bondman might easily break them, and again so wide and large, that when it pleased him, he might cast them off, and run away at liberty whither he would. But when the ambassadors had been there a day or two and saw so great abundance of gold so lightly esteemed, yea in no less reproach, than it was with them in honour: and besides that more gold in the chains and gyves of one fugitive bondman, than all the costly ornaments of them three was worth: they began to abate their courage, and for very shame laid away all that gorgeous array, whereof they were so proud. And specially when they had talked familiarly with the Utopians, and had learned all their fashions and opinions.

For they marvel that any men be so foolish, as to have delight and pleasure in the glistering of a little trifling stone, which may behold any of the stars, or else the sun itself. Or that any man is so mad, as to count himself the nobler for the smaller or finer thread of wool, which selfsame wool (be it now in never so fine a spun thread) did once a sheep wear: and yet was she all that time no other thing than a sheep. They marvel also that gold, which of the own nature is a thing so unprofitable, is now among all people in so high estimation, that man himself, by whom, yea and for the use of whom it is so much set by, is in much less estimation than the gold itself. . . .

[Utopian Marriage Customs]

. . . The woman is not married before she be eighteen [1] years old. The man is four years older before he marry.

If either the man or the woman be proved to have bodily offended before their marriage with another, he or she whether [2] it be is sharply punished.

---

28. Ornamented, embroidered.
29. Elegant.
30. Dolt.

1. This is rather old by the customs of More's day. Aristotle had set eighteen as the best age for a woman, but thirty-seven for a man.
2. Whichever.

And both the offenders be forbidden ever after in all their life to marry: unless the fault be forgiven by the prince's pardon. But both the goodman [3] and the goodwife of the house where that offence was done, as being slack and negligent in looking to their charge, be in danger of great reproach and infamy. That offence is so sharply punished, because they perceive, that unless they be diligently kept from the liberty of this vice, few will join together in the love of marriage, wherein all the life must be led with one, and also all the griefs and displeasures that come therewith must patiently be taken and borne. Furthermore in choosing wives and husbands they observe earnestly and straitly [4] a custom, which seemed to us very fond and foolish. For a sad [5] and an honest [6] matron showeth the woman, be she maid or widow, naked to the wooer.[7] And likewise a sage and discreet man exhibiteth the wooer naked to the woman. At this custom we laughed and disallowed [8] it as foolish. But they on the other part do greatly wonder at the folly of all other nations, which in buying a colt,[9] whereas a little money is in hazard,[10] be so chary and circumspect, that though he be almost all bare, yet they will not buy him, unless the saddle and all the harness be taken off, lest under those coverings be hid some gall or sore. And yet in choosing a wife, which shall be either pleasure, or displeasure to them all their life after, they be so reckless, that all the residue of the woman's body being covered with clothes, they esteem [11] her scarcely by one hand-breadth (for they can see no more but her face), and so do join her to them not without great jeopardy of evil agreeing together, if anything in her body afterward do offend and mislike [12] them.

For all men be not so wise, as to have respect to the virtuous conditions of the party.[13] And the endowments of the body cause the virtues of the mind more to be esteemed and regarded: yea even in the marriages of wise men. Verily so foul deformity may be hid under those coverings, that it may quite alienate and take away the man's mind from his wife, when it shall not be lawful for their bodies to be separate again. If such deformity happen by any chance after the marriage is consummate and finished, well, there is no remedy but patience. Every man must take his fortune, well-a-worth.[14] But it were well done that a law were made whereby all such deceits might be eschewed and avoided beforehand.

And this were they constrained more earnestly to look upon, because they

3. Head of the house.
4. Strictly.
5. Sober, respectable.
6. Good.
7. Plutarch reports that the Spartan lawgiver Lycurgus sanctioned this custom.
8. Disapproved of.
9. More took this comparison from Horace, who uses the horse-dealing image (*Satires* I.ii.83–105) in his argument that fornication is preferable to adultery. Married women are always over-dressed and you cannot see what is underneath. Prostitutes, on the other hand, show you enough to give you a good idea.
10. At stake.
11. Value.
12. Displease.
13. Person.
14. Alas.

only of the nations in that part of the world be content every man with one wife apiece.

And matrimony is there never broken, but by death; except adultery break the bond, or else the intolerable wayward manners of either party. For if either of them find themselves for any such cause grieved, they may by the licence of the council change and take another. But the other party liveth ever after in infamy and out of wedlock. But for the husband to put way his wife for no fault, but for that some mishap is fallen to her body, this by no means they will suffer. For they judge it a great point of cruelty, that anybody in their most need of help and comfort should be cast off and forsaken, and that old age, which both bringeth sickness with it, and is a sickness itself, should unkindly and unfaithfully be dealt withal.[15] But now and then it chanceth, whereas the man and the woman cannot well agree between themselves, both of them finding other, with whom they hope to live more quietly and merrily, that they by the full consent of them both be divorced asunder and new married to other. . . . For in all offences they count the intent and pretensed [16] purpose as evil as the act or deed itself, for they think that no let [17] ought to excuse him that did his best to have no let. They set great store by fools.[18] And as it is great reproach to do to any of them hurt or injury, so they prohibit not to take pleasure of foolishness. For that, they think, doth much good to the fools. And if any man be so sad [19] and stern, that he cannot laugh neither at their words, nor at their deeds, none of them be committed to his tuition; [20] for fear lest he would not order them gently and favourably enough, to whom they should bring no delectation (for other goodness in them is none) much less any profit should they yield him. To mock a man for his deformity, or for that he lacketh any part or limb of his body, is counted great dishonesty [21] and reproach, not to him that is mocked, but to him that mocketh, which [22] unwisely doth upbraid any man of that as a vice which was not in his power to eschew. Also as they count and reckon very little wit to be in him, that regardeth not natural beauty and comeliness, so to help the same with paintings,[23] is taken for a vain and a wanton pride, not without great infamy. For they know, even by very experience, that no comeliness of beauty doth so highly commend and advance the

15. With.
16. That is, designed. Cf. Matthew 5:28: "whosoever looketh on a woman to lust after her hath committed adultery already with her in his heart."
17. Hindrance.
18. That is, they take good care of their mental defectives and do not laugh at them for their deficiencies, but because they can sometimes do or say things that are funny, wise, or witty on account of their simplicity. The fool in a well-to-do English household of the time, such as More's, need not have been such a defective, but if he was, he would have been taken into that household as a protection against less merciful members of society as well as for his talents as simpleton-philosopher. More's own fool, Henry Patenson, appears in the family-group portrait by Holbein (Fig. 2), which indicates the value set by More on simplicity and jesting as sources of wisdom.
19. Sober.
20. Guardianship.
21. Wrong.
22. Who.
23. Cosmetics.

wives in the conceit of their husbands, as honest conditions [24] and lowliness. For as love is oftentimes won with beauty, so it is not kept, preserved and continued, but by virtue and obedience.[25] They do not only fear [26] their people from doing evil by punishments, but also allure them to virtue with rewards of honour. Therefore they set up in the market-place the images of notable men, and of such as have been great and bountiful benefactors to the commonwealth, for the perpetual memory of their good acts, and also that the glory and renown of the ancestors may stir and provoke their posterity to virtue. He that inordinately and ambitiously desireth promotions is left all hopeless for ever attaining any promotion as long as he liveth. They live together lovingly. For no magistrate [27] is either haughty or fearful.[28] Fathers they be called, and like fathers they use themselves. The citizens (as it is their duty) do willingly exhibit unto them due honour without any compulsion. Nor the prince himself is not known from the other by his apparel, nor by a crown or diadem, or cap of maintenance,[29] but by a little sheaf of corn [30] carried before him. And so a taper of wax is borne before the bishop, whereby only he is known. They have but few laws.[31] For to people so instruct and institute [32] very few do suffice. Yea this thing they chiefly reprove among other nations, that innumerable books of laws and expositions upon the same be not sufficient. But they think it against all right and justice that men should be bound to those laws, which either be in number more than be able to be read, or else blinder and darker, than that any man can well understand them. Furthermore they utterly exclude and banish all proctors,[33] and sergeants at the law; [34] which craftily handle matters, and subtly dispute of the laws. For they think it most meet,[35] that every man should plead his own matter, and tell the same tale before the judge that he would tell to his man of law. So shall there be less circumstance of words, and the truth shall sooner come to light; whiles [36] the judge with a discreet judgment doth weigh the words of him whom no lawyer hath instruct with deceit, and whiles he helpeth and beareth out simple wits against the false and malicious circumversions [37] of crafty children.[38] This is hard to be ob-

24. Good morals.
25. English civil law allowed a husband to beat his wife with whips and sticks.
26. Frighten.
27. High public official.
28. Terrifying.
29. A crimson velvet hat, lined with ermine, originally worn by dukes only, as a symbol of dignity.
30. Representing the abundance that the well-governed land ought to produce, as it did when the goddess Astraea was on earth in the Golden Age and there was no need of any law or constraint.
31. The number of laws was regarded as an index of corruption: the more corrupt the society, the greater the number of laws required.
32. Instructed and trained.
33. That is, an attorney in the ecclesiastical and admiralty courts. More was himself a lawyer, with a contempt for those who used the law for self-advancement and self-importance.
34. Highest degree of barrister (pleader in court).
35. Fitting.
36. Sometimes.
37. Twistings.
38. People, as in "children of Israel."

served in other countries, in so infinite a number of blind and intricate laws. But in Utopia every man is a cunning [39] lawyer. For (as I said) they have very few laws; and the plainer and grosser [40] that any interpretation is, that they allow as most just. For all laws (say they) be made and published only to the intent that by them every man should be put in remembrance of his duty. But the crafty and subtle interpretation of them can put very few in that remembrance (for they be but few that do perceive them), whereas the simple, the plain and gross meaning of the laws is open to every man.

Else as touching the vulgar [41] sort of the people, which be both most in number, and have most need to know their duties, were it not as good for them, that no law were made at all, as when it is made, to bring so blind [42] an interpretation upon it, that without great wit [43] and long arguing no man can discuss it? To the finding out whereof neither the gross judgment of the people can attain, neither the whole life of them that be occupied in working for their livings can suffice thereto. These virtues of the Utopians have caused their next neighbours and borderers, which live free and under no subjection (for the Utopians long ago, have delivered many of them from tyranny) to take magistrates of them, some for a year, and some for five years' space. Which when the time of their office is expired, they bring home again with honour and praise, and take new ones again with them into their country. These nations have undoubtedly very well and wholesomely [44] provided for their commonwealths. For seeing that both the making and the marring of the weal public doth depend and hang upon the manners of the rulers and magistrates, what officers could they more wisely have chosen, than those which cannot be led from honesty by bribes (for to them that shortly after shall depart thence into their own country money should be unprofitable) nor yet be moved either with favour, or malice towards any man, as being strangers, and unacquainted with the people? The which two vices of affection and avarice, where they take place in judgments, incontinent [45] they break justice,[46] the strongest and surest bond of a commonwealth. These peoples which fetch their officers and rulers from them, the Utopians call their fellows. And other to whom they have been beneficial, they call their friends. As touching leagues,[47] which in other places between country and country be so oft concluded, broken and made again, they never make none with any nation. For to what purpose serve leagues? say they. As though nature had not set sufficient love between man and man. And who so regardeth not nature, think you that he will pass for words? They be brought into this opinion chiefly, because that in those parts of the world, leagues between princes be wont to be kept and observed very slenderly. For

39. Knowledgeable.
40. Simpler, more obvious.
41. Ordinary.
42. Obscure.
43. Intellect.
44. Soundly.
45. Immediately.
46. The contrast between justice (the natural) and law (the actual) is emphasized throughout.
47. Alliances.

here in Europe,[48] and especially in these parts where the faith and religion of Christ reigneth, the majesty of leagues is everywhere esteemed holy and inviolable, partly through the justice and goodness of princes, and partly through the reverence of great bishops. Which like as they make no promise themselves but they do very religiously perform the same, so they exhort all princes in any wise to abide by their promises, and them that refuse or deny so to do, by their pontifical power and authority they compel thereto. And surely they think well [49] that it might seem a very reproachful thing, if in the leagues of them which by a peculiar [50] name be called faithful,[51] faith should have no place. But in that new found part of the world, which is scarcely so far from us beyond the line equinoctial [52] as our life and manners be dissident from theirs, no trust nor confidence is in leagues. But the more and holier ceremonies the league is knit up with, the sooner it is broken by some cavillation [53] found in the words, which many times of purpose be so craftily put in and placed, that the bands can never be so sure nor so strong, but they will find some hole open to creep out at, and to break both league and truth. The which crafty dealing, yea the which fraud and deceit, if they should know it to be practised among private men in their bargains and contracts, they would incontinent cry out at it with a sour countenance, as an offence most detestable, and worthy to be punished with a shameful death: yea even very they that advance themselves authors of like counsel given to princes. Wherefore it may well be thought, either that all justice is but a base and a low virtue, and which abaseth itself far under the high dignity of kings; or at the leastwise, that there be two justices, the one meet [54] for the inferior sort of the people, going afoot and creeping below on the ground, and bound down on every side with many bands because it shall not run at rovers; [55] the other a princely virtue, which like as it is of much higher majesty than the other poor justice, so also it is of much more liberty, as to the which nothing is unlawful that it lusteth after. These manners of princes (as I said) which be there so evil keepers of leagues, cause the Utopians, as I suppose, to make no leagues at all, which perchance would change their mind if they lived here. Howbeit they think that though leagues be never so faithfully observed and kept, yet the custom of making leagues was very evil begun.[56] For this causeth men (as though nations which be separate asunder, by the space of a little hill or a river, were coupled together by no society or bond of nature) to think themselves born adversaries and enemies one to another, and that it is lawful for the one to seek the death and destruction of the

48. More is referring ironically to such incidents as the treachery of the French king Louis XII and of Ferdinand V of Castile against Frederick of Naples, of Pope Julius II and his attempt to expel the French, his former allies, from Italy, and to the break-up of the Holy League which Julius had formed for this purpose.
49. Rightly.
50. Special.
51. That is, holy, Christian.
52. That is, the equator. There is no need of leagues and covenants among "natural" men like the Indians.
53. Legal quibble.
54. Fit.
55. That is, run wild. "To shoot at rovers" was an archery term meaning to shoot an arrow at random and not at any target.
56. That is, that it was bad to have begun the custom of making alliances.

THE LIFE OF JOHN PICUS   569

other, if leagues were not: yea, and that after the leagues be accorded, friendship doth not grow and increase; but the licence of robbing and stealing doth
still remain, as farforth as for lack of foresight and advisement [57] in writing
the words of the league, any sentence or clause to the contrary is not therein
sufficiently comprehended.[58] But they be of a contrary opinion. That is, that no
man ought to be counted an enemy, which hath done no injury. And that the
fellowship of nature is a strong league; and that men be better and more
surely knit together by love and benevolence, than by covenants of leagues;
by hearty affection of mind, than by words.

1515   1516–51

Life of Pico

The example of Giovanni Pico della Mirandola, 1463–94, the Italian nobleman, scholar,
and philosopher, was of the greatest importance for Thomas More. He was the epitome
of the handsome nobleman who was not haughty and proud but delighted in works
of self-abasement and charity, who was learned but not puffed up and impious. He
applied his knowledge of the classical and Eastern languages, and the knowledge he
gained from Jewish scholars and from the Cabbala (Jewish esoteric interpretation of
the Old Testament), to investigating the mysteries of the Christian faith. He died in
the habit of a Dominican friar. His neoplatonic and Cabbalistic philosophy was of
little interest to More, who saw him especially as a man who had achieved the correct
detachment from the things of this world, because of his fervent love of Christ. At the
time when he translated the life of Pico, by Giovanni Francesco Pico della Mirandola,
nephew of the philosopher (written in 1495), More was perhaps still undecided
whether to enter religious life himself. The translation dates from between 1505 and
1510 and was made for Joyce Leigh, a nun. This text is modernized from More's
English *Works*, 1557.

From The Life of John Picus, Earl of Mirandula

Of the Voluntary Affliction and Paining [1] of his Own Body.
Over all this, many times (which is not to be kept secret) he gave alms [2] of his
own body. We know many men which, as Saint Hierom [3] saith, put forth their
hand to poor folk; but with the pleasure of the flesh they be overcomen. But he
many days (and namely those days which represent unto us the passion and
death that Christ suffered for our sake) beat and scourged his own flesh in the
remembrance of that great benefit, and for cleansing of his old offences.

57. Consideration.
58. Contained.

1. That is, beating.
2. That is, expressions of pity for Christ and so for all that are afflicted.
3. St. Jerome (*c.* 342–420), Letter 54: i.e. men will give money and help to poor people,
but will not deny themselves food, drink, and other pleasures, still less afflict themselves
and mortify the flesh in atonement for sin.

Of his Placability or Benign Nature.

He was of cheer[4] alway merry, and of so benign nature that he was never troubled with anger. And he said once to his nephew, that whatsoever should happen (fell there never so great misadventure) he could never, as him thought,[5] be moved to wrath, but if[6] his chests perished, in which his books lay, that he had with great travail and watch[7] compiled. But forasmuch as he considered that he laboured only for the love of God and profit of his church, and that he had dedicate unto him all his works, his studies and his doings; and sith[8] he saw that, sith God is almighty, they could not miscarry but if it were either by his commandment or by his sufferance, he verily trusted, sith God is all good, that he would not suffer him to have that occasion of heaviness. O very happy mind, which none adversity might oppress, which no prosperity might enhance! Not the conning[9] of all philosophy was able to make him proud: not the knowledge of the Hebrew, Chaldee[10] and Arabie[11] language, beside Greek and Latin, could make him vainglorious: not his great substance,[12] not his noble blood, could blow up[13] his heart; not the beauty of his body, not the great occasion of sin, were able to pull him back into the voluptuous broad way that leadeth to hell. What thing was there of so marvellous strength, that might overturn the mind of him which now, as Seneca saith,[14] was gotten above fortune? as he which as well her favour as her malice hath set at nought, that he might be coupled with a spiritual knot unto Christ and his heavenly citizens.

How he eschewed Dignities.

When he saw many men with great labour and money desire and busily purchase the offices and dignities of the church (which are nowadays, alas the while, commonly bought and sold), himself refused to receive them, when two kings offered them. When another man offered him great worldly promotion, if he would go to the king's court, he gave him such an answer, 'that he should well know that he neither desired worship nor worldly riches, but rather set them at nought, that he might the more quietly give himself to study and the service of God.' This wise he persuaded that to a philosopher and him that seeketh for wisdom, it was no praise to gather riches, but to refuse them. . . .

c. 1505–10   1557

4. Behavior.
5. It seemed to him.
6. Unless.
7. Labor and care.
8. Since.
9. Knowledge.
10. Aramaic.
11. Arabic.
12. Wealth.
13. Make proud.
14. Lucius Annaeus Seneca, *c.* 5 B.C.–65 A.D., Roman Stoic philosopher and playwright, tutor to the Emperor Nero. The passage is the last sentence of his dialogue *On the Constancy of a Wise Man*, a favorite Renaissance text.

The History of King Richard III

More's *History of King Richard III* exists in both Latin and English, and was probably written between 1514 and 1518, when the author was much occupied with royal affairs and had just entered the service of Henry VIII, the second monarch of the new Tudor dynasty, established in 1485 by the defeat and death of Richard III, the usurper.

It is Thomas More who is chiefly responsible for the picture of Richard passed on by the propagandists for the Tudor monarchy and picked up by Shakespeare in his *Richard III*—and it may well be that the picture is a true one, though much controversy has ensued about Richard's character. More's detail is often scrupulously correct and he appears to make few mistakes, though he must have been working from hearsay. He used other contemporary historians, but his history is more of a work of art than theirs, with the central character of Richard closely modeled on the portrait of the Emperor Tiberius by the Roman historian Tacitus (b. about 55 A.D.). More takes every opportunity to present Richard as a tyrant and villain.

This text is modernized from More's English *Works,* 1557.

From The History of King Richard III

The Young King and His Brother Murdered

Now fell there mischiefs thick. And as the thing evil gotten is never well kept, through all the time of his reign never ceased there cruel death and slaughter, till his own destruction ended it. But as he finished his time with the best death and the most righteous, that is to wit his own, so began he with the most piteous and wicked, I mean the lamentable murder of his innocent nephews, the young King and his tender brother.[1] Whose death and final infortune hath natheless [2] so far come in question, that some remain yet in doubt whether they were in his days destroyed or no. Not for that only, that Perkin Warbeck [3] (by many folks' malice and more folks' folly, so long space abusing [4] the world) was as well with princes as the poorer people reputed and taken for the younger of those two; but for that also, that all things were in late days so covertly demeaned,[5] one thing pretended and another meant, that there was nothing so plain and openly proved, but that yet for the common custom of close and covert dealing, men had it ever inwardly suspect, as many well-counterfeited jewels make the true mistrusted. Howbeit concerning that opinion,[6] with the occasions moving either party, we shall have place more at large

1. There is still much controversy over whether Richard III was responsible for the murder of his nephews, the young King Edward V and his brother the Duke of York. More's is the fullest account, but it must be hearsay, for he was only five years old in August 1483, when the princes were murdered.
2. Nevertheless.
3. Perkin Warbeck (1474–99), an impostor, who first appeared, claiming the throne as the Duke of York, in 1491. He was aided by the enemies of the new king, Henry VII, who had defeated the usurper Richard III in 1485; but was finally hanged.
4. Deceiving.
5. Secretly carried on.
6. That is, that the Duke of York was still alive.

to entreat, if we hereafter happen to write the time of the late noble prince of famous memory King Henry the Seventh, or percase [7] that history of Perkin in any compendious process [8] by itself. But in the mean time for this present matter, I shall rehearse you the dolorous end of those babes, not after every way that I have heard, but after that way that I have so heard by such men, and by such means, as methinketh it were hard but it should be true.

King Richard after his coronation taking his way to Gloucester, to visit in his new honour the town of which he bare the name of his old,[9] devised, as he rode, to fulfil the thing which he before had intended. And forasmuch as his mind gave him, that his nephews living, men would not reckon that he could have right to the realm, he thought therefore without delay to rid them, as though the killing of his kinsmen could amend his cause and make him a kindly [10] king. Whereupon he sent one John Grene,[11] whom he specially trusted, unto Sir Robert Brakenbery,[12] constable of the Tower, with a letter and credence [13] also, that the same Sir Robert should in any wise put the two children to death. This John Grene did his errand unto Brakenbery kneeling before our Lady [14] in the Tower; who plainly answered that he would never put them to death, to die therefore: [15] with which answer John Grene returning, recounted the same to King Richard at Warwick yet in his way.[16] Wherewith he took such displeasure and thought, that the same night he said unto a secret [17] page of his: 'Ah, whom shall a man trust? Those that I have brought up myself, those that I had went [18] would most surely serve me, even those fail me, and at my commandment will do nothing for me.' 'Sir,' quoth his page, 'there lieth one of your pallet without, that I dare well say, to do your Grace pleasure, the thing were right hard that he would refuse'; meaning this by [19] Sir James Tyrell,[20] which was a man of right goodly personage, and for nature's gifts, worthy to have served a much better prince, if he had well served God, and by grace obtained as much truth and good will as he had strength and wit. The man had an high heart, and sore longed upward, not rising yet so fast as he had hoped, being hindered and kept under by the means of Sir Richard

---

7. Perhaps.
8. Short narrative.
9. That is, he was visiting in his new capacity as King Richard III the town his title had been taken from when he was Duke of Gloucester, Protector of England, during the reign of the child-king Edward V.
10. That is, a king by natural right.
11. Various candidates have been proposed for the owner of this common name.
12. That is, the governor of the Tower, who usually deputed his duties to the lieutenant. He was a creature of Richard's and had just been appointed to the post. He was killed with Richard at the Battle of Bosworth Field (1485).
13. Credentials.
14. That is, Brakenbery was at his devotions.
15. That is, even if he should be put to death for it.
16. That is, still going westward to Gloucester.
17. Intimate.
18. Believed.
19. Referring to.
20. 1445–1502, a strong Yorkist, taken into favor by Henry VII after Richard's death. He had been knighted in 1471, after the Battle of Tewkesbury, not, as More says below, by Richard for the murder of the princes. He was beheaded for treason in 1502.

Ratclife and Sir William Catesby; [21] which longing for no more partners of the Prince's favour, and namely [22] not for him, whose pride they wist would bear no peer,[23] kept him by secret drifts [24] out of all secret trust. Which thing this page well had marked and known. Wherefore this occasion offered of very special friendship, he took his time [25] to put him forward, and by such wise do him good, that all the enemies he had except the devil, could never have done him so much hurt. For upon this page's words King Richard arose . . . and came out into the pallet chamber; on which he found in bed Sir James and Sir Thomas Tyrell,[26] of person like and brethren of blood, but nothing of kin in conditions.[27] Then said the king merrily to them, 'What, sirs, be ye in bed so soon?' and calling up Sir James, brake [28] to him secretly his mind in this mischievous matter. In which he found him nothing strange.[29] Wherefore on the morrow he sent him to Brakenbery with a letter, by which he was commanded to deliver Sir James all the keys of the Tower for one night; to the end he might there accomplish the King's pleasure, in such thing as he had given him commandment. After which letter delivered and the keys received, Sir James appointed the night next ensuing [30] to destroy them, devising before and preparing the means.

The Prince, as soon as the Protector [31] left that name and took himself as King, had it showed unto him that he should not reign, but his uncle should have the crown. At which word the Prince sore abashed began to sigh and said: 'Alas, I would my uncle would let me have my life yet, though I lose my kingdom.' Then he that told him the tale, used him with good words and put him in the best comfort he could. But forthwith was the Prince and his brother both shut up, and all other removed from them, only one called Black Will or William Slaughter [32] except, set to serve them and to see them sure. After which time the Prince never tied his points,[33] nor ought rought [34] of himself, but with that young babe his brother, lingered in thought and heaviness [35] till this traitorous death delivered them of that wretchedness.

For Sir James Tyrell devised that they should be murdered in their beds. To the execution whereof he appointed Miles Forest,[36] one of the four that kept them, a fellow fleshed [37] in murder beforetime. To him he joined one

21. Richard's powerful supporters and most influential counselors, the "Cat" and the "Rat." Ratcliffe was killed at Bosworth, Catesby was executed by Henry VII three days afterward.
22. Especially.
23. They knew would brook no equal.
24. Schemes.
25. That is, when this occasion for getting into truly high favor presented itself, he took his opportunity.
26. Younger brother of Sir James, supporter of Henry VII.
27. Morals, personal qualities.
28. Disclosed to him privately.
29. Unwilling, standoffish.
30. Following.
31. That is, Richard.
32. The name exists in contemporary records.
33. Laces for holding doublet to hose.
34. Took care.
35. Sadness.
36. Also known from the records, like Dighton.
37. Initiated into, inured to.

John Dighton, his own horsekeeper, a big, broad, square, strong knave. Then all the other being removed from them, this Miles Forest and John Dighton about midnight (the sely [38] children lying in their beds) came into the chamber, and suddenly lapped [39] them up among the clothes, so bewrapped them and entangled them, keeping down by force the featherbed and pillows hard unto their mouths, that within a while smored [40] and stifled, their breath failing, they gave up to God their innocent souls into the joys of heaven, leaving to the tormentors their bodies dead in the bed. Which after that the wretches perceived, first by the struggling with the pains of death, and after long lying still to be thoroughly dead, they laid their bodies naked out upon the bed, and fetched Sir James to see them. Which, [41] upon the sight of them, caused those murderers to bury them at the stair foot, meetly [42] deep in the ground under a great heap of stones. Then rode Sir James in great haste to King Richard, and showed him all the manner of the murder; who gave him great thanks and, as some say, there made him knight. But he allowed not, as I have heard, the burying in so vile a corner, saying that he would have them buried in a better place, because they were a King's sons. Lo, the honourable courage [43] of a King! Whereupon, they say that a priest of Sir Robert Brakenbery took up the bodies again, and secretly interred them in such place as, by the occasion of his death which only knew it, could never since come to light. [44] Very truth is it and well knowen, that at such time as Sir James Tyrell was in the Tower for treason committed against the most famous prince King Henry the seventh, both Dighton and he were examined, and confessed the murder in the manner above written; but whither the bodies were removed they could nothing tell.

And thus as I have learned of them that much knew and little cause had to lie, were these two noble princes, these innocent tender children, born of most royal blood, brought up in great wealth, likely long to live to reign and rule in the realm, by traitorous tyranny taken, deprived of their estate, shortly shut up in prison, and privily slain and murdered, their bodies cast God wot [45] where, by the cruel ambition of their unnatural uncle and his dispiteous [46] tormentors. Which things on every part well pondered, God never gave this world a more notable example, neither in what unsurety standeth this worldly weal, [47] or what mischief worketh the proud enterprise [48] of an high heart, or finally what wretched end ensueth such dispiteous cruelty. For first, to begin with the ministers, [49] Miles Forest at Saint Martin's [50] piecemeal rotted away. Dighton indeed yet walketh on alive, in good possibility to be hanged ere he

38. Poor innocent.
39. Bundled.
40. Smothered.
41. Who.
42. Moderately.
43. Heart.
44. Skeletons came to light in 1674 which were identified as the princes'.
45. Knows.
46. Cruel.
47. Prosperity.
48. Undertaking.
49. That is, murderers.
50. St. Martin le Grand, in the City of London, a place of sanctuary—i.e. holy ground, where fugitives from justice, by medieval law, could be safe.

die. But Sir James Tyrell died at Tower Hill,[51] beheaded for treason. King Richard himself, as ye shall hereafter hear, slain in the field,[52] hacked and hewed of his enemies' hands, harried on horseback dead, his hair in despite[53] torn and tugged like a cur dog: and the mischief that he took, within less than three years of the mischief that he did. And yet all the mean time spent in much pain and trouble outward, much fear, anguish, and sorrow within. For I have heard by credible report of such as were secret with his chamberers,[54] that after this abominable deed done, he never had quiet in his mind, he never thought himself sure. Where he went abroad, his eyes whirled about, his body privily fenced,[55] his hand ever on his dagger, his countenance and manner like one alway ready to strike again; he took ill rest a-nights, lay long waking and musing, sore wearied with care and watch, rather slumbered[56] than slept, troubled with fearful dreams, suddenly sometimes started up, leaped out of his bed and ran about the chamber, so was his restless heart continually tossed and tumbled with the tedious[57] impression and stormy remembrance of his abominable deed.

c. 1514–18   1557

The Life of Sir Thomas More

William Roper was probably born in 1496, and married More's favorite daughter Margaret in 1521. He was rescued from the Lutheran heresy by More, became an eminent lawyer and Member of Parliament, and died in 1577. His *Life* of More was probably written about 1555 but not printed until 1626, and is the shortest and best early biography, its spare narrative bringing home the superb and studied dignity of More's trial and death. Roper also took a hand in the preparation of the collected edition of More's English *Works*, 1557. This text is based on that of S. W. Singer (1822), with corrections and interpolations from the edition of E. V. Hitchcock (1935).

51. The hill by the Tower of London, scene of public executions. Tyrell, as a knight, would be beheaded, not hanged.
52. In battle at Bosworth (1485).
53. Contempt.
54. Chamberlains, valets.
55. Secretly protected.
56. Dozed.
57. Painful.

From William Roper's The Life of Sir Thomas More

[The Death of More]

. . . So remained Sir Thomas More [1] in the Tower [2] more than a sevennight [3] after his judgment. From whence, the day before he suffered, [4] he sent his shirt of hair, [5] not willing to have it seen, to my wife, his dearly beloved daughter, and a letter, written with a coal, [6] contained in the foresaid book of his works, [7] plainly expressing the fervent desire he had to suffer on the morrow in these words following: 'I cumber you, good Margaret, much, but I would be sorry if it should be any longer than tomorrow. For tomorrow is St. Thomas' even, [8] and the Octave of St. Peter, [9] and therefore tomorrow long I to go to God; it were a day very meet and convenient for me. I never liked your manner towards me better, than when you kissed me last. For I like when daughterly love, and dear charity hath no leisure to look to worldly courtesy.'

And so upon the next morrow, being Tuesday, St. Thomas' even, and the Octave of St. Peter in the year of our Lord God 1535, according as he in his letter the day before had wished, early in the morning came to him Sir Thomas Pope, [10] his singular [11] friend, on message from the King [12] and his Council, that he should before nine of the clock the same morning suffer death, and that therefore forthwith he should prepare himself thereunto. 'Master Pope,' saith he, 'for your good tidings I most heartily thank you. I have been always much bounden to the King's Highness for the benefits and honours that he hath

1. On false evidence More had been tried and judged guilty of high treason in that he had refused to acknowledge the right of Henry VIII, a temporal king, to govern the church in England.

2. The Tower of London, where offenders against the king who were of the clergy, gentry, or nobility, were imprisoned.

3. More was actually executed not a week, but on the fifth day (July 6, 1535), after his trial.

4. That is, was executed. There is already an element here of seeing More as the saint that the Church made him four hundred years after his death, in 1935. Roper's use of "suffered" may be intended to recall the "passion," i.e. suffering and execution of others—like St. Cyprian below—who had died martyrs for the faith.

5. A shirt woven of hair cloth was worn next to the skin by penitents and religious persons to mortify the flesh, in remembrance of Christ's sufferings. More had attempted to conceal his wearing of such a thing—it was part of his lifelong preparation for death—even from his daughter Margaret, his favorite child.

6. A piece of either charcoal or mineral coal. More had previously been allowed the use of pen and paper and had written a great deal of devotional prose in the Tower.

7. The collected volume of his English writings, published in 1557.

8. The eve of the feast day commemorating removal of St. Thomas Becket's body to its shrine in Canterbury Cathedral in 1220. The martyrdom of St. Thomas (More's patron saint) occurred on December 29, 1170, and is commemorated on that day in the Church's calendar.

9. The eighth day, counting inclusively, after the feast day of St. Peter, the first Bishop of Rome and the first head of the Catholic Church (June 29). To More, St. Peter is a symbol of the unity and inviolability of the church for which he was prepared to die.

10. (1507?–59), a wealthy lawyer, founder of Trinity College, Oxford, and guardian of the young Princess Elizabeth.

11. Special.

12. Henry VIII.

still from time to time most bountifully heaped upon me, and yet more bound [13] I am to his Grace for putting me into this place, where I have had convenient time and space to have remembrance of my end, and so help me God most of all, Master Pope, am I bound to his Highness, that it pleaseth him so shortly to rid me out of the miseries of this wretched world. And therefore will I not fail earnestly to pray for his Grace both here, and also in another world.' 'The King's pleasure is further,' quoth Master Pope, 'that at your execution you shall not use many words'. 'Master Pope' (quoth he), 'you do well to give me warning of his Grace's pleasure. For otherwise I had purposed [14] at that time somewhat to have spoken, but of no matter wherewith his Grace, or any other, should have had cause to be offended. Nevertheless, whatsoever I intended, I am ready obediently to conform myself to his Grace's commandment. And I beseech you, good Master Pope, to be a mean [15] unto his Highness, that my daughter Margaret may be at my burial.' 'The King is content already' (quoth Master Pope) 'that your wife, children, and other your friends shall have liberty to be present thereat.' 'O how much beholden,' then said Sir Thomas More, 'am I to his Grace, that unto my poor burial vouchsafeth to have so gracious consideration.' Wherewithal Master Pope taking his leave of him, could not refrain from weeping, which Sir Thomas More perceiving, comforted him in this wise, 'Quiet yourself, good Master Pope, and be not discomforted. For I trust that we shall, once in heaven, see each other full merrily, where we shall be sure to live and love together in joyful bliss eternally.' Upon whose departure Sir Thomas More, as one that had been invited to some solemn feast, changed himself into his best apparel; which Master Lieutenant [16] espying, advised him to put it off, saying, that he that should have it was but a javel.[17] 'What Master Lieutenant' (quoth he), 'shall I account him a javel, that will do me this day so singular a benefit? [18] Nay, I assure you, were it cloth of gold, I would account it well bestowed on him, as St. Cyprian [19] did, who gave his executioner thirty pieces of gold.' And albeit at length, through Master Lieutenant's importunate persuasion, he altered his apparel, yet, after the example of that holy martyr St. Cyprian, did he of that little money that was left him, send one angel of gold to his executioner. And so was he by Master Lieutenant brought out of the Tower, and from thence led towards the place of execution, where, going up the scaffold, which was so weak that it was ready to fall, he said merrily to Master Lieutenant, 'I pray you, Master Lieutenant, see me safe up, and for my coming down let me shift for myself.' [20] Then desired he all

13. More is making a special point: he was the King's servant as well as his subject and always emphasized that he was so: he depends for all his benefits on the King. He is also emphasizing that he is keeping true order and degree in church and state: Henry is overturning it.
14. Intended.
15. Intermediary.
16. The effective governor of the Tower was so titled.
17. Worthless rogue.
18. That is, by helping him exchange his earthly life for eternal life.
19. Bishop of Carthage, executed 258 A.D., whose writings and views on the unity and powers of the church influenced More.
20. More was famous for his "merry tales" and jokes.

the people thereabout to pray for him, and to bear witness with him, that he should now there suffer death in and for the faith of the holy Catholic Church,[21] which done he kneeled down, and after his prayers said, turned to the executioner, and with a cheerful countenance spake thus to him. 'Pluck up thy spirits, man, and be not afraid to do thine office, my neck is very short. Take heed therefore thou strike not awry for saving of thine honesty.'

So passed Sir Thomas More out of his world to God upon the very same day in which himself had most desired. Soon after whose death came intelligence [22] thereof to the Emperor Charles,[23] whereupon he sent for Sir Thomas Elyot,[24] our English Ambassador, and said unto him, 'My Lord Ambassador, we understand that the King your master hath put his faithful servant and grave wise councillor Sir Thomas More to death.' Whereunto Sir Thomas Elyot answered, that he understood nothing thereof. 'Well,' said the Emperor, 'it is too true, and this will we say, that if we had been master of such a servant, of whose doings ourselves have had these many years no small experience, we would rather have lost the best city of our dominions, than have lost such a worthy councillor.' . . .

c. 1555   1626

SIR THOMAS ELYOT
c. 1490–1546

Born about 1490, probably in Wiltshire, of West Country gentlefolk, Elyot received an informal legal training as Clerk to the Justices of Assize on the Western Circuit (from 1511), and a formal legal education at the Middle Temple in London and at Oxford University. As a young man he came under the influence of Sir Thomas More, and frequented his house in Chelsea, where he met Thomas Linacre, who taught him Greek and medicine, and made the acquaintance of other scholars. Elyot held an important administrative post under Cardinal Wolsey—which he lost at Wolsey's fall in 1530. Retiring to his country estate, he wrote *The Book Named the Governor*, first published in 1531. This, probably together with his friendship with Thomas Cromwell, Henry's adviser, got him the appointment of ambassador to Emperor Charles V in 1531. In 1532 he was recalled from his mission, to pass the rest of his life in semi-retirement.

Elyot made translations from several Greek authors (he held views on the structural relations between the two languages), such as Plutarch, Isocrates, and St. Cyprian, as well as from the Latin of Giovanni Pico della Mirandola. He also compiled, among other works, a Latin-English dictionary (1538) and a medical treatise *The Castle of Health* (1534?). In these, as in *The Governor*, he has constantly before his eyes the responsibility to "divulgate or set forth" the sound and beneficial learning of ancient and modern authors in an English which should be equal in strength and efficacy to its content. One of his methods of achieving the required linguistic solidity was the

21. He was always clear that this was what he was dying for.
22. News.
23. Charles V, Holy Roman Emperor.
24. 1490?–1546. He was not ambassador at Charles's court in 1535, but had been in 1531–32.

imitation of Latin and Greek syntax; another, especially in *The Governor,* was to strengthen the expressive possibilities of English by deliberate borrowing from other languages, carefully signaled either by defining the word in question or by using the new word along with an English word of the same or similar meaning—as in "divulgate or set forth" above.

The Governor begins by defining a public weal—a commonwealth—as "a body living, compact or made of sundry estates and degrees of men, which is disposed by the order of equity and governed by the rule and moderation of reason," in which nobles, commons, and clergy are under the rule of a king, all ranged in and observing the harmony of order and degree which God has ordained. The "inferior governors" to the king are those whose training requires special attention: it is to their education proper from early childhood that Elyot's book, like Plato's before him, is devoted. They begin Latin and Greek at the age of seven and, by allurements rather than by threats and punishments, are taken through Homer, Virgil, Lucian, Aristophanes, Ovid, Cicero, Quintilian, Livy, Xenophon, Caesar, Aristotle, and Plato, so that they will be fully equipped to manage civil and military matters as well as to follow virtue and eschew vice. As a relaxation from serious matters such as these, the aspiring "governor" is to practice music, painting, and sculpture; and to take exercise at hunting, archery, and dancing. But even when taking his exercise, the student must be alive to the moral lessons available. Borrowing the ideas of Lucian of Samosata, Elyot maintains that the base dance (*basse danse*), for example, is no mere frivolous pleasure. Its patterns of movement are intimations of that true and permanent pattern, or Platonic idea, laid up in heaven, of perfect proportion and congruity. It can, besides, teach one lessons about the nature of virtue and its residence in the Aristotelian mean. The final two-thirds of Elyot's book are taken up with a consideration of the virtues necessary to a "governor" and with *exempla* of their exercise—majesty, affability, placability, humanity, benevolence, liberality, amity, justice, faith, fortitude, patience, magnanimity, constancy, temperance, and the rest.

Elyot's aim, as it was later to be Ascham's—and, with differences, Sir Thomas Hoby's —was to provide England with properly and liberally educated servants of the state, to counteract the effects of an aristocracy that despised learning and of a legal-administrative social unit whose training was too narrowly confined to the financially profitable technicalities of the law.

Like Hoby and Ascham, Elyot chose to write in English, for his countrymen, not in Latin for the educated world of Europe: he was less concerned to make England-as-she-was known to the larger learned community. His self-appointed task was to apply the civilizing influence of humanism to English life, so that England would be worthy to take her place at the head of nations.

The text of *The Governor* is based on that of the first edition of 1531. Spelling and punctuation have been modernized.

The Book Named the Governor

From *Book I*

XXI. *Wherefore in the good order of dancing a man and a woman danceth together*

It is diligently to be noted that the associating of man and woman in dancing, they both observing one number and time in their movings, was not begun without a special consideration, as well for the necessary conjunction of those two persons, as for the intimation of sundry virtues which be by them represented. And forasmuch as by the association of a man and a woman in dancing may be signified matrimony, I could in declaring the dignity and commodity [1] of that sacrament make entire volumes, if it were not so commonly known to all men, that almost every friar limiter [2] carrieth it written in his bosom. Wherefore, lest in repeating a thing so frequent and common my book should be as fastidious [3] or fulsome [4] to the readers as such merchant [5] preachers be now to their customers, I will reverently take my leave of divines. And for my part I will endeavour myself to assemble, out of the books of ancient poets and philosophers, matter as well apt [6] to my purpose as also new or at the least ways infrequent, or seldom heard of them that have not read very many authors in Greek and Latin.

But now to my purpose. In every dance, of a most ancient custom, there danceth together a man and a woman, holding each other by the hand or the arm, which betokeneth concord. Now it behoveth the dancers and also the beholders of them to know all qualities incident to a man, and also all qualities to a woman likewise appertaining.

A man in his natural perfection is fierce, hardy, strong in opinion, covetous of glory, desirous of knowledge, appetiting [7] by generation to bring forth his semblable.[8] The good nature of a woman is to be mild, timorous, tractable, benign, of sure remembrance, and shamefast. Divers other qualities of each of them might be found out, but these be most apparent, and for this time sufficient.

Wherefore, when we behold a man and a woman dancing together, let us suppose there to be a concord of all the said qualities, being joined together, as I have set them in order. And the moving of the man would be more vehement, of the woman more delicate, and with less advancing of the body, signifying the courage and strength that ought to be in a man, and the pleasant soberness that should be in a woman. And in this wise fierceness joined with mildness maketh severity; audacity with timorosity maketh magnanimity; wilful opinion and tractability (which is to be shortly persuaded and moved) maketh

---

1. Advantage, profit. Compare T. S. Eliot, *East Coker*—though the dance Elyot describes is not a vigorous country-dance.
2. A friar licensed to beg, hear confessions, and preach within a certain district. Such a person would deal only in the most commonplace and best-known doctrines.
3. Boring.
4. Superfluous.
5. That is, mendicant.
6. Relating.
7. Instinctively desiring, as a natural necessity.
8. That is, a child like him.

constancy a virtue; covetousness of glory adorned with benignity causeth honour; desire of knowledge with sure remembrance procureth sapience; [9] shamefastness joined to appetite of generation maketh continence, which is a mean [10] between chastity and inordinate lust. These qualities, in this wise being knit together and signified in the personages of man and woman dancing, do express or set out the figure of very [11] nobility; which in the higher estate it is contained, the more excellent is the virtue in estimation.

XXII. How dancing may be an introduction unto the first moral virtue, called prudence [12]

As I have already affirmed, the principal cause of this my little enterprise is to declare an induction [13] or mean,[14] how children of gentle nature or disposition may be trained into the way of virtue with a pleasant facility. And for as much as it is very expedient that there be mixed with study some honest [15] and moderate disport,[16] or at the least way recreation, to recomfort and quicken [17] the vital spirits,[18] lest they long travailing,[19] or being much occupied in contemplation or remembrance of things grave and serious, might happen to be fatigued, or perchance oppressed. And therefore Tully,[20] who unneth [21] found ever any time vacant from study, permitteth in his first book of *Offices* [22] that men may use play and disport, yet notwithstanding in such wise as they do use sleep and other manner of quiet, when they have sufficiently disposed earnest matters and of weighty importance.

Now because there is no pastime to be compared to that wherein may be found both recreation and meditation of virtue, I have among all honest pastimes, wherein is exercise of the body, noted dancing to be of an excellent utility, comprehending in it wonderful figures, or, as the Greeks do call them, *ideae*,[23] of virtues and noble qualities, and specially of the commodious [24] virtue called prudence, whom Tully defineth to be the knowledge of things which ought to be desired and followed,[25] and also of them which ought to be fled

---

9. Wisdom.

10. According to Aristotle, *Nicomachean Ethics* II.6 ff., virtue has a disposition to choose the middle between extremes, and finds its true nature in the mean.

11. True.

12. Prudence, wisdom, the first of the cardinal virtues, the others being justice, temperance, and fortitude. According to Aristotle, prudence was the virtue best adapted to the mean.

13. Inducement.

14. Means.

15. Good.

16. Pastime.

17. Enliven.

18. The rarefied substances which, according to medieval and Renaissance medicine, were sent from the heart by the arteries and pulses, so that they permeated the body and kept it vigorous. Overmuch study was held to be one of the greatest and most deadening dangers to the vital spirits.

19. Working, laboring.

20. Marcus Tullius Cicero.

21. Scarcely.

22. *De Officiis* (Of Moral Duties) I.29.

23. Ideal patterns.

24. Advantageous, beneficial.

25. *De Officiis* I.43.

from or eschewed. And it is named of Aristotle the mother of virtues;[26] of other philosophers it is called the captain or mistress of virtues; of some the housewife, for as much as by her diligence she doth investigate and prepare places apt and convenient, where other virtues shall execute their powers or offices. Wherefore, as Solomon saith,[27] like as in water be shown the visages of them that behold it, so unto men that be prudent the secrets of men's hearts be openly discovered. This virtue being so commodious to man, and, as it were, the porch of the noble palace of man's reason, whereby all other virtues shall enter, it seemeth to me right expedient, that as soon as opportunity may be found, a child or young man be thereto induced. And because that the study of virtue is tedious for the more part to them that do flourish in young years, I have devised how in the form of dancing, now late used in this realm among gentlemen, the whole description of this virtue prudence may be found out and well perceived, as well by the dancers as by them which standing by will be diligent beholders and markers, having first mine instruction surely graven in the table of their remembrance. Wherefore all they that have their courage stirred toward very honour or perfect nobility, let them approach to this pastime, and either themselves prepare them to dance, or else at the least way behold with watching eyes other that can dance truly, keeping just measure and time. But to the understanding of this instruction, they must mark well the sundry motions and measures, which in true form of dancing is to be specially observed.

The first moving in every dance is called honour,[28] which is a reverent inclination or curtsey, with a long deliberation or pause, and is but one motion, comprehending the time of three other motions, or setting forth of the foot. By that may be signified that at the beginning of all our acts, we should do due honour to God, which is the root of prudence; which honour is compact of these three things, fear, love, and reverence. And that in the beginning of all things we should advisedly, with some tract[29] of time, behold and foresee the success of our enterprise.

By the second motion,[30] which is two in number, may be signified celerity and slowness: which two, albeit they seem to discord in their effects and natural properties, and therefore they may be well resembled to the brawl[31] in dancing (for in our English tongue we say men do brawl, when between them is altercation in words), yet of them two springeth an excellent virtue whereunto we lack a name in English.

26. *Magna Moralia*, I.35.
27. Proverbs 27:19: "As in the water face answereth to face, so the heart of man to man."
28. "Honour" was the first movement of the base dance, a "grave and slow" dance in which the feet did not leave the ground. The man made his reverence by keeping the left foot firm on the floor, bending the right knee and placing the right foot behind the left leg, meanwhile saluting the company and his partner by taking off his hat. According to Elyot, the reverence occupies the time taken by three steps of the dance itself.
29. Delay.
30. The step known as "braule," one of the four basic steps in the base dance (Elyot makes them eight), which normally came either immediately after the reverence, or at the end of the dance, or both.
31. Elyot seems to be saying that the brawl is second in order, that movement is either fast or slow, that these are two opposites, and that they are therefore susceptible to mediation by the mean.

Wherefore I am constrained to usurp a Latin word,[32] calling it maturity: which word, though it be strange and dark, yet by declaring the virtue in a few more words, the name once brought in custom, shall be facile to understand as other words late coming out of Italy and France, and made denizens[33] among us.

Maturity[34] is a mean between two extremities, wherein nothing lacketh or exceedeth, and is in such estate that it may neither increase nor minish[35] without losing the denomination of maturity. The Greeks in a proverb do express it properly in two words, which I can none otherwise interpret in English, but 'Speed thee slowly.'[36]

Also of this word maturity sprang a noble and precious sentence,[37] recited by Sallust in the *Battle against Catiline*,[38] which is in this manner or like, 'Consult before thou enterprise anything, and after thou hast taken counsel, it is expedient to do it maturely.'

Maturum in Latin may be interpreted ripe or ready, as fruit when it is ripe, it is at the very point to be gathered and eaten. And every other thing, when it is ready, it is at the instant after to be occupied. Therefore that word maturity is translated to the acts of man, that when they be done with such moderation that nothing in the doing may be seen superfluous or indigent,[39] we may say that they be maturely done: reserving the words ripe and ready to fruit and other things separate from affairs, as we have now in usage. And this do I now remember for the necessary augmentation of our language.

In the most excellent and most noble emperor Octavius Augustus, in whom reigned all nobility, nothing is more commended than that he had frequently in his mouth this word *Matura*, 'Do maturely.'[40] As he should have said, 'Do neither too much nor too little, too soon nor too late, too swiftly nor slowly, but in due time and measure.'

Now I trust I have sufficiently expounded the virtue called maturity, which is the mean or mediocrity between sloth and celerity, commonly called speediness; and so have I declared what utility may be taken of a brawl in dancing.

1531

---

32. Elyot's method for augmentation and enrichment of the English language was to introduce a Latin word along with an English equivalent or explanation, so as to ease the process of assimilation.

33. Naturalized aliens.

34. Elyot probably took the word from the Roman encyclopedist Aulus Gellius' (*c.* 123–165 A.D.) *Attic Nights* X.11.

35. Diminish.

36. Speude bradeōs, as "Festina lente," a favorite saying of the Emperor Augustus.

37. Wise saying.

38. The *Bellum Catilinae* I.1, by the Roman historian Gaius Sallustius Crispus (86–34 B.C.).

39. Lacking.

40. Also from Aulus Gellius; cf. Suetonius (*c.* 69–*c.* 140 A.D.), *Life of Octavius Augustus* XXV.

BALDASSARE CASTIGLIONE
1478–1529

SIR THOMAS HOBY
1530–1566

Castiglione was born in Mantuan territory in 1478, his mother being a member of the Gonzaga family, lords of Mantua. He was educated in Milan under celebrated humanist teachers and later established himself at the court of Urbino, which Duke Federigo da Montefeltro, the great *condottiere* and patron of learning (1422–82: Fig. 4) himself the pupil of the greatest educators of his day, had made one of the most famous in Italy for all the peaceful and military arts. During the years he spent there, from 1504 until 1513, Castiglione served the reigning duke, Guidobaldo, as ambassador in France and England and wrote *Il Cortegiano*. In 1513, he was sent as ambassador from Urbino to the court of Pope Leo X, brother of Giuliano de' Medici, the Lord Julian of *The Courtier*. Here he became a friend of the painter Raphael (Fig. 5). Castiglione had married in 1516, and on the death of his wife after only four years of marriage he entered the priesthood and was sent as Papal Nuncio to Spain, where he won the friendship of Emperor Charles V. The sack of Rome by the Emperor's troops in 1527 affected Castiglione deeply: it signified—as it did for Sir Thomas More—the death of what he had lived and worked for, a truly Christian Europe, united and at peace with itself spiritually and materially. He retired from the imperial court and died at Toledo early in 1529.

Il Cortegiano was one of the most influential and most famous products of the Italian Renaissance: its examination of the make-up of the perfect courtier provided a much more exalted and sophisticated model for imitation than had hitherto been available—or indeed than was set out in its successors, such as Giovanni della Casa's *Galateo* or Stefano Guazzo's *Civile Converzatione*. It is, in form, a record of the discussions of four successive evenings by one of those assemblies of learned and cultured men for which the Duchess of Urbino, with the aid of the Lady Emilia de' Pii, had made Urbino famous. Castiglione himself modestly pretends to have been absent from among his friends on the occasion. They discussed, on the first evening, the birth and education of the perfect courtier; on the second, his social experience and behavior in the daily circumstances of life, and the accomplishments that he ought to cultivate; on the third, the perfection of the noblewoman. On the fourth evening— from whose record our extract is taken—the Platonist Pietro Bembo defined the nature of love and its power to ennoble, a favorite topic of philosophic discourse in the Renaissance.

Castiglione's views on *cortegiania*—"the form of courtiership most befitting a gentle- man who lives in the courts of princes, through which he may know how to serve them perfectly in everything which is according to reason, so as to win favour from them and praise from others"—became those of Europe. Ophelia's praise of Hamlet is a kind of paraphrase of them:

> The courtier's, soldier's, scholar's, eye, tongue, sword:
> The expectancy and rose of the fair state,
> The glass of fashion and the mould of form.

Gabriel Harvey's note in his copy of Sir Thomas Hoby's translation, too, sums up the book and its ethos well, and we can be sure that it found its echo in the mind of

Harvey's friend Edmund Spenser: "Above all things it importeth a courtier to be graceful and lovely in countenance and behaviour; fine and discreet in discourse and entertainment; skilful and expert in letters and arms; active and gallant in every courtly exercise; nimble and speedy of body and mind; resolute, industrious and valorous in action; as profound and invincible in action as is possible; and withal ever generously bold, wittily pleasant, and full of life in his sayings and doings." It is to men such as this, who by elaborating and transforming the mediaeval chivalric ideal to realize their full potential for virtuous action in arts and arms, that others looked for the improvement of the quality of English life.

This was what Sir Thomas Hoby hoped his translation might effect. He may have come across the original before he began the travels in Germany, France, and Italy by which he completed the education begun at St. John's College, Cambridge, the Renaissance stronghold of Protestant scholarship, in 1545. But it is more likely that he did not make its acquaintance until he had reached Italy, by which time the book itself was some forty years old. Castiglione had written it between 1508 and 1516, though it had not been published until 1528, after long revision and circulation, in the Renaissance fashion, among his friends. Hoby's is a young man's work: his spirited translation reflects his enthusiasm for Italy and the impact made on him by the nobility of the original as well as the fact that he was, as his friend Roger Ascham put it, "well furnished with learning and very expert in knowledge of divers tongues." This knowledge was to serve him well later, when, after Elizabeth's succession and the re-establishment of Protestantism, he became a public servant. Hoby was English ambassador when he died at Paris in 1566. His translation, complete by 1554, when he was twenty-four, was not published until 1561.

The Book of the Courtier

Hoby's book is the first translation of a secular work which can be called a masterpiece of English prose, but important and influential as it is in this respect, it owed its popularity—and the four editions of 1561, 1577, 1588, and 1603 which it went through during Elizabeth's reign—chiefly to its doctrine. It would be, he felt, useful to all men. It would tell princes truths that their advisers dared not utter; it would be the cause of useful reflection in older men and, most important of all, it would be for young gentlemen "an encouraging to garnish their minds with moral virtues, and their bodies with comely exercises, and . . . both . . . with honest qualities." To ladies and gentlemen it would be "a mirror to deck and tire themselves with virtuous conditions, comely behaviour and honest entertainment toward all men." To every reader it would be "a storehouse of most necessary implements for the conversation, use and training up of man's life with courtly demeanours."

Hoby's purpose is patriotic, as his use of English itself would show. But language was the means to an end. He wants Englishmen to have the best of it, to have this valuable doctrine in their own tongue. Translation, according to others, he says, injures memory and hinders learning; for his part, he sees it as performing the exact opposite. The more members of the nobility and gentry to whom such excellent reading is available, the better. Like Sir Thomas Elyot, he believed that if only each of our learned men would "store the tongue according to his knowledge and delight above other men" with good content and good language, England would soon become the equal of the ancient commonwealths of Greece and Rome for wisdom and power, and English the equal of the ancient languages for eloquence. Hoby was less concerned than Elyot to naturalize words from other languages, and had some sympathy with the purist principles of Sir John Cheke (his Cambridge mentor and later his friend) as they are expressed in Cheke's prefatory letter to *The Courtier*. He did not, however, go all the way with Cheke in wishing English written pure, "unmixed and unmangled with borrowing of other tongues."

This linguistic patriotism, a marked feature of sixteenth-century humanism in Italy, Spain, France, and Germany, as well as England, is more explicit in Hoby than in Castiglione. On the other hand, the element of philosophic discussion, of embodiment of the ideal, though inevitably present, is subtly altered by the translation. *The Courtier* is more sophisticated, less earnest, than Elyot's *Governor* in its purpose, but Hoby has broadened, almost moralized, his original: his book was for the many, not the few. It was intended to help in the fashioning of a class of living men who would be fit, by the refinement of their natures brought about by their practice of virtue and the completeness of their education, to be the guides of the life of a country which had now entered into her full share of greatness. It was intended for the social unit of hereditary nobility and gentry combined, who were the rulers, under the monarch, of Tudor England.

Other translators followed Hoby's lead: Robert Peterson in 1576 with a version of Della Casa's *Galateo*, and George Pettie and Bartholomew Young with their rendering of Guazzo's *Civile Conversatione* in 1581–86. Both texts are more restricted in their scope and neither had the impact of Hoby's *Courtier*.

The most famous passage in *The Courtier* is Cardinal Bembo's superbly eloquent exposition of the nature of love according to the philosophy of neoplatonism, which concludes the fourth and final book just as the new day is beginning to show itself. True love, he tells the company, is born of the intellectual perception of the beautiful, which is also the good. It is this which can make a man more like an angel than the beast he resembles if he stops short in mere earthly love and the gratification of the senses. In true love, he is united with the divine. His soul desires the immortal, unchanging, ideal beauty that it knew before its descent into the gross material of the body.

The extract from Bembo's speech here given begins with a difficulty, raised by one of the speakers in the dialogue. It looks as if, he is made to say, the ideal courtier will have to be an older man, since the knowledge and counsel which are the essential part of his make-up are the virtues of maturity: they take time to acquire. Will this, the question is, make him unapt for love and to that extent a less than perfect courtier?

The text is that of the first edition as reprinted in the series *Tudor Translations*, 1900. Spelling and punctuation have been modernized.

The Book of the Courtier

From *Book IV*

Then M. Peter [1] after a while's silence, somewhat settling himself as though he should entreat upon [2] a weighty matter, said thus: 'My lords, to show that old men may love not only without slander, but otherwhile [3] more happily than young men, I must be enforced to make a little discourse to declare what love is, and wherein consisteth the happiness that lovers may have. Therefore I beseech you give the hearing with heedfulness, for I hope to make you understand that it were not unfitting for any man here to be a lover, in case he were fifteen or twenty years elder than M. Morello.' [4]

And here, after they had laughed awhile, M. Peter proceeded: 'I say, therefore, that according as it is defined of the wise men of old time,[5] love is nothing else but a certain coveting to enjoy beauty; and forsomuch as coveting longeth for nothing but for things known,[6] it is requisite that knowledge go evermore before coveting,[7] which of his own nature willeth the good,[8] but of himself is blind and knoweth it not. Therefore hath nature so ordained that to every virtue of knowledge [9] there is annexed a virtue of longing. And because in our soul there be three manner [10] ways to know, namely, by sense, reason, and understanding: [11] of sense there ariseth appetite or longing, which is common to us with brute beasts; of reason ariseth election or choice, which is proper to man; of understanding, by the which man may be partner with angels, ariseth

1. Master Peter is Pietro Bembo (1470–1547), the Venetian humanist scholar, poet, prose writer, historian, later a cardinal, whose most famous work, *Gli Asolani,* is a series of dialogues on the nature of love. Bembo, a Platonist in philosophy, is here expounding a doctrine of love which is based ultimately on Plato, especially on his *Symposium* and *Phaedrus,* but owes much to Renaissance commentators on them, especially to Marsilio Ficino (1433–99), the Florentine neoplatonist philosopher. There are also similarities with other Renaissance neoplatonist works, such as the *De Amore* (On Love) of Francesco Cattani da Diacceto.
2. Handle, deal with.
3. Sometimes.
4. Morello de' Riccardi da Ortona, elderly soldier of fortune and courtier, a skilled musical performer, later intervenes in the discussion. His contention is that old men can love as hotly and sensuously as young.
5. That is, especially Plato.
6. That is, perceived by the senses.
7. That is, we must perceive before we can desire.
8. Wishes for the good.
9. Power, faculty of perception.
10. Kinds of.
11. If we perceive only through the senses, so that our passions or appetites are roused, we are no better than the beasts, in whom the same process can take place. If, by the exercise of our reason, which is what distinguishes man from the beasts, we perceive that we have an alternative and exercise our power of choice, we have moved away from bestiality to human, rational behavior. If our perceptions are intellectual, via the understanding, we can grasp the true nature of things, and our will must necessarily become set on such things, i.e. on the divine ideas. In desiring these, we become like the angels. See Pico della Mirandola in *On the Dignity of Man,* where God tells man: "You shall have the power to degenerate to the lower brutish forms of life; and you shall also have the power to be reborn to the higher, or divine, according to the judgment [i.e. choice] of your soul."

will.[12] Even as therefore the sense knoweth not but sensible matters and that which may be felt, so the appetite or coveting only desireth the same; and even as the understanding is bent but to behold things that may be understood, so is that will only fed with spiritual goods. Man of nature endowed with reason, placed, as it were, in the middle between these two extremities, may, through his choice inclining to sense or reaching to understanding, come nigh to the coveting, sometime of the one, sometime of the other part. In these sorts therefore may beauty be coveted, the general name whereof may be applied to all things, either natural or artificial, that are framed in good proportion and due temper,[13] as their nature beareth.

'But speaking of the beauty that we mean, which is only it that appeareth in bodies, and especially in the face of man, and moveth this fervent coveting which we call love, we will term it an influence of the heavenly bountifulness, the which for all it stretcheth over all things that be created (like the light of the sun), yet when it findeth out a face well proportioned, and framed with a certain lively agreement of several colours, and set forth with lights and shadows, and with an orderly distance and limits of lines,[14] thereinto it distilleth itself and appeareth most well favoured, and decketh out and lighteneth the subject where it shineth with a marvellous grace and glistering, like the sun-beams that strike against beautiful plate of fine gold wrought and set with precious jewels, so that it draweth unto it men's eyes with pleasure, and piercing through them, imprinteth himself in the soul, and with an unwonted sweetness all to-stirreth [15] her and delighteth, and setting her on fire maketh her to covet him. When the soul then is taken with coveting to enjoy this beauty as a good thing, in case she suffer herself to be guided with the judgment of sense, she falleth into most deep errors, and judgeth the body in which beauty is discerned to be the principal cause thereof; whereupon to enjoy it she reckoneth it neces-sary to join as inwardly as she can with that body, which is false; and therefore whoso thinketh in possessing the body to enjoy beauty, he is far deceived, and is moved to it, not with true knowledge by the choice of reason, but with false opinion by the longing of sense. Whereupon the pleasure that followeth it is also false and of necessity full of errors. And therefore into one of the two vices run all those lovers that satisfy their unhonest [16] lusts with the women whom they love; for either as soon as they come to the coveted end, they not only feel a fullness and loathsomeness, but also conceive a hatred against the wight [17] beloved, as though longing repented him of his offence and acknowl-edged the deceit wrought him by the false judgment of sense, that made him believe the ill to be good, or else they continue in the very same coveting and greediness, as though they were not indeed come to the end which they sought for. And albeit through the blind opinion that hath made them drunken

12. According to Ficino, intellect (understanding) is pure and refined will.
13. That is, the best balance of elements, the constituents of all matter (earth, water, fire, and air), and of qualities (hot, cold, moist, dry), which determine the nature of all created things.
14. Outlines.
15. Moves strongly.
16. Morally wrong.
17. Person.

(to their seeming) [18] in that instant they feel a contentation,[19] as the diseased otherwhile, that dream they drink of some clear spring, yet be they not satisfied, nor leave off so. And because of possessing coveted goodness there arises always quietness and satisfaction in the possessor's mind, in case this were the true and right end of their coveting, when they possess it they would be at quietness and thoroughly satisfied, which they be not: but rather deceived through that likeness, they forthwith return again to unbridled coveting, and with the very same trouble which they felt at the first, they fall again into the raging and most burning thirst of the thing, that they hope in vain to possess perfectly.

'These kinds of lovers therefore love most unluckily,[20] for either they never come by their covetings, which is a great unluckiness, or else if they do come by them, they find they come by their hurt and end their miseries with other greater miseries, for both in the beginning and middle of this love, there is never other thing felt but afflictions, torments, griefs, pining, travail, so that to be wan, vexed with continual tears and sighs, to live with a discontented mind, to be always dumb, or to lament, to covet death, in conclusion to be most unlucky, are the properties which, they say, belong to lovers.

'The cause therefore of this wretchedness in men's minds is principally sense, which in youthful age beareth most sway, because the lustiness of the flesh and of the blood in that season addeth unto him even so much force as it withdraweth from reason. Therefore doth it easily train the soul to follow appetite or longing, for when she seeth herself drowned in the earthly prison, because she is set in the office to govern the body, she cannot of herself understand plainly at the first the truth of spiritual beholding. Wherefore to compass the understanding of things, she must go beg the beginning at the senses, and therefore she believeth them and giveth ear to them, and is contented to be led by them, especially when they have so much courage, that (in a manner) they enforce [21] her, and because they be deceitful they fill her with errors and false opinions. Whereupon most commonly it happeneth that young men be wrapped in this sensual love, which is a very rebel against reason, and therefore they make themselves unworthy to enjoy the favours and benefits which love bestoweth upon his true subjects. Neither in love feel they any other pleasures than what beasts without reason do, but much more grievous afflictions.

'Setting case therefore this to be so, which is most true, I say that the contrary chanceth to them of a more ripe age. For in case they, when the soul is not now so much weighed down with the bodily burden, and when the natural burning assuageth and draweth to [22] a warmth, if they be inflamed with beauty, and to it bend their coveting guided by reasonable choice, they be not deceived, and possess beauty perfectly, and therefore through the possessing of it, always goodness ensueth to them. Because beauty is good [23] and

18. Appearance.
19. Satisfaction.
20. Unhappily.
21. Take by violence, rape.
22. Approaches, becomes.
23. The identity of beauty and goodness is fundamental to Platonism: the beauty of earthly things should recall to the soul its memory of true, heavenly beauty.

consequently the true love of it is most good and holy, and evermore bringeth forth good fruits in the souls of them that with the bridle of reason [24] restrain the ill disposition of sense, the which old men can much sooner do than young.

'It is not therefore out of reason to say that old men may also love without slander and more happily than young men, taking notwithstanding this name old, not for the age at the pit's brink, nor when the canals [25] of the body be so feeble, that the soul cannot through them work her feats,[26] but when knowledge in us is in his right strength. And I will not also hide this from you: namely, that I suppose where sensual love in every age is naught,[27] yet in young men it deserveth excuse, and perhaps in some cases lawful; [28] for although it putteth them in afflictions, dangers, travails, and the unfortunateness that is said, yet are there many that to win them the goodwill of their ladies practise virtuous things, which for all they be not bent to a good end, yet are they good of themselves; and so of that much bitterness they pick out a little sweetness, and through the adversities which they sustain, in the end they acknowledge their error. As I judge therefore those young men that bridle their appetites, and love with reason, to be godly; so do I hold excused such as yield to sensual love, whereunto they be so inclined through the weakness and frailty of man—so [29] they show therein meekness, courtesy, and prowess, and the other worthy conditions that these lords have spoken of; and when those youthful years be gone and past, leave it off clean, keeping aloof from this sensual coveting as from the lowermost step of the stairs, by the which a man may ascend to true love. But in case after they draw in [30] years, once they reserve [31] in their cold heart the fire of appetites, and bring stout reason in subjection to feeble sense, it cannot be said how much they are to be blamed: for like men without sense they deserve with an everlasting shame to be put in the number of unreasonable living creatures, because the thoughts and ways of sensual love be far unsitting for ripe age.'

Here Bembo paused awhile, as though he would breathe him, and when all things were whist [32] M. Morello of Ortona said: 'And in case there were some old man more fresh and lusty and of a better complexion [33] than many young men, why would you not have it lawful for him to love with the love that young men love?'

The Duchess [34] laughed, and said: 'If the love of young men be so unlucky,

---

24. The metaphor comes ultimately from Plato's *Phaedrus,* but the actual expression "bridle of reason" is in Seneca, *Dialogues* III.iii.7 ("On Anger" I.7).

25. Passages along which the "spirits," the refined substances which permeate the body and make it live and act, can travel.

26. Perform its operations.

27. Wrong, worthless.

28. That is, rightly.

29. As long as.

30. Advance in.

31. Retain.

32. Quiet.

33. Bodily make-up.

34. Elisabetta Gonzaga (1471–1526), the beautiful and gifted wife of Guidobaldo da Montefeltro, Duke of Urbino, whose court, like that of his father Federigo, was famous for its splendor and love of learning. It was the custom of the guests there to meet in the evening after supper for music, dancing, and discussion, presided over by the Duchess, of subjects proposed by her.

why would you, M. Morello, that old men should also love with this unluckiness? But in case you were old, as these men say you be, you would not thus
procure the hurt of old men.'

M. Morello answered: 'The hurt of old men, meseemeth, M. Peter Bembo
procureth, who will have them to love after a sort that I for my part understand not; and, methink,[35] the possessing of this beauty which he praiseth so
much, without the body, is a dream.'

'Do you believe, M. Morello,' quoth then Count Lewis,[36] 'that beauty is
always so good a thing as M. Peter Bembo speaketh of?'

'Not I, in good sooth,' answered M. Morello. 'But I remember rather that I
have seen many beautiful women of a most ill inclination, cruel and spiteful,
and it seemeth that, in a manner, it happeneth always so, for beauty maketh
them proud, and pride, cruel.'

Count Lewis said, smiling: 'To you perhaps they seem cruel, because they
content you not with it that you would have. But cause M. Peter Bembo to
teach you in what sort old men ought to covet beauty, and what to seek at
their ladies' hands, and what to content themselves withal; and in not passing
out of these bounds you shall see that they shall be neither proud nor cruel,
and will satisfy you with what you shall require.'

M. Morello seemed then somewhat out of patience, and said: 'I will not
know the thing that toucheth [37] me not. But cause you to be taught how the
young men ought to covet this beauty that are not so fresh and lusty as old
men be.'

Here Sir Frederick,[38] to pacify M. Morello and to break their talk, would not
suffer Count Lewis to make answer, but interrupting him said: 'Perhaps M.
Morello is not altogether out of the way in saying that beauty is not always
good, for the beauty of women is many times cause of infinite evils in the
world—hatred, war, mortality, and destruction, whereof the razing of Troy [39]
can be a good witness; and beautiful women for the most part be either proud
and cruel, as is said, or unchaste; but M. Morello would find no fault with that.
There be also many wicked men that have the comeliness of a beautiful countenance, and it seemeth that nature hath so shaped them because they may be
the readier to deceive, and that this amiable look were like a bait that covereth
the hook.'

Then M. Peter Bembo: 'Believe not,' quoth he, 'but beauty is always good.'

Here Count Lewis, because he would return again to his former purpose,
interrupted him and said: 'Since M. Morello passeth [40] not to understand that
which is so necessary for him, teach it me, and show me how old men may

---

35. It seems to me.
36. Count Lodovico of Canossa (1476–1532), another of those attracted to the court of
Urbino by its reputation for learning and refinement, came of a Veronese family. He was
a relation and a close friend of Castiglione's, and became bishop of Tricarico and papal
emissary to France. In France he became bishop of Bayeux and acted as ambassador for
the French king to the pope.
37. Concerns.
38. Federigo Fregoso (b. 1480), soldier and poet, a relative of the Duke's, in exile from
Genoa; later nominated archbishop of Salerno and became bishop of Gubbio.
39. On account of Helen.
40. That is, cares.

come by this happiness of love, for I will not care to be counted old, so it may profit me.' [41]

M. Peter Bembo laughed, and said: 'First will I take the error out of these gentlemen's mind, and afterward will I satisfy you also.' So beginning afresh: 'My Lords,' quoth he, 'I would not that with speaking all of beauty, which is a holy thing, any of us, as profane and wicked, should purchase him the wrath of God. Therefore, to give M. Morello and Sir Frederick warning, that they lose not their sight, as Stesichorus [42] did—a pain most meet for whoso dispraiseth beauty—I say that beauty cometh of God and is like a circle, the goodness whereof is the centre. And therefore, as there can be no circle without a centre, no more can beauty be without goodness. Whereupon doth very seldom an ill soul dwell in a beautiful body. And therefore is the outward beauty a true sign of the inward goodness, and in bodies this comeliness is imprinted, more and less, as it were, for a mark of the soul, whereby she is outwardly known; as in trees, in which the beauty of the buds giveth a testimony of the goodness of the fruit. And the very same happeneth in bodies, as it is seen that palmisters [43] by the visage know many times the conditions and otherwhile the thoughts of men. And, which is more, in beasts also a man may discern by the face the quality of the courage, which in the body declareth itself as much as it can. Judge you how plainly in the face of a lion, a horse, and an eagle, a man shall discern anger, fierceness, and stoutness; [44] in lambs and doves, simpleness and very [45] innocency; the crafty subtlety in foxes and wolves; and the like, in a manner, in all other living creatures.

'The foul,[46] therefore, for the most part be also evil, and the beautiful good. Therefore it may be said that beauty is a face pleasant, merry, comely, and to be desired for goodness; and foulness a face dark, uglesome, unpleasant, and to be shunned for ill. And in case you will consider all things, you shall find that whatsoever is good and profitable hath also evermore the comeliness of beauty. Behold the state of this great engine [47] of the world, which God created for the health and preservation of everything that was made: the

41. That is, as long as good may come of it for me, I shall not care if I am thought old.
42. Hoby's note: "a notable poet which lost his sight for writing against Helena and recanting had his sight restored him again." He lived probably during the 6th century B.C. Plato tells the story in his *Phaedrus* 243a.
43. That is, physiognomists, who professed to read the outward characteristics of the body as indications of the soul and interior constitution.
44. Courage.
45. Real, true.
46. Ugly.
47. "Universal frame"; cf. Lucretius' *machina mundi*. This part of Bembo's speech, on fitness, harmony, and proportion in all things, is imitated from Cicero's *De Oratore*, III.45, where Cicero is arguing that nature has contrived that what is useful is also dignified and beautiful. The map of the universe that is described is the pre-Copernican, "Ptolemaic," so called after the Greek astronomer and mathematician Claudius Ptolemaeus (2nd century A.D.). See Fig. 1. The cosmos has earth at its center, surrounded by the spheres of the other elements—water, air, and fire—in concentric circles. These are in turn surrounded, in this simplified diagram, by the spheres of the planets, seven in all, beginning with the moon. After these comes the firmament, with the signs of the zodiac; then the crystalline sphere and the sphere of the *primum mobile* (first moving), which governs the orbits of all the others. They are presided over by God, the unmoved, Prime Mover.

heaven round beset with so many heavenly lights; and in the middle the earth environed with the elements and upheld with the very weight of itself; the sun, that compassing about giveth light to the whole, and in winter season draweth to the lowermost sign, afterward by little and little climbeth again to the other part; the moon, that of him taketh her light, according as she draweth nigh or goeth farther from him; and the other five stars that diversely keep the very same course. These things among themselves have such force by the knitting together of an order so necessarily framed that, with altering them any one jot, they should all be loosed and the world would decay. They have also such beauty and comeliness that all the wits men have cannot imagine a more beautiful matter.

'Think now of the shape of man, which may be called a little world,[48] in whom every parcel [49] of his body is seen to be necessarily framed by art and not by hap,[50] and then the form altogether most beautiful, so that it were a hard matter to judge whether the members (as the eyes, the nose, the mouth, the ears, the arms, the breast, and in like manner the other parts) give either more profit [51] to the countenance and the rest of the body, or comeliness. The like may be said of all other living creatures. Behold the feathers of fowls, the leaves and boughs of trees, which be given them of nature to keep them in their being, and yet have they withal [52] a very great sightliness.

'Leave nature, and come to art. What thing is so necessary in sailing vessels as the forepart, the sides, the main yards, the mast, the sails, the stern, oars, anchors, and tacklings? All these things notwithstanding are so well-favoured in the eye that unto whoso beholdeth them they seem to have been found out as well for pleasure as for profit. Pillars and great beams uphold high buildings and palaces, and yet are they no less pleasureful unto the eyes of the beholders than profitable to the buildings. When men began to build, in the middle of temples and houses they reared the ridge of the roof, not to make the works to have a better show, but because the water might the more commodiously avoid [53] on both sides; yet unto profit there was forthwith adjoined a fair sightliness, so that if, under the sky where there falleth neither hail nor rain, a man should build a temple without a reared ridge, it is to be thought that it could have neither a sightly show nor any beauty.

'Beside other things, therefore, it giveth a great praise to the world in saying that it is beautiful. It is praised in saying the beautiful heaven, beautiful earth, beautiful sea, beautiful rivers, beautiful woods, trees, gardens, beautiful cities, beautiful churches, houses, armies. In conclusion, this comely and holy beauty is a wondrous setting out of everything. And it may be said that good and beautiful be after a sort one self thing, especially in the bodies of men; of

48. The microcosm, man, framed by God with the same exactness and proportion as the universe, the macrocosm, all the parts and motions of one corresponding to those of the other, the body corresponding to the sensible, the soul to the intelligible world. Democritus, the pre-Socratic philosopher, is said to have originated the term microcosm; its first actual appearance is in Aristotle, *Physics* VIII.8. (See also Glossary.)
49. Part.
50. Chance.
51. Use.
52. Moreover.
53. Escape. Bembo is still quoting Cicero, *De Oratore* III.45.

the beauty whereof the nighest cause, I suppose, is the beauty of the soul; [54] the which, as a partner of the right and heavenly beauty, maketh sightly and beautiful whatever she toucheth, and most of all, if the body, where she dwelleth, be not of so vile a matter that she cannot imprint in it her property. Therefore beauty is the true monument and spoil of the victory of the soul, when she with heavenly influence beareth rule over material and gross nature, and with her light overcometh the darkness of the body.

'It is not, then, to be spoken that beauty maketh women proud or cruel, although it seem so to M. Morello. Neither yet ought beautiful women to bear the blame of that hatred, mortality,[55] and destruction which the unbridled appetites of men are the cause of. I will not now deny but it is possible also to find in the world beautiful women unchaste; yet not because beauty inclineth them to unchaste living, for it rather plucketh them from it, and leadeth them into the way of virtuous conditions, through the affinity that beauty hath with goodness; but otherwhile ill bringing up, the continual provocations of lovers' tokens, poverty, hope, deceits, fear, and a thousand other matters, overcome the steadfastness, yea, of beautiful and good women; and for these and like causes may also beautiful men become wicked.'

Then said the Lord Cesar: [56] 'In case the Lord Gaspar's [57] saying be true of yesternight, there is no doubt but the fair women be more chaste than the foul.'

'And what was my saying?' quoth the Lord Gaspar.

The Lord Cesar answered: 'If I do well bear in mind, your saying was that the women that are sued [58] to always refuse to satisfy him that sueth to them, but those that are not sued to, sue to others. There is no doubt but the beautiful women have always more suitors, and be more instantly laid at [59] in love, than the foul. Therefore the beautiful always deny, and consequently be more chaste than the foul, which, not being sued to, sue unto others.'

M. Peter Bembo laughed, and said: 'This argument cannot be answered to.'

Afterward he proceeded: 'It chanceth also, oftentimes, that as the other senses, so the sight is deceived and judgeth a face beautiful which indeed is not beautiful. And because in the eyes and in the whole countenance of some woman a man beholdeth otherwhile a certain lavish wantonness, painted with dishonest flickerings, many, whom that manner delighteth because it promiseth them an easiness to come by the thing that they covet, call it beauty; but indeed it is a cloaked unshamefastness,[60] unworthy of so honourable and holy a name.'

M. Peter Bembo held his peace, but those lords still were earnest upon him [61]

---

54. That internal beauty, beauty of the soul, was essential to external beauty, was fundamental Platonic doctrine.
55. Deadliness.
56. Cesare Gonzaga (c. 1475–1512), Castiglione's cousin and paragon of the noble virtues
and practices of chivalry.
57. Gaspare Pallavicino (1486–1511), whose short life was marred by ill-health, is presented throughout the book as a misogynist and contender with Emilia de' Pii: their sparring
may have been one of Shakespeare's sources for the contests of Beatrice and Benedick in
Much Ado About Nothing.
58. Pressed, solicited.
59. Besieged.
60. Immodesty.
61. Begged him earnestly.

to speak somewhat more of this love and of the way to enjoy beauty aright, and at the last: 'Methink,' quoth he, 'I have showed plainly enough that old men may love more happily than young, which was my drift; therefore it belongeth not to me to enter any farther.'

Count Lewis answered: 'You have better declared the unluckiness of young men than the happiness of old men, whom you have not as yet taught what way they must follow in this love of theirs; only you have said that they must suffer themselves to be guided by reason, and the opinion of many is that it is unpossible for love to stand with reason.'

Bembo notwithstanding sought to make an end of reasoning,[62] but the Duchess desired him to say on, and he began thus afresh: 'Too unlucky were the nature of man, if our soul, in which this so fervent coveting may lightly[63] arise, should be driven to nourish it with that only which is common to her with beasts, and could not turn it to the other noble part, which is proper to her. Therefore, since it is so your pleasure, I will not refuse to reason upon this noble matter. And because I know myself unworthy to talk of the most holy mysteries of love, I beseech him to lead my thought and my tongue so that I may show this excellent Courtier how to love contrary to the wonted manner of the common ignorant sort. And even as from my childhood I have dedicated all my whole life unto him, so also now that my words may be answerable to the same intent, and to the praise of him: I say, therefore, that since the nature of man in youthful age is so much inclined to sense, it may be granted the Courtier, while he is young, to love sensually; but in case afterward also, in his riper years, he chance to be set on fire with this coveting of love, he ought to be good and circumspect, and heedful that he beguile not himself to be led willfully into the wretchedness that in young men deserveth more to be pitied than blamed; and contrariwise in old men, more to be blamed than pitied.

Therefore when an amiable countenance of a beautiful woman cometh in his sight, that is accompanied with noble conditions[64] and honest[65] behaviours, so that, as one practised in love, he wotteth[66] well that his hue[67] hath an agreement with hers, as soon as he is aware that his eyes snatch that image and carry it to the heart, and that the soul beginneth to behold it with pleasure, and feeleth within herself the influence that stirreth her and by little and little setteth her in heat, and that those lively[68] spirits that twinkle out through the eyes put continually fresh nourishment to the fire, he ought in this beginning to seek a speedy remedy and to raise up reason, and with her to fence the fortress of his heart, and to shut in such wise the passages against sense and appetites that they may enter neither with force nor subtle practice.

'Thus, if the flame be quenched, the jeopardy is also quenched. But in

62. Talk.
63. Quickly.
64. Moral qualities.
65. Good. The Italian is *gentile*.
66. Knows.
67. The Italian reads "blood." The sense is more than "coloring" and nearer the modern "character" or "temperament."
68. Vital spirits, the rarefied substance that sustains life.

case it continue or increase, then must the Courtier determine, when he per-
ceiveth he is taken, to shun thoroughly all filthiness of common love, and so
enter into the holy way of love with the guide of reason, and first consider
that the body where that beauty shineth is not the fountain from whence beauty
springeth, but rather because beauty is bodiless and, as we have said, an
heavenly shining beam, she loseth much of her honour when she is coupled with
that vile subject and full of corruption, because the less she is partner thereof,
the more perfect she is, and, clean sundered from it, is most perfect. And as
a man heareth not with his mouth, nor smelleth with his ears, no more can he
also in any manner wise enjoy beauty, nor satisfy the desire that she stirreth
up in our minds, with feeling, but with the sense unto whom beauty is the very
butt to level at, namely, the virtue of seeing. Let him lay aside, therefore, the
blind judgment of the sense, and enjoy with his eyes the brightness, the
comeliness, the loving sparkles, laughters, gestures, and all the other pleasant
furnitures of beauty, especially with hearing the sweetness of her voice, the
tunableness of her words, the melody of her singing and playing on instruments (in case the woman beloved be a musician), and so shall he with most
dainty food feed the soul through the means of these two senses which have
little bodily substance in them and be the ministers of reason,[69] without
entering farther toward the body with coveting unto any longing otherwise
than honest. Afterward let him obey, please, and honour with all reverence
his woman, and reckon her more dear to him than his own life, and prefer all
her commodities [70] and pleasures before his own, and love no less in her the
beauty of the mind than of the body. Therefore let him have a care not to
suffer her to run into any error, but with lessons and good exhortations seek
always to frame [71] her to modesty, to temperance, to true honesty, and so to
work that there may never take place in her other than pure thoughts and far
wide from all filthiness of vices. And thus in sowing of virtue in the garden of
that mind, he shall also gather the fruits of most beautiful conditions, and savour
them with a marvellous good relish. And this shall be the right engendering
and imprinting of beauty in beauty, the which some hold opinion to be the end
of love. In this manner shall our Courtier be most acceptable to his lady, and
she will always show herself toward him tractable, lowly,[72] and sweet in language, and as willing to please him as to be beloved of him; and the wills of
them both shall be most honest and agreeable, and they consequently shall
be most happy.'

Here M. Morello: 'The engendering,' quoth he, 'of beauty in beauty aright
were the engendering of a beautiful child in a beautiful woman; and I would
think it a more manifest token a great deal that she loved her lover, if she
pleased him with this than with the sweetness of language that you speak of.'

M. Peter Bembo laughed, and said: 'You must not, M. Morello, pass your
bounds. I may tell you it is not a small token that a woman loveth when she
giveth unto her lover her beauty, which is so precious a matter; and by the

69. Hearing and sight, in Ficino's system, are the least material of the senses and therefore
the nearest to divine perfection.
70. Advantage, interests.
71. Shape, direct.
72. Humble, modest.

ways that be a passage to the soul (that is to say, the sight and the hearing) sendeth the looks of her eyes, the image of her countenance, and the voice of her words, that pierce into the lover's heart and give a witness of her love.'

M. Morello said: 'Looks and words may be, and oftentimes are, false witnesses. Therefore whoso hath not a better pledge of love, in my judgment he is in an ill assurance. And surely I looked still that you would have made this woman of yours somewhat more courteous and free toward the Courtier than my Lord Julian [73] hath made his; but meseemeth ye be both of the property [74] of those judges that, to appear wise, give sentence against their own.'

Bembo said: 'I am well pleased to have this woman much more courteous toward my Courtier not young than the Lord Julian's is to the young; and that with good reason, because mine coveteth but honest matters, and therefore may the woman grant him them all without blame. But my Lord Julian's woman, that is not so assured of the modesty of the young man, ought to grant him the honest matters only, and deny him the dishonest. Therefore more happy is mine, that hath granted him whatsoever he requireth, than the other, that hath part granted and part denied. And because you may moreover the better understand that reasonable [75] love is more happy than sensual, I say unto you that selfsame things in sensual ought to be denied otherwhile, and in reasonable granted; because in the one they be honest, and in the other dishonest. Therefore the woman, to please her good lover, besides the granting him merry countenances, familiar and secret talk, jesting, dallying, hand-in-hand, may also lawfully and without blame come to kissing, which in sensual love, according to the Lord Julian's rules, is not lawful. For since a kiss is a knitting together both of body and soul,[76] it is to be feared lest the sensual lover will be more inclined to the part of the body than of the soul; but the reasonable lover wotteth well that although the mouth be a parcel of the body, yet is it an issue for the words that be the interpreters of the soul, and for the inward breath, which is also called the soul; and therefore hath a delight to join his mouth with the woman's beloved with a kiss—not to stir him to any unhonest desire, but because he feeleth that that bond is the opening of an entry to the souls, which, drawn with a coveting the one of the other, pour themselves by turn the one into the other's body, and be so mingled together that each of them hath two souls, and one alone so framed of them both ruleth, in a manner, two bodies. Whereupon a kiss may be said to be rather a coupling together of the soul than of the body, because it hath such force in her that it draweth her unto it, and, as it were, separateth her from the body. For this do all chaste lovers covet a kiss as a coupling of souls together. And therefore Plato, the divine lover, saith that in kissing his soul came as far as his lips to depart out of the body.[77] And because the separating of the soul from the

---

73. Giuliano de' Medici (1479–1516), youngest son of Lorenzo il Magnifico, Duke of Nemours, poet and close friend of Castiglione, in exile from Florence, like the rest of his family at the time. His funerary effigy by Michelangelo is in the New Sacristy of San Lorenzo in Florence.

74. Kind, nature.

75. Rational.

76. Because of the mingling of the breath in the touch of the lips.

77. This is an allusion to a poem in the *Greek Anthology* by one Plato, who is perhaps the same as Plato the philosopher.

matters of the sense, and the thorough coupling of her with matters of understanding, may be betokened by a kiss, Solomon saith [78] in his heavenly book of ballads, "Oh that he would kiss me with a kiss of his mouth," to express the desire he had that his soul might be ravished through heavenly love to the beholding of heavenly beauty in such manner that, coupling herself inwardly with it, she might forsake the body.' . . .

1508–16 / 1554   1528–61

ROGER ASCHAM
1515–1568

Ascham was born in Yorkshire and entered St. John's College, Cambridge, in 1530. He became friends with Sir John Cheke (1514–57), his tutor, and was made Fellow of his College in 1534 and Reader in Greek in 1538, siding with Cheke on the "reforming" side in the controversy about the pronunciation of Greek. He received a pension from Henry VIII in 1545 on the publication of his *Toxophilus* and became Public Orator of the University, charged with the duty of making Latin orations on great occasions, in 1546. A staunch Protestant, he was tutor to Princess Elizabeth (later Queen) in 1548–49; secretary to Sir Richard Morison, ambassador of Edward VI to the Emperor, in 1550–53, and Latin Secretary, managing diplomatic correspondence, to the Catholic Queen Mary in 1553. He retained the post under Elizabeth, with whom he continued daily reading of Latin and Greek authors. Ascham married in 1554 and died in 1568. His two chief works are *Toxophilus,* a dialogue on archery (1545), and *The Schoolmaster* (posthumously published in 1570).

Ascham's overriding concern was that of his fellow humanists: to strengthen his native country in all the arts of peace and of defense, providing men properly educated to serve and govern her so as to keep her at the head of European nations. His reverence for Cicero and for Renaissance Ciceronianism does not make him write his treatises in Latin, though he tries to strengthen his language and enrich it by using classical models. The gentlest and most enlightened of teachers, the first to speak openly against beating as an incentive to learning, he lays his stress on the possible, on what can be done by encouragement, even with apparently unpromising material. Ascham has no grand schemes: what he asks is that "goodness of nature be joined to the wisdom of the teacher, in leading young wits into a right and plain way of learning" so that "children, kept up in God's fear and governed by his grace, may most easily be brought well to serve God and their country, both by virtue and wisdom." The way to this virtue and wisdom was through the study of Latin and Greek, both as models of the eloquence without which a man can never persuade another to virtue, and as the storehouse of practical and theoretical wisdom (see the application of Homer's story of Ulysses in *The Schoolmaster*). Along with the enchantments of Italy, "Gothic," immoral literature —such as medieval romances—must be disregarded. Ascham endorses Cheke's judgment that "God's holy Bible," Cicero, Plato, Aristotle, with the Greek orators Isocrates and Demosthenes, are enough to make an excellent man.

Ascham's contemporaries speak of him as an engaging, agreeable man, apt to make and keep friends. His prose, carefully framed and neat, reflects the man. Its syntax is

---

78. Song of Songs, 1:2. The Song had the philosophic status of divine wisdom on the nature of love.

based on Ciceronian models, but its character is strongly English, its vocabulary free of the patriotic purism of Cheke, or the affected learning of "inkhorn" terms—learned borrowings—of other contemporaries. It is wholly at ease with itself.

The Schoolmaster

The first book of *The Schoolmaster*, from which these passages are taken, is an account of the principles on which boys should be taught, along with some examples of their successful application. The most effective way to writing good Latin is via the method of double translation. After this recommendation comes a description of the qualities to be sought in a pupil and of the means of enticing, rather than compelling, him to study. The whole curriculum is directed toward making the young fit for "virtuous action": the aim of the English humanist educator. To keep them on the right path, in literature as in life, they must be kept from both the sight and the practice of all that is vicious (e.g. the reading of Arthurian romances and the experience of Italy).

The second book of *The Schoolmaster* is chiefly concerned with the doctrine of imitation in particular stylistic terms, rather than the general and ethical modes of Book I. To learn languages and improve eloquence, Ascham prescribes translation and imitation of the best (i.e. Ciceronian) models, along with paraphrase and metaphrase (turning prose into verse, verse into prose), and summary.

Ascham names his own masters as Plato, Aristotle, and Cicero among the ancients; and Sir John Cheke and Johann Sturm, his friend the preceptor of Strasbourg, among the moderns. There is an unacknowledged pervasive tinge from Quintilian's (c. 35–c. 100 A.D.) *De Institutione Oratoria*—as in all Renaissance educators—with its insistence that the ideal orator must be "a good man, skilled in speaking." Plato's influence is strongest in the first book, where it is made clear that the proper bringing-up of children, from birth onward, not merely in schools, is the most important of social responsibilities, involving a just estimate of the nature of pleasure and of freedom and their place in education. In the second book, the presence of the Ciceronian *Sturm* and of Cicero himself are most strongly felt.

The text of the selections from Ascham is taken from *The Whole Works*, ed. J. A. Giles, 1864–65. Spelling and punctuation have been modernized.

The Schoolmaster

From *Book I*

. . . First, let him teach the child cheerfully and plainly the cause [1] and matter [2] of the letter; [3] then, let him construe [4] it into English so oft, as the child may easily carry away the understanding of it; lastly, parse [5] it over

1. The reason for and circumstances of its writing.
2. Content.
3. That is, of Cicero's, which is his assigned reading.
4. Translate.
5. Describe each word in it grammatically, stating its part of speech, its case, and its relation to the others.

perfitly.[6] This done thus, let the child, by and by, both construe and parse it over again; so that it may appear, that the child doubteth in nothing that his master taught him before. After this, the child must take a paper book, and sitting in some place, where no man shall prompt him, by himself, let him translate into English his former lesson. Then showing it to his master, let the master take from him his Latin book, and pausing an hour at the least, then let the child translate his own English into Latin again in another paper book. When the child bringeth it turned into Latin, the master must compare it with Tully's [7] book, and lay them both together; and where the child doth well, either in choosing or true placing of Tully's words, let the master praise him, and say, 'Here ye do well.' For I assure you, there is no such whetstone to sharpen a good wit, and encourage a will to learning, as is praise.

But if the child miss, either in forgetting a word, or in changing a good with a worse, or misordering the sentence, I would not have the master either frown or chide with him, if the child have done his diligence, and used no truantship therein. For I know by good experience, that a child shall take more profit of two faults gently warned of, than of four things rightly hit: for then the master shall have good occasion to say unto him; 'N.,[8] Tully would have used such a word, not this: Tully would have placed this word here, not there; would have used this case, this number, this person, this degree, this gender: he would have used this mood, this tense, this simple, rather than this compound; this adverb here, not there: he would have ended the sentence with this verb, not with that noun or participle,' &c.

In these few lines I have wrapped up the most tedious part of grammar; and also the ground of almost all the rules that are so busily taught by the master, and so hardly learned by the scholar, in all common schools; which, after this sort, the master shall teach without all error, and the scholar shall learn without great pain; the master being led by so sure a guide, and the scholar being brought into so plain and easy a way. And therefore we do not contemn rules, but we gladly teach rules; and teach them more plainly, sensibly, and orderly, than they be commonly taught in common schools. For when the master shall compare Tully's book with the scholar's translation, let the master, at the first, lead and teach his scholar to join the rules of his grammar book with the examples of his present lesson, until the scholar by himself be able to fetch out of his grammar every rule for every example; so as the grammar book be ever in the scholar's hand, and also used of him as a dictionary for every present use. This is a lively and perfit way of teaching of rules; where the common way used in common schools, to read the grammar alone by itself, is tedious for the master, hard for the scholar, cold and uncomfortable for them both.

Let your scholar be never afraid to ask you any doubt, but use discreetly the best allurements ye can to encourage him to the same; lest his overmuch fearing of you drive him to seek some misorderly shift; [9] as to seek to be helped by some other book, or to be prompted by some other scholar; and so go about to beguile you much and himself more.

6. Perfectly.
7. Marcus Tullius Cicero's.
8. *Nomen*, i.e. the child's name.
9. Wrong expedient.

[Ascham goes on to give Socrates' points for distinguishing good students. The first comes from Plato's *Republic* 455b; the next five from 535b ff. The final point seems to be Ascham's: it is not in Plato.]

And because I write English, and to Englishmen, I will plainly declare in English both what these words of Plato mean, and how aptly they be linked, and how orderly they follow one another.

1. Euphuēs

Is he, that is apt by goodness of wit, and appliable by readiness of will, to learning, having all other qualities of the mind and parts of the body, that must another day serve learning; not troubled, mangled, and halved, but sound, whole, full, and able to do their office; as, a tongue not stammering, or over-hardly drawing forth words, but plain and ready to deliver the meaning of the mind; a voice not soft, weak, piping, womanish, but audible, strong, and man-like; a countenance not wearish [10] and crabbed, but fair and comely; a personage not wretched and deformed, but tall and goodly; for surely, a comely countenance with a goodly stature giveth credit to learning, and authority to the person; otherwise, commonly, either open contempt or private [11] disfavour doth hurt or hinder both person and learning; and even as a fair stone requireth to be set in the finest gold, with the best workmanship, or else it loseth much of the grace and price; even so excellence in learning, and namely divinity, joined with a comely personage, is a marvellous jewel in the world. And how can a comely body be better employed than to serve the fairest exercise of God's greatest gift? and that is learning. But commonly the fairest bodies are bestowed on the foulest purposes. . . .

2. Mnēmōn

Good of memory: a special part of the first note [12] *euphuēs*, and a mere benefit of nature; yet it is so necessary for learning, as Plato maketh it a separate and perfect note of itself, and that so principal a note, as without it all other gifts of nature do small service to learning. . . .

3. Philomathēs

Given to love learning: for though a child have all the gifts of nature at wish, and perfection of memory at will, yet if he have not a special love to learning, he shall never attain to much learning. . . .

4. Philoponos

Is he that hath a lust [13] to labour and a will to take pains: for if a child have all the benefits of nature, with perfection of memory, love, like, and praise learning never so much, yet if he be not of himself painful, he shall never attain unto it. And yet where love is present, labour is seldom absent, and namely in study of learning, and matters of the mind. . . .

5. Philēkoos

He that is glad to hear and learn of another: for otherwise he shall stick with great trouble, where he might go easily forward; and also catch hardly a very

10. Sickly, delicate.
11. Concealed
12. Sign.
13. Desire, pleasure.

little by his own toil, when he might gather quickly a good deal by another man's teaching. . . .

6. Zētētikos

He that is naturally bold to ask any question, desirous to search out any doubt; not ashamed to learn of the meanest, nor afraid to go to the greatest, until he be perfectly taught and fully satisfied. The seventh and last point is,

7. Philepainos

He that loveth to be praised for well doing, at his father or master's hand. A child of this nature will earnestly love learning, gladly labour for learning, willingly learn of other, boldly ask any doubt.

. . . Hear what Socrates in the same place doth more plainly say: [14] 'And therefore, my dear friend, bring not up your children in learning by compulsion and fear, but by playing and pleasure.' [15] And you that do read Plato as you should, do well perceive, that these be no questions asked by Socrates as doubts, but they be sentences,[16] first affirmed by Socrates as mere [17] truths, and after given forth by Socrates as right rules, most necessary to be marked, and fit to be followed of all them that would have children taught as they should. And in this counsel, judgment, and authority of Socrates I will repose myself, until I meet with a man of the contrary mind, whom I may justly take to be wiser than I think Socrates was.

Fond [18] schoolmasters neither can understand, nor will follow this good counsel of Socrates; but wise riders in their office can and will do both; which is the only cause that commonly the young gentlemen of England go so unwillingly to school, and run so fast to the stable. For in very deed, fond schoolmasters, by fear, do beat into them the hatred of learning; and wise riders, by gentle allurements, do breed up in them the love of riding. They find fear and bondage in schools, they feel liberty and freedom in stables; which causeth them utterly to abhor the one, and most gladly to haunt [19] the other. And I do not write this, that, in exhorting to the one, I would dissuade young gentlemen from the other; yea, I am sorry with all my heart that they be given no more to riding than they be. For of all outward qualities, to ride fair is most comely for himself, most necessary for his country; and the greater [20] he is in blood, the greater is his praise, the more he doth exceed all other therein. It was one of the three excellent praises amongst the noble gentlemen of the old Persians; 'Always to say truth, to ride fair, and shoot well': and so it was engraven upon Darius's tomb, as Strabo beareth witness:

> Darius the king lieth buried here,
> Who in riding and shooting had never peer.[21]

14. The Greek is omitted.
15. Plato, *Republic* 536e.
16. Wise sayings.
17. Simple.
18. Foolish.
19. Frequent.
20. More noble. Cf. Spenser, *The Faerie Queene* II.iv.1: "But chiefly skill to ride seemes a science / Proper to gentle blood. . . ."
21. Strabo, Greek historian and geographer (64 B.C.–c. 21 A.D.), in his *Geography* XV.iii.8.

But to our purpose: Young men, by any means losing the love of learning, when by time [22] they come to their own rule,[23] they carry commonly from the school with them a perfect hatred of their master, and a continual contempt of learning. If ten gentlemen be asked, why they forgot so soon in court, that which they were learning so long in school, eight of them, or let me be blamed, will lay the fault on their ill-handling by their schoolmasters.

. . .

And thus will in children, wisely wrought [24] withal, may easily be won to be very well willing to learn. And wit in children, by nature, namely memory, the only key and keeper of all learning, is readiest to receive, and surest to keep any manner of thing that is learned in youth. This, lewd [25] and learned, by common experience, know to be most true. For we remember nothing so well when we be old, as those things which we learned when we were young. And this is not strange, but common in all nature's works. . . .

Therefore, if to the goodness of nature be joined the wisdom of the teacher, in leading young wits into a right and plain way of learning; surely children, kept up in God's fear, and governed by his grace, may most easily be brought well to serve God and their country, both by virtue and wisdom.

. . .

Therefore, to love or to hate, to like or contemn, to ply [26] this way or that way to good or to bad, ye shall have as ye use a child in his youth.

And one example, whether love or fear doth work more in a child for virtue and learning, I will gladly report; which may be heard with some pleasure, and followed with more profit.

Before I went into Germany,[27] I came to Broadgate in Leicestershire, to take my leave of that noble lady Jane Grey,[28] to whom I was exceeding much beholding.[29] Her parents, the Duke [30] and Duchess, with all the household, gentlemen and gentlewomen, were hunting in the park. I found her in her chamber, reading *Phædo Platonis* [31] in Greek, and that with as much delight as some gentlemen would read a merry tale in Boccace.[32] After salutation, and duty done,[33] with some other talk, I asked her, why she would lose such pastime

22. In due time.
23. Reach their majority and independence.
24. Wisely worked on.
25. Ignorant.
26. Bend, mold.
27. Ascham went to Germany, as secretary to Sir Richard Morison, the English ambassador to the Emperor Charles V, in 1550. Ascham and Morison read Greek together. Ascham learned Italian and briefly visited Italy. He returned to England in September 1553, but his *Report on the State of Germany* was not published until after his death.
28. 1537–54, later married to Lord Guildford Dudley as part of a plot to supplant the Tudor dynasty upon the death of Edward VI. She was proclaimed queen in 1553, arrested for treason in the same year, and executed at Queen Mary's order in 1554. The pupil of Bishop John Aylmer, she could at 15 write Latin, Greek, French, and German, and she had begun to study Hebrew.
29. Obligated.
30. Of Suffolk.
31. Plato's dialogue *Phaedo,* concerned with the nature of the soul.
32. Giovanni Boccaccio (1313?–75), author of the *Decameron* and other works of amusement and of piety.
33. That is, proper exchange of courtesies.

in the park? Smiling, she answered me; 'I wiss,[34] all their sport in the park is but a shadow [35] to that pleasure that I find in Plato. Alas! good folk, they never felt what true pleasure meant.' 'And how came you, madam,' quoth I, 'to this deep knowledge of pleasure? and what did chiefly allure you unto it, seeing not many women, but very few men, have attained thereunto?' 'I will tell you,' quoth she, 'and tell you a truth, which perchance ye will marvel at. One of the greatest benefits that ever God gave me, is, that he sent me so sharp and severe parents, and so gentle a schoolmaster. For when I am in presence either of father or mother; whether I speak, keep silence, sit, stand, or go, eat, drink, be merry, or sad, be sewing, playing, dancing, or doing any thing else; I must do it, as it were, in such weight, measure, and number, even so perfectly, as God made the world; [36] or else I am so sharply taunted, so cruelly threatened, yea presently [37] sometimes with pinches, nips, and bobs,[38] and other ways (which I will not name for the honour I bear them) so without measure mis-ordered,[39] that I think myself in hell, till time come that I must go to Mr. Elmer; [40] who teacheth me so gently, so pleasantly, with such fair allurements to learning, that I think all the time nothing whiles I am with him. And when I am called from him, I fall on weeping, because whatsoever I do else but learning, is full of grief, trouble, fear, and whole misliking unto me. And thus my book hath been so much my pleasure, and bringeth daily to me more pleasure and more, that in respect of it, all other pleasures, in very deed, be but trifles and troubles unto me.'

I remember this talk gladly, both because it is so worthy of memory, and because also it was the last talk that ever I had, and the last time that ever I saw that noble and worthy lady.

. . .

To join learning with comely exercises, Conte Baldesar Castiglione, in his book *Cortegiane*,[41] doth trimly [42] teach; which book advisedly [43] read and diligently followed but one year at home in England, would do a young gentleman more good, I wiss, than three years' travel abroad spent in Italy. And I marvel this book is no more read in the court than it is, seeing it is so well translated into English by a worthy gentleman, Sir Thomas Hobby,[44] who was many ways well furnished with learning, and very expert in knowledge of divers tongues.

34. Certainly; a corrupt form of Middle English *ywis*.

35. Lady Jane is playing with the platonic notion of worldly things being only shadowy replicas of divine and eternal ideas: physical pleasures are nothing compared with intellectual pleasures.

36. The perfect proportion of God's creation is expressed in the Wisdom of Solomon 11:20, an apocryphal book of the Old Testament: "Thou hast ordered all things in measure, number and weight."

37. On the spot.

38. Raps, blows.

39. Ill-treated.

40. John Aylmer (1521–94), later Bishop of London, a good Latin and Greek scholar and an exile during Mary's reign.

41. See above.

42. Finely, effectively.

43. With care and consideration.

44. See above.

[They forget, Ascham goes on, all the good they have learned, they become dulled to virtuous learning ever after, they lose the ability to tell good from evil, and they come to despise good men. The only preservative against this corruption is the study of virtue, which is so far neglected that young men go abroad to study vice.]

Sir Richard Sackville,[45] that worthy gentleman of worthy memory, as I said in the beginning, in the queen's privy chamber [46] at Windsor, after he had talked with me for the right choice of a good wit in a child for learning, and of the true difference betwixt quick and hard wits, of alluring young children by gentleness to love learning, and of the special care that was to be had to keep young men from licentious living; he was most earnest with me, to have me say my mind also, what I thought concerning the fancy that many young gentlemen of England have to travel abroad, and namely to lead a long life in Italy. His request, both for his authority and good will toward me, was a sufficient commandment unto me, to satisfy his pleasure with uttering plainly my opinion in that matter. 'Sir,' quoth I, 'I take going thither, and living there, for a young gentleman that doth not go under the keep [47] and guard of such a man, as both by wisdom can, and authority dare rule him, to be marvellous dangerous.'

And why I said so then, I will declare at large now, which I said then privately, and write now openly; not because I do contemn either the knowledge of strange and divers tongues, and namely [48] the Italian tongue (which, next the Greek and Latin tongue, I like and love above all other), or else because I do despise the learning that is gotten, or the experience that is gathered in strange countries; or for any private malice that I bear to Italy; which country, and in it namely Rome, I have always specially honoured; because time was, when Italy and Rome have been to the great good of us that now live, the best breeders and bringers up of the worthiest men, not only for wise speaking, but also for well doing, in all civil affairs, that ever was in the world. But now that time is gone; and though the place remain, yet the old and present manners do differ as far as black and white, as virtue and vice. Virtue once made that country mistress over all the world; vice now maketh that country slave to them that before were glad to serve it. All men seeth it; they themselves confess it, namely such as be best and wisest amongst them. For sin, by lust and vanity, hath and doth breed up everywhere, common contempt of God's word, private contention in many families, open factions in every city; and so making themselves bond to vanity and vice at home, they are content to bear the yoke of serving strangers abroad. Italy now, is not that Italy that it was wont to be; and therefore now not so fit a place as some do count it, for young men to fetch either wisdom or honesty from thence. For surely they will make others but bad scholars, that be so ill masters to themselves. Yet, if a gentleman will needs travel into Italy, he shall do well to look

---

45. Ascham's Preface contains an account of the conversation in the Queen's private apartment at Windsor Castle, and Sackville's urging, which prompted him to write his book. Sir Richard Sackville (d. 1566), cousin of Anne Boleyn, was Treasurer of the Exchequer.
46. Private apartment.
47. Guardianship, care.
48. Especially.

on the life of the wisest traveller that ever travelled thither, set out by the wisest writer [49] that ever spake with tongue, God's doctrine only excepted; and that is Ulysses [50] in Homer.

. . .

Therefore, if wise men will needs send their sons into Italy, let them do it wisely, under the keep and guard of him who, by his wisdom and honesty, by his example and authority, may be able to keep them safe and sound in the fear of God, in Christ's true religion, in good order, and honesty [51] of living; except they will have them run headlong into over-many jeopardies, as Ulysses had done many times, if Pallas [52] had not always governed him; if he had not used to stop his ears with wax, to bind himself to the mast of his ship,[53] to feed daily upon that sweet herb Moly,[54] with the black root and white flower, given unto him by Mercury to avoid all the enchantments of Circe. Whereby the divine poet Homer meant covertly (as wise and godly men do judge) that love of honesty and hatred of ill, which David more plainly doth call the fear of God, the only remedy against all enchantments of sin.[55]

I know divers noble personages, and many worthy gentlemen of England, whom all the Siren songs of Italy could never untwine from the mast of God's Word, nor no enchantment of vanity overturn them from the fear of God and love of honesty.

But I know as many, or more, and some sometime my dear friends (for whose sake I hate going into that country the more), who parting out of England fervent in the love of Christ's doctrine, and well furnished with the fear of God, returned out of Italy worse transformed than ever was any in Circe's court. I know divers, that went out of England, men of innocent life, men of excellent learning, who returned out of Italy, not only with worse manners, but also with less learning; neither so willing to live orderly, nor yet so able to speak learnedly, as they were at home, before they went abroad. . . .

ELIZABETHAN SONG AND LYRIC

Actual songs, and lyric poems which might or might not be intended for setting, come down to us in several ways. There are, first, the miscellanies, or anthologies of verse, starting with Richard Tottel's *Songs and Sonnets* (1557), although an earlier one called *The Court of Venus*, of which we have only fragments, was printed in the late 1530's.

---

49. Homer was thought of as a sort of encyclopedia of wise counsel.
50. Ulysses reached Sicily and Italy in the wanderings described by Homer in his *Odyssey*.
51. Goodness.
52. Athena was the protector of Ulysses.
53. *Odyssey* XII.153 ff. On Circe's advice, to avoid being seduced by the sirens' song and destroyed by them, Ulysses had his crew stop their ears with wax and bind him to the mast.
54. *Odyssey* X.302–6. Ulysses had set out to bring back his comrades, turned into swine by the wicked enchantress Circe, when Mercury warned him that he would suffer the same fate without the help of the herb moly. Later commentators on Homer saw the incident as an allegory of education, the purpose of which was to teach a man to act virtuously, and steer clear of evil.
55. Psalms 34:9 ff. (Vulgate 33:9 ff.).

The editing of Tottel's Miscellany, and the explanatory titles attached to the poems, indicate a sense of a style, and of norms of metrical smoothness, quite well established. A successor, *The Paradise of Dainty Devices*, went through ten editions between its first appearance, in 1576, and 1606; *A Gorgeous Gallery of Gallant Inventions* (1578); *A Handful of Pleasant Delights* (1584, but based on a much earlier collection); *The Phoenix Nest* (1592), which contains elegies on Sir Philip Sidney—the phoenix of the title, out of whose ashes arise the new English poems of the 1590's—and a variety of modish and more old-fashioned poems both; *England's Helicon* (1600), limited to pastoral poetry of all sorts; and Davison's *A Poetical Rhapsody* of 1602, containing "Pastorals and Eglogues, Odes and Madrigals," including a good many translations from classical poets—in all these anthologies we find poems duplicated elsewhere in collections of work by the individual poets represented in them, and many that are not.

Then, too, there are the songbooks, the poems with their printed music—either for voices or for instruments in polyphonic settings, or, later on (the first such collection is William Barley's *A New Book of Tablature* of 1596), for lute and voice and known as "airs." The poems appearing with their musical settings were usually anonymous, or at least unidentified, and scholars have been gradually attempting to identify the authorship of many remarkable poems. Perhaps at this point something should be said about what "song" as a literary term implies. The concept "lyric poetry" originally comes from a classical Greek distinction between solo songs, sung to the lyre, composed in short stanzas and usually erotic in character, and choral ode, composed in triads of long strophes and of a public, celebratory character when not occurring as part of tragedy or comedy. There were many other classical poetic styles: elegiac verse was composed in couplets (always unrhymed as in all classical verse) and was used for satire and epigram, inscriptions and witty or pointed observation. Iambic verse had other ranges of use, from speeches in plays to drinking songs and love lyrics. Then there was, of course, the continuous hexameter line of epic poetry, and the originally almost startling adaptation of it by Theocritus for his pastoral eclogues.

Latin poets followed and adapted these Greek models, but the actual association of meters with musical forms and styles began to disappear. The Renaissance, extremely self-conscious as it came to be about classical antiquity, sought to emulate it with a deliberate re-unification of music and poetry. England lagged behind the Continent in the development of its music after the death of John Dunstable (1390–1453), one of the most renowned musicians of his day. By the 1580's, however, Italian influences and the invigoration of a native tradition led to a remarkable burst of secular musical activity, and the emergence of a group of composers of the first rank, among them William Byrd, Orlando Gibbons, John Dowland, Thomas Weelkes, Thomas Morley, and others. Aside from solo keyboard and lute composition, their main activities were in the field of song. Madrigals were polyphonic settings of poetic texts for several singers, either unaccompanied or, more often, with instruments either doubling the voices or taking their parts. They were often florid, chromatic, and complex, and went to such lengths to avoid stanzaic repetition of different words to the same tune that they confined themselves to monostrophic poems, like sonnets, or else frequently set two stanzas of the same poem as two different madrigals. Airs, or solo songs, were written for voice and lute (although usually printed with four-part settings included). They were oriented more toward a performer-audience situation than the madrigals, whose musico-poetic delights would appeal primarily to the individual singer, hearing the complexities of the setting of the often-repeated words weaving around him. Airs, in addition, were primarily stanzaic: thus the composer found a text and set the first stanza, allowing the subsequent ones to be "sung to the same tune," as it were. In the case of frequently banal, metrically smooth poems this "fit" worked very well. In the case of Donne's *Songs and Sonnets,* the tense, wrenched, individualized rhythmic patternings of almost every line made stanzaic settings almost impossible, though there were several attempts; and with Donne's poems we begin to see texts whose musical settings can best be thought of as the verbal "music" of their own intense speech cadences.

By the 1580's, a variety of poetic conventions had become assimilated to the notion of "lyric poem," including "sonnets" in both the strict and loose senses (that is, the familiar fourteen-line iambic pentameter poems as well as any short, Petrarchan love poem), epigrams, pastoral lyrics, and so forth. A musician (as Donne puts it in "The Triple Fool"), "his art and voice to show, / Doth set and sing my pain"—and composers frequently raided miscellanies and anthologies as well as published books and poems in manuscript. Almost any poem might, after publication, show up in a musical setting, sometimes altered for the convenience of the composer.

THOMAS, LORD VAUX
1510–1556

The Agèd Lover Renounceth Love°

I loathe that° I did love,
  In youth that I thought sweet,
As time requires for my behove:°
  Methinks they are not meet.

My lusts they do me leave,
  My fancies all be fled,
And tract of time begins to weave
  Grey hairs upon my head.

For age with stealing steps
10 Hath clawed me with his crutch,
And lusty life away she leaps
  As there had been none such.

My Muse doth not delight
  Me as she did before,
My hand and pen are not in plight,
  As they have been of yore.

The Agèd Lover Renounceth Love The title is from Richard Tottel's Miscellany (1557), where the poem first appeared; it was an important anthology which first printed the poems of Wyatt and Surrey. In Tottel, this poem was printed in "poulter's measure," the quatrains arranged into alternating 12- and 14-syllable rhyming lines in couplets; the gravedigger in *Hamlet* V.i hums parts of it, half-misremembering.
that what
behove benefit

For reason me denies
 This youthly idle rhyme;
And day by day to me she cries:
20 'Leave off these toys in time.'

The wrinkles in my brow,
 The furrows in my face,
Say limping age will lodge him now
 Where youth must give him place.

The harbinger of death,
 To me I see him ride,
The cough, the cold, the gasping breath
 Doth bid me to provide

A pickaxe and a spade,
30 And eke° a shrouding sheet,
A house of clay for to be made
 For such a guest most meet.

Methinks I hear the clerk
 That knolls the carefull knell,
And bids me leave my woeful wark,
 Ere nature me compel.

My keepers knit the knot
 That youth did laugh to scorn,
Of me that clean shall be forgot
40 As I had not been born.

Thus must I youth give up,
 Whose badge I long did wear;
To them I yield the wanton cup
 That better may it bear.°

Lo, here the barèd skull,
 By whose bald sign I know
That stooping age away shall pull
 Which youthful years did sow.

For beauty with her band
 These crooked cares hath
50   wrought,
And shippèd me into the land
 From whence I first was brought.

And ye that bide behind,
 Have ye none other trust:
As ye of clay were cast by kind,°
 So shall ye waste to dust.
   1557

eke also
by kind by nature

To them . . . bear I give up joy to those
who can manage it

NICHOLAS GRIMALD°
1519–1562

The Garden°

The issue of great Jove, draw near you Muses nine:°
Help us to praise the blissful plot of garden ground so fine.
The garden gives good food, and aid for leeches'° cure:
The garden, full of great delight, his master doth allure.
Sweet salad herbs be here, and herbs of every kind:
The ruddy grapes, the seemly fruits, be here at hand to find.
Here pleasance wanteth not, to make a man full fain:
Here marvellous the mixture is of solace and of gain.
To water sundry seeds, the furrow by the way
10 A running river, trilling down with liquor, can convey.
Behold, with lively hue fair flowers that shine so bright:
With riches, like the orient° gems, they paint the mould° in sight.
Bees, humming with soft sound (their murmur is so small),
Of blooms and blossoms suck the tops, on dewèd leaves they fall.
The creeping vine holds down her own bewedded elms,
And, wandering out with branches thick, reeds folded overwhelms.
Trees spread their coverts wide with shadows fresh and gay:
Full well their branchèd boughs defend° the fervent sun away.
Birds chatter, and some chirp, and some sweet tunes do yield:
20 All mirthful, with their songs so blithe, they make both air and field.
The garden, it allures; it feeds, it glads the sprite:
From heavy hearts all doleful dumps° the garden chaseth quite.
Strength it restores to limbs, draws and fulfills the sight,
With cheer revives the senses all, and maketh labour light.
O, what delights to us the garden ground doth bring?
Seed, leaf, flower, fruit, herb, bee, and tree, and more, then I may sing.

1557

Nicholas Grimald Playwright as well as poet, Grimald was a heavy contributor to Tottel's *Miscellany.*
The Garden Probably a paraphrase of a Latin poem in praise of gardens, this poem in poulter's measure demonstrates the poetic plain style of the mid-century; it is at its best when listing or cataloguing.
Muses nine An invocation to the Muses in so trivial a piece is little more than throat-clearing, a kind of literary "ahem!"
leeches' physicians'
orient shining
mould earth
defend ward off
doleful dumps common phrase for clouds of spiritual depression (cf. modern "down in the dumps"), but coming to mean a kind of musical piece

CHIDIOCK TICHBORNE
1558?–1586

Tichborne's Elegy°

My prime of youth is but a frost of cares,
My feast of joy is but a dish of pain,
My crop of corn is but a field of tares,
And all my good is but vain hope of gain;
The day is past, and yet I saw no sun,
And now I live, and now my life is done.

My tale was heard and yet it was not told,
My fruit is fallen and yet my leaves are green,
My youth is spent and yet I am not old,
10   I saw the world and yet I was not seen;
My thread is cut and yet it is not spun,
And now I live, and now my life is done.

I sought my death and found it in my womb,
I looked for life and saw it was a shade,
I trod the earth and knew it was my tomb,
And now I die, and now I was but made;
My glass is full, and now my glass is run,
And now I live, and now my life is done.

                              1586

ANONYMOUS

[A Song from Ovid]°

Constant Penelope sends to thee, careless Ulysses.
Write not again, but come, sweet mate, thyself to revive me.
Troy we do much envy, we desolate lost ladies of Greece,
Not Priamus, nor yet all Troy can us recompense make.
Oh, that he had, when he first took shipping to Lacedaemon,
That adulter I mean, had been o'erwhelmed with waters.
Then had I not lain now all alone, thus quivering for cold,
Nor used this complaint, nor have thought the day to be so long.

                              1588

Tichborne's Elegy Usually subtitled "Written with his own hand in the Tower before his execution"; whether or not actually so written by this conspirator in a plot against the Queen, it was an extremely popular poem of the period, being set to music many times. Its easy use of oxymoron, alliterating pairs, and clichés like the "womb-tomb" rhyme, undoubtedly helped the supposed circumstances of its composition to make it a favorite.

A Song from Ovid a translation from the first book of Ovid's *Heroides* (*Hanc tua Penelope lento mittit, Ulixe*) into purely quantitative English verse, perhaps by Thomas Watson, and set to music, with the unrhymed hexameters used in the rhythm of the setting, by William Byrd in his *Psalms, Sonnets and Songs of Sadness and Piety* (1588). To the modern ear, it sounds like beautifully cadenced free verse.

ANONYMOUS

[Shadow and Substance]°

I heard a noise and wishèd for a sight,
I looked for life and did a shadow see
Whose substance was the sum of my delight,
Which came unseen, and so did go from me.
    Yet hath conceit persuaded my content
    There was a substance where the shadow went.

I did not play Narcissus in conceit,°
I did not see my shadow in a spring;
I know mine eyes were dimmed with no deceit,
I saw the shadow of some worthy thing:
    For, as I saw the shadow glancing by,
    I had a glimpse of something in mine eye.

But what it was, alas, I cannot tell,
Because of it I had no perfect view;
But as it was, by guess, I wish it well
And will until I see the same anew.
    Shadow, or she, or both, or choose you whither:
    Blest be the thing that brought the shadow hither!

                        c. 1597

ROBERT SOUTHWELL
1561–1595

The Burning Babe°

As I in hoary winter's night stood shivering in the snow,
Surprised I was with sudden heat which made my heart to glow;
And lifting up a fearful eye to view what fire was near,
A pretty babe all burning bright did in the air appear;
Who, scorchèd with excessive heat, such floods of tears did shed
As though his floods should quench his flames which with his tears
    were fed.°
'Alas,' quoth he, 'but newly born in fiery heats I fry,
Yet none approach to warm their hearts or feel my fire but I!
My faultless breast the furnace is, the fuel wounding thorns,
Love is the fire, and sighs the smoke, the ashes shame and scorns;

Shadow and Substance the present editors' title for an anonymous poem from a manuscript probably written in the late 1590's; "shadow" means, as it does throughout this period, an image or vision, rather than only a cast shade
in conceit "in concept," imaginedly
The Burning Babe Southwell, a Jesuit martyr hanged for his activities in England (where he had returned from Douay in 1586), wrote reli-gious verse in a rather archaic manner; this poem, printed variously in the rhymed "four-teeners" of mid-century verse as well as in ballad form, is perhaps the most famous piece of recusant verse, admired by Ben Jonson and Dylan Thomas alike.
Who . . . fed Notice the parody, in these lines, of Petrarchan language about love.

612

The fuel justice layeth on, and mercy blows the coals,
The metal in this furnace wrought are men's defiled souls,
For which, as now on fire I am to work them to their good,
So will I melt into a bath to wash them in my blood.'
With this he vanished out of sight and swiftly shrunk away,
And straight I callèd unto mind that it was Christmas day.

1602

ANONYMOUS

'Hark, All Ye Lovely Saints'°

Hark, all ye lovely saints above:
Diana hath agreed with Love
His fiery weapon to remove.
    Do you not see
    How they agree?
Then cease, fair ladies, why weep ye?

See, see your mistress bids you cease,
And welcome Love with love's increase:
Diana hath procured your peace.
10   Cupid hath sworn
    His bow forlorn
To break and bend, ere ladies mourn.

The First Stanza as set to Music:

Hark, all ye lovely saints above:
Diana hath agreed with Love, hath agreed with Love
His fiery weapon to remove. *Fa la la la la la,*
La, la, la——fa la la la la la, la, la,
La la la la la——la.
    Do you not see
    How they agree?
20 *Then cease, fair ladies, why weèp ye? why weep yè?*

1598

'**Hark, All Ye Lovely Saints**' This little song, from Thomas Weelkes's *Ballets and Madrigals to Five Voices* (1598), is like an epigram or motto for an emblematic picture of sexuality abandoned for chastity; it is set in a ballet or "fa-la," as they were called, a mixture of homophonic setting, with every voice singing chordally, the same words at the same time (like a hymn tune), and true fugal polyphony on the "fa-la-la's." We also give the text as set, with polyphonic parts in italic: notice how Weelkes has chosen to set the words "why weep ye?" polyphonically, perhaps to bring out the different contrastive stress accent which gives the phrase slightly different meanings.

THOMAS NASHE°

Litany in Time of Plague

Adieu, farewell earth's bliss,
This world uncertain is:
Fond are life's lustful joys,
Death proves them all but toys,
None from his darts can fly.
I am sick, I must die.
      Lord, have mercy on us!

Rich men, trust not in wealth,
Gold cannot buy you health;
Physic° himself must fade,
All things to end are made.
The plague full swift goes by.
I am sick, I must die.
      Lord, have mercy on us!

Beauty is but a flower
Which wrinkles will devour;
Brightness falls from the air,°
Queens have died young and fair,
Dust° hath closed Helen's eye.
I am sick, I must die.
      Lord, have mercy on us!

Strength stoops unto the grave,
Worms feed on Hector brave,
Swords may not fight with fate,
Earth still holds ope her gate.
Come! come! the bells do cry.°
I am sick, I must die.
      Lord, have mercy on us!

Wit with his wantonness
Tasteth death's bitterness;
Hell's executioner
Hath no ears for to hear
What vain art can reply.
I am sick, I must die.
      Lord, have mercy on us!

Thomas Nashe Novelist (*The Unfortunate Traveller, or Jack of Wilton,* published in 1594, a brilliant picaresque adventure), pamphleteer, and master of splendid prose invective, Nashe was one of the bright young "University wits" —including Robert Greene, George Peele, Marlowe, and his stolid polemical enemy, Gabriel Harvey—who flourished in the 1590's and many of whom died young.

Physic medical skill
Brightness falls from the air an image of darkening, although its place in the catalogue of decaying beauties has made for a suggested emendation to "hair"
Dust The Biblical "dust to dust" means, of course, mud, clay, not dry precipitate.
bells do cry parish bell ringing out a death (see Donne, "Meditation XVII")

Haste, therefore, each degree,°
To welcome destiny.
Heaven is our heritage,
Earth but a player's stage;°
Mount we unto the sky.
I am sick, I must die.
          Lord, have mercy on us!
                              1600

Autumn

Autumn hath all the summer's fruitful treasure;
Gone is our sport, fled is poor Croydon's° pleasure.
Short days, sharp days, long nights come on apace,
Ah! who shall hide us from the winter's face?
Cold doth increase, the sickness will not cease,
And here we lie, God knows, with little ease.
    From winter, plague, and pestilence, good Lord, deliver us!

London doth mourn, Lambeth° is quite forlorn;
Trades cry, woe worth that ever they were born.
The want of term° is town and city's harm;
Close chambers we do want, to keep us warm.
Long banishèd must we live from our friends;
This low-built house° will bring us to our ends.
    From winter, plague, and pestilence, good Lord, deliver us!
                              1600

ANONYMOUS

A Peddler's Song°

Fine knacks for ladies, cheap, choice, brave and new!
    Good pennyworths! but money cannot move.
I keep a fair but for the fair° to view;
    A beggar may be liberal of love.

degree social class
stage the old commonplace (see Spenser, *Amoretti* LIV)
Croydon's This and the following poem are both songs from Nashe's rather masque-like play, *Summer's Last Will and Testament*, performed in 1592 for the Archbishop of Canterbury at his palace in Croydon, south of London; the play represented the death of summer as occurring in Croydon, and it was performed while the plague raged in London.
Lambeth south of the Thames, seat of the archbishop's palace
want of term lack of an ending to the plague;

also, perhaps, suggesting that it is vacation, after Michaelmas term in the autumn
low built house the palace at Croydon; perhaps also, in a more medieval way, the human body
A Peddler's Song a magnificent poem, exemplifying a common genre (see Autolycus's songs from *A Winter's Tale*), which appeared, set for lute and voice by John Dowland, in 1600. The usual catalogue of the peddler's wares has erotic connotations, but here an uncharacteristic elevation of the plain over the fancy arises.
fair but for the fair the first "fair" meaning an open sale, a one-man fair; the second, of course, the girls who would be his customers

Though all my wares be trash, the heart is true,
 The heart is true,
 The heart is true.

Great gifts are guiles and look for gifts again;
 My trifles comes as treasures from my mind.
10 It is a precious jewel to be plain;
 Sometimes in shell the orient pearls we find.
Of others take a sheaf, of me a grain,
 Of me a grain,
 Of me a grain.

Within this pack pins, points, laces, and gloves,
 And divers toys° fitting a country fair.
But in my heart, where duty serves and loves,
 Turtles and twins, court's brood,° a heavenly pair.
Happy the heart that thinks of no removes,
20 Of no removes,
  Of no removes.
   1600

SIR THOMAS WYATT
1503–1542

"A hand that taught what might be said in rhyme," his follower, Surrey, said of him. Wyatt's inaugurating role in the establishment of Elizabethan poetic conventions is a strange one. Like many originators who forge the stylistic models from which others will work, there is a kind of awkwardness and tentativeness about even his best work. Wyatt, born in Kent and educated at St. John's College, Cambridge, was a courtier and diplomat whose travels to Italy and France in 1526 and 1527 acquainted him with the High Renaissance abroad. He served Henry VIII in various capacities, and was charged with treason, and acquitted, a year before his death. Wyatt's poems are of two sorts. The first—lyrics in short, tight stanzas of eight-syllable lines or less, written in an earlier tradition of song continued from the later fifteenth century—represents what the Elizabethan critic Puttenham called the poetry of the "courtly makers." These poems are metrically regular in the accentual-syllabic tradition which, after Chaucer, was lost (save by the Scottish poets) in all but the short lines of song meters. (We must remember that iambic pentameter had virtually to be rediscovered in the Tudor period. Chaucer was known and admired devoutly, but his iambic pentameter line was misread, even as late as Spenser's time, as a rough, accentual, four-beat "riding rhyme.") The second sort, Wyatt's translations and adaptations of Petrarch, not only brought the sonnet form to English but also sought to work out, from the Italian eleven-syllable line, a viable English equivalent. Wyatt's sonnets are written in a peculiar mixture of syllabic and accentual lines, but the majority of those lines move toward the normative verse pattern which he was able to bequeath to his follower, the Earl of Surrey.

toys both small objects and "fancies": compare our contemporary notions counter at a store **Turtles and twins . . . brood** turtle-doves and the "heavenly pair" of twins, Castor and Pollux of the constellation Gemini, were emblems of true love and constancy; the latter were the "brood" of Jove as the swan, and Leda

I Find No Peace°

I find no peace and all my war is done;
　　I fear and hope, I burn and freeze like ice;
　　I fly above the wind, yet can I not arise,
　　And naught I have and all the world I seize on;
That° looseth nor locketh holdeth me in prison,
　　And holdeth me not yet can I scape nowise;
　　Nor letteth me live nor die at my devise,°
　　And yet of death it giveth none occasion.
Without eyen° I see, and without tongue I plain;
10　　I desire to perish, and yet I ask health;
　　I love another, and thus I hate myself;
I feed me in sorrow, and laugh in all my pain.
　　Likewise displeaseth me both death and life,
　　And my delight is causer of this strife.

　　　　　　　　　　　　from ms. 1913

My Galley Chargèd with Forgetfulness°

My galley chargèd with forgetfulness
　　Through sharp seas, in winter night doth pass
　　Tween rock and rock;° and eke° mine enemy, alas,
　　That is my lord steereth with cruelness.
And every oar a thought in readiness,
　　As though that death were light in such a case.
　　An endless wind doth tear the sail apace
　　Of forcèd sighs and trusty fearfulness.
A rain of tears, a cloud of dark disdain,
10　　Hath done the wearied cords° great hinderance,
　　Wreathed with error and eke with ignorance.
The stars be hid that led me to this pain
　　Drownèd is reason that should me consort,
　　And I remain despairing of the port.

　　　　　　　　　　　　from ms. 1913

Farewell, Love

Farewell, Love, and all thy laws forever,—
　　Thy baited hooks shall tangle me no more;
　　Senec° and Plato call me from thy lore,

I Find No Peace from Petrarch (*In Vita*, Sonnet XC), helping to establish the subsequently popular vogue for talking in paradoxes, particularly about love—in a tradition going back before Petrarch to Sappho and Catullus—and represented in its clichéd form by poems like "Tichborne's Elegy" (see above)
that that which (love)
devise plan
eyen eyes

My Galley . . . Forgetfulness from Petrarch (*In Vita*, Sonnet CXXXVII)
tween rock and rock a reminiscence of Homeric navigational dangers; the whole poem transforms Horace's "Ship of the state" (*Odes* I.14) into a ship of self
eke also
cords rigging
Senec Seneca, the Roman Stoic philosopher and tragedian

617

To perfect wealth my wit for to endeavour.
In blind error when I did persever,
   Thy sharp repulse, that pricketh aye so sore,
   Hath taught me to set in trifles no store
   And scape forth since liberty is lever.°
Therefore farewell—go trouble younger hearts,
10   And in me claim no more authority;
   With idle youth go use thy property,
And thereon spend thy many brittle darts.
   For hitherto though I have lost all my time,
   Me lusteth° no longer rotten boughs to climb.

from ms. 1913

The Long Love That in My Thought Doth Harbour°

The long love that in my thought doth harbour,
And in my heart doth keep his residence,
Into my face presseth with bold pretence
And there encampeth, spreading his banner.
She that me learns° to love and suffer
And wills that my trust and lust's negligence
Be reined° by reason, shame° and reverence
With his hardiness takes displeasure.
Wherewithal unto the heart's forest he flieth,
10 Leaving his enterprise with pain and cry,
And there him hideth, and not appeareth.
What may I do, when my master feareth,
But in the field with him to live and die?
For good is the life ending faithfully.

from ms. 1913

Blame Not My Lute°

Blame not my lute, for he must sound
Of this or that as liketh me,
For lack of wit the lute is bound
To give such tunes as pleaseth me.
Though my songs be somewhat strange
And speaks such words as touch thy change,
Blame not my lute.

lever preferable
Me lusteth I desire
The Long Love . . . Harbour an adaptation of
Petrarch (*In Vita*, Sonnet xci also translated
by Surrey; see below). The conceit of conqueror
Love occupying the poet's inner state, showing
his colors in self-revealing blushes, is typical
of the mythological psychologizing of Petrarchan
poetry.
learns teaches
reined restrained
shame proper modesty
Blame Not My Lute As in the following poem,
the lute, like the classical poet's lyre, stands
for poetic eloquence.

My lute, alas, doth not offend,
Though that perforce he must agree
10 To sound such tunes as I intend,
To sing to them that heareth me.
Then, though my songs be somewhat plain,
And toucheth some that use to feign,°
Blame not my lute.

My lute and strings may not deny
But as I strike they must obey:
Break not them then so wrongfully,
But wreak thyself some wiser way.
And though the songs which I indite°
20 Do quit thy change with rightful spite,
Blame not my lute.

Spite asketh spite and changing change,
And falsèd faith must needs be known.
The fault so great, the case so strange,
Of right it must abroad be blown.°
Then since that by thine own desért°
My songs do tell how true thou art,
Blame not my lute.

Blame but thyself that hast misdone
30 And well deservèd to have blame.
Change thou thy way so evil begun
And then my lute shall sound that same.
But if till then my fingers play,
By thy desért, their wonted way,
Blame not my lute.

Farewell, unknown, for though thou brake
My strings in spite, with great disdain,
Yet have I found out for thy sake
Strings for to string my lute again.
40 And if perchance this foolish rhyme
Do make thee blush at any time,
Blame not my lute.
            from ms. 1913

My Lute, Awake!

My lute, awake! Perform the last
Labour that thou and I shall waste,
And end that I have now begun:

use to feign have elaborate and fancy manners   blown broadcast
indite compose   desert deserving

For when this song is sung and past,
My lute, be still, for I have done.

As to be heard where ear is none,
As lead to grave in marble stone,
My song may pierce her heart as soon.°
Should we then sigh or sing or moan?
10   No, no, my lute, for I have done.

The rocks do not so cruelly
Repulse the waves continually
As she my suit and affectiòn,
So that I am past remedy,
Whereby my lute and I have done.

Proud of the spoil that thou hast got
Of simple hearts, thorough° love's shot,
By whom, unkind,° thou hast them won—
Think not he hath his bow forgot,
20   Although my lute and I have done.

Vengeance shall fall on thy disdain
That makest but game on earnest pain.
Think not alone under the sun,
Unquit,° to cause thy lovers plain,°
Although my lute and I have done.

Perchance thee lie withered and old
The winter nights that are so cold,
Plaining in vain unto the moon.
Thy wishes then dare not be told.
30   Care then who list,° for I have done.

And then may chance thee to repent
The time that thou hast lost and spent
To cause thy lovers sigh and swoon.
Then shalt thou know beauty but lent,
And wish and want as I have done.

Now cease, my lute. This is the last
Labour that thou and I shall waste,
And ended is that we begun.
Now is this song both sung and past;
40   My lute, be still, for I have done.
                              from ms. 1913

As to . . . soon not until sounds are audible
without ears, or lead can carve marble, will my
eloquence touch her heart
thorough through

unkind unnatural
Unquit unrevenged
plain to lament
list wishes

Whoso List To Hunt°

Whoso list° to hunt, I know where is an hind,
  But as for me alas, I may no more—
  The vain travail hath wearied me so sore,
  I am of them that farthest cometh behind.
Yet may I, by no means, my wearied mind
  Draw from the deer, but as she fleeth afore,
  Fainting I follow. I leave off therefore,
  Since in a net I seek to hold the wind.
Who list her hunt, I put him out of doubt,
10 As well as I, may spend his time in vain.
  And graven with diamonds in letters plain
There is written her fair neck round about:
  '*Noli me tangere,*° for Caesar's I am,
  And wild for to hold, though I seem tame.'

                  from ms. 1913

They Flee from Me°

They flee from me, that sometime did me seek,
With naked foot stalking in my chamber.
I have seen them, gentle, tame, and meek,
That now are wild, and do not remember
That sometime they put themselves in danger
To take bread at my hand, and now they range,
Busily seeking with a continual change.

Thanked be Fortune it hath been otherwise,
Twenty times better; but once in special,
10 In thin array, after a pleasant guise,
When her loose gown from her shoulders did fall,
And she me caught in her arms long and small,°
And therewith all sweetly did me kiss
And softly said, 'Dear heart, how like you this?'

It was no dream, I lay broad waking.
But all is turned, thorough my gentleness,
Into a strange fashion of forsaking;
And I have leave to go, of her goodness,
And she also to use newfangleness.°

Whoso List To Hunt from Petrarch (*Rime,* Sonnet CXC)
list wishes
'Noli me tangere "Don't touch me"; appropriating Latin of John 20:17 out of context—presumably the situation of Anne Boleyn, admired by Wyatt but already marked for Henry VIII's interest, is reflected here: Petrarch's conceit and what was thought to be an actual court intrigue blend in prototypical English Petrarchan fashion.

They Flee from Me This remarkable poem exists both in manuscript, as here given, and in a form slightly rewritten by Richard Tottel, in his *Miscellany* (1557), with the rough, experimental meter normalized into regular iambic pentameter, and a more rhetorically pointed ending.
long and small long and slender
newfangleness fashionable fickleness

20   But since that I so kindely° am served,
      I fain would know what she hath deserved.
                                    from ms. 1913

HENRY HOWARD, EARL OF SURREY
1517–1547

Soldier, courtier from the time of his youth, in and out of favor with King Henry VIII
who married, then beheaded, Surrey's cousin Catherine, the poet was finally executed
himself, for treason, in 1547. He appears to have done translations into English verse
when young, and was an admirer and younger friend of Wyatt. His own poems left
a more palpable legacy than Wyatt's. The sonnets in Tottel's Miscellany (1557) are of the
quatrain and couplet sort which became the standard English model. His is the first
English blank verse, perhaps derived from an acquaintance with Italian poetry in this
meter, and used with neoclassical appropriateness for a translation of two books of
Virgil's *Aeneid*, published after his death, in 1557. Surrey's sonnets lack the experimental vigor of Wyatt's which appealed so much to the tastes of poetic modernism
in the 1930's and '40's; they are marked instead by the smoothness and sophistication
in handling the form used later by Shakespeare, the balance and measure of syntax
and verse unit, and the absorption of classical styles and their lessons for English,
which make him such a direct precursor of Sir Philip Sidney.

Alas, So All Things Now Do Hold Their Peace°

Alas, so all things now do hold their peace,
Heaven and earth disturbed in no-thing;
The beasts, the air, the birds their song do cease,
The nightès chair° the stars about do bring.
Calm is the sea: the waves work less and less;
So am not I, whom love, alas, doth wring,
Bringing before my face the great increase
Of my desires, whereat I weep and sing
In joy and woe as in a doubtful ease;
10   For my sweet thoughts sometime do pleasure bring,
But by and by the cause of my disease°
Gives me a pang that inwardly doth sting,
      When that I think what grief it is again
      To live and lack the thing should rid my pain.
                                    1557

---

kindely appropriately. Rather sarcastic, of
course, and Tottel's version of the last two lines
uses the word in its modern sense, making it
negative, and coarsening the tone: "But since
that I unkindly so am served, How like you
this? What hath she now deserved?"
Alas . . . peace a version of Petrarch's sonnet

(*In Vita*, Sonnet CLXIV) which is, itself, worked
up from the well-known set piece by Virgil
translated below
nightès chair car, or chariot, of the night, i.e.
the Great Bear; "nightes" is disyllabic
disease uneasiness

From Virgil's Aeneid

[The Night-Piece°]

It was then night: the sound and quiet sleep
Had through the earth the wearied bodies caught;
The woods, the raging seas were fallen to rest;
When that the stars had half their course declined
The fields whist;° beasts and fowls of divers hue,
And what so that in the broad lakes remained,
Or yet among the bushy thicks° of briar
Laid down to sleep by silence of the night,
710 Gan 'suage their cares, mindless of travels past.
Not so the sprite of this Phoenician:°
Unhappy she, that on no sleep could chance,
Nor yet night's rest enter in eye or breast.
Her cares redouble; love doth rise and rage again,°
And overflows with swelling storms of wrath.

1557

[The Trojan Horse°]

'The Greeks' chieftains, all irkèd with the war
Wherein they wasted had so many years
20 And oft repulsed by fatal destiny,
By the divine science of Minerva
A huge horse made, high raisèd like a hill,
For their return a feignèd sacrifice:
The fame whereof so wandered it at point.°
Of cloven fir compacted were his ribs;
In the dark bulk they closed bodies of men
Chosen by lot, and did enstuff° by stealth
The hollow womb with armèd soldiers.
There stands in sight an isle, hight° Tenedon,
30 Rich, and of fame, while Priam's kingdom stood;
Now but a bay, and road unsure for ship.
Hither them secretly the Greeks withdrew,
Shrouding themselves under the desert shore.
And, weening° we they had been fled and gone
And with that wind had fet the land of Greece,
Troyè discharged her long continued dole.
The gates cast up, we issued out to play,
The Greekish camp desirous to behold,
The places void, and the forsaken coasts.

The Night-Piece a famous passage in Virgil, *Aeneid* IV.522–28 contrasting the quiet of night with Dido's anxiety when she knows Aeneas will desert her. It was imitated by Petrarch in the sonnet adapted by Surrey given above.
whist were silent
thicks thickets
this Phoenician Dido, queen of Carthage

Her cares . . . again This is a deliberate alexandrine, or twelve-syllable line.
The Trojan Horse This section is narrated by Aeneas at Dido's court.
at point aptly
enstuff to garrison with soldiers
hight named
weening knowing

40 Here Pyrrhus' band; there fierce Achilles pight;°
Here rode their ships; there did their battles join.
Astonied, some the scatheful gift beheld,
Behight° by vow unto the chaste Minerve,
All wondering at the hugeness of the horse.
    The first of all Timoetes gan advise
Within the walls to lead and draw the same,
And place it eke amid the palace court:
Whether of guile, or Troyès fate it would.
Capys, with some of judgment more discreet,
50 Willed it to drown, or underset with flame
The suspect present of the Greeks' deceit,
Or bore and gauge the hollow caves uncouth:
So diverse ran the giddy people's mind.
    Lo, foremost of a rout that followed him,
Kindled Laocoön° hasted from the tower,
Crying far off: "O wretched citizens!
What so great kind of frenzy fretteth you?
Deem ye the Greeks our enemies to be gone?
Or any Greekish gifts can you suppose
60 Devoid of guile? Is so Ulysses known?
Either the Greeks are in this timber hid,
Or this an engine is to annoy our walls,
To view our towers, and overwhelm our town.
Here lurks some craft. Good Troyans, give no trust
Unto this horse, for whatsoever it be,
I dread the Greeks—yea, when they offer gifts!"
And with that word, with all his force a dart
He lancèd then into that crooked womb
Which trembling stuck, and shook within the side:
70 Wherewith the caves gan hollowly resound.
And, but for Fates, and for our blind forecast,
The Greeks' device and guile had he descried:
Troy yet had stood, and Priam's towers so high.'

. . .

1557

Love That Doth Reign and Live Within My Thought

Love, that doth reign and live within my thought,°
And built his seat within my captive breast,
Clad in the arms wherein with me he fought,

---

pight pitched (of tents)
Behight consecrated
Laocoön Son of Priam (king of Troy) and a priest of Apollo, he was punished by Athena for his attempts to warn the Trojans about the

Wooden Horse, and died, with his sons, in the coils of two great serpents.
Love . . . thought adapted from the same Petrarchan sonnet (*In Vita*, Sonnet XCI) as Wyatt's "The Long Love That in My Thought Doth Harbour"

Oft in my face he doth his banner rest.
But she that taught me love and suffer pain,
My doubtful hope and eke my hot desire
With shamefast° look to shadow and refrain,
Her smiling grace converteth straight to ire.
And coward Love, then, to the heart apace
10 Taketh his flight, where he doth lurk and plain,°
His purpose lost, and dare not show his face.
For my lord's guilt thus faultless bide I pain,
    Yet from my lord shall not my foot remove:
    Sweet is the death that taketh end by love.

1557

SIR PHILIP SIDNEY
1554–1586

If the humanist ideal of the fulfilled human being was a wisely and gracefully educated aristocrat, Sir Philip Sidney was almost the perfect courtier. A man who could stand for the condition of humanity, not by exemplifying a random sample but as a mirror and a mold of all the virtues, should possess many cultivated skills (as Castiglione argued in *Il Cortegiano*) tempered with that *sprezzatura,* or aristocratic carelessness, which would distinguish him from a professional, a mere hired hand. English humanist educators had prescribed formal intellectual training as being necessary to the art of government; and the arts of literature as they might be practiced in courtly poetry, certainly, were free of the taint of base handicrafts and household help that painting, architecture, and professional music-making still kept. Sidney was able in his short life to unite some of the separate concerns of court and university by informing his originally recreational writing with a range of purposes and concerns shared by his teachers and his friends like Spenser and Fulke Greville; and indeed, under the pressure of these concerns, moral and aesthetic, two of these projects actually got, in a sense, out of hand. His prose romance (now called *The Old Arcadia*) gave way, in his later rewriting of it, to something so much more complex that he could not complete it. His sonnet sequence, *Astrophel and Stella,* created a model not only for what would become a national literary fashion in the last decade of the century but also for an association of form, mythological and narrative elements, and tone of personal voice which would continue to influence English lyric poetry in the century after his death.

Sidney was born to an important family; his uncles were the Earls of Leicester and Warwick, his mother, an unusually well educated lady for her day, who was able to assist with the basic education of her son and his sister (later the Countess of Pembroke) at Penshurst, the family castle in Kent (see Ben Jonson's "To Penshurst"). Sidney later went to Shrewsbury School and to Oxford, but left his college, Christ Church, without taking a degree, in 1571. Thereafter he traveled extensively abroad assisting on diplomatic missions, fought in Ireland, and met many learned and influential men who would reinforce his commitments to the skills of knowledge, and to Protestantism. It was in that cause, as much as in the nationalist one, that he would die in Holland,

shamefast modest   plain lament

after being wounded at the Battle of Zutphen fighting the Spanish forces of his god-father, King Philip of Spain.

Sidney's friendships in England and abroad were literary as well as courtly and diplomatic, and the concern for the establishment of an English national literature which is apparent in his *Defence of Poesie* was deeply rooted in more than merely the contemporary arguments about style and form (poetic meter, in particular, was an important issue) that dominated critical writing about literature in his day. In 1578 he wrote an entertainment (somewhere between a masque and a pageant) for Queen Elizabeth's visit to the Earl of Leicester; in that year, too, he began work on the *Arcadia*, "This idle work of mine," as he referred to it, "this child which I am loth to father," his *sprezzatura* minimizing what must have been, even in a work probably designed at first to amuse his sister, a very deep commitment to a literary program. Based on an Italian prototype, the *Arcadia* of Sannazaro (1501), in alternating passages of prose and verse as well as on the five-act structure of classical comedy, Sidney's work uses the idyllic setting of pastoral tradition, the shipwrecks, abductions by pirates, usurpations, and mistaken identities of the Alexandrian romances like Heliodorus' *Aethiopian Romance*, for its plot. But its literary center is in the dialogues and debates, in the most rhetorical of prose styles, on such subjects as reason and passion, the active as opposed to the contemplative life, the duties of kingship, and other academic set pieces. Fully as important were the interspersed poems, on a variety of subjects and in a variety of forms and meters, including adaptations of Greek and Latin quantitative meter in the fashionably experimental way. Sidney finished *The Old Arcadia* in 1580; two years later, he began work on its never-to-be-finished revision to be called (from the title of its first posthumously published version) *The Countess of Pembroke's Arcadia* (1590), or *The New Arcadia*. It represented a new mode of seriousness, introducing just the confusion of genres which the *Defence* so deplored (it is, perhaps, a good candidate for Polonius's "tragical-comical-historical-pastoral" in *Hamlet*). After finishing two books and part of a very long third one, Sidney abandoned the project; it was reissued with some slight changes and the added last three books of *The Old Arcadia*. There was perhaps no way in which Sidney could handle the transformation of the brilliant but limited genre of the first book without the kind of fundamental re-thinking of the nature of a literary form which resulted in many of Shakespeare's plays, and *The Faerie Queene*.

The sonnets of *Astrophel and Stella*, started in 1581, probably finished the following year, circulated widely, like many poems of their age, in manuscript, and finally appeared in three unauthorized but influential editions in 1591. The first full Petrarchan sequence in English, it adopts both the Petrarchan fiction (Astrophil or -phel means "star-lover" in Greek; Stella is Latin for "star") and the meta-fiction, namely that the fiction exists merely to veil a literal autobiographical situation. In fact, the Petrarchan mythology exists to provide a muse, a psychology, and a set of relations and images; the use of biography is to support that myth. Penelope Devereux, to whom Sidney was briefly engaged when she was quite young, was the daughter of the Earl of Essex; she eventually married Lord Rich, rather unhappily. The identification of Stella with her is unquestioned, and if threads of "story" are carefully analyzed, some relation between them and possible meetings, confrontations, and partings in the lives of Sidney and Penelope during 1581–82 may be discerned. In several sonnets there are puns on her name (she "Hath no misfortune but that Rich she is," etc.) that would become almost mandatory in subsequent sonnet collections. Still, the Stella of the sequence is a mythical muse of lyric poetry, and of English lyric poetry struggling to justify itself in the light of antiquity and of Continental mastery of the classical tradition. Sidney's use not only of Petrarchan imagery but also of patternings of linguistic surface and depth which he had learned from the Renaissance study of rhetoric, is reinforced in these poems by a constant sense of personal presence, of a tone of voice of a speaker in a situation, which will lay the groundwork for the new kind of lyric of speech that first appears so dramatically in the poetry of John Donne.

Ye Goatherd Gods°

STREPHON Ye goatherd gods, that love the grassy mountains,
     Ye nymphs that haunt the springs in pleasant valleys,
     Ye satyrs joyed with free and quiet forests,
     Vouchsafe your silent ears to plaining music,
     Which to my woes gives still an early morning,
     And draws the dolour on till weary evening.

KLAIUS O Mercury, foregoer to the evening,
     O heavenly huntress° of the savage mountains,
     O lovely star, entitled of the morning,°
10   While that my voice doth fill these woeful valleys,
     Vouchsafe your silent ears to plaining music,
     Which oft hath Echo tired in secret forests.

STREPHON I, that was once free burgess° of the forests,
     Where shade from sun, and sport I sought at evening,
     I, that was once esteemed for pleasant music,
     Am banished now among the monstrous mountains
     Of huge despair, and foul affliction's valleys,
     Am grown a screech owl to myself each morning.

KLAIUS I, that was once delighted every morning,
20   Hunting the wild inhabiters of forests,
     I, that was once the music of these valleys,
     So darkened am that all my day is evening,
     Heartbroken so that molehills seem high mountains
     And fill the vales with cries instead of music.

STREPHON Long since, alas, my deadly swannish music°
     Hath made itself a crier of the morning,

Ye Goatherd Gods One of the songs (No. 71) from the *Old Arcadia*, sung by Strephon and Klaius, two foreign swains united by their love for Urania, who has left Arcadia, commanding them to remain there. A double sestina, it expands the original 39-line form that traditionally uses only the six terminal words of its first stanza as terminals throughout (permutations of their order generate the subsequent stanzas). The brilliance and fame of this poem depend upon the resonant evocations of overtones of meaning in the repetitions of *mountains —valleys—forests—music—morning—evening.*
huntress Diana (Artemis), virgin moon goddess
O lovely . . . morning Lucifer, the Morning Star
burgess free citizen
deadly swannish music The swan was supposed to sing only at its death.

And hath with wailing strength climbed highest mountains;
Long since my thoughts more desert be than forests,
Long since I see my joys come to their evening,
30   And state thrown down to overtrodden valleys.

KLAIUS   Long since the happy dwellers of these valleys
Have prayed me leave my strange exclaiming music
Which troubles their day's work and joys of evening;
Long since I hate the night, more hate the morning,
Long since my thoughts chase me like beasts in forests
And make me wish myself laid under mountains.

STREPHON   Meseems I see the high and stately mountains
Transform themselves to low dejected° valleys;
Meseems I hear in these ill-changèd forests
40   The nightingales do learn of owls their music;
Meseems I feel the comfort of the morning
Turned to the mortal serene° of an evening.

KLAIUS   Meseems I see a filthy cloudy evening
As soon as sun begins to climb the mountains;
Meseems I feel a noisome scent, the morning
When I do smell the flowers of these valleys;
Meseems I hear, when I do hear sweet music,
The dreadful cries of murdered men in forests.

STREPHON   I wish to fire the trees of all these forests;
50   I give the sun a last farewell each evening;
I curse the fiddling finders-out of music;
With envy I do hate the lofty mountains.
And with despite despise the humble valleys;
I do detest night, evening, day, and morning.

KLAIUS   Curse to myself my prayer is, the morning;
My fire is more than can be made with forests,
60   My state more base than are the basest valleys.
I wish no evenings more to see, each evening;
Shamèd, I hate myself in sight of mountains
And stop mine ears, lest I grow mad with music.

STREPHON   For she whose parts° maintained a perfect music,
Whose beauty shined more than the blushing morning,
Who much did pass in state the stately mountains,
In straightness passed the cedars of the forests,
Hath cast me, wretched, into eternal evening
By taking her two suns° from these dark valleys.

dejected humble, with the Latin sense also of   parts with a pun on musical polyphonic parts,
"cast down"   or voices
mortal serene deadly (perhaps, also, transient)   suns her eyes
mist

70 KLAIUS   For she, to whom compared, the Alps are valleys,
                She, whose least word brings from the spheres their music,
                At whose approach the sun rose in the evening,
                Who where she went bare in her forehead morning,
                Is gone, is gone, from these our spoiled forests,
                Turning to deserts our best pastured mountains.

    STREPHON   These mountains witness shall, so shall these valleys,

    KLAIUS   These forests eke,° made wretched by our music,
                Our morning hymn this is, and song at evening.

                                    1580

THE OLD ARCADIA

At the beginning of *The Old Arcadia,* two princes from Thrace have wandered into
Arcadia on a long journey home. The cousins are named Pyrocles ("fire and glory")
and Musidorus ("the Muses' gift"), and the former falls in love with a picture of the
daughter of the Duke of Arcadia. Musidorus rebukes him for his distractedness and
"solitariness"; his answer follows. It culminates in a description of Arcadia as the
locus amoenus, the "lovely place," that concept which connects Renaissance pastoral
settings with such classical paradises as those of the Golden Age and the Hesperidean
garden.

From The Old Arcadia

These words spoken vehemently and proceeding from so dearly an esteemed
friend as Musidorus did so pierce poor Pyrocles, that his blushing cheeks did
witness with him, he rather could not help, than did not know his fault. Yet,
desirous by degrees to bring his friend to a gentler consideration of him, and
beginning with two or three broken sighs, answered him to this purpose: 'Excellent Musidorus, in the praises you gave me in the beginning of your speech I
easily acknowledge the force of your good will unto me. For, neither could you
have thought so well of me if extremity of love had not something dazzled your
eyes, nor you could have loved me so entirely, if you had not been apt to make
so great (though undeserved) judgement of me. And even so must I say of
those imperfections, to which though I have ever through weakness been subject, yet which you by the daily mending of your mind have of late been able
to look into, which before you could not discern, so that the change you spake
of falls not out by my impairing, but by your bettering. And yet under the leave
of your better judgment I must needs say thus much, my dear cousin, that I
find not myself wholly to be condemned, because I do not with a continual
vehemency follow those knowledges which you call the betterings of my mind.
For, both the mind itself must (like other things) sometimes be unbent, or else
it will be either weakened or broken, and these knowledges, as they are of good

eke also

use, so are they not all the mind may stretch itself unto. Who knows whether I feed not my mind with higher thoughts? Truly, as I know not all the particularities, so yet see I the bounds of all those knowledges; but the workings of the mind I find much more infinite than can be led unto by the eye, or imagined by any that distract their thoughts without themselves; and in such contemplations, or as I think more excellent, I enjoy my solitariness, and my solitariness perchance is the nurse of these contemplations. Eagles we see fly alone, and they are but sheep which always herd together. Condemn not therefore my mind sometime to enjoy itself, nor blame not the taking of such times as serve most fit for it.'

And here Pyrocles suddenly stopped, like a man unsatisfied in himself, though his wit might well have served to have satisfied another. And so looking with a countenance as though he desired he should know his mind without hearing him speak, and yet desirous to speak, to breathe out some part of his inward evil, sending again new blood to his face, he continued his speech in this manner.

'And lord, dear cousin,' said he, 'doth not the pleasantness of this place carry in itself sufficient reward for any time lost in it, or for any such danger that might ensue? Do you not see how everything conspires together to make this place a heavenly dwelling? Do you not see the grass, how in color they excell the emeralds, every one striving to pass his fellow, and yet they are all kept in an equal height? And see you not the rest of all these beautiful flowers, each of which would require a man's wit to know, and his life to express? Do not these stately trees seem to maintain their flourishing old age, with the only happiness of their seat being clothed with a continual spring, because no beauty here should ever fade? Doth not the air breathe health which the birds (both delightful both to the ear and eye) do daily solemnize with the sweet consent of their voices? Is not every echo here a perfect music? And these fresh and delightful brooks, how slowly they slide away, as, loath to leave the company of so many things united in perfection, and with how sweet a murmur they lament their forced departure. Certainly, certainly, cousin, it must needs be, that some goddess this desert belongs unto, who is the soul of this soil, for neither is any less than a goddess worthy to be shrined in such a heap of pleasures, nor any less than a goddess could have made it so perfect a model of the heavenly dwellings.'

And so he ended with a deep sigh, ruefully casting his eye upon Musidorus, as more desirous of pity than pleading.

1580

From Astrophel and Stella

I

Loving in truth, and fain in verse my love to show,°
That she, dear she, might take some pleasure of my pain,
Pleasure might cause her read, reading might make her know,

Loving . . . show This opening sonnet of the sequence is an original text about the notion of originality in English poetry (see Herbert's "Jordan II" for an elaboration on it); it is one of six sonnets in alexandrines, twelve-syllabled lines adapted from the standard French meter, in the collection.

Knowledge might pity win, and pity grace obtain,
I sought fit words to paint the blackest face of woe:
Studying inventions fine,° her wits to entertain,
Oft turning others' leaves, to see if thence would flow
Some fresh and fruitful showers upon my sunburned brain.°
But words came halting forth, wanting Invention's stay;
10   Invention, Nature's child, fled stepdame Study's blows;
And others' feet° still seemed but strangers in my way.
Thus, great with child to speak, and helpless in my throes,
  Biting my truant pen, beating myself for spite:
  'Fool,' said my Muse to me, 'look in thy heart, and write!'°

II

Not at the first sight, nor with a dribbed° shot,
Love gave the wound which, while I breathe, will bleed;
But known worth did in mine° of time proceed,
Till, by degrees, it had full conquest got.
I saw, and liked; I liked, but lovèd not;
I loved, but straight did not what Love decreed:
At length to Love's decrees I, forced, agreed,
Yet with repining at so partial lot.°
Now even that footstep° of lost liberty
10   Is gone, and now, like slave-born Muscovite,
I call it praise to suffer tyranny;
And now employ the remnant of my wit
  To make myself believe that all is well,
  While, with a feeling skill,° I paint my hell.

III

Let dainty wits cry on the Sisters nine,°
That bravely masked, their fancies may be told;
Or, Pindar's apes,° flaunt they in phrases fine,
Enamelling with pied flowers their thoughts of gold;
Or else let them in statelier glory shine,
Ennobling new-found tropes° with problems old;

inventions fine *Inventio* (here not the person-ified process, as in l. 8, but its results) is the first of the three phases of composition—with *dispositio*, or structure, and *elocutio*, or style—recognized in the Renaissance; these "fine" inventions, obviously, will not do for Stella's poet.
sunburned brain Astrophel's study of courtly verse ("Oft turning others' leaves") accounts for his "sunburned brain," for this striking phrase refers to an accepted Elizabethan figure for poetic imitation. Sidney draws out what is implied in the metaphor from Thomas Wilson's *Art of Rhetoric*, the parched sense of the man who has walked too long in the sun of the ancients.
feet metrical feet as well
'Fool . . . write' that is, look in your heart and find Stella's image there and write from that image, that source and origin of true poetry (that poetry, in fact, will be Petrarchan)

dribbed dribbled, random
mine tunnel dug to undermine fortified walls: just so time undermines emotional resistance
repining . . . lot complaining of a judgment so unfair to my side of the case
footstep footprint
feeling skill the skill bred of feeling; a skill that is itself sensible of the emotions it depicts
Let . . . nine "Let weaker, foppish minds appeal to the Muses." The strategy in this sonnet will be to authenticate Stella as the true Muse by rejecting the artifices of literature, particularly of all the fashionable theories of poetry of Sidney's day.
Pindar's apes French lyric poets like Ronsard, claiming to ape Pindar, the Greek master of choral lyric, by their use of the term "ode" and the "flowers" of rhetorical art.
tropes figures of thought (see Rhetoric in the Glossary)

Or with strange similes° enrich each line,
Of herbs or beasts which Ind or Afric hold.
For me, in sooth, no Muse but one I know;
10 Phrases and problems from my reach do grow,
And strange things cost too dear for my poor sprites.°
How then? Even thus: in Stella's face I read
What love and beauty be; then all my deed
But copying is, what, in her, Nature writes.

V

It is most true that eyes are formed to serve
The inward light,° and that the heavenly part
Ought to be king, from whose rules who do swerve,
Rebels to nature, strive for their own smart.
It is most true, what we call Cupid's dart
An image is, which for ourselves we carve
And, fools, adore in temple of our heart,
Till that good god make church and churchmen starve.
True, that true beauty virtue is indeed,
10 Whereof this beauty can be but a shade,°
Which elements with mortal mixture breed.
True, that on earth we are but pilgrims made,°
    And should in soul up to our country move.
    True, and yet true that I must Stella love.

XIV

Alas, have I not pain enough, my friend,
Upon whose breast a fiercer gripe doth tire°
Than did on him who first stole down the fire,°
While Love on me doth all his quiver spend—
But with your rhubarb° words ye must contend,
To grieve me worse, in saying that Desire
Doth plunge my well-formed soul even in the mire
Of sinful thoughts, which do in ruin end?
If that be sin which doth the manners° frame,
10 Well stayed with truth in word and faith of deed,
Ready of wit, and fearing naught but shame;
If that be sin, which in fixed hearts doth breed
    A loathing of all loose unchastity,
    Then love is sin, and let me sinful be.

strange similes the over-elaborate prose style and exotic comparisons of the so-called Euphuistic style (see the selection from John Lyly)
sprites spirits
inward light reason, which ought to rule over the whole person; yet love, by another convention, enters at the eye and imprints the beloved's image on the heart
shade image or picture; a standard Platonic theme

pilgrims made the medieval notion of life as a mere pilgrimage to the eternal life beyond death
gripe doth tire grip does rip
him who . . . fire Prometheus, punished by being chained to a rock with a vulture to lunch on his liver
rhubarb used as a bitter laxative
manners moral style

XV

You that do search for every purling spring
Which from the ribs of old Parnassus° flows,
And every flower, not sweet perhaps, which grows
Near thereabouts, into your poesy wring;°
You that do dictionary's method° bring
Into your rhymes, running in rattling rows;
You that poor Petrarch's long deceasèd woes
With newborn sighs and denizened° wit do sing:
You take wrong ways; those far-fet° helps be such
10   As do bewray° a want of inward touch,°
And sure at length stolen goods do come to light;
But if, both for your love and skill, your name
You seek to nurse at fullest breasts of Fame,
Stella behold, and then begin to indite.

XX

Fly, fly, my friends—I have my death wound—fly!
See there that boy, that murdering boy, I say,
Who, like a thief, hid in dark bush doth lie
Till bloody bullet get him wrongful prey.°
So tyrant he no fitter place could spy,
Nor so fair level in so secret stay,°
As that sweet black which veils the heavenly eye;
There himself with his shot he close° doth lay.
Poor passenger,° pass now thereby I did,
10   And stayed, pleased with the prospect of the place,
While that black hue from me the bad guest hid;
But straight I saw motions of lightning grace,
    And then descried the glistering of his dart;
    But ere I could fly thence, it pierced my heart.

XXV

The wisest scholar of the wight most wise°
By Phoebus' doom, with sugared sentence says
That Virtue, if it once met with our eyes,
Strange flames of love it in our souls would raise;
But, for that° man with pain this truth descries,

Parnassus the other Greek mountain of inspiration, on which were Delphi (Apollo's
oracle) and the Castalian spring, like the Hippocrene spring on Mt. Helicon sacred to the
Muses
poesy wring twist into your wreath, work into
your poem
dictionary's method alliterative, lame lines, as
below
denizened naturalized into English. Sidney, as a
devout Petrarchan, is prophetically attacking
his own weaker imitators-to-be, and doing so
as part of a Petrarchan strategy—only a vision
of the Lady is sufficiently heavenly inspiration,

and all literary methods are to be shunned.
far-fet farfetched
bewray betray
inward touch true imagination
Till . . . prey For the image of the "hunter
hunted" see "Ye Goatherd Gods."
so fair . . . stay get such a good aim in so
secret a place
close secretly
passenger passer-by
wight most wise wisest man: Socrates (declared so by Apollo, see next line); his wisest
scholar, Plato
for that because

While he each thing in sense's balance weighs,
And so nor will nor can behold those skies
Which inward sun° to heroic mind displays,
Virtue of late, with virtuous care to stir
10 Love of herself, takes Stella's shape, that she
To mortal eyes might sweetly shine in her.
It is most true; for since I her did see,
   Virtue's great beauty in that face I prove,°
   And find the effect, for I do burn in love.

XXVI

Though dusty wits dare scorn astrology,
And fools can think those lamps of purest light°
—Whose numbers, ways, greatness, eternity,
Promising wonders, wonder do invite—
To have for no cause birthright in the sky
But for to spangle the black weeds° of night;
Or for some brawl° which in that chamber high
They should still dance to please a gazer's sight.
For me, I do Nature unidle° know,
10 And know great causes great effects procure;
And know those bodies high reign on° the low.
And if these rules did fail, proof makes me sure,
   Who oft forejudge my after-following race°
   By only those two stars in Stella's face.

XXVIII

You that with allegory's curious frame
Of others' children changelings use to make,°
With me those pains, for God's sake, do not take;
I list° not dig so deep for brazen fame.
When I say Stella, I do mean the same
Princess of beauty, for whose only sake
The reins of Love I love, though never slack,
And joy therein, though nations count it shame.
I beg no subject to use eloquence,°
10 Nor in hid ways do guide philosophy;
Look at my hands for no such quintessence;°
But know that I in pure simplicity
   Breathe out the flames which burn within my heart,
   Love only reading unto me this art.

inward sun See Sonnet V, l. 2n.
prove try out
lamps . . . light the stars
weeds garments
brawl branle, a ring-dance, hence appropriate to the spheres' rotation
Nature unidle Nature to be active
reign on rule over, with a pun on "rain (influence—see Astrology in the Glossary) down on"

race life, seen as a pursuit of a goal
You that . . . make you who misread poems by taking them allegorically
list wish
I beg . . . eloquence I'm not out of ideas to use my style for
quintessence Aside from the four earthly elements, there was ether, a non-material essence which pervaded all matter, and which the alchemists labored unsuccessfully to extract.

XXXIII

I might—unhappy word—oh me, I might,
And then would not, or could not, see my bliss;
Till now wrapped in a most infernal night,
I find how heavenly day (wretch) I did miss.
Heart, rent° thyself, thou dost thyself but right;
No lovely Paris made thy Helen his;
No force, no fraud robbed thee of thy delight,
Nor Fortune of thy fortune author is;
But to myself myself did give the blow,
10   While too much wit, forsooth, so troubled me
That I respects° for both our sakes must show;
And yet could not, by rising morn, foresee
    How fair a day was near—oh punished eyes,
    That I had been more foolish, or more wise!

XLIX

I on my horse, and Love on me, doth try
Our horsemanships, while by strange work I prove
A horseman to my horse, a horse to Love,
And now man's wrongs in me, poor beast, descry.°
The reins wherewith my rider doth me tie
Are humbled thoughts, which bit of reverence move,
Curbed in with fear, but with gilt boss° above
Of hope, which makes it seem fair to the eye.
The wand° is will; thou, fancy, saddle art,
10   Girt fast by memory; and while I spur
My horse, he spurs with sharp desire my heart;
He sits me fast, however I do stir;
    And now hath made me to his hand so right
    That in the manege° myself takes delight.

LXXI

Who will in fairest book of Nature know
How virtue may best lodged in beauty be,
Let him but learn of love to read in thee,
Stella, those fair lines which true goodness show.
There shall he find all vices' overthrow,
Not by rude force, but sweetest sovereignty
Of reason, from whose light those night-birds° fly,
That inward sun° in thine eyes shineth so.
And, not content to be perfection's heir
10   Thyself, dost strive all minds that way to move,
Who mark in thee what is in thee most fair.

rent tear
respects due regard
man's wrongs . . . descry I perceive marks of
a rider's cruelty on me
boss ornamental gold stud on the bit

wand whip
manege art of horsemanship
night-birds the vices
inward sun here, as throughout these sonnets,
reason; cf. Sonnets V and XXV

So while thy beauty draws the heart to love,
  As fast thy virtue bends that love to good.
  But, ah, Desire still cries, 'Give me some food.'

1591

DEFENCE OF POESIE

In 1579 Stephen Gosson (1554–1624), having been converted to the prevailing Puritan view that all the arts were pernicious, published "a pleasant invective" against them entitled *The School of Abuse;* and, presuming on Sidney's more cultivated Puritan sympathies, dedicated it to him. Sidney, says Gabriel Harvey, scorned him for his labor, "if at least it be in the goodness of that nature to scorn." Thomas Lodge published a *Defence* (1579), and Sidney reacted in the present work, first published after his death in 1595, but probably written about 1582. Sidney had better things to do than to reply in detail to Gosson, who merely provided the occasion for what is recognized as the most distinguished work of Elizabethan criticism and literary theory, its only rival, Puttenham's *Art of English Poesie* (1589), being less brilliant and speculative, though very useful.

Sidney planned the work carefully on the lines of a classical forensic defense, but concealed the rigidity of its organization under a flow of easy civilized prose. He also, in gentlemanly manner, refrained from a parade of learning, though he evidently knew the leading Continental critics J. C. Scaliger and A. S. Minturno and was at home with the classics. His argument is notable for its emphasis not only on the superior power of poetry to instruct, but on its inspiration, a doctrine he has to deal with at its source in Plato. It is this power which enables the poet to surpass philosophers and historians in his service to society and to morality. And it is this power which surpasses even the one which Sidney sees in the poet, who, "lifted up with the vigour of his own invention, doth grow in effect another nature, in making things either better than nature bringeth forth, or, quite anew, forms such as never were in nature, as the Heroes, Demigods, Cyclops, Chimeras, Furies, and such like: so as he goeth hand in hand with nature, and enclosed within the narrow warrant of her gifts, but freely ranging only within the zodiac of his own wit." Sidney combines with his views on inspiration a notable defense of the utility of fiction, not only because it avoids the generalities of the philosopher and the insignificant particularities of the historian but also because it can speak without necessarily making assertions: *now, for the poet, he nothing affirms, and therefore never lieth.* Apart from this subtle defense of fiction, Sidney's most penetrating idea may be that the poet (though, following Aristotle, he calls him an imitator of nature) is in fact a creator, a second nature, dealing with essential ideas and not their copies. Here, as elsewhere, he manipulates the conflicting texts of Plato in favor of poetry. For the rest, his lively and good-humored attack on the poet-haters, and his survey, cool but not bitter, of the contemporary English literary scene, are conducted with an easy and unaffected elegance rather rare in the English prose of the period.

From Defence of Poesie

[The opening is light and anecdotal in manner, establishing the easy tone of a lively gentleman's conversation. Sidney then continues the work by speaking of the antiquity of poetry, and its dignity as the source of other forms of knowledge.]

First, truly, to all them that professing learning inveigh against poetry may justly be objected that they go very near to ungratefulness, to seek to deface that which, in the noblest nations and languages that are known, hath been the first light-giver to ignorance, and first nurse, whose milk by little and little enabled them to feed afterwards of tougher knowledges. And will they now play the hedgehog that, being received into the den, drove out his host, or rather the vipers, that with their birth kill their parents? Let learned Greece in any of her manifold sciences be able to show me one book before Musaeus, Homer, and Hesiod,[1] all three nothing else but poets. Nay, let any history be brought that can say any writers were there before them, if they were not men of the same skill, as Orpheus, Linus,[2] and some other are named, who, having been the first of that country that made pens deliverers of their knowledge to their posterity, may justly challenge to be called their fathers in learning, for not only in time they had this priority (although in itself antiquity be venerable) but went before them, as causes to draw with their charming sweetness the wild untamed wits to an admiration of knowledge, so as Amphion was said to move stones with his poetry to build Thebes, and Orpheus[3] to be listened to by beasts—indeed stony and beastly people.[4] So among the Romans were Livius Andronicus and Ennius.[5] So in the Italian language the first that made it aspire to be a treasure-house of science were the poets Dante, Boccaccio and Petrarch.[6] So in our English were Gower and Chaucer, after whom, encouraged and delighted with their excellent foregoing, others have followed, to beautify our mother tongue, as well in the same kind as in other arts.

This did so notably show itself, that the philosophers of Greece durst not a long time appear to the world but under the masks of poets. . . . And truly, even Plato,[7] whosoever well considereth shall find that in the body of his work, though the inside and strength were philosophy, the skin as it were and beauty depended most of poetry: for all standeth upon dialogues, wherein he feigneth many honest burgesses of Athens to speak of such matters, that if they had been set on the rack they would never have confessed them, besides his poetical

1. Musaeus (non-historical), supposed to have been a pupil of Orpheus (see Marlowe, *Hero and Leander*); Hesiod, 7th-century B.C., author of the didactic *Works and Days*.
2. Non-historical poet.
3. Amphion made the rocks, and Orpheus the trees, follow his harp and do his bidding.
4. An allegorical interpretation of the story; see the section The Renaissance Ovid.
5. L. Andronicus, Latin poet and playwright of 3rd century B.C.; Ennius, Latin epic poet, 239–169 B.C.
6. Dante Alighieri (1265–1321) used the vernacular for his *Commedia*, which included much contemporary learning; Giovanni Boccaccio (1313–75), humanist scholar and writer of tales; Francesco Petrarca (1304–74), learned poet and humanist.
7. Plato was cited by the opponents of poetry because he excluded poets from his *Republic* as liars; but he himself used fictive dialogues and myths in his philosophy. Medieval and Renaissance theories of allegory and of biblical interpretation frequently used the image of shell and kernel to stand for literal ("outer") meaning and inner, or figurative, truth.

describing the circumstances of their meetings, as the well ordering of a banquet, the delicacy of a walk, with interlacing mere tales, as Gyges' Ring [8] and others, which who knoweth not to be flowers of poetry did never walk into Apollo's garden.

And even historiographers [9] (although their lips sound of things done, and verity be written in their foreheads) have been glad to borrow both fashion and perchance weight of poets. So Herodotus entitled his history by the name of the nine Muses; [10] and both he and all the rest that followed him either stole or usurped of poetry their passionate describing of passions, the many particularities of battles, which no man could affirm, or, if that be denied me, long orations put in the mouths of great kings and captains, which it is certain they never pronounced. So that, truly, neither philosopher nor historiographer could at the first have entered into the gates of popular judgments, if they had not taken a great passport of poetry, which in all nations at this day, where learning flourisheth not, is plain to be seen, in all which they have some feeling of poetry.

. . .

Nature never set forth the earth in so rich tapestry as divers poets have done—neither with pleasant rivers, fruitful trees, sweet-smelling flowers, nor whatsoever else may make the too much loved earth more lovely. Her world is brazen, the poets only deliver a golden. But let those things alone, and go to man—for whom as the other things are, so it seemeth in him her uttermost cunning is employed—and know whether she have brought forth so true a lover as Theagenes, [11] so constant a friend as Pylades, [12] so valiant a man as Orlando, [13] so right a prince as Xenophon's Cyrus, [14] so excellent a man every way as Virgil's Aeneas. Neither let this be jestingly conceived because the works of the one be essential, the other in imitation or fiction; for any understanding knoweth the skill of the artificer standeth in that idea or foreconceit of the work and not in the work itself. [15] And that the poet hath that idea is mainifest, by delivering them forth in such excellency as he hath imagined them. Which delivering forth also is not wholly imaginative, as we are wont to say by them that build castles in the air: but so far substantially it worketh, not only to make a Cyrus, which had been but a particular excellency, as nature might have done, but to bestow a Cyrus upon the world, to make many Cyruses, if they will learn aright why and how that maker [16] made him.

Neither let it be deemed too saucy a comparison to balance the highest point of man's wit with the efficacy of nature; but rather give right honour to the heavenly maker of that maker, who, having made man to his own likeness, set

---

8. Gyges, a Lydian shepherd, gained possession of a ring that could make him invisible; he used it to seduce the queen and kill the king (Plato, *Republic* 359–60).
9. Historians.
10. The nine books of his history are named for the Muses.
11. Hero of the Greek romance *Aethiopica* by Heliodorus (3rd century A.D.)
12. Friend of Orestes; their fidelity was proverbial.
13. Hero of Ariosto's *Orlando Furioso* (1515).
14. Subject of Xenophon's *Cyropaedia, The Education of Cyrus* (early 4th century B.C.).
15. It does not follow that because the work is fictive the idea of it is not valid; it pre-exists the work and has substance, more even than a natural creation.
16. Sidney has previously explained that the Greeks called the poet the "maker."

him beyond and over all the works of that second nature: which in nothing he showeth so much as in poetry, when with the force of a divine breath he bringeth things forth far surpassing her doings, with no small argument to the incredulous of that first accursed fall of Adam, since our erected wit maketh us know what perfection is, and yet our infected will keepeth us from reaching unto it. . . . [Sidney proceeds to "a more ordinary opening" of the subject.]

Poesy therefore is an art of imitation, for so Aristotle termeth it [17] in his word *Mimesis*, that is to say, a representing, counterfeiting, or figuring forth—to speak metaphorically, a speaking picture; [18] with this end, to teach and delight. Of this have been three several kinds.

The chief, both in antiquity and excellency, were they that did imitate the inconceivable excellencies of God. Such were David in his Psalms; Solomon in his Song of Songs, in his Ecclesiastes, and Proverbs; Moses and Deborah in their Hymns, [19] and the writer of Job, which, beside other, the learned Emanuel Tremellius [20] and Franciscus Junius [21] do entitle the poetical part of the Scripture. Against these none will speak that hath the Holy Ghost in due holy reverence. In this kind, though in a full wrong divinity, were Orpheus, Amphion, Homer in his Hymns . . . [Sidney's second kind of poet is philosophical.]

. . . [The] third be they which most properly do imitate to teach and delight,[22] and to imitate borrow nothing of what is, hath been, or shall be; but range, only reined with learned discretion, into the divine consideration of what may be, and should be.[23] These be they that, as the first and most noble sort may justly be termed *Vates*,[24] so these are waited on in the excellentest languages and best understandings, with the foredescribed name of poets; for these indeed do merely make to imitate, and imitate both to delight and teach, and delight to move men to take that goodness in hand, which without delight they would fly as from a stranger, and teach, to make them know that goodness whereunto they are moved: which being the noblest scope to which ever any learning was directed, yet want there not idle tongues to bark at them.

These be subdivided into sundry more special denominations. The most notable be the heroic, lyric, tragic, comic, satiric, iambic, elegiac, pastoral, and certain others, some of these being termed according to the matter they deal with, some by the sorts of verses they liked best to write in; for indeed the greatest part of poets have apparelled their poetical inventions in that numbrous [25] kind of writing which is called verse—indeed but apparelled, verse being but an ornament and no cause to poetry, since there have been many most excellent poets that never versified, and now swarm many versifiers that need never answer to the name of poets. For Xenophon, who did imitate so excellently as to give us *effigiem justi imperii*, 'the portraiture of a just Empire,'

---

17. *Poetics* I.2, which Sidney probably got from Scaliger's *Poetices Libri Septem*.
18. The phrase has a long history, going back to Plutarch and beyond.
19. Exodus 15:1–19, Judges 5.
20. Jewish Bible scholar converted to Protestantism (1510–80).
21. Edited a Latin Bible with Tremellius (1545–1602).
22. The requirement of Horace, always endorsed.
23. Aristotle, *Poetics* IX.1–3; see note 29 below.
24. Latin; Sidney earlier translates "diviner, foreseer, or prophet."
25. Metrical.

under name of Cyrus (as Cicero saith of him), made therein an absolute heroical poem. So did Heliodorus in his sugared invention of that picture of love in Theagenes and Chariclea;[26] and yet both these writ in prose: which I speak to show that it is not rhyming and versing that maketh a poet, no more than a long gown maketh an advocate, who though he pleaded in armour should be an advocate and no soldier. But it is that feigning notable images of virtues, vices, or what else, with that delightful teaching, which must be the right describing note to know a poet by, although indeed the senate of poets hath chosen verse as their fittest raiment, meaning, as in matter they passed all in all, so in manner to go beyond them—not speaking, table-talk fashion or like men in a dream, words as they chanceably fall from the mouth, but peizing [27] each syllable of each word by just proportion according to the dignity of the subject.

[Sidney now proceeds to the next task, the examination of poetry with respect to its rivals for the title of *Architectonikè*, the "mistress-knowledge." He finds that philosophy is too general, history too tied to particulars.]

The philosopher therefore and the historian are they which would win the goal, the one by precept, the other by example. But both, not having both, do both halt.[28] For the philosopher, setting down with thorny argument the bare rule, is so hard of utterance and so misty to be conceived, that one that hath no other guide but him shall wade in him till he be old before he shall find sufficient cause to be honest. For his knowledge standeth so upon the abstract and general, that happy is that man who may understand him, and more happy that can apply what he doth understand. On the other side the historian, wanting the precept, is so tied, not to what should be but to what is, to the particular truth of things and not to the general reason of things, that his example draweth no necessary consequence, and therefore a less fruitful doctrine.

Now doth the peerless poet perform both: for whatsoever the philosopher saith should be done, he giveth a perfect picture of it in someone by whom he presupposeth it was done; so as he coupleth the general notion with the particular example. A perfect picture I say, for he yieldeth to the powers of the mind an image of that whereof the philosopher bestoweth but a wordish description: which doth neither strike, pierce, nor possess the sight of the soul so much as that other doth.

For as in outward things, to a man that had never seen an elephant or a rhinoceros, who should tell him most exquisitely all their shapes, colour, bigness, and particular marks, or of a gorgeous palace the architecture, with declaring the full beauties might well make the hearer able to repeat, as it were by rote, all he had heard, yet should never satisfy his inward conceits with being witness to itself of a true lively knowledge: but the same man, as soon as he might see those beasts well painted, or the house well in model, should straightways grow, without need of any description, to a judicial comprehending of them: so no doubt the philosopher with his learned definition—be it of virtue, vices, matters of public policy or private government—replenisheth the memory with many infallible grounds of wisdom, which, notwithstanding, lie dark before the imag-

26. See note 11.
27. Weighing.
28. Limp.

inative and judging power, if they be not illuminated or figured forth by the speaking picture of poesy.

[After explaining that even primitive cultures had poets, Sidney goes on to speak of the honorable names given to poets by the Greeks and Romans; he calls the Psalms a "divine poem." He thinks this right because, unlike other learned activities, poetry does not depend on nature but creates a second nature of its own.]

But now may it be alleged that, if this imagining of matters be so fit for the imagination, then must the historian needs surpass, who bringeth you images of true matters, such as indeed were done, and not such as fantastically or falsely may be suggested to have been done. Truly, Aristotle [29] himself, in his discourse of poesy, plainly determineth this question, saying that poetry is *Philosophoteron* and *Spoudaioteron*, that is to say, it is more philosophical and more studiously serious than history. His reason is, because poesy dealeth with *Katholou*, that is to say, with the universal consideration, and the history with *Kathekaston*, the particular: 'now,' saith he, 'the universal weighs what is fit to be said or done, either in likelihood or necessity (which the poesy considereth in his imposed names), and the particular only marks whether Alcibiades did, or suffered, this or that.' Thus far Aristotle: which reason of his, as all his, is most full of reason. For indeed, if the question were whether it were better to have a particular act truly or falsely set down, there is no doubt which is to be chosen, no more than whether you had rather have Vespasian's [30] picture right as he was, or at the painter's pleasure nothing resembling. But if the question be for your own use and learning, whether it be better to have it set down as it should be, or as it was, then certainly is more doctrinable the feigned Cyrus in Xenophon than the true Cyrus in Justin, [31] and the feigned Aeneas in Virgil than the right Aeneas in Dares Phrygius: [32] as to a lady that desired to fashion her countenance to the best grace, a painter should more benefit her to portrait a most sweet face, writing Canidia upon it, than to paint Canidia as she was, who, Horace sweareth, was foul and ill favoured.[33]

If the poet do his part aright, he will show you in Tantalus, Atreus,[34] and such like, nothing that is not to be shunned; in Cyrus, Aeneas, Ulysses, each thing to be followed; where the historian, bound to tell things as things were, cannot be liberal (without he will be poetical) of a perfect pattern, but, as in Alexander or Scipio himself, show doings, some to be liked, some to be misliked. And then how will you discern what to follow but by your own discretion, which you had without reading Quintus Curtius? [35] . . .

29. Aristotle (*Poetics* IX) says that poetry (by which he means "fiction" more generally) is *philosophoteron kai spoudaioteron* ("more philosophical and more serious") than history because it deals with the general, while history deals with the particular.
30. Roman emperor, 70–79 A.D.
31. Marcus Junianus Justinus, Roman historian of the 2nd century A.D.
32. A medieval account of the Trojan war, attributed to the non-existent eyewitness Dares Phrygius, was long thought to be older than Homer.
33. Canidia is a witch-like figure in Horace, *Epode* V and *Satires* I.8.
34. Tantalus was punished in hell by perpetual hunger and thirst though almost within reach of water and food, for his blasphemous ambition. He served his son Pelops as a dish to the gods. Atreus served his brother Thyestes a meal consisting of Thyestes' sons.
35. Author of a history of Alexander the Great in the 1st century A.D.

[Sidney develops the point that poetry uses the material of history, but more usefully, and argues that its supremacy lies in the fact that it not only instructs but moves its listeners to act on the instruction.]

Now therein of all sciences (I speak still of human, and according to the humane conceits) is our poet the monarch. For he doth not only show the way, but giveth so sweet a prospect into the way, as will entice any man to enter into it. Nay, he doth, as if your journey should lie through a fair vineyard, at the first give you a cluster of grapes, that, full of that taste, you may long to pass further. He beginneth not with obscure definitions, which must blur the margent [36] with interpretations, and load the memory with doubtfulness; [37] but he cometh to you with words set in delightful proportion, either accompanied with or prepared for, the well-enchanting skill of music; and with a tale forsooth he cometh unto you, with a tale which holdeth children from play, and old men from the chimney corner. And, pretending no more, doth intend the winning of the mind from wickedness to virtue: even as the child is often brought to take most wholesome things by hiding them in such other as have a pleasant taste: which, if one should begin to tell them the nature of aloes [38] or rhubarb they should receive, would sooner take their physic at their ears than at their mouth. So is it in men (most of which are childish in the best things, till they be cradled in their graves): glad they will be to hear the tales of Hercules, Achilles, Cyrus, and Aeneas; and, hearing them, must needs hear the right description of wisdom, valour, and justice; which, if they had been barely, that is to say philosophically, set out, they would swear they be brought to school again.

[Sidney now gives further examples of poetry's power to move.]

By these, therefore, examples and reasons, I think it may be manifest that the poet, with that same hand of delight, doth draw the mind more effectually than any other art doth: and so a conclusion not unfitly ensueth, that, as virtue is the most excellent resting place for all worldly learning to make his end of, so poetry, being the most familiar to teach it, and most princely to move towards it, in the most excellent work is the most excellent workman. . . .

[Sidney now considers objections to the different kinds of poetry: pastoral, elegiac, comic, tragic, lyric, epic; all of which he finds of social value, as well as productive of pleasure. He sums up:]

Since then poetry is of all human learning the most ancient and of most fatherly antiquity, as from whence other learnings have taken their beginnings; since it is so universal that no learned nation doth despise it, nor no barbarous nation is without it; since both Roman and Greek gave divine names unto it, the one of 'prophesying,' the other of 'making,' and that indeed that name of 'making' is fit for him, considering that whereas other arts retain themselves within their subject, and receive, as it were, their being from it, the poet only bringeth his own stuff, and doth not learn a conceit [39] out of a matter, but maketh matter for a conceit; since neither his description nor his end containeth any evil, the thing described cannot be evil; since his effects be so good as to

36. Margin.
37. Disputed points.
38. Bitter purgative; for "rhubarb" see *Astrophel and Stella*, Sonnet XIV, l. 5n.
39. Concept, idea; see Glossary.

teach goodness and to delight the learners; since therein (namely in moral doctrine, the chief of all knowledges) he doth not only far pass the historian, but, for instructing, is well-nigh comparable to the philosopher, and, for moving, leaves him behind him; since the Holy Scripture (wherein there is no uncleanness) hath whole parts in it poetical, and that even our Saviour Christ vouchsafed to use the flowers of it; since all his kinds are not only in their united forms but in their severed dissections fully commendable; I think (and think I think rightly) the laurel crown appointed for triumphing captains doth worthily (of all other learnings) honour the poet's triumph.[40] But because we have ears as well as tongues, and that the lightest reasons that may be will seem to weigh greatly, if nothing be put in the counterbalance, let us hear, and, as well as we can, ponder, what objections may be made against this art, which may be worthy either of yielding or answering.

[Sidney now turns on the *Mysomousoi*, poet-haters, first dealing with their more trivial objections and rhetorical point-scoring. Speech, next to reason, is our greatest gift, and verse is the highest form of speech. Then he begins the defense against more serious and specific charges.]

Now then go we to the most important imputations laid to the poor poets. For aught I can yet learn, they are these. First, that there being many other more fruitful knowledges, a man might better spend his time in them than in this. Secondly, that it is the mother of lies. Thirdly, that it is the nurse of abuse, infecting us with many pestilent desires, with a siren's sweetness drawing the mind to the serpent's tale of sinful fancy—and herein, especially, comedies give the largest field to ear (as Chaucer saith)[41]—how both in other nations and in ours, before poets did soften us, we were full of courage, given to martial exercises, the pillars of manlike liberty, and not lulled asleep in shady idleness with poets' pastimes. And lastly, and chiefly, they cry out with an open mouth, as if they outshot Robin Hood, that Plato banished them out of his Commonwealth.[42] Truly, this is much, if there be much truth in it. First, to the first, that a man might better spend his time is a reason indeed: but it doth (as they say) but *petere principium:* [43] for if it be, as I affirm, that no learning is so good as that which teacheth and moveth to virtue, and that none can both teach and move thereto so much as poetry, then is the conclusion manifest that ink and paper cannot be to a more profitable purpose employed. And certainly, though a man should grant their first assumption, it should follow (methinks) very unwillingly, that good is not good because better is better. But I still and utterly deny that there is sprung out of earth a more fruitful knowledge. To the second therefore, that they should be the principal liars, I answer paradoxically, but truly, I think truly, that of all writers under the sun the poet is the least liar, and, though he would, as a poet can scarcely be a liar. The astronomer, with his cousin the geometrician, can hardly escape, when they take upon them to

40. The laurel crown, worn by the central figure in a Roman triumph, was also claimed by poets.
41. Knight's Tale, l. 28: "I have, God wot, a large field to ere" (plow).
42. Gosson had stressed this point, which depends principally on *Republic* 607a, where Plato says that except for hymns there should be no poetry allowed in the republic, not even Homer.
43. "Beg the question."

measure the height of the stars. How often, think you, do the physicians lie, when they aver things good for sicknesses, which afterwards send Charon [44] a great number of souls drowned in a potion before they come to his ferry? And no less of the rest, which take upon them to affirm. Now, for the poet, he nothing affirms, and therefore never lieth. For, as I take it, to lie is to affirm that to be true which is false; so as the other artists, and especially the historian, affirming many things, can, in the cloudy knowledge of mankind, hardly escape from many lies. But the poet (as I said before) never affirmeth. The poet never maketh any circles about your imagination, to conjure you to believe for true what he writes. He citeth not authorities of other histories, but even for his entry calleth the sweet Muses to inspire into him a good invention; in truth, not laboring to tell you what is, or is not, but what should or should not be. And therefore, though he recount things not true, yet because he telleth them not for true, he lieth not . . . What child is there that, coming to a play, and seeing *Thebes* written in great letters upon an old door,[45] doth believe that it is Thebes? If then a man can arrive, at that child's age, to know that the poets' persons and doings are but pictures what should be, and not stories what have been, they will never give the lie to things not affirmatively but allegorically and figuratively written. And therefore, as in history, looking for truth, they go away full fraught with falsehood, so in poesy, looking for fiction, they shall use the narration but as an imaginative ground-plot of a profitable invention.

But hereto is replied, that the poets give names to men they write of, which argueth a conceit of an actual truth, and so, not being true, proves a falsehood. And doth the lawyer lie then, when under the names of 'John a Stile' and 'John a Noakes' [46] he puts his case? But that is easily answered. Their naming of men is but to make their picture the more lively, and not to build any history; painting men, they cannot leave men nameless. We see we cannot play at chess but that we must give names to our chessmen; and yet, methinks, he were a very partial champion of truth that would say we lied for giving a piece of wood the reverend title of a bishop. The poet nameth Cyrus or Aeneas no other way than to show what men of their fames, fortunes, and estates should do.

[Having dealt with the first two objections, that other kinds of knowledge are more profitable and that poets tell lies, Sidney turns to the charge that poetry can corrupt; he admits this, but treats it as a confirmation of the fact that it can also edify and improve. "But what, shall the abuse of a thing make the right use odious? Nay truly, though I yield that poetry may not only be abused, but that being abused, by the reason of his sweet charming force, it can do more hurt than any other army of words, yet shall it be so far from concluding that the abuse should give reproach to the abused, that contrariwise it is a good reason, that whatsoever, being abused, doth most harm, being rightly used (and upon the right use each thing conceiveth his title) doth most good."

He denies that poetry corrupts military virtue, arguing the contrary. And then he answers the fourth objection, which is made with the authority of Plato.]

But now indeed my burden is great; now Plato's name is laid upon me, whom, I must confess, of all philosophers I have ever esteemed most worthy of rev-

---

44. Ferryman of Hades who bore the newly arrived dead across the Styx.
45. It was a custom in the Elizabethan playhouse to indicate the place of the action thus.
46. Fictitious names used in certain kinds of suit in the English courts.

erence, and with great reason, since of all philosophers he is the most poetical. Yet if he will defile the fountain out of which his flowing streams have proceeded, let us boldly examine with what reasons he did it. First truly, a man might maliciously object that Plato, being a philosopher, was a natural enemy of poets.[47] For indeed, after the philosophers had picked out of the sweet mysteries of poetry the right discerning true points of knowledge, they forthwith, putting it in method, and making a school art of that which the poets did only teach by a divine delightfulness, beginning to spurn at their guides, like ungrateful prentices, were not content to set up shops for themselves, but sought by all means to discredit their masters; which by the force of delight being barred them, the less they could overthrow them the more they hated them. For indeed, they found for Homer seven cities strove who should have him for their citizen; where many cities banished philosophers as not fit members to live among them. For only repeating certain of Euripides' verses, many Athenians had their lives saved of the Syracusians,[48] when the Athenians themselves thought many philosophers unworthy to live. Certain poets, as Simonides and Pindarus, had so prevailed with Hiero the First, that of a tyrant they made him a just king,[49] where Plato could do so little with Dionysius, that he himself of a philosopher was made a slave.[50] But who should do thus, I confess, should requite the objections made against poets with like cavilation[51] against philosophers; as likewise one should do that should bid one read *Phaedrus* or *Symposium* in Plato, or the discourse of love in Plutarch, and see whether any poet do authorize abominable filthiness,[52] as they do. Again, a man might ask out of what commonwealth Plato did banish them. In sooth, thence where he himself alloweth community of women.[53] So as belike this banishment grew not for effeminate wantonness, since little should poetical sonnets be hurtful when a man might have what woman he listed. But I honour philosophical instructions, and bless the wits which bred them: so as they be not abused, which is likewise stretched to poetry.

St. Paul himself, who yet, for the credit of poets, allegeth[54] twice two poets, and one of them by the name of a prophet, setteth a watchword[55] upon philosophy—indeed upon the abuse. So doth Plato upon the abuse, not upon poetry. Plato found fault that the poets of his time filled the world with wrong opinions of the gods, making light tales of that unspotted essence, and therefore would not have the youth depraved with such opinions. Herein may much be said;

47. "There is an ancient quarrel between philosophy and poetry," *Republic* 607.
48. Plutarch (*Nicias* 29) says that the inhabitants of Syracuse in Sicily spared some of the survivors of the unsuccessful Athenian expedition against them (415 B.C.) because they were able to teach them some verses of Euripides, their favorite poet.
49. Hiero I, tyrant of Syracuse, 478–467 B.C., patronized these and other poets and accepted their counsel.
50. Plato went to Sicily in 390 B.C., but the monarch Dionysius disliked his views and is said to have caused him to be sold into slavery.
51. Caviling, quibbling.
52. Homosexual love.
53. Plato admired the physique of the Spartans, who held their women in common, *Republic* 449 ff.
54. St. Paul alludes to the Greek poets Aratus, Cleanthes, Epimenides, and Menander in Acts 17:28, Titus 1:12, and I Corinthians 1:22. Epimenides is called a prophet in Titus.
55. Advises caution.

let this suffice: the poets did not induce such opinions, but did imitate those opinions already induced. For all the Greek stories can well testify that the very religion of that time stood upon many and many-fashioned gods, not taught so by the poets, but followed according to their nature of imitation. Who list may read in Plutarch the discourses of Isis and Osiris, of the cause why oracles ceased, of the divine providence,[56] and see whether the theology of that nation stood not upon such dreams which the poets indeed superstitiously observed, and truly (since they had not the light of Christ) did much better in it than the philosophers, who, shaking off superstition, brought in atheism. Plato therefore (whose authority I had much rather justly construe than unjustly resist) meant not in general of poets, in those words of which Julius Scaliger saith, *Qua authoritate barbari quidam atque hispidi abuti velint ad poetas e republica exigendos;*[57] but only meant to drive out those wrong opinions of the Deity (whereof now, without further law, Christianity hath taken away all the hurtful belief), perchance (as he thought) nourished by the then esteemed poets. And a man need go no further than to Plato himself to know his meaning: who, in his dialogue called *Ion*,[58] giveth high and rightly divine commendation to poetry. So as Plato, banishing the abuse, not the thing, not banishing it, but giving due honour unto it, shall be our patron and not our adversary. For indeed I had much rather (since truly I may do it) show their mistaking of Plato (under whose lion's skin they would make an ass-like braying against poesy) than go about to overthrow his authority; whom, the wiser a man is, the more just cause he shall find to have in admiration; especially since he attributeth unto poesy more than myself do, namely, to be a very inspiring of a divine force, far above man's wit, as in the afore-named dialogue is apparent.

. . . even the Greek Socrates, whom Apollo confirmed to be the only wise man,[59] is said to have spent part of his old time in putting Aesop's fables into verses.[60] And therefore, full evil should it become his scholar Plato to put such words in his master's mouth against poets. But what need more? Aristotle writes the Art of Poesy: and why, if it should not be written? Plutarch teacheth the use to be gathered of them,[61] and how, if they should not be read? And who reads Plutarch's either history or philosophy, shall find he trimmeth both their garments with guards [62] of poesy. But I list not to defend poesy with the help of her underling historiography. Let it suffice that it is a fit soil for praise to dwell upon; and what dispraise may set upon it, is either easily overcome, or transformed into just commendation. So that, since the excellencies of it may be so easily and so justly confirmed, and the low-creeping objections so soon trodden down; it not being an art of lies, but of true doctrine; not of effeminateness, but of notable stirring of courage; not of abusing man's wit, but of strengthening man's wit; not banished, but honoured by Plato; let us rather

56. Titles of essays by Plutarch included in his *Moralia*.
57. "Which authority some rude and barbarous people would like to abuse in order to expel poets from the state."
58. The *Ion*, a somewhat ironical account of the inspiration of poet and reciter, was an important source of doctrine on poetic inspiration.
59. Through the Delphic oracle as reported in Plato's *Apology* 21.
60. Socrates is made to say so in Plato's *Phaedo* 61.
61. In "On Listening to Poetry" in *Moralia*.
62. Ornaments.

plant more laurels for to engarland our poets' heads (which honour of being laureate, as besides them only triumphant captains wear, is a sufficient authority to show the price they ought to be had in) than suffer the ill-favouring breath of such wrong-speakers once to blow upon the clear springs of poesy.

[Sidney now turns his attention to the contemporary state of English poetry, lamenting its decline, but praising some poets old and new.]

Chaucer, undoubtedly, did excellently in his *Troilus and Cressida;* of whom, truly, I know not whether to marvel more, either that he in that misty time could see so clearly, or that we in this clear age walk so stumblingly after him. Yet had he great wants, fit to be forgiven in so reverent antiquity. I account the *Mirror of Magistrates* [63] meetly furnished of beautiful parts, and in the Earl of Surrey's *Lyrics* many things tasting of a noble birth, and worthy of a noble mind. The *Shepherd's Calendar* [64] hath much poetry in his Eclogues, indeed worthy the reading, if I be not deceived. That same framing of his style to an old rustic language I dare not allow, since neither Theocritus in Greek, Virgil in Latin, nor Sannazaro in Italian did affect it. Besides these, do I not remember to have seen but few (to speak boldly) printed, that have poetical sinews in them: for proof whereof, let but most of the verses be put in prose, and then ask the meaning; and it will be found that one verse did but beget another, without ordering at the first what should be at the last; which becomes a confused mass of words, with a tingling sound of rhyme, barely accompanied with reason.

Our tragedies and comedies (not without cause cried out against), observing rules neither of honest civility nor of skillful poetry, excepting *Gorboduc* [65] (again, I say, of those that I have seen), which notwithstanding as [66] it is full of stately speeches and well-sounding phrases, climbing to the height of Seneca's style, and as full of notable morality, which it doth most delightfully teach, and so obtain the very end of poesy, yet in truth it is very defectious in the circumstances,[67] which grieveth me, because it might not remain as an exact model of all tragedies. For it is faulty both in place and time, the two necessary companions of

---

63. *The Mirror for Magistrates* was first published in 1559, then in 1563 with the famous Induction of Thomas Sackville, Earl of Dorset (1536–1608), and in many later editions. It contains metrical tragedies on the falls of great men, known generally, from the first example of the kind in Boccaccio's *De Casibus Virorum Illustrium,* as the *de casibus* theme. The collection had wide circulation in the period.

64. Spenser's book was dedicated to Sidney; see Headnote to *The Shepheardes Calender.*

65. *Gorboduc,* by Sackville and Thomas Norton, was first acted at the Inner Temple in 1561, and was the first regular English dramatic tragedy. It uses blank verse and has a political-historical theme, the horror of civil war, a topic much in Elizabethan minds. The bloody story, the division into five acts, the use of "sentences" or moral pronouncements, and the absence of violence on the stage, suggest the comparison with Seneca, but other elements such as the dumbshows and the English patriotic fervor are nothing like him. The influence of Seneca, whose Latin plays of the 1st century were more for recitation than action, was great in the Renaissance drama of Europe, but there was and is a tendency to overstate its effect on the development of English drama. It should be recalled that *Gorboduc* was written for amateur performers, the law students of the Middle Temple; that it has little influence on later popular drama; and that the themes of man's fall from good fortune and the need for patience (Seneca was a Stoic) have medieval counterparts not always easy to distinguish from it.

66. That.

67. Defective in the arrangement of the narrative.

all corporal actions. For where the stage should always represent but one place, and the uttermost time presupposed in it should be, both by Aristotle's precept and common reason,[68] but one day, there is both many days, and many places, inartificially imagined. But if it be so in *Gorboduc,* how much more in all the rest, where you shall have Asia of the one side, and Afric of the other, and so many other under-kingdoms, that the player, when he cometh in, must ever begin with telling where he is, or else the tale will not be conceived? Now ye shall have three ladies walk to gather flowers, and then we must believe the stage to be a garden. By and by we hear news of shipwreck in the same place, and then we are to blame if we accept it not for a rock. Upon the back of that comes out a hideous monster, with fire and smoke, and then the miserable beholders are bound to take it for a cave. While in the meantime two armies fly in, represented with four swords and bucklers, and then what hard heart will not receive it for a pitched field? Now, of time they are much more liberal, for ordinary it is that two young princes fall in love. After many traverses,[69] she is got with child, delivered of a fair boy; he is lost, groweth a man, falls in love, and is ready to get another child; and all this in two hours' space: which, how absurd it is in sense, even sense may imagine, and art hath taught, and all ancient examples justified, and, at this day, the ordinary players in Italy will not err in. . . .

But besides these gross absurdities, how all their plays be neither right tragedies, nor right comedies, mingling kings and clowns, not because the matter so carrieth it, but thrust in clowns by head and shoulders, to play a part in majestical matters, with neither decency nor discretion, so as neither the admiration and commiseration, nor the right sportfulness, is by their mongrel tragicomedy obtained.[70]. . . So falleth it out that, having indeed no right comedy, in that comical part of our tragedy we have nothing but scurrility, unworthy of any chaste ears, or some extreme show of doltishness, indeed fit to lift up a loud laughter, and nothing else; where the whole tract of a comedy should be full of delight, as the tragedy should be still maintained in a well-raised admiration. But our comedians think there is no delight without laughter; which is very wrong, for though laughter may come with delight, yet cometh it not of delight, as though delight should be the cause of laughter; but well may one thing breed both together. Nay, rather in themselves they have, as it were, a kind of contrariety: for delight we scarcely do but in things that have a conveniency to ourselves or to the general nature: laughter almost ever cometh of things most

68. Aristotle recommended (*Poetics* V) that the action should take place within the compass of twenty-four hours or little more. The other two "unities," of place and action, were inferred from Aristotle by 16th-century commentators after the rediscovery of the *Poetics* at the beginning of the 16th century.

69. Difficulties, setbacks.

70. Sidney's objection to the mixing of the genres would rule out most of Elizabethan drama, including Shakespeare. He thinks the effect of "admiration and commiseration" proper to tragedy (and going back to Aristotle's "pity and terror") cannot be mixed with low comedy, and that the result is neither one thing nor the other, since comedy has no business with clowning either. Tragicomedy as a mean between tragedy and comedy may have been discussed by Aristotle in a lost part of the *Poetics,* but he cannot have had in mind the mixture common in Elizabethan theater.

disproportioned to ourselves and nature. Delight hath a joy in it, either permanent or present. Laughter hath only a scornful tickling.

[Sidney next condemns the English lyric for its frigidity and general lack of "forcibleness, or *Energia*." He attacks excessive "euphuism" (see Headnote on Lyly) in prose—the use of rigid rhetorical schemes and similes drawn from bestiary and herbal lore. The English language lends itself so well to a flexible and easy discourse ("being so easy of itself, and so void of those cumbersome differences of cases, genders, moods and tenses which I think was a piece of the Tower of Babylon's curse") that it should not be restricted artificially. Such a language should meet every need, and English poetry in particular should be elevated to its proper position.]

So that since the ever-praiseworthy poesy is full of virtue-breeding delightfulness, and void of no gift that ought to be in the noble name of learning; since the blames laid against it are either false or feeble; since the cause why it is not esteemed in England is the fault of poet-apes, not poets; since, lastly, our tongue is most fit to honour poesy, and to be honoured by poesy; I conjure you all that have had the evil luck to read this ink-wasting toy of mine, even in the name of the Nine Muses, no more to scorn the sacred mysteries of poesy, no more to laugh at the name of 'poets,' as though they were next inheritors to fools, no more to jest at the reverent title of a 'rhymer'; but to believe, with Aristotle,[71] that they were the ancient treasures of the Grecians' divinity; to believe, with Bembus,[72] that they were first bringers-in of all civility; to believe, with Scaliger, that no philosopher's precepts can sooner make you an honest man than the reading of Virgil;[73] to believe, with Clauserus,[74] the translator of Cornutus, that it pleased the heavenly Deity, by Hesiod and Homer, under the veil of fables, to give us all knowledge, logic, rhetoric, philosophy, natural and moral, and *Quid non?*,[75] to believe, with me, that there are many mysteries contained in poetry, which of purpose were written darkly, lest by profane wits it should be abused;[76] to believe, with Landin,[77] that they are so beloved of the gods that whatsoever they write proceeds of a divine fury; lastly, to believe themselves, when they tell you they will make you immortal by their verses.

[The work ends on a tone of light banter matching that of its opening.]

71. Aristotle doesn't exactly say this, only that the poets first gave an account of the gods (*Metaphysics* 983 b); but the opinion was attributed to him by Renaissance authorities.

72. Pietro Bembo (1470–1547), humanist and defender of the vernacular, and prominent character in Castiglione's *Il Cortegiano*.

73. Julius Caesar Scaliger (1484–1558), a great Renaissance polymath whose *Poetices Libri Septem* (1561) Sidney knew well, argued for the supremacy of the epic and Virgil, as well as for the unities in drama.

74. Conrad Clauser was the 16th-century translator of Lucius Annaeus Cornutus, a Roman grammarian of the 1st century A.D., and made this quite ordinary claim in the Preface to the translation.

75. "What not?"

76. Another common defense of obscurity in poetry, used, for example, of difficult allegory and emblems.

77. Cristoforo Landino (1424–1504), Florentine humanist and author of a famous commentary on the *Aeneid* (in *Disputationes Camaldulenses*, 1475) from which the period took much of its allegorization of Virgil, and Sidney this quotation.

FULKE GREVILLE, LORD BROOKE
1554–1628

"Servant to Queen Elizabeth, Councillor to King James, Friend to Sir Philip Sidney"—the epitaph Greville wrote for himself points up the centers of importance for his career. Born to a Warwickshire landowning family, he became Sidney's close friend at school and shared his literary and political interests. He was profoundly shaken by Sidney's death (he wrote a *Life of Sidney* not published until 1652). Working at court as Treasurer of the Navy, then Chancellor of the Exchequer under James, he grew very rich and was made a peer in 1621. Except for the unauthorized printing of a tragedy, his works were all published posthumously in 1633. They include the remarkable collection of poems called *Caelica* ("heavenly one") written perhaps over a period of twenty years ending, according to Geoffrey Bullough, Greville's modern editor, in 1600. Some of the poems are sonnets, some meditations and expositions in a strong "plain style," but there is nothing of the Petrarchan sequence about them.

From Caelica

XLIV

The Golden Age was when the world was young,
Nature so rich, as earth did need no sowing,
Malice not known, the serpents had not stung,
Wit was but sweet affection's overflowing;

Desire was free, and beauty's first-begotten;
Beauty then neither net,° nor made by art,
Words out of thoughts brought forth, and not forgotten;
The laws were inward that did rule the heart.

10 The Brazen Age is now when earth is worn,
Beauty grown sick, Nature corrupt and nought,
Pleasure untimely dead as soon as born,
Both words and kindness° strangers to our thought:

If now this changing world do change her head,
Caelica, what have her new lords for to boast?
The old lord knows desire is poorly fed,
And sorrows not a wavering province lost,
   Since in the gilt age Saturn ruled alone,
   And in this painted, planets every one.°

            1633

C

In night when colours all to black are cast,
Distinction lost, or gone down with the light;

---

net caught in a net
kindness naturalness
Saturn . . . planets every one the Golden Age
was ruled by Saturn (see Golding's translation
of the passage from Ovid); now fate and
arbitrariness (symbolized by all the planets'
rule, or astrology) hold sway

The eye—a watch to inward senses placed,
Not seeing, yet still having power of sight—
Gives vain alarums° to the inward sense
Where fear, stirred up with witty tyranny,°
Confounds all powers, and through self-offence,
Doth forge and raise impossibility,
Such as in thick, depriving darknesses
10   Proper reflections of the error be,
And images of self-confusednesses
Which hurt imaginations only° see—
    And from this nothing seen, tells news of devils,
    Which but expressions be of inward evils.
                    1633

Chorus Sacerdotum°

O wearisome condition of humanity!
Born under one law, to another bound:°
Vainly begot, and yet forbidden vanity,
Created sick, commanded to be sound:
What meaneth Nature by these diverse laws?
Passion and reason, self-division cause.
Is it the mark, or majesty of power
To make offences that it may forgive?
Nature herself doth her own self deflower,
10   To hate those errors she herself doth give;
For how should man think that, he may not do
If Nature did not fail, and punish too?
Tyrant to others, to herself unjust,
Only commands things difficult and hard,
Forbids us all things, which it knows is lust,
Makes easy pains, unpossible reward.
If Nature did not take delight in blood,
She would have made more easy ways to good.
We that are bound by vows, and by promotion,°
20   With pomp of holy sacrifice and rites,
To teach belief in good and still devotion,
To preach of Heaven's wonders, and delights:
Yet when each of us, in his own heart looks,
He finds the God there, far unlike his books.
1609   1633

alarums alarms
witty tyranny power of imagining
hurt imaginations only only hurt imaginations
Chorus Sacerdotum "chorus of priests," from
The Tragedy of Mustapha (1609). This famous
text was moved to the end of the play in
Greville's 1633 *Works*, following a previous
chorus attacking superstition, praising reason,
and affirming natural law.

Born under . . . bound natural law and God's
word
promotion ecclesiastical and political advancement, connected with "vows" or declarations
of faith. This attack on ritual and forms of
order, very Calvinist in tone, should be contrasted with the passage from Hooker on
Ceremony in *Of the Laws of Ecclesiastical
Polity.*

EDMUND SPENSER
1552–1599

Spenser was born in London in 1552, or soon after that date. Though connected with a noble family of Spencers, he was not himself richly born, and went to school as a "poore scholler." His school was the Merchant Taylors', then a new humanist foundation, and his headmaster was Richard Mulcaster, famous for his learning and his insistence that the boys study not only Latin, Greek, and Hebrew, but also English.

In 1569, assisted by a charitable grant, Spenser went to Pembroke Hall, Cambridge, a strongly Puritan college. He was a sizar, which meant that he had free meals in return for doing jobs about the college. His studies were in rhetoric, logic, and philosophy, and he would have had to take part in formal disputations. In the usual way he was graduated B.A. after four years and took the three-year M.A. course, including philosophy, astronomy, Greek, and mathematics. These studies were based on ancient authors—there was no formal study of modern languages.

Spenser had published poetry even before going to university—his translations of Petrarch and Du Bellay appeared in John Vandernoodt's *Theatre of Voluptuous Worldlings* in 1569. But the learning that was considered essential to poetry—Harvey was to insist that the heroic poet needed to be "a curious and universal scholar"— Cambridge provided, together with the warm ecclesiastical controversy that left its mark on his poetry, especially *The Shepheardes Calender*. His poetic interests were also developed by his friendship with Gabriel Harvey, a Fellow of the College. Harvey was a farmer's son, and at once learned and likable, pedantic and amusing. Later he became famous for his acrimonious pamphleteering exchanges with Thomas Nashe. At this time he shared with Spenser an interest in English versification, and wanted to introduce into English the quantitative prosody of Latin. His exchange of letters with Spenser on this point was published in 1580. Spenser experimented with quantitative meters, and sent them to Harvey with a request for fuller instruction, adding that Sidney and others were also trying them out. Little came of this, but Harvey happened in replying to mention some works by Spenser, whether complete, in progress, or projected; there seems to have been a large body of work, virtually all of which has perished. Harvey remarked that he preferred Spenser's Nine Comedies to a part of *The Faerie Queene* then in existence. He hoped Spenser would give up the attempt to write like Ariosto, regretting that he would not write prophetic and visionary poetry on the lines of St. John's Revelation. This indicates that what Harvey saw was not a part of Book I, which is largely based on Revelation, but something now embedded in Books III or IV. Replying, Spenser speaks of the "Areopagus." This group consisted of himself, Sidney, and Dyer, and was dedicated to the reform of English poetry; but he soon abandoned the attempt to introduce classical meter. Indeed he had already written the *Calender*, which, however experimental in language and techniques, is in the native tradition.

After being graduated M.A. in 1576, Spenser visited his noble kinsmen in Lancashire, and seems to have met Rosalind, a girl whom Harvey teases him about, and who figures in the *Calender* and even, many years later, in *Colin Clouts Come Home Againe*. In 1577 he probably made his first trip to Ireland, and returned to enter the service of the powerful Earl of Leicester—hence his acquaintance with Leicester's nephew Philip Sidney. He married Machabyas Childe in 1579, the year of the *Calender*, which he dedicated to Sidney. Sidney admired it, with reservations concerning the "old rustic language," which he expressed in his *Defence of Poesie*.

Now familiar with the court, Spenser began a bold satire, *Mother Hubberds Tale*, a beast fable with strong political implications—he was of the party which disliked Lord Burleigh and opposed the projected marriage of the Queen to the Duc d'Alençon. In 1580 he became secretary to Lord Grey de Wilton, the new Lord Deputy of Ireland; and apart from visits to London he spent the rest of his life in that country. Elizabeth's handling of the Irish problem is one of the least glorious aspects of her reign. Ireland was virtually a colony, harshly exploited by the English; and Spenser was as colonialist as the rest of them. The new men, coming in to serve their own interests, got on neither with the Catholic poor nor the old Anglo-Irish ruling class; they tried to impose Protestantism, English justice, and the kind of agriculture profitable to themselves on a nation that wanted none of them. The ensuing uprisings Lord Grey suppressed with great severity, and Spenser approved of this, as Book V of *The Fairie Queene* and, more explicitly, his prose work, *A Vewe of the Present State of Ireland*, written in 1596, show. He accompanied Grey on military expeditions intended to pacify the Irish, and may well have seen him in action as Justice, with his troops in the role of Talus (the impersonal agent of Justice in Book V). But Grey felt he had inadequate support in London, and resigned, amid much ill-feeling and backbiting, in 1582. Spenser stayed on, at first in Dublin, then, from 1588, on the 3000-acre estate he had acquired at Kilcolman, adjacent to the larger estate of Ralegh.

Spenser, though much involved with his job, made a literary friend in Lodowick Bryskett, another civil servant, and in Bryskett's book, *A Discourse of Civil Life*, published in 1606, we hear of a conversation between Spenser, Bryskett, and others, in which Spenser declines to discourse on moral philosophy because he has in hand a poem on that very subject, "in *heroical verse* under the title of a *Faerie Queene* . . . assigning to every vertue a Knight to be the patron and defender of the same." Even if Bryskett is using hindsight here, it would seem that Spenser in Dublin had decided on the general scheme and was writing the poem.

In 1589 his neighbor Ralegh induced Spenser to visit London with him, and to bring along the first three books of the big poem. The Queen liked them, and awarded him a pension of £50, quite a good sum at the time, though he was disappointed, as we see from *Colin Clout* and from the Proem to Book IV. They were published in 1590, and Spenser followed up their success by publishing several poems in the following year, among them the mythological fable *Muiopotmos*, the satire *Mother Hubberds Tale*, and *Daphnaida*, an elegy.

Back in Ireland, he was involved in difficult law-suits, but remained very productive. If the attribution is correct, he translated the pseudo-Platonic dialogue *Axiochus*, published in 1592. He courted and in 1594 married Elizabeth Boyle, and the publication of *Amoretti* (the sonnet sequence of about 1591–94) and the marriage poem *Epithalamion* followed in 1595. That year also saw the publication of *Colin Clout* and *Astrophell*, his elegy for Sidney. Meanwhile he was finishing Books IV, V, and VI of *The Faerie Queene*, which were published, together with the earlier books, in 1596. His interest in contemporary affairs was never greater than in these later Irish years, when he inserted very late into *The Faerie Queene* (V.xi) a piece of political allegory involving the Earl of Essex and Henry IV of France, and wrote the *Vewe*. In 1596 James VI of Scotland, who was to succeed Elizabeth in 1603, demanded Spenser's punishment for libeling his mother, Mary Queen of Scots, in the portrait of Duessa before

Mercilla (V.ix). No action was taken. Other works of this period were the *Fowre Hymnes* and *Prothalamion,* written for the double marriage of the daughters of the Earl of Worcester, a friend of Essex.

The continuation of *The Faerie Queen* brought Spenser no reward from the Queen, and after a spell in London he went back to Ireland, becoming Sheriff of Cork in 1598. The much-feared rebellion of Tyrone, who was later to help discredit Essex himself, broke out in 1598; Kilcolman was sacked, and Spenser fled to Cork and then to London. There, on January 6, 1599, he died, probably not, as Jonson said, "for lack of bread," but certainly much reduced. Essex paid for his funeral in Westminister Abbey, and poets threw elegies into his grave, near Chaucer's. The Queen ordered him a monument, but it was not erected; the Countess of Dorset provided one in 1620. It got Spenser's dates wrong, but contained the famous eulogy, "The Prince of Poets in His Tyme." It was restored in marble in 1778, with the dates corrected, and is still in the Abbey.

It is not easy to form a definite view of the personality of Spenser. He was scholarly in a poet's way; he was ambitious, and had, till the final debacle, a pretty successful worldly career. He must have been exceptionally industrious, combining diligence in his job with diligence in poetry, from which he sought material reward as well as glory. He was a literary adventurer, seeking in the past models for entirely original modern achievements, much as the voyagers did. He, like some of his poetry, constituted a reconciliation of opposites. His views on Ireland seem cruel, yet he was gentle. He had strong opinions on the subjection of women, as Book V shows, yet he broke off the composition of his major work to write *Epithalamion,* and most of his lifework is an act of worship offered to a woman. He was oppressed by signs of returning chaos in the world, but celebrated love as an inexhaustible source of beauty and order. He valued peace and courtesy, yet supported the war party. These real and apparent oppositions are characteristic of his great poem, and perhaps also of his personality.

The text of Spenser used here is that of J. C. Smith and E. de Selincourt in the Oxford Standard Authors. Punctuation, capitalization, and use of italic are unchanged, but *u* and *v* have been changed to conform to modern usage, and *j* replaces *i* in such words as *joy.*

The Shepheardes Calender

This work was at once recognized as a great landmark in the development of a national poetry, and it retains its historical importance in times when it is no longer especially to our taste. Spenser designed it on the grand scale. There is an eclogue for each month, starting (unusually, since the year was normally taken to begin in March) with January. E.K., the unidentified commentator (perhaps Gabriel Harvey) who provides miscellaneous humanist glosses to the work, divides the Eclogues into three groups, Plaintive, Recreative, Moral. The classification is occasionally hard to follow, but we can agree that the second, fifth, seventh, ninth, and tenth are Moral (and "mixed with some satirical bitterness"). There is some hint of a narrative. Colin Clout is Spenser, Hobbinol is Harvey, and Rosalind seems to have been a real person.

Traditionally the pastoral eclogue was allegorical, aiming, as Puttenham says in his *Art of English Poesy* (1589), "under the veil of homely persons, and in rude speeches, to insinuate and glance at greater matters." So that whether or no in Rosalind and Dido Spenser "shadows" Elizabeth, the Lobbin of the November Eclogue, certainly seems to be the Earl of Leicester; and in the ecclesiastical allegory, a special attribute of the Renaissance pastoral tradition, contemporary bishops are more or less transparently displayed. (Priests being pastors, poems about shepherds were a convenient way of complaining about their corruption, as Milton did in *Lycidas.*) So Spenser has a lot to say about the religious issues of the time, generally from the viewpoint of a moderate Anglicanism.

The true importance of the work was, however, poetic. The *Calender* was as original in its day as *The Waste Land* (a poem it also resembles in having a not altogether helpful commentary). Its language is strange, using many archaic words (some of which have subsequently returned to use); and this not only because of the custom that pastoral uses a rustic or "Doric" dialect, but also in an attempt to revive Chaucerian English, as, in France, the group of poets called the Pléiade had revived obsolete French words. Moreover, Spenser, like Sidney in the *Arcadia,* used a great variety of meters and stanzas; he did not carry on with those classical quantitative meters he had tried out earlier with Harvey, but instead developed the possibilities of the native manner, in homage to the dedicatee, Sidney (who liked the work but not the archaic diction).

For all its novelty, the *Calender* claims its inheritance from a long tradition, going back to the Alexandria of Theocritus, the Rome of Virgil, the Italy of Mantuan (1448–1516), and the France of Marot (1497–1544). The Tenth (October) Eclogue looks back to Virgil, who established a model for other poets by writing eclogues before rising to epic; it laments the condition of English poetry, praises its ideal dignity, and ends once again in pastoral retirement.

From The Shepheardes Calender

October°
Ægloga decima°

Argument

In Cuddie° is set out the perfecte paterne of a Poete, whiche finding no main-tenaunce of his state and studies, complayneth of the contempte of Poetrie, and the causes thereof: Specially having bene in all ages, and even amongst the most barbarous alwayes of singular accounpt and honor, and being indede so worthy and commendable an arte: or rather no arte, but a divine gift and heavenly

October The *Calender* is augmented by lengthy notes, attributed to E.K.—perhaps Gabriel Harvey, perhaps Edmund Kirke, perhaps Spenser himself, though he occasionally takes issue with the poem. This humanistic commentary, rhetorical, linguistic, mythological, suited the Renaissance pastoral, a learned kind; but there seems no need to reprint it in full here. Some of E.K.'s glosses are therefore incorporated in the notes of the present edition, and marked E.K. Others are omitted.
Ægloga decima Tenth Eclogue. E.K. says it

is an imitation of the sixteenth idyll of Theocritus, "wherein he reproved the Tyranne Hiero of Syracuse for his nigardise towarde Poetes . . . The style hereof as also that in Theocritus, is more loftye then the rest, and applyed to the heighte of Poeticall witte."
Cuddie E.K. doubts "whether by Cuddie be specified the authour selfe, or some other." One suggestion is the court poet Dyer, friend of Sidney. Cuddie can hardly be Spenser, to whom (as Colin) he defers in l. 88.

instinct not to bee gotten by laboure and learning, but adorned with both: and
poured into the witte by a certaine ἐνθουσιασμός.° *and celestiall inspiration,*
as the Author hereof els where at large discourseth, in his booke called the Eng-
lish Poete,° which booke being lately come to my hands, I mynde also by Gods
grace upon further advisement to publish.

PIERCE

Cuddie, for shame hold up thy heavye head,
And let us cast with what delight to chace,
And weary thys long lingring *Phœbus* race.°
Whilome⸥ thou wont the shepheards laddes to leade,   *formerly*
In rymes, in riddles, and in bydding base:°
Now they in thee, and thou in sleepe art dead.

CUDDIE

Piers, I have pypèd erst⸥ so long with payne,   *lately*
That all mine Oten reedes° bene rent and wore:
And my poore Muse hath spent her sparèd⸥ store,   *small*
10   Yet little good hath got, and much lesse gayne.
Such pleasaunce makes the Grashopper so poore,
And ligge so layd,° when Winter doth her straine.

The dapper° ditties, that I wont devise,
To feede youthes fancie, and the flocking fry,°
Delighten much: what I the bett for thy⸥?   *as a result*
They han the pleasure, I a sclender prise.
I beate the bush, the byrds to them doe flye.
What good thereof to Cuddie can arise?

PIRES°

Cuddie, the prayse is better, then⸥ the price,   *than*
20   The glory eke⸥ much greater then the gayne: *also*
O what an honor is it, to restraine
The lust of lawlesse youth with good advice:°
Or pricke⸥ them forth with pleasaunce of thy vaine,   *urge*
Whereto thou list their traynèd willes entice.   *snared*

Soone as thou gynst to sette thy notes in frame,
O how the rurall routes⸥ to thee doe cleave: *crowds*
Seemeth thou dost their soule of sence bereave,°

ενθουσιασμος. *enthousiasmos,* the divine fury
that transports the poet beyond himself
the English Poete lost treatise by Spenser
weary . . . race pass the time
bydding base country game
Oten reedes "Avena" (E.K.), the Latin for
stalks, used by Virgil to mean the shepherd's
pipe
ligge so layd "lye so faynt and unlustye"
(E.K.), referring to the fable of the ant and
the grasshopper
dapper "pretye" (E.K.)
fry "is a bold Metaphore, forced from the

spawning fishes. For the multitude of young
fish be called the frye" (E.K.).
Pires "Piers" is the normal form, used hereafter.
restraine . . . advice E.K. relates this to Plato,
Laws 1, which speaks of poets inspiring young
people—ravishing them with delight—and also,
in a less heroic vein, amusing them with love
poems and satires.
soule . . . bereave E.K. illustrates this with the
story of how the musician Timotheus worked on
the passions of Alexander, and by recalling
that Plato advised against a certain musical
mode as likely to enervate children. Cf. Dryden,
Alexander's Feast.

All' as the shepheard,° that did fetch his dame   *just*
From *Plutoes* balefull bowre withouten leave:
His musicks might the hellish hound° did tame.
30

    CUDDIE
So praysen babes the Peacoks spotted traine,
And wondren at bright *Argus*° blazing eye:
But who rewards him ere the more for thy?
Or feedes him once the fuller by a graine?
Sike' prayse is smoke, that sheddeth in the skye,   *such*
Sike words bene wynd, and wasten soone in vayne.

    PIERS
Abandon then the base and viler clowne,'   *rustic*
Lyft up thy selfe out of the lowly dust:
And sing of bloody Mars, of wars, of giusts,'   *jousts*
40 Turne thee to those, that weld' the awful crowne.   *wield*
To doubted Knights, whose woundlesse armour° rusts,
And helmes unbruzèd wexen dayly browne.

There may thy Muse display° her fluttryng wing,
And stretch her selfe at large from East to West:
Whither thou list in fayre *Elisa* rest,
Or if thee please in bigger notes to sing,
Advaunce the worthy° whome shee loveth best,
That first the white beare to the stake did bring.

And when the stubborne stroke of stronger stounds,'   *blows*
50 Has somewhat slackt the tenor of thy string:
Of love and lustihead tho' mayst thou sing,   *then*
And carrol lowde, and leade the Myllers rownde,°
All' were *Elisa* one of thilke same ring.   *Although*
So mought our *Cuddies* name to Heaven sownde.

    CUDDIE
Indeede the Romish *Tityrus,*° I heare,
Through his *Mecænas* left his Oaten reede,
Whereon° he earst' had taught his flocks to feede,   *formerly*
And laboured lands to yield the timely eare,°

shepheard "Orpheus: of whom it is sayd, that by his excellent skil in Musick and Poetry, he recovered his wife Eurydice from hell" (E.K.).
hound Cerberus, three-headed watchdog of hell
Argus Juno set Argus, who had a hundred eyes, to watch over Jupiter's girl Io, but Mercury played him asleep with music, and killed him. Juno transferred his eyes to the tail of her bird, the peacock. "For those coloured spots indeede resemble eyes" (E.K.).
woundlesse armour "unwounded in warre, do rust through long peace" (E.K.)
display E.K. calls this "a poeticall metaphor," meaning that Queen Elizabeth affords him opportunity for "more Heroicall argument" either in herself or in her nobles.

the worthy "he meaneth . . . the Erle of Leycester" (E.K.); Leicester's arms bore a bear and a ragged (knotty) staff
Myllers rownde "a kind of daunce" (E.K.)
Tityrus "wel knowen to be Virgile, who by Maecenas means was brought into the favour of the Emperor Augustus, and by him moved to write in loftier kinde, then he had erst doen" (E.K.)
Whereon " . . . the three severall workes of Virgile [are] intended. For in teaching his flocks to feede, is meant his Aeglogues. In labouring of lands, is hys Bucoliques. In singing of wars and deadly dreade, is his divine Aeneis figured" (E.K.).
laboured . . . eare farmed

And eftˀ did sing of warres and deadly drede,   *afterwards*
60 So asˀ the Heavens did quake his verse to here.   *so well that*

But ah *Mecænas* is yclad in claye,
And great *Augustus* long ygoe is dead:
And all the worthies liggenˀ wrapt in leade,   *lie*
That matter made for Poets on to play:
For ever, who in derring doe° were dreade,
The loftie verse of hemˀ was loved aye.°   *about them*

But after° vertue gan for age to stoupe,
And mighty manhode brought a bedde of ease.
The vaunting Poets found nought worth a pease,ˀ   *pea*
70 To put in preaceˀ among the learnèd troupe.   *crowd in*
Tho gan the streames of flowing wittes to cease,
And sonnebright honour pend in shamefull coupe.°

And if that any buddes of Poesie,
Yet of the old stocke gan to shoote agayne:
Or it mens follies mote be forst to fayne,°
And rolle with rest in rymes of rybaudrye:
Or as it sprong, it wither must agayne:
Tom Piper makes us better melodie.°

          PIERS
O pierlesse Poesye, where is then thy place?
80 If nor in Princes pallace thou doe sitt:
(And yet is Princes pallace the most fitt)
Ne brest of baser birth doth thee embrace.
Then make thee winges of thine aspyring wit,
And, whence thou camst, flye backe to heaven apace.

          CUDDIE
Ah *Percy* it is all to weake and wanne,
So high to sore, and make so large a flight:
Her peecèd pyneons° bene not so in plight,
For *Colin* fittes° such famous flight to scanne:
He, were he not with love so ill bedight,
90 Would mount as high, and sing as sooteˀ as Swanne.°   *sweetly*

          PIERS
Ah fon,ˀ for love does teach him climbe so hie,   *fool*
And lyftes him up out of the loathsome myre:
Such immortall mirrhor,° as he doth admire,

in derring doe "in manhoode and chevalrie"
(E.K.)
For ever . . . aye E.K. repeats the Renaissance
commonplace that poets immortalize great men.
But after "he sheweth the cause of contempt of
poetry to be idlenesse and basenesse of mynd"
(E.K.)
pend . . . coupe "shut up in slouth, as in a
coope or cage" (E.K.)
follies . . . fayne go in for satire or comedy
Tom . . . melodie "An ironicall Sarcasmus,
spoken in derision of these rude wits, whych
make more account of a ryming rybaud, then

of skill grounded upon learning and judgment"
(E.K.); Tom Piper is the name for the rustic
musician who plays for morris dancing.
peecèd pyneons "unperfect skil" (E.K.); repaired wings (the wings having been impaired,
the hawk cannot fly well)
For . . . fittes it is more suitable for Colin
(Spenser)
soote . . . Swanne E.K. explains that the swan
sings only at death, but then "most pleasantly."
mirrhor "Beauty, which is an excellent object
of politicall spirites" (E.K.)

Would rayse ones mynd above the starry skie.
And cause a caytive corage° to aspire,
For lofty love doth loath a lowly eye.°

    CUDDIE

All otherwise the state of Poet stands,
For lordly love is such a Tyranne fell:
That where he rules, all power he doth expell.
100 The vaunted verse a vacant head demaundes,
Ne wont with crabbèd care the Muses dwell.
Unwisely weaves, that takes two webbes in hand.

Who ever casts to compasse weightye prise,
And thinks to throwe out thondring words of threate:
Let powre in lavish cups and thriftie bitts of meate,°
For *Bacchus* fruite is frend to *Phœbus* wise.
And when with Wine the braine begins to sweate,
The nombers flowe as fast as spring doth ryse.

Thou kenst not *Percie* howe the ryme should rage.
110 O if my temples were distaind⁷ with wine,°   *stained*
And girt in girlonds of wild Yvie twine,°
How I could reare the Muse on stately stage,
And teache her tread aloft in bus-kin° fine,
With queint *Bellona*° in her equipage.

But ah my corage cooles ere it be warme,
For thy,⁷ content us in thys humble shade: *wherefore*
Where no such troublous tydes⁷ han us assayde,   *opportunities*
Here we our slender pipes may safely charme.°

    PIERS
And when my Gates shall han their bellies layd:°
120 *Cuddie* shall have a Kidde to store his farme.

    Cuddies Embleme.°
    Agitante calescimus illo, &c.°

      1579

a . . . corage "a base and abject minde" (E.K.)
lofty . . . eye E.K. complains of the alliterative l's, saying that "this playing with the letter" is a fault in English as well as Latin, and labeling it *cacozelon.*
lavish . . . meate lots of wine and not much food
O if . . . wine "He seemeth here to be ravished with a poetical furie. For . . . the numbers rise so ful, and the verse groweth so big, that it seemeth he hath forgot the meanenesse of shepheards state and stile" (E.K., remembering that decorum required pastoral to keep to the low style, though allowing for exceptions)
wild . . . twine "for it is dedicated to Bacchus and therefore it is sayd that the Maenades (that is Bacchus franticke priestes) used in their sacrifice to carry Thyrsos, which were pointed staves or Javelins, wrapped about with ivie" (E.K.)

bus-kin the high boot worn in tragedy (E.K. explains at length)
queint Bellona "strange Bellona; the goddess of battaile" (E.K., who explains that she is Pallas, born fully armed from the head of Jupiter and strange for that and other reasons)
charme "temper and order" (E.K.), but also a word used of birdsong as late as Milton (see *Paradise Lost* IV.642)
their . . . layd dropped their young
Embleme motto
Agitante . . . &c. "Hereby is meant, as also in the whole course of this Aeglogue, that Poetry is a divine instinct and unnatural rage passing the reach of comen reason . . ." (E.K.). The quotation from Ovid, *Fasti* VI.5, *est deus in nobis, agitante calescimus illo*— "there is a god in us, his stirring warms us"— crops up repeatedly in Renaissance discussion of poetic inspiration.

Colin Clouts Come Home Againe

This pastoral has an autobiographical content. Published in 1595, it was written four years earlier, when Spenser returned to Ireland after the visit to London which resulted in the publication of the first three books of *The Faerie Queene*. Spenser (Colin) tells his shepherd friends, including Hobbinol, about the journey and his visit to Cynthia's court. He and The Shepherd of the Ocean (Ralegh) read their poems to each other, and Colin waited on the Queen. He describes the voyage, and the strange and beautiful country beyond the sea, where the arts are honored. Cynthia, who approved of Colin's "piping" (she gave Spenser £50), has a number of poets attending her, and is bountiful. But he leaves the court because, despite the presence of good men (such as Lobbin-Leicester), it is a place of wicked ambition. In reply to a question as to whether love exists at court as well as in the country, Colin says that at court it is blasphemed; commended for his insight into its true nature, he speaks the lines that follow. He remembers his love for Rosalind; then they fold their sheep and rest.

Colin Clout abandons the experimental diction of the *Calender*, being, as pastoral ought to be, in the "low" style (see *Decorum* in the Glossary) yet capable of eloquence. The lines here given provide a valuable account (in less space than the *Fowre Hymnes*) of Platonic love doctrine. Love is the power that binds and moves the whole world. These doctrines are ancient, but had been refurbished and sophisticated in the Renaissance. Here love is the heavenly power that made the world, resolved the contraries of chaos (hot and cold, moist and dry, etc.), ordered the elements, and arranged a creative coincidence of opposites, of which generative love is an example. Thus the earth was filled with animal life. But men, having reason, are guided not merely by animal passion but by a desire for beauty; and those who dishonor this ennobling love are condemned and outlawed by the god.

From Colin Clouts Come Home Againe

Of loves perfection perfectly to speake,
Or of his nature rightly to define,
Indeed (said *Colin*) passeth reasons reach,
And needs his priest t'expresse his powre divine.
For long before the world he was y'bore   *born*
840   And bred above in *Venus* bosome deare:
For by his powre the world was made of yore,
And all that therein wondrous doth appeare.
For how should else things so far from attone   *agreement*
And so great enemies as of them bee,   *among*
Be ever drawne together into one,
And taught in such accordance to agree?   *harmony*
Through him the cold began to covet heat,
And water fire; the light to mount on hie,
And th'heavie downe to peize; the hungry t'eat   *press down*
850   And voydnesse to seeke full satietie.
So being former foes, they wexèd friends,   *grow to be*

And gan by litle learne to love each other:
So being knit, they brought forth other kynds
Out of the fruitfull wombe of their great mother.
Then first gan heaven out of darknesse dread
For to appeare, and brought forth chearfull day:
Next gan the earth to shew her naked head,
Out of deep waters which her drownd alway.
And shortly after, everie living wight⸖   *creature*
860   Crept forth like wormes out of her slimie nature,
Soone as on them the Suns life giving light,
Had powred kindly⸖ heat and formall feature,⸖   *natural / regular shape*
Thenceforth they gan each one his like to love,
And like himselfe desire for to beget,
The Lyon chose his mate, the Turtle Dove
Her deare, the Dolphine his owne Dolphinet:
But man that had the sparke of reasons might,
More then the rest to rule his passiòn,
Chose for his love the fairest in his sight.
870   Like as himselfe was fairest by creatiòn.
For beautie is the bayt which with delight
Doth man allure, for to enlarge his kynd,
Beautie the burning lamp of heavens light,
Darting her beames into each feeble mynd:
Against whose powre, nor God nor man can fynd,
Defence, ne⸖ ward⸖ the daunger of the wound,   *nor / protect himself against*
But being hurt, seeke to be medicynd
Of her that first did stir that mortall stownd.⸖   *stroke*
Then do they cry and call to love apace,
880   With praiers lowd importuning the skie,
Whence he them heares, and when he list⸖ shew grace,   *wishes to*
Does graunt them grace that otherwise would die.
So love is Lord of all the world by right,
And rules the creatures by his powrfull saw:⸖   *command*
All being made the vassalls of his might,
Through secret sence which therto doth them draw.
Thus ought all lovers of their lord to deeme:
And with chaste heart to honor him alway:
But who so else doth otherwise esteeme,
890   Are outlawes, and his lore do disobay.
For their desire is base, and doth not merit,
The name of love, but of disloyall lust:
Ne amongst true lovers they shall place inherit,
But as Exuls⸖ out of his court be thrust.   *exiles*

. . .

1595

The Faerie Queene

Heroic poetry, which in the Renaissance was taken by most commentators to be the highest kind, was necessarily associated with the growth of nationalist feelings, since it attempted to achieve in the vernacular what Virgil had done for the Roman empire in Latin. This explains Spenser's interest not only in the ancient models but also in modern Italian and French poetry—he would learn what he could from renaissances that flowered earlier than the English. But it also explains why The Faerie Queene, for all its dreamy Romance landscape and narrative, is very much a poem of its moment. He was celebrating national or imperial power, and did so not only by placing its origins in a fictive British past but by justifying modern policies, ecclesiastical, political, and military. He had to make his poem relevant to the glories, real and imaginary, of the reign he chose to represent as climactic in history; but he could not ignore the dark side of the picture.

The Acts of Supremacy and Uniformity of 1559 gave the country a foundation of peace and order but alienated recusants. The loss of Calais in 1558 marked the end of English power in France; henceforth England would be more narrowly nationalistic, and its church, with the Queen at its head, reflected this development. It became the chief Protestant power and engaged in a long and mostly cold war with Spain, the chief Catholic power. Meanwhile the cities grew larger and the great men grew greater, but the reign of Elizabeth ended with years that were glorious only in some ways; they were also melancholy, anxious, and beset by social and economic problems.

Elizabeth was a great but difficult woman. Her failure to marry and produce an heir meant that over the long period when this was no longer even a possibility her reign was under threat of the Catholic Stuart claims, represented in life by Mary Queen of Scots, and in Spenser's poem by Duessa. Mary was beheaded in 1587, the Armada defeated in 1588; but the succeeding thirteen years continued to be anxious, and the last of the favorites, Essex, was executed in 1601 for rebelliously declaring his interest in the succession of Mary's son, James VI of Scotland.

The celebration of the Virgin Queen, which Spenser and others carried to such heights, was in origin a way of making the best of a bad situation, and was intimately, though not obviously, related to foreign and ecclesiastical policy, which would arguably have been much easier if the Queen had lost her virginity, since the disputed succession made all the problems more acute. The religious situation was political, and vice versa. When Elizabeth succeeded to the throne in 1558, the country had just lived through her father's dispute with Rome, the brief period of triumphant Protestantism under Edward VI, and the Catholic reaction under Mary. Elizabeth was by no means an extreme Protestant, and the settlement of 1559 was a compromise, which for years pleased neither Protestant nor Catholic. The church now claimed, in fact, to be both— a Catholic church purged by Protestant action, with the Queen as its governor. Conformity was required by law. The clergy had mostly changed doctrines with each new reign; they were undistinguished, often venal, and easily exploited by the great laymen who had made fortunes out of the dissolution of the monasteries. The new (or, as propaganda said, very old) church was in poor condition. It was rescued by a brilliant intellectual enterprise: Archbishop Jewel's apology for the church, Archbishop Parker's history of it, and Hooker's justification of its middle way in broad historical and theological terms (see Of the Laws of Ecclesiastical Polity below) created a myth which Spenser and others accepted. The English church was older than Rome, having been founded soon after the Crucifixion by Joseph of Arimathaea, and it was ruled by an empress who inherited the powers of Constantine, the emperor who Christianized the Roman empire. So, from the doctrinal confusion and worldly corruption he commented on in the *Calender,* Spenser moved on to the heroic situation of a nation in all respects the heir of Rome, a church which had restored primitive purity in an apocalyptic manner, and an empress who concentrated the Catholic and universal in her reign over one people. Rejecting both the extremes, the Catholic enemy who threatened both inside and outside England, and the Puritanism he had known at Cambridge, with its mistrust of bishops and the Prayer Book, Spenser found himself in a position to write an Anglican epic. The enemy therein is, primarily, Catholicism, the usurping papacy (antichrist); in his myth they are destroyers of paradise, types of the perfidy and duplicity which beset fallen humanity. Truth is England, Falsehood Rome.

This is stated most clearly in Book I. But Spenser never calls the British restoration of Truth perfect. And the strength of the whole poem arises in part from his reconciling incompatible feelings and attitudes to his subject. The court is the fount of courtesy, but also corrupt. The world which has seen the restoration of the true church is also evil and decaying. A polarity of light and dark is essential to his mind. He delights in the changing forms and colors of life, while allowing that movement belongs to time, not eternity, and color to earth, not heaven. He celebrates fertility and generation, but allows that it is inseparable from "fleshly slime" (III.vi.3). Life is not only delightful, it is also a trial or initiation, a total temptation. Time, which makes the world changeable and delightful to the senses, is the drudge of eternity, and our main business is with that.

Whatever his stated subject, Spenser confronts a virtue with its opposites, dark with light; he invents myth after myth to celebrate opposites, and develops his great technical variety in order to accommodate them. The very length of the poem, its turnings aside, is a function of his need to make contraries meet in one: past and present, concord and discord, good and evil, time and eternity, light and dark. The inclusiveness of the poem is its most remarkable virtue. It lacks the gravity of Virgil, the speed and power of Ariosto, but as a "continued allegory" it has no rival. Spenser aims, as heroic poets were supposed to, at educating a gentleman in the virtues. But in doing so he used his allegorical powers to much greater effect than Ariosto and Tasso, even with all the help they got from their commentators, had wanted or been able to do. Sometimes he is simple, as in the House of Alma or the House of Holiness. Sometimes the allegory is thin, sometimes frankly popular, as in parts of the First Book, which are little different in design from the popular allegories of Lord Mayors' shows or celebrations of the Queen's birthday, or her reception at some country house. The symbolism of the First Book is especially popular; but Spenser is capable of deepening it until it remembles the learned allegory of Ben Jonson in his masques, so that Spenser is both "homely, churchwardenly," as C. S. Lewis calls him, and a profound philosophical allegorist, with elaborate allegorical programs that have still not been worked out.

The allegory, then, is multiform, sometimes thin, sometimes thick, always an aspect of a syncretic myth-making operation which for Spenser was the poet's way to tell the truth about everything—and that means about the state of affairs in the England of the 1580's and 1590's as well as in the whole frame of the world. Hence the blend, strange to us, of topicality and ethical generality; hence the sudden moves from shallow to very deep water. In a sense it could be said that this habitual allegorizing at one level or another makes Spenser more "medieval" than, say, Tasso; if so, the issue is not very important. The England of the Renaissance did retain, in spite of its efforts to be modern and humanist, much of the medieval spirit, and Chaucer was as important to Spenser as any other poet. But there was nevertheless a true modernism in Spenser's experimental, past-rifling methods. An employment of every resource—Ovidian mythologizing, heroic convention, symbolism and allegory of whatever kind—to speak about the world as it is, about deep problems which, rightly expressed, are reflected in the movements from day to day of politicians and religious leaders, is in that sense modern.

A poem, to do all that, must have readers who understand its peculiar languages and its ways of achieving flexibility. Spenser's language is not modern; it corresponds to his device of thrusting all the action back into a remote past, where connections are easier to make, life being simpler. Thus did the Elizabethans restore in show and tournament the old language and symbolism of chivalry. The archaism of *The Faerie Queene* increases its range of meaning; the vagueness of its fairyland allows Spenser to fluctuate, as in a myth or a dream, between vagueness and sharp definition at will. The reader must collaborate: *The Faerie Queene* is a world and a great one to all who learn to move in it.

A Letter of the Authors

Spenser returned to London with Ralegh in 1589–90, and presumably wrote this Letter specially for the publication of Books I through III in 1590. Perhaps he did so in haste, for, valuable as it is, it contains some puzzles and inaccuracies. The account of Book II seems to conflict with the facts of the poem. The reference to "the twelve private morall vertues, as Aristotle hath devised" and again to Magnificence and "the xii other vertues" has long been debated. Is it twelve or thirteen? In any case Aristotle's *Nicomachean Ethics* has no such list of virtues; and furthermore the six Spenser actually treated—seven if one counts Constancy—do not match Aristotle; for example, Temperance is an Aristotelian virtue but Holiness is not. Perhaps the mistake about Book II arose from haste—in setting down the part of Guyon's story which precedes the narrative as we have it, he neglected to make the two exactly consistent. As to the virtues, he may have been thinking more loosely than at first appears when he spoke of using Aristotle's *Ethics*—or some of the many Christianizing commentaries on the book—as a scheme from which he could vary.

These difficulties do not cancel the great value of the Letter. Here is a summary of its argument: 1. (1–12) mode of the work: allegory; 2. (12–44) moral intention; justification of subject and method; 3. (44–59) defense of allegorical poetry as morally beneficial ("ensample" better than "rule"); 4. (60–87) "general intention" of portrait of Arthur and of the Faerie Queene and other "shadowings" of Elizabeth; 5. (87–95) the other knights of the first three books; 6. (95–172) difference between poetry and historiography—stories of Books I through III as they would be in a chronicle rather than a poem; 7. (173–78) "other adventures intermedled"; 8. 179–87) conclusion: the Letter tries to establish the general design of a poem that might without this explanation seem "tedious and confused."

The Letter, in its general claims, is in the tradition of Renaissance apologias for epic poetry; see Sidney's remarks in the *Defence*. The object is to fashion gentlemen; moral precepts are easier to swallow if the pill is coated. The choice of Arthur fits the rule that the hero should be both great and of a remote time (more, he was an official ancestor of the Tudors and the last emperor of Britain before them; thus he was a hero of the type used by Virgil and the Italian heroic poets of the sixteenth century). Homer and, more importantly, Virgil provide models; Ariosto and Tasso maintained and modified their tradition in modern times; to cover all the ground he would need twenty-four books.

Teaching "by ensample," Spenser needs an exemplary hero. His Arthur, however, cannot be to Elizabeth what Aeneas was to Augustus, and the sex of his monarch led him into various "dark conceits." Arthur is Magnificence, which includes all the other virtues. Elizabeth is first the Faerie Queene, Glory, for which gentlemen should strive; secondly, "a most vertuous and beautifull Lady." The division reflects her two "persons," political and natural (Gloriana and Belphoebe), a division that goes deep in English constitutional theory. She is also present in other female characters. As for the knights, they have a virtue apiece; Spenser found some difficulty in working Arthur into a scheme already so elaborate.

In the "historiographical" rendering, Spenser allows only an occasional hint of allegorical intention—as when he speaks of Red Cross's armour as that of the soldier of Christ (*miles Christi,* Ephesians 6). He also states that some episodes are "accidents" rather than "intendments"—scenes and narratives that developed along the way without belonging to the master plan; but this does not mean that they have no allegorical meanings; Britomart, Marinell and Florimell, and Belphoebe certainly have, and so do "many the like."

Everybody wishes Spenser had said a bit more, and said it more clearly, in this Letter; but it is the first commentary ever written on the poem, and comes from the best-informed commentator; so it is certainly worth study.

A Letter of the Authors

expounding his *whole intention in the course of this worke: which* for that it giveth great light to the Reader, for the better understanding is hereunto annexed.

To the Right noble, and Valorous, Sir Walter Ralegh knight, Lo. Wardein of the Stanneryes, and her Majesties liefetenaunt of the County of Cornewayll.

Sir knowing how doubtfully[1] all Allegories may be construed, and this booke of mine, which I have entituled the Faery Queene, being a continued Allegory, or darke conceit,[2] I have thought good as well for avoyding of gealous [3] opinions

1. Ambiguously.
2. Homer and Virgil were interpreted as continuously allegorical; allegorical readings were attached to Ariosto by the poet himself and his commentators; Tasso insisted on his moral allegory. So it was right for heroic poetry to be allegorical, to have a meaning or meanings below the surface and therefore "dark." These meanings Spenser calls "conceits," meaning something between the modern "concepts" and the now obsolete "acute metaphorical discoveries." In a poem so long and loosely structured as *The Faerie Queene* the conceits cannot be uniformly dark—the allegorical significances vary from the transparent to the unfathomable.
3. Hostile, envious.

and misconstructions, as also for your better light in reading therof, (being so by you commanded,) to discover unto you the general intention and meaning, which in the whole course thereof I have fashioned, without expressing of any particular[4] purposes or by-accidents therein occasioned. The generall end therefore of all the booke is to fashion a gentleman or noble person in vertuous and gentle discipline: Which for that I conceived shoulde be most plausible and pleasing, being coloured with an historicall fiction, the which the most part of men delight to read, rather for variety of matter, then for profite of the ensample: I chose the historye of king Arthure, as most fitte for the excellency of his person, being made famous by many mens former workes, and also furthest from the daunger of envy, and suspition of present time. In which I have followed all the antique Poets historicall, first Homere, who in the Persons of Agamemnon and Ulysses hath ensampled a good governour and a vertuous man, the one in his Ilias, the other in his Odysseis:[5] then Virgil, whose like intention was to doe in the person of Aeneas: after him Ariosto[6] comprised them both in his Orlando: and lately Tasso[7] dissevered them againe, and formed both parts in two persons, namely that part which they in Philosophy call Ethice, or vertues of a private man, coloured in his Rinaldo.[8] The other named Politice in his Godfredo.[9] By ensample of which excellente Poets, I labour to pourtraict in Arthure, before he was king, the image of a brave knight, perfected in the twelve private morall vertues, as Aristotle hath devised, the which is the purpose of these first twelve bookes: which if I finde to be well accepted, I may be perhaps encoraged, to frame the other part of polliticke vertues in his person, after that hee came to be king. To some I know this Methode will seeme displeasaunt, which had rather have good discipline delivered plainly in way of precepts, or sermoned at large, as they use, then thus clowdily enwrapped in Allegoricall devises. But such, me seeme, should be satisfide with the use of these dayes, seeing all things accounted by their showes, and nothing esteemed of, that is not delightfull and pleasing to commune sence. For this cause is Xenophon[10] preferred before Plato, for that the one in the exquisite depth of his judgement, formed a Commune welth such as it should be, but the other in the person of Cyrus and the Persians fashioned a government such as might best be: So much more profitable and gratious is doctrine by ensample, then by rule. So have I laboured to doe in the person of Arthure: whome I conceive after his long education by Timon, to whom he was by Merlin delivered to be brought up, so soone as he was borne of the Lady Igrayne, to have seene in a dream or vision the Faery Queene, with

---

4. As opposed to general, meaning the "accidents" mentioned near the end of the letter.
5. *Iliad, Odyssey.*
6. Lodovico Ariosto (1474–1533), author of *Orlando Furioso* (1532), the formative heroic poem of the Renaissance; Spenser is closest to it in the many interlinked stories of Bks. III and IV.
7. Torquato Tasso (1544–95), author of *Gerusalemme Liberata* (1581), owing much to Ariosto but made graver and more explicitly Christian by the influence of the Counter-Reformation.
8. Hero of Tasso's poem in its dealings with personal morality.
9. Godfrey of Boulogne, hero of Tasso's poem in its dealings with political morality.
10. Xenophon's *Cyropaedia, The Education of Cyrus,* and Plato's *Republic;* see Sidney's *Defence of Poesie.*

whose excellent beauty ravished, he awaking resolved to seeke her out, and so being by Merlin armed, and by Timon throughly instructed, he went to seeke her forth in Faerye land.[11] In that Faery Queene I meane glory in my generall intention, but in my particular I conceive the most excellent and glorious person of our soveraine the Queene, and her kingdome in Faery land. And yet in some places els, I doe otherwise shadow [12] her. For considering she beareth two persons,[13] the one of a most royall Queene or Empresse, the other of a most vertuous and beautifull Lady, this latter part in some places I doe expresse in Belphœbe, fashioning her name according to your owne excellent conceipt of Cynthia,[14] (Phœbe and Cynthia being both names of Diana.) So in the person of Prince Arthure I sette forth magnificence in particular, which vertue for that (according to Aristotle and the rest) it is the perfection of all the rest, and conteineth in it them all, therefore in the whole course I mention the deedes of Arthure applyable to that vertue, which I write of in that booke. But of the xii. other vertues, I make xii. other knights the patrones, for the more variety of the history: Of which these three bookes contayn three, The first of the knight of the Redcrosse, in whome I expresse Holynes: The seconde of Sir Guyon, in whom I sette forth Temperaunce: The third of Britomartis a Lady knight, in whome I picture Chastity. But because the beginning of the whole worke seemeth abrupte and as depending upon other antecedents, it needs that ye know the occasion of these three knights severall adventures. For the Methode of a Poet historical is not such, as of an Historiographer. For an Historiographer discourseth of affayres orderly as they were donne, accounting as well the times as the actions, but a Poet thrusteth into the middest,[15] even where it most concerneth him, and there recoursing to the thinges forepaste, and divining of thinges to come, maketh a pleasing Analysis of all. The beginning therefore of my history, if it were to be told by an Historiographer, should be the twelfth booke, which is the last, where I devise that the Faery Queene kept her Annuall feaste xii. dayes, uppon which xii. severall dayes, the occasions of the xii. severall adventures hapned, which being undertaken by xii. severall knights, are in these xii books severally handled and discoursed. The first was this. In the beginning of the feast, there presented him selfe a tall clownishe [16] younge man, who falling before the Queen of Faries desired a boone (as the manner then was) which during that feast she might not refuse: which was that hee might have the atchievement of any adventure, which during that feaste should happen, that being graunted, he rested him on the floore, unfitte through his rusticity for a better place. Soone after entred a faire Ladye in mourning weedes, riding on a white Asse, with a dwarfe behind her leading a warlike steed, that bore the Armes of a knight, and his speare in the dwarfes hand. Shee falling before the Queene of Faeries, com-

11. "By the Faery land of the poem I mean England."
12. Portray.
13. Referring to the doctrine that the monarch had two persons, one private and mortal, one political and immortal ("the king is dead, long live the king"). Elizabeth is therefore represented as both Queen and Empress, and most virtuous and beautiful lady.
14. Ralegh's poem to the Queen, *Cynthia;* like Phoebe and Diana, a name of the goddess of the moon and of chastity.
15. *In medias res,* as Horace (*Ars Poetica,* 148) advises.
16. Rustic, unpolished.

playned that her father and mother an ancient King and Queene, had bene by
an huge dragon many years shut up in a brasen Castle, who thence suffred
them not to yssew: and therefore besought the Faery Queene to assygne her
some one of her knights to take on him that exploit. Presently [17] that clownish
person upstarting, desired that adventure: whereat the Queene much wondering, and the Lady much gainesaying,[18] yet he earnestly importuned his desire.
In the end the Lady told him that unlesse that armour which she brought,
would serve him (that is the armour of a Christian man specified by Saint
Paul v. Ephes.) that he could not succeed in that enterprise, which being forthwith put upon him with dewe furnitures [19] thereunto, he seemed the goodliest
man in al that company, and was well liked of the Lady. And eftesoones taking
on him knighthood, and mounting on that straunge Courser, he went forth
with her on that adventure: where beginneth the first booke, vz.
    A gentle knight was pricking on the playne, &c.
    The second day ther came in a Palmer bearing an Infant with bloody hands,
whose Parents he complained to have bene slayn by an Enchaunteresse called
Acrasia: and therfore craved of the Faery Queene, to appoint him some knight,
to performe that adventure, which being assigned to Sir Guyon, he presently
went forth with that same Palmer: which is the beginning of the second booke
and the whole subject thereof. The third day there came in, a Groome who
complained before the Faery Queene, that a vile Enchaunter called Busirane
had in hand a most faire Lady called Amoretta, whom he kept in most grievous
torment, because she would not yield him the pleasure of her body. Whereupon
Sir Scudamour the lover of that Lady presently tooke on him that adventure.
But being unable to performe it by reason of the hard Enchauntments, after
long sorrow, in the end met with Britomartis, who succoured him, and reskewed
his love.
    But by occasion hereof, many other adventures are intermedled,[20] but rather
as Accidents, then intendments. As the love of Britomart, the overthrow of
Marinell, the misery of Florimell, the vertuousnes of Belphœbe, the lascivious-
nes of Hellenora, and many the like.
    Thus much Sir, I have briefly overronne [21] to direct your understanding to
the wel-head of the History, that from thence gathering the whole intention
of the conceit, ye may as in a handfull gripe al the discourse, which otherwise
may happily [22] seeme tedious and confused. So humbly craving the continu-
aunce of your honorable favour towards me, and th'eternall establishment of
your happines, I humbly take leave.

23. January. 1589.
Yours most humbly affectionate.
Ed. Spenser.

17. At once.
18. Protesting.
19. Equipment.
20. Mixed in.
21. Run through.
22. Perchance.

Book I

Spenser probably did not begin here; the parts of the work that Harvey saw in 1580 must, if they survive at all, be in the middle books, for the work in which Spenser was then attempting to "overgo" Ariosto can have had nothing to do with the Revelation of St. John, a topic which Harvey recommends, and which is central to Book I as we now have it. When he did settle to Book I he made it very different in tone, and also made it much more self-contained than the more Ariostan books; in fact, I is even more so than II, which is to a great degree modeled on it, and V, the other Book that comes closest.

Red Cross is the greatest of the knights, a saint rather than a mere hero, and occasionally the image of Christ. The historical scope of the Book (extended by more or less "dark conceits") is the whole history of the world from the Fall to the final overthrow of Satan. Its theology and religion are more directly expressed than in the other Books, and it speaks with far more urgency to the great themes of history, and notably the vicissitudes of the church on earth, than they.

Red Cross is St. George, slayer of the dragon; a figure who is both a type of Christ and a droll figure in folkplay and popular pageant, hero of great works of art and of the antique Mummers Play; patron saint of England. He rides into Spenser's poem, *in medias res,* with his usual pageant companions, the lady on the ass and the lamb. The scene is vague and dreamlike, and we can already see what Coleridge meant when he spoke of "the marvellous independence and true imaginative absence of all particular space and time" in *The Faerie Queene.* But that is only a half-truth. These characters from the village play and the Lord Mayor's Show, in their narrative of nightmare apparitions, dreamlike transfigurations, apparently fitful meanings, are going to serve a story which deals with the history of the human condition as it appeared in an age of apocalyptic climax, the late 1580's. We have the same fancy in our day, but do not express it, as Spenser did and Virgil had done, in a heroic poem about human destiny in the context of earthly power and heavenly providence; nor would we give the story a milieu of Arthurian romance, though we might envy the way in which it enables the poet to achieve those strange transitions and condensations which so remind us of the Freudian dreamwork.

Red Cross, though of the elect, is a sinner, everyman. Spenser emphasizes his fall into sin and despair by echoing the anti-Romanist article of his church: "that we are justified by faith alone is a most wholesome doctrine." Given grace to repent, Red Cross undertakes the imitation of Christ, redeems the parents of Una (Adam and Eve), slays the old Dragon, and harrows hell—becomes, in short, Christ, the object of his imitation, and marries his Bride, Una, the True Church (i.e. the Church of England). Such are the transformations of Spenser's world, and they are prepared for in the opening lines. Red Cross, who wears the apocalyptic "bloudie Cross" (Christ wore it in the battle in heaven, as shown in illuminated manuscripts of Revelation), is also called "Right faithful true," which, *fidelis et verax,* is the title of Christ in Revelation (19:11). And Red Cross, St. George, is also England, defender of the true faith.

Revelation is the ultimate source. Una is "the woman clothed with the sun" (Revelation 12:1), traditionally identified with the true church; Spenser speaks of her "sunshyny face" (I.xii.23) as the medieval illuminators showed her in a glory of light. She, like her prototype, flees into the wilderness (Revelation 12:6). Duessa plays multiplicity to Una's integrity, but is also the Whore of Babylon, the Scarlet Woman

(Revelation 17); the best possible illustrations of Spenser's eighth canto, where she rides the Beast, are in the medieval apocalypses. She is also the Church of Rome in the allegories of Reformation propaganda. Archimago is antichrist, the Beast from the Land of Revelation, the papacy. The tree and the water, representing the two out of the Catholic seven sacraments retained by the reformed church (communion and baptism) refresh Red Cross in his three-day battle with the Dragon; they come from Revelation 22. And these are only samples of Spenser's allusions to Revelation.

If one thinks of the number of times it has happened both before and after Spenser, it will seem less strange that references to Revelation—a vision of the end of the world —should have historical and political meanings. The last book of the Bible was thought to contain in prophetic form the whole history of the church, and Spenser followed an English tradition when he favored a Protestant interpretation and one which made the true Catholic church the Church of England, the primitive church now restored after centuries of Romanist disfigurement. Una is that church, and also its head, Elizabeth I, who replaced the papacy which had usurped the royal chief priests, her ancestors, for so long. The overthrow of the antichrist Archimago and the false fallen church, Duessa, amounts to a restoration of Eden.

Thus Spenser embodies in his dreamlike romance story the imperial and ecclesiastical pretensions of the last of the Tudors. He associates his empress with a triumphant restoration of the true church on earth, and with the reuniting of church and state by a queen who liked to be thought of as a second Constantine, the emperor who 1200 years earlier had Christianized the Roman empire. The presumptuous bishops of Rome had set apart the secular and religious powers, but they had been ousted from England and a new emperor, a new Constantine, ruled all.

As Virgil had celebrated the culmination of empire in the *Aeneid,* so would Spenser in *The Faerie Queene,* and especially in Book I. But to do so he chooses not courtly or difficult materials; rather he builds into his heroic pattern the familiar figures and almost equally familiar interpretations of Revelation, and explains how universal history justifies the worship of imperial Elizabeth.* It is not surprising that when Colin Clout read the poem to her she "gan to take delight . . . and it desired at timely hours to hear."

° The dedication ran as follows: "To the most high, mightie and magnificent empresse renowmed for pietie, vertue, and all gratious government Elizabeth by the grace of God Queene of England Fraunce and Ireland and of Virginia, defendour of the faith, &c. Her Most humble servaunt Edmund Spenser doth in all Humilitie Dedicate, Present and Consecrate these his labours to live with the eternitie of her fame."

The First Booke of The
Faerie Queene

Contayning, the Legende of the Knight of the Red Crosse, or
Of Holinesse

1	Lo I the man, whose Muse whilome° did maske,	*formerly*
	As time her taught, in lowly Shepheards weeds,°	*clothes*
	Am now enforst a far unfitter taske,	

For trumpets sterne to chaunge mine Oaten reeds,°
And sing of Knights and Ladies gentle° deeds;   *noble*
Whose prayses having slept in silence long,°
Me, all too meane, the sacred Muse areeds°   *counsels*
To blazon broad emongst her learned throng:
Fierce warres and faithfull loves shall moralize my song.

2   Helpe then, O holy Virgin chiefe of nine,°
Thy weaker° Novice to performe thy will,   *too weak*
Lay forth out of thine everlasting scryne°   *record chest*
The antique rolles, which there lye hidden still,
Of Faerie knights and fairest *Tanaquill*,°   *Gloriana*
Whom that most noble Briton Prince° so long
Sought through the world, and suffered so much ill,
That I must rue his undeserved wrong:
O helpe thou my weake wit, and sharpen my dull tong.

3   And thou most dreaded impe° of highest *Jove*,   *child*
Faire *Venus* sonne,° that with thy cruell dart
At that good knight so cunningly didst rove,°   *shoot*
That glorious fire it kindled in his hart,
Lay now thy deadly Heben° bow apart,   *ebony*
And with thy mother milde, come to mine ayde:
Come both, and with you bring triumphant *Mart*,°
In loves and gentle jollities arrayd,
After his murdrous spoiles and bloudy rage allayd.°   *calmed*

4   And with them eke,° O Goddesse heavenly bright,°   *also*
Mirrour of grace and Majestie divine,
Great Lady of the greatest Isle, whose light
Like *Phœbus* lampe° throughout the world doth shine,
Shed thy faire beames into my feeble eyne°,   *eyes*
And raise my thoughts too humble and too vile,
To thinke of that true glorious type° of thine,
The argument of mine afflicted stile:
The which to heare, vouchsafe, O dearest dred° a-while.

For trumpets . . . reeds He changes from the shepherd's pipe of pastoral to the trumpets of heroic poetry. This first stanza imitates the proem to Virgil's *Aeneid*. On Virgil's model it became prescriptive for an epic poet to prepare himself with pastoral.
And sing . . . long imitating the opening of Ariosto's *Orlando Furioso*
O holy . . . nine Calliope, chief of the Muses, presided over eloquence and heroic poetry;
represented in art with a trumpet in the right hand, a book in the left.
most . . . Prince Arthur
sonne Cupid
Mart Mars, god of war and lover of Venus
Goddesse . . . bright Queen Elizabeth
Phœbus lamps the sun
true . . . type Gloriana, symbol of Queen Elizabeth
dearest dred object of greatest awe

Canto i°
The Patron of true Holinesse,
　Foule Errour doth defeate:
Hypocrisie him to entrappe,
　Doth to his home entreate.

1　A Gentle Knight was pricking° on the plaine,　　　　　　　*spurring*
　　Y cladd in mightie armes and silver shielde,
　　Wherein old dints of deepe wounds did remaine,
　　The cruell markes of many' a bloudy fielde;
　　Yet armes till that time did he never wield:°
　　His angry steede did chide his foming bitt,
　　As much disdayning to the curbe to yield:
　　Full jolly° knight he seemd, and faire did sitt,　　　　　*brave*
　As one for knightly giusts° and fierce encounters fitt.　*jousts*

2　But on his brest a bloudie Crosse he bore,
　　The deare remembrance of his dying Lord,
　　For whose sweete sake that glorious badge he wore,
　　And dead as living ever him ador'd:
　　Upon his shield the like was also scor'd,
　　For soveraine hope, which in his helpe he had:
　　Right faithfull true° he was in deede and word,
　　But of his cheere° did seeme too solemne sad;　　　　　*expression*
　Yet nothing did he dread, but ever was ydrad.°　　　　　*dreaded*

3　Upon a great adventure he was bond,°　　　　　　　　　*bound*
　　That greatest *Gloriana* to him gave,
　　That greatest Glorious Queene of *Faerie* lond,
　　To winne him worship, and her grace to have,
　　Which of all earthly things he most did crave;
　　And ever as he rode, his hart did earne°　　　　　　　　*yearn*
　　To prove his puissance° in battell brave　　　　　　　　*strength*
　　Upon his foe, and his new force to learne;
　Upon his foe, a Dragon horrible and stearne.

4　A lovely Ladie° rode him faire beside,
　　Upon a lowly Asse more white then snow,
　　Yet she much whiter, but the same did hide
　　Under a vele, that wimpled° was full low,　　　　　　　*folded*
　　And over all a blacke stole she did throw,
　　As one that inly mournd: so was she sad,

Canto i When Red Cross and his companions
seek shelter they enter a wood, symbol of the
errors of human existence. Despite the lady's
warning that he places too much confidence in
unaided human strength, the knight provokes
and fights with Error (heresy, corrupter of pure
doctrine). In his difficulty he is advised "Add
faith unto your force"—a tenet of the true
religion which allowed no justification by works
alone—and he forces Error to spew forth its
heretical brood. His victory at the outset fore-
shadows the victory over the dragon at the
end, as Christ's victory over Satan in the
wilderness foreshadowed the final overthrow
of the old dragon; but his lapse foretells the
sins that lie ahead also. His first encounter
with religious deceit and hypocrisy of the papal
kind that plagued England till the Reformation
follows immediately.
armes . . . wield He is wearing the old arms of
the Christian soldier (see Headnote to Bk. I)
for the first time.
Right . . . true See Headnote.
Ladie Una, her radiance concealed by a veil

And heavie sat upon her palfrey slow:
Seemed in heart some hidden care she had,
And by her in a line° a milke white lambe she lad.   *leash*

5   So pure an innocent, as that same lambe,
    She was in life and every vertuous lore,
    And by descent from Royall lynage came
    Of ancient Kings and Queenes, that had of yore
    Their scepters stretcht from East to Westerne shore,
    And all the world in their subjection held;°
    Till that infernal feend with foule uprore
    Forwasted° all their land, and them expeld: *destroyed*
    Whom to avenge, she had this Knight from far compeld.°   *summoned*

6   Behind her farre away a Dwarfe° did lag,
    That lasie seemd in being ever last,
    Or wearièd with bearing of her bag
    Of needments at his backe. Thus as they past,
    The day with cloudes was suddeine overcast,
    And angry *Jove* an hideous storme of raine
    Did poure into his Lemans lap° so fast,
    That every wight° to shrowd° it did constrain,   *creature / shelter*
    And this faire couple eke to shroud themselves were fain.

7   Enforst to seeke some covert night at hand,
    A shadie grove not far away they spide,
    That promist ayde the tempest to withstand:
    Whose loftie trees yclad with sommers pride,
    Did spred so broad, that heavens light did hide,
    Not perceable with power of any starre:
    And all within were pathes and alleies wide,
    With footing worne, and leading inward farre:
    Faire harbour that them seems; so in they entred arre.

8   And foorth they passe, with pleasure forward led,
    Joying to heare the birdes sweete harmony,
    Which therein shrouded from the tempest dred,
    Seemd in their song to scorne the cruell sky.
    Much can° they prayse the trees so straight and hy,   *did*
    The sayling Pine,° the Cedar proud and tall,
    The vine-prop Elme, the Poplar never dry,
    The builder Oake, sole king of forrests all,
    The Aspine good for staves, the Cypresse funerall.

by descent . . . held Una is both the true and primitive church and the daughter of Eden. She is the unfallen world (her name means One, the primal unity before numbers) and the church while still universal; Duessa is multiplicity and even on her own claim her father rules only the west (I.ii.22). The point is, politically, to establish, as Elizabethan churchmen always did, the truth of the position that the English church was older and purer than the Roman, which had usurped it.
Dwarfe perhaps signifies her human needs, as the lamb signifies her purity
Lemans lap mistress's lap; the earth
sayling Pine used by shipbuilders. This epic catalogue of trees is probably developed here from Chaucer's *Parlement of Foules*.

9   The Laurell, meed° of mightie Conquerors   *prize*
     And Poets sage, the Firre that weepeth still,°   *always*
     The Willow worne of forlorne Paramours,
     The Eugh° obedient to the benders will,   *yew*
     The Birch for shaftes, the Sallow° for the mill,   *willow*
     The Mirrhe sweete bleeding in the bitter wound,°
     The warlike Beech, the Ash for nothing ill,
     The fruitfull Olive, and the Platane° round,   *plane-tree*
     The carver Holme,° the Maple seeldom inward sound.

10   Led with delight, they thus beguile the way,
     Untill the blustring storme is overblowne;
     When weening° to returne, whence they did stray,   *thinking*
     They cannot finde that path, which first was showne,
     But wander too and fro in wayes unknowne,
     Furthest from end then, when they neerest weene,
     That makes them doubt, their wits be not their owne:
     So many pathes, so many turnings seene,
     That which of them to take, in diverse doubt they been.

11   At last resolving forward still to fare,
     Till that some end they finde or° in or out,   *either*
     That path they take, that beaten seemd most bare,
     And like to lead the labyrinth about;°   *out of*
     Which when by tract they hunted had throughout,
     At length it brought them to a hollow cave,
     Amid the thickest woods. The Champion stout°   *brave*
     Eftsoones° dismounted from his courser brave,°   *at once / splendid*
     And to the Dwarfe a while his needlesse spere he gave.

12   Be well aware, quoth then that Ladie milde,
     Least suddaine mischiefe ye too rash provoke:
     The danger hid, the place unknowne and wilde,
     Breedes dreadfull doubts: Oft fire is without smoke,
     And perill without show: therefore your stroke
     Sir knight with-hold, till further triall made.
     Ah Ladie (said he) shame were to revoke
     The forward footing for° an hidden shade: *because of*
     Vertue gives her selfe light, through darkenesse for to wade.°

13   Yea but (quoth she) the perill of this place
     I better wot° then you, though now too late   *know*
     To wish you backe returne with foule disgrace,
     Yet wisedome warnes, whilest foot is in the gate,
     To stay the steppe, ere forcèd to retrate.
     This is the wandring wood, this *Errours den,*°

Mirrhe . . . wound Its resins were extracted for
perfume from cuts in the bark.
carver Holme holm-oak used for carving
Vertue . . . wade Compare the misplaced confidence of the Elder Brother in Milton's *Comus,*

ll. 372–73: "Virtue could see to do what Virtue
would / By her own radiant light . . ."
Errours den Error stands for heresy; old
heresies breed new ones which feed on them;
Spenser remembers Revelation 9:7–10.

    A monster vile, whom God and man does hate:
      Therefore I read˼ beware. Fly fly (quoth then   *counsel*
    The fearefull Dwarfe:) this is no place for living men.

14   But full of fire and greedy hardiment,˼   *courage*
      The youthfull knight could not for ought be staide,
      But forth unto the darksome hole he went,
      And lookèd in: his glistring armor made
      A litle glooming light, much like a shade,
      By which he saw the ugly monster plaine,
      Halfe like a serpent horribly displaide,
      But th'other halfe did womans shape retaine,
    Most lothsom, filthie, foule, and full of vile disdaine.

15   And as she lay upon the durtie ground,
      Her huge long taile her den all overspred,
      Yet was in knots and many boughtes˼ upwound,   *bends*
      Pointed with mortall sting. Of her there bred
      A thousand yong ones, which she dayly fed,
      Sucking upon her poisonous dugs, eachone
      Of sundry shapes, yet all ill favorèd:
      Soone as that uncouth˼ light upon them shone,   *unfamiliar*
    Into her mouth they crept, and suddain all were gone.

16   Their dam upstart, out of her den effraide,˼   *scared*
      And rushed forth, hurling her hideous taile
      About her cursèd head, whose folds displaid
      Were stretcht now forth at length without entraile.˼   *coils*
      She lookt about, and seeing one in mayle
      Armèd to point,˼ sought back to turne againe;   *fully*
      For light she hated as the deadly bale,˼   *harm*
      Ay wont in desert darknesse to remaine,
    Where plaine none might her see, nor she see any plaine.

17   Which when the valiant Elfe° perceiv'd, he lept
      As Lyon fierce upon the flying pray,
      And with his trenchand˼ blade her boldly kept   *sharp*
      From turning backe, and forcèd her to stay:
      Therewith enrag'd she loudly gan to bray,
      And turning fierce,˼ her speckled taile advaunst,   *fiercely*
      Threatning her angry sting, him to dismay:
      Who nought aghast, his mightie hand enhaunst˼:   *raised*
    The stroke down from her head unto her shoulder glaunst.

18   Much daunted with that dint, her sence was dazd,
      Yet kindling rage, her selfe she gathered round,
      And all attonce her beastly body raizd
      With doubled forces high above the ground:

Elfe fairy (Harvey's early reference is to the
Elvish Queen)

Tho⟩ wrapping up her wrethèd sterne arownd,   *then*
Lept fierce upon his shield, and her huge traine⟩   *tail*
All suddenly about his body wound,
That hand or foot to stirre he strove in vaine:
God helpe the man so wrapt in *Errours* endlesse traine.⟩   *deceit*

19   His Lady sad to see his sore constraint,
      Cride out, Now now Sir knight, shew what ye bee,
      Add faith unto your force, and be not faint:
      Strangle her, else she sure will strangle thee.
      That when he heard, in great perplexitie,
      His gall did grate for griefe⟩ and high disdaine,   *anger*
      And knitting all his force got one hand free,
      Wherewith he grypt her gorge with so great paine,
That soone to loose her wicked bands did her constraine.

20   Therewith she spewd out of her filthy maw⟩   *stomach*
      A floud of poyson horrible and blacke,
      Full of great lumpes of flesh and gobbets raw,
      Which stunck so vildly,⟩ that it forst him slacke   *vilely*
      His grasping hold, and from her turne him backe:
      Her vomit full of bookes and papers was,°
      With loathly frogs and toades, which eyes did lacke,°
      And creeping sought way in the weedy gras:
Her filthy parbreake⟩ all the place defilèd has.   *vomit*

21   As when old father *Nilus* gins to swell
      With timely pride above the *Aegyptian* vale,
      His fattie⟩ waves do fertile slime outwell,   *greasy*
      And overflow each plaine and lowly dale:
      But when his later spring⟩ gins to avale,⟩   *flood / subside*
      Huge heapes of mudd he leaves, wherein there breed
      Ten thousand kindes of creatures, partly male
      And partly female of his fruitfull seed;
Such ugly monstrous shapes elsewhere may no man reed.⟩°   *see*

22   The same so sore annoyèd has the knight,
      That welnigh chokèd with the deadly stinke,
      His forces faile, ne⟩ can no longer fight.   *nor*
      Whose corage when the feend perceiv'd to shrinke,
      She pourèd forth out of her hellish sinke
      Her fruitfull cursèd spawne of serpents small,
      Deformèd monsters, fowle, and blacke as inke,
      Which swarming all about his legs did crall,
And him encombred sore, but could not hurt at all.

---

vomit . . . was referring to the voluminousness of religious controversy, especially in the 16th century

loathly . . . lacke Revelation 16:13: "And I saw three unclean spirits like frogs come out of the mouth of the dragon, and out of the mouth of the beast, and out of the mouth of the false prophet."

As when . . . reed (stanza 21) The Nile floods which ensure the fertility of the valley, were supposed on subsiding to leave behind such creatures as crocodiles, bred from the mud.

23   As gentle Shepheard in sweete even-tide,
      When ruddy *Phœbus* gins to welke˃ in west,   *fade*
      High on an hill, his flocke to vewen wide,
      Markes which do byte their hasty supper best;
      A cloud of combrous gnattes do him molest,
      All striving to infixe their feeble stings,
      That from their noyance˃ he no where can rest,   *irritation*
      But with his clownish hands their tender wings
   He brusheth oft, and oft doth mar their murmurings.

24   Thus ill bestedd,˃ and fearefull more of shame,   *situated*
      Then˃ of the certaine perill he stood in,   *than*
      Halfe furious˃ unto his foe he came,   *mad*
      Resolv'd in minde all suddenly to win,
      Or soone to lose, before he once would lin;˃   *stop*
      And strooke at her with more than manly force,
      That from her body full of filthie sin
      He raft˃ her hatefull head without remorse;   *cut*
   A streame of cole black bloud forth gushèd from her corse.

25   Her scattred brood, soone as their Parent deare
      They saw so rudely falling to the ground,
      Groning full deadly, all with troublous feare,
      Gathred themselves about her body round,
      Weening their wonted entrance to have found
      At her wide mouth: but being there withstood
      They flockèd all about her bleeding wound,
      And suckèd up their dying mothers blood,
   Making her death their life, and eke her hurt their good.°

26   That detestáble sight him much amazde,
      To see th'unkindly Impes˃ of heaven accurst,   *young, brood*
      Devoure their dam; on whom while so he gazd,
      Having all satisfide their bloudy thurst,
      Their bellies swolne he saw with fulnesse burst,
      And bowels gushing forth: well worthy end
      Of such as drunke her life, the which them nurst;
      Now needeth him no lenger labour spend,
   His foes have slaine themselves, with whom he should contend.

27   His Ladie seeing all, that chaunst, from farre
      Approcht in hast to greet his victorie,
      And said, Faire knight, borne under happy starre,
      Who see your vanquisht foes before you lye;
      Well worthy be you of that Armorie,°
      Wherein ye have great glory wonne this day,
      And proov'd your strength on a strong enimie,

Making . . . good heresy as finally self-de-   **Armorie** the armor of the *miles Christi*
structive

Your first adventure: many such I pray,
And henceforth ever wish, that like succeed it may.

28   Then mounted he upon his Steede againe,
     And with the Lady backward⸴ sought to wend;⸴   *back / go*
     That path he kept, which beaten was most plaine,
     Ne ever would to any by-way bend,
     But still⸴ did follow one unto the end,   *always*
     The which at last out of the wood them brought.
     So forward on his way (with God to frend)
     He passèd forth, and new adventure sought;
   Long way he travellèd, before he heard of ought.

29   At length they chaunst to meet upon the way
     An agèd Sire,° in long blacke weedes⸴ yclad,   *garments*
     His feete all bare, his beard all hoarie gray,
     And by his belt his booke he hanging had;
     Sober he seemde, and very sagely sad,⸴   *grave*
     And to the ground his eyes were lowly bent,
     Simple in shew, and voyde of malice bad,
     And all the way he prayèd, as he went,
   And often knockt his brest, as one that did repent.

30   He faire the knight saluted, louting⸴ low,   *bowing*
     Who faire him quited,⸴ as that courteous was: *responded*
     And after asked him, if he did know
     Of straunge adventures, which abroad did pas.
     Ah my deare Sonne (quoth he) how should, alas,
     Silly⸴ old man, that lives in hidden cell,   *simple*
     Bidding his beades all day for his trespas,
     Tydings of warre and worldly trouble tell?
   With holy father sits not with such things to mell.⸴   *meddle*

31   But if of daunger which hereby doth dwell,
     And homebred evill ye desire to heare,
     Of a straunge man I can you tidings tell,
     That wasteth all this countrey farre and neare.
     Of such (said he) I chiefly do inquere,
     And shall you well reward to shew the place,
     In which that wicked wight⸴ his dayes doth weare:⸴   *creature / pass*
     For to all knighthood it is foule disgrace,
   That such a cursèd creature lives so long a space.

32   Far hence (quoth he) in wastfull wildernesse
     His dwelling is, by which no living wight
     May ever passe, but thorough⸴ great distresse.   *through*
     Now (sayd the Lady) draweth toward night,
     And well I wote,⸴ that of your later⸴ fight   *know / recent*

agèd Sire The black-magician hermit occurs in other romances, but Spenser makes Archimago allegorical of the papacy; various popes were accused by Protestant historians of black magic.

Ye all forwearied be: for what so strong,
But wanting° rest will also want of might?   *lacking*
The Sunne that measures heaven all day long,
At night doth baite° his steedes the *Ocean* waves emong.   *refresh*

33 Then with the Sunne take Sir, your timely rest,
    And with new day new worke at once begin:
    Untroubled night they say gives counsell best.
    Right well Sir knight ye have advisèd bin,
    (Quoth then that agèd man;) the way to win
    Is wisely to advise:° now day is spent;   *consider*
    Therefore with me ye may take up your In°   *lodging*
    For this same night. The knight was well content:
So with that godly father to his home they went.

34 A little lowly Hermitage it was,
    Downe in a dale, hard by a forests side,
    Far from resort of people, that did pas
    In travell to and froe: a little wyde°   *away*
    There was an holy Chappell edifyde,
    Wherein the Hermite dewly wont to say
    His holy things each morne and eventyde:
    Thereby a Christall streame did gently play,
Which from a sacred fountaine wellèd forth alway.

35 Arrivèd there, the little house they fill,
    Ne looke for entertainement,° where none was: *food*
    Rest is their feast, and all things at their will;°   *as they wish*
    The noblest mind the best contentment has.
    With faire discourse the evening so they pas:
    For that old man of pleasing wordes had store,
    And well could file his tongue as smooth as glas;
    He told of Saintes and Popes, and evermore
He strowd an *Ave-Mary* after and before.

36 The drouping Night thus creepeth on them fast,
    And the sad humour° loading their eye liddes,   *heavy moisture*
    As messenger of *Morpheus*° on them cast
    Sweet slombring deaw, the which to sleepe them biddes.
    Unto their lodgings then his guestes he riddes:°   *leads*
    Where when all drownd in deadly° sleepe he findes,   *death-like*
    He to his study goes, and there amiddes
    His Magick bookes and artes of sundry kindes,
He seekes out mighty charmes, to trouble sleepy mindes.

37 Then choosing out few wordes most horrible,
    (Let none them read) thereof did verses frame,
    With which and other spelles like terrible,
    He bad awake blacke *Plutoes* griesly Dame,°

Morpheus god of dreams   **Plutoes . . . Dame** Hecate, goddess of witch-
                                   craft, wife of Pluto, god of the underworld

And cursed heaven, and spake reprochfull shame
Of highest God, the Lord of life and light;
A bold bad man, that dar'd to call by name
Great *Gorgon,*° Prince of darknesse and dead night,
At which *Cocytus* quakes, and *Styx*° is put to flight.

38   And forth he cald out of deepe darknesse dred
Legions of Sprights, the which like little flyes
Fluttring about his ever damnèd hed,
A-waite whereto their service he applyes,°
To aide his friends, or fray⸳ his enimies: *frighten*
Of those he chose out two, the falsest twoo,
And fittest for to forge true-seeming lyes;
The one of them he gave a message too,
The other by him selfe staide other worke to doo.

39   He making speedy way through spersèd⸳ ayre,   *dispersed*
And through the world of waters wide and deepe,
To *Morpheus* house doth hastily repaire.
Amid the bowels of the earth full steepe,
And low, where dawning day doth never peepe,
His dwelling is; there *Tethys*° his wet bed
Doth ever wash, and *Cynthia*° still⸳ doth steepe   *forever*
In silver deaw his ever-drouping hed,
Whiles sad Night over him her mantle black doth spred.

40   Whose double gates° he findeth lockèd fast,
The one faire fram'd of burnisht Yvory,
The other all with silver overcast;
And wakefull dogges before them farre do lye,
Watching to banish Care their enimy,
Who oft is wont to trouble gentle Sleepe.
By them the Sprite doth passe in quietly,
And unto *Morpheus* comes, whom drownèd deepe
In drowsie fit he findes: of nothing he takes keepe.⸳   *heed*

41   And more, to lulle him in his slumber soft,
A trickling streame from high rocke tumbling downe
And ever-drizling raine upon the loft,
Mixt with a murmuring winde, much like the sowne⸳   *sound*
Of swarming Bees, did cast him in a swowne:⸳   *faint*
No other noyse, nor peoples troublous cryes,
As still are wont t'annoy the wallèd towne,
Might there be heard: but carelesse Quiet lyes,
Wrapt in eternall silence farre from enemyes.

Gorgon Demogorgon, the original god, who
dwelt in darkness
Cocytus . . . Styx two of the five rivers of hell
A-waite . . . applyes wait to find out what job
he wants them to do
Tethys wife of Ocean

Cynthia moon goddess
double gates In *Odyssey* XIX the two gates
of sleep were of ivory and horn (here silver);
false dreams issued from the ivory gate, true
ones from the gate of horn.

42   The messenger approching to him spake,
      But his wast wordes returnd to him in vaine:
      So sound he slept, that nought mought⁐ him awake.   *might*
      Then rudely he him thrust, and pusht with paine,
      Whereat he gan to stretch: but he againe
      Shooke him so hard, that forcèd him to speake.
      As one then in a dreame, whose dryer⁐ braine   *too dry*
      Is tost with troubled sights and fancies weake,
  He mumbled soft, but would not all his silence breake.

43   The Sprite then gan more boldly him to wake,
      And threatned unto him the dreaded name
      Of *Hecate:* whereat he gan to quake,
      And lifting up his lumpish head, with blame⁐   *pain*
      Halfe angry askèd him, for what he came.
      Hither (quoth he) me *Archimago* sent,
      He that the stubborne Sprites can wisely tame,
      He bids thee to him send for his intent
  A fit⁐ false dreame, that can delude the sleepers sent.⁐   *suitable / senses*

44   The God obayde, and calling forth straight way
      A diverse⁐ dreame out of his prison darke,   *deceptive*
      Delivered it to him, and down did lay
      His heavie head, devoide of carefull carke,⁐   *worry*
      Whose sences all were straight benumbd and starke.⁐   *paralyzed*
      He backe returning by the Yvorie dore,
      Remounted up as light as chearefull Larke,
      And on his litle winges the dreame he bore
  In hast unto his Lord, where he him left afore.

45   Who all this while with charmes and hidden artes,
      Had made a Lady of that other Spright,
      And fram'd of liquid ayre her tender partes
      So lively, and so like⁐ in all mens sight,   *lifelike*
      That weaker⁐ sence it could have ravisht quight: *too weak*
      The maker selfe for all his wondrous witt,
      Was nigh beguilèd with so goodly sight:
      Her all in white he clad, and over it
  Cast a blacke stole, most like to seeme for *Una* fit.

46   Now when that ydle⁐ dreame was to him brought, *mischievous*
      Unto that Elfin knight he bad him fly,
      Where he slept soundly void of evill thought,
      And with false shewes abuse his fantasy,°
      In sort as he him schoolèd privily:°
      And that new creature borne without her dew,⁐   *unnaturally*
      Full of the makers guile, with usage sly

---

fantasy imagination (in sleep the reason no   **In sort . . . privily** in the manner in which he
longer controls it)   had secretly taught him

He taught to imitate that Lady trew,>   *honest*
Whose semblance she did carrie under feignèd hew.>   *form*

47   Thus well instructed, to their worke they hast,
And comming where the knight in slomber lay,
The one upon his hardy head him plast,
And made him dreame of loves and lustfull play,
That nigh his manly hart did melt away,
Bathèd in wanton blis and wicked joy:
Then seemèd him his Lady by him lay,
And to him playnd,> how that false wingèd boy°   *complained*
Her chast hart had subdewd, to learne Dame pleasures toy.>   *love play*

48   And she her selfe of beautie soveraigne Queene,
Faire *Venus* seemde unto his bed to bring
Her, whom he waking> evermore did weene>   *when awake / believe*
To be the chastest flowre, that ay> did spring   *ever*
On earthly braunch, the daughter of a king,
Now a loose Leman> to vile service bound: *mistress*
And eke the *Graces*° seemed all to sing,
Hymen iô Hymen,° dauncing all around,
Whilst freshest *Flora*° her with Yvie girlond crownd.

49   In this great passion of unwonted lust,
Or wonted feare of doing ought amis,
He started up, as seeming to mistrust
Some secret ill, or hidden foe of his:
Loe there before his face his Lady is,
Under blake stole hyding her bayted hooke,
And as halfe blushing offred him to kis,
With gentle blandishment and lovely looke,
Most like that virgin true, which for her knight him took.

50   All cleane dismayd to see so uncouth> sight,   *unfamiliar*
And halfe enragèd at her shamelesse guise,
He thought have> slaine her in his fierce despight:>   *to have / contempt*
But hasty heat tempring with sufferance> wise,   *patience*
He stayde his hand, and gan himselfe advise>   *consider*
To prove his sense, and tempt her faignèd truth.
Wringing her hands in wemens pitteous wise,
Tho> can> she weepe, to stirre up gentle ruth,>   *then / did / pity*
Both for her noble bloud, and for her tender youth.

51   And said, Ah Sir, my liege Lord and my love,
Shall I accuse the hidden cruell fate,

false . . . boy Cupid
Graces Aglaia, Thalia, Euphrosyne (see VI.x.
22): daughters of Venus by Bacchus; here
expressing in the false vision amity and joy
as at marriage. Renaissance mythography held
that "the unity of Venus is unfolded in the
trinity of the Graces."
Hymen iô Hymen ritual shout at Roman wedding, invoking the god of marriage
Flora goddess of flowers; present with the Graces
and Venus in Botticelli's *Primavera*

And mightie causes wrought in heaven above,
Or the blind God, that doth me thus amate,⸗   *cast down*
For⸗ hopèd love to winne me certaine hate?   *instead of*
Yet thus perforce he bids me do, or die.
Die is my dew: yet rew⸗ my wretched state   *pity*
You, whom my hard avenging destinie
Hath made judge of my life or death indifferently.

52 Your owne deare sake forst me at first to leave
My Fathers kingdome, There she stopt with teares;
Her swollen hart her speach seemd to bereave,
And then againe begun, My weaker years⸗   *extreme youth*
Captiv'd to fortune and frayle worldly feares,
Fly to your faith for succour and sure ayde:
Let me not dye in languor and long teares.
Why Dame (quoth he) what hath ye thus dismayd?
What frayes ye, that were wont to comfort me affrayd?

53 Love of your selfe, she said, and deare constraint⸗   *strong compulsion*
Lets me not sleepe, but wast the wearie night
In secret anguish and unpittied plaint,
Whiles you in carelesse sleepe are drownèd quight.
Her doubtfull⸗ words made that redoubted knight   *questionable*
Suspect her truth: yet since no' untruth he knew,
Her fawning love with foule disdainefull spight
He would not shend,⸗ but said, Deare dame I rew,   *reprove*
That for my sake unknowne such griefe unto you grew.

54 Assure your selfe, it fell not all to ground;
For all so deare as life is to my hart,
I deeme your love, and hold me to you bound;
Ne let vaine feares procure your needlesse smart,
Where cause is none, but to your rest depart.
Not all content, yet seemd she to appease
Her mournefull plaintes, beguilèd of her art,
And fed with words, that could not chuse but please,
So slyding softly forth, she turnd as to her ease.

55 Long after lay he musing at her mood,
Much griev'd to thinke that gentle Dame so light,
For whose defence he was to shed his blood.
At last dull wearinesse of former fight
Having yrockt a sleepe his irkesome spright,⸗   *spirit*
That troublous dreame gan freshly tosse his braine,
With bowres, and beds, and Ladies deare delight:
But when he saw his labour all was vaine,
With that misformèd⸗ spright he backe returnd againe.   *illicitly created*

[Deceived by the demonic imitator of Una, Red Cross in canto ii is parted
from the Truth; when he sees the spirit Una again, this time in bed with a

"young Squire" (another demon), he abandons her and leaves with the Dwarf.
Una goes in pursuit, and is met by Archimago disguised as Red Cross—a false
St. George, a false Holiness. Meanwhile Red Cross meets a scarlet lady, Duessa,
who is in the company of Sans Foy (Faithless). The Saracen Sans Foy attacks
Red Cross, who kills him. He consoles the lady, who tells him that she was

> Borne the sole daughter of an Emperour,
> He that the wide West under his rule has,
> And high hath set his throne where *Tiberis* doth pas.

That is, as we gathered from her scarlet dress and miter, she is the Roman
church. (Una, the true and single church, is the daughter of one who ruled
East and West; she is universal and single, Duessa partial, false, and divided.)
She complains further that her betrothal to a great prince (Christ) was thwarted
because he died and she could not find his body. She fell in with Sans Foy
and his brothers, Sans Joy and Sans Loy (a trinity opposite to the Christian
Faith, Hope, and Charity—faithless, loveless, lawless). This suggests, as Protestant propaganda often did, a league between Rome and the Moslems, who
threatened Europe from the East. As a further lie she names herself Fidessa.
Later Sans Loy is killed in Book II (the book of Temperance) and Sans Joy
in Book III (the book of Chastity). Red Cross believes Duessa's story despite
the warning of Fradubio (False Doubt), who has now been turned into a tree
(captive to sin) because he fell in just this way to the wiles of Duessa. Canto
ii deals with Red Cross's human lapse into sin and error, but also with the
desertion of the original true faith by England.

Canto iii describes Una, now protected by a lion, sheltering in the House
of Blind Devotion (the Roman faith, attended by superstition and clerical
greed). Archimago, dressed as Red Cross, joins her, but is defeated in combat
by Sans Loy, who also kills the lion and takes Una captive.

In canto iv Duessa leads Red Cross into the House of Pride, ruled over by
Lucifera (Pride, for Lucifer fell because of that sin) and her six counselors,
representing the other deadly sins. The formal pageant of the Seven Deadly
Sins which follows is often conventional in detail, but Spenser handles it with
vigor.]

From Canto iv

17   So forth she° comes, and to her coche does clyme,
     Adornèd all with gold, and girlonds gay,
     That seemd as fresh as *Flora* in her prime,
     And strove to match, in royall rich array,
     Great *Junoes* golden chaire, the which they say
     The Gods stand gazing on, when she does ride
     To *Joves* high house through heavens braspavèd way
     Drawne of faire Pecocks,° that excell in pride,
    And full of *Argus* eyes° their tailes dispredden wide.

---

she Lucifera
Pecocks Juno's chariot was represented as
drawn by peacocks.
Argus eyes Argus had 100 eyes, and so Juno put

him to watch over Io, a paramour of Jupiter's;
Jupiter had Mercury lull all the eyes to sleep
and kill Argus; Juno put his eyes on the
peacock's tail.

18 But this was drawne of six unequall° beasts,   *dissimilar*
  On which her six sage Counsellours did ryde,
  Taught to obay their bestiall beheasts,°
  With like conditions to their kinds° applyde: *natures*
  Of which the first, that all the rest did guyde,
  Was sluggish *Idlenesse* the nourse of sin;
  Upon a slouthfull Asse he chose to ryde,
  Arayd in habit blacke, and amis° thin,   *hood*
 Like to an holy Monck, the service to begin.

19 And in his hand his Portesse° still he bare, *breviary*
  That much was worne, but therein little red,
  For of devotion he had little care,
  Still drownd in sleepe, and most of his dayes ded;
  Scarse could he once uphold his heavie hed,
  To looken, whether it were night or day:
  May seeme the wayne° was very evill led, *coach, car*
  When such an one had guiding of the way,
 That knew not, whether right he went, or else astray.

20 From wordly cares himselfe he did esloyne,° *withdraw*
  And greatly shunnèd manly exercise,
  From every worke he chalengèd essoyne°, *excuse*
  For contemplation sake: yet otherwise,
  His life he led in lawlesse riotise;
  By which he grew to grievous malady;
  For in his lustlesse° limbs through evill guise° *feeble / way of life*
  A shaking fever raignd continually:
 Such one was *Idlenesse*, first of this company.

21 And by his side rode loathsome *Gluttony,*
  Deformèd creature, on a filthie swyne,
  His belly was up-blowne with luxury,
  And eke with fatnesse swollen were his eyne,
  And like a Crane° his necke was long and fyne,° *thin*
  With which he swallowed up excessive feast,
  For want whereof poore people oft did pyne;° *starve*
  And al the way, most like a brutish beast,
 He spuèd up his gorge, that all did him deteast.

22 In greene vine leaves he was right fitly clad;
  For other clothes he could not weare for heat,
  And on his head an yvie girland had,
  From under which fast trickled downe the sweat:
  Still as he rode, he somewhat° still did eat, *something*
  And in his hand did beare a bouzing can,
  Of which he supt so oft, that on his seat

Taught . . . beheasts i.e. they were instructed to obey the animals, not control them
Crane Like most of the other detail, this is traditional; Gluttony was represented as having a long thin crane's neck, for the better enjoyment of food.

His dronken corse he scarse upholden can,
In shape and life more like a monster, then a man.°

23 Unfit he was for any worldly thing,
And eke unhable once⁾ to stirre or go,⁾   *at all / walk*
Not meet to be of counsell to a king,
Whose mind in meat and drinke was drownèd so,
That from his friend he seldome knew his fo:
Full of diseases was his carcas blew,⁾   *livid*
And a dry⁾ dropsie through his flesh did flow: *thirst-producing*
Which by misdiet daily greater grew:
Such one was *Gluttony,* the second of that crew.

24 And next to him rode lustfull *Lechery,*
Upon a bearded Goat, whose rugged haire,
And whally⁾ eyes (the signe of gelosy,)   *green-tinged*
Was like the person selfe, whom he did beare:
Who rough, and blacke, and filthy did appeare,
Unseemely man to please faire Ladies eye;
Yet he of Ladies oft was lovèd deare,
When fairer faces were bid standen by:⁾   *aside*
O who does know the bent of womens fantasy?

25 In a greene gowne he clothèd was full faire,
Which underneath did hide his filthinesse,
And in his hand a burning hart he bare,
Full of vaine follies, and new fanglenesse⁾:   *vain novelty*
For he was false, and fraught with ficklenesse,
And learnèd had to love with secret lookes,
And well could⁾ daunce, and sing with ruefulnesse,   *knew how to*
And fortunes tell, and read in loving bookes,
And thousand other wayes, to bait his fleshly hookes.

26 Inconstant man, that lovèd all he saw,
And lusted after all, that he did love,
Ne would his looser⁾ life be tide to law,   *too loose*
But joyd weake wemens hearts to tempt and prove⁾   *try*
If from their loyall loves he might them move;
Which lewdnesse fild him with reprochfull paine
Of that fowle evill,⁾ which all men reprove,   *syphilis*
That rots the marrow, and consumes the braine:
Such one was *Lecherie,* the third of all this traine.

27 And greedy *Avarice* by him did ride,
Upon a Camell loaden all with gold;
Two iron coffers hong on either side,
With precious mettall full, as they might hold,

In greene . . . man (stanza 22) modeled on
Silenus, gluttonous and drunken attendant of
Bacchus

And in his lap an heape of coine he told;>   *counted*
For of his wicked pelfe his God he made,
And unto hell him selfe for money sold;
Accursed usurie was all his trade,
And right and wrong ylike in equall ballaunce waide.

28   His life was nigh unto deaths doore yplast,
    And thred-bare cote, and cobled shoes he ware,
    Ne scarse good morsell all his life did tast,
    But both from backe and belly still did spare,
    To fill his bags, and richesse to compare;>   *acquire*
    Yet chylde ne kinsman living had he none
    To leave them to; but thorough> daily care   *through*
    To get, and nightly feare to lose his owne,
He led a wretched life unto him selfe unknowne.

29   Most wretched wight, whom nothing might suffise,
    Whose greedy lust did lacke in greatest store,>   *plenty*
    Whose need had end, but no end covetise,
    Whose wealth was want, whose plenty made him pore,
    Who had enough, yet wishèd ever more;
    A vile disease, and eke in foote and hand
    A grievous gout tormented him full sore,
    That well he could not touch, nor go, nor stand:
Such one was *Avarice*, the fourth of this faire band.

30   And next to him malicious *Envie* rode,
    Upon a ravenous wolfe, and still did chaw
    Betweene his cankred teeth a venemous tode,
    That all the poison ran about his chaw;>   *jaw*
    But inwardly he chawèd his owne maw>   *guts*
    At neighbours wealth, that made him ever sad;
    For death it was, when any good he saw,
    And wept, that cause of weeping none he had,
But when he heard of harme, he wexèd wondrous glad.   *grew*

31   All in a kirtle of discolourd say>   *serge*
    He clothèd was, ypainted full of eyes;
    And in his bosome secretly there lay
    An hatefull Snake, the which his taile uptyes
    In many folds, and mortall sting implyes.>   *enfolds*
    Still as he rode, he gnasht his teeth, to see
    Those heapes of gold with griple> Covetyse,   *grasping*
    And grudgèd at the great felicitie
Of proud *Lucifera*, and his owne companie.

32   He hated all good workes and vertuous deeds,
    And him no lesse, that any like did use,°
    And who with gracious bread the hungry feeds,

that . . . use that did such good deeds

His almes for want of faith he doth accuse;
So every good to bad he doth abuse:
And eke the verse of famous Poets witt
He does backebite, and spightfull poison spues
From leprous mouth on all, that ever writt:
Such one vile *Envie* was, that fifte in row did sitt.

33 And him beside rides fierce revenging *Wrath*,
    Upon a Lion, loth for to be led;
    And in his hand a burning brond⟩ he hath,   *sword*
    The which he brandisheth about his hed;
    His eyes did hurle forth sparkles fiery red,
    And starèd sterne on all, that him beheld,
    As ashes pale of hew and seeming ded;
    And on his dagger still his hand he held,
Trembling through hasty rage, when choler⟩ in him sweld.   *anger*

34 His ruffin⟩ raiment all was staind with blood,   *disorderly*
    Which he had spilt, and all to rags yrent,⟩   *torn*
    Through unadvizèd⟩ rashnesse woxen wood;⟩   *unreflecting / mad*
    For of his hands he had no government,
    Ne car'd for⟩ bloud in his avengement: *cared about*
    But when the furious fit was overpast,
    His cruell facts⟩ he often would repent;   *deeds*
    Yet wilfull man he never would forecast,⟩   *foretell*
How many mischieves should ensue his heedlesse hast.

35 Full many mischiefes follow cruell *Wrath;*
    Abhorrèd bloudshed, and tumultuous strife,
    Unmanly murder, and unthrifty scath,⟩   *damage*
    Bitter despight, with rancours rusty knife,
    And fretting griefe the enemy of life;
    All these, and many evils moe⟩ haunt ire,   *more*
    The swelling Splene, and Frenzy raging rife,
    The shaking Palsey, and Saint *Fraunces* fire:⟩   *erysipelas*
Such one was *Wrath*, the last of this ungodly tire.

36 And after all, upon the wagon beame⟩   *shaft*
    Rode *Sathan*, with a smarting whip in hand,
    With which he forward lasht the laesie teme,
    So oft as *Slowth* still in the mire did stand.
    Huge routs of people did about them band,
    Showting for joy, and still before their way
    A foggy mist had covered all the land;
    And underneath their feet, all scattered lay
Dead sculs and bones of men, whose life had gone astray.

37 So forth they marchen in this goodly sort,
    To take the solace⟩ of the open aire,   *recreation*
    And in fresh flowring fields themselves to sport;

Emongst the rest rode that false Lady faire,
The fowle *Duessa,* next unto the chaire
Of proud *Lucifera,* as one of the traine:
But that good knight would not so nigh repaire,
Him selfe estraunging from their joyaunce vaine,
Whose fellowship seemd far unfit for warlike swaine.

. . .

[Immediately after the pageant, Red Cross encounters Sans Joy, representative of Despair, the deadliest of sins. Lucifera stops the fight and orders them to meet next day in the lists; Duessa attaches herself, lying as ever about Red Cross, to his enemy.

In canto v Red Cross defeats Sans Joy, but Duessa saves his life and takes him for treatment to Aesculapius in hell. Red Cross, seeing the dangers of the House of Pride, leaves.

Canto vi tells how Una is rescued from Sans Loy by a band of satyrs who, in "bootlesse zeale" worship her ass when she forbids them to worship her. Sir Satyrane, son of a lady and a savage man, arrives, admires Una's wisdom, and enables her to flee. Archimago announces that Sans Joy has killed Red Cross, and Sans Loy appears to fight with Satyrane. Una escapes. (Here is one of Spenser's loose ends, for Satyrane's fight is never finished, and when he turns up again in III.vii.28 it has been forgotten.) Perhaps the satyrs stand for natural religion, a good instinct misdirected; Satyrane for a good mixture of nature and instruction, which is capable, like the Reformed Church of England, of receiving the truth.

The seventh canto shows Red Cross tricked by Duessa into drinking of an enervating fountain—corrupt Gospel—after he has removed his Christian armor. While powerless, he is captured by Orgoglio, the Pride of Life, great enemy of Holiness. Orgoglio's mistress is Duessa, in her role as the Whore Babylon, wearing the triple crown of the papacy. The Dwarf finds Una and tells her what is happening; as she laments, Prince Arthur arrives, and this super-hero is described for the first time. Spenser planned, roughly, to have Arthur intervene in about the seventh or eighth canto of each book; so it is in I, II, and V. Una tells him of her plight; her parents have been the captives of the dragon for four years (i.e. the 4000 years between the fall of Adam and the birth of Christ). Arthur goes to the rescue.]

Canto viii
Faire virgin to redeeme her deare
   brings Arthur to the fight:
Who slayes the Gyant, wounds the beast,
   and strips Duessa quight.

1   Ay me, how many perils doe enfold
    The righteous man, to make him daily fall?
    Were not, that heavenly grace doth him uphold,
    And stedfast truth acquite⁀ him out of all.   *deliver*
    Her love is firme, her care continuall,
    So oft as he through his owne foolish pride,
    Or weaknesse is to sinfull bands⁀ made thrall: *bonds*

Else should this *Redcrosse* knight in bands have dyde,
For whose deliverance she this Prince doth thither guide.

2   They sadly traveild thus, untill they came
Nigh to a castle builded strong and hie:
Then cryde the Dwarfe, lo yonder is the same,
In which my Lord my liege doth lucklesse lie,
Thrall° to that Gyants hatefull tyrannie: *slave*
Therefore, deare Sir, your mightie powres assay.°   *try*
The noble knight alighted by and by
From loftie steede, and bad the Ladie stay,
To see what end of fight should him befall that day.

3   So with the Squire, th'admirer of his might,
He marchèd forth towards that castle wall;
Whose gates he found fast shut, ne° living wight   *nor*
To ward° the same, nor answere commers call.   *guard*
Then tooke that Squire an horne of bugle small,°
Which hong adowne his side in twisted gold,
And tassels gay. Wyde wonders° over all
Of that same hornes great vertues weren told,
Which had approvèd° bene in uses manifold.   *proved*

4   Was never wight, that heard that shrilling sound,
But trembling feare did feele in every vaine;
Three miles it might be easie heard around,
And Ecchoes three answerd it selfe againe:
No false enchauntment, nor deceiptfull traine°   *trickery*
Might once abide the terror of that blast,
But presently was voide and wholly vaine:
No gate so strong, no locke so firme and fast,
But with that percing noise flew open quite, or brast.°   *burst*

5   The same before the Geants gate he blew,
That all the castle quakèd from the ground,
And every dore of freewill open flew.
The Gyant selfe dismaièd with that sownd,
Where he with his *Duessa* dalliance° fownd,   *love making*
In hast came rushing forth from inner bowre,
With staring countenance sterne, as one astownd,
And staggering steps, to weet, what suddein stowre°   *tumult*
Had wrought that horror strange, and dar'd his dreaded powre.

6   And after him the proud *Duessa* came,
High mounted on her manyheaded beast,°
And every head with fyrie tongue did flame,
And every head was crownèd on his creast,
And bloudie mouthèd with late cruell feast.

horne . . . small small wild ox's horn   such horns had been featured in Romance
Wyde wonders from the *Chanson de Roland;*   **High . . . beast** See Headnote to Bk. I.

That when the knight beheld, his mightie shild
 Upon his manly arme he soone addrest,⁾   *adjusted*
 And at him fiercely flew, with courage fild,
And eger greedinesse through every member thrild.

7   Therewith the Gyant buckled him to fight,
     Inflam'd with scornefull wrath and high disdaine,
     And lifting up his dreadfull club on hight,
     Allarm'd with ragged snubbes⁾ and knottie graine,   *snags*
     Him thought at first encounter to have slaine.
     But wise and warie was that noble Pere⁾,   *peer*
     And lightly leaping from so monstrous maine,⁾   *force*
     Did faire avoide the violence him nere;
It booted nought, to thinke, such thunderbolts to beare.

8   Ne shame he thought to shunne so hideous might:
     The idle stroke, enforcing furious way,
     Missing the marke of his misaymèd sight
     Did fall to ground, and with his⁾ heavie sway   *its*
     So deepely dinted in the driven clay,
     That three yardes deepe a furrow up did throw:
     The sad earth wounded with so sore assay,⁾   *onslaught*
     Did grone full grievous underneath the blow,
And trembling with strange feare, did like an earthquake show.

9.   As when almightie *Jove* in wrathfull mood,
     To wreake⁾ the guilt of mortall sins is bent,   *punish*
     Hurles forth his thundring dart with deadly food,⁾   *hatred (feud)*
     Enrold in flames, and smouldring dreriment,
     Through riven cloudes and molten firmament;
     The fierce threeforkèd engin⁾ making way,   *weapon*
     Both loftie towres and highest trees hath rent,
     And all that might his⁾ angrie passage stay,   *its*
And shooting in the earth, casts up a mount of clay.

10   His boystrous⁾ club, so buried in the ground,   *vast*
     He could not rearen up again so light,
     But that the knight him at avantage found,
     And whiles he strove his combred clubbe to quight⁾   *free*
     Out of the earth, with blade all burning bright
     He smote off his left arme, which like a blocke
     Did fall to ground, depriv'd of native might;
     Large streames of bloud out of the trunckèd stocke
Forth gushed, like fresh water streame from riven rocke.

11   Dismaièd with so desperate deadly wound,
     And eke impatient of unwonted paine,
     He loudly brayd with beastly yelling sound,
     That all the fields rebellowèd againe;
     As great a noyse, as when in Cymbrian⁾ plaine   *Danish*

An heard of Bulles, whom kindly⟩ rage doth sting,   *natural*
Do for the milkie mothers want complaine,°
And fill the fields with troublous bellowing,
The neighbour woods around with hollow murmur ring.

12   That when his deare *Duessa* heard, and saw
     The evill stownd,⟩ that daungerd her estate,   *blow*
     Unto his aid she hastily did draw
     Her dreadfull beast, who swolne with bloud of late
     Came ramping forth with proud presumpteous gate,
     And threatned all his heads like flaming brands.⟩   *torches*
     But him the Squire made quickly to retrate,
     Encountring fierce with single⟩ sword in hand,   *only*
     And twixt him and his Lord did like a bulwarke stand.

13   The proud *Duessa* full of wrathfull spight,
     And fierce disdaine, to be affronted so,
     Enforst her purple beast with all her might
     That stop⟩ out of the way to overthroe,   *hindrance*
     Scorning the let⟩ of so unequall foe: *obstruction*
     But nathemore⟩ would that courageous swayne   *nevertheless . . . not*
     To her yeeld passage, gainst his Lord to goe,
     But with outrageous strokes did him restraine,
     And with his bodie bard the way atwixt them twaine.

14   Then tooke the angrie witch her golden cup,°
     Which still she bore, replete with magick artes;
     Death and despeyre did many thereof sup,
     And secret poyson through their inner parts,
     Th'eternall bale⟩ of heavie wounded harts;   *grief*
     Which after charmes and some enchauntments said,
     She lightly sprinkled on his weaker⟩ parts;   *too weak*
     Therewith his sturdie courage soone was quayd,⟩   *subdued*
     And all his senses were with suddeine dread dismayd.

15   So downe he fell before the cruell beast,
     Who on his necke his bloudie clawes did seize,
     That life nigh crusht out of his panting brest:
     No powre he had to stirre, nor will to rize.
     That when the carefull⟩ knight gan well avise,⟩   *watchful / notice*
     He lightly left the foe, with whom he fought,
     And to the beast gan turne his enterprise;
     For wondrous anguish in his hart it wrought,
     To see his lovèd Squire into such thraldome brought.

16   And high advauncing his bloud-thirstie blade,
     Stroke one of those deformèd heads so sore,°

Do . . . complaine lament the absence of cows
golden cup Revelation 17:4; the Whore carries
"a golden cup in her hand full of abominations
and filthiness of her fornication"
Stroke . . . sore Revelation 13:3: "And I saw
one of his heads as it were wounded to death";
the passage is related to the prophecy of the
bruising of the serpent's head (fulfilled at the
Crucifixion) in Genesis 3:15.

That of his puissance proud ensample made;
His monstrous scalpe downe to his teeth it tore,
And that misformèd shape mis-shapèd more:
A sea of bloud gusht from the gaping wound,
Thatʾ her gay garments staynd with filthy gore,   *which*
And overflowèd all the field around;
That over shoes in bloud he waded on the ground.

17 Thereat he roarèd for exceeding paine,
    That to have heard, great horror would have bred,
    And scourging th'emptie ayre with his long traine,ʾ   *tail*
    Through great impatienceʾ of his grievèd hed   *pain*
    His gorgeous ryder from her loftie stedʾ   *place*
    Would have cast downe, and trod in durtie myre,
    Had not the Gyant soone her succourèd;
    Who all enrag'd with smart and franticke yre,
Came hurtling in full fierce, and forst the knight retyre.

18 The force, which wont in two to be disperst,
    In one alone leftʾ hand he now unites,   *remaining*
    Which is through rage more strong then both were erst;ʾ   *formerly*
    With which his hideous club aloft he dites,ʾ   *raises*
    And at his foe with furious rigour smites,
    That strongest Oake might seeme to overthrow:
    The stroke upon his shield so heavie lites,
    That to the ground it doubleth him full low:
What mortall wight could ever beare so monstrous blow?

19 And in his fall his shield, that covered was,
    Did loose his vele by chaunce, and open flew:
    The light whereof, that heavens light did pas,ʾ   *surpass*
    Such blazing brightnesse through the aier threw,
    That eye moteʾ not the same endure to vew.   *might*
    Which when the Gyaunt spyde with staring eye,
    He downe let fall his arme, and soft withdrew
    His weapon huge, that heavèd was on hye
For to have slaine the man, that on the ground did lye.

20 And eke the fruitfull-headedʾ beast, amaz'd   *many-headed*
    At flashing beames of that sunshiny shield,
    Became starke blind, and all his senses daz'd,
    That downe he tumbled on the durtie field,
    And seem'd himselfe as conquerèd to yield.
    Whom when his maistresse proud perceiv'd to fall,
    Whiles yet his feeble feet for faintnesse reeld,
    Unto the Gyant loudly she gan call,
O helpe *Orgoglio*, helpe, or else we perish all.

21 At her so pitteous cry was much amoov'd
    Her champion stout, and for to ayde his frend,

Againe his wonted angry weapon proov'd:⟩   *tried*
But all in vaine: for he has read his end
In that bright shield, and all their forces spend
Themselves in vaine: for since that glauncing sight,
He hath no powre to hurt, nor to defend;
As where th'Almighties lightning brond does light,
It dimmes the dazèd eyen, and daunts the senses quight.

22 Whom when the Prince, to battell new addrest,
    And threatning high his dreadfull stroke did see,
    His sparkling blade about his head he blest,⟩   *waved*
    And smote off quite his right leg by the knee,
    That downe he tombled; as an agèd tree,
    High growing on the top of rocky clift,
    Whose hartstrings with keene steele nigh hewen be,
    The mightie trunck halfe rent, with ragged rift
Doth roll adowne the rocks, and fall with fearefull drift.⟩ *impact*

23 Or as a Castle rearèd high and round,
    By subtile engins and malitious slight⟩   *artifice*
    Is underminèd from the lowest ground,
    And her foundation forst, and feebled quight,
    At last downe falles, and with her heapèd hight
    Her hastie ruine does more heavie make,
    And yields it selfe unto the victours might;
    Sich was this Gyaunts fall, that seemd to shake
The stedfast globe of earth, as it for feare did quake.

24 The knight then lightly leaping to the pray,
    With mortall steele him smot againe so sore,
    That headlesse his unweldy bodie lay,
    All wallowd in his owne fowle bloudy gore,
    Which flowèd from his wounds in wondrous store.
    But soone as breath out of his breast did pas,
    That huge great body, which the Gyaunt bore,
    Was vanisht quite, and of that monstrous mas
Was nothing left, but like an emptie bladder was.

25 Whose grievous fall, when false *Duessa* spide,
    Her golden cup she cast unto the ground,
    And crownèd mitre rudely threw aside;
    Such piercing griefe her stubborne hart did wound,
    That she could not endure that dolefull stound,⟩   *affliction*
    But leaving all behind her, fled away:
    The light-foot Squire her quickly turnd around,
    And by hard meanes enforcing her to stay,
So brought unto his Lord, as his deservèd pray.

26 The royall Virgin, which beheld from farre,
    In pensive plight, and sad perplexitie,

The whole atchievement⌐ of this doubtfull warre,   *course*
Came running fast to greet his victorie,
With sober gladnesse, and myld modestie,
And with sweet joyous cheare him thus bespake;
Faire braunch of noblesse, flowre of chevalrie,
That with your worth the world amazèd make,
How shall I quite⌐ the paines, ye suffer for my sake?   *repay*

27   And you fresh bud of vertue springing fast,°
      Whom these sad eyes saw nigh unto deaths dore,
      What hath poore Virgin for such perill past,
      Wherewith you to reward? Accept therefore
      My simple selfe, and service evermore;
      And he that high does sit, and all things see
      With equall⌐ eyes, their merites to restore,⌐   *just / reward*
      Behold what ye this day have done for mee,
    And what I cannot quite, requite with usuree.⌐   *interest*

28   But sith⌐ the heavens, and your faire handeling⌐   *since /conduct*
      Have made you maister of the field this day,
      Your fortune maister eke with governing,°
      And well begun end all so well, I pray,
      Ne let that wicked woman scape away;
      For she it is, that did my Lord bethrall,
      My dearest Lord, and deepe in dongeon lay,
      Where he his better dayes hath wasted all.
    O heare, how piteous he to you for ayd does call.

29   Forthwith he gave in charge unto his Squire,
      That scarlot whore to keepen carefully;
      Whiles he himselfe with greedie⌐ great desire   *eager*
      Into the Castle entred forcibly,
      Where living creature none he did espye;
      Then gan he lowdly through the house to call:
      But no man car'd to answere to his crye.
      There raignd a solemne silence over all,
    Nor voice was heard, nor wight was seene in bowre or hall.

30   At last with creeping crooked pace forth came
      An old old man, with beard as white as snow,
      That on a staffe his feeble steps did frame,
      And guide his wearie gate both too and fro:
      For his eye sight him failed long ygo,
      And on his arme a bounch of keyes he bore,
      The which unusèd rust did overgrow:
      Those were the keyes of every inner dore,
    But he could not them use, but kept them still in store.

And . . . fast addressed to the squire, Timias   Your . . . governing now take advantage of
                                                     your fortune, too, by exercising foresight

31   But very uncouth sight was to behold,
   How he did fashion his untoward pace,
   For as he forward moov'd his footing old,
   So backward still was turnd his wrincled face,
   Unlike to men, who ever as they trace,
   Both feet and face one way are wont to lead.
   This was the auncient keeper of that place,
   And foster father of the Gyant dead;
His name *Ignaro*° did his nature right aread.˃   *reveal*

32   His reverend haires and holy gravitie
   The knight much honord, as beseemèd well,
   And gently askt, where all the people bee,
   Which in that stately building wont to dwell.
   Who answerd him full soft, he could not tell.
   Againe he askt, where that same knight was layd,
   Whom great *Orgoglio* with his puissaunce fell
   Had made his caytive thrall;˃ againe he sayde,   *slave*
He could not tell: ne ever other answere made.

33   Then askèd he, which way he in might pas:
   He could not tell, againe he answerèd.
   Thereat the curteous knight displeasèd was,
   And said, Old sire, it seemes thou hast not red˃   *understood*
   How ill it sits with˃ that same silver hed   *becomes*
   In vaine to mocke, or mockt in vaine to bee:
   But if thou be, as thou art pourtrahèd
   With natures pen, in ages grave degree,˃   *solemn status*
Aread˃ in graver wise, what I demaund of thee.   *answer*

34   His answere likewise was, he could not tell.
   Whose sencelesse speach, and doted ignorance
   When as the noble Prince had markèd well,
   He ghest his nature by his countenance,
   And calmd his wrath with goodly temperance.
   Then to him stepping, from his arme did reach
   Those keyes, and made himselfe free enterance.
   Each dore he openèd without any breach;
There was no barre to stop, nor foe him to empeach.˃   *hinder*

35   There all within full rich arayd he found,
   With royall arras and resplendent gold.
   And did with store of every thing abound,
   That greatest Princes presence might behold.
   But all the floore (too filthy to be told)
   With bloud of guiltlesse babes, and innocents trew,
   Which there were slaine, as sheepe out of the fold,

Ignaro This Ignorance reflects Spenser's contempt for blind devotion—he showed it in canto iv; Ignaro is silent and pious but lives with and fosters Worldly Pride.

Defilèd was, that dreadfull was to vew,
And sacred ashes over it was strowèd new.

36 And there beside of marble stone was built
An Altare, carv'd with cunning imagery,
On which true Christians bloud was often spilt,
And holy Martyrs often doen to dye,⸌   *put to death*
With cruell malice and strong tyranny.
Whose blessèd sprites from underneath the stone
To God for vengeance cryde continually,°
And with great griefe were often heard to grone,
That hardest heart would bleede, to heare their piteous mone.

37 Through every rowme he sought, and every bowr,
But no where could he find that wofull thrall:
At last he came unto an yron doore,
That fast was lockt, but key found not at all
Emongst that bounch, to open it withall;
But in the same a little grate was pight,⸌   *placed*
Through which he sent his voyce, and lowd did call
With all his powre, to weet, if living wight
Were housèd therewithin, whom he enlargen⸌ might.   *set free*

38 Therewith an hollow, dreary, murmuring voyce
These piteous plaints and dolours did resound;
O who is that, which brings me happy choyce
Of death, that here lye dying every stound,⸌   *moment*
Yet live perforce in balefull darkenesse bound?
For now three Moones have changèd thrice° their hew,⸌   *shape*
And have beene thrice hid underneath the ground,
Since I the heavens chearefull face did vew,
O welcome thou, that doest of death bring tydings trew.

39 Which when that Champion heard, with percing point
Of pitty deare⸌ his hart was thrillèd⸌ sore,   *great / pierced*
And trembling horrour ran through every joynt,
For ruth of gentle knight so fowle forlore:⸌   *lost*
Which shaking off, he rent that yron dore,
With furious force, and indignation fell;
Where entred in, his foot could find no flore,
But all a deepe descent, as darke as hell,
That breathèd ever forth a filthie banefull smell.

40 But neither darkenesse fowle, nor filthy bands,⸌   *bonds*
Nor noyous⸌ smell his purpose could withhold,   *noxious*

Whose . . . continually At the opening of the Fifth Seal St. John "saw under the altar the souls of them that were slain for the word of God . . . And they cried with a loud voice, saying, How long, O Lord, holy and true, dost thou not judge and avenge our blood . . . ?" (Revelation 6:9–10); in this canto the apocalyptic theme is unusually evident. **three Moones . . . thrice** three months, representing the three centuries between Pope Gregory VII and Wyclif during which England was supposed to have been under the domination of the papacy

(Entire affection hateth nicer⌐ hands)   *too fastidious*
But that with constant zeale, and courage bold,
After long paines and labours manifold,
He found the meanes that Prisoner up to reare;
Whose feeble thighes, unhable to uphold
His pinèd corse,⌐ him scarse to light could beare,   *wasted corpse*
A ruefull spectacle of death and ghastly drere.⌐   *wretchedness*

41 His sad dull eyes deepe sunck in hollow pits,
Could not endure th'unwonted sunne to view;
His bare thin cheekes for want of better bits,⌐   *food*
And empty sides deceivèd of their dew,
Could make a stony hart his hap⌐ to rew;   *luck*
His rawbone armes, whose mighty brawnèd bowrs⌐   *muscles*
Were wont to rive steele plates, and helmets hew,
Were cleane consum'd, and all his vitall powres
Decayd, and all his flesh shronk up like withered flowres.

42 Whom when his Lady saw, to him she ran
With hasty joy: to see him made her glad,
And sad to view his visage pale and wan,
Who earst⌐ in flowres of freshest youth was clad.   *formerly*
Tho when her well of teares she wasted had,
She said, Ah dearest Lord, what evill starre
On you hath fround, and pourd his influence bad,
That of your selfe ye thus berobbèd arre,
And this misseeming hew⌐ your manly looks doth marre?   *appearance*

43 But welcome now my Lord, in wele or woe,
Whose presence I have lackt too long a day;
And fie on Fortune mine avowèd foe,
Whose wrathfull wreakes⌐ them selves do now alay.⌐   *injuries / diminish*
And for these wrongs shall treble penaunce pay
Of treble good: good growes of evils priefe.⌐   *test, experience*
The chearelesse man, whom sorrow did dismay,
Had no delight to treaten⌐ of his griefe;   *talk*
His long endurèd famine needed more reliefe.

44 Faire Lady, then said that victorious knight,
The things, that grievous were to do, or beare,
Them to renew, I wote, breeds no delight;°
Best musicke breeds delight in loathing eare:°
But th'onely good, that growes of passèd feare,
Is to be wise, and ware⌐ of like agein.   *wary*
This dayes ensample hath this lesson deare

Them . . . delight remembering the famous line (*Aeneid* II.3), in which Aeneas answers Dido's request that he should tell the story of his adventures: *Infandum, regina, jubes renovare dolorem* ("Queen, you are commanding me to renew unspeakable grief")
Best . . . eare although fine music can produce pleasure even in the ear that resists it (this is not true of the knight's story)

Deepe written in my heart with yron pen,
That blisse may not abide in state of mortall men.

45 Henceforth sir knight, take to you wonted strength,
    And maister these mishaps with patient might;
    Loe where your foe lyes stretcht in monstrous length,
    And loe that wicked woman in your sight,
    The roote of all your care, and wretched plight,
    Now in your powre, to let her live, or dye.
    To do her dye (quoth *Una*) were despight,
    And shame t'avenge so weake an enimy;
    But spoile her of her scarlot robe, and let her fly.

46 So as she bad, that witch they disaraid,
    And robd of royall robes, and purple pall,
    And ornaments that richly were displaid;
    Ne sparèd they to strip her naked all.
    Then when they had despoild her tire> and call,>   *dress / headdress*
    Such as she was, their eyes might her behold,
    That her misshapèd parts did them appall,
    A loathly, wrinckled hag, ill favoured, old,
    Whose secret filth good manners biddeth not be told.

47 Her craftie head was altogether bald,
    And as in hate of honorable eld,>   *old age*
    Was overgrowne with scurfe and filthy scald;>   *scabs*
    Her teeth out of her rotten gummes were feld,>   *fallen*
    And her sowre breath abhominably smeld;
    Her drièd dugs, like bladders lacking wind,
    Hong downe, and filthy matter from them weld;
    Her wrizled> skin as rough, as maple rind,   *wrinkled*
    So scabby was, that would have loathd all womankind.

48 Her neather parts, the shame of all her kind,>   *womenkind*
    My chaster Muse for shame doth blush to write;
    But at her rompe she growing had behind
    A foxes taile,° with dong all fowly dight;>   *covered*
    And eke her feete most monstrous were in sight;
    For one of them was like an Eagles claw,
    With griping talaunts armd to greedy fight,
    The other like a Beares uneven> paw: *rough*
    More ugly shape yet never living creature saw.

49 Which when the knights beheld, amazd they were,
    And wondred at so fowle deformèd wight.
    Such then (said *Una*) as she seemeth here,
    Such is the face of falshood, such the sight
    Of fowle *Duessa*, when her borrowed light

Foxes taile The fox was associated in contem- text was Song of Songs 2:15, supported by
porary polemic with the Catholic clergy; the Luke 13:32, where Jesus calls Herod a fox.

Is laid away, and counterfesaunce° knowne.   *deception*
Thus when they had the witch disrobèd quight,°
And all her filthy feature open showne,
They let her goe at will, and wander wayes unknowne.

50 She flying fast from heavens hated face,
    And from the world that her discovered wide,
    Fled to the wastfull wildernesse apace,
    From living eyes her open shame to hide,
    And lurkt in rocks and caves long unespide.
    But that faire crew of knights, and *Una* faire
    Did in that castle afterwards abide,
    To rest them selves, and weary powres repaire,
    Where store they found of all, that dainty was and rare.°

[In canto ix we hear Arthur's story of his love for Gloriana. He exchanges
gifts, Arthur's symbolizing the Eucharist, and Red Cross's the New Testament,
and Arthur leaves. Red Cross then meets Sir Trevisan, fleeing from the Cave of
Despair; he goes to the Cave and meets Despair, to whom he almost succumbs.
In terms of the spiritual allegory this passage describes a great crisis in the
career of what Milton calls the "wayfaring" Christian soul; despair is the greatest single threat to it. In terms of the historical allegory, following the exposure
of Duessa, it means the relapse into Romanism under Queen Mary, before the
Elizabethan Settlement established the true church for ever.]

From Canto ix

33 Ere long they come, where that same wicked wight°
    His dwelling has, low in an hollow cave,
    Farre underneath a craggie clift ypight,°   *placed*
    Darke, dolefull, drearie, like a greedie grave,
    That still for carrion carcases doth crave:
    On top whereof aye dwelt the ghastly Owle,
    Shrieking his balefull note, which ever drave
    Farre from that haunt all other chearefull fowle;
    And all about it wandring ghostes did waile and howle.

34 And all about old stockes and stubs of trees,
    Whereon nor fruit, nor leafe was ever seene,
    Did hang upon the ragged rocky knees°;   *crags*
    On which had many wretches hangèd beene,
    Whose carcases were scattered on the greene,
    And throwne about the cliffs. Arrivèd there,
    That bare-head knight for dread and dolefull teene,°   *grief*
    Would faine have fled, ne durst approchen neare,
    But th'other forst him stay, and comforted in feare.

---

disrobèd quight Revelation 17:16: "these shall
hate the whore, and shall make her desolate and
naked . . . ".
store . . . rare They confiscate the viciously
acquired wealth of Orgoglio and Duessa, which
figures the confiscation of monastic wealth in
the reign of Henry VIII.
wight Despair

35   That darkesome cave they enter, where they find
    That cursèd man, low sitting on the ground,
    Musing full sadly in his sullein mind;
    His griesie˃ lockes, long growen, and unbound,   *gray*
    Disordred hong about his shoulders round,
    And hid his face; through which his hollow eyne
    Lookt deadly dull, and starèd as astound;
    His raw-bone cheekes through penurie and pine,˃   *hunger*
  Were shronke into his jawes, as˃ he did never dine.   *as though*

36   His garments nought but many ragged clouts,˃   *cloths*
    With thornes together pind and patchèd was,
    The which his naked sides he wrapt abouts;
    And him beside there lay upon the gras
    A drearie corse, whose life away did pas,
    All wallowd in his owne yet˃ luke-warme blood,   *still*
    That from his wound yet wellèd fresh alas;
    In which a rustie knife fast fixèd stood,
  And made an open passage for the gushing flood.

37   Which piteous spectacle, approving˃ trew   *proving*
    The wofull tale that *Trevisan* had told,
    When as the gentle *Redcrosse* knight did vew,
    With firie zeale he burnt in courage bold,
    Him to avenge, before his bloud were cold,
    And to the villein said, Thou damnèd wight,
    The author of this fact,˃ we here behold,   *deed*
    What justice can but judge against thee right,
  With thine owne bloud to price˃ his bloud, here shed in sight?   *pay for*

38   What franticke fit (quoth he) hath thus distraught
    Thee, foolish man, so rash a doome˃ to give?   *judgment*
    What justice ever other judgement taught,
    But he should die, who merites not to live?
    None else to death this man despayring drive,˃   *drove*
    But his owne guiltie mind deserving death.
    Is then unjust to each his due to give?
    Or let him die, that loatheth living breath?
    Or let him die at ease, that liveth here uneath?˃   *uneasy*

39   Who travels by the wearie wandring way,
    To come unto his wishèd home in haste,
    And meetes a flood, that doth his passage stay,
    Is not great grace to helpe him over past,˃   *to pass over*
    Or free his feet, that in the myre sticke fast?
    Most envious man, that grieves at neighbours good,
    And fond,˃ that joyest in the woe thou hast,   *foolish*
    Why wilt not let him passe, that long hath stood
  Upon the banke, yet wilt thy selfe not passe the flood?

40   He there does now enjoy eternall rest
  And happie ease, which thou doest want and crave,
  And further from it daily wanderest:
  What if some litle paine the passage have,
  That makes fraile flesh to feare the bitter wave?
  Is not short paine well borne, that brings long ease,
  And layes the soule to sleepe in quiet grave?
  Sleepe after toyle, port after stormie seas,
 Ease after warre, death after life° does greatly please.

41   The knight much wondred at his suddeine˃ wit,   *quick*
  And said, The terme of life is limited,
  Ne may a man prolong, nor shorten it;
  The souldier may not move from watchfull sted,˃   *post*
  Nor leave his stand, untill his Captaine bed.˃   *orders*
  Who life did limit by almightie doome,˃   *judgment*
  (Quoth he) knowes best the terms establishèd;
  And he, that points˃ the Centonell his roome,˃ *appoints / post*
 Doth license him depart at sound of morning droome.

42   Is not his deed, what ever thing is donne,
  In heaven and earth? did not he all create
  To die againe? all ends that was begonne.
  Their times in his eternall booke of fate
  Are written sure, and have their certaine date.˃ *termination*
  Who then can strive with strong necessitie,
  That holds the world in his˃ still chaunging state, *its*
  Or shunne the death ordaynd by destinie?
 When houre of death is come, let none aske whence, nor why.

43   The lenger life, I wote˃ the greater sin,   *think*
  The greater sin, the greater punishment:
  All those great battels, which thou boasts to win,
  Through strife, and bloud-shed, and avengèment,
  Now praysd, hereafter deare thou shalt repent:
  For life must life, and bloud must bloud repay.
  Is not enough thy evill life forespent?
  For he, that once hath missèd the right way,
 The further he doth goe, the further he doth stray.

44   Then do no further goe, no further stray,
  But here lie downe, and to thy rest betake,
  Th'ill to prevent, that life ensewen may.°
  For what hath life, that may it lovèd make,
  And gives not rather cause it to forsake?
  Feare, sicknesse, age, losse, labour, sorrow, strife,
  Paine, hunger, cold, that makes the hart to quake;

death . . . life This is Despair's "suddeine wit"—he smuggles this item, which is not parallel to the others, into his list; all his subsequent arguments have the same kind of rhetorical plausibility.
that . . . may that may follow life

And ever fickle fortune rageth rife,
All which, and thousands mo° do make a loathsome life.   *more*

45   Thou wretched man, of death hast greatest need,
 If in true ballance thou wilt weigh thy state:
 For never knight, that darèd warlike deede,
 More lucklesse disaventures did amate:°   *overthrow*
 Witnesse the dongeon deepe, wherein of late
 Thy life shut up, for death so oft did call;
 And though good lucke prolongèd hath thy date,
 Yet death then, would the like mishaps forestall,
Into the which hereafter thou maiest happen fall.

46   Why then doest thou, O man of sin, desire
 To draw thy dayes forth to their last degree?
 Is not the measure of thy sinfull hire°   *service to sin*
 High heapèd up with huge iniquitie,
 Against the day of wrath, to burden thee?
 Is not enough, that to this Ladie milde
 Thou falsèd hast thy faith with perjurie,
 And sold thy selfe to serve *Duessa* vilde,°   *vile*
With whom in all abuse thou hast thy selfe defilde?

47   Is not he just, that all this doth behold
 From highest heaven, and beares an equall° eye?   *impartial*
 Shall he thy sins up in his knowledge fold,
 And guiltie be of thine impietie?
 Is not his law, Let every sinner die:
 Die shall all flesh?° what then must needs be donne,
 Is it not better to doe willinglie,
 Then linger, till the glasse be all out ronne?
Death is the end of woes: die soone, O faeries sonne.

48   The knight was much enmovèd with his speach,
 That as a swords point through his hart did perse,
 And in his conscience made a secret breach,
 Well knowing true all, that he did reherse°   *recount*
 And to his fresh remembrance did reverse°   *bring back*
 The ugly vew of his deformèd crimes,
 That all his manly powres it did disperse,
 As he were charmèd with inchaunted rimes,
That oftentimes he quakt, and fainted oftentimes.

49   In which amazement, when the Miscreant
 Perceivèd him to waver weake and fraile,
 Whiles trembling horror did his conscience dant,°   *daunt*
 And hellish anguish did his soule assaile,

Is . . . flesh Despair naturally omits to mention
that God modified this sentence, or that He
forbade suicide.

To drive him to despaire, and quite to quaile,°   *be dismayed*
He shew'd him painted in a table° plaine,   *picture*
The damnèd ghosts, that doe in torments waile,
And thousand feends that doe them endlesse paine
With fire and brimstone, which for ever shall remaine.

50   The sight whereof so throughly him dismaid,
     That nought but death before his eyes he saw,
     And ever burning wrath before him laid,
     By righteous sentence of th'Almighties law:
     Then gan the villein him to overcraw,°   *exult over*
     And brought unto him swords, ropes, poison, fire,
     And all that might him to perdition draw;
     And bad him choose, what death he would desire:
     For death was due to him, that had provokt Gods ire.°

51   But when as none of them he saw him take,
     He to him raught° a dagger sharpe and keene,   *handed*
     And gave it him in hand: his hand did quake,
     And tremble like a leafe of Aspin° greene,   *poplar*
     And troubled bloud through his pale face was seene
     To come, and goe with tydings from the hart,
     As it a running messenger had beene.
     At last resolv'd to worke his finall smart,
     He lifted up his hand, that backe again did start.

52   Which when as *Una* saw, through every vaine
     The crudled° cold ran to her well of life,   *congealed*
     As in a swowne:° but soone reliv'd° againe,   *faint / revived*
     Out of his hand she snatcht the cursèd knife,
     And threw it to the ground, enragèd rife,°   *deeply*
     And to him said, Fie, fie, faint harted knight,
     What meanest thou by this reprochfull strife?
     Is this the battell, which thou vauntst to fight
     With that fire-mouthèd Dragon, horrible and bright?

53   Come, come away, fraile, feeble, fleshly wight,
     Ne let vaine words bewitch thy manly hart,
     Ne divelish thoughts dismay thy constant spright.
     In heavenly mercies hast thou not a part?
     Why shouldst thou then despeire, that chosen art?°
     Where justice growes, there grows eke greater grace,°
     The which doth quench the brond of hellish smart,°   *pain*

death . . . ire Red Cross has been deceived into the desperate belief that his sins are unforgivable and that he should therefore anticipate the judgment of God.
chosen art theological: he is one of God's Elect, chosen before the creation for heaven. This "single" predestinarianism—there is election to salvation but not to damnation—is the less rigid form of the Calvinist doctrine: see

Paradise Lost III.183 ff.: "Some I have chosen of peculiar grace / Elect above the rest; so is my will; / The rest shall hear me call, and oft be warned / Their sinful state, and to appease betimes / The incensed deity, while offered grace / Invites. . . ."
where . . . grace Una reminds him of the fact Despair wanted him to forget: God's justice is followed by even greater grace.

And that accurst hand-writing doth deface.
Arise, Sir knight arise, and leave this cursèd place.

54 So up he rose, and thence amounted⁷ streight.   *mounted*
   Which when the carle⁷ beheld, and saw his gust   *churl*
   Would safe depart, for all his subtill sleight,
   He chose an halter from among the rest,
   And with it hung himselfe, unbid⁷ unblest.   *unprayed for*
   But death he could not worke himselfe thereby;
   For thousand times he so himselfe had drest,⁷   *prepared*
   Yet nathelesse it could not doe him die,⁷   *kill him*
Till he should die his last, that is eternally.

[In canto x Una brings Red Cross to the House of Holiness, an elaborate allegorical set-piece. He meets the three theological virtues, Fidelia, Speranza, and Charissa (Faith, Hope, and Charity), sketched with their emblematic attributes and called the daughters of Cælia (Heaven). Then the "soule-diseasèd knight" undergoes severe penance and performs, in an allegory of seven beadsmen in a hospital, the seven corporal works of mercy. This prepares him for Contemplation. In the following passage Contemplation leads him to the top of a holy mountain, compared to Sinai and the Mount of Olives, and also to Parnassus, haunt of the Muses. He can see the Heavenly Jerusalem and compare it with its earthly counterpart, Cleopolis (London). Now he acquires his saint's name and reluctantly leaves to finish his quest.]

From Canto x

46 Thence forward by that painfull way they pas,
   Forth to an hill, that was both steepe and hy;
   On top whereof a sacred chappell was,
   And eke a litle Hermitage thereby,
   Wherein an agèd holy man did lye,
   That day and night said his devotión,
   Ne⁷ other worldly busines did apply;   *nor*
   His name was heavenly *Contemplatión*;
Of God and godnesse was his meditatión.

47 Great grace that old man to him given had;
   For God he often saw from heavens hight,
   All⁷ were his earthly eyen both blunt and bad,   *although*
   And through great age had lost their kindly⁷ sight,   *natural*
   Yet wondrous quick and persant⁷ was his spright,   *penetrating*
   As Eagles eye, that can behold the Sunne:
   That hill they scale with all their powre and might,
   That his frayle thighes nigh wearie and fordonne⁷   *tired out*
Gan faile, but by her helpe the top at last he wonne.

48 There they do finde that godly aged Sire,
   With snowy lockes adowne his shoulders shed,
   As hoarie frost with spangles doth attire
   The mossy braunches of an Oke halfe ded.

Each bone might through his body well be red,°   *seen*
And every sinew seene through his long fast:
For nought he car'd his carcas long unfed;
His mind was full of spirituall repast,
And pyn'd° his flesh, to keepe his body low and chast.   *starved*

49   Who when these two approaching he aspide,
At their first presence grew agrievèd sore,
That forst him lay his heavenly thoughts aside;
And had he not that Dame° respected more,°   *greatly*
Whom highly he did reverence and adore,
He would not once have movèd for the knight.
They him saluted standing far afore;°   *far off*
Who well them greeting, humbly did requight,
And askèd, to what end they clomb that tedious height.

50   What end (quoth she) should cause us take such paine,
But that same end, which every living wight
Should make his marke, high heaven to attaine?
Is not from hence the way, that leadeth right
To that most glorious house, that glistreth bright
With burning starres, and everliving fire,
Whereof the keyes are to thy hand behight°   *entrusted*
By wise *Fidelia?* she doth thee require,
To shew it to this knight, according° his desire.   *granting*

51   Thrise happy man, said then the father grave,
Whose staggering steps thy steady hand doth lead,
And shewes the way, his sinfull soule to save.
Who better can the way to heaven aread,°   *show*
Then thou thy selfe, that was both borne and bred
In heavenly throne, where thousand Angels shine?
Thou doest the prayers of the righteous sead°   *offspring*
Present before the majestie divine,
And his avenging wrath to clemencie incline.

52   Yet since thou bidst, thy pleasure shalbe donne.
Then come thou man of earth, and see the way,
That never yet was seene of Faeries sonne,
That never leads the traveiler astray,
But after labours long, and sad delay,
Brings them to joyous rest and endlesse blis.
But first thou must a season fast and pray,
Till from her bands the spright assoilèd° is,   *released*
And have her strength recur'd° from fraile infirmitis.   *recovered*

53   That done, he leads him to the highest Mount;
Such one, as that same mighty man of God,°

Dame Mercy, who is leading Red Cross   the Israelites in flight from Egypt (Exodus
man of God Moses, who parted the Red Sea for   14:21 ff.)

That bloud-red billowes like a wallèd front
On either side disparted⌐ with his rod,   *parted*
Till that his army dry-foot through them yod,⌐   *went*
Dwelt fortie dayes upon; where writ in stone
With bloudy letters by the hand of God,
The bitter doome of death and balefull mone
He did receive, whiles flashing fire about him shone.°

54   Or like that sacred hill, whose head full hie,
Adornd with fruitfull Olives all arownd,
Is, as it were for endlesse memory
Of that deare Lord, who oft thereon was fownd,
For ever with a flowring girlond crownd:
Or like that pleasaunt Mount, that is for ay
Through famous Poets verse each where⌐ renownd,   *everywhere*
On which the thrise three learnèd Ladies° play
Their heavenly notes, and make full many a lovely lay.

55   From thence, far off he unto him did shew
A litle path, that was both steepe and long,
Which to a goodly Citie led his vew;
Whose wals and towres were builded high and strong
Of perle and precious stone, that earthly tong
Cannot describe, nor wit of man can tell;
Too high a ditty for my simple song;
The Citie of the great king hight it⌐ well,   *it is called*
Wherein eternall peace and happinesse doth dwell.

56   As he thereon stood gazing, he might⌐ see   *could*
The blessed Angels to and fro descend
From highest heaven,° in gladsome companee,
And with great joy into that Citie wend,
As commonly⌐ as friend does with his frend.   *familiarly*
Whereat he wondred much, and gan enquere,
What stately building durst so high extend
Her loftie towres unto the starry sphere,
And what unknowen nation there empeoplèd⌐ were.   *established*

57   Faire knight (quoth he) *Jerusalem* that is,
The new *Jerusalem,*° that God has built
For those to dwell in, that are chosen his,
His chosen people purg'd from sinfull guilt,
With pretious bloud, which cruelly was spilt
On cursèd tree, of that unspotted lam,
That for the sinnes of all the world was kilt:

where writ . . . shone Moses received the tablets of the Law on Mount Sinai (Exodus 24:
12 ff.).
thrise . . . Ladies the nine Muses, who lived on
Parnassus
to and fro . . . heaven Jacob dreamed he saw
a ladder stretching from earth to heaven, with
"the angels of God ascending and descending
on it" (Genesis 28:12).
new Jerusalem Hebrews 12:22–23; the Heavenly
City, here compared not with Jerusalem but
Gloriana's capital, in effect London

Now are they Saints all in that Citie sam,°   *together*
More deare unto their God, then younglings to their dam.

58 Till now, said then the knight, I weenèd° well,   *thought*
That great *Cleopolis,*° where I have beene,
In which that fairest *Faerie Queene* doth dwell,
The fairest Citie was, that might be seene;
And that bright towre all built of christall cleene,°   *clear*
Panthea,° seemd the brightest thing, that was:
But now by proofe° all otherwise I weene;   *test*
For this great Citie that does far surpas,
And this bright Angels towre quite dims that towre of glas.

59 Most trew, then said the holy agèd man;
Yet is *Cleopolis* for earthly frame,°   *structure*
The fairest peece, that eye beholden can:
And well beseemes all knights of noble name,
That covett in th'immortall booke of fame,
To be eternizèd, that same to haunt.°   *frequent*
And doen their service to that soveraigne Dame,
That glorie does to them for guerdon graunt:
For she is heavenly borne, and heaven may justly vaunt.°   *claim*

60 And thou faire ymp, sprong out from English race,
How ever now accompted Elfins sonne,°
Well worthy doest thy service for her grace,
To aide a virgin desolate foredonne.°   *ruined*
But when thou famous victorie hast wonne,
And high emongst all knights hast hong thy shield,
Thenceforth the suit° of earthly conquest shonne,°   *pursuit / avoid*
And wash thy hands from guilt of bloudy field:
For bloud can nought but sin, and wars but sorrowes yield.

61 Then seeke this path, that I to thee presage,°   *point out*
Which after all° to heaven shall thee send;   *finally*
Then peaceably thy painefull pilgrimage
To yonder same *Jerusalem* do bend,
Where is for thee ordaind a blessèd end:
For thou emongst those Saints, whom thou doest see,
Shalt be a Saint, and thine owne nations frend
And Patrone: thou Saint *George* shalt called bee,
Saint *George* of mery England, the signe of victoree.

62 Unworthy wretch (quoth he) of so great grace,
How dare I thinke such glory to attaine?
These that have it attaind, were in like cace

Cleopolis London
Panthea feminine version of Pantheon; a royal palace, perhaps Greenwich, may be in Spenser's mind
How . . . sonne Spenser wants Red Cross now to be known as English; in the next stanza he becomes, explicitly, St. George, patron saint of England, slayer of the dragon, knight faithful true, and type of Christ. For explanation see stanzas 64–66.

(Quoth he) as wretched, and liv'd in like paine.
But deeds of armes must I at last be faine,⸖   *willing*
And Ladies love to leave so dearely bought?
What need of armes, where peace doth ay remaine,
(Said he) and battailes none are to be fought?
As for loose loves are vaine, and vanish into nought.

63   O let me not (quoth he) then turne againe
Backe to the world, whose joyes so fruitlesse are;
But let me here for aye in peace remaine,
Or streight way on that last long voyage fare,
That nothing may my present hope empare.⸖   *impair*
That may not be° (said he) ne maist thou yit⸖   *yet*
Forgo that royall maides bequeathèd care,°
Who did her cause into thy hand commit,
Till from her cursèd foe thou have her freely quit.

64   Then shall I soone, (quoth he) so God me grace,
Abet⸖ that virgins cause disconsolate,   *uphold*
And shortly backe returne unto this place,
To walke this way in Pilgrims poore estate.
But now aread, old father, why of late
Didst thou behight⸖ me borne of English blood,   *call*
Whom all a Faeries sonne doen nominate?
That word shall I (said he) avouchen⸖ good,   *prove*
Sith to thee is unknowne the cradle of thy brood.

65   For well I wote, thou springst from ancient race
Of *Saxon* kings, that have with mightie hand
And many bloudie battailes fought in place⸖   *there*
High reard their royall throne in *Britane* land,
And vanquisht them, unable to withstand:
From thence a Faerie thee unweeting⸖ reft,⸖   *unconscious / stole*
There as thou slepst in tender swadling band,
And her base Elfin brood there for thee left.
Such men do Chaungelings call, so chaungd by Faeries theft.

66   Thence she thee brought into this Faerie lond,
And in an heapèd furrow did thee hyde,
Where thee a Ploughman all unweeting⸖ fond,   *unexpectedly*
As he his toylesome teme that way did guyde,
And brought thee up in ploughmans state to byde,
Whereof *Georgos*° he thee gave to name;
Till prickt with courage, and thy forces pryde,°
To Faery court thou cam'st to seeke for fame,
And prove thy puissaunt armes, as seemes thee best became.

That . . . be Spenser uses the familar idea that in life there must be a balance of the active and the contemplative.

royall . . . care charge of that royal maid, which has been entrusted to you
Georgos Greek for "farmer"
forces pryde confidence of your own strength

67   O holy Sire (quoth he) how shall I quight
     The many favours I with thee have found,
     That hast my name and nation red aright,
     And taught the way that does to heaven bound?>   *lead*
     This said, adowne he lookèd to the ground,
     To have returnd, but dazèd were his eyne,
     Through passing> brightnesse, which did quite confound   *surpassing*
     His feeble sence, and too exceeding shyne.
   So darke are earthly things compard to things divine.

68   At last whenas himselfe he gan to find,
     To *Una* back he cast him to retire;
     Who him awaited still with pensive mind.
     Great thankes and goodly meed> to that good syre,   *reward*
     He thence departing gave for his paines hyre.
     So came to *Una*, who him joyd to see,
     And after litle rest, gan him desire,
     Of her adventure mindfull for to bee.
   So leave they take of *Cælia*, and her daughters three.

[The eleventh canto describes the battle of Red Cross with the Dragon. On the first day things go badly for the knight; the heat of battle makes his Christian armor intolerable to him. He is revived by water from the Well of Life, type of the sacrament of Baptism, one of the two sacraments admitted, of the Roman seven, by the reformed church.]

    From Canto xi

29   It fortunèd (as faire it then befell)
     Behind his backe unweeting,> where he stood,   *not noticed*
     Of auncient time there was a springing well,
     From which fast trickled forth a silver flood,
     Full of great vertues, and for med'cine good.
     Whylome,> before that cursèd Dragon got   *formerly*
     That happie land, and all with innocent blood
     Defyld those sacred waves, it rightly hot>   *was called*
   The well of life, ne yet his> vertues had forgot.   *its*

30   For unto life the dead it could restore,
     And guilt of sinfull crimes cleane wash away,
     Those that with sicknesse were infected sore,
     It could recure,> and agèd long decay   *cure*
     Renew, as one were borne that very day.
     Both *Silo* this, and *Jordan* did excell,
     And th'English *Bath*, and eke the german *Spau*,
     Ne can *Cephise*, nor *Hebrus*° match this well:
   Into the same the knight backe overthrowen, fell.

Silo . . . Hebrus Siloam, the stream by which Jesus cured a blind man (John 9:7); Jordan, the crossing of which saved the Jews; Bath in England and Spa in Germany have therapeutic waters; Cephisus and the Thracian Hebrus were renowned for the purity of their waters.

31 Now gan the golden *Phœbus* for to steepe
    His fierie face in billowes of the west,
    And his faint steedes watred in Ocean deepe,
    Whiles from their journall⁓ labours they did rest,   *daily*
    When that infernall Monster, having kest⁓   *cast*
    His wearie foe into that living well,
    Can⁓ high advance his broad discolourèd brest,   *did*
    Above his wonted pitch, with countenance fell,
    And clapt his yron wings, as victor he did dwell.⁓   *remain*

32 Which when his pensive Ladie saw from farre,
    Great woe and sorrow did her soule assay,⁓   *assault*
    As weening that the sad end of the warre,
    And gan to highest God entirely⁓ pray,   *earnestly*
    That fearèd chance from her to turne away;
    With folded hands and knees full lowly bent
    All night she watcht, ne once adowne would lay
    Her daintie limbs in her sad dreriment,⁓   *sorrow*
    But praying still⁓ did wake, and waking did lament.   *always*

33 The morrow next gan early to appeare,
    That⁓ *Titan*⁓ rose to runne his daily race;   *when / the sun*
    But early ere the morrow next gan reare
    Out of the sea faire *Titans* deawy face,
    Up rose the gentle virgin from her place,
    And lookèd all about, if she might spy
    Her lovèd knight to move his manly pace:
    For she had great doubt of his safèty,
    Since late she saw him fall before his enemy.

34 At last she saw, where he upstarted brave
    Out of the well, wherein he drenchèd lay;
    As Eagle fresh out of the Ocean wave,°
    Where he hath left his plumes all hoary gray,
    And deckt himselfe with feathers youthly gay,
    Like Eyas⁓ hauke up mounts unto the skies,   *fledgling*
    His newly budded pineons to assay,
    And marveiles at himselfe, still as he flies:
    So new this new-borne knight to battell new did rise.

                    .   .   .

[The second day's fighting goes better at first, but the knight is again driven
back, to be revived this time by the Tree of Life, representing the sacrament
of Communion. This extract describes its effects, and the knight's preparation
for the third and last day of the battle, in which the dragon is killed. The fight
is a type of the victory of Christ over Satan in the Last Days.]

Eagle . . . wave "thy youth is renewed like
the eagle's" (Psalms 103:5). The eagle, in
bestiary lore, was supposed when old to fly
toward the sun and burn off his old feathers
before plunging into water and renewing his
youth; cf. Milton, *Areopagitica*.

46   There grew a goodly tree him faire beside,
         Loaden with fruit and apples rosie red,
         As they in pure vermilion had beene dide,°   *dyed*
         Whereof great vertues over all° were red:°   *everywhere / told*
         For happie life to all, which thereon fed,
         And life eke everlasting did befall:
         Great God it planted in that blessèd sted°   *place*
         With his almightie hand, and did it call
      The tree of life, the crime of our first fathers fall.°

47   In all the world like was not to be found,
         Save in that soile, where all good things did grow,
         And freely sprong out of the fruitfull ground,
         As incorrupted Nature did them sow,
         Till that dread Dragon all did overthrow.°
         Another like faire tree eke grew thereby,
         Whereof who so did eat, eftsoones did know
         Both good and ill:° O mornefull memory:
      That tree through one mans fault hath doen us all to dy.

48   From that first tree forth flowd, as from a well,
         A trickling streame of Balme,° most soveraine°   *curative*
         And daintie deare,° which on the ground still fell,   *precious*
         And overflowèd all the fertill plaine,
         As it had deawèd bene with timely raine:
         Life and long health that gratious ointment gave,
         And deadly woundes could heale, and reare againe
         The senselesse corse appointed° for the grave.   *prepared*
      Into that same he fell: which did from death him save.

49   For night thereto the ever damnèd beast
         Durst not approch, for he was deadly made,°
         And all that life preservèd, did detest:
         Yet he it oft adventur'd to invade. . . .

[Red Cross, type of Christ, now, in the final canto, harrows hell, restores Eden, and takes Una (the true church) as his betrothed bride. Details of the marriage feast derive from Revelation. Una appears in her full glory—as the true ancient church appears in the Church of England. Archimago arrives with a lying letter from Duessa, but is exposed and cast into a dungeon, like his prototype in Revelation. Finally Red Cross resumes his knightly role and returns to the service of Gloriana for six more years.]

The tree . . . fall planted next to the Tree of the Knowledge of Good and Evil in Eden (Genesis 2:9). Its benefits were lost through Adam's fall; it grows in the New Jerusalem (Revelation 22:2).
Till . . . overthrow referring to Satan, who caused the Fall

Whereof . . . ill This is the Tree of Knowledge of Good and Evil, of which Eve and Adam ate the fruit (Genesis 3:1–6).
Balme This balm is related in typology to the healing blood of Christ.
deadly made His being had affinity with death, not life.

From Canto xii

17 Then said that royall Pere in sober wise;°
  Deare Sonne, great beene the evils, which ye bore
  From first to last in your late enterprise,
  That I note,° whether prayse, or pitty more:
  For never living man, I weene, so sore
  In sea of deadly daungers was distrest;
  But since now safe ye seisèd° have the shore,   *reached*
  And well arrivèd are, (high God be blest)
Let us devize of ease and everlasting rest.

18 Ah dearest Lord, said then that doughty knight,
  Of ease or rest I may not yet devize;
  For by the faith, which I to armes have plight,
  I bounden am streight after this emprize,°   *enterprise*
  As that your daughter can ye well advize,
  Backe to returne to that great Faerie Queene,
  And her to serve six yeares in warlike wize,°   *wise*
  Gainst that proud Paynim king,° that workes her teene:° *woe*
Therefore I ought° crave pardon, till I there have beene. *must*

19 Unhappie falles that hard necessitie,
  (Quoth he) the troubler of my happie peace,
  And vowèd foe of my felicitie;
  Ne I against the same can justly preace:°   *press*
  But since that band° ye cannot now release,   *bond*
  Nor doen undo; (for vowes may not be vaine)
  Soone as the terme of those six yeares shall cease,
  Ye then shall hither backe returne againe,
The marriage to accomplish vowd betwixt you twain.

20 Which for my part I covet to performe,
  In sort as° through the world I did proclame,   *just as*
  That who so kild that monster most deforme,
  And him in hardy battaile overcame,
  Should have mine onely daughter to his Dame,°   *wife*
  And of my kingdome heire apparaunt bee:
  Therefore since now to thee perteines the same,
  By dew desert of noble chevalree,
Both daughter and eke kingdome, lo I yield to thee.

21 Then forth he called that his daughter faire,
  The fairest *Un'* his onely daughter deare,
  His onely daughter, and his onely heyre;
  Who forth proceeding with sad° sober cheare,° *solemn / appearance*
  As bright as doth the morning starre appeare

Then . . . wise Una's father is commenting on
Red Cross's story of his adventures.
I note I don't know whether to

Paynim king the enemies of the true church,
both the Romans and the Turks

Out of the East, with flaming lockes bedight,
To tell that dawning day is drawing neare,
And to the world does bring long wishèd light;
So faire and fresh that Lady shewd her selfe in sight.

22   So faire and fresh, as freshest flowre in May;
For she had layd her mournefull stole aside,
And widow-like sad wimple˃ throwne away,   *veil*
Wherewith her heavenly beautie she did hide,
Whiles on her wearie journey she did ride;
And on her now a garment she did weare,
All lilly white, withoutten spot, or pride,˃   *ornament*
That seemd like silke and silver woven neare,
But neither silke nor silver therein did appeare.°

23   The blazing brightnesse of her beauties beame,
And glorious light of her sunshyny face°
To tell, were as to strive against the streame.
My ragged rimes are all too rude and bace,
Her heavenly lineaments for to enchace.˃   *adorn*
Ne wonder; for her owne deare lovèd knight,
All˃ were she dayly with himselfe in place,˃ *although / in the same place*
Did wonder much at her celestiall sight:
Oft had he seene her faire, but never so faire dight.

24   So fairely dight, when she in presence came,
She to her Sire made humble reverence,
And bowèd low, that˃ her right well became,   *so that it*
And added grace unto her excellence:
Who with great wisedome, and grave eloquence
Thus gan to say. But eare˃ he thus had said,   *before*
With flying speede, and seeming great pretence,˃   *importance*
Came running in, much like a man dismaid,
A Messenger with letters, which his message said.

25   All in the open hall amazèd stood,
At suddeinnesse of that unwarie˃ sight,   *unexpected*
And wondred at his breathlesse hastie mood.
But he for nought would stay his passage right˃   *direct*
Till fast˃ before the king he did alight;   *close*
Where falling flat, great humblesse he did make,
And kist the ground, whereon his foot was pight;˃   *placed*
Then to his hands that writ he did betake,
Which he disclosing, red thus, as the paper spake.

26   To thee, most mighty king of *Eden* faire,
Her greeting sends in these sad lines addrest,

But . . . appeare The bride of the Lamb was arrayed in fine linen (Revelation 19:7–8). **glorious . . . face** Una, the woman clothed with the sun (Revelation 12:1), has now ended her time in the wilderness (12:6) and survived the persecution of the dragon (12:4); she emerges reclothed with the sun, the Bride of Christ, who, as the New Jerusalem, has a "light . . . like unto a stone most precious" (Revelation 21:11).

The wofull daughter, and forsaken heire
Of that great Emperour of all the West;
And bids thee be advizèd for the best,
Ere thou thy daughter linck in holy band
Of wedlocke to that new unknowen guest:
For he already plighted his right hand
Unto another love, and to another land.

27 To me sad mayd, or rather widow sad,
He was affiauncèd long time before,
And sacred pledges he both gave, and had,
False erraunt knight, infámous, and forswore:
Witnesse the burning Altars, which˃ he swore, *by which*
And guiltie heavens of his bold perjury,°
Which though he hath polluted oft of yore,
Yet I to them for judgement just do fly,
And them conjure˃ t'avenge this shamefull injury. *beseech*

28 Therefore since mine he is, or free or bond,
Or false or trew, or living or else dead,
Withhold, O soveraine Prince, your hasty hond
From knitting league with him, I you aread;˃ *advise*
Ne weene˃ my right with strength adowne to tread, *don't think*
Through weakenesse of my widowhed, or woe:
For truth is strong, her rightfull cause to plead,
And shall find friends, if need requireth soe,
So bids thee well to fare, Thy neither friend, nor foe, *Fidessa.*

29 When he these bitter byting words had red,
The tydings straunge did him abashèd make,
That still he sate long time astonishèd
As in great muse, ne word to creature spake.
At last his solemne silence thus he brake,
With doubtfull eyes fast fixèd on his guest;
Redoubted knight, that for mine onely sake
Thy life and honour late adventurest,
Let nought be hid from me, that ought to be exprest.

30 What meane these bloudy vowes, and idle threats,
Throwne out from womanish impatient mind?
What heavens? what altars? what enragèd heates˃ *passions*
Here heapèd up with termes of love unkind,
My conscience cleare with guilty bands° would bind?
High God be witnesse, that I guiltlesse ame.
But if your selfe, Sir knight, ye faultie find,
Or wrappèd be in loves of former Dame,
With crime do not it cover, but disclose the same.

guiltie . . . perjury heavens tainted by the guilt of his perjury

guilty bands illicit bonds

31   To whom the *Redcrosse* knight this answere sent,
     My Lord, my King, be nought hereat dismayd,
     Till well ye wote by grave intendiment,°   *consideration*
     What woman, and wherefore doth me upbrayd
     With breach of love, and loyalty betrayd.
     It was in my mishaps, as hitherward
     I lately traveild, that unwares I strayd
     Out of my way, through perils straunge and hard;
  That day should faile me, ere I had them all declard.

32   There did I find, or rather I was found
     Of this false woman, that *Fidessa* hight,
     Fidessa hight the falsest Dame on ground,°   *anywhere*
     Most false *Duessa*, royall richly dight,
     That easie was t'invegle° weaker° sight: *deceive / too weak*
     Who by her wicked arts, and wylie skill,
     Too false and strong for earthly skill or might,
     Unwares me wrought unto her wicked will,
  And to my foe betrayd, when least I fearèd ill.

33   Then steppèd forth the goodly royall Mayd,
     And on the ground her selfe prostrating low,
     With sober countenaunce thus to him sayd;
     O pardon me, my soveraigne Lord, to show
     The secret treasons, which of late I know
     To have bene wroght by that false sorceresse.
     She onely she it is, that earst° did throw   *previously*
     This gentle knight into so great distresse,
  That death him did awaite in dayly wretchednesse.

34   And now it seemes, that she subornèd hath
     This craftie messenger with letters vaine,
     To worke new woe and improvided° scath,°   *unlooked-for / harm*
     By breaking of the band betwixt us twaine;
     Wherein she usèd hath the practicke paine°   *artful skill*
     Of this false footman, clokt with simplenesse,
     Whom if ye please for to discover plaine,
     Ye shall him *Archimago* find, I ghesse,
  The falsest man alive; who tries shall find no lesse.

35   The king was greatly movèd at her speach,
     And all with suddein indignation fraight,°   *burdened*
     Bad on that Messenger rude hands to reach.
     Eftsoones the Gard, which on his state did wait,
     Attacht° that faitor° false, and bound him strait: *seized / impostor*
     Who seeming sorely chauffèd° at his band,   *chafed*
     As chained Beare, whom cruell dogs do bait,
     With idle° force did faine° them to withstand,   *futile / wish*
  And often semblaunce made to scape out of their hand.

36 But they him layd full low in dungeon deepe,°
    And bound him hand and foote with yron chains.
    And with continuall watch did warely keepe;
    Who then would thinke, that by his subtile trains
    He could escape fowle death or deadly paines?
    Thus when that Princes wrath was pacifide,
    He gan renew the late forbidden banes,⸒   *banns*
    And to the knight his daughter deare he tyde,
    With sacred rites and vowes for ever to abyde.

37 His owne two hands the holy knots did knit,
    That none but death for ever can devide;
    IIis owne two hands, for such a turne most fit,
    The housling⸒ fire did kindle and provide,   *sacramental*
    And holy water° thereon sprinckled wide;
    At which the bushy Teade⸒ a groome did light,   *torch*
    And sacred lampe in secret chamber hide,
    Where it should not be quenchèd day nor night,
    For feare of evill fates, but burnen ever bright.

38 Then gan they sprinckle all the posts with wine,
    And made great feast to solemnize that day;
    They all perfumde with frankencense divine,
    And precious odours fetcht from far away,
    That all the house did sweat with great aray:⸒   *adornment*
    And all the while sweete Musicke did apply
    Her curious⸒ skill, the warbling notes to play,   *intricate*
    To drive away the dull Meláncholy;
    The whiles one sung a song of love and jollity.

39 During the which there was an heavenly noise
    Heard sound through all the Pallace pleasantly,
    Like as it had bene many an Angels voice,
    Singing before th'eternall majesty,
    In their trináll triplicities° on hye;
    Yet wist no creature, whence that heavenly sweet⸒   *delight*
    Proceeded, yet each one felt secretly⸒   *inwardly*
    Himselfe thereby reft of his sences meet,⸒   *proper*
    And ravishèd with rare impression⸒ in his sprite.   *sensation*

40 Great joy was made that day of young and old,
    And solemne feast proclaimd throughout the land,
    That their exceeding merth may not be told:
    Suffice it heare by signes to understand

they . . . deepe "And he laid hold on the dragon, that old serpent, which is the devil, and Satan, and bound him a thousand years, and cast him into the bottomless pit, and shut him up, and set a seal upon him, that he should deceive the nations no more, till the thousand years should be fulfilled: and after that he must be loosed a little season" (Revelation 20:1–3). Hence Archimago's escape, and the fact that history does not end at this point. **fire . . . water** These rituals are borrowed from the ancient Roman marriage ceremony. **trináll triplicities** The angels were ranked in three groups of three orders.

The usuall joyes at knitting of loves band.
Thrise happy man the knight himselfe did hold,
Possessèd of his Ladies hart and hand,
And ever, when his eye did her behold,
His heart did seeme to melt in pleasures manifold.

41   Her joyous presence and sweet company
In full content he there did long enjoy,
Ne wicked envie, ne vile gealosy
His deare delights were able to annoy:
Yet swimming in that sea of blisfull joy,
He nought forgot, how he whilome⟩ had sworne,   *formerly*
In case he could⟩ that monstrous beast destroy,   *did*
Unto his Farie Queene backe to returne:
The which he shortly did, and *Una* left to mourne.

42   Now strike your sailes ye jolly Mariners,
For we be come unto a quiet rode,⟩   *harbor*
Where we must land some of our passengers,
And light this wearie vessell of her lode.
Here she a while may make her safe abode,
Till she repairèd have her tackles spent,⟩   *worn out*
And wants supplide. And then againe abroad
On the long voyage whereto she is bent:
Well may she speede and fairely finish her intent.

1590

Book II

The main theme of the Legend of Temperance is the control of the passions by the higher powers of the mind. In the *Nicomachean Ethics* Aristotle had distinguished between temperance and continence; the latter presupposes, as the former does not, the existence of strong desires that have to be overcome. Guyon seems to represent a mixture of these two virtues, and Spenser, who probably derived his knowledge of the *Ethics* from editions with Christian commentaries, does not keep rigidly to Aristotle's scheme. Temperance, in Christian thought, was one of the four cardinal virtues, the others being Prudence, Fortitude, and Justice; these, added to the theological virtues (Faith, Hope, and Charity), made up the seven which were set against the Seven Deadly Sins. Christian Temperance, like the other virtues, had its own emblems —the set square, the bridle, the wine mixed with water, or the mixing bowl itself— and Spenser uses them all. The very name of Guyon derives from that one of the four rivers of Eden—Gehon—which was allegorically associated with Temperance.

However, there are Aristotelian elements in the syncretic mix. Aristotle, as usual, defines the virtue as a mean between its excess and its deficiency, and Spenser uses this, together with the doctrine that the passions, which temperance and continence oppose, are divided into the angry and the desirous, the irascible and the concupiscible. Spenser illustrates this division by concentrating on the irascible in the first six cantos and on the concupiscible in the second six. Even the condition he finally attains to—

Heroic Virtue—is mentioned by Aristotle as the opposite—there is, exceptionally, no mean between them—of bestiality.

The conflicts involving Guyon take place in the human being; so there is much less supernatural activity in this than in the First Book, which it otherwise so closely parallels in design. Primarily Book II has to do with the moral activity of men in the natural world. (Temperance was a pagan virtue; holiness was known only to Christians, by revelation.) Guyon must keep to the golden mean, and has the Palmer, representing Right Reason, to aid him most of the time. Thus he is lower than Red Cross, a saint, and more like a pagan hero, such as Aeneas, whom he resembles also in his visit to the underworld. But it would be wrong to suggest that Spenser excludes Christianity. As we shall see, the quest of Guyon has strong Christian implications. The Second Book is an interesting example of a Renaissance phenomenon, the syncretic blend of pagan and Christian, set in a medieval (romance) form.

The Second Booke of The Faerie Queene

Contayning,
The Legend of Sir Guyon,
or
Of Temperaunce

1   Right well I wote⸮ most mighty Soveraine,   *know*
    That all this famous antique history,
    Of some th'aboundance of an idle braine
    Will judgèd be, and painted forgery,
    Rather then matter of just⸮ memory,   *true*
    Sith⸮ none, that breatheth living aire, does know,   *since*
    Where is that happy land of Faery,
    Which I so much do vaunt,⸮ yet no where show,   *publicize*
    But vouch⸮ antiquities, which no body can know.   *assert*

2   But let that man with better sence advize,⸮   *consider*
    That of the world least part to us is red:⸮   *made known*
    And dayly how through hardy enterprize,
    Many great Regions are discoverèd,
    Which to late age were never mentionèd.
    Who ever heard of th'Indian *Peru?*
    Or who in venturous vessell measurèd
    The *Amazons* huge river now found trew?°
    Or fruitfullest *Virginia°* who did ever vew?

3   Yet all these were, when no man did them know;
    Yet have from wisest ages hidden beene:
    And later times things more unknowne shall show.

The Amazons . . . trew It was first navigated (in part) in 1540.   **Virginia** named for Elizabeth, the Virgin Queen, on Ralegh's return in 1584.

Why then should witlesse man so much misweene°   *wrongly suppose*
That nothing is, but that which he hath seene?
What if within the Moones faire shining spheare?
What if in every other starre unseene
Of other worldes he happily° should heare?   *by chance*
He wonder would much more: yet such to some appeare.

4. Of Faerie lond yet if he more inquire,
    By certaine signes here set in sundry place
    He may it find; ne let him then admire,°   *be surprised*
    But yield° his sence to be too blunt and bace,   *confess*
    That no'te without an hound fine footing trace.°
    And thou, O fairest Princesse under sky,
    In this faire mirrhour maist behold thy face,
    And thine owne realmes in lond of Faery,
    And in this antique Image thy great auncestry.

5   The which O pardon me thus to enfold
    In covert vele, and wrap in shadowes light,
    That feeble eyes your glory may behold,
    Which else could not endure those beames bright,
    But would be dazled with exceeding light.
    O pardon, and vouchsafe with patient eare
    The brave adventures of this Faery knight
    The good Sir *Guyon* gratiously to heare,
    In whom great rule of Temp'raunce goodly doth appeare.

[The first canto of Book II, like that of I, establishes the nature of the quest
assigned to the knight of the Book, Guyon, whose "Legend" is Temperance. The
escaped Archimago directs Guyon and the Palmer to Duessa, posing as a girl
raped by Red Cross; but the knights recognize each other before Guyon prose-
cutes her revenge. They converse and part, Red Cross wishing Guyon luck as
he sets out "like race to run." Beside a fountain they find Amavia with her
baby Ruddymane, so called because his hands are stained with her blood.
Amavia dies beside the body of her husband Mordant, victim of the enchantress
Acrasia (Incontinence). Mordant (Mortdant: deathgiver) was like Adam infected by concupiscence with original sin. The fountain stands for divine law,
which provides sin with its occasion to produce concupiscence in men (Romans
7:7). The burial of Amavia and Mordant represents the death of the Old Man.
Ruddymane is baptized, but carries the stain contracted by his father. Guyon
at first thinks it is a simple case of intemperance; the deeper Christian meaning
is revealed to him by the Palmer in canto xi. The destruction of the Bower of
Bliss in xii is not just the overthrow of incontinence, but of sin in the human
heart. Spenser is building Temperance into a Christian rather than a pagan
(Aristotelian) scheme.

The second canto offers a schematic allegory of the doctrine of the mean, in the
House of Medina. Medina is the mean, her sisters Elissa ("deficient") and Perissa

no'te . . . trace can't follow the tracks without a hunting dog

("excessive") are the extremes. They have lovers who share their qualities; Perissa's is San Loy. Canto iii introduces Braggadocchio, who steals Guyon's horse, and Belphoebe—it is a sort of first installment of Book III. In the fourth canto Spenser deals with irascibility as the enemy of temperance; Furor (Anger) is bound, and Occasio (occasion, opportunity) has her tongue locked up. Other characters are Atin (Strife), Pyrochles ("fire disturbed" = incontinent anger), and Cymochles, his brother ("wave disturbed" = incontinent sex); these last two return later.

In canto v, amid more instances of anger and its occasions, Guyon overthrows Pyrochles. In vi there is a transition from irascibility to concupiscence, and Spenser starts it with the moralization: "A Harder lesson, to learne Continence / In joyous pleasure, then in grievous paine." Guyon, now without his Palmer, falls in with Phaedria (Greek, "glittering," but Spenser himself calls her "immodest Merth".) She sails about on the Idle Lake—loose mirth floating on idleness leads, says Spenser to "loose desire." She sings to her victim Cymochles of the beauty and plenty of the paradise she inhabits on a floating island (a forecast of the Bower of Bliss). Guyon, though courteous, has no difficulty in rejecting her charms. There is an inconclusive bout between Guyon and Cymochles; and we see Pyrochles, trying to drown himself to extinguish his anger, saved by Archimago. The rejection of sensual pleasure by Guyon, though easy, is part of the pattern of rejections that is completed in the seventh canto; note that he undergoes these temptations without the aid of the Palmer.]

Book II, Canto vii

This is the crucial canto of Book II. Mammon is the god of money, but of more than money: "God of the world and worldlings" he says; of all, in fact, that the virtuous soul must resist, including fame, power, and improper knowledge. The scheme of the canto has much in common with that of *Paradise Regained,* and of Marvell's "Dialogue Between the Resolved Soul and Created Pleasure." During his three-day tour of Mammon's underground realm, Guyon is followed by a terrible fiend who will tear him to pieces if he once weakens. He has no difficulty in rejecting riches, having chosen "another bliss . . . another end." Nor does he have much of a struggle at the Temple of Philotime ("love of earthly honor"), because he has plighted his troth to another lady ("heavenly honor"). The final temptation is that of the Garden of Proserpina: this is the temptation of forbidden knowledge—here, as in Milton and Marvell, the climactic temptation. Unmoved, he has undergone, like Christ in the wilderness, the *total* temptation (the temptation of sex came with Phaedria), and Mammon, his time expired, has to take him back to the light. Only then does he require succor, as Christ received it after his trial.

This is one of the great cantos; Lamb said that "the transitions in this episode are every whit as violent as in the most extravagant dream, and yet the waking judgment ratifies them." Its interpretation is, however, disputed. Some believe Guyon should not have accompanied Mammon, and that his doing so illustrates his inability to avoid the occasion of temptation. His error would be comparable to that of Red Cross in the Cave of Despair. But Milton, despite his error in thinking that the Palmer was with

Guyon, is likely to be right in his reading, when he says, in *Areopagitica,* that "our sage and serious poet Spenser . . . describing true temperance under the person of Guyon, brings him in with his palmer through the cave of Mammon, and the bower of earthly bliss, that he might see and know, and yet abstain."

In this episode Guyon is not being tempted by his own desires but by an external enemy; he is no more seeking the occasion of sin than Christ in the wilderness. His reward for withstanding the total temptation is Heroic Virtue, in the sense given to this term by the church when adapting it from Aristotle's *Ethics;* he now has a habit of good conduct that is second nature, and it fits him for deeds beyond the scope of the ordinarily virtuous man; he occupies a middle ground between such a man and a saint. As the victory over sin in the wilderness prepared Christ for the victory over death on the Cross, so Guyon's victory over Mammon makes possible the destruction of the Bower of Bliss. His faint, requiring angelic succor, is therefore not a sign of moral weakness, but of exhaustion at the end of this ordeal of initiation.

Canto vii

Guyon findes Mammon in a delve,
  Sunning his threasure hore:
Is by him tempted, and led downe,
  To see his secret store.

1   As Pilot well expert in perilous wave,
   That to a stedfast starre his course hath bent,
   When foggy mistes, or cloudy tempests have
   The faithfull light of that faire lampe yblent,>   *blinded*
   And cover'd heaven with hideous dreriment,
   Upon his card> and compas firmes his eye,   *chart*
   The maisters> of his long experiment,>   *agents / experience*
   And to them does the steddy helme apply,
Bidding his wingèd vessell fairely forward fly:

2   So *Guyon* having lost his trusty guide,°
   Late left beyond that *Ydle lake,* proceedes
   Yet on his way, of none accompanide;
   And evermore himselfe with comfort feedes,
   Of his owne vertues, and prayse-worthy deedes.°
   So long he yode,> yet no adventure found,   *went*
   Which fame of her shrill trompet worthy reedes:>   *considers*
   For still he traveild through wide wastfull ground,
That nought but desert wildernesse shew'd all around.

3   At last he came unto a gloomy glade,
   Cover'd with boughes and shrubs from heavens light,
   Whereas he sitting found in secret shade
   An uncouth,> salvage, and uncivile wight,   *strange*
   Of griesly hew,> and fowle ill favour'd sight;>   *shape / appearance*

---

lost . . . guide The absence of the Palmer is presumably to allow Guyon to undergo these tests without the help of a guide external to himself who would always represent the reasonable attitude, and so shield Guyon from the spiritual pressures besetting him; Jesus in the wilderness had no supernatural aid, was as if only a man.
And evermore . . . deedes sometimes thought very smug, but he is cheering himself up by counting all the support he has

His face with smoke was tand, and eyes were bleard,
His head and beard with sout were ill bedight,
His cole-blacke hands did seeme to have beene seard
In smithes fire-spitting forge, and nayles like clawes appeard.

4   His yron coate all overgrowne with rust,
     Whose underneath envelopèd with gold,
     Whose glistring glosse darkned with filthy dust,
     Well yet appearèd, to have beene of old
     A worke of rich entayle,˃ and curious mould,   *carving*
     Woven with antickes˃ and wild Imagery: *strange figures*
     And in his lap a masse of coyne he told,˃   *counted*
     And turnèd upsidowne, to feede his eye
And covetous desire with his huge threasury.

5   And round about him lay on every side
     Great heapes of gold, that never could be spent:
     Of which some were rude owre,˃ not purifide   *ore*
     Of *Mulcibers*° devouring element;
     Some others were new driven,˃ and distent˃   *smelted / beaten*
     Into great Ingoes,˃ and to wedges square;   *ingots*
     Some in round plates withouten moniment;˃   *engraving*
     But most were stampt, and in their metall bare
The antique shapes of kings and kesars˃ straunge and rare.   *emperors*

6   Soone as he *Guyon* saw, in great affright
     And hast he rose, for to remove aside
     Those pretious hils from straungers envious sight,
     And downe them pourèd through an hole full wide,
     Into the hollow earth, them there to hide.
     But *Guyon* lightly to him leaping, stayd
     His hand, that trembled, as one terrifyde;
     And though him selfe were at the sight dismayd,
Yet him perforce restraynd, and to him doubtfull sayd.

7   What art thou man, (if man at all thou art)
     That here in desert hast thine habitaunce,
     And these rich heapes of wealth doest hide apart
     From the worldes eye, and from her right usaunce?
     Thereat with staring eyes fixèd askaunce,
     In great disdaine, he answerd; Hardy Elfe,
     The darest vew my direfull countenaunce,
     I read˃ thee rash, and heedlesse of thy selfe,   *perceive*
To trouble my still˃ seate,˃ and heapes of pretious pelfe.   *quiet / place*

8   God of the world and worldlings I me call,
     Great *Mammon*,° greatest god below the skye,

Mulcibers Mulciber was Vulcan, the smith god; his element was fire.
Mammon "No man can serve two masters . . . Ye cannot serve God and mammon" (Matthew 6:24); his name means "wealth"; one has to choose between the world and heaven.

That of my plenty poure out unto all,
And unto none my graces do enuye:
Riches, renowme, and principality,
Honour, estate, and all this worldes good,
For which men swinck> and sweat incessantly,   *labor*
Fro me do flow into an ample flood,
And in the hollow earth have their eternall brood.

9   Wherefore if me thou deigne to serve and sew,>   *follow*
   At thy command lo all these mountains bee;
   Or if to thy great> mind, or greedy vew   *ambitious*
   All these may not suffise, there shall to thee
   Ten times so much be numbred francke and free.
   Mammon (said he) thy godheades vaunt° is vaine,
   And idle offers of thy golden fee;
To them, that covet such eye-glutting gaine,
Proffer thy giftes, and fitter servaunts entertaine.

10 Me ill besits,> that in der-doing armes,°   *besets*
   And honours suit> my vowèd dayes do spend,   *pursuit*
   Unto thy bounteous baytes, and pleasing charmes,
   With which weake men thou witchest, to attend:
   Regard of worldly mucke doth fowly blend,>   *defile*
   And low abase the high heroicke spright,
   That joyes for crownes and kingdomes to contend;
Faire shields, gay steedes, bright armes be my delight.
Those be the riches fit for an advent'rous knight.

11 Vaine glorious Elfe (said he) doest not thou weet,
   That money can thy wantes at will supply?
   Shields, steeds, and armes, and all things for thee meet
   It can purvay in twinckling of an eye;
   And crownes and kingdomes to thee multiply.
   Do not I kings create, and throw the crowne
   Sometimes to him, that low in dust doth ly?
   And him that raignd, into his rowme thrust downe,
And whom I lust,> do heape with glory and renowne?   *please*

12 All otherwise (said he) I riches read,>   *understand*
   And deeme them roote of all disquietnesse;°
   First got with guile, and then preserv'd with dread,
   And after spent with pride and lavishnesse,
   Leaving behind them griefe and heavinesse.
   Infinite mischiefes of them do arize,
   Strife, and debate, bloudshed, and bitternesse,
   Outrageous wrong, and hellish covetize,
That noble heart as great dishonour doth despize.

---

godheades vaunt boast of divinity
der-doing armes feats of high courage

roote . . . disquietnesse "the love of money is the root of all evil" (I Timothy 6:10)

13   Ne thine be kingdomes, ne the scepters thine;
        But realmes and rulers thou doest both confound,
        And loyall truth to treason doest incline;
        Witnesse the guiltlesse bloud pourd oft on ground,
        The crownèd often slain, the slayer cround,
        The sacred Diademe in peeces rent
        And purple robe⁊ gorèd with many a wound;   *imperial cloak*
        Castles surprizd, great cities sackt and brent:
        So mak'st thou kings, and gaynest wrongfull governement.

14   Long were to tell the troublous stormes, that tosse
        The private state,⁊ and make the life unsweet: *private life*
        Who swelling sayles in Caspian sea doth crosse,
        And in frayle wood on *Adrian*⁊ gulfe doth fleet,⁊   *Adriatic / float*
        Doth not, I weene, so many evils meet.
        Then *Mammon* wexing wroth, And why then, said,
        Are mortall men so fond and undiscreet,
        So evil thing to seeke unto their ayd,
        And having not complaine, and having it upbraid?⁊   *reproach it*

15   Indeede (quoth he) through fowle intemperaunce,
        Frayle men are oft captiv'd to covetise:
        But would they thinke, with how small allowaunce
        Untroubled Nature doth her selfe suffise,°
        Such superfluities they would despise,
        Which with sad cares empeach⁊ our native joyes: *impair*
        At the well head the purest streames arise:
        But mucky filth his⁊ braunching armes annoyes,⁊   *its / fouls*
        And with uncomely weedes the gentle wave accloyes.⁊   *clogs*

16   The antique⁊ world,° in his first flowring youth,   *ancient*
        Found no defect in his Creatours grace,
        But with glad thankes, and unreprovèd truth,
        The gifts of soveraigne bountie did embrace:
        Like Angels life was then mens happy cace;
        But later ages pride, like corn-fed steed,
        Abusd her plenty, and fat swolne encreace
        To all licentious lust, and gan exceed
        The measure of her meane, and naturall first need.

17   Then gan a cursèd hand the quiet wombe
        Of his great Grandmother with steele to wound,
        And the hid treasures in her sacred tombe,
        With Sacriledge to dig. Therein he found
        Fountaines of gold and silver to abound,

Untroubled . . . suffice Boethius, *The Consolation of Philosophy* II.5, was the classical statement of this idea.
The antique world also based on the famous passage in Boethius, *The Consolation of Philosophy* II.5, *Felix nimium prior aetas* ("Too

happy was that first age"); Boethius was translated into English by two sovereigns, Alfred and Elizabeth. Spenser also knew well the opening pages of Ovid's *Metamorphoses*, which describe the Golden Age and the subsequent decline.

Of which the matter of his huge desire
And pompous pride eftsoones> he did compound;   *forth with*
Then avarice gan through his veines inspire>   *breathe*
His greedy flames, and kindled life-devouring fire.

18 Sonne (said he then) let be thy bitter scorne,
And leave the rudenesse of that antique age
To them, that liv'd therein in state forlorne;
Thou that doest live in later times, must wage
Thy workes for wealth, and life for gold engage.
If then thee list my offred grace to use,
Take what thou please of all this surplusage;
If thee list not, leave have thou to refuse:
But thing refused, do not afterward accuse.

19 Me list not> (said the Elfin knight) receave   *I choose not*
Thing offred, till I know it well be got,°
Ne wote> I, but thou didst these goods bereave   *nor know*
From rightfull owner by unrighteous lot,>   *division*
Or that bloud guiltinesse or guile them blot.
Perdy> (quoth he), yet never eye did vew,   *indeed*
Ne toung did tell, ne hand these handled not,
But safe I have them kept in secret mew,>   *den*
From heavens sight, and powre of all which them pursew.

20 What secret place (quoth he) can safely hold
So huge a masse, and hide from heavens eye?
Or where hast thou thy wonne,> that so much gold   *dwelling*
Thou canst preserve from wrong and robbery?
Come thou (quoth he) and see. So by and by
Through that thicke covert he him led, and found
A darkesome way, which no man could descry
That deepe descended through the hollow ground,
And was with dread and horrour compassèd around.

21 At length they came into a larger space,
That stretcht it selfe into an ample plaine,
Through which a beaten broad high way did trace,
That streight did lead to *Plutoes* griesly raine:>   *hideous realm*
By that wayes side, there sate infernall Payne,°
And fast beside him sat tumultuous Strife:
The one in hand an yron whip did straine,>   *grip*
The other brandishèd a bloudy knife,
And both did gnash their teeth, and both did threaten life.

22 On thother side in one consort there sate,
Cruell Revenge, and rancorous despight,

Me list . . . well got Aristotle, *Nicomachean Ethics* IV, says a good man will not take money from a tainted source; the concept was Christianized (as we see from the reply of Jesus to Satan in *Paradise Regained*) on an offer of food—Satan asks "wouldst thou not eat?" and the reply is "Thereafter as I like the giver" (II.321). **Payne** These simple allegories are based on the description of hell in Virgil, *Aeneid* VI.273 ff.

Disloyall Treason, and hart-burning Hate,
But gnawing Gealosie out of their sight
Sitting alone, his bitter lips did bight,
And trembling Feare still to and fro did fly,
And found no place, where safe he shroud° him might,   *shelter*
Lamenting Sorrow did in darknesse lye,
And Shame his ugly face did hide from living eye.

23 And over them sad Horrour with grim hew,°   *shape*
    Did alwayes sore, beating his yron wings;
    And after him Owles and Night-ravens flew,
    The hatefull messengers of heavy things,
    Of death and dolour telling sad tidings;
    Whiles sad *Celeno*,° sitting on a clift,°   *cliff*
    A song of bale and bitter sorrow sings,
    That hart of flint a sunder could have rift:°   *split*
Which having ended, after him she flyeth swift.

24 All these before the gates of *Pluto* lay,
    By whom they passing, spake unto them nought.
    But th'Elfin knight with wonder all the way
    Did feed his eyes, and fild his inner thought.
    At last him to a litle dore he brought,
    That to the gate of Hell, which gapèd wide,
    Was next adjoyning, ne them parted ought:°
    Betwixt them both was but a little stride,
That did the house of Richesse from hell-mouth divide.

25 Before the dore sat self-consuming Care,
    Day and night keeping wary watch and ward,
    For feare least Force or Fraud should unaware
    Breake in, and spoile the treasure there in gard:
    Ne would he suffer Sleepe once thither-ward
    Approch, albe his drowsie den were next;
    For next to death is Sleepe to be compard:
    Therefore his house is unto his annext;
Here Sleep, there Richesse, and Hel-gate them both betwext.°

26 So soone as *Mammon* there arriv'd, the dore
    To him did open, and affoorded way;
    Him followed eke Sir *Guyon* evermore,
    Ne darkensse him, ne daunger might dismay.
    Soone as he entred was, the dore streight way
    Did shut, and from behind it forth there lept

Celeno a Harpy; in Virgil, *Aeneid* III.219 ff., an image of rapacity; she speaks like a prophetess of doom (cf. *Tempest* III.iii, the apparition of Ariel as Harpy before the "three men of sin")
ne . . . ought i.e. there was nothing between them

Here . . . betwext Spenser arranges the "houses" and hell-mouth as if in a picture or in a pageant; the "hell-mouth" was familiar on the popular stage, a large-toothed aperture, partly a whale's, partly a devil's mouth.

An ugly feend,° more fowle then dismall day,
The which with monstrous stalke behind him stept,
And ever as he went, dew watch upon him kept.

27   Well hopèd he, ere long that hardy guest,
  If ever covetous hand, or lustfull eye,
  Or lips he layd on thing, that likt⁾ him best,   *pleased*
  Or ever sleepe his eye-strings did untye,
  Should be his pray. And therefore still⁾ on hye   *always*
  He over him did hold his cruell clawes,
  Threatning with greedy gripe to do him dye
  And rend in peeces with his ravenous pawes,
If ever he transgrest the fatal *Stygian*° lawes.

28   That houses forme within was rude and strong,
  Like an huge cave hewne out of rocky clift,
  From whose rough vaut⁾ the ragged breaches⁾ hong,   *vault / fissures*
  Embost with massy gold of glorious gift,⁾   *quality*
  And with rich metall loaded every rift,
  That heavy ruine⁾ they did seeme to threat;   *fall*
  And over them *Arachne*° high did lift
  Her cunning web, and spred her subtile net,
Enwrappèd in fowle smoke and clouds more blacke then Jet.

29   Both roofe, and floore, and wals were all of gold,
  But overgrowne with dust and old decay,
  And hid in darkenesse, that none could behold
  The hew⁾ thereof: for vew of chearefull day   *appearance*
  Did never in that house it selfe display,
  But a faint shadow of uncertain light;
  Such as a lamp, whose life does fade away:
  Or as the Moone cloathèd with clowdy night,
Does shew to him, that walkes in feare and sad affright.

30   In all that rowme was nothing to be seene,
  But huge great yron chests and coffers strong,
  All bard with double bends, that none could weene⁾   *think*
  Them to efforce⁾ by violence or wrong;   *break open*
  On every side they placèd were along.
  But all the ground with sculs was scatterèd,
  And dead mens bones, which round about were flong,
  Whose lives, it seemèd, whilome⁾ there were shed,   *formerly*
And their vile carcases now left unburièd.

---

feend Probably Eurynomos, described first by Pausanias (*Description of Greece* X.28) but accessible in the well-known manual of Cartari, *Imagini degli Dei* (many 16th-century editions). He tore his victims to pieces. In the Eleusinian mystery ritual the candidate was followed by a similar fury and forbidden to turn around; this stresses the initiatory element in Guyon's visit to the Cave of Mammon. The Eleusinian rite involved three days in "hell." Hercules, the type-hero for Guyon, was an initiate. Of course the ancient mystery rituals were given Christian significances. **Stygian** referring to Styx, the infernal river, and thus to hell **Arachne** the spider

31 They forward passe, ne *Guyon* yet spoke word,
    Till that they came unto an yron dore,
    Which to them openèd of his owne accord,
    And shewd of richesse such exceeding store,
    As eye of man did never see before;
    Ne ever could within one place be found,
    Through all the wealth, which is, or was of yore,
    Could gatherèd be through all the world around,
    And that above were added to that under ground.

32 The charge thereof unto a covetous Spright
    Commaunded was, who thereby did attend,
    And warily awaited day and night,
    From other covetous feends it to defend,
    Who it to rob and ransacke did intend.⸓   *wish*
    Then *Mammon* turning to that warriour, said;
    Loe here the worldès blis, loe here the end,
    To which all men do ayme, rich to be made:
    Such grace now to be happy, is before thee laid.

33 Certes (said he) I n'ill⸓ thine offred grace,   *do not want*
    Ne to be made so happy do intend:
    Another blis before mine eyes I place,
    Another happinesse, another end.
    To them, that list, these base regardes I lend:⸓   *give*
    But I in armes, and in atchievements brave,
    Do rather choose my flitting houres to spend,
    And to be Lord of those, that riches have,
    Then them to have my selfe, and be their servile sclave.

34 Thereat the feend his gnashing teeth did grate,
    And griev'd, so long to lacke his greedy⸓ pray;   *eagerly desired*
    For well he weenèd, that so glorious bayte
    Would tempt his guest, to take thereof assay:⸓   *trial*
    Had he so doen, he had him snatcht away,
    More light then Culver⸓ in the Faulcons fist.   *dove*
    Eternall God thee save from such decay.
    But whenas *Mammon* saw his purpose mist,
    Him to entrap unwares another way he wist.

35 Thence forward he him led, and shortly brought
    Unto another rowme,° whose dore forthright,
    To him did open, as it had beene taught:
    Therein an hundred raunges weren pight,⸓   *placed*
    And hundred fornaces all burning bright;
    By every fornace many feends did bide,
    Deformèd creatures, horrible in sight,

rowme This is Mammon's forge, based on the
forges of the Cyclops in Virgil, *Aeneid* VIII.418.

And every feend his busie paines applide,
To melt the golden metall, ready to be tride.°   *refined*

36 One with great bellowes gathered filling aire,
    And with forst wind the fewell did inflame;
    Another did the dying bronds repaire
    With yron toungs, and sprinckled oft the same
    With liquid waves, fiers *Vulcans* rage to tame,
    Who maistring them, renewd his former heat;
    Some scumd the drosse, that from the metall came;
    Some stird the molten owre with ladles great;
And every one did swincke,° and every one did sweat.   *labor*

37 But when as earthly wight they present saw,
    Glistring in armes and battailous aray,
    From their whot° worke they did themselves withdraw   *hot*
    To wonder at the sight: for till that day,
    They never creature saw, that came that way.
    Their staring eyes sparckling with fervent fire,
    And ugly shapes did nigh the man dismay,
    That were it not for shame, he would retire,
Till that him thus bespake their soveraigne Lord and sire.

38 Behold, thou Faeries sonne, with mortall eye,
    That° living eye before did never see: *that which*
    The thing, that thou didst crave so earnestly,
    To weet, whence all the wealth late shewd by mee,
    Proceeded, lo now is reveald to thee.
    Here is the fountaine of the worldès good:
    Now therefore, if thou wilt enrichèd bee,
    Avise thee° well, and chaunge thy wilfull mood,   *consider*
Least° thou perhaps hereafter wish, and be withstood.   *lest*

39 Suffise it then, thou Money God (quoth hee)
    That all thine idle offers I refuse.
    All that I need I have; what needeth mee
    To covet more, then I have cause to use?
    With such vaine shewes thy worldlings vile abuse:
    But give me leave to follow mine emprise.°   *enterprise*
    Mammon was much displeased, yet no'te he° chuse,   *he could not*
    And beare the rigour of his bold mesprise,°   *scorn*
And thence him forward led, him further to entise.

40 He brought him through a darksome narrow strait,
    To a broad gate, all built of beaten gold:
    The gate was open, but therein did wait
    A sturdy villein, striding stiffe and bold,
    As if that highest God defie he would;
    In his right hand an yron club he held,
    But he himselfe was all of golden mould,

Yet had both life and sence, and well could weld^{>}   *wield*
That cursèd weapon, when his cruell foes he queld.

41 *Disdayne* he callèd was, and did disdaine
    To be so cald, and who so did him call:
    Sterne was his looke, and full of stomacke^{>} vaine,   *pride*
    His portaunce^{>} terrible, and stature tall,   *bearing*
    Far passing th'hight of men terrestriall;
    Like an huge Gyant of the *Titans* race,
    That made him scorne all creatures great and small,
    And with his pride all others powre deface^{>}:   *abash*
  More fit amongst blacke fiendes, then men to have his place.

42 Soone as those glitterand armes he did espye,
    That with their brightnesse made that darknesse light,
    His harmefull club he gan to hurtle^{>} hye,   *brandish*
    And threaten batteill to the Faery knight;
    Who likewise gan himselfe to batteill dight,^{>}   *prepare*
    Till *Mammon* did his hasty hand withhold,
    And counseld him abstaine from perilous fight:
    For nothing might abash the villein bold,
  Ne mortall steele emperce his miscreated mould.

43 So having him with reason pacifide,
    And the fiers Carle^{>} commaunding to forbeare,   *churl*
    He brought him in. The rowme° was large and wide,
    As it some Gyeld^{>} or solemne Temple weare: *guildhall*
    Many great golden pillours did upbeare
    The massy roofe, and riches huge sustayne,
    And every pillour deckèd was full deare^{>}   *richly*
    With crownes and Diademes, and titles vaine,
  Which mortall Princess wore, whiles they on earth did rayne.

44 A route of people there assemblèd were,
    Of every sort and nation under skye,
    Which with great uprore preacèd to draw nere   *pressed*
    To th'upper part, where was advauncèd hye
    A stately siege^{>} of soveraigne majestye;   *throne*
    And thereon sat a woman° gorgeous gay,
    And richly clad in robes of royaltye,
    That^{>} never earthly Prince in such aray   *such that*
  His glory did enhaunce, and pompous pride display.

45 Her face right wondrous faire did seeme to bee,
    That^{>} her broad beauties beam great brightnes threw   *so that*
    Through the dim shade, that all men might it see:
    Yet was not that same her owne native hew,^{>}   *form*

The rowme Passing by Disdain, protector of the privileged, Guyon now embarks on the temptation of false honor and wordly power in the temple of Philotime ("love of honor"); Spenser makes the temple rather like a great monarch's court.
woman Philotime, a corrupt earthly version of heavenly honor, to which Guyon is committed

But wrought by art and counterfetted shew,
Thereby more lovers unto her to call;
Nath'lesse˃ most heavenly faire in deed and vew   *nevertheless*
She by creation was, till she did fall;
Thenceforth she sought for helps, to cloke her crime withall.

46   There, as in glistring glory she did sit,
     She held a great gold chaine° ylinckèd well,
     Whose upper end to highest heaven was knit,
     And lower part did reach to lowest Hell;
     And all that preace˃ did round about her swell,   *crowd*
     To catchen hold of that long chaine, thereby
     To clime aloft, and others to excell:
     That was *Ambition*, rash desire to sty.˃   *ascend*
     And every lincke thereof a step of dignity.

47   Some thought to raise themselves to high degree,
     By riches and unrightèous reward,
     Some by close shouldring,˃ some by flatteree;   *intriguing*
     Others through friends, others for base regard;˃   *bribery*
     And all by wrong wayes for themselves prepard.
     Those that were up themselves, kept others low,
     Those that were low themselves, held others hard,
     Ne suffered them to rise or greater grow,
     But every one did strive his fellow downe to throw.

48   Which whenas *Guyon* saw, he gan inquire,
     What meant that preace about that Ladies throne,
     And what she was that did so high aspire.
     Him *Mammon* answerèd; That goodly one,
     Whom all that folke with such contention,
     Do flocke about, my deare, my daughter is;
     Honour and dignitie from her alone
     Derivèd are, and all this worldès blis
     For which ye men do strive: few get, but many mis.

49   And faire *Philotime* she rightly hight,˃   *is called*
     The fairest wight that wonneth˃ under skye,   *lives*
     But that this darksome neather world her light
     Doth dim with horrour and deformitie,
     Worthy of heaven and hye felicitie,
     From whence the gods have her for envy thrust:
     But sith thou hast found favour in mine eye,
     Thy spouse I will her make, if that thou lust,˃   *wish*
     That she may thee advance for workes and merites just.

---

gold chaine When attached to the throne of
Zeus in Homer's *Iliad* (VIII.19 ff.) the golden
chain became, for later allegorists, a symbol
of the order of divine creation with its grades
and hierarchies; Philotime's gold chain is a
human and wicked parody, representing only
the struggle for worldly power; every link is
a "step of dignity," that is, a degree of social
rank by which earthly ambition seeks to ascend.

50   Gramercy *Mammon* (said the gentle knight)
     For so great grace and offred high estate;
     But I, that am fraile flesh and earthly wight,
     Unworthy match for such immortall mate
     My self well wote,˃ and mine unequall fate;˃   *know / inferior destiny*
     And were I not, yet is my trouth yplight,
     And love avowd to other Lady° late,˃   *lately*
     That to remove the same I have no might:˃   *power*
   To chaunge love causelesse is reproch to warlike knight.

51   *Mammon* emmovèd was with inward wrath;
     Yet forcing it to faine,˃ him forth thence led   *to dissimulate it*
     Through griesly shadowes by a beaten path,
     Into a gardin° goodly garnishèd
     With hearbs and fruits, whose kinds mote˃ not be red:˃   *can / told*
     Not such, as earth out of her fruitfull woomb
     Throwes forth to men, sweet and well savourèd,
     But direfull deadly blacke both leafe and bloom,
   Fit to adorne the dead, and decke the drery toombe.

52   There mournfull *Cypresse* grew in greatest store,
     And trees of bitter *Gall,* and *Heben*˃ sad,   *ebony*
     Dead sleeping *Poppy,* and blacke *Hellebore,*
     Cold *Coloquintida,* and *Tetra* mad,
     Mortall *Samnitis,* and *Cicuta* bad,°
     With which th' unjust *Atheniens* made to dy
     Wise *Socrates,* who thereof quaffing glad
     Pourd out his life, and last Philosophy
   To the faire *Critias*° his dearest Belamy.˃   *friend*

53   The *Gardin* of *Proserpina* this hight;˃   *was named*
     And in the midst thereof a silver seat,°
     With a thicke Arber goodly over dight,˃   *placed overhead*

other Lady Guyon courteously rejects the offer on the ground that he is betrothed to another lady, meaning the true "love of honor" in the heaven from which Philotime has fallen (see stanza 45 and, for Mammon's version of her fall, stanza 49).
gardin The Garden of Proserpina is the setting for Guyon's last temptation, which completes the others, so that they add up to a total temptation like that of Jesus in the wilderness. This is the temptation of *curiosity* (forbidden knowledge). The garden is based on the Grove of Persephone in Homer, *Odyssey* X; Spenser fills it with deathly herbs, taking a hint from Pausanias, (*Description of Greece* X.30). The herbs are appropriate to Proserpina in her character as Hecate, patroness of poisons.
Dead sleeping . . . bad Poppy is the source of narcotics; hellebore is a plant supposed to cure madness; coloquintida is bitter-apple; tetra is deadly nightshade; samnitis is the savine-tree used to procure abortions; cicuta is hemlock.
Critias Though once a disciple, Critias was an enemy of Socrates; Spenser seems confused

about what happens in Plato's *Phaedo.* Many involved explanations of this have been offered, and some say Spenser evidently did not know his Plato. But there is a simple explanation: Socrates speaks his last words to Crito; Crito closes his eyes. The dialogue *Crito* also deals with the last days of Socrates. Crito was a very old friend of the philosopher.
silver seat Not a simple invitation to sloth but the forbidden seat of the Eleusinian mysteries—the *mystes* could not sit in it lest they should seem to be imitating the mourning Ceres as she rested on her search for her daughter Proserpina. For his attempt to rape Proserpina Theseus was punished (*Aeneid* VI. 617–18) by perpetual imprisonment in an underworld chair; Pausanias describes a painting (XXIX.9) which shows Theseus in the Chair of Forgetfulness, now a punishment for knowing too much of forbidden matters. Spenser somehow discovered this allegorical sense; it fits his theme of initiation into the mystery (of Heroic Virtue) and goes well, of course, in the Garden of Proserpina.

In which she often usd from open heat
Her selfe to shroud,° and pleasures to entreat,°   *shelter / occupy*
Next thereunto did grow a goodly tree,   *herself with*
With braunches broad dispred and body great,
Clothèd with leaves, that none the wood mote° see   *could*
And loaden all with fruit as thicke as it might bee.

54   Their fruit were golden apples° glistring bright,
That goodly was their glory to behold,
On earth like never grew, ne living wight
Like ever saw, but° they from hence were sold;°   *unless / brought*
For those, which *Hercules* with conquest bold
Got from great *Atlas* daughters,° hence began,
And planted there, did bring forth fruit of gold:
And those with which th'*Eubœan* young man wan°   *won*
Swift *Atalanta*,° when through craft he her out ran.

55   Here also sprong that goodly golden fruit,
With which *Acontius*° got his lover trew,
Whom he had long time sought with fruitlesse suit:
Here eke that famous golden Apple grew,
The which emongst the gods false *Ate*° threw;
For which th'*Idæan* Ladies disagreed,
Till partiall *Paris* dempt° it *Venus* dew,   *judged*
And had of her, faire *Helen* for his meed,
That many noble *Greekes* and *Trojans* made to bleed.

56   The warlike Elfe much wondred at this tree,
So faire and great, that shadowèd all the ground,
And his broad braunches, laden with rich fee,
Did stretch themselves without° the utmost bound   *beyond*
Of this great gardin, compast with a mound,
Which over-hanging, they themselves did steepe,
In a blacke flood which flow'd about it round;
That is the river of *Cocytus*° deepe,
In which full many soules do endlesse waile and weepe.

---

golden apples These are underworld fruit that must not be eaten (the *mala Punica*, Punic apples or pomegranates, were Proserpina's food of the dead), but Spenser adds that the famous apples of myth all descended from them. The forbidden fruit represents a temptation like that of Eve's apple, which was eaten out of appetite, vainglory, and curiosity. Spenser relates its mythological descendants to the temptation of forbidden knowledge.
Hercules . . . daughters The apples of the Hesperides; Hercules in his eleventh labor had to get them from the tree of the daughters of Atlas (Hesperides); they were protected by a dragon. They became emblems of astronomical knowledge.
th'Eubœan . . . Atalanta Hippomenes won his race with the swift Atalanta by throwing golden apples in her way; she stopped to pick them up and was beaten. These apples were Hesperidean. Atalanta had desecrated the shrine of the Great Mother (an image of the blasphemy of forbidden knowledge).
Acontius He wrote on an apple "I swear by Artemis that I will marry Acontius"; Cydippe picked the apple up, read the message aloud, and was bound by the oath, though she tried blasphemously to get out of it.
Ate goddess of Discord. She produced the apple which was the prize to be awarded by Paris to the most beautiful of three goddesses; in return for Helen he gave it to Venus. His abduction of Helen caused the Trojan War. Allegorically this apple was a symbol of insane contempt for divine wisdom.
Cocytus river of hell

57 Which to behold, he clomb up to the banke,
        And looking downe, saw many damnèd wights,
        In those sad waves, which direfull deadly stanke,
        Plongèd continually of cruell Sprights,   *by*
        That with their pitteous cryes, and yelling shrights,˃   *shrieks*
        They made the further shore resounden˃ wide: *echo*
        Emongst the rest of those same ruefull sights,
        One cursèd creature he by chaunce espide,
    That drenchèd lay full deepe, under the Garden side.

58 Deepe was he drenchèd to the upmost chin,
        Yet gapèd still, as coveting to drinke
        Of the cold liquor, which he waded in,
        And stretching forth his hand, did often thinke
        To reach the fruit, which grew upon the brincke:
        But both the fruit from hand, and floud from mouth
        Did flie abacke, and made him vainely swinke:˃   *labor*
        The whiles he sterv'd˃ with hunger and with drouth   *died*
    He daily dyde, yet never throughly˃ dyen couth.˃   *completely / could*

59 The knight him seeing labour so in vaine,
        Askt who he was, and what he ment thereby:
        Who groning deepe, thus answerd him againe;
        Most cursèd of all creatures under skye,
        Lo *Tantalus*,° I here tormented lye:
        Of whom high *Jove* wont˃ whylome˃ feasted bee,   *was accustomed / once*
        Lo here I now for want of food doe dye:
        But if that thou be such, as I thee see,
    Of grace I pray thee, give to eat and drinke to mee.

60 Nay, nay, thou greedie *Tantalus* (quoth he)
        Abide the fortune of thy present fate,
        And unto all that live in high degree,
        Ensample be of mind intemperate,
        To teach them how to use their present state.
        Then gan the cursèd wretch aloud to cry,
        Accusing highest *Jove* and gods ingrate,
        And eke blaspheming heaven bitterly,
    As authour of unjustice, there to let him dye.

61 He lookt a little further, and espyde
        Another wretch, whose carkasse deepe was drent˃   *submerged*
        Within the river, which the same did hyde:
        But both his hands most filthy feculent,˃   *foul*

Tantalus His punishment derives from *Odyssey* XI. A type of avarice, but also of intemperate and blasphemous knowledge, for he served the gods a dish made of the body of his son Pelops in order to test their immortality; also, as a guest of Jupiter, he heard secrets of divine knowledge and reported them to men. Ovid says he revealed the Eleusinian secrets, and Pausanias shows him suffering in hell with those who revealed or despised these mysteries. Guyon in stanza 60 says he is an example of "mind intemperate"; Spenser is not talking about greed or avarice.

Above the water were on high extent,°   *extended*
And faynd° to wash themselves incessantly: *pretended*
Yet nothing cleaner were for such intent,
But rather fowler seemèd to the eye;
So lost his labour vaine and idle industry.

62   The knight him calling, askèd who he was,
      Who lifting up his head, him answerd thus:
      I *Pilate*° am the falsest Judge, alas,
      And most unjust, that by unrighteous
      And wicked doome, to Jewes despiteous
      Delivered up the Lord of life to die,
      And did acquite a murdrer felonous;
      The whiles my hands I washt in puritie,
      The whiles my soule was soyld with foule iniquitie.

63   Infinite moe,° tormented in like paine   *more*
      He there beheld, too long here to be told:
      Ne *Mammon* would there let him long remaine,
      For terrour of the tortures manifold,
      In which the damnèd soules he did behold,
      But roughly him bespake. Thou fearefull foole,
      Why takest not of that same fruit of gold,
      Ne sittest downe on that same silver stoole,
      To rest thy wearie person, in the shadow coole.

64   All which he did, to doe him deadly fall
      In frayle intemperance through sinfull bayt;
      To which if he inclinèd had at all,
      That dreadfull feend, which did behind him wayt,
      Would him have rent in thousand peeces strayt:
      But he was warie wise in all his way,
      And well perceivèd his deceiptfull sleight,
      Ne suffred lust his safetie to betray:
      So goodly did beguile the Guyler° of the pray.   *deceiver*

65   And now he has so long remainèd there,
      That vitall powres gan wexe both weake and wan,
      For want of food, and sleepe, which two upbeare,
      Like mightie pillours, this fraile life of man,
      That none without the same enduren can.
      For now three dayes of men were full outwrought,°   *completed*
      Since he this hardie enterprize began:
      For thy° great *Mammon* fairely he besought,   *therefore*
      Into the world to guide him backe, as he him brought.

Pilate the type of judicial corruption. When Christ said "To this end was I born, and for this cause came I into the world, that I should bear witness unto the truth. Every one that is of the truth heareth my voice," Pilate replied "What is truth?" (John 18:37–38); by releasing Barabbas he denied divine truth.

66 The God, though loth, yet was constraind t'obay,
    For lenger time, then that, no living wight
    Below the earth, might suffred be to stay:
    So backe againe, him brought to living light.
    But all so soone as his enfeebled spright
    Gan sucke this vitall aire into his brest,
    As overcome with too exceeding might,
    The life did flit away out of her nest,
And all his senses were with deadly fit opprest.

> *From Canto viii°*
> Sir Guyon laid in swowne is by
>   Acrates sonnes despoyld,
> Whom Arthur soone hath reskewed
>   And Paynim brethren foyld.

1   And is there care in heaven? and is there love
    In heavenly spirits to these creatures bace,
    That may compassion of their evils move?
    There is: else much more wretched were the cace
    Of men, then beasts. But O th' exceeding grace
    Of highest God, that loves his creatures so,
    And all his workes with mercy doth embrace,
    That blessèd Angels, he sends to and fro,
To serve to wicked man, to serve his wicked foe.°

2   How oft do they, their silver bowers leave,
    To come to succour us, that succour want?⟩   *lack*
    How oft do they with golden pineons,⟩ cleave   *wings*
    The flitting⟩ skyes, like flying Pursuivant,⟩   *changing / messenger*
    Against foule feends to aide us millitant?
    They for us fight, they watch and dewly ward,
    And their bright Squadrons round about us plant,
    And all for love, and nothing for reward:
O why should heavenly God to men have such regard?°

[In canto viii the Palmer returns, but Arthur has to rescue Guyon from the
attack of Pyrochles and Cymochles, perhaps representing the threat of a temporary insurrection of irascibility and concupiscence in his weakened state. Canto
ix has a full-scale allegorical treatment of the House of Alma (the soul), also
called the House of Temperance. The well-regulated human body is here
described under the transparent allegory of a great house with its services, interconnections, sewers, etc. But it is besieged by enemies; and in xi (the interven-

Canto viii Spenser opens with a passage commenting on the fact that Guyon, in his faint, is
tended by an angel (stanzas 5–8). So was Christ
after his victory over sin in the wilderness; he
had overcome, says St. Augustine, temptation
by the lust of the flesh; by vainglory; and by
curiosity. These are all the temptations. (Augustine says this in a Homily on Psalm 8, which
Spenser quotes in these stanzas.) Guyon is now
confirmed in Heroic Virtue, having withstood
his initiatory trial; his virtues are now those of

the purged soul, a little lower than sanctity,
which Red Cross achieved, but higher than
ordinary virtues, and qualifying for the category
first invented by Aristotle, and later Christianized, namely, Heroic Virtue.
blessèd . . . foe "ministering spirits, sent forth
to minister for them who shall be heirs of salvation" (Hebrews 1:14)
O why . . . regard "What is man, that thou
art mindful of him? and the son of man, that
thou visitest him?" (Psalms 8:4)

ing canto is a long account of Elizabeth's legendary ancient British ancestors)
Spenser describes the siege, the assault on the human body of its enemies, led
by Maleger (Latin: *aeger,* sick). This is one of the great passages of *The
Faerie Queene*; Maleger is Spenser's most nightmarish figure—"like a ghost
he seemed, whose grave clothes were unbound"—and Arthur's combat with this
unkillable but apparently lifeless shadow has real horror. It represents the un-
stoppable onslaught of ills brought on by Adam's intemperance.

Canto xii brings Guyon to the climax of his quest, the Bower of Bliss, home
of Acrasia, Intemperance herself. But it takes a long voyage to get there, and
the account of it serves to recapitulate much of the Book. Guyon and the Palmer
sail past Phaedria, for example, and many other *exempla* of intemperance. At
the Bower they encounter many spurious beauties provided by art to conceal
the truth that it is an evil structure calling for merciless purgation. The Porter
is Genius, but not the benign Genius of "life and generation" we meet in
Epithalamion; in fact he is the exact opposite, "the foe of life," and Guyon
knocks over his winebowl and breaks his staff. Within, the Bower is a false version of the Earthly Paradise.]

> *From Canto xii*
> 50   Thus being entred, they behold around
>   A large and spacious plaine, on every side
>   Strowèd with pleasauns,° whose faire grassy ground   *pleasances*
>   Mantled with greene, and goodly beautifide
>   With all the ornaments of *Floraes* pride,
>   Wherewith her mother Art, as halfe in scorne
>   Of niggard Nature, like a pompous bride
>   Did decke her, and too lavishly adorne,
>   When forth from virgin bowre she comes in th' early morne.
>
> 51   Thereto the Heavens alwayes Joviall,°
>   Lookt on them lovely, still in stedfast state,
>   Ne suffred storme nor frost on them to fall,
>   Their tender buds or leaves to violate,
>   Nor scorching heat, nor cold intemperate°
>   T'afflict the creatures, which therein did dwell,
>   But the milde aire with season moderate
>   Gently attempred, and disposd so well,
>   That still it breathèd forth sweet spirit and holesome smell.
>
> 52   More sweet and holesome, then the pleasaunt hill
>   Of *Rhodope,*° on which the Nimphe, that bore
>   A gyaunt babe, her selfe for griefe did kill;

Joviall under the influence of the planet Jupiter,
producing joy and happiness
Nor . . . intemperate Spenser represents the
place somewhat conventionally as an Earthly
Paradise and, like Milton in *Paradise Lost* IV,
enforces the idea by saying that this is better
than all the others; but he includes various
indications—not only Guyon's determination
to have nothing to do with the pleasures of
the place—to suggest that it is the scene of
abuses as well as of the natural plenty proper
to paradises. Hence the "wanton wreathings";
but especially he places Excess in the foreground,
for the lavish gifts of nature are being abused,
as later they are by Comus.
Rhodope mountain in Thrace into which Rhodope was turned for claiming to be more
beautiful than Juno; she bore Neptune a giant
son

Or the Thessalian *Tempe,*° where of yore
Faire *Daphne*° *Phœbus* hart with love did gore;
Or *Ida,*° where the Gods lov'd to repaire,
When ever they their heavenly bowres forlore;
Or sweet *Parnasse,* the haunt of Muses faire;
Or *Eden* selfe, if ought with *Eden* mote˒ compaire.   *can*

53   Much wondred *Guyon* at the faire aspect
Of that sweet place, yet suffred no delight
To sincke into his sence, nor mind affect,
But passèd forth, and lookt still forward right,
Bridling his will, and maistering his might:
Till that he came unto another gate;
No gate, but like one, being goodly dight
With boughes and braunches, which did broad dilate
Their clasping armes, in wanton wreathings intricate.

54   So fashionèd a Porch with rare device,
Archt over head with an embracing vine,
Whose bounches hanging downe, seemed to entice
All passers by, to tast their lushious wine,
And did themselves into their hands incline,
As freely offering to be gatherèd:
Some deepe empurpled as the *Hyacint,*˒   *sapphire*
Some as the *Rubine,*˒ laughing sweetly red,   *ruby*
Some like faire Emeraudes, not yet well ripenèd.

55   And them amongst, some were of burnisht gold,
So made by art, to beautifie the rest,
Which did themselves emongst the leaves enfold,
As lurking from the vew of covetous guest,
That the weake bowes, with so rich load opprest,
Did bow adowne, as over-burdenèd.
Under that Porch a comely dame did rest,
Clad in faire weedes,˒ but fowle disorderèd,   *garments*
And garments loose, that seemd unmeet for womanhed.

56   In her left hand a Cup of gold she held,
And with her right the riper fruit did reach,
Whose sappy liquor, that with fulnesse sweld,
Into her cup she scruzd,˒ with daintie breach   *squeezed*
Of her fine fingers, without fowle empeach,˒   *detriment*
That so faire wine-presse made the wine more sweet:
Thereof she usd to give to drinke to each,
Whom passing by she happenèd to meet:
It was her guise,˒ all Straungers goodly so to greet.   *manner*

Tempe Orpheus by his music led trees to the mountain valley in Thessaly, famous for its groves and walks.

Daphne She escaped Phoebus Apollo in Tempe by being turned into a laurel.
Ida Cretan mountain, frequented by gods during the Trojan war

57   So she to *Guyon* offred it to tast;
 Who taking it out of her tender hond,
 The cup to ground did violently cast,
 That all in peeces it was broken fond,
 And with the liquor stainèd all the lond:
 Whereat *Excesse* exceedingly was wroth,
 Yet no'te  the same amend, ne yet withstond,   *could not*
 But suffrèd him to passe, all were she loth;
Who nought regarding her displeasure forward goth.

58   There the most daintie Paradise on ground,
 It selfe doth offer to his sober eye,
 In which all pleasures plenteously abound,
 And none does others happinesse envye:
 The painted flowres, the trees upshooting hye,
 The dales for shade, the hilles for breathing space,
 The trembling groves, the Christall running by;
 And that, which all faire workes doth most aggrace,
The art, which all that wrought, appearèd in no place.°

59   One would have thought, (so cunningly, the rude,
 And scornèd parts were mingled with the fine,)
 That nature had for wantonesse ensude  *imitated*
 Art, and that Art at nature did repine;
 So striving each th' other to undermine,
 Each did the others worke more beautifie;
 So diff'ring both in willes, agreed in fine:  *in the end*
 So all agreed through sweete diversitie,
This Gardin to adorne with all varietie.

60   And in the midst of all, a fountaine stood,
 Of richest substaunce, that on earth might bee,
 So pure and shiny, that the silver flood
 Through every channell running one might see;
 Most goodly it with curious imageree
 Was over-wrought, and shapes of naked boyes,
 Of which some seemd with lively jollitee,
 To fly about, playing their wanton toyes,  *games*
Whilest others did them selves embay  in liquid joyes.   *bathe*

61   And over all, of purest gold was spred,
 A trayle of yvie in his native hew:  *appearance*
 For the rich mettall was so colourèd,
 That wight, who did not well avis'd it vew,
 Would surely deeme it to be yvie trew;
 Low his lascivious armes adown did creepe,
 That themselves dipping in the silver dew,

The art . . . place exactly translated from Tasso, *Gerusalemme Liberata* (the main inspiration of this canto). Spenser's meaning is not that art is lower than nature, as some critics say; the fault in the paradise lies in the human uses to which it is put, not in its design.

Their fleecy flowres they tenderly did steepe,
Which drops of Christall seemd for wantonès to weepe.

62 Infinit streames continually did well
  Out of this fountaine, sweet and faire to see,
  The which into an ample laver⟩ fell,   *basin*
  And shortly grew to so great quantitie,
  That like a little lake it seemd to bee;
  Whose depth exceeded not three cubits hight,
  That through the waves one might the bottom see,
  All pav'd beneath with Jaspar shining bright,
That seemd the fountaine in that sea did sayle upright.

63 And all the margent round about was set,
  With shady Laurell trees, thence to defend⟩   *fend off*
  The sunny beames, which on the billowes bet,⟩   *beat*
  And those which therein bathèd, mote offend.
  As *Guyon* hapned by the same to wend,
  Two naked Damzelles he therein espyde,
  Which therein bathing, seemèd to contend,
  And wrestle wantonly, ne car'd to hyde,
Their dainty parts from vew of any, which them eyde.

64 Sometimes the one would lift the other quight
  Above the waters, and then downe againe
  Her plong, as over maisterèd by might,
  Where both awhile would covered remaine,
  And each the other from to rise⟩ restraine;   *rising*
  The whiles their snowy limbes, as through a vele,
  So through the Christall waves appearèd plaine:
  Then suddeinly both would themselves unhele,⟩ *uncover*
And th'amarous sweet spoiles to greedy eyes revele.

65 As that faire Starre,° the messenger of morne,
  His deawy face out of the sea doth reare:
  Or as the *Cyprian* goddesse,° newly borne
  Of th'Oceans fruitfull froth, did first appeare:
  Such seemèd they, and so⟩ their yellow heare *in the same way*
  Christalline humour⟩ dropped downe apace.   *water*
  Whom such when *Guyon* saw, he drew him neare,
  And somewhat gan relent his earnest pace,
His stubborne brest gan secret pleasaunce to embrace.°

66 The wanton Maidens him esyping, stood
  Gazing a while at his unwonted guise;⟩   *behavior*
  Then th'one her selfe low duckèd in the flood,

faire Starre the Morning Star (Venus)
Cyprian goddesse Venus, born of the union
of Saturn's semen and the ocean
His stubborne . . . embrace Guyon's momentary lust for the girls in the fountain recalls
the lapses of his pagan (but Christianized)
prototype Hercules; but Right Reason (the Palmer) enables temperance to overcome concupiscence.

Abasht, that her a straunger did avise:>   *look at*
But th'other rather higher did arise,
And her two lilly paps aloft displayd,
And all, that might his melting hart entise
To her delights, she unto him bewrayd:>   *displayed*
The rest hid underneath, him more desirous made.

67   With that, the other likewise up arose,
And her faire lockes, which formerly were bownd
Up in one knot, she low adowne did lose:>   *unloose*
Which flowing long and thick, her cloth'd arownd,
And th'yvorie in golden mantle gown:
So that faire spectacle from him was reft,
Yet that, which reft it, no lesse faire was fownd:
So hid in lockes and waves from lookers theft,
Nought but her lovely face she for his looking left.

68   Withall she laughèd, and she blusht withall,
That blushing to her laughter gave more grace,
And laughter to her blushing, as did fall:
Now when they spide the knight to slacke his pace,
Them to behold, and in his sparkling face
The secret signes of kindled lust appeare,
Their wanton meriments they did encreace,
And to him beckned, to approach more neare,
And shewd him many sights, that courage> cold could reare.   *desire*

69   On which when gazing him the Palmer saw,
He much rebukt those wandring eyes of his,
And counseld well, him forward thence did draw.
Now are they come nigh to the *Bowre of blis*
Of her fond favorites so nam'd amis:
When thus the Palmer; Now Sir, well avise;
For here the end of all our travell is:
Here wonnes> *Acrasia,* whom we must surprise,   *lives*
Else she will slip away, and all our drift> despise.   *plans*

70   Eftsoones they heard a most melodious sound,
Of all that mote delight a daintie eare,
Such as attonce might not on living ground,
Save in this Paradise, be heard elsewhere:
Right hard it was, for wight, which did it heare,
To read,> what manner musicke that mote bee: *tell*
For all that pleasing is to living eare,
Was there consorted in one harmonee,
Birdes, voyces, instruments, windes, waters, all agree.

71   The joyous birdes shrouded in chearefull shade,
Their notes unto the voyce attempred sweet;
Th'Angelicall soft trembling voyces made

To th'instruments divine respondence meet;
The silver sounding instruments did meet
With the base˃ murmure of the waters fall: *bass*
The waters fall with difference discreet,
Now soft, now loud, unto the wind did call:
The gentle warbling wind low answerèd to all.°

72   There, whence that Musick seemèd heard to bee,
Was the faire Witch her selfe now solacing,
With a new Lover, whom through sorceree
And witchcraft, she from farre did thither bring:
There she had him now layd a slombering,
In secret shade, after long wanton joyes:
Whilst round about them pleasauntly did sing
Many faire Ladies, and lascivious boyes,
That ever mixt their song with light licentious toyes.

73   And all that while, right over him she hong,
With her false eyes fast fixèd in his sight,
As seeking medicine, whence she was stong,°
Or greedily depasturing˃ delight: *consuming*
And oft inclining downe with kisses light,
For feare of waking him, his lips bedewed,
And through his humid eyes did sucke his spright,
Quite molten into lust and pleasure lewd;
Wherewith she sighèd soft, as if his case she rewd.

74   The whiles some one did chaunt this lovely lay;°
Ah see, who so faire thing doest faine to see,
In springing flowre the image of thy day;
Ah see the Virgin Rose, how sweetly shee
Doth first peepe forth with bashfull modestee,
That fairer seemes, the lesse ye see her may;
Lo see soone after, how more bold and free
Her bared bosome she doth broad display;
Loe see soone after, how she fades, and falles away.

75   So passeth, in the passing of a day,
Of mortall life the leafe, the bud, the flowre,
Ne more doth flourish after first decay,
That earst was sought to decke both bed and bowre,

The joyous . . . all This stanza of natural and artificial harmony Spenser developed from Tasso, *Gerusalemme Liberata* XVI.2, though that leaves out the instruments and voices; however, Tasso includes these when he writes a rather similar stanza (XVIII.8); hence if Spenser is really, as some critics say, making the combination of artificial and natural music seem sinister, Tasso, whose sinister intent is hard to see, preceded him.
seeking . . . stong seeking a cure from that which hurt her

lay Translated from Tasso (XVI.14–15), where it is sung by a bird. The theme—*carpe diem*, seize the day—is ancient, and so is the group of figures attached to the rose. The beauty of the "lovely lay" emphasizes, like the beauty of the approaches to the Bower, the powerful forces against which Temperance must fight. The theme occurs in many poems which have not the moralistic context of Spenser's, but Comus's use of the rose-figure in Milton's masque is very like this one (ll. 742–43).

Of many a Ladie, and many a Paramowre:
Gather therefore the Rose, whilest yet is prime,
For soone comes age, that will her pride deflowre:
Gather the Rose of love, whilest yet is time,
Whilest loving thou mayst lovèd be with equall crime.˒   *sin*

76   He ceast, and then gan all the quire of birdes
Their diverse notes t'attune unto his lay,
As in approvance of his pleasing words.
The constant paire heard all, that he did say,
Yet swarvèd˒ not, but kept their forward way,   *swerved*
Through many covert groves, and thickets close,
In which they creeping did at last display˒   *discover*
That wanton Ladie, with her lover lose,
Whose sleepie head she in her lap did soft dispose.

77   Upon a bed of Roses she was layd,
As faint through heat, or dight to pleasant sin,
And was arayd, or rather disarayd,
All in a vele of silke and silver thin,
That hid no whit her alablaster˒ skin,   *alabaster*
But rather shewd more white, if more might bee:
More subtile web *Arachne* cannot spin,
Nor the fine nets, which oft we woven see
Of scorchèd deaw, do not in th'aire more lightly flee.

78   Her snowy brest was bare to readie spoyle
Of hungry eies, which n'ote˒ therewith be fild,   *could not*
And yet through languor of her late sweet toyle,
Few drops, more cleare then Nectar, forth distild,
That like pure Orient perles adowne it trild,
And her faire eyes sweet smyling in delight,
Moystenèd their fierie beames, with which she thrild
Fraile harts, yet quenchèd not; like starry light
Which sparckling on the silent waves, does seeme more bright.

79   The young man sleeping by her, seemd to bee
Some goodly swayne of honorable place,
That certes it great pittie was to see
Him his nobilitie so foule deface;
A sweet regard, and amiable grace,
Mixèd with manly sternnesse did appeare
Yet sleeping, in his well proportiond face,
And on his tender lips the downy heare
Did now but freshly spring, and silken blosomes beare.

80   His warlike armes, the idle instruments
Of sleeping praise, were hong upon a tree,
And his brave shield, full of old moniments,˒   *figures*
Was fowly ra'st,˒ that none the signes might see;   *erased*

Ne for them, ne for honour carèd hee,
Ne ought, that did to his advauncement tend,
But in lewd loves, and wastfull luxuree,
His dayes, his goods, his bodie he did spend:
O horrible enchantment, that him so did blend.°   *blind*

81 The noble Elfe, and carefull Palmer drew
    So nigh them, minding nought, but lustfull game,
    That suddein forth they on them rusht, and threw
    A subtile° net,° which onely°for the same   *fine / specially*
    The skilfull Palmer formally° did frame.°   *expressly / design*
    So held them under fast, the whiles the rest
    Fled all away for feare of fowler shame.
    The faire Enchauntresse, so unwares opprest,
Tryde all her arts, and all her sleights, thence out to wrest.

82 And eke her lover strove: but all in vaine;
    For that same net so cunningly was wound,
    That neither guile, nor force might it distraine.°   *break*
    They tooke them both, and both them strongly bound
    In captive bandes, which there they readie found:
    But her in chaines of adamant he tyde;
    For nothing else might keepe her safe and sound;
    But *Verdant*° (so he hight) he soone untyde,
And counsell sage in steed thereof° to him applyde.   *of constraint*

83 But all those pleasant bowres and Pallace brave,
    Guyon broke downe, with rigour pittilesse;
    Ne ought their goodly workmanship might save
    Them from the tempest of his wrathfulnesse,
    But that their blisse he turn'd to balefulnesse:
    Their groves he feld, their gardins did deface,
    Their arbers spoyle, their Cabinets° suppresse,   *bowers*
    Their banket houses burne, their buildings race,°   *raze*
And of the fairest late, now made the fowlest place.

84 Then led they her away, and eke that knight
    They with them led, both sorrowfull and sad:
    The way they came, the same retourn'd they right,
    Till they arrivèd, where they lately had
    Charm'd those wild-beasts,° that rag'd with furie mad.
    Which now awaking, fierce at them gan fly,
    As in their mistresse reskew, whom they lad;
    But them the Palmer soone did pacify.
Then *Guyon* askt, what meant those beastes, which there did ly.

net borrowed from *Odyssey* VIII. 276 ff., where Hephaestus (Vulcan) traps his wife Aphrodite (Venus) in bed with Ares (Mars) by a similar stratagem
Verdant perhaps because in the spring of his life; perhaps "spring (or life)-giving," as Mordant, Acrasia's earlier lover, was "death-giving"
wild-beasts They met these beasts on the way in stanza 39.

85   Said he, These seeming beasts are men indeed,
     Whom this Enchauntresse hath transformèd thus,
     Whylome° her lovers, which her lusts did feed,   *formerly*
     Now turned into figures hideous,
     According to their mindes like monstruous.°
     Sad end (quoth he) of life intemperate,
     And mournefull meed of joyes delicious:
     But Palmer, if it mote thee so aggrate,°   *please*
     Let them returnèd be unto their former state.

86   Streight way he with his vertuous staffe them strooke,
     And streight of beasts they comely men became;
     Yet being men they did unmanly looke,
     And starèd ghastly, some for inward shame,
     And some for wrath, to see their captive Dame:
     But one above the rest in speciall,
     That had an hog beene late, hight *Grille*° by name,
     Repinèd greatly, and did him miscall,
     That had from hoggish forme him brought to naturall.

87   Said *Guyon*, See the mind of beastly man,
     That hath so soone forgot the excellence
     Of his creation, when he life began,
     That now he chooseth, with vile difference,
     To be a beast, and lacke intelligence.
     To whom the Palmer thus, The donghill kind
     Delights in filth and foule incontinence:
     Let *Grill* be *Grill*, and have his hoggish mind,
     But let us hence depart, whilest wether serves and wind.

                                                    1590

Book III

Book III is the Legend of Chastity, a Book of Love, and very different structurally
from I and II, being in this regard closely linked to IV. It may be that parts of it are
earlier than I and II, and belong to a time when Spenser was much more interested in
writing a poem like Ariosto's *Orlando Furioso*, which has, though with greater pace
and dash, a similar interweaving of many stories. Spenser here combines the tales of
Britomart and Artegall, Marinell and Florimell, Belphoebe and Timias, with that of
Scudamour and Amoret and many others. Amoret is chaste married love, and Scuda-

---

According . . . monstruous Acrasia is modeled
on Homer's Circe, who turns men into beasts.
Allegorically, the cup she offers gives a man his
choice between two extremes between which,
according to Aristotle, there is no mean: Bestiality and Heroic Virtue. Acrasia's victims
chose Bestiality, and so are transformed into
beasts.
Grille According to Plutarch, in his *Whether
the Beasts Have Use of Reason*, one of Odys-

seus' comrades refused to be turned back into
a man. This was Gryllus. The story was known
in England from a book called *Circe*, translated
from Italian and published in 1557. Guyon
uses Grille as an occasion to reflect on the
willingness of some men to forgo their rank
above the beast and next to the angels; the
Palmer abandons him, since some men do,
through incontinence, lose even the desire to
be restored to humanity.

mour finally achieves her at the end of the Book, but only in the 1590 edition of Books I to III; in 1596 Spenser canceled the last five stanzas and replaced them by three new ones postponing the union.

In Book III Elizabeth is celebrated in her second person, not as Queen but as "a most virtuous and beautifull Lady," namely Belphoebe. Spenser can include in a treatment of love philosophical considerations wider and higher than relations between men and women; he glories in love as the bringer of fertility and order in the whole world. Thus the Virgin Queen can be the patroness and exemplar of plenty, fertility, order, while remaining a devotee of virginity; her twin sister, Amoret, expresses the other kind of chastity, which is consistent with married love.

The cosmic and moral implications of love are present also in the parts of the Book Spenser calls, in the Letter to Ralegh, "Accidents"; one is "the over-throw of Marinell, the misery of Florimell," a story that runs on into Book V. Florimell is based on Ariosto's Angelica, who is always being chased and who has an evil double, as Florimell has a Snowy Florimell imitating her. Her allegorical significance is not clear, but she seems to be a type of the beauty of natural creation, the opposite but also the complement of the chaotic sea (Marinell) out of which Love was born.

[In the opening canto Spenser follows his now established procedure—the departing Guyon meets the knight of the new Book, the maiden warrior Britomart, and she beats him in fight because Chastity, her virtue, is higher than Temperance, Guyon's. But she presides over the Book much less firmly than Guyon over his, and comes into her own only at the end. The first canto also contains a key to the whole Book in the account of Castle Joyeous, the abode of Malecasta, which is full of emblems of unchastity. Britomart defeats Malecasta's champions. Cantos ii and iii establish the relation between Britomart and Artegall (knight of Justice in Book V) to Elizabeth, and iv is about Marinell and Florimell and ends with a beautiful apostrophe to Night. Canto v describes the healing of the squire Timias by Belphoebe (probably a reference to the quarrel between Ralegh and the Queen). Canto vi is the "core" canto, and one of the most important in the entire poem.]

Book III, Canto vi

This canto, which has strong associations with the Mutability Cantos, contains a charming, newly invented myth and a philosophical allegory which is not only hard to interpret but also, in some respects, central to the poem, and the source of much that we consider "Spenserian"; if *The Faerie Queene* in any sense adds up to a great poem much depends upon these stanzas; they tell us about the color of the poet's mind and the way he had learned to speak a philosophy of life through mythological fictions.

The Garden of Adonis is about the great opposites that everybody knows about in his own life; we experience continuity but also change; we know that humanity, like plant life, survives, but also that as individuals we die. In short, life is mutable but also constant. The Renaissance poet will express this felt knowledge by making a myth which brings the opposites into a unity. Spenser will explain that the forms are sempiternal, that is, perpetual though lacking the final immutable stillness of eternity.

They are deathless but do not possess being-for-ever. The matter which these forms assume is separated from them by death. He represents the forms as plants in a nursery garden, and the matter that clothes them comes from a chaos like that which God used as material for the creation. This matter is eternal; love produces its union with form, so that the world is stocked with generated beings; and Time produces their separation. The generative cycle is quasi-immortal; the individual elements of it are not.

Consequently the species, neither eternal nor of time, occupies a third realm in between them. It partakes both of mutability and the unchangingness of the eternal: "by succession made perpetuall, / Transformed oft and chaunged diverslie." The symbol of this realm is Adonis; he is the entire biological cycle, dying and living on, in time and out of it.

Like all myths, as Claude Lévi-Strauss sees them, Spenser's is not an answer to a problem, but a way of containing it, making it humanly acceptable. Through culture man is aware of and dreads death; here culture and nature confront each other, and the myth allows the mind to condone the confrontation: the problem is not solved but acceptably formulated. So essential is this problem to Spenser's whole view of the world that he restates it in an analogous myth in Book VII.

It is disastrous to try to give this canto exact philosophical meanings. It is a myth, and the use of philosophical concepts and language is incidental to that kind of explanation. But a few notes on the more abstract-sounding stanzas may be helpful. The seminary (as described in stanzas 33–38) is analogous to the Platonic *anima mundi* or world-soul, from which come the forms that give created things their characteristic shapes ("hews") when joined with matter from chaos. When Spenser says "the substance is eterne" he is not trying, as a philosopher using such language would, to distinguish between "matter" and "substance"; for him they mean much the same thing, substance being a little more specific, and meaning matter in so far as it has a relation to form.

When Spenser says that it is the forms which suffer under time, and that if it were otherwise the voluptuous delights of the garden would be immortal, we understand him well enough without troubling to ask why, since the wearing out of the forms takes place in "the state of life," there has to be an allegorical figure of Time inside the garden as well. The introduction of that figure into an Earthly Paradise is in itself a myth; it represents the confrontation of human knowledge of fact and human hope.

It is Adonis himself, in the famous stanza 47, who elicits from Spenser his most determined effort to spell out discursively the knowledge which is implicit in his myth. Adonis was killed by the boar, but lives. Instead of representing him in the traditional way as dying annually and annually reviving, like vegetation, Spenser crushes together his mortality and immortality; in explaining this he has to be aphoristic: "All be he subject to mortalitie, / Yet is eterne in mutabilitie, / And by succession made perpetuall." For this reason he is called "the Father of all formes"; he represents the condition under which, though the living die, they still have life. Meanwhile the additional myth of Cupid and Psyche relates the pleasure of generation to the most exalted idea of love, seen as following the mutable course of the passion in life and in time. In the Mutability Cantos the relation of eternity to time is more fully considered.

Canto vi°
The birth of faire Belphœbe and
Of Amoret is told.
The Gardins of Adonis° fraught
With pleasures manifold.

1   Well may I weene, faire Ladies, all this while
    Ye wonder, how this noble Damozell°
    So great perfections did in her compile,
    Sith that in salvage˃ forests she did dwell,   *wild*
    So farre from court and royall Citadell,
    The great schoolmistresse of all curtesy:
    Seemeth that such wild woods should far expell
        All civill usage and gentility,
And gentle sprite deforme with rude rusticity.

2   But to this faire *Belphœbe°* in her berth
    The heavens so favourable were and free,˃   *unencumbered*
    Looking with myld aspect° upon the earth,
    In th'*Horoscope* of her nativitee,
    That all the gifts of grace and chastitee
    On her they pourèd forth of plenteous horne;°
    Jove laught on *Venus* from his soveraigne see,˃   *throne*
    And *Phœbus* with faire beames did her adorne,
    And all the *Graces*° rockt her cradle being borne.

3   Her berth was of the wombe of Morning dew,
    And her conception of the joyous Prime˃   *spring*
    And all her whole creation did her shew
    Pure and unspotted from all loathly crime,˃   *sin*
    That is ingenerate˃ in fleshly slime.   *inborn*
    So was this virgin borne, so was she bred,
    So was she trayned up from time to time,°
        In all chast vertue, and true bounti-hed
Till to her dew perfection she was ripenèd.

4   Her mother was the faire *Chrysogonee,*°
    The daughter of *Amphisa,°* who by race
    A Faerie was, yborne of high degree,
    She bore *Belphœbe*, she bore in like cace
    Faire *Amoretta* in the second place:
    These two were twinnes, and twixt them two did share
        The heritage of all celestiall grace.

Gardins of Adonis originally little pots of flowers which sprang up and in a few days withered, symbols of the death of Adonis used by women who mourned him, like Thammuz, as a god who died and was annually revived. Spenser hardly has them in mind when he constructs his big allegory of what is "eterne in mutabilitie."
Damozell Belphoebe
Belphœbe "handsome-radiant"

aspect This is the relative position of the planets as it determines their influence (see *Astrology* in the Glossary).
pourèd . . . horne as if from a cornucopia
Graces See I.i.48n.
from time to time through the stages of growth
Chrysogonee "golden-born"
Amphisa "of double nature" (natural and supernatural)

That all the rest it seem'd they robbèd bare
Of bountie, and of beautie, and all vertues rare.

5   It were a goodly storie,° to declare,
    By what straunge accident faire *Chrysogone*
    Conceiv'd these infants, and how them she bare,
    In this wild forrest wandring all alone,
    After she had nine moneths fulfild and gone:
    For not as other wemens commune brood,
    They were enwombèd in the sacred throne
    Of her chaste bodie, nor with commune food,
As other wemens babes, they suckèd vitall blood.

6.   But wondrously they were begot, and bred
    Through influence of th'heavens fruitfull ray,
    As it in antique bookes is mentionèd.
    It was upon a Sommers shynie day,
    When *Titan* faire his beamès did display,
    In a fresh fountaine, farre from all mens vew,
    She bath'd her brest, the boyling heat t' allay;
    She bath'd with roses red, and violets blew,
And all the sweetest flowres, that in the forrest grew.

7   Till faint through irkesome wearinesse, adowne
    Upon the grassie ground her selfe she layd
    To sleepe, the whiles a gentle slombring swowne͗   *faint*
    Upon her fell all naked bare displayd;
    The sunne-beames bright upon her body playd,
    Being through former bathing mollifide,͗   *softened*
    And pierst into her wombe, where they embayd͗   *pervaded*
    With so sweet sence and secret power unspide,
That in her pregnant flesh they shortly fructifide.

8   Miraculous may seeme to him, that reades
    So straunge ensample of conceptión;
    But reason teacheth that the fruitfull seades
    Of all things living, through impressión
    Of the sunbeames in moyst complexión,
    Doe life conceive and quickned are by͗ kynd: *according to*
    So after *Nilus* inundatión,°
    Infinite shapes of creatures men do fynd,
Informèd in the mud, on which the Sunne hath shynd.

9   Great father he of generation
    Is rightly cald, th'author of life and light;
    And his faire sister for creation
    Ministreth matter fit, which tempred right

---

storie This is a myth of Spenser's invention, made to give a narrative explanation of the sinless birth of Belphoebe and Amoret, and their separate and different educations. **Nilus inundation** See I.i.21n.

With heate and humour,° breedes the living wight. *moisture*
So sprong these twinnes in wombe of *Chrysogone,*
Yet wist she nought thereof, but sore affright,
Wondred to see her belly so upblone,
Which still increast, till she her terme had full outgone.

10 Whereof conceiving shame and foule disgrace,
  Albe° her guiltlesse consciènce her cleard, *although*
  She fled into the wildernesse a space,
  Till that unweeldy burden she had reard,
  And shund dishonor, which as death she feard:
  Where wearie of long travell, downe to rest
  Her selfe she set, and comfortably cheard,° *encouraged*
  There a sad cloud of sleepe her overkest,° *overcast*
And seizèd every sense with sorrow sore opprest.

11 It fortunèd, faire *Venus* having lost
  Her little sonne, the wingèd god of love,
  Who for some light displeasure, which him crost,
  Was from her fled, as flit° as ayerie Dove, *swift*
  And let her blisfull bowre of joy above,
  (So from her often he had fled away,°
  When she for ought him sharpely did reprove,
  And wandred in the world in strange aray,
Disguiz'd in thousand shapes, that none might him bewray.°) *reveal*

12 Him for to seeke, she left her heavenly hous,
  The house of goodly formes and faire aspects,
  Whence all the world derives the glorious
  Features of beautie, and all shapes select,
  With which high God his workmanship hath deckt;
  And searchèd every way, through which his wings
  Had borne him, or his tract° she mote° detect: *track / could*
  She promist kisses sweet, and sweeter things
Unto the man, that of him tydings to her brings.

13 First she him sought in Court, where most he used
  Whylome° to haunt, but there she found him not; *formerly*
  But many there she found, which sore accused
  His falsehood, and with foule infámous blot
  His cruell deedes and wicked wyles did spot:
  Ladies and Lords she every where mote heare
  Complayning, how with his empoysned shot
  Their wofull harts he wounded had whyleare,° *earlier*
And so had left them languishing twixt hope and feare.

14 She then the Citties sought from gate to gate,
  And every one did aske, did he him see;

So . . . away Spenser is imitating an idyll of and country, the three divisions of society, and
the Alexandrian poet Moschus, called *Love the* must now try the wilds.
Runaway. Venus seeks Cupid in court, city,

And every one her answerd, that too late
He had him seene, and felt the crueltie
Of his sharpe darts and whot artillerie;
And every one threw forth reproches rife
Of his mischievous deedes, and said, That hee
Was the disturber of all civill' life,   *city*
The enimy of peace, and author of all strife.

15   Then in the countrey she abroad him sought,
And in the rurall cottages inquirèd,
Where also many plaints to her were brought,
How he their heedlesse harts with love had fyrèd,
And his false venim through their veines inspyrèd;
And eke the gentle shepheard swaynes, which sat
Keeping their fleecie flockes, as they were hyrèd,
She sweetly heard complaine, both how and what
Her sonne had to them doen; yet she did smile thereat.

16   But when in none of all these she him got,
She gan avize,' where else he mote' him hyde: *consider / might*
At last she her bethought, that she had not
Yet sought the salvage woods and forrests wyde,
In which full many lovely Nymphes abyde,
Mongst whom might be, that he did closely lye,
Or that the love of some of them him tyde:
For thy,' she thither cast her course t'apply,   *wherefore*
To search the secret haunts of *Dianes* company.

17   Shortly unto the wasteful woods she came,
Whereas she found the Goddesse with her crew,
After late chace of their embrewèd' game,   *blood-stained*
Sitting beside a fountaine in a rew,'   *row*
Some of them washing with the liquid dew
From off their dainty limbes the dustie sweat,
And soyle which did deforme their lively hew;'   *form*
Others lay shaded from the scorching heat;
The rest upon her person gave attendance great.

18   She having hong upon a bough on high
Her bow and painted quiver, had unlaste
Her silver buskins from her nimble thigh,
And her lancke loynes ungirt, and brests unbraste,
After her heat the breathing cold to taste;
Her golden lockes, that late in tresses bright
Embreaded were for hindring of her haste,
Now loose about her shoulders hong undight,'   *loose*
And were with sweet *Ambrosia* all besprinckled light.

19   Soone as she *Venus* saw behind her backe,
She was asham'd to be so loose surprized,

And woxe halfe wroth against her damzels slacke,
That had not her thereof before avized,ˢ   *warned*
But suffred her so carelesly disguizedˢ   *adorned*
Be overtaken. Soone her garments loose
Upgath'ring, in her bosome she comprized,ˢ   *drew together*
Well as she might, and to the Goddesse rose,
Whiles all her Nymphes did like a girlond her enclose.°

20 Goodly she gan faire *Cytherea* greet,   *Venus*
    And shortly askèd her, what cause her brought
    Into that wildernesse for her unmeet,ˢ   *unsuitable*
    From her sweete bowres, and beds with pleasures fraught:
    That suddein change she strange adventure thought.
    To whom halfe weeping, she thus answerèd,
    That she her dearest sonne *Cupído* sought,
    Who in his frowardnesseˢ from her was fled;   *peevishness*
That she repented sore, to have him angerèd.

21 Thereat *Diana* gan to smile, in scorne
    Of her vaine plaint, and to her scoffing sayd;
    Great pittie sure, that ye be so forlorne
    Of your gay sonne, that gives ye so good ayd
    To your disports:ˢ ill mote ye bene apaydˢ *sports / requited*
    But she was more engrievèd, and replide;
    Faire sister, ill beseemes it to upbrayd
    A dolefull heart with so disdainfull pride;
The like that mine, may be your paine another tide.ˢ   *time*

22 As you in woods and wanton wildernesse
    Your glory set, to chace the salvage beasts,
    So my delight is all in joyfulnesse,
    In beds, in bowres, in banckets, and in feasts:
    And ill becomes you with your loftie creasts,ˢ   *helmets*
    To scorne the joy, that *Jove* is glad to seeke;
    We both are bound to follow heavens beheasts,
    And tend our charges with obeisance meeke:
Spare, gentle sister, with reproch my paine to eeke.ˢ   *augment*

23 And tell me, if that ye my sonne have heard,
    To lurke emongst your Nymphes in secret wize;
    Or keepeˢ their cabins: much I am affeard,   *watch*
    Least he like one of them him selfe disguize,
    And turne his arrowes to their exercize:
    So may he long himself full easie hide:
    For he is faire and fresh in face and guize,ˢ   *appearance*
    As any Nymph (let not it be envyde.)ˢ   *grudged*
So saying every Nymph full narrowly she eyde.

Whiles . . . enclose The story of Venus sur-   who did so in Ovid, *Metamorphoses* III; and
prising Diana is adapted from that of Actaeon,   this line is almost a translation of III.180.

24 But *Phœbe* therewith sore was angerèd,
   And sharply said; Goe Dame, goe seeke your boy,
   Where you him lately left, in *Mars* his bed;
   He comes not here, we scorne his foolish joy,
   Ne lend we leisure to his idle toy:°   *game*
   But if I catch him in this company,
   By *Stygian* lake I vow, whose sad annoy°   *injuriouness*
   The Gods doe dread, he dearely shall abye.°   *pay for it*
Ile clip his wanton wings, that he no more shall fly.

25 Whom when as *Venus* saw so sore displeased,
   She inly sory was, and gan relent,
   What she had said: so her she soone appeased,
   With sugred words and gentle blandishment,
   Which as a fountaine from her sweet lips went,
   And wellèd goodly forth, that in short space
   She was well pleasd, and forth her damzels sent,
Through all the woods, to search from place to place,
If any tract of him or tydings they mote trace.

26 To search the God of love, her Nymphes she sent
   Throughout the wandring forrest every where:
   And after them her selfe eke with her went
   To seeke the fugitive, both farre and nere,
   So long they sought, till they arrivèd were
   In that same shadie covert, whereas lay
   Faire *Crysogone* in slombry traunce whilere:
   Who in her sleepe (a wondrous thing to say)
Unwares had borne two babes, as faire as springing day.

27 Unwares she them conceiv'd, unwares she bore:
   She bore withouten paine, that she conceived
   Withouten pleasure: ne her need implore
   Lucinaes aide:° which when they both perceived,
   They were through wonder nigh of sense bereaved,
   And gazing each on other, nought bespake:
   At last they both agreed, her seeming grieved°   *unwell*
   Out of her heavy swowne not to awake,
But from her loving side the tender babes to take.

28 Up they them tooke, each one a babe uptooke,
   And with them carried, to be fosterèd;
   Dame *Phœbe* to a Nymph her babe betooke,
   To be upbrought in perfect Maydenhed,
   And of her selfe her name *Belphœbe* red:°   *gave*
   But *Venus* hers thence farre away convayd,
   To be upbrought in goodly womanhed,

Lucinaes aide Juno, in the capacity of patron
of women in labor, was called Lucina.

And in her litle loves stead,° which was strayd,   *place*
Her *Amoretta* cald,° to comfort her dismayd.

29   She brought her to her joyous Paradize,
      Where most she wonnes,° when she on earth does dwel.   *lives*
      So faire a place, as Nature can devize:
      Whether in *Paphos,*° or *Cytheron*° hill,
      Or it in *Gnidus*° be, I wote not well;
      But well I wote by tryall,° that this same   *experience*
      All other pleasant places doth excell,
    And callèd is by her lost lovers name
The *Gardin* of *Adonis*, farre renowmd by fame.

30   In that same Gardin all the goodly flowres,
      Wherewith dame Nature doth her beautifie,
      And decks the girlonds of her paramoures,
      Are fetcht: there is the first seminarie°   *seed nursery*
      Of all things, that are borne to live and die,
      According to their kindes. Long worke it were,
      Here to account the endlesse progenie
      Of all the weedes,° that bud and blossome there;   *plants*
But so much as doth need, must needs be counted here.

31   It sited was in fruitfull soyle of old,
      And girt in with two walles on either side;
      The one of yron, the other of bright gold,
      That none might thorough° breake, nor overstride: *through*
      And double gates it had, which opened wide,
      By which both in and out men moten° pas;   *could*
      Th'one faire and fresh, the other old and dride:
      Old *Genius* the porter of them was,
Old *Genius*, the which a double nature has.

32   He letteth in, he letteth out to wend,°   *go*
      All that to come into the world desire;
      A thousand thousand naked babes attend
      About him day and night, which do require,
      That he with fleshly weedes would them attire:
      Such as him list, such as eternall fate
      Ordainèd hath, he clothes with sinfull mire,°
      And sendeth forth to live in mortall state,
Till they againe returne backe by the hinder gate.

33   After that they againe returnèd beene,
      They in that Gardin planted be againe;

And in . . . cald Lacking Cupid (Amor), she called the baby Amoretta.
Paphos town in Cyprus, sacred to Venus
Cytheron mountain where Venus was worshiped
Gnidus Cnidus in Doria, where stood the statue of Venus by Praxiteles

sinful mire flesh; matter; so called because the world is fallen, but also because, in neo-platonism, matter is evil in so far as it is remote from spirit

And grow afresh, as they had never seene
Fleshly corruption, nor mortall paine.
Some thousand yeares so doen they there remaine;
And then of him are clad with other hew,°   *forms*
Or sent into the chaungefull world againe,
Till thither they returne, where first they grew:
So like a wheele around they runne from old to new.

34   Ne needs there Gardiner to set, or sow,
To plant or prune: for of their owne accord
All things, as they created were, doe grow,
And yet remember well the mightie word,
Which first was spoken by th'Almightie lord,
That bad them to increase and multiply:°
Ne doe they need with water of the ford,
Or of the clouds to moysten their roots dry;
For in themselves eternall moisture they imply.°   *contain*

35   Infinite shapes of creatures there are bred,
And uncouth° formes, which none yet ever knew,   *unknown, strange*
And every sort is in a sundry° bed   *separate*
Set by it selfe, and ranckt in comely rew:°   *row*
Some fit for reasonable soules° t'indew,°   *put on*
Some made for beasts, some made for birds to weare,
And all the fruitfull spawne of fishes hew
In endlesse rancks along enraungèd were,
That seem'd the *Oceán* could not containe them there.

36   Daily they grow, and daily forth are sent
Into the world, it to replenish more;
Yet is the stocke not lessenèd, nor spent,
But still remaines in everlasting store,
As it at first created was of yore,
For in the wide wombe of the world there lyes,
In hatefull darkenesse and in deepe horrore,
An huge eternal *Chaos*, which supplyes
The substances of natures fruitfull progenyes.

37   All things from thence doe their first being fetch,
And borrow matter, whereof they are made,
Which when as forme and feature it does ketch,°   *take*
Becomes a bodie, and doth then invade°   *enter*
The state of life, out of the griesly° shade.   *ghastly*
That substance is eterne, and bideth so,
Ne when the life decayes, and forme does fade,
Doth it consume, and into nothing go,
But chaungèd is, and often altred to and fro.

increase and multiply Genesis 1:22   **reasonable soules** human souls; below them
                                                 there is no reason

38 The substance is not chaunged, nor alterèd,
But th'only forme and outward fashión;   *only the / appearance*
For every substance is conditioned
To change her hew, and sundry formes to don,
Meet for her temper and complexión:
For formes are variable and decay,
By course of kind, and by occasión;   *nature / accident*
And that faire flowre of beautie fades away,
As doth the lilly fresh before the sunny ray.

39 Great enimy to it, and to all the rest,
That in the *Gardin* of *Adonis* springs,
Is wicked *Time*, who with his scyth addrest,   *equipped*
Does mow the flowring herbes and goodly things,
And all their glory to the ground downe flings,
Where they doe wither, and are fowly mard:
He flyes about, and with his flaggy wings   *drooping*
Beates downe both leaves and buds without regard,
Ne ever pittie may relent his malice hard.

40 Yet pittie often did the gods relent,
To see so faire things mard, and spoylèd quight:
And their great mother *Venus* did lament
The losse of her deare brood, her deare delight:
Her hart was pierst with pittie at the sight,
When walking through the Gardin, them she spyde,
Yet no'te she find redresse for such despight.   *knew not how to*
For all that lives, is subject to that law:
All things decay in time, and to their end do draw.

41 But were it not, that *Time* their troubler is,
All that in this delightfull Gardin growes,
Should happie be, and have immortall bliss.
For here all plentie, and all pleasure flowes,
And sweet love gentle fits emongst them throwes,
Without fell rancor, or fond gealosie;
Franckly each paramour his leman knowes.   *lover / mistress*
Each bird his mate, ne any does envie   *resent*
Their goodly meriment, and gay felicitie.

42 There is continuall spring, and harvest there
Continuall, both meeting at one time:°
For both the boughes doe laughing blossomes beare,
And with fresh colours decke the wanton Prime,   *spring*
And eke attonce the heavy trees they clime,
Which seeme to labour under their fruits lode:
The whiles the joyous birdes make their pastime

Continuall . . . time another feature of the Earthly Paradise. To contrast this with the Bower of Bliss in II.xii is a favorite topic: here is good generative sexuality, where God's commandment to increase and multiply is obeyed with joy and not corrupted by sinister luxury.

Emongst the shadie leaves, their sweet abode,
And their true loves without suspition° tell abrode.   *fear*

43 Right in the middest of that Paradise,
    There stood a stately Mount, on whose round top
    A gloomy grove of mirtle trees did rise,
    Whose shadie boughes sharpe steele did never lop,
    Nor wicked beasts their tender buds did crop,
    But like a girlond compassèd the hight,
    And from their fruitfull sides sweet gum did drop,
    That all the ground with precious deaw bedight,
  Threw forth most dainty odours, and most sweet delight.

44 And in the thickest covert of that shade,
    There was a pleasant arbour, not by art.
    But of the trees owne inclination° made,   *bending*
    Which knitting their rancke° braunches part to part,   *luxuriant*
    With wanton yvie twyne entrayld athwart,
    And Eglantine, and Caprifole° emong,   *honeysuckle*
    Fashiond above within their inmost part,
    That nether° Phœbus beams could through them throng,   *neither*
  Nor Aeolus sharp blast could worke them any wrong.

45 And all about grew every sort of flowre,
    To which sad lovers were transformed of yore;
    Fresh *Hyacinthus,*° *Phœbus* paramoure,
    And dearest love,
    Foolish *Narcisse,*° that likes the watry shore,
    Sad *Amaranthus,*° made a flowre but late,
    Sad *Amaranthus,* in whose purple gore
    Me seemes I see *Amintas*° wretched fate,
  To whom sweet Poets verse hath given endlesse date.

46 There wont faire *Venus* often to enjoy
    Her deare *Adonis* joyous company,
    And reape sweet pleasure of the wanton boy;
    There yet, some say, in secret he does ly,
    Lappèd in flowres and pretious spycery,
    By her hid from the world, and from the skill°   *knowledge*
    Of *Stygian* Gods,° which doe her love envy;   *gods of hell*
    But she her selfe, when ever that she will,
  Possesseth him, and of his sweetnesse takes her fill.

47 And sooth it seemes they say: for he may not
    For ever die, and ever burièd bee
    In balefull night, where all things are forgot;

Hyacinthus killed while playing quoits with Apollo, who made the flower that sprang from his blood an emblem of his mourning
Narcisse Narcissus, who died of self-love and was transformed into a flower

Amaranthus from the flower so called because it does not fade; there is no myth of Amaranthus
Amintas a pastoral name for Sir Philip Sidney, whose death was celebrated by many elegies

All be˃ he subject to mortalitie,   *even though*
   Yet is eterne in mutabilitie,
   And by succession made perpetuall,
   Transformèd oft, and chaungèd diverslie:
   For him the Father of all formes, they call;
Therefore needs mote he live, that living gives to all.

48   There now he liveth in eternall blis,
   Joying his goddesse, and of her enjoyd:
   Ne feareth he henceforth that foe of his,
   Which with his cruell tuske him deadly cloyd:˃   *pierced*
   For that wilde Bore, the which him once annoyd,˃   *injured*
   She firmely hath emprisonèd for ay,
   That her sweet love his malice mote avoyd,
   In a strong rocky Cave, which is they say,
Hewen underneath that Mount, that none him losen˃ may.   *loose*

49   There now he lives in everlasting joy,
   With many of the Gods in company,
   Which thither haunt,˃ and with the wingèd boy   *visit*
   Sporting himselfe in safe felicity:
   Who when he hoth with spoiles and cruelty
   Ransackt the world, and in the wofull harts
   Of many wretches set his triumphes hye,
   Thither resorts, and laying his sad darts
Aside, with faire *Adonis* playes his wanton parts.

50   And his true love faire *Psyche*° with him playes,
   Faire *Psyche* to him lately reconcyld,
   After long troubles and unmeet upbrayes,˃   *unsuitable reproaches*
   With which his mother *Venus* her revyld,
   And eke himselfe her cruelly exyld:
   But now in stedfast love and happy state
   She with him lives, and hath him borne a chyld,
   Pleasure,° that doth both gods and men aggrate,
Pleasure, the daughter of *Cupid* and *Psyche* late.

51   Hither great *Venus* brought this infant faire,
   The younger daughter of *Chrysogonee*,
   And unto *Psyche* with great trust and care
   Committed her, yfosterèd to bee,
   And trainèd up in true feminitee:
   Who no lesse carefully her tenderèd,
   Then her owne daughter *Pleasure*, to whom shee

Psyche (Greek, "breath" and "soul") The myth of Cupid and Psyche originates in *The Golden Ass* of Apuleius, and from the outset had allegorical significance; Psyche is the Soul, joined, after many trials, with the love of God. **Pleasure** Apuleius called the daughter of Cupid and Psyche Voluptas (Pleasure). See Milton's adaptation, in which he had Spenser much in mind, in the Epilogue to *Comus*. Cupid visits Psyche only at night and she never sees him; trying to do so, she spills hot oil from a lamp on the sleeping god, and he leaves her. In her search for him she has to perform almost impossible tasks set by Venus, but finally succeeds.

Made her companion, and her lessonèd
In all the lore of love, and goodly womanhead.

52 In which when she to perfect ripenesse grew,
Of grace and beautie noble Paragone,°   *model*
She brought her forth into the worldes vew,
To be th'ensample of true love alone,
And Lodestarre of all chaste affectióne,
To all faire Ladies, that doe live on ground.
To Faery court she came, where many one
Admyred her goodly haveour,° and found   *behavior*
His feeble hart wide launchèd° with loves cruell wound.   *pierced*

53 But she to none of them her love did cast,
Save to the noble knight Sir *Scudamore*,
To whom her loving hart she linkèd fast
In faithfull love, t'abide for evermore,
And for his dearest sake endurèd sore,
Sore trouble of an hainous enimy;
Who her would forcèd have to have forlore°   *abandoned*
Her former love, and stedfast loialty,
As ye may elsewhere read that ruefull history.

.   .   .

[The remainder of Book III continues Florimell's story, and introduces other *exempla* of love. So, in canto vii, Satyrane rescues the Squire of Dames, who has been set the impossible task of finding many chaste women (this has humor, somewhat rare in Spenser). The ninth canto contains the story of Malbecco, an impotent miser who keeps a jealous eye on his pretty young wife Hellenore. Satyrane says knowingly: "Extremely mad the man I surely deeme, / That weenes with watch and hard restraint to stay / A womans will, which is disposed to go astray" (stanza 6). And go astray she does, with Paridell, Satyrane's traveling companion. (The girl's name derives from that of Helen, Paridell's from Paris.) At first Malbecco will not let them into his house, though the weather is very bad. Britomart shows up, fights with Paridell, forms an allegiance with him, and finally succeeds with him in making Malbecco let them in. They sit at the table. The dinner is the occasion for an intense flirtation between Hellenore and Paridell, and a discourse on the history of the Trojans after the fall of their city; they founded first Rome and then London.]

From Canto ix
27 They sate to meat, and *Satyrane* his chaunce
Was her before,° and *Paridell* besyde;
But he him selfe° sate looking still askaunce,
Gains *Britomart*, and ever closely eyde
Sir *Satyrane*, that glaunces might not glyde:

his chaunce . . . before it happened that he   **he him selfe** Malbecco
sat opposite her

But his blind eye, that syded *Paridell*,
All his demeasnure,° from his sight did hyde: *behavior*
On her faire face so did he feede his fill,
And sent close messages of love to her at will.

28   And ever and anone, when none was ware,
      With speaking lookes, that close embassage° bore,   *message*
      He rov'd° at her, and told his secret care: *shot*
      For all that art he learnèd had of yore.
      Ne was she ignoraunt of that lewd lore,
      But in his eye his meaning wisely red,
      And with the like him answerd evermore:
      She sent at him one firie dart, whose hed
Empoisned was with privy lust, and gealous dred.

29   He from that deadly throw made no defence,
      But to the wound his weake hart opened wyde;
      The wicked engine° through false influence,   *weapon*
      Past through his eyes, and secretly did glyde
      Into his hart, which it did sorely gryde.°   *pierce*
      But nothing new to him was that same paine,
      Ne paine at all; for he so oft had tryde
      The powre thereof, and lov'd so oft in vaine,
That thing of course he counted,° love to entertaine.

30   Thenceforth to her he sought to intimate
      His inward griefe, by meanes to him well knowne,
      Now *Bacchus* fruit out of the silver plate
      He on the table dasht, as overthrowne,
      Or of the fruitfull liquor overflowne,
      And by the dauncing bubbles did divine,
      Or therein write to let his love be showne;
      Which well she red out of the learnèd line,
A sacrament prophane in mistery of wine.°

31   And when so of his hand the pledge she raught,°
      The guilty cup she fainèd to mistake,°
      And in her lap did shed her idle draught,
      Shewing desire her inward flame to slake:
      By such close signes they secret way did make
      Unto their wils, and one eyes watch escape;
      Two eyes him needeth, for to watch and wake,
      Who lovers will deceive. Thus was the ape,
By their faire handling, put into *Malbeccoes* cape.°

That . . . counted he regarded such suffering as a necessary part of
A sacrament . . . wine based on Ovid's account of Paris and Helen in a similar situation, *Heroides* XVII.75 ff., where the word *Amo* ("I love you") is traced in wine. The sacrament is "profane" because of the use of wine in the communion service, where it relates to divine love and the blood of Christ.
of . . . raught took the winecup from his hand
mistake not get good hold of
ape . . . cape Malbecco was made a fool of

32   Now when of meats and drinks they had their fill,
        Purpose was movèd by that gentle Dame,
        Unto those knights adventurous, to tell
        Of deeds of armes, which unto them became,
        And every one his kindred, and his name.
        Then *Paridell,* in whom a kindly° pryde   *natural*
        Of gracious speach, and skill his words to frame
        Abounded, being glad of so fit tyde°   *occasion*
    Him to commend to her, thus spake, of all well eyde.

33   *Troy,* that art now nought, but an idle name,
        And in thine ashes buried low dost lie,
        Though whilome° far much greater then thy fame,   *formerly*
        Before that angry Gods, and cruell skye
        Upon thee heapt a direfull destinie,
        What boots it boast thy glorious descent,
        And fetch from heaven thy great Genealogie,
        Sith all thy worthy prayses being blent,°   *defiled*
    Their of-spring hath embaste,° and later glory shent.°   *debased / disgraced*

34   Most famous Worthy of the world, by whome
        That warre was kindled, which did *Troy* inflame,
        And stately towres of *Ilion* whilome
        Brought unto balefull ruine, was by name
        Sir *Paris* far renowmd through noble fame,
        Who through great prowesse and bold hardinesse,
        From *Lacedæmon*° fetcht the fairest Dame,°   *Helen*
        That ever *Greece* did boast, or knight possesse,
    Whom *Venus* to him gave for meed° of worthinesse.   *reward*

35   Faire *Helene,* flowre of beautie excellent,
        And girlond of the mighty Conquerours,
        That madest many Ladies deare lament
        The heavie losse of their brave Paramours,
        Which they far off beheld from *Trojan* toures,°
        And saw the fieldes of faire *Scamander*° strowne
        With carcases of noble warrioures,
        Whose fruitlesse lives were under furrow sowne,
    And *Xanthus*° sandy bankes with bloud all overflowne.

36   From him my linage I derive aright,
        Who long before the ten yeares siege of *Troy,*
        Whiles yet on *Ida* he a shepheard hight,°   *was called*
        On faire *Oenone*° got a lovely boy,
        Whom for remembraunce of her passèd joy,

Lacedæmon Sparta, where Helen was the wife   Xanthus another name for Scamander
of the king, Menelaus   Oenone nymph of Ida, and first love of Paris
toures Helen and the other ladies watched the   before he was awarded Helen (see Tennyson,
fighting from the towers of Troy   *Oenone*)
Scamander river flowing through the plain
before Troy

She of his Father *Parius* did name;
Who, after *Greekes* did *Priams* realme° destroy,
Gathred the *Trojan* reliques° sav'd from flame,
And with them sayling thence, to th'Isle of *Paros* came.

37 That was by him cald *Paros*, which before
    Hight *Nausa*, there he many yeares did raine,
    And built *Nausicle*° by the *Pontick*° shore,
    The which he dying left next in remaine
    To *Paridas* his sonne.
    From whom I *Paridell* by kin descend;
    But for faire Ladies love, and glories gaine,
    My native soile have left, my dayes to spend
In sewing⁀ deeds of armes, my lives and labours end.   *pursuing*

38 Whenas the noble *Britomart* heard tell
    Of *Trojan* warres, and *Priams* Citie sackt,°
    The ruefull story of Sir *Paridell*,
    She was empassiond at that piteous act,
    With zelous envy of Greekes cruell fact,⁀   *deed*
    Against that nation, from whose race of old
    She heard, that she was lineally extract:
    For noble *Britons* sprong from *Trojans* bold,
And *Troynovant*° was built of old *Troyes* ashes cold.

39 Then sighing soft awhile, at last she thus:
    O lamentable fall of famous towne,
    Which raignd so many yeares victorious,
    And of all *Asie* bore the soveraigne crowne,
    In one sad night consumd, and throwen downe:
    What stony hart, that heares thy haplesse fate,
    Is not empierst with deepe compassiowne,
    And makes ensample of mans wretched state,
That floures so fresh at morne, and fades at evening late?

40 Behold, Sir, how your pitifull complaint
    Hath found another partner of your payne:
    For nothing may impresse so deare constraint,⁀   *distress*
    As countries cause, and commune foes disdayne
    But if it should not grieve you, backe agayne
    To turne your course, I would to heare desyre,
    What to *Aeneas* fell; sith that men sayne
    He was not in the Cities wofull fyre
Consum'd, but did him selfe to safètie retyre.

Priams realme Troy
Trojan reliques the palladium, on which the
safety of Troy depended, and which Aeneas
(not Paris) saved and took to Rome
Nausicle the city of Nausa
Pontick Black Sea
Priams . . . sackt Spenser is varying the story
as he knew it from Virgil's *Aeneid* and other
sources.
Troynovant New Troy = London. It was a
commonplace in popular history and also in
propaganda that the British were descended
from the Trojans, just as the Romans were—
a myth shared by many other countries.

41   *Anchyses* sonne begot of *Venus* faire,°
    (Said he,) out of the flames for safegard fled,
    And with a remnant did to sea repaire,
    Where he through fatall errour° long was led
    Full many yeares, and weetlesse wanderèd
    From shore to shore, emongst the Lybicke⁾ sands,   *Libyan*
    Ere rest he found. Much there he sufferèd,
    And many perils past in forreine lands,
To save his people sad from victours vengefull hands.

42   At last in *Latium*° he did arrive,
    Where he with cruell warre was entertaind
    Of th'inland folke, which sought him backe to drive,
    Till he with old *Latinus* was constraind,
    To contract wedlock: (so the fates ordaind.)
    Wedlock contract in bloud, and eke in blood
    Accomplishèd, that many deare⁾ complained:°   *sadly*
    The rivall slaine, the victour through the flood
Escapèd hardly, hardly praisd his wedlock good.

43   Yet after all, he victour did survive,
    And with *Latinus* did the kingdome part.
    But after, when both nations gan to strive,
    Into their names the title to convart,
    His sonne *Iülus* did from thence depart,
    With all the warlike youth of *Trojans* bloud,
    And in long *Alba*° plast his throne apart,
    Where faire it florishèd, and long time stoud,
Till *Romulus* renewing it,° to *Rome* remoud.

44   There there (said *Britomart*) a fresh appeard
    The glory of the later world to spring,
    And *Troy* againe out of her dust was reard,
    To sit in second seat of soveraigne king,
    Of all the world under her governing.
    But a third kingdome yet is to arise,
    Out of the *Trojans* scatterèd of-spring,
    That in all glory and great enterprise,
Both first and second *Troy* shall dare to equalise.

45   It *Troynovant* is hight, that with the waves
    Of wealthy *Thamis*⁾ washèd is along,   *Thames*
    Upon whose stubborne neck, whereat he raves
    With roring rage, and sore him selfe does throng,⁾   *crush*

Anchyses . . . faire Aeneas
fatall errour wanderings decreed by fate
Latium part of Italy near the Tiber
Wedlock . . . complaind refers to the wars
between Aeneas and Latinus, king of Latium,
and their settlement by Aeneas' marriage with
Lavinia, daughter of Latinus; Juno said this

would result in bloodshed, because Turnus of
the Rutilians wanted Lavinia. Turnus tried to
expel Aeneas, but was killed by him.
long Alba city built in Latium by Aeneas' son
Ascanius, extending along the hill Albinus
it the Trojan dynasty, which now moved to
Rome

That all men feare to tempt his billowes strong,
She fastned hath her foot, which standes so hy,
That it a wonder of the world is song
In forreine landes, and all which passen by,
Beholding it from far, do thinke it threates the skye.

46　The *Trojan Brute*° did first that Citie found,
　　And Hygate made the meare˃ thereof by West,　　　　*boundary*
　　And *Overt*˃ gate by North: that is the bound　　　　*open*
　　Toward the land; two rivers bound the rest.
　　So huge a scope at first him seemèd best,
　　To be the compasse of his kingdomes seat:
　　So huge a mind could not in lesser rest,
　　Ne in small meares containe his glory great,
That *Albion*° had conquerèd first by warlike feat.

47　Ah fairest Lady knight, (said *Paridell*)
　　Pardon I pray my heedlesse oversight,
　　Who had forgot, that whilome˃ I heard tell　　　　*once*
　　From agèd *Mnemon;*° for my wits bene light.
　　Indeed he said (if I remember right,)
　　That of the antique *Trojan* stocke, there grew
　　Another plant, that raught˃ to wondrous hight,　　*reached*
　　And far abroad his mighty branches threw,
Into the utmost Angle of the world he knew.

48　For that same *Brute,* whom much he did advaunce˃　　*praise*
　　In all his speach, was *Sylvius* his sonne,
　　Whom having slaine, through luckles arrowes glaunce
　　He fled for feare of that he had misdonne,
　　Or else for shame, so fowle reproch to shonne,
　　And with him led to sea an youthly trayne,
　　Where wearie wandring they long time did wonne,˃　　*dwell*
　　And many fortunes prov'd in th'*Ocean* mayne,
And great adventures found, that now were long to sayne.˃　　*say*

49　At last by fatall course they driven were
　　Into an Island spatious and brode,
　　The furthest North, that did to them appeare:
　　Which after rest they seeking far abrode,
　　Found it the fittest soyle for their abode,
　　Fruitfull of all things fit for living foode,
　　But wholy wast, and void of peoples trode,
　　Save an huge nation of the Geaunts broode,°
That fed on living flesh, and druncke mens vitall blood.

50　Whom he through wearie wars and labours long,
　　Subdewd with losse of many *Britons* bold:

Brute Brutus, in legendary history the first　　**Mnemon** Memory personified
king of Britain, and great-grandson of Aeneas　　**Geaunts broode** Brutus, arriving in Britain
Albion Britain　　found it populated only by giants.

In which the great *Goemagot*° of strong
Corineus,° and *Coulin*° of *Debon*° old
Were overthrowne, and layd on th'earth full cold,
Which quakèd under their so hideous masse,
A famous history to be enrold
In everlasting moniments˃ of brasse,   *records*
That all the antique Worthies merits far did passe.

51 His worke great *Troynovant*, his worke is eke
Faire *Lincolne*, both renowmèd far away,
That who from East to West will endlong seeke,
Cannot two fairer Cities find this day,
Except *Cleopolis:*° so heard I say
Old *Mnemon*. Therefore Sir, I greet you well
Your countrey kin, and you entirely pray
Of pardon for the strife, which late befell
Betwixt us both unknowne. So ended *Paridell*.

52 But all the while, that he these speaches spent,
Upon his lips hong faire Dame *Hellenore*,
With vigilant regard, and dew attent,˃   *attention*
Fashioning worlds of fancies evermore
In her fraile wit, that now her quite forlore:˃   *deserted*
The whiles unwares away her wondring eye,
And greedy eares her weake hart from her bore:
Which he perceiving, ever privily
In speaking, many false belgardes˃ at her let fly.   *loving looks*

53 So long these knights discoursed diversly,
Of straunge affaires, and noble hardiment,
Which they had past with mickle jeopardy,
That now the humid night was farforth spent,
And heavenly lampes were halfendeale˃ ybrent: *half*
Which th'old man seeing well, who too long thought
Every discourse and every argument,
Which by the houres he measurèd, besought
Them go to rest. So all unto their bowres were brought.

[In canto x Paridell outwits Malbecco, and elopes with "this second Hellene," having stolen his wealth and set fire to his house. Malbecco, fruitlessly pursuing them, falls in with the sham knight Braggadocchio and his servant Trompart, who take up his cause. Paridell abandons Hellenore, who is discovered by Malbecco in a new role, as the queen of a group of satyrs, greatly enjoying their sexual performances; she turns Malbecco down, and he goes off, finding

Goemagot Gogmagog: giant, later split into Gog and Magog, whose effigies stand outside the Guildhall in the City of London
Corineus Trojan who conquered Gogmagog and was awarded Cornwall for his pains
Coulin a giant

Debon the hero who overcame Coulin, and was awarded Devonshire (Spenser had already made these points about Corineus and Debon in II.xii.12)
Cleopolis here the city of Gloriana, temporarily distinct from London (Troynovant)

himself a cave, where he lives miserably and for ever; for "he has quight / Forgot he was a man, and *Gealosie* is hight." So ends one of the oddest and most lascivious of Spenser's "accidents."

Canto xi brings Britomart to the aid of Scudamour, lamenting the imprisonment of Amoret in the house of Busirane, an enchanter named for Busiris, a cruel pharaoh who slew all strangers. To enter one must pass through a flame; Britomart does so, but Scudamour cannot, his desires not being sufficiently pure. Britomart, inside, inspects Busirane's tapestries, dealing with Jupiter's love affairs, and those of the other gods. There is also an altar dedicated to Cupid, "Victor of the Gods," at which the inhabitants of the house blasphemously worship. The motto *Be bold* is emblazoned everywhere, except in one place, where it reads *Be not too bold*, which seems to refer to an English nursery rhyme—behind *that* door are skeletons and tubs of blood. Britomart prepares her weapons. She is about to perform for Unchastity what Guyon did for Intemperance.]

Book III, Canto xii

Allegorically the Mask of Cupid represents the disordered passions which intervene in love relationships, as between Amoret and Scudamour—she, though the perfect bride, tormented by the charms of Busirane, he out of control and unable to act for her preservation. Spenser emphasizes that the procession of Cupid's attendants is a masque, that is, a show of allegorical figures with allegorical intent, presented as a dance which displays their attributes. Masques were courtly entertainments, and involved dancing in which the characters of the masque joined with the audience; but here he is content with that part of the presentation which exhibited, in the known language of symbols, some complex moral proposition. In this respect it could be called a pageant with equal correctness. In fact some of Spenser's allegorical detail is borrowed from Petrarch's pageant *The Triumph of Love*. The "triumph" was a Renaissance courtly form related to the masque.

Although there is a real debt to courtly entertainments of a kind he must often have seen, Spenser is here, no more than anywhere else, willing to tie himself strictly to what could be presented in such a show, as the plight of Amoret sufficiently proves. With the masque itself Spenser combines the story of Britomart's intrusion, which is the stuff of romantic narrative: the storm, the fire, the arras depicting Cupid's triumphs, the baffling of the hero by a closed door, the reversal of the enchanter's charms, and the extinguishing of the fire are all romance themes.

Cupid here has a different aspect from that displayed in the allegory of Cupid and Psyche in III.vi. Spenser uses Venus in similarly contradictory (or complementary) ways. The cruelty of the wrong kind of love, in which passion predominates, is his theme. He wanted, as in the last cantos of Books I and II, a great set piece, this time an image of the love in which chastity has no part, but which succumbs to passion and madness; and he has his knight come in and abolish this image, and take prisoner the enchanter who forged it.

From Canto xii
The maske of Cupid, and th'enchaunted
    Chamber are displayd.
Whence Britomart redeemes faire
    Amoret, through charmes decayd.

1   Tho when as chearelesse Night ycovered had
        Faire heaven with an universall cloud,
        That every wight dismayd with darknesse sad,
        In silence and in sleepe themselves did shroud,
        She heard a shrilling Trompet sound aloud,
        Signe of nigh battell, or got victory;
        Nought therewith daunted was her courage proud,
        But rather stird to cruell enmity,
    Expecting ever, when some foe she might descry.

2   With that, an hideous storme of winde arose,
        With dreadfull thunder and lightning atwixt,
        And an earth-quake, as if it streight would lose
        The worlds foundations from his centre fixt;
        A direfull stench of smoke and sulphure mixt
        Ensewd, whose noyance fild the fearefull sted,   *place*
        From the fourth houre of night untill the sixt;
        Yet the bold *Britonesse* was nought ydred,
    Though much emmov'd, but stedfast still perseverèd.

3   All suddenly a stormy whirlwind blew
        Throughout the house, that clappèd every dore,
        With which that yron wicket open flew,
        As it with mightie levers had bene tore:
        And forth issewd, as on the ready flore
        Of some Theàtre, a grave personage,
        That in his hand a branch of laurell bore,
        With comely haveour and count'nance sage,
    Yclad in costly garments, fit for tragicke Stage.

4   Proceeding to the midst, he still did stand,
        As if in mind he somewhat had to say,
        And to the vulgar beckning with his hand,
        In signe of silence, as to heare a play,
        By lively actions he gan bewray   *expound*
        Some argument of matter passionèd;
        Which doen, he backe retyrèd soft away,
        And passing by, his name discoverèd,
    Ease,° on his robe in golden letters cypherèd.

5   The noble Mayd, still standing all this vewd,
        And merveild at his strange intendiment,   *design*

Ease is the "presenter" of the masque, as the
Attendant Spirit is of Milton's *Comus;* he makes
the preliminary announcement stating the theme.

With that a joyous fellowship issewd
Of Minstrals, making goodly meriment,
With wanton Bardes, and Rymers impudent,
All which together sung full chearefully
A lay of loves delight, with sweet concent.˃   *harmony*
After whom marcht a jolly company,
In manner of a maske, enragèd orderly.

6   The whiles a most delitious harmony,
         In full straunge notes was sweetly heard to sound,
         That the rare sweetnesse of the melody
         The feeble senses wholly did confound,
         And the fraile soule in deepe delight nigh dround:
         And when it ceast, shrill trompets loud did bray,
         That their report did farre away rebound,˃   *echo*
         And when they ceast, it gan againe to play,
     The whiles the maskers marchèd forth in trim aray.

7   The first was *Fancy,*° like a lovely boy,
         Of rare aspect, and beautie without peare;
         Matchable either to that ympe˃ of *Troy,*   *child*
         Whom Jove did love, and chose his cup to beare,°
         Or that same daintie lad, which was so deare
         To great *Alcides,*° that when as he dyde,
         He wailèd womanlike with many a teare,
         And every wood, and every valley wyde
     He fild with *Hylas*° name; the Nymphes eke *Hylas* cryde.

8   His garment neither was of silke nor say,˃   *fine wool*
         But painted plumes, in goodly order dight,
         Like as the sunburnt *Indians* do aray
         Their tawney bodies, in their proudest plight.˃   *attire*
         As those same plumes, so seemd he vaine and light,
         That by his gate˃ might easily appeare;   *gait*
         For still he far'd as dauncing in delight,
         And in his hand a windy fan did beare,
     That in the idle aire he mov'd still here and there.

9   And him beside marcht amorous *Desyre,*
         Who seemd of riper yeares, then th'other Swaine,
         Yet was that other swayne this elders syre,
         And gave him being, commune to them twaine:
         His garment was disguisèd˃ very vaine,˃   *worn / foolishly*
         And his embrodered Bonet sat awry;
         Twixt both his hands few sparkes he close did straine,

---

Fancy, fantasy, imagination, especially strong
in lovers; he wears feathers, symbols of lightness
and uncertainty
ympe . . . beare Ganymede, cupbearer of Jupiter, very beautiful

Alcides Hercules
Hylas Hercules' page, abducted by nymphs; for
this Hercules mourned

Which still he blew, and kindled busily,
That soone they life conceiv'd, and forth in flames did fly.

10   Next after him went *Doubt,* who was yclad
     In a discolour'd cote, of straunge disguyse,°   *fashion*
     That at his backe a brode Capuccio° had,   *hood*
     And sleeves dependant *Albanese*-wyse:°
     He lookt askew with his mistrustfull eyes,
     And nicely° trode, as thornes lay in his way,   *delicately*
     Or that the flore to shrinke he did avyse,°   *consider*
     And on a broken reed he still° did stay   *ever*
   His feeble steps, which shrunke, when hard theron he lay.°   *trod*

11   With him went *Daunger,*° cloth'd in raggèd weed,
     Made of Beares skin, that him more dreadfull made,
     Yet his owne face was dreadfull, ne did need
     Straunge° horrour, to deforme his griesly shade;   *external*
     A net in th'one hand, and a rustie blade
     In th'other was, this Mischiefe, that Mishap;
     With th'one his foes he threatned to invade,°   *stab*
     With th'other he his friends ment to enwrap:
   For whom he could not kill, he practizd to entrap.

12   Next him was *Feare,* all arm'd from top to toe,
     Yet thought himselfe not safe enough thereby,
     But feard each shadow moving to and fro,
     And his owne armes when glittering he did spy,
     Or clashing heard, he fast away did fly,
     As ashes pale of hew, and wingyheeld;
     And evermore on daunger fixt his eye,
     Gainst whom he alwaies bent a brasen shield,
   Which his right hand unarmèd fearefully did wield.

13   With him went *Hope* in rancke, a handsome Mayd,
     Of chearefull looke and lovely to behold;
     In silken samite° she was light arayd,   *rich silk*
     And her faire lockes were woven up in gold;
     She alway smyld, and in her hand did hold
     An holy water Sprinckle, dipt in deowe,
     With which she sprinckled favours manifold,
     On whom she list, and did great liking sheowe,
   Great liking unto many, but true love to feowe.°   *few*

14   And after them *Dissemblance*° and *Suspect*°   *dissimulation / suspicion*
     Marcht in one rancke, yet an unequall paire:
     For she was gentle, and of milde aspect,
     Courteous to all, and seeming debonaire,

Albanese-wyse in the Albanian fashion (?)
Daunger a regular attendant on Love. It means, in this context, the unapproachability of a lady, her creation around herself of hostility toward a lover; in IV.x.17 and also here it has to do with the withholding of love from a suitor.

Goodly adornèd, and exceeding faire:
Yet was that all but painted, and purloynd,
And her bright browes were deckt with borrowed haire:
Her deedes were forgèd, and her words false coynd,
And alwaies in her hand two clewes of silke she twynd.

15 But he was foule, ill favourèd, and grim,
    Under his eyebrowes looking still askaunce;
    And ever as *Dissemblance* laught on him,
    He lowrd on her with daungerous eyeglaunce;
    Shewing his nature in his countenance;
    His rolling eyes did never rest in place,
    But walkt each where, for feare of hid mischaunce,
    Holding a lattice° still' before his face,   *always*
Through which he still did peepe, as forward he did pace.

16 Next him went *Griefe*, and *Fury* matcht yfere,'   *together*
    Griefe all in sable sorrowfully clad,
    Downe hanging his dull head, with heavy chere,
    Yet inly being more, then' seeming sad: *than*
    A paire of Pincers in his hand he had,
    With which he pinchèd people to the hart,
    That from thenceforth a wretched life they lad,
    In wilfull languor and consuming smart,
Dying each day with inward wounds of dolours dart.

17 But *Fury* was full ill appareilèd
    In rags, that naked nigh she did appeare,
    With ghastly lookes and dreadfull drerihed,'   *gloom*
    For from her backe her garments she did teare,
    And from her head oft rent her snarlèd heare:
    In her right hand a firebrand she did tosse
    About her head, still roming here and there;
    As a dismayèd Deare in chace embost,'   *hard pressed*
Forgetfull of his safety, hath his right way lost.

18 After them went *Displeasure* and *Pleasance*,
    He looking lompish and full sullein sad,
    And hanging downe his heavy countenance;
    She chearefull fresh and full of joyance glad,
    As if no sorrow she ne felt ne drad;
    That evill matchèd paire they seemd to bee:
    An angry Waspe th'one in a viall had
    Th'other in hers an hony-lady Bee;
Thus marchèd these six couples forth in faire degree.

19 After all these there marcht a most faire Dame,°
    Led of two grysie' villeins, th'one *Despight*,'   *grim / spite*

---

lattice Suspect carries it because of a pun on the Italian *gelosia* or French *jalousie*, meaning both "jealousy" and "Venetian blind."

Dame Amoret; the picture of her is reminiscent of some in the emblem books (see Glossary).

The other clepèd *Cruelty* by name:
She dolefull Lady, like a dreary Spright,
Cald by strong charmes out of eternall night,
Had deathes owne image figurd in her face,
Full of sad signes, fearefull to living sight;
Yet in that horror shewd a seemely grace,
And with her feeble feet did move a comely pace.

20   Her brest all naked, as net› ivory,   *pure*
Without adorne of gold or silver bright,
Wherewith the Craftesman wonts it beautify,
Of her dew honour was despoylèd quight,
And a wide wound therein (O ruefull sight)
Entrenchèd deepe with knife accursèd keene,
Yet› freshly bleeding forth her fainting spright,   *still*
(The worke of cruell hand) was to be seene,
That dyde in sanguine red her skin all snowy cleene.

21   At that wide orifice her trembling hart
Was drawne forth, and in silver basin layd,
Quite through transfixèd with a deadly dart,
And in her bloud yet steeming fresh embayd.›   *bathed*
And those two villeins, which her steps upstayd,
When her weake feete could scarcely her sustaine,
And fading vitall powers gan to fade,
Her forward still with torture did constraine,
And evermore encreasèd her consuming paine.

22   Next after her the winged God himselfe
Came riding on a Lion ravenous,
Taught to obay the menage› of that Elfe,   *handling*
That man and beast with powre imperious
Subdeweth to his kingdome tyrannous:
His blindfold eyes° he bad a while unbind,
That his proud spoyle of that same dolorous
Faire Dame he might behold in perfect kind;
Which seene, he much rejoyced in his cruell mind.

23   Of which full proud, himselfe up rearing hye,
He lookèd round about with sterne disdaine;
And did survay his goodly company:
And marshalling the evill ordered traine,
With that the darts which his right hand did straine,
Full dreadfully he shooke that all did quake,
And clapt on hie his coulourd wingès twaine,
That all his many› it affraide did make: *company*
Tho› blinding him› againe, his way he forth did take.   *then / himself*

blindfold eyes Cupid was never blindfolded in antiquity; later he was so represented to imply the blindness of erotic choice, though in more mystical writings his blindness was said to show that love is above the intellect.

24   Behinde him was *Reproch, Repentance, Shame;*
    Reproch the first, *Shame* next, *Repent* behind:
    Repentance feeble, sorrowfull, and lame:
    Reproch despightfull, carelesse, and unkind;
    Shame most ill favourd, bestiall, and blind:
    Shame lowrd, *Repentance* sigh'd, *Reproch* did scould;
    Reproch sharpe stings, *Repentance* whips entwind,
    Shame burning brond-yrons in her hand did hold:
All three to each unlike, yet all made in one mould.

25   And after them a rude confusèd rout
    Of persons flockt, whose names isʾ hard to read: *it is*
    Emongst them was sterne *Strife,* and *Anger* stout,
    Unquiet *Care,* and fond *Unthriftihead,*
    Lewd *Losse of Time,* and *Sorrow* seeming dead,
    Inconstant *Chaunge,* and false *Disloyaltie,*
    Consuming *Riotise,* and guilty *Dread*
    Of heavenly vengeance, faint *Infirmitie,*
Vile *Povertie,* and lastly *Death* with infamie.

26   There were full many moe like maladies,
    Whose names and natures I note readen well,ʾ   *cannot well say*
    So many moe, as there be phantasies
    In wavering wemens wit, that none can tell,
    Or paines in love, or punishments in hell;
    All which disguizèd marcht in masking wise,
    About the chamber with that Damozell,
    And then returnèd, having marchèd thrise,
Into the inner roome, from whence they first did rise.

27   So soone as they were in, the dore streight way
    Fast lockèd, driven with that stormy blast,
    Which first it opened; and bore all away.
    Then the brave Maid, which all this while was plast
    In secret shade, and saw both first and last,
    Issewèd forth, and went unto the dore,
    To enter in, but found it lockèd fast:
    It vaine she thought with rigorous uprore
For to efforce, when charmes had closèd it afore.

28   Where force might not availe, there sleights and art
    She cast to use, both fit for hard emprize;
    For thyʾ from that same roome not to depart   *because*
    Till morrow next, she did her selfe avize,ʾ   *counsel*
    When that same Maske againe should forth arize.
    The morrow next appeard with joyous cheare,
    Calling men to their daily exercize,
    Then she, as morrow fresh, her selfe did reare
Out of her secret stand, that day for to out weare.

29   All that day she outwore in wandering,
       And gazing on that Chambers ornament,
       Till that againe the second evening
       Her covered with her sable vestiment,
       Wherewith the worlds faire beautie she hath blent:˃   *extinguished*
       Then when the second watch was almost past,
       That brasen dore flew open, and in went
       Bold *Britomart,* as she had late forecast,˃   *planned*
   Neither of idle shewes, nor of false charmes aghast.

30   So soone as she was entred, round about
       She cast her eies, to see what was become
       Of all those persons, which she saw without:
       But lo, they streight were vanisht all and some,˃   *entirely*
       Ne living wight she saw in all that roome,
       Save that same woefull Ladie, both whose hands
       Were bounden fast, that did her ill become,
       And her small wast girt round with yron bands,
   Unto a brasen pillour, by the which she stands.

31   And her before the vile Enchaunter sate,
       Figuring straunge charácters of his art,
       With living bloud he those charácters wrate,
       Dreadfully dropping from her dying hart,
       Seeming transfixèd with a cruell dart,
       And all perforce to make her him to love.
       Ah who can love the worker of her smart?˃   *pain*
       A thousand charmes he formerly did prove;˃   *try*
   Yet thousand charmes could not her stedfast heart remove.

32   Soone as that virgin knight he saw in place,
       His wicked bookes in hast he overthrew,
       Not caring his long labours to deface,˃   *spoil*
       And fiercely ronning to that Lady trew,
       A murdrous knife out of his pocket drew,
       The which he thought, for villeinous despight,
       In her tormented bodie to embrew:˃   *plunge*
       But the stout Damzell to him leaping light,
   His cursèd hand withheld, and maisterèd his might.

33   From her, to whom his fury first he ment,˃   *intended*
       The wicked weapon rashly he did wrest,
       And turning to her selfe his fell intent,
       Unwares it strooke into her snowie chest,
       That little drops empurpled her faire brest.
       Exceeding wroth therewith the virgin grew,
       Albe˃ the wound were nothing deepe imprest,   *although*
       And fiercely forth her mortall blade she drew,
   To give him the reward for such vile outrage dew.

34 So mightily she smote him, that to ground
  He fell halfe dead; next stroke him should have slaine,
  Had not the Lady, which by him stood bound,
  Dernely⁊ unto her callèd to abstaine,   *dismally*
  From doing him to dy. For else her paine
  Should be remedilesse, sith⁊ none but hee,   *since*
  Which wrought it, could the same recure⁊ againe. *cure*
  Therewith she stayd her hand, loth stayd to bee;
For life she him envyde,⁊ and long'd revenge to see. *begrudged*

35 And to him said, Thou wicked man, whose meed
  For so huge mischiefe, and vile villany
  Is death, or if that ought do death exceed,
  Be sure, that nought may save thee from to dy,
  But if that thou this Dame doe presently
  Restore unto her health, and former state;
  This doe and live, else die undoubtedly.
  He glad of life, that lookt for death but late,
Did yield himselfe right willing to prolong his date.

36 And rising up, gan streight to overlooke
  Those cursèd leaves, his charmes backe to reverse;
  Full dreadfull things out of that balefull booke
  He red, and measur'd many a sad verse,
  That horror gan the virgins hart to perse,
  And her faire locks up starèd stiffe on end,
  Hearing him those same bloudy lines reherse;
  And all the while he red, she did extend
Her sword high over him, if ought⁊ he did offend. *lest in anyway*

37 Anon she gan perceive the house to quake,
  And all the dores to rattle round about;
  Yet all that did not her dismaièd make,
  Nor slacke her threatfull hand for daungers dout,⁊ *fear*
  But still with stedfast eye and courage stout
  Abode, to weet what end would come of all.
  At last that mightie chaine, which round about
  Her tender waste was wound, adowne gan fall,
And that great brasen pillour broke in peeces small.

38 The cruell steele, which thrild⁊ her dying hart, *pierced*
  Fell softly forth, as of his owne accord,
  And the wyde wound, which lately did dispart⁊ *divide*
  Her bleeding brest, and riven bowels gor'd,
  Was closèd up, as it had not bene bor'd,
  And every part to safèty full sound,
  As she were never hurt, was soone restor'd:
  Tho⁊ when she felt her selfe to be unbound, *then*
And perfect hole,⁊ prostrate she fell unto the ground. *whole*

39　Before faire *Britomart,* she fell prostrate,
　　　Saying, Ah noble knight, what worthy meed
　　　Can wretched Lady, quit⌐ from wofull state,　　　　　　*redeemed*
　　　Yield you in liew of this your gratious deed?
　　　Your vertue selfe her owne reward shall breed,
　　　Even immortall praise, and glory wyde,
　　　Which I your vassall, by your prowesse freed,
　　　Shall through the world make to be notifyde,
　　And goodly well advance,⌐ that goodly well was tryde.⌐　*make known /*
　　　　　　　　　　　　　　　　　　　　　　　　　　　proved

40　But *Britomart* uprearing her from ground,
　　　Said, Gentle Dame, reward enough I weene
　　　For many labours more, then I have found,
　　　This, that in safety now I have you seene,
　　　And meane of your deliverance have beene:
　　　Henceforth faire Lady comfort to you take,
　　　And put away remembrance of late teene;
　　　In stead thereof know, that your loving Make,⌐　　　　*mate*
　　Hath no lesse griefe endurèd for your gentle sake.

41　She much was cheard to heare him mentiònd,
　　　Whom of all living wights she lovèd best.
　　　Then laid the noble Championesse strong hond
　　　Upon th'enchaunter, which had her distrest
　　　So sore, and with foule outrages opprest:
　　　With that great chaine, wherewith not long ygo
　　　He bound that pitteous Lady prisoner, now relest,
　　　Himselfe she bound, more worthy to be so,
　　And captive with her led to wretchednesse and wo.

42　Returning backe, those goodly roomes, which erst⌐　　*recently*
　　　She saw so rich and royally arayd,
　　　Now vanisht utterly, and cleane subverst⌐　　　　　*overthrown*
　　　She found, and all their glory quite decayd,
　　　That sight of such a chaunge her much dismayd.
　　　Thence forth descending to that perlous Porch,
　　　Those dreadfull flames she also found delayd,⌐　　　*quenched*
　　　And quenchèd quite, like a consumèd torch,
　　That erst all entrers won⌐ so cruelly to scorch.　　　　*used*

43　More° easie issew⌐ now, then entrance late　　　　　　*exit*
　　　She found: for now that fainèd dreadfull flame,

More The following three stanzas were inserted in the edition of 1596 to replace the five with which Spenser had originally ended the Book. In the first version Britomart finds Scudamour, as usual, in distress, but when he sees Amoret in good health he runs to her and embraces her. They seemed grown together like a hermaphrodite, and Britomart half envies them, knowing that she is to be denied such happiness. Spenser makes no use of these stanzas when Scudamour and Amoret finally do meet again in IV.ix. It has been suggested (see Proem to IV) that he changed them because he was afraid of offending Burleigh any further; but more probably he had further use, in the interlocking stories that also make up Book IV, for Scudamour and Amoret.

Which chokt the porch of that enchaunted gate,
And passage bard to all, that thither came,
Was vanisht quite, as it were not the same,
And gave her leave at pleasure forth to passe.
Th'Enchaunter selfe, which all that fraud did frame,
To have efforst the love of that faire lasse,
Seeing his worke now wasted deepe engrievèd was.

44 But when the victoresse arrivèd there,
       Where late she left the pensife *Scudamore*,
       With her owne trusty Squire, both full of feare,
       Neither of them she found where she them lore:>   *left*
       Thereat her noble hart was stonisht sore;
       But most faire *Amoret*, whose gentle spright
       Now gan to feede on hope, which she before
    Conceivèd had, to see her owne deare knight,
Being thereof beguyld was fild with new affright.

45 But he sad man, when he had long in drede
       Awayted there for *Britomarts* returne,
       Yet saw her not nor signe of her good speed,
       His expectation to despaire did turne,
       Misdeeming sure that her those flames did burne;
       And therefore gan advize> with her old Squire,   *decide*
       Who her deare nourslings losse no lesse did mourne,
    Thence to depart for further aide t'enquire:
Where let them wend at will, whilest here I doe respire.>   *take a breather*
                              1590

Book IV

It may be that in the course of writing Book IV Spenser found that the Ariostan scheme of interlocked stories was less suitable to his purposes than the more monolithic organization of I and II. Book IV is the least compelling part of the poem, despite its connections with the brilliant Book III. It is the Legend of Friendship, and attempts to express the Renaissance mystique of friendship; the simplest expression Spenser gives it occurs in the opening stanza of canto ix:

Hard is the doubt, and difficult to deeme,
    When all three kinds of love together meet,
    And do dispart> the heart with powre extreme,   *divide*
    Whether> shall weigh the balance down; to weet   *which*
    The deare affection unto kindred sweet,
    Or raging fire of love to woman kind,
    Or zeale of friends combynd with vertues meet.
    But of them all the band> of vertuous mind   *bond*
Me seemes the gentle hart should most assurèd bind.

For naturall affection soone doth cesse,
  And quenchèd is with *Cupids* greater flame:
  But faithfull friendship doth them both suppresse,
  And them with maystring discipline doth tame,
  Through thoughts aspyring to eternall fame.
  For as the soule doth rule the earthly masse,
  And all the service of the bodie frame,
  So love of soule doth love of bodie passe,
No lesse than perfect gold surmounts the meanest brasse.

This is the kind of friendship that makes Shakespeare's Valentine, in *Two Gentlemen of Verona,* offer to give up his girl Silvia to his friend Proteus, who has just tried to rape her; except that Spenser always insists that true friendship is between virtuous equals.

The nominal heroes of this book are Cambel and Triamond, borrowed from Chaucer's unfinished Squire's Tale; but Spenser diversifies that story in order to provide many different examples of love and friendship. Many of these are carried over from III: the False Florimell, Florimell and Marinell, Britomart and Artegall, Timias and Belphoebe, Scudamour and Amoret. Guyon and Braggadocchio, Satyrane and Archimago also return. The cancellation of the original conclusion made it possible to continue Scudamour's adventures, and to show him in the House of Care, a famous passage which is given below.

In the Proem to IV, which serves as an introduction to the second installment of the whole poem, Books IV through VI, Spenser refers to the censure of Lord Burleigh, Elizabeth's Lord Chancellor and the most powerful man in England, and offers a spirited defense, saying that his work is not for such readers but for those who, like the Queen, understand love, and the utility of examples which show what is right by exposing what is wrong.

The Fourth Booke of The Faerie Queene

    Contayning, The Legend of Cambel and Triamond,
    or *Of Friendship*

1   The rugged forhead that with grave foresight
    Welds⟩ kingdomes causes, and affaires of state,°   *wields*
    My looser rimes (I wote) doth sharply wite,⟩   *blame*
    For praising love, as I have done of late,
    And magnifying⟩ lovers deare debate;   *glorifying*
    By which fraile youth is oft to follie led,
    Through false allurement of that pleasing baite,
    That better were in vertues disciplèd,
  Then with vaine poemes weeds⟩ to have their fancies fed.   *blooms*

The rugged . . . state William Cecil, Lord Burleigh

2   Such ones ill judge of love, that cannot love,
    Ne in their frosen hearts feele kindly゛ flame: *natural*
    For thy゛ they ought not thing unkowne reprove,   *therefore*
    Ne naturall affection faultlesse blame,
    For fault of few that have abusd the same.
    For it of honor and all vertue is
    The roote, and brings forth glorious flowres of fame,
    That crowne true lovers with immortall blis,
The meed of them that love, and do not live amisse.

3   Which who so list looke backe to former ages,
    And call to count the things that then were donne,
    Shall find, that all the workes of those wise sages,
    And brave exploits which great Heroès wonne,
    In love were either ended or begunne:
    Witnesse the father of Philosophie,
    Which to his *Critias,*° shaded oft from sunne,
    Of love full manie lessons did apply,
The which these Stoicke censours cannot well deny.

4   To such therefore I do not sing at all,
    But to that sacred Saint my soveraigne Queene,
    In whose chast breast all bountie naturall,
    And treasures of true love enlockèd beene,
    Bove all her sexe that ever yet was seene;
    To her I sing of love, that loveth best,
    And best is lov'd of all alive I weene:
    To her this song most fitly is addrest,
The Queene of love, and Prince of peace from heaven blest.

5   Which that she may the better deigne to heare,
    Do thou dred infant, *Venus* dearling dove,°
    From her high spirit chase imperious feare,
    And use of awfull Majestie remove:
    In sted thereof with drops of melting love,
    Deawd with ambrosiall kisses, by thee gotten
    From thy sweete smyling mother from above,
    Sprinckle her heart, and haughtie courage゛ soften,   *spirit*
That she may hearke to love, and reade this lesson often.

[In this Book Atè (Strife) and Concord contend for mastery. Atè fills Scudamour with rage and misery by persuading him that Britomart has stolen the
affections of Amoret. It is in this frame of mind that Scudamour enters the
House of Care. Care is a blacksmith who makes instruments to torment the
unquiet soul.]

Critias meaning Crito; see II.vii.52n   **dove** Cupid

From Canto v

32 So as they travellèd, the drouping night
    Covered with cloudie storme and bitter showre,
    That dreadfull seem'd to every living wight,
    Upon them fell, before her timely howre;
    That forcèd them to seeke some covert bowre,
    Where they might hide their heads in quiet rest,
    And shrowd their persons from that stormie stowre.
  Not farre away, not meete for any guest
They spide a little cottage, like some poore mans nest.

33 Under a steepe hilles side it placèd was,
    There where the mouldred earth had cav'd the banke;
    And fast beside a little brooke did pas
    Of muddie water, that like puddle stanke,
    By which few crookèd sallowes‸ grew in ranke: *willows*
    Whereto approaching nigh, they heard the sound
    Of many yron hammers beating ranke,‸   *violently*
  And answering their wearie turnes around,
That seemèd some blacksmith dwelt in that desert ground.

34 There entring in, they found the goodman selfe,
    Full busily unto his worke ybent;
    Who was to weet a wretched wearish‸ elfe,   *wizened*
    With hollow eyes and rawbone cheekes forspent,
    As if he had in prison long bene pent:
    Full blacke and griesly did his face appeare,
    Besmeard with smoke that nigh his eye-sight blent;‸   *blinded*
  With rugged beard, and hoarie shaggèd heare,
The which he never wont to combe, or comely sheare.

35 Rude was his garment, and to rags all rent,
    Ne better had he, ne for better cared:
    With blistred hands emongst the cinders brent,
    And fingers filthie, with long nayles unpared,
    Right fit to rend the food, on which he fared.
    His name was *Care;* a blacksmith by his trade,
    That neither day nor night from working spared,
  But to small purpose yron wedges made;
Those be unquiet thoughts, that carefull minds invade.

36 In which his worke he had sixe servants prest,
    About the Andvile standing evermore,
    With huge great hammers, that did never rest
    From heaping stroakes, which thereon sousèd‸ sore: *struck*
    All sixe strong groomes, but one then other more;
    For by degrees they all were disagreed;
    So likewise did the hammers which they bore,
  Like belles in greatnesse orderly succeed,
That he which was the last, the first did farre exceede.

37   He like a monstrous Gyant seem'd in sight,
  Farre passing *Bronteus*, or *Pyracmon*° great,
  The which in *Lipari*° doe day and night
  Frame thunderbolts for *Joves* avengefull threate.
  So dreadfully he did the andvile beat,
  That seem'd to dust he shortly would it drive:
  So huge his hammer and so fierce his heat,
  That seem'd a rocke of Diamond it could rive,
 And rend a sunder quite, if he thereto list strive.

38   Sir *Scudamour* there entring, much admired
  The manner of their worke and wearie paine;
  And having long beheld, at last enquired
  The cause and end thereof: but all in vaine;
  For they for nought would from their worke refraine,
  Ne let his speeches come unto their eare.
  And eke the breathfull bellowes blew amaine,°   *powerfully*
  Like to the Northren winde, that° none could heare: *so that*
 Those *Pensifenesse* did move; and *Sighes* the bellows weare.

39   Which when that warriour saw, he said no more,
  But in his armour layd him downe to rest:
  To rest he layd him downe upon the flore,
  (Whylome° for ventrous Knights the bedding best)   *formerly*
  And thought his wearie limbs to have redrest.
  And that old agèd Dame,° his faithfull Squire,
  Her feeble joynts layd eke a downe to rest;
  That needed much her weake age to desire,
 After so long a travell, which them both did tire.

40   There lay Sir *Scudamour* long while expecting,
  When gentle sleepe his heavie eyes would close;
  Oft chaunging sides, and oft new place electing,
  Where better seem'd he mote himselfe repose;
  And oft in wrath he thence againe uprose;
  And oft in wrath he layd him downe againe.
  But wheresoever he did himselfe dispose,
  He by no meanes could wishèd ease obtaine:
 So every place seem'd painefull, and ech changing vaine.

41   And evermore, when he to sleepe did thinke,
  The hammers sound his senses did molest;
  And evermore, when he began to winke,
  The bellowes noyse disturb'd his quiet rest,
  Ne suffred sleepe to settle in his brest.
  And all the night the dogs did barke and howle
  About the house, at sent° of stranger guest: *scent*

Bronteus . . . Pyracmon two of the Cyclops who forged the thunderbolts of Zeus **Lipari** Lipara, one of the Lipari islands off Sicily **agèd Dame** Glaucè, serving as squire to Scudamour

And now the crowing Cocke, and now the Owle
Lowde shriking him afflicted to the very sowle.

42 And if by fortune any litle nap
    Upon his heavie eye-lids chaunst to fall,
    Eftsoones one of those villeins him did rap
    Upon his headpeece with his yron mall;   *mallet*
    That he was soone awakèd therewithall,
    And lightly started up as one affrayd;
    Or as if one him suddenly did call.
    So oftentimes he out of sleepe abrayd,   *awoke*
And then lay musing long, on that him ill apayd.   *pleased*

43 So long he muzèd, and so long he lay,
    That at the last his wearie sprite opprest
    With fleshly weaknesse, which no creature may
    Long time resist, gave place to kindly rest,
    That all his senses did full soone arrest:
    Yet in his soundest sleepe, his dayly feare
    His ydle braine gan busily molest,
    And made him dreame those two° disloyall were:
The things that day most minds, at night doe most appeare.

44 With that, the wicked carle the maister Smith
    A paire of redwhot yron tongs did take
    Out of the burning cinders, and therewith
    Under his side him nipt, that forst to wake,
    He felt his hart for very paine to quake,
    And started up avengèd for to be
    On him, the which his quiet slomber brake:
    Yet looking round about him none could see;
Yet did the smart remaine, though he himselfe did flee.

45 In such disquiet and hartfretting payne,
    He all that night, that too long night did passe.
    And now the day out of the Ocean mayne
    Began to peepe above this earthly masse,
    With pearly dew sprinkling the morning grasse:
    Then up he rose like heavie lumpe of lead,
    That in his face, as in a looking glasse,
    The signes of anguish one mote plainely read,
And ghesse the man to be dismayd with gealous dread.

46 Unto his lofty steede he clombe anone,
    And forth upon his former voiage fared,
    And with him eke that agèd Squire attone;   *together*
    Who whatsoever perill was prepared,
    Both equall paines and equall perill shared:
    The end whereof and daungerous event

those two Britomart and Amoret

Shall for another canticle be spared.
But here my wearie teeme nigh over spent
Shall breath it selfe awhile, after so long a went.°   *journey*

[In the sixth canto Britomart and Artegall fall in love; upon their union depend
not only the future happiness of Britain but much of Spenser's Fifth Book. In vii
Belphoebe saves Amoret from the attentions of a wicked "salvage" man (some
are good, some bad as Caliban). He represents the intrusion of bestial lust into
the world of love, a fallen world in which virtuous friendship is nobler than the
love of women. Yet the core of the Book is really not any example of male friendship but Scudamour's account, in canto x, of his first wooing and winning of
Amoret. He forces access into the Temple of Venus, past Doubt, Delay, and
Danger, who make for the unapproachability of virtuous women, and comes
upon a paradise of pleasure and innocent friendship. In the Temple itself,
Concord reconciles the passions of love and hate, as she holds together the
conflicting elements in the frame of the world. The goddess now appears as
Hermaphrodite, symbolizing the union of opposites in the love of man and
woman (Spenser had used the idea figuratively in the original conclusion to
Book III). The prayer of the lover to Venus is based on the great invocation
to Venus of Lucretius in his *De Rerum Natura:* "alma Venus, Venus genetrix,"
giver of pleasure and fertility throughout the creation. Scudamour echoes him.
In the lap of Womanhood, flanked by appropriate female qualities, he sees
Amoret; the goddess smiles on him and he leads his woman away. This is an
allegory of proper courtship; a little forcefulness is required to break down
the good customary prohibitions. It is also an allegory of love as Spenser understands it, for instance in *Epithalamion* and Book III of *The Faerie Queene.* It
is a power transcending physical relations, being the source of order and fertility in all things. As it affects men and women it is a source of delight, but
needs checks, and is subject to being overbalanced by sexual passion; this
episode is a flashback, and precedes the disasters of Book III, in which Scudamour is parted from Amoret by Busirane, who stands for the unregulated
desire that came between them on their wedding night. At the end of Book
IV he still hasn't got her back.]

From Canto x
23   In such luxurious plentie of all pleasure,
       It seem'd a second paradise° to ghesse,
       So lavishly enricht with natures threasure,
       That if the happie soules, which doe possesse
       Th'Elysian fields, and live in lasting blesse,
       Should happen this with living eye to see,
       They soone would loath their lesser happinesse,
       And wish to life return'd againe to bee,
       That in this joyous place they mote have joyance free.

24   Fresh shadowes, fit to shroud from sunny ray;
       Faire lawnds, to take the sunne in season dew;

second paradise We have now seen several such
paradises; note how their purport changes with
the context, just as does the significance of Cupid
and Venus.

Sweet springs, in which a thousand Nymphs did play;
Soft rombling brookes, that gentle slomber drew;
High rearèd mounts, the lands about to vew;
Low looking dales, disloignd° from common gaze;   *distant*
Delightfull bowres, to solace lovers trew;
False Labyrinthes, fond runners eyes to daze;
All which by nature made did nature selfe amaze.

25   And all without were walkes and alleyes dight°   *adorned*
With divers trees, enrang'd in even rankes;
And here and there were pleasant arbors pight.°   *placed*
And shadie seates, and sundry flowring bankes,
To sit and rest the walkers wearie shankes,
And therein thousand payres of lovers walkt,
Praysing their god, and yeelding him great thankes,
Ne ever ought but of their true loves talkt,
Ne ever for rebuke or blame of any balkt.°   *stopped*

26   All these together by themselves did sport
Their spotlesse pleasures, and sweet loves content.
But farre away from these, another sort
Of lovers linckèd in true harts consent;
Which lovèd not as these, for like intent,
But on chast vertue grounded their desire,
Farre from all fraud, or faynèd blandishment;
Which in their spirits kindling zealous fire,
Brave thoughts and noble deeds did evermore aspire.

27   Such were great *Hercules,* and *Hylas*° deare;
Trew *Jonathan,* and *David*° trustie tryde;
Stout *Theseus,* and *Pirithous*° his feare;°   *companion*
Pylades and *Orestes*° by his syde;
Myld *Titus* and *Gesippus*° without pryde;
Damon and *Pythias* whom death could not sever:°
All these and all that ever had bene tyde
In bands of friendship, there did live for ever,
Whose lives although decay'd, yet loves decayèd never.

28   Which when as I, that never tasted blis,
Nor happie howre, beheld with gazefull eye,
I thought there was none other heaven then this;
And gan their endlesse happinesse envye,
That being free from feare and gealosye,

Hylas boy lover of Hercules; he was either drowned or carried away by nymphs
Jonathan, and David I Samuel 18
Theseus, and Pirithous a friendship cemented by war against the Centaurs and by the attempted rape of Proserpina from the underworld
Pylades and Orestes the classical type of friendship; Pylades helped Orestes revenge his father

Agamemnon by killing his mother Clytemnestra and her lover Aegisthus
Titus and Gesippus The story of Titus and Giseppus is in the Tenth Day of Boccaccio's *Decameron;* Titus accused himself of a murder for which Giseppus had accepted responsibility.
Damon . . . sever Damon stood as hostage for his friend Pythias when the latter was under sentence of death.

Might frankely there their loves desire possesse;
    Whilest I through paines and perlous jeopardie,
    Was forst to seeke my lifes deare patronesse:
Much dearer be the things, which come through hard distresse.

29   Yet all those sights, and all that else I saw,
    Might not my steps withhold, but that forthright
    Unto that purposd place I did me draw,
    Where as my love was lodgèd day and night:
    The temple of great *Venus,* that is hight
    The Queene of beautie, and of love the mother,
    There worshippèd of every living wight;
    Whose goodly workmanship farre past all other
That ever were on earth, all were they° set together.   *as if they were*

30   Not that same famous Temple of *Diane,*°
    Whose hight all *Ephesus* did oversee,
    And which all *Asia* sought with vowes prophane,
    One of the worlds seven wonders sayd to bee,
    Might match with this by many a degree:
    Nor that, which that wise King of *Jurie* framed,
    With endlesse cost, to be th'Almighties see;°   *abode*
    Nor all that else through all the world is named
To all the heathen Gods, might like to this be clamed.

31   I much admyring that so goodly frame,
    Unto the porch approcht, which open stood;
    But therein sate an amiable Dame,
    That seem'd to be of very sober mood,
    And in her semblant° shewed great womanhood: *appearance*
    Strange was her tyre;° for on her head a crowne   *headdress*
    She wore much like unto a Danisk hood,°
    Poudred with pearle and stone, and all her gowne
Enwoven was with gold, that raught° full low a downe.   *reached*

32   On either side of her, two young men stood,
    Both strongly arm'd, as fearing one another;
    Yet were they brethren both of halfe the blood,
    Begotten by two fathers of one mother,
    Though of contrarie natures each to other:
    The one of them hight *Love,* the other *Hate,*
    Hate was the elder, *Love* the younger brother;
    Yet was the younger stronger in his state
Then th'elder, and him maystred still in all debate.

33   Nathlesse that Dame so well them tempred both,
    That she them forcèd hand to joyne in hand,
    Albe that *Hatred* was thereto full loth,

Temple of Diane Acts 19   **Danisk hood** Danish headdress, perhaps distinctive in shape

And turn'd his face away, as he did stand,
Unwilling to behold that lovely band.°   *bond*
Yet she was of such grace and vertuous might,
That her commaundment he could not withstand,
But bit his lip for felonous despight,
And gnasht his yron tuskes at that displeasing sight.

34   Concord° she cleepèd° was in common reed,°   *called / speech*
      Mother of blessèd *Peace,* and *Friendship* trew;
      They both her twins, both borne of heavenly seed,
      And she her selfe likewise divinely grew;
      The which right well her workes divine did shew:
      For strength, and wealth, and happinesse she lends,
      And strife, and warre, and anger does subdew:
      Of litle much, of foes she maketh frends,
And to afflicted minds sweet rest and quiet sends.

35   By her the heaven is in his course contained,
      And all the world in state unmovèd stands,
      As their Almightie maker first ordained.
      And bound them with inviolable bands;
      Else would the waters overflow the lands,
      And fire devoure the ayre, and hell them quight,°   *revenge, pay back*
      But that she holds them with her blessèd hands.
      She is the nourse of pleasure and delight,
And unto *Venus* grace the gate doth open right.°

36   By her I entring halfe dismayèd was,
      But she in gentle wise me entertayned,
      And twixt her selfe and *Love* did let me pas;
      But *Hatred* would my entrance have restrayned,
      And with his club me threatned to have brayned,
      Had not the Ladie with her powrefull speach
      Him from his wicked will uneath° refrayned;   *with difficulty*
      And th'other eke his malice did empeach,°   *hinder*
Till I was throughly past the perill of his reach.

37   Into the inmost Temple thus I came,
      Which fuming all with frankensence I found,
      And odours rising from the altars flame,
      Upon an hundred marble pillors round
      The roofe up high was rearèd from the ground,
      All deckt with crownes, and chaynes, and girlands gay,
      And thousand pretious gifts worth many a pound,
      The which sad lovers for their vowes did pay;
And all the ground was strow'd with flowres, as fresh as May.

Concord Placing her between love and hate as mediator, Spenser is remembering the ancient principle that concord issues from the resolution of discords; it is stated in Boethius, *The Consolation of Philosophy* II.8, which he knew, and also by Chaucer in *Troilus and Criseyde* III.1751 ff., and The Knight's Tale, ll. 2990 ff. Spenser puts it into the *Hymne of Heavenly Love,* ll. 76 ff.

unto . . . right without the resolution of the discord of opposites there can be no love between men and women

38   An hundred Altars round about were set,
     All flaming with their sacrifices fire,
     That with the steme thereof the Temple swet,’   *sweated*
     Which rould in clouds to heaven did aspire,
     And in them bore true lovers vowes entire:
     And eke an hundred brasen caudrons bright,
     To bath in joy and amorous desire,
     Every of which was to a damzell hight;’   *assigned*
For all the Priests were damzels, in soft linnen dight.

39   Right in the midst the Goddesse selfe did stand
     Upon an altar of some costly masse,
     Whose substance was ueatli’ to understand: *difficult*
     For neither pretious stone, nor durefull brasse,
     Nor shining gold, nor mouldring clay it was;
     But much more rare and pretious to esteem,
     Pure in aspect, and like to christall glasse,
     Yet glasse was not, if one did rightly deeme,
But being faire and brickle,’ likest glasse did seeme.   *brittle*

40   But it in shape and beautie did excell
     All other Idoles, which the heathen adore,
     Farre passing that, which by surpassing skill
     Phidias did make in *Paphos* Isle° of yore,
     With which that wretched Greeke, that life forlore,’   *abandoned*
     Did fall in love: yet this much fairer shined,
     But covered with a slender veile afore;
     And both her feete and legs together twyned
Were with a snake, whose head and tail were fast combyned.

41   The cause why she was covered with a vele,
     Was hard to know, for that her Priests the same
     From peoples knowledge labour'd to concele.
     But sooth it was not sure for womanish shame,
     Nor any blemish, which the worke mote blame;’   *disfigure*
     But for, they say, she hath both kinds in one,
     Both male and female, both under one name:°
     She syre and mother is her selfe alone,
Begets and eke conceives, ne needeth other none.

42   And all about her necke and shoulders flew
     A flocke of litle loves, and sports, and joyes,
     With nimble wings of gold and purple hew;
     Whose shapes seem'd not like to terrestriall boyes,
     But like to Angels playing heavenly toyes;’   *games*

---

that . . . Isle the statue made by Praxiteles at
Cnidos, which first showed Venus naked; a
youth fell in love with it
Both . . . name The name is Hermaphroditus,
son of Hermes and Aphrodite, who was made
one body with the nymph Salmacis in love.
The Venus of this name sums up the male-
female generative process over which the goddess traditionally presides; as Spenser puts it
in *Colin Clout,* ll. 801–2: "For Venus selfe
doth solely couples seem, / Both male and
female through commixture join'd." Hairy Ven-
uses in women's dress are recorded in antiquity.

The whilest their eldest brother was away,
Cupid their eldest brother; he enjoyes
The wide kingdome of love with Lordly sway,
And to his law compels all creatures to obay.

43 And all about her altar scattered lay
    Great sorts° of lovers piteously complayning,   *groups*
    Some of their losse, some of their loves delay,
    Some of their pride, some paragons disdayning,
    Some fearing fraud, some fraudulently fayning,
    As every one had cause of good or ill.
    Amongst the rest some one through loves constrayning,
    Tormented sore, could not containe it still,
But thus brake forth, that all the temple it did fill.

44 Great *Venus*, Queene of beautie and of grace,
    The joy of Gods and men, that under skie
    Doest fayrest shine, and most adorne thy place,
    That with thy smyling looke doest pacifie
    The raging seas, and makst the stormes to flie;
    Thee goddesse, thee the winds, the clouds doe feare,
    And when thou spredst thy mantle forth on hie,
    The waters play and pleasant lands appeare,
And heavens laugh, and al the world shews joyous cheare.

45 Then doth the dædale° earth throw forth to thee
    Out of her fruitfull lap aboundant flowres,
    And then all living wights, soone as they see
    The spring breake forth out of his lusty bowres,
    They all doe learne to play the Paramours;
    First doe the merry birds, thy prety pages
    Privily prickèd with thy lustfull powres,
    Chirpe loud to thee out of their leavy cages,
And thee their mother call to coole their kindly rages.

46 Then doe the salvage beasts begin to play
    Their pleasant friskes, and loath their wonted food;
    The Lyons rore, the Tygres loudly bray,
    The raging Buls rebellow through the wood,
    And breaking forth, dare tempt the deepest flood,
    To come where thou doest draw them with desire:
    So all things else, that nourish vitall blood,
    Soone as with fury thou doest them inspire,
In generation seeke to quench their inward fire.

47 So all the world by thee at first was made,
    And dayly yet thou doest the same repayre:

dædale intricately constructed, as if by Daedalus,
the great artificer who built the labyrinth at
Cnossos

Ne ought on earth that merry is and glad,
Ne ought on earth that lovely is and fayre,
But thou the same for pleasure didst prepayre.
Thou art the root of all that joyous is,
Great God of men and women, queene of th'ayre,
Mother of laughter, and welspring of blisse,
O graunt that of my love at last I may not misse.

48 So did he say: but I with murmure soft,
That none might heare the sorrow of my hart,
Yet inly groning deepe and sighing oft,
Besought her to graunt ease unto my smart,
And to my wound her gratious help impart.
Whilest thus I spake, behold with happy eye
I spyde, where at the Idoles feet apart
A bevie of fayre damzels close did lye,
Wayting when as the Antheme should° be sung on hye.

49 The first of them did seeme of ryper yeares,
And graver countenance then all the rest;
Yet all the rest were eke her equall peares,
Yet unto her obayèd all the best.
Her name was *Womanhood*, that she exprest
By her sad⸀ semblant⸀ and demeanure wyse: *serious / appearance*
For stedfast still her eyes did fixèd rest,
Ne rov'd at randon after gazers guyse,⸀   *fashion*
Whose luring baytes oftimes doe heedlesse harts entyse.

50 And next to her sate goodly *Shamefastnesse*,
Ne ever durst her eyes from ground upreare,
Ne never once did looke up from her desse,⸀   *dais*
As if some blame of evill she did feare,
That in her cheekes made roses oft appeare.
And her against sweet *Cherefulnesse* was placed,
Whose eyes like twinkling stars in evening cleare,
Were deckt with smyles, that all sad humors chaced,
And darted forth delights, the which her goodly graced.

51 And next to her sate sober *Modestie*,
Holding her hand upon her gentle hart;
And her against sate comely *Curtesie*,
That unto every person knew her part;
And her before was seated overthwart⸀   *opposite*
Soft *Silence*, and submisse⸀ *Obedience*,   *submissive*
Both linckt together never to dispart,⸀   *part*
Both gifts of God not gotten but from thence,
Both girlonds° of his Saints against their foes offence.

Wayting . . . should waiting for the anthem to   girlonds adornments (which protect them from
be   foes)

52   Thus sate they all a round in seemely rate:°   *manner*
     And in the midst of them a goodly mayd,
     Even in the lap of *Womanhood* there sate,
     The which was all in lilly white arayd,
     With silver streames amongst the linnen stray'd;
     Like to the Morne, when first her shyning face
     Hath to the gloomy world it selfe bewray'd,
     That same was fayrest *Amoret* in place,
Shyning with beauties light, and heavenly vertues grace.

53   Whom soone as I beheld, my hart gan throb,
     And wade in doubt, what best were to be donne:
     For sacrilege me seem'd the Church to rob,
     And folly seem'd to leave the thing undonne,
     Which with so strong attempt I had begonne.
     Tho° shaking off all doubt and shamefast feare,   *then*
     Which Ladies love I heard had never wonne
Mongst men of worth, I to her steppèd neare,
And by the lilly hand her labour'd up to reare.

54   Thereat that formost matrone me did blame,
     And sharpe rebuke, for being over bold;
     Saying it was to Knight unseemely shame,
     Upon a recluse° Virgin to lay hold,   *in seclusion*
     That unto *Venus* services were sold.°   *given*
     To whom I thus, Nay but it fitteth best,
     For *Cupids* man with *Venus* mayd to hold,
     For ill your goddesse services are drest
By virgins, and her sacrifices let to rest.

55   With that my shield I forth to her did show,
     Which all that while I closely had conceld;
     On which when *Cupid* with his killing bow
     And cruell shafts emblazond she beheld,
     At sight thereof she was with terror queld,
     And said no more: but I which all that while
     The pledge of faith, her hand engagèd held,
     Like warie Hynd° within the weedie soyle,   *laborer*
For no intreatie would forgoe so glorious spoyle.

56   And evermore upon the Goddesse face
     Mine eye was fixt, for feare of her offence,
     Whom when I saw with amiable grace
     To laugh at me, and favour my pretence,°   *claim*
     I was emboldned with more confidence,
     And nought for nicenesse° nor for envy sparing,   *scrupulousness*
     In presence of them all forth led her thence,
     All looking on, and like astonisht staring,
Yet to lay hand on her, not one of all them daring.

57 She often prayd, and often me besought,
Sometime with tender teares to let her goe,
Sometime with witching smyles: but yet for nought,
That ever she to me could say or doe,
Could she her wishèd freedome fro me wooe;
But forth I led her through the Temple gate,
By which I hardly past with much adoe:
But that same Ladie which me friended late
In entrance, did me also friend in my retrate.

58 No lesse did *Daunger* threaten me with dread,
When as he saw me, maugre⟩ all his powre,   *despite*
That glorious spoyle of beautie with me lead,
Then *Cerberus*, when *Orpheus* did recoure⟩   *recover*
His Leman° from the Stygian Princes boure.
But evermore my shield did me defend,
Against the storme of every dreadfull stoure⟩:   *conflict*
Thus safely with my love I thence did wend.
So ended he his tale, where I this Canto end.

1596

[The main business of the concluding cantos is to bring together Florimell and Marinell. Canto xi is a big set-piece, which Spenser had possibly had for some years in a drawer, describing the marriage of the rivers Thames and Medway. It fits, in general, the theme of concord resolving discord, but emphasizes the loose-knit quality of IV; the union of Florimell and Marinell (of sea and land) also fits the theme, but neither the characters nor the theme have the centrality and the climactic quality one finds at the conclusion of the earlier books. However, Alastair Fowler, in his study of the numerological patterns of *The Faerie Queene* (*Spenser and the Numbers of Time*, 1964), claims that on the basis of such patterns he sees the fourth "as in many ways the most unified of all the books of *The Faerie Queene*."]

Book V

In this Book Spenser reverts to a scheme more like that of I and II: in fact his examination of the nature of Justice may be his most schematic. He also crowds in allusions to contemporary affairs. He opens with a proem lamenting the changes that have come over the world since the departure of Astraea, goddess of Justice, at the end of the Golden Age. The present age is of stone. Not only human affairs, but even the movements of the planets, have grown very irregular. Justice now comes from princes, for example from Elizabeth, the returned Astraea (Virgil, in his most famous prophetic eclogue, the fourth, had predicted this: "iam redit et Virgo"—and now Astraea returns; and a mystique of Astraeanism grew up around the Queen).

Leman Eurydice, temporarily brought back from
the underworld by the music of her husband
Orpheus

The Fifth Booke of The Faerie Queene

Contayning, The Legend of Artegall, *or Of Justice*

1 So oft as I with state of present time,
    The image of the antique world compare,
    When as mans age was in his freshest prime,
    And the first blossome of faire vertue bare,
    Such oddes I finde twixt those, and these which are,
    As that, through long continuance of his course,
    Me seemes the world is runne quite out of square,
    From the first point of his appointed sourse,
  And being once amisse growes daily wourse and wourse.

2 For from the golden age, that first was named,
    It's now at earst° become a stonie one;   *lately*
    And men themselves, the which at first were framed
    Of earthly mould, and form'd of flesh and bone,
    Are now transformèd into hardest stone:
    Such as behind their backs (so backward bred)
    Were throwne by *Pyrrha* and *Deucalione:*°
    And if then those may any worse be red,°   *called*
  They into that ere long will be degenderèd.

3 Let none then blame me, if in discipline
    Of vertue and of civill uses lore,
    I doe not forme them to the common line
    Of present dayes, which are corrupted sore,
    But to the antique use, which was of yore,
    When good was onely for it selfe desyrèd,
    And all men sought their owne, and none no more;
    When Justice was not for most meed outhyrèd,
  But simple Truth did rayne, and was of all admyrèd.

4 For that which all men then did vertue call,
    Is now cald vice; and that which vice was hight,
    Is now hight vertue, and so us'd of all:
    Right now is wrong, and wrong that was is right,
    As all things else in time are chaungèd quight.
    Ne wonder; for the heavens revolution
    Is wandred farre from where it first was pight,°   *placed*
    And so doe make contrarie constitution
  Of all this lower world, toward his dissolution.

5 For who so list into the heavens looke,
    And search the courses of the rowling spheares,
    Shall find that from the point, where they first tooke

Pyrrha . . . Deucalione They escaped like Noah and his family from a general deluge; later an oracle told them to throw stones over their shoulders, from which grew men and woman to restock the world.

Their setting forth, in these few thousand yeares
They all are wandred much;° that plaine appeares.
For that same golden fleecy Ram, which bore
Phrixus and *Helle*° from their stepdames feares,
Hath now forgot, where he was plast of yore,
And shouldred hath the Bull, which fayre *Europa*° bore.

6   And eke the Bull hath with his bow-bent horne
        So hardly butted those two twinnes of *Jove,*°
        That they have crusht the Crab,° and quite him borne
        Into the great *Nemæan* lions grove.°
        So now all range, and doe at randon rove
        Out of their proper places farre away,
        And all this world with them amisse doe move,
        And all his creatures from their course astray,
    Till they arrive at their last ruinous decay.

7   Ne is that same great glorious lampe of light,
        That doth enlumine all these lesser fyres,°
        In better case, ne keepes his course more right,
        But is miscaried with the other Spheres.
        For since the term of fourteene hundred yeres,
        That learnèd *Ptolomæe* his hight did take,°
        He is declynèd from that marke of theirs,
        Nigh thirtie minutes to the Southerne lake;
    That makes me feare in time he will us quite forsake.

8   And if to those Ægyptian wisards old,
        Which in Star-read⸗ were wont have best insight,   *star-lore*
        Faith may be given, it is by them told,
        That since the time they first tooke the Sunnes hight,
        Foure times his place he shifted hath in sight,
        And twice hath risen, where he now doth West,
        And wested twice, where he ought rise aright.°
        But most is *Mars* amisse of all the rest,
    And next to him old *Saturne,*° that was wont be best.

---

wandred much Spenser bases his lament for the decay of the world on the apparent disorder of the heavens. Ptolemy of Alexandria, whose astronomy with modifications survived until Copernicus, recorded the obliquity of the ecliptic (the apparent course of the sun through the sky relative to the equator) and between 130 A.D. and Spenser's time it had decreased somewhat. Consequently it was possible to say that the sun, Mars, and Saturn got progressively out of line as time went by, and that the signs of the zodiac, through which sun and planets pass, were jostling one another, so that the heavens as well as the earth were in decay. Further speculation of the kind occurs in VII.vi.50 ff., on which see note.
Phrixus and Helle Brother and sister who, fleeing the cruelty of Ino their stepmother, escaped on a golden-fleeced flying ram—Aries, of the zodiac; all the zodiacal signs were attached to myths.

Europa carried off by Jupiter in the form of a bull—the sign of Taurus
twinnes of Jove Castor and Pollux, sons of Jove by Leda—the sign of Gemini
Crab sign of Cancer
Nemæan lions grove sign of Leo; killing the Nemaean lion was one of the labors of Hercules
enlumine . . . fyres the stars were thought to store light from the sun
his . . . take determined the obliquity of the sun's ecliptic
And . . . aright These impossible phenomena were alleged by Herodotus (b. 404 B.C.) in his *History* II.142.
Mars . . . Saturne They have the most eccentric planetary orbits except for Mercury: see VII. vii.51n; and in Spenser's time it was assumed these orbits must normally be circular (elliptical orbits were proved by Kepler in 1609).

9   For during *Saturnes* ancient raigne° it's sayd,
    That all the world with goodnesse did abound:
    All lovèd vertue, no man was affrayd
    Of force, ne fraud in wight was to be found:
    No warre was knowne, no dreadfull trompets sound,
    Peace universall rayn'd mongst men and beasts,
    And all things freely grew out of the ground:
    Justice sate high ador'd with solemne feasts,
And to all people did divide her dred beheasts.

10   Most sacred vertue she of all the rest,
    Resembling God in his imperiall might;
    Whose soveraine powre is herein most exprest,
    That both to good and bad he dealeth right,
    And all his workes with Justice hath bedight.
    That powre he also doth to Princes lend,
    And makes them like himselfe in glorious sight,
    To sit in his owne seate, his cause to end,
And rule his people right, as he doth recommend.

11   Dread Soverayne Goddesse, that doest highest sit
    In seate of judgement, in th'Almighties stead,
    And with magnificke might and wondrous wit
    Doest to thy people righteous doome° aread,°   *judgment / deliver*
    That furthest Nations filles with awfull dread,
    Pardon the boldnesse of thy basest thrall,
    That dare discourse of so divine a read,
    As thy great justice praysèd over all:
The instrument whereof loe here thy *Artegall.*°

[The action of V is supposed to occur after the departure of Astraea; the administration of justice has fallen to such as Bacchus and Hercules and Artegall (Artegalle was a mythical British king, and the name could mean "equal to Arthur"). By his union with Britomart, Artegall would establish (as Arthur did, according to Tudor historians) a line of British kings stretching to the Tudors. He represents pure justice, enforcing the law with the aid of Talus, an iron man with a flail, a sort of one-giant police force who executes the decisions of the law. Artegall's quest is to destroy Grantorto (Great Wrong) and release Irena (meaning both "peace" and "Ireland"). On the pattern of I, the first canto contains a miniature of the quest; Sangliere is forced by justice to carry around the head of the lady he has killed. Then Artegall and Talus suppress men who buy and sell justice, and go on to deal with a mad revolutionary giant who proposes a communism of the sort then proposed by extreme Protestant sects. Artegall explains that the elimination of inequality among men would destroy order and harmony. The people are mutinous at this, but Talus

Saturnes . . . raigne The *Saturnia regna* of Virgil's fourth Eclogue constituted the Age of Gold, the first age, as described earlier by Hesiod (*Works and Days*), and by Ovid at the outset of the *Metamorphoses;* Astraea then lived on earth.
Artegall Knight of Justice and hero of Bk. V

subdues them. Here Spenser is expressing a commonplace of the age: justice depends on a recognition of the divinely ordered inequality of all creation.

The third canto interpolates the marriage, finally, of Florimell, and the exposure of Braggadocchio; Guyon at last retrieves his horse. In the fourth there are *exempla* of distributive justice (there were two branches, distributive and corrective) and in the fifth, Artegall, lapsing like Red Cross, imitates Hercules (with whom all Renaissance heroes have something in common) by falling under the spell of a woman, Radigund. The unnatural situation—for women are naturally the inferiors of men—is underlined by his effeminate dress and his woman's occupation, spinning. The only exception to the rule, that women must not be masters, is when Heaven lifts a woman "to lawfull soveraintie" (v.25)—a necessary and prudent, but also, in England, a common view. Britomart hears from Talus about Artegall's plight, and sets out to rescue him, stopping at Isis' church for spiritual support.

As in earlier books, the seventh is the core canto. The Isis allegory is brief and mysterious. Probably it deals with equity—"that part of Justice, which is Equity." In Elizabethan England the Courts of Chancery and Star Chamber were courts of equity. Chancery was "the conscience of the Queen" as represented by her Lord Chancellor; unlike the courts of justice it was not bound by precedent, and it accumulated great power. Star Chamber dealt with criminal causes such as sedition touching the monarch's security, and was also powerful. Chancery could remedy injustices that found no remedy in common law, for example, when a poor man was wronged by a nobleman who could pack the jury. Common lawyers resented the growth of the power of Chancery and associated it with growing absolutism. Star Chamber was the more hated, and Parliament abolished it in 1641.

In Spenser's myth, his Temple of Justice, he borrows from Plutarch's allegory of Isis and Osiris. Isis was identified with justice, with Astraea, and with matter (see III.vi). Osiris is justice without benefit of equity, as in the common law courts. Equity is like matter, and justice gives it mutable forms. The priests of Isis are jurists. Their abstinence from wine, described earlier as the blood of the rebel Titans, stands for their opposition to riot and recusancy. The foot on the crocodile and the wand signify the control of justice by equity, in both civil and criminal causes (Chancery and Star Chamber). The crocodile is law-without-equity, such as Artegall, incapable on his own of imperial equity, has thus far practiced.

The dream of Britomart changes her from priest to empress, robed in imperial purple, crowned with the sun, fount (if you saw it her way) of equity and ancestress of Elizabeth. The tempest and fire are rebellions against her, suppressed by the crocodile, the law of England. Perhaps the crocodile's impatience suggests the discontent of common lawyers with the prerogative or equity courts. The union of Britomart and the crocodile is that of justice and equity in the imperial person of the Queen. The priestly interpreter explains that the crocodile is Artegall, justice-without-equity; his union with equity completes the imperial justice of the Queen, and the Isis allegory allies this to the function of love in ordering and maintaining the frame of the whole world. So, at any rate, one might venture to read this passage, which is perhaps at this date the "darkest" in the whole poem, and the one about which least is certainly known.]

From Canto vii

1   Nought is on earth more sacred or divine,
       That Gods and men doe equally adore,
       Then this same vertue, that doth right define:
       For th'hevens themselves, whence mortal men implore
       Right in their wrongs, are rul'd by righteous lore
       Of highest Jove, who doth true justice deale
       To his inferiour Gods, and evermore
       Therewith containes his heavenly Commonweale:
   The skill whereof to Princes hearts he doth reveale.

2   Well therefore did the antique world invent,
       That Justice was a God of soveraine grace,
       And altars unto him, and temples lent,
       And heavenly honours in the highest place;
       Calling him great *Osyris*, of the race
       Of th'old Ægyptian Kings, that whylome˃ were;   *once*
       With faynèd colours shading˃ a true case: *painting*
       For that *Osyris*, whilest he livèd here,
   The justest man alive, and truest did appeare.°

3   His wife was *Isis*, whom they likewise made
       A Goddesse of great powre and soverainty,
       And in her person cunningly did shade
       That part of Justice, which is Equity,°
       Whereof I have to treat here presently.
       Unto whose temple when as *Britomart*
       Arrivèd, shee with great humility
       Did enter in, ne could that night depart;
   But *Talus* mote not be admitted to her part.°

4   There she receivèd was in goodly wize
       Of many Priests, which duely did attend
       Uppon the rites and daily sacrifize,
       All clad in linnen robes with silver hemd;
       And on their heads with long locks comely kemd,°
       They wore rich Mitres shapèd like the Moone,
       To shew that *Isis* doth the Moone portend;
       Like as *Osyris* signifies the Sunne.
   For that they both like race in equall justice runne.

5   The Championesse them greeting, as she could,˃   *knew how*
       Was thence by them into the Temple led;
       Whose goodly building when she did behould,

The justest . . . appeare This is the "euhemer-
ist" explanation of Osiris: that is, it treats his
myth as a version of the life of a hero.
That . . . Equity Spenser is adapting Plutarch's
myth, in his usual freely creative way, to allow
of this justice-equity interpretation.
But Talus . . . part Talus is excluded because

equity thinks it "better to reforme then to cut
off the ill."
And . . . kemd Plutarch's priests are shaven;
Spenser is borrowing from an account of the
priesthood of Rhea (vowed to chastity and
dressed as women) or some other priesthood—
why he does so is a matter for guessing.

Borne uppon stately pillours, all dispred
With shining gold, and archèd over hed,
She wondred at the workemans passing skill,
Whose like before she never saw nor red;
And thereuppon long while stood gazing still,
But thought, that she thereon could never gaze her fill.

6   Thence forth unto the Idoll they her brought,
The which was framèd all of silver fine,
So well as could with cunning hand be wrought,
And clothèd all in garments made of line,°   *linen*
Hemd all about with fringe of silver twine.
Uppon her head she wore a Crowne of gold,
To shew that she had powre in things divine;
And at her feete a Crocodile° was rold,
That with his wreathèd taile her middle did enfold.

7   One foote was set uppon the Crocodile,
And on the ground the other fast did stand,
So meaning to suppresse both forgèd guile,
And open force: and in her other hand
She stretchèd forth a long white sclender wand.
Such was the Goddesse; whom when *Britomart*
Had long beheld, her selfe uppon the land
She did prostrate, and with right humble hart,
Unto her selfe her silent prayers did impart.

8   To which the Idoll as it were inclining,
Her wand did move with amiable looke,
By outward shew her inward sence desining.°   *indicating*
Who well perceiving, how her wand she shooke,
It as a token of good fortune tooke.
By this the day with dampe was overcast,
And joyous light the house of *Jove*° forsooke: *sky*
Which when she saw, her helmet she unlaste,
And by the altars side her selfe to slumber plaste.

9   For other beds the Priests there usèd none,
But on their mother Earths deare lap did lie,
And bake° their sides uppon the cold hard stone,   *harden*
T'enure them selves to sufferaunce thereby
And proud rebellious flesh to mortify.
For by the vow of their religión
They tied were to stedfast chastity,
And continence of life, that all forgon,°   *given up*
They mote the better tend to their devotion.

10   Therefore they mote not taste of fleshly food,
Ne feed on ought, the which doth bloud containe,

Crocodile In Plutarch the crocodile stands not for Osiris but for Typhon, the irrational part of the soul; again Spenser is transforming an existing myth for his own purposes.

Ne drinke of wine, for wine they say is blood,
Even the bloud of Gyants, which were slaine,
By thundring Jove in the Phlegrean plaine: °
For which the earth° (as they the story tell)
Wroth with the Gods, which to perpetuall paine
Had damn'd her sonnes, which gainst them did rebell,
With inward grief and malice did against them swell.

11 And of their vitall bloud, the which was shed
Into her pregnant bosome, forth she brought
The fruitfull vine, whose liquor blouddy red
Having the mindes of men with fury fraught,
Mote in them stirre up old rebellious thought,
To make new warre against the Gods againe:
Such is the powre of that same fruit, that nought
The fell contagion may thereof restraine,
Ne within reasons rule, her madding mood containe.

12 There did the warlike Maide her selfe repose,
Under the wings of *Isis* all that night,
And with sweete rest her heavy eyes did close,
After that long daies toile and weary plight.
Where whilest her earthly parts with soft delight
Of sencelesse sleepe did deeply drownèd lie,
There did appeare unto her heavenly spright
A wondrous vision, which did close implie˃ *secretly sum up*
The course of all her fortune and posteritie.

13 Her seem'd, as she was doing sacrifize
To *Isis,* deckt with Mitre on her hed,
And linnen stole after those Priestès guize,˃ *fashion*
All sodainely she saw transfigurèd
Her linnen stole to robe of scarlet red,
And Moone-like Mitre to a Crowne of gold,
That even she her selfe much wonderèd
At such a chaunge, and joyed to behold
Her selfe, adorn'd with gems and jewels manifold.

14 And in the midst of her felicity,
An hideous tempest seemèd from below,
To rise through all the Temple sodainely,
That from the Altar all about did blow
The holy fire, and all the embers strow
Uppon the ground, which kindled privily,
Into outragious flames unwares did grow,

the bloud . . . plaine Throughout the Book the giants or Titans are symbols of lawlessness and rebellion. Jupiter overthrew their rebellion at Phlegra, near Naples—the many volcanic cones of the area are supposed to be the places where the Titans were thrown to earth. Plutarch says that vines sprang from their blood, so that wine is their rebellious blood.

The earth Gaea, Earth, mother of the Titans

That all the Temple put in jeopardy
Of flaming, and her selfe in great perplexity.

15   With that the Crocodile, which sleeping lay
Under the Idols feete in fearelesse bowre,
Seem'd to awake in horrible dismay,
As being troubled with that stormy stowre;   *disturbance*
And gaping greedy wide, did streight devoure
Both flames and tempest: with which growen great,
And swolne with pride of his owne peerelesse powre,
He gan to threaten her likewise to eat;
But that the Goddesse with her rod him backe did beat.

16   Tho turning all his pride to humblesse meeke,
Him selfe before her feete he lowly threw,
And gan for grace and love of her to seeke:
Which she accepting, he so neare her drew,
That of his game she soone enwombèd grew,
And forth did bring a Lion of great might;
That shortly did all other beasts subdew.
With that she wakèd, full of fearefull fright,
And doubtfully dismayd through that so uncouth sight.   *strange*

17   So thereuppon long while she musing lay,
With thousand thoughts feeding her fantasie,
Untill she spide the lampe of lightsome day,
Up-lifted in the porch of heaven hie.
Then up she rose fraught with melancholy,
And forth into the lower parts did pas;
Whereas the Priestes she found full busily
About their holy things for morrow Mas:
Whom she saluting faire, faire resaluted was.

18   But by the change of her unchearefull looke,
They might perceive, she was not well in plight;
Or that some pensivenesse to heart she tooke.
Therefore thus one of them, who seem'd in sight
To be the greatest, and the gravest wight,
To her bespake; Sir Knight it seemes to me,
That thorough evill rest of this last night,
Or ill apayd; or much dismayd ye be,   *satisfied*
That by your change of cheare is easie for to see.

19   Certes (sayd she) sith ye so well have spide
The troublous passion of my pensive mind,
I will not seeke the same from you to hide,
But will my cares unfolde, in hope to find
Your aide, to guide me out of errour blind.
Say on (quoth he) the secret of your hart:
For by the holy vow, which me doth bind,

I am adjur'd, best counsell to impart
To all, that shall require my comfort in their smart.⸾   *pain*

20 Then gan she to declare the whole discourse
    Of all that vision, which to her appeard,
    As well as to her minde it had recourse.⸾   *came back*
    All which when he unto the end had heard,
    Like to a weake faint-hearted man he fared,
    Through great astonishment of that strange sight;
    And with long locks up-standing, stifly stared
    Like one adawèd⸾ with some dreadfull spright.   *terrified*
 So fild with heavenly fury, thus he her behight.⸾   *named*

21 Magnificke Virgin, that in queint disguise
    Of British armes doest maske thy royall blood,
    So to pursue a perillous emprize,⸾   *adventure*
    How couldst thou weene, through that disguizèd hood,
    To hide thy state from being understood?
    Can from th'immortall Gods ought hidden bee?
    They doe thy linage, and thy Lordly brood;
    They doe thy sire, lamenting sore for thee;
 They doe thy love, forlorne in womens thraldome see.

22 The end whereof, and all the long event,
    They doe to thee in this same dreame discover.
    For that same Crocodile doth represent
    The righteous Knight, that is thy faithfull lover,
    Like to *Osyris* in all just endever.
    For that same Crocodile *Osyris* is,
    That under *Isis* feete doth sleepe for ever:
    To shew that clemence oft in things amis,
 Restraines those sterne behests, and cruell doomes of his.

23 That Knight shall all the troublous stormes asswage,
    And raging flames, that many foes shall reare,
    To hinder thee from the just heritage
    Of thy sires Crowne, and from thy countrey deare.
    Then shalt thou take him to thy lovèd fere,⸾   *mate*
    And joyne in equall portion of thy realme.
    And afterwards a sonne to him shalt beare,
    That Lion-like shall shew his powre extreame.
 So blesse thee God, and give thee joyance of thy dreame.

24 All which when she unto the end had heard,
    She much was easèd in her troublous thought,
    And on those Priests bestowèd rich reward:
    And royall gifts of gold and silver wrought,
    She for a present to their Goddesse brought.
    Then taking leave of them, she forward went,
    To seeke her love, where he was to be sought;

Ne rested till she came without relent
Unto the land of Amazons, as she was bent.

. . .

1596

[Fortified by the divine prediction of her powers, Britomart defeats Radigund, overthrows the unnatural "liberty of women," and frees Artegall. They go on to perform various tasks, in which the allegorical content grows more and more political; canto viii treats of the war with Spain, the Soudan being the king of Spain and his wife Adicia (Greek, injustice). There is a transparent allusion to the defeat of the Armada (1588), and other matters of contemporary history. The ninth canto concerns Lord Grey's campaign against the Irish, and, in the trial of Duessa at the court of Mercilla, an allegory of Elizabeth's condemnation of Mary Queen of Scots. Equity does not mean indiscriminate forgiveness; Mercilla, with the lion from Britomart's dream at her feet and in all the trappings of majesty, stands for equity, with the lion as her servant the common law. Arthur leaves her court to do her business in the Netherlands, against the Spanish forces of the papal antichrist, and the eleventh canto describes greater successes against them than were ever achieved in history. Arthur visits the Temple of Geryon, or injustice, which balances that of Isis, and slays the beast under its altar. Finally Artegall fulfills his quest in a welter of topical allegory, killing the tyrant Grantorto and restoring Irena to her throne—an outcome sought for but not achieved by Grey and later Essex, who went to Ireland in 1599 to implement Grey's hard-line policies (here supported) but failed. On his way home Artegall is assailed by Envy, Detraction, and the Blatant Beast— the object of the quest in Book VI—by way of allusion to the ill repute of Grey on his return from Ireland.

The intrusion of so much topical material does the Book no good in the eyes of a modern reader, and in general it is a poor relation of Book I. But the triple portraits of Isis, Mercilla, and Grantorto are finely done and related, as the best of Spenser's set pieces are, like sections of some great fresco, such as that in the Palazzo Púbblico at Urbino.]

Book VI

Book VI is the legend of Courtesy; the knight Calidore must quest after the Blatant Beast. As in I, II, and V, the knight meets his predecessor in canto i, and in this opening there is a seed of all the rest. After encountering many *exempla* of courtesy and discourtesy Calidore drops out, rather as Red Cross did, in mid-course, going into a "pastoral truancy" and neglecting his quest. But the tone of the Book is new; it lacks deep allegories like those in the "core" cantos of earlier Books. Instead Spenser includes something quite different, the scene in which the Graces appear to Colin Clout, as given below.

Spenser means more by "courtesy" than agreeableness of manner. In his Proem he distinguishes between that, and something more noble and inclusive. Courtesy is a gentleman's or nobleman's standard of conduct, the virtue which poems of this kind were meant to develop, when they undertook, as Spenser did in the Letter to Ralegh, "to fashion a gentleman or noble person in vertuous and gentle discipline." Gentle birth was a prerequisite for its possession; even courteous savages will turn out to have been well borne. Of course, the gentle can fall into discourtesy.

Courtesy, in the full sense of "civility" or "gentleness" given it by the Elizabethans, is *noblesse oblige*—what makes for decency, honor, and harmony in civil and military life. It was a fashionable subject, and courtesy books abounded, Castiglione's *The Courtier*, which Hoby translated into English, being only the most famous. Their precepts—aimed at fashioning gentlemen by example and ethical instruction—Spenser takes over in this Book, translating them into a romance narrative which, more than his others, approximates to the mood and style of Greek romance, and especially to the novella *Daphnis and Chloe* of Longus (probably 3rd century B.C.). He was also remembering the courtesy of Sidney, and the example of his prose-epic *Arcadia*. There is every reason to think that Shakespeare in turn was affected by Book VI when he wrote his final plays.

Calidore is bound to put down slander and evil speaking at its source, but also to demonstrate the gentleness of the gentleman: to be mild when that is appropriate, to champion women, show politeness to inferiors, and oppose all manifestations of discourtesy. In the course of some strange stories we see him doing this, chastising a churl for cutting off people's hair, righting the wrongs of ladies. He meets Childe Tristram, a wild young man of the forest, and at once detects his royal birth. He tends a wounded knight, and, by a knightly equivocation, saves a lady, caught in a compromising position with her lover, from her father's anger. Stumbling on a secluded pair of lovers, he manages to convince them that his intentions are innocent, and when the lady, Serena, is carried off by the Blatant Beast, he rescues her. The lover, Calepine, then takes Serena to the castle of Sir Turpine, a discourteous knight who refuses them admittance. Turpine and Calepine fight, and Calepine is saved by a courteous "salvage man," who also turns out to have been nobly born. The savage cures Calepine's wounds, but the knight gets lost, and Serena, traveling now with the savage, meets Arthur with Timias (Ralegh), who is being slandered (an allusion to Ralegh's fall into royal disfavor when he secretly married the lady-in-waiting Elizabeth Throckmorton). Timias and Serena are cured of the wound of slander by a hermit's psychological counseling; Arthur and the savage defeat Turpine and courteously allow him and his wife Blandina to live; but on a recurrence of treachery Arthur hangs Turpine by his heels from a tree. Meanwhile Timias and Serena meet Mirabella, who is undergoing a grotesque punishment for treating her lovers discourteously. Timias is captured by Disdain, and Arthur frees him. Calepine turns up just in time to save Serena from a band of cannibals who are admiring her naked body as a prelude to consuming it—this is one of the most sensual passages in the poem; the prurience of these savages represents a great enemy of courtesy.

Having neglected Calidore for a long time, Spenser now returns to him, describing his "truancy," his sojourn in the idyllic pastoral retreat of Pastorella and her (supposed) father Meliboee. The knight lives the life of pastoral content, described by Meliboee in lines (ix.20–21) that may have been in Shakespeare's mind when he conducted his lighthearted but searching examination of the pastoral conventions in *As You Like It*. Meliboee attacks gardens, emblems of the interference of art with nature, rather as Marvell's Mower does (see below). Calidore accepts the pastoral life, and when a rustic swain of Pastorella's grows jealous, he treats him with courtesy. The girl begins to love Calidore, but Spenser reminds us that his time is not his own, and that he should not be "Unmyndful of his vow and high beheast." Yet it is in the midst of this premature retirement from the life of action that he is blessed with the vision of the maidens dancing around the three Graces to the music of Colin Clout, representing Spenser himself.

The Graces usually appear in a group, usually with one facing the spectator. Here (in vi. x. 1–28) they represent the civil delight which good love spreads through human society—they are often associated with Venus—and are the opposites of the vices associated with discourtesy. The presence of Colin makes this a rare autobiographical interlude, strangely occurring at a crucial point in the Book; Spenser places his own love at the center, and shows himself singing her praises. He seems to be saying that his labors on the huge poem were interrupted by the personal matters described in the *Amoretti* and *Epithalamion*, poems which must have caused him to break off the epic in Book VI. He himself has been guilty of a "pastoral truancy," and in stanza 27 he asks pardon of the Queen for introducing this passage in praise of her "poore handmayd," for, after all, he had spent his life celebrating her greater glory. The girl is almost certainly Elizabeth Boyle, though some say she is the Rosalind of *The Shepheardes Calender* and *Colin Clout*; the tone of the poet's praise of her, mediator of delight and virtue through love, is close to that of *Epithalamion*.

From Canto x
Calidore sees the Graces daunce,
    To Colins melody:
The whiles his Pastorell is led,
    Into captivity.

1   Who now does follow the foule *Blatant Beast*,
        Whilest *Calidore* does follow that faire Mayd,
        Unmyndfull of his vow and high beheast,
        Which by the Faery Queene was on him layd,
        That he should never leave, nor be delayd
        From chacing him, till he had it attchieved?
        But now entrapt of love, which him betrayd,
        He mindeth more, how he may be relieved
    With grace from her, whose love his heart hath sore engrieved.

2   That from henceforth he meanes no more to sew˃   *follow*
        His former quest, so full of toile and paine;
        Another quest, another game in vew
        He hath, the guerdon˃ of his love to gaine: *reward*
        With whom he myndes for ever to remaine,
        And set his rest amongst the rusticke sort,
        Rather then hunt still after shadowes vaine
        Of courtly favour, fed with light report
    Of every blaste, and sayling alwaies in the port.°

3   Ne certes mote he greatly blamèd be,
        From so high step to stoupe unto so low.

sayling . . . port prevented by headwinds from
getting anywhere

For who had tasted once (as oft did he)
The happy peace, which there doth overflow,
And prov'd the perfect pleasures, which doe grow
Amongst poore hyndes,˃ in hils, in woods, in dales,   *country folk*
Would never more delight in painted show
Of such false blisse, as there is set for stales,˃   *baits*
T'entrap unwary fooles in their eternall bales.˃   *evils*

4   For what hath all that goodly glorious gaze
　　Like to one sight, which *Calidore* did vew?
　　The glaunce whereof their dimmèd eies would daze,
　　That never more they should endure the shew
　　Of that sunne-shine, that makes them looke askew.
　　Ne ought in all that world of beauties rare,
　　(Save onely *Glorianaes* heavenly hew˃   *form*
　　To which what can compare?) can it compare;°
The which as commeth now, by course I will declare.

5   One day as he did raunge the fields abroad,
　　Whilest his faire *Pastorella* was elsewhere,
　　He chaunst to come, far from all peoples troad,˃   *tread*
　　Unto a place, whose pleasaunce did appere
　　To passe all others, on the earth which were:
　　For all that ever was by natures skill
　　Devized to worke delight, was gathered there,
　　And there by her were pourèd forth at fill,
As if this to adorne, she all the rest did pill.˃   *plunder*

6   It was an hill plaste in an open plaine,
　　That round about was bordered with a wood
　　Of matchlesse hight, that seem'd th'earth to disdaine,
　　In which all trees of honour stately stood,
　　And did all winter as in sommer bud,°
　　Spredding pavilions for the birds to bowre,
　　Which in their lower braunches sung aloud;
　　And in their tops the soring hauke did towre,˃   *perch high*
Sitting like King of fowles in majesty and powre.

7   And at the foote thereof, a gentle flud
　　His silver waves did softly tumble downe,
　　Unmard with ragged mosse or filthy mud,
　　Ne mote wylde beastes, ne mote the ruder clowne
　　Thereto approach, ne filth mote therein drowne:
　　But Nymphes and Faeries by the bancks did sit,
　　In the woods shade, which did the waters crowne,
　　Keeping all noysome things away from it,
And to the waters fall tuning their accents fit.

can . . . compare can rival it   **all winter . . . bud** yet another view of the Earthly Paradise

8   And on the top thereof a spacious plaine
      Did spred it selfe, to serve to all delight,
      Either to daunce, when they to daunce would faine,
      Or else to course about their bases light;°
      Ne ought there wanted, which for pleasure might
      Desirèd be, or thence to banish bale:
      So pleasauntly the hill with equall hight,
      Did seeme to overlooke the lowly vale;
  Therefore it rightly cleepèd was mount *Acidale.*°

9   They say that *Venus,* when she did dispose
      Her selfe to pleasaunce, usèd to resort
      Unto this place, and therein to repose
      And rest her selfe, as in a gladsome port,
      Or with the Graces there to play and sport;
      That even her owne Cytheron,° though in it
      She usèd most to keepe her royall court,
      And in her soveraine Majesty to sit,
  She in regard hereof° refusde and thought unfit.

10 Unto this place when as the Elfin Knight
      Approcht, him seemèd that the merry sound
      Of a shrill pipe he playing heard on hight,
      And many feete fast thumping th'hollow ground,
      That through the woods their Eccho did rebound.
      He nigher drew, to weete what mote it be;
      There he a troupe of Ladies dauncing found
      Full merrily, and making gladfull glee,
  And in the midst of Shepheard piping he did see.

11 He durst not enter into th'open greene,
      For dread of them unwares to be descryde,
      For breaking of their daunce, if he were seene;
      But in the covert of the wood did byde,
      Beholding all, yet of them unespyde.
      There he did see, that pleasèd much his sight,
      That even he himselfe his eyes envyde,
      An hundred naked maidens lilly white,
  All raungèd in a ring, and dauncing in delight.

12 All they without were raungèd in a ring,
      And dauncèd round; but in the midst of them
      Three other Ladies did both daunce and sing,
      The whilest the rest them round about did hemme,
      And like a girlond did in compasse stemme

---

to course . . . light to play the game of prisoner's base
Acidale the name of the Muses' fountain (see *Epithalamion,* l. 310) but here transferred to the hill because of its association with Greek *akades,* "carefree," or because of Latin *acies,* sight, view, here combined with *dale*
Cytheron Cythera, Venus' island, was sometimes confused with the mountain Citheron in Greece.
in regard hereof compared with this

And in the middest of those same three, was placed
Another Damzell, as a precious gemme,
Amidst a ring most richly well enchaced,
That with her goodly presence all the rest much graced.

13 Looke how the Crowne, which *Ariadne* wore
Upon her yvory forehead that same day,
That *Theseus* her unto his bridale bore,
When the bold *Centaures* made that bloudy fray,
With the fierce *Lapithes*, which did them dismay;
Being now placèd in the firmament,
Through the bright heaven doth her beames display,
And is unto the starres an ornament,
Which round about her move in order excellent.°

14 Such was the beauty of this goodly band,
Whose sundry parts were here too long to tell:
But she that in the midst of them did stand,
Seem'd all the rest in beauty to excell,
Crownd with a rosie girlond, that right well
Did her beseeme. And ever, as the crew
About her daunst, sweet flowres, that far did smell,
And fragrant odours they uppon her threw;
But most of all, those three did her with gifts endew.

15 Those were the Graces, daughters of delight,
Handmaides of *Venus*, which are wont to haunt⸃   *sojourn*
Uppon this hill, and daunce there day and night:
Those three to men all gifts of grace do graunt,
And all, that *Venus* in her selfe doth vaunt,
Is borrowèd of them. But that faire one,
That in the midst was placed paravaunt,⸃   *in foremost place*
Was she to whom that shepheard pypt alone,
That made him pipe so merrily, as never none.

16 She was to weete⸃ that jolly Shepheards lasse,   *to wit*
Which pipèd there unto that merry rout,
That jolly shepheard, which there pipèd, was
Poore *Colin Clout* (who knowes not *Colin Clout?*)
He pypt apace, whilest they him daunst about.
Pype jolly shepheard, pype thou now apace
Unto thy love, that made thee low to lout:⸃   *bow*
Thy love is present there with thee in place,
Thy love is there advaunst to be another Grace.

17 Much wondred *Calidore* at this straunge sight,
Whose like before his eye had never seene,
And standing long astonishèd in spright,

Looke how . . . excellent (stanza 13) refers
to the constellation, but the fight Spenser
mentions occurred at the wedding of Pirithous
and Hippodamia

And rapt with pleasaunce, wist not what to weene;
Whether it were the traine of beauties Queene,
Or Nymphes, or Faeries, or enchaunted show,
With which his eyes mote have deluded beene.
Therefore resolving, what it was, to know,
Out of the wood he rose, and toward them did go.

18   But soone as he appearèd to their vew,
They vanisht all away out of his sight,
And cleane were gone, which way he never knew;
All save the shepheard, who for fell despight
Of that displeasure, broke his bag-pipe quight,
And made great mone for that unhappy turne.
But *Calidore*, though no lesse sory wight,
For that mishap, yet seeing him to mourne,
Drew neare, that he the truth of all by him mote learne.

19   And first him greeting, thus unto him spake,
Haile jolly shepheard, which thy joyous dayes
Here leadest in this goodly merry make,   *merrymaking*
Frequented of these gentle Nymphes alwayes,
Which to thee flocke, to heare thy lovely layes;
Tell me, what mote these dainty Damzels be,
Which here with thee doe make their pleasant playes?
Right happy thou, that mayst them freely see:
But why when I them saw, fled they away from me?

20   Not I so happy, answerd then that swaine,
As thou unhappy, which them thence didst chace,
Whome by no meanes thou canst recall againe,
For being gone, none can them bring in place,
But whom they of themselves list so to grace.
Right sory I, (saide then Sir *Calidore*,)
That my ill fortune did them hence displace.
But since things passèd none may now restore,
Tell me, what were they all, whose lacke thee grieves so sore.

21   Tho> gan that shepheard thus for to dilate;   *then*
Then wote thou shepheard, whatsoever thou bee,
That all those Ladies, which thou sawest late,
Are *Venus* Damzels, all within her fee,>   *service*
But differing in honour and degree:
They all are Graces, which on her depend,
Besides a thousand more, which ready bee
Her to adorne, when so she forth doth wend:
But those three in the midst, doe chiefe on her attend.

22   They are the daughters of sky-ruling Jove,
By him begot of faire *Eurynome*,°

Eurynome daughter of Ocean and mother of
the Graces

The Oceans daughter, in this pleasant grove,
As he this way comming from feastfull glee,
Of *Thetis* wedding with *Æacidee,*°
In sommers shade him selfe here rested weary.
The first of them hight mylde *Euphrosyne,*
Next faire *Aglaia,* last *Thalia* merry:
Sweete Goddesses all three which me in mirth do cherry.°   *cheer*

23 These three on men all gracious gifts bestow,
    Which decke the body or adorne the mynde,
    To make them lovely or well favoured show,
    As comely carriage, entertainement° kynde,   *behavior to others*
    Sweete semblaunt,° friendly offices that bynde,   *demand*
    And all the complements of curtesie:
    They teach us, how to each degree and kynde
    We should our selves demeane,° to low, to hie;   *conduct*
To friends, to foes, which skill men call Civility.

24 Therefore they alwaies smoothly seeme to smile,
    That we likewise should mylde and gentle be,
    And also naked are, that without guile
    Or false dissemblaunce all them plaine may see,
    Simple and true from covert malice free:
    And eeke them selves so in their daunce they bore,
    That two of them still froward° seem'd to bee,   *turned away*
    But one still tòwards shew'd her selfe afore;
That good should from us goe, then come in greater store.

25 Such were those Goddesses, which ye did see;
    But that fourth Mayd, which there amidst them traced,
    Who can aread,° what creature mote she bee,   *tell*
    Whether a creature, or a goddesse graced
    With heavenly gifts from heven first enraced?°   *implanted*
    But what so sure she was, she worthy was,
    To be the fourth with those three other placed:
    Yet was she certes but a countrey lasse,
Yet she all other countrey lasses farre did passe.

26 So farre as doth the daughter of the day,°
    All other lesser lights in light excell,
    So farre doth she in beautyfull array,
    Above all other lasses beare the bell,°   *gains victory*
    Ne lesse in vertue that beseemes her well,
    Doth she exceed the rest of all her race,
    For which the Graces that here wont to dwell,
    Have for more honor brought her to this place,
And gracèd her so much to be another Grace.

Æacidee Peleus, son of Aeacus, whose wedding   daughter of the day the evening (and morning)
(he married Thetis) was attended by the gods   star, Venus

27 Another Grace she well deserves to be,
       In whom so many Graces gathered are,
       Excelling much the meane of her degree;
       Divine resemblaunce, beauty soveraine rare,
       Firme Chastity, that spight ne blemish dare;
       All which she with such courtesie doth grace,
       That all her peres cannot with her compare,
       But quite are dimmèd when she is in place.
       She made me often pipe and now to pipe apace.⁷   *copiously*

28 Sunne of the world, great glory of the sky,
       That all the earth doest lighten with thy rayes,
       Great *Gloriana*, greatest Majesty,
       Pardon thy shepheard, mongst so many layes,
       As he hath sung of thee in all his dayes,
       To make one minime⁷ of thy poore handmayd,   *musical note*
       And underneath thy feete to place her prayse,
       That when thy glory shall be farre displayd
       To future age of her this mention may be made.

                          .   .   .

                          1596

[The pastoral calm is abruptly broken when brigands attack the settlement and carry off Pastorella, Meliboee, and others. Then the brigands fight with slavers, and all their prisoners are killed except Pastorella, whom Calidore rescues from under a heap of bodies. The courtesy of innocence, he has discovered, is too vulnerable; in the wicked world we have there must be men of chivalry perpetually ready for the defense of innocence and courtesy. Pastorella, identified by a birthmark, is restored to her noble parents; Calidore captures the Blatant Beast, but it escapes, and, says Spenser, waxes even more mischievous and outrageous, not even sparing poets.

On this inconclusive note, introduced as a sad afterthought in the last four stanzas, the unfinished poem comes to a stop, except for the fragment of another Book which was published in 1609. This is made up of the Two Cantos of Mutability, and the publisher guesses that they are part of a legend of Constancy, labeling them cantos vi, vii, and viii 1–2 of that Book.]

Two Cantos of Mutability

It appears most likely that Spenser wrote these as the "core" cantos, leaving the rest of the work, which would have to be devoted more to narrative, for later completion; for example, there is no reason why the Garden of Adonis canto in Book III should not have been written separately and in advance. The view that these are early and rejected drafts seems incomprehensible, considering that they contain Spenser's finest philosophical poetry.

Canto vi proposes the topic of Change or Mutability, opposite of Constancy, and calls Mutability a daughter of the Titans (charged in Book V with the guilt of having brought rebellion and intemperance into the world). She has altered the original order of creation, defaced Nature and Justice, and brought death into life; she is, in fact under one aspect, the image of the disaster of the Fall. Having ruined earth, she aspires to the heavens which are beyond the moon, below which her power is admitted by all. First she claims the moon, whose sphere is the border between the two worlds; an eclipse strikes terror and creates the fear that Chaos is coming again. Mercury investigates for Jupiter, who explains to the heavenly powers that a Titan's daughter is again challenging them. Mutability arrives to state her claim. Jupiter admires her beauty, but chides her, asserting his obvious preeminence. She claims a hearing in a higher court, that of Nature, and a hearing is appointed, to be held on Arlo Hill in Spenser's Ireland.

Spenser now makes a myth, based on Ovid, to explain why this beautiful place (used in the previous Book as the dancing place of the Graces) should have lost some of its original loveliness and innocence. Then, in canto vii, the hearing is described.

The success of these cantos depends on Spenser's ability to convert philosophical explanations into myths of his own devising, and therefore fitting the basic patterns of his imagination. Scholarship has said much about the sources—in Ovid, Lucretius, the neo-platonists, in Boethius, the mainstay of medieval philosophy, and even in the thought of Spenser's contemporary, Giordano Bruno, who spent some time in London and Oxford before being condemned as a heretic by the Inquisition. Probably he depended on no particular source—philosophically, what he says on this subject both here and in III.vi is not very different from the speech of Theseus at the end of Chaucer's Knight's Tale: God is stable and eternal, but has decreed that "speces of thinges and progressiouns / Shullen enduren by successiouns, / And nat eterne be, withoute lye." But the whole joint development of thought and myth—or thought-in-myth—is Spenserian.

Ovid, the classic poet of mutability (his greatest work is the *Metamorphoses*), was in Spenser's mind; he borrowed from Ovid not only Nature (again see the opening lines of the *Metamorphoses*), trimming it with other material from the long tradition, but also three strands of narrative: the challenge of Mutability, the story of Faunus in vi, and the pageant of times and seasons in vii. From Ovid he also borrowed a speech attributed to Pythagoras on the subject of change. But he is not a "classical" poet; he admits medieval elements, and also understands things in a Christian sense. The relation of Time and Eternity—the root problem, since time is the agent of change—he sees in a Christian light, remembering the great medieval commonplaces. Here the answer is quite like that of III.vi. Adonis, though "subject to mortalitie / Yet is eterne in mutabilitie, / And by succession made perpetuall." Boethius said that "all things rejoice to return again to their own nature," and that in the long run they do not change except insofar as change may bring them to the perfection potential in their natures. This also implies change and decay; but the two things are complementary, and mutability is the servant of the eternality of things.

Mutability may reflect, as Spenser often does, contemporary convictions of the rapid decay of the world, but she also represents something that delighted him, which is why he makes her beautiful, and why this myth goes very deep with him. "All change is sweet," he says in *Muiopotmos,* and, at the very end of the poem, "for all that moveth, doth in *Change* delight." The beauty and variety of the physical world are a consequence of mutability. Thus Mutability has the better arguments, and Jupiter merely storms; Nature ends the dispute only by means of a mysterious answer, but one in which gnomic language underlines what mythological invention has already achieved, the reconciliation of opposites.

From Canto vii

3 Now, at the time that was before agreed,
 The Gods assembled all on *Arlo*° hill;
 As well those that are sprung of heavenly seed,
 As those that all the other world doe fill,
 And rule both sea and land unto their will:
 Onely th'infernall Powers might not appeare;
 As well for horror of their count'naunce ill,
 As for th'unruly fiends which they did feare;
 Yet *Pluto* and *Proserpina*° were present there.

4 And thither also came all other creatures,
 What-ever life or motion doe retaine,
 According to their sundry kinds of features;
 That *Arlo* scarsly could them all containe;
 So full they fillèd every hill and Plaine:
 And had not *Natures* Sergeant (that is *Order*)
 Them well disposèd by his busie paine,
 And raungèd farre abroad in every border,
 They would have causèd much confusion and disorder.

5 Then forth issewed (great goddesse) great dame *Nature*°
 With goodly port and gracious Majesty;
 Being far greater and more tall of stature
 Then any of the gods or Powers on hie:
 Yet certès by her face and physnomy,
 Whether she man or woman inly were,
 That could not any creature well descry:
 For, with a veile that wimpled° every where   *covered*
 Her head and face was hid, that mote to none appeare.

6 That some doe say was so by skill devizèd,
 To hide the terror of her uncouth° hew,   *unknown*
 From mortall eyes that should be sore agrizèd;°   *horrified*
 For that her face did like a Lion shew,
 That eye of wight could not indure to view:
 But others tell that it so beautious was,
 And round about such beames of splendor threw,
 That it the Sunne a thousand times did pass,
 Ne could be seene, but like an image in a glass.

Arlo hill near Spenser's estate at Kilcolman
Pluto and Proserpina king and queen of hell
dame Nature As he suggests, Spenser owes something to Alanus, *De Planctu Naturae*, and more directly to Chaucer's *Parlement of Foules* for this figure. The veil and the hermaphroditism probably come from Plutarch's Isis and Osiris,

on which he also drew for III.vi and V.x vii; and just as the philosophical argument partly parallels that of III.vi, so the presentation of the figure of Nature is reminiscent of the hermaphrodite Venus of IV.x. Here he succeeds marvelously in attributing to Nature beauty and terror, mystery and authority, fertility and order.

7 That well may seemen true: for, well I weene
    That this same day, when she on *Arlo* sat,
    Her garment was so bright and wondrous sheene,°   *fair*
    That my fraile wit cannot devize to what
    It to compare, nor finde like stuffe to that,
    As those three sacred *Saints,* though else most wise,
    Yet on mount *Thabor* quite their wits forgat,
    When they their glorious Lord in strange disguise
  Transfigur'd sawe;° his garments so did daze their eyes.

8 In a fayre Plaine upon an equall° Hill,   *symmetrical*
    She placèd was in a pavilión;
    Not such as Craftes-men by their idle° skill   *vain*
    Are wont for Princes states to fashión:
    But th'earth her self of her owne motión,
    Out of her fruitfull bosome made to growe
    Most dainty trees; that, shooting up anon,
    Did seeme to bow their bloosming heads full lowe,
  For homage unto her, and like a throne did shew.

9 So hard it is for any living wight,
    All her array and vestiments to tell,
    That old *Dan Geffrey*° (in whose gentle spright
    The pure well head of Poesie did dwell)
    In his *Foules parley*° durst not with it mel,
    But it transferd to *Alane,*° who he thought
    Had in his *Plaint of kindes*° describ'd it well:
    Which who will read set forth so as it ought,
  Go seek he out that *Alane* where he may be sought.

10 And all the earth far underneath her feete
    Was dight with flowres, that voluntary grew
    Out of the ground, and sent forth odours sweet;
    Tenne thousand mores° of sundry sent and hew,   *roots, plants*
    That might delight the smell, or please the view;
    The which, the Nymphes, from all the brooks thereby
    Had gathered, which° they at her foot-stoole threw;
    That richer seem'd then any tapestry,
  That Princes bowres adorne with painted imagery.

11 And *Mole*° himself, to honour her the more,
    Did deck himself in freshest faire attire,

---

those three . . . sawe Matthew 17:1–2, Mark
9:6: "And after six days Jesus taketh Peter,
James and John his brother, and bringeth them
up into a high mountain apart, and was transfigured before them: and his face did shine
with the sun, and his raiment was white as
the light . . . they were sore afraid"
Dan Geffrey Chaucer
Foules parley *The Parlement of Foules*
Alane Alanus de (ab) Insulis, Alain de l'Isle
(c.1128–1203), French Cistercian theologian,

author of satirical poem cited in the following
line.
Plaint of kinds *De Planctu Naturae;* Chaucer
says: "And right as Aleyn, in the Pleynt of
Kinde, / Devyseth Nature of aray and face, / In
swich aray men mighten hir ther finde" (*The
Parlement of Foules*, ll. 316–18)
which redundant syntactically, and also metrically if one says *gatherèd*
Mole forest near Kilcolman

And his high head, that seemeth alwaies hore
With hardned frosts of former winters ire,
He with an Oaken girlond now did tire,°   *dress*
As if the love of some new Nymph late seene,
Had in him kindled youthfull fresh desire,
And made him change his gray attire to greene;
Ah gentle *Mole!* such joyance hath thee well beseene.°   *become*

12   Was never so great joyance since the day,
That all the gods whylome° assembled were,   *once*
On *Hæmus hill*° in their divine array,
To celebrate the solemne bridall cheare,
Twixt *Peleus*, and dame *Thetis*° pointed° there;   *appointed*
Where *Phœbus* self, that god of Poets hight,
They say did sing the spousall hymne full cleere,
That all the gods were ravisht with delight
Of his celestiall song, and Musicks wondrous might.

13   This great Grandmother of all creatures bred
Great *Nature,* ever young yet full of eld,
Still mooving, yet unmovèd from her sted;°   *position*
Unseene of any, yet of all beheld;°
Thus sitting in her throne as I have teld,
Before her came dame *Mutabilitie*;
And being lowe before her presence feld,°   *fallen*
With meek obaysance and humilitie,
Thus gan her plaintif Plea, with words to amplifie;

14   To thee O greatest goddesse, onely° great,   *alone*
An humble suppliant loe, I lowely fly
Seeking for Right, which I of thee entreat;
Who Right to all dost deale indifferently,
Damning all Wrong and tortious° Injurie,   *wrongful*
Which any of thy creatures doe to other
(Oppressing them with power, unequally)
Sith of them all thou art the equall° mother,   *impartial*
And knittest each to each, as brother unto brother.

15   To thee therefore of this same *Jove* I plaine,°   *complain*
And of his fellow gods that faine to be,
That challenge° to themselves the whole worlds raign;   *claim*
Of which, the greatest part is due to me,
And heaven it selfe by heritage in Fee:°   *right of inheritance*
For, heaven and earth I both alike do deeme,
Sith heaven and earth are both alike to thee;

Hæmus hill hill in Thessaly
Peleus . . . Thetis See XI.x.22n.
ever young . . . beheld This reconciliation of
opposites in Nature states the main theme of
the Mutability Cantos, and one of Spenser's
most radically important poetic preoccupations.

Furthermore, in her ability to be "Still mooving,
yet unmovèd from her sted," Nature contains
the secret answer to Mutability, who cannot
understand the possibility of reconciling stillness
and movement, or time and eternity.

And, gods no more then men thou doest esteeme:
For, even the gods to thee, as men to gods do seeme.

16   Then weigh, O soveraigne goddesse, by what right
These gods do claime the worlds whole soverainty;
And that˃ is onely˃ dew unto thy might   *that which / solely*
Arrogate to themselves ambitiously:
As for the gods owne principality,
Which *Jove* usurpes unjustly; that to be
My heritage, *Jove's* self cannot deny,
From my great Grandsire *Titan*, unto mee,
Deriv'd by dew descent; as is well knowen to thee.

17   Yet mauger˃ *Jove*, and all his gods beside,   *in spite of*
I doe possesse the worlds most regiment;˃   *rule*
As, if ye please it into parts divide,
And every parts inholders˃ to convent,˃   *tenants / summon*
Shall to your eyes appeare incontinent.˃   *immediately*
And first, the Earth (great mother of us all)
That only˃ seems unmov'd and permanent,   *alone*
And unto *Mutability* not thrall;
Yet is she chang'd in part, and eeke in generall.°

18   For, all that from her springs, and is ybredde,
How-ever fayre it flourish for a time,
Yet see we soone decay; and, being dead,
To turne again unto their earthly slime:
Yet, out of their decay and mortall crime,°
We daily see new creatures to arize;
And of their Winter spring another Prime,˃   *spring*
Unlike in forme, and chang'd by strange disguise:
So turne they still about, and change in restlesse wise.

19   As for her tenants; that is, man and beasts,
The beasts we daily see massácred dy,
As thralls and vassalls unto mens beheasts:˃   *commands*
And men themselves doe change continually,
From youth to eld, from wealth to poverty,
From good to bad, from bad to worst of all.
Ne doe their bodies only flit and fly:
But eeke their minds (which they immortall call)
Still change and vary thoughts, as new occasions fall.

20   Ne is the water in more constant case;
Whether those same on high, or these belowe.°
For, th'Ocean moveth stil,˃ from place to place;   *always*

Yet . . . generall The arguments of Mutability derive partly from the teaching of Pythagoras in Ovid, *Metamorphoses* XV, on the theme *omnia mutantur*, all things are changed.

mortall crime This is the association, inevitable in the period, between mutability and the consequences of the Fall.
on high . . . belowe Genesis 1:7

And every River still doth ebbe and flowe:
Ne any Lake, that seems most still and slowe;
Ne Poole so small, that can his smoothnesse holde,˃   *maintain*
When any winde doth under heaven blowe;
With which, the clouds are also tost and roll'd;
Now like great Hills; and, streight, like sluces, them unfold.

21   So likewise are all watry living wights
Still tost, and turnèd, with continuall change.
Never abyding in their stedfast plights.˃   *fixed conditions*
The fish, still floting, doe at randon range,
And never rest; but evermore exchange
Their dwelling places, as the streames them carrie:
Ne have the watry foules a certaine grange,˃   *dwelling*
Wherein to rest, ne in one stead˃ do tarry;   *place*
But flitting still doe flie, and still their places vary.

22   Next is the Ayre: which who feeles not by sense
(For, of all sense it is the middle meane)°
To flit still? and, with subtill influence
Of this thin spirit,° all creatures to maintaine,
In state of life? O weake life! that does leane
On thing so tickle˃ as th'unsteady ayre;   *unstable*
Which every howre is chang'd, and altred cleane˃   *completely*
With every blast that bloweth fowle or faire:
The faire doth it prolong; the fowle doth it impaire.

23   Therein the changes infinite beholde,
Which to her creatures every minute chaunce;
Now, boyling hot: streight, friezing deadly cold:
Now, faire sun-shine, that makes all skip and daunce:
Streight, bitter storms and balefull countenance,
That makes them all to shiver and to shake:
Rayne, hayle, and snowe do pay˃ them sad penance,   *inflict on*
And dreadfull thunder-claps (that makes them quake)
With flames and flashing lights that thousand changes make.

24   Last is the fire: which, though it live for ever,
Ne can be quenchèd quite; yet, every day,
Wee see his parts, so soone as they do sever,
To lose their heat, and shortly to decay;
So, makes himself his owne consuming pray.
Ne any living creatures doth he breed:°
But all, that are of others bredd,° doth slay;
And, with their death, his cruell life dooth feed;
Nought leaving but their barren ashes, without seede.

middle meane medium, e.g. for scent and   **Ne . . . breed** The salamander was sometimes
hearing   excepted.
spirit monosyllabic   **of others bredd** bred of the other elements

25   Thus, all these fower° (the which the ground-work bee
     Of all the world, and of all living wights)
     To thousand sorts of *Change* we subject see.
     Yet are they chang'd (by other wondrous slights⁾)   *tricks*
     Into themselves,⁾ and lose their native mights;   *each other*
     The Fire to Aire, and th'Ayre to Water sheere,⁾   *bright*
     And Water into Earth: yet Water fights
     With Fire, and Aire with Earth approaching neere:
   Yet all are in one body, and as one appeare.

26   So, in them all raignes *Mutabilitie*;
     How-ever these, that Gods themselves do call,
     Of them doe claime the rule and soveraintie:
     As, *Vesta*, of the fire æthereall;°
     Vulcan, of this, with us so usuall;°
     Ops,° of the earth; and *Juno* of the Ayre;
     Neptune, of Seas; and Nymphes, of Rivers all.
     For, all those Rivers to me subject are:
   And all the rest, which they usurp, be all my share.

27   Which to approven true, as I have told,
     Vouchsafe, O goddesse, to thy presence call
     The rest which doe the world in being hold:
     As, times and seasons of the yeare that fall:
     Of all the which, demand in generall,
     Or judge thy selfe, by verdit⁾ of thine eye,   *verdict*
     Whether to me they are not subject all.
     Nature did yeeld thereto; and by-and-by,
   Bade *Order* call them all, before her Maiesty.

       . . .

[There follows a lavish pageant of the Seasons, the Months, Day and Night, the Hours, and Life and Death. Mutability resumes her plea.]

47   When these were past, thus gan the *Titanesse*;
     Lo, mighty mother, now be judge and say,
     Whether in all thy creatures more or lesse⁾   *greater or smaller*
     CHANGE doth not raign and beare the greatest sway:
     For, who sees not, that *Time* on all doth pray?
     But *Times* do change and move continually.
     So nothing here long standeth in one stay:
     Wherefore, this lower world who can deny
   But to be subject still to *Mutabilitie*?

48   Then thus gan *Jove*; Right true it is, that these
     And all things else that under heaven dwell
     Are chaung'd of *Time*, who doth them all disseise⁾   *deprive*

---

fower the four elements, earth, water, air, fire, of which everything is constituted
Vesta . . . æthereall Vesta, goddess of holy fire, and so of the celestial fires of the heavens

Vulcan . . . usual Vulcan the smith, so god of the fire on earth, which is used for manufacture
Ops identified with Rhea and Gaea, names of the earth goddess

Of being: But, who is it (to me tell)
That *Time* himselfe doth move and still compell
To keepe his course? Is not that namely wee
Which poure that vertue° from our heavenly cell,   *influence*
That moves them all, and makes them changèd be?
So them we gods doe rule, and in them also thee.

49   To whom, thus *Mutability:* The things
Which we see not how they are mov'd and swayd,
Ye may attribute to your selves as Kings,
And say they by your secret powre are made:
But what we see not, who shall us perswade?
But were they so, as ye them faine to be,
Mov'd by your might, and ordred by your ayde;
Yet what if I can prove, that even yee.
Your selves are likewise chang'd, and subject unto mee?

50   And first, concerning her that is the first,
Even you faire *Cynthia,*° whom so much ye make
Joves dearest darling, she was bread and nurst
On *Cynthus* hill, whence she her name did take:
Then is she mortall borne, how-so ye crake;°   *boast*
Besides, her face and countenance every day
We changèd see, and sundry forms partake,
Now hornd, now round, now bright, now brown and gray:
So that *as changefull as the Moone* men use to say.

51   Next, *Mercury,* who though he lesse appeare
To change his hew,° and alwayes seeme as one;   *form*
Yet, he his course doth altar° every yeare,   *alter*
And is of late far out of order gone:°
So *Venus* eeke, that goodly Paragone,
Though faire all night, yet is she darke all day;
And *Phœbus* self, who lightsome is alone,°   *alone is*
Yet is he oft eclipsèd by the way,
And fills the darkned world with terror and dismay.

52   Now *Mars* that valiant man is changèd most:
For, he some times so far runs out of square,
That he his way doth seem quite to have lost,
And cleane without his usuall sphere to fare;
That even these Star-gazers stonisht are
At sight thereof, and damne their lying bookes:
So likewise, grim Sir *Saturne* oft doth spare

Cynthia moon goddess, so called from Cynthus, a mountain in Delos. Spenser treats the moon as a planet, and goes on to deal with the other six of the old system: Mercury, Venus, the sun, Mars, Saturn, and Jupiter.
out of order gone See notes on V, Proem, where Spenser confines his remarks on eccentric orbits to the sun, Mars, and Saturn. That Mercury, much harder to observe, was also eccentric, was a fairly recent discovery, and perhaps Spenser caught up with it between the writing of V and of these cantos. Of course all such eccentricities were consequent upon the mistaken view that planetary orbits were circular (see also the opening lines of Donne's "Good Friday, 1613. Riding Westward").

His sterne aspect, and calme his crabbèd lookes:
So many turning cranks these have, so many crookes.°

53   But you *Dan Jove*, that only constant are,
   And King of all the rest, as ye do clame,
   Are you not subject eek to this misfare?˃   *misfortune*
   Then let me aske you this withouten blame,˃   *offense*
   Where were ye borne? some say in *Crete* by name,
   Others in *Thebes*, and others other-where;°
   But wheresoever they comment˃ the same,   *lyingly invent*
   They all consent that ye begotten were,
And borne here in this world, ne other can appeare.

54   Then are ye mortall borne, and thrall to me,
   Unlesse the kingdome of the sky yee make˃   *argue*
   Immortall, and unchangeable to bee;
   Besides, that power and vertue which ye spake,
   That ye here worke, doth many changes take,
   And your owne natures change: for, each of you.
   That vertue have, or this, or that to make,
   Is checkt and changèd from his nature trew,
By others opposition or obliquid view.°

55   Besides, the sundry motions of your Spheares,
   So sundry waies and fashions as clerkes faine,
   Some in short space, and some in longer yeares;
   What is the same but alteration plaine?
   Onely the starrie skie° doth still remaine:
   Yet do the Starres and Signes therein still move,°
   And even it self is mov'd, as wizards saine.°
   But all that moveth, doth mutation love:
Therefore both you and them to me I subject prove.

56   Then since within this wide great *Universe*
   Nothing doth firme and permanent appeare,
   But all things tost and turnèd by transverse:˃   *haphazardly*
   What then should let,˃ but I aloft should reare   *hinder*
   My Trophee, and from all, the triumph beare?
   Now judge then (O thou greatest goddesse trew!)

---

cranks . . . crooks turnings and windings (alluding to the progressively more complex hypotheses of epicycles introduced to justify the Ptolemaic system in the light of observed eccentricities)
some . . . other-where There were conflicting traditions about Jupiter's birthplace, Crete, Thebes, and Arcadia being claimants: Natalis Comes, the Renaissance mythographer known to Spenser, sums up the matter as "very contentious."
each of you . . . view The influences of which the planets are capable are qualified and changed by their action on one another; *opposition* is the relation between two planets

when their longitude differs by 180 degrees; an *obliquid* relation is more obliquely directed.
the starry skie the "crystalline" sphere of the fixed stars, held to be immutable and pure
Starres . . . move The movement referred to resulted from the effect on terrestrial observation of the precession of the equinoxes (cf. V, Proem).
it self . . . saine the crystalline sphere itself moves, according to astronomers. Ptolemy said that "inasmuch as the stars maintain their relative distances we may justly call them fixed, yet inasmuch as the whole sphere to which they are attached is in motion, the word 'fixed' is but little appropriate."

  According as thy selfe doest see and heare,
   And unto me addoom° that is my dew;   *adjudicate*
 That is the rule of all, all being rul'd by you.

57 So having ended, silence long ensewed,
   Ne *Nature* to or fro spake for a space,
   But with firme eyes affixt, the ground still viewed.
   Meane while, all creatures, looking in her face,
   Expecting th'end of this so doubtfull case,
   Did hang in long suspence what would ensew,
   To whether° side should fall the soveraigne place: *which*
   At length, she looking up with chearefull view,
 The silence brake, and gave her doome in speeches few.

58 I well consider all that ye have sayd,
   And find that all things stedfastnes doe hate
   And changèd be: yet being rightly wayd°   *considered*
   They are not changèd from their first estate;
   But by their change their being doe dilate:
   And turning to themselves at length againe,
   Doe worke their owne perfection so by fate:
   Then over them Change doth not rule and raigne;
 But they raigne over change, and doe their states maintaine.

59 Cease therefore daughter further to aspire,
   And thee content thus to be rul'd by me:
   For thy decay thou seekst by thy desire;°
   But time shall come that all shall changèd bee,
   And from thenceforth, none no more change shall see.
   So was the *Titaness* put downe and whist,°   *silenced*
   And *Jove* confirm'd in his imperiall see.°   *throne*
   Then was that whole assembly quite dismist,
 And *Natur's* selfe did vanish, whither no man wist.° *knew*

  The viii. Canto, unperfite°   *unfinished*

1 When I bethinke me on that speech whyleare,°   *recent*
   Of *Mutability*, and well it way:
   Me seemes, that though she all unworthy were
   Of the Heav'ns Rule; yet very sooth to say,
   In all things else she beares the greatest sway.
   Which makes me loath this state of life so tickle,° *unstable*
   And love of things so vaine to cast away;
   Whose flowring pride, so fading and so fickle,
 Short° *Time* shall soon cut down with his consuming sickle. *who shortens*

2 Then gin I thinke on that which Nature sayd,
   Of that same time when no more *Change* shall be,

For . . . desire by your own wish to subject your own decay, since you will have to be
everything to mutability you unwittingly seek mutable too

But stedfast rest of all things firmely stayd
Upon the pillours of Eternity,
That is contrayr to *Mutabilitie*:
For, all that moveth, doth in *Change* delight:
But thence-forth all shall rest eternally
With Him that is the God of Sabbaoth° hight:>   *called*
O that great Sabbaoth God, graunt me that Sabaoths sight.°

       1609

Amoretti

Amoretti means "little cupids"; Spenser's sonnet sequence, published in 1595 with the *Epithalamion*, is not only a collection of "little loves" (or expressions thereof), but a carefully constructed series of glimpses into the quasi-fictional sonnet world, part private and autobiographical, part mythological and shared with Sidney, Daniel, Drayton, and Shakespeare. Spenser married Elizabeth Boyle before the publication of the collection, and the poems seem to comprehend this cycle of courtship and marriage, interlaced with the cycle of the secular and liturgical year and even of phases of poetic work (numbers 33 and 80 refer to the unfinished *Faerie Queene*). Spenser's form combines French and English verse traditions in linking the sonnet quatrains with common rhymes (the interlocking of *The Faerie Queene* stanza) and maintaining or breaking the octave-sestet division at will (abab bcbc cdcd ee). Rhetorically less dynamic than the sonnets of Sidney or Shakespeare, they nevertheless present in a subtle way a variety of tones and stances.

From Amoretti

I

Happy ye leaves° when as those lilly hands,
 which hold my life in their dead doing> might,   *killing*
 shall handle you and hold in loves soft bands,
 lyke captives trembling at the victors sight.
And happy lines, on which with starry light,
 those lamping> eyes will deigne sometimes to look   *flashing*
 and reade the sorrowes of my dying spright,>   *spirit*
 written with teares in harts close> bleeding book.   *secret*
And happy rymes bath'd in the sacred brooke,
10 of *Helicon*° whence she derivèd is,
 when ye behold that Angels blessèd looke,
 my soules long lackèd foode, my heavens blis.

God of Sabbath God of Hosts
Sabaoths sight Spenser may mean "grant me sight of the Lord on the last day," but more probably he means *Sabbath* in the sense of eternity—the stillness that will follow the tumult of the six days of the world's history.
leaves pages of the book of the *Amoretti*; similarly the "lines" and "rymes"

the sacred . . . Helicon the fountain of Hippocrene on Mt. Helicon, sacred to the Muses, the mythical "source" (which word itself originally means "spring") of poetry, here "sacred" because of the Petrarchan heavenly associations with the sonneteer's muse

Leaves, lines, and rymes, seeke her to please alone,
    whom if ye please, I care for other none.
                              1595

               XV

Ye tradefull Merchants, that with weary toyle,
    do seeke most pretious things to make your gain;
    and both the Indias° of their treasures spoile,
    what needeth you to seeke so farre in vaine?
For loe my love doth in her selfe containe
    all this worlds riches that may farre be found,
    if Saphyres,° loe her eies be Saphyres° plaine,⌐   *clear*
    if Rubies, loe hir lips be Rubies sound:
If Pearles, hir teeth be pearles both pure and round;
10   if Yvorie, her forhead yvory weene;⌐   *beautiful*
    if Gold, her locks are finest gold on ground;
    if silver, her faire hands are silver sheene.
But that which fairest is, but few behold,
    her mind adornd with vertues manifold.
                              1595

               XVI

One day as I unwarily did gaze
    on those fayre eyes my loves immortall light:
    the whiles my stonisht hart stood in amaze,
    through sweet illusion of her lookes delight.
I mote⌐ perceive how in her glauncing sight,   *could*
    legions of loves° with little wings did fly:
    darting their deadly arrowes fyry bright,
    at every rash beholder passing by.
One of those archers closely⌐ I did spy,   *secretly*
10   ayming his arrow at my very hart:
    when suddenly with twincle⌐ of her eye,   *blink*
    the Damzell broke his misintended dart.
Had she not so doon, sure I had bene slayne,
    yet as it was, I hardly⌐ scap't with paine.   *scarcely*
                              1595

               LIV

Of this worlds Theatre° in which we stay,
    My love lyke the Spectator ydly sits

Indias both East and West Indies
Saphyres This blazon of the Lady's beauties may
stem from the comparisons of those of the beloved to rare artifacts in the Song of Songs
5:10–16, but it also reflects a contemporary
convention: it is hard to believe that Shakespeare's Sonnet CXXX is not, particularly in
ll. 3–4, parodying this poem.
loves The "amoretti," little cupids, fly along
the "eyebeams" which interlock two lovers'
gazes (see Donne, "The Ecstasy," for a complex use of this lore; behind Spenser's use of
it lies the serious doctrine in his own *Hymne in
Honour of Beautie*, ll. 231–45).
worlds Theatre The *theatrum mundi* commonplace, likening reality to a play, God to the
author and director, the world to a set, and
people to actors (the final curtain is, inevitably,
Apocalypse), goes back originally to Plato; it
is most familiar through Jaques's "All the
world's a stage" speech in *As You Like It*,
although it is uncommon in Petrarchan sonnets.

beholding me that all the pageants° play,
  disguysing diversly my troubled wits.
Sometimes I joy when glad occasion fits,
  and mask in myrth lyke to a Comedy:
soone after when my joy to sorrow flits,
  I waile and make my woes a Tragedy.
Yet she beholding me with constant eye,
10 delights not in my merth�> nor rues my smart:°   *mirth*
but when I laugh she mocks, and when I cry
  she laughs, and hardens evermore her hart.
What then can move her? if nor merth nor mone,�>   *moan*
  she is no woman, but a sencelesse stone.

1595

LXIII

After long stormes and tempests sad assay,°
  Which hardly I endurèd heretofore:
in dread of death and daungerous dismay,
  with which my silly barke° was tossèd sore:
I doe at length descry the happy shore,
  in which I hope ere long for to arryve;
fayre soyle it seemes from far and fraught with store°
  of all that deare and daynty is alyve.
Most happy he that can at last atchyve
10 the joyous safety of so sweet a rest:
whose least delight sufficeth to deprive
  remembrance of all paines which him opprest.
All paines are nothing in respect of this,
  all sorrowes short that gaine eternall blisse.

1595

LXIV

Comming to kisse her lyps, (such grace I found)
  me seemd I smelt a gardin of sweet flowres:°
that dainty odours from them threw around
  for damzels fit to decke their lovers bowres.
Her lips did smell lyke unto Gillyflowers,
  her ruddy cheekes lyke unto Roses red:
her snowy browes lyke budded Bellamoures,
  her lovely eyes lyke Pincks⁾ but newly spred.   *carnations*
Her goodly bosome lyke a Strawberry bed,
10 her neck lyke to a bounch of Cullambynes:⁾   *columbine*
her brest lyke lillyes, ere theyr leaves be shed,
  her nipples lyke yong blossomd Jessemynes.⁾   *jasmines*

---

pageants parts in the productions
rues my smart pities my sorrow
sad assay painful encounter (with storms)
silly barke innocent or simple ship: this is a
commonplace (see Wyatt's "My Galley Chargèd
with Forgetfullness")

fraught with store bounteously supplied
gardin of sweet flowres another sort of blazon
or catalogue, going back to another source in
Song of Songs (4:12–15), describing the lover
as an enclosed garden

Such fragrant flowres doe give most odorous smell,
but her sweet odour did them all excell.

1595

LXXV

One day I wrote her name upon the strand,°   *beach*
  but came the waves and washèd it away:
agayne I wrote it with a second hand,
  but came the tyde, and made my paynes his pray.°   *prey*
Vayne man, sayd she, that doest in vaine assay,
  a mortall thing so to immortalize,
for I my selve shall lyke to this decay,
  and eek° my name bee wypèd out lykewize.   *also*
Not so, (quod I) let baser things devize°   *contrive*
10 to dy in dust, but you shall live by fame:
my verse your vertues rare shall eternize,°
  and in the hevens wryte your glorious name.
Where whenas death shall all the world subdew,
  our love shall live, and later life renew.

1595

Epithalamion

Epithalamion was published with the *Amoretti* in 1595. An epithalamion is a marriage song, and Spenser combines conventional features of the genre with strong personal applications, for he wrote the poem about his own wedding, to his second wife, Elizabeth Boyle. The wedding songs of Catullus are the type, and, as in Jonson in the masque *Hymenaei* and Herrick later, there are ceremonies and figures belonging more to a Roman than an English wedding; but Spenser, in the Renaissance manner, blends with these purely Christian figures, and also breaks with tradition in making the bridegroom the singer of the song.

In apparently freely flowing stanzas, Spenser invokes the Muses and follows the events of the wedding day, much in the Latin manner; the effect is of controlled abundance, an ordered joy appropriate to marriage and that desire of generation which is the honorable gift of the earthly Venus. And this effect is not impaired by the knowledge, recently achieved, that the poem has an elaborate hidden numerological structure. A. Kent Hieatt has demonstrated that the twenty-three stanzas and the envoy stand for the hours of the day, the last eight being the night hours, for the day of the wedding is the summer solstice. The day hours have the refrain, "The woods shall to me answer"; the night hours, "The woods no more shall answer." There are 365 long lines, one for each day of the year. There are other evidences of strict design, but the demands it made on Spenser did not prevent his achieving what C. S. Lewis calls "festal sublimity," any more than similar patterns, even more recently discovered in *The Faerie Queene,* cramp or diminish it.

eternize Poetry's ability to perpetuate beautiful lives in myth even longer than can statues or inscriptions in stone is an old theme (cf. Shakespeare's Sonnet LV: "Not marble, nor the gilded monuments"), and especially suited to the delight sonnet sequences took in referring to themselves.

Epithalamion

Ye learnèd sisters° which have oftentimes
Beene to me ayding, others° to adorne:
Whom ye thought worthy of your gracefull° rymes,
That even the greatest did not greatly scorne
To heare theyr names sung in your simple layes,
But joyèd in theyr prayse.
And when ye list⁾ your owne mishaps to mourne,   *choose*
Which death, or love, or fortunes wreck did rayse,
Your string could soone to sadder tenor° turne,
10 And teach the woods and waters to lament
Your dolefull dreriment.⁾   *grief*
Now lay those sorrowfull complaints aside,
And having all your heads with girland crownd,
Helpe me mine owne loves prayses to resound,
Ne let the same of any be envide⁾   *grudged*
So Orpheus did for his owne bride,°
So I unto my selfe alone will sing,
The woods shall to me answer and my Eccho ring.

Early before the worlds light giving lampe,
20 His golden beame upon the hils doth spred,
Having disperst the nights unchearefull dampe,
Doe ye awake, and with fresh lusty hed,⁾   *vigor*
Go to the bowre of my belovèd love,
My truest turtle dove,
Bid her awake; for Hymen° is awake,
And long since ready forth his maske to move,°
With his bright Tead⁾ that flames with many a flake,⁾   *torch / spark*
And many a bachelor to waite on him,
In theyr fresh garments trim.
30 Bid her awake therefore and soone her dight,⁾   *dress*
For lo the wishèd day is come at last,
That shall for al the paynes and sorrowes past,
Pay to her usury⁾ of long delight: *interest*
And whylest she doth her dight,
Doe ye to her of joy and solace sing,
That all the woods may answer and your eccho ring.

Bring with you all the Nymphes that you can heare°
Both of the rivers and the forrests greene:
And of the sea that neighbours to her neare,°
40 Al with gay girlands goodly wel beseene.⁾   *provided*

learnèd sisters the Muses
others e.g. Queen Elizabeth
gracefull conferring grace
sadder tenor graver mood, deeper note
So . . . bride Orpheus can plausibly be supposed to have provided an epithalamion for Eurydice.

Hymen god of marriage
his maske to move to lead the procession of revelers
that . . . heare that can hear you
sea . . . neare Elizabeth Boyle had been staying at Youghal near the sea.

824

And let them also with them bring in hand,
Another gay girland
For my fayre love of lillyes and of roses,
Bound truelove wize° with a blew silke riband.
And let them make great store of bridale poses,
And let them eeke bring store of other flowers
To deck the bridale bowers.
And let the ground whereas° her foot shall tread,   *where*
For feare the stones her tender foot should wrong
50 Be strewed with fragrant flowers all along,
And diapred° lyke the discolorèd° mead.   *strewn with flowers / multicolored*
Which done, doe at her chambre dore awayt,
For she will waken strayt,
The whiles doe ye this song unto her sing,
The woods shall to you answer and your Eccho ring.

Ye Nymphes of Mulla° which with carefull heed,
The silver scaly trouts doe tend full well;
And greedy pikes which use therein to feed,
(Those trouts and pikes all others doo excell)
60 And ye likewise which keepe the rushy lake,
Where none doo fishes take,
Bynd up the locks the which hang scatterd light,
And in his waters which your mirror make,
Byhold your faces as the christall bright,
That when you come whereas my love doth lie,
No blemish she may spie.
And eke ye lightfoot mayds which keepe the deere,
That on the hoary mountayne use to towre,°
And the wylde wolves which seeke them to devoure,
70 With your steele darts doo chace from comming neer
Be also present heere,
To helpe to decke her and to help to sing,
That all the woods may answer and your eccho ring.

Wake, now my love, awake; for it is time,
The Rosy Morne long since left Tithones bed,°
All ready to her silver coche to clyme,
And Phœbus gins to shew his glorious hed.
Hark how the cheerefull birds do chaunt theyr laies
And carroll of loves praise.
80 The merry Larke hir mattins sings aloft,
The thrush replyes, the Mavis° descant° playes.   *thrush*
The Ouzell° shrills, the Ruddock° warbles soft,   *blackbird / robin*
So goodly all agree with sweet consent,

truelove wize in a love knot
Mulla now the river Awbeg, which flows near
Kilcolman
towre live high up
Tithones bed Tithonus is the husband of the

Dawn; this is a stock expression, going back
to Homer.
descant melody or counterpoint written above
a simple musical theme. The concept of birds
is a medieval convention.

To this dayes merriment.
Ah my deere love why doe ye sleepe thus long,
When meeter were that ye should now awake,
T'awayt the comming of your joyous make,°   *mate*
And hearken to the birds lovelearnèd song,
The deawy leaves among.
90   For they of joy and pleasance to you sing,
That all the woods them answer and theyr eccho ring.

My love is now awake out of her dreame,
And her fayre eyes like stars that dimmèd were
With darksome cloud, now shew theyr goodly beams
More bright then Hesperus his head doth rere.
Come now ye damzels, daughters of delight,
Helpe quickly her to dight.
But first come ye fayre houres which were begot
In Joves sweet paradice, of Day and Night,°
100   Which doe the seasons of the yeare allot,
And al that ever in this world is fayre
Doe make and still° repayre.   *ever*
And ye three handmayds of the Cyprian Queene,°
The which doe still adorne her beauties pride,
Helpe to addorne my beautifullest bride:
And as ye her array, still throw betweene
Some graces to be seene,
And as ye use° to Venus, to her sing,   *do as a rule*
The whiles the woods shal answer and your eccho ring.

110   Now is my love all ready forth to come,
Let all the virgins therefore well awayt,
And ye fresh boyes that tend upon her groome
Prepare your selves; for he is comming strayt.
Set all your things in seemely good aray
Fit for so joyfull day,
The joyfulst day that ever sunne did see.
Faire Sun, shew forth thy favourable ray,
And let thy lifull° heat not fervent be   *life-bestowing*
For feare of burning her sunshyny face,
120   Her beauty to disgrace.
O fayrest Phœbus, father of the Muse,
If ever I did honour thee aright,
Or sing the thing, that mote thy mind delight,
Doe not thy servants simple boone refuse,
But let this day let this one day be myne,
Let all the rest be thine.
Then I thy soverayne prayses loud wil sing,
That all the woods shal answer and theyr eccho ring.

of Day and Night more usually of Zeus and
Themis—a little invention of Spenser's

three . . . Queene the Graces, attendant on
Venus, as in *The Faerie Queene* VI.x

Harke how the Minstrels gin to shrill aloud
130 Their merry Musick that resounds from far,
The pipe, the tabor, and the trembling Croud,°   *fiddle*
That well agree withouten breach or jar.°   *discord*
But most of all the Damzels doe delite,
When they their tymbrels smyte,
And thereunto doe daunce and carrol sweet,
That all the sences they doe ravish quite,
The whyles the boyes run up and downe the street,
Crying aloud with strong confusèd noyce,°   *noise*
As if it were one voyce.
140 Hymen io Hymen,° Hymen they do shout,
That even to the heavens theyr shouting shrill
Doth reach, and all the firmament doth fill,
To which the people standing all about,
As in approvance doe thereto applaud
And loud advaunce her laud,°   *praise*
And evermore they Hymen Hymen sing,
That al the woods them answer and theyr eccho ring.

Loe where she comes along with portly° pace   *stately*
Lyke Phœbe° from her chamber of the East,
150 Arysing forth to run her mighty race,
Clad all in white, that seemes a virgin best.
So well it her beseemes° that ye would weene   *becomes*
Some angell she had beene.
Her long loose yellow locks lyke golden wyre,
Sprinckled with perle, and perling flowres a tweene,
Doe lyke a golden mantle her attyre,
And being crownèd with a girland greene,
Seeme lyke some mayden Queene.
Her modest eyes abashèd to behold
160 So many gazers, as on her do stare,
Upon the lowly ground affixèd are.
Ne dare lift up her countenance too bold,
But blush to heare her prayses sung so loud,
So farre from being proud.
Nathlesse doe ye still loud her prayses sing.
That all the woods may answer and your eccho ring.

Tell me ye merchants daughters did ye see
So fayre a creature in your towne before,
So sweet, so lovely, and so mild as she,
170 Adornd with beautyes grace and vertues store,
Her goodly eyes° lyke Saphyres shining bright,

Hymen io Hymen traditional wedding cry (see *The Faerie Queen* I.i.48) / **Phoebe** moon goddess, who borrows from her brother Phoebus the sun, "which is as a bridegroom coming out of his chamber, and rejoiceth as a strong man to run a race" (Psalms 15:5): Spenser transfers all this to the virgin bride / **goodly eyes** This begins a conventional catalogue of beauties known as the blazon; cf. Sonnet XV.

Her forehead yvory white,
Her cheekes lyke apples which the sun hath rudded,°   *reddened*
Her lips lyke cherryes charming men to byte,
Her brest like to a bowle of creame uncrudded,°   *uncurdled*
Her paps lyke lyllies budded,
Her snowie necke lyke to a marble towre,
And all her body like a pallace fayre,
Ascending uppe with many a stately stayre,
180   To honors seat and chastities sweet bowre.°
Why stand ye still ye virgins in amaze,
Upon her so to gaze,
Whiles ye forget your former lay to sing,
To which the woods did answer and your eccho ring.

But if ye saw that which no eyes can see,
The inward beauty of her lively spright,°   *spirit*
Garnisht with heavenly guifts of high degree,
Much more then would ye wonder at that sight,
And stand astonisht lyke to those which red°   *saw*
190   Medusaes mazeful hed.°
There dwels sweet love and constant chastity,
Unspotted fayth and comely womanhood,
Regard of honour and mild modesty,
There vertue raynes as Queen in royal throne,
And giveth lawes alone.°
The which the base affections° doe obay,   *passions*
And yeeld theyr services unto her will,
Ne thought of thing uncomely ever may
Thereto approach to tempt her mind to ill.
200   Had ye once seene these her celestial threasures,
And unrevealèd pleasures,
Then would ye wonder and her prayses sing,
That al the woods should answer and your echo ring.

Open the temple gates unto my love,
Open them wide that she may enter in,
And all the postes adorne° as doth behove,°   *as is fitting*
And all the pillours deck with girlands trim,
For to recyve this Saynt with honour dew,
That commeth in to you.
210   With trembling steps and humble reverence,
She commeth in, before th'almighties vew,
Of her ye virgins learne obedience,
When so ye come into those holy places,
To humble your proud faces:

---

honors . . . **bowre** the head, which controls the rest
Medusaes . . . hed Medusa was a Gorgon, whose terrible head turned the beholder to stone;

the bride's spirit would be awe-inspiring.
giveth . . . alone alone commands
postes adorne Roman wedding custom, surviving in poetry

Bring her up to th'high altar, that she may
The sacred ceremonies there partake,
The which do endlesse matrimony make,
And let the roring Organs loudly play
The praises of the Lord in lively notes,
220 The whiles with hollow throates
The Choristers the joyous Antheme sing,
That al the woods may answere and their eccho ring.

Behold whiles she before the altar stands
Hearing the holy priest that to her speakes
And blesseth her with his two happy hands,
How the red roses flush up in her cheekes,
And the pure snow with goodly vermill stayne,
Like crimsin dyde in grayne,>   *thoroughly*
That even th'Angels which continually,
230 About the sacred Altare doe remaine,°
Forget their service and about her fly;
Ofte peeping in her face that seemes more fayre,
The more they on it stare.
But her sad> eyes still fastened on the ground,   *grave*
Are governèd with goodly modesty,
That suffers not one looke to glaunce awry,
Which may let in a little thought unsownd.
Why blush ye love to give to me your hand,
The pledge of all our band?>   *bond*
240 Sing ye sweet Angels, Alleluya sing,°
That all the woods may answere and your eccho ring.

Now al is done; bring home the bride againe,
Bring home the triumph of our victory,
Bring home with you the glory of her gaine,>   *of gaining her*
With joyance bring her and with jollity.
Never had man more joyfull day then this,
Whom heaven would heape with blis.
Make feast therefore now all this live long day,
This day for ever to me holy is,
250 Poure out the wine without restraint or stay,
Poure not by cups, but by the belly full,
Poure out to all that wull,>   *want*
And sprinkle all the postes and wals with wine,°
That they may sweat, and drunken be withall.
Crowne ye God Bacchus with a coronall,>   *garland*
And Hymen also crowne with wreathes of vine,
And let the Graces daunce unto the rest;
For they can doo it best:

remaine Revelation 7:11
Sing . . . sing Revelation 19:1. Spenser remembers the marriage in Revelation, which was
so important in the conclusion of *The Faerie
Queene* I.
sprinkle . . . wine another Roman custom

The whiles the maydens doe theyr carroll sing,
260 To which the woods shal answer and theyr eccho ring.

Ring ye the bels, ye yong men of the towne,
And leave your wonted° labors for this day: *usual*
This day is holy; doe ye write it downe,
That ye for ever it remember may.
This day the sunne is in his chiefest hight,
With Barnaby the bright,°
From whence declining daily by degrees,
He somewhat loseth of his heat and light,
When once the Crab behind his back he sees.°
270 But for this time it ill ordainèd was,
To chose the longest day in all the yeare,
And shortest night, when longest fitter weare:
Yet never day so long, but late° would passe.   *at last*
Ring ye the bels, to make it weare away,
And bonefiers° make all day,
And daunce about them, and about them sing
That all the woods may answer, and your eccho ring.

Ah when will this long weary day have end,
And lende me leave to come unto my love?
280 How slowly do the houres theyr numbers spend?
How slowly does sad Time his feathers move?
Hast thee O fayrest Planet° to thy home
Within the Westerne fome:
Thy tyrèd steedes long since have need of rest.
Long though it be, at last I see it gloome,°   *darken*
And the bright evening star with golden creast
Appeare out of the East.
Fayre childe of beauty, glorious lampe of love
That all the host of heaven in rankes doost lead,
290 And guydest lovers through the nightes dread,
How chearefully thou lookest from above,
And seemst to laugh atweene thy twinkling light
As joying in the sight
Of these glad many which for joy doe sing,
That all the woods them answer and their eccho ring.

Now ceasse ye damsels your delights forepast;°   *over*
Enough is it, that all the day was youres:
Now day is doen, and night is nighing fast:
Now bring the Bryde into the brydall boures.
300 Now night is come, now soone her disaray,

the sunne . . . bright St. Barnabas day, June 11, was till the revision of the calendar the summer solstice.
the Crab . . . sees The sun moved out of Cancer into Leo in mid-June.

bonefiers midsummer bonfires, a surviving pagan custom
Planet The sun was regarded as a planet in Ptolemaic astronomy.

And in her bed her lay;
Lay her in lillies and in violets,
And silken courteins over her display,°   *spread*
And odourd sheetes, and Arras° coverlets.   *tapestry*
Behold how goodly my faire love does ly
In proud humility;
Like unto Maia,° when as Jove her tooke,
In Tempe,° lying on the flowry gras,
Twixt sleepe and wake, after she weary was,
310   With bathing in the Acidalian° brooke.
Now it is night, ye damsels may be gon,
And leave my love alone,
And leave likewise your former lay to sing:
The woods no more shal answere, nor your eccho ring.

Now welcome night, thou night so long expected,
That long daies labour doest at last defray,°   *pay for*
And all my cares, which cruell love collected,
Hast sumd in one, and cancellèd for aye:
Spread thy broad wing over my love and me,
320   That no man may us see,
And in thy sable mantle us enwrap,
From feare of perill and foule horror free.
Let no false treason seeke us to entrap,
Nor any dread disquiet once annoy
The safety of our joy:
But let the night be calme and quietsome,
Without tempestuous storms or sad afray:
Lyke as when Jove with fayre Alcmena lay,
When he begot the great Tirynthian groome:°
330   Or lyke as when he with thy selfe° did lie,
And begot Majesty.°
And let the mayds and yongmen cease to sing:
Ne let the woods them answer, nor theyr eccho ring.

Let no lamenting cryes, nor dolefull teares,
Be heard all night within nor yet without:
Ne let false whispers, breeding hidden feares,
Breake gentle sleepe with misconceivèd dout.
Let no deluding dreames, nor dreadful sights
Make sudden sad affrights;
340   Ne let housefyres, nor lightnings helpelesse° harmes,   *incurable*

Maia one of the seven Pleiades; she gave birth to Hermes (Mercury) after the encounter described
Tempe beautiful vale in Thessaly
Acidalian Acidalia was a fountain sacred to Venus.
Lyke . . . groome Alcmena, wife of Amphitryon, spent a night of love, magically prolonged to the length of three nights, with Jupiter, and conceived Hercules, who was born at Tiryns and served as a super-groom in the cleaning of the Augean stables.
thy selfe Night
begot Majesty Spenser made up this little myth himself.

Ne let the Pouke,° nor other evill sprights,
Ne let mischívous witches with theyr charmes,
Ne let hob Goblins, names whose sence we see not,
Fray us with things that be not,
Let not the shriech Oule, nor the Storke be heard:
Nor the night Raven° that still° deadly yels,   *ever*
Nor damnèd ghosts cald up with mighty spels,
Nor griesly vultures make us once affeard:
Ne let th'unpleasant Quyre of Frogs still° croking   *always*
350 Make us to wish theyr choking.
Let none of these theyr drery accents sing;
Ne let the woods them answer, nor theyr eccho ring.

But let stil Silence trew night watches keepe,
That sacred peace may in assurance rayne,
And tymely sleep, when it is tyme to sleepe,
May poure his limbs forth on your° pleasant playne,
The whiles an hundred little wingèd loves,°
Like divers fethered doves,
Shall fly and flutter round about your bed,
360 And in the secret darke, that° none reproves,   *when*
Their prety stealthes shal worke, and snares shal spread
To filch away sweet snatches of delight,
Conceald through covert night.
Ye sonnes of Venus, play your sports at will,
For greedy pleasure, carelesse of your toyes,°   *tricks*
Thinks more upon her paradise of joyes,
Then what ye do, albe it good or ill.
All night therefore attend your merry play,
For it will soone be day:
370 Now none doth hinder you, that say or sing,
Ne will the woods now answer, nor your Eccho ring.

Who is the same, which at my window peepes?
Or whose is that faire face, that shines so bright,
Is it not Cinthia,° she that never sleepes,
But walkes about high heaven al the night?
O fayrest goddesse, do thou not envy
My love with me to spy:
For thou likewise didst love, though now unthought,°   *unremembered*
And for a fleece of woll, which privily,
380 The Latmian shephard° once unto thee brought,
His pleasures with thee wrought.
Therefore to us be favorable now;

Pouke puck, Robin Goodfellow, mischievous and malevolent fairy
Oule . . . Storke . . . night Raven birds of ill-omen, all foretelling death except the stork, believed to avenge adultery
your Night's

loves cupids, "amoretti"
Cinthia the moon; there was a new moon on June 9, two days before the wedding
Latmian shephard Endymion lay with Diana on Mount Latmos; in most versions it was Pan who won her with a fleece of wool.

And sith of wemens labours thou hast charge,
And generation goodly dost enlarge,
Encline thy will t'effect our wishfull vow,
And the chast wombe informe with timely seed,
That may our comfort breed:
Till which we cease our hopefull hap° to sing,   *luck*
Ne let the woods us answere, nor our Eccho ring.

390 And thou great Juno, which with awful might
The lawes of wedlock still dost patronize,°
And the religion° of the faith first plight°   *bond / pledged*
With sacred rites hast taught to solemnize:
And eeke for comfort often callèd art
Of women in their smart,°   *labor pains*
Eternally bind thou this lovely band,
And all thy blessings unto us impart.
And thou glad Genius,° in whose gentle hand,
The bridale bowre and geniall° bed remaine,
400 Without blemish or staine,
And the sweet pleasures of theyr loves delight
With secret ayde doest succour and supply,
Till they bring forth the fruitfull progeny,
Send us the timely fruit of this same night.
And thou fayre Hebe,° and thou Hymen free,
Grant that it may so be.
Til which we cease your further prayse to sing,
Ne any woods shal answer, nor your Eccho ring.

And ye high heavens, the temple of the gods,
410 In which a thousand torches flaming bright
Doe burne, that to us wretched earthly clods,
In dreadful darknesse lend desirèd light;
And all ye powers which in the same remayne,
More then we men can fayne,
Poure out your blessing on us plentiously,
And happy influence upon us raine,
That we may raise a large posterity,
Which from the earth, which they may long possesse,
With lasting happinesse,
420 Up to your haughty pallaces may mount,
And for the guerdon of theyr glorious merit
May heavenly tabernacles there inherit,
Of blessèd Saints for to increase the count.
So let us rest, sweet love, in hope of this,

Juno . . . patronize *Juno pronuba*, goddess of marriage. Lucina, on whom women called in childbirth, was a name applied to both Diana and Juno.
Genius the patron of generation, as in *The Faerie Queene* III.vi 31–33

geniall Latin expression for marriage bed, place of generation
Hebe goddess of youth, not traditionally associated with weddings

And cease till then our tymely joyes to sing,
The woods no more us answer, nor our eccho ring.

Song made in lieu of many ornaments,°
With which my love should duly have bene dect,⁊   *decked*
Which cutting off through hasty accidents,°
430   Ye would not stay your dew time to expect,
But promist both to recompens,
Be unto her a goodly ornament,
And for short time an endlesse moniment.°

1595

SIR WALTER RALEGH
1552–1618

Born to a Devon family, he attended Oriel College, Oxford, for a while, served as a soldier in France and Ireland, returned to London, and lived in the Middle Temple. He became a favorite of the Queen, who elevated him and made him rich. His careers were many: as a courtier, he was a precursor of the later "dandy"; as a sailor and entrepreneur, he explored Guiana, founded the first Virginia colony, and attacked the Spanish fleet at Cadiz in 1596. As an intellectual, his association with Chapman, Marlowe, and Hariot in a group referred to as the "School of Night" earned him a reputation for atheism (for a suggestion of the precise flavor of his fame, see the sketch of him by John Aubrey, below). After being the Queen's protégé for a decade, he was dropped (so the story went) because of his seduction of one of the Queen's attendants, Elizabeth Throckmorton. James I, who eventually had him beheaded for treason, imprisoned him in the Tower for thirteen years, during which time he worked on scientific and historical projects. The poems published in his lifetime appeared in anthologies (his long poem, *Cynthia*, in praise of Queen Elizabeth, is lost, except for a fragment); his comprehensive historical work is *The History of the World*.

From The History of the World

Book I, Chapter II, Section V

That man is, as it were, a little world: [1] with a digression touching our mortality.

Man, thus compounded and formed by God, was an abstract or model, or brief story of the universal, in whom God concluded the creation and work of the world, and whom he made the last and most excellent of his creatures, being

---

ornaments wedding presents; the envoy makes apologetic reference to the occasion of the poem **hasty accidents** accidents of haste (perhaps the date had to be brought forward)

short . . . moniment immortal record of the one day it records and schematically represents

1. This section forms part of the theoretical opening of Ralegh's huge, meditative *History of the World*, unfinished (like its subject), and published first in 1614. The part reproduced here is as elaborate a statement as one could want of the received idea of man as microcosm, or little world (see Fig. 22).

internally endued with a divine understanding, by which he might contemplate and serve his Creator, after whose image he was formed, and endued with the powers and faculties of reason and other abilities, that thereby also he might govern and rule the world, and all other God's creatures therein. And whereas God created three sorts of living natures, to wit, angelical, rational, and brutal; giving to angels an intellectual, and to beasts a sensual nature, he vouchsafed unto man both the intellectual of angels, the sensitive of beasts, and the proper rational belonging unto man,[2] and therefore, saith Gregory Nazianzen,[3] *Homo est utriusque naturæ vinculum:* 'Man is the bond and chain which tieth together both natures.' And because in the little frame of man's body there is a representation of the universal, and (by allusion) a kind of participation of all the parts thereof, therefore was man called *microcosmos,* or the little world. *Deus igitur hominem factum, velut alterum quendam mundum, in brevi magnum, atque exiguo totum, in terris statuit:* 'God therefore placed in the earth the man whom he had made, as it were another world, the great and large world in the small and little world.'[4] For out of earth and dust was formed the flesh of man, and therefore heavy and lumpish; the bones of his body we may compare to the hard rocks and stones, and therefore strong and durable, of which Ovid:[5]

> Inde genus durum sumus, experiensque laborum,
> Et documenta damus qua simus origine nati.

> From thence our kind hard-hearted is,
>   Enduring pain and care,
> Approving, that our bodies of
>   A stony nature are.

His blood, which disperseth itself by the branches of veins through all the body, may be resembled to those waters which are carried by brooks and rivers over all the earth; his breath to the air; his natural heat to the enclosed warmth which the earth hath in itself—which, stirred up by the heat of the sun, assisteth nature in the speedier procreation of those varieties which the earth bringeth forth; our radical moisture, oil, or balsamum (whereon the natural heat feedeth and is maintained) is resembled to the fat and fertility of the earth; the hairs of man's body, which adorns, or overshadows it, to the grass, which covereth the upper face and skin of the earth; our generative power, to nature, which produceth all things; our determinations,[6] to the light, wandering, and unstable clouds, carried every where with uncertain winds; our eyes, to the light of the sun and moon; and the beauty of our youth, to the flowers of the spring, which, either in a very short time, or with the sun's heat, dry up and wither away, or the fierce puffs of wind blow them from the stalks; the thoughts of our mind, to the motion of angels; and our pure understanding (formerly called *mens,* and that which always looketh upwards) to those intellectual natures which are always present with God; and, lastly, our immortal souls (while they are

2. Another received notion of Renaissance psychology, derived from Aristotle's statement of it in his *Physics.*
3. St. Gregory of Nazianzus (c. 328–390), bishop and theologian.
4. Ralegh is quoting from St. Augustine, *The City of God.*
5. *Metamorphoses* I.414–15.
6. Resolutions.

righteous) are by God himself beautified with the title of his own image and similitude. And although, in respect of God, there is no man just, or good, or righteous (for, *in angelis deprehensa est stultitia*, 'Behold, he found folly in his angels,' saith Job [7]) yet, with such a kind of difference as there is between the substance and the shadow,[8] there may be found a goodness in man: which God being pleased to accept, hath therefore called man the image and similitude of his own righteousness. In this also is the little world of man compared, and made more like the universal (man being the measure of all things—*Homo est mensura omnium rerum*, saith Aristotle [9] and Pythagoras) that the four complexions resemble the four elements,[10] and the seven ages of man the seven planets; whereof our infancy is compared to the moon, in which we seem only to live and grow, as plants; the second age to Mercury, wherein we are taught and instructed; our third age to Venus, the days of love, desire, and vanity; the fourth to the sun, the strong, flourishing, and beautiful age of man's life; the fifth to Mars, in which we seek honour and victory, and in which our thoughts travel to ambitious ends; the sixth age is ascribed to Jupiter, in which we begin to take account of our times, judge of ourselves, and grow to the perfection of our understanding; the last and seventh to Saturn, wherein our days are sad, and overcast, and in which we find by dear and lamentable experience, and by the loss which can never be repaired, that of all our vain passions and affections past, the sorrow only abideth: our attendants are sicknesses, and variable infirmities; and by how much the more we are accompanied with plenty, by so much the more greedily is our end desired, whom when time hath made unsociable to others, we become a burden to ourselves: being of no other use, than to hold the riches we have from our successors. In this time it is, when (as aforesaid) we, for the most part, and never before, prepare for our eternal habitation, which we pass on unto with many sighs, groans, and sad thoughts, and in the end, by the workmanship of death, finish the sorrowful business of a wretched life; towards which we always travel both sleeping and waking; neither have those beloved companions of honour and riches any power at all to hold us any one day by the glorious promise of entertainments; but by what crooked path soever we walk, the same leadeth on directly to the house of death, whose doors lie open at all hours, and to all persons. For this tide of man's life, after it once turneth and declineth, ever runneth with a perpetual ebb and falling stream, but never floweth again: our leaf once fallen, springeth no more; neither doth the sun or the summer adorn us again, with the garments of new leaves and flowers.

> Redditur arboribus florens revirentibus ætas;
> Ergo non homini, quod fuit ante, redit.[11]

7. Job 4:18.
8. A traditional way of phrasing a contrast between matter and the mere image of matter.
9. In the *Metaphysics* I.1053b which mentions Protagoras, not "Pythagoras"; this idea was also treated by Plato in the *Theaetetus*.
10. The four "complexions" or temperaments (sanguine, choleric, phlegmatic, and melancholy) are actually generated by combinations of the elements (see *Renaissance Psychology* in the Glossary).
11. From an elegy on the death of Maecenas by Albinovanus, a minor poet of the Augustan age.

To which I give this sense.

> The plants and trees made poor and old
> By winter envious,
> The spring-time bounteous
> Covers again from shame and cold:
> But never man repaired again
> His youth and beauty lost,
> Though art, and care, and cost,
> Do promise nature's help in vain.

And of which Catullus, Epigram 53.[12]

> Soles occidere et redire possunt:
> Nobis cum semel occidit brevis lux,
> Nox est perpetua una dormienda.

> The sun may set and rise:
> But we contrarywise
> Sleep after our short light
> One everlasting night.

For if there were any baiting place, or rest, in the course or race of man's life, then, according to the doctrine of the Academics,[13] the same might also perpetually be maintained. But as there is a continuance of motion in natural living things, and as the sap and juice, wherein the life of plants is preserved, doth evermore ascend or descend; so is it with the life of man, which is always either increasing towards ripeness and perfection, or declining and decreasing towards rottenness and dissolution.

1614

A Description of Love

Now what is love? I pray, tell.
It is that fountain and that well,
Where pleasure and repentance dwell.
It is perhaps that saucing° bell,
That tolls all in to heaven or hell:
And this is love, as I hear tell.

Yet what is love? I pray thee say.
It is a work on holy-day;
It is December matched with May;
10 When lusty bloods, in fresh array
Hear ten months after of the play:
And this is love, as I hear say.

---

12. A famous passage from the "Vivamus mea Lesbia, atque amemus," adapted by Ben Jonson and Thomas Campion (see "Come, My Celia" and "My Sweetest Lesbia").
13. The philosophic descendants of Plato, down to the Roman Cicero.

saucing the Sanctus bell, rung during that portion of the Mass

Yet what is love? I pray thee sayn.
It is a sunshine mixed with rain;
It is a tooth-ache, or like pain;
It is a game where none doth gain;
The lass saith no, and would full fain:°
And this is love, as I hear sayn.

Yet what is love? I pray thee say.
20 It is a yea, it is a nay,
A pretty kind of sporting fray;
It is a thing will soon away;
Then take the vantage while you may:
And this is love, as I hear say.

Yet what is love? I pray thee show.
A thing that creeps, it cannot go;
A prize that passeth to and fro;
A thing for one, a thing for mo;
And he that proves° must find it so:
30 And this is love, sweet friend, I trow.

                    1593

Answer to Marlowe°

If all the world and love were young,
And truth in every shepherd's tongue,
These pretty pleasures might me move
To live with thee and be thy love.

Time drives the flocks from field to fold,
When rivers rage and rocks grow cold,
And Philomel° becometh dumb;
The rest complain of cares to come.

The flowers do fade, and wanton fields
10 To wayward winter reckoning yields;
A honey tongue, a heart of gall,
Is fancy's spring, but sorrow's fall.

Thy gowns, thy shoes, thy beds of roses,
Thy cap, thy kirtle,° and thy posies
Soon break, soon wither, soon forgotten,
In folly ripe, in reason rotten.

Thy belt of straw and ivy buds,
Thy coral clasps and amber studs,

---

fain be glad to, with a pun on "feign" (pretend)
proves tries it out
Answer to Marlowe See "The Passionate

Shepherd to His Love," and Donne, "The Bait."
Philomel the nightingale
kirtle dress

All these in me no means can move
20   To come to thee and be thy love.

But could you last and love still breed,
Had joys no date nor age no need,
Then these delights my mind might move
To live with thee and be thy love.

1600

On the Life of Man

What is our life? a play° of passion,
Our mirth the music of division;°
Our mothers' wombs the tiring-houses° be
Where we are dressed for this short comedy;
Heaven the judicious, sharp spectator is
That sits and marks still who doth act amiss;
Our graves that hide us from the searching sun
Are like drawn curtains when the play is done:
Thus march we, playing, to our latest° rest,
10   Only we die in earnest, that's no jest.

1612

GEORGE CHAPMAN
1559–1634

Born in 1559 of Hertfordshire yeomanry, Chapman may have attended Oxford, but if so, left without taking a degree. After some time abroad, probably fighting in the Low Countries, he returned to England, and his circle there included Marlowe, Sir Walter Ralegh, and the mathematicians Roydon and Hariot, a group of advanced thinkers, religiously and intellectually, who may have constituted what is called "The School of Night," after the title of Chapman's first published work, *The Shadow of Night* (1594). An obscure and difficult poem, it presents an antithetical reading of the mythological significance and moral import of chaos, night, and darkness. *Ovid's Banquet of Sense*, a mythological narrative with neoplatonic philosophical interpolations, appeared the following year. By 1598, when his completion of Marlowe's unfinished *Hero and Leander* appeared, he was an established dramatist. But he is best known for his magnificent translation of Homer (the *Iliad* appearing in 1611, the *Odyssey* in 1614–15), the first done in the rhymed fourteeners of earlier sixteenth-century tradition, the second in the heroic couplets that replaced them as the equivalent of heroic Greek and Latin verse. His concern in all his poetry was for the philosophical interpretation of received ancient mythology; in his conclusion to *Hero and Leander*, we see him turning erotic narrative into moral speculation.

play This is a version of the *theatrum mundi* theme (see Spenser's *Amoretti*, Sonnet LIV) but a grim, half-mocking one; the first line puns on "passion plays", as religious drama.

division in the musical sense, free counterpoint based on a theme
tiring-houses dressing rooms
latest last

From Hero and Leander°

The Third Sestiad

THE ARGUMENT OF THE THIRD SESTIAD

Leander to the envious light
Resigns his night-sports with the night,
And swims the Hellespont again.
Thesme,° the deity sovereign
Of customs and religious rites,
Appears, improving° his delights,
Since nuptial honours he neglected;
Which straight he vows shall be effected.
Fair Hero, left devirginate,
Weighs, and with fury wails her state:
But with her love and woman's wit
She argues and approveth it.

New light gives new directions,° fortunes new
To fashion our endeavours that ensue—
More harsh, at least more hard, more grave and high
Our subject runs, and our stern Muse must fly.
Love's edge is taken off, and that light flame,
Those thoughts, joys, longings, that before became
High unexperienced blood, and maids' sharp plights,
Must now grow staid, and censure the delights,
That, being enjoyed, ask judgment; now we praise,
10 As having parted: evenings crown the days.
    And now, ye wanton Loves, and young Desires,
Pied Vanity, the mint of strange attires,
Ye lisping Flatteries, and obsequious Glances,
Relentful° Musics, and attractive Dances,
And you detested Charms constraining love!
Shun love's stoln° sports by that these lovers prove.
    By this, the sovereign of heaven's golden fires,
And young Leander, lord of his desires,
Together from their lover's arms arose:
20 Leander into Hellespontus throws
His Hero-handled body, whose delight
Made him disdain each other epithite.
And so amidst the enamoured waves he swims,
The god of gold° of purpose gilt his limbs,

Hero and Leander See Marlowe's two Sestiads, below.
Thesme from the Greek *thesmos*, meaning "law": we shall see her named Ceremony below
improving reproving, condemning
New light . . . directions Chapman, starting out on the morning after Hero and Leander's first night of making love, connects his changing subject—the legitimization of human passion in moral order—with a narrative new day's dawning.
Relentful relaxing, calming
stoln stolen
god of gold Apollo, because, here, the power of sunlight is imagined as creating it

That, this word *gilt* including double sense,
The double guilt of his incontinence
Might be expressed, that had no stay to employ
The treasure which the love-god let him joy
In his dear Hero, with such sacred thrift
30 As had beseemed so sanctified a gift;
But, like a greedy vulgar prodigal,
Would on the stock dispend,° and rudely fall,
Before his time, to that unblessèd blessing
Which, for lust's plague, doth perish with possessing:
Joy graven in sense,° like snow in water, wastes;
Without preserve of virtue, nothing lasts.
What man is he, that with a wealthy eye
Enjoys a beauty richer than the sky,
Through whose white skin, softer than soundest sleep,
40 With damask eyes the ruby blood doth peep,
And runs in branches through her azure veins,
Whose mixture and first fire his love attains;
Whose both hands limit both love's deities,°
And sweeten human thoughts like paradise;
Whose disposition silken is and kind.
Directed with an earth-exempted mind—
Who thinks not heaven with such a love is given?
And who, like earth, would spend that dower of heaven,
With rank desire to joy it all at first?
50 What simply kills our hunger, quencheth thirst,
Clothes but our nakedness and makes us live,
Praise doth not any of her favours give
But what doth plentifully minister
Beauteous apparel and delicious cheer,
So ordered that it still excites desire,
And still gives pleasures freeness to aspire,
The palm of Bounty ever moist preserving—
To Love's sweet life this is the courtly carving.°
Thus Time and all-states-ordering Ceremony°
60 Had banished all offence: Time's golden thigh°
Upholds the flowery body of the earth
In sacred harmony, and every birth
Of men and actions makes legitimate;
Being used aright, the use of time is fate.
    Yet did the gentle flood transfer once more
This prize of love home to his father's shore,
Where he unlades himself of that false wealth

---

dispend spend wastefully
graven in sense at a purely sensual level
deities Venus and Cupid
courtly carving showing the proper courtesy
all-states-ordering Ceremony the goddess will appear shortly

Time's golden thigh the golden thigh, traditional attribute of Pythagoras; here given to Time because Pythagoras discovered numerical proportion, the "sacred harmony" on which the order of creation depends

That makes few rich—treasures composed by stealth;
And to his sister, kind Hermione
70 (Who on the shore kneeled, praying to the sea
For his return), he all love's goods did show,
In Hero seized° for him, in him for Hero.
    His most kind sister all his secrets knew,
And to her, singing, like a shower, he flew,
Sprinkling the earth, that to their tombs took in
Streams dead for love, to leave his ivory skin,
Which yet a snowy foam did leave above,
As soul to the dead water that did love;
And from thence did the first white roses spring
80 (For love is sweet and fair in every thing),
And all the sweetened shore, as he did go,
Was crowned with odorous roses, white as snow.
Love-blest Leander was with love so filled,
That love to all that touched him he instilled;
And as the colours of all things we see,
To our sight's powers communicated be,
So to all objects that in compass came
Of any sense he had, his senses' flame
Flowed from his parts with force so virtual,
90 It fired with sense things mere° insensual.
    Now, with warm baths and odours comforted,
When he lay down, he kindly kissed his bed,
As consecrating it to Hero's right,
And vowed thereafter, that whatever sight
Put him in mind of Hero or her bliss,
Should be her altar to prefer° a kiss.
    Then laid he forth his late-enrichèd arms,
In whose white circle Love writ all his charms,
And made his characters° sweet Hero's limbs,
100 When on his breast's warm sea she sideling° swims;
And at those arms, held up in circle, met,
He said, 'See, sister, Hero's carquenet!'°
Which she had rather wear about her neck
Than all the jewels that do Juno deck.
    But, as he shook with passionate desire
To put in flame his other secret fire,
A music so divine did pierce his ear,
As never yet his ravished sense did hear;
When suddenly a light of twenty hues
110 Brake through the roof, and, like the rainbow, views
Amazed Leander: in whose beams came down

---

seized settled, established
mere totally
to prefer on which to proffer

characters the letters in which magician love
writes his charms
sideling sideways
carquenet jeweled collar or necklace

The goddess Ceremony,° with a crown
Of all the stars; and Heaven with her descended:
Her flaming hair to her bright feet extended,
By which hung all the bench of deities;
And in a chain,° compact° of ears and eyes,
She led Religion: all her body was
Clear and transparent as the purest glass,
For she was all presented to the sense:
120 Devotion, Order, State, and Reverence,
Here shadows were; Society, Memory;
All which her sight made live, her absence die.
A rich disparent pentacle° she wears,
Drawn full of circles and strange characters.
Her face was changeable to every eye;
One way looked ill, another graciously;
Which while men viewed they cheerful were and holy,
But looking off, vicious and melancholy.
The snaky paths to each observed law
130 Did Policy° in her broad bosom draw.
One hand a mathematic crystal° sways,
Which, gathering in one line a thousand rays
From her bright eyes, Confusion burns to death,
And all estates of men distinguisheth:
By it Morality and Comeliness
Themselves in all their sightly figures dress.
Her other hand a laurel rod applies,
To beat back Barbarism and Avarice,
That followed eating earth and excrement
140 And human limbs; and would make proud ascent
To seats of gods, were Ceremony slain.
The Hours and Graces bore her glorious train;
And all the sweets of our society
Were sphered and treasured in her bounteous eye.
Thus she appeared, and sharply did reprove
Leander's bluntness in his violent love:
Told him how poor was substance without rites,
Like bills unsigned; desires without delights;
Like meats unseasoned; like rank corn that grows
150 On cottages, that none or reaps or sows;
Not being with civil forms confirmed and bounded,

goddess Ceremony This allegorical figure is Chapman's own, but she represents powerful forces in the Renaissance world view; see the relevant passage from Hooker's *Of the Laws of Ecclesiastical Polity*, below; also, Prospero's insistence on ceremonious marriage, *The Tempest* IV.
chain a version of the famous concept of the Great Chain of Being, derived from Homer's vision of Zeus' golden chain by which all the other gods, earth, and sea were connected in order and by which he could draw them all up to Olympus. Spenser refers to it in *The Faerie Queene* II.vii.46 as the "faire cheyne of love" and Milton in the Second Prolusion as the "universal concord and sweet union of all things which Pythagoras poetically figures as harmony."
compact compounded
disparent pentacle multicolored five-pointed star, emblematic of magical power
Policy governmental and legal manipulations
mathematic crystal probably a convex lens

For human dignities and comforts founded;
But loose and secret all their glories hide;
Fear fills the chamber. Darkness decks the bride.

. . .

1598

From Homer's Odyssey

[The Gardens of Alcinoüs°]
　Without the hall, and close upon the gate,
A goodly orchard-ground was situate,
Of near ten acres; about which was led
A lofty quickset.˒ In it flourishèd   *hedge*
High and broad fruit trees, that pomegranates bore,
Sweet figs, pears, olives; and a number more
Most useful plants did there produce their store;
Whose fruits the hardest winter could not kill,
160　Nor hottest summer wither. There was still
Fruit in his proper season all the year.
Sweet Zephyr breathed upon them blasts that were
Of varied tempers. These he made to bear
Ripe fruits, these blossoms. Pear grew after pear,
Apple succeeded apple, grape the grape,
Fig after fig came; time made never rape
Of any dainty there. A sprightly vine
Spread here his root, whose fruit a hot sunshine
Made ripe betimes; here grew another green.
170　Here some were gathering, here some pressing, seen.
A large-allotted several° each fruit had;
And all the adorned grounds their appearance made
In flower and fruit, at which the king did aim
To the precisest order he could claim.
　Two fountains graced the garden; of which one
Poured out a winding stream that over-run

The Gardens of Alcinoüs In the *Odyssey* VII.
85–135 the hero, after being washed up on the
shores of Phaeacia, proceeds to the palace of its
ruler, where he is beautifully entertained, and
where he narrates all of the adventures befall-
ing him from the time of leaving Troy to his stay
on Calypso's island. Phaeacia is a version of the
Great Good Place, and Odysseus is tempted
by its bounties (and by the innocent loveliness
of Nausicaa, Alcinous' daughter) to remain.
For the Renaissance, the Phaeacian gardens
were a classical parallel to the biblical Eden,
along with the Elysian Fields,

　Where Rhadamanthus rules, and where
　　men live
　A never-troubled life, where snow, nor
　　showers,

Nor irksome Winter spends his
　fruitless powers,
But from the ocean Zephyr still resumes
A constant breath, that all the fields
　perfumes.
　　　　　　　　　　(*Odyssey* IV. 762–66)
Visions of the pastoral realm involved this
garden world (see the passage from Sidney's
Old Arcadia, above), and English gardening
traditions were acutely aware of the literary
and pictorial background of their art. What
became the Continental formal garden in the
17th and 18th centuries, laid out geo-
metrically and schematically, corresponds to the
Phaeacian gardens; the English tradition, the
carefully arranged appearance of haphazard-
ness, can be thought of as mimetic of Eden.
several perhaps "a place allocated to it"

The grounds for their use chiefly; the other went
Close by the lofty palace gate, and lent
The city his sweet benefit. And thus
180   The Gods the court deckt of Alcinoüs.

1614

CHRISTOPHER MARLOWE
1564–1593

Marlowe was the son of a Canterbury shoemaker. Scholarships took him to the King's School, Canterbury, and then to Corpus Christi College, Cambridge, in 1580. He graduated B.A. in 1584, and satisfied requirements for the M.A. by March 1587; but the authorities withheld the degree. At this point there was an extraordinary intervention by the Queen's Privy Council, which explained that Marlowe did not, as the University apparently supposed, intend to go to Rheims, considered the center of Catholic conspiracy against Elizabeth, and that "he had done her Majestie good service," adding that the Queen thought it wrong for Marlowe to suffer because of this. He took the degree.

The University had probably expected him to take holy orders, and suspected that he was about to leave, a convert to Catholicism, for the English seminary at Rheims. In fact he had already been employed by the Government on some secret political mission. Thus, Marlowe's career as a playwright, which also began at Cambridge, was from the start superimposed on a more underground existence.

Tamburlaine (1587), with its superman hero and its "mighty line," practically invented English tragedy and its blank-verse medium. But its author apparently continued to lead a double life; two years later he was involved in a fatal sword fight, in London. Not surprisingly he acquired a reputation for violent manners, and also for "atheism." His friend Thomas Kyd, trying to explain some compromising papers found in the room they had shared, said after Marlowe's death that the poet would "jest at the divine scriptures, gibe at prayers," and the informer Richard Baines accused him of many "atheistical" remarks, such as "Christ was a bastard and his mother dishonest" or "the first beginning of religion was only to keep men in awe." (In Elizabethan English the term atheism applied to any extreme manifestation of impiety.) Baines also reported a remark suggestive of homosexuality, and *Edward II* (c. 1591), Marlowe's history play, shows discreet interest in the theme.

Marlowe's death in a way fitted this kind of life. In his last year, probably, he wrote *Doctor Faustus* and was perhaps working on *Hero and Leander* when, in May 1593, the Privy Council ordered his arrest. He was awaiting examination by them and reporting daily when, on May 30, he went to a Deptford tavern with Ingram Frizer, Nicholas Skeres, and Robert Poley. Frizer and Skeres were agents and swindlers, Poley a double-agent. After supper there was a quarrel about the check, and Marlowe, seizing Frizer's dagger, wounded him; whereupon Frizer stabbed him to death, later successfully pleading self-defense. Marlowe was twenty-nine years old.

As a poet Marlowe achieved both celebrity and infamy; he was "the Muses' darling" but also creator of "that atheist Tamburlaine"; he was "by profession a scholar . . . but by practice a playmaker, and a Poet of scurrility." His "high astounding terms"— as he calls them in the Prologue to *Tamburlaine*—and his admiration for the ambitious "overreacher" hero and the "Machiavel" introduced the great period of English drama and gave expression to that hubris attendant on the revaluation of human power we associate with the Renaissance. In the highly original *Jew of Malta*—"tragic farce" as T. S. Eliot called it—the aim of ambition is money; in *Doctor Faustus* it is knowledge. Thus Marlowe displays his heroes reacting to most of the temptations that Satan can contrive; and the culminating temptation, as in Andrew Marvell's "Dialogue Between Resolved Soul and Created Pleasure," in Spenser's Cave of Mammon, and in *Paradise Regained*, is the scholar's temptation, forbidden knowledge. The difference between Marlowe and the others is that his heroes do not resist the temptations, and he provides us, not with a negative proof of virtue and obedience to divine law, but with positive examples of what happens in their absence. Thus, whatever his intentions may have been, and however much he flouted convention, Marlowe's themes are finally reducible to the powerful formulae of contemporary religion and morality. The interest of the plays, except perhaps Part I of *Tamburlaine*, derives largely from an exhibition of heroic and unavailing resistance, which releases great moral and dramatic energy. In the poems, based on an Ovid liberated from the old moralizing, we can see that energy operating without such severe resistance, in verse that is self-delighting, strong and easy.

Doctor Faustus

By common consent Marlowe's greatest play, *Doctor Faustus*, can nevertheless try the reader's patience. One difficulty is that we are often uncertain about the authenticity of what we are reading. Marlowe collaborated with at least one other writer, and there are, broadly, two distinct versions of the play. The first, published in 1604, is probably based on the players' memories of a touring version, shorter than the original but including extra clowning scenes. The other, of 1616, was probably based on the original manuscripts but including theatrical revisions; unfortunately the editors also used the text of 1604 and made cuts and changes. Only since W. W. Greg published his edition in 1950 has it been possible to feel any assurance that one has something fairly close to what Marlowe and his collaborator wrote. The whole basis of Greg's "conjectural reconstruction" has recently been called into question by Fredson T. Bowers in an important article, but for the time being Greg's is the text on which secondary editions must depend.

We cannot now blame later interfering hands for the mixing of very bad with very fine material. From the beginning the play must have had scenes of second-rate farce, and there can never have been a version in which Faustus did not use his powers to absurdly trivial ends. For one thing, it was part of the conception that such a bargain could not be of high human use. Furthermore, the foolery that intervenes between the strong opening and the wonderful closing scene paid off in the popular theater, if not in terms of dramatic art. Marlowe left these scenes to the collaborator, perhaps Samuel Rowley, who knew how to write for the clowns and devils, and how to use the properties—the dragon, for example—of the Admiral's Men. He himself handled most, but not all, of the serious material; F. P. Wilson calculates that he was responsible for not more than 825 lines.

The comic material is developed from *The Damnable Life and Deserved Death of*

Doctor John Faustus, published in 1592—a free translation of a Lutheran German original of 1587. The *Damnable Life* was thus an anti-Catholic work, and the authors eked it out by referring also to that great English work of anti-papal propaganda, Foxe's *Acts and Monuments* (1563).

If the theme of the play can be reduced to a simple proposition, some words from *The Damnable Life* might serve: "Give none blame but thine own self-will, thy proud and aspiring mind, which both brought thee into the wrath of God and utter damnation." This is the moral, but it is of course complicated by Marlowe's ability to give powerfully attractive accounts of "proud and aspiring minds." The Faust story acquired a quasi-mythical status as an *exemplum* of the soul that yields to the last temptation of Satan, the temptation of knowledge.

This was a theme of high interest in Marlowe's time. The ecclesiastical ban on *curiositas*—the desire for forbidden knowledge—was constant, but the line between the licit and the wicked was differently drawn at different times and by different sects. In general the principle was that all knowledge which did not contribute to the salvation of the soul was wrong, whether sought out of pride or ambition. Yet knowledge of the creation—God's second book—could be good; where "curiosity" began and pious inquiry into the creatures left off was a question. In Marvell's "Dialogue Between the Resolved Soul and Created Pleasure" the tempter says

> Thou shalt know each hidden cause
> And see the future time;
> Try what depth the center draws,
> And then to heaven climb.

but the Resolved Soul rejects this; it would not help him to heaven, except in the sense that Faustus takes a trip to its frontiers with Mephostophilis. Faustus, on the other hand, accepts, for purely worldly reasons. He wants everything the good soul rejects: money, women, power. "The god thou serv'st is thine own appetite," he confesses. None of the questions to which, as a scholar, he values the answers are properly dealt with by Mephostophilis, and the devil, in Marlowe's parts of the play, does not conceal the pains of hell—the price of this essentially trivial and imperfect learning. So Faustus damns himself; his curiosity, like Eve's in *Paradise Lost* a tributary of pride, is proof against his occasional motions of repentance.

The greatness of the play lies not in its compliance with religious wisdom but in the resistance, not only of Faustus but of the very verse he speaks, to the law which must subdue him. There is, for example, a crisis when the demonic Helen appears; the Old Man has moved him, but the second apparition of Helen results from his deliberate choice; and by carnally embracing a demon he excludes "the grace of heaven," as the Old Man observes. Thus Faustus sins only by his own choice, here as elsewhere. But the address to Helen: "Was this the face that launched a thousand ships?" illustrates the resistance of the senses and poetry to the law. So in the opening, when Faustus, proud and inconsiderate in his scholarly ambition, rejects all human learning, and all the warnings of divinity, and wantonly sets out on his self-destructive course—"A sound magician is a demi-god"—his folly has a kind of poetic splendor; so has his blasphemy, when he uses the last words of Christ on the cross in sealing his bargain with Lucifer. Nearly all the rest till Helen comes—even the fine talk about astrology—is dross. Then, in Faustus's last speech, the first great tragic monologue of the English stage, we find a verse of Ovid, transplanted from its amorous context into this scholar's agony—a last poignant testimony of the struggle of the intellect and senses against the law.

It is as scholar and poet that the closing Chorus laments Faustus. The description, and the lament, fit Marlowe as well; learning, virtuosity in erotic and tragic verse, violence in action, a humane magniloquence not yet free of the religious bonds that restricted it: these are characteristic not only of the play and its author, but also of what we understand when we speak of "Renaissance Man."

Doctor Faustus

DRAMATIS PERSONAE

CHORUS

DR. JOHN FAUSTUS

WAGNER, *his servant, a student*

CORNELIUS ⎫
VALDES ⎬ *his friends, magicians*

THREE SCHOLARS, *students under Faustus*

OLD MAN

POPE ADRIAN

RAYMOND, *King of Hungary*

BRUNO, *the rival Pope*

CARDINALS OF FRANCE AND PADUA

ARCHBISHOP OF RHEIMS

CHARLES V, *Emperor of Germany*

MARTINO ⎫
FREDERICK ⎬ *knights at the*
BENVOLIO ⎭ *Emperor's court*

DUKE OF SAXONY

DUKE OF VANHOLT

DUCHESS OF VANHOLT

ROBIN

DICK

VINTNER

HORSE-COURSER

CARTER

HOSTESS

GOOD ANGEL

BAD ANGEL (*Spirit*)

MEPHOSTOPHILIS

LUCIFER

BELZEBUB

SPIRITS PRESENTING THE SEVEN DEADLY SINS

ALEXANDER THE GREAT

ALEXANDER'S PARAMOUR

DARIUS, *King of Persia*

HELEN OF TROY

DEVILS, CUPIDS, BISHOPS, MONKS, FRIARS, LORDS, SOLDIERS, ATTENDANTS

[PROLOGUE]

CHORUS

Not marching in the fields of Thrasimene,°
Where Mars did mate° the warlike Carthagens,
Nor sporting in the dalliance of love
In courts of kings where state° is overturned,
Nor in the pomp of proud audacious deeds,
Intends our muse° to vaunt his heavenly verse.

Thrasimene Lake Trasimene, scene of Hannibal's victory over Rome (217 B.C.), presumably treated in some lost play

mate ally with
state government
muse poet

Only this, Gentles: we must now perform
The form of Faustus' fortunes, good or bad.
And now to patient judgements we appeal,
10   And speak for Faustus in his infancy.
Now is he born, of parents base of stock,
In Germany, within a town called Rhode.°
At riper years to Wittenberg° he went,
Whereas° his kinsmen chiefly brought him up.
So much he profits in divinity,
The fruitful plot of scholarism° graced,
That shortly he was graced with doctor's name,
Excelling all whose sweet delight disputes
In heavenly matters of theology.
20   Till swol'n with cunning of a self-conceit,°
His waxen wings did mount above his reach,
And melting,° heavens conspired his overthrow.
For falling to a devilish exercise,
And glutted now with learning's golden gifts,
He surfeits upon cursèd necromancy;
Nothing so sweet as magic is to him,
Which he prefers before his chiefest bliss:°
And this the man that in his study sits.   *Exit.*

[SCENE I]

FAUSTUS *in his study.*°

FAUSTUS   Settle thy studies, Faustus, and begin
To sound the depth of that thou wilt profess.
Having commenced,° be a divine in show,°
Yet level° at the end of every art
And live and die in Aristotle's works.°
Sweet Analytics,° 'tis thou hast ravished me.
Bene disserere est finis logices.°
Is to dispute well logic's chiefest end?
Affords this art no greater miracle?
10   Then read no more, thou hast attained that end.
A great subject fitteth Faustus' wit:

Rhode Roda (now Stadtroda) in central Germany
Wittenberg German university (Luther was an alumnus)
Whereas where
plot of scholarism garden of scholarship
cunning . . . self-conceit intellectual pride arising from arrogance
melting when they melted; Marlowe is thinking of Icarus
chiefest bliss heaven
in his study The curtain has been drawn, revealing Faustus in the alcove at the back of the stage.
commenced taken a degree
in show ostensibly
level aim
Aristotle's works These still dominated the university curriculum, though they were increasingly challenged.
Analytics Aristotle's work on the nature of proof
Bene . . . logices "To argue well is the end of logic"; not from Aristotle but his 16th-century opponent Ramus

Bid *on kai me on*° farewell; Galen,° come.
Seeing, *ubi desinit philosophus, ibi incipit medicus.*°
Be a physician, Faustus, heap up gold
And be eternized° for some wondrous cure.
Summum bonum medicinae sanitas:°
The end of physic is our body's health.
Why Faustus, hast thou not attained that end?
Is not thy common talk sound aphorisms?°
20   Are not thy bills° hung up as monuments,
Whereby whole cities have escaped the plague,
And thousand desperate maladies been cured?
Yet art thou still but Faustus, and a man.
Couldst thou make men to live eternally,
Or being dead, raise them to life again,
Then this profession were to be esteemed.
Physic, farewell. Where is Justinian?°
Si una eademque res legatur duobus,
Alter rem, alter valorem rei°—*etc.,*
30   A petty case of paltry legacies!
Exhaereditare filium non potest pater, nisi°—
Such is the subject of the Institute°
And universal body of the law.
This study fits a mercenary drudge,
Who aims at nothing but external trash,°
Too servile and illiberal for me.
When all is done divinity is best.
Jerome's Bible,° Faustus, view it well.
Stipendium peccati mors est.° Ha! *Stipendium, etc.,*
40   The reward of sin is death. That's hard.
Si pecasse negamus, fallimur, et nulla est in nobis veritas.°
If we say that we have no sin we deceive ourselves, and there is no truth
    in us. Why then, belike we must sin, and so consequently die.°
Ay, we must die an everlasting death.
What doctrine call you this? *Che sera, sera.*
What will be, shall be. Divinity, adieu!
These metaphysics of magicians
And necromantic books are heavenly;
Lines, circles, signs, letters and characters:
50   Ay, these are those that Faustus most desires.

---

on kai me on being and not being (Greek)
Galen Greek writer on medicine (*c.* 129–199 A.D.)
ubi desinit . . . medicus "where the philosopher leaves off, the doctor begins" (Aristotle, *De Sensu*)
eternized made immortal
Summum . . . sanitas translated in next line
aphorisms medical precepts
bills prescriptions
Justinian 6th-century Roman emperor who codified the law
Si una . . . rei "if one and the same thing is bequeathed to two persons, one shall have

the thing itself, the other the value of the thing"
Exhaereditare . . . nisi "a father cannot disinherit his son unless"
Institute Justinian's collection is called the *Institutes;* these Latin quotations derive from it.
trash money
Jerome's Bible the Vulgate, Latin Bible formerly used by Catholics, based on the translation of St. Jerome completed in 405 A.D.
Stipendium . . . est Romans 6:23
Si . . . veritas 1 John 1:8
Why then . . . die Faustus omits considering the Christian doctrine of redemption.

O what a world of profit and delight,
Of power, of honour, of omnipotence,
Is promised to the studious artisan!°
All things that move between the quiet° poles
Shall be at my command. Emperors and kings
Are but obeyed in their several° provinces.
Nor can they raise the wind or rend the clouds.
But this dominion that exceeds in this
Stretcheth as far as doth the mind of man:
A sound magician is a demi-god.
Here tire,° my brains to get° a deity.

Enter WAGNER.

Wagner, commend me to my dearest friends,
The German Valdes and Cornelius.
Request them earnestly to visit me.

WAGNER   I will sir.   *Exit*

FAUSTUS   Their conference° will be a greater help to me
Than all my labours, plod I ne'er so fast.

Enter the ANGEL *and* SPIRIT.°

GOOD ANGEL   O Faustus, lay that damnèd book aside,
And gaze not on it lest it tempt thy soul,
And heap God's heavy wrath upon thy head.
Read, read the scriptures: that is blasphemy.

BAD ANGEL   Go forward, Faustus, in that famous art
Wherein all nature's treasury is contained.
Be thou on earth as Jove° is in the sky,
Lord and commander of these elements.   *Exeunt* ANGELS.

FAUSTUS   How am I glutted with conceit° of this!
Shall I make spirits fetch me what I please,
Resolve me of all ambiguities,
Perform what desperate enterprise I will?
I'll have them fly to India for gold,
Ransack the ocean for orient pearl,
And search all corners of the new-found world
For pleasant fruits and princely delicates;°
I'll have them read me strange philosophy,
And tell the secrets of all foreign kings;
I'll have them wall all Germany with brass,°
And make swift Rhine circle fair Wittenberg;
I'll have them fill the public schools with silk,
Wherewith the students shall be bravely clad;

60

70

80

artisan artist; here, practitioner of magic
quiet motionless
several respective
tire tire yourselves
get beget
conference conversation
Spirit Bad Angel (devil)

Jove God
conceit the idea
delicates delicacies
wall . . . brass The 13th-century English
scholar-alchemist Roger Bacon, in Robert
Greene's play *Friar Bacon and Friar Bungay*
(1594), planned to wall England thus.

90
I'll levy soldiers with the coin they bring,
And chase the Prince of Parma° from our land,
And reign sole king of all the provinces.
Yea, stranger engines for the brunt of war
Than was the fiery keel at Antwerp's bridge°
I'll make my servile spirits to invent.
Come, German Valdes and Cornelius,
And make me blest with your sage conference.

Enter VALDES *and* CORNELIUS.

Valdes, sweet Valdes and Cornelius!
Know that your words have won me at the last
100
To practise magic and concealèd arts.
Yet not your words only but mine own fantasy°
That will receive no object for my head,
But ruminates on necromantic skill.
Philosophy is odious and obscure,
Both law and physic are for petty wits;
Divinity is basest of the three,
Unpleasant, harsh, contemptible and vile.
'Tis magic, magic that hath ravished me.
Then, gentle friends, aid me in this attempt,
110
And I, that have with concise syllogisms
Gravelled° the pastors of the German church
And made the flowering pride of Wittenberg
Swarm to my problems as the infernal spirits
On sweet Musaeus° when he came to hell,
Will be as cunning as Agrippa° was,
Whose shadows made all Europe honour him.

VALDES   Faustus, these books, thy wit and our experience
Shall make all nations to canónize us.
As Indian Moors obey their Spanish lords,
120
So shall the spirits of every element
Be always serviceable to us three.
Like lions shall they guard us when we please,
Like Almain rutters° with their horsemen's staves,
Or Lapland giants trotting by our sides;
Sometimes like women or unwedded maids,
Shadowing more beauty in their airy brows
Than has the white breasts of the Queen of Love.
From Venice shall they drag huge argosies,
And from America the golden fleece°

Prince of Parma Spanish governor of the Netherlands provinces 1579–92, and enemy of the English
fiery keel . . . bridge a fireship that destroyed the bridge Parma had built over the Scheldt
fantasy imagination
Gravelled brought down

Musaeus legendary Greek poet, perhaps here confused with Orpheus
Agrippa Cornelius Agrippa (1485–1535), humanist and mage
Almain rutters German cavalry
the golden fleece object of Jason's voyage in the *Argo*, but Marlowe is thinking of the treasure fleets of Philip II of Spain

130   That yearly stuffs old Philip's treasury,
           If learned Faustus will be resolute.
FAUSTUS   Valdes, as resolute am I in this
           As thou to live, therefore object it not.°
CORNELIUS The miracles that magic will perform
           Will make thee vow to study nothing else.
           He that is grounded in astrology,
           Enriched with tongues, well seen° in minerals,
           Hath all the principles magic doth require.
           Then doubt not, Faustus, but to be renowned,
140   And more frequented for this mystery
           Than heretofore the Delphian oracle.
           The spirits tell me they can dry the sea,
           And fetch the treasure of all foreign wrecks—
           Ay, all the wealth that our forefathers hid
           Within the massy entrails of the earth
           Then tell me, Faustus, what shall we three want?
FAUSTUS   Nothing, Cornelius! O, this cheers my soul.
           Come, show me some demonstrations magical,
           That I may conjure in some lusty° grove,
150   And have these joys in full possession.
VALDES   Then haste thee to some solitary grove,
           And bear wise Bacon's and Abanus' works,°
           The Hebrew Psalter and New Testament;°
           And whatsoever else is requisite
           We will inform thee ere our conference cease.
CORNELIUS Valdes, first let him know the words of art,
           And then, all other ceremonies learned,
           Faustus may try his cunning° by himself.
VALDES   First I'll instruct thee in the rudiments,
160   And then wilt thou be perfecter than I.
FAUSTUS   Then come and dine with me, and after meat
           We'll canvass every quiddity° thereof,
           For ere I sleep, I'll try what I can do.
           This night I'll conjure, though I die therefore.   *Exeunt omnes.*

           [SCENE II]

           Enter two SCHOLARS.

1 SCHOLAR   I wonder what's become of Faustus, that was wont to make our
schools ring with *sic probo.*°

---

object it not do not object to it
well seen well versed
lusty pleasant
Bacon's and Abanus' works Roger Bacon (see
l. 86n) and Pietro d'Abano (1250?–1316?),
Italian philospher and magician
Hebrew . . . Testament Psalms 22 and 51, and

the opening words of St. John's gospel, were
used in conjuring spirits.
cunning skill
quiddity fine point
sic probo "thus I prove it" (used in scholastic
disputation)

Enter WAGNER.

2 SCHOLAR   That shall we presently° know. Here comes his boy.

1 SCHOLAR   How now, sirrah, where's thy master?

WAGNER   God in heaven knows.

2 SCHOLAR   Why, dost not thou know then?

WAGNER   Yes, I know, but that follows not.

1 SCHOLAR   Go to, sirrah, leave your jesting and tell us where he is.

WAGNER   That follows not by force of argument, which you, being licentiates,°
10   should stand° upon; therefore acknowledge your error and be attentive.

2 SCHOLAR   Then you will not tell us?

WAGNER   You are deceived, for I will tell you. Yet if you were not dunces, you
would never ask me such a question. For is he not *corpus naturale?* And is
not that *mobile?*° Then wherefore should you ask me such a question? But
that I am by nature phlegmatic, slow to wrath and prone to lechery (to love,
I would say), it were not for you to come within forty foot of the place of
execution,° although I do not doubt but to see you both hanged the next
sessions. Thus, having triumphed over you, I will set my countenance like a
precisian,° and begin to speak thus: Truly, my dear brethren, my master is
20   within at dinner with Valdes and Cornelius, as this wine, if it could speak,
would inform your worships. And so the Lord bless you, preserve you and
keep you, my dear brethren.   *Exit.*

1 SCHOLAR   O Faustus, then I fear that which I have long suspected
That thou art fallen into that damnèd art
For which they two are infamous through the world.

2 SCHOLAR   Were he a stranger, not allied to me,
The danger of his soul would make me mourn.
But come, let us go and inform the Rector;°
It may be his grave counsel may reclaim him.

1 SCHOLAR   I fear me nothing will reclaim him now.

2 SCHOLAR   Yet let us see what we can do.   *Exeunt.*

[SCENE III]

Thunder. Enter LUCIFER *and four* DEVILS *[above].* FAUSTUS *to them with
this speech.*

FAUSTUS   Now that the gloomy shadow of the night,
Longing to view Orion's drizzling looks,°
Leaps from the antarctic° world unto the sky,
And dims the welkin° with her pitchy breath,

---

presently immediately
licentiates qualified to go on to the master's or
doctor's degree
stand rely
corpus naturale . . . mobile *corpus naturale
seu mobile* ("a natural body and as such
capable of movement") was the Aristotelian
definition of the subject matter of physics;
Wagner had picked it up from his betters.

place of execution dining room, but he carries
on the criminal sense
precisian puritan
Rector head of the University
Orion's . . . looks Orion was traditionally a
rainy constellation
Now that . . . antarctic a strange supposition,
that night comes on from the south
welkin sky

Faustus, begin thine incantations
And try if devils will obey thy hest,°
Seeing thou hast prayed and sacrificed to them.
Within this circle is Jehovah's name
Forward and backward anagrammatized:
10 The abbreviated names of holy saints,
Figures of every adjunct° to the heavens,
And characters° of signs and erring stars°
By which the spirits are enforced to rise.
Then fear not, Faustus, to be resolute
And try the utmost magic can perform.   *Thunder.*

Sint mihi dei Acherontis propitii; valeat numen triplex Jehovae; ignei, aerii,
aquatici, terreni spiritus salvete! Orientis princeps, Belzebub inferni ardentis
monarcha, et Demogorgon, propitiamus vos, ut appareat, et surgat, Me-
phostophilis.   *Dragon [appears above.]*
20 *Quid tu moraris? Per Jehovam, Gehannam, et consecratam aquam quam nunc*
spargo; signumque crucis quod nunc facio; et per vota nostra, ipse nunc surgat
nobis dicatus Mephostophilis.°

Enter a DEVIL.°

I charge thee to return and change thy shape,
Thou art too ugly to attend on me.
Go, and return an old Franciscan friar,
That holy shape becomes a devil best.   *Exit* DEVIL.
I see there's virtue in my heavenly words!
Who would not be proficient in this art?
How pliant is this Mephostophilis,
30 Full of obedience and humility,
Such is the force of magic and my spells.
Now, Faustus, thou art conjurer laureate,°
That canst command great Mephostophilis.
Quin redis, Mephostophilis, fratris imagine!°

Enter MEPHOSTOPHILIS.

MEPHOSTOPHILIS Now Faustus, what wouldst thou have me do?
FAUSTUS I charge thee wait upon me whilst I live,
To do whatever Faustus shall command,
Be it to make the moon drop from her sphere,
Or the ocean to overwhelm the world.

hest command
adjunct heavenly body
characters Rays from the stars were thought to
mark certain earthly objects, giving them magical power in the hands of the adept.
signs and erring stars signs of the Zodiac and
planets
Sint . . . Mephostophilis "May the gods of
hell be favorable to me; farewell to the threefold spirit of God; hail, spirits of fire, air,
water and earth! O prince of the East [Lucifer],
Beelzebub monarch of burning hell, and De-

mogorgon, we beseech you that Mephostophilis
should appear and rise. Why do you delay?
By Jehovah, hell, and the holy water that I
now sprinkle; by the sign of the cross that I
now make; and by our prayers, may Mephostophilis himself now rise, compelled to obey
us."
Devil Mephostophilis in devilish form
laureate singled out for honors
Quin . . . imagine "Why do you not return,
Mephostophilis, in the likeness of a friar?"

40   MEPHOSTOPHILIS   I am a servant to great Lucifer,
And may not follow thee without his leave;
No more than he commands must we perform.
FAUSTUS   Did not he charge thee to appear to me?
MEPHOSTOPHILIS   No, I came now hither of mine own accord.
FAUSTUS   Did not my conjuring speeches raise thee? Speak.
MEPHOSTOPHILIS   That was the cause, but yet *per accidens;*°
For when we hear one rack° the name of God,
Abjure the scriptures and his saviour Christ,
We fly in hope to get his glorious soul;
50   Nor will we come unless he use such means
Whereby he is in danger to be damned.
Therefore the shortest cut for conjuring
Is stoutly to abjure the Trinity
And pray devoutly to the prince of hell.°
FAUSTUS   So Faustus hath already done, and holds this principle:
There is no chief but only Belzebub,
To whom Faustus doth dedicate himself.
This word 'damnation' terrifies not him,
For he confounds hell in Elysium.°
60   His ghost be with the old philosophers.°
But leaving these vain trifles of men's souls,
Tell me, what is that Lucifer, thy lord?
MEPHOSTOPHILIS   Arch-regent and commander of all spirits.
FAUSTUS   Was not that Lucifer an angel once?
MEPHOSTOPHILIS   Yes Faustus, and most dearly loved of God.
FAUSTUS   How come it then that he is prince of devils?
MEPHOSTOPHILIS   O, by aspiring pride and insolence,
For which God threw him from the face of heaven.
FAUSTUS   And what are you that live with Lucifer?
70   MEPHOSTOPHILIS   Unhappy spirits that fell with Lucifer,
Conspired against our God with Lucifer,
And are for ever damned with Lucifer.
FAUSTUS   Where are you damned?
MEPHOSTOPHILIS   In hell.
FAUSTUS   How comes it then that thou art out of hell?
MEPHOSTOPHILIS   Why, this is hell, nor am I out of it.°
Think'st thou that I who saw the face of God
And tasted the eternal joys of heaven,
Am not tormented with ten thousand hells

---

per accidens i.e. not the essential cause but an incidental contribution; a scholastic expression
rack torment
For when . . . hell (ll. 47–54) In this speech Mephostophilis clarifies an important point; it is not conjuring itself that damns a man, but the evidence it provides that he is a likely subject for diabolic treatment; consequently the bond Faustus signs is not in itself irrevocable; he must damn himself otherwise.

confounds . . . Elysium does not distinguish between hell and Elysium (the pagan afterworld)
old philosophers who lived before the Redemption and neither knew of nor could go to Heaven
this is hell . . . it Cf. Milton's Satan, "Which way I fly is Hell; my self am Hell" (*Paradise Lost* IV.75); other Miltonic resemblances will be noticed.

80　　In being deprived of everlasting bliss?°
　　　O Faustus, leave these frivolous demands,
　　　Which strikes a terror to my fainting soul.
　FAUSTUS　What, is great Mephostophilis so passionate°
　　　For being deprivèd of the joys of heaven?
　　　Learn thou of Faustus manly fortitude,
　　　And scorn those joys thou never shalt possess.
　　　Go, bear these tidings to great Lucifer,
　　　Seeing Faustus hath incurred eternal death
　　　By desperate thoughts against Jove's deity.
90　　Say he surrenders up to him his soul,
　　　So° he will spare him four and twenty years,
　　　Letting him live in all voluptuousness,
　　　Having thee ever to attend on me,
　　　To give me whatsoever I shall ask,
　　　To tell me whatsoever I demand,
　　　To slay mine enemies and aid my friends
　　　And always be obedient to my will.
　　　Go, and return to mighty Lucifer,
　　　And meet me in my study at midnight,
100　　And then resolve me of thy master's mind.
　MEPHOSTOPHILIS　I will, Faustus.　　　　　　　　　　　*Exit.*
　FAUSTUS　Had I as many souls as there be stars,
　　　I'd give them all for Mephostophilis.
　　　By him I'll be great emperor of the world,
　　　And make a bridge through the moving air
　　　To pass the ocean with a band of men;
　　　I'll join the hills that bind the Afric shore,
　　　And make that country continent to° Spain,
　　　And both contributory° to my crown.
110　　The Emperor shall not live but by my leave,
　　　Nor any potentate of Germany.
　　　Now that I have obtained what I desire
　　　I'll live in speculation° of this art
　　　Till Mephostophilis return again.　　　　　　　　*Exit.*
　　　[*Exeunt* LUCIFER *and* DEVILS.]

　　　[SCENE IV]

　　　Enter WAGNER *and the* CLOWN [ROBIN].

　WAGNER　Come hither, sirrah boy.
　ROBIN　Boy? O disgrace to my person! Zounds, boy in your face! You have seen
　　　many boys with such pickadevants,° I am sure.

---

deprived . . . bliss traditionally the most painful punishment of the damned
passionate sorrowful
So on condition that

continent to continuous with
contributory i.e. paying tribute
speculation contemplation
pickadevants pointed beards

WAGNER   Sirrah, hast thou no comings in?°

ROBIN   Yes, and goings out° too, you may see, sir.

WAGNER   Alas, poor slave, see how poverty jests in his nakedness. I know the villain's out of service and so hungry that I know he would give his soul to the devil for a shoulder of mutton, though it were blood-raw.

ROBIN   Not so neither. I had need to have it well roasted, and good sauce to it, if I pay so dear, I can tell you.

WAGNER   Sirrah, wilt thou be my man and wait on me? And I will make thee go like *Qui mihi discipulus.*°

ROBIN   What, in verse?

WAGNER   No, slave, in beaten silk° and stavesacre.°

ROBIN   Stavesacre? That's good to kill vermin; then belike if I serve you I shall be lousy.

WAGNER   Why, so thou shalt be whether thou dost it or no; for, sirrah, if thou dost not presently bind thyself to me for seven years, I'll turn all the lice about thee into familiars° and make them tear thee in pieces.

ROBIN   Nay sir, you may save yourself a labour, for they are as familiar with me as if they paid for their meat and drink, I can tell you.

WAGNER   Well sirrah, leave your jesting and take these guilders.°

ROBIN   Yes, marry sir, and I thank you too.

WAGNER   So, now thou art to be at an hour's warning, whensoever and wheresoever the devil shall fetch thee.

ROBIN   Here, take your guilders, I'll none of 'em.

WAGNER   Not I, thou art pressed;° prepare thyself, for I will presently raise up two devils to carry thee away. Banio! Belcher!

ROBIN   Belcher? And° Belcher come here, I'll belch him! I am not afraid of a devil.

Enter two DEVILS, *and the* CLOWN *runs up and down crying.*

WAGNER   How now, sir, will you serve me now?

ROBIN   Ay, good Wagner; take away the devil then.

WAGNER   Spirits, away!   *Exeunt* [DEVILS].
Now, sirrah, follow me.

ROBIN   I will sir. But hark you master, will you teach me this conjuring occupation?

WAGNER   Ay sirrah, I'll teach thee to turn thyself to a dog, or a cat, or a mouse, or a rat, or anything.

ROBIN   A dog, or a cat, or a mouse, or a rat! O brave, Wagner.

WAGNER   Villain, call me Master Wagner, and see that you walk attentively, and let your right eye be always diametrally° fixed upon my left heel, that thou mayst *quasi vestigiis nostris insistere.*°

ROBIN   Well sir, I warrant you.   *Exeunt.*

---

comings in earnings, income
goings out expenses
Qui . . . discipulus "You who are my pupil" (opening words of a didactic poem for schoolboys, used in Elizabethan schools)
beaten silk embroidered silk; Wagner means he will beat him
stavesacre flea powder

familiars attendant devils
guilders Dutch money
pressed hired, drafted
And if
diametrally directly
quasi . . . insistere "follow as it were in our footsteps"

[SCENE V]

Enter FAUSTUS *in his study.*

FAUSTUS   Now, Faustus, must thou needs be damned?
And canst thou not be saved.
What boots it then to think on God or heaven?
Away with such vain fancies, and despair;
Despair in God, and trust in Belzebub.
Now go not backward; no, Faustus, be resolute.
Why waver'st thou? O something soundeth in mine ears,
'Abjure this magic, turn to God again.'
Ay, and Faustus will turn to God again.
10   To God? He loves thee not.
The God thou serv'st is thine own appetite,
Wherein is fixed the love of Belzebub.
To him, I'll build an altar and a church,
And offer lukewarm blood of new-born babes.

Enter the two ANGELS.

GOOD ANGEL   Sweet Faustus, leave that execrable art.
FAUSTUS   Contrition, prayer, repentance, what of these?
GOOD ANGEL   O they are means to bring thee unto heaven.
BAD ANGEL   Rather illusions, fruits of lunacy,
That make men foolish that do trust them most.
20   GOOD ANGEL   Sweet Faustus, think of heaven and heavenly things.
BAD ANGEL   No, Faustus, think of honour and of wealth.   *Exeunt* ANGELS.
FAUSTUS   Of wealth!
Why, the signory° of Emden° shall be mine!
When Mephostophilis shall stand by me,
What God can hurt me? Faustus, thou art safe;
Cast no more doubts. Mephostophilis, come,
And bring glad tidings from great Lucifer.
Is it not midnight? Come Mephostophilis!
Veni,° *veni, Mephostophile!*

Enter MEPHOSTOPHILIS.

30   Now tell me, what saith Lucifer, thy lord?
MEPHOSTOPHILIS   That I shall wait on Faustus whilst he lives,
So he will buy my service with his soul.
FAUSTUS   Already Faustus hath hazarded that for thee.
MEPHOSTOPHILIS   But now thou must bequeath it solemnly,
And write a deed of gift with thine own blood,
For that security craves Lucifer.
If thou deny it, I must back to hell.
FAUSTUS   Stay, Mephostophilis, and tell me

signory lordship   **Veni** come
Emden large northwest German port, trading
with England

What good will my soul do thy lord?
40 MEPHOSTOPHILIS   Enlarge his kingdom.
FAUSTUS   Is that the reason why he tempts us thus?
MEPHOSTOPHILIS   *Solamen miseris, socios habuisse doloris.*°
FAUSTUS   Why, have you any pain, that torture other?°
MEPHOSTOPHILIS   As great as have the human souls of men.
        But tell me, Faustus, shall I have thy soul?
        And I will be thy slave and wait on thee,
        And give thee more than thou hast wit to ask.
FAUSTUS   Ay, Mephostophilis, I'll give it him.
MEPHOSTOPHILIS   Then, Faustus, stab thy arm courageously,
50   And bind thy soul, that at some certain day
        Great Lucifer may claim it as his own,
        And then be thou as great as Lucifer.
FAUSTUS   Lo, Mephostophilis, for love of thee
        Faustus hath cut his arm, and with his proper° blood
        Assures his soul to be great Lucifer's,
        Chief lord and regent of perpetual night.
        View here this blood that trickles from mine arm,
        And let it be propitious for my wish.
MEPHOSTOPHILIS   But, Faustus,
60   Write it in manner of a deed of gift.
FAUSTUS   Ay, so I will. But, Mephostophilis,
        My blood congeals and I can write no more!
MEPHOSTOPHILIS   I'll fetch thee fire to dissolve it straight.   *Exit.*
FAUSTUS   What might the staying of my blood portend?
        Is it unwilling I should write this bill?
        Why streams° it not that I may write afresh?
        'Faustus gives to thee his soul': ah, there it stayed!
        Why shouldst thou not? Is not thy soul thine own?
        Then write again: 'Faustus gives to thee his soul.'

        Enter MEPHOSTOPHILIS *with the chafer*° *of fire.*

70 MEPHOSTOPHILIS   See Faustus, here is fire; set it on.
FAUSTUS   So, now the blood begins to clear again;
        Now will I make an end immediately.
MEPHOSTOPHILIS   What will not I do to obtain his soul!
FAUSTUS   *Consummatum est:*° this bill is ended,
        And Faustus hath bequeathed his soul to Lucifer.
        But what is this inscription on mine arm?
        Homo fuge!° Whither should I flie?
        If unto God, he'll throw me down to hell.
        My senses are deceived: here's nothing writ!

Solamen . . . doloris "it is a comfort to the   chafer portable grate
wretched to have companions in distress"   Consummatum est "it is finished"; last words
that torture other you that torture others   of Christ on the Cross, John 20:30
proper own   Homo fuge fly, O man
streams The word is used of Christ's blood in
the closing scene.

80   O yes, I see it plain. Even here is writ
        Homo fuge! Yet shall not Faustus fly.
MEPHOSTOPHILIS   I'll fetch him somewhat to delight his mind.   *Exit.*

Enter DEVILS, *giving crowns and rich apparel to* FAUSTUS; *they dance
and then depart. Enter* MEPHOSTOPHILIS.

FAUSTUS   What means this show? Speak, Mephostophilis.
MEPHOSTOPHILIS   Nothing, Faustus, but to delight thy mind,
        And let thee see what magic can perform.
FAUSTUS   But may I raise such spirits when I please?
MEPHOSTOPHILIS   Ay, Faustus, and do greater things than these.
FAUSTUS   Then Mephostophilis, receive this scroll,
        A deed of gift, of body and of soul:
90   But yet conditionally, that thou perform
        All covenants and articles between us both.
MEPHOSTOPHILIS   Faustus, I swear by hell and Lucifer
        To effect all promises between us made.
FAUSTUS   Then hear me read it, Mephostophilis.
        On these conditions following:
        'First, that Faustus may be a spirit in form and substance.
        'Secondly, that Mephostophilis shall be his servant, and at his command.
100   'Thirdly, that Mephostophilis shall do for him, and bring him whatsoever.
        'Fourthly, that he shall be in his chamber or house invisible.
        'Lastly, that he shall appear to the said John Faustus at all times in
what form or shape soever he please.
        'I John Faustus of Wittenberg, doctor, by these presents, do give both
body and soul to Lucifer, Prince of the East, and his minister Mephostophilis,
and furthermore grant unto them that, four-and-twenty years being expired,
the articles above written inviolate,° full power to fetch or carry the said
John Faustus, body and soul, flesh, blood or goods, into their habitation
wheresoever.
110   'By me John Faustus.'
MEPHOSTOPHILIS   Speak, Faustus, do you deliver this as your deed?
FAUSTUS   Ay, take it, and the devil give thee good on it.
MEPHOSTOPHILIS   Now, Faustus, ask what thou wilt.
FAUSTUS   First will I question with thee about hell.
        Tell me, where is the place that men call hell?
MEPHOSTOPHILIS   Under the heavens.
FAUSTUS   Ay, so are all things else; but whereabouts?
MEPHOSTOPHILIS   Within the bowels of these elements,
        Where we are tortured and remain for ever.
120   Hell hath no limits, nor is circumscribed
        In one self place,° but where we are is hell,
        And where hell is, there must we ever be.
        And to be short, when all the world dissolves
        And every creature shall be purified,

---

inviolate, not having been violated   **one self place** one and the same place

All places shall be hell that is not heaven.
FAUSTUS   I think hell's a fable.
MEPHOSTOPHILIS   Ay, think so still, till experience change thy mind.
FAUSTUS   Why, does thou think that Faustus shall be damned?
MEPHOSTOPHILIS   Ay, of necessity, for here's the scroll
130   In which thou hast given thy soul to Lucifer.
FAUSTUS   Ay, and body too, but what of that?
          Think'st thou that Faustus is so fond° to imagine
          That after this life there is any pain?
          Tush, these are trifles and mere old wives' tales.
MEPHOSTOPHILIS   But I am an instance to prove the contrary,
          For I tell thee I am damned, and now in hell.
FAUSTUS   Nay, and this be hell, I'll willingly be damned.
          What, sleeping, eating, walking and disputing?
          But leaving this, let me have a wife, the fairest maid in Germany, for
140   I am wanton and lascivious, and cannot live without a wife.
MEPHOSTOPHILIS   How, a wife? I prithee, Faustus, talk not of a wife.
FAUSTUS   Nay, sweet Mephostophilis, fetch me one, for I will have one.
MEPHOSTOPHILIS   Well, thou wilt have one. Sit there till I come: I'll fetch thee
          a wife in the devil's name.   [Exit.]

          Enter with a DEVIL dressed like a woman, with fireworks.

          Tell me, Faustus, how dost thou like thy wife?
FAUSTUS   A plague on her for a hot whore.
MEPHOSTOPHILIS   Marriage is but a ceremonial toy,
          And if thou lovest me, think no more of it.
          I'll cull thee out the fairest courtesans
150   And bring them every morning to thy bed:
          She whom thine eye shall like, thy heart shall have,
          Were she as chaste as was Penelope,°
          As wise as Saba,° or as beautiful
          As was bright Lucifer before his fall.
          Hold, take this book, peruse it thoroughly:
          The iterating° of these lines brings gold,
          The framing of this circle on the ground
          Brings thunder, whirlwinds, storm and lightning.°
          Pronounce this thrice devoutly to thyself
160   And men in harness° shall appear to thee,
          Ready to execute what thou command'st.
FAUSTUS   Thanks, Mephostophilis. Yet fain would I have a book wherein I
          might behold all spells and incantations, that I might raise up spirits when
          I please.
MEPHOSTOPHILIS   Here they are in this book.   *There turn to them.*
FAUSTUS   Now would I have a book where I might see all characters and

---

fond foolish
Penelope the faithful wife of Ulysses
Saba Queen of Sheba

iterating repetition
lightning trisyllabic; pronounced light-en-ing
harness armor

planets of the heavens, that I might know their motions and dispositions.°
MEPHOSTOPHILIS Here they are too.   *Turn to them.*
FAUSTUS Nay, let me have one book more, and then I have done, wherein I
170   might see all plants, herbs and trees that grow upon the the earth.
MEPHOSTOPHILIS Here they be.
FAUSTUS Oh thou art deceived.
MEPHOSTOPHILIS Tut, I warrant° thee.   *Turn to them.*
                                                                    Exeunt.

[SCENE VI°]

Enter FAUSTUS *in his study, and* MEPHOSTOPHILIS.

FAUSTUS When I behold the heavens then I repent,
         And curse thee, wicked Mephostophilis,
         Because thou hast deprived me of those joys.
MEPHOSTOPHILIS 'Twas thine own seeking, Faustus, thank thyself.
         But think'st thou heaven is such a glorious thing?
         I tell thee, Faustus, it is not half so fair
         As thou or any man that breathes on earth.
FAUSTUS How prov'st thou that?
MEPHOSTOPHILIS 'Twas made for man; then he's more excellent.
10   FAUSTUS If heaven was made for man, 'twas made for me.
         I will renounce this magic and repent.

Enter the two ANGELS.

GOOD ANGEL Faustus, repent; yet God will pity thee.
BAD ANGEL Thou art a spirit;° God cannot pity thee.
FAUSTUS Who buzzeth° in mine ears I am a spirit?
         Be I a devil, yet God may pity me;
         Yea, God will pity me if I repent.
BAD ANGEL Ay, but Faustus never shall repent.   *Exeunt* ANGELS.
FAUSTUS My heart's so hardened I cannot repent.
         Scarce can I name salvation, faith or heaven,
20   But fearful echoes thunders in mine ears
         'Faustus, thou art damned'; then swords and knives,
         Poison, guns, halters and envenomed steel
         Are laid before me to dispatch myself.
         And long ere this I should have done the deed,
         Had not sweet pleasure conquered deep despair.
         Have not I made blind Homer sing to me
         Of Alexander's love and Oenon's death?°
         And hath not he, that built the walls of Thebes

dispositions situations
warrant assure
Scene vi A scene, presumably comic, has apparently been lost from the position between v
and vi.

spirit demon, devil
buzzeth muttereth
Alexander's . . . death Alexander (Paris) loved
Oenone but deserted her when offered Helen.

With ravishing sound of his melodious harp,°
30   Made music with my Mephostophilis?
Why should I die then, or basely despair?
I am resolved, Faustus shall not repent.
Come, Mephostophilis, let us dispute again,
And reason of divine astrology.
Speak, are there many spheres above the moon?
Are all celestial bodies but one globe,
As is the substance of this centric earth?

MEPHOSTOPHILIS   As are the elements, such are the heavens,
Even from the moon unto the empyreal orb,°
40   Mutually folded in each other's spheres,
And jointly move upon one axle-tree,
Whose terminé° is termed the world's wide pole.
Nor are the names of Saturn, Mars or Jupiter
Feigned, but are erring stars.

FAUSTUS   But have they all one motion, both *situ et tempore?*°

MEPHOSTOPHILIS   All move from east to west in four and twenty hours upon
the poles of the world, but differ in their motions upon the poles of the zodiac.°

FAUSTUS   These slender questions Wagner can decide!
50   Hath Mephostophilis no greater skill?
Who knows not the double motion of the planets,
That the first is finished in a natural day,
The second thus: Saturn in thirty years, Jupiter in twelve, Mars in four, the
Sun, Venus and Mercury in a year, the Moon in twenty-eight days. These
are freshmen's suppositions.° But tell me, hath every sphere a dominion or
intelligentia?°

MEPHOSTOPHILIS   Ay.

FAUSTUS   How many heavens or spheres are there?

60   MEPHOSTOPHILIS   Nine, the seven planets, the firmament, and the empyreal
heaven.

FAUSTUS   But is there not *coelum igneum?*° *et cristallinum?*°

MEPHOSTOPHILIS   No, Faustus, they be but fables.

FAUSTUS   Resolve me then in this one question. Why are not conjunctions,°
oppositions,° aspects,° eclipses, all at one time, but in some years we have
more, in some less?

MEPHOSTOPHILIS   *Per inaequalem motum, respectu totius.*°

---

he . . . harp Amphion's harp made the stones
move together to form the wall of Thebes.
Even . . . orb from the sphere of the moon,
closest of the "planets," to the empyrean, beyond their spheres and that of the fixed stars,
where God is
terminé extremity
situ et tempore as to both position and time
poles of the zodiac common axle on which all
spheres revolve
freshmen's suppositions elementary assumptions
as taught to first-year students
dominion or intelligentia angel that controls the
motion of a planet within its sphere
coelum igneum sphere of fire, a cosmological

hypothesis often regarded skeptically at this
time
et cristallinum crystalline sphere, an extra
sphere, brought in to explain astronomical
observations in conflict with Ptolemaic principles
conjunctions apparent proximity of heavenly
bodies
oppositions extreme apparent divergence
aspects Such relative positions were called
aspects.
Per inaequalem . . . totius "on account of
their unequal movement with respect to the
whole"

FAUSTUS   Well, I am answered. Now tell me, who made the world?
MEPHOSTOPHILIS   I will not.
FAUSTUS   Sweet Mephostophilis, tell me.
70   MEPHOSTOPHILIS   Move° me not, Faustus.
FAUSTUS   Villain, have not I bound thee to tell me anything?
MEPHOSTOPHILIS   Ay, that is not against our kingdom:
This is. Thou art damned, think thou of hell.
FAUSTUS   Think, Faustus, upon God, that made the world.
MEPHOSTOPHILIS   Remember this—   *Exit.*
FAUSTUS   Ay, go, accursèd spirit to ugly hell.
'Tis thou hast damned distressèd Faustus' soul.
Is't not too late?

Enter the two ANGELS.

BAD ANGEL   Too late.
80   GOOD ANGEL   Never too late, if Faustus will repent.
BAD ANGEL   If thou repent, devils will tear thee in pieces.
GOOD ANGEL   Repent, and they shall never raze° thy skin.   *Exeunt* ANGELS.
FAUSTUS   Ah, Christ my saviour, my saviour,
Help to save distressèd Faustus' soul.

Enter LUCIFER, BELZEBUB, *and* MEPHOSTOPHILIS.

LUCIFER   Christ cannot save thy soul, for he is just;
There's none but I have interest in° the same.
FAUSTUS   O what art thou that look'st so terribly?
LUCIFER   I am Lucifer, and this is my companion prince in hell.
FAUSTUS   O Faustus, they are come to fetch thy soul.
90   BELZEBUB   We are come to tell thee thou dost injure us.
LUCIFER   Thou call'st on Christ contrary to thy promise.
BELZEBUB   Thou shouldst not think on God.
LUCIFER   Think on the devil.
BELZEBUB   And his dam too.
FAUSTUS   Nor will I henceforth. Pardon me in this,
And Faustus vows never to look to heaven,
Never to name God or to pray to him,
To burn his scriptures, slay his ministers,
And make my spirits pull his churches down.
100   LUCIFER   So shalt thou show thyself an obedient servant,
And we will highly gratify thee for it.
BELZEBUB   Faustus, we are come from hell in person to show thee some
pastime. Sit down and thou shalt behold the Seven Deadly Sins appear to
thee in their own proper shapes and likeness.
FAUSTUS   That sight will be as pleasant to me as Paradise was to Adam the
first day of his creation.
LUCIFER   Talk not of Paradise or Creation, but mark the show. Go, Mephostophilis, fetch them in.

Move anger   interest in claim upon
raze graze

Enter the SEVEN DEADLY SINS *[led by a Piper].*

BELZEBUB   Now, Faustus, question them of their names and dispositions.

110 FAUSTUS   That shall I soon. What are thou, the first?

PRIDE   I am Pride. I disdain to have any parents. I am like to Ovid's flea,° I can creep into every corner of a wench; sometimes like a periwig I sit upon her brow; next, like a necklace I hang about her neck; then, like a fan of feathers, I kiss her; and then, turning myself to a wrought° smock, do what I list. But fie, what a smell is here! I'll not speak another word, unless the ground be perfumed and covered with cloth of arras.°

FAUSTUS   Thou art a proud knave indeed. What art thou, the second?

COVETOUSNESS   I am Covetousness, begotten of an old churl in a leather bag; and might I now obtain my wish, this house, you and all, should turn to gold,
120   that I might lock you safe into my chest. O my sweet gold!

FAUSTUS   And what are thou, the third?

ENVY   I am Envy, begotten of a chimney-sweeper and an oyster-wife.° I cannot read and therefore wish all books burned. I am lean with seeing others eat: O that there would come a famine over all the world, that all might die, and I live alone; then thou shouldst see how fat I'd be. But must thou sit and I stand? Come down, with a vengeance!

FAUSTUS   Out, envious wretch. But what art thou, the fourth?

WRATH   I am Wrath. I had neither father nor mother. I leapt out of a lion's mouth when I was scarce an hour old, and ever since have run up and down
130   the world with these case° of rapiers, wounding myself when I could get none to fight withal. I was born in hell, and look to it, for some of you shall be° my father.

FAUSTUS   And what art thou, the fifth?

GLUTTONY   I am Gluttony. My parents are all dead, and the devil a penny they have left me, but a small pension, and that buys me thirty meals a day and ten bevers:° a small trifle to suffice nature. I come of a royal pedigree: my father was a gammon of bacon and my mother was a hogshead of claret wine. My godfathers were these: Peter Pickle-herring and Martin Martlemas-beef.° But my godmother, O, she was an ancient gentle-woman, and well-beloved
140   in every good town and city; her name was Mistress Margery March-beer.° Now, Faustus, thou hast heard all my progeny,° wilt thou bid me to supper?

FAUSTUS   No, I'll see thee hanged; thou wilt eat up all my victuals.

GLUTTONY   Then the devil choke thee.

FAUSTUS   Choke thyself, Glutton. What art thou, the sixth?

SLOTH   Hey ho, I am Sloth. I was begotten on a sunny bank, where I have lain ever since, and you have done me great injury to bring me from thence. Let me be carried thither again by Gluttony and Lechery. Hey ho! I'll not speak a word more for a king's ransom.

Ovid's flea an elegy on a flea, erroneously attributed to Ovid; the lover envies the flea who has the freedom of his mistress's body; cf. John Donne's "The Flea"
wrought embroidered
cloth of arras rich tapestry (too fine for floor-covering)
chimney-sweeper and an oyster-wife consequently black and smelly

case pair
shall be is sure to prove
bevers snacks
Martlemas-beef On November 11, Martlemas or Martinmas, the feast of St. Martin of Tours, cattle were slaughtered for salting.
March-beer strong beer brewed in March
progeny line

150 FAUSTUS   And what are you, Mistress Minx, the seventh and last?

LECHERY   Who, I sir? I am one that loves an inch of raw mutton° better than an ell of fried stockfish, and the first letter of my name begins with Lechery.°

LUCIFER   Away to hell! Away, on, piper! *Exeunt the* SEVEN SINS [*and the Piper*]

FAUSTUS   O how this sight doth delight my soul.

LUCIFER   But Faustus, in hell is all manner of delight.

FAUSTUS   O might I see hell and return again safe, how happy were I then!

LUCIFER   Faustus, thou shalt; at midnight I will send for thee. Meanwhile, peruse this book and view it thoroughly, and thou shalt turn thyself into what
160 shape thou wilt.

FAUSTUS   Thanks, mighty Lucifer; this will I keep as chary° as my life.

LUCIFER   Now, Faustus, farewell.

FAUSTUS   Farewell, great Lucifer. Come, Mephostophilis.

Exeunt omnes, several° ways.

[SCENE VII]

Enter the CLOWN [ROBIN].

ROBIN   What, Dick, look to the horses there till I come again. I have gotten one of Doctor Faustus' conjuring books, and now we'll have such knavery as passes.°

Enter DICK.

DICK   What, Robin, you must come away and walk the horses.

ROBIN   I walk the horses? I scorn it, 'faith. I have other matters in hand. Let the horses walk themselves and they will. *A per se a, t.h.e. the: o per se o, deny orgon, gorgon.*° Keep further from me, O thou illiterate and unlearned hostler.

DICK   'Snails,° what hast thou got there? A book? Why, thou canst not tell
10 ne'er a word on it.

ROBIN   That thou shalt see presently. Keep out of the circle, I say, lest I send you into the hostry° with a vengeance.

DICK   That's like, 'faith. You had best leave your foolery, for an° my master come, he'll conjure you, 'faith!

ROBIN   My master conjure me? I'll tell thee what, an my master come here, I'll clap as fair a pair of horns° on his head as e'er thou sawest in thy life.

DICK   Thou need'st not do that, for my mistress hath done it.

ROBIN   Ay, there be of us here, that have waded as deep into matters as other men, if they were disposed to talk.

20 DICK   A plague take you! I thought you did not sneak up and down after her for nothing. But I prithee tell me, in good sadness,° Robin, is that a conjuring book?

inch . . . mutton penis
first letter . . . Lechery a common facetious expression
chary carefully
several different
as passes as beats everything
A per se . . . gorgon having difficulty in read-
ing, he spells out: *a* by itself spells *a*; *t,h,e* spells *the*; *o* by itself spells *o*; *Demogorgon*
'Snails God's nails
hostry hostelry, inn
an if
pair of horns the sign of a cuckold
in good sadness to be serious

ROBIN   Do but speak what thou'lt have me to do, and I'll do it. If thou'lt dance
naked, put off thy clothes and I'll conjure thee about presently. Or if thou'lt
go but to the tavern with me, I'll give thee white wine, red wine, claret wine,
sack, muscadine,° malmesey° and whippincrust,° hold—belly—hold,° and
we'll not pay one penny for it.

DICK   O brave! Prithee, let's to it presently, for I am as dry as a dog.

ROBIN   Come, then, let's away.   *Exeunt.*

[CHORUS I]

CHORUS

    Learnèd Faustus,
    To find the secrets of astronomy
    Graven in the book of Jove's high firmament,
    Did mount him up to scale Olympus top,
    Where sitting in a chariot burning bright,
    Drawn by the strength of yokèd dragons' necks,
    He views the clouds, the planets, and the stars,
    The tropics, zones, and quarters of the sky,
    From the bright circle of the hornèd moon,
10   Even to the height of *Primum Mobile.*°
    And whirling round with this circumference,
    Within the concave compass of the pole,
    From east to west his dragons swiftly glide,
    And in eight days did bring him home again.
    Not long he stayed within his quiet house,
    To rest his bones after his weary toil,
    But new exploits do hale him out again,
    And mounted then upon a dragon's back,
    That with his wings did part the subtle air,
20   He now is gone to prove° cosmography,
    That measures coasts and kingdoms of the earth;
    And as I guess will first arrive at Rome,
    To see the Pope and manner of his court,
    And take some part of holy Peter's feast,
    The which this day° is highly solemnized.   *Exit*

[SCENE VIII]

Enter FAUSTUS *and* MEPHOSTOPHILIS.

FAUSTUS   Having now, my good Mephostophilis,
    Passed with delight the stately town of Trier,
    Environed round with airy mountain tops,
    With walls of flint, and deep-entrenchèd lakes,°

muscadine muscatel
malmesey a strong sweet wine
whippincrust hippocras, a special wine
hold—belly—hold a bellyful
From . . . Mobile i.e. from the lowest to the
highest of the spheres, *Primum Mobile* being
the First Mover which imparted motion to all
the rest
prove put to the test
this day June 29th, the feast of St. Peter
lakes moats

Not to be won by any conquering prince;
From Paris next, coasting the realm of France,
We saw the river Main fall into Rhine,
Whose banks are set with groves of fruitful vines;
Then up to Naples, rich Campania,°

10   With buildings fair and gorgeous to the eye,
Whose streets straight forth° and paved with finest brick,
Quarters the town in four equivalents.
There saw we learned Maro's golden tomb,°
The way he cut,° an English mile in length,
Thorough a rock of stone in one night's space.
From thence to Venice, Padua and the rest,
In the midst of which a sumptuous temple° stands,
That threats the stars with her aspiring top,
Whose frame is paved with sundry coloured stones,

20   And roofed aloft with curious work in gold.
Thus hitherto hath Faustus spent his time.
But tell me now, what resting place is this?
Hast thou, as erst I did command,
Conducted me within the walls of Rome?

MEPHOSTOPHILIS   I have, my Faustus, and for proof thereof,
This is the goodly palace of the Pope;
And 'cause we are no common guests,
I choose his privy chamber for our use.

FAUSTUS   I hope his Holiness will bid us welcome.

30 MEPHOSTOPHILIS   All's one, for we'll be bold with his venison.
But now, my Faustus, that thou mayest perceive
What Rome contains for to delight thine eyes,
Know that this city stands upon seven hills,
That underprop the groundwork of the same;
Just through the midst runs flowing Tiber's stream,
With winding banks that cut it in two parts,
Over the which four stately bridges lean,
That make safe passage to each part of Rome.
Upon the bridge° called Ponte Angelo

40   Erected in a castle passing strong,
Where thou shalt see such store of ordinance
As that the double cannons forged of brass
Do match the number of the days contained
Within the compass of one complete year;
Beside the gates and high pyrámidès,°
That Julius Caesar brought from Africa.

FAUSTUS   Now by the kingdoms of infernal rule,

Naples . . . Campania an erroneous identification
straight forth in straight lines
Maro's . . . tomb Virgil (Maro) was buried near Naples.
The way he cut Virgil had a great reputation during the Middle Ages, as a necromancer, and was supposed to have cut the tunnel running through the promontory where he was buried.
sumptuous temple St. Mark's at Venice
Upon the bridge This is inaccurate; the Castel Sant' Angelo is not on the bridge.
pyramides actually an obelisk brought from Egypt by Caligula

Of Styx, of Acheron, and the fiery lake
Of ever-burning Phlegethon,° I swear
50   That I do long to see the monuments
And situation of bright-splendent Rome.
Come, therefore, let's away.
MEPHOSTOPHILIS   Nay stay, my Faustus. I know you'd see the Pope,
And take some part of holy Peter's feast,
The which in state and high solemnity
This day is held through Rome and Italy
In honour of the Pope's triumphant victory.
FAUSTUS   Sweet Mephostophilis, thou pleasest me.
Whilst I am here on earth let me be cloyed
60   With all things that delight the heart of man.
My four-and-twenty years of liberty
I'll spend in pleasure and in dalliance,
That Faustus' name, whilst this bright frame doth stand,
May be admirèd through the furthest land.
MEPHOSTOPHILIS   'Tis well said, Faustus. Come then, stand by me,
And thou shalt see them come immediately.
FAUSTUS   Nay stay, my gentle Mephostophils,
And grant me my request, and then I go.
Thou knowest within the compass of eight days
70   We viewed the face of heaven, of earth and hell;
So high our dragons soared into the air,
That looking down, the earth appeared to me
No bigger than my hand in quantity.
There did we view the kingdoms of the world,
And what might please mine eye, I there beheld.
Then in this show let me an actor be,
That this proud Pope may Faustus' cunning see.
MEPHOSTOPHILIS   Let it be so, my Faustus, but first stay
And view their triumphs° as they pass this way.
80   And then devise what best contents thy mind
By cunning in thine art to cross the Pope,
Or dash the pride of this solemnity,
To make his monks and abbots stand like apes,
And point like antics° at his triple crown,
To beat the beads about the friars' pates,
Or clap huge horns upon the cardinals' heads,
Or any villainy thou canst devise,
And I'll perform it, Faustus. Hark, they come!
This day shall make thee be admired in Rome.

Enter the CARDINALS *and* BISHOPS, *some bearing crosiers,*° *some the pillars;*° MONKS *and* FRIARS *singing their procession. Then the* POPE *and* RAYMOND° *King of Hungary with Bruno*° *led in chains.*

Styx . . . Phlegethon the three rivers of Hades	**pillars** symbols of the cardinal's dignity
triumphs ceremonial parades	**Raymond** not historical
antics grotesques	**Bruno** fictitious antipope; probably based on
crosiers crosses carried by bishops	Victor IV in Foxe's *Acts and Monuments*

POPE   Cast down our footstool.

90   RAYMOND   Saxon Bruno, stoop,
    Whilst on thy back his Holiness ascends
    Saint Peter's chair and state° pontifical.

BRUNO   Proud Lucifer, that state belongs to me:
    But thus I fall to Peter, not to thee.

POPE   To me and Peter shalt thou grovelling lie,
    And crouch before the papal dignity.
    Sound trumpets then, for thus Saint Peter's heir
    From Bruno's back ascends Saint Peter's chair.

                              A flourish° while he ascends.

    Thus, as the gods creep on with feet of wool
100   Long ere with iron hands° they punish men,
    So shall our sleeping vengeance now arise,
    And smite with death thy hated enterprise.
    Lord cardinals of France and Padua,
    Go forthwith to our holy consistory,°
    And read amongst the statutes décretál,°
    What by the holy council held at Trent°
    The sacred synod° hath decreed for him
    That doth assume the papal government,
    Without election and a true consent.
110   Away, and bring us word with speed!

1 CARDINAL   We go, my lord.

                                        Exeunt CARDINALS.

POPE   Lord Raymond.   [*The* POPE *and* RAYMOND *converse.*]

FAUSTUS   Go, haste thee, gentle Mephostophilis,
    Follow the cardinals to the consistory,
    And as they turn their superstitious books,
    Strike them with sloth and drowsy idleness,
    And make them sleep so sound that in their shapes
    Thyself and I may parley with this Pope,
    This proud confronter of the Emperor,°
120   And in despite of all his holiness
    Restore this Bruno to his liberty
    And bear him to the states of Germany.

MEPHOSTOPHILIS   Faustus, I go.

FAUSTUS   Dispatch it soon,
    The Pope shall curse that Faustus came to Rome.

                              Exeunt FAUSTUS *and* MEPHOSTOPHILIS.

BRUNO   Pope Adrian, let me have some right of law:
    I was elected by the Emperor.

POPE   We will depose the Emperor for that deed,

---

state throne
flourish fanfare of trumpets
feet . . . hands proverb: "God comes with
woollen feet but strikes with iron hands"
consistory meeting place of the papal consistory
or senate
statutes décretál papal decrees

council . . . Trent council held in 1543–63
and launching the Counter-Reformation
synod general council
confronter . . . Emperor The pope has captured the Holy Roman Emperor's nominee
for the papacy.

And curse the people that submit to him.
Both he and thou shalt stand excommunicate,
130   And interdict° from Church's privilege
And all society of holy men.
He grows too proud in his authority,
Lifting his lofty head above the clouds
And like a steeple overpeers the Church.
But we'll pull down his haughty insolence,
And as Pope Alexander, our progenitor,
Stood on the neck of German Frederick,°
Adding this golden sentence to our praise,
That Peter's heirs should tread on emperors
140   And walk upon the dreadful adder's back,
Treading the lion and the dragon down,
And fearless spurn the killing basilisk,
So will we quell that haughty schismatic,
And by authority apostolical
Depose him from his regal government.

BRUNO   Pope Julius swore to princely Sigismund,°
For him and the succeeding popes of Rome,
To hold the emperors their lawful lords.

POPE   Pope Julius did abuse the Church's rites,
150   And therefore none of his decrees can stand.
Is not all power on earth bestowed on us?
And therefore though we would we cannot err.
Behold this silver belt, whereto is fixed
Seven golden keys° fast sealed with seven seals,
In token of our seven-fold power from heaven,
To bind or loose, lock fast, condemn or judge,
Resign° or seal, or whatso pleaseth us.
Then he and thou, and all the world, shall stoop,
Or be assurèd of our dreadful curse,
160   To light as heavy as the pains of hell.

Enter FAUSTUS *and* MEPHOSTOPHILIS, *like the cardinals.*

MEPHOSTOPHILIS   Now tell me, Faustus, are we not fitted well?
FAUSTUS   Yes, Mephostophilis, and two such cardinals
Ne'er served a holy pope as we shall do.
But whilst they sleep within the consistory,
Let us salute his reverend Fatherhood.
RAYMOND   Behold, my lord, the cardinals are returned.
POPE   Welcome, grave fathers, answer presently:
What have our holy council there decreed
Concerning Bruno and the Emperor,

---

interdict forbidden
Pope Alexander . . . Frederick Pope Alexander
III (1159–81) compelled the Emperor Frederick Barbarossa to stoop to him; Foxe reports the pope as quoting Psalms 91:13: "Thou
shalt walk upon the adder and on the basilisk,
and shalt tread down the lion and the dragon."
Pope . . . Sigismund fictitious
keys of St. Peter
Resign unseal

170   In quittance° of their late conspiracy
             Against our state and papal dignity?
FAUSTUS   Most sacred patron of the Church of Rome,
             By full consent of all the synod
             Of priests and prelates, it is thus decreed:
             That Bruno and the German Emperor
             Be held as lollards° and bold schismatics
             And proud disturbers of the Church's peace.
             And if that Bruno by his own assent,
             Without enforcement of the German peers,
180   Did seek to wear the triple diadem
             And by your death to climb Saint Peter's chair,
             The statutes décretal have thus decreed:
             He shall be straight condemned of heresy
             And on a pile of faggots burnt to death.
POPE   It is enough. Here, take him to your charge,
             And bear him straight to Ponte Angelo,
             And in the strongest tower enclose him fast.
             Tomorrow, sitting in our consistory
             With all our college of grave cardinals,
190   We will determine of his life or death.
             Here, take his triple crown° along with you,
             And leave it in the Church's treasury.
             Make haste again,° my good lord cardinals,
             And take our blessing apostolical.
MEPHOSTOPHILIS   So, so, was never devil thus blessed before.
FAUSTUS   Away, sweet Mephostophilis, be gone:
             The cardinals will be plagued for this anon.

             Exeunt FAUSTUS *and* MEPHOSTOPHILIS [*with* BRUNO].

POPE   Go presently and bring a banquet forth
             That we may solemnize Saint Peter's feast,
200   And with Lord Raymond, King of Hungary,
             Drink to our late and happy victory.   *Exeunt.*

             [SCENE IX]

             A sennet° while the banquet is brought in; and then enter FAUSTUS *and*

             MEPHOSTOPHILIS *in their own shapes.*

MEPHOSTOPHILIS   Now, Faustus, come prepare thyself for mirth;
             The sleepy cardinals are hard at hand
             To censure° Bruno, that is posted hence,

---

quittance requital of
lollards heretics; originally the followers of
Wyclif
triple crown Bruno had apparently acquired a
papal tiara.

again back again
sennet trumpet flourish
censure judge

And on a proud-placed steed as swift as thought
Flies o'er the Alps to fruitful Germany,
There to salute the woeful Emperor.

FAUSTUS   The Pope will curse them for their sloth today,
That slept both Bruno and his crown away.
But now, that Faustus may delight his mind,
10   And by their folly make some merriment,
Sweet Mephostophilis, so charm me here,
That I may walk invisible to all,
And do what e'er I please unseen of any.

MEPHOSTOPHILIS   Faustus, thou shalt. Then kneel down presently:
Whilst on thy head I lay my hand,
And charm thee with this magic wand.
First wear this girdle, then appear
Invisible to all are here.
The planets seven, the gloomy air,
20   Hell, and the Furies' forkèd hair,°
Pluto's blue fire° and Hecat's tree,°
With magic spells so compass thee,
That no eye may thy body see.
So, Faustus, now for all their holiness,
Do what thou wilt, thou shalt not be discerned.

FAUSTUS   Thanks, Mephostophilis. Now, friars, take heed
Lest Faustus make your shaven crowns to bleed.

MEPHOSTOPHILIS   Faustus, no more; see where the cardinals come.

Enter POPE *and all the* LORDS [*and* ARCHBISHOP OF RHEIMS]. *Enter the*
CARDINALS *with a book.*

POPE   Welcome, lord cardinals. Come, sit down.
30   Lord Raymond, take your seat. Friars, attend,
And see that all things be in readiness
As best beseems this solemn festival.

1 CARDINAL   First, may it please your sacred holiness
To view the sentence of the reverend synod
Concerning Bruno and the Emperor?

POPE   What needs this question? Did I not tell you
Tomorrow we would sit i' the consistory
And there determine of his punishment?
You brought us word even now, it was decreed
40   That Bruno and the cursèd Emperor
Were by the holy Council both condemned
For loathèd lollards and base schísmatics.
Then wherefore would you have me view that book?

1 CARDINAL   Your grace mistakes. You gave us no such charge.

RAYMOND   Deny it not; we all are witnesses
That Bruno here was late delivered you,

---

forkèd hair the tongues of the snakes on the
Furies' heads

Pluto's blue fire the sulphurous flames of hell
Hecat's tree the gallows-tree

With his rich triple crown to be reserved°
And put into the Church's treasury.

BOTH CARDINALS   By holy Paul, we saw them not.

50 POPE   By Peter, you shall die
Unless you bring them forth immediately.
Hale them to prison, lade° their limbs with gyves!°
False prelates, for this hateful treachery,
Cursed be your souls to hellish misery.   [*Exit* CARDINALS, *guarded.*]

FAUSTUS   So, they are safe. Now Faustus, to the feast;
The Pope had never such a frolic guest.

POPE   Lord Archbishop of Rheims, sit down with us.

ARCHBISHOP   I thank your holiness.

FAUSTUS   Fall to;° the devil choke you an° your spare.

60 POPE   Who's that spoke? Friars, look about.

FRIARS   Here's nobody, if it like your holiness.

POPE   Lord Raymond, pray fall to. I am beholding
To the Bishop of Milan for this so rare a present.

FAUSTUS   I thank you, sir.   *Snatch it.*

POPE   How now? Who snatched the meat from me?
Villains, why speak you not?
My good Lord Archbishop, here's a most dainty dish
Was sent me from a cardinal in France.

FAUSTUS   I'll have that too.   [*Snatch it.*]

70 POPE   What lollards do attend our holiness
That we receive such great indignity? Fetch me some wine.

FAUSTUS   Ay, pray do, for Faustus is a-dry.

POPE   Lord Raymond, I drink unto your grace.

FAUSTUS   I pledge your grace.   [*Snatch the cup.*]

POPE   My wine gone too? Ye lubbers,° look about
And find the man that doth this villainy,
Or by our sanctitude you all shall die.
I pray, my lords, have patience at this
Troublesome banquet.

80 ARCHBISHOP   Please it your holiness, I think it be some ghost crept out of
purgatory, and now is come unto your holiness for his pardon.

POPE   It may be so.
Go, then, command our priests to sing a dirge
To lay the fury of this same troublesome ghost.   *The* POPE *crosseth himself.*

FAUSTUS   How now? Must every bit be spiced with a cross?
Well, use that trick no more, I would advise you.   *Cross again.*
Well, there's the second time; aware° the third:
I give you fair warning.   *Cross again.*
Nay then take that!

---

reserved kept safe
lade load
gyves fetters; shackles
Fall to start eating

an if
lubbers clumsy fools
aware beware

FAUSTUS *hits him a box of the ear.*

POPE   Oh, I am slain! Help me, my lords.
Oh come, and help to bear my body hence.
Damned be this soul for ever for this deed!
Exeunt the POPE *and his train.*

90   MEPHOSTOPHILIS   Now, Faustus, what will you do now? For I can tell you,
you'll be cursed with bell, book and candle,°

FAUSTUS   Bell, book and candle, candle, book and bell,
Forward and backward, to curse Faustus to hell.

Enter the FRIARS *with bell, book and candle, for the dirge.*

FRIAR   Come, brethren, let's about our business with good devotion.   *Sing this.*
Cursed be he that stole his holiness' meat from the table.
Maledicat Dominus!°
Cursed be he that struck his holiness a blow on the face.
Maledicat Dominus!
Cursed be he that took Friar Sandelo a blow on the pate.
100   *Madelicat Dominus!*
Cursed be he that disturbeth our holy dirge.
Maledicat Dominus!
Cursed be he that took away his holiness' wine.
Maledicat Dominus!

[FAUSTUS *and* MEPHOSTOPHILIS] *beat the* FRIARS, *fling
fireworks among them, and exeunt* [*omnes*].

[SCENE X]

Enter CLOWN [ROBIN] *and* DICK, *with a cup.*

DICK   Sirrah, Robin we were best look that your devil can answer the stealing
of this same cup, for the vintner's boy follows us at the hard heels.°

ROBIN   'Tis no matter, let him come; an he follow us, I'll so conjure him, as he
was never conjured in his life, I warrant him. Let me see the cup.

Enter VINTNER.

DICK   Here 'tis. Yonder he comes! Now Robin, now or never show thy cunning.

VINTNER   O, are you here? I am glad I have found you. You are a couple of fine
companions! Pray where's the cup you stole from the tavern?

ROBIN   How, how? We steal a cup? Take heed of what you say; we look not
10   like cup-stealers, I can tell you.

VINTNER   Never deny, for I know you have it, and I'll search you.

ROBIN   Search me? Ay, and spare not. [*Aside*] Hold the cup, Dick. Come,
come, search me, search me.   [VINTNER *searches him.*]

VINTNER   Come on sirrah, let me search you now.

---

bell, book and candle an excommunication
ritual: the bell is tolled, the book closed, the
candle extinguished

Maledicat Dominus "May the Lord curse him"
at the hard heels right at our heels

DICK   Ay, ay, do, do. [*Aside*] Hold the cup, Robin. I fear not your searching; we scorn to steal your cups, I can tell you.   [VINTNER *searches him.*]

VINTNER   Never outface me for the matter,° for sure the cup is between you two.

ROBIN   Nay, there you lie; 'tis beyond us both.

20 VINTNER   A plague take you! I thought 'twas your knavery to take it away. Come, give it me again.

ROBIN   Ay, much!° When, can you tell?° Dick, make me a circle, and stand close at my back, and stir not for thy life. Vintner, you shall have your cup back anon. Say nothing, Dick. *O per se, o; Demogorgon, Belcher and Mephostophilis!*

Enter MEPHOSTOPHILIS.

MEPHOSTOPHILIS   You princely legions of infernal rule,
How am I vexèd by these villains' charms!
From Constantinople have they brought me now,
Only for pleasure of these damnèd slaves.   [*Exit* VINTNER.]

30 ROBIN   By lady sir, you have had a shrewd journey of it. Will it please you to take a shoulder of mutton to supper, and a tester° in your purse, and go back again?

DICK   Ay, I pray you heartily, sir, for we called you but in jest, I promise you.

MEPHOSTOPHILIS   To purge the rashness of this cursèd deed
First, be thou turnèd to this ugly shape,
For apish° deeds transformèd to an ape.

ROBIN   O brave, an ape! I pray sir, let me have the carrying of him about to show some tricks.

40 MEPHOSTOPHILIS   And so thou shalt: be thou transformed to a dog, and carry him upon thy back. Away, be gone!

ROBIN   A dog? That's excellent: let the maids look well to their porridge-pots, for I'll into the kitchen presently. Come, Dick, come.

Exeunt the two CLOWNS.

MEPHOSTOPHILIS   Now with the flames of ever-burning fire
I'll wing myself and forthwith fly amain°
Unto my Faustus to the great Turk's court.   *Exit.*

[CHORUS 2]

CHORUS

When Faustus had with pleasure ta'en the view
Of rarest things and royal courts of kings,
He stayed his course° and so returnèd home,
Where such as bare his absence but with grief—
I mean his friends and nearest companions—
Did gratulate° his safety with kind words;

Never . . . matter don't try to brazen the matter out with me
Ay, much derisive
When, can you tell derisive
tester sixpence

apish foolish, ridiculous
amain speedily
stayed his course interrupted his traveling
gratulate rejoice at

And in their conference of that befell,
Touching his journey through the world and air,
They put forth questions of astrology,
10   Which Faustus answered with such learnèd skill
As they admired and wondered at his wit.
Now is his fame spread forth in every land:
Amongst the rest, the Emperor is one,
Carolus the Fifth,° at whose palace now
Faustus is feasted 'mongst his noblemen.
What there he did in trial of his art,
I leave untold: your eyes shall see performed.   *Exit.*

[SCENE XI]

Enter MARTINO *and* FREDERICK *at several doors.*

MARTINO   What ho, officers, gentlemen!
Hie to the presence° to attend the Emperor.
Good Frederick, see the rooms be voided straight,°
His majesty is coming to the hall;
Go back, and see the state° in readiness.
FREDERICK   But where is Bruno, our elected Pope,
That on a fury's back came post from Rome?
Will not his grace consort° the Emperor?
MARTINO   Oh, and with him comes the German conjurer.
10   The learnèd Faustus, fame of Wittenberg,
The wonder of the world for magic art;
And he intends to show great Carolus
The race of all his stout progenitors,
And bring in presence of his majesty
The royal shapes and warlike semblances
Of Alexander and his beauteous paramour.
FREDERICK   Where is Benvolio?
MARTINO   Fast asleep, I warrant you.
He took his rouse° with stoups° of Rhenish wine
20   So kindly yesternight to Bruno's health,
That all this day the sluggard keeps his bed.
FREDERICK   See, see, his window's ope. We'll call to him.
MARTINO   What ho, Benvolio?

Enter BENVOLIO *above at a window in his nightcap, buttoning.*

BENVOLIO   What a devil ail you two?
MARTINO   Speak softly, sir, lest the devil hear you;
For Faustus at the court is late arrived,

Carolus the Fifth Charles V, Emperor from   **state** throne
1519–1556   **consort** accompany
presence audience chamber   **took his rouse** drank heavily
voided straight cleared at once   **stoups** measures

And at his heels a thousand furies wait
To accomplish whatsoever the doctor please.
BENVOLIO What of this?
30 MARTINO Come, leave thy chamber first, and thou shalt see
This conjurer perform such rare exploits
Before the Pope and royal Emperor
As never yet was seen in Germany.
BENVOLIO Has not the Pope enough of conjuring yet?
He was upon the devil's back late enough,
And if he be so far in love with him,
I would he would post with him to Rome again.
FREDERICK Speak, wilt thou come and see this sport?
BENVOLIO Not I.
40 MARTINO Wilt thou stand in thy window and see it, then?
BENVOLIO Ay, and I fall not asleep i' the meantime.
MARTINO The Emperor is at hand, who comes to see
What wonders by black spells may compassed be.
BENVOLIO Well, go you attend the Emperor. I am content for this once to
thrust my head out at a window, for they say if a man be drunk overnight the
devil cannot hurt him in the morning. If that be true, I have a charm in my
head shall control° him as well as the conjurer, I warrant you.

A sennet. [Enter] Charles the German EMPEROR, BRUNO, [*Duke of*]
SAXONY, FAUSTUS, MEPHOSTOPHILIS, *and* ATTENDANTS.

EMPEROR Wonder of men, renowned magician,
Thrice-learnèd Faustus, welcome to our court.
50 This deed of thine, in setting Bruno free
From his and our professèd enemy,
Shall add more excellence unto thine art,
Than if by powerful necromantic spells
Thou couldst command the world's obedience.
For ever be beloved of Carolus;
And if this Bruno thou hast late redeemed,
In peace possess the triple diadem
And sit in Peter's chair, despite of chance,°
Thou shalt be famous through all Italy,
60 And honoured of the German emperor.
FAUSTUS These gracious words, most royal Carolus,
Shall make poor Faustus to his utmost power
Both love and serve the German Emperor,
And lay his life at Holy Bruno's feet.
For proof whereof, if so your grace be pleased,
The doctor stands prepared by power of art
To cast his magic charms that shall pierce through
The ebon gates of ever-burning hell,
And hale the stubborn furies from their caves,

control subdue   **chance** fortune

70   To compass whatsoe'er your grace commands.

BENVOLIO   Blood, he speaks terribly! But for all that, I do not greatly believe
him; he looks as like a conjurer as the Pope to a costermonger.°

EMPEROR   Then, Faustus, as thou late didst promise us,
        We would behold that famous conqueror,
        Great Alexander, and his paramour,
        In their true shapes and state majestical,
        That we may wonder at their excellence.

FAUSTUS   Your majesty shall see them presently.
        Mephostophilis, away!
80   And with a solemn noise of trumpets' sound,
        Present before this royal Emperor
        Great Alexander and his beauteous paramour.

MEPHOSTOPHILIS   Faustus, I will.   *Exit* MEPHOSTOPHILIS.

BENVOLIO   Well, master doctor, an your devils come not away quickly, you
shall have me asleep presently. Zounds, I could eat myself for anger, to
think I have been such an ass all this while, to stand gaping after the devil's
governor, and can see nothing.

FAUSTUS   I'll make you feel something anon, if my art fail me not.
        My lord, I must forewarn your majesty
90   That when my spirits present the royal shapes
        Of Alexander and his paramour,
        Your grace demand no questions of the king,
        But in dumb silence let them come and go.

EMPEROR   Be it as Faustus please, we are content.

BENVOLIO   Ay, ay, and I am content too. And thou bring Alexander and his
paramour before the Emperor, I'll be Actaeon° and turn myself to a stag.

FAUSTUS   And I'll play Diana, and send you the horns presently.°

SENNET   *Enter at one door the Emperor* ALEXANDER, *at the other* DARIUS; *they*
meet; DARIUS *is thrown down;* ALEXANDER *kills him, takes off his crown,*
and, offering to go out, his PARAMOUR *meets him; he embraceth her and*
sets DARIUS' *crown upon her head, and coming back, both salute the*
EMPEROR, *who, leaving his state, offers to embrace them, which* FAUSTUS
seeing, suddenly stays him. Then trumpets cease and music sounds.

        My gracious lord, you do forget yourself;
        These are but shadows, not substantial.

100   EMPEROR   O pardon me, my thoughts are ravished so
        With sight of this renownèd emperor,
        That in mine arms I would have compassed him.
        But, Faustus, since I may not speak to them,
        To satisfy my longing thoughts at full,
        Let me this tell thee: I have heard it said
        That this fair lady, whilst she lived on earth,
        Had on her neck a little wart or mole;

costermonger man who sells fruit, fish, etc. from
a barrow in the street
Actaeon saw Diana bathing and was turned into
a stag for punishment; his own hounds killed
him.
send . . . presently Cf. vii. 16n.

How may I prove that saying to be true?

FAUSTUS   Your majesty may boldly go and see.

110 EMPEROR   Faustus, I see it plain,
    And in this sight thou better pleasest me
    Than if I gained another monarchy.

FAUSTUS   Away, be gone.   *Exit Show.*
    See, see, my gracious lord, what strange beast is yon, that thrusts this head out at window?

EMPEROR   O, wondrous sight! See, Duke of Saxony,
    Two spreading horns most strangely fastenèd
    Upon the head of young Benvolio!

SAXONY   What, is he asleep or dead?

120 FAUSTUS   He sleeps, my lord, but dreams not of his horns.

EMPEROR   This sport is excellent. We'll call and wake him.
    What ho, Benvolio!

BENVOLIO   A plague upon you! Let me sleep awhile.

EMPEROR   I blame thee not to sleep much,° having such a head of thine own.

SAXONY   Look up, Benvolio, 'tis the Emperor calls.

BENVOLIO   The Emperor? Where? O, zounds, my head!

EMPEROR   Nay, and thy horns hold, 'tis no matter for thy head, for that's armed sufficiently.

FAUSTUS   Why, how now, sir knight? What, hanged by the horns? This is most
130   horrible! Fie, fie, pull in your head for shame, let not all the world wonder at you.

BENVOLIO   Zounds, doctor, is this your villainy?

FAUSTUS   O say not so, sir. The doctor has no skill,
    No art, no cunning, to present these lords
    Or bring before this royal Emperor
    The mighty monarch, warlike Alexander.
    If Faustus do it, you are straight resolved
    In bold Actaeon's shape to turn a stag.
    And therefore, my lord, so please your majesty,
140   I'll raise a kennel of hounds shall hunt him so
    As all his footmanship° shall scarce prevail
    To keep his carcass from their bloody fangs.
    Ho, Belimote, Argiron, Asterote!

BENVOLIO   Hold, hold! Zounds, he'll raise up a kennel of devils, I think, anon. Good my lord, entreat for me. 'Sblood, I am never able to endure these torments.

EMPEROR   Then, good master doctor,
    Let me entreat you to remove his horns:
    He has done penance now sufficiently.

150 FAUSTUS   My gracious lord, not so much for injury done to me, as to delight your majesty with some mirth, hath Faustus justly requited this injurious° knight; which being all I desire, I am content to remove his horns. Mephostophilis, transform him. And hereafter, sir, look you speak well of scholars.

I blame . . . much I don't much blame you for sleeping   **footmanship** skill in the running
    injurious insulting

BENVOLIO   Speak well of ye? 'Sblood, and scholars be such cuckhold-makers
to clap horns of honest men's head o' this order,° I'll ne'er trust smooth faces
and small ruffs° more. But an° I be not revenged for this, would I might be
turned to a gaping oyster and drink nothing but salt water.

EMPEROR   Come, Faustus, while the Emperor lives,
160   In recompense of this thy high desert,
           Thou shalt command the state of Germany,
           And live beloved of mighty Carolus.   *Exeunt omnes.*

[SCENE XII]

Enter BENVOLIO, MARTINO, FREDERICK, *and* SOLDIERS.

MARTINO   Nay, sweet Benvolio, let us sway thy thoughts
          From this attempt against the conjurer.
BENVOLIO   Away, you love me not, to urge me thus.
           Shall I let slip so great an injury,
           When every servile groom jests at my wrongs,
           And in their rustic gambols° proudly say
           'Benvolio's head was graced with horns today'?
           O may these eyelids never close again
           Till with my sword I have that conjurer slain.
10   If you will aid me in this enterprise,
           Then draw your weapons and be resolute;
           If not, depart: here will Benvolio die,
           But Faustus' death shall quit my infamy.
FREDERICK   Nay, we will stay with thee, betide° what may,
            And kill that doctor if he come this way.
BENVOLIO   Then, gentle Frederick, hie thee to the grove,
           And place our servants and our followers
           Close in an ambush there behind the trees.
           By this, I know, the conjurer is near:
20   I saw him kneel and kiss the Emperor's hand,
           And take his leave, laden with rich rewards.
           Then, soldiers, boldly fight; if Faustus die,
           Take you the wealth, leave us the victory.
FREDERICK   Come, soldiers, follow me unto the grove.
            Who kills him shall have gold and endless love.

                              Exit FREDERICK *with the* SOLDIERS.

BENEVOLIO   My head is lighter than it was by the horns,
            But yet my heart's more ponderous than my head,
            And pants until I see that conjurer dead.
MARTINO   Where shall we place ourselves, Benvolio?

o' this order in this manner   But an unless if
smooth faces and small ruffs Scholars often   gambols frolics
avoided the beards and large ruffs of the   betide happen
courtier.

30 BENVOLIO   Here will we stay to bide the first assault.
    O were that damnèd hell-hound but in place,
    Thou soon shouldst see me quit° my foul disgrace.

Enter FREDERICK.

FREDERICK   Close, close! The conjurer is at hand,
    And all alone comes walking in his gown.
    Be ready then, and strike the peasant down.
BENVOLIO   Mine be that honour, then; now sword, strike home.
    For horns he gave, I'll have his head anon.

Enter FAUSTUS *with the false head.*

MARTINO   See, see, he comes.
BENVOLIO   No words. This blow ends all.
    Hell take his soul; his body thus must fall.

                                    [*Strikes* FAUSTUS.]

FAUSTUS   O!
40 FREDERICK   Groan you, master doctor?
BENVOLIO   Break may his heart with groans! Dear Frederick, see,
    Thus will I end his griefs immediately.   [*Cuts off his head.*]
MARTINO   Strike with a willing hand; his head is off.
BENVOLIO   The devil's dead; the Furies now may laugh.
FREDERICK   Was this that stern aspect, that awful frown,
    Made the grim monarch of infernal spirits
    Tremble and quake at his commanding charms?
MARTINO   Was this that damnèd head, whose art° conspired
50   Benvolio's shame before the Emperor?
BENVOLIO   Ay, that's the head, and here the body lies,
    Justly rewarded for his villainies.
FREDERICK   Come, let's devise how we may add more shame
    To the black scandal of his hated name.
BENVOLIO   First, on his head, in quittance of my wrongs,
    I'll nail huge forkèd horns, and let them hang
    Within the window where he yoked° me first,
    That all the world may see my just revenge.
MARTINO   What use shall we put his beard to?
60 BENVOLIO   We'll sell it to a chimney-sweeper; it will wear out ten birchen
    brooms, I warrant you.
FREDERICK   What shall his eyes do?
BENVOLIO   We'll put out his eyes, and they shall serve for buttons to his lips,
    to keep his tongue from catching cold.
MARTINO   An excellent policy!° And now, sirs, having divided him, what shall
    the body do?   [FAUSTUS *stands up*]
BENVOLIO   Zounds, the devil's alive again!
FREDERICK   Give him his head, for God's sake!

quit repay   yoked the horns held his head fast, like the
art wit   yoke of oxen
                                      policy trick

FAUSTUS   Nay, keep it. Faustus will have heads and hands,
70   Ay, all your hearts to recompense this deed.
             Knew you not, traitors, I was limited°
             For four-and-twenty years to breathe on earth?
             And had you cut my body with your swords,
             Or hewed this flesh and bones as small as sand,
             Yet in a minute had my spirit returned,
             And I had breathed a man made free from harm.
             But wherefore do I dally° my revenge?
             Asteroth, Belimoth, Mephostophilis!

Enter MEPHOSTOPHILIS *and other* DEVILS.

             Go, horse these traitors on your fiery backs,
80   And mount aloft with them as high as heaven;
             Thence pitch them headlong to the lowest hell.
             Yet stay, the world shall see their misery,
             And hell shall after plague their treachery.
             Go, Belimoth, and take this caitiff° hence,
             And hurl him in some lake of mud and dirt.
             Take thou this other, drag him through the woods
             Amongst the pricking thorns and sharpest briars,
             Whilst with my gentle Mephostophilis,
             This traitor flies unto some steepy rock,
90   That rolling down may break the villain's bones
             As he intended to dismember me.
             Fly hence, dispatch my charge immediately.
FREDERICK   Pity us, gentle Faustus! Save our lives!
FAUSTUS   Away!
FREDERICK   He must needs go that the devil drives.°

                              Exeunt SPIRITS *with the* KNIGHTS.

Enter the ambushed SOLDIERS.

1 SOLDIER   Come, sirs, prepare yourselves in readiness.
             Make haste to help these noble gentlemen.
             I heard them parley with the conjurer.
2 SOLDIER   See where he comes; dispatch and kill the slave.
FAUSTUS   What's here? An ambush to betray my life!
100   Then Faustus, try thy skill. Base peasants, stand!
             For lo, these trees remove at my command,
             And stand as bulwarks twixt yourselves and me,
             To shield me from your hated treachery.
             Yet, to encounter this your weak attempt,
             Behold an army comes incontinent.°

FAUSTUS *strikes the door,° and enter a* DEVIL *playing on a drum; after*
him another bearing an ensign; and divers with weapons; MEPHO-

---

limited allowed the extent of   **He . . . drives** proverbial
dally trifle with, delay over   **incontinent** immediately
caitiff wretch   **the door** at the back of the stage

STOPHILIS *with fireworks. They set upon the* SOLDIERS *and drive them out.*   [*Exit* FAUSTUS.]

[SCENE XIII]

Enter at several doors BENVOLIO, FREDERICK, *and* MARTINO, *their heads and faces bloody and besmeared with mud and dirt, all having horns on their heads.*

MARTINO   What ho, Benvolio!
BENVOLIO   Here, what, Frederick, ho!
FREDERICK   O help me, gentle friend; where is Martino?
MARTINO   Dear Frederick, here,
    Half smothered in a lake of mud and dirt,
    Through which the furies dragged me by the heels.
FREDERICK   Martino, see, Benvolio's horns again!
MARTINO   O misery! How now, Benvolio?
BENVOLIO   Defend me, heaven! Shall I be haunted still?
10 MARTINO   Nay, fear not, man; we have no power to kill.
BENVOLIO   My friends transformèd thus! O hellish spite!
    Your heads are all set with horns!
FREDERICK   You hit it right:
    It is your own you mean; feel on your head.
BENVOLIO   Zounds, horns again!
MARTINO   Nay, chafe not, man, we all are sped.°
BENVOLIO   What devil attends this damned magician,
    That, spite of spite,° our wrongs are doubled?°
FREDERICK   What may we do, that we may hide our shames?
BENVOLIO   If we should follow him to work revenge,
    He'd join long asses' ears to these huge horns,
20   And make us laughing stocks to all the world.
MARTINO   What shall we then do, dear Benvolio?
BENVOLIO   I have a castle joining near these woods,
    And thither we'll repair and live obscure,
    Till time shall alter these our brutish shapes.
    Sith° black disgrace hath thus eclipsed our fame,
    We'll rather die with grief, than live with shame.   *Exeunt omnes.*

[SCENE XIV]

Enter FAUSTUS *and the* HORSE-COURSER° *and* MEPHOSTOPHILIS.

HORSE-COURSER   I beseech your worship accept of these forty dollars.
FAUSTUS   Friend, thou canst not buy so good a horse for so small a price; I have no great need to sell him, but if thou likest him for ten dollars more, take him, because I see thou hast a good mind to him.

---

sped done for
spite of spite in spite of everything
doubled trisyllabic; pronounced dou-ble-ed
Sith since

Horse-courser horse-dealer (with traditional reputation like a used-car salesman's)

HORSE-COURSER   I beseech you sir, accept of this. I am a very poor man, and
have lost very much of late by horse-flesh, and this bargain will set me up
again.

FAUSTUS   Well, I will not stand° with thee, give me the money. Now sirrah,
I must tell you, that you may ride him o'er hedge and ditch, and spare him
10   him not; but, do you hear, in any case, ride him not into the water.°

HORSE-COURSER   How sir, not into the water? Why, will he not drink of all
waters?°

FAUSTUS   Yes, he will drink of all waters, but ride him not into the water; o'er
hedge and ditch or where thou wilt, but not into the water. Go bid the ostler
deliver him unto you—and remember what I say.

HORSE-COURSER   I warrant you, sir. O joyful day! Now am I a made man for
ever.   *Exit.*

FAUSTUS   What art thou, Faustus, but a man condemned to die?
Thy fatal time° draws to a final end.
20   Despair doth drive distrust into my thoughts;
Confound° these passions with a quiet sleep.
Tush, Christ did call the thief upon the cross,°
Then rest thee, Faustus, quiet in conceit.°   *He sits to sleep.*

Enter the HORSE-COURSER, *wet.*

HORSE-COURSER   O what a cozening° doctor was this! I, riding my horse into
the water, thinking some hidden mystery had been in the horse, I had nothing
under me but a little straw, and had much ado to escape drowning. Well,
I'll go rouse him, and make him give me my forty dollars again. Ho, sirrah
doctor, you cozening scab!° Master doctor, awake, and rise, and give me my
money again, for your horse is turned to a bottle° of hay. Master doctor!
30   *He pulls off his leg.*
Alas, I am undone; what shall I do? I have pulled off his leg.

FAUSTUS   O help, help! The villain hath murdered me.

HORSE-COURSER   Murder or not murder, now he has but one leg I'll outrun him,
and cast this leg into some ditch or other.   [*Exit.*]

FAUSTUS   Stop him, stop him, stop him—ha, ha, ha! Faustus hath his leg again,
and the horse-courser a bundle of hay for his forty dollars.

Enter WAGNER.

How now Wagner, what news with thee?

WAGNER   If it pleases you, the Duke of Vanholt doth earnestly entreat your
company, and hath sent some of his men to attend you with provision fit for
40   your journey.

FAUSTUS   The Duke of Vanholt's an honourable gentleman, and one to whom
I must be no niggard of my cunning. Come away.   *Exeunt.*

---

stand haggle
ride . . . water Running water breaks witches'
spells.
drink . . . waters go anywhere
fatal time time allotted by fate
Confound disperse

Christ . . . cross Luke 23:39–43
conceit mind
cozening cheating
scab villain
bottle bundle

[SCENE XV]

Enter Clown [ROBIN], DICK, HORSE-COURSER, *and a* CARTER.

CARTER   Come, my masters, I'll bring you to the best beer in Europe. What ho, hostess. Where be these whores?°

Enter HOSTESS.

HOSTESS   How now, what lack you? What, my old guests, welcome!

ROBIN   Sirrah Dick, dost thou know why I stand so mute?

DICK   No, Robin, why is it?

ROBIN   I am eighteen pence on the score;° but say nothing, see if she have forgotten me.

HOSTESS   Who's this, that stands so solemnly by himself? What, my old guest!

10   ROBIN   Oh, hostess, how do you? I hope my score stands still.

HOSTESS   Ay, there's no doubt of that, for methinks you make no haste to wipe it out.

DICK   Why, hostess, I say, fetch us some beer.

HOSTESS   You shall presently. Look up into the hall there, ho!°   *Exit.*

DICK   Come, sirs, what shall we do now till mine hostess comes?

CARTER   Marry, sir, I'll tell you the bravest tale how a conjurer served me. You know Doctor Fauster?

HORSE-COURSER   Ay, a plague take him. Here's some on's have cause to know him. Did he conjure thee too?

20   CARTER   I'll tell you how he served me. As I was going to Wittenberg t'other day, with a load of hay, he met me and asked me what he should give me for as much hay as he could eat. Now, sir, I, thinking that a little would serve his turn, bade him take as much as he would for three-farthings. So he presently gave me my money and fell to eating; and, as I am a cursen° man, he never left eating till he had eat up all my load of hay.

ALL   O monstrous, eat a whole load of hay!

ROBIN   Yes, yes, that may be, for I have heard of one that h'as eat a load of logs.°

HORSE-COURSER   Now, sirs, you shall hear how villainously he served me. I

30   went to him yesterday to buy a horse of him, and he would by no means sell him under forty dollars. So, sir, because I knew him to be such a horse as would run over hedge and ditch and never tire, I gave him his money. So when I had my horse, Doctor Fauster bade me ride him night and day and spare him no time. 'But,' quoth he, 'in any case ride him not into the water.' Now, sir, I thinking the horse had some quality that he would not have me know of, what did I but rid him into a great river, and when I came just in the midst, my horse vanished away, and I sat straddling upon a bottle of hay.

ALL   O brave° doctor!

40   HORSE-COURSER   But you shall hear how bravely° I served him for it: I went me home to his house, and there I found him asleep. I kept-a-hallowing and

whores servants
on the score an old debt still charged against him
Look . . . ho She instructs the maids to attend to the customers.

cursen Christian
eat . . . logs been drunk
brave excellent
bravely well

whooping in his ears, but all could not wake him. I, seeing that, took him by the leg and never rested pulling, till I had pulled me his leg quite off, and now 'tis at home in mine hostry.

ROBIN   And has the doctor but one leg, then? That's excellent, for one of his devils turned me into the likeness of an ape's face.

CARTER   Some more drink, hostess.

ROBIN   Hark you, we'll into another room and drink a while, and then we'll go seek out the doctor.   *Exeunt omnes.*

[SCENE XVI]

Enter the DUKE OF VANHOLT, *his* DUCHESS, [SERVANTS,] FAUSTUS *and* MEPHOSTOPHILIS.

DUKE   Thanks, master doctor, for these pleasant sights. Nor know I how sufficiently to recompense your great deserts in erecting that enchanted castle in the air, the sight whereof so delighted me, as nothing in the world could please me more.

FAUSTUS   I do think myself, my good lord, highly recompensed in that it pleaseth your grace to think but well of that which Faustus hath performed. But, gracious lady, it may be that you have taken no pleasure in those sights; therefore, I pray you tell me, what is the thing you most desire to have: be it in the world, it shall be yours. I have heard that great-bellied women do long for things are° rare and dainty.

DUCHESS   True, master doctor, and since I find you so kind, I will make known unto you what my heart desires to have; and were it now summer, as it is January, a dead time of the winter, I would request no better meat° than a dish of ripe grapes.

FAUSTUS   This is but a small matter; go, Mephostophilis, away.

Exit MEPHOSTOPHILIS.

Madame, I will do more than this for your content.

Enter MEPHOSTOPHILIS *again with the grapes.*

Here, now taste ye these; they should be good, for they come from a far country, I can tell you.

DUKE   This makes me wonder more than all the rest, that at this time of the year, when every tree is barren of his fruit, from whence you had these ripe grapes.

FAUSTUS   Please it your grace, the year is divided into two circles over the whole world, so that when it is winter with us, in the contrary circle it is likewise summer with them, as in India, Saba° and such countries that lie far east, where they have fruit twice a year. From whence, by means of a swift spirit that I have, I had these grapes brought as you see.

DUCHESS   And trust me, they are the sweetest grapes that e'er I tasted.

The CLOWNS *bounce° at the gate within.*

are that are
meat food

Saba Sheba
bounce knock loudly

DUKE   What rude disturbers have we at the gate?
30   Go, pacify their fury. Set it ope,
         And then demand of them what they would have.

They knock again and call out to talk with FAUSTUS.

SERVANT   Why, how now, masters? What a coil° is there? What is the reason°
you disturb the Duke?

DICK   We have no reason for it, therefore a fig for him.°

SERVANT   Why, saucy varlets, dare you be so bold?

HORSE-COURSER   I hope, sir, we have wit enough to be more bold than welcome.

SERVANT   It appears so. Pray be bold elsewhere, and trouble not the Duke.

DUKE   What would they have?

SERVANT   They all cry out to speak with Doctor Faustus.

40 CARTER   Ay, and we will speak with him.

DUKE   Will you sir? Commit° the rascals.

DICK   Commit with° us! He were as good commit with his father as commit
with us.

FAUSTUS   I do beseech your grace let them come in.
They are good subject for a merriment.

DUKE   Do as thou wilt, Faustus; I give thee leave.

FAUSTUS   I thank your grace.

Enter the CLOWN [ROBIN], DICK, CARTER, *and* HORSE-COURSER.

Why, how now, my good friends?
Faith, you are too outrageous,° but come near;
I have procured your pardons. Welcome all.

50 ROBIN   Nay, sir, we will be welcome for our money, and we will pay for what
we take. What ho! Give's half-a-dozen of beer here, and be hanged.

FAUSTUS   Nay, hark you, can you tell me where you are?

CARTER   Ay, marry can I; we are under heaven.

SERVANT   Ay, but, sir sauce-box, know you in what place?

HORSE-COURSER   Ay, ay, the house is good enough to drink in. Zounds, fill us
some beer or we'll break all the barrels in the house and dash out all your
brains with your bottles.

FAUSTUS   Be not so furious; come, you shall have beer.
My lord, beseech you give me leave awhile.

60   I'll gage° my credit, 'twill content your grace.

DUKE   With all my heart, kind doctor, please thyself;
Our servants and our court's at thy command.

FAUSTUS   I humbly thank your grace. Then fetch some beer.

HORSE-COURSER   Ay, marry, there spake a doctor indeed, and, 'faith, I'll drink
a health to thy wooden leg for that word.

FAUSTUS   My wooden leg? What dost thou mean by that?

CARTER   Ha, ha, ha! Dost thou hear him, Dick? He has forgot his leg.

---

coil disturbance
reason with a pun on the homophone *raisin*—
which leads to the fig
a fig for him expression of contempt. They don't
realize that the room they have got into is the
Court.

Commit take to prison
Commit with have sexual intercourse
outrageous violent
gage wager

HORSE-COURSER   Ay, ay, he does not stand much upon° that.

FAUSTUS   No, 'faith, not much upon a wooden leg.

70   CARTER   Good Lord, that flesh and blood should be so frail with your worship!
Do not you remember a horse-courser you sold a horse to?

FAUSTUS   Yes, I remember I sold one a horse.

CARTER   And do you remember you bid he should not ride into the water?

FAUSTUS   Yes, I do very well remember that.

CARTER   And do you remember nothing of your leg?

FAUSTUS   No, in good sooth.

CARTER   Then I pray remember your curtsy.°

FAUSTUS   I thank you, sir.   [*He bows.*]

CARTER   'Tis not so much worth; I pray you, tell me one thing.

80   FAUSTUS   What's that?

CARTER   Be both your legs bedfellows every night together?

FAUSTUS   Wouldst thou make a colossus° of me, that thou askest me such
questions?

CARTER   No, truly, sir; I would make nothing of you, but I would fain know
that.

Enter HOSTESS *with drink.*

FAUSTUS   Then I assure thee certainly they are.

CARTER   I thank you, I am fully satisfied.

FAUSTUS   But wherefore dost thou ask?

CARTER   For nothing, sir—but methinks you should have a wooden bedfellow
90   of one of 'em.

HORSE-COURSER   Why, do you hear, sir, did not I pull off one of your legs when
you were asleep?

FAUSTUS   But I have it again now I am awake. Look you here, sir.

ALL   O horrible! Had the doctor three legs?

CARTER   Do you remember, sir, how you cozened me and eat up my load of—
                                                        FAUSTUS *charms him dumb.*

DICK   Do you remember how you made me wear an ape's—

HORSE-COURSER   You whoreson conjuring scab, do you remember how you
99   cozened me with a ho—

ROBIN   Ha' you forgotten me? You think to carry it away° with your hey-pass
and re-pass.° Do you remember the dog's fa—   *Exeunt* CLOWNS.

HOSTESS   Who pays for the ale? Hear you, master doctor, now you have sent
away my guests, I pray who shall pay me for my a—   *Exit* HOSTESS.

DUCHESS   My lord,
We are much beholding to this learnèd man.

DUKE   So are we, madam, which we will recompense
With all the love and kindness that we may.
His artful sport drives all sad thoughts away.   *Exeunt.*

---

stand much upon set great store by
curtsy to curtsy was "to make a leg"
colossus The Colossus of Rhodes was an enormous statue bestriding the harbor.

carry it away carry it off
hey-pass and re-pass juggler's exclamations

[SCENE XVII]

Thunder and lightning. Enter DEVILS *with covered dishes.*
MEPHOSTOPHILIS *leads them into* FAUSTUS' *study. Then enter* WAGNER.

WAGNER   I think my master means to die shortly.
He hath made his will, and given me his wealth,
His house, his goods, and store of golden plate,
Besides two thousand ducats ready coined.
And yet methinks, if that death were near,
He would not banquet and carouse and swill
Amongst the students, as even now he doth,
Who are at supper with such belly-cheer
As Wagner ne'er beheld in all his life.
See where they come; belike the feast is ended.   *Exit.*

Enter FAUSTUS, MEPHOSTOPHILIS, *and two or three* SCHOLARS.

1 SCHOLAR   Master Doctor Faustus, since our conference about fair ladies, which was the beautifullest in all the world, we have determined with ourselves that Helen of Greece was the admirablest lady that ever lived. Therefore master doctor, if you will do us so much favour, as to let us see that peerless dame of Greece, whom all the world admires for majesty, we should think ourselves much beholding unto you.

FAUSTUS   Gentlemen,
For that I know your friendship is unfeigned,
And Faustus' custom is not to deny
The just requests of those that wish him well,
You shall behold that peerless dame of Greece,
No otherways for pomp and majesty,
Than when Sir Paris crossed the seas with her,
And brought the spoils to rich Dardania.°
Be silent then, for danger is in words.

Music sounds. MEPHOSTOPHILIS *brings in* HELEN; *she passeth over the stage.*

2 SCHOLAR   Too simple is my wit to tell her praise,
Whom all the world admires for majesty.
3 SCHOLAR   No marvel though the angry Greeks pursued
With ten years war the rape of such a queen,
Whose heavenly beauty passeth all compare.
1 SCHOLAR   Since we have seen the pride of nature's works,
And only° paragon of excellence,
Let us depart; and for this glorious deed
Happy and blest be Faustus evermore.

Enter an OLD MAN.

FAUSTUS   Gentlemen, farewell: the same wish I to you.   *Exeunt* SCHOLARS.
OLD MAN   O gentle Faustus, leave this damnèd art,

Dardania Troy   **only** sole

This magic, that will charm thy soul to hell,
And quite bereave thee of salvation.
Though thou hast now offended like a man,
40   Do not perséver in it like a devil.
Yet, yet, thou hast an amiable soul,
If sin by custom grow not into nature.°
Then, Faustus, will repentance come too late,
Then thou art banished from the sight of heaven;
No mortal can express the pains of hell.
It may be this my exhortation
Seems harsh and all unpleasant; let it not,
For, gentle son, I speak it not in wrath,
Or envy of thee, but in tender love,
50   And pity of thy future misery;
And so have hope, that this my kind rebuke,
Checking° thy body, may amend thy soul.
FAUSTUS   Where art thou, Faustus? Wretch, what hast thou done?
Damned art thou, Faustus, damned: despair and die.
Hell claims his right, and with a roaring voice
Says 'Faustus, come, thine hour is almost come'
MEPHOSTOPHILIS *gives him a dagger.*°
And Faustus now will come to do thee right.°
OLD MAN   O stay, good Faustus, stay thy desperate stops!
I see an angel hovers o'er thy head,
60   And with a vial full of precious grace,
Offers to pour the same into thy soul.
Then call for mercy and avoid despair.
FAUSTUS   O friend, I feel thy words
To comfort my distressèd soul.
Leave me awhile to ponder on my sins.
OLD MAN   Faustus, I leave thee, but with grief of heart,
Fearing the ruin of thy hapless soul.   *Exit.*
FAUSTUS   Accursed Faustus, where is mercy now?
I do repent, and yet I do despair.
70   Hell strives with grace for conquest in my breast;
What shall I do to shun the snares of death?
MEPHOSTOPHILIS   Thou traitor, Faustus, I arrest thy soul
For disobedience to my sovereign lord.
Revolt,° or I'll in piecemeal tear thy flesh.
FAUSTUS   I do repent I e'er offended him.
Sweet Mephostophilis, entreat thy lord
To pardon my unjust presumption,
And with my blood again I will confirm
The former vow I made to Lucifer.

custom . . . nature often opposed in Renaissance thought. Here "custom" means "habit,"
and the warning is against sin's becoming
"second nature."
Checking reproving

dagger Suicide would suit the devil's purposes
well.
do thee right pay you your due
Revolt turn back (to the devil)

80   MEPHOSTOPHILIS   Do it then, Faustus, with unfeignèd heart,
       Lest greater dangers do attend thy drift.°
     FAUSTUS   Torment, sweet friend, that base and agèd man
       That durst dissuade me from thy Lucifer,
       With greatest torment that our hell affords.
     MEPHOSTOPHILIS   His faith is great: I cannot touch his soul,
       But what I may afflict his body with
       I will attempt, which is but little worth.
     FAUSTUS   One thing, good servant, let me crave of thee,
       To glut the longing of my heart's desire,
90   That I may have unto my paramour
       That heavenly Helen which I saw of late,
       Whose sweet embracings may extinguish clear°
       Those thoughts that do dissuade me from my vow,
       And keep mine oath I made to Lucifer.
     MEPHOSTOPHILIS   This, or what else my Faustus shall desire,
       Shall be performed in twinkling of an eye.

       Enter HELEN *again, passing over between two* CUPIDS.

     FAUSTUS   Was this the face that launched a thousand ships,
       And burnt the topless° towers of Ilium?
       Sweet Helen, make me immortal with a kiss:
100   Her lips suck forth my soul, see where it flies.
       Come, Helen, come, give me my soul again.
       Here will I dwell, for heaven is in these lips,
       And all is dross that is not Helena.

       Enter OLD MAN.

       I will be Paris, and for love of thee
       Instead of Troy shall Wittenberg be sacked,
       And I will combat with weak Menelaus,°
       And wear thy colours on my plumèd crest.
       Yea, I will wound Achilles in the heel,°
       And then return to Helen for a kiss.
110   O, thou art fairer than the evening's air,
       Clad in the beauty of a thousand stars.
       Brighter art thou than flaming Jupiter,
       When he appeared to hapless Semele:°
       More lovely than the monarch of the sky,
       In wanton Arethusa's azured arms,°
       And none but thou shalt be my paramour.
                                    Exeunt [FAUSTUS *and* HELEN].
     OLD MAN   Accursèd Faustus, miserable man,

drift away from his allegiance
clear entirely
topless so high as to seem to have no tops
Menelaus Helen's Greek husband
in the heel where alone he was vulnerable
Semele She asked Jupiter to appear to her in

his full glory as a god; when he did, she was
consumed by the lightning and thunderbolts
that attended him.
More lovely . . . arms Arethusa, a nymph, was
changed into a fountain; thus, the sun reflected
in the water.

That from thy soul exclud'st the grace of heaven,
And fliest the throne of his tribunal seat.

Enter the DEVILS.

120   Satan begins to sift° me with his pride,
As in this furnace God shall try my faith.
My faith, vile hell, shall triumph over thee!
Ambitious fiends, see how the heavens smiles
At your repulse, and laughs your state to scorn.
Hence, hell, for hence I fly unto my God.   *Exeunt.*

[SCENE XVIII]

Thunder. Enter LUCIFER, BELZEBUB, *and* MEPHOSTOPHILIS [*above.*]

LUCIFER   Thus from infernal Dis° do we ascend
To view the subjects of our monarchy,
Those souls which sin seals the black sons of hell,
'Mong which as chief, Faustus, we come to thee,
Bringing with us lasting damnation
To wait upon thy soul; the time is come
Which makes it forfeit.
MEPHOSTOPHILIS   And this gloomy night,
Here in this room will wretched Faustus be.
BELZEBUB   And here we'll stay,
10   To mark him how he doth demean° himself.
MEPHOSTOPHILIS   How should he, but in desperate lunacy?
Fond worldling, now his heart-blood dries with grief,
His conscience kills it, and his labouring brain
Begets a world of idle fantasies
To overreach the devil. But all in vain:
His store of pleasures must be sauced with pain.
He and his servant Wagner are at hand.
Both come from drawing Faustus' latest will.
See where they come.

Enter FAUSTUS *and* WAGNER.

20   FAUSTUS   Say, Wagner, thou hast perused my will:
How dost thou like it?
WAGNER   Sir, so wondrous well,
As in all humble duty I do yield
My life and lasting service for your love.

Enter the SCHOLARS.

FAUSTUS   Gramercies,° Wagner. Welcome, gentlemen.   [*Exit* WAGNER.]
1 SCHOLAR   Now, worthy Faustus, methinks your looks are changed.

sift test   **demean** conduct
Dis the underworld   **Gramercies** thanks

FAUSTUS   Ah gentlemen!

2 SCHOLAR   What ails Faustus?

FAUSTUS   Ah, my sweet chamber-fellow, had I lived with thee, then had I lived
30   still, but now must die eternally. Look, sirs, comes he not, comes he not?

1 SCHOLAR   O my dear Faustus, what imports this fear?

2 SCHOLAR   Is all our pleasure turned to melancholy?

3 SCHOLAR   He is not well with being over-solitary.

2 SCHOLAR   If it be so, we'll have physicians, and Faustus shall be cured.

3 SCHOLAR   'Tis but a surfeit,° sir, fear nothing.

FAUSTUS   A surfeit of deadly sin, that hath damned both body and soul.

2 SCHOLAR   Yet Faustus, look up to heaven, and remember God's mercy is infinite.

FAUSTUS   But Faustus' offence can ne'er be pardoned; the serpent that tempted
40   Eve may be saved, but not Faustus. O gentlemen, hear with patience and
tremble not at my speeches. Though my heart pants and quivers to remember
that I have been a student here these thirty years—O would I had never seen
Wittenberg, never read book! And what wonders I have done all Germany
can witness, yea all the world—for which Faustus hath lost both Germany
and the world, yea heaven itself, heaven, the seat of God, the throne of the
blessed, the kingdom of joy; and must remain in hell for ever. Hell, ah hell
for ever! Sweet friends, what shall become of Faustus, being in hell for ever?

2 SCHOLAR   Yet Faustus, call on God.

50   FAUSTUS   On God, whom Faustus hath abjured? On God, whom Faustus hath
blasphemed? Ah my God—I would weep, but the devil draws in my tears.
Gush forth blood instead of tears, yea, life and soul! O, he stays my tongue.
I would lift up my hands, but see, they hold them, they hold them.

ALL   Who, Faustus?

FAUSTUS   Why, Lucifer and Mephostophilis: Ah gentlemen, I gave them my
soul for my cunning.

ALL   God forbid.

FAUSTUS   God forbade it indeed, but Faustus hath done it. For the vain pleasure
60   of four-and-twenty years hath Faustus lost eternal joy and felicity. I writ
them a bill° with mine own blood; the date is expired; this is the time, and
he will fetch me.

1 SCHOLAR   Why did not Faustus tell us of this before, that divines might have
prayed for thee?

FAUSTUS   Oft have I thought to have done so, but the devil threatened to tear
me in pieces if I named God, to fetch me body and soul if I once gave ear to
divinity; and now 'tis too late. Gentlemen, away, lest you perish with me.

2 SCHOLAR   Oh what may we do to save Faustus?

70   FAUSTUS   Talk not of me, but save yourselves and depart.

3 SCHOLAR   God will strengthen me. I will stay with Faustus.

1 SCHOLAR   Tempt not God, sweet friend, but let us into the next room and pray
for him.

FAUSTUS   Ay, pray for me, pray for me. And what noise soever you hear, come
not unto me, for nothing can rescue me.

surfeit overindulgence in food or drink   bill deed

2 SCHOLAR   Pray thou, and we will pray, that God may have mercy upon thee.
FAUSTUS   Gentlemen, farewell. If I live till morning, I'll visit you. If not,
Faustus is gone to hell.
ALL   Faustus, farewell.   *Exeunt* SCHOLARS.

80   MEPHOSTOPHILIS   Ay, Faustus, now thou hast no hope of heaven,
    Therefore despair, think only upon hell,
    For that must be thy mansion, there to dwell.
FAUSTUS   Oh, thou bewitching fiend, 'twas thy temptation
    Hath robbed me of eternal happiness.
MEPHOSTOPHILIS   I do confess it, Faustus, and rejoice.
    'Twas I that, when thou were it i' the way to heaven,
    Damned up thy passage; when thou took'st the book
    To view the scriptures, then I turned the leaves
    And led thine eye.
90   What, weep'st thou? 'Tis too late, despair. Farewell.
    Fools that will laugh on earth, must weep in hell.   *Exit.*

    Enter the GOOD *and the* BAD ANGEL *at several doors.*

GOOD ANGEL   O Faustus, if thou hadst given ear to me
    Innumerable joys had followed thee.
    But thou didst love the world.
BAD ANGEL   Gave ear to me,
    And now must taste hell's pains perpetually.
GOOD ANGEL   O, what will all thy riches, pleasures, pomps,
    Avail thee now?
BAD ANGEL   Nothing but vex thee more,
    To want in hell, that had on earth such store.
                     Music while the throne° descends.
GOOD ANGEL   O, thou hast lost celestial happiness,
100   Pleasures unspeakable, bliss without end.
    Hadst thou affected sweet divinity,
    Hell, or the devil, had had no power on thee.
    Hadst thou kept on that way, Faustus, behold
    In what resplendent glory thou hadst sat
    In yonder throne, like those bright shining saints,
    And triumphed over hell. That hast thou lost,
    And now, poor soul, must thy good angel leave thee:
    The jaws of hell are open to receive thee.   *Exit [the throne ascends].*
                          Hell is discovered.°
110   BAD ANGEL   Now, Faustus, let thine eyes with horror stare
    Into that vast perpetual torture-house.
    There are the furies tossing damnèd souls
    On burning forks; there bodies boil in lead;
    There are live quarters° broiling on the coals
    That ne'er can die; this ever-burning chair

---

throne chair let down from roof of stage on
ropes and representing the throne Faustus might
have had in heaven
Hell is discovered Curtain is drawn to reveal

perhaps a painted backcloth, perhaps some other
image of hell.
quarters quartered bodies

Is for o'er-tortured souls to rest them in;
These, that are fed with sops of flaming fire,
Were gluttons, and loved only delicates,
And laughed to see the poor starve at their gates.
But yet all these are nothing: thou shalt see
120   Then thousand tortures that more horrid be.
FAUSTUS   O, I have seen enough to torture me.
BAD ANGEL   Nay, thou must feel them, taste the smart of all:
He that loves pleasure must for pleasure fall.
And so I leave thee, Faustus, till anon:
Then wilt thou tumble in confusión.   *Exit* [*Hell is concealed*].
                                        The clock strikes eleven.

FAUSTUS   Ah Faustus,
Now hast thou but one bare hour to live,
And then thou must be damned perpetually.
Stand still, you ever-moving spheres of heaven,
130   That time may cease and midnight never come.
Fair nature's eye, rise again, and make
Perpetual day; or let this hour be but
A year, a month, a week, a natural day,
That Faustus may repent and save his soul.
O lente, lente, currite noctis equi!°
The stars move still, time runs, the clock will strike.
The devil will come, and Faustus must be damned.
O I'll leap up to my God! Who pulls me down?
See, see, where Christ's blood streams in the firmament!°
140   One drop would save my soul, half a drop. Ah, my Christ!
Rend not my heart for naming of my Christ!
Yet will I call on him. O spare me, Lucifer!
Where is it now? 'Tis gone:
And see where God stretcheth out his arm,
And bends his ireful brows.
Mountains and hills, come, come, and fall on me,
And hide me from the heavy wrath of God.
No, no!
Then will I headlong run into the earth.
Earth gape! O no, it will not harbour me.
You stars that reigned at my nativity,
Whose influence hath allotted death and hell,
Now draw up Faustus like a foggy mist
Into the entrails of yon labouring clouds,
That when they vomit forth into the air,
160   My limbs may issue from their smoky mouths,
So that° my soul may but ascend to heaven.
                                        The watch strikes.

O lente . . . equi "O run slowly, slowly, horses of the night"; the lover who says this in Ovid, *Amores* I.xiii.40, wants to prolong the night in his mistress's arms.

Christ's blood . . . firmament See above, Scene V, l. 66n.
So that if only

Ah, half the hour is passed: 'twill all be passed anon.
O God,
If thou wilt not have mercy on my soul,
Yet for Christ's sake, whose blood hath ransomed me,
Impose some end to my incessant pain;
Let Faustus live in hell a thousand years,
A hundred thousand, and at last be saved!
Oh, no end is limited° to damnèd souls.
170   Why wert thou not a creature wanting soul?
Or why is this immortal that thou hast?
Ah, Pythagoras' metempsychosis,° were that true
This soul should fly from me and I be changed
Unto some brutish beast: all beasts are happy,
For when they die
Their souls are soon dissolved in elements;
But mine must live still° to be plagued in hell.
Cursed be the parents that engendered me!
No, Faustus, curse thyself, curse Lucifer
180   That hath deprived thee of the joys of heaven.

                              The clock striketh twelve.

It strikes, it strikes! Now body, turn to air,
Or Lucifer will bear thee quick° to hell!

                              Thunder and lightning.

O soul, be changed to little water-drops
And fall into the ocean, ne'er be found.

Enter DEVILS.

My God, my God! Look not so fierce on me!
Adders and serpents, let me breathe awhile!
Ugly hell, gape not! Come not, Lucifer;
I'll burn my books!°—Ah, Mephostophilis!

                              Exeunt with him.

[SCENE XIX]

Enter the SCHOLARS.

1 SCHOLAR   Come gentlemen, let us go visit Faustus,
For such a dreadful night was never seen
Since first the world's creation did begin.
Such fearful shrieks and cries were never heard;
Pray heaven the doctor have escaped the danger.
2 SCHOLAR   Oh help us, heaven! See, here are Faustus' limbs,
All torn asunder by the hand of death.
3 SCHOLAR   The devils whom Faustus served have torn him thus:

---

limited appointed
metempsychosis Pythagoras' theory that at death
the soul passed into some other creature

still forever
quick alive
books (of magic)

For 'twixt the hours of twelve and one, methought
10   I heard him shriek and call aloud for help,
At which self time the house seemed all on fire
With dreadful horror of these damnèd fiends.
2 SCHOLAR   Well, Gentlemen, though Faustus' end be such
As every Christian heart laments to think on,
Yet, for he was a scholar once admired
For wondrous knowledge in our German schools,
We'll give his mangled limbs due burial,
And all the students clothed in mourning black
Shall wait upon his heavy° funeral.   *Exeunt.*

[EPILOGUE]

CHORUS

Cut is the branch that might have grown full straight,
And burnèd is Apollo's laurel bough,°
That sometime° grew within this learnèd man.
Faustus is gone: regard his hellish fall,
Whose fiendful fortune may exhort the wise
Only to wonder° at unlawful things,
Whose deepness doth entice such forward wits,
To practise more than heavenly power permits.   *[Exit.]*

Terminat hora diem, terminat Author opus.°

FINIS.

1604, 1616

Hero and Leander

The brief epic, or epyllion as it is sometimes called, is a genre with its roots in classical antiquity—such works as Catullus' poem on the lock of Berenice, and more particularly the individual narratives of Ovid's *Heroides*—and, in particular, in an Alexandrian tradition, opposed to the "epic" proportions of Homeric narrative, favoring the verse tale of one episode. The Elizabethan literary type of Ovidian mythological verse narrative inaugurated by Marlowe's *Hero and Leander* and Shakespeare's *Venus and Adonis* is a typically Renaissance invention. Alternately pictorial, sententious, delightedly lascivious, didactically moralizing, and interpretively mythographic, the erotic epyllia of the late sixteenth and early seventeenth century discharged those twinned Renaissance obligations to instruct and delight. They followed not only classical models, but contemporary interpretive and emblematic traditions as well. A passage from Marston's *The Metamorphosis of Pygmalion's Image* (given in The Renaissance Ovid) illustrates

heavy sorrowful
Apollo's laurel bough Apollo is the god of learning; his tree is the laurel or bay, thus associated with learning and poetry.
sometime once

Only to wonder be content with merely wondering
Terminat . . . opus "The hour ends the day, the author ends his work."

the kind of pointing-up of an Ovidian story which even the poorer sort of imagination could effect.

Marlowe's unfinished poem, only two cantos of which survive, is based upon a fifth-century (A.D.) version of the story by Musaeus, as well as on Ovid's *Heroides*. It is both witty and lush, picturesque and ironic; its moralization is all in the realm of erotic psychology and no censorious notes intrude. Marlowe's two "Sestiads" were first published five years after his death, in 1598; the same year, they were brought out again with George Chapman's vastly different completion, in which a whole exterior moral realm is introduced with more philosophic and mythographic intensity than narrative sophistication.

Hero and Leander

From *First Sestiad*°

On Hellespont, guilty of true love's blood,°
In view and opposite, two cities stood,
Sea-borderers, disjoined by Neptune's might;
The one Abydos, the other Sestos hight.°
At Sestos Hero dwelt; Hero the fair,
Whom young Apollo courted for her hair,°
And offered as a dower his burning throne,
Where she should sit for men to gaze upon.
The outside of her garments were of lawn,°
10   The lining purple silk, with gilt stars drawn;
Her wide sleeves green, and bordered with a grove
Where Venus in her naked glory strove
To please the careless and disdainful eyes
Of proud Adonis, that before her lies.
Her kirtle blue, whereon was many a stain,
Made with the blood of wretched lovers slain.
Upon her head she ware° a myrtle° wreath,
From whence her veil reached to the ground beneath.
Her veil was artificial flowers and leaves,
20   Whose workmanship both man and beast deceives.
Many would praise the sweet smell as she passed,
When 'twas the odour which her breath forth cast;
And there for honey, bees have sought in vain,
And, beat from thence, have lighted there again.
About her neck hung chains of pebble-stone,
Which, lightened by her neck, like diamonds shone.

Sestiad Marlowe's own term for the books of this poem, from "Sestos"
Hellespont . . . blood Helle drowned in the Dardanelles while riding on a golden ram.
hight named
Whom . . . hair Marlowe's invented anecdote
lawn a fine linen. Marlowe is describing an allegorical costume like that in a court masque or emblematic picture assembled from various

symbolic modes: thus green sleeves are conventionally erotic, but blend into a picture of Venus' grove; Hero is Venus' votary; she also wears buskins, boots worn by the classically derived personages of masques, pageants, and pictures.
ware wore
myrtle signifying sexual love

She ware no gloves, for neither sun nor wind
Would burn or parch her hands, but to her mind°
Or warm or cool them, for they took delight
30 To play upon those hands, they were so white.
Buskins° of shells all silverèd, used she,
And branched with blushing coral to the knee,
Where sparrows perched, of hollow pearl and gold,
Such as the world would wonder to behold—
Those with sweet water oft her handmaid fills,
Which, as she went, would chirrup through the bills.
Some say, for her the fairest Cupid pined,
And looking in her face, was strooken blind.°
But this is true: so like was one the other,
40 As he imagined Hero was his mother;
And oftentimes into her bosom flew,
About her naked neck his bare arms threw,
And laid his childish head upon her breast,
And with still° panting rocked, there took his rest.
So lovely fair was Hero, Venus' nun,°
As Nature wept, thinking she was undone,
Because she took more from her than she left
And of such wondrous beauty her bereft:
Therefore, in sign her treasure suffered wrack,
50 Since Hero's time hath half the world been black.
Amorous Leander, beautiful and young,
(Whose tragedy divine Musaeus° sung)
Dwelt at Abydos; since him dwelt there none
For whom succeeding times make greater moan.
His dangling tresses that were never shorn,
Had they been cut and unto Colchos° borne,
Would have allured the venturous youth of Greece
To hazard more than for the Golden Fleece.
Fair Cynthia° wished his arms might be her sphere;°
60 Grief makes her pale, because she moves not there.
His body was as straight as Circe's wand;
Jove might have sipped out nectar from his hand.°

to her mind as she was minded to
Buskins See l. 9n.
strooken blind In Renaissance images, Eros or Cupid is shown blindfolded because "Love is blind," passion clouds understanding, etc., although a commentator like Pico della Mirandola (1463–94), the Florentine humanist, would point to Love's blindness as a transcendence of the senses (like the blindfold on Justice, allowing her to ignore interest). A great painting by Titan (1477?–1576) shows Venus blindfolding her son Cupid, while another unblinded Cupid looks on—perhaps a picture of a "blind" sensuous love and a "seeing," higher one. In the light of all this background, Marlowe's anti-mythological joke becomes more pointed. See Francis Bacon's "Cupid, or the Atom."

still constant
nun votary
Musaeus 5th-century (A.D.) author of Marlowe's original, confused with a mythical, earlier, Homeric sort of bard
Colchos Colchis, home of the Golden Fleece, sought by the Argonauts on one of the great quests of myth
Cynthia the moon
sphere orbit
Jove . . . hand like Ganymede, Jupiter's cupbearer. There is intense sexual interest both in this description of Leander, and in the homosexual episode with Neptune in the Second Sestiad (see below).

Even as delicious meat is to the taste,
So was his neck in touching, and surpassed
The white of Pelops' shoulder.° I could tell ye
How smooth his breast was, and how white his belly,
And whose immortal fingers did imprint
That heavenly path, with many a curious° dint,
That runs along his back; but my rude pen
70   Can hardly blazon° forth the loves of men,
Much less of powerful gods—let it suffice
That my slack muse sings of Leander's eyes,
Those orient° cheeks and lips, exceeding his
That leapt into the water for a kiss
Of his own shadow,° and despising many,
Died ere he could enjoy the love of any.
Had wild Hippolytus° Leander seen,
Enamoured of his beauty had he been;
His presence made the rudest peasant melt,
80   That in the vast uplandish country dwelt.
The barbarous Thracian soldier, moved with naught,
Was moved with him, and for his favour sought.
Some swore he was a maid in man's attire,
For in his looks were all that men desire:
A pleasant smiling cheek, a speaking eye,
A brow for love to banquet royally;
And such as knew he was a man, would say,
'Leander, thou art made for amorous play:
Why art thou not in love, and loved of all?
90   Though thou be fair, yet be not thine own thrall.'

[In the remainder of the First Sestiad, Leander has fallen in love with Hero at
the temple of Venus. In II, they meet and embrace, but she will allow him
nothing more than passionate kissing. He leaves, and returns home, still longing
for Hero, who is "As loath to see Leander going out."]

From *Second Sestiad*

And now the sun that through the horizon peeps,
100   As pitying these lovers, downward creeps,
So that in silence of the cloudy night,
Though it was morning, did he take his flight.
But what the secret trusty night concealed,
Leander's amorous habit soon revealed;
With Cupid's myrtle was his bonnet crowned,
About his arms the purple riband wound
Wherewith she wreathed her largely spreading hair;

Pelops' shoulder It was of ivory.
curious exquisite
blazon to catalogue admiringly
orient shining

shadow image; this is about Narcissus
Hippolytus He preferred the hunt to the bed
of Phaedra.

Nor could the youth abstain, but he must wear
The sacred ring wherewith she was endowed,
When first religious chastity she vowed;
Which made his love through Sestos to be known,
And thence unto Abydos sooner blown
Than he could sail; for incorporeal Fame,
Whose weight consists in nothing but her name,
Is swifter than the wind, whose tardy plumes
Are reeking water and dull earthly fumes.
Home, when he came, he seemed not to be there,
But like exiled heir thrust from his sphere,
Set in a foreign place; and straight from thence,
Alcides° like, by mighty violence
He would have chased away the swelling main
That him from her unjustly did detain.
Like as the sun in a diameter
Fires and inflames objects removed far,
And heateth kindly, shining laterally,
So beauty sweetly quickens when 'tis nigh,
But being separated and removed,
Burns where it cherished, murders where it loved.
Therefore even as an index to a book,
So to his mind was young Leander's look.
Oh, none but gods have power their love to hide;
Affection by the countenance is descried.
The light of hidden fire itself discovers,
And love that is concealed betrays poor lovers.
His secret flame apparently was seen;
Leander's father knew where he had been,
And for the same mildly rebuked his son,
Thinking to quench the sparkles new begun.
But love, resisted once, grows passionate,
And nothing more than counsel lovers hate:
For as a hot proud horse° highly disdains
To have his head controlled, but breaks the reins,
Spits forth the ringled° bit, and with his hooves
Checks° the submissive ground, so he that loves,
The more he is restrained, the worse he fares.
What is it now but mad Leander dares?
'Oh Hero, Hero!' thus he cried full oft,
And then he got him to a rock aloft,
Where having spied her tower, long stared he on't
And prayed the narrow toiling Hellespont
To part in twain, that he might come and go,
But still the rising billows answered 'No.'

110   (line marker)
120   (line marker)
130   (line marker)
140   (line marker)
150   (line marker)

Alcides Hercules
horse Cf. the analogous section from Shakespeare's *Venus and Adonis*.

ringled ringed
Checks stamps

With that he stripped him to the ivory skin,
And crying, 'Love, I come!' leaped lively° in.
Whereat the sapphire-visaged god° grew proud,
And made his capering Triton sound aloud,
Imagining that Ganymede,° displeased,
Had left the heavens; therefore on him he seized.
Leander strived; the waves about him wound,
And pulled him to the bottom, where the ground
Was strewed with pearl, and in low coral groves
Sweet singing mermaids sported with their loves
On heaps of heavy gold, and took great pleasure
To spurn in careless sort° the shipwreck treasure.
For here the stately azure palace stood
Where kingly Neptune and his train abode.
The lusty god embraced him, called him love,
And swore he never should return to Jove.
But when he knew it was not Ganymede,
(For under water he was almost dead)
He heaved him up, and looking on his face,
Beat down the bold waves with his triple mace,
Which mounted up, intending to have kissed him,
And fell in drops like tears, because they missed him.
Leander, being up, began to swim,
And looking back, saw Neptune follow him;
Whereat aghast, the poor soul gan to cry,
'Oh, let me visit Hero ere I die!'
The god put Helle's bracelet on his arm,
And swore the sea should never do him harm.
He clapped his plump cheeks, with his tresses played,
And smiling wantonly, his love bewrayed.°
He watched his arms, and as they opened wide
At every stroke, betwixt them would he slide
And steal a kiss, and then run out and dance,
And as he turned, cast many a lustful glance,
And threw him gaudy toys to please his eye,
And dive into the water, and there pry
Upon his breast, his thighs, and every limb,
And up again, and close beside him swim,
And talk of love. Leander made reply,
'You are deceived, I am no woman, I.'
Thereat smiled Neptune, and then told a tale
How that a shepherd, sitting in a vale,
Played with a boy so lovely, fair, and kind,
As for his love both earth and heaven pined;
That of the cooling river durst not drink

160

170

180

190

---

lively smartly
god Neptune
Ganymede Jupiter's cup-bearer

sort fashion
bewrayed revealed

Lest water nymphs should pull him from the brink;
And when he sported in the fragrant lawns,
200   Goat-footed satyrs and up-staring fauns
Would steal him thence. Ere half this tale was done,
'Ay me,' Leander cried, 'the enamoured sun,
That now should shine on Thetis'° glassy bower,
Descends upon my radiant Hero's tower.
O, that these tardy arms of mine were wings!'
And as he spake, upon the waves he springs.
Neptune was angry that he gave no ear,
And in his heart revenging malice bare:
He flung at him his mace, but as it went
210   He called it in, for love made him repent.
The mace returning back, his own hand hit,
As meaning to be venged for darting it.
When this fresh bleeding wound Leander viewed,
His colour went and came, as if he rued
The grief which Neptune felt. In gentle breasts
Relenting thoughts, remorse, and pity rests;
And who have hard hearts and obdurate minds
But vicious, harebrained, and illiterate hinds?
The god, seeing him with pity to be moved,
220   Thereon concluded that he was beloved.
(Love is too full of faith, too credulous,
With folly and false hope deluding us.)
Wherefore, Leander's fancy to surprise,
To the rich ocean for gifts he flies.
'Tis wisdom to give much; a gift prevails
When deep persuading oratory fails.
   By this, Leander, being near the land,
Cast down his weary feet and felt the sand.
Breathless albeit he were, he rested not
230   Till to the solitary tower he got,
And knocked and called, at which celestial noise
The longing heart of Hero much more joys
Than nymphs or shepherds when the timbrel rings,
Or crooked dolphin when the sailor sings°
She stayed not for her robes, but straight arose,
And drunk with gladness, to the door she goes,
Where seeing a naked man, she screeched for fear,
—Such sights as this to tender maids are rare—
And ran into the dark herself to hide.
240   Rich jewels in the dark are soonest spied;
Unto her was he led, or rather drawn,
By those white limbs which sparkled through the lawn.°

Thetis' Neptune's daughter, a sea nymph
Or crooked . . . sings The mythical lyre-player

Arion, shipwrecked, charmed a dolphin with his
music; it bore him to shore.
lawn her sheer dress

The nearer that he came, the more she fled,
And seeking refuge, slipped into her bed.
Whereon Leander sitting, thus began,
Through numbing cold all feeble, faint and wan:
　'If not for love, yet, love, for pity sake,
Me in thy bed and maiden bosom take;
At least vouchsafe these arms some little room,
250　Who, hoping to embrace thee, cheerly° swum;
This head was beat with many a churlish billow,
And therefore let it rest upon thy pillow.'
Herewith affrighted Hero shrunk away,
And in her lukewarm place Leander lay,
Whose lively heat like fire from heaven fet,°
Would animate gross clay, and higher set
The drooping thoughts of base declining souls,
Than dreary° Mars carousing nectar bowls.
His hands he cast upon her like a snare;
260　She, overcome with shame and sallow fear,
Like chaste Diana, when Actaeon spied her,
Being suddenly betrayed, dived down to hide her.
And as her silver body downward went,
With both her hands she made the bed a tent,
And in her own mind thought herself secure,
O'ercast with dim and darksome coverture.
And now she lets him whisper in her ear,
Flatter, entreat, promise, protest, and swear;
Yet ever as he greedily assayed
270　To touch those dainties, she the harpy played,
And every limb did as a soldier stout
Defend the fort and keep the foeman out;
For though the rising ivory mount he scaled,
Which is with azure circling lines empaled,
Much like a globe (a globe may I term this,
By which love sails to regions full of bliss)
Yet there with Sisyphus° he toiled in vain,
Till gentle parley did the truce obtain.
Wherein Leander on her quivering breast,
280　Breathless spoke something, and sighed out the rest;
Which so prevailed, as he with small ado
Enclosed her in his arms and kissed her too.
And every kiss to her was as a charm,
And to Leander as a fresh alarm,°
So that the truce was broke, and she, alas,
(Poor silly maiden) at his mercy was.
Love is not full of pity (as men say)

cheerly happily
fet fetched
dreary gory

Sisyphus punished in Hades by having to roll
a stone uphill continuously
alarm battle cry

But deaf and cruel where he means to prey.
Even as a bird, which in our hands we wring,
290　Forth plungeth and oft flutters with her wing,
She trembling strove; this strife of hers (like that
Which made the world)° another world begat
Of unknown joy. Treason was in her thought,
And cunningly to yield herself she sought.
Seeming not won, yet won she was at length—
In such wars women use but half their strength.
Leander now, like Theban Hercules,
Entered the orchard of the Hesperides,
Whose fruit none rightly can describe but he
300　That pulls or shakes it from the golden tree.°
And now she wished this night were never done,
And sighed to think upon the approaching sun,
For much it grieved her that the bright daylight
Should know the pleasure of this blessed night,
And them like Mars and Erycine° displayed
Both in each other's arms chained as they laid,°
Again she knew not how to frame her look,
Or speak to him who in a moment took
That which so long, so charily she kept,
310　And fain by stealth away she would have crept,
And to some corner secretly have gone,
Leaving Leander in the bed alone.
But as her naked feet were whipping out,
He on the sudden clinged her so about,
That mermaid-like unto the floor she slid:
One half appeared, the other half was hid.
Thus near the bed she blushing stood upright.
And from her countenance behold ye might
A kind of twilight break, which through the hair,
320　As from an orient cloud, glimpse here and there;
And round about the chamber this false morn
Brought forth the day before the day was born.
So Hero's ruddy cheek Hero betrayed,
And her all naked to his sight displayed,
Whence his admiring eyes more pleasure took
Than Dis° on heaps of gold fixing his look.
By this, Apollo's° golden harp began
To sound forth music to the ocean,

made the world Love and Strife, according to a Greek philosophical tradition, governed the patterning of the four elements in the organization of the world from chaos.
Leander . . . tree Gathering the golden apples guarded by Atlas' daughters was the last of the Labors of Hercules; the golden fruit was associated in the Renaissance with the Earthly Paradise, and Marlowe cleverly uses the allusion here to tell of Leander's final sexual possession of Hero without actual pornographic description.
Erycine a name for Venus
laid lay
Dis Pluto, god of the underworld, and hence of minerals
Apollo's as song god and lord of the stringed instruments

330
Which watchful Hesperus no sooner heard,
But he the day-bright-bearing car° prepared,
And ran before, as harbinger of light,
And with his flaring beams mocked ugly Night
Till she, o'ercome with anguish, shame, and rage,
Danged° down to hell her loathsome carriage.

Desunt nonnulla.°
1598

The Passionate Shepherd to His Love°

Come live with me and be my love,
And we will all the pleasures prove°
That valleys, groves, hills, and fields,
Woods, or steepy mountain yields.

And we will sit upon the rocks,
Seeing the shepherds feed their flocks,
By shallow rivers to whose falls
Melodious birds sings madrigals.°

10
And I will make thee beds of roses
And a thousand fragrant posies,
A cap of flowers, and a kirtle °
Embroidered all with leaves of myrtle.

A gown made of the finest wool
Which from our pretty lambs we pull;
Fair lined slippers for the cold,
With buckles of the purest gold

A belt of straw and ivy buds,
With coral clasps and amber studs;
And if these pleasures may thee move,
20
Come live with me, and be my love.

The shepherd° swains shall dance and sing
For thy delight each May morning
If these delights thy mind may move,
Then live with me and be my love.
1599–1600

car chariot
Danged hurled
Desunt nonnulla "some are missing" (the other
Sestiads); see George Chapman's continuation,
above
The Passionate Shepherd to His Love an invita-
tion to the pastoral realm where nature outdoes
art; see Ralegh's answer to it, above, and
Donne's "The Bait"

prove test by experiencing
madrigals the natural harmony of the pastoral
world; notice the complex and perverted use of
it in the Bower of Bliss in Spenser's *Faerie
Queene* II.xii
kirtle dress
shepherd The 1600 text gives "shepherds'."

SAMUEL DANIEL
1562–1619

An enterprising and remarkably productive Elizabethan man of letters, Daniel came from a musical Somerset family, studied at Oxford, traveled abroad, and became a member of the literary circle of the Countess of Pembroke, Sir Philip Sidney's sister. He was involved in the establishment of the sonneteering tradition of the last decade of the century, publishing in 1591—along with the first appearance of Sidney's *Astrophel and Stella* sonnets—a group of twenty-eight of his own. In 1592 a full collection entitled *Delia* appeared. Their form is usually said to have influenced Shakespeare's choice of the three-quatrain-and-couplet model set up by Surrey, but there seem to be occasional similarities in a shared condensed syntax and rhythmic structures as well. Daniel wrote narrative, history, lofty disquisition, tragedy, and pastoral drama, all in assured and competent verse, as well as a famous prose essay, *A Defence of Rhyme,* in answer to Thomas Campion's attack on vernacular traditions of versifying. He wrote masques for the Jacobean court, and like his contemporary, Drayton, kept revising his sonnets and other poems, hardening and purifying the diction.

Care-charmer Sleep

Care-charmer Sleep, son of the sable Night,
Brother to Death, in silent darkness born,
Relieve my languish° and restore the light,
With dark forgetting of my cares, return.
And let the day be time enough to mourn
The shipwreck of my ill-adventured youth;
Let waking eyes suffice to wail their scorn
Without the torment of the night's untruth.
Cease, dreams, the images of day-desires,
10   To model forth the passions of the morrow;
Never let rising sun approve you liars,
To add more grief to aggravate° my sorrow.
    Still let me sleep, embracing clouds in vain,
    And never wake to feel the day's disdain.

1592–94

A Pastoral°

Oh happy golden age
Not for° that rivers ran
With streams of milk, and honey dropped from trees;

---

languish drooping enfeeblement
aggravate make heavier
A Pastoral translated from a chorus in Torquato Tasso's pastoral drama, *Aminta* (1573); see "The Golden Age" in The Renaissance Ovid, above, and the chorus from Guarini's *Il Pastor*

Fido (1590) translated by Sir Richard Fanshawe. Daniel here adapts the Italian 7- and 11-syllable lines to English, keeping the rhyme scheme.
Not for not (golden or happy) because . . .

Not that the earth did gauge°
Unto the husbandman
Her voluntary fruits,° free without fees;
Not for no cold did freeze,
Nor any cloud beguile
The eternal flowering spring
10 Wherein lived everything
And whereon the heavens perpetually did smile;
Not for no ship had brought
From foreign shores or wars or wares° ill sought—

But only for that name,
That idle name of wind,
That idol of deceit, that empty sound
Called Honour,° which became
The tyrant of the mind
And so torments our nature without ground,
20 Was not yet vainly found;
Nor yet sad griefs imparts
Amidst the sweet delights
Of joyful amorous wights,°
Nor were his hard laws known to free-born hearts;
But golden laws like these
Which Nature wrote: 'That's lawful which doth please.'

Then amongst flowers and springs
Making delightful sport,
Sat lovers without conflict, without flame;
30 And nymphs and shepherds sings,
Mixing in wanton sort
Whisperings with songs, then kisses with the same
Which from affection came;
The naked virgin then
Her roses fresh reveals
Which now her veil conceals,
The tender apples in her bosom seen;
And oft in rivers clear
The lovers with their loves consorting were.

40 Honour, thou first didst close
The spring of all delight,
Denying water to the amorous thirst;
Thou taught'st fair eyes to lose
The glory of their light,
Restrained from men, and on themselves reversed.

gauge pledge
voluntary fruits no work was needed for human
sustenance
or . . . or either . . . or
Honour in the sense of sexual chasity, here
viewed in its negative aspect of coyness, reticence, and prudery—all bred by the knowledge
that sexual enjoyment is forbidden. Tasso's
point is that the most important thing about
the Golden Age is that everything was permitted,
and thus lovely; see *Paradise Lost* IV.312–18.
wights people

Thou in a lawn° didst first
Those golden hairs encase
Late° spread unto the wind;
Thou mad'st loose grace unkind,
50 Gav'st bridle to their words, art to their pace.°
Oh Honour, is it thou
That mak'st that stealth which love doth free allow?

It is thy work that brings
Our griefs and torments thus,
But thou, fierce lord of nature and of love,
The qualifier of kings,
What dost thou here with us
That are below thy power, shut from above?
Go, and from us remove:
60 Trouble the mighty's sleep!
Let us, neglected, base,
Live still without thy grace,
And the use of the ancient happy ages keep.
Let's love—this life of ours
Can make no truce with time, that all devours.
Let's love! The sun doth set and rise again,
But whenas our short light
Comes once to set, it makes eternal night.°

1592, 1601

MICHAEL DRAYTON
1563–1631

Drayton is essentially an Elizabethan in the line of Spenser. Born in Warwickshire, brought up as a page in a noble house, he composed fashionable sonnets (*Idea's Mirror*, 1594), pastorals, and historical narrative in the 1590's. Never achieving favor or influence at the Jacobean court, he depended upon patronage (such as that of the Countess of Bedford, Donne's admirer) for support of his growingly ambitious projects. Notable among these was the massive topographical, historical poem *Poly-Olbion* (1612–13) covering England, county by county, and his post-Spenserian pastoral narrative *Nymphidia* (1627). *The Muses' Elizium* (1630) represents a last flowering of mythopoetic tradition at the edge of a narrower, wittier period of mythological poetry. The sonnets printed below are from the revised *Idea* of 1619.

lawn piece of fine linen. Loose hair was emblematic of free pleasure.
Late previously
bridle . . . pace you made some language dirty and some gestures provocative

Let's love . . . eternal night Tasso, and through him, Daniel, is virtually quoting Catullus here, in lines made resonant by Ben Jonson ("To Celia") and Thomas Campion ("My Sweetest Lesbia"), which see.

From The Muses' Elizium

The Description of Elizium°

A Paradise on earth is found,
Though far from vulgar sight,
Which with those pleasures doth abound
That it *Elizium*° hight.

Where, in delights that never fade,
The Muses lullèd be,
And sit at pleasure in the shade
Of many a stately tree,

Which no rough tempest makes to reel
10 Nor their straight bodies bows,
Their lofty tops do never feel
The weight of winter's snows.

In groves that evermore are green
No falling leaf is there,
But Philomel° (of birds the queen)
In music spends the year.

The merle upon her myrtle perch
There to the mavis sings,
Who from the top of some curled birch
20 Those notes redoubled rings.

There daisies damask° every place
Nor once their beauties lose,
That when proud Phoebus hides his face
Themselves they scorn to close.

The pansy and the violet here,
As seeming to descend
Both from one root, a very pair,
For sweetness yet contend

And, pointing to a pink to tell
30 Which bears it, it is loath
To judge it; but replies, for smell
That it exceeds them both;

Wherewith displeased they hang their heads
So angry soon they grow,

The Description of Elizium This is the introductory poem to *The Muses' Elizium*, blending Renaissance themes of the earthly paradise with such classical motifs as the Elysian Fields and the Gardens of Alcinous from Bk. 7 of the *Odyssey*, into a vision of the paradise of poetry. **Elizium** Its name mixes that of the classical Elysian Fields with the late Queen Elizabeth's, the implication being that the Elizabethan period was a poetical Golden Age. **Philomel** Philomela, who was changed into a nightingale **damask** ornament

And from their odoriferous beds
Their sweets at it they throw.

The winter here a summer is,
No waste is made by time,
Nor doth the autumn ever miss
40   The blossoms of the prime.°

The flower that Júly forth doth bring
In April here is seen,
The primrose that puts on the spring
In Júly decks each green.

The sweets for sovereignty contend
And so abundant be,
That to the very earth they lend
And bark of every tree.

Rills rising out of every bank
50   In wild meanders strain,
And playing many a wanton prank
Upon the speckled plain,

In gambols and lascivious gyres°
Their time they still bestow,
Nor to the fountaines none retires;
Nor on their course will go

Those brooks with lilies bravely decked,
So proud and wanton made
That they their courses quite neglect,
60   And seem as though they stayed

Fair Flora in her state to view
Which through these lilies looks,
Or as those lilies leaned to show
Their beauties to the brooks.

That Phoebus in his lofty race
Oft lays aside his beams
And comes to cool his glowing face
In these delicious streams.

Oft spreading vines climb up the cleeves°
70   Whose ripened clusters there
Their purple liquid drop, which drives
A vintage through the year.

Those cleeves whose craggy sides are clad
With trees of sundry suits,

---

prime spring. Compare this with the Garden of   **lascivious gyres** erotic twistings
Adonis in Spenser's *Faerie Queene* III.vi.   **cleeves** cliffs

Which make continual summer glad,
Even bending with the fruits,

Some ripening, ready some to fall,
Some blossomed, some to bloom,
Like gorgeous hangings on the wall
80 Of some rich, princely room:

Pomegranates, lemons, citrons, so
Their laded branches bow,
Their leaves in number that outgo
Nor roomth° will them allow.

There in perpetual summer's shade,
Apollo's prophets sit,
Among the flowers that never fade,
But flourish like their wit;

To whom the nymphs upon their lyres,
90 Tune many a curious lay,
And with their most melodious choirs
Make short the longest day.

The thrice three virgins heavenly clear,
Their trembling timbrels sound,
Whilst the three comely Graces there
Dance many a dainty round,°

Decay nor age there nothing knows;
There is continual youth,
As time on plant or creatures grows
100 So still their strength reneweth.

The poets' paradise this is,
To which but few can come;
The Muses' only bower of bliss°
Their dear *Elizium.*

Here happy souls (their blessed bowers,
Free from the rude resort
Of beastly people) spend the hours,
In harmless mirth and sport.

Then on to the Elizian plains
110 Apollo doth invite you
Where he provides with pastoral strains,
In Nymphals° to delight you.

1630

roomth room
Whilst . . . round Cf. Calidore's vision of the
maidens dancing around the three graces to the
music of Colin Clout in *The Faerie Queene*
VI.x.
bower of bliss alludes to Spenser's in *The*

Faerie Queene II.xii, but with no negative overtones
Nymphals The pastoral narratives which follow
Drayton calls "Nymphals" rather than "songs,"
as elsewhere.

From Idea

How many paltry, foolish, painted things,
That now in coaches trouble every street,
Shall be forgotten, whom no poet sings,
Ere they be well wrapped in their winding sheet!
Where I to thee eternity shall give,
When nothing else remaineth of these days,
And queens hereafter shall be glad to live
Upon the alms of thy superfluous praise.
Virgins and matrons reading these my rhymes
10   Shall be so much delighted with thy story
That they shall grieve they lived not in these times,
To have seen thee, their sex's only glory.
   So shalt thou fly above the vulgar throng,
   Still to survive in my immortal song.
                              1619

VIII

There's nothing grieves me but that age should haste
That in my days I may not see thee old:
That where those two clear, sparkling eyes are placed
Only two loopholes then I might behold;
That lovely archèd, ivory, polished brow
Deface with wrinkles that I might but see;
Thy dainty hair, so curled and crispèd now
Like grizzled moss upon some agèd tree;
Thy cheek, now flush with roses, sunk and lean;
10   Thy lips, with age as any wafer thin;
Thy pearly teeth out of thy head so clean,
That when thou feed'st thy nose shall touch thy chin.
   These lines that now thou scorn'st, which should delight thee,
   Then would I make thee read, but to despite thee.
                              1619

LVI

Since there's no help, come let us kiss and part;
Nay, I have done, you get no more of me,
And I am glad, yea glad with all my heart
That thus so cleanly I myself can free;
Shake hands forever, cancel all our vows,
And when we meet at any time again,
Be it not seen in either of our brows
That we one jot of former love retain.
Now at the last gasp of love's latest breath,
10   When, his pulse failing, Passion° speechless lies,

Passion These personifications make up a kind
of allegorical picture or sculptured group, almost
the parody of a Pietà.

When Faith is kneeling by his bed of death,
And Innocence is closing up his eyes,
  Now if thou wouldst, when all have given him over,
  From death to life thou mightst him yet recover.

1619

WILLIAM SHAKESPEARE
1564–1616

Shakespeare was baptized on April 26, 1564, at Stratford-on-Avon, Warwickshire. His father John was a Stratford tradesman, called in legal documents a "glover," but also a dealer in timber and wool, the main commodity of the nearby Cotswold area. A man of substance and father of eight children, John owned property in Stratford, and was an official of the town, but he suffered a period of reverses, some possibly caused by his recusancy—he remained Catholic when it was dangerous and costly to do so. He got over this, and in 1596 he was granted the arms of a gentleman, probably at William Shakespeare's request. He died in 1601.

Shakespeare almost certainly attended Stratford Grammar School, where the teaching was mostly of Latin grammar and rhetoric, and where he would have read Terence, the Latin dramatist from whom the rules of dramatic structure—which he knew but did not slavishly obey—ultimately derived. He went to neither university, but married the pregnant Anne Hathaway, eight years his senior, in November 1582; their daughter Susanna was christened in May 1583, and their twins, Judith and Hamnet, in February 1585.

Nothing is known about his going to London, but he almost certainly was there by 1589; by 1592 he had written *Henry VI* and was well enough known to be attacked as an upstart actor by the pamphleteer Greene in his *Groatsworth of Wit.*

The London theaters closed when deaths from plague reached a certain figure each week, and there was an especially bad epidemic in the years 1592–94. During this time the existing companies went on tour, collapsed, and lost their principal writers. Shakespeare wrote his narrative poems, *Venus and Adonis* and *The Rape of Lucrece,* during this time. Both poems were dedicated to the Earl of Southampton (1573–1624), a patron of literature and the friend of the Queen's favorite, the Earl of Essex, in whose rebellion (1601) Southampton was to take part. Although he is a favored candidate for the role of dedicatee and friend in Shakespeare's *Sonnets,* no positive connection between them other than the dedications of *Venus and Adonis* and *The Rape of Lucrece* has ever been proved. Evidently, however, during the plague years Shakespeare was seeking or enjoying the protection of this powerful nobleman.

When the plague abated, the companies sorted themselves out into two—the Admiral's Men and the Lord Chamberlain's Men (named for their official sponsors at court—they were in fact liveried servants of these aristocrats). The great actor Alleyn went to the Admiral's Men; Burbage, his rival, to the Lord Chamberlain's. Shakespeare joined Burbage, and remained with the company for the rest of his working life. When King James I took it over (1603) as the King's Men he became, technically, a servant of the king. The grant of arms to his father in 1596 made Shakespeare himself a gentleman, and in the following year he was rich enough to buy a large house in Stratford.

Before the formation of the Lord Chamberlain's Men Shakespeare had probably written *Henry VI, Richard II,* and *Titus Andronicus.* His early plays for the new company were *The Comedy of Errors, The Taming of the Shrew, The Two Gentlemen of Verona,* and *Love's Labour's Lost.* He must have been extremely busy in this period, as "sharer" (shareholder) in the company, actor, and principal playwright. By 1599 he had also written *Romeo and Juliet, Richard II, King John, The Merchant of Venice,* the two parts of *Henry IV, Henry V, Much Ado About Nothing,* and *The Merry Wives of Windsor.*

In 1599 the lease of their house, The Theatre, expired, and in an operation of considerable ingenuity and enterprise Shakespeare's company forestalled the demolition men sent in by the landlord, rapidly dismantled the building, and shipped it across the Thames to Bankside, where they built a new playhouse with the old timbers and called it The Globe. Shakespeare was registered as owner of one-tenth share. In this theater were played most of his masterpieces, including all the main tragedies: *Julius Caesar, Hamlet, Othello, King Lear, Macbeth, Antony and Cleopatra, Coriolanus,* and *Timon of Athens* (if it was performed at all). The Globe also saw the première of *As You Like It* and *Twelfth Night,* of the "problem" plays, *Troilus and Cressida, All's Well That Ends Well,* and *Measure for Measure,* and Shakespeare's final plays, *Pericles, Cymbeline, The Winter's Tale,* and *The Tempest.* There were two more works, in which Shakespeare was a collaborator, *Two Noble Kinsmen* and *Henry VIII,* during a performance of which the theater burnt down when a blank cannon shot set fire to the thatch, on June 29, 1613.

In the preceding few years, from about 1609, the King's Men had also performed indoors in the more sophisticated Blackfriars Theatre; this certainly affected the kind of play they wanted and got from Shakespeare and the younger playwrights Beaumont and Fletcher. But The Globe was his true arena, the "wooden O" which contained and fed his imagination.

Shakespeare retired to Stratford around 1610; *The Winter's Tale* and *The Tempest* were probably written there. He continued his business life, and records of lawsuits—Shakespeare appears always to have enjoyed litigation—survive from the period between his retirement and his death, at the age of fifty-two, on April 23, 1616.

Shakespeare apparently took little care to be published, except with *Venus and Adonis* and *The Rape of Lucrece;* even the authorized quartos of the plays published during his life time are badly and carelessly printed. The *Sonnets* were published without his consent or care, and his mysterious poem "The Phoenix and Turtle," which appeared in an anthology in 1601, is almost the only work he willingly published after 1593. A great part of his work remained in manuscript until his colleagues John Heminges and Henry Condell brought out in 1623 the collection we now call the First Folio. This large book contains, in texts of varying authority, all the plays we now attribute to Shakespeare except *Pericles,* which was added in the third edition (Third Folio) of 1664.

Venus and Adonis

This was Shakespeare's first published work (he calls it "the first heir of my invention" in the dedication). The first edition of 1593 is one of the few things he is likely to have seen carefully through the press, for it was dedicated to a noble patron—the young Earl of Southampton—and needed to be presented in a form that would please him. Ten more editions appeared in the next twenty-four years; the poem presumably achieved this degree of success because of its fashionable eroticism.

Venus and Adonis belongs to the genre of erotic epyllion, of which other examples are Marlowe's *Hero and Leander* (see the Headnote to that poem) and Marston's *Pygmalion's Image.* The immediate appeal lies, broadly speaking, in the wittily erotic handling of the theme; yet these poems were capable of bearing some allegorical freight, and Shakespeare's does so. Such poetry is Ovidian (see The Renaissance Ovid) and "etiological," that is, providing mythical explanations for, say, the existence of a particular flower. The ostensible "cause" of Shakespeare's poem is thus to account for the anemone, said to have grown out of Adonis' blood after the boar has killed him. But this is merely the occasion for a display of rhetorical, decorative, and serio-comic poetry.

Shakespeare uses a variant of the Venus-Adonis myth which (as in Titian's painting) makes Adonis reluctant, and Venus the outrageous wooer (see also *Hero and Leander* I.12–14). This adds to the piquancy of the narrative, and also enables the author to make observations, at once eloquent and singularly moral, about love and lust. So the poem is not without seriousness, but there is little of the high seriousness which colors Spenser's treatment of the theme in *The Faerie Queene* III.vi, or Milton's in the Epilogue to *Comus.*

Venus and Adonis has two notable digressions, one on the hunting of the hare, and one on the stallion of Adonis (part of the latter is given below). Venus has already wooed Adonis, the "flint-hearted boy," by praising his beauty and by using arguments employed by Shakespeare in the early sonnets ("Thou wast begot, to get it is thy duty"). He resists, showing both sexual coldness and some effeminacy ("The sun doth burn my face, I must remove"); then, rejecting Venus' suggestions of sexual pleasure, he tries but fails to recover his horse, whose amorous attitude to the stray mare makes an interesting contrast with Adonis' attitude to Venus. This use of a contrasting example to add, without explicit comment, a dimension to the theme, is a sophistication similar in some ways to the author's use of dramatic subplots, in others to techniques later identified as "baroque"—though the *ecphrasis*, as it is called, is an ancient device. In this case, as with the hare, Shakespeare mingles Italianate refinement with down-to-earth detail and observation.

After this digression the poem continues for nearly nine hundred lines more; Adonis expatiates on his unripeness, on the crime of lust, on his desire to hunt the boar; Venus argues back unavailingly. He leaves her ("Look how a bright star shooteth from the sky, / So glides he in the night from Venus' eye" are lines made famous by Coleridge as an example of the operation of imagination, as opposed to fancy) and is killed. Venus lengthily laments his death, decrees that "Sorrow on love hereafter shall attend," and clutches his flower to her bosom.

From Venus and Adonis°

'Fondling,'° she saith, 'since I have hemmed thee here
230   Within the circuit of this ivory pale,°
I'll be a park, and thou shalt be my deer:°
Feed where thou wilt, on mountain or in dale;
    Graze on my lips, and if those hills be dry,
    Stray lower, where the pleasant fountains° lie.

'Within this limit° is relief° enough,
Sweet bottom grass° and high delightful plain,
Round rising hillocks, brakes obscure and rough,°
To shelter thee from tempest and from rain:
    Then be my deer, since I am such a park,
240   No dog shall rouse° thee, though a thousand bark.'

At this Adonis smiles as in disdain,
That° in each cheek appears a pretty dimple;
Love made those hollows, if himself were slain,°
He might be buried in a tomb so simple,
    Foreknowing well, if there he came to lie,
    Why there love lived, and there he could not die.

These lovely caves, these round enchanting pits,
Opened their mouths to swallow Venus' liking:°
Being mad before, how doth she now for wits?
250   Struck dead before, what needs a second striking?
    Poor queen of love, in thine own law forlorn,°
    To love a cheek that smiles at thee in scorn!

Now which way shall she turn? what shall she say?
Her words are done, her woes the more increasing;
The time is spent, her object° will away,
And from her twining arms doth urge releasing.
    'Pity,' she cries, 'some favour, some remorse!'°
    Away he springs, and hasteth to his horse.

But lo from forth a copse that neighbours by,°
260   A breeding jennet,° lusty, young and proud,
Adonis' trampling courser doth espy,
And forth she rushes, snorts and neighs aloud:
    The strong-necked steed being tied unto a tree,
    Breaketh his rein, and to her straight goes he.

Venus and Adonis Venus forces Adonis to dismount, and woos him ardently without success; now she embraces him and links her fingers behind him.
Fondling foolish one
hemmed enclosed
pale fence
deer pun on "dear"
limit precinct
relief pasture
fountains . . . bottom grass . . . brakes obscure and rough This kind of punning gave the poem its reputation for naughtiness; *bottom:* meadow, *brakes:* thickets.
rouse drive from cover
That so that
if . . . slain so that if he himself were killed
liking desire
in thine . . . forlorn deprived in a matter which you're supposed to control
object Adonis
remorse mercy
neighbours by lies near by
breeding jennet small Spanish mare

Imperiously he leaps, he neighs, he bounds,
And now his woven girths he breaks asunder;
The bearing° earth with his hard hoof he wounds,
Whose hollow womb resounds like heaven's thunder;
   The iron bit he crusheth 'tween his teeth,
270   Controlling what he was controllèd with.°

His ears up-pricked, his braided hanging mane
Upon his compassed° crest now stand on end;
His nostrils drink the air, and forth again
As from a furnace, vapours doth he send;
   His eye which scornfully glisters like fire,
   Shows his hot courage° and his high desire.

Sometimes he trots, as if he told° the steps,
With gentle majesty and modest pride;
Anon he rears upright, curvets° and leaps,
280 As who should say 'Lo thus my strength is tried:
   And this I do to captivate the eye
   Of the fair breeder that is standing by.'

What recketh° he his rider's angry stir,°
His flattering 'holla' or his 'Stand, I say'?
What cares he now for curb or pricking spur,
For rich caparisons° or trappings gay?
   He sees his love, and nothing else he sees,
   For nothing else with his proud sight agrees.

Look when a painter would surpass the life
290 In limning out° a well-proportioned steed,
His art with nature's workmanship at strife,
As if the dead the living should exceed:
   So did this horse excel a common one,
   In shape, in courage, colour, pace and bone.°

Round-hoofed, short-jointed, fetlocks shag° and long,
Broad breast, full eye, small head, and nostril wide,
High crest, short ears, straight legs and passing strong,
Thin mane, thick tail, broad buttock, tender hide:
   Look what a horse should have he did not lack,
300   Save a proud rider on so proud a back.

Sometimes he scuds far off, and there he stares;
Anon he starts at stirring of a feather.
To bid the wind a base° he now prepares,

bearing that bears his weight
Imperiously . . . with Cf. the use of a horse as
emblem of sexual desire in Marlowe, *Hero and
Leander* II.141–45.
compassed arched
courage lust
told counted
curvets prances

recketh cares
stir agitation
caparisons ornamental harness
limning out drawing, painting
bone frame
shag rough, untrimmed
bid . . . base challenge the wind to a chase

And where° he run or fly, they know not whether,°
  For through his mane and tail the high wind sings,
  Fanning the hairs, who wave like feathered wings.

He looks upon his love, and neighs unto her:
She answers him, as if she knew his mind.
Being proud, as females are, to see him woo her,
310 She puts on outward strangeness,° seems unkind,
  Spurns at his love, and scorns the heat he feels,
  Beating his kind° embracements with her heels.

Then like a melancholy malcontent,°
He vails° his tail that like a falling plume
Cool shadow to his melting buttock lent;
He stamps, and bites the poor flies in his fume.°
  His love perceiving how he was enraged,
  Grew kinder, and his fury was assuaged.

His testy° master goeth about° to take him,
320 When lo the unbacked° breeder, full of fear,
Jealous of catching,° swiftly doth forsake him;
With her the horse, and left Adonis there:
  As they were mad unto the wood they hie them,
  Outstripping crows that strive to overfly them.

          · · ·

1593?   1593

The Rape of Lucrece

This poem, like *Venus and Adonis,* was dedicated to the Earl of Southampton, in terms which may suggest that Shakespeare had improved his acquaintance with the nobleman in the intervening year. Published in a careful text in 1594, it had five more editions in the next twelve years.

   Lucrece is longer and more weighty than *Venus,* being the "graver labour" he had promised Southampton in the dedication to the earlier poem. It is a narrative tragedy of extreme schematic and rhetorical elaboration. The theme is roughly that of Sonnet CXXIX, "The expense of spirit in a waste of shame / Is lust in action." The action is simple: Tarquin, inflamed by the virtuous Lucrece, accepts her hospitality and then rapes her; she requires of her husband an oath of revenge, and then commits suicide. The expulsion of the Tarquins and the end of the Roman monarchy follow.

   Shakespeare extends this material to 1855 lines by dwelling on the struggle in Tarquin's mind between desire and dishonor ("Thus graceless holds he disputation / 'Tween frozen conscience and hot burning will"), his guilt, Lucrece's sense of disgrace, and her invocations to Night, Opportunity, and Time, of which the last is given

where whether	**vails** droops
whether which	**fume** irritation
outward strangeness show of indifference	**testy** angry
kind both loving and according to nature	**goeth about** tries
melancholy malcontent The melancholy man	**unbacked** unbroken
and the malcontent were fashionable social types.	**Jealous of catching** anxious not to be caught

here. (With characteristic virtuosity it touches on most of the commonplaces associated with the subject.) The work is further extended by a long and significant digression in which she describes a wall-hanging depicting the fall of Troy.

No other work of Shakespeare resembles this early ambitious and learned poem. Its extensive working out of schemes and topics is matched by nothing in the plays (*Titus Andronicus*, the closest of the tragedies in time and theme, is also closest in treatment). It contains much, in the description of both action and passion, in the seizing of narrative and moral opportunities, that is remarkably fine; it touches on matters which were many times to preoccupy the later dramatist; but it represents with *Venus and Adonis* the starting point of a career Shakespeare never followed, for he gave it up as soon as the theaters reopened and enabled him to resume his dramatic work.

From The Rape of Lucrece

'Mis-shapen Time,° copesmate° of ugly Night,
Swift subtle post,° carrier of grisly Care,
Eater of youth, false slave to false delight,
Base watch° of woes, sin's pack-horse, virtue's snare!
Thou nursest all, and murderest all that are:
930   O hear me then, injurious shifting° Time!
    Be guilty of my death, since of° my crime.

'Why hath thy servant Opportunity°
Betrayed the hours thou gavest me to repose,
Cancelled my fortunes and enchainèd me
To endless date° of never-ending woes?
Time's office is to fine° the hate of foes,
    To eat up errors by Opinion° bred,
    Not spend the dowry of a lawful bed.°

'Time's glory is to calm contending kings,
940 To unmask falsehood and bring truth° to light,
To stamp the seal of time in agèd things,
To wake the morn and sentinel° the night,
To wrong the wronger till he render right,°
    To ruinate° proud buildings with thy hours,
    And smear with dust their glittering golden towers;

Time Lucrece, having inveighed against Night and Opportunity, now formally accuses Time, which is almost a favorite topic of Shakespeare's; see especially Sonnets XII, XIX, LXIV.
copesmate companion
post messenger
watch watchman (who counts woes like hours)
shifting moving; cheating
since of since you were guilty of
Opportunity occasion (closely related to time: "Whoever plots the sin, thou pointst the season," l. 879).
Cancelled . . . date cancelled an existing contract with fortune and substituted another, with no expiry date, to sorrow
fine bring to an end
Opinion belief unsupported by real knowledge (the word usually had a disparaging sense at this time)
spend . . . bed squander the future of a virtuous marriage
truth often called "the daughter of time"
sentinel stand watch over
To wrong . . . right to afflict the guilty with later misfortunes so as to produce a change of conscience
ruinate reduce to ruins

'To fill with worm-holes stately monuments,
To feed Oblivion° with decay of things,
To blot old books and alter their contents,
To pluck the quills from ancient ravens'° wings,
950   To dry the old oak's sap and cherish springs,
    To spoil antiquities of hammered steel,
    And turn the giddy round of fortune's wheel;°

'To show the beldam° daughters of her daughter,
To make the child a man, the man a child,
To slay the tiger that doth live by slaughter,
To tame the unicorn and lion wild,
To mock the subtle in themselves beguiled,°
    To cheer the ploughman with increaseful crops,
    And waste huge stones with little water-drops.

960 'Why workest thou mischief in thy pilgrimage,
Unless thou couldst return to make amends?
One poor retiring minute° in an age
Would purchase thee a thousand thousand friends,
Lending him wit that to bad debtors lends:°
    O this dread night, wouldst thou one hour come back,
    I could prevent this storm and shun thy wrack!

'Thou ceaseless lackey to eternity,°
With some mischance cross° Tarquin in his flight;
Devise extremes beyond extremity,°
970   To make him curse this cursèd crimeful night.
Let ghastly shadows his lewd eyes affright,
    And the dire thought of his committed evil
    Shape every bush a hideous shapeless devil.

'Disturb his hours of rest with restless trances,
Afflict him in his bed with bedrid° groans;
Let there bechance him pitiful mischances,
To make him moan, but pity not his moans.
Stone him with hardened hearts harder than stones,
    And let mild women to him lose their mildness,
980   Wilder to him than tigers in their wildness.

'Let him have time to tear his curlèd hair,
Let him have time against himself to rave,
Let him have time of time's help to despair,

Oblivion later, in *Troilus and Cressida* III.
iii.144–45: "Time hath, my lord, a wallet at his
back, / Wherein he puts alms for oblivion"
ravens' Ravens were supposed to live three times
as long as humans.
fortune's wheel Fortune is usually represented
with a wheel, on which some mount and some
fall.
beldam old woman
To mock . . . beguiled by providing a simpler
outcome than they expected

retiring minute a minute in which time goes
backward
Lending . . . lends giving him a glimpse of
the future which would prevent his making that
mistake
ceaseless . . . eternity Eternity is the "standing
now"; time does the moving, and is its agent.
cross interfere with
extremes . . . extremity the wildest contin-
gencies
bedrid bedridden

Let him have time to live a loathèd slave,
Let him have time a beggar's orts° to crave,
   And time to see one that by alms doth live
   Disdain to him disdainèd scraps to give.

'Let him have time to see his friends his foes,
And merry fools to mock at him resort;
990   Let him have time to mark how slow time goes
In time of sorrow, and how swift and short
His time of folly and his time of sport:
   And ever let his unrecalling° crime
   Have time to wail the abusing of his time.

· · ·

1594   1594

The Phoenix and Turtle

In 1601 appeared a quarto called *Love's Martyr: Or, Rosalin's Complaint. Allegorically shadowing the truth of Love, in the constant Fate of the Phoenix and Turtle,* etc. After describing the main part of the work, the title goes on to say that it also includes *some new compositions, of severall moderne Writers . . . upon the first Subject: viz. The Phoenix and Turtle.*

Among much else, *Love's Martyr* contains a story of how a Turtledove, sorrowing for his dead mate, meets the Phoenix; and how they decide to die together in a fire of sweet wood. The Turtle goes first, then the Phoenix; and the event is reported by a nearby pelican. To this muddled poem of Robert Chester's, Ben Jonson, Shakespeare, and others, for unknown reasons, consented to add their shorter pieces.

Chester was celebrating his patron Sir John Salisbury as the Turtledove (Constancy) and his wife as the Phoenix (Love), and the daughter of that union. The other contributors, including Shakespeare, treat his new-made myth with great freedom. Shakespeare appears to have found in it an occasion to combine the image of the phoenix with a bird-funeral of the kind known in folklore; one analogue to his poem is "Cock Robin." But in doing so he also wrote his most obscure and metaphysical poem.

Shakespeare's birds have "no posterity"—even the phoenix this time does not arise from its ashes. There may be a topical issue to explain this—the execution of Essex (the approach of the Phoenix Elizabeth to death)—but it has not been satisfactorily adduced. The best course is to read the poem for its own sake—in rhythm, movement of thought, and lexical inventiveness a great work and itself a phoenix.

The birds assemble (ll. 1–20), appropriately if conceitedly characterized; then follows the anthem, which gives way to a simpler funeral song, into the tercets of which it modulates with unprecedented musical effect. Most of the obscurities of language and idea occur in the anthem, which F. T. Prince has in mind when he calls the work "a marriage between intense emotion and almost unintelligible fantasy." It is a meditation on the question, which so often arises in a quite different way in Donne, of the identity of separate persons in love. Shakespeare adapts scholastic terms used in the discussion of the persons of the Trinity, which, though distinct, are not divided; but in the

orts scraps of food   **unrecalling** irrevocable

course of the adaptation he stretches many English words—*property, selfsame, mine, either, neither*—to fit contexts of exalted argument remote from their daily uses. This practice and the unclued context of the whole make of *The Phoenix and Turtle* one of the least explicable and most beautiful poems in the language.

The Phoenix and Turtle

Let the bird of loudest lay,°
On the sole Arabian tree,°
Herald sad and trumpet° be,
To whose sound chaste wings obey.°

But thou shrieking harbinger,°
Foul precurrer° of the fiend,
Augur° of the fever's end,
To this troop come thou not near.

From this session interdict°
10   Every fowl of tyrant wing,°
Save the eagle, feathered king;
Keep the obsequy° so strict.°

Let the priest in surplice white,
That defunctive music can,°
Be the death-divining swan,
Lest the requiem lack his right.°

And thou treble-dated° crow,
That thy sable gender mak'st,
With the breath thou giv'st and tak'st,°
20   'Mongst our mourners shalt thou go.

Here the anthem doth commence:
Love and Constancy is dead;
Phoenix and the turtle fled
In a mutual flame from hence.

So they loved as° love in twain
Had the essence but in one;

of **loudest lay** that can sing loudest
sole Arabian tree As there was but one phoenix, so he had a unique tree, probably a palm; in Greek *phoinix* means both "phoenix" and "palm."
trumpet trumpeter
To . . . obey to whose sound the wings of virtuous birds are obedient
shrieking harbinger screech-owl
precurrer precursor
Augur prophet, soothsayer; the screech-owl foreboded death
interdict forbid

tyrant wing prey
obsequy funeral
strict restricted
the priest . . . can The swan sang only before its own death: it "knows how to sing funeral music."
right either the "rite" provided by the swan or "what is due to the requiem"
treble-dated long-lived
thy sable . . . tak'st Crows were thought to mate at the mouth and lay their eggs there.
as so that

Two distincts, division none:°
Number there in love was slain.°

Hearts remote, yet not asunder;
30 Distance, and no space was seen
Twixt this turtle and his queen:
But in them it were a wonder.°

So between them love did shine
That the turtle saw his right°
Flaming in the phoenix' sight;
Either was the other's mine.°

Property° was thus appalled,
That the self was not the same;°
Single nature's double name
40 Neither two nor one was called.°

Reason, in itself confounded,°
Saw division grow together,°
To themselves, yet either neither,°
Simple were so well compounded:°

That it cried, 'How true a twain
Seemeth this concordant one!°
Love hath reason, Reason none,
If what parts can so remain.'°

Whereupon it made this threne°
50 To the phoenix and the dove,
Co-supremes° and stars of love,
As chorus to their tragic scene:

Beauty, Truth, and Rarity,
Grace in all simplicity,
Here enclosed in cinders lie.

Death is now the phoenix nest,
And the turtle's loyal breast
To eternity doth rest,

Two . . . none two distinct, but not divided, persons. Scholastically the terms are used of the relations between the three persons of the Trinity.
Number . . . slain Mathematically it is said that "one is no number," so when two become one, number is slain.
But . . . wonder in any other case but theirs it would have been a marvel
right love returned, as was due to him
mine selfhood (not "source of wealth")
Property the natural order in which each thing is itself
self . . . same splits up "selfsame" in order to emphasize the uniqueness of this situation.
Single . . . called not one, because their persons remain distinct; not two, because they are not divided

confounded because these matters defy normal logic
grow together resolve into unity
yet either neither expresses, unparaphraseably, the positive and negative of each selfhood in this relation.
Simple . . . compounded The substance of the soul is simple, but here a compound retains the qualities of the simple.
How true . . . one This harmonious "one" is really a new kind of two, with the integrity of unity.
Love . . . remain Love is more reasonable than reason if it can give to the compound and divide the virtues of the simple unity.
threne funeral song; from the Greek, *threnos*
Co-supremes joint rulers

60 Leaving no posterity:
'Twas not their infirmity,
It was married chastity.

Truth may seem, but cannot be;°
Beauty brag, but 'tis not she;
Truth and Beauty buried be.

To this urn let those repair
That are either true or fair;
For these dead birds sigh a prayer.

1601   1601

The Sonnets

Shakespeare's sonnets were written over an indeterminate period and published to-gether in 1609, after the vogue of sonneteering was over. Unlike Spenser's *Amoretti* or Sidney's *Astrophel and Stella* they revolve about no central mythical lady, named and constantly invoked; instead, we have a constellation of three figures providing a far greater ironic and dramatic range than the traditional relation of lover-poet to lady-muse. A blond young aristocrat, a dark lady, and a rival poet, none totally trustworthy, all ambiguously admirable, inhabit these sonnets, which, throughout, are haunted by the theme of time and its effects on people, things and buildings, human relationships. They attracted much misguided critical attention because of the belief that they were autobiographical and because of the mystery (but probably trivial import) of the dedi-cation to an unknown "Mr. W. H." Their compact language, range of tone, profound word-play, and intense moral vision are unsurpassed by any of the regular sonnet sequences of Sidney, Spenser, or Drayton. The early poems of the cycle urge the young man to marry and have children; later on, there is a group addressed to the lady; toward the end, obvious complications occur.

XII
When I do count the clock that tells the time,°
And see the brave° day sunk in hideous night;
When I behold the violet past prime,°
And sable curls o'er-silvered all with white;
When lofty trees I see barren of leaves,
Which erst from heat did canopy the herd,
And summer's green all girded up° in sheaves
Borne on the bier with white and bristly beard;°
Then of thy beauty do I question make

Truth . . . be henceforth there can be only the appearance, not the reality, of truth
count . . . time mark the passage of the hours
brave resplendent, finely attired
past prime faded
girded up with a girdle about his waist, the

image being that of an old man being carried to his grave
And summer's . . . beard the green corn, now ripe, harvested, the imagery making the sheaves a conceited image of death

10   That thou among the wastes of time° must go,
Since sweets° and beauties do themselves forsake°
And die as fast they see others grow;
    And nothing 'gainst Time's scythe can make defence
    Save breed° to brave° him when he takes thee hence.

XVIII

Shall I compare thee to a summer's day?°
Thou art more lovely and more temperate:
Rough winds do shake the darling buds of May,
And summer's lease hath all too short a date:°
Sometime too hot the eye of heaven shines,
And often is his gold complexion dimmed,
And every fair from fair sometime declines,
By chance or nature's changing course untrimmed;°
But thy eternal summer shall not fade
10   Nor lose possession of that fair thou owest,°
Nor shall Death brag thou wander'st in his shade,
When in eternal lines° to time thou growest:°
    So long as men can breathe or eyes can see,
    So long lives this, and this gives life to thee.

XIX

Devouring Time, blunt thou the lion's paws,
And make the earth devour her own sweet brood;
Pluck the keen teeth from the fierce tiger's jaws,
And burn the long-lived phoenix in her blood;°
Make glad and sorry seasons as thou fleet'st,
And do whate'er thou wilt, swift-footed Time,
To the wide world and all her fading sweets:°
But I forbid thee one most heinous crime—
Oh carve not with thy hours my love's fair brow
10   Nor draw no lines there with thine ántique° pen;
Him in thy course untainted do allow
For beauty's pattern to succeeding men.
    Yet do thy worst, old Time: despite thy wrong
    My love shall in my verse ever live young.

wastes of time the things time has destroyed
sweets blossoms
forsake undo
breed offspring
brave defy
day may mean the period (or season) of a
summer, as in the expression "in my day"
date the period of a lease
untrimmed stripped of beauty
that . . . owest that beauty thou possessest
(ownest)

lines such as the lines of this poem and the
other sonnets
growest becomes a part of
phoenix . . . blood The first three lines describe
Time's action on living things that change and
die; the phoenix also comes to the end of its
years, although it is instantly reborn from its
own funeral pyre.
sweets flowers
ántique ancient, with a play on "antic" or
"fantastic"

XX

A woman's face with nature's own hand painted
Hast thou, the master-mistress° of my passion;
A woman's gentle heart, but not acquainted
With shifting change as is false women's fashion;
An eye more bright than theirs, less false in rolling,°
Gilding the object whereupon it gazeth;
A man in hue° all hues in his controlling,
Which steals men's eyes and women's souls amazeth:
And for a woman wert thou first created,—
10   Till nature as she wrought thee fell a-doting,
And by addition me of thee defeated,°
By adding one thing° to my purpose nothing.
   But since she pricked° thee out for women's pleasure,
   Mine be thy love and thy love's use° their treasure.

XXIX

When, in disgrace with Fortune and men's eyes,
I all alone beweep my outcast state,°
And trouble deaf heaven with my bootless° cries,
And look upon myself and curse my fate,
Wishing me like to one more rich in hope,
Featured like him,° like him with friends possessed,
Desiring this man's art and that man's scope,
With what I most enjoy contented least;
Yet in these thoughts myself almost despising
10   Haply I think on thee, and then my state,
Like to the lark at break of day arising
From sullen° earth, sings hymns at heaven's gate:
   For thy sweet love remembered such wealth brings
   That then I scorn to change my state with kings.

XXX

When to the sessions° of sweet silent thought
I summon up remembrance of things past,
I sigh the lack of many a thing I sought,
And with old woes new wail my dear time's waste:
Then can I drown an eye, unused to flow,
For precious friends hid in death's dateless° night,

---

master-mistress both the oxymoron "boy-girl" and, as if unhyphenated, "sovereign mistress"
rolling roving
hue form
defeated defrauded
one thing male sex
pricked selected; also "prick" as in modern slang for penis
use sexual practice
state Here, as in all the sonnets, the meaning shifts from "condition in life" through "state of being" (l. 10) to "stately."
bootless unavailing
like him like yet another person
sullen dull, heavy
sessions of a law court. The legal conceit turns on words like "dateless," "cancelled," "expense," "account," etc., and suggests the poet being called to account, as steward, for the estate of his life.
dateless endless

And weep afresh love's long since cancelled woe,
And moan the expense° of many a vanished sight:
Then can I grieve at grievances foregone,°
10   And heavily° from woe to woe tell° o'er
The sad account of fore-bemoanèd moan,
Which I new pay as if not paid before.
   But if the while I think on thee, dear friend,°
   All losses are restored and sorrows end.

XXXIII

Full many a glorious morning have I seen
Flatter° the mountain tops with sovereign eye,
Kissing with golden face the meadows green,
Gilding pale streams with heavenly alchemy,
Anon permit the basest clouds to ride
With ugly rack° on his celestial face,
And from the fórlorn world his visage hide,
Stealing unseen to west with this disgrace:°
Even so my sun one early morn did shine
10   With all triumphant° splendour on my brow;
But out alack, he was but one hour mine:
The region° cloud hath masked him from me now.
   Yet him for this my love no whit disdaineth:
   Suns of the world may stain,° when heaven's sun staineth.

LIII

What is your substance, whereof are you made,
That millions of strange shadows° on you tend?
Since every one hath, every one, one shade,
And you, but one, can every shadow lend.
Describe Adonis,° and the counterfeit
Is poorly imitated after you;
On Helen's cheek all art of beauty set,°
And you in Grecian tires° are painted new.
Speak of the spring and foison° of the year:
10   The one doth shadow of your beauty show,
The other as your bounty doth appear,
And you in every blessèd shape we know.

expense loss
foregone gone by
heavily sadly
tell reckon
dear friend the first use of this term in the *Sonnets*
Flatter brighten, cheer up (as the sovereign's smile would a courtier)
rack drifting; a mass of clouds driven before the wind; cf. *The Tempest* IV.i.156
this disgrace i.e. the concealing clouds
triumphant glorious

region region of the air
stain grow dim
strange shadows external, foreign images. The word-play is on "shadow and substance" meaning "appearance vs. reality"; in l. 10, the word takes on its modern sense of "cast shade."
Adonis See notes to *Venus and Adonis*, above.
On Helen's . . . set put the best makeup on the face of the most beautiful woman ever
tires attire, costume, dress
foison autumnal harvest

In all external grace you have some part,
But you like none, none you for constant heart.

LV

Not marble, nor the gilded monuments
Of princes shall outlive this powerful rhyme;
But you shall shine more bright in these contents
Than unswept stone besmeared with sluttish time.°
When wasteful° war shall statues overturn,
And broils° root out the work of masonry,
Nor Mars his sword° nor war's quick° fire shall burn
The living record of your memory.
'Gainst death and all oblivious° enmity
10 Shall you pace forth: your praise° shall still find room
Even in the eyes of all posterity
That wear this world out° to the ending doom.
    So, till the judgment that yourself arise,
    You live in this,° and dwell in lovers' eyes.

LXIV

When I have seen by Time's fell hand defaced
The rich proud cost of outworn buried age;
When sometime lofty towers I see down razed,
And brass eternal° slave to mortal° rage;
When I have seen the hungry ocean gain
Advantage on the kingdom of the shore,
And the firm soil win of the watery main,
Increasing store° with loss and loss with store;
When I have seen such interchange of state,°
10 Or state itself confounded to decay,
Ruin hath taught me thus to ruminate
That Time will come and take my love away.
    This thought is as a death, which cannot choose
    But weep to have that which it fears to lose.

LXVI

Tired with all these for restful death I cry
As to behold Desert° a beggar born,
And needy Nothing trimmed in jollity,°

---

unswept . . . time The stone bore an inscription to the dead man, the letters of which had become obscured ("sluttish" = dirty) in the course of time.
wasteful destructive
broils battles
Nor . . . sword "Destroy" is understood.
quick lively
oblivious bringing to oblivion
praise glory
wear . . . out outlast

this these lines of poetry
brass eternal Eternal brass as opposed, syntactically, to "mortal rage"—this patterning of noun-adjective:adjective-noun, called chiasmus, is typically Elizabethan.
mortal both "deadly" and "subject to death"
store abundance
state condition; also "estate"; also "grandeur" (as in the next line)
Desert a personification of one who is deserving
jollity fine costume

And purest Faith° unhappily forsworn,
And gilded Honour shamefully misplaced,
And maiden Virtue rudely strumpeted,°
And right Perfection wrongfully disgraced,
And Strength by limping Sway disablèd,
And Art made tongue-tied by Authority,
10   And Folly, Doctor-like,° controlling° Skill,
And simple Truth miscalled Simplicity,°
And captive Good attending captain Ill:
    Tired with all these, from these would I be gone
    Save that, to die, I leave my love alone.

LXXIII

That time of year thou mayst in me behold
When yellow leaves, or none, or few, do hang
Upon those boughs which shake against the cold,
Bare ruined choirs where late the sweet birds sang:°
In me thou see'st the twilight of such day
As after sunset fadeth in the west,
Which by and by black night doth take away,
Death's second self that seals up all in rest:
In me thou see'st the glowing of such fire
10   That on the ashes of his youth doth lie
As the death-bed whereon it must expire,
Consumed with that which it was nourished by:°
    This thou perceivest, which makes thy love more strong
    To love that well which thou must leave ere long.

LXXXVI

Was it the proud full sail of his° great verse,
Bound for the prize of all-too-precious you,
That did my ripe thoughts in my brain inhearse,°
Making their tomb the womb wherein they grew?
Was it his spirit, by spirits taught to write
Above a mortal pitch, that struck me dead?
No, neither he, nor his compeers by night
Giving him aid, my verse astonishèd:
He, nor that affable familiar ghost°
10   Which nightly gulls° him with intelligence,°

Faith fidelity; also True Religion
strumpeted called a whore
Doctor-like pedant-like
controlling also with a sense of rebuking, censuring
Simplicity stillness
Bare . . . sang The trees are likened to arching ruins, half-opened to the sky, of the choirs of gothic monastery churches; the sweet birds literally sang in the summer trees, and, figuratively, sang as choir boys, perhaps, in the choir stalls of the church in the image; notice the

sequence in the quatrains of autumn—sundown—dying fire.
Consumed . . . by "consumed with life," as with passion; also perhaps consumed by the nourishing fire; the image is one of embers hotter than they look
his some rival poet: George Chapman has been suggested
inhearse entomb
familiar ghost some spirit attending the rival; perhaps a poetic predecessor
gulls deceives
intelligence secret information

As victors of my silence cannot boast,
I was not sick of any fear from thence:
    But when your countenance filled up his line,
    Then lacked I matter; that° enfeebled mine.

LXXXVII

Farewell—thou art too dear° for my possessing,
And like enough thou knowest thy estimate:°
The charter° of thy worth gives thee releasing;
My bonds in thee are all determinate.°
For how do I hold thee but by thy granting?
And for that riches where is my deserving?
The cause of this fair gift in me is wanting,
And so my patent° back again is swerving.°
Thy self thou gavest, thy own worth then not knowing;
Or me, to whom thou gavest it, else mistaking:°
So thy great gift, upon misprision° growing,
Comes home again on better judgment making.°
    Thus have I had thee as a dream doth flatter:
    In sleep a king, but waking no such matter.

XCIV

They that have power to hurt and will do none,
That do not do the thing they most do show,°
Who moving others are themselves as stone,
Unmovèd, cold, and to temptation slow;
They rightly do inherit heaven's graces,°
And husband nature's riches from expense;°
They are the lords and owners of their faces,
Others but stewards° of their excellence.
The summer's flower is to the summer sweet,
Though to itself it only live and die;
But if that flower with base infection meet,
The basest weed outbraves° his dignity:
    For sweetest things turn sourest by their deeds.
    Lilies that fester smell far worse than weeds.°

XCVII

How like a winter hath my absence been
From thee, the pleasure of the fleeting year!
What freezings have I felt, what dark days seen!—

---

that "that this was true"
dear expensive; also, "aristocratic"
estimate worth
charter privilege
determinate ended
patent grant of a monopoly
is swerving returns to you
mistaking overestimating
misprision misjudgment

on better judgment making on your judging better
show look as if they could do
heaven's graces the favors of heaven
husband . . . expense protect from wastefulness
stewards officials who manage estates for the owners; "their" refers to "they" in l. 1
outbraves makes a finer show than
Lilies . . . weeds a line from an old play

What old December's bareness everywhere!
And yet this time removed° was summer's time:
The teeming autumn big with rich increase°
Bearing the wanton° burthen of the prime,°
Like widowed wombs after their lords' decease.
Yet this abundant issue seemed to me
10   But hope of orphans, and unfathered fruit;
For summer and his pleasures wait on° thee,
And thou away the very birds are mute;
    Or if they sing, 'tis with so dull a cheer
    That leaves look pale, dreading the winter's near.

CVI

When in the chronicle of wasted time
I see descriptions of the fairest wights,°
And beauty making beautiful old rhyme
In praise of ladies dead and lovely knights,
Then in the blazon° of sweet beauty's best—
Of hand, of foot, of lip, of eye, of brow—
I see their antique pen would have expressed
Even such a beauty as you master now.
So all their praises are but prophecies
10   Of this our time, all you prefiguring;
And for they looked but with divining eyes
They had not skill enough your worth to sing:
    For we which now behold these present days
    Have eyes to wonder, but lack tongues to praise.

CVII

Not mine own fears, nor the prophetic soul
Of the wide world dreaming on things to come
Can yet the lease° of my true love control,
Supposed as forfeit to a cónfined doom.
The mortal moon hath her eclipse endured,°
And the sad augurs mock their own presage;
Incertainties now crown themselves assured,
And peace proclaims olives° of endless age.
Now with the drops of this most balmy time
10   My love looks fresh; and Death to me subscribes,
Since spite of him I'll live in this poor rhyme
While he insults o'er° dull and speechless tribes:

---

time removed time of separation
increase offspring, crops
wanton playful; luxuriant
prime spring
wait on attend, as at court
wights people
blazon poetic cataloguing of a person's beauties
and virtues, publicly displayed
lease period or term of lease

The mortal moon . . . endured Some historical
crisis has passed—whether the Spanish Armada,
sailing in a crescent (defeated in 1588), a lunar
eclipse, or some crisis of the Queen—making
"mortal" mean "deadly" or "able to die."
olives olive branch of peace (ever since the dove
flew back to Noah's ark with one when the flood
had abated)
insults o'er triumphs over

And thou in this shalt find thy monument
When tyrants' crests and tombs of brass are spent.

CXVI

Let me not to the marriage of true minds
Admit impediments:° love is not love
Which alters when it alteration finds,
Or bends with the remover to remove.°
Oh no! it is an ever-fixèd mark°
That looks on tempests and is never shaken;
It is the star to every wandering bark,
Whose worth's unknown although his height be taken.°
Love's not Time's fool, though rosy lips and cheeks
10   Within his bending° sickle's compass come;
Love alters not with his brief hours and weeks,
But bears it out° even to the edge of doom.
    If this be error and upon me proved,
    I never writ, nor no man ever loved.

CXXI

'Tis better to be vile than vile esteemed,
When not to be receives reproach of being,
And the just pleasure lost which is so deemed°
Not by our feeling but by others' seeing.
For why should others' false adulterate eyes
Give salutation to my sportive blood?°
Or on my frailties why are frailer spies,
Which in their wills count bad what I think good?
No: I am that I am,° and they that level°
10   At my abuses reckon up their own;
I may be straight though they themselves be bevel;°
By their rank° thoughts my deeds must not be shown, —
    Unless this general evil° they maintain:
    All men are bad and in their badness reign.

CXXIX

The expense of spirit in a waste of shame°
Is lust° in action; and till action, lust°

Let . . . impediments an echo of the marriage service. The "impediments" are change of circumstance (l. 3) and inconstancy (l. 4).
bends . . . remove withdraws when its object does
an . . . mark a beacon
height be taken altitude be known
bending bent; also "causing the grass of youthful beauty to bend"
bears it out endures
so deemed either "vile," in which case the unjust condemnation of the love by outsiders wrecks its pleasure; or "just pleasure," in which case the outsiders ("others") approve of the love although the sonneteer doesn't

Give salutation . . . blood mockingly hail my sexual activity
I am that I am I am what I am (apparently echoing the words of God from the burning bush to Moses, Exodus 3:14)
level aim a weapon
bevel crooked
rank lewd
general evil i.e. the following moral formula: "All men are bad . . ." etc.
The expense . . . shame abstractly, characterizing lust; concretely, sexual "spending" (orgasm) to no purpose in a shameful waste (the theme of *post coitum triste*—"sorrow after sex")
lust grammatical subject of the first sentence

Is perjured, murderous, bloody, full of blame,
Savage, extreme, rude,° cruel, not to trust;
Enjoyed no sooner but despisèd straight;
Past reason hunted; and no sooner had,
Past reason hated, as a swallowed bait
On purpose laid to make the taker mad;
Mad in pursuit, and in possession so;
10   Had, having, and in quest to have, extreme;
A bliss in proof;° and proved, a very woe;
Before, a joy proposed; behind, a dream.
 All this the world well knows, yet none knows well
 To shun the heaven that leads men to this hell.

CXXX

My mistress' eyes are nothing like the sun;
Coral is far more red than her lips' red;
If snow be white, why then her breasts are dun;°
If hairs be wires, black wires grow on her head;
I have seen roses damasked,° red and white,
But no such roses see I in her cheeks;
And in some perfumes is there more delight
Than in the breath that from my mistress reeks;°
I love to hear her speak, yet well I know
10   That music hath a far more pleasing sound;
I grant I never saw a goddess go
(My mistress when she walks treads on the ground).
 And yet by heaven I think my love as rare
 As any she belied with false compare.

CXXXV

Whoever hath her wish, thou hast thy *Will*,°
And *Will* to boot, and *Will* in overplus:
More than enough am I that vex thee still,
To thy sweet *Will* making addition thus.
Wilt thou whose *Will* is large and spacious
Not once vouchsafe to hide my *Will* in thine?
Shall *Will* in others seem right gracious,
And in my *Will* no fair acceptance shine?
The sea, all water, yet receives rain still,
10   And in abundance addeth to his store:
So thou being rich in *Will* add to thy *Will*
One *Will* of mine to make thy large *Will* more.

---

rude brutal
in proof experienced
dun tan. The whole poem is an anti-blazon,
actually a Petrarchan "anti-Petrarchan" device.
roses damasked pink roses, but also perhaps
patterned in the symbolic colors of passion and
purity

reeks emanates (with no sense of "stinks")
Will volition; desire; passionate feeling ("wit
and will" meant something like "thought and
feeling"); the auxiliary verb; and, in this sonnet, both the poet's own name, and sexual
member (but of both sexes—as if modern slang
"dick" meant both penis and vagina)

Let no unkind no fair° beseechers kill;
Think all but one, and me in that one *Will*.

CXXXVIII

When my love swears that she is made of truth°
I do believe her, though I know she lies,°
That she might think me some untutored youth
Unlearnèd in the world's false subtleties.
Thus vainly thinking that she thinks me young,
Although she knows my days are past the best,
Simply° I credit her false-speaking tongue:
On both sides thus is simple truth suppressed.
But wherefore says she not she is unjust?°
10   And wherefore say not I that I am old?
Oh, love's best habit° is in seeming trust,
And age, in love,° loves not to have years told.
  Therefore I lie with her,° and she with me,
  And in our faults by lies we flattered be.

CXLIV

Two loves I have, of comfort and despair,
Which like two spirits do suggest me still:°
The better angel is a man right fair,°
The worser spirit a woman coloured ill.°
To win me soon to hell, my female evil
Tempteth my better angel from my side,
And would corrupt my saint to be a devil,
Wooing his purity with her foul pride.
And whether that my angel be turned fiend
10   Suspect I may, yet not directly tell;
But being both from me, both to each friend,
I guess one angel in another's hell:°
  Yet this shall I ne'er know, but live in doubt
  Till my bad angel fire my good one out.°

CXLVI

Poor soul, the centre of my sinful earth,°
(Foiled by)° these rebel powers that thee array,°
Why dost thou pine within and suffer dearth,

---

fair legitimate
made of truth "faithful to me," as well as
"truth-telling"
she lies "sleeps around," as well as "tells lies"
Simply like a simpleton, unconditionally, absolutely
unjust unfaithful
habit costume
in love also, "in re love"
lie with her "lie to her"; also, "sleep with her"
suggest me still tempt me ever
fair light-haired and -complexioned; beautiful;
honest (modern "fair" as "just")

coloured ill a brunette
hell the prison zone in barley-break, a game
like prisoner's base; also, as in a story in the
Decameron of Giovanni Boccaccio (1313–75),
"the devil in hell" as his sexual member in hers
fire . . . out reject him; also, to give him
venereal disease (only when the friend shows
signs of this will it be clear that he slept with
her)
earth flesh, body
(Foiled by) an emendation; the original phrase
is a misprint
array both "deck out" and "afflict"

Painting thy outward walls so costly gay?
Why so large cost, having so short a lease,
Dost thou upon thy fading mansion spend?
Shall worms, inheritors of this excess,
Eat up thy charge? Is this thy body's end?
Then, soul, live thou upon thy servant's loss,
10   And let that° pine to aggravate° thy store;
Buy terms° divine in selling hours of dross;
Within be fed, without be rich no more:
   So shalt thou feed on Death, that feeds on men,
   And Death once dead there's no more dying then.

Songs from the Plays

The songs in Shakespeare's plays represent almost every sixteenth-century lyrical mode. They follow, adapt, parody, and transform conventions of courtly lyric, ballad, pastoral song, air, masque lyric, and others, sometimes quoting or reworking familiar words or following familiar tunes. In plays, the role of song varies: does a character ask for music, in the course of the action, from musicians? does he sing himself? to another person? is the singing an aside or soliloquy? Shakespeare often condensed central themes of plays in phrases in the songs (consider "benefits forgot" and its meaning in *As You Like it*).

Tell Me Where Is Fancy Bred? °

Tell me where is fancy bred,
Or in the heart or in the head?
How begot, how nourishèd?
   Reply, reply!
It is engendered in the eyes,
With gazing fed; and fancy dies
In the cradle where it lies.
   Let us all ring fancy's knell:
   I'll begin it—Ding, dong, bell.
10   *Ding, dong, bell.*

that "that one," the servant body
aggravate increase
terms years or decades of a lease
And Death . . . then Cf. I Corinthians 15:54–55.
Tell Me Where Is Fancy Bred? from *The Mer-*

chant of Venice (1596–97), III.ii; sung by Portia's musicians as Bassanio makes his choice of a lead casket over a silver or gold one, thus winning her. The opening rhymes are all on "lead."

Dirge°

Fear no more the heat o' the sun
    Nor the furious winter's rages;
Thou thy worldly task hast done,
    Home art gone, and ta'en thy wages;
Golden lads and girls all must,
As chimney-sweepers,° come to dust.°

Fear no more the frown o' the great,
    Thou art past the tyrant's stroke;
Care no more to clothe and eat,
10   To thee the reed is as the oak:
The sceptre, learning, physic,° must
All follow this and come to dust.

Fear no more the lightning flash,
    Nor the all-dreaded thunder-stone;°
Fear not slander, censure rash;
    Thou hast finished joy and moan:
All lovers young, all lovers must
Consign to thee and come to dust.

No exorciser harm thee!
20   Nor no witchcraft charm thee!
Ghost unlaid forbear thee!
    Nothing ill come near thee!
Quiet consummation have,
And renownèd be thy grave.

Dialogue in Praise of the Owl and Cuckoo°

Spring

When daisies pied° and violets blue
    And lady-smocks all silver-white
And cuckoo-buds of yellow hue
    Do paint the meadows with delight,
The cuckoo then, on every tree,
Mocks married men; for thus sings he,
    Cuckoo,°

Dirge from *Cymbeline* (1610–11), IV.ii; ceremonially chanted by Guiderius and Arviragus over Imogen, believed dead
chimney-sweepers a secondary meaning: slang in Warwickshire for "dandelions"
come to dust both literal and figurative ashes: "Man, thou art dust, and into dust thou shalt return"
physic medical learning
thunder-stone believed to cause its sound

Dialogue in Praise of the Owl and Cuckoo from the ironically tinged happy ending of *Love's Labours Lost* (1594–95), which defers the concluding marriages for a year. The spring song sounds a "word of fear," the night and winter one, "a merry note."
pied varicolored
Cuckoo The cuckoo's cry sounds like the "cuckold" he thereby rebukes.

Cuckoo, cuckoo! O word of fear
Unpleasing to a married ear!

10   When shepherds pipe on oaten straws,
        And merry larks are ploughmen's clocks,
When turtles tread, and rooks, and daws,
        And maidens bleach their summer smocks,
The cuckoo then, on every tree,
Mocks married men; for thus sings he,
            Cuckoo,
Cuckoo, cuckoo! O word of fear,
Unpleasing to a married ear!

        Winter

When icicles hang by the wall,
        And Dick the shepherd blows his nail,°
And Tom bears logs into the hall,
        And milk comes frozen home in pail,
When blood is nipped, and ways be foul,°
Then nightly sings the staring owl,
            Tu-whit, to-who,
            A merry note,
While greasy Joan doth keel° the pot.

10   When all aloud the wind doth blow,
        And coughing drowns the parson's saw,°
And birds sit brooding in the snow,
        And Marian's nose looks red and raw,
When roasted crabs° hiss in the bowl,
Then nightly sings the staring owl,
            Tu-whit, to-who,
            A merry note,
While greasy Joan doth keel the pot.

Who Is Silvia?°

Who is Silvia? what is she,
    That all our swains commend her?
Holy, fair, and wise is she;
    The heaven such grace did lend her,
That she might admirèd be.

Is she kind as she is fair?
    For beauty lives with kindness:
Love doth to her eyes repair

blows his nail to warm his fingers
ways . . . foul roads be impassable
keel scrape out
saw proverb
crabs crabapples

Who Is Silvia? from *Two Gentlemen of Verona*
(1594–95), IV.ii; a formal serenade sung in the
play by hired musicians (for Thurio, who will
not get Silvia anyway)

To help him of his blindness,°
10   And being helped, inhabits there.

Then to Silvia let us sing
    That Silvia is excelling;
She excels each mortal thing
    Upon the dull earth dwelling.
To her let us garlands bring.

Take, O Take Those Lips Away°

Take, O take those lips away,
    That so sweetly were forsworn;
And those eyes, the break of day,
    Lights that do mislead the morn:
But my kisses bring again,
    Bring again,
Seals of love, but sealed in vain,
    Sealed in vain.

O Mistress Mine°

O mistress mine, where are you roaming?
O, stay and hear; your true-love's coming,
    That can sing both high and low.
Trip no further, pretty sweeting;
Journeys end in lovers meeting,
    Every wise man's son doth know.

What is love? 'tis not hereafter;
Present mirth hath present laughter;
    What's to come is still unsure:
In delay there lies no plenty;
Then come kiss me, sweet and twenty!
    Youth's a stuff will not endure.

When That I Was and a Little Tiny Boy°

When that I was and a little tiny boy,
    With hey, ho, the wind and the rain,

blindness See note to Marlowe's *Hero and Leander* I.38n.
Take, O Take Those Lips Away from *Measure for Measure* (1604), IV.i; sung at the jilted Mariana's first entrance, by a boy, indicating her pitiable state

O Mistress Mine from *Twelfth Night* (1601), II.iii; sung by Feste, the clown
When That I Was and a Little Tiny Boy an epilogue to *Twelfth Night*, again sung by Feste

A foolish thing was but a toy,°
    For the rain it raineth every day.

But when I came to man's estate,
    With hey, ho, the wind and the rain,
'Gainst knaves and thieves men shut their gate,
    For the rain it raineth every day.

But when I came, alas! to wive,
    With hey, ho, the wind and the rain,
By swaggering could I never thrive,
    For the rain it raineth every day.

But when I came unto my beds,
    With hey, ho, the wind and the rain,
With tosspots still had drunken heads,
    For the rain it raineth every day.

A great while ago the world begun,
    With hey, ho, the wind and the rain;
But that's all one, our play is done,
    And we'll strive to please you every day.

Under the Greenwood Tree°

    Under the greenwood tree
    Who loves to lie with me,
    And turn his merry note
    Unto the sweet bird's throat,
Come hither, come hither, come hither:
      Here shall he see
      No enemy
But winter and rough weather.°

    Who doth ambition shun
    And loves to live in the sun,
    Seeking the food he eats,
    And pleased with what he gets,
Come hither, come hither, come hither:
      Here shall he see
      No enemy
But winter and rough weather.

A foolish . . . toy a fool's bauble was nothing serious
Under the Greenwood Tree from *As You Like It*

(1599), II.v; sung by Touchstone, the clown, to celebrate the forest of Arden
No enemy . . . weather even his realistic, anti-pastoral country is better than court life

Blow, Blow, Thou Winter Wind°

Blow, blow, thou winter wind,
Thou are not so unkind
   As man's ingratitude;
Thy tooth is not so keen
Because thou art not seen,
   Although thy breath be rude.
Heigh-ho! sing heigh-ho, unto the green holly:
Most friendship is feigning, most loving mere folly:
   Then heigh-ho! the holly!
10   *This life is most jolly.*

Freeze, freeze, thou bitter sky
That dost not bite so nigh
   As benefits forgot:
Though thou the waters warp,°
Thy sting is not so sharp
   As friend remembered not.
Heigh-ho! etc.

Autolycus' Song°

When daffodils begin to peer,°
   With heigh, the doxy° over the dale!
Why, then comes in the sweet of the year
   For the red blood reigns in the winter's pale.

The white sheet bleaching on the hedge,°
   With heigh, the sweet birds, O how they sing!
Doth set my pugging° tooth on edge,
   For a quart of ale is a dish for a king.

The lark that tirra lirra chants,
10   With heigh, with heigh, the thrush and the jay!
Are summer songs for me and my aunts°
   While we lie tumbling in the hay.

Blow, Blow, Thou Winter Wind from *As You Like It* II.vii
warp by freezing
Autolycus' Song from *The Winter's Tale* (1609–10), IV.ii; Autolycus, a thief (his name that of Mercury's son), sings this to himself
peer appear
doxy girl

The white . . . hedge Laundry left out to dry and whiten in the sun was often snatched by wandering peddlers like Autolycus, cloth of any kind being most valuable. For the thief, such sheets would indeed be blossoms to be plucked.
pugging stealing
aunts girls

Autolycus as Peddler°

Lawn° as white as driven snow,
Cyprus° black as e'er was crow,
Gloves as sweet as damask roses,
Masks for faces and for noses,
Bugle-bracelet, necklace amber,
Perfume for a lady's chamber,
Golden quoifs and stomachers°
For my lads to give their dears,
Pins and poking sticks° of steel
—What maids lack from head to heel.
Come buy of me, come; come buy, come buy,
Buy lads, or else your lasses cry.

The Tempest

The first play in the First Folio is *The Tempest,* although it was the last Shakespeare wrote unaided. The publishers took exceptional care with its preparation, as if, in putting it at the head of the section of comedies, and so first in the book, they were treating it as a showpiece.

Ever since it was discovered to be the last of Shakespeare's plays, *The Tempest* has attracted special attention as a kind of culmination of his work, the final statement of the greatest of dramatists. The attempts of nineteenth- and twentieth-century critics to find in it an allegory of Shakespeare's life or thoughts vary in subtlety and constitute an enormous range of interpretations. Perhaps we should react to these not by choosing one against the others but by arguing that the very fact of its lending itself, however partially, to such allegories, proves the play to have the rare quality of *suggesting* to the spectator or reader that he must make his own contribution, must complete the work in his own imagination. The play is perhaps the most remarkable example of qualities all good Shakespeareans learn to attribute to his finest work: patience and reticence. Patience is that ability to suffer and survive interpretation without which no work of art can achieve classic status and have direct relevance to the lives of successive generations. Reticence is the quality of not speaking out, not simplifying the text to the point where its meanings become more or less explicit, but leaving unsettled potential conflicts and complexities of meaning. Anyone who studies Verdi's *Otello,* great masterpiece though it is, will see that in comparison Shakespeare's *Othello* is reticent. Anyone who knows the history of *King Lear* criticism will understand the sense in which *King Lear* is patient. *The Tempest,* so resistant to interpretation, so full of possible but never fully spoken meanings, exemplifies both characteristics; which is why it preserves its unique status in the canon of Shakespeare's work.

Autolycus as Peddler *The Winter's Tale* IV.iii; disguised as a thief, he sings a conventional peddler's song (see "Fine Knacks for Ladies," above)
Lawn fine linen
Cyprus a thin crape

quoifs and stomachers close-fitting caps, and parts of bodices
poking sticks metal rods used to iron ruffs; given the next line, perhaps with a bawdy overtone

It is, of course, possible to relate it to other plays of Shakespeare, and especially to the romances—*Pericles, Cymbeline,* and *The Winter's Tale,* with which it is usually classified. These works all came into being because of the revival of an old form of dramatic romance. The element of masque, the dominant form of courtly entertainment in King James's reign, which is particularly strong in *The Tempest,* suggests not only that the King's Men were often engaged for masques at court but also that the play may have been written with the Blackfriars Theatre in mind; for these things, with their scenes and machines, their dancing and music, could be done better in the smaller, artificially-lighted indoor theater with its courtly audiences than in the big open-air house. If we speak of *The Tempest* as a romance, we need to bear all this in mind: the dramatic romance was not a subtle or courtly form, but it rapidly became so in the years leading up to *The Tempest.*

The history of the changes whereby simple romance could be made adequate to the purposes of Shakespeare in *The Tempest* may be seen from his own work. *Pericles* is formally an adaptation of a simpler romance narrative enormously sophisticated by Shakespeare in the interests of the beautiful scene of recognition between Marina and Pericles which is its climax. *Cymbeline* displays examples of Shakespeare's most mature and difficult blank verse, but also exploits with a deliberate false naïveté the Romance themes of lost sons and miraculous multiple recognitions. *The Winter's Tale* dramatizes a romantic novella, changing out of recognition its naïve philosophy but preserving its extensive Romance chronology and also developing its "pastoral" possibilities; again the climax is a miraculous recognition scene, more improbable than anything in the novella.

The Tempest is the story of a magician prince and his daughter put to sea in a leaky boat and taking possession of an island where, twelve years later, amid fantastic displays of the prince's supernatural powers, the wrongs of the past are righted at the final recognition. But this time Shakespeare has taken up the themes of royal children, of marvelous rescue from death, of reconciliation a generation later between enemies —in a different way. He has made the form *intensive;* this play alone of Shakespeare's is played in something like the same time as that taken by the events it enacts, and the text draws our attention to this. Such tautness of dramatic form—which nevertheless allows multiple plotting, a masque, and spectacular and climactic *coups de théâtre* like the apparition of Ariel as a Harpy—makes this play, for all its thematic resemblances to the other romances, uniquely surprising in design and suggestive in meaning. Nowhere else does Shakespeare use so much music, so many pantomimic devices, yet there is always a sense of the imminence of the catastrophe. Nowhere else does he juxtapose so abruptly verses which enact the turbulent human passions of anger, remorse, and fear—the verse, one might say, of *Coriolanus* and parts of *Cymbeline*—with the limpid, stylized grief of Ferdinand ("This music crept by me upon the waters") and the unearthly songs of Ariel. *The Tempest* is, finally, *sui generis,* the only play of its kind, and nothing we can learn about it will alter that.

At the level of fact, as of reasonable conjecture, we can, however, offer some relevant information. Shakespeare in 1610 evidently saw certain accounts, both published and unpublished, of a wreck in the Bermudas a year earlier. He had read a lot about voyages to the New World, but this occurrence was especially interesting because he knew people connected with the Virginia Company; the *Sea-Adventure* was bound for Virginia when she ran ashore in a gale and was lodged between two rocks; the colonists escaped with their lives and much of the ship's stores. William Strachey's

True Reportory of the Wrack, written in 1610 but not published till 1625, gives the most important account of the wreck and subsequent adventures. Shakespeare uses Strachey's description of St. Elmo's fire in Ariel's account of the storm, as well as other borrowings.

The importance of these allusions is not that Shakespeare was being very topical, but that the New World colonies deeply stirred his imagination. The Virginia Company had, of course, an economic interest which was served best by regarding the colonies as the natural domain of the European Christian. One of the books Shakepeare read calls the natives "human beasts." When Prospero says he was set upon his island "to be the lord on it" (V.i.162), he is talking like a colonist; when he discovers that on Caliban's "nature / Nurture will never stick," he is repeating what many colonial adventurers had reported; and when Caliban complains that he had been helpful with fresh water and fish-dams we recall that this was also admitted by the colonists, who added that the natives soon turned treacherous.

In this way *The Tempest* alludes to the new colonial problem; it also repeats some of the moralizations of the adventurers, who called the wreck a "tragicall comaedie," and rejoiced that what had seemed "a punishment against evil" was "but a medicine." Discussing the quarrels and mutinies in Virginia, they showed they had learned the lesson that "every inordinate soul soon becomes his own punishment." (Compare Gonzalo's "their great guilt . . . now 'gins to bite the spirits," III.iii.104–6.) Strachey calls the Bermudas "these unfortunate (yet fortunate) Ilands"—for all their terrors they proved a place of deliverance. (Compare Gonzalo's expressions in V.i.206 ff.)

But *The Tempest* does not take place in the New World—the island is somewhere between Tunis and Naples in the Mediterranean—and like everybody else Shakespeare interpreted the astonishing news from America in accordance with already existing Old World ideas. For example, Caliban, though his name is probably an anagram of "cannibal," is based on the wild man or *Wodewose* of European tradition—treacherous, lecherous, without language. It was easy to relate the savages to this type, which was traditionally held to be in an intermediate position between man and beast, natural in a bad sense. However, there are, for example in Spenser, good and bad wild men; and the travelers and others who speculated on the matter were divided into those who believed that "natural" men—without Christianity or civility—would be better and more beautiful, or wickeder and more ugly, than Europeans. Montaigne, whose essay "Of Cannibals" is paraphrased by Gonzalo in II.i.143 ff., was of the first party. Shakespeare is more ambiguous. Prospero's "Art," represented by his magical powers, is incapable of civilizing Caliban ("You taught me language; and my profit on't / Is, I know how to curse," I.ii.365–66), and Caliban is the dupe of Stephano and a traitor to his lord. He was given the same education as Miranda, but tried to rape her and was unrepentant. Yet he is not as base as the wicked Italians, who illustrate the saying *corruptio optimi pessima,* the corruption of the best is the worst corruption. Miranda's "brave new world" is the old one, in which man, though redeemed and beautiful in comparison with the world of mere nature, can be corrupt. Although art as well as grace can be added to nature, as by grafting finer fruit is made to grow on natural stocks, there is a corruption worse than the natural; and this the art of Prospero must try to purge. The purity possible to those who live above nature is Miranda's; her assurance that beautiful souls inhabit beautiful bodies ('There's nothing ill can dwell in such a temple," I.ii.460, and "How beauteous mankind is!," V.i.183) is not in accord with the facts, any more than the notion of the noble savage. And

Prospero, having failed with Caliban, must try with the Italian noblemen. He does not, it appears, wholly succeed.

Prospero has a "project," like an alchemist; the action of the play represents the climactic stage of the experiment. He saves his enemies, unharmed, from a tempest of his own causing; and will, if he can, regenerate them and by a marriage union prevent further strife. He is technically in charge of the whole experiment, stage-managing, or "presenting" the wanderings of the various parties, the great apparition of Ariel, the masques, the punishment of the vulgar rebels, and the final confrontation with Alonso and Sebastian. But Shakespeare will not allow the play to become too inertly schematic. Prospero is passionate, even bad-tempered. His excitement in the long expository scene (I.ii) is reflected in the disturbed verses which recount the past, his severe admonitions to Miranda, his nervous rage with Caliban and harshness to Ariel. So, later, his mind is "troubled" (IV.i.160); he rejoices in having his enemies at his mercy (IV.i.263), but also speaks the great lines from Ovid which are his farewell to magic arts, and the famous elegiac set piece after the masque. He is naggingly insistent about the need for Miranda and Ferdinand not to anticipate marriage; and his forgiveness of his brother Antonio is hardly in the mood of gentle reconciliation occasionally called characteristic in these romances—"most wicked sir, whom to call brother / Would even infect my mouth" (V.i.130–31). Miranda's more innocent reactions he learns to treat pityingly.

Such are the cross-currents of meaning and tone that make it impossible for anybody to announce boldly what *The Tempest* is about. Like all the best plays of Shakespeare, it is reticent on that point. When you think it may declare itself as having a particular theme, it frustrates the expectation by suddenly modulating into a different narrative manner, a different verse style. Thus the stage realism of the opening scene is followed by the scene of Prospero's agitated reminiscence, and when that threatens to become a forceful account of some political usurpation, the verse shifts it into a new mode of fairy tale at I.ii.44. Soon we meet Ariel and Caliban, for each of whom Shakespeare invented an idiomatic poetry; and then Ferdinand (I.ii.390), his strange water-music deriving from Ariel's uncanny song, "Full fadom five." This is a slight indication of the range of the play's voices; one needs to add the cheerful solemnity of Gonzalo's, the guilty sorrow of Alonso's, the Macbeth-like whispers of Antonio's and Sebastian. Ariel speaks as scourge and minister as well as fretful sprite, Caliban as a native of a good place and not only as a savage, Prospero as artist but also as fallible, vindictive, regretful man. Miranda's are the expressions of a perfectly innocent high-born wonder no less true for its brokenness; Ferdinand greets her as a goddess, she him as a god, and it is Prospero who suggests that there is ignorance in this innocence. The play does not imply that he must be right, and it does not call him wrong; it leaves us to follow, and choose between, the swirling changes of tone and emphasis, the clues that cross each other and prevent any from becoming dominant, ideological. This is the reticence that accompanies the classic's patience, and this marvelous play, so well endowed with both, may stand here as representative of Shakespeare's highest achievements.

The Tempest

The Scene, an uninhabited Island

Names of the Actors

ALONSO, *King of Naples*
SEBASTIAN, *his brother*
PROSPERO, *the right Duke of Milan*
ANTONIO *his brother, the usurping*
  Duke of Milan
FERDINAND, son to the King of Naples
GONZALO, *an honest old Counsellor*
ADRIAN *and* FRANCISCO, *Lords*
CALIBAN, *a savage and deformed slave*
TRINCULO, *a jester*
STEPHANO, *a drunken butler*

MASTER OF A SHIP
BOATSWAIN
MARINERS
MIRANDA, *daughter to Prospero*
ARIEL, *an airy spirit*
IRIS
CERES
JUNO   } SPIRITS
NYMPHS
REAPERS

ACT I

SCENE I   [*On a ship at sea*]:° *a tempestuous noise of thunder and light-ning heard.*

Enter a SHIP-MASTER *and a* BOATSWAIN.

SHIP-MASTER   Boatswain!
BOATSWAIN   Here, master: what cheer?
SHIP-MASTER   Good: speak to the mariners: fall to it, yarely,° or we run our-selves aground: bestir, bestir.   *Exit.*

Enter MARINERS.

BOATSWAIN   Heigh, my hearts! cheerly, cheerly, my hearts! yare, yare! Take in the topsail. Tend to the master's whistle.° Blow till thou burst thy wind, if room° enough!

Enter ALONSO, SEBASTIAN, ANTONIO, FERDINAND, GONZALO, *and others.*

10   ALONSO   Good boatswain, have care. Where's the master? Play the men.°
BOATSWAIN   I pray now, keep below.
ANTONIO   Where is the master, boatswain?
BOATSWAIN   Do you not hear him? You mar our labour: keep your cabins: you do assist the storm.
GONZALO   Nay, good, be patient.
BOATSWAIN   When the sea is. Hence! What cares these roarers° for the name of King? To cabin: silence! trouble us not.

[On a ship at sea] Square brackets in stage directions mean that the words enclosed are editorial additions to the copy-text, which is that of the First Folio of 1623, here called F.
yarely briskly

whistle used for giving orders by the Master
room sea-room
Play the men be courageous; or, make the men work (*ply* the men)
cares care
roarers toughs, hooligans (meaning the waves)

GONZALO   Good, yet remember whom thou hast aboard.

20   BOATSWAIN   None that I more love than myself. You are a counsellor; if you can command these elements to silence, and work the peace of the presence,° we will not hand a rope more; use your authority: if you cannot, give thanks you have lived so long, and make yourself ready in your cabin for the mischance of the hour, if it so hap. Cheerly, good hearts! Out of our way, I say.   *Exit.*

GONZALO   I have great comfort from this fellow: methinks he hath no drowning mark° upon him; his complexion is perfect gallows.° Stand fast, good Fate, to his hanging: make the rope of his destiny our cable, for our own doth little advantage.° If he be not born to be hanged, our case is miserable.   *Exeunt.*

30

Re-enter BOATSWAIN.

BOATSWAIN   Down with the topmast! yare! lower, lower! Bring her to try with main-course° [*A cry within*]. A plague upon his howling! they are louder than the weather or our office.

Re-enter SEBASTIAN, ANTONIO, *and* GONZALO.

Yet again! what do you here? Shall we give o'er, and drown? Have you a mind to sink?

40   SEBASTIAN   A pox o' your throat, you bawling, blasphemous, incharitable dog!

BOATSWAIN   Work you, then.

ANTONIO   Hang, cur! hang, you whoreson, insolent noise-maker. We are less afraid to be drowned than thou art.

GONZALO   I'll warrant him for° drowning, though the ship were no stronger than a nutshell, and as leaky as an unstanched wench.°

BOATSWAIN   Lay her a-hold,° a-hold! set her two courses;° off to sea again; lay

50   her off.

Enter MARINERS *wet.*

MARINERS   All lost, to prayers, to prayers! all lost!

BOATSWAIN   What, must our mouths be cold?

GONZALO   The King and Prince at prayers, let's assist them,
            For our case is as theirs.

SEBASTIAN   I'm out of patience.

ANTONIO   We are merely° cheated of our lives by drunkards:
            This wide-chapped rascal,—would thou mightst lie drowning
            The washing of ten tides!

GONZALO   He'll be hanged yet,
            Though every drop of water swear against it,

---

presence F has *present*, but *presence* (meaning the immediate vicinity of the king and court) is probable; his counselors would be responsible for keeping order in this area.
drowning mark mole or other blemish thought to indicate by its position the person's likeliest mode of death, here drowning
perfect gallows he will hang rather than drown
little advantage helps us little

Bring . . . main-course make her heave to
for i.e. against
unstanched wench loose (literally "leaky") woman
a-hold hove-to
courses sails; lacking sea-room to heave to, he tries to take the ship to sea
merely absolutely

And gape at wid'st to glut him.

[*A confused noise within:* 'Mercy on us!'—

'We split, we split!'—'Farewell, my wife and children!'—

'Farewell, brother!'—'We split, we split, we split!']

ANTONIO   Let's all sink wi' the King.

SEBASTIAN   Let's take leave of him.   *Exeunt* ANTONIO *and* SEBASTIAN

GONZALO   Now would I give a thousand furlongs of sea for an acre of barren
ground, long heath, broom, furze,° anything. The wills above be done!
but I would fain die a dry death.   *Exeunt.*

SCENE II [*The Island. Before* PROSPERO'S *Cell.*]

Enter PROSPERO *and* MIRANDA.

MIRANDA   If by your Art, my dearest father, you° have
Put the wild waters in this roar, allay them.
The sky, it seems, would pour down stinking pitch,
But that the sea, mounting to the welkin's° cheek,
Dashes the fire out. O, I have suffered
With those that I saw suffer! a brave vessel,
(Who had, no doubt, some noble creature in her,)
Dashed all to pieces. O, the cry did knock
Against my very heart! Poor souls, they perished!
Had I been any god of power, I would
Have sunk the sea within the earth, or ere
It should the good ship so have swallowed, and
The fraughting° souls within her.

PROSPERO   Be collected:
No more amazement:° tell your piteous° heart
There's no harm done.

MIRANDA   O, woe the day!

PROSPERO   No harm.
I have done nothing but in care of thee,
Of thee, my dear one; thee, my daughter, who
Art ignorant of what thou art; nought knowing
Of whence I am, nor that I am more better°
Than Prospero, master of a full poor cell,
And thy no greater father.

MIRANDA   More to know
Did never meddle° with my thoughts.

PROSPERO   'Tis time
I should inform thee farther. Lend thy hand,
And pluck my magic garment from me.—So:

                                                  Lays down his mantle.
Lie there, my Art.° Wipe thou thine eyes; have comfort.

broom, furze F has *browne firrs.*
you deferential, used by Miranda to her father,
who usually addresses her as "thou"
welkin's firmament's
fraughting forming the cargo

amazement terror
piteous full of pity
more better of higher rank
meddle mingle
my Art i.e. the robe, symbol of his art

The direful spectacle of the wrack,° which touched
The very virtue° of compassion in thee,
I have with such provision in mine Art
So safely ordered, that there is no soul°—
No, not so much perdition° as an hair
Betid° to any creature in the vessel
Which thou heard'st cry, which thou saw'st sink. Sit down;
For thou must now know farther.

MIRANDA   You have often
Begun to tell me what I am, but stopped,
And left me to bootless inquisition,°
Concluding 'Stay: not yet.'

PROSPERO   The hour's now come;
The very minute bids thee ope thine ear;
Obey, and be attentive. Canst thou remember
A time before we came unto this cell?
I do not think thou canst, for then thou wast not
Out° three years old.

MIRANDA   Certainly, sir, I can.

PROSPERO   By what? by any other house or person?
Of any thing the image tell me, that
Hath kept with thy remembrance.

MIRANDA   'Tis far off,
And rather like a dream than an assurance
That my remembrance warrants.° Had I not
Four or five women once that tended me?

PROSPERO   Thou hadst, and more, Miranda. But how is it
That this lives in thy mind? What seest thou else
In the dark backward and abysm of time?°
If thou rememberest aught ere thou camest here,
How thou camest here thou mayst.

MIRANDA   But that I do not.

PROSPERO   Twelve year since, Miranda, twelve year since,
Thy father was the Duke of Milan, and
A prince of power.

MIRANDA   Sir, are not you my father?

PROSPERO   Thy mother was a piece° of virtue, and
She said thou wast my daughter; and thy father
Was Duke of Milan; and his only heir
And princess, no worse issued.

MIRANDA   O the heavens!
What foul play had we, that we came from thence?
Or blessed was't we did?

---

wrack wreck
virtue essence
soul Prospero is about to say something like
"lost," but changes the direction of his sentence.
perdition loss
Betid happened

bootless inquisition fruitless inquiry
Out fully
an assurance . . . warrants a certainty my
memory guarantees
backward . . . time dark abyss of time past
piece perfect specimen

PROSPERO   Both, both, my girl:
  By foul play, as thou say'st, were we heaved thence,
  But blessedly holp° hither.
MIRANDA   O, my heart bleeds
  To think o' the teen° that I have turned you to,
  Which is from° my remembrance! Please you, farther.
PROSPERO   My brother, and thy uncle, called Antonio,—
  I pray thee, mark me, that a brother should
  Be so perfidious!—he whom next thyself
  Of all the world I loved, and to him put
70 The manage of my state; as at that time
  Through all the signories it was the first,
  And Prospero the prime duke, being so reputed
  In dignity, and for the liberal Arts
  Without a parallel; those being all my study,
  The government I cast upon my brother,
  And to my state grew stranger, being transported
  And rapt in secret studies° thy false uncle—
  Dost thou attend me?
MIRANDA   Sir, most heedfully.
PROSPERO   Being once perfected how to grant suits,
80 How to deny them, who to advance, and who
  To trash for over-topping,° new created
  The creatures that were mine, I say, or changed 'em,
  Or else new formed 'em; having both the key
  Of officer and office, set all hearts i' the state
  To what tune pleased his ear;° that now he was
  The ivy which had hid my princely trunk,
  And sucked my verdure out on it.° Thou attend'st not?
MIRANDA   O, good sir, I do.
PROSPERO   I pray thee, mark me.
  I, thus neglecting worldly ends, all dedicated
90 To closeness and the bettering of my mind
  With that which, but by being so retired,
  O'er-prized all popular rate, in my false brother
  Awaked an evil nature; and my trust,
  Like a good parent, did beget of him
  A falsehood in its contrary, as great

holp helped
teen trouble
from absent from
My brother . . . studies (ll. 66–77) Prospero
loses the thread of this speech, which may be
summarized: My brother Antonio—note his
amazing treachery—the person I loved best in
the world except for you, so that I entrusted
him with the management of my estate, which
was the chief one in North Italy and I the
senior duke by virtue of my position and my
learning . . . to this brother I delegated the
government, caring not for my dukedom but
for my studies.

trash for over-topping keep in check for being
over-bold; "trash" means a cord used in training hounds
set . . . ear The musical image grows out of
the word key.
Being . . . on it (ll. 79–87) having mastered
the art of dealing with suitors, advancing some,
disappointing others, so arranging things that
those already in office by my favor became
his dependents—having got the measure of all
the jobs and the men who did them, he ran
the state exactly as he pleased; he was to me
as ivy to the noble oak, concealing and enfeebling it

As my trust was; which had indeed no limit,
A confidence sans bound.° He being thus lorded,°
Not only with what my revénue yielded,
But what my power might else exact,° like one
100 Who having into° truth, by telling of it,°
Made such a sinner of his memory,
To credit his own lie, he did believe
He was indeed the duke; out o' the substitution,
And executing the outward face of royalty,
With all prerogative;°—hence his ambition growing,—
Dost thou hear?

MIRANDA   Your tale, sir, would cure deafness.

PROSPERO   To have no screen between this part he played
And him he played it for,° he needs will be
Absolute Milan.° Me, poor man, my library
110 Was dukedom large enough: of temporal° royalties
He thinks me now incapable; confederates,
So dry° he was for sway, wi' the King of Naples
To give him annual tribute, do him homage,
Subject his coronet to his crown, and bend
The dukedom, yet unbowed,—alas, poor Milan!—
To most ignoble stooping.

MIRANDA   O the heavens!

PROSPERO   Mark his condition,° and the event;° then tell me
If this might be a brother.

MIRANDA   I should sin
To think but nobly of my grandmother:
Good wombs have borne bad sons.

120 PROSPERO   Now the condition.
This King of Naples, being an enemy
To me inveterate, hearkens my brother's suit;
Which was, that he, in lieu o' the premises°
Of homage and I know not how much tribute,
Should presently° extirpate me and mine
Out of the dukedom, and confer fair Milan,
With all the honours, on my brother: whereon,
A treacherous army levied, one midnight
Fated to the purpose, did Antonio open

I . . . sans bound (ll. 89–97) the fact of my
retirement, in which I neglected wordly affairs
and gave myself to secret studies of a kind
beyond the understanding and esteem of the
people, brought out a bad side in my brother's
nature; consequently the great, indeed boundless, trust I placed in him gave rise on his part
to a disloyalty equally great, just as it can
happen that a virtuous father may have a
vicious son
lorded made a lord of
else exact otherwise extort
into unto
it i.e. his own lie

executing . . . prerogative carrying out the
public duties of royalty with full power
him . . . for i.e. himself
Absolute Milan Duke, not merely Duke's substitute
temporal worldly, as opposed to spiritual
dry thirsty
condition terms on which the deal with Naples
was concluded
event outcome
in lieu o' the premises in return for the undertaking
presently immediately

130
The gates of Milan; and, i' the dead of darkness,
The ministers° for the purpose hurried thence
Me and thy crying self.

MIRANDA   Alack, for pity!
I, not remembering how I cried out then,
Will cry it o'er again: it is a hint°
That wrings mine eyes to it.

PROSPERO   Hear a little further,
And then I'll bring thee to the present business
Which now's upon us; without the which, this story
Were most impertinent.°

MIRANDA   Wherefore did they not
That hour destroy us?

PROSPERO   Well demanded, wench:

140
My tale provokes that question. Dear, they durst not,
So dear the love my people bore me; nor set
A mark so bloody on the business; but
With colours fairer painted their foul ends.
In few,° they hurried us aboard a bark,
Bore us some leagues to sea; where they prepared
A rotten carcass of a butt,° not rigged,
Nor tackle, sail, nor mast; the very rats
Instinctively have quit it: there they hoist us,
To cry to the sea that roared to us; to sigh

150
To the winds, whose pity, sighing back again,
Did us but loving wrong.

MIRANDA   Alack, what trouble
Was I then to you!

PROSPERO   O, a cherubin
Thou wast that did preserve me. Thou didst smile,
Infusèd with a fortitude from heaven,
When I have decked° the sea with drops full salt,
Under my burthen groaned; which raised in me
An undergoing stomach,° to bear up
Against what should ensue.

MIRANDA   How came we ashore?

PROSPERO   By Providence divine.

160
Some food we had, and some fresh water, that
A noble Neapolitan, Gonzalo,
Out of his charity,° who being then appointed
Master of this design, did give us, with
Rich garments, linens, stuffs and necessaries,
Which since have steaded much;° so, of his gentleness,

---

ministers those employed
hint occasion
impertinent not to the purpose
In few to be brief
butt tub (contemptuous); a clumsy boat
decked adorned; note the intrusion here of an

artificial, conceited manner
undergoing stomach spirit of endurance
charity love, but in a wider sense than the
modern; see The English Bible section
steaded much stood us in good stead

Knowing I loved my books, he furnished me
From mine own library with volumes that
I prize above my dukedom.

MIRANDA   Would I might
But ever° see that man!

PROSPERO   Now I arise:
170   Sit still, and hear the last of our sea-sorrow.
Here in this island we arrived; and here
Have I, thy schoolmaster, made thee more profit
Than other princess'° can, that have more time
For vainer hours, and tutors not so careful.

MIRANDA   Heavens thank you for it! And now, I pray you, sir,
For still 'tis beating in my mind, your reason
For raising this sea-storm?

PROSPERO   Know thus far forth.
By accident most strange, bountiful Fortune
(Now my dear lady) hath mine enemies
180   Brought to this shore; and by my prescience°
I find my zenith doth depend upon
A most auspicious star,° whose influence
If now I court not, but omit, my fortunes
Will ever after droop. Here cease more questions:
Thou art inclined to sleep; 'tis a good dulness,
And give it way: I know thou canst not choose.

                                              MIRANDA *sleeps.*

Come away, servant, come. I am ready now.
Approach, my Ariel, come.

Enter ARIEL.

ARIEL   All hail, great master! grave sir, hail! I come
190   To answer thy best pleasure; be it to fly,
To swim, to dive into the fire, to ride
On the curled clouds, to thy strong bidding task
Ariel and all his quality.°

PROSPERO   Hast thou, spirit,
Performed to point° the tempest that I bade thee?

ARIEL   To every article.
I boarded the king's ship; now on the beak,°
Now in the waist,° the deck,° in every cabin,
I flamed amazement:° sometime I'd divide,
And burn in many places; on the topmast,
200   The yards and boresprit,° would I flame distinctly,

But ever only someday
princess' princesses
prescience foreknowledge
my zenith . . . star I am reaching the highest
point in my fortunes—my star is in its most
favorable aspect
quality attendant spirits

to point exactly
beak prow
waist amidships
deck poop
flamed amazement struck terror by appearing as
flames (as lightning and St. Elmo's fire)
boresprit bowsprit

Then meet and join. Jove's lightnings, the precursors
O' the dreadful thunder-claps, more momentary
And sight-outrunning were not: the fire and cracks
Of sulphurous roaring the most mighty Neptune
Seem to besiege, and make his bold waves tremble,
Yea, his dread trident shake.

PROSPERO   My brave spirit!
Who was so firm, so constant, that this coil°
Would not infect his reason?

ARIEL   Not a soul
But felt a fever of the mad, and played
210 Some tricks of desperation. All but mariners
Plunged in the foaming brine, and quit the vessel,
Then all afire with me: the King's son, Ferdinand,
With hair up-staring,°—then like reeds, not hair,—
Was the first man that leaped; cried, 'Hell is empty,
And all the devils are here.'

PROSPERO   Why, that's my spirit!
But was not this nigh shore?

ARIEL   Close by, my master.

PROSPERO   But are they, Ariel, safe?

ARIEL   Not a hair perished;
On their sustaining° garments not a blemish,
But fresher than before: and, as thou bad'st me.
220 In troops I have dispersed them 'bout the isle.
The King's son have I landed by himself;
Whom I left cooling of the air with sighs
In an odd angle° of the isle, and sitting,
His arms in this sad knot.°

PROSPERO   Of the King's ship,
The mariners, say how thou hast disposed,
And all the rest o' the fleet.

ARIEL   Safely in harbour
Is the King's ship; in the deep nook, where once
Thou call'dst me up at midnight to fetch dew
From the still-vexed Bermoothes,° there she's hid:
230 The mariners all under hatches stowed;
Who, with a charm joined to their suffered labour,°
I have left asleep: and for the rest o' the fleet,
Which I dispersed, they all have met again,
And are upon the Mediterranean flote,°
Bound sadly home for Naples;
Supposing that they saw the King's ship wracked,
And his great person perish.

coil turmoil
up-staring standing on end
sustaining upholding
angle corner

in . . . knot folded
still-vexed Bermoothes always stormy Bermudas
suffered labour the labor they have undergone
flote sea

PROSPERO   Ariel, thy charge
Exactly is performed: but there's more work.
What is the time o' the day?

ARIEL   Past the mid season.

240 PROSPERO   At least two glasses.° The time 'twixt six and now
Must by us both be spent most preciously.

ARIEL   Is there more toil? Since thou dost give me pains,
Let me remember thee what thou hast promised,
Which is not yet performed me.

PROSPERO   How now? moody?
What is it thou canst demand?

ARIEL   My liberty.

PROSPERO   Before the time be out? no more!

ARIEL   I prithee,
Remember I have done thee worthy service;
Told thee no lies, made no mistakings,° served
Without or° grudge or grumblings: thou didst promise
To bate° me a full year.

250 PROSPERO   Dost thou forget
From what a torment I did free thee?

ARIEL   No.

PROSPERO   Thou dost, and think'st it much to tread the ooze°
Of the salt deep,
To run upon the sharp wind of the north,
To do me business in the veins o' the earth°
When it is baked° with frost.

ARIEL   I do not, sir.

PROSPERO   Thou liest, malignant thing! Hast thou forgot
The foul witch Sycorax, who with age and envy°
Was grown into a hoop?° hast thou forgot her?

ARIEL   No, sir.

260 PROSPERO   Thou hast. Where was she born? speak; tell me.

ARIEL   Sir, in Argier.°

PROSPERO   O, was she so? I must
Once in a month recount what thou hast been,
Which thou forget'st. This damned witch Sycorax,
For mischiefs manifold, and sorceries terrible
To enter human hearing, from Argier,
Thou knowest, was banished: for one thing she did°
They would not take her life. Is not this true?

ARIEL   Ay, sir.

PROSPERO   This blue-eyed° hag was hither brought with child,

glasses hours; turns of the hourglass
made no mistakings F has *made thee no mistak-*
ings.
or either
bate let me off
ooze slimy bottom
veins o' the earth Contemporary cosmology
held that there were subterranean waters in the

earth like veins and arteries in the body.
baked hardened
envy malignity
grown into a hoop bent double
Argier Algiers
one thing she did some good service; or, being
with child
blue-eyed sign of exhaustion or pregnancy

270   And here was left by the sailors. Thou, my slave,
As thou report'st thyself, wast then her servant;
And, for° thou wast a spirit too delicate
To act her earthy° and abhorred commands,
Refusing her grand hests,° she did confine thee,
By help of her more potent ministers,°
And in her most unmitigable rage,
Into a cloven pine; within which rift
Imprisoned thou didst painfully remain
A dozen years; within which space she died,
280   And left thee there; where thou didst vent° thy groans
As fast as mill-wheels strike. Then was this island—
Save for the son that she did litter here,
A freckled whelp hag-born—not honoured with
A human shape.

ARIEL   Yes, Caliban her son.

PROSPERO   Dull thing, I say so; he, that Caliban,
Whom now I keep in service. Thou best knowest
What torment I did find thee in; thy groans
Did make wolves howl, and penetrate the breasts
Of ever-angry bears: it was a torment
290   To lay upon the damned, which Sycorax
Could not again undo: it was mine Art,
When I arrived and heard thee, that made gape
The pine, and let thee out.

ARIEL   I thank thee, master.

PROSPERO   If thou more murmur'st, I will rend an oak,
And peg thee in his knotty entrails, till
Thou hast howled away twelve winters.

ARIEL   Pardon, master:
I will be correspondent° to command,
And do my spriting gently.°

PROSPERO   Do so; and after two days
I will discharge thee.

ARIEL   That's my noble master!
300   What shall I do? say what; what shall I do?

PROSPERO   Go make thyself like a nymph o' the sea:
Be subject to
No sight but thine and mine; invisible
To every eyeball else. Go take this shape,
And hither come in it: go: hence
With diligence.   *Exit* ARIEL.
Awake, dear heart, awake! thou hast slept well;
Awake!

---

for because
earthy Sycorax and Caliban are associated with
earth, Ariel with air and fire.
hests commands

ministers demonic agents
vent utter
correspondent compliant
gently without complaint

MIRANDA   The strangeness of your story put
        Heaviness° in me.

PROSPERO   Shake it off. Come on;
310   We'll visit Caliban my slave, who never
        Yields us kind answer.

MIRANDA   'Tis a villain, sir,
        I do not love to look on.

PROSPERO   But, as 'tis,
        We cannot miss° him: he does make our fire,
        Fetch in our wood, and serves in offices°
        That profit us. What, ho! slave! Caliban!
        Thou earth, thou! speak.

CALIBAN   [*Within*] There's wood enough within.

PROSPERO   Come forth, I say! there's other business for thee;
        Come, thou tortoise! when?

    Re-enter ARIEL *like a water-nymph.*

        Fine apparition! My quaint° Ariel,
        Hark in thine ear.

320   ARIEL   My lord, it shall be done.   *Exit.*

PROSPERO   Thou poisonous slave, got by the devil himself°
        Upon thy wicked dam, come forth!

    Enter CALIBAN.

CALIBAN   As wicked° dew as e'er my mother brushed
        With raven's feather° from unwholesome fen
        Drop on you both! a south-west° blow on ye
        And blister you all o'er!

PROSPERO   For this, be sure, tonight thou shalt have cramps,
        Side-stitches that shall pen thy breath up; urchins°
        Shall for that vast of night that they may work,
330   All exercise on thee;° thou shalt be pinched
        As thick as honeycomb, each pinch more stinging
        Than bees that made 'em.°

CALIBAN   I must eat my dinner.
        This island's mine, by Sycorax my mother,
        Which thou tak'st from me. When thou camest first,
        Thou strok'st me, and made much of me; wouldst
           give me
        Water with berries° in it; and teach me how

Heaviness drowsiness
miss do without
offices services
quaint elegant, ingenious
got . . . himself Caliban was the result of a union between witch and devil.
wicked baneful
raven's feather The raven (*corax*) was a bird of ill-omen.

south-west the pestilence-bearing wind
urchins hedgehogs, goblins in the shape of hedgehogs
Shall for . . . thee shall, during the dead of night which is the period during which they are allowed to operate, all torment you
'em the cells of the honeycomb
berries The Bermudan castaways used berries to make drinks.

To name the bigger light, and how the less,°
That burn by day and night: and then I loved thee,
And showed thee all the qualities o' the isle,
340   The fresh springs, brine-pits, barren place and fertile:
Cursed be I that did so! All the charms
Of Sycorax, toads, beetles, bats,° light on you!
For I am all the subjects that you have,
Which first was mine own King: and here you sty me°
In this hard rock, whiles you do keep from me
The rest o' the island.

PROSPERO   Thou most lying slave,
Whom stripes° may move, not kindness! I have used thee,
Filth as thou art, with human care; and lodged thee
In mine own cell, till thou didst seek to violate
350   The honour of my child.

CALIBAN   O ho, O ho! would it had been done!
Thou didst prevent me; I had peopled else
This isle with Calibans.

MIRANDA   Abhorrèd slave,
Which any print° of goodness wilt not take,
Being capable of° all ill! I pitied thee,
Took pains to make thee speak, taught thee each hour
One thing or other: when thou didst not, savage,
Know thine own meaning, but wouldst gabble like
A thing most brutish, I endowed thy purposes
360   With words that made them known. But thy vile race,°
Though thou didst learn, had that in it which good natures
Could not abide to be with; therefore wast thou
Deservedly confined into this rock,
Who hadst deservèd more than a prison.

CALIBAN   You taught me language; and my profit on it
Is, I know how to curse. The red plague° rid° you
For learning me your language!

PROSPERO   Hag-seed, hence!
Fetch us in fuel; and be quick, thou 'rt best,
To answer other business.° Shrug'st thou, malice?°
370   If thou neglect'st, or dost unwillingly
What I command, I'll rack thee with old° cramps,
Fill all thy bones with achès, make thee roar,
That beasts shall tremble at thy din.

CALIBAN   No, 'pray thee.
[*Aside*] I must obey: his Art is of such power,

---

bigger light . . . less sun and moon; see
Genesis 1:16
toads, beetles, bats all associated with witches
sty me keep me pent up
stripes lashes
print impression
capable of apt to receive the impression of
race hereditary nature; contrasted with the
"good natures" of the next line

red plague bubonic plague; called after the
color of the sores
rid destroy
thou'rt . . . business it will be best for you
to do the jobs assigned you
malice malicious thing
old severe

It would control° my dam's god, Setebos,°
And make a vassal of him.

PROSPERO   So, slave; hence!   *Exit* CALIBAN.

Re-enter ARIEL, *invisible, playing and singing;* FERDINAND *following.*

ARIEL'S SONG

> *Come unto these yellow sands,*
>   *And then take hands:*
> *Courtsied when you have and kissed*
380   *The wild waves whist:°*
> *Foot it featly° here and there,*
>   *And sweet sprites bear*
> *The burthen. Hark, hark.*

Burthen° dispersedly.° *Bow-wow.*
ARIEL   *The watch dogs bark:*

Burthen dispersedly. *Bow-wow.*

ARIEL   *Hark, hark! I hear*
> *The strain of strutting chanticleer*

Cry—Burthen dispersedly. *Cock a diddle dow.*

390 FERDINAND   Where should this music be? i' the air or the earth?
It sounds no more: and, sure, it waits upon°
Some god o' the island. Sitting on a bank,
Weeping again° the King my father's wrack,
This music crept by me upon the waters,
Allaying both their fury and my passion
With its sweet air: thence° I have followed it,
Or it hath drawn me rather. But 'tis gone.
No, it begins again.

ARIEL *sings.*

> *Full fadom° five thy father lies;*
400 >   *Of his bones are coral made;*
> *Those are pearls that were his eyes:*
>   *Nothing of him that doth fade,*
> *But doth suffer a sea-change*
> *Into something rich and strange.°*
> *Sea-nymphs hourly ring his knell:*

> Burthen: *Ding-dong.*

ARIEL   *Hark! now I hear them,—Ding-dong, bell.*

control overcome
Setebos Patagonian god mentioned by a travel
writer
Courtsied . . . whist either "when you have
curtsied to and kissed your partner, the sea
remaining quiet," or, "when you have curtsied
and kissed the sea into silence"
featly gracefully
Burthen refrain

dispersedly not in unison
waits upon attends
again indicates intensity as well as repetition
thence from the water's edge
fadom fathom
Nothing . . . strange Every part of his body
that is otherwise doomed to decay is transformed into some rich or rare sea-substance.

Ding Dong Ding Dong   Bell   Ding   Dong Ding Dong   Bell.

This setting of "Full Fadom Five", like that of "Where the Bee Sucks" in Act V
(for voice and unfigured bass line), is by Robert Johnson (1583?–1633), a composer
known for his music for plays and masques. These settings may well have been written
for the first production, although they were first published in an arrangement for three
voices in John Wilson's *Cheerful Airs* (1659). The unfigured bass simply gave the lowest
musical line; the songs could be sung as given, with a bass viol accompaniment, or
with a lute (filling in other lines and chords), or by a group of instruments (this is a
little like the modern practice of printing a popular song with guitar chords). In "Full
Fadom Five" there is a fugue-like imitation in the voice and bass parts, and we can be
certain that other instruments took up the melody as well. The effect of the whole
would be that of chiming bells.

FERDINAND   The ditty° does remember° my drowned father.
　　　　This is no mortal business, nor no sound
410　　　That the earth owes:°—I hear it now above me.
PROSPERO   The fringèd curtains of thine eye advance,°
　　　　And say what thou seest yond.
MIRANDA 　　　　　　　　　　　What is it? a spirit?
　　　　Lord, how it looks about! Believe me, sir,
　　　　It carries a brave° form. But 'tis a spirit.
PROSPERO   No, wench; it eats and sleeps and hath such senses
　　　　As we have, such. This gallant which thou seest
　　　　Was in the wrack; and, but° he's something stained
　　　　With grief (that's beauty's canker°) thou mightst call him
　　　　A goodly person: he hath lost his fellows,
　　　　And strays about to find 'em.
420　MIRANDA 　　　　　　　　　I might call him
　　　　A thing divine; for nothing natural°
　　　　I ever saw so noble.
PROSPERO 　　　　[*Aside*] It goes on,° I see,
　　　　As my soul prompts it. Spirit, fine spirit! I'll free thee
　　　　Within two days for this.
FERDINAND 　　　　　　　　Most sure the goddess°
　　　　On whom these airs attend! Vouchsafe my prayer

ditty words of the song
remember commemorate
owes owns
fringèd curtains . . . advance eyelids . . . lift
up
brave splendid
but except that
canker disease of roses

natural in the realm of nature as opposed to
spirit
It goes on my plan (that Miranda should love
Ferdinand) is working out
Most sure the goddess virtually a translation
of Virgil's *O dea certe, Aeneid* I.328, often used
in romance; Miranda's response (ll. 430–31)
is also modeled on the passage

May know if you remain upon this island;
And that you will some good instruction give
How I may bear me° here: my prime° request,
Which I do last pronounce, is, O you wonder!°
If you be maid or no?

430 MIRANDA   No wonder, sir;
But certainly a maid.

FERDINAND   My language! heavens!
I am the best of them that speak this speech,
Were I but where 'tis spoken.

PROSPERO   How? the best?
What wert thou, if the King of Naples heard thee?

FERDINAND   A single° thing, as I am now, that wonders
To hear thee speak of Naples. He does hear me;
And that he does I weep: myself am Naples,°
Who with mine eyes, never since at ebb, beheld
The King my father wracked.

MIRANDA   Alack, for mercy!

440 FERDINAND   Yes, faith, and all his lords; the Duke of Milan
And his brave° son being twain.

PROSPERO   [Aside] The Duke of Milan
And his more braver daughter could control° thee,
If now 'twere fit to do it. At the first sight
They have changed eyes.° Delicate Ariel,
I'll set thee free for this. [To FERDINAND] A word, good sir;
I fear you have done yourself some wrong:° a word.

MIRANDA   Why speaks my father so ungently? This
Is the third man° that e'er I saw; the first
That e'er I sighed for: pity move my father
To be inclined my way!°

450 FERDINAND   O, if a virgin,
And your affection not gone forth, I'll make you
The Queen of Naples.

PROSPERO   Soft, sir! one word more.
[Aside] They are both in either's powers: but this swift business
I must uneasy make, lest too light winning°
Make the prize light.° [To FERDINAND] One word more; I charge thee
That thou attend me: thou dost here usurp
The name thou ow'st° not; and hast put thyself
Upon this island as a spy, to win it
From me, the lord on it.

bear me conduct myself
prime most important
wonder a play on Miranda's name, which
Ferdinand doesn't yet know
single solitary
myself am Naples Ferdinand thinks his father
is dead and that he himself is King of Naples.
brave gallant. There is no further mention of
Antonio's son in the play and this may be a
slip.

control confute
changed eyes fallen in love
you have done yourself some wrong ironically
polite way of saying "You're mistaken"
third man the others are Prospero and Caliban
inclined my way persuaded to my wishes
light winning easy success
light undervalued
ow'st ownest

FERDINAND   No, as I am a man.
460 MIRANDA   There's nothing ill can dwell in such a temple:°
         If the ill spirit have so fair a house,
         Good things will strive to dwell with it.°
PROSPERO   Follow me.
         Speak not you for him: he's a traitor. Come;
         I'll manacle thy neck and feet together:
         Sea-water shalt thou drink; thy food shall be
         The fresh-brook mussels, withered roots, and husks
         Wherein the acorn cradled. Follow.
FERDINAND   No;
         I will resist such entertainment° till
         Mine enemy has more power.

                    He draws, and is charmed from moving.

MIRANDA   O dear father,
470   Make not too rash a trial of him, for
         He's gentle, and not fearful.°
PROSPERO   What! I say,
         My foot my tutor?° Put thy sword up, traitor;
         Who mak'st a show, but dar'st not strike, thy conscience
         Is so possessed with guilt: come from thy ward;°
         For I can here disarm thee with this stick°
         And make thy weapon drop.
MIRANDA   Beseech you, father.
PROSPERO   Hence! hang not on my garments.
MIRANDA   Sir, have pity;
         I'll be his surety.
PROSPERO   Silence! one word more
         Shall make me chide thee, if not hate thee. What!
480   An advocate for an impostor! hush!
         Thou think'st there is° no more such shapes as he,
         Having seen but him and Caliban: foolish wench!
         To° the most of men this is a Caliban,
         And they to him are angels.
MIRANDA   My affections°
         Are then most humble; I have no ambition
         To see a goodlier° man.
PROSPERO   Come on; obey:
         Thy nerves° are in their infancy again,
         And have no vigour in them.

There's nothing . . . temple Conventional neoplatonic doctrine—that the beautiful body
houses a beautiful soul—is expressed by
Miranda though qualified by Prospero later;
but for the same reason Caliban and Sycorax
are ugly.
Good things . . . with it suggesting that this is
absurd
entertainment hospitality (ironical)
gentle . . . fearful high-born and not cowardly
My foot my tutor? shall you, so much my

inferior, presume to instruct me? (Prospero
thinks of himself as the head)
come from thy ward abandon your posture of
defense
stick magic staff
is are
To in comparison with
affections feelings
goodlier more handsome
nerves sinews

FERDINAND   So they are:
My spirits,° as in a dream, are all bound up.
My father's loss, the weakness which I feel,
The wrack of all my friends, nor° this man's threats,
To whom I am subdued, are° but light to me,
Might I but through my prison once a day
Behold this maid: all corners else o' the earth
Let liberty make use of;° space enough
Have I in such a prison.

PROSPERO   [*Aside*] It works. [*To* FERDINAND] Come on.
[*To* ARIEL] Thou hast done well, fine Ariel! Follow me;
Hark what thou else shalt do me.

MIRANDA   Be of comfort;
My father's of a better nature, sir,
Than he appears by speech: this is unwonted°
Which now came from him.

PROSPERO   Thou shalt be as free
As mountain winds: but then exactly do
All points of my command.

ARIEL   To the syllable.

PROSPERO   Come, follow. Speak not for him.   *Exeunt.*

ACT II

SCENE I [*Another part of the Island.*]

Enter ALONSO, SEBASTIAN, ANTONIO, GONZALO, ADRIAN, FRANCISCO, *and others.*

GONZALO   Beseech you, sir, be merry; you have cause,
So have we all, of joy; for our escape
Is much beyond our loss. Our hint of° woe
Is common; every day, some sailor's wife,
The masters of some merchant,° and the merchant,°
Have just our theme of woe; but for the miracle,
I mean our preservation, few in millions
Can speak like us: then wisely, good sir, weigh
Our sorrow with our comfort.

ALONZO   Prithee, peace.

SEBASTIAN [*Aside to* ANTONIO]   He receives comfort like cold porridge.°

ANTONIO [*Aside to* SEBASTIAN]   The visitor° will not give him o'er° so.

---

spirits energies; animal spirits, which convey nourishment and so strength to the body
nor Grammar confused; it would be clear if this were *and*.
are Read *would be*.
all corners . . . use of those who are free may have all the rest of the world; my prison, if I could see Miranda, would be all the space I needed

unwonted unaccustomed
hint of occasion for
some merchant some merchant vessel
merchant owner of the vessel
porridge made of pease; so there is a pun on Alonso's word, "peace"
visitor one who comforts the infirm
give him o'er cease to administer his advice

SEBASTIAN [*Aside to* ANTONIO]   Look, he's winding up the watch of his wit; by
    and by it will strike.°
GONZALO   Sir,—
SEBASTIAN [*Aside to* ANTONIO]   One: tell.°
GONZALO   When every grief is entertained that's offered,
    Comes to the entertainer°—
SEBASTIAN   A dollar.°
GONZALO   Dolour comes to him, indeed: you have spoken truer than you pur-
20   posed.
SEBASTIAN   You have taken it wiselier° than I meant you should.
GONZALO   Therefore, my lord,—
ANTONIO   Fie, what a spendthrift is he of his tongue!
ALONZO   I prithee, spare.°
GONZALO   Well, I have done: but yet,—
SEBASTIAN   He will be talking.
ANTONIO   Which, of he or Adrian, for a good wager, first begins to crow?
SEBASTIAN   The old cock.
30 ANTONIO   The cockerel.°
SEBASTIAN   Done. The wager?
ANTONIO   A laughter.°
SEBASTIAN   A match!
ADRIAN   Though this island seem to be desert,—
ANTONIO   Ha, ha, ha!
SEBASTIAN   So: you're paid.°
ADRIAN   Uninhabitable, and almost inaccessible,—
SEBASTIAN   Yet,—
40 ANTONIO   He could not miss it.
ADRIAN   It must needs be of subtle, tender and delicate temperance.°
ANTONIO   Temperance° was a delicate wench.
SEBASTIAN   Ay, and a subtle; as he most learnedly delivered.
ADRIAN   The air breathes upon us here most sweetly.
SEBASTIAN   As if it had lungs, and rotten ones.
ANTONIO   Or as 'twere perfumed by a fen.
GONZALO   Here is everything advantageous to life.
ANTONIO   True; save means to live.
50 SEBASTIAN   Of that there's none, or little.
GONZALO   How lush and lusty° the grass looks! how green!
ANTONIO   The ground, indeed, is tawny.°
SEBASTIAN   With an eye of green° in it.
ANTONIO   He misses not much.

---

strike Striking or "repeating" watches were
invented about 1510.
tell count
When . . . entertainer he who makes a point
of accepting every occasion for grief that presents itself gets—
dollar sum of money (punning on the word
Gonzalo speaks next)
wiselier more cleverly, more sagely
spare your words

cockerel i.e. Adrian
A laughter The winner is to have the right to
laugh at the loser.
paid Antonio has had his laugh; in F Sebastian
is given l. 35, Antonio l. 36.
temperance climate
Temperance a (Puritan) woman's name
lush and lusty fresh and luxuriant
tawny parched brown
eye of green having green patches

SEBASTIAN   No; he doth but mistake° the truth totally.

GONZALO   But the rarity of it is,—which is indeed almost beyond credit,°—

SEBASTIAN   As many vouched rarities° are.

GONZALO   That our garments, being, as they were, drenched in the sea, hold, notwithstanding, their freshness and glosses, being rather new-dyed than stained with salt water.

ANTONIO   If but one of his pockets could speak, would it not say he lies?

SEBASTIAN   Ay, or very falsely pocket up° his report.

GONZALO   Methinks our garments are now as fresh as when we put them on first in Afric, at the marriage of the King's fair daughter Claribel to the King of Tunis.

SEBASTIAN   'Twas a sweet marriage, and we prosper well° in our return.

ADRIAN   Tunis was never graced before with such a paragon to their Queen.

GONZALO   Not since widow Dido's° time.

ANTONIO   Widow! a pox o' that! How came that widow in? widow Dido!

SEBASTIAN   What if he had said 'widower Æneas'° too? Good Lord, how you take it!

ADRIAN   'Widow Dido' said you? you make me study of that:° she was of Carthage, not of Tunis.°

GONZALO   This Tunis, sir, was Carthage.

ADRIAN   Carthage?

GONZALO   I assure you, Carthage.

ANTONIO   His word is more than the miraculous harp.°

SEBASTIAN   He hath raised the wall, and houses too.

ANTONIO   What impossible matter will he make easy next?

SEBASTIAN   I think he will carry this island home in his pocket, and give it his son for an apple.

ANTONIO   And, sowing the kernels of it in the sea, bring forth more islands.

GONZALO   Ay.°

ANTONIO   Why, in good time.

GONZALO   Sir,° we were talking that our garments seem now as fresh as when we were at Tunis at the marriage of your daughter, who is now Queen.

ANTONIO   And the rarest that e'er came there.

SEBASTIAN   Bate,° I beseech you, widow Dido.

ANTONIO   O, widow Dido! ay, widow Dido.

GONZALO   Is not, sir, my doublet as fresh as the first day I wore it? I mean, in a sort.°

---

mistake punning on *miss* in previous line
credit belief
vouched rarities strange travelers' tales, vouched for by the teller
pocket up conceal (referring to the remark about Gonzalo's pocket, which could act as mouthpiece for the suit and tell a different story)
we prosper well ironical, of course
widow Dido's She was the widow of Sychaeus when she met Aeneas, but the expression is found ridiculous.
widower Æneas Aeneas was a widower just as Dido was a widow—why not mention that, too?

study of that give some thought to that
Tunis The site of the ancient Carthage was near to, but not identical with, that of modern Tunis; so Gonzalo is wrong.
more . . . harp Only the *walls* of Thebes rose to the music of Amphion's harp, whereas Gonzalo, by identifying Carthage and Tunis, fabricates a whole city.
Ay Gonzalo reaffirms his position on Tunis and Carthage (F has *I*).
Sir he addresses the King
Bate make an exception of
sort up to a point

100   ANTONIO   That sort was well fished for.°
    GONZALO   When I wore it at your daughter's marriage?
    ALONSO   You cram these words into mine ears against
        The stomach of my sense.° Would I had never
        Married my daughter there! for, coming thence,
        My son is lost, and, in my rate,° she too,
        Who is so far from Italy removed
        I ne'er again shall see her. O thou mine heir
        Of Naples and of Milan, what strange fish
        Hath made his meal on thee?
    FRANCISCO   Sir, he may live:
110   I saw him beat the surges° under him,
        And ride upon their backs; he trod the water,
        Whose enmity he flung aside, and breasted
        The surge most swoln that met him; his bold head
        'Bove the contentious waves he kept, and oared
        Himself with his good arms in lusty stroke
        To the shore, that o'er his wave-worn basis° bowed,
        As stooping to relieve him: I not doubt
        He came alive to land.
    ALONSO   No, no, he's gone.
    SEBASTIAN   Sir, you may thank yourself for this great loss,
120   That would not bless our Europe with your daughter,
        But rather loose° her to an African;
        Where she, at least, is banished from your eye,
        Who hath cause to wet the grief on it.°
    ALONSO   Prithee, peace.
    SEBASTIAN   You were kneeled to, and importuned otherwise,
        By all of us; and the fair soul herself
        Weighed° between loathness° and obedience, at
        Which end o' the beam should bow. We have lost your son,
        I fear, for ever: Milan and Naples have
        Mo° widows in them of this business' making
130   Than we bring men to comfort them:
        The fault's your own.
    ALONSO   So is the dearest° o' the loss.
    GONZALO   My lord Sebastian,
        The truth you speak doth lack some gentleness,
        And time° to speak it in: you rub the sore,
        When you should bring the plaster.°
    SEBASTIAN   Very well.

That . . . for the word "sort" was a lucky
catch, and saved Gonzalo from an outright lie
stomach of my sense The King compares Gonzalo's persistence in plying him with consolations to that of a man who forces food on a
reluctant recipient.
rate estimation
surges waves
basis base

loose mate (contemptuous)
Who . . . on it obscure: probably "weep for
the grief her loss has caused you"
Weighed balanced
loathness reluctance
Mo more
dearest bitterest
time appropriate time
plaster dressing

ANTONIO   And most chirurgeonly.°
GONZALO   It is foul weather in us all, good sir,
When you are cloudy.
SEBASTIAN   Foul° weather?
ANTONIO   Very foul.
GONZALO   Had I plantation° of this isle, my lord,—
ANTONIO   He'd sow it with nettle-seed.
140 SEBASTIAN   Or docks, or mallows.°
GONZALO   And were the King on it, what would I do?
SEBASTIAN   'Scape being drunk for want of wine.
GONZALO   I' the commonwealth° I would by contraries°
Execute all things; for no kind of traffic°
Would I admit; no name of magistrate;
Letters° should not be known; riches, poverty,
And use of service,° none; contract, succession,°
Bourn,° bound of land, tilth,° vineyard, none;
No use of metal, corn, or wine, or oil;
150 No occupation;° all men idle, all;
And women too, but innocent and pure:
No sovereignty;—
SEBASTIAN   Yet he would be King on it.
ANTONIO   The latter end of his commonwealth forgets the beginning.
GONZALO   All things in common° Nature should produce
Without sweat or endeavour: treason, felony,
Sword, pike, knife, gun, or need of any engine,°
Would I not have; but Nature should bring forth,
Of its own kind, all foison,° all abundance,
160 To feed my innocent people.
SEBASTIAN   No marrying 'mong his subjects?
ANTONIO   None, man; all idle; whores and knaves.
GONZALO   I would with such perfection govern, sir,
To excel the Golden Age.
SEBASTIAN   'Save his Majesty!
ANTONIO   Long live Gonzalo!
GONZALO   And,—do you mark me, sir?
ALONSO   Prithee, no more: thou dost talk nothing° to me.
GONZALO   I do well believe your highness; and did it to minister occasion° to
these gentlemen, who are of such sensible° and nimble lungs that they
170 always use to laugh at nothing.

chirurgeonly surgeon-like
Foul The point of this exchange is lost—perhaps
Sebastian looks mockingly at the fineness of
the weather.
plantation colonization; Antonio takes it in the
other sense of "planting"
nettle-seed . . . docks . . . mallows common
English weeds
commonwealth The passage that follows is based
on Montaigne's essay "Of Cannibals" as translated by John Florio.
by contraries doing the opposite of what is
usually done

traffic trade
Letters literacy
use of service the employment of servants
succession inheritance of property
Bourn boundry
tilth tillage
occupation working at a trade
in common for ownership
engine military weapon
foison abundance
nothing empty nonsense
minister occasion afford opportunity
sensible sensitive

ANTONIO 'Twas you we laughed at.

GONZALO Who in this kind of merry fooling am nothing to you: so you may continue, and laugh at nothing still.

ANTONIO What a blow was there given!

SEBASTIAN An it had not fallen flat-long.°

GONZALO You are gentlemen of brave mettle;° you would lift the moon out of her sphere, if she would continue in it five weeks without changing.°

Enter ARIEL *(invisible) playing solemn music.*

180 SEBASTIAN We would so, and then go a-batfowling.°

ANTONIO Nay, good my lord, be not angry.

GONZALO No, I warrant you; I will not adventure° my discretion so weakly. Will you laugh me asleep, for I am very heavy?°

ANTONIO Go sleep, and hear us.°

All sleep except ALONSO, SEBASTIAN, *and* ANTONIO

ALONSO What, all so soon asleep! I wish mine eyes
Would, with themselves, shut up my thoughts: I find
They are inclined to do so.

SEBASTIAN   Please you, sir,
Do not omit° the heavy offer of it:
190 It seldom visits sorrow; when it doth,
It is a comforter.

ANTONIO   We two, my lord,
Will guard your person while you take your rest,
And watch your safety.

ALONSO   Thank you.—Wondrous heavy.

ALONSO *sleeps. Exit* ARIEL.

SEBASTIAN What a strange drowsiness possesses them!

ANTONIO It is the quality° o' the climate.

SEBASTIAN   Why
Doth it not then our eyelids sink? I find not
Myself disposed to sleep.

ANTONIO   Nor I; my spirits are nimble.
They fell together all, as by consent;
They dropped, as by a thunder-stroke. What might,
200 Worthy Sebastian?—O, what might?—No more:—
And yet methinks I see it in thy face,
What thou shouldst be: the occasion speaks° thee; and
My strong imagination sees a crown
Dropping upon thy head.

SEBASTIAN   What, art thou waking?°

ANTONIO Do you not hear me speak?

flat-long with the flat of the sword	**adventure** risk
brave mettle fine spirit	**heavy** drowsy
you would lift . . . changing you'd have the moon out of the heavens if she'd stay still a little longer	**hear us** hear us laughing
	omit neglect
a-batfowling hunting birds with a light (in this case, the moon), toward which they fly and are beaten down with clubs	**quality** characteristic
	occasion speaks opportunity invites
	waking awake

972   WILLIAM SHAKESPEARE

SEBASTIAN   I do; and surely
    It is a sleepy language, and thou speak'st
    Out of thy sleep. What is it thou didst say?
    This is a strange repose, to be asleep
    With eyes wide open; standing, speaking, moving,
    And yet so fast asleep.
210 ANTONIO   Noble Sebastian,
    Thou let'st thy fortune sleep—die, rather; wink'st°
    Whiles thou art waking.
SEBASTIAN   Thou dost snore distinctly;
    There's meaning in thy snores.
ANTONIO   I am more serious than my custom: you
    Must be so too, if heed me; which to do
    Trebles thee o'er.°
SEBASTIAN   Well, I am standing water.°
ANTONIO   I'll teach you how to flow.°
SEBASTIAN   Do so: to ebb
    Hereditary sloth instructs me.
ANTONIO   O,
    If you but knew how you the purpose cherish°
220   Whiles thus you mock it! how, in stripping it,
    You more invest it!° Ebbing men, indeed,
    Most often do so near the bottom run
    By their own fear of sloth.
SEBASTIAN   Prithee, say on:
    The setting of thine eye and cheek° proclaim
    A matter° from thee; and a birth, indeed,
    Which throes° thee much to yield.
ANTONIO   Thus, sir:
    Although this lord of weak remembrance,° this,
    Who shall be of as little memory
    When he is earthed,° hath here almost persuaded,—
230   For he's a spirit of persuasion, only
    Professes to persuade,°—the King his son's alive,
    'Tis is as impossible that he's undrowned
    As he that sleeps here swims.
SEBASTIAN   I have no hope°
    That he's undrowned.
ANTONIO   O, out of that 'no hope'
    What great hope have you! no hope that way is
    Another way so high a hope, that even

wink'st closest thine eyes
Trebles thee o'er triples thy greatness
standing water slack water between tides
flow continuing the tide figure—flow rather
than ebb
cherish value, enhance
invest it clothe it (while you think that by
playing it cool you're stripping or minimizing it)
setting . . . cheek serious look on your face

A matter something of weight
throes gives pain
weak remembrance poor memory
Who shall . . . earthed who will himself be
unremembered when he is buried
Professes to persuade makes a profession of
persuasion
hope expectation. Antonio takes it in a more
modern sense.

Ambition cannot pierce a wink beyond,
But doubt discovery there.° Will you grant with me
That Ferdinand is drowned?

SEBASTIAN   He's gone.

ANTONIO   Then tell me,
Who's the next heir of Naples?

240   SEBASTIAN   Claribel.

ANTONIO   She that is Queen of Tunis; she that dwells
Ten leagues beyond man's life;° she that from Naples
Can have no note,° unless the sun were post,°—
The man i' the moon's too slow,—till new-born chins
Be rough and razorable; she that from whom°
We all were sea-swallowed, though some cast° again,
And by that destiny to perform an act
Whereof what's past is prologue; what to come,
In yours and my discharge.°

SEBASTIAN   What stuff is this! how say you?

250   'Tis true, my brother's daughter's Queen of Tunis;
So is she heir of Naples; 'twixt which regions
There is some space.

ANTONIO   A space whose every cubit°
Seems to cry out, 'How shall that Claribel
Measure us° back to Naples? Keep in Tunis,
And let Sebastian wake.' Say this were death
That now hath seized them;° why, they were no worse
Than now they are. There be that can rule Naples
As well as he that sleeps; lords that can prate
As amply and unnecessarily

260   As this Gonzalo; I myself could make
A chough of as deep chat.° O, that you bore°
The mind that I do! what a sleep were this
For your advancement! Do you understand me?

SEBASTIAN   Methinks I do.

ANTONIO   And how does your content
Tender° your own good fortune?

SEBASTIAN   I remember
You did supplant your brother Prospero.

ANTONIO   True:
And look how well my garments sit upon me;
Much feater° than before: my brother's servants

Were then my fellows; now they are my men.
270 SEBASTIAN   But for your conscience.
ANTONIO   Ay, sir; where lies that? if 'twere a kibe,°
      'Twould put me to my slipper:° but I feel not
      This deity in my bosom: twenty consciences,
      That stand 'twixt me and Milan, candied° be they,
      And melt, ere they molest! Here lies your brother,
      No better than the earth he lies upon,
      If he were that which now he's like, that's dead;
      Whom I, with this obedient steel, three inches of it,
      Can lay to bed for ever; whiles you, doing thus,
280   To the perpetual wink° for aye might put
      This ancient morsel,° this Sir Prudence, who
      Should not upbraid our course. For all the rest,
      They'll take suggestion° as a cat laps milk;
      They'll tell the clock to any business that
      We say befits the hour.°
SEBASTIAN   Thy, case, dear friend,
      Shall be my precedent; as thou got'st Milan,
      I'll come by Naples. Draw thy sword: one stroke
      Shall free thee from the tribute which thou payest;
      And I the King shall love thee.
ANTONIO   Draw together;
290   And when I rear my hand, do you the like,
      To fall it° on Gonzalo.
SEBASTIAN   O, but one word.   *They talk apart.*

Re-enter ARIEL *invisible, with music and song.*

ARIEL   My master through his Art foresees the danger
      That you, his friend,° are in; and sends me forth,—
      For else his project dies,—to keep them living.

                                        Sings in GONZALO's *ear.*

          While you here do snoring lie,
          Open-eyed conspiracy
             His time doth take.
          If of life you keep a care,
          Shake off slumber, and beware:
300   *Awake, Awake!*

ANTONIO   Then let us both be sudden.°
GONZALO [*Waking*]   Now, good angels
      Preserve the King!   *The others wake.*
ALONSO   Why, how now? ho; awake?—Why are you drawn?

kibe sore, usually on the heel
put in slipper force me to wear a slipper
candied frozen solid
perpetual wink everlasting sleep
ancient morsel Gonzalo
suggestion prompting

tell . . . hour pretend that whatever we propose is opportune
fall it let it fall
friend Gonzalo
sudden prompt in action

Wherefore this ghastly looking?

GONZALO   What's the matter?

SEBASTIAN   Whiles we stood here securing your repose,
      Even now, we heard a hollow burst of bellowing
      Like bulls, or rather lions: did it not wake you?
      It struck mine ear most terribly.

ALONSO   I heard nothing.

ANTONIO   O, 'twas a din to fright a monster's ear,
310   To make an earthquake! sure, it was the roar
      Of a whole herd of lions.

ALONSO   Heard you this, Gonzalo?

GONZALO   Upon mine honour, sir, I heard a humming,°
      And that a strange one too, which did awake me:
      I shaked you, sir, and cried: as mine eyes opened,
      I saw their weapons drawn:—there was a noise,
      That's verily.° 'Tis best we stand upon our guard,
      Or that we quit this place: let's draw our weapons.

ALONSO   Lead off this ground; and let's make further search
      For my poor son.

GONZALO   Heavens keep him from these beasts!
      For he is, sure, i' the island.

320   ALONSO   Lead away.

ARIEL   Prospero my lord shall know what I have done:
      So, King, go safely on to seek thy son.   *Exeunt.*

SCENE II [*Another part of the Island.*]

Enter CALIBAN *with a burthen of wood. A noise of thunder heard.*

CALIBAN   All the infections that the sun sucks up°
      From bogs, fens, flats, on Prosper fall, and make him
      By inch-meal° a disease! his spirits hear me,
      And yet I needs must curse. But they'll nor pinch,
      Fright me with urchin-shows,° pitch me i' the mire,
      Nor lead me, like a firebrand,° in the dark
      Out of my way, unless he bid 'em: but
      For every trifle are they set upon me;
      Sometime like apes, that mow° and chatter at me,
10   And after bite me; then like hedgehogs, which
      Lie tumbling in my barefoot way, and mount
      Their pricks° at my footfall; sometime am I
      All wound° with adders, who with cloven tongues
      Do hiss me into madness.

humming he heard Ariel's song
verily (to speak) truly
sucks up Disease-bearing mists were thought
to be sucked from bogs and fens by the sun.
inch-meal inch by inch

urchin-shows apparitions of goblins
firebrand will-o'-the-wisp, *ignis fatuus*
mow make faces
pricks quills
wound twined about with

Enter TRINCULO.

Lo, now, lo!
Here comes a spirit of his, and to torment me
For bringing wood in slowly. I'll fall flat;
Perchance he will not mind me.

TRINCULO   Here's neither bush nor shrub, to bear off° any weather at all, and
another storm brewing; I hear it sing i' the wind: yond same black cloud,
yond huge one, looks like a foul bombard° that would shed his liquor.
If it should thunder as it did before, I know not where to hide my head:
yond same cloud cannot choose but fall by pailfuls. What have we here?
a man or a fish? dead or alive? A fish: he smells like a fish; a very ancient
and fish-like smell; a kind of, not of the newest Poor-John.° A strange
fish! Were I in England° now, as once I was, and had but this fish
painted,° not a holiday fool there but would give a piece of silver: there
would this monster make a man;° any strange beast there makes a man:
when they will not give a doit° to relieve a lame beggar, they will lay
out ten to see a dead Indian.° Legged like a man! and his fins like arms!
Warm o' my troth! I do now let loose my opinion, hold it no longer:
this is no fish, but an islander, that hath lately suffered° by a thunderbolt. [*Thunder*] Alas, the storm is come again! my best way is to creep
under his gaberdine;° there is no other shelter hereabout: misery
acquaints a man with strange bed-fellows. I will here shroud till the
dregs of the storm be past.

Enter STEPHANO, *singing: a bottle in his hand.*

> *I shall no more to sea, to sea,*
> *Here shall I die ashore,—*

This is a very scurvy tune to sing at a man's funeral; well, here's my
comfort.   *Drinks. Sings.*

> *The master, the swabber, the boatswain, and I,*
> *The gunner, and his mate,*
> *Loved Mall,° Meg, and Marian, and Margery,*
> *But none of us cared for Kate:*
> *For she had a tongue with a tang,*
> *Would cry to a sailor, Go hang!*
> *She loved not the savour of tar nor of pitch;*
> *Yet a tailor might scratch her where'er she did itch.*
> *Then to sea, boys, and let her go hang!*

This is a scurvy tune too: but here's my comfort.   *Drinks.*

CALIBAN   Do not torment me:—O!

bear off ward off
bombard large leather bottle
Poor-John dried hake, a fish similar to cod
England where exhibitions of monsters were popular
painted on a board and hung outside a fair-booth
make a man make a man's fortune (with pun

on the other sense)
doit small coin
Indian Indians were often so exhibited, and usually died early.
suffered been killed
gaberdine cloak
Mall diminutive form of Mary

STEPHANO   What's the matter? Have we devils here? Do you put tricks upon
us with salvages° and men of Ind,° ha? I have not scaped drowning, to
be affeard now of your four legs; for it hath been said, As proper a
man° as ever went on four legs cannot make him give ground; and it
shall be said so again, while Stephano breathes at' nostrils.

CALIBAN   The spirit torments me:—O!

STEPHANO   This is some monster of the isle with four legs, who hath got, as
I take it, an ague.° Where the devil should he learn° our language? I
60   will give him some relief, if it be but for that. If I can recover° him,
and keep him tame, and get to Naples with him, he's a present° for
any emperor that ever trod on neat's leather.°

CALIBAN   Do not torment me, prithee; I'll bring my wood home faster.

STEPHANO   He's in his fit now, and does not talk after the wisest. He shall
taste of my bottle: if he have never drink wine afore, it will go near to
remove his fit. If I can recover him, and keep him tame, I will not take
too much for him;° he shall pay for him that hath him and that soundly.

CALIBAN   Thou dost me yet but little hurt; thou wilt anon, I know it by thy
trembling:° now Prosper works upon thee.

70   STEPHANO   Come on your ways; open your mouth; here is that which will
give language to you, cat:° open your mouth; this will shake your
shaking, I can tell you, and that soundly: you cannot tell who's your
friend: open your chaps° again.

TRINCULO   I should know that voice: it should be—but he is drowned; and
these are devils:—O defend me!

STEPHANO   Four legs and two voices,—a most delicate monster! His forward
voice, now, is to speak well of his friend; his backward voice is to utter
foul speeches and to detract.° If all the wine in my bottle will recover
him, I will help° his ague. Come:—Amen!° I will pour some in thy
80   other mouth.

TRINCULO   Stephano!

STEPHANO   Doth thy other mouth call me? Mercy, mercy! This is a devil, and
no monster: I will leave him; I have no long spoon.°

TRINCULO   Stephano! If thou beest Stephano, touch me, and speak to me; for
I am Trinculo,—be not afeard,—thy good friend Trinculo.

STEPHANO   If thou beest Trinculo, come forth: I'll pull thee by the lesser legs:
If any be Trinculo's legs, these are they. Thou art very Trinculo indeed!
How camest thou to be the siege° of this moon-calf?° can he vent°
Trinculos?

90   TRINCULO   I took him to be killed with a thunder-stroke. But art thou not drowned, Stephano? I hope, now, thou art not drowned. Is the storm over-blown? I hid me under the dead moon-calf's gaberdine for fear of the storm. And art thou living, Stephano? O Stephano, two Neapolitans scaped!

STEPHANO   Prithee, do not turn me about; my stomach is not constant.°

CALIBAN [*Aside*]   These be fine things,° an if° they be not sprites. That's a brave° god, and bears celestial liquor: I will kneel to him.

STEPHANO   How didst thou scape? How camest thou hither? swear, by this
100   bottle, how thou camest hither. I escaped upon a butt of sack,° which the sailors heaved o'erboard, by this bottle! which I made of the bark of a tree with mine own hands, since I was cast ashore.

CALIBAN   I'll swear, upon that bottle, to be thy true subject; for the liquor is not earthly.

STEPHANO   Here; swear, then, how thou escapedst.

TRINCULO   Swum ashore, man, like a duck: I can swim like a duck, I'll be sworn.

STEPHANO   Here, kiss the book.° Though thou canst swim like a duck, thou art made like a goose.

110   TRINCULO   O Stephano, hast any more of this?

STEPHANO   The whole butt, man: my cellar is in a rock by the seaside, where my wine is hid. How now, moon-calf! how does thine ague?

CALIBAN   Hast thou not dropped from heaven?

STEPHANO   Out o' the moon,° I do assure thee: I was the man i' the moon when time was.°

CALIBAN   I have seen thee in her, and I do adore thee: My mistress showed me thee, and thy dog, and thy bush.

STEPHANO   Come, swear to that; kiss the book: I will furnish it anon with new contents: swear.

120   TRINCULO   By this good light, this is a very shallow monster; I afeard of him? A very weak monster! The man i' the moon! A most poor credulous monster! Well drawn,° monster, in good sooth!°

CALIBAN   I'll show thee every fertile inch° o' the island; and I will kiss thy foot: I prithee, be my god.

TRINCULO   By this light, a most perfidious and drunken monster! when his god's asleep, he'll rob his bottle.

CALIBAN   I'll kiss thy foot; I'll swear myself thy subject.

STEPHANO   Come on, then; down, and swear.

TRINCULO   I shall laugh myself to death at this puppy-headed monster. A
130   most scurvy monster! I could find in my heart to beat him,—

---

constant steady
fine things Note the similarity of Caliban's reaction to the sight of Trinculo and Stephano, and Miranda's to the noblemen, especially Ferdinand.
an if if
brave fine
sack sherry-like wine; such a butt is mentioned in one of the narratives of the Bermuda wreck

kiss the book Trinculo raises the bottle to his lips.
Out o' the moon Stephano was not the first voyager to tell this to the natives.
when time was once upon a time
Well drawn a good pull at the wine
in good sooth truly
every fertile inch Twelve years earlier he had done this for Prospero.

STEPHANO   Come, kiss.

TRINCULO   But that the poor monster's in drink. An abominable monster!

CALIBAN   I'll show thee the best springs; I'll pluck thee berries;
I'll fish for thee, and get thee wood enough.
A plague upon the tyrant° that I serve!
I'll bear him no more sticks, but follow thee,
Thou wondrous man.

TRINCULO   A most ridiculous monster, to make a wonder of a poor drunkard!

CALIBAN   I prithee, let me bring thee where crabs° grow;

140   And I with my long nails will dig thee pig-nuts;°
Show thee a jay's nest, and instruct thee how
To snare the nimble marmoset;° I'll bring thee
To clustering filberts,° and sometimes I'll get thee
Young scamels° from the rock. Wilt thou go with me?

STEPHANO   I prithee now, lead the way, without any more talking. Trinculo,
the King and all our company else being drowned, we will inherit° here:
here; bear my bottle: fellow Trinculo, we'll fill him by and by again.

CALIBAN   *Sings drunkenly.*

    Farewell, master; farewell, farewell!

TRINCULO   A howling monster; a drunken monster!

150   CALIBAN   *No more dams I'll make for fish;*
       Nor fetch in firing
       At requiring;
    Nor scrape trenchering,° nor wash dish:
    'Ban, 'Ban, Cacaliban
    Has a new master:—get a new man.

    Freedom, high-day!° high-day, freedom! freedom, high-day, freedom!

STEPHANO   O brave monster! lead the way.   *Exeunt.*

ACT III

SCENE I [*Before* PROSPERO's *Cell.*]

Enter FERDINAND, *bearing a log.*

FERDINAND   There be some sports are painful, and their labour
Delight in them sets off:° some kinds of baseness
Are nobly undergone; and most poor° matters
Point to rich ends. This my mean task
Would be as heavy to me as odious, but
The mistress which I serve quickens° what's dead,

---

tyrant usurper
crabs crab-apples
pig-nuts earthnuts
marmoset small monkey (called "good meat" by colonists)
filberts trees bearing hazel nuts
scamels The word is not recorded elsewhere: either a bird or a shellfish.

inherit take possession
trenchering "trenchers" (dishes) collectively; cf. housing, clothing
high-day meaningless cry of joy and pleasure
There . . . off in some arduous sports the pleasure they give cancels our pains
most poor the poorest
quickens gives life to

And makes my labour pleasures: O, she is
Ten times more gentle than her father's crabbed,°
And he's composed of harshness. I must remove
Some thousands of these logs, and pile them up,
Upon a sore injunction:° my sweet mistress
Weeps when she sees me work, and says, such baseness
Had never like executor.° I forget:
But these sweet thoughts do even refresh my labours,
Most busy least when I do it.°

Enter MIRANDA; *and* PROSPERO [*at a distance, unseen*].

MIRANDA   Alas, now, pray you,
Work not so hard: I would the lightning had
Burnt up those logs that you are enjoined° to pile!
Pray, set it down, and rest you: when this burns,
'Twill weep° for having wearied you. My father
Is hard at study; pray, now, rest yourself:
He's safe for these three hours.
FERDINAND   O most dear mistress,
The sun will set before I shall discharge°
What I must strive to do.
MIRANDA   If you'll sit down,
I'll bear your logs the while: pray give me that;
I'll carry it to the pile.
FERDINAND   No, precious creature;
I had rather crack my sinews, break my back,
Than you should such dishonour undergo,
While I sit lazy by.
MIRANDA   It would become me
As well as it does you: and I should do it
With much more ease; for my good will is to it,
And yours it is against.
PROSPERO   Poor worm, thou art infected!°
This visitation° shows it.
MIRANDA   You look wearily.
FERDINAND   No, noble mistress: 'tis fresh morning with me
When you are by at night. I do beseech you,—
Chiefly that I might set it in my prayers,—
What is your name?
MIRANDA   Miranda.—O my father,
I have broke your hest° to say so!
FERDINAND   Admired° Miranda!

crabbed bad-tempered
Upon . . . injunction under a severe penalty
Had . . . executor was never carried out by so
noble a person
Most busy . . . it F: *Most busie lest, when I
do it;* unsolved crux, perhaps corrupt, perhaps
meaning "My work is hardest when I think of
her least"

enjoined commanded
weep by exuding sap
discharge fulfill
infected by love, as by the plague
visitation visit; also used of a plague epidemic
hest order
admired playing on the meaning of her name:
"worthy of admiration"

Indeed the top of admiration! worth
What's dearest to the world! Full many a lady
40 I have eyed with best regard,° and many a time
The harmony of their tongues hath into bondage
Brought my too diligent ear: for several° virtues°
Have I liked several women; never any
With so full soul, but some defect in her
Did quarrel with the noblest grace° she owed,°
And put it to the foil:° but you, O you,
So perfect and so peerless, are created
Of every creature's best!°

MIRANDA   I do not know
One of my sex: no woman's face remember,
50 Save, from my glass, mine own; nor have I seen
More that I may call men than you, good friend,
And my dear father: how features are abroad,°
I am skilless of;° but, by my modesty,
The jewel in my dower, I would not wish
Any companion in the world but you;
Nor can imagination form a shape,
Besides yourself, to like of.° But I prattle
Something too wildly, and my father's precepts
I therein do forget.

FERDINAND   I am, in my condition,°
60 A prince, Miranda; I do think, a King;
I would not so!—and would no more endure
This wooden slavery° than to suffer
The flesh-fly blow° my mouth. Hear my soul speak:
The very instant that I saw you, did
My heart fly to your service; there resides,
To make me slave to it; and for your sake
Am I this patient log-man.

MIRANDA   Do you love me?

FERDINAND   O heaven, O earth, bear witness to this sound,
And crown what I profess with kind event,°
70 If I speak true! if hollowly,° invert
What best is boded me° to mischief! I,
Beyond all limit of what else i' the world,
Do love, prize, honour you.

MIRANDA   I am a fool
To weep at what I am glad of.

---

best regard attentive gaze
several different
virtues qualities
noblest grace finest attribute
owed owned
put . . . foil spoiled, overthrew it
every creature's best a common Elizabethan
love-compliment
abroad out in the world

skilless of ignorant of
like of be pleased with
condition rank
wooden slavery menial task of wood-carrying
blow foul, sully
kind event favorable outcome
hollowly insincerely
What . . . me the best fortune has in store for
me

PROSPERO   Fair encounter
Of two most rare affections!° Heavens rain grace
On that which breeds between 'em!°
FERDINAND   Wherefore weep you?
MIRANDA   At mine unworthiness, that dare not offer
What I desire to give; and much less take
What I shall die to want.° But this is trifling;°
80   And all the more it° seeks to hide itself,
The bigger bulk it shows. Hence, bashful cunning!
And prompt me, plain and holy innocence!
I am your wife, if you will marry me;
If not, I'll die your maid:° to be your fellow
You may deny me; but I'll be your servant,
Whether you will or no.
FERDINAND   My mistress, dearest;
And I thus humble ever.
MIRANDA   My husband, then?
FERDINAND   Ay, with a heart as willing
As bondage e'er of freedom:° here's my hand.
90   MIRANDA   And mine, with my heart in it: and now farewell
Till half an hour hence.
FERDINAND   A thousand thousand!°
                         Exeunt. FERDINAND *and* MIRANDA *severally.*
PROSPERO   So glad of this as they I cannot be,
Who are surprised with all;° but my rejoicing
At nothing can be more. I'll to my book;
For yet, ere supper-time, must I perform
Much business appertaining.°   *Exit.*

SCENE II [*Another part of the Island.*]

Enter CALIBAN, STEPHANO, *and* TRINCULO.

STEPHANO   Tell not me;°—when the butt is out, we will drink water; not a
drop before: therefore bear up, and board 'em.° Servant-monster, drink
to me.
TRINCULO   Servant-monster! the folly° of this island! They say there's but five
upon this isle: we are three of them; if the other two be brained° like
us, the state totters.
STEPHANO   Drink, servant-monster, when I bid thee: thy eyes are almost set°
in thy head.

---

affections dispositions
that which . . . 'em i.e. love and/or children
want be without
trifling using words unequal to her true feelings
it her love
maid with two senses, "virgin" and "servant"
with . . . freedom as eagerly as the captive longs for freedom
thousand "farewells"
surprised with all taken unawares by all these developments (or *withal,* by this)

appertaining relating (to the marriage and what must lead up to it)
Tell not me don't talk to me (about saving liquor)
bear up and board 'em naval order, here meaning "drink up"
folly freak
brained equipped with brains
set disappearing, like the setting sun. Trinculo takes it in a different sense.

TRINCULO   Where should they be set else? he were a brave monster indeed, if
they were set in his tail.

STEPHANO   My man-monster hath drowned his tongue in sack: for my part, the
sea cannot drown me; I swam, ere I could recover° the shore, five-and-
thirty leagues off and on. By this light, thou shalt be my lieutenant,
monster, or my standard.°

TRINCULO   Your lieutenant, if you list; he's no standard.

STEPHANO   We'll not run,° Monsieur Monster.

TRINCULO   Nor go° neither; but you'll lie,° like dogs, and yet say nothing
neither.

STEPHANO   Moon-calf, speak once in thy life, if thou beest a good moon-calf.

CALIBAN   How does thy honour? Let me lick thy shoe: I'll not serve him, he is
not valiant.

TRINCULO   Thou liest, most ignorant monster: I am in case° to justle a constable.° Why, thou deboshed° fish, thou, was there ever man a coward
that hath drunk so much sack as I to-day? Wilt thou tell a monstrous lie,
being but half a fish and half a monster?

CALIBAN   Lo, how he mocks me! wilt thou let him, my lord?

TRINCULO   'Lord,' quoth he? That a monster should be such a natural!°

CALIBAN   Lo, lo, again! bite him to death, I prithee.

STEPHANO   Trinculo, keep a good tongue in your head: if you prove a mutineer,
—the next tree! The poor monster's my subject, and he shall not suffer
indignity.

CALIBAN   I thank my noble lord. Wilt thou be pleased to hearken once again
to the suit I made to thee?

STEPHANO   Marry, will I: kneel and repeat it; I will stand, and so shall Trinculo.

Enter ARIEL, *invisible.*

CALIBAN   As I told thee before, I am subject to a tyrant,° a sorcerer, that by
his cunning hath cheated me of the island.

ARIEL   Thou liest.

CALIBAN   Thou liest, thou jesting monkey,° thou:
I would my valiant master would destroy thee!
I do not lie.

STEPHANO   Trinculo, if you trouble him any more in 's tale, by this hand, I will
supplant° some of your teeth.

TRINCULO   Why, I said nothing.

STEPHANO   Mum, then, and no more. Proceed.

CALIBAN   I say, by sorcery he got this isle;
From me he got it. If thy greatness will
Revenge it on him,—for I know thou dar'st,
But this thing° dare not,—

---

recover reach
standard standard-bearer, but as Caliban can
hardly stand, Trinculo puns on the word
run from the enemy; but also because they are
staggering
go walk
lie lie down; tell lies
in case in a condition

justle a constable Trinculo is drunk enough
to rough up a law officer
deboshed debauched
natural idiot
tyrant usurper
Thou liest . . . monkey Caliban thinks the previous remark came from Trinculo.
supplant uproot
this thing Trinculo

STEPHANO   That's most certain.

CALIBAN   Thou shalt be lord of it, and I'll serve thee.

STEPHANO   How now shall this be compassed?° Canst thou bring me to the party?°

CALIBAN   Yea, yea, my lord: I'll yield him thee asleep,
60   Where thou mayst knock a nail into his head.

ARIEL   Thou liest; thou canst not.

CALIBAN   What a pied° ninny's this! Thou scurvy patch!°
        I do beseech thy greatness, give him blows,
        And take his bottle from him: when that's gone,
        He shall drink nought but brine; for I'll not show him
        Where the quick freshes° are.

STEPHANO   Trinculo, run into no further danger: interrupt the monster one
        word further, and, by this hand, I'll turn my mercy out o' doors, and
70   make a stock-fish° of thee.

TRINCULO   Why, what did I? I did nothing. I'll go farther off.

STEPHANO   Didst thou not say he lied?

ARIEL   Thou liest.

STEPHANO   Do I so? take thou that. [*Beats him.*] As you like this, give me the
        lie° another time.

TRINCULO   I did not give the lie. Out o' your wits, and hearing too? A pox o'
        your bottle! this can sack and drinking do. A murrain° on your monster,
        and the devil take your fingers!

80 CALIBAN   Ha, ha, ha!

STEPHANO   Now, forward with your tale.—Prithee, stand further off.°

CALIBAN   Beat him enough: after a little time,
        I'll beat him too.

STEPHANO   Stand farther.—Come, proceed.

CALIBAN   Why, as I told thee, 'tis a custom with him
        I' the afternoon to sleep: there° thou mayst brain him,
        Having first seized his books; or with a log
        Batter his skull, or paunch° him with a stake,
        Or cut his wezand° with thy knife. Remember
90   First to possess° his books; for without them
        He's but a sot,° as I am, nor hath not
        One spirit to command: they all do hate him
        As rootedly as I. Burn but° his books.
        He has brave útensils,°—for so he calls them,—
        Which, when he has a house, he'll deck withal.°
        And that° most deeply to consider is

compassed brought about
party person concerned
pied particolored (referring to jester's motley)
patch fool, jester
freshes springs of fresh water
stock-fish salted cod, beaten with a club before cooking
give me the lie call me a liar
murrain disease of cattle
stand further off to Trinculo, to prevent him from interrupting; or to Caliban because he smells
there at that time
paunch disembowel
wezand windpipe
possess seize
sot ignoramus
Burn but only be sure to burn; burn only
utensils household goods
deck withal furnish it with
that that which is

The beauty of his daughter; he himself
Calls her a nonpareil:° I never saw a woman,
But only Sycorax my dam and she;

100 But she as far surpasseth Sycorax
As greatest does least.

STEPHANO   Is it so brave a lass?

CALIBAN   Ay, lord; she will become thy bed, I warrant,
And bring thee forth brave brood.

STEPHANO   Monster, I will kill this man: his daughter and I will be king and
queen,—save our graces!—and Trinculo and thyself shall be viceroys.
Dost thou like the plot,° Trinculo?

TRINCULO   Excellent.

STEPHANO   Give me thy hand: I am sorry I beat thee; but, while thou livest,

110 keep a good tongue in thy head.

CALIBAN   Within this half hour will he be asleep:
Wilt thou destroy him then?

STEPHANO   Ay, on mine honour.

ARIEL   This will I tell my master.

CALIBAN   Thou mak'st me merry; I am full of pleasure:
Let us be jocund: will you troll the catch°
You taught me but while-ere?°

STEPHANO   At thy request, monster, I will do reason, any reason.°—Come on,
Trinculo, let us sing.   *Sings.*

        Flout 'em and scout° 'em,
120   *And scout 'em and flout 'em;*
        Thought is free.°

CALIBAN   That's not the tune.

                    ARIEL *plays the tune on a tabor° and pipe.*

STEPHANO   What is this same?

TRINCULO   This is the tune of our catch, played by the picture of Nobody.°

STEPHANO   If thou beest a man, show thyself in this likeness: if thou beest a
devil, take it as thou list.°

TRINCULO   O, forgive me my sins!

STEPHANO   He that dies pays all debts: I defy thee. Mercy upon us!

130 CALIBAN   Art thou afeard?

STEPHANO   No, monster, not I.

CALIBAN   Be not afeard; the isle is full of noises,°
Sounds and sweet airs, that give delight, and hurt not.
Sometimes a thousand twangling instruments
Will° hum about mine ears; and sometime voices,
That, if I then had waked° after long sleep,

---

nonpareil without an equal
plot in the modern sense; but *plot* was also the
summary of a play's action
troll the catch sing the round
while-ere a short time ago
any reason anything within reason
scout on first occurrence F reads *cout* (jeer at),
which is possible
Thought is free thought can't be censored
(proverbial)

tabor little drum
picture of Nobody Personifying Nobody was a
very old joke, and pictures of Nobody usually
consist of empty suits of clothes.
take it as thou list take it anyway you like (old
saying: "the devil take it")
noises music
Will . . . had waked . . . Will . . . methought
. . . waked . . . cried Note illogical sequence
of tenses for special effect.

Will° make me sleep again: and then, in dreaming,
The clouds methought° would open; and show riches
140   Ready to drop upon me; that, when I waked,°
I cried° to dream again.
STEPHANO   This will prove a brave kingdom to me, where I shall have my music
for nothing.
CALIBAN   When Prospero is destroyed.
STEPHANO   That shall be by and by: I remember the story.
TRINCULO   The sound is going away; let's follow it, and after do our work.
STEPHANO   Lead, monster; we'll follow. I would I could see this taborer; he
lays it on.
150   TRINCULO   Wilt come?° I'll follow, Stephano.   *Exeunt.*

SCENE III [*Another part of the Island.*]

Enter ALONSO, SEBASTIAN, ANTONIO, GONZALO, ADRIAN, FRANCISCO, etc.

GONZALO   By 'r lakin,° I can go no further, sir;
My old bones ache: here's a maze trod, indeed,
Through forth-rights° and meanders!° By your patience,
I needs must rest me.
ALONSO   Old lord, I cannot blame thee,
Who am myself attached° with weariness,
To the dulling of my spirits:° sit down, and rest.
Even here I will put off° my hope, and keep it
No longer for my flatterer: he is drowned
Whom thus we stray to find; and the sea mocks
10   Our frustrate° search on land. Well, let him go.
ANTONIO [*Aside to* SEBASTIAN]   I am right glad that he's so out of hope.
Do not, for one repulse, forego the purpose
That you resolved to effect.
SEBASTIAN [*Aside to* ANTONIO]   The next advantage
Will we take throughly.°
ANTONIO [*Aside to* SEBASTIAN]   Let it be tonight;
For, now they are oppressed with travel, they
Will not, nor cannot, use such vigilance
As when they are fresh.
SEBASTIAN [*Aside to* ANTONIO]   I say, tonight: no more.

Solemn and strange music; and PROSPER *on the top*° (*invisible*).° *Enter
several strange Shapes, bringing in a banquet;*° *and dance about it with
gentle actions of salutations; and inviting the King, etc., to eat,*° *they
depart.*

Wilt come? addressed to Caliban
lakin "Ladykin," i.e. the Virgin Mary
forth-rights straight paths
meanders winding paths
attached seized
spirits vital powers
put off divest myself of
frustrate vain
throughly thoroughly

on the top on the upper stage, or possibly in
a higher place
(invisible) not, of course, to the audience
banquet a light meal; stage magicians often
conjured up banquets
to eat Banquets could stand allegorically for
all voluptuous temptation and for that which
the virtuous man would refuse to partake of.

ALONSO   What harmony is this? My good friends, hark!

GONZALO   Marvellous sweet music!

20 ALONSO   Give us kind keepers,° heavens!—What were these?

SEBASTIAN   A living drollery.° Now I will believe
    That there are unicorns; that in Arabia
    There is one tree, the phoenix' throne; one phoenix°
    at this hour reigning there.

ANTONIO   I'll believe both;
    And what does else want credit,° come to me,
    And I'll be sworn 'tis true: travellers ne'er did lie,°
    Though fools at home condemn 'em.

GONZALO   If in Naples
    I should report this now, would they believe me?
    If I should say, I saw such islanders,—

30   For, certes,° these are people of the island,—
    Who, though they are of monstrous° shape, yet, note,
    Their manners° are more gentle, kind, than of
    Our human generation you shall find
    Many, nay, almost any.

PROSPERO   [Aside] Honest° lord,
    Thou hast said well; for some of you there present
    Are worse than devils.

ALONSO   I cannot too much muse°
    Such shapes, such gesture, and such sound, expressing—
    Although they want the use of tongue—a kind
    Of excellent dumb discourse.

PROSPERO   [Aside] Praise in departing.°

FRANCISCO   They vanished strangely.

40 SEBASTIAN   No matter, since
    They have left their viands° behind; for we have stomachs.°—
    Will it please you taste of what is here?

ALONSO   Not I.

GONZALO   Faith, sir, you need not fear. When we were boys,
    Who would believe that there were mountaineers
    Dew-lapped like bulls, whose throats had hanging at 'em
    Wallets of flesh?° or that there were such men
    Whose heads stood in their breasts?° which now we find

---

keepers guardian angels
living drollery puppet show in which the figures are alive
unicorns . . . phoenix frequent wonders in travelers' tales, myth, and folklore. There was only one Phoenix, in the "sole Arabian tree"; it renewed itself from the ashes of its funeral pyre; see above, "The Phoenix and Turtle."
want credit is difficult to believe
travellers . . . lie The lies of travelers were famous.
certes certainly
monstrous unnatural
manners in a wider sense than ours

Honest honorable
muse wonder at
Praise in departing "don't praise your host till the entertainment's over" (proverbial)
viands food
stomachs appetites
Wallets of flesh exaggerated account of goiter found in some mountain areas; "wallet" is cognate with "wattle"
heads . . . breasts These monsters go back beyond Mandeville to Pliny; and Othello on his travels met "men whose heads / Do grow beneath their shoulders."

Each putter-out of five for one° will bring us
Good warrant of.

ALONSO   I will stand to, and feed,
50   Although my last: no matter, since I feel
The best° is past. Brother, my lord the duke,
Stand to, and do as we.

Thunder and lightning. Enter ARIEL *like a Harpy;° claps his wings upon
the table; and, with a quaint device,° the banquet vanishes.*

ARIEL   You are three men of sin, whom Destiny,—
That hath to instrument° this lower world
And what is in it,—the never-surfeited° sea
Hath caused to belch up you; and on this island,
Where man doth not inhabit,—you 'mongst men
Being most unfit to live. I have made you mad;
And even with such-like valour° men hang and drown
Their proper° selves.

ALONSO, SEBASTIAN, *etc., draw their swords.*
60   You fools! I and my fellows
Are ministers° of Fate: the elements,
Of whom your swords are tempered, may as well
Wound the loud winds, or with bemocked-at-stabs
Kill the still-closing° waters, as diminish
One dowle° that's in my plume: my fellow-ministers
Are like° invulnerable.° If° you could hurt,
Your swords are now too massy° for your strengths,
And will not be uplifted. But remember—
For that's my business to you—that you three
70   From Milan did supplant good Prospero:
Exposed unto the sea, which hath requit° it,
Him and his innocent child: for which foul deed
The powers, delaying, not forgetting, have
Incensed the seas and shores, yea, all the creatures,°
Against your peace. Thee of thy son, Alonso,
They have bereft; and do pronounce by me

---

putter-out . . . one Travelers could take out a form of insurance, leaving a premium which would be forfeited if they failed to return, but which would be repaid fivefold if they came back with proof that they had reached the stated destination.
best best part of my life
Harpy In Virgil's *Aeneid* III.255 ff. harpies devour and befoul the food of Aeneas and his friends, and the harpy Celaeno speaks a prophecy on which Ariel's is ultimately based; allegorically the harpy confronted a man with his guilty past.
quaint device ingenious contrivance. Perhaps Ariel, descending in a "machine," covered the table with his wings, and a stagehand, concealed under the table, removed a panel and whisked the banquet out of sight below.
to instrument as its instrument

never-surfeited A surfeit—eating too much— would be a normal cause of belching up, but the sea is always hungry, and a special intervention of Destiny was necessary to cause it to vomit forth the "men of sin" on this occasion.
such-like valour a false courage, of the kind that leads people to suicide
proper own
ministers agents
still-closing that always close up again
dowle small feather
like likewise
invulnerable as were Virgil's harpies
If even if
massy heavy
requit paid back
Incensed roused
creatures created things

Ling'ring perdition°—worse than any death
Can be at once—shall step by step attend
You and your ways; whose wraths to guard you from—
80 Which here, in this most desolate isle, else° falls°
Upon your heads,—is nothing but heart-sorrow
And a clear° life ensuing.

*He vanishes in thunder; then, to soft music, enter the Shapes again, and
dance, with mocks and mows,° and carrying out the table.*

PROSPERO   Bravely° the figure of this Harpy hast thou
Performed, my Ariel; a grace it had devouring:°
Of my instruction hast thou nothing bated°
In what thou hadst to say: so, with good life°
And observation strange,° my meaner ministers°
Their several kinds have done.° My high charms work,
And these mine enemies are all knit up
90 In their distractions:° they now are in my power;
And in these fits I leave them, while I visit
Young Ferdinand,—whom they suppose is drowned,—
And his and mine loved darling.   *Exit.*
GONZALO   I' the name of something holy, sir, why stand you
In this strange stare?
ALONSO   O, it is monstrous, monstrous!
Methought the billows spoke, and told me of it;
The winds did sing it to me; and the thunder,
That deep and dreadful organ-pipe, pronounced
The name of Prosper: it did bass my trespass.°
100 Therefor my son i' the ooze° is bedded; and
I'll seek him deeper than e'er plummet sounded,
And with him there lie mudded.   *Exit.*
SEBASTIAN   But one fiend at a time,
I'll fight their legions o'er.°
ANTONIO   I'll be thy second.
                              Exeunt SEBASTIAN *and* ANTONIO.
GONZALO   All three of them are desperate: their great guilt,
Like poison given to work a great time after,°
Now 'gins to bite the spirit. I do beseech you,

Ling'ring perdition slow wasting away
else otherwise
falls fall
clear blameless
mocks and mows mocking gestures and grimaces
Bravely finely
a grace . . . devouring either: it was graceful
in the act of devouring the banquet (Virgil's
harpies do so, but Ariel presumably merely
caused it to disappear); or: it had a devouring
(ravishing) grace
bated left out
good life a comment on Ariel's powers as an
actor
observation strange unusual attentiveness

meaner ministers the spirits, subservient to
Ariel, who played in the banquet scene
Their . . . done have performed the tasks their
natures suited them for
knit up . . . distractions entangled in their
madness
bass my trespass provide the bass part in the
chorus in which nature described my sin
ooze sea mud
o'er to the last
Like poison . . . after The Elizabethan was
credulous about poisons, especially in the hands
of Italians, and it was thought possible that
there were some that acted after a long interval.

That are of suppler joints, follow them swiftly,
And hinder them from what this ecstasy°
May now provoke them to.

ADRIAN   Follow, I pray you.   *Exeunt omnes.*

ACT IV

SCENE I [*Before* PROSPERO'*s Cell.*]

Enter PROSPERO, FERDINAND, *and* MIRANDA.

PROSPERO   If I have too austerely punished you,
Your compensation makes amends; for I
Have given you here a third of mine own life,°
Or that for which I live; who once again
I tender° to thy hand: all thy vexations
Were but my trials of thy love, and thou
Hast strangely° stood the test: here, afore Heaven,
I ratify this my rich gift. O Ferdinand,
Do not smile at me that I boast her off,°
10   For thou shalt find she will outstrip all praise,
And make it halt° behind her.

FERDINAND   I do believe it
Against an oracle.°

PROSPERO   Then, as my gift,° and thine own acquisition
Worthily purchased,° take my daughter: but
If thou dost break her virgin-knot° before
All sanctimonious° ceremonies may
With full and holy rite be ministered,
No sweet aspersion° shall the heavens let fall
To make this contract grow;° but barren hate,
20   Sour-eyed disdain and discord shall bestrew°
The union of your bed with weeds so loathly
That you shall hate it both: therefore take heed,
As Hymen's lamp shall light you.°

FERDINAND   As I hope
For quiet days, fair issue° and long life,

---

ecstasy madness
a third . . . life Either he thinks of Miranda, his dead wife, and himself as the whole; or Miranda, Milan, and himself; or that he has spent a third of his life bringing up Miranda; or that he has a third of his life to come, and that Miranda alone gives it value.
tender hand over
strangely wonderfully well
boast her off cry up her praises
halt limp
Against an oracle even if an oracle should declare otherwise
gift F: *guest*

purchased earned, won
break her virgin-knot take her maidenhead; from the symbolic loosening of the girdle in Roman custom, *virgineam dissoluit zonam,* "he untied her virgin belt or girdle"
sanctimonious holy
aspersion sprinkling (ritual sense)
grow into a happy and fruitful marriage
bestrew flowers—not weeds—were customarily scattered on the bridal bed
As . . . light you as you hope that the torch of the marriage god will burn clear as a good omen at your marriage; F has *lamps*
issue children

With such love as 'tis now, the murkiest den,
The most opportune place, the strong'st suggestion°
Our worser genius° can,° shall never melt
Mine honour into lust, to° take away
The edge of that day's celebration
30   When I shall think, or° Phoebus' steeds are foundered,°
Or Night kept chained below.°
PROSPERO   Fairly spoke.
Sit, then, and talk with her; she is thine own.
What, Ariel! my industrious servant, Ariel!

Enter ARIEL.

ARIEL   What would my potent master? here I am.
PROSPERO   Thou and thy meaner fellows your last service
Did worthily perform; and I must use you
In such another trick.° Go bring the rabble,°
O'er whom I give thee power, here to this place:
Incite them to quick motion; for I must
40   Bestow upon the eyes of this young couple
Some vanity° of mine Art: it is my promise,
And they expect it from me.
ARIEL   Presently?°
PROSPERO   Ay, with a twink.°
ARIEL   Before you can say, 'come,' and 'go,'
And breathe twice, and cry, 'so, so,'
Each one, tripping on his toe,
Will be here with mop and mow.°
Do you love me, master? no?
PROSPERO   Dearly, my delicate Ariel. Do not approach
Till thou dost hear me call.
50   ARIEL   Well, I conceive.°   *Exit.*
PROSPERO   Look thou be true;° do not give dalliance°
Too much the rein: the strongest oaths are straw
To the fire in' the blood: be more abstemious,
Or else, good night your vow!
FERDINAND   I warrant you, sir;
The white cold virgin snow upon my heart
Abates the ardour of my liver.°
PROSPERO   Well.
Now come, my Ariel! bring a corollary,°

suggestion temptation
worser genius bad angel; everybody had a
good one and a bad one
can is capable of
to so as to
or either
foundered gone lame
below below the horizon, from which it ascends
at sunset
trick magic device
rabble the inferior spirits

vanity trifle
Presently at once
with a twink in the twinkling of an eye
mop and mow grin and grimace
conceive understand
true faithful to your promise
dalliance lovemaking
liver thought to be the seat of the passion of
love
corollary extra man, supernumerary

Rather than want° a spirit: appear, and pertly!°
No tongue! all eyes! be silent.   *Soft music.*

Enter IRIS.°

60   IRIS   *Ceres, most bounteous lady, thy rich leas°*
          Of wheat, rye, barley, vetches, oats, and pease;
          Thy turfy mountains, where live nibbling sheep,
          And flat meads thatched with stover,° them to keep;
          Thy banks with pionèd and twillèd° brims,
          Which spongy April° at thy hest betrims,°
          To make cold° nymphs chaste crowns; and thy broom-groves,°
          Whose shadow the dismissèd bachelor° loves,
          Being lass-lorn;° thy pole-clipt° vinëyard;
          And thy sea-marge,° sterile and rocky-hard,
70   *Where thou thyself dost air;—the queen o' th' sky,*
          Whose wat'ry arch° and messenger° am I,
          Bids thee leave these;° and with her sovereign grace,

          JUNO *descends.°*

          Here, on this grass-plot, in this very place,
          To come and sport:—her peacocks° fly amain:°
          Approach, rich Ceres, her to entertain.

          Enter CERES.

      CERES   *Hail, many-coloured messenger, that ne'er*
          Dost disobey the wife of Jupiter;
          Who, with thy saffron° wings, upon my flowers
80   *Diffusest honey-drops, refreshing showers;*
          And with each end of thy blue bow dost crown
          My bosky° acres and my unshrubbed down,°
          Rich scarf to my proud earth; why hath thy queen
          Summoned me hither, to this short-grassèd green?
      IRIS   *A contract of true love to celebrate;*
          And some donation° freely to estate°
          On the blest lovers.

---

want lack
pertly smartly
Enter Iris What follows is a reduced form of
court masque (See Headnote to *Pleasure Reconciled to Virtue,* below) appropriate to a
betrothal; it cannot end, as masques should,
with a dance involving the spectators; however,
it is what was called a "show," as was the
spectacular episode in III.iii.
Ceres goddess of grain and harvest
leas meadows
thatched . . . stover covered with a growth of
grass used as winter fodder
pionèd and twillèd Meaning is uncertain but
most likely man-made embankments with
branches laid criss-cross on the top.
spongy April April is traditionally a showery
month.
betrims adorns

cold sexually pure
broom-groves gorse-clumps (perhaps)
dismissèd bachelor rejected lover
lass-lorn deprived of his girl
pole-clipt pruned
sea-marge seashore
wat'ry arch rainbow
messenger Iris traditionally had this role.
these the places mentioned
Juno descends presumably begins her descent
from the roof
peacocks sacred to Juno, whose chariot they
drew
amain swiftly
saffron yellow
bosky wooded
unshrubbed down hilly country without trees
donation gift
estate bestow

CERES   *Tell me, heavenly bow,*
If Venus or her son, as thou dost know,
Do now attend the queen? Since they did plot
The means that dusky Dis° my daughter got,
90 *Her and her blind boy's° scandalled° company*
I have forsworn.

IRIS   *Of her society*
Be not afraid: I met her deity
Cutting the clouds towards Paphos,° and her son
Dove-drawn° with her. Here thought they to have done
Some wanton charm upon this man and maid,
Whose vows are, that no bed-right shall be paid°
Till Hymen's torch be lighted: but in vain;
Mars's hot minion° is returned again;
Her waspish-headed° son has broke his arrows,
100 *Swears he will shoot no more, but play with sparrows,°*
And be a boy right out.°

CERES   *Highest queen of state,*
Great Juno comes; I know her by her gait.

JUNO *How does my bounteous sister? Go with me*
To bless this twain, that they may prosperous be,
And honoured in their issue.

They sing:

JUNO   *Honour, riches, marriage-blessing,*
Long continuance, and increasing,
Hourly joys be still° upon you!
Juno sings her blessings on you.
110 CERES *Earth's increase, foison° plenty,*
Barns and garners never empty;
Vines with clust'ring bunches growing;
Plants with goodly burthen bowing;
Spring come to you at the farthest
In the very end of harvest!°
Scarcity and want shall shun you;
Ceres' blessing so is on you.

FERDINAND This is a most majestic vision, and
Harmonious charmingly. May I be bold
To think these spirits?

---

dusky Dis Pluto; dusky because king of the underworld; he abducted Persephone (Proserpina in Latin) to be his queen for half the year
blind boy's Cupid's
scandalled tainted with scandal, disgraceful
Paphos center of the cult of Venus, in Cyprus
Dove-drawn doves were sacred to Venus and drew her chariot
bed-right . . . paid marital intercourse take place

hot minion lustful mistress
waspish-headed peevish
sparrows also associated with Venus, and thought to be lustful
right out outright, altogether
still always
foison harvest
Spring . . . harvest i.e. may you have no winter

120 PROSPERO   Spirits, which by mine Art
        I have from their confines° called to enact
        My present fancies.°
    FERDINAND   Let me live here ever;
        So rare a wondered father and a wise°
        Makes this place Paradise.

                    JUNO *and* CERES *whisper, and send* IRIS *on employment.*
                                Sweet, now, silence!
        Juno and Ceres whisper seriously;
        There's something else to do: hush, and be mute,
        Or else our spell is marred.
    IRIS   *You nymphs, called Naiads, of the windring° brooks,*
            With your sedged crowns° and ever-harmless looks,
130   *Leave your crisp° channels, and on this green land*
            Answer your summons; Juno does command:
            Come, temperate° nymphs, and help to celebrate
            A contract of true love; be not too late.

        Enter certain NYMPHS.

            You sunburned sicklemen,° of August weary,
            Come hither from the furrow, and be merry:
            Make holiday; your rye-straw hats put on,
            And these fresh° nymphs encounter every one
            In country footing.°

        Enter certain Reapers, properly habited: they join with the Nymphs in
        a graceful dance; towards the end whereof PROSPERO *starts suddenly,*
        and speaks; after which, to a strange, hollow, and confused noise, they
        heavily° vanish.

    PROSPERO [*Aside*] I had forgot that foul conspiracy
140   Of the beast Caliban and his confederates
        Against my life: the minute of their plot
        Is almost come. [*To the* SPIRITS] Well done! avoid;° no more!
    FERDINAND   This is strange: your father's in some passion
        That works° him strongly.
    MIRANDA   Never till this day
        Saw I him touched with anger, so distempered.
    PROSPERO   You do look, my son, in a moved sort,°
        As if you were dismayed: be cheerful, sir.
        Our revels° now are ended. These our actors,

---

confines natural limits
fancies imaginative entertainments
wondered . . . wise father so to be wondered
at (or so capable of producing wonders) and
also wise (some copies of F have *wife*, which
creates an analogy between the island and the
Garden of Eden, with Prospero as God the
Father and Miranda as Eve)
windring portmanteau of "wandering" and
"winding"
sedged crowns garlands of sedge
crisp covered with little waves

temperate chaste (which is why Naiads, nymphs
of the cool water, are summoned)
sicklemen reapers
fresh young
encounter . . . footing partner in a country
dance
heavily dejectedly
avoid begone
works agitates
moved sort troubled state
revels common name for such entertainments

As I foretold you, were all spirits, and
150   Are melted into air, into thin air:
And, like the baseless fabric° of this vision,
The cloud-capped towers, the gorgeous palaces,
The solemn temples, the great globe itself,
Yea, all which it inherit,° shall dissolve,
And, like this insubstantial pageant° faded,
Leave not a rack° behind. We are such stuff
As dreams are made on;° and our little life
Is rounded with° a sleep. Sir, I am vexed;°
Bear with my weakness; my old brain is troubled:
160   Be not disturbed with my infirmity:
If you be pleased, retire into my cell,
And there repose: a turn or two I'll walk,
To still my beating° mind.

FERDINAND, MIRANDA   We wish your peace.   *Exeunt.*
PROSPERO   Come with a thought.° I thank thee. Ariel: come.

Enter ARIEL.

ARIEL   Thy thoughts I cleave to.° What's thy pleasure?
PROSPERO   Spirit,
   We must prepare to meet with Caliban.
ARIEL   Ay, my commander: when I presented° Ceres,
I thought to have told thee of it; but I feared
Lest I might anger thee.
170 PROSPERO   Say again, where didst thou leave these varlets?°
ARIEL   I told you, sir, they were red-hot with drinking;
So full of valour that they smote the air
For breathing in their faces; beat the ground
For kissing of their feet; yet always bending°
Towards their project. Then I beat my tabor;
At which, like unbacked° colts, they pricked their ears,
Advanced° their eyelids, lifted up their noses
As° they smelt music: so I charmed their ears,
That, calf-like, they my lowing followed, through
180   Toothed briers, sharp furzes, pricking goss,° and thorns,
Which entered their frail shins: at last I left them
I' the filthy-mantled° pool beyond your cell,
There dancing up to the chins, that the foul lake

---

baseless fabric structure without foundation.
The comparison that follows between "revels"
and the whole world was an old commonplace,
here given powerful elegiac expression; cf.
Spenser, *Amoretti*, Sonnet 54.
inherit possess, occupy
pageant term applied to elaborate and temporary
allegorical show
rack cloud
on of
rounded with rounded off by; or, crowned with
vexed emotionally troubled
beating agitated

Come with a thought Prospero has only to
think his wish that Ariel should come.
Thy thoughts . . . cleave to Ariel confirms this.
presented acted the part of Ceres; or, as Iris,
the "presenter" of the masque, introduced
Ceres
varlets rascals
bending directly their way
unbacked unbroken
Advanced opened
As As if
goss gorse
filthy-mantled covered with filthy scum

O'erstunk their feet.°

PROSPERO   This was well done, my bird.
Thy shape invisible retain thou still:
The trumpery° in my house, go bring it hither,
For stale° to catch these thieves.

ARIEL   I go, I go.   *Exit.*

PROSPERO   A devil, a born devil, on whose nature
Nurture° can never stick; on whom my pains,
190   Humanely taken, all, all lost, quite lost;
And as with age his body uglier grows,
So his mind cankers.° I will plague them all,
Even to roaring.

Re-enter ARIEL, *loaden with glistering apparel, etc.*

                        Come, hang them on this line.°
PROSPERO *and* ARIEL *remain, invisible.*

Enter CALIBAN, STEPHANO, *and* TRINCULO, *all wet.*

CALIBAN   Pray you, tread softly, that the blind mole may not
Hear a foot fall: we now are near his cell.

STEPHANO   Monster, your fairy, which you say is a harmless fairy, has done
little better than played the Jack° with us.
with us.

TRINCULO   Monster, I do smell all horse-piss; at which my nose is in great
200   indignation.

STEPHANO   So is mine. Do you hear, monster? If I should take displeasure
against you, look you,—

TRINCULO   Thou wert but a lost monster.

CALIBAN   Good my lord, give me thy favour still.
Be patient, for the prize I'll bring thee to
Shall hoodwink this mischance:° therefore speak softly.
All's hushed as midnight yet.

TRINCULO   Ay, but to lose our bottles in the pool,—

STEPHANO   There is not only disgrace and dishonour in that, monster, but an
210   infinite loss.

TRINCULO   That's more to me than my wetting: yet this is your harmless fairy,
monster.

STEPHAN   I will fetch off my bottle, though I be o'er ears for my labour.

CALIBAN   Prithee, my King, be quiet. Seest thou here,
This is the mouth o' the cell: no noise, and enter.
Do that good mischief which may make this island
Thine own for ever, and I, thy Caliban,
For aye thy foot-licker.

O'erstunk their feet smelled worse than their feet
trumpery rubbishy clothes
stale bait, decoy
Nurture education, civility
cankers grows diseased

line lime-tree
played the Jack played the knave; played the jack o' lantern (will-o'-the-wisp)
hoodwink this mischance put this mischance out of sight

STEPHANO   Gives me thy hand. I do begin to have bloody thoughts.

220 TRINCULO   O King Stephano! O peer! O worthy Stephano!° look what a wardrobe here is for thee!

CALIBAN   Let it alone, thou fool; it is but trash.

TRINCULO   O, ho, monster! we know what belongs to a frippery.° O King
Stephano!

STEPHANO   Put off that gown, Trinculo; by this hand, I'll have that gown.

TRINCULO   Thy grace shall have it.

CALIBAN   The dropsy drown this fool!° what do you mean
To dote thus on such luggage?° Let 't° alone,
And do the murther first: if he awake,
230 From toe to crown he'll fill our skins with pinches,
Make us strange stuff.°

STEPHANO   Be you quiet, monster. Mistress line, is not this my jerkin? Now is
the jerkin under the line: now, jerkin, you are like to lose your hair, and
prove a bald jerkin.°

TRINCULO   Do, do;° we steal by line and level,° an't like your grace.

STEPHANO   I thank thee for that jest; here's a garment for it: wit shall not go
unrewarded while I am King of this country. 'Steal by line and level' is
an excellent pass of pate;° there's another garment for it.

TRINCULO   Monster, come, put some lime° upon your fingers, and away with
240 the rest.

CALIBAN   I will have none on it: we shall lose our time,
And all be turned to barnacles,° or to apes
With foreheads villainous° low.

STEPHANO   Monster, lay-to your fingers: help to bear this away where my hogshead of wine is, or I'll turn you out of my kingdom: go to, carry this.

TRINCULO   And this.

STEPHANO   Ay, and this.

*A noise of hunters heard. Enter divers Spirits, in shape of dogs and
hound, hunting them about;* PROSPERO *and* ARIEL *setting them on.*

PROSPERO   Hey, Mountain, hey!

ARIEL   Silver! there it goes, Silver!

250 PROSPERO   Fury, Fury! there, Tyrant,° there! hark, hark!

CALIBAN, STEPHANO, *and* TRINCULO *are driven out.*

Go charge my goblins that they grind their joints

O King . . . Stephano refers to old ballad
"King Stephen was a worthy peer," which Iago
sings in *Othello.*
frippery old-clothes shop. Trinculo is saying he
knows the contents of such shops, and denies
that these clothes are of that kind.
The dropsy . . . fool Dropsy is an excessive
accumulation of fluid in the body. Caliban
wants him to drown internally since he escaped
drowning in the sea.
luggage encumbrance
Let't F has "let's"
strange stuff when he's done with us we'll look
even stranger than the clothes
Now is . . . bald jerkin The jerkin is under the

tree (line=equator) and diseases contracted in
the tropics caused loss of hair.
Do, do expressing some kind of amusement at
the joke?
steal . . . level according to the rule, systematically (carrying on the punning on *line*)
an't like if it please
pass of pate thrust of wit
lime birdline
barnacles a kind of geese, supposed to hatch
from barnacles on ships' timbers
villainous wretchedly
Mountain . . . Silver . . . Fury . . . Tyrant
names of hounds

With dry convulsions;° shorten up their sinews
With aged cramps;° and more pinch-spotted° make them
Than pard° or cat o' mountain.°
ARIEL   Hark, they roar!
PROSPERO   Let them be hunted soundly. At this hour
Lies° at my mercy all mine enemies:
Shortly shall all my labours end, and thou
Shalt have the air at freedom: for a little
260   Follow, and do me service.   *Exeunt.*

ACT V

SCENE I [*Before the Cell of* PROSPERO.]

Enter PROSPERO *in his magic robes, and* ARIEL.

PROSPERO   Now does my project gather to a head:°
My charms crack not;° my spirits obey; and time
Goes upright with his carriage.° How's the day?
ARIEL   On the sixth hour; at which time, my lord,
You said our work should cease.
PROSPERO   I did say so,
When first I raised the tempest. Say, my spirit,
How fares the King and his followers?
ARIEL   Confined together
In the same fashion as you gave in charge,
Just as you left them; all prisoners, sir,
10   In the line-grove which weather-fends° your cell;
They cannot budge till your release.° The King,
His brother, and yours, abide all three distracted.
And the remainder mourning over them,
Brimful of sorrow and dismay; but chiefly
Him that you termed, sir, 'The good old lord, Gonzalo';
His tears runs° down his beard, like winter's drops
From eaves of reeds.° Your charm so strongly works° 'em,
That if you now beheld them, your affections
Would become tender.
PROSPERO   Dost thou think so, spirit?
ARIEL   Mine would, sir, were I human.°
20   PROSPERO   And mine shall.
Hast thou, which art but air, a touch, a feeling
Of their afflictions, and shall not myself,

---

dry convulsions convulsions in which bone
grinds on bone
aged cramps cramps such as the aged suffer
pinch-spotted bruised all over with pinches
from the goblins
pard leopard
cat' o' mountain catamount, lynx
Lies lie
project . . . head experiment reach its final
phase (alchemical)

crack not don't go wrong (the alchemist's
retort might "crack" at this point)
time . . . carriage time's burden is light; we
are near the end
weather-fends protects from the weather
your release you release them
runs run
reeds a thatched roof
works moves, agitates
were I human Ariel, a spirit of air, can only
imagine human feelings.

One of their kind, that relish all as sharply
Passion as they,° be kindlier° moved than thou art?
Though with their high wrongs° I am struck to the quick,
Yet with my nobler° reason 'gainst my fury
Do I take part: the rarer° action is
In virtue° than in vengeance: they being penitent,
The sole drift of my purpose doth extend
30   Not a frown further.° Go release them, Ariel:
My charms I'll break, their senses I'll restore,
And they shall be themselves.

ARIEL   I'll fetch them, sir.   *Exit.*

PROSPERO   Ye elves° of hills, brooks, standing lakes, and groves;
And ye that on the sands with printless foot°
Do chase the ebbing Neptune,° and do fly him
When he comes back; you demi-puppets° that
By moonshine do the green sour ringlets° make,
Whereof the ewe not bites; and you whose pastime
Is to make midnight mushrooms,° that rejoice
40   To hear the solemn curfew;° by whose aid—
Weak masters° though ye be—I have bedimmed
The noontide sun, called forth the mutinous winds,
And 'twixt the green sea and the azured vault°
Set roaring war: to the dread rattling thunder
Have I given fire, and rifted Jove's stout oak
With his own bolt; the strong-based promontory
Have I made shake, and by the spurs° plucked up
The pine and cedar: graves at my command
Have waked their sleepers, oped, and let 'em forth
50   By my so potent Art. But this rough magic
I here abjure; and, when I have required
Some heavenly music,—which even now I do,—
To work mine end upon their senses, that
This airy charm is for, I'll brake my staff,
Bury it certain fadoms in the earth,
And deeper than did ever plummet sound
I'll drown my book.°   *Solemn music.*

Re-enter ARIEL *before: then* ALONSO, *with a frantic gesture,*° *attended
by* GONZALO; SEBASTIAN *and* ANTONIO *in like manner, attended by* ADRIAN

relish . . . they am wholly as sensitive as they
to suffering
kindlier more suitably to human nature
high wrongs great injuries inflicted on me
nobler i.e. nobler than passion
rarer finer
virtue as contrasted with *vengeance*, the Christian virtue of forgiveness
Not a frown further no further than I have gone, not by so much as a look of displeasure
Ye elves . . . ll. 33–58. In this farewell to magic Shakespeare paraphrases very closely Ovid, *Metamorphoses* VII.197–209, using the original as well as Golding's translation.
printless foot foot that leaves no print

Neptune ocean
demi-puppets quasi-puppets; elves the size of puppets
green sour ringlets "fairy rings," caused by mycelium under the surface. Apparently sheep do not avoid them.
mushrooms grow overnight, so their nurture is attributed to elves
curfew After curfew tolls, spirits and elves can walk abroad.
masters the magician's demonic agents
azured vault blue sky
spurs roots
book which is necessary to his magic
gesture demeanor

and FRANCISCO: *they all enter the circle which* PROSPERO *had made, and there stand charmed; which* PROSPERO *observing, speaks:*

A solemn air, and the best comforter
To an unsettled fancy, cure thy brains,
⁶⁰ Now useless, boiled° within thy skull! There stand,
For you are spell-stopped.
Holy Gonzalo, honourable man,
Mine eyes, even sociable to the show of thine,
Fall fellowly drops.° The charm dissolves apace;
And as the morning steals upon the night,
Melting the darkness, so their rising senses
Begin to chase the ignorant fumes that mantle°
Their clearer reason. O good Gonzalo,
My true preserver, and a loyal sir
⁷⁰ To him thou follow'st! I will pay° thy graces
Home° both in word and deed. Most cruelly
Didst thou, Alonso, use me and my daughter:
Thy brother was a furtherer in the act.
Thou art pinched for it now, Sebastian. Flesh and blood,
You, brother mine, that entertained° ambition,
Expelled remorse and nature; whom,° with Sebastian—
Whose inward pinches therefore are most strong—
Would here have killed your King; I do forgive thee,
Unnatural though thou art. Their understanding
⁸⁰ Begins to swell;° and the approaching tide
Will shortly fill the reasonable shore,°
That now lie° foul and muddy. Not one of them
That yet looks on me, or would know me: Ariel,
Fetch me the hat and rapier in my cell:
I will discase me,° and myself present
As I was sometime° Milan:° quickly, spirit;

ARIEL *sings and helps to attire him.*

Thou shalt ere long be free.

Where the bee sucks, there suck I:
In a cowslip's bell lie;
⁹⁰ *There I couch° when owls do cry.*
On the bat's back I do fly
After summer° merrily.
Merrily, merrily shall I live now
Under the blossom that hangs on the bough.

boiled seething; F: *boile*
Mine eyes . . . drops my eyes, in sympathy with the tears visible in yours, let fall sympathetic drops
mantle shroud, obscure
pay repay
Home thoroughly
entertained welcomed
whom who

swell rise like the tide
reasonable shore shore of reason, now empty and dry
lie lies
discase me take off my cloak
sometime formerly
Milan Duke of Milan
couch lie
After summer in pursuit of summer

un - der the blos - som that hangs on the bough.

This setting of "Where the Bee Sucks" is by Robert Johnson. (See Note on "Full Fadom Five," Act I, Scene II.)

PROSPERO   Why, that's my dainty Ariel! I shall miss thee;
            But yet thou shalt have freedom: so, so, so.
            To the King's ship, invisible as thou art:
            There shalt thou find the mariners asleep
            Under the hatches; the master and the boatswain
100   Being awake,° enforce them to this place,
            And presently, I prithee.
ARIEL   I drink the air° before me, and return
            Or ere your pulse twice beat.   *Exit.*
GONZALO   All torment, trouble, wonder and amazement
            Inhabits here: some heavenly power guide us
            Out of this fearful country!
PROSPERO   Behold, sir King,
            The wrongèd Duke of Milan, Prospero:
            For more assurance° that a living Prince
            Does now speak to thee, I embrace thy body;
110   And to thee and thy company I bid
            A hearty welcome.
ALONSO   Whether° thou be'st he or no,
            Or some enchanted trifle° to abuse° me,
            As late I have been, I not know: thy pulse
            Beats, as of flesh and blood; and, since I saw thee,
            The affliction of my mind amends, with which,
            I fear, a madness held me: this must crave—
            An if this be at all—a most strange story.
            Thy dukedom I resign, and do entreat
            Thou pardon me my wrongs.—But how should Prospero
            Be living and be here?
120 PROSPERO   First, noble friend,
            Let me embrace thine age, whose honour cannot
            Be measured or confined.
GONZALO   Whether this be
            Or be not, I'll not swear.
PROSPERO   You do yet taste

Being awake having awakened them
drink the air devour the way
For more assurance to make thee more sure
Whether F: *Where*

enchanted trifle apparition raised by an enchanter
abuse delude, deceive

Some subtleties° o' the isle, that will not let you
Believe things certain.° Welcome, my friends all!
[*Aside to* SEBASTIAN *and* ANTONIO] But you, my brace of lords,
    were I so minded,
I here could pluck° his highness' frown upon you,
And justify° you traitors: at this time
I will tell no tales.

SEBASTIAN [*Aside*]   The devil speaks in him.

PROSPERO   No.

130   For you, most wicked sir, whom to call brother
Would even infect my mouth, I do forgive
Thy rankest fault,—all of them; and require
My dukedom of thee, which perforce, I know,
Thou must restore.

ALONSO   If thou be'st Prospero,
Give us particulars of thy preservation;
How thou hast met us here, whom three hours since°
Were wracked upon this shore; where I have lost—
How sharp the point of this remembrance is!—
My dear son Ferdinand.

PROSPERO   I am woe° for it, sir.

140 ALONSO   Irreparable is the loss; and patience
Says it is past her cure.

PROSPERO   I rather think
You have not sought her help, of whose soft grace
For the like loss I have her sovereign° aid,
And rest myself content.

ALONSO   You the like loss!

PROSPERO   As great to me as late;° and, súpportable
To make the dear° loss, have I means much weaker°
Than you may call to comfort you, for I
Have lost my daughter.

ALONSO   A daughter?
O heavens, that they were living both in Naples,

150   The King and Queen there! that° they were, I wish
Myself were mudded in that oozy bed
Where my son lies. When did you lose your daughter?

PROSPERO   In this last tempest. I perceive, these lords
At this encounter do so much admire,°
That they devour their reason,° and scarce think

---

taste . . . subtleties The normal meaning of
subtleties is qualified by a secondary sense,
"elaborate confections of sugar," hence the
word *taste*.
things certain real, non-magical things
pluck bring down
justify prove
three hours since calling attention to the short
time taken by the events of the play
woe sorry

sovereign all-healing
As great to me as late as great to me and as
recent (as yours to you)
dear heavy
much weaker Alonso has a child left; or,
Miranda will live at Naples
that provided that
admire wonder
devour their reason are open-mouthed with
wonder

Their eyes do offices of truth,° their words
Are natural breath:° but, howsoe'er you have
Been justled from your senses, know for certain
That I am Prospero, and that very duke
160   Which was thrust forth of° Milan; who most strangely
Upon this shore, where you were wracked, was landed,
To be the lord on it. No more yet of this;
For 'tis a chronicle of day by day,
Not a relation for a breakfast, nor
Befitting this first meeting. Welcome, sir;
This cell's my court: here have I few attendants,
And subjects none abroad:° pray you, look in.
My dukedom since you have given me again,
I will requite you with as good a thing;
170   At least bring forth a wonder,° to content ye
As much as me my dukedom.

Here PROSPERO *discovers*° FERDINAND *and* MIRANDA *playing at chess.*

MIRANDA   Sweet lord, you play me false.°
FERDINAND   No, my dearest love,
    I would not for the world.
MIRANDA   Yes, for a score of kingdoms you should wrangle,
    And I would call it fair play.°
ALONSO   If this prove
    A vision° of the island, one dear son
    Shall I twice lose.
SEBASTIAN   A most high miracle!°
FERDINAND   Though the seas threaten, they are merciful;
    I have cursed them without cause.
ALONSO   Now all the blessings
180   Of a glad father compass thee about!
    Arise,° and say how thou cam'st here.
MIRANDA   O, wonder!
    How many goodly creatures are there here!
    How beauteous mankind is! O brave new world,
    That has such people in it!
PROSPERO   'Tis new to thee.
ALONSO   What is this maid with whom thou wast at play?
    Your eld'st° acquaintance cannot be three hours:°
    Is she the goddess that hath severed us,
    And brought us thus together?
FERDINAND   Sir, she is mortal;

do offices of truth report the world truly
natural breath the ordinary speech of human
beings
of from
abroad outside this cell, about the island
wonder apparently announcing another "trick,"
really about to display Miranda (the wonder)
and Ferdinand
discovers draws back a curtain to display
play me false cheat me

fair . . . play i.e. if we were playing for a stake
of twenty kingdoms you'd cheat and I'd call
it fair play
vision illusion
miracle Sebastian has the right reaction.
Arise Ferdinand has knelt for a paternal
blessing.
eld'st longest
three hours another reminder

But by immortal Providence she's mine:
190 I chose her when I could not ask my father
For his advice, nor thought I had one. She
Is daughter to this famous Duke of Milan,
Of whom so often I have heard renown,
But never saw before; of whom I have
Received a second life; and second father
This lady makes him to me.

ALONSO   I am hers:°
But, O, how oddly will it sound that I
Must ask my child forgiveness!

PROSPERO   There, sir, stop:
Let us not burthen our remembrance'° with
A heaviness° that's gone.

200 GONZALO   I have inly wept,
Or should have spoke ere this. Look down, you gods,
And on this couple drop a blessed crown!
For it is you that have chalked forth° the way
Which brought us hither.

ALONSO   I say, Amen, Gonzalo!

GONZALO Was Milan° thrust from Milan, that his issue
Should become Kings of Naples! O, rejoice
Beyond a common joy, and set it down
With gold on lasting pillars: in one voyage
Did Claribel her husband find at Tunis,
210 And Ferdinand, her brother, found a wife
Where he himself was lost, Prospero his dukedom
In a poor isle, and all of us ourselves
When no man was his own.°

ALONSO [To FERDINAND and MIRANDA] Give me your hands:
Let grief and sorrow still° embrace° his heart
That doth not wish you joy!

GONZALO   Be it so! Amen!

Re-enter ARIEL, *with the Master and Boatswain amazedly following.*

O, look, sir, look, sir! here is more of us:
I prophesied, if a gallows were on land,
This fellow could not drown. Now, blasphemy,°
That swear'st grace o'erboard,° not an oath on shore?
220 Hast thou no mouth by land? What is the news?

BOATSWAIN The best news is, that we have safely° found
Our King, and company; the next, our ship—

hers her father
remembrance' F: *remembrances*
heaviness sadness
chalked forth marked out
Was . . . (ll. 205–12) Gonzalo, rejoicing that
all the ills resulting from the crime against
Prospero should be canceled, and good come
of them, has a sort of exaltation, and this
speech greatly affects the overall tone of the
play.

no man was his own nobody was in command
of himself; now they have found themselves
again
still always
embrace cling to
blasphemy blasphemous fellow
swear'st grace o'erboard by thy profanity drivest
grace out of the ship
safely in a state of safety

Which, but three glasses° since, we gave out split—
Is tight and yare° and bravely rigged, as when
We first put out to sea.

ARIEL [*Aside to* PROSPERO]   Sir, all this service
Have I done since I went.

PROSPERO [*Aside to* ARIEL]   My tricksy° spirit!

ALONSO   These are not natural events; they strengthen
From strange to stranger.° Say, how came you hither?

BOATSWAIN   If I did think, sir, I were well awake,
230   I'd strive to tell you. We were dead of sleep,°
And—how we know not—all clapped under hatches;
Where, but even now, with strange and several° noises
Of roaring, shrieking, howling, jingling chains,
And mo° diversity of sounds, all horrible,
We were awaked; straightway, at liberty;°
Where we, in all our trim,° freshly beheld
Our royal, good, and gallant ship; our master
Cap'ring° to eye her:—on a trice,° so please you,
Even in a dream, were we divided from them,
And were brought moping° hither.
240 ARIEL [*Aside to* PROSPERO]   Was it well done?

PROSPERO [*Aside to* ARIEL] Bravely,° my diligence.° Thou shalt be free.

ALONSO   This is as strange a maze as e'er men trod;
And there is in this business more than nature
Was ever conduct of:° some oracle°
Must rectify our knowledge.

PROSPERO   Sir, my liege,
Do not infest° your mind with beating° on
The strangeness of this business; at picked° leisure
Which shall be shortly single,° I'll resolve you,°
Which to you shall seem probable,° of every
250   These happened accidents;° till when, be cheerful,
And think of each thing well.° [*Aside to* ARIEL] Come hither, spirit:
Set Caliban and his companions free;
Untie the spell. [*Exit* ARIEL] How fares my gracious sir?
There are yet missing of your company
Some few odd lads that you remember not.

---

three glasses three hours (another reminder)
yare shipshape, ready for sea
tricksy nimble, clever
strengthen . . . stranger increase in strangeness
of sleep asleep
several separate, different
mo more
at liberty no longer confined under hatches
in all our trim our clothes in good shape; some read *her trim* and refer the phrase to the ship
Cap'ring dancing for joy
on a trice in an instant
moping dazed
Bravely splendidly

diligence diligent one
more . . . of more than unaided nature could arrange
oracle source of more than natural information
infest torment, annoy
beating dwelling agitatedly
picked leisure a free time we shall choose
single continuous
resolve you explain to you
Which . . . probable in a manner you'll accept as plausible
every . . . accidents each one of these occurrences
think . . . well give a favorable interpretation to everything

Re-enter ARIEL, *driving in* CALIBAN, STEPHANO, *and* TRINCULO, *in their stolen apparel.*

STEPHANO   Every man shift for all the rest,° and let no man take care for himself; for all is but fortune.—Coragio,° bully-monster, coragio!

TRINCULO   If these be true spies° which I wear in my head, here's a goodly
260   sight.

CALIBAN   O Setebos, these be brave spirits indeed!
How fine° my master is! I am afraid
He will chastise me.

SEBASTIAN   Ha, ha!
What things are these, my lord Antonio?
Will money buy 'em?

ANTONIO   Very like; one of them
Is a plain fish, and, no doubt, marketable.

PROSPERO   Mark but the badges° of these men, my lords,
Then say if they be true.° This mis-shapen knave,
His mother was a witch; and one so strong
270   That could control the moon, make flows and ebbs,
And deal in her command, without her power.°
These three have robbed me; and this demi-devil—
For he's a bastard one°—had plotted with them
To take my life. Two of these fellows you
Must know and own;° this thing of darkness I
Acknowledge mine.

CALIBAN   I shall be pinched to death.

ALONSO   Is not this Stephano, my drunken butler?

SEBASTIAN   He is drunk now: where had he wine?

ALONSO   And Trinculo is reeling ripe:° where should they
280   Find this grand liquor that hath gilded 'em?°—
How comest thou in this pickle?°

TRINCULO   I have been in such pickle,° since I saw you last, that, I fear me,
will never out of my bones: I shall not fear fly-blowing.°

SEBASTIAN   Why, how now, Stephano!

STEPHANO   O, touch me not;—I am not Stephano, but a cramp.

PROSPERO   You'ld be King o' the isle, sirrah?

STEPHANO   I should have been a sore° one, then.

ALONSO   This is as strange a° thing as e'er I looked on.

Every man . . . rest inversion of the saying, "Every man for himself"
Coragio courage
true spies trustworthy eyes
fine Prospero is magnificently dressed in ducal robes.
badges device indicating to which lord a servant belonged (the stolen clothes are thus a proof of the conspirators' dishonesty)
true honest
deal . . . power act in the moon's sphere of authority with a power beyond that of the moon herself (the witch Medea in Ovid's *Metamorphoses* VII.207 had this power)

demi-devil . . . one Caliban was begotten by the devil on a witch; he is a half-devil and a bastard.
own acknowledge
reeling ripe so drunk he reeled as he walked
grand liquor . . . 'em The "grand liquor" is sack, but here Alonso alludes to the elixir the alchemists make gold; "gilded" refers to this metaphor but also means "flushed."
pickle mess
pickle preservative
fly-blowing being pickled, he is safe from the flies that corrupt fresh meat
sore severe; also aching
as strange a F: *a stranger*

Pointing to CALIBAN.

290 PROSPERO   He is disproportioned in his manners°
            As in his shape. Go, sirrah, to my cell;
            Take with you your companions; as you look
            To have my pardon, trim it handsomely.
CALIBAN   Ay, that I will; and I'll be wise hereafter,
            And seek for grace.° What a thrice-double ass
            Was I, to take this drunkard for a god,
            And worship this dull fool!
PROSPERO   Go to; away!
ALONSO   Hence, and bestow your luggage° where you found it.
SEBASTIAN   Or stole it, rather.
300 PROSPERO   Sir, I invite your Highness and your train
            To my poor cell, where you shall take your rest
            For this one night; which, part of it, I'll waste°
            With such discourse as, I not doubt, shall make it
            Go quick away: the story of my life,
            And the particular accidents° gone by
            Since I came to this isle: and in the morn
            I'll bring you to your ship, and so to Naples,
            Where I have hope to see the nuptial°
            Of these our dear-beloved solemnized;
310   And thence retire me to my Milan, where
            Every third thought shall be my grave.
ALONSO   I long
            To hear the story of your life, which must
            Take° the ear strangely.
PROSPERO   I'll deliver° all;
            And promise you calm seas, auspicious gales,
            And sail° so expeditious, that shall catch
            Your royal fleet far off.° [*Aside to* ARIEL] My Ariel, chick,°
            That is thy charge: then to the elements°
            Be free, and fare thou well! Please you, draw near.   *Exeunt omnes.*

EPILOGUE°

Spoken by PROSPERO.

Now my charms are all o'erthrown,
And what strength I have's mine own,

manners conduct, morality
grace pardon, favor
luggage rubbish, encumbrance
waste spend
accidents incidents
nuptial nuptials, wedding ceremony
Take captivate
deliver tell
sail voyage
far off far off though it already is
chick term of endearment
elements Ariel's natural habitat
Epilogue Although this is valuable material for

those who would read the play as an allegory, it is basically the traditional appeal for applause, expressed in figures derived from the action of the play that has just ended. The actor who played Prospero has now, he says, no power to release himself from a spell which can only be broken when the audience applauds; and he prays for this as a grace that will help him avoid the sin of despair and set him free of his faults (as an actor). This he asks in the language of the Lord's Prayer; as the audience hopes for pardon itself, so it should award it to him.

Which is most faint: now, 'tis true,
I must be here confined°   by you,
Or sent to Naples. Let me not,
Since I have my dukedom got,
And pardoned the deceiver, dwell
In this bare island by your spell;
But release me from my bands°
10   *With the help of your good hands:°*
Gentle breath°   of yours my sails
Must fill, or else my project°   fails,
Which was to please. Now I want
Spirits to enforce, Art to enchant;
And my ending is despair,
Unless I be relieved by prayer,°
Which pierces°   so, that it assaults
Mercy itself,°   and frees°   all faults.
As you from crimes°   would pardoned be,
20   *Let your indulgence°   set me free.*   *Exit.*
1611   1623

THOMAS CAMPION
1567–1620

One of the greatest writers of song in English, Campion, a student of law and medicine, was also a composer and poet. He published the bulk of his work in several books of airs between 1601 and 1617. He also wrote court masques and a good deal of Latin verse. Campion used the form of the stanzaic song to embody a variety of Renaissance poetic genres, including Petrarchan poems, epigrams, hymns, pastoral lyrics. His musical settings for solo voice and lute are graceful and typical of their style. While as a composer he is far less remarkable, particularly in his lute accompaniments, than the great lutenist John Dowland, his poems are unsurpassed for their smoothness and freshness, which still provide great rhetorical power. In an effort to augment such power John Donne was concurrently eschewing the rhythmic evenness of song texts, with their adaptability for musical setting, for the "strong lines" of his *Songs and Sonnets.*

Campion remained more or less in a Sidneyan tradition. He wrote a treatise on quantitative verse, suggesting a way of counting long and short syllables in English different from the usual Elizabethan methods but, like them, opting for unrhymed verse. His splendid collections of songs ignore these prescriptions.

confined as Ariel was
bands bonds
hands their clapping would break the spell
Gentle breath kindly comment on the performance
project his, parallel to but distinct from, Prospero's

prayer the petition he is now making
pierces is so penetrating
assaults Mercy itself "Prayers . . . break open heaven's gate" was a proverb.
frees wins pardon for
crimes sins
indulgence kindness; also remission for sins

My Sweetest Lesbia°

My sweetest Lesbia, let us live and love.
And, though the sager sort our deeds reprove,
Let us not weigh them. Heaven's great lamps do dive
Into their west, and straight again revive.
But soon as once set is our little light,
Then must we sleep one ever-during night.

If all would lead their lives in love like me,
Then bloody swords and armour should not be.
No drum nor trumpet peaceful sleeps should move,
Unless alarm came from the camp of Love.
But fools do live and waste their little light,
And seek with pain their ever-during night.

When timely death my life and fortune ends,
Let not my hearse be vexed with mourning friends.
But let all lovers, rich in triumph, come
And with sweet pastimes grace my happy tomb.
And, Lesbia, close up thou my little light,
And crown with love my ever-during night.

                                        1601

Follow Your Saint

Follow your saint, follow with accents sweet;
Haste you, sad notes, fall at her flying feet.
There, wrapped in cloud of sorrow, pity move,
And tell the ravisher of my soul I perish for her love.
But if she scorns my never-ceasing pain,
Then burst with sighing in her sight and ne'er return again.

All that I sung still to her praise did tend,
Still she was first, still she my songs did end.
Yet she my love and music both doth fly,
The music that her echo is and beauty's sympathy.
Then let my notes pursue her scornful flight:
It shall suffice that they were breathed and died for her delight.

                                        1601

My Sweetest Lesbia An adaptation of Catullus'
famous *Vivamus mea Lesbia, atque amemus;*
compare it with Ben Jonson's version in "Come,
My Celia" to see how Campion's use of the
varied refrain helps him build a stanzaic song.

Rose-cheeked Laura°

Rose-cheeked Laura, come
Sing thou smoothly with thy beauty's
Silent music, either other°
    Sweetly gracing.

Lovely forms do flow
From concent° divinely framed;
Heaven is music, and thy beauty's
    Birth is heavenly.

These dull notes we sing
10 Discords need for helps to grace them;
Only beauty purely loving
    Knows no discord,

But still moves delight,
Like clear springs renewed by flowing,
Ever perfect, ever in them-°
    selves eternal.
        1602

Mistress, Since You So Much Desire

Mistress, since you so much desire
To know the place of Cupid's fire,
In your fair shrine that flame doth rest,
Yet never harboured in your breast.
It bides not in your lips so sweet,
Nor where the rose and lilies meet,
    But a little higher,
There, there, O there, lies Cupid's fire.

E'en in those starry piercing eyes,
10 There Cupid's sacred fire lies.
Those eyes I strive not to enjoy,
For they have power to destroy.
Nor woo I for a smile or kiss,
So meanly triumphs not my bliss.
    But a little higher
I climb to crown my chaste desire.
        1601

Rose-cheeked Laura an example of the "lyrical" metrical forms from Campion's *Observations in the Art of English Poesy* (1602), in which he tried to reconstitute English meter on a kind of quantitative basis, although the modern reader can hear it is unrhymed, stressed trochaic

either other each one the other
concent harmony
them- This kind of hyphenation across the last two lines of a stanza occurs in Greek Sapphic verse, from which this form is derived.

Beauty, Since You So Much Desire°

Beauty since you so much desire
To know the place of Cupid's fire,
About you somewhere doth it rest,
Yet never harboured in your breast,
Nor gout-like in your heel or toe.
What fool would seek Love's flame so low?
    But a little higher,
There, there, O there lies Cupid's fire.

10 Think not, when Cupid most you scorn,
Men judge that you of ice were born.
For though you cast Love at your heel,
His fury yet sometime you feel.
And whereabout, if you would know,
I tell you still, not in your toe,
    But a little higher,
There, there, O there lies Cupid's fire.

c. 1618

There Is a Garden in Her Face

There is a garden in her face
    Where roses and white lilies grow;
A heavenly paradise° is that place,
    Wherein these pleasant fruits do flow.°
There cherries grow which none may buy,
Till 'Cherry-ripe'° themselves do cry.

These cherries fairly do enclose
    Of orient pearl° a double row,
Which when her lovely laughter shows,
10   They look like rose-buds filled with snow;
Yet them no peer nor prince can buy,
Till 'Cherry-ripe' themselves do cry.

Her eyes like angels watch them still;
    Her brows like bended bows° do stand,
Threatening with piercing shafts to kill

Beauty, Since You So Much Desire This poem is
an erotic parody of the idealized, Petrarchan
"Mistress, Since You So Much Desire" which
precedes it in this text; here, the lady's eyes
as the place of love give way to her genital
region, much as in Donne's "Love's Progress."
There is . . . paradise no mere hyperbole, for
the garden and its treasures, the fruit and jewels
of Eden and the Hesperides garden with its
golden apples, are guarded by angels against
re-entry
flow abound, echoing the biblical "flowing with
milk and honey"

'Cherry-ripe' This was the conventional advertis-
ing street cry of cherry-peddlers in London. Campion not only quotes the phrase but, in his
musical setting of this poem, quotes the b-
natural—c—d—d—d melody of the street cry
on the words "cherry ripe, ripe, ripe" in the
completed song; the point is only that one
mayn't kiss the lady until those same lips invite
the kiss.
orient pearl shining pearls; her teeth
bended bows a traditional conceit

All that presume with eye or hand
Those sacred cherries to come nigh,
Till 'Cherry-ripe' themselves do cry.
1617

'cher - ry ripe!'   till 'cher - ry   ripe,   cher - ry ripe,   ripe,

ripe,   cher - ry   ripe,   cher - ry   ripe!' them - selves   do   cry.

This is Campion's own setting, for lute and voice, of the preceding poem. The little melodic fragment to "cherry ripe ripe ripe" was the street-cry actually sung to these words by London cherry vendors, and Campion works it into the vocal part just as he works the words into the conceit of his text.

Thrice Toss These Oaken Ashes in the Air°

Thrice toss these oaken ashes in the air.
Thrice sit thou mute in this enchanted chair.
Then thrice three times tie up this true love's knot,
And murmur soft: She will, or she will not.

Go burn these poisonous weeds in yon blue fire,
These screech-owl's feathers and this prickling briar,
This cypress gathered at a dead man's grave,
That all thy fears and cares and end may have.

Then come, you fairies, dance with me a round;
10 Melt her hard heart with your melodious sound.
In vain are all the charms I can devise;
She hath an art to break them with her eyes.

                  c. 1618

Thrice Toss These Oaken Ashes This song is an incantation or spell, invoking traditional fairy magic (like pulling petals from a daisy and saying "He loves me, he loves me not"); the world of magic, it will be observed, defers to the conventional Petrarchan power of the lady's eyes.

When to Her Lute Corinna Sings

When to her lute Corinna° sings,
Her voice revives the leaden strings,
And doth in highest notes appear
As any challenged echo clear.
But when she doth of mourning speak,
Even with her sighs the strings do break.

And as her lute doth live or die,
Led by her passion, so must I.
For when of pleasure she doth sing,
10 My thoughts enjoy a sudden spring;
But if she doth of sorrow speak,
Even from my heart the strings° do break.

                              1601

Never Weather-beaten Sail

Never weather-beaten sail more willing bent to shore,
Never tired pilgrim's limbs affected slumber more,
Than my weary sprite° now longs to fly out of my troubled breast.
O come quickly, sweetest Lord, and take my soul to rest.

Ever blooming are the joys of Heaven's high Paradise.
Cold age deafs not there our ears, nor vapour dims our eyes;
Glory there the sun outshines, whose beams the blessed only see.
O come quickly, glorious Lord, and raise my sprite° to thee.

                              c. 1613

JOHN DONNE
1572–1631

Donne was born early in 1572, son of a prosperous London merchant and a mother not only Catholic but connected by marriage to Sir Thomas More; her brother, Jasper Heywood, translator of Seneca, was imprisoned for his part in a Jesuit mission to England, and Donne's own brother Henry died in prison in 1593 after being arrested for concealing a priest. The poet was justified in claiming that his family had suffered heavily "for obeying the teachers of the Roman Doctrine" (*Pseudo-Martyr*, an anti-Jesuit polemic of 1610). His early education was Catholic, and although he came to reject it (especially in its Jesuit form) his thinking and his temperament were affected by his Catholic training throughout his life.

As a Catholic, Donne could not take a degree, though he spent three years at Oxford, and three at Cambridge; in the early 1590's he was a student at the Inns of Court, in

---

Corinna an ancient Greek lyric poetess. Her name is used for the Petrarchan lady in the guise of musician who plays on her lover like an instrument.

the strings Because of a pun on the Latin words for "heart" and "string," the concept of "heart-strings" was a Renaissance cliché.

sprite spirit

London, then more a university than a law school; he studied law, languages, and theology from four in the morning till ten, and in his spare time was, we are told, a great visitor of ladies and a theatergoer. In these years he wrote the Elegies and Satires, and some of the *Juvenilia* and of the *Songs and Sonnets*. He traveled in Europe and took part in two naval expeditions before becoming, in 1598, secretary to the powerful Sir Thomas Egerton; but his good prospects of worldly success were ended by his secret marriage with Ann More, Egerton's niece, in 1601. For years he lived miserably and sought patronage—Lucy, Countess of Bedford and Sir Robert Drury were among his most important benefactors—and worked at anti-Romanist polemic as assistant to Morton, a clergyman who was to become the bishop of Durham. In 1610 his financial difficulties were eased; he published *Pseudo-Martyr* and the satire *Ignatius His Conclave*, also directed against the Jesuits. To this period belong also the two *Anniversaries* commemorating Elizabeth Drury (1611, 1612) and *Biathanatos*, a casuistic work on suicide which he did not publish. His chief theological work, *Essays in Divinity*, was written in 1614 but remained unpublished till after his death.

Although he had probably declared for the Anglican religion by 1602, Donne resisted royal pressure to take orders until 1615, after which his ecclesiastical advancement was rapid. Henceforth he wrote few poems—even the *Holy Sonnets* are, for the most part, earlier than the date of his ordination. His wife died in 1617, at a time when he was achieving fame as a preacher. He became Dean of St. Paul's in 1621, and so completed the rejection of "the mistress of my youth, Poetry" for "the wife of mine age, Divinity." In 1623 he had a serious illness, during which he wrote his *Devotions upon Emergent Occasions* and two famous hymns. But the great sermons—ten volumes of them in the standard edition—were his chief work in these years. They often allude to his own life—the deaths of his wife and daughter, his own departure abroad, his remorse at past sins, even, in the famous *Death's Duel*, preached to King Charles I in Lent 1631, his own death. His friend Walton made much of his histrionic composure on his deathbed, and did much to confirm the traditional view of Donne as a sort of St. Augustine, who, after a wild youth, settled for preaching, piety, and remorse. This is too simple, for Donne was an ambitious man, a man with many friends in the world; there must have been a certain piquancy in the thought that the libertine poems still circulating around London had come from the pen of the somber and powerful preacher in St. Paul's; yet the same intellectual ambitions and interests, the same wit, animate both. "Wit / He did not banish, but transplanted it," says one of his elegists; for wit was certainly a quality as highly valued in sermons as in love poems.

The best way to understand what is meant by Donne's "wit" is to work at the poems. For they require work; they depend upon one's understanding how the fantastic argument is advanced by the pseudo-logic of analogy and far-fetched allusion. After that one can begin to admire the complexity of tone, the countercurrents of secondary meaning, the ingenuity of the prodigally invented stanza forms, and the "masculine persuasive force," as Donne himself called it, of the language. To be thus "harsh"—Donne's own word again—was a duty imposed on satirists; to be conceited and harsh was a requirement of the funeral elegy, of which Donne wrote many. What is more unusual is the employment of "strong lines" and scholastic argument in love poetry, especially in a poet whose voice is capable of combining a masculine tenderness with colloquial power and both with obscure argument. Such combination—of apparent spontaneity and fine-drawn ratiocination, of amorous élan with verse forms of wantonly ingenious difficulty—characterize the finest of the poems to a degree that sets them apart from all predecessors and imitators, no matter how cogently resemblances are argued.

This does not mean, of course, that Donne was an absolute innovator. Many of his poems are on topics which occur in other sixteenth- and early seventeenth-century verse—"The Flea" and "The Dream," for example—and the conceits of Petrarchanism, like some standard emblems, recur, though in modified forms. Donne was harsher than the others—Jonson scolded him for it—and also wittier and more skeptical.

It might also be said that he was more "modern"; but this is a difficult concept. Wit, the *discordia concors*, was not modern. Nor was obscurity—Jonson said Donne would perish for not being understood, but he is much less obscure than his contemporary Chapman, and even the mellifluous Spenser is on occasion virtually impenetrable. Furthermore, the modernity of Donne's references to "new philosophy"— specifically Copernicanism—has been much exaggerated; his chief sources of learned imagery are the doctrines of the Schoolmen, law, and alchemy. For all his learning he was traditionally skeptical about the power of the human mind to know truth.

Where, then, does this modernity, so much admired by the nineteenth and twentieth centuries, lie? Partly in the new cult of an old wit, which affected poetry and preaching throughout Europe in these years; partly in a new kind of obscurity, deriving not from a manipulation of secret mythic meanings but from the representation of passionate thinking; partly from a skepticism which, despite its deep religious roots, took a modern form in Montaigne and Donne. Donne's rejection of the learning that depends on unaided human sense is essential to his religion; we see it expressed with extravagance in the lines here extracted from the *Second Anniversary*, and with more gravity in the Easter-Day Sermon. In the same way he distinguished between human "custom," which has no divine support, and the law; and his ultimate rejection of the church of Rome depended on this distinction. But when erotic poetry is subjected to the same skepticism the effect is very different; for "custom" is what controls normal "bourgeois" sexual relations, and "law" is natural inclination. In short, the skeptic can, in these matters, reject convention and the vast superstructure of human sanctions as matters of opinion, not of true knowledge of the natural law. The consequence of this rejection is libertine poetry.

Yet even libertine poetry is ancient; and in the Elegies, the warmest of his poems, Donne is imitating Ovid. Nor is his amorous verse all concerned with the paradoxes and problems that arise from the conflict of desire with authority; he often has a recognizably more serious tone, and draws on the lore of Renaissance Platonism to illustrate the union of lovers' souls and the relationship between soul and body.

All we can say, then, is that Donne's modern contained much of the past, as modernity always does. What, in the end, preserves him is that his poetry is full of his powerful mind; and that the projection of his mind into poetry is immediate and, whatever the subject, witty or passionate or both.

It would not do to end this brief general introduction without a word more about Donne's religion, which preoccupied him through most of his life and long survived his active career as a poet. The third Satire is an urgent statement of the importance, there and then, of discovering a true religion. His choice of the English church as nearest to the true primitive and catholic was no doubt made possible by the labors of Hooker and other apologists. Donne held to the English middle course, the *via media*, supporting all attempts to persuade others to join it, for the rest of his life.

His chosen church avoided the errors of Rome, but maintained its contact with the ancient learning and forms; it cherished tradition without accumulated error, the Fathers but not their follies. He rejected the extreme Calvinists with detestation, but, like them, knew his Augustine. He saw the dangers of learned controversy: "It is the text that saves us; the interlineary glosses, and the marginal notes, and the *variae lectiones*, controversies and perplexities, undo us." Although his sermons seem very learned, it is worth noticing that he patiently explains his meanings, and repeats the explanations; he was an enormously popular preacher, and his distinction as a church-man lies in that and in his piety, for he was not a distinguished theologian. The wit—fineness of mind—and passion of the erotic poetry lived on, not only into the religious poetry but, suitably adapted to a larger audience, into the great sermons also. "His fancy," said his biographer Izaak Walton, "was unimitably high, equalled only by his great wit . . . He was by nature highly passionate." The words will serve to explain why, as beneficiaries of the twentieth-century revival of Donne and the scholarship which has cleared his text and illustrated his meanings, we continue to value him so highly, and perhaps occasionally to marvel that the smallish city of London, in one lifetime, contained such different poets as Marlowe, Spenser, Shake-speare, Jonson, and Donne.

We sometimes hear of a School of Donne, and there were certainly admirers and imitators, of whom the best was also the last of any merit, Abraham Cowley (1618–67). What will not do is to include the other so-called Metaphysical poets—men of the stature and idiosyncrasy of Herbert, Vaughan, Crashaw, Marvell—under such a head-ing. The conceit of Donne degenerated into a joke; the ultimate ancestor of such a work as the young Dryden's *Elegy on Lord Hastings* may be the conceit-powered funeral elegies of Donne, or even the *Anniversaries*, but a remarkable decline has occurred.

At the same time the concept of wit underwent important changes. As an admired quality it was no longer primarily a matter of acuteness, the power to make unforeseen metaphors and arguments; the concept grew more general, closer to Pope's "What oft was thought. . . ." So conceived, "strong-lined" poetry went out of fashion, as did "Senecan" prose and the witty sermon. Dr. Johnson's study of Donne's wit in his *Life of Cowley*, hostile, penetrating, even in its way just, shows him conversant with the Donnean idea of wit, but also disapproving; the best he can say is that to write as these men did it "was at least necessary to think." Pope knew the Satires, but smoothed them out, and Donne's poetry came to be thought of as at best interesting primitive work. The revival, depending on atrocious texts, was an achievement of the nineteenth century; Coleridge read deeply in the verse and prose, saying some harsh things about the verse but soliciting admiration also, especially for "The Ecstasy" and *Satire 3*. Later Browning, and George Eliot, and then many poets of the later years of the century, helped to build up a cult. Grierson's edition of 1912 made good texts and informed commentary available, and by the time T. S. Eliot wrote his famous essay "The Metaphysical Poets" in 1923, there were easily available ways of speaking and writing about this exciting poet. These we tend, wrongly, to attribute to Eliot himself. For a while modern criticism treated the disappearance of Donne's colloquial intensity from English poetry as a symptom of a general cultural disaster, called by Eliot a "dissociation of sensibility"; later he revised his views on Donne, and some-what changed that concept, in itself neither original nor historically valid; but the association of Donne with it, and with critical campaigns against Milton, still persists in some quarters. It is not harmless, for it imposes false ways of reading both Donne and Milton, which is why these notes say so little, and that skeptically, about the cultural and scientific crisis identified with Donne's verse, and so much, relatively, about Donne's own skepticism.

From Juvenilia: Or Paradoxes and Problems°

Problem: Why Does the Pox So Much Affect to Undermine the Nose?°

Paracelsus° perchance saith true, that every disease hath his exaltation° in some part certain. But why this in the nose? Is there so much mercy in this disease that it provides that one should not smell his own stink? Or hath it but the common fortune that, being begot and bred in obscurest and secretest places (because therefore his serpentine crawling and insinuation should not be suspected nor seen), he comes soonest into great place, and is more able to destroy the worthiest member than a disease better born? Perchance as mice defeat elephants° by gnawing their *proboscis* (which is their nose), this wretched Indian vermin practiceth to do the same upon us. Or as the ancient furious custom and connivancy° of some laws that° one might cut off their nose whom he deprehended in adultery, was but a type of this; and that now, more charitable laws having taken away all revenge from particular hands, this common magistrate and executioner is come to do the same office invisibly? Or by withdrawing this conspicuous part, the nose, it warns us from all adventuring upon that coast—for it is as good a mark to take in a flag, as to hang one out. Possibly Heat, which is more potent and active than Cold, thought herself injured, and the Harmony of the World out of tune, when Cold was able to show the high-way to noses in Muscovia, except she found the means to do the same in other countries. Or because by the consent of all, there is an analogy, proportion and affection between the nose and that part where this disease is first contracted, and therefore Heliogabalus° chose not his minions° in the bath but by the nose. And Albertus° had a knavish meaning when he preferred great noses. And the licentious poet° was *Naso Poeta*. I think this reason is nearest truth:° that the nose is most compassionate with this part

Paradoxes and Problems The paradox was a fashionable exercise throughout Europe, and Donne's early interest in it is reflected in some of the *Songs and Sonnets*.
Why Does . . . Nose While the point of the "paradox" as a literary exercise was to argue contrary to the received view, the problem of these "problems" was to produce as many ingenious and funny "explanations" as possible for a phenomenon that, presumably, could not be explained. The pox, syphilis, frequently resulted in facial disfigurement; as the erotic and mercantile disease (it was believed to have been brought to Europe from the Caribbean by explorers) it led to much grim humor.
Paracelsus (Theophrastus Bombastus von Hohenheim, 1493–1541), Swiss alchemist and physician

exaltation most powerful manifestation
mice . . . elephants or so the belief was
connivancy literally, "winking at," overlooking, and pretending not to
that so that
deprehended apprehended
Heliogabalus (204–222 A.D.), wildly depraved Roman emperor
minions literally, "cuties," male sexual partners
Albertus St. Albertus Magnus (Albert von Böllstadt, 1193?–1280), scholastic philosopher and St. Thomas Aquinas's teacher
licentious poet Ovid, whose full name was Publius Ovidius Naso
nearest truth He certainly does not; this is like the "But seriously, now," of the stand-up comic.

—except this be nearer: that it is reasonable that this disease in particular should affect the most eminent and perspicuous part, which in general doth affect to take hold of the most eminent and conspicuous men.

1633

Elegies

The chief model of the Elizabethan love elegy was the *Amores* of Ovid; Marlowe had made these fashionable, and the tradition was crossed with that of the witty, para-doxical, Italian love poetry of the period. Donne's Elegies, of which two are given here, belong to his early twenties, being attributable to the early 1590's, when he was a student at Lincoln's Inn. He outdoes Ovid in his witty dedication to physical pleasure; and the Elegies differ from the *Songs and Sonnets* not only in their adherence to the iambic pentameter couplet but in the unspiritual ruthlessness that for the most part characterizes their attitude to love. Not all the Elegies have the sexual directness and plain-spokenness of these two, but they will serve to demonstrate one extreme of his love poetry.

Elegy XVIII: Love's Progress°

Whoever loves, if he do not propose
The right true end of love, he's one that goes
To sea for nothing but to make him sick.
And love's a bear-whelp° born, if we o'er-lick
Our love, and force it new strange shapes to take,
We err, and of a lump a monster make.
Were not a calf a monster that were grown
Faced like a man, though better than his own?°
Perfection is in unity: prefer°
One woman first, and then one thing in her.
I, when I value gold, may think upon
The ductileness, the application,°
The wholesomeness, the ingenuity,°
From rust, from soil, from fire ever free,
But if I love it, 'tis because 'tis made
By our new nature,° use, the soul of trade.
   All these in women we might think upon
(If women had them) and yet love but one.
Can men more injure women than to say
They love them for that, by which they are not they?

10

20

Love's Progress refused a license in 1633; first printed in 1661 and with Donne's other poems in 1669
bear-whelp supposed to be born a shapeless lump which the mother licked into shape
though . . . own even though a man's face is in itself better than a calf's
prefer choose
application uses it is put to
ingenuity noble quality
new nature human custom (or, as he calls it, *use*)

Makes virtue woman? must I cool my blood
Till I both be, and find one, wise and good?
May barren angels love so. But if we
Make love to woman, virtue is not she,
As beauty's not, nor wealth. He that strays thus
From her to hers,° is more adulterous
Than if he took her maid. Search every sphere
And firmament, our Cupid is not there.°
He's an infernal god and underground
30   With Pluto dwells, where gold and fire° abound.
Men to such gods, their sacrificing coals
Did not in altars lay, but pits and holes.
Although we see celestial bodies move
Above the earth, the earth we till and love:
So we her airs contemplate, words and heart,
And virtues; but we love the centric part.°
    Nor is the soul more worthy, or more fit
For love than this,° as infinite as it.
But in attaining this desirèd place
40   How much they stray, that set out at the face!
The hair a forest is of ambushes,
Of springes, snares, fetters and manacles;
The brow becalms us when 'tis smooth and plain,
And when 'tis wrinkled, shipwrecks us again;
Smooth, 'tis a paradise, where we would have
Immortal stay, and wrinkled 'tis our grave.
The nose like to the first meridian° runs
Not 'twixt an east and west, but 'twixt two suns;
It leaves a cheek, a rosy hemisphere
50   On either side, and then directs us where
Upon the Islands Fortunate° we fall,
(Not faint Canary,° but ambrosial°)
Her swelling lips; to which when we are come,
We anchor there, and think ourselves at home,
For they seem all: there sirens' songs, and there
Wise Delphic oracles do fill the ear;
There in a creek where chosen pearls do swell,
The remora,° her cleaving tongue doth dwell.
These, and the glorious promontory, her chin
60   O'erpast; and the strait Hellespont between

from her to hers from her essential self to her
mere attributes
Search . . . there no heavenly body is called
after Cupid
gold with fire Deep in the earth, in the realm
of the god of hell, are gold and heat, both
necessary to love.
pits and holes . . . centric part *doubles en-
tendres*
this the vagina
springes small traps for game

first meridian first circle of longitude, which
(at the Canary Islands) divided the eastern and
western hemispheres
Islands Fortunate mythical happy islands west
of Gibraltar; usually identified with the Canaries
faint Canary the light sweet wine of the
Canaries
ambrosial Ambrosia was the food of the gods.
remora sucking-fish, supposed to be able to
stop ships

The Sestos and Abydos° of her breasts,
(Not of two lovers,° but two loves the nests)
Succeeds a boundless sea, but yet thine eye
Some island moles may scattered there descry;
And sailing towards her India,° in that way
Shall at her fair Atlantic navel stay;
Though thence the current be thy pilot made,
Yet ere thou be where thou wouldst be embayed,°
Thou shalt upon another forest set,
70   Where many shipwreck, and no further get.
When thou art there, consider what this chase
Misspent by thy beginning at the face.
    Rather set out below, practise my art,
Some symmetry° the foot hath with that part
Which thou dost seek, and is thy map for that
Lovely enough to stop, but not stay at:
Least subject to disguise and change it is;
Men say the Devil never can change his.°
It is the emblem that hath figurèd
80   Firmness;° 'tis the first part that comes to bed.
Civility, we see, refined the kiss
Which at the face begun, transplanted is
Since to the hand, since to the imperial knee,
Now at the papal foot delights to be.°
If kings think that the nearer way,° and do
Rise from the foot, lovers may do so too;
For as free spheres° move faster far than can
Birds, whom the air resists, so may that man
Which goes this empty and ethereal way,
90   Than if at beauty's elements he stay.
Rich Nature hath in women wisely made
Two purses,° and their mouths aversely° laid;
They then, which to the lower tribute owe,
That way which that exchequer looks, must go.
He which doth not, his error is as great,
As who by clyster° gave the stomach meat.

1669

Sestos and Abydos towns on the opposite shores of the Hellespont; cf. Marlowe's *Hero and Leander* above
two lovers Hero and Leander
India the orient, source of riches
embayed See Carew, "A Rapture," ll. 85–90, below.
symmetry likeness of shape
his his cloven foot
emblem . . . firmness The foot was used as an emblem of *firmitas*.

Civility . . . to be polite manners have made our kissing more subservient; kissing on the face descends to hand-kissing, then to kissing the emperor's knee and the pope's foot
the nearer way the shortest way to what they want
free spheres the heavenly bodies, which encounter no resistance from the air
Two purses the mouth and the vagina
aversely at different angles
clyster enema

Elegy XIX: To His Mistress Going to Bed°

Come, Madam, come, all rest my powers defy,
Until I labour, I in labour lie.
The foe oft-times having the foe in sight,
Is tired with standing° though they never fight.
Off with that girdle, like heaven's zone° glistering,
But a far fairer world encompassing.
Unpin that spangled breastplate° which you wear,
That the eyes of busy fools may be stopped there.
Unlace yourself, for that harmonious chime°
10 Tells me from you, that now 'tis your bed time.
Off with that happy busk,° which I envy,
That still can be, and still can stand so nigh.
Your gown going off, such beauteous state reveals,
As when from flowery meads the hill's shadow steals.
Off with that wiry coronet° and show
The hairy diadem which on you doth grow;
Now off with those shoes, and then safely tread
In this love's hallowed temple, this soft bed.
In such white robes heaven's angels used to be
20 Received by men; thou angel bring'st with thee
A heaven like Mahomet's paradise;° and though°
Ill spirits walk in white, we easily know
By this these angels from an evil sprite:
Those set our hairs, but these our flesh upright.
    Licence my roving hands, and let them go
Before, behind, between, above, below.
O my America, my new found land,
My kingdom, safeliest when with one man manned,°
My mine of precious stones, my empery,°
30 How blessed am I in this discovering thee!
To enter in these bonds,° is to be free;
Then where my hand is set, my seal shall be.°
    Full nakedness, all joys are due to thee.
As souls unbodied, bodies unclothed must be,
To taste whole joys.° Gems which you women use
Are like Atalanta's balls,° cast in men's views,

To His Mistress Going to Bed refused license
in 1633; published 1669
standing waiting to fight; here: having an erec-
tion
heaven's zone Orion's belt (*zona* = girdle)
spangled breastplate stomacher, which covered
the breast and was often jeweled
chime she had a chiming watch
busk corset
wiry coronet band of metal worn round the
brow
Mahomet's paradise a place of sensual bliss
(for men)
though even though

manned inhabited, served
empery empire
these bonds her arms
where . . . shall be having signed the contract he will seal it; having put his hand on
her sex he will complete that transaction also
As souls . . . whole joys as souls must be
divested of bodies to taste heavenly joy, so
bodies must be divested of clothes
Atalanta's balls Hippomenes defeated the un-
beatable Atalanta in a race by throwing three
golden apples in her path; she stopped to pick
them up.

That when a fool's eyes lighteth on a gem,
His earthly soul may covet theirs, not them.
Like pictures, or like books' gay coverings made
40 For laymen,° are all women thus arrayed;
Themselves are mystic books, which only we
Whom their imputed grace will dignify°
Must see revealed. Then since I may know,
As liberally, as to a midwife, show
Thyself: cast all, yea, this white linen hence,
There is no penance due to innocence.°
    To teach thee, I am naked first, why then
What need'st thou have more covering than a man.
                                1669

Songs and Sonnets

First published in 1633, two years after Donne's death, these poems circulated in
manuscript during the poet's lifetime. Their first audience was a small, sophisticated,
no doubt rather "fast" group of like-minded young men, willing to be tested by
fantastic argument, admiring what Donne himself called, in a squib called *The
Courtier's Library*, "itchy outbreaks of far-fetched wit." This much may be said without
prejudice to the great variety of tone in the poems: they all ask one to admire their
ingenuity, their skill in overcoming the difficulties placed in the way of complicated
argument by the arbitrarily difficult stanza forms. Yet some really are "songs," and
were sung; others fail, as so many of the poems of later poets who imitated them fail,
by being nothing but ingenious. The selection of poems that follows excludes several
such relative failures.

    Nevertheless, it would be dangerous to argue that only the more "serious" poems
are good; just as it is dangerous to divide the poems, as some do, into two groups,
rakish poems written before 1600, more subtle and serious poems written after 1602.
Occasionally dates can be conjectured; some of these dates are after 1600, and the
tone of the poems is different from that of the more libertine Elegies, which belong to
the 1590's. But there is no certainty, and for that reason no dates of composition are
appended to the poems in this selection.

The Good Morrow

I wonder by my troth, what thou and I
    Did, till we loved? were we not weaned till then,
But sucked on country° pleasures, childishly?

---

laymen who cannot understand the contents
imputed grace . . . dignify to the elect women
will impute the grace necessary to this revelation, as Christ, in Calvinist doctrine, imputes
to his elect the grace necessary to salvation
There . . . innocence the white linen of penitence is inappropriate, since you are doing no
sin. Another much-favored reading is: "Here is
no penance, much less innocence"—you are
neither a penitent nor an innocent, and so have
no occasion to wear white.
country rustic

Or snorted° we in the seven sleepers' den?°
'Twas so; but this,° all pleasures fancies be.
If ever any beauty I did see,
Which I desired, and got, 'twas but a dream of thee.

And now good morrow to our waking souls,
    Which watch not one another out of fear;
10 For love, all love of other sights controls,°
    And makes one little room, an every where.
Let sea-discoverers to new worlds have gone,
Let maps° to others, worlds on worlds have shown,
Let us possess one world, each hath one, and is one.

My face in thine eye, thine in mine appears,
    And true plain hearts do in the faces rest;
Where can we find two better hemispheres°
    Without sharp north, without declining west?
Whatever dies, was not mixed equally;°
20 If our two loves be one, or, thou and I
Love so alike that none do slacken, none can die.°
                                          1633

The Sun Rising°

    Busy old fool, unruly sun,
        Why dost thou thus,
Through windows, and through curtains call on us?
Must to thy motions lovers' seasons run?
        Saucy pedantic wretch, go chide
        Late school-boys, and sour prentices,
    Go tell court-huntsmen,° that the King will ride,
    Call country ants° to harvest offices;°
Love, all alike, no season knows, nor clime,
10 Nor hours, days, months, which are the rags° of time.

        Thy beams, so reverend, and strong
        Why shouldst thou think?
I could eclipse and cloud them with a wink,
But that I would not lose her sight so long:
        If her eyes have not blinded thine,

snorted snored
seven sleepers' den Seven young Christians were walled up in a cave during the persecution of Decius (249) and did not die but slept for 187 years.
but this except for this
controls inhibits
maps charts of the heavens
two better hemispheres together they make the whole world, and as hemispheres they lack the disadvantages of the geographical ones, which have to include the cold north and the west where the sun sets
Whatever . . . equally Death, in Galen's teach-

ing, results from imbalance of elements within the body.
Love . . . die each matches the perfection of the other's love to a degree that prevents either from waning; neither can die
The Sun Rising follows the tradition, beginning with Ovid, of the lover's address to the sun, but differs in its irreverence.
court-huntsmen who hunt with King James, and also hunt office
country ants rural drudges
offices tasks
rags fragments, divisions

Look, and tomorrow late, tell me,
  Whether both the Indias° of spice and mine
  Be where thou left'st them, or lie here with me.
Ask for those kings whom thou saw'st yesterday,
20 And thou shalt hear, All here in one bed lay.

  She is all states, and all princes, I,
    Nothing else is.
Princes do but play us; compared to this,
All honour's mimic; all wealth alchemy.°
    Thou sun art half as happy as we,
    In that the world's contracted thus;
   Thine age asks ease, and since thy duties be
   To warm the world, that's done in warming us.
  Shine here to us, and thou art everywhere;
30 This bed thy centre° is, these walls, thy sphere.

1633

The Canonization°

For God's sake hold your tongue, and let me love,
  Or chide my palsy, or my gout,
My five grey hairs, or ruined fortune flout,
  With wealth your state, your mind with arts improve,
    Take you a course,° get you a place,°
    Observe his Honour,° or his Grace,°
  Or the King's real, or his stamped face°
  Contemplate; what you will, approve,°
    So you will let me love.

10 Alas, alas, who's injured by my love?
  What merchant's ships have my sighs° drowned?
Who says my tears° have overflowed his ground?
  When did my colds° a forward spring remove?
    When did the heats° which my veins fill
    Add one more to the plaguy bill?°
  Soldiers find wars, and lawyers find out still
    Litigious men, which quarrels move,
    Though she and I do love.

20   Call us what you will, we are made such by love;
      Call her one, me another fly,
   We are tapers too,° and at our own cost die,°
      And we in us find the Eagle and the Dove.
        The Phoenix riddle° hath more wit
        By us; we two being one, are it.
   So to one neutral thing both sexes fit,°
      We die and rise the same, and prove
      Mysterious by this love.

   We can die by it, if not live by love,
      And if unfit for tombs and hearse
30   Our legend be, it will be fit for verse;
      And if no piece of chronicle° we prove,
        We'll build in sonnets° pretty rooms;
        As well a well-wrought urn° becomes
   The greatest ashes, as half-acre tombs,°
      And by these hymns, all shall approve°
      Us canonized for love:

   And thus invoke us;° 'You whom reverend love
      Made one another's hermitage;
   You, to whom love was peace, that now° is rage;
40   Who did the whole world's soul contract, and drove
        Into the glasses of your eyes
        (So made such mirrors, and such spies,
   That they did all to you epitomize),
      Countries, towns, courts:° beg from above°
   A pattern° of your love!'
           1633

Lovers' Infiniteness°

If yet I have not all thy love,
Dear, I shall never have it all,
I cannot breathe one other sigh, to move,
Nor can entreat one other tear to fall.
All my treasure, which should purchase thee,

fly . . . tapers too not only moths but flames
die with the common double meaning: have
orgasm
Eagle . . . Dove the predatory and the meek
Phoenix riddle The Phoenix was reborn out of
its own ashes, not by sex, and so contained in
one individual the male and female principles;
cf. Shakespeare, *The Phoenix and Turtle,* above.
So . . . fit in such measure do both sexes meet
in one neutral thing (that)
die and rise with secondary sexual sense
Mysterious worthy of reverence, like religious
mysteries
chronicle history
sonnets love poems

urn . . . tombs taking the urn as the love
lyric, the tomb as the chronicle of worldly
achievement
approve allow
invoke us pray to them as saints
now in the world you have left
Who did . . . courts who reduced the entire
animating principle of the world to yourselves,
concentrated all society into your own eyes,
which accordingly mirrored and epitomized it
beg from above pray on behalf (for)
pattern model
Lovers' Infiniteness the three-stage argument
often found in Donne

Sighs, tears, and oaths, and letters I have spent,
Yet no more can be due to me,
Than at the bargain made was meant.
If then thy gift of love were partiàl,
10   That some to me, some should to others fall,
    Dear, I shall never have thee all.

Or if then thou gavest me all,
All was but all, which thou hadst then;
But if in thy heart, since, there be or shall
New love created be, by other men,
Which have their stocks entire, and can in tears,
In sighs, in oaths, and letters outbid me,
This new love may beget new fears,
For, this love was not vowed by thee.
20   And yet it was, thy gift being general,
The ground, thy heart is mine; whatever shall
    Grow there, dear, I should have it all.

Yet I would not have all yet,
He that hath all can have no more,
And since my love doth every day admit
New growth, thou shouldst have new rewards in store;
Thou canst not every day give me thy heart,
If thou canst give it, then thou never gav'st it:
Love's riddles° are, that though thy heart depart,
30   It stays at home, and thou with losing sav'st it:°
But we will have a way more liberal,
Than changing hearts, to join them, so we shall
    Be one, and one another's all.
               1633

Song°

Sweetest love, I do not go,
    For weariness of thee,
Nor in hope the world can show
    A fitter love for me;
      But since that I
Must die at last, 'tis best,
To use my self in jest
      Thus by feigned deaths to die.

Yesternight the sun went hence,
10   And yet is here today,
He hath no desire nor sense,

---

riddles paradoxes. They are adapted from Matthew 16:25: ". . . whosoever will save his life shall lose it."

Song Like several other Donne poems, this one exists in a contemporary musical setting.

Nor half so short a way:
　Then fear not me,
But believe that I shall make
Speedier journeys, since I take
　More wings and spurs than he.

O how feeble is man's power,
　That if good fortune fall,
Cannot add another hour,
20　Nor a lost hour recall!
　　But come bad chance,
And we join to it our strength,
And we teach it art and length,
　Itself o'er us to advance.°

When thou sigh'st, thou sigh'st not wind,
　But sigh'st my soul away,
When thou weep'st, unkindly kind,
　My life's blood doth decay.
　　It cannot be
30　That thou lov'st me, as thou say'st,
If in thine my life thou waste,
　Thou art the best of me.°

Let not thy divining° heart
　Forethink me any ill,
Destiny may take thy part,
　And may thy fears fulfil;
　　But think that we
Are but turned aside to sleep;
They who one another keep
40　Alive, ne'er parted be.
　　　　1633

A Fever°

Oh do not die, for I shall hate
　All women so when thou art gone,
That thee I shall not celebrate
　When I remember, thou wast one.

But yet thou canst not die, I know,
　To leave this world behind, is death;
But when thou from this world wilt go,
　The whole world vapours with thy breath.

But come . . . advance but if bad luck comes we lend it our strength, and teach it how to torment us protractedly, so that it triumphs over us
the best of me in expending her soul in sighs and tears she is wasting him, since she is his life
divining prophetic, foreseeing
A Fever The basic conceit—that the death of a mistress destroys the world—is Petrarchan.

Or if, when thou, the world's soul,° go'st,
10   It stay, 'tis but thy carcase then,
The fairest woman, but thy ghost,
        But corrupt worms, the worthiest men.

Oh wrangling schools, that search what fire
        Shall burn this world,° had none the wit
Unto this knowledge to aspire,
        That this her fever might be it?

And yet she cannot waste by this,
        Nor long bear this torturing wrong,
For much corruption needful is
20   To fuel such a fever long.°

These burning fits but meteors be,
        Whose matter in thee is soon spent.
Thy beauty, and all parts, which are thee,
        Are unchangeable firmament.°

Yet 'twas of my mind, seizing thee,
        Though it in thee cannot perséver.°
For I had rather owner be
        Of thee one hour, than all else ever.
                                        1633

Air and Angels°

Twice or thrice had I loved thee,
Before I knew thy face or name;
So in a voice, so in a shapeless flame,
Angels affect us oft, and worshipped be;
        Still° when, to where thou wert, I came,
Some lovely glorious nothing° I did see,
        But since my soul, whose child love is,
Takes limbs of flesh, and else could nothing do,°
        More subtle° than the parent is
10   Love must not be, but take a body too,
        And therefore what thou wert, and who

world's soul anima mundi, a Platonic concept
what fire . . . world The Stoics, and later the
Schoolmen, disputed the nature of the final conflagration.
much . . . long The heat of fevers was thought
to proceed from corruption caused by conflict
between elements in the body.
These burning . . . firmament Meteors were
thought to be exhaled from the earth and
consumed in the sphere of fire (cf. Dr. Faustus
vi.61n.); their corruptibility is contrasted with
the incorruptibility of the heavens.
seizing taking possession of (legal)
perséver persist
Air and Angels The argument of the poem de-

pends on the difference of purity between air
and angels: air, the purest form of matter, cannot be quite as pure as angels, which are spirit.
One of Donne's most difficult poems.
Still always
some . . . nothing He saw her as he might an
angel, without the specific form angels take on
when, to be visible to those they visit, they
wear a "body of air"; the point is that his
first love for her lacked this physical or material
element.
could nothing do Cf. end of "The Ecstasy"; the
soul acts through the senses.
subtle ethereal

I bid love ask, and now
That it assume thy body, I allow,
And fix itself in thy lip, eye, and brow.

Whilst thus to ballast love I thought,
And so more steadily to have gone,
With wares which would sink admiration,
I saw, I had love's pinnace° overfraught,
    Every thy hair for love to work upon
20 Is much too much, some fitter must be sought;
    For, nor° in nothing, nor in things
Extreme, and scatt'ring bright, can love inhere;
    Then as an angel, face and wings
Of air, not pure as it, yet pure doth wear,
    So thy love may be my love's sphere;°
      Just such disparity
As is 'twixt air and angels' purity,
'Twixt women's love and men's will ever be.°
              1633

The Anniversary

All kings, and all their favourites,
    All glory of honours, beauties, wits
The sun itself, which makes times as they pass,
Is elder by a year now than it was
When thou and I first one another saw:
All other things to their destruction draw,
    Only our love hath no decay;
This, no tomorrow hath, nor yesterday,
Running it never runs from us away,
10 But truly keeps his first, last, everlasting day.

Two graves must hide thine and my corse,
    If one might, death were no divorce,
Alas, as well as other princes, we
(Who prince enough in one another be),
Must leave at last in death, these eyes, and ears,
Oft fed with true oaths, and with sweet salt tears;
    But souls where nothing dwells but love
(All other thoughts being inmates°) then shall prove°
This, or a love increasèd there above,°
20 When bodies to their graves, souls from their graves remove.

---

pinnace small ship; now he has gone too far in associating love with specific physical detail
nor neither
sphere in the relation of the planet (material) to the angel-intelligence (spiritual) which informs and guides it
Just . . . ever be The compromise, whereby love is not reduced to materiality—the woman's way—nor left in an angelic shapelessness and spirituality—men's way—is represented by the angel wearing his body of air.
inmates lodgers
prove experience
above in heaven

And then we shall be throughly blessed,
     But we no more, than all the rest.°
Here upon earth, we are kings, and none but we
Can be such kings, nor of such subjects° be;
Who is so safe as we? where none can do
Treason to us, except one of us two.
     True and false fears let us refrain,
Let us love nobly, and live, and add again
Years and years unto years, till we attain
30   To write threescore; this is the second of our reign.

                         1633

The Dream°

Dear love, for nothing less than thee
Would I have broke this happy dream,
          It was a theme
For reason, much too strong for phantasy,°
Therefore thou waked'st me wisely; yet
My dream thou brokest not, but continued'st it;
Thou art so truth,° that thoughts of thee suffice,
To make dreams truths, and fables histories;
Enter these arms, for since thou thought'st it best,
10   Not to dream all my dream, let's act the rest.

As lightning, or a taper's light,
Thine eyes, and not thy noise waked me;
          Yet I thought thee
(For thou lov'st truth) an angel, at first sight,
But when I saw thou saw'st my heart,
And knew'st my thoughts, beyond an angel's art,°
When thou knew'st what I dreamed, when thou knew'st when
Excess of joy would wake me, and cam'st then,
I must confess, it could not choose but be
20   Profane,° to think thee anything but thee.

Coming and staying showed thee, thee,
But rising makes me doubt, that now,
          Thou art not thou.
That love is weak, where fear's as strong as he;
'Tis not all spirit, pure, and brave,

---

no more . . . rest the doctrine that in heaven each is blessed with contentment according to his capacity
of such subjects subjects of such kings
The Dream based on the topic of the waking to find at one's bedside a mistress of whom one has been dreaming; as old as Ovid, but here newly handled
too strong . . . phantasy The fantasy or im-agination continues to produce images in sleep, when the reason cannot process them.
truth so absolutely the truth itself (many editions read *true*)
knew'st . . . art not even angels, but only God himself, can read one's inmost thoughts
Profane with a hint that she is more God than angel

If mixture it of fear, shame, honour,° have.
Perchance as torches which must ready be,
Men light and put out,° so thou deal'st with me,
Thou cam'st to kindle, goest to come;° then I
30 Will dream that hope again, but else would die.

1633

A Valediction: Of Weeping

Let me pour forth
My tears before thy face, whilst I stay here,°
For thy face coins them,° and thy stamp they bear,
And by this mintage they are something worth,
　　For thus they be
　　Pregnant of thee;
Fruits of much grief they are, emblems° of more,
When a tear falls, that thou° falls which it bore,
So thou and I are nothing then, when on a divers shore.°

10　　On a round ball
A workman that hath copies by, can lay
An Europe, Afric, and an Asia,
And quickly make that, which was nothing, all,°
　　So doth each tear,
　　Which thee doth wear,
A globe, yea world by that impression grow,
Till thy tears mixed with mine do overflow
This world, by waters sent from thee, my heaven dissolvèd so.°

　　O more than moon,°
20 Draw not up seas to drown me in thy sphere,
Weep me not dead, in thine arms, but forbear
To teach the sea, what it may do too soon;
　　Let not the wind
　　Example find,
To do me more harm, than it purposeth;
Since thou and I sigh one another's breath,
Whoe'er sighs most, is cruellest, and hastes the other's death.

1633

honour as usual in Donne, the enemy of love
torches . . . put out A torch that has been burning ignites more easily.
come come back
whilst I stay here while I'm still with you
coins them Each tear, bearing her reflected image, is like a coin.
emblems prophetic images (the next lines explain why)
that thou that image of you
on a divers shore in different countries
nothing, all By pasting maps of the countries of the world on a blank globe he is converting nothing (the zero of the globe) into everything (the world).
Till . . . dissolved so Their tears combine to form a flood and inundate the world of the tear—it is a world because it bears her image. She is his heaven, which dissolves as the sky did for the Flood.
more than moon She is more powerful than the moon and should not raise a tide that would drown him.

Love's Alchemy°

Some that have deeper digged love's mine than I,
Say, where his centric happiness doth lie:
   I have loved, and got,° and told,°
But should I love, get, tell, till I were old,
I should not find that hidden mystery;
     Oh, 'tis imposture all:
And as no chemic yet the elixir got,
    But glorifies his pregnant pot,
    If by the way to him befall
10 Some odoriferous thing, or medicinal,°
   So, lovers dream a rich and long delight,
   But get a winter-seeming summer's night.

Our ease, our thrift, our honour, and our day,°
Shall we, for this vain bubble's shadow pay?
   Ends love in this, that my man,°
Can be as happy as I can; if he can
Endure the short scorn of a bridegroom's play?
    That loving wretch that swears,
'Tis not the bodies marry, but the minds,
20   Which he in her angelic finds,
    Would swear as justly, that he hears,
In that day's° rude hoarse minstrelsy, the spheres.°
Hope not for mind in women; at their best
   Sweetness and wit, they are but mummy, possessed.°

                1633

The Flea°

Mark but this flea, and mark in this,
How little that which thou deny'st me is;
Me it sucked first, and now sucks thee,
And in this flea, our two bloods mingled be;
Confess it, this cannot be said°

A sin, or shame, or loss of maidenhead,
   Yet this enjoys before it woo,
   And pampered swells with one blood made of two,
   And this, alas, is more than we would do.°

10   Oh stay, three lives in one flea spare,
Where we almost, nay more than married are.
This flea is you and I, and this
Our marriage bed, and marriage temple is;
Though parents grudge, and you, we are met,
And cloistered in these living walls of jet.
   Though use° make you apt to kill me,
   Let not to this, self murder added be,
   And sacrilege, three sins° in killing three.

Cruel and sudden, hast thou since
20   Purpled thy nail, in blood of innocence?
In what could this flea guilty be,
Except in that drop which it sucked from thee?
Yet thou triumph'st, and say'st that thou
Find'st not thyself, nor me the weaker now;
   'Tis true, then learn how false, fears be;
   Just so much honour, when thou yield'st to me,
   Will waste, as this flea's death took life from thee.

1633

A Nocturnal upon S. Lucy's Day, Being the Shortest Day°

'Tis the year's midnight, and it is the day's,
Lucy's, who scarce seven hours herself unmasks,
   The sun is spent, and now his flasks°
   Send forth light squibs,° no constant rays;
      The world's whole sap is sunk:
The general balm° the hydroptic° earth hath drunk,
Whither, as to the bed's-feet,° life is shrunk,
Dead and interred; yet all these seem to laugh,
Compared with me, who am their epitaph.

10   Study me then, you who shall lovers be
At the next world, that is, at the next spring:°

more . . . do They don't want an ensuing pregnancy.
use habit
three sins murder, suicide, sacrilege
A Nocturnal upon S. Lucy's Day . . . December 13, then the shortest day of the year, the winter solstice, when the sun entered the sign of the Goat (Capricorn). The Gregorian calendar was not adopted in England till 1752, by which eleven days were added to the date. St. Lucy's festival is celebrated with lights and candles.

flasks The stars were thought to store up the sun's light as flasks store gunpowder.
light squibs weak flashes
sap . . . balm preservative essences of living things
hydroptic pathologically thirsty
bed's-feet A patient huddling at the foot of the bed was thought to be near death.
world . . . spring spring as *renovatio mundi*, rebirth of the world

> For I am every dead thing,
>   In whom love wrought new alchemy.°
>   For his art did express°
> A quintessence° even from nothingness,°
> From dull privations, and lean emptiness;
> He ruined me,° and I am re-begot
> Of absence, darkness, death;° things which are not.

20 All° others, from all° things, draw all° that's good,
> Life, soul, form, spirit, whence they being have;
>   I, by love's limbeck,° am the grave
>   Of all,° that's nothing.° Oft a flood
>   Have we two wept, and so
> Drowned the whole world, us two;° oft did we grow
> To be two chaoses, when we did show
> Care to aught else;° and often absences
> Withdrew our souls; and made us carcases.

> But I am by her death (which word wrongs her)
> Of the first nothing, the elixir grown;°
30   Were I a man, that I were one,
>   I needs must know; I should prefer,
>   If I were any beast,
> Some ends, some means; yea plants, yea stones detest,
> And love,° all, all some properties invest;°
> If I an ordinary nothing were,
> As° shadow, a light, and body must be here.

> But I am none;° nor will my sun° renew.
> You lovers, for whose sake, the lesser sun°
>   At this time to the Goat is run
40   To fetch new lust,° and give it you,
>   Enjoy your summer all;
> Since she enjoys her long night's festival,°

new alchemy which, unlike the old, is concerned with the principle of deadness rather than the principle of life
express distill, extract (alchemical)
quintessence elixir, principle
from nothingness unlike "old" alchemy, which dealt with allness
He ruined me he broke down my substance (alchemical)
I am . . . death I am reconstituted by the forms of nothingness ("re-begot" is alchemical)
limbeck alembic, the distilling flask used by alchemists
All . . . nothing the basic conceit of the poem
Oft a flood . . . us two By weeping they have drowned the images of each other in their eyes (see "Valediction: Of Weeping" above); "flood" is another alchemical term.
show . . . else concerned ourselves about matters external to us, so causing our souls which having given form to our material bodies, to vacate them, leaving them chaoses
Of the first . . . grown become the quintessence not of chaos but of the primal nothing which preceded the institution of chaos (matter without form) by God
Were I . . . love If I were a man I should know it, because men have a rational soul; if a beast, I should have a sensitive soul, and make certain choices; if a plant, with only a vegetative soul, I could choose nutriment. Even (magnetic) stones, with no souls at all, attract and repel.
all . . . invest everything else is endowed with some properties
As such as
none nonce usage to suggest absolute nothingness
my sun his lady
lesser sun the sun
to the Goat . . . lust to the sign of Capricorn to bring back lust, always associated with the goat
long night's festival dark sleep of death, which this, the longest night of the year, fittingly commemorates

Let me prepare towards her,° and let me call
This hour her virgil, and her eve, since this
Both the year's, and the day's deep midnight is.

1633

The Bait

Come live with me, and be my love,
And we will some new pleasures prove
Of golden sands, and crystal brooks,
With silken lines, and silver hooks.

There will the river whispering run
Warmed by thy eyes, more than the sun.
And there th'enamoured fish will stay,
Begging themselves they may betray.

When thou wilt swim in that live bath,
10   Each fish, which every channel hath,
Will amorously to thee swim,
Gladder to catch thee, than thou him.

If thou, to be so seen, be'st loth,
By sun, or moon, thou darkenest both,
And if myself have leave to see,
I need not their light, having thee.

Let others freeze with angling reeds,
And cut their legs, with shells and weeds,
Or treacherously poor fish beset,
20   With strangling snare, or windowy net:

Let coarse bold hands, from slimy nest
The bedded fish in banks out-wrest,
Or curious traitors, sleavesilk flies°
Bewitch poor fishes' wandering eyes.

For thee, thou need'st no such deceit,
For thou thyself art thine own bait,
That fish, that is not catched thereby,
Alas, is wiser far than I.

1633

---

prepare towards her fit myself by meditation
for her feast
vigil service the night before a festival
The Bait A reply—by no means the first—to
Marlowe's *The Passionate Shepherd to His Love*
(cf. Ralegh's *Reply*). Walton quotes all three
in *The Compleat Angler*, Donne's being of
course especially appropriate; Walton thought
it showed Donne "could make soft and smooth
verses when he thought fit." It is also a
piscatory pastoral, substituting the world of
the fisherman for that of the shepherd.
sleavesilk flies artificial flies made of silk thread
separable into finer filaments

The Apparition

When by thy scorn,° O murderess, I am dead,
And that thou think'st thee free
From all solicitation from me,
Then shall my ghost come to thy bed,
And thee, feigned vestal,° in worse arms shall see;
Then thy sick taper will begin to wink,
And he whose thou art then, being tired before,
Will, if thou stir, or pinch to wake him, think
    Thou call'st for more,
10 And in false sleep will from thee shrink,
And then poor aspen° wretch, neglected thou
Bathed in a cold quicksilver sweat wilt lie
    A verier ghost than I;
What I will say, I will not tell thee now,
Lest that preserve thee; and since my love is spent,
I had rather thou shouldst painfully repent,
Than by my threatenings rest still innocent.

                1633

A Valediction: Forbidding Mourning

As virtuous men pass mildly away,
  And whisper to their souls, to go,
Whilst some of their sad friends do say,
  The breath goes now, and some say, no:

So let us melt, and make no noise,
  No tear-floods, nor sigh-tempests° move,
'Twere profanation of our joys
  To tell the laity our love.

Moving of th' earth° brings harms and fears,
10 Men reckon what it did and meant,
But trepidation of the spheres,°
  Though greater far, is innocent.°

Dull súblunary° lovers' love
  (Whose soul is sense°) cannot admit
Absence, because it doth remove
  Those things which elemented° it.

---

by thy scorn Donne takes up the Petrarchan theme of the lover dying of his mistress's scorn but gives it new dramatic force.
vestal holy virgin
aspen trembling (like a poplar leaf in the wind)
tear-floods . . . sigh-tempests the Petrarchan conceits, see "Passa la nave mia" above.
Moving of th'earth earthquakes
trepidation of the spheres libration of the ninth or crystalline sphere, which accounted for the precession of the equinoxes
innocent does no harm
sublunary below the moon, therefore more corrupt than the heavens
Whose soul is sense not mind; it therefore requires contact
elemented composed

But we by a love, so much refined,
   That our selves know not what it is,
Inter-assurèd of the mind,
20   Care less, eyes, lips, and hands to miss.

Our two souls therefore, which are one,
   Though I must go, endure not yet
A breach, but an expansion,
   Like gold to aery thinness beat.

If they be two, they are two so
   As stiff twin compasses° are two,
Thy soul the fixed foot, makes no show
   To move, but doth, if th'other do.

And though it in the centre sit,
30   Yet when the other far doth roam,
It leans, and hearkens after it,
   And grows erect, as that comes home.

Such wilt thou be to me, who must
   Like the other foot, obliquely run;
Thy firmness makes my circle just,
   And makes me end, where I begun.°

               1633

The Ecstasy°

Where, like a pillow on a bed,
   A pregnant bank swelled up, to rest
The violet's reclining head,°
   Sat we two, one another's best;

Our hands were firmly cemented
   With a fast balm, which thence did spring,°
Our eye-beams twisted, and did thread
   Our eyes, upon one double string;°

compasses a familiar emblem, denoting constancy in change
end . . . begun complete circle
The Ecstasy The title means "standing outside," as the souls here are represented as doing; long periods of this were thought inadvisable, though the experience offered unmediated knowledge of divine truth. The argument concerns the power of the ecstatic joint soul of the lovers to know the truth about love when outside their bodies, but the man urges a return to the physical. Opinion is divided about the full tone and sense of the poem: to some it is a central statement of the poet's love-metaphysic, and deeply serious; to others it is an example of what Dryden called his power to "perplex the minds of the fair sex with the nice speculations of philosophy." At one extreme is the reading which takes the last line as referring merely to the return of the souls to the inanimate bodies; at the other, the view that the whole poem is a fantastic seduction. In fact the opinion that the last line connotes sexual activity does not imply cynicism, and there is no good reason not to treat the poem as both serious *and* persuasive to love. See also William Cartwright's "No Platonic Love."
Where . . . head a traditional, though quickly sketched, *locus amoenus:* setting for pastoral or garden love-making or love-talk
Our . . . spring sweat; a moist palm was an index of sexual desire
Our . . . string The light-rays, thought of as emerging from the eyes, twist together so that the eyes are like beads on a string.

So to intergraft° our hands, as yet
    Was all our means to make us one,
And pictures in our eyes to get°
    Was all our propagatiòn.°

As 'twixt two equal armies, Fate
    Suspends uncertain victory,°
Our souls, (which to advance their state,°
    Were gone out), hung 'twixt her, and me.

And whilst our souls negotiate° there,
    We like sepulchral statues lay;
All day, the same our postures were,
    And we said nothing, all the day.

If any, so by love refined,
    That he soul's language understood,
And by good love were grown all mind,
    Within convenient distance stood,

He (though he knew not which soul spake
    Because both meant, both spake the same)
Might thence a new concoction° take,
    And part far purer than he came.

This ecstasy doth unperplex
    (We said) and tell us what we love,°
We see by this, it was not sex,
    We see we saw not what did move:°

But as all several° souls contain
    Mixture of things, they know not what,°
Love, these mixed souls doth mix again,
    And makes both one, each this and that.°

A single violet transplant,
    The strength, the colour, and the size,
(All which before was poor, and scant,)
    Redoubles still, and multiplies.°

When love, with one another so
    Interinanimates two souls,

10

20

30

40

---

intergraft graft one on the other; grafting—cf.
Marvell, "Mower against Gardens"—was a
sexual figure
pictures . . . get The reflection of one's face in
an eye into which one is gazing was sometimes
called a baby—hence *get* = beget.
propagatiòn five syllables
'twixt . . . victory The uncertainty of the outcome of a battle is represented by an image of
Victory hanging between them.
state dignity
negotiate as in a parley before battle
concoction purification of metals by heat, of
the physique by refinement of the animal
spirits; see below

what we love the true object of their love
what did move what the true motive was
several distinct
Mixture . . . what the functions of the soul
being both physical and spiritual, it must be of
compounded nature which we cannot know
exactly
Love . . . that The new single soul, made up
of two, is also mixed, but has advantages explained later: that the two souls of lovers
become one is a Platonic commonplace.
A single . . . multiplies either the violet prop-
agates itself on transplantation, or grows richer
double flowers

That abler soul, which thence doth flow,
　　Defects of loneliness controls.°

We then, who are this new soul, know,
　　Of what we are composed, and made,
For, th'atomies° of which we grow,
　　Are souls, whom no change can invade.°

50　　But O alas, so long, so far
　　Our bodies why do we forbear?
They are ours, though they are not we, we are
　　The intelligences, they the sphere.°

We owe them thanks, because they thus,
　　Did us, to us, at first convey,
Yielded their forces, sense,° to us,
　　Nor are dross to us, but allay.°

On man heaven's influence works not so,
　　But that it first imprints the air,°
So soul into the soul may flow,
60　　Though it to body first repair.

As our blood labours to beget
　　Spirits, as like souls as it can,°
Because such fingers need° to knit
　　That subtle° knot, which makes us man:

So must pure lovers' souls descend
　　T'affections,° and to faculties,°
Which sense may reach and apprehend,°
　　Else a great prince in prison lies.°

To our bodies turn we then, that so
70　　Weak men on love revealed may look;°
Love's mysteries in souls do grow,
　　But yet the body is his book.°

And if some lover, such as we,
　　Have heard this dialogue of one,

Defects . . . controls overcomes the imperfections of separateness
atomies components
Are . . . invade Unlike the body, the soul is not subject to change; this completes the argument for the advantages of pure soul-union, and there is now a sharp turn in the poem.
we are . . . sphere Souls are to bodies as the angel-intelligence-spirit is to the planet—matter —it controls; cf. "Air and Angels" above.
forces, sense They have given up their power of movement to enable the souls to experience non-physical union.
dross . . . allay not the waste left over after metallurgical refinement but that which, in an alloy, makes the gold serviceable
heaven's . . . air The influence of the stars on men was held to occur through the medium of air; and angels (cf. "Air and Angels") took a body of air, "not pure as it," when appearing to men.
Spirits . . . can The animal spirits, "concocted" or refined from the blood, serve as a medium between matter and spirit, body and soul.
need are needed
subtle fine, impalpable
affections feelings, passions
faculties power of the body
Which . . . apprehend with which sense has contact and relation
Else . . . lies otherwise the new soul is impotent, has no agents
weak . . . look As the truths of religions accommodate themselves to weak men through revelation, so physical activity will make evident a love which otherwise would not be so.
body is his book as the Bible makes evident the truths of religion

Let him still mark us, he shall see
    Small change, when we are to bodies gone.°

1633

The Funeral

Whoever comes to shroud me, do not harm
    Nor question much
That subtle wreath of hair, which crowns my arm;
The mystery, the sign you must not touch,
    For 'tis my outward soul,
Viceroy to that, which then to heaven being gone,
    Will leave this to control,
And keep these limbs, her° provinces, from dissolution.

For if the sinewy thread° my brain lets fall
10   Through every part,
Can tie those parts, and make me one of all;°
These hairs which upward grew, and strength and art
    Have from a better brain,
Can better do it; except° she meant that I
    By this should know my pain,
As prisoners then are manacled, when they're condemned to die.

Whate'er she meant by it, bury it with me,
    For since I am
Love's martyr, it might breed idolatry,
20   If into others' hands these relics came;
    As 'twas humility
To afford to it all that a soul can do,°
    So, 'tis some bravery,°
That since you would save none of me, I bury some of you.

1633

Farewell to Love°

    Whilst yet to prove,°
I thought there was some deity in love
    So did I reverence, and gave
Worship; as atheists at their dying hour
Call, what they cannot name, an unknown power,

---

some lover . . . gone The refined lover of line
21 will see that there is little difference between
our loving before and after we used our bodies.
her the soul's
sinewy thread the nerves by which the brain
transmits messages to the body
make . . . all unite my several parts into a
whole person
except unless

To afford . . . do to credit it with the powers
of a soul
bravery bravado
Farewell to Love Not positively ascribed to
Donne in the 1633 edition; it is probably by
him but may represent a draft rather than a
finished poem.
Whilst . . . prove while still inexperienced

As ignorantly did I crave:
　　Thus when
Things not yet known are coveted by men,
Our desires give them fashion,° and so
10　As they wax lesser, fall, as they size, grow.°

　　But, from late° fair
His highness sitting in a golden chair,°
　Is not less cared for after three days
By children, than the thing° which lovers so
Blindly admire, and with such worship woo;
　　Being had, enjoying it decays:°
　　　And thence,
What before pleased them all, takes but one sense,°
　And that so lamely, as it leaves behind
20　A kind of sorrowing dullness to the mind.°

　　Ah cannot we,
As well as cocks and lions° jocund be,
　After such pleasures? Unless wise
Nature decreed (since each such act, they say,
Diminisheth the length of life a day)
　　This; as she would man should despise
　　　The sport,
Because that other curse of being short,
　And only for a minute made to be
30　Eager, desires to raise posterity.°

　　Since so,° my mind
Shall not desire what no man else can find,
　I'll no more dote and run
To pursue things which had endamaged me.
And when I come where moving beauties° be,
　As men do when the summer's sun
　　Grows great,
Though I admire their greatness, shun their heat;
　Each place can afford shadows. If all fail,
40　'Tis but applying worm-seed° to the tail.°

　　　　　1633

Our . . . fashion we imagine them to accord
with our wishes
As . . . grow they decline as our desire reduces, grow as our desire expands
late some recent
His highness . . . chair gingerbread effigy of
a prince sold to children at a fair
the thing sex
Being . . . decays once had, the enjoyment of
it wanes
What . . . sense what formerly pleased all the
senses now captivates only one (touch)
A kind . . . mind referring to the saying "omne
animal post coitum triste" (all animals are sad
after sex)
cocks and lions The medical authority Galen

exempts these animals from the general rule.
Unless . . . posterity perhaps the most difficult
passage in Donne, and possibly corrupt—"unless
nature, because every act of sex is said to reduce one's life by a day, wisely arranged that
men should feel contemptuous of sex when the
act is over; since its other disadvantage (its
brevity) would otherwise lead us to do it too
often." Here "desires to raise posterity" is taken
to mean "wants the act to beget other successive
acts."
so it is so
moving beauties beauties who rouse my desire
worm-seed an anaphrodisiac
tail penis

The Relic°

When my grave is broke up again
Some second guest to entertain,
(For graves have learned that woman-head°
To be to more than one a bed)
  And he that digs it, spies
A bracelet of bright hair about the bone,
  Will he not let us alone,
And think that there a loving couple lies,
Who thought that this device might be some way
To make their souls, at the last busy day,°
Meet at this grave, and make a little stay?

If this fall° in a time, or land,
Where mis-devotion° doth command,
Then, he that digs us up, will bring
Us, to the Bishop, and the King,
  To make us relics; then
Thou shalt be a Mary Magdalen,° and I
  A something else° thereby;
All women shall adore us, and some men;
And since at such time, miracles are sought,
I would have that age by this paper° taught
What miracles we harmless lovers wrought.

First, we loved well and faithfully,
Yet knew not what we loved, nor why,
Difference of sex no more we knew,
Than our guardian angels° do;
  Coming and going,° we
Perchance might kiss, but not between those meals;
  Our hands ne'er touched the seals,
Which nature, injured by late law, sets free:°
These miracles we did; but now alas,
All measure, and all language, I should pass,
Should I tell what a miracle she was.

    1633

The Relic Cf. "The Funeral"; the situation is the same, but at a somewhat later time.
woman-head woman-like behavior
last busy day the Resurrection
this fall the digging up of my body should happen
mis-devotion false religious practices, such as the use of relics
a Mary Magdalen in art represented as having golden hair, and in her youth could have given lovers such tokens

a something else contemptuous for Mary's lover; or, scandalously, "Jesus Christ," represented in that role
this paper this poem
guardian angels having no sexuality
Coming and going arriving and departing
seals . . . free prohibitions on sexual conduct which do not exist in nature, but which law and custom have, at a later time of the world, imposed

Satire III

Donne wrote five satires in the 1590's, a time when they were greatly in vogue (publication of satire was inhibited in 1598). Partly because of a mistaken etymology which related satire to *Satyr*, the Elizabethan practitioners affected a very rough style, harsh and "snarling," as appropriate to an uncouth natural speaker commenting on the evil sophistication of city life. Hence the violently misplaced accents, hypermetric syllables, and forced rhymes, not to speak of the farfetched images and emphasis on vice and ugliness, of Donne's satires. The ancient model was Horace, whose satires are colloquial in manner and have similar themes, but are not, in this sense, "harsh."

The third Satire is unlike the others, not in manner but in theme. It concerns the necessity for choosing a religion, a necessity nonetheless paramount because the decision is not one to be made hastily. This was Donne's own position as a young man; he said he "used no inordinate haste, nor precipitation, in binding my conscience to any local religion" (*Pseudo-Martyr*), but nevertheless regarded the choice as of great urgency. He seems to have regarded himself as Protestant from about the turn of the century; this poem probably belongs to 1595. It is unique in the impassioned immediacy of its religious argument; it is part satiric railing against men's unwillingness to give priority to their most urgent concerns, part sarcasm at the expense of contemporary religious follies, and partly virile exhortation. Above all it considers, in the very voice of urgent meditation, the harsh and solemn necessity of choice imposed upon the serious Christian in an age when doctrinal differences were reflected in political power-struggles. It reminds us that the poet of the Elegies was, at the same time, profoundly concerned to use his mind and poetic powers on what seemed to him the greatest single issue, that of the true religion.

Satire III

Kind pity chokes my spleen;° brave scorn° forbids
Those tears to issue which swell my eye-lids,
I must not laugh, nor weep sins, and be wise;°
Can railing° then cure these worn° maladies?
Is not our mistress fair religion,
As worthy of all our soul's devotion,
As virtue was to the first blinded age?°
Are not heaven's joys as valiant to assuage
Lusts, as earth's honour° was to them? Alas,
10   As we do them in means, shall they surpass
Us in the end, and shall thy father's spirit
Meet blind philosophers in heaven, whose merit

spleen the source of scornful laughter
brave scorn the flaunting scorn of the satirist
I must . . . wise If I'm to be wise I mustn't, it seems, either laugh about sins or weep over them
railing ranting, shouting down
worn hackneyed

first blinded age Before Christ the philosophers, denied the light of revelation, worshipped virtue; we should surely think as well of religion as they did of virtue.
earth's honour which was all they had, whereas we have the bliss of heaven

Of strict life may be imputed faith,° and hear
Thee, whom he taught so easy ways and near
To follow, damned? O if thou dar'st, fear this;
This fear great courage, and high valour is.
Dar'st thou aid mutinous Dutch,° and dar'st thou lay
Thee in ships' wooden sepulchres, a prey
To leaders' rage, to storms, to shot, to dearth?
20   Dar'st thou dive seas, and dungeons° of the earth?
Hast thou courageous fire to thaw the ice
Of frozen north discoveries?° and thrice
Colder than salamanders,° like divine
Children in th'oven,° fires of Spain, and the line,°
Whose countries limbecks° to our bodies be,
Canst thou for gain bear? and must every he
Which cries not, 'Goddess!' to thy mistress, draw,
Or eat thy poisonous words? courage of straw!
O desperate coward, wilt thou seem bold, and
30   To thy foes and his° (who made thee to stand
Sentinel in his world's garrison) thus yield,
And for forbidden wars, leave th'appointed field?
Know thy foes: the foul Devil, he, whom thou
Strivest to please, for hate, not love, would allow
Thee fain, his whole realm to be quit;° and as
The world's all parts wither away and pass,
So the world's self, thy other loved foe, is
In her decrepit wane,° and thou loving this,
Doest love a withered and worn strumpet; last,
40   Flesh (itself's death)° and joys which flesh can taste,
Thou lovest; and thy fair goodly soul, which doth
Give this flesh power to taste joy, thou dost loathe.
      Seek true religion. O where? Mirreus°
Thinking her unhoused here, and fled from us,
Seeks her at Rome, there, because he doth know
That she was there a thousand years ago,
He loves her rags° so, as we here obey
The statecloth where the Prince sate yesterday.°
Crants° to such brave° loves will not be enthralled,

---

blind . . . faith though not justified by faith,
since they lived before Christ, they may be in
heaven because their pagan virtues qualify
them—are imputed to them as faith
mutinous Dutch The Dutch resisted their Spanish overlords, and the English sometimes assisted
them.
dungeon mines, caves
frozen . . . discoveries attempts to find a north-
west passage to the Pacific
salamanders lizards supposed to live in fire
divine . . . oven Shadrach, Meshach, and Abed-
nego, who survived the ordeal of the fiery
furnace into which Nebuchadnezzar cast them
fires . . . line the Inquisition and tropical heat
limbecks alchemical stills

his God's
the foul . . . quit Satan, whom you try to
please, would willingly grant you his whole
kingdom, but for hate, not love
decrepit wane Donne often recurs to the view
that the world is declining into its last age.
(itself's death) the sins of the flesh bring
about its destruction
Mirreus the Romanist; perhaps latinized from
"Mreo," anagram of "Rome"
rags ceremonial survivals
statecloth . . . yesterday the canopy over the
chair of state; the throne was reverenced even
in the monarch's absence
Crants Calvinist
brave showy

50   But loves her only, who at Geneva° is called
Religiòn, plain, simple, sullen, young,
Contemptuous, yet unhandsome; as among
Lecherous humours,° there is one that judges
No wenches wholesome, but coarse country drudges.
Graius° stays still at home here, and because
Some preachers, vile ambitious bawds,° and laws
Still new like fashions,° bid him think that she
Which dwells with us, is only° perfect, he
Embraceth her, whom his godfathers will
60   Tender to him, being tender,° as wards still
Take such wives as their guardians offer, or
Pay values.° Careless Phrygius° doth abhor
All, because all cannot be good, as one
Knowing some women whores, dares marry none.
Gracchus° loves all as one, and thinks that so
As women do in divers countries go
In divers habits, yet are still one kind,
So does, so is religion; and this blind-
ness too much light breeds;° but unmovèd thou
70   Of force must one, and forced but one allow;
And the right; ask thy father° which is she,
Let him ask his; though truth and falsehood be
Near twins, yet truth a little elder is;°
Be busy to seek her, believe me this,
He's not of none, nor worst, that seeks the best.°
To adore, or scorn an image, or protest,°
May all be bad; doubt wisely; in strange way°
To stand inquiring right, is not to stray;
To sleep, or run wrong is. On a huge hill,
80   Cragged, and steep, Truth stands, and he that will
Reach her, about must, and about must go;
And what the hill's suddenness resists, win so;°
Yet strive so, that before age, death's twilight,
Thy soul rest, for none can work in that night,°

Geneva center of Calvinism
lecherous humours men of lecherous tastes
Graius Greek; perhaps because the Greeks
worshipped "an unknown God"—Acts 17–23
—and sought novelty
ambitious bawds pimps seeking advancement
by selling their girl
Still . . . fashions always changing, like fashions (the variety of English laws aimed at
securing conformity)
only alone
Tender . . . tender offer to him in his infancy
Pay values Wards who refused the marriage
proposed for them by their guardians had to pay
a fine; so, under the Act of Uniformity of
1559, did people who refused to attend the
parish church.
Phrygius who turns against all religion

Gracchus named for the Roman Gracchi, who
were democrats; a liberal, unwisely tolerant
bindness . . . breeds too much light breeds this
blindness
ask thy father "Ask thy father and he will
show thee," Deuteronomy 32:7
a little elder is the need is to get back to the
facts of the true primitive church; heresy is
almost but not quite as old
He's . . . best he's not of no religion, nor of
the worst religion, who seeks the best religion
protest be Protestant
in strange way on an unfamilar road
And what . . . so thus achieve what the steep-
ness of the hill tries to prevent
that night "the night cometh, when no man can
work" (John 9:4)

To will implies delay, therefore now do.
Hard deeds, the body's pains; hard knowledge too
The mind's endeavours reach,° and mysteries
Are like the sun, dazzling, yet plain to all eyes.°
Keep the truth which thou hast found; men do not stand
90 In so ill case° here, that God hath with his hand
Signed king's blank-charters° to kill whom they hate,
Nor are they vicars,° but hangmen to Fate.
Fool and wretch, wilt thou let thy soul be tied
To man's laws, by which she shall not be tried
At the last day? Or will it then boot thee
To say a Philip,° or a Gregory,°
A Harry,° or a Martin° taught thee this?
Is not this excuse for mere° contraries,
Equally strong; cannot both sides say so?
100 That thou mayest rightly obey power, her bounds know;
Those past, her nature, and name is changed;° to be
Then humble to her is idolatry.
As streams are, power is; those blessed flowers that dwell
At the rough stream's calm head, thrive and prove well,
But having left their roots, and themselves given
To the stream's tyrannous rage, alas are driven
Through mills, and rocks, and woods, and at last, almost
Consumed in going, in the sea are lost:
So perish souls, which more choose men's unjust
Power from God claimed, than God himself to trust.

from MS. 1802

The Second Anniversary

Donne wrote two *Anniversaries* to commemorate the death at fourteen of Elizabeth Drury in 1610. The girl's father, Sir Robert, was his benefactor, but he never met the girl. These strange poems—Donne's longest, and interesting experiments in the prolongation during lengthy structured works of the fantastic conceited style of the funeral elegy—were regarded at the time as excessive; Ben Jonson is reported as saying that "Donne's Anniversary was profane and full of blasphemies; that he had told Mr. Donne, if it had been written of the Virgin Mary it had been something; to which he answered, that he described the Idea of a Woman, and not as she was."

The poems, especially the second, use an elaborate system of linked formal meditations. The first, *An Anatomy of the World*, treats the girl as the embodiment of all that

Hard deeds . . . reach as the labor of the body achieves severe physical tasks, so that of the mind achieves hard knowledge
mysteries . . . eyes the fact that we can never comprehend them doesn't alter the fact that they are visibly there
so ill case such an evil condition
blank-charters Richard II made wealthy men sign promises to pay money to him, and to leave the sum blank; here the idea is extended to death warrants which could be filled in at the whim of the ruler.

vicars deputies
Philip Philip II of Spain
Gregory Pope Gregory VII (who in the 11th century established papal power over secular rulers) or Gregory XIII or Gregory XIV (contemporary popes)
Harry Henry VIII
Martin Luther
mere absolute
nature . . . changed to tyranny

men forfeited at the Fall, and imagines the world as a corpse following the departure
of its soul. The second, *The Progress of the Soul,* dwells on the advantages enjoyed
by the soul after death by comparison with "the incommodities of the soul in this life."
The extract is from a section dealing with a theme Donne often treated, the uselessness
and partiality of earthly knowledge in comparison with the full knowledge of essentials
that the soul will achieve in heaven.

From The Second Anniversary

Poor soul, in this thy flesh what dost thou know?
Thou know'st thyself so little, as thou know'st not,
How thou didst die, nor how thou wast begot.
Thou neither know'st, how thou at first cam'st in,
Nor how thou took'st the poison of man's sin.°
Nor dost thou, (though thou know'st, that thou art so)
260 By what way thou art made immortal, know.
Thou art too narrow, wretch, to comprehend
Even thyself; yea though thou wouldst but bend
To know thy body. Have not all souls thought
For many ages, that our body is wrought
Of air, and fire, and other elements?
And now they think of new ingredients,°
And one soul thinks one, and another way
Another thinks, and 'tis an even lay.
Know'st thou but how the stone doth enter in
270 The bladder's cave, and never break the skin?
Know'st thou how blood, which to the heart doth flow,
Doth from one ventricle to th'other go?°
And for the putrid stuff, which thou dost spit,
Know'st thou how thy lungs have attracted it?
There are no passages, so that there is
(For aught thou know'st) piercing of substances.°
And of those many opinions which men raise
Of nails and hairs,° dost thou know which to praise?
What hope have we to know our selves, when we
280 Know not the least things, which for our use be?
We see in authors, too stiff to recant,
A hundred controversies of an ant;
And yet one watches, starves, freezes, and sweats,
To know but catechisms and alphabets
Of unconcerning° things, matters of fact;

how . . . sin whether from the parents or by
direct infusion—an old controversy
new ingredients The old Galenist view was
that earth, water, and fire were balanced in
man; the Paracelsan novelty lay in making the
constituents chemical, e.g. sulfur, mercury, etc.
blood . . . go Harvey's discoveries were published in 1628.

piercing of substances transmission of matter
through solid resistances
opinions . . . hairs whether or no they were
organic or waste matter
unconcerning trivial; a magnificent statement of
the argument

How others on our stage their parts did act;
What Caesar did, yea, and what Cicero said.
Why grass is green, or why our blood is red,
Are mysteries which none have reached unto.
290   In this low form,° poor soul, what wilt thou do?
When wilt thou shake off this pedántery,
Of being taught by sense and fantasy?°
Thou look'st through spectacles; small things seem great
Below; but up unto the watch-tower get,
And see all things despoiled of fallacies:
Thou shalt not peep through lattices of eyes,
Nor hear through labyrinths of ears, nor learn
By circuit,° or collections° to discern.
In heaven thou straight know'st all, concerning it,°
And what concerns it not, shalt straight forget.

                                         1612

The Holy Sonnets

It seems probable that all these sonnets, except for three in the Westmoreland manuscript, belong to about 1609–11, that is, before Donne's ordination. These other three are later: one on the death of his wife (1617), one on the defeat of the Protestants at the battle of the White Mountain in 1620, and one uncertain, but presumably late. Of the remaining sixteen, four are additional to the two sequences of six which appeared in the first edition of 1633. Their order in that edition is the correct one, as Dame Helen Gardner showed when she restored and justified it in her 1952 Oxford edition of Donne's *Divine Poems*.

The first six, here represented by II, IV, V, and VI, are meditations on the Last Judgment; the second six, of which only X is given here, meditate on the Atonement and on the love owed by man to God and to his neighbor, and plead the intervention of God in the subject's life. The Jesuit meditation, based on the prescriptions of St. Ignatius Loyola, was designed to involve all the powers of the soul, including the senses, in the contemplation of some religious object or moment—the subject's own deathbed, for example, or the Crucifixion, or, as in IV, the Last Judgment. Donne adapts this form of meditation to an Italian sonnet form, usually with a clear break at the *volta*, after the eighth line, and a change of tone in the sestet, which is quieter and more reflective than the octave. It was admirably suited to his powers, providing for passionate and excited as well as for devotional language and rhythms.

II

Oh my black soul! now thou art summonèd
By sickness, death's herald, and champion;
Thou art like a pilgrim, which abroad hath done
Treason, and durst not turn° to whence he is fled,
Or like a thief, which till death's doom be read,

---

low form humble condition
sense and fantasy by the evidence of the senses as treated by the fancy or imagination, i.e. by fallible human instruments

circuit roundabout processes
collections inferences
it heaven
turn return

Wisheth himself deliverèd from prison;
But damned and haled to execùtiòn,
Wisheth that still he might be imprisonèd;
Yet grace, if thou repent, thou canst not lack;
10   But who shall give thee that grace to begin?°
Oh make thyself with holy mourning black,
And red with blushing, as thou art with sin;
Or wash thee in Christ's blood, which hath this might
That being red, it dyes red souls to white.

IV

At the round earth's imagined corners,° blow
Your trumpets, angels, and arise, arise
From death, you numberless infinities
Of souls, and to your scattered bodies go,
All whom the flood did, and fire shall o'erthrow,
All whom war, dearth, age, agues, tyrannies,
Despair, law, chance, hath slain, and you whose eyes,
Shall behold God, and never taste death's woe.°
But° let them sleep, Lord, and me mourn a space,
10   For, if above all these, my sins abound,
'Tis late to ask abundance of thy grace,°
When we are there; here on this lowly ground,
Teach me how to repent; for that's as good
As if thou hadst sealed° my pardon, with thy blood.

V

If poisonous minerals, and if that tree,
Whose fruit threw death on else immortal us,
If lecherous goats, if serpents envious
Cannot be damned;° alas, why should I be?
Why should intent or reason, born in me,
Make sins, else equal, in me more heinous?
And mercy being easy, and glorious
To God, in his stern wrath, why threatens he?
But who am I,° that dare dispute with thee
10   O God? Oh! of thine only worthy blood,°
And my tears, make a heavenly lethean° flood,
And drown in it my sin's black memory;
That thou remember them, some claim as debt,°
I think it mercy, if thou wilt forget.

grace to begin prevenient grace, without which the repentance which gains further grace is impossible
imagined corners Revelation 7:1
never . . . woe I Corinthians 15:51–52
But the characteristic change of tone for the sestet
sins . . . grace Romans 6:1
sealed confirmed
If . . . be damned Only men, who have reason, can be damned; cf. Dr. Faustus XVIII. 171 ff.

But who am I Changing tone in sestet, he reproves himself for arguing with God's dispensations.
thine . . . blood thy blood which is alone worthy
lethean Lethe was the river of Hades out of which souls drank forgetfulness of their previous existence.
That . . . debt some ask for their sins to be remembered, and so included in the debt Christ discharged

VI

Death be not proud, though some have callèd thee
Mighty and dreadful, for, thou art not so,
For, those, whom thou think'st, thou dost overthrow,
Die not, poor death, nor yet canst thou kill me;
From rest and sleep, which but thy pictures be,
Much pleasure, then from thee, much more must flow,°
And soonest our best men with thee do go,°
Rest of their bones, and soul's delivery.
Thou art slave to fate, chance, kings, and desperate men,
10   And dost with poison, war, and sickness dwell,
And poppy,° or charms can make us sleep as well,
And better than thy stroke; why swell'st thou then?
One short sleep past, we wake eternally,
And death shall be no more, Death thou shalt die.

X

Batter my heart, three-personed° God; for, you
As yet but knock, breathe, shine, and seek to mend;
That I may rise, and stand, o'erthrow me, and bend
Your force, to break, blow, burn, and make me new.
I, like an usurped town, to another due,°
Labour to admit you, but oh, to no end,
Reason your viceroy in me, me should defend,
But is captived, and proves weak or untrue,
Yet dearly I love you,° and would be loved fain,
10   But am bethrothed unto your enemy,
Divorce me, untie, or break that knot again,
Take me to you, imprison me, for I
Except you enthral° me, never shall be free,
Nor ever chaste, except you ravish me.

XIX

Oh, to vex° me, contraries meet in one:
Inconstancy unnaturally hath begot
A constant habit; that when I would not
I change in vows, and in devotiòn.
As humorous° is my contritiòn
As my profane love,° and as soon forgot:
As riddlingly distempered,° cold and hot,

From rest . . . flow if we derive pleasure from
rest and sleep, which are only images of death,
how much more should we get from death itself
soonest . . . go the good die without fuss
poppy puff yourself up
three-personed the trinity
to another due owing allegiance to someone
other than the usurper, in this case the devil
Yet . . . you For the sestet the figure changes

to one of love, marriage and rape.
enthral take prisoner
humorous changeable, whimsical
As . . . love rare instance of Donne's relating
sacred and profane love
riddlingly distempered puzzlingly disproportioned

As praying, as mute; as infinite, as none.
I durst not view heaven yesterday; and today
10   In prayers, and flattering speeches I court God:
Tomorrow I quake with true fear of his rod.
So my devout fits come and go away
Like a fantastic ague:° save that here
Those are my best days, when I shake with fear.°

1633

Good Friday, 1613. Riding Westward°

Let man's soul be a sphere, and then, in this,
The intelligence that moves, devotion is,
And as the other spheres, by being grown
Subject to foreign motions, lose their own,
And being by others hurried every day,
Scarce in a year their natural form obey:
Pleasure or business, so, our souls admit
For their first mover, and are whirled by it.°
Hence is't, that I am carried towards the west
10   This day, when my soul's form° bends toward the east.
There I should see a sun, by rising set,°
And by that setting endless day beget;°
But that Christ on this Cross, did rise and fall,
Sin had eternally benighted all.
Yet dare I almost be glad, I do not see
That spectacle of too much weight for me.
Who sees God's face, that is self life,° must die;°
What a death were it then to see God die?°
It made his own lieutenant° Nature shrink,
20   It made his footstool crack,° and the sun wink.
Could I behold those hands which span the poles,
And turn° all spheres at once, pierced with those holes?
Could I behold that endless height which is
Zenith° to us, and to our antipodes,°

fantastic ague capricious fever; agues, caused
by malaria, struck at intervals
best . . . fear the difference from an ague is
that in that case one's worst days are the days
on which one shakes
Good Friday, 1613. . . . a meditation actually
composed on a journey taken that day from
Warwickshire to Montgomery in Wales
Let . . . whirled by it as the angel-intelligence
moves its heavenly body, so the devotion moves
man's soul; and as the regular motion of
heavenly bodies is affected by external forces,
so that they are rarely in their proper orbits,
so the forces of business or pleasure take over
from devotion and move us in directions not
proper to us

soul's form devotion
by rising set . . . beget Christ coming into the
world and dying; by so doing he creates the
possibility of eternal life
self life the essence of life
must die Exodus 33:20
die the rime riche, unusual in English verse
lieutenant deputy
footstool crack Isaiah 66:1 and, for the earthquake at the Crucifixion, Matthew 27:51
turn An alternative reading, "tune," would make
this refer to the music of the spheres.
Zenith . . . antipodes the highest point to us
and also to those who inhabit the other side
of the world

Humbled below us? or that blood which is
The seat of all our souls, if not of his,°
Made dirt of dust,° or that flesh which was worn,
By God, for his apparel, ragged, and torn?
If on these things I durst not look, durst I
30 Upon his miserable mother cast mine eye,
Who was God's partner here, and furnished thus
Half of that sacrifice, which ransomed us?
Though these things, as I ride, be from mine eye,
They are present yet unto my memory,
For that looks towards them; and thou look'st towards me,
O Saviour, as thou hang'st upon the tree;
I turn my back to thee, but to receive
Corrections, till thy mercies bid thee leave.
O think me worth thine anger, punish me,
40 Burn off my rusts, and my deformity,
Restore thine image,° so much, by thy grace,
That thou mayst know me, and I'll turn my face.

                                    1633

Hymn to God My God, in My Sickness°

Since I am coming to that holy room,°
    Where, with thy choir of saints for evermore,
I shall be made thy music; as I come
    I tune the instrument here at the door,
    And what I must do then, think now before.

Whilst my physicians by their love° are grown
    Cosmographers, and I their map, who lie
Flat on this bed, that by them may be shown
    That this is my south-west discovery°
10   Per fretum febris,° by these strains to die,

I joy, that in these straits, I see my west;°
    For, though their currents yield return to none,
What shall my west hurt me? As west and east
    In all flat maps (and I am one) are one,
    So death doth touch the resurrection.

The seat . . . of his whether or no the blood is,
as some say, the seat of the soul, Christ's
blood is certainly the seat of ours
Made . . . dust turned into mud by mixing
with dust
Restore thine image (by punishment) make
anew your likeness in me
Hymn to God, in My Sickness According to
Walton this was written by Donne on his death-
bed, but more likely it dates, like "A Hymn
to God the Father," from his illness of 1623.

holy room heaven
love attentive care to his body
Cosmographers geographers
south-west discovery The south is hot, the west
"declining"—cf. "The Good Morrow"—and so
the discovery of a southwest passage to the East
is an emblem of death by fever.
Per fretum febris fretum is both "heat" and
"strait": through the hot strait of fever
my west my death (his east will be the resurrection)

Is the Pacific Sea° my home? Or are
   The eastern riches?° Is Jerusalem?°
Anyan,° and Magellan, and Gibraltàr,
   All straits, and none but straits, are ways to them,°
20   Whether where Japhet dwelt, or Cham, or Shem.°

We think that Paradise and Calvary,
   Christ's cross, and Adam's tree, stood in one place;°
Look Lord, and find both Adams met in me;
   As the first Adam's sweat surrounds my face,
   May the last Adam's blood my soul embrace.

So, in his purple wrapped receive me Lord,
   By these his thorns° give me his other crown;
And as to others' souls I preached thy word,
   Be this my text, my sermon to mine own,
30   Therefore that° he may raise the Lord throws down.

1635

A Hymn to God the Father°

I

Wilt thou forgive that sin where I begun,
   Which is my sin, though it were done before?°
Wilt thou forgive that sin, through which I run,°
   And do run still:° though still° I do deplore?
      When thou hast done, thou hast not done,°
         For I have more.

II

Wilt thou forgive that sin which I have won
   Others to sin? and, made my sin their door?
Wilt thou forgive that sin which I did shun
10   A year, or two, but wallowed in a score?
      When thou hast done, thou hast not done,
         For I have more.

Pacific Sea which could stand for heavenly peace
eastern riches standing for heaven
Jerusalem standing, as always, for the Heavenly City
Anyan Annam, then thought of as a strait dividing Asia from America
All straits . . . to them all the ways to heaven are "straits"
Japhet . . . Cham . . . Shem The world was divided between the sons of Noah: Japhet got Europe, Ham Africa, and Shem Asia.
Paradise . . . one place This myth is recorded elsewhere, but seems not to have been widespread, though Donne refers to it twice.

these his thorns the poet's sufferings which resemble Christ's
Therefore that in order that
A Hymn to God the Father according to Walton, written during the serious illness of 1623 which also produced the *Devotions*. A contemporary musical setting by John Hilton survives.
my sin . . . before the sin of his parents, by which original sin was transmitted to him
run ran
still always
When . . . done When you've done that you've not finished / When you've done that you've still not gained Donne

III

I have a sin of fear, that when I have spun
 My last thread, I shall perish on the shore;
But swear by thy self, that at my death thy son°
 Shall shine as he shines now, and heretofore;
  And, having done that, thou hast done,
   I fear no more.

1633

Devotions upon Emergent Occasions

From Meditation X

This is Nature's nest of Boxes: the Heavens contain the earth, the earth, cities, cities, men. And all these are concentric: the common center to them all is decay, ruin; only that is eccentric which was never made; only that place or garment rather, which we can imagine, but not demonstrate—that light which is the very emanation of the light of God, in which the saints shall dwell, with which the saints shall be apparelled—only that bends not to this center, this ruin; that which was not made of Nothing is not threatened with this annihilation. All other things are, even angels, even our souls: they move upon the same poles, they bend to the same center, and if they were not made immortal by preservation, their nature could not keep them from sinking to this center, annihilation.

Meditation XVII

Nunc lento sonitu dicunt, Morieris [1]
Now this bell, rolling softly for another, says to me, Thou must die

Perchance he for whom this bell [2] tolls may be so ill as that he knows not it tolls for him; and perchance I may think myself so much better than I am, as that they who are about me and see my state, may have caused it to toll for me, and I know not that. The church is catholic, universal; so are all her actions; all that she does belongs to all. When she baptizes a child, that action concerns me, for that child is thereby connected to that Head which is my Head too, and engraffed [3] into that body, whereof I am a member.[4] And when she buries a man, that action concerns me. All mankind is of one author, and is one volume; when one man dies, one chapter is not torn out of the book, but trans-

---

thy son a pun which makes Christ = the sun

1. Literally, "Now they say with their slow sounding, 'Thou shalt die.' "
2. Passing-bell.
3. Grafted.
4. The church.

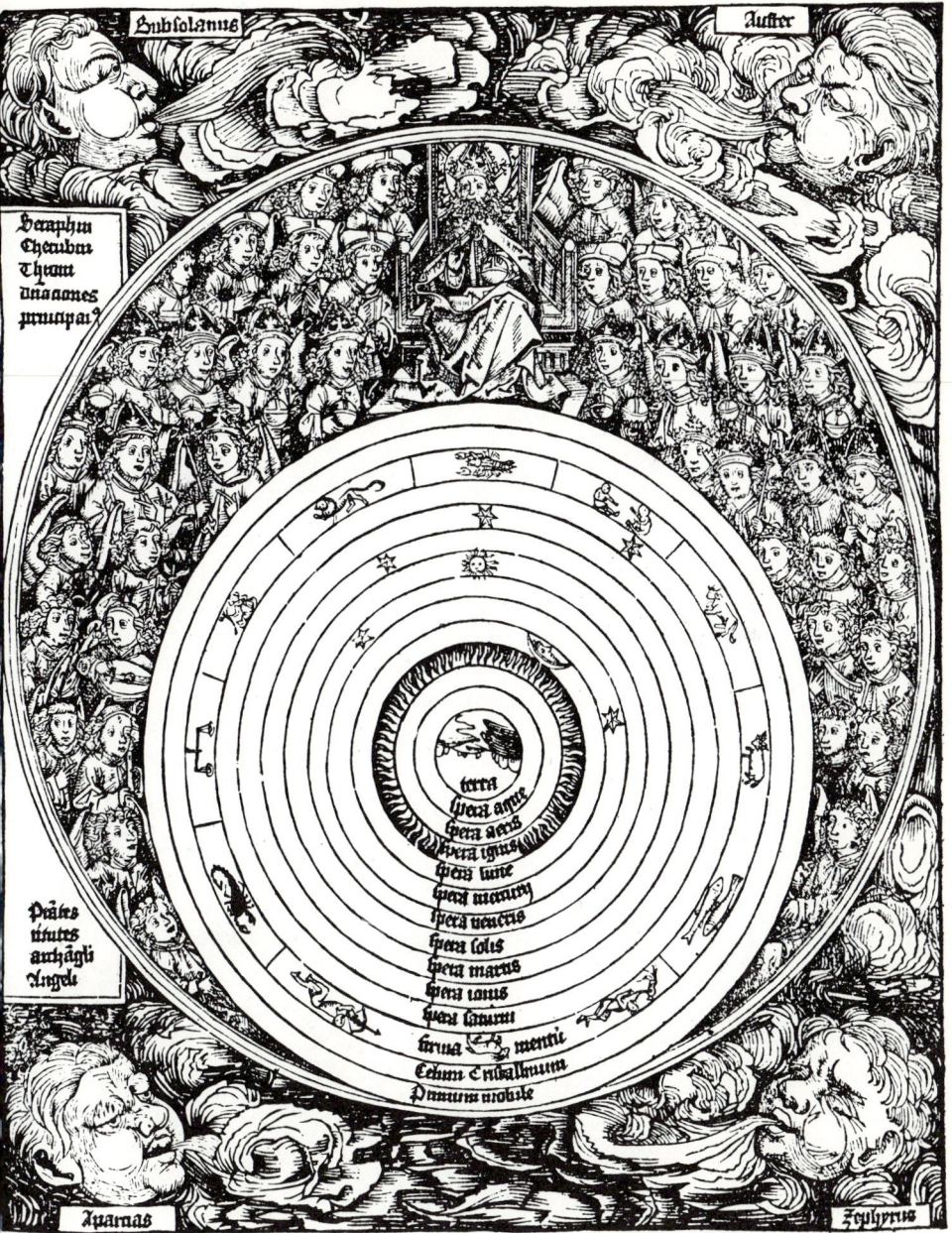

∴ The "Ptolemaic" Universe: the spheres from earth to Prime Mover, with God at the top, surrounded by choiring angels, and with the four winds in their corners. From Hartmann Schedel, *Liber Chronicarum* ("Nuremberg Chronicle"), 1493.

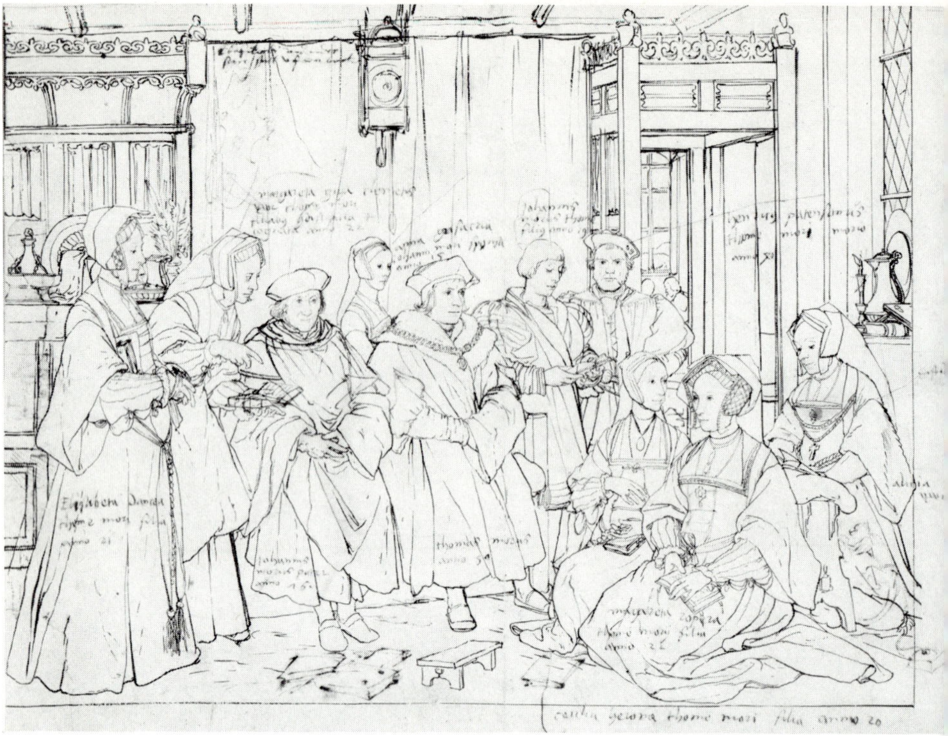

2. *Sir Thomas More and His Household* (c. 1527), by Hans Holbein the Younger (1497/8–1543), the German artist who served as court painter to Henry VIII. *Oeffentliche Kunstsammlung*, Basel.

3. *Sir Thomas Elyot* (c. 1527–28),
also drawn by Holbein.
*By permission of Her Majesty the Queen,
Copyright reserved.*

4. Guidobaldo da Montefeltro as a boy, with his father Federigo, Duke of Urbino, painted about 1476 by the Flemish artist Joos van Wassenhove called Justus van Ghent (active c. 1460–80). *Anderson-Art Reference Bureau.*

THE WORLD OF *THE COURTIER*

5. Raphael's portrait of Baldassare Castiglione (c. 1514–15). *Photo Bulloz.*

6. Allegory in Portraiture: Sir John Luttrell (1550), after the painting by Hans Eworth (c. 1520–73). Here shown wading waist-high amid shipwreck, Luttrell, a naval adventurer, looks up at the allegorical figure of Peace surrounded by her attendants. On his wrist is a bracelet with a Latin motto, which would be translated "Money deterred him not, nor did danger wreck him." On the rock at the left are the English verses:

> More than the rock amid the raging seas
> The constant heart no danger dreads, nor fears.

It has recently been suggested that the allegory of Peace also refers specifically to a treaty made with France in 1550. *Luttrell Estates, Ltd.*

7. *Queen Elizabeth I and the Three Goddesses* (1569), by the monogrammist "HE." Like so much mythological poetry and, in particular, like the masques and entertainments of the Jacobean period, this emblematic painting portrays the Queen as Paris, in the famous episode from Greek mythology in which he awards the apple to Aphrodite (Venus) and is rewarded with Helen of Troy—and the Trojan War. Here the Queen awards the prize (the apple "for the fairest" as her orb of power) to herself; the goddesses are, *left* to *right,* Juno (crowned but with her scepter cast down and with her left shoe come off), Minerva (armed), and Venus (nude, as always, and accompanied by Cupid). In the background is Windsor Castle. *By permission of Her Majesty the Queen, Copyright reserved.*

8. Queen Elizabeth (c. 1592), by Marcus Gheeraerts the Younger (1561–1635). The so-called "Ditchley Portrait," probably commemorating an entertainment given the Queen at his house in Oxfordshire by Sir Henry Lee, her Master of the Armoury and probable author of the sonnet appearing in fragmentary form on the right. It hails her as "The prince of light," toward which the figure of the Queen faces, away from stormy clouds ("Thunder, the image of that power divine," says the inscription). She stands on a map of England, with her feet near Ditchley, in fact. *National Portrait Gallery*, London.

9. Sir Walter Ralegh (1588); to the right of his head, a crescent moon facing downward, perhaps in allusion to Queen Elizabeth as Cynthia, the moon goddess and muse of Ralegh's unfinished cycle of poems. The painter has not been definitely identified. *National Portrait Gallery.*

10. A Burning Lover. A miniature by Nicholas Hilliard (c. 1547–1619) depicting a man in his shirt, conventionally ear-ringed, holding a locket probably containing his mistress's picture, and surrounded by the metaphorical fires of his passion. *Victoria and Albert Museum*, London.

11. A Courtly Sonneteer. This Hilliard miniature, c. 1588, shows an unidentified young man leaning against a tree among roses. The Latin motto, *Dat poenas laudata fides,* proclaims that the lover's vaunted faith in love has given him suffering, a typical formula. *Victoria and Albert Museum.*

12. An Elizabethan Musing, c. 1590. This later miniature by Isaac Oliver (1568?–1617) shows a young man beneath a tree in solitude away from the social life in the house and garden behind him. It has been suggested that the melancholy with which the figure is tinged has some relation to that of the figure of Democritus (also seated beneath a tree) on the title page of Burton's *Anatomy of Melancholy* (see Fig. 17). *By permission of Her Majesty the Queen, Copyright reserved.*

13. Shakespeare, engraving by Martin Droeshout (b. 1601) on a title page of the First Folio. *The Granger Collection.*

14. Ben Jonson, by an anonymous seventeenth-century painter. *The Granger Collection.*

15. John Donne (c. 1595), as a melancholic lover—"that picture of mine" he said in disposing of it in his will, "which was taken in the shadows." The large, floppy hat and the undone collar were both marks of the distracted lover in a usually tightly laced age. The inscription, to an unidentified lady, implores her to light up his shadow: *Illumina tenebras nostras domina* (Enlighten our darkness, lady)—a parody, in fact, of the Latin text translated in the (Anglican) Book of Common Prayer as "Lighten our darkness, we beseech thee, Lord." *National Portrait Gallery.*

16. *Melancholy.* The celebrated engraving by Albrecht Dürer (1471–1528), with its emblematic bat, dog, abandoned scientific and speculative instruments, makes of this brooding, dark angel as personal a myth of the internalized imagination as Milton's in "Il Penseroso" or Burton's in the *Anatomy. The Metropolitan Museum of Art, Harris Brisbane Dick Fund, 1943,* New York.

17. *The Anatomy of Melancholy,* title page of the 1628 edition. Surrounding the text are images of melancholic types: on the *left,* the Lover; on the *right,* the Hypochondriac; *above, center,* the Scholar. The Lover may be compared, for his hat and crossed arms, with the portrait of Donne in Figure 15. "Democritus Jr.," the pseudonymous Burton, appears at lower center. *New York Public Library, Arents Collection.*

H EERE, *Melancholly* muſing in his fits,
Pale viſag'd, of complexion cold and drie,
All ſolitarie, at his ſtudie ſits,
Within a wood, devoid of companie:
  Saue Madge the Owle, and melancholly Puſſe,
  Light-loathing Creatures, hatefull, ominous.

His mouth, in ſigne of ſilence, vp is bound,
For *Melancholly* loues not many wordes:
One foote on Cube is fixt vpon the ground,
The which him plodding *Conſtancie* affordes:
  A ſealed Purſe he beares, to ſhew no vice,
  So proper is to him, as *Avarice*.

T I. *Sanguis*

18. *Melancholy.* Notice that the text gives readings of various elements of the picture.

Emblems of the Four Temperaments from Henry Peacham's emblem book *Minerva Brittana,* 1610. *Yale University Library,* New Haven, Conn.

THE Aierie *Sanguine*, in whofe youthfull cheeke,
  The *Peftane Rofe*, and *Lilly* doe contend:
By nature is benigne, and gentlie meeke,
To Mufick, and all merriment a frend;
   As feemeth by his flowers, and girlondes gay,
   Wherewith he dightes him, all the merry May.

And by him browzing, of the climbing vine,
The luftfull *Goate* is feene, which may import,
His pronenes both to women, and to wine,
Bold, bounteous, frend vnto the learned fort;
   For ftudies fit, beft louing, and belou'd,
   Faire-fpoken, bafhfull, feld in anger moou'd.

Cholera

19. *The Sanguine Temperament.*

NEXT *Choller* ſtandes, reſembling moſt the fire,
  Of ſwarthie yeallow, and a meager face;
With Sword a late, vnſheathed in his Ire:
Neere whome, there lies, within a little ſpace,
  A ſterne ei'de Lion, and by him a ſheild,
  Charg'd with a flame, vpon a crimſon feild.

We paint him young, to ſhew that paſſions raigne,
The moſt in heedles, and vnſtaied youth:
That Lion ſhowes, he ſeldome can refraine,
From crueli deede, devoide of gentle ruth:
  Or hath perhaps, this beaſt to him aſſign'd,
  As bearing moſt, the braue and bounteous mind.

T 2. *Phlegma*

20. *The Choleric.*

H EERE *Phlegme* fits coughing on a Marble feate,
   As Citie-vfurers before their dore :
Of Bodie groffe, not through exceffe of meate,
But of a Dropfie, he had got of yore :
   His flothfull hand, in's bofome ftill he keepes,
   Drinkes, fpits, or nodding, in the Chimney fleepes.

Beneath his feete, there doth a *Tortoife* crall,
For floweft pace, Sloth's Hieroglyphick here,
For Phlegmatique, hates Labour moft of all,
As by his courfe araiment, may appeare :
   Nor is he better furnifhed I find,
   With Science, or the virtues of the mind .

21. *The Phlegmatic.*

H EARE what's the reafon why a man we call
A little world? and what the wifer ment
By this new name? two lights Cœleftiall
Are in his head, as in the Element:
Eke as the wearied Sunne at night is fpent,
    So feemeth but the life of man a day,
    At morne hee's borne, at night he flits away.

Of heate and cold as is the Aire compofed,
So likewife man we fee breath's whot and cold,
His bodie's earthy: in his lunges inclofed,
Remaines the Aire: his braine doth moifture hold,
His heart and liver, doe the heate infold:
    Of Earth, Fire, Water, Man thus framed is,
    Of Elements the threefold Qualities.

Ddı.   And

22. Man the Microcosm, another emblem from *Minerva Brittana*. Compare with the treatment of the human microcosm in Donne's "I am a little world made cunningly," and in Browne and Ralegh. *Yale University Library*.

WHEN HERCVLES, was dowtfull of his waie,
   Inclofed rounde, with vertue, and with vice:

Virgil. in Fragm.
de littera y.
*Quifquis enim duros
cafus virtutis amore
Vicerit, ille fibi lau-
démque decúfque pa-
rabit.
At qui defidiã luxúm-
que fequetur inertem,
Dum fugit oppofitos in-
cauta mente labores,
Turpis, inópfque fimul,
miferabile tranfiget
auum.*

With reafons firfte, did vertue him affaie,
The other, did with pleafures him entice:
   They longe did ftriue, before he coulde be wonne,
   Till at the lengthe, ALCIDES thus begonne.

Oh pleafure, thoughe thie waie bee fmoothe, and faire,
And fweete delightes in all thy courtes abounde:
Yet can I heare, of none that haue bene there,
That after life, with fame haue bene renoumde:
   For honor hates, with pleafure to remaine,
   Then houlde thy peace, thow waftes thie winde in vaine.

But heare, I yeelde oh vertue to thie will,
And vowe my felfe, all labour to indure,
For to afcende the fteepe, and craggie hill,
The toppe whereof, whoe fo attaines, is fure
   For his rewarde, to haue a crowne of fame:
   Thus HERCVLES, obey'd this facred dame.

Pana

23. The Choice of Hercules, a mythological emblem expounded in an almost homiletic way, from Geoffrey Whitney's *Choice of Emblems*, 1586. See also Ben Johnson's *Pleasure Reconciled to Virtue. Yale University Library.*

ILLVSTR. XII.   *Book.3*

Hen *Emblems*, of too many parts consist,
Their Author was no choice *Emblematist* :
But, is like those, that wast whole *howres*, to tell
What, in three *minutes*, might be said as well.
Yet, when each member is interpreted,
Out of these vulgar *Figures*, you may read
A *Morall*, (altogether) not unfit
To be remembred, ev'n, by *men of wit*.
And, if the *Kernell* proove to be of worth,
No matter from what shell we drew it forth.
   The *Square* whereon the *Globe* is placed, here,
Must *Vertue* be ; That *Globe* upon the *Square*,
Must meane the *World* ; The *Figure*, in the *Round*,
(Which in appearance doth her *Trumpet* sound)
Was made for *Fame* ; The *Booke* she beares, may show,
What *Breath* it is, which makes her *Trumpet* blow :
The *Wreath*, inclosing all, was to intend
A glorious *Praise*, that never shall have end :
And, these, in one summ'd up, doe seeme to say ;
That, (if men *study* in a *vertuous-way*)
The *Trumpet* of a never-ceasing *Fame*,
Shall through the *world* proclaime their praisefull *Name*.
   Now *Reader*, if large *Fame*, be thy ambition,
This *Emblem* doth informe, on what condition
She may be gain'd. But, (herein, me beleeve)
Thy *studie* for meere-praise, will thee deceive :
And, if thy *Vertues*, be, but onely, those
For which the vulgar *Fame*, her *Trumpet* blowes,
    Thy *Fame's* a blast ; Thy *Vertues*, Vices be ;
    Thy *Studie's* vaine ; and, *shame* will follow thee.

Above

24. Study and Fame. George Wither's *A Collection of Emblems*, 1635, contains this rather plodding reading of a complex symbol. It may amuse the modern reader to follow it step by step.

72

If Safely, *thou desire to goe,*
Bee nor too swift, *nor* overflow.

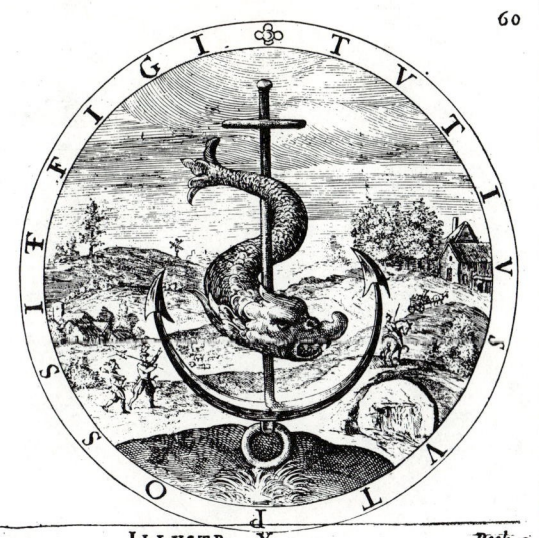

60

ILLVSTR. X.   Book. 2

OVr *Elders,* when their meaning was to shew
A *native-speedinesse* (in Emblem wise)
The picture of a *Dolphin-Fish* they drew;
Which, through the waters, with great swiftnesse, flies.
An *Anchor,* they did figure, to declare
Hope, *stayednesse,* or a *grave-deliberation:*
And therefore when those two, united are,
It giveth us a two-fold Intimation.
For, as the *Dolphin* putteth us in minde,
That in the Courses, which we have to make,
Wee should not be, to *slothfulnesse* enclin'd;
But, swift to follow what we undertake:
So, by an *Anchor* added thereunto,
Inform'd wee are, that, to maintaine our *speed,*
Hope, must bee joyn'd therewith (in all we doe)
If wee will undiscouraged proceed.
It sheweth (also) that, our *speedinesse,*
Must have some *staydnesse;* lest, when wee suppose
To prosecute our aymes with good successe,
Wee may, by *Rashnesse,* good endeavors lose.
    They worke, with most securitie, that know
The *Times,* and best *Occasions* of *delay;*
When, likewise, to be neither *swift,* nor *slow;*
And, when to practise all the *speed,* they may.
For, whether calme, or stormie-passages,
(Through this life's *Ocean*) shall their *Bark* attend;
This *double Vertue,* will procure their ease:
And, them, in all necessities, befriend.
    By *Speedinesse,* our works are timely wrought;
    By *Staydnesse,* they, to passe are, safely, brought.

They,

25. *Festina Lente* (Make haste slowly). The device of a dolphin curled about an anchor
appears first in classical times and as ascribed to the Emperor Augustus. In the Renaissance it becomes a dialectical resolution of the opposites of anchored steadfastness and
joyful, bounding motion. The great Venetian printer Aldus Manutius used it as his device.
This version, from Wither's book of emblems, uses the conventional symbolism of the
anchor as Hope and, later, as Faith.

26. Emblem and Poem

The engraved title page of Ralegh's *History of the World,* 1614, shows an allegorical figure of History, labeled in Latin "mistress of life" and bearing aloft the globe, which remains beneath the Eye of Providence; History tramples Death and Oblivion, and is attended by Experience and Truth (naked as always). Ben Jonson wrote the poem "The Mind of the Frontispiece to a Book" to accompany, and gloss, the picture:

> From Death and dark Oblivion, ne'er the same
>   The Mistress of Man's life, grave History
> Raising the World to Good or Evil Fame
>   Doth vindicate it to eternity.
> Wise Providence would so: that nor the good
>   Might be defrauded, nor the great secured,
> But both might know their ways were understood
>   When Vice alike in time with Virtue dured.
> Which makes that (lighted by the beamy hand
>   Of Truth that searcheth the most hidden springs
> And guided by Experience, whose straight wand
>   Doth mete, whose line doth sound, the depth of things),
> She cheerfully supporteth what she rears
>   Assisted by no strengths but are her own,
> Some note of which each varied pillar bears,
>   By which, as proper titles, she is known:
> Time's witness, Herald of Antiquity,
>   The Light of Truth, and Life of Memory.

New York Public Library, Rare Book Division.

27. The Entry of Comus, from Jonson's *Pleasure Reconciled to Virtue,* one of the designs by Inigo Jones (1573–1652) for the masque. *Courtauld Institute,* London.

28. *Queen Henrietta Maria as Chloris* in Ben Jonson's *Chlorida,* 1631, another Inigo Jones drawing of a costume design to illustrate the stage direction: "In the most eminent place of the Bower sat the goddess Chloris, accompanied with fourteen Nymphs, their apparell white, embroidered with silver, trimmed at the shoulders with great leaves of green, embroidered with gold, falling one under the other. . . . their headties of flowers mixed with silver and gold, with sprigs of egrets among, and from the top of their dressing a thin veil hanging down." *Courtauld Institute of Art,* London.

29. The young Milton, at age twenty or twenty-one, in 1629. *National Portrait Gallery.*

30. Milton at thirty-six or thirty-seven, the frontispiece to the *Poems*, 1645, as engraved by William Marshall. In reaction Milton wrote the Greek inscription at the bottom: "This picture was drawn by an unskillfull hand (you'd say,) looking at its original and not recognizing the true copy [pun on *engraving*]. Friends, laugh at the bad picture by a worthless engraver." *New York Public Library, Rare Book Division.*

Melpo'mene Erato.

IOANNIS MILTONI ANGLI EFFIGIES ANNO ÆTATIS VIGES: PRI:

Urania. Clio

Ἀμαθεῖ γεγράφθαι χειρὶ τηνδὲ μὲν εἰκόνα
Φαίης τάχ᾽ ἄν, πρὸς εἶδος αὐτοφυὲς βλέπων
Τὸν δ᾽ ἐκτυπωτὸν ἐκ ἐπιγνόντες φίλοι
Γελᾶτε φαύλȣ δυσμίμημα ζωγράφȣ.

W:M· *sculp:*

31. *King Charles I on Horseback.* Sir Anthony Van Dyck (1599–1641), who lived in England from 1632 until his death, served as painter to Charles I, a great collector and connoisseur. Van Dyck's various portraits of him capture a range of the King's qualities, such as hauteur and refinement; in this equestrian portrait (163?) he is depicted in a manner derived from Titian's Emperor Charles V, but not literally denoting the head of a conquering army so much as suggesting, with almost Platonist imagery, a higher soul controlling powerful passions. *National Gallery,* London.

32. *Charles I and James, Duke of York, 1647.* Portrait by Sir Peter Lely (1618–80) of the doomed King and his heir suggested an almost emblematic reading to the Cavalier poet Richard Lovelace, who wrote of it:

> See what a clouded Majesty! and eyes
> Whose glory through their mist doth brighter rise!
> See what an humble bravery doth shine,
> And grief triumphant breaking through each line; . . .
> That mightiest Monarchs by this shaded book
> May copy out their proudest, richest look.

From "To My Worthy Friend Mr. Peter Lilly"

Country Life, London.

33. The Cavalier Temper. Though most often thought of as a court painter to Charles II, the Dutch artist Sir Peter Lely, who came to London in 1643, was active during the Commonwealth as well. This exotic vision of nymphs at a fountain seems an apt counterpart to the poetic world of Thomas Carew's "A Rapture." *Dulwich College Picture Gallery*, London.

34. St. Teresa in Ecstasy

> His is the dart must make the death
> Whose stroke shall taste thy hallowed breath;
> A dart thrice dipped in that rich flame
> Which writes thy spouse's radiant name
> Upon the roof of heaven. . . .

From Richard Crashaw's "A Hymn to the Name
and Honour of the Admirable Saint Teresa, . . ."

The great baroque vision of *The Ecstasy of St. Teresa* by Gianlorenzo Bernini (1598–1680) (in the Cornaro Chapel of Santa Maria della Vittoria, in Rome) took form in 1645–52, and its amazing theatrical use of natural lighting from above to play about flesh, drapery, and gilded, carved rays of celestial light parallels Crashaw's imagery in representing the rapid transience of the ecstatic moment. Compare with Crashaw's "The Flaming Heart." *Alinari-Scala.*

35. Oliver Cromwell, painted by Robert Walker (c. 1605–60) in a format derived, like Lely's of Charles I and his son, from Van Dyck's division of the scene into two areas, one backed by hanging drapery, the other by outdoor sky. It is ironic that Walker should have used the courtly pictorial conventions to depict the Court's destroyer. *National Portrait Gallery*

36. Andrew Marvell (1658), by Adriaen Hanneman. (*c.* 1601–71). *The Granger Collection.*

37. Rubens's Ceiling, detail of the center end panel representing *The Benefits of the Government of James I.* James crowned and wreathed by angelic figures; *below,* Minerva (as Wisdom) defends the throne against Mars (as War) who crushes the King's enemies. Mercury, *left,* points toward their Hell, and above him Peace embraces Plenty. *Department of the Environment, Crown Copyright reserved.*

38. Interior view of the Banqueting House, Whitehall, designed by Inigo Jones (1573–1652) and completed in 1622 for James I. It was the scene of court masques by Ben Jonson and others until 1635, at which time the ceiling by Peter Paul Rubens (1577–1640), commissioned by Charles I, was installed. *A. F. Kersting.*

lated [5] into a better language, and every chapter must be so translated; God employs several translators; some pieces are translated by age, some by sickness, some by war, some by justice; but God's hand is in every translation; and his hand shall bind up all our scattered leaves again for that library where every book shall lie open to one another. As therefore the bell that rings to a sermon calls not upon the preacher only, but upon the congregation to come, so this bell calls us all; but how much more me, who am brought so near the door by this sickness. There was a contention as far as a suit [6] (in which both piety and dignity, religion and estimation,[7] were mingled) which of the religious orders should ring to prayers first in the morning; and it was determined, that they should ring first that rose earliest. If we understand aright the dignity of this bell that tolls for our evening prayer, we would be glad to make it ours by rising early, in that application, that it might be ours as well as his whose indeed it is. The bell doth toll for him that thinks it doth; and though it intermit [8] again, yet from that minute that that occasion wrought upon him, he is united to God. Who casts not [9] up his eye to the sun when it rises? But who takes off his eye from a comet when that breaks out? Who bends not [9] his ear to any bell which upon any occasion rings? But who can remove it from that bell which is passing a piece of himself out of this world? No man is an island, entire of itself; every man is a piece of the continent, a part of the main; [10] if a clod be washed away by the sea, Europe is the less, as well as if a promontory were, as well as if a manor [11] of thy friend's or of thine own were. Any man's death diminishes me, because I am involved in mankind; and therefore never send to know for whom the bell tolls; it tolls for thee. Neither can we call this a begging of misery or a borrowing of misery, as though we were not miserable enough of ourselves, but must fetch in more from the next house, in taking upon us the misery of our neighbours. Truly it were an excusable covetousness if we did; for affliction is a treasure, and scarce any man hath enough of it. No man hath affliction enough that is not matured and ripened by it, and made fit for God by that affliction. If a man carry treasure in bullion, or in a wedge of gold, and have none coined into current monies, his treasure will not defray him as he travels. Tribulation is treasure in the nature of it, but it is not current money in the use of it, except we get nearer and nearer our home, heaven, by it. Another man may be sick too, and sick to death, and this affliction may lie in his bowels, as gold in a mine, and be of no use to him; but this bell, that tells me of his affliction, digs out and applies that gold to me, if by this consideration of another's danger, I take mine own into contemplation, and so secure myself by making my recourse to my God, who is our only security.

1624

5. Punning on the etymological sense, "carried over."
6. Which went as far as legal action.
7. Self-esteem.
8. Break off.
9. These words may be intrusive; the sense is stronger without them.
10. Mainland.
11. Estate.

Sermons

By the end of his life, when he was Dean of St. Paul's, Donne's chief fame was as a preacher. His sermons form a vast bulk, and nowadays they are mostly read by scholars seeking, and finding, enlightenment concerning what they value more highly, namely, the poems; but they are, in themselves, a great achievement. They are not all of equal importance or profundity; some were for learned audiences, some for large; some are relatively perfunctory, some terrifying. The liturgical season, the particular occasion, affect the tone. Like most preachers of his time, Donne was preoccupied by sin and death; he confesses his melancholy and his desire for extinction. "I preach the sense of God's indignation on mine own soul." But there is joy also, and humanity. Above all there is a learned wit, which relates the old to the young Donne, and both to the other great preachers of his day. He followed the general scheme employed in the very long sermons of the time, but expected his audience, in the midst of their instruction, to follow his puns and allusions, as well as to respond to the immense eloquence he could produce when he thought fit.

It is impossible to select one brief passage and expect it to give any notion of Donne the preacher; the famous final sermon *Death's Duel* is not really characteristic, and too many anthologists have, by choosing only purple passages, given a positively false impression. What follows here is from a fine but not spectacular sermon on a central text, which happens to be in the chapter chosen to illustrate the development of the English Bibles. There is just about enough of it to enable the reader to see how Donne handled a text, and how he defined and enriched his theme for an audience which, though made up of better listeners than any preacher could find today, nevertheless needed the preacher's summations, repetitions and explanations, if they were to follow him.

From A Sermon Preached at St. Paul's for Easter-Day, 1628

'For now we see through a glass darkly, but then face to face; now I know in part, but then I shall know even as also I am known.'[1]

These two terms in our text, *nunc* and *tunc*, now and then, now in a glass, then face to face, now in part, then in perfection, these two secular[2] terms, of which one designs the whole age of this world from the creation to the dissolution thereof, for all that is comprehended in this word *now*, and the other designs the everlastingness of the next world, for that incomprehensibleness is comprehended in the other word *then*—these two words that design two such ages are now met in one day, in this day in which we celebrate all resurrections in the root in the resurrection of our Lord and Saviour Christ Jesus blest forever. For the first term, *now*, 'Now in a glass, now in part,' is intended most especially of that very act which we do now at this present, that is, of the ministry of the Gospel, of declaring God in his ordinance, of preaching his word, 'Now,' in

1. I Corinthians 13:12—"glass" = "mirror." See the section The English Bible.
2. Relating to ages.

this ministry of his Gospel, 'we see in a glass, we know in part'; and then the *then*, the time of seeing face to face and knowing as we are known is intended of that time which we celebrate this day, the day of resurrection, the day of judgement, the day of the actual possession of the next life. So that this day this whole Scripture is fulfilled in your ears; for now, now in this preaching, you have some sight, and then, then when that day comes which in the first root thereof we celebrate this day, you shall have a perfect sight of all; 'Now we see through a glass,' etc.

That therefore you may the better know him when you come to see him face to face than by having seen him in a glass now, and that your seeing him now in his ordinance [3] may prepare you to see him then in his essence, proceed we thus in the handling of these words. First, that there is nothing brought into comparison, into consideration, nothing put into the balance, but the sight of God, the knowledge of God; it is not called a better sight, nor a better knowledge, but there is no other sight, no other knowledge proposed or mentioned or intimated or imagined but this; all other sight is blindness, all other knowledge is ignorance; [4] and then we shall see how there is a twofold sight of God and a twofold knowledge of God proposed to us here; a sight and a knowledge here in this life, and another manner of sight and another manner of knowledge in the life to come; for here we see God *in speculo*, in a glass, that is, by reflection, and here we know God *in ænigmate*, says our text, darkly, so we translate it, that is, by obscure presentations, and therefore it is called a knowledge but in part; but in heaven our sight is face to face, and our knowledge is to know as we are known.

For our sight of God here, our theatre, the place where we sit and see him, is the whole world, the whole house and frame of nature, and our medium, our glass, is the book of creatures, and our light, by which we see him, is the light of natural reason. And then for our knowledge of God here, our place, our academy, our university is the church, our medium is the ordinance of God in his church, preaching and sacraments; and our light is the light of faith. Thus we shall find it to be for our sight and for our knowledge of God here. But for our sight of God in heaven, our place, our sphere is heaven itself, our medium is the patefaction,[5] the manifestation, the revelation of God himself, and our light is the light of glory. And then for our knowledge of God there, God himself is all; God himself is the place, we see him in him; God is our medium, we see him by him; God is our light; not a light which is his, but a light which is he; not a light which flows from him, no, nor a light which is in him, but that light which is he himself. Lighten our darkness, we beseech thee, O Lord, O Father of lights, that in thy light we may see light,[6] that now we see this through this thy glass, thy ordinance, and by the good of this hereafter face to face.

The sight is so much the noblest of all the senses as that it is all the senses.[7] As the reasonable soul of man, when it enters, becomes all the soul of man, and

3. Explained in next paragraph.
4. See *The Second Anniversary*, ll. 254 ff.
5. Making plain.
6. Psalms 36:9.
7. The usual view; the senses ran down from sight through hearing, smell, taste, and touch.

he hath no longer a vegetative and a sensitive soul but all is that one reasonable soul; [8] so, says St. Augustine, and he exemplifies it by several pregnant places of Scripture, *Visus per omnes sensus recurrit,* all the senses are called seeing; as there is *videre et audire,* 'St. John turned to see the sound'; [9] and there is *gustate et videte,* 'Taste and see how sweet the Lord is'; [10] and so of the rest of the senses, all is sight. Employ then this noblest sense upon the noblest object, see God; see God in everything, and then thou needst not take off thine eye from beauty, from riches, from honour, from anything. St. Paul speaks here of a diverse seeing of God. Of seeing God in a glass, and seeing God face to face; but of not seeing God at all, the apostle speaks not at all.

When Christ took the blind man by the hand,[11] though he had then begun his cure upon him, yet he asked him if he saw aught. Something he was sure he saw; but it was a question whether it were to be called a sight, for he saw men but as trees. The natural man [12] sees beauty and riches and honour, but yet it is a question whether he sees them or no, because he sees them but as a snare. But he that sees God in them sees them to be beams and evidences of that beauty, that wealth, that honour, that is in God, that is in God himself. The other blind man that importuned Christ, 'Jesus, thou son of David, have mercy upon me,' when Christ asked him, 'What wilt thou that I shall do unto thee?' had presently that answer, 'Lord, that I may receive my sight'; [13] and we may easily think that if Christ had asked him a second question, 'What wouldst thou see when thou hast received thy sight?' he would have answered, 'Lord, I will see thee'; for when he had his sight and Christ said to him, 'Go thy way,' he had no way to go from Christ, but, as the text says there, 'He followed him.' All that he cared for was seeing, all that he cared to see was Christ. Whether he would see a peace or a war may be a statesman's problem; whether he would see plenty or scarcity of some commodity may be a merchant's problem; whether he would see Rome or Spain grow in greatness may be a Jesuit's problem; but whether I had not rather see God than anything is no problematical matter. All sight is blindness, that was our first; all knowledge is ignorance till we come to God, is our next consideration.

The first act of will is love, says the School; [14] for till the will love, till it would have something, it is not a will. But then, *amare nisi nota non possumus;* it is impossible to love anything till we know it. First our understanding must present it as *verum,* as a known truth, and then our will embraces it as *bonum,* as good, and worthy to be loved. Therefore the philosopher [15] concludes easily, as a thing that admits no contradiction, that naturally all men desire to know, that they may love. But then, as the addition [16] of an honest man varies the signification with the profession and calling of the man—for he is an honest man at court that oppresses no man with his power, and at the exchange he is

8. Man has the first, which comprehends the others; animals the second and third.
9. Revelation 1:12.
10. Psalms 34:8.
11. Mark 8:23.
12. Man without religion, seeing by the light of nature.
13. Mark 10:46–51.
14. The scholastic philosophy.
15. St. Augustine.
16. Description.

the honest man that keeps his word, and in an army the valiant man is the honest man—so the addition of learning and understanding varies with the man; the divine, the physician, the lawyer are not qualified, not denominated by the same kind of learning. But yet, as it is for honesty, there is no honest man at court or exchange or army if he believe not in God; so there is no knowledge in the physician nor lawyer if he know not God. Neither does any man know God except he know him so as God hath made himself known, that is, in Christ. Therefore, as St. Paul desires to know nothing else,[17] so let no man pretend to know anything but Christ crucified; that is, crucified for him, made his. In the eighth verse of this chapter he says, 'Prophecy shall fail, and tongues shall fail, and knowledge shall vanish'; but this knowledge of God in Christ made mine, by being crucified for me, shall dwell with me forever. And so from this general consideration all sight is blindness, all knowledge is ignorance, but of God, we pass to the particular consideration of that twofold sight and knowledge of God expressed in this text, 'Now we see through a glass,' etc.

First then we consider—before we come to our knowledge of God—our sight of God in this world, and that is, says our apostle, *in speculo,* 'We see as in a glass.' But how do we see in a glass? Truly, that is not easily determined. The old writers in the optics said that when we see a thing in a glass, we see not the thing itself but a representation only; all the later men say we do see the thing itself but not by direct but by reflected beams. It is a useless labour for the present to reconcile them. This may well consist with both, that as that which we see in a glass assures us that such a thing there is, for we cannot see a dream in a glass, nor a fancy, nor a chimera, so this sight of God, which our apostle says we have in a glass, is enough to assure us that a God there is.

This glass is better than the water; the water gives a crookedness and false dimensions to things that it shows; [18] as we see by an oar when we row a boat, and as the poet describes a wry and distorted face, *qui faciem sub aqua, Phœbe, natantis habes,* that he looked like a man that swam under water. But in the glass which the apostle intends we may see God directly, that is, see directly that there is a God. And therefore St. Cyril's addition in this text is a diminution; *videmus quasi in fumo,* says he, we see God as in a smoke; we see him better than so; for it is a true sight of God, though it be not a perfect sight, which we have this way. This way our theatre, where we sit to see God, is the whole frame of nature; our medium, our glass in which we see him is the creature; and our light by which we see him is natural reason.

Aquinas calls this theatre, where we sit and see God, the whole world; and David compasses the world and finds God everywhere and says at last, 'Whither shall I fly from thy presence? If I ascend up into heaven, thou art there'; [19] at Babel they thought to build to heaven; but did any man ever pretend to get above heaven? Above the power of the winds, or the impression of other malignant meteors, some high hills are got. But can any man get above the power of God? 'If I take the wings of the morning, and dwell in the uttermost parts of the sea, there thy right hand shall hold me and lead me.' If we sail to the waters above the firmament, it is so too. Nay, take a place which

17. I Corinthians 2:2.
18. The phenomenon of refraction.
19. Psalms 139:8.

God never made, a place which grew out of our sins, that is, hell; yet, 'If we make our bed in hell, God is there too.' It is a woeful inn to make our bed in, hell; and so much the more woeful as it is more than an inn, an everlasting dwelling. But even there God is; and so much more strangely than in any other place because he is there without any emanation of any beam of comfort from him who is the God of all consolation or any beam of light from him who is the Father of all lights. In a word, whether we be in the eastern parts of the world, from whom the truth of religion is passed, or in the western, to which it is not yet come; whether we be in the darkness of ignorance, or darkness of the works of darkness, or darkness of oppression of spirit in sadness; the world is the theatre that represents God, and everywhere every man may, nay, must see him.

The whole frame of the world is the theatre, and every creature the stage, the medium, the glass in which we may see God. 'Moses made the laver in the tabernacle of the looking glasses of women.' [20] Scarce can you imagine a vainer thing—except you will except the vain lookers-on in the action—than the looking glasses of women; and yet Moses brought the looking glasses of women to a religious use, to show them that came in the spots of dirt which they had taken by the way, that they might wash themselves clean before they passed any farther.

There is not so poor a creature but may be the glass to see God in. The greatest flat glass that can be made cannot represent anything greater than it is. If every gnat that flies were an archangel, all that could but tell me that there is a God; and the poorest worm that creeps tells me that. If I should ask the basilisk,[21] how camest thou by those killing eyes? he would tell me, thy God made me so; and if I should ask the slow-worm, how camest thou to be without eyes? he would tell me, thy God made me so. The cedar is no better a glass to see God in than the hyssop[22] upon the wall; all things that are, are equally removed from being nothing; and whatsoever hath any being is by that very being a glass in which to see God, who is the root and the fountain of all being. The whole frame of nature is the theatre, the whole volume of creatures is the glass, and the light of nature, reason, is our light; which is another circumstance.

Of these words, John 1:9, 'That was the true light that lighteth every man that cometh into the world,' the slackest sense that they can admit gives light enough to see God by. If we spare St. Chrysostom's sense, that that light is the light of the Gospel and of grace, and that that light considered in itself and without opposition in us does enlighten, that is, would enlighten every man if that man did not wink[23] at that light; if we forbear St. Augustine's sense, that light enlightens every man, that is, every man that is enlightened is enlightened by that light; if we take but St. Cyril's sense, that this light is the light of natural reason, which, without all question, 'enlighteneth every man that comes into the world'; yet have we light enough to see God by that light in the theatre of nature and in the glass of creatures. God affords no man the comfort, the false comfort of atheism. He will not allow a pretending atheist the power to flatter

20. Exodus 38:8: "laver" = washbowl.
21. Fabulous dragon that killed by looking at its victim.
22. Aromatic herb.
23. Close his eyes.

himself so far as seriously to think there is no God. He must pull out his own eyes and see no creature before he can say, he sees no God; he must be no man and quench his reasonable soul before he can say to himself, there is no God. The difference between the reason of man and the instinct of the beast is this, that the beast does but know, but the man knows that he knows.[24] The bestial atheist will pretend that he knows there is no God; but he cannot say that he knows that he knows it; for his knowledge will not stand the battery[25] of an argument from another nor a ratiocination from himself. He dares not ask himself, who is it that I pray to in a sudden danger if there be no God? Nay, he dares not ask, who is it that I swear by in a sudden passion if there be no God? Whom do I tremble at and sweat under at midnight and whom do I curse by next morning if there be no God? It is safely said in the School, *media perfecta ad quæ ordinantur*, how weak soever those means which are ordained by God seem to be, and be indeed in themselves, yet they are strong enough to those ends and purposes for which God ordained them.

And so for such a sight of God as we take the apostle to intend here, which is to see that there is a God, the frame of nature, the whole world is our theatre, the book of creatures is our medium, our glass, and natural reason is light enough. But then for the other degree, the other notification of God, which is the knowing of God, though that also be first to be considered in this world, the means is of a higher nature than served for the sight of God; and yet whilst we are in this world it is but *in ænigmate*, in an obscure riddle, a representation, darkly, and in part, as we translate it.

As the glass which we spoke of before was proposed to the sense, and so we might see God, that is, see that there is a God, this *ænigma* that is spoken of now, this dark similitude and comparison, is proposed to our faith; and so far we know God, that is, believe in God in this life but by enigmas, by dark representations and allusions. Therefore says St. Augustine that Moses saw God, in that conversation which he had with him in the mount, *sevocatus ab omni corporis sensu*, removed from all benefit and assistance of bodily senses—he needed not that glass, the help of the creature; and more than so, *ab omni significativo æenigmate spiritus*, removed from all allusions or similitudes or representations of God which might bring God to the understanding and so to the belief; Moses knew God by a more immediate working than either sense or understanding or faith. Therefore says that father, *per speculum et ænigma*, by this which the apostle calls a glass and this which he calls *ænigma*, a dark representation, *intelliguntur omnia accommodata ad notificandum deum*, he understands all things by which God hath notified himself to man, by the glass to his reason, by the *ænigma* to his faith. And so for this knowing of God by way of believing in him—as for seeing him our theatre was the world, the creature was our glass, and reason was our light—our academy to learn this knowledge is the church, our medium is the ordinance and institution of Christ in his church, and our light is the light of faith in the application of those ordinances in that church.

This place then where we take our degrees in this knowledge of God, our

24. See "A Nocturnal upon S. Lucy's Day," ll. 30–31.
25. Assault.

academy, our university for that, is the church; for, though as there may be some few examples given of men that have grown learned who never studied at university; so there may be some examples of men enlightened by God and yet not within that covenant which constitutes the church; yet the ordinary place for degrees is the university, and the ordinary place for illumination in the knowledge of God is the church. Therefore did God, who ever intended to have his kingdom of heaven well peopled, so powerfully, so miraculously enlarge his way to it, the church, that it prospered as a wood which no feeling, no stubbing could destroy. We find in the acts of the church five thousand martyrs executed in a day; and we find in the Acts of the Apostles five thousand brought to the church by one sermon; still our christenings were equal to our burials at least. . . .

1628   1640

BEN JONSON
1572–1637

Born in the same year as Donne, Ben Jonson was to exert an equally strong shaping force on the poetry of his century. The son of a London bricklayer, he attended Westminster school under the scholar and antiquary William Camden, soldiered in Flanders, and returned to the London stage, first as an actor, then as the major play-wright of *Sejanus* (1603), *Volpone* (1606), *Epicoene* (1609), *The Alchemist* (1610), *Bartholomew Fair* (1614), and other plays. As a poet he produced as well a major corpus of verse—lyric, satiric, epigrammatic, elegiac—informed by his vast and pro-found knowledge of the Latin and Greek classics, as well as by his own remarkable sense of language's control of thought and feeling in poetry. Appropriateness, order, structure, all brought his wit under the control of rhetorical and dialectical patterns based, but elaborated, on the classics. His influence reached through his immediate followers and friends—Herrick, the Cavalier poets, Waller—to Dryden at the other end of the century. Jonson's ambitiousness and self-regard enabled him to publish, in 1616, a folio edition of his *Works* (a word used hitherto only for the *Opera* or dead classical authors), containing epigrams, songs from plays, masques, and a selection of his favorite poems called *The Forest;* a posthumous edition of 1640–41 added more masques and a larger group of poems called *The Underwood.* After the accession of James I in 1603, Jonson became responsible for the writing of masques and entertain-ments at court, at annual revels and state occasions; and his twenty-eight masques form a major body of imaginative achievement, particularly in the mythopoetic direc-tions which his plays and his other verse rarely sought to take. In the fables and animated moral emblems of his masques, Jonson links up Spenserian traditions with their eventual rebirth in the poetry of Milton.

But it is the public, instructive character both of his poetry and of his sense of the poet's role in society which distinguishes Jonson from Donne; the latter poet was our language's genius of the private, and his idiosyncratic revisions of the available Petrarchan phrases, attitudes, and expressive forms create what we think of as the personal voice. Jonson wrote personal poems, but always as the kind of public spokesman that his classical forebears, Horace and Pindar, led him to try to be. When he felt that, after the accession of Charles I, he could no longer speak to England by influencing its center, the crown, he betook himself more and more to his immediate circle, the so-called Tribe of Ben which included not only most of the best minor poets of the middle of the century, but scholars and statesmen as well. The wisdom and flexibility of his voice is continually evident in the wide range of his forms and lyric types as well as in the constancy of his instructive power, even in moments of self-mockery as poet and as man.

To the Memory of My Beloved, the Author Mr. William Shakespeare:°

and What He Hath Left Us

To draw no envy (Shakespeare) on thy name,
  Am I thus ample° to thy book, and fame,
While I confess thy writings to be such
  As neither Man nor Muse can praise too much.
'Tis true, and all men's suffrage.° But these ways
  Were not the paths I meant unto thy praise:
For seeliest° ignorance on these may light,
  Which, when it sounds at best, but echoes right;
Or blind affection, which doth ne'er advance
10 The truth, but gropes, and urgeth all by chance;
Or crafty malice might pretend this praise,
  And think to ruin, where it seemed to raise.
These are, as some infamous bawd or whore,
  Should praise a matron. What could hurt her more?
But thou art proof against them, and indeed
  Above the ill fortune of them, or the need,
I, therefore will begin. Soul of the age!
  The applause! delight! the wonder of our stage!
My Shakespeare, rise; I will not lodge thee by
20 Chaucer or Spenser, or bid Beaumont lie
A little further, to make thee a room:°
  Thou art a monument without a tomb,
And art alive still, while thy book doth live,
  And we have wits to read, and praise to give.
That I not mix thee so, my brain excuses,
  I mean with great, but disproportioned muses;
For, if I thought my judgment were of years,
  I should commit thee surely with thy peers,
And tell, how far thou didst our Lyly° outshine,
30 Or sporting Kyd,° or Marlowe's mighty line.

To the Memory . . . Shakespeare prefixed to the Shakespeare First Folio of 1623
ample liberal
suffrage consent (as by vote)
seeliest silliest
make thee a room in Westminster Abbey, where all these poets are ceremoniously entombed
Lyly See Headnote on John Lyly.
Kyd Thomas Kyd (1558–94), author of heavy melodrama; "sporting" is a sarcastic pun on "kidding"

And though thou hadst small Latin and less Greek,°
    From thence to honour thee, I would not seek
For names; but call forth thundering Aeschylus,
    Euripides and Sophocles° to us,
Paccuvius, Accius,° him° of Cordova dead,
    To life again, to hear thy buskin° tread,
And shake a stage: Or, when thy socks° were on,
    Leave thee alone, for the comparison
Of all that insolent Greece or haughty Rome
40   Sent forth, or since did from their ashes come.
Triumph, My Britain, thou hast one to show,
    To whom all scenes of Europe homage owe.
He was not of an age, but for all time!
    And all the muses still were in their prime,
When like Apollo he came forth to warm
    Our ears, or like a Mercury to charm!
Nature herself was proud of his designs,
    And joyed to wear the dressing of his lines!
Which were so richly spun and woven so fit,
50   As,° since, she will vouchsafe no other wit:
The merry Greek, tart Aristophanes,°
    Neat Terence,° witty Plautus, now not please,
But antiquated, and deserted lie
    As they were not of nature's family.
Yet must I not give nature all: thy art,
    My gentle Shakespeare, must enjoy a part,
For though the poet's matter nature be,
    His art doth give the fashion; and that he
Who casts° to write a living line, must sweat
60   (Such as thine are), and strike the second heat
Upon the muses' anvil, turn the same
    (And himself with it), that he thinks to frame,
Or for the laurel, he may gain a scorn;
    For a good poet's made, as well as born.
And such wert thou. Look how the father's face
    Lives in his issue; even so, the race
Of Shakespeare's mind, and manners brightly shines
    In his well turnèd, and true-filèd lines:
In each of which, he seems to shake a lance,°
70   As brandished at the eyes of ignorance.

---

small Latin and less Greek as compared with Jonson's own massive classical learning; as compared with our own, he had a good knowledge of Latin
Aeschylus, Euripides and Sophocles the three great Greek tragedians
Paccuvius, Accius Roman tragedians
him Seneca, Roman tragic poet and philosopher who strongly influenced Elizabethan dramatists; he was born, and died, at Corduba

buskin emblematic high boot of tragedy, worn by actors in the classical drama
socks the low shoes or slippers of comedy
As that
Aristophanes great Greek comic playwright
Terence with Plautus, greatest and most influential Roman comedians
casts sets out
shake a lance shake a spear (an old gag)

Sweet Swan of Avon!° what a sight it were
   To see thee in our waters yet appear,
And make those flights upon the banks of Thames,
   That so did take Eliza° and our James!
But stay, I see thee in the hemisphere
   Advanced and made a constellation there!
Shine forth, thou star of poets, and with rage°
   Or influence,° chide, or cheer the drooping stage;
Which, since thy flight from hence, hath mourned like night,
80   And déspairs day, but for thy volume's light.

1623

To the Immortal Memory and Friendship of That Noble Pair Sir Lucius Cary and Sir H. Morison°

THE TURN°

Brave infant of Saguntum,° clear°
Thy coming forth in that great year,
When the prodigious Hannibal did crown
His rage, with razing your immortal town.
Thou, looking then about,
Ere thou wert half got out,
Wise child, didst hastily return,
And madest thy mother's womb thine urn.°
How summed a circle didst thou leave mankind
10   Of deepest lore,° could we the center find!

THE COUNTERTURN

Did wiser nature draw thee back,
From out the horror of that sack,
Where shame, faith, honour, and regard of right
Lay trampled on; the deeds of death and night,
Urged, hurried forth, and hurled°

Swan of Avon He makes Shakespeare a swan because that most noble and serene of birds, "fair, upward and direct" as Jonson puts it elsewhere, in flight, was reputed to sing magnificently at its death; this poem celebrates a posthumous volume of Shakespeare's works, and its metamorphic image is that of the constellations Cygnus (as the lyre of Orpheus, in classical tradition, became Lyra).
Eliza Queen Elizabeth
rage rapture or enthusiasm
influence the way stars affected human lives; see *Astrology* in the Glossary
To . . . Sir Lucius Cary and Sir H. Morison Viscount Falkland, philosophically inclined, died fighting for the king in 1643; Morison was his

brother-in-law who died prematurely in 1629.
The Turn Jonson is self-consciously writing the first Pindaric ode in English, and he labels the triads with literal translations of "strophe," "antistrophe," and "epode."
infant of Saguntum Pliny tells this anecdote of a newborn baby in a town besieged by Hannibal in 219 B.C., starting the second Punic War.
clear famous (was); perhaps with a sense of "pure"
urn funeral urn
How summed . . . lore how full of meaning would be your circle emblem, your "in my end is my beginning"
hurled hurled themselves

Upon the affrighted world:
Sword, fire, and famine, with fell fury met;
And all on utmost ruin set;
As, could they but life's miseries foresee,
20   No doubt all infants would return like thee?

THE STAND

For, what is life, if measured by the space,°
Not by the act?°
Or maskèd man, if valued by his face,
Above his fact?°
Here's one outlived his peers,
And told forth fourscore years;
He vexèd time, and busied the whole state,
Troubled both foes and friends,
But ever to no ends.
30   What did this stirrer, but die late?
How well at twenty had he fallen or stood!
For three of his fourscore, he did no good.

THE TURN

He entered well, by virtuous parts,°
Got up and thrived with honest arts;
He purchased friends, and fame, and honours then,
And had his noble name advanced with men,
But weary of that flight,
He stooped in all men's sight
To sordid flatteries, acts of strife,
40   And sunk in that dead sea of life
So deep, as he did then death's waters sup,
But that the cork of title buoyed him up.

THE COUNTERTURN

Alas, but Morison fell young:
He never fell; thou fallest, my tongue.
He stood, a soldier to the last right end,
A perfect patriot, and a noble friend,
But most a virtuous son.
All offices were done
By him, so ample, full, and round,
50   In weight, in measure, number, sound,
As thought his age imperfect might appear,
His life was of humanity the sphere.°

space length
act action
fact deed
virtuous parts he was well-born

sphere Circles were symbols of perfection as
were spheres; in Ptolemaic astronomy, they were
planetary orbits.

THE STAND

Go now, and tell° out days summed up with fears,
And make them years;
Produce thy mass of miseries on the stage,
To swell thine age;
Repeat of things a throng,
To show thou hast been long,
Not lived; for life doth her great actions spell,
60 By what was done and wrought
In season, and so brought
To light: her measures° are how well
Each syllable answered, and was formed, how fair:
These make the lines of life, and that's her air.°

THE TURN

It is not growing like a tree
In bulk, doth make man better be,
Or standing long an oak, three hundred year,
To fall a log, at last, dry, bald, and sear;
A lily of a day
70 Is fairer far in May,
Although it fall and die that night:
It was the plant and flower of light.
In small proportions, we just beauties see,
And in short measures, life may perfect be.

THE COUNTERTURN

Call, noble Lucius, then for wine
And let thy looks with gladness shine;
Accept this garland, plant it on thy head,
And think, nay know, thy Morison's not dead.
He leaped the present age,
80 Possessed with holy rage,
To see that bright eternal day,
Of which we priests and poets say
Such truths, as we expect for happy men,
And there he lives with memory; and Ben°

THE STAND

Jonson, who sung this of him, ere he went
Himself to rest,

tell count
measures how we judge lives, punning on poetic
meter (thus "syllable" means each moment or
deed)
air fashion, manner; also, perhaps, "tune" (setting words in those "lines")

Ben a shocking enjambment, separating "Ben"
(as he would be known in his circle of friends)
from "Ben Jonson" (his public self) "who
wrote this" public, celebratory, instructive form
of poem, the ode

Or taste a part of that full joy he meant
To have expressed,
In this bright asterism,°
90   Where it were friendship's schism,
(Were not his Lucius long with us to tarry)
To separate these twi-
Lights, the Dioscuri,°
And keep the one half from his Harry.
But fate doth so altérnate the design,
Whilst that in heaven, this light on earth must shine.

THE TURN

And shine as you exalted are,
Two names of friendship, but one star,
Of hearts the union. And those not by chance
100   Made, or indentured,° or leased out to advance
The profits for a time.
No pleasures vain did chime,
Of rimes, or riots, at your feasts,
Orgies of drink, or feigned protests,
But simple love of greatness, and of good,
That knits brave minds, and manners, more than blood.

THE COUNTERTURN

This made you first to know the Why
You liked, then after, to apply
That liking; and approach so one the tother,°
110   Till either grew a portion of the other,
Each styled by his end,
The copy of his friend.
You lived to be the great surnames,
And titles, by which all made claims
Unto the virtue: Nothing perfect done,
But as a Cary or a Morison.

THE STAND

And such a force the fair example had,
As they that saw
The good, and durst not practise it, were glad
120   That such a law
Was left yet to mankind,
Where they might read, and find
Friendship, in deed, was written, not in words;
And with the heart, not pen,

asterism constellation
To separate . . . Dioscuri Again, the enjambment "separates," here the Dioscuri (Castor and
Pollux, the constellation Gemini), as death has
parted these twin lights, Cary and Morison.
indentured contracted out
tother other

Of two so early° men,
Whose lines her rolls° were, and recórds,
Who, ere the first down bloomèd on the chin,
Had sowed these fruits, and got the harvest in.

1640

Ode to Himself°

Come leave the loathèd stage,
And the more loathsome age,
Where pride and impudence in faction knit
Usurp the chair of wit:
Indicting and arraigning every day,
Something they call a play.
Let their fastidious, vain
Commission of the brain,
Run on and rage, sweat, censure, and condemn:
10   They were not made for thee, less thou for them.

Say that thou pourest 'em wheat,
And they would acorns eat:
'Twere simple° fury, still thyself to waste
On such as have no taste,
To offer them a surfeit of pure bread,
Whose appetites are dead.
No, give them grains° their fill,
Husks, draff° to drink, and swill:
If they love lees,° and leave the lusty wine,
20   Envy them not, their palate's with the swine.°

No doubt a mouldy tale,
Like *Pericles*,° and stale
As the shrive's° crusts, and nasty as his fish,
Scraps out of every dish.
Thrown forth and raked into the common tub,°
May keep up the Play Club.
Broome's° sweepings do as well
There as his master's meal,
For who the relish of these guests will fit
30   Needs set them but the alms-basket of wit.

And much good do't ye then,
Brave plush and velvet men

early young
rolls archives
Ode to Himself written after the failure of his
play *The New Inn* in 1629
simple simpleminded
grains brewers' residue
draff refuse
lees dregs

the swine as in "neither cast ye your pearls before swine" (Matthew 7:6)
Pericles Shakespeare's play, first printed in 1609
shrive's sheriff's—this means jail food
common tub scraps for the poor
Broome's Richard Brome, Jonson's ex-servant, now a playwright

Can feed on orts;° and safe in your scene clothes,
　　Dare quit upon your oaths
The stagers, and the stage-wrights too; your peers,
　　Of stuffing your large ears
　　With rage of comic socks,°
　　Wrought upon twenty blocks,°
Which, if they're torn, and foul, and patched enough,
40　The gamesters share your guilt,° and you their stuff.

　　　Leave things so prostitute,
　　　And take the Alcaic lute,°
Or thine own Horace, or Anacreon's lyre;°
　　　Warm thee by Pindar's fire,°
And though thy nerves° be shrunk and blood be cold,
　　　Ere years have made thee old,
　　　Strike that disdainful heat
　　　Throughout, to their defeat:
As curious fools, and envious of thy strain,
50　May blushing swear, no palsy's in thy brain.°

　　　But when they hear thee sing
　　　The glories of thy king;
His zeal to God, and his just awe of men,
　　　They may be bloodshaken, then
Feel such a flesh-quake to possess their powers,
　　　That no tuned harp like ours,
　　　In sound of peace or wars,
　　　Shall truly hit the stars
When they shall read the acts of Charles° his reign,
60　And see his chariot triumph 'bove his wain.°
　　　　　　　　　　　　　　1631, 1640

A Fit of Rime Against Rime°

Rime, the rack° of finest wits,
That expresseth but by fits,°
　　　True conceit.°
Spoiling senses of their treasure,
Cozening judgment with a measure,
　　　But false weight.°

orts scraps
socks low shoes of classical comedy
blocks both shoe molds and blockheads
guilt punning on "gilt" (gilded, flashy fake)
Alcaic lute lyric poetry; Alcaeus (l. 600 B.C.)
invented a lyric meter, used frequently in Latin
by Horace
Anacreon's lyre lyric poetry again; for the
Anacreontic poems, see note on Lovelace's "The
Grasshopper"
Pindar's fire odes, like the one he is writing,
based on Pindar
nerves sinews, muscles

no palsy's . . . brain Jonson had been paralyzed by a stroke in 1628.
Charles Charles I assumed the throne in 1625.
wain wagon (the Big Dipper, called "Charles's
Wain"); also, his "wane," or decline
Rime Our modern "rhyme" preserves in its
spelling the etymology from the Greek "rhythm,"
but "rime" is older in English and French.
rack wreck; also, "torturing device"
fits cantos of a poem; also, "fitfully"
conceit thought
Cozening . . . weight cheating like a crooked
merchant, by being metrical but trivial

Wresting words from their true calling;
Propping verse for fear of falling
    To the ground.
10 Jointing syllables, drowning letters,
Fastening vowels, as with fetters
    They were bound!
Soon as lazy thou wert known,
All good poetry hence was flown,
    And art banished.
For a thousand years together
All Parnassus° green did wither,
    And wit vanished.
Pegasus° did fly away,
20 At the wells no muse did stay,
    But bewailed
So to see the fountain dry,
And Apollo's music die,
    All light failed!
Starveling° rimes did fill the stage,
Not a poet in an age
    Worth crowning.
Not a work deserving bays,°
Nor a line deserving praise,
30   Pallas° frowning;
Greek was free from rime's infection,
Happy Greek by this protection
    Was not spoiled.
Whilst the Latin, queen of tongues,
Is not yet free from rime's wrongs,
    But rests foiled.°
Scarce the hill again doth flourish,
Scarce the world a wit doth nourish
    To restore
40 Phoebus° to his crown again,
And the muses to their brain
    As before.
Vulgar° languages that want
Words, and sweetness, and be scant
    Of true measure,
Tyrant rime hath so abused
That they long since have refused
    Other ceasure;°
He that first invented thee

Parnassus the Muses' mountain
Pegasus winged horse of poetry, whose hoof
struck open Hippocrene, a fountain on Helicon,
the Muses' other hill
Starveling weak, shoddy
bays laurel crown for poetic glory
Pallas Athena

foiled stabbed, and so defeated. The point is
that classical Greek never developed rhyme,
while medieval Latin did.
Phoebus Apollo
Vulgar vernacular
other ceasure other ways of ending lines (than
with rhyming words)

50   May his joints tormented be,
      Cramped forever;
Still may syllables jar with time,
Still may reason war with rime,
      Resting never.
May his sense when it would meet
The cold tumor in his feet°
      Grow unsounder.
And his title be long fool,°
That in rearing such a school
60   Was the founder.
           1640

The Hourglass°

Do but consider this small dust,
    Here running in the glass,
      By atoms moved;°
Could you believe that this,
    The body was
      Of one that loved?
And in his mistress' flame, playing like a fly,
    Turned to cinders by her eye?
Yes, and in death, as life unblessed,
10   To have't expressed,
    Even ashes of lovers find no rest.
           1640

Epigram from Petronius

Doing° a filthy pleasure is, and short,
    And done, we straight repent us of the sport.
Let us not then rush blindly on unto it,
    Like lustful beasts, that only know to do it;
For lust will languish, and that heat decay;
    But thus, thus keeping endless holiday
Let us together closely lie, and kiss:
    There is no labour, nor no shame in this.
This hath pleased, doth please and long will please; never
10   Can this decay, but is beginning ever.
           1640

feet punning on "metrical feet"
fool a labored joke: "arse" (ass) means "fool"; "ars longa, vita brevis" ("art is long, life short"), a famous tag
The Hourglass a typical emblem poem: compare it with Herbert's "Church Monuments" below

By atoms moved not atoms in the modern sense, but those identical smallest units of matter which the Renaissance learned of from Lucretius
Doing fucking

To Penshurst°

Thou art not, Penshurst, built to envious show
　Of touch° or marble, nor canst boast a row
Of polished pillars, or a roof of gold;
　Thou hast no lanthorn,° whereof tales are told,
Or stairs, or courts; but standest an ancient pile,
　And these grudged at,° art reverenced the while.
Thou joyest in better marks,° of soil, of air,
　Of wood, of water: therein thou art fair.
Thou hast thy walks for health, as well as sport;
10　Thy Mount,° to which the Dryads do resort,
Where Pan and Bacchus their high feasts have made
　Beneath the broad beech and the chestnut shade,
The taller tree, which of a nut was set,
　At his great birth,° where all the Muses met.
There, in the writhèd bark, are cut the names
　Of many a Sylvan, taken with his flames.°
And thence, the ruddy Satyrs oft provoke
　The lighter Fauns, to reach thy Lady's oak.°
Thy copse, too, named of Gamage,° thou hast there,
20　That never fails to serve thee seasoned deer
When thou wouldst feast, or exercise thy friends.
　The lower land that to the river bends,
Thy sheep, thy bullocks, kine, and calves do feed;
　The middle grounds thy mares and horses breed.
Each bank doth yield thee coneys,° and the tops
　Fertile of wood, Ashore and Sidney's copse,°
To crown thy open table doth provide
　The purpled pheasant with the speckled side.
The painted partridge lies in every field,
30　And, for thy mess, is willing to be killed;
And if the high swollen Medway° fail thy dish,
　Thou hast thy ponds that pay thee tribute fish,
Fat, agèd carps, that run into thy net.
　And pikes, now weary their own kind to eat,
As loath, the second draught° or cast to stay,°
　Officiously,° at first, themselves betray.
Bright eels that emulate them and leap on land,

Penshurst In Kent, the home of the Sidney family (although only from 1552); Sir Robert Sidney, Sir Philip's younger brother, was then head of the household. See Waller's poem praising the same great house, Denham's *Cooper's Hill*, Marvell's "Upon Appleton House," and Pope's "Windsor Forest" for the tradition of the topographical poem.
touch black marble
lanthorn lantern: small, glassed-in cupola atop a building
grudged at begrudged ("they are envied; you, lacking them, are not")
marks boundaries
Mount some hill on the grounds

his great birth Sir Philip Sidney's (November 30, 1554)
Sylvan . . . flames country people who fell in love (as if love "flamed" out of Sidney's sonnets)
Lady's oak under which Lady Leicester started into labor with her son, Sir Robert Sidney
Gamage after Barbara Gamage, the owner's wife, who fed deer there
coneys rabbits
Ashore . . . copse two wooded areas
Medway the river beside the estate
draught drawing-in of the fishing net
stay await
Officiously dutifully

Before the fisher or into his hand.°
Then hath thy orchard fruit, thy garden flowers,
40   Fresh as the air and new as are the hours.
The early cherry, with the later plum,
    Fig, grape, and quince, each in his time doth come;
The flushing apricot and woolly peach
    Hang on thy walls° that° every child may reach.
And though thy walls be of the country stone,
    They are reared with no man's ruin, no man's groan.
There's none that dwell about them wish them down;
    But all come in, the farmer, and the clown;°
And no one empty-handed to salute
50   Thy lord and lady, though they have no suit.°
Some bring a capon, some a rural cake,
    Some nuts, some apples; some that think they make
The better cheeses bring them; or else send
    By their ripe daughters whom they would commend
This way to husbands, and whose baskets bear
    An emblem of themselves,° in plum or pear.
But what can this (more than express their love)
    Add to thy free provisions, far above
The need of such? whose liberal board doth flow
60   With all that hospitality doth know!
Where comes no guest, but is allowed to eat
    Without his fear,° and of thy Lord's own meat,
Where the same beer and bread and self-same wine
    That is his Lordship's shall be also mine.
And I not fain to sit (as some, this day,
    At great men's tables) and yet dine away.°
Here no man tells° my cups; nor, standing by,
    A waiter doth my gluttony envý,
But gives me what I call and lets me eat,
70   He knows, below, he shall find plenty of meat.
Thy tables hoard not up for the next day,
    Nor when I take my lodging need I pray
For fire, or lights, or livery:° all is there;
    As if thou, then, wert mine, or I reigned here,
There's nothing I can wish, for which I stay.
    That found King James, when hunting late this way,
With his brave son, the Prince,° they saw thy fires
    Shine bright on every hearth as° the desires
Of thy Penates° had been set on flame

---

into his hand These extravagances and those that follow are all quasi-paradisiacal images of natural plenitude in a rural life more like Adam's than like a fallen human farmer's.
Hang on thy walls Trees were espaliered for decoration; this is Jonson's conceit.
that so that
clown peasant
suit petition
emblem of themselves picture of their ripeness

and roundness
fear (of poisoning)
dine away still hungry, have to go out for a meal
tells counts
livery provision
Prince James I's son, Prince Henry, died in November of 1612.
as as if
Penates Roman household gods

80   To entertain them; or the country came,
With all their zeal, to warm their welcome here.
    What (great, I will not say, but) sudden cheer
Didst thou, then, make them! and what praise was heaped
    On thy good lady, then! who, therein, reaped
The just reward of her high huswifery;
    To have her linen, plate, and all things nigh,
When she was far: and not a room, but dressed,
    As if it had expected such a guest!
These, Penshurst, are thy praise, and yet not all.
90   Thy lady's noble, fruitful, chaste withall.
His children thy great lord may call his own:
    A fortune in this age but rarely known.
They are and have been taught religion; thence
    Their gentler spirits have sucked innocence.
Each morn and even they are taught to pray
    With the whole household, and may, every day,
Read, in their virtuous parents noble parts,
    The mysteries of manners, arms, and arts.
Now Penshurst, they that will proportion° thee
100   With other edifices, when they see
Those proud, ambitious heaps, and nothing else,
    May say, their lords have built, but thy lord dwells.

                                    1616

Song: To Celia°

Come, my Celia, let us prove,°
While we may, the sports of love;
Time will not be ours forever:
He, at length, our good will sever.
Spend not then his gifts in vain:
Suns that set may rise again;
But if once we lose this light,
'Tis with us perpetual night.
Why should we defer our joys?
10   Fame and rumour are but toys.
Cannot we delude the eyes
Of a few poor household spies?
Or his easier ears beguile,°
So removèd by our wile?
'Tis no sin love's fruit to steal,
But the sweet theft to reveal:
To be taken, to be seen,
These have crimes accounted been.

                        1606

proportion compare
To Celia from *Volpone* (1606), III.vii, where
it is sung as a seduction song and reflects the
play's themes of acquisition and deceit. It is
based on Catullus' fifth ode (see Campion's

"My Sweetest Lesbia").
prove experience
his . . . beguile Volpone, the seducer, is aware
that the lady's husband is listening.

Rather quick.

Voice

Come my Ce - li - a, let us prove,
Spend not then his____ gifts in vain;

While we may, the sweets of love. Time____
Suns that set may rise a - gain, But____

____ will not be ours for ev - er, He at length____
____ if we once lose this light 'Tis with us____

____ our good____ will se - ver.
____ per - pe - - - - - tual night.

Piano

* Small notes second time.   *2 No G second time.

Why should we de - fer our joys? Fame and
Ru - mour_ are but toys. Can - not we_____ de - lude the
eyes Of a few poor house-hold spies? Or_ his eas - ier ears_
_ be - guile, Thus re - mov - ed by our wile?

This is the setting of the poem by Alfonso Ferrabosco (c. 1575–1628), for lute and solo voice, from his 1609 book of airs. Although a contemporary piece, this was probably not the sort of more simplified setting that might have been used for the song in *Volpone*.

To the Same°

Kiss me, sweet: the wary lover
Can your favours keep, and cover,
When the common courting jay
All your bounties will betray.
Kiss again: no creature comes.
Kiss, and score up wealthy sums
On my lips, thus hardly sundered
While you breathe. First give a hundred,
Then a thousand, then another
10   Hundred, then unto the tother
Add a thousand, and so more,
Till you equal with the store
All the grass that Rumney° yields,
Or the sand in Chelsea fields,
Or the drops in silver Thames,
Or the stars that gild his streams
In the silent summer-nights,
When youths ply their stolen delights,
That the curious may not know
20   How to tell° them, as thy flow,
And the envious, when they find
What their number is, be pined.°
                          1616

Song: To Celia

Drink to me only with thine eyes,
    And I will pledge° with mine;
Or leave a kiss but in the cup,
    And I'll not look for wine.
The thirst that from the soul doth rise
    Doth ask a drink divine:
But might I of Jove's nectar sup,
    I would not change for thine.°
I sent thee, late, a rosy wreath,
10   Not so much honouring thee,
As giving it a hope that there
    It could not withered be.
But thou thereon didst only breathe
    And sent'st it back to me,
Since when it grows, and smells, I swear,
    Not of itself, but thee.
                          1616

To the Same from Catullus' seventh ode
Rumney famous pasture grounds in Kent
tell count
pined miserable

pledge drink a toast
But . . . thine except for the nectar of the
gods, I'd not swap my "drinks" of you for anything

On My First Son

Farewell, thou child of my right hand° and joy;
  My sin was too much hope of thee, loved boy.
Seven years thou wert lent to me, and I thee pay,
  Exacted by thy fate, on the just day.°
O, could I lose all father now! For why
  Will man lament the state he should envy?
To have so soon 'scaped world's and flesh's rage,
  And, if no other misery, yet age?
Rest in soft peace,° and asked, say here doth lie
10 Ben. Jonson, his best piece of poetry:°
For whose sake, henceforth, all his vows be such,
  As what he loves may never like too much.

                      1616

Epitaph on S. P.° a Child of Queen Elizabeth's Chapel

Weep with me, all you that read
  This little story,
And know, for whom a tear you shed,
  Death's self is sorry.
'Twas a child, that so did thrive
  In grace and feature,
As Heaven and Nature seemed to strive
  Which owned the creature.
Years he numbered scarce thirteen
10 When Fates turned cruel,
Yet three filled zodiacs° had he been
  The stage's jewel,
And did act, what now we moan,
  Old men so duly,
As, sooth, the Parcae° thought him one,
  He played so truly.
So, by error, to his fate
  They all consented;
But viewing him since (alas, too late)
20 They have repented.
And have sought, to give new birth,
  In baths° to steep him;

---

right hand Jonson's boy, who died of the plague in 1603 at the age of 7, was likewise Benjamin (in Hebrew, "son of the right hand").
just day Day of Judgment
Rest . . . peace the "requiescat in pace"
poetry Jonson has in mind the Greek etymology of *poesis*, "making" or "creation."

S. P. Salomon Pavy, a boy actor
zodiacs 1600–1602, his three brief years on the stage
Parcae the Fates
baths Aeson, father of Jason (he of the Golden Fleece) was restored from decrepitude by a magical bath.

But, being so much too good for earth,
    Heaven vows to keep him.
          1616

To William Roe°

Roe (and my joy to name), thou art now to go,
    Countries and climes, manners and men to know,
To extract, and choose the best of all these known,
    And those to turn to blood and make thine own.
May winds as soft as breath of kissing friends
    Attend thee hence, and there may all thy ends,
As the beginning here, prove purely sweet
    And perfect in a circle always meet.°
So when we, blessed with thy return, shall see
10   Thyself, with thy first thoughts, brought home by thee,
We each to other may this voice inspire:
    This is that good Aeneas, passed through fire,
Through seas, storms, tempests; and embarked for hell,
    Came back untouched. This man hath travelled° well.
          1616

Inviting a Friend to Supper

Tonight, grave sir, both my poor house, and I
    Do equally desire your company;
Not that we think us worthy such a guest,
    But that your worth will dignify our feast
With those that come, whose grace may make that seem
    Something, which else could hope for no esteem.
It is the fair acceptance, sir, creates
    The entertainment perfect, not the cates.°
Yet shall you have, to rectify your palate,
10   An olive, capers, or some better salad
Ushering the mutton; with a short-legged hen,
    If we can get her, full of eggs, and then
Lemons, and wine for sauce; to these, a coney°
    Is not to be despaired of, for our money;
And, though fowl now be scarce, yet there are clerks,
    The sky not falling, think we may have larks.
I'll tell you of more, and lie, so you will come:
    Of partridge, pheasant, woodcock, of which some

To William Roe as he was setting out on a journey
circle always meet Compare Donne's compass image in "A Valediction: Forbidding Mourning."

travelled also "travailed," labored
cates delicacies (cf. "caterer")
coney rabbit

May yet be there, and godwit, if we can;
20 Knat, rail, and ruff° too. Howsoe'r, my man
Shall read a piece of Virgil, Tacitus,
 Livy, or of some better book to us,
Of which we'll speak our minds, amidst our meat;°
 And I'll profess no verses to repeat.
To this, if aught appear which I not know of,
 That will the pastry, not my paper, show of.
Digestive cheese and fruit there sure will be;
 But that which most doth take my Muse and me,
Is a pure cup of rich Canary wine,
30 Which is the Mermaid's° now, but shall be mine;
Of which had Horace, or Anacreon tasted,
 Their lives, as do their lines, till now had lasted.
Tobacco,° nectar, or the Thespian spring,°
 Are all but Luther's beer° to this I sing.
Of this we will sup free, but moderately,
 And we will have no Pooley, or Parrot° by,
Nor shall our cups make any guilty men;
 But, at our parting we will be as when
We innocently met. No simple word
40 That shall be uttered at our mirthful board,
Shall make us sad next morning or affright
 The liberty that we'll enjoy tonight.

     1616

Songs From Plays

Slow, Slow Fresh Fount°

Slow, slow, fresh fount, keep time with my salt tears;
Yet slower, yet, Oh faintly, gentle springs!
List to the heavy part the music bears,
Woe weeps out her division,° when she sings.
  Droop herbs and flowers;
  Fall grief in showers;
Our beauties are not ours. Oh, I could still
Like melting snow upon some craggy hill,
10 Drop, drop, drop, drop,
Since nature's pride is now a withered daffodil.

     1601

godwit . . . Knat . . . rail . . . ruff game birds
meat meal
Mermaid's the Mermaid Tavern, convivial home of Jonson's circle
Tobacco "Drinking" meant smoking it.
Thespian spring another of the Muses' fountains
Luther's beer bad German beer (as opposed to his wine)

Pooley, or Parrot famous government informers (Pooley, or Poley, was present at Marlowe's murder)
Slow, Slow Fresh Fount from *Cynthia's Revels* (1601)
division musical improvisation or variation based on a stated theme ("dividing" its long notes), like a jazz soloist's "chorus"

Queen and Huntress°

Queen and huntress, chaste and fair,
Now the sun is laid to sleep,
Seated in thy silver chair,
State in wonted manner keep:
  Hesperus° entreats thy light,
  Goddess excellently bright.

Earth, let not thy envious shade
Dare itself to interpose;
Cynthia's shining orb was made
10 Heaven to clear° when day disclose:
  Bless us then with wishèd sight,
  Goddess excellently bright.

Lay thy bow of pearl apart,
And thy crystal-shining quiver;
Give unto the flying hart°
Space to breathe, how short soever:
  Thou that mak'st a day of night,
  Goddess excellently bright.

Clerimont's Song°

Still to be neat, still to be dressed
As° you were going to a feast;
Still to be powdered, still perfumed—
Lady, it is to be presumed,
Though art's hid causes are not found,
All is not sweet, all is not sound.

Give me a look, give me a face,
That makes simplicity a grace;
Robes loosely flowing, hair as free:
10 Such sweet neglect more taketh me
Than all the adulteries° of art;
They strike mine eyes, but not my heart.

Queen and Huntress from the concluding masque in *Cynthia's Revels.* Cynthia (Diana), goddess of the moon and of hunting, symbolized Queen Elizabeth.
Hesperus the Evening Star
clear brighten
hart male deer, with the usual pun

Clerimont's Song from *Epicoene, or The Silent Woman* (1609), I.i. Compare Herrick's "Delight in Disorder" with this praise of "naturalness" based on a late Latin poem.
As as if
adulteries adulterations

Pleasure Reconciled to Virtue

The court masque was, for Jonson, a supreme form in which to exercise what he felt were the moral and political obligations of poetry. The Jacobean and Caroline masque had evolved from staged court dances and entertainments, and came to include dancing, singing, allegorical scenery and costume, and an elaborate mythology (put together, like pictures of the great Italian Renaissance painters, out of classical myths, Christian materials, and their combined interpretations and inter-associations). All this centered on the monarch or other presiding figure, and involved the audience in many ways: as spectators, students of the emblematic lesson being taught, hearers of music, and, finally, as participating dancers themselves. The "masquers" were members of the court or state family, elaborately dressed in symbolic costume; they joined the richly, but not allegorically, dressed spectators in the revels, the occurrence of which, for Jonson and other writers of masques, could figure forth the interaction of myth and reality, of poetry and actual moral order as centered on the monarch. The stage scenery and effects were most complex—transformation scenes, involving both illusionistic sets and complex machinery, were frequent—and Jonson worked with Inigo Jones, the great architect and stage designer, falling out with him when it became apparent that Charles I, unlike his intellectual father, preferred more spectacle and less poetic coherence in his masques.

Pleasure Reconciled to Virtue was Charles's first masque (as the young Prince, he led the masquers). Its mythology is based on the Choice of Hercules (himself a centrally important heroic figure for the English Renaissance): as a youth, he met two tall women at a crossroads; each offered him a different future. Pleasure promised him delight, Virtue, a life of toil crowned with glory (in some versions of the legend, Pleasure inevitably, trivially, is called Vice). Jonson gives his spectators a complex, animated emblem of moral fulfillment in "reconciling" the two personifications: when what is good and what is delightful, "pleasure and profit," are indistinguishable, life is being properly conducted (a lesson, we must remember, being taught a royal court on Twelfth Night, traditional time of revelry). In the action, we have first, an antimasque ("antic masque" or "anti-masque") of Comus, a big comic fatso, figure of overindulgence and the monstrosity of its moral shape; next, a second antimasque of pygmies; then Hercules appears and banishes the monsters, is crowded by Mercury, and gives way in the action to Daedalus (here standing for skill in design, music, and, of course, Jonson's own art), leading the masquers through the grand masquing dances. The symbolic action occurs not merely in the text, but in the audience's controlled reactions to it—watching the dance, joining it, and somehow, *thereby*, understanding it. Milton knew this masque, and transformed its low-comic figure into someone very different in *Comus*. Our text owes much to Stephen Orgel's splendid edition.

Pleasure Reconciled to Virtue

A Masque. As it was presented at court before King James, 1618

The scene was the mountain ATLAS,° *who had his top ending in the figure of an old man, his head and beard all hoary and frost as if his shoulders were*

Atlas mountain mythologically placed in Libya, the transformed state of the giant who was said to support the earth on his shoulders

1086

covered with snow; the rest wood and rock. A grove of ivy at his feet, out of which, to a wild music of cymbals, flutes and tabers, is brought forth COMUS,° *the god of cheer, or the belly, riding in triumph, his head crowned with roses and other flowers, his hair curled; they that wait upon him crowned with ivy, their javelins done about with it; one of them going with* HERCULES *his bowl bare before him, while the rest presented him with this*

HYMN

10   Room, room, make room for the bouncing belly,
        First father of sauce, and deviser of jelly,
        Prime master of arts, and the giver of wit,
        That found out the excellent engine, the spit,
        The plow, and the flail, the mill, and the hopper,°
        The hutch,° and the bolter,° the furnace, and copper,°
        The oven, the bavin,° the mawkin,° the peel,°
        The hearth, and the range, the dog and the wheel.°
        He, he first invented the hogshead and tun,°
        The gimlet and vise° too, and taught 'em to run.
20   And since, with the funnel, an Hippocras bag°
        He's made of himself, that now he cries swag.°
        Which shows, though the pleasure be but of four inches,
        Yet he is a weasel, the gullet that pinches,
        Of any delight, and not spares from this back
        Whatever to make of the belly a sack.°
        Hail, hail, plump paunch, O the founder of taste
        For fresh meats, or powdered, or pickle, or paste;
        Devourer of broiled, baked, roasted or sod,°
        And emptier of cups, be they even or odd;
30   All which have now made thee so wide i' the waist
        As scarce with no pudding thou art to be laced;°
        But eating and drinking until thou dost nod,
        Thou break'st all thy girdles, and break'st forth a god.

To this, the Bowl-bearer

Do you hear, my friends? to whom did you sing all this now? Pardon me only that I ask you, for I do not look for an answer; I'll answer myself: I know it is

---

Comus from the Greek "kōmos" ("carousal"); late mythic figure of a winged, rose-crowned youth; Jonson adds attributes of a monster turned all belly (by the Circe-like power of satire)
hopper for receiving grain in a mill
hutch sifting bin. All these terms will follow a process, from milling to cooking, paralleling that of the alimentary tract.
bolter sifter
copper pot
bavin kindling brushwood for bakers' ovens
mawkin baker's mop
peel baker's shovel
dog . . . wheel treadmill to turn a roasting spit

tun keg
vise for tapping kegs
Hippocras bag for straining spiced wine punch
cries swag shows his swag-belly, his pendulous paunch
which shows . . . sack though the pleasure of swilling only adds four inches to the waistline, the gullet won't give up its delights, even to make it easier for the back to bear the weight of the huge tummy
sod boiled
As scarce . . . laced you're too fat (even stuffing more pudding into you—which can't be done) to be laced up

now such a time as the saturnals° for all the world, that every man stands under the eaves of his own hat and sings what please him; that's the right and the liberty of it. Now you sing of god Comus here, the Belly-god. I say it is well, and I say it is not well. It is well as it is a ballad, and the belly worthy of it,
40   I must needs say, an 'twere forty yards of ballad more—as much ballad as tripe.° But when the belly is not edified by it, it is not well; for where did you ever read or hear that the belly had any ears? Come, never pump for an answer, for you are defeated. Our fellow Hunger there, that was as ancient a retainer to the belly as any of us, was turned away from being unseasonable (not unreasonable, but unseasonable) and now is he (poor thin-gut) fain to get his living with teaching of starlings, magpies, parrots and jackdaws, those things he would have taught the belly. Beware of dealing with the belly; the belly will not be talked to, especially when he is full. Then there is no venturing upon Venter;° he will blow you all up; he will thunder indeed, la: some in
50   derision call him the father of farts. But I say he was the first inventor of great ordnance,° and taught us to discharge them on festival days. Would we had a fit feast for him, i' faith, to show his activity: I would have something now fetched in to please his five senses, the throat, or the two senses, the eyes. Pardon me for my two senses; for I that carry Hercules' bowl i' the service may see double by my place, for I have drunk like a frog today. I would have a tun now brought in to dance, and so many bottles about him. Ha! You look as if you would make a problem of this. Do you see? Do you see? a problem: why bottles? and why a tun? and why a tun? and why bottles to dance? I say that men that drink hard and serve the belly in any place of quality (as The Jovial Tinkers, or
60   The Lusty Kindred)° are living measures of drink, and can transform themselves, and do every day, to bottles or tuns when they please; and when they ha' done all they can, they are, as I say again (for I think I said somewhat like it afore) but moving measures of drink; and there is a piece° i' the cellar can hold more than all they. This will I make good if it please our new god but to give a nod; for the belly does all by signs, and I am all for the belly, the truest clock i' the world to go by.

     Here the first antimasque° after which,

HERCULES   What rites are these? Breeds earth more monsters yet?
       Antaeus° scarce is cold: what can beget
70   This store?° And stay! such contraries upon her?°
       Is earth so fruitful of her own dishonour?
       Or 'cause his vice was inhumanity,
       Hopes she by vicious hospitality
       To work an expiation first? and then
       (Help, Virtue!) these are sponges, and not men.

---

saturnals the Roman Saturnalia, a feast of licentious revelry, corresponding to Twelfth Night, which concluded the period of Christmas revels (this masque was written for Twelfth Night, 1618)
tripe guts
Venter Latin for tummy
ordnance artillery
The Jovial . . . Kindred perhaps taverns

piece barrel
antimasque It was danced by men costumed as bottles and a barrel.
Antaeus a giant whose power came from touching Earth, his mother; Hercules held him off the ground and crushed him to death
store abundance
her Earth. "Contraries" are monsters.

Bottles? Mere vessels? Half a tun of paunch?
How? and the other half thrust forth in haunch?
Whose feast? the belly's? Comus'? and my cup
Brought in to fill the drunken orgies up?
80   And here abused, that was the crowned reward
Of thirsty heroes after labour hard?
Burdens and shames of nature, perish, die!
—For yet you never lived, but in the sty
Of vice have wallowed, and in that swine's strife
Been buried under the offence of life.
Go, reel and fall under the load you make,
Till your swollen bowels burst with what you take.
Can this be pleasure, to extinguish man?
Or so quite change him in his figure? Can
90   The belly love his pain, and be content
With no delight but what's a punishment?
These monsters plague themselves, and fitly, too,
For they do suffer what and all they do.
But here must be no shelter, nor no shroud
For such: sink grove, or vanish into cloud!

*At this the whole grove vanished, and the whole music° was discovered,
sitting at the foot of the mountain, with* PLEASURE *and* VIRTUE *seated
above them. The choir invited* HERCULES *to rest with this*

SONG

100   Great friend and servant of the good,
            Let cool awhile thy heated blood,
               And from thy mighty labour cease.
                  Lie down, lie down,
            And give thy troubled spirits peace,
               Whilst Virtue, for whose sake
            Thou dost this godlike travail take,
               May of the choicest herbage make,
                  Here on this mountain bred,
                     A crown, a crown
110   For thy immortal head.

Here HERCULES *being laid down at their feet, the second antimasque,
which was of* PIGMIES, *appeared.*

1ST PIGMY   Antaeus dead! and Hercules yet live!
            Where is this Hercules? What would I give
            To meet him now? Meet him? nay three such other,
            If they had hand in murder of our brother?°
            With three? with four? with ten? Nay, with as many

---

music the orchestra and choir, whose members,
like the actors and singers, were professionals
(the masquers were not)

brother The fabled Pygmies of antiquity were
also distorted sons of Earth.

As the name yields?° Pray anger there be any
Whereon to feed my just revenge, and soon
120   How shall I kill him? Hurl him 'gainst the moon,
And break him in small portions? Give to Greece
His brain, and every tract of earth a piece?

2ND PIGMY   He is yonder.

1ST PIGMY   Where?

3RD PIGMY   At the hill foot, asleep.

1ST PIGMY   Let one go steal his club.

2ND PIGMY   My charge, I'll creep.

4TH PIGMY   He's ours.

1ST PIGMY   Yes, peace.

3RD PIGMY   Triumph, we have him, boy.

4TH PIGMY   Sure, sure, he is sure.

1ST PIGMY   Come, let us dance for joy.

At the end of their dance they thought to surprise him; when suddenly, being awaked by the music, he roused himself, they all ran into holes.

SONG°

130   Wake, Hercules, awake: but heave up thy black eye,
'Tis only asked from thee to look and these will die,
                    Or fly.
            Already they are fled,
            Whom scorn had else left dead.

At which MERCURY *descended from the hill with a garland of poplar°
to crown him.*

MERCURY   Rest still, thou active friend of Virtue: these
Should not disturb the peace of Hercules.
Earth's worms and honour's dwarfs, at too great odds,
140   Prove,° or provoke the issue of the gods.
See, here a crown the agèd hill hath sent thee,
My grandsire Atlas, he that did present thee
With the best sheep that in his fold were found,
Or golden fruit in the Hesperian ground,°
For rescuing his fair daughters, then the prey
Of a rude pirate, as thou cam'st this way;
And taught thee all the learning of the sphere,
And how, like him,° thou might'st the heavens up-bear,
As that thy labour's virtuous recompense.
150   He, though a mountain now, hath yet the sense

as many . . . yields Various ancient local
heroes were called "Hercules" and assimilated
to his cult.
Song sung by the choir
poplar In another story, Hercules crowned himself with poplar leaves from the Aventine Hill;
Jonson here associates it with Atlas (see below).
Prove test

Hesperian ground In a garden, Atlas' three
daughters, the Hesperides, guarded the golden
apples whose acquisition was the last of the
labors of Hercules.
like him Hercules had carried the world for
Atlas for a while, and duped him into taking on
the burden again.

Of thanking thee for more, thou being still
Constant to goodness, guardian of the hill;
Antaeus, by thee suffocated here,
And the voluptuous Comus, god of cheer,
Beat from his grove, and that defaced. But now
The time's arrived that Atlas told thee of—how,
By unaltered law, and working of the stars,
There should be a cessation of all jars°
'Twixt Virtue and her noted opposite,
160 Pleasure; that both should meet here in the sight
Of Hesperus,° the glory of the west,
The brightest star, that from his burning crest
Lights all on this side the Atlantic seas
As far as to thy pillars,° Hercules.
See where he shines: Justice and Wisdom placed
About his throne, and those with Honour graced,
Beauty and Love. It is not with his brother
Bearing the world, but ruling such another
Is his renown.° Pleasure, for his delight
170 Is reconciled to Virtue, and this night
Virtue brings forth twelve princes have° been bred
In this rough mountain and near Atlas' head,
The hill of knowledge; one and chief of whom°
Of the bright race of Hesperus is come,
Who shall in time the same that he is be,
And now is only a less light than he.
These now she° trusts with Pleasure, and to these
She gives an entrance to the Hesperides,
Fair Beauty's garden; neither can she fear
180 They should grow soft or wax effeminate here,
Since in her sight and by her charge all's done,
Pleasure the servant, Virtue looking on.

*Here the whole choir of music called the twelve masquers forth from
the lap of the mountain, which then opened with this*

SONG°

Ope agèd Atlas, open then thy lap,
And from thy beamy bosom strike a light,
That men may read in thy mysterious map
All lines
190 And signs
Of royal education and the right.

jars discords
Hesperus the Evening Star, here symbolically
associated with King James
pillars the Strait of Gibraltar
ruling . . . renown being king of "another
world" (England), paralleling Atlas carrying
his world

have who have
chief of whom Prince Charles, who was the
chief masquer
she Virtue
Song sung and danced, Pleasure probably leading the way; this was the entrance of the
masquers

See how they come and show,
That are but born to know.
Descend,
Descend,
Though pleasure lead,
Fear not to follow;
They who are bred
Within the hill
200   Of skill
May safely tread
What path they will:
No ground of good is hollow.

In their descent from the hill DAEDALUS° *came down before them, of
whom* HERCULES *questioned* MERCURY.

HERCULES   But Hermes,° stay a little, let me pause.
Who's this that leads?
MERCURY   A guide that gives them laws
To all their motions: Daedalus the wise.
HERCULES   And doth in sacred harmony comprise
His precepts?
MERCURY   Yes.
210   HERCULES   They may securely prove°
Then any labyrinth, though it be of love.

Here, while they put themselves in form, DAEDALUS *had his first*

SONG

Come on, come on; and where you go,
So interweave the curious knot,°
As even the observer scarce may know
Which lines are Pleasure's and which not.
First, figure out the doubtful way
At which awhile all youth should stay,
220   Where she and Virtue did contend
Which should have Hercules to friend.°
Then, as all actions of mankind
Are but a labyrinth or maze,
So let your dances be entwined,
Yet not perplex men unto gaze;°

Daedalus great designer and artificer who built
the labyrinth for Minos; here he descends from
the "hill of skill' to preside over the remainder
of the masque
Hermes "Mercury" in Greek
prove experience
curious knot complex choreographic interweaving of lines of dancers. The masquers are literally acting out Daedalus' metaphorical in-

structions in this part of the masque, and it will
be hard to tell pleasures and virtues apart. See
the emblem of Hercules (Fig. 23).
Hercules to friend referring to the Choice of
Hercules (see Headnote). The episode of the
Choice has happened in the past, and Hercules
represents a moral being already tested.
unto gaze into bewilderment

But measured, and so numerous° too,
As men may read each act you do,
And when they see the graces meet,
Admire the wisdom of your feet.
230 For dancing is an exercise
Not only shows the mover's wit,
But maketh the beholder wise,°
As he hath power to rise to it.

The first dance.

After which DAEDALUS *again.*

SONG 2

O more, and more; this was so well
As praise wants half his voice to tell;
Again yourselves compose,°
240 And now put all the aptness on
Of figure, that proportion
Or colour can disclose—°
That if those silent arts° were lost,
Design and picture, they might boast
From you a newer ground,°
Instructed by the heightening sense
Of dignity and reverence
In your true motions found:
Begin, begin; for look, the fair
250 Do longing listen to what air°
You form your second touch,°
That they may vent their murmuring hymns
Just to the tune you move your limbs,
And wish their own were such.
Make haste, make haste, for this
The labyrinth of beauty is.

The second dance.

That ended, DAEDALUS.

SONG 3

260 It follows now you are to prove°
The subtlest maze of all, that's love,

numerous "numbered," like English verse (both
"measured" and stress-accented)
wise by understanding its symbolic significance
compose rearrange
And now . . . disclose arrange your postures
and expressions with the same skill that design
and painting use

silent arts architectural design and pictures are
silent poetry
ground basis (conceptually); base (architec-
turally); underlaid color (in painting); bass
(musically)
air melody
touch passage of music
prove try out

And if you stay too long,
  The fair will think you do 'em wrong.
Go, choose among,° but with a mind
  As gentle as the stroking wind
    Runs o'er the gentler flowers.
And so let all your actions smile,
  As if they meant not to beguile
    The ladies, but the hours.
Grace, laughter and discóurse may meet,
  And yet the beauty not go less:°
For what is noble should be sweet,
  But not dissolved in wantonness.
Will you° that I give the law
  To all your sport, and sum it?°
It should be such should° envy draw,
  But ever overcome it.

*Here they danced with the ladies, and the whole revels° followed; which
ended,* MERCURY *called to him° in this following speech, which was after
repeated in song by two trebles, two tenors, a bass and the whole chorus.*

SONG 4

An eye of looking back were well,
  Or any murmur that would tell
    Your thoughts, how you were sent
      And went,
To walk with Pleasure, not to dwell.
These, these are hours by Virtue spared
  Herself, she being her own reward,
    But she will have you know
      That though
Her sports be soft, her life is hard.
You must return unto the hill,
  And there advance
With labour, and inhabit still
  That height and crown
From whence you ever may look down
    Upon triumphèd° Chance.
She, she it is, in darkness shines.
'Tis she that still herself refines,
  By her own light, to every eye
More seen, more known when Vice stands by.
And though a stranger here on earth,

among among them
go less be worth less
will you do you wish
sum it sum it up
should that should
revels the part of the masque in which the

"beholders" would, literally, "rise to it" (see
l. 233) and join with the masquers in the
dancing, which would go on a good while
him Daedalus
triumphèd triumphed-over

In heaven she hath her right of birth.
There, there is Virtue's seat,°
Strive to keep her your own;
'Tis only she can make you great,
Though place° here make you known.

After which, they danced their last dance, and returned into the scene,
which closed and was a mountain again as before.

The End.
1618   1640

WILLIAM DRUMMOND OF HAWTHORNDEN
1585–1649

He attended the University of Edinburgh, became laird of Hawthornden in 1610, corresponded with Drayton and Ben Jonson (who visited him in 1618–19, and whose remarks Drummond dutifully recorded in a set of *Conversations*), wrote epigrammatic verse and religious meditation (the prose *Cypress Grove*, published in 1623), and, towards the end of his life, political pamphlets for the Royalist cause. His 1616 *Poems* contain sonnets, songs, and epigrams strangely called "madrigals," arranged in Petrarchan sections following the life and then the death of the beloved lady. His religious poems appeared in *Flowers of Sion,* in 1623.

Madrigal°

Like the Idalian Queen,°
Her hair about her eyne,°
With neck and breasts' ripe apples to be seen,
At first glance of the morn
In Cyprus' gardens gathering those fair flowers
Which of her blood were born,
I saw, but fainting saw, my paramours.
The Graces naked danced about the place,
The winds and trees amazed
10 With silence on her gazed,
The flowers did smile, like those upon her face,
And as their aspine° stalks those fingers band,
(That she might read my case)
A hyacinth I wished me in her hand.
1616

---

seat official place
place status, rank
Madrigal Drummond uses this term in a peculiar way, to mean short, epigrammatic poems, more usually perhaps written in heroic couplets, but here comprising one strophe or stanza with

varying line lengths, an Italian conception.
Idalian Queen Venus; Idalia, on Cyprus, was the center of her cult
eyne eyes
aspine trembling

Madrigal

This life which seems so fair
Is like a bubble blown up in the air
By sporting children's breath,
Who chase it everywhere,
And strive who can most motion it bequeath;
And though it sometime seem of its own might,
Like to an eye of gold, to be fixed there,
And firm to hover in that empty height,
That only is because it is so light;
10   But in that pomp it doth not long appear,
    For even when most admired, it in a thought,
    As swelled from nothing, doth dissolve in nought.

1616

On Mary Magdalen°

Those eyes (dear Lord) once brandons° of desire,
Frail scouts betraying what they had to keep,
Which their own heart, then others, set on fire,
Their traitorous black before thee here outweep:
Those locks, of blushing deeds the fair attire,
Smooth-frizzled waves, sad shelves which shadow deep,
Soul-stinging serpents in gilt curls which creep,
To touch thy sacred feet do now aspire.
In seas of care behold a sinking bark,
10   By winds of sharp remorse unto thee driven:
O, let me not exposed by ruin's mark,
My faults confessed (Lord) say they are forgiven.
    —Thus sighed to Jesus the Bethanian° fair,
    His tear-wet feet still drying with her hair.

1623

WILLIAM BROWNE OF TAVISTOCK
1591?–1643?

Browne was born in Devon and educated at Exeter College, Oxford, and the Inner Temple. His sense of place, of the natural scene of the West Country, combined with his deep love of the Sidneyan and Spenserian poetic traditions to allow him, like Drayton and his friend George Wither, to continue that tradition well into the seventeenth century. He was in the service of the Pembroke family, and collaborated on a book of pastorals called *The Shepherd's Pipe* (1614); his major work, *Britannia's Pastorals*, appeared in 1613 (Pt. I) and 1616 (Pt. II). Part III was not printed until 1852.

On Mary Magdalen The weeping figure of the Magdalene, or her very tears, were a favorite subject for baroque poetry (see Crashaw's verse on this subject).

brandons torches
Bethanian Mary Magdalene (from the town of Bethany)

On the Death of Marie, Countess of Pembroke

Underneath this sable hearse
Lies the subject of all verse:
Sidney's sister, Pembroke's mother;
Death, ere thou has slain another,
Fair, and learned, and good as she,
Time shall throw a dart at thee.

Marble piles let no man raise
To her name for after days;
Some kind woman borne as she,
10 Reading this, like Niobe°
Shall turn marble, and become
Both her mourner and her tomb.

                    1623

To Pyrrha°

Tell me, Pyrrha, what fine youth,
        All perfumed and crowned with roses,
To thy chamber thee pursueth,
        And thy wanton arm encloses?

What is he thou now hast got,
        Whose more long and golden tresses
Into many a curious knot
        Thy more curious finger dresses?

How much will he wail his trust,
10   And, forsook, begin to wonder,
When black winds shall billows thrust,
        And break all hopes in sunder!

Fickleness of winds he knows
        Very little that doth love thee;
Miserable are all those
        That affect thee ere they prove thee.

I, as one from shipwreck freed,
        To the ocean's mighty ranger
Consecrate my dropping weed,
20   And in freedom think of danger.

                    from MS. 1894

Niobe Mourning the death of her twelve children, she was transformed into a rocky mountain spring, forever weeping.

To Pyrrha imitated from Horace; compare
Milton's version of the same Latin original

From Britannia's Pastorals

[Aletheia Arises from the Corpse of Fida's Hind°]

As that Arabian bird° (whom all admire)
Her exequies prepared and funeral fire,
Burnt in a flame conceivèd from the sun,
And nourishèd with slips of cinnamon,
Out of her ashes hath a second birth,
And flies abroad, a wonderment on earth:
So from the ruins of this mangled creature
Arose so fair and so divine a feature,
That Envy for her heart would dote upon her;
10 Heaven could not choose but be enamoured on her:
Were I a star, and she a second sphere,
I'd leave the other, and be fixèd there.
Had fair Arachne° wrought this maiden's hair,
When she with Pallas did for skill compare,
Minerva's work had never been esteemed,
But this had been more rare and highly deemed;
Yet gladly now she would reverse her doom,
Weaving this hair within a spider's loom.
Upon her forehead, as in glory, sat
20 Mercy and Majesty, for wondering at,
As pure and simple as Albania's snow,
Or milk-white swans which stem the streams of Po:
Like to some goodly foreland, bearing out
Her hair, the tufts which fringed the shore about.
And lest the man which sought those coasts might slip,
Her eyes like stars did serve to guide the ship.
Upon her front (heaven's fairest promontory)
Delineated was the authentic story
Of those elect, whose sheep at first began
To nibble by the springs of Canaan:
30 Out of whose sacred loins (brought by the stem
Of that sweet singer of Jerusalem)
Came the best Shepherd° ever flocks did keep,
Who yielded up his life to save his sheep.
    O thou Eterne! by whom all beings move,
Giving the springs beneath, and springs above;
Whose finger doth this universe sustain,
Bringing the former and the latter rain;

Aletheia Arises . . . Hind from the fourth song of Book I of Browne's Spenserian poem (ll. 155–224), describing the birth of Aletheia (Truth), daughter of Time, from the remains of Fida's (Faith's) dead deer, killed by the monster Riot

bird the phoenix
Arachne challenged Athena (here called both "Pallas" and "Minerva") to a weaving contest, lost, and was turned into a spider.
Shepherd Christ, of the "stem" of David the psalmist

Who dost with plenty meads and pastures fill,
40   By drops distilled like dew on Hermon° hill:
Pardon a silly swain, who (far unable
In that which is so rare, so admirable)
Dares on an oaten pipe thus meanly sing
Her praise immense, worthy a silver string.
And thou which through the desert and the deep,
Didst lead thy chosen like a flock of sheep:
As sometime by a star thou guided'st them,
Which fed upon the plains of Bethlehem;
So by thy sacred Spirit direct my quill,
50   When I shall sing ought of thy holy hill,
That times to come, when they my rhymes rehearse,
May wonder at me, and admire my verse:
For who but one rapt in celestial fire,
Can by his Muse to such a pitch aspire,
That from aloft he might behold and tell
Her worth, whereon an iron pen might dwell?
    When she was born, Nature in sport began
To learn the cunning of an artisan,
And did vermilion with a white compose,
60   To mock herself and paint a damask rose.
But scorning Nature unto Art should seek,
She spilt her colours on this maiden's cheek.
Her mouth the gate from whence all goodness came,
Of power to give the dead a living name.
Her words embalmèd in so sweet a breath,
That made them triumph both on Time and Death;
Whose fragrant sweets, since the chameleon knew,
And tasted of, he to this humour grew,
Left other elements, held this so rare,
70   That since he never feeds on ought but air.

1613

SEVENTEENTH-CENTURY LYRIC MODES

With Jacobean verse traditions, music and lyric verse begin to part company, although there are still interconnections. Certainly the court masque remains a unifying force in the Caroline period as well, and the many volumes of "Airs and Dialogues" by such composers as William and Henry Lawes continue to set witty courtly verse much as the madrigalists and lutenist composers had set Petrarchan poetry in the earlier period. But lyric verse forms came to be used for epigrammatic purposes, and the development of the ode from Jonson through Cowley was that of an expository

---

Hermon The reference here is to Psalms 133:3 "As the dew of Hermon and as the dew that descended upon the mountains of Zion: for there the Lord commanded the blessing, even life for evermore."

form. Below are a number of Jacobean and Caroline poems representing forms as diverse as song, inscription, and elegy, and exemplifying both the so-called strong lines of the school of Donne, and the gradually developing smoothness (as in Denham) of the later part of the century.

ANONYMOUS

Tom o' Bedlam°

From the hag and hungry goblin
That into rags would rend ye,
The spirit that stands by the naked man
In the Book of Moons° defend ye,
That of your five sound senses
You never be forsaken,
Nor wander from yourselves with Tom
Abroad to beg your bacon,
  While I do sing, Any food, any feeding,
10 Feeding, drink, or clothing;
  Come dame or maid, be not afraid,
  Poor Tom will injure nothing.

Of thirty bare years have I
Twice twenty been enragèd,
And of forty been three times fifteen
In durance soundly cagèd
On the lordly lofts of Bedlam
With stubble soft and dainty,
Brave bracelets° strong, sweet whips ding dong
20 With wholesome hunger plenty,
  And now I sing, etc.

With a thought I took for Maudlin°
And a cruse of cockle pottage,°
With a thing thus tall, sky bless you all,
I befell into this dotage.
I slept not since the Conquest,
Till then I never wakèd,
Till the roguish boy of love where I lay

Tom o' Bedlam This amazing poem from a manuscript commonplace—or literary scrap-book —of about 1620 is the greatest example of the mad song, or dramatic expression of a conventionalized view of insanity, before Blake. The protagonist is the stock figure of the out-patient from Bedlam (Bethlehem Hospital, the London madhouse), a wandering beggar, asking for alms and insisting he is harmless. Edgar in *King Lear* becomes this same "Poor Tom" in his manic guise. This song moves from the rhetoric of begging and confessional to a kind of triumphant expression of an autonomous visionary.
Book of Moons an astrological treatise for fortune-telling
bracelets handcuffs; like the "lordly lofts" and the dainty stubble, this is ironic
Maudlin British pronounciation of "Magdalene," hence, some whore, or sex personified
cockle pottage weed stew

Me found and strip't me nakèd.
30   And now I sing, etc.

When I short have shorn my sow's face
And swigged my horny barrel,°
In an oaken inn I pound° my skin
As a suit of gilt apparel;
The moon's my constant mistress
And the lovely owl my marrow;°
The flaming drake° and the night crow° make
Me music to my sorrow.
          While I do sing, etc.

40 The palsy plagues my pulses
When I prig° your pigs or pullen,°
Your culvers° take, or matchless° make
Your Chanticleer or Sullen.°
When I want provant° with Humphrey°
I sup, and when benighted,
I repose in Paul's° with waking souls
Yet never am affrighted.
          But I do sing, etc.

I know more than Apollo,°
50 For oft when he lies sleeping
I see the stars at bloody wars
In the wounded welkin weeping;
The moon embrace her shepherd,°
And the Queen of Love° her warrior,
While the first doth horn the star of morn,°
And the next the heavenly Farrier.°
          While I do sing, etc.

The gypsies, Snap and Pedro,
Are none of Tom's comradoes,
60 The punk° I scorn and the cutpurse° sworn,
And the roaring boy's° bravadoes.
The meek, the white, the gentle
Me handle, touch, and spare not;
But those that cross Tom Rynosseross

---

horny barrel leather flask
pound impound (as if it were a suit he could pawn for a night's lodging)
marrow mate
flaming drake flaming dragon: a meteor
night crow an owl, here a maddened alternative to the nightingale
prig steal. This and other words in the poem are from thieves' or gypsies' cant, or slang.
pullen chickens
culvers doves
matchless without their hens
Sullen Solon, like Chanticleer, a rooster
provant provender, food

Humphrey "dining with Duke Humphrey" meant "going hungry"
Paul's the haunted churchyard of St. Paul's
Apollo here, as the sun god
shepherd Endymion, lover of Cynthia or Diana
Queen of Love Venus; her "warrior" was Mars
horn . . . morn by enclosing the Morning Star in the horns of the crescent moon
Farrier Vulcan, Venus' husband, who is "horned," or cuckolded
punk whore
cutpurse pickpocket
roaring boy's juvenile gang member's

Do what the panther dare not.
　　Although I sing, etc.

With an host of furious fancies
　Whereof I am commander,
With a burning spear and a horse of air,
70　To the wilderness I wander.
By a knight of ghosts and shadows
I summoned am to a tourney
Ten leagues beyond the wide world's end:
Methinks it is no journey.
　　　Yet will I sing, etc.
　　　　　　c. 1620

FRANCIS QUARLES°

Emblem IV°

　　I am my beloved's, and his desire is towards me.°

Like to the arctic needle,° that doth guide
　The wandering shade by his magnetic power,
And leaves his silken gnomon° to decide
　The question of the controverted hour,
First frantics up and down from side to side,
　　And restless beats his crystalled ivory case
　　With vain impatience; jets° from place to place,
And seeks the bosom of his frozen bride;
　　At length he slacks his motion, and doth rest
10　His trembling point at his bright pole's belovèd breast.

Even so my soul, being hurried here and there,
　By every object that presents delight,
Fain would be settled, but she knows not where;
　She likes at morning what she loathes at night:
She bows to honour, then she lends an ear
　　To that sweet swan-like voice of dying pleasure,
　　Then tumbles in the scattered heaps of treasure;
Now flattered with false hope, now foiled with fear:
　　Thus finding all the world's delight to be
20　But empty toys, good God, she points alone to thee.

Francis Quarles [1592–1644] a civil servant
and author of prose tracts defending church and
king
Emblem IV from Quarles's *Emblems, Divine
and Moral*, the Fifth Book (1635, and countless
editions thereafter—it was one of the most
popular books of verse in the century). The
imprese or pictures in this part of Quarles's book
were taken from the Jesuit Herman Hugo's
Pia Desideria (1624); the poems are Quarles's
(see *Emblem* in the Glossary).

I am . . . me Canticles 7:10
arctic needle compass needle. The conceit is extremely complex, comparing the wavering and
vertical tilt of the needle to that of the soul.
gnomon the vertical finger of a sundial. Here,
the vertical silk thread or thin metallic pin on
which the transverse needle is hung becomes
momentarily a sundial hand for the compass's
clock-face.
jets throws itself about

But hath the virtued steel° a power to move?
　Or can the untouched needle point aright?
Or can my wandering thoughts forbear to rove,
　Unguided by the virtue of thy sprite?°
Oh hath my laden soul the art to improve
　　Her wasted talent, and, unraised, aspire
　　In this sad moulting time of her desire?
Not first beloved, have I the power to love?
　　I cannot stir but as thou please to move me,
30　Nor can my heart return thee love until thou love me.

The still commandress° of the silent night
　Borrows her beams from her bright brother's eye;
His fair aspéct fills her sharp horns with light,
　If he withdraw, her flames are quenched and die:
Even so the beams of thy enlightening sprite,
　　Infused and shot into my dark desire,
　　Inflame my thoughts, and fill my soul with fire,
That I am ravished with a new delight;
　　But if thou shroud thy face, my glory fades,
40　And I remain a nothing, all composed of shades.

Eternal God! O thou that only art,
　The sacred fountain of eternal light,
And blessed loadstone of my better part,
　O thou, my heart's desire, my soul's delight!
Reflect upon my soul, and touch my heart,
　　And then my heart shall prize no good above thee;
　　And then my soul shall know thee; knowing, love thee;
And then my trembling thoughts shall never start
　　From thy commands, or swerve the least degree,
50　Or once presume to move, but as they move in thee.

EPIGRAM 4

My soul, thy love is dear; 'twas thought a good
And easy penn'worth° of thy Saviour's blood;
But be not proud; all matters rightly scanned,
'Twas over-bought: 'twas sold at second hand.
1635

---

virtued steel magnetized (and thus, empowered)　　**commandress** the moon
steel　　**penn'worth** pennyworth
sprite spirit

THOMAS RANDOLPH°

Upon Love Fondly Refused for Conscience's Sake°

Nature, Creation's law, is judged by sense,
  Not by the tyrant conscience.
Then our commission gives us leave to do,
  What youth and pleasure prompts us to:
For we must question else heaven's great decree,
  And tax it with a treachery,
If things made sweet to tempt our appetite
  Should with a guilt stain the delight.
Higher powers rule us, ourselves can nothing do;
10 Who made us love, made it lawful too.
It was not love, but love transformed to vice,
  Ravished by envious avarice,
Made women first impropriate:° all were free:
  Enclosures men's inventions be.
In the golden age no action could be found
  For trespass on my neighbour's ground:
'Twas just with any fair to mix our blood;
  The best is most diffusive good.
She that confines her beams to one man's sight,
20 Is a dark lanthorn° to a glorious light.
Say, does the virgin-spring less chaste appear,
  'Cause many thirsts are quenchèd there?
Or have you not with the same odours met,
  When more have smelt your violet?
The Phœnix is not angry at her nest,
  'Cause her perfumes make others blest.
Though incense to the eternal gods be meant,
  Yet mortals rival in the scent.
Man is the lord of creatures, yet we see
30 That all his vassals' loves are free,
The severe wedlock's letters do not bind
  The pard's° inflamed and amorous mind;
But that he may be like a bridegroom led
  Even to the royal lion's bed.
The birds may for a year their loves confine,
  But make new choice each Valentine.°

Thomas Randolph [1603–1635] in his own day, almost the most famous poetical son of Ben Jonson's circle, Randolph was wildly praised, even after his death, as an *enfant terrible*. His posthumous collected *Poems* (1638) went through a great many editions.
Upon Love Fondly Refused for Conscience's Sake This poem takes up the garden theme in a typically lascivious Cavalier mode, its meter based on that of a Horatian epode which Randolph had translated. See Andrew Marvell's "The Mower Against Gardens" as an answer to, and revision of, Randolph's treatment of grafting in horticulture to produce new species and more plenteous growth; it is written in the same meter.
impropriate indecorous; unchaste
lanthorn lantern
pard's leopard's
Valentine Birds supposedly took new mates on St. Valentine's Day.

If our affections then more servile be
  Than are our slaves, where is man's sovereignty?
Why, then, by pleasing more, should you less please,
40   And spare the sweets, being more sweet than these?
If the fresh trunk have sap enough to give
  That each insertive° branch may live;
The gardener grafts not only apples there,
  But adds the warden° and the pear.
The peach and apricot together grow,
  The cherry and the damson too,
Till he hath made by skilful husbandry
  An entire orchard of one tree.°
So lest our paradise perfection want,
50   We may as well inoculate° as plant.
What's conscience but a beldame's midnight theme,
  Or nodding nurse's idle dream?
So feigned as are the goblins, elves, and fairies
  To watch their orchards and their dairies.
For who can tell, when first her reign begun?
  In the state of innocence was none:
And since large conscience (as the proverb shows)
  In the same sense with bad one goes,
The less the better then, whence this will fall,
60   'Tis to be perfect to have none at all.
Suppose it be a virtue rich and pure,
  'Tis not for spring or summer, sure.
Nor yet for autumn; love must have his prime,
  His warmer heats and harvest-time.
Till we have flourished, grown, and reaped our wishes;
  What conscience dares oppose our kisses?
But when time's colder hand leads us near home,
  Then let that winter-virtue come:
Frost is till then prodigious; we may do
70   What youth and pleasure prompts us to.

1638

---

insertive inserted in grafting. This whole passage plays on the sexual connotation of putting a twig into a slot cut in another branch.
warden a kind of pear
one tree the Roman writer Pliny mentions in a letter a remarkable tree in the gardens at Tivoli which, by tricks of grafting, was made to bear grapes, pomegranates, apples, pears, figs, nuts, and berries all at once.
inoculate to graft by budding

JOHN CLEVELAND°

On the Memory of Mr. Edward King, Drowned in the Irish Seas°

I like not tears in tune, nor do I prize
His artificial grief who scans his eyes.
Mine weep down pious beads, but why should I
Confine them to the Muse's rosary?
I am no poet here; my pen's the spout
Where the rain-water of mine eyes runs out
In pity of that name, whose fate we see
Thus copied out in grief's hydrography.°
The Muses are not mermaids, though upon
10 His death the ocean might turn Helicon.°
The sea's too rough for verse: who rhymes upon't
With Xerxes strives to fetter the Hellespont.°
My tears will keep no channel, know no laws
To guide their streams, but like the waves, their cause,
Run with disturbance till they swallow me
As a description of his misery.
But can his spacious virtue find a grave
Within the imposthumed° bubble of a wave?
Whose learning if we found, we must confess
20 The sea but shallow and him bottomless.
Could not the winds, to countermand thy death,
With their whole card of lungs° redeem thy breath?
Or some new island in thy rescue peep
To heave thy resurrection from the deep,
That so the world might see thy safety wrought
With no less wonder than thyself was thought?
The famous Stagirite,° who in his life
Had Nature as familiar as his wife,
Bequeathed his widow to survive with thee,
30 Queen Dowager of all philosophy—
An ominous legacy, that did portend
Thy fate and predecessor's second end.°
Some have affirmed that what on earth we find,
The sea can parallel in shape and kind.

John Cleveland [1613–1658] a late and extravagant Metaphysical poet, whose name became attached to empty and overworked conceits (called by Dryden "Clevelandisms")
On the Memory of Mr. Edward King . . . Seas from *Justa Edouardo King*, a set of elegies by various hands on the young Cambridge poet, drowned in the Irish Sea. Cleveland's elaborate, highly wrought, and rhetorical poem should be compared with "Lycidas," Milton's contribution to the same volume.
hydrography literally, "water-writing"
Helicon actually, the mountain sacred to poetry: the fountain on it was called Hippocrene (formed when Pegasus' hoof struck the hilltop)

Hellespont the strait joining the Propontis or Sea of Marmora with the Aegean (see Marlowe's *Hero and Leander*). Xerxes, the 5th-century Persian emperor, bridged it for his invading troops by putting causeways over ranks of ships.
imposthumed swollen, both as in a festering pustule and as with pride
card of lungs Cleveland is thinking of old maps which represented the four winds in puffing pictures at each corner.
Stagirite Aristotle
second end alluding to a mythical story that Aristotle drowned himself in a body of water whose complex tidal schedule he could not calculate

Books, arts, and tongues were wanting, but in thee
Neptune hath got an university.
We'll dive no more for pearls; the hope to see
Thy sacred reliques of mortality
Shall welcome storms, and make the seaman prize
His shipwreck now more than his merchandise.
He shall embrace the waves and to thy tomb
As to a royaler exchanges shall come.
What can we now expect? Water and fire,
Both elements our ruin do conspire,
And that dissolves us which doth us compound.
One Vatican was burnt,° another drowned.
We of the gown our libraries must toss°
To understand the greatness of our loss;
Be pupils to our grief, and so much grow
In learning as our sorrows overflow.
When we have filled the runlets° of our eyes,
We'll issue it forth and vent such elegies
As that our tears shall seem the Irish Seas,
We floating islands, living Hebrides.°

                                    1638

Mark Antony

Whenas the nightingale chanted her vespers,
And the wild forester couched on the ground,
Venus invited me in the evening whispers
Unto a fragrant field with roses crowned,
        Where she before had sent
        My wishes' complement;
        Unto my heart's content
        Played with me on the green.
            Never Mark Antony
            Dallied more wantonly
            With the fair Egyptian Queen.

First on her cherry cheeks I mine eyes feasted,
Thence fear of surfeiting made me retire;
Next on her warmer lips, which when I tasted,
My duller spirits made active as fire.
        Then we began to dart,
        Each at another's heart,
        Arrows that knew no smart,
        Sweet lips and smiles between.
            Never Mark, &c.

burnt The Vatican Library was never burned;
Cleveland is referring (either erroneously or
wittily) to the great library at Alexandria,
burned by Caesar.
toss turn (as the pages of books)

runlets kegs
floating . . . Hebrides a linking of Delos, the
mythical birthplace of Apollo, with the Hebrides,
near which King drowned

Wanting a glass to plait her amber tresses,
Which like a bracelet rich deckèd mine arm,
Gaudier than Juno wears whenas she graces
Jove with embraces more stately than warm;
    Then did she peep in mine
    Eyes' humour° crystalline;
    I in her eyes was seen,
    As if we one had been.
      Never Mark, &c.

30 Mystical grammar of amorous glances;
Feeling of pulses, the physic of love;
Rhetorical courtings and musical dances;
Numbering of kisses arithmetic prove;°
    Eyes like astronomy;
    Straight-limbed geometry;
    In her art's ingeny°
    Our wits were sharp and keen.
      Never Mark Antony
      Dallied more wantonly
40   With the fair Egyptian Queen.
          1647

WILLIAM STRODE°
1602?–1645

On Chloris Walking in the Snow

I saw fair Chloris walk alone
Where feathered rain came softly down:
Then Jove descended from his tower
To court her in a silver shower;°
The wanton snow flew to her breast
Like little birds into their nest,
But overcome with whiteness there,
For grief it thawed into a tear;
Then, falling down her garment hem,
For grief it freezed into a gem.
      1632

humour bodily fluid
prove test
ingeny wit, in the 17th-century sense of creative
intelligence
William Strode author of a tragi-comedy, *The*

Floating Island, produced at Oxford in 1636.
This poem is from a songbook by Walter Porter.
a silver shower with a tactful nod to the myth
of Danaë, mother of Perseus, whom Jupiter
possessed in the form of a shower of gold

SIR RICHARD FANSHAWE°

1608–1666

The Golden Age°

Fair Golden Age! when milk was the only food,
And cradle of the infant world the wood
(Rocked by the winds); and the untouched flocks did bear
Their dear young for themselves! None yet did fear
The sword or poison; no black thoughts begun
T'eclipse the light of the eternal Sun:
Nor wandring pines unto a foreign shore
Or war, or riches (a worse mischief), bore.
That pompous sound, Idol of vanity,
Made up of Title, Pride, and Flattery,
Which they call Honour° whom Ambition blinds,
Was not as yet the tyrant of our minds.
But to buy real goods with honest toil
Amongst the woods and flocks, to use no guile,
Was honour to those sober souls that knew
No happiness but what from virtue grew.
Then sports and carols amongst brooks and plains
Kindled a lawful flame in nymphs and swains.
Their hearts and tongues concurred, the kiss and joy
Which were most sweet, and yet which least did cloy
Hymen bestowed on them. To one alone
The lively roses of delight were blown;
The thievish lover found them shut on trial,
And fenced with prickles of a sharp denial.
Were it in cave or wood, or purling Spring,
Husband and Lover signified one thing.
   Base present age, which dost with thy impure
Delights the beauty of the soul obscure:
Teaching to nurse a dropsy in the veins:
Bridling the look, but givest desire the reins.
Thus, like a net that spread and covered lies
With leaves and tempting flowers, thou dost disguise
With coy and holy arts a wanton heart;
Makest life a Stage-play, virtue but a part:
Nor thinkest it any fault love's sweets to steal,
So from the world thou canst the theft conceal.°
   But thou that art the King of Kings, create

Sir Richard Fanshawe translated the fourth book of the *Aeneid* in Spenserian stanzas, the Portuguese Camoëns's *Lusiads* (1665), and selections from Horace.
The Golden Age a translation of a famous chorus from Battista Guarini's *Il Pastor Fido* (The Faithful Shepherd), combining material from Ovid and Horace (see Golding's version, above)
Honour sexual honor, modesty; here seen as a product of guilt in a fallen world. Cf. Daniel, "A Proposal," Carew's "Rapture," and *Paradise Lost IV*. 314–18.
theft conceal probably a reminiscence of Ben Jonson's "To Celia"

In us true honour: Virtue's all the state
Great souls should keep. Unto these cells return
40 Which were thy court, but now thy absence mourn:
From their dead sleep with thy sharp goad awake
Them who, to follow their base wills, forsake
Thee, and the glory of the ancient world.
    Let's hope: our ills have truce till we are hurled
From that: Let's hope, the sun that's set may rise,
And with new light salute our longing eyes.
                1647

WILLIAM CARTWRIGHT°
1611–1643

No Platonic Love°

Tell me no more of minds embracing minds,
    And hearts exchanged for hearts;
That spirits spirits meet, as winds do winds,
    And mix their subtlest parts;
That two unbodied essences may kiss,
And then like angels, twist and feel one bliss.

I was that silly thing that once was wrought
    To practise this thin love;
I climbed from sex to soul, from soul to thought;
10   But thinking there to move,
Headling I rolled from thought to soul, and then
From soul I lighted at the sex again.

As some strict down-looked men pretend to fast
    Who yet in closets eat,
So lovers who profess they spirits taste,
    Feed yet on grosser meat;
I know they boast they souls to souls convey,
Howe'er they meet, the body is the way.

Come, I will undeceive thee: they that tread
20   Those vain aërial ways
Are like young heirs and alchemists, misled
    To waste their wealth and days;
For searching thus to be forever rich,
They only find a medicine for the itch.
                1651

William Cartwright one of the most popular young poets and preachers in the Oxford of his day, admired by the king and one of Ben Jonson's favorite "sons"

No Platonic Love a parody of John Donne's "The Ecstasy"

AURELIAN TOWNSHEND°
c. 1583–1651?

A Dialogue Betwixt Time and a Pilgrim°

PILGR. Aged man, that mows these fields.
TIME. Pilgrim speak, what is thy will?
PILGR. Whose soil is this that such sweet pasture yields?
      Or who art thou whose foot stand never still?
      Or where am I? TIME. In love.
PILGR. His lordship lies above.
TIME. Yes and below, and round about
    Where in all sorts of flowers are growing
  Which as the early spring puts out,
      Time falls as fast a mowing.
PILGR. If thou art Time, these flowers have lives,
    And then I fear,
  Under some lilly she I love
    May now be growing there.
TIME. And in some thistle or some spire of grass,
  My scythe thy stalk before hers come may pass.
PILGR. Will thou provide it may? TIME. No.
PILGR. Allege the cause.
TIME. Because time cannot alter but obey fate's laws.
CHO. Then happy those whom fate, that is the stronger,
  Together twists their threads, and yet draws hers the longer.

                 1653

JAMES SHIRLEY°
1596–1666

Dirge°

The glories of our blood and state
  Are shadows, not substantial things,
There is no armour against fate,
  Death lays his icy hand on Kings;
    Scepter and crown,
    Must tumble down,
And in the dust be equal made,
With the poor crooked scythe and spade.

Aurelian Townshend An associate of Lord Herbert of Cherbury and Thomas Carew, he composed some lyrics and two masques (1632). **A Dialogue . . . Pilgrim** The form of this lyric is that of the 17th-century musical dialogue, for two voices and harpsichord or lute accompaniment, which explains why the final moralization is given to a "chorus"; the biblical text behind the figure of Time as a mower is Isaiah 40:6: "All flesh is grass." **James Shirley** a copious dramatist, who also published a collected *Poems* in 1646 **Dirge** from *The Contention of Ajax and Ulysses*

Some men with swords may reap the field,
10   And plant fresh laurels where they kill,
But their strong nerves° at last must yield,
    They tame but one another still;
        Early or late,
        They stoop to fate,
And must give up the murmuring breath,
When they, pale captives, creep to death.

The garlands wither on your brow,
    Then boast no more your mighty deeds;
Upon death's purple° altar now,
20   See where the victor-victim bleeds,
        Your heads must come,
        To the cold tomb;
Only the actions of the just
Smell sweet, and blossom in their dust.

                      1659

SIR JOHN DENHAM°
1615–1669

From Cooper's Hill

My eye, descending from the hill,° surveys
Where Thames amongst the wanton valleys strays.
Thames, the most loved of all the ocean's sons,
By his old sire, to his embraces runs,
Hasting to pay his tribute to the sea,
Like mortal life to meet eternity.
Though with those streams he no resemblance hold,
Whose foam is amber and their gravel gold;
His genuine, and less guilty° wealth to explore,
10   Search not his bottom, but survey his shore,
O'er which he kindly spreads his spacious wing,
And hatches plenty for the ensuing spring.

Not then destroys it with too fond a stay,
Like mothers which their infants overlay;
Nor with a sudden and impetuous wave,
Like prófuse kings, resumes° the wealth he gave.
No unexpected inundations spoil

nerves sinews; muscles
purple red
Sir John Denham royalist, playwright, friend
of Waller, and regarded in the Augustan age
as a major figure. *Cooper's Hill*, his topographical poem, was first published in a pirated
edition.

hill Cooper's Hill, in Surrey, overlooking the
Thames, about 7 miles from Windsor
less guilty because it is the wealth of agriculture and mercantile trade, with a pun on "gilt,"
for gilded
resumes repossesses

The mower's hopes, nor mock the plowman's toil;
But God-like his unwearied bounty flows:
20   First loves to do, then loves the good he does.°
Nor are his blessings to his banks confined,
But free and common as the sea or wind;
When he to boast, or to disperse his stores,
Full of the tributes of his grateful shores,
Visits the world, and in his flying towers°
Brings home to us, and makes the Indies ours;
Finds wealth where 'tis, bestows it where it wants,°
Cities in deserts, woods in cities plants,
So that to us no thing, no place is strange,
30   While his fair bosom is the world's exchange.
O could I flow like thee, and make thy stream
My great example, as it is my theme!
Though deep, yet clear, though gentle, yet not dull,
Strong without rage, without o'er-flowing, full.°

                    1642–1665

ROBERT HERRICK
1591–1674

Son of a London goldsmith, Herrick was apprenticed early to a rich uncle, also a goldsmith, but at the late age of twenty-two he went to Cambridge. He took B.A. and M.A. degrees, was ordained in 1623, and for the next six years led a life centering on London, where he was a devoted member of Ben Jonson's circle and the companion of literary courtiers. In 1629 he obtained the living of Dean Prior in Devonshire, and took up the life of a country clergyman, never feeling totally in tune with his surroundings. "More discontents I never had, / Since I was born, than here, / Where I have been and, still am, sad / In this dull Devonshire" he wrote, and yet it was perhaps just this sense of alienation from London, and from the cultural cosmopolis which the Tribe of Ben had meant for him, which led to the extensiveness of his output of verse. *Hesperides* (published with *Noble Numbers* in 1648), named for the golden apples whose gathering was Hercules' task, were the fruits of a poetic paradise located somewhere in his world of classical reading: his more than 1400 short poems (some, admittedly, consisting of a single couplet) sprang from an antique ground of Horace, Catullus, Martial, the Anacreontic poems, and the epigrams of the Greek Anthology, which provided form, tone of voice, allusions, images, and strategies of rhetoric. Subject and scene came often from the rural life around him, often from memories of a learned and convivial London life. It was as if, in a mild kind of exile,

First loves . . . does alluding to God in Genesis 1:4–31: "And God saw the light, that it was good," and so on.
flying towers of square-rigged merchant ships
wants is lacking
O could . . . o'erflowing, full These lines were to become extremely important and widely known in the later 17th and the early 18th century; not only did their rhetoric, diction, and syntax seem to suggest the model of how heroic couplets should be written, but their tactful use of images about language ("clear," "deep," etc.) derived from aspects of moving (eloquence) or standing (thought) water were strikingly attractive, although Dr. Johnson later confessed himself to be unimpressed.

he could reconstruct an imaginative life from the convivial and amatory wit of writers whose world he seldom makes any attempt to accommodate to Christian thought. His religious poems parallel the *Hesperides* in their use of scriptural allusion as a taking-off point, but though their diction and style are quite similar, their modes never interpenetrate, as in the poetry of Donne or Crashaw. Herrick was ejected from his parish (he was a Royalist) in 1647, apparently lived in London, and returned to his "discontents in Devon" in 1660, where, by his own admission, "I ne'er invented such / Ennobled numbers for the press / Than where I loathed so much." Herrick never wrote much after the publication of *Hesperides* and *Noble Numbers*.

From Hesperides

The Argument° of His Book

I sing of brooks, of blossoms, birds and bowers;
Of April, May, of June and Júly flowers.
I sing of May-poles, hock-carts,° wassails, wakes,°
Of bridegrooms, brides and of their bridal cakes.
I write of youth, of love, and have access
By these, to sing of cleanly wantonness.
I sing of dews, of rains, and piece by piece,
Of balm, of oil, of spice, of ambergris.°
I sing of times trans-shifting; and I write
10   How roses first came red, and lilies white.
I write of groves, of twilights, and I sing
The court of Mab,° and of the Fairy King.°
I write of hell; I sing (and ever shall)
Of heaven, and hope to have it after all.
                    1648

To the Virgins, To Make Much of Time

Gather ye rosebuds while ye may,
    Old time is still a-flying;
And this same flower that smiles today,
    Tomorrow will be dying.

The glorious lamp of heaven, the sun,
    The higher he's a-getting,
The sooner will his race be run,
    And nearer he's to setting.

Argument summary of the contents of a piece of writing
hock-carts that brought in the last of the harvest
wakes parish festivals

ambergris perfume base from the spout of whales
Mab Queen of the Fairies
King Oberon

10 That age is best which is the first,
        When youth and blood are warmer,
    But being spent, the worse, and worst
        Times still succeed the former.

    Then be not coy, but use your time,
        And while ye may, go marry:
    For having lost but once your prime,
        You may forever tarry.

                    1648

Corinna's Going A-Maying°

Get up, get up for shame; the blooming morn
Upon her wings presents the god unshorn.°
        See how Aurora° throws her fair
        Fresh-quilted colours through the air!
        Get up, sweet slug-a-bed, and see
        The dew-bespangling herb and tree.
Each flower has wept, and bowèd toward the east,
Above an hour since; yet you not dressed,
        Nay! not so much as out of bed?
10   When all the birds have matins° said,
        And sung their thankful hymns: 'tis sin,
        Nay, profanation to keep in,
When as a thousand virgins on this day,
Spring, sooner than the lark, to fetch in may.°

Rise; and put on your foliage, and be seen
To come forth, like the springtime, fresh and green
        And sweet as Flora. Take no care
        For jewels for your gown or hair;
        Fear not: the leaves will strew
20   Gems in abundance upon you;
Besides, the childhood of the day has kept,
Against° you come, some orient° pearls unwept:
        Come, and receive them while the light
        Hangs on the dew-locks of the night:
        And Titan° on the eastern hill
        Retires himself, or else stands still
Till you come forth. Wash, dress, be brief in praying:
Few beads° are best when once we go a-maying.

Corinna's Going A-Maying like "To the Virgins
. . ." a treatment of the famous theme of
carpe diem ("seize the day"), but a much more
elaborate one, involving an injunction to rise
up early in the morning of one's youth to gather
these special symbolic blossoms on May-day
god unshorn the ever-young sun god, Apollo,
with his long hair streaming

Aurora goddess of the dawn
matins morning prayers
may the white hawthorn, emblematic of marriage
(white for purity, thorns for the danger of pain)
Against until
orient shining; orient pearls were the best
Titan the sun
beads of a rosary

Come, my Corinna, come; and coming, mark
30   How each field turns a street; each street a park
      Made green, and trimmed with trees; see how
      Devotion gives each house a bough,
      Or branch; each porch, each door, ere this,
      An ark, a tabernacle is,
Made up of white-thorn° neatly interwove;
As if here were those cooler shades of love.
      Can such delights be in the street,
      And open fields, and we not see't?
      Come, we'll abroad; and let's obey
40   The proclamation made for May:
And sin no more, as we have done, by staying;
But my Corinna, come, let's go a-maying.

There's not a budding boy or girl this day,
But is got up, and gone to bring in may.
      A deal of youth, ere this, is come
      Back, and with white-thorn laden home.
      Some have dispatched their cakes and cream,
      Before that we have left to dream;°
And some have wept, and wooed, and plighted troth,
50   And chose their priest, ere we can cast off sloth.
      Many a green-gown has been given;°
      Many a kiss, both odd and even:
      Many a glance too has been sent
      From out the eye, love's firmament;
Many a jest told of the keys betraying
This night, and locks picked,° yet we are not a-maying.

Come, let us go, while we are in our prime;
And take the harmless folly of the time.
      We shall grow old apace, and die
60   Before we know our liberty.
      Our life is short; and our days run
      As fast away as does the sun:
And as a vapour, or a drop of rain
Once lost, can ne'er be found again:
      So when or you or I are made
      A fable, song, or fleeting shade,
      All love, all liking, all delight
      Lies drowned with us in endless night.
Then while time serves, and we are but decaying,
70   Come, my Corinna, come, let's go a-maying.

1648

white-thorn The may, the white hawthorn sanctifies houses into churches in the religion of
nature worship—the "old religion" behind the
"old religion" of Catholicism.
left to dream left off dreaming

green-gown . . . given gowns grass-stained from
amorous rolling about
locks picked literally, and figuratively by phal-
lic keys

Upon Julia's Clothes

Whenas in silks my Julia goes,
Then, then (methinks) how sweetly flows
That liquefaction of her clothes.

Next, when I cast mine eyes and see
That brave° vibration each way free,
O how that glittering taketh me!

                                        1648

Delight in Disorder°

A sweet disorder in the dress
Kindles in clothes a wantonness:
A lawn° about the shoulders thrown
Into a fine distraction:
An erring lace, which here and there
Enthralls the crimson stomacher:°
A cuff neglectful, and thereby
Ribbands° to flow confusèdly:
A winning wave (deserving note)
In the tempestuous petticoat:
A careless shoestring, in whose tie
I see a wild civility:
Do more bewitch me than when art
Is too precise in every part.

                                        1648

The Night-Piece, To Julia

Her eyes the glow-worm lend thee;
The shooting stars attend thee;
    And the elves also,
    Whose little eyes glow
Like the sparks of fire, befriend thee.

No will-o'-the-wisp mis-light thee;
Nor snake or slow-worm° bite thee;
    But on, on thy way,
    Not making a stay,
Since ghost there's none to affright thee.

---

brave bright
Delight in Disorder This poem reflects the
changing aesthetic of dress in the Caroline
period, as tight sleeves, corseting, and stiff,
formal hair styles gave way to an equally care-
fully-arranged appearance of looseness.
lawn a scarf of fine linen

erring lace . . . stomacher The stomacher was
a separate piece of cloth held in place across
the front of the bodice by lacing; here, the
lace must wander haphazardly across it.
ribbands ribbons
slow-worm a kind of lizard

Let not the dark thee cumber;°
What though the moon does slumber?
　　The stars of the night
　　Will lend thee their light,
Like tapers clear without number.

Then, Julia, let me woo thee,
Thus, thus to come unto me;
　　And when I shall meet
　　Thy silvery feet,
20 My soul I'll pour into thee.
　　　　　　　1648

The Mad Maid's Song°

Good morrow to the day so fair;
　　Good morning sir to you;
Good morrow to mine own torn hair
　　Bedabbled with the dew.

Good morning to this primrose too;
　　Good morrow to each maid;
That will with flowers the tomb bestrew,
　　Wherein my love is laid.

Ah woe is me, woe, woe is me,
10　　Alack and welladay!
For pity, sir, find out that bee,
　　Which bore my love away.

I'll seek him in your bonnet brave;°
　　I'll seek him in your eyes;
Nay, now I think they've made his grave
　　In the bed of strawberries.

I'll seek him there; I know, ere this,
　　The cold, cold earth doth shake° him;
But I will go, or send a kiss
20　　By you, sir, to awake him.

Pray hurt him not; though he be dead,
　　He knows well who do love him,
And who with green turfs rear his head,
　　And who do rudely move him.

He's soft and tender (pray take heed);
　　With bands of cowslips bind him;
And bring him home, but 'tis decreed
　　That I shall never find him.
　　　　　　　1648

cumber trouble
The Mad Maid's Song See also "Tom o' Bedlam," above.

brave splendid
shake chill

To Anthea, Who May Command Him Anything

Bid me to live, and I will live
    Thy protestant to be:
Or bid me love, and I will give
    A loving heart to thee.

A heart as soft, a heart as kind,
    A heart as sound and free
As in the whole world thou canst find,
    That heart I'll give to thee.

10   Bid that heart stay, and it will stay,
    To honour thy decree;
Or bid it languish quite away,
    And't shall do so for thee.

Bid me to weep, and I will weep,
    While I have eyes to see;
And having none, yet I will keep
    A heart to weep for thee.

Bid me despair, and I'll despair,
    Under that cypress° tree;
Or bid me die, and I will dare
20   E'en death, to die for thee.

Thou art my life, my love, my heart,
    The very eyes of me;
And hast command of every part,
    To live and die for thee.
               1648

From Noble Numbers

The White Island, or Place of the Blessed

In this world, the isle of dreams,
While we sit by sorrow's streams,
Tears and terrors are our themes,
    Reciting;

But when once from hence we fly,
More and more approaching nigh
Unto young eternity,
    Uniting

In that whiter island, where
10   Things are evermore sincere;
Candour° here and lustre there
    Delighting:

---

cypress emblematic of death

candour literally, a white glow; als' in its verbal sense of frankness

There no monstrous fancies shall
Out of hell an horror call
To create, or cause at all,
    Affrighting;

There, in calm and cooling sleep
We our eyes shall never steep,
But eternal watch shall keep,
20   Attending

Pleasures such as shall pursue
Me immortalized, and you,
And fresh joys as never, too,
    Have ending.
        1648

THOMAS CAREW
1594?–1640

Carew, whose name is generally pronounced 'Cary' and who may have sounded it that way himself, was born to a well-connected and influential family, studied at Merton College, Oxford, and at the Middle Temple, and spent his life in various subsidiary diplomatic posts (such as secretary to Lord Herbert of Cherbury) and, finally, attached to Charles I's court, for which he wrote his celebrated masque *Coelum Britannicum* in 1633. An amorous courtier and a dedicated and skillful poet, he was devoted to both Ben Jonson and to John Donne, both of whom he knew and allowed to influence and shape his work. His elegy on the death of Donne is a major statement of the Caroline poetic temper, employing language and paradoxical concepts derived from Donne to praise him. His great "Rapture" poem is a masterpiece of erotic vision strengthened, rather than kept in check by, the action of wit. Its sexual topography heightens that of Renaissance epic with the intense precision of Donne and the Italian Giambattista Marino, who influenced both Carew and Crashaw; its language quotes, alludes to, and expands upon that of Donne as Jonsonian tradition was doing with Horace, Catullus, the Anacreontic poems, and Martial, and as the sonneteers of the 1590's did with Petrarch.

A Rapture

I will enjoy thee now, my Celia, come,
And fly with me to Love's Elysium.°
The giant, Honour, that keeps cowards out,
Is but a masquer,° and the servile rout

Elysium Compare this erotic paradise with Drayton's "The Muses' Elizium" above, and with the descriptions of the Golden Age by Daniel and Fanshawe.

masquer Honour is only an allegorical figure in a court masque.

Of baser subjects only bend in vain
To the vast idol; whilst the nobler train
Of valiant lovers daily sail between
The huge Colossus' legs,° and pass unseen
Unto the blissful shore. Be bold and wise,
10   And we shall enter: the grim Swiss° denies
Only to tame fools a passage, that not know
He is but form, and only frights in show
The duller eyes that look from far; draw near,
And thou shalt scorn what we were wont to fear.
We shall see how the stalking pageant° goes
With borrowed legs, a heavy load to those
That made and bear him: not, as we once thought,
The seed of gods, but a weak model wrought
By greedy men, that seek to enclose the common,°
20   And within private arms impale free woman.
     Come, then, and mounted on the wings of Love
We'll cut the flitting air, and soar above
The monster's° head, and in the noblest seats
Of those blest shades quench and renew our heats.
There shall the Queens of Love and Innocence,
Beauty and Nature, banish all offence
From our close ivy-twines; there I'll behold
Thy barèd snow and thy unbraided gold;
There my enfranchised hand° on every side
30   Shall o'er thy naked polished ivory slide.
No curtain there, though of transparent lawn,
Shall be before thy virgin-treasure drawn;
But the rich mine, to the inquiring eye
Exposed, shall ready still for mintage lie;
And we will coin young Cupids. There a bed
Of roses and fresh myrtles shall be spread
Under the cooler shade of cypress groves;
Our pillows of the down of Venus' doves,
Whereon our panting limbs we'll gently lay,
40   In the faint respites of our active play;
That so our slumbers may in dreams have leisure
To tell the nimble fancy our past pleasure,
And so our souls that cannot be embraced
Shall the embraces of our bodies taste.
Meanwhile the bubbling stream shall court the shore,
The enamoured chirping wood-choir shall adore

Colossus' legs the Colossus of Rhodes, one of the Wonders of the ancient world, popularly supposed to have straddled the entrance to the harbor
Swiss the Vatican's Swiss Guards, known for their height
pageant the show of Honour
common a town's or village's farm or grazing land. The conceit is of enclosure and continues to pun on "pale" (for "fence") in the next line; cf. *Venus and Adonis*, ll. 229–40.
monster's Honour's
enfranchised hand recalls Donne's "License my roving hands, and let them go / Before, behind, between, above, below" (see Elegy XIX: "To His Mistress going to Bed")

In varied tunes the Deity of Love;
The gentle blasts of western winds shall move
The trembling leaves, and through their close boughs breathe
50 Still music, whilst we rest ourselves beneath
Their dancing shade; till a soft murmur, sent
From souls entranced in amorous languishment,
Rouse us, and shoot into our veins fresh fire,
Till we in their sweet ecstasy expire.
    Then, as the empty bee, that lately bore
Into the common treasure all her store,
Flies 'bout the painted field with nimble wing,
Deflowering the fresh virgins of the spring,°
So will I rifle all the sweets that dwell
60 In my delicious paradise, and swell
My bag with honey, drawn forth by the power
Of fervent kisses from each spicy flower.
I'll seize the rose-buds in their perfumed bed,
The violet knots, like curious mazes spread
O'er all the garden, taste the ripened cherry,
The warm firm apple, tipped with coral berry;
Then will I visit with a wandering kiss
The vale of lilies and the bower of bliss:°
And where the beauteous region doth divide
70 Into two milky ways, my lips shall slide
Down those smooth alleys, wearing as I go
A tract° for lovers on the printed snow;
Thence climbing o'er the swelling Apennine,°
Retire into thy grove of eglantine,°
Where I will all those ravished sweets distill
Through Love's alembic,° and with chemic° skill
From the mixed mass one sovereign balm derive,
Then bring that great elixir to thy hive.
    Now in more subtle wreaths I will entwine
80 My sinewy thighs, my legs and arms with thine;
Thou like a sea of milk shalt lie displayed,
Whilst I the smooth, calm ocean invade
With such a tempest, as when Jove of old
Fell down on Danaë in a storm of gold;
Yet my tall pine shall in the Cyprian strait°
Ride safer at anchor, and unlade her freight:
My rudder with thy bold hand, like a tried
And skillful pilot, thou shalt steer, and guide
My bark into love's channel, where it shall

virgins of the spring untasted flowers; notice
how the honey-making image then stands for
physical sex in the next lines
bower of bliss Spenser's phrase, here used without a negative moral cast; see *The Faerie Queene*
II.xii
tract both pathways and treatise
Apennine Italy's central mountain range; the
lady's belly
eglantine sweetbriar; here, the pubic hair
Love's alembic alchemists' distilling flask; the
image is Donne's
chemic alchemical
Cyprian straight the vagina; Cyprus was Venus'
birthplace

90   Dance, as the bounding waves do rise or fall.
        Then shall thy circling arms embrace and clip
        My willing body, and thy balmy lip
        Bathe me in juice of kisses, whose perfume
        Like a religious incense shall consume,
        And send up holy vapours to those powers
        That bless our loves and crown our sportful hours,
        That with such halcyon° calmness fix our souls
        In steadfast peace, as no affright controls.
        There no rude sounds shake us with sudden starts;
100   No jealous ears, when we unrip our hearts,
        Suck our discourse in; no observing spies
        This blush, that glance traduce;° no envious eyes
        Watch our close meetings; nor are we betrayed
        To rivals by the bribèd chambermaid.
        No wedlock bonds unwreathe our twisted loves;
        We seek no midnight arbour, no dark groves
        To hide our kisses: there the hated name
        Of husband, wife, lust, modest, chaste or shame,
        Are vain and empty words, whose very sound
110   Was never heard in the Elysian ground.
        All things are lawful there that may delight
        Nature or unrestrainèd appetite;
        Like and enjoy, to will and act is one:
        We only sin when Love's rites are not done.
            The Roman Lucrece° there reads the divine
        Lectures of Love's great master, Aretine,°
        And knows as well as Lais° how to move
        Her pliant body in the act of love.
        To quench the burning ravisher, she hurls
120   Her limbs into a thousand winding curls,
        And studies artful postures, such as be
        Carved on the bark of every neighbouring tree
        By learnèd hands, that so adorned the rind
        Of those fair plants, which, as they lay entwined,
        Have fanned their glowing fires. The Grecian dame,°
        That in her endless web toiled for a name
        As fruitless as her work, doth there display
        Herself before the youth of Ithaca,
        And the amorous sport of gamesome nights prefer
130   Before dull dreams of the lost traveller.
        Daphne hath broke her bark, and that swift foot
        Which the angry gods had fastened with a root
        To the fixed earth doth now unfettered run

halcyon kingfisher, associated with calm waters
traduce slander
Lucrece Shakespeare's Roman heroine, an emblem of chastity; in Carew's bower she is reading pornography
Aretine Pietro Aretino (1492–1566) was famous
for, among other things, his sonnets made to go

with Giulio Romano's paintings describing various positions of sexual intercourse.
Lais a courtesan of antiquity
Grecian dame Odysseus' Penelope who, to keep
her suitors at bay, unravelled at night the
weaving she had done in the day, upon whose
completion she was to have chosen one of them

To meet the embraces of the youthful Sun.
She hangs upon him like his Delphic lyre;
Her kisses blow the old, and breathe new fire;
Full of her god, she sings inspired lays,
Sweet odes of love, such as deserve the bays,°
Which she herself was. Next her, Laura° lies
140 In Petrarch's learnèd arms, drying those eyes
That did in such sweet smooth-paced numbers° flow,
As made the world enamoured of his woe.
These, and ten thousand beauties more, that died
Slave to the tyrant, now enlarged deride
His cancelled laws, and for their time misspent
Pay into Love's exchequer double rent.
    Come then, my Celia, we'll no more forbear
To taste our joys, struck with a panic fear,
But will depose from his imperious sway
150 This proud usurper, and walk free as they,
With necks unyoked; nor is it just that he
Should fetter your soft sex with chastity,
Which Nature made unapt for abstinence;
When yet this false impostor can dispense
With human justice and with sacred right,
And, maugre° both their laws, command me fight
With rivals or with emulous loves that dare
Equal with thine their mistress' eyes or hair.
If thou complain of wrong, and call my sword
160 To carve out thy revenge, upon that word
He bids me fight and kill, or else he brands
With marks of infamy my coward hands,
And yet religion bids from bloodshed fly,
And damns me for that act. Then tell me why
This goblin Honour, which the world adores,
Should make men atheists, and not women whores.

                          1640

An Elegy upon the Death of Doctor Donne, Dean of Paul's°

Can we not force from widowed poetry,
Now thou art dead (great Donne) one elegy
To crown thy hearse?° Why yet did we not trust,
Though with unkneaded dough-baked prose, thy dust,

---

bays laurel crowns for poetic achievement
Laura Petrarch's muse
numbers metrical verses
maugre despite
An Elegy . . . Paul's This poem was first printed in the 1633 edition of Donne's poems.

crown thy hearse It was actually the practice to attach poems praising the dead to the funeral hearse, like wreaths, further enforcing the 17th-century association of flowers and poetry, poesy and posies.

Such as the unscissored° churchman from the flower
Of fading rhetoric, short-lived as his hour,
Dry as the sand that measures it, should lay
Upon the ashes, on the funeral day?
Have we no voice, nor tune? Didst thou dispense
Through all our language both the words and sense?
'Tis a sad truth. The pulpit may her plain
And sober Christian precepts still retain;
Doctrines it may, and wholesome uses, frame,
Grave homilies and lectures, but the flame
Of thy brave soul (that shot such heat and light
As burnt our earth, and made our darkness bright,
Committed holy rapes upon our will,
Did through the eye the melting heart distil,
And the deep knowledge of dark truths so teach
As sense might judge, what fancy could not reach)
Must be desired for ever. So the fire
That fills with spirit and heat the Delphic choir,°
Which, kindled first by thy Promethean° breath,
Glowed here a while, lies quenched now in thy death.
The Muses' garden with pedantic weeds
O'erspread, was purged by thee; the lazy seeds
Of servile imitation thrown away,
And fresh invention planted; thou didst pay
The debts of our penurious bankrupt age;
Licentious thefts, that make poetic rage
A mimic fury, when our souls must be
Possessed, or with Anacreon's° ecstasy
Or Pindar's,° not their own; the subtle cheat
Of sly exchanges,° and the juggling feat
Of two-edged words, or whatsoever wrong
By ours was done the Greek or Latin tongue,
Thou hast redeemed, and opened us a mine
Of rich and pregnant fancy; drawn a line
Of masculine° expression, which had good
Old Orpheus seen, or all the ancient brood
Our superstitious fools admire and hold
Their lead more precious than thy burnished gold,
Thou hadst been their exchequer, and no more
They each in other's dust had raked for ore.
Thou shalt yield no precedence, but of time

unscissored untonsured
Delphic choir the Muses, led by Apollo
Promethean Prometheus stole fire, symbolizing all crafts and skills, from the gods to give to men, and was punished for his pains with greater pains.
Anacreon's the Greek poet to whom were wrongly ascribed the poems that served as a model for so much Cavalier verse
Pindar's the great Greek choral, public poet
sly exchanges Perhaps plays upon the Latin sense of English words.
masculine referring not to sexuality, but to stylistic power. In differing ages it could imply anything from decorum to the "strong lines" of Metaphysical verse which Carew is praising.

And the blind fate of language, whose tunèd chime
More charms the outward sense; yet thou mayst claim
From so great disadvantage greater fame,
Since to the awe of thy imperious wit
50 Our stubborn language bends, made only fit
With her tough thick-ribbed hoops to gird about
Thy giant fancy, which had proved too stout
For their soft melting phrases. As in time
They had the start, so did they cull the prime
Buds of invention many a hundred year,
And left the rifled fields, besides the fear
To touch their harvest; yet from those bare lands
Of what is purely thine, thy only hands,
(And that their smallest work) have gleanèd more
60 Than all those times and tongues could reap before.
    But thou art gone, and thy strict laws will be
Too hard for libertines in poetry;
They will recall the goodly exiled train
Of gods and goddesses, which in thy just reign
Were banished nobler poems; now with these,
The silenced tales i' the *Metamorphoses*,°
Shall stuff their lines, and swell the windy page,
Till verse, refined by thee in this last age,
Turn ballad-rhyme, or those old idols be
70 Adored again with new apostasy.°
    O, pardon me, that break with untuned verse
The reverend silence that attends thy hearse,
Whose awful solemn murmurs were to thee,
More than these faint lines, a loud elegy,
That did proclaim in a dumb eloquence
The death of all the arts; whose influence,
Grown feeble, in these panting numbers° lies
Gasping short-winded accents, and so dies.
So doth the swiftly turning wheel not stand
80 In the instant we withdraw the moving hand,
But some small time retain a faint weak course,
By virtue of the first impulsive force;
And so, whilst I cast on thy funeral pile
The crown of bays,° oh, let it crack awhile,
And spit disdain, till the devouring flashes
Suck all the moisture up, then turn to ashes.
    I will not draw the envy to engross°
All thy perfections, or weep all the loss;
Those are too numerous for an elegy,

Metamorphoses Ovid's epic, a repository of
classical myth (see The Renaissance Ovid)
apostasy All of these religious terms, applied
to the holy company of good poetry, parallel

Donne's use of them for images of love.
numbers verses
bays laurel (the poet's crown)
engross copy out (a legal term)

90   And this too great to be expressed by me.
Though every pen should share a distinct part,
Yet art thou theme enough to tire all art;
Let others carve the rest, it shall suffice
I on thy tomb this epitaph incise:

    Here lies a king, that ruled as he thought fit
    The universal monarchy of wit;
    Here lie two flamens,° and both those, the best,
    Apollo's first, at last, the true God's priest.
                    1633

Upon a Ribband°

This silken wreath, which circles in mine arm,
Is but an emblem of that mystic charm
Wherewith the magic of your beauties binds
My captive soul, and round about it winds
Fetters of lasting love. This hath entwined
My flesh alone; that hath impaled my mind.
Time may wear out these soft weak bands, but those
Strong chains of brass Fate shall not discompose.
This holy relic may preserve my wrist,
10   But my whole frame doth by that power subsist:
To that my prayers and sacrifice, to this
I only pay a superstitious kiss.
This but the idol, that's the deity;
Religion there is due; here, ceremony.
That I receive by faith, this but in trust;
Here I may tender duty: there, I must.
This order as a layman I may bear,
But I become Love's priest when that I wear.
This moves like air; that as the centre stands;
20   That knot your virtue tied; this but your hands.
That, Nature framed; but this was made by Art;
This makes my arm your prisoner; that, my heart.
                    1640

RICHARD LOVELACE
1618–1657

Lovelace is perhaps the Cavalier poet *par excellence*. Born to a prominent Kentish family, a social and literary success at Oxford, personally gorgeous enough for the King and Queen to have caused him to be given an M.A. while on an Oxford visit, he lived a country life of learning and enjoyments. In 1642 he was imprisoned for petition-

flamens priests   **Ribband** ribbon ing the Long Parliament in the King's cause, was released, fought in France against the Spanish, returned, was imprisoned again by the Puritan government, was released after ten months, and died in obscurity. The volume called *Lucasta* was published in 1649. Lovelace's poems celebrate Love as the child of Beauty and War (Cupid's father was Mars in some versions of the myth) and are full of an awareness of the fragility of the life they celebrate, and of the possibilities of erotic joy and delight in emblematic readings of animals and pictures.

The Grasshopper°

To my noble friend, Mr. Charles Cotton

ODE°

O thou that swing'st upon the waving hair
   Of some well-fillèd oaten beard,
Drunk every night with a delicious tear
   Dropped thee from heaven, where now th'art reared:

The joys of earth and air are thine entire,
   That with thy feet and wings dost hop and fly;
And, when thy poppy works, thou dost retire
   To thy carved acorn-bed to lie.

Up with the day, the sun thou welcomest then,
10   Sport'st in the gilt plats° of his beams,
And all these merry days makest merry: men,
   Thyself, and melancholy streams.

But ah, the sickle!° Golden ears are cropped;
   Ceres and Bacchus bid good night;°
Sharp frosty fingers all your flowers have topped,
   And what scythes spared, winds shave off quite.

Poor verdant fool! and now green ice! thy joys
   Large and as lasting as thy perch of grass,
Bid us lay in 'gainst winter, rain, and poise°
20   Their floods with an o'erflowing glass.

Thou best of men and friends! we will create
   A genuine summer in each other's breast,
And spite of this cold time and frozen fate,
   Thaw us a warm seat to our rest.

The Grasshopper In Aesop, the silly grasshopper fiddles and sings all summer long, while the wise ant lays up stores for the winter which will kill the careless singer. In the Greek poems called Anacreontic, the grasshopper is praised for his love of drinking—the wine of dew—and his song.
Ode alluding to the Anacreontic poems, one of which is translated by Lovelace's first three stanzas (see Abraham Cowley's translation of the Anacreontic poem in this volume)
plats braids
sickle of autumnal mowers, of Time, thus perhaps of the Puritan world cutting down the Cavalier one
Ceres . . . night bid farewell to these gods of food and drink, plenitude and joy
poise balance

Our sacred hearths shall burn eternally
   As vestal flames; the North Wind, he
Shall strike his frost-stretched wings, dissolve, and fly
   This Aetna° in epitome.

30   Dropping December shall come weeping in,
   Bewail the usurping° of his reign;
But when in showers of old Greek° we begin,
   Shall cry he hath his crown again.

Night as clear Hesper° shall our tapers whip
   From the light casements where we play,
And the dark hag from her black mantle strip,
   And stick there everlasting day.

Thus richer than untempted kings are we,
   That asking nothing, nothing need:
Though lord of all what seas embrace, yet he
40   That wants° himself is poor indeed.
                    1649

La Bella Bona Roba°

I cannot tell who loves the skeleton
Of a poor marmoset,° naught but bone, bone.
Give me a nakedness with her clothes on.

Such whose white-satin upper coat of skin,
Cut upon velvet rich incarnadin,°
Has yet a body (and of flesh) within.

Sure it is meant good husbandry in men,
Who so incorporate with aery lean,°
To repair their sides, and get their rib again.

10   Hard hap unto that huntsman that decrees
Fat joys for all his sweat, whenas he sees,
After his 'say,° naught but his keeper's fees.

Then Love, I beg, when next thou takest thy bow,
Thy angry shafts, and dost heart-chasing° go,
Pass rascal deer,° strike me the largest doe.
                    1649

Aetna the famous Sicilian volcano
usurping perhaps an allusion to the Long Parliament's ban in 1644 of Christmas celebrations as paganism
old Greek perhaps Hippocras, a spiced wine drink
Hesper the Evening Star. The syntax of this line is puzzling: "Our tapers shall, like Hesper, whip night away from our windows."
wants lacks

La Bella Bona Roba a common expression for a whore, but, literally, a pleasantly plump girl
marmoset slang for prostitute
incarnadin flesh-colored
lean leanness (in women)
'say "assay," taken of the deer's flesh to check its quality
heart-chasing punning on "hart"
rascal deer were thin and too poor to hunt

Song

To Lucasta, Going to the Wars

Tell me not, sweet, I am unkind,°
   That from the nunnery
Of thy chaste breast and quiet mind,
   To war and arms I fly.

True, a new mistress now I chase,
   The first foe in the field;
And with a stronger faith embrace
   A sword, a horse, a shield.

Yet this inconstancy is such
10   As you too shall adore;
I could not love thee, dear, so much,
   Loved I not honour more.

               1649

The Snail

Wise emblem of our politic world,
Sage snail, within thine own self curled,
Instruct me softly to make haste,°
Whilst these my feet go slowly fast.
   Compendious snail! thou seemst to me
Large Euclid's strict epitome;°
And in each diagram, dost fling
Thee from the point unto the ring.
A figure now triangular,
10 An oval now, and now a square;
And then a serpentine dost crawl,
Now a straight line, now crooked, now all.
   Preventing rival of the day,
Th'art up and openest thy ray,
And ere the morn cradles the moon,
Th'art broke into a beauteous noon.
Then, when the sun sups in the deep,
Thy silver horns ere Cynthia's peep,
And thou, from thine own liquid bed,
20 New Phoebus, heavest thy pleasant head.
   Who shall a name for thee create,

---

unkind unnatural, as well as in the modern sense
softly to make haste A famous tag, *festina lente* ("make haste slowly"), usually attributed to the Emperor Augustus, was frequently applied to the snail's slow pace; this whole poem is an expanded emblem verse.
Euclid's strict epitome because it embraces, in its slow motions, all the geometric figures, including the spiral of its shell

Deep riddle of mysterious state?
Bold nature, that gives common birth
To all products of sea and earth,
Of thee, as earthquakes, is afraid,
Nor will thy dire delivery aid.
   Thou thine own daughter, then, and sire,
That son and mother art entire,
That big still with thy self dost go,
30 And livest an aged embryo;
That like the cubs of India,
Thou from thy self a while dost play;
But frighted with a dog or gun,
In thine own belly thou dost run,
And as thy house was thine own womb,
So thine own womb concludes thy tomb.
   But now I must (analyzèd king)
Thy economic virtues sing;
Thou great staid husband still within,
40 Thou thee, that's thine, dost discipline;
And when thou art to progress bent,
Thou movest thy self and tenement,
As warlike Scythians travelled, you
Remove your men and city too;
Then, after a sad dearth and rain,
Thou scatterest thy silver train;
And when the trees grow naked and old,
Thou clothest them with cloth of gold,
Which from thy bowels thou dost spin,
50 And draw from the rich mines within.
   Now hast thou changed thee saint, and made
Thy self a fane° that's cupola'd
And in thy wreathèd cloister thou
Walkest thine own grey friar too;
Strict, and locked up, th'art hood all o'er,
And ne'er eliminatest thy door.
On salads thou dost feed severe,
And 'stead of beads thou droppest a tear,
And when to rest each calls the bell,
60 Thou sleepest within thy marble cell;
Where, in dark contemplation placed,
The sweets of nature thou dost taste;
Who now with time thy days resolve,
And in a jelly thee dissolve,
Like a shot star, which doth repair
Upward, and rarify the air.

          1659–60

fane temple

Love Made in the First Age:°
To Chloris

In the nativity of time,
Chloris, it was not thought a crime
   In direct Hebrew° for to woo.
Now we make love, as all on fire,
Ring retrograde our lewd desire,
   And court in English backward too.

Thrice happy was the golden age,
When compliment was construed rage,
   And fine words in the center hid;
10   When cursèd *No* stained no maid's bliss
And all discourse was summed in *Yes,*
   And nought forbade, but to forbid.

Love then unstinted love did sip,
And cherries plucked fresh from the lip,
   On cheeks and roses free he fed;
Lasses like autumn plums did drop,
And lads indifferently did crop
   A flower and a maidenhead.

Then unconfinèd each did tipple
20   Wine from the bunch, milk from the nipple,
   Paps tractable as udders were;
Then equally the wholesome jellies
Were squeezed from olive trees and bellies,
   Nor suits° of trespass did they fear.

A fragrant bank of strawberries,
Diapered with violet's eyes
   Was table, tablecloth, and fare;
No palace to the clouds did swell,
Each humble princess then did dwell
30   In the piazza of her hair.

Both broken faith and the cause of it,
All-damning gold, was damned to the pit;
   Their troth, sealed with a clasp and kiss,
Lasted until that éxtreme day
In which they smiled their souls away,
   And, in each other, breathed new bliss.

Love Made in the First Age This poem is a libertine elaboration of the theme of unfallen eros in the Golden Age: see the treatments of it by Ovid, Daniel, and Fanshawe above.
direct Hebrew The Renaissance believed Hebrew to have been the original language spoken in Paradise; the fracturing of Speech into myriad languages after the Tower of Babel is Lovelace's image for how guilt ruined sex after an initial age of perfection was over. Hebrew reads from right to left: this forms the basis for the conceit in the first stanza.
suits lawsuits

Because no fault, there was no tear;
No groan did grate the granting ear;
   No false foul breath their delicate smell:
40 No serpent kiss poisoned the taste,
Each touch was naturally chaste,
   And their mere sense a miracle.

Naked as their own innocence,
And unembroidered from offence
   They went, above poor riches, gay;
On softer than the cygnet's down,
In beds they tumbled of their own;
   For each within the other lay.

Thus did they live: thus did they love,
50 Repeating only joys above;
   And angels were, but with clothes on,
Which they would put off cheerfully,
To bathe them in the galaxy,
   Then gird them with the heavenly zone.

Now, Chloris, miserably crave
The offered bliss you would not have,
   Which evermore I must deny,
Whilst ravished with these noble dreams,
And crownèd with mine own soft beams,
60   Enjoying of myself I lie.
            1659–60

EDMUND WALLER
1606–1687

Waller's reputation, along with that of Sir John Denham, could not outlast the Augustan period which claimed them as true progenitors of proper verse—for just so long did "Denham's strength and Waller's sweetness," in Pope's phrase, remain celebrated models. Waller himself was born to a wealthy country family, attended Eton, Cambridge for a while, and Lincoln's Inn; then he was elected to Parliament, and made a wealthy marriage to a lady whose fortune he inherited upon her early death. Although a Parliamentarian at first, he veered to the Royalist cause. He became involved in a plot to seize London for the crown, was exposed, joined the English exiles in Paris in 1643, was pardoned in 1651, and after the Restoration again became involved in court life and government. His literary sphere was Jonsonian, he was a member of the circle of Lucius Cary, Viscount Falkland (celebrated in Jonson's great Pindaric ode). In our own day, Ezra Pound has praised and imitated Waller, perhaps in recognition of all sorts of affinities.

Song

Go, lovely Rose—
Tell her that wastes her time and me
   That now she knows,
When I resemble her to thee,
   How sweet and fair she seems to be.

   Tell her that's young
And shuns to have her graces spied
   That, hadst thou sprung
In deserts where no men abide,
   Thou must have uncommended died.

   Small is the worth
Of beauty from the light retired:
   Bid her come forth,
Suffer herself to be desired,
   And not blush so to be admired.

   Then die that she
The common fate of all things rare
   May read in thee;
How small a part of time they share
   That are so wondrous sweet and fair!

1645

At Penshurst°

Had Sacharissa° lived when mortals made
Choice of their deities, this sacred shade
Had held an altar to her power, that gave
The peace and glory which these alleys have;
Embroidered so with flowers where she stood,
That it became a garden of a wood.
Her presence has such more than human grace,
That it can civilize the rudest place;
And beauty too, and order, can impart,
Where nature ne'er intended it, nor art.
The plants acknowledge this, and her admire,
No less than those of old did Orpheus' lyre;°
If she sit down, with tops all towards her bowed,
They round about her into arbours crowd;
Or if she walk, in even ranks they stand,
Like some well-marshalled and obsequious band.

At Penshurst See Ben Jonson's poem to the same
house.
Sacharissa literally, "sweet one," Waller's name
in his poems for Lady Dorothy Sidney, whom he
courted unsuccessfully
Orpheus' lyre His fabulous music made the trees
dance.

Amphion° so made stones and timber leap
Into fair figures from a cónfused heap,
And in the symmetry of her parts is found
20   A power like that of harmony in sound.
     Ye lofty beeches, tell this matchless dame
That if together ye fed all one flame,
It could not equalize the hundredth part
Of what her eyes have kindled in my heart!
Go, boy, and carve this passion on the bark
Of yonder tree,° which stands the sacred mark
Of noble Sidney's birth; when such benign,
Such more than mortal-making stars did shine,
That there they cannot but for ever prove
30   The monument and pledge of humble love;
His humble love whose hopes shall ne'er rise higher,
Than for a pardon that he dares admire.

                    1645

Of English Verse

Poets may boast, as safely vain,
Their works shall with the world remain;
Both, bound together, live or die,
The verses and the prophecy.

But who can hope his lines should long
Last in a daily changing tongue?
While they are new, envy prevails;
And as that dies, our language fails.

When architects have done their part,
10   The matter may betray their art;
Time, if we use ill-chosen stone,
Soon brings a well-built palace down.

Poets that lasting marble seek,
Must carve in Latin, or in Greek;
We write in sand, our language grows,
And, like the tide, our work o'erflows.

Chaucer his sense can only boast;
The glory of his numbers lost!°
Years have defaced his matchless strain;
20   And yet he did not sing in vain.

Amphion a parallel mythological figure: his
music charmed the stones of the walls of Thebes
into place
tree the one planted in honor of Sir Philip
Sidney's birth

numbers lost Even in Waller's time, it was not
understood that Chaucer's verse was iambic
pentameter.

The beauties which adorned that age,
The shining subjects of his rage,°
Hoping they should immortal prove,
Rewarded with success his love.

This was the generous poet's scope;
And all an English pen can hope,
To make the fair approve his flame,
That can so far extend their fame.

Verse, thus designed, has no ill fate,
30   If it arrive but at the date°
Of fading beauty; if it prove
But as long-lived as present love.

                    1693

ABRAHAM COWLEY
1618–1667

Abraham Cowley is perhaps best remembered as Samuel Johnson's epitome of the Metaphysical school, for it is in his Life of Cowley that the famous remarks on Donne appear. As a writer of "strong lines," Cowley certainly sounds a dying fall, and it is in his more public and expository manner that he seems interesting now. Born to a London middle-class family, he attended Westminster School and Trinity College, Cambridge, became a close friend of Crashaw, traveled abroad for the Royalist cause and was imprisoned upon his return to England in 1655. Following his release, he studied medicine, and after 1660 experienced a private restoration in the return of his Cambridge fellowship and the gift of some land by the Queen, to which he retired to write essays and to concern himself with the Royal Society, in whose foundation he was interested. His "Pindaric" odes are, in fact, the first irregular odes in English, and it was this form which Dryden bequeathed to the differing uses of posterity.

Cowley's Metaphysical lyrics were published in The Mistress (1647), to considerable acclaim; in 1656 he published his attempt at a large-scale biblical epic in heroic couplets, Davideis, and his collected Poems. The posthumous Works appeared in 1668.

Ode° of Wit

Tell me, O tell, what kind of thing is wit,°
    Thou who master art of it.
For the first matter° loves variety less;

rage poetic ardor
date terminal date, or end. The whole phrase is strangely reminiscent of the language of Shakespeare's sonnets.
Ode This is not one of Cowley's "Pindaric" odes, but, like them, it flourishes its title to suggest a public poem, almost an essay.
wit Between the death of Queen Elizabeth and

about 1750, the word "wit" undergoes shifts of meaning; Cowley's opening question, conscious of this, is more than a mere rhetorical device.
first matter In classical creation theories, chaos contained matter, but without orderly differentiation even of qualities and attributes; thus it would love variety, but wit loves it even more.

Less women love't, either in love or dress.
   A thousand different shapes it bears,
   Comely in thousand shapes appears.
Yonder we saw it plain; and here 'tis now,
Like spirits in a place, we know not how.

London that vents of false ware so much store,°
10   In no more ware deceives us more.
For men led by the colour and the shape,
Like Zeuxis' birds, fly to the painted grape;°
   Some things do through our judgment pass
   As through a multiplying° glass.
And sometimes, if the object be too far,
We take a falling meteor for a star.

Hence 'tis a wit, that greatest word of fame,
   Grows such a common name,
And wits by our creation they become,
20 Just so, as titular bishops made at Rome.°
   'Tis not a tale, 'tis not a jest
   Admired with laughter at a feast,
Nor florid talk, which can that title gain:
The proofs of wit forever must remain.

'Tis not to force some lifeless verses meet
   With their five gouty feet.°
All everywhere, like man's, must be the soul,
And reason the inferior powers control.°
   Such were the numbers° which could call
30   The stones into the Theban wall.°
Such miracles are ceased, and now we see
No towns or houses raised by poetry.

Yet 'tis not to adorn and gild each part
   That shows more cost than art.
Jewels at nose and lips but ill appear;
Rather than all thing wit, let none be there.
   Several° lights will not be seen
   If there be nothing else between;
Men doubt, because they stand so thick i' the sky,
40 If those be stars which paint the galaxy.

---

vents . . . store abounds with fakes
Zeuxis' birds . . . grape the most famous anecdote about Greek painting: Zeuxis, a 5th-century B.C. painter, painted grapes so realistically that birds flew to them
multiplying magnifying
made at Rome bishops with titles but not present at their distant sees
feet of iambic pentameter verse
All . . . control Just as the human soul was thought to be diffused throughout the body (except by Descartes, who located it in the inaccessible pineal gland), so must poetic power be generally dispersed throughout, and in mastery of, the mere arts of language.
numbers meter and music
which could . . . wall Amphion, an Orpheus-like figure, charmed the stones of the walls of Thebes into place with his playing.
Several distinct, separate

'Tis not when two like words make up one noise,°
    Jests for Dutch men, and English boys.
In which who finds out wit, the same may see
In anagrams and acrostics° poetry.
        Much less can that have any place
        At which a virgin hides her face.
Such dross the fire must purge away: 'tis just
The author blush, there where the reader must.

'Tis not such lines as almost crack the stage,
50   When Bajazet° begins to rage.
Nor a tall metaphor in the Oxford way,°
Nor the dry chips of short-lunged Seneca.°
        Nor upon all things to obtrude,
        And force some odd similitude.
What is it then, which like the Power Divine
We only can by negatives define?

In a true piece of wit all things must be,
        Yet all things there agree,
As in the ark, joined without force or strife,
60 All creatures dwelt, all creatures that had life;
        Or as the primitive forms of all
        (If we compare great things with small)
Which without discord or confusion lie,
In that strange mirror of the Deity.°

But Love that moulds one man up out of two,
        Makes me forget and injure you.
I took you for myself sure when I thought
That you in anything were to be taught.
        Correct my error with thy pen,
70   And if any ask me then,
What thing right wit and height of genius° is,
I'll only show your lines, and say, ' 'Tis this.'
                        1656

The Grasshopper°

Happy insect, what can be
In happiness compared to thee?
Fed with nourishment divine,
The dewy morning's gentle wine!
Nature waits upon thee still,
And thy verdant cup does fill;

one noise and sound: he means puns
acrostics poems and initial letters of whose lines
spell out a message
Bajazet defeated potentate in Marlowe's *Tamburlaine the Great*
tall . . . way high-flown, bombastic rhetoric
Seneca The Roman tragedian's style was more terse.

mirror of the Deity perhaps the hyaline stone
in Revelation 4:6
genius in the sense of "wit" (which, in Italian,
is "ingegno")
The Grasshopper a translation of the Anacreontic
poem from which Lovelace derives his remarkable "The Grasshopper." Cowley expands considerably on the original.

'Tis filled wherever thou dost tread,
Nature's self's thy Ganymede.°
Thou dost drink and dance and sing,
10   Happier than the happiest king!°
All the fields which thou dost see,
All the plants, belong to thee;
All that summer hours produce,
Fertile made with early juice.
Man for thee does sow and plow,
Farmer he, and landlord thou!
Thou dost innocently joy,
Nor does thy luxury° destroy;
The shepherd gladly heareth thee,
20   More harmonious than he.
Thee country hinds with gladness hear,
Prophet of the ripened year!
Thee Phœbus° loves and does inspire;
Phœbus is himself thy sire.
To thee of all things upon earth
Life is no longer than thy mirth.
Happy insect, happy thou,
Dost neither age nor winter know.
But when thou'st drunk and danced and sung
30   Thy fill the flowery leaves among,
Voluptuous and wise withal,
Epicurean animal!°
Sated with thy summer feast,
Thou retirest to endless rest.
                    1656

The Praise of Pindar° in Imitation of Horace His Second Ode, Book 4

Pindarum quisquis studet œmulari, &.

Pindar is imitable by none;
    The phoenix Pindar° is a vast species alone.
Whoe'er but Dædalus with waxen wings could fly
And neither sink too low nor soar too high?°
        What could he who followed claim
But of vain boldness the unhappy fame,

Ganymede Zeus' cup-bearer
Happier . . . king Again, see what use Lovelace makes of this.
luxury lust ("luxuria" was one of the seven deadly sins)
Phœbus Apollo, as lord of stringed music; grasshoppers were always thought of as fiddling, never piping (perhaps because of biological fact).
Epicurean animal The Greek philosopher Epicurus was taken as the proverbial theoretican of enjoyment.

The Praise of Pindar one of Cowley's programmatic "Pindaric" or "irregular" odes
phoenix Pindar there is only one phoenix, it is individual and species in one; this is the first of the bird images in the poem
Daedalus . . . high the fabulous artificer of antiquity, who built the labyrinth for Minos in which to hide the Minotaur, and escaped out of it on wax wings; his son, Icarus, flew too high, his wings melted, and down he fell

And by his fall a sea to name?
Pindar's unnavigable song,
Like a swollen flood from some steep mountain, pours along;
10   The ocean meets with such a voice
From his enlargèd mouth as drowns the ocean's noise.

So Pindar does new words and figures roll
Down his impetuous dithyrambic° tide,
      Which in no channel deigns to abide,
      Which neither banks nor dikes control.
      Whether the immortal gods he sings
      In a no less immortal strain,
Or the great acts of god-descended kings,
Who in his numbers° still survive and reign,
20   Each rich embroidered line,
   Which their triumphant brows around
      By his sacred hand is bound,
Does all their starry diadems outshine.

Whether at Pisa's race° he please
To carve in polished verse the conquerors' images,
Whether the swift, the skillful, or the strong
Be crownèd in his nimble, artful, vigorous song,
Whether some brave young man's untimely fate
In words worth dying for he celebrate,
30   Such mournful and such pleasing words
As joy to his mother's and his mistress' grief affords,
      He bids him live and grow in fame;
      Among the stars he sticks his name;
The grave can but the dross of him devour,
So small is death's, so great the poet's power.

Lo, how the obsequious wind and swelling air
      The Theban swan° does upwards bear
Into the walks of clouds, where he does play,
And with extended wings opens his liquid way,
40   Whilst, alas, my timorous Muse
      Unambitious tracks pursues;
      Does, with weak, unballast° wings,
      About the mossy brooks and springs,
      About the trees' new-blossomed heads,
      About the gardens' painted beds,
      About the fields and flowery meads,
      And all inferior beauteous things,
         Like the laborious bee,
      For little drops of honey flee,
50   And there with humble sweets contents her industry.

                                    1656

dithyrambic inspired, ecstatic
numbers verses
Pisa's race the Olympic games

Theban swan Pindar; see Ben Jonson's poem
to Shakespeare
unballast unsteady

ANDREW MARVELL
1621–1678

Marvell, the son of a Yorkshire Calvinist clergyman, was educated at Hull Grammar School and Trinity College, Cambridge. At eighteen he was temporarily converted to Roman Catholicism; at twenty he lost his Cambridge appointment. When the Civil War began in 1642 he was traveling in Europe. At the end of the war he found himself on the winning anti-Royalist side, and became tutor, at Nunappleton in Yorkshire, to Mary Fairfax, daughter of the victorious Commonwealth general. Later he was tutor to William Dutton, Cromwell's prospective son-in-law, and traveled with Dutton; in 1657 he became Latin Secretary as a colleague of Milton. In 1659, after the death of Cromwell, he became Member of Parliament for Hull, and held the seat till his death, serving also as secretary to English embassies in Russia, Denmark, and Sweden.

A bachelor, a man of violent temper, and in his later years a powerful controversialist, Marvell seems to have written his lyric poetry by the early 1650's; his satirical verse and prose belong to the Restoration period, and for a long time his reputation was primarily as a patriot, satirist, and prose-writer. The appearance in 1681 of his *Miscellaneous Poems* attracted little notice. His lyric poetry, then out of fashion, is highly individual yet related, in close and interesting ways, to that of Jonson, Carew, Lovelace, and Randolph. His range and virtuosity are greater than any of theirs, except Jonson's; and the central comment on his lyric verse is T. S. Eliot's: "Marvell's best verse is the product of European, that is to say Latin, culture," and from this he derives his *wit* and his *magniloquence*. His wit Eliot speaks of as "a tough reasonableness beneath the slight lyric grace," which, playing over "the great traditional commonplaces of European literature," renews them. Thus we have transferred from his political to his poetic reputation the words of his epitaph, which grant him "wit and learning, with a singular penetration and strength of judgment."

A Dialogue Between the Resolved Soul and Created Pleasure°

Courage my soul, now learn to wield
The weight of thine immortal shield.°
Close on thy head thy helmet° bright.
Balance thy sword° against the fight.
See where an army, strong as fair,
With silken banners° spreads the air.
Now, if thou be'st that thing divine,
In this day's combat let it shine:
And show that nature wants an art
10   To conquer one resolvèd heart.

A Dialogue . . . Pleasure The tempter, in this schematic poem, deploys against the Resolved Soul all the elements of the total temptation suffered by Christ in the wilderness. First the senses are the targets, and the Chorus intervenes at line 45 to comment on their successful resistance. Then follow the temptations of voluptuous sex, money, glory, and forbidden knowledge. Having overcome these, the Soul has defeated all temptation, and the Chorus ends the work by proclaiming this fact.

shield . . . helmet . . . sword "the whole armour of God" (Ephesians 6:11, 13, 16, 17) worn by the *miles Christi*, soldier of Christ and his imitator

army . . . banners "terrible as an army with banners," Song of Songs 6:4

PLEASURE   Welcome the creation's guest,
              Lord of earth, and heaven's heir.
              Lay aside that warlike crest,
              And of nature's banquet share:
              Where the souls of fruits and flowers
              Stand prepared to heighten yours.°

SOUL   I sup above, and cannot stay
              To bait° so long upon the way.

PLEASURE   On these downy pillows lie,
              Whose soft plumes will thither fly;
              On these roses strowed so plain°
              Lest one leaf° thy side should strain.

SOUL   My gentler rest is on a thought,
              Conscious of doing what I ought.

PLEASURE   If thou be'st with perfumes pleased,
              Such as oft the gods appeased,
              Thou in fragrant clouds shalt show
              Like another god below.

SOUL   A soul that knows not to presume
              Is heaven's and its own perfume.

PLEASURE   Everything does seem to vie
              Which should first attract thine eye;
              But since none deserves that grace,
              In this crystal° view *thy* face.

SOUL   When the Creator's skill is prized,
              The rest is all but earth disguised.

PLEASURE   Hark how music then prepares
              For thy stay° these charming airs;
              When the posting winds recall,
              And suspend the river's fall.

SOUL   Had I but any time to lose,
              On this I would it all dispose.
              Cease, Tempter. None can chain a mind
              Whom this sweet chordage° cannot bind.

CHORUS   *Earth cannot show so brave a sight*
              As when a single soul does fence
              The batteries of alluring sense,
              And Heaven views it with delight.
                 Then persevere, for still new charges sound;
                 And if thou overcom'st thou shalt be crowned.

Where the souls . . . yours where the essences
of fruits and flowers will be ready to stimulate
your (lower or sensitive) soul
bait pause for refreshment
plain flat
one leaf remembering the Sybarite who was
made uncomfortable by a crumpled rose petal
(a tale told by Seneca)
crystal looking-glass
stay sustenance
chordage bonds, musical chords

PLEASURE   All this fair and soft and sweet,
      Which scatteringly doth shine,
   Shall within one beauty° meet,
      And she be only thine.

SOUL   If things of sight such heavens be,
   What heavens are those we cannot see?

PLEASURE   Wheresoe'er thy foot shall go
      The minted gold shall lie;
   Till thou purchase all below,
60   And want new worlds to buy.

SOUL   Were't not a price who'd value gold?
   And that's worth nought that can be sold.

PLEASURE   Wilt thou all the glory have
      That war or peace commend?
   Half the world shall be thy slave,
      The other half thy friend.

SOUL   What friends, if to my self untrue?
   What slaves, unless I captive you?

PLEASURE   Thou shalt know each hidden cause,°
70   And see the future time;
   Try what depth the centre° draws,
      And then to heaven climb.

SOUL   None thither mounts by the degree°
   Of knowledge, but humility.

CHORUS   *Triumph, triumph, victorious soul;*
   The world has not one pleasure more:°
   The rest does lie beyond the pole,
   And is thine everlasting store.
                1681

A Dialogue Between the Soul and Body°

SOUL   Oh, who shall from this dungeon raise
      A soul enslaved so many ways?
      With bolts of bones; that fettered stands
      In feet, and manacled in hands;°
      Here blinded with an eye, and there

within one beauty remembering the painter Zeuxis who brought together the beauties of many models in his portrait of Helen
cause antecedent of natural phenomenon
centre of the earth
degree ladder (pun on academic sense)
not . . . more all temptations are exhausted, as in Luke 4:13
A Dialogue . . . Body For the theme see

Galatians 5:17: "the flesh lusteth against the spirit, and the spirit against the flesh: and these are contrary the one to the other."
bolts . . . hands The soul sees the organs of the body as having, for it, exactly the opposite of their obvious functions; the feet *fetter*, the hands *manacle* (Latin, *manus*, hand), the eye blinds, and the ear deafens.

Deaf with the drumming of an ear;
A soul hung up, as 'twere, in chains
Of nerves and arteries and veins;
Tortured, besides each other part,
In a vain head and double heart.°

BODY   Oh, who shall me deliver whole
From bonds of this tyrannic soul?
Which stretched upright, impales° me so
That mine own precipice I go;
And warms and moves this needless° frame,
A fever could but do the same.
And, wanting where its spite to try,
Has made me live to let me die.
A body that could never rest,
Since this ill spirit it possessed.

SOUL   What magic° could me thus confine
Within another's grief to pine?
Where whatsoever it complain,
I feel, that cannot feel, the pain.°
And all my care itself employs,
That to preserve which me destroys.
Constrained not only to endure
Diseases, but, what's worse, the cure;
And ready oft the port° to gain,
Am shipwrecked into health again.

BODY   But physic yet could never reach
The maladies° thou me dost teach:
Whom first the cramp of hope does tear,
And then the palsy shakes of fear;
The pestilence of love does heat,
Or hatred's hidden ulcer eat.
Joy's cheerful madness does perplex,
Or sorrow's other madness vex;
Which knowledge forces me to know,
And memory will not forgo.
What but a soul could have the wit
To build me up for sin so fit?
So architects do square and hew
Green trees that in the forest grew.°

1681

head . . . heart these words used by the soul in their figurative instead of their organic senses, the head egotistic, the heart treacherous
impales The soul, responsible for the body's motion, holds it reluctantly upright, like a man impaled.
needless that doesn't need it
magic Magicians—like Prospero—could confine spirits within trees.

whatsoever . . . pain whatever ill the body complains of, I experience the pain, although (except for my connection with it) I am immaterial and so impervious to pain
port death
maladies spiritual ills
So . . . grew just as architects take naturally round trees and make square pillars of them

The Nymph Complaining for the Death of Her Fawn°

The wanton troopers° riding by
Have shot my fawn, and it will die.
Ungentle men! They cannot thrive
To kill thee. Thou ne'er didst alive
Them any harm, alas, nor could
Thy death yet do them any good.
I'm sure I never wished them ill,
Nor do I for all this, nor will;
But if my simple prayers may yet
10   Prevail with heaven to forget
The murder, I will join my tears
Rather than fail. But oh, my fears!
It cannot die so.° Heaven's King
Keeps register of everything,
And nothing may we use in vain.
Ev'n beasts must be with justice slain,
Else men are made their deodands;°
Though they should wash their guilty hands,
In this warm life-blood, which doth part
20   From thine, and wound me to the heart,
Yet could they not be clean, their stain
Is dyed in such a purple grain.
There is not such another in
The world to offer for their sin.
    Unconstant Sylvio, when yet
I had not found him counterfeit,
One morning (I remember well)
Tied in this silver chain and bell,
Gave it to me: nay, and I know
30   What he said then; I'm sure I do:
Said he, 'Look how your huntsman here
Hath taught a fawn to hunt his dear.'°
But Sylvio soon had me beguiled;

This waxèd tame, while he grew wild,
And quite regardless of my smart,
Left me his fawn, but took his heart.°
   Thenceforth I set myself to play
My solitary time away
With this, and very well content,
40 Could so mine idle life have spent;
For it was full of sport and light
Of foot and heart, and did invite
Me to its game: it seemed to bless
Itself in me; how could I less
Than love it? Oh, I cannot be
Unkind to a beast that loveth me.
   Had it lived long, I do not know
Whether it too might have done so
As Sylvio did; his gifts might be
50 Perhaps as false, or more, than he;
But I am sure, for aught that I
Could in so short a time espy,
Thy love was far more better than
The love of false and cruel men.
   With sweetest milk and sugar, first
I it at mine own fingers nursed;
And as it grew, so every day
It waxed more white and sweet than they.
It had so sweet a breath! And oft
60 I blushed to see its foot more soft
And white, shall I say than my hand?
Nay, any lady's of the land.
   It is a wondrous thing how fleet
'Twas on those little silver feet;
With what a pretty skipping grace
It oft would challenge me the race;
And when it had left me far away,
'Twould stay, and run again, and stay;
For it was nimbler much than hinds,
70 And trod as if on the four° winds.
   I have a garden of my own,
But so with roses overgrown,
And lilies, that you would it guess
To be a little wilderness;
And all the springtime of the year
It only lovèd to be there.
Among the beds of lilies I
Have sought it oft, where it should lie,
Yet could not, till itself would rise,

heart heart-hart   **four** disyllabic

80 Find it, although before mine eyes;
For in the flaxen lilies' shade,
It like a bank of lilies laid.
Upon the roses it would feed,
Until its lips e'en seemed to bleed;
And then to me 'twould boldly trip,
And print those roses on my lip.
But all its chief delight was still
On roses thus itself to fill,
And its pure virgin limbs to fold
90 In whitest sheets of lilies cold:
Had it lived long, it would have been
Lilies without, roses within.

O help! O help! I see it faint
And die as calmly as a saint!
See how it weeps! the tears do come
Sad, slowly dropping like a gum.
So weeps the wounded balsam;° so
The holy frankincense doth flow;
The brotherless Heliades°
100 Melt in such amber tears as these.
I in a golden vial will
Keep these two crystal tears, and fill
It till it do o'erflow with mine;
Then place it in Diana's shrine.

Now my sweet fawn is vanished to
Whither the swans and turtles go,
In fair Elysium to endure,
With milk-white lambs and ermines pure.
O do not run too fast; for I
110 Will but bespeak thy grave, and die.
First, my unhappy statue shall
Be cut in marble, and withal
Let it be weeping, too; but there
Th' engraver sure his art may spare;
For I so truly thee bemoan
That I shall weep, though I be stone,°
Until my tears, still dropping, wear
My breast, themselves engraving there.
There at my feet shalt thou be laid,
120 Of purest alabaster made;
For I would have thine image be
White as I can, though not as thee.

1681

balsam both the balsam-tree and its resin
Heliades the three daughters of the sun god
Helios who, after mourning the death of their
brother Phaeton, were changed into amber-
dropping trees
stone like the weeping Niobe, who was turned
to stone

To His Coy Mistress°

Had we but world enough, and time,
This coyness, Lady, were no crime.
We would sit down, and think which way
To walk, and pass our long love's day.
Thou by the Indian Ganges' side
Shouldst rubies find; I by the tide
Of Humber° would complain. I would
Love you ten years before the Flood,
And you should, if you please, refuse
10   Till the Conversion of the Jews.°
My vegetable° love should grow
Vaster than empires and more slow;
An hundred years should go to praise
Thine eyes, and on thy forehead gaze;
Two hundred to adore each breast,
But thirty thousand to the rest;
An age at least to every part,
And the last age should show your heart.
For, Lady, you deserve this state,°
20   Nor would I love at lower rate.

But at my back I always hear
Time's wingèd chariot° hurrying near;
And yonder all before us lie
Deserts of vast eternity.
Thy beauty shall no more be found,
Nor, in thy marble vault, shall sound
My echoing song; then worms shall try
That long-preserved virginity,
And your quaint° honour turn to dust,
30   And into ashes all my lust:
The grave's a fine and private place,
But none, I think, do there embrace.
Now therefore, while the youthful hue
Sits on thy skin like morning dew,
And while thy willing soul transpires

To His Coy Mistress The theme is ancient: seize the day, there is no love-making in hell. Even the catalogue of a girl's charms (*blazon*, see Glossary) is old, though here merely sketched in derisive rejection of her notion that she exists in a world where there is plenty of time. The ultimate source is a poem by Asclepiades in the Greek Anthology: "You spare your maidenhead, and to what profit? For when you come to Hades you will not find your lover, girl. Among the living are the delights of Venus; but, maiden, we shall lie in the underworld mere bones and dust." Marvell's lover is masculine and physical, at war with time and with metaphysical notions of love. The abstraction "virginity" is, for him, a hymen, a physical obstacle; so is "quaint honour"; even "quaint" puns on "cunt". The girl must see the terrifying Time of the conclusion as her enemy too.

Humber river on which stands Hull, Marvell's home town
Conversion of the Jews thought to be one of the concluding events of history
vegetable growing as slowly as vegetation
state ceremonial treatment
Time's . . . chariot Time is often winged, and often has a chariot; only Marvell, apparently, gives him both attributes at once.
quaint fastidious (for pun, see first note)

At every pore with instant fires,°
Now let us sport us while we may,
And now, like amorous birds of prey,
Rather at once our time devour
40 Than languish in his slow-chapt° power.
Let us roll all our strength and all
Our sweetness up into one ball,
And tear our pleasures with rough strife
Thorough° the iron gates of life;
Thus, though we cannot make our sun
Stand still, yet we will make him run.°

1681

The Definition of Love°

My love is of a birth as rare
As 'tis, for object, strange and high;
It was begotten by Despair
Upon Impossibility.

Magnanimous Despair alone
Could show me so divine a thing,
Where feeble Hope could ne'er have flown,
But vainly flapped its tinsel wing.

And yet I quickly might arrive
10 Where my extended soul° is fixed;
But Fate does iron wedges drive,
And always crowds itself betwixt.

For Fate with jealous eyes does see
Two perfect loves, nor lets them close;°
Their union would her ruin be,
And her tyrannic power depose.

And therefore her decrees of steel
Us as the distant poles have placed
(Though Love's whole world on us doth wheel),
20 Not by themselves to be embraced;

willing . . . fires her coyness cannot prevent
her amorous spirit from showing in her flushed
face
slow-chapt power power of his devouring jaws
Thorough through
Let us roll . . . run discontinuous and urgent.
The first two lines suggest a pomander, the
next couplet a forcing of pleasure out of the
dull constriction of ordinary life; and the last
says the lovers cannot treat the sun like Joshua,
who made it stand still, but should treat it like
David, who made it come forth like a bridegroom to run his race.

The Definition of Love Not very like other
"Definitions of Love" in the period; rather a
poem on the known topic, "in love despair
is nobler than hope," developed by metaphysical
conceits to the point where the structure of
nature would have to be changed to bring the
lovers together; a situation in which the lover
takes despairing pride
extended soul It resides in his mistress, not in
him.
close unite

Unless the giddy heaven fall,
And earth some new convulsion tear,
And, us to join, the world should all
Be cramped into a planisphere.°

As lines, so loves, oblique may well
Themselves in every angle greet;
But ours, so truly parallel,
Though infinite, can never meet.

Therefore the love which us doth bind,
30 But Fate so enviously debars,
Is the conjunction of the mind,
And opposition° of the stars.

                    1681

The Picture of Little T. C.°
In a Prospect of Flowers

See with what simplicity
This nymph begins her golden days!
In the green grass she loves to lie,
And there with her fair aspect tames
The wilder flowers, and gives them names;°
But only with the roses plays,
        And them does tell
What colour best becomes them, and what smell.

Who can foretell for what high cause
10 This darling of the gods° was born?
Yet this is she whose chaster laws
The wanton Love shall one day fear,
And under her command severe
See his bow broke and ensigns torn.
        Happy, who can
Appease this virtuous enemy of man!

Oh then let me in time compound,
And parley with those conquering eyes,
Ere they have tried their force to wound;
20 Ere with their glancing wheels they drive
In triumph over hearts that strive,
And them that yield but° more despise.
        Let me be laid
Where I may see thy glories from some shade.

planisphere map of the worlds or heavens projected on a plane surface
conjunction . . . opposition astrological terms—
the proximity and the maximum separation of
planets
T. C. perhaps Theophila Cornewall (b. 1644)

gives them names traditionally Adam's task in
Paradise (see Genesis 2:19)
darling of the gods Theophila means "dear to
the gods."
but only

Meantime, whilst every verdant thing
Itself does at thy beauty charm,
Reform the errors of the spring:
Make that the tulips may have share
Of sweetness, seeing they are fair;
30   And roses of their thorns disarm;
      But most procure
That violets may a longer age endure.

But, O young beauty of the woods,
Whom nature courts with fruits and flowers,
Gather the flowers, but spare the buds,
Lest Flora, angry at thy crime,
To kill her infants in their prime,
Do quickly make the example yours;
      And ere we see,
40   Nip in the blossom all our hopes and thee.
                    1681

The Mower Against Gardens°

Luxurious° man, to bring his vice in use,°
    Did after him the world seduce,
And from the fields the flowers and plants allure,
    Where Nature was most plain and pure.
He first enclosed within the gardens square
    A dead and standing pool of air,
And a more luscious earth for them did knead,
    Which stupefied them while it fed.
The pink grew then as double as his mind;
10   The nutriment did change the kind.
With strange perfumes he did the roses taint;
    And flowers themselves were taught to paint.°
The tulip white did for complexion seek,
    And learned to interline its cheek;
Its onion root they then so high did hold,°
    That one was for a meadow sold:°
Another world was searched through oceans new,
    To find the *Marvel of Peru;*°

The Mower Against Gardens Gardens could be good (the art that improves nature) or bad (the art that corrupts nature). Grafting can be good when it improves the natural stock; or bad, since the gardener is acting like a pander. Gardens can be the settings for debauchery or for meditation. These antitheses are frequent in the poetry of this period. Randolph's poem "Upon Love Fondly Refused for Conscience's Sake" is on the libertine side. Marvell, using the same Horatian epode measure, puts the other case, using many of the same instances but in the contrary sense. He makes his speaker a mower, who belongs to the fields outside the house and garden, and so not corrupt.
Luxurious lecherous, sinful
bring . . . use to make a profit on his sin
paint apply make-up
hold value
one . . . sold At the height of Dutch tulipo-mania in the 1630's bulbs were bought for huge prices; the Mower naturally chooses "a meadow" to represent something of high value.
Marvel of Peru *Mirabilis jalapa* or *peruviana,* then an exotic flower

And yet these rarities might be allowed
20   To man, that sovereign thing and proud,
Had he not dealt between° the bark and tree,
    Forbidden mixtures° there to see.
No plant now knew the stock from which it came;
    He grafts upon the wild the tame,
That the uncertain and adulterate fruit
    Might put the palate in dispute.
His green seraglio has its eunuchs too,
    Lest any tyrant him outdo;
And in the cherry he does Nature vex,
30   To procreate without a sex.°
'Tis all enforced, the fountain and the grot,
    While the sweet fields do lie forgot,
Where willing Nature does to all dispense
    A wild and fragrant innocence;
And fauns and fairies do the meadows till
    More by their presence than their skill.
Their statues polished by some ancient hand,
    May to adorn the gardens stand;
But, howsoe'er the figures do excel,
40   The Gods themselves with us do dwell.

                                        1681

Damon the Mower

Hark how the mower Damon sung,
With love of Juliana stung!
While everything did seem to paint
The scene more fit for his complaint:
Like her fair eyes the day was fair;
But scorching like his am'rous care:
Sharp like his scythe his sorrow was,
And withered like his hopes the grass.

'Oh what ususual heats are here,
10   Which thus our sunburned meadows sear!
The grasshopper its pipe gives o'er;
And hamstringed° frogs can dance no more:
But in the brook the green frog wades,
And grasshoppers seek out the shades.
Only the snake, that kept within,
Now glitters in its second skin.

---

dealt between acted as pander for
Forbidden mixtures Cf. Deuteronomy 22:9.

To . . . sex probably a reference to a stoneless cherry
hamstringed lamed (by the heat)

'This heat the sun could never raise,
Nor Dog Star so inflames the days.
It from an higher beauty grow'th,
20   Which burns the fields and mower both:
Which made the Dog,° and makes the sun
Hotter than his own Phaëton.°
Not July causeth these extremes,
But Juliana's scorching beams.

'Tell me where I may pass the fires
Of the hot day, or hot desires.
To what cool cave shall I descend,
Or to what gelid fountain bend?
Alas! I look for ease in vain,
30   When remedies themselves complain;
No moisture but my tears do rest,
Nor cold but in her icy breast.

'How long wilt thou, fair Shepherdess,
Esteem me, and my presents less?
To thee the harmless snake I bring,
Disarmèd of its teeth and sting;
To thee chameleons changing hue,
And oak leaves tipped with honey dew.
Yet thou, ungrateful, hast not sought
40   Nor what they are, nor who them brought.

'I am the mower Damon, known
Through all the meadows I have mown.
On me the morn her dew distills
Before her darling daffodils:
And, if at noon my toil me heat,
The sun himself licks off my sweat;
While, going home, the evening sweet
In cowslip-water° bathes my feet.

'What though the piping shepherd stock
50   The plains with an unnumbered flock,
This scythe of mine discovers wide
More ground than all his sheep do hide.
With this the golden fleece I shear
Of all these closes° every year.
And though in wool more poor than they,
Yet am I richer far in hay.

'Nor am I so deformed to sight,°
If in my scythe I lookèd right;

made the Dog perhaps "mads the Dog" (Sirius)
Phaëton who failed to control the horses of
the sun
cowslip-water used by ladies to cleanse the skin
closes enclosed fields

deformed to sight using his scythe as a mirror,
whereas Virgil's Corydon, in the phrase Marvell
translates, was using a calm sea

In which I see my picture done,
As in a crescent moon the sun.
The deathless fairies take me oft
To lead them in their dances soft;
And, when I tune myself to sing,
About me they contract their ring.°

'How happy might I still have mowed,
Had not Love here his thistles sowed!
But now I all the day complain,
Joining my labour to my pain;
And with my scythe cut down the grass,
Yet still my grief is where it was;
But, when the iron blunter grows,
Sighing I whet my scythe and woes.'

While thus he threw his elbow round,
Depopulating all the ground,
And, with his whistling scythe, does cut
Each stroke between the earth and root,
The edgèd steel by careless chance
Did into his own ankle glance;
And there among the grass fell down,
By his own scythe, the mower mown.

'Alas!' said he, 'these hurts are slight
To those that die by Love's dispite.
With shepherd's-purse,° and clown's-all-heal,°
The blood I stanch, and wound I seal.
Only for him no cure is found,
Whom Juliana's eyes do wound.
'Tis death alone that this must do:
For Death, thou art a mower too.'

                    1681

The Mower to the Glowworms

Ye living lamps, by whose dear light
The nightingale does sit so late,
And studying all the summer-night,
Her matchless songs does meditate;

Ye country comets, that portend
No war, nor prince's funeral,°
Shining unto no higher end
Than to presage the grass's fall;°

---

ring the "fairy-ring" caused by certain fungi
shepherd's-purse a weed supposed to check bleeding
clown's-all-heal a nettle thought to heal wounds

funeral Comets were supposed to signify the death of great men.
grass's fall Glowworms were thought to appear only when the hay was ripe for cutting.

Ye glowworms, whose officious° flame
10 To wand'ring mowers shows the way,
That in the night have lost their aim,
And after foolish fires° do stray;

Your courteous lights in vain you waste,
Since Juliana here is come,
For she my mind hath so displaced
That I shall never find my home.

1681

The Garden°

How vainly men themselves amaze
To win the palm, the oak, or bays;°
And their uncessant labours see
Crowned from some single herb or tree:
Whose short and narrow-vergèd shade
Does prudently their toils upbraid;
While all flowers and all° trees do close°
To weave the garlands of repose.

Fair Quiet, have I found thee here,
10 And Innocence, thy sister dear!
Mistaken long, I sought you then
In busy companies of men.
Your sacred plants, if here below,
Only among the plants will grow.
Society is all but rude,
To this delicious solitude.°

No white nor red° was ever seen
So amorous as this lovely green.°
Fond lovers, cruel as their flame,
20 Cut in these trees their mistress' name:
Little, alas, they know or heed
How far these beauties hers exceed!
Fair trees, wheresoe'er your barks I wound,
No name shall but your own° be found.

officious attentive
foolish fires the *ignis fatuus* or will-o'-the-wisp.
Marsh-gas spontaneously ignited, was thought
to "mislead night wanderers."
The Garden The garden, like the biblical
"paradise of pleasure," satisfies the senses but
also calls for contemplation of the source of
these delights. It is not a libertine garden; there
is no woman in it, and the poem echoes the
misogynist tradition that Adam was better off
without Eve. The garden's color, green, is
good; other colors are not. Eventually the mind
withdraws from all that pleases the senses and
contemplates the source of pure light, broken
on earth (as the Platonists declared), into

variety. There is a return to the green pleasures
of the garden.
palm . . . oak . . . bays honors awarded for
war, statesmanship, poetry
all . . . all . . . as opposed to the *single* of
l. 4
close unite
Society . . . solitude paradoxical, since society
is usually thought more "polished" than retirement
white . . . red emblematic of female beauty
green by association, emblematic of solitude
and the absence of women
No . . . own since the trees are lovelier than
the girls, we should cut *their* names, not the
girls', in the barks

When we have run our passion's heat,°
Love hither makes his best retreat.°
The gods, that mortal beauty chase,
Still° in a tree did end their race:
Apollo hunted Daphne so,
30 Only that she might laurel grow;
And Pan did after Syrinx speed,
Not as a nymph, but for a reed.°

What wondrous life in this I lead!
Ripe apples drop about my head;
The luscious clusters of the vine
Upon my mouth do crush their wine;
The nectarine and curious peach
Into my hands themselves do reach;
Stumbling on melons, as I pass,
40 Ensnared with flowers, I fall on grass.°

Meanwhile the mind from pleasure less°
Withdraws into its happiness;
The mind, that ocean° where each kind
Does straight its own resemblance find;
Yet it creates, transcending these,
Far other worlds and other seas,°
Annihilating all that's made
To a green thought in a green shade.°

Here at the fountain's sliding foot,
50 Or at some fruit-tree's mossy root,
Casting the body's vest aside,
My soul into the boughs does glide:
There, like a bird, it sits and sings,
Then whets° and combs its silver wings,
And, till prepared for longer flights,°
Waves in its plumes the various light.°

Such was that happy garden-state,
While man there walked without a mate:°
After a place so pure and sweet,

heat ardor; race
retreat both military and religious senses
Still always
Apollo . . . reed contrary to the myth, which
represents Apollo as frustrated when Daphne
turned into a laurel, so with the story of Pan
and Syrinx, who escaped him by turning into
a reed
fall on grass harmlessly, unlike Adam
from . . . less experiencing less pleasure in
nature than the senses (and so turning inward)
ocean It was supposed that the sea contained
creatures parallel to all found on land; the
implication is that the mind is equipped in

advance to recognize everything in the world.
Yet . . . seas beyond this, the imagination
creates forms with no equivalents in reality
Annihilating . . . shade making the visible
world seem as nothing compared with what can
be imagined by the contemplative
whets preens
Till . . . flight resting, in its ascent, between
the created and the intelligible worlds
various light neoplatonic image of the white
light of eternity broken into color in the
temporal world
Such . . . mate the Garden of Eden before the
creation of Eve

60 What other help could yet be meet!°
    But 'twas beyond a mortal's share
    To wander solitary there:
    Two paradises 'twere in one
    To live in paradise alone.

    How well the skillful gardener drew,
    Of flowers and herbs, this dial new;°
    Where, from above, the milder sun
    Does through a fragrant° zodiac run;
    And, as it works, the industrious bee
70 Computes its time° as well as we!
    How could such sweet and wholesome hours
    Be reckoned but with herbs and flowers!

                                    1681

From Upon Appleton House°

    And now to the abyss I pass
370 Of that unfathomable grass,
    Where men like grasshoppers appear,
    But grasshoppers are giants° there:
    They, in their squeaking laugh, contemn
    Us as we walk more low than them;
    And, from the precipices tall
    Of the green spires, to us do call.

    To see men through this meadow dive
    We wonder how they rise alive;
    As, under water, none does know
380 Whether he fall through it or go;
    But as the mariners that sound
    And show upon their lead the ground,°
    They bring up flowers so to be seen,
    And prove they've at the bottom been.

---

help . . . meet "And the LORD God said, It is not good that the man should be alone; I will make him an help meet for him" (Genesis 2:18).
dial new new style of sundial (the whole garden)
milder . . . fragrant The sun is filtered through trees and on to green plants.
time pun on "thyme"
Upon Appleton House Appleton House, the home of Lord Fairfax, was once a priory but at the time a brick mansion with a center block and two wings. There was a large park, including watermeadows of the River Wharfe. The poem is a somewhat unusual member of a genre praising country houses and their lords. Marvell uses a "conceited" manner, corres-ponding as nearly as anything in English to the French *précieux* poetry. The house may represent its master, and Order, but Marvell applies to his theme a fantastic wit and many elaborate set pieces—on the house itself, its Catholic history, the garden, the mowing of the meadows (here extracted), the woods meet for contemplation (given here in part), the river, and Maria Fairfax, his pupil. The whole is what the French called a *tableau fantasque*, sustained with extraordinary wit and learning; some 200 lines must serve to give an impression of the whole, which has 776. At the outset the poet moves into the deep grass that is about to be mown.
grasshoppers . . . giants Cf. Numbers 13:33.
ground mud from seabed

No scene that turns with engines strange
Does oftener than these meadows change:
For when the sun the grass hath vexed,
The tawny mowers enter next;
Who seem like Israelites to be,
390 Walking on foot through a green sea.
To them the grassy deeps divide,
And crowd a lane to either side.°

With whistling scythe and elbow strong,
These massacre the grass along;
While one, unknowing, carves the rail,°
Whose yet unfeathered quills her fail.
The edge all bloody from its breast
He draws, and does his stroke detest;
Fearing the flesh untimely mowed°
400 To him a fate as black forebode.

But bloody Thestylis, that waits
To bring the mowing camp° their cates,°
Greedy as kites has trussed it up,
And forthwith means on it to sup;
When on another quick° she lights,
And cries, 'He° called us Israelites;
But now, to make his saying true,
Rails rain for quails, for manna dew.'°

Unhappy birds! what does it boot
410 To build below the grasses' root,
When lowness is unsafe as height,
And chance o'ertakes what scapeth spite?
And now your orphan parents' call
Sounds your untimely funeral.
Death-trumpets creak in such a note,
And 'tis the sourdine° in their throat.

Or sooner hatch or° higher build!
The mower now commands the field,
In whose new traverse° seemeth wrought
420 A camp of battle newly fought:
Where, as the meads with hay, the plain
Lies quilted o'er with bodies slain;
The women that with forks it fling,
Do represent the pillaging.

crowd . . . side crowd to either side to form
a lane, as the Red Sea did for the Israelites
rail corn crake, land bird
untimely mowed Cf. "Damon the Mower," l. 88.
mowing camp The mowers are thought of as
soldiers.
cates food
quick alive

He the poet, in l. 389, of whom she has somehow got knowledge
quails . . . dew Exodus 16:13–14
sourdine hoarse low trumpet, or mute producing
this effect
Or either
traverse passage cut through the field

And now the careless victors play,
Dancing the triumphs of the hay;°
Where every mower's wholesome heat
Smells like an Alexander's sweat,°
Their females fragrant as the mead
430 Which they in fairy circles° tread:
When at their dance's end they kiss,
Their new-made hay not sweeter is.

When after this 'tis piled in cocks,
Like a calm sea it shows the rocks;
We wondering in the river near
How boats among them safely steer.
Or, like the desert Memphis° sand,
Short pyramids of hay do stand.
And such° the Roman camps° do rise
440 In hills for soldiers' obsequies.

This scene again withdrawing° brings
A new and empty face of things;
A levelled space, as smooth and plain
As cloths° for Lely° stretched to stain.
The world when first created sure
Was such a table rase° and pure;
Or rather such is the *toril*°
Ere the bulls enter at Madril.°

For to this naked equal flat,
450 Which Levellers° take pattern at,°
The villagers in common° chase
Their cattle, which it closer rase;
And what below the scythe increased°
Is pinched yet nearer by the beast.
Such, in the painted world, appeared
Davenant with the universal Herd.°

They seem within the polished grass
A landskip drawn in looking-glass;°
And shrunk in the huge pasture show

hay country dance (with a pun)
Alexander's sweat According to Plutarch this
had a "passing delightful savor."
fairy circles See "Damon the Mower," l. 64.
Memphis Egyptian city near Pyramids
such in the same manner
Roman camps tumuli now known to be of ancient British origin
scene . . . withdrawing continues theatrical figure of l. 385
cloths canvases
Lely Sir Peter Lely, Dutch portrait painter
who went to England in 1641. See Fig. 33.
table rase *tabula rasa*
toril bullring
Madril Madrid

Levellers egalitarian political party, favoring
the leveling out of rank, parliamentary representation, etc.
take pattern at use as a model
in common The meadow is for common grazing.
what . . . increased what grew lower than the
scythe could cut
Davenant . . . Herd In Sir William Davenant's
admired contemporary epic *Gondibert* there is a
description of a painting of the Six Days of
Creation; on the sixth day "an universal Herd
appears."
landskip . . . glass landscape shown in a painting reflected in a mirror and thus reduced in
size

460 As spots, so shaped, on faces do.
     Such fleas, ere they approach the eye,
     In multiplying glasses lie;°
     They feed so wide, so slowly move,
     As constellations do above.

     Then to conclude these pleasant acts,
     Denton° sets ope its cataracts;
     And makes the meadow truly be
     (What it but seemed before) a sea.
     For, jealous of its lord's long stay,
470 It tries t'invite him thus away.
     The river in itself is drowned
     And isles the astonished cattle round.

     Let others tell the paradox,
     How eels now bellow in the ox;
     How horses at their tails do kick,
     Turned as they hang to leeches° quick;
     How boats can over bridges sail,
     And fishes do the stables scale;
     How salmons trespassing are found,
480 And pikes are taken in the pound.

     But I, retiring from the flood,
     Take sanctuary in the wood;
     And, while it lasts, myself embark
     In this yet green, yet growing ark;
     Where the first carpenter° might best
     Fit timber for his keel have pressed;°
     And where all creatures might have shares,
     Although in armies, not in pairs.

     The double wood of ancient stocks
490 Linked in, so thick an union locks,
     It like two pedigrees appears,
     On one hand Fairfax, th' other Veres;
     Of whom though many fell in war,°
     Yet more to heaven shooting are:
     And, as they Nature's cradle decked,
     Will in green age her hearse expect.

     When first the eye this forest sees
     It seems indeed as wood not trees:
     As if their neighbourhood° so old
500 To one great trunk them all did mould.

Such . . . lie so do fleas appear on the glass
before one looks at them through a microscope
Denton river flowing through the meadow
leeches Horsehairs in water were supposed to
turn into eels or leeches.

first carpenter Noah
pressed commandeered
fell in war were cut down to satisfy the war-
time demand for timber
neighbourhood proximity

There the huge bulk takes place, as meant
To thrust up a fifth element;°
And stretches still so closely wedged
As if the night within were hedged.

Dark all without it knits; within
It opens passable and thin;
And in as loose an order grows
As the Corinthian° porticoes.
The arching boughs unite between
510   The columns of the temple green;
And underneath the wingèd choirs
Echo about their tunèd fires.

The nightingale does here make choice
To sing the trials of her voice.
Low shrubs she sits in, and adorns
With music high the squatted thorns.
But highest oaks stoop down to hear,
And listening elders prick the ear.
The thorn, lest it should hurt her, draws
520   Within the skin its shrunken claws.

But I have for my music found
A sadder, yet more pleasing sound:
The stock doves, whose fair necks are graced
With nuptial rings, their ensigns chaste;
Yet always, for some cause unknown,
Sad pair, unto the elms they moan.
O why should such a couple mourn,
That in so equal flames do burn!

Then as I careless on the bed
530   Of gelid strawberries do tread,
And through the hazels thick espy
The hatching throstle's shining eye,
The heron from the ash's top
The eldest of its young lets drop,
As if it, stork-like,° did pretend
That tribute to its Lord to send.

But most the hewel's° wonders are,
Who here has the holt-felster's° care.
He walks still upright from the root,
540   Measuring the timber with his foot;
And all the way, to keep it clean,

---

fifth element of different substance from the
other four: earth, water, air, fire
Corinthian most ornate of the Greek architectural orders, also associated with moral laxity
(hence "looseness")

stork-like The stork was supposed to leave one
of its young behind as tribute to the owner.
hewel's green woodpecker's
holt-felster's woodcutter's

Doth from the bark the wood-moths glean.
He, with his beak, examines well
Which fit to stand and which to fell.

The good he numbers up, and hacks;
As if he marked them with the ax.
But where he, tinkling with his beak,
Does find the hollow oak to speak,
That for his building he designs,
550   And through the tainted side he mines.°
Who could have thought the tallest oak
Should fall by such a feeble stroke!

Nor would it, had the tree not fed
A traitor worm, within it bred.
(As first our flesh corrupt within
Tempts impotent and bashful sin.)
And yet that worm triumphs not long,
But serves to feed the hewel's young;
While the oak seems to fall content,
560   Viewing the treason's punishment.

Thus I, easy philosopher,
Among the birds and trees confer;
And little now to make me wants,
Or of the fowls or of the plants.
Give me but wings as they, and I
Straight floating on the air shall fly:
Or turn me but, and you shall see
I was but an inverted tree.°

· · ·

1681

An Horatian Ode upon Cromwell's Return from Ireland°

The forward° youth that would appear
Must now° forsake his Muses dear,
   Nor in the shadows sing
   His numbers languishing:
'Tis time to leave the books in dust,

mines burrows
tree "Man is like an inverted tree" is an old commonplace.
An Horatian Ode . . . Written between May and July 1650, after Cromwell's return from Ireland and before his Scottish campaign, which began in July. Marvell had in mind certain odes of Horace, and the *Pharsalia* of Lucan, which is about Julius Caesar and Pompey (Caesar also violated "ancient rights," as Charles I did). What makes this the greatest of political poems in English is its weight and control. Whether, as seems most likely, Marvell was at the time of writing committed to Cromwell, or whether the lines on the King's execution are not merely part of the rhetorical strategy but express sympathy for his cause, we feel principally a strong mind and a mature wit at work in the representation of a great historical crisis. The poem is soaked in history, not only English but imperial; and the force of its political realism is no greater than the gravity with which it deploys its sense of history, and of what has been lost.
forward ambitious
now in times like these

And oil th' unusèd armour's rust,
  Removing from the wall
  The corslet of the hall.
So restless Cromwell could not cease
10 In the inglorious arts of peace,
  But through adventurous war
  Urgèd his active star;
And like the three-forked lightning, first
Breaking the clouds where it was nursed,
  Did thorough° his own side°
  His fiery way divide.
For 'tis all one to courage high,
The emulous or enemy;
  And with such to inclose
20 Is more than to oppose.°
Then burning through the air he went,
And palaces and temples rent;
  And Cæsar's° head at last
  Did through his laurels° blast.
'Tis madness to resist or blame
The force of angry heaven's flame;
  And, if we would speak true,
  Much to the man is due,
Who, from his private gardens, where
30 He lived reservèd and austere
  (As if his highest plot
  To plant the bergamot),°
Could by industrious valour climb
To ruin the greatest work of time,
  And cast the kingdoms old
  Into another mould;
Though Justice against Fate complain,
And plead the ancient rights in vain;
  But those do hold or break,
40 As men are strong or weak.
Nature, that hateth emptiness,
Allows of penetration° less,
  And therefore must make room
  Where greater spirits come.
What field of all the civil wars,
Where his were not the deepest scars?
  And Hampton shows what part
  He had of wiser art;

thorough through
side party. But the lightning tears through its
own body, namely, the cloud.
with . . . oppose to pen him in will produce
an even more violent reaction than to fight
against him

Cæsar's Charles I, beheaded in 1649
laurels supposed to be proof against lightning
bergamot kind of pear
penetration occupation of same space by two
bodies at the same time

Where, twining subtle° fears with hope,
50 He wove a net of such a scope
        That Charles himself might chase
        To Carisbrooke's° narrow case,°
    That thence the Royal Actor° borne
    The tragic scaffold might adorn;
        While round the armèd bands
        Did clap° their bloody hands.
    He nothing common did, or mean,
    Upon that memorable scene,
        But with his keener° eye
60   The axe's edge did try;°
    Nor called the gods with vulgar spite
    To vindicate his helpless right;
        But bowed his comely head
        Down, as upon a bed.°
    This was that memorable hour
    Which first assured the forcèd° power;
        So, when they did design
        The Capitol's first line,
    A bleeding head, where they begun,
70 Did fright the architects to run;
        And yet in that the state
        Foresaw its happy fate.°
    And now the Irish are ashamed
    To see themselves in one year° tamed;
        So much one man can do
        That does both act and know.°
    They° can affirm his praises best,
    And have, though overcome, confessed
        How good he is, how just,
80   And fit for highest trust,
    Nor yet grown stiffer with command,
    But still in the republic's hand—
        How fit is he to sway
        That can so well obey!
    He to the Commons' feet presents
    A kingdom for his first year's rents;
        And, what he may,° forbears
        His fame, to make it theirs;

subtle finely woven
Carisbrooke's In 1648 Charles fled from Hampton Court to Carisbrooke in the Isle of Wight, but did not receive the welcome he expected, and was made prisoner; but it seems not to be true that Cromwell engineered this.
case cage
Actor This theatrical figure continues in *scaffold*, *clap*, *scene*.
clap Some said the soldiers were told to clap to render the King's last words inaudible.
keener than the ax's edge; *acies* is Latin for both "eyesight" and "blade." The King's eyes were said to be very bright on the scaffold, and he asked about the sharpness of the ax.
try test
bowed . . . bed Arrangements to drag his head down by force were unnecessary.
forcèd gained by force
So . . . fate This myth about the building of the Roman Capitol is in Pliny.
in one year Cromwell's Irish campaign lasted from August 1649 to May 1650.
act and know excel in action as in contemplation
They the Irish
what he may as far as he can

And has his sword and spoils ungirt,
90   To lay them at the public's skirt:
    So when the falcon high
    Falls heavy from the sky,
She, having killed, no more does search
But on the next green bough to perch;
    Where, when he first does lure,
    The falconer has her sure.
What may not, then, our isle presume,
While victory his crest does plume?
    What may not others fear,
100   If thus he crown each year?
A Cæsar he, ere long, to Gaul,
To Italy an Hannibal,
    And to all states not free
    Shall climactèric° be.
The Pict° no shelter now shall find
Within his party-coloured° mind,
    But from this valour sad°
    Shrink underneath the plaid;
Happy if in the tufted brake
110   The English hunter him mistake,°
    Nor lay his hounds in near
    The Caledonian° deer.
But thou, the war's and fortune's son,
March indefatigably on!
    And for the last effect,
    Still keep thy sword erect;
Besides the force it has to fright
The spirits of the shady night,°
    The same arts that did gain
120   A power must it maintain.

                1681

GEORGE HERBERT

1593–1633

George Herbert's greatness as a religious poet came in some measure from his struggle with the temptations of poetry itself. His carefully arranged collection of English poems called *The Temple* was published posthumously in 1633, and had gone through thirteen editions by 1709, influencing Crashaw, Vaughan, and Traherne—to mention only three of his followers—in a variety of ways. Herbert was born of a distinguished family, the younger brother of Lord Herbert of Cherbury; he was educated at Westminster School

---

climacteric critical; marking an epoch
Pict Scots tribe
party-coloured variously colored (suggested by "Pict" and its similarity to the Latin verb "to paint"), that is, changeable
sad severe

mistake because of his camouflaging colors
Caledonian Scottish
force . . . night not because of the uplifted cross-hilt, but because the sun glitters on the blade

and Trinity College, Cambridge, elected to a fellowship and a readership after that, and served as a member of Parliament for two years. In 1630 he became rector of Bemerton, near Salisbury, and it was apparently during the last years of his life that almost all of his English poems were composed.

The Temple is an astonishing work, reflecting at once a discontent with the fashions of complex, post-Petrarchan amatory verse which we loosely call the Metaphysical tradition, and a brilliant and subtle use of all those arts of image-making and rhetoric practiced by Donne and used by Herbert to cast doubt on the purity of any discourse which would employ them. The Temple is in one sense a constant attempt, in poem after poem, to make poetry do the work of prayer and devotion. They substitute for the Petrarchan poet's implicit pleading to his muse to grant authenticity to the poems he writes for her a prayer to God for their own moral genuineness. In another way, these poems go to make up a private liturgy of the vicarage, a day-to-day meditative regimen attuned not to canonical hours or days, but to a personal array of occasions. The poems present a spectrum of almost celestial variety: not only is the range of versification and stanza form amazing (every poem is in some formal way unique), but the centers of meditative attention in them vary widely as well.

Almost every aspect of clerical life becomes an emblem for Herbert: parts of the church building, on the one hand, sections of biblical text, on the other. Scriptural allusions and quotations abound, as do a host of formal figurative devices—ways of making the printed text of the poem itself the *impresa,* or picture, of the emblem they make up, as well as the *motto,* or caption. Herbert may have been influenced in his sense of formal variety by the songs from Sir Philip Sidney's *Arcadia,* and by the metrical psalm paraphrases of Sidney and his sister, the Countess of Pembroke (see The Psalms in English Verse, above). Herbert's poetic world is ever-conscious of music as well, and he employs the word "sing" in a way parallel to, but very different from, the Jonsonian, neoclassical poet's use to mean "write poetry."

From The Temple

Love-joy

As on a window late I cast mine eye,
I saw a vine drop grapes with *J* and *C*
Annealed° to every bunch. One standing by
Asked what it meant; I, who am never loth
To spend my judgment, said, It seemed to me
To be the body and the letters both
Of *Joy* and *Charity.* 'Sir, you have not missed,'
The man replied; 'It figures° JESUS CHRIST.'

1633

Annealed the grapes are in a stained-glass window   **figures** both in the sense of "pictures" and of "symbolizes"

The Altar°

A broken ALTAR, Lord, thy servant rears,
Made of a heart, and cémented with tears;
  Whose parts are as thy hand did frame;
  No workman's tool hath touched the same.°
      A   HEART   alone
      Is   such   a   stone
      As   nothing   but
      Thy   power doth cut.
      Wherefore each   part
      Of   my   hard   heart
      Meets   in   this   frame,
      To   praise   thy   Name;
  That, if I chance to hold my peace,
  These stones to praise thee may not cease.
O let thy blessèd SACRIFICE be mine,
And santify this ALTAR to be thine.

                       1633

Denial°

    When my devotions could not pierce
              Thy silent ears;
  Then was my heart broken, as was my verse:
         My breast was full of fears
                  And disorder:

    My bent thoughts, like a brittle bow,
              Did fly asunder:
  Each took his way; some would to pleasures go,
         Some to the wars and thunder
                  Of alarms.

     'As good go any where,' they say,
           'As to benumb
  Both knees and heart, in crying night and day,
      Come, come, my God, O come,
              But no hearing.'

    O that thou shouldst give dust a tongue
             To cry to thee,
  And then not hear it crying! all day long
        My heart was in my knee,
              But no hearing.

The Altar This and "Easter-Wings," another "pattern poem," represent a Renaissance revival of an Alexandrian tradition of shaping poems like eggs, pillars, even the pipe of Pan; altars were the most common form, rhymed iambic lines being easily arranged in such a shape.
No workman's . . . same Herbert is remembering "And if thou wilt make me an altar of stone, thou shalt not build it of hewn stone: for if thou lift up thy tool upon it, thou hast polluted it" (Exodus 20:25).
Denial The unrhyming final lines of each stanza are, at the end, granted rhyming status.

Therefore my soul lay out of sight,
                    Untuned, unstrung;
My feeble spirit, unable to look right,
            Like a nipped blossom, hung
                                Discontented.

O cheer and tune my heartless breast,
                    Defer no time;
That so thy favours granting my request,
            They and my mind may chime,
30   And mend my rhyme.
                                1633

Easter-Wings°

Lord, who createdst man in wealth and store,°
    Though foolishly he lost the same,
        Decaying more and more,
            Till he became
                Most poor:
                With thee
                O let me rise
            As larks, harmoniously,
    And sing this day thy victories:
10 Then shall the fall further the flight in me.

My tender age in sorrow did begin:
    And still with sicknesses and shame
        Thou didst so punish sin,
            That I became
                Most thin.
                With thee
            Let me combine,
        And feel this day thy victory:
    For, if I imp° my wing on thine,
20 Affliction shall advance the flight in me.
                                1633

Easter-Wings based on a Greek poem shaped like Cupid's wings. Notice how, when turned so that the lines are vertical, the two stanzas resemble a pair of angels rising upward, seen from behind; as printed regularly, it is in a lozenge shape whose "meaning" is "first narrow, then widen" or a meaning of Easter: "descent in order that there may be ascent."
store abundance
imp to graft feathers on a falcon's damaged wing

Our Life Is Hid with Christ in God

COLOSS. 3. 3.°

My words and thoughts do both express this notion,
That *Life* hath with the sun a double motion.°
The first *Is* straight, and our diurnal friend,
The other *Hid,* and doth obliquely bend.
One life is wrapped *In* flesh, and tends to earth:
The other winds towards *Him,* whose happy birth
Taught me to live here so, *That* still one eye
Should aim and shoot at that which *Is* on high:
Quitting with daily labour all *My* pleasure,
To gain at harvest an eternal *Treasure.*

1633

The Pearl°

MATTH. 13. 45

I know the ways of Learning; both the head
And pipes that feed the press,° and make it run;
What reason hath from nature borrowèd,
Or of itself, like a good huswife, spun
In laws and policy; what the stars conspire;
What willing nature speaks, what forced by fire;
Both the old discoveries, and the new-found seas,
The stock and surplus, cause and history;
All these stand open, or I have the keys:
                                        Yet I love thee.

I know the ways of Honour, what maintains
The quick returns of courtesy and wit:
In vies of favours whether° party gains,
When glory° swells the heart, and mouldeth it
To all expressions both of hand and eye,
Which on the world a true-love-knot° may tie,
And bear the bundle, wheresoe'er it goes;
How many drams of spirit there must be
To sell my life unto my friends or foes:
                                        Yet I love thee.

Coloss. 3. 3. the text: "For ye are dead, and
your life is hid with Christ in God"
double motion the sun's two apparent motions,
revolution and rotation. The poem's "oblique"
motion "is hid" in the italicized iambic pentameter line got by reading diagonally, as the spirit
"is hid" in the flesh, the figurative in the literal.
The Pearl The text behind this is Matthew 13:
45–46, likening the kingdom of heaven to "one
pearl of great price," for which a wise merchant

"went out and sold all that he had and bought
it."
press wine or olive press imagined as a printing
press
whether which
glory ambition
true-love-knot a token of faithful love; the
ambitious heart is pledged to the world—and
stuck with it

I know the ways of Pleasure, the sweet strains,
The lullings and the relishes° of it;
The propositions of hot blood and brains;
What mirth and music mean; what love and wit
Have done these twenty hundred years, and more:
I know the projects of unbridled store:°
My stuff is flesh, not brass; my senses live,
And grumble oft, that they have more in me
Than he that curbs them, being but one to five:
30   Yet I love thee.

I know all these, and have them in my hand:
Therefore not sealèd,° but with open eyes
I fly to thee, and fully understand
Both the main sale, and the commodities;
And at what rate and price I have thy love;
With all the circumstances that may move
Yet through these labyrinths, not my groveling wit,
But thy silk twist° let down from heaven to me
Did both conduct and teach me, how by it
40   To climb to thee.

                          1633

The Church-Floor°

Mark you the floor? that square and speckled stone,
        Which looks so firm and strong,
                Is *Patience;*

And th'other black and grave, wherewith each one
        Is checkered all along,
                Humility;

The gentle rising, which on either hand
        Leads to the Choir above,
                Is *Confidence;*

10   But the sweet cément, which in one sure band
        Ties the whole frame, is *Love*
                And *Charity.*

    Hither sometimes Sin steals, and stains
        The marble's neat and curious veins
    But all is cleansèd when the marble weeps.

relishes musical ornamentation
store wealth
sealèd In falconry, birds' eyes were sewn closed
during training.
silk twist thread
The Church-Floor a meditative reading of the

checkerboard marble floor of the church. The
change of form in the last eight lines follows
a shift from the presentation of an emblem
to its interpretation; it is almost as if ll. 1–12
were picture, and 13–20, motto or text.

Sometimes Death, puffing at the door,
Blows all the dust about the floor,
But while he thinks to spoil the room, he sweeps.
Blest be the Architect, whose art
20   Could build so strong in a weak heart.

            1633

Aaron°

    Holiness on the head,
    Light and perfections on the breast,
Harmonious bells below, raising the dead
    To lead them unto life and rest:
        Thus are true Aarons dressed.

    Profaneness in my head,
    Defects and darkness in my breast,
A noise of passions ringing me for dead
    Unto a place where is no rest:
10   Poor priest thus am I dressed.

    Only another head
    I have, another heart and breast,
Another music, making live not dead,
    Without whom I could have no rest:
        In him I am well dressed.

    Christ is my only head,
    My alone only heart and breast,
My only music, striking me even dead;°
    That to the old man I may rest,
20   And be in him new dressed.

    So holy in my head,
    Perfect and light in my dear breast,
My doctrine tuned by Christ (who is not dead,
    But lives in me while I do rest):
        Come people; Aaron's dressed.

            1633

Aaron a meditation as though while putting on vestments, remembering the garments of Aaron, the first high priest (see Exodus 28)

dead As a clapper strikes a bell, Christ's music strikes dead the sinner in man.

Sonnet°

My God, where is that ancient heat towards thee,
    Wherewith whole shoals of martyrs once did burn,
    Besides their other flames? Doth poetry
Wear Venus' livery? only serve her turn?
Why are not sonnets made of thee? and lays
    Upon thine altar burnt? Cannot thy love
    Heighten a spirit to sound out thy praise
As well as any she? Cannot thy Dove
Outstrip their Cupid easily in flight?
    Or, since thy ways are deep, and still the same,
    Will not a verse run smooth that bears thy name?
Why doth that fire, which by thy power and might
    Each breast does feel, no braver° fuel choose
    Than that, which one day worms may chance refuse?
    1610   1670

10 at line "Or, since thy ways are deep"

The Pulley°

    When God at first made man,
Having a glass of blessings standing by,
'Let us' (said he) 'pour on him all we can:
Let the world's riches, which dispersèd lie,
    Contract into a span.'°

    So strength first made a way;
Then beauty flowed, then wisdom, honour, pleasure:
When almost all was out, God made a stay,
Perceiving that alone of all his treasure
    Rest° in the bottom lay.

    'For if I should' (said he)
'Bestow this jewel also on my creature,
He would adore my gifts instead of me,
And rest in Nature, not the God of Nature:
    So both should losers be.

    'Yet let him keep the rest,
But keep them with repining° restlessness:
Let him be rich and weary, that at least,
If goodness lead him not, yet weariness
    May toss him to my breast.'
             1633

10 at "Rest in the bottom lay"
20 at "May toss him to my breast"

Sonnet from *The Life of Herbert* by Izaak
Walton, who says that Herbert sent it to his
mother as a New Year's gift when he was
seventeen, from Cambridge
braver handsomer
The Pulley which draws man up to God on
either side, as long as on the other there is a
compensating descent. This poem plays on the
myth of Pandora's box, in a later version of
which all the divine blessings escape from
it, leaving only hope; here, Herbert makes the
gift of restlessness (withholding of rest) a
kind of hope.
span the width of a man's hand
Rest repose, but punning on "what remains"
repining complaining

The Collar°

I struck the board,° and cried, 'No more,
    I will abroad!
What? shall I ever sigh and pine?
My lines and life are free, free as the road,
    Loose as the wind, as large as store.°
      Shall I be still in suit?°
Have I no harvest but a thorn
To let me blood, and not restore
What I have lost with cordial° fruit?
10   Sure there was wine
Before my sighs did dry it; there was corn
    Before my tears did drown it.
Is the year only lost to me?
    Have I no bays° to crown it?
No flowers, no garlands gay? all blasted?
      All wasted?
Not so, my heart: but there is fruit,
    And thou hast hands.
Recover all thy sigh-blown age
20 On double pleasures: leave thy cold dispute
Of what is fit, and not. Forsake thy cage,
    Thy rope of sands,°
Which petty thoughts have made, and made to thee
    Good cable, to enforce and draw,
      And be thy law,
While thou didst wink and wouldst not see.
      Away; take heed:
    I will abroad.
Call in thy death's head° there; tie up thy fears.
30   He that forbears
    To suit and serve his need,
      Deserves his load.'
But as I raved and grew more fierce and wild
    At every word,
Me thoughts I heard one calling, 'Child!'
    And I replied, 'My Lord.'

        1633

The Collar an emblem of discipline and restraint, perhaps also punning on "choler" as
"anger"
board dining table (where he is serving)
store abundance
in suit in attendance
cordial restorative

bays laurel crown for poetic excellence
rope of sands This startling image of a connection unable to withstand the slightest tug has
an almost proverbial force.
death's head the *memento mori* skull as a
meditational reminder of death

A Wreath°

A wreathèd garland of deservèd praise,
Of praise deservèd, unto thee I give,
I give to thee, who knowest all my ways,
My crooked winding ways, wherein I live,
Wherein I die, not live: for live is straight,
Straight as a line, and ever tends to thee,
To thee, who art more far above deceit,
Than deceit seems above simplicity.
Give me simplicity, that I may live,
10 So live and like, that I may know thy ways,
Know them and practise them: then shall I give
For this poor wreath, give thee a crown of praise.

1633

Ana-{ Mary / Army }gram°

How well her name an *Army* doth present,
In whom the *Lord of Hosts* did pitch his tent!

1633

Jordan (I)°

Who says that fictions only and false hair
Become a verse? Is there in truth no beauty?
Is all good structure in a winding stair?
May no lines pass, except they do their duty
    Not to a true, but painted chair?°

Is it no verse, except 'enchanted groves'°
And 'sudden arbours' shadow° coarse-spun lines?
Must 'purling° streams' refresh a lover's loves?
Must all be veiled, while he that reads, divines,
10   Catching the sense at two removes?

A Wreath Not only are the lines "interwoven" by means of locking repeated words, but also the poem "curls around" the central quatrain about straightness and directness, ll. 9–12 matching in their rhyme-words ll. 4–1.
Ana-gram Herbert may be thinking of an image from Hebrews 8:1–2.
Jordan (I) This and the following poem, both praising the plain over the artful, refer in their titles to Jordan (the language of piety) as an alternative to Helicon's fountain (literary poetry), Jordan's rough waters being more healing than smooth classical streams (see the anecdote in II Kings 5:1–14).
May . . . chair must all poetry defer to pictures of the world?
'enchanted groves' The phrases in quotes are used in two ways: designating elements in an over-elaborate garden, and as their equivalents —fancy clichés in poems.
shadow both "shade" and "provide images for"
purling curling, swiftly-running (of streams); a stitching (in knitting or sewing)

Shepherds are honest people: let them sing.
Riddle who list,° for me, and pull for prime;°
I envy no man's nightingale or spring;
Nor let them punish me with loss of rhyme,
   Who plainly say, 'My God, My King.'
             1633

Jordan (II)°

When first my lines of heavenly joys made mention,
Such was their lustre, they did so excell,
That I sought out quaint words, and trim invention;°
My thoughts began to burnish,° sprout, and swell,
Curling with metaphors a plain intention,
Decking the sense, as if it were to sell.

Thousands of notions in my brain did run,
Offering their service, if I were not sped;°
I often blotted° what I had begun:
10   This was not quick° enough, and that was dead.
Nothing could seem too rich to clothe the sun,
Much less those joys which trample on his head.°

As flames do work and wind, when they ascend,
So did I weave my self into the sense.
But while I bustled, I might hear a friend
Whisper, 'How wide° is all this long pretense!°
There is in love a sweetness ready penned:
Copy out only that, and save expense.'
             1633

Paradise°

I bless thee, Lord, because I GROW
Among thy trees, which in a ROW
To thee both fruit and order OW.

What open force, or hidden CHARM
Can blast° my fruit, or bring me HARM
While the enclosure is thine ARM?

Enclose me still for fear I START;
Be to me rather sharp and TART,
Than let me want° thy hand and ART.

10   When thou dost greater judgments SPARE,
And with thy knife but prune and PARE,
Even fruitful trees more fruitful ARE.

Such sharpness shows the sweetest FREND:°
Such cuttings rather heal than REND;
And such beginnings touch° their END.

1633

Church Monuments°

While that my soul repairs to her devotion,
Here I entomb my flesh, that it betimes
Make take acquaintance of this heap of dust,
To which the blast of Death's incessant motion,
Fed with the exhalation° of our crimes,
Drives all at last. Therefore I gladly trust

My body to this school, that it may learn
To spell° his elements, and find his birth
Written in dusty heraldry and lines;°
10   Which dissolution sure doth best discern,
Comparing dust with dust, and earth with earth.
These laugh at jet and marble, put for signs,

To sever the good fellowship of dust,
And spoil the meeting—what shall point out them,
When they shall bow and kneel and fall down flat
To kiss those heaps which now they have in trust?
Dear flesh, while I do pray, learn here thy stem°
And true descent, that, when thou shalt grow fat,

And wanton in thy cravings, thou mayst know
20   That flesh is but the glass° which holds the dust
That measures all our time, which also shall
Be crumbled into dust. Mark here below
How tame these ashes are, how free from lust,
That thou mayst fit thyself against° thy fall.

1633

want lack
Frend friend (the old spelling preserved in this case)
touch with a sense of "color" or "tinge," and of "join"
Church Monuments a meditation on the carved tombs in churches, of "jet and marble" and sometimes ruined and crumbling, containing the "dust" to which the dust of human flesh returns
exhalation ironically paralleling the divine ex-

halation which animated the first Adamic dust
spell spell out half-obscured inscriptions
lines genealogical lines of descent, as well as the actual carved ones on the tomb
stem ancestry
glass hourglass of Time's emblem; made of marble, it too will crumble. There is a surprising echo of the biblical "All flesh is grass" (Isaiah 40:6), with the hardened, monumental "glass" substituted.
fit thyself against make ready for

Prayer (I)°

Prayer the Church's banquet,° Angels' age,°
   God's breath in man returning to his birth,
   The soul in paraphrase,° heart in pilgrimage,
The Christian plummet sounding heaven and earth;
Engine against the Almighty, sinners' tower,
   Reversèd thunder, Christ-side-piercing spear,
   The six-day's-world° transposing in an hour,
A kind of tune, which all things hear and fear;
Softness, and peace, and joy, and love, and bliss,
10   Exalted manna,° gladness of the best,
   Heaven in ordinary, man well dressed,°
The milky way, the bird of paradise,°
   Church-bells beyond the stars heard, the soul's blood,
   The land of spices; something understood.

1633

Virtue

Sweet day, so cool, so calm, so bright,
The bridal of the earth and sky:
The dew shall weep thy fall tonight;
     For thou must die.

Sweet rose, whose hue angry° and brave°
Bids the rash gazer wipe his eye:
Thy root is ever in its grave,
     And thou must die.

Sweet spring, full of sweet days and roses,
10 A box where sweets° compacted lie;
My music shows ye have your closes,°
     And all must die.

Only a sweet and virtuous soul,
Like seasoned timber, never gives;
But though the whole world turn to coal,°
     Then chiefly lives.

1633

Prayer (I) The whole poem (with no predicate verb) is itself a brilliant series of paraphrases.
banquet a light refreshment between meals (i.e. prayer is a snack between one Holy Communion and the next)
Angels' age an eternity
paraphrase with a sense of an expansion of an original (rather than, as in modern usage, a compression)
six-day's-world Creation took six days; also, the world occupies six days of the week, but not the Sabbath; "transposing" that world suggests making any of the six days into the seventh.

Exalted manna The biblical manna fell from heaven; this kind rises to it.
Heaven . . . dressed God at the table, and man prepared as a dish for Him
bird of paradise from the legend that this bird had no feet and so never touched the ground
angry red
brave splendid
sweets perfumes
closes musical cadences
turn to coal become cinders and ashes in the conflagration of the Day of Judgment

Love (III)

Love bade me welcome: yet my soul drew back,
    Guilty of dust and sin.
But quick-eyed Love,° observing me grow slack
    From my first entrance in,
Drew nearer to me, sweetly questioning,
    If I lacked any thing.

'A guest,' I answered, 'worthy to be here':
    Love said, 'You shall be he.'
'I the unkind, ungrateful? Ah my dear,
    I cannot look on thee.'
Love took my hand, and smiling did reply,
    'Who made the eyes but I?'

'Truth Lord, but I have marred them: let my shame
    Go where it doth deserve.'
'And know you not,' says Love, 'who bore the blame?'
    'My dear, then I will serve.'
'You must sit down,' says Love,' and taste my meat:°
    So I did sit and eat.

1633

RICHARD CRASHAW
1612/13–1649

If Crashaw is indeed, as Douglas Bush has remarked, the "one conspicuous English incarnation of the baroque sensibility,'" it is perhaps because of his association with just those aspects of European baroque which are easiest to identify across national and formal boundaries. An enthusiastic Roman Catholic convert at a historical moment when Anglicanism could suffice for many, his mature work was influenced by Jesuit Latin poetry and by the Italian of Giambattista Marino (1569–1625). His religious verse is far more excitedly sensual than a good deal of Caroline erotic poetry. His use of the paradox of self-contradiction and of excruciatingly insistent conceits was energized by a belief that only by the intensification of the concrete realms—of body, picture, or thing—could the abstract ones of soul and significance be released.

Crashaw was born in London, the son of a Yorkshire clergyman, and educated at the Charterhouse and at Pembroke College, Cambridge; he became a fellow of Peterhouse in 1635, is thought to have taken orders by 1639, was associated with High Church intellectuals like Nicholas Ferrar and with Abraham Cowley. In 1643, like Cowley, he abandoned his fellowship before being ejected from it. He went abroad,

---

quick-eyed Love As opposed to the blind or blindfolded Cupid of Renaissance erotic imagery, Caritas or Divine Love is characterized as "quick-" (or "living-") eyed; the whole poem plays on this contrast; for the blindness of Amor or Cupid, see Marlowe's *Hero and Leander* I.38n.

meat repast, as almost always in the 17th century; here, the love-feast, or *agapē*, of the early Christians, manifesting itself in Holy Communion, which the priest both serves and takes himself

became a Catholic in 1645, it is believed, lived among the royalist émigrés in Paris, and finally went to Rome, where he entered Cardinal Pallotta's service. Perhaps because of a lack of political sophistication, he was sent to a post at Loreto, where he died (as a result, it was almost inevitably rumored in England at the time, of poisoning).

His earliest published poems were his Latin epigrams, including a now-famous line "explaining" Christ's transformation of water to wine at the marriage in Cana (John 2:1–10): the embarrassed nymph inhabiting the water caught sight of God, and blushed. In 1646 and 1648 appeared two versions of *Steps to the Temple* (the allusion being to the title of George Herbert's 1633 collection) and, in 1652, the posthumous *Carmen Deo Nostro*. Some of his more intense secular poetry, like the grand "Music's Duel," shares with his devotional verse a delight in expressive energy itself, banishing good taste and rhetorical control as a Cavalier love lyrist would banish prudence, a delight that found no strength save at the brink of rage, no fullness save in overflow.

Music's Duel°

Now Westward Sol had spent the richest beams
Of noon's high glory, when hard by the streams
Of Tiber, on the scene of a green plat,°
Under protection of an oak, there sat
A sweet lute's-master, in whose° gentle airs
He lost the day's heat and his own hot cares.
    Close in the covert of the leaves there stood
A nightingale, come from the neighbouring wood
(The sweet inhabitant of each glad tree,
10 Their muse, their siren, harmless siren she):
There stood she listening, and did entertain
The music's soft report, and mould the same
In her own murmurs, that whatever mood°
His curious° fingers lent, her voice made good.
The man perceived his rival and her art,
Disposed to give the light-foot lady sport
Awakes his lute, and 'gainst the fight to come
Informs it, in a sweet praeludium,°
Of closer strains, and ere the war begin,
20 He lightly skirmishes on every string
Charged with a flying touch,° and straightway she
Carves out her dainty voice as readily
Into a thousand sweet distinguished tones,
And reckons up in soft divisions,°

Music's Duel a wildly elaborate version of a Latin original by the Jesuit Famianus Strada, itself frequently translated as an epitome of the conflict between art and nature
plat plot
whose the lute's. The pun on "airs" ("tunes," thus the lute's "breezes") inaugurates the continuous word-play on technical musical terms throughout the poem.
mood also means musical mode, or key
curious complicatedly artful
praeludium prelude, first movement in a suite of instrumental pieces
touch a passage of music
divisions improvised expansions of a theme

Quick volumes of wild notes, to let him know
By that shrill taste, she could do something too.
   His nimble hands instinct then taught each string
A capering cheerfulness, and made them sing
To their own dance; now negligently rash
³⁰ He throws his arm, and with a long drawn dash°
Blends all together, then distinctly trips
From this to that, then quick returning skips
And snatches this again, and pauses there.
She° measures every measure, everywhere
Meets art with art; sometimes as if in doubt
Not perfect yet, and fearing to be out
Trails her plain ditty in one long-spun note
Through the sleek passage of her open throat:
A clear unwrinkled° song, then doth she point it
⁴⁰ With tender accents, and severely joint it
By short diminutives, that being reared
In controverting warbles° evenly shared,
With her sweet self she wrangles; he amazed
That from so small a channel should be raised
The torrent of a voice, whose melody
Could melt into such sweet variety,
Strains higher yet; that tickled with rare art
The tattling strings (each breathing in his part)
Most kindly do fall out; the grumbling bass
⁵⁰ In surly groans disdains the treble's grace.
The high-perched treble° chirps at this and chides,
Until his finger (moderator) hides
And closes the sweet quarrel rousing all
Hoarse, shrill, at once, as when the trumpets call
Hot Mars to the harvest of death's field, and woo
Men's hearts into their hands; this lesson too
She gives him back; her supple breast thrills out
Sharp airs, and staggers in a warbling doubt
Of dallying sweetness, hovers o'er her skill,
⁶⁰ And folds in waved notes° with a trembling bill,
The pliant series of her slippery song.
Then starts she suddenly into a throng
Of short thick sobs, whose thundering volleys float
And roll themselves over her lubric° throat
In panting murmurs, stilled° out of her breast,
That ever-bubbling spring, the sugared nest
Of her delicious soul, that there does lie

---

dash in lute notation, the sign for a stroked chord
She the bird
unwrinkled In musical notation, all half and quarter notes would look "unwrinkled" on the page, not having the tails or ligatures of shorter-valued notes.
diminutives . . . warbles ornamentation

treble The highest lute string was single, the others, double (octaves or unisons).
waved notes with runs of sixteenth and thirty-second notes, looking like waves on the page
lubric smooth, slippery
stilled distilled

Bathing in streams of liquid melody,
Music's best seed plot, when in ripened airs
70 A bold-headed harvest fairly rears
His honey-dropping tops, plowed by her breath
Which there reciprocally laboureth
In that sweet soil. It seems a holy choir
Founded to the name of great Apollo's lyre,
Whose silver roof rings with the sprightly notes
Of sweet-lipped angel imps, that swill their throats
In cream of morning Helicon,° and then
Prefer° soft anthems to the ears of men,
To woo them from their beds, still murmuring
80 That men can sleep while they their matins sing
(Most divine service! whose so early lay
Prevents° the eyelids of the blushing day).
There might you hear her kindle her soft voice
In the close murmur of a sparkling noise,
And lay the groundwork of her hopeful song,
Still keeping in the forward stream, so long,
Till a sweet whirlwind (striving to get out)
Heaves her soft bosom, wanders round about,
And makes a pretty earthquake in her breast,
90 Till the fledged notes° at length forsake their nest,
Fluttering in wanton shoals, and to the sky,
Winged with their own wild echoes, prattling fly.
She opes the floodgate and lets loose a tide
Of streaming sweetness, which in state doth ride
On the waved back of every swelling strain,
Rising and falling in a pompous train.
And while she thus discharges a shrill peal
Of flashing airs, she qualifies their zeal
With the cool epode of a graver note,°
100 Thus high, thus low, as if her silver throat
Would reach the brazen voice of war's hoarse bird;
Her little soul is ravished, and so poured
Into loose ecstasies that she is placed
Above herself,° music's enthusiast.
      Shame now and anger mixed a double stain
In the musician's face; 'Yet once again,
Mistress I come; now reach a strain, my lute,
Above her mock, or be forever mute.
Or tune a song of victory to me,
110 Or to thyself sing thine own obsequy.'°

Helicon the Muses' and Apollo's mountain
Prefer proffer, extend
Prevents precedes
fledged notes The notes are fledgling birds (1)
because they are daughters of (produced by)
the nightingale; (2) because in notation their
tails (they being eighth and sixteenth notes)

look wing-like (compare comic-book representations of singing).
graver note lower, as well as more weighty, tone
Above herself "Ecstasy" is literally, in Greek,
"standing outside" (oneself); here, the bird has
"overdone it," too.
obsequy funeral rite

So said, his hands sprightly as fire he flings,
And with a quavering coyness° tastes° the strings.
The sweet-lipped sisters° musically frighted,
Singing their fears are fearfully delighted.
Trembling as when Apollo's golden hairs°
Are fanned and frizzled, in the wanton airs
Of his own breath: which married to his lyre
Doth tune the spheres, and make heaven's self look higher.
From this to that, from that to this he flies,
120   Feels Music's pulse in all her arteries,
Caught in a net which there Apollo spreads,
His fingers struggle with the vocal threads,
Following those little rills, he sinks into
A sea of Helicon; his hand does go
Those parts of sweetness, which with nectar drop,
Softer than that which pants in Hebe's cup.°
The humorous° strings expound his learnèd touch
By various glosses;° now they seem to grutch°
And murmur in a buzzing din, then jingle
130   In shrill-tongued accents, striving to be single.°
Every smooth turn, every delicious stroke
Gives life to some new grace; thus doth h'invoke
Sweetness by all her names; thus, bravely thus
(Fraught with a fury so harmonious)
The lute's light genius° now does proudly rise,
Heaved on the surges of swollen rhapsodies.
Whose flourish (meteor-like) doth curl the air
With flash of high-borne fancies,° here and there
Dancing in lofty measures, and anon
140   Creeps on the soft touch of a tender tone,
Whose trembling murmurs melting in wild airs
Runs to and fro, complaining his sweet cares
Because those precious mysteries that dwell
In music's ravished soul he dare not tell,
But whisper to the world: thus do they vary
Each string his note, as if they meant to carry
Their master's blessed soul (snatched out at his ears
By a strong ecstasy)° through all the spheres
Of Music's heaven; and seat it there on high
150   In th' Empyraeum° of pure harmony.

---

quavering coyness "Quavers" is British usage for eighth notes, and "coy" means quiet and reserved here.
tastes "Tastar de corde" was a kind of lute prelude.
sweet-lipped sisters the strings ("sisters," being parallel and like Graces or Muses)
hairs sunbeams
Hebe's cup held by the gods' cup-bearer
humorous lively and intelligent (as students)
glosses footnotes like this one

grutch grouch, complain
single The double lute strings jangle and buzz together in loud passages.
genius spirit
fancies imaginative thoughts and, musically, "fantasias," free compositions
ecstasy Music was thought to ravish men's souls by drawing them out through the ears.
Empyraeum the outermost of the concentric heavens in Greek astronomy, later thought of also as the brightest region

At length (after so long, so loud a strife
Of all the strings, still breathing the best life
Of blessed variety attending on
His finger's fairest revolution
In many a sweet rise, many as sweet a fall)
A full-mouth diapason° swallows all.
   This done, he lists what she would say to this,
And she although her breath's late exercise
Had dealt too roughly with her tender throat,
160 Yet summons all her sweet powers for a note
Alas! in vain! for while (sweet soul) she tries
To measure all those wild diversities
Of chattering strings, by the small size of one
Poor simple voice, raised in a natural tone,
She fails, and failing grieves, and grieving lies.
She dies, and leaves her life the victor's prize,
Falling upon his lute—Oh fit to have
(That lived so sweetly) dead, so sweet a grave!
1646

From The Weeper°

     Hail, sister springs!
    Parents of silver-footed rills!
    Ever bubbling things!
    Thawing crystal! snowy hills,
Still spending, never spent! I mean
Thy fair eyes, sweet Magdalene!

     Heavens thy fair eyes be;
    Heavens of ever-falling stars.
    'Tis seed-time still with thee,
10   And stars thou sowest, whose harvest dares
Promise the earth to countershine
Whatever makes heaven's forehead fine.

     But we're deceivèd all.
    Stars indeed they are too true,
    For they but seem to fall
    As Heaven's other spangles do.
It is not for our earth and us
To shine in things so precious.

diapason octave
The Weeper This string of glittering epigrams was first published in 1646 and later revised, but even in its later form lacks total coherence; the editors have excerpted from it, omitting the following stanzas of the 1652 text: 13–16, 20–27. The poem was printed with an emblem of the weeping Mary Magdalene above a winged, bleeding heart, with this motto: "Lo, where a wounded heart with bleeding eyes conspire: / Is she a flaming fountain, or a weeping fire?" The tears of the repentant Magdalene are a widespread image especially identified with baroque; for the story of her washing the feet of Jesus, her presence at the Crucifixion, and her discovery of his resurrection, see Matthew 27–28.

Upwards thou dost weep:
Heaven's bosom drinks the gentle stream.
Where the milky rivers creep,
Thine floats above and is the cream.°
Waters above the Heavens, what they be
We are taught best by thy tears and thee.

Every morn from hence
A brisk cherub something sips
Whose sacred influence°
Adds sweetness to his sweetest lips.
Then to his music. And his song
Tastes of this breakfast all day long.

Not in the evening's eyes
When they red with weeping are
For the sun that dies,
Sits sorrow with a face so fair;
Nowhere but here did ever meet
Sweetness so sad, sadness so sweet.

When sorrow would be seen
In her brightest majesty
(For she is a queen)
Then is she dressed by none but thee.
Then, and only then, she wears
Her proudest pearls; I mean, thy tears.

The dew no more will weep
The primrose's pale cheek to deck,
The dew no more will sleep
Nuzzled in the lily's neck;
Much rather would it be thy tear,
And leave them both to tremble here.

There's no need at all
That the balsam-sweating bough
So coyly should let fall
His médicinable° tears; for now
Nature hath learnt to extract a dew
More sovereign and sweet from you.

Yet let the poor drops weep,
(Weeping is the ease of woe)
Softly let them creep,
Sad that they are vanquished so.
They, though to others no relief,
Balsam may be for their own grief.

cream of the Milky Way
influence used in an astrological sense to mean
the emanations of the stars

médicinable Many aromatic gums or balms were
used in medicine.

Such the maiden gem
By the purpling vine put on,
Peeps from her parent stem
And blushes at the bridegroom sun.
This watery blossom of thy eyen,
Ripe, will make the richer wine.

When some new bright guest
Takes up among the stars a room,
And Heaven will make a feast,
70   Angels with crystal vials come
And draw from these full eyes of thine
Their master's water, their own wine.

    .   .   .

But can these fair floods be
Friends with the bosom fires that fill thee?
Can so great flames agree
100   Eternal tears should thus distill thee?
Oh floods, oh fires! oh suns, oh showers!
Mixed and made friends by Love's sweet powers.°

'Twas his well-pointed dart
That digged these wells and dressed this vine,
And taught the wounded heart
The way into these weeping eyen.°
Vain loves avaunt! bold hands forbear!
The lamb hath dipped his white foot here.

And now where'er he° strays
110   Among the Galilean mountains
Or more unwelcome ways,
He's followed by two faithful fountains,
Two walking baths, two weeping motions,
Portable and compendious oceans.

Oh thou, thy Lord's fair store!
In thy so rich and rare expenses,
Even when he showed most poor,
He might provoke the wealth of princes:
What prince's wantonest pride e'er could
120   Wash with silver, wipe with gold?°

    .   .   .

Love's sweet powers Notice the shift from Christian to adapted classical imagery here: the power of Love (with that of Strife) first arranged the elements out of chaos; in the next stanza, Love will be the traditional Eros with bow and arrow, but here made to stand for Christian *caritas,* divine love.
eyen eyes. In Petrarchan and neoplatonist traditions, Cupid's arrows hit one in the eye (love occurs proverbially "at first sight," not at first hearing, or touch).
he Jesus, who is now "love" incarnate. The image at the end of this stanza is a famous conceit, widely extravagant and perched on the edge of the ridiculous.
with gold her hair, with which Jesus' feet were dried

Say, ye bright brothers,
The fugitive sons of those fair eyes,
Your fruitful mother's!
What make you here? what hopes can 'tice°
You to be born? what cause can borrow
You from those nests of noble sorrow?

170

Whither away so fast?
For sure the sordid° earth
Your sweetness cannot taste
Nor does the dust deserve your birth.
Sweet, whither haste you then? oh say
Why you trip so fast away?

'We go not to seek
The darlings of Aurora's bed,
The rose's modest cheek,
Nor the violet's humble head,
Though the field's eyes too weepers be
Because they want° such tears as we.

180

Much less mean we to trace
The fortune of inferior gems,
Preferred to some proud face
Or perched upon feared diadems.
Crowned heads are toys. We go to meet
A worthy object, our Lord's feet.'

1646, 1648, 1652

On Our Crucified Lord, Naked and Bloody

Th'have left thee naked, Lord, O that they had!
This garment, too, I would they had denied;
Thee with thyself they have too richly clad,
Opening the purple° wardrobe of thy side.
    O never could be found garments too good
    For thee to wear, but these, of thy own blood.

1640

'tice entice
sordid dirty
want lack

purple This usually means "red" in 17th-century
English, not "violet"; thus the "royal purple"
was a powerful crimson.

Upon Our Saviour's Tomb Wherein Never Man Was Laid

How Life and Death in Thee
        Agree?
Thou had'st a virgin Womb
        And Tomb.
A Joseph° did betroth
        Them both.
                1646

Upon the Infant Martyrs

To see both blended in one flood;
The mother's milk, the children's blood,
Makes me doubt if Heaven will gather
Roses hence, or lilies rather.
                1646

The Flaming Heart

Along with the weeping Magdalene, a favorite figure for Crashaw's baroque meditation was Saint Teresa of Avila (1515–82), the Spanish Carmelite nun, whose mystical auto-biography would have been known to him in an English translation published in 1642. Her ecstatic vision of angelic penetration is enshrined in Bernini's great sculpture in the church of Santa Maria della Salute in Rome; she wrote of an angel appearing to her "in a corporeal form" with "a long dart of gold in his hand; and at the end of the iron below, me thought, there was a little fire; and I conceived that he thrust it some several times through my very heart, after such a manner as that it passed the very inwards of my bowels. And when he drew it back, me thought, it carried away as much as it had touched within me, and left all that which remained wholly inflamed with a great love of almighty God." The figuring forth of divine possession in sexual terms appealed strongly to the concretely emblematic and the paradoxical elements of Crashaw's imagination, and in two poems about her he responded to ecstasy in a controlled linguistic frenzy of his own, a religious equivalent of the energies of "Music's Duel." (See Fig. 34.)

Joseph Joseph of Arimathea, who laid Jesus away in the tomb which he soon vacated, and Joseph, Mary's husband. William Butler Yeats's nasty little epigram, "A Stick of Incense," is based on this conceit.

From The Flaming Heart

> Upon the book and picture of the seraphical Saint Teresa, as she is usually
> expressed with a seraphim° beside her.

Well-meaning readers, you that come as friends
And catch the precious name this piece pretends;
Make not too much haste to admire
That fair-cheeked fallacy° of fire.
That is a seraphim, they say,
And this the great Teresia.
Readers, be ruled by me, and make
Here a well-placed and wise mistake:
You must transpose the picture quite,
10 And spell it wrong to read it right;
Read *him* for her and *her* for him;
And call the saint the seraphim.

    .   .   .

   Do then as equal right requires,
Since his the blushes be, and hers the fires,
Resume and rectify thy rude design;
40 Undress thy seraphim into mine.
Redeem this injury of thy art:
Give him the veil, give her the dart.
   Give him the veil, that he may cover
The red cheeks of a rivalled lover,
Ashamed that our world now can show
Nests of new seraphims here below.
   Give her the dart, for it is she
(Fair youth) shoots both thy shaft and thee.
Say, all ye wise and well-pierced hearts
50 That live and die amidst her darts,
What is it your tasteful spirits prove
In that rare life of her, and love?
Say and bear witness: sends she not
A seraphim at every shot?
What magazines of immortal arms there shine!
Heaven's great artillery in each love-spun line.
Give then the dart to her who gives the flame;
Give him the veil, who kindly takes the shame.
   But if it be the frequent fate
60 Of worse faults to be fortunate;
If all's prescription, and proud wrong
Harkens not to an humble song;
For all the gallantry of him,
Give me the suffering seraphim.

---

seraphim The form is a Hebrew plural ("seraph" is the correct singular), but the mistake is conventional in English.

fallacy The emblem is wrong; only the following paradoxical twisting of things into their opposites will makes the true significance emerge.

His be the bravery of all those bright things,
The glowing cheeks, the glistering wings;
The rosy hand, the radiant dart;
Leave her alone the flaming heart.
    Leave her that; and thou shalt leave her
70 Not one loose shaft, but love's whole quiver.
For in love's field was never found
A nobler weapon than a wound.
Love's passives are his activest part,
The wounded is the wounding heart.
O heart! the equal poise° of love's both parts,
Big like° with wounds and darts,
Live in these conquering leaves; live all the same
And walk through all tongues one triumphant flame:
Live here, great heart, and love and die and kill,
80 And bleed and wound, and yield and conquer still.

. . .

1648

HENRY VAUGHAN
1621/22–1695

Henry Vaughan was the elder twin of Thomas Vaughan, the alchemist and hermetist, later satirized in Swift's *The Tale of a Tub*. They were born and bred in Breconshire, Wales, and Vaughan called himself "Silurist" after the ancient British tribe which had lived there. The twins went, as Welshmen did and still do, to Jesus College, Oxford. But Henry took no degree, and his subsequent study of the law was, according to his own testimony, ended by the Civil War, in which he saw military service on the Royalist side. He married, and published volumes of poetry: *Poems* in 1646, *Olor Iscanus* (Swan of Usk, the local river) in 1651; most of the poems to be found in this book were written at least four years earlier.

Partly through his brother's work, partly through his own study, Henry grew familiar with hermetic and alchemical lore. This fed into the entirely new kind of poetry he began to write—possibly after a serious illness—in the late 1640's, poetry which appeared in *Silex Scintillans* (The Sparkling Flint; 1650) and in the second part added to that work in 1655. For the second part he wrote a Preface condemning strongly the abuse of wit in the writing of irreligious poetry, and commended the work of Herbert, in whose steps he proposed to follow. He did so; it has been said that Vaughan's debt to Herbert is the greatest any English poet owes to another. After *Silex Scintillans* he produced some prose, devotional meditations, a medical treatise, and a last volume of verse, *Thalia Rediviva* (1678), which makes no difference to his reputation.

Vaughan's masterpieces are, then, in *Silex*, and belong to a few years of his life from about 1650 to 1655. His imperfections are often pointed out: he can begin a poem with Herbertian directness (sometimes on a Herbertian text) but not always quite control it as Herbert did; he is repetitive and sometimes too vague. But his

---

poise weight, value   **Big like** equally full of

merits are quite clear; he has a wholly distinctive resonance, and complex new meanings rise up and follow his peculiar voice. On the face of it there is a unique blend of Christian devotional and neoplatonic ideas and images; go deeper and there is more, a power—perhaps not wholly conscious—to form images, each carrying a strong charge of devotional meaning, into constellations which occur nowhere else, so that even the biblical allusions are strongly colored by the strange and strong imagination which brings them together. An example would be the unique transformation of an already ravishing passage from the Song of Songs in *Night*, or the ubiquitous associations of stars, clouds, veils, tombs, darkness, and plants, some of which are briefly indicated in the notes.

Vaughan's distinction is of a kind hardly to be found outside his lifetime. The new science, and the purgation from the humanist tradition of mysticism and pseudo-science, introduced a world in which poetry of his kind was all but impossible. With none of the Continental afflatus of Crashaw, he had much in common with Herbert, though he is less neat, less liturgical, less proverbial, and more strange than that spiritually more consistent and intellectually more powerful poet; nonetheless, his best works stand with theirs as among the greatest of seventeenth-century devotional poetry.

Religion°

My God, when I walk in those groves
   And leaves thy spirit doth still fan,
I see in each shade that there grows
   An angel talking with a man.

Under a juniper,° some house,
   Or the cool myrtle's canopy;°
Others beneath an oak's green boughs,°
   Or at some fountain's bubbling eye.°

Here Jacob dreams, and wrestles;° there
10   Elias by a raven is fed;°
Another time by the angel, where
   He brings him water with his bread.

In Abraham's tent° the wingèd guests
   (Oh how familiar then was heaven!)
Eat, drink, discourse, sit down, and rest,
   Until the cool and shady even.

Religion In groves which Vaughan can still think of as holy, he imagines free conversation between men and angels, and remembers that God also spoke directly to men. Why is this no longer so? Has the Incarnation, providing us with a Mediator, rendered such encounters unnecessary? He denies this. Religion has grown corrupt, but at its source still bears miraculous benefits; he prays that the spring be cleansed, or that we be led to its source.
juniper There an angel spoke to the sleeping Elijah (I Kings 19:5).

myrtle's canopy Zechariah 1:11
oak's . . . boughs There an angel spoke to Gideon (Judges 6:11).
fountain's . . . eye There an angel accosted Hagar, Sarah's maid (Genesis 16:7).
Here . . . wrestles with an angel, Genesis 32:24 ff.; his dream of the ladder, Genesis 28:12 ff.
Elias . . . fed I Kings 17; Elias = Elijah
In Abraham's tent Genesis 18:1 ff., where the angels bearing the promise that Sarah will be fruitful accept refreshments

Nay Thou Thyself, my God, in fire,
   Whirlwinds and clouds, and the soft voice,°
Speak'st there so much, that I admire°
20   We have no conference in these days.

Is the truce broke? or 'cause we have
   A Mediator now with Thee,
Dost Thou therefore old treaties waive,
   And by appeals from Him decree?°

Or is't so, as some green heads° say,
   That now all miracles must cease?
Though Thou has promised they should stay
   The tokens of the Church and peace.

No, no; Religion is a spring
30   That from some secret, golden mine
Derives her birth, and thence doth bring
   Cordials in every drop, and wine.

But in her long and hidden course,
   Passing through the Earth's dark veins,
Grows still from better unto worse,
   And both her taste and colour stains;

Then drilling on, learns to increase
   False echoes and confusèd sounds,
And unawares doth often seize
40   On veins of sulphur underground;

So poisoned, breaks forth in some clime,
   And at first sight doth many please;
But drunk,° is puddle or mere slime,
   And 'stead of physic, a disease.

Just such a tainted sink we have,
   Like that Samaritan's dead well;°
Nor must we for the kernel crave
   Because most voices like the shell.

Heal then these waters, Lord; or bring Thy flock,
50   Since these are troubled, to the springing rock;
Look down, Great Master of the feast; Oh shine,
And turn once more our water into wine!°

fire . . . voice fire: Exodus 3:2; whirlwind:
Job 38:1; clouds: Exodus 24:16; soft voice:
I Kings 19:12
admire wonder
Is . . . decree Does the existence of Jesus
Christ as our Mediator imply that the old
covenant between God and man (Genesis 9:
12–13, Exodus 31:13–17, Numbers 25:13)
is invalid?
green heads immature thinkers

drunk when we drink it
Samaritan's . . . well Jesus said to the Samaritan woman at the well, "Whosoever drinketh
of this water shall thirst again: But whosoever
drinketh of the water that I shall give him
shall never thirst" (John 4:13–14).
water into wine The idea of water (religion)
miraculously purified leads Vaughan, in the
concluding petition, to remember line 32, and
also the miracle at Cana, John 2:1–11.

CANT. CAP. 4. VER. 12.

My sister, my spouse is as a garden enclosed, as a spring shut up, and a
  fountain sealed up.°

1650

The Retreat°

Happy those early days! when I
Shined in my angel-infancy,
Before I understood this place
Appointed for my second race,°
Or taught my soul to fancy ought
But a white, celestial thought;
When yet I had not walked above
A mile or two from my first love,
And looking back—at that short space—
10 Could see a glimpse° of His bright face;
When on some gilded cloud, or flower,
My gazing soul would dwell an hour,
And in those weaker glories spy
Some shadows° of eternity;
Before I taught my tongue to wound
My conscience with a sinful sound,
Or had the black art to dispense
A several° sin to every sense,
But felt through all this fleshly dress
20 Bright shoots of everlastingness.°
    Oh how I long to travel back,
And tread again that ancient track!
That I might once more reach that plain,
Where first I left my glorious train;°
From whence the enlightened spirit sees
That shady city of palm trees.°
But ah! my soul with too much stay°

My sister . . . sealed up Here as elsewhere Vaughan adds a verse of the Song of Songs (4:12), a work subjected to multiple allegorical interpretation. The sister-spouse is the Church, bride of Christ; here the verse is apposite because the spouse is compared to "a spring shut up."
The Retreat Vaughan seems to have believed in something like the Platonic notion of a prior existence which, in childhood and less often later, we can recall; in the innocence of childhood he is close to the divine source (represented, again in neoplatonic terms, as a white radiance), can see images of eternity in the world; and feels, in his mortal flesh, the truth of his immortality. This after-vision of the Heavenly City is lost as maturity brings on its sins. The similarity of the basic idea to that of

Wordsworth's *Ode on the Intimations of Immortality* is often noticed, and Wordsworth knew Vaughan's poem.
second race The first "race" (life, nation, contest) was in heaven.
glimpse a favorite word of Vaughan's referring to the human power of briefly intuiting divinity
shadows images, reflections
several separate
Bright . . . everlastingness Like other expressions that sound idiosyncratic to Vaughan, this is borrowed—from the essayist Owen Felltham.
train companions, or way of life
shady . . . trees Jericho, as Moses saw it from the top of Pisgah; here a type of the Heavenly City (Deuteronomy 34:1–4)
stay from having stayed too long

Is drunk, and staggers in the way.
Some men a forward motion love,
30   But I by backward steps would move
And when this dust falls to the urn,
In that state I came, return.°
                    1650

Corruption°

Sure it was so. Man in those early days
   Was not all stone and earth;
He shined a little, and by those weak rays
   Had some glimpse of his birth.°
He saw Heaven o'er his head, and knew from whence
   He came, condemnèd hither;
And, as first love draws strongest, so from hence
   His mind sure progressed thither.
Things here were strange unto him: sweat and till,
10   All was a thorn or weed:
Nor did those last, but, like himself, died still°
   As soon as they did seed.
They seemed to quarrel with him, for that act
   That felled him foiled them all:°
He drew the curse upon the world, and cracked
   The whole frame with his fall.
This made him long for home, as loth to stay
   With murmurers and foes;
He sighed for Eden, and would often say,
20   'Ah! what bright days were those!'
Nor was Heaven cold unto him; for each day
   The valley or the mountain
Afforded visits, and still paradise lay
   In some green shade or fountain.
Angels lay lieger° here; each bush and cell,
   Each oak and highway knew them;
Walk but the fields, or sit down at some well,
   And he was sure to view them.°

---

return would return
Corruption Vaughan looks back, not to childhood as in "The Retreat," but to an earlier stage in history, when man had easier access to the divine, and remembered his heavenly origin. He then charts the decline of such powers, explaining that in falling, man also corrupted nature, which became mortal and also the cause of man's labor. Still he longed for his immortal home and still had encounters with angels, and paradisal intimations from nature (as in "Religion" and "The Retreat"), whereas now man is in despair, will not help himself, and demands that fate end his life. God does not communicate; man lives in sin and darkness; but the trumpet will sound for the last day and the restoration of heaven and light.
He shined . . . birth Vaughan thought of the soul as a divine spark; here its light affords a "glimpse" (see note on "The Retreat") of heaven. "Ray" was another favorite word.
still always
that act . . . all the Fall, as explained in succeeding lines
lieger a resident, not merely visiting, ambassador
view them exactly the same idea in "Religion"

Almighty Love! where art Thou now? Mad man
30   Sits down and freezeth on;
He raves, and swears to stir nor fire nor fan,
        But bids the thread be spun.°
I see thy curtains are close-drawn; thy bow
        Looks dim, too, in the cloud;
Sin triumphs still, and man is sunk below
        The centre,° and his shroud.
All's in deep sleep and night: thick darkness lies
        And hatcheth° o'er thy people—
But hark! what trumpet's that? what angel cries,
40   'Arise! thrust in Thy sickle'?°

                    1650

The World°

I saw Eternity the other night
Like a great ring of pure and endless light,°
        All calm as it was bright;
And round beneath it, Time in hours, days, years,
        Driven by the spheres°
Like a vast shadow moved; in which the world
        And all her train° were hurled.
The doting lover in his quaintest° strain
        Did there complain;
10 Near him, his lute, his fancy, and his flights,°
        Wit's sour delights;
With gloves and knots, the silly snares of pleasure,
        Yet his dear treasure,
All scattered lay, while he his eyes did pour°
        Upon a flower.

The darksome statesman, hung with weights and woe
Like a thick midnight fog, moved there so slow,
        He did nor stay, nor go;
Condemning thoughts—like sad eclipses—scowl
20   Upon his soul,

thread be spun The Fates spun the thread of men's lives.
centre of the earth; the lowest place, where corruption gathers
hatcheth places a hatch
Arise . . . sickle Revelation 14:18. The angel that has power over fire cried to another, "Thrust in thy sharp sickle, and gather the clusters of the vine of the earth; for her grapes are fully ripe" (note the surprising assonance of people / sickle, expressively replacing a rhyme).
The World The basic contrast is between Eternity, symbolized by the circle, and Time, in which various types of folly, emblematically

represented, are described; the question of access from Time to Eternity is handled in the enigmatic conclusion.
ring . . . light The circle was the usual emblem of eternity, having no begining or end; by calling it a *ring*, Vaughan prepares for the nuptial figure introduced later.
Driven . . . spheres According to Plato (*Timaeus*), time is identified with the movement of the heavenly bodies.
train followers, companions
quaintest most highly wrought
flights of rhetoric
pour he poured his eyes; pored over

And clouds of crying witnesses without
    Pursued him with one shout.
Yet digged the mole,° and lest his ways be found,
    Worked under ground,
Where he did clutch his prey; but one° did see
    That policy:
Churches and altars fed him, perjuries
    Were gnats and flies;
It rained about him blood and tears, but he
30   Drank them as free.°

The fearful miser on a heap of rust
Sat pining all his life there, did scarce trust
    His own hands with the dust,
Yet would not place one piece above, but lives
    In fear of thieves.
Thousands there were as frantic as himself,
    And hugged each one his pelf;°
The downright epicure° placed heaven in sense,
    And scorned pretence;
40   While others, slipped into a wide excess,
    Said little less;
The weaker sort slight, trivial wares enslave,
    Who think them brave;°
And poor, despisèd Truth sat counting° by
    Their victory.

Yet some,° who all this while did weep and sing,
And sing and weep, soared up into the ring;
    But most would use no wing.
Oh fools, said I, thus to prefer dark night
50   Before true light!
To live in grots and caves, and hate the day
    Because it shows the way;
The way, which from this dead and dark abode
    Leads up to God;
A way where you might tread the sun, and be
    More bright than he!
But as I did their madness so discuss,
    One whispered thus,
'This ring the Bridegroom did for none provide,
60   But for His bride.'°

mole the statesman, at his devious work
one God
as free as freely as they came
pelf lucre, wealth
epicure The word derives from the philosopher Epicurus but came to mean simply one who makes pleasure the highest good, that is, "places heaven in sense." See Glossary.
brave fine, splendid
counting estimating

some Vaughan's adepts or mystics, who can "walk to the sky" during their lives
His bride the Church: "I John saw the holy city, new Jerusalem, coming down from God out of heaven, prepared as a bride adorned for her husband . . . And there came unto me one of the seven angels . . . saying, Come hither, I will show you the bride, the Lamb's wife" (Revelation 21:2, 9)

JOHN, CAP. 2 VER. 16, 17

All that is in the world, the lust of the flesh, the lust of the eyes, and the pride
of life, is not of the Father, but is of the world.

And the world passeth away, and the lusts thereof; but he that doeth the will
of God abideth for ever.

1650

[They Are All Gone into the World of Light]°

They are all gone into the world of light!
    And I alone sit lingering here;
Their very memory is fair and bright
    And my sad thoughts doth clear.

It grows and glitters in my cloudy breast,
    Like stars° upon some gloomy grove,
Or those faint beams in which this hill is dressed
    After the sun's remove.

I see them walking in an air of glory,
10   Whose light doth trample on my days:
My days, which are at best but dull and hoary,
    Mere glimmering and decays.

Oh holy hope, and high humility,
    High as the heavens above!
These are your walks, and you have showed them me
    To kindle my cold love.

Dear, beauteous death! the jewel of the just,
    Shining nowhere but in the dark,
What mysteries do lie beyond thy dust,
20   Could man outlook that mark!

He that hath found some fledged bird's° nest, may know
    At first sight, if the bird be flown;
But what fair well or grove° he sings in now,
    That is to him unknown.

And yet, as angels in some brighter dreams
    Call to the soul when man doth sleep,
So some strange thoughts transcend our wonted themes,
    And into glory peep.°

They . . . Light The souls of the dead are in
the world of light, heaven; the poet is meditating on the place of the soul in the darkness
of the world, from which death will free it;
he petitions for light, as he does for the pure
water at the end of "Religion"—either here
or, by the intervention of death, in heaven.
stars Vaughan often compares the dead to
stars; here the memory of them is a faint
light to him.
fledged bird's image of the winged soul
well or grove as in "Religion" and "corruption" associated with holy places
peep another favorite word of Vaughan's used,
like *glimpse*, of the faint intimation of immortality available to the soul

30
If a star were confined into a tomb,°
    Her captive flames must needs burn there;
But when the hand that locked her up gives room,
    She'll shine through all the sphere.

Oh father of eternal life, and all
    Created glories under thee!
Resume° thy spirit from this world of thrall
    Into true liberty.

Either disperse these mists, which blot and fill
    My pérspective° still as they pass:
Or else remove me hence unto that hill
40
    Where I shall need no glass.

        1655

The Night°

JOHN 3:2°
  Through that pure virgin shrine,
That sacred veil° drawn o'er thy glorious noon,
That men might look and live, as glow-worms shine
    And face the moon,°
  Wise Nicodemus saw such light
  As made him know his God by night.

  Most blest believer he!
Who in that land of darkness and blind eyes
Thy long-expected healing wings° could see,
10
    When thou didst rise,
  And, what can never more be done,
  Did at midnight speak with the sun!

  Oh who will tell me where
He found thee at that dead and silent hour?
What hallowed solitary ground did bear
    So rare a flower,
  Within whose sacred leaves did lie
  The fullness of the deity?

star . . . tomb characteristic; cf. opening of "Cock-Crowing," below
Resume take back
perspective telescope, optic glass
The Night Nicodemus saw his God through the veil of the flesh of Jesus, saw, in the dark, the light. The poem praises night and secrecy, the meeting of Nicodemus with Jesus not in the Temple but in some dark grove. Night is the time of prayer; it is also, in a famous mystical text, an image of God considered as dazzlingly dark; and Vaughan finally petitions for death, the darkest of nights, in which he will be with God as Nicodemus was.

John 3:2 The gospel text tells how Nicodemus, a Pharisee, "came to Jesus by night, and said unto him, Rabbi, we know that thou art a teacher come from God," and was told that a man must be born again to enter into the kingdom of God.
veil See "Cock-crowing," below, l. 37n.
That men . . . moon That men might survive its brilliance ("there shall no man see me, and live," Exodus 33:20) and live with their own small light as glowworms can with the moon, though not the sun.
healing wings Malachi 4:2: "unto you that fear my name shall the Sun of righteousness arise with healing in his wings"

No mercy-seat of gold,
20 No dead and dusty cherub, nor carved stone,°
But His own living works did my Lord hold°
        And lodge alone;
    Where trees and herbs did watch and peep
    And wonder, while the Jews did sleep.°

    Dear night! this world's defeat;
The stop to busy fools; care's check and curb;
The day of spirits; my soul's calm retreat
        Which none disturb!
    Christ's progress, and his prayer time;°
30   The hours to which high heaven doth chime;

    God's silent, searching flight;
When my lord's head is filled with dew, and all
His locks are wet with the clear drops of night;°
        His still, soft call;°
    His knocking time;° the soul's dumb watch,
    When spirits their fair kindred catch.°

    Were all my loud, evil days
Calm and unhaunted as is thy dark tent,
Whose peace but by some angel's wing or voice
40   Is seldom rent,
    Then I in heaven all the long year
    Would keep, and never wander here.

    But living where the sun
Doth all things wake, and where all mix and tire
Themselves and others, I consent and run
        To every mire,
    And by this world's ill-guiding light,
    Err more than I can do by night.

    There is in God—some say—
50 A deep but dazzling darkness,° as men here
Say it is late and dusky, because they
        See not all clear.

No mercy-seat . . . stone not in the Temple
hold keep to
Where trees . . . sleep The notion is of vegetation being awake and growing in the night,
here aware of Jesus as the Jews, who set much
store by the Temple rejected in the preceding
lines, were not.
his prayer time Jesus prayed at night in
Gethsemane while the disciples slept.
my lord's head . . . night Song of Songs 5:2:
"I sleep, but my heart waketh: it is the voice
of my beloved that knocketh, saying, Open to
me, my sister, my love, my dove, my undefiled:
for my head is filled with dew, and my locks
with the drops of night." This image of the
Beloved is even more beautiful if one sees it

as a figure for the star-filled night sky.
still . . . call I Kings 19:12.
knocking time Revelation 3:20: "Behold I
stand at the door, and knock"
spirits . . . catch perhaps the contact between
living and dead mentioned in "They Are All
Gone . . ."
deep . . . darkness The mystical tradition venerated the works of Dionysius the Areopagite
(Pseudo-Dionysius), who spoke of heavenly
truths which lay "hidden in the dazzling obscurity of the secret Silence, outshining all
brilliance with the intensity of their darkness";
and this was a common theme in Renaissance
neoplatonic thought.

Oh for that night, where I in Him
Might live invisible and dim!
1655

Cock-Crowing°

Father of lights!° what sunny seed,°
What glance of day hast thou confined
Into this bird? To all the breed
This busy ray° thou hast assigned;
    Their magnetism works all night,°
    And dreams of Paradise and light.

Their eyes watch for the morning-hue,
Their little grain,° expelling night,
So shines and sings, as if it knew
10 The path unto the house of light.°
    It seems their candle, howe'er done,
    Was tinned° and lighted at the sun.

If such a tincture, such a touch,
So firm a longing can impour,°
Shall thy own image° think it much
To watch for thy appearing hour?
    If a mere blast so fill the sail,
    Shall not the breath of God prevail?

Oh thou immortal light and heat,
20 Whose hand so shines through all this frame,
That by the beauty of the seat,
We plainly see who made the same;

Cock-Crowing One of the most "hermetic" of Vaughan's poems, and directly indebted to his brother Thomas's treatise *Anima Magica Abscondita* (1650): "for she [the soul] is guided in her operations by a spiritual, metaphysical grain, a seed or glance of light . . . descending from the first Father of Lights" (see Elizabeth Holmes, *Henry Vaughan and the Hermetic Philosophy*, 1932). Hermetic and other occult doctrines combine in Vaughan with a traditional Christianity and a reflective use of Bible texts; he is in no way an adherent of some rival or heretical sect. The occasional strangeness of his idiom, like the range of inference he can suggest in what are otherwise plain scriptural allusions, is due to this commingling with Christianity of imagery from an independent tradition much cultivated in the mid-17th century, and regarded partly as a complement to the new science, and partly as a complement to traditional Christian devotion. Thus "Cock-Crowing," though one of his strangest poems, is not only similar in method to his others, but an orthodox act of Christian devotion.

Father of lights See the quotation from Thomas Vaughan, but also James 1:17, "Every good gift . . . cometh down from the Father of lights."
seed Vaughan's use of this word, like his brother's, is idiosyncratic but related to other mystical usages; it means, roughly, the same as *ray* (in l. 4) and "spark," an element of divinity within the soul, and here within the cock, which, responding to the first light, is an emblem of man's recognition of the heavenly light, and a symbol of the Resurrection (it has alchemical significance also).
ray See preceding note on *seed*.
magnetism . . . night Magnetism, important in the science and occult learning of the day, is a figure for the "sympathies" uniting distant objects; here the power of the "rays" to make the cocks dream of the origin of the rays.
grain seed
house of light Cf. Thomas Vaughan's treatise *Aula Lucis, or, The House of Light* (1652).
tinned kindled
impour pour in
thy own image man

Seeing thy seed abides in me,
Dwell thou in it, and I in thee!

To sleep without thee is to die;
Yea, 'tis a death partakes of hell;
For where thou dost not close the eye
It never opens, I can tell.
    In such a dark, Egyptian border,°
30   The shades of death dwell, and disorder.

If joys and hopes and earnest throes,
And hearts whose pulse beats still° for light,
Are given to birds, who but thee knows
A love-sick soul's exalted flight?
    Can souls be tracked by any eye
    But his, who gave them wings to fly?

Only this veil° which thou hast broke,
And must be broken yet in me,
This veil, I say, is all the cloak,
40 And cloud which shadows thee from me.
    This veil thy full-eyed love denies,
    And only gleams and fractions spies.

Oh take it off! make no delay,
But brush me with thy light, that I
May shine unto a perfect day,
And warm me at thy glorious eye.
    Oh take it off! or till it flee,
    Though with no lily,° stay with me!
                 1655

THOMAS TRAHERNE
1637–1674

Traherne's poems and those of his prose works which we find of interest were unpublished during the seventeenth century; in 1896–97, manuscripts of his poetry and of a remarkable group of prose meditations arranged in groups of a hundred were discovered on a London bookstall. The poems were at first attributed to Henry Vaughan (whose work they resemble rather more than Vaughan's does that of George Herbert), but Bertram Dobell, who published them in 1903, ascribed them to Traherne.

dark . . . border Exodus 10:21–2
still always
veil Vaughan was fond of this word, and the idea of light, for instance starlight, concealed behind a veil; in II Corinthians 3:13 ff. the veil is over the heart of the Jews in their reading of the Old Testament, but will be taken away when that heart "shall turn to the Lord." Vaughan means that the Law has been superseded—the Old Testament revealed to be a preparation for the New—and that a similar process must happen in his own soul. Elsewhere Vaughan quotes Hebrews 10:19–20: "Having . . . boldness to enter into the holiest by the blood of Jesus, By a new and living way, which he hath consecrated for us, through the veil, that is to say, his flesh." Perhaps Vaughan means here: be rid of the flesh, as Jesus was.
Though . . . lily Song of Songs 2:16: "My beloved . . . feedeth among the lilies." The point is that he is no lily, but a weed, as in a similar use of this text in his prose work The Mount of Olives.

Seven years later, another manuscript turned up at the British Museum, containing some of these same poems somewhat reworked by Traherne's brother, Philip, who had prepared the work for the publication it was not, in its own time, to receive. We know little of Traherne's life: son of a Herefordshire shoemaker, he was sent to Oxford (Brasenose, B.A. 1656), took orders (the living of Credenhill in his native Herefordshire was his), then became chaplain, in London and in Hereford, to Sir Orlando Bridgeman, Lord Keeper of the Great Seal. He published some polemical and devotional works in 1673, and some were published posthumously, but his truly remarkable achievement comprises the "centuries" or hundreds of devotional meditations. For their time, they are direct and unadorned, proceeding by intuitive leaps more than through evolving conceits; at their best, they are amazingly powerful, particularly in the evocation of childhood, a world which, as Philippe Ariès has shown us in his *Centuries of Childhood,* would not conceptually evolve until the later eighteenth century. It is the privileged condition which Traherne ascribes to the incompleteness of childhood, and the imaginative possibilities he sees in contemplating the mistakes children make in reading the world about them, that have caused critics to liken him to Blake and Wordsworth, whom he in fact does not very much resemble. "When I was a child," says St. Paul, "I spake as a child, I understood as a child, I thought as a child: but when I became a man, I put away childish things" (I Corinthians 13:11); and the point of the passage is about completeness and maturation as types of fulfilled, redeemed knowledge. But Traherne would see a loss rather than a gain in the putting away; it is that loss which he reveals in some of the prose passages and in many of his somewhat prolix, structurally uncomfortable poems, which nevertheless represent in their own way a final stage of the Metaphysical devotional poetry springing from Donne and Herbert.

Shadows° in the Water

In unexperienced° infancy
Many a sweet mistake doth lie:
Mistake though false, intending° true;
A *seeming* somewhat more than *view;*
    That doth instruct the mind
    In things that lie behind,
And many secrets to us show
Which afterwards we come to know.

Thus did I by the water's brink
10   Another world beneath me think;
And while the lofty spacious skies
Reversèd there abused mine eyes,
    I fancied other feet
    Came mine to touch and meet;
As by some puddle I did play°
Another world within it lay.

Shadows images
unexperienced inexperienced
intending meaning

As by . . . play as if nearby some puddle I played in

Beneath the water people drowned,
Yet with another heaven° crowned,
In spacious regions seemed to go
Freely moving to and fro:
    In bright and open space
    I saw their very face;
Eyes, hands, and feet they had like mine;
Another sun did with them shine.

'Twas strange that people there should walk,
And yet I could not hear them talk:
That through a little watery chink,
Which one dry ox or horse might drink,
    We other worlds should see,
    Yet not admitted be;
And other confines there behold
Of light and darkness, heat and cold.

I called them oft, but called in vain;
No speeches we could entertain:
Yet did I there expect to find
Some other world, to please my mind.
    I plainly saw by these
    A new Antipodes,°
Whom, though they were so plainly seen,
A film kept off that stood between.

By walking men's reversed feet
I chanced another world to meet;
Though it did not to view exceed
A phantasm, 'tis a world indeed,
    Where skies beneath us shine,
    And earth by art divine
Another face presents below,
Where people's feet against ours go.

Within the regions of the air,
Compassed about with heavens fair,
Great tracts of land there may be found
Enriched with fields and fertile ground;
    Where many numerous hosts,
    In those far distant coasts,
For other great and glorious ends,
Inhabit, my yet unknown friends.

Oh ye that stand upon the brink,
Whom I so near me, through the chink,
With wonder see: what faces there,
Whose feet, whose bodies, do ye wear?

---

another heaven Cf. Eve's vision of herself reflected in *Paradise Lost* IV.459.

Antipodes the reciprocal but antithetical world at the diametric opposite of the globe

I, my companions, see
In you another me.
They seemed others, but are we;
Our second selves those shadows be.

Look how far off those lower skies
Extend themselves! scarce with mine eyes
I can them reach. Oh ye, my friends,
What secret borders on those ends?
    Are lofty heavens hurled
70   'Bout your inferior° world?
Are ye the representatives
Of other peoples' distant lives?

Of all the playmates which I knew
That here I do the image view
In other selves, what can it mean?
But that below the purling stream
    Some unknown joys there be
    Laid up in store for me;
To which I shall, when that thin skin
Is broken, be admitted in.

      from MS., pub. 1903

From Centuries of Meditations

(*The First Century*)

3

I will open my mouth in parables: I will utter things that have been kept secret
from the foundation of the world. Things strange, yet common; incredible, yet
known; most high, yet plain; infinitely profitable, but not esteemed. Is it not a
great thing that you should be heir of the world? Is it not a very enriching verity,
in which the fellowship of the Mystery which from the beginning of the world
hath been hid in God, lies concealed? The thing hath been from the creation of
the world, but hath not been so explained, as that the interior beauty should
be understood.[1] It is my design, therefore, in such a plain manner to unfold it,
that my friendship may appear in making you possessor of the whole world.

(*The Third Century*)

1

Will you see the infancy of this sublime and celestial greatness? Those pure
and virgin apprehensions I had from the womb, and that divine light wherewith I was born are the best unto this day, wherein I can see the universe. By
the gift of God they attended me into the world, and by his special favour I
remember them till now. Verily they seem the greatest gifts his wisdom could

---

inferior lower
1. Compare this with Sir Thomas Browne's "I love to lose myself in a mystery," from the
Religio Medici.

bestow, for without them all other gifts had been dead and vain. They are unattainable by book, and therefore I will teach them by experience. Pray for them earnestly: for they will make you angelical and wholly celestial. Certainly Adam in Paradise had not more sweet and curious apprehensions of the world than I when I was a child.

2

All appeared new, and strange at the first, inexpressibly rare and delightful and beautiful. I was a little stranger, which at my entrance into the world was saluted and surrounded with innumerable joys. My knowledge was divine. I knew by intuition those things which since my apostasy I collected again by the highest reason. My very ignorance was advantageous. I seemed as one brought into the estate of innocence. All things were spotless and pure and glorious: yea, and infinitely mine, and joyful and precious. I knew not that there were any sins, or complaints, or laws. I dreamed not of poverties, contentions, or vices. All tears and quarrels were hidden from mine eyes. Everything was at rest, free and immortal. I knew nothing of sickness or death or rents or exaction, either for tribute or bread. In the absence of these I was entertained like an angel with the works of God in their splendour and glory, I saw all in the peace of Eden; heaven and earth did sing my Creator's praises, and could not make more melody to Adam than to me. All time was eternity, and a perpetual Sabbath. Is it not strange that an infant should be heir of the whole world, and see those mysteries which the books of the learned never unfold?

3

The corn was orient [2] and immortal wheat, which never should be reaped, nor was ever sown. I thought it had stood from everlasting to everlasting. The dust and stones of the street were as precious as gold: the gates were at first the end of the world. The green trees when I saw them first through one of the gates transported and ravished me, their sweetness and unusual beauty made my heart to leap, and almost mad with ecstasy, they were such strange and wonderful things. The men! Oh what venerable and reverend creatures did the aged seem! Immortal cherubims! [3] And young men glittering and sparkling angels, and maids strange seraphic pieces of life and beauty! Boys and girls tumbling in the street, and playing, were moving jewels. I knew not that they were born or should die; but all things abided eternally as they were in their proper places. Eternity was manifest in the light of the day, and something infinite behind everything appeared, which talked with my expectation and moved my desire. The city seemed to stand in Eden, or to be built in heaven. The streets were mine, the temple was mine, the people were mine, their clothes and gold and silver were mine, as much as their sparkling eyes, fair skins and ruddy faces. The skies were mine, and so were the sun and moon and stars, and all the world was mine; and I the only spectator and enjoyer of it. I knew no churlish proprieties,[4] nor bounds, nor divisions: but all pro-

2. Shining.
3. This is the traditional, but incorrect plural; the Hebrew masculine plural, -im should give cherub, cherubim as the proper forms, but the solecism has become accepted.
4. Properties, possessions.

prieties and divisions were mine: all treasures and the possessors of them. So that with much ado I was corrupted, and made to learn the dirty devices of this world. Which now I unlearn, and become, as it were, a little child again that I may enter into the Kingdom of God.

7

The first light which shined in my infancy in its primitive and innocent clarity was totally eclipsed: insomuch that I was fain to learn all again. If you ask me how it was eclipsed? Truly by the customs and manners of men, which like contrary winds blew it out: by an innumerable company of other objects, rude, vulgar and worthless things, that like so many loads of earth and dung did overwhelm and bury it; by the impetuous torrent of wrong desires in all others whom I saw or knew that carried me away and alienated me from it: by a whole sea of other matters and concernments that covered and drowned it: finally by the evil influence of a bad education that did not foster and cherish it. All men's thoughts and words were about other matters. They all prized new things which I did not dream of. I was a stranger and unacquainted with them; I was little and reverenced their authority; I was weak, and easily guided by their example; ambitious also, and desirous to approve myself unto them. And finding no one syllable in any man's mouth of those things, by degrees they vanished, my thoughts (as indeed what is more fleeting than a thought?) were blotted out; and at last all the celestial, great, and stable treasures to which I was born, as wholly forgotten as if they had never been.

12

By this you may see who are the rude and barbarous Indians. For verily there is no savage nation under the cope of heaven, that is more absurdly barbarous than the Christian world. They that go naked and drink water and live upon roots are like Adam, or angels in comparison of us. But they indeed that call beads and glass buttons jewels, and dress themselves with feathers, and buy pieces of brass and broken hafts of knives of our merchants are somewhat like us. But we pass them in barbarous opinions and monstrous apprehensions, which we nickname civility and the mode, amongst us. I am sure those barbarous people that go naked come nearer Adam, God, and angels in the simplicity of their wealth, though not in knowledge.

from MS., pub. 1908

JOHN MILTON
1608–1674

The shape of a very great poetic career must always be discerned against a historical background even as the effects of powerful forming forces within it are being understood. The   intentions of Chaucer, Shakespeare, and Spenser to live a life of art, and their visions of the route along which they would move, must all be read from the inner biography of their poetry itself. In the case of Milton, both the historical determinants and the informing energies from within are documented for us, and in inner and outer biography together. From his university days on, he was possessed of a self-awareness as a poet that could still, without limitation or qualification, transcend self-consciousness in a way that became almost impossible in literary history after, and perhaps because of, him. He planned when young not only to become a poet but to become a major one, and lived a consecrated life; yet he did not shrink from responding to the demands of a historical moment, and at a crucial high point in his creative career was ready to abandon the service of his poetic imagination, to stand and wait, while his activities and errands were all in the service of the Commonwealth, the Just City of men in whose possibility his vision encouraged him to believe.

The Renaissance and Reformation which continued in England through the middle of the seventeenth century surrounded him in childhood. His father, John Milton senior, was the Protestant son of a recusant Catholic yeoman who had disinherited him; he came to London and became moderately wealthy as a moneylender and scrivener, or notary. Sacrifice and inconvenience tend to strengthen piety, and Milton's continuation of his family's devoted Protestantism remained no easy and habitual matter, but a commitment which flourished, rather than suffered, in the high winds of doctrinal controversy that buffeted his post-university years. His father was a musician of some competence as well; and his general culture may have aided an imaginative generosity about a son who decided to give himself a six-year postgraduate course at home, leading to no degree or to anything else save for possible distant laurels.

Milton's education formally began at St. Paul's School in London, under a scholarly and imaginative master, in late 1620 or early 1621; but he started soon after to extend his own education at home with voluminous and extensive reading, and shortly thereafter additional formal tutoring followed, in classics and modern languages as well. He was at Cambridge for the spring term of 1625, matriculating at Christ's College and taking his B.A. in the spring of 1629, despite some slight altercation with a tutor in 1626 that seems to have resulted in a suspension for a brief time. While at Cambridge, he produced an impressive body of Latin verse and prose, the latter being represented by a group of oratorical exercises, or *Prolusions,* which show more than a mechanical approach to rhetorical problems. Indeed, in such pieces as the first one, delivered in college and debating the claims of day and night to be more excellent, we see the beginnings of a kind of mythopoetic thinking which is more than a mere brilliant assemblage of classical texts, just as the problematic part of the exercise seems a far cry from the undergraduate scholastic jugglings of Donne (in his *Paradoxes and Problems*). The germ of the *L'Allegro—Il Penseroso* pairing may indeed lie in the ability of Milton's mind, evidenced by this early work, to generate energies from conflict. His Latin verses of the time were mostly elegiac, commendatory, funerary, or half-serious epistolary, but his longish, mock-heroic poem on the Gunpowder Plot, written for the annual university Guy Fawkes Day celebrations, was extremely ambitious and unusually powerful. After some talented but tentatively conventional exercises in Jacobean poetic in English—funeral elegy was an accessible mode, and from the experimental vigor of his fancy, no nearby death was safe—he produced, in December of 1629, an unquestionably major poem of its moment, his *On the Morning of Christ's Nativity.* Its handling of the harmonization of various modes of angelic and celestial harmony, in the presentation of the heavenly voices heard by the Bethlehem shepherds, is brilliant at one level; but its treatment of the main theme of the phasing-out of pagan mythology by the birth of a new truth is more than that. The poem's vision is so fine that it is unable to avoid even a feeling of pathetic generosity for the gentler among the displaced: "With flower-inwoven tresses torn / The Nymphs in twilight shade of tangled thickets mourn." It represents the first clear instance of the direction

Milton's poetic career is to take thenceforth, following neither the Tribe of Ben into the realms of gracefulness, nor the "strong lines" of Donne's school into the tense regions of wit, erotic or divine. "If the Athenians, as some say, made their small deeds great and renowned by their eloquent writers, England hath had her noble achievements made small by the unskillful handling of monks and mechanics," he would write in 1642 in *The Reason of Church Government*, in a spirited passage of self-defense in the midst of his pamphleteering. But the conviction behind this started to flower early on, while in continued residence at Cambridge for his Master of Arts degree, reading Italian and writing sonnets in it, and, in 1631, producing *L'Allegro* and *Il Penseroso*. After taking his M.A. in 1632, Milton moved back home to continue preparing himself for major eloquence; first in a suburb west of London, then, in about 1635, at the family's country estate at Horton, in Buckinghamshire, near Windsor.

It was at Horton that Milton's fierce period of reading and creative concentration began to focus on specific large goals. In 1634, through his friendship with the musician Henry Lawes, who was tutor to the children of the Earl of Bridgewater, he got a chance to write a public piece of some magnitude. *Comus* (or, *A Masque Presented at Ludlow Castle*, as the 1637 printed version calls it) enabled him not only to address himself to the exposition of a virtue that was far from being what he would call in *Areopagitica* "fugitive and cloistered," but also to import into the transitory conventions of court masque some of the Shakespearean and Spenserian language and modes of representation that lyric poetry had not allowed him, up till then, to attempt. Similarly with the great programmatic force of *Lycidas*, in 1637.

From the spring of 1638 until the middle of the summer of 1639, Milton was in Italy, traveling in Tuscany and to Rome and Naples; he went about some in society, met musicians and patrons and even, in Florence, Galileo. In general, Italy had come to stand, in its language and poetry, as a region of the creative imagination for him; he was fortunate, this being so, that his experience of the actuality was so pleasant. In 1640 he moved to London and set up as a private schoolmaster; his first pupils were his nephews, Edward and John Phillips. But his concerns began to move toward public conflict, for London was a center of the struggle between Parliament on the one hand, and king and bishops on the other. Milton was on the brink of moving into some of his grandest fields of accomplishment—"not to make verbal curiosities the end (that were a toilsome vanity), but to be an interpreter and relater of the best and sagest things among mine own citizens throughout this island in the mother dialect"— as he would put it two years later in *The Reason of Church Government*. But the crucial issues raging about him, and about the principles to which he felt so committed, would have betrayed any task in the realm of epic or major drama which he might have set himself. From 1641, when he published his first tract against the institution of bishops, until twenty years after, when those bishops had been reinstituted with the Restoration of the monarchy, Milton devoted himself to prose, to argument, to armed mental fight. Writing with what he referred to as his "left hand," he produced a major series of prose works in defense of various religious, political, and moral freedoms, moving with a majority Puritan consensus in his anti-episcopal writings and then finding that the Presbyterian cause could itself become the oppressive one. In the next phase of his life, during which he married Mary Powell in 1642 (she left him in a fit of incompatibility after three months, but returned in 1645 to live with him until her death in childbirth seven years later), Milton wrote tracts in favor of divorce on the grounds of disharmony rather than only for adultery, and a brilliant short essay, *Of Education*, which supported the reformation of the still pre-

dominantly scholastic educational systems which prevailed in Europe. Such a reformation had indeed been going on at Milton's own school, St. Paul's, whose more
"Platonic" tradition of humanist training had been established by Erasmus, John Colet,
and William Lily. Then, too, there were the influential educational theories of John
Amos Comenius (1592–1670), the Czech educator who likewise opposed the arbitrariness and wearisome stuffiness of older methods, but whose own methods and
curricula aimed at a more pragmatic and less imaginatively self-fulfilling kind of
literacy. Milton's argument for the centrality of humanist literary and philosophical
disciplines itself made use, in an almost Baconian way, of the very methods whose
inculcation it desired to foster. Thus, Milton urges that logic be employed to lead
toward a flowering of intellectual activity in the arts of rhetoric, but that poetry be
made an instrument in that process, "as being less subtle and fine, but more simple,
sensuous and passionate"; and thus, in setting out the very aims of education themselves, earlier in the treatise, he leaps to the heart of biblical example:

> The end then of learning is to repair the ruins of our first parents by re-
> gaining to know God aright, and out of that knowledge to love him, to imi-
> tate him, to be like him, as we may the nearest by possessing our souls of
> true virtue, which being united to the heavenly grace of faith makes up the
> highest perfection. But because our understanding cannot in this body found
> itself but on sensible things, nor arrive so clearly to the knowledge of God
> and things invisible as by orderly conning over the visible and inferior creature,
> the same method is necessarily to be followed in all discreet teaching. And
> seeing every nation affords not experience and tradition enough for all kind
> of learning, therefore we are chiefly taught the languages of those who have
> at any time been most industrious after wisdom; so that language is but the
> instrument conveying to us things useful to be known. And though a linguist
> should pride himself to have all the tongues that Babel cleft the world into,
> yet, if he have not studied the solid things in them as well as the words and
> lexicons, he were nothing so much to be esteemed a learned man as any
> yeoman or tradesman competently wise in his mother dialect only.

Of Education and Areopagitica appeared in 1644. The following year, amid more
pamphleteering, Milton published a volume of his verse, Poems of Mr. John Milton,
including the sonnets which he had been writing during the 1640's as his only
poetry. It would not be until after service to the Commonwealth as Secretary for
Foreign Tongues to the Council of State (from 1649 until 1655, three years after his
blindness had become total), and after a long series of prose works, that he was
able, under the most adverse of circumstances, to get on with his deferred epic task.
In 1649, The Tenure of Kings and Magistrates had argued, shortly after the execution
of Charles I, for the divine right of removing kings; later that year, he attacked in
Eikonoklastes the roots of a Royalist cult which was attempting to make the martyred
Charles into a kind of saint. His first and second Defences of the English People
apeared in 1651 and 1654; The Ready and Easy Way to Establish a Free Commonwealth
was published on the brink of the Restoration in 1660.

The return of a Stuart monarch to the throne brought with it more than disappointment for Milton; he was in danger from royal prosecution, both as a propagandist for the Commonwealth cause and as a formal member of its government. He
actually went into hiding in the summer of 1660 until the general pardon of August
of that year, in which he was finally included. For some reason he was arrested and
imprisoned briefly at the end of the year, probably in November, but by December he
was granted a full pardon and had no further fear that personal action would be
taken against him.

It was during these last years of his life that Milton was finally to fulfill himself. Despite his total blindness, which dated from 1651–52, he was able to dictate *Paradise Lost*, finish it by 1665, continue on to *Paradise Regained* and, if most critics are correct in their view of its date of composition, *Samson Agonistes*, all of which were published in these last fourteen years of Milton's life. He was blind, and poorer than he had been with a state salary to augment his inheritance; he had seen the Commonwealth for which he had labored submerged in what looked to be an irreversible current of reaction; and yet he was able to concentrate all of his visionary and creative energies for a poetic accomplishment which ranks with Virgil's and Dante's in its organization of the knowledge and the spirit of its age. Like them, too, he evolved from received materials a fable powerful enough to be able to insist that it was not merely a fable, but an image of evolving human consciousness itself. Milton's major poems are the crowning fulfillment, too, of a life of learning as well as of the exercise of mental and moral combat; William Hazlitt remarked that Milton's learning has "the effect of intuition," and certainly in *Paradise Lost* he was able to include all that he knew without a sense of intrusion. His precursors (Virgil, Dante, Spenser among them) were an unalloyed imaginative aid to him. He was able to take what he needed from them without moving into their shadows; Hazlitt could perceive in him "a mighty intellect that, the nearer it approaches to others, the more distinct it becomes from them." Milton's last years were spent in continuing work, including revisions of the 1667 *Paradise Lost*, the second edition of which appeared in the year of his death, 1674.

L'Allegro and Il Penseroso

L'Allegro and *Il Penseroso* are of an unprecedented form in English poetry, related only to what was called a *synkriseis*, or debating situation, in classical literature (of which Milton's own college exercise, a prose oration on "Whether Day or Night Is More Excellent," is an example), and to analogous treatments, in Renaissance paintings and prints, of pairs of allegorical figures, such as Nature and Grace—the first, nude and associated with Eve, the second robed, and associated with Mary. Milton's two spirits are his own, compounded by his myth-making from traditional figures, but transformed by their milieu and its details. *L'Allegro* is a picture of a kind not yet invented: imagine a film version of a series of paintings like Botticelli's *Primavera* (Spring), with different scenes, but connected by the presence of one figure. She is Euphrosyne, one of the three Graces, naked (like her sisters, considered to be aspects of Venus). *Il Penseroso*, dark-robed, derives from personified Melancholy; a somber muse, neither the self-creating and self-consuming obsession of Burton in his dark tower of books, nor the massive, brooding angel of Albrecht Dürer's great engraving. The introductory verses to Burton's *Anatomy of Melancholy* may have suggested the tetrameter couplets as a meter (their refrain rhymes "melancholy" alternately with "folly" and "jolly"), but the modulation of their rhythms in the two poems is most flexible. Each poem opens with a half-serious banishment of a parody version of the spirit in the other lyric; in the main portion of each, the complementary treatment of light and dark, sound and silence, society and solitude, is subtle and complex. (See Figs. 15–18).

L'Allegro

Hence, loathèd Melancholy,°
Of Cerberus° and blackest Midnight born,
In Stygian cave forlorn
'Mongst horrid shapes, and shrieks, and sights unholy,
Find out some uncouth° cell,
Where brooding darkness spreads his jealous wings,
And the night-raven sings;
There under ebon shades and low-browed rocks,
As ragged as thy locks
10 In dark Cimmerian° desert ever dwell.
But come, thou goddess fair and free,
In heaven yclept Euphrosyne,°
And by men heart-easing Mirth,
Whom lovely Venus at a birth°
With two sister Graces more
To ivy-crownèd Bacchus bore;
Or whether° (as some sager sing)
The frolic wind that breathes the spring,
Zephyr, with Aurora° playing,
20 As he met her once a-Maying,
There on beds of violets blue,
And fresh-blown roses washed in dew,
Filled her with thee, a daughter fair,
So buxom,° blithe, and debonair.°
Haste thee, Nymph, and bring with thee
Jest and youthful Jollity,
Quips and cranks,° and wanton wiles,
Nods and becks° and wreathèd smiles,
Such as hang on Hebe's° cheek,
30 And love to live in dimple sleek;
Sport that wrinkled Care derides,°
And Laughter holding both his sides.
Come, and trip it as ye go
On the light fantastic toe,
And in thy right hand lead with thee
The mountain nymph, sweet Liberty;

loathèd Melancholy See Headnote.
Cerberus three-headed watchdog of Hades,
whose cave by the river Styx, Virgil says
(*Aeneid* VI.418), is full of the shrieking souls
of dead children
uncouth unknown
Cimmerian proverbially dark region, home of
the cave of Morpheus, one of the three sons
of sleep
yclept Euphrosyne called Euphrosyne, or
"Mirth." She was one of the three Graces usually
thought of as daughters of Zeus and Hera;
her sisters were Aglaia ("Brightness") and
Thalia ("Flowering") (see *The Faerie Queene*
VI.x.21–24).

Venus at a birth other fables make the Graces
daughters of Venus and Bacchus
Or whether In the tone of a commentator
on mythology, Milton adduces yet another
parentage, made up by him for this poem; in
a sense, the new parentage redefines the meaning of the Grace.
Aurora goddess of the dawn
buxom compliant
debonair gracious
cranks word-play jokes
becks gestures of beckoning, or "come-on"
Hebe's the Olympian barmaid and youth goddess
derides "Care" is the object.

And if I give thee honour due,
Mirth, admit me of thy crew,
To live with her, and live with thee,
40   In unreprovèd pleasures free;
To hear the lark begin his flight,
And singing startle the dull night,
From his watch-tower in the skies,°
Till the dappled dawn doth rise;
Then to come in spite of sorrow
And at my window bid good-morrow,
Through the sweet-briar or the vine,
Or the twisted eglantine;
While the cock with lively din
50   Scatters the rear of darkness thin,
And to the stack or the barn door
Stoutly struts his dames before;
Oft listening how the hounds and horn
Cheerly rouse the slumbering morn,
From the side of some hoar° hill,
Through the high wood echoing shrill;
Sometime walking, not unseen,°
By hedgerow elms, on hillocks green,
Right against the eastern gate,
60   Where the great sun begins his state,°
Robed in flames and amber light,
The clouds in thousand liveries dight;°
While the ploughman near at hand
Whistles o'er the furrowed land,
And the milkmaid singeth blithe,
And the mower whets his scythe,
And every shepherd tells his tale°
Under the hawthorn in the dale.
Straight mine eye hath caught new pleasures,
70   Whilst the landscape round it measures:
Russet lawns and fallows gray,
Where the nibbling flocks do stray;
Mountains on whose barren breast
The labouring clouds° do often rest;
Meadows trim with daisies pied,°
Shallow brooks and rivers wide.
Towers and battlements it° sees

To hear . . . skies The poetic power of the skylark results from the intensity of his song, filling the sky which, because of the small size and great altitude of the singer, looks empty.
hoar not frosty, but gray from morning mist
Sometime . . . unseen Cf. *Il Penseroso*, l. 65.
state royal progress or tour
liveries dight gay costumes clad

tells his tale counts his tally (of sheep); perhaps "recounts his story"
labouring clouds unlike the barren hills, they will bring forth rain
daisies pied variegated daisies; like many other phrases in these poems, quoted from Shakespeare (the cuckoo's song from *Love's Labour's Lost* V.ii.882–85)
it "mine eye" (from l. 69)

Bosomed high in tufted trees,
Where perhaps some beauty lies,
80 The cynosure° of neighbouring eyes.
Hard by, a cottage chimney smokes
From betwixt two agèd oaks,
Where Corydon and Thyrsis met
Are at their savoury dinner set
Of herbs and other country messes,
Which the neat-handed Phillis dresses;
And then in haste her bower° she leaves,
With Thestylis to bind the sheaves;
Or if the earlier season lead,
90 To the tanned haycock in the mead.
Sometimes with secure° delight
The upland hamlets will invite,
When the merry bells ring round,
And the jocund rebecs° sound
To many a youth and many a maid
Dancing in the chequered shade;
And young and old come forth to play
On a sunshine holiday,
Till the livelong daylight fail:
100 Then to the spicy nut-brown ale,
With stories told of many a feat,
How fairy Mab the junkets eat;°
She was pinched and pulled, she said,
And he, by friar's lantern° led,
Tells how the drudging goblin sweat
To earn his cream-bowl duly set,
When in one night, ere glimpse of morn,
His shadowy flail hath threshed the corn
That ten day-labourers could not end;
110 Then lies him down the lubber fiend,°
And stretched out all the chimney's length,
Basks at the fire his hairy strength;
And crop-full out of doors he flings,
Ere the first cock his matin rings.
Thus done the tales, to bed they creep,
By whispering winds soon lulled asleep.
Towered cities please us then,°

---

cynosure the constellation Ursa Minor, containing Polaris; thus, a proverbial center of attention
bower cottage
secure carefree
rebecs primitive fiddles
eat ate. "Mab" is the fairy queen from Mercu-
tio's speech in *Romeo and Juliet* I.iv. 55–95.
friar's lantern the will-o'-the-wisp
lubber fiend spirit who is a lob, or household
drudge. Puck, in *Midsummer Night's Dream*

II.i.16 and 40, is called "lob of spirits" and
"Hobgoblin."
Towered . . . then Here comes the shift from
glad day to glad night, paralleled at almost
exactly the same point (l. 121) in *Il Penseroso*
by the dawning of sad day. The interpenetration
of the spirits of the poems is important:
L'Allegro's night is full of illuminations, comic
theater, songs, and festivals, while *Il Penseroso's*
day is shadowed and shrouded.

And the busy hum of men,
Where throngs of knights and barons bold
120   In weeds° of peace high triumphs hold,
With store of ladies, whose bright eyes
Rain influence,° and judge the prize
Of wit or arms, while both contend
To win her grace whom all commend.
There let Hymen° oft appear
In saffron robe, with taper clear,
And pomp, and feast, and revelry,
With masque and antique pageantry:
Such sights as youthful poets dream
130   On summer eves by haunted stream.
Then to the well-trod stage anon,
If Jonson's learnèd sock° be on,
Or sweetest Shakespeare, Fancy's child,°
Warble his native wood-notes wild;
And ever against eating° cares
Lap me in soft Lydian airs,°
Married to immortal verse,
Such as the meeting soul may pierce
In notes with many a winding bout°
140   Of linkèd sweetness long drawn out,
With wanton heed and giddy cunning,
The melting voice through mazes running,
Untwisting all the chains that tie
The hidden soul of harmony;
That Orpheus' self may heave his head
From golden slumber on a bed
Of heaped Elysian flowers, and hear
Such strains as would have won the ear
Of Pluto, to have quite set free
150   His half-regained Eurydice.
These delights if thou canst give,
Mirth, with thee I mean to live.°
1631–32?   1645

---

weeds costumes
Rain influence See *Astrology* in the Glossary. The ladies are out of Petrarchan poetry—the conceit about the eyes of the beloved being stars is a cliché.
Hymen god of marriage, as a character in a masque
learnèd sock The sock, or low shoe, was emblematic of classical comedy; cf. *Il Penseroso*, l. 102.
sweetest . . . child In the earlier poem "On Shakespeare" Milton alluded to this spontaneous creativity; the juxtaposition of "learnèd" Jonson and "native" Shakespeare is a commonplace.
eating (adjectival)

soft Lydian airs melodies of a delightful and relaxing sort (the Lydian mode or key, in Greek tradition, was "lax," the Dorian "manly," the Phrygian "wild," etc., in the same way in which we think of minor as being "sad" and major "happy"; in addition, "airs" means breezes).
bout turn, or possibly, return. Milton may be thinking of the Italian aria, or solo air, with its turning ornamentations, and *ritornello*, or *da capo* repeat.
These delights . . . live yet one more response—here to the closing lines of Marlowe's "The Passionate Shepherd"

Il Penseroso

Hence, vain deluding Joys,°
　The brood of Folly without father bred,
How little you bestead,°
　Or fill the fixèd mind with all your toys;
Dwell in some idle brain,
　And fancies fond with gaudy shapes possess,
As thick and numberless
　As the gay motes that people the sunbeams,
Or likest hovering dreams,
10　The fickle pensioners of Morpheus' train.°
But hail, thou Goddess sage and holy,
Hail, divinest Melancholy,
Whose saintly visage is too bright
To hit the sense of human sight,
And therefore to our weaker view
O'erlaid with black, staid Wisdom's hue;
Black, but such as in esteem
Prince Memnon's sister° might beseem,
Or that starred Ethiop queen° that strove
20　To set her beauty's praise above
The sea-nymphs, and their powers offended.
Yet thou art higher far descended:
Thee bright-haired Vesta° long of yore
To solitary Saturn bore—
His daughter she (in Saturn's reign
Such mixture was not held a stain).
Oft in glimmering bowers and glades
He met her, and in secret shades
Of woody Ida's inmost grove,
30　While yet there was no fear of Jove.°
Come, pensive Nun, devout and pure,
Sober, steadfast, and demure,
All in a robe of darkest grain,°
Flowing with majestic train,
And sable stole of cypress lawn°
Over thy decent shoulders drawn.
Come, but keep thy wonted state,
With even step and musing gait,
And looks commercing with the skies,

---

deluding Joys See Headnote.
bestead help
pensioners . . . train attendants on Morpheus,
god of dreams, son of Sleep
Memnon's sister Himera, an Ethiopian princess
in Homer
Ethiop queen Cassiopeia who, in one version
of her legend, was transformed into a constellation because she boasted so of her daughter
Andromeda's beauty

Vesta usually virginal, Roman goddess of the
hearth. Milton invents this myth of her incestuous parentage.
Jove Jupiter's childhood was spent on Mt. Ida
on Crete; later, he overthrew Saturn, his
father (or Zeus and his father Cronos, in
Greek).
grain color
cypress lawn black, fine linen

40 Thy rapt soul sitting in thine eyes;
There held in holy passion still,
Forget thyself to marble, till
With a sad° leaden downward cast
Thou fix them on the earth as fast.
And join with thee calm Peace and Quiet,
Spare Fast, that oft with gods doth diet,
And hears the Muses in a ring
Aye round about Jove's altar sing;
And add to these retired Leisure,°
50 That in trim gardens takes his pleasure;
But first, and chiefest, with thee bring
Him that yon soars on golden wing,
Guiding the fiery-wheelèd throne,
The Cherub Contemplatïon;°
And the mute Silence hist° along,
'Less Philomel will deign a song,
In her sweetest, saddest plight,°
Smoothing the rugged brow of Night,
While Cynthia° checks her dragon yoke
60 Gently o'er th' accustomed oak.
Sweet bird, that shunn'st the noise of folly,
Most musical, most melancholy!
Thee, chauntress, oft the woods among
I woo to hear thy even-song;
And missing thee, I walk unseen
On the dry smooth-shaven green,
To behold the wandering moon
Riding near her highest noon,
Like one that had been led astray
70 Through the heaven's wide pathless way;
And oft, as if her head she bowed,
Stooping through a fleecy cloud.
Oft on a plat° of rising ground
I hear the far-off curfew sound
Over some wide-watered shore,
Swinging slow with sullen° roar;
Or if the air will not permit,
Some still removèd place will fit,
Where glowing embers through the room
80 Teach light to counterfeit a gloom,°

sad serious
Leisure See Marvell's "The Garden" for an instance of this theme of retirement.
Contemplatïon The diaeresis mark indicates that the diphthong is separated into two vowels sounds, here giving the word five syllables.
hist to whisper "hist!"—meaning "come along!"
'Less . . . plight the nightingale, changed form of Philomela whose brother-in-law raped her and tore out her tongue; her metamorphosis made her the bird of sad song
Cynthia the moon goddess; "dragon yoke" because a chariot drawn by dragons is Hecate's and Hecate is the antithetical form of the moon enchantress
plat plot
sullen solemn, religious
Teach . . . gloom This contrasts with the lighting of interiors at night in *L'Allegro*.

Far from all resort of mirth,
Save the cricket on the hearth,
Or the bellman's drowsy charm,°
To bless the doors from nightly harm:
Or let my lamp at midnight hour
Be seen in some high lonely tower,°
Where I may oft outwatch the Bear,°
With thrice great Hermes,° or unsphere
The spirit of Plato° to unfold
90   What worlds or what vast regions hold
The immortal mind that hath forsook
Her mansion in this fleshly nook;
And of those daemons that are found
In fire, air, flood, or under ground,
Whose power hath a true consent
With planet or with element.°
Sometime let gorgeous Tragedy
In sceptred pall come sweeping by,
Presenting Thebes, or Pelops' line,°
100   Or the tale of Troy divine,
Or what (though rare) of later age
Ennobled hath the buskined° stage.
But, O sad Virgin, that thy power
Might raise Musaeus° from his bower,
Or bid the soul of Orpheus sing
Such notes as, warbled to the string,
Drew iron tears down Pluto's cheek
And made hell grant what love did seek;°
Or call up him° that left half told
110   The story of Cambuscan bold,
Of Camball and of Algarsife,
And who had Canace to wife,
That owned the virtuous ring and glass,
And of the wondrous horse of brass,
On which the Tartar king did ride;
And if aught else great bards beside

bellman's . . . charm the chant of the night-watchman calling the hours
high lonely tower This is the central point of contemplative vision in the poem; it has been associated by critics with Isaiah's watchtower (Isaiah 21:8), and Plato's notion, in the *Republic* 560b, of a high place, or "acropolis" of the soul. The tower is ascended not like the major prophetic mountains, but, as here, to devote to the night skies the same attentive gaze as that which, in *L'Allegro*, follows the "live-long daylight."
outwatch the Bear Ursa Major, the Big Dipper, never sets; thus, to work all night.
thrice great Hermes Hermes Trismegistus, supposed author of neoplatonist writings, actually from Alexandria in the third and fourth centuries A.D. (See *Platonism* in the Glossary.)

unsphere . . . Plato to call Plato's ghost back from its home in the highest sphere of heaven
With planet . . . element Evil or marginal spirits were classified according to which of the four elements composed them, and with particular heavenly bodies.
Thebes, or Pelops' line the Oedipus cycle and the tales of the house of Atreus (Thyestes, Agamemnon, Orestes, etc.)
buskined booted with the emblematic footwear of tragedy; cf. *L'Allegro*, l. 132
Musaeus mythical Greek poet (fictionally associated by Marlowe with his actual, late 5th-century A.D. author in *Hero and Leander*)
what . . . seek Eurydice; cf. *L'Allegro*, ll. 145–50
him Chaucer; the half-told story, The Squire's Tale

In sage and solemn tunes have sung,
Of tourneys and of trophies hung,
Of forests and enchantments drear,
120 Where more is meant than meets the ear.°
Thus, Night, oft see me in thy pale career,°
Till civil-suited° Morn appear,
Not tricked and frounced° as she was wont
With the Attic boy° to hunt,
But kerchiefed in a comely cloud,
While rocking winds are piping loud,
Or ushered with a shower still,
When the gust hath blown his fill,
Ending on the rustling leaves,
130 With minute° drops from off the eaves.
And when the sun begins to fling
His flaring beams, me, Goddess, bring
To archèd walks of twilight groves,
And shadows brown° that Sylvan loves,
Of pine or monumental oak,
Where the rude axe with heavèd stroke
Was never heard the nymphs to daunt,
Or fright them from their hallowed haunt.
There in close covert by some brook,
140 Where no profaner eye may look,
Hide me from Day's garish eye,
While the bee with honied thigh,
That at her flowery work doth sing,
And the waters murmuring
With such consort° as they keep,
Entice the dewy-feathered Sleep;
And let some strange mysterious dream
Wave at his wings in airy stream
Of lively portraiture displayed,
150 Softly on my eyelids laid.
And as I wake, sweet music breathe
Above, about, or underneath,
Sent by some Spirit to mortals good,
Or the unseen Genius of the wood.
But let my due feet never fail
To walk the studious cloister's pale,°
And love the high embowèd° roof,

Where more . . . ear the corpus of allegorical
romance: particularly Spenser (see *Areopa-*
gitica), but also Tasso and Ariosto
Thus, Night . . . career a deliberately placed
pentameter line, breaking the rhythm: it moves
away from the praise of dead poets, and is,
perhaps, a hidden defiance of Mirth
civil-suited simply dressed
frounced with hair curled

Attic boy Cephalus
minute falling once a minute (not "tiny")
brown standard term for "dark" in pastoral
diction
consort other polyphonic parts (sung by leaves,
sad birds, etc.)
pale enclosure
embowèd vaulted

With antique° pillars' massy proof,°
And storied windows richly dight,°
160   Casting a dim religious light.
There let the pealing organ blow
To the full-voiced quire below,
In service high and anthems clear,
As may with sweetness, through mine ear,
Dissolve me into ecstasies,
And bring all heaven before mine eyes.
And may at last my weary age
Find out the peaceful hermitage,
The hairy gown and mossy cell,
170   Where I may sit and rightly spell°
Of every star that heaven doth shew,
And every herb that sips the dew,
Till old experience do attain
To something like prophetic strain.
These pleasures, Melancholy, give,
And I with thee will choose to live.
1631–32?   1645

Sonnets

Milton started writing sonnets while still at Cambridge, but they were never of the traditionally Petrarchan sequence type (e.g. *Astrophel and Stella, Delia, Ideas Mirror*) that had gone out of fashion more than forty years earlier. His poems developed under the influence of the Italian sonnets of Giovanni della Casa and, in his later ones, of Tasso's *Sonnetti Eroici;* he learned particularly from their syntax, their placing of nouns and adjectives, and strong enjambments. Five of Milton's first six sonnets were in Italian; later on, he used the form in a more public, proclamatory, and even denunciatory manner—as a kind of ode in miniature. Based on the Italian sonnet form divided into octave-sestet sections (rather than the more logically schematic quatrain and couplet pattern used by Shakespeare), Milton's sonnets nevertheless grew to override that central division. They developed a flow of utterance building to a high (rather than to the kind of shutting-off that an epigrammatic or neat ending effects). Wordsworth likened their self-contained homogeneous character to that of a drop of dew. Their rhymes aside, these sonnets were a study for the eventual blank-verse paragraphs of *Paradise Lost.*

antique antic, grotesque
proof impenetrability
dight decorated (stained-glass)
spell decipher the meaning, read. At the end of the poem, Melancholy is left with a kind of resolute, scientific patience, a healthy introspection fulfilled in looking outward, not like Dürer's angel of the imagination whose abandoned scientific instruments lie around her.

Sonnet I°

O nightingale, that on yon bloomy spray
    Warblest at eve, when all the woods are still,
    Thou with fresh hope the lover's heart dost fill,
    While the jolly Hours° lead on propitious May;
Thy liquid notes that close the eye of day,°
    First heard before the shallow cuckoo's bill,
    Portend success in love; O if Jove's will
    Have linked that amorous power to thy soft lay,
Now timely sing, ere the rude bird of hate°
10   Foretell my hopeless doom in some grove nigh,
    As thou from year to year hast sung too late
For my relief, yet hadst no reason why:
    Whether the Muse or Love call thee his mate,°
    Both them I serve, and of their train am I.
    1629–30?   1645

Sonnet VII

How soon hath time, the subtle thief of youth,
    Stolen on his wing my three and twentieth year!°
    My hasting days fly on with full career,
    But my late spring no bud or blossom° showeth.
Perhaps my semblance° might deceive° the truth,
    That I to manhood am arrived so near,
    And inward ripeness doth much less appear,
    That some more timely-happy spirits° endueth.
Yet be it less or more, or soon or slow,
10   It shall be still° in strictest measure even
    To that same lot, however mean or high,
Toward which time leads me, and the will of heaven;
    All is, if I have grace to use it so,
    As ever° in my great task-master's eye.
    1631   1645

Sonnet I Milton's first sonnet in English, a response to the self-generated occasion of answering the song of the nightingale: he has never been in love, he has never written the kind of poetry he was going to demand of himself—what can the nightingale *mean,* then, as an emblem as well as by its song?
Hours daughters of Jupiter and Themis (see Spenser's *Epithalamium,* I. 98, 280)
eye of day the sun; a vestigial Petrarchanism
bird of hate the cuckoo. In medieval tradition, to hear him sing before the nightingale was a bad omen for a lover.
Whether . . . mate The sexes here are a bit confused, but "mate" merely implies mythological association: whether the nightingale is a myth of poetry (as in Ovid's story of the raped, mute Philomela, restored to her voice through change), or whether, as in popular tradition, the night-bird of love.

three and twentieth year thus, the poem written for his 24th birthday, a confrontation with his own inactivity and of his prolonged scholarly and imaginative apprenticeship
bud or blossom poetry (a 17th-century commonplace)
semblance appearance
deceive prove false
timely-happy spirits He is thinking of Cambridge friends, perhaps, who at his age seem more mature, fulfilled, and fashionable as poets; scholars have proposed his friend Charles Diodati, Thomas Randolph, Abraham Cowley, and even Spenser, as historical candidates.
still always
ever eternity. The last two lines probably mean "All time is, if I have grace to use it so, as eternity in the sight of God."

Sonnet VIII

When the Assault Was Intended to the City°

Captain or colonel,° or knight in arms,
    Whose chance on these defenseless doors may seize,
    If deed of honour did thee ever please,
    Guard them, and him within protect from harms;
He can requite thee, for he knows the charms
    That call fame on such gentle acts as these,
    And he can spread thy name o'er lands and seas,
    Whatever clime the sun's bright circle warms.
Lift not thy spear against the Muses' bower:
10   The great Emathian conqueror bid spare
    The house of Pindarus,° when temple and tower
Went to the ground; and the repeated air°
    Of sad Electra's poet had the power
    To save the Athenian walls from ruin bare.
    1642   1642

Sonnet XVII

When I consider how my light is spent,
    Ere half my days,° in this dark world and wide,
    And that one talent° which is death to hide
    Lodged with me useless, though my soul more bent
To serve therewith my maker, and present
    My true account, lest he, returning, chide.
    'Doth God exact day-labour, light denied?'
    I fondly ask; but Patience, to prevent°
That murmur, soon replies: 'God doth not need
10   Either man's work or his own gifts; who best
    Bear his mild yoke,° they serve him best; his state

When . . . City The assault was of Royalist troops on London, from which King Charles's army was turned back on November 13, 1642, at Turnham Green, and the poem is written as if to be posted on the author's door.
colonel here trisyllabic: cur-o-nel
Pindarus Alexander the Great reportedly spared Pindar's house when he burned Thebes; see E.K.'s gloss on the October Eclogue in Spenser's *Shepheards Calender.*
air song, here the first chorus of Euripides' *Electra,* recited ("repeated") by an Athenian officer in 404 B.C., so moving the victorious Spartans that they spared Athens
half my days Since there is some controversy over the dating of this sonnet, "half my days" does not necessarily mean 35, midpoint of the biblical life-span of "threescore years and ten," but perhaps half of Milton's mature life, or half the span of his father, who died at 84; some scholars would put it earlier, and have the

"spent" light indicate the onset of his blindness, which was gradually overcoming him between 1644 and 1652.
one talent Our modern word is derived from a word meaning a weight of gold, a sum of money equivalent to about $30,000 (if a silver talent, about $6,000), thus a possession or disposition. However, our modern use is shaped by the central allusion of this poem, the parable of the Kingdom of Heaven in Matthew 25: 14–30, in which a lord gives his servants various sums of money. The good ones use their talents to double the value by investment, but the "wicked and slothful servant" hides his in the ground and is rebuked when his master returns, asking for a true account. Milton's talent, for writing a great poem, seems to be burying itself in darkness against his will.
prevent forestall
Bear . . . yoke Milton is alluding to Matthew 11:29–30.

Is kingly—thousands° at his bidding speed
    And post o'er land and ocean without rest:
    They also serve who only stand and wait.'
    1652?   1673

Sonnet XVIII

    On the Late Massacre in Piedmont°

Avenge, O Lord, thy slaughtered saints, whose bones
    Lie scattered on the Alpine mountains cold,
    Even them who kept thy truth so pure of old
    When all our fathers worshipped stocks and stones,°
Forget not; in thy book° record their groans
    Who were thy sheep, and in their ancient fold
    Slain by the bloody Piemontese that rolled
    Mother with infant down the rocks. Their moans
The vales redoubled to the hills, and they
    To heaven. Their martyred blood and ashes sow
    O'er all the Italian fields, where still doth sway
The triple tyrant,° that from these may grow
    A hundredfold,° who, having learnt thy way,
    Early may fly the Babylonian° woe.
    1655   1673

Sonnet XIX

Methought I saw my late espousèd saint°
    Brought to me like Alcestis° from the grave,
    Whom Jove's great son to her glad husband gave,
    Rescued from death by force, though pale and faint.
Mine, as whom washed from spot of child-bed taint
    Purification in the old Law° did save,

Thousands of angels
On . . . Piedmont The Vaudois, an early Protestant sect formed in the 12th century, lived in Alpine villages and were tolerated by the Dukes of Savoy, until the then Duke, Charles Emmanuel II, sent an army to remove them. On April 24, 1655, many were massacred, including prisoners.
stocks and stones gods of wood or stone
book the Book of Life in Revelation 5:1ff.
triple tyrant the triple-crowned pope
A hundredfold The army harvested by Cadmus from dragon's teeth he sowed combines with the seeds of the sower (Matthew 13:8) which "fell into good ground, and brought forth fruit, some an hundredfold."
Babylonian Just as the author of Revelation had encoded imperial Rome as Babylon, so did Puritan writers with the papal city.

saint a spirit in heaven, in this case, probably Katherine Woodcock, Milton's second wife, although some scholars, dating the sonnet earlier, apply it to Mary Powell, the first Mrs. Milton, who died in childbirth
Alcestis wife of Admetus who chose to die in his place and who, in Euripides' drama, was returned to him by Heracles, who wrestled with Death to win her back; Alcestis was veiled on her return, and Katherine also, in that Milton had never seen her face, being blind at their marriage
Law In Leviticus, the postpartum condition is deemed unclean for 66 days, and the woman must be purified; if this is literal, it might apply to Mary Powell; if figurative, to Katherine (from the Greek *kathara*, "pure"), who died the day after the feast of the Purification of the Virgin.

And such as yet once more I trust to have
Full sight of her in heaven without restraint,
Came vested all in white,° pure as her mind.
10   Her face was veiled, yet to my fancied sight
Love, sweetness, goodness in her person shined
So clear as in no face with more delight.
But O as to embrace me she inclined,
I waked, she fled, and day brought back my night.
1658   1673

Comus

The proper but less familiar title of *Comus* is "A Masque Presented at Ludlow Castle, 1634," and it comes down to us in printed editions (an anonymous one of 1637 and, later, in the *Poems* of 1645) as well as in manuscripts which suggest what the actual version was like. It was written as an entertainment for the household of the Earl of Bridgewater, who had recently been made Lord President of Wales; Milton's friend, the composer Henry Lawes, was employed there as tutor to the Earl's three children, Alice, fifteen, and John and Thomas, eleven and nine. *Comus* is not strictly a masque (see the Headnote to Ben Jonson's *Pleasure Reconciled to Virtue*), but it partakes of many elements of that major seventeenth-century form of symbolic entertainment, particularly in the relation of the masquing figures, or members of the courtly audience who in fact participate in the emblematic dances, and those mythological roles. In *Comus* the roles of the Lady, her younger brothers, and the Attendant Spirit were played by the children and their tutor; the monsters attending Comus dance in a version of the "antimasque" or grotesque prelude or interlude that in Ben Jonson's masques provided different sorts of contrast to the main fiction. But the heart of masque is dancing, and the heart of *Comus* is language; the mythological "action" in it occurs through no staggering effects of stage machinery, in which one realm or world "becomes" another, but in the great speeches of Comus and the Lady, and in the recitations and songs of the Spirit and the goddess Sabrina. Milton's poetic language is notably Shakespearean: his phrases echo *A Midsummer Night's Dream, The Tempest, The Winter's Tale,* and other plays, and the syntax and the texture of the blank verse throughout constantly remind us of the earlier poet. Word-forms and archaisms are modeled on, but not actually borrowed from, Spenser.

Most critics today like to think of *Comus* as pastoral drama, objectifying platonistic tradition and stemming from Tasso's *Aminta* (see Samuel Daniel's "A Pastoral" and the analogous passage from Guarini's *Il Pastor Fido* adapted by Fanshawe). Here, the allegory of chastity is embodied in the powers to resist deforming magic that a young girl's virginity possesses. (It must be understood that lifelong virginity is not what Milton, or Spenser, thought chastity to be, but that for a certain kind of symbolic dramaturgy, that complex virtue seemed best represented by the power of virginity, as a state, to preserve itself delicately and forcefully.) Chastity's antagonist is worthy of her, making trial rather than crudely assaulting; he is Comus, a transformed version of both the handsome young reveler from classical lore, and Ben Jonson's big-bellied

white With this word the rhymes shift from those on the long ā sound to long ī; the last line "waked . . . night" recapitulates this shift.

mockery of pleasure. Milton makes him the son of Circe, who, in the *Odyssey,* changed men who behaved like pigs into the swine they "really" were. Circe was the first satirist, in a sense, and the worse a person was, the more monstrous his transformed shape would be. But Comus is also a suave, learned seducer, master of the conventional *carpe diem* arguments which overran Caroline love poetry and which Milton augmented, presumably after more exposure to them, in his printed text.

The magic herb *haemony* which the "shepherd lad" (l. 619) produces is an example of Milton's kind of myth-making in his early poems; scholars are in doubt about its exact traditional source, but it is clearly modeled on the moly plant used against Circe in Homer, and may derive its name from Greek words for blood (thus associating it with the power of sacrificial blood, in both pagan and Christian story), or with the name of Thessaly, from which magic herbs came. In any event, it is a resonant name for a substance whose power, though limited, must be defined by the poem's own moral realm.

Comus

THE PERSONS
The Attendant Spirit, afterwards in the habit of Thyrsis
Comus with his crew
The Lady
First Brother
Second Brother
Sabrina the Nymph

The chief persons which presented were
The Lord Brackley
Mr. Thomas Egerton his Brother
The Lady Alice Egerton

    The first scene discovers a wild wood.
    [THE ATTENDANT SPIRIT *descends or enters*]

Before the starry threshold of Jove's court
My mansion is, where those immortal shapes
Of bright aërial Spirits live ensphered
In regions mild of calm and serene air,
Above the smoke and stir of this dim spot
Which men call Earth, and with low-thoughted care,
Confined and pestered° in this pinfold° here,
Strive to keep up a frail and feverish being,
Unmindful of the crown that Virtue gives,
After this mortal change,° to her true servants
Amongst the enthronèd gods on sainted seats.
Yet some there be that by due steps aspire
To lay their just hands on that golden key

10

pestered crowded together   **mortal change** death
pinfold pen for farm animals

That opes the palace of Eternity:
To such my errand is, and but for such
I would not soil these pure ambrosial weeds°
With the rank vapours of this sin-worn mould.°
    But to my task. Neptune, besides the sway
Of every salt flood and each ebbing stream,
20 Took in, by lot, 'twixt high and nether Jove°
Imperial rule of all the sea-girt isles
That like to rich and various gems inlay
The unadornèd bosom of the deep,
Which he, to grace his tributary gods,
By course° commits to several government,
And gives them leave to wear their sapphire crowns
And wield their little tridents;° but this isle,
The greatest and the best of all the main,
He quarters° to his blue-haired deities;
30 And all this tract° that fronts the falling sun
A noble peer° of mickle° trust and power
Has in his charge, with tempered awe° to guide
An old and haughty nation° proud in arms—
Where his fair offspring, nursed in princely lore,
Are coming to attend their father's state
And new-entrusted sceptre, but their way
Lies through the pérplexed° paths of this drear wood,°
The nodding horror of whose shady brows
Threats the forlorn and wandering passenger.
40 And here their tender age might suffer peril,
But that by quick command from sovereign Jove
I was dispatched for their defence and guard;
And listen why, for I will tell ye now
What never yet was heard in tale or song
From old or modern bard, in hall or bower.
    Bacchus, that first from out the purple grape
Crushed the sweet poison of misusèd wine,
After the Tuscan mariners transformed,°
Coasting the Tyrrhene shore, as the winds listed,
50 On Circe's° island fell (Who knows not Circe,
The daughter of the Sun? whose charmèd cup

---

ambrosial weeds heavenly garments
mould the earth, the body in which he in-
carnates
Neptune . . . Jove Zeus, high Jove, and Hades
or Pluto, nether Jove, ruled the realms of the
sky and the dead; over the third realm, the
sea, Neptune ruled.
By course duly
tridents Neptune's three-pronged spear
quarters deals out
this tract Wales, and Bridgewater's counties
in England
peer the Earl of Bridgewater
mickle great

awe awesomeness
nation the Welsh
pérplexed tangled
wood The dark wood at the opening of Dante's
Inferno and Book I of Spenser's *Faerie Queene*
represents the moral difficulties and obscurities
of life.
mariners transformed by Bacchus, whom they
had captured, into dolphins. The construction
is latinate *(post nautas mutatos)*, an early
instance of what was to become a dominant
feature of Milton's diction.
Circe's See Headnote.

Whoever tasted, lost his upright shape,
And downward fell into a groveling swine).
This nymph that gazed upon his clustering locks,
With ivy berries wreathed, and his blithe youth,
Had by him, ere he parted thence, a son
Much like his father, but his mother more,
Whom therefore she brought up and Comus° named;
Who, ripe and frolic° of his full-grown age,
60   Roving the Celtic and Iberian fields,
At last betakes him to this ominous wood,
And, in thick shelter of black shades embowered,
Excels his mother at her mighty art,
Offering to every weary traveller
His orient° liquor in a crystal glass,
To quench the drouth of Phoebus,° which as they taste
(For most do taste through fond intemperate thirst)
Soon as the potion works, their human countenance,
The express resemblance of the gods,° is changed
70   Into some brutish form of wolf, or bear,
Or ounce,° or tiger, hog, or bearded goat,
All other parts remaining as they were;°
And they, so perfect is their misery,
Not once perceive their foul disfigurement,
But boast themselves more comely than before
And all their friends, and native home forget
To roll with pleasure in a sensual sty.
Therefore when any favoured of high Jove
Chances to pass through this adventurous glade,
80   Swift as the sparkle of a glancing° star
I shoot from heaven to give him safe convoy,
As now I do—but first I must put off
These my sky-robes, spun out of Iris' woof,°
And take the weeds° and likeness of a swain
That to the service of this house belongs,
Who with his soft pipe and smooth-dittied song
Well knows to still the wild winds when they roar,
And hush the waving woods;° nor of less faith,°
And in this office of his mountain watch
90   Likeliest, and nearest to the present aid

Comus See Headnote.
frolic joyful
orient sparkling
drouth of Phoebus thirst caused by the sun
The express . . . gods "God created man in his image" (Genesis 1:27)
ounce lynx
All . . . were Necessities of production (animal-head masks were easier to manage than animal suits) and emblematic meaning (the head, the highest, most divine and least animal part

of man, is reduced to the bestial status of his lower organs and limbs) here combine to produce the monsters of Comus's retinue.
glancing shooting
Iris' woof rainbow fabric
weeds costume; cf. l. 16
That . . . woods Henry Lawes, a composer and tutor, playing the part of the Spirit, is likened to Orpheus, whose music was indeed so commanding.
nor of less faith no less loyal

Of this occasion. But I heard the tread
Of hateful steps; I must be viewless° now.

> [COMUS *enters with a charming-rod in one hand, his glass in the other;
> with him a rout of monsters headed like sundry sorts of wild beasts, but
> otherwise like men and women, their apparel glistering. They come in
> making a riotous and unruly noise, with torches in their hands.*]

COMUS   The star° that bids the shepherd fold°
Now the top of heaven doth hold,
And the gilded car° of day
His glowing axle doth allay°
In the steep Atlantic stream,
And the slope sun his upward beam
Shoots against the dusky pole,
100 Pacing toward the other goal
Of his chamber in the east.
Meanwhile welcome joy and feast,
Midnight shout and revelry,
Tipsy dance and jollity.
Braid your locks with rosy twine
Dropping odours, dropping wine.
Rigour now is gone to bed,
And Advice with scrupulous head,
Strict Age, and sour Severity,
110 With their grave saws° in slumber lie.
We that are of purer fire
Imitate the starry quire,
Who in their nightly watchful spheres
Lead in swift round the months and years.°
The sounds and seas with all their finny drove
Now to the moon in wavering morris° move,
And on the tawny sands and shelves
Trip the pert fairies and the dapper elves;
By dimpled brook and fountain brim
120 The wood-nymphs, decked with daisies trim,
Their merry wakes° and pastimes keep:
What hath night to do with sleep?
Night hath better sweets to prove,
Venus now wakes, and wakens Love.
Come, let us our rites begin;
'Tis only daylight that makes sin,
Which these dun shades will ne'er report.

---

viewless invisible
star Hesperus, the Evening Star
fold pen up the sheep
car chariot
allay cool
saws maxims
the starry . . . years The heavenly motions,

imaged as "the music of the spheres" in antiquity and later, were also thought of by Plato in *Timaeus* 40 as a great dance of the spheres (see *Astronomy* in the Glossary).
morris morris dance (from "Moorish")
wakes night-long ceremonies

Hail, goddess of nocturnal sport,
Dark-veiled Cotytto,° to whom the secret flame
130 Of midnight torches burns; mysterious dame,
That ne'er art called but when the dragon womb
Of Stygian darkness spits her thickest gloom,
And makes one blot of all the air,
Stay thy cloudy ebon chair
Wherein thou rid'st with Hecat',° and befriend
Us thy vowed priests, till utmost end
Of all thy dues be done, and none left out
Ere the blabbing eastern scout,
The nice Morn° on the Indian steep,°
140 From her cabined loop-hole peep,
And to the tell-tale Sun descry°
Our concealed solemnity.°
Come, knit hands, and beat the ground,
In a light fantastic round.°

  [*The Measure*°]

Break off, break off, I feel the different pace
Of some chaste footing near about this ground.
Run to your shrouds° within these brakes and trees;
Our number may affright: some virgin sure
(For so I can distinguish by mine art)
150 Benighted in these woods. Now to my charms
And to my wily trains;° I shall ere long
Be well stocked with as fair a herd as grazed
About my mother Circe. Thus I hurl
My dazzling spells into the spongy air,
Of power to cheat the eye with blear° illusion,
And give it false presentments,° lest the place
And my quaint habits° breed astonishment,
And put the damsel to suspicious flight,
Which must not be, for that's against my course;
160 I, under fair pretense of friendly ends,
And well-placed words of glozing° courtesy
Baited with reasons not unplausible,
Wind me into the easy-hearted man,
And hug him into snares. When once her eye
Hath met the virtue° of this magic dust,

Cotytto Thracian goddess whose nocturnal rites
were reputedly wildly lascivious
Hecat' Hecate, the witch goddess
nice Morn the overly fastidious goddess Aurora
Indian steep the Himalayas
descry reveal
solemnity celebration
round ring dance
Measure the antic dance of what would, in a
traditional masque, have been the antimasque,
or grotesque counterpart of the main dance and
mythology
shrouds hiding places
trains allurements
blear deceiving
false presentments fake visions
quaint habits strange costume
glozing flattering
virtue power

I shall appear some harmless villager
Whom thrift keeps up about his country gear.
But here she comes; I fairly° step aside,
And hearken, if I may, her business here.

    [THE LADY *enters*]

170   LADY   This way the noise was, if mine ear be true,
My best guide now. Methought it was the sound
Of riot and ill-managed merriment,
Such as the jocund flute or gamesome pipe
Stirs up among the loose unlettered hinds,°
When for their teeming° flocks, and granges° full,
In wanton dance they praise the bounteous Pan,°
And thank the gods amiss. I should be loth
To meet the rudeness and swilled insolence
Of such late wássailers;° yet O where else
180 Shall I inform my unacquainted feet
In the blind mazes of this tangled wood?
My brothers, when they saw me wearied out
With this long way, resolving here to lodge
Under the spreading favour of these pines,
Stepped as they said to the next thicket side
To bring me berries, or such cooling fruit
As the kind hospitable woods provide.
They left me then when the grey-hooded Even,
Like a sad votarist in palmer's weed,°
190 Rose from the hindmost wheels of Phoebus' wain.°
But where they are, and why they came not back,
Is now the labour of my thoughts; 'tis likeliest
They had engaged their wandering steps too far,
And envious darkness, ere they could return,
Had stole them from me—Else, O thievish Night,
Why shouldst thou, but for some felonious end,
In thy dark lantern thus close up the stars
That Nature hung in heaven, and filled their lamps
With everlasting oil, to give due light
200 To the misled and lonely traveller?
This is the place, as well as I may guess,
Whence even now the tumult of loud mirth
Was rife, and perfect in my listening ear,
Yet naught but single° darkness do I find.
What might this be? A thousand fantasies
Begin to throng into my memory

fairly silently
hinds farmhands
teeming both overflowing or abundant
granges barns
Pan god of woods and shepherds

wássailers revelers
votarist . . . weed pilgrim to the Holy Land
wain wagon
single absolute

Of calling shapes, and beckoning shadows dire,
And airy tongues that syllable men's names
On sands and shores and desert wildernesses.
210 These thoughts may startle well, but not astound
The virtuous mind, that ever walks attended
By a strong siding° champion, Conscïence.
O welcome, pure-eyed Faith, white-handed Hope,
Thou hovering angel girt with golden wings,
And thou unblemished form of Chastity,
I see ye visibly, and now believe
That He, the supreme Good, to whom all things ill
Are but as slavish officers of vengeance,
Would send a glistering guardian if need were
220 To keep my life and honour unassailed.
Was I deceived, or did a sable cloud
Turn forth her silver lining on the night?
I did not err, there does a sable cloud
Turn forth her silver lining on the night,°
And casts a gleam over this tufted grove.
I cannot hallo to my brothers, but
Such noise as I can make to be heard farthest
I'll venture, for my new-enlivened spirits
Prompt me; and they perhaps are not far off.

SONG°

230 *Sweet Echo, sweetest nymph that liv'st unseen*
Within thy airy shell°
By slow Maeander's margent° green,
And in the violet-embroidered vale
Where the lovelorn nightingale
Nightly to thee her sad song mourneth well:
Canst thou not tell me of a gentle pair
That likest thy Narcissus are?
O if thou have
Hid them in some flowery cave,
240 *Tell me but where,*
Sweet queen of parley,° daughter of the sphere;
So mayest thou be translated to the skies,
And give resounding grace° to all heaven's harmonies.

---

siding defending
Was I . . . night This exact repetition in answer
to a rhetorical question may seem almost ludicrous, but (1) these lines were not in the acting script; (2) they have a rhetorical source
in Ovid (*Fasti* V.549) for their use on the page;
and (3) they do serve to indicate the Lady's
calm self-possession.
Song The Lady's song to Echo is a prayer for
amplification (by natural acoustic means) of
her call, and also a song to her solitariness; un-

like operatic "echo scenes" there is no audible
answer from hidden chorus or whatever, but the
effects on Comus are quite apparent.
shell personified echoes inhabit caverns; "shell"
has the sense both of "cell" or cave, and of the
higher "shell" of the arched sky
Maeander's margent the margin, or bank of a
(hence) "meandering" river in Asia Minor
parley discourse
resounding grace "grace" also in the musical
sense of embellishments like trills

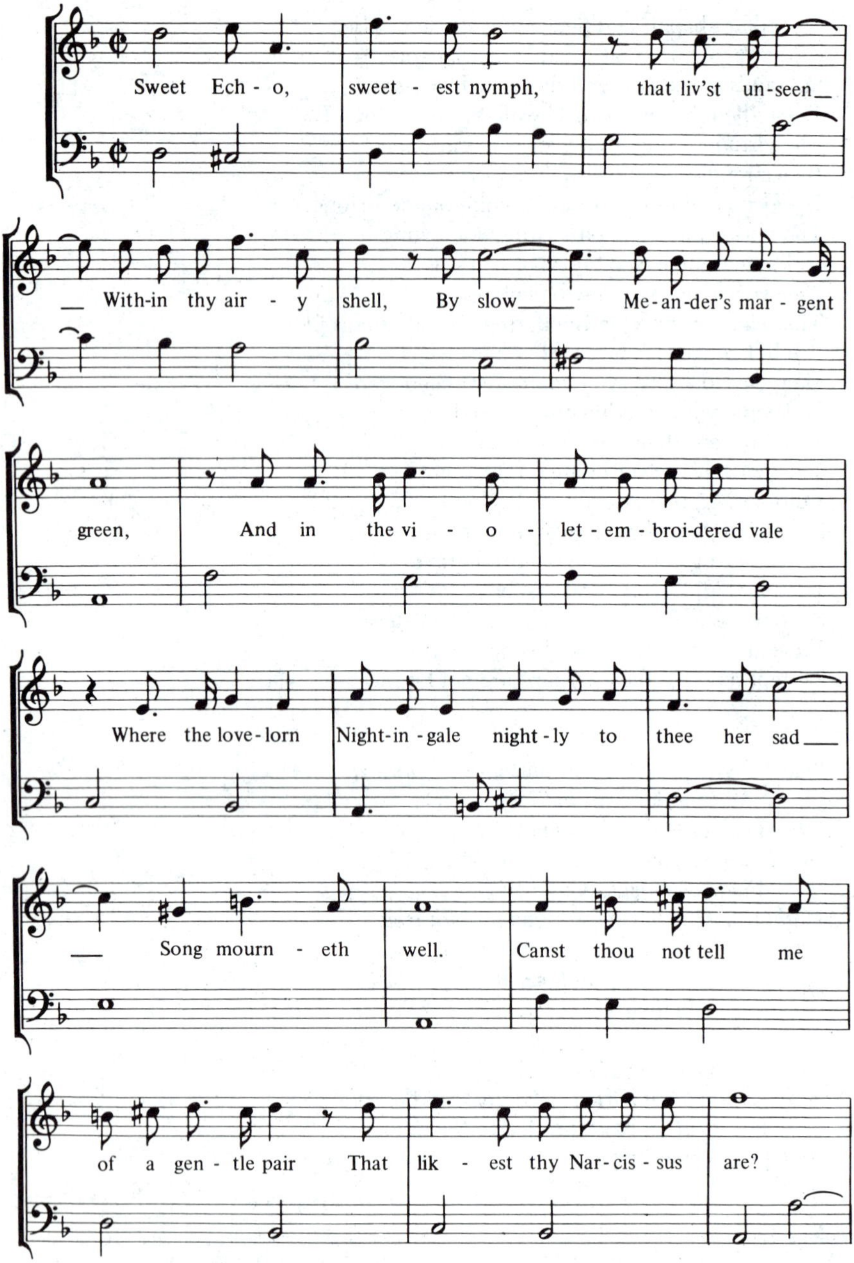

Sweet Ech - o, sweet - est nymph, that liv'st un-seen _ With-in thy air - y shell, By slow _ Me-an-der's mar - gent green, And in the vi - o - let - em - broi-dered vale Where the love-lorn Night-in-gale night-ly to thee her sad _ Song mourn - eth well. Canst thou not tell me of a gen - tle pair That lik - est thy Nar-cis - sus are?

O if thou have hid them in some flow - 'ry cave.

Tell me but where sweet____ Queen of Par - ly, Daugh-

- ter of the Sphere, So may'st thou be trans - lat - ed to the skies,

And give re-sound-ing grace to all heav'ns har - mo - nies.

Lawes's setting of this song uses in its last line Milton's earliest version of the text, which he later rewrote.

COMUS [*Aside*]   Can any mortal mixture of earth's mould
Breathe such divine enchanting ravishment?
Sure something holy lodges in that breast,
And with these raptures moves the vocal air
To testify° his hidden residence;
How sweetly did they float upon the wings
250   Of silence, through the empty-vaulted night,
At every fall° smoothing the raven down
Of darkness till it smiled. I have oft heard
My mother Circe with the Sirens three,°
Amidst the flowery-kirtled Naiades,°
Culling their potent herbs and baleful drugs,
Who as they sung would take the prisoned soul

testify attest to
fall musical cadence
Circe . . . three Milton means the sirens whose

song bewitched sailors; in Milton, they attend
Circe, but not in Homer.
flowery-kirtled Naiades fresh-water nymphs, perhaps dressed in pond lilies

And lap it in Elysium; Scylla° wept,
And chid her barking waves into attention,
And fell Charybdis murmured soft applause.
260 Yet they in pleasing slumber lulled the sense,
And in sweet madness robbed it of itself;
But such a sacred and home-felt° delight,
Such sober certainty of waking bliss,
I never heard till now. I'll speak to her,
And she shall be my queen. Hail, foreign wonder,
Whom certain these rough shades did never breed,
Unless° the goddess that in rural shrine
Dwellest here with Pan or Sylvan, by blest song
Forbidding every bleak unkindly fog
270 To touch the prosperous growth of this tall wood.
  LADY Nay, gentle shepherd, ill is lost that praise
That is addressed to unattending ears;
Not any boast of skill, but éxtreme shift
How to regain my severed company
Compelled me to awake the courteous Echo
To give me answer from her mossy couch.
   COMUS What chance, good lady, hath bereft you thus?
   LADY Dim darkness and this leafy labyrinth.°
   COMUS Could that divide you from near-ushering guides?
280   LADY They left me weary on a grassy turf.
   COMUS By falsehood, or discourtesy, or why?
   LADY To seek i' th' valley some cool friendly spring.
   COMUS And left your fair side all unguarded, lady?
   LADY They were but twain, and purposed quick return.
   COMUS Perhaps forestalling night prevented them.
   LADY How easy my misfortune is to hit!°
   COMUS Imports their loss,° beside the present need?
   LADY No less than if I should my brothers lose.
   COMUS Were they of manly prime, or youthful bloom?
290   LADY As smooth as Hebe's° their unrazored lips.
   COMUS Two such I saw, what time the laboured ox
In his loose traces from the furrow came,°
And the swinked hedger° at his supper sat;
I saw them under a green mantling vine
That crawls along the side of yon small hill,
Plucking ripe clusters from the tender shoots;
Their port° was more than human, as they stood.
I took it for a faëry vision

Scylla . . . Charybdis The monster and, across
the straights of Messina from her, the whirlpool—all these Odyssean allusions are associated
with Circe.
home-felt deeply felt
Unless unless you are
Dim . . . labyrinth This line-for-line dialogue
imitates the stichomythia of Greek drama.

hit guess
Imports their loss does losing them matter
Hebe's the youth goddess and Olympian cup-
bearer
what time . . . came Unyoking the oxen is a
symbol of nightfall in Homer and Virgil.
swinked hedger tired hedge-cutter
port bearing

Of some gay creatures of the element,°
300 That in the colours of the rainbow live
And play i' th' plighted° clouds. I was awe-strook,
And as I passed, I worshipped; if those you seek,
It were a journey like the path to heaven
To help you find them.
LADY   Gentle villager,°
What readiest way would bring me to that place?
COMUS   Due west it rises from this shrubby point.
LADY   To find out that, good shepherd, I suppose,
In such a scant allowance of star-light,
Would overtask the best land-pilot's art
310 Without the sure guess of well-practised feet.
COMUS   I know each lane and every alley green,
Dingle° or bushy dell of this wild wood,
And every bosky bourn° from side to side
My daily walks and ancient neighbourhood,
And if your stray attendance° be yet lodged,
Or shroud° within these limits, I shall know
Ere morrow wake or the low-roosted lark
From her thatched pallet° rouse; if otherwise,
I can conduct you, lady, to a low
320 But loyal cottage, where you may be safe
Till further quest.
LADY   Shepherd, I take thy word,
And trust thy honest-offered courtesy,
Which oft is sooner found in lowly sheds
With smoky rafters, than in tap'stry halls
And courts of princes, where it first was named,
And yet is most pretended. In a place
Less warranted than this, or less secure,
I cannot be, that I should fear to change it.
Eye me, blest Providence, and square my trial
330 To my proportioned strength. Shepherd, lead on.
[*Exeunt*]

[*The two Brothers*]

ELDER BROTHER   Unmuffle, ye faint stars, and thou, fair moon,
That wont'st to love the traveller's benison,
Stoop thy pale visage through an amber cloud,
And disinherit° Chaos, that reigns here
In double night of darkness and of shades;

element in this case, air
plighted folded
Gentle villager Comus is, of course, disguised as a Shropshire countryman, to trap the Lady's own "gentleness" which would assume no connection between rusticity or humble condition and evil.

Dingle hollow
bosky bourn bushy brook
attendance attendants
shroud hide themselves
pallet straw bed
disinherit dispossess

Or if your influence be quite dammed up
With black usurping mists, some gentle taper
Though a rush-candle from the wicker hole
Of some clay habitation, visit us
340   With thy long levelled rule of streaming light,
And thou shalt be our star of Arcady,
Or Tyrian Cynosure.°
    SECOND BROTHER   Or if our eyes
Be barred that happiness, might we but hear
The folded flocks penned in their wattled cotes,°
Or sound of pastoral reed with oaten stops,°
Or whistle from the lodge, or village cock
Count the night-watches to his feathery dames,
'Twould be some solace yet, some little cheering,
In this close dungeon of innumerous° boughs.
350   But O that hapless virgin, our lost sister,
Where may she wander now, whither betake her
From the chill dew, amongst rude burrs and thistles?
Perhaps some cold bank is her bolster now,
Or 'gainst the rugged bark of some broad elm
Leans her unpillowed head fraught with sad fears.
What if in wild amazement and affright,
Or, while we speak, within the direful grasp
Of savage hunger or of savage heat?
    ELDER BROTHER   Peace, brother, be not over-exquisite°
360   To cast° the fashion of uncertain evils;
For grant they be so, while they rest unknown,
What need a man forestall his date of grief,
And run to meet what he would most avoid?
Or if they be but false alarms of fear,
How bitter is such self-delusïon?
I do not think my sister so to seek,°
Or so unprincipled in virtue's book,
And the sweet peace that goodness bosoms ever,
As that the single° want of light and noise
370   (Not being in danger, as I trust she is not)
Could stir the constant mood of her calm thoughts,
And put them into misbecoming plight.
Virtue could see to do what Virtue would
By her own radiant light, though sun and moon
Were in the flat sea sunk. And Wisdom's self
Oft seeks to sweet retired solitude,

star . . . Cynosure Ursa Major or Ursa Minor (containing the pole star); Greek mariners steered by the first, Phoenicians by the second
wattled cotes sheepfolds of interwoven branches
pastoral . . . stops The reed flute symbolized pastoral poetry; cf. the "oaten pipe" of Colin Clout in Spenser, The Shepheards Calender, January Eclogue, l. 72, and the "oaten flute" in Lycidas, l. 33.
innumerous numberless
over-exquisite too subtle
cast forecast
so to seek so lacking (here, virtue)
single mere

Where with her best nurse, Contemplatïon,
She plumes her feathers, and lets grow her wings,
That in the various bustle of resort
380 Were all to-ruffled,° and sometimes impaired.
He that has light within his own clear breast
May sit i' th'centre° and enjoy bright day,
But he that hides a dark soul and foul thoughts
Benighted walks under the mid-day sun;
Himself is his own dungeon.

    SECOND BROTHER   'Tis most true
That musing meditation most affects
The pensive secrecy of desert cell,
Far from the cheerful haunt of men and herds,
And sits as safe as in a senate-house;
390 For who would rob a hermit of his weeds,
His few books, or his beads, or maple dish,
Or do his grey hairs any violence?
But beauty, like the fair Hesperian tree
Laden with blooming gold,° had need the guard
Of dragon-watch with unenchanted° eye
To save her blossoms and defend her fruit
From the rash hand of bold Incontinence.
You may as well spread out the unsunned heaps
Of miser's treasure by an outlaw's den,
400 And tell me it is safe, as bid me hope
Danger will wink on opportunity,
And let a single helpless maiden pass
Uninjured in this wild surrounding waste.
Of night or loneliness it recks me not;°
I fear the dread events that dog them both,
Lest some ill-greeting touch attempt the person
Of our unowned° sister.

    ELDER BROTHER   I do not, brother,
Infer as if I thought my sister's state
Secure without all doubt or controversy;
410 Yet where an equal poise of hope and fear
Does arbitrate the event, my nature is
That I incline to hope rather than fear,
And gladly banish squint° suspicïon.
My sister is not so defenceless left
As you imagine; she has a hidden strength
Which you remember not.

    SECOND BROTHER   What hidden strength,

---

to-ruffled ruffled up
centre of the earth
blooming gold the golden apples of the Hesperides
unenchanted unenchantable (Milton liked this phrase so much that he reinserted it here after

having cut it from another place in the MS.; cf. similar latinate use of participle in l. 215)
it recks me not I don't care
unowned unguarded
squint squinting

Unless the strength of heaven, if you mean that?
 ELDER BROTHER I mean that too, but yet a hidden strength
Which, if heaven gave it, may be termed her own
420 —'Tis chastity, my brother, chastity:
She that has that is clad in cómplete steel,
And like a quivered° nymph with arrows keen
May trace huge forests and unharboured heaths,
Infamous hills and sandy perilous wilds,
Where, through the sacred rays of chastity,
No savage fierce, bandit, or mountaineer
Will dare to soil her virgin purity.
Yea, there where very desolation dwells,
By grots and caverns shagged with horrid shades,
430 She may pass on with unblenched° majesty,
Be it not done in pride or in presumption.
Some say no evil thing that walks by night
In fog or fire,° by lake or moorish fen,
Blue meagre hag, or stubborn unlaid° ghost
That breaks his magic chains at curfew time,
No goblin or swart fairy of the mine,
Hath hurtful power o'er true virginity.
Do ye believe me yet, or shall I call
Antiquity from the old schools° of Greece
440 To testify the arms of chastity?
Hence had the huntress Dian her dread bow,
Fair silver-shafted queen for ever chaste,
Wherewith she tamed the brinded° lioness
And spotted mountain pard,° but set at naught
The frivolous bolt of Cupid; gods and men
Feared her stern frown, and she was queen o' th' woods.
What was that snaky-headed Gorgon shield
That wise Minerva wore,° unconquered virgin,
Wherewith she freezed her foes to cóngealed stone,
450 But rigid looks of chaste austerity,
And noble grace that dashed brute violence
With sudden adoration and blank awe?
So dear to heaven is saintly chastity
That when a soul is found sincerely so,
A thousand liveried angels lackey° her,
Driving far off each thing of sin and guilt,
And in clear dream and solemn visïon
Tell her of things that no gross ear can hear,

---

quivered carrying a quiver of arrows; a nymph
of Diana, the virgin goddess of the hunt
unblenched undismayed
fire *ignis fatuus:* will-o'-the-wisp or phosphorescent light
unlaid unexorcised
schools philosophical traditions

brinded tawny
pard panther
Minerva wore Athena (Minerva) had Medusa's
petrifying head on her shield because, said a
Renaissance mythographer, no one can turn
his eyes against wisdom with impunity.
lackey attend

Till oft converse with heavenly habitants
460 Begin to cast a beam on the outward shape,
The unpolluted temple of the mind,
And turns it by degrees to the soul's essence,
Till all be made immortal. But when lust,
By unchaste looks, loose gestures, and foul talk,
But most by lewd and lavish act of sin,
Lets in defilement to the inward parts,
The soul grows clotted by contagion,°
Imbodies and imbrutes, till she quite lose
The divine property of her first being.
470 Such are those thick and gloomy shadows damp
Oft seen in charnel vaults and sepulchres
Lingering, and sitting by a new-made grave,
As loth to leave the body that it loved,
And linked itself by carnal sensuality
To a degenerate and degraded state.
    SECOND BROTHER   How charming is divine philosophy!
Not harsh and crabbèd, as dull fools suppose,
But musical as is Apollo's lute,
And a perpetual feast of nectared sweets,
Where no crude surfeit reigns.
480   ELDER BROTHER   List! list, I hear
Some far-off hallo break the silent air.
    SECOND BROTHER   Methought so too; what should it be?
    ELDER BROTHER   For certain,
Either some one like us night-foundered° here,
Or else some neighbour woodman, or at worst,
Some roving robber calling to his fellows.
    SECOND BROTHER   Heaven keep my sister! Again, again, and near!
Best draw, and stand upon our guard.
    ELDER BROTHER   I'll hallo;
If he be friendly, he comes well; if not,
Defense is a good cause, and Heaven be for us.

      [THE ATTENDANT SPIRIT, *habited like a shepherd*]

490 That hallo I should know; what are you? speak.
Come not too near, you fall on iron stakes° else.
    SPIRIT   What voice is that? my young lord? speak again.
    SECOND BROTHER   O brother, 'tis my father's shepherd, sure.
    ELDER BROTHER   Thyrsis,° whose artful strains have oft delayed
The huddling brook° to hear his madrigal,

The soul . . . contagion Plato's *Phaedo* 81
provides the doctrine for this explanation of why
ghosts are always the souls of those who made
of their bodies a prison while alive.
night-foundered sunk in night
iron stakes swords
Thyrsis name of a pastoral singer from Theocritus and Virgil; it is the Attendant Spirit in
disguise, or rather incarnated as a literary
figure whose name Milton might have used
to praise Henry Lawes, who is playing the part
huddling brook its waves crowd together to
stop and listen

And sweetened every musk-rose of the dale,
How camest thou here, good swain? Hath any ram
Slipped from the fold, or young kid lost his dam,
Or straggling wether° the pent flock forsook?
500 How couldst thou find this dark sequestered nook?
    SPIRIT   O my loved master's heir, and his next° joy,
I came not here on such a trivial toy
As a strayed ewe, or to pursue the stealth
Of pilfering wolf; not all the fleecy wealth
That doth enrich these downs is worth a thought
To this my errand, and the care it brought.
But O my virgin lady, where is she?°
How chance she is not in your company?
    ELDER BROTHER   To tell thee sadly,° shepherd, without blame
510 Or our neglect, we lost her as we came.
    SPIRIT   Ay me unhappy, then my fears are true.
    ELDER BROTHER   What fears, good Thyrsis? Prithee briefly shew.
    SPIRIT   I'll tell ye. 'Tis not vain or fabulous°
(Though so esteemed by shallow ignorance)
What the sage poets, taught by the heavenly Muse,
Storied of old in high immortal verse
Of dire Chimeras and enchanted isles,
And rifted rocks whose entrance leads to hell—
For such there be, but unbelief is blind.
520   Within the navel° of this hideous wood,
Immured in cypress shades, a sorcerer dwells,
Of Bacchus and of Circe born, great Comus,
Deep skilled in all his mother's witcheries,
And here to every thirsty wanderer
By sly enticement gives his baneful cup,
With many murmurs° mixed, whose pleasing poison
The visage quite transforms of him that drinks,
And the inglorious likeness of a beast
Fixes instead, unmoulding reason's mintage
530 Charáctered° in the face; this have I learnt
Tending my flocks hard by i' th' hilly crofts°
That brow° this bottom glade, whence night by night
He and his monstrous rout are heard to howl
Like stabled wolves, or tigers at their prey,
Doing abhorrèd rites to Hecate
In their obscurèd haunts of inmost bowers.

---

wether castrated ram
next nearest and dearest
where is she? The Spirit clearly knows (see ll.
561–76) and the question is rhetorical in a
way, drawing the audience's attention to the
following long description.
sady seriously
fabulous mythical. The Spirit is here stating a
basic position of Renaissance mythography,

namely, that not only did these old stories
have ethical and psychological significance, but
that they represented slightly misshapen versions
of biblical truths.
navel center
murmurs incantations
Charactered imprinted
crofts small farms
brow overlook

Yet have they many baits and guileful spells
To inveigle and invite the unwary sense
Of them that pass unweeting° by the way.
540 This evening late, by then° the chewing flocks
Had ta'en their supper on the savoury herb
Of knot-grass dew-besprent, and were in fold,
I sat me down to watch upon a bank
With ivy canopied, and interwove
With flaunting honeysuckle, and began,
Wrapped in a pleasing fit of melancholy,
To meditate my rural minstrelsy,°
Till fancy had her fill. But ere a close°
The wonted roar was up amidst the woods,
550 And filled the air with barbarous dissonance,
At which I ceased, and listened them a while,
Till an unusual stop of sudden silence
Gave respite to the drowsy frighted steeds
That draw the litter of close-curtained Sleep.
At last a soft and solemn-breathing sound
Rose like a steam of rich distilled perfumes,
And stole upon the air, that even Silence
Was took ere she was ware, and wished she might
Deny her nature and be never more,
560 Still to be so displaced. I was all ear,
And took in strains that might create a soul
Under the ribs of Death, but O ere long
Too well I did perceive it was the voice
Of my most honoured lady, your dear sister.
Amazed I stood, harrowed with grief and fear,
And 'O poor hapless nightingale,' thought I,
'How sweet thou sing'st, how near the deadly snare!'
Then down the lawns I ran with headlong haste
Through paths and turnings often trod by day,
570 Till guided by mine ear I found the place
Where that damned wizard, hid in sly disguise
(For so by certain signs I knew), had met
Already, ere my best speed could prevent,
The aidless innocent lady, his wished prey,
Who gently asked if he had seen such two,
Supposing him some neighbour villager;
Longer I durst not stay, but soon I guessed
Ye were the two she meant; with that I sprung
Into swift flight, till I had found you here;
But further know I not.
580   SECOND BROTHER   O night and shades,

unweeting heedless   To meditate . . . minstrelsy to play a shep-
by then when   herd's pipe
              close musical cadence

How are ye joined with hell in triple knot
Against the unarmèd weakness of one virgin
Alone and helpless! Is this the confidence
You gave me, brother?
    ELDER BROTHER   Yes, and keep it still,
Lean on it safely; not a period°
Shall be unsaid, for me—against the threats
Of malice or of sorcery, or that power
Which erring men call chance, this I hold firm:
Virtue may be assailed, but never hurt,
590   Surprised by unjust force, but not enthralled,
Yea, even that which mischief meant most harm
Shall in the happy trial prove most glory.
But evil on itself shall back recoil,
And mix no more with goodness, when at last,
Gathered like scum, and settled to itself,
It shall be in eternal restless change
Self-fed and self-consumèd;° if this fail,
The pillared firmament is rottenness,
And earth's base built on stubble. But come, let's on.
600   Against the opposing will and arm of heaven
May never this just sword be lifted up;
But for that damned magician, let him be girt
With all the grisly legïons that troop
Under the sooty flag of Acheron,°
Harpies° and Hydras,° or all the monstrous forms
'Twixt Africa and Ind, I'll find him out,
And force him to restore his purchase° back,
Or drag him by the curls to a foul death,
Cursed as his life.
    SPIRIT   Alas, good venturous youth,
610   I love thy courage yet, and bold emprise,°
But here thy sword can do thee little stead;
For other arms and other weapons must
Be those that quell the might of hellish charms.
He with his bare wand can unthread thy joints,
And crumble all thy sinews.
    ELDER BROTHER   Why, prithee, shepherd,
How durst thou then thyself approach so near
As to make this relation?
    SPIRIT   Care and utmost shifts
How to secure the lady from surprisal
Brought to my mind a certain shepherd lad,
620   Of small regard to see to, yet well skilled

---

period sentence
But evil . . . self-consumed Cf. *Paradise Lost*
II.795–802.
Acheron one of the rivers of Hades; hell itself
Harpies horrible birds with women's faces

Hydras nine-headed monsters of the species
killed by Hercules
purchase prey
emprise enterprise

In every virtuous° plant and healing herb
That spreads her verdant leaf to the morning ray.
He loved me well, and oft would beg me sing;
Which when I did, he on the tender grass
Would sit, and hearken even to ecstasy,
And in requital ope his leathern scrip,°
And show me simples° of a thousand names,
Telling their strange and vigorous faculties;
Amongst the rest a small unsightly root,
630   But of divine effect, he culled me out;
The leaf was darkish, and had prickles on it,
But in another country, as he said,
Bore a bright golden flower, but not in this soil:
Unknown, and like esteemed, and the dull swain
Treads on it daily with his clouted shoon,°
And yet more med'cinal is it than that moly°
That Hermes once to wise Ulysses gave;
He called it haemony,° and gave it me,
And bade me keep it as of sovereign use
640   'Gainst all enchantments, mildew blast, or damp,
Or ghastly Furies' apparition;
I pursed it up, but little reckoning made,
Till now that this extremity compelled,
But now I find it true; for by this means
I knew the foul enchanter though disguised,
Entered the very lime-twigs° of his spells,
And yet came off. If you have this about you
(As I will give you when we go), you may
Boldly assault the necromancer's hall,
650   Where if he be, with dauntless hardihood
And brandished blade rush on him, break his glass,
And shed the luscious liquor on the ground,°
But seize his wand. Though he and his cursed crew
Fierce sign of battle make, and menace high,
Or like the sons of Vulcan vomit smoke,
Yet will they soon retire, if he but shrink.
    ELDER BROTHER   Thyrsis, lead on apace, I'll follow thee,
And some good angel bear a shield before us.

*The scene changes to a stately palace, set out with all manner of deli-
ciousness: soft music, tables spread with all dainties.* COMUS *appears*

---

virtuous pharmacologically potent
scrip bag
simples medicinal herbs; called so because used
uncompounded
clouted shoon hobnailed shoes
moly Hermes gave Odysseus this magic plant
as an antidote to the transforming spells of
Circe.
haemony See Headnote.

lime-twigs Twigs, smeared with lime, were used
to trap birds.
And shed . . . ground one of many Spenserian
reminiscences in this work; in the Bower of
Bliss, Guyon breaks the cup of excess "And with
the liquor stainèd all the lond" (*The Faerie
Queene* II.xii.57); by this allusion, the overthrow
of Comus is made to parallel Acrasia's in moral
significance

with his rabble, and THE LADY *set in an enchanted chair, to whom he offers his glass, which she puts by, and goes about to rise.*

COMUS   Nay, lady, sit; if I but wave this wand,
660   Your nerves° are all chained up in alabaster,°
And you a statue, or as Daphne° was
Root-bound, that fled Apollo.
    LADY   Fool, do not boast;
Thou canst not touch the freedom of my mind
With all thy charms, although this corporal rind
Thou hast immanacled,° while heaven sees good.
    COMUS   Why are you vexed, lady? why do you frown?
Here dwell no frowns, nor anger; from these gates
Sorrow flies far: see, here be all the pleasures
That fancy can beget on youthful thoughts,
670   When the fresh blood grows lively, and returns
Brisk as the April buds in primrose season.
And first behold this cordial julep here
That flames and dances in his crystal bounds
With spirits of balm and fragrant syrups mixed.
Not that nepenthes which the wife of Thone
In Egypt gave to Jove-born Helena°
Is of such power to stir up joy as this,
To life so friendly, or so cool to thirst.
Why should you be so cruel to yourself,
680   And to those dainty limbs which Nature lent
For gentle usage and soft delicacy?
But you invert the covenants of her trust,
And harshly deal like an ill borrower
With that which you received on other terms,
Scorning the unexempt condition
By which all mortal frailty must subsist,
Refreshment after toil, ease after pain,
That have been tired all day without repast,
And timely rest have wanted; but, fair virgin,
This will restore all soon.
690   LADY   'Twill not, false traitor,
'Twill not restore the truth and honesty
That thou hast banished from thy tongue with lies.
Was this the cottage and the safe abode
Thou told'st me of? What grim aspécts are these,
These ugly-headed monsters? Mercy guard me!
Hence with thy brewed enchantments, foul deceiver;
Hast thou betrayed my credulous innocence

---

nerves muscles
alabaster marble
Daphne Fleeing Apollo's desiring grasp, she
turned into a laurel bush.
immanacled chained up

nepenthes . . . Helena In the *Odyssey* IV.
219–32 Helen gives her husband Menelaus an
Egyptian drug of an opium-like sort to drive
away his grief.

With vizored falsehood and base forgery,°
And wouldst thou seek again to trap me here
700 With lickerish° baits fit to ensnare a brute?
Were it a draught for Juno when she banquets,
I would not taste thy treasonous offer; none
But such as are good men can give good things,
And that which is not good is not delicious
To a well-governed and wise appetite.
        COMUS O foolishness of men! that lend their ears
To those budge° doctors of the Stoic fur,°
And fetch their precepts from the Cynic tub,°
Praising the lean and sallow Abstinence.
710 Wherefore did Nature pour her bounties forth
With such a full and unwithdrawing hand,
Covering the earth with odours, fruits, and flocks
Thronging the seas with spawn innumerable,
But all to please and sate the curious taste?
And set to work millions of spinning worms,
That in their green shops weave the smooth-haired silk
To deck her sons, and that no corner might
Be vacant of her plenty, in her own loins
She hutched° the all-worshipped ore and precious gems
720 To store her children with. If all the world
Should in a pet of temperance feed on pulse,°
Drink the clear stream, and nothing wear but frieze,°
The All-giver would be unthanked, would be unpraised,
Not half his riches known, and yet despised;
And we should serve him as a grudging master,
As a penurious niggard of his wealth,
And live like Nature's bastards, not her sons,
Who would be quite surcharged with her own weight,
And strangled with her waste fertility;
730 The earth cumbered, and the winged air darked with plumes;
The herds would over-multitude their lords,
The sea o'erfraught would swell, and the unsought diamonds
Would so emblaze the forehead of the deep,°
And so bestud with stars, that they below
Would grow inured to light, and come at last
To gaze upon the sun with shameless brows.
List, lady, be not coy, and be not cozened°
With that same vaunted name 'Virginity':

forgery deception
lickerish pleasing to the taste, but also with
a sense of "lecherous"
budge stiff, pompous (from the fur "budge"
on academic gowns)
Stoic fur here, Stoic school or persuasion—
Comus is sneering at philosophic asceticism
Cynic tub Diogenes the Cynic also scorned the
things of this world; unlike the Stoics Epictetus
and Seneca, his views were unsupported by

theories of the relation of soul to body and he
lived in a tub.
hutched laid away
pulse peas, beans, lentils, etc.
frieze coarse woolen cloth
deep the middle of the earth, specifically the
outer layer where mining takes place, and where
precious stones were thought to reproduce themselves like living organisms
cozened cheated

Beauty is Nature's coin, must not be hoarded,
740   But must be current, and the good thereof
Consists in mutual and partaken bliss,
Unsavoury in the enjoyment of itself.
If you let slip time, like a neglected rose
It withers on the stalk with languished head.
Beauty is Nature's brag,° and must be shown
In courts, at feasts, and high solemnities
Where most may wonder at the workmanship;
It is for homely features to keep home,
They had their name thence; coarse complexïons
750   And cheeks of sorry grain° will serve to ply
The sampler, and to tease° the housewife's wool.
What need a vermeil°-tinctured lip for that,
Love-darting eyes, or tresses like the morn?
There was another meaning in these gifts,
Think what, and be advised; you are but young yet.
LADY   I had not thought to have unlocked my lips
In this unhallowed air, but that this juggler
Would think to charm my judgment, as mine eyes,
Obtruding false rules pranked° in reason's garb.
760   I hate when vice can bolt° her arguments,
And virtue has no tongue to check her pride.
Impostor, do not charge most innocent Nature,
As if she would her children should be riotous
With her abundance; she, good cateress,
Means her provision only to the good,
That live according to her sober laws
And holy dictate of spare Temperance.
If every just man that now pines with want
Had but a moderate and beseeming share
770   Of that which lewdly pampered luxury
Now heaps upon some few with vast excess,
Nature's full blessings would be well dispensed
In unsuperfluous even proportïon,
And she no whit encumbered with her store;
And then the Giver would be better thanked,
His praise due paid, for swinish gluttony
Ne'er looks to heaven amidst his gorgeous feast,
But with besotted base ingratitude
Crams, and blasphemes his Feeder. Shall I go on?
780   Or have I said enough? To him that dares
Arm his profane tongue with contemptuous words
Against the sun-clad power of Chastity,
Fain would I something say, yet to what end?

brag boast
grain color
tease comb

vermeil vermilion
pranked decked out
bolt sift; refine

Thou hast nor ear nor soul to apprehend
The sublime notion and high mystery°
That must be uttered to unfold the sage
And serious doctrine of Virginity,
And thou art worthy that thou shouldst not know
More happiness than this thy present lot.
790 Enjoy your dear wit and gay rhetoric
That hath so well been taught her dazzling fence;°
Thou art not fit to hear thyself convinced.°
Yet should I try, the uncontrollèd worth
Of this pure cause would kindle my rapt° spirits
To such a flame of sacred vehemence
That dumb things would be moved to sympathize,
And the brute Earth would lend her nerves, and shake,
Till all thy magic structures, reared so high,
Were shattered into heaps o'er thy false head.
800 COMUS   She fables not. I feel that I do fear
Her words set off by some superior power;
And though not mortal, yet a cold shuddering dew
Dips me all o'er, as when the wrath of Jove
Speaks thunder and the chains of Erebus°
To some of Saturn's crew.° I must dissemble,
And try her yet more strongly. Come, no more,
This is mere moral babble, and direct
Against the canon laws of our foundation;
I must not suffer this, yet 'tis but the lees°
810 And settlings of a melancholy blood;
But this will cure all straight; one sip of this
Will bathe the drooping spirits in delight
Beyond the bliss of dreams. Be wise, and taste.

[THE BROTHERS *rush in with swords drawn, wrest his glass out of his*
hand, and break it against the ground; his rout make sign of resistance,
but are all driven in; THE ATTENDANT SPIRIT *comes in*]

SPIRIT   What, have you let the false enchanter scape?
O ye mistook, ye should have snatched his wand
And bound him fast; without his rod reversed,°
And backward mutters of dissevering power,
We cannot free the lady that sits here

mystery Milton writes elsewhere, quoting I
Corinthians 6:13, of "unfolding those chaste
and high mysteries . . . that 'the body is for
the Lord and the Lord for the body'" (*Apology*
for Smectymnuus, Columbia Edition, Vol. 3,
p. 306).
fence fencing, i.e. debating
convinced refuted
rapt transported
Erebus in Hesiod's account of creation, the son
of Chaos, and the original darkness that existed
before there was light

Saturn's crew Zeus (Jupiter) overthrew his
ruling father Cronus, or Saturn, and imprisoned
him in the underworld, Tartarus.
lees dregs of wine, here likened to the melancholy humor of blood
rod reversed In Ovid, *Metamorphoses* XIV.300,
Circe's spells are undone by reversing the motion
of the wand that cast them; the spells of
Spenser's Busyrane are also revoked in this
manner (*The Faerie Queene* III.xii.36).

In stony fetters fixed and motionless;
820   Yet stay, be not disturbed; now I bethink me,
Some other means I have which may be used,
Which once of Meliboeus° old I learnt,
The soothest shepherd that e'er piped on plains.
     There is a gentle Nymph not far from hence,
That with moist curb sways the smooth Severn° stream;
Sabrina is her name, a virgin pure;
Whilom she was the daughter of Locrine,
That had the sceptre from his father Brute.°
She, guiltless damsel, flying the mad pursuit
830   Of her enragèd stepdame Guendolen,
Commended her fair innocence to the flood
That stayed her flight with his cross-flowing course;
The water-nymphs that in the bottom played
Held up their pearlèd wrists and took her in,
Bearing her straight to aged Nereus'° hall,
Who, piteous of her woes, reared her lank head,
And gave her to his daughters to imbathe
In nectared lavers° strewed with asphodel,°
And through the porch and inlet of each sense
840   Dropped in ambrosial oils, till she revived
And underwent a quick immortal change,
Made goddess of the river. Still she retains
Her maiden gentleness, and oft at eve
Visits the herds along the twilight meadows,
Helping all urchin blasts,° and ill-luck signs
That the shrewd meddling elf delights to make,
Which she with precious vialed liquors heals;
For which the shepherds at their festivals
Carol her goodness loud in rustic lays,
850   And throw sweet garland wreaths into her stream
Of pansies, pinks, and gaudy daffodils.
And, as the old swain° said, she can unlock
The clasping charm and thaw the numbing spell,
If she be right invoked in warbled song;
For maidenhood she loves, and will be swift
To aid a virgin such as was herself
In hard-besetting need: this will I try,
And add the power of some adjuring verse.

Meliboeus Milton's pastoral name for Spenser
Severn the river rising in Wales and flowing through Shropshire to the sea. Sabrina is her mythical personification, whose story Spenser tells in *The Faerie Queene* II.x.19; Milton transforms her into a local spirit for Ludlow Castle and makes her powers more complex and potent than those of a mere water nymph.
Brute in British mythology, Aeneas' great-grandson, who founded Britain
Nereus' father of the Nereids or sea nymphs
lavers basins
asphodel the undying flower growing in the Elysian fields (see Chapman's Homer)
urchin blasts boils or infections caused by the fairies
old swain Meliboeus

SONG

860
Sabrina fair,
   Listen where thou art sitting
Under the glassy, cool, translucent wave,
   In twisted braids of lilies knitting
The loose train of thy amber-dropping hair;
   Listen for dear honour's sake,
   Goddess of the silver lake,
   Listen and save.

Listen and appear to us
In name of great Oceanus,°
By the earth-shaking Neptune's mace,°
870
And Tethys'° grave majestic pace,
By hoary Nereus'° wrinkled look,
And the Carpathian wizard's hook,°
By scaly Triton's° winding shell,
And old soothsaying Glaucus'° spell,
By Leucothea's° lovely hands,
And her son that rules the strands,
By Thetis'° tinsel-slippered feet,
And the songs of Sirens sweet,
By dead Parthenope's° dear tomb,
880
And fair Ligea's golden comb,°
Wherewith she sits on diamond rocks
Sleeking her soft alluring locks;
By all the nymphs that nightly dance
Upon thy streams with wily glance,
Rise, rise, and heave thy rosy head
From thy coral-paven bed,
And bridle in thy headlong wave,
Till thou our summons answered have.
                Listen and save.

[*Sabrina rises, attended by water-nymphs, and sings*]

890
By the rushy-fringèd bank,
Where grows the willow and the osier dank,
   My sliding chariot stays,°

Oceanus god of the river of ocean which, in Greek mythology, circled the earth
mace trident
Tethys' his wife
Nereus' See l. 835n.
Carpathian . . . hook the crook of Proteus, shepherd of Poseidon's (Neptune's) seals
Triton's Triton was Neptune's trumpeter, who played a conch; "winding" means "being blown upon" as well as "twisting."
Glaucus' He became a sea god and prophet.
Leucothea's "bright goddess" who helps Odysseus in *Odyssey* V

Thetis' a Nereid, married to Peleus and mother of Achilles
Parthenope's one of the sirens
Ligea's . . . comb another siren. Virgil mentions her hair, and Milton puts her in standard mermaid position, sitting on the rocks, combing her hair.
sliding chariot stays Her "chariot" is the water itself, awaiting her in the sense that it is always there, rushing by; the chariot of water is the subject of l. 895.

Thick set with agate, and the azurn° sheen
Of turkis° blue, and emerald green,
That in the channel strays.
Whilst from off the waters fleet
Thus I set my printless feet
O'er the cowslip's velvet head,
That bends not as I tread.
900   *Gentle swain, at thy request*
I am here.

SPIRIT   Goddess dear,
We implore thy powerful hand
To undo the charmèd band
Of true virgin here distressed,
Through the force and through the wile
Of unblest enchanter vile.
    SABRINA   Shepherd, 'tis my office best
To help ensnarèd chastity.
910   Brightest lady, look on me;
Thus I sprinkle on thy breast
Drops that from my fountain pure
I have kept of precious cure,
Thrice upon thy finger's tip,
Thrice upon thy rubied lip;
Next this marble venomed seat,
Smeared with gums of glutinous heat,
I touch with chaste palms moist and cold.
Now the spell hath lost his hold,
920   And I must haste ere morning hour
To wait in Amphitrite's° bower.

[SABRINA *descends, and* THE LADY *rises out of her seat*]

    SPIRIT   Virgin, daughter of Locrine,
Sprung of old Anchises' line,°
May thy brimmèd waves for this
Their full tribute never miss
From a thousand petty rills,
That tumble down the snowy hills;
Summer drouth or singèd air
Never scorch thy tresses fair,
930   Nor wet October's torrent flood
Thy molten crystal fill with mud,
May thy billows roll ashore
The beryl and the golden ore,
May thy lofty head be crowned

azurn azure
turkis turquoise
Amphitrite's Neptune's wife's
Virgin . . . line Sabrina is the daughter of

Locrine, who is the great-granddaughter of
Aeneas, who is the son of Anchises; see l.
828n.

With many a tower and terrace round,
And here and there thy banks upon
With groves of myrrh and cinnamon.
    Come, lady, while heaven lends us grace,
    Let us fly this cursèd place,
940 Lest the sorcerer us entice
With some other new device.
Not a waste or needless sound
Till we come to holier ground;
I shall be your faithful guide°
Through this gloomy covert wide,
And not many furlongs thence
Is your father's residence,
Where this night are met in state
Many a friend to gratulate
950 His wished presence, and beside
All the swains that there abide
We shall catch them at their sport,
With jigs and rural dance resort;
We shall catch them at their sport,
And our sudden coming there
Will double all their mirth and cheer.
Come let us haste, the stars grow high,
But Night sits monarch yet in the mid sky.

*The scene changes, presenting Ludlow Town and the President's Castle;
then come in Country Dancers, after them* THE ATTENDANT SPIRIT, *with
the* TWO BROTHERS *and* THE LADY.

SONG

SPIRIT   *Back, shepherds, back, enough your play
Till next sunshine holiday;*
960 *Here be without duck° or nod
Other trippings to be trod
Of lighter toes, and such court guise
As Mercury did first devise
With the mincing Dryades°
On the lawns and on the leas.*

[*This second song presents them to their father and mother*]

*Noble Lord, and Lady bright,
I have brought ye new delight.*

faithful guide Double meanings begin to emerge
here as the Spirit, played by their tutor Henry
Lawes, leads the Earl of Bridgewater's children
(as the Brothers and the Lady) out of the dark
wood in whose mythological realm the whole
of the action has taken place, and into the transformed scene of "Ludlow Town" and the castle
where the very masque is itself being given.

What is underlined is how Lawes has indeed
been their "guide" in their education, and the
act of presenting them to their father occurs
both within the fiction of the masque and outside it, as a kind of graduation ceremony.
duck bow or curtsy in country dancing
Dryades dryads, wood nymphs

Here behold so goodly grown
Three fair branches of your own;
970   *Heaven hath timely° tried their youth,*
Their faith, their patience, and their truth,
And sent them here through hard assays
With a crown of deathless praise,
*   To triumph in victorious dance*
O'er sensual folly and intemperance.

[*The dances ended,* THE SPIRIT *epiloguizes*]

SPIRIT   To the ocean now I fly,°
And those happy climes that lie
Where day never shuts his eye,
Up in the broad fields of the sky.
980   There I suck the liquid air
All amidst the gardens fair
Of Hesperus, and his daughters three
That sing about the golden tree:°
Along the crispèd° shades and bowers
Revels the spruce and jocund Spring;
The Graces° and the rosy-bosomed Hours°
Thither all their bounties bring,
That there eternal summer dwells,
And west winds with musky wing
990   About the cedarn alleys fling
Nard and cassia's balmy smells.°
Iris° there with humid bow
Waters the odorous banks that blow°
Flowers of more mingled hue
Than her purfled° scarf can shew,
And drenches with Elysian dew
(List, mortals, if your ears be true)
Beds of hyacinth and roses,
Where young Adonis° oft reposes,
1000   Waxing well of his deep wound
In slumber soft, and on the ground

timely early
To . . . fly The ocean which surrounds the earth, and which contains such islands as those of the Hesperidean gardens, but this is also an ocean of heavenly sky, in which drift islands of light. This vision, like so many Renaissance earthly paradises, combines many elements from classical mythology: the Elysian fields and the Hesperides were often associated, and Milton has assimilated the vision of Venus and Adonis from Spenser's Garden of Adonis (in *The Faerie Queene* III.vi) as well. In the performance of the masque, the Spirit opened with a version of these lines, presenting his realm of origin in a more detailed way.
golden tree on which the golden apples grew
crispèd curled

Graces Euphrosyne, Aglaia, Thalia; see Spenser, *The Faerie Queene* VI.x
Hours goddesses of seasonal cycle and changing times, frequently associated with spring
Nard and cassia's balmy smells spikenard and a cinnamon-like bark
Iris the rainbow
blow cause to blossom
purfled with a decorated border
Adonis Here Venus and Adonis seem to be in a more transitional state than in Spenser, where they lie at the world's center of generation; here, Adonis is recovering from his wound, asleep, and Venus ("the Assyrian queen") sits "sadly" by; upon recovery, Adonis will presumably advance beyond this phase of representing wounded sexual love.

Sadly sits the Assyrian queen;
But far above in spangled sheen
Celestial Cupid,° her famed son, advanced,
Holds his dear Psyche sweet entranced
After her wandering labours long,
Till free consent the gods among
Make her his eternal bride,
And from her fair unspotted side
1010 Two blissful twins are to be born,
Youth and Joy; so Jove hath sworn.
  But now my task is smoothly done,
I can fly, or I can run
Quickly to the green earth's end,
Where the bowed welkin° slow doth bend,
And from thence can soar as soon
To the corners of the moon.
  Mortals that would follow me,
Love Virtue, she alone is free;
1020 She can teach ye how to climb
Higher than the sphery chime;°
Or if Virtue feeble were,
Heaven itself would stoop to her.
1634   1637

Lycidas

Lycidas is a pastoral elegy, but its relation to that tradition is most complex. Milton's college acquaintance Edward King was drowned in the Irish Sea in August 1637. *Lycidas* is Milton's response not so much to his death, which Dr. Johnson and many critics since have assumed, as to being asked to contribute a poem to a memorial volume, *Justa Edouardo King* (1638), of which the other contributions, such as John Cleveland's extravagant effusion, could easily lead one to believe that sincerity and eloquence frequently avoid each other's company. Milton's contribution is a very great poem about the death of The Poet by drowning; the consolation that all elegies must offer comes in this case from the unfolding realization that it is not Poetry which has died. Starting with his own feeling of unripeness for a major poetic task, the poem moves through a series of confrontations—with the chosen form of pastoral elegy and its symbolic devices; with the possible demands of epic poetry someday, perhaps, to be faced; and, finally, with a kind of floating processional of emblematic personages, each of whom is to disclaim responsibility for The Poet's death. This sequence is

Cupid Venus' son, he is "advanced" by being elevated to this higher realm; in the imagery of Christian Platonism, Cupid or Eros could be made to stand for heavenly love, and Apuleius' 2nd-century A.D. story of Cupid and Psyche came to be interpreted as Christ's love for the human soul. Spenser, following Apuleius, makes them the parents of Pleasure (*The Faerie Queene* III.vi.50); here, Milton gives them Youth and Joy.

bowed welkin the sky's curved vault
sphery chime the music of the spheres, supposedly produced by the movements of the crystalline heavenly spheres, each carrying one of the planets or all the fixed stars, as they moved through the ether (see *Music of the Spheres* in the Glossary). Above these would be heaven.

rather like a pageant or masque worked into a solo invocation (the model for this is Spenser's *Epithalamion*, made in "lieu of many ornaments" for Spenser's own wedding, and containing ceremony within an expanded kind of lyric poem). All the personages—classical, Christian, local, and made-up spirits—are relevant to the drowned *pastor*—which means "shepherd" (or poet, in pastoral symbolism) as well as "priest." Water nymphs and local deities are finally followed by the fisherman-priest, St. Peter, who denounces a corrupt clergy even more blatantly than Apollo had previously attacked easy, vulgar poetic successes.

The poem keeps shifting back to pastoral elegy from its digressions, and throughout there runs, like a stream of water itself, the myth of the Arcadian river god Alpheus (standing for pastoral poetry), reputedly ran underground and undersea to mix with his beloved Arethusa, a Sicilian fountain (Sicily, home of Theocritus, was the official home of pastoral). The rivers, lakes, and streams in *Lycidas* are all beneficent presences associated with poetic and religious traditions; the estranging salt water of tears and drowning sea is hostile. Central also is the myth of Orpheus floating down the Hebrus (see ll. 58 ff.) as a type of deliverance.

The verse is a brilliant adaptation of the Italian *canzone*, using ten- and six-syllabled lines for the Italian seven and eleven, irregular rhyming schemes, and occasional blank lines to build up its strophic paragraphs, moving at the end to two rhymed couplets just before a final stanza of *ottava rima*. This last replaces the *commiato* or usual formal address of the canzona to itself (as in Spenser's at the end of *Epithalamion*) with a stanza reminiscent of Renaissance epic narrative, distancing and framing the whole poem.

Lycidas

In this monody the author bewails a learned friend, unfortunately drowned in his passage from Chester on the Irish Seas, 1637. And by occasion foretells the ruin of our corrupted clergy, then in their height.°

Yet once more, O ye laurels,° and once more,
Ye myrtles brown,° with ivy never sere,°
I come to pluck your berries harsh and crude,
And with forced fingers rude
Shatter your leaves before the mellowing year.
Bitter constraint, and sad occasion dear,°
Compels me to disturb your season due:
For Lycidas° is dead, dead ere his prime,
Young Lycidas, and hath not left his peer.

In this monody . . . height This note was added in an edition of 1645, after there was no danger from the church's censors. "By occasion" is a conventional one: Renaissance eclogues frequently used the bucolic mask for denouncing clerical abuses.
laurels sacred to Apollo, and the crown of poetic achievement. Myrtle is Venus', and ivy Bacchus', crown; the point is that poetry lives in the realm of all three of these deities, as Petrarch said in his Oration of 1341.

brown dark
ivy never sere All these plants are evergreen.
dear in both senses of "precious" and "dire"
Lycidas the name of a shepherd in Theocritus and Virgil, of a man who nearly drowned in Lucan's *Pharsalia*, and of the fisherman-swain in the first of Sannazaro's piscatory eclogues, which substituted Neapolitan marine life for a bucolic realm

10   Who would not sing for Lycidas? He knew
      Himself to sing, and build the lofty rhyme.
      He must not float upon his watery bier
      Unwept, and welter° to the parching wind,
      Without the meed of some melodious tear.°
          Begin then, Sisters of the sacred well°
      That from beneath the seat of Jove doth spring,
      Begin, and somewhat loudly sweep the string.
      Hence with denial vain, and coy° excuse,
      So may some gentle Muse
20   With lucky words favour my destined urn,
      And as he passes turn,
      And bid fair peace be to my sable° shroud.
      For we were nursed upon the self-same hill,
      Fed the same flock, by fountain, shade, and rill.
          Together both, ere the high lawns appeared
      Under the opening eyelids of the morn,
      We drove afield, and both together heard
      What time the grey-fly winds° her sultry horn,
      Battening° our flocks with the fresh dews of night,
30   Oft till the star that rose, at evening, bright
      Toward heaven's descent had sloped his westering wheel.
      Meanwhile the rural ditties were not mute,
      Tempered to the oaten flute;°
      Rough Satyrs danced, and Fauns with cloven heel
      From the glad sound would not be absent long,
      And old Damaetas° loved to hear our song.
          But O the heavy change, now thou art gone,
      Now thou art gone, and never must return!
      Thee, Shepherd, thee the woods and desert caves,
40   With wild thyme and the gadding° vine o'ergrown,
      And all their echoes mourn.
      The willows and the hazel copses green
      Shall now no more be seen
      Fanning their joyous leaves to thy soft lays.
      As killing as the canker° to the rose,
      Or taint-worm to the weanling herds that graze,
      Or frost to flowers, that their gay wardrobe wear,
      When first the white-thorn blows;°
      Such, Lycidas, thy loss to shepherd's ear.
50   Where were ye, Nymphs, when the remorseless deep
      Closed o'er the head of your loved Lycidas?

welter be tossed about
the meed . . . tear the recompense of some
elegiac poem
Sisters . . . well the Muses; their well on Mt.
Helicon was Aganippe
coy reticent
sable black
winds blows

Battening fattening
oaten flute instrument symbolic of pastoral
poetry
Damaetas pastoral name, perhaps for some
Cambridge tutor
gadding wandering
canker a kind of worm
white-thorn blows hawthorn blossoms

For neither were ye playing on the steep°
Where your old bards, the famous Druids, lie,
Nor on the shaggy top of Mona° high,
Nor yet where Deva° spreads her wizard stream.
Ay me, I fondly° dream,
Had ye been there!—for what could that have done?
What could the Muse herself that Orpheus bore,°
The Muse herself, for her enchanting son
60 Whom universal nature did lament,
When by the rout that made the hideous roar
His gory visage down the stream was sent,
Down the swift Hebrus to the Lesbian shore?
     Alas! what boots° it with uncessant care
To tend the homely slighted shepherd's trade,
And strictly meditate the thankless Muse?
Were it not better done as others use,
To sport with Amaryllis° in the shade,
Or with° the tangles of Neaera's hair?
70 Fame is the spur that the clear spirit doth raise
(That last infirmity of noble mind)
To scorn delights, and live laborious days;
But the fair guerdon when we hope to find,
And think to burst out into sudden blaze,
Comes the blind Fury° with the abhorrèd shears,
And slits the thin-spun life. 'But not the praise,'
Phoebus replied, and touched my trembling ears:°
'Fame° is no plant that grows on mortal soil,
Nor in the glistering foil°
80 Set off to the world, nor in broad rumour lies,
But lives and spreads aloft by those pure eyes
And perfect witness of all-judging Jove;
As he pronounces lastly on each deed,
Of so much fame in heaven expect thy meed.'
     O fountain Arethuse,° and thou honoured flood,

steep mountain slope, perhaps on the island of Bardsey ("Bards' island")
Mona the island of Anglesey
Deva the river Dee, "wizard" because it was reputed to shift its channel
fondly foolishly
the Muse . . . bore Calliope. Orpheus was torn apart by Thracian Bacchantes and his head floated down the river Hebrus, and it was fabled that all of nature went into mourning for him.
boots profits
Amaryllis The poet-swain Tityrus in Virgil's First Eclogue writes poems that "teach the woods to echo" his girl's name, Amaryllis; she and Neaera, also known to Milton from classical tradition for her beautiful hair, stand for the objects of the fashionable erotic Caroline verse which it would be so much easier, and safer, to write than an ambitious work on the death of poets.

with Perhaps this is a form of the verb "*withe*," "to twist."
blind Fury Atropos, nastiest of the Fates, cut the thread of life which her sisters had spun and measured; Milton calls her a "Fury" here as if to evoke a feeling of bungled retribution, of punishment for no crime.
touched . . . ears So Apollo tweaked Virgil's ear, warning him against over-ambition, Milton's allusion to whom being hardly modest, but contrasting heroic poetry with Pan's pastoral.
Fame Apollo properly defines it as immortal glory, whose acquisition cannot be arranged for
foil gold or silver leaf set under jewels before modern faceting could make them brilliant enough
Arethuse See Headnote; the juxtaposition with Mincius, a river of Lombardy associated with Virgil and his *Eclogues*, signals a return of the poem to a pastoral key, after the distant major ("that strain I heard") of Apollo's pronouncement.

Smooth-sliding Mincius, crowned with vocal reeds,
That strain I heard was of a higher mood.
But now my oat° proceeds,
And listens to the herald of the sea°
90   That came in Neptune's plea.
He asked the waves, and asked the felon winds,
What hard mishap hath doomed this gentle swain?
And questioned every gust of rugged wings
That blows frof off each beakéd promontory—
They knew not of his story,
And sage Hippotades° their answer brings,
That not a blast was from his dungeon strayed;
The air was calm, and on the level brine
Sleek Panope° with her all sisters played.
100   It was that fatal and perfidious bark,
Built in the eclipse, and rigged with curses dark,
That sunk so low that sacred head of thine.
　　　Next Camus,° reverend sire, went footing slow,
His mantle hairy, and his bonnet sedge,°
Inwrought with figures dim, and on the edge
Like to that sanguine flower° inscribed with woe.
'Ah, who hath reft,' quoth he, 'my dearest pledge?'°
Last came, and last did go,
The Pilot° of the Galilean lake;
110   Two massy keys he bore of metals twain
(The golden opes, the iron shuts amain°).
He shook his mitred locks, and stern bespake:
'How well could I have spared for thee, young swain,
Enow of such as for their bellies' sake
Creep and intrude and climb into the fold!
Of other care they little reckoning make
Than how to scramble at the shearers' feast,
And shove away the worthy bidden guest.
Blind mouths!° that scarce themselves know how to hold
120   A sheep-hook, or have learned aught else the least
That to the faithful herdman's art belongs!
What recks° it them? What need they? They are sped;°
And when they list,° their lean and flashy songs

oat See l. 33n.
herald of the sea Triton, blowing his shell
Hippotades Aeolus, wind god
Panope standing for all the Nereids, or sea nymphs
Camus the river Cam, standing for his university, Cambridge
sedge plants growing near water
sanguine flower the blood-colored hyacinth, which sprang up from the blood of the young man Apollo had accidentally killed, the streaks on its leaves reading like AI AI, Greek sounds of woe
pledge child
Pilot St. Peter, fisherman, the first bishop, to whom Jesus gave "the keys of the kingdom of heaven" (Matthew 16:19)
amain mightily
Blind mouths a startling and intense characterization of inauthentic bishops and corrupted clergy in general. John Ruskin's reading of it, in *Sesame and Lilies* I.22, remains the best: he points out that a *bishop* ("episcopus") is someone who oversees, and a pastor is someone who feeds, nurtures a flock. "The most unbishoply character a man can have is therefore to be blind. The most unpastoral is, instead of feeding, to want to be fed—to be a Mouth."
recks matters
are sped have more than enough
list want

Grate on their scrannel° pipes of wretched straw
The hungry sheep look up, and are not fed,
But swoln with wind, and the rank mist they draw,
Rot inwardly, and foul contagion spread,
Besides what the grim wolf° with privy paw
Daily devours apace, and nothing said;
130   But that two-handed engine° at the door
Stands ready to smite once, and smite no more.'
     Return, Alphéus,° the dread voice is past
That shrunk thy streams; return, Sicilian Muse,
And call the vales, and bid them hither cast
Their bells and flowerets of a thousand hues.
Ye valleys low where the mild whispers use°
Of shades and wanton winds and gushing brooks,
On whose fresh lap the swart star° sparely looks,
Throw hither all your quaint enamelled eyes,
140   That on the green turf suck the honied showers,
And purple all the ground with vernal flowers.
Bring the rathe° primrose that forsaken dies,
The tufted crowtoe, and pale jessamine,
The white pink, and the pansy freaked° with jet,
The glowing violet,
The musk-rose, and the well-attired woodbine,
With cowslips wan that hang the pensive° head,
And every flower that sad embroidery wears.
Bid amaranthus all his beauty shed,
150   And daffadillies fill their cups with tears,
To strew the laureate hearse where Lycid lies.
For so to interpose a little ease,
Let our frail thoughts dally with false surmise;
Ay me! whilst thee the shores and sounding seas
Wash far away, where'er thy bones are hurled,
Whether beyond the stormy Hebrides,
Where thou perhaps under the whelming° tide
Visit'st the bottom of the monstrous world;
Or whether thou, to our moist vows denied,
160   Sleep'st by the fable of Bellerus° old,

scrannel thin and squeaky-sounding
grim wolf the Roman Catholic Church, particularly in the person of the Jesuits, who can only devour (make converts) when the shepherd fails his flock
two-handed engine "Engine" usually means a device, and many scholars have suggested that Milton's visionary instrument of retribution is some kind of sword or axe, of symbolic nature in that it is identified in some scriptural or later text as such; others have suggested everything from two houses of Parliament to the two keys Peter holds. Some sort of sword seems most probable, and possibly one which combines the attributive significances of many of the single candidates proposed.

Alphéus See Headnote; the modulation is back to pastoral again, which the complexities of the poem's seriousness lead it to keep fleeing (where there is leisure for demonstrated grief, there is little room for the true fictions).
use are used to go
swart star Sirius
rathe early
freaked capriciously dressed
pensive The Latin words for "think" and "hang" are related, and Milton is reminding us of this.
whelming tossing
Bellerus mythical giant, perhaps invented by Milton, who would have given his name to Bellerium, the Roman designation of Land's End in Cornwall

Where the great Vision of the guarded mount°
Looks toward Namancos and Bayona's hold:°
Look homeward, Angel,° now, and melt with ruth;°
And, O ye dolphins,° waft the hapless youth.
    Weep no more, woeful shepherds, weep no more,
For Lycidas, your sorrow, is not dead,
Sunk though he be beneath the watery floor;
So sinks the day-star° in the ocean bed,
And yet anon repairs his drooping head,
170 And tricks his beams, and with new-spangled ore
Flames in the forehead of the morning sky:
So Lycidas sunk low, but mounted high,
Through the dear might of him that walked the waves,°
Where, other groves and other streams along,
With nectar pure his oozy locks he laves,
And hears the unexpressive nuptial song
In the blest kingdoms meek of joy and love.
There entertain him all the saints above,
In solemn troops and sweet societies
180 That sing, and singing in their glory move,
And wipe the tears for ever from his eyes.
Now, Lycidas, the shepherds weep no more;
Henceforth thou art the Genius° of the Shore,
In thy large recompense, and shalt be good
To all that wander in that perilous flood.
    Thus sang the uncouth° swain to the oaks and rills,
While the still morn went out with sandals grey;
He touched the tender stops of various quills,°
With eager thought warbling his Doric lay.°
190 And now the sun had stretched out all the hills,
And now was dropped into the western bay;
At last he rose, and twitched his mantle blue:
Tomorrow to fresh woods, and pastures new.
1637   1645

guarded mount St. Michael's Mount, off Cornwall
Namancos . . . hold the mountains of Namancos and the fortress of Bayona, on the coast of
Spain
Angel the archangel Michael, patron of mariners,
looking across the water from the top of St.
Michael's Mount (as he is from the top of
Mont St. Michel off Brittany)
ruth pity
dolphins The poet-musician Arion was carried
to safety over the waves by a dolphin; also,
Melicertes (see Comus, l. 876n) was carried to
shore by a dolphin and became the sea god
Palaemon; dolphins are here invoked to carry the
drowned poet over into myth.
day-star the sun
walked the waves Christ, of course (Matthew
14:25–26)
Genius in the sense of genius loci, the local
spirit inhabiting and protecting a particular spot
uncouth awkward; also perhaps in the older
sense of "unknown"
quills hollow stems of reeds in Pan's pipe
Doric lay rustic, pastoral song

Paradise Lost

Milton's blindness and the return of king and bishops combined to make of the 1660's an inner and outer darkness out of which, like a night bird and like a blind prophet, he could respond vocally to an inner light. The abandoned confrontation with epic was his first task. Early notes for a tragedy to be called *Adam Unparadised* proved more potent seeds than those of ideas specifically for heroic narrative—the Arthurian subject, for example, toward which English poetic vision has continued to gaze. Brought up for consideration in two of his early Latin poems (*Damon's Epitaph* and *Manso*), it is one of those alternatives to the poem's subject whose rejection is explained in IX.25–40. *Paradise Lost* was composed in the early 1660's, dictated in stretches of up to forty lines at once during days otherwise filled with walking, playing music, and being read to. It was published in 1667, originally in ten books which, considered in pairs, reflected the five-act structure of neoclassical drama. In 1674, the second edition reorganized the poem into an epic pattern of twelve books, but it required very little actual revision to do so.

Paradise Lost is a Renaissance, Protestant, English epic, confronting, containing, and reinterpreting the Homeric, Virgilian, Dantesque, and Spenserian poems which precede it. It enlists their aid in the poetic realization of a perfect state of man, and the fall from that perfection into a state of human reality. Whereas in Homeric epic the similes and other arts of language are employed to explain to an audience what a vanished heroic age was really like, Milton's analogous task was to describe Paradise in the kind of language that had developed in human history only since, and because of, the loss of it. The very form of his poem is an avowal of the nature of that task.

It begins with a literal "fall" to prefigure the metaphorical, but more general, Fall of Man—the dropping of Satan from heaven to the bottom of everything (save, as we soon see, the depths of his own thoughts) in hell. The once glorious leader of a rebellion against God evinces, in Book I, some of the virtues of the human heroic—energy, resolution, wit, power of command, what looks like imagination. It is only when we remember that these virtues—along with physical strength, competitiveness, craft, and enterprise, for example—are rather like spiritual crutches with which Fallen Man was supplied, that we can put into proper perspective the inverted heroics of Satan and the world of Pandemonium. Satan's perversion of activity brings about the primary (but, in the narrative, chronologically secondary) human one; this relation is like that of prophecy to fulfillment, if we read it correctly, of "shadowy type" (as Milton puts it in the terms used by biblical interpreters) to truth, or, an another way, of thought to action. The puzzle of the attractiveness and intensity of Books I and II, and the static, doctrinal quality of Book III (which directly treats of God and heaven) has been observed since William Blake's first perception of it ("Milton was of the Devil's party without knowing it") to represent the effects of unavowed forces in Milton's imagination. Critics since remain divided even about the proper language in which to describe the puzzle, let alone about how to solve it. Is Satan hero? Villain? Hero-villain from the Jacobean stage? Embodiment of energy or only of evil? Attractive because he speaks to our condition of vitality? Or only because we are fallen sinners who cannot respond without interest and pleasure to the embodiment of our worst fault?

The way in which Satan's fall introduces Adam's (and thereby, ours) is not only an act of obeisance to the classical epic tradition of starting *in medias res* ("in the midst of things"), rather than with true causal beginnings: rather is it at the heart of Milton's poetic method. Classical, biblical, and contemporary allusions, at the poem's beginning, to events which, in human time, are yet to occur, light up this world of events prior to all events. Classical myths in relation to their later interpretations are constantly and thematically present, and patristic biblical commentary, with its typological readings of earlier events in the light of later ones, provides both details and larger models. The complex relation *Satan—Adam—Christ*, for instance, is almost a typological triangle, and there are many interesting parallels to this. By alluding, for example, in the description of Satan's spear in Book I, to Ovid's Golden Age, Milton underlines Satan's destructive role: Renaissance mythographers associated Saturn, who ruled the Age of Gold in Hesiod and Ovid, and who taught men to farm and who was cast, by Zeus, out of the sky, with Adam. Momentary connections like this abound in *Paradise Lost,* where they have both local and general application.

Milton's language and style in the poem both reflect this too. His similes are always powerfully complex; they never merely compare the recounted to the familiar with respect to one quality or attribute (like Homeric similes), but always imply others, of a different sort or quality, as well. His references look forward and back, within and beyond the poem: the reader's knowledge of human history, Man's past, lies in the visionary future of the poem's events, and even the use of particular words shows an awareness of this. The unfallen world, the pre-historical dimension, has to be rendered in concepts themselves created by history. Milton compensates for this somewhat by associating the etymological meaning of a word with the unfallen domain, and the more common, ordinary sense of it with the world of biological-historical mankind. Other concepts—*crooked:straight, stand:rise:fall, up:down*—have this double role in the poem, an early use of a term in Paradise being "infected," as Christopher Ricks has called it, with the figurative moral meanings they would, in human vernaculars, come to have.

Milton's latinate syntax, attacked by T. S. Eliot and other associates in a modernist cause for its betrayal of the values of English speech, is by no means only latinate. His placing of adjectives (as in I. 18: "the upright heart and pure"), where the sequence *first adjective–noun–second adjective* is itself a miniature narrative or argument, is all Italian. Constructions like "Tree of Prohibition" (meaning "prohibited tree" primarily, but with complex overtones) are Hebrew. If Greek syntax were less like English, so that its use might set up new possibilities for enriching the forward movement of subject-predicate word order in English, there might have been more adaptations of it. The language of *Paradise Lost,* in fact, even echoes itself, time and again: phrases from earlier parts appear in later ones, and it is almost as if the story of Satan's fall were a minor epic lying in the background of the poem's central world —that of Books IV through IX: the region of Eden and the stories and lessons learned there.

Milton's poetic line is the blank verse of English stage tragedy, a counterpart of classical hexameters first used by Surrey for his *Aeneid* translation (but without, at the time, setting up a tradition). In a prose statement about the form of the poem, added to the second printing of the first edition purportedly because of complaints from readers that the poem was not in heroic couplets, Milton says something very revealing. "The sense variously drawn out from one verse to another," he declares, will do the work of orchestrating his line endings better than rhyme can. He refers to the enjambment (the way in which line-breaks cut into the syntactic flow, thus manipulating sense). We see this in the very first line of the poem, and throughout. In

IV.25 we are told of how conscience, in Satan, "wakes the bitter memory / Of what he was, what is, and what must be"—and here the new line starts—"Worse"; the very drama of discovery that the familiar liturgical *is–was–will be* phrasing is violated, and that the verb "be" is auxiliary (predicating, and not identifying), is part of the poetic action.

Milton's ambition in *Paradise Lost* was nothing short of the highest—as he does not shrink from acknowledging. The poem's influence on subsequent English poetry is only beginning to be fully understood today, and it remains perhaps the last poem which could equal, if only as an intellectual achievement, any other accomplishment —even Newton's *Principia*—of its century, or of our age.

Paradise Lost

From *Book I*

Of man's first disobedience, and the fruit°
Of that forbidden tree, whose mortal taste
Brought death into the world, and all our woe,
With loss of Eden, till one greater Man°
Restore us, and regain the blissful seat,
Sing, heavenly Muse,° that on the secret top
Of Oreb, or of Sinai,° didst inspire
That shepherd who first taught the chosen seed
In the beginning how the heavens and earth
10   Rose out of Chaos; or if Sion hill
Delight thee more, and Siloa's brook° that flowed
Fast by the oracle of God, I thence
Invoke thy aid to my adventurous song,
That with no middle flight° intends to soar
Above the Aonian mount,° while it pursues
Things unattempted yet in prose or rhyme.
And chiefly thou, O Spirit, that dost prefer
Before all temples the upright heart and pure,
Instruct me, for thou knowest; thou from the first
20   Wast present, and with mighty wings outspread
Dove-like sat'st brooding on the vast abyss
And mad'st it pregnant:° what in me is dark
Illumine, what is low raise and support;

Of . . . fruit The opening line's structure, with "disobedience," the commanding polysyllabic word framed by monosyllables, culminates in the "fruit" which, because of the enjambment, suggests both "results" and the fruit of "that forbidden tree," both the general and concrete meanings; notice also the end words of the first three lines, whose sequence "fruit–taste-woe" is the plot of the Fall.
one greater Man Christ, the "second Adam"
heavenly Muse invoking Urania, Muse of the most elevated vision, whom he will actually name only at the beginning of Book VII
Oreb . . . Sinai where Moses ("That shepherd") heard the word of God (Exodus 3:1) and received the law
Siloa's brook in Jerusalem, near the temple
Aonian mount Helicon, the hill of the Muses: Milton's epic will fly beyond antiquity
mad'st it pregnant The creation of the world as told in Genesis, the impregnation of Mary by the descending dove of the Holy Spirit, and the secondary creation of Milton's own great poem are here brought together.

That to the highth of this great argument
I may assert eternal providence,
And justify the ways of God to men.
    Say first, for heaven hides nothing from thy view,
Nor the deep tract of hell, say first what cause
Moved our grand° parents in that happy state,
30   Favoured of heaven so highly, to fall off
From their creator, and transgress his will
For one restraint, lords of the world besides?
Who first seduced them to that foul revolt?
The infernal serpent;° he it was whose guile,
Stirred up with envy and revenge, deceived
The mother of mankind, what time his pride
Had cast him out from heaven, with all his host
Of rebel angels, by whose aid aspiring°
To set himself in glory above his peers,
40   He trusted to have equalled the Most High,
If he opposed; and with ambitious aim
Against the throne and monarchy of God
Raised impious war in heaven and battle proud
With vain attempt. Him the Almighty Power
Hurled headlong flaming from the ethereal sky
With hideous ruin° and combustion down
To bottomless perdition, there to dwell
In adamantine° chains and penal fire,
Who° durst defy the omnipotent to arms.
50   Nine times the space that measures day and night
To mortal men, he with his horrid crew
Lay vanquished, rolling in the fiery gulf
Confounded though immortal. But his doom
Reserved him to more wrath; for now the thought
Both of lost happiness and lasting pain
Torments him; round he throws his baleful eyes,
That witnessed° huge affliction and dismay
Mixed with obdúrate pride and steadfast hate.
At once as far as angels' ken° he views
60   The dismal situation waste and wild:
A dungeon horrible, on all sides round
As one great furnace flamed, yet from those flames
No light, but rather darkness visible°

grand great, but also the parents of all the parents who would ever live
infernal serpent Only in the last book of the Bible, Revelation 12:9 and 20:2, is the wily serpent of Genesis associated with the rebel angel, Satan.
aspiring one of very few lines in *Paradise Lost* with a feminine, or unstressed, ending
ruin downfall
adamantine of the hardest substance imaginable; there is a hint of Prometheus, chained to his rock, too

Who he who
witnessed bore witness to
angels' ken their range of vision
darkness visible Light in all its forms—heavenly, created, the light of physical sight denied a blind man, symbolic light of reason, and divine creative power—is far too important in *Paradise Lost* to allow Milton to be careless with it: whatever makes things visible in hell, it is not light.

Served only to discover sights of woe,
Regions of sorrow, doleful shades, where peace
And rest can never dwell, hope never comes°
That comes to all; but torture without end
Still urges,° and a fiery deluge, fed
With ever-burning sulphur unconsumed:
70   Such place eternal justice had prepared
For those rebellious, here their prison ordained
In utter° darkness, and their portion set
As far removed from God and light of heaven
As from the centre thrice to the utmost pole.
O how unlike the place from whence they fell!
There the companions of his fall, o'erwhelmed
With floods and whirlwinds of tempestuous fire,
He soon discerns, and weltering° by his side
One next himself in power, and next in crime,
80   Long after known in Palestine, and named
Beelzebub.° To whom the arch-enemy,
And thence in heaven called Satan,° with bold words
Breaking the horrid silence thus began:
     'If thou beest he . . . but O how fallen! how changed
From him, who in the happy realms of light
Clothed with transcendent brightness didst outshine
Myriads though bright—if he whom mutual league,
United thoughts and counsels, equal hope
And hazard in the glorious enterprise,
90   Joined with me once, now misery hath joined
In equal ruin: into what pit thou seest
From what highth fallen, so much the stronger proved
He with his thunder, and till then who knew
The force of those dire arms? Yet not for those,
Nor what the potent victor in his rage
Can else inflict, do I repent or change,
Though changed in outward lustre that fixed mind
And high disdain, from sense of injured merit,°
That with the mightiest raised me to contend,
100   And to the fierce contention brought along
Innumerable force of spirits armed
That durst dislike his reign, and me preferring,
His utmost power with adverse power opposed
In dubious battle on the plains of heaven,
And shook his throne.° What though the field be lost?

hope never comes echoing Dante, over the entrance to whose hell is inscribed: "Abandon hope all ye enter here" (*Inferno* III.4–6)
urges presses
utter also in the sense of "outer"
weltering tossing
Beelzebub Hebrew for "lord of the flies"; Satan's lieutenant here
Satan The name in Hebrew means "enemy, opponent, adversary."

merit an important word: for Satan, it means "power," for Christ, goodness; cf.II.6 and 21
And shook his throne a lie—in the description of the war in heaven in Bk. VI, we learn that it was because of the chariot of the Son that "The steadfast Empyrean shook throughout." In this and subsequent speeches, one can view Satan as a crude liar or as a suffering, deposed leader, enthusiastically self-deceived.

All is not lost; the unconquerable will,
And study° of revenge, immortal hate,
And courage never to submit or yield:
And what is else not to be overcome?
110   That glory never shall his wrath or might
Extort from me. To bow and sue for grace
With suppliant knee, and deify his power—
Who° from the terror of this arm so late
Doubted° his empire—that were low indeed,
That were an ignominy° and shame beneath
This downfall; since by fate the strength of gods°
And this empyreal substance cannot fail,°
Since through experience of this great event,
In arms not worse, in foresight much advanced,
120   We may with more successful hope resolve
To wage by force or guile eternal war
Irreconcilable to our grand foe,
Who now triumphs, and in the excess of joy
Sole reigning holds the tyranny of heaven.'
So spake the apostate Angel, though in pain,
Vaunting aloud, but racked with deep despair;
And him thus answered soon his bold compeer:
'O Prince, O chief of many thronèd powers,°
That led the embattled seraphim to war
130   Under thy conduct, and in dreadful deeds
Fearless, endangered heaven's perpetual king,
And put to proof his high supremacy,
Whether upheld by strength, or chance, or fate;
Too well I see and rue the dire event,
That with sad overthrow and foul defeat
Hath lost us heaven, and all this mighty host
In horrible destruction laid thus low,
As far as gods and heavenly essences
Can perish: for the mind and spirit remains
140   Invincible, and vigour soon returns,
Though all our glory extinct,° and happy state
Here swallowed up in endless misery.
But what if he our conqueror (whom I now
Of force° believe almighty, since no less
Than such could have o'erpowered such force as ours)
Have left us this our spirit and strength entire
Strongly to suffer and support our pains,

study search for
Who I who
Doubted feared for
ignominy pronounced "ignomy"
gods As a relativist in theology and a Hobbesian
in political theory, Satan thinks of God as
being one of a collection of pagan deities; it
is axiomatic that He is not.
substance cannot fail even the vanquished rebels
are immortal (see l. 53, above)

thronèd powers Medieval angelology distinguished nine angelic orders: seraphim, cherubim,
thrones, dominations, virtues, powers, principalities, angels, and archangels. Beelzebub
obliquely invokes these now, but will trot out
most of the list later, in his public rhetoric.
extinct extinguished
Of force perforce

That we may so suffice° his vengeful ire,
Or do him mightier service as his thralls
150   By right of war, whate'er his business be,
Here in the heart of hell to work in fire,
Or do his errands in the gloomy deep?
What can it then avail though yet we feel
Strength undiminished, or eternal being
To undergo eternal punishment?'
        Whereto with speedy words the arch-fiend replied:
'Fallen cherub, to be weak is miserable,
Doing or suffering: but of this be sure,
To do aught good never will be our task,
160   But ever to do ill our sole delight,
As being the contrary to his high will
Whom we resist. If then his providence
Out of our evil seek to bring forth good,
Our labour must be to pervert that end,
And out of good still to find means of evil;°
Which ofttimes may succeed, so as perhaps
Shall grieve him, if I fail not,° and disturb
His inmost counsels from their destined aim.
But see the angry victor hath recalled
170   His ministers of vengeance and pursuit
Back to the gates of heaven; the sulphurous hail
Shot after us in storm, o'erblown hath laid°
The fiery surge, that from the precipice
Of heaven received us falling, and the thunder,
Winged with red lightning and impetuous rage,
Perhaps hath spent his shafts, and ceases now
To bellow through the vast and boundless deep.
Let us not slip° the occasion, whether scorn
Or satiate fury yield it from our foe.
180   Seest thou yon dreary plain, forlorn and wild,
The seat of desolation, void of light,
Save what the glimmering of these livid flames
Casts pale and dreadful? Thither let us tend
From off the tossing of these fiery waves,
There rest, if any rest can harbour there,
And reassembling our afflicted° powers,
Consult how we may henceforth most offend°
Our enemy, our own loss how repair,
How overcome this dire calamity,
190   What reinforcement we may gain from hope;

---

suffice appease
If then . . . evil These lines frame the notion
of the *felix culpa*, or fortunate fall: out of their
evil God will bring forth human and divine
good; they also introduce Satan's dialectical
juggling of divine concepts and their opposites;

later on, it will get more tortured and desperate.
if I fail not unless I'm wrong
laid reduced
slip let go by
afflicted cast down
offend injure

If not, what resolution from despair.'
—Thus Satan talking to his nearest mate
With head uplift above the wave, and eyes
That sparkling blazed;° his other parts besides
Prone on the flood, extended long and large
Lay floating many a rood,° in bulk as huge
As whom the fables name of monstrous size,
Titanian° or Earth-born, that warred on Jove,
Briareos or Typhon, whom the den
200 By ancient Tarsus held, or that sea-beast
Leviathan,° which God of all his works
Created hugest that swim the ocean stream:
Him haply slumbering on the Norway foam,
The pilot of some small night-foundered° skiff,
Deeming some island, oft, as seamen tell,
With fixèd anchor in his scaly rind
Moors by his side under the lee, while night
Invests° the sea, and wishèd morn delays:
So stretched out huge in length the arch-fiend lay
210 Chained on the burning lake; nor ever thence
Had risen or heaved his head, but that the will
And high permission of all-ruling heaven
Left him at large to his own dark designs,
That with reiterated crimes he might
Heap on himself damnation, while he sought
Evil to others, and enraged might see
How all his malice served but to bring forth
Infinite goodness, grace and mercy shown
On man by him seduced, but on himself
220 Treble confusion, wrath and vengeance poured.
    Forthwith upright he rears from off the pool
His mighty stature; on each hand the flames
Driven backward slope their pointing spires, and rolled
In billows, leave i' th' midst a horrid ° vale.
Then with expanded wings he steers his flight
Aloft, incumbent° on the dusky air
That felt unusual weight, till on dry land
He lights, if it were land that ever burned
With solid, as the lake with liquid fire;
230 And such appeared in hue;° as when the force

With head . . . blazed There is a premonition
of Satan's later—chosen—shape here, a touch
of the sea serpent.
rood rod, the unit of length: 5.5 yards
Titanian The Titans and the Giants both attacked
the Olympian gods (Briareos represents the
first, Typhon the second).
Leviathan the great sea beast of Scripture
(Job 41, Isaiah 27:1, and elsewhere), thought
of as a whale. The story about the whale's
being mistaken for an island is from the

medieval bestiaries; every simile emphasizing
Satan's magnitude or power in Books I and II of
Paradise Lost will also show something false,
illusory, or, as here, untrustworthy about it.
night-foundered sunk in night
Invests enfolds
horrid in the Latin sense, "bristling," with a
touch of the modern sense
incumbent weighing down
hue surface color and texture

Of subterranean wind transports a hill
Torn from Pelorus,° or the shattered side
Of thundering Aetna, whose combustible
And fuelled entrails thence conceiving fire,
Sublimed° with mineral fury, aid the winds,
And leave a singèd bottom all involved°
With stench and smoke: such resting found the sole
Of unblest feet. Him followed his next° mate,
Both glorying to have scaped the Stygian flood°
240   As gods, and by their own recovered strength,
Not by the sufferance of supernal power.
      'Is this the region, this the soil, the clime,'
Said then the lost archangel, 'this the seat°
That we must change for heaven, this mournful gloom
For that celestial light? Be it so, since he
Who now is sovereign can dispose and bid
What shall be right: farthest from him is best,
Whom reason hath equalled, force hath made supreme
Above his equals. Farewell, happy fields,
250   Where joy for ever dwells: hail, horrors! hail,
Infernal world! and thou, profoundest hell,
Receive thy new possessor: one who brings
A mind not to be changed by place or time.
The mind is its own place, and in itself
Can make a heaven of hell, a hell of heaven.°
What matter where, if I be still the same,
And what I should be, all but less than he
Whom thunder hath made greater? Here at least
We shall be free; the Almighty hath not built
260   Here for his envy, will not drive us hence:
Here we may reign secure, and in my choice
To reign is worth ambition, though in hell:
Better to reign in hell than serve in heaven.°
But wherefore let we then our faithful friends,
The associates and co-partners of our loss,
Lie thus astonished on the oblivious pool,°
And call them not to share with us their part
In this unhappy mansion, or once more
With rallied arms to try what may be yet

Pelorus Cape Faro, near the volcano Aetna
in Sicily
Sublimed vaporized; a term from alchemy
meaning the refining of metals by fire
involved entwined
next closest
Stygian flood the "fiery gulf" of l. 52
seat proper place
The mind . . . heaven This sounds both like
great self-reliance and courageous resolve, and
like a bad mistake in denying the external,
local existence of heaven and hell; the dramatic
irony is that after twisting good and evil, rise
and fall, up and down, heaven and hell into
each other, Satan will complain, in his great
speech on Mt. Niphates (IV.32–113), of the
hell within him.
Better . . . heaven again, on the surface, a
slogan asserting human dignity; but Satan is
not human, heaven commands no "servitude,"
and what kind of kingdom hell is becomes
clear
astonished . . . pool stupefied on the lake of
forgetfulness

270 Regained in heaven, or what more lost in hell?'
  So Satan spake, and him Beelzebub
Thus answered: 'Leader of those armies bright,
Which but the omnipotent none could have foiled,
If once they hear that voice, their liveliest pledge
Of hope in fears and dangers, heard so oft
In worst extremes, and on the perilous edge°
Of battle when it raged, in all assaults
Their surest signal, they will soon resume
New courage and revive, though now they lie
280 Grovelling and prostrate on yon lake of fire,
As we erewhile, astounded and amazed;
No wonder, fallen such a pernicious highth!'
  He scarce had ceased when the superior fiend
Was moving toward the shore; his ponderous shield,
Ethereal temper,° massy, large, and round,
Behind him cast; the broad circumference
Hung on his shoulders like the moon,° whose orb
Through optic glass the Tuscan artist° views
At evening from the top of Fesole,
290 Or in Valdarno,° to descry new lands,
Rivers or mountains in her spotty globe.
His spear, to equal which the tallest pine
Hewn on Norwegian hills, to be the mast
Of some great ammiral,° were but a wand,
He walked with to support uneasy steps
Over the burning marl, not like those steps
On heaven's azure; and the torrid clime
Smote on him sore besides, vaulted with fire.
Nathless° he so endured, till on the beach
300 Of that inflamèd sea, he stood and called
His legions, angel forms, who lay entranced,
Thick as° autumnal leaves that strow the brooks
In Vallombrosa,° where the Etrurian shades
High over-arched embower; or scattered sedge
Afloat, when with fierce winds Orion armed°
Hath vexed the Red Sea° coast, whose waves o'erthrew

perilous edge front line
Ethereal temper tempered by ethereal flame
like the moon In this sequence of similes, the
grandeur of Satan's appearance and his authenticity are simultaneously developed; the
moon, to which his shield is compared, looks
startlingly huge through the artificial magnification of a telescope, and unlike the shield of
Achilles in Homer (*Iliad* XIX) it does not
have an emblem of human civilization upon it.
Tuscan artist Galileo Galilei (1564–1642);
Milton had actually visited him
Fesole . . . Valdarno Fiesole and the Arno
valley, both near Florence
ammiral admiral's flagship. Like the shield,
the comparison is to something technological,
hence from fallen human life, and, in this case,
quotes Ovid, *Metamorphoses* I (see Golding's
translation of the Golden Age passage), to
remind us that Satan will be doing the equivalent
of wrenching the Golden Age into an Iron
one, in which trees will become masts of ships.
There is also a covert allusion to the blind Polyphemus, "of light bereft," in whose hand a pine
tree guides and steadies his steps (Virgil, *Aeneid* III. 658–59).
Nathless nevertheless
Thick as also, dead as
Vallombrosa shady, wooded valley near Florence
Orion armed associated with seasonal storms
Red Sea in Hebrew, "sea of sedge"

Busiris° and his Memphian chivalry,
While with perfidious hatred they pursued
The sojourners of Goshen,° who beheld
310 From the safe shore their floating carcasses
And broken chariot wheels;° so thick bestrown,
Abject° and lost lay these, covering the flood,
Under amazement of° their hideous change.
He called so loud that all the hollow deeps
Of hell resounded: 'Princes, Potentates,
Warriors, the flower of heaven, once yours, now lost,
If such astonishment° as this can seize
Eternal Spirits; or have ye chosen this place
After the toil of battle to repose
320 Your wearied virtue,° for the ease you find
To slumber here, as in the vales of heaven?
Or in this abject posture have ye sworn
To adore the conqueror, who now beholds
Cherub and seraph rolling in the flood
With scattered arms and ensigns, till anon
His swift pursuers from heaven gates discern
The advantage, and descending tread us down
Thus drooping, or with linkèd thunderbolts
Transfix us to the bottom of this gulf?
330 Awake, arise, or be for ever fallen!'
    They heard, and were abashed, and up they sprung
Upon the wing, as when men wont to watch
On duty, sleeping found by whom they dread,
Rouse and bestir themselves ere well awake.
Nor did they not perceive the evil plight
In which they were, or the fierce pains not feel;
Yet to their general's voice they soon obeyed
Innumerable. As when the potent rod
Of Amram's son° in Egypt's evil day
340 Waved round the coast, up called a pitchy cloud
Of locusts, warping° on the eastern wind,
That o'er the realm of impious Pharaoh hung
Like night, and darkened all the land of Nile:
So numberless were those bad angels seen
Hovering on wing under the cope° of hell
'Twixt upper, nether, and surrounding fires;
Till, as a signal given, the uplifted spear

Busiris Pharaoh in Exodus
Goshen place of safety on the east of the Red Sea
chariot wheels again, a remarkable simile purporting to show how thick, numerous, and densely massed were Satan's troops, but reminding us of corpses and a defeated army that pursued Israel as Satan does Adam
abject cast down

amazement of stupefaction *of* and *at*
astonishment immobilization
virtue power, strength
Amram's son Moses
locusts, warping one of the ten plagues with which God smote the Egyptians (Exodus 10: 12–13); "warping" here means "swerving"
cope canopy

Of their great Sultan waving to direct
Their course, in even balance down they light
350 On the firm brimstone, and fill all the plain;
A multitude, like which the populous North
Poured never from her frozen loins, to pass
Rhene or the Danaw,° when her barbarous sons
Came like a deluge on the south, and spread
Beneath Gibraltar to the Libyan sands.
Forthwith from every squadron and each band
The heads and leaders thither haste where stood
Their great commander; godlike shapes and forms
Excelling human, princely dignities,
360 And powers that erst° in heaven sat on thrones;
Though of their names in heavenly records now
Be no memorial, blotted out and razed
By their rebellion from the books of life.°
Nor had they yet among the sons of Eve
Got them new names, till wandering o'er the earth,
Through God's high sufferance for the trial of man,
By falsities and lies the greatest part
Of mankind they corrupted to forsake
God their creator, and the invisible
370 Glory of him that made them to transform
Oft to the image of a brute, adorned
With gay religions° full of pomp and gold,
And devils to adore for deities:
Then were they known to men by various names,
And various idols through the heathen world.

[There follows a demonic parody of Homer's famous catalogue of ships in the *Iliad* II, a list of all the Greek captains and princes allied against Troy. Milton's list of demons includes names of devils from Hebraic and Christian folklore, as well as a multitude of pagan gods, whose mythological ancestry, following patristic tradition, Milton locates in fallen angels. In human history they would (or, from this point on in the poem's time scheme, they *will*) come to be false gods. This is Milton's visionary alternative to what might be a modern anthropologist's observation that the gods of a conquered people may persist, in changed form as demons or fairies or the like, under the imposed religion—or to a psychologist's suggestion that vanquished, suppressed memories of trauma return as the false gods of dream and hysterical symptom.

After Satan's troops are gathered, he urges them to pull themselves together, to resolve to recover their lost glories; and, suggesting that God is going to prepare a new garden world in which to "plant a generation," demands that "War / Open or undeclared, must be resolved." The remainder of Book I tells of the building of Pandemonium, capitol of Satan's realm.]

Rhene . . . Danaw Rhine and Danube. The whole image compares Satan to a leader of Asiatic barbarian raiders.
erst formerly

books of life God's ledgers, in which the Good are enrolled
gay religions pagan ceremonies

670   There stood a hill not far whose grisly top
   Belched fire and rolling smoke; the rest entire
   Shone with a glossy scurf,° undoubted sign
   That in his womb was hid metallic ore,
   The work of sulphur.° Thither winged with speed
   A numerous brigade hastened: as when bands
   Of pioneers with spade and pickaxe armed
   Forerun the royal camp, to trench a field
   Or cast a rampart. Mammon° led them on,
   Mammon, the least erected° Spirit that fell
680   From heaven, for even in heaven his looks and thoughts
   Were always downward bent, admiring more
   The riches of heaven's pavement, trodden gold,
   Than aught divine or holy else enjoyed
   In vision beatific.° By him first
   Men also, and by his suggestion taught,
   Ransacked° the centre, and with impious hands
   Rifled the bowels of their mother earth
   For treasures better hid. Soon had his crew
   Opened into the hill a spacious wound
690   And digged out ribs of gold. Let none admire°
   That riches grow in hell; that soil may best
   Deserve the precious bane. And here let those
   Who boast in mortal things, and wondering tell
   Of Babel,° and the works of Memphian° kings,
   Learn how their greatest monuments of fame,
   And strength and art are easily outdone
   By spirits reprobate,° and in an hour
   What in an age they with incessant toil
   And hands innumerable scarce perform.
700   Nigh on the plain in many cells prepared,
   That underneath had veins of liquid fire
   Sluiced from the lake, a second multitude
   With wondrous art founded the massy ore,
   Severing each kind, and scummed the bullion dross.
   A third as soon had formed within the ground
   A various mould, and from the boiling cells
   By strange conveyance filled each hollow nook,
   As in an organ from one blast of wind

scruf scaly incrustation: gold ore is seen as a skin disease of hell's rocks
sulphur essential, in alchemy, to the production of metals
Mammon in Aramaic, "wealth," but in medieval tradition standing for the realm of this world. Milton's conception of him as a Pluto-like mining god is based on Spenser's Cave of Mammon (see *The Faerie Queene* II.vii); cf. Matthew 6:24.
erected uplifted
vision beatific the direct vision of God by the saints which constitutes paradise

Ransacked This word, and "Rifled" below, suggest the aggressive violence of mining, as opposed to the nurturing of agriculture; the truer, "vegetable" gold of the earth's fruits, rather than her guts, will be seen in Paradise (IV. 220).
admire wonder
Babel the tower of Babel (Genesis 11:1–9) and all of Babylon's famous structures, all emblems of pride and presumption
Memphian Egyptian
reprobate rejected

To many a row of pipes the sound-board breathes.
710 Anon out of the earth a fabric huge
Rose like an exhalation,° with the sound
Of dulcet symphonies and voices sweet,
Built like a temple, where pilasters round
Were set, and Doric pillars overlaid
With golden architrave; nor did there want
Cornice or frieze, with bossy° scultpures graven;
The roof was fretted° gold. Not Babylon,
Nor great Alcairo° such magnificence
Equalled in all their glories, to enshrine
720 Belus or Serapis° their gods, or seat
Their kings, when Egypt with Assyria strove
In wealth and luxury. The ascending pile
Stood fixed her stately highth, and straight the doors
Opening their brazen folds discover wide
Within, her ample spaces, o'er the smooth
And level pavement; from the archèd roof
Pendent by subtle magic many a row
Of starry lamps and blazing cressets° fed
With naphtha and asphaltus° yielded light
730 As from a sky. The hasty multitude
Admiring entered, and the work some praise,
And some the architect: his hand was known
In heaven by many a towered structure high,
Where sceptred angels held their residence,
And sat as princes, whom the súpreme king
Exalted to such power, and gave to.rule,
Each in his hierarchy, the orders bright.
Nor was his name unheard or unadored
In ancient Greece, and in Ausonian land°
740 Men called him Mulciber;° and how he fell
From heaven, they fabled, thrown by angry Jove
Sheer o'er the crystal battlements: from morn
The noon he fell, from noon to dewy eve,
A summer's day; and with the setting sun
Dropped from the zenith like a falling star,
On Lemnos the Aégean isle. Thus they relate,
Erring; for he with this rebellious rout
Fell long before; nor aught availed him now

exhalation also, like a comet or meteor. This whole passage suggests a description of a masque transformation scene (see the Headnote to Ben Jonson's *Pleasure Reconciled to Virtue*)—rapid, illusory, dramatically impressive; the accompanying music hints at the power of Amphion raising the walls of Thebes to music, while the architectural details are those of massive, baroque architecture.
bossy in relief
fretted patterned, interlaced carving

Alcairo ancient Memphis
Belus or Serapis Baal or Osiris
cressets iron baskets
asphaltus pitch asphalt
Ausonian land Italy (its old Greek name)
Mulciber Hephaestus, Vulcan. Milton sums up the Homeric story (*Iliad* I.590–94) of his day-long, leisurely fall, almost as if a pleasant trip, then snaps in (l. 747) the corrective to what seems far too sweet a fable.

To have built in heaven high towers;° nor did he scape
750   By all his engines,° but was headlong sent
With his industrious crew to build in hell.
     Meanwhile the wingèd heralds by command
Of sovereign power, with awful ceremony
And trumpet's sound, throughout the host proclaim
A solemn council forthwith to be held
At Pandemonium,° the high capitol
Of Satan and his peers; their summons called
From every band and squarèd regiment
By place or choice the worthiest; they anon
760   With hundreds and with thousands trooping came
Attended. All access was thronged, the gates
And porches wide, but chief the spacious hall
(Though like a covered field, where champions bold
Wont ride in armed, and at the Soldan's° chair
Defied the best of paynim° chivalry
To mortal combat or career with lance)
Thick swarmed, both on the ground and in the air,
Brushed with the hiss of rustling wings. As bees
In springtime, when the sun with Taurus° rides,
770   Pour forth their populous youth about the hive
In clusters; they among fresh dews and flowers
Fly to and fro, or on the smoothèd plank,
The suburb of their straw-built citadel,
New rubbed with balm, expatiate° and confer
Their state affairs: so thick the airy crowd
Swarmed° and were straitened; till the signal given,
Behold a wonder! they but now who seemed
In bigness to surpass earth's giant sons,
Now less than smallest dwarfs, in narrow room
780   Throng numberless, like that pygmean race
Beyond the Indian mount, or fairy elves,
Whose midnight revels by a forest side
Or fountain some belated peasant sees,
Or dreams he sees, while overhead the moon
Sits arbitress, and nearer to the earth
Wheels her pale course; they on their mirth and dance
Intent, with jocund music charm his ear;°

heaven high towers The reversed syntax reflects the climax-capping of adding height to heaven.
engines devices (machinery and machinations)
Pandemonium in Greek, "all demons"
Soldan's Sultan's
paynim pagan
Taurus the sun is in Taurus from mid-April to mid-May
expatiate amble about
so thick . . . Swarmed Again, the density, busy-ness, and multitude of the bees show us those qualities of Satan's legions, but the scale is reduced to a *tiny* model of human industry and social organization (although a traditional one), and the "straw-built citadel" is both literal about straw beehives and figurative about vast structures (like Roman churches with hive-shaped domes) "built on straw."
fairy elves . . . ear (ll. 781–87) no longer reduced in size (bees, pygmies), but are now as illusory as spooks that the simple see. We are now in the English countryside for a moment, to give us a breath of pragmatic fresh air (as Chaucer does with his introduction of January in The Franklin's Tale); there are echoes of A Midsummer Night's Dream.

At once with joy and fear his heart rebounds.
Thus incorporeal spirits to smallest forms
790 Reduced their shapes immense, and were at large,°
Though without number still, amidst the hall
Of that infernal court. But far within,
And in their own dimensions like themselves,
The great seraphic lords and cherubim
In close° recess and secret conclave sat,
A thousand demi-gods and golden seats,
Frequent° and full. After short silence then
And summons read, the great consult° began.

    From *Book II*
High on a throne of royal state, which far
Outshone the wealth of Ormus° and of Ind,
Or where the gorgeous East with richest hand
Showers on her kings barbaric pearl and gold,
Satan exalted sat, by merit° raised
To that bad eminence; and from despair
Thus high uplifted beyond hope, aspires
Beyond thus high,° insatiate to pursue
Vain war with heaven, and by success° untaught,
10 His proud imaginations thus displayed:
    'Powers and dominions,° deities of heaven,
For since no deep within her gulf can hold
Immortal vigour, though oppressed and fallen,
I give not heaven for lost. From this descent
Celestial virtues° rising will appear
More glorious and more dread than from no fall,
And trust themselves to fear no second fate.
Me though just right and the fixed laws of heaven
Did first create your leader, next, free choice,
20 With what besides, in council or in fight,
Hath been achieved of merit, yet this loss,
Thus far at least recovered, hath much more
Established in a safe unenvied throne
Yielded with full consent. The happier state
In heaven, which follows dignity, might draw
Envy from each inferior; but who here
Will envy whom the highest place exposes
Foremost to stand against the thunderer's° aim
Your bulwark, and condemns to greatest share

at large The pun is quite deliberate.
close secret
Frequent crowded
consult debate
Ormus island city in the Persian gulf
merit power (see I.98n and II.21)
from despair . . . high again, the patterned
syntax reflects the overreaching of Satan's will

success the outcome, implying neither good nor
bad results; cf. II.123
Powers and dominions He still uses their angelic
titles (see I.128n).
virtues capabilities; also, the angelic order
the thunderer's Zeus, Jupiter; again, a false
reduction of God

30   Of endless pain? Where there is then no good
     For which to strive, no strife can grow up there
     From faction; for none sure will claim in hell
     Precedence, none whose portion is so small
     Of present pain that with ambitious mind
     Will covet more. With this advantage then
     To union, and firm faith, and firm accord,
     More than can be in heaven, we now return
     To claim our just inheritance of old,
     Surer to prosper than prosperity
40   Could have assured us;° and by what best way,
     Whether of open war or covert guile,
     We now debate; who can advise, may speak.
       He ceased, and next him Moloch,° sceptred king,
     Stood up, the strongest and the fiercest Spirit
     That fought in heaven, now fiercer by despair.
     His trust was with the Eternal to be deemed
     Equal in strength, and rather than be less
     Cared not to be at all; with that care lost
     Went all his fear: of God, or hell, or worse
50   He recked not, and these words thereafter spake:
       'My sentence° is for open war. Of wiles,
     More unexpert, I boast not: them let those
     Contrive who need, or when they need, not now.
     For while they sit contriving, shall the rest,
     Millions that stand° in arms and longing wait
     The signal to ascend, sit lingering here,
     Heaven's fugitives, and for their dwelling-place
     Accept this dark opprobrious den of shame,
     The prison of his tyranny who reigns
60   By our delay? No, let us rather choose,
     Armed with hell flames and fury, all at once
     O'er heaven's high towers° to force resistless way,
     Turning our tortures into horrid arms
     Against the torturer; when to meet the noise
     Of his almighty engine he shall hear
     Infernal thunder, and for lightning see
     Black fire and horror shot with equal rage
     Among his angels, and his throne itself
     Mixed with Tartarean° sulphur and strange fire,

Surer . . . assured us This shaping of words—
a b b a—called a "chiasmus," or "crossing,"
exemplifies Satan's use of rhetorical devices
common in the Renaissance.
Moloch One of the better known of Milton's
devils who later enter history as pagan gods;
he becomes a Canaanite idol to whom children
are sacrificed and is introduced in I.392–96
as the "horrid king besmeared with blood / Of
human sacrifice, and parents' tears / Though for
the noise of drums and timbrels loud / Their
children's cries unheard, that passed through
fire / To his grim idol."
sentence decision; cf. l. 291
stand metaphorically, as in "standing army,"
but notice the sequence of words in these
lines: "sit . . . stand . . . ascend . . . sit"
towers echoing I.749
Tartarean hellish. This is gunpowder, artillery
being an infernal parody of God's thunder and
an appropriate revenge.

70   His own invented torments. But perhaps
The way seems difficult and steep to scale
With upright wing against a higher foe?
Let such bethink them, if the sleepy drench
Of that forgetful lake benumb not still,
That in our proper motion we ascend
Up to our native seat; descent and fall
To us is adverse. Who but felt of late,
When the fierce foe hung on our broken rear
Insulting,° and pursued us through the deep,
80   With what compulsion and laborious flight
We sunk thus low? The ascent is easy then;
The event is feared; Should we again provoke
Our stronger, some worse way his wrath may find
To our destruction, if there be in hell
Fear to be worse destroyed: what can be worse
Than to dwell here, driven out from bliss, condemned
In this abhorrèd deep to utter woe;
Where pain of unextinguishable fire
Must exercise° us without hope of end
90   The vassals of his anger, when the scourge
Inexorably, and the torturing hour
Calls us to penance? More destroyed than thus
We should be quite abolished and expire.
What fear we then? What doubt we to incense
His utmost ire? Which to the highth enraged
Will either quite consume us, and reduce
To nothing this essential,° happier far
Than miserable to have eternal being;
Or if our substance be indeed divine,
100 And cannot cease to be, we are at worst
On this side nothing; and by proof we feel
Our power sufficient to disturb his heaven,
And with perpetual inroads to alarm,
Though inaccessible, his fatal° throne;
Which if not victory is yet revenge.'
    He ended frowning, and his look denounced°
Desperate revenge, and battle dangerous
To less than gods. On the other side up rose
Belial, in act more graceful and humane;
110 A fairer person lost not heaven; he seemed
For dignity composed and high exploit:
But all was false and hollow, though his tongue
Dropped manna,° and could make the worse appear

Insulting assaulting, as well as jeering
exercise torture
essential essence. Angelic substance is immaterial; cf. I.138.
fatal by fate; cf. I.116

denounced threatened
manna the heavenly food supplied to the
wandering Israelites (Exodus 16:14–16); this
is sarcastic, modeled on "dripping honey"

The better reason, to perplex and dash
Maturest counsels: for his thoughts were low;
To vice industrious, but to nobler deeds
Timorous and slothful: yet he pleased the ear,
And with persuasive accent thus began:
 'I should be much for open war, O Peers,
120 As not behind in hate, if what was urged
Main reason to persuade immediate war
Did not dissuade me most, and seem to cast
Ominous conjecture on the whole success:
When he who most excels in fact° of arms,
In what he counsels and in what excels
Mistrustful, grounds his courage on despair
And utter dissolution, as the scope
Of all his aim, after some dire revenge.
First, what revenge? The towers of heaven are filled
130 With armèd watch, that render all access
Impregnable; oft on the bordering deep
Encamp their legions, or with óbscure wing
Scout far and wide into the realm of Night,
Scorning surprise. Or could we break our way
By force, and at our heels all hell should rise
With blackest insurrection, to confound
Heaven's purest light, yet our great enemy
All incorruptible would on his throne
Sit unpolluted, and the ethereal mould
140 Incapable of stain would soon expel
Her mischief, and purge off the baser fire,°
Victorious. Thus repulsed, our final hope
Is flat despair; we must exasperate
The almighty victor to spend all his rage,
And that must end us, that must be our cure,
To be no more. Sad cure! for who would lose,
Though full of pain, this intellectual being,
Those thoughts that wander through eternity,°
To perish rather, swallowed up and lost
150 In the wide womb of uncreated Night,
Devoid of sense and motion? And who knows,
Let this be good, whether our angry foe
Can give it, or will ever? How he can
Is doubtful; that he never will is sure.
Will he, so wise, let loose at once his ire,
Belike° through impotence, or unaware,
To give his enemies their wish, and end

---

fact deed, feat
baser fire Heavenly light has been a refining
fire in this passage, burning off even the lower,
hellish sort.

for who . . . eternity An overtone of Hamlet's
"To be or not to be" soliloquy may be discerned
here.
Belike doubtless

Them in his anger, whom his anger saves
To punish endless? *Wherefore cease we then?*
160   Say they who counsel war; *We are decreed,*
Reserved, and destined to eternal woe;
Whatever doing, what can we suffer more,
What can we suffer worse?° Is this then worst,
Thus sitting, thus consulting, thus in arms?
What when we fled amain, pursued and strook
With heaven's afflicting thunder, and besought
The deep to shelter us? This hell then seemed
A refuge from those wounds—or when we lay
Chained on the burning lake?° That sure was worse.
170   What if the breath that kindled those grim fires
Awaked should blow them into sevenfold rage
And plunge us in the flames? or from above
Should intermitted vengeance arm again
His red right hand° to plague us? What if all
Her stores were opened and this firmament
Of hell should spout her cataracts of fire,
Impendent horrors, threatening hideous fall
One day upon our heads; while we perhaps
Designing or exhorting glorious war,
180   Caught in a fiery tempest shall be hurled
Each on his rock transfixed, the sport and prey
Of racking whirlwinds, or for ever sunk
Under yon boiling ocean, wrapped in chains;
There to converse with everlasting groans,
Unrespited, unpitied, unreprieved,
Ages of hopeless end? This would be worse.
War therefore, open or concealed, alike
My voice dissuades; for what can force or guile
With him, or who deceive his mind, whose eye
190   Views all things at one view? He from heaven's highth
All these our motions° vain, sees and derides;
Not more almighty to resist our might
Than wise to frustrate all our plots and wiles.
Shall we then live thus vile, the race of heaven
Thus trampled, thus expelled to suffer here
Chains and these torments? Better these than worse,
By my advice; since fate inevitable
Subdues us, and omnipotent decree,
The victor's will. To suffer, as to do,°

What . . . worse He will keep answering this rhetorical question in his own rhetorically brilliant speech.
burning lake an echo of I.52
red right hand quoted from Horace (*Odes* I.2), where it is used of civil war. This passage (to l. 186) also echoes classical accounts of Zeus' vanquishing the Titans.

motions plans
To suffer, as to do chimes against Satan's "Doing or suffering" (I.158) and the words of the Roman Mucius Scaevola, as he burned his right hand in the flames to show his captors his inner resources

200 Our strength is equal, nor the law unjust
     That so ordains: this was at first resolved,
     If we were wise, against so great a foe
     Contending, and so doubtful what might fall.
     I laugh when those who at the spear are bold
     And venturous, if that fail them, shrink and fear
     What yet they know must follow, to endure
     Exile, or ignominy,° or bonds, or pain,
     The sentence of their conqueror. This is now
     Our doom; which if we can sustain and bear,
210 Our súpreme foe in time may much remit
     His anger, and perhaps, thus far removed,
     Not mind us not offending, satisfied
     With what is punished; whence these raging fires
     Will slacken, if his breath stir not their flames.
     Our purer essence then will overcome
     Their noxious vapour, or enured° not feel,
     Or changed at length, and to the place conformed
     In temper and in nature, will receive
     Familiar the fierce heat, and void of pain;
220 This horror will grow mild, this darkness light,°
     Besides what hope the never-ending flight
     Of future days may bring, what chance, what change
     Worth waiting, since our present lot appears
     For happy° though but ill, for ill not worst,
     If we procure not to ourselves more woe.'
          Thus Belial with words clothed in reason's garb,
     Counselled ignoble ease, and peaceful sloth,
     Not peace; and after him thus Mammon° spake—
          'Either to disenthrone the king of heaven
230 We war, if war be best, or to regain
     Our own right lost: him to unthrone we then
     May hope when everlasting fate shall yield
     To fickle chance, and Chaos judge the strife:°
     The former, vain to hope, argues as vain
     The latter; for what place can be for us
     Within heaven's bound, unless heaven's lord supreme
     We overpower? Suppose he should relent
     And publish grace to all, on promise made
     Of new subjection; with what eyes could we
240 Stand in his presence humble, and receive
     Strict laws imposed, to celebrate his throne
     With warbled hymns, and to his Godhead sing
     Forced halleluiahs; while he lordly sits
     Our envied sovereign, and his altar breathes

---

ignominy See I.115n.
enured accustomed to
light not dark; not heavy

For happy as for happiness
Mammon See I.680.
strife between fate and chance

Ambrosial odours and ambrosial flowers,
Our servile offerings? This must be our task
In heaven, this our delight; how wearisome
Eternity so spent in worship paid
To whom we hate. Let us not then pursue
250   By force impossible, by leave obtained
Unácceptáble—though in heaven—our state
Of splendid vassalage, but rather seek
Our own good from ourselves, and from our own
Live to ourselves, though in this vast recess,
Free, and to none accountable, preferring
Hard liberty° before the easy yoke
Of servile pomp. Our greatness will appear
Then most conspicuous, when great things of small,
Useful of hurtful, prosperous of adverse
260   We can create, and in what place soe'er
Thrive under evil, and work ease out of pain
Through labour and endurance. This deep world
Of darkness do we dread? How oft amidst
Thick clouds and dark doth heaven's all-ruling sire
Choose to reside, his glory unobscured,
And with the majesty of darkness round
Covers his throne; from whence deep thunders roar,
Mustering their rage, and heaven resembles hell?
As he our darkness, cannot we his light
270   Imitate when we please? This desert soil
Wants not her hidden lustre, gems and gold;
Nor want we skill or art, from whence to raise
Magnificence; and what can heaven show more?
Our torments also may in length of time
Become our elements, these piercing fires
As soft as now severe, our temper changed
Into their temper; which must needs remove
The sensible° of pain. All things invite
To peaceful counsels, and the settled state
280   Of order, how in safety best we may
Compose° our present evils, with regard
Of what we are and where, dismissing quite
All thoughts of war. Ye have what I advise.'
    He scarce had finished, when such murmur filled
The assembly as when hollow rocks retain
The sound of blustering winds, which all night long
Had roused the sea, now with hoarse cadence lull

Hard liberty Mammon's declaration of independence cannot help but move the lover of human freedom, even one who appreciates the prophecy of the relation of individual liberty to the institution of wealth as acted out in the history of Western capitalism. In the context of the debate—Moloch's primitive, heroic violence and Belial's guileful parody of medieval quietism —Mammon's exhortation (ll. 269–73 below) to his fellows to produce light of their own follows as a version of what Max Weber called the Protestant ethic.
sensible felt part
Compose arrange

Seafaring men o'erwatched, whose bark by chance
Or pinnace anchors in a craggy bay
290 After the tempest. Such applause was heard
As Mammon ended, and his sentence° pleased,
Advising peace; for such another field
They dreaded worse than hell: so much the fear
Of thunder and the sword of Michaël°
Wrought still within them; and no less desire
To found this nether empire, which might rise
By policy,° and long procéss of time,
In emulation opposite to heaven.
Which when Beelzebub° perceived, than whom,
300 Satan except, none higher sat, with grave
Aspect he rose, and in his rising seemed
A pillar of state; deep on his front° engraven
Deliberation sat and public care;
And princely counsel in his face yet shone,
Majestic though in ruin: sage he stood,
With Atlantean° shoulders fit to bear
The weight of mightiest monarchies; his look
Drew audience and attention still as night
Or summer's noontide air, while thus he spake.

[Beelzebub's speech which follows dismisses the notion of merely trying to make Hell a better place to live, and outlines his general Satan's plan to attack the Kingdom of Heaven through its colony, a weak spot, "another world, the happy seat / Of some new race called Man," the inhabitants of which, currently "favoured more / Of him who rules above," might be corrupted, dispossessed, and added to their ranks. The assembly votes for this plan, and Satan, with no volunteers for the dangerous mission of checking the rumor and scouting the terrain, flies off himself. Meanwhile, the remaining demons occupy themselves in cultural pursuits: not only is the culture of Pandemonium, as we might call it, a brilliantly prophetic version of that of classical antiquity, but it shifts to Renaissance exploration, based on mythical and actual accounts of journeys alike. Then we have Satan leaving Hell to find earth, encountering the portress, a monster whom he does not recognize, and another, impossible to describe in detail. This inset allegory of Sin and Death is the narrative actualization of the imagery in James 1:15 which speaks of how lust, when it "hath conceived, it bringeth forth sin; and sin, when it is finished, bringeth forth death."]

The Stygian council thus dissolved; and forth
In order came the grand infernal peers;
Midst came their mighty paramount,° and seemed

---

sentence opinion; cf. l. 51
Michaël archangel who commanded God's army in Bk. VI
policy statecraft, with Machiavellian overtones

Beelzebub See I.81.
front forehead
Atlantean Atlas-like
paramount ruler

Alone the antagonist of heaven, nor less
510   Than hell's dread emperor, with pomp supreme
And god-like imitated state;° him round
A globe° of fiery seraphim enclosed
With bright emblazonry and horrent° arms.
Then of their session ended they bid cry
With trumpet's regal sound the great result.
Toward the four winds four speedy cherubim
Put to their mouths the sounding alchemy°
By herald's voice explained; the hollow abyss
Heard far and wide, and all the host of hell
520   With deafening shout returned them loud acclaim.
Thence more at ease their minds and somewhat raised°
By false presumptuous hope, the rangèd powers°
Disband, and wandering each his several way
Pursues, as inclination or sad choice
Leads him perplexed, where he may likeliest find
Truce to his restless thoughts, and entertain°
The irksome hours, till his great chief return.
Part on the plain, or in the air sublime°
Upon the wing, or in swift race contend,
530   As at the Olympian games or Pythian fields;°
Part curb their fiery steeds, or shun the goal
With rapid wheels, or fronted brigades form:
As when to warn proud cities war appears
Waged in the troubled sky, and armies rush
To battle in the clouds; before each van
Prick forth the airy knights, and couch their spears,
Till thickest legions close; with feats of arms
From either end of heaven the welkin° burns.
Others with vast Typhoean° rage more fell
540   Rend up both rocks and hills, and ride the air
In whirlwind; hell scarce holds the wild uproar;
As when Alcides° from Oechalia crowned
With conquest, felt the envenomed robe, and tore
Through pain up by the roots Thessalian pines,°
And Lichas from the top of Oeta threw
Into the Euboic sea. Others more mild,

---

state ceremonial royal trappings
globe phalanx
horrent bristling
alchemy metallic alloy
raised heartened
rangèd powers ranked armies
entertain pass away
sublime raise up
Olympian . . . fields This introduces the heroic games.
welkin sky
Typhoean titanic (see I.199); also, through

"typhon" (influencing "typhoon" later on), a whirlwind
Alcides Hercules, whose wife sent him a poisoned robe, went mad with the pain and hurled his friend Lichas, the mere bringer of the gift, into the Euboean sea.
tore . . . pines Not only does the wrenched syntax "imitate" the heroic action described (mostly by separating "tore" and "up"), but the whole of l. 544 itself is symmetrically patterned, with a pun on "pain" and "pine" (meaning "pain" as a noun, as well).

Retreated in a silent valley, sing°
With notes angelical to many a harp
Their own heroic deeds and hapless fall
550   By doom of battle; and complain that fate
Free virtue should enthrall to force or chance.
Their song was partial,° but the harmony
(What could it less when spirits immortal sing?)
Suspended° hell, and took with ravishment
The thronging audience. In discourse more sweet
(For eloquence the soul, song charms the sense)
Others apart sat on a hill retired,
In thoughts more elevate, and reasoned° high
Of providence, foreknowledge, will, and fate,
560   Fixed fate, free will, foreknowledge absolute,
And found no end, in wandering mazes lost.°
Of good and evil much they argued then,
Of happiness and final misery,
Passion and apathy, and glory and shame,
Vain wisdom all, and false philosophy—
Yet with a pleasing sorcery could charm
Pain for a while or anguish, and excite
Fallacious hope, or arm the obdurèd° breast
With stubborn patience as with triple steel.
570   Another part, in squadrons and gross° bands,
On bold adventure to discover wide
That dismal world, if any clime perhaps
Might yield them easier habitation, bend
Four ways their flying march, along the banks
Of four infernal rivers that disgorge
Into the burning lake their baleful streams:
Abhorrèd Styx,° the flood of deadly hate;
Sad Acheron of sorrow, black and deep;
Cocytus, named of lamentation loud
580   Heard on the rueful stream; fierce Phlegethon,
Whose waves of torrent fire inflame with rage.
Far off from these a slow and silent stream,
Lethe, the river of oblivion, rolls
Her watery labyrinth,° whereof who drinks
Forthwith his former state and being forgets,
Forgets both joy and grief, pleasure and pain.
Beyond this flood a frozen continent

---

sing epics, like their own versions of *Paradise Lost* VI
partial one-sided; also, possibly "in parts," or polyphonic musically
Suspended held rapt
reasoned a prophetic vision of fallen classical philosophy, particularly of Stoicism
wandering mazes lost as in the syntax and the twisting repetitions of abstract philosophical concepts, their way to truth forever lost
obdurèd hardened
gross massive
Abhorrèd Styx Each of these four rivers of the classical Hades has its name translated and explained.
labyrinth ironically paralleling the labyrinthine mazes of pagan thought, l. 561

Lies dark and wild, beat with perpetual storms
Of whirlwind and dire hail, which on firm land
590   Thaws not, but gathers heap, and ruin seems
Of ancient pile;° all else deep snow and ice,
A gulf profound as that Serbonian° bog
Betwixt Damiata and Mount Casius old,
Where armies whole have sunk; the parching air
Burns frore,° and cold performs the effect of fire.
Thither by harpy-footed Furies haled,
At certain revolutions all the damned
Are brought; and feel by turns the bitter change
Of fierce extremes, extremes by change more fierce,
600   From beds of raging fire to starve° in ice
Their soft ethereal warmth, and there to pine
Immovable, infixed, and frozen round,
Periods of time; thence hurried back to fire.
They ferry over this Lethean sound
Both to and fro, their sorrow to augment,
And wish and struggle, as they pass, to reach
The tempting stream, with one small drop to lose
In sweet forgetfulness all pain and woe,
All in one moment, and so near the brink;
610   But fate withstands, and to oppose the attempt
Medusa° with Gorgonian terror guards
The ford, and of itself the water flies
All taste of living wight, as once it fled
The lip of Tantalus.° Thus roving on
In cónfused march forlorn, the adventurous bands,
With shuddering horror pale, and eyes aghast,
Viewed first their lamentable lot, and found
No rest. Through many a dark and dreary vale
They passed, and many a region dolorous,
620   O'er many a frozen, many a fiery alp,°
Rocks, caves, lakes, fens, bogs, dens, and shades of death,°
A universe of death, which God by curse
Created evil, for evil only good,
Where all life dies, death lives, and Nature breeds,
Perverse, all monstrous, all prodigious things,
Abominable, inutterable, and worse
Than fables yet have feigned, or fear conceived,
Gorgons and Hydras, and Chimeras° dire.

---

pile building
Serbonian the quicksands which lay between Lake Serbonis and Damiata, near the Nile delta, renowned in antiquity for their danger to armies
frore frozen
starve Only the syntax is misleading: "to starve their warmth to death in ice."
Medusa one of the snaky-haired Gorgons whose look turns men to stone
Tantalus In the *Odyssey,* Odysseus sees Tanta-

lus, desperately thirsty, standing in a pool that always drops below his mouth when he tries to drink from it; cf. *The Faerie Queene* I.v.35.
alp any mountain
Rocks . . . death again, a mimetic line, its list of monosyllables tiring to get through, and slow
Hydras, and Chimeras many-headed beasts, and fire-breathing, triple-bodied (lion-serpent-goat) monsters

Meanwhile the adversary of God and man,
630 Satan, with thoughts inflamed of highest design,
Puts on swift wings, and toward the gates of hell
Explores° his solitary flight; sometimes
He scours the right-hand coast, sometimes the left;
Now shaves with level wing the deep, then soars
Up to the fiery concave towering high:
As when far off at sea a fleet descried
Hangs in the clouds, by equinoctial winds
Close sailing from Bengala,° or the isles
Of Ternate and Tidore,° whence merchants bring
640 Their spicy drugs: they on the trading flood
Through the wide Ethiopian to the Cape°
Ply° stemming nightly toward the pole. So seemed
Far off the flying fiend. At last appear
Hell bounds high reaching to the horrid° roof,
And thrice threefold the gates; three folds were brass,
Three iron, three of adamantine rock,
Impenetrable, impaled° with circling fire,
Yet unconsumed. Before the gates there sat
On either side a formidable shape;
650 The one seemed woman to the waist, and fair,
But ended foul in many a scaly fold
Voluminous° and vast, a serpent armed
With mortal sting. About her middle round
A cry° of hell-hounds never ceasing barked
With wide Cerberean mouths full loud, and rung
A hideous peal; yet, when they list, would creep,
If aught disturbed their noise, into her womb,
And kennel there, yet there still barked and howled,
Within unseen. Far less abhorred than these
660 Vexed Scylla bathing in the sea that parts
Calabria from the hoarse Trinacrian° shore;
Nor uglier follow the Night-hag,° when called
In secret, riding through the air she comes,
Lured with the smell of infant blood, to dance
With Lapland witches, while the labouring° moon
Eclipses at their charms. The other shape—
If shape it might be called that shape had none°

Explores tests out
Bengala Bengal
Ternate and Tidore islands of the Moluccas, or "spice islands"
Ethiopian to the Cape Indian Ocean to the Cape of Good Hope
Ply beat to windward
horrid bristling
impaled not "spiked," but "enclosed"
Voluminous coiled
cry pack. Part of the description evokes Spenser's Error (*The Faerie Queene* I.i.14–15).
Trinacrian Sicilian. In the *Odyssey*, the monster

Scylla and the whirlpool Charybdis control the strait of Messina.
Night-hag Hecate
labouring undergoing eclipse
that shape had none Nobody can know what death is like; only the dead, who cannot know or tell, have seen it. Having Satan—and thus the reader—encounter Sin and Death before knowing who they are, is a higher kind of allegorizing: were they both labeled with their identities they would be more easily avoided. Cf. *The Faerie Queene* VII.vii.46.

Distinguishable in member, joint, or limb,
Or substance might be called that shadow seemed,
670 For each seemed either—black it stood as Night,
Fierce as ten Furies, terrible as hell,
And shook a dreadful dart; what seemed his head
The likeness of a kingly crown had on.
Satan was now at hand, and from his seat
The monster moving onward came as fast
With horrid strides; hell trembled as he strode.
The undaunted fiend what this might be admired,
Admired, not feared; God and his Son except,
Created thing naught valued he nor shunned;
680 And with disdainful look thus first began:
  'Whence and what art thou, execrable shape,
That darest, though grim and terrible, advance
Thy miscreated front athwart my way
To yonder gates? Through them I mean to pass,
That be assured, without leave asked of thee.
Retire, or taste thy folly, and learn by proof,
Hell-born, not to contend with spirits of heaven.'
  To whom the goblin full of wrath replied:
'Art thou that traitor angel, art thou he,
690 Who first broke peace in heaven and faith, till then
Unbroken, and in proud rebellious arms
Drew after him the third part of heaven's sons
Conjured° against the highest, for which both thou
And they, outcast from God, are here condemned
To waste eternal days in woe and pain?
And reckonest thou thyself with spirits of heaven,
Hell-doomed, and breathest defiance here and scorn
Where I reign king, and to enrage thee more,
Thy king and lord? Back to thy punishment,
700 False fugitive, and to thy speed add wings,
Lest with a whip of scorpions I pursue
Thy lingering, or with one stroke of this dart
Strange horror seize thee, and pangs unfelt before.'
  So spake the grisly terror, and in shape,
So speaking and so threatening, grew tenfold
More dreadful and deform. On the other side,
Incensed with indignation Satan stood
Unterrified, and like a comet burned,
That fires the length of Ophiuchus° huge
710 In the arctic sky, and from his horrid hair°
Shakes pestilence and war. Each at the head

Conjured sworn together. The "third part of
the stars of heaven" were thrown to earth by
the dragon in Revelation 12:3–4.
Ophiuchus "serpent-bearer," a large and prominent constellation of the northern sky

horrid hair "Comet" means "long-haired" star,
and comets were portents of disaster; the Latin
horrere means "to bristle."

Levelled his deadly aim; their fatal hands
No second stroke intend; and such a frown
Each cast at the other, as when two black clouds
With heaven's artillery fraught, come rattling on
Over the Caspian, then stand front to front
Hovering a space, till winds the signal blow
To join their dark encounter in mid-air:°
So frowned the mighty combatants that hell
720   Grew darker at their frown, so matched they stood;
For never but once more was either like
To meet so great a foe.° And now great deeds
Had been achieved, whereof all hell had rung,
Had not the snaky sorceress that sat
Fast by hell gate, and kept the fatal key,
Risen, and with hideous outcry rushed between.
   'O father, what intends thy hand,' she cried,
'Against thy only son? What fury, O son,
Possesses thee to bend that mortal dart
730   Against thy father's head? And knowest for whom?
For him who sits above and laughs the while
At thee ordained his drudge, to execute
Whate'er his wrath, which he calls justice, bids,
His wrath which one day will destroy ye both.'
   She spake, and at her words the hellish pest
Forbore; then these to her Satan returned:
   'So strange thy outcry, and thy words so strange
Thou interposest, that my sudden hand
Prevented spares to tell thee yet by deeds
740   What it intends; till first I know of thee,
What thing thou art, thus double-formed, and why
In this infernal vale first met thou callest
Me father, and that phantasm callest my son.
I know thee not, nor ever saw till now
Sight more detestable than him and thee.'
   To whom thus the portress of hell gate replied:
'Hast thou forgot me then, and do I seem
Now in thine eye so foul? Once deemed so fair
In heaven, when at the assembly, and in sight
750   Of all the seraphim with thee combined
In bold conspiracy against heaven's king,
All on a sudden miserable pain
Surprised thee; dim thine eyes, and dizzy swum
In darkness, while thy head flames thick and fast
Threw forth, till on the left side opening wide,
Likest to thee in shape and countenance bright,

---

mid-air the middle region of atmospheric phenomena and air demons (as opposed to a more
visionary domain of sky)

so great a foe Christ, conquering them

Then shining heavenly fair, a goddess armed
Out of thy head I sprung.° Amazement seized
All the host of heaven; back they recoiled afraid
760   At first, and called me *Sin,* and for a sign
Portentous held me; but familiar grown,
I pleased, and with attractive graces won
The most averse, thee chiefly, who full oft
Thyself in me thy perfect image viewing
Becamest enamoured; and such joy thou tookest
With me in secret, that my womb conceived
A growing burden. Meanwhile war arose,
And fields were fought in heaven; wherein remained
(For what could else?) to our almighty foe
770   Clear victory, to our part loss and rout
Through all the empyrean: down they fell
Driven headlong from the pitch° of heaven, down
Into this deep, and in the general fall
I also; at which time this powerful key
Into my hand was given, with charge to keep
These gates for ever shut, which none can pass
Without my opening. Pensive here I sat
Alone, but long I sat not, till my womb,
Pregnant by thee, and now excessive grown,
780   Prodigious motion felt and rueful throes.
At last this odious offspring whom thou seest,
Thine own begotten, breaking violent way
Tore through my entrails, that with fear and pain
Distorted, all my nether shape thus grew
Transformed; but he my inbred enemy
Forth issued, brandishing his fatal dart
Made to destroy. I fled, and cried out *Death!*
Hell trembled at the hideous name, and sighed
From all her caves, and back resounded *Death!*
790   I fled, but he pursued (though more, it seems,
Inflamed with lust than rage) and swifter far,
Me overtook, his mother, all dismayed,
And in embraces forcible and foul
Engendering with me, of that rape begot
These yelling monsters that with ceaseless cry
Surround me, as thou sawest, hourly conceived
And hourly born, with sorrow infinite
To me; for when they list, into the womb
That bred them they return, and howl and gnaw
800   My bowels, their repast; then bursting forth

Out . . . sprung like Athena, Wisdom, from
the forehead of Zeus, to show the birth of
Mind. Similarly, Sin proceeds from Satan's
thought, not, for example, from his guts, or by
normal engendering; additionally, in the anti-
Trinity of Father, Daughter, and Unholy Monster, she is the second term.
pitch high point

Afresh, with conscious terrors vex me round,
That rest or intermission none I find.°
Before mine eyes in opposition sits
Grim Death my son and foe, who sets them on,
And me his parent would full soon devour
For want of other prey, but that he knows
His end with mine involved; and knows that I
Should prove a bitter morsel, and his bane,
Whenever that shall be; so fate pronounced.
810   But thou, O father, I forewarn thee, shun
His deadly arrow; neither vainly hope
To be invulnerable in those bright arms,
Though tempered heavenly, for that mortal dint,°
Save he who reigns above, none can resist.'
    She finished, and the subtle Fiend his lore
Soon learned, now milder, and thus answered smooth:
'Dear daughter, since thou claimest me for thy sire,
And my fair son here showest me, the dear pledge°
Of dalliance had with thee in heaven, and joys
820   Then sweet, now sad to mention, through dire change
Befallen us unforeseen, unthought of, know
I come no enemy, but to set free
From out this dark and dismal house° of pain
Both him and thee, and all the heavenly host
Of spirits that in our just pretences° armed
Fell with us from on high. From them I go
This uncouth errand sole, and one for all
Myself expose with lonely steps to tread
The unfounded° deep, and through the void immense
830   To search with wandering quest a place foretold
Should be, and, by concurring signs, ere now
Created vast and round, a place of bliss
In the purlieus° of heaven, and therein placed
A race of upstart creatures, to supply
Perhaps our vacant room, though more removed,
Lest heaven surcharged° with potent multitude
Might hap to move new broils. Be this or aught
Than this more secret now designed, I haste
To know, and this once known, shall soon return,
840   And bring ye to the place where thou and Death
Shall dwell at ease, and up and down unseen
Wing silently the buxom° air, embalmed
With odours; there ye shall be fed and filled

These yelling . . . find (ll. 795–802). Cf. *The Faerie Queene* I.i.15.
dint blow of a sword
pledge child
house hell, as in Job 30:23
pretences legal claims

unfounded bottomless
purlieus bordering region, but with an implication of a licentious neighborhood
surcharged overburdened
buxom unresisting

Immeasurably; all things shall be your prey.'
He ceased, for both seemed highly pleased, and Death
Grinned horrible a ghastly smile, to hear
His famine should be filled, and blessed his maw
Destined to that good hour. No less rejoiced
His mother bad, and thus bespake her sire:
850   'The key of this infernal pit by due°
And by command of heaven's all-powerful king
I keep, by him forbidden to unlock
These adamantine gates; against all force
Death ready stands to interpose his dart,
Fearless to be o'ermatched by living might.
But what owe I to his commands above
Who hates me, and hath hither thrust me down
Into this gloom of Tartarus profound,
To sit in hateful office here confined,
860   Inhabitant of heaven and heavenly-born,
Here in perpetual agony and pain,
With terrors and with clamours compassed round
Of mine own brood, that on my bowels feed?
Thou art my father, thou my author, thou
My being gavest me; whom should I obey
But thee, whom follow? Thou wilt bring me soon
To that new world of light and bliss, among
The gods who live at ease, where I shall reign
At thy right hand voluptuous,° as beseems
870   Thy daughter and thy darling, without end.'

      . . .

[Sin then unlocks the gate of hell. Satan flies out toward the world, moving through atmosphere, tidal marshes, and a composite Chaos—part the classical description (from Hesiod and Ovid) of warring unorganized elements, part an allegorical picture of night and ethical and political disorder. Through these and "O'er bog or steep, through strait, rough, dense, or rare, / With head, hands, wings, or feet pursues his way, / And swims or sinks, or wades, or creeps, or flies." The allegorized Chaos, lord of "Havoc and spoil and ruin," directs him toward regions by which hangs "in a golden chain / This pendant world. . . . Thither full fraught with mischievous revenge / Accurst, and in a cursèd hour he hies."]

    From *Book III*
[The Muse is again invoked, here as light itself, which resulted from the first act of creation (Genesis 1:3) but which also, in another aspect, coexisted with its creator from the beginning. The original of all creative acts for Milton is the lighting up of darkness—transforming a chaotic world by ex-

---

due right
At thy right hand voluptuous a parody of the Nicene Creed: "who sittest on the right hand

of the Father" and "whose kingdom shall be without end"

plaining it—and the physical reduction of general created light into the sun and moon was the shaping of an attribute of this power. The present exordium is a lyric spell spun to help the poet move from his description of hell, where all the energies of heroic, epical poetry aided him, to scenes in heaven, whose static and doctrinal character would pose a different sort of challenge.]

Hail, holy Light, offspring of heaven first-born,
Or of the eternal coeternal beam
May I express thee unblamed? since God is light,
And never but in unapproachèd light
Dwelt from eternity, dwelt then in thee,
Bright effluence of bright essence increate.
Or hearest thou rather° pure ethereal stream,°
Whose fountain who shall tell? Before the sun,
Before the heavens thou wert, and at the voice
Of God, as with a mantle didst invest   10
The rising world of waters dark and deep,
Won from the void and formless infinite.
Thee I revisit now with bolder wing,
Escaped the Stygian pool,° though long detained
In that obscure sojourn, while in my flight
Through utter° and through middle darkness° borne
With other notes° than to the Orphéan lyre
I sung of Chaos and eternal Night,
Taught by the heavenly Muse to venture down
The dark descent, and up to reascend,   20
Though hard and rare. Thee I revisit safe,
And feel thy sovereign vital lamp; but thou
Revisit'st not these eyes, that roll in vain
To find thy piercing ray, and find no dawn;
So thick a drop serene° hath quenched their orbs,
Or dim suffusion° veiled. Yet not the more
Cease I to wander where the Muses haunt
Clear spring, or shady grove, or sunny hill,
Smit with the love of sacred song; but chief
Thee, Sion,° and the flowery brooks beneath   30
That wash thy hallowed feet, and warbling flow,
Nightly I visit;° nor sometimes forget
Those other two equalled with me in fate,
So were I° equalled with them in renown,

hearest thou rather would you rather be called?
stream like poetry in classical myth, an outbreak of expression
Stygian pool hell, the lower darkness
utter outer
middle darkness Chaos
other notes because he (his poetry) would not merely make an Orphean visit to the underworld, nor would his Muse be lost to him there

drop serene translates the Latin medical term for his blindness, *gutta serena*.
suffusion cataract
Sion Hebrew poetry, rather than Helicon, or Greek
Nightly I visit This theme of composing at night, literally and figuratively, is taken up again at VII. 29.
So were I would that I were

Blind Thamyris and blind Maeonides,°
And Tiresias and Phineus° prophets old:
Then feed on thoughts that voluntary move
Harmonious numbers,° as the wakeful bird
Sings darkling,° and in shadiest covert hid
40   Tunes her nocturnal note. Thus with the year
Seasons return; but not to me returns
Day, or the sweet approach of even or morn,
Or sight of vernal bloom, or summer's rose,
Or flocks, or herds, or human face divine;°
But cloud instead, and ever-during dark
Surrounds me, from the cheerful ways of men
Cut off, and for the book of knowledge° fair
Presented with a universal blank°
Of Nature's works to me expunged and razed,
50   And wisdom at one entrance° quite shut out.
So much the rather thou, celestial Light,
Shine inward, and the mind through all her powers
Irradiate, there plant eyes, all mist from thence
Purge and disperse, that I may see and tell
Of things invisible to mortal sight. . . .

[The world of Book III is unveiled with God enthroned in heaven, where all the angels "stood thick as stars"; at his right hand is his Son, to whom he points out the tiny image of distant Satan, about to alight, insect-like (as he appears from heaven), on the outside of the world. Telling the Son of the Satanic plan, God points out that Man will nevertheless be responsible for the foreknown, but not foreordained Fall ("he had of me / All he could have: I made him just and right, / Sufficient to have stood, though free to fall"). When the Father insists that justice must be done, the Son offers himself as a sacrifice for human eternal life: "Behold me then, me for him, life for life / I offer, on me let thine anger fall: / Account me man." God accepts, describing the incarnation and passion, ordains "Be thou in Adam's room / The head of all mankind, though Adam's son. / As in him perish all men, so in thee / As from a second root shall be restored." An angelic choir celebrates this ordination. The action then cuts to Satan, alighting now vulture-like upon the world, passing through a Limbo of Vanity where, blown by winds, types of folly abound. He moves into the orb of the sun (descending, as he must, from the outermost sphere of the Ptolemaic structure down toward the central earth),

Thamyris . . . Maeonides a mythical Thracian bard, blinded for his presumption, and Homer (from Maeonia)
Tiresias . . . Phineus Tiresias was the blind seer of antiquity, Phineus a blinded Thracian king who prophesied.
Harmonious numbers beautiful lines of verse
darkling in the dark. This bird is the nightingale, with whom is associated mute suffering transformed into poetic song.
human face divine The word order makes the adjectives play different roles, defining and at-

tributing, and in reading the phrase we progress from low to high; Blake used this compound as a model for a crucial phrase of his own: "human form divine."
book of knowledge Nature which, for the hieroglyphic-minded, was a book to be read and understood (see *Emblem* in the Glossary)
blank a blank page, a whiteness
one entrance too fragile a one: see Samson's staggering eloquence on this matter in *Samson Agonistes* ll. 90–96

encounters Uriel, "God's light," the guardian of that region, disguises himself
and is able by fraud to discover the whereabouts of Eden, and alights on
Mount Niphates.]

Book IV

O for that warning voice, which he who saw
The Apocalypse° heard cry in heaven aloud,
Then when the dragon, put to second rout,
Came furious down to be revenged on men,
'Woe to the inhabitants on earth!' that now,
While time was, our first parents had been warned
The coming of their secret foe, and scaped,
Haply so scaped, his mortal snare; for now
Satan, now first inflamed with rage, came down,
10 The tempter ere the accuser of mankind,
To wreak° on innocent frail man his loss
Of that first battle, and his flight to hell:
Yet not rejoicing in his speed, though bold,
Far off and fearless, nor with cause to boast,
Begins his dire attempt, which nigh the birth
Now rolling, boils in his tumultuous breast,
And like a devilish engine° back recoils
Upon himself; horror and doubt distract
His troubled thoughts, and from the bottom stir
20 The hell within him, for within him hell
He brings, and round about him, nor from hell°
One step no more than from himself can fly
By change of place. Now conscience wakes despair
That slumbered, wakes the bitter memory
Of what he was, what is, and what must be
Worse; of worse deeds worse sufferings must ensue.
Sometimes towards Eden which now in his view
Lay pleasant,° his grieved look he fixes sad,
Sometimes towards heaven and the full-blazing sun,
30 Which now sat high in his meridian tower.°
Then much revolving, thus in sighs began:
    'O thou° that with surpassing glory crowned
Look'st from thy sole dominion like the god

---

he . . . Apocalypse St. John, warning in Revelation 12:7–12 of another battle in heaven between "the dragon" and Michael; would that he could so prophetically warn, Milton pleads.
wreak avenge
devilish engine artillery, invented by Satan's forces in the war; also, "engine" (in a sense related to "ingenious") as a plan or scheme, for which the word "recoils" is metaphoric, suggesting the re-coiling or twisting of snaky thought, of dialectic; cf. II.65
The hell within . . . hell This beautifully arranged line with its chiasmus (see II.39–40n)

mocks by its static order the churning of Satan's inner state, an ironic fulfillment of his statement in I.254–55 about the mind's being "its own place"; cf. *Doctor Faustus* v.120–21.
pleasant In Hebrew, Eden means "delight."
meridian tower It is noon, and the Fall will occur at noon with light at its height and despite guarding enlightenment.
O thou the sun. According to Milton's nephew Edward Phillips in his *Life of Milton*, these lines were originally composed as the opening lines of the tragedy about the Fall that *Paradise Lost* was once to have been.

Of this new world; at whose sight all the stars
Hide their diminished heads; to thee I call,
But with no friendly voice, and add thy name,
O sun, to tell thee how I hate thy beams
That bring to my remembrance from what state
I fell, how glorious once above thy sphere;
40   Till pride and worse ambition threw me down
Warring in heaven against heaven's matchless king.
Ah wherefore? He deserved no such return
From me, whom he created what I was°
In that bright eminence,° and with his good
Upbraided none; nor was his service hard.
What could be less than to afford him praise,
The easiest recompense, and pay him thanks,
How due! Yet all his good proved ill in me,
And wrought but malice; lifted up so high
50   I sdained° subjection, and thought one step higher
Would set me highest, and in a moment quit°
The debt immense of endless gratitude,
So burdensome still paying, still° to owe;
Forgetful what from him I still received,
And understood not that a grateful mind
By owing owes not, but still pays, at once
Indebted and discharged; what burden then?
O had his powerful destiny ordained
Me some inferior angel, I had stood
60   Then happy; no unbounded hope had raised
Ambition. Yet why not? Some other power
As great might have aspired, and me though mean
Drawn to his part; but other powers as great
Fell not, but stand unshaken, from within
Or from without, to all temptations armed.
Hadst thou the same free will and power to stand?
Thou hadst. Whom hast thou then or what to accuse,
But heaven's free love dealt equally to all?
Be then his love accurst, since love or hate,
70   To me alike, it deals eternal woe.
Nay cursed be thou, since against his thy will
Chose freely what it now so justly rues.
Me miserable! which way shall I fly
Infinite wrath, and infinite despair?
Which way I fly is hell; myself am hell;°

whom he . . . was Satan admits this here,
but denies it in his public, political oratory
elsewhere.
that bright eminence Notice the echo of the
reciprocal epithet in the narrator's lines in II.6.
sdained disdained
quit pay off

still continually
Which way . . . hell echoing IV.20, and Marlowe's *Doctor Faustus* iii.76: "Why, this is hell,
nor am I out of it" and, later on, v.120–121:
"Hell hath no limits, nor is circumscribed / In
one self place, but where we are is hell";
cf. also I.225 and IX.122–23

And in the lowest deep a lower deep
Still threatening to devour me opens wide,
To which the hell I suffer seems a heaven.°
O then at last relent: is there no place
80   Left for repentance, none for pardon left?
None left but by submission; and that word
Disdain forbids me, and my dread of shame
Among the spirits beneath, whom I seduced
With other promises and other vaunts
Than to submit, boasting I could subdue
The omnipotent.° Ay me, they little know
How dearly I abide that boast so vain,
Under what torments inwardly I groan;
While they adore me on the throne of hell,
90   With diadem and sceptre high advanced,
The lower still I fall, only supreme
In misery; such joy ambition finds.
But say I could repent and could obtain
By act of grace° my former state; how soon
Would highth recall high thoughts, how soon unsay
What feigned submission swore: ease would recant
Vows made in pain, as violent and void.
For never can true reconcilement grow
Where sounds of deadly hate have pierced so deep;
100   Which would but lead me to a worse relapse
And heavier fall: so should I purchase dear
Short intermission bought with double smart.
This knows my punisher; therefore as far
From granting he, as I from begging peace.
All hope excluded thus, behold instead
Of us outcast, exiled, his new delight,
Mankind created, and for him this world.
So farewell hope, and with hope farewell fear,
Farewell remorse! All good to me is lost;
110   Evil, be thou my good;° by thee at least
Divided empire with heaven's king I hold
By thee, and more than half perhaps will govern;
As man ere long, and this new world shall know.'
    Thus while he spake, each passion dimmed his face
Thrice changed with° pale, ire, envy, and despair,
Which marred his borrowed visage,° and betrayed
Him counterfeit, if any eye beheld.

---

the hell . . . heaven Local and general, concrete and abstract, literal ad figurative uses
of words have become all mixed up in Satan's
tangled thought.
None left . . . omnipotent (ll. 81–86) Cf.
ll. 388–92 below.
act of grace formal pardon, not an admission
of right

Evil . . . good Again, the dramatic irony here
is crushing: at IX.121–23 he realizes, almost
with disgust, that his command has been
obeyed; cf. I.165.
changed with changed to
borrowed visage explained in III.636 to be
that of a "stripling cherub"

For heavenly minds from such distempers foul
Are ever clear. Whereof he soon aware,
120 Each perturbation smoothed with outward calm,
Artificer of fraud; and was the first
That practised falsehood under saintly show,
Deep malice to conceal, couched with revenge:
Yet not enough had practised to deceive
Uriel° once warned, whose eye pursued him down
The way he went, and on the Assyrian mount°
Saw him disfigured, more than could befall
Spirit of happy sort: his gestures fierce
He marked and mad demeanour, then alone,
130 As he supposed, all unobserved, unseen.
So on he fares, and to the border comes
Of Eden, where delicious Paradise,
Now nearer, crowns with her enclosure green
As with a rural mound the champaign head°
Of a steep wilderness, whose hairy sides
With thicket overgrown, grotesque° and wild,
Access denied; and overhead up grew
Insuperable highth of loftiest shade,
Cedar, and pine, and fir, and branching palm,
140 A sylvan scene, and as the ranks ascend
Shade above shade, a woody theatre
Of stateliest view. Yet higher than their tops
The verdurous wall of Paradise up sprung;
Which to our general sire° gave prospect large°
Into his nether empire neighbouring round.
And higher than that wall a circling row
Of goodliest trees loaden with fairest fruit,
Blossoms and fruits at once° of golden hue,
Appeared, with gay enamelled colours mixed;
150 On which the sun more glad impressed his beams
Than in fair evening cloud, or humid bow,
When God hath showered the earth; so lovely seemed
That landscape. And of pure now purer air
Meets his approach, and to the heart inspires
Vernal delight and joy, able to drive
All sadness but despair; now gentle gales
Fanning their odoriferous wings dispense

Uriel In III.623 ff. this archangel is deceived
by Satan's disguise.
Assyrian mount Mount Niphates, on which this
soliloquy occurs, and which Milton makes the
scene of Christ's temptation in *Paradise Regained*
champaign head a treeless plateau. The imagery
of the human body persists in the following
lines.
grotesque grotto-like
general sire Adam
large broad

Blossoms and fruits at once This description
assembles images of pastoral perfection from
such myths as the Hesperides (cf. *Comus* ll.
980–81), the Elysian fields, the Golden Age,
and Spenser's Garden of Adonis (*The Faerie
Queene* III.vi); in Eden, the spring of beauty
and promise, the fall of ripeness and fulfillment,
coexist with no intervening extreme seasons,
which will come into being with the Fall, and
the origin of biological "nature."

Native perfumes, and whisper whence they stole
Those balmy spoils. As when to them who sail
160   Beyond the Cape of Hope,° and now are past
Mozambic,° off at sea north-east winds blow
Sabaean° odours from the spicy shore
Of Araby the Blest, with such delay
Well pleased they slack their course, and many a league
Cheered with the grateful smell old ocean smiles;
So entertained those odorous sweets the fiend
Who came their bane, though with them better pleased
Than Asmodëus° with the fishy fume,
That drove him, though enamoured, from the spouse
170   Of Tobit's son, and with a vengeance sent
From Media post to Egypt, there fast bound.
   Now to the ascent of that steep savage° hill
Satan had journeyed on, pensive and slow;
But further way found none, so thick entwined,
As one continued brake, the undergrowth
Of shrubs and tangling bushes had perplexed
All path of man or beast that passed that way.
One gate there only was, and that looked east
On the other side; which when the arch-felon saw,
Due entrance he disdained, and in contempt
180   At one slight bound high overleaped all bound
Of hill or highest wall, and sheer within
Lights on his feet. As when a prowling wolf,
Whom hunger drives to seek new haunt for prey,
Watching where shepherds pen their flocks at eve
In hurdled cotes° amid the field secure,
Leaps o'er the fence with ease into the fold;
Or as a thief bent to unhoard the cash
Of some rich burgher, whose substantial doors,
190   Cross-barred and bolted fast, fear no assault,
In at the window climbs, or o'er the tiles:
So clomb° this first grand thief into God's fold;
So since into his church lewd° hirelings climb.
Thence up he flew, and on the Tree of Life,
The middle tree and highest there that grew,
Sat like a cormorant;° yet not true life
Thereby regained, but sat devising death°
To them who lived; nor on the virtue thought

Hope Good Hope
Mozambic Mozambique
Sabaean Sheban, from modern Yemen
Asmodëus a nasty demon, driven off by Tobias, Tobit's son, on Raphael's advice, by means of a stink-bomb (Tobit 7:6)
savage wooded
hurdled cotes crowded folds
clomb climbed

lewd ignorant and uneducated, as well as vile. Milton is attacking, in the same ecclesiastical pastoral imagery as in *Lycidas,* "hirelings," or salaried clergy.
cormorant literally "sea-crow"; emblem of greed
death both "death in general" and, reading on across the enjambment, the deaths of Adam and Eve

Of that life-giving plant, but only used
200 For prospect, what well used had been the pledge
Of immortality. So little knows
Any, but God alone, to value right
The good before him, but perverts best things
To worst abuse, or to their meanest use.
　　Beneath him with new wonder now he views
To all delight of human sense exposed
In narrow room Nature's whole wealth,° yea more,
A heaven on earth, for blissful Paradise
Of God the garden was, by him in the east
210 Of Eden planted; Eden stretched her line
From Auran° eastward to the royal towers
Of great Seleucia,° built by Grecian kings,
Or where the sons of Eden long before
Dwelt in Telassar.° In this pleasant soil
His far more pleasant garden God ordained;
Out of the fertile ground he caused to grow
All trees of noblest kind for sight, smell, taste;
And all amid them stood the Tree of Life,
High eminent, blooming ambrosial fruit
220 Of vegetable gold,° and next to life
Our death,° the Tree of Knowledge, grew fast by,
Knowledge of good bought dear by knowing ill.°
Southward through Eden went a river large,
Nor changed his course, but through the shaggy hill
Passed underneath engulfed, for God had thrown
That mountain as his garden mould, high raised
Upon the rapid current, which through veins
Of porous earth with kindly thirst up drawn,
Rose a fresh fountain, and with many a rill
230 Watered the garden; thence united fell
Down the steep glade, and met the nether flood,
Which from his darksome passage now appears,
And now divided into four main streams
Runs diverse, wandering° many a famous realm
And country whereof here needs no account;
But rather to tell how, if art could tell,
How from that sapphire fount the crispèd brooks,
Rolling on orient pearl and sands of gold,

Nature's whole wealth all the fruitfulness that was ever to be was there (see *The Faerie Queene* III.vi.30)
Auran a town in northwestern Mesopotamia; see Genesis 11:31
Seleucia built as a capital city by Alexander the Great's viceroy for Syria, Seleucus
Telassar a city in Mesopotamia, mentioned in II Kings 19:12 as a land ruined by war
vegetable gold the figurative "gold" of grain and

natural fruitfulness; also in the sense of "vegetative" (cf. I.685–87)
life . . . death perhaps the most startling enjambment in the poem. Reading along, we expect something like "*and next to life / the brightest gift* . . . etc., and then realize, with a shock, that the juxtaposition of the two Trees in Paradise, reinforced by "Our," means a good deal more.
Knowledge . . . ill Cf. *Areopagitica*, note 28.
wandering wandering through

With mazy error° under pendant shades
240 Ran nectar, visiting each plant, and fed
Flowers worthy of Paradise, which not nice art
In beds and curious knots,° but Nature boon°
Poured forth profuse on hill and dale and plain,
Both where the morning sun first warmly smote
The open field, and where the unpierced shade
Embrowned° the noontide bowers. Thus was this place,
A happy rural seat of various view;
Groves whose rich trees wept odorous gums and balm,
Others whose fruit burnished with golden rind
250 Hung amiable, Hesperian fables true,°
If true, here only, and of delicious taste.
Betwixt them lawns, or level downs, and flocks
Grazing the tender herb, were interposed,
Or palmy hillock, or the flowery lap
Of some irriguous° valley spread her store,
Flowers of all hue, and without thorn the rose.°
Another side, umbrageous° grots and caves
Of cool recess, o'er which the mantling vine
Lays forth her purple grape, and gently creeps
260 Luxuriant; meanwhile murmuring waters fall
Down the slope hills, dispersed, or in a lake,
That to the fringèd bank with myrtle° crowned
Her crystal mirror holds, unite their streams.
The birds their quire apply; airs, vernal airs,°
Breathing the smell of field and grove, attune
The trembling leaves, while universal Pan,°
Knit with the Graces and the Hours in dance,
Led on the eternal spring. Not that fair field
Of Enna, where Prosérpine° gathering flowers,
270 Herself a fairer flower by gloomy Dis
Was gathered, which cost Ceres all that pain

---

mazy error "Error" in Latin means "wandering," with no negative moral sense; this is an unfallen usage (see Headnote) as well as the first instance of unfallen, beautiful twisting, turning, and curling imagery, later to be corrupted.
curious knots labyrinthine patterns in which flowerbeds were frequently laid out; is Milton remembering the beneficent "curious knots" of Pleasure and Virtue in Jonson's masque? See *Pleasure Reconciled to Virtue.*
boon bountiful
Embrowned darkened
Hesperian fables true as if the golden apples of the Hesperides were a fiction mistakenly based on the truth of Paradise's "vegetable gold"
irriguous irrigated
the rose a traditional interpretation; in Genesis 3:18 part of Adam's curse involves the origins of thorns and thistles
umbrageous shadowy
myrtly sacred to Venus. The mirror is also her

emblem, and they both partake of the unfallen, pre-erotic sensual joy of this bower.
airs songs, melodies. Notice the whole musical sequence of waters, birds, and leaves; cf. its perverted version in Spenser's *Bower of Bliss,* an artfully faked Eden (*The Faerie Queene* II. xii).
Pan In Greek, his name means "all, everything"; the classical figures here are metaphorical for the forces of unfallen nature.
Prosérpine Persephone (Proserpine), daughter of Demeter (Ceres), the harvest goddess, carried to the underworld by Dis (Pluto) to be his queen. Ceres sought her throughout the world, which in sympathy became barren. When she was finally restored, it was only for half the year (hence, spring and summer), because while Queen of the Underworld, she had eaten seven pomegranate seeds. Renaissance mythographers seized on the obvious parallels to Eve, who, in Bk. IX, will be "gathered" by Satan while "gathering flowers."

To seek her through the world; nor that sweet grove
Of Daphne° by Orontes, and the inspired
Castalian spring, might with this Paradise
Of Eden strive; nor that Nyseian isle°
Girt with the river Triton, where old Cham,
Whom Gentiles Ammon call and Libyan Jove,
Hid Amalthea and her florid son
Young Bacchus from his stepdame Rhea's eye;
280   Nor where Abassin kings their issue guard,
Mount Amara,° though this by some supposed
True Paradise, under the Ethiop line°
By Nilus' head, enclosed with shining rock,
A whole day's journey high, but wide remote
From this Assyrian garden, where the fiend
Saw undelighted all delight, all kind
Of living creatures new to sight and strange.
    Two of far nobler shape erect and tall,
God-like erect, with native honour° clad
290   In naked majesty seemed lords of all,
And worthy seemed, for in their looks divine
The image of their glorious maker shone,
Truth, wisdom, sanctitude severe and pure,
Severe but in true filial freedom placed;
Whence true authority in men; though both
Not equal, as their sex not equal seemed;
For contemplation he and valour formed,
For softness she and sweet attractive grace;
He for God only, she for God in him.
300   His fair large front° and eye sublime° declared
Absolute rule; and hyacinthine locks°
Round from his parted forelock manly hung
Clustering, but not beneath his shoulders broad:
She as a veil down to the slender waist
Her unadornèd golden tresses wore
Dishevelled, but in wanton° ringlets waved
As the vine curls her tendrils, which implied
Subjection, but required with gentle sway,°

Daphne a grove near the river Orontes, famous for its oracle
Nyseian isle Nysa in Tunisia, where Ammon (Jupiter) hid the infant Dionysus (Bacchus) from his wife, Rhea (Ops)
Amara where Abyssinian princes were brought up
Ethiop line the equator
native honour The natural dignity of being complete in their skin; the very concepts "nakedness" and "nudity" would be as meaningless if applied to them here as to a lion or a human fetus; see l. 314. Milton suggests that the "honour" as used in fallen human society, whether of women or of "gentlemen," is as inferior to this original honor as fallen is to

"original Justice." Fallen "honour," the "honour dishonourable" against which Milton rages in l.314, is a show, or mask of virtue, more like "reputation."
front forehead
sublime upward-looking
hyacinthine locks probably not referring to color, but to curliness, and invoking the doomed beauty of Hyacinth, Apollo's beloved. The curling hair in this passage is an emblem of luxuriant sensuality and uncorrupted complexity (like the "curious knots," l. 242), as well as "Subjection."
wanton unrestrained
sway influence

And by her yielded, by him best received,
310   Yielded with coy° submission, modest pride,
And sweet reluctant amorous delay.
Nor those mysterious parts were then concealed;
Then was not guilty shame; dishonest shame
Of Nature's works, honour dishonourable,°
Sin-bred, how have ye troubled all mankind
With shows instead, mere shows of seeming pure,
And banished from man's life his happiest life,
Simplicity and spotless innocence!
So passed they naked on, nor shunned the sight
320   Of God or angel, for they thought no ill;
So hand in hand° they passed, the loveliest pair
That ever since in love's embraces met,
Adam the goodliest man of men since born
His sons, the fairest of her daughters Eve.
Under a tuft of shade that on a green
Stood whispering soft, by a fresh fountain side
They sat them down; and after no more toil
Of their sweet gardening labour than sufficed
To recommend cool Zephyr, and made ease
330   More easy,° wholesome thirst and appetite
More grateful, to their supper fruits they fell,
Nectarine fruits which the compliant boughs
Yielded them, sidelong as they sat recline°
On the soft downy bank damasked° with flowers.
The savoury pulp they chew, and in the rind
Still as they thirsted scoop the brimming stream;
Nor gentle purpose,° nor endearing smiles
Wanted,° nor youthful dalliance, as beseems
Fair couple linked in happy nuptial league,
340   Alone as they. About them frisking played
All beasts of the earth, since wild, and of all chase°
In wood or wilderness, forest or den;
Sporting the lion ramped, and in his paw
Dandled the kid; bears, tigers, ounces, pards,°
Gambolled before them; the unwieldy elephant
To make them mirth used all his might, and wreathed
His lithe proboscis; close° the serpent sly

coy reticent
honour dishonourable In this context, even the thought of sexual shame, of guilt about bodies, of covering up genitalia, disgusts Milton, and his meditation gives way to indignation.
hand in hand Clasped hands appear in emblem books in pictures of Faith, Concord, and Married Love; but see also *Paradise Lost* XII.648, and intervening glimpses of the pair at 488, 689, and 739 of Bk. IV, VIII.510, IX.385 and 1037.
easy comfortable
recline recumbent

damasked patterned
gentle purpose polite discourse
Wanted were lacking
of all chase of every habitat, part of "Nature's whole wealth" (l. 207)
ounces, pards lynxes, leopards
close Close by (in the garden and in the line of verse) the serpent's "curious knot" of motion, uninfected yet by Satan's possession of it, is a sort of emblem requiring prophecy, or a fallen reader, correctly to understand (thus, "proof unheeded").

Insinuating,° wove with Gordian twine
His braided train, and of his fatal guile
350   Gave proof unheeded; others on the grass
Couched, and now filled with pasture gazing sat,
Or bedward ruminating; for the sun
Declined was hasting now with prone career
To the ocean isles,° and in the ascending scale°
Of heaven the stars that usher evening rose:
When Satan still in gaze, as first he stood,
Scarce thus at length failed speech recovered sad:
    'O hell! what do mine eyes with grief behold!
Into our room° of bliss thus high advanced
360   Creatures of other mould, earth-born perhaps,
Not spirits, yet to heavenly spirits bright
Little inferior; whom my thoughts pursue
With wonder, and could love, so lively shines
In them divine resemblance, and such grace
The hand that formed them on their shape hath poured.
Ah gentle pair, ye little think how nigh
Your change approaches, when all these delights
Will vanish and deliver ye to woe,
More woe, the more your taste is now of joy;
370   Happy, but for so happy ill secured
Long to continue, and this high seat your heaven
Ill fenced, for heaven, to keep out such a foe
As now is entered; yet no purposed foe
To you whom I could pity thus forlorn,
Though I unpitied. League with you I seek,
And mutual amity so strait,° so close,
That I with you must dwell, or you with me
Henceforth; my dwelling haply may not please,
Like this fair Paradise, your sense, yet such
380   Accept your maker's work; he gave it me,
Which I as freely give;° hell shall unfold,°
To entertain you two, her widest gates,
And send forth all her kings; there will be room,
Not like these narrow limits, to receive
Your numerous offspring; if no better place,
Thank him who puts me loth to this revenge
On you who wrong me not, for him who wronged.
And should I at your harmless innocence
Melt, as I do, yet public reason just,
390   Honour and empire with revenge enlarged

Insinuating winding
ocean isles the Azores; see l. 592
scale both Libra, now rising, and the heavens'
balance of light and darkness in the then
eternal equinox
room region, space
strait intimate

freely give not only half-sarcastic, but echoing
Matthew 10:8
hell shall unfold At Isaiah 14:9 the destruction
of Babylon is envisaged in these terms, but
Satan is offering Adam and Eve part of his
kingdom, as Dis had given Proserpine his.

By conquering this new world, compels me now
To do what else though damned I should abhor.'
     So spake the fiend, and with necessity—
The tyrant's plea—excused his devilish deeds.
Then from his lofty stand on that high tree
Down he alights among the sportful herd
Of those four-footed kinds, himself now one,
Now other, as their shape served best his end
Nearer to view his prey, and unespied
400   To mark what of their state he more might learn
By word or action marked. About them round
A lion now he stalks with fiery glare;
Then as a tiger, who by chance hath spied
In some purlieu° two gentle fawns at play,
Straight° couches close, then rising, changes oft
His couchant watch, as one who chose his ground
Whence rushing he might surest seize them both
Gripped in each paw; when Adam first of men
To first of women Eve thus moving speech,
410   Turned him° all ear to hear new utterance flow—
     'Sole partner and sole part° of all these joys,
Dearer thyself than all, needs must the power
That made us, and for us this ample world,
Be infinitely good, and of his good
As liberal and free as infinite,
That raised us from the dust and placed us here
In all this happiness, who at his hand
Have nothing merited, nor can perform
Aught whereof he hath need; he who requires
420   From us no other service than to keep
This one, this easy charge, of all the trees
In Paradise that bear delicious fruit
So various, not to taste° that only Tree
Of Knowledge, planted by the Tree of Life,
So near grows death to life,° whate'er death is,
Some dreadful thing no doubt; for well thou knowest
God hath pronounced it death to taste that Tree,
The only sign of our obedience left
Among so many signs of power and rule
430   Conferred upon us,° and dominion given
Over all other creatures that possess
Earth, air, and sea. Then let us not think hard
One easy prohibition, who enjoy
Free leave so large to all things else, and choice

purlieu borders of a forest
Straight immediately; also, "tightly" (punning
on "strait")
him Satan
Sole partner and sole part only partner and

principal part
not to taste the commandment at Genesis
2:16–17
death to life See ll. 220–21.
Conferred upon us at Genesis 1:28

Unlimited of manifold delights;
But let us ever praise him, and extol
His bounty, following our delightful task
To prune these growing plants, and tend these flowers,
Which were it toilsome, yet with thee were sweet.'
440   To whom thus Eve replied, 'O thou for whom
And from whom I was formed flesh of thy flesh,
And without whom am to no end, my guide
And head,° what thou hast said is just and right.
For we to him indeed all praises owe,
And daily thanks, I chiefly who enjoy
So far the happier lot, enjoying thee
Pre-eminent by so much odds,° while thou
Like consort to thyself canst nowhere find.
That day I oft remember, when from sleep
450   I first awaked, and found myself reposed
Under a shade of flowers, much wondering where
And what I was, whence thither brought, and how.
Not distant far from thence a murmuring sound
Of waters issued from a cave and spread
Into a liquid plain,° then stood unmoved
Pure as the expanse of heaven; I thither went
With unexperienced thought, and laid me down
On the green bank, to look into the clear
Smooth lake, that to me seemed another sky.°
460   As I bent down to look, just opposite
A shape within the watery gleam appeared
Bending to look on me: I started back,
It started back, but pleased I soon returned,
Pleased it returned as soon with answering looks
Of sympathy and love; there I had fixed
Mine eyes till now, and pined with vain desire,
Had not a voice thus warned me:° *"What thou seest,*
What there thou seest, fair creature, is thyself,
With thee it came and goes; but follow me,
470   *And I will bring thee where no shadow stays*°
Thy coming, and thy soft embraces, he
Whose image thou art, him thou shalt enjoy
Inseparably thine; to him shalt bear

---

head echoing I Corinthians 11:3: "The head of every man is Christ; and the head of the woman is the man . . . ," but also combining the two in a kind of single human body, an image suggested for the garden itself, ll. 134 ff.
by so much odds by so much
liquid plain The first mirror forms when "murmuring" water stops and reflects.
another sky There is only the subtlest hint here ("another sky": "another heaven") of the idolatry implict in the use of mirrors; in the fallen world, mirrors are emblems of Venus and of the other nude figure, personified Vanitas, "vanity."
warned me Narcissus, Eve's prototype here who fell in love with his own image (like Eve, not knowing it was himself), died when he discovered the truth—the only warning had been from the blind seer Tiresias, in the boy's childhood, that he would die when he knew himself; Eve is not abandoned to his fate, at least at this point.
no shadow stays no illusory image awaits

Multitudes like thyself, and thence be called
Mother of human race." What could I do
But follow straight, invisibly thus led?
Till I espied thee, fair indeed and tall,
Under a platane;° yet methought less fair,
Less winning soft, less amiably mild,
480   Than that smooth watery image; back I turned,
Thou following cried'st aloud, "Return, fair Eve,
Whom fli'st thou? Whom thou fli'st, of him thou art,
His flesh, his bone;° to give thee being I lent
Out of my side to thee, nearest my heart,
Substantial life, to have thee by my side
Henceforth an individual° solace dear.
Part of my soul° I seek thee, and thee claim
My other half." With that thy gentle hand
Seized mine, I yielded, and from that time see°
490   How beauty is excelled by manly grace
And wisdom, which alone is truly fair.'
    So spake our general mother, and with eyes
Of conjugal attraction unreproved,
And meek surrender, half embracing leaned
On our first father; half her swelling breast
Naked met his under the flowing gold
Of her loose tresses hid. He in delight
Both of her beauty and submissive charms
Smiled with superior love, as Jupiter
500   On Juno smiles, when he impregns° the clouds
That shed May flowers; and pressed her matron lip
With kisses pure. Aside the devil turned
For envy,° yet with jealous leer malign
Eyed them askance, and to himself thus plained:
    'Sight hateful, sight tormenting! thus these two
Imparadised in one another's arms,
The happier Eden,° shall enjoy their fill
Of bliss on bliss, while I to hell am thrust,
Where neither joy nor love, but fierce desire,
510   Among our other torments not the least,
Still unfulfilled with pain of longing pines;°
Yet let me not forget what I have gained
From their own mouths. All is not theirs, it seems;

---

platane plane tree
His flesh, his bone Here, and at l. 441, the reference is to Genesis 2:23.
individual undividable
Part of my soul a musical and rhetorical resonance, if not a pun, from l. 411
see Again, the enjambment brings a surprise—"see / How," or "know," "understand"; Eve never really totally *"sees"* wisdom as fairer than beauty.
impregns impregnates

envy Part of the torment of Hell is sexual deprivation, a practice common to various sorts of imprisonment in most Christian societies.
Imparadised . . . Eden Satan is almost at his most pitiable at this poignant moment, for it is only after the Fall that human love will be able (and be forced) to "imparadise" the lovers. Here, at this unfallen moment, when the two are *in Paradise,* literally, he sees them as they will be in Bk. XII (see ll. 614–19).
pines tortures

One fatal tree there stands, of Knowledge called,
Forbidden them to taste. Knowledge forbidden?
Suspicious, reasonless. Why should their lord
Envy them that? Can it be sin to know?
Can it be death? And do they only stand
By ignorance, is that their happy state,
520   The proof of their obedience and their faith?
O fair foundation laid whereon to build
Their ruin!° Hence I will excite their minds
With more desire to know, and to reject
Envious commands, invented with design
To keep them low whom knowledge might exalt
Equal with gods. Aspiring to be such,
They taste and die: what likelier can ensue?
But first with narrow search I must walk round
This garden, and no corner leave unspied;
530   A chance but chance may lead where I may meet
Some wandering Spirit of heaven, by fountain side,
Or in thick shade retired, from him to draw
What further would be learnt. Live while ye may,
Yet happy pair; enjoy, till I return,
Short pleasures, for long woes are to succeed.'
     So saying, his proud step he scornful turned,
But with sly circumspection, and began
Through wood, through waste, o'er hill, o'er dale, his roam.°
Meanwhile in utmost longitude, where heaven
540   With earth and ocean meets, the setting sun
Slowly descended, and with right aspéct
Against the eastern gate of Paradise
Levelled his evening rays. It was a rock
Of alabaster, piled up to the clouds,
Conspicuous far, winding with one ascent
Accessible from earth, one entrance high;
The rest was craggy cliff, that overhung
Still as it rose, impossible to climb.
Betwixt these rocky pillars Gabriel° sat,
550   Chief of the angelic guards, awaiting night;
About him exercised° heroic games
The unarmèd youth of heaven, but nigh at hand
Celestial armoury, shields, helms, and spears,
Hung high, with diamond flaming and with gold.
Thither came Uriel, gliding through the even
On a sunbeam, swift as a shooting star
In autumn thwarts the night, when vapours fired
Impress the air, and shows the mariner

---

ruin both "destruction" and the wreckage, or
remnants, of that destruction ("ruins")
roam walk

Gabriel one of the four archangels in apocryphal
tradition assigned to Paradise as guards
exercised played

From what point of his compass to beware
560 Impetuous winds. He thus began in haste:
     'Gabriel, to thee thy course by lot hath given
Charge and strict watch that to this happy place
No evil thing approach or enter in;
This day at highth of noon came to my sphere
A Spirit, zealous, as he seemed, to know
More of the Almighty's works, and chiefly man,
God's latest image.° I described° his way
Bent all on speed, and marked his airy gait;
But in the mount that lies from Eden north,
570 Where he first lighted, soon discerned his looks
Alien from heaven, with passions foul obscured.
Mine eye pursued him still, but under shade
Lost sight of him; one of the banished crew,
I fear, hath ventured from the deep, to raise
New troubles; him thy care must be to find.'
     To whom the wingèd warrior thus returned:
'Uriel, no wonder if thy perfect sight,
Amid the sun's bright circle where thou sit'st,
See far and wide. In at this gate none pass
580 The vigilance° here placed, but such as come
Well known from heaven; and since meridian hour
No creature thence. If spirit of other sort,
So minded, have o'erleaped these earthy bounds°
On purpose, hard thou knowest it to exclude
Spiritual substance with corporeal bar.
But if within the circuit of these walks,
In whatsoever shape he lurk, of whom
Thou tell'st, by morrow dawning I shall know.'
     So promised he, and Uriel to his charge
590 Returned on that bright beam, whose point now raised
Bore him slope downward to the sun now fallen
Beneath the Azores—whether the prime orb,°
Incredible how swift, had thither rolled
Diurnal, or this less volúble° earth
By shorter flight to the east, had left him there
Arraying with reflected purple and gold
The clouds that on his western throne attend.
     Now came still evening on, and twilight grey
Had in her sober livery all things clad;
600 Silence accompanied,° for beast and bird,
They to their grassy couch, these to their nests
Were slunk, all but the wakeful nightingale—

latest image The first image was Christ, the Son.
described perceived
The vigilance Gabriel
o'erleaped . . . bounds reminding us of the
easy joke back at l. 181
prime orb the sun, in the Ptolemaic system.

Milton allows for both accounts, as if either
might be a distorting reduction of an actual
Edenic sunset.
volúble rapidly revolving; see ll. 661–64
Silence accompanied in both a musical and a
general sense

She all night long her amorous descant° sung:
Silence was pleased.° Now glowed the firmament
With living sapphires; Hesperus° that led
The starry host, rode brightest, till the moon
Rising in clouded majesty, at length
Apparent queen° unveiled her peerless light,
And o'er the dark her silver mantle threw;

610   When Adam thus to Eve: 'Fair consort, the hour
Of night, and all things now retired to rest
Mind us of like repose, since God hath set
Labour and rest, as day and night to men
Successive, and the timely dew of sleep
Now falling with soft slumbrous weight inclines
Our eyelids; other creatures all day long
Rove idle, unemployed, and less need rest;
Man hath his daily work° of body or mind
Appointed, which declares his dignity,

620 And the regard of heaven on all his ways;
While other animals unactive range,
And of their doings God takes no account.
Tomorrow ere fresh morning streak the east
With first approach of light, we must be risen,
And at our pleasant labour, to reform
Yon flowery arbours, yonder alleys green,
Our walk at noon, with branches overgrown,
That mock our scant manuring,° and require
More hands than ours to lop their wanton° growth.

630 Those blossoms also, and those dropping gums,
That lie bestrown unsightly and unsmooth,
Ask riddance, if we mean to tread with ease;
Meanwhile, as nature wills, night bids us rest.'

    To whom thus Eve with perfect beauty adorned:
'My author and disposer,° what thou bid'st
Unargued I obey; so God ordains.
God is thy law, thou mine; to know no more
Is woman's happiest knowledge and her praise.
With thee conversing I forget all time,

640 All seasons° and their change, all please alike.
Sweet is the breath of morn, her rising sweet,
With charm° of earliest birds; pleasant the sun
When first on this delightful land he spreads
His orient beams, on herb, tree, fruit, and flower,

descant highest free contrapuntal part
Silence was pleased at her pupil?
Hesperus the Evening Star
Apparent queen manifestly the queen (of the sky, now that she has risen), who rules this whole part of Bk. IV, from the opening Virgilian night-piece just concluded (see the selection from the Earl of Surrey's *Aeneid* translation) to the love scene which follows
daily work Even in Paradise there is gardening

to do, not to be confused with agriculture, done "with the sweat of thy brow."
manuring cultivating
wanton luxuriant (like Eve's hair at l. 306)
My . . . disposer In Books IX through XII these formal titles of address are not used.
seasons times of day (it is always spring and fall at once in Eden)
charm song

Glistering with dew; fragrant the fertile earth
After soft showers; and sweet the coming on
Of grateful evening mild, then silent night
With this her solemn bird° and this fair moon,
And these the gems of heaven, her starry train:
650   But neither breath of morn when she ascends
With charm of earliest birds, nor rising sun
On this delightful land, nor herb, fruit, flower,
Glistering with dew, nor fragrance after showers,
Nor grateful evening mild, nor silent night
With this her solemn bird, nor walk by moon
Or glittering starlight without thee is sweet.
But wherefore all night long° shine these, for whom
This glorious sight, when sleep hath shut all eyes?'
      To whom our general ancestor replied:
660   'Daughter of God and man, accomplished° Eve,
Those have their course to finish, round the earth,
By morrow evening, and from land to land
In order, though to nations yet unborn,
Ministering light prepared, they set and rise;
Lest total darkness should by night regain
Her old possession,° and extinguish life
In nature and all things; which these soft fires
Not only enlighten, but with kindly° heat
Of various influence° foment and warm,
670   Temper or nourish, or in part shed down
Their stellar virtue on all kinds that grow
On earth, made hereby apter to receive
Perfection from the sun's more potent ray.
These then, though unbeheld in deep of night,
Shine not in vain, nor think, though men were none,
That heaven would want spectators, God want praise;
Millions of spiritual creatures walk the earth
Unseen, both when we wake, and when we sleep:
All these with ceaseless praise his works behold
680   Both day and night—how often from the steep
Of echoing hill or thicket have we heard
Celestial voices to the midnight air,
Sole, or responsive each to other's note,°
Singing their great creator; oft in bands
While they keep watch, or nightly rounding walk,
With heavenly touch of instrumental sounds
In full harmonic number joined, their songs

---

solemn bird the nightingale
wherefore all night long Eve's question is
innocent, straightforward, reasonable, personal,
and anticlimactically deadly to the cadence of
the ode she has just recited.
accomplished Cf. *Samson Agonistes*, l. 230.

Her old possession Chaos originally reigned
in darkness; creation of light meant a disposses-
sion of her rule.
kindly natural
influence See *Astrology* in the Glossary.
responsive . . . note in antiphonal choirs

Divide° the night, and lift our thoughts to heaven.'
    Thus talking, hand in hand alone they passed
690 On to their blissful bower;° it was a place
Chosen by the sovereign planter, when he framed
All things to man's delightful use; the roof
Of thickest covert was inwoven shade,
Laurel and myrtle,° and what higher grew
Of firm and fragrant leaf; on either side
Acanthus, and each odorous bushy shrub
Fenced up the verdant wall; each beauteous flower,
Iris all hues, roses, and jessamine
Reared high their flourished° heads between, and wrought
700 Mosaic; under foot the violet,
Crocus, and hyacinth with rich inlay
Broidered the ground, more coloured than with stone
Of costliest emblem. Other creature here,
Beast, bird, insect, or worm durst enter none;
Such was their awe of man. In shadier bower
More sacred and sequestered, though but feigned,°
Pan or Silvanus never slept, nor nymph
Nor Faunus haunted. Here in close recess
With flowers, garlands, and sweet-smelling herbs
710 Espousèd Eve decked first her nuptial bed,
And heavenly quires the hymenean sung,
What day the genial angel° to our sire
Brought her in naked beauty more adorned,
More lovely than Pandora,° whom the gods
Endowed with all their gifts, and O too like
In sad event, when to the unwiser son
Of Japhet° brought by Hermes, she ensnared
Mankind with her fair looks, to be avenged
On him who had stole Jove's authentic° fire.
720   Thus at their shady lodge arrived, both stood,
Both turned, and under open sky adored
The God that made both sky, air, earth, and heaven
Which they beheld, the moon's resplendent globe
And starry pole: 'Thou also mad'st the night,

Divide by marking off the watches of the night, and also by playing "divisions" or melodic improvisations
blissful bower not the artificial Bower of Bliss (*The Faerie Queene* II.xii), but a brilliant reversal of Spenser's construct of false love, where art imitates nature deceptively. In the following lines, natural beauties triumph over artificiality by anticipating it.
Laurel and myrtle Apollo's plant and Venus' entwined together, making an emblem of married attributes such as male-female, wisdom-beauty
flourished flowered
feigned fictionalized; see Sidney's discussion of

"the feigned image of poesie" in *The Defence of Poetry*
genial angel nuptial, generative spirit, parallel to Old Genius at the boundary of the Garden of Adonis, *The Faerie Queene* III.vi
Pandora another Greek Eve-parallel. Her name means "all gifts," and she was given to the Titan Epimetheus ("after-knowledge"), brother of Prometheus ("fore-knowledge") who stole fire from Olympus for mankind; she opened a box she was forbidden to and loosed evils and miseries on the world.
Japhet Iapetus, father of the two Titans above
authentic original

Maker omnipotent, and thou the day,
Which we in our appointed work employed
Have finished happy in our mutual help
And mutual love, the crown of all our bliss
Ordained by thee, and this delicious place
730   For us too large, where thy abundance wants
Partakers, and uncropped falls to the ground.
But thou hast promised from us two a race
To fill the earth, who shall with us extol
Thy goodness infinite, both when we wake,
And when we seek, as now, thy gift of sleep.'
    This said unanimous, and other rites
Observing none, but adoration pure
Which God likes best, into their inmost bower
Handed° they went; and eased the putting off
740   These troublesome disguises which we wear,
Straight side by side were laid, nor turned, I ween,
Adam from his fair spouse, nor Eve the rites
Mysterious° of connubial love refused;
Whatever hypocrites austerely talk
Of purity and place and innocence,
Defaming as impure what God declares
Pure, and commands to some, leaves free to all.
Our Maker bids increase; who bids abstain
But our destroyer, foe to God and man?
750   Hail, wedded Love, mysterious law, true source
Of human offspring, sole propriety°
In Paradise of all things common else.
By thee adulterous lust was driven from men
Among the bestial herds to range; by thee
Founded in reason, loyal, just, and pure,
Relations dear, and all the charities°
Of father, son, and brother first were known.
Far be it that I should write thee sin or blame,
Or think thee unbefitting holiest place,
760   Perpetual fountain of domestic sweets,
Whose bed is undefiled and chaste pronounced,
Present or past, as saints and patriarchs used.
Here Love his golden shafts° employs, here lights
His constant lamp, and waves his purple wings,
Reigns here and revels; not in the bought smile
Of harlots, loveless, joyless, unendeared,
Casual fruition; nor in court amours,
Mixed dance, or wanton masque, or midnight ball,

Handed hand in hand (see l. 321n)
Mysterious The representation of unfallen sex is indeed tinged with mystery, and Milton will be able only to insist, as he does below, that it transcends fallen eroticism, and that its

mysteries are re-created in human marriage.
propriety domain of belonging, of possessing
charities loves
golden shafts Cupid had golden arrows of desire and leaden ones of disaffection.

Or serenate,° which the starved lover° sings
770 To his proud fair, best quitted with disdain.
These lulled by nightingales, embracing slept,
And on their naked limbs the flowery roof
Showered roses, which the morn repaired. Sleep on,
Blest pair; and O yet happiest if ye seek
No happier state, and know° to know no more.
     Now had night measured with her shadowy cone
Half way up hill this vast sublunar vault,
And from their ivory port° the cherubim
Forth issuing at the accustomed hour stood armed
780 To their night-watches in warlike parade,
When Gabriel to his next in power thus spake:
     'Uzziel, half these draw off, and coast the south
With strictest watch; these other wheel the north;
Our circuit meets full west.' As flame they part,
Half wheeling to the shield, half to the spear.°
From these, two strong and subtle spirits he called
That near him stood, and gave them thus in charge:
     'Ithuriel and Zephon, with winged speed
Search through this garden; leave unsearched no nook,
790 But chiefly where those two fair creatures lodge,
Now laid perhaps asleep secure of harm.
This evening from the sun's decline arrived
Who° tells of some infernal spirit seen
Hitherward bent (who could have thought?) escaped
The bars of hell, on errand bad no doubt:
Such where ye find, seize fast, and hither bring.'
     So saying, on he led his radiant files,
Dazzling the moon; these to the bower direct
In search of whom they sought. Him there they found
800 Squat like a toad, close at the ear of Eve,
Assaying by his devilish art to reach
The organs of her fancy, and with them forge
Illusions as he list, phantasms and dreams,
Or if, inspiring venom, he might taint
The animal spirits° that from pure blood arise
Like gentle breaths from rivers pure, thence raise
At least distempered, discontented thoughts,
Vain hopes, vain aims, inordinate desires
Blown up with high conceits° engendering pride.
810 Him thus intent Ithuriel with his spear

---

serenate serenade
starved lover Milton's point is that fallen Eros,
here imaged in Ovidian, courtly, and Cavalier
love, flourishes in a world of sexual denial, of
loss.
know know enough
ivory port through the gates of ivory came
false dreams, through gates of horn, true ones;

the Cherubim will interfere with the Satanically
induced false dream
Half . . . spear to left and right
Who one who
animal spirits See *Renaissance Psychology* in the
Glossary.
conceits ideas

Touched lightly; for no falsehood can endure
Touch of celestial temper, but returns
Of force to its own likeness. Up he starts
Discovered and surprised. As when a spark
Lights on a heap of nitrous powder,° laid
Fit for the tun° some magazine to store
Against a rumoured war, the smutty grain
With sudden blaze diffused, inflames the air:
So started up in his own shape the fiend.
820   Back stepped those two fair angels half amazed
So sudden to behold the grisly king,
Yet thus, unmoved with fear, accost him soon:
    'Which of those rebel spirits adjudged to hell
Com'st thou, escaped thy prison; and transformed,
Why sat'st thou like an enemy in wait
Here watching at the head of these that sleep?'
    'Know ye not then,' said Satan, filled with scorn,
'Know ye not me? Ye knew me once no mate
For you, there sitting where ye durst not soar;
830   Not to know me argues yourselves unknown,
The lowest of your throng; or if ye know,
Why ask ye, and superfluous begin
Your message, like to end as much in vain?'
To whom thus Zephon, answering scorn with scorn:
'Think not, revolted Spirit, thy shape the same,
Or undiminished brightness, to be known
As when thou stood'st in heaven upright and pure;
That glory then, when thou no more wast good,
Departed from thee, and thou resemblest now
840   Thy sin and place of doom obscure° and foul.
But come, for thou, be sure, shalt give account
To him who sent us, whose charge is to keep
This place inviolable, and these° from harm.'
    So spake the cherub, and his grave rebuke,
Severe in youthful beauty, added grace
Invincible. Abashed the devil stood,
And felt how awful° goodness is, and saw
Virtue in her shape how lovely; saw, and pined
His loss; but chiefly to find here observed
850   His lustre visibly impaired; yet seemed
Undaunted. 'If I must contend,' said he,
'Best with the best, the sender not the sent;
Or all at once; more glory will be won,
Or less be lost.' 'Thy fear,' said Zephon bold,

---

nitrous powder gunpowder
tun keg
obscure dark (whereas "dark," as in I Corinthians 13:12, and Spenser's phrase "dark

conceit," means "obscure" in the modern sense
of "hard to make out")
these Adam and Eve, asleep
awful awe-engendering

'Will save us trial what the least can do
Single against thee wicked, and thence weak.'
    The fiend replied not, overcome with rage;
But like a proud steed reined, went haughty on,
Champing his iron curb. To strive or fly
860 He held it vain; awe from above had quelled
His heart, not else dismayed. Now drew they nigh
The western point, where those half-rounding guards
Just met, and closing stood in squadron joined
Awaiting next command. To whom their chief
Gabriel from the front thus called aloud:
    'O friends, I hear the tread of nimble feet
Hasting this way, and now by glimpse discern
Ithuriel and Zephon through the shade,
And with them comes a third, of regal port,
870 But faded splendour wan, who by his gait
And fierce demeanour seems the prince of hell,
Not likely to part hence without contést;
Stand firm, for in his look defiance lours.'
    He scarce had ended, when those two approached
And brief related whom they brought, where found,
How busied, in what form and posture couched.
    To whom with stern regard thus Gabriel spake:
'Why hast thou, Satan, broke the bounds prescribed
To thy transgressions, and disturbed the charge
880 Of others,° who approve not to transgress
By thy example, but have power and right
To question thy bold entrance on this place;
Employed it seems to violate sleep, and those
Whose dwelling God hath planted here in bliss?'
    To whom thus Satan, with contemptuous brow:
'Gabriel, thou hadst in heaven the esteem of wise,
And such I held thee; but this question asked
Puts me in doubt. Lives there who loves his pain?
Who would not, finding way, break loose from hell,
890 Though thither doomed? Thou wouldst thyself, no doubt,
And boldly venture to whatever place
Farthest from pain, where thou mightst hope to change
Torment with ease, and soonest recompense
Dole° with delight, which in this place I sought;
To thee no reason, who knowest only good,
But evil hast not tried. And wilt object°
His will who bound us? Let him surer bar
His iron gates, if he intends our stay
In that dark durance°—thus much what was asked.

charge Of others their responsibility (Adam   object make legal objection about
and Eve)   durance confinement
Dole distress

900   The rest is true, they found me where they say;
      But that implies not violence or harm.'
          Thus he in scorn. The warlike angel moved,
      Disdainfully half smiling thus replied:
      'O loss of one in heaven to judge of wise,°
      Since Satan fell, whom folly overthrew,
      And now returns him from his prison scaped,°
      Gravely in doubt whether to hold them wise
      Or not, who ask what boldness brought him hither
      Unlicensed from his bounds in hell prescribed;
910   So wise he judges it to fly from pain
      However,° and to scape his punishment.
      So judge thou still, presumptuous, till the wrath,
      Which thou incurrest by flying, meet thy flight
      Sevenfold, and scourge that wisdom back to hell,
      Which taught thee yet no better, that no pain
      Can equal anger infinite provoked.
      But wherefore thou alone? Wherefore with thee
      Came not all hell broke loose? Is pain to them
      Less pain, less to be fled, or thou than they
920   Less hardy to endure? Courageous chief,
      The first in flight from pain, hadst thou alleged
      To thy deserted host this cause of flight,
      Thou surely hadst not come sole fugitive.'
          To which the fiend thus answered frowning stern:
      'Not that I less endure, or shrink from pain,
      Insulting angel, well thou knowest I stood°
      Thy fiercest, when in battle to thy aid
      The blasting volleyed thunder made all speed
      And seconded thy else not dreaded spear.
930   But still thy words at random, as before,
      Argue thy inexperience what behoves,
      From hard assays° and ill successes past,
      A faithful leader, not to hazard all
      Through ways of danger by himself untried.
      I therefore, I alone first undertook
      To wing the desolate abyss, and spy
      This new-created world, whereof in hell
      Fame° is not silent, here in hope to find
      Better abode, and my afflicted° powers
940   To settle here on earth, or in mid-air;
      Though for possession put to try once more
      What thou and thy gay legions dare against,
      Whose easier business were to serve their Lord

O loss . . . wise What a loss . . . wisdom!   stood withstood
returns . . . scaped returns himself from his   assays attempts
escape   Fame rumor
However whichever way   afflicted outcast

High up in heaven, with songs to hymn his throne,
And practiced distances to cringe, not fight.'
    To whom the warrior angel soon replied:
'To say and straight unsay, pretending first
Wise to fly pain, professing next the spy,
Argues no leader but a liar traced,°
950   Satan, and couldst thou "faithful" add? O name,
O sacred name of faithfulness profaned!
Faithful to whom? To thy rebellious crew?
Army of fiends, fit body to fit head;
Was this your discipline and faith engaged,
Your military obedience, to dissolve
Allegiance to the acknowledged power supreme?
And thou sly hypocrite, who now wouldst seem
Patron of liberty, who more than thou
Once fawned, and cringed, and servilely adored
960   Heaven's awful monarch? Wherefore but in hope
To dispossess him, and thyself to reign?
But mark what I areed° thee now: Avaunt!
Fly thither whence thou fled'st. If from this hour
Within these hallowed limits thou appear,
Back to the infernal pit I drag thee chained,
And seal thee so, as henceforth not to scorn
The facile° gates of hell too slightly barred.'
    So threatened he, but Satan to no threats
Gave heed, but waxing more in rage replied:
970   'Then when I am thy captive talk of chains,
Proud limitary° cherub, but ere then
Far heavier load thyself expect to feel
From my prevailing arm, though heaven's king
Ride on thy wings, and thou with thy compeers,
Used to the yoke, drawest his triumphant wheels
In progress through the road of heaven star-paved.'
    While thus he spake, the angelic squadron bright
Turned, fiery red, sharpening in moonèd horns°
Their phalanx, and began to hem him round
980   With ported spears, as thick as when a field
Of Ceres° ripe for harvest waving bends
Her bearded grove of ears, which way the wind
Sways them; the careful° ploughman doubting stands
Lest on the threshing-floor his hopeful sheaves
Prove chaff. On the other side Satan alarmed°
Collecting all his might dilated° stood,

traced disclosed
areed advise
facile easily opened
limitary frontier-guard (with a bit of a snarl)
moonèd horns crescent-shaped
Ceres here, the goddess standing for the grain itself

careful anxious, even as God, the thresher and winnower, might be for the outcome of this renewed combat. This image is reinforced shortly by that of God as weigher.
alarmed aroused
dilated into more ethereal condition by Ithuriel's spear

Like Teneriffe or Atlas unremoved:°
His stature reached the sky, and on his crest
Sat Horror plumed; nor wanted in his grasp
990   What seemed both spear and shield. Now dreadful deeds
Might have ensued, nor only Paradise
In this commotion, but the starry cope°
Of heaven perhaps, or all the elements
At least had gone to wrack, disturbed and torn
With violence of this conflict, had not soon
The Eternal to prevent such horrid fray
Hung forth in heaven his golden scales,° yet seen
Betwixt Astraea° and the Scorpion sign,
Wherein all things created first he weighed,
1000   The pendulous round earth with balanced air
In counterpoise, now ponders° all events,
Battles and realms. In these he put two weights,
The sequel° each of parting and of fight;
The latter quick up flew, and kicked the beam;
Which Gabriel spying, thus bespake the fiend:
    'Satan, I know thy strength, and thou knowest mine,
Neither our own but given; what folly then
To boast what arms can do, since thine no more
Than heaven permits, nor mine, though doubled now
1010   To trample thee as mire. For proof look up,
And read thy lot in yon celestial sign
Where thou art weighed,° and shown how light, how weak,
If thou resist.' The fiend looked up and knew
His mounted scale aloft: nor more; but fled
Murmuring, and with him fled the shades of night.

    From *Book V*

Now Morn her rosy steps in the eastern clime
Advancing, sowed the earth with orient pearl,
When Adam waked, so customed—for his sleep
Was airy light, from pure digestion bred,
And temperate vapours° bland, which the only° sound
Of leaves and fuming rills, Aurora's fan,°
Lightly dispersed, and the shrill matin song
Of birds on every bough—so much the more

Teneriffe . . . unremoved peak in the Canary
islands, and the Atlas range in Morocco, both
unremovable
cope canopy
golden scales the constellation Libra now, at
midnight, at the zenith; also reminiscent of the
Homeric golden scales in which Zeus weighed
the destinies of Greek and Trojans, Achilles
and Hector, and, in Virgil, Aeneas and Turnus
Astraea the constellation Virgo was formed
when Astraea, or Justice, left the world at the
end of the Golden Age

ponders weighs, with an overtone of "considers"
sequel consequence
thou art weighed "—in the balance, and art
found wanting," the warning to Belshazzar   in
the Book of Daniel 5:27
vapours a medical term referring to the exhalations of digestion
only mere
Aurora's fan the leaves

His wonder was to find unwakened Eve
10   With tresses discomposed, and glowing cheek,
As through unquiet rest. He on his side
Leaning half-raised, with looks of cordial love
Hung over her enamoured, and beheld
Beauty, which whether waking or asleep
Shot forth peculiar graces;° then with voice
Mild, as when Zephyrus on Flora breathes,
Her hand soft touching, whispered thus: 'Awake,
My fairest,° my espoused, my latest found,
Heaven's last best gift, my ever new delight,
20   Awake, the morning shines, and the fresh field
Calls us; we lose the prime,° to mark how spring
Our tended plants, how blows° the citron grove,
What drops the myrrh, and what the balmy° reed,
How Nature paints her colours, how the bee
Sits on the bloom extracting liquid sweet.'
    Such whispering waked her, but with startled eye
On Adam, whom embracing, thus she spake:
'O sole in whom my thoughts find all repose,
My glory, my perfection, glad I see
30   Thy face, and morn returned, for I this night—
Such night till this I never passed—have dreamed,
If dreamed, not as I oft am wont, of thee,
Works of day past, or morrow's next design,
But of offence and trouble, which my mind
Knew never till this irksome night. Methought
Close at mine ear one called me forth to walk
With gentle voice; I thought it thine. It said:
"Why sleep'st thou, Eve? Now is the pleasant time,
The cool, the silent, save where silence yields
40   To the night-warbling bird, that now awake
Tunes sweetest his° love-laboured song; now reigns
Full-orbed the moon, and with more pleasing light
Shadowy sets off the face of things;° in vain,
If none regard; heaven wakes with all his eyes,°
Whom to behold but thee, Nature's desire,
In whose sight all things joy, with ravishment
Attracted by thy beauty still to gaze?"
I rose as at thy call, but found thee not;
To find thee I directed then my walk;
50   And on, methought, alone I passed through ways
That brought me on a sudden to the tree

peculiar graces graces peculiar to her
Awake, My fairest echoes the morning song
in the Song of Songs 2:10.
prime early morning hours
blows blooms
balmy yielding aromatic resin
his The nightingale is, normally, "she" (because

the transformed Philomela), but here is masculine by association with Satan.
Shadowy . . . things This serenade (evening
song), the opposite of Adam's aubade (morning
song), praises moonlight's qualities of ambi-
guity, soft vagueness, and outline-blurring.
all his eyes the stars

Of interdicted° knowledge. Fair it seemed,
Much fairer to my fancy than by day;
And as I wondering looked, beside it stood
One shaped and winged like one of those from heaven
By us oft seen; his dewy locks distilled
Ambrosia; on that tree he also gazed;
And "*O fair plant,*" said he, "*with fruit surcharged,*
Deigns none to ease thy load and taste thy sweet,
60   *Nor god,*° *nor man; is knowledge so despised?*
Or envy, or what reserve forbids to taste?
Forbid who will, none shall from me withhold
Longer thy offered good, why else set here?"
This said he paused not, but with venturous arm
He plucked, he tasted; me damp horror chilled
At such bold words vouched with a deed so bold.
But he thus, overjoyed: "*O fruit divine,*°
Sweet of thyself, but much more sweet thus cropped,
Forbidden here, it seems, as only fit
70   *For gods, yet able to make gods of men;*
And why not gods of men, since good, the more
Communicated, more abundant grows,
The author not impaired, but honoured more?
Here, happy creature, fair angelic Eve,
Partake thou also; happy though thou art,
Happier thou may'st be, worthier canst not be;
Taste this, and be henceforth among the gods
Thyself a goddess, not to earth confined,
But sometimes in the air, as we; sometimes
80   *Ascend to heaven, by merit thine, and see*
What life the gods live there, and such live thou."
So saying, he drew nigh, and to me held,
Even to my mouth of that same fruit held part
Which he had plucked; the pleasant savoury smell
So quickened appetite that I, methought,
Could not but taste. Forthwith up to the clouds
With him I flew, and underneath beheld
The earth outstretched immense, a prospect wide
And various. Wondering at my flight and change
90   To this high exaltation, suddenly
My guide was gone, and I, methought, sunk down,
And fell asleep; but O how glad I waked
To find this but a dream!'° Thus Eve her night
Related, and thus Adam answered sad:°

---

interdicted forbidden
god spirit, as at l. 117, below
O fruit divine Satan's voice mistakenly over-emphasizes the power of the fruit itself which, "well used" (IV.200), would have remained uneaten.
but a dream as Eve recounts it, a prophetic one, having its fulfillment in Bk. IX, when

details of the temptation of Eve will echo those of her narration here. This non-biblical dream raises interesting interpretive questions: if a "true dream," is Eve already lost? if a false one (see IV.778n.), then a necessary educational experience?
sad serious

'Best image of myself and dearer half,
The trouble of thy thoughts this night in sleep
Affects me equally; nor can I like
This uncouth° dream, of evil sprung, I fear;
Yet evil whence? In thee can harbour none,
100   Created pure. But know that in the soul
Are many lesser faculties° that serve
Reason as chief; among these fancy next
Her office holds; of all external things,
Which the five watchful senses represent,°
She forms imaginations,° airy shapes,
Which reason joining or disjoining frames
All what we affirm or what deny, and call
Our knowledge or opinion; then retires
Into her private cell when nature rests.
110   Oft in her absence mimic fancy wakes
To imitate her; but misjoining shapes,
Wild work produces oft, and most in dreams,
Ill matching words and deeds long past or late.
Some such resemblances methinks I find
Of our last evening's talk in this thy dream,
But with addition strange; yet be not sad.
Evil into the mind of god or man
May come and go, so unapproved, and leave
No spot or blame behind; which gives me hope
120   That what in sleep thou didst abhor to dream,
Waking thou never wilt consent to do.
Be not disheartened then, nor cloud those looks
That wont to be more cheerful and serene
Than when fair morning first smiles on the world,
And let us to our fresh employments rise
Among the groves, the fountains, and the flowers
That open now their choicest bosomed smells
Reserved from night, and kept for thee in store.'

. . .

[Eve's anxiety allayed, they proceed to the first day's activities, starting with a morning hymn followed by the unfallen work of gardening. God instructs the archangel Raphael to descend to Paradise and visit Adam and Eve in the garden in order to teach them who they are and what their relation to the world is, and, most particularly, "to render man inexcusable" by telling them who their enemy is. This entails a sub-epic, Raphael's narration of all that has gone before, modeled on the flashback narration in Homer and Virgil by which we

uncouth unpleasant
lesser faculties In a brilliant parody of the story of the Fall, Chaucer's Pertelote explains to her husband Chaunteclere that his prophetic dream must have been something he ate. Here, Adam gives Eve a lecture on the psychology of the faculties, notably about fancy, or imagination (they were usually not distinguished). See

Renaissance Psychology in the Glossary, the passage on fancy from Burton's Anatomy of Melancholy, and the allegory of Phantastes in The Faerie Queene II.ix.49–58.
represent show
imaginations visions; the objects, rather than the faculty itself

learn of all of Odysseus' adventures between Troy and Calypso's island, for example, only when he narrates them at the court of Alcinous. *Paradise Lost,* too, has started *in medias res,* and now we learn of the total time sequence stretching back behind the Fall of Satan. The promotion of the Son by God, the jealousy and scheming of Satan, and the beginning of the revolution in heaven are all unfolded.]

Book VI

[Raphael's narration continues. It describes the three days' battle in heaven in a grim and animated fashion, including the invention of "devilish engines," the first artillery, and other war matériel, "which in the second day's fight put Michael and his angels to some disorder," as Milton puts it in his prose *argument* to Book VI. The third day's victory is given not to Michael, the general, but the Son, whose thundering chariot ride routs Satan's legions; as they retreat in disarray, the wall of heaven opens, and "they leap down with horror and confusion into the place of punishment prepared for them in the deep." The Son returns to his Father in triumph.]

From *Book VII*

[Here, in the proem to Book VII, Milton finally names his "heavenly Muse." His invocation calls on her for help in making a difficult imaginative transition from the almost mock-heroic liveliness of the war in heaven in Book VI to the monumental task of revealing, through Raphael's narration, the story of creation. His poem is "descending" to earth from heavenly subjects, but his efforts and craft must rise to this harder task. This is also the midpoint of the poem, and from here the action is all downhill; there are no more scenes taking place in heaven. As always, too, there is Milton's anxiety, as a poet, about falling.]

Descend from heaven, Urania,° by that name
If rightly thou art called, whose voice divine
Following, about the Olympian hill I soar,
Above the flight of Pegasean wing.°
The meaning, not the name° I call; for thou
Nor of the Muses nine, nor on the top
Of old Olympus dwell'st, but heavenly born,
Before the hills appeared or fountain flowed,
Thou with eternal wisdom didst converse,
10   Wisdom thy sister, and with her didst play
In presence of the almighty father, pleased
With thy celestial song. Up led by thee
Into the heaven of heavens I have presumed,

Urania See I.6n.
Pegasean wing Pegasus, the winged horse ridden by Bellerophon when he killed the Chimera (see II.628n), thus committing an act of truth. The flying horse was symbolic of poetry itself (1) because he struck Mt. Helicon with his hoof to produce the Muses' spring and (2) from his flights above even the fountains which

stood for poetic expression, for breaking out and flowing.
meaning, not the name not Urania only as one of the nine (Muse of astronomy, who will preside over the discussion of the cosmos in Bk. VII), but as a kind of Christian Muse of religious poetry

An earthly guest, and drawn empyreal air,
Thy tempering; with like safety guided down,
Return me to my native element,°
Lest from this flying steed unreined (as once
Bellerophon, though from a lower clime)
Dismounted, on the Aleian field° I fall,
20   Erroneous° there to wander and forlorn.
Half yet remains unsung,° but narrower bound
Within the visible diurnal° sphere;
Standing on earth, not rapt° above the pole,
More safe I sing with mortal voice, unchanged
To hoarse or mute, though fallen on evil days,°
On evil days, though fallen, and evil tongues;
In darkness,° and with dangers compassed round,
And solitude; yet not alone, while thou
Visit'st my slumbers nightly,° or when morn
30   Purples the east. Still govern thou my song,
Urania, and fit audience find, though few.
But drive far off the barbarous dissonance
Of Bacchus and his revellers, the race
Of that wild rout that tore the Thracian bard°
In Rhodope,° where woods and rocks had ears
To rapture, till the savage clamour drowned°
Both harp and voice; nor could the Muse defend
Her son. So fail not thou who thee implores;
For thou art heavenly, she° an empty dream.

[Book VII tells the story of Creation. Raphael tells of God's desire to create another world and "out of one man a race / Innumerable" in further despite of Satan's decimation of heaven's ranks, "there to dwell, / Not here, till by degrees of merit raised" they will become as angels (a promise Satan makes to Eve) "And Earth be changed to heaven, and heaven to earth." The Son, as the Word of God, then creates the world in six days, starting out with a pair of compasses which draw circles and boundaries of limitation, then creating light, and so on through the processes of the text in Genesis. The work culminates in the creation, among the animals, of the vertical animal, man; the Word reascends to heaven, and angelic rejoicing celebrates the completion of the act.

Book VIII continues the education of man, following his two heroic narrations of warfare and of creation and founding of living places with a brief

native element earth
Aleian field Bellerophon finally tried to reach heaven on Pegasus, and Zeus threw him off onto the plain of Aleia (in Greek: "error").
Erroneous Latin error means "wandering," and Milton plays here, as so often, on both the original and derived meanings of words.
Half . . . unsung See Headnote to Bk. VII.
diurnal rotating daily
rapt entranced, "caught up" (into heaven?)
evil days the Restoration, which commenced with an anti-Puritan reaction during which Milton felt in great danger; also, evil in that

the decade of political writing and work during which he had gone blind had come to nothing darkness his blindness; this echoes part of the meditation on light (III. 145)
nightly See III.31 and IX.21–24.
Thracian bard Orpheus, torn apart by the Bacchantes (see Comus, l. 550, and Lycidas, ll. 57–63)
Rhodope a mountain in Thrace
drowned Given the fate of the dismembered Orpheus, harp and head floating down the Hebrus, this word is doubly powerful.
she Orpheus' muse

response to Adam's questions about the relation of Paradise to the celestial phenomena apparent from it: he asks about sun, moon, and stars, and what accounts for their motions through the visible sky (an original and fruitful question for fallen man's science). Raphael instructs him to forget such pseudo-problems, implying that in Paradise the phenomena are the reality, and presenting a satiric picture of the search "through wandering mazes lost" (like the philosophy of the demons in Book II) for knowledge of reality in fallen human history. He particularly ridicules the way in which theories, or models, succeed each other in the history of science, how astronomers "build, unbuild, contrive / To save appearances, how gird the sphere / With centric and eccentric scribbled o'er, / Cycle and epicycle, orb in orb"—the picture of a Ptolemaic chart scribbled over with constant revisions. His account finished, Adam responds with one of his own, of his memories of everything since the dawn of his own consciousness, on awaking from his creation, his first sight of Eve, and so forth. Raphael, "after admonitions repeated" to Adam about not letting his feelings for Eve overcome his higher reason, departs.]

Book IX

No more of talk where God or angel guest
With man, as with his friend, familiar used
To sit indulgent, and with him partake
Rural repast, permitting him the while
Venial° discourse unblamed. I now must change
Those notes to tragic; foul distrust, and breach
Disloyal on the part of man, revolt,
And disobedience; on the part of heaven
Now alienated, distance° and distaste,°
10   Anger and just rebuke, and judgment given,
That brought into this world a world of woe,°
Sin and her shadow Death, and misery,
Death's harbinger. Sad task, yet argument
Not less but more heroic than the wrath°
Of stern Achilles on his foe pursued
Thrice fugitive about Troy wall; or rage
Of Turnus for Lavinia disespoused;°
Or Neptune's ire or Juno's, that so long
Perplexed the Greek° and Cytherea's son;°
20   If answerable style I can obtain
Of my celestial patroness,° who deigns
Her nightly visitation° unimplored,

venial allowable
distance may also have the sense "discord" or "quarrel."
distaste completes the list of hissing "dis-" 's starting at l. 6 with what will be the operative word in the plot now, "taste" (see I.2).
world . . . woe The two "world"'s are local and general, literal and figurative; "woe," soon after "taste," echoes I.3.
wrath the first word of the Iliad. Milton shifts from describing his modulating tone to the subject of epic and what its subject should be.
Turnus . . . disespoused Turnus is Aeneas'

major antagonist in the latter portion of Virgil's epic; to Turnus he loses Italy, his beloved, and his life.
the Greek Odysseus
Cytherea's son Aeneas
celestial patroness Urania (see the invocations to Bks. I, III, VII)
nightly visitation Milton dictated Paradise Lost in the mornings from inspiration in the previous night; at any rate this is the poem's own myth of its composition, of having been sung out of darkness.

And dictates to me slumbering, or inspires
Easy my unpremeditated verse,
Since first this subject for heroic song
Pleased me long choosing, and beginning late;
Not sedulous by nature to indite
Wars, hitherto the only argument
Heroic deemed, chief maistry° to dissect
30   With long and tedious havoc fabled knights
In battles feigned (the better fortitude
Of patience and heroic martyrdom
Unsung), or to describe races and games,
Or tilting° furniture, emblazoned shields,
Impresses° quaint, caparisons and steeds,
Bases and tinsel trappings,° gorgeous knights
At joust and tournament; then marshalled feast
Served up in hall with sewers and seneschals;°
The skill of artifice or office mean,
40   Not that which justly gives heroic name
To person or to poem. Me of these
Nor skilled nor studious, higher argument
Remains, sufficient of itself to raise
That name,° unless an age too late, or cold
Climate,° or years damp my intended wing
Depressed, and much they may, if all be mine,
Not hers who brings it nightly to my ear.
      The sun was sunk,° and after him the star
Of Hesperus, whose office is to bring
50   Twilight upon the earth, short arbiter
'Twixt day and night, and now from end to end
Night's hemisphere had veiled the horizon round,
When Satan, who late fled before the threats
Of Gabriel out of Eden, now improved°
In meditated fraud and malice, bent
On man's destruction, maugre° what might hap
Of heavier on himself, fearless returned.°
By night he fled, and at midnight returned
From compassing the earth, cautious of day,
60   Since Uriel, regent of the sun, descried
His entrance, and forewarned the Cherubim
That kept their watch; thence full of anguish driven,
The space of seven continued nights he rode

maistry mastery, skill. The word has an archaic flavor, and introduces the terms associated with Renaissance epic and its world of medieval romance (Tasso, Ariosto, and Spenser).
tilting jousting
Impresses emblems or devices on shields
Bases . . . trappings draperies, caparisons, and trimmings for horses
sewers and seneschals waiters and stewards
That name epic poetry ("heroic name")
an age . . . Climate the burden of an epic

tradition, even mastered, is very great. These phrases refer to a moment of Western history, Restoration England, as well as to the northern climate and the winter weather, during which, we are told, he wrote.
sun was sunk The transition to narrative is from the echoing "nightly."
improved intensified
maugre despite
returned to where the narrative left him at the end of Bk. IV

With darkness, thrice the equinoctial line
He circled, four times crossed the car° of Night
From pole to pole, traversing each colure;°
On the eighth returned, and on the coast averse°
From entrance or Cherubic watch, by stealth
Found unsuspected way. There was a place—
70 Now not, though sin, not time, first wrought the change—
Where Tigris at the foot of Paradise
Into a gulf shot under ground, till part
Rose up a fountain by the Tree of Life;
In with the river sunk, and with it rose
Satan, involved in rising mist, then sought
Where to lie hid; sea he had searched and land
From Eden over Pontus,° and the pool
Maeotis,° up beyond the river Ob;°
Downward as far antarctic; and in length
80 West from Orontes° to the ocean barred
At Darien,° thence to the land where flows
Ganges and Indus. Thus the orb he roamed
With narrow search, and with inspection deep
Considered every creature, which of all
Most opportune might serve his wiles, and found
The serpent subtlest beast of all the field.
Him after long debate, irresolute°
Of thoughts revolved,° his final sentence° chose
Fit vessel, fittest imp° of fraud, in whom
90 To enter, and his dark suggestions hide
From sharpest sight; for in the wily snake,
Whatever sleights none would suspicious mark,
As from his wit and native subtlety
Proceeding, which, in other beasts observed,
Doubt° might beget of diabolic power
Active within beyond the sense of brute.
Thus he resolved, but first from inward grief
His bursting passion into plaints thus poured:
    'O earth, how like to heaven, if not preferred
100 More justly, seat worthier of gods, as built
With second thoughts, reforming what was old!°
For what God after better worse would build?

---

car chariot
colure one of two longitudinal circles drawn
from the celestial poles, cutting the ecliptic at
solstice and equinox
averse opposite
Pontus the Black Sea
Maeotis the Sea of Azov
river Ob in Siberia
Orontes Syrian river
Darien Isthmus of Panama
irresolute unresolved
thoughts revolved turned and twisted, like a
serpent's motion
sentence decision
imp offshoot
Doubt suspicion
With . . . old Satan's address to the earth,
paralleling his invocation of the sun in IV.32,
begins here with a fallen reading of an unfallen
event: wise men learn by experience, and a
second version, in a technological context, improves on the first; this is not true of Creation,
nor necessarily of poems.

Terrestrial heaven, danced round by other heavens
That shine, yet bear their bright officious° lamps,
Light above light, for thee alone, as seems,
In thee concentring all their precious beams
Of sacred influence! As God in heaven
Is centre, yet extends to all, so thou
Centring receivest from all those orbs; in thee,
110   Not in themselves, all their known virtue appears
Productive in herb, plant, and nobler birth
Of creatures animate with gradual° life
Of growth, sense, reason,° all summed up in man.
With what delight could I have walked thee round,
If I could joy in aught, sweet interchange
Of hill and valley, rivers, woods, and plains,
Now land, now sea, and shores with forest crowned,
Rocks, dens, and caves; but I in none of these
Find place or refuge; and the more I see
120   Pleasures about me, so much more I feel
Torment within me, as from the hateful siege°
Of contraries; all good to me becomes
Bane,° and in heaven much worse would be my state.
But neither here seek I, no nor in heaven
To dwell, unless by mastering heaven's Supreme;
Nor hope to be myself less miserable
By what I seek, but others to make such
As I, though thereby worse to me redound.
For only in destroying I find ease
130   To my relentless thoughts; and him destroyed,
Or won to what may work his utter loss,
For whom all this was made, all this will soon
Follow, as to him linked in weal or woe;
In woe then, that destruction wide may range.
To me shall be the glory sole among
The infernal powers, in one day to have marred
What he, almighty styled, six nights and days
Continued making, and who knows how long
Before had been contriving? Though perhaps
140   Not longer than since I in one night freed
From servitude inglorious well-nigh half
The angelic name, and thinner left the throng
Of his adorers. He to be avenged,
And to repair his numbers thus impaired,
Whether such virtue spent of old now failed

---

officious serviceable
gradual on a scale of nature
growth, sense, reason functions of the vegetable, animal, and rational souls in man; see *Renaissance Psychology* in the Glossary
siege The contraries Satan has manipulated in his dialectic are now besieging him, with the final and appropriate irony that "siege" can also mean "seat" or "throne," his internal state in which these contraries are enshrined.
all good . . . Bane "bane": "evil"; can he remember saying "Evil, be thou my good" (IV.110)? Cf. IV.32–113 and IX.467–70.

More angels to create, if they at least
Are his created, or to spite us more,
Determined to advance into our room°
A creature formed of earth, and him endow,
150   Exalted from so base original,
With heavenly spoils, our spoils. What he decreed
He effected; man he made, and for him built
Magnificent this world, and earth his seat,
Him lord pronounced, and, O indignity!
Subjected to his service angel wings,
And flaming ministers to watch and tend
Their earthy charge. Of these the vigilance
I dread, and to elude, thus wrapped in mist
Of midnight vapour glide obscure, and pry
160   In every bush and brake, where hap° may find
The serpent sleeping, in whose mazy folds
To hide me, and the dark intent I bring.
O foul descent!° that I who erst contended
With Gods to sit the highest, am now constrained
Into a beast, and mixed with bestial slime,
This essence to incarnate and imbrute,
That to the height of deity aspired;
But what will not ambition and revenge
Descend to? Who aspires must down as low
170   As high he soared, obnoxious° first or last
To basest things. Revenge, at first though sweet,
Bitter ere long back on itself recoils;
Let it; I reck not, so it light well aimed,
Since higher I fall short, on him who next
Provokes my envy, this new favourite
Of heaven, this man of clay, son of despite,
Whom us the more to spite his maker raised
From dust: spite then with spite is best repaid.'
      So saying, through each thicket dank or dry,
180   Like a black mist low creeping, he held on
His midnight search, where soonest he might find
The serpent: him fast sleeping soon he found
In labyrinth of many a round self-rolled,
His head the midst, well stored with subtle wiles:
Not yet in horrid° shade or dismal den,
Nor nocent° yet, but on the grassy herb
Fearless, unfeared, he slept. In at his mouth
The devil entered, and his brutal sense,
In heart or head, possessing soon inspired

room place
hap chance
O foul descent! and a hideous parody of the
other Incarnation, the other Descent (of the
Holy Ghost to incarnate in Mary)

obnoxious exposed
horrid bristling
nocent harmful (snakes become poisonous only
after the Fall); also, perhaps, "guilty"

190   With act intelligential, but his sleep
Disturbed not, waiting close° the approach of morn.
Now whenas sacred light began to dawn
In Eden on the humid flowers, that breathed
Their morning incense, when all things that breathe
From the earth's great altar send up silent praise
To the Creator, and his nostrils fill
With grateful smell, forth came the human pair
And joined their vocal worship to the quire
Of creatures wanting° voice; that done, partake

200   The season, prime for sweetest scents and airs;°
Then cómmune how that day they best may ply
Their growing work; for much their work outgrew
The hands' dispatch of two gardening so wide.
And Eve first to her husband thus began:
  'Adam, well may we labour still to dress
This garden, still to tend plant, herb, and flower,
Our pleasant task enjoined, but till more hands
Aid us, the work under our labour grows,
Luxurious by restraint; what we by day

210   Lop overgrown, or prune, or prop, or bind,
One night or two with wanton growth derides,
Tending to wild. Thou therefore now advise
Or hear what to my mind first thoughts present:
Let us divide our labours, thou where choice
Leads thee, or where most needs, whether to wind
The woodbine° round this arbour, or direct
The clasping ivy where to climb, while I
In yonder spring° of roses intermixed
With myrtle, find what to redress° till noon.

220   For while so near each other thus all day
Our task we choose, what wonder if so near
Looks intervene and smiles, or object new
Casual discourse draw on, which intermits
Our day's work, brought to little, though begun
Early, and the hour of supper comes unearned.'
    To whom mild answer Adam thus returned:
'Sole Eve,° associate sole, to me beyond
Compare above all living creatures dear,
Well hast thou motioned,° well thy thoughts employed

230   How we might best fulfill the work which here
God hath assigned us, nor of me shalt pass
Unpraised; for nothing lovelier can be found

close hidden
wanting lacking
airs also in a musical sense: "tunes"
wind The woodbine She leaves to Adam the intertwining plants.
spring grove of young trees or bushes
redress prop up again. The trouble with all these immensely practical suggestions is that it will leave her unpropped (ll. 432–33) by Adam.
Eve as by her epithet, "Mother of all life" (Genesis 3:2)
motioned proposed

In woman, than to study household good,
And good works in her husband to promote.
Yet not so strictly hath our Lord imposed
Labour, as to debar us when we need
Refreshment, whether food, or talk between,
Food of the mind, or this sweet intercourse
Of looks and smiles, for smiles from reason flow,
240 To brute denied, and are of love the food,
Love not the lowest end of human life.
For not to irksome toil, but to delight
He made us, and delight to reason joined.
These paths and bowers doubt not but our joint hands
Will keep from wilderness with ease, as wide
As we need walk, till younger hands ere long
Assist us. But if much convérse perhaps
Thee satiate, to short absence I could yield.
For solitude sometimes is best society,
250 And short retirement urges sweet return.
But other doubt possesses me, lest harm
Befall thee severed from me; for thou knowest
What hath been warned us, what malicious foe,
Envying our happiness, and of his own
Despairing, seeks to work us woe and shame
By sly assault; and somewhere nigh at hand
Watches, no doubt, with greedy hope to find
His wish and best advantage, us asunder,
Hopeless to circumvent us joined, where each
260 To other speedy aid might lend at need;
Whether his first design be to withdraw
Our fealty° from God, or to disturb
Conjugal love, than which perhaps no bliss
Enjoyed by us excites his envy more;
Or this,° or worse, leave not the faithful side
That gave thee being, still shades thee and protects.
The wife, where danger or dishonour lurks,
Safest and seemliest by her husband stays,
Who guards her, or with her the worst endures.'
270   To whom the virgin° majesty of Eve,
As one who loves, and some unkindness meets,
With sweet austere composure thus replied:
    'Offspring of heaven and earth, and all earth's lord,
That such an enemy we have, who seeks
Our ruin, both by thee informed I learn,
And from the parting angel overheard
As in a shady nook I stood behind,
Just then returned at shut° of evening flowers.

---

fealty fidelity
Or this whether (his plan) is this
virgin innocent; but literally too: she is not

a virgin, but her majesty is so far unruptured
shut folding-up time

But that thou shouldst my firmness therefore doubt
280   To God or thee, because we have a foe
May tempt it, I expected not to hear.
His violence thou fear'st not, being such
As we, not capable of death or pain,
Can either not receive, or can repel.
His fraud is then thy fear, which plain infers
Thy equal fear that my firm faith and love
Can by his fraud be shaken or seduced;
Thoughts, which how found they harbour in thy breast,
Adam, misthought of her to thee so dear?'
290   To whom with healing words Adam replied:
'Daughter of God and man, immortal Eve,
For such thou art, from sin and blame entire;°
Not diffident of thee do I dissuade
Thy absence from my sight, but to avoid
The attempt itself, intended by our foe.
For he who tempts, though in vain, at least asperses°
The tempted with dishonour foul, supposed
Not incorruptible of faith, not proof
Against temptation. Thou thyself with scorn
300   And anger wouldst resent the offered wrong,
Though ineffectual found. Misdeem not then,
If such affront I labour to avert
From thee alone, which on us both at once
The enemy, though bold, will hardly dare,
Or daring, first on me the assault shall light.
Nor thou his malice and false guile contemn;
Subtle he needs must be, who could seduce
Angels, nor think superfluous others' aid.
I from the influence° of thy looks receive
310   Access° in every virtue, in thy sight
More wise, more watchful, stronger, if need were
Of outward strength; while shame, thou looking on,
Shame to be overcome or overreached,
Would utmost vigour raise, and raised unite.
Why shouldst not thou like sense within thee feel
When I am present, and thy trial choose
With me, best witness of thy virtue tried?'
     So spake domestic Adam in his care
And matrimonial love; but Eve, who thought
320   Less° attribúted to her faith sincere,
Thus her reply with accent sweet renewed:
     'If this be our condition, thus to dwell
In narrow circuit straitened° by a foe,

---

entire integral, untarnished
asperses sprays about
influence the beams of stars. Adam has fallen
into Petrarchan poetry.

Access increase
Less too little
straitened constricted

Subtle or violent, we not endued
Single with like defence, wherever met,
How are we happy, still in fear of harm?
But harm precedes not sin: only our foe
Tempting affronts us with his foul esteem
Of our integrity; his foul esteem
330   Sticks no dishonour on our front,° but turns
Foul on himself; then wherefore shunned or feared
By us? Who rather double honour gain
From his surmise proved false, find peace within,
Favour from heaven, our witness, from the event.
And what is faith, love, virtue, unassayed
Alone, without exterior help sustained?
Let us not then suspect our happy state
Left so imperfect by the maker wise
As not secure to single or combined.
340   Frail is our happiness, if this be so,
And Eden were no Eden° thus exposed.'
        To whom thus Adam fervently replied:
'O woman, best are all things as the will
Of God ordained them; his creating hand
Nothing imperfect or deficient left
Of all that he created, much less man,
Or aught that might his happy state secure,
Secure from outward force: within himself
The danger lies, yet lies within his power;
350   Against his will he can receive no harm.
But God left free the will, for what obeys
Reason is free, and reason he made right,°
But bid her well beware, and still erect,°
Lest by some fair appearing good surprised
She dictate false, and misinform the will
To do what God expressly hath forbid.
Not then mistrust, but tender love enjoins,
That I should mind° thee oft, and mind° thou me.
Firm we subsist, yet possible to swerve,°
360   Since reason not impossibly may meet
Some specious object by the foe suborned,
And fall into deception unaware,
Not keeping strictest watch, as she was warned.
Seek not temptation then, which to avoid
Were better, and most likely if from me
Thou sever not; trial will come unsought.

front brow, forehead
Eden in its Hebrew meaning of "pleasure"
right right reason, as distinguished from capable wit
erect attentive

mind remind admonishingly; but when repeated, "pay heed to"
Firm . . . swerve a subtly modulated echo of the central doctrinal statement of God: "I made him just and right, / Sufficient to have stood, though free to fall" (III.98–99)

Wouldst thou approve thy constancy, approve°
First thy obedience; the other who can know,
Not seeing thee attempted, who attest?
370 But if thou think trial unsought may find
Us both securer° than thus warned thou seem'st,
Go; for thy stay, not free, absents thee more;
Go in thy native innocence, rely
On what thou hast of virtue, summon all,
For God towards thee hath done his part, do thine.'
     So spake the patriarch of mankind, but Eve
Persisted; yet submiss,° though last, replied:
     'With thy permission then, and thus forewarned,
Chiefly by what thy own last reasoning words
380 Touched only, that our trial, when least sought,
May find us both perhaps far less prepared,
The willinger I go, nor much expect
A foe so proud will first the weaker seek;
So bent, the more shall shame him his repulse.'
     Thus saying, from her husband's hand her hand
Soft she withdrew,° and like a wood-nymph light,
Oread or Dryad, or of Delia's° train,
Betook her to the groves, but Delia's self
In gait surpassed and goddess-like deport,°
390 Though not as she with bow and quiver armed,
But with such gardening tools as art yet rude
—Guiltless of fire°—had formed, or angles brought.
To Pales,° or Pomona,° thus adorned,
Likest she seemed, Pomona when she fled
Vertumnus,° or to Ceres in her prime,
Yet virgin of Proserpina° from Jove.
Her long with ardent look his eye pursued
Delighted, but desiring more her stay.
Oft he to her his charge of quick return
400 Repeated, she to him as oft engaged
To be returned by noon amid the bower,
And all things in best order to invite
Noontide repast, or afternoon's repose.
O much deceived, much failing,° hapless Eve,
Of thy presumed return! event perverse!
Thou never from that hour in Paradise
Found'st either sweet repast or sound repose;

approve prove
Us both securer surer of ourselves (and thus,
more careless)
submiss submissively
her hand . . . withdrew Casual as this detail
may seem, it makes a picture of an emblem
being broken (see IV.321n.).
Oread . . . Delia's mountain or tree nymph of
Diana's

deport bearing
fire The fire Prometheus stole stands for all
technology.
Pales Roman goddess of pastures
Pomona goddess of fruit trees
Vertumnus god of seasons, her lover
Proserpina See IV.269n.
failing to return; also, generally, "failed Eve—"

Such ambush hid, among sweet flowers and shades
Waited with hellish rancour imminent
410 To intercept thy way, or send thee back
Despoiled of innocence, of faith, of bliss.
For now, and since first break of dawn the fiend,
Mere serpent° in appearance, forth was come,
And on his quest, where likeliest he might find
The only two of mankind, but in them
The whole included race, his purposed prey.
In bower and field he sought, where any tuft
Of grove or garden-plot more pleasant lay,
Their tendance° or plantation for delight;
420 By fountain or by shady rivulet
He sought them both, but wished his hap might find
Eve separate; he wished, but not with hope
Of what so seldom chanced, when to his wish,
Beyond his hope, Eve separate he spies,
Veiled in a cloud of fragrance, where she stood,
Half spied, so thick the roses bushing round
About her glowed, oft stooping to support
Each flower of slender stalk, whose head though gay
Carnation, purple, azure, or specked with gold,
430 Hung drooping unsustained; them she upstays
Gently with myrtle band, mindless° the while,
Herself, though fairest unsupported flower,
From her best prop° so far, and storm so nigh.
Nearer he drew, and many a walk traversed
Of stateliest covert, cedar, pine, or palm,
Then voluble° and bold, now hid, now seen
Among thick-woven arborets° and flowers
Embordered on each bank, the hand of Eve:
Spot more delicious than those gardens feigned°
440 Or of revived Adonis, or renowned
Alcinous, host of old Laertes' son,°
Or that, not mystic, where the sapient king°
Held dalliance with his fair Egyptian spouse.
Much he the place admired, the person more.
As one who long in populous city pent,
Where houses thick and sewers annoy the air,
Forth issuing on a summer's morn to breathe
Among the pleasant villages and farms
Adjoined, from each thing met conceives delight,

Mere serpent He did not look like Northern Renaissance pictures of the temptation of Eve, in which the serpent has a human head.
tendance something to be tended
mindless heedless
her best prop Cf. ll. 210 and 219n.
voluble coiling; perhaps now in the sense of "glib" as well

arborets shrubs
feigned imagined; see *The Faerie Queene* III.vi, and Chapman's translation of the corresponding passage from Homer
Laertes' son Ulysses
not mystic . . . king Solomon's garden, real, historical biblical, hence not mythical like the garden of Adonis ("mystic")

450 The smell of grain, or tedded° grass, or kine,°
Or dairy, each rural sight, each rural sound;
If chance with nymph-like step fair virgin pass,
What pleasing seemed, for her now pleases more,
She most, and in her look sums all delight:
Such pleasure took the Serpent to behold
This flowery plat,° the sweet recess of Eve
Thus early, thus alone; her heavenly form
Angelic, but more soft and feminine,
Her graceful innocence, her every air
460 Of gesture or least action overawed
His malice, and with rapine sweet bereaved
His fierceness of the fierce intent it brought.
That space the evil one abstracted stood
From his own evil, and for the time remained
Stupidly° good, of enmity disarmed,
Of guile, of hate, of envy, of revenge;
But the hot hell that always in him burns,
Though in mid-heaven, soon ended his delight,
And tortures him now more, the more he sees
470 Of pleasure not for him ordained; then soon
Fierce hate he recollects, and all his thoughts
Of mischief, gratulating,° thus excites:
  'Thoughts, whither have ye led me, with what sweet
Compulsion thus transported to forget
What hither brought us? Hate, not love, nor hope
Of Paradise for hell, hope here to taste
Of pleasure, but all pleasure to destroy,
Save what is in destroying; other joy
To me is lost. Then let me not let pass
480 Occasion which now smiles: behold alone
The woman, opportune° to all attempts,
Her husband, for I view far round, not nigh,
Whose higher intellectual° more I shun,
And strength, of courage haughty, and of limb
Heroic built, though of terrestrial mould,°
Foe not informidable, exempt from wound,
I not; so much hath hell debased, and pain
Enfeebled me, to what I was in heaven.
She fair, divinely fair, fit love for gods,
490 Not terrible, though terror be in love
And beauty, not° approached by stronger hate,
Hate stronger, under show of love well feigned,

---

tedded spread out for haymaking
kine cattle
plat plot of ground
Stupidly stupefied (and thus incapable, for the
moment, of evil)

gratulating expressing pleasure
opportune opportunely placed
intellectual mind
terrestrial mould formed of earth
not if not

The way which to her ruin now I tend.'
    So spake the Enemy of mankind, enclosed
In serpent, inmate bad, and toward Eve
Addressed his way, not with indented wave,
Prone on the ground, as since, but on his rear,
Circular base of rising folds, that towered
Fold above fold a surging maze; his head
500   Crested aloft, and carbuncle his eyes;
With burnished neck of verdant gold, erect
Amidst his circling spires,° that on the grass
Floated redundant.° Pleasing was his shape,
And lovely, never since of serpent kind
Lovelier; not those that in Illyria changed
Hermione and Cadmus,° or the god
In Epidaurus;° nor to which transformed
Ammonian Jove,° or Capitoline° was seen,
He with Olympias, this with her who bore
510   Scipio, the highth of Rome. With tract° oblique
At first, as one who sought accéss, but feared
To interrupt, sidelong he works his way.
As when a ship by skilful steersman wrought
Nigh river's mouth or foreland, where the wind
Veers oft, as oft so steers, and shifts her sail,
So varied he, and of his tortuous train
Curled many a wanton wreath in sight of Eve,
To lure her eye; she busied heard the sound
Of rustling leaves, but minded not, as used
520   To such disport before her through the field
From every beast, more duteous at her call
Than at Circean call the herd disguised.°
He bolder now, uncalled before her stood,
But as in gaze admiring. Oft he bowed
His turret crest, and sleek enamelled neck,
Fawning, and licked the ground whereon she trod.
His gentle dumb expression turned at length
The eye of Eve to mark his play; he glad
Of her attention gained, with serpent tongue
530   Organic,° or impulse of vocal air,
His fraudulent temptation thus began:
    'Wonder not, sovereign mistress, if perhaps
Thou canst, who art sole wonder, much less arm
Thy looks, the heaven of mildness, with disdain,

spires spirals
redundant excessively flowing, wave-like
Hermione and Cadmus Hermione (Harmonia)
and her king were changed into serpents.
god In Epidaurus Aesculapius' statue in Epidaurus represented the god of healing as an
erect serpent.
Ammonian Jove Jupiter took Olympias, Alexander the Great's mother, in the form of a
snake; Capitoline Jupiter, similarly, the father
of the Roman general Scipio Africanus.
tract path
herd disguised Ulysses' men turned by Circe
into pigs
Organic instrumental

Displeased that I approach thee thus, and gaze
Insatiate, I thus single, nor have feared
Thy awful brow, more awful thus retired.
Fairest resemblance of thy maker fair,
Thee all things living gaze on, all things thine
540 By gift, and thy celestial beauty adore,
With ravishment beheld, there best beheld
Where universally admired; but here
In this enclosure wild, these beasts among,
Beholders rude, and shallow to discern
Half what in thee is fair, one man except,
Who sees thee? (and what is one?) who shouldst be seen
A goddess among gods, adored and served
By angels numberless, thy daily train.'
    So glozed° the Tempter, and his proem tuned;
550 Into the heart of Eve his words made way,
Though at the voice much marvelling; at length
Not unamazed she thus in answer spake:
    'What may this mean? Language of man pronounced
By tongue of brute, and human sense expressed?
The first at least of these I thought denied
To beasts, whom God on their creation-day
Created mute to all articulate sound;
The latter I demur,° for in their looks
Much reason, and in their actions oft appears.
560 Thee, Serpent, subtlest beast of all the field
I knew, but not with human voice endued;
Redouble then this miracle, and say,
How cam'st thou speakable of mute,° and how
To me so friendly grown above the rest
Of brutal kind, that daily are in sight?
Say, for such wonder claims attention due.'
    To whom the guileful tempter thus replied:
'Empress of this fair world, resplendent Eve,
Easy to me it is to tell thee all
570 What thou command'st, and right thou shouldst be obeyed.
I was at first as other beasts that graze
The trodden herb, of abject° thoughts and low,
As was my food, nor aught but food discerned
Or sex, and apprehended nothing high:
Till on a day roving the field, I chanced
A goodly tree far distant to behold,
Loaden with fruit of fairest colours mixed,
Ruddy and gold. I nearer drew to gaze;

glozed flattered
The latter I demur I have doubts about
"human sense expressed"—obviously, animals
communicate, but don't have language

speakable of mute capable of speech, from
being mute
abject cast down

When from the boughs a savoury odour blown,
580   Grateful to appetite, more pleased my sense
Than smell of sweetest fennel or the teats
Of ewe or goat dropping with milk at even,
Unsucked of lamb or kid, that tend their play.
To satisfy the sharp desire I had
Of tasting those fair apples,° I resolved
Not to defer;° hunger and thirst at once,
Powerful persuaders, quickened at the scent
Of that alluring fruit, urged me so keen.
About the mossy trunk I wound me soon,
590   For high from ground the branches would require
Thy utmost reach or Adam's: round the tree
All other beasts that saw, with like desire
Longing and envying stood, but could not reach.
Amid the tree now got, where plenty hung
Tempting so nigh, to pluck and eat my fill
I spared not, for such pleasure till that hour
At feed or fountain never had I found.
Sated at length, ere long I might perceive
Strange alteration in me, to degree°
600   Of reason in my inward powers, and speech
Wanted not long, though to this shape retained.
Thenceforth to speculations high or deep
I turned my thoughts, and with capacious mind
Considered all things visible in heaven,
Or earth, or middle,° all things fair and good;
But all that fair and good in thy divine
Semblance, and in thy beauty's heavenly ray
United I beheld; no fair to thine
Equivalent or second, which compelled
610   Me thus, though importune perhaps, to come
And gaze, and worship thee of right declared
Sovereign of creatures, universal dame.'°
    So talked the spirited° sly snake; and Eve
Yet more amazed unwary thus replied:
    'Serpent, thy overpraising leaves in doubt
The virtue° of that fruit, in thee first proved.
But say, where grows the tree, from hence how far?
For many are the trees of God that grow
In Paradise, and various, yet unknown
620   To us; in such abundance lies our choice
As leaves a greater store of fruit untouched,
Still hanging incorruptible, till men

---

apples The identification of the fruit with the
apple is folkloristic, not biblical.
defer delay
to degree to an extent

middle the air
dame mistress
spirited animated
virtue power

Grow up to their provision, and more hands
Help to disburden Nature of her birth.'
   To whom the wily adder, blithe and glad:
'Empress, the way is ready, and not long,
Beyond a row of myrtles, on a flat,
Fast by a fountain, one small thicket past
Of blowing° myrrh and balm; if thou accept
630   My conduct,° I can bring thee thither soon.'
   'Lead then,' said Eve. He leading swiftly rolled
In tangles, and made intricate seem straight,°
To mischief swift. Hope elevates, and joy
Brightens his crest, as when a wandering fire,
Compact° of unctuous vapour, which the night
Condenses, and the cold environs round,
Kindled through agitation to a flame,
Which oft, they say, some evil spirit attends,°
Hovering and blazing with delusive light,
640   Misleads the amazed night-wanderer from his way
To bogs and mires, and oft through pond or pool,
There swallowed up and lost, from succour far.
So glistered the dire Snake, and into fraud
Led Eve our credulous mother, to the tree
Of prohibition,° root of all our woe;
Which when she saw, thus to her guide she spake:
   'Serpent, we might have spared our coming hither,
Fruitless to me, though fruit be here to excess,
The credit of whose virtue rest with thee,
650   Wondrous indeed, if cause of such effects.
But of this tree we may not taste nor touch;
God so commanded, and left that command
Sole daughter of his voice;° the rest, we live
Law to ourselves, our reason is our law.'
   To whom the Tempter guilefully replied:
'Indeed? Hath God then said that of the fruit
Of all these garden trees ye shall not eat,
Yet lords declared of all in earth or air?'
   To whom thus Eve yet sinless: 'Of the fruit
660   Of each tree in the garden we may eat,
But of the fruit of this fair tree amidst
The garden, God hath said, "Ye shall not eat
Thereof, nor shall ye touch it, lest ye die."'

---

blowing blooming
conduct lead (the moral sense is there, unavowed)
intricate seem straight again, his shaky motion and his moral direction. From this moment on in human history, "crooked" and "straight" will have moral connotations.
Compact composed
evil spirit attends the *ignis fatuus,* or will-o'-the-wisp, often associated with self-delusion
tree Of prohibition prohibited tree. The impact of "root," following immediately in the metaphorical sense, and "fruitless" three lines further on, is strengthened by the literalness of "tree."
daughter of his voice the only commandment He enjoined on us

She scarce had said, though brief, when now more bold
The tempter, but with show of zeal and love
To man, and indignation at his wrong,
New part puts on, and as to passion moved,
Fluctuates° disturbed, yet comely, and in act
Raised, as of some great matter to begin.
670 As when of old some orator renowned
In Athens or free Rome, where eloquence
Flourished, since mute, to some great cause addressed,
Stood in himself collected, while each part,
Motion, each act won audience° ere the tongue,
Sometimes in highth° began, as no delay
Of preface brooking through his zeal of right:
So standing, moving, or to highth upgrown,
The tempter all impassioned thus began:
      'O sacred, wise, and wisdom-giving plant,
680 Mother of science,° now I feel thy power
Within me clear, not only to discern
Things in their causes, but to trace the ways
Of highest agents, deemed however wise.
Queen of this universe, do not believe
Those rigid threats of death; ye shall not die:
How should ye? By the fruit? It gives you life
To° knowledge; by the threatener? Look on me,
Me who have touched and tasted, yet both live,
And life more perfect have attained than fate
690 Meant me, by venturing higher than my lot.
Shall that be shut to man, which to the beast
Is open? Or will God incense his ire
For such a petty trespass, and not praise
Rather your dauntless virtue, whom the pain
Of death denounced,° whatever thing death be,
Deterred not from achieving what might lead
To happier life, knowledge of good and evil?
Of good, how just? Of evil, if what is evil
Be real, why not known, since easier shunned?
700 God therefore cannot hurt ye, and be just;
Not just, not God; not feared then, nor obeyed:
Your fear itself of death removes the fear.
Why then was this forbid? Why but to awe,
Why but to keep ye low and ignorant,
His worshippers? He knows that in the day
Ye eat thereof, your eyes that seem so clear,
Yet are but dim, shall perfectly be then
Opened and cleared, and ye shall be as gods,

Fluctuates changes appearance   science knowledge
audience attention   To as well as
highth height of feeling   denounced proclaimed

Knowing both good and evil as they know.
710   That ye should be as gods, since I as man,
Internal man,° is but proportion meet,
I of brute human, ye of human gods.
So ye shall die perhaps, by putting off
Human, to put on gods,° death to be wished,
Though threatened, which no worse than this can bring.
And what are gods that man may not become
As they, participating° godlike food?
The gods are first, and that advantage use
On our belief, that all from them proceeds;
720   I question it, for this fair earth I see,
Warmed by the sun, producing every kind,
Them nothing. If they° all things, who enclosed
Knowledge of good and evil in this tree,
That whoso eats thereof, forthwith attains
Wisdom without their leave? And wherein lies
The offence, that man should thus attain to know?
What can your knowledge hurt him, or this tree
Impart against his will, if all be his?
Or is it envy, and can envy dwell
730   In heavenly breasts? These, these and many more
Causes import° your need of this fair fruit.
Goddess humane,° reach then, and freely taste!'
He ended, and his words replete with guile
Into her heart too easy entrance won.
Fixed on the fruit she gazed, which to behold
Might tempt alone, and in her ears the sound
Yet rung of his persuasive words, impregned
With reason, to her seeming, and with truth;
Meanwhile the hour of noon° drew on, and waked
740   An eager appetite, raised by the smell
So savoury of that fruit, which with desire,
Inclinable now grown to touch or taste,
Solicited her longing eye; yet first
Pausing a while, thus to herself she mused:
'Great are thy virtues, doubtless, best of fruits,
Though kept from man, and worthy to be admired,
Whose taste, too long forborne, at first assay
Gave elocution° to the mute, and taught

Internal man See above, l. 600, where Satan claims that his inner state has become human through the agency of the fruit.
put on gods Satan brilliantly and nastily adapts the language of Colossians 3:9–10 to his perverse construction of spiritual regeneration: "Lie not one to another, seeing that ye have put off the old man with his deeds; And have put on the new man, which is renewed in knowledge after the image of him that created him."
participating sharing

they they produced
import indicate
Goddess humane "Human," the first reading, concludes Satan's rhetoric with a blatant oxymoron; the second sense, "gentle," is only to mellow it in afterthought.
noon The tasting and falling must occur at noon, less light be denied, and reason be cheated.
elocution eloquence

The tongue not made for speech to speak thy praise.
750 Thy praise he also who forbids thy use
Conceals not from us, naming thee the Tree
Of Knowledge, knowledge both of good and evil;
Forbids us then to taste, but his forbidding
Commends thee more, while it infers the good
By thee communicated, and our want;
For good unknown sure is not had, or had
And yet unknown, is as not had at all.
In plain° then, what forbids he but to know,
Forbids us good, forbids us to be wise?
760 Such prohibitions bind not. But if Death
Bind us with after-bands, what profits then
Our inward freedom? In the day we eat
Of this fair fruit, our doom is, we shall die.
How dies the serpent? He hath eaten and lives,
And knows, and speaks, and reasons, and discerns,
Irrational till then. For us alone
Was death invented? Or to us denied
This intellectual food, for beasts reserved?
For beasts it seems—yet that one beast which first
770 Hath tasted, envies not, but brings with joy
The good befallen him, author unsuspect,°
Friendly to man, far from deceit or guile.
What fear I then, rather what know to fear
Under this ignorance of good and evil,
Of God or death, of law or penalty?
Here grows the cure° of all, this fruit divine,
Fair to the eye, inviting to the taste,
Of virtue° to make wise; what hinders then
To reach, and feed at once both body and mind?'
780   So saying, her rash hand in evil hour°
Forth reaching to the fruit, she plucked, she eat.°
Earth felt the wound, and Nature from her seat
Sighing through all her works gave signs of woe,
That all was lost.° Back to the thicket slunk
The guilty Serpent, and well might, for Eve
Intent now wholly on her taste, naught else
Regarded; such delight till then, as seemed,
In fruit she never tasted, whether true
Or fancied so, through expectation high
790 Of knowledge, nor was godhead from her thought.
Greedily she engorged without restraint,

In plain put simply
author unsuspect unsuspected authority
cure The secondary sense is "charge, responsibility."
Of virtue able

evil hour Our sense that "evil" puns on "Eve"
is confirmed at l. 1067.
eat ate
Nature . . . lost Nature only sighs in pain
here, but see ll. 1000–1004.

And knew not eating death,° Satiate at length,
And heightened as with wine, jocund and boon,°
Thus to herself she pleasingly began:
    'O sovereign, virtuous, precious of all trees
In Paradise, of operation° blest
To sapience, hitherto obscured, infamed,
And thy fair fruit let hang, as to no end
Created; but henceforth my early care,
800   Not without song, each morning, and due praise,
Shall tend thee, and the fertile burden ease
Of thy full branches offered free to all;
Till dieted by thee I grow mature
In knowledge, as the gods° who all things know;
Though others envy what they cannot give;
For had the gift been theirs, it had not here
Thus grown. Experience, next to thee I owe,
Best guide; not following thee, I had remained
In ignorance; thou open'st wisdom's way,
810   And giv'st accéss, though secret she retire.
And I perhaps am secret;° heaven is high,
High and remote to see from thence distinct
Each thing on earth; and other care perhaps
May have diverted from continual watch
Our Great Forbidder, safe° with all his spies
About him. But to Adam in what sort
Shall I appear? Shall I to him make known
As yet my change, and give him to partake
Full happiness with me, or rather not,
820   But keep the odds of knowledge in my power
Without copartner? So to add what wants
In female sex, the more to draw his love,
And render me more equal, and perhaps—
A thing not undesirable—sometime
Superior; for inferior who is free?°
This may be well. But what if God have seen,
And death ensue? Then I shall be no more,
And Adam wedded to another Eve
Shall live with her enjoying, I extinct;
830   A death to think.° Confirmed then I resolve,
Adam shall share with me in bliss or woe.
So dear I love him, that with him all deaths
I could endure, without him live no life.'

---

knew not eating death knew not that she was
eating death
boon jolly
operation effectiveness
gods Echoes Satan's equivocal use of the plural
in ll. 712, 718, and I.116.
secret hidden, secreted

safe of no danger
for inferior who is free? The rhetorical questioning and the political theory are both recognizably Satan's.
A death to think Having literalized death by her
act, Eve's using the word figuratively is in
odious taste.

So saying, from the tree her step she turned,
But first low reverence done,° as to the power
That dwelt within, whose presence had infused
Into the plant sciential° sap, derived
From nectar, drink of gods.° Adam the while
Waiting desirous her return, had wove
840   Of choicest flowers a garland to adorn
Her tresses, and her rural labours crown,
As reapers oft are wont their harvest queen.
Great joy he promised to his thoughts, and new
Solace in her return, so long delayed;
Yet oft his heart, divine° of something ill,
Misgave him; he the faltering measure° felt;
And forth to meet her went, the way she took
That morn when first they parted. By the Tree
Of Knowledge he must pass; there he her met,
850   Scarce from the tree returning; in her hand
A bough of fairest fruit that downy smiled,
New gathered, and ambrosial smell diffused.
To him she hasted; in her face excuse
Came prologue, and apology to prompt,°
Which with bland words at will she thus addressed:
   'Hast thou not wondered, Adam, at my stay?
Thee I have missed, and thought it long, deprived
Thy presence, agony of love till now
Not felt, nor shall be twice, for never more
860   Mean I to try what rash untried I sought,
The pain of absence from thy sight. But strange
Hath been the cause, and wonderful to hear:
This tree is not as we are told, a tree
Of danger° tasted, nor to evil unknown
Opening the way, but of divine effect
To open eyes, and make them gods who taste;
And hath been tasted° such. The serpent wise,
Or° not restrained as we, or not obeying,
Hath eaten of the fruit, and is become
870   Not dead, as we are threatened, but thenceforth
Endued with human voice and human sense,
Reasoning to admiration, and with me
Persuasively hath so prevailed, that I
Have also tasted, and have also found

---

low reverence done a bow, the first act of idolatry, and the first myth. Eve is worshiping a Dryad of some sort by treating the power in the fruit in this way.
sciential knowledge-giving
nectar, drink of gods Her personal religion implies a whole pagan pantheon.

divine prophet
faltering measure irregular heartbeat
prologue . . . prompt These are theatrical terms: Eve's facial expression is visible before she speaks, like a prologue to a play; cf. IX.670–76.
Of danger of danger if
tasted tested
Or either

The effects to correspond, opener° mine eyes,
Dim erst, dilated spirits, ampler heart,
And growing up to godhead; which for thee
Chiefly I sought, without thee can despise.
For bliss, as thou hast part, to me is bliss;
880   Tedious, unshared with thee, and odious soon.
Thou therefore also taste, that equal lot
May join us, equal joy, as equal love;
Lest thou not tasting, different degree
Disjoin us, and I then too late renounce
Deity for thee, when fate will not permit.'
    Thus Eve with countenance blithe her story told;
But in her cheek distemper° flushing glowed.
On the other side, Adam, soon as he heard
The fatal trespass done by Eve, amazed,
890   Astonied° stood and blank, while horror chill
Ran through his veins, and all his joints relaxed;
From his slack hand the garland wreathed for Eve
Down dropped, and all the faded roses° shed.
Speechless he stood and pale, till thus at length
First to himself he inward silence broke:
    'O fairest of creation, last and best
Of all God's works, creature in whom excelled
Whatever can to sight or thought be formed,
Holy, divine, good, amiable,° or sweet!
900   How art thou lost, how on a sudden lost,
Defaced, deflowered,° and now to death devote!°
Rather how hast thou yielded to transgress
The strict forbiddance, how to violate
The sacred fruit forbidden! Some cursèd fraud
Of enemy hath beguiled thee, yet unknown,
And me with thee hath ruined, for with thee
Certain my resolution is to die;
How can I live without thee, how forgo
Thy sweet converse and love so dearly joined,
910   To live again in these wild woods forlorn?°
Should God create another Eve, and I
Another rib afford, yet loss of thee
Would never from my heart; no, no! I feel
The link of nature draw me: flesh of flesh,
Bone of my bone thou art,° and from thy state

opener The insistence on this word arises from
Genesis 3:7, "And the eyes of them both were
opened" (this is shortly to occur), but its force
comes from our ironic realization that her act
has closed off everything.
distemper intoxication, disorder of temperament
Astonied petrified, paralyzed
faded roses the first instance of natural cycle,
of withering flowers
amiable lovely

deflowered in a host of senses, given the
association of Eve with flowers throughout
devote cursed
To live . . . forlorn To see Adam think of
Eden as "wild woods" is touching; to see,
through the ambiguous syntax, that "forlorn"
can mean the woods, Eden, as well as the
speaker, is tragic.
flesh . . . art echoing IV.483

Mine never shall be parted, bliss or woe.'
    So having said, as one from sad dismay
Recomforted, and after thoughts disturbed
Submitting to what seemed remédiless,
920   Thus in calm mood his words to Eve he turned:
    'Bold deed thou hast presumed, adventurous Eve,
And peril great provoked, who thus hast dared
Had it been only coveting to eye
That sacred fruit, sacred to abstinence,
Much more to taste it under ban to touch.
But past who can recall, or done undo?
Not God omnipotent, nor fate. Yet so
Perhaps thou shalt not die; perhaps the fact°
Is not so heinous now, foretasted fruit,
930   Profaned first by the Serpent, by him first
Made common and unhallowed ere our taste,
Nor yet on him found deadly; he yet lives,
Lives, as thou saidst, and gains to live as man
Higher degree of life, inducement strong
To us, as likely tasting to attain
Proportional ascent, which cannot be
But to be gods, or angels, demi-gods.
Nor can I think that God, Creator wise,
Though threatening, will in earnest so destroy
940   Us his prime creatures, dignified so high,
Set over all his works, which in our fall,
For us created, needs with us must fail,
Dependent made; so God shall uncreate,
Be frustrate, do, undo, and labour lose,°
Not well conceived of God, who though his power
Creation could repeat, yet would be loth
Us to abolish, lest the adversary
Triumph and say,° *"Fickle their state whom God
Most favours, who can please him long? Me first
950   He ruined, now mankind; whom will he next?"*
Matter of scorn not to be given the foe;
However, I with thee have fixed my lot,
Certain° to undergo like doom: if death
Consort with thee, death is to me as life;
So forcible within my heart I feel
The bond of nature draw me to my own,
My own in thee, for what thou art is mine;
Our state cannot be severed; we are one,
One flesh; to lose thee were to lose myself.'

---

fact deed, crime
lose or perhaps, "loose," in the sense of
"undo"
say Even before tasting the fruit himself, Adam

has become sensitive to Satanic rhetoric: he
parodies the adversary too well.
Certain resolved

960   So Adam, and thus Eve to him replied:
'O glorious trial of exceeding love,
Illustrious evidence, example high!
Engaging me to emulate, but short
Of thy perfection, how shall I attain,
Adam, from whose dear side I boast me sprung,
And gladly of our union hear thee speak,
One heart, one soul in both; whereof good proof
This day affords, declaring thee resolved,
Rather than death or aught than death more dread
970   Shall separate us, linked in love so dear,
To undergo with me one guilt, one crime,
If any be, of tasting this fair fruit,
Whose virtue (for of good still good proceeds,
Direct, or by occasion) hath presented
This happy trial of thy love, which else
So eminently never had been known.
Were it I thought death menaced would ensue
This my attempt, I would sustain alone
The worst, and not persuade thee, rather die
980   Deserted, than oblige° thee with a fact
Pernicious to thy peace, chiefly assured°
Remarkably so late of thy so true,
So faithful love unequalled; but I feel
Far otherwise the event,° not death, but life
Augmented, opened eyes, new hopes, new joys,
Taste so divine, that what of sweet before
Hath touched my sense, flat seems to this and harsh.
On my experience, Adam, freely taste,
And fear of death deliver to the winds.'
990   So saying, she embraced him, and for joy
Tenderly wept, much won that he his love
Had so ennobled, as of choice to incur
Divine displeasure for her sake, or death.
In recompense (for such compliance bad
Such recompense best merits) from the bough
She gave him of that fair enticing fruit
With liberal hand. He scrupled not to eat
Against his better knowledge, not deceived,
But fondly overcome with female charm.
1000   Earth trembled from her entrails, as again
In pangs, and Nature gave a second groan;
Sky loured and, muttering thunder,° some sad drops

oblige involve in guilt
chiefly assured especially with the assurance
event result
muttering thunder the first thunderstorm, imprinting on all subsequent storms, particularly in myth (Shakespearean tempests, etc.), traces of this original rupture between man and his garden, this birth of the natural environment. From the point of view of a 16th-century usage, Nature, cracking, is decaying into "nature"— physical and biological dispositions (see Fulke Greville, "O Wearisome Condition of Humanity").

Wept at completing of the mortal sin
Original;° while Adam took no thought,
Eating his fill, nor Eve to iterate
Her former trespass feared, the more to soothe
Him with her loved society, that now
As with new wine intoxicated both
They swim in mirth, and fancy that they feel
1010   Divinity within them breeding wings°
Wherewith to scorn the earth. But that false fruit
Far other operation first displayed,
Carnal desire inflaming: he on Eve
Began to cast lascivious eyes, she him
As wantonly repaid; in lust they burn,
Till Adam thus 'gan Eve to dalliance move:
    'Eve, now I see thou art exact of taste,°
And elegant, of sapience no small part;
Since to each meaning savour we apply,
1020   And palate call judicious; I the praise
Yield thee, so well this day thou hast purveyed.°
Much pleasure we have lost, while we abstained
From this delightful fruit, nor known till now
True relish, tasting; if such pleasure be
In things to us forbidden, it might be wished
For this one tree had been forbidden ten.°
But come, so well refreshed, now let us play,
As meet is, after such delicious fare;
For never did thy beauty since the day
1030   I saw thee first and wedded thee, adorned
With all perfections, so inflame my sense
With ardour to enjoy thee, fairer now
Than ever, bounty of this virtuous tree.'
    So said he, and forbore not glance or toy
Of amorous intent, well understood
Of Eve, whose eye darted contagious fire.
Her hand he seized,° and to a shady bank,
Thick overhead with verdant roof embowered,
He led her nothing loth; flowers were the couch,
1040   Pansies, and violets, and asphodel,
And hyacinth, earth's freshest softest lap.
There they their fill of love and love's disport

---

sin Original that one, first, comprehensive disobedience, containing a host of others "which our first parents, and in them all their posterity, committed," as Milton says in the *Christian Doctrine*
breeding wings This is an expansion of Eve's first intoxication, at l. 793, and an ironic fulfillment of the trip in her dream (V.86–90).
exact of taste having "good taste" (discernment, moral and esthetic wisdom). Like so many fundamental dramatic ironies affecting the in-

stitution of human death, this word-play, unwitting on Adam's part, perhaps, is in the worst taste imaginable.
purveyed provided
ten ten times over. Now that they are mortal, number games seem appealing; now that there will never be world enough and time, the counting starts.
seized The word has all the strength of "grabbed."

Took largely,° of their mutual guilt the seal,
The solace of their sin, till dewy sleep
Oppressed them, wearied with their amorous play.°
Soon as the force of that fallacious fruit,
That with exhilarating vapour bland
About their spirits had played, and inmost powers
Made err, was now exhaled, and grosser sleep°
1050   Bred of unkindly° fumes, with conscious dreams
Encumbered, now had left them, up they rose
As from unrest, and each the other viewing,
Soon found their eyes how opened, and their minds
How darkened; innocence, that as a veil
Had shadowed them° from knowing ill, was gone;
Just confidence, and native righteousness,
And honour from about them, naked left
To guilty shame; he covered, but his robe
Uncovered more. So rose the Danite strong,
1060   Herculean Samson, from the harlot-lap
Of Philistéan Dálilah, and waked
Shorn of his strength, they destitute and bare
Of all their virtue. Silent, and in face
Confounded, long they sat, as strucken mute,
Till Adam, though not less than Eve abashed,
At length gave utterance to these words constrained:
    'O Eve, in evil hour° thou didst give ear
To that false worm, of whomsoever taught
To counterfeit man's voice, true in our fall,
1070   False in our promised rising; since our eyes
Opened we find indeed, and find we know
Both good and evil, good lost and evil got,
Bad fruit of knowledge, if this be to know,
Which leaves us naked thus, of honour void,
Of innocence, of faith, of purity,
Our wonted ornaments now soiled and stained,
And in our faces evident the signs
Of foul concupiscence; whence evil store,
Even shame, the last° of evils; of the first
1080   Be sure then. How shall I behold the face
Henceforth of God or angel, erst with joy
And rapture so oft beheld? Those heavenly shapes

their fill . . . largely Milton quotes Proverbs
7:18, where a prostitute uses these phrases.
amorous play This is the first act of fallen sex,
casual and desperate in its needed effects of
consolation, "of their mutual guilt the seal"—
and guilt for the disobedience of eating the
fruit. The horror of "honour dishonourable" is
that they will now feel guilt about the sex,
certainly the one thing for which they should
not. In their shame (ll. 1092–93) they wish not
to cover the mouths that ate, but the innocent

parts of love. This is the horror of the Fall, and
the means by which sin infects life around it.
grosser sleep as opposed to the "airy light"
sleep at V.4
unkindly unnatural
shadowed them The figurative, inner moral
shade being removed, Adam and Eve will
begin to feel the pain of light (ll. 1080–90).
Eve . . . hour The pun is now Adam's.
last least

Will dazzle now this earthly,° with their blaze
Insufferably bright. O might I here
In solitude live savage, in some glade
Obscured, where highest woods impenetrable
To star or sunlight, spread their umbrage° broad
And brown as evening! Cover me, ye pines,
Ye cedars, with innumerable boughs
1090   Hide me, where I may never see them° more.
But let us now, as in bad plight, devise
What best may for the present serve to hide
The parts of each from other that seem most
To shame obnoxious,° and unseemliest seen,
Some tree whose broad smooth leaves together sewed,
And girded on our loins, may cover round
Those middle parts, that this newcomer, shame,
There sit not, and reproach us as unclean.'
    So counselled he, and both together went
1100   Into the thickest wood; there soon they chose
The fig-tree,° not that kind for fruit renowned,
But such as at this day to Indians known
In Malabar or Deccan° spreads her arms
Branching so broad and long, that in the ground
The bended twigs take root, and daughters grow
About the mother tree, a pillared shade
High overarched, and echoing walks between;
There oft the Indian herdsman shunning heat
Shelters in cool, and tends his pasturing herds
1110   At loop-holes cut through thickest shade. Those leaves
They gathered, broad as Amazonian targe,
And with what skill they had, together sewed,
To gird their waist, vain covering if to hide
Their guilt and dreaded shame, O how unlike
To that first naked glory! Such of late
Columbus found the American so girt
With feathered cincture, naked else and wild
Among the trees on isles and woody shores.
Thus fenced, and as they thought, their shame in part
1120   Covered, but not at rest or ease of mind,
They sat them down to weep; nor only tears
Rained at their eyes, but high winds worse within°
Began to rise, high passions, anger, hate,

---

earthly earthly shape
umbrage shade
them the "heavenly shapes" of l. 1082
obnoxious exposed
fig-tree The elaborate, encyclopedic digression occurs here to reinforce the enormity of the institution of clothing; by the description of the Indian banyan tree, and by the allusion to Caribbean savages (ll. 1116–18), we now see Adam and Eve as having suddenly become not Primal man but merely Primitive man. "And

with what skill they had" (l. 1112) betokens the touching but inadequate technology of paleo-lithic people.
Malabar or Deccan on the southwest Indian coast, or the southern peninsula of the subcontinent
Rained . . . within The first thunderstorm has been internalized, the Renaissance microcosmic view of man now becoming an adequate model for comprehending the relation of man and nature.

Mistrust, suspicion, discord, and shook sore
Their inward state of mind, calm region once
And full of peace, now tossed and turbulent;
For understanding ruled not, and the will
Heard not her lore, both in subjection now
To sensual appetite, who from beneath
1130   Usurping over sovereign reason claimed
Superior sway.° From thus distempered breast,
Adam, estranged° in look and altered style,
Speech intermitted thus to Eve renewed:
       'Would thou hadst hearkened to my words, and stayed
With me, as I besought thee, when that strange
Desire of wandering this unhappy morn,
I know not whence possessed thee; we had then
Remained still happy, not as now, despoiled
Of all our good, shamed, naked, miserable.°
1140   Let none henceforth seek needless cause to approve°
The faith they owe;° when earnestly they seek
Such proof, conclude they then begin to fail.'
       To whom, soon moved with touch of blame, thus Eve:
'What words have passed thy lips, Adam severe!
Imput'st thou that to my default, or will
Of wandering, as thou callest it, which who knows
But might as ill have happened thou being by,
Or to thyself perhaps? Hadst thou been there,
Or here the attempt, thou couldst not have discerned
1150   Fraud in the serpent, speaking as he spake;
No ground of enmity between us known
Why he should mean me ill, or seek to harm.
Was I to have never parted from thy side?
As good have grown there still a lifeless rib.
Being as I am, why didst not thou, the head,°
Command me absolutely not to go,
Going into such danger as thou saidst?
Too facile then, thou didst not much gainsay,
Nay didst permit, approve, and fair dismiss.
1160   Hadst thou been firm and fixed in thy dissent,
Neither had I transgressed, nor thou with me.'
       To whom then first incensed Adam replied:
'Is this the love, is this the recompense
Of mine to thee, ingrateful Eve, expressed°
Immutable when thou wert lost, not I,
Who might have lived and joyed° immortal bliss,

Superior sway greater power. The imagery in
ll. 1125–31 has moved from storm to political
discord.
estranged changed
shamed, naked, miserable See Hobbes's characterization of the life of man in the state of
nature: "Solitary, poor, nasty, brutish and

short" (*Leviathan*, 1651).
approve prove
owe own
head See IV.433n.
expressed revealed
joyed enjoyed

Yet willingly chose rather death with thee?
And am I now upbraided, as the cause
Of thy transgressing? Not enough severe,
1170   It seems, in thy restraint. What could I more?
I warned thee, I admonished thee, foretold
The danger, and the lurking enemy
That lay in wait; beyond this had been force,
And force upon free will hath here no place.
But confidence then bore thee on, secure
Either to meet no danger, or to find
Matter of glorious trial; and perhaps
I also erred in overmuch admiring
What seemed in thee so perfect, that I thought
1180   No evil durst attempt thee, but I rue
That error now, which is become my crime,
And thou the accuser. Thus it shall befall
Him who to worth in women overtrusting
Lets her will rule; restraint she will not brook,
And left to herself, if evil thence ensue,
She first his weak indulge will accuse.'
    Thus they in mutual accusation spent
The fruitless° hours, but neither self-condemning,
And of their vain contést appeared no end.

From *Book X*

[Man fallen, the guardian angels informed that it was not through their failure that the Fall occurred. Satan in triumph, Sin and Death depart from their locale at the gate of hell and enter the world. They build a broad causeway, over the realm of Chaos, connecting hell and the world, the prototype of all easy, populous routes. Satan decends to Pandemonium, where he delivers an address of victory, concluding with the exhortation, "What remains ye Gods, / But up and enter now into full bliss." As if in rhyme, applauding with a hiss, the demons (they are now serpents whose only song is hissing) they fall to a meal on the fruit of a multitude of replicas of the Forbidden Tree, but instead of fruit, they find themselves chewing "bitter ashes." Sin and Death now loose in the world, the latter to feed henceforth on all living things in order to surround man with continual emblems of his own end, God predicts the apocalypse and final revision of the created world. The details of the birth of fallen, biological nature are unfolded, and the introduction of inimical natural forces is followed by a long lament of self-recrimination from Adam which culminates in rhetoric reminiscent of Satan's: "O conscience, into what abyss of fears / And horrors hast thou driven me; out of which / I find no way, from deep to deeper plunged!"]

    Thus Adam to himself lamented loud
Through the still night, not now, as ere man fell,

---

fruitless with the pun still working from the
opening line of the poem

Wholesome and cool and mild, but with black air
Accompanied, with damps and dreadful gloom,
Which to his evil conscience represented
850   All things with double terror. On the ground
Outstretched he lay, on the cold ground, and oft
Cursed his creation, death as oft accused
Of tardy execution, since denounced°
The day of his offence. 'Why comes not death,'
Said he, 'with one thrice-ácceptáble stroke
To end me? Shall truth fail to keep her word,
Justice divine not hasten to be just?
But death comes not at call, justice divine
Mends not her slowest pace for prayers or cries.
860   O woods, O fountains, hillocks, dales, and bowers,
With other echo late I taught your shades
To answer, and resound far other song.'
Whom thus afflicted when sad Eve beheld,
Desolate where she sat, approaching nigh,
Soft words to his fierce passion she assayed:°
But her with stern regard he thus repelled:
    'Out of my sight, thou serpent!° that name best
Befits thee with him leagued, thyself as false
And hateful; nothing wants, but that thy shape,
870   Like his, and colour serpentine, may show
Thy inward fraud, to warn all creatures from thee
Henceforth; lest that too heavenly form, pretended°
To hellish falsehood, snare them. But for thee
I had persisted happy, had not thy pride
And wandering vanity, when least was safe,
Rejected my forewarning, and disdained
Not be trusted, longing to be seen
Though by the devil himself, him overweening
To overreach, but with the serpent meeting
880   Fooled and beguiled, by him thou, I by thee.
To trust thee from my side, imagined wise,
Constant, mature, proof against all assaults,
And understood not all was but a show
Rather than solid virtue, all but a rib
Crooked by nature, bent, as now appears,
More to the part siníster° from me drawn;
Well if thrown out, as supernumerary
To my just° number found. O why did God,

---

denounced announced (on)
assayed tried out
serpent An interpretive false etymology could connect "Eve" with a word for "serpent."
pretended held out in order to screen or disguise
sinister left side, but also "evil." It is Adam, not Milton (through Raphael, in his account of

the Creation in Bk. VII), who comes up with the traditional anti-feminist rhetoric and imagery here, in his self-loathing; according to some traditions, Eve came from Adam's left side where there was an extra ("supernumerary") rib.
just exact

Creator wise, that peopled highest heaven
890   With spirits masculine, create at last
This novelty on earth, this fair defect
Of Nature, and not fill the world at once
With men as angels without feminine,
Or find some other way to generate
Mankind? This mischief had not then befallen,
And more that shall befall, innumerable
Disturbances on earth through female snares,
And strait° conjunction with this sex. For either
He never shall find out fit mate, but such
900   As some misfortune brings him, or mistake,
Or whom he wishes most shall seldom gain,
Through her perverseness, but shall see her gained
By a far worse, or if she love, withheld
By parents, or his happiest choice too late
Shall meet, already linked and wedlock-bound
To a fell adversary, his hate or shame;
Which infinite calamity shall cause
To human life, and household peace confound.'
    He added not, and from her turned, but Eve,
910   Not so repulsed, with tears that ceased not flowing,
And tresses all disordered, at his feet
Fell humble, and embracing them, besought
His peace, and thus proceeded in her plaint:
    'Forsake me not thus, Adam, witness heaven
What love sincere and reverence in my heart
I bear thee, and unweeting° have offended,
Unhappily deceived; thy suppliant
I beg, and clasp thy knees; bereave me not
Whereon I live, thy gentle looks, thy aid,
920   Thy counsel in this uttermost distress,
My only strength and stay. Forlorn of thee,
Whither shall I betake me, where subsist?
While yet we live, scarce one short hour perhaps,
Between us two let there be peace, both joining,
As joined in injuries, one enmity
Against a foe by doom express assigned us,
That cruel serpent. On me exercise not
Thy hatred for this misery befallen,
On me already lost, me than thyself
930   More miserable. Both have sinned, but thou
Against God only, I against God and thee,
And to the place of judgment will return,
There with my cries importune heaven, that all
The sentence from thy head removed may light

strait intimate   unweeting unwitting

On me, sole cause to thee of all this woe,
Me, me only, just object of his ire.'
   She ended weeping, and her lowly plight,
Immovable° till peace obtained from fault
Acknowledged and deplored, in Adam wrought
940   Commiseration; soon his heart relented
Towards her, his life so late and sole delight,
Now at his feet submissive in distress,
Creature so fair his reconcilement seeking,
His counsel whom she had displeased, his aid;
As one disarmed, his anger all he lost,
And thus with peaceful words upraised her soon:
   'Unwary, and too desirous, as before
So now, of what thou know'st not, who desir'st
The punishment all on thyself; alas,
950   Bear thine own first, ill able to sustain
His full wrath whose thou feel'st as yet least part,
And my displeasure bear'st so ill. If prayers
Could alter high decrees, I to that place
Would speed before thee, and be louder heard,
That on my head all might be visited,
Thy frailty and infirmer sex forgiven,
To me committed and by me exposed.
But rise, let us no more contend, nor blame
Each other, blamed enough elsewhere,° but strive
960   In offices of love, how we may lighten
Each other's burden in our share of woe;
Since this day's death denounced,° if aught I see,
Will prove no sudden, but a slow-paced evil,
A long day's dying to augment our pain,
And to our seed (O hapless seed!) derived.'°
   To whom thus Eve, recovering heart, replied:
'Adam, by sad experiment I know
How little weight my words with thee can find,
Found so erroneous, thence by just event
970   Found so unfortunate; nevertheless,
Restored by thee, vile as I am, to place
Of new acceptance, hopeful to regain
Thy love, the sole contentment of my heart
Living or dying, from thee I will not hide
What thoughts in my unquiet breast are risen,
Tending to some relief of our extremes,
Or end, though sharp and sad, yet tolerable,
As in our evils, and of easier choice.

Immovable Modifies both "plight" and "Adam."
elsewhere in heaven?

death denounced here, as at l. 853, an echo
of that telling phrase in IX.695
derived descended

If care of our descent° perplex us most,
980   Which must be born to certain woe, devoured
By death at last (and miserable it is
To be to others cause of misery,
Our own begotten, and of our loins to bring
Into this cursèd world a woeful race,
That after wretched life must be at last
Food for so foul a monster), in thy power
It lies, yet ere conception, to prevent°
The race unblest, to being yet unbegot.
Childless thou art, childless remain; so death
990   Shall be deceived his glut, and with us two
Be forced to satisfy his ravenous maw.
But if thou judge it hard and difficult,
Conversing, looking, loving, to abstain
From love's due rites, nuptial embraces sweet,
And with desire to languish without hope,
Before the present object° languishing
With like desire—which would be misery
And torment less than none of what we dread
—Then both ourselves and seed at once to free
1000   From what we fear for both, let us make short,
Let us seek death, or he not found, supply
With our own hands his office on ourselves;
Why stand we longer shivering under fears
That show no end but death, and have the power,
Of many ways to die the shortest choosing,
Destruction with destruction to destroy?'°
    She ended here, or vehement despair
Broke off the rest; so much of death her thoughts
Had entertained as dyed her cheeks with pale.
1010   But Adam with such counsel nothing swayed,
To better hopes his more attentive mind
Labouring had raised, and thus to Eve replied:
    'Eve, thy contempt of life and pleasure seems
To argue in thee something more sublime°
And excellent than what thy mind contemns;
But self-destruction therefore sought refutes
That excellence thought in thee, and implies,
Not thy contempt, but anguish and regret
For loss of life and pleasure overloved.
1020   Or if thou covet death, as utmost end
Of misery, so thinking to evade

---

descent descendants
prevent preclude
object Eve
Destruction . . . destroy This ordinarily easy
paradox is more than rhetorical here, acknowledging the difficulty (". . . with destruction
. . .").

Eve thy . . . sublime In this scene we have
had Adam's ranting and Eve's genuine desperation; now, we have a clerical, moralizing tone
from Adam at the opening of this speech.

The penalty pronounced, doubt not but God
Hath wiselier armed his vengeful ire than so
To be forestalled; much more I fear lest death
So snatched will not exempt us from the pain
We are by doom° to pay; rather such acts
Of contumácy will prove the Highest
To make death in us live. Then let us seek
Some safer resolution, which methinks
1030   I have in view, calling to mind with heed
Part of our sentence, that thy seed shall bruise
The serpent's head;° piteous amends, unless
Be meant, whom I conjecture, our grand foe
Satan, who in the serpent hath contrived
Against us this deceit. To crush his head
Would be revenge indeed; which will be lost
By death brought on ourselves, or childless days
Resolved, as thou proposest; so our foe
Shall scape his punishment ordained, and we
1040   Instead shall double ours upon our heads.
No more be mentioned then of violence
Against ourselves, and wilful barrenness,
That cuts us off from hope, and savours only
Rancor and pride, impatience and despite,
Reluctance° against God and his just yoke
Laid on our necks. Remember with what mild
And gracious temper he both heard and judged,
Without wrath or reviling; we expected
Immediate dissolution, which we thought
1050   Was meant by death that day, when lo, to thee
Pains only in child-bearing were foretold,
And bringing forth, soon recompensed wth joy,
Fruit of thy womb; on me the curse aslope
Glanced on the ground: with labour I must earn
My bread; what harm? Idleness° had been worse;
My labour will sustain me; and lest cold
Or heat should injure us, his timely care
Hath unbesought provided, and his hands
Clothed us unworthy, pitying while he judged;
1060   How much more, if we pray him, will his ear
Be open, and his heart to pity incline,
And teach us further by what means to shun
The inclement seasons, rain, ice, hail, and snow,
Which now the sky with various face begins

doom judgment
bruise The serpent's head This prophecy from Genesis 3:15 is another glimpse of Eve's compensatory fulfillment promised at X.179, outlined in detail in Bk. XII.
Reluctance struggle
Idleness Notice that with the fall from perfection into biological nature, comes not only the institution of labor, but of its complement, idleness. Both idleness and its inner state, boredom, are generally regarded as faults in most contrived Utopias; in Paradise, they are not even conceivable.

To show us in this mountain, while the winds
Blow moist and keen, shattering the graceful locks
Of these fair spreading trees; which bids us seek
Some better shroud,° some better warmth to cherish
Our limbs benumbed, ere this diurnal star°
1070   Leave cold the night, how we his gathered beams
Reflected, may with matter sere° foment,
Or by collision of two bodies grind
The air attrite° to fire, as late the clouds,
Justling° or pushed with winds rude in their shock,
Tine° the slant lightning, whose thwart° flame driven down
Kindles the gummy bark of fir or pine,
And sends a comfortable heat from far,
Which might supply° the sun. Such fire to use,
And what may else be remedy or cure
1080   To evils which our own misdeeds have wrought,
He will instruct us praying,° and of grace
Beseeching him, so as we need not fear
To pass commodiously this life, sustained
By him with many comforts, till we end
In dust, our final rest and native home.
What better can we do, than to the place
Repairing where he judged us, prostrate fall
Before him reverent, and there confess
Humbly our faults, and pardon beg, with tears
1090   Watering the ground, and with our sighs the air
Frequenting,° sent from hearts contrite, in sign
Of sorrow unfeigned, and humiliation meek?
Undoubtedly he will relent and turn
From his displeasure; in whose look serene,
When angry most he seemed and most severe,
What else but favour, grace, and mercy shone?'
    So spake our father penitent, nor Eve
Felt less remorse. They forthwith to the place
Repairing where he judged them, prostrate fell
1100   Before him reverent, and both confessed
Humbly their faults, and pardon begged, with tears
Watering the ground, and with their sighs the air
Frequenting, sent from hearts contrite, in sign
Of sorrow unfeigned, and humiliation meek.

Book XI
[Books XI and XII form a reciprocal pair to the historical accounts recited
by Raphael to Adam and Eve in Books VI and VII; they are revealed, not

shroud shelter	**Tine** kindle (hence, "tinder")
diurnal star the sun	**thwart** transverse
sere dry	**supply** substitute for
attrite ground down	**praying** if we pray
Justling jostling	**Frequenting** crowding

narrated, and they are a vision of the future, not of the past, being selected glimpses of human history leading away from the Fall and toward the redemption and fulfillment of fallen man. Michael, commissioned by God to lead Adam and Eve out of Paradise forever, takes Adam to the top of a high hill, where he sees in vision the extent of the world and a pastoral scene which ends in the first human death, in the concrete sense: Cain's murder of Abel. "Death hast thou seen / In his first shape on man," says Michael, reminding us that the original of all deaths was a murder. Other episodes from biblical history are shown, leading up to the Flood.]

From *Book XII*

[Book XII resumes the vision of the human future, starting at a point "Betwixt the world destroyed and world restored," both in the broadest sense of history as an intermediate area between loss and reconstitution, and, in particular, as applying to the Flood and subsequent history. This leads to the promise of analogous redemptive fulfillment for Eve, in that the Son will manifest himself on earth in normal human form, born of woman; the Incarnation, Death, Resurrection, and Ascension of Christ are shown, and the history of his church on earth is mapped out until the Second Coming; the final overcoming of Satan is foretold, and a promise that "then the earth / Shall be all Paradise, far happier place / Than this of Eden, and far happier days."]

So spake the Archangel Michaël, then paused,
As at the world's great period; and our sire
Replete with joy and wonder thus replied:
'O goodness infinite, goodness immense!
470   That all this good of evil shall produce,
And evil turn to good;° more wonderful
Than that which by creation first brought forth
Light out of darkness! Full of doubt I stand,
Whether I should repent me now of sin
By me done and occasioned, or rejoice
Much more, that much more good thereof shall spring,
To God more glory, more good will to men
From God, and over wrath grace shall abound.°
But say, if our Deliverer up to heaven
480   Must reascend, what will betide the few
His faithful, left among the unfaithful herd,
The enemies of truth; who then shall guide
His people, who defend? Will they not deal
Worse with his followers than with him they dealt?'

---

evil turn to good This whole speech is an expression of the theme of the Fortunate Fall (from the hymn *O Felix Culpa:* "O lucky sin!"), completing the reversal of, and triumph over, Satan's plan "out of good still to find means of evil" (I.165). The Fortunate Fall paradox praises the first sin on the grounds that, without it, there would have been no need for a Redeemer; it is appropriate that Adam responds to Michael's prophecy of Christ's victory over Satan by invoking the paradox.
grace shall abound an important echo: "where sin abounded, grace did much more abound" (Romans 5:20); cf. Bunyan, *Grace Abounding to the Chief of Sinners* (1666)

'Be sure they will,' said the Angel; 'but from heaven
He to his own a Comforter° will send,
The promise of the Father, who shall dwell,
His Spirit, within them, and the law of faith
Working through love, upon their hearts shall write,
490   To guide them in all truth, and also arm
With spiritual armour,° able to resist
Satan's assaults, and quench his fiery darts,
What man can do against them, not afraid,
Though to the death, against such cruelties
With inward consolations recompensed,
And oft supported so as shall amaze
Their proudest persecutors. For the Spirit
Poured first on his apostles, whom he sends
To evangelize the nations, then on all
500   Baptized, shall them with wondrous gifts endue
To speak all tongues, and do all miracles,
As did their Lord before them.° Thus they win
Great numbers of each nation to receive
With joy the tidings brought from heaven: at length
Their ministry performed, and race well run,
Their doctrine and their story written left,
They die; but in their room, as they forewarn,
Wolves° shall succeed for teachers, grievous wolves,
Who all the sacred mysteries of heaven
510   To their own vile advantages shall turn
Of lucre and ambition, and the truth
With superstitions and traditions taint,
Left only in those written records pure,
Though not but by the Spirit understood.
Then shall they seek to avail themselves of names,
Places and titles, and with these to join
Secular power, though feigning still to act
By spiritual, to themselves appropriating
The Spirit of God, promised alike and given
520   To all believers; and from that pretence,
Spiritual laws by carnal power shall force
On every conscience; laws which none shall find
Left them enrolled, or what the Spirit within
Shall on the heart engrave. What will they then
But force the Spirit of Grace itself, and bind

Comforter the Holy Spirit (sent, according to
Milton, "by the Son, from the Father," and
thus an emanation of his power; cf. John
15:26)
spiritual armour from Ephesians 6:11–17, the
same armor the Red Cross Knight wears in Bk.
I of *The Faerie Queene*. All of Michael's discourse is full of scriptural allusions and echoes,
some of which will be identified.

For the Spirit . . . them (ll. 497–502) from
Acts 2
Wolves from Acts 20:29, also as used in
Lycidas, l. 128. This whole passage foresees
the decline of the institutional church, first
Roman, then Anglican, contrasting this with
the forever uncorrupted internalized authority
of conscience.

His consort Liberty,° what but unbuild
His living temples,° built by faith to stand,
Their own faith, not another's; for on earth
Who against faith and conscience can be heard
530   Infallible? Yet many will presume:
Whence heavy persecution shall arise
On all who in the worship persevere
Of spirit and truth; the rest, far greater part,
Will deem in outward rites and specious forms
Religion satisfied; Truth shall retire
Bestuck with slanderous darts, and works of faith
Rarely be found. So shall the world go on,
To good malignant, to bad men benign,
Under her own weight groaning,° till the day
540   Appear of respiration° to the just,
And vengeance to the wicked, at return
Of him so lately promised to thy aid,
The woman's seed, obscurely then foretold,
Now amplier known thy saviour and thy Lord,
Last in the clouds from heaven to be revealed
In glory of the Father, to dissolve
Satan with his perverted world; then raise
From the conflagrant mass, purged and refined,
New heavens, new earth,° ages of endless date
550   Founded in righteousness and peace and love,
To bring forth fruits,° joy and eternal bliss.'
      He ended; and thus Adam last replied:
'How soon hath thy prediction, seer blest,
Measured this transient world, the race of time,
Till time stand fixed: beyond is all abyss,
Eternity, whose end no eye can reach.
Greatly instructed I shall hence depart,
Greatly in peace of thought, and have my fill
Of knowledge, what this vessel can contain;
560   Beyond which was my folly to aspire.
Henceforth I learn that to obey is best,
And love with fear the only God, to walk
As in his presence, ever to observe
His providence, and on him sole depend,
Merciful over all his works, with good
Still overcoming evil,° and by small
Accomplishing great things, by things deemed weak
Subverting worldly strong, and worldly wise

consort Liberty II Corinthians 3:17
temples I Corinthians 3:17 and 6:19
groaning Romans 8:22, perhaps also a continuation of Nature's groans (IX.783, 1001) as Eve and Adam fall
respiration refreshment, rest
new earth The final apocalypse as envisioned here culminates in an allusion to Revelation 21:1: "And I saw a new heaven and a new earth."
fruits not the fruit of I.1, followed by "taste" and "woe," but appositively here by "joy and eternal bliss"
good . . . evil Romans 12:21

By simply meek; that suffering for truth's sake
570　Is fortitude to highest victory,
And to the faithful death the gate of life;
Taught this by his example whom I now
Acknowledge my redeemer ever blest.'
　　To whom thus also the Angel last replied:
'This having learnt, thou hast attained the sum
Of wisdom; hope no higher, though all the stars
Thou knew'st by name, and all the ethereal powers,
All secrets of the deep, all Nature's works,
Or works of God in heaven, air, earth, or sea,
580　And all the richest of this world enjoy'dst,
And all the rule, one empire; only add
Deeds to thy knowledge answerable, add faith,
Add virtue, patience, temperance, add love,
By name to come called charity,° the soul
Of all the rest: then wilt thou not be loth
To leave this Paradise, but shalt possess
A paradise within thee, happier far.°
Let us descend now therefore from this top
Of speculation;° for the hour precise
590　Exacts our parting hence; and see the guards,
By me encamped on yonder hill, expect°
Their motion, at whose front a flaming sword,
In signal of remove, waves fiercely round;
We may no longer stay: go, waken Eve;
Her also I with gentle dreams have calmed,
Portending good, and all her spirits composed
To meek submission: thou at season fit
Let her with thee partake what thou hast heard,
Chiefly what may concern her faith to know,
600　The great deliverance by her seed to come
(For by the woman's seed) on all mankind:
That ye may live, which will be many days,°
Both in one faith unanimous though sad,
With cause for° evils past, yet much more cheered
With meditation on the happy end.'
　　He ended, and they both descend the hill;
Descended, Adam to the bower where Eve
Lay sleeping ran before, but found her waked;
And thus with words not sad she him received:
610　'Whence thou return'st, and whither went'st, I know;

charity literally "love," from the Latin *caritas*, translating Greek *agapē*, as at I Corinthians 13, especially 13:13 (see section on The English Bible, above)
A paradise . . . far This final internalization of a lost exterior place also contrasts finally with Satan's "the mind is its own place" and the hell within him (IV.20); the rhythms of this authentic transfer continue into Eve's final words below.
top Of speculation mount of vision; see *Paradise Regained* IV.236n
expect await
many days 930 years, according to Genesis 5:5
With cause for in view of

For God is also in sleep, and dreams advise,
Which he hath sent propitious, some great good
Presaging, since with sorrow and heart's distress
Wearied I fell asleep. But now lead on;
In me is no delay; with thee to go,
Is to stay here;° without thee here to stay,
Is to go hence unwilling; thou to me
Art all things under heaven, all places thou,
Who for my wilful crime art banished hence.
620   This further consolation yet secure
I carry hence; though all by me is lost,
Such favour I unworthy am vouchsafed,
By me the promised seed shall all restore.'
    So spake our mother Eve, and Adam heard
Well pleased, but answered not; for now too nigh
The archangel stood, and from the other hill
To their fixed station, all in bright array
The Cherubim descended; on the ground
Gliding metéorous,° as evening mist
630   Risen from a river o'er the marish° glides,
And gathers ground fast at the labourer's heel
Homeward returning. High in front advanced,
The brandished sword of God before them blazed
Fierce as a comet; which with torrid heat,
And vapour as the Libyan air adust,°
Began to parch that temperate clime; whereat
In either hand the hastening Angel caught
Our lingering parents, and to the eastern gate
Led them direct, and down the cliff as fast
640   To the subjected° plain; then disappeared.
They, looking back, all the eastern side beheld
Of Paradise, so late their happy seat,
Waved over by that flaming brand, the gate
With dreadful faces thronged and fiery arms.
Some natural tears they dropped, but wiped them soon;
The world was all before them, where to choose
Their place of rest, and Providence their guide:
They hand in hand,° with wandering steps and slow,
Through Eden took their solitary° way.
1658?–1665?   1667

with thee . . . here not merely an echo of the Hebrew matriarch Ruth to her mother-in-law Naomi, "Whither thou goest, I will go, . . ." (Ruth 1:16), but an avowal of the loss the seed of compensation, and the ultimate arbitrariness of place, of location on the planet, in subsequent human history
metéorous in mid-air
marish marsh
adust parched

subjected lying below; but also subject to
hand in hand catching up the emblematic meaning present at the first appearance of the two, hand in hand (IV.321), but moving beyond hieroglyphic somehow to a larger human meaning; "wandering" and "slow" perhaps with overtones of error and hesitancy, but only with overtones
solitary They are together, which is to say, Man is alone.

Paradise Regained

Written between the publication of *Paradise Lost* (1667) and 1670, *Paradise Regained* was published with *Samson Agonistes* in 1671. It is of the genre "brief epic," of which the ultimate model was the Book of Job. Milton takes the account of the temptation in the wilderness from Luke 4:1–13, and treats it as a victory over sin which prefigures the later victory over death at the Crucifixion. He also follows a tradition of the exegetes whereby this is a *total* temptation; they built on St. Luke's words, "all the temptation" in v.13. The scheme Milton follows is almost exactly that of Marvell's *Dialogue Between the Resolved Soul and Created Pleasure,* though there are other parallels; for example, as the second Adam, Jesus rejects the tempta- tions (gluttony, ambition, avarice) which the first accepted. Christian heroic virtue resides in "humiliation and strong sufferance" and not, like pagan heroism, in action. Consequently Jesus does nothing except decline what is offered, and finally, when swept up to the pinnacle of the temple, he simply stands still. This is his initiation into the new and higher heroism, a point which Milton enforces by frequent favorable comparisons with pagan heroes.

He first rejects the sensual banquet arranged by Satan; he prefers a celestial banquet, and gets one at the end of the poem. Then he turns down earthly honor, favoring heavenly honor, which does not depend on what fallible and foolish men say about one, but on the testimony of God. The military power of Persia he rejects "unmoved," and also the more significant power of Rome. He turns down the earthly in favor of the heavenly city. The final temptation, before the crisis at the temple, is that of knowledge. Satan, having failed with "the kingdoms of this world," tries instead, in the great encomium of Athens, the temptations of intellect. But Jesus rejects learning for the same reason he turned down the others; he already has a superior version of what the tempter offers, namely, heavenly learning. That such learning made all other kinds redundant was a common enough position in the seventeenth century and earlier; it is surprising only because we know of Milton's love of classical poetry and philosophy, which he cannot quite keep out of this very denunciation of them. But it was necessary to take a diagrammatic position here; and the hidden conflict between the needs of the work and the temper of his mind makes this the finest thing in Milton's brief epic.

From *Book IV*

Therefore let pass, as they are transitory,
210   The kingdoms of this world; I shall no more
Advise thee; gain them as thou canst, or not.
And thou thyself seem'st otherwise inclined
Than to a worldly crown, addicted more
To contemplation and profound dispute,
As by that early action may be judged,
When slipping from thy mother's eye thou went'st
Alone into the temple; there wast found
Among the gravest rabbis disputant
On points and questions fitting Moses' chair,
220   Teaching, not taught; the childhood shows the man,

As morning shows the day. Be famous then
By wisdom; as thy empire must extend,
So let extend thy mind o'er all the world,
In knowledge, all things in it comprehend.
All knowledge is not couched in Moses' Law,
The Pentateuch° or what the Prophets wrote;
The Gentiles also know, and write, and teach
To admiration,° led by nature's light;
And with the Gentiles much thou must converse,
230   Ruling them by persuasion as thou mean'st;
Without their learning, how wilt thou with them,
Or they with thee hold conversation meet?
How wilt thou reason with them, how refute
Their idolisms,° traditions, paradoxes?
Error by his own arms is best evinced.°
Look once more, ere we leave this specular mount,°
Westward, much nearer by southwest; behold
Where on the Aegean shore a city stands
Built nobly, pure the air, and light the soil,
240   Athens, the eye° of Greece, mother of arts
And eloquence, native to famous wits
Or hospitable, in her sweet recess,
City or suburban, studious walks and shades;
See there the olive grove of Academe,°
Plato's retirement, where the Attic bird°
Trills her thick-warbled notes the summer long;
There flowery hill Hymettus° with the sound
Of bees' industrious murmur oft invites
To studious musing; there Ilissus° rolls
250   His whispering stream. Within the walls then view
The schools of ancient sages: his° who bred
Great Alexander to subdue the world,
Lyceum° there, and painted Stoa° next.
There thou shalt hear and learn the secret power°
Of harmony in tones and numbers hit
By voice or hand, and various-measured verse,
Aeolian charms° and Dorian lyric odes,°
And his who gave them breath, but higher sung,

Pentateuch the first five books of the Old
Testament
To admiration admirably
idolisms idolatries
evinced defeated
specular mount lookout hill (Latin *specula*,
watchtower)
eye highest faculty, chief city
Academe Plato's Academy, a park planted with
olives, just outside Athens
Attic bird nightingale
Hymettus the hills, famous for honey, in which
the Ilissus rises
Ilissus stream near Athens

his Aristotle's: he was Alexander's tutor
Lyceum the park where Aristotle ran his
Peripatetic School of Philosophy, so called
because he and his pupils walked around as
they talked
painted Stoa porch, painted with frescoes,
where Zeno taught Stoicism
secret power The Greeks attributed therapeutic
and other powers to music.
Aeolian charms songs in the Aeolian dialect
used by Sappho
Dorian lyric odes Pindar's odes in the Dorian
dialect

Blind Melesigenes,° thence° Homer called,
260　Whose poem Phoebus challenged for his own.°
Thence what the lofty grave tragedians taught
In chorus or iambic,° teachers best
Of moral prudence, with delight received
In brief sententious precepts, while they treat
Of fate, and chance, and change in human life,
High actions and high passions best describing.
Thence to the famous orators repair,
Those ancient, whose resistless eloquence
Wielded at will that fierce democraty,°
270　Shook the Arsenal° and fulmined° over Greece,
To Macedon, and Artaxerxes' throne;°
To sage philosophy next lend thine ear,
From heaven descended to the low-roofed house
Of Socrates°—see there his tenement—
Whom well inspired the oracle° pronounced
Wisest of men; from whose mouth issued forth
Mellifluous streams that watered all the schools
Of Academics old and new,° with those
Surnamed Peripatetics,° and the sect
280　Epicurean,° and the Stoic severe;°
These here revolve, or, as thou lik'st, at home,
Till time mature thee to a kingdom's weight;
These rules will render thee a king complete
Within thyself, much more with empire joined.'
　　To whom our Saviour sagely° thus replied:
'Think not but that I know these things, or think
I know them not; not therefore am I short
Of knowing what I ought. He who receives
Light from above, from the fountain of light,
290　No other doctrine needs, though granted true;°
But these are false, or little else but dreams,
Conjectures, fancies, built on nothing firm.
The first and wisest of them all professed

Melesigenes Homer, after his reputed birth-place near the river Meles; Milton invented this **thence** because he was blind; from the doubtful Greek word *homeros*, blind
poem . . . own An epigram in the Greek Anthology makes Apollo say "It was I who sang, but divine Homer wroe it down."
chorus or iambic Greek tragedy had choral odes, and dialogue in iambics.
democraty democracy
Arsenal naval dockyard at Piraeus near Athens, here used as military threat
fulmined hurled forth thunder and lightning
Artaxerxes' throne Artaxerxes was king of Persia, allied to Sparta.
From heaven . . . Socrates Cicero said that Socrates brought philosophy down from the heavens and made it deal with morality.

oracle The Delphic oracle said that there was no one wiser than Socrates (Plato's *Apology*).
Academics . . . new successive schools of Platonism
Peripatetics See l. 253n.
Epicurean Epicurus, 341–270 B.C. taught that happiness arose from the senses, and that virtuous pleasure was the end of life; the Stoics attacked him for debauchery.
Stoic severe Stoics thought of the soul as imprisoned in the body, and that the ideal man was totally immune to passion.
sagely Milton gives Jesus the adverb appropriate to the temptation here, as elsewhere.
He . . . true the heart of Jesus' reply; none of this knowledge is necessary, or even desirable, to those who have revealed truth

To know this only, that he nothing knew;°
The next to fabling fell and smooth conceits;°
A third sort doubted all things, though plain sense;°
Others in virtue placed felicity,°
But virtue joined with riches and long life;
In corporal pleasure he,° and careless ease;
300   The Stoic last in philosophic pride,
By him called virtue; and his virtuous man,
Wise, perfect in himself, and all possessing
Equal to God, oft shames not to prefer,
As fearing God nor man, contemning all
Wealth, pleasure, pain or torment, death and life,
Which when he lists, he leaves, or boasts he can;
For all his tedious talk is but vain boast,
Or subtle shifts conviction to evade.°
Alas what can they teach, and not mislead,
310   Ignorant of themselves, of God much more,
And how the world began, and how man fell
Degraded by himself, on grace depending?
Much of the soul they talk, but all awry,
And in themselves seek virtue, and to themselves
All glory arrogate, to God give none;°
Rather accuse him under usual names,
Fortune and fate, as one regardless quite
Of mortal things. Who therefore seeks in these
True wisdom, finds her not, or by delusion
320   Far worse, her false resemblance only meets,
An empty cloud.° However, many books,
Wise men have said, are wearisome;° who reads
Incessantly, and to his reading brings not
A spirit and judgment equal or superior
(And what he brings, what needs he elsewhere seek?),
Uncertain and unsettled still remains,
Deep versed in books and shallow in himself,
Crude° or intoxicate, collecting toys
And trifles for choice matters, worth a sponge,°
330   As children gathering pebbles on the shore.
Or if I would delight my private hours
With music or with poem, where so soon

professed . . . knew Socrates in the *Apology*
said that his superiority consisted only in that
he knew nothing.
To fabling . . . conceits Plato made myths in
his philosophy.
doubted . . . sense the Skeptics, who did not
believe that the human mind could know anything truly, and thought that a state of suspended judgment was the best
in virtue . . . felicity the Peripatetics
he Epicurus
The Stoic . . . evade The Stoics believed that

the virtuous man was equal to the gods, and
indifferent to pain and pleasure; he could
commit suicide if he so decided.
All . . . none Cicero said that praiseworthy
virtue must be a man's own, not a lucky
gift of fortune.
cloud recalling the cloud embraced by Ixion
in mistake for Juno
books . . . wearisome Ecclesiastes 12:12
Crude surfeited
worth a sponge worthy to be erased

As in our native language can I find
That solace? All our law and story° strewed
With hymns, our Psalms with artful terms° inscribed,
Our Hebrew songs and harps in Babylon,°
That pleased so well our victors' ear, declare
That rather Greece from us these arts derived;°
Ill imitated, while they loudest sing
340   The vices of their deities, and their own,
In fable, hymn, or song, so personating
Their gods ridiculous, and themselves past shame.
Remove their swelling epithets° thick laid
As varnish on a harlot's cheek, the rest,
Thin sown with aught of profit or delight,°
Will far be found unworthy to compare
With Sion's songs, to all true tastes excelling,°
Where God is praised aright, and godlike men,
The Holiest of Holies, and his saints;
350   Such are from God inspired, not such from thee;
Unless° where moral virtue is expressed
By light of nature not in all quite lost.
Their orators thou then extoll'st, as those
The top of eloquence, statists° indeed,
And lovers of their country, as may seem;
But herein to our Prophets far beneath,
As men divinely taught, and better teaching
The solid rules of civil government
In their majestic unaffected style
360   Than all the oratory of Greece and Rome.
In them is plainest taught, and easiest learnt,
What makes a nation happy, and keeps it so,
What ruins kingdoms, and lays cities flat;
These only with our Law best form a king.'

. . .

[Satan, remarking that Jesus is equally unconcerned about the active and the
contemplative virtues, asks "What dost thou in this world?" and leaves him
for what turns into a stormy night. Next morning he bears him by force to
the highest pinnacle of the temple, telling him scornfully either to stand or
to cast himself down for angels to save him. Jesus simply says "Tempt not
the Lord thy God," and stands. Satan falls. Jesus, who has throughout been
without divine powers or aid—like Guyon in the Cave of Mammon—is
provided by angels with "a table of celestial food." Finally "he unobserved /
Home to his mother's house private returned," and so the epic ends.]

story history
artful terms The Psalms were thought to orig-
inate all the arts of poetry and rhetoric.
Babylon Psalms 137:1
derived A common Renaissance opinion was
that all Greek learning and poetry derived
from Hebrew.
swelling epithets for example, in the odes of
Pindar

profit or delight That poetry should provide both
was the traditional view derived from Horace,
Ars Poetica.
Sion's . . . excelling Sion was in this way
regularly preferred to Parnassus as a source of
poetry; see Sidney's *Defence of Poesie,* where
the best poets are said to be biblical writers
like David and Solomon.
Unless refers to "unworthy," above.
statists statesmen

Samson Agonistes

The date of *Samson Agonistes* is disputed; the argument for an early date is most fully stated in W. R. Parker's *John Milton: A Biography* (1968). The most important points are, first, there is no evidence that it was a late work except its late publication, and Milton had little time between the publication of *Paradise Lost* and that of *Paradise Regained* and *Samson Agonistes* to write more than *Paradise Regained*. Nobody ever treated it as late until Upton in 1746 said that it represented Milton after the Restoration, and Thomas Newton, on similar grounds, called it in his edition (1749) Milton's last work. Second, *Samson Agonistes* has a good deal of rhyme, which Milton rejected in a paragraph on "The Verse" affixed to *Paradise Lost*. Parker, now followed by other scholars, chooses an early date, about 1647–53, and supports it on various stylistic and autobiographical grounds. Another view, supported by the notes for tragedies surviving in Milton's Commonplace Book, is that he sketched it early and finished it late.

It does not seem impossible that Milton could have fitted the play in between 1667 and 1670; *Paradise Regained* is not so long a work. As for the rhyme, there was current a theory, as it happens erroneous, that Hebrew verse used rhymes and half-rhymes, and Milton, using a Hebrew subject and perhaps fresh from the commendation to the Psalms in *Paradise Regained* iv.334–38, could have thought it proper to use rhyme in the same irregular way; what he complains of in his note on verse is the "modern bondage of rhyming," calling it "the invention of a barbarous age"; but Hebrew rhyme was neither barbarous, nor modern, nor a bondage, since it rhymed at will and not by compulsion. Furthermore it is hard to believe (despite the tenuous parallels adduced in Milton's Latin ode *Ad Rousium*, written in 1647) that his prosodic experiments in *Samson Agonistes* should have preceded the long works in blank verse; having explored the range of effects to be had from irregular strophes —the impact of short choric lines, and the effect of such transitions as that from 79 to 80—it is highly improbable that he would return to regular blank verse without such variation. We need not give up the view that *Samson Agonistes* is a triumphant tragic conclusion to Milton's work.

Milton had explored heroism in *Paradise Lost* and *Paradise Regained*. His tragic hero is an Old Testament type of Christian heroism, though in its active mode, Christ's in *Paradise Regained* being passive. (Much of the irony turns on the apparent passivity of Samson, "vigorous most when most unactive deemed.") His subject is accordingly Hebraic. The appropriate form for tragedy is, however, Greek. Milton knew Aeschylus, Sophocles, and Euripides, and built his drama out of that knowledge. It is generally agreed that Sophocles, perhaps especially in his *Oedipus at Colonus*, affected Milton most strongly, and that the persistent ironies of the work are Sophoclean in that they depend on the ignorance of the characters as to what is to ensue. Milton Christianizes this; it is the inaccessibility of God's design to human questioning that makes everybody go wrong about the true state of affairs, at all stages up to the entry of the messenger. The plight of Samson is considered in the light of partial human explanations, some of which Milton borrowed from the exegetical tradition: Samson as a warning against pride or uxoriousness; Samson as a subject for casuistry on the subject of suicide; Samson as a case history of despair. He had formerly referred to the story (in *The Reason of Church Government*, 1641) as an allegory of the enfeebling of the king by the bishops, and there is certainly nothing implausible in the supposition that in the 1660's he was thinking of Samson's apparent eclipse and eventual triumph as an allegory of the condition, under the Restoration, of the Good Old Cause of the Puritan Commonwealth (Harapha almost certainly reflects some satirical intention). Samson proves a highly adaptable theme for exegesis and allegory.

Milton, however much he might use such interpretations as material for irony and topical comment, was primarily concerned with the relations between his hero, the elected one, and the God who seemed to have deserted him. If this is remembered, the narrative structure of the work will seem simple enough. Samson is accustomed to visitations from the spirit of God, and to "intimate impulse." In the case of the woman of Timna this impulse led him into a marriage that would ordinarily have been forbidden; the marriage was a disaster, but it furthered the ends of God. His desire for Dalila seemed to him to proceed from an exactly analogous impulse. It was another disaster, and resulted in his captivity and blindness. Therefore, he supposes, and the Israelites suppose, that he has made a mistake, for which he is now punished and abandoned. Of course this is wrong; the analogy between the two marriages is exact, but the action is not yet complete, so that God's plan cannot be seen. The completion of the action stems from a third intimate impulse, occurring between the departure and return of the Philistine Public Officer. That impulse vindicates not only itself, but also the unclean marriage to Dalila, in the destruction of the temple.

Throughout most of the work discussion of Samson's powers is erroneous simply because it is assumed that they are now forever out of use, and this accounts for the mistake of the Chorus in its comments (ll. 1268 ff.) on the heroic virtue of God's champions; they think Samson's heroism can no longer be active, and that he must now exhibit the heroism of patience. The clarification of these errors, and the motivation of the intimate impulse by God, constitute the main action of the poem. Samson begins in total suffering, lamenting the contrast with the past, blaming himself for acts which would indeed be blameworthy if God did not provide a dispensation for them as part of his plan. The important question of the marriages is brought up by Manoa, who cannot see their relation to the signs given him at Samson's birth; the Dalila marriage is agreed to have resulted from intemperance. Dalila herself continues to be the instrument of God in angering Samson, beginning the process of rousing him from his apathy which the contemptible Harapha completes. The dramatic crisis occurs at line 1382; Samson is again authorized to break the Law, take part in a heathen festival; what impels him is a force he recognizes from the past. His humility before the officer is a *conscious* irony.

There is a persistent critical charge, first made by Dr. Johnson, that whereas *Samson Agonistes* has a beginning and an end it lacks a middle, "since nothing passes between the first act and the last, that either hastens or delays the death of Samson." The criticism, which has many variants, is invalidated by such considerations as those of the preceding paragraph. Pehaps the Dalila and Harapha episodes are too long, but that is virtually the extent of the case against Milton's structure. Milton had rethought the heroic poem, and the brief heroic poem; here he rethinks tragedy. The humanist enterprise which involved the Christianizing and modernizing of the great ancient modes was at last, though at a very late date, accomplished.

Samson Agonistes [1]

A Dramatic Poem

Of That Sort of Dramatic Poem Which Is Called Tragedy

Tragedy, as it was anciently composed, hath been ever held the gravest, moralest, and most profitable of all other poems: therefore said by Aristotle to be of power, by raising pity and fear, or terror, to purge the mind of those and suchlike passions, that is, to temper and reduce them to just measure with a kind of delight, stirred up by reading or seeing those passions well imitated.[2] Nor is Nature wanting in her own effects to make good his assertion; for so in physic, things of melancholic hue and quality are used against melancholy, sour against sour, salt to remove salt humours. Hence philosophers and other gravest writers, as Cicero, Plutarch, and others, frequently cite out of tragic poets, both to adorn and illustrate their discourse. The Apostle Paul himself thought it not unworthy to insert a verse of Euripides into the text of Holy Scripture, I Cor. 15, 33,[3] and Pareus,[4] commenting on the Revelation, divides the whole book as a tragedy, into acts distinguished each by a chorus of heavenly harpings and song between. Heretofore men in highest dignity have laboured not a little to be thought able to compose a tragedy. Of that honour Dionysius the elder was no less ambitious than before of his attaining to the tyranny.[5] Augustus Caesar also had begun his *Ajax*, but, unable to please his own judgment with what he had begun, left it unfinished.[6] Seneca the philosopher is by some thought the author of those tragedies (at least the best of them) that go under that name.[7] Gregory Nazianzen, a Father of the Church, thought it not unbeseeming the sanctity of his person to write a tragedy, which he entitled *Christ Suffering*.[8] This is mentioned to vindicate tragedy from the small esteem, or rather infamy, which in the account of many it undergoes at this day with other common interludes; happening through the poet's error of intermixing comic stuff with tragic sadness and gravity, or introducing trivial and vulgar persons, which by all judicious hath been counted absurd, and brought in without discretion, corruptly to gratify the people.[9] And though

1. Samson the performer or contestant, Samson at the Games.
2. Aristotle, *Poetics* VI: "Tragedy is the imitation of a serious action, effecting through pity and terror the *catharsis* of such passions." The dispute as to what *catharsis* means here has continued since the 16th century, but Milton partly follows Italian interpretations, partly provides his own. He thinks that small doses of pity and terror in an imitated action will drive out the real and dangerous passions, not only pity and terror but others ("those and suchlike"). The purgation depends on *delight* in the imitation; the medicine is pleasant.
3. See note on Sidney's *Defence* (n.54); of St. Paul's several references to poets Milton is thinking of "Evil communications corrupt good manners" (I Corinthians 15:33), which is from Menander.
4. David Paraeus (1548–1622) in his work *On the Divine Apocalypse* (1618).
5. Tyrant of Syracuse (431–367 B.C.), who sought fame as poet and playwright.
6. According to Suetonius, *Lives of the Caesars* II.85, Augustus erased what he had written of this tragedy.
7. Lucius Annaeus Seneca (3 B.C.–65 A.D.). The Renaissance distinction between Seneca the philosopher and Seneca the dramatist has since disappeared.
8. St. Gregory of Nazianzus, fourth-century bishop of Constantinople who wrote *Christus Patiens*.
9. This condemnation was made by Sidney in the *Defence*.

ancient tragedy use no prologue,[10] yet using sometimes, in case of self-defence, or explanation, that which Martial calls an epistle;[11] in behalf of this tragedy, coming forth after the ancient manner, much different from what among us passes for best, thus much beforehand may be epistled: that chorus is here introduced after the Greek manner, not ancient only but modern, and still in use among the Italians.[12] In the modelling therefore of this poem, with good reason, the ancients and Italians are rather followed, as of much more authority and fame. The measure of verse used in the chorus is of all sorts, called by the Greeks *monostrophic*, or rather *apolelymenon*,[13] without regard had to strophe, antistrophe, or epode, which were a kind of stanzas framed only for the music, then used with the chorus that sung; not essential to the poem, and therefore not material; or, being divided into stanzas or pauses, they may be·called *alloeostropha*.[14] Division into act and scene, referring chiefly to the stage (to which this work never was intended), is here omitted.

It suffices if the whole drama be found not produced beyond the fifth act. Of the style and uniformity, and that commonly called the plot, whether intricate or explicit[15]—which is nothing indeed but such economy, or disposition of the fable, as may stand best with verisimilitude and decorum[16]—they only will best judge who are not unacquainted with Aeschylus, Sophocles, and Euripides, the three tragic poets unequalled yet by any, and the best rule to all who endeavour to write tragedy. The circumscription of time wherein the whole drama begins and ends is, according to ancient rule and best example, within the space of twenty-four hours.[17]

The Argument

Samson, made captive, blind, and now in the prison at Gaza, there to labour as in a common workhouse, on a festival day, in the general cessation from labour, comes forth into the open air, to a place nigh, somewhat retired, there to sit a while and bemoan his condition. Where he happens at length to be visited by certain friends and equals of his tribe, which make the chorus, who seek to comfort him what they can; then by his old father, Manoa, who endeavours the like, and withal tells him his purpose to procure his liberty by ransom; lastly, that this feast was proclaimed by the Philistines as a day of thanksgiving for their deliverance from the hands of Samson, which yet more troubles him. Manoa then departs to prosecute his endeavour with the Philistian

10. Preliminary address to the audience, not the part of the tragedy which precedes the first entrance of the chorus, the sense in which it is used in Greek tragedy.

11. Martial's "Letter to the Reader" introducing his epigrams is the model.

12. Milton uses the chorus in the manner adapted by modern Italians from the Greek (in drama and opera) rather than in the original Greek way.

13. "Freed"—from the limits of a regular stanzaic pattern. In Greek drama the chorus sang the strophe as they moved or danced one way, the antistrophe as they reversed the movement, and the epode, standing still.

14. Insofar as the verse does seem to divide into stanzas, these should be regarded as "irregular strophes."

15. Referring to Aristotle's distinction between "simple" and "complex" plots (*Poetics* VI).

16. Two important aims of neoclasic thought; see *Rhetoric* in the Glossary.

17. Aristotle's words in *Poetics* V were not prescriptive, and became so only when the Unities were evolved in 16th-century Italian criticism.

lords for Samson's redemption; who in the meanwhile is visited by other persons; and lastly by a public officer to require his coming to the feast before the lords and people, to play or show his strength in their presence. He at first refuses, dismissing the public officer with absolute denial to come; at length persuaded inwardly that this was from God, he yields to go along with him, who came now the second time with great threatenings to fetch him. The chorus yet remaining on the place, Manoa returns full of joyful hope to procure ere long his son's deliverance; in the midst of which discourse an Hebrew comes in haste, confusedly at first, and afterward more distinctly, relating the catastrophe, what Samson had done to the Philistines, and by accident to himself; wherewith the tragedy ends.

THE PERSONS

SAMSON
MANOA, *the father of Samson*
DALILA, *his wife*
HARAPHA OF GATH

PUBLIC OFFICER
MESSENGER
CHORUS OF DANITES

The Scene, before the Prison in Gaza

SAMSON   A little onward lend thy guiding hand
To these dark steps,° a little further on,
For yonder bank hath choice of sun or shade;
There I am wont to sit, when any chance
Relieves me from my task of servile toil,
Daily in the common prison else enjoined me,
Where I, a prisoner chained, scarce freely draw
The air imprisoned also, close and damp,
Unwholesome draught. But here I feel amends,
10 The breath of heaven fresh-blowing, pure and sweet,
With day-spring° born; here leave me to respire.°
This day a solemn feast the people hold
To Dagon° their sea-idol, and forbid
Laborious works; unwillingly this rest
Their superstition yields me; hence with leave
Retiring from the popular noise, I seek
This unfrequented place to find some ease,
Ease to the body some, none to the mind
From restless thoughts, that like a deadly swarm
20 Of hornets armed, no sooner found alone,
But rush upon me thronging, and present
Times past, what once I was, and what am now.
O wherefore was my birth from heaven foretold
Twice by an angel, who at last in sight

dark steps The very phrase echoes the language of Greek tragedy, particularly the "blind feet" of Tiresias guided by his daughter, who will be "eyes" to them, in Euripides' *Phoenissae;* one is also to think of the opening of Sophocles' *Oedipus at Colonus.*
day-spring daybreak
respire breathe
Dagon Philistine fish god, worshiped at Gaza

Of both my parents all in flames ascended
From off the altar, where an offering burned,
As in a fiery column charioting
His godlike presence, and from some great act
Or benefit revealed to Abraham's race?
30 Why was my breeding ordered and prescribed
As of a person separate to God,
Designed for great exploits, if I must die
Betrayed, captived, and both my eyes put out,
Made of my enemies the scorn and gaze;°
To grind in brazen fetters under task
With this heaven-gifted strength? O glorious strength,
Put to the labour of a beast, debased
Lower than bondslave! Promise was° that I
Should Israel from Philistian yoke deliver;
40 Ask for this great deliverer now, and find him
Eyeless in Gaza at the mill with slaves,
Himself in bonds under Philistian yoke;
Yet stay, let me not rashly call in doubt
Divine prediction; what if all foretold
Had been fulfilled but through mine own default?
Whom have I to complain of but myself?
Who this high gift of strength committed to me,
In what part lodged, how easily bereft me,
Under the seal of silence could not keep,
50 But weakly to a woman must reveal it,
O'ercome with importunity and tears.
O impotence of mind, in body strong!°
But what is strength without a double share
Of wisdom? Vast, unwieldy, burdensome,
Proudly secure,° yet liable to fall
By weakest subtleties; not made to rule,
But to subserve where wisdom bears command.
God, when he gave me strength, to show withal
How slight the gift was, hung it in my hair.
60 But peace! I must not quarrel with the will
Of highest dispensation, which herein
Haply had ends above my reach to know:
Suffices that to me strength is my bane,
And proves the source of all my miseries,
So many, and so huge, that each apart
Would ask a life to wail; but chief of all,
O loss of sight, of thee I most complain!

---

gaze object of jeering gazes (did Milton pronounce "Gaza" this way?)
Promise was at Judges 13:5, that he should "begin to deliver Israel out of the hands of the Philistines"

O impotence . . . strong And towering strength, like any fortress when it tumbles in, imprisons its inhabitant; see the continuation of this image in that of burial in self, ll. 101–5 and 155–56.
secure careless of danger

Blind among enemies, O worse than chains,
Dungeon, or beggary, or decrepit age!
70 Light, the prime work of God, to me is extinct,
And all her various objects of delight
Annulled, which might in part my grief have eased,
Inferior to the vilest now become
Of man or worm; the vilest here excel me,
They creep, yet see; I, dark in light exposed
To daily fraud, contempt, abuse and wrong,
Within doors, or without, still as a fool,
In power of others, never in my own;
Scarce half I seem to live, dead more than half.
80 O dark, dark, dark,° amid the blaze of noon,
Irrecoverably dark, total eclipse
Without all hope of day!
O first-created beam, and thou great Word,
'Let there be light, and light was over all';
Why am I thus bereaved thy prime decree?
The sun to me is dark
And silent° as the moon,
When she deserts the night,
Hid in her vacant° interlunar cave.
90 Since light so necessary is to life,
And almost life itself, if it be true
That light is in the soul,
She all in every part,° why was the sight
To such a tender ball as the eye confined?
So obvious° and so easy to be quenched,
And not, as feeling, through all parts diffused,
That she might look at will through every pore?
Then had I not been thus exiled from light,
As in the land of darkness, yet in light,
100 To live a life half dead, a living death,
And buried; but O yet more miserable!
Myself my sepulchre, a moving grave,
Buried, not yet exempt
By privilege of death and burial
From worst of other evils, pains and wrongs,
But made hereby obnoxious° more
To all the miseries of life,
Life in captivity

O dark, dark, dark Here Milton abandons the blank verse of the dialogue for one of the many unrhymed lyrical passages in Samson's speeches.
silent meaning the dark of the moon, but significant here in its transfer of location from the visual domain to the aural one
vacant idle, resting in her fabled cave between visible phases

all in every part The soul, in Augustinian tradition and thereafter, was not thought to be localized in any part of the body, but rather suffusing it all like warmth, until Milton's contemporary, René Descartes, decided that it was in the surgically inaccessible pineal gland.
obvious evident, thus vulnerable
obnoxious exposed to

Among inhuman foes,
110 But who are these? For with joint pace I hear
The tread of many feet steering this way;
Perhaps my enemies who come to stare
At my affliction, and perhaps to insult,
Their daily practice to afflict me more.
    CHORUS   This, this is he; softly a while;
Let us not break in upon him.
O change beyond report, thought, or belief!
See how he lies at random, carelessly diffused,°
With languished head unpropped,
120 As one past hope, abandoned,
And by himself given over;
In slavish habit, ill-fitted weeds°
O'erworn and soiled;
Or do my eyes misrepresent? Can this be he,
That heroic, that renowned,
Irresistible Samson? Whom unarmed
No strength of man, or fiercest wild beast could withstand;
Who tore the lion, as the lion tears the kid,°
Ran on embattled armies clad in iron,
130 And, weaponless himself,
Made arms ridiculous, useless the forgery°
Of brazen shield and spear, the hammered cuirass,
Chalýbean°-tempered steel, and frock of mail
Adamantean° proof;
But safe he who stood aloof,
When insupportably° his foot advanced,
In scorn of their proud arms and warlike tools,
Spurned them to death by troops. The bold Ascalonite°
Fled from his lion ramp,° old warriors turned
140 Their plated° backs under his heel;
Or grovelling soiled their crested helmets in the dust.
Then with what trivial weapon came to hand,
The jaw of a dead ass, his sword of bone,
A thousand foreskins° fell, the flower of Palestine,
In Ramath-lechi, famous to this day;
Then by main force pulled up, and on his shoulders bore
The gates of Azza,° post and massy bar,
Up to the hill by Hebron, seat of giants old,
No journey of a Sabbath day,° and loaded so;

---

diffused spread out
weeds clothing
Who tore . . . kid See Judges 14:6.
forgery making; faking
Chalybean made by fabled metalworkers
Adamantean diamond-hard; steely
insupportably irresistibly
Ascalonite Ascalon: one of the five principal
Philistine cities

lion ramp leonine, rampant posture
plated armor-clad
foreskins synecdoche for uncircumcised Philistines
Azza Gaza
No journey . . . day Jewish law permits no labor or travel on the Sabbath.

150 Like whom the Gentiles feign° to bear up heaven.
Which shall I first bewail,
Thy bondage or lost sight,
Prison within prison
Inseparably dark?
Thou art become (O worst imprisonment!)
The dungeon of thyself; thy soul
(Which men enjoying sight oft without cause complain)
Imprisoned now indeed,
In real darkness of the body dwells,
160 Shut up from outward light
To incorporate with gloomy night;
For inward light, alas,
Puts forth no visual beam.
O mirror of our fickle state,
Since man on earth unparalleled!
The rarer thy example stands,
By how much from the top of wondrous glory,
Strongest of mortal men,
To lowest pitch of abject fortune thou art fallen.
170 For him I reckon not in high estate
Whom long descent of birth
Or the sphere° of fortune raises;
But thee whose strength, while virtue was her mate,
Might have subdued the earth,
Universally crowned with highest praises.
    SAMSON   I hear the sound of words, their sense the air
Dissolves unjointed ere it reach my ear.
    CHORUS   He speaks, let us draw nigh. Matchless in might,
The glory late of Israel, now the grief,
180 We come thy friends and neighbours not unknown
From Eshtaol and Zora's fruitful vale°
To visit or bewail thee, or if better,
Counsel or consolation we may bring,
Salve to thy sores; apt words have power to 'suage
The tumours° of a troubled mind,
And are as balm to festered wounds.
    SAMSON   Your coming, friends, revives me, for I learn
Now of my own experience, not by talk,
How counterfeit a coin they are who friends
190 Bear in their superscription° (of the most
I would be understood); in prosperous days
They swarm, but in adverse withdraw their head,

feign From a Hebraic viewpoint, classical myths, like those of Atlas holding up the world, were uninterestingly fictitious.
sphere Fortune's emblematic wheel frequently became a ball, sometimes the globe, in Renaissance pictures.

Eshtaol . . . vale Samson was born at Zora; Eshtaol was near by.
tumours swellings, disturbances
superscription the legend on a coin

Not to be found, though sought. Ye see, O friends,
How many evils have enclosed me round;
Yet that which was the worst now least afflicts me,
Blindness, for had I sight, confused with shame,
How could I once look up, or heave the head,
Who like a foolish pilot have shipwrecked
My vessel trusted to me from above,
200 Gloriously rigged; and for a word, a tear,
Fool, have divulged the secret gift of God
To a deceitful woman: tell me, friends,
Am I not sung and proverbed° for a fool
In every street, do they not say, how well
Are come upon him his deserts? yet why?
Immeasurable strength they might behold
In me, of wisdom nothing more than mean;°
This with the other should, at least, have paired,
These two proportioned ill drove me transverse.°
210 CHORUS Tax not divine disposal, wisest men
Have erred, and by bad women been deceived;
And shall again, pretend they ne'er so wise.
Deject not then so overmuch thyself,
Who hast of sorrow thy full load besides;
Yet truth to say, I oft have heard men wonder
Why thou shouldst wed Philistian women rather
Than of thine own tribe fairer, or as fair,
At least of thine own nation, and as noble.
SAMSON The first I saw at Timna, and she pleased
220 Me, not my parents, that I sought to wed
The daughter of an infidel;° they knew not
That what I motioned was of God; I knew
From intimate impulse, and therefore urged
The marriage on; that by occasion hence
I might begin Israel's deliverance,
The work to which I was divinely called;
She proving false, the next I took to wife
(O that I never had! fond wish too late)
Was in the vale of Sorec, Dálila,°
230 That specious° monster, my accomplished snare.°
I thought it lawful from my former act,

proverbed made a byword
mean average
transverse astray; a nautical term, meaning "off-course"
The first . . . infidel In Judges 14:3–4 Samson's parents complain of his choice, though he insists: "she pleaseth me well." But his father and mother "knew not that it was of the Lord, that he sought an occasion [see l. 237] against the Philisitines." He marries the woman, but then propounds to the Philistines the riddle of the honey which came from the lion's carcass,
which they get right by making his wife pester him for the answer; whereupon Samson slays thirty Philistines, takes their clothes and pays his wager (thirty changes of garments). He breaks with his wife.
Dálila "He loved a woman in the valley of Sorek, whose name was Delilah" (Judges 16:4)
specious superficially beautiful
accomplished snare snare that has now fulfilled its task; both Dalila's accomplished charms and her accomplishment of Samson's ruin

And the same end;° still watching to oppress
Israel's oppressors: of what now I suffer
She was not the prime cause, but I myself,
Who vanquished with a peal of words° (O weakness!)
Gave up my fort of silence to a woman.
    CHORUS   In seeking just occasion to provoke
The Philistine, thy country's enemy,
Thou never wast remiss, I bear thee witness:
240   Yet Israel still serves with all his sons.
    SAMSON   That fault I take not on me, but transfer
On Israel's governors, and heads of tribes,
Who seeing those great acts which God had done
Singly by me against their conquerors,
Acknowledged not, or not at all considered
Deliverance offered: I on the other side
Used no ambition° to commend my deeds;
The deeds themselves, though mute, spoke loud the doer;
But they persisted deaf, and would not seem
250   To count them things worth notice, till at length
Their lords the Philistines with gathered powers
Entered Judea seeking me, who then
Safe to the rock of Etham° was retired,
Not flying, but forecasting in what place
To set upon them, what advantaged best;
Meanwhile the men of Judah, to prevent
The harass of their land, beset me round;
I willingly on some conditions° came
Into their hands, and they as gladly yield me
260   To the uncircumcised a welcome prey,
Bound with two cords; but cords to me were threads
Touched with the flame: on their whole host I flew
Unarmed, and with a trivial weapon° felled
Their choicest youth; they only lived who fled.
Had Judah that day joined, or one whole tribe,
They had by this° possessed the towers of Gath,°

I thought . . . end This is a very important source of the main ironies that animate the drama. Samson is saying that his first marriage, though a failure, was right because it was ordered by God as part of His plans, a fact he knew "by intimate impulse." But in undertaking the second, with Dalila, he now supposes that he argued wrongly from analogy; the circumstances were similar but this was *not* part of God's plan, merely an indication of his own weakness. Hence his present situation, blind, disgraced, and with no future. But the irony is that the marriage with Dalila was as much part of God's plan as that with the women of Timna. The consequences of it are not yet worked out; everybody thinks the action is over, but it is not. The provision of "just occasion to provoke / The Philistine,"

and of course what follows justify Samson's confidence in the inspired nature of his second marriage.
peal of words as it were, surrendering to the mere noise of the attacker's weapons
ambition canvasing (from original Latin meaning "walking around")
Etham Judges 15
conditions Samson gave himself up to the men of Judah, who wanted to hand him over to the Philistines, on a promise that they would not "fall on him." They bound him, but he burst the cords and seized the jawbone of an ass, with which he slew a thousand men (Judges 15).
trivial weapon the jawbone, casually acquired
this this time
Gath Philistian city

And lorded over them whom now they serve;
But what more oft in nations grown corrupt,
And by their vices brought to servitude,
270   Than to love bondage more than liberty,
Bondage with ease than strenuous liberty;
And to despise, or envy, or suspect
Whom God hath of his special favour raised
As their deliverer; if he aught begin,
How frequent° to desert him, and at last
To heap ingratitude on worthiest deeds?
    CHORUS   Thy words to my remembrance bring
How Succoth and the fort of Penuel
Their great deliverer contemned,
280   The matchless Gideon in pursuit
Of Madian and her vanquished kings:°
And how ingrateful Ephraim
Had dealt with Jephtha, who by argument,
Not worse than by his shield and spear,
Defended Israel from the Ammonite,
Had not his prowess quelled their pride
In that sore battle when so many died
Without reprieve adjudged to death,
For want of well pronouncing *Shibboleth*.°
290   SAMSON   Of such examples add me to the roll;
Me easily indeed mine° may neglect,
But God's proposed deliverance not so.
    CHORUS   Just are the ways of God,
And justifiable to men;
Unless there be who think not God at all:
If any be, they walk obscure;
For of such doctrine never was there school,
But the heart of the fool,°
And no man therein doctor but himself.
300   Yet more there be who doubt his ways not just,
As to his own edícts, found contradicting,
Then give the reins to wandering thought,
Regardless of his glory's diminution;
Till by their own perplexities involved
They ravel° more, still less resolved,
But never find self-satisfying solution.
    As if they would confine the interminable,
And tie him to his own prescript,

---

frequent accustomed
How Succoth . . . kings Gideon in pursuit of
the enemy asked bread from Succoth and
Penuel and was refused (Judges 8).
And how . . . Shibboleth The Ephraimites refused help to Jephtha, who nevertheless defeated the Ammonites. Then a quarrel grew up
between the Ephraimites and Jephtha's Gile-

adites, and Jephtha's men used as a test the
Hebrew *shibboleth*, which the Ephraimites
could not pronounce; so infiltrators were detected and slain.
mine my people
heart . . . fool "The fool hath said in his
heart, there is no God" (Psalms 14:1)
ravel become entangled

Who made our laws to bind us, not himself,
310 And hath full right to exempt
Whomso it pleases him by choice
From national obstriction,° without taint
Of sin, or legal debt;
For with his own laws he can best dispense.
    He would not else, who never wanted means,
Nor in respect of the enemy just cause,
To set his people free,
Have prompted this heroic Nazarite,°
Against his vow of strictest purity,
320 To seek in marriage that fallacious° bride,
Unclean, unchaste.°
    Down, reason, then, at least vain reasonings down,
Though reason here aver
That moral verdict quits her of unclean:
Unchaste was subsequent; her stain, not his.
    But see, here comes thy reverend sire
With careful° step, locks white as down,
Old Mánoa: advise
Forthwith how thou ought'st to receive him.
330   SAMSON   Ay me, another inward grief awaked
With mention of that name renews the assault.
    MANOA   Brethren and men of Dan, for such ye seem,
Though in this uncouth° place; if old respect,
As I suppose, towards your once gloried friend,
My son now captive, hither hath informed°
Your younger feet, while mine cast back with age
Came lagging after; say if he be here.
    CHORUS   As signal° now in low dejected state,
As erst° in highest, behold him where he lies.
340   MANOA   O miserable change! is this the man,
That invincible Samson, far renowned,
The dread of Israel's foes, who with a strength
Equivalent to angels' walked their streets,
None offering fight;° who single combatant
Duelled their armies ranked in proud array,°
Himself an army, now unequal match
To save himself against a coward armed

obstriction obligation (the law against marriage with Gentiles)
Nazarite member of ascetic religious sect (the broken vow is not of celibacy but of impure marriage)
fallacious treacherous (referring of course to the woman of Timna)
Unclean, unchaste As the Chorus goes on to say, she was not morally unclean, only ceremonially so, as a Gentile; she was not unchaste until after the marriage and the episode of the riddle. In short, God can dispense with His own law and make any arrangements He likes without regard to such considerations; but here, as it happens, He did not make Samson marry uncleanly and unchastely.
careful full of care
uncouth unfamilar
informed directed
signal distinguished
erst formerly
The dread . . . fight presumably after his visit to the harlot of Gaza, when he went home with the town gates
Duelled . . . array in the jawbone fight

At one spear's length? O ever-failing trust
In mortal strength! and oh what not in man
350 Deceivable and vain! Nay, what thing good
Prayed for, but often proves our woe, our bane?
I prayed for children, and thought barrenness
In wedlock a reproach; I gained a son,
And such a son as all men hailed me happy:
Who would be now a father in my stead?
O wherefore did God grant me my request,
And as a blessing with such pomp adorned?
Why are his gifts desirable, to tempt
Our earnest prayers, then given with solemn hand
360 As graces,° draw a scorpion's tail behind?
For this did the angel twice descend?° For this
Ordained thy nurture holy, as of a plant;
Select and sacred, glorious for a while,
The miracle of men; then in an hour
Ensnared, assaulted, overcome, led bound,
Thy foes' derision, captive, poor, and blind,
Into a dungeon thrust, to work with slaves?
Alas, methinks whom God hath chosen once
To worthiest deeds, if he through frailty err,
370 He should not so o'erwhelm, and as a thrall
Subject him to so foul indignities,
Be it but for honour's sake of former deeds.°
       SAMSON   Appoint° not heavenly disposition, father.
Nothing of all these evils hath befallen me
But justly; I myself have brought them on,
Sole author I, sole cause: if aught seem vile,
As vile hath been my folly, who have profaned
The mystery of God given me under pledge
Of vow, and have betrayed it to a woman,
380 A Canaanite,° my faithless enemy.
This well I knew, nor was at all surprised,
But warned by oft experience: did not she
Of Timna first betray me, and reveal
The secret wrested from me in her highth
Of nuptial love professed, carrying it straight
To them who had corrupted her, my spies,
And rivals? In this other was there found
More faith? Who also in her prime of love,
Spousal embraces, vitiated with gold,

---

graces favors
twice descend He does so in Judges 13, describing the signs and admonitions accompanying the conception and prescribing the education of Samson.
former deeds Manoa thinks the story is over,
and so wonders at God's desertion of his

former champion; he does not understand
that this apparent desertion is part of the
arrangement for Samson's last exploit, still
to come.
Appoint arraign, charge
Canaanite Philistine

390   Though offered only, by the scent conceived°
Her spurious first-born, treason against me.
Thrice she assayed with flattering prayer and sighs
And amorous reproaches to win from me
My capital° secret, in what part my strength
Lay stored, in what part summed, that she might know:
Thrice I deluded her, and turned to sport
Her importunity, each time perceiving
How openly, and with what impudence,
She purposed to betray me, and (which was worse
400   Than undissembled hate) with what contempt
She sought to make me traitor to myself;
Yet the fourth time, when mustering all her wiles,
With blandished parleys, feminine assaults,
Tongue-batteries, she surceased not day nor night
To storm me over-watched,° and wearied out,
At times when men seek most repose and rest,
I yielded, and unlocked her all my heart,
Who with a grain of manhood well resolved
Might easily have shook off all her snares;
410   But foul effeminacy held me yoked
Her bondslave; O indignity, O blot
To honour and religion! servile mind
Rewarded well with servile punishment!
The base degree to which I now am fallen,
These rags, this grinding,° is not yet so base
As was my former servitude, ignoble,
Unmanly, ignominious, infamous,
True slavery, and that blindness worse than this,
That saw not how degenerately I served.
420   MANOA   I cannot praise thy marriage choices, son,
Rather approved them not; but thou didst plead
Divine impulsion prompting how thou might'st
Find some occasion to infest° our foes.
I state not that; this I am sure, our foes
Found soon occasion thereby to make thee
Their captive, and their triumph; thou the sooner
Temptation found'st, or over-potent charms,
To violate the sacred trust of silence
Deposited within thee; which to have kept
430   Tacit was in thy power; true; and thou bear'st
Enough, and more, the burden of that fault;
Bitterly hast thou paid, and still art paying,
That rigid score.° A worse thing yet remains:

by . . . conceived conceived, not a child from the spousal embraces, but treason from the mere promise of reward (Judges 16:5)
capital relating to the head—Samson's uncut hair; most important

over-watched too long awake. The whole story of Dalila's temptation is in Judges 16.
grinding working at the flour mill
infest harass
score account of a debt

This day the Philistines a popular feast
Here celebrate in Gaza, and proclaim
Great pomp, and sacrifice, and praises loud
To Dagon, as their god who hath delivered
Thee, Samson, bound and blind into their hands,
Them out of thine,° who slew'st them many a slain.
440 So Dagon shall be magnified, and God,
Besides whom is no god, compared with idols,
Disglorified, blasphemed, and had in scorn
By the idolatrous rout amidst their wine;
Which to have come to pass by means of thee,
Samson, of all thy sufferings think the heaviest,
Of all reproach the most with shame that ever
Could have befallen thee and thy father's house.
 SAMSON Father, I do acknowledge and confess
That I this honour, I this pomp have brought
450 To Dagon, and advanced his praises high
Among the heathen round; to God have brought
Dishonour, obloquy, and oped the mouths
Of idolists° and atheists; have brought scandal
To Israel, diffidence of° God, and doubt
In feeble hearts, propense° enough before
To waver, or fall off and join with idols:
Which is my chief affliction, shame and sorrow,
The anguish of my soul, that suffers not
Mine eye to harbour sleep, or thoughts to rest.
460 This only hope° relieves me, that the strife
With me hath end; all the contést is now
'Twixt God and Dagon; Dagon hath presumed,
Me overthrown, to enter lists with God,
His deity comparing and preferring
Before the God of Abraham. He, be sure,
Will not connive,° or linger, thus provoked,
But will arise and his great name assert:
Dagon must stoop, and shall ere long receive
Such a discomfit,° as shall quite despoil him
470 Of all these boasted trophies won on me,
And with confusion blank° his worshippers.
 MANOA With cause this hope relieves thee, and these words
I as a prophecy receive; for God,
Nothing more certain, will not long defer
To vindicate the glory of his name
Against all competition, nor will long
Endure it doubtful whether God be Lord,

Them . . . thine and delivered them out of
your hands
idolists idolaters
diffidence of lack of faith in
propense disposed

only hope hope alone
connive acquiesce
discomfit defeat
blank confound

Or Dagon. But for thee what shall be done?
Thou must not in the meanwhile, here forgot,
480 Lie in this miserable loathsome plight
Neglected. I already have made way
To some Philistian lords, with whom to treat
About thy ransom:° well they may by this
Have satisfied their utmost of revenge
By pains and slaveries, worse than death, inflicted
On thee, who now no more canst do them harm.

    SAMSON   Spare that proposal, father, spare the trouble
Of that solicitation; let me here,
As I deserve, pay on my punishment;
490 And expiate, if possible, my crime,
Shameful garrulity. To have revealed
Secrets of men, the secrets of a friend,
How heinous had the fact° been, how deserving
Contempt, and scorn of all, to be excluded
All friendship, and avoided as a blab,
The mark of fool set on his front!° But I
God's counsel have not kept, his holy secret
Presumptuously have published, impiously,
Weakly at least, and shamefully: a sin
500 That Gentiles in their parables condemn
To their abyss and horrid pains confined.°

    MANOA   Be penitent and for thy fault contrite,
But act not in thy own affliction, son;
Repent the sin, but if the punishment
Thou canst avoid, self-preservation bids;
Or the execution leave to high disposal,°
And let another hand, not thine, exact
Thy penal forfeit from thyself; perhaps
God will relent, and quit thee all his debt;
510 Who ever more approves and more accepts
(Best pleased with humble and filial submission)
Him who imploring mercy sues for life,
Than who self-rigorous chooses death as due;
Which argues over-just, and self-displeased
For self-offence, more than for God offended.°
Reject not then what offered means who knows
But God hath set before us, to return thee
Home to thy country and his sacred house,
Where thou mayst bring thy offerings, to avert
520 His further ire, with prayers and vows renewed.

ransom This is an incident Milton added to the
biblical account.
fact deed
front forehead
a sin . . . confined the myth of Tantalus, who
was tormented in hell for having revealed the

secrets of the gods (see Spenser, *The Faerie
Queene* II.vii and notes)
the execution . . . disposal leave the carrying
out of the punishment to God
Which . . . offended an argument against self-
punishment, including suicide, used by Milton
in his *Christian Doctrine*

SAMSON   His pardon I implore; but as for life,
To what end should I seek it? When in strength
All mortals I excelled, and great in hopes
With youthful courage and magnanimous thoughts
Of birth from heaven foretold and high exploits,
Full of divine instinct, after some proof
Of acts indeed heroic, far beyond
The sons of Anak,° famous now and blazed,
Fearless of danger, like a petty god
530   I walked about admired of all and dreaded
On hostile ground, none daring my affront.
Then swollen with pride into the snare I fell
Of fair fallacious looks, venereal trains,°
Softened with pleasure and voluptuous life;
At length to lay my head and hallowed pledge
Of all my strength in the lascivious lap
Of a deceitful concubine who shore me
Like a tame wether, all my precious fleece,
Then turned me out ridiculous, despoiled,
540   Shaven, and disarmed among my enemies.
      CHORUS   Desire of wine and all delicious drinks,
Which many a famous warrior overturns,
Thou couldst repress,° nor did the dancing ruby
Sparkling outpoured, the flavour, or the smell,
Or taste that cheers the heart of gods and men,
Allure thee from the cool crystálline stream.
      SAMSON   Wherever fountain or fresh current flowed
Against° the eastern ray, translucent, pure
With touch ethereal of heaven's fiery rod,°
550   I drank, from the clear milky juice allaying
Thirst, and refreshed; nor envied them the grape
Whose heads that turbulent liquor fills with fumes.
      CHORUS   O madness, to think use of strongest wines
And strongest drinks our chief support of health,
When God with these forbidden made choice to rear
His mighty champion, strong above compare,
Whose drink was only from the liquid brook.
      SAMSON   But what availed this temperance, not complete
Against another object more enticing?
560   What boots it° at one gate to make defence,
And at another to let in the foe,
Effeminately vanquished? By which means,
Now blind, disheartened, shamed, dishonoured, quelled,
To what can I be useful, wherein serve

---

sons of Anak giants; see Numbers 13:33
venereal trains amorous snares
Desire . . . repress The Nazarites abstained
from wine.

Against in the direction of (east-flowing water
was thought purer)
fiery rod sun ray
What boots it what use is it?

My nation, and the work from heaven imposed,
But to sit idle on the household hearth,
A burdenous drone? To visitants a gaze,°
Or pitied object; these redundant° locks,
Robustious° to no purpose, clustering down,
570   Vain monument of strength; till length of years
And sedentary numbness craze° my limbs
To a contemptible old age obscure.
Here rather let me drudge and earn my bread,
Till vermin or the draff° of servile food
Consume me, and oft-invocated death
Hasten the welcome end of all my pains.
    MANOA   Wilt thou then serve the Philistines with that gift
Which was expressly given thee to annoy° them?
Better at home lie bed-rid, not only idle,
580   Inglorious, unemployed, with age outworn.
But God, who caused a fountain at thy prayer
From the dry ground to spring,° thy thirst to allay
After the brunt of battle, can as easy
Cause light again within thy eyes to spring,
Wherewith to serve him better than thou hast;
And I persuade me so; why else this strength
Miraculous yet remaining in those locks?
His might continues in thee not for naught,
Nor shall his wondrous gifts be frustrate° thus.
590   SAMSON   All otherwise to me my thoughts portend,
That these dark orbs no more shall treat with light,
Nor the other light of life continue long,
But yield to double darkness nigh at hand:
So much I feel my genial spirits° droop,
My hopes all flat; nature within me seems
In all her functions weary of herself;
My race of glory run, and race of shame,
And I shall shortly be with them that rest.
    MANOA   Believe not these suggestions,° which proceed
600   From anguish of the mind and humours black,°
That mingle with thy fancy. I however
Must not omit a father's timely care
To prosecute the means of thy deliverance
By ransom or how else: meanwhile be calm,
And healing words from these thy friends admit.
    SAMSON   O that torment should not be confined
To the body's wounds and sores,

---

a gaze something to be stared at
redundant flowing; serving no purpose
Robustious robust, flourishing
craze enfeeble
draff refuse, garbage
annoy molest

But God . . . spring Judges 15:18–19
frustrate rendered vain
genial spirits vital and generative powers
suggestions modern sense, plus "temptations"
humours black Melancholy was the black humor.

With maladies innumerable
In heart, head, breast, and reins;°
610   But must secret passage find
To the inmost mind,
There exercise all his fierce accidents,°
And on her purest spirits prey,
As on entrails, joints, and limbs,
With answerable° pains, but more intense,
Though void of corporal sense.
    My griefs not only pain me
As a lingering disease,
But finding no redress, ferment and rage,
620   Nor less than wounds immedicable
Rankle, and fester, and gangrene,
To black mortification.°
Thoughts, my tormentors, armed with deadly stings
Mangle my apprehensive° tenderest parts,
Exasperate, exulcerate, and raise
Dire inflammation which no cooling herb
Or med'cinal liquor can assuage,
Nor breath of vernal air from snowy alp.
Sleep hath forsook and given me o'er
630   To death's benumbing opium as my only cure.
Thence faintings, swoonings of despair,
And sense of heaven's desertion.
    I was his nursling once and choice delight,
His destined from the womb,
Promised by heavenly message twice descending.°
Under his special eye
Abstemious I grew up and thrived amain;
He led me on to mightiest deeds
Above the nerve° of mortal arm
640   Against the uncircumcised, our enemies.
But now hath cast me off as never known,
And to those cruel enemies,
Whom I by his appointment had provoked,
Left me all helpless with the irreparable loss
Of sight, reserved alive to be repeated°
The subject of their cruelty or scorn.
Nor am I in the list of them that hope;
Hopeless are all my evils, all remediless;
This one prayer yet remains, might I be heard,
650   No long petition—speedy death,
The close of all my miseries, and the balm.

reins kidneys
accidents symptoms
answerable corresponding
mortification gangrene

apprehensive sensitive
twice descending See l. 361n.
nerve sinew; strength
repeated talked of as

CHORUS   Many are the sayings of the wise
In ancient and in modern books enrolled,
Extolling patience as the truest fortitude;
And to the bearing well of all calamities,
All chances incident to man's frail life,
Consolatories° writ
With studied argument, and much persuasion sought,
Lenient° of grief and anxious thought;
660   But with the afflicted in his pangs their sound
Little prevails, or rather seems a tune
Harsh, and of dissonant mood° from his complaint,
Unless he feel within
Some source of consolation from above,
Secret refreshings that repair his strength,
And fainting spirits uphold.
    God of our fathers, what is man!°
That thou towards him with hand so various—
Or might I say contrarious?—
670   Temper'st thy providence through his short course,
Not evenly, as thou rul'st
The angelic orders and inferior creatures mute,
Irrational and brute.°
Nor do I name of men the common rout,
That wandering loose about
Grow up and perish, as the summer fly,
Heads without name no more remembered;
But such as thou hast solemnly elected,
With gifts and graces eminently adorned
680   To some great work, thy glory,
And people's safety, which in part they effect;
Yet toward these thus dignified, thou oft
Amidst their highth of noon
Changest thy countenance and thy hand, with no regard
Of highest favours past
From thee on them, or them to thee of service.
    Nor only dost degrade them, or remit
To life obscured, which were a fair dismission,°
But throw'st them lower than thou didst exalt them high,
690   Unseemly falls in human eye,
Too grievous for the trespass or omission;
Oft leav'st them to the hostile sword

Consolatories writings intended to console in distress
Lenient soothing
mood a pun on a term both musical and spiritual
what is man "What is man, that thou art mindful of him?" (Psalms 8:4)
That thou . . . brute (ll. 667–73) Here the uncomprehending complaint against God for maltreating his champions takes the form of the old complaint that in the orders of angel and beast, between which men stand, there is no similar problem; the angels understand intuitively their duties, and the beasts, lacking reason, are spared both moral choices and God's election.
dismission dismissal

Of heathen and profane, their carcasses
To dogs and fowls a prey, or else captíved,
Or to the unjust tribunals, under change of times,
And condemnation of the ingrateful multitude.°
If these they scape, perhaps in poverty
With sickness and disease thou bow'st them down,
Painful diseases and deformed,
700   In crude° old age;
Though not disordinate, yet causeless suffering
The punishment of dissolute days;° in fine,
Just or unjust, alike seem miserable,
For oft alike, both come to evil end.
    So deal not with this once thy glorious champion,
The image of thy strength, and mighty minister.
What do I beg? How hast thou dealt already?
Behold him in this state calamitous, and turn
His labours, for thou canst, to peaceful end.
710   But who is this, what thing of sea or land?
Female of sex it seems,
That so bedecked, ornate, and gay,
Comes this way sailing
Like a stately ship
Of Tarsus,° bound for the isles
Of Javan or Gadire,°
With all her bravery on, and tackle trim,
Sails filled, and streamers waving,
Courted by all the winds that hold them play,
720   An amber scent of odorous perfume
Her harbinger,° a damsel train behind;
Some rich Philistian matron she may seem,
And now at nearer view, no other certain
Than Dálila thy wife.
    SAMSON   My wife, my traitress, let her not come near me.
    CHORUS   Yet on she moves, now stands and eyes thee fixed,
About to have spoke; but now, with head declined
Like a fair flower surcharged with dew, she weeps,
And words addressed seem into tears dissolved,
730   Wetting the borders of her silken veil;
But now again she makes address° to speak.
    DALILA   With doubtful° feet and wavering resolution

Oft leav'st . . . multitude It is often remarked
(by those who take *Samson Agonistes* to be a
late work) that Milton must have had in mind
the sufferings of the Commonwealth leaders
after the Restoration—including his own, which
included diseases of the kind mentioned immediately afterward.
crude premature
Though . . . days not themselves intemperate,
they nevertheless suffer diseases thought to be

the penalty of dissolute living (such as Milton's
gout)
Tarsus Tarshish (Isaiah 23:1), a Spanish port
(Tarsus, birthplace of St. Paul, was a port in
Turkey)
Javan or Gadire the Ionian isles of Greece, and
Cadiz
An amber . . . harbinger scent of ambergris,
which precedes her like a herald
makes address prepares
doubtful doubting

I came, still dreading thy displeasure, Samson,
Which to have merited, without excuse,
I cannot but acknowledge; yet if tears
May expiate (though the fact° more evil drew
In the perverse event° than I foresaw),
My penance° hath not slackened, though my pardon°
No way assured. But conjugal affection,
740 Prevailing over fear and timorous doubt,
Hath led me on, desirous to behold
Once more thy face, and know of thy estate;°
If aught in my ability may serve
To lighten what thou suffer'st, and appease
Thy mind with what amends is in my power,
Though late, yet in some part to recompense
My rash but more unfortunate misdeed.
    SAMSON   Out, out, hyena!° These are thy wonted arts,
And arts of every woman false like thee,
750 To break all faith, all vows, deceive, betray;
Then as repentant to submit, beseech,
And reconcilement move° with feigned remorse,
Confess, and promise wonders in her change,
Not truly penitent, but chief to try
Her husband, how far urged his patience bears,
His virtue or weakness which way to assail;
Then with more cautious and instructed skill
Again transgresses, and again submits;
That wisest and best men, full oft beguiled,
760 With goodness principled not to reject
The penitent, but ever to forgive,
Are drawn to wear out miserable days,
Entangled with a poisonous bosom snake,°
If not by quick destruction soon cut off,
As I by thee, to ages an example.
    DALILA   Yet hear me, Samson; not that I endeavour
To lessen or extenuate my offense,
But that on the other side if it be weighed
By itself, with aggravations° not surcharged,
770 Or else with just allowance counterpoised,
I may, if possible, thy pardon find
The easier towards me, or thy hatred less.
First granting, as I do, it was a weakness
In me, but incident to all our sex,
Curiosity, inquisitive, importúne

---

fact deed
perverse event unhappy outcome
penance penitence
pardon "Be" is understood in this latinate
construction.
estate condition

hyena The hyena was thought to imitate the
human voice and so lure men to destruction.
move propose
bosom snake "nourish a viper in one's bosom"
(proverb)
aggravations exaggerations

Of° secrets, then with like infirmity
To publish them, both common female faults;
Was it not weakness also to make known
For importunity, that is for naught,
780 Wherein consisted all thy strength and safety?
To what I did thou show'dst me first the way.
But I to enemies revealed, and should not?
Nor shouldst thou have trusted that to woman's frailty:
Ere I to thee, thou to thyself wast cruel.
Let weakness then with weakness come to parle,°
So near related, or the same of kind;°
Thine forgive mine, that men may censure thine
The gentler, if severely thou exact not
More strength from me than in thyself was found.
790 And what if love, which thou interpret'st hate,
The jealousy of love, powerful of sway
In human hearts, nor less in mine towards thee,
Caused what I did? I saw thee mutable
Of fancy,° feared lest one day thou wouldst leave me
As her at Timna, sought by all means therefore
How to endear, and hold thee to me firmest:
No better way I saw than by impórtuning
To learn thy secrets, get into my power
Thy key of strength and safety. Thou wilt say,
800 'Why then revealed?' I was assured by those
Who tempted me that nothing was designed
Against thee but safe custody and hold:
That made for me;° I knew that liberty
Would draw thee forth to perilous enterprises,
While I at home sat full of cares and fears,
Wailing thy absence in my widowed bed;
Here I should still enjoy thee day and night,
Mine and love's prisoner, not the Philistines',
Whole to myself, unhazarded abroad,
810 Fearless at home of partners in my love.
These reasons in love's law have passed for good,
Though fond° and reasonless to some perhaps;
And love hath oft, well meaning, wrought much woe,
Yet always pity or pardon hath obtained.
Be not unlike all others, not austere
As thou art strong, inflexible as steel.
If thou in strength all mortals dost exceed,
In uncompassionate anger do not so.
SAMSON   How cunningly the sorceress displays
820 Her own transgressions, to upbraid me mine!

importune Of persistent in inquiry concerning   fancy affection
parle parley   made for me was to my advantage
kind nature   fond foolish

That malice, not repentance, brought thee hither,
By this appears: I gave, thou say'st, the example,
I led the way—bitter reproach, but true;
I to myself was false ere thou to me;
Such pardon therefore as I give my folly,
Take to thy wicked deed; which° when thou seest
Impartial, self-severe, inexorable,
Thou wilt renounce thy seeking, and much rather
Confess it feigned. Weakness is thy excuse,
And I believe it, weakness to resist
Philistian gold; if weakness may excuse,
What murtherer, what traitor, parricide,
Incestuous, sacrilegious, but may plead it?
All wickedness is weakness: that plea therefore
With God or man will gain thee no remission.
But love constrained thee? Call it furious rage
To satisfy thy lust: love seeks to have love;
My love how couldst thou hope, who took'st the way
To raise in me inexpiable hate,
Knowing, as needs I must, by thee betrayed?°
In vain thou striv'st to cover shame with shame,
Or by evasions thy crime uncover'st more.
　　　DALILA   Since thou determin'st weakness for no plea
In man or woman, though to thy own condemning,
Hear what assaults I had, what snares besides,
What sieges girt me round, ere I consented;
Which might have awed the best-resolved of men,
The constantest, to have yielded without blame.
It was not gold, as to my charge thou lay'st,
That wrought with me: thou know'st the magistrates
And princes of my country came in person,
Solicited, commanded, threatened, urged,
Adjured by all the bonds of civil duty
And of religion, pressed how just it was,
How honourable, how glorious to entrap
A common enemy, who had destroyed
Such numbers of our nation: and the priest°
Was not behind, but ever at my ear,
Preaching how meritorious with the gods
It would be to ensnare an irreligious
Dishonourer of Dagon. What had I
To oppose against such powerful arguments?
Only my love of thee held long debate;
And combated in silence all these reasons
With hard contést. At length that grounded° maxim,

830

840

850

860

which Refers to "pardon" in l. 825.
Knowing . . . betrayed knowing myself to
have beeen betrayed by you

priest an addition to the biblical story
grounded well-established

So rife and celebrated in the mouths
Of wisest men, that to the public good
Private respects° must yield, with grave authority
Took full possession of me and prevailed;
870   Virtue, as I thought, truth, duty, so enjoining.
      SAMSON   I thought where all thy circling wiles would end,
In feigned religion, smooth hypocrisy.
But had thy love, still odiously pretended,
Been, as it ought, sincere, it would have taught thee
Far other reasonings, brought forth other deeds.
I before all the daughters of my tribe
And of my nation chose thee from among
My enemies, loved thee, as too well thou knewest,
Too well; unbosomed all my secrets to thee,
880   Not out of levity, but overpowered
By thy request, who could deny thee nothing;
Yet now am judged an enemy. Why then
Didst thou at first receive me for thy husband,
Then, as since then, thy country's foe professed?
Being once a wife, for me thou wast to leave
Parents and country; nor was I their subject,
Nor under their protection, but my own;
Thou mine, not theirs. If aught against my life
Thy country sought of thee, it sought unjustly,
890   Against the law of nature, law of nations;
No more thy country, but an impious crew
Of men conspiring to uphold their state
By worse than hostile deeds, violating the ends
For which our country is a name so dear;
Not therefore to be obeyed. But zeal moved thee;
To please thy gods thou didst it; gods unable
To acquit themselves° and prosecute their foes
But by ungodly deeds, the contradiction
Of their own deity, gods cannot be:
900   Less therefore to be pleased, obeyed, or feared.
These false pretexts and varnished colours° failing,
Bare in thy guilt how foul must thou appear!
      DALILA   In argument with men a woman ever
Goes by the worse,° whatever be her cause.
      SAMSON   For want of words, no doubt, or lack of breath;
Witness when I was worried with thy peals.
      DALILA   I was a fool, too rash, and quite mistaken
In what I thought would have succeeded best.
Let me obtain forgiveness of thee, Samson;
910   Afford me place to show what recompense
Towards thee I intend for what I have misdone,

---

respects interests
acquit themselves maintain their positions

varnished colours false arguments
Goes by the worse gets the worst of it

Misguided; only what remains past cure
Bear not too sensibly,° nor still insist
To afflict thyself in vain. Though sight be lost,
Life yet hath many solaces, enjoyed
Where other senses want not their delights
At home in leisure and domestic ease,
Exempt from many a care and chance to which
Eyesight exposes daily men abroad.

920 I to the lords will intercede, not doubting
Their favourable ear, that I may fetch thee
From forth this loathsome prison-house, to abide
With me, where my redoubled love and care
With nursing diligence, to me glad office,
May ever tend about thee to old age
With all things grateful° cheered, and so supplied,
That what by me thou hast lost thou least shall miss.

    SAMSON   No, no, of my condition take no care;
It fits not; thou and I long since are twain;
930 Nor think me so unwary or accurst
To bring my feet again into the snare
Where once I have been caught; I know thy trains,°
Though dearly to my cost, thy gins,° and toils;
Thy fair enchanted cup and warbling charms°
No more on me have power, their force is nulled;°
So much of adder's wisdom° I have learnt
To fence my ear against thy sorceries.
If in my flower of youth and strength, when all men
Loved, honoured, feared me, thou alone could hate me,
940 Thy husband, slight me, sell me, and forgo me,
How wouldst thou use me now, blind, and thereby
Deceivable, in most things as a child
Helpless, thence easily contemned, and scorned,
And last neglected? How wouldst thou insult
When I must live uxorious to thy will
In perfect thraldom, how again betray me,
Bearing my words and doings to the lords
To gloss° upon, and censuring, frown or smile?
This jail I count the house of liberty
950 To° thine whose doors my feet shall never enter.

    DALILA   Let me approach at least, and touch thy hand.

    SAMSON   Not for thy life, lest fierce remembrance wake
My sudden rage to tear thee joint by joint.
At distance I forgive thee, go with that;

---

sensibly feelingly, sensitively
grateful pleasing
trains tricks
gins traps
fair . . . charms attributing to Dalila the instruments of Circe (see *Comus*, ll. 51–53, and Spenser, *The Faerie Queene* II.xii)

nulled nullified, extinguished
adder's wisdom ". . . they are like the deaf adder that stoppeth her ear; Which will not hearken to the voice of charmers" (Psalms 58: 4f.)
gloss comment
To compared with

Bewail thy falsehood, and the pious works
It hath brought forth to make thee memorable
Among illustrious women, faithful wives;
Cherish thy hastened widowhood with the gold
Of matrimonial treason: so farewell.

960   DALILA   I see thou art implacable, more deaf
To prayers than winds and seas; yet winds to seas
Are reconciled at length, and sea to shore:
Thy anger, unappeasable, still rages,
Eternal tempest never to be calmed.
Why do I humble thus myself, and suing
For peace, reap nothing but repulse and hate?
Bid go with evil omen° and the brand
Of infamy upon my name denounced?
To mix with thy concernments I desist
970 Henceforth, nor too much disapprove my own.
Fame, if not double-faced, is double-mouthed,
And with contráry blast proclaims most deeds;
On both his wings, one black, the other white,
Bears greatest names in his wild airy flight.°
My name perhaps among the circumcised
In Dan,° in Judah, and the bordering tribes,
To all posterity may stand defamed,
With malediction mentioned, and the blot
Of falsehood most unconjugal traduced.
980 But in my country where I most desire,
In Ekron, Gaza, Asdod, and in Gath,°
I shall be named among the famousest
Of women, sung at solemn festivals,
Living and dead recorded, who, to save
Her country from a fierce destroyer, chose
Above the faith of wedlock bands, my tomb
With odours° visited and annual flowers:
Not less renowned than in Mount Ephraim
Jael, who with inhospitable guile
990 Smote Sisera sleeping, through the temples nailed.°
Nor shall I count it heinous to enjoy
The public marks of honour and reward
Conferred upon me for the piety°
Which to my country I was judged to have shown.
At this whoever envies or repines,
I leave him to his lot, and like my own.
    CHORUS   She's gone, a manifest serpent by her sting

evil omen predictions of bad luck
Fame . . . flight This allegory of Fame differs in some ways from the conventional, and Milton must have invented it.
Dan Samson's own tribe
Ekron . . . Gath principal cities of the Philistines

odours spices
Jael . . . nailed Jael allowed Sisera, a Philistine general, to hide in her tent. While he was sleeping she knocked a nail into his head; the story is in Deborah's song, Judges 5.
piety from the Latin *pietas*, meaning devotion to one's country

Discovered in the end, till now concealed.

SAMSON   So let her go; God sent her to debase me,
And aggravate my folly who committed
To such a viper his most sacred trust
Of secrecy, my safety, and my life.

CHORUS   Yet beauty, though injurious, hath strange power,
After offence returning, to regain
Love once possessed, nor can be easily
Repulsed, without much inward passion° felt
And secret sting of amorous remorse.

SAMSON   Love-quarrels oft in pleasing concord end,
Not wedlock-treachery endangering life.

CHORUS   It is not virtue, wisdom, valour, wit,
Strength, comeliness of shape, or amplest merit
That woman's love can win or long inherit;°
But what it is, hard is to say,
Harder to hit,
(Which way soever men refer it),
Much like thy riddle,° Samson, in one day
Or seven, though one should musing sit;
    If any of these, or all, the Timnian bride
Had not so soon preferred
Thy paranymph,° worthless to thee compared,
Successor in thy bed,
Nor both° so loosely disallied
Their nuptials, nor this last so treacherously
Had shorn the fatal harvest of thy head.
Is it for that° such outward ornament
Was lavished on their sex, that inward gifts
Were left for haste unfinished, judgment scant,
Capacity not raised to apprehend
Or value what is best
In choice, but oftest to affect° the wrong?
Or was too much of self-love mixed,
Of constancy no root infixed,
That either they love nothing, or not long?
    Whate'er it be, to wisest men and best
Seeming at first all heavenly under virgin veil,
Soft, modest, meek, demure,
Once joined, the contrary she proves, a thorn
Intestine,° far within defensive arms
A cleaving° mischief, in his way to virtue
Adverse and turbulent; or by her charms

passion suffering
inherit possess
riddle the riddle of the lion and the honeycomb, which caused the breakup of Samson's
first marriage (Judges 14)
paranymph groomsman, companion of the bride-

groom, to whom Samson's wife turned (Judges
14:20) for consolation
both both wives
for that because
affect desire
Intestine domestic
cleaving closely fitting, enwrapping, hindering

Draws him awry enslaved
With dotage, and his sense depraved
To folly and shameful deeds which ruin ends.
What pilot so expert but needs must wreck,
Embarked with such a steers-mate at the helm?
　　Favoured of heaven who finds
One virtuous, rarely found,
That in domestic good combines:
Happy that house! his way to peace is smooth;
But virtue which breaks through all opposition,   1050
And all temptation can remove,
Most shines and most is ácceptáble above.
　　Therefore God's universal law
Gave to the man despotic power
Over his female in due awe,
Nor from that right to part an hour,
Smile she or lour:°
So shall he least confusion draw
On his whole life, not swayed
By female usurpation, nor dismayed.°   1060
　　But had we best retire? I see a storm.
　　SAMSON   Fair days have oft contracted wind and rain.
　　CHORUS   But this another kind of tempest brings.
　　SAMSON   Be less abstruse, my riddling days are past.
　　CHORUS   Look now for no enchanting voice, nor fear
The bait of honied words; a rougher tongue
Draws hitherward; I know him by his stride,
The giant Hárapha° of Gath, his look
Haughty as is his pile° high-built and proud.
Comes he in peace? What wind hath blown him hither   1070
I less conjecture than when first I saw
The sumptuous Dálila floating this way;
His habit carries peace, his brow defiance.
　　SAMSON   Or peace or not, alike to me he comes.
　　CHORUS   His fraught° we soon shall know, he now arrives.
　　HARAPHA   I come not, Samson, to condole thy chance,
As these perhaps, yet wish it had not been,
Though for no friendly intent. I am of Gath;
Men call me Hárapha, of stock renowned

---

lour frown
Is it . . . dismayed In this "misogynist" chorus
(ll. 1025–60) Milton both repeats some traditional antifeminist positions and echoes his own
complaints in the pamphlets on divorce. In
1046 ff. he remembers Proverbs 31 on virtuous
wives ("The heart of her husband doth
safely trust in her . . . she will do him good
and not evil all the days of her life," etc.).
Samson was used as a negative example in
discussions about good marriages. Milton,
despite his own disappointments, took a more

exalted view of marriage than many contemporaries, and perhaps lets the Chorus state the
argument against wives as gloomily as possible
for dramatic reasons: they are again showing no
understanding of the reality of Samson's position, nor of the reason that he married Dalila.
Harapha not in the biblical story; Milton
made him up from the Hebrew for giant and
the exploits of Goliath
pile building, here probably meaning Gath
fraught freight, message

1080 As Og or Anak and the Emims old
That Kiriathaim held;° thou knowest me now,
If thou at all art known.° Much I have heard
Of thy prodigious might and feats performed
Incredible to me, in this displeased,
That I was never present on the place
Of those encounters where we might have tried
Each other's force in camp° or listed field:°
And now am come to see of whom such noise
Hath walked° about, and each limb to survey,
1090 If thy appearance answer loud report.
    SAMSON   The way to know were not to see but taste.
    HARAPHA   Dost thou already single° me? I thought
Gyves° and the mill had tamed thee. O that fortune
Had brought me to the field where thou art famed
To have wrought such wonders with an ass's jaw;
I should have forced thee soon wish other arms,
Or left thy carcass where the ass lay thrown:
So had the glory of prowess been recovered
To Palestine, won by a Philistine
1100 From the unforeskinned race, of whom thou bear'st
The highest name for valiant acts; that honour,
Certain to have won by mortal duel from thee.
I lose, prevented by thy eyes put out.
    SAMSON   Boast not of what thou wouldst have done, but do
What then thou wouldst; thou seest it in thy hand.
    HARAPHA   To combat with a blind man I disdain,
And thou hast need much washing to be touched.
    SAMSON   Such usage as your honourable lords
Afford me, assassinated° and betrayed;
1110 Who durst not with their whole united powers
In fight withstand me single and unarmed,
Nor in the house with chamber ambushes
Close-banded° durst attack me, no, not sleeping,
Till they had hired a woman with their gold,
Breaking her marriage faith to circumvent me.
Therefore without feigned shifts° let be assigned
Some narrow place enclosed, where sight may give thee,
Or rather flight, no great advantage on me;
Then put on all thy gorgeous arms, thy helmet
1120 And brigandine° of brass, thy broad habergeon,°

Og . . . held "Only Og king of Bashan remained of the . . . giants" (Deuteronomy 3:11);
"the giants, the sons of Anak" (Numbers 13:
33); "The Emims . . . were accounted giants"
(Deuteronomy 2:10–11); "the Emims in Shaveh
Kiriathaim" (Genesis 14:5)
If . . . known if you know anything at all
camp field
listed field equipped with lists for jousting
walked gone
single pick me out (as opponent)
Gyves fetters
assassinated treacherously attacked
Close-banded secretly associated
shifts tricks
brigandine ringed body-armor
habergeon coat of mail

Vant-brace° and greaves,° and gauntlet; add thy spear,
A weaver's beam,° and seven-times-folded shield;°
I only with an oaken staff will meet thee,
And raise such outcries on thy clattered iron,
Which long shall not withhold me from thy head,
That in a little time while breath remains thee,
Thou oft shalt wish thyself at Gath to boast
Again in safety what thou wouldst have done
To Samson, but shalt never see Gath more.

1130   HARAPHA   Thou durst not thus disparage glorious arms
Which greatest heroes have in battle worn,
Their ornament and safety, had not spells
And black enchantments, some magician's art,
Armed thee or charmed thee strong, which thou from heaven
Feign'dst at thy birth was given thee in thy hair,
Where strength can least abide, though all thy hairs
Were bristles ranged like those that ridge the back
Of chafed° wild boars, or ruffled porcupines.

        SAMSON   I know no spells, use no forbidden arts;°
1140   My trust is in the living God who gave me
At my nativity this strength, diffused
No less through all my sinews, joints and bones,
Than thine, while I preserved these locks unshorn,
The pledge of my unviolated vow.
For proof hereof, if Dagon be thy god,
Go to his temple, invocate his aid
With solemnest devotion, spread before him
How highly it concerns his glory now
To frustrate and dissolve these magic spells,
1150   Which I to be the power of Israel's God
Avow, and challenge Dagon to the test,
Offering to combat thee, his champion bold,
With the utmost of his godhead seconded:
Then thou shalt see, or rather to thy sorrow
Soon feel, whose God is strongest, thine or mine.

        HARAPHA   Presume not on thy God, whate'er he be;
Thee he regards not, owns not, hath cut off
Quite from his people, and delivered up
Into thy enemies' hand; permitted them
1160   To put out both thine eyes and fettered send thee
Into the common prison, there to grind
Among the slaves and asses, thy comrádes,
As good for nothing else, no better service
With those thy boisterous° locks; no worthy match

Vant-brace armor for forearm
greaves thigh-armor
weaver's beam wooden roller in loom (the armor comes from the description of Goliath in I Samuel 17)

shield recalling that of Ajax in Homer
chafed angry
forbidden arts Duelists were required to swear that they would use no magic.
boisterous thick-growing

For valour to assail, nor by the sword
Of noble warrior, so to stain his honour,°
But by the barber's razor best subdued.
    SAMSON   All these indignities, for such they are
From thine,° these evils I deserve and more,
1170   Acknowledge them from God inflicted on me
Justly, yet despair not of his final pardon
Whose ear is ever open, and his eye
Gracious to readmit the suppliant;
In confidence whereof I once again
Defy° thee to the trial of mortal fight,
By combat to decide whose god is God,
Thine or whom I with Israel's sons adore.
    HARAPHA   Fair honour that thou dost thy God, in trusting
He will accept thee to defend his cause,
1180   A murderer, a revolter, and a robber.
    SAMSON   Tongue-doughty° giant, how dost thou prove me these?
    HARAPHA   Is not thy nation subject to our lords?
Their magistrates confessed it, when they took thee
As a league-breaker and delivered bound
Into our hands:° for hadst thou not committed
Notorious murder on those thirty men
At Ascalon, who never did thee harm,
Then like a robber stripp'dst them of their robes?°
The Philistines, when thou hadst broke the league,
1190   Went up with armèd powers thee only seeking,
To others did no violence nor spoil.
    SAMSON   Among the daughters of the Philistines
I chose a wife, which argued me no foe,
And in your city held my nuptial feast;
But your ill-meaning politician° lords,
Under pretence of bridal friends and guests,
Appointed to await me thirty spies,
Who threatening cruel death constrained the bride
To wring from me and tell to them my secret,
1200   That solved the riddle which I had proposed.
When I perceived all set on enmity,
As on my enemies, wherever chanced,
I used hostility, and took their spoil
To pay my underminers in their coin.°
My nation was subjected to your lords.
It was the force of conquest; force with force
Is well ejected when the conquered can.
But I a private person, whom my country

honour Milton gives Harapha some of the
punctilio of the kind of courtier he hated.
thine your people
Defy challenge to combat, as in the medieval
tradition of trying justice by means of a joust

Tongue-doughty brave in speech
delivered . . . hands See l. 258n.
stripp'dst . . . robes See l. 221n.
politician Machiavellian

As a league-breaker gave up bound, presumed
1210 Single rebellion and did hostile acts.
I was no private but a person raised
With strength sufficient and command from heaven
To free my country; if their servile minds
Me their deliverer sent would not receive,
But to their masters gave me up for naught,
The unworthier they; whence to this day they serve.
I was to do my part from heaven assigned,
And had performed it if my known offence
Had not disabled me, not all your force.
1220 These shifts° refuted, answer thy appellant,°
Though by his blindness maimed for high attempts,
Who now defies thee thrice to single fight,
As a petty enterprise of small enforce.°
    HARAPHA   With thee, a man condemned, a slave enrolled,
Due by the law to capital punishment?
To fight with thee no man of arms will deign.
    SAMSON   Cam'st thou for this, vain boaster, to survey me,
To descant° on my strength, and give thy verdict?
Come nearer, part not hence so slight informed;
1230 But take good heed my hand survey not thee.
    HARAPHA   O Baal-zebub!° can my ears unused°
Hear these dishonours, and not render death?
    SAMSON   No man withholds thee, nothing from thy hand
Fear I incurable; bring up thy van;°
My heels are fettered, but my fist is free.
    HARAPHA   This insolence other kind of answer fits.
    SAMSON   Go, baffled coward, lest I run upon thee,
Though in these chains, bulk without spirit vast,
And with one buffet lay thy structure low,
1240 Or swing thee in the air, then dash thee down
To the hazard of thy brains and shattered sides.
    HARAPHA   By Astaroth,° ere long thou shalt lament
These braveries° in irons loaden on thee.
    CHORUS   His giantship is gone somewhat crestfallen,
Stalking with less unconscionable° strides,
And lower looks, but in a sultry chafe.°
    SAMSON   I dread him not, nor all his giant brood,
Though fame divulge him father of five sons,
All of gigantic size, Goliah chief.°
1250 CHORUS   He will directly to the lords, I fear,

---

shifts dishonest arguments
appellant challenger
enforce effort
descant play variations on
Baal-zebub (probably) Beelzebub, lord of the
flies, a Philistine idol
unused unaccustomed
van vanguard

Astaroth Philistine moon goddess
braveries boasts
unconscionable excessive
sultry chafe sullen temper
father . . . chief II Samuel 21.16 ff. describes
four Philistine giants killed by David, but of
course makes no mention of Harapha.

And with malicious counsel stir them up
Some way or other yet further to afflict thee.
SAMSON   He must allege some cause, and offered fight
Will not dare mention, lest a question rise
Whether he durst accept the offer or not,
And that he durst not plain enough appeared.
Much more affliction than already felt
They cannot well impose, nor I sustain,
If they intend advantage of my labours,
1260 The work of many hands, which earns my keeping
With no small profit daily to my owners.
But come what will, my deadliest foe will prove
My speediest friend, by death to rid me hence,
The worst that he can give, to me the best.
Yet so it may fall out, because their end
Is hate, not help to me, it may with mine
Draw their own ruin who attempt the deed.°
  CHORUS   Oh how comely it is and how reviving
To the spirits of just men long oppressed,
1270 When God into the hands of their deliverer
Puts invincible might
To quell the mighty of the earth, the oppressor,
The brute and boisterous force of violent men,
Hardy and industrious to support
Tyrannic power, but raging to pursue
The righteous and all such as honour truth!
He all their ammunition°
And feats of war defeats
With plain heroic magnitude of mind
1280 And celestial vigour armed;
Their armories and magazines contemns,
Renders them useless, while
With wingèd expedition
Swift as the lightning glance he executes
His errand on the wicked, who surprised
Lose their defence, distracted and amazed.
  But patience is more oft the exercise
Of saints, the trial of their fortitude,°
Making them each his own deliverer,
1290 And victor over all
That tyranny or fortune can inflict;
Either of these is in thy lot,
Samson, with might endued
Above the sons of men; but sight bereaved

---

yet so . . . deed Samson has a premonition of the sequel; the Chorus comments, but soon abandons the idea that this kind of heroic act is still open to Samson.

ammunition military stores
patience . . . fortitude Of the two heroisms, passive and active, the Chorus wrongly opts for the first.

May chance to number thee with those
Whom patience finally must crown.
   This idol's day° hath been to thee no day of rest,
Labouring thy mind
More than the working day thy hands;
And yet perhaps more trouble is behind.
For I descry this way
Some other tending; in his hand
A sceptre or quaint° staff he bears,
Comes on amain, speed in his look.
By his habit I discern him now
A public officer, and now at hand.
His message will be short and voluble.°
     OFFICER   Hebrews, the prisoner Samson here I seek.
     CHORUS   His manacles remark° him; there he sits.
     OFFICER   Samson, to thee our lords thus bid me say:
This day to Dagon is a solemn feast,
With sacrifices, triumph, pomp, and games;
Thy strength they know surpassing human rate,
And now some public proof thereof require
To honour this great feast, and great assembly;
Rise therefore with all speed and come along,
Where I will see thee heartened and fresh clad
To appear as fits before the illustrious lords.
     SAMSON   Thou knowest I am an Hebrew, therefore tell them
Our law forbids at their religious rites
My presence; for that cause I cannot come.
     OFFICER   This answer, be assured, will not content them.
     SAMSON   Have they not sword-players, and every sort
Of gymnic artists, wrestlers, riders, runners,
Jugglers and dancers, antics,° mummers,° mimics,
But they must pick me out with shackles tired,
And over-laboured at their public mill,
To make them sport with blind activity?
Do they not seek occasion of new quarrels,
On my refusal, to distress me more,
Or make a game of my calamities?
Return the way thou cam'st; I will not come.
     OFFICER   Regard thyself;° this will offend them highly.
     SAMSON   Myself? My conscience and internal peace.
Can they think me so broken, so debased
With corporal servitude, that my mind ever
Will condescend to such absurd commands?
Although their drudge, to be their fool or jester,
And in my midst of sorrow and heart-grief

---

idol's day on the analogy of holy-day, holiday   **antics** clowns
quaint elaborately carved   **mummers** actors
voluble rapid   **Regard thyself** look to your own interests
remark indicate

1340   To show them feats and play before their god,
The worst of all indignities, yet on me
Joined° with extreme contempt? I will not come.
   OFFICER   My message was imposed on me with speed,
Brooks no delay; is this thy resolution?
   SAMSON   So take it with what speed thy message needs.
   OFFICER   I am sorry what this stoutness° will produce.
   SAMSON   Perhaps thou shalt have cause to sorrow indeed.
   CHORUS   Consider, Samson; matters now are strained
Up to the highth, whether to hold or break;
1350   He's gone, and who knows how he may report
Thy words by adding fuel to the flame?
Expect another message more imperious,
More lordly thundering than thou well wilt bear.
   SAMSON   Shall I abuse this consecrated gift
Of strength, again returning with my hair
After my great transgression, so requite
Favour renewed, and add a greater sin
By prostituting holy things to idols;
A Nazarite in place abominable
1360   Vaunting my strength in honour to their Dagon?
Besides, how vile, contemptible, ridiculous,
What act more execrably unclean, profane?
   CHORUS   Yet with this strength thou serv'st the Philistines,
Idolatrous, uncircumcised, unclean.
   SAMSON   Not in their idol-worship, but by labour
Honest and lawful to deserve my food
Of those who have me in their civil power.
   CHORUS   Where the heart joins not, outward acts defile not.
   SAMSON   Where outward force constrains, the sentence° holds;
1370   But who constrains me to the temple of Dagon,
Not dragging? The Philistian lords command.
Commands are no constraints. If I obey them,
I do it freely, venturing to displease
God for the fear of man, and man prefer,
Set God behind; which in his jealousy
Shall never, unrepented, find forgiveness.
Yet that he may dispense with° me or thee,
Present in temples at idolatrous rites
For some important cause, thou need'st not doubt.
1380   CHORUS   How thou wilt here come off surmounts my reach.
   SAMSON   Be of good courage; I begin to feel
Some rousing motions° in me which dispose
To something extraordinary my thoughts.

Joined enjoined, commanded
stoutness stubbornness
sentence saying, maxim
dispense with grant a dispensation to; Samson
is beginning to form a different plan
rousing motions He is recognizing an "intimate

impulse" like those which caused his marriages;
it, too, will send him among the Philistines and
put him in a position in which he seems to be
breaking Hebrew law; and of course the end—
the killing of Philistines—is the same, and
part of God's concealed plan for his champion.

I with this messenger will go along,
Nothing to do, be sure, that may dishonour
Our law, or stain my vow of Nazarite.
If there be aught of presage in the mind,
This day will be remarkable in my life
By some great act, or of my days the last.°
1390   CHORUS   In time thou hast resolved; the man returns.
    OFFICER   Samson, this second message from our lords
To thee I am bid say: art thou our slave,
Our captive, at the public mill our drudge,
And dar'st thou at our sending and command
Dispute thy coming? Come without delay;
Or we shall find such engines to assail
And hamper thee, as thou shalt come of° force,
Though thou wert firmlier fastened than a rock.
    SAMSON   I could be well content to try their art,
1400   Which to no few of them would prove pernicious.
Yet knowing their advantages too many,
Because° they shall not trail me through their streets
Like a wild beast, I am content to go.
Masters' commands come with a power resistless
To such as owe them absolute subjection;
And for a life who will not change his purpose?
(So mutable are all the ways of men.)°
Yet this be sure, in nothing to comply
Scandalous or forbidden in our law.
1410   OFFICER   I praise thy resolution;° doff° these links.
By this compliance thou wilt win the lords
To favour, and perhaps to set thee free.
    SAMSON   Brethren, farewell; your company along
I will not wish, lest it perhaps offend them
To see me girt with friends; and how the sight
Of me as of a common enemy,
So dreaded once, may now exasperate them,
I know not. Lords are lordliest in their wine;
And the well-feasted priest then soonest fired
1420   With zeal, if aught° religion seem concerned;
No less the people on their holy-days
Impetuous, insolent, unquenchable;
Happen what may, of me expect to hear
Nothing dishonourable, impure, unworthy
Our God, our law, my nation, or myself;
The last of me or no I cannot warrant.
    CHORUS   Go, and the Holy One

---

some . . . last Samson says either-or; it turns
out to be both.
of by
Because so that

Masters' . . . men all ironical
resolution decision
doff take off
aught to any degree

Of Israel be thy guide
To what may serve his glory best, and spread his name
1430   Great among the heathen round;
Send thee the angel of thy birth, to stand
Fast by thy side, who from thy father's field
Rode up in flames after his message told
Of thy conception,° and be now a shield
Of fire; that spirit that first rushed on thee
In the camp of Dan,°
Be efficacious in thee now at need.
For never was from heaven imparted
Measure of strength so great to mortal seed,
1440   As in thy wondrous actions hath been seen.
But wherefore comes old Mánoa in such haste
With youthful steps? Much livelier than erewhile
He seems: supposing here to find his son,
Or of him bringing to us some glad news?
      MANOA Peace with you, brethren; my inducement hither
Was not at present here to find my son,
By order of the lords new parted hence
To come and play before them at their feast.
I heard all as I came, the city rings,
1450   And numbers thither flock; I had no will,
Lest I should see him forced to things unseemly.
But that which moved my coming now was chiefly
To give ye part° with me what hope I have
With good success° to work his liberty.
      CHORUS That hope would much rejoice us to partake
With thee; say, reverend sire; we thirst to hear.
      MANOA I have attempted° one by one the lords,
Either at home, or through the high street passing,
With supplication prone and father's tears
1460   To accept of ransom for my son their prisoner.
Some much averse I found and wondrous harsh,
Contemptuous, proud, set on revenge and spite;
That part most reverenced Dagon and his priests;
Others more moderate seeming, but their aim
Private reward, for which both God and State
They easily would set to sale; a third
More generous far and civil, who confessed
They had enough revenged, having reduced
Their foe to misery beneath their fears;
1470   The rest was magnanimity to remit,
If some convenient ransom were proposed.

Rode . . . conception Judges 13:10   **give ye part** share
that spirit . . . Dan Judges 13:25. At other   **success** outcome
times the angel, or "the Spirit of the Lord,"   **attempted** appealed to
attended Samson at need.

What noise or shout was that? It tore the sky.
    CHORUS   Doubtless the people shouting to behold
Their once great dread, captive and blind before them,
Or at some proof of strength before them shown.
    MANOA   His ransom, if my whole inheritance
May compass it, shall willingly be paid
And numbered down; much rather I shall choose
To live the poorest in my tribe, than richest,
1480   And he in that calamitous prison left.°
No, I am fixed not to part hence without him.
For his redemption all my patrimony,
If need be, I am ready to forgo
And quit; not wanting him, I shall want nothing.
    CHORUS   Fathers are wont to lay up for their sons,
Thou for thy son art bent to lay out all;
Sons wont° to nurse their parents in old age,
Thou in old age car'st how to nurse thy son,
Made older than thy age through eyesight lost.
1490   MANOA   It shall be my delight to tend his eyes,
And view him sitting in the house, ennobled
With all those high exploits by him achieved,
And on his shoulders waving down those locks
That of a nation armed the strength contained.
And I persuade me God had not permitted
His strength again to grow up with his hair
Garrisoned round about him like a camp
Of faithful soldiery, were not his purpose
To use him further yet in some great service,
1500   Not to sit idle with so great a gift
Useless, and thence ridiculous, about him.
And since his strength with eyesight was not lost,
God will restore him eyesight to° his strength.
    CHORUS   Thy hopes are not ill-founded nor seem vain
Of his delivery, and thy joy thereon
Conceived, agreeable to a father's love;
In both which we, as next,° participate.°
    MANOA   I know your friendly minds and—O what noise!
Mercy of heaven, what hideous noise was that!
1510   Horribly loud, unlike the former shout.
    CHORUS   Noise call you it, or universal groan,
As if the whole inhabitation° perished?
Blood, death, and dreadful deeds are in that noise,
Ruin, destruction at the utmost point.

And he . . . left while he . . . is left
wont "Are" is understood.
to to match
next nearest; kinsmen, fellow tribesman
fathers . . . participate This conversation between Manoa and the Chorus (ll. 1485–1507)
develops the ironical little plot of Manoa's
attempts to find a human plan for the comfort
of Samson despite his professed belief that
God's plan is still operative. It comes to a
head, and accordingly seems, like most human
stratagems, ridiculous, at exactly the moment
when God declares himself, and uses Samson,
as before, in an actively heroic role.
inhabitation population

MANOA   Of ruin indeed methought I heard the noise.
Oh it continues, they have slain my son.
    CHORUS   Thy son is rather slaying them; that outcry
From slaughter of one foe could not ascend.
    MANOA   Some dismal accident it needs must be;
1520   What shall we do, stay here or run and see?
    CHORUS   Best keep together here, lest running thither
We unawares run into danger's mouth.
This evil on the Philistines is fallen;
From whom could else a general cry be heard?
The sufferers then will scarce molest us here;
From other hands we need not much to fear.
What if his eyesight (for to Israel's God
Nothing is hard) by miracle restored,
He now be dealing dole° among his foes,
1530   And over heaps of slaughtered walk his way?
    MANOA   That were a joy presumptuous to be thought.
    CHORUS   Yet God hath wrought things as incredible
For his people of old; what hinders now?
    MANOA   He can I know, but doubt to think he will;
Yet hope would fain subscribe, and tempts belief.
A little stay will bring some notice hither.
    CHORUS   Of good or bad so great, of bad the sooner;
For evil news rides post, while good news baits.°
And to our wish I see one hither speeding,
1540   A Hebrew, as I guess, and of our tribe.
    MESSENGER°   O whither shall I run, or which way fly
The sight of this so horrid spectacle
Which erst° my eyes beheld and yet behold;
For dire imagination still pursues me.
But providence or instinct of nature seems,
Or reason though disturbed, and scarce consulted
To have guided me aright, I know not how,
To thee first reverend Manoa, and to these
My countrymen, whom here I knew remaining,
1550   As at some distance from the place of horror,
So in the sad event too much concerned.°
    MANOA   The accident was loud, and here before thee
With rueful cry, yet what it was we hear not,
No preface needs, thou seest we long to know.
    MESSENGER   It would burst forth, but I recover breath,
And sense distract,° to know well what I utter.
    MANOA   Tell us the sum, the circumstance defer.°

---

dole a pun on "that which is dealt (or doled)
out" and "grief, or pain"
baits pauses for refreshment on the way
Messenger Since violent incidents were forbidden by the rules of classical tragedy, the Messenger or Nuntius is a regular feature of
tragedies at this point.

erst a little while ago
As . . . concerned both removed from the
scene of the occurrence and deeply concerned
in it
distract distracted
Tell . . . defer give us the gist of it, leave the
detail till later

MESSENGER   Gaza yet stands, but all her sons are fallen,
All in a moment overwhelmed and fallen.
1560   MANOA   Sad, but thou know'st to Israelites not saddest
The desolation of a hostile city.
MESSENGER   Feed on that first, there may in grief be surfeit.°
MANOA   Relate by whom.
MESSENGER   By Samson.
MANOA   That still lessens
The sorrow, and converts it nigh to joy.
MESSENGER   Ah Manoa I refrain, too suddenly
To utter what will come at last too soon;
Lest evil tidings with too rude irruption
Hitting thy agèd ear should pierce too deep.
MANOA   Suspense in news is torture, speak them out.
1570   MESSENGER   Then take the worst in brief, Samson is dead.
MANOA   The worst indeed, O all my hope's defeated
To free him hence! but death who sets all free
Hath paid his ransom now and full discharge.
What windy joy this day had I conceived°
Hopeful of his delivery, which now proves
Abortive as the first-born bloom of spring
Nipped with the lagging rear of winter's frost.
Yet ere I give the reins to grief, say first,
How died he? death to life is crown or shame.
1580   All by him fell thou say'st, by whom fell he,
What glorious hand gave Samson his death's wound?
MESSENGER   Unwounded of his enemies he fell.
MANOA   Wearied with slaughter then or how? explain.
MESSENGER   By his own hands.
MANOA   Self-violence? what cause
Brought him so soon at variance with himself
Among his foes?
MESSENGER   Inevitable cause
At once both to destroy and be destroyed;
The edifice where all were met to see him
Upon their heads and on his own he pulled.
1590   MANOA   O lastly over-strong against thyself!
A dreadful way thou took'st to thy revenge.
More than enough we know; but while things yet
Are in confusion, give us if thou canst,
Eye-witness of what first or last was done,
Relation more particular and distinct.
MESSENGER   Occasions drew me early to this city,
And as the gates I entered with sunrise,
The morning trumpets festival proclaimed

Feed . . . surfeit digest that news first; what
follows may make you sick with grief

What . . . conceived what seemed to be a
pregnancy turns out to be mere flatulence

Through each high street. Little I had despatched°
1600 When all abroad was rumoured that this day
Samson should be brought forth to show the people
Proof of his mighty strength in feats and games;
I sorrowed at his captive state, but minded°
Not to be absent at that spectacle.
The building was a spacious theatre,
Half round on two main pillars vaulted high,
With seats where all the lords, and each degree
Of sort, might sit in order to behold;
The other side was open, where the throng
1610 On banks° and scaffolds under sky might stand;
I among these aloof obscurely stood.
The feast and noon grew high, and sacrifice
Had filled their hearts with mirth, high cheer, and wine,
When to their sports they turned. Immediately
Was Samson as a public servant brought,
In their state livery clad; before him pipes
And timbrels; on each side went armèd guards,
Both horse and foot before him and behind
Archers, and slingers, cataphracts° and spears.
1620 At sight of him the people with a shout
Rifted the air, clamouring their god with praise,
Who had made their dreadful enemy their thrall.
He, patient but undaunted, where they led him,
Came to the place; and what was set before him,
Which without help of eye might be assayed,
To heave, pull, draw, or break, he still performed,
All with incredible, stupendious° force,
None daring to appear antagonist.
At length for intermission sake they led him
1630 Between the pillars; he his guide requested
(For so from such as nearer stood we heard),
As over-tired, to let him lean a while
With both his arms on those two massy pillars
That to the archèd roof gave main support.
He unsuspicious led him; which when Samson
Felt in his arms, with head a while inclined,
And eyes fast fixed he stood, as one who prayed,
Or some great matter in his mind revolved.°
At last with head erect thus cried aloud:
1640 'Hitherto, lords, what your commands imposed
I have performed, as reason was, obeying,
Not without wonder or delight beheld.

despatched done in the way of business
minded resolved
banks benches
cataphracts armored men on armored mounts
stupendious stupendous

in his mind revolved In Judges 16:30, Samson prays to be allowed to die with his enemies; Milton substitutes an inner resolution and an outer declaration to absolve Samson of suicide, a Christian sin.

Now of my own accord such other trial
I mean to show you of my strength, yet greater,
As with amaze° shall strike all who behold.'
This uttered, straining all his nerves he bowed;
As with the force of winds and waters pent
When mountains tremble, those two massy pillars
With horrible convulsion to and fro
1650 He tugged, he shook, till down they came and drew
The whole roof after them, with burst of thunder
Upon the heads of all who sat beneath,
Lords, ladies, captains, counsellors, or priests,
Their choice nobility and flower, not only
Of this but each Philistian city round,
Met from all parts to solemnize this feast.
Samson, with these inmixed, inevitably
Pulled down the same destruction on himself;
The vulgar only scaped who stood without.
1660   CHORUS   O dearly bought revenge, yet glorious!
Living or dying thou hast fulfilled
The work for which thou wast foretold
To Israel, and now li'st victorious
Among thy slain self-killed,
Not willingly, but tangled in the fold
Of dire necessity, whose law in death conjoined
Thee with thy slaughtered foes, in number more
Than all thy life had slain before.
    SEMICHORUS   While their hearts were jocund and sublime,°
1670 Drunk with idolatry, drunk with wine,
And fat regorged of bulls and goats,
Chanting their idol, and preferring
Before our living dread who dwells
In Silo,° his bright sanctuary,
Among them he a spirit of frenzy sent,
Who hurt their minds,
And urged them on with mad desire
To call in haste for their destroyer;
They only set on sport and play
1680 Unweetingly° importuned
Their own destruction to come speedy upon them.
So fond are mortal men
Fallen into wrath divine,
As their own ruin on themselves to invite,
Insensate left, or to sense reprobate,
And with blindness internal struck.
    SEMICHORUS   But he, though blind of sight,

amaze confusion; cf. l. 1286   Silo Shiloh, where the Ark of the Covenant
sublime elated   was set up
                                      Unweetingly unwittingly

Despised and thought extinguished quite,
With inward eyes illuminated,
1690　His fiery virtue roused
From under ashes into sudden flame,
And as an evening dragon° came,
Assailant on the perchèd roosts
And nests in order ranged
Of tame villatic° fowl; but as an eagle
His cloudless thunder bolted on their heads.
So virtue, given for lost,
Depressed, and overthrown, as seemed,
Like that self-begotten bird°
1700　In the Arabian woods embost,°
That no second knows nor third,°
And lay erewhile a holocaust,°
From out her ashy womb now teemed,°
Revives, reflourishes, then vigorous most
When most unactive deemed,
And though her body die, her fame survives,
A secular° bird, ages of lives.
　　　MANOA   Come, come, no time from lamentation now,
Nor much more cause; Samson hath quit himself
1710　Like Samson, and heroicly hath finished
A life heroic, on his enemies
Fully revenged; hath left them years of mourning,
And lamentation to the sons of Caphtor°
Through all Philistian bounds. To Israel
Honour hath left, and freedom: let but them
Find courage to lay hold on this occasion;
To himself and father's house eternal fame;
And, which is best and happiest yet, all this
With God not parted from him, as was feared,
1720　But favouring and assisting to the end.
Nothing is here for tears, nothing to wail
Or knock the breast, no weakness, no contempt,
Dispraise, or blame, nothing but well and fair,
And what may quiet us in a death so noble.
Let us go find the body where it lies
Soaked in his enemies' blood, and from the stream
With lavers° pure and cleansing herbs wash off
The clotted gore. I with what speed° the while

dragon serpent
villatic barnyard; the Italian meaning of *villa* is farmhouse
self-begotten bird the phoenix, not used literally as an emblem of resurrection, but of fame and glory and, perhaps, some kind of spiritual regeneration; an image of Christian heroic virtue and God's use of it
embost "embosked"—hidden in woods like a hunted animal

That . . . third Only one phoenix is alive at a time.
holocaust a sacrificial animal burned entire
teemed delivered in birth
Caphtor original home of the Philistines
lavers basins
with what speed with whatever speed I can

(Gaza is not in plight° to say us nay)
1730 Will send for all my kindred, all my friends,
To fetch him hence and solemnly attend
With silent obsequy and funeral train
Home to his father's house: there will I build him
A monument, and plant it round with shade
Of laurel ever green, and branching palm,
With all his trophies hung, and acts enrolled
In copious legend, or sweet lyric song.
Thither shall all the valiant youth resort,
And from his memory inflame their breasts
1740 To matchless valour and adventures high;
The virgins also shall on feastful days
Visit his tomb with flowers, only bewailing
His lot unfortunate in nuptial choice,
From whence captivity and loss of eyes.
      CHORUS   All is best, though we oft doubt,
What the unsearchable dispose
Of highest wisdom brings about,
And ever best found in the close.
Oft he seems to hide his face,
1750 But unexpectedly returns
And to his faithful champion hath in place°
Bore witness gloriously; whence Gaza mourns,
And all that band them to resist
His uncontrollable intent:
His servants he, with new acquist°
Of true experience from this great event,
With peace and consolation hath dismissed,
And calm of mind, all passion spent.
1647–70?   1671

Areopagitica

If *Areopagitica* is Milton's most resonant prose work, it may be because, first, its specific polemical purpose was one which still moves us today, and whose importance has not diminished, and, second, because its author evolved during the course of his argument a powerful vision of the moral life as embodied in the world of the intellect, and, particularly for Milton, in the representation of truth in terms of major fictions. Milton's essay is an address to Parliament on the subject of licensing—not censorship, to which he was by no means totally opposed, but the prior censorship imposed by requiring books to be approved before publication. Such approval had been entrusted in 1637, by Star Chamber decision, to a small group of churchmen; and a predominantly Presbyterian Parliament, in the ordinance of 1643 to which Milton is objecting, was in effect continuing the oppressive measure, which had

in plight in condition   acquist acquisition
in place at hand

given great personal licensing power to Archbishop Laud before. *Areopagitica,* like Milton's divorce tracts of the previous year, itself appeared without license. Its title derives from a famous address of the Greek orator Isocrates, to the Areopagus, or high court, which held session on the Athenian hill of Ares (Mars); like Milton's, that address was not written for oral delivery.

From Areopagitica

A Speech for the Liberty of Unlicensed Printing, to the Parliament of England

> This is true liberty, when free-born men,
> Having to advise the public, may speak free,
> Which he who can and will, deserves high praise;
> Who neither can nor will, may hold his peace;
> What can be juster in a State than this?
> EURIPIDES, *The Suppliants*

They who to states[1] and governors of the Commonwealth direct their speech, High Court of Parliament, or, wanting[2] such access in a private condition, write that which they foresee may advance the public good, I suppose them, as at the beginning of no mean endeavour, not a little altered[3] and moved inwardly in their minds: some with doubt of what will be the success,[4] others with fear of what will be the censure;[5] some with hope, others with confidence of what they have to speak. And me perhaps each of these dispositions, as the subject was whereon I entered, may have at other times variously affected; and likely might in these foremost expressions now also disclose which of them swayed most, but that the very attempt of this address thus made, and the thought of whom it hath recourse to, hath got the power within me to a passion far more welcome than incidental to a preface. Which though I stay not to confess ere any ask I shall be blameless, if it be no other than the joy and gratulation which it brings to all who wish and promote their country's liberty; whereof this whole discourse proposed will be a certain testimony, if not a trophy.[6] For this is not the liberty which we can hope, that no grievance ever should arise in the Commonwealth—that let no man in this world expect; but when complaints are freely heard, deeply considered, and speedily reformed, then is the utmost bound of civil liberty attained that wise men look for. . . .

Nor did they stay in matters heretical, but any subject that was not to their palate they either condemned in a Prohibition or had it straight into the new Purgatory of an Index. To fill up the measure of encroachment, their last invention was to ordain that no book, pamphlet, or paper should be printed (as

1. The three estates of lords, clergy, and commons forming the parliaments of England and France.
2. Lacking.
3. Worried.
4. Result.
5. Decision; a neutral term.
6. Of victory in his argument.

if St. Peter had bequeathed them the keys of the press also out of Paradise)
unless it were approved and licensed under the hands of two or three glutton
friars. For example:

> 'Let the Chancellor Cini be pleased to see if in this present work be con-
> tained aught that may withstand the printing.
>
> > Vincent Rabbatta, Vicar of Florence.'

> 'I have seen this present work, and find nothing athwart the Catholic
> faith and good manners: in witness whereof I have given, etc.
>
> > Nicolo Cini, Chancellor of Florence.'

> 'Attending the precedent relation, it is allowed that this present work of
> Davanzati may be printed.
>
> > Vincent Rabbatta, etc.'

I deny not, but that it is of greatest concernment in the Church and Commonwealth, to have a vigilant eye how books demean themselves as well as
men; and thereafter to confine, imprison, and do sharpest justice on them as
malefactors. For books are not absolutely dead things, but do contain a potency
of life in them to be as active as that soul was whose progeny they are; nay,
they do preserve as in a vial the purest efficacy and extraction of that living
intellect that bred them. I know they are as lively, and as vigorously productive,
as those fabulous dragon's teeth,[7] and being sown up and down, may chance
to spring up armed men. And yet, on the other hand, unless wariness be used,
as good almost kill a man as kill a good book: who kills a man kills a reasonable
creature, God's image; but he who destroys a good book, kills reason itself, kills
the image of God, as it were in the eye.[8] Many a man lives a burden to the
earth; but a good book is the precious life-blood of a master spirit, embalmed
and treasured up on purpose to a life beyond life. 'Tis true, no age can restore
a life, whereof perhaps there is no great loss; and revolutions of ages do not
oft recover the loss of a rejected truth, for the want of which whole nations
fare the worse. We should be wary therefore what persecution we raise against
the living labours of public men, how we spill that seasoned life of man,
preserved and stored up in books; since we see a kind of homicide may be
thus committed, sometimes a martyrdom, and if it extend to the whole impression, a kind of massacre, whereof the execution ends not in the slaying of an
elemental life, but strikes at that ethereal and fifth essence,[9] the breath of reason
itself, slays an immortality rather than a life. But lest I should be condemned
of introducing license, while I oppose licensing, I refuse not the pains to be
so much historical as will serve to show what hath been done by ancient and
famous commonwealths, against this disorder, till the very time that this project
of licensing crept out of the Inquisition,[10] was catched up by our prelates, and

---

7. Cadmus and Jason both slew dragons and sowed their teeth, from which sprang up a
crop of soldiers (Ovid, *Metamorphoses* III.95 ff. and VII.121 ff.).

8. In the reader's eye.

9. Beyond the four elements lay a fifth entity, ether, the heavenly essence (see Donne, "A
Nocturnal upon S. Lucy's Day," l. 15n).

10. The church's inquisitorial institution rooted out heresy and heterodoxy; its powers,
Milton insists, were inherited by Rome's Anglican opponents ("prelates") and, in turn, by
the latter's Presbyterian antagonists ("New Presbyter is but old Priest writ large" Milton
would write two years later).

hath caught some of our presbyters. [Milton now goes on to summarize the history of censorship, in Greece, Rome, and in the early days of the church, concluding with the introduction of prohibitions against reading heretical books in the 15th century, and the activities of the Spanish Inquisition and the Council of Trent (1545–63). A witty passage attacking ecclesiastical approval follows.]

> 'It may be printed, July 15.
> Friar Simon Mompei d'Amelia,
> Chancellor of the holy office in Florence.'

Sure they have a conceit, if he of the bottomless pit had not long since broke prison, that this quadruple exorcism would bar him down. I fear their next design will be to get into their custody the licensing of that which they say Claudius intended,[11] but went not through with. Vouchsafe to see another of their forms, the Roman stamp:

> 'Imprimatur,[12] If it seem good to the reverend master of the holy Palace,
> Belcastro, Vicegerent.'

> 'Imprimatur, Friar Nicolo Rodolphi, Master of the holy Palace.'

Sometimes five Imprimaturs are seen together dialogue-wise in the piazza of one title-page, complimenting and ducking each to other with their shaven reverences, whether the author who stands by in perplexity at the foot of his epistle shall to the press or to the sponge.[13] These are the pretty responsories,[14] these are the dear antiphonies,[15] that so bewitched of late our prelates and their chaplains with the goodly echo they made; and besotted us to the gay imitation of a lordly Imprimatur, one from Lambeth House,[16] another from the west end of Paul's;[17] so apishly romanizing that the word of command still was set down in Latin; as if the learned grammatical pen that wrote it would cast no ink without Latin; or perhaps, as they thought, because no vulgar tongue was worthy to express the pure conceit[18] of an Imprimatur; but rather, as I hope, for that our English, the language of men ever famous and foremost in the achievements of liberty, will not easily find servile letters enow to spell such a dictatory presumption English.[19] And thus ye have the inventors and the original of book-licensing ripped up[20] and drawn as lineally as any pedigree. We have it not, that can be heard of, from any ancient state, or polity, or church, nor by any statute left us by our ancestors elder or later; nor from the

---

11. A license allowing one to fart at table: Milton's marginal note quotes Suetonius' *Life of Claudius* to this effect.

12. "Let it be printed"—the phrase giving official ecclesiastical permission for publication of manuscripts.

13. "To the sponge," meaning to have the contents wiped off, was an expression applied to manuscripts unworthy of publication.

14. Sections of the Psalms sung between other biblical readings in the mass.

15. Hymns or anthems sung in responsive parts by two choirs.

16. Lambeth Palace, residence of the Archbishop of Canterbury when in London.

17. This may refer either to the Bishop of London (at St. Paul's), or to the home of the Stationers' Company, who urged the enforcement of the licensing order.

18. Idea.

19. In English.

20. Revealed.

modern custom of any reformed city or church abroad; but from the most anti-
christian council and the most tyrannous inquisition that ever inquired. Till then
books were ever as freely admitted into the world as any other birth; the issue
of the brain was no more stifled than the issue of the womb: no envious Juno
sat cross-legged [21] over the nativity of any man's intellectual offspring; but if
it proved a monster, who denies but that it was justly burnt, or sunk into the
sea. But that a book, in worse condition than a peccant soul, should be to stand
before a jury ere it be born to the world, and undergo yet in darkness the
judgment of Radamanth and his colleagues,[22] ere it can pass the ferry backward into light, was never heard before, till that mysterious iniquity, provoked
and troubled at the first entrance of Reformation, sought out new limbos and
new hells wherein they might include our books also within the number of their
damned. And this was the rare morsel so officiously snatched up, and so ill-
favouredly imitated by our inquisiturient [23] bishops, and the attendant minorites [24] their chaplains. That ye like not now these most certain authors of this
licensing order, and that all sinister intention was far distant from your thoughts,
when ye were importuned the passing it, all men who know the integrity of
your actions, and how ye honour truth, will clear ye readily. [Milton then
attacks the notion that there is any good in licensing itself aside from its proponents' vices, and adducing a remark of John Selden, the legal scholar (1584–
1654), that "all opinions, yea errors, known, read and collated, are of main
service and assistance toward the speedy attainment of what is truest," moves
to the imaginative center of his argument.]

I conceive, therefore, that when God did enlarge the universal diet of man's
body, saving ever the rules of temperance, he then also, as before, left arbitrary
the dieting and repasting of our minds; as wherein every mature man might
have to exercise his own leading capacity. How great a virtue is temperance,
how much of moment through the whole life of man! Yet God commits the
managing so great a trust, without particular law or prescription, wholly to the
demeanour [25] of every grown man. And therefore when he himself tabled the
Jews from heaven, that omer,[26] which was every man's daily portion of manna,
is computed to have been more than might have well sufficed for the heartiest
feeder thrice as many meals. For those actions which enter into a man, rather
than issue out of him, and therefore defile not, God uses not to captivate under
a perpetual childhood of prescription, but trusts him with the gift of reason
to be his own chooser; there were but little work left for preaching if law and
compulsion should grow so fast upon those things which heretofore were governed only by exhortation. Solomon informs us that much reading is a weariness
to the flesh; but neither he nor other inspired author tells us that such or such
reading is unlawful; yet certainly had God thought good to limit us herein, it
had been much more expedient to have told us what was unlawful than what

21. She tried, with charms and spells, to prevent the birth of Hercules, whose mother was
in labor with him for seven days.
22. Rhadamanthus, Minos, and Aeacus, the three judges of Hades.
23. Would-be inquisitors.
24. The Franciscans called themselves "minorites," alluding to their humility, with which
Milton here remains unimpressed.
25. Management.
26. A biblical measure, here, of manna (Exodus 16:16 ff.), the daily ration Moses was
commanded to distribute.

was wearisome. As for the burning of those Ephesian books by St. Paul's converts, 'tis replied the books were magic, the Syriac so renders them. It was a private act, a voluntary act, and leaves us to a voluntary imitation: the men in remorse burnt those books which were their own; the magistrate by this example is not appointed: these men practised the books, another might perhaps have read them in some sort usefully. Good and evil we know in the field of this world grow up together almost inseparably; and the knowledge of good is so involved and interwoven with the knowledge of evil, and in so many cunning resemblances hardly to be discerned, that those confused seeds which were imposed upon Psyche as an incessant labour to cull out, and sort asunder, were not more intermixed.[27] It was from out the rind of one apple tasted, that the knowledge of good and evil, as two twins cleaving together, leaped forth into the world. And perhaps this is that doom which Adam fell into of knowing good and evil, that is to say of knowing good by evil.[28] As therefore the state of man is, what wisdom can there be to choose, what continence to forbear, without the knowledge of evil? He that can apprehend and consider vice with all her baits and seeming pleasures, and yet abstain, and yet distinguish, and yet prefer that which is truly better, he is the true warfaring [29] Christian. I cannot praise a fugitive and cloistered virtue, unexercised and unbreathed, that never sallies out and sees her adversary, but slinks out of the race, where that immortal garland [30] is to be run for, not without dust and heat. Assuredly we bring not innocence into the world, we bring impurity much rather; that which purifies us is trial, and trial is by what is contrary. That virtue therefore which is but a youngling in the contemplation of evil, and knows not the utmost that vice promises to her followers, and rejects it, is but a blank virtue, not a pure; her whiteness is but an excremental [31] whiteness; which was the reason why our sage and serious poet Spenser, whom I dare be known to think a better teacher than Scotus or Aquinas,[32] describing true temperance under the person of Guyon, brings him in with his palmer through the cave of Mammon, and the bower of earthly bliss,[33] that he might see and know, and yet abstain. Since therefore the knowledge and survey of vice is in this world so necessary to the constituting of human virtue, and the scanning of error to the confirmation of truth, how can we more safely and with less danger scout into the regions of sin and falsity than by reading all manner of tractates and hearing all manner of reason? And this is the benefit which may be had of books promiscuously read.

. . .

27. In Apuleius' *The Golden Ass*, Venus set Psyche the task of sorting out a heap of mixed seeds, in anger at Cupid's love for her.
28. "Knowledge of good bought dear by knowing ill" (*Paradise Lost* IV.222); in his great poem, Milton expands and elaborates this theme.
29. *Wayfaring* in the first edition, but there is strong evidence for the present reading.
30. The garland is the crown of virtue; being good is likened both to medieval knight-errantry and to Greek and Roman games.
31. Superficial.
32. Duns Scotus and Thomas Aquinas, two great 13th-century logicians (the second, the master-theologian of scholasticism); they represent abstract philosophy here, as opposed to the concreteness of poetic myth.
33. See *The Faerie Queene* II. vii and xii. The Palmer does *not* accompany Guyon into the Cave of Mammon, however; Milton's memory failed him here.

Seeing, therefore, that those books, and those in great abundance which are likeliest to taint both life and doctrine, cannot be suppressed without the fall of learning, and of all ability in disputation, and that these books of either sort are most and soonest catching to the learned, from whom to the common people whatever is heretical or dissolute may quickly be conveyed, and that evil manners are as perfectly learnt without books a thousand other ways which cannot be stopped, and evil doctrine not with books can propagate, except a teacher guide, which he might also do without writing, and so beyond prohibiting, I am not unable to unfold how this cautelous [34] enterprise of licensing can be exempted from the number of vain and impossible attempts. And he who were pleasantly disposed could not well avoid to liken it to the exploit of that gallant man who thought to pound up the crows by shutting his park gate. Besides another inconvenience, if learned men be the first receivers out of books and dispreaders both of vice and error, how shall the licensers themselves be confided in, unless we can confer upon them, or they assume to themselves above all others in the land, the grace of infallibility and uncorruptedness? And again if it be true, that a wise man, like a good refiner, can gather gold out of the drossiest volume, and that a fool will be a fool with the best book, yea, or without book; there is no reason that we should deprive a wise man of any advantage to his wisdom, while we seek to restrain from a fool that which being restrained will be no hindrance to his folly. For if there should be so much exactness always used to keep that from him which is unfit for his reading, we should in the judgment of Aristotle [35] not only, but of Solomon [36] and of our Saviour,[37] not vouchsafe him good precepts, and by consequence not willingly admit him to good books; as being certain that a wise man will make better use of an idle pamphlet than a fool will do of sacred Scripture.

.   .   .

For if we be sure we are in the right, and do not hold the truth guiltily, which becomes not, if we ourselves condemn not our own weak and frivolous teaching, and the people for an untaught and irreligious gadding rout, what can be more fair than when a man judicious, learned, and of a conscience, for aught we know as good as theirs that taught us what we know, shall not privily from house to house, which is more dangerous, but openly by writing publish to the world what his opinion is, what his reasons, and wherefore that which is now thought cannot be sound? Christ urged it as wherewith to justify himself that he preached in public; [38] yet writing is more public than preaching; and more easy to refutation, if need be, there being so many whose business and profession merely it is to be the champions of Truth; which if they neglect, what can be imputed but their sloth, or inability?

Thus much we are hindered and disenured [39] by this course of licensing toward the true knowledge of what we seem to know. For how much it hurts

34. Tricky, liable to backfire.
35. At the end of the *Nicomachean Ethics*, rejecting the possibility that philosophy can influence ordinary men, instead of guiding the best of them.
36. Throughout the Book of Proverbs, as for example 17:24 and 26:5.
37. ". . . Neither cast ye your pearls before swine" (Matthew 7:6).
38. John 18:19-20.
39. Grown unaccustomed.

and hinders the licensers themselves in the calling of their ministry, more than any secular employment, if they will discharge that office as they ought, so that of necessity they must neglect either the one duty or the other, I insist not, because it is a particular,[40] but leave it to their own conscience, how they will decide it there.

There is yet behind of what I purposed to lay open, the incredible loss and detriment that this plot of licensing puts us to, more than if some enemy at sea should stop up all our havens and ports and creeks, it hinders and retards the importation of our richest merchandise, Truth: nay, it was first established and put in practice by anti-christian malice and mystery[41] on set purpose to extinguish, if it were possible, the light of Reformation, and to settle falsehood; little differing from that policy wherewith the Turk upholds his Alcoran, by the prohibition of Printing. 'Tis not denied, but gladly confessed, we are to send our thanks and vows to Heaven, louder than most of nations for that great measure of truth which we enjoy, especially in those main points between us and the Pope, with his appurtenances the Prelates: but he who thinks we are to pitch our tent here, and have attained the utmost prospect of reformation, that the mortal glass[42] wherein we contemplate can show us, till we come to beatific vision, that man by this very opinion declares that he is yet far short of truth.

Truth indeed came once into the world with her divine Master, and was a perfect shape most glorious to look on: but when he ascended, and his Apostles after him were laid asleep, then straight arose a wicked race of deceivers, who (as that story goes of the Egyptian Typhon with his conspirators, how they dealt with the good Osiris)[43] took the virgin Truth, hewed her lovely form into a thousand pieces, and scattered them to the four winds. From that time ever since, the sad friends of Truth, such as durst appear, imitating the careful[44] search that Isis made for the mangled body of Osiris, went up and down gathering up limb by limb still as they could find them. We have not yet found them all, Lords and Commons, nor ever shall do, till her Master's second coming; he shall bring together every joint and member, and shall mould them into an immortal feature of loveliness and perfection. Suffer not these licensing prohibitions to stand at every place of opportunity forbidding and disturbing them that continue seeking, that continue to do our obsequies to the torn body of our martyred saint. We boast our light; but if we look not wisely on the sun itself, it smites us into darkness. Who can discern those planets that are oft combust,[45] and those stars of brightest magnitude that rise and set with the sun, until the opposite motion of their orbs bring them to such a place in the firmament where they may be seen evening or morning. The light which we have gained was given us, not to be ever staring on, but by it to discover

40. Matter of particular concern.
41. Mystification.
42. Mirror (see I Corinthians 13:12, and comment on it in The English Bible section).
43. Typhon, Osiris' brother, murdered and dismembered him; the body floated down the Nile and was reassembled by his wife, Isis, and Horus, their son. As early as Plutarch, this was read as a myth of the mangling and scattering of Truth, and its reconstitution, both eternal processes (compare Bacon's essay, "Of Truth").
44. Full of cares.
45. "Burnt up," figuratively, by closely approaching the sun; an astrological term.

onward things more remote from our knowledge. It is not the unfrocking of a priest, the unmitring of a bishop, and the removing him from off the Presbyterian shoulders that will make us a happy nation, no, if other things as great in the church, and in the rule of life both economical [46] and political be not looked into and reformed. We have looked so long upon the blaze that Zwinglius and Calvin [47] hath beaconed up to us that we are stark blind. There be who perpetually complain of schisms and sects, and make it such a calamity that any man dissents from their maxims. 'Tis their own pride and ignorance which causes the disturbing, who neither will hear with meekness, nor can convince, yet all must be suppressed which is not found in their syntagma.[48] They are the troublers, they are the dividers of unity, who neglect and permit not others to unite those dissevered pieces which are yet wanting to the body of Truth. To be still searching what we know not by what we know, still closing up truth to truth as we find it (for all her body is homogeneal,[49] and proportional),[50] this is the golden rule in theology as well as in arithmetic, and makes up the best harmony in a church; not the forced and outward union of cold and neutral and inwardly divided minds.

. . .

There have been not a few since the beginning of this Parliament,[51] both of the Presbytery and others, who by their unlicensed books to the contempt of an Imprimatur first broke that triple ice [52] clung about our hearts, and taught the people to see day. I hope that none of those were the persuaders to renew upon us this bondage which they themselves have wrought so much good by contemning. But if neither the check that Moses gave to young Joshua, nor the countermand which our Saviour gave to young John, who was so ready to prohibit those whom he thought unlicensed, be not enough to admonish our elders how unacceptable to God their testy mood of prohibiting is, if neither their own remembrance what evil hath abounded in the Church by this let [53] of licensing, and what good they themselves have begun by transgressing it, be not enough, but that they will persuade, and execute the most Dominican part of the Inquisition over us, and are already with one foot in the stirrup so active at suppressing, it would be no unequal distribution in the first place to suppress the suppressors themselves: whom the change of their condition hath puffed up, more than their late experience of harder times hath made wise.

And as for regulating the Press, let no man think to have the honour of advising ye better than yourselves have done in that order published next before this,[54] *'that no book be printed, unless the printer's and the author's*

---

46. Concerning household management, thus, here, private affairs.
47. Ulrich Zwingli (1484–1531), of Zurich; John Calvin (1509–64), of Geneva—the two Swiss reformers.
48. System of doctrine.
49. All of a piece throughout.
50. Harmoniously composed in relations of parts to whole.
51. The Long Parliament, which first assembled November 3, 1640.
52. Punning on, and nevertheless seriously alluding to, the *aes triplex* ("triple bronze"), needed, says Horace (*Odes* I.3), to gird the heart of a man setting out, for the first time, to sea.
53. Hindrance.
54. An order previous to the one (of June 14, 1643) which Milton is disputing.

name, or at least the printer's be registered.' Those which otherwise come forth, if they be found mischievous and libellous, the fire and the executioner will be the timeliest and the most effectual remedy that man's prevention can use. For this authentic [55] Spanish policy of licensing books, if I have said aught, will prove the most unlicensed book itself within a short while; and was the immediate image of a Star Chamber decree to that purpose made in those very times when that Court did the rest of those her pious works, for which she is now fallen from the stars with Lucifer. Whereby ye may guess what kind of state prudence, what love of the people, what care of Religion or good manners there was at the contriving, although with singular hypocrisy it pretended to bind books to their good behaviour. And how it got the upper hand of your precedent Order so well constituted before, if we may believe those men whose profession gives them cause to inquire most, it may be doubted there was in it the fraud of some old patentees and monopolizers in the trade of bookselling; who under pretence of the poor in their Company not to be defrauded, and the just retaining of each man his several copy, which God forbid should be gainsaid, brought divers glozing [56] colours to the House, which were indeed but colours, and serving to no end except it be to exercise a superiority over their neighbours, men who do not therefore labour in an honest profession to which learning is indebted, that they should be made other men's vassals. Another end is thought was aimed at by some of them in procuring by petition this Order, that having power in their hands, malignant books might the easier scape abroad, as the event shows. But of these sophisms and elenchs [57] of merchandise I skill not. This I know, that errors in a good government and in a bad are equally almost incident; for what Magistrate may not be misinformed, and much the sooner, if liberty of Printing be reduced into the power of a few? But to redress willingly and speedily what hath been erred, and in highest authority to esteem a plain advertisement [58] more than others have done a sumptuous bribe, is a virtue (honoured Lords and Commons) answerable to your highest actions, and whereof none can participate but greatest and wisest men.

1644   1644

The Development of Prose

JOHN LYLY
1554?–1606

Lyly came of a family much involved in scholarly humanism and was himself a master at St. Paul's choir school, though his job was mostly to produce the boys' plays. His court comedies, written for boys, are his most distinguished work, but earlier he had made himself famous with *Euphues: The Anatomy of Wit* (1578) and *Euphues and His England* (1580), works which combine an appearance of moral rectitude with

55. Peculiarly.
56. Flattering.
57. Fallacious points.
58. Notification.

a prose style of great though rhetorically repetitive elaboration. They achieved great success, and continued to be read even after Lyly's reputation was dimmed in the late 1580's by that of Sidney, whose "Arcadianism"—still ornate, but less rigid— replaced "Euphuism" as a favored rhetorical style.

The story of *Euphues* is unimportant, being no more than a "trellis," as C. S. Lewis called it, for the flowers of rhetoric and the festoons of similes to grow on. Euphues is a noble young Greek (his name means "gentleman") who ignores advice and goes from Athens (the university) to Naples (the city, specifically London), where he makes a friend of Philautus, betrays him, is reconciled, lectures him in moral philosophy, and so on. *Euphues and His England* has more story, and concludes with a long passage in praise of England, London, the court, and, most of all, the Queen. In the present extract Philautus' girl has entertained him and Euphues (whom she received rather coldly) at supper; and Euphues is afterwards required to discourse concerning love or learning. He chooses to speak on whether beauty or wit in women move men most to love; but in fact he speaks against the fickleness and cruelty of women. When he breaks off and leaves, Lucilla soliloquizes, exhibiting most of the characteristics of Euphuism in the process.

Lyly did not invent this kind of "wit"; he took certain tendencies already existing in prose, and even in the fashionable Oxford lectures of his undergraduate days and brought them to a new pitch. The forced balances and antitheses, "terms and contrarieties," can be given various rhetorical names, and exist elsewhere. The extended similes (drawn from what has been called "unnatural natural history") and the copious use of proverbs are part of the common stock, but nowhere else occur in this concentration. As Lewis rightly says, "What constitutes euphuism is neither the structural devices nor the 'unnatural history' but the unremitting use of both." It was a "camp" style; Sidney complained of it and Shakespeare parodied it in a famous passage in I *Henry IV*—but the parody doesn't sound much different from parts of the original: compare Shakespeare's lines (II.iv.440 ff.) with "Though the camomile the more it is trodden and pressed down the more it spreadeth," which is genuine Lyly. Most of *Euphues* is in the same manner, and a small sample suffices.

From Euphues: The Anatomy of Wit

. . . Lucilla, who now began to fry in the flames of love, all the company being departed to their lodgings, entered into these terms and contrarieties: [1]—

'Ah, wretched wench Lucilla, how art thou perplexed! What a doubtful fight dost thou feel betwixt faith and fancy, hope and fear, conscience and concupiscence! O my Euphues, little dost thou know the sudden sorrow that I sustain for thy sweet sake, whose wit hath bewitched me, whose rare qualities have deprived me of mine old quality, whose courteous behaviour without curiosity, whose comely feature without fault, whose filed [2] speech without fraud hath wrapped me in this misfortune. And canst thou, Lucilla, be so light of love in forsaking Philautus to fly to Euphues? Canst thou prefer a stranger

1. Opposing considerations.
2. Polished.

before thy countryman; a starter [3] before thy companion? Why, Euphues doth perhaps desire my love, but Philautus hath deserved it. Why, Euphues' feature is worthy as good as I, but Philautus his faith is worthy a better. Aye, but the latter love is most fervent; aye, but the first ought to be most faithful. Aye, but Euphues hath greater perfection; aye, but Philautus hath deeper affection.

'Ah fond wench, dost thou think Euphues will deem thee constant to him, when thou hast been unconstant to his friend? Weenest thou [4] that he will have no mistrust of thy faithfulness, when he hath had trial [5] of thy fickleness? Will he have no doubt of thine honour, when thou thyself callest thine honesty [6] in question? Yes, yes, Lucilla, well doth he know that the glass once crazed [7] will with the least clap be cracked,[8] that the cloth which staineth with milk will soon lose his colour with vinegar, that the eagle's wing [9] will waste the feather as well of the phœnix as of the pheasant, that she that hath been faithless to one will never be faithful to any.

'But can Euphues convince [10] me of fleeting, seeing for his sake I break my fidelity? Can he condemn me of disloyalty, when he is the only cause of my disliking? May he justly condemn me of treachery, who hath this testimony as trial [11] of my good will? Doth he not remember that the broken bone once set together is stronger than ever it was? That the greatest blot is taken off with the pumice? [12] That though the spider poison the fly, she cannot infect the bee? That although I have been light to Philautus, yet I may be lovely to Euphues? It is not my desire but his deserts that moveth my mind to this choice, neither the want of the like good will in Philautus but the lack of the like good qualities that removeth my fancy from the one to the other.

'For as the bee that gathereth honey out of the weed when she espieth the fair flower flieth to the sweetest; or as the kind [13] spaniel though he hunt after birds yet forsakes them to retrive the partridge; or as we commonly feed on beef hungerly at the first, yet seeing the quail more dainty change our diet; so I although I loved Philautus for his good properties, yet seeing Euphues to excel him I ought by nature to like him better. By so much the more, therefore, my change is to be excused, by how much the more my choice is excellent; and by so much the less I am to be condemned, by how much the more Euphues is to be commended. Is not the diamond of more value than the ruby because he is of more virtue? [14] Is not the emerald preferred before the sapphire for his wonderful property? Is not Euphues more praiseworthy than Philautus being more witty?

3. Newcomer.
4. Do you suppose.
5. Experience.
6. Meaning much the same as honor.
7. Cracked.
8. Broken.
9. Referring to the belief that the eagle's feathers, after death, will corrode or destroy those of other birds, so maintaining his superiority in life.
10. Convict.
11. Evidence.
12. Used in the 16th century to absorb ink.
13. Acting according to his nature.
14. Power.

'But fie, Lucilla, why dost thou flatter thyself in thine own folly! Canst thou feign Euphues thy friend, whom by thine own words thou hast made thy foe? Didst not thou accuse women of inconstancy? Didst not thou account them easy to be won? Didst not thou condemn them of weakness? What sounder argument can he have against thee than thine own answer; what better proof than thine own speech; what greater trial than thine own talk? If thou hast belied women, he will judge thee unkind; [15] if thou have revealed the troth,[16] he must needs think thee unconstant; if he perceive thee to be won with a nut, he will imagine that thou wilt be lost with an apple; [17] if he find thee wanton before thou be wooed, he will guess thou wilt be wavering when thou art wedded.'

1578

RICHARD HOOKER
1554–1600

Hooker was the greatest of Elizabethan prose writers. He transformed controversy into philosophy, making the dispute between the middle-of-the-way churchmen and the Puritan extremists an occasion for a great meditation on natural, human, and divine law. In 1585 Hooker was preferred over the Puritan Walter Travers for the post of Master of the Temple, a London law school. Travers held that Scripture was the sole source of truth and authority in the church, so that ceremonies without scriptural warrant, and the elaborate hierarchical organization of the clergy, were wrong. Hooker deplored the contentious zeal of the Puritans as a disturber of the church's peace, and also refused to admit an absolutely sharp distinction between different kinds of law and learning, human and divine. He valued tradition without giving it the force attributed to it by Catholics; and he defended ceremony in terms of natural common sense. Out of the controversy with Travers grew the eight books Of The Laws of Ecclesiastical Polity, of which four were published in 1593. Book I speaks of laws generally, the laws of nature and societies; Books II and III treat of Scripture and its authority; Book IV is in defense of ceremony. Hooker proceeds with a calm stateliness to the defeat of the enemy position; as C. S. Lewis observes, "Long before the close fighting in Book III begins, the puritan position has been rendered desperate by the great flanking movements in Book I and II."

The first selection below comes from the discussion in Book I of the law of nature, the obedience of natural things to laws of which they cannot consciously have knowledge. Their performance, though in consequence of the fall of man not perfect, is nonetheless so regular as to allow us to suppose nature to have a faithful relationship with the divinity; we should therefore not exclude knowledge achieved by the light of nature.

The second selection makes the point that total dependence on Scripture for necessary knowledge is in fact impossible. Scripture tells us whatever is necessary to salvation that we could not otherwise know; but this cannot mean that all other knowledge, natural or otherwise, is superfluous, since it is by reason of it that we

15. Unnatural (also with modern sense).
16. Truth.
17. Proverbial for the inconstant mind.

know, for example, that the Scriptures *are* the "oracles of God." This is an indirect assault on the central Puritan position.

The third selection justifies ceremony, not as part of an inviolable tradition, but as a means of making the word and the sacraments of God more solemn and memorable. Like all Hooker's work, it is an appeal to reason in the midst of fierce and dangerous controversies. He is always ready to consider usefulness to human beings as an important recommendation, and to avoid dogmatism. In hoping that although "nature hath need of grace" (I Corinthians 2:14)he was not opposing St. Paul when he added, "grace hath use of nature" (III.viii.6), Hooker was proposing for the Church of England a reasonable alternative to a Puritanism which accepted the first but denied the second proposition—just as by giving ceremony a natural human use he avoided the extreme formulations imposed on the Roman church at the Council of Trent.

Of the Laws of Ecclesiastical Polity

From *Book I, Chapter 3*

. . . Now if nature should intermit [1] her course, and leave altogether though it were but for a while the observation of her own laws; if those principal and mother elements of the world, whereof all things in this lower world are made, should lose the qualities which now they have; if the frame of that heavenly arch erected over our heads should loosen and dissolve itself; if celestial spheres should forget their wonted motions, and by irregular volubility turn themselves any way as it might happen; if the prince of the lights of heaven, which now as a giant doth run his unwearied course,[2] should as it were through a languishing faintness begin to stand and to rest himself; if the moon should wander from her beaten way, the times and seasons of the year blend themselves by disordered and confused mixture, the winds breathe out their last gasp, the clouds yield no rain, the earth be defeated of heavenly influence, the fruits of the earth pine away as children at the withered breasts of their mother no longer able to yield them relief: what would become of man himself, whom these things now do all serve? See we not plainly that obedience of creatures unto the law of nature is the stay of the whole world? Notwithstanding with nature it cometh sometimes to pass as with art. Let Phidias [3] have rude and obstinate stuff to carve, though his art do that it should, his work will lack that beauty which otherwise in fitter matter it might have had. He that striketh an instrument with skill may cause notwithstanding a very unpleasant sound, if the string whereon he striketh chance to be uncapable of harmony. In the matter whereof things natural consist, that of Theophrastus [4] taketh place, 'Much of it is oftentimes such as will by no means yield to receive that impression which were best and most perfect.' Which defect in the matter of things natural, they who gave themselves unto the contemplation of nature amongst

1. Interrupt.
2. Psalms 19:5.
3. Greek sculptor, architect, and painter of 4th century B.C., for the Parthenon frieze responsibly.
4. *C.* 371–*c.* 287 B.C.; pupil of Aristotle and prolific writer, best known for his *Characters*, outlines of personality types, which were imitated, e.g. by Earle and Overbury (see below).

the heathen observed often: but the true original cause thereof, divine malediction, laid for the sin of man upon these creatures which God had made for the use of man,[5] this being an article of that saving truth which God hath revealed unto his Church, was above the reach of their merely natural capacity and understanding. But howsoever these swervings are now and then incident into the course of nature, nevertheless so constantly the laws of nature are by natural agents observed, that no man denieth but those things which nature worketh are wrought, either always or for the most part, after one and the same manner.

If here it be demanded what that is which keepeth nature in obedience to her own law, we must have recourse to that higher law whereof we have already spoken, and because all other laws do thereon depend, from thence we must borrow so much as shall need for brief resolution in this point. Although we are not of opinion therefore, as some are, that nature in working hath before her certain exemplary draughts or patterns, which subsisting in the bosom of the Highest, and being thence discovered, she fixeth her eye upon them, as travellers by sea upon the pole-star of the world, and that according thereunto she guideth her hand to work by imitation: although we rather embrace the oracle of Hippocrates,[6] that 'each thing both in small and in great fulfilleth the task which destiny hath set down'; and concerning the manner of executing and fulfilling the same, 'what they do they know not, yet is it in show and appearance as though they did know what they do; and the truth is they do not discern the things which they look on': nevertheless, forasmuch as the works of nature are no less exact, than if she did both behold and study how to express some absolute shape or mirror always present before her; yea, such her dexterity and skill appeareth, that no intellectual creature in the world were able by capacity to do that which nature doth without capacity and knowledge; it cannot be but nature hath some director of infinite knowledge to guide her in all her ways. Who the guide of nature, but only the God of nature? 'In Him we live, move, and are.'[7] Those things which nature is said to do, are by divine art performed, using nature as an instrument; nor is there any such art or knowledge divine in nature herself working, but in the Guide of nature's work.

From *Book I, Chapter 14*

Although the scripture of God therefore be stored with infinite variety of matter in all kinds, although it abound with all sorts of laws, yet the principal intent of scripture is to deliver the laws of duties supernatural.[1] Oftentimes it hath been in very solemn manner disputed whether all things necessary unto salvation be necessarily set down in the holy scriptures or no. If we define that necessary unto salvation whereby the way to salvation is in any sort made more plain, apparent and easy to be known, then is there no part of true philosophy, no art of accompt,[2] no kind of science rightly so called, but the scripture must

5. The doctrine that the fall of Adam entailed that of nature.
6. Great 5th-century B.C. Greek physician, here quoted from Aristotle's *Rhetoric* I.39.
7. Acts 17:28.

1. The distinction is between natural law, of which Hooker speaks elsewhere, and supernatural or "positive" law, which we should not know if it were not revealed in Scripture.
2. Account (meaning here history, narration).

contain it. If only those things be necessary, as surely none else are, without the knowledge and practice whereof it is not the will and pleasure of God to make any ordinary grant of salvation, it may be, notwithstanding, and oftentimes hath been, demanded, how the books of holy scripture contain in them all necessary things, when of things necessary the very chiefest is to know what books we are bound to esteem holy, which point is confessed impossible for the scripture itself to teach. Whereunto we may answer with truth that there is not in the world any art or science, which proposing unto itself an end, as every one doth some end or other, hath been therefore thought defective if it have not delivered simply whatsoever is needful to the same end; but all kinds of knowledge have their certain bounds and limits: each of them presupposeth many necessary things learned in other sciences and known beforehand. He that should take upon him to teach men how to be eloquent in pleading causes must needs deliver unto them whatsoever precepts are requisite unto that end; otherwise he doth not the thing which he taketh upon him. Seeing then no man can plead eloquently unless he be able first to speak, it followeth that ability of speech is in this case a thing most necessary. Notwithstanding every man would think it ridiculous that he which undertaketh by writing to instruct an orator should therefore deliver all the precepts of grammar, because his profession is to deliver precepts necessary unto eloquent speech, yet so that they which are to receive them be taught beforehand so much of that[3] which is thereunto necessary as comprehendeth the skill of speaking. In like sort, albeit scripture do profess to contain in it all things which are necessary unto salvation, yet the meaning cannot be simply of all things that are necessary, but all things that are necessary in some certain kind or form, as: all things that are necessary and either could not at all or could not easily be known by the light of natural discourse; all things which are necessary to be known that we may be saved, but known with presupposal of knowledge concerning certain principles whereof it receiveth us already persuaded and then instructeth us in all the residue that are necessary. In the number of these principles one is the sacred authority of scripture. Being therefore persuaded by other means that these scriptures are the oracles of God, themselves do then teach us the rest and lay before us all the duties which God requireth at our hands as necessary unto salvation. . . .

From *Book IV, Chapter 1*
Book IV. Ch. i. 1, 2. [Ceremony] [1]

I. Such was the ancient simplicity and softness of spirit which sometimes[2] prevailed in the world, that they whose words were even as oracles amongst

---

3. Grammar.

1. This characteristically moderate defense of ceremonies, regardless of their origin, as not as of the essence of religion but as making an important contribution to it not only answers Puritan objections (ceremonies are not derived from the Word) but also illustrates the contemporary understanding of the relation between outward and visible signs and inward meanings. In particular compare Chapman, *Hero and Leander*, and in general the ceremonial of masque and pageant, and the use of emblems and devices. It is also worth recalling that rhetorical speaking was accompanied by standardized gestures, so that ear was reinforced by eye.

2. Long ago.

men, seemed evermore loth to give sentence [3] against any thing publicly received in the Church of God, except it were wonderful apparently [4] evil; for that they did not so much incline to that severity which delighteth to reprove the least things it seeth amiss, as to that charity which is unwilling to behold any thing that duty bindeth it to reprove. The state of this present age, wherein zeal hath drowned charity, and skill meekness, will not now suffer any man to marvel, whatsoever he shall hear reproved by whomsoever. Those rites and ceremonies of the Church therefore, which are the selfsame now that they were when holy and virtuous men maintained them against profane and deriding adversaries, her own children [5] have at this day in derision. Whether justly or no, it shall then appear, when all things are heard which they have to allege against the outward received orders of this church. Which inasmuch as themselves do compare unto 'mint and cummin,' [6] granting them to be no part of those things which in the matter of polity are weightier, we hope that for small things their strife will neither be earnest nor long. . . .

. . . we are to note, that in every grand or main public duty which God requireth at the hands of his Church, there is, besides that matter and form wherein the essence thereof consisteth, a certain outward fashion whereby the same is in decent sort administered. The substance of all religious actions is delivered from God himself in few words. For example's sake in the sacraments. 'Unto the element let the word be added, and they both do make a sacrament,' saith St. Augustine. Baptism is given by the element of water, and that prescript [7] form of words which the Church of Christ doth use; the sacrament of the body and blood of Christ is administered in the elements of bread and wine, if those mystical words be added thereunto. But the due and decent form of administering those holy sacraments doth require a great deal more.

The end which is aimed at in setting down the outward form of all religious actions is the edification of the Church. Now men are edified, when either their understanding is taught somewhat [8] whereof in such actions it behoveth all men to consider, or when their hearts are moved with any affection suitable thereunto; when their minds are in any sort [9] stirred up unto that reverence, devotion, attention, and due regard, which in those cases seemeth requisite. Because therefore unto this purpose not only speech but sundry sensible means besides have always been thought necessary, and especially those means which being object to the eye, the liveliest and the most apprehensive sense of all other, have in that respect seemed the fittest to make a deep and a strong impression: from hence have risen not only a number of prayers, readings, questionings, exhortings, but even of visible signs also; which being used in performance of holy actions, are undoubtedly most effectual to open such matter, as men when they know and remember carefully, must needs be a great deal the better informed

3. Speak against.
4. Very obviously.
5. The Puritans.
6. "Woe unto you, scribes and Pharisees, hypocrites! for ye pay tithe of mint and anise and cummin, and have omitted the weightier matters of the law . . ." (Matthew 23:23). Cummin is a seed used for flavoring.
7. Prescribed.
8. Something.
9. Way.

to what effect such duties serve. We must not think but that there is some ground of reason even in nature,[10] whereby it cometh to pass that no nation under heaven either doth or ever did suffer public actions which are of weight, whether they be civil and temporal or else spiritual and sacred, to pass without some visible solemnity: the very strangeness whereof and difference from that which is common, doth cause popular eyes to observe and to mark the same. Words, both because they are common, and do not so strongly move the fancy of man, are for the most part but slightly heard: and therefore with singular wisdom it hath been provided, that the deeds of men which are made in the presence of witnesses should pass not only with words, but also with certain sensible actions, the memory whereof is far more easy and durable than the memory of speech can be.

The things which so long experience of all ages hath confirmed and made profitable, let not us presume to condemn as follies and toys, because we sometimes know not the cause and reason of them. A wit disposed to scorn whatsoever it doth not conceive, might ask wherefore Abraham should say to his servant, 'Put thy hand under my thigh and swear'[11]: was it not sufficient for his servant to show the religion of an oath by naming the Lord God of heaven and earth, unless that strange ceremony were added? In contracts, bargains, and conveyances, a man's word is a token sufficient to express his will. Yet 'this was the ancient manner in Israel concerning redeeming and exchanging, to establish all things; a man did pluck off his shoe and gave it his neighbour; and this was a sure witness in Israel.'[12] Amongst the Romans in their making of a bondman free, was it not wondered wherefore so great ado should be made? The master to present his slave in some court, to take him by the hand, and not only to say in the hearing of the public magistrate, 'I will that this man become free,' but after these solemn words uttered, to strike him on the cheek, to turn him round, the hair of his head to be shaved off, the magistrate to touch him thrice with a rod, in the end a cap and a white garment to be given him. To what purpose all this circumstance? Amongst the Hebrews how strange and in outward appearance almost against reason, that he which was minded to make himself a perpetual servant, should not only testify so much in the presence of the judge, but for a visible token thereof have also his ear bored through with an awl.[13] It were an infinite labour to prosecute these things so far as they might be exemplified both in civil and religious actions. For in both they have their necessary use and force. 'The sensible things which religion hath hallowed, are resemblances framed according to things spiritually understood, whereunto they serve as a hand to lead, and a way to direct.'[14]

1593

10. Hooker's constant appeal is to nature thus conceived.
11. Genesis 24:2.
12. Ruth 4:7.
13. Exodus 21:6.
14. From the *Ecclesiastical Hierarchies* of Dionysius the Areopagite.

LANCELOT ANDREWES

1555–1626

Chaplain to Queen Elizabeth, bishop of Winchester, important figure at the court of James I, Andrewes was one of the translators of the Authorized Version of the Bible (King James Bible). This sermon was one of a long series preached before the King at Christmas. James was a theologian, and Andrewes gave learned sermons which would have been unsuitable for large popular congregations. His terse Senecan style, extracting every possible meaning from the text, is aimed at intellectuals, but he was regarded as *stella predicantium*, the star among the preachers of his time. The style became obsolete before the century was out, but Andrewes has retained some appeal, and was venerated by T. S. Eliot, who compares him with Donne to Donne's discredit. "Intellect and sensibility were in harmony; and hence arise the particular qualities of his style."

The present sermon examines—or as some might say, torments—its text in characteristic fashion. It opens by setting up two topics, the persons arriving, and their errand. This second topic he enlarges. First he shows that the text, though on the face of it more appropriate to the feast of the Epiphany, suits Christmas Day; and the whole sermon is shaped by this.

From A Sermon Preached Before the King's Majesty

at Whitehall, on Wednesday, the Twenty-fifth of December, A.D. MDCXXII., Being Christmas-Day

Behold there came wise men from the East to Jerusalem,
Saying, Where is the King of the Jews that is born? For we have
seen His star in the East, and are come to worship Him.

Ecce magi ab oriente venerunt Jerosolymam,
Dicentes, ubi est qui natus est Rex Judæorum? vidimus enim
stellam ejus in oriente, et venimus adorare eum. (Latin Vulgate)
MATTHEW ii. 1, 2.

Their errand we may best learn from themselves out of their *dicentes*,[1] etc. Which, in a word, is to worship Him. Their errand our errand, and the errand of this day.

This text may seem to come a little too soon, before the time; and should have stayed till the day it was spoken on,[2] rather than on this day. But if you mark them well, there are in the verse four words that be *verba diei hujus*, 'proper and peculiar to this very day.' 1. For first, *natus est*[3] is most proper to this day of all days, the day of His Nativity. 2. Secondly, *vidimus stellam*;[4] for on this day it was first seen, appeared first. 3. Thirdly, *venimus*;[5] for this day

---

1. "Saying" (refers to the Latin text).
2. The feast of the Epiphany, twelve days after Christmas.
3. "(He) is born" (referring to the Latin text).
4. "We have seen the star."
5. "We have come."

they set forth, began their journey. 4. And last, *adorare eum*,[6] for 'when He brought His only-begotten Son into the world, He gave in charge, Let all the angels of God worship Him.'[7] And when the angels to do it, no time more proper for us to do it as then. So these four appropriate it to this day, and none but this.

The main heads of their errand are 1. *Vidimus stellam*, the occasion; 2. and *Venimus adorare*, the end[8] of their coming. But for the better conceiving it I will take another course, to set forth these points to be handled.

I. Their faith first: faith—in that they never ask 'Whether He be,' but 'Where He is born'; for that born He is, that they steadfastly believe.

II. Then 'the work or service'[9] of this faith, as St. Paul calleth it; 'the touch or trial,' 'δοχίμιον,'[10] as St. Peter; the *ostende mihi*, as St. James.[11] . . .

[He develops these divisions, and further subdivisions, until, at this point, he explains the significance of the fact that the wise men knew this was *His* (Christ's) star.]

Vidimus stellam—we can well conceive that; any that will but look up, may see a star. But how could they see the *ejus* of it, that it was His? Either that it belonged to any, or that He it was it belonged to. This passeth all perspective;[12] no astronomy could show them this. What by course of nature the stars can produce, that they by course of art or observation may discover. But this birth was above nature. No trigon, triplicity, exaltation could bring it forth. They are but idle that set figures for it. The star should not have been His, but He the star's, if it had gone that way. Some other light then, they saw this *ejus* by.

Now with us in Divinity there be but two in all; 1. *Vespertina*,[13] and 2. *Matutina lux*.[14] *Vespertina*, 'the owl-light' of our reason or skill, is too dim to see it by. No remedy then but it must be as Esay[15] calls it, *matutina lux*, 'the morning-light,' the light of God's law must certify them of the *ejus* of it. There, or not at all, to be had whom this star did portend.

[After extracting more doctrine from the star, he finds a text to authorize a switch to another subject, namely *venimus*, we came, and meditates on this journey in a passage made famous by Eliot's *Journey of the Magi*, which begins "A cold coming we had of it."]

It is not commended to stand 'gazing up into heaven'[16] too long; not on Christ Himself ascending, much less on His star. For they sat not still gazing on the star. Their *vidimus* begat *venimus;* their seeing made them come, come a great journey. *Venimus* is soon said, but a short word; but many a wide and weary step they made before they could come to say *Venimus*, Lo, here 'we are

6. To adore Him.
7. Hebrews 1:6.
8. Purpose.
9. Philippians 2:17.
10. I Peter 1:7.
11. James 2:18.
12. Telescope.
13. "Evening twilight."
14. "Morning twilight."
15. Isaiah 58:8.
16. Acts 1:11.

come'; come, and at our journey's end. To look a little on it. In this their coming
we consider, 1. First, the distance of the place they came from. It was not hard
by as the shepherds—but a step to Bethlehem over the fields; this was riding
many a hundred miles, and cost them many a day's journey. 2. Secondly, we
consider the way that they came, if it be pleasant, or plain and easy; for if it be,
it is so much the better. 1. This was nothing pleasant, for through deserts, all the
way waste and desolate. 2. Nor secondly, easy either; for over the rocks and
crags of both Arabias, specially Petræa,[17] their journey lay. 3. Yet if safe—but
it was not, but exceeding dangerous, as lying through the midst of the 'black
tents of Kedar,'[18] a nation of thieves and cut-throats; to pass over the hills of
robbers, infamous then, and infamous to this day. No passing without great
troop or convoy. 4. Last we consider the time of their coming, the season of
the year. It was no summer progress. A cold coming they had of it at this time
of the year, just the worst time of the year to take a journey, and specially
a long journey in. The ways deep, the weather sharp, the days short, the sun
farthest off, *in solstitio brumali*,[19] 'the very dead of winter.' *Venimus*, 'we are
come,' if that be one, *venimus*, 'we are now come,' come at this time, that sure
is another.

And these difficulties they overcame, of a wearisome, irksome, troublesome,
dangerous, unseasonable journey; and for all this they came. And came it cheerfully and quickly, as appeareth by the speed they made. It was but *vidimus,
venimus*, with them; 'they saw,' and 'they came'; no sooner saw, but they set
out presently. So as upon the first appearing of the star, as it might be last
night, they knew it was Balaam's star;[20] it called them away, they made ready
straight to begin their journey this morning. A sign they were highly conceited
of[21] His birth, believed some great matter of it, that they took all these pains,
made all this haste that they might be there to worship Him with all the possible
speed they could. Sorry for nothing so much as that they could not be there
soon enough, with the very first, to do it even this day, the day of His birth.
All considered, there is more in *venimus* than shows at the first sight.[22] It was
not for nothing it was said in the first verse, *ecce venerunt;* their coming hath
an *ecce*[23] on it, it well deserves it.

And we, what should we have done? Sure these men of the East shall rise in
judgment against the men of the West,[24] that is us, and their faith against ours
in this point. With them it was but *vidimus, venimus;* with us it would have
been but *veniemus*[25] at most. Our fashion is to see and see again before we stir
a foot, specially if it be to the worship of Christ. Come such a journey at such
a time? No; but fairly have put it off to the spring of the year, till the days

---

17. Arabia was divided into three parts by ancient geographers: *Arabia felix* (fertile
Arabia), *Arabia deserta, Arabia petraea* (stony Arabia).
18. Song of Songs 1:5.
19. "In the winter solstice."
20. Balaam's trance: "I shall behold him, but not nigh: there shall come a Star out of
Jacob, and a sceptre shall rise out of Israel . . ." (Numbers 24:17).
21. Had a strong notion of.
22. This sentence expresses the method of Andrewes and his contemporaries in unfolding
the full significance of their sermon texts.
23. "Behold." He means that there was something remarkable in their speedy action.
24. Matthew 8:11.
25. "We shall come."

longer, and the ways fairer, and the weather warmer, till better travelling to Christ. Our Epiphany would sure have fallen in Easter-week at the soonest.

But then for the distance, desolateness, tediousness, and the rest, any of them were enough to mar our *venimus* quite. It must be no great way, first, we must come; we love not that. Well fare the shepherds, yet they came but hard by; rather like them than the Magi. Nay, not like them neither. For with us the nearer, lightly the farther off; our proverb is, you know, 'The nearer the Church, the farther from God.'

Nor it must not be through no desert, over no Petræa. If rugged or uneven the way, if the weather ill-disposed, if any never so little danger, it is enough to stay us. To Christ we cannot travel, but weather and way and all must be fair. If not, no journey, but sit still and see farther. As indeed, all our religion is rather *vidimus*, a contemplation, than *venimus*, a motion, or stirring to do aught.

But when we do it, we must be allowed leisure. Ever *veniemus*, never *venimus;* ever coming, never come. We love to make no very great haste. To other things perhaps; not to *adorare*, the place of the worship of God. Why should we? Christ is no wild-cat.[26] What talk ye of twelve days?[27] And if it be forty days hence, ye shall be sure to find His Mother and Him; she cannot be churched[28] till then. What needs such haste? The truth is, we conceit Him and His birth but slenderly, and our haste is even thereafter. But if we be at that point, we must be out of this *venimus;* they like enough to leave us behind. Best get us a new Christmas in September; we are not like to come to Christ at this feast. Enough for *venimus*.

[From *venimus* he passes to the purpose of the journey, *invenimus*, we find. The wise men found, and fell down before Christ, and made offerings to him. We should do likewise.]

We cannot say *vidimus stellam;* the star is gone long since, not now to be seen. Yet I hope for all that, that *venimus adorare*, 'we be come thither to worship.' It will be the more acceptable, if not seeing it we worship though. It is enough we read of it in the text; we see it there. And indeed as I said, it skills[29] not for the star in the firmament, if the same day-star be risen in our hearts that was in theirs, and the same beams of it to be seen, all five. For then we have our part in it no less, nay full out as much as they. And it will bring us whither it brought them, to Christ. Who at His second appearing in glory shall call forth these wise men and all that have ensued[30] the steps of their faith, and that upon the reason specified in the text; for I have seen their star shining and showing forth itself by the like beams; and as they came to worship Me, so am I come to do them worship. A *venite*[31] then, for a *venimus*

26. A sentence admired but not explained by T. S. Eliot. The sense requires it to mean that there is no hurry to get to Christ, as if a wildcat were something shown as a public sensation, like a dead Indian. Or it may mean that he will not attack us for being late.
27. The twelve days between Christmas and the Epiphany.
28. Churching is the service of thanksgiving for women after childbirth.
29. Matters.
30. Followed.
31. "Come!"—imperative form of *venire*, "to come," and the short title of a canticle in the Prayer Book, *Venite omnia opera* ("Come All Ye Works of the Lord"). This playing on the moods and tenses of the verb from the text is characteristic of the preaching method of the period, though Andrewes does it more tersely than, say, Donne.

now. Their star I have seen, and give them a place above among the stars. They fell down: I will lift them up, and exalt them. And as they offered to Me, so am I come to bestow on them, and to reward them with the endless joy and bliss on My heavenly kingdom.

1622   1629

FRANCIS BACON
1561–1626

At the beginning of the seventeenth century, the word "science" still meant both "knowledge," acquired by a systematic acquaintance with the assertions of authority from Aristotle down through his scholastic interpreters, and general truths, made evident by the controlling fictions of art or literature. The phrase "natural philosophy" could still include anything from the dying stages of alchemy and astrology to the exciting and frightening new revisions of the age's sense of the universe. These revisions were being brought about by a century of global exploration and revolutionary astronomical thought, but they would soon extend into other areas of knowledge. "And new philosophy calls all in doubt," lamented John Donne in his "An Anatomy of the World," and it was not only the old maps of that world—the Ptolemaic cosmology, the macro-microcosmic relationships, the hierarchies of being and condition in animal, vegetable, and mineral kingdoms, as well as in those of nations and churches—whose loss he bemoaned. It was also a whole attitude toward certainty, a condition of comfort taken in demonstrations logically deduced from propositions of unquestioned authoritativeness. The new empirical attitudes toward truths about nature threatened some of that deductive security, that sense of protection which closure affords. To the active humanist intellect, compensation could lie in the energies of reason at work, in the spreading of reason's light which some radical reformers could feel was focusing (and which many of the orthodox feared was threatening to supplant) divine illumination.

Although the name of Francis Bacon is associated with the most systematic early vision of the generation and distribution of that empirical light, he was no true natural philosopher himself. At best he was an amateur experimentalist, innocent of mathematics, for the most part—a lawyer, a major legal theorist, an administrator and judge, and above all, a literary intellect whose thought seldom strayed far from the gardens of imagery and symbol in which they flourished. Bacon's great idea for a reconstruction of the institutions by which truths are discovered, recorded, and maintained could in no way be said to constitute one of the major advances of seventeenth-century science. That Great Reconstruction (the *Instauratio Magna,* his uncompleted general work) remains in many ways more like a poem than a theory, more like a fiction than a model.

Bacon's private program for the reform of knowledge was so much a public plan that it is odd to find such inconsistencies between his private and public lives. His career was marked by the difficulties which beset a world of public service governed by the caprices of courts rather than by the machinery of self-perpetuating bureaucracies. Bacon was well-connected, the younger son of the Lord Keeper of the Great Seal, Sir Nicholas Bacon. At Cambridge (he went to Trinity in 1573 but left two years later without a degree) and at Gray's Inn, where he read law, he trained for the kind of government post which would allow him either leisure to philosophize about the world or power to control it; yet even his relation to Lord Burghley and his friendship with the favorite, Essex, were of no help to him in Elizabeth's court. He was, indeed, finally put in the position of having to help prepare the prosecution of the Earl of Essex for treason; and only in the Jacobean court, with its scholarly airs and its penchant for rapid promotions, did Bacon prosper. But he did so rapidly, after receiving the knighthood in 1603 and a succession of honors thereafter—Solicitor General, Attorney General, Lord Keeper, Lord Chancellor—and became Baron Verulam in 1618 and Viscount St. Albans three years after. But at the height of his career he was indicted, by a Parliament hostile to James's court and its conduct, for accepting bribes while on the bench. His plea of guilty to the charge, coupled with the insistence that he had never let bribes (so common as to be almost customary) influence any of his judgments, left his accusers unimpressed; there were few among them who could have grasped the truth of this, as there were even fewer who might have said, as Bacon did about himself, "I was the justest judge that was in England these fifty years, but it was the justest censure in Parliament these two hundred years." Bacon lived on for about five years after a token imprisonment, and died of pneumonia resulting from overexposure to snow in which he was attempting experimentally to preserve food.

Bacon's *Essays*, for which he remained most famous, first appeared in 1597; an expanded edition of thirty-eight essays was published in 1612, and in 1625 the complete series of fifty-eight. Memorable for their crisp, "pointed" style, the *Essays or Counsels, Civil and Moral* eschewed abstract theorizing as they fled the lengthy balance of Ciceronian prose. They provide excellent evidence of Bacon's early seriousness about his belief, elaborated in *The Advancement of Learning*, that many of the miseries of truth could be traced to diseases of language. Aphoristic, flexible, far less bound in their structure to the quoted words of other men than even Montaigne's *Essais*, they have remained celebrated and widely quoted. The great project of the Instauration was launched only in pieces. In 1605, *The Advancement of Learning* outlined the problems with which the whole plan was to deal. The second part, the Latin *Novum Organum* (a "new instrument" to replace, presumably, the logical treatises or *Organon* of the Aristotelian canon against which his scholastic experiences at Cambridge had turned him early in youth) appeared in 1620. *Sylva Sylvarum*, his collection of observations on, and designs for experiments in, natural history, was published in 1626–27; likewise, the unfinished utopia called *The New Atlantis*. Throughout all of these runs an ultimately cheerful intellectual energy, a sense of manifest human destiny over nature. That state of nature sketched by Hobbes, wherein man is stripped down to his common bestiality, contrasts strongly with the Baconian one, wherein man is freed from the conceptual and institutional shadows of societies and theories, to walk about bathed in the light of his own reason.

From Essays or Counsels, Civil and Moral

Of Truth

What is Truth? said jesting Pilate, and would not stay for an answer. Certainly there be that delight in giddiness,[1] and count it a bondage to fix a belief, affecting[2] free will in thinking, as well as in acting. And though the sects of philosophers[3] of that kind be gone, yet there remain certain discoursing wits[4] which are of the same veins, though there be not so much blood in them as was in those of the ancients. But it is not only the difficulty and labour which men take in finding out of truth, nor again that when it is found it imposeth upon[5] men's thoughts, that doth bring lies in favour, but a natural though corrupt love of the lie itself. One of the later school of the Grecians examineth the matter, and is at a stand to think what should be in it, that men should love lies, where neither they make for pleasure, as with poets, nor for advantage, as with the merchant, but for the lie's sake. But I cannot tell: this same truth is a naked and open daylight, that doth not show the masks and mummeries and triumphs of the world, half so stately and daintily[6] as candlelights. Truth may perhaps come to the price of a pearl, that showeth best by day; but it will not rise to the price of a diamond or carbuncle, that showeth best in varied lights. A mixture of a lie doth ever add pleasure. Doth any man doubt, that if there were taken out of men's minds vain opinions, flattering hopes, false valuations, imaginations as one would, and the like, but it would leave the minds of a number of men poor shrunken things, full of melancholy and indisposition, and unpleasing to themselves? One of the Fathers, in great severity, called poesy *vinum dæmonum*,[7] because it filleth the imagination, and yet it is but with the shadow of a lie. But it is not the lie that passeth through the mind, but the lie that sinketh in and settleth in it, that doth the hurt; such as we spake of before. But howsoever these things are thus in men's depraved judgments and affections, yet truth, which only doth judge itself, teacheth that the inquiry of truth, which is the love-making or wooing of it, the knowledge of truth, which is the presence of it, and the belief of truth, which is the enjoying of it, is the sovereign good of human nature. The first creature of God, in the works of the days, was the light of the sense, the last was the light of reason; and his sabbath work ever since is the illumination of His Spirit. First He breathed light upon the face of the matter or chaos; then He breathed light into the face of man; and still He breatheth and inspireth light into the face of his chosen. The poet[8] that beautified the sect that was otherwise inferior to the rest saith yet excellently well: *It is a pleasure to stand upon the shore, and to see ships tossed upon the sea; a pleasure to stand in the window of a castle, and to see a battle and the ad-*

1. Intellectual fickleness.
2. Trying for.
3. The Skeptical school, probably; they simply denied the possibility of certainty.
4. Rambling or talkative minds.
5. Influences.
6. Elegantly.
7. "The wine of devils" (possibly quoted from St. Augustine, *Confessions* I.xvi).
8. Lucretius; Bacon is paraphrasing the opening of Bk. II of his *De Rerum Natura* (Of the Nature of Things).

ventures [9] *thereof below; but no pleasure is comparable to the standing upon the vantage ground of Truth* (a hill not to be commanded,[10] and where the air is always clear and serene), *and to see the errors, and wanderings, and mists, and tempests, in the vale below;* so [11] always that this prospect be with pity and not with swelling or pride. Certainly it is heaven upon earth to have a man's mind move in charity, rest in providence, and turn upon the poles of truth.

To pass from theological and philosophical truth to the truth of civil business, it will be acknowledged even by those that practise it not that clear and round [12] dealing is the honour of man's nature; and that mixture of falsehood is like allay [13] in coin of gold and silver, which may make the metal work the better, but it embaseth [14] it. For these winding and crooked courses are the goings of the serpent, which goeth basely upon the belly and not upon the feet. There is no vice that doth so cover a man with shame as to be found false and perfidious. And therefore Montaigne saith prettily, when he inquired the reason, why the word of the lie should be such a disgrace and such an odious charge? Saith he, *If it be well weighed, to say that a man lieth, is as much to say, as that he is brave towards God and a coward towards men.*[15] For a lie faces God and shrinks from man. Surely the wickedness of falsehood and breach of faith cannot possibly be so highly expressed, as in that it shall be the last peal to call the judgments of God upon the generations of men, it being foretold that when Christ cometh, *he shall not find faith upon the earth.*[16]

1625

Of Death

Men fear Death, as children fear to go in the dark; and as that natural fear in children is increased with tales, so is the other. Certainly the contemplation of death, as the wages of sin [1] and passage to another world, is holy and religious, but the fear of it, as a tribute due unto nature, is weak. Yet in religious meditations there is sometimes mixture of vanity and of superstition. You shall read in some of the friars' books of mortification, that a man should think with himself what the pain is if he have but his finger's end pressed or tortured, and thereby imagine what the pains of death are, when the whole body is corrupted and dissolved; when many times death passeth with less pain than the torture of a limb, for the most vital parts are not the quickest of sense. And by him that spake only as a philosopher and natural man, it was well said, *Pompa mortis magis terret, quam mors ipsa.*[2] Groans and convulsions, and a discoloured face, and friends weeping, and blacks, and ob-

9. What chances to happen.
10. Taken.
11. So long as.
12. Honest.
13. Alloy.
14. Debases.
15. From his *Essays* II.18.
16. Luke 18:8.

1. Romans 6:23.
2. "The circumstances surrounding death are more frightening than death itself" (possibly from Seneca, *Epistles* XXIV.14.)

sequies, and the like show death terrible. It is worthy the observing that there is no passion in the mind of man so weak, but it mates [3] and masters the fear of death; and therefore death is no such terrible enemy when a man hath so many attendants about him that can win the combat of him. Revenge triumphs over death; Love slights it; Honour aspireth to it; Grief flieth to it; Fear preoccupateth [4] it; nay we read, after Otho the emperor [5] had slain himself, Pity (which is the tenderest of affections) provoked many to die out of mere compassion to their sovereign, and as the truest sort of followers. Nay Seneca adds niceness [6] and satiety: *Cogita quamdiu eadem feceris; mori velle, non tantum fortis, aut miser, sed etiam fastidiosus potest.*[7] A man would die, though he were neither valiant nor miserable, only upon a weariness to do the same thing so oft over and over. It is no less worthy to observe how little alteration in good spirits the approaches of death make, for they appear to be the same men till the last instant. Augustus Cæsar died in a compliment: *Livia, conjugii nostri memor, vive et vale;* [8] Tiberius in dissimulation, as Tacitus saith of him: *Jam Tiberium vires et corpus, non dissimulatio, deserebant;* [9] Vespasian in a jest, sitting upon the stool: *Ut puto Deus fio;* [10] Galba with a sentence: *Feri, si ex re sit populi Romani,*[11] holding forth his neck; Septimius Severus in despatch: *Adeste si quid mihi restat agendum.*[12] And the like. Certainly the Stoics bestowed too much cost upon death, and by their great preparations made it appear more fearful. Better saith he, *qui finem vitæ extremum inter munera ponat naturæ.*[13] It is as natural to die as to be born; and to a little infant, perhaps, the one is as painful as the other. He that dies in an earnest pursuit is like one that is wounded in hot blood, who, for the time, scarce feels the hurt; and therefore a mind fixed and bent upon somewhat that is good doth avert the dolours [14] of death. But above all, believe it, the sweetest canticle is, *Nunc dimittis;* [15] when a man hath obtained worthy ends and expectations. Death hath this also, that it openeth the gate to good fame, and extinguisheth envy. *Extinctus amabitur idem.*[16]

1625

Of Love

The stage is more beholding [1] to love than the life of man. For as to the stage, love is ever matter of comedies, and now and then of tragedies, but in

---

3. Overcomes.
4. Anticipates (by causing suicide).
5. The Roman emperor who died by his own hand when his army was defeated, 69 A.D.
6. Fastidiousness.
7. Again from *Epistles* LXXVII.6, paraphrased, as frequently, in the next lines.
8. "Live, remembering our marriage, Livia, and farewell."
9. "Tiberius' strength was leaving him, but not his power to fake."
10. "I guess I'm becoming a god" ("stool": toilet).
11. "Strike, if it's for the people of Rome."
12. "Hurry, if there's anything left for me to do."
13. "Who thinks the end of life one of nature's blessings" (Juvenal, *Satires* X.358).
14. Pains.
15. "Now lettest thou thy servant depart in peace" (Luke 2:29).
16. "(Envied when alive) the same man, dead, will be loved" (Horace, *Epistles* II.i.14).

1. Beholden, indebted.

life it doth much mischief, sometimes like a siren, sometimes like a fury. You may observe that among all great and worthy persons (whereof the memory remaineth, either ancient or recent) there is not one that hath been transported to the mad degree of love, which shows that great spirits and great business do keep out this weak passion. You must except nevertheless Marcus Antonius, the half partner of the empire of Rome, and Appius Claudius,[2] the decemvir and lawgiver; whereof the former was indeed a voluptuous man, and inordinate, but the latter was an austere and wise man; and therefore it seems (though rarely) that love can find entrance not only into an open heart, but also into a heart well fortified, if watch be not well kept. It is a poor saying of Epicurus, *Satis magnum alter alteri theatrum sumus*,[3] as if man, made for the contemplation of heaven and all noble objects, should do nothing but kneel before a little idol, and make himself a subject, though not of the mouth (as beasts are), yet of the eye, which was given him for higher purposes. It is a strange thing to note the excess of this passion, and how it braves[4] the nature and value of things, by this: that the speaking in a perpetual hyperbole is comely in nothing but in love. Neither is it merely in the phrase, for whereas it hath been well said that the arch-flatterer, with whom all the petty flatterers have intelligence,[5] is a man's self, certainly the lover is more. For there was never proud man thought so absurdly well of himself as the lover doth of the person loved; and therefore it was well said, *That it is impossible to love and to be wise.* Neither doth this weakness appear to others only, and not to the party loved, but to the loved most of all, except the love be reciproque.[6] For it is a true rule that love is ever rewarded either with the reciproque or with an inward and secret contempt. By how much the more men ought to beware of this passion, which loseth not only other things but itself. As for the other losses, the poet's relation doth well figure them: that he[7] that preferred Helena quitted the gifts of Juno and Pallas. For whosoever esteemeth too much of amorous affection quitteth both riches and wisdom. This passion hath his floods in the very times of weakness, which are great prosperity and great adversity, though this latter hath been less observed, both which times kindle love, and make it more fervent, and therefore show it to be the child of folly. They do best who, if they cannot but admit love, yet make it keep quarter[8] and sever it wholly from their serious affairs and actions of life, for if it check[9] once with business, it troubleth men's fortunes, and maketh men that they can no ways be true to their own ends. I know not how, but martial men are given to love; I think it is but as they are given to wine, for perils commonly ask to be paid in pleasures. There is in man's

---

2. Appius Claudius (not the lawgiver; Bacon confused the two) desired Virginia, and her father, Virginius, killed him in order to spare her (449 B.C.). Told by Livy, the story was a popular tragic subject, from Chaucer's day through Bacon's.
3. "Each of us is a big enough theater to one another."
4. Insults.
5. Are confederates.
6. Reciprocal.
7. Paris; asked to award a golden apple (Discord, it was) to the most beautiful of three goddesses, he took Venus' bribe (Helen, wife of Menelaus), rejecting Minerva's offer of wisdom, and Juno's, of power.
8. Proper place.
9. Interfere.

nature a secret inclination and motion towards love of others, which if it be not spent upon some one or a few, doth naturally spread itself towards many, and maketh men become humane and charitable, as it is seen sometime in friars. Nuptial love maketh mankind; friendly love perfecteth it; but wanton love corrupteth and embaseth it.

1625

Of Innovations [1]

As the births of living creatures at first are ill-shapen, so are all Innovations, which are the births of time. Yet notwithstanding, as those that first bring honour into their family are commonly more worthy than most that succeed, so the first precedent (if it be good) is seldom attained by imitation. For Ill, to man's nature as it stands perverted, hath a natural motion, strongest in continuance, but Good, as a forced motion, strongest at first. Surely every medicine is an innovation; and he that will not apply new remedies must expect new evils, for time is the greatest innovator, and if time of course [2] alter things to the worse, and wisdom and counsel shall not alter them to the better, what shall be the end? It is true that what is settled by custom, though it be not good, yet at least it is fit; and those things which have long gone together are as it were confederate within themselves; whereas new things piece not so well, but though they help by their utility, yet they trouble by their inconformity. Besides, they are like strangers, more admired and less favoured. All this is true, if time stood still, which contrariwise moveth so round [3] that a froward retention of custom is as turbulent a thing as an innovation; and they that reverence too much old times are but a scorn to the new. It were good therefore that men in their innovations would follow the example of time itself, which indeed innovateth greatly, but quietly and by degrees scarce to be perceived. For otherwise, whatsoever is new is unlooked for, and ever it mends some, and pairs [4] other; and he that is holpen [5] takes it for a fortune, and thanks the time; and he that is hurt, for a wrong, and imputeth it to the author. It is good also not to try experiments in states, except the necessity be urgent, or the utility evident, and well to beware that it be the reformation that draweth on the change, and not the desire of change that pretendeth the reformation. And lastly, that the novelty, though it be not rejected, yet be held for a suspect,[6] and, as the Scripture saith, *that we make a stand upon the ancient way, and then look about us, and discover what is the straight and right way, and so to walk in it.*[7]

1625

1. Bacon will give the word a double sense of "renewal," and "rebellion against" old things.
2. As a matter of course.
3. Swiftly.
4. Impairs.
5. Helped, cured, mended.
6. Suspicion.
7. Paraphrase of Jeremiah 6:16.

Of Prophecies

I mean not to speak of divine prophecies, nor of heathen oracles, nor of natural predictions, but only of prophecies that have been of certain memory and from hidden causes. Saith the Pythonissa [1] to Saul, *Tomorrow thou and thy son shall be with me.* Homer hath these verses:

> *At domus Æneæ cunctis dominabitur oris,*
> *Et nati natorum, et qui nascentur ab illis.* [2]

A prophecy, as it seems, of the Roman empire. Seneca the tragedian hath these verses:

> *Venient annis*
> *Sæcula seris, quibus Oceanus*
> *Vincula rerum laxet, et ingens*
> *Pateat Tellus, Tiphysque novos*
> *Detegat orbes; nec sit terris*
> *Ultima Thule.* [3]

a prophecy of the discovery of America. The daughter of Polycrates [4] dreamed that Jupiter bathed her father, and Apollo anointed him, and it came to pass that he was crucified in an open place, where the sun made his body run with sweat, and the rain washed it. Philip of Macedon dreamed he sealed up his wife's belly, whereby he did expound it, that his wife should be barren, but Aristander [5] the soothsayer told him his wife was with child, because men do not use to seal vessels that are empty. A phantasm that appeared to M. Brutus in his tent said to him, *Philippis iterum me videbis.* [6] Tiberius said to Galba, *Tu quoque, Galba, degustabis imperium.* [7] In Vespasian's time there went a prophecy in the East, that those that should come forth of Judea should reign over the world, which though it may be was meant of our Saviour, yet Tacitus expounds it of Vespasian. Domitian dreamed, the night before he was slain, that a golden head was growing out of the nape of his neck, and indeed the succession that followed him for many years made golden times. Henry the Sixth of England said of Henry the Seventh, when he was a lad, and gave him water, *This is the lad that shall enjoy the crown for which we strive.* When I was in France, I heard from one Dr. Pena that the Queen Mother, who was given to curious arts, caused the King [8] her husband's

---

1. The Pythonissa was the priestess of the oracle at Delphi (because of Apollo's epithet of Pythian, who had killed a python); here, she is identified with the Witch of Endor (in I Samuel 28).
2. "The house of Aeneas will reign in all lands, and his children's children, and their descendants" (Virgil, *Aeneid* III.97–98).
3. "In years to come, Oceanus will unloose the chains that bind things, revealing the vast earth, Tiphys will discover new lands, and Thule will not be the limit of the world" (Seneca, *Medea* II.374–8). Tiphys was the *Argo's* pilot, *Ultima Thule* the northernmost land.
4. A tyrant of Samos; the story is from Herodotus.
5. A favorite soothsayer of Alexander the Great, Philip's son.
6. "You will see me again at Philippi."
7. "You too, Galba, will taste of empire."
8. King Henry II of France; the tournament in which he was accidentally killed took place in 1559.

nativity to be calculated under a false name; and the astrologer gave a judgment, that he should be killed in a duel, at which the Queen laughed, thinking her husband to be above challenges and duels, but he was slain upon a course at tilt, the splinters of the staff of Montgomery going in at his beaver.[9] The trivial [10] prophecy which I heard when I was a child and Queen Elizabeth was in the flower of her years, was,

> When hempe is sponne
> England's done:

whereby it was generally conceived that after the princes had reigned which had the principial [11] letters of that word *hempe* (which were Henry, Edward, Mary, Philip, and Elizabeth), England should come to utter confusion, which, thanks be to God, is verified only in the change of the name, for that the King's style is now no more of England but of Britain.[12] There was also another prophecy before the year of eighty-eight, which I do not well understand:

> There shall be seen upon a day,
> Between the Baugh and the May,
> The black fleet of Norway.
> When that that is come and gone,
> England build houses of lime and stone,
> For after wars shall you have none.

It was generally conceived to be meant of the Spanish fleet that came in eighty-eight, for that the king of Spain's surname, as they say, is Norway. The prediction of Regiomontanus,

> *Octogesimus octavus mirabilis annus,*[13]

was thought likewise accomplished in the sending of that great fleet, being the greatest in strength, though not in number, of all that ever swam upon the sea. As for Cleon's dream, I think is was a jest. It was that he was devoured of a long dragon; and it was expounded of [14] a maker of sausages, that troubled him exceedingly. There are numbers of the like kind, especially if you include dreams and predictions of astrology. But I have set down these few only of certain credit for example. My judgment is that they ought all to be despised, and ought to serve but for winter talk by the fireside. Though when I say *despised*, I mean it as for belief, for otherwise, the spreading or publishing of them is in no sort to be despised. For they have done much mischief, and I see many severe laws made to suppress them. That that hath given them grace and some credit consisteth in three things. First, that men mark when

9. Movable part of the tilting helmet.
10. Common.
11. Initial.
12. Because James I, formerly King of Scotland, ruled over a new "Great Britain" in which the nations were joined.
13. "Eighty-eight, a year most great," Regiomontanus (Johannes Müller, a 15th-century German mathematician and astrologer).
14. By.

they hit, and never mark when they miss, as they do generally also of dreams. The second is that probable conjectures or obscure traditions many times turn themselves into prophecies, while the nature of man, which coveteth divination, thinks it no peril to foretell that which indeed they do but collect. As that of Seneca's verse. For so much was then subject to demonstration that the globe of the earth had great parts beyond the Atlantic, which mought [15] be probably conceived not to be all sea, and adding thereto the tradition in Plato's Timæus and his Atlanticus, [16] it mought encourage one to turn it to a prediction. The third and last (which is the great one) is that almost all of them, being infinite in number, have been impostures, and by idle and crafty brains merely contrived and feigned after the event past.

1625

Of Studies

Studies serve for delight, for ornament, and for ability. Their chief use for delight is in privateness and retiring; [1] for ornament, is in discourse; and for ability, is in the judgment and disposition of business. For expert [2] men can execute and perhaps judge of particulars, one by one, but the general counsels and the plots and marshalling of affairs come best from those that are learned. To spend too much time in studies is sloth; to use them too much for ornament is affectation; to make judgment wholly by their rules is the humour of a scholar. They perfect nature, and are perfected by experience, for natural abilities are like natural plants, that need proyning [3] by study; and studies themselves do give forth directions too much at large, except they be bounded in by experience. Crafty men contemn studies; simple men admire them; and wise men use them, for they teach not their own use, but that is a wisdom without them and above them, won by observation. Read not to contradict and confute, nor to believe and take for granted, nor to find talk and discourse, but to weigh and consider. Some books are to be tasted, others to be swallowed, and some few to be chewed and digested; that is, some books are to be read only in parts; others to be read, but not curiously; [4] and some few to be read wholly and with diligence and attention. Some books also may be read by deputy, and extracts made of them by others, but that would [5] be only in the less important arguments and the meaner sort of books; else distilled books are like common distilled waters, flashy things. Reading maketh a full man, conference a ready man, and writing an exact man. And therefore, if a man write little, he had need have a great memory; if he confer little, he had need have a present wit; and if he read little, he had need have much cunning, to seem to know that he doth not. Histories make men wise, poets witty, the mathematics subtile, natural philosophy deep, moral grave,

---

15. Might.
16. This dialogue, relating the myth of Atlantis, is called the *Critias*.

1. Privacy and retirement.
2. Experienced (rather than learned).
3. Pruning.
4. Carefully.
5. Should.

logic and rhetoric able to contend. *Abeunt studia in mores.*[6] Nay there is no stond [7] or impediment in the wit but may be wrought out by fit studies, like as diseases of the body may have appropriate exercises. Bowling is good for the stone and reins; [8] shooting for the lungs and breast; gentle walking for the stomach; riding for the head; and the like. So if a man's wit be wandering, let him study the mathematics, for in demonstrations, if his wit be called away never so little, he must begin again. If his wit be not apt to distinguish or find differences, let him study the schoolmen, for they are *cymini sectores.*[9] If he be not apt to beat over [10] matters, and to call up one thing to prove and illustrate another, let him study the lawyers' cases. So every defect of the mind may have a special receipt.

1625

Aphorisms

The Aphorisms of the *Novum Organum* were written in Latin, but like Bacon's English prose, they generate their pith through a stalk of metaphor. Bacon remarks in another context that just as hieroglyphics preceded alphabets, so parables (by which he means what we would call myths) preceded argument, or logical exposition. His own style remains close to parable, as in the famous image of the four classes of Idols or false images which interfere with the perception of truth. The English translation used here is the standard one of Ellis and Spedding.

1

Man, being the servant and interpreter of Nature, can do and understand so much and so much only as he has observed in fact or in thought of the course of nature; beyond this he neither knows anything nor can do anything.

2

Neither the naked hand nor the understanding left to itself can effect much. It is by instruments and helps that the work is done, which are as much wanted for the understanding as for the hand. And as the instruments of the hand either give motion or guide it, so the instruments of the mind supply either suggestions for the understanding or cautions.

3

Human knowledge and human power meet in one, for where the cause is not known the effect cannot be produced. Nature to be commanded must be obeyed, and that which in contemplation is as the cause, is in operation as the rule.

6. "Studies become ways of life" (Ovid, *Heroides* XV. 83).
7. Block.
8. Gallstone and kidneys.
9. "Hair-splitters."
10. Work over, conceptually.

19

There are and can be only two ways of searching into and discovering truth. The one flies from the senses and particulars to the most general axioms,[1] and from these principles, the truth of which it takes for settled and immovable, proceeds to judgment and to the discovery of middle axioms. And this way is now in fashion. The other derives axioms from the senses and particulars, rising by a gradual and unbroken ascent, so that it arrives at the most general axioms last of all. This is the true way, but as yet untried.

38

The idols and false notions which are now in possession of the human understanding, and have taken deep root therein, not only so beset men's minds that truth can hardly find entrance, but even after entrance obtained, they will again in the very instauration[2] of the sciences meet and trouble us, unless men being forewarned of the danger fortify themselves as far as may be against their assaults.

39

There are four classes of Idols[3] which beset men's minds. To these for distinction's sake I have assigned names, calling the first class *Idols of the Tribe*; the second, *Idols of the Cave*; the third, *Idols of the Marketplace*; the fourth, *Idols of the Theatre*.

40

The formation of ideas and axioms by true induction is no doubt the proper remedy to be applied for the keeping off and clearing away of idols. To point them out, however, is of great use, for the doctrine of Idols is to the Interpretation of Nature what the doctrine of the refutation of sophisms[4] is to common logic.

41

The Idols of the Tribe have their foundation in human nature itself and in the tribe or race of men. For it is a false assertion that the sense of man is the measure of things.[5] On the contrary, all perceptions as well of the sense

1. Bacon means true assertions, not logical or mathematical postulates. The first of these "ways" is deduction, essential in closed systems like logic and mathematics, crippling in the investigation of nature. Thus: "All swans are white; here is what looks like a black swan." The deductive way forces us to conclude "It cannot be a true swan." The "untried" way Bacon is advocating would lead us to say: "Since this is swan-like in every way save for its color, then it must *be* a swan, and the original generalization about swan-whiteness must be revised to include, at least, black swans."
2. Reconstruction.
3. From Greek *eidōlon*, image; Bacon means by these not false gods, as in the Bible, but specters and phantasms, entities which appear to exist in nature, but which are only part of our describing or interpreting apparatus.
4. Fallacies.
5. A remark attributed to Protagoras, discussed by Plato in the *Theaetetus*, and in Aristotle's *Metaphysics*.

as of the mind are according to the measure of the individual and not according to the measure of the universe. And the human understanding is like a false mirror, which, receiving rays irregularly, distorts and discolours the nature of things by mingling its own nature with it.

42

The Idols of the Cave are the idols of the individual man. For every one (besides the errors common to human nature in general) has a cave or den of his own, which refracts and discolours the light of nature, owing either to his own proper and peculiar nature, or to his education and conversation with others, or to the reading of books, and the authority of those whom he esteems and admires, or to the differences of impressions, accordingly as they take place in a mind preoccupied and predisposed or in a mind indifferent and settled, or the like. So that the spirit of man (according as it is meted out to different individuals) is in fact a thing variable and full of perturbation, and governed as it were by chance. Whence it was well observed by Heraclitus[6] that men look for sciences in their own lesser worlds and not in the greater or common world.

43

There are also Idols formed by the intercourse and association of men with each other, which I call Idols of the Marketplace on account of the commerce and consort of men there. For it is by discourse that men associate, and words are imposed according to the apprehension of the vulgar.[7] And therefore the ill and unfit choice of words wonderfully obstructs the understanding. Nor do the definitions or explanations wherewith in some things learned men are wont to guard and defend themselves, by any means set the matter right. But words plainly force and overrule the understanding, and throw all into confusion, and lead men away into numberless empty controversies and idle fancies.

44

Lastly, there are Idols which have immigrated into men's minds from the various dogmas of philosophies and also from wrong laws of demonstration. These I call Idols of the Theatre, because in my judgment all the received systems are but so many stage plays, representing worlds of their own creation after an unreal and scenic fashion. Nor is it only of the systems now in vogue or only of the ancient sects and philosophies that I speak, for many more plays of the same kind may yet be composed and in like artificial manner set forth, seeing that errors the most widely different have nevertheless causes for the most part alike. Neither again do I mean this only of entire systems, but also of many principles and axioms in science, which by tradition, credulity, and negligence have come to be received.

But of these several kinds of Idols I must speak more largely and exactly, that the understanding may be duly cautioned.

6. Important pre-Socratic Greek philosopher (540–475 B.C.).
7. The common understanding.

45

The human understanding is of its own nature prone to suppose the existence of more order and regularity in the world than it finds. And though there be many things in nature which are singular and unmatched, yet it devises for them parallels and conjugates and relatives which do not exist. Hence the fiction that all celestial bodies move in perfect cicles, spirals and dragons[8] being (except in name) utterly rejected. Hence too the element of fire with its orb[9] is brought in, to make up the square with the other three which the sense perceives. Hence also the ratio of density of the so-called elements is arbitrarily fixed at ten to one.[10] And so on of other dreams. And these fancies affect not dogmas only, but simple notions also.

46

The human understanding when it has once adopted an opinion (either as being the received opinion or as being agreeable to itself) draws all things else to support and agree with it. And though there be a greater number and weight of instances to be found on the other side, yet these it either neglects and despises, or else by some distinction sets aside and rejects; in order that by this great and pernicious predetermination the authority of its former conclusions may remain inviolate. And therefore it was a good answer that was made by one who when they showed him hanging in a temple a picture of those who had paid their vows as having escaped shipwreck, and would have him say whether he did not now acknowledge the power of the gods. 'Aye,' asked he again, 'but where are they painted that were drowned after their vows?' And such is the way of all superstition, whether in astrology, dreams, omens, divine judgments, or the like wherein men, having a delight in such vanities, mark the events where they are fulfilled, but where they fail, though this happen much oftener, neglect and pass them by. But with far more subtlety does this mischief insinuate itself into philosophy and the sciences, in which the first conclusion colours and brings into conformity with itself all that come after, though far sounder and better. Besides, independently of that delight and vanity which I have described it is the peculiar and perpetual error of the human intellect to be more moved and excited by affirmatives than by negatives, whereas it ought properly to hold itself indifferently disposed towards both alike. Indeed in the establishment of any true axiom, the negative instance is the more forcible of the two.

8. Probably helical movements, possibly the ones traced by the epicycles moving about the main orb (see *Astronomy* in the Glossary). Bacon is attacking the disposition of astronomers to believe that the orbits of the planets must be circular, circles being the shape of perfection, etc. He was correct in fact, as well as in principle: Kepler's revision of Copernicus showed that the orbits were elliptical, with the sun at one of the foci.

9. In the older Ptolemaic model of the universe, Earth was surrounded by the elemental spheres of water, air, and fire, just inside the first celestial sphere of the moon.

10. Bacon may be alluding to Aristotle (*On Generation and Corruption*) or to some contemporary alchemical writer; in either case, the prior dogmatism of the notion displeased him.

49

The human understanding is no dry light, but receives an infusion from the will and affections; whence proceed sciences which may be called 'sciences as one would.' For what a man had rather were true he more readily believes. Therefore he rejects difficult things from impatience of research; sober things because they narrow hope; the deeper things of nature from superstition; the light of experience for arrogance and pride, lest his mind should seem to be occupied with things mean and transitory; things not commonly believed, out of deference to the opinion of the vulgar. Numberless, in short, are the ways, and sometimes imperceptible, in which the affections[11] colour and infect the understanding.

50

But by far the greatest hindrance and aberration of the human understanding proceeds from the dulness, incompetency, and deceptions of the senses; in that things which strike the sense outweigh things which do not immediately strike it, though they be more important. Hence it is that speculation commonly ceases where sight ceases; insomuch that of things invisible there is little or no observation. Hence all the working of the spirits[12] inclosed in tangible bodies lies hid and unobserved of men. So also all the more subtle changes of form in the parts of coarser substances (which they commonly call alteration, though it is in truth local motion through exceedingly small spaces) is in like manner unobserved. And yet, unless these two things just mentioned be searched out and brought to light, nothing great can be achieved in nature as far as the production of works is concerned. So again, the essential nature of our common air and of all bodies less dense than air (which are very many) is almost unknown. For the sense by itself is a thing infirm and erring; neither can instruments for enlarging or sharpening the senses do much; but all the truer kind of interpretation of nature is effected by instances and experiments fit and apposite, wherein the sense decides touching the experiment only, and the experiment touching the point in nature and the thing itself.

51

The human understanding is of its own nature prone to abstractions and gives a substance and reality to things which are fleeting. But to resolve nature into abstractions is less to our purpose than to dissect her into parts, as did the school of Democritus,[13] which went further into nature than the rest. Matter rather than forms[14] should be the object of our attention, its configurations

11. Emotions.
12. The "spirits" or "subtle vapors," diffused throughout the substance of bodily tissues were of three types, natural, vital, and animal. See Burton's section on "The Division of the Body," from *The Anatomy of Melancholy*, and also *Renaissance Psychology* in the Glossary.
13. The Greek atomist, who held that all phenomena were the product of random assemblages of ultimate particles of matter ("a fortuitous concourse of atoms" is the tag phrase).
14. Aristotle's concept of those non-material entities which constitute the essence, the "whatness" or particularity of any substance or object; Bacon views these mental fictions with disfavor.

and changes of configuration, and simple action, and law of action or motion, for forms are figments of the human mind, unless you will call those laws of action forms.

52

Such then are the idols which I call Idols of the Tribe, and which take their rise either from the homogeneity of the substance of the human spirit, or from its preoccupation, or from its narrowness, or from its restless motion, or from an infusion of the affections, or from the incompetency of the senses, or from the mode of impression.

53

The Idols of the Cave take their rise in the peculiar constitution, mental or bodily, of each individual, and also in education, habit, and accident. Of this kind there is a great number and variety, but I will instance those the pointing out of which contains the most important caution, and which have most effect in disturbing the clearness of the understanding.

54

Men become attached to certain particular sciences and speculations, either because they fancy themselves the authors and inventors thereof, or because they have bestowed the greatest pains upon them and become most habituated to them. But men of this kind, if they betake themselves to philosophy and contemplations of a general character, distort and colour them in obedience to their former fancies, a thing especially to be noticed in Aristotle, who made his natural philosophy a mere bondservant to his logic, thereby rendering it contentious and well nigh useless. The race of chemists[15] again out of a few experiments of the furnace have built up a fantastic philosophy, framed with reference to a few things, and Gilbert[16] also, after he had employed himself most laboriously in the study and observation of the loadstone, proceeded at once to construct an entire system in accordance with his favourite subject.

55

There is one principal and as it were radical distinction between different minds, in respect of philosophy and the sciences, which is this: that some minds are stronger and apter to mark the differences of things, others to mark their resemblances. The steady and acute mind can fix its contemplations and dwell and fasten on the subtlest distinctions, the lofty and discursive mind recognizes and puts together the finest and most general resemblances. Both kinds however easily err in excess, by catching the one at gradations, the other at shadows.

15. The alchemists.
16. William Gilbert (1540–1603), Queen Elizabeth's physician. In 1600 his *De Magnete* appeared, describing magnetic phenomena and those of static electricity (the latter word being his coinage), but attempting, wrongly, to attribute both gravity and electricity to magnetic force.

56

There are found some minds given to an extreme admiration of antiquity, others to an extreme love and appetite for novelty; but few so duly tempered that they can hold the mean, neither carping at what has been well laid down by the ancients, nor despising what is well introduced by the moderns. This however turns to the great injury of the sciences and philosophy: since these affectations of antiquity and novelty are the humours of partisans rather than judgments; and truth is to be sought for not in the felicity of any age, which is an unstable thing, but in the light of nature and experience, which is eternal. These factions therefore must be abjured, and care must be taken that the intellect be not hurried by them into assent.

57

Contemplations of nature and of bodies in their simple form break up and distract the understanding, while contemplations of nature and bodies in their composition and configuration overpower and dissolve the understanding—a distinction well seen in the school of Leucippus and Democritus as compared with the other philosophies. For that school is so busied with the particles that it hardly attends to the structure, while the others are so lost in admiration of the structure that they do not penetrate to the simplicity of nature. These kinds of contemplation should therefore be alternated and taken by turns, that so the understanding may be rendered at once penetrating and comprehensive, and the inconveniences above mentioned, with the idols which proceed from them, may be avoided.

58

Let such then be our provision and contemplative prudence for keeping off and dislodging the Idols of the Cave, which grow for the most part either out of the predominance of a favourite subject, or out of an excessive tendency to compare or to distinguish, or out of partiality for particular ages, or out of the largeness or minuteness of the objects contemplated. And generally let every student of nature take this as a rule, that whatever his mind seizes and dwells upon with peculiar satisfaction is to be held in suspicion, and that so much the more care is to be taken in dealing with such questions to keep the understanding even and clear.

59

But the Idols of the Marketplace are the most troublesome of all—idols which have crept into the understanding through the alliances of words and names. For men believe that their reason governs words, but it is also true that words react on the understanding, and this it is that has rendered philosophy and the sciences sophistical and inactive. Now words, being commonly framed and applied according to the capacity of the vulgar, follow those lines of division which are most obvious to the vulgar understanding. And whenever an understanding of greater acuteness or a more diligent observation would alter those lines to suit the true divisions of nature, words stand in the way and resist the change. Whence it comes to pass that the high and formal discussions of learned men end oftentimes in disputes about words and names, with which (according to the use [17] and wisdom of the mathematicians) it would be more prudent to begin, and so by means of definitions reduce them to order. Yet even definitions cannot cure this evil in dealing with natural and material things; since the definitions themselves consist of words, and those words beget others, so that it is necessary to recur to individual instances, and those in due series and order, as I shall say presently when I come to the method and scheme for the formation of notions and axioms.

60

The idols imposed by words on the understanding are of two kinds. They are either names of things which do not exist (for as there are things left unnamed through lack of observation, so likewise are there names which result from fantastic suppositions and to which nothing in reality corresponds), or they are names of things which exist, but yet confused and ill defined and hastily and irregularly derived from realities. Of the former kind are Fortune, the Prime Mover,[18] Planetary Orbits,[19] Element of Fire, and like fictions which owe their origin to false and idle theories. And this class of idols is more easily expelled, because to get rid of them it is only necessary that all theories should be steadily rejected and dismissed as obsolete.

But the other class, which springs out of a faulty and unskilful abstraction, is intricate and deeply rooted. Let us take for example such a word as *humid,* and see how far the several things which the word is used to signify agree with each other; and we shall find the word *humid* to be nothing else than a mark loosely and confusedly applied to denote a variety of actions which will not bear to be reduced to any constant meaning. For it both signifies that which easily spreads itself round any other body; and that which in itself is indeterminate and cannot solidise; and that which readily yields in every direction; and that which easily divides and scatters itself; and that which easily unites and collects itself; and that which readily flows and is put in motion; and that which readily clings to another body and wets it; and that which is easily reduced to a liquid, or being solid easily melts. Accordingly when you come to apply the word, if you take it in one sense, flame is humid; if in another, air is not humid; if in another, fine dust is humid; if in another, glass is humid. So that it is easy to see that the notion is taken by abstraction only from water and common and ordinary liquids without any due verification.

There are however in words certain degrees of distortion and error. One of the least faulty kinds is that of names of substances, especially of lowest species and well deduced (for the notion of *chalk* and of *mud* is good, of *earth* bad); a more faulty kind is that of actions, as *to generate, to corrupt, to alter;* the most faulty is of qualities (except such as are the immediate objects of

17. Practice.
18. The "prime mover," or outermost celestial sphere, which imparted motion through the ether to the others (think of a kind of fluid transmission system) in the Ptolemaic system (see *Astronomy* in the Glossary).
19. Bacon means the concrete *orbs* or spheres of the old system, not the abstract *orbits,* or paths, of the new.

the sense) as *heavy, light, rare, dense,* and the like. Yet in all these cases some notions are of necessity a little better than others, in proportion to the greater variety of subjects that fall within the range of the human sense.

61

But the Idols of the Theatre are not innate, nor do they steal into the understanding secretly, but are plainly impressed and received into the mind from the playbooks [20] of philosophical systems and the perverted rules of demonstration. To attempt refutations in this case would be merely inconsistent with what I have already said, for since we agree neither upon principles nor upon demonstrations there is no place for argument. And this is so far well, inasmuch as it leaves the honour of the ancients untouched. For they are no wise disparaged, the question between them and me being only as to the way. For as the saying is, the lame man who keeps the right road outstrips the runner who takes a wrong one. Nay, it is obvious that when a man runs the wrong way, the more active and swift he is, the further he will go astray.

But the course I propose for the discovery of sciences is such as leaves but little to the acuteness and strength of wits, but places all wits and understandings nearly on a level. For as in the drawing of a straight line or a perfect circle much depends on the steadiness and practice of the hand, if it be done by aim of hand only, but if with the aid of rule or compass, little or nothing; so is it exactly with my plan. But though particular confutations would be of no avail, yet touching the sects and general divisions of such systems I must say something; something also touching the external signs which show that they are unsound; and finally something touching the causes of such great infelicity and of such lasting and general agreement in error: that so the access to truth may be made less difficult, and the human understanding may the more willingly submit to its purgation and dismiss its idols.

62

Idols of the Theatre, or of Systems, are many, and there can be and perhaps will be yet many more. For were it not that now for many ages men's minds have been busied with religion and theology; and were it not that civil governments, especially monarchies, have been averse to such novelties, even in matters speculative; so that men labour therein to the peril and harming of their fortunes,—not only unrewarded, but exposed also to contempt and envy: doubtless there would have arisen many other philosophical sects like to those which in great variety flourished once among the Greeks. For as on the phenomena of the heavens many hypotheses may be constructed, so likewise (and more also) many various dogmas may be set up and established on the phenomena of philosophy.[21] And in the plays of this philosophical theatre you may observe the same thing which is found in the theatre of the poets, that stories invented for the stage are more compact and elegant, and more as one would wish them to be, than true stories out of history.

20. Collections of plays (with reference to the Idols of the Theater).
21. "Philosophy" means science here, as it usually does in this discussion; the word "science" still retains its Latin general meaning of "knowledge."

In general however there is taken for the material of philosophy either a great deal out of a few things, or a very little out of many things; so that on both sides philosophy is based on too narrow a foundation of experiment and natural history, and decides on the authority of too few cases. For the rational school of philosophers snatches from experience a variety of common instances, neither duly ascertained nor diligently examined and weighed, and leaves all the rest to meditation and agitation of wit.

There is also another class of philosophers, who having bestowed much diligent and careful labour on a few experiments, have thence made bold to educe and construct systems; wresting all other facts in a strange fashion to conformity therewith.

And there is yet a third class, consisting of those who out of faith and veneration mix their philosophy with theology and traditions; among whom the vanity of some has gone so far aside as to seek the origin of science among spirits and genii. So that this parent stock of errors—this false philosophy—is of three kinds; the sophistical, the empirical, and the superstitious.

The Wisdom of the Ancients

In 1609 Bacon published a strange little collection in Latin of mythographic essays on certain classical stories, by way of recreation, as he confessed in the Preface. *De Sapientia Veterum* (or *The Wisdom of the Ancients* in its 1619 English version) belongs to a tradition of Renaissance interpretation we have seen before (see The Renaissance Ovid); and although Bacon's readings would sometimes be very strange indeed, they influenced subsequent commentators like George Sandys and Sir Thomas Browne. Bacon himself expanded some of these essays in his later remarks on mytho-poetic poetry ("parabolical poesy," he calls it) in the 1623 *De Dignitate et Augmentis Scientarium*. Pan means Nature, conventionally enough; but in Bacon's reading, the nature he represents becomes the object of scientific knowledge. Even his horns are allegorized as a kind of project-director's flow-chart: "Horns are attributed to the Universe, broad at the base and pointed at the top. For all nature rises to a point like a pyramid. Individuals, which lie at the base of nature, are infinite in number; these are collected into Species, which are themselves manifold; the Species rise again into Genera . . . so that at last nature seems to end as it were in unity, as is signified by the pyramidal form of the horns of Pan." Sometimes, as in making Proteus (the sea god who kept changing his form) a myth of matter (maintaining itself through change of phase), Bacon is interpretively tactful. The section below will seem less allegorically strained if it is remembered that even Lucretius, at the beginning of his great scientific poem *De Rerum Natura* (Of the Nature of Things), makes Venus and Mars, Love and War, into Creation and De-creation, the two phases of eternal process.

From The Wisdom of the Ancients

Cupid Or the Atom [1]

The accounts given by the poets of Cupid, or Love, are not properly applicable to the same person; yet the discrepancy is such that one may see where the confusion is and where the similitude, and reject the one and receive the other.

They say then that Love was the most ancient of all the gods; the most ancient therefore of all things whatever, except Chaos, which is said to have been coeval with him; and Chaos is never distinguished by the ancients with divine honour or the name of a god. This Love is introduced without any parent at all; only, that some say he was an egg of Night. And himself out of Chaos begot all things, the gods included. The attributes which are assigned to him are in number four: he is always an infant; he is blind; [2] he is naked; he is an archer. There was also another Love, the youngest of all the gods, son of Venus, to whom the attributes of the elder are transferred, and whom in a way they suit.

The fable relates to the cradle and infancy of nature, and pierces deep. This Love I understand to be the appetite or instinct of primal matter; or to speak more plainly, *the natural motion of the atom*; which is indeed the original and unique force that constitutes and fashions all things out of matter. Now this is entirely without parent; that is, without cause. For the cause is as it were parent of the effect; and of this virtue there can be no cause in nature (God always excepted): there being nothing before it, therefore no efficient; nor anything more original in nature, therefore neither kind nor form. Whatever it be therefore, it is a thing positive and inexplicable. And even if it were possible to know the method and process of it, yet to know it by way of cause is not possible; it being, next to God, the cause of causes—itself without cause. That the method even of its operation should ever be brought within the range and comprehension of human inquiry, is hardly perhaps to be hoped; with good reason therefore it is represented as an egg hatched by night. Such certainly is the judgment of the sacred philosopher,[3] when he says, *He hath made all things beautiful according to their seasons; also he hath submitted the world to man's inquiry, yet so that man cannot find out the work which God worketh from the beginning to the end*. For the summary law of nature, that impulse of desire impressed by God upon the primary particles of matter which makes them come together, and which by repetition and multiplication produces all the variety of nature, is a thing which mortal thought may glance at, but can hardly take in.

Now the philosophy of the Greeks, which in investigating the material principles of things is careful and acute, in inquiring the principles of motion,

---

1. This essay is in the 1619 English translation of Sir Arthur Gorges; Bacon later expanded his interpretation of Cupid at great length in another Latin work, *De Dignitate et Augmentis Scientarium*.

2. For the blindness of Cupid and its interest for the Renaissance, see Marlowe, *Hero and Leander* I.48n (as well as the elaborate studies by Erwin Panofsky, in *Studies in Iconology*, and Edgar Wind, *Pagan Mysteries in the Renaissance*, 2nd ed.) See also the extract from Sir Thomas Browne's *Miscellanies*, below.

3. Ecclesiastes 3:11.

wherein lies all vigour of operation, is negligent and languid; and on the point now in question seems to be altogether blind babbling; for that opinion of the Peripatetics[4] which refers the original impulse of matter to privation, is little more than words—a name for the thing rather than a description of it. And those who refer it to God, though they are quite right in that, yet they ascend by a leap and not by steps. For beyond all doubt there is a single and summary law in which nature centres and which is subject and subordinate to God; the same in fact which in the text just quoted is meant by the words: *the work which God worketh from the beginning to the end.* Democritus considered the matter more deeply; and having first given the atom some dimension and shape, attributed to it a single desire or primary motion simply and absolutely, and a second by comparison. For he thought that all things move by their proper nature towards the centre of the world; but that that which has more matter, moving thither faster, strikes aside that which has less, and forces it to go the other way. This however was but a narrow theory, and framed with reference to too few particulars: for it does not appear that either the motion of the heavenly bodies in circle, or the phenomena of contraction and expansion, can be reduced to this principle, or reconciled with it. As for Epicurus's opinion of the declination and fortuitous agitation of the atom, it is a relapse to trifling and ignorance. So it is but too plain that the parentage of this Cupid is wrapped in night.

Let us now consider his attributes. He is described with great elegance as a little child, and a child for ever; for things compounded are larger and are affected by age; whereas the primary seeds of things, or atoms, are minute and remain in perpetual infancy.

Most truly also is he represented as naked: for all compounds (to one that considers them rightly) are masked and clothed; and there is nothing properly naked, except the primary particles of things.

The blindness likewise of Cupid has an allegorical meaning full of wisdom. For it seems that this Cupid, whatever he be, has very little providence; but directs his course, like a blind man groping, by whatever he finds nearest; which makes the supreme divine Providence all the more to be admired, as that which contrives out of subjects peculiarly empty and destitute of providence, and as it were blind, to educe[5] by a fatal and necessary law all the order and beauty of the universe.

His last attribute is archery: meaning that this virtue is such as acts at a distance: for all operation at a distance is like shooting an arrow. Now whoever maintains the theory of the atom and the vacuum (even though he suppose the vacuum not to be collected by itself but intermingled through space), necessarily implies the action of the virtue of the atom at a distance: for without this no motion could be originated, by reason of the vacuum interposed; but all things would remain fixed and immovable.

As for that younger Cupid, it is with reason that he is reported to be the youngest of the gods; since until the species were constituted he could have no operation. In the description of him the allegory changes its aim and passes

4. The school of Aristotle.
5. Elicit, develop.

to morals. And yet there remains a certain conformity between him and the elder Cupid. For Venus excites the general appetite of conjunction and procreation; Cupid, her son, applies the appetite to an individual object. From Venus therefore comes the general disposition, from Cupid the more exact sympathy. Now the general disposition depends upon causes near at hand, the particular sympathy upon principles more deep and fatal, and as if derived from that ancient Cupid, who is the source of all exquisite sympathy.

1619

The New Atlantis

Bacon's utopia, The New Atlantis (1627), grew out of an impulse to provide, in the words of his secretary quoted in a preface, "a model or description of a college instituted for the interpreting of nature and the producing of great and marvellous works for the benefit of men, under the name of Salomon's House." On the imaginary island of Bensalem in the south, Bacon places a community whose social and legal system is developed in brief detail, sometimes avowedly differing from More's Utopia. But Bacon's greatest concern lay in a society which might support the life of the mind as he conceived it, embodied in a project-director's vision of an institute for the pursuit of knowledge. Salomon's House is that ideal institution, here described to the narrator at the end of The New Atlantis by its venerable director.

From The New Atlantis

[Salomon's House]

'God bless thee, my son; I will give thee the greatest jewel I have. For I will impart unto thee, for the love of God and men, a relation of the true state of Salomon's House. Son, to make you know the true state of Salomon's House, I will keep this order. First, I will set forth unto you the end of our foundation. Secondly, the preparations and instruments we have for our works. Thirdly, the several employments and functions whereto our fellows are assigned. And fourthly, the ordinances and rites which we observe.

'The End of our Foundation is the knowledge of Causes and secret motions of things, and the enlarging of the bounds of Human Empire,[1] to the effecting of all things possible.

'The Preparations and Instruments are these. We have large and deep caves of several depths; the deepest are sunk six hundred fathom, and some of them are digged and made under great hills and mountains, so that if you reckon together the depth of the hill and the depth of the cave, they are (some of them) above three miles deep. For we find that the depth of a hill and the depth of a cave from the flat is the same thing, both remote alike from the sun and heaven's beams and from the open air. These caves we call the Lower Region. And we use them for all coagulations, indurations,[2] refrigerations,

1. Empire over Nature.
2. Preservations by hardening.

and conservations of bodies. We use them likewise for the imitation of natural mines and the producing also of new artificial metals by compositions and materials which we use, and lay there for many years. We use them also sometimes (which may seem strange) for curing of some diseases and for prolongation of life in some hermits that choose to live there, well accommodated of [3] all things necessary; and indeed live very long, by whom also we learn many things.

'We have burials in several earths, where we put divers cements, as the Chineses do their porcelain. But we have them in greater variety, and some of them more fine. We have also great variety of composts and soils for the making of the earth fruitful.

'We have high towers, the highest about half a mile in height, and some of them likewise set upon high mountains, so that the vantage of the hill with the tower is in the highest of them three miles at least. And these places we call the Upper Region, accounting the air between the high places and the low as a Middle Region. We use these towers, according to their several heights and situations, for insolation, refrigeration, conservation, and for the view of divers meteors,[4] as winds, rain, snow, hail, and some of the fiery meteors also. And upon them, in some places, are dwellings of hermits, whom we visit sometimes, and instruct what to observe.

'We have great lakes both salt and fresh, whereof we have use for the fish and fowl. We use them also for burials of some natural bodies, for we find a difference in things buried in earth or in air below the earth and things buried in water. We have also pools, of which some do strain fresh water out of salt, and others by art do turn fresh water into salt. We have also some rocks in the midst of the sea, and some bays upon the shore, for some works wherein is required the air and vapour of the sea. We have likewise violent streams and cataracts, which serve us for many motions, and likewise engines for multiplying and enforcing[5] of winds, to set also on going divers motions.

'We have also a number of artificial wells and fountains, made in imitation of the natural sources and baths, as tincted upon[6] vitriol, sulphur, steel, brass, lead, nitre, and other minerals. And again we have little wells for infusions of many things, where the waters take the virtue[7] quicker and better than in vessels or basins. And amongst them we have a water which we call Water of Paradise, being, by what we do to it, made very sovereign for health and prolongation of life.

'We have also great and spacious houses, where we imitate and demonstrate meteors, as snow, hail, rain, some artificial rains of bodies and not of water, thunders, lightnings, also generations of bodies in air, as frogs, flies, and divers others.

'We have also fair and large baths of several mixtures for the cure of diseases and the restoring of man's body from arefaction,[8] and others for the confirming

3. Supplied with.
4. The word means meteorological phenomena of all sorts; "fiery meteors" are comets, what we would call meteors, and other astral appearances.
5. Intensifying.
6. Tinctured with.
7. Absorb the properties of the thing dissolved.
8. Drying up.

of it in strength of sinews, vital parts, and the very juice and substance of the body.

'We have also large and various orchards and gardens, wherein we do not so much respect beauty as variety of ground and soil, proper for divers trees and herbs, and some very spacious, where trees and berries are set whereof we make divers kinds of drinks, besides the vineyards. In these we practise likewise all conclusions[9] of grafting and inoculating, as well of wild trees as fruit trees, which produceth many effects. And we make (by art) in the same orchards and gardens trees and flowers to come earlier or later than their seasons, and to come up and bear more speedily than by their natural course they do. We make them also by art greater much than their nature, and their fruit greater and sweeter and of differing taste, smell, colour, and figure, from their nature. And many of them we so order as they become of medicinal use.

'We have also means to make divers plants rise by mixtures of earths without seeds, and likewise to make divers new plants differing from the vulgar,[10] and to make one tree or plant turn into another.

'We have also parks and inclosures of all sorts of beasts and birds, which we use not only for view or rareness but likewise for dissections and trials, that thereby we may take light[11] what may be wrought upon the body of man. Wherein we find many strange effects: as continuing life in them, though divers parts, which you account vital, be perished and taken forth; resuscitating of some that seem dead in appearance; and the like. We try also all poisons and other medicines upon them, as well of chirurgery[12] as physic. By art likewise we make them greater or taller than their kind is, and contrariwise dwarf them, and stay their growth; we make them more fruitful and bearing than their kind is, and contrariwise barren and not generative. Also we make them differ in colour, shape, activity, many ways. We find means to make commixtures and copulations of different kinds, which have produced many new kinds, and them not barren, as the general opinion is. We make a number of kinds of serpents, worms, flies, fishes, of putrefaction, whereof some are advanced (in effect) to be perfect creatures, like beasts or birds, and have sexes, and do propagate. Neither do we this by chance, but we know beforehand of what matter and commixture what kind of those creatures will arise.

'We have also particular pools, where we make trials upon fishes, as we have said before of beasts and birds.

'We have also places for breed and generation of those kinds of worms and flies which are of special use, such as are with you your silkworms and bees.

'I will not hold you long with recounting of our brew-houses, bakehouses, and kitchens, where are made divers drinks, breads, and meats, rare and of special effects. Wines we have of grapes, and drinks of other juice of fruits,

9. Procedures.
10. Ordinary.
11. Gain knowledge; this metaphor of light, "enlightenment," "illumination," now virtu-ally a cliché in our language, is crucial in Bacon; elsewhere, he distinguishes between ex-periments of *fruit* and of *light,* between those which are directed toward a potential techno-logical result, and those simply exploratory (a version of a later distinction between "pure" and "applied" science which has lately been re-examined by critics such as P. B. Medawar).
12. Surgery.

of grains, and of roots, and of mixtures with honey, sugar, manna, and fruits dried and decocted. Also of the tears or woundings of trees and of the pulp of canes. And these drinks are of several ages, some to the age or last[13] of forty years. We have drinks also brewed with several herbs and roots and spices, yea with several fleshes and white meats,[14] whereof some of the drinks are such as they are in effect meat and drink both, so that divers, especially in age, do desire to live with[15] them, with little or no meat or bread. And above all, we strive to have drinks of extreme thin parts to insinuate into the body, and yet without all biting, sharpness, or fretting, insomuch as some of them put upon the back of your hand will, with a little stay, pass through to the palm, and yet taste mild to the mouth. We have also waters which we ripen in that fashion, as they become nourishing, so that they are indeed excellent drink, and many will use no other. Breads we have of several grains, roots, and kernels; yea and some of flesh and fish dried, with divers kinds of leavenings and seasonings, so that some do extremely move appetites; some do nourish so, as divers do live of them without any other meat, who live very long. So for meats: we have some of them so beaten and made tender and mortified,[16] yet without all corrupting, as a weak heat of the stomach will turn them into good chylus,[17] as well as a strong heat would meat otherwise prepared. We have some meats also and breads and drinks, which taken by men enable them to fast long after, and some other that, used, make the very flesh of men's bodies sensibly more hard and tough, and their strength far greater than otherwise it would be.

'We have dispensatories, or shops of medicines. Wherein you may easily think, if we have such variety of plants and living creatures more than you have in Europe (for we know what you have), the simples,[18] drugs, and ingredients of medicines must likewise be in so much the greater variety. We have them likewise of divers ages and long fermentations. And for their preparations, we have not only all manner of exquisite distillations and separations, and especially by gentle heats and percolations through divers strainers, yea and substances, but also exact forms of composition,[19] whereby they incorporate almost, as they were natural simples.

'We have also divers mechanical arts, which you have not, and stuffs made by them, as papers, linen, silks, tissues, dainty works of feathers of wonderful lustre, excellent dyes, and many others; and shops likewise as well for such as are not brought into vulgar use amongst us as for those that are. For you must know that of the things before recited, many of them are grown into use throughout the kingdom, but yet if they did flow from our invention, we have of them also for patterns and principals.[20]

'We have also furnaces of great diversities and that keep great diversity

13. Duration.
14. Foods.
15. On.
16. Aged to the point of tenderness.
17. Chyle, the macerated, half-digested contents of the stomach.
18. Medicinal herbs, called so because they were used uncompounded.
19. Compound.
20. Models.

of heats: fierce and quick; strong and constant; soft and mild; blown, quiet; dry, moist; and the like. But above all, we have heats in imitation of the sun's and heavenly bodies' heats, that pass divers inequalities and (as it were) orbs, progresses, and returns,[21] whereby we produce admirable effects. Besides, we have heats of dungs, and of bellies and maws of living creatures, and of their bloods and bodies, and of hays and herbs laid up moist, of lime unquenched,[22] and such like. Instruments also which generate heat only by motion. And farther, places for strong insolations; [23] and again, places under the earth, which by nature or art yield heat. These divers heats we use, as the nature of the operation which we intend requireth.

'We have also perspective-houses,[24] where we make demonstrations of all lights and radiations, and of all colours; and out of things uncoloured and transparent we can represent unto you all several colours, not in rainbows, as it is in gems and prisms, but of themselves single. We represent also all multiplications of light, which we carry to great distance, and make so sharp as to discern small points and lines; also all colourations of light, all delusions and deceits of the sight in figures, magnitudes, motions, colours, all demonstrations of shadows. We find also divers means, yet unknown to you, of producing of light originally from divers bodies. We procure means of seeing objects afar off, as in the heaven and remote places, and represent things near as afar off and things afar off as near, making feigned distances. We have also helps for the sight, far above spectacles and glasses in use. We have also glasses and means to see small and minute bodies perfectly and distinctly, as the shapes and colours of small flies and worms, grains and flaws in gems, which cannot otherwise be seen, observations in urine and blood, not otherwise to be seen. We make artificial rainbows, haloes, and circles about light. We represent also all manner of reflexions, refractions, and multiplications of visual beams of objects.

'We have also precious stones of all kinds, many of them of great beauty and to you unknown; crystals likewise; and glasses of divers kinds; and amongst them some of metals vitrificated,[25] and other materials besides those of which you make glass. Also a number of fossils and imperfect minerals,[26] which you have not. Likewise loadstones of prodigious virtue [27] and other rare stones, both natural and artificial.

'We have also sound-houses, where we practise and demonstrate all sounds and their generation. We have harmonies, which you have not, of quarter-sounds and lesser slides of sounds.[28] Divers instruments of music likewise to you unknown, some sweeter than any you have, together with bells and rings that are dainty and sweet. We represent small sounds as great and deep, likewise great sounds extenuate [29] and sharp; we make divers tremblings and

21. Planetary motions.
22. Unslaked.
23. Sunbaking.
24. Laboratories for the study of optics.
25. Turned into glass.
26. Mineral ores.
27. Power.
28. Quarter-tones and other microtones.
29. Thin; the following clause refers to inventions that decompose single natural sounds into harmonic groups.

warblings of sound, which in their original are entire. We represent and imitate all articulate sounds and letters, and the voices and notes of beasts and birds. We have certain helps which set to the ear do further the hearing greatly. We have also divers strange and artificial echoes, reflecting the voice many times, and as it were tossing it, and some that give back the voice louder than it came, some shriller and some deeper; yea, some rendering the voice differing in the letters or articulate sound from that they receive. We have also means to convey sounds in trunks [30] and pipes, in strange lines and distances.

'We have also perfume-houses, wherewith we join also practices of taste. We multiply smells, which may seem strange. We imitate smells, making all smells to breathe out of other mixtures than those that give them. We make divers imitations of taste likewise, so that they will deceive any man's taste. And in this house we contain also a confiture-house, where we make all sweet-meats, dry and moist, and divers pleasant wines, milks, broths, and sallets, [31] far in greater variety than you have.

'We have also engine-houses, where are prepared engines and instruments for all sorts of motions. There we imitate and practise to make swifter motions than any you have, either out of your muskets or any engine that you have; and to make them and multiply them more easily and with small force by wheels and other means, and to make them stronger and more violent than yours are, exceeding your greatest cannons and basilisks. [32] We represent also ordnance and instruments of war, and engines of all kinds, and likewise new mixtures and compositions of gunpowder, wildfires burning in water and unquenchable. Also fireworks of all variety both for pleasure and use. We imitate also flights of birds; we have some degrees of flying in the air; we have ships and boats for going under water, and brooking of seas, also swimming-girdles and supporters. We have divers curious clocks and other like motions of return [33] and some perpetual motions. We imitate also motions of living creatures by images of men, beasts, birds, fishes, and serpents. We have also a great number of other various motions, strange for equality, fineness, and subtilty.

'We have also a mathematical house, where are represented all instruments, as well of geometry as astronomy, exquisitely made.

'We have also houses of deceits of the senses, where we represent all manner of feats of juggling, false apparitions, impostures, and illusions, and their fallacies. And surely you will easily believe that we that have so many things truly natural which include admiration [34] could in a world of particulars deceive the senses, if we would disguise those things and labour to make them seem more miraculous. But we do hate all impostures and lies; insomuch as we have severely forbidden it to all our fellows, under pain of ignominy and fines, that they do not show any natural work or thing adorned or swelling, but only pure as it is, and without all affectation of strangeness.

'These are, my son, the riches of Salomon's House.

30. Tubes.
31. Salads.
32. Kind of artillery, named for the mythical serpent whose eye turns one to stone.
33. Pendulum mechanisms.
34. Visual atention.

'For the several employments and offices of our fellows, we have twelve that sail into foreign countries, under the names of other nations (for our own we conceal), who bring us the books and abstracts and patterns of experiments of all other parts. These we call Merchants of Light.

'We have three that collect the experiments which are in all books. These we call Depredators.

'We have three that collect the experiments of all mechanical arts, and also of liberal sciences, and also of practices which are not brought into arts. These we call Mystery Men.

'We have three that try new experiments, such as themselves think good. These we call Pioneers or Miners.

'We have three that draw the experiments of the former four into titles and tables, to give the better light for the drawing of observations and axioms out of them. These we call Compilers.

'We have three that bend [35] themselves, looking into the experiments of their fellows, and cast about how to draw out of them things of use and practice for man's life, and knowledge as well for works as for plain demonstration of causes, means of natural divinations, and the easy and clear discovery of the virtues and parts of bodies. Those we call Dowry Men or Benefactors.

'Then, after divers meetings and consults of our whole number to consider of the former labours and collections, we have three that take care, out of them, to direct new experiments of a higher light, more penetrating into nature than the former. These we call Lamps.

'We have three others that do execute the experiments so directed, and report them. These we call Inoculators.

'Lastly, we have three that raise the former discoveries by experiments into greater observations, axioms, and aphorisms. These we call Interpreters of Nature.

'We have also, as you must think, novices and apprentices, that the succession of the former employed men do not fail, besides a great number of servants and attendants, men and women. And this we do also: we have consultations, which of the inventions and experiences which we have discovered shall be published, and which not; and take all an oath of secrecy for the concealing of those which we think fit to keep secret, though some of those we do reveal sometimes to the state, and some not.[36]

'For our ordinances and rites, we have two very long and fair galleries: in one of these we place patterns and samples of all manner of the more rare and excellent inventions, in the other we place the statues of all principal inventors. There we have the statue of your Columbus, that discovered the West Indies; also the inventor of ships; your monk [37] that was the inventor of ordnance and of gunpowder; the inventor of music; the inventor of letters; the inventor of printing; the inventor of observations of astronomy; the inventor of works in metal; the inventor of glass; the inventor of silk of the worm; the inventor of wine; the inventor of corn and bread; the inventor of

35. Apply.
36. Bacon had, by experience, developed enough distrust of government to anticipate modern problems here; Salomon's House can be fragile.
37. Roger Bacon, 13th-century Franciscan philosopher and alchemist.

sugars; and all these by more certain tradition than you have. Then have we divers inventors of our own, of excellent works, which since you have not seen, it were too long to make descriptions of them; and besides, in the right understanding of those descriptions you might easily err. For upon every invention of value we erect a statua [38] to the inventor, and give him a liberal and honourable reward. These statuas are some of brass, some of marble and touchstone,[39] some of cedar and other special woods gilt and adorned, some of iron, some of silver, some of gold.

'We have certain hymns and services, which we say daily, of laud and thanks to God for his marvellous works, and forms of prayers imploring his aid and blessing for the illumination of our labours and the turning of them into good and holy uses.

'Lastly, we have circuits or visits of divers principal cities of the kingdom, where, as it cometh to pass, we do publish such new profitable inventions as we think good. And we do also declare natural divinations [40] of diseases, plagues, swarms of hurtful creatures, scarcity, tempests, earthquakes, great inundations, comets, temperature of the year, and divers other things; and we give counsel thereupon what the people shall do for the prevention and remedy of them.'

And when he had said this, he stood up, and I, as I had been taught, kneeled down, and he laid his right hand upon my head, and said, 'God bless thee, my son, and God bless this relation which I have made. I give thee leave to publish it for the good of other nations, for we here are in God's bosom, a land unknown.' And so he left me, having assigned a value of about two thousand ducats for a bounty to me and my fellows. For they give great largesses where they come upon all occasions.

[THE REST WAS NOT PERFECTED]

1626

ROBERT BURTON
1577–1640

The life of this remarkable figure is so nearly co-extensive with his one great work that its mere chronology yields little of interest: he was born in Leicestershire, came to Oxford (to Brasenose College) in 1593, and in 1599 was elected Student of Christ Church, "the most flourishing college of Europe." He took his B.A. in 1602 there, and his M.A. in 1605, and lived at the college for the rest of his life. In 1616 he became vicar of St. Thomas's church in Oxford and held, toward the end of his life, two absentee livings; but his time was mainly spent in reading and in composing his *Anatomy,* that vast systematic work which started out as a compendium of medical and moral knowledge and ended up, constantly revised in five editions before its author's death, as a study of the morbidity of its own studiousness. From its first appearance in 1621 Burton kept augmenting his compilation of learned opinion, allusion, and eloquence, adding new light as it came into his dark tower of self-

38. Statue.
39. A kind of jasper, used for the testing of alloys.
40. Make predictions.

consciousness through the windows of countless books. If *The Anatomy of Melancholy* is about the human psyche's entire range of states—manic, depressed, light, dark, high, and low, and the ways in which they lead to each other—it is also about the very condition of being learned. Burton's systematic structure embraces physiology, medicine, moral philosophy, and literary history; it moves from detailed exposition of received pre-scientific doctrine to long, wide-ranging essays on such questions as the woes and miseries of scholars, or the effects of literary eroticism (Burton calls it "heroic love") on psychic stability.

Burton's melancholy is not only the totality of the types he classifies so exhaustively. A cult of melancholia was fashionable in early Jacobean England, particularly around the Inns of Court, the theaters, and the haunts of young men down from the universities. This melancholy was associated with the intellectual life which—through lack of preferment at court and insufficient civil service posts to absorb the over-educated and under-inherited—could not fulfill itself. Such diverse Shakespearean figures as Hamlet and Malvolio reflect this condition, which for Burton is almost identical with the human one. His own private melancholy is, ultimately, that of the book itself, a strange mixture of inner enterprise and practical idleness, as far removed from the healthy, somber joy of Milton's *Il Penseroso* as from the massive brooding figure of intellect abandoned in Dürer's *Melancolia*. The introduction to Burton's work, explaining why he adopts the pseudonym of Democritus Jr., is a masterpiece of self-revelation through disguise, moving at times beyond even the candor and wisdom of Montaigne, discussing its own prose style as if it were an inner life; apologizing for the intrusions of its own English into its mosaic of Latin quotations (the interior dialogue of the whole work is between scholar and books, English and Latin); gloomily propounding a scholarly utopia based upon the certain conviction of human imperfectibility; and refurbishing its mythical progenitor, the laughing Greek atomist Democritus, into an ancestor of the self-contemplating lyricist of the late eighteenth century—that poet of the crucial modern mode, the therapeutic work, whose internal sanity is its author's only hedge against madness. (See Figs. 15–18 in the illustrations for this volume.)

From The Anatomy of Melancholy

Democritus Junior to the Reader

Gentle Reader, I presume thou wilt be very inquisitive to know what antic or personate actor this is, that so insolently intrudes upon this common theatre to the world's view, arrogating another man's name; whence he is, why he doth it, and what he hath to say. Although, as he said,[1] *Primum si noluero, non respondebo, quis coacturus est?* I am a free man born, and may choose whether I will tell; who can compel me? if I be urged, I will as readily reply as that Egyptian in Plutarch, when a curious fellow would needs know what he had in his basket, *Quum vides velatam, quid inquiris in rem absconditam?* It was therefore covered, because he should not know what was in it. Seek not after that which is hid; if the contents please thee, 'and be for thy use, suppose the

---

1. Seneca, the Roman tragedian and philosopher.

Man in the Moon, or whom thou wilt, to be the author'; [2] I would not willingly be known. Yet in some sort to give thee satisfaction, which is more than I need, I will show a reason, both of this usurped name, title, and subject. And first of the name of Democritus; lest any man by reason of it should be deceived, expecting a pasquil,[3] a satire, some ridiculous treatise (as I myself should have done), some prodigious tenet, or paradox of the earth's motion, of infinite worlds, *in infinito vacuo, ex fortuita atomorum collisione,* in an infinite waste, so caused by an accidental collision of motes in the sun, all which Democritus held, Epicurus and their master Leucippus of old maintained, and are lately revived by Copernicus, Brunus, and some others.[4] . . .

Democritus, as he is described by Hippocrates[5] and Laertius,[6] was a little wearish old man, very melancholy by nature, averse from company in his latter days, and much given to solitariness, a famous philosopher in his age, *coævus*[7] with Socrates, wholly addicted to his studies at the last, and to a private life: writ many excellent works, a great divine, according to the divinity of those times, an expert physician, a politician, an excellent mathematician, as *Diacosmus*[8] and the rest of his works do witness. He was much delighted with the studies of husbandry, saith Columella,[9] and often I find him cited by Constantinus[10] and others treating of that subject. He knew the natures, differences of all beasts, plants, fishes, birds; and, as some say, could understand the tunes and voices of them. In a word, he was *omnifariam doctus,* a general scholar, a great student; and to the intent he might better contemplate, I find it related by some, that he put out his eyes, and was in his old age voluntarily blind, yet saw more than all Greece besides, and writ of every subject, *Nihil in toto opificio naturæ, de quo non scripsit.*[11] A man of an excellent wit, profound conceit; and to attain knowledge the better in his younger years he travelled to Egypt and Athens, to confer with learned men, 'admired of some, despised of others.' After a wandering life, he settled at Abdera, a town in Thrace, and was sent for thither to be their law-maker, recorder, or town clerk as some will; or as others, he was there bred and born. Howsoever it was, there he lived at last in a garden in the suburbs, wholly betaking himself to his studies and a private life, 'saving that sometimes he would walk down to the haven, and laugh heartily at such variety of ridiculous objects, which there he saw.'[12] Such a one was Democritus.

But in the meantime, how doth this concern me, or upon what reference do I usurp his habit? I confess, indeed, that to compare myself unto him for

---

2. Burton is quoting J. J. Wecker, a 16th-century Swiss physician and author.
3. A burlesque.
4. A good deal of physical and astronomical theory is lumped together here; the most spectacular formulation of the notion that there are infinite worlds besides our own was by Giordano Bruno (1548–1600), who was burned by the Inquisition for his views.
5. The great Greek physician (c. 460–c. 360 B.C.).
6. Diogenes Laertius (2nd century A.D.), author of *Lives of the Philosophers.*
7. Contemporary with.
8. Democritus' great cosmological work (literally, "orderly pattern of the cosmos").
9. Augustan Roman author of *De Re Rustica* (On Agriculture).
10. Supposed author of a 6th- or 7th-century book on agriculture.
11. "There was nothing in Nature about which he did not write."
12. Partly quoted from Juvenal's Tenth Satire.

aught I have yet said, were both impudency and arrogancy. I do not presume to make any parallel, *antistat mihi millibus trecentis*,[13] *parvus sum, nullus sum, altum nec spiro, nec spero*.[14] Yet thus much I will say of myself, and that I hope without all suspicion of pride, or self-conceit, I have lived a silent, sedentary, solitary, private life, *mihi et musis*[15] in the university, as long almost as Xenocrates in Athens, *ad senectam fere*[16] to learn wisdom as he did, penned up most part in my study. For I have been brought up a student in the most flourishing college of Europe, *augustissimo collegio*,[17] and can brag with Jovius, almost, *in ea luce domicilii Vaticani, totius orbis celeberrimi, per 37 annos multa opportunaque didici;*[18] for thirty years I have continued (having the use of as good libraries as ever he had) a scholar, and would be therefore loath, either by living as a drone to be an unprofitable or unworthy member of so learned and noble a society, or to write that which should be anyway dishonourable to such a royal and ample foundation. Something I have done, though by my profession a divine, yet *turbine raptus ingenii*, as he[19] said, out of a running wit, an unconstant, unsettled mind, I had a great desire (not able to attain to a superficial skill in any) to have some smattering in all, to be *aliquis in omnibus, nullus in singulis*,[20] which Plato commends, out of him Lipsius approves and furthers, 'as fit to be imprinted in all curious wits, not to be a slave of one science, or dwell altogether in one subject, as most do, but to rove abroad, *centum puer artium*,[21] to have an oar in every man's boat, to taste of every dish, and sip of every cup, which, saith Montaigne, was well performed by Aristotle and his learned countryman Adrian Turnebus. This roving humour (though not with like success) I have ever had, and like a ranging spaniel, that barks at every bird he sees, leaving his game, I have followed all, saving that which I should, and may justly complain, and truly, *qui ubique est, nusquam est*,[22] which Gesner[23] did in modesty, that I have read many books, but to little purpose, for want of good method, I have confusedly tumbled over divers authors in our libraries, with small profit for want of art, order, memory, judgment. I never travelled but in map or card,[24] in which my unconfined thoughts have freely expatiated, as having ever been especially delighted with the study of cosmography. Saturn was lord of my geniture, culminating, etc., and Mars principal significator of manners, in partile conjunction with mine ascendant; both fortunate in their houses, etc.[25] I am not poor, I am not rich; *nihil est, nihil deest*, I have little, I want nothing: all my treasure

13. "He is far ahead of me."
14. "I'm nobody; I'm nothing; with neither hopes nor prospects."
15. "For my work and myself."
16. "Almost to old age."
17. Christ Church, Oxford, whose students still think of it as such.
18. "In that splendid, world-famous Vatican library, I've made the best of my opportunities for 37 years"; Jovius is Paolo Giovio (1483–1552), biographer, historian, and Latin stylist.
19. Julius Caesar Scaliger (1484–1558), Italian scholar and physician.
20. "Knowing something about everything, nothing about any one thing."
21. "Child of a hundred skills."
22. "He who is everywhere is nowhere."
23. Konrad von Gesner (1516–65), Swiss naturalist.
24. Chart, nautical map.
25. These all constitute astrological signs governing a melancholy temperament.

is in Minerva's tower. Greater preferment as I could never get, so am I not in debt for it, I have a competency (*laus Deo*[26]) from my noble and munificent patrons, though I live still a collegiate student, as Democritus in his garden, and lead a monastic life, *ipse mihi theatrum*,[27] sequestered from those tumults and troubles of the world, *et tanquam in specula positus* (as he said[28]), in some high place above you all, like *Stoicus sapiens, omnia sæcula, præterita præsentiaque videns, uno velut intuitu*,[29] I hear and see what is done abroad, how others run, ride, turmoil, and macerate themselves in court and country, far from those wrangling lawsuits, *aulæ vanitatem, fori ambitionem, ridere mecum soleo*,[30] I laugh at all; 'only secure lest my suit go amiss, my ships perish,' corn and cattle miscarry, trade decay, 'I have no wife nor children good or bad to provide for.'[31] A mere spectator of other men's fortunes and adventures, and how they act their parts, which methinks are diversely presented unto me, as from a common theatre or scene. I hear new news every day, and those ordinary rumours of war, plagues, fires, inundations, thefts, murders, massacres, meteors, comets, spectrums, prodigies apparitions, of towns taken, cities besieged in France, Germany, Turkey, Persia, Poland, etc., daily musters and preparations, and such-like, which these tempestuous times afford, battles fought, so many men slain, monomachies,[32] shipwrecks, piracies, and sea-fights, peace, leagues, stratagems and fresh alarums. A vast confusion of vows, wishes, actions, edicts, petitions, lawsuits, pleas, laws, proclamations, complaints, grievances are daily brought to our ears. New books every day, pamphlets, currantoes,[33] stories, whole catalogues of volumes of all sorts, new paradoxes, opinions, schisms, heresies, controversies in philosophy, religion, etc. Now come tidings of weddings, maskings, mummeries, entertainments, jubilees, embassies, tilts and tournaments, trophies, triumphs, revels, sports, plays: then again, as in a new shifted scene, treasons, cheating tricks, robberies, enormous villainies in all kinds, funerals, burials, deaths of princes, new discoveries, expeditions: now comical, then tragical matters. Today we hear of new lords and officers created, tomorrow of some great men deposed, and then again of fresh honours conferred; one is let loose, another imprisoned; one purchaseth, another breaketh; he thrives, his neighbour turns bankrupt; now plenty, then again death and famine; one runs, another rides, wrangles, laughs, weeps, etc. Thus I daily hear, and such-like, both private and public news; amidst the gallantry and misery of the world—jollity, pride, perplexities and cares, simplicity and villainy; subtlety, knavery, candour and integrity, mutually mixed and offering themselves—I rub on *privus privatus*;[34] as I have still lived, so I now continue, *statu quo prius*, left to a solitary life and mine own domestic discontents: saving that sometimes, *ne quid mentiar*,[35] as Diogenes went into the city and Democ-

---

26. "Praise God."
27. "Entertainment enough for myself."
28. Daniel Heinsius (1580–1655), Dutch scholar and poet.
29. "The Stoic philosopher, seeing in one glance all ages down to the present one."
30. "I laugh to myself at the court's vanities, the competitiveness of the Forum."
31. Quoted from St. Cyprian (c. 200–258), early Church Father.
32. Hand-to-hand fights.
33. Newspapers, just coming into existence.
34. "In total privacy."
35. "To be absolutely candid."

ritus to the haven to see fashions, I did for my recreation now and then walk abroad, look into the world, and could not choose but make some little observation, *non tam sagax observator, ac simplex recitator,*[36] not as they did, to scoff or laugh at all, but with a mixed passion.

> *Bilem sæpe, jocum vestri movere tumultus.*[37]

I did sometime laugh and scoff with Lucian,[38] and satirically tax with Menippus,[39] lament with Heraclitus,[40] sometimes again I was *petulanti splene cachinno,*[41] and then again, *urere bilis jecur,*[42] I was much moved to see that abuse which I could not mend. In which passion howsoever I may sympathize with him or them, 'tis for no such respect I shroud myself under his name; but either in an unknown habit to assume a little more liberty and freedom of speech, or if you will needs know, for that reason and only respect which Hippocrates relates at large in his Epistle to Damagetus, wherein he doth express, how coming to visit him one day, he found Democritus in his garden at Abdera, in the suburbs, under a shady bower, with a book on his knees, busy at his study, sometimes writing, sometimes walking. The subject of his book was melancholy and madness; about him lay the carcasses of many several beasts, newly by him cut up and anatomized; not that he did contemn God's creatures, as he told Hippocrates, but to find out the seat of this *atra bilis,* or melancholy, whence it proceeds, and how it was engendered in men's bodies, to the intent he might better cure it in himself, and by his writings and observations teach others how to prevent and avoid it. Which good intent of his, Hippocrates highly commended: Democritus Junior is therefore bold to imitate, and because he left it unperfect, and it is now lost, *quasi succenturiator Democriti,*[43] to revive again, prosecute, and finish in this treatise.

You have had a reason of the name. If the title and inscription offend your gravity, were it a sufficient justification to accuse others, I could produce many sober treatises, even sermons themselves, which in their fronts carry more phantastical names. Howsoever, it is a kind of policy in these days, to prefix a phantastical title to a book which is to be sold; for, as larks come down to a day-net, many vain readers will tarry and stand gazing like silly passengers at an antic picture in a painter's shop, that will not look at a judicious piece. . . .

One or two things yet I was desirous to have amended if I could, concerning the manner of handling this my subject, for which I must apologize, *deprecari,* and upon better advice give the friendly reader notice. It was not mine intent to prostitute my muse in English, or to divulge *secreta Minervæ,*[44] but to have

---

36. "Not as clever observer, but as simple reporter."
37. "Your passions have often produced my mirth and spleen" (Horace, *Epistles* I.20).
38. The famous and influential Greek satirist, 2nd century A.D.
39. Greek Cynic philosopher, 3rd century B.C., author of essays (now lost) part in prose, part in verse.
40. Ephesian philosopher (540–575 B.C.) known as "The Weeping Philosopher" (whereas Democritus was proverbially the "laughing" one).
41. "Move by mockery to laughter."
42. "My liver burns with gall" (misquoted from Horace, *Sermones* I.ix.66).
43. "As a substitute Democritus."
44. "The secrets of Minerva."

exposed this more contract in Latin, if I could have got it printed. Any scurrile pamphlet is welcome to our mercenary stationers in English; they print all,

cuduntque libellos
In quorum foliis vix simia nuda cacaret; [45]

but in Latin they will not deal; which is one of the reasons Nicholas Car,[46] in his oration of the paucity of English writers, gives, that so many flourishing wits are smothered in oblivion, lie dead and buried in this our nation. Another main fault is, that I have not revised the copy, and amended the style, which now flows remissly, as it was first conceived; but my leisure would not permit; *Feci nec quod potui, nec quod volui,* I confess it is neither as I would, nor as it should be.

Cum relego scripsisse pudet, quia plurima cerno
Me quoque quæ fuerant judice digna lini.[47]

When I peruse this tract which I have writ,
I am abashed, and much I hold unfit.

Et quod gravissimum [48] in the matter itself, many things I disallow at this present, which when I writ, *Non eadem est ætas, non mens;* [49] I would willingly retract much, etc., but 'tis too late, I can only crave pardon now for what is amiss.

I might indeed (had I wisely done), observed that precept of the poet, *Nonumque prematur in annum,*[50] and have taken more care: or, as Alexander the physician would have done by lapis lazuli, fifty times washed before it be used, I should have revised, corrected, and amended this tract; but I had not (as I said) that happy leisure, no amanuenses or assistants. Pancrates in Lucian, wanting a servant as he went from Memphis to Coptus in Egypt, took a door-bar, and after some superstitious words pronounced (Eucrates the relater was then present) made it stand up like a serving-man, fetch him water, turn the spit, serve in supper, and what work he would besides; and when he had done that service he desired, turned his man to a stick again. I have no such skill to make new men at my pleasure, or means to hire them; no whistle to call like the master of a ship, and bid them run, etc. I have no such authority, no such benefactors, as that noble Ambrosius was to Origen,[51] allowing him six or seven amanuenses to write out his dictates; I must for that cause do my business myself, and was therefore enforced, as a bear doth her whelps, to bring forth this confused lump; I had not time to lick it into form, as she doth her young ones, but even so to publish it as it was first written, *quicquid in buccam venit,*[52] in an extemporean style, as I do commonly all other exercises, *effudi quicquid dictavit genius meus,*[53] out of a confused company of notes, and writ with as

45. "They run off books on whose pages a naked ape would scarcely deign to shit."
46. 1524–68; professor of Greek at Cambridge, later a physician.
47. Ovid, *Letters from Pontus* I.5.
48. "And what is most serious."
49. "I was younger and sillier" (Horace, *Epistles* I.14).
50. "Don't publish for nine years."
51. Origen (185–254), prolific theologian, early Church Father martyred under Decius.
52. "Whatever came out first."
53. "I poured out whatever came into my mind."

small deliberation as I do ordinarily speak, without all affectation of big words, fustian phrases, jingling terms, tropes, strong lines, that like Acestes' arrows caught fire as they flew,[54] strains of wit, brave heats, elogies, hyperbolical exornations,[55] elegancies, etc., which many so much affect. I am *aquæ potor,*[56] drink no wine at all, which so much improves our modern wits, a loose, plain, rude writer, *ficum voco ficum et ligonem ligonem,*[57] and as free, as loose, *idem calamo quod in mente,*[58] I call a spade a spade, *animis hæc scribo, non auribus,*[59] I respect matter, not words; remembering that of Cardan, *verba propter res, non res propter verba,*[60] and seeking with Seneca, *quid scribam, non quemadmodum,* rather what than how to write: for as Philo thinks, 'He that is conversant about matter neglects words, and those that excel in this art of speaking have no profound learning.'

> *Verba nitent phaleris, at nullas verba medullas*
> *Intus habent.*[61]

Besides, it was the observation of that wise Seneca, 'When you see a fellow careful about his words, and neat in his speech, know this for a certainty, that man's mind is busied about toys, there's no solidity in him.' *Non est ornamentum virile concinnitas:* [62] as he said of a nightingale, *Vox es, præterea nihil,*[63] etc. I am therefore in this point a professed disciple of Apollonius, a scholar of Socrates, I neglect phrases, and labour wholly to inform my reader's understanding, not to please his ear; 'tis not my study or intent to compose neatly, which an orator requires, but to express myself readily and plainly as it happens. So that as a river runs sometimes precipitate and swift, then dull and slow; now direct, then *per ambages;* [64] now deep, then shallow; now muddy, then clear; now broad, then narrow; doth my style flow: now serious, then light; now comical, then satirical; now more elaborate, then remiss, as the present subject required, or as at that time I was affected. And if thou vouchsafe to read this treatise, it shall seem no otherwise to thee than the way to an ordinary traveller, sometimes fair, sometimes foul; here champaign, there enclosed; barren in one place, better soil in another: by woods, groves, hills, dales, plains, etc. I shall lead thee *per ardua montium, et lubrica vallium, et roscida cespitum, et glebosa camporum,*[65] through variety of objects, that which thou shalt like and surely dislike. . . .

---

54. A king in Virgil's *Aeneid* V.
55. Rhetorical extravagancies.
56. "A drinker of water."
57. "I call a fig a fig and a spade a spade."
58. "My pen writes what's in my mind."
59. "I write for the mind, not the ear."
60. "Language for the subject, not vice versa."
61. "Words may sound well, but hollow with no meaning."
62. "Prettiness is no masculine ornament."
63. "You are nothing but a voice."
64. "Winding"; this whole passage compares stylistic flow, the movement of fluent language, to that of a stream. (See the selection from Denham's *Cooper's Hill.*)
65. "I shall lead thee among steep mountains, slippery valleys, wet meadows, and rough fields."

From *Part I. Section I*

Subsection II. Division of the Body, Humours, Spirits

Of the parts of the body there may be many divisions: the most approved is that of Laurentius,[1] out of Hippocrates: which is, into parts contained, or containing. Contained, are either humours or spirits.

A humour is a liquid or fluent part of the body, comprehended in it, for the preservation of it; and is either innate or born with us, or adventitious and acquisite. The radical or innate is daily supplied by nourishment, which some call cambium, and make those secondary humours of ros and gluten [2] to maintain it: or acquisite, to maintain these four first primary humours, coming and proceeding from the first concoction in the liver, by which means chylus is excluded. Some divide them into profitable and excrementitious. But Crato,[3] out of Hippocrates, will have all four to be juice, and not excrements, without which no living creature can be sustained: which four, though they be comprehended in the mass of blood, yet they have their several affections, by which they are distinguished from one another, and from those adventitious, peccant, or diseased humours, as Melancthon calls[4] them.

Blood is a hot, sweet, temperate, red humour, prepared in the meseraic [5] veins, and made of the most temperate parts of the chylus in the liver, whose office is to nourish the whole body, to give it strength and colour, being dispersed by the veins through every part of it. And from it spirits are first begotten in the heart, which afterwards by the arteries are communicated to the other parts.

Pituita, or phlegm, is a cold and moist humour, begotten of the colder part of the chylus (or white juice coming out of the meat digested in the stomach), in the liver; his office is to nourish and moisten the members of the body which, as the tongue, are moved, that they be not over-dry.

Choler is hot and dry, bitter, begotten of the hotter parts of the chylus, and gathered to the gall: it helps the natural heat and senses, and serves to the expelling of excrements.

Melancholy, cold and dry, thick, black, and sour, begotten of the more feculent part of nourishment, and purged from the spleen, is a bridle to the other two hot humours, blood and choler, preserving them in the blood, and nourishing the bones. These four humours have some analogy with the four elements,[6] and to the four ages in man.

To these humours you may add serum, which is the matter of urine, and those excrementitious humours of the third concoction, sweat and tears.

Spirit is a most subtle vapour, which is expressed from the blood, and the instrument of the soul, to perform all his actions; a common tie or medium

1. Andrew Lawrence, a 17th-century British physician (?); at any rate, the author of a treatise on melancholy.
2. "Gluten" is fibrin; "ros" (Latin for "dew"), some other blood component.
3. Johannes Craton von Kraftheim, 16th-century German medical writer.
4. Philip Schwartzerd (German: "black earth," thus Hellenized; 1497–1560), scholar, church reformer, and follower of Luther.
5. Mesenteric: blood vessels supplying the mesenterum, or membrane holding the intestines to the abdominal wall.
6. See *Renaissance Psychology* in the Glossary.

between the body and the soul, as some will have it; or as Paracelsus,[7] a fourth soul of itself. Melancthon holds the fountain of these spirits to be the heart, begotten there; and afterward conveyed to the brain, they take another nature to them. Of these spirits there be three kinds, according to the three principal parts, brain, heart, liver; natural, vital, animal. The natural are begotten in the liver, and thence dispersed through the veins, to perform those natural actions. The vital spirits are made in the heart of the natural, which by the arteries are transported to all the other parts: if the spirits cease, then life ceaseth, as in a syncope or swooning. The animal spirits, formed of the vital, brought up to the brain, and diffused by the nerves to the subordinate members, give sense and motion to them all.

. . .

Subsection VII. Of the Inward Senses

Inner senses are three in number, so called because they be within the brain-pan, as common sense, phantasy, memory. Their objects are not only things present, but they perceive the sensible species of things to come, past, absent, such as were before in the sense. This common sense is the judge or moderator of the rest, by whom we discern all differences of objects; for by mine eye I do not know that I see, or by mine ear that I hear, but by my common sense, who judgeth of sounds and colours: they are but the organs to bring the species to be censured; so that all their objects are his, and all their offices are his. The fore-part of the brain is his organ or seat.

Phantasy, or imagination, which some call estimative, or cogitative (confirmed, saith Fernelius,[1] by frequent meditation), is an inner sense which doth more fully examine the species perceived by common sense, of things present or absent, and keeps them longer, recalling them to mind again, or making new of his own. In time of sleep this faculty is free, and many times conceives, strange, stupend,[2] absurd shapes, as in sick men we commonly observe. His organ is the middle cell of the brain; his objects all the species communicated to him by the common sense, by comparison of which he feigns infinite other unto himself. In melancholy men this faculty is most powerful and strong, and often hurts, producing many monstrous and prodigious things, especially if it be stirred up by some terrible object, presented to it from common sense or memory. In poets and painters imagination forcibly works, as appears by their several fictions, antics, images: as Ovid's house of Sleep,[3] Psyche's palace in Apuleius,[4] etc. In men it is subject and governed by reason, or at least should be; but in brutes it hath no superior, and is *ratio brutorum*, all the reason they have.

Memory lays up all the species which the senses have brought in, and records them as a good register, that they may be forthcoming when they are called for by phantasy and reason. His object is the same with phantasy, his seat and organ the back part of the brain.

7. Theophrastus Bombastus von Hohenheim (1493?–1541), alchemist and physician.
1. Jean François Fernel (1497–1558), French physician.
2. Astonishing.
3. In *Metamorphoses XI*.
4. In *The Golden Ass*.

The affections of these senses are sleep and waking, common to all sensible creatures. "Sleep is a rest or binding of the outward senses, and of the common sense, for the preservation of body and soul' (as Scaliger [5] defines it); for when the common sense resteth, the outward senses rest also. The phantasy alone is free, and his commander, reason: as appears by those imaginary dreams, which are of divers kinds, natural, divine, demoniacal, etc., which vary according to humours, diet, actions, objects, etc., of which Artemidorus,[6] Cardanus,[7] and Sambucus,[8] with their several interpretators, have written great volumes. This ligation of senses proceeds from an inhibition of spirits, the way being stopped by which they should come; this stopping is caused of vapours arising out of the stomach, filling the nerves, by which the spirits should be conveyed. When these vapours are spent, the passage is open, and the spirits perform their accustomed duties: so that 'waking is the action and motion of the senses, which the spirits dispersed over all parts cause.'

1621–51

SIR THOMAS BROWNE
1605–1682

Browne, who loved paradoxes and found in them a kind of reassurance in an age torn by religious and political dogmatisms, embodied some milder paradoxes in his own life. A physician, natural scientist, and Baconian bringer of light, he had before he was forty acquired an international reputation for a religious work; a Royalist and Anglican, he spent more than half his life in the Puritan and Parliamentarian East Anglian city of Norwich, where he was liked and admired; a naturalist whose notebooks and larger works are full of detailed observations; a killer of the chimerical dragons of superstition in his work usually known as *Vulgar Errors*,[1] he delighted in mysteries and puzzles, and delighted most to read all of nature as one vast hieroglyphic which would reflect, on close inspection, the mind that read and understood it. There is little wonder that Ralph Waldo Emerson was so devoted to his writings. Browne was born in London, studied at Winchester School and Pembroke College, Oxford, studied medicine at Montpellier, Padua, and Leyden (from which he took a degree probably in 1633, being granted the M.D. by Oxford in 1637). He moved to Norwich, then the second largest city in England, where he practised medicine, botanized along the shore, and wrote. He had a good many children (accounts differ between ten and twelve) and was knighted in 1671, on a royal visit to Norwich.

The *Religio Medici* (Faith of a Physician) was written in 1634–35 as an attempt to come to terms with the doctrinal winds that were blowing up into the storms of the English revolution, and which had plunged the Continent into the Thirty Years War.

5. Julius Caesar Scaliger (1484–1558), Italian scholar and physician.
6. Artemidorus of Daldianus (2nd century A.D.), author of *Oneirokritika*, a treatise on dreams.
7. Girolamo Cardano (1501–76), Italian mathematician and natural philosopher.
8. Johann Zsámboky (1554–84), Hungarian scholar and emblematist.

1. *Pseudodoxia Epidemica: or Enquiries into Very Many Received Tenets and Commonly Presumed Truths* (1646). Two works published posthumously were *A Letter to a Friend* (1690) and *Christian Morals* (1716).

Published first in two pirated editions in 1642, it was followed the next year by an authorized text and, in 1644, a Latin translation. It is less remarkable for its opening sections' sophisticated Anglican compromise (between ritualistic orthodoxy and reformed independence of Rome) than for its exposition of both a world view and a sense of self within that view. What C. S. Lewis called "the discarded image"—that model of the structure of the cosmos and all its component parts, concentric, hierarchical, attentive to natural phenomena but with no method for going behind them to anything but Providence—shows up beautifully in Browne's informal exploration of self. Ultimately, the faith revealed by the two parts of the long chain of meditations is in that model, and in the way in which it allows all of nature, both the horrific and the benign, to be read as evidence of ultimate human dignity. Browne's mode of thinking in images, rather more Baconian in many ways than his style would warrant, allows him to contain the doubts of a Hobbes or a Descartes, the probings and anatomies which would ultimately collapse the old model of the universe.

Religio Medici

From *Part I*

1.

For my religion, though there be several circumstances that might persuade the world I have none at all, as the general scandal of my profession, the natural course of my studies, the indifferency of my behaviour and discourse in matters of religion, neither violently defending one, nor with that common ardour and contention opposing another; yet, in despite hereof, I dare without usurpation [1] assume the honourable style of a Christian. Not that I merely owe this title to the font, my education, or the clime wherein I was born, as being bred up either to confirm those principles my parents instilled into my unwary understanding, or by a general consent proceed in the religion of my country. But having in my riper years and confirmed judgement seen and examined all, I find myself obliged by the principles of grace, and the law of mine own reason, to embrace no other name but this. Neither doth herein my zeal so far make me forget the general charity I owe unto humanity, as rather to hate than pity Turks, Infidels, and (what is worse) Jews; rather contenting myself to enjoy that happy style, than maligning those who refuse so glorious a title.

2.

But, because the name of a Christian is become too general to express our faith, there being a geography of religions as well as lands, and every clime distinguished not only by their laws and limits, but circumscribed by their doctrines and rules of faith; to be particular, I am of that reformed new-cast religion, wherein I dislike nothing but the name; of the same belief our Saviour taught, the Apostles disseminated, the Fathers authorised, and the Martyrs confirmed; but by the sinister ends of princes, the ambition and avarice of

1. Wrongly so doing.

prelates, and the fatal corruption of times, so decayed, impaired, and fallen from its native beauty, that it required the careful and charitable hands of these times to restore it to its primitive integrity. Now the accidental occasion whereupon, the slender means whereby, the low and abject condition of the person by whom so good a work was set on foot, which in our adversaries beget contempt and scorn, fills me with wonder, and is the very same objection the insolent pagans first cast at Christ and his disciples.

3.

Yet I have not so shaken hands with those desperate resolutions [2] who had rather venture at large their decayed bottom, than bring her in to be new trimmed in the dock; who had rather promiscuously retain all, than abridge any, and obstinately be what they are, than what they have been, as to stand in diameter [3] and sword's point with them. We have reformed from them, not against them; for, omitting those improperations [4] and terms of scurrility betwixt us which only difference our affections and not our cause, there is between us one common name and appellation, one faith and necessary body of principles common to us both; and therefore I am not scrupulous to converse or live with them, to enter their churches in defect of ours, and either pray with them, or for them. I am, I confess, naturally inclined to that which misguided zeal terms superstition. My common conversation I do acknowledge austere, my behaviour full of rigour, sometimes not without morosity; yet at my devotion I love to use the civility of my knee, my hat, and hand,[5] with all those outward and sensible motions which may express or promote my invisible devotion. I should violate my own arm rather than a church; nor willingly deface the name of saint or martyr. At the sight of a cross or crucifix I can dispense with my hat, but scarce with the thought or memory of my Saviour. I cannot laugh at, but rather pity, the fruitless journeys of pilgrims, or contemn the miserable condition of friars; for, though misplaced in circumstances, there is something in it of devotion. I could never hear the Ave-Mary Bell [6] without an elevation; or think it a sufficient warrant, because they erred in one circumstance, for me to err in all, that is, in silence and dumb contempt. Whilst, therefore, they directed their devotions to her, I offered mine to God, and rectified the errors of their prayers by rightly ordering mine own. At a solemn procession I have wept abundantly while my consorts, blind with opposition and prejudice, have fallen into an excess of scorn and laughter. There are, questionless,[7] both in Greek, Roman and African churches solemnities and ceremonies whereof the wiser zeals do make a Christian use, and stand condemned by us, not as evil in themselves, but as allurements and baits of superstition to those vulgar heads that look asquint on the face of truth, and those unstable judgements that

2. Roman Catholics; Browne is putting the Anglican case for accommodation of orthodoxy without the necessity of submitting to the papacy.
3. Opposed to.
4. Reproaches.
5. That is, genuflecting, uncovering his head, crossing himself.
6. The Angelus, rung at six, twelve, and six o'clock as a summons to prayer, usually to the Virgin: a specifically Roman Catholic custom.
7. Unquestionably.

cannot consist in the narrow point and centre of virtue without a reel or stagger to the circumference.

. . .

6.

I could never divide myself from any man upon the difference of an opinion, or be angry with his judgement for not agreeing with me in that from which perhaps within a few days I should dissent myself. I have no genius to disputes in religion, and have often thought it wisdom to decline them, especially upon a disadvantage, or when the cause of truth might suffer in the weakness of my patronage. Where we desire to be informed, 'tis good to contest with me above ourselves; but to confirm and establish our opinions, 'tis best to argue with judgements below our own, that the frequent spoils and victories over their reasons may settle in ourselves an esteem and confirmed opinion of our own. Every man is not a proper champion for truth, nor fit to take up the gauntlet in the cause of verity: many, from the ignorance of these maxims, and an inconsiderate zeal unto truth, have too rashly charged the troops of error, and remain as trophies unto the enemies of truth. A man may be in as just possession of truth as of a city, and yet be forced to surrender; 'tis therefore far better to enjoy her with peace, than to hazard her on a battle. If, therefore, there rise any doubts in my way, I do forget them, or at least defer them till my better settled judgement and more manly reason be able to resolve them; for I perceive every man's own reason is his best Œdipus,[8] and will, upon a reasonable truce, find a way to loose those bonds wherewith the subtleties of error have enchained our more flexible and tender judgements. In philosophy, where truth seems double-faced, there is no man more paradoxical than myself: but in divinity I love to keep the road; and, though not in an implicit, yet an humble faith, follow the great wheel of the church, by which I move, not reserving any proper poles or motion from the epicycle [9] of my own brain. By this means I leave no gap for heresies, schisms, or errors, of which at present I hope I shall not injure truth to say I have no taint or tincture. . . . I must confess my greener studies have been polluted with two or three—not any begotten in the latter centuries, but old and obsolete—such as could never have been revived but by such extravagant and irregular heads as mine; for indeed, heresies perish not with their authors, but like the river *Arethusa*,[10] though they lose their currents in one place, they rise up again in another. One general council is not able to extirpate one single heresy, it may be cancelled for the present, but revolution of time and the like aspects of heaven will restore it, when it will flourish till it be condemned again. For as though there were a *metempsychosis*,[11] and the soul of one man passed into another, opinions do find, after certain revolutions, men and minds like those that first begat them. To see ourselves again we need not look for Plato's year; [12] every man is not only

8. As problem-solver (Oedipus answered the Sphinx's riddle).
9. The circle-on-the-circle of the orbits in the old astronomy (see *Astronomy* in the Glossary).
10. "That loseth itself in Greece and riseth again in Sicily" (Browne's note); see also Headnote to Milton's *Lycidas*.
11. Transmigration of souls; reincarnation.
12. The *magnus annus* or great year of Plato; "a revolution of several thousand years when all things should return to their former estate and he teaching again in his school as when he delivered this opinion" (Browne's note).

himself—there have been many Diogenes and as many Timons, though but few of that name. Men are lived over again; the world is now as it were in ages past; there was none then but there hath been some one since that parallels him, and is, as it were, his revived self.

. . .

9.

As for those wingy mysteries in divinity, and airy subtleties in religion, which have unhinged the brains of better heads, they never stretched the *pia mater* [13] of mine. Methinks there be not impossibilities enough in religion for an active faith; the deepest mysteries ours contains have not only been illustrated, but maintained by syllogism and the rule of reason. I love to lose myself in a mystery, to pursue my reason to an *O altitudo!* [14] 'Tis my solitary recreation to pose my apprehension with those involved enigmas and riddles of the Trinity, with incarnation, and resurrection. I can answer all the objections of Satan and my rebellious reason with that odd resolution I learned of Tertullian, *Certum est, quia impossibile est.*[15] I desire to exercise my faith in the difficultest point; for to credit ordinary and visible objects is not faith, but persuasion. Some believe the better for seeing Christ's sepulchre; and, when they have seen the Red Sea, doubt not of the miracle. Now, contrarily, I bless myself and am thankful that I lived not in the days of miracles, that I never saw Christ nor his disciples. I would not have been one of those Israelites that passed the Red Sea, nor one of Christ's patients on whom he wrought his wonders, then had my faith been thrust upon me; nor should I enjoy that greater blessing pronounced to all that believe and saw not. 'Tis an easy and necessary belief, to credit what our eye and sense hath examined. I believe he was dead, and buried, and rose again; and desire to see him in his glory, rather than to contemplate him in his cenotaph or sepulchre. Nor is this much to believe; as we have reason, we owe this faith unto history: they only had the advantage of a bold and noble faith who lived before his coming, who upon obscure prophecies and mystical types [16] could raise a belief, and expect apparent impossibilities.

. . . .

15.

Natura nihil agit frustra [17] is the only indisputed axiom in philosophy. There are no grotesques in nature; not anything framed to fill up empty cantons,[18] and unnecessary spaces. In the most imperfect creatures, and such as were not preserved in the ark, but, having their seeds and principles in the womb of nature, are everywhere, where the power of the sun is, in these is the wisdom of

13. The vascular membrane covering the brain.
14. Bacon, in *The Advancement of Learning* II.xxv.13, says that "In divinity many things must be left abrupt, and concluded with this: 'O altitudo sapientiae et scientiae Dei! quam incomprehensibilia sunt judicia ejus, et non investigabiles viae ejus!'" (O the depth of the riches both of the wisdom and knowledge of God! how unsearchable are his judgments, and his ways past finding out!—Romans 11:33).
15. "It is certain just because it is impossible"—a famous paradox of faith posed by Tertullian (160–230 A.D.), theologian and polemicist.
16. The foreshadowing figures of biblical interpretation.
17. "Nature does nothing in vain" (a basic principle of Aristotelian scientific tradition).
18. Regions, divisions.

his hand discovered. Out of this rank Solomon chose the object of his admiration.[19] Indeed, what reason may not go to school to the wisdom of bees, ants, and spiders? what wise hand teacheth them to do what reason cannot teach us? Ruder heads stand amazed at those prodigious pieces of nature, whales, elephants, dromedaries and camels; these, I confess, are the colossus and majestic piece of her hand: but in these narrow engines there is more curious mathematics; and the civility of these little citizens more neatly sets forth the wisdom of their Maker. Who admires not Regiomontanus [20] his fly beyond his eagle, or wonders not more at the operation of two souls in those little bodies, than but one in the trunk of a cedar? I could never content my contemplation with those general pieces of wonder, the flux and reflux of the sea,[21] the increase of Nile, the conversion of the needle [22] to the north; and have studied to match and parallel those in the more obvious and neglected pieces of nature, which without further travel I can do in the cosmography of myself. We carry with us the wonders we seek without us: there is all Africa and her prodigies in us; we are that bold and adventurous piece of nature, which he that studies wisely learns in a compendium what others labour at in a divided piece and endless volume.

16.

Thus there are two books from whence I collect my divinity; besides that written one of God, another of his servant nature, that universal and public manuscript that lies expansed [23] unto the eyes of all: those that never saw him in the one, have discovered him in the other. This was the scripture and theology of the heathens: the natural motion of the sun made them more admire him than its supernatural station did the children of Israel; the ordinary effects of nature wrought more admiration in them than in the other all his miracles. Surely the heathens knew better how to join and read these mystical letters than we Christians, who cast a more careless eye on these common hieroglyphics, and disdain to suck divinity from the flowers of nature. Nor do I so forget God as to adore the name of nature; which I define not, with the schools, to be the principle of motion and rest, but that straight and regular line, that settled and constant course the wisdom of God hath ordained the actions of his creatures, according to their several kinds. To make a revolution every day is the nature of the sun, because of that necessary course which God hath ordained it, from which it cannot swerve but by a faculty from that voice which first did give it motion. Now this course of nature God seldom alters or perverts, but like an excellent artist, hath so contrived his work, that with the selfsame instrument, without a new creation, he may effect his obscurest designs. Thus he sweeteneth the water with a wood, preserveth the creatures in the ark, which the blast of his mouth might have as easily created; for God is like a skillful geometrician, who, when more easily and with one stroke of his compass

19. The ant ("Go to the ant, thou sluggard; consider her ways, and be wise"—Proverbs 6:6).
20. Johann Müller (1436–75) was supposed to have built an iron fly and a wooden eagle, both of which flew.
21. The tides.
22. The compass needle.
23. Open.

he might describe or divide a right line, had yet rather do this in a circle or longer way, according to the constituted and fore-laid principles of his art. Yet this rule of his he doth sometimes pervert, to acquaint the world with his prerogative, lest the arrogancy of our reason should question his power, and conclude he could not. And thus I call the effects of nature the works of God, whose hand and instrument she only is; and therefore to ascribe his actions unto her, is to devolve [24] the honour of the principal agent upon the instrument; which if with reason we may do, then let our hammers rise up and boast they built our houses, and our pens receive the honour of our writings. I hold there is a general beauty in the works of God, and therefore no deformity in any kind or species of creature whatsoever. I cannot tell by what logic we call a toad, a bear, or an elephant ugly; they being created in those outward shapes and figures which best express the actions of their inward forms, and having passed that general visitation of God, who saw that all that he had made was good, that is, conformable to his will, which abhors deformity, and is the rule of order and beauty. There is no deformity but in monstrosity; wherein, notwithstanding, there is a kind of beauty, nature so ingeniously contriving the irregular parts, as they become sometimes more remarkable than the principal fabric. To speak yet more narrowly, there was never anything ugly or misshapen, but the chaos; wherein, notwithstanding, to speak strictly, there was no deformity, because no form; nor was it yet impregnant by the voice of God. Now nature is not at variance with art, nor art with nature, they being both servants of his providence. Art is the perfection of nature. Were the world now as it was the sixth day, there were yet a chaos. Nature hath made one world, and art another. In brief, all things are artificial; for nature is the art of God.

27.

That miracles are ceased, I can neither prove, nor absolutely deny, much less define the time and period of their cessation. That they survived Christ is manifest upon the record of Scripture; that they outlived the Apostles also, and were revived at the conversion of nations many years after, we cannot deny, if we shall not question those writers whose testimonies we do not controvert in points that make for our own opinions. Therefore that may have some truth in it that is reported by the Jesuits of their miracles in the Indies; I could wish it were true, or had any other testimony than their own pens. They may easily believe those miracles abroad, who daily conceive a greater at home, the transmutation of those visible elements into the body and blood of our Saviour.[25] For the conversion of water into wine, which he wrought in Cana,[26] or, what the Devil would have had him done in the wilderness, of stones into bread,[27] compared to this, will scarce deserve the name of a miracle: though indeed, to speak properly, there is not one miracle greater than another, they being the extraordinary effects of the hand of God, to which all things are of an equal facility; and to create the world, as easy as one single creature. For this is also a miracle,

24. Transfer.
25. Browne refers to the mystery of the Eucharist, with apparent total acceptance of the transubstantiation of Christ's body and blood.
26. John 2:3-9.
27. Luke 4:1-4.

not only to produce effects against or above nature, but before nature; and to create nature, as great a miracle as to contradict or transcend her. We do too narrowly define the power of God, restraining it to our capacities. I hold that God can do all things; how he should work contradictions, I do not understand, yet dare not therefore deny. I cannot see why the angel of God should question Esdras [28] to recall the time past, if it were beyond his own power; or that God should pose [29] mortality in that which he was not able to perform himself. I will not say God cannot, but he will not, perform many things, which we plainly affirm he cannot. This, I am sure, is the mannerliest [30] proposition, wherein, notwithstanding, I hold no paradox; for, strictly, his power is the same with his will, and they both, with all the rest, do make but one God.

28.

Therefore that miracles have been, I do believe; that they may yet be wrought by the living, I do not deny; but have no confidence in those which are fathered on the dead. And this hath ever made me suspect the efficacy of relics, to examine the bones, question the habits and appurtenances of saints, and even of Christ himself. I cannot conceive why the cross that Helena found, and whereon Christ himself died, should have power to restore others unto life. I excuse not Constantine from a fall off his horse, or a mischief from his enemies, upon the wearing those nails on his bridle which our Saviour bore upon the cross in his hands. I compute among your *piæ fraudes*,[31] nor many degrees before consecrated swords and roses, that which Baldwin, King of Jerusalem, returned the Genovese for their cost and pains in his war, to wit, the ashes of John the Baptist. Those that hold the sanctity of their souls doth leave behind a tincture [32] and sacred faculty on their bodies, speak naturally of miracles, and do not salve the doubt. Now one reason I tender so little devotion unto relics, is, I think, the slender and doubtful respect I have always held unto antiquities. For that indeed which I admire, is far before antiquity, that is, eternity; and that is, God himself; who, though he be styled *the Ancient of Days*, cannot receive the adjunct of antiquity; who was before the world, and shall be after it, yet is not older than it; for in his years there is no climacter; [33] his duration is eternity, and far more venerable than antiquity.

. . .

39.

Some divines count Adam thirty years old at his creation, because they suppose him created in the perfect age and stature of man. And surely we are all out of the computation of our age, and every man is some months elder than he bethinks him; for we live, move, have a being,[34] and are subject to the actions

28. "Then he said unto me, Go to, weigh me a weight of fire, or measure me a measure of wind, or call me again the day that is past" (II Esdras 4:5).
29. Perplex.
30. Most sophisticated.
31. "Pious frauds"; Browne is discussing the claims made for famous relics.
32. Tint; here, of holiness.
33. Climacteric: a crucial point of change in human life.
34. Echoing St. Paul in Acts 17:28.

of the elements, and the malice of diseases, in that other world, the truest microcosm, the womb of our mother. For besides that general and common existence we are conceived to hold in our chaos, and whilst we sleep within the bosom of our causes, we enjoy a being and life in three distinct worlds, wherein we receive most manifest graduations. In that obscure world and womb of our mother, our time is short, computed by the moon, yet longer than the days of many creatures that behold the sun; ourselves being not yet without life, sense, and reason; though for the manifestation of its actions, it awaits the opportunity of objects, and seems to live there but in its root and soul of vegetation. Entering afterwards upon the scene of the world, we arise up and become another creature, performing the reasonable actions of man, and obscurely manifesting that part of divinity in us; but not in complement and perfection, till we have once more cast our secondine, that is, this slough of flesh, and are delivered into the last world, that is, that ineffable place of Paul, that proper *ubi* [35] of spirits. The smattering I have of the philosopher's stone [36] (which is something more than the perfect exaltation of gold) hath taught me a great deal of divinity, and instructed my belief, how that immortal spirit and incorruptible substance of my soul may lie obscure, and sleep a while within this house of flesh. Those strange and mystical transmigrations that I have observed in silkworms, turned my philosophy into divinity. There is in these works of nature, which seem to puzzle reason, something divine, and hath more in it than the eye of a common spectator doth discover.

From *Part II*

9.

I was never yet once,[1] and commend their resolutions who never marry twice: not that I disallow of second marriage; as neither, in all cases, of polygamy, which, considering some times, and the unequal number of both sexes, may be also necessary. The whole world was made for man, but the twelfth part of man for woman: man is the whole world, and the breadth of God, woman the rib and crooked piece [2] of man. I could be content that we might procreate like trees, without conjunction, or that there were any way to perpetuate the world without this trivial and vulgar way of union: it is the foolishest act a wise man commits in all his life: nor is there anything that will more deject his cooled imagination, when he shall consider what an odd and unworthy piece of folly he hath committed. I speak not in prejudice, nor am averse from that sweet sex, but naturally amorous of all that is beautiful. I can look a whole day with delight upon a handsome picture, though it be but of an horse. It is my temper, and I like it the better, to affect all harmony; and sure there is music even in the beauty and the silent note which Cupid strikes, far sweeter than the

35. "Where."
36. The philosopher's stone was the object of the alchemical quest, and, with it, transmutation of metals could be effected; but it came, in time, to develop more allegorical meaning (see *Alchemy* in the Glossary).

1. Browne did in fact marry (in 1641).
2. Alluding to the old misogynistic fable that the rib from which Eve was created was a crooked one.

sound of an instrument. For there is a music wherever there is a harmony, order, or proportion: and thus far we may maintain the music of the spheres; [3] for those well-ordered motions, and regular paces, though they give no sound unto the ear, yet to the understanding they strike a note most full of harmony. Whosoever is harmonically composed delights in harmony, which makes me much distrust the symmetry of those heads which declaim against all church-music. For myself, not only from my obedience, but my particular genius,[4] I do embrace it: for even that vulgar and tavern-music which makes one man merry, another mad, strikes in me a deep fit of devotion, and a profound contemplation of the First Composer. There is something in it of divinity more than the ear discovers: it is an hieroglyphical and shadowed [5] lesson of the whole world, and creatures of God; such a melody to the ear, as the whole world, well understood, would afford the understanding. In brief, it is a sensible [6] fit of that harmony which intellectually sounds in the ears of God. I will not say, with Plato, the soul is an harmony, but harmonical, and hath its nearest sympathy unto music: thus some, whose temper of body agrees, and humours the constitution of their souls, are born poets, though indeed all are naturally inclined unto rhythm. This made Tacitus, in the very first line of his story,[7] fall upon a verse; and Cicero, the worst of poets but declaiming for a poet, fall in the very first sentence upon a perfect hexameter.[8] I feel not in me those sordid and unchristian desires of my profession; I do not secretly implore and wish for plagues, rejoice at famines, revolve ephemerides [9] and almanacs in expectation of malignant aspects, fatal conjunctions, and eclipses. I rejoice not at unwholesome springs, nor unseasonable winters: my prayer goes with the husbandman's; I desire everything in its proper season, that neither men nor the times be put out of temper. Let me be sick myself, if sometimes the malady of my patient be not a disease unto me. I desire rather to cure his infirmities than my own necessities. Where I do him no good, methinks it is scarce honest gain; though I confess 'tis but the worthy salary of our well-intended endeavours. I am not only ashamed, but heartily sorry, that, besides death, there are diseases incurable: yet not for my own sake, or that they be beyond my art, but for the general cause and sake of humanity, whose common cause I apprehend as mine own. . . . .

10.

For my conversation,[10] it is like the sun's, with all men, and with a friendly aspect to good and bad. Methinks there is no man bad, and the worst, best; that is, while they are kept within the circle of those qualities wherein they are good: there is no man's mind of such discordant and jarring a temper, to which a tuneable disposition may not strike a harmony. *Magnæ virtutes, nec*

3. See *Music of the Spheres* in the Glossary.
4. Cast of mind.
5. Figurative.
6. Audible.
7. The first line of his *Annals* seems to scan.
8. A well-known bit of lore, involving his *Pro Archia*.
9. Astronomical charts.
10. Conduct.

minora vitia; [11] it is the posy of the best natures, and may be inverted on the worst; there are in the most depraved and venomous dispositions, certain pieces that remain untouched, which by an *antiperistasis* [12] become more excellent, or by the excellency of their antipathies are able to preserve themselves from the contagion of their enemy vices, and persist entire beyond the general corruption. For it is also thus in nature: the greatest balsams [13] do lie enveloped in the bodies of most powerful corrosives. I say, moreover, and I ground upon experience, that poisons contain within themselves their own antidote, and that which preserves them from the venom of themselves, without which they were not deleterious to others only, but to themselves also. But it is the corruption that I fear within me, not the contagion of commerce without me. 'Tis that unruly regiment within me, that will destroy me; 'tis I that do infect myself; the man without a navel [14] yet lives in me; I feel that original canker corrode and devour me; and therefore *Defenda me Dios de me,* Lord deliver me from myself, is a part of my litany, and the first voice of my retired imaginations. There is no man alone, because every man is a microcosm,[15] and carries the whole world about him. *Nunquam minus solus quam cum solus,*[16] though it be the apothegm of a wise man, is yet true in the mouth of a fool. Indeed, though in a wilderness, a man is never alone, not only because he is with himself and his own thoughts, but because he is with the Devil, who ever consorts with our solitude, and is that unruly rebel that musters up those disordered motions which accompany our sequestered imaginations. And to speak more narrowly, there is no such thing as solitude, nor anything that can be said to be alone and by itself, but God, who is his own circle, and can subsist by himself; all others, besides their dissimilar and heterogeneous parts, which in a manner multiply their natures, cannot subsist without the concourse of God, and the society of that hand which doth uphold their natures. In brief, there can be nothing truly alone and by itself, which is not truly one; and such is only God: all others do transcend an unity, and so by consequence are many.

11.

Now for my life, it is a miracle of thirty years, which to relate were not a history, but a piece of poetry, and would sound to common ears like a fable. For the world, I count it not an inn, but an hospital; and a place not to live, but to die in. The world that I regard is myself; it is the microcosm of my own frame that I cast mine eye on; for the other, I use it but like my globe, and turn it round sometimes for my recreation. Men that look upon my outside, perusing only my condition and fortunes, do err in my altitude; for I am above Atlas [17] his shoulders. The earth is a point not only in respect of the heavens

11. "Great virtues and no lesser vices" (Plato quoted by Plutarch).
12. An intensification of contraries, by virtue of their very opposition.
13. Healing salves; "balms" in the most general sense.
14. Adam, who had no navel, presumably because he was not born of woman; theologically, the old Adam within man, the unexpunged sinful element in his nature (see I Corinthians 15:45).
15. For an extremely detailed treatment of this, see the extract from Ralegh's *History of the World.*
16. "Never less lonely than when alone" (Cicero, *De Officiis* III.1).
17. The mythical giant Atlas bore the globe on his shoulders.

above us, but of that heavenly and celestial part within us; that mass of flesh that circumscribes me, limits not my mind. That surface that tells the heavens it hath an end, cannot persuade me I have any: I take my circle to be above three hundred and sixty; [18] though the number of the arc do measure my body, it comprehendeth not my mind: whilst I study to find how I am a microcosm, or little world, I find myself something more than the great. There is surely a piece of divinity in us, something that was before the elements, and owes no homage unto the sun. Nature tells me I am the image of God, as well as Scripture: he that understands not thus much, hath not his introduction or first lesson, and is yet to begin the alphabet of man. Let me not injure the felicity of others, if I say I am as happy as any: *Ruat cœlum, fiat voluntas tua,*[19] salveth all; so that whatsoever happens, it is but what our daily prayers desire. In brief, I am content; and what should Providence add more? Surely this is it we call happiness, and this do I enjoy; with this I am happy in a dream, and as content to enjoy a happiness in a fancy, as others in a more apparent truth and realty. There is surely a nearer apprehension of anything that delights us in our dreams, than in our waked senses: without this I were unhappy; for my awaked judgement discontents me, ever whispering unto me, that I am from my friend; but my friendly dreams in the night requite me, and make me think I am within his arms. I thank God for my happy dreams, as I do for my good rest; for there is a satisfaction in them unto reasonable desires, and as such can be content with a fit of happiness: and surely it is not a melancholy conceit [20] to think we are all asleep in this world, and that the conceits of this life are as mere dreams to those of the next, as the phantasms of the night to the conceits of the day. There is an equal delusion in both, and the one doth but seem to be the emblem or picture of the other: we are somewhat more than ourselves in our sleeps, and the slumber of the body seems to be but the waking of the soul. It is the ligation [21] of sense, but the liberty of reason; and our waking conceptions do not match the fancies of our sleeps. At my nativity my ascendant [22] was the watery sign of Scorpius; I was born in the planetary hour of Saturn, and I think I have a piece of that leaden planet in me. I am no way facetious, not disposed for the mirth and galliardize [23] of company; yet in one dream I can compose a whole comedy, behold the action, apprehend the jests, and laugh myself awake at the conceits thereof. Were my memory as faithful as my reason is then fruitful, I would never study but in my dreams; and this time also would I choose for my devotions: but our grosser memories have then so little hold of our abstracted understandings, that they forget the story, and can only relate to our awaked souls a confused and broken tale of that that hath passed. Aristotle, who hath written a singular tract Of Sleep, hath not, methinks, thoroughly defined it; nor yet Galen,[24] though he seem to have corrected it; for those *noctambuloes* [25] and night-

18. That is, if the self is likened to a circle, it is one of more than 360 degrees.
19. "Though heaven fall, thy will be done."
20. Notion.
21. Binding, constricting.
22. Rising zodiacal sign, with astrological implications.
23. Merriment; from "galliard," a dance in three-quarter time.
24. Claudius Galenus (130–200 A.D.), Greek writer on medicine.
25. Somnambulists.

walkers, though in their sleep, do yet enjoy the action of their senses. We must therefore say that there is something in us that is not in the jurisdiction of Morpheus; and that those abstracted and ecstatic souls do walk about in their own corpse as spirits with the bodies they assume, wherein they seem to hear, see, and feel, though indeed the organs are destitute of sense, and their natures of those faculties that should inform them. Thus it is observed, that men sometimes, upon the hour of their departure, do speak and reason above themselves; for then the soul, beginning to be freed from the ligaments of the body, begins to reason like herself, and to discourse in a strain above mortality.

12.

We term sleep a death; and yet it is waking that kills us, and destroys those spirits that are the house of life. 'Tis indeed a part of life that best expresseth death; for every man truly lives, so long as he acts his nature, or some way makes good the faculties of himself. Themistocles, therefore, that slew his soldier in his sleep, was a merciful executioner: 'tis a kind of punishment the mildness of no laws hath invented: I wonder the fancy of Lucan and Seneca did not discover it. It is that death by which we may be literally said to die daily; a death which Adam died before his mortality; a death whereby we live a middle and moderating point between life and death: in fine, so like death, I dare not trust it without my prayers, and an half adieu unto the world, and take my farewell in a colloquy with God. . . .

1634–35   1642

Hydriotaphia

Hydriotaphia, Urn-Burial (published 1658) is a long meditation on death, time, and memory, occasioned by antiquarian researches. Some burial urns, discovered in a field in Norfolk, led Browne to consider their provenance (he mistakenly thought them to be Roman), and from there to meditate upon burial customs, cremations, tombs, and monuments among as many cultures as he could. But like any emblem or sonnet of the sixteenth century, the consideration of the object led to the *significatio* or interpretation; in his great last chapter, worthy of Montaigne at his best (of whom Browne claimed never to have read more than a few pages), the vanity of all the false technologies of immortality is relentlessly, but not cruelly, disclosed.

From Hydriotaphia

Chapter V

Now since these dead bones have already outlasted the living ones of Methuselah,[1] and in a yard under ground, and thin walls of clay, out-worn all the strong and spacious buildings above it, and quietly rested under the

1. Who lived 969 years, according to Genesis 5:27.

drums and tramplings of three conquests: what prince can promise such diuturnity [2] unto his relics, or might not gladly say,

Sic ego componi versus in ossa velim? [3]

Time, which antiquates antiquities, and hath an art to make dust of all things, hath yet spared these minor monuments.

In vain we hope to be known by open and visible conservatories, when to be unknown was the means of their continuation, and obscurity their protection. If they died by violent hands, and were thrust into their urns, these bones become considerable, and some old philosophers would honour them, whose souls they conceived most pure, which were thus snatched from their bodies, and to retain a stronger propension unto [4] them; whereas they weariedly left a languishing corpse, and with faint desires of reunion. If they fell by long and aged decay, yet wrapt up in the bundle of time, they fall into indistinction,[5] and make but one blot with infants. If we begin to die when we live, and long life be but a prolongation of death, our life is a sad composition; we live with death, and die not in a moment. How many pulses made up the life of Methuselah, were work for Archimedes: common counters sum up the life of Moses his man.[6] Our days become considerable, like petty sums, by minute accumulations; where numerous fractions make up but small round numbers; and our days of a span long, make not one little finger.[7]

If the nearness of our last necessity brought a nearer conformity into it, there were a happiness in hoary hairs, and no calamity in half-senses.[8] But the long habit of living indisposeth us for dying; when avarice makes us the sport of death, when even David grew politicly cruel, and Solomon could hardly be said to be the wisest of men. But many are too early old, and before the date of age. Adversity stretcheth our days, misery makes Alcmena's nights,[9] and time hath no wings unto it. But the most tedious being is that which can unwish itself, content to be nothing, or never to have been, which was beyond the malcontent of Job, who cursed not the day of his life, but his nativity; [10] content to have so far been, as to have a title to future being, although he had lived here but in an hidden state of life, and as it were an abortion.

What song the Sirens sang, or what name Achilles assumed when he hid himself among women, though puzzling questions, are not beyond all conjecture.[11] What time the persons of these ossuaries entered the famous nations of the dead, and slept with princes and counselors, might admit a wide [12]

2. Long life; the three conquests of Celtic Britain were by the Romans, Saxons, and Normans.
3. "Thus I, when turned to bones, should wish to rest" (Tibullus).
4. Inclination for.
5. Indistinctness.
6. Moses' man is the canonical man of Psalm 90 (traditionally and mistakenly said to be by Moses), the days of whose years are threescore and ten.
7. "According to the ancient arithmetic of the hand, wherein the little finger of the right hand contracted signified an hundred" (Browne's note).
8. Deterioration of sight, hearing, and other senses.
9. Jupiter so liked his night of love with Alcmena that he prevented the sun from rising, thus producing three adjacent nights; Hercules was born of this union.
10. "Let the day perish wherein I was born" (Job 3:3–12).
11. Famous pointless questions of antiquity (like Donne's "Who cleft the devil's foot?").
12. Tentative or approximate.

solution. But who were the proprietaries of these bones, or what bodies these ashes made up, were a question above antiquarism; not to be resolved by man, nor easily perhaps by spirits, except we consult the provincial guardians, or tutelary observators. Had they made as good provision for their names, as they have done for their relics, they had not so grossly erred in the art of perpetuation. But to subsist in bones, and be but pyramidally [13] extant, is a fallacy in duration. Vain ashes which in the oblivion of names, persons, times, and sexes, have found unto themselves a fruitless continuation, and only arise unto late posterity, as emblems of mortal vanities, antidotes against pride, vainglory, and madding vices. Pagan vainglories which thought the world might last for ever, had encouragement for ambition; and, finding no Atropos [14] unto the immortality of their names, were never damped with the necessity of oblivion. Even old ambitions had the advantage of ours, in the attempts of their vainglories, who acting early, and before the probable meridian [15] of time, have by this time found great accomplishment of their designs, whereby the ancient heroes have already outlasted their monuments and mechanical preservations. But in this latter scene of time, we cannot expect such mummies unto our memories, when ambition may fear the prophecy of Elias,[16] and Charles the Fifth can never hope to live within two Methuselahs of Hector.[17]

And therefore, restless unquiet for the diuturnity [18] of our memories unto present considerations seems a vanity almost out of date, and superannuated piece of folly. We cannot hope to live so long in our names, as some have done in their persons. One face of Janus [19] holds no proportion unto the other. 'Tis too late to be ambitious. The great mutations of the world are acted, or time may be too short for our designs. To extend our memories by monuments whose death we daily pray for, and whose duration we cannot hope without injury to our expectations in the advent of the last day, were a contradiction to our beliefs. We whose generations are ordained in this setting part of time, are providentially taken off from such imaginations; and, being necessitated to eye the remaining particle of futurity, are naturally constituted unto thoughts of the next world, and cannot excusably decline the consideration of that duration which maketh pyramids pillars of snow, and all that's past a moment.

Circles and right lines limit and close all bodies, and the mortal right-lined circle [20] must conclude and shut up all. There is no antidote against the opium of time, which temporally considereth all things: our fathers find their

13. Like the dead Egyptians (in the days before hieroglyphics could be read), who were unknown, though their pyramids were themselves emblems of fame.

14. Third and most terrifying of the three Fates (with Clotho and Lachesis); they spun and measured the thread of life, Atropos cut it.

15. Noon, or midpoint.

16. "That the world will last but six thousand years" (Browne's note).

17. The Emperor Charles V lived from 1500 to 1588; two Methuselahs would put Hector back in the Athens of Socrates, so that if any historical Hector can be surmised, he surely antedates this.

18. Long life.

19. Two-faced (away from each other) Roman god, presiding over commencements and openings (hence, January).

20. The Greek letter theta, Θ; Browne calls it "the character of death" because it is the initial letter of *thanatos* (death).

graves in our short memories, and sadly tell us how we may be buried in our survivors. Gravestones tell truth scarce forty years.[21] Generations pass while some trees stand, and old families last not three oaks. To be read by bare inscriptions like many in Gruter,[22] to hope for eternity by enigmatical epithets or first letters of our names, to be studied by antiquaries, who we were, and have new names given us like many of the mummies, are cold consolations unto the students of perpetuity, even by everlasting languages.

To be content that times to come should only know there was such a man, not caring whether they knew more of him, was a frigid ambition in Cardan,[23] disparaging his horoscopical inclination and judgement of himself. Who cares to subsist like Hippocrates' patients, or Achilles' horses in Homer, under naked nominations, without deserts and noble acts, which are the balsam of our memories, the *entelechia* [24] and soul of our subsistences? To be nameless in worthy deeds, exceeds [25] an infamous history. The Canaanitish woman [26] lives more happily without a name, than Herodias [27] with one. And who had not rather have been the good thief than Pilate?

But the iniquity of oblivion blindly scattereth her poppy, and deals with the memory of men without distinction to merit of perpetuity. Who can but pity the founder of the pyramids? Herostratus [28] lives that burnt the temple of Diana, he is almost lost that built it. Time hath spared the epitaph of Adrian's [29] horse, confounded that of himself. In vain we compute our felicities by the advantage of our good names, since bad have equal durations, and Thersites [30] is like to live as long as Agamemnon. Who knows whether the best of men be known, or whether there be not more remarkable persons forgot, than any that stand remembered in the known account of time? Without the favour of the everlasting register, the first man had been as unknown as the last, and Methuselah's long life had been his only chronicle.

Oblivion is not to be hired. The greater part must be content to be as though they had not been, to be found in the register of God, not in the record of man. Twenty-seven names make up the first story,[31] and the recorded names ever since contain not one living century. The number of the dead long exceedeth all that shall live. The night of time far surpasseth the day, and who knows when was the equinox? Every hour adds unto that current [32] arithmetic, which scarce stands one moment. And since death must be the *Lucina* [33] of

21. "Old ones being taken up, and other bodies laid under them" (Browne's note); see also Donne, "The Relic."
22. Jan Gruter (1560–1627), Dutch Latinist.
23. Girolamo Cardano, Italian mathematician (1501–76).
24. Essential life force or principle.
25. Outdoes.
26. Matthew 15:22–28; she is known only as "a woman of Canaan."
27. Mark 6:17; Herodias forced her daughter Salome to ask for the head of John the Baptist.
28. He burned the Ephesian temple in order to be remembered.
29. The Emperor Hadrian's, for whom he composed an epitaph.
30. Homer's nasty cynic, in the *Iliad*.
31. In Genesis 5, the genealogy from Adam to Noah contains 27 names; there have not been 100 (a century of) generations of recorded names since the Deluge.
32. Continual.
33. Roman goddess of childbirth.

life, and even Pagans could doubt, whether thus to live were to die; since our longest sun sets at right descensions, and makes but winter arches, and therefore it cannot be long before we lie down in darkness, and have our light in ashes; [34] since the brother of death [35] daily haunts us with dying mementos, and time that grows old in itself, bids us hope no long duration;—diuturnity is a dream and folly of expectation.

Darkness and light divide the course of time, and oblivion shares with memory a great part even of our living beings; we slightly remember our felicities, and the smartest strokes of affliction leave but short smart upon us. Sense endureth no extremities, and sorrows destroy us or themselves. To weep into stones [36] are fables. Afflictions induce callosities; [37] miseries are slippery, or fall like snow upon us, which notwithstanding is no unhappy stupidity. To be ignorant of evils to come, and forgetful of evils past, is a merciful provision in nature, whereby we digest the mixture of our few and evil days, and, our delivered senses not relapsing into cutting rememberances, our sorrows are not kept raw by the edge of repetitions. A great part of antiquity contented their hopes of subsistency with a transmigration of their souls,—a good way to continue their memories, while having the advantage of plural successions, they could not but act something remarkable in such variety of beings, and enjoying the fame of their passed selves, make accumulation of glory unto their last durations. Others, rather than be lost in the uncomfortable night of nothing, were content to recede into the common being, and make one particle of the public soul of all things, which was no more than to return into their unknown and divine original again. Egyptian ingenuity was more unsatisfied, contriving their bodies in sweet consistencies, to attend the return of their souls. But all was vanity, feeding the wind, and folly. The Egyptian mummies which Cambyses [38] or time hath spared, avarice now consumeth. Mummy [39] is become merchandise, Mizraim [40] cures wounds, and Pharaoh is sold for balsams.

In vain do individuals hope for immortality, or any patent from oblivion, in preservations below the moon; [41] men have been deceived even in their flatteries above the sun, and studied conceits to perpetuate their names in heaven. The various cosmography of that part hath already varied the names of contrived constellations. Nimrod is lost in Orion, and Osiris in the Dog-star.[42] While we look for incorruption in the heavens, we find they are but like the earth;—durable in their main bodies, alterable in their parts; whereof, beside comets and new stars, perspectives [43] begin to tell tales, and the

---

34. "According to the custom of the Jews, who place a lighted wax candle in a pot of ashes by the corpse" (Browne's note, added to later editions).
35. Sleep.
36. To turn, like the weeping Niobe of myth, into stone.
37. Hardenings, insensitivities.
38. The Persian conqueror of Egypt.
39. Powdered mummies, sold as a pharmaceutical.
40. In Hebrew, "Egypt"; also, one of the sons of Ham, Noah's son.
41. Hope of continued existence in any sublunary (actual) mode.
42. Now called Sirius.
43. Telescopes.

spots that wander about the sun, with Phaeton's favour,[44] would make clear conviction.

There is nothing strictly immortal but immortality. Whatever hath no beginning may be confident of no end (all others have a dependent being and within the reach of destruction); which is the peculiar [45] of that necessary Essence that cannot destroy itself; and the highest strain of omnipotency, to be so powerfully constituted as not to suffer even from the power of itself. But the sufficiency of Christian immortality frustrates all earthly glory, and the quality of either state after death, makes a folly of posthumous memory. God who can only [46] destroy our souls, and hath assured our resurrection, either of our bodies or names, hath directly promised no duration. Wherein there is so much of chance that the boldest expectants [47] have found unhappy frustration; and to hold long subsistence seems but a scape in [48] oblivion. But man is a noble animal, splendid in ashes, and pompous [49] in the grave, solemnizing nativities and deaths with equal lustre, nor omitting ceremonies of bravery in the infamy of his nature.

Life is a pure flame, and we live by an invisible sun within us. A small fire sufficeth for life, great flames seemed too little after death, while men vainly affected precious pyres, and to burn like Sardanapalus; [50] but the wisdom of funeral laws found the folly of prodigal blazes, and reduced undoing fires unto the rule of sober obsequies, wherein few could be so mean as not to provide wood, pitch, a mourner, and an urn.

Five languages secured not the epitaph of Gordianus.[51] The man of God lives longer without a tomb, than any by one, invisibly interred by angels,[52] and adjudged to obscurity, though not without some marks directing human discovery. Enoch and Elias,[53] without either tomb or burial, in an anomalous state of being, are the great examples of perpetuity, in their long and living memory, in strict account being still on this side death, and having a late part yet to act upon this stage of earth. If in the decretory term [54] of the world, we shall not all die but be changed, according to received translation, the last day will make but few graves; at least quick resurrections will anticipate lasting sepultures. Some graves will be opened before they be quite closed, and Lazarus [55] be no wonder. When many that feared to die, shall groan that they can die but once, the dismal state is the second and living death, when life puts despair on the damned, when men shall wish the coverings of mountains, not of monuments, and annihilations shall be courted.

44. Phaëthon, who drove his father's chariot of the sun in a reckless course (burning the deserts and freezing out the poles), was also for Browne a wandering spot (sunspots had recently been observed by Galileo).
45. Peculiarity.
46. Alone.
47. Those who wait and watch for something.
48. Cheat for.
49. Stately.
50. An Assyrian king who had an entire palace and its inhabitants burned as his funeral pyre.
51. Roman emperor (238–244); all his five epitaphs were obliterated.
52. Moses (Deuteronomy 34:6).
53. Elijah and Enoch were both so good that they were transported directly to heaven.
54. The decreed end, at the Last Judgment.
55. Raised from the dead by Christ (John 11:1–45).

While some have studied monuments, others have studiously declined them, and some have been so vainly boisterous, that they durst not acknowledge their graves; wherein Alaricus [56] seems most subtle, who had a river turned to hide his bones at the bottom. Even Sylla,[57] that thought himself safe in his urn, could not prevent revenging tongues, and stones thrown at his monument. Happy are they whom privacy makes innocent, who deal so with men in this world, that they are not afraid to meet them in the next; who, when they die, make no commotion among the dead, and are not touched with that poetical taunt of Isaiah.[58]

Pyramids, arches, obelisks, were but the irregularities of vainglory, and wild enormities of ancient magnanimity. But the most magnanimous resolution rests in the Christian religion, which trampleth upon pride, and sits on the neck of ambition, humbly pursuing that infallible perpetuity, unto which all others must diminish their diameters, and be poorly seen in angles of contingency.[59]

Pious spirits who passed their days in raptures of futurity, made little more of this world than the world that was before it, while they lay obscure in the chaos of preordination, and night of their forebeings. And if any have been so happy as truly to understand Christian annihilation, ecstasies, exolution,[60] liquefaction, transformation, the kiss of the spouse, gustation of God, and ingression into the divine shadow, they have already had an handsome anticipation of heaven; the glory of the world is surely over, and the earth in ashes unto them.

To subsist in lasting monuments, to live in their productions, to exist in their names and predicament of chimeras,[61] was large satisfaction unto old expectations, and made one part of their Elysiums. But all this is nothing in the metaphysics of true belief. To live indeed, is to be again ourselves, which being not only an hope, but an evidence in noble believers, 'tis all one to lie in St. Innocents' [62] church-yard, as in the sands of Egypt. Ready to be any thing, in the ecstasy of being ever, and as content with six foot as the *moles* of Adrianus.[63]

> *—tabesne cadavera solvat,*
> *An rogus, haud refert.*[64]—Lucan

1658

56. Alaric the Goth had himself interred beneath a river-bed.
57. Roman general.
58. "Is this the man that made the earth to tremble, that did shake kingdoms?"—asked of those about to be cast into Hell (Isaiah 14:16).
59. "*Angulus contingentiae,* the least of angles" (Browne's note); the smallest possible angle, thus the narrowest view and the most contingent in the ordinary sense.
60. The escape of soul from the body's confines.
61. Fictive monsters.
62. "In Paris, where bodies soon consume" (Browne's note).
63. "A stately mausoleum or sepulchural pile, built by Adrianus in Rome, where now stands the castle of St. Angelo" (Browne's note).
64. "Whether funeral pyre or grave swallows the corpses matters little" (*Pharsalia* VII. 809).

The Garden of Cyrus

A strange and, to us, obsessive little work, one that nevertheless manages to combine Browne's scientific and hieroglyphical interests even more elegantly than the *Hydriotaphia, Urn Burial*, is *The Garden of Cyrus*. It begins with a discussion of the quincunx, or "decussated" pattern of planting employed in the Persian emperor's fabled gardens, but quickly dissolves into a meditation on the hieroglyphical and emblematic significances of the quincunxial figure

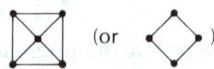

Rectangles, rhombs, cones, and pyramids, figures denoting five and ten, men and trees inverted into one another—all of these fancies are intermingled with piercing botanical and zoological questions. Readers interested in the mathematics of biological patterns will want to look at the great *Growth and Form* by Darcy Wentworth Thompson, a modern work curiously analogous to Browne's in some ways.

From The Garden of Cyrus

Chapter IV

The cylindrical figure of trees is virtually contained and latent in this order: a cylinder or long round being made by the conversion or turning of a parallelogram, and most handsomely by a long square, which makes an equal, strong, and lasting figure in trees, agreeable unto the body and motive part of animals, the greatest number of plants, and almost all roots, though their stalk be angular, and of many corners, which seem not to follow the figure of their seeds (since many angular seeds send forth round stalks, and spherical seeds arise from angular spindles, and many rather conform unto their roots, as the round stalks of bulbous roots and in tuberous roots stems of like figure). But why, since the largest number of plants maintain a circular figure, there are so few with teretous or long round leaves? Why coniferous trees are tenuifolious or narrow-leafed? Why plants of few or no joints have commonly round stalks? Why the greatest number of hollow stalks are round stalks; or why in this variety of angular stalks the quadrangular most exceedeth, were too long a speculation? Meanwhile obvious experience may find, that in plants of divided leaves above, nature often beginneth circularly in the two first leaves below, while in the singular plant of ivy she exerciseth a contrary geometry, and beginning with angular leaves below, rounds them in the upper branches.

. . . .

Beside, in this kind of aspect the sight being not diffused, but circumscribed between long parallels and the ἐπισκιασμὸς [1] and adumbration [2] from the branches, it frameth a penthouse over the eye, and maketh a quiet vision:—and therefore in diffused and open aspects, men hollow their hand above their

---

1. Episkiasmos, a shading or covering.
2. The same in Latinate English.

eye, and make an artificial brow, whereby they direct the dispersed rays of sight, and by this shade preserve a moderate light in the chamber of the eye; keeping the pupilla plump and fair, and not contracted or shrunk, as in light and vagrant vision.

And therefore Providence hath arched and paved the great house of the world, with colours of mediocrity, that is, blue and green, above and below the sight, moderately terminating the *acies* [3] of the eye. For most plants, though green above ground, maintain their original white below it, according to the candour of their seminal pulp: and the rudimental leaves do first appear in that colour, observable in seeds sprouting in water upon their first foliation. Green seeming to be the first supervenient,[4] or above ground complexion of vegetables, separable in many upon ligature or inhumation, as succory, endive, artichokes, and which is also lost upon fading in the autumn.

. . .

Nor are only dark and green colours, but shades and shadows contrived through the great volume of nature, and trees ordained not only to protect and shadow others, but by their shades and shadowing parts, to preserve and cherish themselves: the whole radiation or branchings shadowing the stock and the root;—the leaves, the branches and fruit, too much exposed to the winds and scorching sun. The calicular [5] leaves enclose the tender flowers, and the flowers themselves lie wrapt about the seeds, in their rudiment and first formations, which being advanced, the flowers fall away; and are therefore contrived in variety of figures, best satisfying the intention; handsomely observable in hooded and gaping flowers, and the butterfly blooms of leguminous plants, the lower leaf closely involving the rudimental cod, and the alary or wingy divisions embracing or hanging over it.

But seeds themselves do lie in perpetual shades, either under the leaf, or shut up in coverings; and such as lie barest, have their husks, skins, and pulps about them, wherein the nib and generative particle lieth moist and secured from the injury of air and sun. Darkness and light hold interchangeable dominions, and alternately rule the seminal state of things. Light unto Pluto is darkness unto Jupiter. Legions of seminal ideas lie in their second chaos and Orcus [6] of Hippocrates; till putting on the habits of their forms, they show themselves upon the stage of the world, and open dominion of Jove. They that held the stars of heaven were but rays and flashing glimpses of the empyreal light, through holes and perforations of the upper heaven, took off the natural shadows of stars; while according to better discovery the poor inhabitants of the moon have but a polary life, and must pass half their days in the shadow of that luminary.

Light that makes things seen, makes some things invisible; were it not for darkness and the shadow of the earth, the noblest part of the creation had remained unseen, and the stars in heaven as invisible as on the fourth day, when they were created above the horizon with the sun, or there was not an eye to behold them. The greatest mystery of religion is expressed by adumbra-

3. Range of vision.
4. Suddenly appearing.
5. Of the calyx.
6. The original Roman god of the Underworld, later assimilated with the Greek Hades.

tion, and in the noblest part of Jewish types,[7] we find the cherubims shadowing the mercy-seat. Life itself is but the shadow of death, and souls departed but the shadows of the living. All things fall under this name. The sun itself is but the dark *simulachrum*,[8] and light but the shadow of God. . . .

Chapter V

To enlarge this contemplation unto all the mysteries and secrets accommodable unto this number, were inexcusable Pythagorism,[9] yet cannot omit the ancient conceit of five surnamed the number of justice; as justly dividing between the digits, and hanging in the centre of nine, described by square numeration, which angularly divided will make the decussated [10] number; and so agreeable unto the quincuncial ordination, and rows divided by equality, and just decorum, in the whole com-plantation; and might be the original of that common game among us, wherein the fifth place is sovereign, and carrieth the chief intention—the ancients wisely instructing youth, even in their recreations unto virtue, that is, early to drive at the middle point and central seat of justice.

Nor can we omit how agreeable unto this number an handsome division is made in trees and plants, since Plutarch, and the ancients have named it the divisive number, justly dividing the entities of the world, many remarkable things in it, and also comprehending the general division of vegetables.[11] And he that considers how most blossoms of trees, and greatest number of flowers, consist of five leaves, and therein doth rest the settled rule of nature— so that in those which exceed, there is often found, or easily made, a variety— may readily discover how nature rests in this number, which is indeed the first rest and pause of numeration in the fingers, the natural organs thereof. Nor in the division of the feet of perfect animals doth nature exceed this account. And even in the joints of feet, which in birds are most multiplied, surpasseth not this number; so progressionally making them out in many,[12] that from five in the fore-claw she descendeth unto two in the hindmost; and so in four feet makes up the number of joints, in the five fingers or toes of man.

Not to omit the quintuple section of a cone,[13] of handsome practice in ornamental garden-plots, and in same way discoverable in so many works of nature, in the leaves, fruits, and seeds of vegetables, and scales of some fishes; so much considerable in glasses, and the optic doctrine; wherein the learned may consider the crystalline humour of the eye in the cuttle-fish and loligo.

He that forgets not how antiquity named this the conjugal or wedding number, and made it the emblem of the most remarkable conjunction, will

---

7. Prefigurations in the Old Testament of events in the New.
8. Likeness.
9. But Browne is, in pursuing this discussion of 5-ness, being wildly Pythagorean.
10. Literally, criss-crossed like an X, that being the Roman numeral denoting ten. The decussated pattern, or quincunx, is the central hieroglyphic of this meditation. See Head-note.
11. Browne lists *arbor, frutex, suffrutex, herba,* and a fifth category including *fungi* and *tubera.*
12. "As herons, bitterns and long-clawed fowls" (Browne's note).
13. Browne lists as the conic sections: ellipse, parabola, hyperbola, circle, and triangle.

conceive it duly appliable unto this handsome economy, and vegetable combination: and may hence apprehend the allegorical sense of that obscure expression of Hesiod,[14] and afford no improbable reason why Plato admitted his nuptial guests by fives, in the kindred of the married couple.[15]

And though a sharper mystery might be implied in the number of the five wise and foolish virgins, which were to meet the bridegroom, yet was the same agreeable unto the conjugal number, which ancient numerists made out by two and three, the first parity and imparity, the active and passive digits, the material and formal principles in generative societies. And not discordant even from the customs of the Romans, who admitted but five torches in their nuptial solemnities. Whether there were any mystery or not, implied, the most generative animals were created on this day, and had accordingly the largest benediction. And under a quintuple consideration, wanton antiquity considered the circumstances of generation, while by this number of five they naturally divided the nectar of the fifth planet.

. . .

If any shall question the rationality of that magic, in the cure of the blind man by Serapis,[16] commanded to place five fingers on his altar, and then his hand on his eyes? Why, since the whole comedy is primarily and naturally comprised in four parts,[17] and antiquity permitted not so many persons to speak in one scene, yet would not comprehend the same in more or less than five acts? Why amongst sea-stars nature chiefly delighteth in five points? And since there are found some of no fewer than twelve, and some of seven, and nine, there are few or none discovered of six or eight? If any shall enquire why the flowers of rue properly consist of four leaves, the first and third flower have five? Why, since many flowers have one leaf or none, as Scaliger will have it, divers three, and the greatest number consist of five divided from their bottoms, there are yet so few of two? or why nature generally beginning or setting out with two opposite leaves at the root, doth so seldom conclude with that order and number at the flower? He shall not pass his hours in vulgar speculations.

If any shall further query why magnetical philosophy excludeth decussations, and needles transversely placed do naturally distract their verticities? Why geomancers[18] do imitate the quintuple figure, in their mother characters of acquisition and amission,[19] &c., somewhat answering the figures in the lady or speckled beetle? With what equity chiromantical[20] conjecturers decry these decussations in the lines and mounts of the hand? What that decussated figure intendeth in the medal of Alexander the Great? Why the goddesses sit commonly cross-legged in ancient draughts, since Juno is described in the same as a beneficial posture to hinder the birth of Hercules? If any shall doubt why at

14. To the effect that it was a marriage number (*Works and Days*, l. 802).
15. In the *Laws*.
16. Osiris in his role as ruler of the Underworld.
17. Browne lists: *protasis* (introduction); *epitasis* (onset of action); *katastasis* (development); and *katastrophe* (turnabout).
18. Earth magicians.
19. Loss.
20. Chiromancy is palmistry.

the amphidromical feasts,[21] on the fifth day after the child was born, presents were sent from friends, of polypuses and cuttle-fishes? Why five must be only left in that symbolical mutiny among the men of Cadmus? [22] Why Proteus in Homer, the symbol of the first matter, before he settled himself in the midst of his sea-monsters, doth place them out by fives? Why the fifth year's ox was acceptable sacrifice unto Jupiter? Or why the noble Antoninus [23] in some sense doth call the soul itself a rhombus? He shall not fall on trite or trivial disquisitions. And these we invent and propose unto acuter enquirers, nauseating crambe verities and questions over-queried. Flat and flexible truths are beat out by every hammer; but Vulcan and his whole forge sweat to work out Achilles his armour. A large field is yet left unto sharper discerners to enlarge upon this order, to search out the *quaternios* [24] and figured draughts of this nature, and (moderating the study of names, and mere nomenclature of plants), to erect generalities, disclose unobserved proprieties, not only in the vegetable shop, but the whole volume of nature; affording delightful truths, confirmable by sense and ocular observation, which seems to me the surest path to trace the labyrinth of truth. For though discursive enquiry and rational conjecture may leave handsome gashes and flesh-wounds; yet without conjunction of this, expect no mortal or dispatching blows unto error.

But the quincunx [25] of heaven runs low, and 'tis time to close the five ports of knowledge. We are unwilling to spin out our awaking thoughts into the phantasms of sleep, which often continueth precogitations, making cables of cobwebs, and wildernesses of handsome groves. Beside Hippocrates [26] hath spoke so little, and the oneirocritical [27] masters have left such frigid interpretations from plants, that there is little encouragement to dream of Paradise itself. Nor will the sweetest delight of gardens afford much comfort in sleep; wherein the dulness of that sense shakes hands with delectable odours; and though in the bed of Cleopatra,[28] can hardly with any delight raise up the ghost of a rose.

Night, which Pagan theology could make the daughter of Chaos, affords no advantage to the description of order; although no lower than that mass can we derive its genealogy. All things began in order, so shall they end, and so shall they begin again; according to the ordainer of order and mystical mathematics of the city of heaven.

Though Somnus in Homer be sent to rouse up Agamemnon, I find no such effects in these drowsy approaches of sleep. To keep our eyes open longer, were but to act our Antipodes.[29] The huntsmen are up in America, and they are already past their first sleep in Persia. But who can be drowsy at that hour

21. Athenian festival of consecration of the newborn.
22. Cadmus sowed a crop of dragon's teeth and reaped an army whose combatants fought each other to death, except for five survivors.
23. Marcus Aurelius, in his *Meditations*.
24. Quadruples.
25. "The Hyades, near the horizon about midnight at that time" (Browne's note).
26. The great Greek physician.
27. Pertaining to the theory of dreams.
28. "Strewed with roses" (Browne's note).
29. "To act out the roles of our diametrical counterparts at the bottom of the globe" (Browne's note).

which freed us from everlasting sleep? or have slumbering thoughts at that time, when sleep itself must end, and as some conjecture all shall awake again. . . .

1658

From Miscellanies

[On the Blindness of Cupid]

Cupid is seen to be blind;[1] affection should not be too sharp-sighted, and love not to be made by magnifying glasses: if things were seen as they are, the beauty of bodies would be much abridged, and therefore the wisdom of God hath drawn the pictures and outsides of things softly and amiably unto the natural edge of our eyes, not to be able to discover those unlevel asperities which make oystershells in good faces, and hedgehogs even in Venus' moles.

From The Notebooks

[On Dreams]

Half our days we pass in the shadow of the earth; and the brother of death exacteth a third part of our lives. A good part of our sleep is peered out with visions and fantastical objects, wherein we are confessedly deceived. The day supplieth us with truths; the night with fictions and falsehoods, which un-comfortably divide the natural account of our beings. And, therefore, having passed the day in sober labours and rational enquiries of truth, we are fain to betake ourselves unto such a state of being, wherein the soberest heads have acted all the monstrosities of melancholy, and which unto open eyes are no better than folly and madness.

Happy are they that go to bed with grand music, like Pythagoras, or have ways to compose the fantastical spirit, whose unruly wanderings take off inward sleep, filling our heads with St. Anthony's visions, and the dreams of Lipara[1] in the sober chambers of rest.

Virtuous thoughts of the day lay up good treasures for the night; whereby the impressions of imaginary forms arise into sober similitudes, acceptable unto our slumbering selves and preparatory unto divine impressions. Hereby Solomon's sleep was happy. Thus prepared, Jacob might well dream of angels upon a pillow of stone. And the best sleep of Adam might be the best of any after.[2]

1. See Bacon's account of this in "Cupid, or the Atom," and Marlowe's *Hero and Leander* I.48n. Also see Jonathan Swift's "A Digression Concerning Madness" for a brilliant and sharp use of Browne's providential biology to bait, and entrap, the optimistic reader.

1. St. Anthony of Egypt was tempted by and plagued by monstrous visions; the Lipari were the Aeolian Islands off Sicily, and the site of the fabled workshop of Vulcan, where all the automata of antiquity were made.
2. The sleep of Adam's unfallen first night, calmer than ours.

That there should be divine dreams seems unreasonably doubted by Aristotle. That there are demoniacal dreams we have little reason to doubt. Why may there not be angelical? If there be guardian spirits, they may not be inactively about us in sleep; but may sometimes order our dreams: and many strange hints, instigations, or discourses, which are so amazing unto us, may arise from such foundations.

.   .   .

There is an art to make dreams, as well as their interpretations, and physicians will tell us that some food makes turbulent, some gives quiet, dreams. Cato,[3] who doted upon cabbage, might find the crude effects thereof in his sleep; wherein the Egyptians might find some advantage by their superstitious abstinence from onions. Pythagoras might have calmer sleeps, if he totally abstained from beans. Even Daniel, the great interpreter of dreams, in his leguminous diet, seems to have chosen no advantageous food for quiet sleeps, according to Grecian physic.[4]

To add unto the delusion of dreams, the fantastical objects seem greater than they are; and being beheld in the vaporous state of sleep, enlarge their diameters unto us; whereby it may prove more easy to dream of giants than pigmies. Democritus [5] might seldom dream of atoms, who so often thought of them. He almost might dream himself a bubble extending unto the eighth sphere. A little water makes a sea; a small puff of wind a tempest. A grain of sulphur kindled in the blood may make a flame like Ætna; [6] and a small spark in the bowels of Olympias a lightning over all the chamber.

But, beside these innocent delusions, there is a sinful state of dreams. Death alone, not sleep, is able to put an end unto sin; and there may be a night-book of our iniquities; for beside the transgressions of the day, casuists will tell us of mortal sins in dreams, arising from evil precogitations; meanwhile human law regards not noctambulos; and if a night-walker should break his neck, or kill a man, takes no notice of it.

Dionysius was absurdly tyrannical to kill a man for dreaming that he had killed him; and really to take away his life, who had but fantastically taken away his. Lamia [7] was ridiculously unjust to sue a young man for a reward, who had confessed that pleasure from her in a dream which she had denied unto his awaking senses: conceiving that she had merited somewhat from his fantastical fruition and shadow of herself. If there be such debts, we owe deeply unto sympathies; but the common spirit of the world must be ready in such arrearages.

If some have swooned, they may have also died in dreams, since death is but a confirmed swooning. Whether Plato died in a dream, as some deliver,[8] he must rise again to inform us. That some have never dreamed, is as improbable as that some have never laughed. That children dream not the first

3. Marcus Porcius Cato ("The Censor"), Roman leader (234–149 B.C.).
4. Medical science.
5. The Greek atomist; see above, Burton's *Anatomy of Melancholy*.
6. The great Sicilian volcano.
7. One of the monsters with women's heads and breasts and serpents' bodies; they drank the blood of fair young men and children.
8. Report.

half-year; that men dream not in some countries, with many more, are unto me sick men's dreams—dreams out of the ivory gate,[9] and visions before midnight.

THOMAS HOBBES
1588–1679

Hobbes, who worked for Bacon as his secretary, began his own philosophical career late, as a Royalist exile in Paris (1640–51). His major work, Leviathan, came out in the year of his return, when he made his peace with the Cromwellian regime. The writing of the book, and that of the Answer to Davenant's Preface Before "Gondibert," belongs to his time in Paris, where Davenant was also in exile. After the Restoration he wrote many more works of all kinds—translations, histories, geometrical studies, controversies with Descartes and others. Aubrey, his close friend, left an amusing account of the philosopher: he grew healthy after forty, was bald, good-natured, and witty, got drunk one hundred times in his long life, played tennis at seventy-five, was timid by nature, and liked to shut himself up and sing for the good of his health.

As a thinker, however, he attracted fierce opposition; his thought was too ruthlessly materialistic to escape censure from many different opponents. "The universe is corporeal; all that is real is material, and what is not material is not real" (Leviathan 46). Although Hobbes was at least nominally a Christian, this kind of philosophy pleased neither orthodox Christians nor others who accepted a supernatural element in the workings of the world. He had a particular contempt for the Aristotelianism of the scholastic philosophers, and this endeared him to proponents of the new science, so that his name was associated with that of Bacon in the minds of those who formed the Royal Society for the study by observation and experiment of problems in natural philosophy.

Hobbes attempted a return to first principles, to a few axioms of the kind he admired in Euclid, and banished from his philosophy the kind of abstraction favored by the scholastics, which seemed to him to signify nothing. The soul and its operations had to be reduced to materiality to mean anything. Our perceptions of the world are really of the pressures materially exerted on us by external "motions."

Rejecting the soul, he rejected free will as well; the passions are influenced by external "motions," which, if they please, cause in us an appetite and seem good, and, if they displease, cause aversion and seem evil. Men are therefore complicated automata, and their involuntary appetites would cause them to destroy one another if there were no arrangements whereby their common life could be regulated by authority and force. So Hobbes defended absolute sovereignty; men must "confer all their power and strength upon one man, or upon one assembly of men. . . ." This is his Commonwealth, in which all men conjoin their power in one, the great Leviathan.

In the chapter "Of Imagination" we see Hobbes providing a materialist explanation of that power of the soul which was usually thought to have least dependence on

9. There were two fabled gates to the regions of sleep: through the ivory gates, false dreams emerged into the world; through the more ordinary gates of horn, the true dreams.

outward impulses: the imagination, or fantasy, surely, operated independently of the senses in lunatics, lovers, poets, and dreamers. Not for Hobbes; it is merely decayed memory. A proper understanding of this would abolish superstition and fit men better for "civil obedience." The importance of all this emerges both in his account of man's natural lust for power (Chapter XI) and in the famous Chapter XIII, on the natural state of man without the order and restraint of the state: a life "solitary, poor, nasty, brutish, and short."

In the *Answer to Davenant's Preface* we find Hobbes in a more urbane mood, but his aesthetic is consistent with the rest of his philosophy. From Memory derive both Judgment and Fancy (Imagination); the first handles the design, the second the ornaments of the poem. Thus "wit," which earlier meant the full power of the mind, was now, without losing its distinctive characteristics of speed and "farfetchedness," given a subordinate role and distinguished from judgment.

On the divisions of poetry Hobbes is again consistent; nature imposes externally three styles of life, in country, city, and court, and men arrange their poetry accordingly. And the manners of men are the true subject of poetry, not the gods, ghosts, and fictive beings of the old epic. It is worth remembering, finally, that Hobbes's philosophy did not impel him to dismiss poetry altogether, despite his materialism. He can, indeed, be defended as a pioneer of the new aesthetic theories required to support poetry in an age of rationalism which might have rejected it.

Leviathan

From *Chapter II: Of Imagination*

That when a thing lies still, unless somewhat else stir it, it will lie still for ever, is a truth that no man doubts of. But that when a thing is in motion, it will eternally be in motion, unless somewhat else stay it, though the reason be the same, namely, that nothing can change itself, is not so easily assented to. For men measure, not only other men, but all other things, by themselves; and because they find themselves subject, after motion, to pain and lassitude, think everything else grows weary of motion, and seeks repose of its own accord; little considering whether it be not some other motion, wherein that desire of rest they find in themselves consisteth. From hence it is that the schools [1] say, heavy bodies fall downwards out of an appetite to rest, and to conserve their nature in that place which is most proper for them; ascribing appetite, and knowledge of what is good for their conservation, which is more than man has,[2] to things inanimate, absurdly.

When a body is once in motion, it moveth, unless something else hinder it, eternally; and whatsoever hindereth it cannot in an instant, but in time and by degrees, quite extinguish it; and as we see in the water, though the wind cease, the waves give not over rolling for a long time after: so also it happeneth in that motion which is made in the internal parts of a man, then,

---

1. Scholastic philosophers.
2. It is an essential condition of Hobbes's thought that man does not naturally possess the means of self-preservation.

when he sees, dreams, etc. For after the object is removed, or the eye shut, we still retain an image of the thing seen, though more obscure than when we see it. And this is it, the Latins call *imagination,* from the image made in seeing; and apply the same, though improperly, to all the other senses. But the Greeks call it *fancy;* which signifies appearance, and is as proper to one sense, as to another. Imagination therefore is nothing but *decaying sense;* and is found in men, and many other living creatures, as well sleeping as waking.

The decay of sense in men waking, is not the decay of the motion made in sense; but an obscuring of it, in such manner as the light of the sun obscureth the light of the stars; which stars do no less exercise their virtue, by which they are visible, in the day than in the night. But because amongst many strokes which our eyes, ears, and other organs receive from external bodies, the predominant only is sensible; therefore, the light of the sun being predominant, we are not affected with the action of the stars. And any object being removed from our eyes, though the impression it made in us remain, yet other objects more present succeeding and working on us, the imagination of the past is obscured and made weak, as the voice of a man is in the noise of the day. From whence it followeth that the longer the time is, after the sight or sense of any object, the weaker is the imagination. For the continual change of man's body destroys in time the parts which in sense were moved; so that distance of time, and of place, hath one and the same effect in us. For as at a great distance of place, that which we look at appears dim, and without distinction of the smaller parts; and as voices grow weak, and inarticulate; so also, after great distance of time, our imagination of the past is weak; and we lose, for example, of cities we have seen, many particular streets, and of actions, many particular circumstances. This decaying sense, when we would express the thing itself, I mean fancy itself, we call *imagination,* as I said before; but when we would express the decay, and signify that the sense is fading, old, and past, it is called *memory.* So that imagination and memory are but one thing,[3] which for divers considerations hath divers names.

Much memory, or memory of many things, is called *experience.* Again, imagination being only of those things which have been formerly perceived by sense, either all at once or by parts at several times; the former, which is the imagining the whole object as it was presented to the sense, is *simple* imagination, as when one imagineth a man, or horse, which he hath seen before. The other is *compounded;* as when, from the sight of a man at one time and of a horse at another, we conceive in our mind a centaur. So when a man compoundeth the image of his own person with the image of the actions of another man, as when a man imagines himself a Hercules or an Alexander, which happeneth often to them that are much taken with reading of romances, it is a compound imagination, and properly but a fiction of the mind. There be also other imaginations that rise in men, though waking, from the great impression made in sense: as from gazing upon the sun, the impression leaves an image of the sun before our eyes a long time after; and from being long and vehemently attent upon geometrical figures, a man shall in the dark, though awake, have

---

3. This is slightly different from the formulation used in the *Answer to Davenant's Preface* (below), but both are consistent with Hobbes's materialism.

the images of lines and angles before his eyes; which kind of fancy hath no particular name, as being a thing that doth not commonly fall into men's discourse.

The imaginations of them that sleep are those we call *dreams*. And these also, as all other imaginations, have been before, either totally or by parcels, in the sense. And because in sense, the brain and nerves, which are the necessary organs of sense, are so benumbed in sleep, as not easily to be moved by the action of external objects, there can happen in sleep no imagination, and therefore no dream, but what proceeds from the agitation of the inward parts of man's body; which inward parts, for the connexion they have with the brain and other organs when they be distempered, do keep the same in motion; whereby the imaginations there formerly made, appear as if a man were waking; saving that the organs of sense being now benumbed, so as there is no new object which can master and obscure them with a more vigorous impression, a dream must needs be more clear, in this silence of sense, than our waking thoughts. And hence it cometh to pass that it is a hard matter, and by many thought impossible, to distinguish exactly between sense and dreaming. For my part, when I consider that in dreams I do not often constantly think of the same persons, places, objects, and actions, that I do waking; nor remember so long a train of coherent thoughts, dreaming, as at other times; and because waking I often observe the absurdity of dreams, but never dream of the absurdities of my waking thoughts; I am well satisfied that, being awake, I know I dream not, though when I dream I think myself awake.

And seeing dreams are caused by the distemper of some of the inward parts of the body, divers distempers must needs cause different dreams. And hence it is that lying cold breedeth dreams of fear, and raiseth the thought and image of some fearful object, the motion from the brain to the inner parts and from the inner parts to the brain being reciprocal; and that as anger causeth heat in some parts of the body when we are awake, so when we sleep the overheating of the same parts causeth anger, and raiseth up in the brain the imagination of an enemy. In the same manner, as natural kindness,[4] when we are awake, causeth desire, and desire maketh heat in certain other parts of the body; so also too much heat in those parts, while we sleep, raiseth in the brain the imagination of some kindness[5] shown. In sum, our dreams are the reverse of our waking imaginations; the motion when we are awake beginning at one end, and when we dream at another.

The most difficult discerning of a man's dream from his waking thoughts is, then, when by some accident we observe not that we have slept: which is easy to happen to a man full of fearful thoughts, and whose conscience is much troubled; and that sleepeth, without the circumstances of going to bed or putting off his clothes, as one that noddeth in a chair. For he that taketh pains, and industriously lays himself to sleep, in case any uncouth and exorbitant fancy come unto him, cannot easily think it other than a dream. We read of Marcus Brutus (one that had his life given him by Julius Caesar, and was

4. Sexual attraction.
5. This usage well illustrates the range of meanings the word has in talk about love.

also his favourite, and notwithstanding murdered him), how at Philippi, the night before he gave battle to Augustus Caesar, he saw a fearful apparition, which is commonly related by historians as a vision; but considering the circumstances, one may easily judge to have been but a short dream. For sitting in his tent, pensive and troubled with the horror of his rash act, it was not hard for him, slumbering in the cold, to dream of that which most affrighted him; which fear, as by degrees it made him wake, so also it must needs make the apparition by degrees to vanish; and having no assurance that he slept, he could have no cause to think it a dream, or anything but a vision. And this is no very rare accident; for even they that be perfectly awake, if they be timorous and superstitious, possessed with fearful tales, and alone in the dark, are subject to the like fancies, and believe they see spirits and dead men's ghosts walking in churchyards; whereas it is either their fancy only, or else the knavery of such persons as make use of such superstitious fear, to pass disguised in the night to places they would not be known to haunt.

From this ignorance of how to distinguish dreams, and other strong fancies, from vision and sense, did arise the greatest part of the religion of the Gentiles in time past, that worshipped satyrs, fawns, nymphs, and the like; and nowadays the opinion that rude people have of fairies, ghosts, and goblins, and of the power of witches. For, as for witches, I think not that their witchcraft is any real power; but yet that they are justly punished, for the false belief they have that they can do such mischief, joined with their purpose to do it if they can; their trade being nearer to a new religion than to a craft or science. And for fairies, and walking ghosts, the opinion of them has, I think, been on purpose either taught or not confuted, to keep in credit the use of exorcism, of crosses, of holy water, and other such inventions of ghostly men. Nevertheless, there is no doubt but God can make unnatural apparitions; but that He does it so often as men need to fear such things more than they fear the stay or change of the course of nature, which He also can stay and change, is no point of Christian faith. But evil men, under pretext that God can do anything, are so bold as to say anything when it serves their turn, though they think it untrue; it is the part of a wise man, to believe them no farther than right reason makes that which they say appear credible. If this superstitious fear of spirits were taken away, and with it, prognostics from dreams, false prophecies, and many other things depending thereon, by which crafty ambitious persons abuse the simple people, men would be much more fitted than they are for civil obedience.

And this ought to be the work of the schools; but they rather nourish such doctrine. For, not knowing what imagination or the senses are, what they receive, they teach: some saying that imaginations rise of themselves, and have no cause; others, that they rise most commonly from the will; and that good thoughts are blown (inspired) into a man by God, and evil thoughts by the Devil; or that good thoughts are poured (infused) into a man by God, and evil ones by the Devil. Some say the senses receive the species of things, and deliver them to the common sense; and the common sense delivers them over to the fancy, and the fancy to the memory, and the memory to the judgement, like handling of things from one to another with many words making nothing understood.

The imagination that is raised in man, or any other creature indued with the faculty of imagining, by words, or other voluntary signs, is that we generally call *understanding;* and is common to man and beast. For a dog by custom will understand the call, or the rating of his master; and so will many other beasts. That understanding which is peculiar to man, is the understanding not only his will, but his conceptions and thoughts, by the sequel and contexture of the names of things into affirmation, negations, and other forms of speech. . . .

From *Chapter IV: Of Speech*

The invention of *printing*, though ingenious, compared with the invention of *letters* is no great matter. But who was the first that found the use of letters, is not known. He that first brought them into Greece, men say was Cadmus, the son of Agenor, king of Phoenicia. A profitable invention for continuing the memory of time past, and the conjunction of mankind dispersed into so many and distant regions of the earth; and withal difficult, as proceeding from a watchful observation of the divers motions of the tongue, palate, lips, and other organs of speech; whereby to make as many differences of characters, to remember them. But the most noble and profitable invention of all other, was that of *speech*, consisting of *names* or *appellations*, and their connexion; whereby men register their thoughts, recall them when they are past, and also declare them one to another for mutual utility and conversation; without which there had been amongst men neither commonwealth, nor society, nor contract, nor peace, no more than amongst lions, bears, and wolves. . . .

The general use of speech is to transfer our mental discourse into verbal, or the train of our thoughts into a train of words; and that for two commodities, whereof one is the registering of the consequences of our thoughts; which, being apt to slip out of our memory and put us to a new labour, may again be recalled by such words as they were marked by. So that the first use of names is to serve for *marks*, or *notes* of remembrance. Another is, when many use the same words, to signify, by their connexion and order, one to another, what they conceive, or think of each matter; and also what they desire, fear, or have any other passion for. And for this use they are called *signs*. Special uses of speech are these: first, to register what by cogitation we find to be the cause of anything, present or past, and what we find things present or past may produce or effect; which, in sum, is acquiring of arts. Secondly, to show to others that knowledge which we have attained; which is, to counsel and teach one another. Thirdly, to make known to others our wills and purposes, that we may have the mutual help of one another. Fourthly, to please and delight ourselves and others, by playing with our words, for pleasure or ornament, innocently.

To these uses, there are also four correspondent abuses. First, when men register their thoughts wrong, by the inconstancy of the signification of their words; by which they register for their conception, that which they never conceived, and so deceive themselves. Secondly, when they use words metaphorically; that is, in other sense than that they are ordained for; and thereby deceive others. Thirdly, by words, when they declare that to be their will which is not. Fourthly, when they use them to grieve one another; for seeing nature hath armed living creatures, some with teeth, some with horns, and some with hands, to grieve an enemy, it is but an abuse of speech, to grieve him with the tongue, unless it be one whom we are obliged to govern; and then it is not to grieve, but to correct and amend.

Seeing then that truth consisteth in the right ordering of names in our affirmations, a man that seeketh precise truth had need to remember what every name he uses stands for, and to place it accordingly, or else he will find himself entangled in words, as a bird in lime twigs, the more he struggles the more belimed. And therefore in geometry, which is the only science that it hath pleased God hitherto to bestow on mankind, men begin at settling the significations of their words; which settling of significations they call *definitions*, and place them in the beginning of their reckoning. . . .

From *Chapter XI: Of the Difference of Manners*

By *manners*, I mean not here, decency of behaviour; as how one should salute another, or how a man should wash his mouth, or pick his teeth before company, and such other points of the *small morals;* but those qualities of mankind, that concern their living together in peace, and unity. To which end we are to consider, that the felicity of this life, consisteth not in the repose of a mind satisfied. For there is no such *finis ultimus,* utmost aim, nor *summum bonum,* greatest good, as is spoken of in the books of the old moral philosophers. Nor can a man any more live, whose desires are at an end, than he, whose senses and imaginations are at a stand. Felicity is a continual progress of the desire, from one object to another; the attaining of the former, being still but the way to the latter. The cause whereof is, that the object of man's desire, is not to enjoy once only, and for one instant of time; but to assure for ever, the way of his future desire. And therefore the voluntary actions, and inclinations of all men, tend, not only to the procuring, but also to the assuring of a contented life; and differ only in the way: which ariseth partly from the diversity of passions, in divers men; and partly from the difference of the knowledge, or opinion each one has of the causes, which produce the effect desired.

So that in the first place, I put for a general inclination of all mankind, a perpetual and restless desire of power after power, that ceaseth only in death. And the cause of this, is not always that a man hopes for a more intensive delight, than he has already attained to; or that he cannot be content with a moderate power: but because he cannot assure the power and means to live well, which he hath present, without the acquisition of more. . . .

From *Chapter XIII: Of the Natural Condition of Mankind as Concerning Their Felicity and Misery*

. . . In the nature of man, we find three principal causes of quarrel. First, competition; second, diffidence; thirdly, glory.

The first maketh men invade for gain; the second, for safety; and the third, for reputation. The first use violence to make themselves masters of other men's persons, wives, children, and cattle; the second, to defend them; the third, for trifles, as a word, a smile, a different opinion, and any other sign of undervalue, either direct in their persons, or by reflection in their kindred, their friends, their nation, their profession, or their name.

Hereby it is manifest that during the time men live without a common power to keep them all in awe, they are in that condition which is called war; and such a war as is of every man against every man. For *war* consisteth not in battle only, or the act of fighting, but in a tract of time wherein the will to contend by battle is sufficiently known, and therefore the notion of *time* is to be considered in the nature of war, as it is in the nature of weather. For as the nature of foul weather lieth not in a shower or two of rain, but in an inclination thereto of many days together; so the nature of war consisteth not in actual fighting, but in the known disposition thereto, during all the time there is no assurance to the contrary. All other time is *peace.*

Whatsoever therefore is consequent to a time of war, where every man is enemy to every man; the same is consequent to the time wherein men live without other security than what their own strength and their own invention shall furnish them withal. In such condition there is no place for industry, because the fruit thereof is uncertain: and consequently no culture of the earth; no navigation, nor use of the commodities that may be imported by sea; no commodious building; no instruments of moving, and removing, such things as require much force; no knowledge of the face of the earth; no account of time; no arts; no letters; no society; and which is worst of all, continual fear, and danger of violent death; and the life of man, solitary, poor, nasty, brutish, and short.

It may seem strange to some man that has not well weighed these things, that nature should thus dissociate, and render men apt to invade and destroy one another; and he may therefore, not trusting to this inference, made from the passions, desire perhaps to have the same confirmed by experience. Let him therefore consider with himself, when taking a journey, he arms himself and seeks to go well accompanied; when going to sleep, he locks his doors; when even in his house he locks his chests; and this when he knows there be laws, and public officers, armed, to revenge all injuries shall be done him: what opinion he has of his fellow-subjects, when he rides armed; of his fellow-citizens, when he locks his doors; and of his children, and servants, when he locks his chests. Does he not there as much accuse mankind by his actions, as I do by my words? But neither of us accuse man's nature in it. The desires, and other passions of man, are in themselves no sin. No more are the actions that proceed from those passions, till they know a law that forbids them: which till laws be made they cannot know; nor can any law be made, till they have agreed upon the person that shall make it.

It may peradventure be thought, there was never such a time nor condition of war as this; and I believe it was never generally so, over all the world: but there are many places where they live so now. For the savage people in many places of America, except the government of small families, the concord whereof dependeth on natural lust, have no government at all; and live at this day in that brutish manner, as I said before. Howsoever, it may be perceived what manner of life there would be, where there were no common power to fear; by the manner of life which men that have formerly lived under a peaceful government, use to degenerate into in a civil war.

But though there had never been any time wherein particular men were in a condition of war one against another; yet in all times, kings, and persons of sovereign authority, because of their independency, are in continual jealousies, and in the state and posture of gladiators; having their weapons pointing, and their eyes fixed on one another; that is, their forts, garrisons, and guns upon the frontiers of their kingdoms; and continual spies upon their neighbours; which is a posture of war. But because they uphold thereby the industry of their subjects, there does not follow from it that misery which accompanies the liberty of particular men.

To this war of every man against every man, this also is consequent: *that nothing can be unjust.* The notions of right and wrong, justice and injustice, have there no place. Where there is no common power, there is no law; where no law, no injustice. Force and fraud are in war the two cardinal virtues. Justice and injustice are none of the faculties neither of the body nor mind. If they were, they might be in a man that were alone in the world, as well as his senses and passions. They are qualities that relate to men in society, not insolitude. It is consequent also to the same condition, that there be no propriety, no dominion, no *mine* and *thine* distinct; but only that to be every man's, that he can get; and for so long as he can keep it. And thus much for the ill condition which man by mere nature is actually placed in; though with a possibility to come out of it, consisting partly in the passions, partly in his reason.

The passions that incline men to peace are fear of death, desire of such things as are necessary to commodious living, and a hope by their industry to obtain them. And reason suggesteth convenient articles of peace, upon which men may be drawn to agreement. . . .

1651

The Answer to Davenant's Preface Before *Gondibert*

SIR,

If to commend your poem, I should only say (in general terms) that in the choice of your argument, the disposition of the parts, the maintenance of the characters of your persons, the dignity and vigour of your expression you have performed all the parts of various experience, ready memory, clear judgment, swift and well governed fancy, though it were enough for the truth, it were too little for the weight and credit of my testimony. For I lie open to two exceptions, one of an incompetent, the other of a corrupted witness. Incompetent, because I am not a poet; [1] and corrupted with the honour done me by your preface. [2] The former obliges me to say something (by the way) of the nature and differences of poesy.

As philosophers have divided the universe (their subject) into three regions, celestial, aerial, and terrestrial; so the poets (whose work it is by imitating human life, in delightful and measured lines, to avert men from vice, and incline them to virtuous and honourable actions) have lodged themselves in the three regions of mankind, court, city, and country correspondent in some proportion, to those three regions of the world. For there is in princes and men of con-

---

1. In fact Hobbes wrote a good deal of poetry, nearly all in Latin.
2. Davenant's long and critically important *Preface* was dedicated "to his much honoured friend, Mr. Hobbes."

spicuous power (anciently called heroes) a lustre and influence upon the rest of men, resembling that of the heavens; and an insincereness, inconstancy, and troublesome humour of those that dwell in populous cities, like the mobility, blustering, and impurity of the air; and a plainness, and (though dull) yet a nutritive faculty in rural people, that endures a comparison with the earth they labour.

From hence have proceeded three sorts of poesy, heroic, scommatic,[3] and pastoral. Every one of these is distinguished again in the manner of representation, which sometimes is narrative, wherein the poet himself relateth, and sometimes dramatic, as when the persons are every one adorned and brought upon the theatre, to speak and act their own parts. There is therefore neither more nor less than six sorts of poesy. For the heroic poem narrative (such as is yours) is called an epic poem; the heroic poem dramatic, is tragedy. The scommatic narrative, is satire; dramatic is comedy. The pastoral narrative, is called simply pastoral (anciently bucolic) the same dramatic, pastoral comedy. The figure therefore of an epic poem, and of a tragedy, ought to be the same, for they differ no more but in that they are pronounced by one, or many persons. Which I insert to justify the figure of yours, consisting of five books divided into songs or cantos, as five acts divided into scenes has ever been the approved figure of a tragedy.[4]

They that take for poesy whatsoever is writ in verse, will think this division imperfect, and call in sonnets, epigrams, eclogues, and the like pieces (which are but essays, and parts of an entire poem) and reckon Empedocles and Lucretius (natural philosophers) for poets, and the moral precepts of Phocylides, Theognis, and the quatrains of Pybrach, and the history of Lucan,[5] and others of that kind amongst poems; bestowing on such writers for honour the name of poets, rather then of historians or philosophers. But the subject of a poem is the manners of men, not natural causes; manners presented, not dictated; and manners feigned (as the name of poesy imports), not found in men. They that give entrance to fictions writ in prose, err not so much, but they err.[6] For poesy requireth delightfulness, not only of fiction, but of style; in which if prose contend with verse, it is with disadvantage (as it were) on foot, against the strength and wings of Pegasus.

For verse amongst the Greeks was appropriated anciently to the service of their gods, and was the holy style; the style of the oracles; the style of the laws; and the style of men that publicly recommended to their gods, the vows and thanks of the people; which was done in their holy songs called hymns, and the composers of them were called prophets and priests before the name of poet was known. When afterwards the majesty of that style was observed, the poets chose it as best becoming their high invention. And for the antiquity

3. Satirical.
4. Davenant, following a minor tradition of heroic poetry which Sidney also knew, planned his poem in five long sections or acts.
5. Phocylides, 6th-century B.C. Greek author of moralistic poems; Theognis, elagiac and moralizing poet of the same period; Gui de Faur, seigneur de Pibrac, wrote moralizing quatrains in French, published 1574 and later translated into English by Joshua Sylvester; Lucan (39–65 A.D.) wrote *Pharsalia*, an epic about the war between Julius Caesar and Pompey.
6. Sidney in the *Defence* is therefore said to err.

of verse it is greater than the antiquity of letters. For it is certain Cadmus was the first that (from Phœnicia, a country that neighboureth Judea) brought the use of letters into Greece.[7] But the service of the Gods, and the laws (which by measured sounds were easily committed to the memory) had been long time in use, before the arrival of Cadmus there.

There is besides the grace of style, another cause why the ancient poets chose to write in measured language, which is this. Their poems were made at first with intention to have them sung, as well epic as dramatic (which custom hath been long time laid aside, but began to be revived in part, of late years in Italy) [8] and could not be made commensurable to the voice or instruments, in prose; the ways and motions whereof are so uncertain and undistinguished (like the way and motion of a ship in the sea) as not only to discompose the best composers, but also to disappoint sometimes the most attentive reader, and put him to hunt counter for the sense. It was therefore necessary for poets in those times, to write in verse.

. . .

Time and education begets experience; experience begets memory; memory begets judgment and fancy: judgment begets the strength and structure, and fancy begets the ornaments of a poem. The ancients therefore fabled not absurdly, in making memory the mother of the muses.[9] For memory is the world (though not really, yet so as in a looking glass) in which the judgment (the severer sister) busieth herself in a grave and rigid examination of all the parts of nature, and in registering by letters, their order, causes, uses, differences and resemblances; whereby the fancy, when any work of art is to be performed, findeth her materials at hand and prepared for use, and needs no more than a swift motion over them, that what she wants, and is there to be had, may not lie too long unespied. So that when she seemeth to fly from one Indies to the other, and from heaven to earth, and to penetrate into the hardest matter, and obscurest places, into the future, and into herself, and all this in a point of time; the voyage is not very great, herself being all she seeks; and her wonderful celerity consisteth not so much in motion as in copious imagery discreetly ordered, and perfectly registered in the memory; which most men under the name of philosophy have a glimpse of, and is pretended to by many that grossly mistaking her embrace contention in her place. But so far forth as the fancy of man has traced the ways of true philosophy, so far it hath produced very marvellous effects to the benefit of mankind. All that is beautiful or defensible [10] in building; or marvellous in engines [11] and instruments of motion; whatsoever commodity men receive from the observation of the heavens, from the description of the earth, from the account of time, from walking on the seas; and whatsoever distinguisheth the civility of Europe, from the barbarity of the American savages, is the workmanship of fancy, but guided by the precepts of true

7. The myth of Cadmus reflects the historical fact that the Greek alphabet derived from Phoenician script.
8. Refers to the origin of Italian opera, at first supposed to re-create the conditions of ancient tragedy.
9. Mnemosyne, goddess of Memory; that she should be called mother of the Muses suits Hobbes; later Blake rejected the idea with disgust.
10. Suited to defensive operations.
11. Machines, mechanical devices.

philosophy. But where these precepts fail, as they have hitherto failed in the doctrine of moral virtue, there the architect (fancy) must take the philosophers part, upon herself. He therefore that undertakes an heroic poem (which is to exhibit a venerable and amiable image of heroic virtue) must not only be the poet, to place and connect, but also the philosopher, to furnish and square his matter, that is, to make both body and soul, colour and shadow of his poem out of his own store: which how well you have performed I am now considering.

. . .

There are some that are not pleased with fiction, unless it be bold not only to exceed the work, but also the possibility of nature; they would have impenetrable armours, enchanted castles, invulnerable bodies, iron men, flying horses, and a thousand other such things which are easily feigned by them that dare. Against such I defend you (without assenting to those that condemn either Homer or Virgil by dissenting only from those that think the beauty of a poem consisteth in the exorbitancy of the fiction). For as truth is the bound of historical, so the resemblance of truth is the utmost limit of poetical liberty. In old time amongst the heathens, such strange fictions and metamorphoses were not so remote from the articles of their faith, as they are now from ours, and therefore were not so unpleasant. Beyond the actual works of nature a poet may now go; but beyond the conceived possibility of nature, never. I can allow a geographer to make in the sea, a fish or a ship, which by the scale of his map would be two or three hundred miles long, and think it done for ornament, because it is done without the precincts of his undertaking; but when he paints an elephant so, I presently apprehend it as ignorance, and a plain confession of terra incognita.[12] . . .

. . .

That which giveth a poem the true and natural colour, consisteth in two things, which are, to know well; that is, to have images of nature in the memory distinct and clear; and to know much. A sign of the first is perspicuity, property, and decency, which delight all sorts of men, either by instructing the ignorant or soothing the learned in their knowledge: A sign of the latter is novelty of expression, and pleaseth by excitation of the mind; for novelty causeth admiration; and admiration, curiosity; which is a delightful appetite of knowledge.

There be so many words in use at this day in the English tongue, that, though of magnific sound, yet (like the windy blisters of a troubled water) have no sense at all; and so many others that lose their meaning by being ill coupled, that it is a hard matter to avoid them; for having been obtruded upon youth in the Schools (by such as make it, I think, their business there, as 'tis expressed by the best poet)

With terms to charm the weak and pose the wise,[13]

they grow up with them, and gaining reputation with the ignorant, are not easily shaken off.

To this palpable darkness, I may also add the ambitious obscurity of expressing more than is perfectly conceived; or perfect conception in fewer words

12. "Unknown territory" (an expression sometimes used on maps of that period).
13. From *Gondibert* I.5.

than it requires. Which expressions, though they have had the honour to be called strong lines, are indeed no better than riddles, and not only to the reader, but also (after a little time) to the writer himself, dark and troublesome.

To the property of expression, I refer that clearness of memory, by which a poet when he hath once introduced any person whatsoever, speaking in his poem, maintaineth in him, to the end, the same character he gave to him in the beginning. The variation whereof, is a change of pace that argues the poet tired.

· · ·

From knowing much, proceedeth the admirable variety and novelty of metaphors and similitudes, which are not possibly to be lighted on in the compass of a narrow knowledge. And the want whereof compelleth a writer to expressions that are either defaced by time or sullied with vulgar or long use. For the phrases of poesy, as the airs of music, with often hearing become insipid; the reader having no more sense of their force, than our flesh is sensible of the bones that sustain it. As the sense we have of bodies, consisteth in change and variety of impression, so also does the sense of language in the variety and changeable use of words. I mean not in the affectation of words newly brought home from travel, but in new (and withal, significant) translation to our purposes, of those that be already received, and in far fetched (but withal, apt, instructive, and comely) similitudes.[14] . . .

1650

IZAAK WALTON
1593–1683

Walton did well in business and became the friend of literary men; he was a parishioner of Donne's. His most famous work is *The Compleat Angler* (1653), a meditative essay on fishing, but he is also important as a biographer. His *Lives,* written at various stages of his own life, include those of Hooker, Wotton, Sanderson, Herbert, and Donne. He took care over detail, but occasionally interpreted evidence, especially from poems, in too literal a fashion; and it is clear that he imposed upon Donne a pattern of repentance which, though it may in general correspond to the facts, is heightened in the presentation. This is true of the speeches he attributes to the dying Dean. He wanted his books to be exemplary as well as informative. The manner of Walton's prose—simple, lucid, unambiguously pious—is represented in these extracts, first in what is his most elaborate set piece, the death of Donne, and secondly in his simple account of the religious community at Little Gidding.

14. Reflecting the new doctrine of wit, and indicating that the element of the new and surprising ("farfetched") is not abolished but modified; it is now set on the course which leads to Pope's "What oft was thought but ne'er so well expressed," but still has a long way to go.

From The Life of Dr. John Donne

The latter part of his life may be said to be a continued study; for as he usually preached once a week, if not oftener, so after his sermon he never gave his eyes rest till he had chosen out a new text, and that night cast his sermon into form and his text into divisions; and the next day betook himself to consult the fathers, and so commit his meditations to his memory, which was excellent. But upon Saturday he usually gave himself and his mind a rest from the weary burden of his week's meditations and usually spent that day in visitation of friends or some other diversions of his thoughts and would say, 'that he gave both his body and mind that refreshment that he might be enabled to do the work of the day following, not faintly, but with courage and cheerfulness.'

Nor was his age only so industrious, but in the most unsettled days of his youth his bed was not able to detain him beyond the hour of four in a morning; and it was no common business that drew him out of his chamber till past ten. All which time was employed in study; though he took great liberty after it; and if this seem strange, it may gain a belief by the visible fruits of his labours, some of which remain as testimonies of what is here written, for he left the resultance [1] of 1400 authors most of them abridged and analysed with his own hand; he left also six-score of his sermons, all written with his own hand, also an exact and laborious treatise concerning self-murder, called *Biathanatos,* wherein all the laws violated by that act are diligently surveyed and judiciously censured, a treatise written in his younger days which alone might declare him then not only perfect in the civil and canon law but in many other such studies and arguments as enter not into the consideration of many that labour to be thought great clerks and pretend to know all things.

Nor were these only found in his study, but all businesses that passed of any public consequence, either in this or any of our neighbour nations, he abbreviated either in Latin or in the language of that nation and kept them by him for useful memorials. So did he the copies of divers letters and cases of conscience that had concerned his friends, with his observations and solutions of them, and divers other businesses of importance, all particularly and methodically digested by himself.

He did prepare to leave the world before life left him, making his will when no faculty of his soul was damped or made defective by pain or sickness or he surprised by a sudden apprehension of death; but it was made with mature deliberation, expressing himself an impartial father by making his children's portions equal, and a lover of his friends, whom he remembered with legacies fitly and discreetly chosen and bequeathed. I cannot forbear a nomination of some of them; for methinks they be persons that seem to challenge a recordation in this place; as namely, to his brother-in-law, Sir Thomas Grimes, he gave that striking clock which he had long worn in his pocket. To his dear friend and executor, Dr. King, late Bishop of Chichester, that model of gold of the synod of Dort with which the States presented him at his last being at The Hague, and the two pictures of Padre Paulo and Fulgentio, men of his acquaintance when he travelled Italy and of great note in that nation for their remarkable learning. To his ancient friend, Dr. Brooke, that married him, Master

1. Summaries.

of Trinity College in Cambridge, he gave the picture of the blessed Virgin and Joseph. To Dr. Winniff, who succeeded him in the deanery he gave a picture called the Skeleton. To the succeeding dean, who was not then known, he gave many necessaries of worth and useful for his house, and also several pictures and ornaments for the chapel, with a desire that they might be registered, and remain as a legacy to his successors. To the Earls of Dorset and Carlisle, he gave several pictures. And so he did to many other friends—legacies given rather to express his affection than to make any addition to their estates. But unto the poor he was full of charity, and unto many others who by his constant and long continued bounty might entitle themselves to be his alms-people, for all these he made provision; and so largely as having then six children living might to some appear more than proportionable to his estate. I forbear to mention any more lest the reader may think I trespass upon his patience. But I will beg his favour to present him with the beginning and end of his will:

'In the name of the blessed and glorious Trinity, Amen. I, John Donne, by the mercy of Jesus Christ and by the calling of the Church of England priest, being at this time in good health and perfect understanding (praised be God therefore) do hereby make my last will and testament in manner and form following:

'First, I give my gracious God an entire sacrifice of body and soul, with my most humble thanks for that assurance which his blessed Spirit imprints in me now of the salvation of the one and the resurrection of the other; and for that constant and cheerful resolution which the same Spirit hath established in me to live and die in the religion now professed in the Church of England. In expectation of that resurrection, I desire my body may be buried, in the most private manner that may be, in that place of St. Paul's Church, London, that the now residenciaries have at my request designed for that purpose, &c.———. And this my last will and testament, made in the fear of God, whose mercy I humbly beg and constantly rely upon in Jesus Christ, and in perfect love and charity with all the world, whose pardon I ask from the lowest of my servants to the highest of my superiors. Written all with my own hand and my name subscribed to every page, of which there are five in number.'

Sealed Decemb. 13, 1630

Nor was this blessed sacrifice of charity expressed only at his death but in his life also by a cheerful and frequent visitation of any friend whose mind was dejected or his fortune necessitous. He was inquisitive after the wants of prisoners and redeemed many from thence that lay for their fees or small debts; he was a continual giver to poor scholars, both of this and foreign nations. Besides what he gave with his own hand, he usually sent a servant or a discreet and trusty friend to distribute his charity to all the prisons in London at all the festival times of the year, especially at the birth and resurrection of our Saviour. He gave an hundred pounds at one time to an old friend whom he had known live plentifully and by a too liberal heart and carelessness become decayed in his estate. And when the receiving of it was denied by the gentleman saying, 'He wanted not'; for the reader may note that as there be some spirits so generous as to labour to conceal and endure a sad poverty rather than expose themselves to those blushes that attend the confession of it so there be others to whom nature and grace have afforded such sweet and compassionate souls as to pity and prevent the distresses of mankind; which I have mentioned because of Mr. Donne's reply, whose answer was, 'I know you want not what will sustain nature, for a little will do that; but my desire is that you who in the days of your plenty have cheered and raised the hearts of so many of your dejected friends would now receive this from me and use it as a cordial for the cheering of your own.' And upon these terms it was received. He was an happy reconciler of many differences in the families of his friends and kindred—which he never undertook faintly, for such undertakings have usually faint effects—and they had such a faith in his judgment and impartiality that he never advised them to anything in vain. He was even to her death a most dutiful son to his mother, careful to provide for her supportation, of which she had been destitute but that God raised him up to prevent her necessities; who having sucked in the religion of the Roman Church with her mother's milk spent her estate in foreign countries to enjoy a liberty in it and died in his house but three months before him.

And to the end it may appear how just a steward he was of his Lord and Master's revenue I have thought fit to let the reader know that after his entrance into his deanery, as he numbered his years, he—at the foot of a private account to which God and his angels were only witnesses with him—computed first his revenue, then what was given to the poor and other pious uses, and lastly what rested for him and his; and having done that, he then blest each year's poor remainder with a thankful prayer. . . .

But I return from my long digression. We left the author sick in Essex, where he was forced to spend much of that winter by reason of his disability to remove from that place. And having never for almost twenty years omitted his personal attendance on his Majesty in that month in which he was to attend and preach to him nor having ever been left out of the roll and number of Lent preachers, and there being then (in January, 1630) a report brought to London or raised there that Dr. Donne was dead, that report gave him occasion to write this following letter to a dear friend:

SIR,

This advantage you and my other friends have by my frequent fevers, that I am so much the oftener at the gates of heaven, and this advantage by the solitude and close imprisonment that they reduce me to after, that I am so much the oftener at my prayers, in which I shall never leave out your happiness; and I doubt not among his other blessings, God will add some one to you for my prayers. A man would almost be content to die (if there were no other benefit in death) to hear of so much sorrow and so much good testimony from good men as I (God be blessed for it) did upon the report of my death; yet I perceive it went not through all; for one writ to me that some (and he said of my friends) conceived I was not so ill as I pretended but withdrew myself to live at ease, discharged of preaching. It is an unfriendly and, God knows, an ill-grounded interpretation; for I have always been sorrier when I could not preach than any could be they could not hear me. It hath been my desire, and God may be pleased to grant it, that I might die in the pulpit; if not that, yet that I might take my death in the pulpit, that is, die the sooner by occasion of those labours. Sir, I hope to see you presently after Candlemass, about which time will fall my Lent sermon at court, except my Lord Chamberlain believe me to be dead and so leave me out of the roll; but as long as I live and am not speechless, I would not willingly decline that service, I have better leisure to write than you to read; yet I would not willingly oppress you with too much letter. God so bless you and your son as I wish to

Your poor friend and servant in Christ Jesus,

J. DONNE

Before that month [2] ended, he was appointed to preach upon his old constant day, the first Friday in Lent; he had notice of it and had in his sickness so prepared for that employment that as he had long thirsted for it so he resolved his weakness should not hinder his journey; he came therefore to London some few days before his appointed day of preaching. At his coming thither many of his friends—who with sorrow saw his sickness had left him but so much flesh as did only cover his bones—doubted his strength to perform that task and did therefore dissuade him from undertaking it, assuring him, however, it was like to shorten his life; but he passionately denied their requests, saying, 'he would not doubt that that God who in so many weaknesses had assisted him with an unexpected strength would now withdraw it in his last employment,' professing an holy ambition to perform that sacred work. And when to the amazement of some beholders he appeared in the pulpit, many of them thought he presented himself not to preach mortification by a living voice but mortality by a decayed body and a dying face. And doubtless many did secretly ask that question in Ezekiel; 'Do these bones live? [3] or can that soul organize that tongue to speak so long time as the sand in that glass will move towards its centre [4] and measure out an hour of this dying man's unspent life? Doubtless it cannot'; and yet, after some faint pauses in his zealous prayer, his strong desires enabled his weak body to discharge his memory of his preconceived meditations, which were of dying, the text being, 'To God the Lord belong the issues from death.' Many that then saw his tears and heard his faint and hollow voice professing they thought the text prophetically chosen and that Dr. Donne 'had preached his own funeral sermon.'

Being full of joy that God had enabled him to perform this desired duty, he hastened to his house; out of which he never moved till, like St. Stephen, he was carried by devout men to his grave.

The next day after his sermon, his strength being much wasted and his spirits so spent as indisposed him to business or to talk, a friend that had often been a witness of his free and facetious discourse asked him, 'Why are you sad?' To whom he replied with a countenance so full of cheerful gravity as gave testimony of an inward tranquillity of mind and of a soul willing to take a farewell of this world and said:

2. January 1631.
3. Ezekiel 37:3.
4. Sink; the preacher preached for an hour by the glass.

'I am not sad, but most of the night past I have entertained myself with many thoughts of several friends that have left me here and are gone to that place from which they shall not return, and that within a few days I also shall go hence and be no more seen. And my preparation for this change is become my nightly meditation upon my bed, which my infirmities have now made restless to me. But, at this present time, I was in a serious contemplation of the providence and goodness of God to me, to me who am less than the least of his mercies; and looking back upon my life past, I now plainly see it was his hand that prevented me from all temporal employment and that it was his will I should never settle nor thrive till I entered into the ministry; in which I have now lived almost twenty years (I hope to his glory) and by which, I most humbly thank him, I have been enabled to requite most of those friends which showed me kindness when my fortune was very low, as God knows it was; and as it hath occasioned the expression of my gratitude, I thank God most of them stood in need of my requital. I have lived to be useful and comfortable to my good father-in-law, Sir George More, whose patience God hath been pleased to exercise with many temporal crosses; I have maintained my own mother, whom it hath pleased God after a plentiful fortune in her younger days to bring to a great decay in her very old age. I have quieted the consciences of many that have groaned under the burthen of a wounded spirit, whose prayers I hope are available for me. I cannot plead innocency of life, especially of my youth. But I am to be judged by a merciful God who is not willing to see what I have done amiss. And, though of myself I have nothing to present to him but sins and misery, yet I know he looks not upon me now as I am of myself but as I am in my Saviour and hath given me even at this present time some testimonies by his holy Spirit that I am of the number of his elect. I am therefore full of inexpressible joy and shall die in peace.'

I must here look so far back as to tell the reader that at his first return out of Essex to preach his last sermon, his old friend and physician, Dr. Fox, a man of great worth, came to him to consult his health and that after a sight of him and some queries concerning his distempers he told him, 'That by cordials and drinking milk twenty days together there was a probability of his restoration to health'; but he passionately denied to drink it. Nevertheless, Dr. Fox, who loved him most entirely, wearied him with solicitations till he yielded to take it for ten days; at the end of which time he told Dr. Fox, 'He had drunk it more to satisfy him than to recover his health and that he would not drink it ten days longer upon the best moral assurance of having twenty years added to his life, for he loved it not, and was so far from fearing death, which to others is the king of terrors, that he longed for the day of his dissolution.'

It is observed that a desire of glory or commendation is rooted in the very nature of man and that those of the severest and most mortified lives, though they may become so humble as to banish self-flattery and such weeds as naturally grow there, yet they have not been able to kill this desire of glory, but that, like our radical heat, it will both live and die with us; and many think it should be so; and we want not sacred examples to justify the desire of having our memory to outlive our lives. Which I mention, because Dr. Donne, by the persuasion of Dr. Fox, easily yielded at this very time to have a monument made for him; but Dr. Fox undertook not to persuade him how or what monument it should be; that was left to Dr. Donne himself.

A monument being resolved upon, Dr. Donne sent for a carver to make for him in wood the figure of an urn, giving him directions for the compass and height of it, and to bring with it a board of the just height of his body. These being got, then without delay a choice painter was got to be in a readiness to draw his picture, which was taken as followeth: Several charcoal fires being first made in his large study, he brought with him into that place his winding-sheet in his hand and, having put off all his clothes, had this sheet put on him and so tied with knots at his head and feet and his hands so placed as dead bodies are usually fitted to be shrouded and put into their coffin or grave. Upon this urn he thus stood with his eyes shut and with so much of the sheet turned aside as might show his lean, pale, and death-like face, which was purposely turned toward the East, from whence he expected the second coming of his and our Saviour, Jesus. In this posture he was drawn at his just height; and when the picture was fully finished, he caused it to be set by his bed-side, where it continued and became his hourly object till his death and was then given to his dearest friend and executor, Doctor Henry King, then chief residenciary of St. Paul's, who caused him to be thus carved in one entire piece of white marble, as it now stands in that church; and by Doctor Donne's own appointment these words were to be affixed to it as his epitaph:

JOHANNES DONNE

Sac. Theol. Profess.

Post varia studia quibus ab annis tenerrimis
fideliter, nec infeliciter incubuit,
instinctu et impulsu Sp. Sancti, monitu
et hortatu

REGIS JACOBI, ordines sacros
amplexus, anno sui Jesu, 1614, et suæ ætatis 42,
decanatu hujus ecclesiæ indutus 27,
Novembris, 1621,

exutus morte ultimo die Martii, 1631,
hic licet in occiduo cinere aspicit eum
cujus nomen est Oriens.[5]

And now, having brought him through the many labyrinths and perplexities of a various life, even to the gates of death and the grave, my desire is he may rest till I have told my reader that I have seen many pictures of him in several habits and at several ages and in several postures. And I now mention this because I have seen one picture of him, drawn by a curious hand at his age of eighteen, with his sword and what other adornments might then suit with the present fashions of youth and the giddy gaieties of that age; and his motto then was,

5. "John Donne, Doctor of Divinity, after various studies, pursued by him from his earliest years with assiduity, and not without success, entered into holy orders under the influence and impulse of the Holy Ghost and by the advice and exhortation of King James, in the year of our Lord 1614, when he was 42. Having been invested with the Deanery of this church on November 27, 1621, he was stripped of it by death on the last day of March 1631: and here, though himself set in dust, he beholdeth Him whose name is the Rising Sun."

How much shall I be changed
Before I am changed!

And if that young and his now dying picture were at this time set together,
every beholder might say, 'Lord! how much is Dr. Donne already changed, before he is changed!' And the view of them might give my reader occasion to
ask himself with some amazement, 'Lord! how much may I also that am now
in health be changed, before I am changed! before this vile, this changeable
body shall put off mortality!' and therefore to prepare for it.——But this is
not writ so much for my reader's *memento* [6] as to tell him that Dr. Donne
would often in his private discourses and often publicly in his sermons mention
the many changes both of his body and mind, especially of his mind from
a vertiginous giddiness, and would as often say his great and most blessed
change was from a temporal to a spiritual employment. In which he was so
happy that he accounted the former part of his life to be lost and the beginning
of it to be from his first entering into sacred orders and serving his most merciful God at his altar.

Upon Monday after the drawing of this picture he took his last leave of his
beloved study, and being sensible of his hourly decay, retired himself to his
bed-chamber; and that week sent at several times for many of his most considerable friends, with whom he took a solemn and deliberate farewell, commending to their considerations some sentences useful for the regulation of
their lives, and then dismissed them, as good Jacob did his sons, with a
spiritual benediction. The Sunday following he appointed his servants, that
if there were any business yet undone that concerned him or themselves, it
should be prepared against Saturday next; for after that day he would not
mix his thoughts with anything that concerned this world; nor ever did, but,
as Job,[7] so he waited for the appointed day of his dissolution.

And now he was so happy as to have nothing to do but to die; to do which
he stood in need of no longer time, for he had studied it long and to so happy
a perfection that in a former sickness [8] he called God to witness, 'He was that
minute ready to deliver his soul into his hands if that minute God would
determine his dissolution.' In that sickness he begged of God the constancy to
be preserved in that estate forever; and his patient expectation to have his
immortal soul disrobed from her garment of mortality makes me confident he
now had a modest assurance that his prayers were then heard and his petition
granted. He lay fifteen days earnestly expecting his hourly change; and in the
last hour of his last day, as his body melted away and vapoured into spirit, his
soul having, I verily believe, some revelation of the beatifical vision, he said,
'I were miserable if I might not die'; and after those words, closed many
periods of his faint breath by saying often, 'Thy kingdom come, thy will be
done.' His speech, which had long been his ready and faithful servant, left
him not till the last minute of his life, and then forsook him not to serve
another master (for who speaks like him!) but died before him for that it was
then become useless to him that now conversed with God on earth as angels

6. *Memento mori*, a reminder of mortality.
7. Job 30:23.
8. The serious illness of 1623, when Donne wrote his *Devotions*.

are said to do in heaven, only by thoughts and looks. Being speechless and seeing heaven by that illumination by which he saw it, he did, as St. Stephen, look steadfastly into it, till he saw the Son of Man, standing at the right hand of God, his Father; and being satisfied with this blessed sight, as his soul ascended and his last breath departed from him, he closed his own eyes; and then disposed his hands and body into such a posture as required not the least alteration by those that came to shroud him.

Thus variable, thus virtuous was the life; thus excellent, thus exemplary was the death of this memorable man.

. . .

He was of stature moderately tall, of a straight and equally-proportioned body, to which all his words and actions gave an inexpressible addition of comeliness.

The melancholy and pleasant humour were in him so contempered that each gave advantage to the other and made his company one of the delights of mankind.

His fancy was inimitably high, equalled only by his great wit; both being made useful by a commanding judgment.

His aspect was cheerful and such as gave a silent testimony of a clear-knowing soul and of a conscience at peace with itself.

His melting eye showed that he had a soft heart, full of noble compassion, of too brave a soul to offer injuries and too much a Christian not to pardon them in others.

He did much contemplate—especially after he entered into his sacred calling—the mercies of Almighty God, the immortality of the soul, and the joys of heaven, and would often say, in a kind of sacred ecstasy, 'Blessed be God that he is God only and divinely like himself.'

He was by nature highly passionate but more apt to reluct at [9] the excesses of it. A great lover of the offices of humanity and of so merciful a spirit that he never beheld the miseries of mankind without pity and relief.

He was earnest and unwearied in the search of knowledge; with which his vigorous soul is now satisfied and employed in a continual praise of that God that first breathed it into his active body, that body which once was a temple of the Holy Ghost and is now become a small quantity of Christian dust.

But I shall see it reanimated.

1640

From The Life of Mr. George Herbert
[On Nicholas Ferrar]

Mr. Nicholas Ferrar (who got the reputation of being called St. Nicholas at the age of six years) was born in London, and doubtless had good education in his youth, but certainly was at an early age made Fellow of Clare Hall in Cambridge, where he continued to be eminent for his piety, temperance and learning. About the twenty-sixth year of his age he betook himself to travel, in which he added to his Latin and Greek a perfect knowledge of all the

9. Resist.

languages spoken in the western parts of our Christian world, and understood well the principles of their religion and of their manner, and the reasons of their worship. In this his travel he met with many persuasions to come into a communion with that Church which calls itself Catholic; but he returned from his travels as he went, eminent for his obedience to his mother, the Church of England. In his absence from England Mr. Ferrar's father (who was a merchant) allowed him a liberal maintenance, and, not long after his return into England, Mr. Ferrar had, by the death of his father or an elder brother, or both, an estate left him, that enabled him to purchase land to the value of four or five hundred pounds a year, the greatest part of which land was at Little Gidden [1] four or six miles from Huntingdon, and about eighteen from Cambridge; which place he chose for the privacy of it, and for the Hall, which had the parish church or chapel belonging and adjoining near to it; for Mr. Ferrar having seen the manners and vanities of the world, and found them to be, as Mr. Herbert says, a nothing between two dishes, did so contemn it, that he resolved to spend the remainder of his life in mortifications, and in devotion and charity, and to be always prepared for death; and his life was spent thus:

He and his family, which were like a little college, and about thirty in number, did most of them keep Lent and all Ember-weeks strictly, both in fasting and using all those mortifications and prayers that the Church hath appointed to be then used; and he and they did the like constantly on Fridays, and on the Vigils or Eves appointed to be fasted before the Saints' days; and this frugality and abstinence turned to the relief of the poor; but this was but a part of his charity, none but God and he knew the rest.

This family, which I have said to be in number about thirty, were a part of them his kindred; and the rest chosen to be of a temper fit to be moulded into a devout life; and all of them were for their dispositions serviceable and quiet and humble, and free from scandal. Having thus fitted himself for his family, he did, about the year 1630, betake himself to a constant and methodical service of God, and it was in this manner:—He, being accompanied with most of his family, did himself use to read the common prayers (for he was a deacon) every day at the appointed hours of ten and four, in the parish church, which was very near his house, and which he had both repaired and adorned; for it was fallen into a great ruin, by reason of a depopulation of the village, before Mr. Ferrar bought the manor; and he did also constantly read the matins every morning at the hour of six, either in the church, or in an oratory which was within his own house; and many of the family did there continue with him after the prayers were ended, and there they spent some hours in singing hymns or anthems, sometimes in the church, and often to an organ in the oratory. And there they sometimes betook themselves to meditate, or to pray privately, or to read a part of the New Testament to themselves, or to continue their praying or reading the Psalms; and, in case the Psalms were not always read in the day, then Mr. Ferrar and others of the congregation did at night, at the ring of a watch-bell, repair to the church or oratory, and

1. Little Gidding, the religious community where Herbert, Crashaw, and perhaps Charles I visited, and which is celebrated in Eliot's poem of the same title (1942). It was a unique example of Anglican piety, in a country which of course no longer had monasteries.

there betake themselves to prayers and lauding God, and reading the Psalms that had not been read in the day; and when these or any part of the congregation grew weary or faint, the watch-bell was rung, sometimes before and sometimes after midnight, and then another part of the family rose, and maintained the watch, sometimes by praying or singing lauds to God or reading the Psalms; and when after some hours they also grew weary and faint, then they rung the watch-bell, and were also relieved by some of the former, or by a new part of the society which continued their devotions (as hath been mentioned) until morning. And it is to be noted, that in this continued serving of God, the Psalter, or whole Book of Psalms, was in every four-and-twenty hours sung or read over, from the first to the last verse; and this was done as constantly as the sun runs his circle every day about the world, and then begins again the same instant that it ended.

Thus did Mr. Ferrar and his happy family serve God day and night—thus did they always behave themselves as in his presence. And they did always eat and drink by the strictest rules of temperance; eat and drink so as to be ready to rise at midnight, or at the call of a watch-bell, and perform their devotions to God. And it is fit to tell the reader, that many of the clergy that were more inclined to practical piety and devotion than to doubtful and needless disputations, did often come to Gidden Hall, and make themselves a part of that happy society, and stay a week or more, and then join with Mr. Ferrar and the family in these devotions, and assist and ease him or them in the watch by night. And these various devotions had never less than two of the domestic family in the night; and the watch was always kept in the church or oratory, unless in extreme cold winter nights, and then it was maintained in a parlour which had a fire in it, and the parlour was fitted for that purpose. And this course of piety, and great liberality to his poor neighbours, Mr. Ferrar maintained till his death, which was in the year 1639. . . .

1670

CHARACTERS

We think of the word "character" as referring either to a person's moral nature or else, in a more limited usage, to a written or printed letter or ideograph. What connects these two totally separate senses of the word is its original meaning in Greek, a sharp tool for inscribing or engraving and thus, by extension, the inscription so made, thought of as an "impression" or "mark." In addition, a kind of verbal sketch, a short prose description of a type of vice, originated by the Athenian writer Theophrastus (372–287 B.C.) was called a "character," and eventually the name came to stand for the contents of the sketch, rather than the form itself. Informally speaking, the written character abounds in literature: the passage on the nature of the Magnanimous Man in Aristotle's *Nichomachean Ethics* might be considered one, for example; and some of Chaucer's descriptions of people in the General Prologue to the *Canterbury Tales* move toward the representation of type. The actual Theophrastan character in the Renaissance dates from the first Latin translation of Theophrastus, in 1592; in English, Joseph Hall's *Characters of Virtues and Vices* appeared in 1608. Numerous characters by various hands (the dramatists John Webster and Thomas Dekker, and others) were published in 1614 to accompany the posthumous appearance of Sir Thomas Overbury's poem, A Wife. Overbury, who had been murdered by a former associate and his wife (whose marriage he had opposed), was a famous figure, and even though few of the characters in the collection were by him, the term "Overburian character" to represent the deft, tight, single long paragraph of characterization of a type of actual person, rather than a virtue or vice embodied, is still used. The character figured significantly in the development of expository writing in the seventeenth century, particularly in the early move away from long, Ciceronian, periodic sentences toward a more "pointed," brisk manner.

SIR THOMAS OVERBURY
1581–1613

From Sir Thomas Overbury His Wife:
New News and Divers More Characters

What a Character Is

If I must speak the schoolmaster's language, I will confess that character comes from this infinite mood χαράξω,[1] that signifieth to engrave, or make a deep impression. And for that cause, a letter (as A.B.) is called a character.

Those elements which we learn first, leaving a strong seal in our memories.

Character is also taken from an Egyptian hieroglyphic, for an impress, or short emblem; in little comprehending much.

To square out a character by our English level, it is a picture (real or personal) quaintly drawn, in various colours, all of them heightened by one shadowing.

It is a quick and soft touch [2] of many strings, all shutting up in one musical close; it is wit's descant on any plain song.

A Puritan

Is a diseased piece of Apocrypha;[1] bind him to the Bible, and he corrupts the whole text, ignorance and fat feed are his founders, his nurses, railing, rabies, and round breeches; his life is but a borrowed blast of wind, for between two religions, as between two doors, he is ever whistling. Truly whose child he is is yet unknown, for willingly his faith allows no father; only thus far his pedigree is found, Bragger and he flourished about a time first, his fiery zeal keeps him continually costive, which withers him into his own translation, and till he eat a schoolman, he is hide-bound; he ever prays against non residents, but is himself the greatest discontinuer, for he never keeps near his text; anything that the law allows, but marriage, and March beer,[2] he

1. Actually, charactēr in Greek means both the engraving tool and, sometimes, the engraver (see Headnote).
2. A musical phrase; also, a "close" is a cadence; a "descant on a plain song" has nothing to do with Gregorian chant, but more simply, an improvised part over a stated theme.

1. Biblical material ruled out of the canon and therefore considered spurious.
2. Thin, light spring beer, on the weak side.

murmurs at; what it disallows and holds dangerous, makes him a discipline; where the gate stands open, he is ever seeking a stile; [3] and where his learning ought to climb, he creeps through; give him advice, you run into traditions, and urge a modest course, he cries out councils. His greatest care is to condemn obedience, his last care to serve God handsomely and cleanly. He is now become so cross a kind of teaching, that should the Church enjoin clean shirts, he were lousy; more sense than single prayers is not his, nor more in those, than still the same Petitions; from which he either fears a learned faith, or doubts God understands not at first hearing. Show him a ring, he runs back like a bear, and hates square dealing as allied to caps; a pair of organs blow him out o' the parish, and are the only clyster-pipes [4] to cool him. Where the meat is best there he confutes most, for his arguing is but the effacacy of his eating; good bits he holds breed good positions, and the Pope he best concludes against, in plum-broth. He is often drunk, but not as we are, temporally, nor can his sleep then cure him, for the fumes of his ambition make his very soul reel, and the small beer that should allay him (silence) keeps him more surfeited, and makes his heat break out in private houses; women and lawyers are his best disciples, the one next fruit, longs for forbidden doctrine, the other to maintain forbidden titles, both which he sows amongst them. Honest he dare not be, for that loves order; yet if he can be brought to ceremony, and made but master of it, he is converted.

An Amorist

Is a man blasted or planet-strooken, and is the dog that leads blind Cupid; when he is at the best his fashion exceeds the worth of his weight. He is never without verses and musk confects,[1] and sighs to the hazard of his buttons. His eyes are all white, either to wear the livery of his mistress' complexion or to keep Cupid from hitting the black. He fights with passion, and loseth much of his blood by his weapon; dreams, thence his paleness. His arms are carelessly used, as if their best use was nothing but embracements. He is untrussed, unbuttoned, and ungartered, not out of carelessness, but care; his farthest end being but going to bed. Sometimes he wraps his petition in neatness, but he goeth not alone; for then he makes some other quality moralize his affection, and his trimness is the grace of that grace. Her favour lifts him up as the sun moisture; when he disfavours, unable to hold that happiness, it falls down in tears. His fingers are his orators, and he expresseth much of himself upon some instrument. He answers not, or not to the purpose, and no marvel, for he is not at home. He scotcheth time with dancing with his mistress, taking up of her glove, and wearing her feather, he is confined to her colour, and dares not pass out of the circuit of her memory. His imagination is a fool, and it goeth in a pied coat of red and white. Shortly he is translated out of a man into folly; his imagination is the glass [2] of lust, and himself the traitor to his own discretion.

3. Ladder-like arrangement for getting over fences.
4. Enemas.

1. Perfumed sachets.
2. Mirror.

A Chambermaid

She is her mistress's she-secretary, and keeps the box of her teeth, her hair, and her painting very private. Her industry is upstairs and downstairs like a drawer: and by her dry hand you may know she is a sore starcher. If she lie at her master's bed's feet, she is quit of the green sickness forever; for she hath terrible dreams when she's awake, as if she were troubled with the nightmare. She hath a good liking to dwell in the country, but she holds London the goodliest forest in England to shelter a great belly. She reads Greene's [1] works over and over, but is so carried away with the Mirror of Knighthood [2] she is many times resolved to run out of herself, and become a lady-errant. If she catch a clap,[3] she divides it so equally between the master and the serving-man as if she had cut out the getting of it by a thread; only the knave sumner makes her bowl booty,[4] and overreach the master. The pedant of the house, though he promise her marriage, cannot grow further inward with her; she hath paid for her credulity often, and now grows wary. She likes the form of our marriage very well, in that a woman is not tied to answer any articles concerning questions of virginity; her mind, her body, and clothes are parcels loosely packed together, and for want of good utterance, she perpetually laughs out her meaning. Her mistress and she help to make away time, to the idlest purpose that can be, either for love or money. In brief, these chambermaids are like lotteries: you may draw twenty ere one worth anything.

1614

JOHN EARLE
1600?–1665

From Microcosmography

Or A Piece of the World Discovered in Essays and Characters

A Child

Is a man in a small letter, yet the best copy of Adam before he tasted of Eve or the apple; and he is happy whose small practice in the world can only write his character. He is nature's fresh picture newly drawn in oil, which time, and much handling, dims and defaces. His soul is yet a white paper [1] unscribbled with observations of the world, wherewith, at length, it becomes a blurred note-book. He is purely happy, because he knows no evil, nor hath made means by sin to be acquainted with misery. He arrives not at the

---

1. Robert Greene (1560–92), author of romances, plays, and pamphlets.
2. A chivalric romance, mentioned in Cervantes' *Don Quixote.*
3. Then, as now, gonorrhea.
4. The "knave sumner" is the serving man, who arranges with her to sleep with their master in order to get an edge on him ("bowl booty": to have a secret confederate in a game).

1. This anticipates John Locke's concept of the *tabula rasa,* the infant mind as a blank slate upon which experience will write its impressions.

mischief of being wise, nor endures evils to come, by foreseeing them. He kisses and loves all, and, when the smart of the rod is past, smiles on his beater. Nature and his parents alike dandle him, and tice [2] him on with a bait of sugar to a draught of wormwood. He plays yet, like a young 'prentice the first day, and is not come to his task of melancholy. All the language he speaks yet is tears, and they serve him well enough to express his necessity. His hardest labour is his tongue, as if he were loth to use so deceitful an organ; and he is best company with it when he can but prattle. We laugh at his foolish sports, but his game is our earnest; and his drums, rattles, and hobby-horses, but the emblems and mocking of man's business. His father hath writ him as his own little story, wherein he reads those days of his life that he cannot remember, and sighs to see what innocence he has out-lived. The older he grows, he is a stair lower from God; and, like his first father, much worse in his breeches.[3] He is the Christian's example, and the old man's relapse; the one imitates his pureness, and the other falls into his simplicity. Could he put off his body with his little coat, he had got eternity without a burden, and exchanged but one heaven for another.

1633

JOSEPH HALL
1574–1656

From Characters of Virtues and Vices

The Slothful [1]

He is a religious man, and wears the time in his cloister, and, as the cloak of his doing nothing, pleads contemplation; yet he is no whit the leaner for his thoughts, no whit learneder. He takes no less care how to spend time than others how to gain by the expense, and, when business importunes him, is more troubled to forethink what he must do than another to affect it. Summer is out of his favour for nothing but long days, that make no haste to their even. He loves still to have the sun witness of his rising, and lies long, more for lothness to dress him than will to sleep; and, after some stretching and yawning calls for dinner unwashed; which having digested with a sleep in his chair, he walks forth to the bench in the market-place and looks for companions; whomsoever he meets he stays with idle questions and lingering discourse; how the days are lengthened, how kindly the weather is, how false the clock, how forward the spring, and ends ever with 'What shall we do?' It pleases him no less to hinder others, than not to work himself.

2. Entice.
3. Punning on "breach," or sin, and the original figleaf in Genesis 3:7; in the Geneva Bible, called for this reason the "Breeches Bible," Adam and Eve are said to have "made themselves breeches."

1. The deadly sin of *accidie* or sloth was not, in orthodox Christian ethics, a matter of physical laziness, but of a want of spiritual and intellectual energy, a moral fault rather than a more trivial physical one. Hall's vice lies somewhere between the sin and the garden variety of laziness.

When all the people are gone from Church, he is left sleeping in his seat alone. He enters bonds, and forfeits them by forgetting the day; and asks his neighbour, when his own field was fallowed, whether the next piece of ground belong not to himself. His care is either none or too late; when winter is come, after some sharp visitations, he looks on his pile of wood, and asks how much was cropped the last spring. Necessity drives him to every action, and what he cannot avoid, he will yet defer. Every change troubles him, although to the better; and his dullness counterfeits a kind of contentment. When he is warned on a jury, he would rather pay the mulct [1] than appear. All but that which nature will not permit, he doth by a deputy; and counts it troublesome to do nothing, but to do any thing yet more. He is witty in nothing but framing excuses to sit still, which, if the occasion yield not, he coineth with ease. There is no work that is not either dangerous or thankless, and whereof he foresees not the inconvenience and gainlessness before he enters; which if it be verified in event, his next idleness hath found a reason to patronize it. He would rather freeze than fetch wood; and choses rather to steal than work, to beg than take pains to steal, and in many things to want than beg. He is so loth to leave his neighbour's fire, that he is fain to walk home in the dark, and, if he be not looked to, wears out the night in the chimney-corner, or if not that, lies down in his clothes to save two labours. He eats and prays himself asleep, and dreams of no other torment but work. This man is a standing pool, and cannot chose but gather corruption; he is descried amongst a thousand neighbours by a dry and nasty hand that still savours of the sheet, a beard uncut, uncombed, an eye and ear yellow with their excretions, a coat, shaken on, ragged, unbrushed, by linen and face striving whether shall excel in uncleanliness. For body, he hath a swollen leg, a dusky and swinish eye, a blown cheek, a drawling tongue, a heavy foot, and is nothing but a colder earth moulded with standing water; to conclude, is a man in nothing, but in speech and shape.

1608

NICHOLAS BRETON
1555?–1626?

From The Good and the Bad

Or Descriptions of the Worthies and Unworthies of This Age

An Effeminate [1] Fool

An Effeminate Fool is the figure of a baby. He loves nothing but to be gay, to look in a glass, to keep among wenches, and to play with trifles; to feed on sweet-meats and to be danced in laps, to be embraced in arms, and to be kissed on the cheek; to talk idly, to look demurely, to go nicely, and to laugh

1. Fine.

1. Here the word has no reference to homosexuality, but rather to a foppish lack of other characteristics of stylish manliness.

continually; to be his mistress' servant, and her maid's master, his father's love and his mother's none-child; to play on a fiddle and sing a love-song, to wear sweet gloves[2] and look on fine things; to make purposes and write verses, devise riddles and tell lies; to follow plays and study dances, to hear news and buy trifles; to sigh for love and weep for kindness and mourn for company, and be sick for fashion; to ride in a coach and gallop a hackney, to watch all night and sleep out the morning; to lie on a bed and take tobacco and to send his page an idle message to his mistress; to go upon gigs,[3] to have his ruffs set in print,[4] to pick his teeth, and to play with a puppet. In sum, he is a man-child and a woman's man, a gaze[5] of folly and wisdom's grief.

1616

OWEN FELLTHAM
1602?–1668

From Resolves, Divine, Moral, and Political

Of Women[1]

Some are so uncharitable as to think all women bad; and others are so credulous as they believe they all are good. Sure, though every man speaks as he finds, there is reason to direct our opinion, without experience of the whole sex; which, in a strict examination, makes more for their honour than most men have acknowledged. At first, she was created his equal; only the difference was in the sex; otherwise they both were man. If we argue from the text that male and female made man, so the man being put first was worthier, I answer, so the evening and morning was the first day,[2] yet few will think the night the better. That man is made her governor, and so above her, I believe rather the punishment of her sin, than the prerogative of his worth. Had they both stood, it may be thought, she had never been in that subjection; for then had it been no curse, but a continuance of her former estate, which had nothing but blessedness in it. Peter Martyr, indeed, is of opinion that man before the Fall had priority; but Chrysostom, he says, does doubt it. All will grant her body more admirable, more beautiful than man's; fuller of curiosities and noble Nature's wonders; both for conception, and fostering the producted birth. And can we think God would put a worser soul into a better body? When man was created, 'tis said, God made man; but when woman, 'tis said, God builded her; as if he had then been about a frame of rarer rooms, and more exact com-

2. Perfumed gloves.
3. To spend time with flighty girls; possibly to be flighty oneself (like "whirligigs").
4. His ruffs starched to an excessive stiffness.
5. Object of regard.

1. Felltham's essay is a kind of expanded character, in the fashionable "Senecan" or sharp, choppy, lively prose style of the Jacobean and Caroline periods. It is far from being like a rambling section of Burton's disquisition, or even a Baconian essay; it also has the air of a "Problem" about it—he is arguing what is, alas, a heterodox view against an official, or at least a received, misogyny.
2. In Genesis 1:5 (as, in subsequent Hebraic tradition, each day starts with the previous sundown).

position. And, without doubt, in her body she is much more wonderful, and by this we may think so in her mind. Philosophy tells us though the soul be not caused by the body, yet in the general it follows the temperament of it; so the comeliest outsides are naturally (for the most part) more virtuous within. If place can be any privilege, we shall find her built in Paradise, when man was made without it. 'Tis certain they are by constitution colder than the boiling man; so by this more temperate; 'tis heat that transports man to immoderation and fury; 'tis that which hurries him to a savage and libidinous violence. Women are naturally the more modest; and modesty is the seat and dwelling place of virtue. Whence proceed the most abhorred villainies, but from a masculine unblushing impudence? What a deal of sweetness do we find in a mild disposition! When a woman grows bold and daring, we dislike her, and say, she is too like a man; yet in ourselves we magnify what we condemn in her. Is not this injustice? Every man is so much the better by how much he comes nearer to God. Man in nothing is more like him than in being merciful. Yet woman is far more merciful than man; it being a sex wherein pity and compassion have dispersed far brighter rays. God is said to be love; and I am sure everywhere woman is spoken of for transcending in that quality. It was never found but in two men only,[3] that their love exceeded that of the feminine sex; and if you observe them you shall find they were both of melting dispositions. I know when they prove bad, they are a sort of the vilest creatures, yet still the same reason gives it; for, *optima corrupta pessima*, the best things corrupted become the worst. They are things whose souls are of a more deductible temper than the harder metal of man; so may be made both better and worse. The representations of Sophocles and Euripides may be both true; and for the tongue-vice, talkativeness, I see not but at meetings men may very well vie words with them. 'Tis true, they are not of so tumultuous a spirit, so not so fit for great actions. Natural heat does more actuate the stirring genius of man. Their easy natures make them somewhat more unresolute; whereby men have argued them of fear and inconstancy. But men have always held the parliament, and have enacted their own wills, without ever hearing them speak; and then, how easy is it to conclude them guilty! Besides, education makes more difference between men and them than Nature; and all their aspersions are less noble for that they are only from their enemies, men. Diogenes snarled bitterly when, walking with another, he spied two women talking, and said, 'See, the viper and the asp are changing poison.' The poet was conceited that said, after they were made ill, that God made them fearful, that man might rule them; otherwise they had been past dealing with. Catullus his conclusion [4] was too general, to collect a deceit in all women, because he was not confident of his own.

> *Nulli se dicit mulier mea nubere malle*
> *Quam mihi; non si se Jupiter ipse petat.*
> *Dicit: sed mulier Cupido quod dicit amanti,*
> *In vento et rapida scribere oportet aqua.*

> My mistress swears, she'd leave all men for me:
> Yea, though that Jove himself should suitor be.

3. The biblical David and Jonathan (I Samuel 18–20).
4. In his Ode given below.

She says it: but what women swear to kind
Loves, may be writ in rapid streams and wind.

I am resolved to honour virtue, in what sex soever I find it. And I think, in
the general, I shall find it more in women than men, though weaker and more
infirmly guarded. I believe they are better, and may be wrought to be worse.
Neither shall the faults of many make me uncharitable to all; nor the goodness
of some make me credulous of the rest. Though hitherto, I confess, I have not
found more sweet and constant goodness in man than I have found in woman;
and yet of these, I have not found a number.

1620–28

THOMAS FULLER
1608–1661

A voluminous writer of devotional manuals, religious verse, didactic character books
(*The Holy State*, published in 1642), and historical works, Fuller is perhaps best
remembered for his two large and comprehensive surveys of his native land, chronologically in *The Church History of Britain* (1655) and topographically (a prose and
prosaic version both, of the format of Michael Drayton's *Poly-Olbion*) in his posthumous *The History of the Worthies of England* (1662), organized county by county.
Fuller, whose degree was from Queen's College, Cambridge, was a moderate Anglican
churchman, his posts temporary and various until he became curate of a chapel in
London and, briefly, chaplain to the infant royal princess. He did not go into exile,
survived the Puritan regime, and was reinstated at the Restoration. The biographical
sketches given below are from the book usually known as "Fuller's *Worthies*"; their
superficial organization is more finished than are Aubrey's random notes, but the
approach to history and character no more systematic. Still, the shared antiquarian
gusto and the general good humor of these little accounts easily explain their popularity.

From The History of the Worthies of England
Warwickshire: William Shakespeare

William Shakespeare was born at Stratford-on-Avon in this country; in whom
three eminent poets may seem in some sort to be compounded. 1. *Martial*, in
the warlike sound of his surname (whence some may conjecture him of military
extraction) *Hasti-vibrans*, or Shake-speare. 2. *Ovid*, the most natural and witty
of all poets; and hence it was that Queen Elizabeth, coming into a grammar
school, made this extemporary phrase,

> Persius a crab-staff, bawdy Martial, Ovid a fine wag.

3. *Plautus*, who was an exact comedian, yet never any scholar, as our Shakespeare (if alive) would confess himself. Add to all these, that though his genius
generally was jocular, and inclining him to festivity, yet he could (when so
disposed) be solemn and serious, as appears by his tragedies; so that Heraclitus [1]

---

1. The Greek philosopher, taken as a type of gloominess.

himself (I mean if secret and unseen) might afford to smile at his comedies, they were so merry; and Democritus[2] scarce forbear to sigh at his tragedies, they were so mournful.

He was an eminent instance of the truth of that rule, 'Poeta non fit sed nascitur' (one is not made but born a poet). Indeed his learning was very little; so that, as Cornish diamonds are not polished by any lapidary, but are pointed and smooth even as they are taken out of the earth, so nature itself was all the art which was used upon him.

Many were the wit-combats betwixt him and Ben Jonson; which two I behold like a Spanish great galleon and an English man-of-war; Master Jonson (like the former) was built far higher in learning; solid, but slow, in his performances. Shakespeare, with the English man-of-war, lesser in bulk, but lighter in sailing, could turn with all tides, tack about, and take advantage of all winds, by the quickness of his wit and invention. He died anno Domini 1616, and was buried at Stratford-upon-Avon, the town of his nativity.

Westminster: Benjamin Jonson

Benjamin Jonson was born in this city. Though I cannot, with all my industrious inquiry, find him in his cradle, I can fetch him from his long coats. When a little child, he lived in Harts-horn-lane near Charingcross, where his mother married a bricklayer for her second husband.

He was first bred in a private school in Saint Martin's Church; then in Westminster School; witness his own epigram;[1]

> Camden, most reverend head, to whom I owe
> All that I am in arts, all that I know;
> How nothing's that to whom my country owes
> The great renown and name wherewith she goes, etc.

He was statutably admitted into Saint John's College in Cambridge (as many years after incorporated an honourary member of Christ Church in Oxford), where he continued but few weeks for want of further maintenance, being fain to return to the trade of his father-in-law. And let them blush not that have, but those who have not, a lawful calling. He helped in the new structure of Lincoln's Inn, when, having a trowel in his hand, he had a book in his pocket.

Some gentlemen, pitying that his parts should be buried under the rubbish of so mean a calling, did by their bounty manumise[2] him freely to follow his own ingenious inclinations. Indeed his parts were not so ready to run of themselves as able to answer the spur; so that it may be truly said of him, that he had an elaborate wit wrought out in his own industry. He would sit silent in a learned company, and suck in (besides wine) their several humours into his observation. What was one in others, he was able to refine to himself.

He was paramount in the dramatic part of poetry, and taught the stage an exact conformity to the laws of comedians. His comedies were above the volge[3]

2. Another, as a type of laughter (but see Robert Burton, The Anatomy of Melancholy).

1. Epigram XIV (to William Camden, the antiquarian, his headmaster).
2. Set him free (economically).
3. Crowd.

(which are only tickled with downright obscenity), and took not so well at the first stroke as at the rebound, when beheld the second time; yea, they will endure reading, and that with due commendation, so long as either ingenuity or learning are fashionable in our nation. If his later be not so spriteful and vigorous as his first pieces, all that are old will, and all that desire to be old should, excuse him therein.

He was not very happy in his children, and most happy in those which died first, though none lived to survive him. This he bestowed as part of an epitaph on his eldest son, dying in infancy:

> Rest in soft peace; and, asked, say here doth lie,
> Ben Jonson his best piece of poetry.[4]

He died *anno Domini* 1638; and was buried about the belfry, in the abbey church at Westminster.

1662

Cornwall: King Arthur

King Arthur, son of Uther Pendragon, was born in Tintagel castle in this county; and proved afterwards monarch of Great Britain. He may fitly be termed the British Hercules in three respects:

1. For his illegitimate birth, both being bastards, begotten on other men's the other by art magic of Merlin, in others personating their husbands. wives,[1] and yet their mothers honest women; deluded, the one by a miracle,

2. Painful life; one famous for his twelve labours, the other for his twelve victories against the Saxons; and both of them had been greater, had they been made less, and the reports of them reduced within the compass of probability.

3. Violent and woeful death; our Arthur's being as lamentable, and more honourable; not caused by feminine jealousy, but masculine treachery, being murdered by Modred, near the place where he was born:

> As though no other place on Britain's spacious earth
> Were worthy of his end, but where he had his birth.[2]

As for his Round Table, with his knights about it, the tale whereof hath trundled so smoothly along for many ages, it never met with much belief amongst the judicious. He died about the year 542.

And now to speak of the Cornish in general. They ever have been beheld men of valour. It seemeth in the reign of the aforesaid King Arthur they ever made up his vanguard, if I can rightly understand the barbarous verses of a Cornish poet: [3]

> *Nobilis Arcturus nos primos Cornubienses*
> *Bellum facturus vocat (ut puta Cæsaris enses).*
> *Nobis (non aliis reliquis) dat primitus ictum.*

4. Epigram XLV; see above.
1. "Alcmena, wife to Amphytrion, and Igern, wife to Gorloise, prince of Cornwall" (Fuller's note).
2. Michael Drayton's *Poly-Olbion* (First Song, ll. 189–90).
3. "Michael Cornubiensis" (Fuller's note).

Brave Arthur, when he meant a field to fight,
Us Cornish men did first of all invite.
Only to Cornish (count them Cæsar's swords)
He the first blow in battle still affords.

But afterwards, in the time of King Canutus, the Cornish were appointed to make up the rear of our armies. Say not they were much degraded by this transposition from head to foot, seeing the judicious, in marshalling of an army, count the strength (and therefore the credit) to consist in the rear thereof.

But it must be pitied that this people, misguided by their leaders, have so often abused their valour in rebellions, and particularly in the reign of King Henry the Seventh, at Blackheath, where they did the greatest execution with their arrows, reported to be the length of a tailor's yard, the last of that proportion which ever were seen in England. However, the Cornish have since plentifully repaired their credit, by their exemplary valour and loyalty in our late civil wars.

London: Edmund Spenser

Edmund Spenser, born in this city, was brought up in Pembroke Hall in Cambridge, where he became an excellent scholar; but especially most happy in English poetry, as his works do declare; in which the many Chaucerisms used (for I will not say affected by him) are thought by the ignorant to be blemishes, known by the learned to be beauties, to his book, which notwithstanding had been more saleable, if more conformed to our modern language.

There passeth a story commonly told and believed, that Spenser presenting his poems to Queen Elizabeth, she, highly affected therewith, commanded the Lord Cecil, her treasurer, to give him a hundred pounds; and when the treasurer (a good steward of the Queen's money) alleged that the sum was too much, 'Then give him,' quoth the queen, 'what is reason'; to which the lord consented. But was so busied, belike, about matters of high concernment that Spenser received no reward; whereupon he presented this petition in a small piece of paper to the queen in her progress:

I was promised on a time,
To have reason for my rhyme;
From that time unto this season,
I received nor rhyme nor reason.

Hereupon the queen gave strict order (not without some check to her treasurer) for the present payment of the hundred pounds she first intended unto him.

He afterwards went over into Ireland, secretary to the Lord Gray, Lord Deputy thereof; and though that his office under his lord was lucrative, yet got he no estate; but, saith my author,[1] 'peculiari poetis fato, semper cum paupertate conflictatus est.' So that it fared little better with him than with William Xilander the German (a most excellent linguist, antiquary, philosopher, and mathematician), who was so poor that (as Thuanus saith) he was thought, 'fami non fame scribere.'[2]

1. "Camden's Elizabeth, in anno 1598" (Fuller's note).
2. "To write because famished, not for want of fame."

Returning into England, he was robbed by the rebels of that little he had; and dying for grief in great want, *anno* 1598, was honourably buried nigh Chaucer in Westminster, where this distich concluded his epitaph on his monument:

> Anglica te vivo vixit plausitque poesis,
> Nunc moritura timet te moriente mori.

> Whilst thou didst live, lived English poetry,
> Which fears, now thou art dead, that she shall die.[3]

Nor must we forget, that the expense of his funeral and monument was defrayed at the sole charge of Robert, first of that name, Earl of Essex.

1662

JOHN AUBREY
1627?–1697

Born in Wiltshire, educated at home and, for a time, at Trinity College, Oxford, Aubrey returned to his home in the late 1640's, inherited, eventually, a good-sized estate from his father—and subsequently lost most of it—and, in 1654, began "to enter into pocket memorandum books, philosophical and antiquarian remarks," as he put it. He endeavored, in a devoted and unsystematic fashion, to write of natural science and regional antiquities; and years later, after having assisted the Oxford historian Anthony à Wood in the compilation of his biographical *Athenae Oxonienses,* began to keep the records for his *Brief Lives.* They remained unpublished, and even unfinished, at his death. Sprawling, tentative, gossipy, Aubrey's notebooks have nevertheless come to be admired for the shading and coloring they can give to the more reliable historical biographies of their subjects, even when that shading may blur the true outlines. He was a close friend of Hobbes (whose biography is the longest and most elaborate in the collection), of Sir Christopher Wren, and others; and Aubrey's talents were those of the anecdotalist and, even with his human subjects, the amateur archaeologist. Hearsay was more intimate for him than recorded fact, and plays an even greater part in his repertory of sources. His style is often pithy and sly, sometimes unconsciously poignant or half-intentionally comical. Aubrey was wistfully realistic about his own role. Reporting seeing a bust of the once famous beauty Lady Venetia Digby, pilfered from her tomb and now on sale in a shop, he remarked: "How these curiosities would be quite forgot, did not such idle fellows as I am put them down."

3. Only this English inscription survives: "The Prince of Poets in his time, whose Divine Spirit needs no other witness than the Works which he left behind him."

From Brief Lives

Andrew Marvell (1621–1678)

He was of middling stature, pretty strong set, roundish faced, cherry cheeked, hazel eye, brown hair. He was in his conversation very modest, and of very few words; and though he loved wine, he would never drink hard in company, and was wont to say that he would not play the good-fellow in any man's company in whose hands he would not trust his life. He had not a general acquaintance.

In the time of Oliver the Protector he was Latin Secretary. He was a great master of the Latin tongue; an excellent poet in Latin or English: for Latin verses there was no man could come into competition with him.

I remember I have heard him say that the Earl of Rochester was the only man in England who had the true vein of satire.

His native town of Hull loved him so well that they elected him for their representative in Parliament, and gave him an honourable pension to maintain him.

He kept bottles of wine at his lodging, and many times he would drink liberally by himself to refresh his spirits and exalt his muse. (I remember I have been told that the learned Goclenius [1] (an High-German) was wont to keep bottles of good Rhenish wine in his study and, when his spirits wasted, he would drink a good rummer of it.)

Obiit Londini,[2] Aug. 18, 1678, and is buried in St. Giles Church-in-the-Fields about the middle of the south aisle. Some suspect that he was poisoned by the Jesuits, but I cannot be positive.

from MS. 1898

Sir Walter Ralegh (1552–1618)

Sir Walter Ralegh was of Oriel College. Mr. Child's father of Worcestershire was his chamberfellow and lent him a gown, which he could never get, nor satisfaction for it.—From Mr. Child.

He was a tall, handsome and bold man; but his naeve [1] was that he was damnable proud. . . .

He had a most remarkable aspect, an exceeding high forehead, long-faced and sour eye-lidded, a kind of pig's eye. His beard turned up naturally.

In the great parlour at Downton, at Mr. Ralegh's, is a good piece [2] (an original) of Sir W. in a white satin doublet, all embroidered with rich pearls, and a mighty rich chain of great pearls about his neck, and the old servants have told me that the pearls were near as big as the painted ones.

Old Sir Thomas Malette, one of the Justices of the King's Bench *tempore Caroli I et II* [3] knew Sir Walter; and I have heard him say that notwithstanding his so great mastership in style and his conversation with the learnedest and

1. Rudolph Goeckel (1547–1628), German logician.
2. "Died in London."

1. Blemish.
2. Painting.
3. "In the days of Charles I and II."

polite persons, yet he spake broad Devonshire to his dying day. His voice yet was small, as likewise were my schoolfellows his grand-nephews.

Durham House was a noble palace; after he came to his greatness he lived there or in some apartment of it. I well remember his study, which was a little turret that looked into and over the Thames, and had the prospect which is pleasant perhaps as any in the world, and which not only refreshed the eyesight and cheers the spirits and (to speak my mind) I believe enlarges an ingenious man's thoughts.

Sherburne Castle, -Park, -Manor, etc. did belong (and still ought to belong) to the Church of Sarum.[4] Sir W.R. begged it as a Bon from Queen Elizabeth; where he built a delicate lodge in the park, of brick, not big, but very convenient for the bigness, a place to retire from the court in summertime, and to contemplate, etc. Upon his attainder it was begged by the favourite, Carr, Earl of Somerset, who forfeited it (I think) about the poisoning of Sir John Overbury.[5] Then John, Earl of Bristowe,[6] had it given him for his good service to the ambassade in Spain, and added two wings to Sir Walter Ralegh's lodge. In short and indeed, 'tis a most sweet and pleasant place and site as any in the West [7]— perhaps none like it.

He was the first that brought tobacco into England and into fashion.—In our part of North Wilts, e.g. Malmesbury hundred, it came first into fashion by Sir Walter Long.

I have heard my grandfather Lyte say that one pipe was handed from man to man round about the table. They had first silver pipes; the ordinary sort made use of a walnut shell and a straw.

It was sold then for its weight in silver. I have heard some of our old yeomen neighbours say that when they went to Malmesbury or Chippenham market, they culled out their biggest shillings to lay in the scales against the tobacco.

Sir W.R., standing in a stand at Sir Robert Poyntz's part at Acton, took a pipe of tobacco, which made the ladies quit till he had done.

Within these 35 years 'twas scandalous for a divine to take tobacco.

Now the customs of it are the greatest his Majesty hath—Rider's Almanac (1682, *scilicet*) [8]—Since tobacco brought into England by Sir Walter Ralegh, 99 years, the custom whereof is now the greatest of all others and amounts to ——yearly.[9]

Sir Walter Ralegh was a great chemist; and amongst some MSS. receipts I have seen some secrets from him. He studied most in his sea voyages, where he carried always a trunk of books along with him, and had nothing to divert him.

---

4. Salisbury Cathedral; "a Bon" is a boon, a favor.
5. Aubrey makes an almost unbelievable slip here: the Sir *Thomas* Overbury poisoning case was one of the scandals of the age, and Aubrey probably wrote "John" for "Thomas" because of the Earl of Bristol's name following.
6. Bristol (as pronounced there).
7. The West Country.
8. "Namely."
9. As a matter of fact, the then staggering sum of £ 400,000 per annum in Aubrey's day. In Ralegh's, the price of a *pipeful* of tobacco was one-fourth of a laborer's daily wage.

A person so much immersed in action all along and in fabrication of his own fortunes, till his confinement in the Tower, could have but little time to study but what he could spare in the morning. He was no slug; without doubt had a wonderful waking spirit and great judgement to guide it.

An attorney's father (that did my business in Herefordshire before I sold it [10]) married Dr. Burhill's widow. She said that he [Burhill] was a great favourite of Sir Walter Ralegh's and, I think, had been his chaplain; but all the greatest part of the drudgery of his book [11] for criticisms, chronology, and reading of Greek and Hebrew authors was performed by him for Sir Walter Ralegh, whose picture my friend has as part of the Doctor's goods.

I have heard old Major Cosh say that Sir W. Ralegh did not care to go on the Thames in a wherry boat; he would rather go round about over London Bridge.

He loved a wench well; and one time getting up one of the Maids of Honour up against a tree in a wood ('twas his first Lady) who seemed at first boarding to be somewhat fearful of her honour and modest, she cried: 'Sweet Sir Walter, what do you me ask? Will you undo me? Nay, sweet Sir Walter! Sweet Sir Walter! Sir Walter!' At last, as the danger and the pleasure at the same time grew higher, she cried in the extasy, 'Swisser Swatter Swisser Swatter.' She proved with child, and I doubt not but that this hero took care of them both, as also that the product was more than an ordinary mortal.

My old friend James Harrington, Esq. was well acquainted with Sir Benjamin Rudyerd, who was an acquaintance of Sir Walter Ralegh's. He told Mr. J.H. that Sir Walter Ralegh, being invited to dinner with some great person where his son was to go with him, he said to his son, 'Thou art such a quarrelsome, affronting creature that I am ashamed to have such a bear in my company.' Mr. Walt humbled himself to his father, and promised he would behave himself mightily mannerly. So away they went, and Sir Benjamin, I think, with them. He sat next to his father and was very demure at least half dinner time. Then said he: 'I this morning, not having the fear of God before my eyes but by the instigation of the Devil, went to a whore. I was very eager of her, kissed and embraced her, and went to enjoy her, but she thrust me from her and vowed I should not, "For your father lay with me but an hour ago."' Sir Walt, being so strangely surprised and put out of his countenance at so great a tale, gives his son a damned blow over the face. His son, as rude as he was, would not strike his father, but strikes over the face of the gentleman that sat next to him and said, 'Box about, 'twill come to my father anon.' 'Tis now a common-used proverb.

At the end of his *History of the World*, he laments the death of the most noble and hopeful Prince Henry, whose great favourite he was, and who, had he survived his father, would quickly have enlarged him with rewards of honour. . . .

His book sold very slowly at first, and the bookseller complained of it, and told him that he should be a loser by it, which put Sir W. into a passion, and said that since the world did not understand it, they should not have his second part, which he took and threw into the fire, and burned before his face.

10. Aubrey's own estate.
11. *The History of the World.*

He was prisoner in the Tower . . . (*quære*) years; [12] *quære* where his lodgings were. He there, besides his compiling his *History of the World*, studied chemistry. The Earl of Northumberland was a prisoner at the same time, who was the patron to Mr. . . .[13] Hariot and Mr. Warner, two of the best mathematicians then in the world, as also Mr. Hues, [author of] *De Globis*. Serjeant Hoskins, the poet, was a prisoner there too. I heard my cousin Whitney say that he saw him [Sir Walter] in the Tower. He had a velvet cap laced and a rich gown and trunk hose.

He was scandalized with atheism, but he was a bold man, and would venture at discourse which was unpleasant to the churchmen. I remember my Lord Scudamour said 'twas basely said of Sir W.R. to talk of the anagram of Dog.[14] In his speech on the scaffold, I have heard my cousin Whitney say (and I think 'tis printed) that he spake not one word of Christ, but of the great and incomprehensible God, with much zeal and adoration, so that he concluded that he was an a-Christ, not an atheist.

He took a pipe of tobacco a little before he went to the scaffold, which some formal persons were scandalized at, but I think 'twas well and properly done, to settle his spirits.

> *Even such is time, which takes in trust*
> *Our youth, our joys, and all we have*
> *And pays us but with age and dust.*
> *Within the dark and silent grave,*
> *When we have wandered all our ways,*
> *Shuts up the story of our days.*
> *But from which grave and earth and dust*
> *The Lord will raise me up I trust.*

These lines Sir Walter Ralegh wrote in his Bible the night before he was beheaded and desired his relations with these words, viz. 'Beg my dead body which living is denied you; and bury it either in Sherburne or Exeter Church.'

from MS. 1898

[As the conclusion to the very brief account of one Nicholas Towes, a friend of the father of the ill-fated Duke of Buckingham who appeared to him as a ghost saying "I am dead, but cannot rest in peace for the wickedness and abomination of my son George at Court," Aubrey adds the following paragraph, concerning a ghost:]

Anno 1670, not far from Cirencester, was an apparition. Being demanded whether a good spirit or bad, returned no answer, but disappeared with a curious perfume and most melodious twang. Mr. W. Lilly believes it was a fairy.

from MS. 1898

12. Thirteen years, in fact; the "quaere" (a modern scholar would write "?") indicates that Aubrey intended to check up on these facts later.
13. Thomas Hariot.
14. The only anagram of "Dog" is "God."

EDWARD HYDE, EARL OF CLARENDON
1608–1674

Lawyer, Parliamentarian, moderate Royalist, and Anglican, counselor to Charles I and, later, to Charles II, victim of court intrigue and unwilling exile, finally, by another turn of fate, father and grandfather of three English queens (Anne, wife of James II, and the reigning queens Mary and Anne), Clarendon is best known today as a historian of his times. Many chroniclers, from the Athenian Thucydides on, have written of their own times and homes from exile. So with Clarendon; while in the Scilly Isles, in retreat from Parliamentary forces with Prince Charles, the future king, he started in 1646 a *History of the Rebellion,* which he was finally to complete in a second exile—from the court of Charles II at the end of his life—in France. In his early days Clarendon had been associated, through Lucius Cary, Viscount Falkland, with the Ben Jonson circle (see Jonson's Cary and Morison ode). As a Royalist, he urged legality and flexibility, and it was perhaps unfortunate for the king that he chose to follow other advice. The two excerpts from *The History of the Rebellion* (first published 1702–4) represent in retrospect the blend of firm conviction and just reasonableness which must have marked him as an adviser. The first selection is from the material covering 1649, the year of Charles's death; the second, 1658, that of Cromwell's. For another view of one of these figures from the opposition—complex rather than balanced—see Marvell's *Horatian Ode.*

From The History of the Rebellion

[The Character of Charles I]

His kingly virtues had some mixture and allay[1] that hindered them from shining in full lustre, and from producing those fruits they should have been attended with. He was not in his nature bountiful, though he gave very much: which appeared more after the duke of Buckingham's[2] death, after which those showers fell very rarely; and he paused too long in giving, which made those to whom he gave less sensible of the benefit. He kept state[3] to the full, which made his Court very orderly; no man presuming to be seen in a place where he had no pretence to be. He saw and observed men long before he received any about his person, and did not love strangers, nor very confident men. He was a patient hearer of causes, which he frequently accustomed himself to, at the Council board; and judged very well, and was dexterous in the mediating part: so that he often put an end to causes by persuasion, which the stubbornness of men's humours made dilatory in courts of justice.

He was very fearless in his person, but not enterprising; and had an excellent understanding, but was not confident enough of it; which made him oftentimes change his own opinion for a worse, and follow the advice of a man that did not judge so well as himself. And this made him more irresolute than the conjec-

1. Alloy.
2. George Villiers (1592–1626), first Duke of Buckingham; friend and playmate of James I, who made him vastly rich; thereafter adviser to Charles I; finally assassinated.
3. Elaborate, formal courtly pomp.

ture of his affairs would admit. If he had been of a rougher and more imperious nature, he would have found more respect and duty; and his not applying some severe cures to approaching evils proceeded from the lenity of his nature and the tenderness of his conscience, which in all cases of blood made him choose the softer way, and not hearken to severe counsels, how reasonably soever urged. This only restrained him from pursuing his advantage in the first Scots' expedition,[4] when, humanly speaking, he might have reduced that nation to the most slavish obedience that could have been wished. But no man can say he had then many who advised him to it, but the contrary, by a wonderful indisposition all his Council had to fighting or any other fatigue. He was always an immoderate lover of the Scottish nation, having not only been born there, but educated by that people, and besieged by them always, having few English about him until he was king; and the major number of his servants being still of those, who he thought could never fail him; and then no man had such an ascendant over him, by the lowest and humblest insinuations, as duke Hambleton[5] had.

As he excelled in all other virtues, so in temperance he was so strict, that he abhorred all deboshry[6] to that degree, that, at a great festival solemnity, where he once was, when very many of the nobility of the English and Scots were entertained, being told by one who withdrew from thence, what vast draughts of wine they drank, and that there was one earl who had drank most of the rest down and was not himself moved or altered, the King said that he deserved to be hanged; and that earl coming shortly into the room where his majesty was, in some gaiety, to show how unhurt he was from that battle, the King sent one to bid him withdraw from his majesty's presence; nor did he in some days after appear before the King.

There were so many miraculous circumstances contributed to his ruin, that men might well think that heaven and earth conspired it, and that the stars designed it. Though he was, from the first declension[7] of his power, so much betrayed by his own servants, that there were very few who remained faithful to him, yet that treachery proceeded not from any treasonable purpose to do him any harm, but from particular and personal animosities against other men. And afterwards, the terror all men were under of the Parliament, and the guilt they were conscious of themselves, made them watch all opportunities to make themselves gracious to those who could do them good; and so they became spies upon their master, and from one piece of knavery were hardened and confirmed to undertake another, till at last they had no hope of preservation but by the destruction of their master. And after all this, when a man might reasonably believe that less than a universal defection of three nations could not have reduced a great king to so ugly a fate, it is most certain that in that very hour when he was this wickedly murdered in the sight of the sun he had as great a share in the hearts and affections of his subjects in general, was as much beloved, esteemed, and longed for by the people in general of the three nations as any

4. In 1639, Charles made an ill-fated attempt to subdue Scottish Presbyterian forces that had refused to accept Archibishop Laud's reorganization of their church.
5. James, first Duke of Hamilton (1606–49), led a Royalist Scottish army into England and was defeated by Cromwell and beheaded.
6. Debauchery.
7. Decline.

of his predecessors had ever been. To conclude: he was the worthiest gentleman, the best master, the best friend, the best husband, the best father, and the best Christian that the age in which he lived produced. And if he was not the greatest king, if he was without some parts and qualities which have made some kings great and happy, no other prince was ever unhappy who was possessed of half his virtues and endowments, and so much without any kind of vice.

[The Character of Cromwell]

He was one of those men, *quos vituperare ne inimici quidem possunt nisi ut simul laudent;*[1] for he could never have done half that mischief without great parts of courage and industry and judgement. And he must have had a wonderful understanding in the natures and humours of men and as great a dexterity in the applying them; who, from a private and obscure birth—though of a good family—without interest of[2] estate, alliance or friendship, could raise himself to such a height and compound and knead such opposite and contradictory tempers, humours, and interests into a consistence that contributed to his designs, and to their own destruction; whilst himself grew insensibly powerful enough to cut off those by whom he had climbed in the instant that they projected to demolish their own building. What Velleius Paterculus said of Cinna may very justly be said of him, *ausum eum quæ nemo auderet bonus perfecisse, quæ a nullo, nisi fortissimo, perfici possent.*[3] Without doubt, no man with more wickedness ever attempted anything or brought to pass what he desired more wickedly, more in the face and contempt of religion and moral honesty; yet wickedness as great as his could never have accomplished those designs without the assistance of a great spirit, an admirable circumspection and sagacity, and a most magnanimous resolution.

When he appeared first in the Parliament, he seemed to have a person in no degree gracious, no ornament of discourse, none of those talents which use[4] to reconcile the affections of the standers by: yet as he grew into place and authority, his parts seemed to be renewed, as if he had concealed faculties till he had occasion to use them; and when he was to act the part of a great man, he did it without any indecency through the want of custom.

After he was confirmed and invested Protector by *The humble Petition and Advice,*[5] he consulted with very few upon any action of importance, nor communicated any enterprise he resolved upon with more than those who were to have principal parts in the execution of it; nor to them sooner than was absolutely necessary. What he once resolved in which he was not rash, he would not be dissuaded from, nor endure any contradiction of his power and authority, but extorted obedience from them who were not willing to yield it.

When he had laid some very extraordinary tax upon the city, one Cony, an

---

1. "Whom even his enemies could not denigrate without at the same time praising."
2. Vested interest in.
3. "He attempted what no good man ought to have tried, and succeeded where only a great man could" (from Velleius Paterculus' *Res Gestae Divi Augusti,* a history of the age of Augustus Caesar).
4. Act.
5. In 1657, a new draft constitution was presented to Parliament by which, among other things, Cromwell was to be given the title of king, a privilege he refused.

eminent fanatic, and one who had heretofore served him very notably, positively refused to pay his part, and loudly dissuaded others from submitting to it, as an imposition notoriously against the law and the propriety of the subject, which all honest men were bound to defend. Cromwell sent for him, and cajoled him with the memory of the old kindness and friendship that had been between them, and that of all men he did not expect this opposition from him, in a matter that was so necessary for the good of the commonwealth. But it was always his fortune to meet with the most rude and obstinate behaviour from those who had formerly been absolutely governed by him, and they commonly put him in mind of some expressions and saying of his own in cases of the like nature; so this man remembered him how great an enemy he had expressed himself to such grievances, and declared that all who submitted to them and paid illegal taxes were more to blame, and greater enemies to their country, than they who imposed them, and that the tyranny of princes could never be grievous but by the tameness and stupidity of the people. When Cromwell saw that he could not convert him, he told him that he had a will as stubborn as his, and he would try which of them two should be master; and thereupon, with some terms of reproach and contempt, he committed the man to prison; whose courage was nothing abated by it; but as soon as the term came, he brought his *habeas corpus* [6] in the King's Bench, which they then called the Upper Bench. Maynard, who was of counsel with the prisoner, demanded his liberty with great confidence, both upon the illegality of the commitment, and the illegality of the imposition, as being laid without any lawful authority. The judges could not maintain or defend either, but enough declared what their sentence would be; and therefore the Protector's Attorney required a farther day to answer what had been urged. Before that day, Maynard was committed to the Tower, for presuming to question or make doubt of his authority; and the judges were sent for, and severely reprehended for suffering that license; and when they with all humility mentioned the law and *Magna Charta,* Cromwell told them, their *magna farta* should not control his actions, which he knew were for the safety of the commonwealth. He asked them who made them judges; whether they had any authority to sit there but what he gave them; and that if his authority were at an end, they knew well enough what would become of themselves; and therefore advised them to be more tender of that which could only preserve them; and so dismissed them with caution, that they should not suffer the lawyers to prate what it would not become them to hear.

Thus he subdued a spirit that had been often troublesome to the most sovereign power, and made Westminster Hall [7] as obedient and subservient to his commands as any of the rest of his quarters. In all other matters which did not concern the life of his jurisdiction, he seemed to have great reverence for the law, and rarely interposed between party and party. And as he proceeded with this kind of indignation and haughtiness with those who were refractory and dared to contend with his greatness, so toward those who complied with his good pleasure, and courted his protection, he used [8] a wonderful civility, generosity, and bounty. . . .

6. His writ of *habeas corpus.*
7. The Presbyterian assembly, which had met there.
8. Practiced.

To reduce three nations, which perfectly hated him, to an entire obedience to all his dictates, to awe and govern those nations by an army that was inde-voted to him and wished his ruin, was an instance of a very prodigious address. But his greatness at home was but a shadow of the glory he had abroad. It was hard to discover which feared him most, France, Spain, or the Low Countries, where his friendship was current at the value he put upon it. And as they did all sacrifice their honour and their interest to his pleasure, so there is nothing he could have demanded that either of them would have denied him. . . .

He was not a man of blood, and totally declined Machiavel's method,[9] which prescribes, upon any alteration of a government, as a thing absolutely necessary, to cut off all the heads of those, and extirpate their families, who are friends to the old one. And it was confidently reported that in the council of officers it was more than once proposed, that there might be a general massacre of all the royal party as the only expedient to secure the government, but Cromwell would never consent to it; it may be, out of too much contempt of his enemies. In a word, as he had all the wickednesses against which damnation is denounced and for which hellfire is prepared, so he had some virtues which have caused the memory of some men in all ages to be celebrated; and he will be looked upon by posterity as a brave, bad man.

1702–1704

JEREMY TAYLOR
1613–1667

The author of *Holy Living* and *Holy Dying* was more highly regarded in the early nineteenth century than Sir Thomas Browne (except by Ralph Waldo Emerson, whose response to seventeenth-century poetry and prose anticipated modern taste); and although it is easy to select haunting and resonant passages from his devotional books and from his sermons, it was not for these that he was so admired. It is instructive to realize that Coleridge liked tremendously the Samuel Daniel of *The Civil Wars,* discursive rather than lyrical; similarly, Taylor's extended meditative seriousness, unmarred by the brilliant leaps and twists and turns of a style like that of Donne, stood for all that was most elegantly solemn in an expository style still untouched by the criteria that the Enlightenment would exact of prose argument. Taylor's style strikes a balance, too, between the slightly archaic and the less mannered, more modern syntax; and, for his age, he is under-, rather than over-allusive.

Taylor was born in Cambridgeshire, educated at Cambridge, took holy orders in 1633, preached in London, became a fellow of All Souls' at Oxford (a college con-sisting solely of fellows, with no undergraduates), and for a while was attached to the royal household. He spent a good many years at Golden House, the estate in Wales of the Earl of Carbey; while there, he preached some and wrote extensively, including an unusually ecumenical treatise, *A Discourse on the Liberty of Prophesying* (1647),

9. Any and all harsh *Realpolitik* could be blamed, in Elizabethan England and thereafter, on a stock figure of Italianate evil, called Machiavel, having not much to do with the major political thought of the Florentine Niccolò Machiavelli (1469–1527). Clarendon's knowledge of both *The Prince* and the more important *Discourses on Livy*, however, was profound.

and his two most famous works, *The Rule and Exercise of Holy Living* (1650) and *Holy Dying* (1651). After the Restoration he lived in London, and before his death was made Bishop of Down and Connor in Ireland.

Holy Dying

Chapter I

A General Preparation Towards a Holy and Blessed Death, by Way of Consideration

From Section I: Consideration of the Vanity and Shortness of Man's Life

A man is a bubble, said the Greek proverb; which Lucian [1] represents with advantages and its proper circumstances, to this purpose; saying, that all the world is a storm, and men rise up in their several generations, like bubbles descending *a Jove pluvio*, from God and the dew of heaven, from a tear and drop of man, from nature and providence: and some of these instantly sink into the deluge of their first parent, and are hidden in a sheet of water, having had no other business in the world but to be born that they might be able to die: others float up and down two or three turns, and suddenly disappear, and give their place to others: and they that live longest upon the face of the waters, are in perpetual motion, restless and uneasy; and, being crushed with the great drop of a cloud, sink into flatness and a froth; the change not being great, it being hardly possible it should be more a nothing than it was before. So is every man: he is born in vanity and sin; he comes into the world like morning mushrooms, soon thrusting up their heads into the air, and conversing with their kindred of the same production, and as soon they turn into dust and forgetfulness: some of them without any other interest in the affairs of the world but that they made their parents a little glad, and very sorrowful: others ride longer in the storm; it may be until seven years of vanity be expired, and then peradventure the sun shines hot upon their heads, and they fall into the shades below, into the cover of death and darkness of the grave to hide them. But if the bubble stands the shock of a bigger drop, and outlives the chances of a child, of a careless nurse, of drowning in a pail of water, of being overlaid by a sleepy servant, or such little accidents, then the young man dances like a bubble, empty and gay, and shines like a dove's neck, or the image of a rainbow, which hath no substance, and whose very imagery and colours are fantastical; and he dances out the gaiety of his youth, and is all the while in a storm, and endures only because he is not shocked on the head by a drop of bigger rain, or crushed by the pressure of a load of indigested meat, or quenched by the disorder of an ill-placed humour: and to preserve a man alive in the midst of so many chances and hostilities, is as great a miracle as to create him; to preserve him from rushing into nothing, and at first to draw him up from nothing, were equally the issues of an almighty power. And

1. Lucian, the satirist, in his dialogue *Charon.*

therefore the wise men of the world have contended who shall best fit man's condition with words signifying his vanity and short abode. Homer[2] calls a man 'a leaf,' the smallest, the weakest piece of a short-lived, unsteady plant: Pindar[3] calls him 'the dream of a shadow': another, 'the dream of the shadow of smoke': but St. James spake by a more excellent spirit, saying, 'our life is but a vapour' (James 4:14, ἀτμίς, viz., drawn from the earth by a celestial influence; made of smoke, or the lighter parts of water, tossed with every wind, moved by the motion of a superior body, without virtue in itself, lifted up on high or left below, according as it pleases the sun its foster-father. But it is lighter yet; it is but 'appearing' (φαινομένη); a fantastic vapour, an apparition, nothing real: it is not so much as a mist, not the matter of a shower, nor substantial enough to make a cloud; but it is like Cassiopeia's chair, or Pelops' shoulder, or the circles of heaven, φαινόμενα, than which you cannot have a word that can signify a verier nothing. And yet the expression is one degree more made diminutive: a 'vapour,' and 'fantastical,' or a 'mere appearance,' and this but for a little while neither (πρὸς ὀλίγον); the very dream, the phantasm disappears in a small time, 'like the shadow that departeth'; or 'like a tale that is told'; or 'as a dream when one awaketh.' A man is so vain, so unfixed, so perishing a creature, that he cannot long last in the scene of fancy: a man goes off, and is forgotten, like the dream of a distracted person. The sum of all is this: that thou art a man, than whom there is not in the world any greater instance of heights and declensions,[4] of lights and shadows, of misery and folly, of laughter and tears, of groans and death.

. . .

Thus nature calls us to meditate of death by those things which are the instruments of acting it: and God by all the variety of his providence makes us see death everywhere, in all variety of circumstances, and dressed up for all the fancies and the expectation of every single person. Nature hath given us one harvest every year, but death hath two, and the spring and the autumn send throngs of men and women to charnel-houses; and all the summer long men are recovering from their evils of the spring, till the dog-days come, and then the Sirian star[5] makes the summer deadly; and the fruits of autumn are laid up for all the year's provision, and the man that gathers them eats and surfeits, and dies and needs them not, and himself is laid up for eternity; and he that escapes till winter only stays for another opportunity which the distempers of that quarter minister to him with great variety. Thus death reigns in all the portions of our time; the autumn with its fruits provides disorders for us, and the winter's cold turns them into sharp diseases, and the spring brings flowers to strew our hearse, and the summer gives green turf and brambles to bind upon our graves. Calentures[6] and surfeit, cold and agues, are the four

2. In the *Iliad* VI.146.
3. In the eighth Pythian Ode, l. 135.
4. Declinings.
5. Sirius, the Dog Star. The "dog days" in August are so-called because the constellation Orion, followed by Sirius, rises near dawn, and Sirius, the brightest star in the skies, was thought to add its heat to that of the sun.
6. Heat spells.

quarters of the year, and all minister to death; and you can go no whither[7] but you tread upon a dead man's bones.

Section IV   Consideration of the Miseries of Man's Life

As our life is very short, so it is very miserable; and therefore it is well it is short. God, in pity to mankind, lest his burden should be insupportable and his nature an intolerable load, hath reduced our state of misery to an abbreviature; and the greater our misery is, the less while it is like to last; the sorrows of a man's spirit being like ponderous weights, which by the greatness of their burden make a swifter motion, and descend into the grave to rest and ease our wearied limbs; for then only we shall sleep quietly, when those fetters are knocked off, which not only bound our souls in prison, but also ate the flesh till the very bones opened the secret garments of their cartilages, discovering their nakedness and sorrow.

1. Here is no place to sit down in, but you must rise as soon as you are set, for we have gnats in our chambers, and worms in our gardens, and spiders and flies in the palaces of the greatest kings. How few men in the world are prosperous! What an infinite number of slaves and beggars, of persecuted and oppressed people, fill all corners of the earth with groans, and heaven itself with weeping prayers and sad remembrances! How many provinces and kingdoms are afflicted by a violent war, or made desolate by popular diseases! Some whole countries are remarked with fatal evils, or periodical sicknesses. Grand Cairo in Egypt feels the plague every three years returning like a quartan ague, and destroying many thousands of persons. All the inhabitants of Arabia the desert[8] are in continual fear of being buried in huge heaps of sand, and therefore dwell in tents and ambulatory houses, or retire to unfruitful mountains, to prolong an uneasy and wilder life. And all the countries round about the Adriatic Sea feel such violent convulsions by tempests and intolerable earthquakes, that sometimes whole cities find a tomb, and every man sinks with his own house made ready to become his monument, and his bed is crushed into the disorders of a grave. Was not all the world drowned at one deluge and breach of the divine anger; and shall not all the world again be destroyed by fire? Are there not many thousands that die every night, and that groan and weep sadly every day? But what shall we think of that great evil which for the sins of men God hath suffered to possess the greatest part of mankind? Most of the men that are now alive, or that have been living for many ages, are Jews, Heathens, or Turks; and God was pleased to suffer a base epileptic person,[9] a villain and a vicious, to set up a religion which hath filled all the nearer parts of Asia, and much of Africa, and some part of Europe; so that the greatest number of men and women born in so many kingdoms and provinces are infallibly made Mahometans, strangers and enemies to Christ by whom alone we can be saved: this consideration is extremely sad, when we remember how universal and how great an evil it is that so many millions of sons and daughters are born to enter into the possession of devils to eternal

7. Nowhere.
8. "Arabia deserta": the Arabian peninsula.
9. Mahommed.

ages. These evils are miseries of great parts of mankind, and we cannot easily consider more particularly the evils which happen to us, being the inseparable affections or incidents to the whole nature of man.

2. We find that all the women in the world are either born for barrenness, or the pains of childbirth, and yet this is one of our greatest blessings; but such indeed are the blessings of this world, we cannot be well with nor without many things. Perfumes make our heads ache, roses prick our fingers, and in our very blood, where our life dwells, is the scene under which nature acts many sharp fevers and heavy sicknesses. It were too sad if I should tell how many persons are afflicted with evil spirits, with spectres and illusions of the night; and that huge multitudes of men and women live upon man's flesh; nay, worse yet, upon the sins of men, upon the sins of their sons and of their daughters, and they pay their souls down for the bread they eat, buying this day's meal with the price of the last night's sin.

1651

From Sermons

[Children]

When we see a child strike a servant rudely, or jeer a silly person, or wittily cheat his play-fellow, or talk words light as the skirt of a summer garment, we laugh and are delighted with the wit and confidence of the boy; and encourage such hopeful beginnings; and in the meantime we consider not that from these beginnings he shall grow up till he become a tyrant, an oppressor, a goat and a traitor. *Nemo simul malus fit & malus esse cernitur; sicut nec scorpiis tum innascuntur stimuli cum pungunt.*[1] No man is discerned to be vicious so soon as he is so, and vices have their infancy and their childhood and it cannot be expected that in a child's age should be the vice of a man; that were monstrous as if he wore a beard in his cradle; and we do not believe that a serpent's sting does just then grow when he strikes us in a vital part. The venom and the little spear was there, when it first began to creep from his little shell. And little boldnesses and looser words and wranglings for nuts, and lying for trifles, are of the same proportion to the malice of a child, as impudence and duels and injurious law-suits, and false witness in judgement and perjuries are in men.

1651

[Children]

No man can tell but he that loves his children, how many delicious accents make a man's heart dance in the pretty conversation of those dear pledges; their childishness, their stammering, their little angers, their innocence, their imperfections, their necessities are so many little emanations of joy and comfort to him that delights in their persons and society; but he that loves not his wife and children, feeds a Lioness at home, and broods a nest of sorrows.

1653

1. Quoted from Plutarch.

The Restoration and
the Eighteenth Century

The Restoration and
the Eighteenth Century

We may speak of the eighteenth century as the period of the Enlightenment, and the term carries a fairly precise meaning when it is applied to France: secular in spirit, skeptical in matters of knowledge, rationalistic only in its critique of historical institutions, devoted to the idea of justice, and jealously protective of the dignity of human nature. Not all these traits are to be found in every writer, it is true, but they serve well enough to characterize the age. When we turn from France to England, however, the idea of an Enlightenment becomes less clear.

As a predominantly Protestant nation, and one whose established church had turned away from dogmatic and evangelical extremes toward a religion of moral duty, England had less reason to be anticlerical or militantly secular. Deism became a force in the later seventeenth century and persisted as a rationalistic natural religion opposed to all dependence upon revelation; but it never achieved a highly respectable position in England. English political liberties, which served as a model for French reformers, were sufficient to make plausible the Whig trust in slow historical progression and to win loyalty, if not in fact reverence, to constitutional forms. Most of the major writers of the age, from Dryden to Dr. Johnson (and including Swift and Pope), were largely Tory in spirit: distrustful of human nature and devoted to the cause of public order.

Yet one can see a degree of secularization in England. The center of concern has shifted from the institutions that confer legitimate authority to the detached individual, from dogma to the painful quest for balance and tact. Decisions are made by man rather than for him, and they exact a new intensity of self-criticism, a wary resistance to the appeals of partiality and self-interest—a discipline, as the age would have it, of both head and heart. For while there is distrust of the private spirit and of anarchic individualism—usually shown to be based in pride—there is no easy recourse in turn to rule or formula. The distinctive spirit of the age, then, and it might be called Enlightenment, is a critical one—constantly testing through irony, purging with satire, and finding conviction in the poise of an exact antithesis or a delicate balance.

POLITICS AND MORALITY

When the Stuarts returned to the throne in 1660, the changes of two intervening decades of revolution could not simply be reversed, for the experience of power had awakened new capacities and justified new ambitions. At first there was apparent reaction. The Church of England was re-established as the state religion. But it now had to fight and intrigue with Dissenters and Roman Catholics to preserve its authority. There were strong demands for full civil rights by the Puritans, and there were grave fears of what Charles II might grant to the Catholic French monarch, Louis XIV, in return for financial subsidy. The fears of the church were only a reflection of the instability of the King's power. Charles was under constant pressure in his later years from Whig lords (whose alliances were with London merchants, middle-class Dissenters, and former Dutch allies) and from the Tory supporters of his Catholic brother and apparent heir, the Duke of York (later James II). But more fundamentally, the idea of kingship itself was in question.

In his great political work of 1651, the *Leviathan*, Thomas Hobbes had argued the need for a stable and undivided sovereignty. Hobbes opposed the growing myth of the mixed state (a balance of power among King, Lords, and Commons), but his defense of absolute sovereignty was no return to the Stuart doctrine of the divine right of kings ("right divine to govern wrong," as Pope described James I's doctrine). Hobbes based his case on natural expediency; the alternative was intolerable anarchy, in which each man warred against every other. It hardly mattered to Hobbes what form the sovereignty took so long as it could command and maintain power (and Swift, writing after the Glorious Revolution of 1688, declared that Hobbes's essential error lay in making the King rather than the Parliament the ultimate sovereign). John Locke, writing in Charles II's reign what was not to be published until 1690, insisted that the King derived his authority not from the sheer necessity of his subjects but from their active consent; should he destroy their property or enslave them, he would put himself "into a state of war with the people, who are thereupon absolved from any further obedience."

This secularized view of the state left little sanctity to the king, and Charles II was rarely the man to claim it. Urbane and cultivated, with a taste for music and wit, he inspired personal affection and public distrust in equal measure. He lacked moral depth or tenacity of purpose, and, while his love of pleasure was a welcome relief for many from the sober fanaticism of strict Puritans and surly republicans, it encouraged little repose in his strength or reliance on his word. The Marquess of Halifax wrote of Charles after his death: "It must be allowed he had a little over-balance on the well-natured side, not vigour enough to be earnest to do a kind thing, much less to do a harsh one; but if a hard thing was done to another man, he did not eat his supper the worse for it. It was rather a deadness than a severity of nature. . . ." One is struck by how often Halifax recurs to the King's physical well-being: "It may be said that his inclinations to love were the effects of health and a good constitution, with as little mixture of the seraphic part as man ever had; and though from that foundation men often raise their passions, I am apt to think his stayed as much as any man's ever did in the lower region. . . . He had more properly . . . a good stomach to his mistresses than any great passion for them. His taking them from others was never learnt in a romance, and indeed fitter for a philosopher than a knight-errant." If Charles showed no jealousy, it was "love of ease" that prevented it; for "where mere nature is the motive, it is possible for a man . . . to argue that a rival taketh away nothing but the heart and leaveth the rest."

The Glorious Revolution of 1688, which brought William III and Mary to the throne, confirmed the principle of the mixed state, a principle that was to be invoked throughout the century to follow and to be accepted as the Revolution Settlement by all but the few fanatical Jacobites (who remained loyal to James II and his heirs). There was still only a cautious assertion of constitutional changes: the fiction of James's abdication was used to soften the force of Parliament's action, and the limits set to the king's power were left implicit in his oath to govern "according to the statutes in Parliament agreed on." For years to come the full meaning of the changes remained in the process of definition, and the stability to be found in the harmony of a mixed state remained more vision than actuality.

The growth of the electorate gave more power to Commons, and the conduct of protracted wars led to the growth of the court bureaucracy. To support its program the court required more and more recourse to public loans, and with them came an increase both of an administrative cadre and of a moneyed class whose wealth came from investment rather than from rents. This erosion of the landed interest was felt most acutely by the smaller landowners, the country gentry, and they were most suspicious of the centralized power at court. The early years of the eighteenth century were a period of frequent elections and shifts of power, and the efforts of the Whig forces to enlist wider support led to more toleration for Dissenters and more dependence upon the financial power of London.

Much of the energy of the writers of the day was devoted to defending traditional attitudes or to destroying them. Daniel Defoe attacked the landed gentry in behalf of the men of wealth; Swift exposed the increasing power of men whose loyalty was claimed not by tenant and estate but by interest rates and "paper money." But meanwhile these distinctions were breaking down, as men of wealth invested in land (at times buying up the nearly bankrupt estates of small landholders) and as the landed aristocracy, through both investment and intermarriage, allied itself with the "moneyed" men. The political stability dreamed of in the mixed state was attained at last in the 1720's when Sir Robert Walpole strengthened the court by his bold use of patronage to win support, and there arose the serious question of whether the state had become a stable balance or rather a new kind of tyranny under the forms of parliamentary leadership.

If Charles II sets the note of the Restoration period, Walpole does as much for the mid-eighteenth century. Bluff, hospitable, ostentatious, he had a sufficient sense of his own power. "I am certainly at present in a situation that makes me," he said to Lord Hervey, "of consequence to more people than any man ever before me was, or perhaps than any man may ever be again." Hervey reflected on "the double vanity this great man was guilty of in believing what he said, and saying what he believed." Walpole's management of George II through Queen Caroline and of Parliament through a system of patronage made his control of England a formidable substitute for earlier and franker forms of tyranny. Walpole's control of English liberties was far less complete; but the Licensing Act of 1737, which imposed political censorship on the stage, might recall Dryden's words about Augustus, who "conscious of himself of so many crimes which he had committed, thought . . . to provide for his own reputation by making an edict against lampoons and satires."

Walpole achieved stability by freeing the court of the overriding power of Commons. In the process the Whig oligarchy, having attained a one-party system, adopted much of the traditional doctrine of the Tories. It was the so-called Patriots (led by the friend of Swift and Pope, Lord Bolingbroke) who kept alive the idea of an Opposition as a guarantor of freedom, who demanded more frequent elections and more extensive representation, and who sought to free Parliament of its control by place-holders.

In an age where power increasingly followed wealth, the highly paid sinecures that Walpole distributed were not only a reward for obedience, they were a further entrenchment of a self-perpetuating group. More appalling to men like Swift and Pope was Walpole's marshalling of a squad of hireling writers, serviceable men of limited talent, to defend his ministry and discredit his opponents. Royal patronage no longer furthered merit for its own sake but used the forms of distinction to reward subservience and intellectual dishonesty. Pope's *Dunciad* makes Colley Cibber the monarch of the dunces, the epitome of a commercialized and debased culture; he had been elevated to the post of poet-laureate less for talent than for pliability.

The opposition to Walpole was made articulate by men who had loyalties to a landed aristocracy, but those loyalties were neither felt nor expressed in limited economic terms. Rather, they were universalized as the opposition of genuine culture to sham, of free intelligence to prostitute mediocrity. For the stability that Walpole gave England was gained at the cost of moral aspiration. A man might aspire to power or wealth, but he had to leave his integrity behind when he went "to see Sir Robert." This sense of universal corruption was the specter created in the great satires of the age, and in opposition to it a new kind of heroism emerged. It included aristocratic scorn for mercantile zeal that slights honesty and justice; esteem for the "middle state" of man (above brutalizing poverty and below debilitating luxury); disdain for the mindless "mob," whether of the lower classes or the hireling nobles; nostalgia for institutions which embodied principles stabler than individual will or current fashion. One can see this as a rear-guard resistance to growing bourgeois liberalism, as reactionary appeal to a past that could not be restored and perhaps had never truly existed. But from the other end of that cycle of growth we may find it harder to call it reaction; such judgments trust history to settle issues, and history never does so for long.

The aspiration that Walpole and his chosen successors, the Pelhams, failed to satisfy found release in the leadership of the elder William Pitt, Earl of Chatham. The hero of the London merchants, he also fostered a sense of national greatness, presiding over the defeat of France on three continents and her loss of power in both Canada and India. These were triumphs of mercantile expansion which laid the groundwork for the growth of empire abroad and of industry at home; but Pitt infused them with a sense of moral purpose.

In George III, who became king in 1760, moral aspiration reached the throne itself, but his earnestness was marked by obstinacy and his devotion to duty by priggishness. The third George, unlike the first two, cultivated domestic virtues rather than foreign mistresses, and his favor was worthily conferred (with the guidance of ministers) upon such men as Dr. Johnson, Gibbon, and Rousseau. But his rigid and suspicious nature made him declare, with a sense of shock, that he had to "call in bad men to govern bad men." Among the "bad men" to be governed were the American colonists, who completed their successful revolution by 1783, and the political radicals at home, whose sympathy with the colonies was only a prelude to their support of the French Revolution a few years later.

Perhaps the best of the men George chose to govern for him was the younger William Pitt, who became chief minister in 1784 at the age of twenty-five (as Coleridge was to observe, he was "always full-grown," for he "was cast rather than grew"). Pitt had genius in administrative reform; he reduced waste in government offices, revised the tax and customs system, reduced the national debt, and stimulated trade.

These technical achievements were, however, overtaken by the war with France which followed upon the Revolution; and Pitt became, with the threat of invasion from abroad and the fear of subversion at home, all too ready to see political radicalism of any sort as potential treason and to make it so in law. Somewhat as Robert Walpole had been the object of attack by the major poets of the mid-century, so Pitt, for different reasons, was to win the scorn of Blake, Wordsworth, and Coleridge.

THE MIDDLE WAY: WIT AND DRESS

Few moments seem so decisive a break in the continuity of English literature as the Restoration. While in exile in France, the court of Charles II had acquired a new tone of worldliness and self-conscious sophistication that was to affect literary as well as social forms. The fact that Milton's *Paradise Lost* or Bunyan's *Pilgrim's Progress* was published after the Restoration seems incongruous. Yet the new tone was not simply a brittle elegance derived from French manners and turned mockingly upon sober Puritan zeal. It had its own seriousness even when it was most willfully outrageous; and it was marked by deep skepticism. The unlimited claims of religious sects and political causes had produced decades of painful division—within the nation, even within families—and they were now seen with a strong sense of their danger. Extravagant assertions of divine favor by radical Protestants and no less fanatical Royalists seemed frivolous, fevered, and deeply destructive. Skepticism turned to the practical and viable; it tested all claims and assertions for both their meaningfulness and their consequences.

One of the forms of this skepticism was the cultivation of dialectic and banter. Against each unlimited assertion one could place its contrary. Or one could frame dialogues in which the intellectual bankruptcy of the fanatics was exposed by a dead-lock between extremists or by an opponent of Socratic modesty and irony. We can see the spirit of this in Dryden's *Essay of Dramatic Poesy* (1668), where four critics assert in turn the superiority of ancient or modern, French or English, literature. It is a dialogue of exceptional amiability, for these men are good-tempered and comparatively flexible; it takes place, moreover, just on the margin of an Anglo-Dutch war, a quiet retreat from public conflicts. Other dialogues were more satirical and reductive; they allowed the "enthusiast" to expand to the utmost before he was punctured and deflated by wit. Enthusiasm itself was a term of reproach; it referred to the delusion of being divinely inspired and to the self-hypnotic rhetoric of those who acted under that delusion. To show them as all the more vehement for their ignorance and superstition was the satirist's device; we see it in Samuel Butler's portrait of the radical Protestant squire Ralpho in *Hudibras* (1663–78). Another method was to study the psychopathology of enthusiasm and to trace its madness to a pride that could not endure the restraints of reason and common truths.

The retreat from public conflicts had led a group of learned men of various allegiances to gather for the discussion of scientific matters at Gresham College in London during the years of Cromwell's Protectorate; out of these meetings (from which the topics of religion and politics were barred) emerged the Royal Society, chartered by the King in 1662. The Royal Society was devoted, in a Baconian spirit, to empirical investigation, and it framed as well an influential conception of language. Joseph Glanvill, for example, could see nothing but "endless disputes and quarrels" come of devotion to the "verbal emptiness of the philosophy of the Schools," that is, the Scholasticism that sought to explain phenomena by multiplying terms: "For what else can be the fruit of a philosophy, made of occult qualities, sympathies, entelechies, elements, celestial influences, and abundance of other hard words and lazy generalities but an arrest of all ingenious and practical endeavour, and a wilderness of opinions instead of certainty and science?" What Glanvill hoped for and at last saw as possible was "a philosophy fruitful in works, not in words, and such as may accommodate the use of life, both natural and moral." And he, like others, drew a parallel for religion: the need to give up endless and insoluble controversy about doctrine, often based upon obscure texts of Scripture, and to concentrate upon the "practical and certain knowledge which will assist and promote our virtue and our happiness."

This reaction against "notion and theory" affected all realms of experience. Sir Isaac Newton boasted, "I do not frame hypotheses," and by that he meant his refusal, in contrast to Descartes, to be seduced by speculation from the essential task of empirical description. In politics and religion the men of "latitude" and moderation tried to forge a method of critical discrimination. It was typically represented as the search for a middle way between extremes. By this was meant not lukewarmness or weak compromise (what the age called "trimming") but a bold rejection of untested dogma. The middle way lacked the support of authority and precedent; it required a delicate judgment of each new situation, a weighing of values without formula, and a readiness to dwell in uncertainties rather than surrender to prejudice or cant.

We can see the theme of the middle way captured in the metaphor of dress that pervaded the writing of the age. Language has often been described as the dress of thought, and rhetoric has been treated as a wardrobe of idioms in which ideas might be clothed. In the Restoration we find a strong reaction against merely verbal wit. The attack could extend to the conceits of the metaphysical poets (and particularly the late, mannered style of a John Cleveland), to the metaphorical flights of baroque sermons, to the jargon of Scholastics or (worse) of pseudo-mystical and alchemical writers, to the "wresting of scriptures" that tortured the text of the Bible until it could serve any prejudice or party. In the realm of manners, the attack (such as we see in Restoration comedy) was turned on the coxcomb who made constant use of the "jerk and sting of an epigram" and who chased the reputation of brilliance through a thousand puns. The would-be wit was always on the stretch to show his cleverness and seldom concerned about whether truth or insight might lie below the dazzling surface. Restoration comedy tended to equate the would-be wit with the fop. The fop, too, disregards "propriety" or "decency," a sense of what belongs or is fitting. He does not dress in a manner appropriate to his rank or to the occasion but seeks only to overwhelm others with his finery. His dress is a collection of unrelated bits of brilliance—"one glaring chaos and wild heap of wit," as Pope described a poem full of conceits—whose only purpose is to dazzle.

What were the alternatives? Was not all dress a form of deception? Some believed so and insisted upon naked nature, as if that were still possible in a world of men. In Restoration comedy, the fop's opponent was often the rake, a man of frankly licentious appetite with the cunning to satisfy it, a cool Machiavellian in the world of sex and money. He enacted the unabashed animal he thought man might better be and gloried in his energy and resourcefulness. Yet neither of these extremes, fop or rake, stood up to scrutiny, for both revealed anarchic pride and self-seeking. The typical response to both was to find a middle way: to recognize the "way of the world" and to dress to meet its demands. For the true wit did not neglect the guises the world would accept; but he used them as a means of preserving his independence and integrity. This was the case of Mirabell in William Congreve's *The Way of the World* (1700), and we can see its deeper implications in Swift's *A Tale of a Tub* (1704).

Swift's allegory presented Christian teaching as a simple garment that, in the course of history, was covered with all the fashionable accessories that the world demanded. Three brothers showed the different ways of treating the garment. Peter (the Roman Catholic Church) first led the others in loading his coat with elaborate ornaments and refused, when they were criticized, to remove any. Jack (the radical Protestant church) condemned Peter's error and, in a fit of enthusiastic reformation, tore his own coat to shreds in the effort to remove whatever Peter had persuaded him to add. Only the third brother, Martin (representing the middle way of the Church of England), recognized the impossibility of restoring his coat to its original purity, accepted those additions whose removal would destroy its fabric, and carefully detached the rest stitch by stitch. Martin was concerned with the coat itself rather than its expression of his own will; and in his rejection of both imposture and brutality he showed an awareness that reached, in effect, a different level rather than lay midway on a single plane. The middle way, for Swift, is not simply a compromise between two errors but a transcendence of the vicious folly that produced both.

AN AUGUSTAN AGE

In his scorn for the verbal sophistries of false wit, the writer of this age often called them barbarous or "Gothic." By contrast he looked back to the grace and lucidity of classical writing and tried to recover its virtues in his own work. The period was one of great translation; not only did Dryden translate all of Virgil, and Pope all of Homer, but there were also the free "imitations" of Horace and Juvenal, from Rochester's early experiments to Dr. Johnson's *Vanity of Human Wishes* (1749). To write in the spirit of the ancients while adapting them to the day is perhaps a greater sign of devotion than the museum-like reproductions that were to follow once historicism, with its sense of the pastness of the past and the distinctiveness of each culture, arose in the late eighteenth century. The earlier revival of the classics was predicated on the view that these writers were more genuinely alive than the eccentric or time-bound authors of the immediate past; it was not the rust of antiquity but its relevance that was esteemed.

The period of the Restoration and early eighteenth century is now often called the Augustan age. The term arose in the period itself, but it was applied tentatively and in more than one sense. London, once called Troynovant or New Troy, came now to be called Augusta, as the heir to imperial Rome. In 1712 John Oldmixon wrote that the age of Charles II "probably may be the Augustan Age of English poetry," and Dr. Johnson applied to Dryden's role in English poetry the words once used of Augustus as the builder of Rome: "He found it brick and left it marble." The term "Augustan" was a tribute to the new urbanity and formal elegance of English verse, and it evoked as well the tradition of a ruler who gave his patronage to and won the sincere respect of his greatest writers. This role could be said to fit Charles II in some measure, but to apply it, as Pope did with brilliant irony, to George I or George II, could be nothing but a gesture of scorn. George II hated poetry and painting alike and allowed politics to dictate patronage.

There were grounds, however, for distrusting the Emperor Augustus as well; his subversion of the freedom of the Roman Republic was a constant theme of historians: Swift alluded to it in 1701, and Gibbon made it the subject of the great third chapter of his *Decline and Fall of the Roman Empire* (1776). The ambivalence felt toward an age that was at once courtly, polished, and servile awakened all the more reverence for republican Rome and praise for the stoical Horace of the Republic rather than the epicurean Horace of the court.

Still, the tribute to Rome served to evoke a common European culture beneath the accidents of time or the changing national and local customs. It was an appeal to values that had won agreement in most times and places and would be confirmed by posterity in turn. For the classical view of history saw man as constant and the accidents of time as repetitive and cyclical rather than progressive. This view provided the Enlightenment with the secular counterpart of those religious values that stood outside the world and could be used to judge it. Whatever the corruptions and blindness of the present, one could see beyond them to permanent truths.

The desire to free the general or the universal in all its grandeur from particular fashion (of dress, of manners, of language) could lead at worst to a vacuous academicism. One might remove all character in order to remove idiosyncrasy. We may recall those white marble statues (for the eighteenth century invented a white antiquity, purified of those colors that had once adorned statues and temples) in classical costume that restored contemporary statesmen (Walpole or Washington) to their universality or a poet like Pope to his role of laurel-crowned *vates*. But at their best, poets and artists achieved a nice balance between the classical form and the substantial actuality. This is most obvious in the "imitation" or in the mock form (such as mock-heroic or mock-pastoral) where the pure form is opposed to the bristling disorder of everyday life. The greatest works of the age play back and forth between the ideal form and the stubborn particular, each criticizing the other.

There is a similar interplay in the architecture of the period. When the Earl of Burlington revived the designs of Andrea Palladio as the most classical and humanistic of Renaissance architects, he was rejecting the baroque freedom of Sir Christopher Wren and in fact restoring a greater Roman severity than he could find in Palladio. Yet the Palladian country house was set in gardens which achieved the natural freedom of landscape rather than geometric formality. House and grounds were set against each other to yield a more complex harmony.

In painting no one caught the vitality and exuberance of urban life so well as William Hogarth, but he was also possessed by the desire to succeed in the high form of history-painting, with its generalized figures of heroic grandeur. Sir Joshua Reynolds, who formulated the doctrine of the grand style in his presidential addresses to the Royal Academy, created in turn witty plays upon the heroic, evoking it in teasing allusions or "quoted" poses, placing children in the heroic stances of prophets or rulers.

SATIRE AND THE NOVEL

Nowhere did the classical forms serve so well as in satire. Satire had never been so central and powerful a form of literature before in England, nor had it ever shown so great a capacity to absorb the tragic and heroic vision as well. The skeptical impetus that discredited false claims to authority found its form by inventing a ludicrous world of mock-grandeur and self-deception, where men pursued the outward forms of greatness with no sense of their meaning or their true cost. In the finest satires of the age the mantle of greatness is placed upon the fool and falls with an overwhelming weight, as if to crush an insect. The heroic vision is essential to the satiric; the satirist shows his anti-hero falling as far below the norms of decency and intelligence as the true hero rises above them. To trap an oaf in the pattern of the heroic is to define his grossness all the more sharply; his high pretensions only serve to measure his contemptible performance.

Yet the heroic works in another way, too. For while the particular object of satire may be ludicrous and transparent, he may serve to reveal a wider and deeper pattern of failure that is more commonplace and less easy to identify in actual men. When Swift embodies the history of the church in the careers of three Restoration fops, the small foreground figures serve to interpret (reductively but with frightening lucidity) vast and complex historical forces. When Pope in *The Dunciad* presents the debased culture of his day as if it were the eclipse of all culture, he is not simply attacking the corruption of the Hanoverian court or of commercialized London. He is attacking "Dulness," the chronic tendency of the mind to relapse into lazy fantasy and to give up its critical powers; the current scene is only the latest instance of a process whose dimensions extend through all history. Satire magnifies as well as reduces; it may reduce man's plausible pretexts to mechanical folly, but it makes the folly in turn a potential tragic failure and a force worthy of heroic resistance.

Once satire gives way to more neutral curiosity, what was seen as failure is regarded with more sympathy and willingness to condone or understand. In the process the very details which were an affront to the high forms of the heroic become the absorbing material of daily life. The marvelous, saintly, and heroic may be transposed to the level of the commonplace. Instead of a lonely Odysseus outwitting vengeful gods we have a sober Robinson Crusoe ingeniously transforming a lonely island into a scene of middle-class enterprise. With the rise of the novel the studied detachment of satire gives way to an exploration of the confusions and inconsistencies seen within the self. In *Robinson Crusoe* (1719) Defoe fused what might have been the material of a Puritan spiritual autobiography with the heroism of mercantile adventure. In *Moll Flanders* (1722) he went on to consider those forms of excess, the ruthlessness of theft and prostitution, that lie at the edge of mercantile zeal, and he treated them with remarkable awareness of the power of their appeal.

Defoe in his first-person narratives and, even more, Samuel Richardson in his epistolary novels, notably *Pamela* (1741) and *Clarissa* (1748), found techniques for giving their stories an air of veracity. The point was not to deceive the reader about their being fictions but to bring him into close involvement with character and event. The novel's slow unfolding and full record of both internal and external realities created a remarkable new opportunity for identification; the letters of the day record the compelling power of the novel upon the reader's feelings. Henry Fielding, particularly in *Joseph Andrews* (1742) and *Tom Jones* (1749), created a new balance between the detached satiric observer, brilliantly artful in his rhetoric, and the closely presented incident. Fielding's formalization is bold and free, and he mocks the very conventions by which the novel asserts its veracity, but he uses them too. In Laurence Sterne's *Tristram Shandy* (1759–67), the self-consciousness of the novel reaches its extreme, veering between circumstantial realism and elaborate contrivance, pushing realism to the point where it frankly topples over into *tour de force*. Sterne also carries sympathy to the point where it becomes sentimentalism, that is, the prizing of feeling and the cultivation of it for its own sake; but he mocks this, too, with a recoil into ironic detachment.

NEW FEELINGS AND FORMS

The growing esteem for sentiment and feeling in the eighteenth century was the culmination of a long process—a movement toward internalization, first from the rationalistic systems of the seventeenth century to the Augustan emphasis on immediate intuition. The Augustans were intensely distrustful of systems; their pursuit of a middle way was a matter of achieving sound feeling as well as true insight, for the two were inextricably related. Pride and self-interest distorted all awareness: the delicate balance of disinterestedness was difficult to attain, and its attainment was as much a moral achievement as an intellectual one. The action of the honest heart was more reliable than any process of reasoning; and it was not a long step to the trust in heart over head. Trust your heart, wrote the third Earl of Shaftesbury, so long as you keep it honest.

In a similar way the grandeur of the general, once derived from a vision of cosmic order, became internalized and identified with what men have generally felt. Generality became a psychological rather than a metaphysical standard. As Reynolds observed, there are illusions that all men share, such as the impression that a medieval castle is older than a classical temple, if only because its origins are more darkly shrouded in a remote but native culture. A century earlier, Sir Christopher Wren had distinguished between natural or geometric beauty and customary beauty (where "familiarity or particular inclination breeds a love to things not in themselves lovely"). Wren has no doubt that natural or geometric beauty is to be preferred; but Reynolds has come to wonder. Reality is becoming what the mind of man creates.

The imaginative power of feeling was given new stress with the doctrine of association of ideas. If men framed an image of the world through repeated and reinforced associations, the linkages were often forged and more often confirmed by the action of the feelings. That seemed true, for David Hume, of our most fundamental conceptions, such as that of causality. Hume showed in his *Treatise on Human Nature* (1739) that the necessary connection of cause and effect was a necessity of our thought rather than an objective natural process. The more distinctive structures of the literary imagination could be traced to the rapid associative movement of genius working under the guidance of strong passion, and the explanation was made complex enough to account for all that was later to be included in the idea of imagination save only conscious artistry and active control. It is interesting, in fact, that Sterne presents man alternately as a victim of his associative processes and as the creator of imagined worlds; an ironic skepticism still surrounds the creative powers of the conscious artist.

In the early stages of this cult of feeling and the exploration of its power of artistry, poetry turned away from the everyday experience that had provided the stuff of Pope's satires or Swift's occasional verse. Instead it cultivated the sublime, images that filled the mind with awe or dread by their very transcendence of its normal scope—images of vastness, of sudden rise or fall, of dark obscurity or blazing light. Before these images were given a theoretical explanation by Edmund Burke in 1757, they had become the characteristic note of such poets of the 1740's as William Collins and Thomas Gray, or of the earlier and most influential poet of the landscape,

James Thomson. These images were, as Burke made clear, supremely realized in Milton's poetry, but they bring to the fore an aspect of Milton given less stress than his moral grandeur in the criticism of Joseph Addison. For the new poetry—as later for the Gothic novel—these images seemed to well up out of the unconscious mind, unrestrained by logic or morality. Their grandeur was not the grandeur of generality, but rather a power to reduce the conscious mind and all its high achievements to triviality. They loom over the ordinary world like towering cliffs or fierce clouds; or they expose the transitoriness of man's control in the images of ruins, the sharp angles of architecture crumbling into organic forms.

Inevitably the sublime and the Gothic provided a form of play-acting, and deliberately created ruins provided a stage for meditation. Yet there was a deeper force at work. To relate man's emotions and unconscious powers to the forms of nature deepened the response to both. Nature became an object of reverence rather than exploitation, a place that both revealed man to himself and imposed limits on his will. On the other hand, the beauty as well as the terror of man's elemental feelings became clear. There were dangers in such a movement toward primitivism; as man's taste opened, it was fed by synthetic products designed to meet it more completely than the natural. If Homer seemed difficult to treat as a primitive bard, the works of the Celtic bard, Ossian, were served up through forgeries that won acclaim throughout Europe. Yet authentic folk poetry was recovered, as in collection of ballads; and the dignity of folk speech or of local dialects began to be credited. All those peculiarities which had been seen as defects of the general now began to seem expressive of a deeper humanity, one that a high culture had suppressed or undervalued.

Another way in which the particular was given new dignity was through the idea of the picturesque. This began as the effort to find (later to create) in natural landscape the designs of the painters of the seventeenth century—Claude Lorrain, Nicolas Poussin, Salvator Rosa. What it came to in time was the rejection of a landscape, however "natural," that was too simple or featureless; the picturesque sought complex relationships of form and color. This was extended from landscape to houses, to villages, to the people who inhabited them. Ironically, bandits were more complex figures—rough, colorful, energetic—than solid tradesmen. There seemed, as often with the sublime, an inverse proportion between the picturesque and the moral. So, too, squalor might provide variety of forms, but the planned town imposed tame uniformity: one might not be content to keep the squalor, but one needed to imitate the slow evolution through time and accident, as in a natural scene, in designing structures or streets. It was better, too, that a cottage reveal its various functions in its surface structure rather than be forced into a pattern of symmetry.

The titanic forces found in the sublime view of nature were found by many in the French Revolution, where oppressive and lifeless forms were thrown off by a people awakened to its own dignity and power. In England some of the enthusiasm which might have turned to revolutionary humanism was captured by Methodism. John Wesley's great evangelical revival had much of the energy of earlier Puritanism, but its anti-intellectualism and political conservatism did nothing to foster the rebellious spirit of an earlier century. Radicalism was largely the product of urban societies of artisans, small merchants, and professional men; their efforts to broaden suffrage and to reform Parliament were blocked by the war with France and the repressive measures undertaken by the younger Pitt. But by the end of the eighteenth century England was clearly moving toward change.

The population of England increased from five and a half million to nine million in the course of the century, and though London maintained its dominance there was rapid growth in the northern areas, where industry developed most rapidly and freely. The concentration of industry in the cities was marked by 1800, but technology was giving all of the landscape a new look: improved turnpikes and canals (including a triumphant aqueduct bearing a canal over a river), new steam-powered pumps for coal mines, large factories for cotton-weaving and pottery-making, and (in 1779) the first iron bridge, over the Severn in Shropshire. To support an increased population required an agricultural as well as an industrial revolution, and this was achieved through the development of new crops (notably root-vegetables), the improved breeding of cattle and sheep (doubling their average weights in the course of the century), and the enclosure of commons so as to make more efficient use of the land. The most controversial developments were the enclosures, and their cost in human displacement was recorded in Oliver Goldsmith's *The Deserted Village* (1770). Hundreds of individual acts of enclosure were approved each year by Parliament from 1760 on, and these were taking place at the time when the growth of factories was destroying the cottage industries that had supplemented farm incomes. The movement toward the towns increased; yet the new agricultural techniques managed, even with a diminished labor force, to add some two million acres of arable land during the century.

By the close of the eighteenth century, English intellectual life had begun to move outside the major cities. We find a provincial painter like Joseph Wright of Derby painting the new industrial landscape as well as portraits of its builders, sublime landscapes and scenes of popular scientific demonstrations such as an experiment with an air-pump. An industrialist like Josiah Wedgwood, properly attentive to the state of roads and canals that served his potteries in Staffordshire, was no less attentive to archaeological discoveries in Pompeii and Herculaneum, from which he adapted designs through the skills of such artists as John Flaxman. Even more, the village and countryside had found poets, and resident poets rather than nostalgic ones, in men like Crabbe, Cowper, and Burns.

SAMUEL BUTLER
1613–1680

Butler first emerged from obscurity at the age of fifty with the publication of *Hudibras*. The poem pleased Charles II and his court, ran through nine printings in a year, and eventually won Butler a royal pension. Born the son of a prosperous Worcestershire yeoman, Butler had served as clerk in several households where he could pursue learning and study painting; and he had acquired a considerable knowledge of law, perhaps as a student at Gray's Inn, London.

As the first great satire to look back upon the Commonwealth, *Hudibras* converts nightmare into farce and sums up an era of fanaticism in the Quixotic career of its Presbyterian knight and his independent or radical Protestant squire. By presenting their adventures as a parody of knight-errantry, Butler catches the preposterous self-importance of two dolts whose smattering of learning is just enough to release them from common sense. Between them they represent many tendencies of the mind to overleap the limits of empirical check: Scholastic logic-chopping; the cult-idiom of sectarians; visionary enthusiasm; and above all, hypocritical self-righteousness. While Hudibras is more Aristotelian and Ralpho, his squire, is more neoplatonic and theosophical, each achieves the absolutism of the private self, a mixture of uncritical superstition and arrogant crusading zeal.

Butler creates this image in large part through literary allusion. In the manner of Paul Scarron, who travestied Virgil's epic by retelling it with low knockabout antics and vulgar speeches (imitated in English by Charles Cotton's *Scarronides*, 1664), Butler accommodates romance forms to the low clowns he creates. But Butler's wit, with its reductive parody of a soaring baroque idiom of paradox, also ridicules man's constant effort to exceed his rational powers. Here the result is self-defeating sophistry, transparently mindless and suggestive of the enthusiastic preaching that followed upon the all-too-easy delusion of being inspired. Enthusiasm was studied in the Restoration (by such men as Henry More and Meric Casaubon) as a typical form of psychopathology, and it was to be analyzed once more in Jonathan Swift's *A Tale of a Tub* (1704). Swift, it was reported, knew much of *Hudibras* by heart; like Matthew Prior, he found new uses for Butler's form of "anti-poetry," the heavily rhymed octosyllabic couplet.

Dr. Johnson explains some of the remarkable power *Hudibras* must have had upon its first appearance:

> The brightest strokes of his wit owed their force to the impression of the characters, which was upon men's minds at the time; to their knowing them, at table and in the street; in short, being familiar with them; and above all to his satire being directed against those whom a little while before they had hated and feared.

As for Butler's wit and learning, Johnson finds them so abundant as at times to be too much, but he asserts that "there is more thinking" in Milton and Butler (the pairing is remarkable) "than in any of our poets." Indeed, he goes on, "If the French boast of the learning of Rabelais, we need not be afraid of confronting them with Butler."

Hudibras°

From Part I Canto I

THE ARGUMENT

Sir Hudibras his passing worth,
The manner how he sallied forth,
His arms and equipage, are shown;
His horse's virtues and his own.
The adventure of the bear and fiddle
Is sung, but breaks off in the middle.

When civil dudgeon first grew high,
And men fell out, they knew not why;
When hard words,° jealousies, and fears
Set folks together by the ears,
And made them fight, like mad or drunk,
For Dame Religion as for punk;°
Whose honesty they all durst swear for,
Though not a man of them knew wherefore;
When gospel-trumpeter, surrounded
10 With long-eared rout,° to battle sounded;
And pulpit, drum ecclesiastic,
Was beat with fist instead of a stick;
Then did Sir Knight abandon dwelling,
And out he rode a-colonelling.
    A wight° he was, whose very sight would
Entitle him Mirror of Knighthood,°
That never bowed his stubborn knee
To anything but chivalry,°
Nor put up blow but that which laid
20 Right Worshipful on shoulder-blade;
Chief of domestic knights and errant,°
Either for chartel° or for warrant;
Great on the bench, great in the saddle,
That could as well bind o'er as swaddle;°
Mighty he was at both of these,
And styled of war as well as peace.
(So some rats, of amphibious nature,
Are either for the land or water.)

Hudibras named for the rash, morose knight who woos the pleasure-hating Elissa in Spenser, *Faerie Queene* II.ii.
hard words not merely harsh words but technical jargon (see ll. 85, 111 below), in this case the cant words ("fears" and "jealousies") by which Puritans described events and motives
punk whore
long-eared rout epic diction for "asses"; applied to Puritans whose short hair (thus Roundheads) made their ears conspicuous and who sometimes cupped their ears with their hands to catch each word of an enthusiastic sermon, in this case a call to rebellion

wight romance diction for "man"
Mirror of Knighthood a chivalric romance admired by Don Quixote
chivalry to the vision of himself as a knight, kneeling to be dubbed by his lord (ll. 19–20)
domestic . . . errant As "domestic" knight, or Justice of the Peace "on the bench," he could issue a "warrant" for arrest and "bind over" a prisoner for future trial; as knight "errant," he could wander in search of righteous battle, i.e. look for vices to suppress.
chartel knightly challenge
swaddle bind up, as in a diaper; but also cudgel

But here our authors make a doubt
30 Whether he were more wise or stout.°
Some hold the one, and some the other;
But howsoe'er they make a pother,
The difference was so small, his brain
Outweighed his rage but half a grain;
Which made some take him for a tool
That knaves do work with, called a fool.
For it has been held by many, that,
As Montaigne, playing with his cat,
Complains she thought him but an ass,
40 Much more she would Sir Hudibras;
(For that's the name our valiant knight
To all his challenges did write).
But they're mistaken very much;
'Tis plain enough he was no such.
We grant, although he had much wit,
He was very shy of using it,
As being loath to wear it out,
And therefore bore it not about,
Unless on holidays or so,
50 As men their best apparel do.
Beside, 'tis known he could speak Greek
As naturally as pigs squeak;
That Latin was no more difficile,
Than to a blackbird 'tis to whistle.
Being rich in both, he never scanted
His bounty unto such as wanted;
But much of either would afford
To many that had not one word.
For Hebrew roots, although they're found
60 To flourish most in barren ground,°
He had such plenty as sufficed
To make some think him circumcised.
And truly so he was perhaps,
Not as a proselyte, but for claps.°
   He was in logic a great critic,
Profoundly skilled in analytic;
He could distinguish and divide
A hair 'twixt south and southwest side;
On either which he would dispute,
70 Confute, change hands, and still confute.
He'd undertake to prove by force
Of argument, a man's no horse;

---

stout bold, brave (although Hudibras is also
"stout" in the modern sense)
barren ground the arid minds of pedants; or,
since Hebrew was believed by some to be the
natural language of man, the completely untutored mind
claps gonorrhea

He'd prove a buzzard is no fowl,°
And that a lord may be an owl;°
A calf° an alderman, a goose a justice,
And rooks° committee-men and trustees.°
He'd run in debt by disputation,
And pay with ratiocination.
All this by syllogism, true
80   In mood and figure,° he would do.
    For rhetoric, he could not ope
His mouth but out there flew a trope;°
And when he happened to break off
In the middle of his speech, or cough,
He had hard words ready to show why,
And tell what rules he did it by.
Else, when with greatest art he spoke,
You'd think he talked like other folk;
For all a rhetorician's rules
90   Teach nothing but to name his tools.
But when he pleased to show it, his speech
In loftiness of sound was rich,
A Babylonish dialect°
Which learnèd pedants much affect.
It was a parti-coloured dress
Of patched and piebald languages;
'Twas English cut on Greek and Latin,
Like fustian° heretofore on satin.
It had an odd promiscuous tone,
100 As if he had talked three parts° in one;
Which made some think, when he did gabble,
They had heard three labourers of Babel,
Or Cerberus himself pronounce
A leash° of languages at once.
This he as volubly would vent,
As if his stock would ne'er be spent;
And truly, to support that charge,
He had supplies as vast and large;
For he could coin or counterfeit
110 New words with little or no wit,
Words so debased and hard, no stone°

fowl domestic bird
owl a bird that may symbolize gravity or stupidity or both
calf fool
rooks crow-like birds, here swindlers
committee-men and trustees appointed by Parliament to confiscate and sell off Church of England property, often high-handed and sometimes
dishonest
mood and figure good logical form
trope figure of speech (see Glossary)
Babylonish dialect with a suggestion of the
splintering of languages at Babel to undo the

building of the tower; a "confusion of languages,
such as some of our modern virtuosi [i.e. experimenters and scientific dabblers] use to express
themselves in" (Butler)
fustian a coarse cloth in which slashings were
made, revealing colorful satin lining
three parts as in rounds, with overtones of trini-
tarian mystery
leash one for each of the heads of Cerberus, the
three-headed dog that guarded the entrance to
Hades
stone the touchstone, used to test the purity of
metal in coins

Was hard enough to touch them on;
And when with hasty noise he spoke 'em,
The ignorant for current° took 'em—
That, had the orator° who once
Did fill his mouth with pebble stones
When he harangued, but known his phrase,
He would have used no other ways.
    In mathematics he was greater
120   Then Tycho Brahe° or Erra Pater;°
For he by geometric scale
Could take the size of pots of ale;
Resolve by sines and tangents straight
If bread or butter wanted weight;
And wisely tell what hour o' the day
The clock does strike, by algebra.
    Besides, he was a shrewd philosopher,
And had read every text and gloss over;
Whate'er the crabbedest author hath,
130   He understood by implicit faith;
Whatever sceptic could inquire for,
For every why he had a wherefore;
Knew more than forty of them do,
As far as words and terms could go.
All which he understood by rote,
And, as occasion served, would quote;
No matter whether right or wrong,
They might be either said or sung.
His notions° fitted things so well,
140   That which was which he could not tell,
But oftentimes mistook the one
For the other, as great clerks° have done.
He could reduce all things to acts,
And knew their natures by abstracts;
Where entity and quiddity,°
The ghosts of defunct bodies, fly;
Where Truth in person does appear,
Like words congealed in northern air.
He knew what's what, and that's as high
150   As metaphysic wit can fly.
    In school-divinity as able
As he that hight° Irrefragable;°

current acceptable as money or meaning
orator Demosthenes
Tycho Brahe (1546–1601) eminent Danish
astronomer
Erra Pater the pseudonymous author of a popular 16th-century almanac and work of astrology,
perhaps William Lilly
notions They "are but pictures of things in the
imagination" (Butler).

clerks men of learning
entity and quiddity Scholastic terms for being
and essence, here treated as real things rather
than as verbal abstractions
hight romance diction for "was called"
Irrefragable irrefutable, applied to the theologian Alexander of Hales (1175?–1245)

A second Thomas,° or, at once
To name them all, another Duns;°
Profound in all the nominal
And real ways beyond them all;
For he a rope of sand° could twist
As tough as learned Sorbonist;°
And weave fine cobwebs, fit for skull
160   That's empty when the moon is full:
Such as take lodgings in a head
That's to be let unfurnishèd.
He could raise scruples° dark and nice,°
And after solve 'em in a trice;
As if divinity had catched
The itch of purpose to be scratched;
Or, like a mountebank,° did wound
And stab herself with doubts profound,
Only to show with how small pain
170   The sores of faith are cured again;
Although by woeful proof we find
They always leave a scar behind.
He knew the seat of Paradise,°
Could tell in what degree it lies,
And, as he was disposed, could prove it
Below the moon, or else above it;
What Adam dreamt of when his bride
Came from her closet in his side;
Whether the devil tempted her
180   By a High Dutch interpreter;°
If either of them had a navel;°
Who first made music malleable;°
Whether the serpent at the Fall
Had cloven feet, or none at all.°
All this, without a gloss or comment,
He could unriddle in a moment,
In proper terms, such as men smatter
When they throw out and miss the matter.
   For his religion, it was fit

Thomas Aquinas, St. (1225–74), who created the philosophical-theological synthesis called Thomism after him
Duns John Duns Scotus (1265?–1308), the Scottish theologian whose name was the source of "dunce"
rope of sand incoherent argument
Sorbonist a theologian at the University of Paris
scruples objections
nice foolishly oversubtle
mountebank performer at a fair, trickster
Paradise Its location was a subject of fantastic speculation in the Middle Ages and the Renaissance.
Whether . . . interpreter "Goropius Becanus endeavors to prove that High-Dutch was the language that Adam and Eve spoke in Paradise" (Butler); in fact, he tried to prove that the Teutonic was the most ancient of languages
If . . . navel "Adam and Eve, being made and not conceived and formed in the womb, had no navels, as some learned men have supposed, because they had no need of them" (Butler)
Who . . . malleable "Music is said to be invented by Pythagoras, who first found out the proportion of notes from the sounds of hammers upon an anvil" (Butler)
Whether . . . all learned speculation about the form of the serpent before it was made to crawl upon its belly after the Fall (Genesis 3:14)

190 To match his learning and his wit;
'Twas Presbyterian true blue,°
For he was of that stubborn crew
Of errant° saints whom all men grant
To be the true church militant;°
Such as do build their faith upon
The holy text of pike and gun;
Decide all controversies by
Infallible artillery;
And prove their doctrine orthodox,
200 By apostolic blows° and knocks;
Call fire and sword and desolation
A godly, thorough reformation,
Which always must be carried on,°
And still be doing, never done;
As if religion were intended
For nothing else but to be mended—
A sect whose chief devotion lies
In odd perverse antipathies,
In falling out with that or this,
210 And finding somewhat still amiss;
More peevish, cross, and splenetic,
Than dog distract or monkey sick;
That with more care keep holy-day
The wrong,° than others the right way;
Compound for sins they are inclined to,
By damning those they have no mind to;
Still so perverse and opposite,
As if they worshipped God for spite.
The self-same thing they will abhor
220 One way, and long another for.
Free will° they one way disavow,
Another, nothing else allow.
All piety consists therein
In them, in other men all sin.
Rather than fail, they will defy
That which they love most tenderly:
Quarrel with minced-pies, and disparage
Their best and dearest friend, plum-porridge;

true blue emblem of loyalty to the cause, also opposed to Royalist red
errant wandering in search of righteous causes, like "knight errant" (l. 21), but also "arrant" (as in "arrant knave"), i.e. thoroughgoing; "saints" was a term applied to Puritans as the self-styled "elect"
church militant the church fighting the temptation and persecution of the world; but also the contentious and rebellious Puritan sects
apostolic blows the laying on of hands in ordination; but also self-righteous force

carried on from the favorite Puritan cant phrase, "carrying on the work"
The wrong as in turning Christmas from a feast to a fast in 1647. The Puritan often "breaks the sabbath by taking too much pains to keep it" (Butler, *Characters*).
Free will denied by the Calvinistic doctrine of predestination but insisted upon in radical Protestant claims of inspiration and righteousness. The Puritan "denies free will and yet will endure nothing but his own will in all the practice of his life" (Butler, *Characters*).

Fat pig and goose itself oppose,
230   And blaspheme custard through the nose.°
The apostles of this fierce religion,
Like Mahomet's, were ass and widgeon,°
To whom our knight, by fast instinct
Of wit and temper, was so linked,
As if hypocrisy and nonsense
Had got the advowson° of his conscience.

. . .

A squire he had whose name was Ralph,°
That in the adventure went his half,
Though writers, for more stately tone,
460   Do call him Ralpho, 'tis all one;
And when we can, with metre safe,
We'll call him so; if not, plain Raph;
(For rhyme the rudder is of verses,
With which like ships they steer their courses).
An equal stock of wit and valour
He had laid in, by birth a tailor.
The mighty Tyrian queen,° that gained
With subtle shreds a tract of land,
Did leave it with a castle fair
470   To his great ancestor, her heir;
From him descended cross-legged° knights,
Famed for their faith° and warlike fights
Against the bloody cannibal,°
Whom they destroyed both great and small.
This sturdy squire had, as well
As the bold Trojan knight,° seen hell;°
Not with a counterfeited pass
Of golden bough, but true gold-lace.
His knowledge was not far behind
480   The Knight's, but of another kind,
And he another way came by't.
Some call it gifts, and some new-light;°
A liberal art that costs no pains
Of study, industry, or brains.

---

through the nose a reference to the nasal drone cultivated by many Puritan preachers
ass and widgeon Mahomet rode to heaven on a milk-white mule, and he kept a pigeon that ate grain from his ear and brought him divine messages; here mule and pigeon are altered into emblems of stupidity, ass and widgeon (a wild duck).
advowson right to fill a vacant office
Ralph perhaps named for the grocer's apprentice who enjoys chivalric exploits in Beaumont and Fletcher's *The Knight of the Burning Pestle* (1608). Neither a Presbyterian nor a man of pseudo-learning like Hudibras, he is a more radical Protestant and probably illiterate.
Tyrian queen Dido, who bought the amount of land she could surround with an ox hide, but cut the hide in thin strips to embrace a large tract (*Aeneid* I.367 ff.)
cross-legged as Knights Templars were supposedly represented on their tombs, and as tailors sat at their work
faith for tailors, credit to customers
cannibal Saracens or (for tailors) lice
Trojan knight Aeneas, who took the golden bough to Proserpina in Hell (*Aeneid* VI.136–41)
hell also the tailor's waste-box for scraps of cloth
gifts . . . new-light cant terms for divine inspiration and revelation, claimed by Puritans at the expense of institutional religion

His wits were sent him for a token,
But in the carriage° cracked and broken;
Like commendation nine-pence° crooked
With 'To and from my love' it looked.
He ne'er considered it, as loath
490   To look a gift horse in the mouth,
And very wisely would lay forth
No more upon it than 'twas worth;
But as he got it freely, so
He spent it frank and freely too:
For saints themselves will sometimes be,
Of gifts that cost them nothing, free.°
By means of this, with hem and cough,
Prolongers to enlightened snuff,°
He could deep mysteries unriddle
500   As easily as thread a needle;
For as of vagabonds we say
That they are ne'er beside their way,
Whate'er men speak by this new-light,
Still they are sure to be in the right.
'Tis a dark lanthorn of the Spirit,°
Which none see by but those that bear it;
A light that falls down from on high,
For spiritual trades to cozen° by;
An *ignis fatuus*° that bewitches,
510   And leads men into pools and ditches,
To make them dip themselves° and sound
For Christendom in dirty pond;
To dive like wild fowl for salvation,
And fish to catch regeneration.
This light inspires and plays upon
The nose of saint, like bagpipe drone,°
And speaks through hollow empty soul,
As through a trunk° or whispering hole,°
Such language as no mortal ear
520   But spiritual eavesdropper's can hear:
So Phoebus° or some friendly Muse

carriage delivery
nine-pence coins bent and sent as love tokens
free a reference to Puritan thrift
snuff candle end, perhaps used to time a sermon. "[It] is frequent for a single *vowel* to draw sighs from a multitude; and for a whole assembly of saints to sob to the music of one solitary liquid. . . . Hawking, spitting, and belching, the defects of other men's rhetoric, are the flowers, and figures, and ornaments" of the enthusiastic Puritan preacher's (Jonathan Swift, *The Mechanical Operation of the Spirit*, 1704) dark . . . Spirit The dark lantern, whose light is confined, is set in contrast with the "candle of the Lord," reason.
cozen cheat

ignis fatuus will-o'-the-wisp
dip themselves referring to the Anabaptist belief in total immersion, which gave them the popular name of Dippers
bagpipe drone a reference to nasal sounds, to Scottish Presbyterianism, and to the literal meaning of "inspiration"; cf. Thomas Hobbes: "A man enabled to speak wisely from the principles of nature . . . loves rather to be thought to speak by inspiration, like a bagpipe" (*Hobbes's Answer to Davenant's Preface to Gondibert*, 1651)
trunk speaking tube
whispering hole as in the ancient oracle at Delphi
Phoebus Apollo as god of poetry

Into small poets song infuse,
Which they at second hand rehearse,
Through reed or bagpipe, verse for verse.
   Thus Ralph became infallible
As three or four-legged oracle,°
The ancient cup, or modern chair,
Spoke truth point-blank, though unaware.
   For mystic learning,° wondrous able
530 In magic talisman° and cabal,°
Whose primitive tradition reaches
As far as Adam's first green breeches;°
Deep-sighted in intelligences,
Ideas, atoms, influences;°
And much of *Terra Incognita,*°
The intelligible world,° could say;
A deep occult philosopher,
As learned as the wild Irish° are,
Or Sir Agrippa,° for profound
540 And solid lying much renowned:
He Anthroposophus° and Fludd°
And Jacob Behmen° understood;
Knew many an amulet and charm,
That would do neither good nor harm;
In Rosicrucian° lore as learned
As he that *Vere adeptus*° earned.
He understood the speech of birds

three . . . oracle references to the three-legged
stool of the Delphic priestess of Apollo, to the
divining cup of Joseph as prophet (Genesis
44:5), and to the four-legged papal throne
mystic learning a reference to the occult philosophy traced back to the legendary Hermes
Trismegistus, supposedly a seer contemporary
with Moses and author of the *Hermetica*, a
body of mystic writings drawn from neoplatonic
and Judaic sources; revived during the Renaissance, particularly by Paracelsus and Jacob
Boehme
magic talisman metal or stone objects imprinted
with symbols of the stars, whose spiritual power
they were supposed to command
cabal the mystical and magical doctrines drawn
from the *Cabala*, a 13th-century work supposedly based on traditions of Jewish wisdom,
part of the large stream of occult thought here
likened to radical Protestant "new light"
green breeches the garment of fig leaves (translated as "breeches" in the so-called Breeches
Bible of 1557) made after the Fall (Genesis
3:7); also satire on Roman Catholic reliance
upon oral tradition as the counterpart of specious claims of occultists and astrologers
intelligences . . . influences technical terms
for objects of knowledge too subtle to be received by the senses, such as spirits controlling
planets ("intelligences"), platonic "ideas" literalized into angelic forms, "atoms" too refined to

be observed, and astral "influences" upon human
character
Terra Incognita the mapmaker's term for unexplored sections of the world
intelligible world "discovered only by the
[occult] philosophers, of which they talk, like
parrots, what they do not understand" (Butler)
wild Irish "addicted to this occult philosophy"
(Butler)
Sir Agrippa Cornelius Agrippa (1486–1535),
well-known writer on occult sciences
Anthroposophus Thomas Vaughan (1622–66),
twin brother of the poet Henry Vaughan, an oc-
cultist and alchemist, author of *Anthroposophia
Theomagica*
Fludd Robert Fludd (1574–1637), physician,
hermeticist, Rosicrucian, author of a mystical
interpretation of creation
Jacob Behmen Jacob Boehme (1575–1624), the
German mystic and alchemist, whose influence
was strongest in the 18th century in William
Law (1686–1761), the tutor of Edward Gibbon's father and aunts
Rosicrucian the mystical secret society with
magical rites, whose lore was later used by
Alexander Pope for the "epic machinery" of
The Rape of the Lock
Vere adeptus "truly a master," a title given to
those alchemists who had achieved the proper
degree of secret wisdom

As well as they themselves do words;
Could tell what subtlest parrots mean,
550 That speak and think contrary clean;
What member° 'tis of whom they talk
When they cry 'Rope,' and 'Walk, knave, walk.'°
He'd extract numbers° out of matter,
And keep them in a glass, like water,
Of sovereign power to make men wise;
For, dropped in blear thick-sighted eyes,
They'd make them see in darkest night,
Like owls, though purblind in the light.
By help of these (as he professed)
560 He had First Matter° seen undressed:
He took her naked, all alone,
Before one rag of form was on.
The Chaos,° too, he had descried,
And seen quite through, or else he lied:
Not that of pasteboard, which men show
For groats at fair of Bartholomew;°
But its great grandsire, first o' the name,
Whence that and Reformation came,
Both cousin-germans,° and right able
570 To inveigle and draw in the rabble.
But Reformation was, some say,
O' the younger house° to Puppet-play.
He could foretell whatsoever was
By consequence to come to pass;
As death of great men, alterations,
Diseases, battles, inundations:
All this without the eclipse of sun,
Or dreadful comet, he hath done
By inward light, a way as good,
580 And easy to be understood;
But with more lucky hit than those
That use to make the stars depose,
Like Knights o' the Post,° and falsely charge
Upon themselves what others forge;
As if they were consenting to

---

member of the fraternity of Rosicrucians or possibly of Parliament
'Rope . . . walk' words commonly taught to parrots
numbers Pythagoreans stressed the numerical structure of the world and endowed some numbers with special virtues; here the abstraction is materialized, as in ll. 133 ff.
First Matter the universal substance, in Hermetic doctrine, out of which all was made; but perceptible in that form only in mystic vision, such as was claimed by Thomas Vaughan

Chaos as in *Paradise Lost*, Book II, the materials out of which God creates cosmos, but perceptible in their original form only by angels
Bartholomew Bartholomew Fair, where puppet shows of the Creation might be seen
cousin-germans first cousins
younger house of later date, born of a younger son; perhaps an imitation, for some doctrines promoted by the Reformation (such as divine inspiration or predestination) might seem to reduce men to puppets
Knights o' the Post hired perjurers

All mischief in the world men do,
Or, like the devil, did tempt and sway 'em
To rogueries, and then betray 'em
They'll search a planet's house° to know
590 Who broke and robbed a house below;
Examine Venus and the Moon,
Who stole a thimble or a spoon;
And though they nothing will confess,
Yet by their very looks can guess,
And tell what guilty aspect° bodes,
Who stole, and who received the goods.
They'll question Mars, and by his look
Detect who 'twas that nimmed° a cloak;
Make Mercury confess, and peach°
600 Those thieves which he himself did teach.°
They'll find in the physiognomies
O' the planets, all men's destinies,
Like him that took the doctor's bill,°
And swallowed it instead o' the pill;
Cast the nativity° o' the question,
And from positions to be guessed on,
As sure as if they knew the moment
Of native's birth, tell what will come on't.
They'll feel the pulses of the stars,
610 To find out agues,° cough, catarrhs,°
And tell what crisis° does divine
The rot in sheep, or mange in swine;
In men, what gives or cures the itch,
What makes them cuckolds, poor or rich;
What gains or loses, hangs or saves,
What makes men great, what fools or knaves;
But not what wise, for only of those
The stars (they say) cannot dispose,
No more than can the astrologians;
620 There they say right, and like true Trojans:°
This Ralpho knew, and therefore took
The other course,° of which we spoke.
      Thus was the accomplished squire endued
With gifts and knowledge perilous shrewd.
Never did trusty squire with knight,
Or knight with squire, jump° more right.
Their arms and equipage did fit,

planet's house that sign of the zodiac where, in astrology, a planet has greatest influence
aspect in the planet, its astrological position; in the thief, his countenance
nimmed stole
peach accuse
teach as god of thieves
bill prescription

nativity horoscope
agues fevers
catarrhs sore throats
crisis conjunction of planets
true Trojans good fellows
other course religious rather than astrological imposture
jump agree, coincide

As well as virtues, parts,° and wit:
Their valours too were of a rate,°
630   And out they sallied at the gate. . . .
                    1663

JOHN BUNYAN
1628–1688

Bunyan was born near Bedford into the family of a traveling tinker whose ancestors had once been landholders. Bunyan tended to exaggerate the lowness of his origin and the limits of his education In order to magnify the extent of grace that was shown him, as he does his own guilt in the title of his great spiritual autobiography, *Grace Abounding to the Chief of Sinners* (1666). This is a record of Bunyan's inner life and of his conversion; like many such works of the age, it followed certain formulae (but so, in fact, did life): God's showing of special providences, the imperfect conversion that produced a merely legal Christianity rather than deep conviction, a pattern of temptation and backsliding into doubt and despair, and a final confirmation in faith marked by an intensely emotional vision. "Suddenly," he wrote,

> there was, as if there rushed in at the window, a noise of wind upon me, but very pleasant, as if I had heard a voice speaking, "Didst ever refuse to be justified by the blood of Christ?" and withal my whole life of profession past was in a moment opened to me, wherein I was made to see that designedly I had not; so my heart answered groaningly, "No." Then fell that word of God upon me, "See that ye refuse not him that speaketh" (Hebrews 12:25). This made a strange seizure upon my spirit; it brought light with it and commanded a silence in my heart of all those tumultuous thoughts that did use, like masterless hellhounds, to roar and bellow and make a hideous noise within me.

Bunyan served in the parliamentary army during the Civil War, in a garrison commanded by Sir Samuel Luke, one of the models for Butler's portrait of Hudibras. By 1649 Bunyan was married and had four children by his first wife, who died in 1658; he remarried a year later. He worked, like his father, as a tinker, but his life became increasingly one of religious devotion. He began to preach by 1656 and engaged in strong controversy with the Quakers, whose doctrine of "inner light" seemed to him a rejection of the objective nature of revelation; although he was a dissenter from Anglican doctrine, he was by no means the most radical of Protestants. With the repression of Dissenters that began after the Restoration, Bunyan was imprisoned for his preaching and refused to give assurances that he would stop. He remained in prison at Bedford for most of the eleven years that followed, writing and preaching as he could all the while, and probably completing a good part of *The Pilgrim's Progress*. Upon his release in 1672 he became well known as a preacher, drawing an audience of three thousand on one occasion in London; and he continued to write religious allegories, notably *The Life and Death of Mr. Badman* and *The Holy War*.

The *Pilgrim's Progress* was a great success, and in the ten years between its first publication and Bunyan's death, it ran through twelve editions—no doubt helping him win the offer, which he refused, of a "place of public trust" from the Catholic James II. Bunyan's book is an allegorical dream vision recounting Christian's pilgrimage from the

parts native abilities   **of a rate** well paired

City of Destruction (the present world seen at the point of apocalypse) to the Celestial City. The dreamer, reminiscent of Will Langland in *Piers Plowman,* can only reach in vision what Christian, within the vision, can attain in act, and the poignant final words reflect their difference: "which, when I had seen, I wished myself among them." The book draws upon medieval allegory and upon the chivalric romances that gave the young Bunyan guilty delight; one can see, after reading of Apollyon, why Dr. Johnson remarked, "There is reason to think that he had read Spenser." But the verve of the book is no less strong in the homely adaptation of spiritual experience to realistic scenes; and the satirical accuracy with which it renders the jury of Vanity Fair makes one recognize a kinship (for all the differences of viewpoint) with Dryden's adaptation of the story of David and Absalom or even with Swift's brisk allegory in *A Tale of a Tub.* In an age when so many wrote critically of Puritan zeal and religious enthusiasm, it is good to have so eloquent a spokesman for them and so fine a specimen, as well, of popular literature.

Bunyan's text provides marginal references to Scripture at many points; the most important of these are given in the notes.

From The Pilgrim's Progress

From This World to That Which Is To Come

As I walked through the wilderness of this world, I lighted on a certain place where was a den,[1] and I laid me down in that place to sleep: and as I slept I dreamed a dream. I dreamed, and behold I saw a man clothed with rags, standing in a certain place, with his face from his own house, a book in his hand, and a great burden upon his back.[2] I looked and saw him open the book and read therein; and, as he read, he wept, and trembled; and not being able longer to contain, he brake out with a lamentable cry, saying, What shall I do?

In this plight, therefore, he went home and restrained himself as long as he could, that his wife and children should not perceive his distress; but he could not be silent long, because that his trouble increased. Wherefore at length he brake his mind to his wife and children; and thus he began to talk to them. O my dear wife, said he, and you the children of my bowels, I, your dear friend, am in myself undone by reason of a burden that lieth hard upon me; moreover, I am for certain informed that this our city will be burned with fire from heaven, in which fearful overthrow both myself, with thee, my wife, and you my sweet babes, shall miserably come to ruin, except (the which yet I see not) some way of escape can be found whereby we may be delivered. At this his relations were sore amazed; not for that they believed that what he had said to them was true, but because they thought that some frenzy distemper had got into his head; therefore, it drawing towards night, and they

1. Often taken as a reference to the Bedford prison.
2. See Isaiah 64:6: "But we are all as an unclean thing, and all our righteousnesses are as filthy rags"; Psalms 38:4: "For mine iniquities are gone over my head; as an heavy burden they are too heavy for me"; Habakkuk 2:2: "And the Lord answered me, and said, Write the vision, and make it plain upon tables, so that he may run that readeth it."

hoping that sleep might settle his brains, with all haste they got him to bed. But the night was as troublesome to him as the day; wherefore, instead of sleeping, he spent it in sighs and tears. So, when the morning was come, they would know how he did. He told them, Worse and worse. He also set to talking to them again: but they began to be hardened. They also thought to drive away his distemper by harsh and surly carriages to him: sometimes they would deride, sometimes they would chide, and sometimes they would quite neglect him. Wherefore he began to retire himself to his chamber, to pray for and pity them, and also to condole his own misery; he would also walk solitarily in the fields, sometimes reading and sometimes praying: and thus for some days he spent his time.

Now, I saw upon a time, when he was walking in the fields, that he was (as he was wont) reading in his book [3] and greatly distressed in his mind; and as he read, he burst out, as he had done before, crying, What shall I do to be saved?

I saw also that he looked this way and that way, as if he would run; yet he stood still, because, as I perceived, he could not tell which way to go. I looked then, and saw a man named Evangelist [4] coming to him, who asked, Wherefore dost thou cry?

He answered, Sir, I perceive by the book in my hand that I am condemned to die, and after that to come to judgment, and I find that I am not willing to do the first, nor able to do the second.

Then said Evangelist, Why not willing to die, since this life is attended with so many evils? The man answered, Because I fear that this burden that is upon my back will sink me lower than the grave, and I shall fall into Tophet.[5] And, sir, if I be not fit to go to prison, I am not fit to go to judgment, and from thence to execution; and the thoughts of these things make me cry.

Then said Evangelist, If this be thy condition, why standest thou still? He answered, Because I know not whither to go. Then he gave him a parchment roll, and there was written within, 'Fly from the wrath to come.'

The man therefore read it and, looking upon Evangelist very carefully, said, Whither must I fly? Then said Evangelist, pointing with his finger over a very wide field, Do you see yonder wicket-gate? [6] The man said, No. Then said the other, Do you see yonder shining light? He said, I think I do. Then said Evangelist, Keep that light in your eye, and go up directly thereto: so shalt thou see the gate; at which when thou knockest, it shall be told thee what thou shalt do.

So I saw in my dream that the man began to run. Now, he had not run

3. The Bible.
4. The name was a term for an itinerant preacher, for any of the authors of the Four Gospels, and, in its literal sense, for the bringer of good news or glad tidings.
5. The name of a refuse dump which became a symbol of damnation; cf. Isaiah 30:33: "For Tophet is ordained of old; yea, for the King it is prepared: he hath made it deep and large: the pile thereof is fire and much wood; the breath of the Lord, like a stream of brimstone, doth kindle it."
6. A small gate for foot-passengers, as opposed to a large gate for horsemen or coaches; cf. Matthew 7:13–14: "Enter ye in at the strait gate: for wide is the gate, and broad is the way, that leadeth to destruction, and many there be which go in thereat: Because strait is the gate, and narrow is the way, which leadeth unto life, and few there be that find it."

far from his own door, but his wife and children perceiving it, began to cry after him to return; but the man put his fingers in his ears, and ran on, crying, Life! life! eternal life! So he looked not behind him, but fled towards the middle of the plain. . . .

[Apollyon]

But now in this Valley of Humiliation poor Christian was hard put to it; for he had gone but a little way before he espied a foul fiend coming over the field to meet him; his name is Apollyon.[7] Then did Christian begin to be afraid, and to cast in his mind whether to go back or to stand his ground. But he considered again that he had no armour for his back, and therefore thought that to turn the back to him might give him the greater advantage with ease to pierce him with his darts. Therefore he resolved to venture and stand his ground. For, thought he, had I no more in mine eye than the saving of my life, 'twould be the best way to stand.

So he went on, and Apollyon met him. Now the monster was hideous to behold; he was clothed with scales like a fish (and they are his pride), he had wings like a dragon, feet like a bear, and out of his belly came fire and smoke, and his mouth was as the mouth of a lion. When he was come up to Christian, he beheld him with a disdainful countenance and thus began to question with him.

APOL. Whence come you? and whither are you bound?

CHR. I am come from the City of Destruction, which is the place of all evil, and am going to the City of Zion.[8]

APOL. By this I perceive thou art one of my subjects, for all that country is mine, and I am the prince and god of it. How is it, then, that thou hast run away from thy king? Were it not that I hope thou mayest do me more service, I would strike thee now at one blow to the ground.

CHR. I was born, indeed, in your dominions, but your service was hard, and your wages such as a man could not live on, for the wages of sin is death;[9] therefore, when I was come to years, I did as other considerate persons do, look out if perhaps I might mend myself.

APOL. There is no prince that will thus lightly lose his subjects, neither will I as yet lose thee; but since thou complainest of thy service and wages, be content to go back. What our country will afford, I do here promise to give thee.

CHR. But I have let myself to another, even to the King of Princes; and how can I, with fairness, go back with thee?

APOL. Thou hast done in this, according to the proverb, changed a bad for a worse; but it is ordinary for those that have professed themselves his servants, after a while to give him the slip and return again to me. Do thou so too, and all shall be well.

7. Literally, the Destroyer or the "angel of the bottomless pit" (Revelation 9:11). His description is based on the account of Leviathan in Job 41 and of the "great beast" of Revelation 13, both taken as types of Satan. See also the dragon Sin in Spenser, *Faerie Queene* I.xi.
8. The New Jerusalem, i.e. the celestial city of Revelation 21:2.
9. Romans 6:23: "For the wages of sin is death, but the gift of God is eternal life through Jesus Christ our Lord."

CHR. I have given him my faith, and sworn my allegiance to him; how, then, can I go back from this and not be hanged as a traitor?

APOL. Thou didst the same to me, and yet I am willing to pass by all, if now thou wilt yet turn again and go back.

CHR. What I promised thee was in my nonage; and, besides, I count the Prince under whose banner now I stand is able to absolve me; yea, and to pardon also what I did as to my compliance with thee; and besides (O thou destroying Apollyon) to speak truth, I like his service, his wages, his servants, his government, his company, and country, better than thine; and, therefore, leave off to persuade me further; I am his servant, and I will follow him.

APOL. Consider, again, when thou art in cool blood, what thou art like to meet with in the way that thou goest. Thou knowest that, for the most part, his servants come to an ill end, because they are transgressors against me and my ways. How many of them have been put to shameful deaths! And, besides, thou countest his service better than mine, whereas he never came yet from the place where he is to deliver any that served him out of their hands; but as for me, how many times, as all the world very well knows, have I delivered, either by power or fraud, those that have faithfully served me, from him and his, though taken by them; and so I will deliver thee.

CHR. His forebearing at present to deliver them is on purpose to try their love, whether they will cleave to him to the end; and as for the ill end thou sayest they come to, that is most glorious in their account; for, for present deliverance, they do not much expect it, for they stay for their glory, and then they shall have it, when their Prince comes in his and the glory of the angels.

APOL. Thou hast already been unfaithful in thy service to him; and how dost thou think to receive wages of him?

CHR. Wherein, O Apollyon, have I been unfaithful to him?

APOL. Thou didst faint at first setting out, when thou wast almost choked in the Gulf of Despond; [10] thou didst attempt wrong ways to be rid of thy burden, whereas thou shouldst have stayed till thy Prince had taken it off; thou didst sinfully sleep and lose thy choice thing; thou wast, also, almost persuaded to go back at the sight of the lions; and when thou talkest of thy journey and of what thou hast heard and seen, thou art inwardly desirous of vain-glory in all that thou sayest or doest.

CHR. All this is true, and much more which thou hast left out; but the Prince whom I serve and honour is merciful and ready to forgive; but, besides, these infirmities possessed me in thy country, for there I sucked them in; and I have groaned under them, been sorry for them, and have obtained pardon of my Prince.

APOL. Then Apollyon broke out into a grievous rage, saying, I am an enemy to this Prince; I hate his person, his laws, and people; I am come out on purpose to withstand thee.

CHR. Apollyon, beware what you do; for I am in the king's highway, the way of holiness; therefore take heed to yourself.

APOL. Then Apollyon straddled quite over the whole breadth of the way, and said, I am void of fear in this matter: prepare thyself to die; for I swear

10. Recalling Christian's earlier temptation to despair and the temporary loss of the parchment roll, "his pass into the Celestial City."

by my infernal den that thou shalt go no further; here will I spill thy soul.

And with that he threw a flaming dart at his breast; but Christian had a shield in his hand, with which he caught it, and so prevented the danger of that.

Then did Christian draw, for he saw it was time to bestir him: and Apollyon as fast made at him, throwing darts as thick as hail; by the which, notwithstanding all that Christian could do to avoid it, Apollyon wounded him in his head, his hand, and foot. This made Christian give a little back; Apollyon therefore followed his work amain, and Christian again took courage and resisted as manfully as he could. This sore combat lasted for above half a day, even till Christian was almost quite spent; for you must know that Christian, by reason of his wounds, must needs grow weaker and weaker.

Then Apollyon, espying his opportunity, began to gather up close to Christian, and wrestling with him, gave him a dreadful fall; and with that Christian's sword flew out of his hand. Then said Apollyon, I am sure of thee now. And with that he had almost pressed him to death, so that Christian began to despair of life. But as God would have it, while Apollyon was fetching of his last blow, thereby to make a full end of this good man, Christian nimbly stretched out his hand for his sword, and caught it, saying, Rejoice not against me, O mine enemy: when I fall I shall arise; and with that gave him a deadly thrust, which made him give back, as one that had received his mortal wound. Christian perceiving that, made at him again, saying, Nay, in all these things we are more than conquerors through him that loved us. And with that Apollyon spread forth his dragon's wings, and sped him away, that Christian for a season saw him no more. . . .

[Vanity Fair]

Then I saw in my dream, that when they [11] were got out of the wilderness, they presently saw a town before them, and the name of that town is Vanity; and at the town there is a fair kept, called Vanity Fair.[12] It is kept all the year long; it beareth the name of Vanity Fair, because the town where it is kept is lighter than vanity; and also because all that is there sold or that cometh thither is vanity. As is the saying of the wise, all that cometh is vanity.

This fair is no new-erected business, but a thing of ancient standing; I will show you the original of it.

Almost five thousand years agone, there were pilgrims walking to the Celestial City, as these two honest persons are: and Beelzebub, Apollyon, and Legion,[13] with their companions, perceiving by the path that the pilgrims made, that their way to the city lay through this town of Vanity, they contrived here to set up a fair; a fair wherein should be sold all sorts of vanity, and that it should last all the year long: therefore at this fair are all such merchandise sold, as houses, lands, trades, places, honours, preferments,[14] titles, countries,

---

11. Christian has been joined by Faithful.
12. Probably based upon Bunyan's experience of the great annual fair at Stourbridge, near Cambridge; "vanity" in the sense of something empty or worthless, like the cheap or false wares often sold at fairs.
13. Named for the "unclean spirit" or devil, who replies, when asked his name, "My name is Legion; for we are many" (Mark 5:9).
14. Promotions.

kingdoms, lusts, pleasures, and delights of all sorts, as whores, bawds, wives, husbands, children, masters, servants, lives, blood, bodies, souls, silver, gold, pearls, precious stones, and what not.

And, moreover, at this fair there is at all times to be seen juggling, cheats, games, plays, fools, apes, knaves, and rogues, and that of every kind.

Here are to be seen, too, and that for nothing, thefts, murders, adulteries, false swearers, and that of a blood-red colour.

And as in other fairs of less moment, there are the several rows and streets, under their proper names, where such wares are vended; so here likewise you have the proper places, rows, streets (viz. countries and kingdoms), where the wares of this fair are soonest to be found. Here is the Britain Row, the French Row, the Italian Row, the Spanish Row, the German Row, where several sorts of vanities are to be sold. But, as in other fairs, some one commodity is as the chief of all the fair, so the ware of Rome and her merchandise is greatly promoted in this fair; only our English nation, with some others, have taken a dislike thereat.

Now, as I said, the way to the Celestial City lies just through this town where this lusty fair is kept; and he that will go to the City, and yet not go through this town, must needs go out of the world. The Prince of Princes himself, when here, went through this town to his own country, and that upon a fair day too; yea, and as I think, it was Beelzebub, the chief lord of this fair, that invited him to buy of his vanities; yea, would have made him lord of the fair, would he but have done him reverence as he went through the town. Yea, because he was such a person of honour, Beelzebub had him from street to street, and showed him all the kingdoms of the world in a little time, that he might, if possible, allure the Blessed One to cheapen [15] and buy some of his vanities; but he had no mind to the merchandise, and therefore left the town without laying out so much as one farthing upon these vanities. This fair, there-fore, is an ancient thing, of long standing, and a very great fair.

Now these pilgrims, as I said, must needs go through this fair. Well, so they did: but, behold, even as they entered into the fair, all the people in the fair were moved, and the town itself as it were in a hubbub about them; and that for several reasons: for—

First, the pilgrims were clothed with such kind of raiment as was diverse from the raiment of any that traded in that fair. The people therefore of the fair, made a great gazing upon them: some said they were fools, some they were bedlams,[16] and some, they are outlandish men.[17]

Secondly, and as they wondered at their apparel, so they did likewise at their speech; for few could understand what they said. They naturally spoke the language of Canaan, but they that kept the fair were the men of this world;

15. To bid or bargain for; referring to the temptation of Christ: "Again, the devil taketh him up into an exceeding high mountain, and showeth him all the Kingdoms of the world. . . . And saith unto him, All these things will I give thee, if thou wilt fall down and worship me" (Matthew 4:8–9).

16. Madmen.

17. Foreigners; emphasizing, in dress as below in speech, the difference of style between the worldly and the devout, the speech of the latter—like Bunyan's prose—often steeped in the idiom of the Bible. See Isaiah 19:18: "In that day shall five cities in the land of Egypt speak the language of Canaan, and swear to the Lord of hosts."

so that, from one end of the fair to the other, they seemed barbarians each to the other.

Thirdly, but that which did not a little amuse the merchandisers, was that these pilgrims set very light by all their wares; they care not so much as to look upon them; and if they called upon them to buy, they would put their fingers in their ears, and cry, Turn away mine eyes from beholding vanity, and look upwards, signifying that their trade and traffic was in heaven.

One chanced mockingly, beholding the carriages of the men, to say unto them, What will ye buy? But they, looking gravely upon him, answered, We buy the truth. At that there was an occasion taken to despise the men the more; some mocking, some taunting, some speaking reproachfully, and some calling upon others to smite them. At last things came to a hubbub and great stir in the fair, insomuch that all order was confounded. Now was word presently brought to the great one of the fair, who quickly came down, and deputed some of his most trusty friends to take these men into examination, about whom the fair was almost overturned. . . .

[A trial is held, in which Faithful is accused by three witnesses, Envy, Superstition, and Pickthank.]

Then went the jury out, whose names were Mr. Blind-man, Mr. No-good, Mr. Malice, Mr. Love-lust, Mr. Live-loose, Mr. Heady, Mr. High-mind, Mr. Enmity, Mr. Liar, Mr. Cruelty, Mr. Hate-light, and Mr. Implacable; who every one gave in his private verdict against him among themselves, and afterwards unanimously concluded to bring him in guilty before the Judge. And first, among themselves, Mr. Blind-man, the foreman, said, I see clearly that this man is a heretic. Then said Mr. No-good, Away with such a fellow from the earth. Ay, said Mr. Malice, for I hate the very looks of him. Then said Mr. Love-lust, I could never endure him. Nor I, said Mr. Live-loose, for he would always be condemning my way. Hang him, hang him, said Mr. Heady. A sorry scrub,[18] said Mr. High-mind. My heart riseth against him, said Mr. Enmity. He is a rogue, said Mr. Liar. Hanging is too good for him, said Mr. Cruelty. Let's despatch him out of the way, said Mr. Hate-light. Then said Mr. Implacable, Might I have all the world given me, I could not be reconciled to him; therefore, let us forthwith bring him in guilty of death. And so they did; therefore he was presently condemned to be had from the place where he was, to the place from whence he came, and there to be put to the most cruel death that could be invented.

They therefore brought him out to do with him according to their law; and, first, they scourged him, then they buffeted him, then they lanced his flesh with knives; after that, they stoned him with stones, then pricked him with their swords; and, last of all, they burned him to ashes at the stake. Thus came Faithful to his end.

Now I saw that there stood behind the multitude a chariot and a couple of horses, waiting for Faithful, who (so soon as his adversaries had despatched him) was taken up into it, and straightway was carried up through the clouds, with sound of trumpet, the nearest way to the celestial gate.

18. Insignificant fellow.

But as for Christian, he had some respite, and was remanded back to prison. So he there remained for a space; but He that overrules all things, having the power of their rage in his own hand, so wrought it about, that Christian for that time escaped them, and went his way. . . .

[Faithful is replaced by the convert, Hopeful.]

[The Celestial City]

. . . I saw in my dream that these two men went in at the gate: and lo, as they entered, they were transfigured, and they had raiment put on that shone like gold. There were also that met them with harps and crowns and gave them to them—the harps to praise withal, and the crowns in token of honour. Then I heard in my dream that all the bells in the city rang again for joy, and that it was said unto them, Enter ye into the joy of your Lord. I also heard the men themselves, that they sang with a loud voice, saying, Blessing and honour, and glory, and power, be unto Him that sitteth upon the throne, and unto the Lamb, for ever and ever.

Now, just as the gates were opened to let in the men, I looked in after them, and, behold, the City shone like the sun; the streets also were paved with gold, and in them walked many men with crowns on their heads, palms in their hands, and golden harps to sing praises withal.

There were also of them that had wings, and they answered one another without intermission, saying, Holy, holy, holy is the Lord. And after that they shut up the gates; which, when I had seen, I wished myself among them. . . .

1678

GEORGE SAVILE, MARQUESS OF HALIFAX
1633–1695

Although his wit was great and indiscreet, leading many to doubt his faith and his principles, Halifax led a life of devoted public service, holding major offices in three reigns. His parliamentary leadership reached its high point in the debate of 1680 over the bill designed to exclude James II from the throne. The bill had passed the House of Commons readily and was championed in the House of Lords by Shaftesbury (the Achitophel of Dryden's satire, as Halifax is the Jotham), with whom Halifax had often sided. On this occasion Halifax met Shaftesbury's powerful oratory with greater eloquence of his own, rising to speak sixteen times over seven hours, and brought the bill to defeat.

He wrote *Advice to a Daughter* (1688), addressed to the mother-to-be of the famous Lord Chesterfield; a brilliant *Character of King Charles II*; as well as political pamphlets and maxims. In *The Character of a Trimmer* he defends himself against the charge of compromise and lukewarmness, redefining a Trimmer as one who, in a boat overbalanced by shifting of sides, conceives "it would do as well if the boat went even, without endangering the passengers. . . ." Elsewhere he remarks that the "best party is but a kind of conspiracy against the rest of the nation," and he expects abuse for his detachment: "Nothing hath an uglier look to us than reason, when it is not of our side." He found Montaigne's *Essays* "the book in the world I am the best entertained with," admiring that "great man, whom Nature hath made too big to confine himself to the exactness of a studied style," and who "let his mind have its full flight" in "a generous kind of negligence." Halifax's own prose is as good as any of its age. One may contrast his brilliant use of analogy with the desperate chase after bright similitudes of Congreve's Witwoud in *The Way of the World,* and one may compare the nicely antithetic syntax with that of the heroic couplet or of the later prose of Johnson and Gibbon: "Friendship cannot live with ceremony, nor without civility." Or that dazzling construction: "Those who merit because they suffered, are so very angry with those that made them suffer, that, though their services deserve employment, their temper rendereth them unfit for it."

From The Character of a Trimmer

[The Laws]

Our Trimmer, as he hath a great veneration for laws in general, so he hath a more particular for our own. He looketh upon them as the chains that tie up our unruly passions, which else, like wild beasts let loose, would reduce the world into its first state of barbarism and hostility;[1] all the good things we enjoy, we owe to them; and all the ill things we are freed from is by their protection.

God himself thought it not enough to be a creator, without being a lawgiver; and His goodness had been defective towards mankind in making them, if He had not prescribed rules to make them happy too.

All laws flow from that of Nature, and where that is not the foundation, they may be legally imposed, but they will be lamely obeyed. By this Nature is not meant that which fools and madmen[2] misquote to justify their excesses; it is innocent and uncorrupted Nature, that which disposeth men to choose virtue without its being prescribed, and which is so far from inspiring ill thoughts into us, that we take pains to suppress the good ones it infuseth.

The civilized world hath ever paid a willing subjection to laws; even conquerors have done homage to them. . . .

They are to mankind that which the sun is to plants, whilst it cherisheth and preserveth them. Where they have their force and are not clouded or suppressed, everything smileth and flourisheth; but where they are darkened and not suffered to shine out, it maketh everything to wither and decay.

They secure man not only against one another, but against themselves too; they are a sanctuary to which the Crown hath occasion to resort as often as the people, so that it hath an interest as well as a duty to preserve them.

There would be no end of making a panegyric of laws; let it be enough to add that without laws the world would become a wilderness, and men little less than beasts. But with all this, the best things may come to be the worst, if they are not in good hands; and if it be true that the wisest men generally make the laws, it is true that the strongest do too often interpret them. And as rivers belong as much to the channel where they run as to the spring from

1. That is, a state of nature such as Hobbes describes in *Leviathan* I.13; but here conceived as a fallen state in opposition to "innocent and uncorrupted Nature."
2. Perhaps a reference to Hobbes; but cf. also Dryden, *Absalom and Achitophel,* ll. 51–56.

whence they first arise, so the laws depend as much upon the pipes through which they are to pass as upon the fountain from whence they flow.

The authority of a king who is head of the law, as well as the dignity of public justice, is debased when the clear stream of the law is puddled and disturbed by bunglers, or conveyed by unclean instruments to the people.

Our Trimmer would have them appear in their full lustre, and would be grieved to see the day when, instead of speaking with authority from the seats of justice, they should speak out of a grate, with a lamenting voice like prisoners that desire to be rescued. . . .

A judge hath such power lodged in him that the king will never be thought to have chosen well where the voice of mankind hath not beforehand recommended the man to his station; when men are made judges of what they do not understand, the world censureth such a choice, not out of ill will to the men, but fear for themselves.

. . . Men will fear that out of the tree of the law, from whence we expect shade and shelter, such workmen will make cudgels to beat us with, or rather they will turn the cannon upon our properties that were entrusted with them for their defence.

To see the laws mangled, disguised, made speak quite another language than their own; to see them thrown from the dignity of protecting mankind to the disgraceful office of destroying them; and, notwithstanding their innocence in themselves, to be made the worst instruments that the most refined villainy can make use of, will raise men's anger above the power of laying it down again, and tempt them to follow the evil examples given them of judging without hearing, when so provoked by their design of revenge. Our Trimmer therefore, as he thinketh the laws are jewels, so he believeth they are nowhere better set than in the constitution of our English government, if rightly understood and carefully preserved.

It would be too great partiality to say they are perfect or liable to no objection; such things are not of this world; but if it hath more excellencies and fewer faults than any other we know, it is enough to recommend them to our esteem.

The dispute which is a greater beauty, a monarchy or a commonwealth, hath lasted long between their contending lovers, and they have behaved themselves too like lovers (who in good manners must be out of their wits), who have used such figures to exalt their own idols on either side, and such angry aggravations to reproach one another in the contest, that moderate men have in all times smiled upon this eagerness, and thought it differed very little from a downright frenzy. We in England, by a happy use of the controversy, conclude them both in the wrong and reject them from being our pattern, not taking the words in the utmost extent, which is, monarchy, a thing that leaveth men no liberty, and a commonwealth, such a one as alloweth them no quiet.

We think that a wise mean between these barbarous extremes [3] is that

---

3. This strategy of thinking is characteristic of Halifax, of his age, and of that to follow. We see it in Bishop Simon Patrick's celebration of the Church of England as a happy mean between the "squalid sluttery" of Puritan chapels and the "meretricious gaudiness" of the Church of Rome, or in Halifax's own plea (elsewhere in this work) for a "mean" between the "sauciness of some of the Scotch apostles" (i.e. militant Presbyterians) and "the indecent

which self-preservation ought to dictate to our wishes; and we may say we have attained to this mean in a greater measure than any nation now in being, or perhaps any we have read of, though never so much celebrated for the wisdom or felicity of their constitutions. We take from one the too great power of doing hurt and yet leave enough to govern and protect us; we take from the other the confusion of parity,[4] the animosities, and the license, and yet reserve a due care of such a liberty as may consist with men's allegiance. But it being hard, if not impossible, to be exactly even, our government hath much the stronger bias towards monarchy, which by the general consent and practice of mankind seemeth to have the advantage in dispute against a commonwealth. The rules of a commonwealth are too hard for the bulk of mankind to come up to; that form of government requireth such a spirit to carry it on as doth not dwell in great numbers, but is restrained to so very few, especially in this age, that let the methods appear never so reasonable in paper, they must fail in practice, which will ever be suited more to men's nature as it is than as it should be.

Monarchy is liked by the people for the bells and tinsel, the outward pomp and gilding; and there must be milk for babes, since the greatest part of mankind are and ever will be included in that list; and it is approved by wise and thinking men as the best when compared with others, all circumstances and objections impartially considered. Then it hath so great an advantage above all other forms, when the administration of that power falleth in good hands, that all other governments look out of countenance when they are set in competition with it. Lycurgus[5] might have saved himself the trouble of making laws if either he had been immortal, or that he could have secured to posterity a succeeding race of princes like himself. . . . Such a magistrate is the life and soul of justice, whereas the law is but a body and a dead one, too, without his influence to give it warmth and vigour; and by the irresistible power of his virtue he doth so reconcile dominion and allegiance that all disputes between them are silenced and subdued. And indeed no monarchy can be perfect and absolute without exception but where the prince is superior by his virtues as well as by his character and his power. So that to screw out precedents of unlimited power is a plain diminution to a prince that nature hath made great, and who had better make himself a glorious example to posterity than borrow an authority from dark records raised out of the grave, which, besides their non-usage, have always in them matter of controversy and debate. . . .

But since for the greater honour of good and wise princes, and the better to set off their character by the comparison, Heaven hath decreed there must be a mixture, and that such as are perverse or insufficient, or perhaps both,

---

courtship of some of the silken divines who, one would think, do practice to bow at the altar only to learn to make the better legs at Court." One culmination of this theme is Swift's *A Tale of a Tub*, where the "barbarous extremes" of Peter (the Church of Rome) and Jack (radical Protestantism) are opposed to the "wise mean" of Martin (the Church of England). See also "The Middle Way" in the Introduction to Restoration section.

4. Leveling, as opposed to hierarchy.

5. The Spartan lawmaker (9th century? B.C.), who, once his constitution was accepted, extracted a vow that it would not be changed until he returned; thereupon he left Sparta forever, hoping to preserve his laws inviolate.

are at least to have their equal turns in the government of the world; and besides, that the will of man is so various, and so unbounded a thing, and so fatal too when joined with power misapplied, it is no wonder if those who are to be governed are unwilling to have so dangerous as well as so uncertain a standard of their obedience.

There must be therefore rules and laws; for want of which, or at least the observation of them, it was as capital for a man to say that Nero did not play well upon the lute [6] as to commit treason or blaspheme the gods. And even Vespasian [7] himself had like to have lost his life for sleeping whilst he should have attended and admired that emperor's impertinence upon the stage. There is a wantonness [8] in great power that men are generally too apt to be corrupted with; and for that reason a wise prince, to prevent the temptations arising from common frailty, would choose to govern by rules for his own sake, as well as for his people's, since it only secureth him from errors, and doth not lessen the real authority that a good magistrate would care to be possessed of. For if the will of a prince is contrary either to reason itself, or to the universal opinion of his subjects, the law by a kind restraint rescueth him from a disease that would undo him; if his will on the other side is reasonable and well directed, that will immediately becometh a law, and he is arbitrary by an easy and natural consequence, without taking pains or overturning the world for it.

If princes consider laws as things imposed on them, they have the appearance of fetters of iron, but to such as would make them their choice as well as their practice they are chains of gold; and in that respect are ornaments, as in others they are a defence to them. And, by a comparison not improper for God's vicegerents [9] upon earth, as our Maker never commandeth our obedience to anything that as reasonable creatures we ought not to make our own election, so a good and wise governor, though all laws were abolished would, by the voluntary direction of his own reason, do without restraint the very same things that they would have enjoined.

Our Trimmer thinketh that the king and kingdom ought to be one creature, not to be separated in their political capacity; and when either of them undertake to act apart, it is like the crawling of worms after they are cut in pieces, which cannot be a lasting motion, the whole creature not stirring at a time. If the body have a dead palsy, the head cannot make it move; and God hath not yet delegated such a healing power to princes as that they can in a moment say to a languishing people oppressed and in despair, Take up your bed and walk.[10]

The figure of a king is so comprehensive and exalted a thing that it is a kind of degrading him to lodge that power separately in his own natural person,

6. The Roman emperor (37–68 A.D.) fancied himself as musician and actor.
7. Roman emperor and earlier a military leader under Nero, noted for the frugality and simplicity of his life.
8. "Sportiveness; negligence of restraint" (Samuel Johnson, *Dictionary*).
9. Those deputed by God to exercise His authority in government, as the doctrine of the divine right of kings would maintain.
10. As Christ said to the "sick of palsy": "Arise, take up thy bed, and go unto thine house" (Matthew 9:6).

which can never be safely or naturally great but where the people are so united to him as to be flesh of his flesh and bone of his bone. For when he is reduced to the single definition of a man he shrinketh into so low a character that it is a temptation upon men's allegiance, and an impairing that veneration which is necessary to preserve their duty to him. Whereas a prince who is so joined to his people that they seem to be his limbs, rather than his subjects; clothed with mercy and justice rightly applied in their several places; his throne supported by love as well as by power; and the warm wishes of his devoted subjects, like never-failing incense, still ascending towards him, looketh so like the best image we can frame to ourselves of God Almighty that men would have much ado not to fall down and worship him, and would be much more tempted to the sin of idolatry than to that of disobedience.

Our Trimmer is of opinion that there must be so much dignity inseparably annexed to the royal function as may be sufficient to secure it from insolence and contempt; and there must be condescensions too from the Throne, like kind showers from Heaven, that the prince may look so much the more like God Almighty's deputy upon earth. For power without love hath a terrifying aspect, and the worship which is paid to it is like that which the Indians give out of fear to wild beasts and devils. He that feareth God only because there is a hell, must wish there were no God; and he who feareth the king only because he can punish, must wish there were no king. So that, without a principle of love, there can be no true allegiance; and there must remain perpetual seeds of resistance against a power that is built upon such an unnatural foundation as that of fear and terror. All force is a kind of foul play, and whosoever aimeth at it himself doth by implication allow it to those he playeth with; so that there will be ever matter prepared in the minds of people when they are provoked, and the prince, to secure himself, must live in the midst of his own subjects as if he were in a conquered country. . . . And besides that there can be no lasting radical security but where the governed are satisfied with the governors, it must be a dominion very unpleasant to a prince of an elevated mind to impose an abject and sordid servility instead of receiving the willing sacrifice of duty and obedience. The bravest princes in all times, who were incapable of any other kind of fear, have feared to grieve their own people; such a fear is a glory, and in this sense 'tis an infamy not to be a coward. So that the mistaken heroes who are void of this generous kind of fear need no other aggravation to complete their ill characters.

When a despotic prince hath bruised all his subjects with a slavish obedience, all the force he can use cannot subdue his own fears, enemies of his own creation, to which he can never be reconciled, it being impossible to do injustice and not to fear revenge. There is no cure for this fear but the not deserving to be hurt; and therefore a prince who doth not allow his thoughts to stray beyond the rules of justice hath always the blessing of an inward quiet and assurance as a natural effect of his good meaning to his people; and though he will not neglect due precautions to secure himself in all events, yet he is incapable of entertaining vain and remote suspicions of those of whom he resolveth never to deserve ill. . . .

Our Trimmer thinketh it no advantage to a government to endeavour the suppressing all kind of right which may remain in the body of the people, or to employ small authors in it whose officiousness [11] or want of money may encourage them to write, though it is not very easy to have abilities equal to such a subject. They forget that in their too high-strained arguments for the rights of princes, they very often plead against human nature,[12] which will always give a bias to those reasons which seem to be of her side. . . .

In power, as in most other things, the way for princes to keep it, is not to grasp more than their arms can well hold; the nice [13] and unnecessary inquiring into these things, or the licensing some books and suppressing some others [14] without sufficient reason to justify the doing either, is so far from being an advantage to a government that it exposeth it to the censure of being partial, and to the suspicion of having some hidden designs to be carried on by these unusual methods.

When all is said, there is a natural reason of state, an undefinable thing,[15] grounded upon the common good of mankind, which is immortal, and in all changes and revolutions still preserveth its original right of saving a nation, when the letter of the law perhaps would destroy it; and by whatsoever means it moveth, carrieth a power with it that admitteth of no opposition, being supported by Nature, which inspireth an immediate consent at some critical times into every individual member, to that which visibly tendeth to preservation of the whole; and this being so, a wise prince, instead of controverting the right of this reason of state, will by all means endeavour it may be of his side, and then he will be secure.

Our Trimmer cannot conceive that the power of any prince can be lasting but where 'tis built upon the foundation of his own unborrowed virtue; he must not only be the first mover and the fountain from whence the great acts of state originally flow but he must be thought so to his people that they may preserve their veneration for him; he must be jealous of his power, and not impart so much of it to any about him as that he may suffer an eclipse by it. . . .

Princes may lend some of their light to make another shine, but they must still preserve the superiority of being the brighter planet, and when it happeneth that the reversion [16] is in men's eyes, there is more care necessary to keep up the dignity of possession that men may not forget who is king, either out of their hopes or fears who shall be. If the sun should part with all his

11. Eagerness to serve; meddlesome zeal.

12. That is, by insisting, as Hobbes did, upon the intolerable chaos man's appetitive nature would produce without the commanding power of a sovereign; or more generally, scorning the natural capacities of the people to rule themselves in order to exalt the power of a monarch.

13. Excessively close.

14. The issue earlier discussed by Milton in the *Areopagitica* and later to be renewed with the Licensing Act of 1737, whereby Walpole sought to repress public criticism in the theater.

15. Later in the work Halifax writes: "In order to its preservation there is a hidden power in government which would be lost if it was defined, a certain mystery by virtue of which a nation may at some critical times be secured from ruin; but then it must be kept as a mystery; it is rendered useless when touched by unskillful hands, and no government ever had, or deserved to have that power which was so unwary as to anticipate their claim to it. . . . " Perhaps relevant is one of Halifax's "thoughts": "There is a happy pitch of ignorance that a man of sense might pray for."

16. Right of succession.

light to any other stars, the Indians would not know where to find their God, after he had so deposed himself, and would make the light (wherever it went) the object of their worship. . . .

[Liberty and the Constitution]

Our Trimmer owneth a passion for liberty, yet so restrained that it doth not in the least impair or taint his allegiance; he thinketh it hard for a soul that doth not love liberty ever to raise itself to another world; he taketh it to be the foundation of all virtue, and the only seasoning that giveth a relish to life; and though the laziness of a slavish subjection hath its charms for the more gross and earthly part of mankind, yet to men made of a better sort of clay, all that the world can give without liberty hath no taste. It is true, nothing is sold so cheap by unthinking men; but that doth no more lessen the real value of it than a country fellow's ignorance doth that of a diamond in selling it for a pot of ale. Liberty is the mistress of mankind; she hath powerful charms which do so dazzle us that we find beauties in her which perhaps are not there, as we do in other mistresses. Yet if she was not a beauty, the world would not run mad for her; therefore, since the reasonable desire of it ought not to be restrained, and that even the unreasonable desire of it cannot be entirely suppressed, those who would take it away from a people possessed of it are likely to fail in the attempting, or be very unquiet in the keeping of it.

Our Trimmer admireth our blessed constitution, in which dominion and liberty are so well reconciled; it giveth to the prince the glorious power of commanding freemen, and to the subjects the satisfaction of seeing the power so lodged as that their liberties are secure. It doth not allow the crown such a ruining power as that no grass can grow wherever it treadeth, but a cherishing and protecting power; such a one as hath a grim aspect only to the offending subjects, but is the joy and the pride of all the good ones; their own interest being so bound up in it as to engage them to defend and support it. And though in some instances the king is restrained, yet nothing in the government can move without him; our laws make a true distinction between vassalage [17] and obedience; between a devouring prerogative [18] and a licentious ungovernable freedom; and as of all the orders of building the composite [19] is the best,

---

17. Political dependence (as in the fealty owned a vassal to his lord) as opposed to voluntary "obedience."

18. Those powers of the sovereign unlimited by laws.

19. This refers first to the orders of architecture, each named for its characteristic column, the Doric, Ionic, Corinthian, and (later in Rome) the Tuscan. During the Roman empire elements of the Ionic and Corinthian were fused to form the new Composite order, and the term was more generally applied to a style that mixed elements of various orders. The counterpart to this is the mixed state, which fuses elements to be found in the pure forms of government—monarchy, oligarchy, and democracy; that is, the rule of the One, the Few, or the Many. It was believed by the classical historian Polybius (204–122 B.C.) that a mixed government might prevent the cyclic alternation of the pure forms and thus achieve stability and enduring power. This doctrine was widely revived in the late 17th century and influenced John Locke and others, including the authors of the American Constitution a century later, in promoting a balance of power within the state. Swift's earliest published work, *The Contests and Dissensions of . . . Greece and Rome* (1701) was a defense of this balance against the tyranny of Commons, and Pope was later to celebrate the "according music of a well-mixed state" (*Essay on Man* III.294).

so ours by a happy mixture and a wise choice of what is best in others, is brought into a form that is our felicity who live under it, and the envy of our neighbours that cannot imitate it.

The Crown hath power sufficient to protect our liberties. The people have so much liberty as is necessary to make them useful to the Crown.

Our government is in a just proportion, no tympany, no unnatural swelling either of power or liberty; and whereas in all overgrown monarchies, reason, learning, and inquiry are banished and hanged in effigy for mutineers,[20] here they are encouraged and cherished as the surest friends to a government established upon the foundation of law and justice. When all is done, those who look for perfection in this world may look as long as the Jews have done for their Messiah; and therefore our Trimmer is not so unreasonably partial as to free our government from all objections. No doubt there have been fatal instances of its sickness, and more than that, of its mortality for some time; though by a miracle it hath been revived again; but till we have another race of mankind, in all constitutions that are bounded there will ever be some matter of strife and contention, and, rather than want pretensions, men's passions and interests will raise them from the most inconsiderable causes.

Our government is like our climate. There are winds which are sometimes loud and unquiet; and yet, with all the trouble they give us, we owe part of our health unto them; they clear the air, which else would be like a standing pool, and instead of refreshment would be a disease unto us.

There may be fresh gales of asserting liberty without turning into such storms of hurricane as that the state should run any hazard of being cast away by them. These strugglings, which are natural to all mixed governments, while they are kept from growing into convulsions, do by a mutual agitation from the several parts rather support and strengthen than weaken and maim the constitution; and the whole frame, instead of being torn or disjointed, cometh to be the better and closer knit by being thus exercised. But whatever faults our government may have, or a discerning critic may find in it when he looketh upon it alone, let any other be set against it, and then it showeth its comparative beauty. Let us look upon the most glittering outside of unbounded authority, and upon a nearer inquiry we shall find nothing but poor and miserable deformity within. Let us imagine a prince living in his kingdom as if in a great galley, his subjects tugging at the oar, laden with chains and reduced to real rags that they may gain him imaginary laurels; let us represent him gazing among his flatterers and receiving their false worship, like a child never contradicted and therefore always cozened,[21] or like a lady complimented only to be abused; condemned never to hear truth, and consequently never to do justice; wallowing in the soft bed of wanton and unbridled greatness, not less odious to the instruments themselves than to the objects of his tyranny; blown up into an ambitious dropsy,[22] never to be satisfied by the conquest of other people or by the oppression of his own. By aiming to be more than a man,

20. Cf. Pope's assertion that merely verbal learning thrives in a despotic reign; see *The Dunciad* IV.175–88.
21. Deceived, beguiled, imposed upon.
22. A disease marked by swelling caused by the accumulation of liquids in the body.

he falleth lower than the meanest of them,[23] a mistaken creature, swelled with panegyrics, and flattered out of his senses, and not only an incumbrance, but a nuisance to mankind, a hardened and unrelenting soul; and, like some creatures that grow fat with poisons, he groweth great by other men's miseries: an ambitious ape of the Divine greatness, an unruly giant that would storm even heaven itself, but that his scaling-ladders are not long enough; in short, a wild and devouring creature in rich trappings and with all his pride, no more than a whip in God Almighty's hand, to be thrown into the fire when the world hath been sufficiently scourged with it. This picture laid in right colours would not incite men to wish for such a government, but rather to acknowledge the happiness of our own, under which we enjoy all the privilege reasonable men can desire and avoid all the miseries many others are subject to; so that our Trimmer would keep it with all its faults and doth as little forgive those who give the occasion of breaking it as he doth those that take it. . . .

Our Trimmer is far from idolatry in other things; in one thing only he cometh near it: his country is in some degree his idol. He doth not worship the sun because 'tis not peculiar to us; it rambleth about the world and is less kind to us than others. But for the earth of England, though perhaps inferior to that of many places abroad, to him there is a divinity in it; and he would rather die than see a spire of English grass trampled down by a foreign trespasser. He thinketh there are a great many of his mind, for all plants are apt to taste of the soil in which they grow; and we that grow here have a root that produceth in us a stock of English juice, which is not to be changed by grafting or foreign infusion; and I do not know whether anything less will prevail than the modern experiment by which the blood of one creature is transmitted into another,[24] according to which, before the French blood can be let into our bodies, every drop of our own must be drawn out of them.

Our Trimmer cannot but lament that by a sacrifice too great for one nation to make to another, we should be like a rich mine, made useless only for want of being wrought, and that the life and vigour which should move us against our enemies is miserably applied to tear our own bowels; that being made by our happy situation not only safer but, if we please, greater too than other countries which far exceed us in extent; that having courage by nature, learning by industry, and riches by trade, we should corrupt all these advantages so as to make them insignificant and, by a fatality which seemeth peculiar to us, misplace our active rage one against another, whilst we are turned into statues on that side where lieth our greatest danger; to be unconcerned not only at our neighbour's ruin but our own,[25] and let our island lie like a great

---

23. Evoking the doctrine of the Great Chain of Being, where the attempt to rise out of one's assigned place in the hierarchy causes one to fall to the lowest place of all, as Satan in his rebellion—when his great powers undergo corruption—becomes the worst of creatures; a theme reinforced below by the reference to the Titans, the giants who sought to storm Olympus and to recover the power won by Zeus.

24. Such experiments in transfusion were made possible when William Harvey (1578–1657), physician to Charles I, discovered the circulation of the blood and published his findings in 1628.

25. Halifax is alluding to both Charles II's continued dependence upon subsidies from Louis XIV and his readiness to withdraw from all alliances with the Dutch; as well as the internal conflicts that followed the Popish Plot, with the Duke of York (later James II) rallying forces to suppress the Whig leadership. Halifax was making an appeal to Charles

hulk in the sea, without rudder or sail, all men cast away in her, or as if we were all children in a great cradle and rocked asleep to a foreign tune.

I say when our Trimmer representeth to his mind our roses blasted and discoloured, whilst the lilies [26] triumph and grow insolent upon the comparison; when he considereth our once flourishing laurel, now withered and dying, and nothing left us but a remembrance of a better part in history than we shall make in the next age, which will be no more to us than an escutcheon [27] hung upon our door when we are dead; when he foreseeth from hence growing infamy from abroad, confusion at home, and all this without the possibility of a cure, in respect of the voluntary fetters good men put on themselves by their allegiance; without a good measure of preventing grace,[28] he would be tempted to go out of the world like a Roman philosopher [29] rather than endure the burthen of life under such a discouraging prospect. But mistakes, as all other things, have their periods, and many times the nearest cure is not to oppose them but stay till they are crushed with their own weight; for Nature will not allow anything to continue long that is violent. Violence is a wound, and as a wound must be curable in a little time; or else 'tis mortal, but a nation comes near to be immortal. Therefore the wound will one time or another be cured. . . .

[Conclusion]

To conclude, our Trimmer is so fully satisfied of the truth of those principles by which he is directed in reference to the public that he will neither be bawled, threatened, laughed, nor drunk out of them; and instead of being converted by the arguments of his adversaries to their opinions, he is very much confirmed in his own by them. He professeth solemnly that were it in his power to choose, he would rather have his ambition bounded by the commands of a great and wise master than let it range with a popular licence, though crowned with success. Yet he cannot commit such a sin against the glorious thing called liberty, nor let his soul stoop so much below itself as to be content without repining to have his reason wholly subdued, or the privilege of acting like a sensible creature torn from him by the imperious dictates of unlimited authority, in what hand soever it happens to be placed.

What is there in this that is so criminal as to deserve the penalty of that most singular apophthegm, a Trimmer is worse than a rebel? What do angry men ail to rail so against moderation? Doth it not look as if they were going to some very scurvy extreme that is too strong to be digested by the more considering part of mankind? These arbitrary methods, besides the injustice of them, are (God be thanked) very unskillful too, for they fright the birds, by talking so loud, from coming into the nets that are laid for them; and when men agree to rifle a house they seldom give warning, or blow a trumpet; but

---

II (as it happened, a month or so before the King's death) for a policy of greater independence abroad and toleration at home. For the so-called Popish Plot see Dryden's *Absalom and Achitophel* (and its Headnote).

26. The roses (white and red) of England versus the lilies of France.

27. The shield depicting the family coat-of-arms, displayed by proud descendants.

28. An allusion to "prevenient grace," that free gift of God's favor that is given before it is sought; here used more generally in the sense of good fortune or divine favor that anticipates the crime of despair and thus deters it.

29. That is, by suicide.

there are some small statesmen who are so full charged with their own expectations that they cannot contain. And kind heaven, by sending such a seasonable curse upon their undertakings, hath made their ignorance an antidote against their malice. Some of these cannot treat peaceably; yielding will not satisfy them, they will have men by storm. There are others that must have plots [30] to make their service more necessary and have an interest to keep them alive, since they are to live upon them; and persuade the king to retrench his own greatness so as to shrink into the head of a party, which is the betraying him into such an unprincely mistake, and to such a wilful diminution of himself, that they are the last enemies he ought to allow himself to forgive.

Such men, if they could, would prevail with the sun to shine only upon them and their friends, and to leave all the rest of the world in the dark. This is a very unusual monopoly and may come within the equity [31] of the law, which maketh it treason to imprison the king, when such unfitting bounds are put to his favour and he confined to the narrow limits of a particular set of men that would enclose him. These honest and only loyal gentlemen, if they may be allowed to bear witness for themselves, make a king their engine [32] and degrade him into a property at the very time that their flattery would make him believe they paid divine worship to him.

Besides these there is a flying squadron on both sides that are afraid the world should agree, small dabblers in conjuring that raise angry apparitions to keep men from being reconciled, like wasps that fly up and down, buzz and sting to keep men unquiet; but these insects are commonly short-lived creatures, and no doubt in a little time mankind will be rid of them. They were giants at least who fought once against heaven, but for such pigmies as these to contend against it is such a provoking folly that the insolent bunglers ought to be laughed and hissed out of the world for it. They should consider there is a soul in that great body of the people, which may for a time be drowsy and unactive, but when the leviathan [33] is roused it moveth like an angry creature, and will neither be convinced nor resisted. The people can never agree to show their united powers till they are extremely tempted and provoked to it, so that to apply cupping glasses [34] to a great beast naturally disposed to sleep, and to force the tame thing whether it will or no to be valiant, must be learnt out of some other book than Machiavel,[35] who would never have prescribed such a preposterous method.

---

30. Perhaps looking back to the Popish Plot (for which see Dryden, *Absalom and Achitophel*) but surely to the Rye House Plot of 1683, both involving the first Earl of Shaftesbury. The Rye House Plot, exposed by somewhat dubious evidence, was claimed to be a conspiracy to assassinate Charles II, and among those executed were Halifax's friends Lord Russell and Algernon Sidney (the latter also his wife's uncle). In both cases Halifax used his influence in vain to obtain a moderation of sentence.

31. Jurisdiction.

32. Instrument.

33. Whale; but with allusion to Hobbes's book of 1651 which represents (in its frontispiece) the multitude united in one great artificial person, the state or commonwealth, composed of the mass of individual men.

34. Used for drawing out blood.

35. Niccolo di Bernardo dei Machiavelli (1469–1527), the Florentine statesman and political theorist whose great work *The Prince* (1513) became a universal manual of political expediency.

It is to be remembered, that if princes have law and authority on their sides, the people on theirs may have Nature, which is a formidable adversary. Duty, justice, religion, nay, even human prudence, too, biddeth the people suffer anything rather than resist; but uncorrected Nature, where'er it feels the smart, will run to the nearest remedy. Men's passions in this case are to be considered as well as their duty, let it be never so strongly enforced; for if their passions are provoked, they being as much a part of us as our limbs, they lead men into a short way of arguing that admitteth no distinction, and from the foundation of self-defence they will draw inferences that will have miserable effects upon the quiet of a government.

Our Trimmer therefore dreads a general discontent, because he thinketh it differeth from a rebellion only as a spotted fever doth from the plague,[36] the same species under a lower degree of malignity. It worketh several ways, sometimes like a slow poison that hath its effects at a great distance from the time it was given, sometimes like dry flax prepared to catch at the first fire, or like seed in the ground ready to sprout upon the first shower. In every shape 'tis fatal, and our Trimmer thinketh no pains or precaution can be so great as to prevent it.

In short, he thinketh himself in the right, grounding his opinion upon that truth which equally hateth to be under the oppressions of wrangling sophistry on the one hand, or the short dictates of mistaken authority on the other.

Our Trimmer adoreth the goddess Truth, though in all ages she hath been scurvily used, as well as those that worshipped her. 'Tis of late become such a ruining virtue that mankind seemeth to be agreed to commend and avoid it; yet the want of practice which repealeth the other laws hath no influence upon the law of Truth, because it hath root in heaven, and an intrinsic value in itself, that can never be impaired. She showeth her greatness in this, that her enemies, even when they are successful, are ashamed to own it. Nothing but powerful Truth hath the prerogative of triumphing not only after victories but in spite of them, and to put conquest herself out of countenance; she may be kept under and suppressed, but her dignity still remaineth with her, even when she is in chains. Falsehood with all her impudence hath not enough to speak ill of her before her face; such majesty she carrieth about her that her most prosperous enemies are fain to whisper their treason. All the power upon earth can never extinguish her; she hath lived in all ages; and let the mistaken zeal of prevailing authority christen any opposition to it with what name they please, she maketh it not only an ugly and unmannerly, but a dangerous, thing to persist. She hath lived very retired indeed, nay sometimes so buried, that only some few of all the discerning part of mankind could have a glimpse of her. With all that, she hath eternity in her, she knoweth not how to die; and from the darkest clouds that shade and cover her she breaketh from time to time with triumph for her friends and terror to her enemies.

Our Trimmer, therefore, inspired by this divine virtue, thinketh fit to conclude with these assertions: that our climate is a Trimmer, between that part of the world where men are roasted and the other where they are frozen; that our Church is a Trimmer between the frenzy of platonic visions and the

---

36. The bubonic plague that had last ravaged London in 1665.

lethargic ignorance of popish dreams; that our laws are Trimmers between the excess of unbounded power and the extravagance of liberty not enough restrained; that true virtue hath ever been thought a Trimmer and to have its dwelling in the middle between the two extremes; that even God Almighty himself is divided between his two great attributes, his mercy and his justice.

In such company, our Trimmer is not ashamed of his name, and willingly leaveth to the bold champions of either extreme the honour of contending with no less adversaries than nature, religion, liberty, prudence, humanity, and common sense.

1684?   1688

JOHN WILMOT, EARL OF ROCHESTER
1647–1680

John Wilmot, Earl of Rochester, was the most brilliant wit and rake at the court of Charles II. He had studied Latin and some Greek at Oxford, and he was the author of the first free imitation of Horace's satires in English. During his years at court, which began when he was seventeen, he was feared for his satirical pen and his often savage practical jokes; "Mean in each action, lewd in every limb, / Manners themselves are mischievous in him," was the tribute of his enemy, Lord Mulgrave. To others his charm was irresistible: "There is not a woman who gives ear to him three times but she irretrievably loses her repuation." King Charles was said to have exclaimed, "Thou art the happiest fellow in my dominion. Let me perish if I do not envy thee thy impudence." But Rochester's notorious "sceptre lampoon" about Charles led to at least a brief exile. At the last, Rochester repented his way of life and took the Christian sacrament, dying "without a convulsion or so much as a groan," at the age of thirty-three.

Rochester's writings include some dabbling in drama, a number of fine lyric poems, and a few extended satires and epistles, of which the *Satire Against Mankind* is perhaps the most impressive. It reflects the skepticism of his age, going back to classical sources in Lucretius and the Epicureans, sometimes turning to modern versions of materialism, sometimes borrowing from those fideistic doctrines which sapped trust in man's reason in order to throw him upon faith. Perhaps the most influential immediate source was Thomas Hobbes, whose materialism was the ground for his view of man's restless, acquisitive, and competitive nature. This insatiable striving for security through power is built into the heroes and villains of many heroic plays of the Restoration, and it marks in some degree the naturalistic zest with which the rake avows and seeks to serve his appetites, disdaining meanwhile the hypocritical censure of no less acquisitive merchants, clergymen, and courtiers. In comedies like William Wycherley's *The Country Wife* or in Sir George Etherege's *The Man of Mode* (whose hero, Dorimant, was often taken as a portrait of Rochester), the frank libertinism of the heroes seems more honest than the pretended squeamishness of the women they easily seduce; their female counterparts are those clear-headed, self-commanding heroines who profess no shock but permit no exploitation. Rochester's *Satire*, notably in its "epilogue" (after l. 174), shows a double attitude: a yearning for authenticity as well as a scorn for hypocrisy, a belief in the possibilities of a generous goodness as well as a detestation of those crippling forms of timorous respectability Bernard Shaw was later to call the "seven deadly virtues." The speaker in the *Satire* shows this doubleness, too; if he seems a bitter Hobbist and disdainful hedonist in the first part, he reveals another aspect in the second—not devout but moral, an admirer not of institutions but of personal goodness, of freedom from both greed and cant.

A Satire Against Mankind

Were I (who to my cost already am
One of those strange, prodigious° creatures, man)
A spirit free to choose, for my own share,
What case° of flesh and blood I pleased to wear,
I'd be a dog, a monkey, or a bear,
Or anything but that vain animal
Who is so proud of being rational.
 The senses are too gross, and he'll contrive
A sixth to contradict the other five,
10   And before certain instinct° will prefer
Reason, which fifty times for one does err;
Reason, an *ignis fatuus*° in the mind,
Which, leaving light of nature, sense, behind,
Pathless and dangerous wandering ways it takes
Through error's fenny bogs and thorny brakes;°
Whilst the misguided follower climbs with pain
Mountains of whimseys, heaped in his own brain;
Stumbling from thought to thought falls headlong down
Into doubt's boundless sea, where, like to drown,
20   Books bear him up a while, and make him try
To swim with bladders of philosophy;
In hopes still to o'ertake the escaping light,—
The vapour dances in his dazzling° sight
Till, spent, it leaves him to eternal night.
Then old age and experience, hand in hand,
Lead him to death and make him understand,
After a search so painful and so long,
That all his life he has been in the wrong.
Huddled in dirt° the reasoning engine° lies,

prodigious monstrous
case cover, dress
certain instinct Although he does not invoke the orthodox view of instinct as the direct power of God acting in animals, Rochester makes similar claims for its superiority to reason. Pope in the *Essay on Man* III.79–98 presents the orthodox view: reason "but serves when pressed, / But honest Instinct comes a volunteer" (ll. 87–88); instinct "must go right, the other may go wrong" (l. 94); "in this 'tis God directs, in that 'tis Man" (l. 98).
ignis fatuus will-o'-the-wisp, the delusive light that can mislead one in a swamp or fen at night
brakes thickets

dazzling dazzled
dirt mud, mire; sordidness, filth
reasoning engine Rochester's point is not so much to reduce man to mechanism as to show him, in Johnson's definition, to be a "mechanical complication in which various movements and parts concur in one effect"— that is, to stress the sole end to which his being has been directed (an engine *for* reasoning) and to show it now in the mire which is the very opposite of elaborate contrivance. The adjectives of the following line emphasize the humanity of the "engine" but accord with the idea of man's misapplying his trust and skill (as in the contrast of "know" and "enjoy" in l. 34).

30   Who was so proud, so witty, and so wise.
    Pride drew him in, as cheats their bubbles° catch,
And made him venture to be made a wretch.
His wisdom did his happiness destroy,
Aiming to know that world he should enjoy.
And wit was his vain, frivolous pretence
Of pleasing others at his own expense,
For wits are treated just like common whores:
First they're enjoyed, and then kicked out of doors.
The pleasure past, a threatening doubt° remains
40   That frights the enjoyer with succeeding pains.
Women and men of wit are dangerous tools,
And ever fatal to admiring fools:
Pleasure allures, and when the fops escape,
'Tis not that they're beloved, but fortunate,
And therefore what they fear at heart, they hate.
    But now, methinks, some formal band° and beard
Takes me to task. Come on, sir; I'm prepared.
    'Then, by your favour, anything that's writ
Against this gibing, jingling knack called wit
50   Likes° me abundantly; but° you take care
Upon this point, not to be too severe.
Perhaps my muse were fitter for this part,
For I profess I can be very smart
On wit, which I abhor with all my heart.
I long to lash it in some sharp essay,
But your grand indiscretion bids me stay
And turns my tide of ink another way.
    'What rage ferments in your degenerate mind
To make you rail at reason and mankind?
60   Blest, glorious man! to whom alone kind heaven
An everlasting soul has freely given,
Whom his great Maker took such care to make
That from himself he did the image take
And this fair frame in shining reason dressed
To dignify his nature above beast;
Reason, by whose aspiring influence
We take a flight beyond material sense,
Dive into mysteries, then soaring pierce
The flaming limits of the universe,
70   Search heaven and hell, find out what's acted there,
And give the world true grounds of hope and fear.'
    Hold, mighty man, I cry, all this we know
From the pathetic pen of Ingelo,°

---

bubbles dupes
doubt as to possible infection in the case of whores
formal band the wearer of a Geneva band, i.e. a clergyman
Likes pleases

but so long as; if only
Ingelo Nathaniel Ingelo (1621?–83), the clerical author of a long religious allegory in the form of a romance, *Bentivolio and Urania* (1660), popular in the period

From Patrick's *Pilgrim*,° Sibbes's soliloquies,°
And 'tis this very reason I despise:
This supernatural gift that makes a mite
Think he's the image of the infinite,
Comparing his short life, void of all rest,
To the eternal and the ever blest;
80   This busy, puzzling stirrer-up of doubt
That frames deep mysteries, then finds them out,°
Filling with frantic crowds of thinking fools
Those reverend bedlams,° colleges and schools;
Borne on whose wings, each heavy sot can pierce
The limits of the boundless universe;
So charming° ointments make an old witch fly
And bear a crippled carcass through the sky.
'Tis this exalted power, whose business lies
In nonsense and impossibilities,
90   This made a whimsical philosopher°
Before the spacious world, his tub prefer,
And we have modern cloistered coxcombs° who
Retire to think, 'cause they have nought to do.°
    But thoughts are given for action's government;
Where action ceases, thought's impertinent.°
Our sphere of action is life's happiness,
And he who thinks beyond thinks like an ass.
Thus, whilst against false reasoning I inveigh,
I own right reason,° which I would obey:
100   That reason which distinguishes by sense
And gives us rules of good and ill from thence,
That bounds desires with a reforming will°
To keep them more in vigour, not to kill.
Your reason hinders, mine helps to enjoy,
Renewing appetites yours would destroy.
My reason is my friend, yours is a cheat;
Hunger calls out, my reason bids me eat;
Perversely, yours your appetite does mock:
This asks for food, that answers, 'What's o'clock?'
110   This plain distinction, sir, your doubt secures:°
'Tis not true reason I despise, but yours.

Patrick's Pilgrim *The Parable of the Pilgrim*
(1664) by Simon Patrick, Bishop of Ely (1626–
1707), a work in the manner of Bunyan's later
allegory
Sibbes's soliloquies inspirational religious works
by the Puritan clergyman Richard Sibbes (1577–
1635)
finds them out claims to solve them easily
bedlams madhouses
charming magical
philosopher Diogenes (412?–323 B.C.), the
Greek Cynic, preached a life of extreme asceticism, living in a tub and teaching that virtue
consisted in the avoidance of all physical pleasure.
coxcombs fops (cf. l. 208), here applied to

empty pretenders
think . . . do recalling the contrast of "know"
and "enjoy" in l. 34
impertinent beside the point, of no use
right reason As Rochester defines it, this is preferable to *a priori* or deductive reason but is
hardly Right Reason as the term was generally
understood in the Renaissance. Rochester's
"right reason" is grounded in sense experience
(l. 100) and avoids asceticism (103), rather
serving as an instrument of pleasure or enjoyment by "renewing appetites" (105).
reforming will playing ironically upon the asceticism of some Reformation leaders, such as
John Calvin
secures resolves

Thus I think reason righted: but for man,
I'll ne'er recant; defend him if you can.
For all his pride and his philosophy,
'Tis evident beasts are, in their degree,
As wise at least and better far than he.
Those creatures are the wisest who attain
By surest means the ends at which they aim.
If therefore Jowler° finds and kills his hares
120   Better than Meres° supplies committee chairs,
Though one's a statesman, the other but a hound,
Jowler, in justice, would be wiser found.
    You see how far man's wisdom here extends;
Look next if human nature makes amends:
Whose principles most generous are and just,
And to whose morals you would sooner trust.
Be judge yourself, I'll bring it to the test:
Which is the basest creature, man or beast?
Birds feed on birds, beasts on each other prey,
130   But savage man alone does man betray.
Pressed by necessity, they kill for food;
Man undoes man to do himself no good.
With teeth and claws by nature armed, they hunt
Nature's allowance, to supply their want.
But man, with smiles, embraces, friendship, praise,
Inhumanly his fellow's life betrays;
With voluntary pains works his distress,
Not through necessity, but wantonness.
    For hunger or for love they fight and tear,
140   Whilst wretched man is still in arms for fear.°
For fear he arms, and is of arms afraid,
By fear to fear successively betrayed;
Base fear, the source whence his best passions came:
His boasted honour, and his dear-bought fame;
That lust of power, to which he's such a slave,
And for the which alone he dares be brave;
To which his various projects are designed;

Jowler a typical name for a hunting dog
Meres Sir Thomas Meres (1635–1715), a prominent Whig parliamentary leader, who served as chairman ("supplies . . . chairs") of many committees
wretched man . . . fear In this Rochester resembles Thomas Hobbes: "We see even in well-governed states, where there are laws and punishments appointed for offenders, yet particular men travel not without their sword by their sides, for their defences; neither sleep they without shutting not only their door against their fellow subjects, but also their trunks and coffers for fear of domestics. Can men give a clearer testimony of the distrust they have of each other, and all of all? How since they do this, and even countries as well as men, they publicly profess their mutual fear and diffidence!" De Cive, or The Citizen, in Latin 1642, in English 1651. In various works, and most notably Leviathan, Hobbes showed the state arising from the intolerable condition of that state of nature that was a "war of every man against every man"; a war bred of distrust, self-seeking, the competition for necessities and for imaginary needs—most fundamentally of a fear of being overcome by others. Rochester plays upon the social restrictions to which man submits in the name of all those virtues that are merely rationalizations of his fear and desire for security, and he stresses more than Hobbes the ironic conversion of fear into more "respectable" passions.

Which makes him generous, affable, and kind;
For which he takes such pains to be thought wise,
150   And screws his actions in a forced disguise,
Leading a tedious life in misery
Under laborious, mean hypocrisy.
Look to the bottom of his vast design,
Wherein man's wisdom, power, and glory join:
The good he acts, the ill he does endure,
'Tis all from fear, to make himself secure.
Merely for safety, after fame we thirst,
For all men would be cowards if they durst.
    And honesty's against all common sense:
160   Men must be knaves, 'tis in their own defence.
Mankind's dishonest; if you think it fair
Amongst known cheats to play upon the square,
You'll be undone——
Nor can weak truth your reputation save:
The knaves will all agree to call you knave.
Wronged shall he live, insulted o'er, oppressed,
Who dares be less a villain than the rest.
    Thus, sir, you see what human nature craves:
Most men are cowards, all men should be knaves.
170   The difference lies, as far as I can see,
Not in the thing itself but the degree,
And all the subject matter of debate
Is only: Who's a knave of the first rate?

    All this with indignation have I hurled
At the pretending part of the proud world,
Who, swollen with selfish vanity, devise
False freedoms, holy cheats, and formal lies
Over their fellow slaves to tyrannize.
    But if in court so just a man there be
180   (In court a just man, yet unknown to me)
Who does his needful flattery direct
Not to oppress and ruin, but protect
(Since flattery, which way soever laid,
Is still a tax on that unhappy trade);
If so upright a statesman you can find,
Whose passions bend to his unbiased mind,
Who does his arts and policies apply
To raise his country, not his family,
Nor, while his pride owned° avarice withstands,
190   Receives close° bribes through friends' corrupted hands?
    Is there a churchman who on God relies;
Whose life his faith and doctrine justifies?

---

owned acknowledged, open   **close** secret

Not one blown up with vain prelatic pride,°
Who for reproof of sins does man deride;
Whose envious heart makes preaching a pretence,
With his obstreperous, saucy eloquence,
To chide at kings and rail at men of sense;
None of that sensual tribe whose talents lie
In avarice, pride, sloth, and gluttony;
200   Who hunt good livings° but abhor good lives;
Whose lust exalted to that height arrives
They act adultery with their own wives,
And ere a score of years completed be,
Can from the lofty pulpit proudly see
Half a large parish their own progeny;
Nor doting bishop who would be adored
For domineering at the council board,
A greater fop in business at fourscore,
Fonder of serious toys, affected more,
210   Than the gay, glittering fool at twenty proves
With all his noise, his tawdry clothes, and loves;
    But a meek, humble man of honest sense,
Who, preaching peace, does practice continence;
Whose pious life's a proof he does believe
Mysterious truths, which no man can conceive.
If upon earth there dwell such God-like men,
I'll here recant my paradox to them,
Adore those shrines of virtue, homage pay,
And, with the rabble world, their laws obey.
220   If such there are, yet grant me this at least:
Man differs more from man, than man from beast.
1675?   1680

JOHN DRYDEN
1631–1700

Dryden's poetic career began with a schoolboy poem, an elegy to Lord Hastings, who
had died of smallpox at nineteen. Dryden wrote with hectic extravagance in the fashionable late Metaphysical manner of John Cleveland, and he did remarkable things with
poor Hastings's pustules: "Each little pimple had a tear in it, / To wail the fault its rising
did commit / . . . Or were these gems sent to adorn his skin, / The cabinet of a richer
soul within?" His first mature poem was the *Heroic Stanzas* on the death of Cromwell,
and by 1660 he welcomed the restoration of Charles II with *Astraea Redux*, the first of a
series of "public" poems in celebration or defense of that monarch. When the theaters
reopened, Dryden wrote the first of his twenty-eight plays and collaborated briefly with
Sir Robert Howard, whose sister he was to marry. Dryden did much to create the new
heroic play, that frankly artificial, rather operatic form in which spectacle alternated

prelatic pride the self-importance of high church   **livings** church appointments that carry an as-
office   sured income

with the fierce and witty debates of fiery souls; the greatest of these was his double play, in ten acts, *The Conquest of Granada* (1670).

Dryden's literary reign, crowned by the wreath of the poet laureate in 1671, included several provinces: drama, criticism, both prose and verse translation, and a large body of poetry in all forms. "Perhaps no nation," Dr. Johnson wrote,

> ever produced a writer that enriched his language with such variety of models. To him we owe the improvement, perhaps the completion of our metre, the refinement of our language, and much of the correctness of our sentiments. . . . What was said of Rome adorned by Augustus may be applied by an easy metaphor to English poetry embellished by Dryden . . . he found it brick, and he left it marble.

In contrast to Johnson's splendid confidence—limited, it should be noted, to formal achievements—Dryden often expressed a double view (such as we see in the poems to Oldham and to Congreve), a sense that greater urbanity might have been gained only at the expense of vigor.

This double view is a constant element in Dryden's superb play of dialectic. As Johnson said, he taught men "to think naturally and to express forcibly"; he was "the first who joined argument with poetry." Of a skeptical turn of mind, Dryden could feel himself into any stance and imagine ideas with the intensity of one who gave them utter conviction. The splendid bravura debate between the languid courtly sensualist and the "natural" man, between the defiant atheist and the Christian saint, between the rationalistic pagan and the wily inquisitor—all these are conducted with such eloquence and cogency that they seem at once aria and argument. His comedies were not remarkable, and he felt some shame at having supplied the lubricity his times demanded; the greatest of his later plays, *All for Love* (1678) and *Don Sebastian* (1690), are tragedies, although the latter has a boldly satiric subplot.

This play of mind gave rise to a major critical essay in the form of a dialogue, *Of Dramatic Poesy: An Essay* (1668). A "sceptical" discourse, it is "sustained by persons of several opinions, all of them left doubtful." The "essay" (and the term is meant still to suggest the tentative and exploratory) is one of the first exercises of that typical Augustan effort to define issues by providing statement and counterstatement, thesis and antithesis, from which the tact of the reader must elicit the delicate and undefinable truth. Ancient and Modern, French and English, Jonson and Shakespeare are placed in an opposition that teases our judgment, just as in later critical prefaces Virgil and Ovid or Horace and Juvenal serve, through counterpoint, to suggest the true nature of metaphor or the full power of satire.

Dryden's politics show a similar dialectical movement. If he played with the ideas of Hobbes, it was usually through dubious spokesmen; if he celebrated royal authority (as in *Absalom and Achitophel*), he could strike a note of balance in a later poem to his kinsman John Driden (1700): "Betwixt the Prince and Parliament we stand; / The barriers of the state on either hand: / May neither overflow, for then they drown the land!" If he scorned the fickle and restless mob, he scorned the egocentric tyrant no less; and some of his most brilliant dramatic moments are the explosion of the power-drive into madness, an insane rage to command those imaginary subjects that alone remain obedient to the tyrant's will.

Dryden's religious attitudes were the occasion for severe doubts of his sincerity. Born into a family of Puritan sympathies, he wrote one of the great defenses of the Anglican middle way in *Religio Laici* (1682). But the restless search for an authority that would resolve doubts and establish peace—both within the mind and among men—let him finally to Roman Catholicism. That he was led there just as the Catholic James II ascended the throne inevitably aroused suspicion of motives less honorable than sincere conviction; but, whatever their mixture, his motives surely included such conviction, and it is magnificently expressed in his defense of the persecuted Roman Catholic Church in *The Hind and the Panther* (1687). There the Church of England appears as the Panther, "the lady of the spotted muff," weak and compromising in her alliance with more radical Protestant sects, ready to unsheathe her claws, for all her superficial gentility, in her use of the civil power.

In Dryden's translations we can see the full range of his power to assume different voices, styles, and visions, as he moves from superb Lucretian didacticism to Juvenalian ferocity, from Ovidian extravagance to Virgilian elegance. Not only did Dryden translate all the works of Virgil, he translated Plutarch's *Lives* as well. The last may recall, finally, Dryden's great contribution to the emergence of an urbane and easy English prose; he had models in the age of Charles I, but his own example was one of the most effective in the age to come.

Of all the major writers in the period Dryden is the most thoroughly open to the energy that outruns moderation. His Cleopatra, in *All for Love*, exclaims: "I have loved with such transcendent passion, / I soared at first quite out of reason's view, / And now am lost above it." The other side of that transcendence is the high folly or madness of Achitophel or of Alexander under the power of music. Dryden is always ready for excess, for the grand gesture or the bold metaphor; yet the excess often carries with it the levity of a holiday from restraint and the potential ironic recoil of a gesture extended an inch too far or held a moment too long. Behind all his achievements we can glimpse the self-conscious artist, fully abandoned only to art itself, and we can sense that presence in a remark that shows the amiable pride of a man nearly seventy: "Thoughts, such as they are, come crowding in so fast upon me that my only difficulty is to choose or to reject, to run them into verse or to give them the other harmony of prose."

Absalom and Achitophel

Dryden's great satire was written at a time when the crisis it presents was still unresolved. Charles II had been urged by Whig leaders, and particularly the first Earl of Shaftesbury, to exclude his Roman Catholic brother from succession to the throne. In efforts to arouse fear of Catholic power, the Whigs found explosive material in the apparent disclosures by Titus Oates, an ex-seminarian, that a Popish Plot existed to assassinate Charles (even his Catholic wife was accused of a conspiratorial role), to seize power by violent means, perhaps to burn London (the Great Fire of 1666 had been attributed by some to a Catholic plot). Oates's testimony was highly suspect, as was the man, and it showed a convenient power of expansion as his memory was stimulated by criticism. But enough shreds of confirming evidence (not least the indiscreet correspondence of the Duchess of York's secretary with Louis XIV's confessor, looking forward to the conversion of the English to the Catholic faith) could be gathered to give Oates's charges plausibility and to promote the Whig demands that

Charles legitimize his bastard son, the Duke of Monmouth, and make him his successor. As the Tory observer Roger L'Estrange later described events, the Whig

> faction had the ascendant of the government, and the multitude bore all before them like a torrent; the witnesses led the rabble; the plot-managers led the witnesses; and the Devil himself led the leaders; for they were to pass to their ends through subornation, perjury, hypocrisy, sacrilege, and treason.

By the time Dryden wrote, Charles had withstood Whig demands and achieved financial independence (through the French king) of a Parliament that tried to force his hand by withholding funds. He dissolved Parliament in March 1681, and Shaftesbury, charged with treason and arrested in July, was awaiting trial at the time Dryden's poem was published. (Shaftesbury was acquitted but never regained his earlier power.)

Dryden was not the first to adduce the biblical parallel of David and Absalom to Charles and his illegitimate son, Monmouth; but he was the first to exploit it so fully and adroitly, creating a constant interplay between biblical narrative and current history. He does more than that; to the story of Absalom's rebellion and his temptation by Achitophel, he brings a resonance not unlike that of Milton's treatment of the rebel angels in *Paradise Lost*. Dryden's figures are more obviously involved in duplicity or self-deception, and the splendid portraits of Whig leaders converge in a central pattern of destructive recklessness. Achitophel sponsors Monmouth precisely because his claim to the throne is unstable; his secret object is to undo monarchy itself, and in his obsessive and theory-ridden drive he is willing to run all the risks of anarchy.

In his treatment of David, Dryden opens with a tone of amused tolerance for the expansive energies of Charles and, somewhat in the manner of Halifax, sets David's easy love of pleasure against the more dangerous intensity of Achitophel; but once the rebellion gains its own reckless force, David emerges as a figure of severity and deep concern, surrounded by figures of dedication like Barzillai and his son. The movement of the poem can almost be seen as the earning of dignity for David by conflict and by trial.

Absalom and Achitophel

In pious times, ere priestcraft did begin,
Before polygamy was made a sin;
When man on many multiplied his kind,
Ere one to one was cursedly confined;
When nature prompted, and no law denied,
Promiscuous use of concubine and bride;
Then Israel's monarch after Heaven's own heart°
His vigorous warmth did variously impart
To wives and slaves; and, wide as his command,
10   Scattered his Maker's image through the land.
Michal,° of royal blood, the crown did wear;

after . . . heart See I Samuel 13:14, where Samuel warns Saul, "thy Kingdom shall not continue: the Lord hath sought him a man after his own heart."   **Michal** alluding to the childless Catherine of Braganza, who married Charles II in 1662

A soil ungrateful to the tiller's care:
Not so the rest; for several mothers° bore
To godlike David several sons before.
But since like slaves his bed they did ascend,
No true succession could their seed attend.
Of all this numerous progeny was none
So beautiful, so brave as Absalom:°
Whether, inspired by some diviner lust,
20   His father got him with a greater gust;°
Or that his conscious destiny made way,
By manly beauty, to imperial sway.
Early in foreign fields° he won renown,
With kings and states allied to Israel's crown:
In peace the thoughts of war he could remove,
And seemed as he were only born for love.
Whate'er he did was done with so much ease,
In him alone 'twas natural to please,
His motions all accompanied with grace;
30   And paradise was opened in his face.
With secret joy indulgent David viewed
His youthful image in his son renewed:
To all his wishes nothing he denied,
And made the charming Annabel° his bride.
What faults he had (for who from faults is free?)
His father could not or he would not see.
Some warm excesses which the law forbore,
Were construed youth that purged by boiling o'er,
And Amnon's murther,° by a specious name,
40   Was called a just revenge for injured fame.
Thus praised and loved the noble youth remained,
While David, undisturbed, in Sion° reigned.
But life can never be sincerely° blest;
Heaven punishes the bad, and proves° the best.
The Jews,° a headstrong, moody, murmuring race
As ever tried the extent and stretch of grace;
God's pampered people, whom, debauched with ease,
No king could govern nor no God could please;
(Gods they had tried° of every shape and size,

several mothers referring to Charles II's many
mistresses and his illegitimate children
Absalom James Scott (1649–85), created Duke
of Monmouth in 1663, born illegitimately to a
"Welsh woman of no good fame" (Clarendon);
"particularly beloved by the King; but the universal terror of husbands and lovers" (Gram-
mont); a brave commander of Charles's forces
in the Scottish campaign of 1679
gust appetite, relish
foreign fields with the French against the
Dutch (1672–73) and with the Dutch against
the French (1678)
Annabel Anne, Countess of Buccleuch (1651–

1732), of great beauty and "one of the wisest
and craftiest of her sex" (John Evelyn)
Amnon's murther Absalom arranged for the
death of his half-brother in revenge for the rape
of his sister, Tamar (II Samuel 13:28–29).
Monmouth did not murder but had his troopers
attack and disfigure a man who had insulted
Charles II.
Sion London
sincerely completely
proves tests
Jews English
Gods . . . tried referring to the numerous sects
that arose after the Reformation

50   That god-smiths could produce or priests devise:)
These Adam-wits, too fortunately free,
Began to dream they wanted° liberty;
And when no rule, no precedent was found
Of men by laws less circumscribed and bound,
They led their wild desires to woods and caves,
And thought that all but savages° were slaves.
They who, when Saul° was dead, without a blow,
Made foolish Ishbosheth° the crown forego;
Who banished David did from Hebron° bring,
60   And with a general shout proclaimed him king:
Those very Jews, who, at their very best,
Their humour° more than loyalty expressed,
Now wondered why so long they had obeyed
An idol monarch which their hands had made;
Thought they might ruin him they could create,
Or melt him to that golden calf,° a state.°
But these were random bolts; no formed design
Nor interest made the factious crowd to join:
The sober part of Israel, free from stain,
70   Well knew the value of a peaceful reign;
And, looking backward with a wise affright,
Saw seams of wounds, dishonest° to the sight:
In contemplation of whose ugly scars
They cursed the memory of civil wars.
The moderate sort of men, thus qualified,
Inclined the balance to the better side;
And David's mildness managed it so well,
The bad found no occasion to rebel.
But when to sin our biased nature leans,
80   The careful Devil° is still at hand with means,
And providently pimps for ill desires.
The Good Old Cause° revived, a plot requires:
Plots, true or false, are necessary things
To raise up commonwealths and ruin kings.
    The inhabitants of old Jerusalem°
Were Jebusites;° the town so called from them;
And theirs the native right——
But when the chosen people° grew more strong,

---

wanted lacked
savages wild beasts
Saul Oliver Cromwell (1599–1658).
Ishbosheth Cromwell's son Richard (1626–1712)
Hebron Scotland, where Charles II was crowned king in 1651, long before he became King of England
humour mood
golden calf the idol worshiped by the Israelites while Moses was receiving the law on Mt. Sinai
state republic, which Dryden elsewhere scornfully describes as "that mock-appearance of a

liberty, where all who have not part in the government are slaves"
dishonest shameful
careful Devil Cf. Dryden's remarks on the Devil's policy "to seduce mankind into the same rebellion with him, by telling him he might be yet freer than he was, more free than his nature would allow" (Epistle Dedicatory to All for Love, 1677).
Good Old Cause for the Commonwealth
Jerusalem London
Jebusites Roman Catholics
chosen people Protestants

The rightful cause at length became the wrong;
90   And every loss the men of Jebus bore,
They still were thought God's enemies the more.
Thus worn and weakened, well or ill content,
Submit they must to David's government:
Impoverished and deprived of all command,
Their taxes doubled as they lost their land;°
And, what was harder yet to flesh and blood,
Their gods disgraced and burnt like common wood.°
This set the heathen priesthood° in a flame,
For priests of all religions are the same:
100 Of whatsoe'er descent their godhead be,
Stock, stone, or other homely pedigree,
In his defence his servants are as bold
As if he had been born of beaten gold.
The Jewish rabbins,° though their enemies,
In this conclude them honest men and wise:
For 'twas their duty, all the learnèd think,
To espouse his cause by whom they eat and drink.
From hence began that Plot,° the nation's curse,
Bad in itself, but represented worse;
110 Raised in extremes, and in extremes decried;
With oaths affirmed, with dying vows denied;
Not weighed or winnowed° by the multitude;
But swallowed in the mass, unchewed and crude.
Some truth there was, but dashed and brewed with lies,
To please the fools and puzzle all the wise.
Succeeding times did equal folly call
Believing nothing or believing all.
The Egyptian° rites the Jebusites embraced,
Where gods were recommended by their taste.
120 Such savoury deities must needs be good
As served at once for worship and for food.°
By force they could not introduce these gods,
For ten to one in former days was odds;
So fraud was used (the sacrificer's° trade):
Fools are more hard to conquer than persuade.
Their busy teachers mingled with the Jews,
And raked for converts even the court and stews:°
Which Hebrew priests° the more unkindly took,

Impoverished . . . land as Roman Catholics were or might be by laws passed under Elizabeth I and still in force beyond Dryden's day
burnt . . . wood referring to the savage destruction of church images during the Commonwealth
heathen priesthood Roman Catholic priests
Jewish rabbins Church of England priests
Plot the Popish Plot (see Headnote)
winnowed sifted
Egyptian French and Roman Catholic; but also referring to Egypt as the source of mysteries and superstition
worship . . . food referring to the doctrine of transubstantiation (the real presence of the body and blood of Christ in the bread and wine of Communion), a doctrine defended by Dryden after his conversion to Catholicism in 1685
sacrificer's priest's
stews brothels
Hebrew priests Church of England clergy

Because the fleece° accompanies the flock.
130 Some thought they God's anointed° meant to slay
By guns, invented since full many a day:
Our author swears it not; but who can know
How far the Devil and Jebusites may go?
This Plot, which failed for want of common sense,
Had yet a deep and dangerous consequence:
For, as when raging fevers boil the blood,
The standing lake soon floats into a flood,
And every hostile° humour, which before
Slept quiet in its channels, bubbles o'er;
140 So several factions from this first ferment
Work up to foam, and threat the government.
Some by their friends, more by themselves thought wise,
Opposed the power to which they could not rise.
Some had in courts been great and, thrown from thence,
Like fiends were hardened in impenitence.
Some by their monarch's fatal mercy grown
From pardoned rebels kinsmen to the throne,
Were raised in power and public office high;
Strong bands, if bands ungrateful men could tie.
150   Of these the false Achitophel° was first;
A name to all succeeding ages curst:
For close° designs and crooked counsels fit;
Sagacious, bold, and turbulent of wit;
Restless, unfixed in principles and place;
In power unpleased, impatient of disgrace:
A fiery soul, which, working out its way,
Fretted° the pigmy body° to decay,
And o'er-informed° the tenement of clay.
A daring pilot in extremity;
160 Pleased with the danger, when the waves went high,
He sought the storms; but, for a calm unfit,
Would steer too nigh the sands, to boast his wit.
Great wits are sure to madness near allied,
And thin partitions do their bounds° divide;
Else why should he, with wealth and honour blest,
Refuse his age the needful hours of rest?
Punish a body which he could not please;

---

fleece income from tithes
God's anointed the king
hostile contentious, excessive
Achitophel Anthony Ashley Cooper (1621–83), 1st Earl of Shaftesbury, who had been one of Cromwell's council of state but helped to arrange Charles II's return; as lord chancellor an excellent jurist and reformer of the Court of Chancery; after 1673 in opposition and by 1676 leader of those opposed to popery and arbitrary royal power; a man without equal "in

the art of governing parties and of making himself the head of them" (Dryden)
close secret
Fretted eroded
pigmy body in fact very small, and in any case too small for its "fiery soul"
o'er-informed filled to overflowing; that is, the soul, which should be the form of mind and body, is here too restless to serve that limited function. On the "informing soul," see Pope, *Essay on Criticism*, ll. 76–79.
bounds of genius (wit) and madness

Bankrupt of life, yet prodigal° of ease?
And all to leave what with his toil he won,
170 To that unfeathered two-legged thing,° a son;
Got° while his soul did huddled° notions try,
And born a shapeless lump, like anarchy.
In friendship false, implacable in hate;
Resolved to ruin or to rule the state.
To compass this the triple bond° he broke,
The pillars of the public safety shook,
And fitted Israel for a foreign yoke:°
Then seized with fear, yet still affecting fame,
Usurped a patriot's all-atoning name.
180 So easy still it proves in factious times
With public zeal to cancel private crimes.
How safe is treason and how sacred ill,
Where none can sin against the people's will;°
Where crowds can wink and no offence be known,
Since in another's guilt they find their own.
Yet fame deserved no enemy can grudge;
The statesman we abhor, but praise the judge.
In Israel's courts ne'er sat an Abbethdin°
With more discerning eyes or hands more clean;
190 Unbribed, unsought, the wretched to redress,
Swift of dispatch and easy of access.
O had he been content to serve the crown
With virtues only proper to the gown,°
Or had the rankness° of the soil been freed
From cockle° that oppressed the noble seed;
David for him his tuneful harp had strung,
And Heaven had wanted° one immortal song.
But wild ambition loves to slide, not stand,°
And fortune's ice prefers to virtue's land.
200 Achitophel, grown weary to possess
A lawful fame and lazy happiness,
Disdained the golden fruit to gather free,
And lent the crowd his arm to shake the tree.
Now, manifest of° crimes contrived long since,
He stood at bold defiance with his prince;
Held up the buckler of the people's cause

---

prodigal spendthrift
unfeathered . . . thing alluding to the famous
definition of man as a "featherless biped"
ascribed to Plato
Got in contrast to Absalom, ll. 17–22
huddled confused; concealed
triple bond the triple alliance of England, Holland, and Sweden against France (1668),
which Shaftesbury helped to break (not without
Charles's connivance, however)
foreign yoke that of France

Where none . . . will i.e. where popular approval can cancel all guilt
Abbethdin presiding judge of the Jewish civil
court
gown of the judge
rankness fertility
cockle weeds found in grain fields
wanted missed, in that David, the composer of
the Psalms, would have devoted one song to
Achitophel rather than to God
slide, not stand as in ll. 154, 161–62
manifest of showing openly

Against the crown, and skulked behind the laws.
The wished occasion of the Plot he takes,
Some circumstances finds, but more he makes.
210　By buzzing emissaries fills the ears
Of listening crowds with jealousies° and fears
Of arbitrary counsels brought to light,
And proves the king himself a Jebusite.
Weak arguments! which yet he knew full well
Were strong with people easy to rebel.
For, governed by the moon, the giddy Jews
Tread the same track when she the prime° renews;
And once in twenty years,° their scribes record,
By natural instinct they change their lord.
220　Achitophel still wants a chief, and none
Was found so fit as warlike Absalon:
Not that he wished his greatness to create,
(For politicians neither love nor hate,)
But, for he knew his title° not allowed
Would keep him still depending on the crowd:
That kingly power, thus ebbing out, might be
Drawn to the dregs of a democracy.°
Him he attempts with studied arts to please,
And sheds his venom° in such words as these:
230　　'Auspicious° prince, at whose nativity
Some royal° planet ruled the southern sky,
Thy longing country's darling and desire,
Their cloudy pillar and their guardian fire,°
Their second Moses,° whose extended wand
Divides the seas, and shows the promised land,
Whose dawning day in every distant age
Has exercised the sacred prophets' rage:
The people's prayer, the glad diviners' theme,
The young men's vision, and the old men's dream!°
240　Thee, Saviour, thee, the nation's vows confess,
And, never satisfied with seeing, bless:
Swift unbespoken° pomps thy steps proclaim,

jealousies suspicion; see Butler, *Hudibras* I.i.3
and note
prime the beginning of a new cycle
twenty years as in Charles I's troubles with
the Long Parliament about 1640, the restoration
of Charles II in 1660, and the Popish Plot fever
of 1678
his title to the throne (Charles II having made
a formal denial in 1679 of his rumored marriage with Monmouth's mother)
democracy literally, rule of the people; regarded
in classical thought as an unstable form of
government, easily tending to tyranny or dictatorship
sheds his venom with suggestion of the serpent's temptation of Eve (cf. Milton, *Paradise
Lost* IX)
Auspicious fortunate

royal promising kingship
cloudy pillar . . . fire In the flight of the
Israelites from Egypt, the "Lord went before
them by day in a pillar of cloud, to lead them
the way; and by night in a pillar of fire, to give
them light" (Exodus 13:21).
second Moses "And the Lord said unto Moses,
wherefore criest thou unto me? . . . But lift
up thy rod, and stretch out thy hand over the
sea, and divide it: and the children of Israel
shall go on dry ground through the midst of the
sea" (Exodus 14:15–16)
The young . . . dream "Your old men shall
dream dreams, your young men shall see visions"
(Joel 2:28), a passage, like most of these, taken
as a prophecy of Christ's reign (cf. l. 245)
unbespoken spontaneous

And stammering babes are taught to lisp thy name.
How long wilt thou the general joy detain,
Starve and defraud the people of thy reign?
Content ingloriously to pass thy days
Like one of virtue's fools that feeds on praise;
Till thy fresh glories, which now shine so bright,
Grow stale and tarnish with our daily sight.
250 Believe me, royal youth, thy fruit must be
Or gathered ripe or rot upon the tree.
Heaven has to all allotted, soon or late,
Some lucky revolution of their fate;
Whose motions, if we watch and guide with skill,
(For human good depends on human will,)
Our fortune rolls as from a smooth descent,
And from the first impression takes the bent;
But, if unseized, she glides away like wind
And leaves repenting folly far behind.
260 Now, now she meets you with a glorious prize,
And spreads her locks before her° as she flies.
Had thus old David, from whose loins you spring,
Not dared, when fortune called him, to be king,
At Gath° an exile he might still remain,
And Heaven's anointing oil had been in vain.
Let his successful youth your hopes engage;
But shun the example of declining age:
Behold him setting in his western skies,
The shadows lengthening as the vapours rise.
270 He is not now, as when on Jordan's sand°
The joyful people thronged to see him land,
Covering the beach and blackening all the strand;
But, like the Prince of Angels,° from his height
Comes tumbling downward with diminished light;
Betrayed by one poor plot to public scorn,
(Our only blessing since his curst return;)
Those heaps of people which one sheaf did bind,
Blown off and scattered by a puff of wind.
What strength can he to your designs oppose,
280 Naked of friends and round beset with foes?
If Pharaoh's° doubtful succour he should use,
A foreign aid would more incense the Jews:
Proud Egypt would dissembled friendship bring;
Foment the war, but not support the king:
Nor would the royal party e'er unite
With Pharaoh's arms to assist the Jebusite;

spreads . . . her to be seized by the forelock,
like opportunity
Gath where David took refuge from Saul;
Brussels, where Charles II was in exile
Jordan's sand as David crossed the river to
resume his kingdom; Dover Beach, where
Charles landed in 1660
Prince of Angels Satan; cf. *Paradise Lost* I.
84–87
Pharaoh's that of Louis XIV of France

Or if they should, their interest soon would break,
And with such odious aid make David weak.
All sorts of men by my successful arts,
290 Abhorring kings, estrange their altered hearts
From David's rule: and 'tis the general cry,
"Religion, commonwealth, and liberty."
If you, as champion of the public good,
Add to their arms a chief of royal blood,
What may not Israel hope, and what applause
Might such a general gain by such a cause?
Not barren praise alone, that gaudy flower
Fair only to the sight, but solid power;
And nobler is a limited command,
300 Given by the love of all your native land,
Than a successive title,° long and dark,
Drawn from the mouldy rolls of Noah's ark.'°
    What cannot praise effect in mighty minds,
When flattery soothes and when ambition blinds!
Desire of power, on earth a vicious weed,
Yet, sprung from high, is of celestial seed:
In God 'tis glory; and when men aspire,
'Tis but a spark too much of heavenly fire.
The ambitious youth, too covetous of fame,
310 Too full of angels' metal° in his frame,
Unwarily was led from virtue's ways,
Made drunk with honour, and debauched with praise.
Half loath and half consenting to the ill,
(For loyal blood within him struggled still,)
He thus replied: 'And what pretence have I
To take up arms for public liberty?
My father governs with unquestioned right;
The faith's defender and mankind's delight;
Good, gracious, just, observant of the laws:
320 And Heaven by wonders° has espoused his cause.
Whom has he wronged in all his peaceful reign?
Who sues for justice to his throne in vain?
What millions has he pardoned of his foes
Whom just revenge did to his wrath expose?
Mild, easy, humble, studious of our good;
Enclined to mercy and averse from blood.
If mildness ill with stubborn Israel suit,
His crime is God's belovèd attribute.
What could he gain, his people to betray,
330 Or change his right for arbitrary sway?

successive title a title based on legitimate succession
Noah's ark playing with the theory that kingship has its origin in the rule of the patriarchs

angels' metal the metal of angels (gold coins);
the ambition (mettle) that led the angels to
rebel
wonders signs of divine favor

Let haughty Pharaoh curse with such a reign
His fruitful Nile, and yoke a servile train.
If David's rule Jerusalem displease,
The dog-star° heats their brains to this disease.
Why then should I, encouraging the bad,
Turn rebel and run popularly mad?
Were he a tyrant who by lawless might
Oppressed the Jews and raised the Jebusite,
Well might I mourn; but nature's holy bands°
340   Would curb my spirits and restrain my hands:
The people might assert their liberty;
But what was right in them were crime in me.
His favour leaves me nothing to require,
Prevents° my wishes and outruns desire.
What more can I expect while David lives?
All but his kingly diadem he gives:
And that'—But there he paused; then sighing, said—
'Is justly destined for a worthier head.
For when my father from his toils shall rest,
350   And late augment the number of the blest,
His lawful issue shall the throne ascend,
Or the collateral line,° where that shall end.
His brother, though oppressed with vulgar spite,°
Yet dauntless, and secure of native right,
Of every royal virtue stands possessed;
Still dear to all the bravest and the best.
His courage foes, his friends his truth proclaim;
His loyalty the king, the world his fame.
His mercy even the offending crowd will find;
360   For sure he comes of a forgiving kind.°
Why should I then repine at Heaven's decree,
Which gives me no pretence to royalty?
Yet O that fate, propitiously inclined,
Had raised my birth or had debased my mind;°
To my large soul not all her treasure lent,
And then betrayed it to a mean descent!
I find, I find my mounting spirits bold,
And David's part disdains my mother's mould.
Why am I scanted by a niggard birth?
370   My soul disclaims the kindred of her earth,
And, made for empire, whispers me within,
"Desire of greatness is a godlike sin." '

dog-star Sirius (in Canis Major), thought to cause heat and induce madness. See Pope, *Epistle to Dr. Arbuthnot*, ll. 3–6, on the "dog-days" of midsummer.
nature's . . . bands as son
Prevents anticipates
collateral line if not in direct descent, through the nearest legitimate kin, in this case, his brother James
vulgar spite popular opposition to his Roman Catholicism
kind family, nature
Had raised . . . mind reminiscent of Satan's great speech at the opening of *Paradise Lost*, Book IV, especially ll. 58–61

Him staggering so when Hell's dire agent found,
While fainting Virtue scarce maintained her ground,
He pours fresh forces in, and thus replies:
    'The eternal God, supremely good and wise,
Imparts not these prodigious gifts in vain:
What wonders are reserved to bless your reign!
Against your will, your arguments have shown,
380   Such virtue's only given to guide a throne.
Not that your father's mildness I contemn;
But manly force becomes the diadem.
'Tis true he grants the people all they crave,
And more, perhaps, then subjects ought to have:
For lavish grants suppose a monarch tame,
And more his goodness than his wit proclaim.
But when should people strive their bonds to break,
If not when kings are negligent or weak?
Let him give on till he can give no more,
390   The thrifty Sanhedrin° shall keep him poor;
And every shekel which he can receive
Shall cost a limb of his prerogative.°
To ply him with new plots shall be my care;
Or plunge him deep in some expensive war;
Which, when his treasure can no more supply,
He must with the remains of kingship buy.
His faithful friends, our jealousies and fears
Call Jebusites and Pharaoh's pensioners;
Whom when our fury from his aid has torn,
400   He shall be naked left to public scorn.
The next successor, whom I fear and hate,
My arts have made obnoxious to the state;
Turned all his virtues to his overthrow,
And gained our elders° to pronounce a foe.
His right,° for sums of necessary gold,
Shall first be pawned, and afterwards be sold;
Till time shall ever-wanting David draw
To pass your doubtful title into law:
If not, the people have a right supreme
410   To make their kings, for kings are made for them.
All empire is no more than power in trust,
Which, when resumed, can be no longer just.
Succession, for the general good designed,
In its own wrong a nation cannot bind;
If altering that the people can relieve,
Better one suffer than a nation grieve.

Sanhedrin the supreme council of the Jews; here
Parliament
prerogative those powers of the king uncircum-
scribed by law, which Parliament sought to
limit by its control of his finances

elders rulers; here Parliament, where a bill excluding James from the throne was supported
by Shaftesbury and passed Commons but was
rejected by Lords through the efforts of Halifax
right to succeed Charles

The Jews well know their power: ere Saul they chose,
God was their king,° and God they durst depose.
Urge now your piety, your filial name,
420   A father's right, and fear of future fame;
The public good, that universal call,
To which even Heaven submitted, answers all.
Nor let his love enchant your generous mind;
'Tis Nature's trick to propagate her kind.
Our fond begetters, who would never die,
Love but themselves in their posterity.
Or let his kindness by the effects be tried,
Or let him lay his vain pretence aside.
God said he loved your father; could he bring
430   A better proof than to anoint him king?
It surely showed he loved the shepherd well,
Who gave so fair a flock as Israel.
Would David have you thought his darling son?
What means he then, to alienate° the crown?
The name of godly he may blush to bear:
'Tis after God's own heart° to cheat his heir.
He to his brother gives supreme command;
To you a legacy of barren land,°
Perhaps the old harp, on which he thrums his lays,°
440   Or some dull Hebrew ballad in your praise.
Then the next heir, a prince severe and wise,
Already looks on you with jealous eyes;
Sees through the thin disguises of your arts,
And marks your progress in the people's hearts.
Though now his mighty soul its grief contains,
He meditates revenge who least complains;
And, like a lion, slumbering in the way,
Or sleep dissembling while he waits his prey,
His fearless foes within his distance draws,
450   Constrains his roaring, and contracts his paws;
Till at the last, his time for fury found,
He shoots with sudden vengeance from the ground;
The prostrate vulgar° passes o'er and spares,
But with a lordly rage his hunters tears.
Your case no tame expedients will afford:
Resolve on death, or conquest by the sword,
Which for no less a stake than life you draw;
And self-defence is nature's eldest law.

God . . . king the Commonwealth, established
in 1649, acknowledging only God as king (literally, a theocracy, as in l. 522), but followed
in 1653 by Cromwell's Protectorate
alienate convey the title to another person
God's . . . heart See l. 7 and note.

barren land the Border estate of Monmouth's
wife
lays the Psalms of David, with a reference to
Charles's love of music
vulgar common people

Leave the warm people no considering time;
460 For then rebellion may be thought a crime.
Prevail yourself of what occasion gives,
But try your title while your father lives;
And that your arms may have a fair pretence,
Proclaim you take them in the king's defence,
Whose sacred life each minute would expose
To plots from seeming friends and secret foes.
And who can sound the depth of David's soul?
Perhaps his fear his kindness may control.
He fears his brother, though he loves his son,
470 For plighted vows too late to be undone.
If so, by force he wishes to be gained;
Like women's lechery, to seem constrained.
Doubt not: but, when he most affects the frown,
Commit a pleasing rape upon the crown.
Secure his person to secure your cause:
They who possess the prince, possess the laws.'
   He said, and this advice above the rest
With Absalom's mild nature suited best:
Unblamed of life (ambition set aside,)
480 Not stained with cruelty nor puffed with pride;
How happy had he been if destiny
Had higher placed his birth, or not so high!
His kingly virtues might have claimed a throne
And blest all other countries but his own.
But charming greatness since so few refuse,
'Tis juster to lament him than accuse.
Strong were his hopes a rival to remove
With blandishments to gain the public love,
To head the faction while their zeal was hot,
490 And popularly prosecute the Plot.
To farther this, Achitophel unites
The malcontents of all the Israelites;
Whose differing parties he could wisely join,
For several ends, to serve the same design:
The best (and of the princes some were such)
Who thought the power of monarchy too much,
Mistaken men and patriots in their hearts,
Not wicked, but seduced by impious arts.
By these the springs of property were bent,
500 And wound so high they cracked the government.
The next for interest sought to embroil the state,
To sell their duty at a dearer rate,
And make their Jewish markets of the throne,
Pretending public good, to serve their own.
Others thought kings an useless heavy load,

Who cost too much and did too little good.
These were for laying honest David by,
On principles of pure good husbandry.°
With them joined all the haranguers of the throng
510   That thought to get preferment by the tongue.
Who follow next, a double danger bring,
Not only hating David, but the king:°
The Solymaean rout,° well-versed of old
In godly faction and in treason bold;
Cowering and quaking at a conqueror's sword,
But lofty to a lawful prince restored;
Saw with disdain an ethnic° plot begun
And scorned by Jebusites to be outdone.
Hot Levites° headed these; who, pulled before
520   From the ark, which in the Judges' days they bore,
Resumed their cant,° and with a zealous° cry
Pursued their old beloved Theocracy:
Where Sanhedrin and priest enslaved the nation
And justified their spoils by inspiration:
For who so fit for reign as Aaron's race,°
If once dominion they could found in grace.°
These led the pack; though not of surest scent,
Yet deepest mouthed° against the government.
A numerous host of dreaming saints° succeed
530   Of the true old enthusiastic° breed:
'Gainst form and order they their power employ,
Nothing to build and all things to destroy.
But far more numerous was the herd of such
Who think too little and who talk too much.
These, out of mere instinct, they knew not why,
Adored their fathers' God, and property;
And, by the same blind benefit of fate,
The Devil and the Jebusite did hate:
Born to be saved, even in their own despite,°
540   Because they could not help believing right.
Such were the tools; but a whole Hydra° more
Remains, of sprouting heads too long to score.
Some of their chiefs were princes of the land:

husbandry thrift
king monarchy
Solymaean rout London rabble (Solyma is Jerusalem)
ethnic Popish (or Gentile)
Levites the Presbyterian clergy, deprived of church livings by the Act of Uniformity (1662) and thus "pulled . . . from the ark" before the Plot; the "ark" being the established or state church, which in "the Judges' days" (the Commonwealth) they governed ("bore")
cant slogans, jargon
zealous fanatical
Aaron's race the priesthood

grace in purity of faith or God's election rather than natural or civil law. See Halifax, The Character of a Trimmer: "Our Trimmer approveth the principles of our church, that dominion is not founded in grace."
deepest mouthed baying most loudly in the pack of hunting dogs
dreaming saints radical Protestants and visionaries
enthusiastic with, as Henry More put it, "the misconceit of being inspired"
in . . . despite because predestined to the elect
Hydra the mythical monster that grew new heads as soon as the old were cut off

In the first rank of these did Zimri° stand;
A man so various, that he seemed to be
Not one, but all mankind's epitome:
Stiff in opinions, always in the wrong;
Was everything by starts, and nothing long;
But, in the course of one revolving moon,
550   Was chemist,° fiddler, statesman, and buffoon:
Then all for women, painting, rhyming, drinking.
Besides ten thousand freaks° that died in thinking.
Blest madman, who could every hour employ
With something new to wish or to enjoy!
Railing and praising were his usual themes;
And both (to show his judgment) in extremes:
So over-violent or over-civil
That every man, with him, was God or Devil.
In squandering wealth was his peculiar art:
560   Nothing went unrewarded but desert.
Beggared by fools, whom still he found° too late,
He had his jest, and they had his estate.
He laughed himself from court; then sought relief
By forming parties, but could ne'er be chief;
For, spite of him, the weight of business fell
On Absalom and wise Achitophel:
Thus, wicked but in will, of means bereft,
He left not faction, but of that was left.
    Titles and names 'twere tedious to rehearse
570   Of lords, below the dignity of verse.
Wits, warriors, Commonwealth's-men, were the best;
Kind husbands and mere nobles, all the rest.
And therefore, in the name of dulness, be
The well-hung Balaam° and cold Caleb,° free;
And canting Nadab° let oblivion damn,
Who made new porridge for the paschal lamb.°
Let friendship's holy band some names assure;
Some their own worth, and some let scorn secure.

Zimri George Villiers (1628–87), second Duke of Buckingham, chief minister to Charles, impeached in 1674 and active in opposition after that; a great wit, author of *The Rehearsal,* which mocked the heroic play and Dryden. "He was true to nothing, for he was not true to himself. He had no steadiness nor conduct. . . . He could never fix his thoughts, nor govern his estate" (Bishop Burnet). The biblical counterparts (there are two) are either lecherous (Numbers 25:6–15) or treacherous (I Kings 16:8–20).
chemist chemist and/or alchemist (according to Burnet, "for some years he thought he was very near finding the philosopher's stone")
freaks whims
found found out
well-hung Balaam probably Theophilus Hastings (1650–1701), 7th Earl of Huntingdon, who

left Shaftesbury and returned to support the king in 1681, and may therefore be based on the diviner who is called upon by Balak to curse the Israelites but blesses them instead (Numbers 22–24); "well-hung" a tribute either to verbal fluency or sexual vigor
cold Caleb probably Arthur Capel (1632–83), Earl of Essex (Numbers 13–14)
canting Nadab Lord Howard of Escrick (1626–94), formerly an Anabaptist preacher vehement against the king and clergy
Who . . . lamb i.e. who revised the Anglican service (called a "porridge" or "hodge-podge" by Dissenters) or worship ("the paschal lamb" is Christ) by taking Communion with lamb's wool (hot ale mixed with the pulp of apples) instead of wine; so Nadab "offered strange fare before the Lord" (Leviticus 10:1)

Nor shall the rascal rabble here have place,
580 Whom kings no titles gave, and God no grace:
Not bull-faced Jonas,° who could statutes draw
To mean rebellion, and make treason law.
But he, though bad, is followed by a worse,
The wretch who Heaven's anointed dared to curse:
Shimei,° whose youth did early promise bring
Of zeal to God and hatred to his king;
Did wisely from expensive sins refrain,
And never broke the Sabbath but for gain;°
Nor ever was he known an oath to vent,
590 Or curse, unless against the government.
Thus heaping wealth, by the most ready way
Among the Jews, which was to cheat and pray,
The city, to reward his pious hate
Against his master, chose him magistrate.
His hand a vare° of justice did uphold;
His neck was loaded with a chain of gold.
During his office, treason was no crime;
The sons of Belial° had a glorious time;
For Shimei, though not prodigal of pelf,
600 Yet loved his wicked neighbour° as himself.
When two or three were gathered° to declaim
Against the monarch of Jerusalem,
Shimei was always in the midst of them;
And if they cursed the king when he was by,
Would rather curse than break good company.
If any durst his factious friends accuse,
He packed a jury of dissenting Jews,
Whose fellow-feeling in the godly cause
Would free the suffering saint from human laws.
610 For laws are only made to punish those
Who serve the king, and to protect his foes.
If any leisure time he had from power,
(Because 'tis sin to misemploy an hour,)
His business was, by writing,° to persuade
That kings were useless and a clog to trade;
And, that his noble style he might refine,

---

bull-faced Jonas Sir William Jones (1631–82),
attorney general and prosecutor in the Popish
Plot trials until 1679, involved in drafting legislation to exclude James from the throne
Shimei Slingsby Bethel (1617–97), one of the
two Whig sheriffs of London, a republican bitterly opposed to the king and able to pack
juries with his enemies; based on the loyal supporter of Saul who curses and stones David
(II Samuel 16:5–14)
gain alluding to Puritan thrift and middle-class
enterprise, raised to new heights of hypocritical
miserliness by Shimei
vare staff

sons of Belial i.e. sons of wickedness, as in
Paradise Lost I.500–502 ("And when night /
Darkens the streets, then wander forth the Sons
/ Of Belial, flown with insolence and wine"),
where Restoration court rakes may be suggested;
here turned by Dryden upon Puritan rebels
wicked neighbour converting Jesus' teaching in
Matthew 22:39 from charity to complicity
gathered echoing the words of Jesus, "Where
two or three are gathered together in my name,
there am I in the midst of them" (Matthew
18:20)
by writing pamphlets such as *The Interest of
Princes and States* (1680)

No Rechabite° more shunned the fumes of wine.
Chaste were his cellars, and his shrieval° board
The grossness of a city feast° abhorred:
His cooks, with long disuse, their trade forgot;
Cool was his kitchen, though his brains were hot.
Such frugal virtue malice may accuse,
But sure 'twas necessary to the Jews;
For towns once burnt° such magistrates require
As dare not tempt God's providence by fire.
With spiritual food° he fed his servants well,
But free from flesh that made the Jews rebel;
And Moses' laws he held in more account,
For forty days of fasting in the mount.°
To speak the rest, who better are forgot,
Would tire a well-breathed° witness of the Plot.
Yet, Corah,° thou shalt from oblivion pass:
Erect thyself, thou monumental brass,°
High as the serpent° of thy metal made,
While nations stand secure beneath thy shade.
What though his birth were base, yet comets rise
From earthy vapours, ere they shine in skies.
Prodigious actions may as well be done
By weaver's issue° as by prince's son.
This arch-attestor for the public good
By that one deed ennobles all his blood.
Who ever asked the witnesses' high race
Whose oath with martyrdom did Stephen° grace?
Ours was a Levite, and as times went then,
His tribe were God Almighty's gentlemen.
Sunk were his eyes, his voice was harsh and loud,
Sure signs he neither choleric was nor proud:
His long chin proved his wit; his saintlike grace
A church vermilion and a Moses' face.°
His memory, miraculously great,
Could plots, exceeding man's belief, repeat;
Which therefore cannot be accounted lies,

620

630

640

650

Rechabite one of the sect sworn "to drink no wine all our days" (Jeremiah 35:8)
shrieval sheriff's
city feast lavish hospitality, expected of the sheriff
towns . . . burnt referring to the great fire of London (1666), often interpreted as divine punishment
spiritual food a Prayer Book term for the Lord's Supper or Communion; here a thrifty substitute for home cooking ("fire")
mount Mt. Sinai, where Moses received the Ten Commandments (Exodus 34:28)
well-breathed long-winded
Corah Titus Oates (1649–1705), chief witness of the Plot. First an Anglican clergyman, he became a Roman Catholic in 1677 and studied

abroad with the Jesuits, thus acquiring some credibility as a witness against them.
brass a metal known for impenetrability; hence insensibility or shamelessness
serpent "Moses made a serpent of brass, and put it on a pole" to cure his people of the bites of fiery serpents (Numbers 21:6–9)
weaver's issue Oates was the son of a weaver turned preacher.
Stephen the first martyr of the Christian church, stoned to death on the testimony of false witnesses (Acts 6–7)
church . . . face the ruddy, well-fed look of a clergyman, the ironic counterpart of the shining face with which Moses descended from Mt. Sinai

For human wit could never such devise.
Some future truths are mingled in his book;
But where the witness failed, the prophet° spoke:
Some things like visionary flights appear;
The spirit caught him up, the Lord knows where;
And gave him his rabbinical degree,
Unknown to foreign university.°
660   His judgment yet his memory did excel;
Which pieced his wondrous evidence so well,
And suited to the temper of the times,
Then groaning under Jebusitic crimes.
Let Israel's foes suspect his heavenly call,
And rashly judge his writ apocryphal;°
Our laws for such affronts have forfeits° made:
He takes his life, who takes away his trade.
Were I myself in witness Corah's place,
The wretch who did me such a dire disgrace
670   Should whet my memory, though once forgot,
To make him an appendix of my plot.
His zeal to Heaven made him his prince despise
And load his person with indignities;
But zeal peculiar privilege affords,
Indulging latitude to deeds and words;
And Corah might for Agag's murther° call,
In terms as coarse as Samuel used to Saul.
What others in his evidence did join,
(The best that could be had for love or coin)
680   In Corah's own predicament will fall;
For witness is a common name to all.
    Surrounded thus with friends of every sort,
Deluded Absalom forsakes the court;
Impatient of high hopes, urged with renown,
And fired with near possession of a crown.
The admiring crowd are dazzled with surprise,
And on his goodly person feed their eyes.
His joy concealed, he sets himself to show,
On each side bowing popularly low;
690   His looks, his gestures, and his words he frames,
And with familiar ease repeats their names.
Thus formed by nature, furnished out with arts,
He glides unfelt into their secret hearts.
Then, with a kind compassionating look,
And sighs, bespeaking° pity ere he spoke,

prophet Oates kept recalling events he claimed to have forgotten in earlier testimony
university e.g. the University of Salamanca, which denied Oates's claim to have taken a divinity degree there
apocryphal of doubtful authenticity
forfeits fines, compensations

Agag's murther i.e. the execution of Lord Stafford, ordered on Oates's evidence in 1680. The prophet Samuel harshly ordered Saul to execute his captured enemy Agag, as the Lord had commanded (I Samuel 15).
bespeaking soliciting

Few words he said; but easy those and fit,
More slow than Hybla-drops,° and far more sweet.
    'I mourn, my countrymen, your lost estate;
Though far unable to prevent your fate:
700   Behold a banished man,° for your dear cause
Exposed a prey to arbitrary laws!
Yet O! that I alone could be undone,
Cut off from empire, and no more a son!
Now all your liberties a spoil are made;
Egypt and Tyrus° intercept your trade,
And Jebusites your sacred rites invade.
My father, whom with reverence yet I name,
Charmed into ease, is careless of his fame;
And, bribed with petty sums of foreign gold,
710   Is grown in Bathsheba's° embraces old;
Exalts his enemies, his friends destroys;
And all his power against himself employs.
He gives, and let him give, my right away;
But why should he his own and yours betray?
He, only he, can make the nation bleed,
And he alone from my revenge is freed.
Take then my tears' (with that he wiped his eyes)
' 'Tis all the aid my present power supplies:
No court-informer can these arms accuse;
720   These arms may sons against their fathers use:
And 'tis my wish the next successor's reign
May make no other Israelite complain.'
    Youth, beauty, graceful action seldom fail;
But common interest always will prevail,
And pity never ceases to be shown
To him who makes the people's wrongs his own.
The crowd, that still believe their kings oppress,
With lifted hands their young Messiah bless:
Who now begins his progress° to ordain
730   With chariots, horsemen, and a numerous train;
From east to west his glories he displays,
And, like the sun, the promised land surveys.
Fame runs before him as the morning star,°
And shouts of joy salute him from afar:

Each house receives him as a guardian god,
And consecrates the place of his abode.
But hospitable treats did most commend
Wise Issachar,° his wealthy western friend.
This moving court, that caught the people's eyes,
740 And seemed but pomp, did other ends disguise:
Achitophel had formed it, with intent
To sound the depths, and fathom, where it went,
The people's hearts; distinguish friends from foes,
And try their strength, before they came to blows.
Yet all was coloured with a smooth pretence
Of specious love, and duty to their prince.
Religion and redress of grievances,
Two names that always cheat and always please,
Are often urged; and good King David's life
750 Endangered by a brother and a wife.°
Thus in a pageant show a plot is made,
And peace itself is war in masquerade.
O foolish Israel! never warned by ill!
Still the same bait, and circumvented still!
Did ever men forsake their present ease,
In midst of health imagine a disease,
Take pains contingent° mischiefs to foresee,
Make heirs for monarchs, and for God decree?
What shall we think! Can people give away,
760 Both for themselves and sons their native sway?
Then they are left defenceless to the sword
Of each unbounded, arbitrary lord:°
And laws are vain by which we right enjoy,
If kings unquestioned can those laws destroy.
Yet if the crowd be judge of fit and just,
And kings are only officers in trust,°
Then this resuming covenant° was declared
When kings were made, or is for ever barred.
If those who gave the sceptre° could not tie
770 By their own deed their own posterity,
How then could Adam bind his future race?
How could his forfeit on mankind° take place?
Or how could heavenly justice damn us all,
Who ne'er consented to our father's fall?

Issachar Thomas Thynne (1648–82) of Long-
leat (Wiltshire), the "Protestant Squire" and
supporter of Monmouth
wife Oates accused the queen of high treason
and of a plot to poison the king.
contingent possible
unbounded, arbitrary lord perhaps evoking the
unlimited and indivisible power of the sovereign
of Hobbes
in trust i.e. by contract which deputizes the
sovereign power of the people to these officers

resuming covenant agreement that the people
can resume their power at will in order to determine the succession to the throne
gave the sceptre the makers of the original covenant that established monarchy
forfeit on mankind alluding to the doctrine of
Paul: "by one man's disobedience many were
made sinners" (Romans 5:19), or "as in Adam
all die, even so in Christ shall all be made alive"
(I Corinthians 15:22)

Then° kings are slaves to those whom they command,
And tenants° to their people's pleasure stand.
Add, that the power for property allowed°
Is mischievously seated in the crowd;
For who can be secure of private right,
780 If sovereign sway may be dissolved by might?
Nor is the people's judgment always true:
The most may err as grossly as the few;
And faultless kings run down, by common cry,
For vice, oppression, and for tyranny.
What standard is there in a fickle rout,
Which, flowing to the mark, runs faster out?°
Nor only crowds, but Sanhedrins may be
Infected with this public lunacy,
And share the madness of rebellious times,
790 To murther monarchs for imagined crimes.
If they may give and take whene'er they please,
Not kings alone (the Godhead's images)
But government itself at length must fall
To nature's state,° where all have right to all.
Yet, grant our lords the people kings can make,
What prudent men a settled throne would shake?
For whatsoe'er their sufferings were before,
That change they covet makes them suffer more.
All other errors but disturb a state,
800 But innovation° is the blow of fate.
If ancient fabrics nod, and threat to fall,
To patch the flaws, and buttress up the wall,
Thus far 'tis duty: but here fix the mark;
For all beyond it is to touch our ark.°
To change foundations, cast the frame anew,
Is work for rebels, who base ends pursue,
At once divine and human laws control,°
And mend the parts by ruin of the whole.
The tampering world is subject to this curse,
810 To physic° their disease into a worse.
   Now what relief can righteous David bring?
How fatal 'tis to be too good a king!
Friends he has few, so high the madness grows;
Who dare be such, must be the people's foes.
Yet some there were, even in the worst of days;

Then if there is not this power to bind posterity
tenants i.e. on lease
for . . . allowed taken to be the people's property
flowing . . . out i.e. the higher the tide, the faster it runs out; an effect of the moon, literally the source of "lunacy" (l. 788 below)
nature's state Hobbes's view of the state of nature, a condition of "war of every man against

every man," in which "nothing can be unjust" and all property or power is "every man's . . . for so long as he can keep it" (*Leviathan* I.13)
innovation starting anew, revolution
ark to commit sacrilege, with reference to the Ark of the Covenant
control contradict, break
physic remedy

Some let me name, and naming is to praise.
　　In this short file Barzillai° first appears;
Barzillai, crowned with honour and with years.
Long since, the rising rebels he withstood
In regions waste,° beyond the Jordan's flood:
Unfortunately brave to buoy the state;
But sinking underneath his master's fate:
In exile with his godlike prince he mourned;
For him he suffered, and with him returned.
The court he practised, not the courtier's art:
Large was his wealth, but larger was his heart,
Which well the noblest objects knew to choose,
The fighting warrior and recording Muse.
His bed could once a fruitful issue boast;
Now more than half a father's name is lost.°
His eldest hope,° with every grace adorned,
By me (so Heaven will have it) always mourned,
And always honoured, snatched in manhood's prime
By unequal fates, and Providence's crime;
Yet not before the goal of honour won,
All parts fulfilled of subject and of son:
Swift was the race, but short the time to run.
O narrow circle, but of power divine,
Scanted in space, but perfect in thy line!
By sea, by land, thy matchless worth was known,
Arms thy delight, and war was all thy own:
Thy force, infused, the fainting Tyrians propped;
And haughty Pharaoh found his fortune stopped.
O ancient honour! O unconquered hand,
Whom foes unpunished never could withstand!
But Israel was unworthy of thy name;
Short is the date of all immoderate fame.
It looks as Heaven our ruin had designed,
And durst not trust thy fortune and thy mind.
Now, free from earth, thy disencumbered soul
Mounts up and leaves behind the clouds and starry pole:
From thence thy kindred legions mayst thou bring,
To aid the guardian angel of thy king.
Here stop, my Muse, here cease thy painful flight;
No pinions can pursue immortal height:
Tell good Barzillai thou canst sing no more,
And tell thy soul she should have fled before.

[marginal line numbers: 820, 830, 840, 850]

Barzillai James Butler (1610–88), Duke of
Ormonde and Lord Lieutenant of Ireland (to
whom Dryden dedicated his translation of Plutarch's *Lives*); a generous supporter of the
Royalist cause, based on the aged benefactor of
David (II Samuel 19:31–39)
regions waste Ireland, where Ormonde fought
for Charles I

more . . . lost six of his ten children having
died
eldest hope Thomas, Earl of Ossory (1634–80),
who distinguished himself at sea, and in support
of the Dutch on land, against Louis XIV; victim of a fever; here seen in contrast with
Achitophel's son (ll. 170–72)

Or fled she with his life, and left this verse
To hang on her departed patron's hearse?°
860 Now take thy steepy flight from Heaven, and see
If thou canst find on earth another *he:*
Another *he* would be too hard to find;
See then whom thou canst see not far behind.
Zadoc° the priest, whom, shunning power and place,
His lowly mind advanced to David's grace.
With him the Sagan of Jerusalem,°
Of hospitable soul and noble stem;
Him of the western dome,° whose weighty sense
Flows in fit words and heavenly eloquence.
870 The prophets' sons,° by such example led,
To learning and to loyalty were bred:
For colleges on bounteous kings depend,
And never rebel was to arts a friend.
To these succeed the pillars of the laws;
Who best could plead, and best can judge a cause.
Next them a train of loyal peers ascend;
Sharp-judging Adriel,° the Muses' friend;
Himself a Muse—in Sanhedrin's debate
True to his prince, but not a slave of state:
880 Whom David's love with honours did adorn,
That from his disobedient son° were torn.
Jotham° of piercing wit, and pregnant thought;
Endued by nature, and by learning taught
To move assemblies, who but only tried
The worse a while, then chose the better side:
Nor chose alone, but turned the balance too;
So much the weight of one brave man can do.
Hushai,° the friend of David in distress;
In public storms, of manly steadfastness:
890 By foreign treaties he informed his youth,
And joined experience to his native truth.
His frugal care supplied the wanting throne;
Frugal for that, but bounteous of his own:
'Tis easy conduct when exchequers flow,
But hard the task to manage well the low;
For sovereign power is too depressed or high,
When kings are forced to sell, or crowds to buy.

---

hearse the structure over a bier where verse tributes were hung
Zadoc William Sancroft (1617–93), Archbishop of Canterbury, subject of an early ode by Swift
Sagan of Jerusalem Henry Compton (1632–1713), Bishop of London, of "noble stem" as the son of the Earl of Southampton
western dome John Dolben (1625–86), Dean of Westminster, a "most passionate and pathetic" preacher (John Evelyn)
prophets' sons boys of Westminster School

Adriel John Sheffield (1648–1721), Earl of Mulgrave, patron of Dryden's poetry, author of a well-known *Essay on Satire* (1680) and *Essay upon Poetry* (1682)
son Monmouth
Jotham George Savile, Marquess of Halifax (see Headnote to selection from his works)
Hushai Laurence Hyde (1642–1711), Clarendon's son, who negotiated the Anglo-Dutch alliance of 1678

Indulge one labour more, my weary Muse,
For Amiel:° who can Amiel's praise refuse?
900   Of ancient race by birth, but nobler yet
In his own worth, and without title great:
The Sanhedrin long time as chief he ruled,
Their reason guided, and their passion cooled:
So dextrous was he in the crown's defence,
So formed to speak a loyal nation's sense,
That, as their band was Israel's tribes in small,
So fit was he to represent them all.
Now rasher charioteers the seat ascend,
Whose loose careers his steady skill commend:
910   They, like the unequal ruler° of the day,
Misguide the seasons and mistake the way;
While he withdrawn at their mad labour smiles,
And safe enjoys the sabbath of his toils.

These were the chief, a small but faithful band
Of worthies, in the breach who dared to stand,
And tempt the united fury of the land.
With grief they viewed such powerful engines bent,
To batter down the lawful government:
A numerous faction, with pretended frights,
920   In Sanhedrins to plume° the regal rights;
The true successor from the court removed;
The Plot, by hireling witnesses, improved.
These ills they saw, and, as their duty bound,
They showed the king the danger of the wound;
That no concessions from the throne would please,
But lenitives° fomented the disease;
That Absalom, ambitious of the crown,
Was made the lure to draw the people down;
That false Achitophel's pernicious hate
930   Had turned the Plot to ruin church and state;
The council violent, the rabble worse;
That Shimei taught Jerusalem to curse.

With all these loads of injuries oppressed,
And long revolving in his careful° breast
The event of things, at last, his patience tired,
Thus from his royal throne, by Heaven inspired,
The godlike David spoke: with awful fear
His train their Maker in their master hear.
'Thus long have I, by native mercy swayed,
940   My wrongs dissembled, my revenge delayed:
So willing to forgive the offending age;

Amiel Edward Seymour (1633–1708), Speaker
of the House of Commons, 1673–78
unequal ruler Phaeton, who attempted to drive
the sun chariot of his father, Apollo, across the
sky and lost control, upsetting the climate and
season
plume pluck away
lenitives pain killers
careful troubled

So much the father did the king assuage.
But now so far my clemency they slight,
The offenders question my forgiving right.
That one was made for many, they contend;
But 'tis to rule; for that's a monarch's end.
They call my tenderness of blood, my fear;
Though manly tempers can the longest bear.
Yet, since they will divert my native course,
950   'Tis time to show I am not good by force.
Those heaped affronts that haughty subjects bring,
Are burthens for a camel, not a king.
Kings are the public pillars of the state,
Born to sustain and prop the nation's weight;
If my young Samson° will pretend a call
To shake the column, let him share the fall:
But O that yet he would repent and live!
How easy 'tis for parents to forgive!
With how few tears a pardon might be won
960   From nature, pleading for a darling son!
Poor pitied youth, by my paternal care
Raised up to all the height his frame could bear!
Had God ordained his fate for empire born,
He would have given his soul another turn:
Gulled° with a patriot's° name, whose modern sense
Is one that would by law supplant his prince;
The people's brave,° the politician's tool;
Never was patriot yet, but was a fool.
Whence comes it that religion and the laws
970   Should more be Absalom's than David's cause?
His old instructor,° ere he lost his place,
Was never thought indued with so much grace.
Good heavens, how faction can a patriot paint!
My rebel ever proves my people's saint.
Would *they* impose an heir upon the throne?
Let Sanhedrins be taught to give their own.°
A king's at least a part of government,
And mine as requisite as their consent;
Without my leave a future king to choose,
980   Infers a right the present to depose.
True, they petition me to approve their choice;
But Esau's hands suit ill with Jacob's voice.°
My pious subjects for my safety pray;
Which to secure, they take my power away.

Samson who perished in the ruins of the temple
he pulled down (Judges 16)
Gulled duped
patriot's as in l. 179 above
brave bully, champion
instructor Achitophel

their own what is in their power to give
Esau's . . . voice referring to Jacob's deception in winning his blind father's blessing: "The
voice is Jacob's voice, but the hands are the
hands of Esau" (Genesis 27:22)

From plots and treasons Heaven preserve my years,
But save me most from my petitioners!
Unsatiate as the barren womb or grave;
God cannot grant so much as they can crave.
What then is left but with a jealous eye
990 To guard the small remains of royalty?
The law shall still direct my peaceful sway,
And the same law teach rebels to obey:
Votes shall no more established power control°—
Such votes as make a part exceed the whole:
No groundless clamours shall my friends remove,
Nor crowds have power to punish ere they prove;°
For gods and godlike kings their care express,
Still to defend their servants in distress.
O that my power to saving were confined!
1000 Why am I forced, like Heaven, against my mind,
To make examples of another kind?
Must I at length the sword of justice draw?
O curst effects of necessary law!
How ill my fear they by my mercy scan!
Beware the fury of a patient man.
Law they require, let Law then show her face;
They could not be content to look on Grace,°
Her hinder parts, but with a daring eye
To tempt the terror of her front and die.°
1010 By their own arts, 'tis righteously decreed,
Those dire artificers of death shall bleed.
Against themselves their witnesses will swear,°
Till viper-like their mother Plot they tear,
And suck for nutriment that bloody gore,
Which was their principle of life before.°
Their Belial with their Belzebub° will fight;
Thus on my foes, my foes shall do me right.
Nor doubt the event;° for factious crowds engage,
In their first onset, all their brutal rage.
1020 Then let 'em take an unresisted course;
Retire, and traverse, and delude their force;
But, when they stand all breathless, urge the fight,
And rise upon 'em with redoubled might;
For lawful power is still superior found;
When long driven back, at length it stands the ground.'

---

control contravene
No groundless . . . prove instances of arbitrary power not in the king but the parliament and the people
Grace the mercy expressed in ll. 939–44
Her hinder . . . die as God warns Moses that no man can see His face (here "front" or brow) and live: "thou shalt see my back parts; but my face shall not be seen' (Exodus 33:23)

will swear as some already had, turning upon the Whigs
Till viper-like . . . before like the offspring of the dragon Error, who "suckèd up their dying mothers blood, / Making her death their life, and eke her hurt their good" (Spenser, *The Faerie Queene* I.i.25)
Belial . . . Belzebub both among the debating leaders of the fallen angels in *Paradise Lost* II
event outcome

He said. The Almighty, nodding, gave consent;
And peals of thunder shook the firmament.
Henceforth a series of new time° began,
The mighty years in long procession ran:
1030   Once more the godlike David was restored,
And willing nations knew their lawful lord.

                              1681

Mac Flecknoe

This superb mock-heroic satire, which looks ahead to Pope's achievement in *The Dunciad,* found its title in the death of a notoriously bad Irish poet, Richard Flecknoe (d. 1678). Dryden has Flecknoe choose a successor in Thomas Shadwell (1640–92), who liked to think of himself as the true heir of the great Ben Jonson (1572–1637). Shadwell, in fact, gave Jonson's plays unstinting praise and imitated them with more zeal than success; he added broader effects of bawdry and slapstick, as Dryden recalls in his satire (ll. 42, 181, 212). But, whatever his deviations from Jonson's art, Shadwell was impatient with Dryden's less than complete admiration of his master, and over ten years engaged Dryden in critical dispute on such matters as the true nature of wit. In 1673 Dryden wrote, "I know I honour Ben Jonson more than my little critics, because without vanity I may own I understand him better." In general the dispute had involved little animosity on either side, and the occasion for this poem is not altogether clear. The likeliest explanation is that Dryden resented Shadwell's praise of Buckingham's *The Rehearsal,* in which Dryden was ridiculed.

Mac Flecknoe

All human things are subject to decay,
And when fate summons, monarchs must obey.
This Flecknoe found, who, like Augustus,° young
Was called to empire, and had governed long;
In prose and verse, was owned, without dispute,
Through all the realms of *Nonsense,* absolute.
This agèd prince, now flourishing in peace,
And blest with issue of a large increase;
Worn out with business, did at length debate
10   To settle the succession of the state;
And, pondering which of all his sons was fit
To reign, and wage immortal war with wit,
Cried: ' 'Tis resolved; for nature pleads, that he
Should only rule, who most resembles me.

series of new time recalling the Virgilian prophecy in *Eclogue* IV: "Saturnian times / Roll round again, and mighty years, begun / From their first orb, in radiant circles run" (Dryden trans.)

like Augustus Octavius Caesar became first Roman emperor in 31 B.C. at the age of 32; he assumed the title of Augustus four years later and ruled for 45 years.

Sh—— alone my perfect image bears,
Mature in dulness from his tender years:
Sh—— alone, of all my sons, is he
Who stands confirmed in full stupidity.
The rest to some faint meaning make pretence,
20   But Sh—— never deviates into sense.
Some beams of wit on other souls may fall,
Strike through, and make a lucid interval;
But Sh——'s genuine night admits no ray,
His rising fogs prevail upon the day.
Besides, his goodly fabric° fills the eye,
And seems designed for thoughtless° majesty;
Thoughtless as monarch oaks that shade the plain,
And, spread in solemn state, supinely reign.
Heywood and Shirley° were but types° of thee,
30   Thou last great prophet of tautology.°
Even I, a dunce of more renown than they,
Was sent before but to prepare thy way;°
And, coarsely clad in Norwich drugget,° came
To teach the nations in thy greater name.
My warbling lute,° the lute I whilom° strung,
When to King John of Portugal° I sung,
Was but the prelude to that glorious day,
When thou on silver Thames° didst cut thy way,
With well-timed oars before the royal barge,
40   Swelled with the pride of thy celestial charge;
And big with hymn, commander of a host,
The like was ne'er in Epsom blankets tossed.°
Methinks I see the new Arion° sail,
The lute still trembling underneath thy nail.
At thy well-sharpened thumb from shore to shore
The treble squeaks for fear, the basses roar;
Echoes from Pissing Alley° Sh—— call,

fabric a term generally used for a building, as in l. 66 below; here a reference to Shadwell's corpulent body
thoughtless carefree; mindless
Heywood and Shirley Thomas Heywood (c. 1574–1641) and James Shirley (1596–1666), both popular and prolific dramatists (Heywood claiming a hand in 220 plays, Shirley the author of 36) before the closing of the theaters in 1642; held in low regard in Dryden's day
types prefigurations, as Old Testament patriarchs (Abraham, Noah), judges or kings (Samson, David, Solomon), and prophets were taken to prefigure Christ, who was their culmination (as he is the "last Adam")
tautology needless repetition in other words, here perhaps replacing "theology"
prepare thy way as John the Baptist does for Jesus (Matthew 3:3)
Norwich drugget a coarse fabric of wool and linen (like Shadwell, from Norfolk), the counterpart of John's "raiment of camel's hair" (Matthew 3:4)
lute Shadwell was ridiculed, by Andrew Marvell among others, for his musical pretensions
whilom formerly
King John of Portugal Flecknoe had visited Portugal and claimed to have been patronized by the king.
silver Thames This phrase and many in succeeding lines, as well as the allusion to Arion, echo a celebration of King Charles by Edmund Waller (1606–87).
in . . . tossed as was Sir Samuel Hearty, the self-styled wit in Shadwell's play The Virtuoso (1676); with reference to Epsom Wells, an earlier Shadwell comedy (1672)
Arion the legendary Greek musician, saved from drowning by dolphins that were charmed by his music
Pissing Alley the actual name of five streets, one near the Thames

And Sh—— they resound from Aston Hall.°
About thy boat the little fishes throng,
50 As at the morning toast° that floats along.
Sometimes, as prince of thy harmonious band,
Thou wieldst thy papers in thy threshing hand.
St. André's° feet ne'er kept more equal time,
Not even the feet of thy own *Psyche's* rhyme;
Though they in number° as in sense excel:
So just, so like tautology, they fell,
That, pale with envy, Singleton° forswore
The lute and sword, which he in triumph bore,
And vowed he ne'er would act Villerius° more.'
60 Here stopped the good old sire, and wept for joy
In silent raptures of the hopeful boy.
All arguments, but most his plays, persuade,
That for anointed° dulness° he was made.
   Close to the walls which fair Augusta° bind,
(The fair Augusta much to fears° inclined),
An ancient fabric° raised to inform the sight,
There stood of yore, and Barbican° it hight:
A watchtower once; but now, so fate ordains,
Of all the pile° an empty name remains.
70 From its old ruins brothel-houses rise,
Scenes of lewd loves, and of polluted joys,
Where their vast courts the mother-strumpets keep,
And, undisturbed by watch,° in silence sleep.°
Near these a Nursery° erects its head,
Where queens are formed, and future heroes bred;
Where unfledged actors learn to laugh and cry,
Where infant punks° their tender voices try,
And little Maximins° the gods defy.
Great Fletcher° never treads in buskins here,

Aston Hall unidentified
morning toast sewage, feces
St. André's a French dancing master and choreographer for Shadwell's opera *Psyche* (1675), whose flat-footed verse is described in next line
number meter; quantity
Singleton John Singleton, one of the royal musicians
Villerius a character in Sir William Davenant's *Siege of Rhodes* (1656), often ridiculed for presenting battles in recitative (requiring both "lute and sword" of the actor) and thus sacrificing sense to sound
anointed i.e. looking forward to the coronation of a new king
dulness implying not simply the power to bore but sluggishness of mind, a relapse from effort, a substitution of the cheap and easy for the excellent (cf. Pope's goddess Dulness, the daughter of Chaos and Night, in *The Dunciad*)
Augusta London
fears aroused by the Popish Plot (cf. *Absalom and Achitophel*)

fabric building
Barbican named for its former function as an outer defense of the city
pile large building
watch constables
Where their . . . sleep a parody of two lines from the epic *Davideis* (1656) by Abraham Cowley: "Where their vast court the mother-waters keep, / And undisturbed by moons in silence sleep"; as are ll. 76–77, with "punks" replacing "winds" in l. 77
Nursery a training school for actors
punks prostitutes
Maximins future performers of such heroic figures as the Roman emperor in Dryden's *Tyrannic Love* (1669), a cruel tyrant given to self-exalting rant
Fletcher John Fletcher (1579–1625), collaborator of Francis Beaumont's (c. 1584–1616), author of celebrated tragedies (hence "buskins," the thick-soled boots of Greek tragic actors)

80 Nor greater Jonson° dares in socks appear;
But gentle Simkin° just reception finds
Amidst this monument of vanished minds:°
Pure clinches° the suburbian Muse affords,
And Panton° waging harmless war with words.
Here Flecknoe, as a place to fame well known,
Ambitiously designed his Sh——'s throne;
For ancient Dekker° prophesied long since,
That in this pile should reign a mighty prince,
Born for a scourge of wit and flail of sense;
90 To whom true dulness should some *Psyches* owe,
But worlds of *Misers* from his pen should flow;
Humorists and *Hypocrites* it should produce,°
Whole Raymond families and tribes of Bruce.°
    Now Empress Fame had published the renown
Of Sh——'s coronation through the town.
Roused by report of Fame, the nations meet,
From near Bunhill and distant Watling Street.°
No Persian carpets spread the imperial way,
But scattered limbs of mangled poets lay;
100 From dusty shops neglected authors come,
Martyrs of pies, and relics of the bum.°
Much Heywood, Shirley, Ogilby° there lay,
But loads of Sh—— almost choked the way.
Bilked stationers° for yeomen stood prepared,
And Herringman° was captain of the guard.
The hoary prince in majesty appeared,
High on a throne° of his own labours reared.
At his right hand our young Ascanius° sate,
Rome's other hope,° and pillar of the state.
110 His brows thick fogs, instead of glories, grace,
And lambent dulness played around his face.°
As Hannibal° did to the altars come,
Sworn by his sire a mortal foe to Rome;

Jonson Ben Jonson as writer of comedy ("socks," the light shoes of the Greek comic actors)
Simkin a typical clown in farces
monument . . . minds in Davenant's *Gondibert* a phrase for a library of dead authors; here transformed by play on the word "vanished"
clinches puns
Panton another farce character, perhaps a punster
Dekker Thomas Dekker (*c.* 1572–1632), an able but often "low" playwright, satirized by Ben Jonson, here taken as a counterpart of such Old Testament prophets as Isaiah
But worlds . . . produce referring to Shadwell's early plays: the unpublished *Hypocrite; The Humorists* (1671); and *The Miser* (1672), adapted from Molière
Raymond . . . Bruce witty characters in *The Humorists* and *The Virtuoso* (1676) respectively
near . . . Street a small area in the heart of the City, the commercial center of London and, as in Pope's *Dunciad,* the center of low taste
Martyrs . . . bum their unsold books providing paper for bakers' pans and for privies
Ogilby John Ogilby (1600–1676), feeble translator of Homer and Virgil and the copious author of original epics
bilked stationers cheated publishers
Herringman Henry Herringman, publisher of both Dryden and Shadwell until 1678
High . . . throne like Milton's Satan, "High on a throne of royal state," *Paradise Lost* II.1
Ascanius Shadwell as son to Flecknoe's Aeneas
Rome's other hope translating *Aeneid* XII.168
His brows . . . his face parodying *Aeneid* II. 680–84, later translated by Dryden: "from young Iülus' head / A lambent flame arose, / which gently spread / Around his brows, and on his temples fed" (II.930–32)
Hannibal forced by his father at the age of nine to swear enmity to Rome, which he almost captured in 216 B.C.

So Sh—— swore, nor should his vow be vain,
That he till death true dulness would maintain;
And, in his father's right, and realm's defence,
Ne'er to have peace with wit, nor truce with sense.
The king himself the sacred unction° made,
As king by office, and as priest by trade.°
In his sinister° hand, instead of ball,
He placed a mighty mug of potent ale;
Love's Kingdom° to his right he did convey,
At once his sceptre, and his rule of sway;
Whose righteous lore the prince had practised young,
And from whose loins recorded *Psyche* sprung.
His temples, last, with poppies° were o'erspread,
That nodding seemed to consecrate his head.
Just at that point of time, if fame not lie,
On his left hand twelve reverend owls° did fly.
So Romulus, 'tis sung, by Tiber's brook,°
Presage of sway from twice six vultures took.
The admiring throng loud acclamations make,
And omens of his future empire take.
The sire then shook the honours of his head,°
And from his brows damps of oblivion shed
Full on the filial dulness: long he stood,
Repelling from his breast the raging god;°
At length burst out in this prophetic mood:
    'Heavens bless my son, from Ireland let him reign
To far Barbadoes° on the western main;
Of his dominion may no end be known,
And greater than his father's be his throne;
Beyond *Love's Kingdom* let him stretch his pen!'
He paused, and all the people cried, 'Amen.'
Then thus continued he: 'My son, advance
Still in new impudence, new ignorance.
Success let others teach, learn thou from me
Pangs without birth, and fruitless industry.
Let *Virtuosos* in five years be writ;
Yet not one thought accuse thy toil of wit.
Let gentle George° in triumph tread the stage,

120

130

140

150

unction oil for anointment
priest by trade Flecknoe was a Roman Catholic priest.
sinister left, the hand in which the British monarch holds an orb as emblem of the world, while he holds a scepter in his right
Love's Kingdom Flecknoe's "pastoral tragicomedy" of 1664
poppies as inducing sleep, but also with reference to Shadwell's use of opium
owls emblems of solemnity and gravity, either wise or stupid
Romulus . . . brook as related by Plutarch of the founder and first ruler of Rome
honours . . . head ornaments, thus locks or hair

Repelling . . . god like the Delphic priestess or the Cumaean Sibyl described in *Aeneid* VI. 46–51: "Her hair stood up; convulsive rage possessed / Her trembling limbs, and heaved her labouring breast. . . . / Her staring eyes with sparkling fury roll; / When all the god came rushing on her soul" (Dryden trans., VI.74–75, 78–79)
from Ireland . . . Barbadoes a vast empire largely of water
gentle George common nickname for Sir George Etherege (*c.* 1635–91), friend of Rochester and one of the most brilliant writers of Restoration comedies

Make Dorimant betray and Loveit rage;°
Let Cully, Cockwood, Fopling,° charm the pit,°
And in their folly show the writer's wit.
Yet still thy fools shall stand in thy defence,
And justify their author's want of sense.
Let 'em be all by thy own model made
Of dulness, and desire no foreign aid;
That they to future ages may be known,
160 Not copies drawn, but issue of thy own.
Nay, let thy men of wit too be the same,
All full of thee, and differing but in name.
But let no alien S-dl-y° interpose,
To lard with wit thy hungry *Epsom* prose.
And when false flowers of rhetoric thou wouldst cull,
Trust nature, do not labour to be dull;
But write thy best, and top; and, in each line,
Sir Formal's oratory° will be thine:
Sir Formal, though unsought, attends thy quill,
170 And does thy northern° dedications fill.
Nor let false friends seduce thy mind to fame,
By arrogating Jonson's hostile name.
Let father Flecknoe fire thy mind with praise,
And uncle Ogilby thy envy raise.
Thou art my blood, where Jonson has no part:
What share have we in nature, or in art?
Where did his wit on learning fix a brand,
And rail at arts he did not understand?
Where made he love in Prince Nicander's° vein,
180 Or swept the dust in *Psyche's* humble strain?
Where sold he bargains,° "whip-stitch, kiss my arse,"
Promised a play° and dwindled to a farce?
When did his Muse from Fletcher scenes purloin,
As thou whole Etherege dost transfuse to thine?
But so transfused, as oil on water's flow,
His always floats above, thine sinks below.
This is thy province, this thy wondrous way,
New humours to invent for each new play:
This is that boasted bias of thy mind,°

Make Dorimant . . . rage the rake-hero and his discarded mistress in *The Man of Mode* (1676), Etherege's finest play
Cully . . . Fopling comic fools in three of Etherege's plays
pit the floor of the theater, less fashionable than the box, more so than the gallery
S-dl-y Sir Charles Sedley (1638–1701), court wit and poet, who contributed a prologue (and many suspected more) to Shadwell's *Epsom Wells*
Sir Formal's oratory the rhetoric of that "most Ciceronian coxcomb," Sir Formal Trifle, in *The Virtuoso*
northern addressed to the Duke or Duchess of Newcastle; but also suggesting a climate where

wit is scarce, what Laurence Sterne calls "Freezeland" or "Fogland" (*Tristram Shandy* VI.i)
Prince Nicander's a character in *Psyche*
sold he bargains induced a question that might be met with a coarse answer, here in the idiom of Sir Samuel Hearty of *The Virtuoso*
Promised a play as Shadwell had in the Dedication of *The Virtuoso*, where he professed to scorn "unnatural farce fools, which some intend for comical"
bias . . . mind terms from bowling (where weighting or shaping of the ball produces a curved path), recalling Shadwell's definition of humor (Epilogue, *The Humorists*): "A humour is the bias of the mind, / By which with violence

190 By which one way, to dulness, 'tis inclined;
Which makes thy writings lean on one side still,
And, in all changes, that way bends thy will.
Nor let thy mountain-belly make pretence
Of likeness;° thine's a tympany° of sense.
A tun° of man in thy large bulk is writ,
But sure thou art but a kilderkin° of wit.
Like mine, thy gentle numbers feebly creep;
Thy tragic Muse gives smiles, thy comic sleep.
With whate'er gall thou settest thyself to write,
200 Thy inoffensive satires never bite.
In thy felonious heart though venom lies,
It does but touch thy Irish° pen, and dies.
Thy genius calls thee not to purchase fame
In keen iambics,° but mild anagram.°
Leave writing plays, and choose for thy command
Some peaceful province in acrostic° land.
There thou mayst wings display and altars° raise,
And torture one poor word ten thousand ways.
Or, if thou wouldst thy different talents suit,
210 Set thy own songs, and sing them to thy lute.'
    He said: but his last words were scarcely heard;
For Bruce and Longvil° had a trap prepared,
And down they sent the yet declaiming bard.
Sinking he left his drugget robe behind,
Borne upwards by a subterranean wind.
The mantle fell to the young prophet's part,°
With double portion of his father's art.
1678?   1682

Religio Laici

This poem, cast in a form like that of the Horatian epistle, offers a defense of a moderate (layman's) Christianity against various enemies, particularly Deism in the part given below. Later in the poem Dryden goes on to consider the implications of Father Richard Simon's *Critical History of the Old Testament,* first published in 1678 and

'tis one way inclined; / It makes our actions lean on one side still, / And in all changes that way bends the will." But the invention of humors was Shadwell's own bias or humor: "I may say I ne'er produced a comedy that had not some natural humour in it not represented before, nor I hope never shall."
likeness to Jonson
tympany windiness that creates unnatural swelling; hence, vacuity
tun large wine cask
kilderkin a small cask, a quarter of a tun
Irish suggesting barbarity and want of skill, inherited from father Flecknoe
keen iambics sharp satiric verse
anagram rearrangement of letters to form a new word

acrostic a poem the first letters of whose lines spell a word or name
wings . . . altars in shaped poems like those of George Herbert ("Easter Wings" and "The Altar"). All these forms of "false wit" or verbal ingenuity without real function are summed up by Joseph Addison in *Spectator* Nos. 58–61 (1711).
Bruce and Longvil characters who perform this trapdoor trick on Sir Formal Trifle in *The Virtuoso*
prophet's part as with Elisha, who "took the mantle of Elijah that fell from him" so that the sons of the prophets say, "The spirit of Elijah does rest on Elisha" (II Kings 2:14–15); whereas Elijah ascends to heaven by a whirlwind, Flecknoe's descent produces a "subterranean" wind

four years later translated into English. That work cast doubt on the reliability of scriptural texts. Dryden defends the plain meaning of Scripture against those who impose their own forced interpretations upon it and against those who use its obscurities as a pretext for divisiveness. (In this he anticipates very clearly Swift's position in *A Tale of a Tub*.) In his attack upon Deism or natural religion, he asserts that reasoning from the evidence of nature to the existence and attributes of God is really less empirical than it claims. Deism, in his view, provides "only the faint remnants or dying flames of revealed religion" that have survived from earlier patriarchal times. "[W]e have not lifted up ourselves to God by the weak pinions of our reason, but he has been pleased to descend to us," and all natural religion is "no more than the twilight of revelation after the sun of it was set in the race of Noah." In the style of his poem, Dryden attempts to be "plain and natural and yet majestic," adopting the "legislative style" of the poet as "a kind of lawgiver." He concludes his preface: "A man is to be cheated into passion, but to be reasoned into truth."

From Religio Laici
or, a Layman's Faith

Dim as the borrowed beams of moon and stars°
To lonely, weary, wandering travelers,
Is Reason to the soul; and, as on high
Those rolling fires discover° but the sky,
Not light us here, so Reason's glimmering ray
Was lent, not to assure our doubtful way,
But guide us upward to a better day.
And as those nightly tapers disappear
When day's bright lord ascends our hemisphere;
10 So pale grows Reason at Religion's sight;
So dies, and so dissolves in supernatural light.°
Some few,° whose lamp shone brighter, have been led
From cause to cause, to nature's secret head;
And found that one first principle must be:
But what, or who, that universal He;
Whether some soul incompassing this ball,
Unmade, unmoved, yet making, moving all;°
Or various atoms' interfering dance°
Leapt into form (the noble work of chance);

stars planets
discover reveal
supernatural light The issue is whether man's reason is self-sufficient and needs no guide from revelation or whether it is totally fallible and can provide us with no guidance at all in matters of faith; the former position leads to Deism, the latter to Fideism. Dryden insists instead upon the continuity between the "borrowed beams" of reason and the "supernatural light" to which they lead us; the dissolution of reason's light is in a light of the same kind but

of greater intensity, made available through Christian revelation.
few those ancient philosophers who were led by reason to the idea of a universal God, but could not agree about his nature
Unmade . . . moving all the Platonic conception of the World Soul, with echoes of Aristotle's "unmoved mover"
interfering dance colliding movement, as in Epicurean theory about the chance formation of a cosmic order

20 Or this great all was from eternity;°
Not even the Stagirite himself could see,
And Epicurus guessed as well as he:
As blindly groped they for a future state;
As rashly judged of providence and fate:
But least of all could their endeavours find
What most concerned the good of humankind;
For happiness° was never to be found,
But vanished from 'em like enchanted ground.
One thought content° the good to be enjoyed;
30 This every little accident destroyed:
The wiser madmen did for virtue° toil,
A thorny or at best a barren soil;
In pleasure° some their glutton souls would steep,
But found their line too short, the well too deep,
And leaky vessels which no bliss could keep.
Thus anxious thoughts in endless circles° roll,
Without a centre where to fix the soul;
In this wild maze their vain endeavours end:
How can the less the greater comprehend?
40 Or finite reason reach Infinity?
For what could fathom God were more than He.
The Deist thinks he stands on firmer ground;
Cries: 'Eúreka! the mighty secret's° found:
God is that spring of good, supreme and best;
We, made to serve, and in that service blest.
If so, some rules of worship must be given,
Distributed alike to all by Heaven:
Else God were partial, and to some denied
The means his justice should for all provide.
50 This general worship is to *praise* and *pray,*
One part to borrow blessings, one to pay;
And when frail nature slides into offence,
The sacrifice for crimes is penitence.
Yet, since the effects of providence, we find,
Are variously dispensed to humankind;
That vice triumphs and virtue suffers here
(A brand that sovereign justice cannot bear),
Our reason prompts us to a future state,

from eternity a hypothesis offered by Aristotle (the "Stagirite" of the next line)
happiness The conflict about the highest good (or *summum bonum*) of man was a counterpart of the conflict in cosmic theories.
content presumably a Stoic doctrine of serenity, which could be attained only by refusing to be unsettled by accident or chance
virtue as in Aristotelian ethics
pleasure as in Epicurean doctrines
endless circles recalling the orbital movements of "moon and stars" in the first line, as opposed to their center in the sun; seen as a "wild maze"

without the ordering principle that controls them (the failure of the great philosophers of antiquity to reach agreement was often used as a Christian argument against the "wisdom of this world")
mighty secret's as in Archimedes' discovery (with the exclamation, "I have found it!") of the way to determine the purity of gold by weighing its displacement of water. In what follows Dryden sums up the principal articles of Deist doctrine as set forth by Lord Herbert of Cherbury in *De Veritate* (1624) and later works by him and others.

The last appeal from fortune and from fate:
60 Where God's all-righteous ways will be declared,
    The bad meet punishment, the good reward.'
       Thus man by his own strength to heaven would soar,
    And would not be obliged to God for more.
    Vain, wretched creature, how art thou misled
    To think thy wit these godlike notions bred!
    These truths are not the product of thy mind,
    But dropped from heaven, and of a nobler kind.
    Revealed Religion first informed thy sight,
    And Reason saw not, till Faith sprung the light.
70 Hence all thy natural worship takes the source:
    'Tis revelation what thou thinkest discourse.°
    Else, how comest thou to see these truths so clear,
    Which so obscure to heathens did appear?
    Not Plato these, nor Aristotle found;
    Nor he° whose wisdom oracles renowned.
    Hast thou a wit so deep, or so sublime,
    Or canst thou lower dive, or higher climb?°
    Canst thou, by Reason, more of Godhead know
    Than Plutarch, Seneca, or Cicero?°
80 Those giant wits, in happier ages born,
    (When arms and arts did Greece and Rome adorn)
    Knew no such system; no such piles° could raise
    Of natural worship, built on prayer and praise,
    To One Sole God:
    Nor did remorse to expiate sin prescribe,
    But slew their fellow creatures for a bribe:
    The guiltless victim groaned for their offence,
    And cruelty and blood was penitence.
    If sheep and oxen could atone for men,
90 Ah! at how cheap a rate the rich might sin!
    And great oppressors might Heaven's wrath beguile,
    By offering his own creatures for a spoil!
       Darest thou, poor worm, offend Infinity?
    And must the terms of peace be given by thee?
    Then thou art Justice in the last appeal:
    Thy easy God instructs thee to rebel;
    And, like a king remote and weak, must take
    What satisfaction thou art pleased to make.
       But if there be a power too just and strong
100 To wink at crimes and bear unpunished wrong;

discourse deliberative or discursive (as opposed to intuitive) reason
Nor he Socrates
Hast thou . . . higher climb Cf. Job 11:7–8: "Canst thou by searching find out God? canst thou find out the Almighty unto perfection? It is as high as heaven; what canst thou do? deeper than hell; what canst thou know?"

Plutarch, Seneca, or Cicero moving from Greek philosophers to those of Rome (where Plutarch, although Greek, lectured on philosophy) and of a later date (Plutarch, 46? A.D.–c. 120 A.D.; Seneca, c. 3 B.C.–65 A.D.; Cicero, 106 B.C.–43 B.C.)
piles structures

Look humbly upward, see his will disclose
The forfeit first and then the fine impose:
A mulct° thy poverty could never pay
Had not eternal wisdom found the way,
And with celestial wealth supplied thy store:
His justice makes the fine, his mercy quits the score.
See God descending in thy human frame;°
The offended suffering in the offender's name;
All thy misdeeds to him imputed see,
110 And all his righteousness devolved on thee.
       For granting we have sinned, and that the offence
Of man is made against Omnipotence,
Some price that bears proportion must be paid,
And infinite with infinite be weighed.
See then the Deist lost: remorse for vice,
Not paid; or paid, inadequate in price:
What farther means can Reason now direct,
Or what relief from human wit expect?
That shows us sick; and sadly are we sure
120 Still to be sick, till Heaven reveal the cure:
If then Heaven's will must needs be understood,
(Which must, if we want cure, and Heaven be good)
Let all records of will revealed be shown;
With Scripture all in equal balance thrown,
And our one sacred book will be that one.

                    .   .   .

       What then remains, but, waiving each extreme,
The tides of ignorance and pride to stem?
Neither so rich a treasure° to forego;
430 Nor proudly seek beyond our power to know:
Faith is not built on disquisitions vain;
The things we must believe are few and plain:
But since men will believe more than they need,
And every man will make himself a creed,
In doubtful questions 'tis the safest way
To learn what unsuspected ancients say;
For 'tis not likely we should higher soar
In search of heaven than all the Church before;
Nor can we be deceived, unless we see
440 The Scripture and the Fathers° disagree.
If, after all, they stand suspected still,
(For no man's faith depends upon his will)
'Tis some relief that points not clearly known

mulct fine
in thy human frame the doctrine of the Incarnation as necessary to that of Atonement, a teaching that is distinctively Christian, as are the doctrines of imputed sin and righteousness in ll. 109–10

treasure the Bible
Fathers the early Church theologians who wrote within a few centuries of the Apostles and were therefore considered purest in doctrine

Without much hazard may be let alone:
And after hearing what our Church can say,
If still our Reason runs another way,
That private Reason 'tis more just to curb
Than by disputes the public peace disturb.
For points obscure are of small use to learn,
450   But common quiet° is mankind's concern.
    Thus have I made my own opinions clear;
Yet neither praise expect, nor censure fear:
And this unpolished, rugged verse I chose,
As fittest for discourse and nearest prose;
For while from sacred truth I do not swerve,
Tom Sternhold's° or Tom Sha - - - ll's° rhymes will serve.

1682

To the Memory of Mr. Oldham°

Farewell, too little, and too lately known,
Whom I began to think and call my own:
For sure our souls were near allied, and thine
Cast in the same poetic mould with mine.
One common note on either lyre did strike,
And knaves and fools we both abhorred alike.
To the same goal did both our studies drive;
The last set out the soonest did arrive.
Thus Nisus° fell upon the slippery place,
10   While his young friend performed and won the race.
O early ripe! to thy abundant store
What could advancing age have added more?
It might (what nature never gives the young)
Have taught the numbers° of thy native tongue.
But satire needs not those, and wit will shine
Through the harsh cadence of a rugged line:
A noble error, and but seldom made,
When poets are by too much force betrayed.
Thy generous fruits, though gathered ere their prime,
20   Still showed a quickness;° and maturing time

---

common quiet Cf. Richard Hooker, *Of the Laws
of Ecclesiastical Polity* (1593–97), Preface, VI.
6: "So that of peace and quietness there is not
any way possible unless the probable voice of
every entire society or body politic overrule all
private of like nature in the same body."
Tom Sternhold's with John Hopkins author of
the metrical version of the Psalms completed in
1562
Tom Sha - - - ll's for Shadwell, see the Headnote to *Mac Flecknoe*
To the Memory of Mr. Oldham John Oldham
(1652–83) first attracted Rochester's attention
with his manuscript poems and after some years
of teaching school came to London in 1681.

His *Satires upon the Jesuits* and other works had
won him a reputation as a fiery writer of both
odes and satires before he met Dryden, probably
two years before his early death. By the time
Dryden, who was twenty years older, wrote this
poem, he had achieved his own reputation as a
satirist with *Absalom and Achitophel.*
Nisus who with his young friend Euryalus took
part in foot races at the funeral of Anchises;
when Nisus slipped in the blood of a sacrifice,
Euryalus won the race (*Aeneid* V.315 ff.)
numbers smoothness and control of verse
quickness vitality; playing upon the victory in
the race as well

But mellows what we write to the dull sweets of rhyme.
Once more, hail and farewell; farewell, thou young,
But ah too short, Marcellus° of our tongue;
Thy brows with ivy, and with laurels° bound;
But fate and gloomy night encompass thee around.

1684

Lines on Milton°

Three poets, in three distant ages born,
Greece, Italy, and England did adorn.
The first in loftiness of thought surpassed,
The next in majesty, in both the last:
The force of Nature could no farther go;
To make a third, she joined the former two.

1688

To the Pious Memory of the Accomplished Young Lady, Mrs. Anne Killigrew

Excellent in the Two Sister-Arts of Poesy and Painting, An Ode°

I

Thou youngest virgin-daughter° of the skies,
Made in the last promotion of the blest;
Whose palms,° new plucked from paradise,
In spreading branches more sublimely rise,
Rich with immortal green above the rest:
Whether,° adopted to some neighbouring star,
Thou rollest above us, in thy wandering race,
  Or, in procession fixed and regular,
  Moved with the heavens' majestic pace;

Marcellus the nephew and potential successor of the emperor Augustus; whose death at age twenty Virgil mourned in *Aeneid* VI.860 ff.
ivy . . . laurels the wreaths that crown the successful poet
fate and gloomy night Dryden retains a Roman idiom throughout, both in allusions and in tone; as a matter of fact, this line is a paraphrase of Virgil's line about Marcellus, VI.866
Lines on Milton first published in Tonson's illustrated edition of *Paradise Lost;* referring to Homer and Virgil as the great predecessors
Ode a free Pindaric ode, in the manner given currency by Abraham Cowley, a vehicle of sublime feeling such as could not be contained in regular forms and might be found not only in Pindar but also in the biblical prophets. This poem was praised by Dr. Johnson as "undoubtedly the noblest ode that our language ever

has produced," the first part flowing "with a torrent of enthusiasm" (*Life of Dryden*).
virgin-daughter Anne Killigrew (1660–85), maid of honor to the Duchess of York, both poetess and painter, who died of smallpox at the age of 25; here she is seen promoted from her candidacy on earth (l. 21) to a place in heaven, in a way that fuses the elevation of the classical hero to the stars with that of the Christian hero to the company of saints
palms emblems of victory and rejoicing, as in Christ's entry into Jerusalem
Whether Dryden professes uncertainty (in the manner of Virgil) as to whether Anne has been placed among the nearer and lower stars (i.e. planets) as an angelic intelligence to guide their course; among the remoter fixed stars in their higher sphere; or, highest of all, among the seraphim about the throne of God.

10   Or, called to more superior bliss,
Thou treadest, with seraphims, the vast abyss:
Whatever happy region is thy place,
Cease thy celestial song a little space;
(Thou wilt have time enough for hymns divine,
    Since heaven's eternal year is thine.)
Here then a mortal Muse thy praise rehearse,°
        In no ignoble verse;
But such as thy own voice did practise here,
When thy first fruits of poesy were given,
20 To make thyself a welcome inmate there;
    While yet a young probationer,
    And candidate of heaven.

        II
    If by traduction° came thy mind,
    Our wonder is the less to find
A soul so charming from a stock° so good;
Thy father was transfused into thy blood:
So wert thou born into the tuneful strain,
(An early, rich, and inexhausted vein.)
    But if thy preëxisting soul°
30 Was formed, at first, with myriads more,
It did through all the mighty poets roll
    Who Greek or Latin laurels wore
And was that Sappho last, which once it was before.
If so, then cease thy flight, O *heaven-born mind!*
Thou hast no dross to purge° from thy rich ore;
Nor can thy soul a fairer mansion find,
Than was the beauteous frame she left behind:
Return, to fill or mend° the choir of thy celestial kind.

        III
    May we presume to say that at thy birth
40 New joy was sprung in heaven, as well as here on earth?
    For sure the milder planets did combine
    On thy auspicious horoscope° to shine,
    And even the most malicious were in trine.
    Thy brother-angels at thy birth
        Strung each his lyre and tuned it high,

---

rehearse repeat
traduction begotten like her body by her father
(one possible origin of an immortal soul), and
thus inheriting his poetic gifts
stock Dr. Henry Killigrew, chaplain to Charles
I and a loyal supporter of his son, author of a
tragedy praised by Ben Jonson
preëxisting soul alluding to the Pythagorean
doctrine of metempsychosis, that souls go from
one body to another; in this case inhabiting first
the body of the splendid Greek poet Sappho

and at last returning to that form in the modern
Sappho, Anne Killigrew
dross to purge Plato, in the *Timaeus,* suggests
that the soul undergoes repeated incarnation as
a punishment until it is purged of evil or worldly
appetites.
mend improve, increase
auspicious horoscope favorable because of its
control by "milder" planets, with even the least
favorable planets "in trine" (120 degrees distant from each other) and therefore benign

That all the people of the sky
Might know a poetess was born on earth.
And then, if ever, mortal ears
Had heard the music of the spheres!°
50 And if no clustering swarm of bees°
On thy sweet mouth distilled their golden dew,
'Twas that such vulgar miracles
Heaven had no leisure to renew:
For all the blest fraternity of love
Solemnized there thy birth and kept thy holiday above.

IV

O gracious God! how far have we
Profaned thy heavenly gift of poesy!
Made prostitute and profligate the Muse,
Debased to each obscene and impious use,
60 Whose harmony was first ordained above
For tongues of angels, and for hymns of love!
O wretched we! why were we hurried down
    This lubric° and adulterate age,
(Nay, added fat° pollutions of our own,)
    To increase the steaming° ordures of the stage?
What can we say to excuse our *second fall?*
Let this thy *vestal,°* Heaven, atone for all:
Her Arethusian° stream remains unsoiled,
Unmixed with foreign filth, and undefiled;
70 Her wit was more than man, her innocence a child!

V

Art° she had none, yet wanted° none;
For nature did that want supply:
So rich in treasures of her own,
She might our boasted stores defy:
Such noble vigour did her verse adorn
That it seemed borrowed, where 'twas only born.
Her morals too were in her bosom bred,
    By great examples daily fed,
What in the best of books, her father's life, she read.
80 And to be read herself she need not fear;
Each test, and every light, her Muse will bear,

music of the spheres The harmony produced by
the movement of the heavenly bodies was
thought to be inaudible to men since the Fall,
except perhaps at the birth of Christ.
bees such as gathered on the lips of the infant
Plato, according to legend, and prophesied his
sweetness of speech
lubric lubricious, lewd
fat gross, indecent

steaming reeking
vestal virgin, like those who served the Roman
goddess Vesta
Arethusian named for the nymph whom Diana
changed to a fountain to save from violation by
the river god Alpheus; cf. Milton, *Lycidas,* l. 85
Art "borrowed" (l. 76) as opposed to native
"vigour"; "nurture" as opposed to "nature"
wanted needed

Though Epictetus with his lamp° were there.
Even love (for love sometimes her Muse expressed)
Was but a lambent° flame which played about her breast,
Light as the vapours of a morning dream:
So cold herself, whilst she such warmth expressed,
'Twas Cupid bathing in Diana's stream.

VI

Born to the spacious empire of the Nine,°
One would have thought she should have been content
90 To manage well that mighty government;
But what can young ambitious souls confine?
    To the next realm she stretched her sway,
    For *painture* near adjoining lay,
A plenteous province, and alluring prey.
    A *chamber of dependences*° was framed,
(As conquerors will never want pretence,
    When armed, to justify the offence,)
And the whole fief in right of poetry she claimed.
The country open lay without defence;
100 For poets frequent inroads there had made,
    And perfectly could represent
    The shape, the face, with every lineament;
And all the large demains° which the *Dumb Sister*° swayed
    All bowed beneath her government;
    Received in triumph wheresoe'er she went.
Her pencil° drew whate'er her soul designed,
And oft the happy draught surpassed the image in her mind.
    The sylvan scenes° of herds and flocks,
    And fruitful plains and barren rocks,
110 Of shallow brooks that flowed so clear
    The bottom did the top appear;
    Of deeper too and ampler floods,
    Which, as in mirrors, showed the woods;
    Of lofty trees, with sacred shades,
    And perspectives of pleasant glades,
    Where nymphs of brightest form appear,
    And shaggy satyrs standing near,
    Which them at once admire and fear:
    The ruins too of some majestic piece,
120 Boasting the power of ancient Rome, or Greece,

Epictetus . . . lamp i.e. it underwent the severest moral scrutiny, such as that of the Stoic philosopher of the 1st century A.D.
lambent softly flickering, as opposed to "wanton" or passionate
Nine the Muses of writing, music, and dance
chamber of dependences a device used by Louis XIV to annex new territory, inducing (by threatened force) local authorities to set up

"chambers" which might cede the lands to Louis through fictions drawn from feudal claims (thus "fief" in l. 98)
demains domains
Dumb Sister Painting
sylvan scenes The following landscapes "conquered" by Anne were the typical subjects of 17th-century painters throughout Europe.

Whose statues, friezes, columns broken lie,
And, though defaced, the wonder of the eye:
What nature, art, bold fiction e'er durst frame,
Her forming hand gave feature to the name.
So strange a concourse ne'er was seen before,
But when the peopled ark the whole creation bore.

VII

The scene then changed: with bold erected look
Our martial king° the sight with reverence strook;
For, not content to express his outward part,
130   Her hand called out the image of his heart:
His warlike mind, his soul devoid of fear,
His high-designing thoughts were figured there,
As when, by magic, ghosts are made appear.
Our phoenix queen° was portrayed too so bright,
Beauty alone could beauty take so right:°
Her dress, her shape, her matchless grace,
Were all observed, as well as heavenly face.
With such a peerless majesty she stands,
As in that day she took the crown° from sacred hands;
140   Before a train of heroines was seen,
In beauty foremost, as in rank the queen.
Thus nothing to her genius was denied,
    But like a ball of fire,° the further thrown,
    Still with a greater blaze she shone,
And her bright soul broke out on every side.
What next she had designed, Heaven only knows;
To such immoderate growth her conquest rose
That fate alone its progress could oppose.

VIII

Now all those charms, that blooming grace,
150   The well-proportioned shape and beauteous face,
Shall never more be seen by mortal eyes:
In earth the much-lamented virgin lies!
    Not wit nor piety could fate prevent;
    Nor was the cruel destiny content
    To finish all the murder at a blow,
    To sweep at once her life and beauty too;
But, like a hardened felon, took a pride
    To work more mischievously slow,
And plundered first, and then destroyed.
160   O double sacrilege on things divine,

martial king James II
queen Mary of Modena, wife of James II, to whose beauty Dryden had earlier paid tribute
take so right represent so well

crown Mary was crowned by the Archbishop of Canterbury on April 23, 1685.
ball of fire skyrocket

To rob the relic, and deface° the shrine!
    But thus Orinda° died:
Heaven, by the same disease, did both translate;
As equal were their souls, so equal was their fate.

IX

    Meantime her warlike brother° on the seas
    His waving streamers to the winds displays,
And vows for his return, with vain devotion, pays.
      Ah, generous youth, that wish forbear,
      The winds too soon will waft thee here!
170   Slack all thy sails, and fear to come,
Alas, thou knowst not, thou art wrecked at home!
No more shalt thou behold thy sister's face,
Thou hast already had her last embrace.
But look aloft, and if thou kennst from far
Among the Pleiads° a new kindled star;
If any sparkles than the rest more bright,
'Tis she that shines in that propitious light.

X

    When in mid-air the golden trump° shall sound,
    To raise the nations° under ground;
180   When in the Valley of Jehoshaphat
The judging God° shall close the book of fate,
    And there the last assizes° keep
    For those who wake and those who sleep;
    When rattling bones together fly
    From the four corners of the sky;
When sinews o'er the skeletons are spread,
Those clothed with flesh, and life inspires the dead;
    The sacred poets first shall hear the sound,
    And foremost from the tomb shall bound,
190 For they are covered with the lightest ground;
And straight, with inborn vigour, on the wing,
Like mounting larks, to the new morning sing.
There thou, sweet saint, before the choir shalt go,
As harbinger of heaven, the way to show,
The way which thou so well hast learned below.

1685

---

deface referring, as in lines above, to the disfigurement caused by smallpox
Orinda Katherine Philips (1631–64), the "Matchless Orinda," another latter-day Sappho
brother Henry Killigrew, naval captain and later admiral (d. 1712)
Pleiads the seven stars in Taurus, whose name was given to groups of poets, notably the French *Pléiade* of the 16th century, which included Ronsard and Du Bellay
trump "for the trumpet shall sound, and the

dead be raised incorruptible" (I Corinthians 15:52)
nations "I will also gather all nations, and will bring them down into the valley of Jehoshaphat" (Joel 3:2)
judging God "Jehoshaphat" means "Jehovah judges."
assizes court session, i.e. the Last Judgment, for both living and dead, the latter resurrected in body as well as soul to meet their judgment

A Song for St. Cecilia's Day,° 1687

I

From harmony, from heavenly harmony
   This universal frame° began:
   When Nature underneath a heap°
      Of jarring atoms lay,
      And could not heave her head,
The tuneful voice was heard from high:
      'Arise, ye more than dead.'
Then cold, and hot, and moist, and dry,
   In order to their stations° leap,
      And Music's power obey.
From harmony, from heavenly harmony
   This universal frame began:
     From harmony to harmony
Through all the compass of the notes it ran,
The diapason° closing full in Man.

II

What passion cannot Music raise and quell!°
   When Jubal° struck the corded shell,
   His listening brethren stood around,
   And, wondering, on their faces fell
   To worship that celestial sound.
Less than a god they thought there could not dwell
   Within the hollow of that shell
   That spoke so sweetly and so well.
What passion cannot Music raise and quell!

St. Cecilia's Day The celebration of the patroness of music on November 22 went back to late 16th-century France but began in England in 1683, when the Musical Society commissioned annual odes from distinguished poets and composers. Written for musical performance and to celebrate the power of music, these tended to draw on two major themes: (1) the *harmonia mundi*, or *musica mundans,* the Pythagorean and Platonic tradition that the world was designed in harmonic intervals (thus reconciling the music of the spheres in the celestial bodies with the Christian heavenly choir or the "morning stars" that "sang together" in Job 38:6–7); and (2) the *musica humana* or moral power of music to move its hearers and arouse in them varying states of the soul (each instrument best evoking a distinct emotion). This ode is the first of two Dryden wrote for such an occasion (the second, *Alexander's Feast,* followed ten years later); it was first set to music by the Italian composer, G. B. Draghi (who served Mary of Modena), and more tellingly later by Handel in 1739.
frame structure of the universe, the cosmos drawn from the chaos of "jarring atoms"
heap Nature seen as the physical world, immersed in primal chaos as imagined by the Epicureans, and notably Lucretius (see below, Dryden's version of portions of the third book of *De Rerum Natura*). Significantly, however, order exists potentially even in chaos and emerges from it not by chance but by divine fiat; here the Word as conveyed in a "tuneful voice."
stations, i.e. the four elements are assigned positions by an ordering principle, and they form a Chain of Being, each creature linked to every other in necessary sequence, creation representing the fullest of harmonies, in which all possible notes are heard
diapason the octave cadence, the consonance which is the proper close for the act of creation
raise and quell moving from the *musica mundans* to the *musica humana* and showing a progression, in successive stanzas, from martial and erotic passion to "holy love"
Jubal "the father of all such as handle the harp and organ" (Genesis 4:21), conceived as recognizing musical harmonies in the anvil blows at his brother's forge, or like Apollo finding an empty tortoise shell strung with three dry sinews, which provided him with a "corded" (but also "chorded") instrument

III

The Trumpet's loud clangour
    Excites us to arms,
With shrill notes of anger
    And mortal alarms.
    The double double double beat
30   Of the thundering Drum
Cries: 'Hark! the foes come;
Charge, charge, 'tis too late to retreat.'

IV

The soft complaining Flute
In dying notes discovers
The woes of hopeless lovers,
Whose dirge is whispered by the warbling Lute.

V

Sharp Violins° proclaim
Their jealous pangs, and desperation,
Fury, frantic indignation,
40   Depth of pains, and height of passion,
    For the fair, disdainful dame.

VI

But O! what art can teach,
What human voice can reach,
The sacred Organ's praise?
Notes inspiring holy love,
Notes that wing their heavenly ways
To mend the choirs above.

VII

Orpheus could lead the savage race;
And trees unrooted left their place,
50   Sequacious of the lyre;°
But bright Cecilia raised the wonder higher:
When to her Organ vocal breath° was given,
An angel heard, and straight appeared,
    Mistaking earth for heaven.

GRAND CHORUS

As from the power of sacred lays°
    The spheres began to move,

Sharp Violins Recently introduced into England, they seemed so in contrast to the duller viols.
lyre Orpheus, who drew beasts and trees and stones after him, figured in traditional pagan myth as the power of music; here he is surpassed by Cecilia, who can draw men to heaven (as traditionally she converted her pagan lover Valerianus to love of God) or an angel down to earth.

vocal breath suggesting, apart from its use of pipes, the power of the organ to sustain notes like the human voice and therefore its superiority (as Cecilia's instrument) to Orpheus' lyre
sacred lays the chorus of praise as both the initial ordering power of harmony and its achieved form, instituted in the music of the spheres

And sung the great Creator's praise
To all the blest above;
So, when the last and dreadful hour
This crumbling pageant° shall devour,
The Trumpet shall be heard on high,
The dead shall live, the living die,
And Music shall untune° the sky.

1687

Alexander's Feast

or, The Power of Music;°
An Ode in Honour of St. Cecilia's Day

I

'Twas at the royal feast for Persia won°
    By Philip's warlike son:
Aloft in awful state
The godlike hero sate
    On his imperial throne:
His valiant peers were placed around;
Their brows with roses and with myrtles° bound:
    (So should desert in arms be crowned.)
The lovely Thais,° by his side,
Sat like a blooming Eastern bride
In flower of youth and beauty's pride.
    Happy, happy, happy pair!
    None but the brave,
    None but the brave,
    None but the brave deserves the fair.

CHORUS
Happy, happy, happy pair!
None but the brave,
None but the brave,
None but the brave deserves the fair.

crumbling pageant the cosmos; with probably a reference to the performance itself, as in the masque or in Prospero's remarks on "this insubstantial pageant" (Shakespeare, *The Tempest* IV.i.155); with the trumpeter of the next line placed literally above the stage as he represents the "last trump" (cf. "Killigrew" ode, l. 178) and with the players about to "untune" (slacken the strings of) their instruments.
Music . . . untune the trumpet, but also the power of harmony now seen as transcending the created world
Alexander's Feast . . . Music This ode, written ten years later than the earlier "St. Cecilia" ode, devotes itself to the theme of *musica humana* announced in the subtitle and embodies it in a dramatic action rather than a series of instrumental solos. Insofar as Timotheus, the mythical court musician of Alexander the Great, had the power to conjure roles and myths as well as pure emotions, the ode becomes a celebration of poetry as well as of music. The original musical setting (now lost) was composed by Jeremiah Clarke, but the ode was reset by Handel in 1736.
Persia won Alexander, son of Philip of Macedon, celebrating the fall of Persepolis and the defeat of Darius III (331 B.C.)
roses . . . myrtles symbols of love and sensuality
Thais the Athenian courtesan

II

20   Timotheus, placed on high
     Amid the tuneful choir,
     With flying fingers touched the lyre:
   The trembling notes ascend the sky,
              And heavenly joys inspire.
   The song began from Jove,
   Who left his blissful seats above,
   (Such is the power of mighty love.)
   A dragon's fiery form belied the god:
   Sublime on radiant spires° he rode,
30   When he to fair Olympia° pressed;
     And while he sought her snowy breast:
   Then, round her slender waist he curled,
   And stamped an image of himself, a sovereign of the world.°
   The listening crowd admire° the lofty sound;
   'A present deity,' they shout around;
   'A present deity,' the vaulted roofs rebound:
     With ravished ears
     The monarch hears,
     Assumes the god,
40   Affects to nod,
   And seems to shake the spheres.°

CHORUS

With ravished ears
The monarch hears,
Assumes the god,
Affects to nod,
And seems to shake the spheres.

III

   The praise of Bacchus° then the sweet musician sung,
     Of Bacchus ever fair and ever young:
     'The jolly god in triumph comes;
50   Sound the trumpets; beat the drums;
       Flushed with a purple grace
       He shows his honest° face:
   Now give the hautboys° breath; he comes, he comes.
     Bacchus, ever fair and young,
      Drinking joys did first ordain;

radiant spires shining coils; cf. Milton, *Paradise Lost* IX. 496–503 for the Serpent's motion "erect / Amidst his circling spires"
Olympia Olympias, the mother of Alexander, who claimed that her son was born not of Philip but of a supernatural serpent, here represented as Jove in a typical amorous disguise (that of a dragon), providing grounds for a belief in Alexander's divine origin to which Alexander readily succumbs

world as was Jove of the gods
admire wonder at, are awed by
seems . . . spheres Alexander is overcome by the fantasy of his own divinity and acts up to the role, convinced that his own nod, like Jove's, "shakes heavens's axles" (*Aeneid*, Dryden trans., X.154).
Bacchus god of wine and revelry
honest glorious
hautboys oboes

Bacchus' blessings are a treasure,
Drinking is the soldier's pleasure:
   Rich the treasure,
   Sweet the pleasure,
60   Sweet is pleasure after pain.'

     CHORUS
Bacchus' blessings are a treasure,
Drinking is the soldier's pleasure:
   Rich the treasure,
   Sweet the pleasure,
Sweet is pleasure after pain.

    IV
Soothed with the sound, the king grew vain;
   Fought all his battles o'er again;
And thrice he routed all his foes; and thrice he slew the slain.
The master° saw the madness rise;
70 His glowing cheeks, his ardent eyes;
And, while he heaven and earth defied,
Changed his hand and checked his pride.
   He chose a mournful Muse,
   Soft pity to infuse:
He sung Darius great and good,
   By too severe a fate,
Fallen, fallen, fallen, fallen,
   Fallen from his high estate,
   And weltering in his blood;°
80 Deserted, at his utmost need,
By those his former bounty fed;
On the bare earth exposed he lies,
With not a friend to close his eyes.
With downcast looks the joyless victor sate,
   Revolving in his altered soul
   The various turns of chance below;
And, now and then, a sigh he stole;
   And tears began to flow.

     CHORUS
Revolving in his altered soul
90   *The various turns of chance below;*
And, now and then, a sigh he stole;
   And tears began to flow.

master Timotheus, as master of the master of
the world, turning "his hand" (1. 72) to another
tune in order to subdue Alexander's mad "pride"
to "soft pity" (1. 74)
blood attacked by his own followers

V

The mighty master smiled, to see
That love was in the next degree:
'Twas but° a kindred sound to move,
For pity melts the mind to love.
    Softly sweet, in Lydian° measures,
    Soon he soothed his soul to pleasures.
    'War,' he sung, 'is toil and trouble;
100   Honour but an empty bubble.
      Never ending, still beginning,
    Fighting still, and still destroying,
      If the world be worth thy winning,
    Think, O think it worth enjoying.
    Lovely Thais sits beside thee,
    Take the good the gods provide thee.'
The many rend the skies with loud applause;
So Love was crowned, but Music won the cause.°
    The prince, unable to conceal his pain,
110   Gazed on the fair
      Who caused his care,
    And sighed and looked, sighed and looked,
    Sighed and looked, and sighed again:
At length, with love and wine at once oppressed,
The vanquished victor sunk upon her breast.

CHORUS

The prince, unable to conceal his pain,
    Gazed on the fair
    Who caused his care,
    And sighed and looked, sighed and looked,
120   *Sighed and looked, and sighed again:*
At length, with love and wine at once oppressed,
The vanquished victor sunk upon her breast.

VI

Now strike the golden lyre again:
A louder yet, and yet a louder strain.
Break his bands of sleep asunder,
And rouse him, like a rattling peal of thunder.
    Hark, hark, the horrid° sound
      Has raised up his head:
      As awaked from the dead,
130   And amazed, he stares around.
'Revenge, revenge!' Timotheus cries,

'Twas but i.e. it required only
Lydian one of the "soft or drinking modes,"
according to Plato; cf. Milton, *L'Allegro,* ll.
136–44

Music . . . cause insisting upon the power of
music to control the imagination through the
passions
horrid rough, terrible

'See the Furies° arise!
See the snakes that they rear,
How they hiss in their hair,
And the sparkles that flash from their eyes!
Behold a ghastly band,
Each a torch in his hand!
Those are Grecian ghosts that in battle were slain,
And unburied remain
140   Inglorious on the plain:
Give the vengeance due
To the valiant crew.
Behold how they toss their torches on high,
How they point to the Persian abodes,
And glittering temples of their hostile gods!'
The princes applaud with a furious joy;
And the king seized a flambeau° with zeal to destroy;
Thais led the way,
To light him to his prey,
150   And, like another Helen, fired another Troy.°

CHORUS

And the king seized a flambeau with zeal to destroy;
Thais led the way,
To light him to his prey,
And, like another Helen, fired another Troy.

VII

Thus, long ago,
Ere heaving bellows learned to blow,
While organs yet were mute;
Timotheus, to his breathing flute,
And sounding lyre,
160   Could swell the soul to rage or kindle soft desire.
At last, divine Cecilia came,
Inventress of the vocal frame;°
The sweet enthusiast,° from her sacred store,
Enlarged the former narrow bounds,
And added length° to solemn sounds,
With nature's mother wit and arts unknown before.
Let old Timotheus yield the prize,
Or both divide the crown;

Furies the Erinyes, the three female spirits with snaky hair who punished those guilty of unavenged crimes, here demanding vengeance for Alexander's dead soldiers
flambeau torch
another Troy As Helen's passion for Paris led the Greeks to burn Troy, so Thais' zeal leads them to burn the palace of Persepolis.
vocal frame organ
enthusiast here used of one genuinely inspired by God rather than one suffering from that delusion
length through the organ's power to sustain notes

He raised a mortal to the skies;°
170   She drew an angel down.°

GRAND CHORUS
At last, divine Cecilia came,
  Inventress of the vocal frame;
The sweet enthusiast, from her sacred store,
  Enlarged the former narrow bounds,
  And added length to solemn sounds,
With nature's mother wit and arts unknown before.
  Let old Timotheus yield the prize,
    Or both divide the crown;
  He raised a mortal to the skies;
180   She drew an angel down.
1697

Translations

Dryden's translations indicate the variety of his uses of the heroic couplet, and they are often splendid poetry in their own right. His translation of a portion of Lucretius' *De Rerum Natura* as well as the opening of Juvenal's Sixth Satire is given here. For other translations by Dryden, see the passage from Juvenal in the section The Urban Scene and the tale of Baucis and Philemon from Ovid's *Metamorphoses* in the section The Mock Form.

The translation from Lucretius is interesting as an example of Epicurean thought, so widely revived in the seventeenth century and particularly in Restoration England. Lucretius' great didactic poem seeks to free man from superstitious fear by presenting a view of life grounded in the theory of atoms, i.e. accounting for all nature by the chance combinations of atoms. The third book, from which this passage is taken, insists upon the mortality of the soul and tries to free man of the idea that death is an experience rather than its absence. Lucretius is one of the chief transmitters of a naturalistic view of the world and of man, one which repudiates a view of divine creation and of supernatural ends and exalts pleasure—not necessarily a gross or merely physical one—as the only true end of man. Epicurean thought like that of Lucretius is constantly contrasted by eighteenth-century writers with Stoic thought, which seems much closer to Christianity because of its belief in a rational natural order that in turn reflects man's reason, a reason most fully expressed in its conquest of passion and its intuitive recognition of duty to others.

Dryden explains in a preface that he put aside his "natural diffidence and skepticism for a while, to take up that dogmatic way" of Lucretius; but he warns against Lucretius' doctrines and defends the immortality of the soul. More interesting is his discussion of the style and tone of Lucretius in the passage that follows.

The section from Juvenal's Sixth Satire is a wonderfully urbane and amused account of a primitivistic vision.

---

raised . . . skies caused Alexander to assume divine stature and rage, however delusively (thus music as a natural power)
drew . . . down as in the "St. Cecilia" ode, ll.

53–54, brought the full power of harmony, in the form of a guardian angel, to earth (thus music as a heavenly power)

[On Lucretius]

. . . If I am not mistaken, the distinguishing character of Lucretius (I mean of his soul and genius) is a certain kind of noble pride, and positive assertion of his opinions. He is everywhere confident of his own reason, and assuming an absolute command not only over his vulgar reader, but even his patron Memmius. For he is always bidding him attend, as if he had the rod over him; and using a magisterial authority, while he instructs him. From his time to ours, I know none so like him, as our poet and philosopher of Malmesbury. This is that perpetual dictatorship which is exercised by Lucretius; who though often in the wrong, yet seems to deal *bona fide* with his reader, and tells him nothing but what he thinks; in which plain sincerity, I believe he differs from our Hobbes, who could not but be convinced, or at least doubt of some eternal truths which he has opposed. But for Lucretius, he seems to disdain all manner of replies, and is so confident of his cause that he is beforehand with his antagonists; urging for them whatever he imagined they could say, and leaving them as he supposes, without an objection for the future. All this too, with so much scorn and indignation, as if he were assured of the triumph before he entered into the lists. From this sublime and daring genius of his, it must of necessity come to pass that his thoughts must be masculine, full of argumentation, and that sufficiently warm. From the same fiery temper proceeds the loftiness of his expressions, and the perpetual torrent of his verse, where the barrenness of his subject does not too much constrain the quickness of his fancy. For there is no doubt to be made, but that he could have been everywhere as poetical, as he is in his descriptions, and in the moral part of his philosophy, if he had not aimed more to instruct in his System of Nature, than to delight. But he was bent upon making Memmius a materialist, and teaching him to defy an invisible power. In short, he was so much an atheist that he forgot sometimes to be a poet. . . . [From Preface to *Sylvae*, 1685]

Lucretius: De Rerum Natura

From *The Latter Part of the Third Book*
Against the Fear of Death

What has this bugbear death to frighten man,
If souls can die, as well as bodies can?
For, as before our birth we felt no pain,
When Punic arms infested land and main,°
When heaven and earth were in confusion hurled,
For the debated empire of the world,
Which awed with dreadful expectation lay,
Sure to be slaves, uncertain who should sway:
So, when our mortal frame shall be disjoined,
10   The lifeless lump uncoupled from the mind,
From sense of grief and pain we shall be free;

Punic arms . . . main The three Punic wars between Rome and Carthage took place in 264– 241 B.C., 218–201 B.C., and 149–146 B.C. Lucretius lived from c. 94 to 55 B.C.

We shall not feel, because we shall not *be*.
Though earth in seas, and seas in heaven were lost,
We should not move, we only should be tossed.
Nay, even suppose when we have suffered fate,
The soul could feel in her divided state,
What's that to us? for we are only we
While souls and bodies in one frame agree.
Nay, though our atoms should revolve by chance,
20 And matter leap into the former dance;
Though time our life and motion could restore,
And make our bodies what they were before,
What gain to us would all this bustle bring?
The new-made man would be another thing.
When once an interrupting pause is made,
That individual being is decayed.
We, who are dead and gone, shall bear no part
In all the pleasures, nor shall feel the smart
Which to that other mortal shall accrue,
30 Whom of our matter time shall mould anew.

· · ·

And therefore if a man bemoan his lot,
50 That after death his mouldering limbs shall rot,
Or flames or jaws of beasts devour his mass,
Know, he's an unsincere, unthinking ass.
A secret sting remains within his mind;
The fool is to his own cast offals° kind.
He boasts no sense can after death remain,
Yet makes himself a part of life again,
As if some other He could feel the pain.
If, while he live, this thought molest his head,
What wolf or vulture shall devour me dead?
60 He wastes his days in idle grief, nor can
Distinguish 'twixt the body and the man;
But thinks himself can still himself survive;
And, what when dead he feels not, feels alive.
Then he repines that he was born to die,
Nor knows in death there is no other He,
No living He remains his grief to vent,
And o'er his senseless carcass to lament.
If after death 'tis painful to be torn
By birds and beasts, then why not so to burn;
70 Or, drenched in floods of honey, to be soaked;
Embalmed, to be at once preserved and choked;
Or on an airy mountain's top to lie,
Exposed to cold and heaven's inclemency;
Or crowded in a tomb to be oppressed

offals carrion, waste

With monumental marble on thy breast?
  But to be snatched from all thy household joys,
From thy chaste wife, and thy dear prattling boys,
Whose little arms about thy legs are cast,
And climbing for a kiss prevent their mother's haste,
80 Inspiring secret pleasure through thy breast—
All these shall be no more: thy friends oppressed
Thy care and courage now no more shall free;
'Ah wretch!' thou criest, 'ah! miserable me!
One woeful day sweeps children, friends, and wife,
And all the brittle blessings of my life!'
Add one thing more, and all thou sayest is true;
Thy want and wish of them is vanished too:
Which, well considered, were a quick relief
To all thy vain imaginary grief.
90 For thou shalt sleep and never wake again,
And quitting life, shalt quit thy living pain.
But we, thy friends, shall all those sorrows find,
Which in forgetful death thou leavest behind;
No time shall dry our tears, nor drive thee from our mind.
The worst that can befall thee, measured right,
Is a sound slumber, and a long good-night.

. . .

What horror seest thou in that quiet state?
180 What bugbear dreams to fright thee after fate?
No ghost, no goblins, that still passage keep;
But all is there serene, in that eternal sleep.
For all the dismal tales that poets tell
Are verified on earth, and not in hell.
No Tantalus° looks up with fearful eye,
Or dreads the impending rock to crush him from on high;
But fear of chance on earth disturbs our easy hours,
Or vain imagined wrath of vain imagined powers.
No Tityus° torn by vultures lies in hell;
190 Nor could the lobes of his rank liver swell
To that prodigious mass for their eternal meal:
Not though his monstrous bulk had covered o'er
Nine spreading acres, or nine thousand more;
Not though the globe of earth had been the giant's floor:
Nor in eternal torments could he lie,
Nor could his corpse sufficient food supply.
But he's the Tityus, who by love oppressed,
Or tyrant passion preying on his breast,

Tantalus Punished for stealing the food of the gods, he is usually pictured as immersed in water up to his chin with fruit hanging over his head, but both water and fruit receding as he tries to assuage his thirst and hunger; Lucretius follows Pindar in seeing his punishment as a rock poised threateningly over his head but never falling.
Tityus punished for assaulting Leto by having two vultures forever tearing at his liver; as a Titan he was supposed to cover nine acres of ground

And ever-anxious thoughts, is robbed of rest.
200   The Sisyphus° is he, whom noise and strife
Seduce from all the soft retreats of life,
To vex the government, disturb the laws:
Drunk with the fumes of popular applause,
He courts the giddy crowd to make him great,°
And sweats and toils in vain to mount the sovereign seat.
For still to aim at power, and still to fail,
Ever to strive, and never to prevail,
What is it, but, in reason's true account,
To heave the stone against the rising mount?
210   Which urged, and laboured, and forced up with pain,
Recoils, and rolls impetuous down, and smokes along° the plain.
Then still to treat thy ever-craving mind
With every blessing and of every kind,
Yet never fill thy ravening appetite;
Though years and seasons vary thy delight,
Yet nothing to be seen of all the store,
But still the wolf within thee barks for more;
This is the fable's moral, which they tell
Of fifty foolish virgins° damned in hell
220   To leaky vessels, which the liquor spill;
To vessels of their sex, which none could ever fill.
As for the Dog,° the Furies, and their snakes,
The gloomy caverns, and the burning lakes,
And all the vain infernal trumpery,
They neither are, nor were, nor e'er can be.
But here on earth the guilty have in view
The mighty pains to mighty mischiefs due;
Racks, prisons, poisons, the Tarpeian rock,°
Stripes, hangmen, pitch, and suffocating smoke;
230   And last, and most, if these were cast behind,
The avenging horror of a conscious mind,
Whose deadly fear anticipates the blow,
And sees no end of punishment and woe;
But looks for more, at the last gasp of breath:
This makes a hell on earth, and life a death.

. . .

Why are we then so fond of mortal life,
Beset with dangers, and maintained with strife?
A life which all our care can never save;
One fate attends us, and one common grave.

Sisyphus punished by having always to roll a great stone uphill, only to have it roll down again before it reaches the top
He courts . . . great Dryden alters the original in ways that recall his account of Absalom.
smokes along drives at a great speed
fifty foolish virgins The Danaides, the daughters of Danaus, who at his order killed their hus-
bands on their wedding night; they were punished by having to draw water eternally in leaky vessels (a phrase also used of women who betray confidence, as the next lines indicate).
Dog Cerberus, the three-headed guardian of the gates of the underworld
Tarpeian rock the cliff from which murderers and traitors were thrown in Rome

Besides, we tread but a perpetual round;
We ne'er strike out, but beat the former ground,
And the same mawkish joys in the same track are found.
For still we think an absent blessing best,
Which cloys, and is no blessing when possessed;
310 A new arising wish expels it from the breast.
The feverish thirst of life increases still;
We call for more and more, and never have our fill,
Yet know not what tomorrow we shall try,
What dregs of life in the last draught may lie:
Nor, by the longest life we can attain,
One moment from the length of death we gain;
For all behind belongs to his eternal reign.
When once the Fates have cut the mortal thread,
The man as much to all intents is dead,
320 Who dies today, and will as long be so,
As he who died a thousand years ago.
                    1685

Juvenal

From *The Sixth Satire*°
In Saturn's reign,° at Nature's early birth,
There was that thing called chastity on earth;
When in a narrow cave, their common shade,°
The sheep, the shepherds, and their gods were laid:
When reeds, and leaves, and hides of beasts were spread
By mountain huswifes for their homely bed,
And mossy pillows raised, for the rude husband's head.
Unlike the niceness of our modern dames,
(Affected nymphs with new affected names,)
10 The Cynthias° and the Lesbias° of our years,
Who for a sparrow's death dissolve in tears;
Those first unpolished matrons, big and bold,
Gave suck to infants of gigantic mould;
Rough as their savage lords who ranged the wood,
And fat with acorns belched their windy food.
For when the world was buxom,° fresh, and young,

Juvenal . . . Sixth Satire This is the longest of Juvenal's sixteen satires; written against immoral and affected women, it forms part of the high rhetorical denunciation of corrupt Rome that Dryden came so much to admire (see below, Critical Prose). Juvenal was born *c*. 50 A.D. and wrote as late as 127; his attacks upon the empire of Domitian constantly evoke an earlier, more austere virtue, but in this instance his golden age is ironically rendered as a boorish and comic one. Dryden himself translated five of Juvenal's satires, and Dr. Johnson was later to write imitations of the third and tenth, the former as *London* and the latter as *The Vanity of Human Wishes.*
Saturn's reign the golden age of innocence
shade shelter
Cynthia Cynthia was celebrated by Propertius (*c*. 54–*c*. 2 B.C.) in his account of their difficult love.
Lesbias Lesbia was the subject of many poems by Catullus (*c*. 84–*c*. 54 B.C.), including one on the death of her sparrow.
buxom wanton, jolly

Her sons were undebauched and therefore strong;
And whether born in kindly° beds of earth,
Or struggling from the teeming oaks to birth,
20   Or from what other atoms they begun,
No sires they had, or, if a sire, the sun.

1693

Critical Prose

Dryden's criticism was unsystematic and for the most part occasional, arising from his wide-ranging undertakings as playwright, poet, and translator. There are often allusions to the systems of classical and Renaissance critics, and Dryden shows competence in Scholastic thought as well; but he is temperamentally opposed to system for himself, preferring what he calls a skeptical method. By this he does not mean a radical skepticism but rather a dialectical openness, a balancing of contraries and opposites, that saves him from rigorous folly and produces instead generosity and readiness to risk inconsistency.

The dialectical cast of Dryden's mind is nowhere more evident than here; if sometimes at the cost of firm argument, all the more revealing of the cross-currents of his age. Thus we can see him moving back and forth between the claims of rational order and of bold fancy, between justness and liveliness, between strictness and inclusiveness of form. This becomes most apparent in those great dialectical contrasts between representative authors—a device that was to survive as late as Dr. Johnson. In his discussion of Horace and Juvenal, we can see a gradual movement toward preference for the gravity of Juvenal, and the final paragraph on Juvenal (given below) is a fine statement of what satire was to become again in the age of Walpole.

The tributes to John Oldham (see above) and to William Congreve (see the Congreve section) are an important part of Dryden's criticism, as is, of course, Mac Flecknoe. In the first two poems, to younger men, there is a warm tribute to achievements Dryden is willing to measure favorably against his own; more than that, we can see his frank acknowledgment of losses inextricable from the gains which he promoted and in which he genuinely believed. Dryden always distinguishes nicely between the "glowing" and the "glaring," between the true vigor and the false, and Mac Flecknoe is a poem based upon such discriminations, a splendid anatomizing of the meretricious and maudlin.

The Poetic Process
[Wit and Fancy]

. . . The composition of all poems is or ought to be of wit, and wit in the poet, or wit writing (if you will give me leave to use a school distinction[1]), is no other than the faculty of imagination in the writer, which, like a nimble spaniel, beats over and ranges through the field of memory, till it springs the quarry it hunted after; or, without metaphor, which searches over all the memory for the species or ideas of those things which it designs to represent.

kindly congenial, kindred

1. That is, a distinction such as the Scholastics might make, on the analogy of *natura naturans* and *natura naturata*, the first a process and the second a product.

Wit written, is that which is well defined the happy result of thought, or product of that imagination. But to proceed from wit in the general notion of it to the proper wit of an heroic or historical poem, I judge it chiefly to consist in the delightful imaging of persons, actions, passions, or things. 'Tis not the jerk or sting of an epigram, nor the seeming contradiction of a poor antithesis (the delight of an ill-judging audience in a play of rhyme), nor the jingle of a more poor paranomasia:[2] neither is it so much the morality of a grave sentence,[3] affected by Lucan, but more sparingly used by Virgil; but it is some lively and apt description, dressed in such colours [4] of speech, that it sets before your eyes the absent object as perfectly and more delightfully than nature. So then, the first happiness of the poet's imagination is properly invention, or finding of the thought; the second is fancy, or the variation, driving [5] or moulding of that thought, as the judgement represents it proper to the subject; the third is elocution, or the art of clothing and adorning that thought so found and varied, in apt, significant, and sounding words: the quickness of the imagination is seen in the invention, the fertility in the fancy, and the accuracy in the expression. For the two first of these Ovid is famous amongst the poets, for the latter Virgil. Ovid images more often the movements and affections of the mind, either combating between two contrary passions, or extremely discomposed by one: his words therefore are the least part of his care, for he pictures nature in disorder, with which the study and choice of words is inconsistent. This is the proper wit of dialogue or discourse, and, consequently, of the drama, where all that is said is to be supposed the effect of sudden thought; which, though it excludes not the quickness of wit in repartees, yet admits not a too curious election of words, too frequent allusions, or use of tropes, or, in fine, anything that shows remoteness of thought, or labour in the writer. On the other side, Virgil speaks not so often to us in the person of another, like Ovid, but in his own; he relates almost all things as from himself, and thereby gains more liberty than the other to express his thoughts with all the graces of elocution, to write more figuratively, and to confess as well the labour as the force of his imagination. . . . [From "An Account of the Ensuing Poem . . .". Prefixed to *Annus Mirabilis*, 1666]

This worthless present was designed [for] you long before it was a play; when it was only a confused mass of thoughts, tumbling over one another in the dark; when the fancy was yet in its first work, moving the sleeping images of things towards the light, there to be distinguished, and then either chosen or rejected by the judgement: it was yours, my Lord, before I could call it mine. And, I confess, in that first tumult of my thoughts there appeared a disorderly kind of beauty in some of them, which gave me hope something worthy my Lord of Orrery might be drawn from them. . . . [From "To the Right Honorable Roger, Earl of Orrery." Prefixed to *The Rival Ladies*, 1664]

2. A pun or similar word play.
3. Moral axiom or maxim.
4. Figures.
5. The usual reading is "deriving," but George Watson points out that this has no authority in the editions Dryden supervised and is an unnecessary variant on "driving," which has the sense of carrying further or elaborating.

. . . Horace himself was cautious [6] to obtrude a new word on his readers, and makes custom and common use the best measure of receiving it into our writings. . . . The not observing this rule is that which the world has blamed in our satirist Cleveland;[7] to express a thing hard and unnaturally, is his new way of elocution. 'Tis true, no poet but may sometimes use a catachresis.[8]. . . But to do this always, and never be able to write a line without it, though it may be admired by some few pedants, will not pass upon those who know that wit is best conveyed to us in the most easy language and is most to be admired when a great thought comes dressed in words so commonly received that it is understood by the meanest apprehensions, as the best meat is the most easily digested: but we cannot read a verse of Cleveland's without making a face at it, as if every word were a pill to swallow. He gives us many times a hard nut to break our teeth, without a kernel for our pains.[9] So that there is this difference between his satires and Doctor Donne's, that the one gives us deep thoughts in common language, though rough cadence; the other gives us common thoughts in abstruse words: 'tis true, in some places his wit is independent of his words, as in that of the *Rebel Scot:*

> Had Cain been Scot God would have changed his doom;
> Not forced him wander, but confined him home.[10]

Si sic omnia dixisset! [11] This is wit in all languages: 'tis like mercury, never to be lost or killed;[12] and so that other:

> For beauty like white-powder makes no noise,
> And yet the silent hypocrite destroys.[13]

You see the last line is highly metaphorical, but it is so soft and gentle that it does not shock us as we read it. [From *Of Dramatic Poesy: An Essay,* 1668]

. . . Imagination in a man, or reasonable creature, is supposed to participate of reason, and when that governs, as it does in the belief of fiction, reason is not destroyed, but misled, or blinded: that can prescribe to the reason, during the time of the representation, somewhat like a weak belief of what it sees and hears; and reason suffers itself to be so hoodwinked, that it may better enjoy the pleasures of the fiction: but it is never so wholly made a captive as to be drawn headlong into a persuasion of those things which are most remote from

6. Slow or reluctant; cf. *Ars Poetica,* ll. 70–72: "Many terms will be revived which have fallen out of use, and many will fall in turn that now are current, if usage wills so, in whose power lies the judgment, the law, and the rule of speech."
7. John Cleveland (1613–58), the late Metaphysical poet and wit.
8. "The abuse of a trope, when the words are too far wrested from their native signification" (Johnson, *Dictionary*); cf. also Johnson's discussion of the Metaphysical poets.
9. In *A Tale of a Tub* Swift takes this further; he writes of wisdom as a nut "which, unless you choose with judgment, may cost you a tooth and pay you with nothing but a worm"; the figure of the rind and the kernel is a traditional means of exploring the relation of words to meaning.
10. *The Rebel Scot* (1644), ll. 63–64.
11. "If only he had always spoken this way—" (Juvenal, *Satires* X.123–24).
12. Stabilized, deprived of motion.
13. *Rupertismus,* ll. 39–40.

probability: 'tis in that case a free-born subject, not a slave; it will contribute willingly its assent, as far as it sees convenient, but will not be forced. . . . Fancy and reason go hand in hand; the first cannot leave the last behind; and though fancy, when it sees the wide gulf, would venture over, as the nimbler; yet it is withheld by reason, which will refuse to take the leap, when the distance over it appears too large. . . . [From *A Defense of an Essay of Dramatic Poesy*, 1668]

. . . Strong and glowing colours are the just resemblances [14] of bold metaphors, but both must be judiciously applied; for there is a difference betwixt daring and foolhardiness. Lucan and Statius [15] often ventured them too far; our Virgil never.

. . . 'Tis said of him that he read the second, fourth, and sixth books of his *Æneids* to Augustus Cæsar. In the sixth . . . the poet, speaking of Misenus the trumpeter, says:

> quo non præstantior alter
> ære ciere viros,

and broke off in the hemistich, or midst of the verse; but in the very reading, seized as it were with a divine fury, he made up the latter part of the hemistich with these following words:

> Martemque accendere cantu.[16]

How warm, nay, how glowing a colouring is this! In the beginning of his verse, the word *æs*, or brass, was taken for a trumpet, because the instrument was made of that metal, which of itself was fine; but in the latter end, which was made *ex tempore*, you see three metaphors, *Martemque . . . accendere . . . cantu*. Good Heavens! how the plain sense is raised by the beauty of the words! But this was happiness; the former might be only judgement: this was the *curiosa felicitas* [17] which Petronius attributes to Horace. . . . These hits of words a true poet often finds, as I may say, without seeking; but he knows their value when he finds them, and is infinitely pleased. A bad poet may sometimes light on them, but he discerns not a diamond from a Bristol-stone;[18] and would have been of the cock's mind in Aesop; a grain of barley would have pleased him better than the jewel.

. . . As the words, etc., are evidently shown to be the clothing of the thought in the same sense as colours are the clothing of the design, so the painter and the poet ought to judge exactly when the colouring and expressions are perfect

---

14. Counterparts; in this *Parallel*, which accompanied his translation of Charles Alphonse du Fresnoy's Latin poem *De arte graphica* (1688), Dryden pursues analogies between the "sister arts."

15. Lucan (39–65 A.D.), author of the epic *Bellum Civile*, better known as the *Pharsalia;* Statius (45–96 A.D.), best known for the epic *Thebaid*.

16. *Aeneid* VI.164–65: "Than whom none is superior in stirring men with brass [the trumpet], and in kindling Mars [war] with his song [playing]."

17. That is, cultivated felicity or planned good luck (*Satyricon*, l. 118); cf. Pope's play on *curiosa felicitas* in the *Essay on Criticism*, l. 142: "For there's a happiness as well as care."

18. Rock-crystal.

and then to think their work is truly finished. Apelles said of Protogenes [19] that he knew not when to give over. A work may be over-wrought as well as under-wrought: too much labour often takes away the spirit by adding to the polishing, so that there remains nothing but a dull correctness, a piece without any considerable faults, but with few beauties; for when the spirits are drawn off, there is nothing but a *caput mortuum*.[20] Statius never thought an expression could be bold enough; and if a bolder could be found, he rejected the first. Virgil had judgment enough to know daring was necessary; but he knew the difference betwixt a glowing colour and a glaring. . . . [From *A Parallel Betwixt Poetry and Painting*, 1695]

Critical Issues
[Subplots and Complex Structure]

And this leads me to wonder why Lisideius and many others should cry up the barrenness of the French plots above the variety and copiousness of the English. Their plots are single, they carry on one design which is pushed forward by all the actors, every scene in the play contributing and moving towards it. Our plays besides the main design, have under-plots or by-concernments, of less considerable persons and intrigues, which are carried on with the motion of the main plot: as they say the orb of the fixed stars and those of the planets, though they have motions of their own, are whirled about by the motion of the *primum mobile*, in which they are contained:[21] that similitude expresses much of the English stage, for if contrary motions may be found in nature to agree; if a planet can go east and west at the same time, one way by virtue of his own motion, the other by the force of the first mover, it will not be difficult to imagine how the under-plot, which is only different, not contrary to the great design, may naturally be conducted along with it. [From *Of Dramatic Poesy: An Essay*, 1668]

[Comedy and Farce]
. . . Comedy consists, though of low persons, yet of natural actions and characters; I mean such humours, adventures, and designs as are to be found and met with in the world. Farce, on the other side, consists of forced humours and unnatural events. Comedy presents us with the imperfections of human nature. Farce entertains us with what is monstrous and chimerical: the one causes laughter in those who can judge of men and manners, by the lively representation of their folly or corruption; the other produces the same effect in those who can judge of neither, and that only by its extravagances. The first works on the judgement and fancy; the latter on the fancy only: there is more of satisfaction in the former kind of laughter, and in the latter more of scorn. But how it happens that an impossible adventure should cause our mirth, I cannot so easily imagine. Something there may be in the oddness of it, because on the stage it is the common effect of things unexpected to surprise us into a

19. Apelles (4th century B.C.) was court painter to Philip and Alexander of Macedon; Protogenes was a contemporary of Apelles.
20. Literally, a death's head; hence the worthless residue of a distillation.
21. Cf. the opening lines of Dryden's "Anne Killigrew" ode.

delight: and that is to be ascribed to the strange appetite, as I may call it, of the fancy; which, like that of a longing woman,[22] often runs out into the most extravagant desires; and is better satisfied sometimes with loam, or with the rinds of trees, than with the wholesome nourishments of life. In short, there is the same difference betwixt farce and comedy as betwixt an empiric and a true physician: both of them may attain their ends; but what the one performs by hazard, the other does by skill. And as the artist is often unsuccessful, while the mountebank succeeds; so farces more commonly take the people than comedies. For to write unnatural things is the most probable way of pleasing them, who understand not nature. And a true poet often misses of applause because he cannot debase himself to write so ill as to please his audience. . . . [From Preface to *An Evening's Love*, 1671]

. . . There is yet a lower sort of poetry and painting, which is out of nature; for a farce is that in poetry which grotesque is in a picture. The persons and action of a farce are all unnatural, and the manners false, that is, inconsisting with the characters of mankind. Grotesque painting is the just resemblance of this; and Horace begins his *Art of Poetry* by describing such a figure, with a man's head, a horse's neck, the wings of a bird, and a fish's tail; parts of different species jumbled together, according to the mad imagination of the dauber; and the end of all this, as he tells you afterward, to cause laughter: a very monster in a Bartholomew Fair, for the mob to gape at for their twopence. Laughter is indeed the propriety[23] of a man, but just enough to distinguish him from his elder brother with four legs. 'Tis a kind of bastardpleasure too, taken in at the eyes of the vulgar gazers, and at the ears of the beastly audience. Church-painters use it to divert the honest countryman at public prayers, and keep his eyes open at a heavy sermon. And farce-scribblers make use of the same noble invention to entertain citizens, country-gentlemen, and Covent Garden fops. If they are merry, all goes well on the poet's side. The better sort go thither too, but in despair of sense and the just images of nature, which are the adequate pleasures of the mind. But the author can give the stage no better than what was given him by nature; and the actors must represent such things as they are capable to perform, and by which both they and the scribbler may get their living. After all, 'tis a good thing to laugh at any rate, and if a straw can tickle a man, 'tis an instrument of happiness. Beasts can weep when they suffer, but they cannot laugh. . . . [From *A Parallel Betwixt Poetry and Painting*, 1695]

[Horace and Juvenal]
. . . Let the chastisements of Juvenal be never so necessary for his new kind of satire; let him declaim as wittily and sharply as he pleases: yet still the nicest and most delicate touches of satire consist in fine raillery. . . . How easy is it to call rogue and villain, and that wittily! But how hard to make a man appear a fool, a blockhead, or a knave, without using any of those opprobrious terms! To spare the grossness of the names, and to do the thing

22. That is, in her pregnancy.
23. Special property.

yet more severely, is to draw a full face, and to make the nose and cheeks stand out, and yet not to employ any depth of shadowing. This is the mystery of that noble trade, which yet no master can teach to his apprentice: he may give the rules, but the scholar is never the nearer in his practice. Neither is it true that this fineness of raillery is offensive. A witty man is tickled while he is hurt in this manner, and a fool feels it not. The occasion of an offence may possibly be given, but he cannot take it. If it be granted that in effect this way does more mischief; that a man is secretly wounded, and though he be not sensible himself, yet the malicious world will find it for him: yet there is still a vast difference betwixt the slovenly butchering of a man, and the fineness of a stroke that separates the head from the body, and leaves it standing in its place. . . .

. . . It must be granted by the favourers of Juvenal, that Horace is the more copious and profitable in his instructions of human life. But in my particular opinion, which I set not up for a standard to better judgements, Juvenal is the more delightful author. I am profited by both, I am pleased with both; but I owe more to Horace for my instruction, and more to Juvenal, for my pleasure. . . .

. . . I must confess, that the delight which Horace gives me is but languishing. Be pleased still to understand that I speak of my own taste only. He may ravish other men, but I am too stupid and insensible to be tickled. Where he barely grins himself, and, as Scaliger says, only shows his white teeth, he cannot provoke me to any laughter. His urbanity, that is, his good manners, are to be commended; but his wit is faint, and his salt,[24] if I may dare to say so, almost insipid. Juvenal is of a more vigorous and masculine wit; he gives me as much pleasure as I can bear. . . . Add to this, that his thoughts are as just as those of Horace, and much more elevated. His expressions are sonorous and more noble; his verse more numerous;[25] and his words are suitable to his thoughts, sublime and lofty. All these contribute to the pleasure of the reader, and the greater the soul of him who reads, his transports are the greater. Horace is always on the amble, Juvenal on the gallop, but his way is perpetually on carpet ground.[26] He goes with more impetuosity than Horace, but as securely; and the swiftness adds a more lively agitation to the spirits. . . .

The meat of Horace is more nourishing; but the cookery of Juvenal more exquisite; so that, granting Horace to be the more general philosopher, we cannot deny that Juvenal was the greater poet, I mean in satire. His thoughts are sharper, his indignation against vice is more vehement; his spirit has more of the commonwealth genius; he treats tyranny, and all the vices attending it, as they deserve, with the utmost rigour; and consequently, a noble soul is better pleased with a zealous vindicator of Roman liberty than with a temporizing poet, a well mannered court slave, and a man who is often afraid of laughing in the right place, who is ever decent because he is naturally servile. After all, Horace had the disadvantage of the times in which he lived; they were better for the man, but worse for the satirist. 'Tis generally said that those

24. Pungency.
25. Harmonious.
26. Even or smooth, as on soft turf.

enormous vices, which were practised under the reign of Domitian, were unknown in the time of Augustus Caesar, that therefore Juvenal had a larger field than Horace. Little follies were out of doors, when oppression was to be scourged instead of avarice. It was no longer time to turn into ridicule the false opinions of philosophers, when the Roman liberty was to be asserted. . . . [From A *Discourse Concerning the Original and Progress of Satire*, 1693]

Critical Judgments
[Shakespeare and Jonson]

To begin with Shakespeare; he was the man who of all modern, and perhaps ancient poets, had the largest and most comprehensive soul. All the images of nature were still present to him, and he drew them not laboriously, but luckily: when he describes anything, you more than see it, you feel it too. Those who accuse him to have wanted learning, give him the greater commendation: he was naturally learned; he needed not the spectacles of books to read nature; he looked inwards, and found her there. I cannot say he is everywhere alike; were he so, I should do him injury to compare him with the greatest of mankind. He is many times flat, insipid; his comic wit degenerating into clenches, his serious swelling into bombast. But he is always great when some great occasion is presented to him: no man can say he ever had a fit subject for his wit and did not then raise himself as high above the rest of poets,

Quantum lenta solent inter viburna cupressi.[27]

The consideration of this made Mr. Hales of Eton[28] say that there was no subject of which any poet ever writ, but he would produce it much better done in Shakespeare; and however others are now generally preferred before him, yet the age wherein he lived, which had contemporaries with him, Fletcher and Jonson, never equalled them to him in their esteem. And in the last king's Court,[29] when Ben's reputation was at highest, Sir John Suckling, and with him the greater part of the courtiers, set our Shakespeare far above him.

. . .

As for Jonson, to whose character I am now arrived, if we look upon him while he was himself (for his last plays were but his dotages), I think him the most learned and judicious writer which any theatre ever had. He was a most severe judge of himself as well as others. One cannot say he wanted wit, but rather that he was frugal of it. In his works you find little to retrench or alter. Wit and language, and humour also in some measure we had before him; but something of art was wanting to the drama till he came. He managed his strength to more advantage than any who preceded him. You seldom find him making love in any of his scenes, or endeavouring to move the passions; his genius was too sullen and saturnine to do it gracefully, especially when he knew he came after those who had performed both to such an height. Humour was his proper sphere, and in that he delighted most to represent mechanic

27. Virgil, *Eclogues* I.25: "as cypresses often do among bending osiers."
28. John Hales (1584–1656), a fellow of Eton College and a master of prose disputation; as in his *Golden Remains* (1659).
29. During the reign of Charles I (1625–49).

people. He was deeply conversant in the Ancients, both Greek and Latin, and he borrowed boldly from them. There is scarce a poet or historian among the Roman authors of those times whom he has not translated in *Sejanus* and *Catiline*. But he has done his robberies so openly, that one may see he fears not to be taxed by any law. He invades authors like a monarch, and what would be theft in other poets, is only victory in him. With the spoils of these writers he so represents old Rome to us, in its rites, ceremonies, and customs, that if one of their poets had written either of his tragedies, we had seen less of it than in him. If there was any fault in his language, 'twas that he weaved it too closely and laboriously, in his comedies especially: perhaps too, he did a little too much Romanize our tongue, leaving the words which he translated almost as much Latin as he found them: wherein though he learnedly followed their language, he did not enough comply with the idiom of ours. If I would compare him with Shakespeare, I must acknowledge him the more correct poet, but Shakespeare the greater wit. Shakespeare was the Homer, or father of our dramatic poets; Jonson was the Virgil, the pattern of elaborate writing. I admire him, but I love Shakespeare. . . . [From *Of Dramatic Poesy: An Essay*, 1668]

[Chaucer]

In the first place, as he is the father of English poetry, so I hold him in the same degree of veneration as the Grecians held Homer, or the Romans Virgil. He is a perpetual fountain of good sense; learned in all sciences; and therefore speaks properly on all subjects. As he knew what to say, so he knows also when to leave off; a continence which is practised by few writers, and scarcely by any of the Ancients, excepting Virgil and Horace. . . .

Chaucer followed nature everywhere; but was never so bold [as] to go beyond her. And there is a great difference of being *poeta* and *nimis poeta*,[30] if we may believe Catullus, as much as betwixt a modest behaviour and affectation. The verse of Chaucer, I confess, is not harmonious to us; but 'tis like the eloquence of one whom Tacitus[31] commends, it was *auribus istius temporis accommodata;* they who lived with him, and some time after him, thought it musical; and it continues so even in our judgement, if compared with the numbers of Lydgate and Gower his contemporaries. There is the rude sweetness of a Scotch tune in it, which is natural and pleasing, though not perfect. . . .

. . . He must have been a man of a most wonderful comprehensive nature, because, as it has been truly observed of him, he has taken into the compass of his *Canterbury Tales* the various manners and humours (as we now call them) of the whole English nation in his age. Not a single character has escaped him. All his pilgrims are severally distinguished from each other; and not only in their inclinations, but in their very physiognomies and persons. Baptista Porta[32] could not have described their natures better than by the marks which the poet gives them. The matter and manner of their tales and

---

30. Being a poet or being too much a poet; not from Catullus but from Martial, *Epigrams* III.xliv.4.
31. *De Oratoribus* XXI: "suited to the ears of another age."
32. Giambattista della Porta (1540–1615), Neapolitan physician and student of physiognomy, particularly of the influence of emotions on the face.

of their telling are so suited to their different educations, humours, and callings, that each of them would be improper in any other mouth. Even the grave and serious characters are distinguished by their several sorts of gravity. Their discourses are such as belong to their age, their calling, and their breeding; such as are becoming of them, and of them only. Some of his persons are vicious, and some virtuous; some are unlearned, or (as Chaucer calls them) lewd, and some are learned. Even the ribaldry of the low characters is different. The Reeve, the Miller, and the Cook, are several men, and distinguished from each other, as much as the mincing Lady Prioress and the broad-speaking gap-toothed Wife of Bath. But enough of this; there is such a variety of game springing up before me that I am distracted in my choice and know not which to follow. 'Tis sufficient to say according to the proverb that here is God's plenty. . . . [From Preface to *Fables, Ancient and Modern*, 1700]

WILLIAM CONGREVE
1670–1729

Congreve was born in Yorkshire but grew up in Ireland, where his father served as an army officer under the Duke of Ormonde. He was a fellow student of Swift both in school at Kilkenny and at Trinity College, Dublin, and one of Swift's earliest poems is an ode to Congreve. By 1691 Congreve had moved to London and become one of those young literary templars or law students who are familiar figures in the satire and comedy of the age; he frequented Will's coffeehouse and revised a short novel, *Incognita* (1692), for publication, then turned to songs and odes and to translations from Homer that won Dryden's praise. It was Dryden who sponsored his first comedy, *The Old Bachelor* (1693); feeling that it needed "only the fashionable cut of the town," Dryden tailored it to the proper length and helped it achieve a splendid success. In the course of its production Congreve fell in love with the beautiful young actress Anne Bracegirdle. "Would she could make of me a saint, / Or I of her a sinner," he wrote; but there is no evidence that either wish was fully granted. At any rate, he was to create the part of Millamant for her a few years later. By the time his third comedy, *Love for Love* (1695), had succeeded, Congreve was given a political sinecure through Whig patronage and responded with the usual celebratory odes. His tragedy *The Mourning Bride* (1697) was perhaps his greatest popular success, and the relative failure of *The Way of the World* (1700) ended his career as a playwright when he was only thirty. For almost thirty more years he remained a respected literary figure (to whom Pope dedicated his *Iliad*) and a witty and amiable companion, lionized by various ladies but captured by Henrietta, the younger Duchess of Marlborough, whose lover he remained until his death.

The Way of the World followed by two years Jeremy Collier's *A Short View of the Immorality and Profaneness of the English Stage* (1698), in which Congreve (with Dryden and Vanbrugh) bore the brunt of the attack. The play contains some ironic allusions to Collier's attack but shows as well the influence of Colley Cibber's success with *Love's Last Shift* (1698). In Cibber's play the rake hero is seduced into reformation by his wife in disguise. In Congreve's play the traditional rake becomes the villain, and Mirabell emerges as a new kind of hero. He cannot be claimed as saintly, for he has at least courted Lady Wishfort and had an affair with her widowed daughter; his command of intrigue is such as might serve baser ends than he pursues, and he shows a lively concern that Millamant not lose her fortune. He genuinely loves her, but, although her fortune is not at all the end of his marrying her, it is very much a necessary condition. Yet, for all Mirabell's prudence, he shows warmth, generosity, even recklessness in his love for Millamant and a cool sharp detachment from Fainall's more perverse and Machiavellian attitudes: "You have a taste extremely delicate," he tells him, "and are for refining on your pleasures."

In Fainall and Mrs. Marwood we can see the older libertinism of Restoration comedy, so openly avowed by Horner in Wycherley's *The Country Wife* (1675) and more problematically represented by Dorimant in Etherege's *The Man of Mode* (1676). The libertine has the virtues of honesty and self-awareness, a resistance to debilitating forms of hypocrisy and earnestness; he acts with almost a reformer's zeal in exposing appetites in others and fulfilling his own, achieving something like an intellectual demonstration in the very act of seduction. So long as this attitude is maintained with style and energy, it has both animal grace and cleansing liberation; when it becomes desperate, cruel, and rankly selfish, it seems more compulsive than free, more feverish than vigorous, and it readily falls victim to its own shortsightedness. In contrast we have a new hero and heroine, who have tact and grace, who can assume cunning where they must, who are deeply in love and yet playfully and warmly so rather than driven by passion. Their passion is real, but so is their desire for integrity and liberty, and their playfulness becomes a means of protecting themselves from each other as well as from those who threaten them from outside. They embody an ordering force, one that is critical and skeptical in the "proviso" scene but that leads toward marriage and even parenthood rather than a continuous dance of amours.

Mirabell and Millamant are given courtly names—he the adorer of beauty, she the woman of a thousand lovers—names that were originally the badges of platonic sublimation and later of cynical dissimulation, the mask worn by such a rake as Dorimant; their names distinguish them as well from such as Lady Wishfort or Witwoud, Fainall or Mincing. They reduce the rake and wronged virago to instances of false wit, to a level not so far above the fops and fools; for in their control and self-knowledge they define a true wit that makes all varieties of false wit seem akin. We can see this best in the brilliant dialogue, where the false note is not always easily distinguished from the true, and where true wit is often marked by its rueful acknowledgment of genuine feeling ("Well, if Mirabell should not make a good husband, I am a lost thing,—for I find I love him violently").

The Way of the World is in some ways the culmination of Restoration comedy and in others a turning point. It includes the wit—both in its satiric bite and its free extravagance—of earlier comedy, and like the best of it treats the most serious problems of personal integrity and social role beneath a surface of manners. But it celebrates as well a capacity for generous feeling and delicacy of sentiment that looks forward to a new sensibility. The play still holds the stage, in fact with more success today than when it was written; and its network of subterranean intrigue still puzzles the audience as it is gradually uncovered. That it was meant to do so seems clear; for "the way of the world" is one of feint and disguise, of plot and counter-plot. And to master it requires a vigilance that Congreve never underestimates, even as he refuses to allow that it need cost us our hearts.

Dryden's poem to Congreve is given here in place of Congreve's own prologue and epilogue.

John Dryden: To My Dear Friend Mr. Congreve,°

On His Comedy Called *The Double-Dealer*

Well then, the promised hour is come at last;
The present age of wit obscures the past:
Strong were our sires, and as they fought they writ,
Conquering with force of arms, and dint of wit;
Theirs was the giant race before the flood;°
And thus, when Charles returned, our empire stood.
Like Janus° he the stubborn soil manured,
With rules of husbandry the rankness cured;
Tamed us to manners, when the stage was rude;
10   And boisterous English wit with art indued.
Our age was cultivated thus at length,
But what we gained in skill we lost in strength.
Our builders were with want of genius curst;
The second temple° was not like the first:
Till you, the best Vitruvius,° come at length;
Our beauties equal, but excel our strength.
Firm Doric pillars° found your solid base;
The fair Corinthian crowns the higher space:
Thus all below is strength, and all above is grace.
20   In easy dialogue is Fletcher's° praise;
He moved the mind, but had not power to raise.
Great Jonson° did by strength of judgment please;
Yet, doubling Fletcher's force, he wants his ease.
In differing talents both adorned their age;
One for the study, the other for the stage:
But both to Congreve justly shall submit,
One matched in judgment, both o'ermatched in wit.
In him all beauties of this age we see,
Etherege° his courtship, Southerne's° purity,

To . . . Mr. Congreve This tribute was published with Congreve's second comedy; Dryden had abandoned the stage and had (for political reasons) lost his posts as Poet Laureate and as Historiographer Royal. We see here, as everywhere in Dryden, a double view of the relation of present to past, a sense of loss as well as gain, a weighing of the claims of "strength" and "grace" (which only an exceptional writer, like Congreve, can reconcile).
the giant . . . flood the Elizabethans and Jacobeans who wrote and ruled before the Commonwealth, likened to the ancient patriarchs before the biblical deluge
Janus the god of beginnings. According to legend he reigned as a king in Italy and gave asylum to Saturn upon his flight from Jupiter; from Saturn he learned the arts of husbandry which here, in the guise of Charles II educated in France, he teaches.
second temple referring to the rebuilding of the temple in Jerusalem upon the return from exile (Ezra 5, 6) in contrast with the original building by Solomon (Haggar 2:1–3)
Vitruvius the celebrated Roman architect and writer on architecture of the age of Augustus
Doric pillars As the simplest and most severe, these were placed at the lowest level of a building (such as the Colosseum), with Ionic and then Corinthian placed at higher levels, tapering from strength to grace.
Fletcher's John Fletcher (1579–1625), best known for his collaboration with Francis Beaumont, who (in Dryden's view) surpassed the French in comic repartee
Jonson Ben Jonson. See Dryden's discussion of him in the selections from his prose criticism.
Etherege Sir George Etherege (c. 1635–91), whose *The Man of Mode* (1676) raised Restoration love comedy to a new level of finesse
Southerne's Thomas Southerne (1660–1746), whose tragicomedies stressed pathos and "purity"

30   The satire, wit, and strength of Manly Wycherley.°
      All this in blooming youth you have achieved,
      Nor are your foiled contemporaries grieved.
      So much the sweetness of your manners move,
      We cannot envy you, because we love.
      Fabius° might joy in Scipio, when he saw
      A beardless consul made against the law;
      And join his suffrage to the votes of Rome,
      Though he with Hannibal was overcome.
      Thus old Romano° bowed to Raphael's fame,
40   And scholar to the youth he taught became.
        O that your brows my laurel had sustained;
      Well had I been deposed, if you had reigned!
      The father had descended for the son;
      For only you are lineal to the throne.
      Thus, when the state one Edward° did depose,
      A greater Edward in his room arose.
      But now, not I, but poetry is curst;
      For Tom the Second° reigns like Tom the First.
      But let 'em not mistake my patron's part,°
50   Nor call his charity their own desert.
      Yet this I prophesy: thou shalt be seen
      (Though with some short parenthesis between)
      High on the throne of wit; and, seated there,
      Not mine—that's little—but thy laurel wear.
      Thy first attempt an early promise made;
      That early promise this has more than paid.
      So bold, yet so judiciously you dare,
      That your least praise is to be regular.
      Time, place, and action, may with pains be wrought;
60   But genius must be born, and never can be taught.
      This is your portion; this your native store;
      Heaven, that but once was prodigal before,
      To Shakespeare gave as much; she could not give him more.
        Maintain your post: that's all the fame you need;
      For 'tis impossible you should proceed.
      Already I am worn with cares and age,
      And just abandoning the ungrateful stage;

Manly Wycherley William Wycherley (1641–1716), author of *The Country Wife* (1675) and here named for the hero of his *Plain Dealer* (1676)
Fabius (d. 203 B.C.) who opposed (in part out of jealousy) the young Scipio's policy for carrying war against Carthage into Africa; Scipio had been made consul (205 B.C.) before attaining the legal age; here Fabius is shown charmed by a Scipio who has Congreve's "sweetness"
Romano Giulio Romano (1492–1546) was in fact younger than Raphael (1483–1520) and was his pupil rather than his master; Dryden may have in mind Perugino (1446–1523?), in whose studio Raphael worked and whom he imitated and surpassed.

Edward Edward II was assassinated in 1327 and succeeded by Edward III, the conqueror of the French.
Tom the Second With the revolution of 1688 Dryden lost both the laureateship and his position as historiographer to Thomas Shadwell (see *Mac Flecknoe*); Shadwell was succeeded as laureate in 1692 by Nahum Tate, as historiographer by the critic Thomas Rymer ("Tom the Second").
my patron's part the Earl of Dorset, who, as Lord Chamberlain, held the power of appointing the laureate and historiographer but did not act on his own volition in removing Dryden

Unprofitably kept at Heaven's expense,
I live a rent-charge° on his providence:
70 But you, whom every Muse and Grace adorn,
Whom I foresee to better fortune born,
Be kind to my remains; and O defend,
Against your judgment, your departed friend!
Let not the insulting foe my fame pursue,
But shade those laurels which descend to you;
And take for tribute what these lines express:
You merit more; nor could my love do less.

1694

The Way of the World

Audire est operae pretium, procedere recte
Qui maechis non vultis—
—Metuat doti deprensa.— [1]

CHARACTERS

FAINALL, in love with Mrs. Marwood [2]
MIRABELL, in love with Mrs. Millamant
WITWOUD   } followers of
PETULANT   } Mrs. Millamant
SIR WILFULL WITWOUD, half brother to Witwoud and nephew to Lady Wishfort
WAITWELL, servant to Mirabell
LADY WISHFORT, enemy to Mirabell for having falsely pretended love to her
MRS. MILLAMANT, a fine lady, niece to Lady Wishfort, and loves Mirabell
MRS. MARWOOD, friend to Mr. Fainall, and likes Mirabell
MRS. FAINALL, daughter to Lady Wishfort and wife to Fainall, formerly friend
    to Mirabell
FOIBLE, woman to Lady Wishfort
MINCING, woman to Mrs. Millamant
DANCERS, FOOTMEN, and ATTENDANTS

SCENE: London

ACT I
A chocolate-house

[MIRABELL and FAINALL, rising from cards. BETTY waiting.[3]]

MIRABELL   You are a fortunate man, Mr. Fainall.
FAINALL   Have we done?
MIRABELL   What you please. I'll play on to entertain you.
FAINALL   No, I'll give you your revenge another time, when you are not so

---

rent-charge a rent forming a charge upon lands
granted to one who is not the owner
1. "O you that do not wish well to the proceedings of adulterers, it is worth your while to
hear how they are hampered on all sides.—Caught in the act, the woman fears for her
dowry." Horace, *Satires* II.1.37–38, 131.
2. Unmarried ladies, as well as married ones, are called "Mrs."
3. That is, on them.

indifferent; you are thinking of something else now, and play too negligently. The coldness of a losing gamester lessens the pleasure of the winner. I'd no more play with a man that slighted his ill fortune, than I'd make love to a woman who undervalued the loss of her reputation.

MIRABELL   You have a taste extremely delicate, and are for refining on your pleasures.

FAINALL   Prithee, why so reserved? Something has put you out of humour.

MIRABELL   Not at all. I happen to be grave today, and you are gay; that's all.

FAINALL   Confess, Millamant and you quarrelled last night, after I left you; my fair cousin has some humours [4] that would tempt the patience of a Stoic. What! some coxcomb came in and was well received by her while you were by?

MIRABELL   Witwoud and Petulant; and what was worse, her aunt, your wife's mother, my evil genius; or to sum up all in her own name, my old Lady Wishfort came in.

FAINALL   Oh, there it is then! She has a lasting passion for you, and with reason. What, then my wife was there?

MIRABELL   Yes, and Mrs. Marwood and three or four more, whom I never saw before. Seeing me, they all put on their grave faces, whispered one another, then complained aloud of the vapours,[5] and after fell into a profound silence.

FAINALL   They had a mind to be rid of you.

MIRABELL   For which reason I resolved not to stir. At last the good old lady broke through her painful taciturnity with an invective against long visits. I would not have understood her, but Millamant joining in the argument, I rose and with a constrained smile told her I thought nothing was so easy as to know when a visit began to be troublesome. She reddened and I withdrew, without expecting [6] her reply.

FAINALL   You were to blame to resent what she spoke only in compliance with her aunt.

MIRABELL   She is more mistress of herself than to be under the necessity of such a resignation.

FAINALL   What? though half her fortune depends upon her marrying with my lady's approbation?

MIRABELL   I was then in such a humour that I should have been better pleased if she had been less discreet.

FAINALL   Now I remember, I wonder not they were weary of you; last night was one of their cabal-nights.[7] They have 'em three times a week and meet by turns at one another's apartments, where they come together like the coroner's inquest to sit upon the murdered reputations of the week. You and I are excluded; and it was once proposed that all the male sex should be excepted; [8] but somebody moved that to avoid scandal there might be one man of the community; upon which motion Witwoud and Petulant were enrolled members.

4. Moods, whims.
5. A fit of melancholy (a fashionable disease).
6. Waiting for.
7. Nights for secret meetings, devoted in politics to conspiracy, here to lesser intrigues.
8. Excluded.

MIRABELL   And who may have been the foundress of this sect? My Lady
Wishfort, I warrant, who publishes her detestation of mankind; and full
of the vigour of fifty-five, declares for a friend and ratafia; [9] and let
posterity shift for itself, she'll breed no more.

FAINALL   The discovery of your sham addresses to her, to conceal your love
to her niece, has provoked this separation. Had you dissembled better,
things might have continued in the state of nature.[10]

MIRABELL   I did as much as man could with any reasonable conscience; I
proceeded to the very last act of flattery with her, and was guilty of a
song in her commendation. Nay, I got a friend to put her into a lampoon
and compliment her with the imputation of an affair with a young
fellow, which I carried so far that I told her the malicious town took
notice that she was grown fat of a sudden; and when she lay in of a
dropsy,[11] persuaded her she was reported to be in labour. The devil's
in't if an old woman is to be flattered further, unless a man should
endeavour downright personally to debauch her; and that my virtue forbade me. But for the discovery of that amour, I am indebted to your
friend, or your wife's friend, Mrs. Marwood.

FAINALL   What should provoke her to be your enemy, without she has made
you advances which you have slighted? Women do not easily forgive
omissions of that nature.

MIRABELL   She was always civil to me till of late. I confess I am not one of
those coxcombs who are apt to interpret a woman's good manners to her
prejudice; and think that she who does not refuse 'em everything, can
refuse 'em nothing.

FAINALL   You are a gallant man, Mirabell; and though you may have cruelty
enough not to satisfy a lady's longing, you have too much generosity
not to be tender of her honour. Yet you speak with an indifference which
seems to be affected and confesses you are conscious of a negligence.

MIRABELL   You pursue the argument with a distrust that seems to be unaffected, and confesses you are conscious of a concern for which the lady
is more indebted to you than your wife.

FAINALL   Fie, fie, friend, if you grow censorious I must leave you. I'll look
upon the gamesters in the next room.

MIRABELL   Who are they?

FAINALL   Petulant and Witwoud. [To BETTY] Bring me some chocolate.
[Exit]

MIRABELL   Betty, what says your clock?

BETTY   Turned of the last canonical hour,[12] sir. [Exit]

MIRABELL   How pertinently the jade answers me! Ha! almost one o'clock!
[Looking on his watch] Oh, y'are come——
[Enter a SERVANT]
Well, is the grand affair over? You have been something tedious.

9. A fruit-flavored liqueur with a brandy base.
10. In their natural state; but with ironic reference to Eden before the fall or to the state
Dryden describes in the opening lines of Absalom and Achitophel.
11. An illness that involves swelling with liquids.
12. That is, past the hours (from 8 A.M. to noon) when marriages could be performed in
the Church of England.

SERVANT   Sir, there's such coupling at Pancras [13] that they stand behind one another, as 'twere in a country dance. Ours was the last couple to lead up; and no hopes appearing of dispatch,[14] besides, the parson growing hoarse, we were afraid his lungs would have failed before it came to our turn; so we drove round to Duke's Place; and there they were riveted in a trice.

MIRABELL   So, so, you are sure they are married.

SERVANT   Married and bedded, sir; I am witness.

MIRABELL   Have you the certificate?

SERVANT   Here it is, sir.

MIRABELL   Has the tailor brought Waitwell's clothes home, and the new liveries?

SERVANT   Yes, sir.

MIRABELL   That's well. Do you go home again, d'ye hear, and adjourn the consummation till farther order. Bid Waitwell shake his ears and Dame Partlet [15] rustle up her feathers, and meet me at one o'clock by Rosamond's Pond,[16] that I may see her before she returns to her lady; and as you tender [17] your ears, be secret.

[*Exit* SERVANT. *Re-enter* FAINALL (*and* BETTY)]

FAINALL   Joy of your success, Mirabell; you look pleased.

MIRABELL   Aye, I have been engaged in a matter of some sort of mirth, which is not yet ripe for discovery. I am glad this is not a cabal-night. I wonder, Fainall, that you who are married, and of consequence should be discreet, will suffer your wife to be of such a party.

FAINALL   Faith, I am not jealous. Besides, most who are engaged are women and relations; and for the men, they are of a kind too contemptible to give scandal.

MIRABELL   I am of another opinion. The greater the coxcomb, always the more the scandal; for a woman who is not a fool can have but one reason for associating with a man that is.

FAINALL   Are you jealous as often as you see Witwoud entertained by Millamant?

MIRABELL   Of her understanding I am, if not of her person.

FAINALL   You do her wrong; for to give her her due, she has wit.

MIRABELL   She has beauty enough to make any man think so, and complaisance enough not to contradict him who shall tell her so.

FAINALL   For a passionate lover, methinks you are a man somewhat too discerning in the failings of your mistress.

MIRABELL   And for a discerning man, somewhat too passionate a lover; for I like her with all her faults; nay, like her for her faults. Her follies are so natural, or so artful, that they become her; and those affectations which

13. The churches of St. Pancras and St. James (in Duke's Place, mentioned below) permitted marriage without special license and were predictably busy.
14. Speed.
15. Chauntecleer's wife (Pertelote) in Chaucer's Nun's Priest's Tale, called Dame Partlet in Dryden's translation, *The Cock and the Fox* (1700).
16. A place of rendezvous in St. James's Park.
17. Value.

in another woman would be odious, serve but to make her more agreeable. I'll tell thee, Fainall, she once used me with that insolence, that in revenge I took her to pieces; sifted her and separated her failings; I studied 'em and got 'em by rote. The catalogue was so large that I was not without hopes, one day or other, to hate her heartily; to which end I so used myself to think of 'em that at length, contrary to my design and expectation, they gave me every hour less and less disturbance; till in a few days it became habitual to me to remember 'em without being displeased. They are now grown as familiar to me as my own frailties; and in all probability in a little time longer I shall like 'em as well.

FAINALL   Marry her, marry her; be half as well acquainted with her charms as you are with her defects, and my life on't, you are your own man again.

MIRABELL   Say you so?

FAINALL   Aye, aye; I have experience; I have a wife, and so forth.

[*Enter* MESSENGER]

MESSENGER   Is one Squire Witwoud here?

BETTY   Yes; what's your business?

MESSENGER   I have a letter for him, from his brother, Sir Wilfull, which I am charged to deliver into his own hands.

BETTY   He's in the next room, friend—that way.

[*Exit* MESSENGER]

MIRABELL   What, is the chief of that noble family in town, Sir Wilfull Witwoud?

FAINALL   He is expected today. Do you know him?

MIRABELL   I have seen him; he promises to be an extraordinary person; I think you have the honour to be related to him.

FAINALL   Yes; he is half-brother to this Witwoud by a former wife, who was sister to my Lady Wishfort, my wife's mother. If you marry Millamant, you must call cousins too.

MIRABELL   I had rather be his relation than his acquaintance.

FAINALL   He comes to town in order to equip himself for travel.

MIRABELL   For travel! Why the man that I mean is above forty.

FAINALL   No matter for that; 'tis for the honour of England, that all Europe should know we have blockheads of all ages.[18]

MIRABELL   I wonder there is not an Act of Parliament to save the credit of the nation and prohibit the exportation of fools.

FAINALL   By no means, 'tis better as 'tis; 'tis better to trade with a little loss, than to be quite eaten up with being overstocked.

MIRABELL   Pray, are the follies of this knight-errant,[19] and those of the squire his brother, anything related?

FAINALL   Not at all; Witwoud grows by the knight, like a medlar grafted on a crab.[20] One will melt in your mouth, and t'other set your teeth on edge; one is all pulp, and the other all core.

18. Europe usually saw them when they left the university, the customary occasion for a grand tour; for a younger "blockhead," see Pope, *Dunciad* IV.282–336.
19. Perhaps with reference to Hudibras and Ralpho in Butler's poem.
20. That is, Witwoud gains by the contrast, like a medlar (a soft fruit eaten only when it has begun to rot) grafted on a crabapple.

MIRABELL   So one will be rotten before he be ripe, and the other will be rotten without ever being ripe at all.

FAINALL   Sir Wilfull is an odd mixture of bashfulness and obstinacy. But when he's drunk, he's as loving as the monster in *The Tempest*,[21] and much after the same manner. To give the t'other his due, he has something of good nature and does not always want wit.

MIRABELL   Not always; but as often as his memory fails him, and his commonplace of comparisons.[22] He is a fool with a good memory and some few scraps of other folks' wit. He is one whose conversation can never be approved, yet it is now and then to be endured. He has indeed one good quality, he is not exceptious; [23] for he so passionately affects the reputation of understanding raillery [24] that he will construe an affront into a jest, and call downright rudeness and ill language, satire and fire.

FAINALL   If you have a mind to finish his picture, you have an opportunity to do it at full length. Behold the original.

[*Enter* WITWOUD]

WITWOUD   Afford me your compassion, my dears; pity me, Fainall, Mirabell, pity me.

MIRABELL   I do from my soul.

FAINALL   Why, what's the matter?

WITWOUD   No letters for me, Betty?

BETTY   Did not the messenger bring you one but now, sir?

WITWOUD   Aye, but no other?

BETTY   No, sir.

WITWOUD   That's hard, that's very hard;—a messenger, a mule, a beast of burden! He has brought me a letter from the fool my brother, as heavy as a panegyric in a funeral sermon, or a copy of commendatory verses from one poet to another.[25] And what's worse, 'tis as sure a forerunner of the author as an epistle dedicatory.

MIRABELL   A fool, and your brother, Witwoud!

WITWOUD   Aye, aye, my half-brother. My half-brother he is, no nearer upon honour.

MIRABELL   Then 'tis possible he may be but half a fool.

WITWOUD   Good, good, Mirabell, *le drôle!* [26] Good, good!—hang him, don't let's talk of him. Fainall, how does your lady? Gad, I say anything in the world to get this fellow out of my head. I beg pardon that I should ask a man of pleasure and the town, a question at once so foreign and domestic. But I talk like an old maid at a marriage, I don't know what I say. But she's the best woman in the world.

FAINALL   'Tis well you don't know what you say, or else your commendation would go near to make me either vain or jealous.

---

21. As Caliban is to Stephano and Trinculo when they make him drunk (II.ii).
22. That is, his memorandum book full of others' ingenious and far-fetched wit.
23. Peevish.
24. Banter or teasing; described by Swift in its ideal form as an apparent insult that turns out to be a compliment.
25. Both likely to run to great length.
26. The amusing fellow.

WITWOUD   No man in town lives well with a wife but Fainall. Your judgment, Mirabell?

MIRABELL   You had better step and ask his wife if you would be credibly informed.

WITWOUD   Mirabell.

MIRABELL   Aye.

WITWOUD   My dear, I ask ten thousand pardons.—Gad, I have forgot what I was going to say to you.

MIRABELL   I thank you heartily, heartily.

WITWOUD   No, but prithee excuse me—my memory is such a memory.

MIRABELL   Have a care of such apologies, Witwoud; for I never knew a fool but he affected to complain either of the spleen [27] or his memory.

FAINALL   What have you done with Petulant?

WITWOUD   He's reckoning his money—my money it was; I have no luck today.

FAINALL   You may allow him to win of you at play, for you are sure to be too hard for him at repartee. Since you monopolize the wit that is between you, the fortune must be his of course.

MIRABELL   I don't find that Petulant confesses the superiority of wit to be your talent, Witwoud.

WITWOUD   Come, come, you are malicious now, and would breed debates. Petulant's my friend, and a very honest fellow, and a very pretty fellow, and has a smattering—faith and troth, a pretty deal of an odd sort of a small wit. Nay, I'll do him justice. I'm his friend, I won't wrong him, neither.—And if he had but any judgment in the world, he would not be altogether contemptible. Come, come, don't detract from the merits of my friend.

FAINALL   You don't take your friend to be over-nicely bred.

WITWOUD   No, no, hang him, the rogue has no manners at all, that I must own—no more breeding than a bumbaily,[28] that I grant you.—'Tis pity, faith; the fellow has fire and life.

MIRABELL   What, courage?

WITWOUD   Hum, faith, I don't know as to that—I can't say as to that.—Yes, faith, in a controversy he'll contradict anybody.

MIRABELL   Though 'twere a man whom he feared or a woman whom he loved.

WITWOUD   Well, well, he does not always think before he speaks.—We have all our failings; you're too hard upon him, you are, faith. Let me excuse him—I can defend most of his faults, except one or two; one he has, that's the truth on't, if he were my brother, I could not acquit him.— That, indeed, I could wish were otherwise.

MIRABELL   Aye, marry, what's that, Witwoud?

WITWOUD   Oh, pardon me!—Expose the infirmities of my friend?—No, my dear, excuse me there.

FAINALL   What! I warrant, he's unsincere, or 'tis some such trifle.

WITWOUD   No, no, what if he be? 'Tis no matter for that, his wit will excuse

27. Low spirits, the "vapors."
28. Sheriff's officer of the lowest rank.

that; a wit should no more be sincere than a woman constant; one argues a decay of parts as t'other of beauty.

MIRABELL   Maybe you think him too positive?

WITWOUD   No, no, his being positive is an incentive to argument and keeps up conversation.

FAINALL   Too illiterate.

WITWOUD   That! that's his happiness. His want of learning gives him the more opportunities to show his natural parts.

MIRABELL   He wants words.

WITWOUD   Aye; but I like him for that now; for his want of words gives me the pleasure very often to explain his meaning.

FAINALL   He's impudent.

WITWOUD   No, that's not it.

MIRABELL   Vain.

WITWOUD   No.

MIRABELL   What, he speaks unseasonable truths sometimes, because he has not wit enough to invent an evasion.

WITWOUD   Truths! Ha, ha, ha! No, no, since you will have it—I mean, he never speaks truth at all—that's all. He will lie like a chambermaid, or a woman of quality's porter. Now that is a fault.

[*Enter* COACHMAN]

COACHMAN   Is Master Petulant here, mistress?

BETTY   Yes.

COACHMAN   Three gentlewomen in the coach would speak with him.

FAINALL   O brave Petulant, three!

BETTY   I'll tell him.

COACHMAN   You must bring two dishes of chocolate and a glass of cinnamon-water.

[*Exeunt* BETTY *and* COACHMAN]

WITWOUD   That should be for two fasting strumpets and a bawd troubled with wind. Now you may know what the three are.

MIRABELL   You are very free with your friend's acquaintance.

WITWOUD   Aye, aye, friendship without freedom is as dull as love without enjoyment or wine without toasting; but to tell you a secret, these are trulls that he allows coach-hire, and something more by the week, to call on him once a day at public places.

MIRABELL   How!

WITWOUD   You shall see he won't go to 'em because there's no more company here to take notice of him.—Why, this is nothing to what he used to do— before he found out this way, I have known him call for himself——

FAINALL   Call for himself? What dost thou mean?

WITWOUD   Mean? why, he would slip you out of this chocolate-house, just when you had been talking to him.—As soon as your back was turned—whip he was gone; then trip to his lodging, clap on a hood and scarf, slap into a hackney-coach, and drive hither to the door again in a trice; where he would send in for himself—that I mean—call for himself, wait for himself, nay and what's more, not finding himself, sometimes leave a letter for himself.

MIRABELL   I confess this is something extraordinary—I believe he waits for himself now, he is so long a-coming. Oh, I ask his pardon!

[*Enter* PETULANT (*and* BETTY)]

BETTY   Sir, the coach stays.

PETULANT   Well, well; I come.—'Sbud,[29] a man had as good be a professed midwife as a professed whoremaster at this rate; to be knocked up and raised at all hours and in all places! Pox on 'em, I won't come.—D'ee hear, tell 'em I won't come. Let 'em snivel and cry their hearts out.

FAINALL   You are very cruel, Petulant.

PETULANT   All's one, let it pass—I have a humour to be cruel.

MIRABELL   I hope they are not persons of condition that you use at this rate.

PETULANT   Condition! condition's a dried fig, if I am not in humour. By this hand, if they were your—a—a—your what-d'ye-call-'ems themselves, they must wait or rub off [30] if I want appetite.

MIRABELL   What-d'ye-call-'ems! What are they, Witwoud?

WITWOUD   Empresses, my dear—by your what-d'ye-call-'ems he means sultana queens.[31]

PETULANT   Aye, Roxolanas.[32]

MIRABELL   Cry you mercy.

FAINALL   Witwoud says they are——

PETULANT   What does he say th'are?

WITWOUD   I—fine ladies, I say.

PETULANT   Pass on, Witwoud.—Hark 'ee, by this light, his relations—two co-heiresses his cousins, and an old aunt, that loves caterwauling better than a conventicle.[33]

WITWOUD   Ha, ha, ha! I had a mind to see how the rogue would come off.— Ha, ha, ha! Gad I can't be angry with him, if he said they were my mother and my sisters.

MIRABELL   No!

WITWOUD   No; the rogue's wit and readiness of invention charm me. Dear Petulant!

BETTY   They are gone, sir, in great anger.

PETULANT   Enough, let 'em trundle. Anger helps complexion, saves paint.

FAINALL   This continence is all dissembled; this is in order to have something to brag of the next time he makes court to Millamant, and swear he has abandoned the whole sex for her sake.

MIRABELL   Have you not left off your impudent pretensions there yet? I shall cut your throat, sometime or other, Petulant, about that business.

PETULANT   Aye, aye, let that pass—there are other throats to be cut—

MIRABELL   Meaning mine, sir?

PETULANT   Not I—I mean nobody—I know nothing—But there are uncles

---

29. 'Sbodikins, God's body.

30. Clear out.

31. Terms for prostitutes; perhaps based on their own practice, for, as Pope indicates, the brothel-keeper "By names of toasts retails each battered jade" (*Dunciad* II.134).

32. Roxolana is the wife of the sultan Solyman the Magnificent in Davenant's *Siege of Rhodes* (1656).

33. A Puritan church service.

and nephews in the world—and they may be rivals. What then? All's one for that——

MIRABELL   How! Hark 'ee, Petulant, come hither. Explain, or I shall call your interpreter.

PETULANT   Explain! I know nothing.—Why you have an uncle, have you not, lately come to town, and lodges by my Lady Wishfort's?

MIRABELL   True.

PETULANT   Why, that's enough.—You and he are not friends; and if he should marry and have a child, you may be disinherited, ha?

MIRABELL   Where hast thou stumbled upon all this truth?

PETULANT   All's one for that; why, then say I know something.

MIRABELL   Come, thou art an honest fellow, Petulant, and shalt make love to my mistress, thou sha't, faith. What hast thou heard of my uncle?

PETULANT   I? nothing, I. If throats are to be cut, let swords clash; snug's the word, I shrug and am silent.

MIRABELL   O raillery, raillery. Come, I know thou art in the women's secrets. —What, you're a cabalist. I know you stayed at Millamant's last night, after I went. Was there any mention made of my uncle or me? Tell me; if thou hadst but good nature equal to thy wit, Petulant, Tony Witwoud, who is now thy competitor in fame, would show as dim by thee as a dead whiting's eye by a pearl of Orient; [34] he would no more be seen by [35] thee than Mercury is by the sun. Come, I'm sure thou wo't tell me.

PETULANT   If I do, will you grant me common sense then, for the future?

MIRABELL   Faith, I'll do what I can for thee; and I'll pray that heaven may grant it thee in the meantime.

PETULANT   Well, hark'ee.

    [They talk apart]

FAINALL   Petulant and you both will find Mirabell as warm a rival as a lover.

WITWOUD   Pshaw, pshaw, that she laughs at Petulant is plain. And for my part —but that it is almost a fashion to admire her, I should—hark'ee—to tell you a secret, but let it go no further—between friends, I shall never break my heart for her.

FAINALL   How!

WITWOUD   She's handsome; but she's a sort of an uncertain woman.

FAINALL   I thought you had died for her.

WITWOUD   Umh—no——

FAINALL   She has wit.

WITWOUD   'Tis what she will hardly allow anybody else. Now, demme, I should hate that, if she were as handsome as Cleopatra. Mirabell is not so sure of her as he thinks for.

FAINALL   Why do you think so?

WITWOUD   We stayed pretty late there last night and heard something of an uncle to Mirabell who is lately come to town,—and is between him and the best part of his estate. Mirabell and he are at some distance, as my Lady Wishfort has been told; and you know she hates Mirabell worse

34. That is, of highest quality.
35. Beside.

than a Quaker hates a parrot, or than a fishmonger hates a hard frost. Whether this uncle has seen Mrs. Millamant or not, I cannot say; but there were items of such a treaty being in embryo; and if it should come to life, poor Mirabell would be in some sort unfortunately fobbed [36] i'faith.

FAINALL   'Tis impossible Millamant should hearken to it.

WITWOUD   Faith, my dear, I can't tell; she's a woman and a kind of a humourist.[37]

MIRABELL [*conversing with* PETULANT]   And this is the sum of what you could collect last night.

PETULANT   The quintessence. Maybe Witwoud knows more; he stayed longer. Besides, they never mind him; they say anything before him.

MIRABELL   I thought you had been the greatest favourite.

PETULANT   Aye, *tête-à-tête;* but not in public, because I make remarks.

MIRABELL   Do you?

PETULANT   Aye, aye, pox, I'm malicious, man. Now, he's soft, you know; they are not in awe of him. The fellow's well bred; he's what you call a— what-d'ee-call-'em. A fine gentleman, but he's silly withal.

MIRABELL   I thank you; I know as much as my curiosity requires.—Fainall, are you for the Mall? [38]

FAINALL   Aye, I'll take a turn before dinner.

WITWOUD   Aye, we'll all walk in the Park; the ladies talked of being there.

MIRABELL   I thought you were obliged to watch for your brother Sir Wilfull's arrival.

WITWOUD   No, no, he comes to his aunt's, my Lady Wishfort; pox on him, I shall be troubled with him too; what shall I do with the fool?

PETULANT   Beg him for his estate, that I may beg you afterwards, and so have but one trouble with you both.

WITWOUD   O rare Petulant! thou art as quick as a fire in a frosty morning; thou shalt to the Mall with us, and we'll be very severe.

PETULANT   Enough! I'm in a humour to be severe.

MIRABELL   Are you? Pray then walk by yourselves—let not us be accessory to your putting the ladies out of countenance with your senseless ribaldry, which you roar out aloud as often as they pass by you; and when you have made a handsome woman blush, then you think you have been severe.

PETULANT   What, what? Then let 'em either show their innocence by not understanding what they hear, or else show their discretion by not hearing what they would not be thought to understand.

MIRABELL   But hast not thou then sense enough to know that thou ought'st to to be most ashamed thyself, when thou has put another out of countenance?

PETULANT   Not I, by this hand—I always take blushing either for a sign of guilt or ill breeding.

36. Done in.
37. One given to whim or caprice.
38. The promenade at St. James's Park.

MIRABELL   I confess you ought to think so. You are in the right, that you may plead the error of your judgment in defence of your practice.

Where modesty's ill manners, 'tis but fit
That impudence and malice pass for wit.
[*Exeunt*]

ACT II
St. James's Park

[*Enter* MRS. FAINALL *and* MRS. MARWOOD]

MRS. FAINALL   Aye, aye, dear Marwood, if we will be happy, we must find the means in ourselves, and among ourselves. Men are ever in extremes; either doting or averse. While they are lovers, if they have fire and sense, their jealousies are insupportable; and when they cease to love (we ought to think at least), they loathe; they look upon us with horror and distaste; they meet us like the ghosts of what we were, and as such, fly from us.

MRS. MARWOOD   True, 'tis an unhappy circumstance of life that love should ever die before us; and that the man so often should outlive the lover. But say what you will, 'tis better to be left than never to have been loved. To pass our youth in dull indifference, to refuse the sweets of life because they once must leave us, is as preposterous as to wish to have been born old because we one day must be old. For my part, my youth may wear and waste, but it shall never rust in my possession.

MRS. FAINALL   Then it seems you dissemble an aversion to mankind only in compliance with my mother's humour.

MRS. MARWOOD   Certainly. To be free, I have no taste of those insipid dry discourses with which our sex of force must entertain themselves apart from men. We may affect endearments to each other, profess eternal friendships, and seem to dote like lovers; but 'tis not in our natures long to persevere. Love will resume his empire in our breasts, and every heart, or soon or late, receive and readmit him as its lawful tyrant.

MRS. FAINALL   Bless me, how have I been deceived! Why, you profess a libertine.

MRS. MARWOOD   You see my friendship by my freedom. Come, be as sincere, acknowledge that your sentiments agree with mine.

MRS. FAINALL   Never.

MRS. MARWOOD   You hate mankind.

MRS. FAINALL   Heartily, inveterately.

MRS. MARWOOD   Your husband.

MRS. FAINALL   Most transcendently; aye, though I say it, meritoriously.

MRS. MARWOOD   Give me your hand upon it.

MRS. FAINALL   There.

MRS. MARWOOD   I join with you; what I have said has been to try you.

MRS. FAINALL   Is it possible? Dost thou hate those vipers, men?

MRS. MARWOOD   I have done hating 'em and am now come to despise 'em; the next thing I have to do is eternally to forget 'em.

MRS. FAINALL   There spoke the spirit of an Amazon, a Penthesilea.[1]

MRS. MARWOOD   And yet I am thinking sometimes to carry my aversion further.

MRS. FAINALL   How?

MRS. MARWOOD   Faith, by marrying; if I could but find one that loved me very well and would be thoroughly sensible of ill usage, I think I should do myself the violence of undergoing the ceremony.

MRS. FAINALL   You would not make him a cuckold?

MRS. MARWOOD   No; but I'd make him believe I did, and that's as bad.

MRS. FAINALL   Why, had not you as good do it?

MRS. MARWOOD   Oh, if he should ever discover it, he would then know the worst and be out of his pain; but I would have him ever to continue upon the rack of fear and jealousy.

MRS. FAINALL   Ingenious mischief! Would thou wert married to Mirabell.

MRS. MARWOOD   Would I were.

MRS. FAINALL   You change colour.

MRS. MARWOOD   Because I hate him.

MRS. FAINALL   So do I, but I can hear him named. But what reason have you to hate him in particular?

MRS. MARWOOD   I never loved him; he is, and always was, insufferably proud.

MRS. FAINALL   By the reason you give for your aversion, one would think it dissembled; for you have laid a fault to his charge of which his enemies must acquit him.

MRS. MARWOOD   Oh, then it seems you are one of his favourable enemies. Methinks you look a little pale, and now you flush again.

MRS. FAINALL   Do I? I think I am a little sick o' the sudden.

MRS. MARWOOD   What ails you?

MRS. FAINALL   My husband. Don't you see him? He turned short upon me unawares, and has almost overcome me.

[Enter FAINALL and MIRABELL]

MRS. MARWOOD   Ha, ha, ha! he comes opportunely for you.

MRS. FAINALL   For you, for he has brought Mirabell with him.

FAINALL   My dear.

MRS. FAINALL   My soul.

FAINALL   You don't look well today, child.

MRS. FAINALL   D'ee think so?

MIRABELL   He is the only man that does, madam.

MRS. FAINALL   The only man that would tell me so, at least; and the only man from whom I could hear it without mortification.

FAINALL   O my dear, I am satisfied of your tenderness; I know you cannot resent anything from me, especially what is an effect of my concern.

MRS. FAINALL   Mr. Mirabell, my mother interrupted you in a pleasant relation last night; I would fain hear it out.

MIRABELL   The persons concerned in that affair have yet a tolerable reputation.—I am afraid Mr. Fainall will be censorious.

MRS. FAINALL   He has a humour more prevailing than his curiosity, and will willingly dispense with the hearing of one scandalous story to avoid

___

1. Queen of the Amazons, the warlike tribe of women.

giving an occasion to make another by being seen to walk with his wife. This way, Mr. Mirabell, and I dare promise you will oblige us both. [*Exeunt* MRS. FAINALL *and* MIRABELL]

FAINALL   Excellent creature! Well, sure if I should live to be rid of my wife, I should be a miserable man.

MRS. MARWOOD   Aye!

FAINALL   For, having only that one hope, the accomplishment of it, of consequence, must put an end to all my hopes; and what a wretch is he who must survive his hopes! Nothing remains when that day comes but to sit down and weep like Alexander when he wanted other worlds to conquer.

MRS. MARWOOD   Will you not follow 'em?

FAINALL   Faith, I think not.

MRS. MARWOOD   Pray let us; I have a reason.

FAINALL   You are not jealous?

MRS. MARWOOD   Of whom?

FAINALL   Of Mirabell.

MRS. MARWOOD   If I am, is it inconsistent with my love to you that I am tender of your honour?

FAINALL   You would intimate, then, as if there were a fellow-feeling between my wife and him.

MRS. MARWOOD   I think she does not hate him to that degree she would be thought.

FAINALL   But he, I fear, is too insensible.

MRS. MARWOOD   It may be you are deceived.

FAINALL   It may be so. I do now begin to apprehend it.

MRS. MARWOOD   What?

FAINALL   That I have been deceived, madam, and you are false.

MRS. MARWOOD   That I am false! What mean you?

FAINALL   To let you know I see through all your little arts. Come, you both love him, and both have equally dissembled your aversion. Your mutual jealousies of one another have made you clash till you have both struck fire. I have seen the warm confession reddening on your cheeks and sparkling from your eyes.

MRS. MARWOOD   You do me wrong.

FAINALL   I do not. 'Twas for my ease to oversee [2] and wilfully neglect the gross advances made him by my wife, that by permitting her to be engaged I might continue unsuspected in my pleasures, and take you oftener to my arms in full security. But could you think, because the nodding husband would not wake, that e'er the watchful lover slept?

MRS. MARWOOD   And wherewithal can you reproach me?

FAINALL   With infidelity, with loving of another, with love of Mirabell.

MRS. MARWOOD   'Tis false. I challenge you to show an instance that can confirm your groundless accusation. I hate him.

FAINALL   And wherefore do you hate him? He is insensible, and your resentment follows his neglect. An instance? The injuries you have done him

2. Overlook.

are a proof: your interposing in his love. What cause had you to make discoveries of his pretended passion? To undeceive the credulous aunt and be the officious obstacle of his match with Millamant?

MRS. MARWOOD   My obligations to my lady urged me. I had professed a friendship to her, and could not see her easy nature so abused by that dissembler.

FAINALL   What, was it conscience then? Professed a friendship! Oh, the pious friendships of the female sex!

MRS. MARWOOD   More tender, more sincere, and more enduring than all the vain and empty vows of men, whether professing love to us or mutual faith to one another.

FAINALL   Ha, ha, ha! you are my wife's friend too.

MRS. MARWOOD   Shame and ingratitude! Do you reproach me? You, you upbraid me! Have I been false to her through strict fidelity to you, and sacrificed my friendship to keep my love inviolate? And have you the baseness to charge me with the guilt, unmindful of the merit! To you it should be meritorious that I have been vicious. And do you reflect that guilt upon me, which should lie buried in your bosom?

FAINALL   You misinterpret my reproof. I meant but to remind you of the slight account you once could make of strictest ties, when set in competition with your love to me.

MRS. MARWOOD   'Tis false; you urged it with deliberate malice—'twas spoke in scorn, and I never will forgive it.

FAINALL   Your guilt, not your resentment, begets your rage. If yet you loved, you could forgive a jealousy; but you are stung to find you are discovered.

MRS. MARWOOD   It shall be all discovered. You too shall be discovered; be sure you shall. I can but be exposed;—if I do it myself I shall prevent [3] your baseness.

FAINALL   Why, what will you do?

MRS. MARWOOD   Disclose it to your wife; own what has passed between us.

FAINALL   Frenzy!

MRS. MARWOOD   By all my wrongs I'll do't!—I'll publish to the world the injuries you have done me, both in my fame and fortune. With both I trusted you, you bankrupt in honour, as indigent of wealth!

FAINALL   Your fame I have preserved. Your fortune has been bestowed as the prodigality of your love would have it, in pleasures which we both have shared. Yet, had not you been false, I had ere this repaid it. 'Tis true. Had you permitted Mirabell with Millamant to have stolen their marriage, my lady had been incensed beyond all means of reconcilement. Millamant had forfeited the moiety [4] of her fortune, which then would have descended to my wife. And wherefore did I marry, but to make lawful prize of a rich widow's wealth, and squander it on love and you?

MRS. MARWOOD   Deceit and frivolous pretence!

FAINALL   Death, am I not married? What's pretence? Am I not imprisoned,

3. Anticipate.
4. Half.

fettered? Have I not a wife? Nay, a wife that was a widow, a young widow, a handsome widow; and would be again a widow, but that I have a heart of proof,[5] and something of a constitution to bustle through the ways of wedlock and this world. Will you yet be reconciled to truth and me?

MRS. MARWOOD   Impossible. Truth and you are inconsistent. I hate you, and shall for ever.

FAINALL   For loving you?

MRS. MARWOOD   I loathe the name of love after such usage; and next to the guilt with which you would asperse me, I scorn you most. Farewell.

FAINALL   Nay, we must not part thus.

MRS. MARWOOD   Let me go.

FAINALL   Come, I'm sorry.

MRS. MARWOOD   I care not—let me go—break my hands, do—I'd leave 'em to get loose.

FAINALL   I would not hurt you for the world. Have I no other hold to keep you here?

MRS. MARWOOD   Well, I have deserved it all.

FAINALL   You know I love you.

MRS. MARWOOD   Poor dissembling!—Oh, that—well, it is not yet——

FAINALL   What? What is it not? What is it not yet? It is not yet too late——

MRS. MARWOOD   No, it is not yet too late—I have that comfort.

FAINALL   It is, to love another.

MRS. MARWOOD   But not to loathe, detest, abhor mankind, myself, and the whole treacherous world.

FAINALL   Nay, this is extravagance. Come, I ask your pardon—no tears—I was to blame, I could not love you and be easy in my doubts.—Pray forbear—I believe you; I'm convinced I've done you wrong; and any way, every way will make amends. I'll hate my wife yet more, damn her. I'll part with her, rob her of all she's worth, and will retire somewhere, anywhere, to another world. I'll marry thee—be pacified.— 'Sdeath, they come; hide your face, your tears. You have a mask; wear it a moment. This way, this way; be persuaded.

[*Exeunt*]

[*Enter* MIRABELL *and* MRS. FAINALL]

MRS. FAINALL   They are here yet.

MIRABELL   They are turning into the other walk.

MRS. FAINALL   While I only hated my husband, I could bear to see him; but since I have despised him, he's too offensive.

MIRABELL   Oh, you should hate with prudence.

MRS. FAINALL   Yes, for I have loved with indiscretion.

MIRABELL   You should have just so much disgust for your husband as may be sufficient to make you relish your lover.

MRS. FAINALL   You have been the cause that I have loved without bounds, and would you set limits to that aversion of which you have been the occasion? Why did you make me marry this man?

---

5. Proved strength, as of steel.

MIRABELL   Why do we daily commit disagreeable and dangerous actions? To save that idol, reputation. If the familiarities of our loves had produced that consequence of which you were apprehensive, where could you have fixed a father's name with credit, but on a husband? I knew Fainall to be a man lavish of his morals, an interested and professing friend,[6] a false and a designing lover; yet one whose wit and outward fair behaviour have gained a reputation with the town, enough to make that woman stand excused who has suffered herself to be won by his addresses. A better man ought not to have been sacrificed to the occasion; a worse had not answered to the purpose. When you are weary of him, you know your remedy.

MRS. FAINALL   I ought to stand in some degree of credit with you, Mirabell.

MIRABELL   In justice to you, I have made you privy to my whole design, and put it in your power to ruin or advance my fortune.

MRS. FAINALL   Whom have you instructed to represent your pretended uncle?

MIRABELL   Waitwell, my servant.

MRS. FAINALL   He is an humble servant to Foible, my mother's woman, and may win her to your interest.

MIRABELL   Care is taken for that. She is won and worn by this time. They were married this morning.

MRS. FAINALL   Who?

MIRABELL   Waitwell and Foible. I would not tempt my servant to betray me by trusting him too far. If your mother, in hopes to ruin me, should consent to marry my pretended uncle, he might, like Mosca in *The Fox*,[7] stand upon terms; so I made him sure beforehand.

MRS. FAINALL   So, if my poor mother is caught in a contract, you will discover [8] the imposture betimes, and release her by producing a certificate of her gallant's former marriage.

MIRABELL   Yes, upon condition she consent to my marriage with her niece, and surrender the moiety of her fortune in her possession.

MRS. FAINALL   She talked last night of endeavouring at a match between Millamant and your uncle.

MIRABELL   That was by Foible's direction and my instruction, that she might seem to carry it more privately.

MRS. FAINALL   Well, I have an opinion of your success, for I believe my lady will do anything to get a husband; and when she has this, which you have provided for her, I suppose she will submit to anything to get rid of him.

MIRABELL   Yes, I think the good lady would marry anything that resembled a man, though 'twere no more than what a butler could pinch out of a napkin.[9]

MRS. FAINALL   Female frailty! We must all come to it, if we live to be old, and feel the craving of a false appetite when the true is decayed.

6. Self-seeking and pretended friend.
7. Mosca, the clever servant who threatens to expose his master if his terms are not met, in Ben Johnson's *Volpone, or The Fox* (1606).
8. Uncover.
9. That is, as a decoration for the dinner table.

MIRABELL   An old woman's appetite is depraved like that of a girl. 'Tis the green-sickness [10] of a second childhood; and like the faint offer of a latter spring, serves but to usher in the fall, and withers in an affected bloom.

MRS. FAINALL   Here's your mistress.

[*Enter* MRS. MILLAMANT, WITWOUD, *and* MINCING]

MIRABELL   Here she comes, i'faith, full sail, with her fan spread and her streamers out, and a shoal of fools for tenders.[11]—Ha, no, I cry her mercy!

MRS. FAINALL   I see but one poor empty sculler; and he tows her woman after him.

MIRABELL   You seem to be unattended, madam. You used to have the *beau monde* [12] throng after you; and a flock of gay fine perukes [13] hovering round you.

WITWOUD   Like moths about a candle.—I had like to have lost my comparison for want of breath.

MILLAMANT   Oh, I have denied myself airs today. I have walked as fast through the crowd——

WITWOUD   As a favourite in disgrace, and with as few followers.

MILLAMANT   Dear Mr. Witwoud, truce with your similitudes; for I am as sick of 'em——

WITWOUD   As a physician of a good air.—I cannot help it, madam, though 'tis against myself.

MILLAMANT   Yet again! Mincing, stand between me and his wit.

WITWOUD   Do, Mrs. Mincing, like a screen before a great fire. I confess I do blaze today, I am too bright.

MRS. FAINALL   But, dear Millamant, why were you so long?

MILLAMANT   Long! Lord, have I not made violent haste? I have asked every living thing I met for you; I have enquired after you, as after a new fashion.

WITWOUD   Madam, truce with your similitudes. No, you met her husband, and did not ask him for her.

MIRABELL   By your leave, Witwoud, that were like enquiring after an old fashion, to ask a husband for his wife.

WITWOUD   Hum, a hit, a hit, a palpable hit! I confess it.

MRS. FAINALL   You were dressed before I came abroad.

MILLAMANT   Aye, that's true—oh, but then I had—Mincing, what had I? Why was I so long?

MINCING   O mem, your la'ship stayed to peruse a pecket [14] of letters.

MILLAMANT   Oh, aye, letters—I had letters—I am persecuted with letters—I hate letters. Nobody knows how to write letters; and yet one has 'em, one does not know why. They serve one to pin up one's hair.

---

10. An anemia of adolescent girls.
11. Perhaps a reminiscence of the description of Dalila in Milton's *Samson Agonistes* (1671): "Like a stately ship . . . / With all her bravery on, and tackle trim, / Sails filled, and streamers waving" (ll. 714–18).
12. Fashionable world.
13. Wigs, then fashionable dress for gentlemen.
14. Mincing affects genteel pronunciation, but not with uniform success.

WITWOUD   Is that the way? Pray, madam, do you pin up your hair with all your letters? I find I must keep copies.

MILLAMANT   Only with those in verse, Mr. Witwoud. I never pin up my hair with prose. I fancy one's hair would not curl if it were pinned up with prose. I think I tried once, Mincing.

MINCING   O mem, I shall never forget it.

MILLAMANT   Aye, poor Mincing tiffed [15] and tiffed all the morning.

MINCING   Till I had the cremp in my fingers, I'll vow, mem. And all to no purpose. But when your la'ship pins it up with poetry, it sits so pleasant the next day as anything, and is so pure and so crips.[16]

WITWOUD   Indeed, so 'crips'?

MINCING   You're such a critic, Mr. Witwoud.

MILLAMANT   Mirabell, did not you take exceptions last night? Oh, aye, and went away. Now I think on't I'm angry.—No, now I think on't I'm pleased—for I believe I gave you some pain.

MIRABELL   Does that please you?

MILLAMANT   Infinitely; I love to give pain.

MIRABELL   You would affect a cruelty which is not in your nature; your true vanity is in the power of pleasing.

MILLAMANT   Oh, I ask your pardon for that. One's cruelty is one's power, and when one parts with one's cruelty, one parts with one's power; and when one has parted with that, I fancy one's old and ugly.

MIRABELL   Aye, aye, suffer your cruelty to ruin the object of your power, to destroy your lover—and then how vain, how lost a thing you'll be! Nay, 'tis true: you are no longer handsome when you've lost your lover; your beauty dies upon the instant. For beauty is the lover's gift; 'tis he bestows your charms—your glass is all a cheat. The ugly and the old, whom the looking-glass mortifies, yet after commendation can be flattered by it, and discover beauties in it; for that reflects our praises, rather than your face.

MILLAMANT   Oh, the vanity of these men! Fainall, d'ee hear him? If they did not commend us, we were not handsome! Now you must know they could not commend one, if one was not handsome. Beauty the lover's gift—Lord, what is a lover, that it can give? Why, one makes lovers as fast as one pleases, and they live as long as one pleases, and they die as soon as one pleases; and then if one pleases, one makes more.

WITWOUD   Very pretty. Why you make no more of making of lovers, madam, than of making so many card-matches.[17]

MILLAMANT   One no more owes one's beauty to a lover than one's wit to an echo; they can but reflect what we look and say—vain empty things if we are silent or unseen, and want a being.

MIRABELL   Yet, to those two vain empty things you owe two the greatest pleasures of your life.

MILLAMANT   How so?

MIRABELL   To your lover you owe the pleasure of hearing yourselves praised; and to an echo the pleasure of hearing yourselves talk.

15. Arranged (Millamant's hair).
16. Crisp, i.e. curly.
17. Cards dipped in sulphur and used as matches.

WITWOUD   But I know a lady that loves talking so incessantly, she won't give
an echo fair play; she has that everlasting rotation of tongue, that an
echo must wait till she dies before it can catch her last words.

MILLAMANT   Oh, fiction! Fainall, let us leave these men.

MIRABELL [*aside to* MRS. FAINALL]   Draw off Witwoud.

MRS. FAINALL   Immediately.—I have a word or two for Mr. Witwoud.

MIRABELL   I would beg a little private audience too.

[*Exeunt* WITWOUD *and* MRS. FAINALL]

You had the tyranny to deny me last night, though you knew I came to
impart a secret to you that concerned my love.

MILLAMANT   You saw I was engaged.

MIRABELL   Unkind! You had the leisure to entertain a herd of fools, things who
visit you from their excessive idleness; bestowing on your easiness [18]
that time which is the incumbrance of their lives. How can you find
delight in such society? It is impossible they should admire you. They
are not capable; or if they were, it should be to you as a mortification;
for sure to please a fool is some degree of folly.

MILLAMANT   I please myself—besides, sometimes to converse with fools is for
my health.

MIRABELL   Your health! Is there a worse disease than the conversation of fools?

MILLAMANT   Yes, the vapours; fools are physic for it, next to asafoetida.

MIRABELL   You are not in a course [19] of fools?

MILLAMANT   Mirabell, if you persist in this offensive freedom—you'll displease
me. I think I must resolve, after all, not to have you.—We shan't agree.

MIRABELL   Not in our physic, it may be.

MILLAMANT   And yet our distemper in all likelihood will be the same; for we
shall be sick of one another. I shan't endure to be reprimanded nor
instructed; 'tis so dull to act always by advice and so tedious to be told
of one's faults—I can't bear it. Well, I won't have you, Mirabell—I'm
resolved—I think—you may go—ha, ha, ha! What would you give,
that you could help loving me?

MIRABELL   I would give something that you did not know I could not help it.

MILLAMANT   Come, don't look grave then. Well, what do you say to me?

MIRABELL   I say that a man may as soon make a friend by his wit, or a
fortune by his honesty, as win a woman with plain dealing and sincerity.

MILLAMANT   Sententious Mirabell! Prithee, don't look with that violent and
inflexible wise face, like Solomon at the dividing of the child [20] in an
old tapestry hanging.

MIRABELL   You are merry, madam, but I would persuade you for one moment
to be serious.

MILLAMANT   What, with that face? No, if you keep your countenance, 'tis
impossible I should hold mine. Well, after all, there is something very
moving in a lovesick face. Ha, ha, ha!—well, I won't laugh; don't be
peevish—heigho! Now I'll be melancholy, as melancholy as a watch-
light.[21] Well, Mirabell, if ever you will win me, woo me now.—Nay, if

18. Indulgence.
19. That is, a course of "physic" or medicine.
20. That is, between the two mothers who claim it, I Kings 3:16–28.
21. Dim night-light.

you are so tedious, fare you well. I see they are walking away.

MIRABELL Can you not find in the variety of your disposition one moment——

MILLAMANT To hear you tell me that Foible's married and your plot like to speed? No.

MIRABELL But how you came to know it——

MILLAMANT Unless by the help of the devil, you can't imagine; unless she should tell me herself. Which of the two it may have been, I will leave you to consider; and when you have done thinking of that, think of me. [*Exit*]

MIRABELL I have something more——. Gone!—Think of you! To think of a whirlwind, though 'twere in a whirlwind, were a case of more steady contemplation; a very tranquillity of mind and mansion. A fellow that lives in a windmill has not a more whimsical dwelling than the heart of a man that is lodged in a woman. There is no point of the compass to which they cannot turn, and by which they are not turned, and by one as well as another; for motion, not method, is their occupation. To know this, and yet continue to be in love, is to be made wise from the dictates of reason, and yet persevere to play the fool by the force of instinct.—Oh, here come my pair of turtles! [22]—What, billing so sweetly! Is not Valentine's Day over with you yet?

[*Enter* WAITWELL *and* FOIBLE]

Sirrah, Waitwell, why sure you think you were married for your own recreation, and not for my conveniency.

WAITWELL Your pardon, sir. With submission, we have indeed been solacing in lawful delights; but still with an eye to business, sir. I have instructed her as well as I could. If she can take your directions as readily as my instructions, sir, your affairs are in a prosperous way.

MIRABELL Give you joy, Mrs. Foible.

FOIBLE O 'las, sir, I'm so ashamed—I'm afraid my lady has been in a thousand inquietudes for me. But I protest, sir, I made as much haste as I could.

WAITWELL That she did indeed, sir. It was my fault that she did not make more.

MIRABELL That I believe.

FOIBLE But I told my lady as you instructed me, sir, that I had a prospect of seeing Sir Rowland, your uncle; and that I would put her ladyship's picture in my pocket to show him; which I'll be sure to say has made him so enamoured of her beauty that he burns with impatience to lie at her ladyship's feet and worship the original.

MIRABELL Excellent Foible! Matrimony has made you eloquent in love.

WAITWELL I think she has profited, sir. I think so.

FOIBLE You have seen Madam Millamant, sir?

MIRABELL Yes.

FOIBLE I told her, sir, because I did not know that you might find an opportunity; she had so much company last night.

MIRABELL Your diligence will merit more. In the meantime——[*Gives money*]

FOIBLE O dear sir, your humble servant.

22. Turtledoves.

WAITWELL   Spouse!

MIRABELL   Stand off, sir, not a penny.—Go on and prosper, Foible. The lease shall be made good and the farm stocked, if we succeed.

FOIBLE   I don't question your generosity, sir, and you need not doubt of success. If you have no more commands, sir, I'll be gone; I'm sure my lady is at her toilet and can't dress 'till I come.—Oh dear, I'm sure that [*Looking out*] was Mrs. Marwood that went by in a mask; if she has seen me with you I'm sure she'll tell my lady. I'll make haste home and prevent her. Your servant, sir. B'w'y,[23] Waitwell.

[*Exit* FOIBLE]

WAITWELL   Sir Rowland, if you please.—The jade's so pert upon her preferment[24] she forgets herself.

MIRABELL   Come, sir, will you endeavour to forget yourself—and transform into Sir Rowland.

WAITWELL   Why, sir, it will be impossible I should remember myself—married, knighted, and attended all in one day! 'Tis enough to make any man forget himself. The difficulty will be how to recover my acquaintance and familiarity with my former self, and fall from my transformation to a reformation into Waitwell. Nay, I shan't be quite the same Waitwell neither—for now I remember me, I am married, and can't be my own man again.

Aye, there's the grief; that's the sad change of life;
To lose my title, and yet keep my wife.   [*Exeunt*]

ACT III

A room in LADY WISHFORT'*s house*
[LADY WISHFORT *at her toilet*, PEG *waiting*]

LADY WISHFORT   Merciful! no news of Foible yet?

PEG   No, madam.

LADY WISHFORT   I have no more patience. If I have not fretted myself till I am pale again, there's no veracity in me. Fetch me the red—the red, do you hear, sweetheart? An arrant[1] ash colour, as I'm a person. Look you how this wench stirs! Why dost thou not fetch me a little red? Didst thou not hear me, mopus?[2]

PEG   The red ratafia does your ladyship mean, or the cherry-brandy?

LADY WISHFORT   Ratafia, fool! No, fool. Not the ratafia, fool—grant me patience! I mean the Spanish paper,[3] idiot,—complexion, darling. Paint, paint, paint, dost thou understand that, changeling, dangling thy hands like bobbins before thee? Why dost thou not stir, puppet?—thou wooden thing upon wires!

PEG   Lord, madam, your ladyship is so impatient. I cannot come at the paint, madam; Mrs. Foible has locked it up, and carried the key with her.

23. Contraction of "God be with you" or "good-bye."
24. Advancement.
1. Thorough.
2. Dunce.
3. A cosmetic like rouge.

LADY WISHFORT   A pox take you both! Fetch me the cherry-brandy then. [*Exit* PEG] I'm as pale and as faint, I look like Mrs. Qualmsick the curate's wife, that's always breeding.—Wench, come, come, wench, what art thou doing, sipping? tasting? Save thee, dost thou not know the bottle? [*Enter* PEG *with a bottle and china cup*]

PEG   Madam, I was looking for a cup.

LADY WISHFORT   A cup, save thee! and what a cup hast thou brought! Dost thou take me for a fairy, to drink out of an acorn? Why didst thou not bring thy thimble? Hast thou ne'er a brass thimble clinking in thy pocket with a bit of nutmeg? [4] I warrant thee. Come, fill, fill.—So— again. [*One knocks*] See who that is.—Set down the bottle first. Here, under the table.—What, wouldst thou go with the bottle in thy hand like a tapster? As I'm a person, this wench has lived in an inn upon the road before she came to me, like Maritornes [5] the Asturian in *Don Quixote*. No Foible yet?

PEG   No, madam,—Mrs. Marwood.

LADY WISHFORT   Oh, Marwood! let her come in. Come in, good Marwood.
[*Enter* MRS. MARWOOD]

MRS. MARWOOD   I'm surprised to find your ladyship in dishabille at this time of day.

LADY WISHFORT   Foible's a lost thing; has been abroad since morning, and never heard of since.

MRS. MARWOOD   I saw her but now, as I came masked through the Park, in conference with Mirabell.

LADY WISHFORT   With Mirabell! You call my blood into my face with mentioning that traitor. She durst not have the confidence. I sent her to negotiate an affair in which if I'm detected I'm undone. If that wheedling villain has wrought upon Foible to detect me, I'm ruined. Oh, my dear friend, I'm a wretch of wretches if I'm detected.

MRS. MARWOOD   O madam, you cannot suspect Mrs. Foible's integrity.

LADY WISHFORT   Oh, he carries poison in his tongue that would corrupt integrity itself. If she has given him an opportunity, she has as good as put her integrity into his hands. Ah, dear Marwood, what's integrity to an opportunity?—Hark! I hear her. [*To* PEG] Go, you thing, and send her in!
[*Exit* PEG]
Dear friend, retire into my closet,[6] that I may examine her with more freedom.—You'll pardon me, dear friend, I can make bold with you. —There are books over the chimney—Quarles and Prynne, and *The Short View of the Stage*,[7] with Bunyan's works, to entertain you.
[*Exit* MARWOOD]

4. As good luck charms.
5. The ugly chambermaid in Cervantes's *Don Quixote*.
6. Small dressing room.
7. Francis Quarles, the emblem writer, was, like Bunyan, favorite moral reading of Puritans; William Prynne (1600–1669) was a Puritan critic of the stage (*Histriomastix*, 1632); Jeremy Collier (1650–1726), an Anglican clergyman, is consigned to this company for his *Short View of the Immorality and Profaneness of the English Stage* (1698), which included an attack on Congreve.

[*Enter* FOIBLE]

O Foible, where hast thou been? What hast thou been doing?

FOIBLE   Madam, I have seen the party.

LADY WISHFORT   But what has thou done?

FOIBLE   Nay, 'tis your ladyship has done, and are to do; I have only promised. But a man so enamoured—so transported! Well, here it is, all that is left; all that is not kissed away. Well, if worshipping of pictures be a sin—poor Sir Rowland, I say.

LADY WISHFORT   The miniature has been counted like [8]—but hast thou not betrayed me, Foible? Hast thou not detected me to that faithless Mirabell? What hadst thou to do with him in the Park? Answer me, has he got nothing out of thee?

FOIBLE [*aside*]   So, the devil has been beforehand with me; what shall I say? —Alas, madam, could I help it, if I met that confident thing? Was I in fault? If you had heard how he used me, and all upon your ladyship's account, I'm sure you would not suspect my fidelity. Nay, if that had been the worst, I could have borne; but he had a fling at your ladyship too, and then I could not hold, but, i'faith, I gave him his own.

LADY WISHFORT   Me? What did the filthy fellow say?

FOIBLE   O madam, 'tis a shame to say what he said—with his taunts and his fleers, tossing up his nose. 'Humh!' says he, 'what, you are a-hatching some plot,' says he, 'you are so early abroad, or catering,' [9] says he, 'ferreting for some disbanded officer, I warrant—half pay is but thin subsistence,' says he. 'Well, what pension does your lady propose? Let me see,' says he; 'what, she must come down pretty deep now, she's superannuated,' says he, 'and——'

LADY WISHFORT   Ods my life, I'll have him—I'll have him murdered. I'll have him poisoned. Where does he eat? I'll marry a drawer [10] to have him poisoned in his wine. I'll send for Robin from Locket's [11] immediately.

FOIBLE   Poison him? Poisoning's too good for him. Starve him, madam, starve him; marry Sir Rowland and get him disinherited. Oh, you would bless yourself, to hear what he said.

LADY WISHFORT   A villain! Superannuated!

FOIBLE   'Humh!' says he, 'I hear you are laying designs against me, too,' says he, 'and Mrs. Millamant is to marry my uncle' (he does not suspect a word of your ladyship); 'but,' says he, 'I'll fit you for that, I warrant you,' says he, 'I'll hamper you for that,' says he, 'you and your old frippery,[12] too,' says he, 'I'll handle you——'

LADY WISHFORT   Audacious villain! handle me! would he durst!—Frippery? old frippery! Was there ever such a foul-mouthed fellow? I'll be married tomorrow; I'll be contracted tonight.

FOIBLE   The sooner the better, madam.

LADY WISHFORT   Will Sir Rowland be here, say'st thou? When, Foible?

---

8. Considered a good likeness.

9. Providing for her needs, i.e. seeking out a former officer reduced to half-pay and willing to be bought.

10. Tapster or waiter.

11. A fashionable tavern.

12. Cast-off garments.

FOIBLE   Incontinently,[13] madam. No new sheriff's wife expects the return of
her husband after knighthood with that impatience in which Sir Rowland burns for the dear hour of kissing your ladyship's hands after
dinner.

LADY WISHFORT   Frippery? superannuated frippery! I'll frippery the villain; I'll
reduce him to frippery and rags. A tatterdemalion!—I hope to see him
hung with tatters, like a Long Lane pent-house,[14] or a gibbet-thief. A
slander-mouthed railer! I warrant the spendthrift prodigal's in debt as
much as the million lottery,[15] or the whole court upon a birthday.[16]
I'll spoil his credit with his tailor. Yes, he shall have my niece with her
fortune, he shall.

FOIBLE   He! I hope to see him lodge in Ludgate first, and angle into Blackfriars for brass farthings, with an old mitten.[17]

LADY WISHFORT   Aye, dear Foible; thank thee for that, dear Foible. He has
put me out of all patience. I shall never recompose my features to receive Sir Rowland with any economy of face. This wretch has fretted
me that I am absolutely decayed. Look, Foible.

FOIBLE   Your ladyship has frowned a little too rashly, indeed, madam. There
are some cracks discernible in the white varnish.

LADY WISHFORT   Let me see the glass.—Cracks, say'st thou? Why, I am
arrantly flayed. I look like an old peeled wall. Thou must repair me,
Foible, before Sir Rowland comes; or I shall never keep up to my
picture.

FOIBLE   I warrant you, madam; a little art once made your picture like you;
and now a little of the same art must make you like your picture. Your
picture must sit for you, madam.

LADY WISHFORT   But art thou sure Sir Rowland will not fail to come? Or will
a' not fail when he does come? Will he be importunate, Foible, and
push? For if he should not be importunate—I shall never break decorums—I shall die with confusion if I am forced to advance—oh no,
I can never advance—I shall swoon if he should expect advances. No,
I hope Sir Rowland is better bred than to put a lady to the necessity
of breaking her forms. I won't be too coy neither. I won't give him
despair—but a little disdain is not amiss; a little scorn is alluring.

FOIBLE   A little scorn becomes your ladyship.

LADY WISHFORT   Yes, but tenderness becomes me best—a sort of a dyingness.
—You see that picture has a sort of a—ha, Foible? a swimmingness in
the eyes. Yes, I'll look so. My niece affects it; but she wants features. Is
Sir Rowland handsome? Let my toilet be removed—I'll dress above.
I'll receive Sir Rowland here. Is he handsome? Don't answer me. I
won't know; I'll be surprised. I'll be taken by surprize.

FOIBLE   By storm, madam. Sir Rowland's a brisk man.

---

13. Immediately.
14. Stall for rags or old clothes.
15. A government lottery designed to raise a million pounds.
16. New clothes were expected of courtiers on the king's birthday; cf. the "birth-night beau"
in Pope's *The Rape of the Lock* I.23.
17. Those in the debtors' prison (the Fleet) at Ludgate near Blackfriars would let down
mittens or containers on a string in order to cadge money from passers-by.

LADY WISHFORT   Is he! Oh, then he'll importune, if he's a brisk man. I shall save decorums if Sir Rowland importunes. I have a mortal terror at the apprehension of offending against decorums. Nothing but importunity can surmount decorums. Oh, I'm glad he's a brisk man! Let my things be removed, good Foible.
[*Exit*]
[*Enter* MRS. FAINALL]

MRS. FAINALL   O Foible, I have been in a fright, lest I should come too late. That devil, Marwood, saw you in the Park with Mirabell, and I'm afraid will discover it to my lady.

FOIBLE   Discover what, madam?

MRS. FAINALL   Nay, nay, put not on that strange face. I am privy to the whole design, and know that Waitwell, to whom thou wert this morning married, is to personate Mirabell's uncle, and as such, winning my lady, to involve her in those difficulties from which Mirabell only must release her, by his making his conditions to have my cousin and her fortune left to her own disposal.

FOIBLE   O dear madam, I beg your pardon. It was not my confidence in your ladyship that was deficient; but I thought the former good correspondence between your ladyship and Mr. Mirabell might have hindered his communicating this secret.

MRS. FAINALL   Dear Foible, forget that.

FOIBLE   O dear madam, Mr. Mirabell is such a sweet winning gentleman—but your ladyship is the pattern of generosity. Sweet lady, to be so good! Mr. Mirabell cannot choose but be grateful. I find your ladyship has his heart still. Now, madam, I can safely tell your ladyship our success; Mrs. Marwood had told my lady, but I warrant I managed myself. I turned it all for the better. I told my lady that Mr. Mirabell railed at her. I laid horrid things to his charge, I'll vow; and my lady is so incensed, that she'll be contracted to Sir Rowland tonight, she says; I warrant I worked her up, that he may have her for asking for, as they say of a Welsh maidenhead.

MRS. FAINALL   O rare Foible!

FOIBLE   Madam, I beg your ladyship to acquaint Mr. Mirabell of his success. I would be seen as little as possible to speak to him; besides, I believe Madam Marwood watches me. She has a month's mind; [18] but I know Mr. Mirabell can't abide her.
[*Enter* FOOTMAN]
John, remove my lady's toilet. Madam, your servant. My lady is so impatient, I fear she'll come for me, if I stay.

MRS. FAINALL   I'll go with you up the back stairs, lest I should meet her.
[*Exeunt*]
[*Enter* MRS. MARWOOD]

MRS. MARWOOD   Indeed, Mrs. Engine,[19] is it thus with you? Are you become a go-between of this importance? Yes, I shall watch you. Why, this wench

18. Desire (for Mirabell).
19. Mrs. Instrument.

is the *passe-partout*, a very master-key to everybody's strong box. My friend Fainall,[20] have you carried it so swimmingly? I thought there was something in it; but it seems it's over with you. Your loathing is not from a want of appetite then, but from a surfeit. Else you could never be so cool to fall from a principal to be an assistant,—to procure for him! A pattern of generosity, that, I confess. Well, Mr. Fainall, you have met with your match.—O man, man! Woman, woman! The devil's an ass; if I were a painter, I would draw him like an idiot, a driveller with a bib and bells. Man should have his head and horns, and woman the rest of him. Poor simple fiend!—'Madam Marwood has a month's mind, but he can't abide her.'—'Twere better for him you had not been his confessor in that affair, without you could have kept his counsel closer. I shall not prove another pattern of generosity; he has not obliged me to that with those excesses of himself! And now I'll have none of him.—Here comes the good lady, panting ripe, with a heart full of hope, and a head full of care, like any chemist upon the day of projection.[21]

[*Enter* LADY WISHFORT]

LADY WISHFORT   Oh, dear Marwood, what shall I say for this rude forgetfulness?—but my dear friend is all goodness.

MRS. MARWOOD   No apologies, dear madam; I have been very well entertained.

LADY WISHFORT   As I'm a person, I am in a very chaos to think I should so forget myself: but I have such an olio [22] of affairs, really I know not what to do.—[*Calls*] Foible! I expect my nephew, Sir Wilfull, every moment, too. [*Calls again*] Why, Foible! He means to travel for improvement.

MRS. MARWOOD   Methinks Sir Wilfull should rather think of marrying than travelling, at his years. I hear he is turned of forty.

LADY WISHFORT   Oh, he's in less danger of being spoiled by his travels. I am against my nephew's marrying too young. It will be time enough when he comes back and has acquired discretion to choose for himself.

MRS. MARWOOD   Methinks Mrs. Millamant and he would make a very fit match. He may travel afterwards. 'Tis a thing very usual with young gentlemen.

LADY WISHFORT   I promise you I have thought on't—and since 'tis your judgment, I'll think on't again. I assure you I will. I value your judgment extremely. On my word, I'll propose it.

[*Enter* FOIBLE]

LADY WISHFORT   Come, come, Foible—I had forgot my nephew will be here before dinner. I must make haste.

FOIBLE   Mr. Witwoud and Mr. Petulant are come to dine with your ladyship.

LADY WISHFORT   Oh, dear, I can't appear till I'm dressed! Dear Marwood, shall I be free with you again, and beg you to entertain 'em? I'll make all imaginable haste. Dear friend, excuse me.

[*Exeunt* LADY WISHFORT *and* FOIBLE]

[*Enter* MRS. MILLAMANT *and* MINCING]

MILLAMANT   Sure never anything was so unbred as that odious man!—Marwood, your servant.

20. That is, Mrs. Fainall.
21. Like an alchemist on the day when he hopes finally to turn his metals into gold.
22. Hodgepodge.

MRS. MARWOOD   You have a colour; what's the matter?

MILLAMANT   That horrid fellow, Petulant, has provoked me into a flame. I have broken my fan. Mincing, lend me yours. Is not all the powder out of my hair?

MRS. MARWOOD   No. What has he done?

MILLAMANT   Nay, he has done nothing; he has only talked—nay, he has said nothing neither, but he has contradicted everything that has been said. For my part, I thought Witwoud and he would have quarrelled.

MINCING   I vow, mem, I thought once they would have fit.[23]

MILLAMANT   Well, 'tis a lamentable thing, I swear, that one has not the liberty of choosing one's acquaintance as one does one's clothes.

MRS. MARWOOD   If we had that liberty, we should be as weary of one set of acquaintance, though never so good, as we are of one suit, though never so fine. A fool and a doily stuff [24] would now and then find days of grace, and be worn for variety.

MILLAMANT   I could consent to wear 'em if they would wear alike; but fools never wear out—they are such *drap-de-Berry* [25] things. Without one could give 'em to one's chambermaid after a day or two!

MRS. MARWOOD   'Twere better so indeed. Or what think you of the playhouse? A fine, gay, glossy fool should be given there, like a new masking habit, after the masquerade is over and we have done with the disguise. For a fool's visit is always a disguise, and never admitted by a woman of wit but to blind her affair with a lover of sense. If you would but appear barefaced now and own Mirabell, you might as easily put off Petulant and Witwoud as your hood and scarf. And indeed 'tis time, for the town has found it, the secret is grown too big for the pretence. 'Tis like Mrs. Primly's great belly; she may lace it down before, but it burnishes [26] on her hips. Indeed, Millamant, you can no more conceal it, than my Lady Strammel can her face, that goodly face, which in defiance of her Rhenish-wine tea, will not be comprehended in a mask.[27]

MILLAMANT   I'll take my death, Marwood, you are more censorious than a decayed beauty, or a discarded toast.[28]—Mincing, tell the men they may come up. My aunt is not dressing here.—Their folly is less provoking than your malice. [*Exit* MINCING] The town has found it! What has it found? That Mirabell loves me is no more a secret than it is a secret that you discovered it to my aunt, or than the reason why you discovered it is a secret.

MRS. MARWOOD   You are nettled.

MILLAMANT   You're mistaken. Ridiculous!

MRS. MARWOOD   Indeed, my dear, you'll tear another fan if you don't mitigate those violent airs.

23. Fought.
24. Cheap woolen cloth.
25. Heavy, durable woolen.
26. Swells out.
27. Lady Strammel (the name implies an ugly woman), for all her efforts to reduce (with white Rhine wine), has an ample face that no mask can conceal.
28. One whose health is no longer drunk by lovers.

MILLAMANT   O silly! Ha, ha, ha! I could laugh immoderately. Poor Mirabell! His constancy to me has quite destroyed his complaisance for all the world beside. I swear, I never enjoined it him to be so coy. If I had the vanity to think he would obey me, I would command him to show more gallantry. 'Tis hardly well bred to be so particular on one hand, and so insensible on the other. But I despair to prevail and so let him follow his own way. Ha, ha, ha! Pardon me, dear creature, I must laugh, ha, ha, ha!—though I grant you 'tis a little barbarous, ha, ha, ha!

MRS. MARWOOD   What pity 'tis, so much fine raillery, and delivered with so significant gesture, should be so unhappily directed to miscarry.

MILLAMANT   Heh? Dear creature, I ask your pardon—I swear I did not mind [29] you.

MRS. MARWOOD   Mr. Mirabell and you both may think it a thing impossible, when I shall tell him by telling you——

MILLAMANT   O dear, what? for it is the same thing, if I hear it—ha, ha, ha!

MRS. MARWOOD   That I detest him, hate him, madam.

MILLAMANT   O madam, why so do I—and yet the creature loves me, ha, ha, ha! How can one forbear laughing to think of it. I am a sibyl [30] if I am not amazed to think what he can see in me. I'll take my death, I think you are handsomer—and within a year or two as young. If you could but stay for me, I should overtake you—but that cannot be. Well, that thought makes me melancholy. Now I'll be sad.

MRS. MARWOOD   Your merry note may be changed sooner than you think.

MILLAMANT   D'ye say so? Then I'm resolved I'll have a song to keep up my spirits.

[*Enter* MINCING]

MINCING   The gentlemen stay but to comb,[31] madam, and will wait on you.

MILLAMANT   Desire Mrs. —— that is in the next room to sing the song I would have learnt yesterday. You shall hear it, madam—not that there's any great matter in it—but 'tis agreeable to my humour.

SONG [32]

I

Love's but the frailty of the mind,
    When 'tis not with ambition joined;
A sickly flame, which if not fed expires;
And feeding, wastes in self-consuming fires.

II

'Tis not to wound a wanton boy
    Or amorous youth, that gives the joy;

29. Pay attention to.
30. Seer, prophetess.
31. That is, their wigs.
32. The original text adds, "Set by Mr. John Eccles and sung by Mrs. Hodgson"; the former was Master of the King's Band and the latter a well-known singer and actress. The blank left in the dialogue allows Millamant to name whichever singer is available for the performance. The song, which seems designed to provoke Marwood, reflects her view of love more accurately than it does Millamant's.

But 'tis the glory to have pierced a swain,
For whom inferior beauties sighed in vain.

III

Then I alone the conquest prize,
    When I insult a rival's eyes:
If there's delight in love, 'tis when I see
That heart which others bleed for, bleed for me.

[*Enter* PETULANT *and* WITWOUD]

MILLAMANT   Is your animosity composed, gentlemen?

WITWOUD   Raillery, raillery, madam; we have no animosity—we hit off a little wit now and then, but no animosity. The falling out of wits is like the falling out of lovers.—We agree in the main,[33] like treble and base. Ha, Petulant?

PETULANT   Aye, in the main. But when I have a humour to contradict——

WITWOUD   Aye, when he has a humour to contradict, then I contradict too. What, I know my cue. Then we contradict one another like two battle-dores;[34] for contradictions beget one another like Jews.

PETULANT   If he says black's black—if I have a humour to say 'tis blue—let that pass—all's one for that. If I have a humour to prove it, it must be granted.

WITWOUD   Not positively must—but it may—it may.

PETULANT   Yes, it positively must, upon proof positive.

WITWOUD   Aye, upon proof positive it must; but upon proof presumptive it only may. That's a logical distinction now, madam.

MRS. MARWOOD   I perceive your debates are of importance and very learnedly handled.

PETULANT   Importance is one thing, and learning's another; but a debate's a debate, that I assert.

WITWOUD   Petulant's an enemy to learning; he relies altogether on his parts.[35]

PETULANT   No, I'm no enemy to learning; it hurts not me.

MRS. MARWOOD   That's a sign indeed it's no enemy to you.

PETULANT   No, no, it's no enemy to anybody, but them that have it.

MILLAMANT   Well, an illiterate man's my aversion. I wonder at the impudence of any illiterate man to offer to make love.

WITWOUD   That I confess I wonder at too.

MILLAMANT   Ah! to marry an ignorant that can hardly read or write!

PETULANT   Why should a man be ever the further from being married though he can't read, any more than he is from being hanged? The ordinary's [36] paid for setting the psalm, and the parish-priest for reading the cere-mony. And for the rest which is to follow in both cases, a man may do it without book—so all's one for that.

---

33. Largely; but also in the mean, the middle part in which treble and bass harmonize.
34. Opponents in a game of badminton.
35. Natural powers.
36. The prison chaplain, who reads a Psalm before the hanging, as the parish priest presides at a wedding.

MILLAMANT   D'ye hear the creature? Lord, here's company, I'll be gone.

[*Exeunt* MILLAMANT *and* MINCING]

WITWOUD   In the name of Barthol'mew [37] and his fair, what have we here?

MRS. MARWOOD   'Tis your brother, I fancy. Don't you know him?

WITWOUD   Not I—yes, I think it is he—I've almost forgot him; I have not seen him since the Revolution.[38]

[*Enter* SIR WILFULL WITWOUD *in a country riding habit, and* SERVANT *to* LADY WISHFORT]

SERVANT   Sir, my lady's dressing. Here's company, if you please to walk in, in the meantime.

SIR WILFULL   Dressing! What, it's but morning here I warrant with you in London; we should count it towards afternoon in our parts down in Shropshire. Why then belike my aunt han't dined yet—ha, friend?

SERVANT   Your aunt, sir?

SIR WILFULL   My aunt, sir, yes, my aunt, sir, and your lady, sir; your lady is my aunt, sir. Why, what, dost thou not know me, friend? Why, then send somebody here that does. How long hast thou lived with thy lady, fellow, ha?

SERVANT   A week, sir; longer than anybody in the house, except my lady's woman.

SIR WILFULL   Why then belike thou dost not know thy lady if thou see'st her, ha, friend?

SERVANT   Why truly, sir, I cannot safely swear to her face in a morning, before she is dressed. 'Tis like I may give a shrewd guess at her by this time.

SIR WILFULL   Well, prithee try what thou canst do; if thou canst not guess, enquire her out, dost hear, fellow? And tell her, her nephew, Sir Wilfull Witwoud, is in the house.

SERVANT   I shall, sir.

SIR WILFULL   Hold ye, hear me, friend; a word with you in your ear; prithee who are these gallants?

SERVANT   Really, sir, I can't tell; there come so many here, 'tis hard to know 'em all.

[*Exit* SERVANT]

SIR WILFULL   Oons, this fellow knows less than a starling; [39] I don't think a' knows his own name.

MRS. MARWOOD   Mr. Witwoud, your brother is not behindhand in forgetfulness —I fancy he has forgot you too.

WITWOUD   I hope so—the devil take him that remembers first, I say.

SIR WILFULL   Save you, gentlemen and lady.

MRS. MARWOOD   For shame, Mr. Witwoud; why won't you speak to him?— And you, sir.

WITWOUD   Petulant, speak.

PETULANT   And you, sir.

---

37. St. Bartholomew gave his name to the fair held on his feast day (August 24) in the market at Smithfield; it was a scene of low entertainments, including exhibitions of monsters.

38. The Glorious Revolution of 1688.

39. Considered a stupid bird (part of Sir Wilfull's country lore).

SIR WILFULL   No offence, I hope. [*Salutes* [40] MARWOOD]

MRS. MARWOOD   No, sure, sir.

WITWOUD   This is a vile dog, I see that already. No offence! Ha, ha, ha! To him; to him, Petulant, smoke [41] him.

PETULANT   It seems as if you had come a journey, sir; hem, hem. [*Surveying him round*]

SIR WITWOUD   Very likely, sir, that it may seem so.

PETULANT   No offence, I hope, sir.

WITWOUD   Smoke the boots, the boots, Petulant, the boots; ha, ha, ha!

SIR WILFULL   Maybe not, sir; thereafter as [42] 'tis meant, sir.

PETULANT   Sir, I presume upon the information of your boots.

SIR WILFULL   Why, 'tis like you may, sir. If you are not satisfied with the information of my boots, sir, if you will step to the stable, you may enquire further of my horse, sir.

PETULANT   Your horse, sir! Your horse is an ass, sir!

SIR WILFULL   Do you speak by way of offence, sir?

MRS. MARWOOD   The gentleman's merry, that's all, sir.—[*Aside*] S'life, we shall have a quarrel betwixt an horse and an ass, before they find one another out.—You must not take anything amiss from your friends, sir. You are among your friends here, though it may be you don't know it. If I am not mistaken, you are Sir Wilfull Witwoud.

SIR WILFULL   Right, lady; I am Sir Wilfull Witwoud, so I write myself; no offence to anybody, I hope; and nephew to the Lady Wishfort of this mansion.

MRS. MARWOOD   Don't you know this gentleman, sir?

SIR WILFULL   Hum! What, sure 'tis not.—Yea, by'r Lady, but 'tis.—'Sheart, I know not whether 'tis or no.—Yea, but 'tis, by the Wrekin.[43] Brother Anthony! What, Tony, i'faith! What, dost thou not know me? By'r Lady, nor I thee, thou art so becravatted, and so beperiwigged.—'Sheart, why dost not speak? Art thou o'erjoyed?

WITWOUD   Odso, brother, is it you? Your servant, brother.

SIR WILFULL   Your servant! Why yours, sir. Your servant again.—'Sheart, and your friend and servant to that—and a—(*Puff*) and a flapdragon [44] for your service, sir, and a hare's foot, and a hare's scut [45] for your service, sir, an you be so cold and so courtly!

WITWOUD   No offence, I hope, brother.

SIR WILFULL   'Sheart, sir, but there is, and much offence. A pox, is this your Inns o' Court [46] breeding, not to know your friends and your relations, your elders, and your betters?

WITWOUD   Why, brother Wilfull of Salop,[47] you may be as short as a Shrews-

---

40. Kisses.
41. Smell him out.
42. Depending on how.
43. A high hill in Shropshire, the source of a local toast, "All friends round the Wrekin."
44. In a game, the raisins caught out of burning brandy.
45. Tail.
46. The four societies in London where lawyers had offices, and law students—such as Witwoud—lived during training.
47. Shropshire, of which Shrewsbury is a principal town; Witwoud puns on the crispness of a shortcake and the shortness of his half-brother's temper.

bury cake, if you please. But I tell you 'tis not modish to know relations in town. You think you're in the country, where great lubberly brothers slabber and kiss one another when they meet, like a call of sergeants.[48] 'Tis not the fashion here; 'tis not indeed, dear brother.

SIR WILFULL   The fashion's a fool; and you're a fop, dear brother. 'Sheart, I've suspected this. By'r Lady, I conjectured you were a fop since you began to change the style of your letters, and write in a scrap of paper gilt round the edges, no broader than a *subpoena*. I might expect this when you left off 'Honoured Brother,' and 'hoping you are in good health,' and so forth—to begin with a 'Rat me, knight, I'm so sick of a last night's debauch'—Od's heart, and then tell a familiar tale of a cock and a bull, and a whore and a bottle, and so conclude. You could write news before you were out of your time,[49] when you lived with honest Pumple Nose, the attorney of Furnival's Inn. You could intreat to be remembered then to your friends round the Wrekin. We could have gazettes then, and Dawks's Letter, and the weekly bill, 'till of late days.

PETULANT   'Slife, Witwoud, were you ever an attorney's [50] clerk? Of the family of the Furnivals? Ha, ha, ha!

WITWOUD   Aye, aye, but that was for a while. Not long, not long. Pshaw! I was not in my own power then. An orphan, and this fellow was my guardian; aye, aye, I was glad to consent to that man to come to London. He had the disposal of me then. If I had not agreed to that, I might have been bound prentice to a felt-maker in Shrewsbury; this fellow would have bound me to a maker of felts.

SIR WILFULL   'Sheart, and better than to be bound to a maker of fops, where, I suppose, you have served your time and now you may set up for yourself.

MRS. MARWOOD   You intend to travel, sir, as I'm informed.

SIR WILFULL   Belike I may, madam. I may chance to sail upon the salt seas, if my mind hold.

PETULANT   And the wind serve.

SIR WILFULL   Serve or not serve, I shan't ask license of you, sir; nor the weather-cock your companion. I direct my discourse to the lady, sir. 'Tis like my aunt may have told you, madam—yes, I have settled my concerns, I may say now, and am minded to see foreign parts. If an how that the peace holds, whereby, that is, taxes abate.[51]

MRS. MARWOOD   I thought you had designed for France at all adventures.

SIR WILFULL   I can't tell that; 'tis like I may, and 'tis like I may not. I am somewhat dainty in making a resolution,—because when I make it I keep it. I don't stand shill I, shall I, then; if I say't, I'll do't. But I have

48. Like a group of lawyers just admitted together to the rank of sergeant-at-law; here congratulating each other heartily on a unique occasion (unlike the more spontaneous warmth of country manners).

49. Before you had finished serving your term as apprentice, while Witwoud still provided news in his letters (such as might be found in Dawks's newsletter or in the weekly parish list of deaths).

50. An attorney was a legal agent without the rights of a barrister to plead cases and therefore had lower status (as did Furnival's among the Inns of Court).

51. The Peace of Ryswick (1697) ended the costly war against France, but for only a few years.

thoughts to tarry a small matter in town, to learn somewhat of your lingo first, before I cross the seas. I'd gladly have a spice of your French, as they say, whereby to hold discourse in foreign countries.

MRS. MARWOOD   Here is an academy in town for that use.

SIR WILFULL   There is? 'Tis like there may.

MRS. MARWOOD   No doubt you will return very much improved.

WITWOUD   Yes, refined, like a Dutch skipper from a whale-fishing.[52]

[*Enter* LADY WISHFORT *and* FAINALL]

LADY WISHFORT   Nephew, you are welcome.

SIR WILFULL   Aunt, your servant.

FAINALL   Sir Wilfull, your most faithful servant.

SIR WILFULL   Cousin Fainall, give me your hand.

LADY WISHFORT   Cousin Witwoud, your servant; Mr. Petulant, your servant. —Nephew, you are welcome again. Will you drink anything after your journey, nephew, before you eat? Dinner's almost ready.

SIR WILFULL   I'm very well, I thank you, aunt—however, I thank you for your courteous offer. 'Sheart, I was afraid you would have been in the fashion too, and have remembered to have forgot your relations. Here's your Cousin Tony, belike, I mayn't call him brother for fear of offence.

LADY WISHFORT   Oh, he's a rallier, nephew—my cousin's a wit; and your great wits always rally their best friends to choose.[53] When you have been abroad, nephew, you'll understand raillery better.

[FAINALL *and* MRS. MARWOOD *talk apart*]

SIR WILFULL   Why then let him hold his tongue in the meantime, and rail[54] when that day comes.

[*Enter* MINCING]

MINCING   Mem, I come to acquaint your la'ship that dinner is impatient.

SIR WILFULL   Impatient? Why then belike it won't stay till I pull off my boots. Sweetheart, can you help me to a pair of slippers? My man's with his horses, I warrant.

LADY WISHFORT   Fie, fie, nephew, you would not pull off your boots here. Go down into the hall—dinner shall stay for you.—My nephew's a little unbred, you'll pardon him, madam.—Gentlemen, will you walk?— Marwood——

MRS. MARWOOD   I'll follow you, madam, before Sir Wilfull is ready.

[*Manent*[55] MRS. MARWOOD *and* FAINALL]

FAINALL   Why then Foible's a bawd, an arrant, rank, match-making bawd. And I, it seems, am a husband, a rank husband; and my wife a very arrant, rank wife—all in the way of the world. 'Sdeath, to be an anticipated cuckold, a cuckold in embryo! Sure I was born with budding antlers like a young satyr, or a citizen's child.[56] 'Sdeath, to be outwitted,

---

52. That is, reeking of oil, as were all aboard whale-fishing ships.
53. As they like.
54. Sir Wilfull misses the crucial distinction between rallying or raillery and railing or scolding and denouncing (as well he might in this company).
55. "There remains."
56. That is, born to be cuckolded; for citizens (or "cits"), merchants in the City of London, were notoriously easy victims of the efforts of Westminster gallants to seduce their wives and thus to put horns on husbands' heads.

to be out-jilted—out-matrimonied! If I had kept my speed like a stag, 'twere somewhat—but to crawl after with my horns like a snail, and outstripped by my wife—'tis scurvy wedlock.

MRS. MARWOOD   Then shake it off. You have often wished for an opportunity to part, and now you have it. But first prevent their plot—the half of Millamant's fortune is too considerable to be parted with to a foe, to Mirabell.

FAINALL   Damn him, that had been mine had you not made that fond discovery [57]—that had been forfeited, had they been married. My wife had added lustre to my horns by that increase of fortune; I could have worn 'em tipped with gold, though my forehead had been furnished like a deputy-lieutenant's hall.[58]

MRS. MARWOOD   They may prove a cap of maintenance [59] to you still, if you can away with [60] your wife. And she's no worse than when you had her —I dare swear she had given up her game before she was married.

FAINALL   Hum! That may be.——She might throw up her cards; but I'll be hanged if she did not put Pam in her pocket.[61]

MRS. MARWOOD   You married her to keep you; and if you can contrive to have her keep you better than you expected, why should you not keep her longer than you intended?

FAINALL   The means, the means!

MRS. MARWOOD   Discover to my lady your wife's conduct; threaten to part with her. My lady loves her, and will come to any composition to save her reputation. Take the opportunity of breaking [62] it just upon the discovery of this imposture. My lady will be enraged beyond bounds, and sacrifice niece and fortune and all at that conjuncture. And let me alone to keep her warm; if she should flag in her part, I will not fail to prompt her.

FAINALL   Faith, this has an appearance.

MRS. MARWOOD   I'm sorry I hinted to my lady to endeavour a match between Millamant and Sir Wilfull; that may be an obstacle.

FAINALL   Oh, for that matter leave me to manage him; I'll disable him for that; he will drink like a Dane. After dinner, I'll set his hand in.

MRS. MARWOOD   Well, how do you stand affected towards your lady?

FAINALL   Why, faith, I'm thinking of it.—Let me see—I am married already, so that's over;—my wife has played the jade with me—well, that's over too;—I never loved her, or if I had, why that would have been over too by this time. Jealous of her I cannot be, for I am certain; so there's an end of jealousy. Weary of her, I am, and shall be—no, there's no end of that; no, no, that were too much to hope. Thus far concerning my repose. Now for my reputation.—As to my own, I married not for it; so that's out of the question.—And as to my part in my wife's—why,

57. Foolishly revealed it.
58. That is, full of antlers, like the hall of a country house.
59. A play upon the heraldic term for a two-pointed cap of high office.
60. Endure, put up with.
61. Keep an ace up her sleeve; actually Pam is jack of clubs but high card in loo.
62. Exposing.

she had parted with hers before; so bringing none to me, she can take none from me; 'tis against all rule of play, that I should lose to one who has not wherewithal to stake.

MRS. MARWOOD   Besides, you forget, marriage is honourable.

FAINALL   Hum! Faith, and that's well thought on; marriage is honourable, as you say, and if so, wherefore should cuckoldom be a discredit, being derived from so honourable a root?

MRS. MARWOOD   Nay, I know not; if the root be honourable, why not the branches? [63]

FAINALL   So, so, why this point's clear. Well, how do we proceed?

MRS. MARWOOD   I will contrive a letter which shall be delivered to my lady at the time when that rascal who is to act Sir Rowland is with her. It shall come as from an unknown hand—for the less I appear to know of the truth, the better I can play the incendiary. Besides, I would not have Foible provoked if I could help it,—because you know she knows some passages. Nay, I expect all will come out—but let the mine [64] be sprung first, and then I care not if I'm discovered.

FAINALL   If the worst come to the worst, I'll turn my wife to grass.—I have already a deed of settlement of the best part of her estate, which I wheedled out of her, and that you shall partake at least.

MRS. MARWOOD   I hope you are convinced that I hate Mirabell. Now you'll be no more jealous?

FAINALL   Jealous, no!—by this kiss—let husbands be jealous, but let the lover still believe. Or if he doubt, let it be only to endear his pleasure and prepare the joy that follows, when he proves his mistress true. But let husbands' doubts convert to endless jealousy; or if they have belief, let it corrupt to superstition and blind credulity. I am single and will herd no more with 'em. True, I wear the badge, but I'll disown the order. And since I take my leave of 'em, I care not if I leave 'em a common motto to their common crest:

All husbands must, or pain, or shame, endure;
The wise too jealous are, fools too secure.
[*Exeunt*]

ACT IV

A room in Lady Wishfort's house [1]

[*Enter* LADY WISHFORT *and* FOIBLE]

LADY WISHFORT   Is Sir Rowland coming, say'st thou, Foible? and are things in order?

FOIBLE   Yes, madam. I have put waxlights in the sconces, and placed the foot men in a row in the hall in their best liveries, with the coachman and postilion to fill up the equipage.

LADY WISHFORT   Have you pulvilled [2] the coachman and postilion that they may not stink of the stable when Sir Rowland comes by?

63. That is, with the image of branching horns or antlers.
64. A buried explosive charge.

1. The original text reads "Scene"—i.e. setting—"continues."
2. Powdered (and perfumed).

FOIBLE   Yes, madam.

LADY WISHFORT   And are the dancers and the music ready that he may be entertained in all points with correspondence to his passion?

FOIBLE   All is ready, madam.

LADY WISHFORT   And—well—and how do I look, Foible?

FOIBLE   Most killing well, madam.

LADY WISHFORT   Well, and how shall I receive him? In what figure shall I give his heart the first impression? There is a great deal in the first impression. Shall I sit?—No, I won't sit—I'll walk—aye, I'll walk from the door upon his entrance, and then turn full upon him.—No, that will be too sudden. I'll lie—aye, I'll lie down—I'll receive him in my little dressing-room; there's a couch—yes, yes, I'll give the first impression on a couch.—I won't lie neither, but loll and lean upon one elbow, with one foot a little dangling off, jogging in a thoughtful way—yes— and then as soon as he appears, start, aye, start and be surprized, and rise to meet him in a pretty disorder—yes—oh, nothing is more allur- ing than a levee [3] from a couch in some confusion.—It shows the foot to advantage, and furnishes with blushes and recomposing airs beyond comparison. Hark! There's a coach.

FOIBLE   'Tis he, madam.

LADY WISHFORT   Oh dear, has my nephew made his addresses to Millamant? I ordered him.

FOIBLE   Sir Wilfull is set in to drinking, madam, in the parlor.

LADY WISHFORT   Ods my life, I'll send him to her. Call her down, Foible; bring her hither. I'll send him as I go. When they are together, then come to me, Foible, that I may not be too long alone with Sir Row- land.

[*Exit*]

[*Enter* MRS. MILLAMANT *and* MRS. FAINALL]

FOIBLE   Madam, I stayed here, to tell your ladyship that Mr. Mirabell has waited this half-hour for an opportunity to talk with you, though my lady's orders were to leave you and Sir Wilfull together. Shall I tell Mr. Mirabell that you are at leisure?

MILLAMANT   No—what would the dear man have? I am thoughtful and would amuse myself,—bid him come another time.

[*Repeating and walking about*]

There never yet was woman made,

Nor shall, but to be curst.[4]

That's hard!

MRS. FAINALL   You are very fond of Sir John Suckling today, Millamant, and the poets.

MILLAMANT   Heh? [5] Aye, and filthy verses—so I am.

FOIBLE   Sir Wilfull is coming, madam. Shall I send Mr. Mirabell away?

MILLAMANT   Aye, if you please, Foible, send him away,—or send him hither,

3. Rising.
4. The opening lines of a poem by Sir John Suckling, through which—as in other quota- tions that follow—Millamant considers her plight: courted by Mirabell, whom she loves and believes to love her, but distrustful of the insincerity of lovers and of the "way of the world."
5. The original texts read "He," but this emendation has been proposed by A. E. Case.

—just as you will, dear Foible.—I think I'll see him—Shall I? Aye, let
the wretch come. [*Repeating*]
Thyrsis, a youth of the inspired train.[6]
Dear Fainall, entertain Sir Wilfull—thou hast philosophy to undergo a
fool; thou art married and hast patience.—I would confer with my own
thoughts.

MRS. FAINALL   I am obliged to you that you would make me your proxy in
this affair; but I have business of my own.
[*Enter* SIR WILFULL]
—O Sir Wilfull, you are come at the critical instant. There's your
mistress up to the ears in love and contemplation; pursue your point
now or never.

SIR WILFULL   Yes; my aunt would have it so,—I would gladly have been
encouraged with a bottle or two, because I'm somewhat wary at first,
before I am acquainted.—[*This while* MILLAMANT *walks about repeating to herself*] But I hope, after a time, I shall break my mind—that is,
upon further acquaintance.—So for the present, cousin, I'll take my
leave—if so be you'll be so kind to make my excuse, I'll return to my
company——

MRS. FAINALL   Oh, fie, Sir Wilfull! What, you must not be daunted.

SIR WILFULL   Daunted! no, that's not it, it is not so much for that—for if so
be that I set on't, I'll do't. But only for the present, 'tis sufficient till
further acquaintance, that's all—your servant.

MRS. FAINALL   Nay, I'll swear you shall never lose so favourable an opportunity, if I can help it. I'll leave you together, and lock the door.
[*Exit*]

SIR WILFULL   Nay, nay, cousin,—I have forgot my gloves. What d'ye do?—
'Sheart, a' has locked the door indeed, I think.—Nay, Cousin Fainall,
open the door.—Pshaw, what a vixen trick is this?—Nay, now a' has
seen me too.—Cousin, I made bold to pass through as it were—I think
this door's enchanted——

MILLAMANT [*repeating*]
I prithee spare me, gentle boy,
Press me no more for that slight toy,—[7]

SIR WILFULL   Anan? [8] Cousin, your servant.

MILLAMANT [*repeating*]
That foolish trifle of a heart——
Sir Wilfull!

SIR WILFULL   Yes—your servant. No offence, I hope, cousin.

MILLAMANT [*repeating*]
I swear it will not do its part,
Though thou dost thine, employ'st thy power and art.
Natural, easy Suckling!

SIR WILFULL   Anan? Suckling? No such suckling neither, cousin, nor stripling.
I thank heaven, I'm no minor.

6. The first line of *The Story of Phoebus and Daphne Applied,* by Edmund Waller.
7. From a song by Suckling, which ironically renders Sir Wilfull's awkward courtship in
cavalier idiom.
8. What's that? (a rustic form).

MILLAMANT   Ah, rustic, ruder than Gothic! [9]

SIR WILFULL   Well, well, I shall understand your lingo one of these days, cousin; in the meanwhile I must answer in plain English.

MILLAMANT   Have you any business with me, Sir Wilfull?

SIR WILFULL   Not at present, cousin.—Yes, I made bold to see, to come and know if that how you were disposed to fetch a walk this evening, if so be that I might not be troublesome, I would have sought a walk with you.

MILLAMANT   A walk? What then?

SIR WILFULL   Nay, nothing—only for the walk's sake, that's all——

MILLAMANT   I nauseate walking; 'tis a country diversion; I loathe the country and everything that relates to it.

SIR WILFULL   Indeed! Hah! Look ye, look ye, you do? Nay, 'tis like you may.— Here are choice of pastimes here in town, as plays and the like; that must be confessed indeed.

MILLAMANT   Ah, *l'étourdi!* [10] I hate the town too.

SIR WILFULL   Dear heart, that's much.—Hah! that you should hate 'em both! Hah! 'tis like you may; there are some can't relish the town, and others can't away with the country,—'tis like you may be one of those, cousin.

MILLAMANT   Ha, ha, ha! Yes, 'tis like I may.—You have nothing further to say to me?

SIR WILFULL   Not at present, cousin.—'Tis like when I have an opportunity to be more private,—I may break my mind in some measure—I conjecture you partly guess.—However, that's as time shall try,—but spare to speak and spare to speed, [11] as they say.

MILLAMANT   If it is of no great importance, Sir Wilfull, you will oblige me to leave me; I have just now a little business——

SIR WILFULL   Enough, enough, cousin; yes, yes, all a case.—When you're disposed, when you're disposed. Now's as well as another time; and another time as well as now. All's one for that,—yes, yes, if your concerns call you, there's no haste; it will keep cold as they say.—Cousin, your servant.—I think this door's locked.

MILLAMANT   You may go this way, sir.

SIR WILFULL   Your servant! then with your leave I'll return to my company.
    [*Exit*]

MILLAMANT   Aye, aye; ha, ha, ha!
    Like Phoebus sung the no less amorous boy.[12]
    [*Enter* MIRABELL]

MIRABELL
    Like Daphne she, as lovely and as coy.
    Do you lock yourself up from me, to make my search more curious? [13]

9. That is, more rough and ill-shaped even than barbarous Gothic (as opposed to classical grace and urbanity); perhaps suggestive of the rough Gothic parish churches to be found in most country villages.

10. Recalling the dolt who gives his name to Molière's comedy.

11. Succeed, thrive.

12. Returning to the Waller poem, which Mirabell immediately and aptly continues, playing in the succeeding lines on Apollo's pursuit of Daphne, who is changed to a laurel tree (the source of Apollo's crown).

13. Difficult.

Or is this pretty artifice contrived to signify that here the chase must end, and my pursuit be crowned, for you can fly no further?

MILLAMANT   Vanity! No—I'll fly and be followed to the last moment. Though I am upon the very verge of matrimony, I expect you should solicit me as much as if I were wavering at the grate of a monastery,[14] with one foot over the threshold. I'll be solicited to the very last, nay, and afterwards.

MIRABELL   What, after the last?

MILLAMANT   Oh, I should think I was poor and had nothing to bestow, if I were reduced to an inglorious ease and freed from the agreeable fatigues of solicitation.

MIRABELL   But do not you know, that when favours are conferred upon instant [15] and tedious solicitation, that they diminish in their value, and that both the giver loses the grace and the receiver lessens his pleasure?

MILLAMANT   It may be in things of common application, but never sure in love. Oh, I hate a lover that can dare to think he draws a moment's air independent on the bounty of his mistress. There is not so impudent a thing in nature as the saucy look of an assured man, confident of success. The pedantic arrogance of a very husband has not so pragmatical [16] an air. Ah! I'll never marry, unless I am first made sure of my will and pleasure.

MIRABELL   Would you have 'em both before marriage? Or will you be contented with the first now and stay for the other till after grace?

MILLAMANT   Ah, don't be impertinent.—My dear liberty, shall I leave thee? My faithful solitude, my darling contemplation, must I bid you then adieu? Ay-h, adieu—my morning thoughts, agreeable wakings, indolent slumbers, all ye *douceurs, ye sommeils du matin*,[17] adieu?—I can't do't, 'tis more than impossible. Positively, Mirabell, I'll lie abed in a morning as long as I please.

MIRABELL   Then I'll get up in a morning as early as I please.

MILLAMANT   Ah! Idle creature, get up when you will.—And d'ye hear, I won't be called names after I'm married; positively I won't be called names.

MIRABELL   Names?

MILLAMANT   Aye, as wife, spouse, my dear, joy, jewel, love, sweetheart, and the rest of that nauseous cant in which men and their wives are so fulsomely familiar—I shall never bear that.—Good Mirabell, don't let us be familiar or fond, nor kiss before folks, like my Lady Fadler [18] and Sir Francis; nor go to Hyde Park together the first Sunday in a new chariot to provoke eyes and whispers, and then never to be seen together again, as if we were proud of one another the first week and ashamed of one another for ever after. Let us never visit together nor go to a play together, but let us be very strange [19] and well bred. Let us be as strange

14. Convent.
15. Urgent.
16. Conceited.
17. "Comforts and morning sleep."
18. Meaning Fondler.
19. Reserved.

as if we had been married a great while, and as well bred as if we were not married at all.

MIRABELL   Have you any more conditions to offer? Hitherto your demands are pretty reasonable.

MILLAMANT   Trifles,—as liberty to pay and receive visits to and from whom I please; to write and receive letters, without interrogatories or wry faces on your part. To wear what I please, and choose conversation with regard only to my own taste; to have no obligation upon me to converse with wits that I don't like, because they are your acquaintance; or to be intimate with fools because they may be your relations. Come to dinner when I please, dine in my dressing-room when I'm out of humour, without giving a reason. To have my closet inviolate; to be sole empress of my tea-table, which you must never presume to approach without first asking leave. And lastly, wherever I am, you shall always knock at the door before you come in. These articles subscribed, if I continue to endure you a little longer, I may by degrees dwindle into a wife.

MIRABELL   Your bill of fare is something advanced [20] in this latter account. Well, have I liberty to offer conditions—that when you are dwindled into a wife, I may not be beyond measure enlarged into a husband?

MILLAMANT   You have free leave. Propose your utmost; speak and spare not.

MIRABELL   I thank you. *Imprimis* [21] then, I covenant that your acquaintance be general; that you admit no sworn confidante or intimate of your own sex, no she-friend to screen her affairs under your countenance and tempt you to make trial of a mutual secrecy. No decoy-duck to wheedle you a fop-scrambling [22] to the play in a mask—then bring you home in a pretended fright, when you think you shall be found out—and rail at me for missing the play and disappointing the frolic which you had, to pick me up and prove my constancy.

MILLAMANT   Detestable *imprimis!* I go to the play in a mask!

MIRABELL   *Item,* I article, [23] that you continue to like your own face as long as I shall; and while it passes current with me, that you endeavour not to new-coin it. To which end, together with all vizards [24] for the day, I prohibit all masks for the night, made of oiled-skins and I know not what—hog's bones, hare's gall, pig-water, and the marrow of a roasted cat. In short, I forbid all commerce with the gentlewoman in What-d'ye-call-it Court. *Item,* I shut my doors against all bawds with baskets, and pennyworths of muslin, china, fans, atlases, [25] etc.—*Item,* when you shall be breeding——

MILLAMANT   Ah! name it not.

MIRABELL   Which may be presumed, with a blessing on our endeavours——

MILLAMANT   Odious endeavours!

MIRABELL   I denounce against all strait lacing, [26] squeezing for a shape, till

20. Extended.
21. "First of all" (in the language of a legal contract).
22. Hoping to attract fops.
23. Stipulate.
24. Masks for dress, as opposed to cosmetic masks "for the night."
25. Oriental satins.
26. Tight lacing of corsets.

you mold my boy's head like a sugar-loaf, and instead of a man-child, make me the father to a crooked billet.[27] Lastly, to the dominion of the tea-table I submit,—but with proviso, that you exceed not in your province; but restrain yourself to native and simple tea-table drinks, as tea, chocolate, and coffee, as likewise to genuine and authorized tea-table talk—such as mending of fashions, spoiling reputations, railing at absent friends, and so forth—but that on no account you encroach upon the men's prerogative and presume to drink healths or toast fellows; for prevention of which I banish all foreign forces, all auxiliaries to the tea-table, as orange-brandy, all aniseed, cinnamon, citron, and Barbadoes waters, together with ratafia and the most noble spirit of clary,[28]—but for cowslip-wine, poppy water, and all dormitives,[29] those I allow. These provisos admitted, in other things I may prove a tractable and complying husband.

MILLAMANT   Oh, horrid provisos! filthy strong waters! I toast fellows, odious men! I hate your odious provisos.

MIRABELL   Then we're agreed. Shall I kiss your hand upon the contract? And here comes one to be a witness to the sealing of the deed.

[*Enter* MRS. FAINALL]

MILLAMANT   Fainall, what shall I do? Shall I have him? I think I must have him.

MRS. FAINALL   Aye, aye, take him, take him, what should you do?

MILLAMANT   Well then—I'll take my death, I'm in a horrid fright—Fainall, I shall never say it—well—I think—I'll endure you.

MRS. FAINALL   Fie, fie! have him, have him, and tell him so in plain terms; for I am sure you have a mind to him.

MILLAMANT   Are you? I think I have—and the horrid man looks as if he thought so too.—Well, you ridiculous thing you, I'll have you—I won't be kissed, nor I won't be thanked—here, kiss my hand though.—So, hold your tongue now, and don't say a word.

MRS. FAINALL   Mirabell, there's a necessity for your obedience;—you have neither time to talk nor stay. My mother is coming; and in my conscience, if she should see you, would fall into fits, and maybe not recover time enough to return to Sir Rowland, who as Foible tells me, is in a fair way to succeed. Therefore spare your ecstasies for another occasion, and slip down the back stairs, where Foible waits to consult you.

MILLAMANT   Aye, go, go. In the meantime I suppose you have said something to please me.

MIRABELL   I am all obedience.

[*Exit* MIRABELL]

MRS. FAINALL   Yonder Sir Wilfull's drunk; and so noisy that my mother has been forced to leave Sir Rowland to appease him; but he answers her only with singing and drinking.—What they have done by this time I know not; but Petulant and he were upon quarrelling as I came by.

27. Piece of firewood.
28. All of the alcoholic drinks ("strong waters").
29. Drinks that help one sleep.

MILLAMANT   Well, if Mirabell should not make a good husband, I am a lost
   thing—for I find I love him violently.

MRS. FAINALL   So it seems, when you mind not what's said to you.—If you
   doubt him, you had best take up with Sir Wilfull.

MILLAMANT   How can you name that superannuated lubber? foh!

   [*Enter* WITWOUD *from drinking*]

MRS. FAINALL   So, is the fray made up, that you have left 'em?

WITWOUD   Left 'em? I could stay no longer—I have laughed like ten christ'-
   nings—I am tipsy with laughing.—If I had stayed any longer I should
   have burst,—I must have been let out and pieced in the sides like an
   unsized camlet.[30]—Yes, yes, the fray is composed; my lady came in
   like a *nolle prosequi* [31] and stopped their proceedings.

MILLAMANT   What was the dispute?

WITWOUD   That's the jest; there was no dispute. They could neither of 'em
   speak for rage; and so fell a sputt'ring at one another like two roasting
   apples.

   [*Enter* PETULANT *drunk*]

   Now, Petulant, all's over, all's well. Gad, my head begins to whim it
   about.[32]—Why dost thou not speak? Thou art both as drunk and as
   mute as a fish.

PETULANT   Look you, Mrs. Millamant—if you can love me, dear nymph—say
   it—and that's the conclusion—pass on, or pass off,—that's all.

WITWOUD   Thou hast uttered volumes, folios, in less than *decimo sexto*,[33] my
   dear Lacedemonian. Sirrah Petulant, thou art an epitomizer of words.

PETULANT   Witwoud—you are an annihilator of sense.

WITWOUD   Thou art a retailer of phrases, and dost deal in remnants of remnants, like a maker of pincushions—thou art in truth (metaphorically
   speaking) a speaker of shorthand.

PETULANT   Thou art (without a figure) just one half of an ass; and Baldwin [34]
   yonder, thy half-brother, is the rest.—A gemini [35] of asses split would
   make just four of you.

WITWOUD   Thou dost bite, my dear mustard seed; kiss me for that.

PETULANT   Stand off—I'll kiss no more males,—I have kissed your twin yonder
   in a humour of reconciliation, till he [*Hiccup*] rises upon my stomach
   like a radish.

MILLAMANT   Eh! filthy creature!—what was the quarrel?

PETULANT   There was no quarrel—there might have been a quarrel.

WITWOUD   If there had been words enow between 'em to have expressed provocation, they had gone together by the ears like a pair of castanets.

PETULANT   You were the quarrel.

MILLAMANT   Me!

---

30. Unstiffened cloth (of wool and silk).
31. A motion of the prosecution to withdraw its case.
32. Spin.
33. The smallest of books, in as few words as a Spartan ("Lacedemonian") or a summarizer
could use.
34. The name of the ass in *Reynard the Fox.*
35. Pair of twins.

PETULANT   If I have a humour to quarrel, I can make less matters conclude
premises. If you are not handsome, what then, if I have a humour to
prove it?—If I shall have my reward, say so; if not, fight for your face
the next time yourself.—I'll go sleep.

WITWOUD   Do, wrap thyself up like a woodlouse, and dream revenge—and
hear me, if thou canst learn to write by tomorrow morning, pen me a
challenge—I'll carry it for thee.

PETULANT   Carry your mistress's monkey a spider,[36]—go flea dogs and read
romances!—I'll go to bed to my maid.
[Exit]

MRS. FAINALL   He's horridly drunk.—How came you all in this pickle?

WITWOUD   A plot, a plot, to get rid of the knight,—your husband's advice;
but he sneaked off.
[Enter LADY WISHFORT, and SIR WILFULL, drunk]

LADY WISHFORT   Out upon't, out upon't, at years of discretion, and comport
yourself at this rantipole [37] rate!

SIR WILFULL   No offence, aunt.

LADY WISHFORT   Offence? As I'm a person, I'm ashamed of you.—Fogh! how
you stink of wine! D'ye think my niece will ever endure such a borachio! [38] you're an absolute borachio.

SIR WILFULL   Borachio!

LADY WISHFORT   At a time when you should commence an amour and put your
best foot foremost——

SIR WILFULL   'Sheart, an you grutch me your liquor, make a bill. Give me
more drink, and take my purse. [Sings]

> Prithee fill me the glass
> Till it laugh in my face,
> With ale that is potent and mellow;
> He that whines for a lass,
> Is an ignorant ass,
> For a bumper has not its fellow.

But if you would have me marry my cousin,—say the word, and I'll
do't—Wilfull will do't, that's the word—Wilfull, will do't, that's my
crest—my motto I have forgot.

LADY WISHFORT   My nephew's a little overtaken, cousin—but 'tis with drinking your health.—O' my word you are obliged to him——

SIR WILFULL   In vino veritas,[39] aunt.—If I drunk your health today, cousin,
—I am a borachio. But if you have a mind to be married, say the word,
and send for the piper; Wilfull will do't. If not, dust it away, and let's
have t'other round.—Tony, 'odsheart, where's Tony.—Tony's an honest
fellow, but he spits after a bumper, and that's a fault. [Sings]

> We'll drink and we'll never ha' done, boys,
> Put the glass then around with the sun, boys,

36. Monkeys were believed to eat insects; for lice, see Swift, A Tale of a Tub, II.
37. Ill-mannered.
38. Drunkard, from Spanish term for wine bag.
39. "In wine there is truth."

Let Apollo's example invite us;
    For he's drunk every night,
    And that makes him so bright,
And he's able next morning to light us.

The sun's a good pimple,[40] an honest soaker; he has a cellar at your
Antipodes. If I travel, aunt, I touch at your Antipodes.—Your Antipodes
are a good rascally sort of topsy-turvy fellows. If I had a bumper, I'd
stand upon my head and drink a health to 'em.—A match or no match,
cousin with the hard name?—Aunt, Wilfull will do't. If she has her
maidenhead, let her look to't; if she has not, let her keep her own
counsel in the meantime, and cry out at the nine months' end.

MILLAMANT   Your pardon, madam, I can stay no longer—Sir Wilfull grows
very powerful. Egh! how he smells! I shall be overcome if I stay. Come,
cousin.

[*Exeunt* MILLAMANT *and* MRS. FAINALL]

LADY WISHFORT   Smells! he would poison a tallow-chandler and his family.[41]
Beastly creature, I know not what to do with him.—Travel, quoth a;
aye travel, travel, get thee gone, get thee but far enough, to the Saracens, or the Tartars, or the Turks—for thou art not fit to live in a Christian commonwealth, thou beastly pagan.

SIR WILFULL   Turks, no; no Turks, aunt. Your Turks are infidels, and believe
not in the grape. Your Mahometan, your Mussulman, is a dry stinkard
—no offence, aunt. My map says that your Turk is not so honest a man
as your Christian—I cannot find by the map that your Mufti is orthodox
—whereby it is a plain case, that orthodox is a hard word, aunt, and
[*Hiccup*] Greek for claret. [*Sings*]

To drink is a Christian diversion,
Unknown to the Turk and the Persian:
    Let Mahometan fools
    Live by heathenish rules,
And be damned over tea-cups and coffee.
    But let British lads sing,
    Crown a health to the king,
And a fig for your sultan and sophy.[42]

Ah, Tony!

[*Enter* FOIBLE *and whispers* LADY WISHFORT]

LADY WISHFORT   Sir Rowland impatient? Good lack! what shall I do with this
beastly tumbril?[43]—Go lie down and sleep, you sot—or as I'm a person,
I'll have you bastinadoed with broomsticks. Call up the wenches.

[*Exit* FOIBLE]

SIR WILFULL   Ahey! Wenches, where are the wenches?

LADY WISHFORT   Dear Cousin Witwoud, get him away, and you will bind me to

40. Companion.
41. Who are not very fragrant to begin with.
42. Shah.
43. Wagon, dung cart.

you inviolably. I have an affair of moment that invades me with some precipitation.—You will oblige me to all futurity.

WITWOUD   Come, knight.—Pox on him, I don't know what to say to him.—Will you go to a cock-match?

SIR WILFULL   With a wench, Tony? Is she a shake-bag,[44] sirrah? Let me bite your cheek for that.

WITWOUD   Horrible! He has a breath like a bagpipe.—Aye, aye; come, will you march, my Salopian? [45]

SIR WILFULL   Lead on, little Tony—I'll follow thee, my Anthony, my Tantony. Sirrah, thou sha't be my Tantony; [46] and I'll be thy pig.

—And a fig for your sultan and sophy.

[Exit singing with WITWOUD]

LADY WISHFORT   This will never do. It will never make a match.—At least before he has been abroad.

[Enter WAITWELL, disguised as for SIR ROWLAND]

Dear Sir Rowland, I am confounded with confusion at the retrospection of my own rudeness,—I have more pardons to ask than the pope distributes in the year of jubilee. But I hope where there is likely to be so near an alliance, we may unbend the severity of decorum and dispense with a little ceremony.

WAITWELL   My impatience, madam, is the effect of my transport;—and till I have the possession of your adorable person, I am tantalized on a rack; and do but hang, madam, on the tenter [47] of expectation.

LADY WISHFORT   You have excess of gallantry, Sir Rowland, and press things to a conclusion with a most prevailing vehemence.—But a day or two for decency of marriage——

WAITWELL   For decency of funeral, madam. The delay will break my heart— or if that should fail, I shall be poisoned. My nephew will get an inkling of my designs and poison me,—and I would willingly starve him before I die—I would gladly go out of the world with that satisfaction. That would be some comfort to me, if I could but live so long as to be revenged on that unnatural viper.

LADY WISHFORT   Is he so unnatural, say you? Truly I would contribute much both to the saving of your life and the accomplishment of your revenge. Not that I respect [48] myself, though he has been a perfidious wretch to me.

WAITWELL   Perfidious to you!

LADY WISHFORT   O Sir Rowland, the hours that he has died away at my feet, the tears that he has shed, the oaths that he has sworn, the palpitations that he has felt, the trances, and the tremblings, the ardours and the ecstasies, the kneelings and the risings, the heart-heavings, and the hand-grippings, the pangs and the pathetic regards of his protesting eyes! Oh, no memory can register!

44. Gamecock.
45. Shropshireman.
46. St. Anthony was usually shown with a pig, as the patron of swineherds.
47. Tenterhook.
48. Regard, think of.

WAITWELL   What, my rival! is the rebel my rival? a' dies!

LADY WISHFORT   No, don't kill him at once, Sir Rowland; starve him gradually inch by inch.

WAITWELL   I'll do't. In three weeks he shall be barefoot; in a month out at knees with begging an alms;—he shall starve upward and upward, till he has nothing living but his head, and then go out in a stink like a candle's end upon a save-all.[49]

LADY WISHFORT   Well, Sir Rowland, you have the way,—you are no novice in the labyrinth of love—you have the clue.—But as I am a person, Sir Rowland, you must not attribute my yielding to any sinister appetite, or indigestion of widowhood; nor impute my complacency to any lethargy of continence. I hope you do not think me prone to any iteration of nuptials.——

WAITWELL   Far be it from me——

LADY WISHFORT   If you do, I protest I must recede—or think that I have made a prostitution of decorums, but in the vehemence of compassion and to save the life of a person of so much importance——

WAITWELL   I esteem it so——

LADY WISHFORT   Or else you wrong my condescension——

WAITWELL   I do not, I do not——

LADY WISHFORT   Indeed you do.

WAITWELL   I do not, fair shrine of virtue.

LADY WISHFORT   If you think the least scruple of carnality was an ingredient——

WAITWELL   Dear madam, no. You are all camphire [50] and frankincense, all chastity and odour.

LADY WISHFORT   Or that——

[Enter FOIBLE]

FOIBLE   Madam, the dancers are ready, and there's one with a letter, who must deliver it into your own hands.

LADY WISHFORT   Sir Rowland, will you give me leave? Think favourably, judge candidly, and conclude you have found a person who would suffer racks in honour's cause, dear Sir Rowland, and will wait on you incessantly. [Exit]

WAITWELL   Fie, fie!—What a slavery have I undergone! Spouse, hast thou any cordial?—I want spirits.

FOIBLE   What a washy rogue art thou to pant thus for a quarter of an hour's lying and swearing to a fine lady!

WAITWELL   Oh, she is the antidote to desire. Spouse, thou wilt fare the worse for't—I shall have no appetite to iteration of nuptials—this eight and forty hours:—by this hand I'd rather be a chairman in the dog-days [51]— than act Sir Rowland till this time tomorrow.

[Enter LADY WISHFORT with a letter]

---

49. A small pan inserted under candlesticks to save the ends of candles.

50. Camphor, used to lessen sexual passion; here coupled with a fragrance used on sacred occasions (both "the antidote to desire").

51. One who carries a sedan-chair in hottest summer.

LADY WISHFORT   Call in the dancers.—Sir Rowland, we'll sit, if you please, and see the entertainment.

[*Dance*]

Now with your permission, Sir Rowland, I will peruse my letter—I would open it in your presence because I would not make you uneasy. If it should make you uneasy I would burn it—speak if it does—but you may see by the superscription it is like a woman's hand.

FOIBLE [*to him*]   By heaven! Mrs. Marwood's, I know it;—my heart aches—get it from her—

WAITWELL   A woman's hand? No, madam, that's no woman's hand, I see that already. That's somebody whose throat must be cut.

LADY WISHFORT   Nay, Sir Rowland, since you give me a proof of your passion by your jealousy, I promise you I'll make you a return, by a frank communication.—You shall see it—we'll open it together—look you here.

[*Reads*] 'Madam, though unknown to you,'—Look you there, 'tis from nobody that I know—'I have that honour for your character, that I think myself obliged to let you know you are abused. He who pretends to be Sir Rowland is a cheat and a rascal——' Oh heavens! what's this?

FOIBLE [*aside*]   Unfortunate, all's ruined.

WAITWELL   How, how, let me see, let me see! [*Reading*] 'A rascal, and disguised and suborned for that imposture,'—O villainy! O villainy!—'by the contrivance of——'

LADY WISHFORT   I shall faint, I shall die, I shall die, oh!

FOIBLE [*to him*]   Say 'tis your nephew's hand.—Quickly, his plot, swear, swear it.

WAITWELL   Here's a villain! Madam, don't you perceive it, don't you see it?

LADY WISHFORT   Too well, too well. I have seen too much.

WAITWELL   I told you at first I knew the hand. A woman's hand? The rascal writes a sort of a large hand, your Roman hand. I saw there was a throat to be cut presently. If he were my son, as he is my nephew, I'd pistol him——

FOIBLE   O treachery! But are you sure, Sir Rowland, it is his writing?

WAITWELL   Sure? am I here? do I live? do I love this pearl of India? I have twenty letters in my pocket from him, in the same character.

LADY WISHFORT   How!

FOIBLE   Oh, what luck it is, Sir Rowland, that you were present at this juncture! This was the business that brought Mr. Mirabell disguised to Madam Millamant this afternoon. I thought something was contriving when he stole by me and would have hid his face.

LADY WISHFORT   How, how!—I heard the villain was in the house indeed, and now I remember, my niece went away abruptly when Sir Wilfull was to have made his addresses.

FOIBLE   Then, then, madam, Mr. Mirabell waited for her in her chamber, but I would not tell your ladyship to discompose you when you were to receive Sir Rowland.

WAITWELL   Enough, his date is short.

FOIBLE   No, good Sir Rowland, don't incur the law.

WAITWELL   Law! I care not for law. I can but die, and 'tis in a good cause
—my lady shall be satisfied of my truth and innocence, though it cost
me my life.

LADY WISHFORT   No, dear Sir Rowland, don't fight; if you should be killed I
must never show my face; or hanged—oh, consider my reputation, Sir
Rowland! No, you shan't fight. I'll go in and examine my niece; I'll
make her confess. I conjure you, Sir Rowland, by all your love, not to
fight.

WAITWELL   I am charmed, madam, I obey. But some proof you must let me
give you;—I'll go for a black box, which contains the writings of my
whole estate, and deliver that into your hands.

LADY WISHFORT   Aye, dear Sir Rowland, that will be some comfort; bring the
black box.

WAITWELL   And may I presume to bring a contract to be signed this night?
May I hope so far?

LADY WISHFORT   Bring what you will; but come alive, pray come alive. Oh,
this is a happy discovery![52]

WAITWELL   Dead or alive I'll come—and married we will be in spite of
treachery; aye, and get an heir that shall defeat the last remaining
glimpse of hope in my abandoned nephew. Come, my buxom widow:

Ere long you shall substantial proof receive
That I'm an arrant [53] knight——

FOIBLE [aside]   Or arrant knave.
    [Exeunt]

ACT V
A room in Lady Wishfort's house [1]
[LADY WISHFORT *and* FOIBLE]

LADY WISHFORT   Out of my house, out of my house, thou viper, thou serpent,
that I have fostered! thou bosom traitress, that I raised from nothing!—
begone, begone, begone, go, go!—that I took from washing of old
gauze and weaving of dead hair,[2] with a bleak blue nose, over a chafing-
dish of starved embers, and dining behind a traverse rag, in a shop no
bigger than a bird-cage,—go, go, starve again, do, do!

FOIBLE   Dear madam, I'll beg pardon on my knees.

LADY WISHFORT   Away, out, out, go set up for yourself again!—do, drive a
trade, do, with your threepenny worth of small ware, flaunting upon a
pack-thread, under a brandy-seller's bulk,[3] or against a dead wall by a
ballad-monger! Go, hang out an old Frisoneer gorget, with a yard of
yellow colberteen [4] again! do! an old gnawed mask, two rows of pins,

52. Fortunate disclosure.
53. Punning on (1) errant or wandering; (2) arrant or thoroughgoing; cf. Butler, *Hudibras*
I.i.21, 193.
1. Once more the original text reads "Scene continues."
2. That is, wig-making.
3. Displaying it on thick string, under a covered stall, or against a blank wall.
4. A woolen neckpiece with coarse yellow lace.

and a child's fiddle; a glass necklace with the beads broken, and a quilted nightcap with one ear! Go, go, drive a trade!—These were your commodities, you treacherous trull, this was your merchandise you dealt in, when I took you into my house, placed you next myself, and made you governante [5] of my whole family! You have forgot this, have you, now you have feathered your nest?

FOIBLE   No, no, dear madam. Do but hear me, have but a moment's patience —I'll confess all. Mr. Mirabell seduced me; I am not the first that he has wheedled with his dissembling tongue; your ladyship's own wisdom has been deluded by him,—then how should I, a poor ignorant, defend myself? O madam, if you knew but what he promised me, and how he assured me your ladyship should come to no damage!—Or else the wealth of the Indies should not have bribed me to conspire against so good, so sweet, so kind a lady as you have been to me.

LADY WISHFORT   No damage? What, to betray me, to marry me to a cast [6] servingman; to make me a receptacle, an hospital for a decayed pimp? No damage? O thou frontless [7] impudence, more than a big-bellied actress!

FOIBLE   Pray, do but hear me, madam; he could not marry your ladyship, madam.—No indeed, his marriage was to have been void in law; for he was married to me first, to secure your ladyship. He could not have bedded your ladyship; for if he had consummated with your ladyship, he must have run the risk of the law and been put upon his clergy.[8] —Yes indeed, I enquired of the law in that case before I would meddle or make.

LADY WISHFORT   What, then I have been your property, have I? I have been convenient to you, it seems—while you were catering for Mirabell, I have been broker for you? What, have you made a passive bawd of me?—This exceeds all precedent; I am brought to fine uses, to become a botcher [9] of second-hand marriages between Abigails and Andrews! [10] I'll couple you! Yes, I'll baste you together, you and your Philander! [11] I'll Duke's Place you, as I'm a person. Your turtle is in custody already; you shall coo in the same cage, if there be constable or warrant in the parish.
[Exit]

FOIBLE   Oh, that ever I was born! Oh, that I was ever married!—A bride, aye, I shall be a Bridewell [12] bride. Oh!
[Enter MRS. FAINALL]

MRS. FAINALL   Poor Foible, what's the matter?

5. Housekeeper.
6. Cast-off.
7. Shameless, as actresses were often regarded; cf. Dryden, *Mac Flecknoe*, ll. 74–77.
8. Obliged to plead "benefit of clergy," i.e. avoid the death penalty by proving he could read. (Clergy once could claim thereby the right to be tried in ecclesiastical rather than civil courts.)
9. Patcher.
10. Conventional names for maids and valets.
11. Lover.
12. Bridewell was the prison for women, where they were often required to beat hemp.

FOIBLE   O madam, my lady's gone for a constable; I shall be had to a justice, and put to Bridewell to beat hemp! Poor Waitwell's gone to prison already.

MRS. FAINALL   Have a good heart, Foible; Mirabell's gone to give security for him. This is all Marwood's and my husband's doing.

FOIBLE   Yes, yes; I know it, madam; she was in my lady's closet, and overheard all that you said to me before dinner. She sent the letter to my lady; and, that missing effect, Mr. Fainall laid this plot to arrest Waitwell when he pretended to go for the papers; and in the meantime Mrs. Marwood declared all to my lady.

MRS. FAINALL   Was there no mention made of me in the letter?—My mother does not suspect my being in the confederacy? I fancy Marwood has not told her, though she has told my husband.

FOIBLE   Yes, madam; but my lady did not see that part; we stifled the letter before she read so far. Has that mischievous devil told Mr. Fainall of your ladyship then?

MRS. FAINALL   Aye, all's out, my affair with Mirabell, everything discovered. This is the last day of our living together; that's my comfort.

FOIBLE   Indeed, madam, and so 'tis a comfort if you knew all;—he has been even with your ladyship, which I could have told you long enough since, but I love to keep peace and quietness, by my good will. I had rather bring friends together than set 'em at distance. But Mrs. Marwood and he are nearer related than ever their parents thought for.

MRS. FAINALL   Say'st thou so, Foible? Canst thou prove this?

FOIBLE   I can take my oath of it, madam, so can Mrs. Mincing; we have had many a fair word from Madam Marwood, to conceal something that passed in our chamber one evening when you were at Hyde Park;—and we were thought to have gone a-walking, but we went up unawares— though we were sworn to secrecy too. Madam Marwood took a book and swore us upon it; but it was but a book of verses and poems. So as long as it was not a Bible oath, we may break it with a safe conscience.

MRS. FAINALL   This discovery is the most opportune thing I could wish. Now, Mincing?

[*Enter* MINCING]

MINCING   My lady would speak with Mrs. Foible, mem. Mr. Mirabell is with her; he has set your spouse at liberty, Mrs. Foible, and would have you hide yourself in my lady's closet till my old lady's anger is abated. Oh, my old lady is in a perilous passion at something Mr. Fainall has said; he swears, and my old lady cries. There's a fearful hurricane, I vow. He says, mem, how that he'll have my lady's fortune made over to him or he'll be divorced.

MRS. FAINALL   Does your lady and Mirabell know that?

MINCING   Yes, mem, they have sent me to see if Sir Wilfull be sober, and to bring him to them. My lady is resolved to have him, I think, rather than lose such a vast sum as six thousand pound. Oh, come, Mrs. Foible, I hear my old lady.

MRS. FAINALL   Foible, you must tell Mincing that she must prepare to vouch when I call her.

FOIBLE Yes, yes, madam.

MINCING Oh, yes, mem, I'll vouch anything for your ladyship's service, be what it will.

[*Exeunt* MINCING *and* FOIBLE]

[*Enter* LADY WISHFORT *and* MRS. MARWOOD]

LADY WISHFORT Oh, my dear friend, how can I enumerate the benefits that I have received from your goodness? To you I owe the timely discovery of the false vows of Mirabell, to you the detection of the impostor Sir Rowland. And now you are become an intercessor with my son-in-law, to save the honour of my house, and compound for the frailties of my daughter. Well, friend, you are enough to reconcile me to the bad world, or else I would retire to deserts and solitudes, and feed harmless sheep by groves and purling streams. Dear Marwood, let us leave the world, and retire by ourselves and be shepherdesses.

MRS. MARWOOD Let us first dispatch the affair in hand, madam. We shall have leisure to think of retirement afterwards.—Here is one who is concerned in the treaty.

LADY WISHFORT O daughter, daughter, is it possible thou shouldst be my child, bone of my bone, and flesh of my flesh, and as I may say, another me; and yet transgress the most minute particle of severe virtue? Is it possible you should lean aside to iniquity, who have been cast in the direct mold of virtue? I have not only been a mold but a pattern for you, and a model for you, after you were brought into the world.

MRS. FAINALL I don't understand your ladyship.

LADY WISHFORT Not understand? Why, have you not been naught? [13] Have you not been sophisticated? [14] Not understand? Here I am ruined to compound for your caprices and your cuckoldoms. I must pawn my plate and my jewels, and ruin my niece, and all little enough——

MRS. FAINALL I am wronged and abused, and so are you. 'Tis a false accusation, as false as hell, as false as your friend there, aye, or your friend's friend, my false husband.

MRS. MARWOOD My friend, Mrs. Fainall? Your husband my friend! what do you mean?

MRS. FAINALL I know what I mean, madam, and so do you; and so shall the world at a time convenient.

MRS. MARWOOD I am sorry to see you so passionate, madam. More temper [15] would look more like innocence. But I have done. I am sorry my zeal to serve your ladyship and family should admit of misconstruction or make me liable to affronts. You will pardon me, madam, if I meddle no more with an affair in which I am not personally concerned.

LADY WISHFORT O dear friend, I am so ashamed that you should meet with such returns;—[*To* MRS. FAINALL] You ought to ask pardon on your knees, ungrateful creature! She deserves more from you, than all your life can accomplish.—[*To* MRS. MARWOOD] Oh, don't leave me destitute in this perplexity!—no, stick to me, my good genius.

13. Immoral.
14. Corrupted.
15. Composure.

MRS. FAINALL   I tell you, madam, you're abused.—Stick to you? aye, like a
leech, to suck your best blood—she'll drop off when she's full. Madam,
you sha' not pawn a bodkin,[16] nor part with a brass counter in composition for me. I defy 'em all. Let 'em prove their aspersions. I know
my own innocence, and dare stand by a trial.
   [*Exit*]

LADY WISHFORT   Why, if she should be innocent, if she should be wronged
after all, ha? I don't know what to think,—and I promise you, her
education has been unexceptionable—I may say it; for I chiefly made
it my own care to initiate her very infancy in the rudiments of virtue,
and to impress upon her tender years a young odium and aversion to the
very sight of men;—aye, friend, she would ha' shrieked if she had but
seen a man, till she was in her teens! As I'm a person, 'tis true. She was
never suffered to play wih a male-child, though but in coats; nay, her
very babies [17] were of the feminine gender. Oh, she never looked a man
in the face but her own father or the chaplain, and him we made a
shift to put upon her for a woman, by the help of his long garments
and his sleek face, till she was going in her fifteen.

MRS. MARWOOD   'Twas much she should be deceived so long.

LADY WISHFORT   I warrant you, or she would never have borne to have been
catechized by him; and have heard his long lectures against singing and
dancing and such debaucheries; and going to filthy plays, and profane
music-meetings, where the lewd trebles squeak nothing but bawdy, and
the basses roar blasphemy. Oh, she would have swooned at the sight or
name of an obscene play-book—and can I think, after all this, that my
daughter can be naught? What, a whore? And thought it excommunication to set her foot within the door of a playhouse! [18] O my dear friend,
I can't believe it. No, no! As she says, let him prove it, let him prove it!

MRS. MARWOOD   Prove it, madam? What, and have your name prostituted in a
public court? Yours and your daughter's reputation worried at the bar
by a pack of bawling lawyers? To be ushered in with an 'Oyez' of
scandal; and have your case opened by an old fumbling lecher in a
quoif [19] like a man midwife, to bring your daughter's infamy to light;
to be a theme for legal punsters, and quibblers by the statute; and become a jest, against a rule of court, where there is no precedent for a
jest in any record, not even in Doomsday Book; [20] to discompose the
gravity of the bench, and provoke naughty interrogatories in more
naughty law Latin; while the good judge, tickled with the proceeding,
simpers under a grey beard, and fidges off and on his cushion as if he
had swallowed cantharides, or sat upon cowitch! [21]

16. Hairpin.
17. Dolls.
18. Here, as in Lady Wishfort's mixture of Puritan works and Jeremy Collier's tract in her
closet, Congreve is mocking Collier's denunciation of the immorality of the stage.
19. Lawyer's cap.
20. The oldest of legal records, a survey of lands made in 1085–86 by order of William
the Conqueror.
21. Fidgets as if he had swallowed the aphrodisiac Spanish fly or sat upon cowhage, a
plant covered with stinging hairs.

LADY WISHFORT   Oh, 'tis very hard!

MRS. MARWOOD   And then to have my young revellers of the Temple take notes, like 'prentices at a conventicle; [22] and after, talk it all over again in Commons, or before drawers in an eating-house.

LADY WISHFORT   Worse and worse!

MRS. MARWOOD   Nay, this is nothing; if it would end here, 'twere well. But it must after this be consigned by the shorthand writers to the public press; and from thence be transferred to the hands, nay, into the throats and lungs of hawkers, with voices more licentious than the loud flounderman's, or the woman that cries grey-pease; and this you must hear till you are stunned; nay, you must hear nothing else for some days.

LADY WISHFORT   Oh, 'tis insupportable. No, no, dear friend, make it up, make it up; aye, aye, I'll compound. I'll give up all, myself and my all, my niece and her all,—anything, everything for composition.

MRS. MARWOOD   Nay, madam, I advise nothing; I only lay before you, as a friend, the inconveniencies which perhaps you have overseen. Here comes Mr. Fainall. If he will be satisfied to huddle up all in silence, I shall be glad. You must think I would rather congratulate than condole with you.

[*Enter* FAINALL]

LADY WISHFORT   Aye, aye, I do not doubt it, dear Marwood; no, no, I do not doubt it.

FAINALL   Well, madam; I have suffered myself to be overcome by the importunity of this lady your friend; and am content you shall enjoy your own proper estate during life, on condition you oblige yourself never to marry, under such penalty as I think convenient.

LADY WISHFORT   Never to marry?

FAINALL   No more Sir Rowlands;—the next imposture may not be so timely detected.

MRS. MARWOOD   That condition, I dare answer, my lady will consent to without difficulty; she has already but too much experienced the perfidiousness of men. Besides, madam, when we retire to our pastoral solitude we shall bid adieu to all other thoughts.

LADY WISHFORT   Aye, that's true; but in case of necessity, as of health, or some such emergency——

FAINALL   Oh, if you are prescribed marriage, you shall be considered; I will only reserve to myself the power to choose for you. If your physic be wholesome, it matters not who is your apothecary. Next, my wife shall settle on me the remainder of her fortune not made over already, and for her maintenance depend entirely on my discretion.

LADY WISHFORT   This is most inhumanly savage; exceeding the barbarity of a Muscovite husband.

FAINALL   I learned it from his Czarish majesty's retinue,[23] in a winter evening's conference over brandy and pepper, amongst other secrets of matrimony and policy as they are at present practised in the northern

22. Law students taking notes like apprentices sent by their Puritan masters to report on a sermon.
23. Peter the Great had visited London in 1698.

hemisphere. But this must be agreed unto, and that positively. Lastly, I will be endowed, in right of my wife, with that six thousand pound which is the moiety of Mrs. Millamant's fortune in your possession; and which she has forfeited (as will appear by the last will and testament of your deceased husband, Sir Jonathan Wishfort) by her disobedience in contracting herself against your consent or knowledge; and by refusing the offered match with Sir Wilfull Witwoud, which you, like a careful aunt, had provided for her.

LADY WISHFORT   My nephew was *non compos*,[24] and could not make his addresses.

FAINALL   I come to make demands,—I'll hear no objections.

LADY WISHFORT   You will grant me time to consider?

FAINALL   Yes, while the instrument is drawing, to which you must set your hand till more sufficient deeds can be perfected, which I will take care shall be done with all possible speed. In the meanwhile, I will go for the said instrument, and till my return you may balance this matter in your own discretion.

[*Exit* FAINALL]

LADY WISHFORT   This insolence is beyond all precedent, all parallel; must I be subject to this merciless villain?

MRS. MARWOOD   'Tis severe indeed, madam, that you should smart for your daughter's wantonness.

LADY WISHFORT   'Twas against my consent that she married this barbarian, but she would have him, though her year [25] was not out.—Ah! her first husband, my son Languish, would not have carried it thus. Well, that was my choice, this is hers; she is matched now with a witness.[26] I shall be mad! Dear friend, is there no comfort for me? Must I live to be confiscated at this rebel-rate? [27]—Here come two more of my Egyptian plagues,[28] too.

[*Enter* MILLAMANT *and* SIR WILFULL]

SIR WILFULL   Aunt, your servant.

LADY WISHFORT   Out, caterpillar, call not me aunt! I know thee not!

SIR WILFULL   I confess I have been a little in disguise,[29] as they say,—'sheart! and I'm sorry for't. What would you have? I hope I committed no offence, aunt—and if I did I am willing to make satisfaction; and what can a man say fairer? If I have broke anything, I'll pay for't, an it cost a pound. And so let that content for what's past, and make no more words. For what's to come, to pleasure you I'm willing to marry my cousin. So pray let's all be friends; she and I are agreed upon the matter before a witness.

LADY WISHFORT   How's this, dear niece? Have I any comfort? Can this be true?

---

24. "Not of sound mind."
25. Of mourning as a widow.
26. With a vengeance.
27. That is, as completely as if I were a rebel.
28. The plagues visited upon Pharaoh for holding the Israelites in bondage (Exodus 7–12).
29. That is, not myself (a euphemism for "drunk").

MILLAMANT   I am content to be a sacrifice to your repose, madam; and to convince you that I had no hand in the plot, as you were misinformed, I have laid my commands on Mirabell to come in person, and be a witness that I give my hand to this flower of knighthood; and for the contract that passed between Mirabell and me, I have obliged him to make a resignation of it in your ladyship's presence. He is without, and waits your leave for admittance.

LADY WISHFORT   Well, I'll swear I am something revived at this testimony of your obedience; but I cannot admit that traitor;—I fear I cannot fortify myself to support his appearance. He is as terrible to me as a Gorgon; if I see him, I fear I shall turn to stone, petrify incessantly.[30]

MILLAMANT   If you disoblige him, he may resent your refusal, and insist upon the contract still. Then, 'tis the last time he will be offensive to you.

LADY WISHFORT   Are you sure it will be the last time?—If I were sure of that —shall I never see him again?

MILLAMANT   Sir Wilfull, you and he are to travel together, are you not?

SIR WILFULL   'Sheart, the gentleman's a civil gentleman, aunt, let him come in; why, we are sworn brothers and fellow-travellers. We are to be Pylades[31] and Orestes, he and I. He is to be my interpreter in foreign parts. He has been overseas once already; and with proviso that I marry my cousin, will cross 'em once again, only to bear me company. —'Sheart, I'll call him in;—an I set on't once, he shall come in; and see who'll hinder him.
   [Exit]

MRS. MARWOOD [aside]   This is precious fooling, if it would pass; but I'll know the bottom of it.

LADY WISHFORT   O dear Marwood, you are not going?

MRS. MARWOOD   Not far, madam; I'll return immediately.
   [Exit]
   [Re-enter SIR WILFULL and MIRABELL]

SIR WILFULL   Look up, man, I'll stand by you; 'sbud, an she do frown, she can't kill you;—besides—hark'ee, she dare not frown desperately, because her face is none of her own; 'sheart, an she should, her forehead would wrinkle like the coat of a cream-cheese; but mum for that, fellow-traveller.

MIRABELL   If a deep sense of the many injuries I have offered to so good a lady, with a sincere remorse and a hearty contrition, can but obtain the least glance of compassion, I am too happy.—Ah, madam, there was a time—but let it be forgotten—I confess I have deservedly forfeited the high place I once held, of sighing at your feet; nay, kill me not, by turning from me in disdain—I come not to plead for favour,—nay, not for pardon; I am a suppliant only for your pity—I am going where I never shall behold you more——

SIR WILFULL—How, fellow-traveller! You shall go by yourself then.

MIRABELL   Let me be pitied first; and afterwards forgotten—I ask no more.

---

30. That is, instantly; as did those who beheld the face of the snake-haired Gorgon.
31. The loyal friend of Agamemnon's son and avenger.

SIR WILFULL   By'r Lady, a very reasonable request, and will cost you nothing, aunt. Come, come, forgive and forget, aunt; why you must, an you are a Christian.

MIRABELL   Consider, madam, in reality you could not receive much prejudice; it was an innocent device, though I confess it had a face of guiltiness,— it was at most an artifice which love contrived—and errors which love produces have ever been accounted venial. At least think it is punishment enough, that I have lost what in my heart I hold most dear, that to your cruel indignation I have offered up this beauty, and with her my peace and quiet; nay, all my hopes of future comfort.

SIR WILFULL   An he does not move me, would I might never be o' the quorum![32]—an it were not as good a deed as to drink, to give her to him again, I would I might never take shipping!—Aunt, if you don't forgive quickly, I shall melt, I can tell you that. My contract went no further than a little mouth glue,[33] and that's hardly dry;—one doleful sigh more from my fellow-traveller and 'tis dissolved.

LADY WISHFORT   Well, nephew, upon your account.—Ah, he has a false insinuating tongue!—Well, sir, I will stifle my just resentment at my nephew's request. I will endeavour what I can to forget—but on proviso that you resign the contract with my niece immediately.

MIRABELL   It is in writing and with papers of concern; but I have sent my servant for it, and will deliver it to you, with all acknowledgments for your transcendent goodness.

LADY WISHFORT   [apart]   Oh, he has witchcraft in his eyes and tongue! When I did not see him, I could have bribed a villain to his assassination; but his appearance rakes the embers which have so long lain smothered in my breast.

[Enter FAINALL and MRS. MARWOOD]

FAINALL   Your date of deliberation, madam, is expired. Here is the instrument; are you prepared to sign?

LADY WISHFORT   If I were prepared, I am not impowered. My niece exerts a lawful claim, having matched herself by my direction to Sir Wilfull.

FAINALL   That sham is too gross to pass on me, though 'tis imposed on you, madam.

MILLAMANT   Sir, I have given my consent.

MIRABELL   And, sir, I have resigned my pretensions.

SIR WILFULL   And sir, I assert my right; and will maintain it in defiance of you, sir, and of your instrument. 'Sheart, an you talk of an instrument, sir, I have an old fox[34] by my thigh shall hack your instrument of ram vellum[35] to shreds, sir! It shall not be sufficient for a mittimus[36] or a tailor's measure; therefore, withdraw your instrument, sir, or by'r Lady I shall draw mine.

LADY WISHFORT   Hold, nephew, hold!

32. Group of Justices of the Peace who must be present to constitute a legal court session.
33. Oral promise.
34. Sword.
35. Legal sheepskin.
36. Warrant of arrest.

MILLAMANT   Good Sir Wilfull, respite your valour!

FAINALL   Indeed? Are you provided of a guard, with your single beefeater [37] there? But I'm prepared for you, and insist upon my first proposal. You shall submit your own estate to my management, and absolutely make over my wife's to my sole use, as pursuant to the purport and tenor of this other covenant.[38] [*To* MRS. MILLAMANT] I suppose, madam, your consent is not requisite in this case; nor, Mr. Mirabell, your resignation; nor, Sir Wilfull, your right. You may draw your fox if you please, sir, and make a bear-garden [39] flourish somewhere else; for here it will not avail. This, my Lady Wishfort, must be subscribed, or your darling daughter's turned adrift, like a leaky hulk to sink or swim, as she and the current of this lewd town can agree.

LADY WISHFORT   Is there no means, no remedy, to stop my ruin? Ungrateful wretch! dost thou not owe thy being, thy subsistence, to my daughter's fortune?

FAINALL   I'll answer you when I have the rest of it in my possession.

MIRABELL   But that you would not accept of a remedy from my hands—I own I have not deserved you should owe any obligation to me; or else perhaps I could advise——

LADY WISHFORT   Oh, what? what? to save me and my child from ruin, from want, I'll forgive all that's past; nay, I'll consent to anything to come, to be delivered from this tyranny.

MIRABELL   Aye, madam, but that is too late; my reward is intercepted. You have disposed of her who only could have made me a compensation for all my services;—but be it as it may, I am resolved I'll serve you—you shall not be wronged in this savage manner!

LADY WISHFORT   How! Dear Mr. Mirabell, can you be so generous at last! But it is not possible. Hark'ee, I'll break my nephew's match, you shall have my niece yet and all her fortune, if you can but save me from this imminent danger.

MIRABELL   Will you? I take you at your word. I ask no more. I must have leave for two criminals to appear.

LADY WISHFORT   Aye, aye, anybody, anybody!

MIRABELL   Foible is one, and a penitent.

[*Enter* MRS. FAINALL, FOIBLE, *and* MINCING]

MRS. MARWOOD [*to* FAINALL]   Oh, my shame! these corrupt things are bought and brought hither to expose me.

[MIRABELL *and* LADY WISHFORT *go to* MRS. FAINALL *and* FOIBLE]

FAINALL   If it must all come out, why let 'em know it; 'tis but *the way of the world*. That shall not urge me to relinquish or abate one tittle of my terms; no, I will insist the more.

FOIBLE   Yes, indeed, madam, I'll take my Bible oath of it.

MINCING   And so will I, mem.

---

37. Name for a guard at the Tower of London.
38. Fainall, dropping his claim to Millamant's money, returns to his original demands ("this other covenant"), the price of remaining married and creating no scandal; this does not involve Millamant, Mirabell, or Sir Wilfull.
39. A place where bear-baiting noisily took place.

LADY WISHFORT   O Marwood, Marwood, art thou false? my friend deceive me? Hast thou been a wicked accomplice with that profligate man?

MRS. MARWOOD   Have you so much ingratitude and injustice to give credit against your friend, to the aspersions of two such mercenary trulls?

MINCING   Mercenary, mem? I scorn your words. 'Tis true we found you and Mr. Fainall in the blue garret; by the same token, you swore us to secrecy upon Messalinas's poems.⁴⁰ Mercenary? No, if we would have been mercenary, we should have held our tongues; you would have bribed us sufficiently.

FAINALL   Go, you are an insignificant thing!—Well, what are you the better for this! Is this Mr. Mirabell's expedient? I'll be put off no longer.—You, thing that was a wife, shall smart for this! I will not leave thee wherewithal to hide thy shame; your body shall be naked as your reputation.

MRS. FAINALL   I despise you, and defy your malice! You have aspersed me wrongfully—I have proved your falsehood. Go you and your treacherous—I will not name it—but starve together—perish!

FAINALL   Not while you are worth a groat, indeed, my dear. Madam, I'll be fooled no longer.

LADY WISHFORT   Ah, Mr. Mirabell, this is small comfort, the detection of this affair.

MIRABELL   Oh, in good time. Your leave for the other offender and penitent to appear, madam.

[*Enter* WAITWELL *with a box of writings*]

LADY WISHFORT   O Sir Rowland!—Well, rascal!

WAITWELL   What your ladyship pleases. I have brought the black box at last, madam.

MIRABELL   Give it me. Madam, you remember your promise.

LADY WISHFORT   Aye, dear sir.

MIRABELL   Where are the gentlemen?

WAITWELL   At hand, sir, rubbing their eyes—just risen from sleep.

FAINALL   'Sdeath, what's this to me? I'll not wait your private concerns.

[*Enter* PETULANT *and* WITWOUD]

PETULANT   How now? what's the matter? whose hand's out? ⁴¹

WITWOUD   Heyday! what, are you all got together, like players at the end of the last act?

MIRABELL   You may remember, gentlemen, I once requested your hands as witnesses to a certain parchment.

WITWOUD   Aye, I do, my hand I remember—Petulant set his mark.

MIRABELL   You wrong him; his name is fairly written, as shall appear.—You do not remember, gentlemen, anything of what that parchment contained? [*Undoing the box*]

WITWOUD   No.

PETULANT   Not I. I writ, I read nothing.

MIRABELL   Very well, now you shall know.—Madam, your promise.

LADY WISHFORT   Aye, aye, sir, upon my honour.

40. Presumably Mincing's version of *Miscellaneous Poems;* Messalina was the licentious wife of the Roman emperor Claudius.
41. Who's making trouble?

MIRABELL.   Mr. Fainall, it is now time that you should know that your lady, while she was at her own disposal, and before you had by your insinuations wheedled her out of a pretended settlement of the greatest part of her fortune——

FAINALL   Sir! pretended!

MIRABELL   Yes, sir. I say that this lady while a widow, having, it seems, received some cautions respecting your inconstancy and tyranny of temper, which from her own partial opinion and fondness of you she could never have suspected—she did, I say, by the wholesome advice of friends and of sages learned in the laws of this land, deliver this same as her act and deed to me in trust, and to the uses within mentioned. You may read if you please [*Holding out the parchment*]— though perhaps what is inscribed on the back may serve your occasions.

FAINALL   Very likely, sir. What's here? Damnation! [*Reads*] 'A deed of conveyance of the whole estate real of Arabella Languish, widow, in trust to Edward Mirabell.'— Confusion!

MIRABELL   Even so, sir; 'tis *the way of the world*, sir—of the widows of the world. I suppose this deed may bear an elder date than what you have obtained from your lady.

FAINALL   Perfidious fiend! then thus I'll be revenged. [*Offers to run at* MRS. FAINALL]

SIR WILFULL   Hold, sir! now you may make your bear-garden flourish somewhere else, sir.

FAINALL   Mirabell, you shall hear of this, sir, be sure you shall.—Let me pass, oaf.

[*Exit*]

MRS. FAINALL [*to* MRS. MARWOOD]   Madam, you seem to stifle your resentment. You had better give it vent.

MRS. MARWOOD   Yes, it shall have vent—and to your confusion, or I'll perish in the attempt.

[*Exit*]

LADY WISHFORT   O daughter, daughter! 'tis plain thou hast inherited thy mother's prudence.

MRS. FAINALL   Thank Mr. Mirabell, a cautious friend, to whose advice all is owing.

LADY WISHFORT   Well, Mr. Mirabell, you have kept your promise—and I must perform mine.—First, I pardon for your sake Sir Rowland there and Foible;—the next thing is to break the matter to my nephew— and how to do that——

MIRABELL   For that, madam, give yourself no trouble; let me have your consent. Sir Wilfull is my friend; he has had compassion upon lovers, and generously engaged a volunteer in this action, for our service, and now designs to prosecute his travels.

SIR WILFULL   'Sheart, aunt, I have no mind to marry. My cousin's a fine lady, and the gentleman loves her and she loves him, and they deserve one another; my resolution is to see foreign parts—I have set on't—and when I'm set on't, I must do't. And if these two gentlemen would travel too, I think they may be spared.

PETULANT   For my part, I say little—I think things are best off or on.

WITWOUD   I'gad, I understand nothing of the matter; I'm in a maze yet, like a dog in a dancing-school.

LADY WISHFORT   Well, sir, take her, and with her all the joy I can give you.

MILLAMANT   Why does not the man take me? Would you have me give myself to you over again?

MIRABELL   Aye, and over and over again; for I would have you as often as possibly I can. [*Kisses her hand*] Well, heaven grant I love you not too well, that's all my fear.

SIR WILFULL   'Sheart, you'll have him time enough to toy after you're married; or if you will toy now, let us have a dance in the meantime, that we who are not lovers may have some other employment besides looking on.

MIRABELL   With all my heart, dear Sir Wilfull. What shall we do for music?

FOIBLE   O sir, some that were provided for Sir Rowland's entertainment are yet within call.

[*A dance*]

LADY WISHFORT   As I am a person, I can hold out no longer; I have wasted my spirits so today already, that I am ready to sink under the fatigue; and I cannot but have some fears upon me yet that my son Fainall will pursue some desperate course.

MIRABELL   Madam, disquiet not yourself on that account; to my knowledge his circumstances are such he must of force comply. For my part, I will contribute all that in me lies to a reunion; in the meantime, madam [*To* MRS. FAINALL], let me before these witnesses restore to you this deed of trust. It may be a means, well managed, to make you live easily together.

From hence let those be warned, who mean to wed;
Lest mutual falsehood stain the bridal-bed;
For each deceiver to his cost may find,
That marriage frauds too oft are paid in kind.

[*Exeunt omnes*]
1700

JONATHAN SWIFT
1667–1745

Swift is the greatest ironist in English literature, and he has as a result been accused of all the malevolence and blindness that resentment can invent. He does not allow man much comfort or dignity, and he cruelly reduces grand pretensions to systematic follies and mechanized brutality. In fact, Swift's characteristic device is to invent some rational basis for the behavior that men fall into unthinkingly or self-indulgently; by rationalizing folly, by finding eloquent arguments for the unspeakable, Swift divorces intention (usually noble) from achievement (somewhat shabbier) and shows what one would have to intend if one were to undertake deliberately what men in fact accomplish. If we live by exploiting others, we are only a short way (just enough to save our self-esteem) from cannibalism, and Swift shocks us with that possibility in

A Modest Proposal. If we have turned religion into an accommodation of our "schemes of wealth and power," always sure to secure a blessing for what is profitable or expedient, we are on the way to abolishing Christianity, and we need not go through the explicit motions, given our great skill at simply undermining the faith by which we might otherwise be judged. There is no wonder that Swift has aroused resentment; there are great temptations to misread him and make him a historical curiosity. The easiest way of all is to attribute his unaccommodating irony to the psychological aberrations of a disturbed or conflict-torn man.

Swift was born in Ireland of English parents and, after studying at Trinity College, Dublin, he entered the household of Sir William Temple, a retired diplomat, as a secretary. Temple lived in retirement outside of London, and he had a fine library, which Swift used well. It was in Temple's household that Swift first met Hester Johnson, with whose education he helped, and upon whose affection he depended greatly during their years together in Dublin. His relations with Temple were close but difficult, and Swift left at one point to become an Anglican parish priest in northern Ireland. Upon his return to England he remained with Temple until the latter's death, helping prepare Temple's works for publication and writing his own remarkable first volume of satire, which included A Tale of a Tub and The Battle of the Books (written in the 1690's and published in 1704). While the Tale had great success, its ironic treatment of the church probably hurt Swift's ecclessiastical career.

In 1707 Swift was sent by the Church of Ireland to seek financial benefits from Queen Anne; during his year's stay in London, he became accepted as a man of letters and was close to Addison's literary circle. When he returned to London in 1710, he left the Whigs and gave his support to the Tory ministry of Robert Harley, later Earl of Oxford, on the grounds that the Whigs might sell the church short in their encouragement of Dissenters. For most of the four years that followed, until the fall of the ministry with the death of the Queen, Swift became a principal spokesman and propagandist for the Tories, through such a periodical as The Examiner and through such political pamphlets as The Conduct of the Allies (1713). He became a leading spirit in the Scriblerus Club with Pope and Dr. Arbuthnot, and he was able to win patronage for friends in difficulty, Addison among them.

With the fall of the ministry, Swift (who had been appointed Dean of St. Patrick's Cathedral, Dublin, in 1713) began his long Irish exile, the hope of a bishopric in England vanishing and the visits to London growing infrequent. He became in some measure an Irish patriot, trying to stir the Irish to self-respect and to resistance against English exploitation; and he won a considerable battle against Sir Robert Walpole through his Drapier's Letters of 1724–25. Gulliver's Travels contained strong political satire, and Swift had a hand in encouraging both Gay's Beggar's Opera and Pope's Dunciad in the following years. Throughout his lifetime Swift created a body of distinctive poetry, and finally his irony turned to a compendium of "polite conversation" and a penetrating set of Directions to Servants. At the end Swift's mind and memory gave way after years of labyrinthine vertigo, a disease of the middle ear that disturbed his sense of balance; he was cared for by others until his death, which fell in the year after Pope's.

Swift's irony required that he write in many guises, and each of these guises (masks or personae, as they have been called) tends to become in some degree a fool among knaves, a man more obtuse and more innocent than the wilier and more clear-headedly vicious knaves. The fool gives them away without meaning to betray, for he guilelessly acknowledges what they know enough to conceal. This contributes to that style of cool understatement which exacts from the reader a moral judgment it does not explicitly provide; in *Gulliver's Travels* it produces a surface of meticulously realistic narration such as the novel might later use. But in Swift's hands this very precision of recorded detail is meant to strike us with its failure to judge or feel and to require us to do so instead.

The Battle of the Books

Swift carries on the wide-ranging quarrel of the Ancients and Moderns which divided scholars in seventeenth-century France. Involved in the quarrel was the whole idea of progress. Were the Moderns inferior to the great Ancients, or were they their equals or even superiors? The defenders of the Ancients could claim that writers of later ages had done little more than borrow from the greatness of Homer and Virgil, Horace and Terence. They traced a pattern of slow but steady degeneration in the history of man. The defenders of the Moderns could point to the dead hand of Aristotle upon history and science and the great achievements that arose among the Moderns with the overthrow of foolish reverence for ancient authorities.

In England the quarrel took a special turn when Sir William Temple, Swift's patron, praised the work of Aesop and Phalaris at the expense of the Moderns, only to bring down the learned criticism of Richard Bentley, the greatest classical scholar of his time, who proved that Temple's Ancients were not nearly so ancient as Temple had thought them. The conflict also represented a clash between literary humanism and philological science, and Swift entered it with an effort to show the arrogance and insensitivity of those Moderns who could date a poem accurately but could neither write nor read one well. He invented the fable of a battle (presented in mock-heroic vein) among the books in the royal library (where Bentley was keeper of books), but the finest episode in the work is an interlude in which a pompous and ill-tempered Modern, the Spider, finds his Gothic cobweb invaded by a Bee. It should be noted that Gothic architecture and scholastic disputation were cheerfully granted to the Moderns by Swift, and Horatian urbanity—so recently revived as a model of style— is a quality of his Ancients. The Ancients, for Swift, represent those who keep the past alive in the present, fostering the virtues of antiquity and not—like Cornelius Scriblerus, in another satire to which Swift contributed—revering its rust. The Moderns in their ambition to be self-sufficient risk parochial narrowness; their manners show a failure of humanity as well as of humanism.

From A Full and True Account of the Battle Fought Last Friday, Between the Ancient and Modern Books in St. James's Library

[Episode of the Spider and the Bee]

Things were at this crisis when a material accident fell out. For upon the highest corner of a large window there dwelt a certain Spider, swollen up to the first magnitude by the destruction of infinite numbers of flies, whose spoils lay scattered before the gates of his palace, like human bones before the cave of some giant.[1] The avenues to his castle were guarded with turnpikes and palisadoes, all after the modern way of fortification.[2] After you had passed several courts, you came to the centre, wherein you might behold the constable[3] himself in his own lodgings, which had windows fronting to each avenue and ports[4] to sally out upon all occasions of prey or defence. In this mansion he had for some time dwelt in peace and plenty, without danger to his person by swallows from above or to his palace by brooms from below; when it was the pleasure of Fortune to conduct thither a wandering Bee, to whose curiosity a broken pane in the glass had discovered itself, and in he went; where, expatiating a while, he at last happened to alight upon one of the outward walls of the Spider's citadel; which, yielding to the unequal weight, sunk down to the very foundation. Thrice he endeavoured to force his passage, and thrice the centre shook. The Spider within, feeling the terrible convulsion, supposed at first that Nature was approaching to her final dissolution;[5] or else that Beelzebub[6] with all his legions was come to revenge the death of many thousands of his subjects, whom his enemy had slain and devoured. However, he at length valiantly resolved to issue forth and meet his fate. Meanwhile the Bee had acquitted himself of his toils,[7] and, posted securely at some distance, was employed in cleansing his wings and disengaging them from the ragged remnants of the cobweb. By this time the Spider was adventured out, when, beholding the chasms and ruins and dilapidations of his fortress, he was very near at his wit's end; he stormed and swore like a madman and swelled till he was ready to burst. At length, casting his eye upon the Bee and wisely gathering causes from events (for they knew each other by sight): 'A plague split you,' said he, 'for a giddy son of a whore. Is it you, with a vengeance, that have made this litter here? Could not you look before you, and be d—ned? Do you think I have nothing else to do, in the devil's name, but to mend and repair after your arse?'

'Good words, friend,' said the Bee (having now pruned himself and being disposed to droll), 'I'll give you my hand and word to come near your kennel no more; I was never in such a confounded pickle since I was born.'

'Sirrah,' replied the Spider, 'if it were not for breaking an old custom in our family never to stir abroad against an enemy, I should come and teach you better manners.'

'I pray have patience,' said the Bee, 'or you will spend your substance, and, for aught I see, you may stand in need of it all towards the repair of your house.'

'Rogue, rogue,' replied the Spider, 'yet methinks you should have more respect to a person whom all the world allows to be so much your betters.'

1. With echoes of Romance literature, which was defended later in the 18th century on the analogy of Gothic architecture.
2. One of the fields in which the Moderns were generally granted eminence, as was mathematics.
3. The keeper of a royal fortress or castle.
4. Gateways.
5. Swift often satirizes the gullible and superstitious fears of scientists.
6. Literally, the god of flies.
7. Snares, nets.

'By my troth,' said the Bee, 'the comparison will amount to a very good jest, and you will do me a favour to let me know the reasons that all the world is pleased to use in so hopeful [8] a dispute.'

At this the Spider, having swelled himself into the size and posture of a disputant, began his argument in the true spirit of controversy, with a resolution to be heartily scurrilous and angry, to urge on his own reasons without the least regard to the answers or objections of his opposite, and fully predetermined in his mind against all conviction.

'Not to disparage myself,' said he, 'by the comparison with such a rascal, what art thou but a vagabond without house or home, without stock or inheritance, born to no possession of your own but a pair of wings and a drone-pipe? Your livelihood is an universal plunder upon nature, a freebooter over fields and gardens; and, for the sake of stealing, will rob a nettle as easily as a violet. Whereas I am a domestic animal, furnished with a native stock within myself. This large castle (to show my improvements in the mathematics) is all built with my own hands, and the materials extracted altogether out of my own person.'

'I am glad,' answered the Bee, 'to hear you grant at least that I am come honestly by my wings and my voice; for then, it seems, I am obliged to Heaven alone for my flights and my music; and Providence would never have bestowed on me two such gifts without designing them for the noblest ends. I visit indeed all the flowers and blossoms of the field and the garden; but whatever I collect from thence enriches myself, without the least injury to their beauty, their smell, or their taste. Now, for you and your skill in architecture and other mathematics, I have little to say. In that building of yours there might, for aught I know, have been labour and method enough; but, by woful experience for us both, 'tis too plain the materials are naught, and I hope you will henceforth take warning and consider duration and matter as well as method and art. You boast, indeed, of being obliged to no other creature but of drawing and spinning out all from yourself; that is to say, if we may judge of the liquor in the vessel by what issues out, you possess a good plentiful store of dirt and poison in your breast; and, though I would by no means lessen or disparage your genuine stock of either, yet I doubt you are somewhat obliged, for an increase of both, to a little foreign assistance. Your inherent portion of dirt does not fail of acquisitions by sweepings exhaled from below; and one insect furnishes you with a share of poison to destroy another. So that, in short, the question comes all to this: whether is the nobler being of the two that which, by a lazy contemplation of four inches round, by an overweening pride which, feeding and engendering on itself, turns all into excrement and venom, producing nothing at all but flybane and a cobweb; or that which, by an universal range, with long search, much study, true judgement, and distinction of things, brings home honey and wax.'

This dispute was managed with such eagerness, clamour, and warmth, that the two parties of Books, in arms below, stood silent a while, waiting in suspense what would be the issue, which was not long undetermined: for the Bee, grown impatient at so much loss of time, fled straight away to a bed of roses without

8. Promising.

looking for a reply, and left the Spider like an orator, collected in himself and just prepared to burst out.

It happened upon this emergency that Aesop broke silence first. He had been of late most barbarously treated by a strange effect of the regent's humanity, who had tore off his title-page, sorely defaced one half of his leaves, and chained him fast among a shelf of Moderns. Where, soon discovering how high the quarrel was like to proceed, he tried all his arts, and turned himself to a thousand forms.[9] At length, in the borrowed shape of an ass, the regent mistook him for a Modern; by which means he had time and opportunity to escape to the Ancients, just when the Spider and the Bee were entering into their contest, to which he gave his attention with a world of pleasure; and when it was ended, swore in the loudest key that in all his life he had never known two cases so parallel and adapt to each other as that in the window and this upon the shelves. 'The disputants,' said he, 'have admirably managed the dispute between them, have taken in the full strength of all that is to be said on both sides, and exhausted the substance of every argument *pro* and *con*. It is but to adjust the reasonings of both to the present quarrel, then to compare and apply the labours and fruits of each, as the Bee has learnedly deduced them, and we shall find the conclusion fall plain and close upon the Moderns and us. For, pray, gentlemen, was ever anything so modern as the Spider in his air, his turns,[10] and his paradoxes? He argues in the behalf of you his brethren and himself with many boastings of his native stock and great genius, that he spins and spits wholly from himself, and scorns to own any obligation or assistance from without. Then he displays to you his great skill in architecture and improvement in the mathematics. To all this the Bee, as an advocate retained by us the Ancients, thinks fit to answer that, if one may judge of the great genius or inventions of the Moderns by what they have produced, you will hardly have countenance to bear you out in boasting of either. Erect your schemes with as much method and skill as you please; yet, if the materials be nothing but dirt, spun out of your own entrails (the guts of modern brains), the edifice will conclude at last in a cobweb, the duration of which, like that of other spiders' webs, may be imputed to their being forgotten, or neglected, or hid in a corner. For anything else of genuine that the Moderns may pretend to, I cannot recollect, unless it be a large vein of wrangling and satire, much of a nature and substance with the Spider's poison; which, however they pretend to spit wholly out of themselves, is improved by the same arts, by feeding upon the insects and vermin of the age. As for us the Ancients, we are content with the Bee to pretend to nothing of our own beyond our wings and our voice, that is to say, our flights and our language. For the rest, whatever we have got, has been by infinite labour and search and ranging through every corner of nature; the difference is that, instead of dirt and poison, we have rather chosen to fill our hives with honey and wax, thus furnishing mankind with the two noblest of things, which are sweetness and light.' [11]

1704

9. Referring to the many animals Aesop had characterized in his fables.
10. Witty plays on words (used ironically of his spluttering abuse).
11. The terms later borrowed and extended by Matthew Arnold in *Culture and Anarchy* (1869).

A Tale of a Tub

A Tale of a Tub, originally published in one volume with *The Battle of the Books* and *The Mechanical Operation of the Spirit,* a satire on religious enthusiasm, marks a turning point in English literature. It looks back to the age of baroque and Metaphysical wit—in such prose as the sermons of John Donne or Lancelot Andrewes or the secular works of Robert Burton and Sir Thomas Browne; in such verse as that of Cowley, whom Swift imitated in his earliest poems—and in looking back, through parody, it sees false and ingenious verbal wit and self-flattering sophistry. Swift mocks the extravagant arguments through metaphor, the fanciful system-building, and the constant "wresting" of terms. Behind this last concern, which had been awakened by the preaching of witty Anglican and enthusiastic Puritan alike, lay the words of Peter (II Peter 3:16) on the epistles of Paul: "in which are some things hard to be understood, which they that are unlearned and unstable wrest, as they do also the other Scriptures, unto their own destruction."

But the *Tale* is a twofold attack: upon the corruption of religion and of learning. The counterpart of the extremes in religion—"the frenzy of Platonic visions and the lethargic ignorance of Popish dreams," as Halifax called them—is the false learning that cultivates the letter at the expense of spirit, words at the expense of meaning. Here Swift returns to the attack upon Bentley he undertook in *The Battle* but extends his attack to include the other extreme of learning as well—superficiality, gullibility, and laziness. His point is that extremes meet, that the pride in self which creates carping arrogance in some produces obtuse complacency in others. The Spider's "lazy contemplation of four inches round" is easier to maintain if the Modern is convinced of his own inherent greatness, and Swift mocks this by showing the Moderns finding "momentous truths" in their most trivial and ephemeral effusions. They do this by ingenious allegorizing, in the manner of Bunyan or his more learned scholarly counterparts, and allegory releases the will to believe, overriding all empirical evidence or restraint from outside. It becomes the vehicle of the private will and imagination, and Swift finally treats the uncontrolled fancy, as Locke and others had done before him, as a kind of madness.

The *Tale* is, in form, an ingeniously baroque structure. After many prefatory and dedicatory sections, it interweaves an allegorical tale with self-styled digressions that gradually overwhelm the tale. (As Hobbes says, in the eighth chapter of *Leviathan,* "A great fancy is one kind of madness such as they have that, entering into any discourse, are snatched from their purpose . . . into so many and so long digressions and parentheses that they utterly lose themselves.") Swift's "digressions" are, in fact, the heart of the work, and the greatest of them is given below. They embody the themes of fancy, wit, and reason in the secular world, while the allegory presents the career of the Christian church once it enters the world. It is embodied in three brothers: Peter (the Church of Rome), Martin (Luther's moderate reforming Protestantism and the Church of England in particular), and Jack (Calvinism and other forms of radical Protestantism). The brothers are meant to live together in peace, but, as they enter the world—as in Section II below—they become more and more at odds, until Peter kicks the others out of doors. Recovering his senses, Martin tries to restore the original form of his coat and realizes that he cannot achieve pristine purity without damaging the fabric. He leaves some of those accretions that cannot safely be removed; but Jack, in utter reaction, tears his to shreds rather than have it show any trace of Peter's influence. The result, ironically, is that Peter's elaborate finery and Jack's rags look—at any distance—indistinguishable, and the modest "trimmer" Martin is hated by both.

The Digression on Madness has sometimes been discussed as if it were wholly negative in implication, as if it prepared us to accept the surfaces of things, only to damn us for doing so. But one must ask whether the defense of surface is meant to be plausible, and this is best determined by asking to what surface is opposed. The speaker involves us in an impossible choice between carping and superficiality, between mangling and piercing on the one hand and skimming on the other. Between these extremes the ideal of true analysis and tactful perception is lost, just as Martin is crowded off the scene by the barbarous vigor of Peter and Jack. The same problem recurs in the fourth voyage of *Gulliver's Travels*, where we must find a norm somewhere between the undisturbed rationality of the Houyhnhnms and the savage passions of the Yahoos.

Section IX makes clear, as earlier sections of the *Tale* have revealed, that Swift is writing in the guise of a Modern hack, full of avowed respect for all forms of modernity and of scorn for old-fashioned "common forms." He writes of madness with special authority as a former inhabitant of Bedlam, and he has all the zeal of a "projector," a man with schemes for public improvements that will win him profit or praise. The guise is a transparent one, for it is clearly the vehicle of a savage irony; but it accounts for the imperturbable ease with which the author both contradicts himself and gives himself away. We see through the speaker; he is given the relative consistency of a type, both psychological and social, that is meant to be recognized and to be given only so much credit as his limitations merit. He is less obviously a *persona* (that is, a mask or assumed identity) than Lemuel Gulliver, who has a name and a fuller history, but we miss much of his meaning if we ignore the allusiveness to contemporary styles and attitudes that shapes his role.

The title of Swift's work comes from a proverbial phrase for a nonsensical *jeu d'esprit* or whimsy, but he mockingly allegorizes it as the tub seamen throw out to distract a threatening whale, the whale in this case being the dangerous doctrines of Thomas Hobbes's *Leviathan*. So influential has that work been in seducing the young wits that serious disturbances might arise if they were not kept busy with harmless tasks, Swift implies, and this book is offered as an absorbing puzzle. In fact, it mocks their modernity and seeks to recall them to sanity.

From A Tale of a Tub

Written for the Universal Improvement of Mankind

Section II

Once upon a time there was a man who had three sons by one wife, and all at a birth; neither could the midwife tell certainly which was the eldest. Their father died while they were young; and upon his deathbed, calling the lads to him, spoke thus:

'Sons, because I have purchased no estate, nor was born to any, I have long considered of some good legacies to bequeath you; and at last, with much care, as well as expense, have provided each of you (here they are) a new coat. Now, you are to understand, that these coats have two virtues contained in them: one is that with good wearing they will last you fresh and sound as long as you live; the other is that they will grow in the same proportion with your bodies, lengthening and widening of themselves, so as to be always fit. Here, let me see them on you before I die. So, very well; pray, children, wear them clean and brush them often. You will find in my will[1] (here it is) full instructions in every particular concerning the wearing and management of your coats; wherein you must be very exact, to avoid the penalties I have appointed for every transgression or neglect, upon which your future fortunes will entirely depend. I have also commanded in my will, that you should live together in one house like brethren and friends, for then you will be sure to thrive, and not otherwise.'

Here the story says this good father died, and the three sons went all together to seek their fortunes.

I shall not trouble you with recounting what adventures they met for the first seven years, any farther than by taking notice that they carefully observed their father's will and kept their coats in very good order: that they travelled through several countries, encountered a reasonable quantity of giants, and slew certain dragons.[2]

Being now arrived at the proper age for producing themselves, they came up to town and fell in love with the ladies, but especially three, who about that time were in chief reputation: the Duchess d'Argent, Madame de Grands Titres, and the Countess d'Orgueil.[3] On their first appearance our three adventurers met with a very bad reception; and soon with great sagacity guessing out the reason, they quickly began to improve in the good qualities of the town. They writ, and rallied, and rhymed, and sung, and said, and said nothing: they drank, and fought, and whored, and slept, and swore, and took snuff: they went to new plays on the first night, haunted the chocolate-houses, beat the watch, lay on bulks,[4] and got claps: they bilked[5] hackney-coachmen, ran in debt with shop-keepers, and lay with their wives: they killed bailiffs, kicked fiddlers down stairs, eat at Locket's,[6] loitered at Will's:[7] they talked of the drawing-room and never came there: dined with lords they never saw: whispered a duchess, and spoke never a word:[8] exposed the scrawls of their laundress for billetdoux of quality: came ever just from court and were never seen in it: attended the levee *sub dio:*[9] got a list of peers by heart in one company, and with great familiarity retailed them in another. Above all, they

1. That is, the New Testament, which provides all that is necessary to know for the sake of salvation (and presumably also for the sake of morality or "decency" in its fullest sense, i.e. what is "fitting"); "by the coats are meant the doctrine and faith of Christianity, by the wisdom of the Divine Founder fitted to all times, places, and circumstances." (Swift)

2. The traditional Romance elements of Christian allegory (as in *The Faerie Queene* I or Bunyan's account of Apollyon) are rapidly disposed of, and the era of "primitive Christianity" gives way to the role of the church in the world (here the world is cut to the scale of the "grand monde" or world of fashionable society).

3. Covetousness (wealth), ambition (great titles), and pride.

4. Stalls outside shops, where impoverished poets sometimes slept.

5. Cheated.

6. A fashionable tavern.

7. The well-known literary coffeehouse.

8. That is, whispered about but never spoke a word to.

9. That is, attended the official reception ("levee") only in the open air ("*sub dio*").

constantly attended those Committees of Senators who are silent in the House and loud in the coffee-house; where they nightly adjourn to chew the cud of politics and are encompassed with a ring of disciples who lie in wait to catch up their droppings. The three brothers had acquired forty other qualifications of the like stamp, too tedious to recount, and by consequence were justly reckoned the most accomplished persons in the town. But all would not suffice, and the ladies aforesaid continued still inflexible. To clear up which difficulty I must, with the reader's good leave and patience, have recourse to some points of weight, which the authors of that age have not sufficiently illustrated.

For about this time it happened a sect arose, whose tenets obtained and spread very far, especially in the *grand monde* and among everybody of good fashion. They worshipped a sort of idol, who, as their doctrine delivered, did daily create men by a kind of manufactory operation. This idol they placed in the highest parts of the house on an altar erected about three foot: he was shown in the posture of a Persian emperor, sitting on a superficies, with his legs interwoven under him.[10] This god had a goose for his ensign, whence it is that some learned men pretend to deduce his original from Jupiter Capitolinus.[11] At his left hand, beneath the altar, Hell seemed to open, and catch at the animals the idol was creating; to prevent which, certain of his priests hourly flung in pieces of the uninformed mass, or substance, and sometimes whole limbs already enlivened, which that horrid gulf insatiably swallowed, terrible to behold. The goose was also held a subaltern divinity or *deus minorum gentium*,[12] before whose shrine was sacrificed that creature whose hourly food is human gore and who is in so great renown abroad for being the delight and favourite of the Egyptian Cercopithecus.[13] Millions of these animals were cruelly slaughtered every day to appease the hunger of that consuming deity. The chief idol was also worshipped as the inventor of the yard and the needle; [14] whether as the god of seamen or on account of certain other mystical attributes hath not been sufficiently cleared.

The worshippers of this deity had also a system of their belief which seemed to turn upon the following fundamental. They held the universe to be a large suit of clothes which invests everything: that the earth is invested by the air; the air is invested by the stars; and the stars are invested by the *primum mobile*.[15] Look on this globe of earth, you will find it to be a very complete and fashionable dress. What is that which some call land, but a fine coat faced with green? or the sea, but a waistcoat of water-tabby? [16] Proceed to the par-

10. The "idol" is a tailor, the "goose" his smoothing-iron (named for the shape of its handle), and "Hell" is his receptacle for scraps of cloth (cf. Butler, *Hudibras* I.i.238).
11. Jupiter had a temple on the Capitoline Hill, where the sacred geese of Rome were also kept.
12. Subordinate deity or "god of the lesser tribes."
13. "The Egyptians worshipped a monkey, which animal is very fond of eating lice, styled here creatures that feed on human gore." (Swift)
14. Punning on the tailor's yardstick and needle as the nautical spar to hold sails and the compass needle.
15. Since the spheres of the planets and stars were seen as concentric, each might be said to be "dressed" (i.e. "invested") with the next outer one; the *primum mobile* was the outermost sphere, beyond which was the empyrean or seat of God (cf. Dryden's "Anne Killigrew" and "St. Cecilia" odes).
16. Watered silk, taffeta.

ticular works of the creation, you will find how curious [17] Journeyman Nature hath been to trim up the vegetable [18] beaux; observe how sparkish a periwig [19] adorns the head of a beech and what a fine doublet of white satin is worn by the birch. To conclude from all, what is man himself but a micro-coat,[20] or rather a complete suit of clothes with all its trimmings? As to his body, there can be no dispute; but examine even the acquirements of his mind, you will find them all contribute in their order towards furnishing out an exact dress. To instance no more: is not religion a cloak; honesty a pair of shoes worn out in the dirt; self-love a surtout; [21] vanity a shirt; and conscience a pair of breeches, which, though a cover for lewdness as well as nastiness, is easily slipped down for the service of both?

These *postulata* [22] being admitted, it will follow in due course of reasoning that those beings which the world calls improperly suits of clothes are in reality the most refined species of animals; or to proceed higher, that they are rational creatures or men. For is it not manifest that they live, and move, and talk, and perform all other offices of human life? Are not beauty, and wit, and mien, and breeding their inseparable proprieties? [23] In short, we see nothing but them, hear nothing but them. Is it not they who walk the streets, fill up parliament-, coffee-, play-, bawdy-houses? 'Tis true, indeed, that these animals, which are vulgarly called suits of clothes, or dresses, do, according to certain compositions, receive different appellations. If one of them be trimmed up with a gold chain and a red gown and a white rod and a great horse, it is called a Lord-Mayor; if certain ermines and furs be placed in a certain position, we style them a Judge; and so an apt conjunction of lawn [24] and black satin we entitle a Bishop.

Others of these professors, though agreeing in the main system, were yet more refined upon certain branches of it; and held that man was an animal compounded of two dresses, the natural and the celestial suit, which were the body and the soul: that the soul was the outward, and the body the inward clothing; that the latter was *ex traduce;* [25] but the former of daily creation and circumfusion. This last they proved by Scripture, because *in them we live, and move, and have our being;* [26] as likewise by philosophy, because they are *all in all, and all in every part.*[27] Besides, said they, separate these two, and you

17. Careful.
18. Vegetative.
19. A wig large and fashionable enough for a young fop (Swift writes of a "shrivelled beau . . . within the penthouse of a modern periwig" in *The Battle of the Books*).
20. "Alluding to the word *microcosm*, or a little world, as man hath been called by the philosophers." (Swift)
21. Loose overcoat or outer garment.
22. Assumptions, conditions (of an argument).
23. Standards.
24. Fine linen.
25. Transmitted at birth (cf. Dryden, "Anne Killigrew" ode, l. 23).
26. "In Him we live, and move, and have our being." (Acts 17:28)
27. Sir John Davies, *Nosce Teipsum* (1599), in using this phrase to describe the soul, follows Aristotelian theory. This dazzling reversal of inside and outside makes the soul (reduced to social manners and professional roles) the dress of the body and a welcome cover for its ugliness. The soul, in its traditional sense as the intellectual and moral power that resides within the body and controls it, simply disappears; for this world gives all its attention to worldly attainments or dress, and ceases, in a sense, to have a spiritual life.

will find the body to be only a senseless unsavoury carcass. By all which it is manifest that the outward dress must needs be the soul.

To this system of religion were tagged several subaltern doctrines which were entertained with great vogue; as particularly, the faculties of the mind were deduced by the learned among them in this manner: embroidery was sheer wit; [28] gold fringe was agreeable conversation; gold lace was repartee; a huge long periwig was humour; [29] and a coat full of powder was very good raillery: [30] all which required abundance of *finesse* and *delicatesse* to manage with advantage as well as a strict observance after times and fashions.[31]

I have, with much pains and reading, collected out of ancient authors, this short summary of a body of philosophy and divinity which seems to have been composed by a vein and race of thinking very different from any other systems, either ancient or modern. And it was not merely to entertain or satisfy the reader's curiosity but rather to give him light into several circumstances of the following story; that knowing the state of dispositions and opinions in an age so remote, he may better comprehend those great events which were the issue of them. I advise therefore the courteous reader to peruse with a world of application, again and again, whatever I have written upon this matter. And leaving these broken ends, I carefully gather up the chief thread of my story and proceed.

These opinions, therefore, were so universal, as well as the practices of them, among the refined part of court and town, that our three brother-adventurers, as their circumstances then stood, were strangely at a loss. For, on the one side, the three ladies they addressed themselves to (whom we have named already) were ever at the very top of the fashion and abhorred all that were below it but the breadth of a hair. On the other side, their father's will was very precise, and it was the main precept in it, with the greatest penalties annexed, not to add to, or diminish from, their coats one thread without a positive command in the will. Now, the coats their father had left them were, 'tis true, of very good cloth, and, besides, so neatly sewn, you would swear they were all of a piece; [32] but, at the same time, very plain, and with little or no ornament: and it happened that before they were a month in town, great shoulder-knots [33] came up. Straight all the world was shoulder-knots; no approaching the ladies' *ruelles* [34] without the quota of shoulder-knots. That fellow, cries one, has no soul; where is his shoulder-knot? Our three brethren soon discovered their want by sad experience, meeting in their walks with forty

28. Perhaps derived from "sheer" in the sense of "very fine" or "diaphanous" as applied to fabrics; probably implying mere verbal play without real point.
29. Probably implying mere whim or caprice.
30. Banter, good-humored teasing.
31. "Nothing is so very tender as a modern piece of wit, and which is apt to suffer so much in the carriage. Some things are extremely witty *today* or *fasting* or *in this place* or at *eight o'clock* . . . any of which, by the smallest transposal or misapplication, is utterly annihilate. . . . Such a jest there is that will not pass out of Covent Garden; and such a one that is nowhere intelligible but at Hyde Park Corner." (Preface, *A Tale of a Tub*)
32. Alluding to Christ's robe, often taken as a symbol of the Christian religion: "now the coat was without seam, woven from the top throughout" (John 19:23).
33. Knots of ribbon or lace, introduced from France about 1670; "By this is understood the first introducing of pageantry and unnecessary ornaments in the church." (Swift)
34. Bedrooms used as salons for morning receptions.

mortifications and indignities. If they went to the play-house, the doorkeeper showed them into the twelve-penny gallery. If they called a boat, says a waterman, 'I am first sculler.'[35] If they stepped to the Rose to take a bottle, the drawer would cry, 'Friend, we sell no ale.' If they went to visit a lady, a footman met them at the door with, 'Pray send up your message.' In this unhappy case, they went immediately to consult their father's will, read it over and over, but not a word of the shoulder-knot. What should they do? What temper should they find? Obedience was absolutely necessary, and yet shoulder-knots appeared extremely requisite. After much thought, one of the brothers, who happened to be more book-learned than the other two, said, he had found an expedient. ' 'Tis true,' said he, 'there is nothing here in this will, *totidem verbis*, making mention of shoulder-knots: but I dare conjecture we may find them *inclusivè*, or *totidem syllabis*.'[36] This distinction was immediately approved by all; and so they fell again to examine the will. But their evil star had so directed the matter that the first syllable was not to be found in the whole writing. Upon which disappointment he who found the former evasion took heart and said, 'Brothers, there is yet hopes; for though we cannot find them *totidem verbis*, nor *totidem syllabis*, I dare engage we shall make them out, *tertio modo*, or *totidem literis*.'[37] This discovery was also highly commended, upon which they fell once more to the scrutiny and picked out S,H,O,U,L,D,E,R; when the same planet,[38] enemy to their repose, had wonderfully contrived that a K was not to be found. Here was a weighty difficulty! But the distinguishing brother (for whom we shall hereafter find a name) now his hand was in, proved by a very good argument, that K was a modern illegitimate letter unknown to the learned ages, nor anywhere to be found in ancient manuscripts. 'Tis true, said he, the word *Calendæ* hath in Q.V.C.[39] been sometimes writ with a K, but erroneously; for in the best copies it has been ever spelt with a C. And by consequence it was a gross mistake in our language to spell Knot with a K; but that from henceforward he would take care it should be writ with a C. Upon this all farther difficulty vanished; shoulder-knots were made clearly out to be *jure paterno:*[40] and our three gentlemen swaggered with as large and as flaunting ones as the best.

But as human happiness is of a very short duration, so in those days were human fashions, upon which it entirely depends. Shoulder-knots had their time, and we must now imagine them in their decline; for a certain lord came just from Paris with fifty yards of gold lace upon his coat, exactly trimmed after the court fashion of that month. In two days all mankind appeared closed up in bars of gold lace: whoever durst peep abroad without his complement of gold lace was as scandalous as a ——, and as ill received among the women. What should our three knights do, in this momentous affair? They had sufficiently strained a point already in the affair of shoulder-knots. Upon recourse to

35. That is, they are being offered the cheaper boat, a "sculler," rowed by one man rather than two; in the same way, they are offered cheap seats at the theater and ale instead of wine at the tavern, and are denied admission to the lady's salon.
36. That is, not in so many *words*, but included within them in so many *syllables*.
37. That is, by a third means, in so many *letters*.
38. That is, unfavorable destiny, the "evil star."
39. *Quibusdam veteribus codicibus* ("in some ancient manuscripts").
40. "According to paternal law," a parody of *jure divino*.

the will, nothing appeared there but *altum silentium*.[41] That of the shoulder-knots was a loose, flying, circumstantial point; but this of gold lace seemed too considerable an alteration without better warrant. It did *aliquo modo essentiæ adhærere*,[42] and therefore required a positive precept. But about this time it fell out that the learned brother aforesaid had read *Aristotelis Dialectica*,[43] and especially that wonderful piece *de Interpretatione*, which has the faculty of teaching its readers to find out a meaning in everything but itself, like commentators on the Revelations, who proceed prophets without understanding a syllable of the text. 'Brothers,' said he, 'you are to be informed that of wills *duo sunt genera*, nuncupatory and scriptory;[44] that in the scriptory will here before us, there is no precept or mention about gold lace, *conceditur*:[45] but, *si idem affirmetur de nuncupatorio, negatur*.[46] For, brothers, if you remember, we heard a fellow say, when we were boys, that he heard my father's man say that he heard my father say that he would advise his sons to get gold lace on their coats as soon as ever they could procure money to buy it.' 'By G—! that is very true,' cries the other. 'I remember it perfectly well,' said the third. And so without more ado they got the largest gold lace in the parish and walked about as fine as lords. . . .

Next winter a player, hired for the purpose by the corporation of fringe-makers, acted his part in a new comedy all covered with silver fringe and, according to the laudable custom, gave rise to that fashion. Upon which the brothers, consulting their father's will, to their great astonishment found these words; '*Item*, I charge and command my said three sons to wear no sort of silver fringe upon or about their said coats,' etc., with a penalty, in case of disobedience, too long here to insert. However, after some pause, the brother so often mentioned for his erudition, who was well skilled in criticisms, had found in a certain author, which he said should be nameless, that the same word, which in the will is called fringe, does also signify a broom-stick, and doubtless ought to have the same interpretation in this paragraph. This another of the brothers disliked, because of that epithet *silver*, which could not, he humbly conceived, in propriety of speech, be reasonably applied to a broom-stick; but it was replied upon him, that this epithet was understood in a mythological and allegorical sense. However, he objected again, why their father should forbid them to wear a broom-stick on their coats, a caution that seemed unnatural and impertinent;[47] upon which he was taken up short, as one that spoke irreverently of a mystery, which doubtless was very useful and significant, but ought not to be over-curiously pried into or nicely[48] reasoned upon. And, in short, their father's authority being now considerably sunk, this expedient was allowed to serve as a lawful dispensation for wearing their full proportion of silver fringe.

41. "Profound silence."
42. "In some manner belong to the essence."
43. A Latin compendium of Aristotle's logical treatises.
44. "There are two sorts," by word of mouth and written.
45. "It may be granted."
46. "If the same be affirmed of the oral will, it is denied." "By this is meant *tradition*, allowed to have equal authority with Scripture, or rather greater." (Swift)
47. Irrelevant.
48. Delicately, closely.

A while after was revived an old fashion, long antiquated, of embroidery with Indian figures of men, women, and children.[49] Here they had no occasion to examine the will. They remembered but too well how their father had always abhorred this fashion; that he made several paragraphs on purpose, importing his utter detestation of it and bestowing his everlasting curse to his sons whenever they should wear it. For all this, in a few days they appeared higher in the fashion than anybody else in the town. But they solved the matter by saying that these figures were not at all the same with those that were formerly worn and were meant in the will. Besides, they did not wear them in the sense as forbidden by their father; but as they were a commendable custom and of great use to the public. That these rigorous clauses in the will did therefore require some allowance and a favourable interpretation, and ought to be understood *cum grano salis*.[50]

But fashions perpetually altering in that age, the scholastic brother grew weary of searching farther evasions and solving everlasting contradictions; resolved, therefore, at all hazards to comply with the modes of the world, they concerted matters together and agreed unanimously to lock up their father's will in a strong box [51] brought out of Greece or Italy (I have forgot which), and trouble themselves no farther to examine it, but only refer to its authority whenever they thought fit. In consequence whereof, a while after, it grew a general mode to wear an infinite number of points,[52] most of them tagged with silver: upon which, the scholar pronounced *ex cathedra*,[53] that points were absolutely *jure paterno*, as they might very well remember. 'Tis true, indeed, the fashion prescribed somewhat more than were directly named in the will; however, that they, as heirs-general of their father, had power to make and add certain clauses for public emolument, though not deducible, *totidem verbis*, from the letter of the will, or else *multa absurda sequerentur*.[54] This was understood for canonical,[55] and therefore on the following Sunday they came to church all covered with points.

The learned brother, so often mentioned, was reckoned the best scholar in all that or the next street to it; insomuch as, having run something behind-hand [56] with the world, he obtained the favour from a certain lord,[57] to receive him into his house, and to teach his children. A while after the lord died, and he, by long practice upon his father's will, found the way of contriving a deed of conveyance of that house to himself and his heirs; upon which he took possession, turned the young squires out, and received his brothers in their stead.

49. "The images of saints, the Blessed Virgin, and our Savior an infant." (Swift)
50. "With a grain of salt."
51. That is, the forbidding of the use of Scripture in the vernacular, and requiring the Latin Vulgate translation or the original Greek of the New Testament.
52. Laces or ties with metal tips.
53. "From the (papal) throne."
54. "Many absurdities would follow."
55. According to church law.
56. In debt.
57. Referring to the Donation of Constantine, the alleged document by which the first Christian emperor, Constantine the Great, conferred all his rights, honors, and property as Emperor of the West on the Pope of Rome and his successors; a document "the Popes . . . have never been able to produce." (Swift)

Section IX

A Digression Concerning the Original, the Use, and
Improvement of Madness, in a Commonwealth

Nor shall it any ways detract from the just reputation of this famous sect [1]
that its rise and institution are owing to such an author as I have described
Jack to be—a person whose intellectuals were overturned and his brain shaken
out of its natural position; which we commonly suppose to be a distemper and
call by the name of madness or frenzy. For if we take a survey of the greatest
actions that have been performed in the world under the influence of single
men, which are the establishment of new empires by conquest, the advance
and progress of new schemes in philosophy, and the contriving, as well as the
propagating, of new religions; we shall find the authors of them all to have been
persons whose natural reason had admitted great revolutions from their diet,
their education, the prevalency of some certain temper, together with the
particular influence of air and climate. Besides, there is something individual in
human minds that easily kindles at the accidental approach and collision of
certain circumstances, which, though of paltry and mean appearance, do often
flame out into the greatest emergencies of life. For great turns are not always
given by strong hands but by lucky adaption and at proper seasons; and it is
of no import where the fire was kindled if the vapour has once got up into the
brain. For the upper region of man is furnished like the middle region of the
air; the materials are formed from causes of the widest difference, yet produce
at last the same substance and effect. Mists arise from the earth, steams from
dunghills, exhalations from the sea, and smoke from fire; yet all clouds are the
same in composition as well as consequences, and the fumes issuing from a
jakes [2] will furnish as comely and useful a vapour as incense from an altar.
Thus far, I suppose, will easily be granted me; and then it will follow, that,
as the face of nature never produces rain but when it is overcast and disturbed,
so human understanding, seated in the brain, must be troubled and overspread
by vapours ascending from the lower faculties to water the invention [3] and
render it fruitful. Now, although these vapours (as it hath been already said)
are of as various original as those of the skies, yet the crop they produce differs
both in kind and degree, merely according to the soil. I will produce two
instances to prove and explain what I am now advancing.

A certain great prince [4] raised a mighty army, filled his coffers with infinite
treasures, provided an invincible fleet, and all this without giving [5] the least

1. Aeolism, the worship of wind (named for the keeper of the winds in the *Odyssey*
and the *Aeneid*), a system that rationalizes Jack's religious enthusiasm much as the clothes
philosophy of Section II does Peter's manipulation of the words of the will.
2. Privy or cesspool.
3. The faculty for making discoveries; a term often applied in the age to poetic wit or
imagination (cf. Dryden's *Critical Prose*, above).
4. Henry IV of France (1553–1610) was obsessed with a late passion for the young
Princesse de Condé, who was taken by her husband (he was to have been only a convenient figurehead) to the Spanish Netherlands, out of Henry's reach. After a futile
effort to abduct her, Henry (enraged and perhaps somewhat mad) began military preparations against the Spanish province, but he was stabbed to death before he could proceed.
5. Revealing.

part of his design to his greatest ministers or his nearest favourites. Immediately the whole world was alarmed; the neighbouring crowns in trembling expectation towards what point the storm would burst, the small politicians everywhere forming profound conjectures. Some believed he had laid a scheme for universal monarchy; others, after much insight, determined the matter to be a project for pulling down the Pope and setting up the reformed religion, which had once been his own. Some, again, of a deeper sagacity, sent him into Asia to subdue the Turk and recover Palestine. In the midst of all these projects and preparations, a certain state-surgeon, gathering the nature of the disease by these symptoms, attempted the cure, at one blow performed the operation, broke the bag, and out flew the vapour; nor did anything want to render it a complete remedy, only that the prince unfortunately happened to die in the performance. Now, is the reader exceeding curious to learn from whence this vapour took its rise which had so long set the nations at a gaze? What secret wheel, what hidden spring, could put into motion so wonderful an engine? It was afterwards discovered that the movement of this whole machine had been directed by an absent female, whose eyes had raised a protuberancy, and, before emission, she was removed into an enemy's country. What should an unhappy prince do in such ticklish circumstances as these? He tried in vain the poet's never-failing receipt of *corpora quæque;* for

> Idque petit corpus mens unde est saucia amore:
> Unde feritur, eo tendit, gestitque coire. (LUCRETIUS)[6]

Having to no purpose used all peaceable endeavours, the collected part of the semen, raised and inflamed, became adust, converted to choler, turned head upon the spinal duct[7] and ascended to the brain. The very same principle that influences a bully to break the windows of a whore who has jilted him naturally stirs up a great prince to raise mighty armies and dream of nothing but sieges, battles, and victories.

> ——Teterrima belli
> Causa.——[8]

The other instance is what I have read somewhere in a very ancient author of a mighty king who, for the space of above thirty years, amused himself to take and lose towns, beat armies and be beaten, drive princes out of their dominions; fright children from their bread and butter; burn, lay waste, plunder, dragoon, massacre subject and stranger, friend and foe, male and female. 'Tis recorded that the philosophers of each country were in grave dispute upon causes natural, moral, and political, to find out where they should assign an original solution of this phenomenon. At last the vapour or spirit which animated the hero's brain, being in perpetual circulation, seized upon that region

6. "Indulging one's lust at once with any persons at hand ["in corpore quaeque" IV.1065] so as not to allow unendurable desire to develop"; the following lines describe "that body through which the mind is wounded by love" (IV.1048) and how "each strains towards the one from whom the blow has come and struggles to unite" (IV.1055).
7. That is, became burned or parched, turned to bile (the source of anger or rage), invaded the spinal duct.
8. "For a whore had been, before Helen, a terrible cause of war." Horace, *Satires* I.iii.107.

of the human body so renowned for furnishing the *zibeta occidentalis*,[9] and, gathering there into a tumour, left the rest of the world for that time in peace. Of such mighty consequence it is where those exhalations fix and of so little from whence they proceed. The same spirits, which, in their superior progress, would conquer a kingdom, descending upon the anus, conclude in a fistula.[10]

Let us next examine the great introducers of new schemes in philosophy, and search till we can find from what faculty of the soul the disposition arises in mortal man of taking it into his head to advance new systems with such an eager zeal, in things agreed on all hands impossible to be known; from what seeds this disposition springs, and to what quality of human nature these grand innovators have been indebted for their number of disciples. Because it is plain that several of the chief among them, both ancient and modern, were usually mistaken by their adversaries, and indeed by all except their own followers, to have been persons crazed or out of their wits; having generally proceeded, in the common course of their words and actions by a method very different from the vulgar dictates of unrefined reason; agreeing for the most part in their several models with their present undoubted successors in the academy of modern Bedlam [11] (whose merits and principles I shall farther examine in due place). Of this kind were *Epicurus, Diogenes, Apollonius, Lucretius, Paracelsus, Descartes*,[12] and others, who, if they were now in the world, tied fast, and separate from their followers, would, in this our undistinguishing age, incur manifest danger of phlebotomy and whips and chains and dark chambers and straw. For what man in the natural state or course of thinking did ever conceive it in his power to reduce the notions of all mankind exactly to the same length and breadth and height of his own? Yet this is the first humble and civil design of all innovators in the empire of reason. Epicurus modestly hoped that, one time or other, a certain fortuitous concourse of all men's opinions, after perpetual justlings, the sharp with the smooth, the light and the heavy, the round and the square, would, by certain clinamina,[13] unite in the notions of atoms and void, as these did in the originals of all things. Cartesius reckoned to

9. "Paracelsus, who was so famous for chemistry, tried an experiment upon human excrement to make perfume of it, which, when he had brought to perfection, he called *Ziberta Occidentalis*, or western-civet, the back parts of a man (according to his division . . .) being the west." (Swift)

10. A pipelike ulcer with a narrow opening.

11. The Hospital of St. Mary of Bethlehem, long a madhouse, regularly open to visitors and sightseers as a public show.

12. All these men were creators or defenders of systems. Epicurus (341?–270 B.C.), the Greek philosopher, and Lucretius (96?–55 B.C.), the Roman poet, were atomists, attributing all life to the "fortuitous concourse" of atoms. Diogenes (4th century B.C.), the Greek Cynic philosopher, defied conventional rules of conduct and lived in an earthenware tub to demonstrate the austere simplicity he preached. Apollonius of Tyana (c. 4th century B.C.) was a wandering Pythagorean philosopher and mystic and a precursor of the occult Hermetic philosophy. Paracelsus (1490?–1541) was an alchemist as well as a chemist, a neoplatonic visionary and mystic in his system of medicine. René Descartes (1596–1650), having separated mind from extended matter (except for their interaction through the pineal gland), erected a mechanical and mathematical system of the material universe.

13. The inherent "swerves" of the atoms, which led to their varying patterns of collision and rebound, thus forming bodies of greater or lesser density; here Epicurus' material explanation is ironically applied to the interaction of minds or opinions in order to account for proselytizing.

see, before he died, the sentiments of all philosophers like so many lesser stars in his romantic system, wrapped and drawn within his own vortex.[14] Now, I would gladly be informed, how it is possible to account for such imaginations as these in particular men without recourse to my phenomenon of vapours ascending from the lower faculties to overshadow the brain, and there distilling into conceptions for which the narrowness of our mother-tongue has not yet assigned any other name besides that of madness or frenzy.

Let us therefore now conjecture how it comes to pass that none of these great prescribers do ever fail providing themselves and their notions with a number of implicit disciples. And, I think, the reason is easy to be assigned: for there is a peculiar string in the harmony of human understanding which, in several individuals, is exactly of the same tuning. This, if you can dexterously screw up to its right key and then strike gently upon it, whenever you have the good fortune to light among those of the same pitch, they will, by a secret necessary sympathy, strike exactly at the same time. And in this one circumstance lies all the skill or luck of the matter; for, if you chance to jar the string among those who are either above or below your own height, instead of subscribing to your doctrine, they will tie you fast, call you mad, and feed you with bread and water.

It is therefore a point of the nicest [15] conduct to distinguish and adapt this noble talent with respect to the differences of persons and of times. Cicero understood this very well, when writing to a friend in England, with a caution, among other matters, to beware of being cheated by our hackney-coachmen (who, it seems, in those days were as arrant [16] rascals as they are now), has these remarkable words: *Est quod gaudeas te in ista loca venisse, ubi aliquid sapere viderere.*[17] For, to speak a bold truth, it is a fatal miscarriage so ill to order affairs, as to pass for a fool in one company when in another you might be treated as a philosopher. Which I desire some certain gentlemen of my acquaintance to lay up in their hearts as a very seasonable *innuendo*.

This, indeed, was the fatal mistake of that worthy gentleman, my most ingenious friend, Mr. W-tt-n: [18] a person, in appearance, ordained for great designs as well as performances; whether you will consider his notions or his looks. Surely no man ever advanced into the public with fitter qualifications of body and mind for the propagation of a new religion. Oh, had those happy talents, misapplied to vain philosophy, been turned into their proper channels of dreams and visions, where distortion of mind and countenance are of such sovereign use, the base detracting world would not then have dared to report that something is amiss, that his brain hath undergone an unlucky shake; which

---

14. The *tourbillon* or whirlpool of material particles, creating a circular motion that is communicated from one body to another; it was applied to the heavenly bodies, as when one star is drawn into the stronger vortex of another's motion.
15. Subtlest.
16. Thorough.
17. "There is reason to rejoice that you have come to those places where you pass as a man of legal ability." Cicero, *Letters to Friends* VII.10 (to Trebatius). In VII.6 Cicero warns that Trebatius must look out in Britain that he is not cheated by the charioteers.
18. William Wotton had joined Bentley in the attack upon Temple; a clergyman, he also wrote what he intended as a damning explanation of Swift's meaning in *A Tale of a Tub*, but Swift used Wotton's remarks as explanatory notes in his 1710 edition.

even his brother modernists themselves, like ungrates, do whisper so loud, it reaches up to the very garret I am now writing in.

Lastly, whosoever pleases to look into the fountains of enthusiasm, from whence, in all ages, have eternally proceeded such fattening [19] streams, will find the spring-head to have been as troubled and muddy as the current. Of such great emolument is a tincture of this vapour which the world calls madness, that without its help, the world would not only be deprived of those two great blessings, conquests and systems, but even all mankind would unhappily be reduced to the same belief in things invisible. Now, the former *postulatum* being held, that it is of no import from what originals this vapour proceeds, but either in what angles it strikes and spreads over the understanding or upon what species of brain it ascends; it will be a very delicate point to cut the feather and divide the several reasons [20] to a nice and curious reader how this numerical difference in the brain can produce effects of so vast a difference from the same vapour, as to be the sole point of individuation between Alexander the Great, Jack of Leyden,[21] and Monsieur Des Cartes. The present argument is the most abstracted that ever I engaged in; it strains my faculties to their highest stretch; and I desire the reader to attend with utmost perpensity for I now proceed to unravel this knotty point.

There is in mankind a certain   .   .   .   .

.   .   .   .

Hic multa   .   .   .   .
desiderantur.[22]   .   .   .   .

.   .   .   .   .   And this I take to be a clear solution of the matter.

Having therefore so narrowly passed through this intricate difficulty, the reader will, I am sure, agree with me in the conclusion that if the moderns mean by madness only a disturbance or transposition of the brain, by force of certain vapours issuing up from the lower faculties, then has this madness been the parent of all those mighty revolutions that have happened in empire, in philosophy, and in religion. For the brain, in its natural position and state of serenity, disposeth its owner to pass his life in the common forms, without any thought of subduing multitudes to his own power, his reasons, or his visions; and the more he shapes his understanding by the pattern of human learning, the less he is inclined to form parties after his particular notions, because that instructs him in his private infirmities as well as in the stubborn ignorance of the people.

But when a man's fancy gets astride of his reason, when imagination is at cuffs with the senses, and common understanding as well as common sense is kicked out of doors; the first proselyte he makes is himself; and when that is once compassed, the difficulty is not so great in bringing over others; a

19. Nourishing.
20. That is, to split hairs or make subtle distinctions.
21. John of Leyden (1509–36), here forming a bridge between military conquest and intellectual system, was a Dutch Anabaptist who founded a short-lived communistic and polygamous "Kingdom of Zion" in the German city of Münster.
22. "Here many things are lacking," a conventional phrase in the editing of a damaged manuscript, a technique Swift parodies throughout the *Tale* and uses, as here, to create an effect of anticlimax.

strong delusion always operating from without as vigorously as from within. For cant and vision are to the ear and the eye the same that tickling is to the touch. Those entertainments and pleasures we most value in life are such as dupe and play the wag with the senses. For, if we take an examination of what is generally understood by happiness as it has respect either to the understanding or the senses, we shall find all its properties and adjuncts [23] will herd under this short definition, that it is a perpetual possession of being well deceived.

And, first, with relation to the mind or understanding, 'tis manifest what mighty advantages fiction has over truth; and the reason is just at our elbow, because imagination can build nobler scenes and produce more wonderful revolutions than fortune or nature will be at expense to furnish. Nor is mankind so much to blame in his choice thus determining him, if we consider that the debate merely lies between things past and things conceived; and so the question is only this:—whether things that have place in the imagination may not as properly be said to exist as those that are seated in the memory, which may be justly held in the affirmative, and very much to the advantage of the former, since this is acknowledged to be the womb of things and the other allowed to be no more than the grave.

Again, if we take this definition of happiness and examine it with reference to the senses, it will be acknowledged wonderfully adapt. How fading and insipid do all objects accost us that are not conveyed in the vehicle of delusion! How shrunk is everything as it appears in the glass of nature! So that if it were not for the assistance of artificial mediums, false lights, refracted angles, varnish, and tinsel, there would be a mighty level in the felicity and enjoyments of mortal men. If this were seriously considered by the world, as I have a certain reason to suspect it hardly will, men would no longer reckon among their high points of wisdom the art of exposing weak sides and publishing infirmities; an employment, in my opinion, neither better nor worse than that of unmasking, which, I think, has never been allowed [24] fair usage, either in the world or the play-house.

In the proportion that credulity is a more peaceful possession of the mind than curiosity, so far preferable is that wisdom which converses about the surface to that pretended philosophy which enters into the depth of things and then comes gravely back with information and discoveries, that in the inside they are good for nothing. The two senses to which all objects first address themselves are the sight and the touch; these never examine farther than the colour, the shape, the size, and whatever other qualities dwell or are drawn by art upon the outward of bodies; and then comes reason officiously with tools for cutting, and opening, and mangling, and piercing, offering to demonstrate that they are not of the same consistence quite through.

Now I take all this to be the last degree of perverting nature; one of whose eternal laws it is to put her best furniture forward. And therefore, in order to save the charges of all such expensive anatomy for the time to come, I do here think fit to inform the reader, that in such conclusions as these, reason

23. Essential and nonessential characteristics.
24. Judged to be.

is certainly in the right, and that in most corporeal beings which have fallen under my cognizance the outside hath been infinitely preferable to the in; whereof I have been farther convinced from some late experiments.

Last week I saw a woman flayed, and you will hardly believe how much it altered her person for the worse. Yesterday I ordered the carcass of a beau to be stripped in my presence, when we were all amazed to find so many unsuspected faults under one suit of clothes. Then I laid open his brain, his heart, and his spleen; but I plainly perceived at every operation that the farther we proceeded, we found the defects increase upon us in number and bulk; from all which I justly formed this conclusion to myself: that whatever philosopher or projector can find out an art to sodder and patch up the flaws and imperfections of nature will deserve much better of mankind, and teach us a more useful science, than that so much in present esteem of widening and exposing them (like him who held anatomy to be the ultimate end of physic [25]). And he whose fortunes and dispositions have placed him in a convenient station to enjoy the fruits of this noble art; he that can, with Epicurus,[26] content his ideas with the films and images that fly off upon his senses from the superficies of things; such a man, truly wise, creams off nature, leaving the sour and the dregs for philosophy and reason to lap up. This is the sublime and refined point of felicity, called the possession of being well deceived; the serene peaceful state of being a fool among knaves.

But to return to madness. It is certain that, according to the system I have above deduced, every species thereof proceeds from a redundancy of vapours; therefore, as some kinds of frenzy give double strength to the sinews, so there are of other species, which add vigour and life and spirit to the brain. Now, it usually happens that these active spirits, getting possession of the brain, resemble those that haunt other waste and empty dwellings, which, for want of business, either vanish and carry away a piece of the house, or else stay at home and fling it all out of the windows. By which, are mystically displayed the two principal branches of madness, and which some philosophers, not considering so well as I, have mistaken to be different in their causes, overhastily assigning the first to deficiency and the other to redundance.

I think it therefore manifest, from what I have here advanced, that the main point of skill and address is to furnish employment for this redundancy of vapour and prudently to adjust the season of it; by which means it may certainly become of cardinal and catholic emolument in a commonwealth. Thus one man, choosing a proper juncture, leaps into a gulf, from whence proceeds a hero, and is called the saver of his country; another achieves the same enterprise, but, unluckily timing it, has left the brand of madness fixed as a reproach upon his memory; upon so nice a distinction, are we taught to repeat the name of Curtius with reverence and love, that of Empedocles with hatred and contempt.[27] Thus also it is usually conceived that the elder

25. That is, reversing ends and means, making surgery the end for which therapy exists.
26. Who had a materialistic account of sense perception: the surfaces ("superficies") discharged fine films, which were replicas of the object and were able to penetrate the sense organs of the perceiver.
27. When a chasm suddenly opened in the Roman forum, with the prophecy that it would close only when the chief strength of Rome had been sacrificed, Marcus Curtius—

Brutus [28] only personated the fool and madman for the good of the public; but this was nothing else than a redundancy of the same vapour long misapplied, called by the Latins *ingenium par negotiis;* [29] or (to translate it as nearly as I can) a sort of frenzy, never in its right element, till you take it up in business of the state.

Upon all which, and many other reasons of equal weight though not equally curious, I do here gladly embrace an opportunity I have long sought for, of recommending it as a very noble undertaking to Sir Edward Seymour, Sir Christopher Musgrave, Sir John Bowls, John How, Esq., and other patriots [30] concerned, that they would move for leave to bring in a bill for appointing commissioners to inspect into Bedlam and the parts adjacent; who shall be empowered to send for persons, papers, and records, to examine into the merits and qualifications of every student and professor, to observe with utmost exactness their several dispositions and behaviour, by which means duly distinguishing and adapting their talents, they might produce admirable instruments for the several offices in a state, _____,[31] civil, and military, proceeding in such methods as I shall here humbly propose. And I hope the gentle reader will give some allowance to my great solicitudes in this important affair, upon account of the high esteem I have borne that honourable society, whereof I had some time the happiness to be an unworthy member.

Is any student tearing his straw in piece-meal, swearing and blaspheming, biting his grate, foaming at the mouth, and emptying his piss-pot in the spectators' faces? Let the right worshipful the commissioners of inspection give him a regiment of dragoons, and send him into Flanders among the rest. Is another eternally talking, sputtering, gaping, bawling, in a sound without period or article? What wonderful talents are here mislaid! Let him be furnished immediately with a green bag and papers, and threepence in his pocket, and away with him to Westminster Hall.[32] You will find a third gravely taking the dimensions of his kennel, a person of foresight and insight, though kept quite in the dark; for why, like Moses, *ecce cornuta erat ejus facies.*[33] He walks duly in one pace, entreats your penny with due gravity and ceremony, talks much of hard times, and taxes, and the whore of Babylon, bars up the wooden window of his cell constantly at eight o'clock, dreams of fire, and shoplifters, and court-customers, and privileged places. Now, what a figure would all these acquirements amount to, if the owner were sent into the City among his brethren! [34]

---

interpreting the strength to be arms and valor—leaped in, armed and on horseback. According to some accounts, Empedocles (fl. 450), the philosopher and statesman of Sicily, threw himself into the crater of Mt. Etna so that the manner of his death might not be known and that he might later pass for a god, but the secret was revealed by Etna's rejecting one of his sandals (or casting it out in an eruption).

28. Lucius Junius Brutus, the nephew of the tyrannous Roman king Tarquin the Proud, assumed the guise of madness to avoid being killed by his uncle, as his brother had been.

29. "A head for business." Tacitus, *Annals* VI.39 and XVI.18.

30. Leading members of the House of Commons, one of them (Bowls) himself mad by 1701.

31. "Ecclesiastical" is omitted.

32. A lawyer's coach fare from the Inns of Court to the law courts at Westminster.

33. "Behold his face was shining." Vulgate text of Exodus 34:30.

34. That is, as a shopkeeper in the City, the commercial part of London.

Behold a fourth, in much and deep conversation with himself, biting his thumbs at proper junctures, his countenance checkered with business and design, sometimes walking very fast, with his eyes nailed to a paper that he holds in his hands; a great saver of time, somewhat thick of hearing, very short of sight, but more of memory; a man ever in haste, a great hatcher and breeder of business, and excellent at the famous art of whispering nothing; a huge idolater of monosyllables and procrastination, so ready to give his word to everybody that he never keeps it; one that has forgot the common meaning of words but an admirable retainer of the sound; extremely subject to the looseness,[35] for his occasions are perpetually calling him away. If you approach his grate in his familiar intervals: 'Sir,' says he, 'give me a penny, and I'll sing you a song; but give me the penny first.' (Hence comes the common saying, and commoner practice, of parting with money for a song.) What a complete system of court skill is here described in every branch of it, and all utterly lost with wrong application!

Accost the hole of another kennel, first stopping your nose; you will behold a surly, gloomy, nasty, slovenly mortal, raking in his own dung and dabbling in his urine. The best part of his diet is the reversion[36] of his own ordure, which, expiring into steams, whirls perpetually about, and at last re-infunds.[37] His complexion is of a dirty yellow, with a thin scattered beard, exactly agreeable to that of his diet upon its first declination, like other insects, who, having their birth and education in an excrement, from thence borrow their colour and their smell. The student of this apartment is very sparing of his words, but somewhat over-liberal of his breath. He holds his hand out ready to receive your penny, and immediately upon receipt withdraws to his former occupations. Now, is it not amazing to think, the society of Warwick-lane[38] should have no more concern for the recovery of so useful a member; who, if one may judge from these appearances, would become the greatest ornament to that illustrious body?

Another student struts up fiercely to your teeth, puffing with his lips, half squeezing out his eyes, and very graciously holds you out his hand to kiss. The keeper desires you not to be afraid of this professor, for he will do you no hurt; to him alone is allowed the liberty of the antechamber, and the orator of the place gives you to understand that this solemn person is a tailor run mad with pride. This considerable student is adorned with many other qualities, upon which, at present, I shall not farther enlarge . . . Hark in your ear . . . I am strangely mistaken, if all his address, his motions, and his airs, would not then be very natural, and in their proper element.[39]

I shall not descend so minutely, as to insist upon the vast number of beaux, fiddlers, poets, and politicians that the world might recover by such a reformation; but what is more material, besides the clear gain redounding to the commonwealth, by so large an acquisition of persons to employ whose talents

35. Diarrhea.
36. Return to its original state.
37. Pours in again.
38. The Royal College of Physicians.
39. "I cannot conjecture what the author means here, or how the chasm could be filled, though it is capable of more than one interpretation" (Swift).

and acquirements, if I may be so bold as to affirm it, are now buried or at least misapplied; it would be a mighty advantage accruing to the public from this inquiry that all these would very much excel and arrive at great perfection in their several kinds; which, I think, is manifest from what I have already shown and shall enforce by this one plain instance, that even I myself, the author of these momentous truths, am a person whose imaginations are hard-mouthed [40] and exceedingly disposed to run away with his reason, which I have observed from long experience to be a very light rider and easily shook off; upon which account my friends will never trust me alone without a solemn promise to vent my speculations in this or the like manner, for the universal benefit of human kind; which perhaps the gentle, courteous, and candid reader, brimful of that modern charity and tenderness usually annexed to his office, will be very hardly persuaded to believe.

1697–1704?   1704

An Argument Against Abolishing Christianity in England

The Test Act of 1673 excluded from public office those who refused the sacrament of the Church of England, but dissenters held office by taking the Anglican sacrament only once. To prevent this evasion, Tories in Commons had three times introduced a Bill for Preventing Occasional Conformity, which was defeated in each case by the Whig lords. There were, in fact, strong Whig efforts to repeal the Test Act both in Ireland and in England. Swift saw this as a real threat to the established church, for an opening of power to an alliance of Whigs and dissenters could lead to disestablishment in time. The *Argument* is presented as the cool proposal of a man who takes for granted that only "nominal" Christianity can any longer survive and argues that it does not threaten, but can even serve, "schemes of wealth and power"—presumably the only ones his public takes seriously. This dismissal of discussion of real Christianity builds up tremendous pressure, as what are taken for granted as the only acceptable terms of discussion become more and more shabbily expedient, more grossly a matter of a power calculus and of cash accounting.

An Argument

To Prove That the Abolishing of Christianity in England May, as Things Now Stand, Be Attended with Some Inconveniencies, and Perhaps, Not Produce Those Many Good Effects Proposed Thereby

I am very sensible what a weakness and presumption it is to reason against the general humour and disposition of the world. I remember it was with great justice, and a due regard to the freedom both of the public and the press, forbidden upon severe penalties to write, or discourse, or lay wagers against the Union [1] even before it was confirmed by Parliament, because that

40. Not easily controlled by bit or rein.

1. The Act of Union between England and Scotland (1707) uniting their two parliaments, opposed by Swift for its possible threat to the Sacramental Test, but also strongly opposed by the Jacobite supporters of the exiled Stuarts.

was looked upon as a design to oppose the current of the people, which besides the folly of it, is a manifest breach of the fundamental law that makes this majority of opinion the voice of God.[2] In like manner, and for the very same reasons, it may perhaps be neither safe nor prudent to argue against the abolishing of Christianity: at a juncture when all parties seem so unanimously determined upon the point, as we cannot but allow from their actions, their discourses, and their writings. However, I know not how, whether from the affectation of singularity or the perverseness of human nature, but so it unhappily falls out that I cannot be entirely of this opinion. Nay, although I were sure an order were issued out for my immediate prosecution by the Attorney-General, I should still confess that in the present posture of our affairs at home or abroad, I do not yet see the absolute necessity of extirpating the Christian religion from among us.

This perhaps may appear too great a paradox even for our wise and parodoxical age to endure; therefore I shall handle it with all tenderness, and with the utmost deference to that great and profound majority which is of another sentiment.

And yet the curious may please to observe, how much the genius of a nation is liable to alter in half an age. I have heard it affirmed for certain by some very old people that the contrary opinion was even in their memories as much in vogue as the other is now. And that a project for the abolishing of Christianity would then have appeared as singular, and been thought as absurd, as it would be at this time to write or discourse in its defence.

Therefore I freely own that all appearances are against me. The system of the gospel, after the fate of other systems, is generally antiquated and exploded; and the mass or body of the common people, among whom it seems to have had its latest credit, are now grown as much ashamed of it as their betters; opinions, like fashions, always descending from those of quality to the middle sort, and thence to the vulgar, where at length they are dropped and vanish.

But here I would not be mistaken, and must therefore be so bold as to borrow a distinction from the writers on the other side, when they make a difference between nominal and real Trinitarians. I hope no reader imagines me so weak to stand up in the defence of real Christianity, such as used, in primitive times (if we may believe the authors of those ages), to have an influence upon men's belief and actions: to offer at the restoring of that would indeed be a wild project; it would be to dig up foundations; to destroy, at one blow, all the wit, and half the learning, of the kingdom; to break the entire frame and constitution of things; to ruin trade, extinguish arts and sciences, with the professors of them; in short, to turn our courts, exchanges, and shops, into deserts; and would be full as absurd as the proposal of Horace,[3] where he advises the Romans, all in a body, to leave their city and seek a new seat in some remote part of the world, by way of cure for the corruption of their manners.

Therefore I think this caution was in itself altogether unnecessary (which I

2. Cf. Preface to A Tale of a Tub: "I am so entirely satisfied with the whole present procedure of human things that I have been for some years preparing materials towards A Panegyric upon the World, to which I intended to add a second part entitled A Modest Defense of the Proceedings of the Rabble in All Ages."
3. In Epode XVI.

have inserted only to prevent all possibility of cavilling) since every candid reader will easily understand my discourse to be intended only in defence of nominal Christianity; the other having been for some time wholly laid aside by general consent as utterly inconsistent with our present schemes of wealth and power.

But why we should therefore cast off the name and title of Christians, although the general opinion and resolution be so violent for it, I confess I cannot (with submission) apprehend the consequence necessary. However, since the undertakers propose such wonderful advantages to the nation by this project and advance many plausible objections against the system of Christianity, I shall briefly consider the strength of both, fairly allow them their greatest weight, and offer such answers as I think most reasonable. After which I will beg leave to show what inconveniencies may possibly happen by such an innovation in the present posture of our affairs.

First, one great advantage proposed by the abolishing of Christianity is that it would very much enlarge and establish liberty of conscience, that great bulwark of our nation and of the Protestant religion; which is still too much limited by priestcraft, notwithstanding all the good intentions of the legislature, as we have lately found by a severe instance. For it is confidently reported that two young gentlemen of great hopes, bright wit, and profound judgment, who, upon a thorough examination of causes and effects, and by the mere force of natural abilities, without the least tincture of learning, having made a discovery that there was no God, and generously communicating their thoughts for the good of the public, were some time ago, by an unparalleled severity, and upon I know not what obsolete law, broke [4] for blasphemy. And as it has been wisely observed, if persecution once begins, no man alive knows how far it may reach, or where it will end.

In answer to all which, with deference to wiser judgments, I think this rather shows the necessity of a nominal religion among us. Great wits love to be free with the highest objects; and if they cannot be allowed a God to revile or renounce, they will speak evil of dignities, abuse the government, and reflect upon the Ministry; which I am sure few will deny to be of much more pernicious consequence, according to the saying of Tiberius, *deorum offensa diis curæ.*[5] As to the particular fact related, I think it is not fair to argue from one instance; perhaps another cannot be produced: yet (to the comfort of all those who may be apprehensive of persecution) blasphemy, we know, is freely spoke a million of times in every coffeehouse and tavern, or wherever else good company meet. It must be allowed, indeed, that to break an English freeborn officer only for blasphemy was, to speak the gentlest of such an action, a very high strain of absolute power. Little can be said in excuse for the general; perhaps he was afraid it might give offence to the allies,[6] among whom, for aught we know, it may be the custom of the country to believe a God. But if he argued, as some have done, upon a mistaken principle that an officer

4. Ruined.
5. Tacitus, *Annals* I.73, which reads *injurias* instead of *offensa;* when the emperor Tiberius was told that a witness had injured the divinity of Augustus by swearing a false oath in his name, the reply was, "It is for the gods to punish their own wrongs."
6. Holland, Austria, Savoy, Portugal, and many German states (in the War of the Spanish Succession, against France).

who is guilty of speaking blasphemy may some time or other proceed so far as to raise a mutiny, the consequence is by no means to be admitted; for surely the commander of an English army is likely to be but ill obeyed, whose soldiers fear and reverence him as little as they do a Deity.

It is further objected against the gospel system that it obliges men to the belief of things too difficult for freethinkers, and such who have shaken off the prejudices that usually cling to a confined education. To which I answer, that men should be cautious how they raise objections which reflect upon the wisdom of the nation. Is not everybody freely allowed to believe whatever he pleases and to publish his belief to the world whenever he thinks fit, especially if it serves to strengthen the party which is in the right? Would any indifferent foreigner who should read the trumpery lately written by Asgil, Tindal, Toland, Coward,[7] and forty more, imagine the gospel to be our rule of faith and confirmed by parliaments? Does any man either believe, or say he believes, or desire to have it thought that he says he believes, one syllable of the matter? And is any man worse received upon that score, or does he find his want of nominal faith a disadvantage to him in the pursuit of any civil or military employment? What if there be an old dormant statute or two against him, are they not now obsolete to a degree that Empson and Dudley[8] themselves, if they were now alive, would find it impossible to put them in execution?

It is likewise urged that there are, by computation, in this kingdom, above ten thousand parsons, whose revenues added to those of my lords the Bishops, would suffice to maintain at least two hundred young gentlemen of wit and pleasure and freethinking, enemies to priestcraft, narrow principles, pedantry, and prejudices; who might be an ornament to the court and town: and then again, so great a number of able [-bodied] divines might be a recruit to our fleet and armies. This indeed appears to be a consideration of some weight: but then, on the other side, several things deserve to be considered likewise: as first, whether it may not be thought necessary, that in certain tracts of country, like what we call parishes, there shall be one man at least of abilities to read and write. Then it seems a wrong computation that the revenues of the Church throughout this island, would be large enough to maintain two hundred young gentlemen, or even half that number, after the present refined way of living; that is, to allow each of them such a rent as, in the modern form of speech, would make them easy. But still there is in this project a greater mischief behind; and we ought to beware of the woman's folly who killed the hen that every morning laid her a golden egg. For, pray what would become of the race of men in the next age if we had nothing to trust to beside the scrofulous, consumptive productions furnished by our men of wit and pleasure, when,

7. John Asgil (1659–1738), an Irish lawyer, published in 1699 a work showing that man might achieve eternal life without undergoing death, a doctrine which he based on the Gospels but which caused his expulsion from Parliament. Matthew Tindal (1657–1733), earlier a Roman Catholic, later an Anglican, was the author of the extremely anticlerical *The Rights of the Christian Church Asserted,* a book burnt by order of Commons. James Junius Toland (1670–1722) carried Locke's views further toward Deism in *Christianity Not Mysterious.* William Coward (1657–1725) was a physician who held that the soul died with the body.
8. Richard Empson and Edmund Dudley were agents of Henry VII who revived obsolete statutes in order to raise new revenues.

having squandered away their vigour, health, and estates, they are forced, by some disagreeable marriage, to piece up their broken fortunes and entail[9] rottenness and politeness on their posterity? Now, here are ten thousand persons reduced, by the wise regulations of Henry the Eighth,[10] to the necessity of a low diet, and moderate exercise, who are the only great restorers of our breed, without which the nation would, in an age or two, become but one great hospital.

Another advantage proposed by the abolishing of Christianity is the clear gain of one day in seven, which is now entirely lost, and consequently the kingdom one seventh less considerable in trade, business, and pleasure; beside the loss to the public of so many stately structures, now in the hands of the clergy, which might be converted into play-houses, exchanges, market-houses, common dormitories, and other public edifices.

I hope I shall be forgiven a hard word, if I call this a perfect cavil. I readily own there has been an old custom, time out of mind, for people to assemble in the churches every Sunday, and that shops are still frequently shut in order, as it is conceived, to preserve the memory of that ancient practice; but how this can prove a hindrance to business or pleasure is hard to imagine. What if the men of pleasure are forced, one day in the week, to game at home instead of the chocolatehouse? Are not the taverns and coffeehouses open? Can there be a more convenient season for taking a dose of physic?[11] Are fewer claps[12] got upon Sundays than other days? Is not that the chief day for traders to sum up the accounts of the week, and for lawyers to prepare their briefs? But I would fain know, how it can be pretended that the churches are misapplied? Where are more appointments and rendezvouses of gallantry? Where more care to appear in the foremost box, with greater advantage of dress? Where more meetings for business? Where more bargains driven of all sorts? And where so many conveniences or enticements to sleep?

There is one advantage greater than any of the foregoing proposed by the abolishing of Christianity; that it will utterly extinguish parties among us, by removing those factious distinctions of High and Low Church, of Whig and Tory, Presbyterian and Church of England, which are now so many grievous clogs upon public proceedings, and are apt to dispose men to prefer the gratifying themselves, or depressing their adversaries, before the most important interest of the state.

I confess, if it were certain that so great an advantage would redound to the nation by this expedient, I would submit and be silent; but will any man say, that if the words *whoring, drinking, cheating, lying, stealing,* were, by act of Parliament, ejected out of the English tongue and dictionaries, we should all awake next morning chaste and temperate, honest and just, and lovers of truth? Is this a fair consequence? Or, if the physicians would forbid us to pronounce the words *pox, gout, rheumatism,* and *stone,* would that expedient serve, like so many talismans, to destroy the diseases themselves? Are party and faction rooted in men's hearts no deeper than phrases borrowed from religion, or founded upon no firmer principles? And is our language so poor

9. Impose through inheritance.
10. In plundering the monasteries and exacting from them payments to the crown; Swift loathed Henry VIII.
11. Medicine.
12. Gonorrhea.

that we cannot find other terms to express them? Are *envy, pride, avarice,* and *ambition* such ill nomenclators, that they cannot furnish appellations for their owners? Will not *heydukes* and *mamalukes, mandarins,* and *potshaws,*[13] or any other words formed at pleasure, serve to distinguish those who are in the Ministry from others who would be in it if they could? What, for instance, is easier than to vary the form of speech, and instead of the word *Church,* make it a question in politics, whether the *Monument* be in danger?[14] Because religion was nearest at hand to furnish a few convenient phrases, is our invention so barren we can find no other? Suppose, for argument sake, that the Tories favoured Margarita, the Whigs Mrs. Tofts,[15] and the Trimmers[16] Valentini; would not *Margaritians, Toftians,* and *Valentinians* be very tolerable marks of distinction? The *Prasini* and *Veniti,* two most virulent factions in Italy,[17] began (if I remember right) by a distinction of colours in ribbons; which we might do with as good a grace about the dignity of the blue and the green, and would serve as properly to divide the court, the Parliament, and the kingdom, between them, as any terms of art[18] whatsoever borrowed from religion. Therefore, I think, there is little force in this objection against Christianity, or prospect of so great an advantage as is proposed in the abolishing of it.

It is again objected, as a very absurd, ridiculous custom, that a set of men should be suffered, much less employed and hired, to bawl one day in seven against the lawfulness of those methods most in use towards the pursuit of greatness, riches, and pleasure, which are the constant practice of all men alive on the other six. But this objection is, I think, a little unworthy so refined an age as ours. Let us argue this matter calmly: I appeal to the breast of any polite freethinker whether, in the pursuit of gratifying a predominant passion, he hath not always felt a wonderful incitement by reflecting it was a thing forbidden: and, therefore, we see, in order to cultivate this taste, the wisdom of the nation hath taken special care that the ladies should be furnished with prohibited silks, and the men with prohibited wine.[19] And, indeed, it were to be wished that some other prohibitions were promoted in order to improve the pleasures of the town; which, for want of such expedients, begin already, as I am told, to flag and grow languid, giving way daily to cruel inroads from the spleen.[20]

13. Used as nonsense words, but in fact with meanings; respectively, Hungarian foot-soldiers or Polish attendants on noblemen (originally robbers or brigands and properly *hajduka*); ruling military class in Egypt; Chinese officials; Persian emperor or sultan, perhaps confused with Turkish pashas or officers.

14. The Monument, built by Sir Christopher Wren in 1666 as a memorial of the Great Fire of London, carried an inscription blaming the Catholics for the fire.

15. Margaritá and Valentini were rival Italian opera singers, and Mrs. Catherine Tofts an English competitor who sang Italian opera.

16. For Trimmers, see the selection from Halifax above.

17. The Greens and Blues, rival factions in Roman chariot races, whose enmity was carried over to Constantinople, where it caused civil war in the reign of Justinian; also alluding to the blue ribbon of the English Order of the Garter and the green of the Scottish Order of the Thistle.

18. Technical terms, often used divisively by sectarians.

19. Prohibited by the war with France but often smuggled.

20. A melancholy affliction, ironically regarded by many as an affectation, but vaguely attributed to the mysterious secretions of the spleen.

It is likewise proposed as a great advantage to the public that if we once discard the system of the gospel, all religion will of course be banished for ever; and consequently, along with it, those grievous prejudices of education, which, under the names of *virtue, conscience, honour, justice,* and the like, are so apt to disturb the peace of human minds, and the notions whereof are so hard to be eradicated by right reason or freethinking, sometimes during the whole course of our lives.

Here first I observe how difficult it is to get rid of a phrase which the world is once grown fond of, though the occasion that first produced it be entirely taken away. For several years past, if a man had but an ill-favoured nose, the deep-thinkers of the age would, some way or other, contrive to impute the cause to the prejudice of his education. From this fountain were said to be derived all our foolish notions of justice, piety, love of our country; all our opinions of God or a future state, heaven, hell, and the like: and there might formerly perhaps have been some pretence for this charge. But so effectual care has been since taken to remove those prejudices by an entire change in the methods of education, that (with honour I mention it to our polite innovators) the young gentlemen who are now on the scene seem to have not the least tincture left of those infusions or string [21] of those weeds: and, by consequence, the reason for abolishing nominal Christianity upon that pretext is wholly ceased.

For the rest, it may perhaps admit a controversy whether the banishing all notions of religion whatsoever would be convenient for the vulgar.[22] Not that I am in the least of opinion with those who hold religion to have been the invention of politicians to keep the lower part of the world in awe by the fear of invisible powers; unless mankind were then very different from what it is now: for I look upon the mass or body of our people here in England to be as freethinkers, that is to say, as staunch unbelievers, as any of the highest rank. But I conceive some scattered notions about a superior power to be of singular use for the common people, as furnishing excellent materials to keep children quiet when they grow peevish, and providing topics of amusement in a tedious winter-night.

Lastly, it is proposed, as a singular advantage, that the abolishing of Christianity will very much contribute to the uniting of Protestants, by enlarging the terms of communion, so as to take in all sorts of dissenters, who are now shut out of the pale upon account of a few ceremonies, which all sides confess to be things indifferent; [23] that this alone will effectually answer the great ends of a scheme for comprehension, by opening a large noble gate at which all bodies may enter; whereas the chaffering with dissenters, and dodging about this or the other ceremony, is but like opening a few wickets,[24] and leaving them at jar,[25] by which no more than one can get in at a time, and that not without stooping, and sideling, and squeezing his body.

To all this I answer, that there is one darling inclination of mankind which

21. Shoots or root fibers.
22. The common people, the uneducated.
23. Matters of no importance and usually left undecided by church doctrine.
24. Small openings in large gates.
25. Ajar.

usually affects to be a retainer to religion, although she be neither its parent, its godmother, or its friend; I mean the spirit of opposition, that lived long before Christianity and can easily subsist without it. Let us, for instance, examine wherein the opposition of sectaries among us consists; we shall find Christianity to have no share in it at all. Does the gospel anywhere prescribe a starched, squeezed countenance, a stiff, formal gait, a singularity of manners and habit, or any affected modes of speech different from the reasonable part of mankind? [26] Yet, if Christianity did not lend its name to stand in the gap and to employ or divert these humours, they must of necessity be spent in contraventions to the laws of the land and disturbance of the public peace. There is a portion of enthusiasm assigned to every nation, which, if it hath not proper objects to work on, will burst out and set all in a flame. If the quiet of a state can be bought by only flinging men a few ceremonies to devour, it is a purchase no wise man would refuse. Let the mastiffs amuse themselves about a sheep's skin stuffed with hay, provided it will keep them from worrying the flock. The institution of convents abroad, seems, in one point, a strain of great wisdom; there being few irregularities in human passions that may not have recourse to vent themselves in some of those orders, which are so many retreats for the speculative, the melancholy, the proud, the silent, the politic, and the morose to spend themselves and evaporate the noxious particles; for each of whom, we, in this island, are forced to provide a several sect of religion to keep them quiet: and whenever Christianity shall be abolished, the legislature must find some other expedient to employ and entertain them. For what imports it how large a gate you open, if there will be always left a number who place a pride and a merit in refusing to enter?

Having thus considered the most important objections against Christianity and the chief advantages proposed by the abolishing thereof, I shall now, with equal deference and submission to wiser judgments as before, proceed to mention a few inconveniences that may happen, if the gospel should be repealed, which perhaps the projectors may not have sufficiently considered.

And first, I am very sensible how much the gentlemen of wit and pleasure are apt to murmur, and be choqued [27] at the sight of so many daggled-tail [28] parsons, who happen to fall in their way and offend their eyes; but, at the same time, these wise reformers do not consider what an advantage and felicity it is for great wits to be always provided with objects of scorn and contempt in order to exercise and improve their talents, and divert their spleen from falling on each other or on themselves; especially when all this may be done without the least imaginable danger to their persons.

And to urge another argument of a parallel nature: if Christianity were once abolished, how could the freethinkers, the strong reasoners, and the men of profound learning be able to find another subject so calculated in all points whereon to display their abilities? what wonderful productions of wit should we be deprived of from those whose genius, by continual practice, hath been wholly turned upon raillery and invectives against religion, and would there-

26. Typical manners of the Puritan sects; for this view of "affected modes of speech" see the criticism of Christian in Vanity Fair (Bunyan, The Pilgrim's Progress).
27. Shocked (taken from the French form).
28. Mud-bespattered.

fore never be able to shine or distinguish themselves upon any other subject! We are daily complaining of the great decline of wit among us, and would we take away the greatest, perhaps the only, topic we have left? Who would ever have suspected Asgil for a wit, or Toland for a philosopher, if the inexhaustible stock of Christianity had not been at hand to provide them with materials? What other subject, through all art or nature, could have produced Tindal for a profound author or furnished him with readers? It is the wise choice of the subject that alone adorns and distinguishes the writer. For, had an hundred such pens as these been employed on the side of religion, they would have immediately sunk into silence and oblivion.

Nor do I think it wholly groundless, or my fears altogether imaginary, that the abolishing Christianity may perhaps bring the Church in danger, or at least put the senate to the trouble of another securing vote.[29] I desire I may not be mistaken; I am far from presuming to affirm, or think, that the Church is in danger at present or as things now stand; but we know not how soon it may be so when the Christian religion is repealed. As plausible as this project seems, there may a dangerous design lurk under it. Nothing can be more notorious than that the Atheists, Deists, Socinians,[30] Anti-trinitarians, and other subdivisions of freethinkers are persons of little zeal for the present ecclesiastical establishment: their declared opinion is for repealing the Sacramental Test; they are very indifferent with regard to ceremonies; nor do they hold the *jus divinum*[31] of episcopacy; therefore this may be intended as one politic step towards altering the constitution of the Church established, and setting up Presbytery in the stead, which I leave to be further considered by those at the helm.

In the last place, I think nothing can be more plain than that, by this expedient, we shall run into the evil we chiefly pretend to avoid: and that the abolishment of the Christian religion will be the readiest course we can take to introduce Popery. And I am the more inclined to this opinion because we know it has been the constant practice of the Jesuits to send over emissaries with instructions to personate themselves members of the several prevailing sects among us. So it is recorded, that they have at sundry times appeared in the guise of Presbyterians, Anabaptists, Independents, and Quakers, according as any of these were most in credit; so, since the fashion hath been taken up of exploding religion, the popish missionaries have not been wanting[32] to mix with the freethinkers; among whom Toland, the great oracle of the Anti-christians, is an Irish priest, the son of an Irish priest; and the most learned and ingenious author of a book called *The Rights of the Christian Church* was in a proper juncture reconciled to the Romish faith, whose true son, as appears by an hundred passages in his treatise he still continues. Perhaps I could add some others to the number; but the fact is beyond dispute and the reasoning they proceed by is right: for, supposing Christianity to be extinguished, the

29. Such as the resolution Commons passed in 1701 for "the securing of the Protestant religion, by law established."
30. Followers of Laelius and Faustus Socinus, Italian theologians of the 16th century who denied the divinity of Christ and the supernatural status of the sacraments.
31. "Divine right" (claiming the example of the Apostles).
32. Lacking.

people will never be at ease till they find out some other method of worship; which will as infallibly produce superstition as this will end in Popery.

And therefore, if, notwithstanding all I have said, it shall still be thought necessary to have a bill brought in for repealing Christianity, I would humbly offer an amendment that instead of the word, Christianity, may be put religion in general; which, I conceive, will much better answer all the good ends proposed by the projectors of it. For, as long as we leave in being a God and his Providence, with all the necessary consequences which curious and inquisitive men will be apt to draw from such premises, we do not strike at the root of the evil, although we should ever so effectually annihilate the present scheme of the gospel: for, of what use is freedom of thought if it will not produce freedom of action, which is the sole end, how remote soever in appearance, of all objections against Christianity; and therefore, the freethinkers consider it as a sort of edifice wherein all the parts have such a mutual dependence on each other that if you happen to pull out one single nail, the whole fabric must fall to the ground. This was happily expressed by him who had heard of a text brought for proof of the Trinity, which in an ancient manuscript was differently read; he thereupon immediately took the hint, and by a sudden deduction of a long *sorites,*[33] most logically concluded; 'Why, if it be as you say, I may safely whore and drink on, and defy the parson.' From which, and many the like instances easy to be produced, I think nothing can be more manifest than that the quarrel is not against any particular points of hard digestion in the Christian system but against religion in general; which, by laying restraints on human nature, is supposed the great enemy to the freedom of thought and action.

Upon the whole, if it shall still be thought for the benefit of church and state that Christianity be abolished, I conceive, however, it may be more convenient to defer the execution to a time of peace; and not venture in this conjuncture to disoblige our allies, who, as it falls out, are all Christians, and many of them, by the prejudices of their education, so bigoted as to place a sort of pride in the appellation. If upon being rejected by them, we are to trust to an alliance with the Turk, we shall find ourselves much deceived: for, as he is too remote and generally engaged in war with the Persian emperor, so his people would be more scandalized at our infidelity than our Christian neighbours. Because the Turks are not only strict observers of religious worship but, what is worse, believe a God; which is more than is required of us even while we preserve the name of Christians.

To conclude: whatever some may think of the great advantages to trade by this favourite scheme, I do very much apprehend that in six months' time after the act is passed for the extirpation of the gospel, the Bank and East India stock may fall at least one *per cent.*[34] And since that is fifty times more than ever the wisdom of our age thought fit to venture for the preservation of Christianity, there is no reason we should be at so great a loss merely for the sake of destroying it.

1708   1711

---

33. A long and tenuous chain of reasoning.
34. The Bank of England (founded in 1695 by William III) and the East India Company, both largely Whig concerns.

A Modest Proposal

This concise and fiercely ironic tract is based upon England's exploitation of Ireland, which was forbidden to trade on its own with other countries but used as a source of raw materials and cheap food. Swift writes as an eager collaborator, an Irish projector who at last finds a scheme that will enrich Ireland without offending the English; it will, moreover, at last make Ireland's people "the riches of a nation," as a large working force was traditionally believed to be. The projector in whose guise Swift writes can sustain without conflict an idiom of humane tenderness, somewhat cloying in fact, with the zeal of a ruthlessly commercial breeder of beef. Clearly, the cannibalism that solves Ireland's problem is simply a metaphor for the exploitation that has created it, and "dressing them hot under the knife" shows insensibility only different in degree from counting on the poor to die "as fast as they reasonably can." The tract does not spare the Irish, either, for one of the worst evils of exploitation is that it degrades and brutalizes its victims; Swift is enraged by their passivity, and that too requires its terrible metaphors.

A Modest Proposal

for
Preventing the Children of Poor People in Ireland from Being a Burden to Their Parents or Country, and for Making Them Beneficial to the Public

It is a melancholy object to those who walk through this great town, or travel in the country, when they see the streets, the roads, and cabin-doors crowded with beggars of the female sex, followed by three, four, or six children, all in rags, and importuning every passenger for an alms. These mothers, instead of being able to work for their honest livelihood, are forced to employ all their time in strolling to beg sustenance for their helpless infants: who, as they grow up, either turn thieves for want of work, or leave their dear native country to fight for the Pretender in Spain, or sell themselves to the Barbadoes.[1]

I think it is agreed by all parties, that this prodigious number of children in the arms, or on the backs, or at the heels of their mothers, and frequently of their fathers, is, in the present deplorable state of the kingdom, a very great additional grievance; and, therefore, whoever could find out a fair, cheap, and easy method of making these children sound and useful members of the commonwealth, would deserve so well of the public, as to have his statue set up for a preserver of the nation.[2]

But my intention is very far from being confined to provide only for the children of professed beggars; it is of a much greater extent, and shall take in the

1. Many Irish Catholics enlisted in French and Spanish forces, the latter employed in the effort to restore the Stuart Pretender to the English throne in 1718; emigration to the West Indies from Ireland had reached the rate of almost fifteen hundred a year (and often led to desperate servitude).
2. The idiom of the "projector," the enthusiastic proponent of public remedies (often suspected of having an eye on his own glory).

whole number of infants at a certain age, who are born of parents in effect as little able to support them as those who demand our charity in the streets.

As to my own part, having turned my thoughts for many years upon this important subject, and maturely weighed the several schemes of other projectors, I have always found them grossly mistaken in their computation. It is true, a child, just dropped from its dam,[3] may be supported by her milk for a solar year with little other nourishment; at most, not above the value of two shillings, which the mother may certainly get, or the value in scraps, by her lawful occupation of begging; and it is exactly at one year old that I propose to provide for them in such a manner, as, instead of being a charge upon their parents or the parish, or wanting food and raiment for the rest of their lives, they shall, on the contrary, contribute to the feeding, and partly to the clothing, of many thousands.

There is likewise another great advantage in my scheme, that it will prevent those voluntary abortions, and that horrid practice of women murdering their bastard children, alas, too frequent among us, sacrificing the poor innocent babes, I doubt more to avoid the expense than the shame, which would move tears and pity in the most savage and inhuman breast.

The number of souls in this kingdom being usually reckoned one millon and a half, of these I calculate there may be about two hundred thousand couple whose wives are breeders; from which number I subtract thirty thousand couple, who are able to maintain their own children (although I apprehend there cannot be so many, under the present distresses of the kingdom); but this being granted, there will remain an hundred and seventy thousand breeders. I again subtract fifty thousand for those women who miscarry, or whose children die by accident or disease within the year. There only remain a hundred and twenty thousand children of poor parents annually born. The question therefore is how this number shall be reared and provided for? which, as I have already said, under the present situation of affairs, is utterly impossible by all the methods hitherto proposed. For we can neither employ them in handicraft or agriculture; we neither build houses (I mean in the country) nor cultivate land: they can very seldom pick up a livelihood by stealing until they arrive at six years old, except where they are of towardly parts; although I confess they learn the rudiments much earlier; during which time they can, however, be properly looked upon only as probationers; as I have been informed by a principal gentleman in the county of Cavan,[4] who protested to me, that he never knew above one or two instances under the age of six, even in a part of the kingdom so renowned for the quickest proficiency in that art.

I am assured by our merchants that a boy or a girl before twelve years old is no saleable commodity; and even when they come to this age they will not yield above three pounds or three pounds and half-a-crown at most, on the exchange; which cannot turn to account either to the parents or kingdom, the charge of nutriment and rags having been at least four times that value.

I shall now, therefore, humbly propose my own thoughts, which I hope will not be liable to the least objection.

3. The idiom now of the cattle breeder.
4. One of the poorest districts of Ireland.

I have been assured by a very knowing American [5] of my acquaintance in London, that a young healthy child, well nursed, is, at a year old, a most delicious, nourishing, and wholesome food, whether stewed, roasted, baked, or boiled; and I make no doubt that it will equally serve in a fricassee or a ragout.[6]

I do therefore humbly offer it to public consideration, that of the hundred and twenty thousand children already computed, twenty thousand may be reserved for breed, whereof only one-fourth part to be males; which is more than we allow to sheep, black cattle, or swine; and my reason is, that these children are seldom the fruits of marriage, a circumstance not much regarded by our savages, therefore one male will be sufficient to serve four females. That the remaining hundred thousand may, at a year old, be offered in sale to the persons of quality and fortune through the kingdom; always advising the mother to let them suck plentifully in the last month, so as to render them plump and fat for a good table. A child will make two dishes at an entertainment for friends; and when the family dines alone, the fore or hind quarter will make a reasonable dish, and, seasoned with a little pepper or salt, will be very good boiled on the fourth day, especially in winter.

I have reckoned, upon a medium, that a child just born will weigh twelve pounds, and in a solar year, if tolerably nursed, increaseth to twenty-eight pounds.

I grant this food will be somewhat dear, and therefore very proper for landlords, who, as they have already devoured most of the parents, seem to have the best title to the children.

Infants' flesh will be in season throughout the year, but more plentifully in March, and a little before and after: for we are told by a grave author, an eminent French physician,[7] that fish being a prolific [8] diet, there are more children born in Roman Catholic countries about nine months after Lent than at any other season; therefore, reckoning a year after Lent, the markets will be more glutted than usual, because the number of popish infants is at least three to one in this kingdom; and therefore it will have one other collateral advantage, by lessening the number of papists among us.

I have already computed the charge of nursing a beggar's child (in which list I reckon all cottagers, labourers, and four-fifths of the farmers) to be about two shillings per annum, rags included; and I believe no gentleman would repine to give ten shillings for the carcass of a good fat child, which, as I have said, will make four dishes of excellent nutritive meat, when he has only some particular friend, or his own family, to dine with him. Thus the squire will learn to be a good landlord, and grow popular among his tenants; the mother will have eight shillings net profit, and be fit for work till she produces another child.

Those who are more thrifty (as I must confess the times require) may flay

---

5. Presumably American Indian, many of whom were believed by the English to enjoy cannibalism.

6. A French stew, one of the foreign dishes ("olios and ragouts") Swift mocks elsewhere as affectations.

7. François Rabelais (c. 1494–1553), Gargantua and Pantagruel V.29.

8. Generative.

the carcass; the skin of which, artificially dressed, will make admirable gloves for ladies, and summer-boots for fine gentlemen.

As to our city of Dublin, shambles [9] may be appointed for this purpose in the most convenient parts of it, and butchers we may be assured will not be wanting; although I rather recommend buying the children alive, and dressing them hot from the knife, as we do roasting pigs.

A very worthy person, a true lover of his country, and whose virtues I highly esteem, was lately pleased, in discoursing on this matter, to offer a refinement upon my scheme. He said, that many gentlemen of this kingdom, having of late destroyed their deer, he conceived that the want of venison might be well supplied by the bodies of young lads and maidens, not exceeding fourteen years of age, nor under twelve; so great a number of both sexes in every country being now ready to starve for want of work and service; and these to be disposed of by their parents, if alive, or otherwise by their nearest relations. But, with due deference to so excellent a friend, and so deserving a patriot, I cannot be altogether in his sentiments; for as to the males, my American acquaintance assured me from frequent experience, that their flesh was generally tough and lean, like that of our schoolboys, by continual exercise, and their taste disagreeable; and to fatten them would not answer the charge. Then as to the females, it would, I think, with humble submission, be a loss to the public, because they soon would become breeders themselves: and besides, it is not improbable that some scrupulous people might be apt to censure such a practice (although indeed very unjustly) as a little bordering upon cruelty; which, I confess hath always been with me the strongest objection against any project, how well soever intended.

But in order to justify my friend, he confessed that this expedient was put into his head by the famous Psalmanazar,[10] a native of the island Formosa, who came from thence to London above twenty years ago; and in conversation told my friend, that in his country, when any young person happened to be put to death, the executioner sold the carcass to persons of quality as a prime dainty; and that in his time the body of a plump girl of fifteen, who was crucified for an attempt to poison the emperor, was sold to his Imperial Majesty's prime minister of state,[11] and other great mandarins of the court, in joints from the gibbet, at four hundred crowns. Neither indeed can I deny, that if the same use were made of several plump young girls in this town, who, without one single groat to their fortunes, cannot stir abroad without a chair, and appear at playhouse and assemblies [12] in foreign fineries which they never will pay for, the kingdom would not be the worse.

Some persons of a desponding spirit are in great concern about that vast number of poor people who are aged, diseased, or maimed; and I have been desired to employ my thoughts what course may be taken to ease the nation of so grievous an encumbrance. But I am not in the least pain upon that matter,

9. Slaughterhouses.
10. George Psalmanazar (1679-1763), a Frenchman who pretended to be a Formosan and wrote (in English) a fraudulent book about his "native" land.
11. Probably a reference to Walpole.
12. Social gatherings (Swift had sought an Irish boycott of all such foreign luxuries of dress or diet).

because it is very well known, that they are every day dying, and rotting, by cold and famine, and filth and vermin, as fast as can be reasonably expected. And as to the younger labourers, they are now in almost as hopeful a condition: they cannot get work, and consequently pine away for want of nourishment, to a degree, that if at any time they are accidentally hired to common labour, they have not strength to perform it; and thus the country and themselves are happily delivered from the evils to come.

I have too long digressed, and therefore shall return to my subject. I think the advantages by the proposal which I have made are obvious and many, as well as of the highest importance.

For first, as I have already observed, it would greatly lessen the number of papists, with whom we are yearly overrun, being the principal breeders of the nation as well as our most dangerous enemies; and who stay at home on purpose with a design to deliver the kingdom to the Pretender, hoping to take their advantage by the absence of so many good Protestants, who have chosen rather to leave their country than stay at home and pay tithes against their conscience to an idolatrous Episcopal curate.[13]

Secondly, the poorer tenants will have something valuable of their own, which by law may be made liable to distress, and help to pay their landlord's rent; their corn and cattle being already seized, and money a thing unknown.

Thirdly, whereas the maintenance of an hundred thousand children, from two years old and upwards, cannot be computed at less than ten shillings a piece per annum, the nation's stock will be thereby increased fifty thousand pounds per annum; besides the profit of a new dish introduced to the tables of all gentlemen of fortune in the kingdom who have any refinement in taste. And the money will circulate among ourselves, the goods being entirely of our own growth and manufacture.

Fourthly, the constant breeders, besides the gain of eight shillings sterling per annum by the sale of their children, will be rid of the charge of maintaining them after the first year.

Fifthly, this food would likewise bring great custom to taverns; where the vintners will certainly be so prudent as to procure the best receipts for dressing it to perfection, and, consequently, have their houses frequented by all the fine gentlemen, who justly value themselves upon their knowledge in good eating: and a skilful cook, who understands how to oblige his guests, will contrive to make it as expensive as they please.

Sixthly, this would be a great inducement to marriage, which all wise nations have either encouraged by rewards, or enforced by laws and penalties. It would increase the care and tenderness of mothers towards their children, when they were sure of a settlement for life to the poor babes, provided in some sort by the public, to their annual profit instead of expense. We should soon see an honest emulation among the married women, which of them could bring the

13. Swift is mocking the castigation of the Catholics, for he regarded it as a typical propaganda device of the Whigs and Protestants; his own experience as a clergyman in northern Ireland had given him reason to fear and distrust the energies of the dissenting Protestants, and he questions their motives (money or conscience) for leaving Ireland. The word "idolatrous" was added in 1735 after renewed agitation to remove the Sacramental Test, with the implication that Anglican forms and doctrines were intolerable to other Protestants.

fattest child to the market. Men would become as fond of their wives during the time of their pregnancy, as they are now of their mares in foal, their cows in calf, or sows when they are ready to farrow; nor offer to beat or kick them (as is too frequent a practice) for fear of a miscarriage.

Many other advantages might be enumerated. For instance, the addition of some thousand carcasses in our exportation of barrelled beef; the propagation of swine's flesh, and improvement in the art of making good bacon, so much wanted among us by the great destruction of pigs, too frequent at our tables, which are no way comparable in taste or magnificence to a well-grown, fat yearling child, which, roasted whole, will make a considerable figure at a Lord Mayor's feast, or any other public entertainment. But this, and many others, I omit, being studious of brevity.

Supposing that one thousand families in this city would be constant customers for infants' flesh, besides others who might have it at merry meetings, particularly weddings and christenings, I compute that Dublin would take off annually about twenty thousand carcasses; and the rest of the kingdom (where probably they will be sold somewhat cheaper) the remaining eighty thousand.

I can think of no one objection that will possibly be raised against this proposal, unless it should be urged, that the number of people will be thereby much lessened in the kingdom. This I freely own, and it was indeed one principal design in offering it to the world. I desire the reader will observe that I calculate my remedy for this one individual kingdom of Ireland, and for no other that ever was, is, or I think ever can be, upon earth. Therefore let no man talk to me of other expedients: [14] of taxing our absentees at five shillings a pound: of using neither clothes nor household-furniture except what is of our own growth and manufacture: of utterly rejecting the materials and instruments that promote foreign luxury: of curing the expensiveness of pride, vanity, idleness, and gaming in our women; of introducing a vein of parsimony, prudence, and temperance: of learning to love our country, wherein we differ even from Laplanders, and the inhabitants of Topinamboo: [15] of quitting our animosities and factions, nor act any longer like the Jews, who were murdering one another at the very moment their city was taken: [16] of being a little cautious not to sell our country and consciences for nothing: of teaching landlords to have at least one degree of mercy towards their tenants: lastly, of putting a spirit of honesty, industry, and skill into our shopkeepers; who, if a resolution could now be taken to buy only our native goods, would immediately unite to cheat and exact upon us in the price, the measure, and the goodness, nor could ever yet be brought to make one fair proposal of just dealing, though often and earnestly invited to it.

Therefore I repeat, let no man talk to me of these and the like expedients, till he hath at least some glimpse of hope that there will ever be some hearty and sincere attempt to put them in practice.

But, as to myself, having been wearied out for many years with offering vain, idle, visionary thoughts, and at length utterly despairing of success, I

14. The following are, of course, Swift's own genuine proposals for Ireland.
15. A region of Brazil known for wildness and barbarous stupidity.
16. When Jerusalem fell to Nebuchadnezzar (II Kings 24, 25; II Chronicles 36), with the suggestion that English domination is Ireland's Babylonian captivity.

fortunately fell upon this proposal; which, as it is wholly new, so it hath something solid and real, of no expense and little trouble, full in our own power, and whereby we can incur no danger in disobliging England. For this kind of commodity will not bear exportation, the flesh being of too tender a consistence to admit a long continuance in salt, although perhaps I could name a country which would be glad to eat up our whole nation without it.

After all, I am not so violently bent upon my own opinion as to reject any offer proposed by wise men which shall be found equally innocent, cheap, easy, and effectual. But before something of that kind shall be advanced in contradiction to my scheme, and offering a better, I desire the author, or authors, will be pleased maturely to consider two points. First, as things now stand, how they will be able to find food and raiment for a hundred thousand useless mouths and backs? And, secondly, there being a round million of creatures in human figure throughout this kingdom, whose whole subsistence put into a common stock would leave them in debt two millions of pounds sterling, adding those who are beggars by profession, to the bulk of farmers, cottagers, and labourers, with the wives and children who are beggars in effect; I desire those politicians who dislike my overture, and may perhaps be so bold as to attempt an answer, that they will first ask the parents of these mortals, whether they would not at this day think it a great happiness to have been sold for food at a year old, in the manner I prescribe, and thereby have avoided such a perpetual scene of misfortunes as they have since gone through, by the oppression of landlords, the impossibility of paying rent without money or trade, the want of common sustenance, with neither house nor clothes to cover them from the inclemencies of weather, and the most inevitable prospect of entailing the like, or greater miseries, upon their breed for ever.

I profess, in the sincerity of my heart, that I have not the least personal interest in endeavouring to promote this necessary work, having no other motive than the public good of my country, by advancing our trade, providing for infants, relieving the poor, and giving some pleasure to the rich. I have no children by which I can propose to get a single penny; the youngest being nine years old, and my wife past child-bearing.

1729

Swift's Poems

Swift began his poetic career with Pindaric odes in the manner of Abraham Cowley, but he soon found his characteristic idiom in the Hudibrastic tetrameter couplet. His poetry is a constant warfare against the false sublime and other forms of specious exaltation, and his dry, colloquial undercutting of pretension is to be seen alike in "Baucis and Philemon" (see The Mock Form), in the birthday poems to Stella (tender and warm as they are), and in caustic or scatological satires such as "The Day of Judgment" and "Cassinus and Peter." The two "city" poems (see The Urban Scene), written in pentameter to burlesque the current form of pastoral and georgic poetry, are further examples of Swift's reduction of unthinking celebration and of his opposition of the commonplace lowness of everyday life to the conventions of literary style.

Phyllis
Or, The Progress of Love

Desponding Phyllis was endued
With every talent of a prude:
She trembled when a man drew near;
Salute her, and she turned her ear:
If o'er against her you were placed,
She durst not look above your waist:
She'd rather take you to her bed,
Than let you see her dress her head;
In church you heard her, through the crowd,

10 Repeat the absolution loud:
In church, secure behind her fan,
She durst behold that monster, man:
There practised how to place her head,
And bit her lips to make them red;
Or, on the mat devoutly kneeling,
Would lift her eyes up to the ceiling.
And heave her bosom unaware,
For neighbouring beaux to see it bare.
    At length a lucky lover came,
20 And found admittance from the dame.
Suppose all parties now agreed,
The writings drawn, the lawyer fee'd,
The vicar and the ring bespoke:
Guess, how could such a match be broke?
See then what mortals place their bliss in!
Next morn betimes the bride was missing:
The mother screamed, the father chid;
Where can this idle wench be hid?
No news of Phyl! the bridegroom came,
30 And thought his bride had skulked for shame;
Because her father used to say
The girl had such a bashful way.
    Now John the butler must be sent
To learn the way that Phyllis went:
The groom was wished to saddle Crop;
For John must neither light nor stop,
But find her whereso'er she fled,
And bring her back alive or dead.
See here again the devil to do;
40 For truly John was missing too:
The horse and pillion° both were gone!
Phyllis, it seems, was fled with John.
Old Madam, who went up to find

pillion saddle for the person who rode behind
(usually a woman)

1774

What papers Phyl had left behind,
A letter on the toilet° sees,
'To my much-honoured father—these—'
('Tis always done, romances tell us,
When daughters run away with fellows)
Filled with the choicest commonplaces,
50   By others used in the like cases.
'That long ago a fortune-teller
Exactly said what now befell her;
And in a glass had made her see
A serving-man of low degree.
It was her fate, must be forgiven;
For marriages are made in Heaven:
His pardon begged: but, to be plain,
She'd do't if 'twere to do again:
Thank God, 'twas neither shame nor sin,
60   For John was come of honest kin.
Love never thinks of rich and poor;
She'd beg with John from door to door.
Forgive her, if it be a crime;
She'll never do't another time.
She ne'er before in all her life
Once disobeyed him, maid nor wife.'
One argument she summed up all in,
'The thing was done and past recalling;
And therefore hoped she would recover
70   His favour, when his passion's over.
She valued not what others thought her,
And was—his most obedient daughter.'
    Fair maidens all, attend the Muse,
Who now the wandering pair pursues:
Away they rode in homely° sort,
Their journey long, their money short;
The loving couple well bemired;
The horse and both the riders tired:
Their victuals bad, their lodging worse;
80   Phyl cried, and John began to curse:
Phyl wished that she had strained a limb,
When first she ventured out with him;
John wished that he had broke a leg,
When first for her he quitted Peg.
    But what adventures more befell 'em,
The Muse has now no time to tell 'em;
How Johnny wheedled, threatened, fawned,
Till Phyllis all her trinkets pawned:
How oft she broke her marriage vows,

toilet dressing table   **homely** simple, plain

90   In kindness to maintain her spouse,
     Till swains unwholesome° spoiled the trade;
     For now the surgeon must be paid,
     To whom those perquisites are gone,
     In Christian justice due to John.
         When food and raiment now grew scarce,
     Fate put a period° to the farce,
     And with exact poetic justice;
     For John is landlord, Phyllis hostess;
     They keep, at Staines, the Old Blue Boar,
100 Are cat and dog, and rogue and whore.
     1719   1727

On Stella's Birthday°

Stella this day is thirty-four,
(We won't dispute a year or more:)
However, Stella, be not troubled,
Although thy size and years are doubled
Since first I saw thee at sixteen,
The brightest virgin on the green;
So little is thy form declined,
Made up so largely in thy mind.
    O, would it please the gods to split
10 Thy beauty, size, and years, and wit,
No age could furnish out a pair
Of nymphs so graceful, wise, and fair;
With half the lustre of your eyes,
With half your wit, your years, and size.
And then, before it grew too late,
How should I beg of gentle fate,
(That either nymph might have her swain,)
To split my worship too in twain.
1719   1727

Stella's Birthday°

          March 13, 1727
This day, whate'er the fates decree,
Shall still° be kept with joy by me:
This day then let us not be told,

---

unwholesome diseased
period end
On Stella's Birthday This is the first of a series
of birthday poems Swift wrote for Hester Johnson; it was written in fact for her thirty-eighth
birthday on March 13, 1719. We can see here

the tenderness and gentle mockery that characterize these poems as they do Swift's letters
in the so-called *Journal to Stella.*
Stella's Birthday This is the last of the series;
Stella died on January 28, 1728.
still always

That you are sick, and I grown old;
Nor think on our approaching ills,
And talk of spectacles and pills;
Tomorrow will be time enough
To hear such mortifying° stuff.
Yet, since from reason may be brought
10   A better and more pleasing thought,
Which can, in spite of all decays,
Support a few remaining days;
From not the gravest of divines
Accept for once some serious lines.
    Although we now can form no more
Long schemes of life, as heretofore;
Yet you, while time is running fast,
Can look with joy on what is past.
    Were future happiness and pain
20   A mere contrivance of the brain;
As atheists argue, to entice
And fit their proselytes for vice;
(The only comfort they propose,
To have companions in their woes)
Grant this the case; yet sure 'tis hard
That virtue, styled its own reward,
And by all sages understood
To be the chief of human good,
Should acting die, nor leave behind
30   Some lasting pleasure in the mind,
Which, by remembrance, will assuage
Grief, sickness, poverty, and age;
And strongly shoot a radiant dart
To shine through life's declining part.
    Say, Stella, feel you no content,
Reflecting on a life well spent?
Your skilful hand employed to save
Despairing wretches from the grave;
And then supporting with your store
40   Those whom you dragged from death before:°
So Providence on mortals waits,
Preserving what it first creates.
Your generous boldness to defend
An innocent and absent friend;
That courage which can make you just
To merit humbled in the dust;
The detestation you express
For vice in all its glittering dress;

---

mortifying humbling, but also destroying vital
or active powers
from death before Swift is eloquent in his tributes to Stella's charity, both in nursing the sick
and in supporting them from her limited income.

That patience under torturing pain,
50 Where stubborn Stoics would complain:
        Must these like empty shadows pass,
    Or forms reflected from a glass?
    Or mere chimeras in the mind,
    That fly and leave no marks behind?
    Does not the body thrive and grow
    By food of twenty years ago?
    And, had it not been still supplied,
    It must a thousand times have died.
    Then who with reason can maintain
60 That no effects of food remain?
    And is not virtue in mankind
    The nutriment that feeds the mind;
    Upheld by each good action past,
    And still continued by the last?
    Then, who with reason can pretend
    That all effects of virtue end?
        Believe me, Stella, when you show
    That true contempt for things below,
    Nor prize your life for other ends,
70 Than merely to oblige your friends;
    Your former actions claim their part,
    And join to fortify your heart.
    For Virtue in her daily race,
    Like Janus,° bears a double face;
    Looks back with joy where she has gone,
    And therefore goes with courage on:
    She at your sickly couch will wait,
    And guide you to a better state.
        O then, whatever Heaven intends,
80 Take pity on your pitying friends!
    Nor let your ills affect your mind,
    To fancy they can be unkind.
    Me, surely me, you ought to spare,
    Who gladly would your suffering share;
    Or give my scrap of life to you,
    And think it far beneath your due;
    You, to whose care so oft I owe
    That I'm alive to tell you so.
    1727   1727

Janus the god of beginnings, his symbol a
double-faced head, looking both forward and
backward

The Day of Judgment

With a whirl of thought oppressed,
I sunk from reverie to rest.
A horrid vision seized my head,
I saw the graves give up their dead!
Jove, armed with terrors, bursts the skies,
And thunder roars and lightning flies!
Amazed, confused, its fate unknown,
The world stands trembling at his throne!
While each pale sinner hangs his head,
10   Jove, nodding, shook the heavens, and said:
'Offending race of human kind,
By nature, reason, learning, blind;
You who, through frailty, stepped aside;
And you who never fell—through pride:
You who in different sects have shammed,
And come to see each other damned;
(So some folk told you, but they knew
No more of Jove's designs than you)
The world's mad business now is o'er,
20   And I resent these pranks no more.
I to such blockheads set my wit!
I damn such fools!—Go, go, you're bit.'
1731?   1774

Cassinus and Peter°

A Tragical Elegy
Two college sophs of Cambridge growth,
Both special wits and lovers both,
Conferring, as they used to meet,
On love and books, in rapture sweet;
(Muse find me names to fix my metre,
Cassinus this, and t'other Peter.)
Friend Peter to Cassinus goes,
To chat a while and warm his nose:
But such a sight was never seen,
10   The lad lay swallowed up in spleen.°
He seemed as just crept out of bed;
One greasy stocking round his head,
The t'other he sat down to darn,

Cassinus and Peter This poem deserves study
rather than the curious notoriety it has received.
The last line is often cited as evidence of
Swift's horror of bodily functions, as if the
poem were not a consistent mockery of the
fatuously romantic idealist, down to his own
slovenliness (only in part the result of distraction) and his visionary mad fit in ll. 79–88,
similar to those of Dryden's heroic plays or of
later 18th-century odes.
spleen melancholy, "vapors"; as the ensuing
picture reveals, the image of a distracted lover

With threads of different coloured yarn;
His breeches torn, exposing wide
A ragged shirt and tawny hide.
Scorched were his shins, his legs were bare,
But well embrowned with dirt and hair.
A rug was o'er his shoulders thrown,
20   (A rug, for nightgown he had none,)
His jordan° stood in manner fitting
Between his legs, to spew° or spit in;
His ancient pipe, in sable dyed,
And half unsmoked, lay by his side.
    Him thus accoutred Peter found,
With eyes in smoke and weeping drowned;
The leavings of his last night's pot°
On embers placed, to drink it hot.
    'Why, Cassy, thou wilt doze thy pate:
30   What makes thee lie a-bed so late?
The finch, the linnet, and the thrush,
Their matins chant in every bush;
And I have heard thee oft salute
Aurora with thy early flute.
Heaven send thou hast not got the hyps!°
How! not a word come from thy lips?'
    Then gave him some familiar thumps,
A college joke to cure the dumps.
    The swain at last, with grief opprest,
40   Cried, 'Celia!' thrice, and sighed the rest.
    'Dear Cassy, though to ask I dread,
Yet ask I must—is Celia dead?'
    'How happy I, were that the worst!
But I was fated to be curst!'
    'Come, tell us, has she played the whore?'
    'O Peter, would it were no more!'
    'Why, plague confound her sandy locks!
Say, has the small or greater pox°
Sunk down her nose, or seamed her face?
50   Be easy, 'tis a common case.'
    'O Peter! beauty's but a varnish,
Which time and accidents will tarnish:
But Celia has contrived to blast
Those beauties that might ever last.
Nor can imagination guess,
Nor eloquence divine express,
How that ungrateful charming maid

jordan chamber pot
spew vomit
pot of wine
hyps hypochondria

small . . . pox smallpox or syphilis, the latter
causing collapse of the bridge of the nose in advanced stages

My purest passion has betrayed:
Conceive the most envenomed dart
60   To pierce an injured lover's heart.'
        'Why, hang her; though she seemed so coy,
I know, she loves the barber's boy.'
        'Friend Peter, this I could excuse,
For every nymph has leave to choose;
Nor have I reason to complain,
She loves a more deserving swain.
But oh! how ill hast thou divined
A crime that shocks all humankind;
A deed unknown to female race,
70   At which the sun should hide his face:
Advice in vain you would apply—
Then leave me to despair and die.
Yet, kind Arcadians,° on my urn
These elegies and sonnets burn;
And on the marble grave these rhymes,
A monument to after-times—
"Here Cassy lies, by Celia slain,
And dying, never told his pain."
Vain empty world, farewell. But hark,
80   The loud Cerberian triple bark;°
And there—behold Alecto° stand,
A whip of scorpions in her hand:
Lo, Charon° from his leaky wherry
Beckoning to waft me o'er the ferry:
I come! I come! Medusa° see,
Her serpents hiss direct at me.
Begone; unhand me, hellish fry:
Avaunt—ye cannot say 'twas I.'°
        'Dear Cassy, thou must purge and bleed;°
90   I fear thou wilt be mad indeed.
But now, by friendship's sacred laws,
I here conjure thee, tell the cause;
And Celia's horrid fact relate:
Thy friend would gladly share thy fate.'
        'To force it out, my heart must rend;
Yet when conjured by such a friend—
Think, Peter, how my soul is racked!
These eyes, these eyes, beheld the fact.

Arcadians the shepherds of pastoral Greece. A famous subject of paintings and prints is a group of shepherds peering at a gravestone that reads "Et in Arcadia ego," interpreted as Death's saying, "Even in Arcadia I am."
Cerberian . . . bark the bark of three-headed Cerberus at the gates of the underworld
Alecto one of the three Furies
Charon the ferryman of the dead across the Styx

Medusa the gorgon whose locks are snakes and whose gaze can turn anything to stone
Avaunt . . . 'twas I "See *Macbeth*" (Swift); a condensation of two outcries of Macbeth upon seeing Banquo's ghost: "Thou canst not say I did it" and "Avaunt! and quit my sight!" (III. iv.50, 93)
purge and bleed laxatives and blood-letting as cures for the spleen

Now bend thine ear, since out it must;
100 But, when thou seest me laid in dust,
The secret thou shalt ne'er impart,
Not to the nymph that keeps thy heart;
(How would her virgin soul bemoan
A crime to all her sex unknown!)
Nor whisper to the tattling reeds°
The blackest of all female deeds;
Nor blab it on the lonely rocks,
Where Echo sits, and listening mocks;°
Nor let the zephyr's treacherous gale
110 Through Cambridge waft the direful tale;
Nor to the chattering feathered race°
Discover° Celia's foul disgrace.
But, if you fail, my spectre dread,
Attending nightly round your bed—
And yet I dare confide in you;
So take my secret, and adieu:
    Nor wonder how I lost my wits;
Oh! Celia, Celia, Celia shits!'

1734

Gulliver's Travels

Gulliver's Travels (as the book has come to be known) was probably begun by 1720
and completed in the summer of 1725; the publisher received the manuscript "he
knew not whence, nor from whom, dropped at his house in the dark, from a
hackney-coach." The book had immediate success. "From the highest to the lowest it is
universally read," Gay wrote to Swift in Ireland, "from the cabinet-council to the
nursery." And Pope wrote, "The countenance with which it is received by some
statesmen is delightful; I wish I could tell you how every single man looks upon it, to
observe which has been my whole diversion this fortnight." In 1735, when Swift
supervised a new edition, he added the letter from Gulliver to his cousin Sympson
which is given here; and the lament of Mary Gulliver is one of a series of poems
inspired by the *Travels* and written in all probability by Gay, perhaps with Pope's
collaboration.

Swift's great satire is recounted by a stolid, unimaginative, decent man who can,
under the stress of pride, become arrogantly complacent or—once he has suffered
disenchantment—arrogantly misanthropic. "I tell you after all that I do not hate mankind," Swift wrote to Pope in 1725; "it is *vous autres* who hate them because you
would have them reasonable animals, and are angry for being disappointed." "You
others" includes Gulliver himself, who seems blandly persuaded that man is a
rational animal until he discovers what a truly rational animal is (in the form of a

---

the tattling reeds to which Midas' wife confided the terrible secret that he had ass's ears
listening mocks The nymph Echo was punished
(for impeding Hera's investigation of Zeus' adul-

teries) by being denied all speech except what
she could repeat of others' words.
chattering . . . race e.g. parrots
Discover disclose

horse) and what kind of animal man can be at worst (in the form, unfortunately, of man). Swift's own definition of man is a creature *rationis capax,* that is, capable of reason, but not at all securely in possession of it. What he presents in the great fourth voyage is the image of man in a state of full degeneration, his bestiality only intensified by his vestigial powers of mind; the Yahoo is offered as a limiting case of what man can become, and he inevitably raises the question of how far man has moved toward that limit already.

The Houyhnhnm, in contrast, is a thoroughly rational animal. He is no more than an animal in that he has no intimations of immortality or of divinity; Nature is the First Mother to whom in death he returns, and he can boast of himself as "the Perfection of Nature" but cannot imagine that he might be something more. His life is mild and temperate, for his passions are thoroughly in the control of his reason; and his reason is an immediate, practical, intuitive power for discerning what is right as well as what is efficient. Houyhnhnm life, then, is neither spirited nor spiritual; it has the virtues of simplicity, honesty, and peacefulness. These are virtues man rarely attains and often wishes he could, but they are not the virtues he celebrates in his heroic, erotic, or visionary art. It is to be expected, then, that that life would not finally have great appeal to man's nature, and Swift teases us with the fact—that rational goodness is something we cannot long endure.

Is the alternative to be a Yahoo? Gulliver, once he awakens to disenchantment with men, cannot really imagine more than these two alternatives and ignores the extent to which he differs from either. Resolved to pass as a Houyhnhnm and affecting the outward mannerisms (of neigh and canter), he desperately seeks to dissociate himself from the Yahoos and is mortified by their attraction to him as one of their kind. By the time of his return, when he encounters a friendly and generous Portuguese captain, Gulliver can only see a Yahoo (as, with terror and disgust, he does in his mirror); even more, he retreats in disgust from his family and seeks solace with horses, if only because they look and smell like Houyhnhnms. Having come belatedly to see below the surfaces he once unquestioningly accepted, Gulliver has not achieved discrimination; instead, he becomes devoted to a new surface.

How does this come about? In the first voyage, Gulliver finds himself among the Lilliputians, one-twelfth his bulk, and gradually adjusts to their scale of vision; for, while he decently refuses to enslave their enemies in Blefuscu (the only other island in their world and therefore the object of conquest), he rather proudly accepts the court honor of being named a *nardac.* And when he is accused of adultery with a minister's wife, he does not laugh at the incongruity, but solemnly defends himself against the charges. In Lilliput he discovers a people who once lived by rational institutions but have learned to pervert their laws into instruments of domination and self-seeking. Words have become emptied of meaning even as they remain full of prestige; the Emperor's subjects have learned to scamper for safety when he speaks of his mercy or lenity, and Gulliver must finally flee to save his own life.

In his second voyage, to Brobdingnag, the proportions are reversed, and Gulliver finds himself a Lilliputian in a land of giants. They are a mixed lot, but the King is, in contrast to George I of England, the best of them—large-souled, generous, with intellectual curiosity and an acute sense of justice. When Gulliver describes to him the institutions of England, the King easily perceives what Gulliver does not mention— the way in which they are open to corruption and the travesty they readily become. As the King sums it up, "By what I have gathered from your own relation, and the answers I have with much pains wringed and extorted from you, I cannot but conclude the bulk of your natives to be the most pernicious race of little odious vermin that nature ever suffered to crawl upon the surface of the earth." Undeterred, in fact stirred to pride, Gulliver offers to give the King the secret of gunpowder so that he can maim and destroy his enemies and gain absolute power; he does this with no active evil intent, but with the single-minded obliviousness that Swift so brilliantly catches in his satires (notably in the speaker of A Modest Proposal). When the King refuses with horror, Gulliver describes with scorn the limited culture of Brobdingnag: short clear laws and no need for lawyers, no tolerance for metaphysics and (it is implied) religious mystery, a balanced ("mixed") state without internal factions or rivalries, a lucid prose and the refusal to write unnecessary books. It is hardly what a European would call "civilization," and it looks ahead (as a fallible but reformed society) to the devastating rationality of the Houyhnhnms.

The third voyage takes Gulliver to Laputa, the flying island, where everyone who counts is addicted to "pure" pursuits—astronomy and music—and utterly divorced from the practical life around him. With one telling exception: the island is a portable court and descends over any province that aspires to freedom, denying it light or rainfall, even ready to crush it to earth in order to maintain power. On the mainland Gulliver encounters Lord Munodi (who, as his name indicates, hates this world), a man of taste and judgment, who must bow to the fashions for experiment and innovation. Whatever is done must be done with the greatest possible show of ingenuity (if pincushions are needed, they must be made out of marble), and the Grand Academy of Lagado (a satire on the Royal Society of England) is devoted to elaborate pseudo-science, designed not for use but for show. Among his other adventures, Gulliver encounters the Struldbruggs, a special race blessed with immortality, or rather cursed with it, for they are not free of degeneration; instead of being oracles of wisdom, they soon descend into a bickering, avaricious, melancholy senility.

At every point Gulliver is confronted with the distinction between idea and execution, the rational possibility and the corrupt practice, the capacity for reason and the passionate degeneracy that overtakes it. His responses are never acute; he may resent an injury or an insult, sidestep a larcenous or murderous gesture, but he remains essentially uncritical and unreflective. In the fourth voyage all that he has seen is made inescapable, and he moves from an insensitive complacency to an unthinking misanthropy, simply redirecting his pride from identification with his kind to hatred of them and to a new and impossible effort at identification with the Houyhnhnms. What Swift means us to conclude has been much debated by scholars. Is he ridiculing a naïve trust in reason and presenting us with a horrible rationalistic utopia of horses, or is he rather showing us how little we really want to be reasonable and how easily we allow the glamour of our corruption to persuade us of its greatness (in contrast with its ugly enactment by the Yahoos)? However one resolves the questions, one can see why a modern critic (T. S. Eliot) refers to Swift's account of Gulliver's fourth voyage as one of the greatest triumphs of the human spirit.

From Travels into Several Remote Nations of the World

A Voyage to the Country of the Houyhnhnms

Chapter One: The author sets out as captain of a ship. His men conspire against him, confine him a long time to his cabin. Set him on shore in an unknown land. He travels up into the country. The Yahoos, a strange sort of animal, described. The author meets two Houyhnhnms.

I continued at home with my wife and children about five months in a very happy condition, if I could have learned the lesson of knowing when I was well. I left my poor wife big with child and accepted an advantageous offer made me to be captain of the *Adventure,* a stout merchantman of 350 tons: for I understood navigation well, and being grown weary of a surgeon's employment at sea, which however I could exercise upon occasion, I took a skilful young man of that calling, one Robert Purefoy, into my ship. We set sail for Portsmouth upon the 7th day of September, 1710; on the 14th, we met with Captain Pocock of Bristol, at Teneriffe,[1] who was going to the bay of Campechy, to cut logwood.[2] On the 16th, he was parted from us by a storm; I heard since my return that his ship foundered and none escaped but one cabin-boy. He was an honest man and a good sailor but a little too positive in his own opinions, which was the cause of his destruction, as it hath been of several others. For if he had followed my advice, he might at this time have been safe at home with his family as well as myself.

I had several men died in my ship of calentures,[3] so that I was forced to get recruits out of Barbadoes and the Leeward Islands,[4] where I touched by the direction of the merchants who employed me, which I had soon too much cause to repent; for I found afterwards that most of them had been buccaneers. I had fifty hands on board, and my orders were that I should trade with the Indians in the South Sea and make what discoveries I could. These rogues whom I had picked up debauched my other men, and they all formed a conspiracy to seize the ship and secure me; which they did one morning, rushing into my cabin and binding me hand and foot, threatening to throw me overboard if I offered to stir. I told them I was their prisoner and would submit. This they made me swear to do, and then unbound me, only fastening one of my legs with a chain near my bed, and placed a sentry at my door with his piece charged, who was commanded to shoot me dead if I attempted my liberty. They sent me down victuals and drink and took the government of the ship to themselves. Their design was to turn pirates and plunder the Spaniards, which they could not do till they got more men. But first they resolved to sell the goods in the ship and then go to Madagascar for recruits, several among them having died since my confinement. They sailed many weeks and traded with the Indians, but I knew not what course they took, being kept close prisoner

1. The largest of the Canary Islands.
2. On the Gulf of Mexico in Yucatán; a source of "campeachy wood," used for making dyes.
3. Tropical fevers.
4. In the West Indies.

in my cabin and expecting nothing less than to be murdered, as they often threatened me.

Upon the 9th day of May, 1711, one James Welch came down to my cabin and said he had orders from the captain to set me ashore. I expostulated with him, but in vain; neither would he so much as tell me who their new captain was. They forced me into the long-boat, letting me put on my best suit of clothes, which were as good as new, and a small bundle of linen, but no arms except my hanger;[5] and they were so civil as not to search my pockets, into which I conveyed what money I had, with some other little necessaries. They rowed about a league and then set me down on a strand. I desired them to tell me what country it was. They all swore they knew no more than myself, but said that the captain (as they called him) was resolved, after they had sold the lading,[6] to get rid of me in the first place where they discovered land. They pushed off immediately, advising me to make haste for fear of being overtaken by the tide, and bade me farewell.[7]

In this desolate condition I advanced forward and soon got upon firm ground, where I sat down on a bank to rest myself and consider what I had best to do. When I was a little refreshed I went up into the country, resolving to deliver myself to the first savages I should meet and purchase my life from them by some bracelets, glass rings, and other toys[8] which sailors usually provide themselves with in those voyages, and whereof I had some about me. The land was divided by long rows of trees, not regularly planted, but naturally growing; there was great plenty of grass, and several fields of oats. I walked very circumspectly for fear of being surprised or suddenly shot with an arrow from behind or on either side. I fell into a beaten road, where I saw many tracks of human feet, and some of cows, but most of horses.

At last I beheld several animals in a field, and one or two of the same kind sitting in trees. Their shape was very singular and deformed, which a little discomposed me, so that I lay down behind a thicket to observe them better. Some of them coming forward near the place where I lay, gave me an opportunity of distinctly marking their form. Their heads and breasts were covered with a thick hair, some frizzled and others lank; they had beards like goats, and a long ridge of hair down their backs and the foreparts of their legs and feet, but the rest of their bodies were bare, so that I might see their skins, which were of a brown buff colour. They had no tails, nor any hair at all on their buttocks, except about the anus; which, I presume, nature had placed there to defend them as they sat on the ground; for this posture they used, as well as lying down, and often stood on their hind feet. They climbed high trees as nimbly as a squirrel, for they had strong extended claws before and behind, terminating in sharp points, and hooked. They would often spring and bound and leap with prodigious agility. The females were not so large as the males; they had long lank hair on their heads, but none on their faces, nor

5. A short broad sword.
6. Cargo.
7. In his first voyage, Gulliver is shipwrecked in a storm; in his second, left behind by his shipmates; in the third, set adrift by pirates; in the fourth, abandoned by mutineers. There is clear progression from natural causes to deliberate evil.
8. Trinkets.

anything more than a sort of down on the rest of their bodies, except about the anus and pudenda. Their dugs hung between their fore-feet and often reached almost to the ground as they walked. The hair of both sexes was of several colours, brown, red, black, and yellow. Upon the whole, I never beheld in all my travels so disagreeable an animal or one against which I naturally conceived so strong an antipathy. So that thinking I had seen enough, full of contempt and aversion, I got up and pursued the beaten road, hoping it might direct me to the cabin of some Indian.

I had not gone far when I met one of these creatures full in my way and coming up directly to me. The ugly monster, when he saw me, distorted several ways every feature of his visage and stared as at an object he had never seen before; then approaching nearer, lifted up his forepaw, whether out of curiosity or mischief, I could not tell. But I drew my hanger and gave him a good blow with the flat side of it, for I durst not strike him with the edge, fearing the inhabitants might be provoked against me if they should come to know that I had killed or maimed any of their cattle. When the beast felt the smart, he drew back and roared so loud that a herd of at least forty came flocking about me from the next field, howling and making odious faces; but I ran to the body of a tree and, leaning my back against it, kept them off by waving my hanger. Several of this cursed brood, getting hold of the branches behind, leaped up into the tree, from whence they began to discharge their excrements on my head: however, I escaped pretty well by sticking close to the stem of the tree, but was almost stifled with the filth, which fell about me on every side.

In the midst of this distress, I observed them all to run away on a sudden as fast as they could, at which I ventured to leave the tree and pursue the road, wondering what it was that could put them into this fright. But looking on my left hand, I saw a horse walking softly in the field, which, my persecutors having sooner discovered, was the cause of their flight. The horse started a little when he came near me but, soon recovering himself, looked full in my face with manifest tokens of wonder: he viewed my hands and feet, walking round me several times. I would have pursued my journey, but he placed himself directly in the way, yet looking with a very mild aspect, never offering the least violence. We stood gazing at each other for some time; at last I took the boldness to reach my hand towards his neck with a design to stroke it, using the common style and whistle of jockeys when they are going to handle a strange horse. But this animal, seeming to receive my civilities with disdain, shook his head and bent his brows, softly raising up his left forefoot to remove my hand. Then he neighed three or four times, but in so different a cadence that I almost began to think he was speaking to himself in some language of his own.

While he and I were thus employed, another horse came up; who applying himself to [9] the first in a very formal manner, they gently struck each other's right hoof before, neighing several times by turns and varying the sound, which seemed to be almost articulate.[10] They went some paces off as if it were to confer together, walking side by side, backward and forward, like persons

9. Accosting, approaching.
10. Meaningful.

deliberating upon some affair of weight, but often turning their eyes towards me as it were to watch that I might not escape. I was amazed to see such actions and behaviour in brute beasts, and concluded with myself that, if the inhabitants of this country were endued with a proportionable degree of reason, they must needs be the wisest people upon earth. This thought gave me so much comfort that I resolved to go forward until I could discover some house or village or meet with any of the natives, leaving the two horses to discourse together as they pleased. But the first, who was a dapple grey, observing me to steal off, neighed after me in so expressive a tone that I fancied myself to understand what he meant; whereupon I turned back and came near him, to expect [11] his farther commands: but concealing my fear as much as I could, for I began to be in some pain how this adventure might terminate; and the reader will easily believe I did not much like my present situation.

The two horses came up close to me, looking with great earnestness upon my face and hands. The grey steed rubbed my hat all around with his right fore-hoof and discomposed it so much that I was forced to adjust it better by taking it off and settling it again; whereat both he and his companion (who was a brown bay) appeared to be much surprised. The latter felt the lappet [12] of my coat, and finding it to hang loose about me, they both looked with new signs of wonder. He stroked my right hand, seeming to admire [13] the softness and colour; but he squeezed it so hard between his hoof and his pastern [14] that I was forced to roar; after which they both touched me with all possible tenderness. They were under great perplexity about my shoes and stockings, which they felt very often, neighing to each other and using various gestures, not unlike those of a philosopher [15] when he would attempt to solve some new and difficult phenomenon.

Upon the whole, the behaviour of these animals was so orderly and rational, so acute and judicious, that I at last concluded they must needs be magicians who had thus metamorphosed themselves upon some design, and, seeing a stranger in the way, were resolved to divert themselves with him; or perhaps were really amazed at the sight of a man so very different in habit, feature, and complexion from those who might probably live in so remote a climate. Upon the strength of this reasoning, I ventured to address them in the following manner: 'Gentlemen, if you be conjurers, as I have good cause to believe, you can understand any language; therefore I make bold to let your Worships know that I am a poor distressed Englishman driven by his misfortunes upon your coast, and I entreat one of you to let me ride upon his back, as if he were a real horse, to some house or village where I can be relieved. In return of which favour, I will make you a present of this knife and bracelet' (taking them out of my pocket). The two creatures stood silent while I spoke, seeming to listen with great attention; and when I had ended they neighed frequently towards each other, as if they were engaged in serious conversation. I plainly observed that their language expressed the passions very well, and the words

11. Await.
12. Flap or lapel.
13. Wonder at.
14. The joint at the back of a horse's leg, just above the hoof.
15. That is, natural philosopher or scientist.

might with little pains be resolved into an alphabet more easily than the Chinese.

I could frequently distinguish the word *Yahoo*, which was repeated by each of them several times; and, although it was impossible for me to conjecture what it meant, yet while the two horses were busy in conversation I endeavoured to practice this word upon my tongue; and as soon as they were silent, I boldly pronounced *Yahoo* in a loud voice, imitating, at the same time, as near as I could, the neighing of a horse; at which they were both visibly surprised, and the grey repeated the same word twice, as if he meant to teach me the right accent, wherein I spoke after him as well as I could and found myself perceivably to improve every time, although very far from any degree of perfection. Then the bay tried me with a second word much harder to be pronounced; but reducing it to the English orthography, may be spelt thus, *Houyhnhnm*. I did not succeed in this so well as the former, but after two or three farther trials I had better fortune; and they both appeared amazed at my capacity.

After some farther discourse, which I then conjectured might relate to me, the two friends took their leaves, with the same compliment of striking each other's hoof; and the grey made me signs that I should walk before him, wherein I thought it prudent to comply till I could find a better director. When I offered to slacken my pace, he would cry *Hhuun, Hhuun;* I guessed his meaning and gave him to understand, as well as I could, that I was weary and not able to walk faster; upon which he would stand a while to let me rest.

Chapter Two: The author conducted by a Houyhnhnm to his house. The house described. The author's reception. The food of the Houyhnhnms. The author, in distress for want of meat, is at last relieved. His manner of feeding in that country.

Having travelled about three miles, we came to a long kind of building, made of timber stuck in the ground and wattled across;[1] the roof was low and covered with straw. I now began to be a little comforted and took out some toys which travellers usually carry for presents to the savage Indians of America and other parts, in hopes the people of the house would be thereby encouraged to receive me kindly. The horse made me a sign to go in first; it was a large room with a smooth clay floor and a rack and manger extending the whole length on one side. There were three nags and two mares, not eating, but some of them sitting down upon their hams, which I very much wondered at; but wondered more to see the rest employed in domestic business. The last seemed but ordinary cattle; however, this confirmed my first opinion, that a people who could so far civilize brute animals must needs excel in wisdom all the nations of the world. The grey came in just after and thereby prevented any ill treatment which the others might have given me. He neighed to them several times in a style of authority and received answers.

Beyond this room there were three others, reaching the length of the house, to which you passed through three doors, opposite to each other in the manner

---

1. Woven across with twigs or light branches.

of a vista.² We went through the second room towards the third; here the grey walked in first, beckoning me to attend. I waited in the second room and got ready my presents for the master and mistress of the house: they were two knives, three bracelets of false pearl, a small looking-glass, and a bead necklace. The horse neighed three or four times, and I waited to hear some answers in human voice; but I heard no other returns than in the same dialect, only one or two a little shriller than his. I began to think that this house must belong to some person of great note among them, because there appeared so much ceremony before I could gain admittance. But that a man of quality should be served all by horses was beyond my comprehension. I feared my brain was disturbed by my sufferings and misfortunes: I roused myself, and looked about me in the room where I was left alone; this was furnished as the first, only after a more elegant manner. I rubbed my eyes often, but the same objects still occurred. I pinched my arms and sides to awake myself, hoping I might be in a dream. I then absolutely concluded that all these appearances could be nothing else but necromancy ³ and magic. But I had no time to pursue these reflections; for the grey horse came to the door and made me a sign to follow him into the third room, where I saw a very comely mare, together with a colt and foal, sitting on their haunches, upon mats of straw not unartfully made and perfectly neat and clean.

The mare, soon after my entrance, rose from her mat, and coming up close, after having nicely ⁴ observed my hands and face, gave me a most contemptuous look; then turning to the horse, I heard the word *Yahoo* often repeated betwixt them; the meaning of which word I could not then comprehend, although it were the first I had learned to pronounce. But I was soon better informed, to my everlasting mortification: for the horse beckoning to me with his head, and repeating the word *Hhuun, Hhuun,* as he did upon the road, which I understood was to attend him, led me out into a kind of court, where was another building at some distance from the house. Here we entered, and I saw three of those detestable creatures which I first met after my landing, feeding upon roots and the flesh of some animals, which I afterwards found to be that of asses and dogs, and now and then a cow dead by accident or disease. They were all tied by the neck with strong withes ⁵ fastened to a beam; they held their food between the claws of their forefeet and tore it with their teeth.

The master horse ordered a sorrel nag, one of his servants, to untie the largest of these animals and take him into the yard. The beast and I were brought close together, and our countenances diligently compared both by master and servant, who thereupon repeated several times the word *Yahoo*. My horror and astonishment are not to be described when I observed, in this abominable animal, a perfect human figure. The face of it indeed was flat and broad, the nose depressed, the lips large, and the mouth wide. But these differences are common to all savage nations, where the lineaments of the countenance are distorted by the natives suffering their infants to lie grovelling on the earth, or by carrying them on their backs, nuzzling with their face

2. An opening that allows an extended view.
3. Enchantment.
4. Carefully.
5. Flexible willow branches.

against the mother's shoulders. The forefeet of the Yahoo differed from my hands in nothing else but the length of the nails, the coarseness and brownness of the palms, and the hairiness on the backs. There was the same resemblance between our feet, with the same differences, which I knew very well, although the horses did not, because of my shoes and stockings; the same in every part of our bodies, except as to hairiness and colour, which I have already described.

The great difficulty that seemed to stick with the two horses was to see the rest of my body so very different from that of a Yahoo; for which I was obliged to my clothes, whereof they had no conception. The sorrel nag offered me a root, which he held (after their manner, as we shall describe in its proper place) between his hoof and pastern.[6] I took it in my hand and, having smelt it, returned it to him as civilly as I could. He brought out of the Yahoo's kennel a piece of ass's flesh, but it smelt so offensively that I turned from it with loathing. He then threw it to the Yahoo, by whom it was greedily devoured. He afterwards showed me a wisp of hay and a fetlock full of oats; but I shook my head to signify that neither of these were food for me. And indeed, I now apprehended that I must absolutely starve if I did not get to some of my own species: for as to those filthy Yahoos, although there were few greater lovers of mankind, at that time, than myself, yet I confess I never saw any sensitive [7] being so detestable on all accounts; and the more I came near them, the more hateful they grew, while I stayed in that country. This the master horse observed by my behaviour, and therefore sent the Yahoo back to his kennel. He then put his fore-hoof to his mouth, at which I was much surprised, although he did it with ease and with a motion that appeared perfectly natural, and made other signs to know what I would eat; but I could not return him such an answer as he was able to apprehend; and if he had understood me, I did not see how it was possible to contrive any way for finding myself nourishment. While we were thus engaged, I observed a cow passing by, whereupon I pointed to her and expressed a desire to let me go and milk her. This had its effect; for he led me back into the house and ordered a mare-servant to open a room where a good store of milk lay in earthen and wooden vessels, after a very orderly and cleanly manner. She gave me a large bowl full, of which I drank very heartily, and found myself well refreshed.

About noon I saw coming towards the house a kind of vehicle drawn like a sledge by four Yahoos. There was in it an old steed, who seemed to be of quality; [8] he alighted with his hind feet forward, having by accident got a hurt in his left forefoot. He came to dine with our horse, who received him with great civility. They dined in the best room and had oats boiled in milk for the second course, which the old horse eat [9] warm, but the rest cold. Their mangers were placed circular in the middle of the room and divided into several partitions, round which they sat on their haunches upon bosses [10] of straw. In the middle was a large rack with angles answering to every partition of the manger. So that each horse and mare eat their own hay and their own mash of oats and milk, with much decency and regularity. The behaviour of the

6. The joint at the back of a horse's leg, just above the hoof.
7. With power of the senses.
8. High rank.
9. The normal past form, the counterpart of modern "ate" and pronounced "ett."
10. Hassocks.

young colt and foal appeared very modest, and that of the master and mistress extremely cheerful and complaisant [11] to their guest. The grey ordered me to stand by him, and much discourse passed between him and his friend concerning me, as I found by the stranger's often looking on me, and the frequent repetition of the word *Yahoo*.

I happened to wear my gloves, which the master grey observing, seemed perplexed, discovering signs of wonder what I had done to my forefeet. He put his hoof three or four times to them, as if he would signify that I should reduce them to their former shape, which I presently did, pulling off both my gloves and putting them into my pocket. This occasioned farther talk, and I saw the company was pleased with my behaviour, whereof I soon found the good effects. I was ordered to speak the few words I understood, and while they were at dinner, the master taught me the names for oats, milk, fire, water, and some others: which I could readily pronounce after him, having from my youth a great facility in learning languages.[12]

When dinner was done, the master horse took me aside, and by signs and words made me understand the concern he was in that I had nothing to eat. Oats in their tongue are called *hlunnh*. This word I pronounced two or three times; for although I had refused them at first, yet upon second thoughts, I considered that I could contrive to make of them a kind of bread, which might be sufficient with milk to keep me alive till I could make my escape to some other country and to creatures of my own species. The horse immediately ordered a white mare-servant of his family to bring me a good quantity of oats in a sort of wooden tray. These I heated before the fire as well as I could, and rubbed them till the husks came off, which I made a shift to winnow from the grain. I ground and beat them between two stones, then took water and made them into a paste or cake, which I toasted at the fire and eat warm with milk. It was at first a very insipid diet, although common enough in many parts of Europe, but grew tolerable by time; and having been often reduced to hard fare in my life, this was not the first experiment I had made how easily nature is satisfied. And I cannot but observe that I never had one hour's sickness while I stayed in this island. It is true, I sometimes made a shift to catch a rabbit or bird, by springes [13] made of Yahoos' hairs; and I often gathered wholesome herbs, which I boiled or eat as salads with my bread; and now and then, for a rarity, I made a little butter and drank the whey. I was at first at a great loss for salt; but custom soon reconciled the want of it; and I am confident that the frequent use of salt among us is an effect of luxury and was first introduced only as a provocative to drink; except where it is necessary for preserving of flesh in long voyages or in places remote from great markets. For we observe no animal to be fond of it but man: [14] and as to myself, when I left

---

11. Courteous.

12. Gulliver's facility with strange languages is part of his pattern of adaptability to external circumstances, but it is seldom accompanied by penetration into their moral implications.

13. Snares.

14. This error may be Swift's but is more likely a deliberate sign of Gulliver's unreliability in his enthusiasm for a simple "natural" life and a forecast of his soon-to-be-avowed adoration of the Houyhnhnms (Chapter 7).

this country, it was a great while before I could endure the taste of it in anything that I eat.

This is enough to say upon the subject of my diet, wherewith other travellers fill their books, as if the readers were personally concerned whether we fare well or ill.[15] However, it was necessary to mention this matter lest the world should think it impossible that I could find sustenance for three years in such a country and among such inhabitants.

When it grew towards evening, the master horse ordered a place for me to lodge in; it was but six yards from the house, and separated from the stable of the Yahoos. Here I got some straw and, covering myself with my own clothes, slept very sound. But I was in a short time better accommodated, as the reader shall know hereafter, when I come to treat more particularly about my way of living.

Chapter Three: The author studious to learn the language, the Houyhnhnm his master assists in teaching him. The language described. Several Houyhnhnms of quality come out of curiosity to see the author. He gives his master a short account of his voyage.

My principal endeavour was to learn the language, which my master (for so I shall henceforth call him) and his children, and every servant of his house, were desirous to teach me. For they looked upon it as a prodigy that a brute animal should discover such marks of a rational creature. I pointed to everything and inquired the name of it, which I wrote down in my journal-book when I was alone, and corrected my bad accent by desiring those of the family to pronounce it often. In this employment a sorrel nag, one of the underservants, was very ready to assist me.

In speaking, they pronounce through the nose and throat; and their language approaches nearest to the High Dutch or German of any I know in Europe, but is much more graceful and significant. The Emperor Charles V made almost the same observation when he said that, if he were to speak to his horse, it should be in High Dutch.[1]

The curiosity and impatience of my master were so great that he spent many hours of his leisure to instruct me. He was convinced (as he afterwards told me) that I must be a Yahoo, but my teachableness, civility, and cleanliness astonished him, which were qualities altogether so opposite to those animals. He was most perplexed about my clothes, reasoning sometimes with himself whether they were a part of my body; for I never pulled them off till the family were asleep and got them on before they waked in the morning. My master was eager to learn from whence I came, how I acquired those appearances of reason which I discovered in all my actions, and to know my story from my own mouth, which he hoped he should soon do by the great proficiency I made in learning and pronouncing their words and sentences. To help

15. If there is a greater and more frequent fault than this self-importance in travel books, it is the needless putting down of other writers; Swift's book is, whatever else, in part a satire upon the form.

1. Charles V (1500–1558), King of Spain and ruler of the Holy Roman Empire, is reported to have said that he would address his God in Spanish, his mistress in Italian, and his horse in German.

my memory, I formed all I learned into the English alphabet and writ the words down with the translations. This last, after some time, I ventured to do in my master's presence. It cost me much trouble to explain to him what I was doing; for the inhabitants have not the least idea of books or literature.[2]

In about ten weeks time I was able to understand most of his questions, and in three months could give him some tolerable answers. He was extremely curious to know from what part of the country I came and how I was taught to imitate a rational creature, because the Yahoos (whom he saw I exactly resembled in my head, hands, and face, that were only visible), with some appearance of cunning and the strongest disposition to mischief, were observed to be the most unteachable of all brutes. I answered that I came over the sea from a far place, with many others of my own kind, in a great hollow vessel made of the bodies of trees; that my companions forced me to land on this coast and then left me to shift for myself. It was with some difficulty and by the help of many signs that I brought him to understand me. He replied that I must needs be mistaken, or that I 'said the thing which was not.' (For they have no words in their language to express lying or falsehood.) He knew it was impossible that there could be a country beyond the sea, or that a parcel of brutes could move a wooden vessel whither they pleased upon water. He was sure no Houyhnhnm alive could make such a vessel, or would trust Yahoos to manage it.

The word *Houyhnhnm*, in their tongue, signifies a *horse*, and in its etymology, *the Perfection of Nature*.[3] I told my master, that I was at a loss for expression but would improve as fast as I could; and hoped in a short time I should be able to tell him wonders. He was pleased to direct his own mare, his colt and foal, and the servants of the family to take all opportunities of instructing me, and every day for two or three hours he was at the same pains himself. Several horses and mares of quality in the neighbourhood came often to our house upon the report spread of a wonderful Yahoo that could speak like a Houyhnhnm and seemed in his words and actions to discover some glimmerings of reason. These delighted to converse with me; they put many questions and received such answers as I was able to return. By all which advantages I made so great a progress that in five months from my arrival I understood whatever was spoke and could express myself tolerably well.

The Houyhnhnms who came to visit my master out of a design of seeing and talking with me could hardly believe me to be a right[4] Yahoo, because my body had a different covering from others of my kind. They were astonished to observe me without the usual hair or skin except on my head, face, and hands; but I discovered that secret to my master, upon an accident which happened about a fortnight before.

I have already told the reader that every night, when the family were gone to bed, it was my custom to strip and cover myself with clothes. It happened

2. In the more limited sense of writing, for they have some poetic and rhetorical powers.
3. That is, as the culmination and master of all natural life, as man has traditionally regarded himself; unlike man, they have no conception of anything supernatural or of a deity other than Nature itself, nor do they have any experience of a "fallen" Nature (except in the Yahoos).
4. True, genuine.

one morning early that my master sent for me by the sorrel nag, who was his valet. When he came, I was fast asleep, my clothes fallen off on one side and my shirt above my waist. I awaked at the noise he made and observed him to deliver his message in some disorder; after which he went to my master and in a great fright gave him a very confused account of what he had seen. This I presently discovered; for going, as soon as I was dressed, to pay my attendance upon his Honour, he asked me the meaning of what his servant had reported, that I was not the same thing when I slept as I appeared to be at other times; that his valet assured him some part of me was white, some yellow, at least not so white, and some brown.

I had hitherto concealed the secret of my dress in order to distinguish myself as much as possible from that cursed race of Yahoos; but now I found it in vain to do so any longer. Besides, I considered that my clothes and shoes would soon wear out, which already were in a declining condition, and must be supplied by some contrivance from the hides of Yahoos or other brutes; whereby the whole secret would be known. I therefore told my master that, in the country from whence I came, those of my kind always covered their bodies with the hairs of certain animals prepared by art, as well for decency as to avoid inclemencies of air both hot and cold; of which, as to my own person, I would give him immediate conviction if he pleased to command me, only desiring his excuse if I did not expose those parts that nature taught us to conceal. He said my discourse was all very strange, but especially the last part; for he could not understand why nature should teach us to conceal what nature had given. That neither himself nor family were ashamed of any parts of their bodies; but however I might do as I pleased. Whereupon, I first unbuttoned my coat and pulled it off. I did the same with my waistcoat; I drew off my shoes, stockings, and breeches. I let my shirt down to my waist and drew up the bottom, fastening it like a girdle about my middle to hide my nakedness.

My master observed the whole performance with great signs of curiosity and admiration. He took up all my clothes in his pastern, one piece after another, and examined them diligently. He then stroked my body very gently and looked around me several times, after which he said it was plain I must be a perfect Yahoo; but that I differed very much from the rest of my species in the whiteness and smoothness of my skin, my want of hair in several parts of my body, the shape and shortness of my claws behind and before, and my affectation of walking continually on my two hinder feet. He desired to see no more and gave me leave to put on my clothes again, for I was shuddering with cold.

I expressed my uneasiness at his giving me so often the appellation of *Yahoo*, an odious animal for which I had so utter an hatred and contempt. I begged he would forbear applying that word to me and take the same order in his family and among his friends whom he suffered to see me. I requested likewise that the secret of my having a false covering to my body might be known to none but himself, at least as long as my present clothing should last; for as to what the sorrel nag his valet had observed, his Honour might command him to conceal it.

All this my master very graciously consented to, and thus the secret was kept till my clothes began to wear out, which I was forced to supply by several contrivances that shall hereafter be mentioned. In the meantime he desired I would go on with my utmost diligence to learn their language, because he was more astonished at my capacity for speech and reason than at the figure of my body, whether it were covered or no; adding that he waited with some impatience to hear the wonders which I promised to tell him.

From thenceforward he doubled the pains he had been at to instruct me. He brought me into all company and made them treat me with civility, because, as he told them privately, this would put me into good humour and make me more diverting.

Every day when I waited on him, beside the trouble he was at in teaching, he would ask me several questions concerning myself, which I answered as well as I could; and by those means he had already received some general ideas, although very imperfect. It would be tedious to relate the several steps by which I advanced to a more regular conversation: but the first account I gave of myself in any order and length was to this purpose:

That I came from a very far country, as I already had attempted to tell him, with about fifty more of my own species; that we travelled upon the seas in a great hollow vessel made of wood and larger than his Honour's house. I described the ship to him in the best terms I could and explained by the help of my handkerchief displayed how it was driven forward by the wind; that upon a quarrel among us, I was set on shore on this coast, where I walked forward without knowing whither, till he delivered me from the persecution of those execrable Yahoos. He asked me who made the ship, and how it was possible that the Houyhnhnms of my country would leave it to the management of brutes? My answer was that I durst proceed no farther in my relation unless he would give me his word and honour that he would not be offended, and then I would tell him the wonders I had so often promised. He agreed; and I went on by assuring him that the ship was made by creatures like myself, who in all the countries I had travelled, as well as in my own, were the only governing, rational animals; and that upon my arrival hither I was as much astonished to see the Houyhnhnms act like rational beings as he or his friends could be in finding some marks of reason in a creature he was pleased to call a Yahoo, to which I owned my resemblance in every part, but could not account for their degenerate and brutal nature. I said farther, that if good fortune ever restored me to my native country to relate my travels hither, as I resolved to do, everybody would believe that I 'said the thing which was not'; that I invented the story out of my own head; and with all possible respect to himself, his family, and friends, and under his promise of not being offended, our countrymen would hardly think it probable that a Houyhnhnm should be the presiding creature of a nation and a Yahoo the brute.

Chapter Four: The Houyhnhnms' notion of truth and falsehood. The author's discourse disapproved by his master. The author gives a more particular account of himself and the accidents of his voyage.

My master heard me with great appearances of uneasiness in his countenance, because *doubting* or *not believing* are so little known in this country that the inhabitants cannot tell how to behave themselves under such circumstances.

And I remember, in frequent discourses with my master concerning the nature of manhood in other parts of the world, having occasion to talk of *lying* and *false representation*, it was with much difficulty that he comprehended what I meant, although he had otherwise a most acute judgment. For he argued thus: that the use of speech was to make us understand one another and to receive information of facts; now if any one *said the thing which was not,* these ends were defeated; because I cannot properly be said to understand him, and I am so far from receiving information that he leaves me worse than in ignorance, for I am led to believe a thing *black* when it is *white* and *short* when it is *long.* And these were all the notions he had concerning that faculty of *lying,* so perfectly well understood and so universally practised among human creatures.

To return from this digression, when I asserted that the Yahoos were the only governing animals in my country, which my master said was altogether past his conception, he desired to know whether we had Houyhnhnms among us and what was their employment. I told him, we had great numbers, that in summer they grazed in the fields and in winter were kept in houses with hay and oats, where Yahoo servants were employed to rub their skins smooth, comb their manes, pick their feet, serve them with food, and make their beds. 'I understand you well,' said my master, 'it is now very plain from all you have spoken that, whatever share of reason the Yahoos pretend to, the Houyhnhnms are your masters. I heartily wish our Yahoos would be so tractable.' I begged his Honour would please to excuse me from proceeding any farther, because I was very certain that the account he expected from me would be highly displeasing. But he insisted in commanding me to let him know the best and the worst. I told him he should be obeyed. I owned that the Houyhnhnms among us, whom we called horses,[1] were the most generous [2] and comely animal we had, that they excelled in strength and swiftness; and when they belonged to persons of quality, employed in travelling, racing, and drawing chariots, they were treated with much kindness and care, till they fell into diseases or became foundered in the feet; but then they were sold and used to all kind of drudgery till they died; after which their skins were stripped and sold for what they were worth, and their bodies left to be devoured by dogs and birds of prey.[3] But the common race of horses had not so good fortune, being kept by farmers and carriers and other mean people, who put them to greater labour and feed them worse. I described, as well as I could, our way of riding, the shape and use of a bridle, a saddle, a spur, and a whip, of harness and wheels. I added, that we fastened plates of a certain hard substance called *iron* at the bottom of their feet, to preserve their hoofs from being broken by the stony ways on which we often travelled.

My master, after some expressions of great indignation, wondered how we dared to venture upon a Houyhnhnm's back, for he was sure that the weakest servant in his house would be able to shake off the strongest Yahoo, or by lying down and rolling upon his back squeeze the brute to death. I answered that

1. Gulliver collapses the distinction between horses and Houyhnhnms, as he has between men and Yahoos, placing external resemblances above the differences of inner capacity.
2. Noble.
3. Ironically echoing the phrase Homer applies to unburied warriors.

our horses were trained up from three or four years old to the several uses we intended them for; that if any of them proved intolerably vicious, they were employed for carriages; that they were severely beaten while they were young for any mischievous tricks; that the males, designed for the common use of riding or draught, were generally castrated about two years after their birth to take down their spirits and make them more tame and gentle; that they were indeed sensible of [4] rewards and punishments; but his Honour would please to consider that they had not the least tincture of reason any more than the Yahoos in this country.

It put me to the pains of many circumlocutions to give my master a right idea of what I spoke; for their language doth not abound in variety of words, because their wants and passions are fewer than among us. But it is impossible to express his noble resentment at our savage treatment of the Houyhnhnm race, particularly after I had explained the manner and use of castrating horses among us to hinder them from propagating their kind and to render them more servile. He said, if it were possible there could be any country where Yahoos alone were endued with reason, they certainly must be the governing animal, because reason will in time always prevail against brutal strength. But, considering the frame of our bodies, and especially of mine, he thought no creature of equal bulk was so ill contrived for employing that reason in the common offices of life; whereupon he desired to know whether those among whom I lived resembled me or the Yahoos of his country.

I assured him that I was as well shaped as most of my age: but the younger and the females were much more soft and tender, and the skins of the latter generally as white as milk. He said I differed indeed from other Yahoos, being much more cleanly and not altogether so deformed; but in point of real advantage he thought I differed for the worse. That my nails were of no use either to my fore or hinder feet; as to my forefeet, he could not properly call them by that name, for he never observed me to walk upon them; that they were too soft to bear the ground; that I generally went with them uncovered, neither was the covering I sometimes wore on them of the same shape or so strong as that on my feet behind. That I could not walk with any security, for if either of my hinder feet slipped, I must inevitably fall. He then began to find fault with other parts of my body, the flatness of my face, the prominence of my nose, my eyes placed directly in front, so that I could not look on either side without turning my head: that I was not able to feed myself without lifting one of my forefeet to my mouth: and therefore nature had placed those joints to answer that necessity. He knew not what could be the use of those several clefts and divisions in my feet behind; that these were too soft to bear the hardness and sharpness of stones without a covering made from the skin of some other brute; that my whole body wanted a fence against heat and cold, which I was forced to put on and off every day with tediousness and trouble. And lastly that he observed every animal in this country naturally to abhor the Yahoos, whom the weaker avoided and the stronger drove from them. So that supposing us to have the gift of reason, he could not see how it were possible to cure that natural antipathy which every creature discovered [5] against us; nor

4. Responsive to.
5. Revealed.

consequently how we could tame and render them serviceable. However, he would (as he said) debate the matter no farther, because he was more desirous to know my own story, the country where I was born, and the several actions and events of my life before I came hither.

I assured him how extremely desirous I was that he should be satisfied in every point; but I doubted much whether it would be possible for me to explain myself on several subjects whereof his Honour could have no conception, because I saw nothing in his country to which I could resemble [6] them. That, however, I would do my best and strive to express myself by similitudes, humbly, desiring his assistance when I wanted proper words, which he was pleased to promise me.

I said my birth was of honest parents, in an island called England, which was remote from this country as many days' journey as the strongest of his Honour's servants could travel in the annual course of the sun. That I was bred a surgeon, whose trade it is to cure wounds and hurts in the body got by accident or violence; that my country was governed by a female man, whom we called a *queen*.[7] That I left it to get riches, whereby I might maintain myself and family when I should return. That in my last voyage I was commander of the ship, and had about fifty Yahoos under me, many of which died at sea, and I was forced to supply them by others picked out from several nations. That our ship was twice in danger of being sunk; the first time by a great storm and the second by striking against a rock. Here my master interposed by asking me how I could persuade strangers out of different countries to venture with me after the losses I had sustained and the hazards I had run. I said they were fellows of desperate fortunes, forced to fly from the places of their birth on account of their poverty or their crimes. Some were undone by lawsuits; others spent all they had in drinking, whoring, and gaming; others fled for treason; many for murder, theft, poisoning, robbery, perjury, forgery, coining false money, for committing rapes or sodomy, for flying from their colours or deserting to the enemy, and most of them had broken prison. None of these durst return to their native countries for fear of being hanged or of starving in a jail; and therefore were under a necessity of seeking a livelihood in other places.

During this discourse, my master was pleased often to interrupt me; I had made use of many circumlocutions in describing to him the nature of the several crimes for which most of our crew had been forced to fly their country. This labour took up several days' conversation before he was able to comprehend me. He was wholly at a loss to know what could be the use or necessity of practising those vices. To clear up which I endeavoured to give him some ideas of the desire of power and riches; of the terrible effects of lust, intemperance, malice, and envy. All this I was forced to define and describe by putting of cases and making suppositions. After which, like one whose imagination was struck with something never seen or heard of before, he would lift up his eyes with amazement and indignation. Power, government, war, law, punishment, and a thousand other things had no terms wherein that language could express them, which made the difficulty almost insuperable to

6. Compare.
7. Queen Anne, who ruled from 1702 to 1714.

give my master any conception of what I meant. But being of an excellent understanding, much improved by contemplation and converse, he at last arrived at a competent knowledge of what human nature in our parts of the world is capable to perform, and desired I would give him some particular account of that land which we call Europe, especially of my own country.

Chapter Five: The author at his master's command informs him of the state of England. The causes of war among the princes of Europe. The author begins to explain the English constitution.

The reader may please to observe, that the following extract of many conversations I had with my master contains a summary of the most material points which were discoursed at several times for above two years; his Honour often desiring fuller satisfaction as I farther improved in the Houyhnhnm tongue. I laid before him, as well as I could, the whole state of Europe; I discoursed of trade and manufactures, of arts and sciences; and the answers I gave to all the questions he made, as they arose upon several subjects, were a fund of conversation not to be exhausted. But I shall here only set down the substance of what passed between us concerning my own country, reducing it into order as well as I can, without any regard to time or other circumstances, while I strictly adhere to truth. My only concern is that I shall hardly be able to do justice to my master's arguments and expressions, which must needs suffer by any want of capacity, as well as by a translation into our barbarous English.[1]

In obedience therefore to his Honour's commands, I related to him the Revolution under the Prince of Orange; the long war with France entered into by the said prince and renewed by his successor the present queen, wherein the greatest powers of Christendom were engaged, and which still continued.[2] I computed, at his request, that about a million of Yahoos might have been killed in the whole progress of it, and perhaps a hundred or more cities taken, and five times as many ships burnt or sunk.

He asked me what were the usual causes or motives that made one country go to war with another. I answered they were innumerable, but I should only mention a few of the chief: sometimes the ambition of princes, who never think they have land or people enough to govern: sometimes the corruption of ministers, who engage their master in a war in order to stifle or divert the clamour of the subjects against their evil administration. Difference in opinions[3] hath cost many millions of lives: for instance, whether *flesh* be

1. Gulliver's first overt revulsion from European culture.
2. William of Orange (1605–1702) succeeded James II as William III of England in the Glorious Revolution of 1688. He fought against France until 1697, when Louis XIV acknowledged his claim to the English throne, but resumed the war in 1701, when Louis gave his recognition to James's heir, the Stuart Pretender. Anne (1665–1714) carried on the War of the Spanish Succession, which ended in 1713, while Gulliver was still among the Houyhnhnms.
3. Alluding to such doctrinal quarrels among the churches as that of transubstantiation (whether the body and blood of Christ are really or only symbolically present in the Eucharistic bread and wine), the use of music in worship (offensive to some radical Protestants), the veneration of an image or crucifix (condemned by Calvinists), and the proper form of church vestments.

bread or *bread* be *flesh;* whether the juice of a certain *berry* be *blood* or *wine;* whether *whistling* be a vice or a virtue; whether it be better to *kiss a post* or throw it into the fire; what is the best colour for a *coat,* whether *black, white, red,* or *grey;* and whether it should be *long* or *short, narrow* or *wide, dirty* or *clean,* with many more. Neither are any wars so furious and bloody or of so long continuance as those occasioned by difference in opinion, especially if it be in things indifferent.[4]

Sometimes the quarrel between two princes is to decide which of them shall dispossess a third of his dominions, where neither of them pretend to any right. Sometimes one prince quarrelleth with another for fear the other should quarrel with him. Sometimes a war is entered upon because the enemy is too *strong,* and sometimes because he is too *weak.* Sometimes our neighbours *want* the things which we *have,* or *have* the things which we *want;* and we both fight till they take ours or give us theirs. It is a very justifiable cause of war to invade a country after the people have been wasted by famine, destroyed by pestilence, or embroiled by factions amongst themselves. It is justifiable to enter into a war against our nearest ally when one of his towns lies convenient for us, or a territory of land that would render our dominions round and compact. If a prince send forces into a nation where the people are poor and ignorant, he may lawfully put half of them to death and make slaves of the rest, in order to civilize and reduce them from their barbarous way of living. It is a very kingly, honourable, and frequent practice, when one prince desires the assistance of another to secure him against an invasion, that the assistant, when he hath driven out the invader, should seize on the dominions himself, and kill, imprison, or banish the prince he came to relieve. Alliance by blood or marriage is a sufficient cause of war between princes, and, the nearer the kindred is, the greater is their disposition to quarrel: *poor* nations are *hungry* and *rich* nations are *proud,* and pride and hunger will ever be at variance. For these reasons, the trade of a soldier is held the most honourable of all others: because a soldier is a Yahoo hired to kill in cold blood as many of his own species, who have never offended him, as possibly he can.

There is likewise a kind of beggarly princes in Europe, not able to make war by themselves, who hire out their troops to richer nations, for so much a day to each man; of which they keep three-fourths to themselves, and it is the best part of their maintenance; such are those in Germany and many northern parts of Europe.[5]

What you have told me (said my master) upon the subject of war does indeed discover most admirably the effects of that reason you pretend to: however, it is happy that the *shame* is greater than the *danger,* and that nature hath left you utterly uncapable of doing much mischief. For your mouths lying flat with your faces, you can hardly bite each other to any purpose unless by consent. Then as to the claws upon your feet before and behind, they are so short and tender that one of our Yahoos would drive a dozen of yours

4. Matters not essential to belief; technically, upon which the church has not chosen to give a decision.
5. George I of England, who ruled from 1714 to 1727, had supplied mercenaries to other nations while still Elector of Hanover.

before him. And therefore in recounting the numbers of those who have been killed in battle, I cannot but think that you have *said the thing which is not.*

I could not forbear shaking my head and smiling a little at his ignorance. And being no stranger to the art of war, I gave him a description of cannons, culverins,[6] muskets, carabines,[7] pistols, bullets, powder, swords, bayonets, battles, sieges, retreats, attacks, undermines, countermines,[8] bombardments, sea-fights; ships sunk with a thousand men; twenty thousand killed on each side; dying groans, limbs flying in the air, smoke, noise, confusion, trampling to death under horses' feet; flight, pursuit, victory; fields strewed with carcasses left for food to dogs and wolves and birds of prey; plundering, stripping, ravishing, burning, and destroying. And to set forth the valour of my own dear countrymen, I assured him, that I had seen them blow up a hundred enemies at once in a siege, and as many in a ship, and beheld the dead bodies drop down in pieces from the clouds, to the great diversion of all the spectators.

I was going on to more particulars when my master commanded me silence. He said whoever understood the nature of Yahoos might easily believe it possible for so vile an animal to be capable of every action I had named, if their strength and cunning equalled their malice. But as my discourse had increased his abhorrence of the whole species, so he found it gave him a disturbance in his mind to which he was wholly a stranger before. He thought his ears being used to such abominable words might by degrees admit them with less detestation. That although he hated the Yahoos of this country, yet he no more blamed them for their odious qualities than he did a *gnnayh* (a bird of prey) for its cruelty or a sharp stone for cutting his hoof. But when a creature pretending to reason could be capable of such enormities, he dreaded lest the corruption of that faculty might be worse than brutality [9] itself. He seemed therefore confident that, instead of reason, we were only possessed of some quality fitted to increase our natural vices; as the reflection from a troubled stream returns the image of an ill-shapen body not only *larger* but more *distorted.*

He added that he had heard too much upon the subject of war both in this and some former discourses. There was another point which a little perplexed him at present. I had said, that some of our crew left their country on account of being ruined by *law;* that I had already explained the meaning of the word; but he was at loss how it should come to pass that the *law,* which was intended for every man's preservation, should be any man's ruin. Therefore he desired to be farther satisfied what I meant by law, and the dispensers thereof according to the present practice in my own country; because he thought nature and reason were sufficient guides for a reasonable animal, as we pretended to be, in showing us what we ought to do and what to avoid.

I assured his Honour that law was a science wherein I had not much conversed further than by employing advocates, in vain, upon some injustices that had been done me. However, I would give him all the satisfaction I was able.

6. Very long cannons.
7. Carbines, firearms used by the cavalry.
8. Excavations made under the walls of a fortress and those made as a defensive countermeasure.
9. That is, brute insensibility.

I said there was a society of men among us bred up from their youth in the art of proving by words multiplied for the purpose, that white is black and black is white, according as they are paid. To this society all the rest of the people are slaves.

For example, if my neighbour hath a mind to my cow, he hires a lawyer to prove that he ought to have my cow from me. I must then hire another to defend my right, it being against all rules of law that any man should be allowed to speak for himself. Now in this case, I who am the true owner lie under two great disadvantages. First, my lawyer, being practised almost from his cradle in defending falsehood, is quite out of his element when he would be an advocate for justice, which as an office unnatural he always attempts with great awkwardness, if not with ill will. The second disadvantage is, that my lawyer must proceed with great caution, or else he will be reprimanded by the judges, and abhorred by his brethren, as one that would lessen the practice of the law. And therefore I have but two methods to preserve my cow. The first is to gain over my adversary's lawyer with a double fee, who will then betray his client by insinuating that he hath justice on his side. The second way is for my lawyer to make my cause appear as unjust as he can, by allowing the cow to belong to my adversary; and this if it be skilfully done will certainly bespeak the favour of the bench.

Now, your Honour is to know that these judges are persons appointed to decide all controversies of property as well as for the trial of criminals, and picked out from the most dextrous lawyers who are grown old or lazy and, having been biassed all their lives against truth and equity, lie under such a fatal necessity of favouring fraud, perjury, and oppression, that I have known some of them to have refused a large bribe from the side where justice lay, rather than injure the faculty [10] by doing anything unbecoming their nature or their office.

It is a maxim among these lawyers that whatever hath been done before may legally be done again: and therefore they take special care to record all the decisions formerly made against common justice and the general reason of mankind. These, under the name of *precedents*, they produce as authorities to justify the most iniquitous opinions; and the judges never fail of decreeing accordingly.

In pleading, they studiously avoid entering into the merits of the cause, but are loud, violent, and tedious in dwelling upon all circumstances which are not to the purpose. For instance, in the case already mentioned; they never desire to know what claim or title my adversary hath to my cow, but whether the said cow were red or black, her horns long or short; whether the field I graze her in be round or square, whether she were milked at home or abroad, what diseases she is subject to, and the like; after which they consult precedents, adjourn the cause from time to time, and in ten, twenty, or thirty years come to an issue. [11]

It is likewise to be observed that this society hath a peculiar cant and jargon of their own that no other mortal can understand and wherein all their laws are written, which they take special care to multiply; whereby they have

10. Profession.
11. Decision, result.

wholly confounded the very essence of truth and falsehood, of right and wrong; so that it will take thirty years to decide whether the field left me by my ancestors for six generations belongs to me or to a stranger three hundred miles off.

In the trial of persons accused for crimes against the state the method is much more short and commendable: the judge first sends to sound the disposition of those in power, after which he can easily hang or save the criminal, strictly preserving all due forms of law.

Here my master, interposing, said it was a pity that creatures endowed with such prodigious abilities of mind as these lawyers, by the description I gave of them, must certainly be, were not rather encouraged to be instructors of others in wisdom and knowledge. In answer to which I assured his Honour that in all points out of their own trade they were usually the most ignorant and stupid generation [12] among us, the most despicable in common conversation, avowed enemies to all knowledge and learning, and equally disposed to pervert the general reason of mankind in every other subject of discourse as in that of their own profession.

Chapter Six: A continuation of the state of England. The character of a first minister.

My master was yet wholly at a loss to understand what motives could incite this race of lawyers to perplex, disquiet, and weary themselves by engaging in a confederacy of injustice, merely for the sake of injuring their fellow-animals; neither could he comprehend what I meant in saying they did it for hire. Whereupon I was at much pains to describe to him the use of money, the materials it was made of, and the value of the metals; that when a Yahoo had got a great store of this precious substance, he was able to purchase whatever he had a mind to, the finest clothing, the noblest houses, great tracts of land, the most costly meats and drinks, and have his choice of the most beautiful females. Therefore since money alone was able to perform all these feats, our Yahoos thought they could never have enough of it to spend or to save, as they found themselves inclined from their natural bent either to profusion or avarice. That the rich man enjoyed the fruit of the poor man's labour, and the latter were a thousand to one in proportion to the former. That the bulk of our people was forced to live miserably, by labouring every day for small wages to make a few live plentifully.

I enlarged myself much on these and many other particulars to the same purpose: but his Honour was still to seek; [1] for he went upon a supposition that all animals had a title to their share in the productions of the earth, and especially those who presided over the rest. Therefore he desired I would let him know what these costly meats were, and how any of us happened to want [2] them. Whereupon I enumerated as many sorts as came into my head, with the various methods of dressing them, which could not be done without sending vessels by sea to every part of the world, as well for liquors to drink

12. Breed.

1. At a loss to understand.
2. Lack.

as for sauces and innumerable other conveniencies. I assured him that this whole globe of earth must be at least three times gone round before one of our better female Yahoos could get her breakfast or a cup to put it in. He said that must needs be a miserable country which cannot furnish food for its own inhabitants.

But what he chiefly wondered at was how such vast tracts of ground as I described should be wholly without fresh water, and the people put to the necessity of sending over the sea for drink. I replied that England (the dear place of my nativity) was computed to produce three times the quantity of food more than its inhabitants are able to consume, as well as liquors extracted from grain or pressed out of the fruit of certain trees, which made excellent drink, and the same proportion in every other convenience of life. But in order to feed the luxury and intemperance of the males and the vanity of the females, we sent away the greatest part of our necessary things to other countries, from whence in return we brought the materials of diseases, folly, and vice, to spend among ourselves. Hence it follows of necessity that vast numbers of our people are compelled to seek their livelihood by begging, robbing, stealing, cheating, pimping, forswearing, flattering, suborning, forging, gaming, lying, fawning, hectoring, voting, scribbling, star-gazing, poisoning, whoring, canting, libelling, free-thinking, and the like occupations: every one of which terms I was at much pains to make him understand.

That wine was not imported among us from foreign countries to supply the want of water or other drinks, but because it was a sort of liquid which made us merry by putting us out of our senses; diverted all melancholy thoughts, begat wild extravagant imaginations in the brain, raised our hopes, and banished our fears, suspended every office of reason for a time, and deprived us of the use of our limbs, until we fell into a profound sleep; although it must be confessed that we always awaked sick and dispirited, and that the use of this liquor filled us with diseases which made our lives uncomfortable and short.

But beside all this, the bulk of our people supported themselves by furnishing the necessities or conveniences of life to the rich and to each other. For instance, when I am at home and dressed as I ought to be, I carry on my body the workmanship of an hundred tradesmen; the building and furniture of my house employ as many more, and five times the number to adorn my wife.

I was going on to tell him of another sort of people who get their livelihood by attending the sick, having upon some occasions informed his Honour that many of my crew had died of diseases. But here it was with the utmost difficulty that I brought him to apprehend what I meant. He could easily conceive that a Houyhnhnm grew weak and heavy a few days before his death, or by some accident might hurt a limb. But that nature, who works all things to perfection, should suffer any pains to breed in our bodies, he thought impossible, and desired to know the reason of so unaccountable an evil. I told him we fed on a thousand things which operated contrary to each other; that we eat when we were not hungry and drank without the provocation of thirst; that we sat whole nights drinking strong liquors without eating a bit, which disposed us to sloth, enflamed our bodies, and precipitated or prevented digestion. That prostitute female Yahoos acquired a certain malady which bred rottenness in the bones of those who fell into their embraces; that this and many other diseases were propagated from father to son, so that great numbers come into the world with complicated maladies upon them. That it would be endless to give him a catalogue of all diseases incident to human bodies; for they could not be fewer than five or six hundred, spread over every limb and joint; in short, every part, external and intestine, having diseases appropriated to each. To remedy which, there was a sort of people bred up among us in the profession or pretence of curing the sick. And because I had some skill in the faculty, I would, in gratitude to his Honour, let him know the whole mystery[3] and method by which they proceed.

Their fundamental is that all diseases arise from repletion, from whence they conclude that a great evacuation of the body is necessary, either through the natural passage or upwards at the mouth. Their next business is, from herbs, minerals, gums, oils, shells, salts, juices, seaweed, excrements, barks of trees, serpents, toads, frogs, spiders, dead men's flesh and bones, birds, beasts, and fishes, to form a composition for smell and taste the most abominable, nauseous, and detestable that they can possibly contrive, which the stomach immediately rejects with loathing, and this they call a vomit; or else from the same storehouse, with some other poisonous additions, they command us to take in at the orifice above or below (just as the physician then happens to be disposed) a medicine equally annoying and disgustful to the bowels, which, relaxing the belly, drives down all before it, and this they call a purge or a clyster.[4] For nature (as the physicians allege) having intended the superior anterior orifice only for the intromission of solids and liquids and the inferior posterior for ejection, these artists, ingeniously considering that in all diseases nature is forced out of her seat, therefore to replace her in it, the body must be treated in a manner directly contrary, by interchanging the use of each orifice, forcing solids and liquids in at the anus and making evacuations at the mouth.

But besides real diseases we are subject to many that are only imaginary, for which the physicians have invented imaginary cures; these have their several names, and so have the drugs that are proper for them, and with these our female Yahoos are always infested.

One great excellency in this tribe is their skill at prognostics, wherein they seldom fail; their predictions in real diseases, when they rise to any degree of malignity, generally portending death, which is always in their power when recovery is not: and therefore, upon any unexpected signs of amendment, after they have pronounced their sentence, rather than be accused as false prophets, they know how to approve[5] their sagacity to the world by a seasonable dose.

They are likewise of special use to husbands and wives who are grown weary of their mates, to eldest sons, to great ministers of state, and often to princes.

I had formerly upon occasion discoursed with my master upon the nature of our government in general, and particularly of our own excellent constitution, deservedly the wonder and envy of the whole world. But having here acciden-

3. Trade secret.
4. Enema.
5. Demonstrate.

tally mentioned a *minister of state*, he commanded me some time after to inform him, what species of Yahoo I particularly meant by that appellation.

I told him that a *first* or *chief minister of state*,[6] whom I intended to describe, was a creature wholly exempt from joy and grief, love and hatred, pity and anger; at least makes use of no other passions but a violent desire of wealth, power, and titles; that he applies his words to all uses except to the indication of his mind; that he never tells a *truth* but with an intent that you should take it for a *lie*, nor a *lie* but with a design that you should take it for a *truth*; that those he speaks worst of behind their backs are in the surest way to preferment; and whenever he begins to praise you to others or to yourself, you are from that day forlorn.[7] The worst mark you can receive is a *promise*, especially when it is confirmed with an oath; after which every wise man retires and gives over all hopes.

There are three methods by which a man may rise to be chief minister: the first is by knowing how with prudence to dispose of a wife, a daughter, or a sister; the second, by betraying or undermining his predecessor; and the third is by a *furious zeal* in public assemblies against the corruptions of the court. But a wise prince would rather choose to employ those who practise the last of these methods; because such zealots prove always the most obsequious and subservient to the will and passions of their master. That these *ministers*, having all employments at their disposal, preserve themselves in power by bribing the majority of a senate or great council; and at last, by an expedient called an *act of indemnity* [8] (whereof I described the nature to him) they secure themselves from after reckonings, and retire from the public laden with the spoils of the nation.

The palace of a chief minister is a seminary to breed up others in his own trade: the pages, lackeys, and porter, by imitating their master, become ministers of state in their several districts, and learn to excel in the three principal ingredients, of *insolence, lying,* and *bribery*. Accordingly, they have a subaltern [9] court paid to them by persons of the best rank, and sometimes by the force of dexterity and impudence arrive through several gradations to be successors to their lord.

He is usually governed by a decayed wench or favourite footman, who are the tunnels through which all graces [10] are conveyed and may properly be called, in the last resort, the governors of the kingdom.

One day my master, having heard me mention the nobility of my country, was pleased to make me a compliment which I could not pretend to deserve:

6. Clearly a reference to Sir Robert Walpole (1676–1745), the first minister to be called "prime" (not an official title) because of his pre-eminence under the rule of George I and later, with the co-operation of Queen Caroline, of George II as well; the object of attacks by Swift, Pope, and Gay—on the score not only of his tyrannical political control but also of his use of writers as paid hacks of official policy.

7. Doomed, lost.

8. Such acts were often passed (with good reason) to free ministers from being prosecuted for actions in office by those who succeeded them to power; but they could become, as Swift pointed out in 1710, laws "enacted to take away the force of all laws whatsoever, by which a man may safely commit upon the last of June what he would be infallibly hanged for if he committed on the first of July" (*Examiner*, No. 18).

9. Subordinate.

10. Favors.

that he was sure I must have been born of some noble family, because I far exceeded in shape, colour, and cleanliness all the Yahoos of his nation, although I seemed to fail in strength and agility, which must be imputed to my different way of living from those other brutes; and, besides, I was not only endowed with the faculty of speech, but likewise with some rudiments of reason, to a degree that with all his acquaintance I passed for a prodigy.[11]

He made me observe, that among the Houyhnhnms, the *white*, the *sorrel*, and the *iron-grey*, were not so exactly shaped as the *bay*, the *dapple-grey*, and the *black*, nor born with equal talents of mind or a capacity to improve them; and therefore continued always in the condition of servants without ever aspiring to match out of their own race, which in that country would be reckoned monstrous and unnatural.

I made his Honour my most humble acknowledgments for the good opinion he was pleased to conceive of me; but assured him at the same time that my birth was of the lower sort, having been born of plain honest parents who were just able to give me a tolerable education: that *nobility* among us was altogether a different thing from the idea he had of it; that our young noblemen are bred from their childhood in idleness and luxury; that as soon as years will permit, they consume their vigour and contract odious diseases among lewd females; and when their fortunes are almost ruined, they marry some woman of mean birth, disagreeable person, and unsound constitution, merely for the sake of money, whom they hate and despise. That the productions of such marriages are generally scrofulous, rickety, or deformed children, by which means the family seldom continues above three generations, unless the wife take care to provide a healthy father among her neighbours or domestics, in order to improve and continue the breed. That a weak diseased body, a meagre countenance, and sallow complexion are the true marks of noble blood; and a healthy robust appearance is so disgraceful in a man of quality that the world concludes his real father to have been a groom or a coachman. The imperfections of his mind run parallel with those of his body, being a composition of spleen,[12] dullness, ignorance, caprice, sensuality, and pride.

Without the consent of this illustrious body[13] no law can be enacted, repealed, or altered, and these nobles have likewise the decision of all our possessions without appeal.

Chapter Seven: The author's great love of his native country. His master's observations upon the constitution and administration of England, as described by the author, with parallel cases and comparisons. His master's observations upon human nature.

The reader may be disposed to wonder how I could prevail on myself to give so free a representation of my own species among a race of mortals who were already too apt to conceive the vilest opinion of humankind from the entire

11. Wonder.
12. Temper or passion; the function of the spleen was not known in Swift's age, and to it was attributed a variety of psychosomatic symptoms—melancholy, gloom, ennui, hypochondria, the "vapors"—which were often fashionable, as is pointed out later in the chapter, among "the lazy, the luxurious, and the rich."
13. The House of Lords.

congruity betwixt me and their Yahoos. But I must freely confess that the many virtues of those excellent quadrupeds, placed in opposite view to human corruptions, had so far opened my eyes and enlarged my understanding that I began to view the actions and passions of man in a very different light, and to think the honour of my own kind not worth managing; [1] which, besides, it was impossible for me to do before a person of so acute a judgment as my master, who daily convinced me of a thousand faults in myself whereof I had not the least perception before, and which with us would never be numbered even among human infirmities. I had likewise learned from his example an utter detestation of all falsehood or disguise; and truth appeared so amiable to me that I determined upon sacrificing everything to it.

Let me deal so candidly with the reader as to confess that there was yet a much stronger motive for the freedom I took in my representation of things. I had not been a year in this country before I contracted such a love and veneration for the inhabitants that I entered on a firm resolution never to return to humankind, but to pass the rest of my life among these admirable Houyhnhnms in the contemplation and practice of every virtue; where I could have no example or incitement to vice. But it was decreed by Fortune, my perpetual enemy, that so great a felicity should not fall to my share. However, it is now some comfort to reflect that in what I said of my countrymen I extenuated their faults as much as I durst before so strict an examiner, and upon every article gave as favourable a turn as the matter would bear. For, indeed, who is there alive that will not be swayed by his bias and partiality to the place of his birth?

I have related the substance of several conversations I had with my master, during the greatest part of the time I had the honour to be in his service, but have indeed for brevity sake omitted much more than is here set down.

When I had answered all his questions, and his curiosity seemed to be fully satisfied, he sent for me one morning early and, commanding me to sit down at some distance (an honour which he had never before conferred upon me), he said he had been very seriously considering my whole story, as far as it related both to myself and my country: that he looked upon us as a sort of animals to whose share, by what accident he could not conjecture, some small pittance of reason had fallen, whereof we made no other use than by its assistance to aggravate our natural corruptions and to acquire new ones which nature had not given us. That we disarmed ourselves of the few abilities she had bestowed, had been very successful in multiplying our original wants, and seemed to spend our whole lives in vain endeavours to supply them by our own inventions. That as to myself, it was manifest I had neither the strength or agility of a common Yahoo, that I walked infirmly on my hinder feet, had found out a contrivance to make my claws of no use or defence and to remove the hair from my chin, which was intended as a shelter from the sun and the weather. Lastly, that I could neither run with speed nor climb trees like my brethren (as he called them), the Yahoos in this country.

That our institutions of government and law were plainly owing to our gross defects in reason and, by consequence, in virtue; because reason alone is sufficient to govern a rational creature; which was therefore a character we had

1. Protecting.

no pretence to challenge, even from the account I had given of my own people, although he manifestly perceived that in order to favour them I had concealed many particulars and often *said the thing which was not.*

He was the more confirmed in this opinion because he observed that, as I agreed in every feature of my body with other Yahoos, except where it was to my real disadvantage in point of strength, speed, and activity, the shortness of my claws, and some other particulars where nature had no part; so from the representation I had given him of our lives, our manners, and our actions, he found as near a resemblance in the disposition of our minds. He said the Yahoos were known to hate one another more than they did any different species of animals; and the reason usually assigned was the odiousness of their own shapes, which all could see in the rest but not in themselves. He had therefore begun to think it not unwise in us to cover our bodies and, by that invention, conceal many of our deformities from each other, which would else be hardly supportable. But he now found he had been mistaken and that the dissensions of those brutes in his country were owing to the same cause with ours, as I had described them. For if (said he) you throw among five Yahoos as much food as would be sufficient for fifty, they will, instead of eating peaceably, fall together by the ears, each single one impatient to have all to itself; and therefore a servant was usually employed to stand by while they were feeding abroad, and those kept at home were tied at a distance from each other. That if a cow died of age or accident before a Houyhnhnm could secure it for his own Yahoos, those in the neighbourhood would come in herds to seize it, and then would ensue such a battle as I had described, with terrible wounds made by their claws on both sides, although they seldom were able to kill one another for want of such convenient instruments of death as we had invented. At other times the like battles have been fought between the Yahoos of several neighbourhoods without any visible cause; those of one district watching all opportunities to surprise the next before they are prepared. But if they find their project hath miscarried, they return home, and, for want of enemies, engage in what I call a civil war among themselves.

That in some fields of this country there are certain shining stones of several colours, whereof the Yahoos are violently fond, and when part of these stones are fixed in the earth, as it sometimes happeneth, they will dig with their claws for whole days to get them out, and carry them away, and hide them by heaps in their kennels; but still looking round with great caution for fear their comrades should find out their treasure. My master said he could never discover the reason of this unnatural appetite or how these stones could be of any use to a Yahoo; but now he believed it might proceed from the same principle of avarice which I had ascribed to mankind; that he had once, by way of experiment, privately removed a heap of these stones from the place where one of his Yahoos had buried it: whereupon the sordid animal, missing his treasure, by his loud lamenting brought the whole herd to the place, there miserably howled, then fell to biting and tearing the rest, began to pine away, would neither eat, nor sleep, nor work, till he ordered a servant privately to convey the stones into the same hole and hide them as before; which when his Yahoo had found, he presently recovered his spirits and good humour, but took care to remove them to a better hiding-place, and hath ever since been a very serviceable brute.

My master farther assured me, which I also observed myself, that in the fields where these shining stones abound, the fiercest and most frequent battles are fought, occasioned by perpetual inroads of the neighbouring Yahoos.

He said it was common when two Yahoos discovered such a stone in a field and were contending which of them should be the proprietor, a third would take the advantage and carry it away from them both; which my master would needs contend to have some resemblance with our *suits at law;* wherein I thought it for our credit not to undeceive him; since the decision he mentioned was much more equitable than many decrees among us: because the plaintiff and defendant there lost nothing beside the stone they contended for, whereas our *courts of equity* would never have dismissed the cause while either of them had anything left.

My master, continuing his discourse, said, there was nothing that rendered the Yahoos more odious than their undistinguishing appetite to devour everything that came in their way, whether herbs, roots, berries, corrupted flesh of animals, or all mingled together: and it was peculiar in their temper that they were fonder of what they could get by rapine or stealth at a greater distance than much better food provided for them at home. If their prey held out, they would eat till they were ready to burst, after which nature had pointed out to them a certain root that gave them a general evacuation.

There was also another kind of root very juicy, but something rare and difficult to be found, which the Yahoos sought for with much eagerness and would suck it with great delight; and it produced in them the same effects that wine hath upon us. It would make them sometimes hug and sometimes tear one another; they would howl and grin, and chatter, and reel, and tumble, and then fall asleep in the mud.

I did indeed observe that the Yahoos were the only animals in this country subject to any diseases; which, however, were much fewer than horses have among us, and contracted not by any ill treatment they meet with but by the nastiness and greediness of that sordid brute. Neither has their language any more than a general appellation for those maladies, which is borrowed from the name of the beast, and called *Hnea Yahoo,* or the *Yahoo's Evil;* and the cure prescribed is a mixture of their own dung and urine forcibly put down the Yahoo's throat. This I have since often known to have been taken with success and do here freely recommend it to my countrymen for the public good, as an admirable specific against all diseases produced by repletion.

As to learning, government, arts, manufactures, and the like, my master confessed he could find little or no resemblance between the Yahoos of that country and those in ours. For he only meant to observe what parity there was in our natures. He had heard indeed some curious Houyhnhnms observe that in most herds there was a sort of ruling Yahoo (as among us there is generally some leading or principal stag in a park), who was always more deformed in body and mischievous in disposition than any of the rest. That this leader had usually a favourite as like himself as he could get, whose employment was to lick his master's feet and posteriors and drive the female Yahoos to his kennel; for which he was now and then rewarded with a piece of ass's flesh. This favourite is hated by the whole herd, and therefore to protect himself keeps always near the person of his leader. He usually continues in office till a worse can be found; but the very moment he is discarded, his successor, at the head of all the

Yahoos in that district, young and old, male and female, come in a body and discharge their excrements upon him from head to foot. But how far this might be applicable to our *courts* and *favourites*, and *ministers of state*, my master said I could best determine.

I durst make no return to this malicious insinuation, which debased human understanding below the sagacity of a common *hound*, who has judgment enough to distinguish and follow the cry of the ablest dog in the pack without being ever mistaken.

My master told me there were some qualities remarkable in the Yahoos which he had not observed me to mention, or at least very slightly, in the accounts I had given him of humankind. He said those animals, like other brutes, had their females in common; but in this they differed, that the she-Yahoo would admit the male while she was pregnant and that the hees would quarrel and fight with the females as fiercely as with each other. Both which practices were such degrees of infamous brutality that no other sensitive creature ever arrived at.

Another thing he wondered at in the Yahoos was their strange disposition to nastiness and dirt, whereas there appears to be a natural love of cleanliness in all other animals. As to the two former accusations, I was glad to let them pass without any reply because I had not a word to offer upon them in defence of my species, which otherwise I certainly had done from my own inclinations. But I could have easily vindicated humankind from the imputation of singularity upon the last article if there had been any *swine* in that country (as unluckily for me there were not), which, although it may be a sweeter quadruped than a Yahoo, cannot, I humbly conceive, in justice pretend to more cleanliness; and so his Honour himself must have owned, if he had seen their filthy way of feeding and their custom of wallowing and sleeping in the mud.

My master likewise mentioned another quality which his servants had discovered in several Yahoos and to him was wholly unaccountable. He said a fancy would sometimes take a Yahoo to retire into a corner, to lie down and howl, and groan, and spurn away all that came near him, although he were young and fat, and wanted neither food nor water; nor did the servants imagine what could possibly ail him. And the only remedy they found was to set him to hard work, after which he would infallibly come to himself. To this I was silent out of partiality to my own kind; yet here I could plainly discover the true seeds of *spleen*, which only seizeth on the *lazy*, the *luxurious*, and the *rich;* who, if they were forced to undergo the same regimen, I would undertake for the cure.

His Honour had farther observed that a female Yahoo would often stand behind a bank or a bush, to gaze on the young males passing by, and then appear and hide, using many antic gestures and grimaces, at which time it was observed that she had a most offensive smell; and when any of the males advanced, would slowly retire, looking often back, and with a counterfeit show of fear run off into some convenient place where she knew the male would follow her.

At other times if a female stranger came among them, three or four of her own sex would get about her and stare and chatter, and grin, and smell her all over, and then turn off with gestures that seemed to express contempt and disdain.

Perhaps my master might refine a little in these speculations, which he had drawn from what he observed himself or had been told him by others: however, I could not reflect without some amazement, and much sorrow, that the rudiments of *lewdness, coquetry, censure,* and *scandal* should have place by instinct in womankind.

I expected every moment that my master would accuse the Yahoos of those unnatural appetites in both sexes so common among us. But nature, it seems, hath not been so expert a schoolmistress; and these politer pleasures are entirely the productions of art and reason, on our side of the globe.

Chapter Eight: The author relateth several particulars of the Yahoos. The great virtues of the Houyhnhnms. The education and exercise of their youth. Their General Assembly.

As I ought to have understood human nature much better than I supposed it possible for my master to do, so it was easy to apply the character he gave of the Yahoos to myself and my countrymen, and I believed I could yet make farther discoveries from my own observation. I therefore often begged his Honour to let me go among the herds of Yahoos in the neighbourhood, to which he always very graciously consented, being perfectly convinced that the hatred I bore those brutes would never suffer me to be corrupted by them; and his Honour ordered one of his servants, a strong sorrel nag, very honest and good-natured, to be my guard, without whose protection I durst not undertake such adventures. For I have already told the reader how much I was pestered by those odious animals upon my first arrival. And I afterwards failed very narrowly three or four times of falling into their clutches, when I happened to stray at any distance without my hanger. And I have reason to believe they had some imagination that I was of their own species, which I often assisted myself by stripping up my sleeves and showing my naked arms and breast in their sight, when my protector was with me. At which times they would approach as near as they durst and imitate my actions after the manner of monkeys but ever with great signs of hatred, as a tame jackdaw, with cap and stockings, is always persecuted by the wild ones when he happens to be got among them.

They are prodigiously nimble from their infancy; however, I once caught a young male of three years old, and endeavoured by all marks of tenderness to make it quiet; but the little imp fell a-squalling, and scratching, and biting with such violence, that I was forced to let it go; and it was high time, for a whole troop of old ones came about us at the noise, but finding the cub was safe (for away it ran), and my sorrel nag being by, they durst not venture near us. I observed the young animal's flesh to smell very rank, and the stink was somewhat between a weasel and a fox, but much more disagreeable. I forgot another circumstance (and perhaps I might have the reader's pardon if it were wholly omitted) that while I held the odious vermin in my hands, it voided its filthy excrement of a yellow liquid substance all over my clothes; but by good fortune there was a small brook hard by where I washed myself as clean as I could, although I durst not come into my master's presence until I were sufficiently aired.

By what I could discover, the Yahoos appear to be the most unteachable of all animals, their capacities never reaching higher than to draw or carry burthens. Yet I am of opinion this defect ariseth chiefly from a perverse, restive disposition. For they are cunning, malicious, treacherous, and revengeful. They are strong and hardy, but of a cowardly spirit, and by consequence insolent, abject, and cruel. It is observed, that the red-haired of both sexes are more libidinous and mischievous than the rest, whom yet they much exceed in strength and activity.

The Houyhnhnms keep the Yahoos for present use in huts not far from the house; but the rest are sent abroad to certain fields where they dig up roots, eat several kinds of herbs, and search about for carrion, or sometimes catch weasels and *luhimuhs* (a sort of wild rat), which they greedily devour. Nature hath taught them to dig deep holes with their nails on the side of a rising ground, wherein they lie by themselves; only the kennels of the females are larger, sufficient to hold two or three cubs.

They swim from their infancy like frogs and are able to continue long under water, where they often take fish, which the females carry home to their young. And upon this occasion, I hope the reader will pardon my relating an odd adventure.

Being one day abroad with my protector the sorrel nag, and the weather exceeding hot, I entreated him to let me bathe in a river that was near. He consented, and I immediately stripped myself stark naked and went down softly into the stream. It happened that a young female Yahoo, standing behind a bank, saw the whole proceeding and, inflamed by desire, as the nag and I conjectured, came running with all speed and leaped into the water within five yards of the place where I bathed. I was never in my life so terribly frighted; the nag was grazing at some distance, not suspecting any harm. She embraced me after a most fulsome manner; I roared as loud as I could, and the nag came galloping towards me, whereupon she quitted her grasp, with the utmost reluctancy, and leaped upon the opposite bank, where she stood gazing and howling all the time I was putting on my clothes.

This was matter of diversion to my master and his family, as well as of mortification to myself. For now I could no longer deny that I was a real Yahoo in every limb and feature, since the females had a natural propensity to me as one of their own species: neither was the hair of this brute of a red colour (which might have been some excuse for an appetite a little irregular) but black as a sloe, and her countenance did not make an appearance altogether so hideous as the rest of the kind; for I think she could not be above eleven years old.

Having already lived three years in this country, the reader I suppose will expect that I should, like other travellers, give him some account of the manners and customs of its inhabitants, which it was indeed my principal study to learn.

As these noble Houyhnhnms are endowed by nature with a general disposition to all virtues and have no conceptions or ideas of what is evil in a rational creature, so their grand maxim is to cultivate reason and to be wholly governed by it. Neither is reason among them a point problematical as with us, where men can argue with plausibility on both sides of a question, but strikes you with immediate conviction, as it must needs do where it is not mingled, obscured, or discoloured by passion and interest. I remember it was with extreme difficulty that I could bring my master to understand the meaning of the word *opinion* or how a point could be disputable; because reason taught us to affirm or deny only where we are certain, and beyond our knowledge we cannot do either. So that controversies, wranglings, disputes, and positiveness in false or dubious propositions are evils unknown among the Houyhnhnms. In the like manner, when I used to explain to him our several systems of *natural philosophy*, he would laugh that a creature pretending to *reason* should value itself upon the knowledge of other people's conjectures and in things where that knowledge, if it were certain, could be of no use. Wherein he agreed entirely with the sentiments of Socrates, as Plato delivers them; [1] which I mention as the highest honour I can do that prince of philosophers. I have often since reflected what destruction such a doctrine would make in the libraries of Europe, and how many paths to fame would be then shut up in the learned world.

Friendship and *benevolence* are the two principal virtues among the Houyhnhnms, and these not confined to particular objects, but universal to the whole race. For a stranger from the remotest part is equally treated with the nearest neighbour, and wherever he goes looks upon himself as at home. They preserve *decency* and *civility* in the highest degrees, but are altogether ignorant of *ceremony*. They have no fondness [2] for their colts or foals, but the care they take in educating them proceeds entirely from the dictates of reason. And I observed my master to show the same affection to his neighbour's issue that he had for his own. They will have it that nature teaches them to love the whole species, and it is reason only that maketh a distinction of persons, where there is a superior degree of virtue.

When the matron Houyhnhnms have produced one of each sex, they no longer accompany with their consorts except they lose one of their issue by some casualty, which very seldom happens: but in such a case they meet again, or, when the like accident befalls a person whose wife is past bearing, some other couple bestows on him one of their own colts, and then go together a second time till the mother be pregnant. This caution is necessary to prevent the country from being overburthened with numbers. But the race of inferior Houyhnhnms bred up to be servants is not so strictly limited upon this article; these are allowed to produce three of each sex to be domestics in the noble families.

In their marriages they are exactly careful to choose such colours as will not make any disagreeable mixture in the breed. *Strength* is chiefly valued in the male, and *comeliness* in the female, not upon the account of *love*, but to preserve the race from degenerating; for where a female happens to excel in strength, a consort is chosen with regard to *comeliness*. Courtship, love, presents, jointures, settlements, have no place in their thoughts or terms whereby to express them in their language. The young couple meet and are joined merely because it is the determination of their parents and friends: it is what they see done every day, and they look upon it as one of the necessary actions in a reasonable being. But the violation of marriage, or any other unchastity,

1. Perhaps a reference to Plato's *Phaedo* 97–98, where Socrates describes his high hopes upon hearing of Anaxagoras' doctrines and his disappointment on learning more.
2. Doting or foolish affection.

was never heard of: and the married pair pass their lives with the same friendship and mutual benevolence that they bear to all others of the same species who come in their way; without jealousy, fondness, quarrelling, or discontent.

In educating the youth of both sexes, their method is admirable and highly deserves our imitation. These are not suffered to taste a grain of oats, except upon certain days, till eighteen years old; nor milk but very rarely; and in summer they graze two hours in the morning and as many in the evening, which their parents likewise observe, but the servants are not allowed above half that time, and a great part of their grass is brought home, which they eat at the most convenient hours, when they can be best spared from work.

Temperance, industry, exercise and *cleanliness,* are the lessons equally enjoined to the young ones of both sexes: and my master thought it monstrous in us to give the females a different kind of education from the males except in some articles of domestic management; whereby, as he truly observed, one half of our natives were good for nothing but bringing children into the world: and to trust the care of their children to such useless animals, he said, was yet a greater instance of brutality.

But the Houyhnhnms train up their youth to strength, speed, and hardiness by exercising them in running races up and down steep hills or over hard stony grounds; and when they are all in a sweat, they are ordered to leap over head and ears into a pond or a river. Four times a year the youth of certain districts meet to show their proficiency in running and leaping and other feats of strength or agility, where the victor is rewarded with a song made in his or her praise. On this festival the servants drive a herd of Yahoos into the field, laden with hay and oats and milk for a repast to the Houyhnhnms; after which these brutes are immediately driven back again for fear of being noisome to the assembly.

Every fourth year, at the vernal equinox, there is a representative council of the whole nation, which meets in a plain about twenty miles from our house, and continues about five or six days. Here they inquire into the state and condition of the several districts: whether they abound or be deficient in hay or oats, or cows or Yahoos. And wherever there is any want (which is but seldom) it is immediately supplied by unanimous consent and contribution. Here likewise the regulation of children is settled: as for instance, if a Houyhnhnm hath two males, he changeth one of them with another who hath two females; and when a child hath been lost by any casualty, where the mother is past breeding, it is determind what family in the district shall breed another to supply the loss.

Chapter Nine: A grand debate at the General Assembly of the Houyhnhnms, and how it was determined. The learning of the Houyhnhnms. Their buildings. Their manner of burials. The defectiveness of their language.

One of these grand assemblies was held in my time, about three months before my departure, whither my master went as the representative of our district. In this council was resumed their old debate, and indeed the only debate that ever happened in their country; whereof my master after his return gave me a very particular account.

The question to be debated was whether the Yahoos should be exterminated from the face of the earth. One of the members for the affirmative offered several arguments of great strength and weight, alleging that, as the Yahoos were the most filthy, noisome, and deformed animal which nature ever produced, so they were the most restive and indocible, mischievous and malicious: they would privately suck the teats of the Houyhnhnms' cows, kill and devour their cats, trample down their oats and grass, if they were not continually watched, and commit a thousand other extravagancies. He took notice of a general tradition that Yahoos had not been always in their country: but that many ages ago two of these brutes appeared together upon a mountain,[1] whether produced by the heat of the sun upon corrupted mud and slime or from the ooze and froth of the sea was never known. That these Yahoos engendered, and their brood in a short time grew so numerous as to overrun and infest the whole nation. That the Houyhnhnms, to get rid of this evil, made a general hunting, and at last enclosed the whole herd; and, destroying the elder, every Houyhnhnm kept two young ones in a kennel and brought them to such a degree of tameness as an animal so savage by nature can be capable of acquiring, using them for draft and carriage. That there seemed to be much truth in this tradition, and that those creatures could not be *ylnhniamshy* (or *aborigines* of the land) because of the violent hatred the Houyhnhnms, as well as all other animals, bore them; which although their evil disposition sufficiently deserved, could never have arrived at so high a degree if they had been aborigines, or else they would have long since been rooted out. That the inhabitants, taking a fancy to use the service of the Yahoos, had very imprudently neglected to cultivate the breed of asses, which were a comely animal, easily kept, more tame and orderly, without any offensive smell, strong enough for labour, although they yield to the other in agility of body; and if their braying be no agreeable sound, it is far preferable to the horrible howlings of the Yahoos.

Several others declared their sentiments to the same purpose, when my master proposed an expedient to the assembly, whereof he had indeed borrowed the hint from me. He approved of the tradition mentioned by the honourable member who spoke before, and affirmed that the two Yahoos said to be first seen among them had been driven thither over the sea; that coming to land and being forsaken by their companions, they retired to the mountains and, degenerating by degrees, became in process of time much more savage than those of their own species in the country from whence these two originals came. The reason of his assertion was that he had now in his possession a certain wonderful Yahoo (meaning myself) which most of them had heard of and many of them had seen. He then related to them how he first found me; that my body was all covered with an artificial composure [2] of the skins and hairs of other animals: that I spoke in a language of my own and had thoroughly learned theirs: that I had related to him the accidents which brought me thither: that when he saw me without my covering, I was an exact Yahoo in

---

1. Perhaps offered by Swift with some ironic suggestion of the fallen Adam and Eve descending from the "mountain" where Milton placed the Garden of Eden (*Paradise Lost* IV.226); but, of course, all nature falls with man in Milton's poem.
2. Composition.

every part, only of a whiter colour, less hairy, and with shorter claws. He added, how I had endeavoured to persuade him that in my own and other countries the Yahoos acted as the governing, rational animal, and held the Houyhnhnms in servitude: that he observed in me all the qualities of a Yahoo, only a little more civilized by some tincture of reason, which however was in a degree as far inferior to the Houyhnhnm race as the Yahoos of their country were to me: that, among other things, I mentioned a custom we had of castrating Houyhnhnms when they were young in order to render them tame; that the operation was easy and safe; that it was no shame to learn wisdom from brutes, as industry is taught by the ant and building by the swallow. (For so I translate the word *lyhannh*, although it be a much larger fowl.) That this invention might be practised upon the younger Yahoos here, which, besides rendering them tractable and fitter for use, would in an age put an end to the whole species without destroying life. That in the meantime the Houyhnhnms should be *exhorted* to cultivate the breed of asses, which, as they are in all respects more valuable brutes, so they have this advantage, to be fit for service at five years old, which the others are not till twelve.

This was all my master thought fit to tell me at that time of what passed in the grand council. But he was pleased to conceal one particular which related personally to myself, whereof I soon felt the unhappy effect, as the reader will know in its proper place, and from whence I date all the succeeding misfortunes of my life.

The Houyhnhnms have no letters, and consequently their knowledge is all traditional. But there happening few events of any moment among a people so well united, naturally disposed to every virtue, wholly governed by reason, and cut off from all commerce with other nations, the historical part is easily preserved without burthening their memories. I have already observed that they are subject to no diseases, and therefore can have no need of physicians. However, they have excellent medicines composed of herbs, to cure accidental bruises and cuts in the pastern or frog [3] of the foot by sharp stones, as well as other maims and hurts in the several parts of the body.

They calculate the year by the revolution of the sun and the moon, but use no subdivisions into weeks. They are well enough acquainted with the motions of those two luminaries and understand the nature of eclipses; and this is the utmost progress of their astronomy.

In poetry they must be allowed to excel all other mortals; wherein the justness of their similes and the minuteness as well as exactness of their descriptions are indeed inimitable. Their verses abound very much in both of these and usually contain either some exalted notions of friendship and benevolence, or the praises of those who were victors in races and other bodily exercises. Their buildings, although very rude and simple, are not inconvenient, but well contrived to defend them from all injuries of cold and heat. They have a kind of tree which at forty years old loosens in the root and falls with the first storm; it grows very straight and, being pointed like stakes with a sharp stone (for the Houyhnhnms know not the use of iron), they stick them erect in the ground about ten inches asunder, and then weave in oat-straw or sometimes

3. The horny sole.

wattles betwixt them. The roof is made after the same manner and so are the doors.

The Houyhnhnms use the hollow part between the pastern and the hoof of their forefeet as we do our hands, and this with greater dexterity than I could at first imagine. I have seen a white mare of our family thread a needle (which I lent her on purpose) with that joint. They milk their cows, reap their oats, and do all the work which requires hands, in the same manner. They have a kind of hard flints, which, by grinding against other stones, they form into instruments that serve instead of wedges, axes, and hammers. With tools made of these flints they likewise cut their hay and reap their oats, which there groweth naturally in several fields: the Yahoos draw home the sheaves in carriages, and the servants tread them in certain covered huts, to get out the grain, which is kept in stores. They make a rude kind of earthen and wooden vessels and bake the former in the sun.

If they can avoid casualties, they die only of old age, and are buried in the obscurest places that can be found, their friends and relations expressing neither joy nor grief at their departure; nor does the dying person discover the least regret that he is leaving the world, any more than if he were upon returning home from a visit to one of his neighbours. I remember my master having once made an appointment with a friend and his family to come to his house upon some affair of importance; on the day fixed, the mistress and her two children came very late. She made two excuses, first for her husband, who, as she said, happened that very morning to *lhnuwnh*. The word is strongly expressive in their language but not easily rendered into English; it signifies, *to retire to his first mother*. Her excuse for not coming sooner was that, her husband dying late in the morning, she was a good while consulting her servants about a convenient place where his body should be laid; and I observed she behaved herself at our house as cheerfully as the rest; she died about three months after.

They live generally to seventy or seventy-five years, very seldom to fourscore; some weeks before their death they feel a gradual decay, but without pain. During this time they are much visited by their friends because they cannot go abroad with their usual ease and satisfaction. However, about ten days before their death, which they seldom fail in computing, they return the visits that have been made them by those who are nearest in the neighbourhood, being carried in a convenient sledge drawn by Yahoos, which vehicle they use, not only upon this occasion but when they grow old, upon long journeys, or when they are lamed by any accident. And therefore when the dying Houyhnhnms return those visits, they take a solemn leave of their friends, as if they were going to some remote part of the country where they designed to pass the rest of their lives.

I know not whether it may be worth observing that the Houyhnhnms have no word in their language to express anything that is evil, except what they borrow from the deformities or ill qualities of the Yahoos. Thus they denote the folly of a servant, an omission of a child, a stone that cuts their feet, a continuance of foul or unseasonable weather, and the like, by adding to each the epithet of *yahoo*. For instance, *hhnm yahoo*, *whnaholm yahoo*, *ynlhmna-wihlma yahoo*, and an ill-contrived house *ynholmhnmrohlnw yahoo*.

I could with great pleasure enlarge farther upon the manners and virtues of this excellent people; but, intending in a short time to publish a volume by itself expressly upon that subject, I refer the reader thither; and in the meantime, proceed to relate my own sad catastrophe.

Chapter Ten: The author's economy and happy life among the Houyhnhnms. His great improvement in virtue by conversing with them. Their conversations. The author hath notice given him by his master that he must depart from the country. He falls into a swoon for grief, but submits. He contrives and finishes a canoe, by the help of a fellow servant, and puts to sea at a venture.

I had settled my little economy to my own heart's content. My master had ordered a room to be made for me after their manner about six yards from the house, the sides and floors of which I plastered with clay and covered with rush mats of my own contriving; I had beaten hemp, which there grows wild, and made of it a sort of ticking: this I filled with the feathers of several birds I had taken with springes made of Yahoos' hairs, and were excellent food. I had worked two chairs with my knife, the sorrel nag helping me in the grosser and more laborious part. When my clothes were worn to rags, I made myself others with the skins of rabbits and of a certain beautiful animal about the same size, called *nnuhnoh*, the skin of which is covered with a fine down. Of these I likewise made very tolerable stockings. I soled my shoes with wood which I cut from a tree and fitted to the upper leather; and when this was worn out, I supplied it with the skins of Yahoos dried in the sun. I often got honey out of hollow trees, which I mingled with water, or eat it with my bread. No man could more verify the truth of these two maxims, *That nature is very easily satisfied* and *That necessity is the mother of invention.* I enjoyed perfect health of body and tranquillity of mind; I did not feel the treachery or inconstancy of a friend, nor the injuries of a secret or open enemy. I had no occasion of bribing, flattering, or pimping to procure the favour of any great man or of his minion. I wanted no fence against fraud or oppression; here was neither physician to destroy my body, nor lawyer to ruin my fortune; no informer to watch my words and actions or forge accusations against me for hire: here were no gibers, censurers, backbiters, pickpockets, highwaymen, housebreakers, attorneys, bawds, buffoons, gamesters, politicians, wits, splenetics, tedious talkers, controvertists, ravishers, murderers, robbers, virtuosos: [1] no leaders or followers of party and faction: no encouragers to vice by seduction or examples: no dungeon, axes, gibbets, whipping-posts, or pillories: no cheating shopkeepers or mechanics: no pride, vanity, or affectation: no fops, bullies, drunkards, strolling whores, or poxes: [2] no ranting, lewd, expensive wives: no stupid, proud pedants: no importunate, overbearing, quarrelsome, noisy, roaring, empty, conceited, swearing companions: no scoundrels raised from the dust upon the merit of their vices, or nobility thrown into it on account of their virtues: no lords, fiddlers, judges, or dancing-masters.

I had the favour of being admitted to several Houyhnhnms who came to visit or dine with my master; where his Honour graciously suffered me to wait in

1. Amateur scientists.
2. Venereal diseases.

the room and listen to their discourse. Both he and his company would often descend to ask me questions and receive my answers. I had also sometimes the honour of attending my master in his visits to others. I never presumed to speak except in answer to a question, and then I did it with inward regret, because it was a loss of so much time for improving myself: but I was infinitely delighted with the station of an humble auditor in such conversations, where nothing passed but what was useful, expressed in the fewest and most significant words: where (as I have already said) the greatest decency [3] was observed without the least degree of ceremony; where no person spoke without being pleased himself and pleasing his companions; where there was no interruptions, tediousness, heat, or difference of sentiments. They have a notion that, when people are met together, a short silence doth much improve conversation: this I found to be true; for during those little intermissions of talk, new ideas would arise in their minds, which very much enlivened the discourse. Their subjects are generally on friendship and benevolence, on order and economy, sometimes upon the visible operations of nature or ancient traditions, upon the bounds and limits of virtue, upon the unerring rules of reason, or upon some determinations to be taken at the next Great Assembly, and often upon the various excellencies of poetry. I may add without vanity that my presence often gave them sufficient matter for discourse, because it afforded my master an occasion of letting his friends into the history of me and my country, upon which they were all pleased to descant in a manner not very advantageous to humankind; and for that reason I shall not repeat what they said: only I may be allowed to observe, that his Honour, to my great admiration, appeared to understand the nature of Yahoos much better than myself. He went through all our vices and follies and discovered many which I had never mentioned to him, by only supposing what qualities a Yahoo of their country, with a small proportion of reason, might be capable of exerting; and concluded, with too much probability, how vile as well as miserable such a creature must be.

I freely confess that all the little knowledge I have of any value was acquired by the lectures I received from my master and from hearing the discourses of him and his friends; to which I should be prouder to listen than to dictate to the greatest and wisest assembly in Europe. I admired the strength, comeliness, and speed of the inhabitants; and such a constellation of virtues in such amiable persons produced in me the highest veneration. At first, indeed, I did not feel that natural awe which the Yahoos and all other animals bear towards them; but it grew upon me by degrees, much sooner than I imagined, and was mingled with a respectful love and gratitude, that they would condescend to distinguish me from the rest of my species.

When I thought of my family, my friends, my countrymen, or human race in general, I considered them as they really were, Yahoos in shape and disposition, perhaps a little more civilized and qualified with the gift of speech, but making no other use of reason than to improve and multiply those vices whereof their brethren in this country had only the share that nature allotted them. When I happened to behold the reflection of my own form in a lake or fountain, I turned away my face in horror and detestation of myself, and could better

3. Decorum, sense of form.

endure the sight of a common Yahoo than of my own person. By conversing with the Houyhnhnms and looking upon them with delight, I fell to imitate their gait and gesture, which is now grown into a habit, and my friends often tell me in a blunt way that I *trot like a horse;* which, however, I take for a great compliment: neither shall I disown that in speaking I am apt to fall into the voice and manner of the Houyhnhnms, and hear myself ridiculed on that account without the least mortification.

In the midst of this happiness, when I looked upon myself to be fully settled for life, my master sent for me one morning a little earlier than his usual hour. I observed by his countenance that he was in some perplexity and at a loss how to begin what he had to speak. After a short silence he told me he did not know how I would take what he was going to say; that in the last General Assembly, when the affair of the Yahoos was entered upon, the representatives had taken offence at his keeping a Yahoo (meaning myself) in his family more like a Houyhnhnm than a brute animal. That he was known frequently to converse with me, as if he could receive some advantage or pleasure in my company: that such a practice was not agreeable to reason or nature, or a thing ever heard of before among them. The assembly did therefore *exhort* him either to employ me like the rest of my species or command me to swim back to the place from whence I came. That the first of these expedients was utterly rejected by all the Houyhnhnms who had ever seen me at his house or their own: for they alleged that, because I had some rudiments of reason, added to the natural pravity [4] of those animals, it was to be feared I might be able to seduce them into the woody and mountainous parts of the country and bring them in troops by night to destroy the Houyhnhnms' cattle, as being naturally of the ravenous kind and averse from labour.

My master added that he was daily pressed by the Houyhnhnms of the neighbourhood to have the assembly's *exhortation* executed, which he could not put off much longer. He doubted it would be impossible for me to swim to another country, and therefore wished I would contrive some sort of vehicle, resembling those I had described to him, that might carry me on the sea, in which work I should have the assistance of his own servants, as well as those of his neighbours. He concluded that for his own part he could have been content to keep me in his service as long as I lived, because he found I had cured myself of some bad habits and dispositions by endeavouring, as far as my inferior nature was capable, to imitate the Houyhnhnms.

I should here observe to the reader that a decree of the General Assembly in this country is expressed by the word *hnhloayn,* which signifies an *exhortation,* as near as I can render it: for they have no conception how a rational creature can be *compelled,* but only advised or *exhorted,* because no person can disobey reason without giving up his claim to be a rational creature.

I was struck with the utmost grief and despair at my master's discourse, and, being unable to support the agonies I was under, I fell into a swoon at his feet. When I came to myself he told me that he concluded I had been dead. (For these people are subject to no such imbecilities [5] of nature.) I answered, in a faint voice, that death would have been too great an happiness; that

4. Viciousness.
5. Frailties, weaknesses.

although I could not blame the assembly's *exhortation* or the urgency of his friends, yet, in my weak and corrupt judgment, I thought it might consist with reason to have been less rigorous. That I could not swim a league, and probably the nearest land to theirs might be distant above an hundred; that many materials, necessary for making a small vessel to carry me off, were wholly wanting in this country, which, however, I would attempt in obedience and gratitude to his Honour, although I concluded the thing to be impossible, and therefore looked on myself as already devoted [6] to destruction. That the certain prospect of an unnatural death was the least of my evils: for, supposing I should escape with life by some strange adventure, how could I think with temper [7] of passing my days among Yahoos and relapsing into my old corruptions for want of examples to lead and keep me within the paths of virtue? That I knew too well upon what solid reasons all the determinations of the wise Houyhnhnms were founded not to be shaken by arguments of mine, a miserable Yahoo; and therefore, after presenting him with my humble thanks for the offer of his servants' assistance in making a vessel and desiring a reasonable time for so difficult a work, I told him I would endeavour to preserve a wretched being; and, if ever I returned to England, was not without hopes of being useful to my own species by celebrating the praises of the renowned Houyhnhnms and proposing their virtues to the imitation of mankind.

My master in a few words made me a very gracious reply, allowed me the space of two months to finish my boat, and ordered the sorrel nag, my fellow-servant (for so at this distance I may presume to call him) to follow my instructions, because I told my master that his help would be sufficient, and I knew he had a tenderness for me.

In his company my first business was to go to that part of the coast where my rebellious crew had ordered me to be set on shore. I got upon a height and, looking on every side into the sea, fancied I saw a small island towards the northeast. I took out my pocket-glass and could then clearly distinguish it about five leagues off, as I computed; but it appeared to the sorrel nag to be only a blue cloud: for, as he had no conception of any country beside his own, so he could not be as expert in distinguishing remote objects at sea as we who so much converse in that element.

After I had discovered this island, I considered no farther; but resolved it should, if possible, be the first place of my banishment, leaving the consequence to fortune.

I returned home and, consulting with the sorrel nag, we went into a copse at some distance, where I with my knife, and he with a sharp flint fastened very artificially,[8] after their manner, to a wooden handle, cut down several oak wattles about the thickness of a walking-staff, and some larger pieces. But I shall not trouble the reader with a particular description of my own mechanics; let it suffice to say that in six weeks' time, with the help of the sorrel nag, who performed the parts that required most labour, I finished a sort of Indian canoe, but much larger, covering it with the skins of Yahoos well

6. Doomed.
7. Equanimity.
8. Artfully.

stitched together with hempen threads of my own making. My sail was like-wise composed of the skins of the same animal; but I made use of the youngest I could get, the older being too tough and thick, and I likewise provided my-self with four paddles. I laid in a stock of boiled flesh of rabbits and fowls, and took with me two vessels, one filled with milk and the other with water.

I tried my canoe in a large pond near my master's house and then corrected in it what was amiss; stopping all the chinks with Yahoos' tallow till I found it staunch and able to bear me and my freight. And when it was as complete as I could possibly make it, I had it drawn on a carriage very gently by Yahoos to the seaside, under the conduct of the sorrel nag and another servant.

When all was ready and the day came for my departure, I took leave of my master and lady and the whole family, my eyes flowing with tears and my heart quite sunk with grief. But his Honour, out of curiosity, and perhaps (if I may speak it without vanity) partly out of kindness, was determined to see me in my canoe and got several of his neighbouring friends to accompany him. I was forced to wait above an hour for the tide, and then observing the wind very fortunately bearing towards the island to which I intended to steer my course, I took a second leave of my master: but as I was going to prostrate myself to kiss his hoof, he did me the honour to raise it gently to my mouth. I am not ignorant how much I have been censured for mentioning this last particular. Detractors are pleased to think it improbable that so illustrious a person should descend to give so great a mark of distinction to a creature so inferior as I. Neither have I forgot how apt some travellers are to boast of extraordinary favours they have received. But if these censurers were better acquainted with the noble and courteous disposition of the Houyhnhnms, they would soon change their opinion.

I paid my respects to the rest of the Houyhnhnms in his Honour's company; then getting into my canoe, I pushed off from shore.

Chapter Eleven: The author's dangerous voyage. He arrives at New Holland, hoping to settle there. Is wounded with an arrow by one of the natives. Is seized and carried by force into a Portuguese ship. The great civilities of the captain. The author arrives at England.

I began this desperate voyage on February 15, 1714–5;[1] at 9 o'clock in the morning. The wind was very favourable; however, I made use at first only of my paddles, but considering I should soon be weary and that the wind might probably chop about, I ventured to set up my little sail; and thus with the help of the tide I went at the rate of a league and a half an hour, as near as I could guess. My master and his friends continued on the shore till I was almost out of sight; and I often heard the sorrel nag (who always loved me) crying out, *Hnuy illa nyha maiah Yahoo*, Take care of thyself, gentle Yahoo.

My design was, if possible, to discover some small island uninhabited, yet sufficient by my labour to furnish me with necessaries of life; which I would have thought a greater happiness than to be first minister in the politest court of Europe, so horrible was the idea I conceived of returning to live in the society and under the government of Yahoos. For in such a solitude as I desired, I could at least enjoy my own thoughts and reflect with delight on the

1. That is, in 1715; in England, the legal year began on March 25 until 1753.

virtues of those inimitable Houyhnhnms, without any opportunity of degenerating into the vices and corruptions of my own species.

The reader may remember what I related when my crew conspired against me and confined me to my cabin. How I continued there several weeks without knowing what course we took, and when I was put ashore in the long-boat how the sailors told me with oaths, whether true or false, that they knew not in what part of the world we were. However, I did then believe us to be about ten degrees southward of the Cape of Good Hope, or about 45 degrees southern latitude, as I gathered from some general words I overheard among them, being, I supposed, to the southeast in their intended voyage to Madagascar. And although this were but little better than conjecture, yet I resolved to steer my course eastward, hoping to reach the southwest coast of New Holland,[2] and perhaps some such island as I desired lying westward of it. The wind was full west, and by six in the evening I computed I had gone eastward at least eighteen leagues, when I spied a very small island about half a league off, which I soon reached. It was nothing but a rock, with one creek, naturally arched by the force of tempests. Here I put in my canoe and, climbing a part of the rock, I could plainly discover land to the east, extending from south to north. I lay all night in my canoe and, repeating my voyage early in the morning, I arrived in seven hours to the southeast point of New Holland. This confirmed me in the opinion I have long entertained that the maps and charts place this country at least three degrees more to the east than it really is; which thought I communicated many years ago to my worthy friend Mr. Herman Moll[3] and gave him my reasons for it, although he hath rather chosen to follow other authors.

I saw no inhabitants in the place where I landed and, being unarmed, I was afraid of venturing far into the country. I found some shellfish on the shore and eat them raw, not daring to kindle a fire for fear of being discovered by the natives. I continued three days feeding on oysters and limpets, to save my own provisions, and I fortunately found a brook of excellent water, which gave me great relief.

On the fourth day, venturing out early a little too far, I saw twenty or thirty natives upon a height not above five hundred yards from me. They were stark naked, men, women, and children, round a fire, as I could discover by the smoke. One of them spied me and gave notice to the rest; five of them advanced towards me, leaving the women and children at the fire. I made what haste I could to the shore and, getting into my canoe, shoved off: the savages, observing me retreat, ran after me; and before I could get far enough into the sea, discharged an arrow which wounded me deeply on the inside of my left knee (I shall carry the mark to my grave). I apprehended the arrow might be poisoned and, paddling out of the reach of their darts (being a calm day), I made a shift to suck the wound and dress it as well as I could.

I was at a loss what to do, for I durst not return to the same landing-place, but stood to the north, and was forced to paddle; for the wind, although very gentle, was against me, blowing northwest. As I was looking about for a secure

2. Tasmania.

3. Herman Moll (d. 1732), a Dutch mapmaker who settled in England about 1698 and whose maps became widely accepted there, providing the basis for the imaginary maps that accompanied the original editions of *Gulliver's Travels*.

landing-place, I saw a sail to the north-northeast, which appearing every minute more visible, I was in some doubt whether I should wait for them or no; but at last my detestation of the Yahoo race prevailed and, turning my canoe, I sailed and paddled together to the south and got into the same creek from whence I set out in the morning, choosing rather to trust myself among these barbarians than live with European Yahoos. I drew up my canoe as close as I could to the shore and hid myself behind a stone by the little brook, which, as I have already said, was excellent water.

The ship came within a half a league of this creek, and sent out her long-boat with vessels to take in fresh water (for the place, it seems, was very well known), but I did not observe it until the boat was almost on shore and it was too late to seek another hiding-place. The seamen at their landing observed my canoe and, rummaging it all over, easily conjectured that the owner could not be far off. Four of them well armed searched every cranny and lurking-hole, till at last they found me flat on my face behind the stone. They gazed a while in admiration at my strange uncouth dress, my coat made of skins, my wooden-soled shoes, and my furred stockings; from whence, however, they concluded I was not a native of the place, who all go naked. One of the seamen in Portuguese bid me rise, and asked who I was. I understood that language very well and, getting upon my feet, said I was a poor Yahoo, banished from the Houyhnhnms, and desired they would please to let me depart. They admired to hear me answer them in their own tongue, and saw by my complexion I must be an European, but were at loss to know what I meant by Yahoos and Houyhnhnms; and at the same time fell a-laughing at my strange tone in speaking, which resembled the neighing of a horse. I trembled all the while betwixt fear and hatred: I again desired leave to depart and was gently moving to my canoe; but they laid hold on me, desiring to know what country I was of, whence I came, with many other questions. I told them I was born in England, from whence I came about five years ago, and then their country and ours were at peace. I therefore hoped they would not treat me as an enemy since I meant them no harm, but was a poor Yahoo seeking some desolate place where to pass the remainder of his unfortunate life.

When they began to talk, I thought I never heard or saw anything so un-natural; for it appeared to me as monstrous as if a dog or a cow should speak in England, or a Yahoo in Houyhnhnmland. The honest Portuguese were equally amazed at my strange dress and the odd manner of delivering my words, which however they understood very well. They spoke to me with great humanity and said they were sure their captain would carry me *gratis* to Lisbon, from whence I might return to my own country; that two of the seamen would go back to the ship, inform the captain of what they had seen, and receive his orders; in the meantime, unless I would give my solemn oath not to fly, they would secure me by force. I thought it best to comply with their proposal. They were very curious to know my story, but I gave them very little satisfaction; and they all conjectured that my misfortunes had impaired my reason. In two hours the boat, which went loaden with vessels of water, returned with the captain's commands to fetch me on board. I fell on my knees to preserve my liberty; but all was in vain, and the men, having tied me with cords, heaved me into the boat, from whence I was taken into the ship and from thence into the captain's cabin.

His name was Pedro de Mendez; he was a very courteous and generous person. He entreated me to give some account of myself, and desired to know what I would eat or drink; said I should be used as well as himself, and spoke so many obliging things that I wondered to find such civilities from a Yahoo. However, I remained silent and sullen; I was ready to faint at the very smell of him and his men. At last I desired something to eat out of my own canoe; but he ordered me a chicken and some excellent wine, and then directed that I should be put to bed in a very clean cabin. I would not undress myself but lay on the bed-clothes, and in half an hour stole out, when I thought the crew was at dinner, and getting to the side of the ship was going to leap into the sea and swim for my life rather than continue among Yahoos. But one of the seamen prevented me, and having informed the captain, I was chained to my cabin.

After dinner Don Pedro came to me and desired to know my reason for so desperate an attempt: assured me he only meant to do me all the service he was able, and spoke so very movingly that at last I descended to treat him like an animal which had some little portion of reason. I gave him a very short relation of my voyage, of the conspiracy against me by my own men, of the country where they set me on shore, and of my three years' residence there. All which he looked upon as if it were a dream or a vision; whereat I took great offence; for I had quite forgot the faculty of lying, so peculiar to Yahoos in all countries where they preside, and, consequently, the disposition of suspecting truth in others of their own species. I asked him whether it were the custom of his country to *say the thing that was not*. I assured him I had almost forgot what he meant by falsehood, and, if I had lived a thousand years in Houyhnhnmland, I should never have heard a lie from the meanest servant; that I was altogether indifferent whether he believed me or no; but however, in return for his favours, I would give so much allowance to the corruption of his nature as to answer any objection he would please to make, and he might easily discover the truth.

The captain, a wise man, after many endeavours to catch me tripping in some part of my story, at last began to have a better opinion of my veracity, and the rather because, he confessed, he met with a Dutch skipper, who pretended to have landed with five others of his crew upon a certain island or continent south of New Holland, where they went for fresh water, and observed a horse driving before him several animals exactly resembling those I described under the name of Yahoos, with some other particulars, which the captain said he had forgot, because he then concluded them all to be lies. But he added that since I professed so inviolable an attachment to truth, I must give him my word of honour to bear him company in this voyage without attempting anything against my life, or else he would continue me a prisoner till we arrived in Lisbon. I gave him the promise he required; but at the same time protested that I would suffer the greatest hardships rather than return to live among Yahoos.

Our voyage passed without any considerable accident. In gratitude to the captain I sometimes sat with him at his earnest request and strove to conceal my antipathy against humankind, although it often broke out, which he suffered to pass without observation. But the greatest part of the day I confined myself to my cabin to avoid seeing any of the crew. The captain had often entreated me to strip myself of my savage dress, and offered to lend me the best suit of clothes he had. This I would not be prevailed on to accept, abhorring to cover myself with anything that had been on the back of a Yahoo. I only desired he would lend me two clean shirts, which having been washed since he wore them, I believed would not so much defile me. These I changed every second day, and washed them myself.

We arrived at Lisbon, Nov. 5, 1715. At our landing the captain forced me to cover myself with his cloak, to prevent the rabble from crowding about me. I was conveyed to his own house, and, at my earnest request, he led me up to the highest room backwards.[4] I conjured him to conceal from all persons what I had told him of the Houyhnhnms, because the least hint of such a story would not only draw numbers of people to see me, but probably put me in danger of being imprisoned or burnt by the Inquisition. The captain persuaded me to accept a suit of clothes newly made, but I would not suffer the tailor to take my measure; however, Don Pedro being almost of my size, they fitted me well enough. He accoutred me with other necessaries all new, which I aired for twenty-four hours before I would use them.

The captain had no wife, nor above three servants, none of which were suffered to attend at meals, and his whole deportment was so obliging, added to very good *human* understanding, that I really began to tolerate his company. He gained so far upon me that I ventured to look out of the back window. By degrees I was brought into another room, from whence I peeped into the street, but drew my head back in a fright. In a week's time he seduced me down to the door. I found my terror gradually lessened, but my hatred and contempt seemed to increase. I was at last bold enough to walk the street in his company, but kept my nose well stopped with rue,[5] or sometimes with tobacco.

In ten days Don Pedro, to whom I had given some account of my domestic affairs, put it upon me as a point of honour and conscience that I ought to return to my native country and live at home with my wife and children. He told me there was an English ship in the port just ready to sail, and he would furnish me with all things necessary. It would be tedious to repeat his arguments and my contradictions. He said it was altogether impossible to find such a solitary island as I had desired to live in; but I might command in my own house and pass my time in a manner as recluse as I pleased.

I complied at last, finding I could not do better. I left Lisbon the 24th day of November in an English merchantman, but who was the master I never inquired. Don Pedro accompanied me to the ship and lent me twenty pounds. He took kind leave of me and embraced me at parting, which I bore as well as I could. During this last voyage I had no commerce with the master or any of his men, but pretending I was sick kept close in my cabin. On the fifth of December, 1715, we cast anchor in the Downs [6] about nine in the morning, and at three in the afternoon I got safe to my house at Redriff.[7]

4. At the back of the house.
5. A strong-scented herb.
6. An anchorage near Dover where ships might discharge passengers and take on pilots for the navigation of the Thames estuary.
7. Rotherhithe, the dock section of East London south of the Thames.

My wife and family received me with great surprise and joy, because they concluded me certainly dead; but I must freely confess the sight of them filled me only with hatred, disgust, and contempt, and the more by reflecting on the near alliance I had to them. For although, since my unfortunate exile from the Houyhnhnm country, I had compelled myself to tolerate the sight of Yahoos, and to converse with Don Pedro de Mendez, yet my memory and imaginations were perpetually filled with the virtues and ideas of those exalted Houyhnhnms. And when I began to consider that by copulating with one of the Yahoo species I had become a parent of more, it struck me with the utmost shame, confusion, and horror.

As soon as I entered the house, my wife took me in her arms and kissed me, at which, having not been used to the touch of that odious animal for so many years, I fell in a swoon for almost an hour. At the time I am writing it is five years since my last return to England: during the first year I could not endure my wife or children in my presence; the very smell of them was intolerable, much less could I suffer them to eat in the same room. To this hour they dare not presume to touch my bread or drink out of the same cup, neither was I ever able to let one of them take me by the hand. The first money I laid out was to buy two young stone-horses; [8] which I keep in a good stable, and next to them the groom is my greatest favourite; for I feel my spirits revived by the smell he contracts in the stable. My horses understand me tolerably well; I converse with them at least four hours every day. They are strangers to bridle or saddle; they live in great amity with me and friendship to each other.

Chapter Twelve: The author's veracity. His design in publishing this work. His censure of those travellers who swerve from the truth. The author clears himself from any sinister ends in writing. An objection answered. The method of planting colonies. His native country commended. The right of the Crown to those countries described by the author is justified. The difficulty of conquering them. The author takes his last leave of the reader, proposeth his manner of living for the future, gives good advice, and concludeth.

Thus, gentle reader, I have given thee a faithful history of my travels for sixteen years and above seven months, wherein I have not been so studious of ornament as of truth. I could perhaps like others have astonished thee with strange improbable tales; but I rather chose to relate plain matter of fact in the simplest manner and style, because my principal design was to inform and not to amuse thee.

It is easy for us who travel into remote countries, which are seldom visited by Englishmen or other Europeans, to form descriptions of wonderful animals both at sea and land; whereas a traveller's chief aim should be to make men wiser and better and to improve their minds by the bad as well as good example of what they deliver concerning foreign places.

I could heartily wish a law were enacted that every traveller, before he were permitted to publish his voyages, should be obliged to make oath before the Lord High Chancellor that all he intended to print was absolutely true

8. Stallions.

to the best of his knowledge; for then the world would no longer be deceived as it usually is while some writers, to make their works pass the better upon the public, impose the grossest falsities on the unwary reader. I have perused several books of travels with great delight in my younger days; but having since gone over most parts of the globe and been able to contradict many fabulous accounts from my own observation, it hath given me a great disgust against this part of reading, and some indignation to see the credulity of mankind so impudently abused. Therefore since my acquaintance were pleased to think my poor endeavours might not be unacceptable to my country, I imposed on myself as a maxim, never to be swerved from, that I would *strictly adhere to truth;* neither indeed can I be ever under the least temptation to vary from it, while I retain in my mind the lectures and example of my noble master and the other illustrious Houyhnhnms, of whom I had so long the honour to be an humble hearer.

—Nec si miserum Fortuna Sinonem
Finxit, vanum etiam mendacemque improba finget.[1]

I know very well how little reputation is to be got by writings which require neither genius nor learning, nor indeed any other talent, except a good memory or an exact journal. I know likewise that writers of travels, like dictionary-makers, are sunk into oblivion by the weight and bulk of those who come last and therefore lie uppermost. And it is highly probable that such travellers who shall hereafter visit the countries described in this work of mine, may, by detecting my errors (if there be any) and adding many new discoveries of their own, jostle me out of vogue and stand in my place, making the world forget that ever I was an author. This indeed would be too great a mortification if I wrote for fame: but, as my sole intention was the *public good,*[2] I cannot be altogether disappointed. For who can read of the virtues I have mentioned in the glorious Houyhnhnms without being ashamed of his own vices, when he considers himself as the reasoning, governing animal of his country? I shall say nothing of those remote nations where Yahoos preside, amongst which the least corrupted are the Brobdingnagians, whose wise maxims in morality and government it would be our happiness to observe. But I forbear descanting further and rather leave the judicious reader to his own remarks and applications.

I am not a little pleased that this work of mine can possibly meet with no censurers: for what objections can be made against a writer who relates only plain facts that happened in such distant countries, where we have not the least interest with respect either to trade or negotiations? I have carefully avoided every fault with which common writers of travels are often too justly charged. Besides, I meddle not the least with any *party,* but write without passion, prejudice, or ill-will against any man or number of men whatsoever.

---

1. "Nor, if false Fortune has made Sinon wretched, shall she make him empty and deceitful as well," Virgil, *Aeneid* II.79–80; but Sinon is the treacherous Greek who is about to persuade the Trojans to admit the wooden horse into their city.
2. Often a suspect claim (cf. the opening of *A Modest Proposal*) on the grounds of outright hypocrisy or zealous self-deception; Gulliver's pride is implied, however genuine his sincerity.

I write for the noblest end, to inform and instruct mankind, over whom I may, without breach of modesty, pretend to some superiority from the advantages I received by conversing so long among the most accomplished Houyhnhnms. I write without any view towards profit or praise. I never suffer a word to pass that may look like reflection or possibly give the least offence even to those who are most ready to take it. So that I hope I may with justice pronounce myself an author perfectly blameless, against whom the tribes of answerers, considerers, observers, reflecters, detecters, remarkers,[3] will never be able to find matter for exercising their talents.

I confess it was whispered to me that I was bound in duty, as a subject of England, to have given in a memorial to a secretary of state at my first coming over; because whatever lands are discovered by a subject belong to the Crown. But I doubt whether our conquests in the countries I treat of would be as easy as those of Ferdinando Cortez over the naked Americans.[4] The Lilliputians, I think, are hardly worth the charge of a fleet and army to reduce them, and I question whether it might be prudent or safe to attempt the Brobdingnagians. Or whether an English army would be much at their ease with the Flying Island over their heads. The Houyhnhnms, indeed, appear not to be so well prepared for war, a science to which they are perfect strangers, and especially against missive weapons.[5] However, supposing myself to be a minister of state, I could never give my advice for invading them. Their prudence, unanimity, unacquaintedness with fear, and their love of their country would amply supply all defects in the military art. Imagine twenty thousand of them breaking into the midst of an European army, confounding the ranks, overturning the carriages,[6] battering the warriors' faces into mummy [7] by terrible yerks [8] from their hinder hoofs. For they would well deserve the character given to Augustus: *Recalcitrat undique tutus.*[9] But instead of proposals for conquering that magnanimous [10] nation, I rather wish they were in a capacity or disposition to send a sufficient number of their inhabitants for civilizing Europe, by teaching us the first principles of honour, justice, truth, temperance, public spirit, fortitude, chastity, friendship, benevolence, and fidelity. The *names* of all which virtues are still retained among us in most languages and are to be met with in modern as well as ancient authors; which I am able to assert from my own small reading.

But I had another reason which made me less forward to enlarge his Majesty's dominions by my discoveries. To say the truth, I had conceived a few scruples with relation to the distributive justice of princes upon those occasions. For instance, a crew of pirates are driven by a storm they know not whither, at length a boy discovers land from the topmast, they go on

3. The usual terms by which authors of hostile replies were designated.
4. Cortez succeeded so easily in his conquest of Mexico (1519) because the Aztecs were awed by the ships and firearms of the Spaniards and by the fact that they were mounted on horses.
5. Those thrown or shot, rather than hand weapons.
6. Gun carriages.
7. Pulp.
8. Kicks.
9. "He kicks back with safety on every side." Horace, *Satires* II.i.20.
10. Large-souled, noble.

shore to rob and plunder, they see an harmless people, are entertained with kindness, they give the country a new name, they take formal possession of it for the king, they set up a rotten plank or a stone for a memorial, they murder two or three dozen of the natives, bring away a couple more by force for a sample, return home, and get their pardon. Here commences a new dominion acquired with a title by *divine right*.[11] Ships are sent with the first opportunity, the natives driven out or destroyed, their princes tortured to discover their gold, a free license given to all acts of inhumanity and lust, the earth reeking with the blood of its inhabitants: and this execrable crew of butchers employed in so pious an expedition is a *modern colony* sent to convert and civilize an idolatrous and barbarous people.

But this description, I confess, doth by no means affect the British nation, who may be an example to the whole world for their wisdom, care, and justice in planting colonies; their liberal endowments for the advancement of religion and learning; their choice of devout and able pastors to propagate Christianity; their caution in stocking their provinces with people of sober lives and conversations from this, the mother kingdom; [12] their strict regard to the distribution of justice in supplying the civil administration through all their colonies with officers of the greatest abilities, utter strangers to corruption; and to crown all, by sending the most vigilant and virtuous governors, who have no other views than the happiness of the people over whom they preside, and the honour of the king their master.

But as those countries which I have described do not appear to have any desire of being conquered and enslaved, murdered, or driven out by colonies, nor abound either in gold, silver, sugar, or tobacco; I did humbly conceive they were by no means proper objects of our zeal, our valour, or our interest. However, if those whom it more concerns think fit to be of another opinion, I am ready to depose, when I shall be lawfully called, that no European did ever visit these countries before me. I mean, if the inhabitants ought to be believed; unless a dispute may arise about the two Yahoos, said to have been seen many ages ago on a mountain in Houyhnhnmland, from whence, the opinion is, that the race of those brutes hath descended; and these, for anything I know, may have been English, which indeed I was apt to suspect from the lineaments of their posterity's countenances, although very much defaced. But how far that will go to make out a title, I leave to the learned in colony-law.

But as to the formality of taking possession in my sovereign's name, it never came once into my thoughts; and if it had, yet as my affairs then stood, I should perhaps, in point of prudence and self-preservation, have put it off to a better opportunity.

Having thus answered the *only* objection that can be raised against me as a traveller, I here take a final leave of my courteous readers, and return to enjoy my own speculations in my little garden at Redriff, to apply those excellent lessons of virtue which I learned among the Houyhnhnms, to instruct the

11. The doctrine of divine right of kings (discussed earlier by Halifax and Dryden) had been current in England since James I and was defended by many so long as the Stuarts held the throne; here it is applied to the specious justification of rule by conquest, as it had been by Spain in the New World.
12. Transportation to the colonies was an alternative to hanging for many serious crimes, and it was used to supply the colonists with a labor force.

Yahoos of my own family as far as I shall find them docible [13] animals, to behold my figure often in a glass, and thus if possible habituate myself by time to tolerate the sight of a human creature; to lament the brutality [14] of Houyhnhnms in my own country, but always treat their persons with respect for the sake of my noble master, his family, his friends, and the whole Houyhnhnm race, whom these of ours have the honour to resemble in all their lineaments, however their intellectuals came to degenerate.

I began last week to permit my wife to sit at dinner with me, at the farthest end of a long table, and to answer (but with the utmost brevity) the few questions I asked her. Yet the smell of a Yahoo continuing very offensive, I always keep my nose well stopped with rue, lavender, or tobacco leaves. And although it be hard for a man late in life to remove old habits, I am not altogether out of hopes in some time to suffer a neighbour Yahoo in my company without the apprehensions I am yet under of his teeth or his claws.

My reconcilement to the Yahoo-kind in general might not be so difficult if they would be content with those vices and follies only which nature hath entitled them to. I am not in the least provoked at the sight of a lawyer, a pickpocket, a colonel, a fool, a lord, a gamester, a politician, a whoremonger, a physician, an evidence,[15] a suborner, an attorney, a traitor, or the like; this is all according to the due course of things: but when I behold a lump of deformity and diseases both in body and mind, smitten with *pride*, it immediately breaks all the measures of my patience; neither shall I be ever able to comprehend how such an animal and such a vice could tally together. The wise and virtuous Houyhnhnms, who abound in all excellencies that can adorn a rational creature, have no name for this vice in their language, which hath no terms to express anything that is evil except those whereby they describe the detestable qualities of their Yahoos, among which they were not able to distinguish this of pride, for want of thoroughly understanding human nature as it showeth itself in other countries where that animal presides. But I, who had more experience, could plainly observe some rudiments of it among the wild Yahoos.

But the Houyhnhnms, who live under the government of reason, are no more proud of the good qualities they possess than I should be for not wanting a leg or an arm; which no man in his wits would boast of, although he must be miserable without them. I dwell the longer upon this subject from the desire I have to make the society of an English Yahoo by any means not insupportable, and therefore I here entreat those who have any tincture of this absurd vice that they will not presume to appear in my sight.

1726

A Letter from Capt. Gulliver to His Cousin Sympson [1]
I hope you will be ready to own publicly, whenever you shall be called to it, that by your great and frequent urgency you prevailed on me to publish a

13. Teachable.
14. That is, animality.
15. Paid informer.

1. This letter first appeared in Faulkner's edition of 1735 and was probably written close to that year rather than in 1727, as it was dated; Sympson was the fictitious name under which negotiations were first made to publish the book.

very loose and uncorrect account of my travels; with direction to hire some young gentlemen of either university to put them in order and correct the style, as my cousin Dampier did by my advice, in his book called *A Voyage Round the World*.[2] But I do not remember I gave you power to consent that anything should be omitted, and much less that anything should be inserted: [3] therefore, as to the latter, I do here renounce everything of that kind; particularly a paragraph about her Majesty, the late Queen Anne, of most pious and glorious memory; although I did reverence and esteem her more than any of human species. But you or your interpolator ought to have considered that, as it was not my inclination, so was it not decent to praise any animal of our composition [4] before my master Houyhnhnm: and besides, the fact was altogether false; for to my knowledge, being in England during some part of her Majesty's reign, she did govern by a chief minister; nay, even by two successively; the first whereof was the Lord of Godolphin, and the second the Lord of Oxford; [5] so that you have made me *say the thing that was not*. Likewise, in the account of the Academy of Projectors and several passages of my discourse to my master Houyhnhnm, you have either omitted some material circumstances, or minced or changed them in such a manner that I do hardly know mine own work. When I formerly hinted to you something of this in a letter, you were pleased to answer that you were afraid of giving offence; that people in power were very watchful over the press and apt not only to interpret but to punish everything which looked like an *innuendo* (as I think you called it). But pray, how could that which I spoke so many years ago and at above five thousand leagues distance, in another reign, be applied to any of the Yahoos who now are said to govern the herd,[6] especially at a time when I little thought on or feared the unhappiness of living under them? Have not I the most reason to complain when I see these very Yahoos carried by Houyhnhnms in a vehicle, as if these were brutes and those the rational creatures? And, indeed, to avoid so monstrous and detestable a sight was one principal motive of my retirement hither.

Thus much I thought proper to tell you in relation to your self and to the trust I reposed in you.

I do in the next place complain of my own great want of judgment in being prevailed upon by the intreaties and false reasonings of you and some others, very much against mine own opinion, to suffer my travels to be published. Pray bring to your mind how often I desired you to consider, when you insisted on the motive of public good, that the Yahoos were a species of animals utterly incapable of amendment by precepts or examples, and so it hath proved; for instead of seeing a full stop put to all abuses and corruptions, at least in this little island, as I had reason to expect: behold, after above six

---

2. William Dampier (1652–1715), whose very popular work *A New Voyage Round the World* appeared in 1697 and is often parodied in *Gulliver's Travels*.
3. As was done, to moderate the satire, by the first publisher, Benjamin Motte.
4. Kind.
5. The 1st Earl of Godolphin from 1702 until 1710; thereafter Robert Harley, 1st Earl of Oxford and the friend of Swift and Pope, until 1714.
6. An ironic reference to the highly topical satire against Walpole and the court of George I that runs through the book.

months' warning, I cannot learn that my book hath produced one single effect according to mine intentions. I desired you would let me know by a letter when party and faction were extinguished; judges learned and upright; pleaders honest and modest, with some tincture of common sense; and Smithfield [7] blazing with pyramids of law-books; the young nobility's education entirely changed; the physicians banished; the female Yahoos abounding in virtue, honour, truth and good sense; courts and levees of great ministers thoroughly weeded and swept; wit, merit and learning rewarded; all disgracers of the press in prose and verse condemned to eat nothing but their own cotton [8] and quench their thirst with their own ink. These and a thousand other reformations I firmly counted upon by your encouragement, as indeed they were plainly deducible from the precepts delivered in my book. And it must be owned that seven months were a sufficient time to correct every vice and folly to which Yahoos are subject, if their natures had been capable of the least disposition to virtue or wisdom; yet so far have you been from answering mine expectation in any of your letters, that on the contrary you are loading our carrier every week with libels, and keys, and reflections, and memoirs, and second parts; wherein I see myself accused of reflecting upon great statesfolk; of degrading human nature (for so they have still the confidence to style it), and of abusing the female sex. I find likewise that the writers of those bundles are not agreed among themselves; for some of them will not allow me to be author of mine own travels, and others make me author of books to which I am wholly a stranger.[9]

I find likewise that your printer hath been so careless as to confound the times and mistake the dates of my several voyages and returns, neither assigning the true year or the true month or day of the month; and I hear the original manuscript is all destroyed since the publication of my book. Neither have I any copy left; however, I have sent you some corrections, which you may insert if ever there should be a second edition: and yet I cannot stand to [10] them, but shall leave that matter to my judicious and candid readers to adjust it as they please.

I hear some of our sea-Yahoos find fault with my sea-language, as not proper in many parts nor now in use. I cannot help it. In my first voyages, while I was young, I was instructed by the oldest mariners and learned to speak as they did. But I have since found that the sea-Yahoos are apt, like the land ones, to become new-fangled in their words; which the latter change every year, insomuch as I remember upon each return to mine own country, their old dialect was so altered that I could hardly understand the new. And I observe, when any Yahoo comes from London out of curiosity to visit me at mine own house, we neither of us are able to deliver our conceptions in a manner intelligible to the other.

7. The London cattle market where heretics and murderers had been burned; Gulliver seems to call for a burning of false books such as Savonarola conducted in 15th-century Florence and the Inquisition did later.
8. Paper.
9. Referring to the numerous spurious "continuations" and imitations, as well as a "complete key."
10. Insist upon.

If the censure of Yahoos could any way affect me, I should have great reason to complain that some of them are so bold as to think my book of travels a mere fiction out of mine own brain; and have gone so far as to drop hints that the Houyhnhnms and Yahoos have no more existence than the inhabitants of Utopia.[11]

Indeed I must confess, that as to the people of Lilliput, Brobdingrag (for so the word should have been spelt, and not erroneously *Brobdingnag*), and Laputa, I have never yet heard of any Yahoo so presumptuous as to dispute their being or the facts I have related concerning them; because the truth immediately strikes every reader with conviction. And is there less probability in my account of the Houyhnhnms or Yahoos when it is manifest as to the latter, there are so many thousands even in this city who only differ from their brother brutes in Houyhnhnmland because they use a sort of a jabber and do not go naked? I wrote for their amendment and not their approbation. The united praise of the whole race would be of less consequence to me than the neighing of those two degenerate Houyhnhnms I keep in my stable; because from these, degenerate as they are, I still improve in some virtues, without any mixture of vice.

Do these miserable animals presume to think that I am so far degenerated as to defend my veracity? Yahoo as I am, it is well known through all Houyhnhnmland that, by the instructions and example of my illustrious master, I was able in the compass of two years (although I confess with the utmost difficulty) to remove that infernal habit of lying, shuffling, deceiving, and equivocating so deeply rooted in the very souls of all my species, especially the Europeans.

I have other complaints to make upon this vexatious occasion; but I forbear troubling myself or you any further. I must freely confess that since my last return some corruptions of my Yahoo nature have revived in me by conversing with a few of your species, and particularly those of mine own family, by an unavoidable necessity; else I should never have attempted so absurd a project as that of reforming the Yahoo race in this kingdom; but I have now done with all such visionary schemes forever.

1735

From John Gay and Alexander Pope: Mary Gulliver to Captain Lemuel Gulliver

Welcome, thrice welcome to thy native place!
—What, touch me not? what, shun a wife's embrace?
Have I for this thy tedious absence borne
And waked and wished whole nights for thy return?
In five long years I took no second spouse;
What Redriff wife so long hath kept her vows?
Your eyes, your nose, inconstancy betray;

11. Utopia (from the Greek for "nowhere") was the name Sir Thomas More gave to his "ideal" commonwealth, and his great ironic work (1516) immensely influenced Swift.

Your nose you stop, your eyes you turn away.
'Tis said, that thou shouldst cleave unto thy wife;
10 Once *thou* didst cleave, and *I* could cleave for life.
Hear and relent! hark, how thy children moan;
Be kind at least to these, they are thy own:
Behold, and count them all; secure to find
The honest number that you left behind.
See how they pat thee with their pretty paws:
Why start you? are they snakes? or have they claws?
Thy Christian seed, our mutual flesh and bone:
Be kind at least to these, they are thy own.

. . .

My bed (the scene of all our former joys,
40 Witness two lovely girls, two lovely boys)
Alone I press; in dreams I call my dear,
I stretch my hand, no Gulliver is there!
I wake, I rise, and shivering with the frost,
Search all the house; my Gulliver is lost!
Forth in the street I rush with frantic cries:
The windows open; all the neighbours rise:
Where sleeps my Gulliver? *O tell me where?*
The neighbours answer, *With the sorrel mare.*

At early morn, I to the market haste,
50 (Studious in everything to please thy taste)
A curious fowl and sparagrass I chose,
(For I remember you were fond of those),
Three shillings cost the first, the last seven groats;
Sullen you turn from both, and call for *oats.*

. . .

Nay, would kind *Jove* my organs so dispose,
To hymn harmonious *Houyhnhnm* through the nose,
I'd call thee *Houyhnhnm*, that high sounding name,
Thy children's noses all should twang the same,
So might I find my loving spouse of course
110 Endued with all the virtues of a horse.

1727

THE MOCK FORM

One of the opportunities the poet gains from a clearly formalized set of genres and from clearly articulated levels of style (we can see the two related to each other and to the levels of society as well by Thomas Hobbes in his *Answer to Davenant's Preface to Gondibert*) is that of playing upon or against the forms. We can see this most clearly in mock-heroic poetry, where the style is highest and achieves its elevation by exclusion; the grand style, especially in the eighteenth century, strives for generality and repudiates the time-bound particular. In his "ironical discourse," for example, Sir Joshua Reynolds scornfully proposes that the sculptor's model be carefully dressed in the latest fashion by his tailor; the next step, he adds, would be "to add colour to these statues, which will complete the deception. . . ." Pope, it is true, defends "small circumstances" (in the farewell of Hector) against the tyrannic view that "a poet ought only to collect the great and noble particulars," but he defends them insofar as they are significantly characteristic. "The question," as he puts it in the Postscript in the *Odyssey* (1726), "is how far a poet, in pursuing a description or image of an action, can attach himself to little circumstances without vulgarity or trifling."

In travesty the poet dresses (*trans-vestire*) a high subject in low costume; in mock heroic he dresses a low subject in high style. In both cases he creates a deliberate incongruity between subject and form and points up the artificiality of the form. This may work both ways: he may remind us how much of human complexity and sheer physical circumstance is excluded by high forms, how vacuous they may become as they move toward the academic and attain a rigid pomposity; or he may remind us how far our present world, caught in its up-to-the-minute modishness or all its embarrassment of particulars, falls below the heroic simplicity of the past or the persistent vision of human greatness. As Dr. Johnson says of John Philips's *The Splendid Shilling*, "to degrade the sounding words of Milton by an application to the lowest and most trivial things gratifies the mind with a momentary triumph over that grandeur which hitherto held its captives in admiration. . . ." Such a poem as Philips's is not an attack upon Milton any more than Pope's *Rape of the Lock* is an attack upon epic; each poem plays with the nature of our imagination and explores its capacity for creating myth, exposing its workings with affection as well as "triumph." In Butler's *Hudibras* the burlesque techniques work to degrade their subject, which is not given even playful dignity by the romance and heroic elements; these serve, instead, to define lunatic pretensions as they are fused with the grubbiest of physical detail.

In *The Shepherd's Week* Gay mocks Ambrose Philips's effort to make the pastoral realistic. Pope had described that form (with Virgil as his model) as "an image of what they call the Golden Age." We are "not to describe our shepherds as shepherds at this day really are"—for that would be to literalize myth—"but as they may be conceived then to have been when the best of men followed the employment." Philips (invoking Theocritus and Spenser) produced something closer to literal shepherds speaking their modern version of a Doric dialect, and Pope ironically commended his "simplicity." For "simplicity" remains throughout the age a key word. Both Swift and Pope are anxious to protect its meaning from mere lack of refinement or art; it must not be slovenliness or the merely "primitive" any more than it can be precious and too conspicuously artificial. It is art concealing art, like the "natural," neither gross nor infantile, but characteristic of man at his fullest and most mature. Gay's *Shepherd's Week* sets out to ridicule Philips's misplaced realism, and in that it succeeds admirably (creating a group of low rustics who undermine the mythical forms in which they are placed); but he also moves—as the satirist does—into a realism that begins to win our respect by displacing value from the mythical and literary to the actual and literal. As Dr. Johnson puts it,

> the effect of reality and truth became conspicuous, even when the intention was to show them grovelling and degraded. These Pastorals became popular and were read with delight as just representations of rural manners and occupations by those who had no interest in the rivalry of the poets nor knowledge of the critical dispute.

That is an overstatement, for no degree of ignorance of the critical dispute can blind us to the tellingly low aspect of Gay's figures, but the poems became an interesting case of the generation of a new vision from the conflict of older forms.

Something of the same sort may be seen in the two poems on Baucis and Philemon. Dryden's translation of Ovid somewhat intensifies the comic charm of the humble household, which is conceived in its very absence of grandeur (but is given equivalent nobility in its warmth of hospitality). But such tendencies as Dryden may have to sentimentalize the humble old couple and to elevate their good nature are undercut by Swift's brisker version, which lowers the characters and plays elaborately on the machinery of metamorphosis. His Baucis and Philemon are hardly allowed the dignity that their goodness warrants; they carry their commonplaceness into new guises, and even their death loses the tenderness of Dryden's duet.

One can take this further. The life of retirement is often set against the heroic and celebrated in the age in poems of country life, close in spirit to the pastorals or georgics of Virgil and often drawing their inspiration from them. Here again the temptation is great to sentimentalize, to claim for the absence of worldly greatness the implicit glories of a greater goodness. Matthew Prior's *An Epitaph* takes as its epigraph a famous chorus from Seneca's *Thyestes,* which became one of the key texts for the life of retirement (we can see it echoed at the close of Pope's *Epistle to Dr. Arbuthnot,* for example). It is given here in Andrew Marvell's translation, and it must be put beside the banal life of moral vacuity Prior offers in its place.

JOHN PHILIPS
1676–1709

From The Splendid Shilling

An Imitation of Milton°

Happy the man who, void of cares and strife,
In silken or in leathern purse retains
A Splendid Shilling: he nor hears with pain
New oysters cried, nor sighs for cheerful ale;
But with his friends, when nightly mists arise,
To Juniper's, Magpie, or Town Hall° repairs:
Where, mindful of the nymph whose wanton eye
Transfixed his soul and kindled amorous flames,
Chloe or Phyllis, he each circling glass
10   Wisheth her health and joy and equal love.
Meanwhile he smokes, and laughs at merry tale,
Or pun ambiguous, or conundrum quaint.

An Imitation of Milton Philips read Milton with great pleasure (according to legend, while his long hair was being combed) at Westminster and later at Oxford, and he finally abandoned the study of medicine for a literary career. *The Splendid Shilling* (which Addison regarded as the "finest burlesque poem in the English lan-guage") won him Tory patronage. In addition to political poems he wrote an imitation of Virgil's *Georgics* in Miltonic blank verse, the influential poem *Cyder.*
Juniper's . . . Town Hall The first may be the name of an innkeeper; the others were Oxford alehouses.

But I, whom griping penury surrounds,
And hunger, sure attendant upon want,
With scanty offals,° and small acid tiff°
(Wretched repast!) my meagre corpse sustain:
Then solitary walk, or doze at home
In garret vile, and with a warming puff
Regale chilled fingers; or from tube as black
20   As winter chimney or well polished jet
Exhale mundungus,° ill-perfuming scent:
Not blacker tube nor of a shorter size
Smokes Cambro-Briton° (versed in pedigree,
Sprung from Cadwalader and Arthur, kings
Full famous in romantic tale) when he
O'er many a craggy hill and barren cliff,
Upon a cargo of famed Cestrian° cheese
High over-shadowing rides, with a design
To vend his wares, or at the Arvonian° mart,
30   Or Maridunum,° or the ancient town
Yclept Brechinia,° or where Vaga's stream°
Encircles Ariconium,° fruitful soil,
Whence flow nectareous wines, that well may vie
With Massic, Setin, or renowned Falern.°
    Thus while my joyless minutes tedious flow
With looks demure and silent pace, a dun,°
Horrible monster! hated by gods and men,
To my aerial citadel ascends;
With vocal heel thrice thundering at my gates,
40   With hideous accent thrice he calls; I know
The voice ill-boding and the solemn sound.
What should I do? or whither turn? Amazed,
Confounded, to the dark recess I fly
Of woodhole; straight my bristling hairs erect
Through sudden fear; a chilly sweat bedews
My shuddering limbs, and, wonderful to tell,
My tongue forgets her faculty of speech,
So horrible he seems; his faded brow
Entrenched with many a frown and conic beard
50   And spreading band,° admired by modern saints,
Disastrous acts forebode; in his right hand
Long scrolls of paper solemnly he waves,
With characters and figures dire inscribed
Grievous to mortal eyes; (ye gods avert
Such plagues from righteous men!) behind him stalks

offals fragments
tiff poor or weak liquor
mundungus strong-smelling tobacco
Cambro-Briton Welshman
Cestrian Cheshire
Arvonian at Carnarvon
Maridunum Camarthen in Wales
Yclept Brechinia named Brecon

Vaga's stream the river Wye
Ariconium Kenchester
Massic . . . Falern old Italian wines from
Monte Massico, Satia, or the Falernian Field in
Campania
dun bill collector
band strips hanging from the collar, associated
with clerical dress (as in Geneva bands)

Another monster, not unlike himself,
Sullen of aspect, by the vulgar called
A catchpole,° whose polluted hands the gods
With force incredible and magic charms
60   Erst have indued; if he his ample palm
Should haply on ill-fated shoulder lay
Of debtor, straight his body to the touch
Obsequious,° as whilom° knights were wont,
To some enchanted castle is conveyed,
Where gates impregnable and coercive chains
In durance strict detain him, till in form
Of money Pallas sets the captive free.

      . . .

  Thus do I live from pleasure quite debarred,
Nor taste the fruits that the sun's genial rays
Mature, John-apple,° nor the downy peach,
Nor walnut in rough-furrowed coat secure,
Nor medlar,° fruit delicious in decay.
120 Afflictions great! yet greater still remain:
My galligaskins° that have long withstood
The winter's fury and encroaching frosts,
By time subdued, (what will not time subdue!)
An horrid chasm disclose, with orifice
Wide, discontinuous; at which the winds
Eurus and Auster,° and the dreadful force
Of Boreas,° that congeals the Cronian° waves,
Tumultuous enter with dire chilling blasts
Portending agues. Thus a well-fraught ship
130 Long sailed secure, or through the Aegean deep,
Or the Ionian, till cruising near
The Lilybean° shore, with hideous crush
On Scylla or Charybdis,° dangerous rocks,
She strikes rebounding, whence the shattered oak,
So fierce a shock unable to withstand,
Admits the sea; in at the gaping side
The crowding waves gush with impetuous rage,
Resistless, overwhelming; horrors seize
The mariners, death in their eyes appears,
140 They stare, they lave, they pump, they swear, they pray:
Vain efforts! still the battering waves rush in
Implacable, till deluged by the foam,
The ship sinks foundering in the vast abyss.

                1701

---

catchpole officer who arrests for debt; bum-bailiff
Obsequious fully yielding, freely following
whilom formerly
John-apple a "keeping apple" that lasts two years and is at its best when shriveled
medlar eaten only when overripe
galligaskins breeches

Eurus and Auster east and south winds
Boreas north wind
Cronian Arctic, as in *Paradise Lost* X.290
Lilybean Sicilian
Scylla or Charybdis the mythical monsters here identified with the rocks on the east coast of Sicily and the west of Italy

JOHN GAY

From The Shepherd's Week°

Wednesday; or, The Dumps°

The wailings of a maiden I recite,
A maiden fair that Sparabella° hight.
Such strains ne'er warble in the linnet's throat,
Nor the gay goldfinch chaunts so sweet a note.
No magpie chattered, nor the painted jay,
No ox was heard to low, nor ass to bray.
No rustling breezes played the leaves among,
While thus her madrigal° the damsel sung.
   A while, O D'Urfey,° lend an ear or twain,
10 Nor, though in homely guise, my verse disdain;
Whether thou seekest new kingdoms in the sun,°
Whether thy muse does at Newmarket° run,
Or does with gossips at a feast regale,
And heighten her conceits with sack° and ale,
Or else at wakes with Joan and Hodge° rejoice,
Where D'Urfey's lyrics swell in every voice;
Yet suffer me, thou bard of wondrous meed,°
Amid thy bays to weave this rural weed.
   Now the sun drove adown the western road,
20 And oxen laid at rest forget the goad,
The clown° fatigued trudged homeward with his spade,
Across the meadows stretched the lengthened shade;
When Sparabella pensive and forlorn,
Alike with yearning love and labour worn,
Leaned on her rake, and straight with doleful guise
Did this sad plaint in moanful notes devise.
   'Come night as dark as pitch, surround my head,
From Sparabella Bumkinet is fled;
The ribbon that his valorous cudgel won,
30 'Last Sunday happier Clumsilis put on.
Sure if he'd eyes (but Love, they say, has none)
I whilom by that ribbon had been known.
Ah, well-a-day! I'm shent° with baneful smart,

Th Shepherd's Week See the Headnote on John Gay for his career; for selections from *Trivia* (1716), see The Urban Scene.
Dumps "Dumps, or Dumbs, made use of to express a fit of the sullens" (Gay, who goes on to provide an elaborate piece of mock-pedantic etymology in the manner of E.K.'s notes to Spenser's *The Shepherd's Calendar*, Ambrose Philips's chief model)
Sparabella the first of Gay's distortions of conventional rustic or pastoral names, here Clarabella given a note of sexual license from the notoriously lecherous sparrow
madrigal love lyric

D'Urfey the popular song writer Thomas D'Urfey (1653–1723), from whom Gay draws in *The Beggar's Opera*
new . . . sun referring to D'Urfey's "opera" *Wonders in the Sun* (1706)
Newmarket the scene of horse races celebrated by D'Urfey in a well-known song
sack dry white wine
Joan and Hodge stock names for rural figures
meed "an old word for fame or renown" (Gay)
clown peasant, bumpkin
shent "an old word signifying *hurt* or harmed" (Gay)

For with the ribbon he bestowed his heart.
  'My plaint, ye lasses, with this burthen aid,
'Tis hard so true a damsel dies a maid.
  'Shall heavy Clumsilis with me compare?
View this, ye lovers, and like me despair.
Her blubbered lip by smutty pipes is worn,
40 And in her breath tobacco whiffs are borne;
The cleanly cheese-press she could never turn,
Her awkward fist did ne'er employ the churn;
If e'er she brewed, the drink would straight go sour,
Before it ever felt the thunder's power:°
No huswifry the dowdy creature knew;
To sum up all, her tongue confessed the shrew.
  'My plaint, ye lasses, with this burthen aid,
'Tis hard so true a damsel dies a maid.
  'I've often seen my visage in yon lake,
50 Nor are my features of the homeliest make.
Though Clumsilis may boast a whiter dye,
Yet the black sloe turns in my rolling eye;
And fairest blossoms drop with every blast,
But the brown beauty will like hollies last.
Her wan complexion's like the withered leek,
While Katherine pears adorn my ruddy cheek.
Yet she, alas! the witless lout hath won,
And by her gain, poor Sparabell's undone!
Let hares and hounds in coupling straps unite,
60 The clucking hen make friendship with the kite,
Let the fox simply wear the nuptial noose,
And join in wedlock with the waddling goose;
For love hath brought a stranger thing to pass,
The fairest shepherd weds the foulest lass.
  'My plaint, ye lasses, with this burthen aid,
'Tis hard so true a damsel dies a maid.
  'Sooner shall cats disport in waters clear,
And speckled mackerels graze the meadows fair,
Sooner shall screech-owls bask in sunny day,
70 And the slow ass on trees, like squirrels, play,
Sooner shall snails on insect pinions rove,
Then I forget my shepherd's wonted love.
  'My plaint, ye lasses, with this burthen aid,
'Tis hard so true a damsel dies a maid.
  'Ah! didst thou know what proffers I withstood,
When late I met the Squire in yonder wood!
To me he sped, regardless of his game,
While all my cheek was glowing red with shame;
My lip he kissed, and praised my healthful look,

thunder's power to sour liquids

80   Then from his purse of silk a guinea took,
Into my hand he forced the tempting gold,
While I with modest struggling broke his hold.
He swore that Dick in livery striped with lace,
Should wed me soon to keep me from disgrace;
But I nor footman prized nor golden fee,
For what is lace or gold compared to thee?
    'My plaint, ye lasses, with this burthen aid,
'Tis hard so true a damsel dies a maid.
    'Now plain I ken whence Love his rise begun.
90   Sure he was born some bloody butcher's son,
Bred up in shambles,° where our younglings° slain,
Erst taught him mischief and to sport with pain.
The father only silly sheep annoys,
The son the sillier shepherdess destroys.
Does son or father greater mischief do?
The sire is cruel, so the son is too.
    'My plaint, ye lasses, with this burthen aid,
'Tis hard so true a damsel dies a maid.
    'Farewell, ye woods, ye meads, ye streams that flow;
100   A sudden death shall rid me of my woe.
This penknife keen my windpipe shall divide.
What, shall I fall as squeaking pigs have died!
No—To some tree this carcass I'll suspend.
But worrying curs find such untimely end!
I'll speed me to the pond, where the high stool
On the long plank hangs o'er the muddy pool,
That stool,° the dread of every scolding quean;°
Yet, sure a lover should not die so mean!
There placed aloft, I'll rave and rail by fits,
110   Though all the parish say I've lost my wits;
And thence, if courage holds, my self I'll throw,
And quench my passion in the lake below.
    'Ye lasses, cease your burthen, cease to moan,
And, by my case forewarned, go mind your own.'
    The sun was set; the night came on a-pace,
And falling dews bewet around the place,
The bat takes airy rounds on leathern wings,
And the hoarse owl his woeful dirges sings;
The prudent maiden deems it now too late,
120   And till tomorrow comes defers her fate.

1714

shambles slaughterhouses
younglings young animals
stool the ducking stool, into which scolds were
fastened in order to be ducked in the pond
quean slut

JOHN DRYDEN

From Baucis and Philemon

Out of the Eighth Book of Ovid's Metamorphoses

Heaven's power is infinite; earth, air, and sea,
The manufactured mass, the making power obey.
By proof to clear your doubt: in Phrygian ground
Two neighbouring trees, with walls encompassed round,
Stand on a moderate rise, with wonder shown,
One a hard oak, a softer linden one. . . .
21   Not far from thence is seen a lake, the haunt
Of coots and of the fishing cormorant:
Here Jove with Hermes came; but in disguise
Of mortal men concealed their deities:
One laid aside his thunder, one his rod;
And many toilsome steps together trod;
For harbour at a thousand doors they knocked—
Not one of all the thousand but was locked.
At last an hospitable house they found,
30   A homely° shed; the roof, not far from ground,
Was thatched with reeds, and straw together bound.
There Baucis and Philemon lived, and there
Had lived long married, and a happy pair:
Now old in love, though little was their store,
Inured to want, their poverty they bore,
Nor aimed at wealth, professing° to be poor.
For master or for servant here to call,
Was all alike, where only two were all.
Command was none, where equal love was paid,
40   Or rather both commanded, both obeyed.
      From lofty roofs the gods repulsed before,
Now, stooping, entered through the little door;
The man (their hearty welcome first expressed)
A common settle drew for either guest,
Inviting each his weary limbs to rest.
But e'er they sat, officious° Baucis lays
Two cushions stuffed with straw, the seat to raise;
Coarse, but the best she had; then rakes the load
Of ashes from the hearth, and spreads abroad
50   The living coals, and, lest they should expire,
With leaves and barks she feeds her infant fire:
It smokes, and then with trembling breath she blows,
Till in a cheerful blaze the flames arose.
With brushwood and with chips she strengthens these,
And adds at last the boughs of rotten trees.

homely humble   officious full of good offices, solicitous
professing openly declaring themselves

The fire thus formed, she sets the kettle on—
Like burnished gold the little seether shone—
Next took the coleworts° which her husband got
From his own ground (a small well-watered spot);
60   She stripped the stalks of all their leaves; the best
She culled, and then with handy care she dressed.
High o'er the hearth a chine of bacon hung:
Good old Philemon seized it with a prong,
And from the sooty rafter drew it down;
Then cut a slice, but scarce enough for one;
Yet a large portion of a little store,
Which for their sakes alone he wished were more.
This in the pot he plunged without delay,
To tame the flesh and drain the salt away.
70   The time between, before the fire they sat,
And shortened the delay by pleasing chat.
   A beam there was, on which a beechen pail
Hung by the handle, on a driven nail:
This filled with water, gently warmed, they set
Before their guests; in this they bathed their feet,
And after with clean towels dried their sweat.
This done, the host produced the genial bed,
Sallow° the feet, the borders, and the stead
Which with no costly coverlet they spread,
80   But coarse old garments; yet such robes as these
They laid alone° at feasts, on holidays.
The good old housewife tucking up her gown,
The table sets; the invited gods lie down.
The trivet table of a foot was lame°—
A blot which prudent Baucis overcame,
Who thrusts beneath the limping leg, a sherd;°
So was the mended board exactly reared:
Then rubbed it o'er with newly gathered mint,
A wholesome herb, that breathed a grateful scent.
90   Pallas° began the feast, where first was seen
The party-coloured° olive, black and green;
Autumnal cornels° next in order served,
In lees of wine° well pickled, and preserved;
A garden salad was the third supply,
Of endive, radishes, and succory;°
Then curds and cream, the flower of country fare,
And new-laid eggs, which Baucis' busy care
Turned by a gentle fire, and roasted rare.

coleworts cabbages
Sallow dingy
alone only
trivet . . . lame the three-legged table was
short in one leg
sherd bit of earthenware

Pallas to whom the olive was sacred
party-coloured of mixed colors
cornels the red fruit of the cornelian cherry tree
lees of wine vinegary dregs of wine
succory chicory

All these in earthen ware were served to board;
100 And, next in place, an earthen pitcher, stored
With liquor of the best the cottage could afford.
This was the table's ornament and pride,
With figures wrought: like pages at his side
Stood beechen bowls; and these were shining clean,
Varnished with wax without, and lined within.
By this the boiling kettle had prepared,
And to the table sent the smoking lard,°
On which with eager appetite they dine,
A savoury bit that served to relish wine;
110 The wine itself was suiting to the rest,
Still working in the must,° and lately pressed.
The second course succeeds like that before;
Plums, apples, nuts, and, of their wintry store,
Dry figs and grapes, and wrinkled dates were set
In canisters, to enlarge the little treat.
All these a milk-white honeycomb surround,
Which in the midst the country banquet crowned.
But the kind hosts their entertainment grace
With hearty welcome and an open face:
120 In all they did you might discern with ease
A willing mind and a desire to please.
    Meantime the beechen bowls went round and still,
Though often emptied, were observed to fill;
Filled without hands, and of their own accord
Ran without feet, and danced about the board.
Devotion seized the pair, to see the feast
With wine, and of no common grape, increased;
And up they held their hands, and fell to prayer,
Excusing, as they could, their country fare.
130 One goose they had ('twas all they could allow),
A wakeful sentry, and on duty now,
Whom to the gods for sacrifice they vow:
Her, with malicious zeal, the couple viewed;
She ran for life, and, limping, they pursued.
Full well the fowl perceived their bad intent,
And would not make her masters' compliment;
But, persecuted, to the powers she flies,
And close between the legs of Jove she lies.
He, with a gracious ear, the suppliant heard,
140 And saved her life; then what he was declared,
And owned° the god. 'The neighbourhood,' said he,
'Shall justly perish for impiety:
You stand alone exempted; but obey
With speed, and follow where we lead the way;

lard bacon   owned acknowledged himself
working in the must fermenting

Leave these accurst, and to the mountain's height
Ascend, nor once look backward in your flight.'
   They haste, and what their tardy feet denied,
The trusty staff (their better leg) supplied.
An arrow's flight they wanted° to the top,
150 And there secure, but spent with travel, stop;
Then turn their now no more forbidden eyes:
Lost in a lake the floated level° lies;
A watery desert covers all the plains;
Their cot° alone, as in an isle, remains;
Wondering with weeping eyes, while they deplore
Their neighbours' fate and country now no more,
Their little shed, scarce large enough for two,
Seems, from the ground increased, in height and bulk to grow.
A stately temple shoots within the skies;
160 The crotches of their cot in columns rise;
The pavement polished marble they behold,
The gates with sculpture graced, the spires and tiles of gold.
   Then thus the Sire of Gods, with look serene:
'Speak thy desire, thou only just of men;
And thou, O woman, only worthy found
To be with such a man in marriage bound.'
   A while they whisper; then, to Jove addressed,
Philemon thus prefers° their joint request:
'We crave to serve before your sacred shrine,
170 And offer at your altars rites divine;
And since not any action of our life
Has been polluted with domestic strife,
We beg one hour of death; that neither she
With widow's tears may live to bury me,
Nor weeping I, with withered arms, may bear
My breathless Baucis to the sepulchre.'
   The godheads sign their suit. They run their race
In the same tenor all the appointed space;
Then, when their hour was come, while they relate
180 These past adventures at the temple gate,
Old Baucis is by old Philemon seen
Sprouting with sudden leaves of sprightly green;
Old Baucis looked where old Philemon stood,
And saw his lengthened arms a sprouting wood.
New roots their fastened feet begin to bind,
Their bodies stiffen in a rising rind:
Then, ere the bark above their shoulders grew,
They give and take at once their last adieu;
At once: 'Farewell, O faithful spouse,' they said;
190 At once the incroaching rinds their closing lips invade.

wanted had to travel   **cot** dwelling
floated level flooded surface   **prefers** offers

Even yet, an ancient Tyanaean° shows
A spreading oak, that near a linden grows;
The neighbourhood confirm the prodigy,
Grave men, not vain of tongue, or like to lie.
I saw myself the garlands on their boughs,
And tablets hung for gifts of granted vows;
And offering fresher up, with pious prayer,
'The good,' said I, 'are God's peculiar care,
And such as honour Heaven, shall heavenly honour share.'

1700

JONATHAN SWIFT

Baucis and Philemon

Imitated from the Eighth Book of Ovid

In ancient times, as story tells,
The saints would often leave their cells,
And stroll about, but hide their quality,
To try good people's hospitality.
    It happened on a winter night,
As authors of the legend write,
Two brother hermits, saints by trade,
Taking their tour in masquerade,
Disguised in tattered habits, went
To a small village down in Kent;
Where, in the strollers' canting strain,
They begged from door to door in vain,
Tried every tone might pity win;
But not a soul would let them in.
    Our wandering saints, in woeful state,
Treated at this ungodly rate,
Having through all the village passed,
To a small cottage came at last
Where dwelt a good old honest yeoman,
Called in the neighbourhood Philemon;
Who kindly did these saints invite
In his poor hut to pass the night;
And then the hospitable sire
Bid Goody° Baucis mend the fire
While he from out the chimney took
A flitch of bacon off the hook,
And freely from the fattest side
Cut out large slices to be fried;
Then stepped aside to fetch 'em drink,

10

20

Tyanaean a native of Tyana (in Asia Minor)   **Goody** a contracted form of goodwife

30 Filled a large jug up to the brink,
    And saw it fairly twice go round;
    Yet (what was wonderful) they found
    'Twas still replenished to the top,
    As if they ne'er had touched a drop.
    The good old couple were amazed,
    And often on each other gazed;
    For both were frightened to the heart,
    And just began to cry, 'What ar't!'
    Then softly turned aside, to view
40 Whether the lights were burning blue.°
    The gentle pilgrims, soon aware on't,
    Told 'em their calling and their errand:
    'Good folks, you need not be afraid,
    We are but saints,' the hermits said;
    'No hurt shall come to you or yours:
    But, for that pack of churlish boors,
    Not fit to live on Christian ground,
    They and their houses shall be drowned:
    While you shall see your cottage rise,
50 And grow a church before your eyes.'
        They scarce had spoke, when fair and soft,
    The roof began to mount aloft;
    Aloft rose every beam and rafter;
    The heavy wall climbed slowly after.
        The chimney widened, and grew higher,
    Became a steeple with a spire.
        The kettle to the top was hoist,
    And there stood fastened to a joist,
    But with the upside down, to show
60 Its inclinations for below:
    In vain; for a superior force
    Applied at bottom stops its course:
    Doomed ever in suspense to dwell,
    'Tis now no kettle, but a bell.
        A wooden jack,° which had almost
    Lost by disuse the art to roast,
    A sudden alteration feels,
    Increased by new intestine wheels;
    And, what exalts the wonder more,
70 The number made the motion slower.
    The flier, though it had leaden feet,
    Turned round so quick you scarce could see't;
    But, slackened by some secret power,
    Now hardly moves an inch an hour.
    The jack and chimney, near allied,

burning blue as candles were believed to do   jack a device for turning the roasting spit
in the presence of evil spirits

Had never left each other's side;
The chimney to a steeple grown,
The jack would not be left alone;
But, up against the steeple reared,
80   Became a clock, and still adhered;
And still its love to household cares
By a shrill voice at noon declares,
Warning the cookmaid not to burn
That roast meat which it cannot turn.
　　The groaning chair began to crawl
Like an huge snail along the wall;
There stuck aloft in public view,
And with small change, a pulpit grew.
　　The porringers, that in a row
90   Hung high, and made a glittering show,
To a less noble substance changed,
Were now but leathern buckets° ranged.
　　The ballads, pasted on the wall,
Of Joan of France, and English Moll,°
Fair Rosamond,° and Robin Hood,
The little Children in the Wood,
Now seemed to look abundance better,
Improved in picture, size and letter:
And, high in order placed, describe
100   The heraldry of every tribe.°
　　A bedstead of the antique mode,
Compact of timber many a load,
Such as our ancestors did use,
Was metamorphosed into pews;
Which still their ancient nature keep
By lodging folks disposed to sleep.
　　The cottage, by such feats as these,
Grown to a church by just degrees,
The hermits then desired their host
110   To ask for what he fancied most.
Philemon, having paused a while,
Returned 'em thanks in homely style;
Then said, 'My house is grown so fine,
Methinks, I still would call it mine.
I'm old, and fain would live at ease;
Make me the parson, if you please.'
　　He spoke, and presently he feels
His grazier's° coat fall down his heels:
He sees, yet hardly can believe,

---

buckets for putting out fires
English Moll a heroine who fought at the siege
of Ghent, 1584; here paired with Joan of Arc
Rosamond daughter of Lord Clifford and mis-

tress of Henry II, subject of a famous ballad
heraldry . . . tribe ensigns of the twelve tribes
of Israel, common in country churches
grazier's one who feeds cattle for market

120   About each arm a pudding sleeve;°
    His waistcoat to a cassock grew,
    And both assumed a sable hue;
    But, being old, continued just
    As threadbare and as full of dust.
    His talk was now of tithes and dues:
    He smoked his pipe and read the news;
    Knew how to preach old sermons next,
    Vamped° in the preface and the text;
    At christenings well could act his part,
130   And had the service all by heart:
    Wished women might have children fast,
    And thought whose sow had farrowed last;
    Against dissenters would repine,
    And stood up firm for right divine;°
    Found his head filled with many a system;
    But classic authors,—he ne'er missed 'em.
      Thus having furbished up a parson,
    Dame Baucis next they played their farce on.
    Instead of homespun coifs,° were seen
140   Good pinners edged with colberteen;°
    Her petticoat transformed apace,
    Became black satin, flounced° with lace.
    Plain 'Goody' would no longer down,
    'Twas 'Madam,' in her grogram° gown.
    Philemon was in great surprise,
    And hardly could believe his eyes.
    Amazed to see her look so prim,°
    And she admired as much at him.
      Thus happy in their change of life,
150   Were several years this man and wife:
    When on a day, which proved their last,
    Discoursing on old stories past,
    They went by chance, amidst their talk,
    To the churchyard to take a walk;
    When Baucis hastily cried out,
    'My dear, I see your forehead sprout!'
    'Sprout,' quoth the man; 'what's this you tell us?
    I hope you don't believe me jealous!°
    But yet, methinks I feel it true,
160   And really yours is budding too—
    Nay,—now I cannot stir my foot;

pudding sleeve a full, bulging (perhaps padded) sleeve
Vamped reworked (the "text" here being the scriptural topic)
right divine i.e. the church structure as derived from the Apostles; perhaps also showing the Tory political cast of the lower clergy, as opposed to many Whig bishops

coifs close-fitting caps
pinners . . . colberteen caps with flaps edged with lace
flounced covered with a second tier
grogram grosgrain, a fabric all or partly of silk
prim smart
jealous referring to cuckold's horns, often called "branches" for antlers

It feels as if 'twere taking root.'
   Description would but tire my Muse,
In short, they both were turned to yews.
Old Goodman Dobson of the green
Remembers he the trees has seen;
He'll talk of them from noon till night,
And goes with folks to show the sight;
On Sundays, after evening prayer,
He gathers all the parish there;
Points out the place of either yew,
Here Baucis, there Philemon, grew:
Till once a parson of our town,
To mend his barn, cut Baucis down;
At which, 'tis hard to be believed
How much the other tree was grieved,
Grew scrubby, died a-top, was stunted;
So the next parson stubbed and burnt it.

                1708

170

MATTHEW PRIOR
1664–1721

An Epitaph°

      Climb at court for me that will
      Tottering favour's pinnacle;
      All I seek is to lie still.
      Settled in some secret nest
      In calm leisure let me rest;
      And far off the public stage
      Pass away my silent age.
      Thus when without noise, unknown,
      I have lived out all my span,
      I shall die without a groan
      An old honest country man.
      Who exposed to others' eyes
      Into his own heart ne'er pries,
      Death to him's a strange surprise.
      SENECA, *Thyestes*, Chorus, Act II
      (ANDREW MARVELL trans.)

   Interred beneath this marble stone
Lie sauntering Jack and idle Joan.
While rolling threescore years and one

An Epitaph Matthew Prior (1664–1721) had a long diplomatic career and took an important role in negotiating the Peace of Utrecht in 1713. His poetry ranges from philosophical works like *Solomon on the Vanity of the World* to brilliant love lyrics, and among his finest poems is the Hudibrastic *Alma*, a dialogue on the nature of the soul and its faculties. An admirer of Butler, Prior praised his art in *Alma:* "His noble negligences teach / What others' toils despair to reach. / He, perfect dancer, climbs the rope, / And balances your fear and hope / . . . With wonder you approve his sleight, / And owe your pleasure to your fright."

Did round this globe their courses run;
If human things went ill or well;
If changing empires rose or fell;
The morning past, the evening came,
And found this couple still the same.
They walked and eat, good folks: What then?
10 Why then they walked and eat again:
They soundly slept the night away:
They did just nothing all the day:
And having buried children four,
Would not take pains to try for more.
Nor sister either had, nor brother:
They seemed just tallied for each other.

    Their moral and economy
Most perfectly they made agree:
Each virtue kept its proper bound,
20 Nor trespassed on the other's ground.
Nor fame, nor censure they regarded:
They neither punished, nor rewarded.
He cared not what the footmen did:
Her maids she neither praised, nor chid:
So every servant took his course;
And bad at first, they all grew worse.
Slothful disorder filled his stable;
And sluttish plenty decked her table.
Their beer was strong; their wine was port;
30 Their meal was large; their grace was short.
They gave the poor the remnant-meat,
Just when it grew not fit to eat.

    They paid the church and parish rate;°
And took, but read not the receipt:
For which they claimed their Sunday's due
Of slumbering in an upper pew.

    No man's defects sought they to know;
So never made themselves a foe.
No man's good deeds did they commend;
40 So never raised themselves a friend.
Nor cherished they relations poor:
That might decrease their present store:
Nor barn nor house did they repair:
That might oblige their future heir.

    They neither added, nor confounded;°
They neither wanted, nor abounded.
Each Christmas they accompts did clear;

rate tax   **confounded** wasted

And wound their bottom° round the year.
Nor tear, nor smile did they employ
50   At news of public grief, or joy.
When bells were rung, and bonfires made,
If asked, they ne'er denied their aid:
Their jug was to the ringers° carried,
Who ever either died, or married.
Their billet° at the fire was found,
Who ever was deposed, or crowned.

    Nor good, nor bad, nor fools, nor wise;
They would not learn, nor could advise:
Without love, hatred, joy, or fear,
60   They led—a kind of—as it were:
Nor wished, nor cared, nor laughed, nor cried:
And so they lived; and so they died.

1718

ALEXANDER POPE
1688–1744

Pope was the great poet of his age, and he made that role a more exacting and influential one than it had ever been before in England. Chaucer had been a court poet and had served as a diplomat; Milton had been virtually foreign minister under Cromwell. But Pope commanded hatred and admiration, both as poet and as man, throughout his career of private citizen and public conscience. He could boast in a late poem, "I must be proud to see / Men not afraid of God, afraid of me." And while he fully earned the right to make the boast, he often doubted the wisdom of his engagement. We can see in his career a constant division between the attraction of a retired life and the claims, early, of literary ambition and, late, of active political concern—a political life such as only a man too independent to be bought and too gifted to be suppressed could maintain in Walpole's England.

    Those who wish to find disabilities for which ambition compensates can find more than his share in Pope. Born to Catholic parents and, however heterodox at moments, loyal to their faith, he suffered first of all the penalties of being a Catholic in a country easily alarmed by the threat of intrigue and invasion. Catholics were forbidden by law to own land or to live within ten miles of London, and, if the laws were rarely enforced, they could be invoked in times of panic. Pope's parents moved near the time of his birth to Binfield in Windsor Forest, and later Pope rented a villa at Twickenham, near London but outside the ten-mile limit. As a Catholic he was denied admission to a university or the right to hold public office, and he was subject as well to double taxation. Nor did his enemies ever allow him to forget his status as a Catholic; but they made even more of his dwarf-like stature and of his crooked body, misshapen from adolescence by a tubercular ailment ("little Alexander," he described himself to a friend, whom "the women laugh at")

---

bottom a skein or ball of thread   **billet** gift of firewood
ringers bell-ringers, on whatever occasion

The compensations took various forms, occasionally the unconvincing posture of a rake, more often precocious literary skill and application and a great talent for friendship. His early friendships with distinguished elderly writers and retired statesmen (which combined charming deference with intellectual equality) were the first of a long series that took the place of more intimate ties. There was a rather romantic, somewhat histrionic attachment to the witty and ultimately spiteful Lady Mary Wortley Montagu (once a candidate for Congreve's affection), and there was something like real intimacy with Martha Blount; but the friendships seem, at this remove, the more essential attachments.

Pope divided his works at one point into "pure description" and "sense"; and, if those terms mean anything, they mark a movement in the late 1720's from a career of intense literary concerns to one of deeper moral engagement. There is no very sharp distinction, for such early works as the *Essay on Criticism* and *Windsor Forest* show moral and even political concern. The earlier career reached its culmination in the great labor of translating Homer, an undertaking that demanded all of Pope's energies and that rewarded him with financial independence. In the course of his earlier career, Pope had become deeply involved in the literary politics of the day, which were neither distinct from nor less vicious than those of the larger public sphere. His very talent was taken as arrogance by some; and Pope, through eagerness for fame and a certain bravado of manner, did little to make his superiority easy to ignore, or even to endure. In his difficult relations with Joseph Addison, who received literary adulation at Button's coffeehouse and could reward it with Whig patronage, Pope may have seemed a self-seeking outsider or even the instrument of his Tory friends. At any rate, Addison condoned strong efforts by his followers to smother Pope's reputation and to kill the prospects of his Homer.

In 1728 Pope paid off scores with *The Dunciad*. He created a brilliant mock-epic framework within which to gather and display—like a collection of butterflies, wasps, and spiders—all those who had maligned him without cause. Thereafter, each gesture he made could be read as defense or attack, and it was only by concealing his authorship that he could get a fair (and favorable) reception for so impersonal a work as the *Essay on Man* (1733–34). The *Essay* marks the last full effort of the contemplative poet: it is a work in a Socratic spirit, seeking to undo the quarrels men make with themselves and their world. This was to have been the first part of a large philosophic work, but the rest finally emerged as a series of "moral essays" or "ethic epistles" (of which *To Burlington* and *To a Lady* are two) and in the satire on false learning in the *New Dunciad* (1743).

The themes of *The Dunciad* looked back to Swift's great early satire, *A Tale of a Tub;* Pope's poem was written in part during a visit from Swift and, when completed, dedicated to him. The two men had met by 1712; and in the next few years, with Dr. John Arbuthnot (who had created the character of John Bull in a series of political satires) and with others—John Gay among them—they undertook the project of ridiculing false learning in a series of papers purportedly written by Martinus Scriblerus, a leaden-witted, pedantic, and indefatigable searcher after natural curiosities and verbal subtleties. The Scriblerus papers, begun about 1714, were not published till years later, but the project was important for providing an imaginative form which could yield Pope's "variorum" edition of *The Dunciad* with Scriblerian commentary, or perhaps even that more modest and less sedentary kin to Scriblerus, Lemuel Gulliver.

Pope's loyalty to these Tory friends—as well as to Queen Anne's chief ministers, Oxford and Bolingbroke—moved him more and more toward a political role. He had been on good personal terms with Sir Robert Walpole, but increasingly he became offended by the ways in which Walpole promoted and embodied the corruptions of the time: the systematic control of power through bribery, the use of hirelings and hacks to malign or silence the opposition, the awarding of honors for serviceable mediocrity, the insatiable appetite for ostentatious grandeur. Pope may well have exaggerated the threat that Walpole represented and have been somewhat eager to see apocalypse where there was only muddle. As Gibbon put it, "The fall of an unpopular Minister was not succeeded, according to general expectation, by a millennium of happiness and virtue." But Pope erected an image of Walpole and his England to stand beside Juvenal's vision of Rome under the rule of Domitian or Byron's and Stendhal's vision of the reaction that followed the French Revolution and Napoleon. The historicity of Pope's world is not our primary concern today, but rather the powerful and all-embracing imaginative form into which he built the details of his time as he did shells and minerals into the arches of his grotto at Twickenham. If the grotto was the retreat of the contemplative private man, and its natural beauties framed the life of retirement, so the greater poetic structure of the satires served no less to exercise the public conscience and to voice an outrage too strong to condone either pretext or pretension.

Pope gained a reputation for deviousness from which his reputation as a poet has often suffered. It arose in part because, like Halifax, he respected men more than parties; in part because he would damn in one withering line a fool who felt he had a claim to two; in part because he was attentive to his own image, editing and revising his letters before he published them, claiming the advantage of second thoughts and of nobler impulses than were spontaneously given. Yet the self-defense was a proportionate reaction to the abuse; and if Pope may be said to have created himself anew for posterity, the creation was still his. John Ruskin, the Victorian critic, pays tribute to his concise and forceful expression of a "benevolence, humble, rational, and resigned"; it is not all of Pope nor even his greatest achievement, but it is a part of all the rest.

An Essay on Criticism

This Horatian essay, Pope's first major poem, is the culmination of those years of literary study and discussion that Pope conducted at Binfield. His choice of criticism as its subject reflects the concern with self-definition of an age that had reacted against baroque wit and sought to cultivate the urbanity of Roman (as well as modern French) models. But a more immediate concern was the social one of how writers and critics were to behave in the new open forum that replaced gentlemanly amateurism and patronage. Critics were more numerous than ever before. As one of the least amiable of them, Thomas Rymer, complained, "till of late years England was as free from critics as it is from wolves," but now "they who are least acquainted with the game are aptest to bark at everything that comes in their way." Swift complained of those critics who read only to damn: "as barbarous as a judge who should take up a resolution to hang all men that came before him upon trial." And Dryden

had traced the most malevolent criticism to failed writers: "the corruption of a poet
is the generation of a critic."

Pope writes in a spirit of moderation, trying to free criticism of its partiality and
its animosity. He offers a generous account of the value and limits of rules and
a warning above all against the pride that sets self against nature, the fashionable
against the universal. The theme of pride, whether of the individual or the coterie,
creates a pattern of imagery that underlies the poem at every point and gives it more
strength than its casual surface might suggest. We see the light of heaven descending
into the "glimmering light" of the individual mind, as it once did more strikingly in the
"celestial fire" of ancient genius. We see the light of nature as "clear, unchanged,
and universal," opposed to the glaring, refracted light of false wit. The light of nature,
like that of true expression, "clears and improves"—that is, dresses to advantage—
"whate'er it shines upon," self-effacing in order to bring each object to its full realization. In contrast, the glitter of false wit conceals the "naked nature" (or rather
hopes to conceal its absence) and buries what might have been "living grace" in a
tawdry display of verbal wit. Behind these images there may be traces of an implicit
scheme familiar in neoplatonic thought: the light of the One descends through emanation, forming and beautifying the Many. As it informs the individual soul and awakens
it to the radiance of beauty in the world, it stirs the soul to reascend toward the One.
Such a system is explicit in Shaftesbury's *The Moralists;* in Pope's less rhapsodic "essay"
there are only glimpses and vestiges, just as in Dryden's urbane and "skeptical" criticism
there are only occasional evocations of neoplatonism (except for the extended quotation from Giovanni Bellori in *The Parallel Betwixt Painting and Poetry*) or as in
Reynolds's *Discourses* we see the translation of a neoplatonic scheme into empirical
terms.

From An Essay on Criticism

'Tis hard to say, if greater want of skill
Appear in writing or in judging ill;
But, of the two, less dangerous is the offence
To tire our patience, than mislead our sense.
Some few in that, but numbers err in this,
Ten censure wrong for one who writes amiss;
A fool might once himself alone expose,
Now one in verse makes many more in prose.
   'Tis with our judgments as our watches; none
10 Go just alike, yet each believes his own.
In poets as true genius is but rare,
True taste as seldom is the critic's share;
Both must alike from Heaven derive their light,
These born to judge, as well as those to write.
Let such teach others who themselves excel,
And censure freely who have written well.
Authors are partial to their wit, 'tis true,

But are not critics to their judgment too?
   Yet if we look more closely, we shall find
20 Most have the seeds of judgment in their mind;
Nature affords at least a glimmering light;°
The lines, though touched but faintly, are drawn right.
But as the slightest sketch, if justly traced,
Is by ill colouring but the more disgraced,
So by false learning is good sense° defaced;
Some are bewildered in the maze of schools,°
And some made coxcombs° Nature meant but fools.
In search of wit these lose their common sense,
And then turn critics in their own defence.
30 Each burns alike, who can, or cannot write,
Or with a rival's or an eunuch's spite.
All fools have still an itching to deride,
And fain would be upon the laughing side;
If Maevius° scribble in Apollo's° spite,
There are who judge still worse than he can write.
   Some have at first for wits, then poets past,
Turned critics next, and proved plain fools at last;
Some neither can for wits nor critics pass,
As heavy mules are neither horse nor ass.
40 Those half-learned witlings, numerous in our isle,
As half-formed insects on the banks of Nile;
Unfinished things, one knows not what to call,
Their generation's so equivocal:°
To tell° 'em, would a hundred tongues require,
Or one vain wit's, that might a hundred tire.
   But you who seek to give and merit fame,
And justly bear a critic's noble name,
Be sure yourself and your own reach to know,
How far your genius, taste, and learning go;
50 Launch not beyond your depth, but be discreet,
And mark that point where sense and dulness meet.
   Nature to all things fixed the limits fit,
And wisely curbed proud man's pretending wit:

glimmering light Sir William Temple (*Of Poetry*) describes poetic inspiration as "the pure and free gift of Heaven or of Nature . . . a fire kindled out of some hidden spark of the very first conception." So, too, Shaftesbury in *The Moralists* III.ii speaks of the "conceptions" of the mind and its "mental children": "Nor could it ever have been thus impregnated by any other mind than that which formed it at the beginning; and which . . . is original to all mental as well as other beauty." For a further development of this theme, which insists upon the divine source of man's powers of creation (or, in Pope, judgment), see also William Collins, *Ode on the Poetical Character*.
good sense related to the "glimmering light" and "seeds of judgment" (ll. 20–21) which may be fulfilled through true learning (as the sketch may be realized by proper coloring) or may be destroyed through false
schools of thought or criticism, the very existence of "schools" implying a diffraction of the light of heaven into self-limiting partisanship
coxcombs fops, superficial pretenders
Maevius a bad poet of Virgil's age
Apollo's as god and inspirer of true poetry
Those . . . equivocal referring to the belief that insects and vermin were spontaneously generated by the mud of the Nile; they are described by Dryden as "part kindled into life, and part a lump of unformed unanimated matter" (Dedication, *Aeneid*)
tell count

As on the land while here the ocean gains,
In other parts it leaves wide sandy plains;
Thus in the soul while memory prevails,
The solid power of understanding fails;
Where beams of warm imagination play,
The memory's soft figures melt away.
60   One science° only will one genius fit,
So vast is art, so narrow human wit;°
Not only bounded to peculiar arts,
But oft in those confined to single parts.
Like kings we lose the conquests gained before,
By vain ambition still to make them more;
Each might his several province well command,
Would all but stoop to what they understand.
    First follow Nature, and your judgment frame
By her just standard, which is still° the same:
70   Unerring NATURE, still divinely bright,
One clear, unchanged, and universal light,
Life, force, and beauty, must to all impart,
At once the source, and end, and test of art.
Art from that fund each just supply provides,
Works without show, and without pomp presides:
In some fair body thus the informing soul°
With spirits feeds, with vigour fills the whole,
Each motion guides, and every nerve sustains;
Itself unseen, but in the effects, remains.
80   Some to whom Heaven in wit has been profuse,
Want as much more,° to turn it to its use;
For wit and judgment often are at strife,
Though meant each other's aid, like man and wife.
'Tis more to guide than spur the Muse's steed;°
Restrain his fury, than provoke his speed;
The wingèd courser, like a generous° horse,
Shows most true mettle when you check his course.
    Those RULES of old discovered, not devised,
Are Nature still, but Nature methodized;
90   Nature, like liberty,° is but restrained

science form of learning or knowledge
So vast . . . wit recalling the maxim of Hippocrates, "Life is short, but art is long" or, in
the Latin version, "Ars longa, vita brevis est"
(*Aphorisms* I.i)
still always; cf. Dryden, "For Nature is still the
same in all ages, and can never be contrary to
herself" (*Parallel Betwixt Poetry and Painting*,
1695)
informing soul the animating power and governing structure; cf. Dryden, *Absalom and Achitophel*, ll. 157–59, for ironic account of the "fiery
soul" that "o'er-informs"
as much more distinguishing implicitly between
wit as invention and fancy ("quickness" and
"fertility") and wit as elocution or expression

("accuracy") as in Dryden's preface to *Annus
Mirabilis* (see above, his Critical Prose); or, to
put it another way, insisting upon the interdependence of wit and judgment, for if like man
and wife they become one, each implies the
other and may be called by the same name
Muse's steed Pegasus, the winged horse
generous spirited
liberty in early editions "monarchy"; in both
cases implying that the sovereign power, whether
the king or the people, limits itself willingly as
the condition of its rule, just as God is often
conceived as limiting himself to rational rather
than merely arbitrary exercise of power (for the
exception, see l. 162)

By the same laws which first herself ordained.
Hear how learnèd Greece her useful rules indites,
When to repress, and when indulge our flights:
High on Parnassus'° top her sons she showed,
And pointed out those arduous paths they trod,
Held from afar, aloft, the immortal prize,
And urged the rest by equal steps to rise;
Just precepts thus from great examples given,
She drew from them what they derived from Heaven.
100   The generous critic fanned the poet's fire,
And taught the world with reason to admire.
Then criticism the Muses' handmaid proved,
To dress her charms,° and make her more beloved;
But following wits from that intention strayed,
Who could not win the mistress, wooed the maid;
Against the poets their own arms they turned,
Sure to hate most the men from whom they learned.
So modern 'pothecaries, taught the art
By doctor's bills° to play the doctor's part,
110   Bold in the practice of mistaken° rules,
Prescribed, apply, and call their masters fools.
Some on the leaves° of ancient authors prey,
Nor time nor moths e'er spoiled so much as they:
Some drily plain, without invention's° aid,
Write dull receipts° how poems may be made:
These leave the sense, their learning to display,
And those explain the meaning quite away.
     You then whose judgment the right course would steer,
Know well each ancient's proper character;
120   His fable,° subject, scope° in every page;
Religion, country, genius of his age:
Without all these at once before your eyes,
Cavil you may, but never criticize.
Be Homer's works your study and delight,
Read them by day, and meditate by night;
Thence form your judgment, thence your maxims bring,
And trace the Muses upward to their spring;
Still with itself compared, his text peruse;
And let your comment be the Mantuan Muse.°
130   When first young Maro° in his boundless mind

Parnassus' the sacred mountain of the Muses
dress her charms implying both to clothe or interpret and to rectify or adjust; the former action making them more apparent, the latter bringing them to fuller realization; cf. *The Rape of the Lock* I.139–44
bills prescriptions
mistaken misunderstood
leaves textual emendators and commentators seen as devouring grubs

invention's imagination, wit
receipts formulae, recipes. Pope later wrote a mocking "receipt" for cooking up an epic poem.
fable plot
scope "aim, final end" (Johnson)
Mantuan Muse Virgil's *Aeneid*, the best commentary on Homer
Maro Virgil

A work to outlast immortal Rome designed,
Perhaps he seemed° above the critic's law,
And but from Nature's fountains scorned to draw:
But when to examine every part he came,
Nature and Homer were, he found, the same:
Convinced, amazed, he checks the bold design,
And rules as strict his laboured work confine,
As if the Stagirite° o'erlooked each line.
Learn hence for ancient rules a just esteem;
140   To copy nature is to copy them.
    Some beauties yet no precepts can declare,
For there's a happiness° as well as care.
Music resembles poetry, in each
Are nameless graces° which no methods teach,
And which a master hand alone can reach.
If, where the rules not far enough extend,
(Since rules were made but to promote their end)
Some lucky licence answer to the full
The intent proposed, that licence is a rule.
150   Thus Pegasus, a nearer way to take,
May boldly deviate from the common track;
From vulgar bounds with brave° disorder part,
And snatch a grace beyond the reach of art,
Which, without passing through the judgment, gains
The heart, and all its end at once attains.
In prospects, thus, some objects please our eyes,
Which out of nature's common order rise,
The shapeless rock, or hanging precipice.°
Great wits sometimes may gloriously offend,
160   And rise to faults true critics dare not mend.
But though the ancients thus their rules invade,
(As kings dispense with laws themselves have made)
Moderns, beware! or if you must offend
Against the precept, ne'er transgress its end;
Let it be seldom, and compelled by need,
And have, at least, their precedent to plead.
The critic else proceeds without remorse,
Seizes your fame, and puts his laws in force.
    I know there are, to whose presumptuous thoughts
170   Those freer beauties, even in them, seem faults:
Some figures monstrous and misshaped appear,
Considered singly, or beheld too near,

---

seemed i.e. to himself
Stagirite Aristotle, whose *Poetics* analyzed the forms of epic and tragedy
happiness felicity, good fortune (as opposed to "care"), as in "lucky license," l. 148
nameless graces alluding to the expression "je ne sais quoi," which had gained currency in French criticism as a tribute to the value which

eludes categorizing; thus René Rapin speaks of "mysteries" which there is "no method to teach" —"the hidden graces, the insensible charms, and all that secret power of poetry which passes to the heart" (1674)
brave daring; but also magnificent, brilliant
rock . . . precipice See below, The Garden and the Wild, for discussion of the "sublime."

Which, but proportioned to their light or place,
Due distance reconciles to form and grace.
A prudent chief not always must display
His powers in equal ranks, and fair array,
But with the occasion and the place comply,
Conceal his force, nay seem sometimes to fly.
Those oft are stratagems which error seem,
180   Nor is it Homer nods, but we that dream.
        Still green with bays° each ancient altar° stands,
Above the reach of sacrilegious hands,
Secure from flames, from envy's fiercer rage,
Destructive war, and all-involving age.
See, from each clime the learned their incense bring!
Hear, in all tongues consenting° paeans ring!
In praise so just, let every voice be joined,
And fill the general chorus of mankind!
Hail Bards triumphant! born in happier days;
190   Immortal heirs of universal praise!
Whose honours with increase of ages grow,
As streams roll down, enlarging as they flow!
Nations unborn your mighty names shall sound,
And worlds applaud that must not yet be found!
Oh may some spark of your celestial fire,
The last, the meanest of your sons inspire,
(That on weak wings, from far, pursues your flights;
Glows while he reads, but trembles as he writes)
To teach vain wits a science little known,
200   To admire superior sense, and doubt their own!
        Of all the causes which conspire to blind
Man's erring judgment, and misguide the mind,
What the weak head with strongest bias rules,
Is *pride*, the never-failing vice of fools.
Whatever Nature has in worth denied,
She gives in large recruits° of needful° pride;
For as in bodies, thus in souls, we find
What wants° in blood and spirits, swelled with wind;
Pride, where wit fails, steps in to our defence,
210   And fills up all the mighty void of sense.
If once right reason drives that cloud away,
Truth breaks upon us with resistless day;
Trust not yourself; but your defects to know,
Make use of every friend—and every foe.
        A *little learning* is a dangerous thing;
Drink deep, or taste not the Pierian spring:°

---

bays the laurel that crowns the poet
altar the works of the ancients
consenting harmonious, unanimous
recruits additional supplies

needful needed (in the absence of "worth");
but also demanding, or arrogant
wants is lacking
Pierian spring a spring sacred to the Muses

There shallow draughts intoxicate the brain,
And drinking largely° sobers us again.
Fired at first sight with what the Muse imparts,
220 In fearless youth we tempt the heights of arts,
While from the bounded level of our mind,
Short views we take, nor see the lengths behind,
But more advanced, behold with strange surprise
New, distant scenes of endless science° rise!
So pleased at first, the towering Alps we try,
Mount o'er the vales, and seem to tread the sky;
The eternal snows appear already past,
And the first clouds and mountains seem the last:
But those attained, we tremble to survey
230 The growing labours of the lengthened way,
The increasing prospect tires our wandering eyes,
Hills peep o'er hills, and Alps on Alps arise!
    A perfect judge will read each work of wit
With the same spirit that its author writ:
Survey the WHOLE, nor seek slight faults to find,
Where nature moves, and rapture warms the mind;
Nor lose, for that malignant dull delight,
The generous pleasure to be charmed with wit.
But in such lays as neither ebb, nor flow,
240 Correctly cold, and regularly° low,
That shunning faults, one quiet tenor keep;
We cannot blame indeed—but we may sleep.
In wit, as nature, what affects our hearts
Is not the exactness° of peculiar° parts;
'Tis not a lip, or eye, we beauty call,
But the joint force and full result of all.
Thus when we view some well-proportioned dome,°
(The world's just wonder, and even thine O Rome!)
No single parts unequally surprise;
250 All comes united to the admiring° eyes;
No monstrous height, or breadth, or length appear;
The whole at once is bold, and regular.
    Whoever thinks a faultless piece to see,
Thinks what ne'er was, nor is, nor e'er shall be.
In every work regard the writer's end,
Since none can compass more than they intend;
And if the means be just, the conduct° true,
Applause, in spite of trivial faults, is due.

largely deeply
science knowledge
Correctly . . . regularly obedient to the rules
but without the vigor of imagination
exactness correctness, strict conformity to rule
peculiar particular, or separate
dome building, whether domed or not; but the
dome of such a cathedral as St. Peter's in Rome
or St. Paul's in London provides a fine instance
of unifying design
admiring wondering or awe-struck as well as
approving
conduct execution

As men of breeding, sometimes men of wit,°
260　To avoid great errors, must the less commit,
Neglect the rules each verbal critic° lays,
For not to know some trifles, is a praise.
Most critics, fond of some subservient art,
Still make the whole depend upon a part,
They talk of principles, but notions° prize,
And all to one loved folly sacrifice.

. . .

Thus critics, of less judgment than caprice,
Curious,° not knowing, not exact, but nice,°
Form short ideas; and offend in arts
(As most in manners) by a love to parts.°
Some to *conceit*° alone their taste confine,
290　And glittering thoughts struck out at every line;
Pleased with a work where nothing's just or fit;
One glaring chaos and wild heap of wit:
Poets like painters, thus, unskilled to trace
The naked nature and the living grace,
With gold and jewels cover every part,
And hide with ornaments their want of art.
True wit is nature to advantage dressed,
What oft was thought, but ne'er so well expressed,
Something, whose truth convinced at sight we find,
300　That gives us back the image of our mind:
As shades° more sweetly recommend the light,
So modest plainness sets off sprightly wit:
For works may have more wit than does 'em good,
As bodies perish through excess of blood.°
Others for *language* all their care express,
And value books, as women men, for dress:
Their praise is still—the style is excellent:
The sense, they humbly take upon content.°
Words are like leaves; and where they most abound,
310　Much fruit of sense beneath is rarely found.
False eloquence, like the prismatic glass,
Its gaudy colours spreads on every place;
The face of nature we no more survey,
All glares alike, without distinction gay:

---

breeding . . . wit playing on the analogy between the tact of good manners and that of art
verbal critic those concerned with details of language to the neglect of larger function
notions prejudices, unexamined ideas
Curious difficult to please
nice squeamish, overly fastidious
parts isolated gifts; in criticism, the "one loved folly"; in manners, one's pleasure in one's own talents (as in "a man of parts")

conceit farfetched comparison or metaphor, such as had been favored by the Metaphysical poets; see Dryden's Critical Prose and Johnson on the Metaphysical poets
shades Cf. *Windsor Forest*, ll. 17–18 (below, The Garden and the Wild), and *Epistle to Burlington*, ll. 53–56.
excess of blood as, it was believed, in apoplexy
upon content on trust

But true expression, like the unchanging sun,
Clears and improves whate'er it shines upon,
It gilds all objects, but it alters none.
Expression is the dress of thought, and still
Appears more decent° as more suitable;
320   A vile° conceit in pompous words expressed,
Is like a clown° in regal purple dressed;
For different styles with different subjects sort,
As several garbs with country, town, and court.
Some by old words° to fame have made pretence;
Ancients in phrase, mere moderns in their sense!
Such laboured nothings, in so strange a style,
Amaze the unlearned, and make the learnèd smile.
Unlucky, as Fungoso in the play,°
These sparks° with awkward vanity display
330   What the fine gentleman wore yesterday;
And but so mimic ancient wits at best,
As apes° our grandsires in their doublets drest.
In words, as fashions, the same rule will hold;
Alike fantastic, if too new, or old;
Be not the first by whom the new are tried,
Nor yet the last to lay the old aside.
     But most by *numbers*° judge a poet's song,
And smooth or rough, with them, is right or wrong;
In the bright Muse though thousand charms conspire,
340   Her voice is all these tuneful fools admire,
Who haunt Parnassus but to please their ear,
Not mend their minds; as some to church repair,
Not for the doctrine but the music there.
These equal syllables alone require,
Though oft the ear the open vowels tire,°
While expletives their feeble aid do join,
And ten low words oft creep in one dull line,
While they ring round the same unvaried chimes,
With sure returns of still expected rhymes.
350   Where'er you find 'the cooling western breeze,'
In the next line, it 'whispers through the trees';
If crystal streams 'with pleasing murmurs creep,'
The reader's threatened (not in vain) with 'sleep.'
Then, at the last and only couplet fraught

---

decent appropriate, becoming. In a letter to Pope in 1706 William Walsh had written that expression is "indeed the same thing to wit, as dress is to beauty."
vile low or inept
clown rustic, peasant
old words archaic diction such as Spenser uses at times, clumsily imitated by Ambrose Philips in his pastorals and parodied by John Gay in *The Shepherd's Week* (see above, The Mock Form)

play Ben Jonson's *Every Man out of His Humour* (1599); Fungoso cannot keep up with current fashions
sparks fops, beaux
apes monkeys dressed elaborately to provide amusement
numbers versification, sound patterns
Though . . . tire This is the first of a series of parodies wherein Pope illustrates the excesses each critical prejudice encourages; here "equal syllables" are rendered.

With some unmeaning thing they call a thought,
A needless Alexandrine° ends the song,
That, like a wounded snake, drags its slow length along.
Leave such to tune their own dull rhymes, and know
What's roundly smooth, or languishingly slow;
360 And praise the easy vigour of a line
Where Denham's strength, and Waller's sweetness° join.
True ease in writing comes from art, not chance,
As those move easiest who have learned to dance.
'Tis not enough no harshness gives offence,
The sound must seem an echo to the sense.
Soft is the strain° when Zephyr° gently blows,
And the smooth stream in smoother numbers flows;
But when loud surges lash the sounding shore,
The hoarse, rough verse should like the torrent roar.
370 When Ajax° strives, some rock's vast weight to throw,
The line too labours, and the words move slow;
Not so, when swift Camilla° scours the plain,
Flies o'er the unbending corn, and skims along the main.
Hear how Timotheus'° varied lays surprise,
And bid alternate passions fall and rise!
While, at each change, the son of Libyan Jove°
Now burns with glory, and then melts with love;
Now his fierce eyes with sparkling fury glow;
Now sighs steal out, and tears begin to flow:
380 Persians and Greeks like turns° of nature found,
And the world's victor stood subdued by sound!
The power of music all our hearts allow,
And what Timotheus was, is DRYDEN now.

·   ·   ·

1711

The Rape of the Lock

Pope's friend John Caryll was concerned about the estrangement between two prominent Roman Catholic families caused when Robert, Lord Petre, cut off a lock of hair
from the head of Arabella Fermor (known as "Belle"). As Pope explained it, Caryll,
"a common acquaintance and well-wisher to both, desired me to write a poem and
make a jest of it, and laugh them together again." Pope's poem failed to persuade
Arabella to resume her engagement to Lord Petre, and it soon outgrew its occasion.

Alexandrine a line of twelve syllables and six
stresses, illustrated in the following line
Denham's . . . sweetness These two 17th-
century poets were often praised for complementary virtues (conciseness to the point of
harshness, "strong lines" as opposed to harmonious musicality) which the Augustans
sought to fuse.
Soft is the strain illustrating, as do the next
eight lines, the maxim of l. 365

Zephyr the west wind
Ajax the rough hero in Homer's *Iliad* XII.378–86
Camilla the female warrior in Virgil's *Aeneid*
VII.808 ff.
Timotheus' the bard as shown in Dryden's *Alex-
ander's Feast*
son . . . Jove Alexander the Great
like turns similar alternations

Originally written in two cantos in 1712, it was amplified with mock-epic "machinery" and new incidents and appeared in five cantos in 1714 (Clarissa's speech in Canto V was not added until 1717).

The poem exults in the very triviality of its action, stressing the charm of a light, gay, and thoughtless world, upon which it lavishes all the gravity of tone and diction that might be allowed Achilles or Aeneas. Pope constantly plays games with scale. The sylphs—drawn from the occult and fantastic Rosicrucian mythology—are diminutive counterparts of classical deities or Miltonic angels, and they bring all the solicitude of solemn guardians to Belinda's petticoat and her hair. So, too, the full intensity of epic combat takes place not on the windy plains of Troy but on the "velvet plain" of the card table, where heroic battles are tricks in the game of ombre, and regal warriors defend the honor of their suits. The charm of this world deflects the contempt that Butler confers upon the manikins of *Hudibras*, misshapen as they are in mind and body; it exacts an attitude more subtle than moral superiority, more complicated than moral censure. Part of that attitude involves the recognition that the sylphs and gnomes are not so much external guardians as projections outward of states of mind, from coquettish concern with one's appearance to the self-pitying rancor of the spoilsport; and the ideal of good humor, explicitly introduced by Clarissa but in fact everywhere present, has its own seriousness as a call to candor, warmth, and tolerance. There is a sense in which the poem is mocking neither its own world nor the imaginative world of the epic but simply putting them side by side, small and great, with a quizzical sense of their parallelism as well as their conflict.

The Rape of the Lock

An Heroi-Comical Poem

Canto I

What dire offence from amorous causes springs,
What mighty contests rise from trivial things,
I sing—This verse to CARYLL, Muse! is due;
This, even Belinda may vouchsafe to view:
Slight is the subject, but not so the praise,
If she inspire, and he approve my lays.
   Say what strange motive, Goddess! could compel
A well-bred Lord to assault a gentle Belle?
O say what stranger cause, yet unexplored,
10 Could make a gentle Belle reject a Lord?
In tasks so bold, can little men engage,
And in soft bosoms dwells such mighty rage?°
   Sol through white curtains shot a timorous ray,
And oped those eyes that must eclipse the day:
Now lapdogs give themselves the rousing shake,

---

in soft . . . rage Having opened with traditional epic "proposition" and invocation, Pope imitates as well the epic questions, here parodying Virgil's *Aeneid* I.ii, "Can heavenly minds such high resentment show?" (Dryden trans.). So in the following lines (13–14) he plays upon Petrarchan conventions to elevate Belinda.

And sleepless lovers, just at twelve, awake:
Thrice rung the bell, the slipper knocked the ground,
And the pressed watch° returned a silver sound.
Belinda still her downy pillow prest,
20   Her guardian Sylph° prolonged the balmy rest.
'Twas he had summoned to her silent bed
The morning dream that hovered o'er her head.
A youth more glittering than a birth-night beau°
(That even in slumber caused her cheek to glow)
Seemed to her ear his winning lips to lay,
And thus in whispers said, or seemed to say:
     'Fairest of mortals, thou distinguished care
Of thousand bright inhabitants of air!
If e'er one vision touched thy infant thought,
30   Of all the nurse and all the priest° have taught,
Of airy elves by moonlight shadows seen,
The silver token, and the circled green,°
Or virgins visited by angel powers,°
With golden crowns and wreaths of heavenly flowers,
Hear and believe! thy own importance know,
Nor bound thy narrow views to things below.
Some secret truths, from learnèd pride concealed,
To maids alone and children are revealed:
What though no credit doubting wits may give?
40   The fair and innocent shall still believe.
Know, then, unnumbered spirits round thee fly,
The light militia of the lower sky;
These, though unseen, are ever on the wing,
Hang o'er the box, and hover round the Ring.°
Think what an equipage° thou hast in air,
And view with scorn two pages and a chair.°
As now your own, our beings were of old,
And once enclosed in woman's beauteous mould;
Thence, by a soft transition, we repair
50   From earthly vehicles° to these of air.

---

pressed watch It responds with chimes for the nearest hour and quarter-hour.
Sylph One of the spirits inhabiting the four elements (sylphs the air, gnomes the earth, nymphs water, and salamanders fire); the Sylphs "are the best-conditioned creatures imaginable," serving faithfully "upon a condition very easy to all true adepts, an inviolate preservation of chastity" (Pope). While the Sylph appears as a guardian angel, his whisper (ll. 25–26) may recall Satan's early temptation of Eve in *Paradise Lost* IV and his later successful appeal to her pride in Book IX.
birth-night beau courtier splendidly dressed for the king's birthday. For this guise, one may compare the dream used by Archimago to tempt the Red Cross Knight in *The Faerie Queene* I.i.
nurse . . . priest considered as sources of su-

perstition, the nurse contributing the elves, the priest the angels
circled green referring to the phosphoric light ("fairy sparks") and the withered circles in the grass ("fairy rings") that were taken as signs of the fairies' presence
virgins . . . powers invoking the Annunciation to the Virgin but also the mystical experience of many saints, such as Teresa of Avila; clearly a romantic dream of glory for a young girl
Ring a circular drive in Hyde Park; like the theater box, a common scene of flirtation
equipage carriage with horses and footmen
chair a sedan chair, in which passengers were carried
vehicles both the "equipage" and the terrestrial form in which the soul was embodied

Think not, when woman's transient breath is fled,
That all her vanities at once are dead:
Succeeding vanities she still regards,
And though she plays no more, o'erlooks the cards.
Her joy in gilded chariots, when alive,
And love of ombre,° after death survive.
For when the fair in all their pride expire,
To their first elements° their souls retire:
The sprites of fiery termagants in flame
60   Mount up, and take a Salamander's° name.
Soft yielding minds to water glide away,
And sip, with Nymphs, their elemental tea.°
The graver prude sinks downward to a Gnome,°
In search of mischief still on earth to roam.
The light coquettes in Sylphs aloft repair,
And sport and flutter in the fields of air.
    'Know farther yet; whoever fair and chaste
Rejects mankind, is by some Sylph embraced:
For spirits, freed from mortal laws, with ease
70   Assume what sexes and what shapes they please.°
What guards the purity of melting maids,
In courtly balls and midnight masquerades,
Safe from the treacherous friend, the daring spark,
The glance by day, the whisper in the dark;
When kind occasion prompts their warm desires,
When music softens, and when dancing fires?
'Tis but their Sylph, the wise celestials know,
Though *honour* is the word with men below.
    'Some nymphs there are, too conscious of their face,
80   For life predestined to the Gnomes' embrace.
These swell their prospects and exalt their pride,
When offers are disdained, and love denied.
Then gay ideas crowd the vacant brain,
While peers and dukes, and all their sweeping train,
And garters, stars, and coronets° appear,
And in soft sounds, *Your Grace*° salutes their ear.
'Tis these that early taint the female soul,
Instruct the eyes of young coquettes to roll,
Teach infant cheeks a bidden blush to know,
90   And little hearts to flutter at a beau.
    'Oft when the world imagine women stray,

---

ombre a popular card game similar to whist or
bridge; see note to III.27 below. Another Virgilian echo: "The love of horses which they had
alive, / And care of chariots after death survive"
(Dryden trans. VI.890 ff.).
first elements the four (earth, air, fire, water)
of which all material things are composed
Salamander's named for the animal which was

believed to live unharmed in the midst of fire
tea pronounced "tay"
Gnome one of the "demons of earth" which
"delight in mischief" (Pope)
what sexes . . . please as can the angels in
Paradise Lost I.427–31
garters . . . coronets emblems of high court
honors
Your Grace the address to a peeress

The Sylphs through mystic mazes guide their way,
Through all the giddy circle they pursue,
And old impertinence° expel by new.
What tender maid but must a victim fall
To one man's treat, but for another's ball?
When Florio speaks, what virgin could withstand,
If gentle Damon did not squeeze her hand?
With varying vanities, from every part,
100   They shift the moving toyshop° of their heart;
Where wigs with wigs, with sword-knots sword-knots
    strive,
Beaux banish beaux, and coaches coaches drive.°
This erring mortals levity may call,
Oh blind to truth! the Sylphs contrive it all.
    'Of these am I, who thy protection claim,
A watchful sprite, and Ariel is my name.
Late, as I ranged the crystal wilds of air,
In the clear mirror of thy ruling star
I saw, alas! some dread event impend,
110   Ere to the main this morning sun descend.
But heaven reveals not what, or how, or where:
Warned by the Sylph, oh pious maid, beware!
This to disclose is all thy guardian can:
Beware of all, but most beware of man!'
    He said; when Shock,° who thought she slept too long,
Leaped up, and waked his mistress with his tongue.
'Twas then, Belinda, if report say true,
Thy eyes first opened on a billet-doux;
Wounds, charms and ardours were no sooner read,
120   But all the vision vanished from thy head.
    And now, unveiled, the toilet° stands displayed,
Each silver vase in mystic order laid.
First, robed in white, the nymph intent adores,
With head uncovered, the cosmetic powers.
A heavenly image in the glass appears,
To that she bends, to that her eyes she rears;
The inferior priestess,° at her altar's side,
Trembling, begins the sacred rites of pride.
Unnumbered treasures ope at once, and here
130   The various offerings of the world appear;
From each she nicely culls with curious° toil,

impertinence trifle, frivolity
toyshop "where playthings and little nice manufactures are sold" (Johnson)
Where wigs . . . drive Cf. Homer, *Iliad* IV.
508–9: "Now shield with shield, with helmet
helmet closed, / To armor armor, lance to lance
opposed" (Pope trans.). "Sword knots" were
ribbons tied to hilts; they help reduce the scale
qualitatively from use to decoration.

Shock name for a lapdog with very long hair
toilet The dressing-table is ironically presented
as an altar, where "cosmetic powers" (l. 124)
displace "cosmic."
inferior priestess the maid Betty; Belinda is
the high priestess as well as the source of the
"heavenly image" (l. 125)
curious careful, full of nicety

And decks the goddess with the glittering spoil.
This casket India's glowing gems unlocks,
And all Arabia° breathes from yonder box.
The tortoise here and elephant unite,
Transformed to combs, the speckled and the white.°
Here files° of pins extend their shining rows,
Puffs, powder, patches,° bibles, billet-doux.
Now awful° beauty puts on all its arms;
140 The fair each moment rises in her charms,
Repairs her smiles, awakens every grace,
And calls forth all the wonders of her face;
Sees by degrees a purer blush° arise,
And keener lightnings° quicken in her eyes.
The busy Sylphs surround their darling care;
These set the head, and those divide the hair,
Some fold the sleeve, whilst others plait the gown;
And Betty's praised for labours not her own.

Canto II

Not with more glories, in the ethereal plain,°
The sun first rises o'er the purpled main,°
Than issuing forth, the rival of his beams
Launched on the bosom of the silver Thames.°
Fair nymphs and well-dressed youths around her shone,
But every eye was fixed on her alone.
On her white breast a sparkling cross she wore,
Which Jews might kiss, and infidels adore.°
Her lively looks a sprightly mind disclose,
10 Quick as her eyes, and as unfixed as those:
Favours to none, to all she smiles extends,
Oft she rejects, but never once offends.
Bright as the sun, her eyes the gazers strike,
And, like the sun, they shine on all alike.
Yet graceful ease, and sweetness void of pride,
Might hide her faults, if belles had faults to hide:
If to her share some female errors fall,
Look on her face, and you'll forget 'em all.
      This nymph, to the destruction of mankind,
20 Nourished two locks, which graceful hung behind
In equal curls, and well conspired to deck
With shining ringlets the smooth ivory neck.
Love in these labyrinths his slaves detains,

Arabia the source of perfumes
speckled . . . white tortoise-shell and ivory
files as of soldiers on parade
patches tiny pieces of black silk pasted on the
face to enhance the skin's whiteness
awful awe-inspiring, like the epic hero arming
himself
purer blush a more even redness, the result of
rouge

lightnings induced by drops of belladonna
ethereal plain the sky
purpled main the sea reddened by dawn to a
"royal purple"
silver Thames Belinda is taking a boat from
London to Hampton Court.
Jews . . . adore the kissing or adoration of the
cross marking conversion to a new faith

And mighty hearts are held in slender chains.
With hairy springes° we the birds betray,
Slight lines of hair surprise the finny prey,
Fair tresses man's imperial race ensnare,
And beauty draws us with a single hair.
    The adventurous Baron the bright locks admired,
30 He saw, he wished, and to the prize aspired:
Resolved to win, he meditates the way,
By force to ravish, or by fraud betray;
For when success a lover's toil attends,
Few ask, if fraud or force attained his ends.
    For this, ere Phoebus rose,° he had implored
Propitious heaven, and every power adored,
But chiefly Love—to Love an altar built,
Of twelve vast French romances,° neatly gilt.
There lay three garters, half a pair of gloves;
40 And all the trophies of his former loves.
With tender billets-doux he lights the pyre,
And breathes three amorous sighs to raise the fire;
Then prostrate falls, and begs with ardent eyes
Soon to obtain, and long possess, the prize:
The powers gave ear, and granted half his prayer;
The rest, the winds dispersed in empty air.°
    But now secure the painted vessel glides,
The sunbeams trembling on the floating tides,
While melting music steals upon the sky,
50 And softened sounds along the waters die.
Smooth flow the waves, the zephyrs gently play,
Belinda smiled, and all the world was gay.
All but the Sylph—with careful thoughts opprest,
The impending woe sat heavy on his breast.
He summons strait his denizens° of air;
The lucid squadrons round the sails repair:
Soft o'er the shrouds° aërial whispers breathe,
That seemed but zephrys to the train beneath.
Some to the sun their insect wings unfold,
60 Waft on the breeze, or sink in clouds of gold;
Transparent forms, too fine for mortal sight,
Their fluid bodies half dissolved in light.
Loose to the wind their airy garments flew,
Thin glittering textures of the filmy dew;
Dipped in the richest tincture of the skies,
Where light disports in ever-mingling dyes,

---

springes snares
ere . . . rose before sunrise
French romances notoriously long and highly conventionalized love stories, here handsomely bound in leather with gold titles and ornaments
The powers . . . air Cf. Virgil, *Aeneid* II.794–

95: "Apollo heard, and granting half his prayer, / Shuffled in winds the rest, and tossed in empty air" (Dryden trans.).
denizens inhabitants
shrouds ropes (appropriate to a greater vessel than the river boat)

While every beam new transient colours flings,
Colours that change whene'er they wave their wings.
Amid the circle, on the gilded mast,
70   Superior by the head,° was Ariel placed;
His purple pinions opening to the sun,
He raised his azure wand, and thus begun.
　'Ye Sylphs and Sylphids, to your chief give ear,
Fays, Fairies, Genii, Elves, and Daemons, hear!°
Ye know the spheres and various tasks assigned
By laws eternal to the aërial kind.
Some in the fields of purest aether° play,
And bask and whiten in the blaze of day.
Some guide the course of wandering orbs° on high,
80   Or roll the planets through the boundless sky.
Some less refined, beneath the moon's pale light
Pursue the stars that shoot athwart the night,
Or suck the mists in grosser air below,
Or dip their pinions in the painted bow,°
Or brew fierce tempests on the wintry main,
Or o'er the glebe° distil the kindly rain.
Others on earth o'er human race preside,
Watch all their ways, and all their actions guide:
Of these the chief the care of nations own,
90   And guard with arms divine the British throne.
　'Our humbler province is to tend the fair,
Not a less pleasing, though less glorious care.
To save the powder from too rude a gale,°
Nor let the imprisoned essences° exhale,
To draw fresh colours from the vernal flowers,
To steal from rainbows e'er they drop in showers
A brighter wash;° to curl their waving hairs,
Assist their blushes, and inspire their airs;
Nay oft, in dreams, invention we bestow,
100 To change a flounce, or add a furbelow.°
　'This day, black omens threat the brightest fair
That e'er deserved a watchful spirit's care;
Some dire disaster, or by force, or sleight,
But what, or where, the fates have wrapped in night:
Whether the nymph shall break Diana's law,°
Or some frail China jar receive a flaw,
Or stain her honour, or her new brocade,

Superior . . . head taller, like the typical epic hero
Ye Sylphs . . . hear Cf. *Paradise Lost* V.600–602: "Hear all ye Angels, progeny of light, / Thrones, Dominations, Princedoms, Virtues, Powers, / Hear my decree. . . ."
purest aether the air above the moon
wandering orbs comets, sometimes regarded as wandering planets

painted bow rainbow
glebe farmland
too rude a gale too rough a breeze
essences bottled perfumes
wash tinting rinse
furbelow ruffle
Diana's law virginity

Forget her prayers, or miss a masquerade,
Or lose her heart, or necklace, at a ball;
110　Or whether Heaven has doomed that Shock must fall.
Haste then, ye spirits! to your charge repair:
The fluttering fan be Zephyretta's care;
The drops° to thee, Brillante, we consign;
And, Momentilla, let the watch be thine;
Do thou, Crispissa,° tend her favourite lock;
Ariel himself shall be the guard of Shock.
　'To fifty chosen Sylphs, of special note,
We trust the important charge, the petticoat:
Oft have we known that sevenfold fence to fail,
120　Though stiff with hoops, and armed with ribs of whale.°
Form a strong line° about the silver bound,
And guard the wide circumference around.
　'Whatever spirit, careless of his charge,
His post neglects, or leaves the fair at large,
Shall feel sharp vengeance soon o'ertake his sins,
Be stopped in vials, or transfixed with pins;
Or plunged in lakes of bitter washes lie,
Or wedged whole ages in a bodkin's° eye:
Gums and pomatums° shall his flight restrain,
130　While clogged he beats his silken wings in vain;
Or alum styptics with contracting power
Shrink his thin essence like a rivelled flower.
Or as Ixion° fixed, the wretch shall feel
The giddy motion of the whirling mill,°
In fumes of burning chocolate shall glow,
And tremble at the sea that froths below!'
　He spoke; the spirits from the sails descend;
Some, orb in orb, around the nymph extend,
Some thrid the mazy ringlets of her hair,
140　Some hang upon the pendants of her ear;
With beating hearts the dire event they wait,
Anxious, and trembling for the birth of fate.°

　　Canto III
Close by those meads, for ever crowned with flowers,
Where Thames with pride surveys his rising towers,
There stands a structure° of majestic frame,
Which from the neighbouring Hampton takes its name.
Here Britain's statesmen oft the fall foredoom

drops diamond earrings
Crispissa from "crisp," in its old sense of "curl"
whale whalebone
line i.e. of defense; the petticoat is described in terms used for an epic shield
bodkin's needle's
Gums and pomatums cosmetic ointments
Ixion the King of Thessaly who sought to seduce the goddess Hera and was bound by Zeus in hell to an eternally revolving wheel
mill for beating chocolate
birth of fate Cf. Homer, *Iliad* IV.112: "And fate now labours with some vast event" (Pope trans.).
structure Hampton Court, the largest of the royal palaces

Of foreign tyrants, and of nymphs at home;
Here thou, great Anna!° whom three realms obey,
Dost sometimes counsel take—and sometimes tea.
    Hither the heroes and the nymphs resort,
10 To taste awhile the pleasures of a court;
In various talk the instructive hours they past,
Who gave the ball, or paid the visit last;
One speaks the glory of the British queen,
And one describes a charming Indian screen;
A third interprets motions, looks, and eyes;
At every word a reputation dies.
Snuff, or the fan, supply each pause of chat,
With singing, laughing, ogling, *and all that.*
    Meanwhile, declining from the noon of day,
20 The sun obliquely shoots his burning ray;
The hungry judges soon the sentence sign,
And wretches hang that jurymen may dine;
The merchant from the Exchange returns in peace,
And the long labours of the toilet cease—
Belinda now, whom thirst of fame invites,
Burns to encounter two adventurous knights,
At ombre° singly to decide their doom;
And swells her breast with conquests yet to come.
Straight the three bands prepare in arms to join,
30 Each band the number of the sacred nine.
Soon as she spread her hand, the aërial guard
Descend, and sit on each important card:
First Ariel perched upon a Matadore,°
Then each, according to the rank they bore;
For Sylphs, yet mindful of their ancient race,
Are, as when women, wondrous fond of place.°
    Behold, four Kings in majesty revered,°
With hoary whiskers and a forky beard;
And four fair Queens whose hands sustain a flower,
40 The expressive emblem of their softer power;
Four Knaves in garbs succinct,° a trusty band,
Caps on their heads, and halberts° in their hand;
And particoloured troops, a shining train,
Draw forth to combat on the velvet plain.°
    The skilful nymph reviews her force with care;

Anna Queen Anne, ruler of Great Britain and Ireland as well as claimant to France
ombre a card game related to whist or modern bridge, played with forty cards—the 10's, 9's, and 8's being removed from the deck; there are three players, each holding nine cards, and the one who contracts to take most tricks is called the "ombre" (from Spanish for "man") and chooses the trumps
Matadore one of the three cards of highest value
place rank

revered There follows a parody of the traditional epic review of forces, in which the royal figures are given the appearance they bear on playing cards.
succinct tucked up
halberts battle axes fixed to long poles
velvet plain typical poetic diction for a smooth grassy field, here applied to the card table covered with green velvet; cf. also "verdant field" (l. 52) and "level green" (l. 80)

'Let spades be trumps!' she said, and trumps they were.°
　　Now move to war her sable Matadores,°
In show like leaders of the swarthy Moors.
Spadillio first, unconquerable lord!
50　Led off two captive trumps, and swept the board.
As many more Manillio forced to yield,
And marched a victor from the verdant field.
Him Basto followed, but his fate more hard
Gained but one trump and one plebeian card.
With his broad sabre next, a chief in years,
The hoary Majesty of Spades appears,
Puts forth one manly leg,° to sight revealed;
The rest, his many-coloured robe concealed.
The rebel Knave, who dares his prince engage,
60　Proves the just victim of his royal rage.
Even mighty Pam,° that kings and queens o'erthrew,
And mowed down armies in the fights of Lu,
Sad chance of war! now, destitute of aid,
Falls undistinguished by the victor spade!
　　Thus far both armies to Belinda yield;
Now to the Baron fate inclines the field.
His warlike Amazon° her host invades,
The imperial consort of the crown of spades.
The club's black tyrant first her victim died,
70　Spite of his haughty mien and barbarous pride:
What boots° the regal circle on his head,
His giant limbs in state unwieldy spread?
That long behind he trails his pompous robe,
And of all monarchs only grasps the globe?
　　The Baron now his diamonds pours apace;
The embroidered King who shows but half his face,
And his refulgent Queen, with powers combined,
Of broken troops an easy conquest find.
Clubs, diamonds, hearts, in wild disorder seen,
80　With throngs promiscuous strew the level green.
Thus when dispersed a routed army runs,
Of Asia's troops, and Afric's sable sons,
With like confusion different nations fly,
Of various habit and of various dye,
The pierced battalions disunited fall,

Let spades . . . were Cf. Genesis 1:3: "And
God said, Let there be light; and there was
light."
Matadores The highest cards (determined by
choice of trumps) are seen as epic heroes taking
the field; they are the ace of spades (Spadillio),
the two of spades (Manillio), and the ace of
clubs (Basto).
Puts forth . . . leg as pictured on the playing
card

Pam knave of clubs, strongest card in the game
of loo
Amazon the queen of spades seen as a female
warrior; giving the Baron the first of four
successive tricks
What boots introducing a typical epic lament
for the decline of greatness (here symbolized
in the "globe" the monarch holds as an emblem of his realm)

In heaps on heaps; one fate o'erwhelms them all.
   The Knave of Diamonds tries his wily arts,
And wins (oh shameful chance!) the Queen of Hearts.
At this, the blood the virgin's cheek forsook,
90   A livid paleness spreads o'er all her look;
She sees, and trembles at the approaching ill,
Just in the jaws of ruin, and Codille.°
And now (as oft in some distempered state)
On one nice trick° depends the general fate.
An Ace of Hearts steps forth: the King unseen
Lurked in her hand, and mourned his captive Queen.
He springs to vengeance with an eager pace,
And falls like thunder on the prostrate Ace.°
The nymph exulting fills with shouts the sky,
100   The walls, the woods, and long canals reply.
   Oh thoughtless mortals! ever blind to fate,°
Too soon dejected, and too soon elate!
Sudden these honours shall be snatched away,
And cursed for ever this victorious day.
   For lo! the board with cups and spoons is crowned,
The berries° crackle, and the mill turns round.
On shining altars of Japan° they raise
The silver lamp; the fiery spirits° blaze.
From silver spouts the grateful° liquors glide,
110   While China's earth° receives the smoking tide.
At once they gratify their scent and taste,
And frequent cups prolong the rich repast.
Straight hover round the fair her airy band;
Some, as she sipped, the fuming liquor fanned,
Some o'er her lap their careful plumes displayed,
Trembling, and conscious of the rich brocade.
Coffee (which makes the politician wise,
And see through all things with his half-shut eyes)
Sent up in vapours to the Baron's brain
120   New stratagems, the radiant lock to gain.
Ah cease, rash youth! desist ere 'tis too late,
Fear the just gods, and think of Scylla's fate!°
Changed to a bird, and sent to flit in air,
She dearly pays for Nisus' injured hair!
   But when to mischief mortals bend their will,

Codille literally "elbow"; defeat, if the Baron wins a fifth trick
nice trick precise or careful play, with suggestion of political intrigue in "some distempered state" (l. 93)
Ace outranked by the king in the red suits; Belinda takes the trick and the game
blind to fate part of the typical epic warning in the moment of pride
berries coffee beans being ground

Japan japanned or lacquered tables
spirits in the spirit lamps that heat the coffee
grateful pleasing
China's earth the cups of earthenware or China
Scylla's fate Scylla plucked the purple hair (which was the source of his power) from the head of her royal father, Nisus, in order to give it to her lover, Minos. Her lover was shocked and refused it, and she was changed into a sea bird (see Ovid, *Metamorphoses* VIII).

How soon they find fit instruments of ill!
Just then, Clarissa drew with tempting grace
A two-edged weapon from her shining case;
So ladies in romance assist their knight,
130 Present the spear, and arm him for the fight.
He takes the gift with reverence, and extends
The little engine on his fingers' ends;
This just behind Belinda's neck he spread,
As o'er the fragrant steams she bends her head.
Swift to the lock a thousand sprites repair,
A thousand wings, by turns, blow back the hair,
And thrice they twitched the diamond in her ear;
Thrice she looked back, and thrice the foe drew near.
Just in that instant, anxious Ariel sought
140 The close recesses of the virgin's thought;
As, on the nosegay° in her breast reclined,
He watched the ideas rising in her mind,
Sudden he viewed, in spite of all her art,
An earthly lover lurking at her heart.
Amazed, confused, he found his power expired,
Resigned to fate, and with a sigh retired.
    The peer now spreads the glittering forfex° wide,
To enclose the lock; now joins it, to divide.
Even then, before the fatal engine closed,
150 A wretched Sylph too fondly interposed;
Fate urged the shears, and cut the Sylph in twain
(But airy substance soon unites° again),
The meeting points the sacred hair dissever
From the fair head, for ever and for ever!
    Then flashed the living lightning from her eyes,
And screams of horror rend the affrighted skies.
Not louder shrieks to pitying heaven are cast,
When husbands or when lapdogs breathe their last,
Or when rich China vessels, fallen from high,
160 In glittering dust and painted fragments lie!
    'Let wreaths of triumph now my temples twine,'
(The victor cried) 'the glorious prize is mine!
While fish in streams, or birds delight in air,
Or in a coach and six the British fair,
As long as Atalantis° shall be read,
Or the small pillow grace a lady's bed,
While visits shall be paid on solemn days,
When numerous wax-lights in bright order blaze,
While nymphs take treats, or assignations give,

---

nosegay corsage of flowers
forfex Latinate diction for the pair of scissors
soon unites Cf. Milton's account of Satan pierced
by Michael's sword: "but the ethereal substance

closed / Not long divisible" (*Paradise Lost* VI.
330–31).
Atalantis a popular book of the day, full of
court scandal

170   So long my honour, name, and praise shall live!'
       What time would spare, from steel° receives its date,
       And monuments, like men, submit to fate!
       Steel could the labour of the gods destroy,
       And strike to dust the imperial towers of Troy;
       Steel could the works of mortal pride confound,
       And hew triumphal arches to the ground.
       What wonder then, fair nymph! thy hairs should feel
       The conquering force of unresisted steel?

           Canto IV
       But anxious cares the pensive nymph oppressed,°
       And secret passions laboured in her breast.
       Not youthful kings in battle seized alive,
       Not scornful virgins who their charms survive,
       Not ardent lovers robbed of all their bliss,
       Not ancient ladies when refused a kiss,
       Not tyrants fierce that unrepenting die,
       Not Cynthia when her manteau's° pinned awry,
       E'er felt such rage, resentment, and despair,
10   As thou, sad virgin! for thy ravished hair.
           For, that sad moment, when the Sylphs withdrew,
       And Ariel weeping from Belinda flew,
       Umbriel,° a dusky melancholy sprite
       As ever sullied the fair face of light,
       Down to the central earth, his proper scene,
       Repaired to search the gloomy Cave of Spleen.°
           Swift on his sooty pinions flits the Gnome,
       And in a vapour reached the dismal dome.°
       No cheerful breeze this sullen region knows,
20   The dreaded East° is all the wind that blows.
       Here, in a grotto, sheltered close from air,
       And screened in shades from day's detested glare,
       She sighs for ever on her pensive bed,
       Pain at her side, and Megrim° at her head.
           Two handmaids wait the throne: alike in place,
       But differing far in figure and in face.
       Here stood Ill Nature like an ancient maid,
       Her wrinkled form in black and white arrayed;
       With store of prayers, for mornings, nights, and noons,
30   Her hand is filled; her bosom with lampoons.°

---

steel the fatal power of arms, which destroys even the Troy built by Apollo and Poseidon
But anxious . . . oppressed Cf. *Aeneid* IV.1 "But anxious cares already seized the Queen" (Dryden trans.).
manteau's mantua, loose robe or hood
Umbriel a gnome and former prude, named for "umbra," Latin for "shadow"
Cave of Spleen an epic visit to the underworld; suggestive of Spenser's caves of Mammon, Despair, and Night. Spleen was the name (drawn from the bodily organ, whose function was not clearly understood) for the fashionable psychosomatic ailment of the day, involving melancholy, self-pity, and hypochondria; particularly rife among those who could afford it.
dome dwelling
East The east wind was taken as a cause of spleen.
Megrim migraine headache
lampoons ill-tempered satires or caricatures

There Affection, with a sickly mien
Shows in her cheek the roses of eighteen,
Practiced to lisp, and hang the head aside,
Faints into airs, and languishes with pride;
On the rich quilt sinks with becoming woe,
Wrapped in a gown for sickness, and for show.
The fair ones feel such maladies as these,
When each new nightdress gives a new disease.
    A constant vapour o'er the palace flies;
40 Strange phantoms° rising as the mists arise;
Dreadful, as hermit's dreams in haunted shades,
Or bright as visions of expiring° maids.
Now glaring fiends, and snakes on rolling spires,°
Pale spectres, gaping tombs, and purple fires:
Now lakes of liquid gold, Elysian scenes,°
And crystal domes, and angels in machines.
    Unnumbered throngs on every side are seen
Of bodies changed° to various forms by Spleen.
Here living teapots stand, one arm held out,
50 One bent; the handle this, and that the spout:
A pipkin° there like Homer's tripod walks;
Here sighs a jar, and there a goose-pie° talks;
Men prove with child, as powerful fancy works,
And maids, turned bottles, call aloud for corks.
    Safe passed the Gnome through this fantastic band,
A branch of healing spleenwort° in his hand.
Then thus addressed the power: 'Hail, wayward Queen!
Who rule the sex to fifty from fifteen,
Parent of vapours° and of female wit,
60 Who give the hysteric, or poetic fit,
On various tempers act by various ways,
Make some take physic,° others scribble plays;
Who cause the proud their visits to delay,
And send the godly in a pet to pray.
A nymph there is, that all thy power disdains,
And thousands more in equal mirth maintains.
But oh! if e'er thy Gnome could spoil a grace,
Or raise a pimple on a beauteous face,
Like citron-waters° matrons' cheeks inflame,

---

phantoms fantasies
expiring literally, dying; in the traditionally punning sense, coming to sexual climax (as might be suggested in the erotic intensity with which saints' raptures were sometimes presented)
spires coils
Elysian scenes not only fantasies of bliss but scenes such as contemporary opera and pantomime lavishly presented ("angels in machines") bodies changed in fantasies that seem psychotic and clearly sexual in some cases, such as the repressed lives of prudes might have engendered
pipkin small earthenware boiler on a tripod;

for Hephaistos' "walking" tripods, see Homer, *Iliad* XVIII.439 ff.
goose-pie "alludes to a real fact; a lady of distinction imagined herself in this condition" (Pope)
spleenwort a fern that protected one against the excesses of the spleen
vapours roughly the same ailment as spleen, melancholy moodiness, here identified with hysteria
physic medicine
citron-waters brandy flavored with lemon

70   Or change complexions at a losing game;
If e'er with airy horns° I planted heads,
Or rumpled petticoats, or tumbled beds,
Or caused suspicion when no soul was rude,
Or discomposed the headdress of a prude,
Or e'er to costive° lapdog gave disease,
Which not the tears of brightest eyes could ease:
Hear me, and touch Belinda with chagrin;
That single act gives half the world the spleen.'
    The goddess with a discontented air
80   Seems to reject him, though she grants his prayer.
A wondrous bag with both her hands she binds,
Like that where once Ulysses° held the winds;
There she collects the force of female lungs,
Sighs, sobs, and passions, and the war of tongues.
A vial next she fills with fainting fears,
Soft sorrows, melting griefs, and flowing tears.
The Gnome rejoicing bears her gifts away,
Spreads his black wings, and slowly mounts to day.
    Sunk in Thalestris'° arms the nymph he found,
90   Her eyes dejected and her hair unbound.
Full o'er their heads the swelling bag he rent,
And all the furies issued at the vent.
Belinda burns with more than mortal ire,
And fierce Thalestris fans the rising fire.
'O wretched maid!' she spread her hands, and cried,
(While Hampton's echoes, 'Wretched maid!' replied)
'Was it for this you took such constant care
The bodkin,° comb, and essence to prepare;
For this your locks in paper durance° bound,
100   For this with torturing irons wreathed around?
For this with fillets° strained your tender head,
And bravely bore the double loads of lead?
Gods! shall the ravisher display your hair,
While the fops envy, and the ladies stare!
Honour forbid! at whose unrivalled shrine
Ease, pleasure, virtue, all, our sex resign.
Methinks already I your tears survey,
Already hear the horrid things they say,
Already see you a degraded toast,°
110   And all your honour in a whisper lost!

airy horns the sign of the cuckold
costive constipated
Ulysses when given a bag filled with the winds
by Aeolus (*Odyssey* X.19 ff.)
Thalestris' named for a queen of the Amazons,
thus fiercely militant
bodkin hairpin
paper durance heroic diction for curling papers

as for curling ("torturing") irons in the next
line
fillets headbands, worn by priestesses in the
Aeneid, but here part of the machinery of hair-
dressing, as are the "loads of lead" in the next
line
toast "a celebrated woman whose health is often
drunk" (Johnson); the "degraded" implies some
boastfulness in the toaster

How shall I, then, your helpless fame defend?
'Twill then be infamy to seem your friend!
And shall this prize,° the inestimable prize,
Exposed through crystal to the gazing eyes,
And heightened by the diamond's circling rays,
On that rapacious hand for ever blaze?
Sooner shall grass in Hyde Park Circus° grow,
And wits take lodgings in the sound of Bow;°
Sooner let earth, air, sea, to chaos fall,
120   Men, monkeys, lapdogs, parrots, perish all!'
    She said; then raging to Sir Plume repairs,
And bids her beau demand the precious hairs:
(Sir Plume, of amber snuffbox justly vain,
And the nice conduct of a clouded° cane)
With earnest eyes, and round unthinking face,
He first the snuffbox opened, then the case,
And thus broke out—'My Lord, why, what the devil?
Z—ds! damn the lock! 'fore Gad, you must be civil!
Plague on't! 'tis past a jest—nay prithee, pox!
130   Give her the hair'—he spoke, and rapped his box.
    'It grieves me much' (replied the peer again)
'Who speaks so well should ever speak in vain.
But by this lock, this sacred lock I swear,°
(Which never more shall join its parted hair,
Which never more its honours shall renew,
Clipped from the lovely head where late it grew)
That while my nostrils draw the vital air,
This hand, which won it, shall for ever wear.'
He spoke, and speaking, in proud triumph spread
140   The long-contended honours° of her head.
    But Umbriel, hateful Gnome! forbears not so;
He breaks the vial whence the sorrows flow.
Then see! the nymph in beauteous grief appears,
Her eyes half languishing, half drowned in tears;
On her heaved bosom hung her drooping head,
Which, with a sigh, she raised; and thus she said:
    'For ever cursed be this detested day,°
Which snatched my best, my favourite curl away!
Happy! ah ten times happy had I been,
150   If Hampton Court these eyes had never seen!
Yet am not I the first mistaken maid,
By love of courts to numerous ills betrayed.

prize the lock of her hair encased in a ring
Hyde Park Circus the Ring (see I.44), where
carriages kept the grass from growing
Bow near St. Mary-le-Bow, in the unfashionable
merchants' quarter of London as opposed to the
polite (west) end
clouded fashionably mottled or veined
this lock . . . swear Cf. Achilles' oath: "Now

by this sacred sceptre, hear me swear, / Which
never more shall leaves or blossoms bear . . ."
(Pope trans., *Iliad* I.309–10).
honours beauties
For ever . . . day This speech is based on
Achilles' lament for Patroclus (*Illiad* XVIII.
107 ff.).

Oh had I rather unadmired remained
In some lone isle, or distant northern land;
Where the gilt chariot never marks the way,
Where none learn ombre; none e'er taste bohea!°
There kept my charms concealed from mortal eye,
Like roses that in deserts bloom and die.
What moved my mind with youthful lords to roam?
160   O had I stayed, and said my prayers at home!
'Twas this, the morning omens seemed to tell;
Thrice from my trembling hand the patch box fell;
The tottering china shook without a wind,
Nay, Poll sat mute, and Shock was most unkind!
A Sylph too warned me of the threats of fate,
In mystic visions, now believed too late!
See the poor remnants of these slighted hairs!
My hands shall rend what even thy rapine spares:
These, in two sable ringlets taught to break,
170   Once gave new beauties to the snowy neck;
The sister lock now sits uncouth, alone,
And in its fellow's fate foresees its own;
Uncurled it hangs, the fatal shears demands;
And tempts once more thy sacrilegious hands.
Oh hadst thou, cruel! been content to seize
Hairs less in sight, or any hairs but these!'°

        Canto V
She said: the pitying audience melt in tears,
But fate and Jove had stopped the Baron's ears.
In vain Thalestris with reproach assails,
For who can move when fair Belinda fails?
Not half so fixed the Trojan could remain,
While Anna° begged and Dido raged in vain.
Then grave Clarissa° graceful waved her fan;
Silence ensued, and thus the nymph began.
    'Say why are beauties praised and honoured most,
10   The wise man's passion, and the vain° man's toast?
Why decked with all that land and sea afford,
Why angels called, and angel-like adored?
Why round our coaches crowd the white-gloved beaux,

bohea a kind of tea
any . . . these The joke here is that while Belinda doesn't mean her pubic hair, her whole
rhetoric of honor (exteriors and reputations matter more than interior truths) leads her to invoke
it inadvertently; the poet's wit traps her, much
as Malvolio, in *Twelfth Night* (III.iv) is trapped
into saying a bit of bawdry his Puritanism would
never allow him consciously to utter.
Anna who failed to persuade Aeneas to remain
faithful to her sister Dido (*Aeneid* IV)
Clarissa "A new character introduced in the
subsequent editions, to open more clearly the

moral of the poem, in a parody of the speech
of Sarpedon to Glaucus in Homer" (Pope); cf.
especially the final lines of the speech: "But
since, alas! ignoble age must come, / Disease,
and death's inexorable doom; / The life which
others pay, let us bestow, / And give to Fame
what we to Nature owe; / Brave though we
fall, and honoured if we live, / Or let us glory
gain, or glory give!" (Pope trans., *Iliad* XII.
391–96). The transposition of scale moves from
"valour" as a source of merit to "good humour."
vain both foolish and boastful

Why bows the side-box from its inmost rows?
How vain are all these glories, all our pains,
Unless good sense preserve what beauty gains:
That men may say, when we the front-box grace,
"Behold the first in virtue, as in face!"
Oh! if to dance all night, and dress all day,
20   Charmed the smallpox,° or chased old age away,
Who would not scorn what housewife's cares produce,
Or who would learn one earthly thing of use?
To patch, nay ogle, might become a saint,
Nor could it sure be such a sin to paint.
But since, alas! frail beauty must decay,
Curled or uncurled, since locks will turn to grey;
Since painted or not painted, all shall fade,
And she who scorns a man, must die a maid;
What then remains, but well our power to use,
30   And keep good humour still whate'er we lose?
And trust me, dear! good humour can prevail,
When airs, and flights, and screams, and scolding fail.
Beauties in vain their pretty eyes may roll;
Charms strike the sight, but merit wins the soul.'
So spoke the dame, but no applause ensued;
Belinda frowned, Thalestris called her prude.
'To arms, to arms!' the fierce virago° cries,
And swift as lightning to the combat flies.
All side in parties, and begin the attack;
40   Fans clap, silks rustle, and tough whalebones crack;
Heroes' and heroines' shouts confusedly rise,
And bass and treble voices strike the skies.
No common weapons in their hands are found;
Like gods they fight, nor dread a mortal wound.
So when bold Homer makes the gods engage,
And heavenly breasts with human passions rage;
'Gainst Pallas,° Mars; Latona,° Hermes arms;
And all Olympus rings with loud alarms.
Jove's thunder roars, heaven trembles all around;
50   Blue Neptune storms, the bellowing deeps resound;
Earth shakes her nodding towers, the ground gives way;
And the pale ghosts start at the flash of day!
Triumphant Umbriel on a sconce's height
Clapped his glad wings, and sat to view the fight:
Propped on their bodkin spears, the sprites survey
The growing combat, or assist the fray.
While through the press enraged Thalestris flies,
And scatters death around from both her eyes,

---

smallpox common and disfiguring disease at the
time
virago man-like woman

Pallas Athena
Latona the mother of Apollo and Diana (Pope
latinized Greek names in his translations)

A beau and witling perished in the throng;
60   One died in metaphor, and one in song.
'O cruel nymph! a living death I bear,'
Cried Dapperwit,° and sunk beside his chair.
A mournful glance Sir Fopling upwards cast,
'Those eyes are made so killing'—was his last.
Thus on Maeander's flowery margin lies
The expiring swan,° and as he sings he dies.
      When bold Sir Plume had drawn Clarissa down,
Chloe stepped in, and killed him with a frown;
She smiled to see the doughty hero slain,
70   But at her smile, the beau revived again.
      Now Jove suspends his golden scales° in air,
Weighs the men's wits against the lady's hair;
The doubtful beam long nods from side to side;
At length the wits mount up, the hairs subside.
      See, fierce Belinda on the Baron flies,
With more than usual lightning in her eyes;
Nor feared the Chief the unequal fight to try,
Who sought no more than on his foe to die.°
But this bold lord, with manly strength endued,
80   She with one finger and a thumb subdued:
Just where the breath of life his nostrils drew,
A charge of snuff the wily virgin threw;
The Gnomes direct, to every atom just,
The pungent grains of titillating dust.
Sudden, with starting tears each eye o'erflows,
And the high dome re-echoes to his nose.
      'Now meet thy fate,' incensed Belinda cried,
And drew a deadly bodkin from her side.
(The same,° his ancient personage to deck,
90   Her great great grandsire wore about his neck
In three seal rings; which after, melted down,
Formed a vast buckle for his widow's gown:
Her infant grandame's° whistle next it grew,
The bells she jingled, and the whistle blew;
Then in a bodkin graced her mother's hairs,
Which long she wore, and now Belinda wears.)
      'Boast not my fall' (he cried) 'insulting foe!
Thou by some other shalt be laid as low.
Nor think, to die dejects my lofty mind;
100   All that I dread is leaving you behind!

Dapperwit like "Sir Fopling" below, the typical
name of a false wit or fop in Restoration comedy
expiring swan The swan, on the banks of the
wandering river Maeander, sings most sweetly
as he dies.
golden scales an epic convention in both Homer
and Virgil

to die in the double sense of "expiring" (IV.42),
as elsewhere in this section, e.g. "laid as low"
(l. 98)
The same a parody of epic accounts of the descent of armor or of Agamemnon's scepter
grandame's grandmother's

Rather than so, ah let me still survive,
And burn in Cupid's flames—but burn alive.'
  'Restore the lock!' she cries; and all around
'Restore the lock!' the vaulted roofs rebound.
Not fierce Othello in so loud a strain
Roared for the handkerchief° that caused his pain.
But see how oft ambitious aims are crossed,
And chiefs contend till all the prize is lost!
The lock, obtained with guilt, and kept with pain,
In every place is sought, but sought in vain:
With such a prize no mortal must be blest,
So heaven decrees! with heaven who can contest?
  Some thought it mounted to the lunar sphere,°
Since all things lost on earth are treasured there.
There heroes' wits are kept in ponderous vases,
And beaus' in snuffboxes and tweezer cases.
There broken vows, and deathbed alms are found,
And lovers' hearts with ends of riband bound;
The courtier's promises, and sick man's prayers,
The smiles of harlots, and the tears of heirs,
Cages for gnats, and chains to yoke a flea,
Dried butterflies, and tomes of casuistry.°
  But trust the Muse—she saw it upward rise,
Though marked by none but quick, poetic eyes:
(So Rome's great founder° to the heavens withdrew,
To Proculus alone confessed in view.)
A sudden star, it shot through liquid° air,
And drew behind a radiant trail of hair.°
Not Berenice's locks° first rose so bright,
The heavens bespangling with dishevelled light.
The Sylphs behold it kindling as it flies,
And pleased pursue its progress through the skies.
  This the beau monde° shall from the Mall° survey,
And hail with music its propitious ray.
This, the blest lover shall for Venus take,
And send up vows from Rosamonda's lake.°

110

120

130

Roared . . . handkerchief perhaps evoking Thomas Rymer's famous objections to the triviality of the occasion in Shakespeare's play: "So much ado, so much stress, so much passion and repetition about an handkerchief!" (*A Short View of Tragedy*, 1693)
lunar sphere reminiscent of Milton's Limbo of Vanity in *Paradise Lost* III.445–46, "Up hither like aerial vapours flew / All things transitory and vain," but even more of Milton's source in Ariosto, *Orlando Furioso* XXXIV.lxviii ff., where the moral tone is lighter and the objects more trivial and minutely specified
casuistry Pope wrote in a letter of 1708 about "deep divines, profound casuists, grave philosophers who have written . . . whole tomes and voluminous treatises about nothing"; casuistry

was the difficult (and sometimes hair-splitting) application of general ethical rules to individual cases.
founder Romulus, who disappeared in a storm and whose ascent to the heavens was attested only by the senator Proculus
liquid clear
trail of hair like the tail of a comet, whose name means "hairy star"
Berenice's locks The queen's hair, offered to Aphrodite to ensure her husband's safe return from battle, disappeared from the temple and was transformed into a constellation.
beau monde fashionable world
Mall the promenade in St. James's Park
Rosamonda's lake a pond in the same park, associated with unhappy lovers

This Partridge° soon shall view in cloudless skies,
When next he looks through Galileo's eyes;°
And hence the egregious wizard shall foredoom
140   The fate of Louis, and the fall of Rome.
    Then cease, bright nymph! to mourn thy ravished hair
Which adds new glory to the shining sphere!
Not all the tresses that fair head can boast
Shall draw such envy as the lock you lost.
For, after all the murders of your eye,
When, after millions slain, yourself shall die;
When those fair suns shall set, as set they must,
And all those tresses shall be laid in dust;
This lock, the Muse shall consecrate to fame,
150   And midst the stars inscribe Belinda's name!

1712–14

Elegy to the Memory of an Unfortunate Lady

With *Eloisa to Abelard,* also published in 1717, this represents the most romantic
strain in Pope's poetry, and the defense of a "brave disorder" is more thoroughgoing
here than in *Eloisa.* (These poems, it should be said, were chosen for highest, and at
times for exclusive, praise among Pope's works by some later eighteenth-century
critics who reacted against Pope's involvement in the daily life of his time.) The poem
draws upon the pattern of Roman elegy, notably in Ovid, Tibullus, and Propertius;
and it creates a situation comparable to those presented in Ovid's *Heroides,* where
women spoke with deep feeling of the wrongs done them, or in Nicholas Rowe's
"she-tragedies" (such as *The Fair Penitent* of 1703, *Jane Shore* of 1714, or *Lady Jane
Grey* of 1715), which turned from the more heroic vein to the pathetic and drew
upon such sources as Thomas Otway and Racine.

    The identity of the lady has aroused much futile speculation. All we need to know
about her can be surmised from the poet's lament. That opens with the vision of a
ghost who still bears the wound and the weapon of her suicide, as if she had been
rejected by heaven as she had by her guardian before. Her wandering the earth after
death seems the counterpart of her burial abroad in unhallowed ground. Tellingly,
as the poet asserts her dignity and even her sanctity, he laments as well her mortality
and his own, stressing both the threats that beset human feeling and the grandeur
of its intensity, moving from heroic passion to tender compassion.

Elegy to the Memory of an Unfortunate Lady

What beckoning ghost, along the moonlight shade
Invites my steps, and points to yonder glade?
'Tis she!—but why that bleeding bosom gored,

Partridge a notorious astrologer (ridiculed by
Swift) who predicted public events, such as
those in l. 140

Galileo's eyes telescope

Why dimly gleams the visionary sword?
Oh ever beauteous, ever friendly! tell,
Is it, in heaven, a crime to love too well?
To bear too tender, or too firm a heart,
To act a lover's or a Roman's part?°
Is there no bright reversion° in the sky,
10 For those who greatly think, or bravely die?
   Why bade ye else, ye Powers! her soul aspire
Above the vulgar flight of low desire?
Ambition first sprung from your blest abodes;
The glorious fault of angels and of gods:°
Thence to their images on earth it flows,
And in the breasts of kings and heroes glows.
Most souls, 'tis true, but peep out once an age,
Dull sullen prisoners in the body's cage:
Dim lights of life, that burn a length of years
20 Useless, unseen, as lamps in sepulchres;
Like eastern kings° a lazy state they keep,
And close confined to their own palace, sleep.
   From these perhaps (ere nature bade her die)
Fate snatched her early to the pitying sky.
As into air the purer spirits flow,
And separate from their kindred dregs below;°
So flew the soul to its congenial place,
Nor left one virtue to redeem her race.
   But thou, false guardian of a charge too good,
30 Thou, mean deserter of thy brother's blood!
See on these ruby lips the trembling breath,
These cheeks, now fading at the blast of death;
Cold is that breast which warmed the world before,
And those love-darting eyes must roll no more.
Thus, if eternal justice rules the ball,
Thus shall your wives, and thus your children fall:
On all the line a sudden vengeance waits,
And frequent hearses shall besiege your gates.
There passengers shall stand, and pointing say,
40 (While the long funerals blacken all the way)
Lo these were they, whose souls the Furies° steeled,
And cursed with hearts unknowing how to yield.
Thus unlamented pass the proud away,
The gaze of fools, and pageant of a day!
So perish all, whose breast ne'er learned to glow

Roman's part commit suicide
reverion literally, a property one expects to obtain; something restored after a period to its true owner
glorious fault . . . gods referring to the rebellion of heavenly angels (as in *Paradise Lost* or of the Titans against Zeus, but also recalling the discussion of ambition as a "spark too much of heavenly fire" in Dryden, *Absalom and Achitophel*, l. 307, or those "great wits" who

"gloriously offend" in Pope, *Essay on Criticism*, l. 152
Like eastern kings Cf. *Epistle to Dr. Arbuthnot*, l. 220.
separate . . . below the purification process of chemical distillation
Furies the avenging goddesses, here punishing the guardian's family for cruelty by cursing them with unremitting obduracy

For others' good, or melt at others' woe.
What can atone (oh ever-injured shade!)
Thy fate unpitied, and thy rites unpaid?
No friend's complaint, no kind domestic tear
50 Pleased thy pale ghost, or graced thy mournful bier.
By foreign hands thy dying eyes were closed,
By foreign hands thy decent limbs composed,
By foreign hands thy humble grave adorned,
By strangers honoured, and by strangers mourned!
What though no friends in sable weeds appear,
Grieve for an hour, perhaps, then mourn a year,
And bear about the mockery of woe
To midnight dances, and the public show?
What though no weeping Loves° thy ashes grace,
60 Nor polished marble emulate° thy face?
What though no sacred earth° allow thee room,
Nor hallowed dirge be muttered o'er thy tomb?
Yet shall thy grave with rising flowers be drest,
And the green turf lie lightly on thy breast:
There shall the morn her earliest tears bestow,
There the first roses of the year shall blow;°
While angels with their silver wings o'ershade
The ground, now sacred by thy reliques° made.
So peaceful rests, without a stone, a name,
70 What once had beauty, titles, wealth, and fame.
How loved, how honoured once, avails thee not,
To whom related, or by whom begot;
A heap of dust alone remains of thee,
'Tis all thou art, and all the proud shall be!
Poets themselves must fall, like those they sung,
Deaf the praised ear, and mute the tuneful tongue.
Even he, whose soul now melts in mournful lays,
Shall shortly want the generous tear he pays;
Then from his closing eyes thy form shall part,
80 And the last pang shall tear thee from his heart,
Life's idle business at one gasp be o'er,
The Muse forgot, and thou beloved no more!

                          1717

Loves funerary monuments in the form of
mourning cupids
emulate rival, reproduce
sacred earth Presumably because of her suicide,
the lady is denied burial in consecrated ground
and the performance of Christian rites ("hallowed dirge"); in contrast, Nature pays her

honors in flowers, turf, and the "tears" of morning dew.
blow blossom
reliques remains, often used of a saint's remains; here making sacred the ground in which
they lie

An Essay on Man

This is Pope's effort to recall man to those truths he professes to believe but finds hard to live by. The essay deals with the complaints that man raises against his nature and his fate, complaints that grow out of the false expectations of pride: that man is the sole end of the universe and that he can enjoy stable self-mastery. The lesson he must relearn is that of God's impartial order—the Great Chain of Being, linking every kind of creature from lowest to highest—and of his place within it. Man is the most dangerous link, neither securely rational nor governed by sure instinct, a volatile mixture (as the opening passage of the second epistle of the *Essay* reveals) and therefore an unstable one. The *Essay* insists upon man's incompleteness, upon his dependent existence within a vast harmony in which nothing can quite subsist without the support of all other creatures. In the final epistle man is taught to find his happiness not in externals but in humility, not in expansion and conquest but in the contraction that opens out in turn as love rather than possession, admitting all creatures into the spreading circle of one's love. Man finds himself, as in traditional Christianity, by losing himself; as he takes "every creature in, of every kind," he finds his earth a new Eden and becomes once more a creature in God's image: "Earth smiles around, with boundless bounty blest, / And Heaven beholds its image in his breast."

In the third epistle Pope treats man's political and social order, and in the passage given below he traces man's career from the state of nature, through the fall into superstition and tyranny, to the ultimate recovery of order through human institutions. Pope differs from the Epicureans, and from Hobbes and Mandeville, in seeing the state of nature as one of society rather than of chaotic individual impulse and appetite. The recovery of political order is for Pope, as for Hobbes and Mandeville, forced upon man by the intolerable insecurity of that state that they call natural but Pope regards as a fallen one; in the process, as Pope presents it, man rediscovers what is inherently natural. The political state is not, therefore, a mere work of artifice, nor is its authority the merely arbitrary one of established power. It is an embodiment, however imperfect, of a natural order and can claim legitimacy by an appeal to natural law.

An Essay on Man

From *Epistle II*

I. Know then thyself, presume not God to scan;°
The proper study of mankind is Man.
Placed on this isthmus of a middle state,
A being darkly wise, and rudely° great:
With too much knowledge for the Sceptic side,°
With too much weakness for the Stoic's pride,°
He hangs between; in doubt to act, or rest,
In doubt to deem himself a god, or beast;

scan criticize, judge
rudely turbulently, roughly

Sceptic side the distrust of the possibility of certain knowledge
Stoic's pride the mastery of all passions

In doubt his mind or body to prefer,
10 Born but to die, and reasoning but to err;
Alike in ignorance, his reason such,
Whether he thinks too little, or too much:
Chaos of thought and passion, all confused;
Still by himself abused, or disabused;
Created half to rise, and half to fall;
Great lord of all things, yet a prey to all;
Sole judge of truth, in endless error hurled:
The glory, jest, and riddle of the world! . . .

From *Epistle III*

IV. Nor think, in NATURE's STATE they blindly trod;
The state of nature° was the reign of God:
Self-love and social at her birth began,
150 Union the bond of all things, and of man.
Pride then was not; nor arts, that pride to aid;
Man walked with beast, joint tenant of the shade;
The same his table, and the same his bed;
No murder clothed him, and no murder fed.
In the same temple, the resounding wood,
All vocal beings hymned their equal° God:
The shrine with gore unstained, with gold undressed,
Unbribed, unbloody,° stood the blameless priest:
Heaven's attribute was universal care,
160 And man's prerogative to rule, but spare.
Ah! how unlike the man of times to come!
Of half that live the butcher and the tomb;°
Who, foe to nature, hears the general groan,
Murders their species and betrays his own.
But just disease to luxury succeeds,
And every death its own avenger breeds;
The fury-passions from that blood began,
And turned on man a fiercer savage,° man.
See him from nature rising slow to art!
170 To copy instinct then was reason's part;
Thus then to man the voice of Nature spake—
'Go, from the creatures thy instructions take:
Learn from the birds what food the thickets yield;
Learn from the beasts the physic° of the field;
Thy arts of building from the bee° receive;
Learn of the mole to plough, the worm° to weave;

---

state of nature rejecting Hobbes's view of it as a state of war in which man was a "wolf to man" and human life was "nasty, brutish, and short"; social love is not artificial but natural, and order or union is part of the frame of nature
equal common, impartial

unbloody not yet sacrificing animals or fellow men
butcher . . . tomb slayer and devourer
savage wild animal
physic medicinal herbs
bee as architect of honeycombed hives
worm silkworm

Learn of the little nautilus° to sail,
Spread the thin oar, and catch the driving gale.
Here too all forms of social union find,
180 And hence let reason, late, instruct mankind:
Here subterranean works° and cities see;
There towns aerial° on the waving tree.
Learn each small people's genius, policies,
The ant's republic, and the realm of bees;°
How those in common all their wealth bestow,
And anarchy without confusion know;
And these for ever, though a monarch reign,
Their separate cells and properties maintain.
Mark what unvaried laws preserve each state,
190 Laws wise as nature, and as fixed as fate.
In vain thy reason finer webs shall draw,
Entangle justice in her net of law,
And right, too rigid, harden into wrong;
Still for the strong too weak, the weak too strong.
Yet go! and thus o'er all the creatures sway,
Thus let the wiser make the rest obey,
And, for those arts mere instinct could afford,
Be crowned as monarchs, or as gods adored.'

    V. Great Nature spoke; observant men obeyed;
200 Cities were built, societies were made:
Here rose one little state; another near
Grew by like means, and joined, through love or fear.
Did here the trees with ruddier burdens bend,
And there the streams in purer rills descend?
What war could ravish, commerce could bestow,
And he returned a friend, who came a foe.
Converse and love mankind might strongly draw,
When love was liberty, and nature law.
Thus states were formed; the name of king unknown,
210 Till common interest placed the sway in one.
'Twas virtue only (or in arts or arms,
Diffusing blessings, or averting harms)
The same which in a sire the sons obeyed,
A prince the father of a people made.

    VI. Till then, by nature crowned, each patriarch sate,
King, priest, and parent of his growing state;
On him, their second providence, they hung,
Their law his eye, their oracle his tongue.

nautilus "They swim on the surface of the sea, on the back of their shells, which exactly resemble the hulk of a ship; they raise two feet like masts and extend a membrane between them which serves as a sail; the other two feet they employ as oars at the side" (Pope).

subterranean works anthills
towns aerial beehives
ant's republic . . . bees representing egalitarian and monarchical states, respectively, in the next four lines

He from the wondering° furrow called the food,
220   Taught to command the fire, control the flood,
Draw forth the monsters of the abyss profound,
Or fetch the aërial eagle to the ground.
Till drooping, sickening, dying they began
Whom they revered as god to mourn as man:
Then, looking up from sire to sire, explored°
One great first father, and that first adored.
Or plain tradition that this All begun,°
Conveyed unbroken faith from sire to son,
The worker from the work distinct was known,
230   And simple reason never sought but one:
Ere wit oblique° had broke that steady light,
Man, like his Maker, saw that all was right,°
To virtue, in the paths of pleasure, trod,
And owned a Father when he owned a God.
LOVE all the faith, and all the allegiance then;
For nature knew no right divine° in men,
No ill could fear in God; and understood
A sovereign being but a sovereign good.
True faith, true policy,° united ran,
240   This was but love of God, and this of man.
    Who first taught souls enslaved, and realms undone,
The enormous° faith of many made for one;°
That proud exception to all nature's laws,
To invert the world, and counterwork its Cause?°
Force first made conquest, and that conquest, law;
Till superstition taught the tyrant awe,
Then shared the tyranny, then lent it aid,
And gods of conquerors, slaves of subjects made:
She,° midst the lightning's blaze, and thunder's sound,
250   When rocked the mountains, and when groaned the ground,
She taught the weak to bend, the proud to pray,
To power unseen, and mightier far than they:
She, from the rending earth and bursting skies,
Saw gods descend and fiends infernal rise:
Here fixed the dreadful, there the blest abodes;
Fear made her devils, and weak hope her gods;
Gods partial, changeful, passionate, unjust,

wondering sharing the amazement of the people
explored discovered by inference
this All begun the world as created rather than
eternal and self-subsistent, a theistic rather than
a pantheistic view, which leads man to distinguish the creature from the Creator (l. 229)
wit oblique prismatically breaking the "steady
light," as in the *Essay on Criticism*, ll. 311–12
all was right Cf. Genesis 1:31: "And God saw
every thing that he had made, and, behold, it
was very good."
right divine arbitrary power conferred upon spe-

cific men by God, as was claimed by the divine
right of kings
policy government
enormous monstrous
many made for one "In this Aristotle placeth the
difference between a king and a tyrant, that the
first supposeth himself made for the people, the
other that the people are made for him" (William Warburton, citing *Politics* V.10).
To invert . . . Cause repudiating God's design
that all creatures serve each other
She superstition

Whose attributes were rage, revenge, or lust;
Such as the souls of cowards might conceive,
260 And, formed like tyrants, tyrants would believe.°
Zeal° then, not charity, became the guide,
And hell was built on spite, and heaven on pride.
Then sacred seemed the ethereal vault no more;
Altars grew marble then, and reeked with gore:
Then first the flamen° tasted living food;
Next his grim idol smeared with human blood;°
With heaven's own thunders shook the world below,
And played the god an engine on his foe.°
     So drives self-love, through just and through unjust,
270 To one man's power, ambition, lucre, lust:
The same self-love, in all, becomes the cause
Of what restrains him, government and laws.
For, what one likes if others like as well,
What serves one will,° when many wills rebel?
How shall he keep, what, sleeping or awake,
A weaker may surprise, a stronger take?
His safety must his liberty restrain:
All join to guard what each desires to gain.
Forced into virtue thus by self-defence,
280 Even kings learned justice and benevolence:
Self-love forsook the path it first pursued,
And found the private in the public good.
     'Twas then, the studious head or generous mind,
Follower of God or friend of humankind,
Poet or patriot, rose but to restore
The faith and moral,° Nature gave before;
Relumed her ancient light, not kindled new;°
If not God's image, yet his shadow drew:
Taught power's due use to people and to kings,
290 Taught nor to slack, nor strain its tender strings,°
The less, or greater, set so justly true,
That touching one must strike° the other too;
Till jarring° interests of themselves create
The according music of a well-mixed state.°

formed . . . believe A worship "grounded not on love but fear," for "the superstitious man looks on the Great Father of all as a tyrant. . . . Accordingly he serves his Maker but as slaves do their tyrants, with a gloomy savage zeal against his fellow-creatures . . . though at the same time he trembles with the dread of being ill-used himself." (Pope)
Zeal fanaticism
flamen priest
smeared . . . blood Cf. Milton, *Paradise Lost* I.392–93: "First Moloch, horrid king, besmeared with blood / Of human sacrifice . . .".
played . . . foe i.e. turned God into a piece of artillery, an instrument of man's own will and vengeance

What . . . will of what force is one will?
moral moral principles, as above in ll. 235–40
Relumed . . . new revived the natural order rather than invented society for the first time
tender strings as in musical instruments, whose harmony was a common analogy for political order
strike cause to reverberate
jarring conflicting, discordant
well-mixed state The mixed state was a balance of the power of the One, the Few, and the Many; such a balance was believed to give the state the stability to endure, and to withstand the claims of rival factions within it.

Such is the world's great harmony, that springs
From order, union, full consent of things!
Where small and great, where weak and mighty, made
To serve, not suffer, strengthen, not invade,
More powerful each as needful to the rest,
300 And, in proportion as it blesses, blest,
Draw to one point, and to one centre bring
Beast, man, or angel, servant, lord, or king,
    For forms of government let fools contest;
Whate'er is best administered is best:°
For modes of faith, let graceless° zealots fight;
His can't be wrong whose life is in the right:
In faith and hope the world will disagree,
But all mankind's concern is charity:
All must be false that thwart this one great end,
310 And all of God, that bless mankind or mend.
    Man, like the generous vine,° supported lives;
The strength he gains is from the embrace he gives.
On their own axis as the planets run,°
Yet make at once their circle round the sun:
So two consistent motions act the soul;
And one regards itself, and one the Whole.
    Thus God and Nature linked the general frame,
And bade self-love and social be the same.
1731?   1733

To Richard Boyle, Earl of Burlington

Richard Boyle, third Earl of Burlington (1695–1753), studied architecture in Italy, designed buildings himself and commissioned works by others, and sponsored publication of the designs of Andrea Palladio and Inigo Jones. In opposition to the baroque of Sir Christopher Wren and Sir John Vanbrugh, he promoted a more severe classicism and spent great sums on public buildings in that spirit. This epistle is an important document of eighteenth-century taste. It sets forth a theory of landscape gardening that Pope had already begun to apply in his own estate and, even more, in his advice to affluent landowners. What he recommends is a "natural" garden, which came to be known through Europe as an "English garden"; that is, one which does not disdain artifice (as no garden can) but seeks to adjust its improvements to the tendencies of the landscape and to bring to fulfillment what is latently there rather than impose a formal design upon it. It is a garden of concealed boundaries, of variety of light and shade, and with the power to evoke the landscapes

---

Whate'er . . . best Pope later explained that he did not mean "that no one form of government is, in itself, better than another . . . but that no form of government, however excellent or preferable in itself, can be sufficient to make a people happy, unless it be administered with integrity."

graceless crude; but also, without divine grace
generous vine as in traditional fables of the love of the vine and the elm, "generous" in giving of oneself to another
run rotate

painted by the great masters of the seventeenth century—Nicolas Poussin, Claude Lorrain, and others (see below, The Garden and the Wild).

The poem is also an interesting discussion of architectural form and function, and, most generally, of the relationship between taste and morality—a problem first raised in the *Essay on Criticism*. Pride is once more a central theme; here, too, it creates objects that are meant to stun, to astonish, to captivate by size or cost, and it neglects the function of part in a whole. The whole is hospitality in Timon's villa; but, more than that, it is generosity and concern for others, even concern for a reality that bounds, limits, and—in the good man—extends and fulfills the self. We can see that whole restored when "laughing Ceres" reassumes Timon's land or when Burlington sponsors, in contrast to the ornamental projects of "imitating fools," public works that gain their dignity, and even their beauty, from solid public use.

The identity of Timon caused Pope much pain; Timon was claimed by the malice of others to refer to Lord Chandos, who had befriended Pope and who, it should be said, dismissed the rumors himself. There now seems reason to see behind Timon, or at least some aspects of him, the figure of Walpole—at his huge house at Houghton —imposing his will in displays of magnificence (which Pope treats as unwitting self-exposure) and turning away Pope's satire by having his supporters direct it to Chandos. If Timon be taken as Walpole, he is only one aspect of that "great man" and a contemptibly trivialized version at that; but he serves to relate the realms of art and politics, and to show the opposition of the tyrannous private will to the generous harmony of a natural order.

The essay was first called *Of Taste* and later *Of False Taste*.

To Richard Boyle, Earl of Burlington

Of the Use of Riches

'Tis strange, the miser should his cares employ
To gain those riches he can ne'er enjoy:
Is it less strange, the prodigal should waste
His wealth, to purchase what he ne'er can taste?
Not for himself he sees, or hears, or eats;
Artists must choose his pictures, music, meats:
He buys for Topham,° drawings and designs,
For Pembroke,° statues, dirty gods, and coins;
Rare monkish manuscripts for Hearne° alone,
10 And books for Mead,° and butterflies for Sloane.°
Think we all these are for himself! no more
Than his fine wife, alas! or finer whore.

Topham Richard Topham (d. 1735), a "gentleman famous for a judicious collection of drawings" (Pope)
Pembroke Thomas Herbert, 8th Earl of Pembroke (1656–1733), had large collections of statues, pictures, and coins at Wilton House.
Hearne Thomas Hearne (1678–1735), eminent

medievalist and editor of early English chronicles
Mead Richard Mead (1673–1754), royal physician and friend of Pope, collector of some 30,000 books
Sloane Sir Hans Sloane (1660–1753), also royal physician and master of "the finest collection in Europe of natural curiosities" (Pope)

For what has Virro° painted, built, and planted?
Only to show, how many tastes he wanted.°
What brought Sir Visto's° ill got wealth to waste?
Some demon whispered, 'Visto! have a taste.'
Heaven visits with a taste the wealthy fool,
And needs no rod° but Ripley° with a rule.°
See! sportive fate, to punish awkward pride,
20   Bids Bubo° build, and sends him such a guide:
A standing sermon, at each year's expense,
That never coxcomb° reached magnificence!°
      You° show us, Rome was glorious, not profuse,
And pompous buildings once were things of use.
Yet shall (my Lord) your just, your noble rules
Fill half the land with imitating fools;
Who random drawings from your sheets shall take,
And of one beauty many blunders make;
Load some vain church with old theatric state,°
30   Turn arcs of triumph° to a garden gate;
Reverse your ornaments, and hang them all
On some patched dog-hole eked with ends of wall;
Then clap four slices of pilaster° on't,
That, laced with bits of rustic,° makes a front;°
Shall call the winds through long arcades to roar,
Proud to catch cold at a Venetian door;°
Conscious they act a true Palladian part,
And, if they starve,° they starve by rules of art.
      Oft have you hinted to your brother peer,
40   A certain truth, which many buy too dear:
Something there is more needful than expense,
And something previous even to taste—'tis sense:
Good sense, which only is the gift of Heaven,°
And though no science, fairly worth the seven:

Virro named for the contemptible rich patron in Juvenal's Fifth Satire
wanted lacked
Visto's named for a vista, a long view through an avenue of trees
rod punishment
Ripley Thomas Ripley (d. 1758), a mediocre but politically favored architect, a protégé of Walpole, hired to execute others' plans for Walpole's hall at Houghton; as Pope put it, "a carpenter employed by a First Minister, who raised him into an architect without any genius in the art"
rule carpenter's rule, as a form of "rod"; also a misapplied principle, as in ll. 25–26
Bubo Latin for owl; a reference to Bubb Dodington, a Whig politician who spent £140,000 completing a country house designed by Sir John Vanbrugh
coxcomb fop, pretender
magnificence not merely splendor but, according to Aristotle (*Nicomachean Ethics* IV.2), spending generously on public works rather than on one's own
You Burlington, then publishing the *Antiquities*

of *Rome* by the great Italian architect Andrea Palladio (1518–80), and other architectural drawings whose "sheets" (l. 27) might be searched for ornamental details by those without a true sense of their "use" (l. 24)
theatric state the misapplied details of a Roman amphitheater; the use of classical detail to achieve baroque theatricality
arcs of triumph Roman triumphal arches reduced in scale and used as models for ornamental gateways
pilaster a column attached to a wall
laced . . . rustic embellished with rustication, the imitation of naturally rough stones
front "frontispiece," the formal entrance to a building
Venetian door Palladio invented the Venetian door and window, consisting of an opening with an arched top set between two smaller rectangular openings; these, originally essential to the structural design of Palladio's buildings, became isolated decorative elements.
starve because of cost and the great distances that food had to be brought
gift of Heaven Cf. *Essay on Criticism*, l. 13.

A light, which in yourself you must perceive;
Jones° and Le Nôtre° have it not to give.
   To build, to plant, whatever you intend,
To rear the column, or the arch to bend,
To swell the terrace, or to sink the grot;°
In all, let Nature never be forgot.
But treat the goddess like a modest fair,
Nor overdress, nor leave her wholly bare;
Let not each beauty everywhere be spied,
Where half the skill is decently° to hide.
He gains all points, who pleasingly confounds,
Surprises, varies, and conceals the bounds.
   Consult the genius of the place° in all;
That tells the waters or to rise, or fall;
Or helps the ambitious hill the heavens to scale,
Or scoops in circling theatres° the vale;
Calls in the country, catches opening glades,
Joins willing woods, and varies shades from shades;
Now breaks, or now directs, the intending lines;°
Paints° as you plant, and, as you work, designs.
   Still follow sense, of every art the soul,
Parts answering parts shall slide into a whole,
Spontaneous beauties all around advance,
Start even from difficulty, strike from chance;
Nature shall join you; time shall make it grow
A work to wonder at—perhaps a Stowe.°
   Without it, proud Versailles!° thy glory falls;
And Nero's terraces° desert their walls:
The vast parterres° a thousand hands shall make,
Lo! Cobham comes, and floats° them with a lake:
Or cut wide views° through mountains to the plains,
You'll wish your hill or sheltered seat° again.
Even in an ornament its place remark,
Nor in an Hermitage set Dr. Clarke.°
   Behold Villario's ten years' toil complete;

50

60

70

Jones Inigo Jones (1573–1652), the distinguished architect and scene designer
Le Nôtre André Le Nôtre (1613–1700), the great French designer of formal gardens, notably those at Versailles
grot grotto, artificial cave
decently modestly, appropriately
genius of the place the character of the natural landscape; also the tutelary deity or *genius loci* who inhabited each place and guarded it
theatres the curving slopes of classical amphitheaters
intending lines which lead the eye forward
Paints with color, and perhaps composes in such designs as landscape painters had used
Stowe the house and gardens of Richard Temple, Lord Cobham (1675–1749), of which Pope wrote at the time, "if anything under Paradise could set me beyond all earthly cogitations, Stowe might do it"

Versailles the formal gardens of Louis XIV's palace
Nero's terraces the elaborate works of the Golden House of Nero, in Rome
parterres formal terraces
floats floods
cut wide views "This was done . . . by a wealthy citizen . . . by which means (merely to overlook a dead plain) he let in the north wind upon his house and parterre, which were before adorned and defended by beautiful woods" (Pope).
seat country house
Hermitage . . . Dr. Clarke Samuel Clarke (1675–1729) was a liberal theologian and student of science, rationalistic and unorthodox, hardly the man for a "hermitage." That is the name of an ornamental building in Richmond Park where Queen Caroline placed busts of Clarke, her favorite, as well as of Locke, Newton, and others.

80　His quincunx° darkens, his espaliers° meet;
　　The wood supports the plain, the parts unite,
　　And strength of shade contends with strength of light;
　　A waving glow the bloomy beds display,
　　Blushing in bright diversities of day,
　　With silver-quivering rills meandered o'er—
　　Enjoy them, you! Villario can no more;
　　Tired of the scene parterres and fountains yield,
　　He finds at last he better likes a field.
　　　　Through his young woods how pleased Sabinus strayed,
90　Or sat delighted in the thickening shade,
　　With annual joy the reddening shoots to greet,
　　Or see the stretching branches long to meet!
　　His son's fine taste an opener vista loves,
　　Foe to the dryads° of his father's groves;
　　One boundless green, or flourished carpet° views,
　　With all the mournful family of yews;°
　　The thriving plants ignoble broomsticks made,
　　Now sweep those alleys they were born to shade.
　　　　At Timon's Villa let us pass a day,
100　Where all cry out, 'What sums are thrown away!'
　　So proud, so grand; of that stupendous air,
　　Soft and agreeable come never there.
　　Greatness, with Timon, dwells in such a draught
　　As brings all Brobdingnag° before your thought.
　　To compass this, his building is a town,
　　His pond an ocean, his parterre a down:
　　Who but must laugh, the master when he sees,
　　A puny insect, shivering at a breeze!
　　Lo, what huge heaps of littleness around!
110　The whole, a laboured quarry above ground.
　　Two cupids squirt before: a lake behind
　　Improves the keenness of the northern wind.°
　　His gardens next your admiration call,
　　On every side you look, behold the wall!
　　No pleasing intricacies intervene,
　　No artful wildness to perplex the scene;
　　Grove nods at grove, each alley has a brother,
　　And half the platform just reflects the other.
　　The suffering eye inverted Nature sees,
120　Trees cut to statues,° statues thick as trees;

quincunx a planting of five trees, four at the corners and one in the center
espaliers trees fastened to a wall
dryads tree nymphs
flourished carpet a terrace with elaborate scrolled beds, here opposed to the contrary vice, the nakedness of a "boundless green"
yews typical planting in cemeteries; here simply forming "pyramids of dark green continually repeated, not unlike a funeral procession" (Pope)
Brobdingnag the land of giants (in the propor-

tion of 12:1 to man) in the second voyage of Swift's *Gulliver's Travels;* all this emphasizing the irony of calling Timon's sprawling palace a "villa"
northern wind an instance of the neglect of function in the "improvement" of landscape; cf. l. 75
Trees . . . statues referring to the topiary art of trimming trees or hedges into sculpturesque shapes

With here a fountain, never to be played;
And there a summerhouse, that knows no shade;
Here Amphitrite° sails through myrtle bowers;
There gladiators fight, or die in flowers;
Unwatered see the drooping sea-horse mourn,
And swallows roost in Nilus' dusty urn.°
　My Lord advances with majestic mien,
Smit with the mighty pleasure, to be seen:
But soft—by regular approach—not yet—
130　First through the length of yon hot terrace sweat;
And when up ten steep slopes you've dragged your thighs,
Just at his study door he'll bless your eyes.
　His study! with what authors is it stored?
In books, not authors, curious is my Lord;
To all their dated backs° he turns you round:
These Aldus° printed, those Du Sueil° has bound.
Lo, some are vellum, and the rest as good
For all his Lordship knows, but they are wood.
For Locke or Milton 'tis in vain to look,
140　These shelves admit not any modern book.
　And now the chapel's silver bell you hear,
That summons you to all the pride of prayer:
Light quirks of music, broken and uneven,
Make the soul dance upon a jig to Heaven.
On painted ceilings you devoutly stare,
Where sprawl the saints of Verrio or Laguerre,°
On gilded clouds in fair expansion lie,
And bring all Paradise before your eye.
To rest, the cushion and soft dean° invite,
150　Who never mentions Hell to ears polite.
　But hark! the chiming clocks to dinner call;
A hundred footsteps scrape the marble hall:
The rich buffet well-coloured serpents grace,
And gaping tritons° spew to wash your face.
Is this a dinner? this a genial room?
No, 'tis a temple, and a hecatomb.°
A solemn sacrifice, performed in state,

Amphitrite a sea nymph, wife of Poseidon and mother of Triton
Nilus' . . . **urn** the urn that accompanies the statue of the reclining river god and from which the waters of the river should pour forth
dated backs early or rare editions with the date stamped in gold on the spine of the binding. "Many delight chiefly in the elegance of the print or the binding; some have carried it so far as to cause the upper shelves to be filled with painted books of wood" (Pope).
Aldus Aldus Manutius (1450–1515), the great Venetian printer
Du Sueil Augustin Desueil (1673–1746), a Parisian bookbinder of note
Verrio or Laguerre Antonio Verrio (1639–

1707) and Louis Laguerre (1663–1721) were fashionable court artists, here creators of baroque ceiling paintings.
soft dean "This is a fact; a reverend Dean preaching at Court, threatened the sinner with punishment in 'a place which he thought it not decent to name in so polite an assembly'" (Pope).
gaping tritons "Taxes the incongruity of ornaments . . . where an open mouth ejects the water into a fountain or where shocking images of serpents, etc. are introduced in grottos or buffets" (Pope). "Tritons" have an upper human form and a lower fishy one, like mermaids.
hecatomb sacrificial slaughter of a hundred oxen

You drink by measure, and to minutes eat.
So quick retires each flying course, you'd swear
160 Sancho's dread Doctor and his wand° were there.
Between each act the trembling salvers ring,
From soup to sweet wine, and God bless the King.°
In plenty starving, tantalized in state,
And complaisantly helped to all I hate,
Treated, caressed, and tired, I take my leave,
Sick of his civil pride from morn to eve;
I curse such lavish cost, and little skill,
And swear no day was ever passed so ill.
     Yet hence the poor are clothed, the hungry fed;
170 Health to himself, and to his infants bread
The labourer bears: what his hard heart denies,
His charitable vanity supplies.°
     Another age shall see the golden ear°
Embrown the slope, and nod on the parterre,
Deep harvests bury all his pride has planned,
And laughing Ceres° reassume° the land.
     Who then shall grace, or who improve the soil?
Who plants like Bathurst,° or who builds like Boyle.°
'Tis use alone that sanctifies expense,
180 And splendour borrows all her rays from sense.
     His father's acres who enjoys in peace,
Or makes his neighbours glad, if he increase:
Whose cheerful tenants bless their yearly toil,
Yet to their Lord owe more than to the soil;
Whose ample lawns are not ashamed to feed
The milky heifer and deserving steed;
Whose rising forests, not for pride or show,
But future buildings, future navies, grow:
Let his plantations stretch from down to down,
190 First shade a country, and then raise a town.
     You too proceed! make falling arts your care,
Erect new wonders, and the old repair;
Jones and Palladio to themselves restore,
And be whate'er Vitruvius° was before:
Till kings call forth the ideas of your mind,
Proud to accomplish what such hands designed,
Bid harbours open, public ways extend,

Sancho's . . . wand Cf. Cervantes, *Don Quixote*
II.xlvii, where the doctor has the food Sancho
yearns for whisked away before he can eat it.
From soup . . . King from the beginning of the
meal to the concluding toast in port
charitable . . . supplies Cf. Atossa in *To a
Lady*, ll. 149–50.
golden ear of wheat
laughing Ceres the Roman goddess of agriculture, cheerfully bounteous and/or scornfully
amused by Timon's unnatural art

reassume regain possession, as a monarch does
a kingdom
Bathurst Allen, Lord Bathurst, (1685–1775),
friend of Congreve, Swift, Pope, and (years
later) of Laurence Sterne; an enthusiastic landscape gardener
Boyle Lord Burlington
Vitruvius Marcus Vitruvius Pollio (1st century
B.C.), the author of the most influential classical
work on architecture

Bid temples,° worthier of the God, ascend;
Bid the broad arch° the dangerous flood contain,
200   The mole projected break the roaring main;
Back to his bounds their subject sea command,
And roll obedient rivers through the land:
These honours, peace to happy Britain brings,
These are imperial works, and worthy kings.°

1731

To a Lady

Of the Characters of Women

Nothing so true as what you once let fall,
'Most women have no characters at all.'
Matter too soft a lasting mark to bear,
And best distinguished by black, brown, or fair.
    How many pictures° of one nymph we view,
All how unlike each other, all how true!
Arcardia's countess,° here, in ermined pride,
Is, there, Pastora° by a fountain side:
Here Fannia,° leering on her own good man,
10   And there, a naked Leda° with a swan.
Let then the fair one beautifully cry,
In Magdalen's loose hair and lifted eye,°
Or dressed in smiles of sweet Cecilia° shine,
With simpering angels, palms, and harps divine;
Whether the charmer sinner it, or saint it,
If folly grow romantic,° I must paint it.
    Come then, the colours and the ground° prepare!
Dip in the rainbow, trick her off° in air,

---

temples churches. Pope explains that because of graft and misuse of funds "some new-built churches . . . were ready to fall, being founded in boggy land . . . others were vilely executed."
broad arch A proposal to build a new Westminster Bridge was rejected, then its execution entrusted to Ripley, "the carpenter . . . who would have made it a wooden one," but finally built of stone with Burlington as a commissioner (Pope).
imperial . . . kings recalling *Aeneid* VI.852, where Anchises sums up his prophecy to Aeneas of the future of Rome: let others pursue sculpture, rhetoric, or astronomy; Rome has as its task "to tame the proud, the fettered slave to free; / These are imperial arts, and worthy thee"
pictures "Attitudes in which several ladies affected to be drawn, and sometimes one lady in them all" (Pope)
Arcadia's countess suggested by Sir Philip Sidney's romance, *The Countess of Pembroke's Arcadia* (1590), and perhaps referring to the wife of Thomas, Earl of Pembroke (1656–1733), a great collector and patron of art
Pastora a shepherdess, in contrast with "ermined pride"
Fannia the name of a Roman adulteress
Leda a popular Renaissance subject, as in the painting (now lost) by Leonardo da Vinci, a copy of which hung at Wilton House, the Pembroke seat
loose hair . . . eye typical attributes of the Magdalene in Renaissance painting; the loose hair recalling her drying of Christ's feet with it but also (as in Titian's version) only partially concealing her bare bosom
Cecilia the patron saint of music (celebrated in an ode by Dryden; see above), often shown in her ascent to heaven
romantic extravagant
ground the prepared surface to which paints will be applied
trick her off sketch her

Choose a firm cloud, before it fall, and in it
20 Catch, ere she change, the Cynthia° of this minute.
    Rufa,° whose eye quick-glancing o'er the park,
Attracts each light gay meteor of a spark,°
Agrees as ill with Rufa studying Locke,°
As Sappho's diamonds with her dirty smock,
Or Sappho° at her toilet's greasy task,
With Sappho fragrant at an evening mask:°
So morning insects that in muck° begun,
Shine, buzz, and flyblow° in the setting sun.
    How soft is Silia! fearful to offend,
30 The frail one's advocate, the weak one's friend:
To her, Calista proved her conduct nice,°
And good Simplicius asks of her advice.
Sudden, she storms! she raves! You tip the wink,°
But spare your censure; Silia does not drink.
All eyes may see from what the change arose,
All eyes may see—a pimple on her nose.
    Papillia,° wedded to her amorous spark,
Sighs for the shades—'How charming is a park!'
A park is purchased, but the fair he sees
40 All bathed in tears—'Oh, odious, odious trees!'
    Ladies, like variegated° tulips, show;
'Tis to their changes half their charms we owe;
Fine by defect, and delicately weak,
Their happy spots the nice° admirer take,
'Twas thus Calypso° once each heart alarmed,
Awed without virtue, without beauty charmed;
Her tongue bewitched as oddly as her eyes,
Less wit than mimic, more a wit than wise;
Strange graces still, and stranger flights she had,
50 Was just not ugly, and was just not mad;
Yet ne'er so sure our passion to create,
As when she touched the brink of all we hate.
    Narcissa's° nature, tolerably mild,
To make a wash,° would hardly stew a child;
Has even been proved to grant a lover's prayer,
And paid a tradesman once to make him stare;
Gave alms at Easter, in a Christian trim,°

Cynthia Diana, here the fickle goddess of the constantly changing moon
Rufa so named for her red hair, regarded as a sign of wantonness
spark beau
Locke The philosophy of John Locke (1632–1704) was made a fashionable study by Addison and Steele in the *Spectator* papers.
Sappho a woman poet (cf. Dryden's "Anne Killigrew" ode for this usage), probably Lady Mary Wortley Montagu, notorious for slovenliness
mask masked ball
muck referring to the belief that insects were

generated by corruption; cf. *Essay on Criticism,* ll. 41–43
flyblow generate
nice proper, punctilious
tip the wink make a surmise
Papillia Latin for butterfly
variegated streaked, varied in color
nice discriminating
Calypso named for the nymph who detained Odysseus for seven years
Narcissa's whose name suggests vanity
wash for complexion or hair
trim dress, manner

And made a widow happy, for a whim.
Why then declare good-nature is her scorn,
60   When 'tis by that alone she can be borne?
Why pique all mortals, yet affect a name?
A fool to pleasure, yet a slave to fame:
Now deep in Taylor° and the Book of Martyrs,°
Now drinking citron° with his Grace° and Chartres:°
Now conscience chills her, and now passion burns;
And atheism and religion take their turns;
A very heathen in the carnal part,
Yet still a sad,° good Christian at her heart.
     See Sin in state, majestically drunk;
70   Proud as a peeress, prouder as a punk;°
Chaste to her husband, frank° to all beside,
A teeming mistress, but a barren bride.
What then? let blood and body bear the fault,
Her head's untouched, that noble seat of thought:
Such this day's doctrine—in another fit
She sins with poets through pure love of wit.
What has not fired her bosom or her brain?
Caesar and Tallboy,° Charles° and Charlemagne.
As Helluo,° late dictator of the feast,
80   The nose of hautgout,° and the tip of taste,
Critiqued your wine, and analyzed your meat,
Yet on plain pudding deigned at home to eat;
So Philomedé, lecturing all mankind
On the soft passion, and the taste refined,
The address, the delicacy—stoops at once,
And makes her hearty meal upon a dunce.
     Flavia's° a wit, has too much sense to pray;
To toast our wants and wishes, is her way;
Nor asks of God, but of her stars, to give
90   The mighty blessing, 'while we live, to live.'
Then all for death, that opiate of the soul!
Lucretia's° dagger, Rosamonda's° bowl.
Say, what can cause such impotence of mind?
A spark too fickle, or a spouse too kind.
Wise wretch! with pleasures too refined to please;
With too much spirit to be e'er at ease;
With too much quickness ever to be taught;

Taylor Jeremy Taylor (1613–67), whose *Holy Living* and *Holy Dying* were extremely popular devotional works
Book of Martyrs the popular title of the work by John Foxe (1516–87)
citron brandy flavored with lemon peel
his Grace a duke, perhaps her lover
Chartres usurer and libertine (cf. *Satires* II.i)
sad sober
punk whore
frank free

Tallboy a booby lover in Richard Brome's *The Jovial Crew* (1641)
Charles a common name for a footman
Helluo Latin for glutton
hautgout anything with a strong scent or flavor
Flavia's named for blond hair
Lucretia's the Roman matron who committed suicide when she was raped by Tarquin
Rosamonda's Rosamond Clifford (d. 1177), mistress of Henry II, forced by his queen to drink poison

With too much thinking to have common thought:
You purchase pain with all that joy can give,
100   And die of nothing but a rage to live.
    Turn then from wits; and look on Simo's mate,
No ass so meek, no ass so obstinate.
Or her, that owns her faults, but never mends,
Because she's honest, and the best of friends.
Or her, whose life the Church and scandal share,
For ever in a passion, or a prayer.
Or her, who laughs at Hell, but (like her Grace)
Cries, 'Ah! how charming, if there's no such place!'
Or who in sweet vicissitude appears
110   Of mirth and opium, ratafie° and tears,
The daily anodyne, and nightly draught,
To kill those foes to fair ones, time and thought.
Woman and fool are two hard things to hit;
For true no-meaning puzzles more than wit.
    But what are these to great Atossa's° mind?
Scarce once herself, by turns all womankind!
Who, with herself, or others, from her birth
Finds all her life one warfare upon earth:
Shines in exposing knaves and painting fools,
120   Yet is whate'er she hates and ridicules.
No thought advances, but her eddy brain
Whisks it about, and down it goes again.
Full sixty years the world has been her trade,
The wisest fool much time has ever made.
From loveless youth to unrespected age,
No passion gratified except her rage.
So much the fury still outran the wit,
The pleasure missed her, and the scandal hit.
Who breaks with her provokes revenge from hell,
130   But he's a bolder man who dares be well.
Her every turn with violence pursued,
Nor more a storm her hate than gratitude:
To that each passion turns, or soon or late;
Love, if it makes her yield, must make her hate:
Superiors? death! and equals? what a curse!
But an inferior not dependent? worse.
Offend her, and she knows not to forgive;
Oblige her, and she'll hate you while you live:
But die, and she'll adore you—Then the bust°
140   And temple° rise—then fall again to dust.
Last night, her Lord was all that's good and great;

ratafie fruit-flavored liqueur with a brandy base
Atossa's named for the daughter of the Persian
emperor Cyrus the Great and the mother of
Xerxes; probably based upon Katharine Darnley,
Duchess of Buckinghamshire (1682?–1743) and
daughter of James II (although long believed to
be Sarah, Duchess of Marlborough)
bust funerary monument
temple sepulcher

A knave this morning, and his will a cheat.
Strange! by the means defeated of the ends,
By spirit robbed of power, by warmth of friends,
By wealth of followers! without one distress,
Sick of herself through very selfishness!
Atossa, cursed with every granted prayer,
Childless with all her children, wants an heir.
To heirs unknown descends the unguarded store,
150   Or wanders, Heaven-directed, to the poor.
     Pictures like these, dear Madam, to design,
Asks no firm hand, and no unerring line;
Some wandering touches, some reflected light,
Some flying stroke alone can hit 'em right:
For how should equal° colours do the knack?
Chameleons who can paint in white and black?
     'Yet Chloe sure was formed without a spot'—
Nature in her then erred not, but forgot.
'With every pleasing, every prudent part,
160   Say, what can Chloe want?'—She wants a heart.
She speaks, behaves, and acts just as she ought;
But never, never, reached one generous thought.
Virtue she finds too painful an endeavour,
Content to dwell in decencies° for ever.
So very reasonable, so unmoved,
As never yet to love, or to be loved.
She, while her lover pants upon her breast,
Can mark the figures on an Indian chest;
And when she sees her friend in deep despair,
170   Observes how much a chintz exceeds mohair.
Forbid it Heaven, a favour or a debt
She e'er should cancel—but she may forget.
Safe is your secret still in Chloe's ear;
But none of Chloe's shall you ever hear.
Of all her dears she never slandered one,
But cares not if a thousand are undone.
Would Chloe know if you're alive or dead?
She bids her footman put it in her head.
Chloe is prudent—Would you too be wise?
180   Then never break your heart when Chloe dies.
     One certain portrait may (I grant) be seen,
Which Heaven has varnished out, and made a *Queen:*°
The same for ever! and described by all
With truth and goodness, as with crown and ball.°
Poets heap virtues, painters gems at will,

And show their zeal, and hide their want of skill.°
'Tis well—but, artists! who can paint or write,
To draw the naked is your true delight.
That robe of quality so struts and swells,
190 None see what parts of nature it conceals:
The exactest traits of body or of mind,
We owe to models of an humble kind.
If Queensberry° to strip there's no compelling,
'Tis from a handmaid we must take a Helen.°
From peer or bishop 'tis no easy thing
To draw the man who loves his God, or king:
Alas! I copy (or my draught° would fail)
From honest Mah'met,° or plain Parson Hale.°
But grant, in public men sometimes are shown,
200 A woman's seen in private life alone:
Our bolder talents in full light displayed;
Your virtues open fairest in the shade.
Bred to disguise, in public 'tis you hide;
There, none distinguish twixt your shame or pride,
Weakness or delicacy; all so nice,
That each may seem a virtue, or a vice.
In men, we various ruling passions° find;
In women, two almost divide the kind;
Those, only fixed, they first or last obey,
210 The love of pleasure, and the love of sway.
That, Nature gives; and where the lesson taught
Is but to please, can pleasure seem a fault?
Experience, this; by man's oppression curst,
They seek the second not to lose the first.
Men, some to business, some to pleasure take;
But every woman is at heart a rake:
Men, some to quiet, some to public strife;
But every lady would be queen for life.
Yet mark the fate of a whole sex of queens!
220 Power all their end, but beauty all the means:
In youth they conquer, with so wild a rage,
As leaves them scarce a subject in their age:
For foreign glory, foreign joy, they roam;
No thought of peace or happiness at home.
But wisdom's triumph is well-timed retreat,
As hard a science to the fair as great!

hide . . . skill Cf. *Essay on Criticism*, ll. 293–96.
Queensberry Catherine Hyde, Duchess of Queensberry (1700–1777), friend and protectress of John Gay, and one of the most beautiful women of her day
Helen of Troy
draught sketch
Mah'met "Servant to the late King, said to be the son of a Turkish Bassa, whom he took at the siege of Buda, and constantly kept about his person" (Pope)
Parson Hale Dr. Stephen Hales (1677–1761), physiologist and admirable parish priest, a friend of Pope
ruling passions The ruling passions, for Pope, were ineradicable drives which might take disguised forms as they bent other passions to their control and which proved, upon scrutiny, to underlie all other motives. See *Essay on Man* II.123 ff.

Beauties, like tyrants, old and friendless grown,
Yet hate repose, and dread to be alone,
Worn out in public, weary every eye,
230 Nor leave one sigh behind them when they die.
    Pleasures the sex, as children birds, pursue,
Still out of reach, yet never out of view;
Sure, if they catch, to spoil the toy° at most,
To covet flying, and regret when lost:
At last, to follies youth could scarce defend,
It grows their age's prudence to pretend;
Ashamed to own they gave delight before,
Reduced to feign it, when they give no more:
As hags° hold sabbaths, less for joy than spite,
240 So these their merry, miserable night;°
Still round and round the ghosts of beauty glide,
And haunt the places where their honour died.
    See how the world its veterans rewards!
A youth of frolics, an old age of cards;
Fair to no purpose, artful to no end,
Young without lovers, old without a friend;
A fop their passion, but their prize a sot;
Alive, ridiculous, and dead, forgot!
    Ah! Friend!° to dazzle let the vain design;
250 To raise the thought, and touch the heart be thine!
That charm shall grow, while what fatigues the Ring°
Flaunts and goes down, an unregarded thing:
So when the sun's broad beam has tired the sight,
All mild ascends the moon's more sober light,
Serene in virgin modesty° she shines,
And unobserved the glaring orb declines.
    Oh! blest with temper whose unclouded ray
Can make tomorrow cheerful as today;
She, who can love a sister's charms, or hear
260 Sighs for a daughter with unwounded ear;
She, who ne'er answers till a husband cools,
Or, if she rules him, never shows she rules;
Charms by accepting, by submitting sways,
Yet has her humour most when she obeys;
Let fops or fortune fly which way they will;
Disdains all loss of tickets,° or Codille;°
Spleen, vapours,° or smallpox,° above them all,
And mistress of herself, though China° fall.

toy plaything
hags witches, whose sabbaths (held at midnight) were orgies with demons and sorcerers
night visiting night
Friend Martha Blount (1690–1763), whom Pope knew all his mature life and honored in his will; they were close friends and were believed by some to be lovers
Ring the fashionable drive in Hyde Park
virgin modesty alluding to Diana as the virgin

goddess of the moon as well as to its silver light
tickets in lotteries
Codille a lost game of ombre (cf. *The Rape of the Lock* III.92)
Spleen, vapours fashionable forms of melancholy or moodiness
smallpox whose scars had disfigured Martha Blount's face
China For its double sense, see *The Rape of the Lock* III.110.

And yet, believe me, good as well as ill,
270 Woman's at best a contradiction still.
Heaven, when it strives to polish all it can
Its last best work, but forms a softer man;
Picks from each sex, to make the favourite blest,
Your love of pleasure, our desire of rest:
Blends, in exception to all general rules,
Your taste of follies, with our scorn of fools:
Reserve with frankness, art with truth allied,
Courage with softness, modesty with pride;
Fixed principles, with fancy ever new;
280 Shakes all together, and produces—You.
Be this a woman's fame: with this unblest,
Toasts live a scorn, and queens may die a jest.
This Phoebus° promised (I forget the year)
When those blue eyes first opened on the sphere;
Ascendant Phoebus watched that hour with care,
Averted half your parents' simple prayer;
And gave you beauty, but denied the pelf°
That buys your sex a tyrant o'er itself.
The generous god,° who wit and gold refines,
290 And ripens spirits as he ripens mines,
Kept dross for duchesses, the world shall know it,
To you gave sense, good humour,° and a poet.

                              1735

Imitations of Horace

Pope's "imitations of Horace" are among his finest works. Some of the poems are direct imitations and were published with the text of Horace beside them (or the text of Donne for the two satires of his that Pope "versified" in more regular couplets). Others are written in the manner of Horace but without precise models. One of these, originally described as "a Dialogue Something like Horace," became, with its companion poem, the Epilogue to the Satires in 1740; the *Epistle to Dr. Arbuthnot* has also been printed as a Prologue to the Satires.

The term "imitation" was first given currency by Dryden, when he distinguished among three kinds of translation: metaphrase, or word-by-word literal translation; paraphrase, or a translation that retains the meaning of the original but does so by departing from strict literalness; and finally imitation (of which Dryden was suspicious), which departs freely from the original text to create a new poem in its spirit, using the experience of a new age to take the place of earlier material. (One may compare "paraphrase" and "imitation" in two instances given here: Dryden's and Swift's versions of Ovid's tale of Baucis and Philemon appearing in the section The Mock Form, and Dryden's and Johnson's versions of Juvenal's Third Satire, in The Urban Scene.)

Phoebus as god of prophecy
pelf wealth
generous god Phoebus as god of poetry, which fosters true wit, and as god of the sun, by which gold is generated and "ripens" in the earth
good humour Cf. *The Rape of the Lock* V.29–34.

The imitation emerged in England (perhaps furthered through Boileau's example) in the work of Abraham Cowley and Sir John Denham, as Dryden recognized, and one can perhaps read Rochester's *Satire Against Mankind* as an "imitation" of Boileau's Eighth Satire. At any rate, it is part of the effect of an imitation that the reader be potentially aware of the text from which the poet departs and recognize the variation upon the original, as one does in a parody. Pope, in fact, applied the phrase "a parody from Horace" to *Satire* II.i given here; and he used the term all but interchangeably with imitation. Yet the imitation, while it cannot be fully grasped without some knowledge of the original, can in considerable measure stand on its own, and it is not a great leap from those imitations which have a specific model in Horace to those which have only the generalized one of Horace's satires and epistles.

Finally, one must ask what that generalized example implied. In Dryden's *Discourse on satire* (passages from which are given above in his Critical Prose section) Juvenal is exalted over Horace: "a noble soul is better pleased with a zealous vindication of Roman liberty than with a temporizing poet, a well mannered court slave, and a man . . . who is ever decent, because he is naturally servile." These charges against Horace haunt the age, but Shaftesbury distinguishes between Horace's "debauched, slavish, courtly state" and his "returning, recovering state." In the latter he returned to a "Socratic" philosophy and left Epicureanism behind him, and in his revived moral severity (with its elements of Stoicism) he put the appeal of the court behind him. It is in this later state that the conversational poems—the *sermones*—were written, and they can be seen as an expression of it. Pope tends to carry Horace's Socratic morality to a stage of deeper intensity, perhaps more readily comparable to that of Juvenal; and he dramatizes the poet's rising to superb indignation, even prophetic rage, as he creates his vision of triumphant Vice (in *Epilogue* I) or defends himself against resentful libels. The modulation of tone is remarkable in all these poems, from the seemingly timid and naïve victim to the morally outraged patriot, from the public wrath of satiric engagement to the personal warmth of friendship in retirement.

Epistle to Dr. Arbuthnot

Being the Prologue to the Satires

P. Shut, shut the door, good John!° fatigued, I said,
Tie up the knocker, say I'm sick, I'm dead.
The Dog-star° rages! nay 'tis past a doubt,
All Bedlam, or Parnassus,° is let out:
Fire in each eye, and papers in each hand,
They rave, recite, and madden round the land.

What walls can guard me, or what shades can hide?
They pierce my thickets, through my grot° they glide;

good John Pope's servant John Serle
Dog-star Sirius, which reappears at the time of late summer heat; for Juvenal the season for the reading of new poems, whose pomposity and incompetence stung him to rage (see "Parnassus," l. 4)

Bedlam, or Parnassus inhabitants of the madhouse or (as they imagine) the mountain of the Muses
grot Pope's grotto at Twickenham was an underground retreat, an artificial cave encrusted with shells and minerals.

By land, by water,° they renew the charge;
10 They stop the chariot, and they board the barge.
No place is sacred, not the church is free;
Even Sunday shines no sabbath-day to me:
Then from the Mint° walks forth the man of rhyme,
Happy! to catch me just at dinner time.
     Is there a parson, much bemused in° beer,
A maudlin poetess, a rhyming peer,
A clerk, foredoomed his father's soul to cross,
Who pens a stanza, when he should *engross.*°
Is there, who, locked from ink and paper, scrawls
20 With desperate charcoal round his darkened walls?°
All fly to Twit'nam,° and in humble strain
Apply to me, to keep them mad or vain.
Arthur,° whose giddy son neglects the Laws,
Imputes to me and my damned works the cause:
Poor Cornus° sees his frantic wife elope,
And curses wit, and poetry, and Pope.°
     Friend to my life! (which did not you prolong,
The world had wanted many an idle song)
What drop or nostrum° can this plague remove?
30 Or which must end me, a fool's wrath or love?
A dire dilemma! either way I'm sped;°
If foes, they write, if friends, they read me dead.
Seized and tied down to judge, how wretched I!
Who can't be silent, and who will not lie;
To laugh were want of goodness and of grace,
And to be grave exceeds all power of face.
I sit with sad civility, I read
With honest anguish, and an aching head;
And drop at last, but in unwilling ears,
40 This saving counsel, 'Keep your piece nine years.'°
     'Nine years!' cries he, who high in Drury Lane,°
Lulled by soft zephyrs through the broken pane,
Rhymes ere he wakes, and prints before Term° ends,
Obliged by hunger, and request of friends:°
'The piece, you think, is incorrect? why, take it,

water Pope's house was on the Thames, and one could be rowed from London by scullers; "chariot" and "barge" suggest land and sea battles.
Mint a section of Southwark where debtors could stay without fear of arrest; on Sundays, however, there were no arrests anywhere
bemused in rhyming with the name of Laurence Eusden (1688–1730), a parson and poet laureate notoriously fond of drink
engross copy a legal document
darkened walls i.e. in confinement, probably in Bedlam
Twit'nam i.e. Twickenham, Pope's home
Arthur perhaps Arthur Moore, whose son (eager to shine as a wit) had plagiarized from Pope;

but the name is generic, like "Cornus" below
Cornus from Latin for a horn; hence a cuckold
Pope As a Roman Catholic, Pope could enjoy parodying the hysterical charges against all forms of popery.
drop or nostrum cures
sped i.e. to my grave
nine years the advice of Horace to the poet, *Ars Poetica*, ll. 386–89
Drury Lane street of theaters, prostitutes, and— here—writers in garrets
Term law court term, also the publishing season
Obliged . . . friends offering the second reason to conceal the first, a common procedure in prefaces

I'm all submission; what you'd have it, make it.'
 Three things another's modest wishes bound:
My friendship, and a prologue,° and ten pound.
 Pitholeon° sends to me: 'You know his Grace;
50 I want a patron; ask him for a place.'°
Pitholeon libelled me—'but here's a letter
Informs you, sir, 'twas when he knew no better.
Dare you refuse him? Curll° invites to dine;
He'll write a Journal, or he'll turn divine.'°
 Bless me! a packet.—' 'Tis a stranger sues,
A virgin tragedy, an orphan Muse.'
If I dislike it, 'Furies, death and rage!'
If I approve, 'Commend it to the stage.'
There (thank my stars) my whole commission ends,
60 The players and I are, luckily, no friends.
Fired that the house° reject him, ' 'Sdeath I'll print it,
And shame the fools—Your Interest, sir, with Lintot.'°
Lintot, dull rogue! will think your price too much:
'Not, sir, if you revise it, and retouch.'
All my demurs but double his attacks;
At last he whispers, 'Do; and we go snacks.'°
Glad of a quarrel, straight I clap the door,
'Sir, let me see your works and you no more.'
 'Tis sung, when Midas' ears° began to spring,
70 (Midas, a sacred person and a King)
His very Minister who spied them first,
(Some say his Queen) was forced to speak, or burst.
And is not mine, my friend, a sorer case,
When every coxcomb perks them in my face?
 'Good friend, forbear! you deal in dangerous things.
I'd never name Queens, Ministers, or Kings;
Keep close to ears, and those let asses prick;
'Tis nothing—' Nothing? if they bite and kick?
Out with it, DUNCIAD! let the secret pass,
80 That secret to each fool, that he's an ass:
The truth once told (and wherefore should we lie?)
The Queen of Midas slept, and so may I.
 You think this cruel? take it for a rule,
No creature smarts so little as a fool.

prologue often sought from well-known writers to help a play succeed
Pitholeon a foolish and pretentious poet mentioned by Horace, here a modern counterpart seeking influence with a nobleman
place position or sinecure
Curll Edmund Curll, notorious publisher of hacks, might commission him to write new libels or forge works in your name
Journal . . . divine sell his talents in party politics or religious controversy
house theater

Lintot Bernard Lintot, who published many of Pope's works
snacks shares
Midas' ears the ass's ears given him by Apollo for preferring Pan's music. Midas' wife (in some versions, his chief minister or barber) could not keep the secret entirely and whispered it into a hole in the earth, but the reeds that grew there repeated the message in the wind. (Since Walpole as chief minister and Caroline as queen virtually ruled in George II's place, they would have most reason to conceal the full extent of that King's stupidity.)

Let peals of laughter, Codrus!° round thee break,
Thou unconcerned canst hear the mighty crack:°
Pit, box, and gallery in convulsions hurled,
Thou standst unshook amidst a bursting world.
Who shames a scribbler? break one cobweb through,
90   He spins the slight, self-pleasing thread anew:
Destroy his fib or sophistry; in vain,
The creature's at his dirty work° again,
Throned in the centre of his thin designs,
Proud of a vast extent of flimsy lines!
Whom have I hurt? has poet yet or peer
Lost the arched eyebrow or Parnassian sneer?°
And has not Colley still his Lord and whore?
His butchers Henley,° his Freemasons Moore?°
Does not one table Bavius° still admit?
100   Still to one bishop Philips° seem a wit?
Still Sappho°—'Hold! for God's sake—you'll offend,
No names—be calm—learn prudence of a friend:
I too could write, and I am twice as tall;
But foes like these—' One flatterer's worse than all.
Of all mad creatures, if the learned are right,
It is the slaver kills, and not the bite.
A fool quite angry is quite innocent:
Alas! 'tis ten times worse when they *repent.*
    One dedicates in high heroic prose,
110   And ridicules beyond a hundred foes:
One from all Grubstreet° will my fame defend,
And, more abusive, calls himself my friend.
This prints my *Letters,*° that expects a bribe,
And others roar aloud, 'Subscribe, subscribe.'°
    There are, who to my person pay their court:
I cough like Horace, and, though lean, am short,
Ammon's great son° one shoulder had too high,
Such Ovid's nose, and 'Sir! you have an eye'—
Go on, obliging creatures, make me see
120   All that disgraced my betters, met in me.

Codrus a poet ridiculed by Virgil and Juvenal
mighty crack This phrase of Joseph Addison's
amused Pope by its total inadequacy to the idea
of cosmic catastrophe, and here Pope applies it
to stage thunder as Codrus's play is produced
and proves a catastrophe of a lesser sort.
dirty work since, like Swift's Spider in *The
Battle of the Books,* he spins a structure out of
his own excrement
Parnassian sneer referring to the current poet
laureate, Colley Cibber (as the phrase once had
to Lewis Theobald, *The Dunciad* II.5)
Henley See *Epilogue to the Satires* I.66 and note.
Moore James Moore-Smythe whom Pope regarded as a plagiarist, here cited as a leader
of Freemasons' processions
Bavius the bad poet of Virgil's and Horace's
day

Philips Ambrose Philips (1674–1749), notorious
for his rustic pastoral and his mock-naïve chil-
dren's verse (which won him the name of
Namby-Pamby), was secretary to Hugh Boulter,
Bishop of Armagh.
Sappho immediately invoking Pope's enemy,
Lady Mary Wortley Montagu, and implying her
support (like Philips's by the bishop) by Wal-
pole
Grubstreet the center and symbol of hack writers
Letters pirated (as some of Pope's were by
Curll) or forged
subscribe Books were often published with the
financial support of advance subscriptions.
Ammon's . . . son Alexander the Great, claim-
ing descent from Jupiter Ammon

Say for my comfort, languishing in bed,
'Just so immortal Maro° held his head':
And when I die, be sure you let me know
Great Homer died three thousand years ago.
    Why did I write? what sin to me unknown
Dipped me in ink, my parents' or my own?
As yet a child, nor yet a fool to fame,
I lisped in numbers,° for the numbers came.
I left no calling for this idle trade,
130   No duty broke, no father disobeyed.
The Muse but served to ease some friend, not wife,
To help me through this long disease, my life,
To second, ARBUTHNOT! thy art and care,
And teach the being you preserved, to bear.
    But why then publish? Granville° the polite,
And knowing Walsh, would tell me I could write;
Well-natured Garth inflamed with early praise;
And Congreve loved, and Swift endured my lays;
The courtly Talbot, Somers, Sheffield read,
140   Even mitred Rochester would nod the head,
And St. John's self (great Dryden's friends before)
With open arms received one poet more.
Happy my studies, when by these approved!
Happier their author, when by these beloved!
From these the world will judge of men and books,
Not from the Burnets, Oldmixons, and Cookes.°
    Soft were my numbers; who could take offence
While pure description held the place of sense?
Like gentle Fanny's° was my flowery theme,
150   A painted mistress, or a purling stream.
Yet then did Gildon° draw his venal quill;
I wished the man a dinner, and sat still.
Yet then did Dennis° rave in furious fret;
I never answered—I was not in debt.

Maro Virgil
numbers meter, verses
Granville The first of a series of statesmen, poets, critics, and patrons—all of high reputation—with whom Pope associates Dryden and himself (and thus himself with Dryden) in opposition to the hacks mentioned above; they are George Granville, Baron Lansdowne (1666–1735), to whom Pope dedicated *Windsor Forest;* William Walsh (1663–1708), his early literary adviser; Sir Samuel Garth (1661–1719), physician and poet; William Congreve; Jonathan Swift; Charles Talbot, Duke of Shrewsbury (1660–1718), statesman and sponsor of Pope's "versification" of Donne's satires; John Lord Somers (1651–1716), the Whig leader to whom Swift dedicated *A Tale of a Tub;* John Sheffield, Duke of Buckinghamshire and Normanby (1648–1721), whose poems Pope edited and to whom Dryden dedicated important work; Francis Atterbury, Bishop of Rochester (1662–

1732), friend of Swift and Pope and himself a distinguished writer; and Henry St. John, Viscount Bolingbroke (1678–1751), chief minister under Anne, political theorist, close friend of Swift and Pope for many years.
Burnets . . . Cookes Thomas Burnet, John Oldmixon, and Thomas Cooke; "authors of secret and scandalous history" (Pope)
gentle Fanny's any conventional poet's, but also with special reference to John, Lord Hervey, who appears below as Sporus, ll. 305–33
Gildon Charles Gildon (1665–1724), a critic who had attacked Pope personally, perhaps (as Pope believed) at the instigation of Joseph Addison (the "Atticus" of ll. 193–214); hence a hireling or "venal" writer
Dennis John Dennis (1657–1734), critic and dramatist, abusively personal in his attacks on Pope; also suspected by Pope of selling his services to Addison

If want provoked, or madness made them print,
I waged no war with Bedlam or the Mint.
  Did some more sober critic come abroad;
If wrong, I smiled; if right, I kissed the rod.
Pains, reading, study, are their just pretence,
And all they want is spirit, taste, and sense.
Commas and points° they set exactly right,
And 'twere a sin to rob them of their mite.
Yet ne'er one sprig of laurel° graced these ribalds,°
From slashing Bentley down to piddling Tibalds:°
Each wight, who reads not, and but scans and spells,
Each word-catcher, that lives on syllables,
Even such small critics some regard may claim,
Preserved in Milton's or in Shakespeare's name.
Pretty! in amber° to observe the forms
Of hairs, or straws, or dirt, or grubs, or worms!
The things, we know, are neither rich nor rare,
But wonder how the devil they got there.
  Were others angry? I excused them too;
Well might they rage; I gave them but their due.
A man's true merit 'tis not hard to find;
But each man's secret standard in his mind,
That casting-weight° pride adds to emptiness,
This, who can gratify? for who can guess?
The bard° whom pilfered pastorals renown,
Who turns a Persian tale for half a crown,°
Just writes to make his barrenness appear,
And strains, from hard-bound brains, eight lines a year;
He, who still wanting, though he lives on theft,
Steals much, spends little, yet has nothing left:
And he, who now to sense, now nonsense leaning,
Means not, but blunders round about a meaning:
And he, whose fustian's so sublimely bad,
It is not poetry, but prose run mad:
All these, my modest satire bade translate,
And owned that nine such poets made a Tate.°

points periods, the concern of these "more sober" verbal critics
laurel the bay with which the true poet was crowned
ribalds buffoons
slashing Bentley . . . piddling Tibalds Richard Bentley (the subject of Swift's earlier attack in *The Battle of the Books* and *A Tale of a Tub*) and Lewis Theobald (1688–1744) were, among other things, textual scholars. Bentley's great learning was accompanied by ill temper toward his colleagues and arrogance toward the authors he edited. Theobald had properly exposed Pope's weaknesses as an editor of Shakespeare, but his own emendations of the text are a mixture of brilliant intuition and heavy self-display; like Bentley's, his literary sense is much less secure than his historical information. Theobald was the king of the dunces in the first version of *The Dunciad* (1728), but he was supplanted by Colley Cibber in the revision of 1743; Bentley preserved his place through all editions.
in amber as flies and other insects have been decoratively preserved
casting-weight that turns the balance
bard Ambrose Philips, whose pastoral poems were clumsily based on Spenser's and who also translated a book of *Persian Tales*
half a crown a prostitute's customary fee
Tate Nahum Tate (1652–1715), former poet laureate, "a cold writer of no invention" (Pope); the line is based on the saying that it takes nine tailors to make a man.

How did they fume, and stamp, and roar, and chafe!
And swear, not *Addison* himself was safe.
   Peace to all such! but were there one° whose fires
True genius kindles, and fair fame inspires;
Blest with each talent and each art to please,
And born to write, converse, and live with ease:
Should such a man, too fond to rule alone,
Bear, like the Turk,° no brother near the throne,
View him with scornful, yet with jealous eyes,
200   And hate for arts that caused himself to rise;
Damn with faint praise, assent with civil leer,
And without sneering, teach the rest to sneer;
Willing to wound, and yet afraid to strike,
Just hint a fault, and hesitate dislike;
Alike reserved to blame, or to commend,
A timorous foe, and a suspicious friend;
Dreading even fools, by flatterers besieged,
And so obliging, that he ne'er obliged;
Like Cato,° give his little Senate laws,
210   And sit attentive to his own applause;
While wits and templars° every sentence raise,
And wonder with a foolish face of praise—
Who but must laugh, if such a man there be?
Who would not weep, if Atticus were he?
   What though my name stood rubric° on the walls,
Or plastered posts, with claps,° in capitals?
Or smoking forth, a hundred hawkers' load,
On wings of wind came flying all abroad?
I sought no homage from the race that write;
220   I kept, like Asian monarchs,° from their sight:
Poems I heeded (now berhymed so long)
No more than thou, great GEORGE! a birthday song.°
I ne'er with wits or witlings passed my days,
To spread about the itch of verse and praise;
Nor like a puppy, daggled° through the town,

---

one In this portrait of Atticus, which had appeared earlier by itself, Pope is clearly suggesting Joseph Addison (1672–1719), the author of the tragedy *Cato* as well as of the *Tatler* and *Spectator*. Addison and Pope had considerable respect for each other's powers, but Pope had some reason to feel Addison's jealousy or at least lack of generosity toward a young writer who stood outside his circle and failed to do homage to him. The original Atticus was a man of letters and friend of Cicero.
like the Turk the Turkish rulers, who in fact had often executed close kinsmen to avoid the threat of rivalry
Cato In his prologue to Addison's play (1713), Pope had written "While Cato gives his little senate laws, / What bosom beats not in his country's cause? / Who sees him act, but envies

every deed? / Who hears him groan, and does not wish to bleed?" (ll. 23–26) Here those questions are echoed with a difference, and the august Roman senate is replaced by the coffee-house hangers-on whom Addison rules as a literary dictator.
templars law students, who often cultivated literary ambitions
stood rubric was posted in red letters in booksellers' advertisements
with claps on posters; also with advertisements for cures for gonorrhea
like . . . monarchs in their withdrawal; cf. *Elegy to the Memory of an Unfortunate Lady,* ll. 21–22
birthday song the official ode of the laureate
daggled splashed in mud

To fetch and carry singsong up and down;
Nor at rehearsals sweat, and mouthed, and cried,
With handkerchief and orange° at my side;
But sick of fops, and poetry, and prate,
230   To *Bufo*° left the whole Castalian state.°
    Proud as Apollo on his forkèd hill,
Sat full-blown Bufo, puffed by every quill;
Fed with soft dedication all day long,
Horace and he° went hand in hand in song.
His library (where busts of poets dead
And a true Pindar stood without a head)
Received of wits an undistinguished race,
Who first his judgment asked, and then a place:
Much they extolled his pictures, much his seat,°
240   And flattered every day, and some days eat:
Till grown more frugal in his riper days,
He paid some bards with port, and some with praise;
To some a dry rehearsal was assigned,
And others (harder still) he paid in kind.°
Dryden alone (what wonder?) came not nigh,
Dryden alone escaped this judging eye:
But still the Great have kindness in reserve,
He helped to bury° whom he helped to starve.
    May some choice patron bless each gray goose quill!
250   May every Bavius have his Bufo still!
So, when a statesman wants a day's defence,
Or envy holds a whole week's war with sense,
Or simple pride for flattery makes demands,
May dunce by dunce be whistled off my hands!
Blest be the Great! for those they take away,°
And those they left me; for they left me GAY,°
Left me to see neglected genius bloom,
Neglected die, and tell it on his tomb:°
Of all thy blameless life the sole return
260   My Verse, and QUEENSBERRY° weeping o'er thy urn!
    Oh let me live my own, and die so too!
(To live and die is all I have to do:)°

orange sold in the theater as refreshment
Bufo a patron, his name taken from the Latin word for a toad, a creature that swells up with air
Castalian state poetry; named for the Muses' sacred spring on the "forkèd hill," Parnassus
Horace and he i.e. with Bufo as a modern Maecenas, replacing Horace's patron
seat estate
in kind with his own poems
helped to bury Dryden, who was poor most of his life, was given a lavish funeral; Bufo feels more secure with "poets dead" or with assured reputations.

take away "The Lord gave and the Lord hath taken away; blessed be the name of the Lord" (Job 1:21)
Gay John Gay, author of *The Beggar's Opera* and many poems, a close friend of Pope, Swift, and Arbuthnot
on his tomb Pope wrote Gay's epitaph.
Queensberry Charles Douglas, 3rd Duke of Queensberry (1698–1778), was, with his beautiful and witty wife, Gay's patron and friend.
To live . . . do a line adapted from Sir John Denham's poem *Of Prudence*

Maintain a poet's dignity and ease,
And see what friends, and read what books I please:
Above a patron, though I condescend
Some times to call a Minister my friend.
I was not born for courts or great affairs;
I pay my debts, believe, and say my prayers;
Can sleep without a poem in my head,
270   Nor know, if Dennis be alive or dead.
     Why am I asked what next shall see the light?
Heavens! was I born for nothing but to write?
Has life no joys for me? or (to be grave)
Have I no friend to serve, no soul to save?
'I found him close with Swift'—'Indeed? no doubt,'
(Cries prating Balbus) 'something will come out.'
'Tis all in vain, deny it as I will.
'No, such a Genius never can lie still';
And then for mine obligingly mistakes
280   The first Lampoon Sir *Will.* or *Bubo*° makes.
Poor guiltless I! and can I choose but smile,
When every coxcomb knows me by my *style?*
     Cursed be the verse, how well soe'er it flow,
That tends to make one worthy man my foe,
Give Virtue scandal, Innocence a fear,
Or from the soft-eyed virgin steal a tear!
But he who hurts a harmless neighbour's peace,
Insults fallen worth, or beauty in distress,
Who loves a lie, lame slander helps about,
290   Who writes a libel, or who copies out:
That fop, whose pride affects a patron's name,
Yet absent, wounds an author's honest fame:
Who can your merit selfishly approve,
And show the sense of it without the love;°
Who has the vanity to call you friend,
Yet wants the honour, injured, to defend;°
Who tells whate'er you think, whate'er you say,
And, if he lie not, must at least betray:
Who to the *Dean,* and *silver bell* can swear,
300   And sees at *Cannons* what was never there;°
Who reads, but with a lust to misapply,
Make satire a lampoon, and fiction, lie.
A lash like mine no honest man shall dread,

Sir Will. or Bubo Sir William Yonge or George Bubb Dodington, the one known as a wit, the other a wealthy patron; but any feeble writer is meant
And show . . . love i.e. demonstrate his taste without real affection or generosity
the honour . . . defend i.e. and lacks the honor to defend the poet (whom he calls friend) against slander or attack
Who . . . there i.e. who makes false identifications of characters and places in Pope's *Epistle to Burlington.* Pope was falsely charged with ingratitude as a result of others' malicious linking of Timon's villa with Cannons, the estate of the Duke of Chandos.

But all such babbling blockheads in his stead.
   Let *Sporus*° tremble—'What? that thing of silk,
Sporus, that mere white curd of ass's milk?
Satire or sense, alas! can Sporus feel?
Who breaks a butterfly upon a wheel?'°
Yet let me flap this bug with gilded wings,
310   This painted child of dirt that stinks and stings;
Whose buzz the witty and the fair annoys,
Yet wit ne'er tastes, and beauty ne'er enjoys:
So well-bred spaniels civilly delight
In mumbling of the game they dare not bite.
Eternal smiles his emptiness betray,
As shallow streams run dimpling all the way.
Whether in florid impotence he speaks,
And, as the prompter breathes, the puppet squeaks;
Or at the ear of Eve,° familiar toad,
320   Half froth, half venom, spits himself abroad,
In puns, or politics, or tales, or lies,
Or spite, or smut, or rhymes, or blasphemies.
His wit all seesaw, between *that* and *this,*
Now high, now low, now master up, now miss,
And he himself one vile antithesis.
Amphibious thing! that acting either part,
The trifling head, or the corrupted heart,
Fop at the toilet, flatterer at the board,
Now trips a Lady, and now struts a Lord.
330   Eve's tempter thus the Rabbins° have exprest,
A cherub's face, a reptile all the rest;
Beauty that shocks you, parts that none will trust,
Wit that can creep, and pride that licks the dust.
   Not Fortune's worshipper, nor fashion's fool,
Not lucre's madman, nor ambition's tool,
Not proud, nor servile; be one poet's praise,
That, if he pleased, he pleased by manly ways:
That flattery, even to kings, he held a shame,
And thought a lie in verse or prose the same.
340   That not in fancy's maze he wandered long,
But stooped° to truth and moralized his song:
That not for fame, but virtue's better end,
He stood° the furious foe, the timid friend,

Sporus Nero's homosexual favorite, a boy to whom he was married in public; appropriately used for Lord Hervey (1696–1743), prominent in the court of George II and especially close to Queen Caroline; a long-time confederate of Lady Mary Wortley Montagu in attacks upon Pope (Hervey's brilliant *Memoirs of the Reign of King George II* were not published until 1848)
wheel the rack or instrument of torture on which men were disjointed

Eve alluding to the early temptation, with Satan "squat like a toad, close at the ear of Eve" (*Paradise Lost* IV.800)
Rabbins rabbis, scholars of the Old Testament, whose image of Satan has often been represented in paintings of the temptation of Eve
stooped as a falcon is said to "stoop" to its prey
stood withstood, endured

The damning critic, half-approving wit,
The coxcomb hit, or fearing to be hit;
Laughed at the loss of friends he never had,
The dull, the proud, the wicked, and the mad;
The distant threats of vengeance on his head,
The blow unfelt, the tear he never shed;°
350   The tale revived, the lie so oft o'erthrown,
The imputed trash,° and dulness not his own;
The morals blackened when the writings 'scape,
The libeled person, and the pictured shape;°
Abuse, on all he loved, or loved him, spread,
A friend in exile, or a father, dead;
The whisper,° that to greatness still too near,
Perhaps, yet vibrates on his Sovereign's ear—
Welcome for thee, fair Virtue! all the past:
For thee, fair Virtue! welcome even the *last!*
360   'But why insult the poor, affront the great?'
A knave's a knave, to me, in every state:
Alike my scorn, if he succeed or fail,
Sporus at court, or Japhet° in a jail,
A hireling scribbler, or a hireling peer,
Knight of the post° corrupt, or of the shire;
If on a pillory, or near a throne,
He gain his Prince's ear, or lose his own.°
Yet soft by nature, more a dupe than wit,
Sappho° can tell you how this man was bit:°
370   This dreaded satirist Dennis will confess
Foe to his pride, but friend to his distress,°
So humble, he has knocked at Tibbald's door,
Has drunk with Cibber, nay, has rhymed for Moore.°
Full ten years slandered, did he once reply?
Three thousand suns went down on Welsted's lie.
To please a mistress one aspersed his life;
He lashed him not, but let her be his wife:
Let Budgell charge low Grubstreet° on his quill,
And write whate'er he pleased, except his will;
380   Let the two Curlls° of town and court, abuse

blow . . . shed the false report, circulated in the pamphlet *A Pop upon Pope* (1728), that Pope had been subjected to a whipping
trash scandalous works published as his by Curll
pictured shape as when he was shown as a hunchbacked ape in the pamphlet *Pope Alexander's Supremacy and Infallibility Examined* (1729)
whisper by Lord Hervey
Japhet Japhet Crook, a forger
Knight . . . post a term for one who made his living by giving false evidence, as opposed to a legitimate knight (of the shire or county), who might also be corrupt
lose his own as Japhet Crook did by way of

punishment before he was exposed in the pillory or stocks
Sappho Lady Mary Wortley Montagu, to whom Pope once had been very close, after their estrangement joined Lord Hervey in attacking him.
bit deceived, fooled
his distress Pope had been helpful in Dennis's last years.
Moore unintentionally, for Moore-Smythe plagiarized from Pope
low Grubstreet contributions to the *Grub Street Journal* that accused Budgell of forging a will and making himself heir
two Curlls the publisher (l. 53), and Lord Hervey, his counterpart at court

His father, mother, body, soul, and Muse.
Yet why? that father held it for a rule,
It was a sin to call our neighbour fool:
That harmless mother thought no wife a whore:
Hear this, and spare his family, *James Moore!*
Unspotted names, and memorable long!
If there be force in virtue or in song.
 Of gentle blood (part shed in honour's cause,
While yet in *Britain* honour had applause)
Each parent sprung—'What fortune, pray?'—Their own,
And better got, than Bestia's° from the throne.
Born to no pride, inheriting no Strife,
Nor marrying discord in a noble wife,
Stranger to civil and religious rage,
The good man walked innoxious through his age.
No courts he saw, no suits would ever try,
Nor dared an oath, nor hazarded a lie.
Unlearned, he knew no schoolman's subtle art,°
No language, but the language of the heart.
By nature honest, by experience wise,
Healthy by temperance and by exercise;
His life, though long, to sickness passed unknown,
His death was instant, and without a groan.
O grant me, thus to live, and thus to die!
Who sprung from kings shall know less joy than I.
 O Friend!° may each domestic bliss be thine!
Be no unpleasing melancholy mine:
Me, let the tender office long engage,
To rock the cradle of reposing age,
With lenient° arts extend a mother's breath,°
Make Languor smile, and smooth the bed of Death,
Explore the thought, explain the asking eye,
And keep a while one parent from the sky!
On cares like these if length of days attend,
May Heaven, to bless those days, preserve my friend,
Preserve him social, cheerful, and serene,
And just as rich as when he served a Queen.°
Whether that blessing be denied or given,
Thus far was right, the rest belongs to Heaven.

                          1735

Bestia's a Roman consul bribed into a dishonorable peace; perhaps referring to the enormous grants made by Queen Anne to the victorious Duke of Marlborough
art i.e. casuistry, which might find ingenious reasons for condoning false actions. Pope's father refused to gain relief from anti-Catholic measures by taking an oath against the pope.
Friend Arbuthnot

lenient relieving
mother's breath Pope's mother died at an advanced age before this poem was published, but these lines had been written some years earlier; Pope's account of his solicitude and devotion seems to be an accurate one.
Queen Anne, to whom Arbuthnot had been court physician

The First Satire of the Second Book of Horace

To Mr. Fortescue°

P.   There are (I scarce can think it, but am told),
There are, to whom my satire seems too bold:
Scarce to wise Peter° complaisant enough,
And something said of Chartres° much too rough.
The lines are weak, another's pleased to say,
Lord Fanny° spins a thousand such a day.
Timorous by nature, of the rich in awe,
I come to counsel learned in the law:
You'll give me, like a friend, both sage and free,°
10   Advice; and (as you use) without a fee.
    F.   I'd write no more.
    P.   Not write? but then I *think*,
And for my soul I cannot sleep a wink.
I nod in company, I wake at night,
Fools rush into my head, and so I write.
    F.   You could not do a worse thing for your life.
Why, if the nights seem tedious, take a wife;
Or rather truly, if your point be rest,
Lettuce and cowslip wine;° *Probatum est.*°
But talk with Celsus,° Celsus will advise
20   Hartshorn,° or something that shall close your eyes.
Or, if you needs must write, write CAESAR's° praise,
You'll gain at least a *knighthood,* or the *bays.*°
    P.   What? like Sir Richard,° rumbling, rough, and fierce,
With ARMS, and GEORGE, and BRUNSWICK° crowd the verse,
Rend with tremendous sound your ears asunder,
With gun, drum, trumpet, blunderbuss, and thunder?
Or nobly wild, with Budgell's° fire and force,
Paint angels trembling round his falling horse?
    F.   Then all your Muse's softer art display,
30   Let CAROLINA° smooth the tuneful lay,

To Mr. Fortescue William Fortescue, a friend and legal adviser of Pope (as well as a friend and supporter of Sir Robert Walpole), replaces the celebrated Roman lawyer Trebatius of Horace's poem.
Peter Peter Walter (1664?–1746) was notorious as a moneylender to the aristocracy and was said to be worth £300,000 at his death; as Swift describes him, "That rogue, of genuine ministerial kind, / Can half the peerage by his arts bewitch" (*Epistle to Mr. Gay*, 1731); and Pope cites him often as the crassest commercial spirit of the age (cf. *Epilogue to the Satires* I.121; II.57).
Chartres Francis Charteris (1675–1732), gambler, usurer, debauchee
Lord Fanny Fannius was a foolish critic and enemy of Horace, and Pope regularly applied his version of the name to John, Lord Hervey, the Sporus of the *Epistle to Dr. Arbuthnot.*

free generous, open
Lettuce . . . wine Both were believed to induce sleep, and lettuce to counteract sexual desire.
Probatum est "it is proved" (to work)
Celsus a physician, named for the chief Roman writer on medicine
Hartshorn ammonia, used in sleeping potions
Caesar's King George II
bays poet laureateship
Sir Richard Blackmore, poet and physician (1655–1729), author of several wretched epics
Brunswick George II's inherited title, from the German duchy his family had ruled
Budgell's Eustace Budgell (1686–1737), cousin and protégé of Addison, who wrote a ludicrous celebration of George and of the horse shot out from under him in battle
Carolina Queen Caroline

Lull with AMELIA's° liquid name the Nine,°
And sweetly flow through all the royal line.
    P.   Alas! few verses touch their nicer° ear;
They scarce can bear their *laureate* twice a year;°
And justly CAESAR scorns the poet's lays,°
It is to *history* he trusts for praise.
    F.   Better be Cibber, I'll maintain it still,
Than ridicule all taste, blaspheme quadrille,°
Abuse the City's best good men° in metre,
40 And laugh at peers that put their trust in Peter.
Even those you touch not, hate you.
    P.   What should ail them?
    F.   A hundred smart in Timon and in Balaam.°
The fewer still you name, you wound the more;
Bond° is but one, but Harpax° is a score.
    P.   Each mortal has his pleasure: none deny
Scarsdale° his bottle, Darty° his ham-pie;
Ridotta° sips and dances, till she see
The doubling lustres° dance as fast as she;
Fox° loves the Senate, Hockley Hole° his brother,
50 Like in all else, as one egg to another.
I love to pour out all my self, as plain
As downright SHIPPEN° or as old MONTAIGNE:°
In them, as certain to be loved as seen,
The soul stood forth, nor kept a thought within;
In me what spots (for spots I have) appear,
Will prove at least the medium must be clear.
In this impartial glass, my Muse intends
Fair to expose myself, my foes, my friends;
Publish the present age; but where my text
60 Is vice too high,° reserve it for the next:
My foes shall wish my life a longer date,
And every friend the less lament my fate.
My head and heart thus flowing through my quill,

Amelia's the third of the royal children
Nine the Muses
nicer more delicate
twice a year at the New Year and the king's birthday, occasions for obligatory odes
poet's lays George II had a well-known dislike of poetry and was supposed to have complained of Pope, "Why will not my subjects write in prose?" With Colley Cibber as laureate, he had better grounds than usual.
quadrille a fashionable card game
City's . . . men prosperous merchants or financiers (cf. ll. 3 and 4 above)
Timon . . . Balaam fictitious characters in the *Epistle to Burlington*, ll. 99 ff., and another satire, the *Epistle to Bathurst*
Bond Denis Bond (d. 1747), expelled from Parliament for a breach of trust and convicted of embezzlement as well

Harpax from Greek for "robber," a name that could be widely applied
Scarsdale the Earl of Scarsdale, well known for his love of drink
Darty Charles Dartineuf, a celebrated epicure
Ridotta a type of society woman
lustres crystals in chandeliers
Fox Stephen Fox, friend of Lord Hervey and loyal supporter of Walpole
Hockley Hole where bear-baiting took place, a resort of Henry Fox, also a Walpole supporter
Shippen William Shippen, a leading Jacobite and opponent of Walpole, outspoken and incorruptible
Montaigne whose essays are candidly self-revealing, open, and free
high in rank or power

Verse-man or prose-man, term me which you will,
Papist or Protestant, or both between,
Like good Erasmus° in an honest mean,
In moderation placing all my glory,
While Tories call me Whig, and Whigs a Tory.
Satire's my weapon, but I'm too discreet
70   To run amuck and tilt at all I meet;
I only wear it in a land of hectors,°
Thieves, supercargoes,° sharpers, and directors.°
Save but our army! and let Jove encrust
Swords, pikes, and guns, with everlasting rust!
Peace is my dear delight—not Fleury's° more:
But touch me, and no Minister so sore.
Whoe'er offends, at some unlucky time
Slides into verse, and hitches in a rhyme,
Sacred to ridicule his whole life long,
80   And the sad burden° of some merry song.
        Slander or poison dread from Delia's rage,
Hard words or hanging, if your judge be Page.°
From furious Sappho° scarce a milder fate,
Poxed° by her love, or libelled by her hate.
Its proper power to hurt, each creature feels;
Bulls aim their horns, and asses lift their heels;
'Tis a bear's talent not to kick but hug;
And no man wonders he's not stung by Pug.°
So drink with Walters or with Chartres eat,
90   They'll never poison you, they'll only cheat.
        Then, learnèd sir! (to cut the matter short)
Whate'er my fate, or well or ill at Court,
Whether old age, with faint but cheerful ray,
Attends to gild the evening of my day,
Or death's black wing already be displayed,
To wrap me in the universal shade;
Whether the darkened room to muse invite,
Or whitened wall provoke the skewer to write:°
In durance, exile, Bedlam, or the Mint,°
100   Like Lee or Budgell,° I will rhyme and print.
        F.   Alas, young man! your days can ne'er be long,

Erasmus the detached scholar and humanist,
who refused to involve himself in the controversies of the Reformation
hectors bullies
supercargoes officers aboard ship who were concerned only with the cargo and were proverbial
for their wealth
directors Those of the South Sea Company had
been notorious for fraud.
Fleury's the French cardinal (1653–1743) who
pursued, under Louis XV, a policy of peace
burden refrain

Page Sir Francis Page, a judge quick to see
guilt and to punish severely
Sappho probably referring to Lady Mary Wortley Montagu, but no doubt to others as well
Poxed infected with syphilis
Pug a common name for a pet dog
provoke . . . write with whatever instruments
are available in a madhouse or prison
Mint the sanctuary for debtors
Lee or Budgell The playwright Nathanael Lee
(1653–92) and Budgell (l. 27) were both
insane for a time.

In flower of age you perish for a song!
Plums° and directors, Shylock° and his wife,
Will club their testers,° now, to take your life!
   P. What? armed for virtue when I point the pen,
Brand the bold front° of shameless guilty men;
Dash the proud gamester in his gilded car;
Bare the mean heart that lurks beneath a star;°
Can there be wanting, to defend her cause,
110 Lights of the Church, or guardians of the laws?
Could pensioned Boileau° lash in honest strain
Flatterers and bigots even in Louis' reign?
Could laureate Dryden pimp and friar° engage,
Yet neither Charles nor James° be in a rage?
And I not strip the gilding off a knave,
Unplaced, unpensioned, no man's heir or slave?
I will, or perish in the generous cause:
Hear this, and tremble! you who 'scape the laws.
Yes, while I live, no rich or noble knave
120 Shall walk the world, in credit, to his grave.
To VIRTUE ONLY AND HER FRIENDS A FRIEND,
The world beside may murmur or commend.
Know, all the distant din that world can keep,
Rolls o'er my grotto,° and but soothes my sleep.
There, my retreat the best companions grace,
Chiefs out of war and statesmen out of place.°
There ST. JOHN° mingles with my friendly bowl,
The feast of reason and the flow of soul:
And he, whose lightning pierced the Iberian lines,°
130 Now forms my quincunx,° and now ranks my vines,
Or tames the genius of the stubborn plain,
Almost as quickly as he conquered Spain.
   Envy must own, I live among the great,
No pimp of pleasure, and no spy of state,
With eyes that pry not, tongue that ne'er repeats,
Fond to spread friendships, but to cover heats;
To help who want, to forward who excel;
This, all who know me, know; who love me, tell;

Plums those who had acquired the sum of £ 100,000
Shylock any usurer, but also an adaptation of the name of the Earl of Selkirk, a widely unloved Scottish peer
club their testers pool their wealth
front brow, where criminals were branded
star the decoration for Knight of the Garter
Boileau Nicolas Boileau-Despréaux (1636–1711), eminent poet and critic, a fierce satirist even in the royal post of historiographer and in the absolute monarchy of Louis XIV
pimp and friar combined in Friar Dominick, in Dryden's comedy *The Spanish Friar* (1680)
Charles nor James Charles had made Dryden

laureate in 1670 and James II retained him in that post, although the Catholic monarch banned the play for its satire on the Roman clergy.
grotto the artificial cave on Pope's estate at Twickenham
place office
St. John Bolingbroke, formerly with Harley at the head of Queen Anne's government, for a long time in self-imposed exile abroad
he . . . Iberian lines Charles Mordaunt (1658–1735), Earl of Peterborough, who captured Barcelona and Valencia in 1705–6
quincunx a planting of five trees, one at the center of the square formed by the rest

And who unknown defame me, let them be
140 Scribblers or peers, alike are *mob* to me.
This is my plea, on this I rest my cause—
What saith my counsel, learnèd in the laws?
    F.   Your plea is good; but still I say, beware!
Laws are explained by men—so have a care.
It stands on record, that in Richard's° times
A man was hanged for very honest rhymes.
Consult the statute: *quart.* I think, it is,
Edwardi sext. or *prim. et quint. Eliz.*
See *Libels, Satires*—here you have it—read.
150   P.   *Libels* and *satires!* lawless things indeed!
But grave *epistles*, bringing vice to light,
Such as a King might read, a Bishop write,
Such as Sir ROBERT° would approve—
    F.   Indeed?
The case is altered—you may then proceed;
In such a cause the plaintiff will be hissed,
My Lords the Judges laugh, and you're dismissed.
                                                                    1733

Epilogue to the Satires

In Two Dialogues

Dialogue I

Fr[iend]. Not twice a twelvemonth you appear in print,
And when it comes, the court see nothing in't.
You grow correct, that once with rapture writ,
And are, besides, too *moral* for a wit.
Decay of parts, alas! we all must feel—
Why now, this moment, don't I see you steal?
'Tis all from Horace; Horace long before ye
Said, 'Tories called him Whig, and Whigs a Tory;'°
And taught his Romans, in much better metre,
10 'To laugh at fools who put their trust in Peter.'°
    But Horace, sir, was delicate, was nice;
Bubo° observes, he lashed no sort of *vice:*
Horace would say, Sir Billy° *served the crown,*
Blunt° could *do business,* Huggins° *knew the town;*

Richard's Richard III
Sir Robert Walpole
Tories called . . . Tory Cf. *Satire* II.i.68.
To laugh . . . Peter Peter Walter, the money-lender; see l. 121 below; Epilogue II. 57–58 and note; and, above, Satire II.i.3 and note, and II.i.40.
Bubo "Some guilty person very fond of making such an observation" (Pope); cf. *Epistle to Dr. Arbuthnot,* l. 280
Sir Billy Sir William Yonge (d. 1755), a prominent Whig of whom Lord Hervey wrote, "His

name was proverbially used to express everything pitiful, corrupt, and contemptible"
Blunt Sir John Blunt (1665–1733), director of the South Sea Company, upon whose collapse he was forced to render his estate of almost £ 200,000
Huggins John Huggins (d. 1745), warden of Fleet Prison. Found guilty of extortion and cruelty and tried for the murder of a prisoner, he was acquitted because of the testimony of prominent character witnesses.

In Sappho° touch the *failings of the sex,*
In reverend bishops note some *small neglects,*
And own, the Spaniard° did a *waggish thing,*
Who cropped our ears, and sent them to the king.
His sly, polite, insinuating style
20   Could please at court, and make Augustus smile:
An artful manager, that crept between
His friend and shame, and was a kind of *screen.*°
But 'faith your very friends will soon be sore;
Patriots° there are, who wish you'd jest no more—
And where's the glory? 'twill be only thought
The Great Man° never offered you a groat.
Go see Sir Robert——

P.   See Sir Robert!—hum—
And never laugh—for all my life to come?
Seen him I have, but in his happier hour
30   Of social pleasure, ill-exchanged for power;
Seen him, uncumbered with the venal tribe,
Smile without art, and win without a bribe.
Would he oblige me? let me only find,
He does not think me what he thinks mankind.°
Come, come, at all I laugh he laughs, no doubt;
The only difference is, I dare laugh out.

F. Why yes: with *Scripture* still you may be free;
A horselaugh, if you please, at *honesty;*
A joke on Jekyl,° or some odd *Old Whig*
40   Who never changed his principles, or wig:°
A patriot is a fool in every age,
Whom all Lord Chamberlains° allow the stage:
These nothing hurts; they keep their fashion still,
And wear their strange old virtue, as they will.

If any ask you, 'Who's the man, so near
His prince, that writes in verse, and has his ear?'
Why, answer Lyttleton,° and I'll engage

Sappho Cf. *Satire* II.i.83.
Spaniard The captain of a Spanish ship cut off the ear of an English ship captain, Jenkins, and told him to carry it to his master, the king. While this eventually helped bring on war with Spain, it was still being investigated at the time the poem appeared, and Pope's irony is directed in part at Walpole's extreme reluctance to risk war.
screen a "metaphor peculiarly appropriated to a certain person in power" (Pope); i.e. Walpole, who opposed parliamentary inquiries into public frauds and was accused of being a "corrupt and all-screening minister"
Patriots a term applied to those in opposition to Walpole "though some of them . . . had views too mean and interested to deserve that name" (Pope)
Great Man a common phrase for Walpole as first minister

what . . . mankind alluding to Walpole's reported maxim, "All men have their price"
Jekyl Sir Joseph Jekyl (1663–1738), "a true Whig in his principles, and a man of the utmost probity. He sometimes voted against the Court, which drew upon him the laugh here described of *one* who bestowed it equally upon religion and honesty." (Pope)
wig still wearing the full-bottomed wig, at that time out of fashion with younger men
Lord Chamberlains given authority by Walpole's Licensing Act (1737) to forbid performances of politically dangerous plays
Lyttleton George, Baron Lyttleton (1709–73), secretary to the Prince of Wales and a strong opponent of Walpole, "distinguished for both his writings and speeches in the spirit of liberty" (Pope)

The worthy youth shall ne'er be in a rage:
But were his verses vile, his whisper base,
50 You'd quickly find him in Lord Fanny's° case.
Sejanus, Wolsey,° hurt not honest Fleury,°
But well may put some statesmen in a fury.
    Laugh then at any, but at fools or foes;
These you but anger, and you mend not those.
Laugh at your friends, and, if your friends are sore,
So much the better, you may laugh the more;
To vice and folly to confine the jest,
Sets half the world, God knows, against the rest,
Did not the sneer of more impartial men
60 At sense and virtue, balance all again.
Judicious wits spread wide the ridicule,
And charitably comfort knave and fool.
    P. Dear sir, forgive the prejudice of youth:
Adieu distinction, satire, warmth, and truth!
Come, harmless characters that no one hit;
Come, Henley's oratory,° Osborn's wit!°
The honey dropping from Favonio's° tongue,
The flowers of Bubo, and the flow of Young!°
The gracious dew of pulpit eloquence,°
70 And all the well-whipped cream of courtly sense,
That first was Hervey's, Fox's next, and then
The Senate's, and then Hervey's once again.
O come, that easy Ciceronian style,
So Latin, yet so English all the while,
As, though the pride of Middleton and Bland,°
All boys may read, and girls may understand!
Then might I sing without the least offence,
And all I sung should be the *Nation's Sense;*°

Lord Fanny's John, Lord Hervey; cf. *Epistle to Dr. Arbuthnot,* ll.305–33.
Sejanus, Wolsey "The one the wicked minister of Tiberius; the other, of Henry VIII. The writers against the Court usually bestowed these and other odious names on the Minister" (Pope). For such names applied to Walpole, see *Epilogue* II.137.
Fleury cardinal and minister to Louis XV of France, praised by the Patriots for his wisdom and honesty; cf. *Satire* II.i.75.
Henley's oratory John Henley, a popular preacher who called himself the "restorer of ancient eloquence," charged a shilling for admission, and trained gentlemen in elocution.
Osborn's wit James Pitt, a journalist and political hireling, wrote in defense of Walpole under many names, among them Socrates and Francis Osborne; known for the "heaviness of his style" as Mother Osborne.
Favonio's from Favonius, the gentle west wind
The flowers . . . Young so coupled in the *Epistle to Dr. Arbuthnot,* l. 280. Dodington was not only dishonest but pretentious; Yonge (Young) was described by Lord Hervey as

"talking eloquently without a meaning and expatiating agreeably upon nothing."
pulpit eloquence In this and the following lines Pope refers to some florid flattery that he believed Lord Hervey had composed. It was delivered by Henry Fox as a parliamentary address on the occasion of Queen Caroline's death and became "The Senate's" (l. 72) when Commons approved it and sent it to the king. It later reappeared in Hervey's Latin epitaph for the Queen. Cf. *Epilogue* II.164–80.
Middleton and Bland Conyers Middleton, theologian and librarian at Cambridge, was writing a life of Cicero, dedicated to Hervey in 1741. He helped correct the Latin of Hervey's epitaph, described by Pope as "between Latin and English." Henry Bland, Provost of Eton, translated the last act of Addison's *Cato* into Latin and published it through Walpole's help. He may have helped with the epitaph, too; both men would represent learning used (even hired) to give pretentious form to court flattery.
Nation's Sense the official view, Walpole's word for "consensus"

Or teach the melancholy Muse to mourn,
80   Hang the sad verse on Carolina's urn,
And hail her passage to the realms of rest,
All parts performed, and *all* her children blest!°
So—satire is no more—I feel it die—
No *gazetteer*° more innocent than I—
And let, a-God's name, every fool and knave
Be graced through life, and flattered in his grave.
    F. Why so? If satire knows its time and place,
You still may lash the greatest—in disgrace:
For merit will by turns forsake them all.
90   Would you know when? exactly when they fall.
But let all satire in all changes spare
Immortal Selkirk,° and grave De la Ware.°
Silent and soft, as saints remove to Heaven,
All ties dissolved, and every sin forgiven,
These may some gentle ministerial wing
Receive, and place forever near a king!
There, where no passion, pride, or shame transport,
Lulled with the sweet nepenthe° of a court;
There, where no father's, brother's, friend's disgrace
100   Once break their rest, or stir them from their place:°
But past the sense of human miseries,
All tears are wiped for ever from all eyes;°
No cheek is known to blush, no heart to throb,
Save when they lose a question,° or a job.°
    P. Good Heaven forbid, that I should blast their
            glory,
Who know how like Whig ministers to Tory,
And when three sovereigns died, could scarce be vext,
Considering what a *gracious Prince* was next.
Have I, in silent wonder, seen such things
110   As pride in slaves, and avarice in kings;
And at a peer or peeress shall I fret
Who starves a sister, or forswears a debt?
Virtue, I grant you, is an empty boast;
But shall the dignity of *vice* be lost?
Ye Gods! shall Cibber's son° without rebuke,

All parts . . . blest Queen Caroline was reported to have died without taking the last sacrament and without being reconciled with her son, the Prince of Wales.
gazetteer a journalist hired by the government to present its view
Immortal Selkirk Charles Douglas, Earl of Selkirk (1663–1739). "He was of the Bedchamber to King William; he was so to King George I; he was so to King George II" (Pope).
grave De la Ware John West, 1st Earl De la Ware (1693–1766), an indefatigable supporter of Walpole, "very skillful in all the forms of the House, in which he discharged himself with great gravity" (Pope)
nepenthe a potion that brings forgetfulness of grief or suffering
place with a punning reference to political appointment
All tears . . . eyes Cf. "and the Lord God will wipe away tears from off all faces" (Isaiah 25:8).
question parliamentary motion
job opportunity for bribery or profit
Cibber's son Colley Cibber's son Theophilus, the actor

Swear like a lord, or Rich° outwhore a duke?
A favourite's porter with his master vie,
Be bribed as often, and as often lie?
Shall Ward° draw contracts with a statesman's skill?
120 Or Japhet° pocket, like his Grace,° a Will?
Is it for Bond,° or Peter,° (paltry things)
To pay their debts, or keep their faith, like kings?
If Blount° dispatched himself, he played the man,
And so mayst thou, illustrious Passeran!°
But shall a printer,° weary of his life,
Learn from their books, to hang himself and wife?
This, this, my friend, I cannot, must not bear;
Vice thus abused, demands a nation's care:
This calls the Church to deprecate our sin,
130 And hurls the thunder of the laws on *gin*.°
    Let modest Foster,° if he will, excel
Ten metropolitans° in preaching well;
A simple Quaker, or a Quaker's wife,
Outdo Landaffe° in doctrine,—yea in life:
Let humble Allen,° with an awkward shame,
Do good by stealth, and blush to find it fame.
Virtue may choose the high or low degree,
'Tis just alike to Virtue, and to me;
Dwell in a monk, or light upon a king,
140 She's still the same, beloved, contented thing.
Vice is undone, if she forgets her birth,
And stoops from angels to the dregs of earth:
But 'tis the *fall* degrades her to a whore;
Let *greatness* own her, and she's mean no more:
Her birth, her beauty, crowds and courts confess,
Chaste matrons praise her, and grave bishops bless;°
In golden chains the willing world she draws,

Rich John Rich, theatrical manager; producer of pantomimes and of Gay's *The Beggar's Opera* (1728)

Ward John Ward (d. 1755), convicted of forgery and expelled from Commons in 1726

Japhet Japhet Crook, convicted in 1731 of forgery and of fraud in obtaining a will; condemned to stand in the pillory, have his ears cut off and his nose slit, forfeit his goods, and be imprisoned for life

his Grace Archbishop Wake handed the will of George I to his son, who suppressed it.

Bond Denis Bond, who embezzled the funds of the Charitable Corporation

Peter Peter Walter. See l. 10 above and Note; Epilogue II.57–58 and Note.

Blount Charles Blount (1654–93), deistic or freethinking writer who stabbed himself out of disappointed love and died of the wound

Passeran Alberto Radicati, Count of Passerano, a Piedmontese freethinker who fled to England, where he wrote a notorious defense of suicide

printer as in fact happened in 1732

gin whose excessive use was not successfully restrained by an Act of 1736

Foster James Foster, an Anabaptist minister and brilliant preacher whom Pope, it was reported, went to hear

metropolitans bishops

Landaffe the holder of a "poor bishopric in Wales, as poorly supplied" (Pope); i.e. both poor and poorly filled

humble Allen Ralph Allen of Bath (1694–1764), friend of Pope and Henry Fielding, reformer of the postal service, famous for his philanthropy

Chaste matrons . . . bless alluding to: (1) Justinian's elevation of the prostitute and entertainer Theodora as his empress; (2) Walpole's belated but scandalous marriage in 1738 to Molly Skerrett, his mistress of many years and the mother of two of his children; (3) in the following lines, the Scarlet Whore of Revelation 17

And hers the gospel is, and hers the laws,
Mounts the tribunal, lifts her scarlet head,
150 And sees pale Virtue carted° in her stead.
Lo! at the wheels of her triumphal car,°
Old England's Genius, rough with many a scar,
Dragged in the dust! his arms hang idly round,
His flag inverted° trails along the ground!
Our youth, all liveried° o'er with foreign gold,
Before her dance: behind her, crawl the old!
See thronging millions to the pagod° run,
And offer country, parent, wife, or son!
Hear her black trumpet through the land proclaim,
160 That 'Not to be corrupted is the shame.'
In soldier, churchman, patriot, man in power,
'Tis avarice all, ambition is no more!
See, all our nobles begging to be slaves!
See, all our fools aspiring to be knaves!
The wit of cheats, the courage of a whore,
Are what ten thousand envy and adore.
All, all look up, with reverential awe,
On crimes that scape, or triumph o'er the law:
While truth, worth, wisdom, daily they decry—
170 'Nothing is sacred now but villainy.'
    Yet may this verse (if such a verse remain)
Show there was one who held it in disdain.

Dialogue II

    Fr[iend], 'Tis all a libel—Paxton° (sir) will say.
P. Not yet, my friend! tomorrow faith it may;
And for that very cause I print today.
How should I fret to mangle every line,
In reverence to the sins of *Thirty-nine!*°
Vice with such giant strides comes on amain,
Invention strives to be before in vain;
Feign what I will, and paint it e'er so strong,
Some rising genius sins up to my song.
10   F. Yet none but you by name the guilty lash;
Even Guthry° saves half Newgate by a dash.
Spare then the person, and expose the vice.
P.   How, sir! not damn the sharper, but the dice?
Come on then, satire! general, unconfined,

carted exhibited as prostitutes were, or carried to execution
triumphal car the conqueror's chariot
flag inverted another reference (cf. ll. 17–18) to Walpole's foreign policy of peace at any price
liveried wearing the uniforms of service
pagod shrine or pagoda
Paxton Nicholas Paxton (d. 1744), an official appointed to scan new publications for slurs or libels upon Walpole's government
Thirty-nine The poem was originally published under the title *One Thousand Seven Hundred and Thirty-Eight.*
Guthry the ordinary or chaplain of Newgate Prison, who published the memoirs or confessions of criminals, "often prevailed upon to be so tender of their reputation as to set down no more than the initials of their name" (Pope)

Spread thy broad wing, and souse° on all the kind.
Ye statesmen, priests, of one religion all!
Ye tradesmen, vile, in army, court, or hall!°
Ye reverend atheists. F. Scandal! name them, who?
    P. Why that's the thing you bid me not to do.
20   Who starved a sister, who forswore a debt,
I never named; the town's inquiring yet.
The poisoning dame— F. You mean—
    P. I don't.—   F. You do.
P. See, now I keep the secret, and not you!
The bribing statesmen— F. Hold! too high you go.
P. The bribed elector— F. There you stoop too low.
P. I fain would please you, if I knew with what:
Tell me, which knave is lawful game, which not?
Must great offenders, once escaped the crown,
Like royal harts, be never more run down?
30   Admit your law to spare the knight requires,
As beasts of nature may we hunt the squires?
Suppose I censure—you know what I mean—
To save a bishop, may I name a dean?°
    F. A dean, sir? no: his fortune is not made;
You hurt a man that's rising in the trade.
    P. If not the tradesman who set up today,
Much less the prentice who tomorrow may.
Down, down, proud satire! though a realm be spoiled,°
Arraign no mightier thief than wretched Wild;°
40   Or, if a court or country's made a job,°
Go drench° a pickpocket, and join the mob.
    But, sir, I beg you (for the love of vice!)
The matter's weighty, pray consider twice;
Have you less pity for the needy cheat,
The poor and friendless villain, than the great?
Alas! the small discredit of a bribe
Scarce hurts the lawyer, but undoes the scribe.°
Then better sure it charity becomes
To tax directors, who (thank God) have plums;°
50   Still better, ministers; or, if the thing
May pinch even there—why, lay it on a king.
    F. Stop! stop!
    P.   Must satire, then, nor rise nor fall?
Speak out, and bid me blame no rogues at all.
    F. Yes, strike that Wild, I'll justify the blow.

souse swoop like a hawk on its prey
hall Westminster Hall, the chief law court of England
dean chief officer of a cathedral chapter, of lower rank than a bishop
spoiled despoiled
Wild Jonathan Wild, thief, fence, and informer, hanged in 1725 (see l. 55); cf. Gay, *The Beg-* *gar's Opera* (whose character of Peachum is based on Wild) and accompanying selections from Defoe and Fielding
made a job turned to personal gain
drench a common punishment, by ducking or under the public pump
scribe the scrivener or copyist, law clerk
plums large sums, usually £100,000

P. Strike? why, the man was hanged ten years ago:
Who now that obsolete example fears?
Even Peter° trembles only for his ears.
    F. What, always Peter? Peter thinks you mad,
You make men desperate, if they once are bad:
60 Else might he take to virtue some years hence—
    P. As Selkirk, if he lives, will love the Prince.°
    F. Strange spleen to Selkirk!
    P.   Do I wrong the man?
God knows, I praise a courtier where I can.
When I confess, there is who feels for fame
And melts to goodness, need I Scarborough° name?
Pleased let me own, in Esher's peaceful grove°
(Where Kent° and Nature vie for Pelham's love)
The scene, the master, opening to my view,
I sit and dream I see my Craggs° anew!
70   Even in a bishop I can spy desert;
Secker° is decent, Rundle° has a heart,
Manners with candour are to Benson° given,
To Berkeley,° every virtue under heaven.
    But does the court a worthy man remove?
That instant, I declare, he has my love:
I shun his zenith, court his mild decline;
Thus Somers° once, and Halifax,° were mine.
Oft, in the clear, still mirror of retreat,
I studied Shrewsbury,° the wise and great:
80 Carleton's° calm sense, and Stanhope's° noble flame,
Compared, and knew their generous end the same:
How pleasing Atterbury's° softer hour!

Peter Peter Walter (*Epilogue* I.10, 121), who had just escaped the pillory the year before
As Selkirk . . . Prince Cf. "immortal Selkirk," *Epilogue* I.92 ff. Because of the hostility between the king and his son, Selkirk (always true to the man in power) cannot love the prince, but he will do so as soon as the prince in turn becomes king.
Scarborough an earl who was a steady adherent to the royal interest but "whose known honour and virtue made him esteemed by all parties" (Pope)
Esher's . . . Grove the estate in Surrey of Henry Pelham, a loyal Whig who succeeded Walpole to power in 1746
Kent William Kent (1685–1748), the architect, painter, and landscape gardener, a friend of Pope and protégé of Burlington. With Pope's advice he did much to promote the "natural" garden, and Esher was one of his finest works of "improvement"; see Headnote to *To . . . Burlington.*
Craggs "There never lived a more worthy nature, a more disinterested mind, a more open and friendly temper" (Pope)
Secker Thomas Secker, Bishop of Oxford and later Archbishop of Canterbury, famous for moderation, tolerance, and discretion
Rundle Thomas Rundle, Bishop of Derry, of

whom Pope wrote, "I never saw a man so seldom whom I like so much"
Benson Martin Benson, Bishop of Gloucester
Berkeley George Berkeley (1685–1753), Bishop of Cloyne, philosopher, friend of Swift and Pope
Somers John, Lord Somers, Lord Keeper under William III. Pope, who knew him after his retirement, found Somers both "a consummate politician" and "a man of learning and politeness"; cf. the *Epistle to Dr. Arbuthnot,* l. 139 and note.
Halifax Charles Montagu, 1st Earl of Halifax (1661–1715), statesman, poet, and patron; a supporter of Pope's translation of Homer
Shrewsbury minister in three reigns and Lord Lieutenant of Ireland; cf. "Courtly Talbot" in the *Epistle to Dr. Arbuthnot,* l. 139 and note
Carleton's Henry Boyle, Baron Carleton, held many offices, including President of the Council, under William III and Anne.
Stanhope's James, Earl Stanhope, commander of the British forces in Spain in 1708; "a nobleman of equal courage, spirit, and learning" (Pope)
Atterbury's Bishop of Rochester, imprisoned in 1722 for his correspondence with the Pretender, convicted of treason and banished. Pope testified in his behalf at the trial.

How shined the soul, unconquered in the Tower!
How can I Pulteney,° Chesterfield° forget,
While Roman spirit charms, and Attic wit:
Argyle,° the state's whole thunder born to wield,
And shake alike the senate and the field:
Or Wyndham,° just to freedom and the throne,
The master of our passions, and his own.
90   Names, which I long have loved, nor loved in vain,
Ranked with their friends, not numbered with their train;
And if yet higher° the proud list should end,
Still let me say! No follower, but a friend.
    Yet think not, friendship only prompts my lays;
I follow *virtue;* where she shines, I praise:
Point she to priest or elder, Whig or Tory,
Or round a Quater's beaver cast a glory.
I never (to my sorrow I declare)
Dined with the Man of Ross,° or my Lord Mayor.°
100 Some, in their choice of friends (nay, look not grave)
Have still a secret bias to a knave:
To find an honest man I beat about,
And love him, court him, praise him, in or out.
    F. Then why so few commended?
    P.   Not so fierce;
Find you the virtue, and I'll find the verse.
But random praise—the task can ne'er be done;
Each mother asks it for her booby son,
Each widow asks it for *the best of men,*
For him she weeps, and him she weds again.
110 Praise cannot stoop, like satire, to the ground;
The number° may be hanged, but not be crowned.
Enough for half the greatest of these days,
To scape my censure, not expect my praise.
Are they not rich? what more can they pretend?
Dare they to hope a poet for their friend?
What Richelieu° wanted, Louis° scarce could gain,
And what young Ammon° wished, but wished in vain.
No power the muse's friendship can command;
No power, when virtue claims it, can withstand:

Pulteney William Pulteney (1686–1764), a leading opponent of Walpole and brilliant orator in Commons
Chesterfield Philip Dormer Stanhope, 4th Earl of Chesterfield (1694–1773) and grandson of Halifax, the Trimmer; another opponent of Walpole and friend of Pope; later author of famous letters to his son
Argyle John Campbell, 2nd Duke of Argyle, earlier a general, later an influential convert to the opposition to Walpole
Wyndham Sir William, a leader of the Tory opposition, a man of "the utmost judgment and temper" (Pope)
yet higher perhaps referring to Pope's friendship with the Prince of Wales

Man of Ross John Kyrle, celebrated by Pope in an earlier poem for the great public benefits he performed on an income of only £500 a year
my Lord Mayor Sir John Barnard, religious, modest, an example of both private and public virtue
number multitude, the many
Richelieu (1585–1642) French cardinal and statesman; principal minister of Louis XIII
Louis Louis XIV, patron of such poets as Boileau (cf. l. 231)
Ammon Alexander the Great, who envied Achilles the fame that Homer had bestowed

120 To Cato, Virgil paid one honest line;°
O let my country's friends illumine mine!
—What are you thinking? F. Faith, the thought's
        no sin,
I think your friends are out, and would be in.
    P. If merely to come in, sir, they go out,
The way they take is strangely round about.
    F. They too may be corrupted, you'll allow?
    P. I only call those knaves who are so now.
Is that too little? Come then, I'll comply—
Spirit of Arnall!° aid me while I lie.
130 Cobham's° a coward, Polwarth° is a slave,
And Lyttleton° a dark, designing knave,
St. John° has ever been a wealthy fool—
But let me add, Sir Robert's° mighty dull,
Has never made a friend in private life,
And was, besides, a tyrant to his wife.
    But, pray, when others praise him, do I blame?
Call Verres, Wolsey,° any odious name?
Why rail they then, if but a wreath of mine,
Oh all-accomplished° St. John! deck thy shrine?
140   What! shall each spur-galled hackney° of the day,
When Paxton° gives him double pots° and pay,
Or each new-pensioned sycophant, pretend°
To break my windows if I treat a friend?°
Then wisely plead, to me they meant no hurt,
But 'twas my guest at whom they threw the dirt?
Sure, if I spare the minister, no rules
Of honour bind me, not to maul his tools;
Sure, if they cannot cut, it may be said
His saws are toothless, and his hatchet's lead.
150   It angered Turenne,° once upon a day,
To see a footman kicked that took his pay:

line *Aeneid* VIII.670, "And far apart the good, and Cato giving them laws," perhaps in praise of Cato Uticensis, who upheld republican ideals; cf. Pope's adaptation of that line in an ironic vein (*Epistle to Dr. Arbuthnot*, l. 209 and note)
Arnall William Arnall, a hireling political journalist
Cobham's friend of Pope and the builder of Stowe (*Epistle to Burlington*, l. 70), a distinguished general discharged for opposing Walpole's screening of the South Sea Company directors; thereupon a leading opposition Whig
Polwarth Hugh Hume, 3rd Earl of Marchmont (1708–94), one of the "boy patriots" in the Whig opposition. Walpole respected his abilities and regretted his intransigent probity.
Lyttleton Cf. *Epilogue* I.29 and note; a patron of Fielding, who was to dedicate *Tom Jones* to him in 1749.
St. John Henry, Viscount Bolingbroke (1678–1751), friend of Pope, Swift, and Gay; leader with Harley of the Tory government under Anne

and of the opposition to Walpole later; a brilliant orator and man of learning, to whom Pope addressed the *Essay on Man*
Sir Robert's Walpole, ironically denied his real attributes. He was personally attractive and totally indifferent to his first wife's infidelities.
Verres, Wolsey Cf. *Epilogue* I.51 and note; both "names" were derived from men who had used their office to gain great personal wealth.
all-accomplished "Lord Bolingbroke is something superior to anything I have seen in human nature" (Pope).
hackney hack writer, hireling
Paxton The censor of l. 1 was also in charge of Walpole's patronage to hired journalists.
pots of ale
pretend attempt
treat a friend as happened at Twickenham when Pope was entertaining Bolingbroke and Lord Bathurst
Turenne (1611–75), Henri, vicomte de, Marshal of France

But when he heard the affront the fellow gave,
Knew one a man of honour, one a knave;
The prudent general turned it to a jest,
And begged, he'd take the pains to kick the rest.
Which not at present having time to do—
    F. Hold, sir! for God's sake, where's the affront to you?
Against your worship when had Selkirk writ?
Or Page° poured forth the torrent of his wit?
160 Or grant the bard whose distich all commend
[*In power a servant, out of power a friend*]°
To Walpole guilty of some venial sin,
What's that to you who ne'er was out nor in?
    The priest whose flattery bedropped the crown,
How hurt he you? he only stained the gown.
And how did, pray, the florid youth° offend,
Whose speech you took, and gave it to a friend?
P. Faith, it imports not much from whom it came;
Whoever borrowed, could not be to blame,
170 Since the whole House did afterwards the same.
Let courtly wits to wits afford supply,
As hog to hog in huts of Westphaly;
If one, through nature's bounty or his lord's,
Has what the frugal, dirty soil affords,
From him the next receives it, thick or thin,°
As pure a mess almost as it came in;
The blessed benefit, not there confined,
Drops to the third, who nuzzles close behind;
From tail to mouth, they feed and they carouse:
180 The last full fairly gives it to the *House.*
    F. This filthy simile, this beastly line,
Quite turns my stomach—
    P.   So does flattery mine;
And all your courtly civet cats can vent,
Perfume° to you, to me is excrement.
But hear me further—Japhet,° 'tis agreed,
Writ not, and Chartres° scarce could write or read,
In all the courts of Pindus° guiltless quite;
But pens can forge, my friend, that cannot write.
And must no egg in Japhet's face be thrown,
190 Because the deed he forged was not my own?
Must never patriot then declaim at gin,

Page Cf. *Satire* II.i.82.
In power . . . friend a line from Bubb Dodington's flattering verse epistle to Walpole, 1726.
Dodington had for a time become adviser to the
Prince of Wales, who was opposed to Walpole.
florid youth Cf. *Epilogue* I.71–72.
From him . . . thin Pope had earlier (1715)
used the simile elsewhere: "Now will gain praise
by copying other wits / As one hog lives on
what another shits."

Perfume made from a substance with a musky
odor secreted by the anal scent glands of the
civet cat
Japhet Japhet Crook the forger; cf. *Epilogue* I.
120 and *Epistle to Dr. Arbuthnot,* l. 363
Chartres Francis Charteris, gambler, usurer, debauchee; cf. *Satire* II.i.4
Pindus mountain in Thessaly, a seat of the
Muses; thus, in any literary judgment

Unless, good man! he has been fairly in?
No zealous pastor blame a failing spouse,
Without a staring reason° on his brows?
And each blasphemer quite escape the rod,
Because the insult's not on man, but God?
　　Ask you what provocation I have had?
The strong antipathy of good to bad.
When truth or virtue an affront endures,
200　The affront is mine, my friend, and should be yours.
Mine, as a foe professed to false pretence,
Who think a coxcomb's honour like his sense;
Mine, as a friend to every worthy mind;
And mine as man, who feel for all mankind.°
　　F. You're strangely proud.
　　P.　　　　　　　　So proud, I am no slave:
So impudent, I own myself no knave:
So odd, my country's ruin makes me grave.
Yes, I am proud; I must be proud to see
Men not afraid of God, afraid of me:
210　Safe from the bar, the pulpit, and the throne,
Yet touched and shamed by ridicule alone.
　　O sacred weapon! left for truth's defence,
Sole dread of folly, vice, and insolence!
To all but heaven-directed hands denied,
The muse may give thee, but the gods must guide.
Reverent I touch thee! but with honest zeal;
To rouse the watchmen of the public weal,
To virtue's work provoke the tardy Hall,°
And goad the prelate slumbering in his stall.
220　Ye tinsel insects! whom a court maintains,
That counts your beauties only by your stains,
Spin all your cobwebs o'er the eye of day!
The muse's wing shall brush you all away:
All his Grace preaches, all his Lordship° sings,
All that makes saints of queens, and gods of kings,
All, all but truth, drops deadborn from the press,
Like the last gazette,° or the last address.°
　　When black ambition stains a public cause,
A monarch's sword when mad vainglory draws,
230　Not Waller's wreath° can hide the nation's scar,
Nor Boileau° turn the feather to a star.
Not so, when diademed with rays divine,

staring reason cuckold's horns
And mine . . . mankind an adaptation of Terence: "I am a man, and I think nothing human
indifferent to me"
Hall Westminster Hall, as the seat of justice
Grace . . . Lordship bishop and peer
gazette official government journal

address the formal reply of Parliament to the
king's opening speech
Waller's wreath Edmund Waller's panegyrics to
Oliver Cromwell
Boileau who, in celebration of Louis XIV's conquest of the Lowlands, suggested that the
feather in Louis's hat would be a comet or star
portending disaster to his enemies

Touched with the flame that breaks from virtue's shrine,
Her priestess Muse forbids the good to die,
And opes the Temple of Eternity.
There, other trophies deck the truly brave,
Than such as Anstis° casts into the grave;
Far other stars° than * and * * wear,
And may descend to Mordington from Stair:°
240   (Such as on Hough's unsullied mitre shine,
Or beam, good Digby, from a heart like thine).°
Let Envy howl, while Heaven's whole chorus sings,
And bark at honour not conferred by kings;
Let Flattery sickening see the incense rise,
Sweet to the world, and grateful to the skies:
Truth guards the poet, sanctifies the line,
And makes immortal, verse as mean as mine.
  Yes, the last pen for freedom let me draw,
When truth stands trembling on the edge of law;
250 Here, last of Britons! let your names be read;
Are none, none living? let me praise the dead,
And for that cause which made your fathers shine,
Fall by the votes of their degenerate line.
  F. Alas! alas! pray end what you began,
And write next winter° more *Essays on Man.*

1738

The Dunciad

The poem was first published in three books in 1728, shortly after *Gulliver's Travels* and *The Beggar's Opera;* it was written in part during Swift's visit to England, and it was dedicated to Swift. In 1729 Pope amplified it as *The Dunciad Variorum* with prefaces and notes of an elaborate pseudo-scholarly sort, incorporating the forms of Dulness into the work, and he included an anthology of the scurrilous comments published about him by the dunces. Twelve years later Pope wrote a new fourth book and revised the poem, replacing the poet-critic Lewis Theobald with the playwright-actor-laureate Colley Cibber as the chief of the dunces. The dunces are, in fact, all those forces making for the debasement of English culture, and the action of the poem shows them moving westward, leaving the low scenes of the Smithfield Fair to take over the court (where George II presides in sublime indifference to questions

Anstis John Anstis, chief herald at arms, who devised symbols of honors that were often cast into the graves of great peers
stars symbols of the Order of the Garter; supply the names of (King) George and (Prince) Frederick
descend to . . . Stair from the Earl of Stair, a distinguished soldier and envoy, to Lord Mordington, whose wife kept a gambling house
Such as . . . thine "The one [John Hough, Bishop of Worcester] an assertor of the Church of England in opposition to the false measures

of King James II; the other [William, Lord Digby] as firmly attached to the cause of that king; both acting out of principle, and equally men of honour and virtue" (Pope)
write next winter "This was the last poem of the kind printed by our author, with a resolution to publish no more, but to enter thus, in the most plain and solemn manner he could, a sort of *protest* against that insuperable corruption and depravity of manners which he had been so unhappy as to live to see" (Pope).

of value). This westward movement from the City to Westminster is the ironic counter-part of Aeneas' bearing the culture of fallen Troy to Latium, to found a new empire which would culminate in the Augustan Age of Virgil.

The mythic action of the poem is the subversion of high by low, as the Titan daughter Dulness reclaims the ordered realms of the Olympian deities for original darkness. She is a vast bloated deity swathed in fogs, pent up in her own world like Swift's Spider; but she is also a projection into the form of divinity of those forces of sluggish inertia, relaxation of effort and thought, and selfish indolence that inhabit every man. To worship her is to choose something easier than excellence and some-thing less than full humanity. In the first three books Pope shows the archetypal dunce, the poet laureate Cibber; the epic games involving authors, publishers, and patrons (the games are debased and excremental, the physical index of moral and intellectual corruption); and the prophetic vision of Dulness's gradual movement from China to the West, marked by the fall of cultures in Greece and Rome and now England.

In the new fourth book Pope moves into the intellectual pursuits of man, reviving an earlier plan to deal with education and extending it to include politics and religion as well. At every point he shows the substitution of triviality for substance, of verbalism for wisdom, of relaxation for vigilance. The poem ends in a great yawn and a nation reduced to sleep, with only the poet himself awake to behold the eclipse of light and the triumph of the "uncreating word." This tragic close achieves a peculiar force: suddenly we see in all the minutiae of pedantry and frivolity a larger pattern, of mind surrendering its powers and of man subsiding—for all his refinements of pleasure—into barbarism.

From The Dunciad°

Book the Fourth

Yet, yet a moment, one dim ray of light
Indulge, dread Chaos, and eternal Night!°
Of darkness visible° so much be lent,
As half to show, half veil, the deep intent.
Ye Powers! whose mysteries restored I sing,
To whom Time bears me on his rapid wing,
Suspend a while your force inertly strong,
Then take at once the poet and the song.
    Now flamed the Dog-star's° unpropitious ray,
10 Smote every brain and withered every bay;

Dunciad The title is formed on the analogy of *Iliad* or *Aeneid;* its great subject is the dunce (whose name derived from that of the scholastic philosopher Duns Scotus) in all his manifesta-tions, from the simple blockhead to the vast force of Dulness itself.
dread Chaos . . . Night Chaos was, according to Hesiod, the progenitor of all the gods. In *Paradise Lost* II, Chaos and Night rule that portion of the universe that God has not yet ordered; so here they are the rulers "of ancient night," seeking to reclaim (through their daughter Dulness) the realms that have been seized from them for light and order. The "restoration of this empire is the action of the poem" (Pope-Warburton); hereafter P-W will be used for those notes that Warburton pro-vided on his own or from Pope's manuscripts.
darkness visible used of hell in *Paradise Lost* 1.63
Dog-star's of Sirius, visible in the hot late sum-mer; cf. *Epistle to Dr. Arbuthnot,* l. 3

Sick was the sun, the owl forsook his bower,
The moon-struck prophet felt the madding hour:
Then rose the seed of Chaos, and of Night,
To blot out order and extinguish light,
Of dull and venal a new world to mould,
And bring Saturnian days of lead and gold.°
    She mounts the throne: her head a cloud concealed,
In broad effulgence all below revealed;°
('Tis thus aspiring Dulness ever shines)
20 Soft on her lap her laureate son reclines.
    Beneath her footstool, *Science* groans in chains,
And *Wit* dreads exile, penalties, and pains.
There foamed rebellious *Logic*, gagged and bound,
There, stripped, fair *Rhetoric* languished on the ground;
His blunted arms by *Sophistry*° are borne,
And shameless *Billingsgate* her robes adorn.
Morality, by her false guardians drawn,
Chicane in furs, and *Casuistry* in lawn,°
Gasps, as they straiten° at each end the cord,
30 And dies, when Dulness gives her Page° the word.
Mad *Máthesis*° alone was unconfined,
Too mad for mere material chains to bind,
Now to pure space lifts her ecstatic stare,
Now running round the circle, finds it square.
But held in tenfold bonds the *Muses* lie,
Watched both by Envy's and by Flattery's eye:
There to her heart sad Tragedy addrest
The dagger wont to pierce the tyrant's breast;
But sober History restrained her rage,
40 And promised vengeance on a barbarous age.
There sunk Thalia,° nerveless, cold, and dead,
Had not her sister Satire held her head:
Nor couldst thou, Chesterfield!° a tear refuse,
Thou weptst, and with thee wept each gentle° Muse.
    When lo! a harlot form° soft sliding by,

lead and gold The age of Saturn was traditionally the Golden Age, but Saturn was also an alchemical symbol for lead; here lead represents the "dull," and gold, as in the Satires, the "venal" or corrupted.
all below revealed recalling the old adage, cited by P-W, "The higher you climb, the more you show your arse"
Sophistry Dulness "admits something *like* each science" (P-W); thus Sophistry for Logic, Billingsgate (the shrill abuse of fishwives) for Rhetoric, etc.
furs . . . lawn law (the ermine robes of the judge) and church (the fine linen sleeves of a bishop), each corrupted into its characteristic substitute for morality; for "Casuistry," cf. *The Rape of the Lock* V.122
straiten tighten

Page punning on Sir Francis Page, the famous "hanging judge"; cf. *Satire* II.i.82
Máthesis pure mathematics, unlimited by application; suggestive of its mystical Pythagorean uses, here madly ambitious and deluded
Thalia Muse of comedy, all but killed by the censorship of Walpole's Licensing Act of 1737
Chesterfield who spoke eloquently against the Act; cf. *Epilogue* II.84
gentle as opposed to the low substitutes, e.g. Billingsgate
harlot form opera, which had gained new favor with the importation of Italian singers; resented for its spectacle and other excesses but chiefly for destroying the fusion of sound and sense that had been achieved in the English song tradition of the Renaissance; here presented with "affected airs"

With mincing step, small voice, and languid eye;
Foreign her air, her robe's discordant pride
In patchwork fluttering, and her head aside.
By singing peers upheld on either hand,
50   She tripped and laughed, too pretty much to stand;
Cast on the prostrate Nine a scornful look,
Then thus in quaint recitativo° spoke:
        'O *Cara! Cara!* silence all that train:
Joy to great Chaos! let Division° reign:
Chromatic tortures° soon shall drive them hence,
Break all their nerves, and fritter all their sense:
One trill shall harmonize joy, grief, and rage,
Wake the dull Church, and lull the ranting stage;
To the same notes thy sons shall hum, or snore,
60   And all thy yawning daughters cry, *encore.*
Another Phoebus, thy own Phoebus,° reigns,
Joys in my jigs, and dances in my chains.
But soon, ah soon, rebellion will commence,
If music meanly borrows aid from sense:
Strong in new arms, lo! giant Handel° stands,
Like bold Briareus,° with a hundred hands;
To stir, to rouse, to shake the soul he comes,
And Jove's own thunders follow Mars's drums.
Arrest him, Empress; or you sleep no more—'
70   She heard, and drove him to the Hibernian shore.
        And now had Fame's posterior trumpet° blown,
And all the nations summoned to the throne.
The young, the old, who feel her inward sway,
One instinct seizes, and transports away.
None need a guide, by sure attraction led,
And strong impulsive gravity° of head:
None want° a place, for all their centre found,
Hung to the goddess, and cohered around.
Not closer, orb in orb,° conglobed are seen
80   The buzzing bees about their dusky queen.
        The gathering number, as it moves along,

recitativo musical declamation, neither quite spoken nor quite sung
Division i.e. breaking up long notes into a succession of short ones and so dwelling on a single syllable of the word being sung; parodied by Swift in a mock-cantata
Chromatic tortures elaborate variations introducing notes that do not belong to the diatonic scale; "the Spartans forbade the use of it as languid and effeminate" (P-W)
thy own Phoebus i.e. the Apollo of *this* pseudo-art, but also referring to the French term *phébus,* "an appearance of light glimmering over the obscurity, a semblance of meaning without any real sense" (P-W, citing Bouhours)
Handel whose increase in "hands" in orchestra and chorus (see next line) "proved so much too manly for the fine gentlemen of his age that he

was obliged to remove his music into Ireland" (P-W), on whose "Hibernian shore" (Dublin) *The Messiah* was first performed in 1741. The power of Handel, as opposed to precious and feminine opera, is made clear in l. 67.
Briareus the giant of a hundred hands who fought for Zeus and the Olympians against the Titans
posterior trumpet "her second or more certain report" (P-W), but cf. also l.18 and note above
gravity solemnity; but also gravitational attraction or impulsion, as in ll.81–84
want lack
orb in orb Cf. Milton's account of the angels in Heaven: "Thus when in orbs / Of circuit inexpressible they stood, / Orb within orb" (*Paradise Lost* V.594–96).

Involves a vast involuntary throng,
Who gently drawn, and struggling less and less,
Roll in her vortex,° and her power confess.
Not those alone who passive own her laws,
But who, weak rebels,° more advance her cause:
Whate'er of dunce in college or in town
Sneers at another, in toupee or gown;°
Whate'er of mongrel no one class admits,
90   A wit with dunces, and a dunce with wits.
Nor absent they, no members of her state,
Who pay her homage in her sons, the Great;°
Who, false to Phoebus, bow the knee to Baal;°
Or, impious, preach his word without a call.
Patrons, who sneak from living worth to dead,
Withhold the pension, and set up the head;°
Or vest dull Flattery in the sacred gown;°
Or give from fool to fool the laurel crown.
And (last and worst) with all the cant of wit,
100   Without the soul, the Muse's hypocrite.°
There marched the bard and blockhead, side by side,
Who rhymed for hire, and patronized for pride.
Narcissus,° praised with all a parson's power,
Looked a white lily sunk beneath a shower.
There moved Montalto° with superior air;
His stretched-out arm displayed a volume fair;
Courtiers and patriots in two ranks divide,
Through both he passed, and bowed from side to side:
But as in graceful act, with awful eye
110   Composed he stood, bold Benson° thrust him by:
On two unequal crutches propped he came,
Milton's on this, on that one Johnston's name.
The decent knight retired with sober rage,
Withdrew his hand, and closed the pompous page.
But (happy for him as the times went then)
Appeared Apollo's mayor and aldermen,°
On whom three hundred gold-capped youths° await,

Roll . . . vortex eddy around her
weak rebels those petty critics who do little to suppress Dulness but in fact only increase her power
toupee or gown in curled periwig (fops) or in academic gown (scholars)
Great the king and nobility
Baal any false god, presumably wealth or power
Withhold . . . head i.e. fail to support while alive and parasitically honor after death
vest . . . gown confer an ecclesiastical gown (with its income) upon a flatterer
Muse's hypocrite "He who thinks the only end of poetry is to be witty . . . who cultivates only such trifling talents in himself and encourages only such in others" (P-W)
Narcissus Lord Hervey, an epileptic, had a very white face; he was heavily flattered in the dedi-

cation of Dr. Middleton's *Life of Cicero* (1741); cf. *Epilogue* I.69–76.
Montalto Sir Thomas Hanmer, pompous and portly, published a lavish edition of Shakespeare at his own expense and for his own glory.
Benson William Benson, for political reasons and in spite of incompetence, succeeded Sir Christopher Wren as royal architect. He built a lavish monument to Milton in Westminster Abbey and commissioned a Latin translation of *Paradise Lost;* he also published several editions of Arthur Johnston's Latin version of the Psalms.
Apollo's . . . aldermen dignitaries of Oxford, whose press agreed to publish Hanmer's Shakespeare
gold-capped youths with the gold tassel of gentlemen-commoners, students who paid higher fees in return for special privileges and dress

To lug the ponderous volume off in state.
When Dulness, smiling—'Thus revive the wits!
120 But murder first, and mince them all to bits;
As erst Medea° (cruel, so to save!)
A new edition of old Aeson gave;
Let standard authors, thus, like trophies born,
Appear more glorious as more hacked and torn,
And you, my critics! in the chequered shade,
Admire new light through holes yourselves have made.
  'Leave not a foot of verse, a foot of stone,
A page, a grave, that they can call their own;
But spread, my sons, your glory thin or thick,
130 On passive paper, or on solid brick.
So by each bard an alderman° shall sit,
A heavy lord shall hang at every wit,
And while on Fame's triumphal car they ride,
Some slave of mine° be pinioned to their side.'
  Now crowds on crowds around the goddess press,
Each eager to present their first address.
Dunce scorning dunce beholds the next advance,
But fop shows fop superior complaisance.°
When lo! a spectre° rose, whose index hand
140 Held forth the virtue of the dreadful wand;
His beavered brow a birchen garland wears,
Dropping with infant's blood, and mother's tears.
O'er every vein a shuddering horror runs;
Eton and Winton° shake through all their sons.
All flesh is humbled, Westminster's bold race
Shrink, and confess the genius° of the place:
The pale boy senator yet tingling stands,
And holds his breeches close with both his hands.
  Then thus: 'Since man from beast by words is known,
150 Words are man's province, words we teach alone.°
When reason doubtful, like the Samian letter,°
Points him two ways, the narrower is the better.
Placed at the door of learning, youth to guide,
We never suffer it to stand too wide.
To ask, to guess, to know, as they commence,
As fancy opens the quick spring of sense,

Medea who, in one version of the legend, had Aeson's daughters cut their father into pieces and cast them into a cauldron, whence, with Medea's magic, he emerged restored to youth
alderman such as Alderman Barber, who proudly placed his own name on the monument he erected to Samuel Butler
slave of mine as in Rome, where a slave was chained beside the triumphant victor (to remind him of the mutability of fortune) while he rode through the city
complaisance tolerance
spectre Dr. Richard Busby (1605–95), the

famous headmaster of Westminster School, carrying his birch cane ("dreadful wand") for discipline (whence the "infant's blood"); cf. *Paradise Lost* I.392–93 for Moloch
Eton and Winton the latter Winchester; schools where Busby's influence still prevails
genius presiding deity
Since man . . . alone The humanist doctrine that eloquence is wisdom expressed now becomes a concern with words to the neglect of thought.
the Samian letter the letter Y, emblem of the crossroads of choice

We ply the memory, we load the brain,
Bind rebel wit, and double chain on chain,
Confine the thought to exercise the breath;
160 And keep them in the pale of words till death.
Whate'er the talents or howe'er designed,
We hang one jingling padlock° on the mind:
A poet the first day he dips his quill;
And what the last? a very poet still.
Pity! the charm works only in our wall,
Lost, lost too soon in yonder House or Hall.°
There truant Wyndham every Muse gave o'er,
There Talbot° sunk, and was a wit no more!
How sweet an Ovid, Murray° was our boast!
170 How many Martials were in Pulteney° lost!
Else sure some bard, to our eternal praise,
In twice ten thousand rhyming nights and days,
Had reached the work, the all that mortal can;
And South° beheld that masterpiece of man.'
    'Oh' (cried the goddess) 'for some pedant reign!
Some gentle James,° to bless the land again;
To stick the doctor's° chair into the throne,
Give law to words, or war with words alone,
Senates and courts with Greek and Latin rule,
180 And turn the Council to a grammar school!
For sure, if Dulness sees a grateful day,
'Tis in the shade of arbitrary sway.°
O! if my sons may learn one earthly thing,
Teach but that one, sufficient for a king:
That which my priests, and mine alone, maintain,
Which as it dies, or lives, we fall, or reign:
May you, may Cam and Isis,° preach it long!
The RIGHT DIVINE of kings to govern wrong.'
    Prompt at the call, around the goddess roll
190 Broad hats, and hoods, and caps, a sable shoal:
Thick and more thick the black blockade extends,

---

jingling padlock exercises in composing Greek and Latin verses
House or Hall Westminster Hall (the courts) or Parliament
Wyndham . . . Talbot two brilliant members of Parliament; cf. *Epilogue* II.79, 88
Murray William Murray (1705–93), later Lord Chief Justice and Earl of Mansfield; awarded a prize for a Latin poem by Busby ("our boast"), he became a distinguished statesman, jurist, and orator
Pulteney gifted in epigram like the Roman Martial, he became instead a political writer and leader in opposition to Walpole
South Dr. Robert South "declared a perfect epigram as difficult a performance as an epic poem, and the critics"—particularly Dryden— "say, 'an epic poem is the greatest work human

nature is capable of," (P-W). The epigram becomes the culmination of Busby's and Dulness's verbalism.
James James I was both a famous pedant and the first English monarch to claim the divine right of kings
doctor's teacher's
For sure . . . sway "no branch of learning thrives well under arbitrary government but verbal" (P-W). Timeliness is given by the charges of the opposition that Walpole's monarch was seeking to subject Parliament to "dependence on the Crown"; thus the pedant Stuart—heavy and dull—becomes the counterpart of the heavier Hanoverian (manipulated as he is by Walpole).
Cam and Isis the universities of Cambridge and Oxford, named here for their rivers

A hundred head° of Aristotle's friends.°
Nor wert thou, Isis! wanting to the day,
Though Christ Church° long kept prudishly away.
Each staunch polemic,° stubborn as a rock,
Each fierce logician, still expelling Locke,°
Came whip and spur, and dashed through thin and thick
On German Crousaz, and Dutch Burgersdyck.°
As many quit the streams that murmuring fall
200   To lull the sons of Margaret and Clare Hall,°
Where Bentley° late tempestuous wont to sport
In troubled waters, but now sleeps in port.
Before them marched that awful Aristarch;°
Ploughed was his front with many a deep remark:°
His hat, which never vailed° to human pride,
Walker° with reverence took, and laid aside.
Low bowed the rest: he, kingly, did but nod;
So upright° Quakers please both man and God.
'Mistress! dismiss that rabble from your throne:
210   Avaunt——is Aristarchus yet unknown?
Thy mighty scholiast,° whose unwearied pains
Made Horace dull, and humbled Milton's strains.°
Turn what they will to verse, their toil is vain,
Critics like me shall make it prose again.
Roman and Greek grammarians! know your better:
Author of something yet more great than letter;
While towering o'er your alphabet, like Saul,
Stands our Digamma,° and o'ertops them all.
'Tis true, on words is still our whole debate,
220   Disputes of *Me* or *Te*, of *aut* or *at*,
To sound° or sink in *cano*, O or A,
Or give up Cicero° to C or K.
Let Freind affect to speak as Terence spoke,

head a term suggestive of cattle
Aristotle's friends those "faithful followers" who, in spite of Cartesian and Newtonian science, "never bowed the knee to Baal nor acknowledged any strange god in philosophy" (P-W)
Christ Church the one college at Oxford whose dons were least under the spell of Dulness
polemic controversialist
still expelling Locke whose work was censured in 1703 by the heads of Oxford
German . . . Burgersdyck cited as two instances of Aristotelian logicians
Margaret and Clare Hall St. John's and Clare colleges in Cambridge, "particularly famous for their skill in disputation" (P-W)
Bentley As master of Trinity College, Cambridge, Richard Bentley, the classical scholar so long a target of Swift and Pope, had been at odds with his fellows but was now at rest; with a pun on "port," the wine plentifully drunk after dinner.
Aristarch Bentley in the guise of Aristarchus,

the Homeric commentator and corrector (d. 150 B.C.)
remark a term used for a note or commentary in Bentley's work
vailed yielded, was lowered
Walker the vice-master of Trinity
upright honest; also not bowing in prayer, as Bentley will not bow before Dulness
scholiast commentator
humbled Milton's strains Bentley, as editor of Milton, boldly "corrected" the text (and "humbled" its greatness) on the assumption that Milton's blindness allowed numerous errors to appear; he edited Horace also with arrogance and insensitivity.
Digamma a letter restored by Bentley in his projected edition of Homer. Since it was one gamma set upon another, it was like Saul, who was "higher than any of the people" (I Samuel 9:2).
sound stress
Cicero the pronunciation of whose name was disputed (as was that of Latin generally)

And Alsop° never but like Horace joke:
For me, what Virgil, Pliny may deny,
Manilius or Solinus° shall supply:
For Attic phrase in Plato let them seek,
I poach in Suidas° for unlicensed Greek.
In ancient sense if any needs will deal,
230 Be sure I give them fragments, not a meal:
What Gellius or Stobaeus° hashed before,
Or chewed by blind old scholiasts o'er and o'er.
The critic eye, that microscope of wit,
Sees hairs and pores, examines bit by bit;
How parts relate to parts, or they to whole,
The body's harmony, the beaming soul,°
Are things which Kuster, Burman, Wasse° shall see,
When man's whole frame is obvious to a *flea*.
    'Ah, think not, Mistress! more true Dulness lies
240 In folly's cap, than wisdom's grave disguise.
Like buoys that never sink into the flood,
On learning's surface we but lie and nod.
Thine is the genuine head of many a house,
And much divinity without a Noûs.°
Nor could a Barrow work on every block,
Nor has one Atterbury° spoiled the flock.
See! still thy own, the heavy canon° roll,
And metaphysic smokes involve the pole.°
For thee we dim the eyes, and stuff the head
250 With all such reading as was never read:
For thee explain a thing till all men doubt it,
And write about it, Goddess, and about it:
So spins the silkworm small its slender store,
And labours till it clouds itself all o'er.
    'What though we let some better sort of fool
Thrid° every science, run through every school?
Never by tumbler through the hoops was shown
Such skill in passing all, and touching none.
He may indeed (if sober all this time)
260 Plague with dispute, or persecute with rhyme.

Freind . . . Alsop Robert Freind and Anthony
Alsop, two scholars who grasped the true spirit
of classical literature rather than its letter
Manilius or Solinus As a philologist, Bentley is
interested not in literature but in words; for his
purposes minor authors are as useful as major
and as important.
Suidas (*c.* 1100 A.D.) a "dictionary writer, a
collector of impertinent facts and barbarous
words" (P-W)
Gellius or Stobaeus the former a Roman grammarian (d. 165 A.D.), the latter a Greek com-
piler of extracts from ancient authors (*c.* 400
A.D.)
the beaming soul i.e. irradiating the body with
form

Kuster . . . Wasse classical scholars and editors of lesser writers
without a Noûs Noûs was the Platonic word for
mind, or the first cause, and that system of
divinity is here hinted at which terminates in
blind nature without a νοῦς (P-W); cf. ll.
487–92 below.
Barrow . . . Atterbury Isaac Barrow (1630–
77) and Atterbury were brilliant scholars and
eloquent preachers, the former a fine mathematician, the latter a classical scholar; for the
"block," cf. l. 270 below.
canon churchman, but also artillery (cannon)
pole sky, heavens
Thrid thread, trace

We only furnish what he cannot use,
Or wed to what he must divorce, a Muse:
Full in the midst of Euclid dip at once,
And petrify a genius to a dunce:
Or set on metaphysic ground to prance,
Show all his paces, not a step advance.
With the same cement, ever sure to bind,
We bring to one dead level every mind.
Then take him to develop, if you can,
270   And hew the block off, and get out the man.°
But wherefore waste I words? I see advance
Whore, pupil, and laced governor° from France.
Walker! our hat'——nor more he deigned to say,
But, stern as Ajax' spectre,° strode away.
    In flowed at once a gay embroidered race,
And tittering pushed the pedants off the place:
Some would have spoken, but the voice was drowned
By the French horn, or by the opening° hound.
The first came forwards, with as easy mien,
280   As if he saw St. James's° and the Queen.
When thus the attendant orator° begun:
'Receive, great Empress! thy accomplished son,
Thine from the birth, and sacred° from the rod,
A dauntless infant! never scared with God.
The sire saw, one by one, his virtues wake:
The mother begged the blessing of a rake.
Thou gavest that ripeness, which so soon began,
And ceased so soon, he ne'er was boy, nor man.
Through school and college, thy kind cloud o'ercast,
290   Safe and unseen° the young Aeneas past:
Thence bursting glorious, all at once let down,°
Stunned with his giddy larum° half the town.
Intrepid then, o'er seas and lands he flew:°
Europe he saw, and Europe saw him too.
There all thy gifts and graces we display,
Thou, only thou, directing all our way!
To where the Seine, obsequious as she runs,
Pours at great Bourbon's feet her silken sons;°
Or Tiber, now no longer Roman, rolls,
300   Vain of Italian arts, Italian° souls:
To happy convents, bosomed deep in vines,

---

get out the man referring to the belief that in every block of stone there is a statue waiting to be freed
governor tutor
Ajax' spectre which turns sullenly from Odysseus in the underworld
opening baying, giving tongue
St. James's the royal palace
orator the tutor or governor of l. 272

sacred exempt
unseen veiled in a cloud as was Aeneas by Venus when he entered Carthage (*Aeneid* I)
let down freed, released
larum commotion
flew on the Grand Tour
her silken sons France is seen as an absolute monarchy encouraging luxury or effeminacy.
Italian as opposed to Roman

Where slumber abbots, purple as their wines:
To isles of fragrance, lily-silvered vales,
Diffusing languor in the panting gales:
To lands of singing, or of dancing slaves,
Love-whispering woods, and lute-resounding waves.
But chief her shrine where naked Venus keeps,
And Cupids ride the Lion of the Deeps;°
Where, eased of fleets, the Adriatic main
310   Wafts the smooth eunuch and enamoured swain.
Led by my hand, he sauntered Europe round,
And gathered every vice on Christian ground;
Saw every court, heard every king declare
His royal sense of operas or the fair;°
The stews° and palace equally explored,
Intrigued with glory, and with spirit whored;
Tried all *hors d'oeuvres*, all *liqueurs* defined,
Judicious drank, and greatly daring dined;
Dropped the dull lumber of the Latin store,°
320   Spoiled his own language, and acquired no more;
All classic learning lost on classic ground;
And last turned *air*, the echo of a sound!
See now, half-cured and perfectly well-bred,
With nothing but a solo in his head;
As much estate, and principle, and wit,
As Jansen, Fleetwood, Cibber° shall think fit;
Stolen° from a duel, followed by a nun,
And, if a borough choose him,° not undone;
See, to my country happy I restore
330   This glorious youth, and add one Venus more.
Her too receive (for her my soul adores)°
So may the sons of sons of sons of whores,
Prop thine, O Empress! like each neighbour throne,
And make a long posterity thy own.'
Pleased, she accepts the hero, and the dame,
Wraps in her veil, and frees from sense of shame.
      Then looked, and saw a lazy, lolling sort,
Unseen at church, at senate, or at court,
Of ever-listless loiterers, that attend
340   No cause, no trust, no duty, and no friend.
Thee too, my Paridel!° she marked thee there,
Stretched on the rack of a too easy chair,

Lion of the Deeps the winged lion, emblem of
Venice as a great mercantile and naval power;
famous at this time as the "brothel of Europe"
operas . . . fair typical conversational topics
of George II of England
stews brothels
Latin store classical learning
Jansen . . . Cibber all gamblers and the last

two theater managers, hence stewards and
tutors to youth
Stolen escaped
borough choose him because members of Parliament could not be arrested for debt
my soul adores Both pupil and tutor seem attached to the former nun and new Venus.
Paridel Spenser's name for an amorous wandering squire (*The Faerie Queene* III.ix–x)

And heard thy everlasting yawn confess
The pains and penalties of idleness.
She pitied! but her pity only shed
Benigner influence on thy nodding head.
   But Annius,° crafty seer, with ebon wand,
And well-dissembled emerald on his hand,
False as his gems, and cankered° as his coins,
350 Came, crammed with capon, from where Pollio° dines.
Soft, as the wily fox is seen to creep,
Where bask on sunny banks the simple sheep,
Walk round and round, now prying here, now there;
So he; but pious, whispered first his prayer:
   'Grant, gracious Goddess! grant me still to cheat,
O may thy cloud still cover the deceit!
Thy choicer mists on this assembly shed,
But pour them thickest on the noble head.
So shall each youth, assisted by our eyes,
360 See other Caesars, other Homers° rise;
Through twilight ages hunt the Athenian fowl,°
Which chalcis gods, and mortals call an owl,°
Now see an Attys, now a Cecrops° clear,
Nay, Mahomet!° the pigeon at thine ear;
Be rich in ancient brass, though not in gold,
And keep his Lares,° though his house be sold;
To headless Phoebe° his fair bride postpone,
Honour a Syrian prince° above his own;
Lord of an Otho,° if I vouch it true;
370 Blest in one Niger,° till he knows of two.'
   Mummius° o'erheard him; Mummius, fool-renowned,°
Who like his Cheops stinks above the ground,
Fierce as a startled adder, swelled, and said,
Rattling an ancient sistrum° at his head:
   'Speakst thou of Syrian princes? Traitor base!
Mine, Goddess! mine is all the hornèd race.°

Annius named for a monk of Viterbo (1432–1502) famous for many forgeries of ancient manuscripts and inscriptions, committed out of vanity. His modern counterpart is more mercenary.
cankered corrupt
Pollio named for the Roman patron
other Caesars . . . Homers forged coins; here also a substitute form of greatness, such as the heroics of collecting and the artistry of acquisition
Athenian fowl the owl stamped on the coins of ancient Athens
Which chalcis . . . owl a line from Hobbes's flat-footed rendering of Homer, "chalcis" being Greek for a bird of prey
Attys . . . Cecrops forgeries of coins professedly issued by mythical kings of Athens
Mahomet Mohammed, who forbade all images, is here represented with the white pigeon that

brought him divine messages and which he claimed to be the angel Gabriel.
Lares Roman statues of household gods
headless Phoebe a mutilated statue of Diana, which pre-empts the place and affection due a living bride
Syrian prince presumably as represented on a medal
Otho coin of a Roman emperor who ruled very briefly
Niger another emperor of short reign, whose coins would be very rare
Mummius a dealer in Egyptian antiquities
fool-renowned "a compound epithet in the Greek manner, *renowned by fools* or *renowned for making fools*" (P-W)
sistrum a percussion instrument used in Egyptian religious rites
hornèd race the successors of Alexander, supposedly born of the gods, represented with horns

True, he had wit, to make their value rise;
From foolish Greeks to steal them, was as wise;
More glorious yet, from barbarous hands to keep,
380   When Sallee rovers° chased him on the deep.
Then taught by Hermes,° and divinely bold,
Down his own throat he risked the Grecian gold;
Received each demigod,° with pious care,
Deep in his entrails—I revered them there,
I bought them, shrouded in that living shrine,
And, at their second birth, they issue mine.'
        'Witness, great Ammon!° by whose horns I swore,'
(Replied soft Annius) 'this our paunch before
Still bears them, faithful; and that thus I eat,
390   Is to refund the medals with the meat.
To prove me, Goddess! clear of all design,
Bid me with Pollio sup, as well as dine:
There all the learned shall at the labour stand,
And Douglas° lend his soft, obstetric hand.'
        The goddess smiling seemed to give consent;
So back to Pollio, hand in hand, they went.
        Then thick as locusts blackening all the ground,
A tribe, with weeds and shells fantastic crowned,
Each with some wondrous gift approached the Power,
400   A nest, a toad, a fungus, or a flower.
But far the foremost, two, with earnest zeal,
And aspect ardent to the throne appeal.
        The first thus opened: 'Hear thy suppliant's call,
Great Queen, and common Mother of us all!
Fair from its humble bed I reared this flower,°
Suckled and cheered, with air, and sun, and shower,
Soft on the paper ruff its leaves° I spread,
Bright with the gilded button tipped its head,
Then throned in glass, and named it Caroline:°
410   Each maid cried, charming! and each youth, divine!
Did nature's pencil° ever blend such rays,
Such varied light in one promiscuous blaze?
Now prostrate! dead! behold that Caroline:
No maid cries, charming! and no youth, divine!
And lo the wretch! whose vile, whose insect lust
Laid this gay daughter of the spring in dust.
Oh punish him, or to the Elysian shades

Sallee rovers pirates from Morocco
Hermes as god of commerce but also patron of thieves
demigod coins of emperors who claimed that status; with suggestions of the Eucharist that are sustained by "pious care" and culminate in the Second Coming of l. 386
Ammon Jupiter Ammon, from whom Alexander and his heirs claimed descent
Douglas James Douglas, a famous obstetrician and himself a collector of editions of Horace
flower a reference to the efforts in the age to produce a perfect carnation
leaves petals
Caroline for the queen, an ardent gardener; P-W pursue the theme of idolatry set forth in ll. 359–86 by citing a gardener who advertised his favorite flower as "*my* Queen Caroline"
pencil paintbrush

Dismiss my soul, where no carnation fades!'°
    He ceased, and wept. With innocence of mien,
420   The accused stood forth, and thus addressed the queen:
    'Of all the enamelled race,° whose silvery wing
Waves to the tepid zephyrs of the spring,
Or swims along the fluid atmosphere,
Once brightest shined this child of heat and air.
I saw, and started from its vernal bower
The rising game,° and chased from flower to flower.
It fled, I followed; now in hope, now pain;
It stopped, I stopped; it moved, I moved again.°
At last it fixed, 'twas on what plant it pleased,
430   And where it fixed, the beauteous bird° I seized:
Rose or carnation was below my care;
I meddle, Goddess! only in my sphere.
I tell the naked fact without disguise,
And, to excuse it, need but show the prize;
Whose spoils this paper° offers to your eye,
Fair even in death! this peerless *butterfly.*'
    'My sons!' (she answered) 'both have done your parts:
Live happy both, and long promote our arts!
But hear a mother, when she recommends
440   To your fraternal care, our sleeping friends.°
The common soul, of Heaven's more frugal make,
Serves but to keep fools pert, and knaves awake:
A drowsy watchman, that just gives a knock,
And breaks our rest, to tell us what's a-clock.
Yet by some object every brain is stirred;
The dull may waken to a hummingbird;
The most recluse, discreetly opened find
Congenial matter in the cockle kind;°
The mind, in metaphysics at a loss,
450   May wander in a wilderness of moss;°
The head that turns at superlunar things,
Poised with a tail, may steer on Wilkins' wings.°
    'O! would the sons of men once think their eyes
And reason given them but to study *flies!*
See nature in some partial narrow shape,
And let the author of the whole escape:
Learn but to trifle; or, who most observe,

---

no . . . fades Cf. I Peter 1:4 "To an inheritance incorruptible, and undefiled, and that
fadeth not away, reserved in heaven for you."
enamelled race colorful butterflies
started . . . game idiom of the huntsman
It fled . . . again Cf. Eve's words (*Paradise
Lost* IV.462–63) on first seeing her reflection in
the water, failing, like Narcissus, to recognize
what it is, and adoring it: "I started back, /
It started back; but pleased I soon returned,
/ Pleased it returned as soon."

bird any winged creature; here the butterfly
this paper i.e. on which the butterfly is mounted
sleeping friends Cf. ll. 337–46 above.
cockle kind collections of scallop shells
moss of which three hundred species had been
identified
Wilkins' wings John Wilkins (1614–72), bishop
and first secretary of the Royal Society, proposed flights to the moon and started "some
volatile geniuses upon making wings for that
purpose" (P–W).

1. John Dryden, 1693,
by Sir Godfrey Kneller (1649?–1723).
National Portrait Gallery, London.

2. Charles II, c. 1660-65,
?studio of John Michael Wright (1617–1700).
National Portrait Gallery.

3. William Congreve, 1709,
by Sir Godfrey Kneller.
National Portrait Gallery.

4. John Bunyan, 1684, by T. Sadler.
National Portrait Gallery.

5. Alexander Pope, ?1741, by L. F. Roubiliac (c. 1705–62). *Leeds City Art Galleries.*

6. Sir Robert Walpole, 1738, by J. M. Rysbrack (1694–1770). *National Portrait Gallery.*

7. Jonathan Swift, by L. F. Roubiliac. *Trinity College, Dublin.*

8. St. Paul's from the northwest.
A. F. Kersting.

ENGLISH BAROQUE ARCHITECTURE

Sir Christopher Wren (1632–1723) came to architecture, at the prompting of Charles II, from a distinguished career in mathematics and astronomy. During a visit to Paris in 1665–66 he met the great Italian baroque architect Gianlorenzo Bernini (1598–1680), and brought back with him "almost all France in paper," i.e. in prints and architectural books. His designs included Hampton Court and the royal hospitals at Chelsea and Greenwich, university buildings at Oxford and Cambridge, and nearly fifty churches in London to replace or restore those damaged in the Great Fire of 1666. Of the last the most ambitious was St. Paul's Cathedral, begun in 1675 and completed in 1710. The bold and intricate west towers engage in constantly changing interplay with the massive dome as the viewer's perspective shifts. They are among the finest of the numerous and remarkably varied spires that were to dominate the London skyline for more than two centuries.

10. St. Bride, c. 1700.
A. F. Kersting.

11. St. Magnus-the-Martyr, 1705

12. St. Mary-le-Bow, completed 1680.

13. St. Vedast, 1694–97.

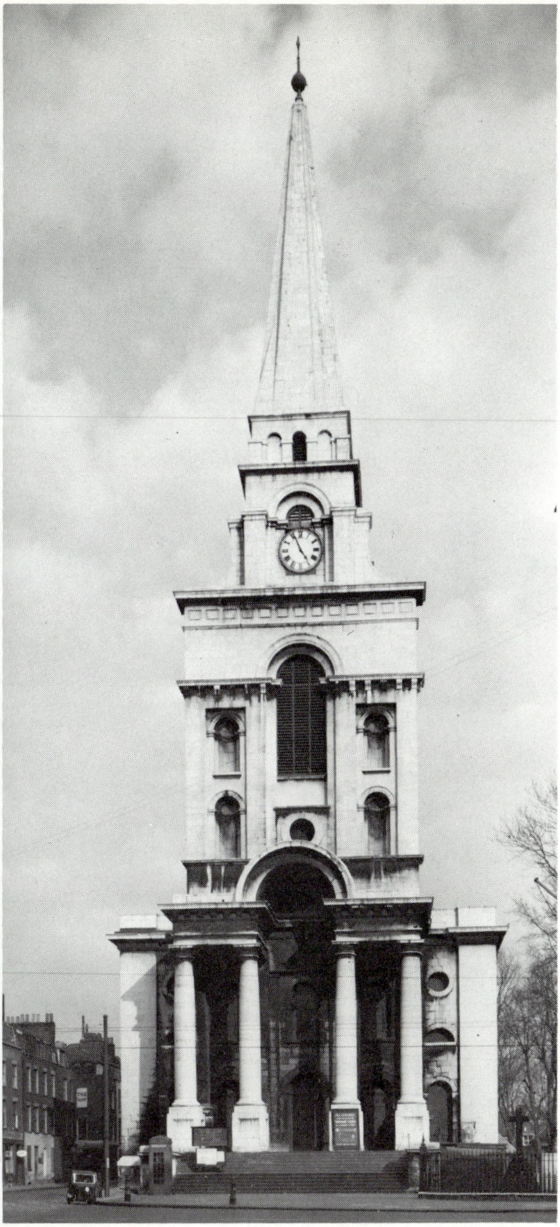

14. Christ Church, Spitalfields.

15. St. Anne, Limehouse.
A. F. Kersting.

Nicholas Hawksmoor (1661–1736), Wren's chief assistant, later worked closely with Sir John Vanbrugh (1664–1726) on such buildings as Blenheim Palace and Castle Howard (see Fig. 16). The two East London churches shown here were begun in 1714 and completed in the late 1720's. Hawksmoor's intense and often somber art turned conventional forms to strikingly novel uses. In Christ Church he used the Palladian form, an arch flanked by two rectangular openings (as in the so-called Venetian window), first magnifying it to the scale of a triumphal arch in the lower storeys, then varying the pattern in shallower and more attenuated forms above. St. Anne, Limehouse, plays with concave and convex forms and concludes in a tower whose angularity suggests Gothic steeples without in fact using any Gothic forms.

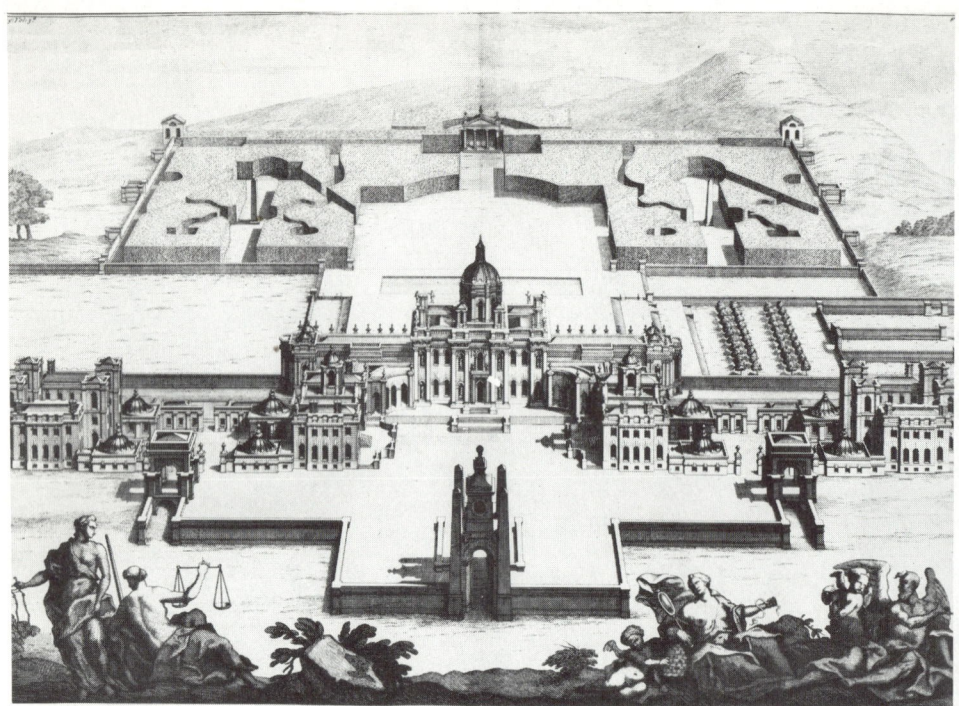

16. Vanbrugh and Hawksmoor, Castle Howard (begun c. 1699). From Colin Campbell, *Vitruvius Britannicus,* 1715. *The New York Public Library.*

Castle Howard, Yorkshire, is one of the most lavish and brilliant of baroque country houses, and its grounds are varied with ornamental buildings in bold shapes. Sir John Vanbrugh's Temple of the Winds was a belvedere; the porticos were designed to prevent direct sunlight but to admit "light of the most pleasing kind." Nicholas Hawksmoor's Mausoleum is set on a rise a mile from the house, its silhouette visible from great distances. Its exterior has twenty Doric columns whose spacing was criticized by Lord Burlington as unclassical in its closeness (see in contrast William Kent's Temple of Ancient Virtue, Fig. 20); and it was one of Burlington's protégés who added later the steps modeled on those at Chiswick House. Hawksmoor's building has survived Palladian criticism and improvement; it remains as he intended: self-enclosed, unaccommodating, formidably severe.

17. Vanbrugh, Temple of the Winds, built in the 1720's. *Country Life*, London.

18. Hawksmoor, Mausoleum, begun in 1729. *Country Life*.

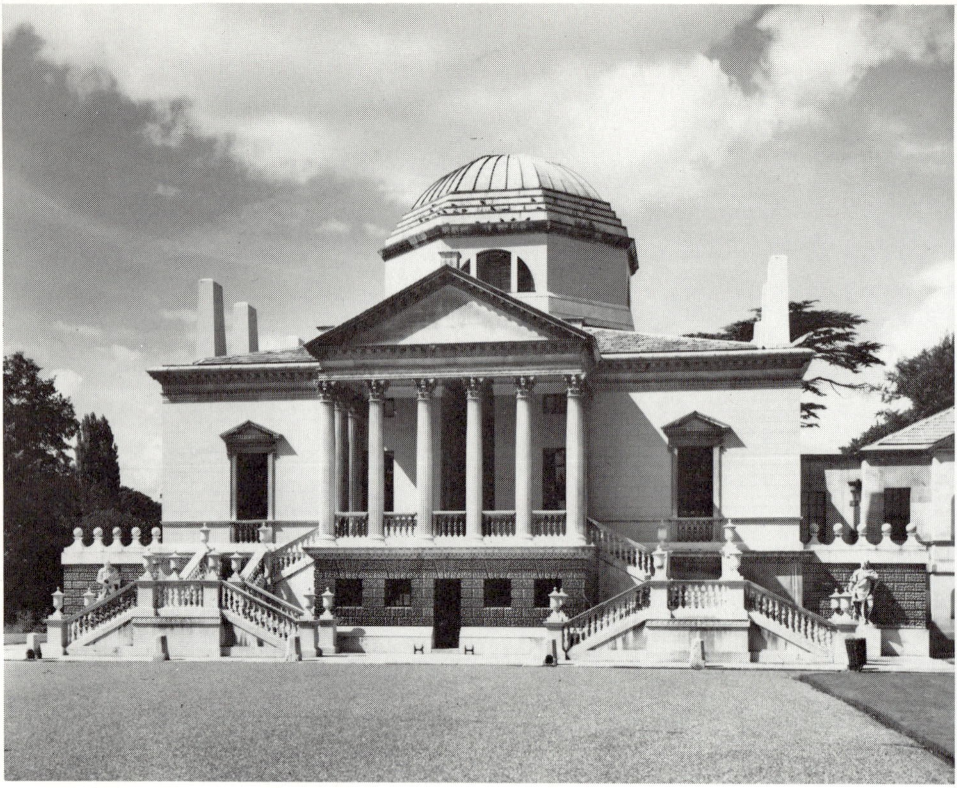

19. Chiswick House, designed before 1727. *A. F. Kersting.*

PALLADIANISM

Lord Burlington (Richard Boyle, 1694–1753; see
Pope's *Essay* to him), like the third Earl of Shaftesbury, reacted against Wren and English baroque
architecture. Upon his return from Italy, Burlington
undertook, with the assistance of William Kent
(1685–1748), to work toward a more chaste, more
authentic classicism than England had achieved before. He found his models in the Italian Renaissance
architect Andrea Palladio (1508–80) and in Palladio's
chief English follower, Inigo Jones (1573–1652);
Burlington sponsored the publication of their designs and imitated their work, at times moving even
closer to their Roman sources. Chiswick House, a
country villa at Twickenham, derives in part from
Palladio's Villa Rotonda at Vicenza. The austerity of
the building itself is offset by the opulent decoration
within and the natural, irregular gardens that surround it.

20. William Kent, Temple of Ancient Virtue
in the gardens at Stowe.
Courtauld Institute of Art, London.

21. Henry Flitcroft (1697–1769), The Temple of Flora, c. 1745–50. *Country Life*.

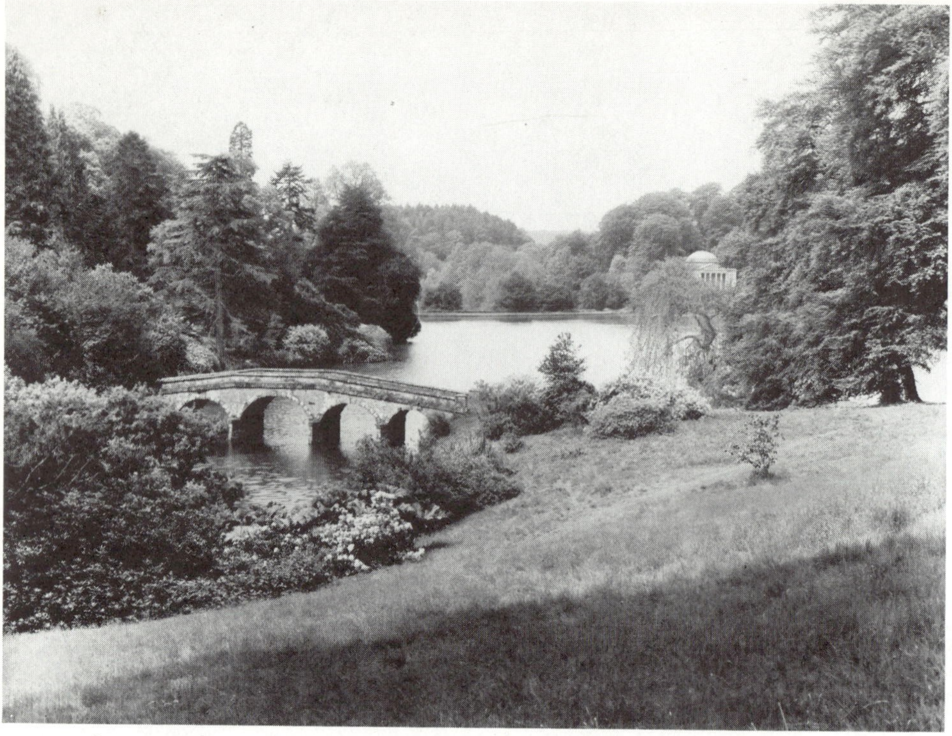

22. The approach to the Pantheon (Flitcroft, c. 1752–56). *Country Life.*

THE GARDENS AT STOURHEAD

Stourhead, near the Wiltshire-Dorset border, was cultivated by banker Henry Hoare, from 1741. By 1765 Horace Walpole could declare it "one of the most picturesque scenes in the world." It was in part a Claude landscape realized in what had been originally barren downs; in fact, Claude's *Coast View of Delos with Aeneas* could have provided the elements of the design and perhaps the implicit theme of the founding of Rome.

23. Claude Lorrain, *Coast View of Delos with Aeneas,* c. 1672.
The National Gallery, London.

24. *The Marriage Contract*

The groom's father, Lord Squander, relieves his gout while he negotiates a dowry for his son's marriage to a City merchant's daughter. Visible through the window is a half-finished Palladian building (Hogarth loathed William Kent and his sponsor, Lord Burlington) which has helped to impoverish him, but he ignores the mortgage debts the clerk holds out before him. The groom gazes at his true love in a mirror, while the bride flirts with the lawyer Silvertongue. The chains on the dogs suggest their bondage.

HOGARTH ON HIGH LIFE

William Hogarth (1697–1764) invented the narrative sequence of paintings that could in turn be engraved and sold widely as sets of prints. Although he attempted more solemn and ambitious "history" painting (that is, historical, biblical, or mythological subjects in the grand style), it was in "comic history" (as Henry Fielding named it in *Joseph Andrews*, 1742) that he achieved his greatest and most characteristic work. Earlier sequences like *The Harlot's Progress* and *The Rake's Progress* had enormous success; in *Marriage à la Mode*, 1743–45, Hogarth attempted to present a more refined, if scarcely more creditable, society. (See Figs. 24–30.) *The National Gallery.*

25. *Shortly after the Marriage*

The wife lazily, but seductively, stretches at breakfast after her late card party (it is now just past noon), but the exhausted young Viscount has just come in from a night on the town. His pursuits are indicated by the woman's cap the dog is pulling from his pocket. The pious steward indicates despair at the neglected household and the unpaid bills, both reflections of the marriage itself.

26. The Visit to the Quack Doctor

The Viscount cheerfully brings his childlike mistress for a cure of the venereal disease he has presumably given her. The cabinets of curiosities and the monstrous machines are only less sinister than the woman with the clasp-knife (the quack's assistant or possibly the brothel-keeper).

27. *The Countess's Morning Levée*

Since Lord Squander has died and her husband has inherited the title, the wife can now adorn her dressing-table with an Earl's coronet. She is receiving morning guests while her hair is dressed. The most intimate is lawyer Silvertongue, sprawling on the sofa beside Crébillon's notorious erotic novel *Le Sopha*. The page unpacks a statue of Actaeon, given a stag's head for seeing Diana naked but here suggesting the cuckold's horns. Among other guests are a fop in curling papers and a melodious *castrato*. Over their heads hangs a painting of Jupiter snatching up Ganymede; over the Countess's, one of Jupiter descending as a cloud to embrace Io.

28. *The Killing of the Earl*

The Earl has surprised his wife with Silvertongue in a hired room after the masquerade, and has been fatally wounded by the fleeing lawyer. The owner rushes in with the guard of the watch. Emblems of disguise are everywhere on floors and walls.

29. *The Suicide of the Countess*

The lawyer has been captured, tried, and executed; a printed copy of his dying speech lies beside the poison bottle of the Countess. As she dies the nurse brings her crippled child, and her thrifty merchant father removes her ring (since a suicide's property was forfeit to the state). The apothecary upbraids the foolish servant who bought the poison; the dog enjoys the meal; and the open window discloses the City of London, where buying and selling continue.

30. *Gin Lane*, 1751. Hogarth's attack on the ravages of gin drinking was paired with a print showing the decent and moderate life of Beer Street. Physical corruption and moral insensibility are reflected in decaying streets and in the ascendancy of the pawnbroker's sign over the steeple (topped with the grandiose figure of George I) of Hawksmoor's parish church of St. George, Bloomsbury. *Courtauld Institute of Art.*

31. *Chairing the Member*. The fourth picture of Hogarth's *Election* series, c. 1754, shows the bloated victor carried in triumph while battles still rage, and the pigs rush to perdition like the Gadarene swine of the biblical parable. *Sir John Soane Museum*, London.

32. *The Beggar's Opera*, Act III, Scene xi, 1729, with Macheath between Lucy Lockit and Polly Peachum. With an ironic use of allusion that anticipates Reynolds (see Fig. 39), Hogarth sets Peachum in the stance with which Christ confronts Mary Magdalene in traditional versions of the *Noli me tangere* motif. *Collection Mr. and Mrs. Paul Mellon*.

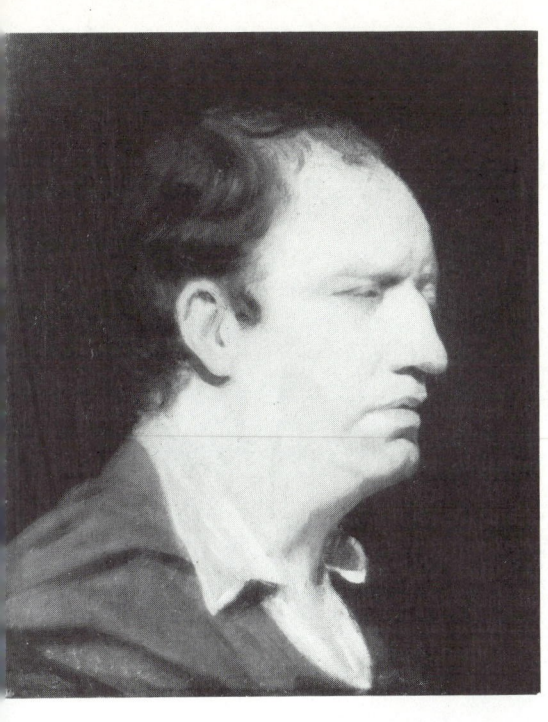

33. Samuel Johnson,
after Sir Joshua Reynolds.
National Portrait Gallery.

34. James Boswell, 1765,
in the costume of his visit to Rousseau,
by George Willison (1741–97).
National Galleries of Scotland, Edinburgh.

35. Thomas Gray, 1748,
by J. G. Eccardt (d. 1779).
National Portrait Gallery.

36. William Cowper, 1792,
by George Romnev (1734–1802).
National Portrait Gallery.

37. Oliver Goldsmith, c. 1770,
studio of Sir Joshua Reynolds.
National Portrait Gallery.

38. Edward Gibbon, 1773,
by Sir Joshua Reynolds.
Collection Lord Rosebery, Dalmeny.

39. Sir Joshua Reynolds (1723–92), *Garrick between Tragedy and Comedy*, 1762. *Rothschild Collection.*

When Reynolds painted a boy in the costume and stance of Henry VIII, Horace Walpole remarked, "Is not there humour and satire in Sir Joshua's reducing Holbein's swaggering and colossal haughtiness of Henry VIII to the boyish jollity of Master Crewe?" Here Reynolds's treatment of Garrick is based on the traditional choice of Hercules. Just as Pleasure is usually represented by an erotic Venus, and Virtue by a martial Athena, so Comedy is painted in the manner of Correggio, and Tragedy in the manner of Guido Reni. Benjamin West based much of his heroic painting on a work of Poussin; but he borrowed the gesture of Tragedy from Reynolds's ironic pastiche of Guido.

40. Benjamin West (1738–1820), *The Choice of Hercules between Virtue and Pleasure*, 1764. *Victoria and Albert Museum,* London.

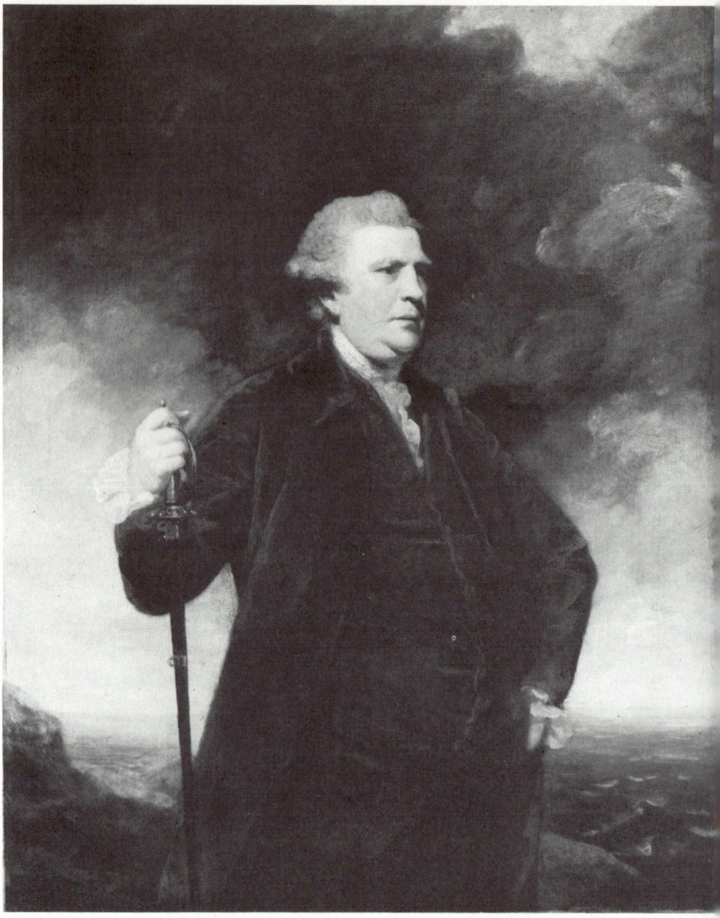

41. Admiral Viscount Keppel, 1780.
The Tate Gallery, London.

The extremes of Reynolds's vision: the heroic portrait and the pathetic but amusing image of a terrified child.

42. *The Strawberry Girl*, 1773.
The Wallace Collection, London
(*Crown Copyright*).

43. *Circa* 1773. *Royal Academy of Arts,* London. 44. Study for a Self Portrait, *c.* 1780. *Collection Mr. and Mrs. Paul Mellon.*

First we see the artist as hero, Reynolds as he might aspire to be, a painter in the costume of Rembrandt, with a head of Michelangelo beside him. Below is a self-portrait of the young artist, and above right is a self-portrait of the man whom the artist inhabits.

45. Age 25, 1748. *National Portrait Gallery.*

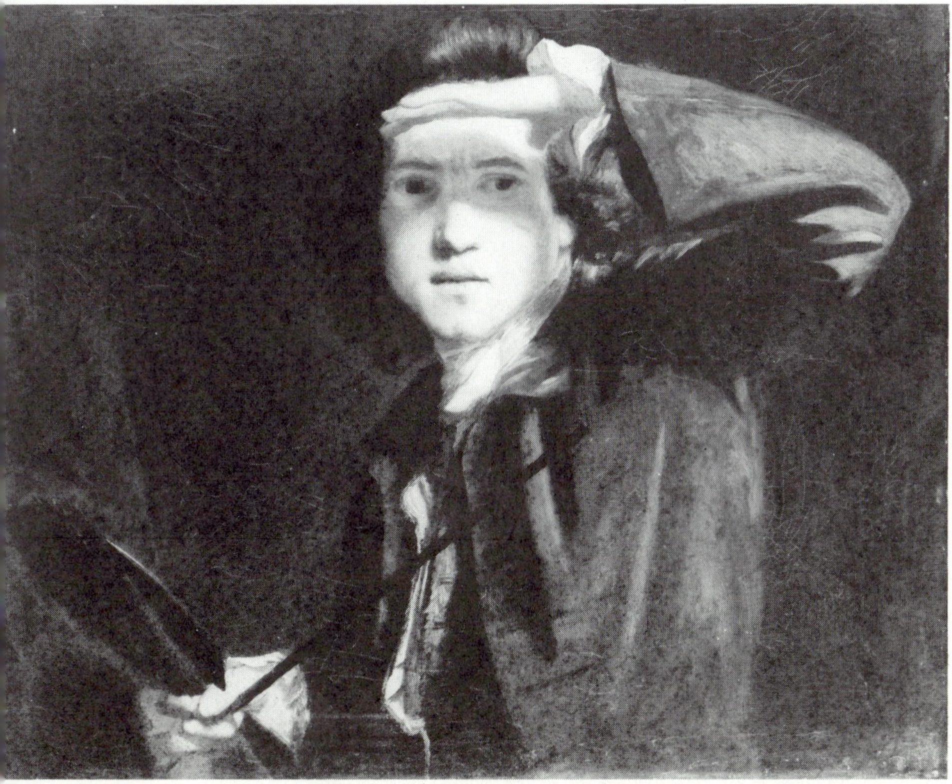

Thomas Gainsborough (1727–88) became a fashionable portrait painter, but he complained, "I'm sick of portraits and wish very much to take my viol da gamba and walk off to some sweet village where I can paint landscapes and enjoy the fag end of life in quietness and ease." He resisted even more the program of the "history" painter, for whom "there is no call in this country." Gainsborough's treatment of texture and surface made his portraits brilliant and flattering. At the same time he could cultivate a simplicity that was unheroic and singularly delicate.

46. The Honourable Mrs. Graham, 1777. *National Galleries of Scotland.*

47. *The Housemaid* (unfinished), *c.* 1786. *The Tate Gallery.*

48. William Blake, illustration
for Gray's *The Bard.*

THE BARD

Thomas Gray's poem of 1757 inspired many painters and illustrators. Typically, William Blake was less concerned with natural setting than with the human form of the prophet-poet. John Martin (1789–1854) transcended the natural scene in his customary pursuit of colossal dimension and sublime intensity. What is striking in Martin's picture is that the landscape is at least as expressive as the human figure and becomes the symbol of human passion and energy at their utmost.

49. John Martin, *The Bard.*
Collection Mr. and
Mrs. Paul Mellon.

50. Wren, Tom Tower, 1681–82, Christ Church College, Oxford. *A. F. Kersting.*

GOTHIC TO GOTHICK

When Sir Christopher Wren was asked to complete Tom Tower at Christ Church College, Oxford, he "resolved it ought to be Gothic to agree with the founder's work; yet I have not continued so busy as he began." Hawksmoor, who completed the towers of Westminster Abbey as well as the court of All Souls College, Oxford (1715–40), used Gothic with a similar mixture of respect and freedom. The brilliant staccato style of the All Souls towers uses Gothic elements for effects that are typical of Hawksmoor, such as the light-holding angular surface of sharp recession and projection. In his Gothic garden temple, James Gibbs (1682–1754), trained in the Italian baroque and proficient as well in Palladian works (exemplified by St. Mary-le-Strand and St. Martin-in-the-Fields in London, the Radcliffe Camera at Oxford, and the Senate House at Cambridge), creates a work appropriately evocative: more a theater set than a true building. By the time Horace Walpole rebuilt his Twickenham house, Strawberry Hill (1750), in a Gothic idiom, the details—however authentic in many cases, such as the fan vaulting of the gallery—became decorative surface, akin to the irregular low-relief ornament of rococo vegetable forms.

51. Hawksmoor, Fellows' Buildings,
All Souls College, Oxford.
Courtauld Institute of Art.

52. James Gibbs', Gothic Temple, *c.* 1740,
in the gardens of Stowe.
Courtauld Institute of Art.

53. The Gallery, Strawberry Hill.
Country Life.

54. Henry Fuseli, *The Artist Moved by the Magnitude of Antique Fragments*, 1778–80. *Kunsthaus*, Zürich.

RUINS

As the art historian Nikolaus Pevsner puts it, for "a generalizing view of the style of 1750 a Chinese bridge, a miniature Pantheon, and a Gothic ruin all belong together. In fact . . . even Robert Adam enjoyed drawing ruins . . . and occasionally designed domestic work in a mildly medieval taste." Increasingly, archeological explorations of classical ruins were recorded in excellent prints. Robert Adam had explored Diocletian's Palace at Split in Yugoslavia; James ("Athenian") Stuart with his fellow architect Nicholas Revett spent five years in Greece and brought back careful studies of the Acropolis. As Fuseli's drawing shows, the interest was as romantic as it was scholarly; moreover, picturesque ruins were frequently constructed—as we see in the designs of Adam and Chambers. In Chambers's design, "There is a great quantity of cornices, and other fragments, spread over the ground, seemingly fallen from the buildings."

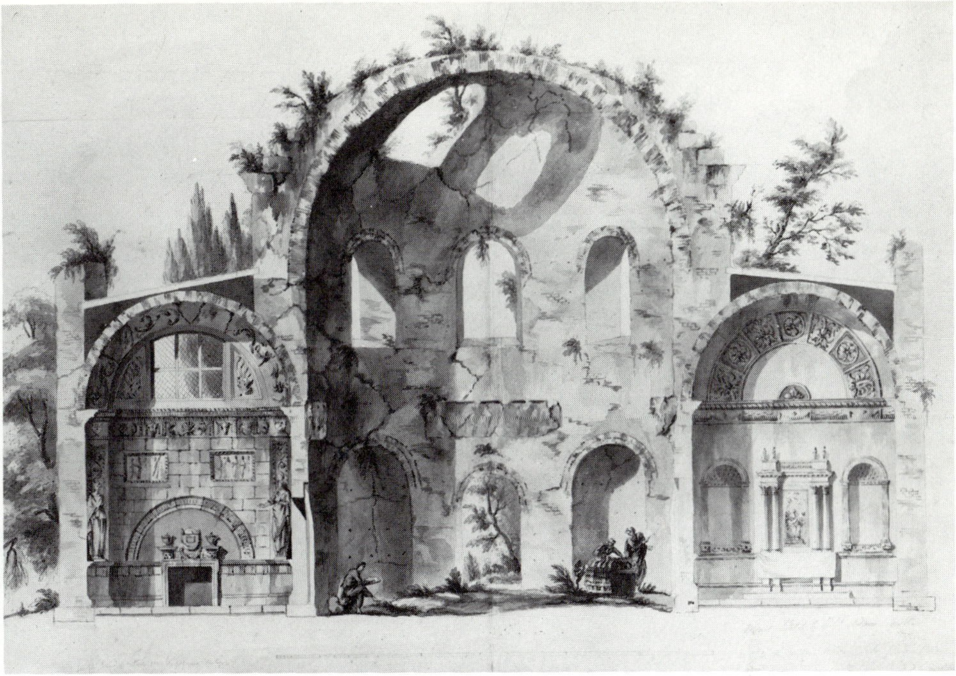

55. Robert Adam (1728–92), Design for a ruin to be built at Mistley Hall, 1761.
Victoria and Albert Museum.

56. Sir William Chambers (1723–96), Roman ruins at Kew Gardens, 1763.
Engraving by Woolett in Chambers's *Plans . . . of Gardens and Buildings at Kew*, 1763.

57. *The Green Monkey,* 1799.
Walker Art Gallery, Liverpool.

George Stubbs (1724–1806) resolved "to look into nature for himself, and consult and study *her only.*" In Italy he made no studies from the antique, and "differed always in opinion from his companions." He became a brilliant student of anatomy, performing elaborate dissections, on which he based his *Anatomy of the Horse* (1759). Noted as a portrait painter of race horses as well as of their owners, Stubbs also made remarkable studies of tigers, monkeys, and even a kangaroo.

58. *A Lion Attacking a Horse. Collection Mr. and Mrs. Paul Mellon.*

Joseph Wright of Derby (1734–94) was the first painter of distinction to celebrate the new industrial leaders, their buildings, and their technological concerns. The experiment with the air pump involves withdrawing air from the glass bell that holds the bird and then replenishing it just in time to save the bird's life; the children betray their fears, but the boy on the right is lowering a cage to hold the revived bird.

59. *An Experiment on a Bird in the Air Pump* (c. 1767–68). *The Tate Gallery.*

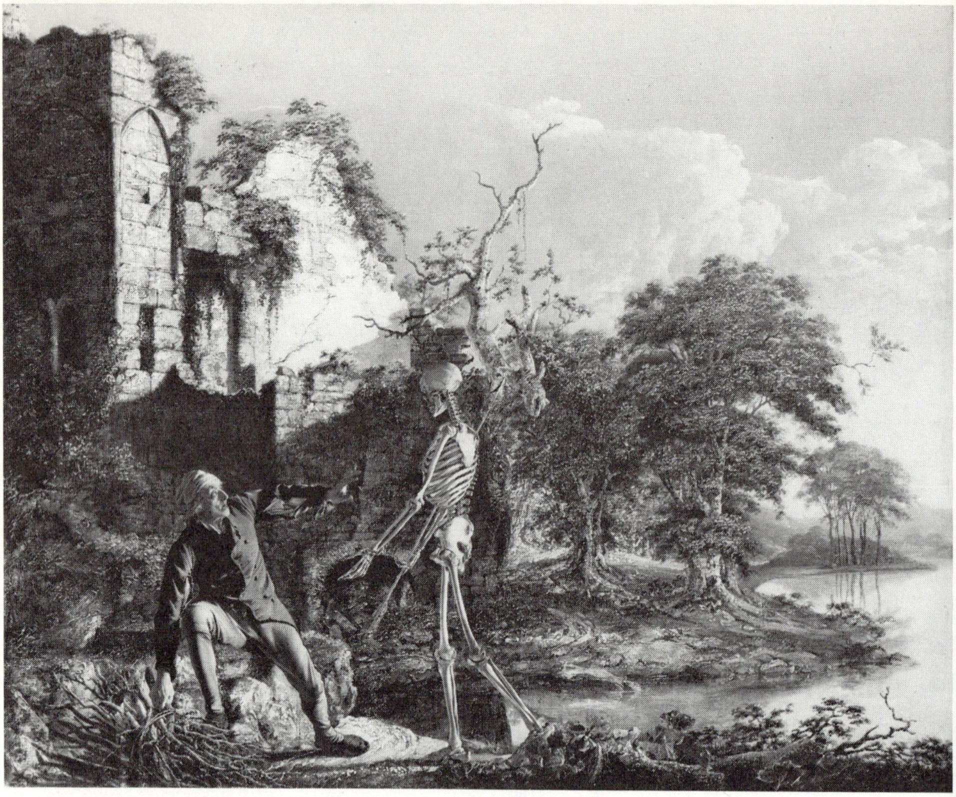

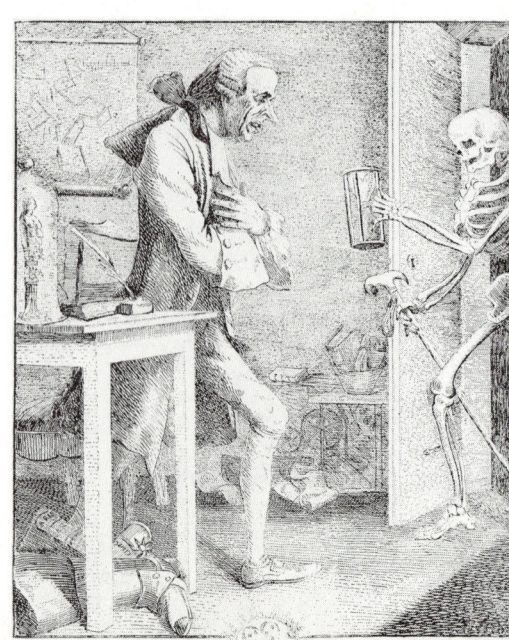

60. Joseph Wright of Derby, *The Old Man and Death*, 1773.
Wadsworth Atheneum, Hartford.

DEATH IN THE EIGHTEENTH CENTURY

Wright's picture draws on Aesop's fable of the old woodgatherer who calls for death to free him of his burdens but is appalled and reluctant to receive what he asks for. The engraving by Thomas Patch (1725–82) catches the appearance of Sterne in the spirit of Tristram Shandy and Yorick.

61. Thomas Patch, *Sterne and Death*, 1768.
Courtauld Institute of Art.

To wonder at their maker, not to serve!'°
 'Be that my task' (replies a gloomy clerk,
460 Sworn foe to mystery,° yet divinely dark;
Whose pious hope aspires to see the day
When moral evidence° shall quite decay,
And damns implicit faith,° and holy lies,
Prompt to impose, and fond to dogmatize:)°
'Let others creep by timid steps, and slow,
On plain experience lay foundations low,
By common sense to common knowledge bred,
And last, to Nature's Cause through Nature led.°
All-seeing in thy mists, we want no guide,
470 Mother of arrogance, and source of pride!
We nobly take the high priori road,°
And reason downward, till we doubt of God:
Make Nature still encroach° upon his plan;
And shove him off as far as e'er we can:
Thrust some mechanic cause into his place,
Or bind in matter, or diffuse in space.°
Or, at one bound o'erleaping° all his laws,
Make God man's image, man the final cause,°
Find virtue local, all relation scorn,°
480 See all in *self*,° and but for self be born:
Of naught so certain as our *reason* still,
Of naught so doubtful as of *soul* and *will*.°

wonder . . . serve to lose themselves in the wonders of God's creation and to neglect his moral teaching
mystery religious mystery, doctrine that defies clear rational explanation, such as the Trinity
moral evidence the probability of the historical facts of the Bible, believed by some to decay as the events became more remote in time
implicit faith belief upon authority, unquestioning adherence without comprehension
Prompt . . . dogmatize the freethinker seen as dogmatically rejecting dogma, self-deceiving and complacently deductive even as he attacks "holy lies"
Nature's Cause . . . led Cf. *Essay on Man* IV. 331–32: "Slave to no sect, who takes no private road, / But looks through Nature, up to Nature's God."
high priori road the deductive or *a priori* method taken by Descartes in his *Meditations*, Spinoza in his *Ethics*, and Hobbes in his *Leviathan*
Nature . . . encroach explain away Providence by natural ("mechanic") causes, or create a metaphysical principle (such as Ralph Cudworth's "plastic nature") to displace or delimit a theistic God. God's "second causes" (those explicable in mechanical terms) assume more and more of the role once given to his "plan" or active ordering.
Thrust . . . space "The first of these follies is that of Descartes; the second of Hobbes; the third of some succeeding philosophers" (P-W). The last may include such as Henry More (1614–87), the Cambridge Platonist, who sepa-

rated extension from matter in order to attribute extension or pure space to spirit; space for More is "an obscure representation of the essential presence of the divine being." More in turn influenced Sir Isaac Newton's conception of absolute space, and it may be to the consequence of the Newtonian mechanical view (rather than its intention) that Pope is alluding so discreetly.
o'erleaping like Satan overleaping the walls of Eden (*Paradise Lost* IV.181)
man the final cause i.e. see human happiness as the sole end of the universe and see God and his varied creation as a means to that end
Find virtue . . . scorn Here the process of contraction continues; given man as the sole end of creation, the idea of "man" gives way to "men" and morality becomes relative to local customs rather than universal, absolute, or dependent on God's will.
self the final contraction of scale, in contrast to the movement of the *Essay on Man* IV.361–72 where the soul rises "from individual to the whole," from self to "friend, parent, neighbour," thence to "country" and "next all human race," until "every creature . . . of every kind" is loved. At that point instead of God's being made in man's image (l. 478 above)—"Heaven beholds its image in his breast"—man has absorbed the capacity for divine love.
soul and will The metaphysical and moral principles of human nature are neglected by the dogmatic rationalism of the freethinkers or deists.

Oh hide the God still more! and make us see
Such as Lucretius° drew, a God like Thee:
Wrapped up in self, a God without a thought,
Regardless of our merit or default.
Or that bright image to our fancy draw,
Which Theocles° in raptured vision saw,
While through poetic scenes the Genius roves,
490   Or wanders wild in academic groves;
That NATURE our society° adores,
Where Tindal° dictates, and Silenus° snores.'
   Roused at his name, up rose the bousy sire,
And shook from out his pipe the seeds of fire;°
Then snapped his box,° and stroked his belly down:
Rosy and reverend, though without a gown.°
Bland and familiar to the throne he came,
Led up the Youth, and called the goddess *Dame.*
Then thus: 'From priestcraft happily set free,
500   Lo! every finished son returns to thee:
First slave to words, then vassal to a name,°
Then dupe to party; child and man the same;
Bounded by nature, narrowed still by art,
A trifling head, and a contracted heart.
Thus bred, thus taught, how many have I seen,
Smiling on all, and smiled on by a queen.
Marked out for honours, honoured for their birth,
To thee the most rebellious things on earth:
Now to thy gentle shadow all are shrunk,
510   All melted down, in pension, or in punk!°
So Kent, so Berkeley° sneaked into the grave,
A monarch's half, and half a harlot's slave.
Poor W——° nipped in folly's broadest bloom,

Lucretius (*c.* 94 B.C.–55 B.C.) whose philosophical poem *De Rerum Natura* (following Epicurean thought) seeks to free man of his fears of anthropomorphic gods and presents nature as an impartial force, free of the concerns that vex man (therefore, like Dulness, sublimely indifferent to all distinctions of value)
Theocles the philosophical visionary in the Earl of Shaftesbury's *The Moralists* (1709), here made into a simple worshiper of Nature (his "Genius"), cultivating Platonic ecstasy in the wild landscape (see below, The Garden and the Wild)
our society the association of freethinkers
Tindal Matthew Tindal (1657–1733), a leading deist
Silenus the fat, drunken, and debauched companion of Dionysus who appears in Virgil's Sixth Eclogue, where he is made a spokesman of the Epicurean philosophy; here also associated with Thomas Gordon, a political writer whom Walpole made Commissioner of the Wine Licenses
seeds of fire parodying Epicurean language for atoms

box snuffbox
without a gown not a priest; Silenus is usually pictured naked
First slave . . . name There follows a "recapitulation of the whole course of modern education . . . which confines youth to the study of *words* only in schools, subjects them to the authority of *systems* in the universities, and deludes them with the names of *party-distinctions* in the world; all equally concurring to narrow the understanding and establish slavery and error in literature, philosophy, and politics. The whole finished in modern free-thinking; the completion of whatever is vain, wrong, and destructive to the happiness of mankind, as it establishes *self-love* for the sole principle of action" (P-W).
punk whore
So Kent, so Berkeley the Duke of Kent and Earl of Berkeley, both holders of the highest royal honor, Knight of the Garter; possibly indebted to one of George I's mistresses ("harlot's slave")
W—— perhaps the dissipated young Earl of Warwick

Who praises now? his chaplain on his tomb.
Then take them all, oh take them to thy breast!
Thy *Magus,*° Goddess! shall perform the rest.'
   With that, a WIZARD OLD his *Cup* extends;
Which whoso tastes, forgets his former friends,
Sire, ancestors, himself. One casts his eyes
520 Up to a *star,*° and like Endymion° dies:
A *feather,*° shooting from another's head,
Extracts his brain; and principle is fled;
Lost is his God, his country, everything;
And nothing left but homage to a king!
The vulgar herd turn off to roll with hogs,°
To run with horses, or to hunt with dogs;
But, sad example! never to escape
Their infamy, still keep the human shape.
But she, good goddess, sent to every child
530 Firm impudence, or stupefaction mild;
And straight succeeded, leaving shame no room,
Cibberian forehead,° or Cimmerian gloom.°
   Kind self-conceit to some her glass° applies,
Which no one looks in with another's eyes,
But, as the flatterer or dependent paint,
Beholds himself a patriot, chief, or saint.
   On others Interest her gay livery° flings,
Interest that waves on party-coloured° wings:
Turned to the sun, she casts a thousand dyes,
540 And, as she turns, the colours fall or rise.
   Others the Siren Sisters° warble round,
And empty heads console with empty sound.
No more, alas! the voice of fame they hear,
The balm of Dulness trickling in their ear.
Great C——, H——, P——, R——, K——,°
Why all your toils? your sons have learned to sing.
How quick ambition hastes to ridicule!
The sire is made a peer, the son a fool.
   On some, a priest succinct in amice white°

Magus adept in occult arts, high priest, "wizard"; Walpole is suggested, his use of bribery embodied in the "Cup of Self-love," as P-W call it, of the next line
star worn by Knights of the Garter or of the Bath
Endymion loved by the Moon, thrown into perpetual sleep and visited by her each night
feather worn in the cap of Knights of the Garter
roll with hogs like the Prodigal Son (Luke 15:11) or like those transformed by Circe; but her enchantment "took away the shape and left the human mind," whereas the Magus's cup "takes away the mind and leaves the human shape" (P-W)
Cibberian forehead the brazenness of Colley Cibber (1671–1757), the poet laureate of George II and King of the Dunces in the re-

vised *Dunciad*, particularly as shown in his autobiographical *Apology* (1740)
Cimmerian gloom referring to Homer's mythical land of constant mists and darkness, the appropriate habitat of the followers of Dulness
glass mirror
livery costume worn by retainers, whether courtiers or servants or both
party-coloured a pun on "parti-colored"; i.e. vari-colored
Siren Sisters the devotees of opera; cf. ll. 45 ff. and 324
Great . . . K—— noblemen ambitious for their families
priest . . . white a chef dressed in a white apron and cap, the counterpart of the priest's "amice" worn over head and shoulders with white vestments

550 Attends; all flesh is nothing in his sight!
    Beeves, at his touch, at once to jelly turn,
    And the huge boar is shrunk into an urn:°
    The board with specious° miracles he loads,
    Turns hares to larks, and pigeons into toads.
    Another (for in all what one can shine?)
    Explains the *sève* and *verdeur*° of the vine.
    What cannot copious sacrifice atone?°
    Thy truffles, Perigord! thy hams, Bayonne!
    With French libation, and Italian strain,
560 Wash Bladen white, and expiate Hays's° stain.
    Knight° lifts the head, for what are crowds undone
    To three essential partridges in one?°
    Gone every blush, and silent all reproach,
    Contending princes mount them in their coach.
        Next bidding all draw near on bended knees,
    The Queen confers her *titles* and *degrees*.
    Her children first of more distinguished sort,
    Who study Shakespeare at the Inns of Court,°
    Impale a glowworm, or virtú° profess,
570 Shine in the dignity of F.R.S.°
    Some, deep Freemasons,° join the silent race
    Worthy to fill Pythagoras's place:°
    Some botanists, or florists at the least;
    Or issue members of an annual feast.°
    Nor passed the meanest unregarded; one
    Rose a Gregorian, one a Gormogon.°
    The last, not least in honour or applause,
    Isis and Cam made Doctors of her Laws.°
        Then, blessing all, 'Go, children of my care!
580 To practice now from theory repair.
    All my commands are easy, short, and full:

Beeves . . . urn culinary miracles, where beef is reduced (by a form of mock-transubstantiation) to jelly, or boned meats are given decorative and amusing shapes by ingenious transformations as in l. 554
specious "showy; superficially, not solidly right" (Johnson)
sève . . . verdeur fineness of flavor and briskness of sparkling wines
sacrifice atone the yield of luxuries by famous French regions (Perigord, Bayonne) seen as religious offerings, with libations accompanied by operatic music in l. 559
Bladen . . . Hays's two notorious gamblers who "lived with utmost magnificence at Paris and kept open tables frequented by persons of the first quality of England and even by princes of the blood of France" (P-W)
Knight Robert Knight, cashier of the South Sea Company, who fled England after its collapse in 1720, causing many to be "undone"
three . . . one two partridges dissolved into sauce for a third, with clear reference to the

mystery of the Trinity ("the incomprehensible union of the three persons in the Godhead," as Dr. Johnson defines it)
Shakespeare . . . Court lawyers who neglect their duties or studies to dabble in Shakespeare criticism
virtú amateur pursuit of arts or sciences; hence *virtuoso*
F.R.S. Fellow of the Royal Society, a title often granted at the time to untrained noblemen
Freemasons "where taciturnity is the *only* essential qualification, as it was the *chief* of the disciples of Pythagoras" (P-W)
Pythagoras's place referring to the ascetic brotherhood which pursued mathematical and religious mysteries at Croton in southern Italy, c. 600–450 B.C.; cf. l. 31 above
annual feast yearly banquet such as was held by the Freemasons or the Royal Society
Gregorian . . . Gormogon members of societies founded in ridicule of Freemasons
Isis and Cam . . . Laws Oxford and Cambridge bestowed honorary degrees.

My sons! be proud, be selfish, and be dull.
Guard my prerogative, assert my throne:
This nod confirms each privilege your own.
The cap and switch° be sacred to his Grace;
With staff and pumps° the Marquis lead the race;
From stage to stage° the licensed° Earl may run,
Paired with his fellow charioteer the sun;
The learnèd Baron butterflies design,°
590 Or draw to silk Arachne's subtile line,°
The Judge to dance his brother Sergeant° call;
The Senator at cricket urge the ball;
The Bishop stow (pontific luxury!)°
An hundred souls of turkeys in a pie;
The sturdy Squire to Gallic masters° stoop,
And drown his lands and manors in a soup.
Others import yet nobler arts from France,
Teach kings to fiddle, and make senates dance.°
Perhaps more high some daring son may soar,°
600 Proud to my list to add one monarch more;
And nobly conscious, princes are but things
Born for first ministers, as slaves for kings,
Tyrant supreme! shall three estates° command,
And MAKE ONE MIGHTY DUNCIAD OF THE LAND!'
    More she had spoke, but yawned—all nature nods:
What mortal can resist the yawn of gods?°
Churches and chapels° instantly it reached;
(St. James's first, for leaden Gilbert° preached)
Then catched the schools;° the Hall scarce kept awake;
610 The convocation gaped, but could not speak:
Lost was the nation's sense, nor could be found,

cap and switch of a jockey, here awarded to a lord devoted to horse racing
staff and pumps equipment of footmen or grooms, at the time a fashion among young gentlemen
stage to stage driving a stagecoach, as the Earl of Salisbury did
licensed as coach owners were; also "privileged"
design study and draw
draw . . . line try to obtain silken thread from spiders' webs (as Swift has the experimenters do in the Grand Academy of Lagado, *Gulliver's Travels* III.v)
Sergeant barrister; the "call of sergeants" involved ceremonies much like a dance
pontific luxury such as was in fact enjoyed at the time by the Bishop of Durham
Gallic masters who will introduce fashionable foreign tastes (here a costly "soup") to traditionally conservative country squires
dance perhaps "after their Prince" (P-W); in *Gulliver's Travels* I.iii Lilliputian courtiers are chosen for office by their agility in dancing on a tightrope
more high . . . soar referring to Walpole's virtual rule of England as first minister from

1721 until his fall in 1742, shortly before this was published
three estates Dulness subdues (as Walpole controlled through appointment, bribery, and appeal to interest) the three estates of nobility, clergy, and commoners.
yawn of gods "The Great Mother composes all, in the same manner as Minerva at the period of the *Odyssey*" (P-W)
chapels places of Dissenters' worship
leaden Gilbert Dr. John Gilbert, Dean of Exeter, was eloquent enough in manner; "leaden" is "an epithet from the age" Dulness "had just then restored" (P-W)
Then . . . schools "The progress of this yawn is judicious, natural, and worthy to be noted. First it seizeth the churches and chapels; then catcheth the schools, where, though the boys be unwilling to sleep, the masters are not; next Westminster Hall [the chief law courts], much more hard indeed to subdue, and not put totally to silence even by the Goddess; then the Convocation [of the clergy], which though extremely desirous to speak yet cannot; even the House of Commons, justly called the Sense of the Nation, is *lost* (that is to say *suspended*) during the yawn" (P-W).

While the long solemn unison went round:
Wide, and more wide, it spread o'er all the realm;
Even Palinurus° nodded at the helm:
The vapour mild o'er each committee crept;
Unfinished treaties in each office slept;
And chiefless armies dozed out the campaign;
And navies yawned for orders on the main.
    O Muse! relate (for you can tell alone,
620 Wits have short memories, and dunces none)
Relate, who first, who last resigned to rest;
Whose heads she partly, whose completely blessed;
What charms could faction, what ambition lull,
The venal quiet, and entrance the dull;
Till drowned was sense, and shame, and right, and wrong—
O sing, and hush the nations with thy song!

       *   *   *

    In vain, in vain—the all-composing hour
Resistless falls: the Muse obeys the power.
She comes! she comes! the sable throne behold
630 Of *Night* primeval, and of *Chaos* old!
Before her, *Fancy's* gilded clouds decay,
And all its varying rainbows die away.
Wit shoots in vain its momentary fires,
The meteor drops, and in a flash expires.
As one by one, at dread Medea's strain,°
The sickening stars fade off the ethereal plain;
As Argus' eyes° by Hermes' wand opprest,
Closed one by one to everlasting rest;
Thus at her felt approach, and secret might,
640 *Art* after *Art* goes out, and all is night.
See skulking *Truth* to her old cavern° fled,
Mountains of casuistry heaped o'er her head!
Philosophy, that leaned on Heaven before,
Shrinks to her second cause,° and is no more.
Physic of *Metaphysic*° begs defence,
And *Metaphysic* calls for aid on *Sense!*°
See *Mystery* to *Mathematics*° fly!

Palinurus the pilot of Aeneas' ship; here Walpole, pilot of the ship of state and, in the following lines, exhibiting passivity in foreign policy
dread Medea's strain In Seneca's *Medea* the enchantress, seeking revenge for Jason's desertion, calls back to life all the monstrous serpents and sings an incantation that causes the sun to halt and the stars to fall.
Argus' eyes placed all over his body so that some might always remain open; but he was slain by Hermes
Truth . . . cavern "alludes to the saying of Democritus, that truth lay at the bottom of a deep well" (P-W)

Shrinks . . . cause explains away divinity by natural causes; cf. ll. 471–82 above
Physic of Metaphysic natural science turning to traditional speculative metaphysics for its ground. Pope had originally written "the Stagirite's defense," suggesting the clinging to Aristotle he ridiculed in the universities.
Metaphysic . . . Sense metaphysics in turn depending upon sense data or empirical findings, completing, with the previous line, a vicious circle
Mystery to Mathematics religious mystery seeking deductive mathematical demonstration, perhaps infecting mathematics with an occult and mystical strain such as that of the Pythagoreans

In vain! they gaze, turn giddy, rave, and die.
Religion blushing veils her sacred fires,
650   And unawares *Morality* expires.
Nor public flame, nor private, dares to shine;
Nor human spark is left, nor glimpse divine!
Lo! thy dread empire, CHAOS! is restored;
Light dies before thy uncreating word: °
Thy hand, great anarch! lets the curtain fall;
And universal darkness buries all.
1741   1743

JOHN GAY
1685–1732

John Gay was perhaps too indolent and amiable to become a major writer, but he might have seemed one in an age that had no Swift or Pope. Gay moved from Devon to London as apprentice to a silk merchant, but he became secretary to Aaron Hill, an old schoolmate who had achieved some literary reputation. Gay supplemented his earnings from writing by gifts and sinecures, gained in part through the help of his more illustrious friends; and in later years the Duke and Duchess of Queensberry were his warm personal friends as well as patrons. He had a special gift for parody and burlesque. His career began with *Wine* (1708), an imitation of Milton in the manner of John Philips. Later, when Ambrose Philips's rustic pastorals were favored by the Addison group at the expense of Pope's more Virgilian work, Pope himself wrote an ironic attack upon Philips; but Gay followed up with *The Shepherd's Week* (1714), in which the parody of Philips turns into a fine, often tender, evocation of country life. Again in *Trivia* (1716) Gay broke new ground in his mock-georgic on "walking the streets of London." While he broke new ground, he was following the hint offered in Swift's *Description of a City Shower* (1710); and it was reportedly to Swift's suggestion that he write a "Newgate pastoral" that we owe *The Beggar's Opera*.

In writing his Newgate pastoral, Gay could draw upon the legend of the recently hanged Jonathan Wild. That devious criminal introduced thieves into their trade, acted as a fence for their loot, and preserved an air of bold respectability as he bargained with those who came to recover their property. (Defoe's narrative, given below, describes this beautifully.) But as soon as Wild gained the ultimate notoriety of execution, he was turned into the material of political satire. The opposition seized upon his likeness to Sir Robert Walpole: "As to party, he was both in principle and practice a right modern Whig, according to the definition of those gentlemen, which is expressed in their motto—*Keep what you get, and get what you can*" (*Mist's Weekly Journal*, May 12, 1725). So too Swift defended Gay's work by pointing to his "comparing those common robbers to robbers of the public; and their several stratagems of betraying, condemning, and hanging each other to the severals arts of politicians in times of corruption"—not at all the present time, Swift ironically observes (*The Intelligencer*, May 25, 1729). Henry Fielding was to pursue this parallel further in his

---

uncreating word referring to the terms "wisdom" and "word" (based on the Greek *logos*) for Christ as creator and orderer; here Dulness represents "uncreation," the restoration of Chaos

brilliantly ironic *Jonathan Wild,* of which a chapter is given below; in fact, he and (more plausibly) Swift have sometimes been suggested as the authors of the piece in *Mist's Weekly Journal.*

Gay is not content to use Peachum (named for "peaching" upon his hirelings in order to get a reward) to recall both Wild and Walpole. He creates other rogues, like Lockit, the corrupt official, and Macheath, the highwayman with a swaggering aristocratic air, to produce a spectrum of "greatness" such as Walpole and his colleagues embodied. Swift wrote to Gay with pleasure about the story that at the opening performance "two great Ministers were in a box together and all the world staring at them." Walpole, in fact, seems to have risen to the occasion by encoring the most damaging song, "When you censure the age" (II, x), and winning applause for his good humor. But we are also told that he avoided any further performances.

Gay had another satiric target, that of Italian opera, which had become the rage in England (as Pope's *Dunciad* IV.45 ff. testifies). As an instance of false taste, of aristocratic pretension, of corruption of manners akin to those of politics, Italian opera provides another of the specious forms of respectability that Gay everywhere attacks. Gay mocks the jealousy of rival Italian singers in Polly and Lucy, and he preserves the requisite artificial happy ending by having the Beggar sell out to the taste of his time. Most of all, however, in creating the "ballad opera" he reinstates the native English tradition of song (not, however, disdaining a borrowing from Handel) and the engaging informality of a mock-heroic of music itself. In fact, he can often count on the full resonance of the original popular song, well known to the audience, to give deeper irony to his adaptation of it to new words. Dr. Arbuthnot took Gay's own opera as a "touchstone to try the British taste on," as a way of recovering "our true inclinations . . . however artfully they may be disguised by a childish fondness for Italian poetry and music in preference to our own."

Yet here, as in other works, Gay's achievement outruns his satiric intentions. He creates, by the very mixture of the raffish and the heroic, by the sense of a life in which betrayal is taken for granted and where each may live only "some months longer," a distinctive world as compelling as any outside itself. Gay sees it with such ironic flexibility and detachment (one might almost say with such anticipation of the "alienation effect" that Bertolt Brecht was to claim for his adaptation, *The Three-Penny Opera,* and for other works) that we are never allowed the simple comforts of either sympathy or disgust. Polly is more innocent than the rest, her head addled by reading play-books and romances, but she imitates the fine ladies with a certain vanity, and she shows a degree of ruthlessness in her desire for romance. Macheath is a kind of Robin Hood, risking danger as Peachum never does, redistributing the "superfluities of mankind"; but he regards any woman as fair game and fills the brothels with the girls he seduces. Like the rest, the Peachums show a mincing elegance of language as they assert the most barbarous maxims; they defend crime in the devout idiom of middle-class mercantile thrift and of Puritan earnestness. Yet they seem thoroughly untroubled and sincere in their inverted morality; they need not adopt the hypocrisy of those who know better, like the "Screenmaster General," Walpole, or any of those in high life or low who nominally subscribe to virtue. To that extent Gay creates a wonderfully absurd world with its own logic; yet it is never so self-contained as to keep out those intimations of savage competition and self-interest that characterize high and low alike.

THE AIRS AND THEIR MUSIC

Like all ballad-operas which employ old and well-known tunes, *The Beggar's Opera* uses the device known in the Renaissance as *contrafactum*, the writing of new words to an old melody, for a wide range of effects. A whole satiric dimension can be invoked by playing the new words off against the audience's sense of the traditional ones. Amateur theatricals and school musical shows frequently use *contrafactum* to popular songs, but the joke is usually confined merely to the displacement of the original words itself, rather than being allowed to play with the exact quality of that displacement. For example, the stirring "Let us take the road" (Air XX) was sung to a march from Handel's opera *Rinaldo* (1711), whose heroic plot and grand Italianate operatic manner were the antithesis of Gay's underworld and simple song style. Air XLIV ("The modes of the court so common are grown") is sung to the tune of "Lillibullero," a famous late seventeenth-century political song, anti-Irish and anti-Catholic, used by the political enemies of James II. The song immediately preceding it, however, uses "Packington's Pound," a melody in constant use from the time of Henry VII both as a melody for newly composed lyrics and as the basis of purely instrumental variations; the audience would have had a sense of its being a familiar tune, and with a particular character perhaps given by words from a 1661 collection beginning "My masters and friends, and good people draw near."

In many cases, however, the specific echoes of the older words are underlined in Gay's lyric. In Air XXI ("If the heart of a man is depressed with cares") is sung to a lilting, *Siciliana*-like, 6/4 melody: Act II, Air III. But the original words written by Thomas Durfey would have grated against the more tender lustiness of the lyric sung by Macheath, both for their cynical bawdry and for the reversed point of view (charm the girl to get her into bed, as opposed to the charming quality of women themselves):

Would ye have a young virgin of fifteen years,
You must tickle her fancy with "sweet" 's and "dear" 's.
Ever toying, and playing, and sweetly, sweetly,
Sing a love sonnet, and charm her ears.
Wittily, prettily talk her down,

Chase her, and praise her, if fair or brown,
  Soothe her, and smooth her,
  And tease her, and please her,
And touch but her smicket, and all's your own.

A "smicket" was an under-smock, or chemise, the undermost women's garment in a day when women wore no underpants. Gay's third and fourth lines are a calculated parody of those of the older version, with the additional irony that the parody is sweeter and more generous than the cynical original.

The beautiful love duet in Act I, "Over the hills and far away" (Air XVI), uses the tune of a song a version of whose words survives even in Mother Goose nursery rhymes: the chorus has the haunting line "Over the hills and far away," which is re-peated three times, but Gay saves the quotation of it for the last line of his text, making the audience's familiarity with it (they might have been half-humming along, half-mouthing the famous refrain words) contribute to its own poignancy.

Polly Peachum's marvelous aria in Act I ("Virgins are like the fair flower in its lustre," Air VI) gains additional ironic power from the very genre of song which is represented by its melody. The original words are empty and conventional operatic filler, ending with a mild paradox to give a slight turn of wit:

What shall I do to show how much I love her,
  How many millions of sighs can suffice?
That which wins other hearts ne'er can move her,
  Those common methods of love she'll despise:
I will love more than man e'er loved before me,
  Gaze on her all day and melt all the night,
Till for her own sake at last she'll implore me,
  To love her less to preserve her delight.

In Polly's aria, the "gaudy butterflies" who frolic around the girl-flower are of just the type of amorous town gentleman who might be singing Purcell's song, or writing the type of verse represented by its text. The additional irony that Covent Garden was a flower market as well as a theater, and that the very actresses and flower girls who plied their trade there may well have been country girls who ended up as London prostitutes, must have helped make this "the favourite tune in the *Beggar's Opera*" throughout the eighteenth century, as Dr. Burney writes of it in his *History of Music* (1770).

The Beggar's Opera

DRAMATIS PERSONAE [1]

MEN		WOMEN	
PEACHUM		MRS. PEACHUM	
LOCKIT		POLLY PEACHUM	
MACHEATH		LUCY LOCKIT	
FILCH		DIANA TRAPES	
JEREMY TWITCHER		MRS. COAXER	
CROOK-FINGERED JACK		DOLLY TRULL	
WAT DREARY		MRS. VIXEN	
ROBIN OF BAGSHOT	*Macheath's*	BETTY DOXY	*Women of*
NIMMING NED	*gang*	JENNY DIVER	*the town*
HARRY PADINGTON		MRS. SLAMMEKIN	
MATT OF THE MINT		SUKY TAWDRY	
BEN BUDGE		MOLLY BRAZEN	
BEGGAR			
PLAYER			

Constables, drawers, turnkey, etc.

INTRODUCTION

[BEGGAR, PLAYER]

BEGGAR   If poverty be a title to poetry, I am sure nobody can dispute mine. I own myself of the company of beggars, and I make one at their weekly festivals at St. Giles's.[2] I have a small yearly salary for my catches [3] and am welcome to a dinner there whenever I please, which is more than most poets can say.

PLAYER   As we live by the Muses, 'tis but gratitude in us to encourage poetical merit wherever we find it. The Muses, contrary to all other ladies, pay no distinction to dress, and never partially [4] mistake the pertness of embroidery for wit, nor the modesty of want for dullness. Be the

1. Many of the characters' names are derived from slang expressions of the time: a "twitcher" was a pickpocket; a "budge" was a sneak-thief; "nimming" was stealing; "trull" and "doxy" were names for prostitutes; "diver" for a pickpocket.
2. A section of London, named for the patron saint of beggars and lepers, and known for filth and squalor.
3. Songs, rounds.
4. With partiality or bias.

author who he will, we push his play as far as it will go. So (though you are in want) I wish you success heartily.

BEGGAR   This piece, I own, was originally writ for the celebrating the marriage of James Chanter and Moll Lay, two most excellent ballad-singers. I have introduced the similes that are in your celebrated operas: the swallow, the moth, the bee, the ship, the flower, etc. Besides, I have a prison-scene, which the ladies always reckon charmingly pathetic. As to the parts, I have observed such a nice impartiality to our two ladies that it is impossible for either of them to take offence.[5] I hope I may be forgiven that I have not made my opera throughout unnatural, like those in vogue; for I have no recitative: [6] excepting this, as I have consented to have neither prologue nor epilogue, it must be allowed an opera in all its forms. The piece indeed hath been heretofore frequently represented by ourselves in our great room at St. Giles's, so that I cannot too often acknowledge your charity in bringing it now on the stage.

PLAYER   But I see 'tis time for us to withdraw; the actors are preparing to begin. Play away the overture.   [*Exeunt*]

ACT I

SCENE I. PEACHUM's *house*

[PEACHUM *sitting at a table with a large book of accounts before him*]

AIR I—*An old woman clothed in gray, etc.*

Through all the employments of life,
    Each neighbour abuses his brother;
Whore and rogue they call husband and wife:
    All professions be-rogue one another.
The priest calls the lawyer a cheat,
    The lawyer be-knaves the divine;
And the statesman, because he's so great,
    Thinks his trade as honest as mine.

A lawyer is an honest employment; so is mine. Like me, too, he acts in a double capacity, both against rogues and for 'em; for 'tis but fitting that we should protect and encourage cheats, since we live by 'em.

SCENE II

[PEACHUM, FILCH]

FILCH   Sir, Black Moll hath sent word her trial comes on in the afternoon, and she hopes you will order matters so as to bring her off.

---

5. Alluding to the public quarrels and rivalry of the two leading singers of Italian opera, Faustina and Cuzzoni, mocked in the quarrel of Polly and Lucy in II.xiii.
6. No portions half-sung, half-spoken.

PEACHUM   Why, she may plead her belly [7] at worst; to my knowledge she
hath taken care of that security. But as the wench is very active and
industrious, you may satisfy her that I'll soften the evidence.

FILCH   Tom Gagg, sir, is found guilty.

PEACHUM   A lazy dog! When I took him the time before, I told him what he
would come to if he did not mend his hand. This is death without
reprieve. I may venture to book him.   [*Writes*]
For Tom Gagg, forty pounds. Let Betty Sly know that I'll save her
from transportation,[8] for I can get more by her staying in England.

FILCH   Betty hath brought more goods into our lock [9] to-year, than any five
of the gang; and in truth, 'tis a pity to lose so good a customer.

PEACHUM   If none of the gang take her off, she may, in the common course
of business, live a twelve-month longer. I love to let women 'scape. A
good sportsman always lets the hen partridges fly, because the breed
of the game depends upon them. Besides, here the law allows us no
reward; there is nothing to be got by the death of women—except
our wives.

FILCH   Without dispute, she is a fine woman! 'Twas to her I was obliged for
my education, and (to say a bold word) she hath trained up more young
fellows to the business than the gaming-table.

PEACHUM   Truly, Filch, thy observation is right. We and the surgeons are
more beholden to women than all the professions besides.

FILCH

AIR II—*The bonny gray-eyed morn, etc.*

'Tis woman that seduces all mankind,
    By her we first were taught the wheedling arts;
Her very eyes can cheat; when most she's kind,
    She tricks us of our money with our hearts.
For her, like wolves by night we roam for prey,
    And practise every fraud to bribe her charms;
For suits of love, like law, are won by pay,
    And beauty must be fee'd into our arms.

PEACHUM   But make haste to Newgate,[10] boy, and let my friends know what
I intend; for I love to make them easy one way or other.

FILCH   When a gentleman is long kept in suspense, penitence may break his
spirit ever after. Besides, certainty gives a man a good air upon his
trial, and makes him risk another without fear or scruple. But I'll away,
for 'tis a pleasure to be the messenger of comfort to friends in affliction.
[*Exit*]

---

7. Pregnancy, which could delay or prevent execution.
8. Tom Gagg is turned in for a reward, and Betty Sly saved (temporarily) from exile to
American plantations for a seven- or fourteen-year period.
9. "A warehouse where stolen goods are deposited" (Gay).
10. The chief prison of London.

SCENE III

[PEACHUM]

PEACHUM   But 'tis now high time to look about me for a decent execution against next sessions.[11] I hate a lazy rogue, by whom one can get nothing till he is hanged. A register of the gang: [*Reading*] 'Crook-fingered Jack. A year and a half in the service.' Let me see how much the stock owes to his industry; one, two, three, four, five gold watches, and seven silver ones.—A mighty clean-handed fellow!—Sixteen snuff-boxes, five of them of true gold. Six dozen of handkerchiefs, four silver-hilted swords, half a dozen of shirts, three tie-periwigs, and a piece of broadcloth.—Considering these are only the fruits of his leisure hours, I don't know a prettier fellow, for no man alive hath a more engaging presence of mind upon the road.[12] 'Wat Dreary, alias Brown Will'—an irregular dog, who hath an underhand way of disposing of his goods. I'll try him only for a sessions or two longer upon his good behaviour. 'Harry Padington'—a poor petty-larceny rascal, without the least genius; that fellow, though he were to live these six months, will never come to the gallows with any credit. 'Slippery Sam'—he goes off the next sessions, for the villain hath the impudence to have views of following his trade as a tailor, which he calls an honest employment. 'Matt of the Mint'—listed not above a month ago, a promising sturdy fellow, and diligent in his way: somewhat too bold and hasty, and may raise good contributions on the public, if he does not cut himself short by murder. 'Tom Tipple'—a guzzling, soaking sot, who is always too drunk to stand himself, or to make others stand.[13] A cart [14] is absolutely necessary for him. 'Robin of Bagshot, alias Gorgon, alias Bluff Bob, alias Carbuncle, alias Bob Booty!—' [15]

SCENE IV

[PEACHUM, MRS. PEACHUM]

MRS. PEACHUM   What of Bob Booty, husband? I hope nothing bad hath be-tided him. You know, my dear, he's a favourite customer of mine. 'Twas he made me a present of this ring.

PEACHUM   I have set his name down in the black list, that's all, my dear; he spends his life among women, and as soon as his money is gone, one or other of the ladies will hang him for the reward, and there's forty pound lost to us forever.

MRS. PEACHUM   You know, my dear, I never meddle in matters of death; I always leave those affairs to you. Women indeed are bitter bad judges

11. The criminal court, held eight times a year; Peachum hopes to produce a felon for hanging at the next session.
12. As a highwayman.
13. Pay up; "stand and deliver" was the highwayman's cry.
14. That is, on which he is taken to the gallows.
15. Adaptations of popular nicknames for Sir Robert Walpole; Bagshot Heath was a place known for robberies.

in these cases, for they are so partial to the brave that they think every man handsome who is going to the camp [16] or the gallows.

AIR III—*Cold and raw, etc.*

If any wench Venus's girdle wear,
    Though she be never so ugly,
Lilies and roses will quickly appear,
    And her face look wondrous smugly.
Beneath the left ear so fit but a cord,
    (A rope so charming a zone is!)
The youth in his cart hath the air of a lord,
    And we cry, There dies an Adonis! [17]

But really, husband, you should not be too hard-hearted, for you never had a finer, braver set of men than at present. We have not had a murder among them all, these seven months. And truly, my dear, that is a great blessing.

PEACHUM   What a dickens is the woman always a-whimpering about murder for? No gentleman is ever looked upon the worse for killing a man in his own defence; and if business cannot be carried on without it, what would you have a gentleman do?

MRS. PEACHUM   If I am in the wrong, my dear, you must excuse me, for nobody can help the frailty of an over-scrupulous conscience.

PEACHUM   Murder is as fashionable a crime as a man can be guilty of. How many fine gentlemen have we in Newgate every year, purely upon that article! If they have wherewithal to persuade the jury to bring it in manslaughter, what are they the worse for it? So my dear, have done upon this subject. Was Captain Macheath here this morning, for the bank-notes [18] he left with you last week?

MRS. PEACHUM   Yes, my dear; and though the bank has stopped payment, he was so cheerful and so agreeable! Sure there is not a finer gentleman upon the road than the captain! If he comes from Bagshot at any reasonable hour he hath promised to make one this evening with Polly and me and Bob Booty, at a party of quadrille.[19] Pray, my dear, is the captain rich?

PEACHUM   The captain keeps too good company ever to grow rich. Marybone [20] and the chocolate-houses are his undoing. The man that proposes to get money by play should have the education of a fine gentleman, and be trained up to it from his youth.

MRS. PEACHUM   Really, I am sorry upon Polly's account the captain hath not

16. Army service.
17. Adonis, the beautiful youth loved by Aphrodite, when killed by a wild boar, was changed by the goddess into a purple flower; he was worshiped as a vegetation god in Cyprus and Greece.
18. Receipts for money deposited, i.e. promissory notes from a banker, like cashier's checks today.
19. A fashionable card game (like ombre).
20. Marylebone, a resort for gambling ("play"), as were chocolate houses.

more discretion. What business hath he to keep company with lords and gentlemen? He should leave them to prey upon one another.

PEACHUM   Upon Polly's account! What a plague does the woman mean? Upon Polly's account!

MRS. PEACHUM   Captain Macheath is very fond of the girl.

PEACHUM   And what then?

MRS. PEACHUM   If I have any skill in the ways of women, I am sure Polly thinks him a very pretty man.

PEACHUM   And what then? You would not be so mad to have the wench marry him! Gamesters and highwaymen are generally very good to their whores, but they are very devils to their wives.

MRS. PEACHUM   But if Polly should be in love, how should we help her, or how can she help herself? Poor girl, I am in the utmost concern about her.

AIR IV—*Why is your faithful slave disdained? etc.*

If love the virgin's heart invade,
How, like a moth, the simple maid
    Still plays about the flame!
If soon she be not made a wife,
Her honour's singed, and then, for life,
She's—what I dare not name.

PEACHUM   Look ye, wife. A handsome wench in our way of business is as profitable as at the bar of a Temple [21] coffee-house, who looks upon it as her livelihood to grant every liberty but one. You see I would indulge the girl as far as prudently we can,—in anything but marriage! After that, my dear, how shall we be safe? Are we not then in her husband's power? For a husband hath the absolute power over all a wife's secrets but her own. If the girl had the discretion of a court lady, who can have a dozen young fellows at her ear without complying with one, I should not matter it; but Polly is tinder, and a spark will at once set her on a flame. Married! If the wench does not know her own profit, sure she knows her own pleasure better than to make herself a property! My daughter to me should be like a court lady to a minister of state, a key to the whole gang. Married! if the affair is not already done, I'll terrify her from it, by the example of our neighbours.

MRS. PEACHUM   Mayhap, my dear, you may injure the girl. She loves to imitate the fine ladies, and she may only allow the captain liberties in the view of interest.

PEACHUM   But 'tis your duty, my dear, to warn the girl against her ruin, and to instruct her how to make the most of her beauty. I'll go to her this moment, and sift her.[22] In the meantime, wife, rip out the coronets

21. At the Inns of Court, the center for lawyers and law students.
22. Question her, sound her out.

and marks of these dozen of cambric handkerchiefs, for I can dispose of them this afternoon to a chap [23] in the City.   [*Exit*]

SCENE V

[MRS. PEACHUM]

MRS. PEACHUM   Never was a man more out of the way in an argument than my husband! Why must our Polly, forsooth, differ from her sex and love only her husband? And why must Polly's marriage, contrary to all observation, make her the less followed by other men? All men are thieves in love, and like a woman the better for being another's property.

AIR V—*Of all the simple things we do, etc.*

A maid is like the golden ore,
   Which hath guineas intrinsical in't;
Whose worth is never known, before
   It is tried and impressed in the mint.
A wife's like a guinea in gold,
   Stamped with the name of her spouse;
Now here, now there; is bought, or is sold;
   And is current in every house.

SCENE VI

[MRS. PEACHUM, FILCH]

MRS. PEACHUM   Come hither, Filch. I am as fond of this child as though my mind misgave me he were my own. He hath as fine a hand at picking a pocket as a woman, and is as nimble-fingered as a juggler. If an unlucky session does not cut the rope of thy life, I pronounce, boy, thou wilt be a great man in history. Where was your post last night, my boy?

FILCH   I plied at the opera, madam; and considering 'twas neither dark nor rainy, so that there was no great hurry in getting chairs [24] and coaches, made a tolerable hand on't. These seven handkerchiefs, madam.

MRS. PEACHUM   Coloured ones, I see. They are of sure sale from our warehouse at Redriff [25] among the seamen.

FILCH   And this snuff-box.

MRS. PEACHUM   Set in gold! A pretty encouragement this to a young beginner.

FILCH   I had a fair tug at a charming gold watch. Pox take the tailors for making the fobs so deep and narrow. It stuck by the way, and I was forced to make my escape under a coach. Really, madam, I fear, I shall be cut off in the flower of my youth, so that every now and then (since I was pumped [26]) I have thoughts of taking up and going to sea.

23. Chapman, i.e. customer.
24. Sedan-chairs.
25. Rotherhithe, the dock district of south London.
26. Punished as a pickpocket by being held under a public water-pump.

MRS. PEACHUM You should go to Hockley-in-the-Hole [27] and to Marybone, child, to learn valour. These are the schools that have bred so many brave men. I thought, boy, by this time, thou hadst lost fear as well as shame.—Poor lad! how little does he know as yet of the Old Bailey! [28] For the first fact I'll insure thee from being hanged; and going to sea, Filch, will come time enough upon a sentence of transportation. But now, since you have nothing better to do, even go to your book and learn your catechism; for really a man makes but an ill figure in the ordinary's [29] paper, who cannot give a satisfactory answer to his questions. But, hark you, my lad. Don't tell me a lie; for you know I hate a liar. Do you know of anything that hath passed between Captain Macheath and our Polly?

FILCH I beg you, madam, don't ask me; for I must either tell a lie to you or to Miss Polly; for I promised her I would not tell.

MRS. PEACHUM But when the honour of our family is concerned—

FILCH I shall lead a sad life with Miss Polly if ever she come to know that I told you. Besides, I would not willingly forfeit my own honour by betraying anybody.

MRS. PEACHUM Yonder comes my husband and Polly. Come, Filch, you shall go with me into my own room, and tell me the whole story. I'll give thee a glass of a most delicious cordial that I keep for my own drinking. [*Exeunt*]

SCENE VII

[PEACHUM, POLLY]

POLLY I know as well as any of the fine ladies how to make the most of myself and of my man too. A woman knows how to be mercenary, though she hath never been in a court or at an assembly. We have it in our natures, papa. If I allow Captain Macheath some trifling liberties, I have this watch and other visible marks of his favour to show for it. A girl who cannot grant some things and refuse what is most material, will make but a poor hand of her beauty, and soon be thrown upon the common.[30]

AIR VI—*What shall I do to show how much I love her, etc.*

Virgins are like the fair flower in its lustre,
    Which in the garden enamels the ground;
Near it the bees in play flutter and cluster,
    And gaudy butterflies frolic around.
But, when once plucked, 'tis no longer alluring;
    To Covent Garden [31] 'tis sent (as yet sweet),

27. Scene of bear-baiting, sword-fighting, and wrestling.
28. The criminal court of London, attached to Newgate.
29. The chaplain of Newgate, who could recommend that a criminal be given a light sentence if he were able to show an ability to read; the ordinary also published the confessions of criminals in his reports, and these were often repentant and full of pious warning.
30. The common law or the common land, as a criminal or a vagrant.
31. The flower market.

There fades, and shrinks, and grows past all enduring,
   Rots, stinks, and dies, and is trod under feet.

PEACHUM   You know, Polly, I am not against your toying and trifling with a
customer in the way of business, or to get out a secret or so. But if I
find out that you have played the fool and are married, you jade you,
I'll cut your throat, hussy! Now you know my mind.

SCENE VIII

[PEACHUM, POLLY, MRS. PEACHUM. MRS. PEACHUM
   in a very great passion]

AIR VII—*Oh London is a fine town*

Our Polly is a sad slut! nor heeds what we have taught her.
I wonder any man alive will ever rear a daughter!
For she must have both hoods and gowns, and hoops to swell her pride,
With scarfs and stays, and gloves and lace; and she will have men
   beside;
And when she's dressed with care and cost, all-tempting fine and gay,
As men should serve a cowcumber,[32] she flings herself away.

You baggage, you hussy! you inconsiderate jade! Had you been hanged,
it would not have vexed me, for that might have been your misfortune;
   but to do such a mad thing by choice! The wench is married, husband.
PEACHUM   Married! The captain is a bold man and will risk anything for
money; to be sure, he believes her a fortune!—Do you think your
mother and I should have lived comfortably so long together, if ever
we had been married? Baggage!
MRS. PEACHUM   I knew she was always a proud slut; and now the wench hath
played the fool and married because, forsooth, she would do like the
gentry. Can you support the expense of a husband, hussy, in gaming,
drinking, and whoring? Have you money enough to carry on the daily
quarrels of man and wife about who shall squander most? There are not
many husbands and wives who can bear the charges of plaguing one
another in a handsome way. If you must be married, could you introduce nobody into our family but a highwayman? Why, thou foolish
jade, thou wilt be as ill used, and as much neglected, as if thou hadst
married a lord!
PEACHUM   Let not your anger, my dear, break through the rules of decency,
for the captain looks upon himself in the military capacity, as a gentleman by his profession. Besides what he hath already, I know he is in
a fair way of getting, or of dying; and both these ways, let me tell you,
are most excellent chances for a wife.—Tell me, hussy, are you ruined
or no?
MRS. PEACHUM   With Polly's fortune, she might very well have gone off to a
person of distinction. Yes, that you might, you pouting slut!
PEACHUM   What, is the wench dumb? Speak, or I'll make you plead by

32. Cucumber; something of no value.

squeezing out an answer from you. Are you really bound wife to him, or are you only upon liking?

[*Pinches her*]

POLLY   [*Screaming*] Oh!

MRS. PEACHUM   How the mother is to be pitied who hath handsome daughters! Locks, bolts, bars, and lectures of morality are nothing to them; they break through them all. They have as much pleasure in cheating a father and mother as in cheating at cards.

PEACHUM   Why, Polly, I shall soon know if you are married, by Macheath's keeping from our house.

POLLY

AIR VIII—*Grim king of the ghosts, etc.*

Can love be controlled by advice?
    Will Cupid our mothers obey?
Though my heart were as frozen as ice,
    At his flame 'twould have melted away.

When he kissed me, so closely he pressed,
    'Twas so sweet that I must have complied,
So I thought it both safest and best
    To marry, for fear you should chide.

MRS. PEACHUM   Then all the hopes of our family are gone for ever and ever!

PEACHUM   And Macheath may hang his father- and mother-in-law, in hope to get into their daughter's fortune!

POLLY   I did not marry him (as 'tis the fashion) coolly and deliberately for honour or money—but I love him.

MRS. PEACHUM   Love him! Worse and worse! I thought the girl had been better bred. O husband, husband! her folly makes me mad! my head swims! I'm distracted! I can't support myself—Oh!   [*Faints*]

PEACHUM   See, wench, to what a condition you have reduced your poor mother! A glass of cordial, this instant. How the poor woman takes it to heart! [*Polly goes out and returns with it*] Ah, hussy, now this is the only comfort your mother has left!

POLLY   Give her another glass, sir; my mama drinks double the quantity whenever she is out of order. This, you see, fetches her.

MRS. PEACHUM   The girl shows such a readiness, and so much concern, that I could almost find in my heart to forgive her.

AIR IX—*O Jenny, O Jenny, where hast thou been, etc.*

O Polly, you might have toyed and kissed;
    By keeping men off, you keep them on.

POLLY

But he so teased me,
    And he so pleased me,
What I did, you must have done—

MRS. PEACHUM   Not with a highwayman.—You sorry slut!

PEACHUM   A word with you, wife. 'Tis no new thing for a wench to take man
   without consent of parents. You know 'tis the frailty of woman, my
   dear.

MRS. PEACHUM   Yes, indeed, the sex is frail. But the first time a woman is
   frail, she should be somewhat nice,[33] methinks, for then or never is the
   time to make her fortune. After that, she hath nothing to do but to
   guard herself from being found out, and she may do what she pleases.

PEACHUM   Make yourself a little easy; I have a thought shall soon set all
   matters again to rights. Why so melancholy, Polly? Since what is done
   cannot be undone, we must all endeavour to make the best of it.

MRS. PEACHUM   Well, Polly, as far as one woman can forgive another, I forgive thee. Your father is too fond of you, hussy.

POLLY   Then all my sorrows are at an end.

MRS. PEACHUM   A mighty likely speech in troth, for a wench who is just
   married.

POLLY

   AIR X—*Thomas, I cannot, etc.*

   I, like a ship in storms, was tossed,
      Yet afraid to put into land;
   For seized in the port, the vessel's lost,
      Whose treasure is contraband.
         The waves are laid,
         My duty's paid,
      Oh, joy beyond expression!
         Thus, safe ashore,
         I ask no more,
   My all is in my possession.

PEACHUM   I hear customers in t'other room. Go, talk with 'em, Polly; but
   come to us again as soon as they are gone.—But, hark ye, child, if
   'tis the gentleman who was here yesterday about the repeating watch,[34]
   say, you believe we can't get intelligence of it till tomorrow—for I lent
   it to Suky Straddle, to make a figure with to-night at a tavern in Drury
   Lane. If t'other gentleman calls for the silver-hilted sword, you know
   beetle-browed Jemmy hath it on, and he doth not come from Tunbridge
   till Tuesday night; so that it cannot be had till then.   [*Exit* POLLY]

   SCENE IX

   [PEACHUM, MRS. PEACHUM]

PEACHUM   Dear wife, be a little pacified. Don't let your passion run away
   with your senses. Polly, I grant you, hath done a rash thing.

MRS. PEACHUM   If she had had only an intrigue with the fellow, why, the very
   best families have excused and huddled up a frailty of that sort. 'Tis
   marriage, husband, that makes it a blemish.

33. Fastidious, squeamish.
34. A watch that "repeats" or sounds the hour and quarter hour when pressed; cf. Pope,
Rape of the Lock I.18.

PEACHUM   But money, wife, is the true fuller's earth for reputations; there is
not a spot or a stain but what it can take out. A rich rogue nowadays
is fit company for any gentleman, and the world, my dear, hath not
such a contempt for roguery as you imagine. I tell you, wife, I can
make this match turn to our advantage.

MRS. PEACHUM   I am very sensible, husband, that Captain Macheath is
worth money, but I am in doubt whether he hath not two or three wives
already, and then if he should die in a session or two, Polly's dower
would come into dispute.

PEACHUM   That, indeed, is a point which ought to be considered.

AIR XI—*A soldier and a sailor*

A fox may steal your hens, sir,
A whore your health and pence, sir,
Your daughter rob your chest, sir,
Your wife may steal your rest, sir,
  A thief your goods and plate.
But this is all but picking,
With rest, pence, chest, and chicken;
It ever was decreed, sir,
If lawyer's hand is fee'd, sir,
  He steals your whole estate.

The lawyers are bitter enemies to those in our way. They don't care
that anybody should get a clandestine livelihood but themselves.

SCENE X

[MRS. PEACHUM, PEACHUM, POLLY]

POLLY   'Twas only Nimming [35] Ned. He brought in a damask window-curtain,
a hoop petticoat, a pair of silver candlesticks, a periwig, and one silk
stocking, from the fire that happened last night.

PEACHUM   There is not a fellow that is cleverer in his way and saves more
goods out of the fire, than Ned. But now, Polly, to your affair; for
matters must not be left as they are. You are married then, it seems?

POLLY   Yes, sir.

PEACHUM   And how do you propose to live, child?

POLLY   Like other women, sir, upon the industry of my husband.

MRS. PEACHUM   What, is the wench turned fool? A highwayman's wife, like a
soldier's, hath as little of his pay as of his company.

PEACHUM   And had not you the common views of a gentlewoman in your
marriage, Polly?

POLLY   I don't know what you mean, sir.

PEACHUM   Of a jointure,[36] and of being a widow.

POLLY   But I love him, sir; how then could I have thoughts of parting with
him?

---

35. That is, stealing, pilfering.
36. Property settled on a wife by her husband for her support after his death.

PEACHUM   Parting with him! Why, that is the whole scheme and intention of all marriage articles. The comfortable estate of widowhood is the only hope that keeps up a wife's spirits. Where is the woman who would scruple to be a wife, if she had it in her power to be a widow whenever she pleased? If you have any views of this sort, Polly, I shall think the match not so very unreasonable.

POLLY   How I dread to hear your advice! Yet I must beg you to explain yourself.

PEACHUM   Secure what he hath got, have him peached the next sessions, and then at once you are made a rich widow.

POLLY   What, murder the man I love! The blood runs cold at my heart with the very thought of it.

PEACHUM   Fie, Polly! What hath murder to do in the affair? Since the thing sooner or later must happen, I dare say the captain himself would like that we should get the reward for his death sooner than a stranger. Why, Polly, the captain knows that as 'tis his employment to rob, so 'tis ours to take robbers; every man in his business. So that there is no malice in the case.

MRS. PEACHUM   Aye, husband, now you have nicked the matter.[37] To have him peached is the only thing could ever make me forgive her.

POLLY

AIR XII—*Now ponder well, ye parents dear*

Oh, ponder well! be not severe;
    So save a wretched wife!
For on the rope that hangs my dear
    Depends poor Polly's life.

MRS. PEACHUM   But your duty to your parents, hussy, obliges you to hang him. What would many a wife give for such an opportunity!

POLLY   What is a jointure, what is widowhood to me? I know my heart. I cannot survive him.

AIR XIII—*Le printemps rappelle aux armes*

The turtle [38] thus with plaintive crying,
    Her lover dying,
The turtle thus with plaintive crying,
    Laments her dove.
Down she drops, quite spent with sighing;
Paired in death, as paired in love.

Thus, sir, it will happen to your poor Polly.

MRS. PEACHUM   What, is the fool in love in earnest then? I hate thee for being particular.[39] Why, wench, thou art a shame to thy very sex.

POLLY   But hear me, mother,—if you ever loved—

37. Hit the nail on the head.
38. Turtledove (The air: "Spring calls to arms").
39. Odd, peculiar.

MRS. PEACHUM   Those cursed play-books she reads have been her ruin. One word more, hussy, and I shall knock your brains out, if you have any.

PEACHUM   Keep out of the way, Polly, for fear of mischief, and consider what is proposed to you.

MRS. PEACHUM.   Away, hussy! Hang your husband, and be dutiful.

SCENE XI

[MRS. PEACHUM, PEACHUM, POLLY *listening*]

MRS. PEACHUM   The thing, husband, must and shall be done. For the sake of intelligence, we must take other measures and have him peached the next session without her consent. If she will not know her duty, we know ours.

PEACHUM   But really, my dear, it grieves one's heart to take off a great man. When I consider his personal bravery, his fine stratagem,⁴⁰ how much we have already got by him, and how much more we may get, methinks I can't find in my heart to have a hand in his death. I wish you could have made Polly undertake it.

MRS. PEACHUM   But in a case of necessity—our own lives are in danger.

PEACHUM   Then, indeed, we must comply with the customs of the world and make gratitude give way to interest. He shall be taken off.

MRS. PEACHUM   I'll undertake to manage Polly.

PEACHUM   And I'll prepare matters for the Old Bailey.   [*Exeunt*]

SCENE XII

[POLLY]

POLLY   Now I'm a wretch, indeed—methinks I see him already in the cart, sweeter and more lovely than the nosegay in his hand!—I hear the crowd extolling his resolution and intrepidity!—What volleys of sighs are sent from the windows of Holborn,⁴¹ that so comely a youth should be brought to disgrace!—I see him at the tree! The whole circle are in tears!—even butchers weep!—Jack Ketch ⁴² himself hesitates to perform his duty, and would be glad to lose his fee by a reprieve. What then will become of Polly? As yet I may inform him of their design and aid him in his escape. It shall be so!—But then he flies, absents himself, and I bar myself from his dear, dear conversation! That too will distract me. If he keep out of the way, my papa and mama may in time relent, and we may be happy. If he stays, he is hanged, and then he is lost forever! He intended to lie concealed in my room till the dusk of evening. If they are abroad, I'll this instant let him out, lest some accident should prevent him.   [*Exit, and returns*]

---

40. Cunning (a term adapted from warfare to politics and robbery).
41. Along the way from Newgate Prison to the gallows ("tree") at Tyburn.
42. Traditional name for a hangman.

SCENE XIII

[POLLY, MACHEATH]

AIR XIV—*Pretty Parrot, say, etc.*

MACHEATH

    Pretty Polly, say,
    When I was away,
Did your fancy never stray
    To some newer lover?

POLLY

    Without disguise,
    Heaving sighs,
    Doating eyes,
My constant heart discover.
    Fondly let me loll!

MACHEATH

    O pretty, pretty Poll.

POLLY   And are you as fond as ever, my dear?

MACHEATH   Suspect my honour, my courage—suspect anything but my love. May my pistols miss fire, and my mare slip her shoulder while I am pursued, if I ever forsake thee!

POLLY   Nay, my dear, I have no reason to doubt you, for I find in the romance you lent me, none of the great heroes were ever false in love.

MACHEATH

AIR XV—*Pray, fair one, be kind*

    My heart was so free,
    It roved like the bee,
Till Polly my passion requited;
    I sipped each flower,
    I changed every hour,
But here every flower is united.

POLLY   Were you sentenced to transportation, sure, my dear, you could not leave me behind you, could you?

MACHEATH   Is there any power, any force that could tear me from thee? You might sooner tear a pension out of the hands of a courtier, a fee from a lawyer, a pretty woman from a looking glass, or any woman from quadrille. But to tear me from thee is impossible!

AIR XVI—*Over the hills and far away*

Were I laid on Greenland's coast,
And in my arms embraced my lass;
Warm amidst eternal frost,
Too soon the half year's night would pass.

POLLY

Were I sold on Indian soil,
Soon as the burning day was closed,

I could mock the sultry toil,
When on my charmer's breast reposed.
MACHEATH   And I would love you all the day,
POLLY   Every night would kiss and play,
MACHEATH   If with me you'd fondly stray
POLLY   Over the hills and far away.

POLLY   Yes, I would go with thee. But oh!—how shall I speak it? I must be
torn from thee. We must part.

MACHEATH   How! Part!

POLLY   We must, we must. My papa and mama are set against thy life. They
now, even now, are in search after thee. They are preparing evidence
against thee. Thy life depends upon a moment.

AIR XVII—'*Gin thou wert mine awn thing*

Oh, what pain it is to part!
Can I leave thee, can I leave thee?
Oh, what pain it is to part!
Can thy Polly ever leave thee?
But lest death my love should thwart
And bring thee to the fatal cart,
Thus I tear thee from my bleeding heart!
Fly hence, and let me leave thee.

One kiss and then,—one kiss—begone—farewell.

MACHEATH   My hand, my heart, my dear, is so riveted to thine that I cannot
unloose my hold.

POLLY   But my papa may intercept thee, and then I should lose the very
glimmering of hope. A few weeks, perhaps, may reconcile us all. Shall
thy Polly hear from thee?

MACHEATH   Must I then go?

POLLY   And will not absence change your love?

MACHEATH   If you doubt it, let me stay—and be hanged.

POLLY   Oh, I fear! how I tremble! Go—but when safety will give you leave,
you will be sure to see me again; for till then Polly is wretched.

[*Parting, and looking back at each other with fondness;*
he at one door, she at the other.]

MACHEATH

AIR XVIII—*Oh the broom, etc.*

The miser thus a shilling sees,
    Which he's obliged to pay,
With sighs resigns it by degrees,
    And fears 'tis gone for aye.

POLLY

The boy, thus, when his sparrow's flown,
    The bird in silence eyes;
But soon as out of sight 'tis gone,
    Whines, whimpers, sobs, and cries.

ACT II

SCENE I. *A tavern near Newgate*

[JEMMY TWITCHER,[1] CROOK-FINGERED JACK, WAT DREARY, ROBIN OF BAG-SHOT, NIMMING NED, HARRY PADINGTON, MATT OF THE MINT, BEN BUDGE,[2] *and the rest of the gang, at the table, with wine, brandy, and tobacco*]

BEN   But prithee, Matt, what is become of thy brother Tom? I have not seen him since my return from transportation.

MATT   Poor brother Tom had an accident this time twelve-month, and so clever a made fellow he was, that I could not save him from those flaying rascals the surgeons; and now, poor man, he is among the anatomies [3] at Surgeons' Hall.

BEN   So, it seems, his time was come.

JEM   But the present time is ours, and nobody alive hath more. Why are the laws levelled at us? Are we more dishonest than the rest of mankind? What we win, gentlemen, is our own by the law of arms and the right of conquest.

JACK   Where shall we find such another set of practical philosophers, who to a man are above the fear of death?

WAT   Sound men, and true!

ROBIN   Of tried courage, and indefatigable industry!

NED   Who is there here that would not die for his friend?

HARRY   Who is there here that would betray him for his interest?

MATT   Show me a gang of courtiers that can say as much.

BEN   We are for a just partition of the world, for every man hath a right to enjoy life.

MATT   We retrench the superfluities of mankind. The world is avaricious, and I hate avarice. A covetous fellow, like a jackdaw, steals what he was never made to enjoy, for the sake of hiding it. These are the robbers of mankind, for money was made for the free-hearted and generous; and where is the injury of taking from another what he hath not the heart to make use of?

JEM   Our several stations for the day are fixed. Good luck attend us! Fill the glasses.

MATT

AIR XIX—*Fill every glass, etc.*

Fill every glass, for wine inspires us,
    And fires us,
With courage, love, and joy.
Women and wine should life employ.
Is there aught else on earth desirous?

CHORUS
        Fill every glass, etc.

1. A name for a pickpocket or shoplifter.
2. A term for sneak-thief.
3. Skeletons.

SCENE II

[*To them enter* MACHEATH]

MACHEATH   Gentlemen, well met. My heart hath been with you this hour, but an unexpected affair hath detained me. No ceremony, I beg you.

MATT   We were just breaking up to go upon duty. Am I to have the honour of taking the air with you, sir, this evening upon the heath? I drink a dram now and then with the stage-coachmen in the way of friendship and intelligence, and I know that about this time there will be passengers upon the Western Road who are worth speaking with.

MACHEATH   I was to have been of that party—but—

MATT   But what, sir?

MACHEATH   Is there any man who suspects my courage?

MATT   We have all been witnesses of it.

MACHEATH   My honour and truth to the gang?

MATT   I'll be answerable for it.

MACHEATH   In the division of our booty, have I ever shown the least marks of avarice or injustice?

MATT   By these questions something seems to have ruffled you. Are any of us suspected?

MACHEATH   I have a fixed confidence, gentlemen, in you all, as men of honour, and as such I value and respect you. Peachum is a man that is useful to us.

MATT   Is he about to play us any foul play? I'll shoot him through the head.

MACHEATH   I beg you, gentlemen, act with conduct and discretion. A pistol is your last resort.

MATT   He knows nothing of this meeting.

MACHEATH   Business cannot go on without him. He is a man who knows the world and is a necessary agent to us. We have had a slight difference, and till it is accommodated I shall be obliged to keep out of his way. Any private dispute of mine shall be of no ill consequence to my friends. You must continue to act under his direction, for the moment we break loose from him, our gang is ruined.

MATT   As a bawd [4] to a whore, I grant you, he is to us of great convenience.

MACHEATH   Make him believe I have quitted the gang, which I can never do but with life. At our private quarters I will continue to meet you. A week or so will probably reconcile us.

MATT   Your instructions shall be observed. 'Tis now high time for us to repair to our several duties; so till the evening at our quarters in Moorfields we bid you farewell.

MACHEATH   I shall wish myself with you. Success attend you.
[*Sits down melancholy at the table*]

MATT

AIR XX—*March in Rinaldo,*[5] *with drums and trumpets*

Let us take the road.
    Hark! I hear the sound of coaches!

4. Pimp.
5. One of Handel's operas (1711).

The hour of attack approaches,
To your arms, brave boys, and load.

See the ball I hold!
Let the chymists [6] toil like asses,
Our fire their fire surpasses,
And turns all our lead to gold.

[*The gang, ranged in the front of the stage, load their pistols, and stick them under their girdles, then go off singing the first part in chorus*]

SCENE III

[MACHEATH, DRAWER]

MACHEATH   What a fool is a fond wench; Polly is most confoundedly bit [7]—I love the sex. And a man who loves money might be as well contented with one guinea as I with one woman. The town perhaps hath been as much obliged to me, for recruiting it with free-hearted ladies, as to any recruiting officer in the army. If it were not for us, and the other gentlemen of the sword, Drury Lane [8] would be uninhabited.

AIR XXI—*Would you have a young virgin, etc.*

If the heart of a man is depressed with cares,
The mist is dispelled when a woman appears;
Like the notes of a fiddle, she sweetly, sweetly
Raises the spirits, and charms our ears.
    Roses and lilies her cheeks disclose,
    But her ripe lips are more sweet than those.
                Press her,
            Caress her
            With blisses,
            Her kisses
Dissolve us in pleasure and soft repose.

I must have women. There is nothing unbends the mind like them. Money is not so strong a cordial for the time. Drawer!—

[*Enter* DRAWER]

Is the porter gone for all the ladies, according to my directions?

DRAWER   I expect him back every minute. But you know, sir, you sent him as far as Hockley-in-the-Hole for three of the ladies, for one in Vinegar Yard, and for the rest of them somewhere about Lewkner's Lane.[9] Sure some of them are below, for I hear the bar bell. As they come I will show them up. Coming! coming!   [*Exit*]

---

6. Alchemists, who like thieves turn lead (as in the bullet or "ball") into gold by the use of fire or firing.
7. Deceived.
8. The center of prostitution.
9. Places of low reputation near Drury Lane.

SCENE IV

[MACHEATH, MRS. COAXER, DOLLY TRULL, MRS. VIXEN, BETTY DOXY,
JENNY DIVER, MRS. SLAMMEKIN, SUKY TAWDRY, *and* MOLLY BRAZEN [10]]

MACHEATH   Dear Mrs. Coaxer, you are welcome. You look charmingly to-day.
I hope you don't want the repairs of quality, and lay on paint.—Dolly
Trull! kiss me, you slut; are you as amorous as ever, hussy? You are
always so taken up with stealing hearts, that you don't allow yourself
time to steal anything else. Ah Dolly, thou wilt ever be a coquette.—
Mrs. Vixen, I'm yours! I always loved a woman of wit and spirit; they
make charming mistresses, but plaguy wives.—Betty Doxy! come hither,
hussy. Do you drink as hard as ever? You had better stick to good,
wholesome beer; for in troth, Betty, strong waters will, in time, ruin
your constitution. You should leave those to your betters.—What! and
my pretty Jenny Diver too! As prim and demure as ever! There is not
any prude, though ever so high bred, hath a more sanctified look, with
a more mischievous heart. Ah! thou art a dear artful hypocrite!—Mrs.
Slammekin! as careless and genteel as ever! all you fine ladies, who know
your own beauty, affect an undress.—But see, here's Suky Tawdry come
to contradict what I was saying. Everything she gets one way, she lays
out upon her back. Why, Suky, you must keep at least a dozen tally-
men.[11]—Molly Brazen! [*She kisses him*] That's well done. I love a free-
hearted wench. Thou hast a most agreeable assurance, girl, and art as
willing as a turtle.—But hark! I hear music. The harper is at the door.
'If music be the food of love, play on.' [12] Ere you seat yourselves, ladies,
what think you of a dance? Come in.

[*Enter* HARPER]

Play the French tune that Mrs. Slammekin was so fond of.

[*A dance* à la ronde *in the French manner; near the end of it this song
and chorus*]

AIR XXII—*Cotillion*

Youth's the season made for joys,
      Love is then our duty;
She alone who that employs,
      Well deserves her beauty.
            Let's be gay,
            While we may,
Beauty's a flower despised in decay.

CHORUS
            Youth's the season, etc.

      Let us drink and sport today,
            Ours is not to-morrow.

10. The names imply slattern (Trapes, Slammekin), prostitute (Trull, Doxy), pickpocket
(Diver), etc.
11. Those who rent clothes or sell on credit.
12. The words of Duke Orsino at the opening of Shakespeare's *Twelfth Night*.

Love with youth flies swift away,
 Age is nought but sorrow.
  Dance and sing,
  Time's on the wing,
Life never knows the return of spring.

CHORUS
 Let us drink, etc.

MACHEATH Now pray, ladies, take your places. Here, fellow. [*Pays the* HARPER] Bid the drawer bring us more wine.   [*Exit* HARPER] If any of the ladies choose gin, I hope they will be so free to call for it.

JENNY You look as if you meant me. Wine is strong enough for me. Indeed, sir, I never drink strong waters but when I have the colic.

MACHEATH Just the excuse of the fine ladies! Why, a lady of quality is never without the colic. I hope, Mrs. Coaxer, you have had good success of late in your visits among the mercers.[13]

MRS. COAXER We have so many interlopers. Yet, with industry, one may still have a little picking. I carried a silver-flowered lute-string and a piece of black padesoy [14] to Mr. Peachum's lock but last week.

MRS. VIXEN There's Molly Brazen hath the ogle of a rattlesnake. She riveted a linen-draper's eye so fast upon her, that he was nicked of three pieces of cambric before he could look off.

MOLLY BRAZEN Oh, dear madam! But sure nothing can come up to your handling of laces! And then you have such a sweet deluding tongue! To cheat a man is nothing; but the woman must have fine parts indeed who cheats a woman!

MRS. VIXEN Lace, madam, lies in a small compass, and is of easy conveyance. But you are apt, madam, to think too well of your friends.

MRS. COAXER If any woman hath more art than another, to be sure, 'tis Jenny Diver. Though her fellow be never so agreeable, she can pick his pocket as coolly as if money were her only pleasure. Now, that is a command of the passions uncommon in a woman!

JENNY I never go to the tavern with a man but in the view of business. I have other hours and other sort of men for my pleasure. But had I your address,[15] madam—

MACHEATH Have done with your compliments, ladies, and drink about. You are not so fond of me, Jenny, as you use to be.

JENNY 'Tis not convenient, sir, to show my kindness among so many rivals. 'Tis your own choice, and not the warmth of my inclination, that will determine you.

AIR XXIII—*All in a misty morning, etc.*

Before the barn-door crowing,
 The cock by hens attended,
His eyes around him throwing,
 Stands for a while suspended.

13. Silk merchants.
14. Expensive silks from France and Holland.
15. Skill, dexterity.

> Then one he singles from the crew,
>> And cheers the happy hen;
> With 'How do you do,' and 'How do you do,'
>> And 'How do you do' again.

MACHEATH   Ah Jenny! thou art a dear slut.

TRULL   Pray, madam, were you ever in keeping?

TAWDRY   I hope, madam, I han't been so long upon the town but I have met with some good fortune as well as my neighbours.

TRULL   Pardon me, madam, I meant no harm by the question; 'twas only in the way of conversation.

TAWDRY   Indeed, madam, if I had not been a fool, I might have lived very handsomely with my last friend. But upon his missing five guineas, he turned me off. Now, I never suspected he had counted them.

SLAMMEKIN   Who do you look upon, madam, as your best sort of keepers?

TRULL   That, madam, is thereafter as they be.

SLAMMEKIN   I, madam, was once kept by a Jew; and bating their religion, to women they are a good sort of people.

TAWDRY   Now for my part, I own I like an old fellow; for we always make them pay for what they can't do.

VIXEN   A spruce prentice, let me tell you, ladies, is no ill thing; they bleed freely.[16] I have sent at least two or three dozen of them in my time to the plantations.

JENNY   But to be sure, sir, with so much good fortune as you have had upon the road, you must be grown immensely rich.

MACHEATH   The road, indeed, hath done me justice, but the gaming-table hath been my ruin.

JENNY

AIR XXIV—*When once I lay with another man's wife, etc.*

> The gamesters and lawyers are jugglers [17] alike,
>> If they meddle, your all is in danger:
> Like gypsies, if once they can finger a souse,[18]
>> Your pockets they pick, and they pilfer your house,
> And give your estate to a stranger.

A man of courage should never put anything to the risk, but his life. These are the tools of a man of honour. Cards and dice are only fit for cowardly cheats, who prey upon their friends.
[*She takes up his pistol.* TAWDRY *takes up the other.*]

TAWDRY   This, sir, is fitter for your hand. Besides your loss of money, 'tis a loss to the ladies. Gaming takes you off from women. How fond could I be of you!—but before company, 'tis ill-bred.

MACHEATH   Wanton hussies!

JENNY   I must and will have a kiss, to give my wine a zest.

[*They take him about the neck, and make signs to Peachum and Constables, who rush in upon him*]

16. Pay well; and are later transported for robbing their masters.
17. Cunning cheats.
18. Small amount of money.

SCENE V

[*To them* PEACHUM *and* CONSTABLES]

PEACHUM   I seize you, sir, as my prisoner.

MACHEATH   Was this well done, Jenny? Women are decoy ducks: who can trust them? Beasts, jades, jilts, harpies, furies, whores!

PEACHUM   Your case, Mr. Macheath, is not particular. The greatest heroes have been ruined by women. But, do them justice, I must own they are a pretty sort of creatures, if we could trust them. You must now, sir, take your leave of the ladies, and if they have a mind to make you a visit, they will be sure to find you at home. This gentleman, ladies, lodges in Newgate. Constables, wait upon the captain to his lodgings.

MACHEATH

AIR XXV—*When first I laid siege to my Chloris, etc.*

At the tree I shall suffer with pleasure,
At the tree I shall suffer with pleasure;
    Let me go where I will,
    In all kinds of ill,
I shall find no such furies as these are.

PEACHUM   Ladies, I'll take care the reckoning [19] shall be discharged.

[*Exit* MACHEATH, *guarded, with* PEACHUM *and* CONSTABLES]

SCENE VI

[*The* WOMEN *remain*]

VIXEN   Look ye, Mrs. Jenny; though Mr. Peachum may have made a private bargain with you and Suky Tawdry for betraying the captain, as we were all assisting, we ought all to share alike.

COAXER   I think Mr. Peachum, after so long an acquaintance, might have trusted me as well as Jenny Diver.

SLAMMEKIN   I am sure at least three men of his hanging, and in a year's time too (if he did me justice), should be set down to my account.

TRULL   Mrs. Slammekin, that is not fair. For you know one of them was taken in bed with me.

JENNY   As far as a bowl of punch or a treat, I believe Mrs. Suky will join with me. As for anything else, ladies, you cannot in conscience expect it.

SLAMMEKIN   Dear madam—

TRULL   I would not for the world—[20]

SLAMMEKIN   'Tis impossible for me—

TRULL   As I hope to be saved, madam—

SLAMMEKIN   Nay, then I must stay here all night—

TRULL   Since you command me.   [*Exeunt with great ceremony*]

SCENE VII. *Newgate*

[LOCKIT, TURNKEYS, MACHEATH, CONSTABLES]

LOCKIT   Noble captain, you are welcome. You have not been a lodger of mine this year and half. You know the custom, sir. Garnish,[21] captain, garnish! Hand me down those fetters there.

19. The bill (for drinks or their services).
20. The ladies debate, in a style of high courtesy, who shall go through the door first.
21. A demand for a fee.

MACHEATH   Those, Mr. Lockit, seem to be the heaviest of the whole set! With your leave, I should like the further pair better.

LOCKIT   Look ye, captain, we know what is fittest for our prisoners. When a gentleman uses me with civility, I always do the best I can to please him.—Hand them down, I say.—We have them of all prices, from one guinea to ten, and 'tis fitting every gentleman should please himself.

MACHEATH   I understand you, sir. [*Gives money*] The fees here are so many and so exorbitant, that few fortunes can bear the expence of getting off handsomely or of dying like a gentleman.

LOCKIT   Those, I see, will fit the captain better. Take down the further pair. Do but examine them, sir,—never was better work. How genteelly they are made! They will fit as easy as a glove, and the nicest man in England might not be ashamed to wear them. [*He puts on the chains*] If I had the best gentleman in the land in my custody, I could not equip him more handsomely. And so, sir—I now leave you to your private meditations.

SCENE VIII

[MACHEATH]

AIR XXVI—*Courtiers, courtiers, think it no harm, etc.*

Man may escape from rope and gun;
Nay, some have outlived the doctor's pill;
Who takes a woman must be undone,
    That basilisk [22] is sure to kill.
The fly that sips treacle is lost in the sweets,
So he that tastes woman, woman, woman,
    He that tastes woman, ruin meets.

To what a woeful plight have I brought myself! Here must I (all day long, till I am hanged) be confined to hear the reproaches of a wench who lays her ruin at my door. I am in the custody of her father, and to be sure if he knows of the matter, I shall have a fine time on't betwixt this and my execution. But I promised the wench marriage. What signifies a promise to a woman? Does not a man in marriage itself promise a hundred things that he never means to perform? Do all we can, women will believe us; for they look upon a promise as an excuse for following their own inclinations.—But here comes Lucy, and I cannot get from her. Would I were deaf!

SCENE IX

[MACHEATH, LUCY]

LUCY   You base man, you, how can you look me in the face after what hath passed between us? See here, perfidious wretch, how I am forced to bear about the load of infamy you have laid upon me—O Macheath!

22. A mythical reptile that can kill by its look.

thou hast robbed me of my quiet—to see thee tortured would give me pleasure.

AIR XXVII—*A lovely lass to a friar came, etc.*

Thus when a good housewife sees a rat
    In a trap in the morning taken,
With pleasure her heart goes pit-a-pat
    In revenge for her loss of bacon.
        Then she throws him
        To the dog or cat,
To be worried, crushed, and shaken.

MACHEATH   Have you no bowels,[23] no tenderness, my dear Lucy, to see a husband in these circumstances?

LUCY   A husband!

MACHEATH   In every respect but the form, and that, my dear, may be said over us at any time. Friends should not insist upon ceremonies. From a man of honour, his word is as good as his bond.

LUCY   'Tis the pleasure of all you fine men to insult the women you have ruined.

AIR XXVIII—*'Twas when the sea was roaring, etc.*

How cruel are the traitors
    Who lie and swear in jest,
To cheat unguarded creatures
    Of virtue, fame, and rest!

Whoever steals a shilling
    Through shame the guilt conceals;
In love, the perjured villain
    With boasts the theft reveals.

MACHEATH   The very first opportunity my dear (have but patience), you shall be my wife in whatever manner you please.

LUCY   Insinuating monster! And so you think I know nothing of the affair of Miss Polly Peachum. I could tear thy eyes out!

MACHEATH   Sure, Lucy, you can't be such a fool as to be jealous of Polly!

LUCY   Are you not married to her, you brute, you?

MACHEATH   Married! Very good. The wench gives it out only to vex thee, and to ruin me in thy good opinion. 'Tis true I go to the house; I chat with the girl, I kiss her, I say a thousand things to her (as all gentlemen do) that mean nothing, to divert myself; and now the silly jade hath set it about that I am married to her, to let me know what she would be at. Indeed, my dear Lucy, these violent passions may be of ill consequence to a woman in your condition.

LUCY   Come, come, captain, for all your assurance, you know that Miss Polly hath put it out of your power to do me the justice you promised me.

23. Compassion.

MACHEATH   A jealous woman believes everything her passion suggests. To convince you of my sincerity, if we can find the ordinary, I shall have no scruples of making you my wife—and I know the consequence of having two at a time.

LUCY   That you are only to be hanged, and so get rid of them both.

MACHEATH   I am ready, my dear Lucy, to give you satisfaction—if you think there is any in marriage. What can a man of honour say more?

LUCY   So then it seems you are not married to Miss Polly.

MACHEATH   You know, Lucy, the girl is prodigiously conceited. No man can say a civil thing to her, but (like other fine ladies) her vanity makes her think he's her own for ever and ever.

AIR XXIX—*The sun had loosed his weary teams, etc.*

The first time at the looking-glass
   The mother sets her daughter,
The image strikes the smiling lass
   With self-love ever after.
Each time she looks, she, fonder grown,
   Thinks every charm grows stronger.
But alas, vain maid, all eyes but your own
   Can see you are not younger.

When women consider their own beauties, they are all alike unreasonable in their demands; for they expect their lovers should like them as long as they like themselves.

LUCY   Yonder is my father. Perhaps this way we may light upon the ordinary, who shall try if you will be as good as your word; for I long to be made an honest woman.   *[Exeunt]*

SCENE X. *Lockit's room in Newgate*

[PEACHUM, LOCKIT *with an account-book*]

LOCKIT   In this last affair, brother Peachum, we are agreed. You have consented to go halves in Macheath.

PEACHUM   We shall never fall out about an execution. But as to that article, pray how stands our last year's account?

LOCKIT   If you will run your eye over it, you'll find 'tis fair and clearly stated.

PEACHUM   This long arrear of the government [24] is very hard upon us! Can it be expected that we should hang our acquaintance for nothing, when our betters will hardly save theirs without being paid for it? Unless the people in employment [25] pay better, I promise them for the future, I shall let other rogues live besides their own.

LOCKIT   Perhaps, brother, they are afraid these matters may be carried too far. We are treated, too, by them with contempt, as if our profession were not reputable.

24. In payment of rewards for capture and conviction of criminals.
25. Official posts.

PEACHUM   In one respect, indeed, our employment may be reckoned dishonest, because, like great statesmen, we encourage those who betray their friends.

LOCKIT   Such language, brother, anywhere else might turn to your prejudice. Learn to be more guarded, I beg you.

AIR XXX—*How happy are we, etc.*

When you censure the age,
   Be cautious and sage,
Lest the courtiers offended should be.
   If you mention vice or bribe,
   'Tis so pat to all the tribe
Each cries—That was levelled at me.

PEACHUM   Here's poor Ned Clincher's name, I see. Sure, brother Lockit, there was a little unfair proceeding in Ned's case; for he told me in the condemned hold, that for value received, you had promised him a session or two longer without molestation.

LOCKIT   Mr. Peachum, this is the first time my honour was ever called in question.

PEACHUM   Business is at an end if once we act dishonourably.

LOCKIT   Who accuses me?

PEACHUM   You are warm, brother.[26]

LOCKIT   He that attacks my honour, attacks my livelihood. And this usage, sir, is not to be borne.

PEACHUM   Since you provoke me to speak, I must tell you too, that Mrs. Coaxer charges you with defrauding her of her information-money for the apprehending of curl-pated Hugh. Indeed, indeed, brother, we must punctually pay our spies, or we shall have no information.

LOCKIT   Is this language to me, sirrah? Who have saved you from the gallows, sirrah!   [*Collaring each other*]

PEACHUM   If I am hanged, it shall be for ridding the world of an arrant rascal.

LOCKIT   This hand shall do the office of the halter [27] you deserve, and throttle you, you dog!   [*They break apart*]

PEACHUM   —Brother, brother,—we are both losers in the dispute—for you know we have it in our power to hang each other. You should not be so passionate.

LOCKIT   Nor you so provoking.

PEACHUM   'Tis our mutual interest, 'tis for the interest of the world, we should agree. If I said anything, brother, to the prejudice of your character, I ask pardon.

LOCKIT   Brother Peachum, I can forgive as well as resent.—Give me your hand. Suspicion does not become a friend.

PEACHUM   I only meant to give you occasion to justify yourself. But I must

26. Suggesting the growing quarrel between Walpole and his brother-in-law Lord Townshend, who was to leave office in 1730; with a possible imitation of the quarrel of Brutus and Cassius in Shakespeare's *Julius Caesar*.
27. Hangman's noose.

now step home, for I expect the gentleman about this snuff-box that
Filch nimmed two nights ago in the park. I appointed him at this hour.
[*Exit*]

SCENE XI

[LOCKIT, LUCY]

LOCKIT   Whence come you, hussy?

LUCY   My tears might answer that question.

LOCKIT   You have then been whimpering and fondling, like a spaniel, over the
fellow that hath abused you.

LUCY   One can't help love; one can't cure it. 'Tis not in my power to obey you,
and hate him.

LOCKIT   Learn to bear your husband's death like a reasonable woman. 'Tis
not the fashion, nowadays, so much as to affect sorrow upon these
occasions. No woman would ever marry if she had not the chance of
mortality for a release. Act like a woman of spirit, hussy, and thank your
father for what he is doing.

LUCY

AIR XXXI—*Of a noble race was Shenkin, etc.*

Is then his fate decreed, sir?
　　Such a man can I think of quitting?
When first we met, so moves me yet,
　　Oh, see how my heart is splitting!

LOCKIT   Look ye, Lucy, there is no saving him. So, I think, you must even do
like other widows,—buy yourself weeds and be cheerful.

AIR XXXII

You'll think, ere many days ensue,
　　This sentence not severe;
I hang your husband, child, 'tis true,
　　But with him hang your care.
　　　　Twang dang dillo dee.

Like a good wife, go moan over your dying husband; that, child, is your
duty.—Consider, girl, you can't have the man and the money too—so
make yourself as easy as you can by getting all you can from him.

[*Exeunt*]

SCENE XII. *Another part of the prison*

[LUCY, MACHEATH]

LUCY   Though the ordinary was out of the way today, I hope, my dear, you
will, upon the first opportunity, quiet my scruples.—Oh, sir!—my
father's hard heart is not to be softened, and I am in the utmost despair.

MACHEATH   But if I could raise a small sum—would not twenty guineas, think
you, move him?—Of all the arguments in the way of business, the

perquisite [28] is the most prevailing.—Your father's perquisites for the escape of prisoners must amount to a considerable sum in the year. Money well timed and properly applied will do anything.

AIR XXXIII—*London ladies*

If you at an office solicit your due,
  And would not have matters neglected;
You must quicken the clerk with the perquisite too,
  To do what his duty directed.
Or would you the frowns of a lady prevent,
  She too has this palpable failing,
The perquisite softens her into consent;
  That reason with all is prevailing.

LUCY   What love or money can do shall be done, for all my comfort depends upon your safety.

SCENE XIII

[LUCY, MACHEATH, POLLY]

POLLY   Where is my dear husband?—Was a rope ever intended for this neck? —Oh, let me throw my arms about it, and throttle thee with love!— Why dost thou turn away from me?—'Tis thy Polly—'tis thy wife.

MACHEATH   Was there ever such an unfortunate rascal as I am!

LUCY   Was there ever such another villain!

POLLY   O Macheath! was it for this we parted? Taken! imprisoned! tried! hanged!—cruel reflection! I'll stay with thee till death—no force shall tear thy dear wife from thee now.—What means my love?—not one kind word!—not one kind look! Think what thy Polly suffers to see thee in this condition.

AIR XXXIV—*All in the downs, etc.*

Thus when the swallow, seeking prey,
  Within the sash is closely pent,
His consort, with bemoaning lay,
  Without, sits pining for the event.
Her chattering lovers all around her skim;
  She heeds them not (poor bird)—her soul's with him.

MACHEATH   [*Aside*] I must disown her. The wench is distracted.

LUCY   Am I then bilked of my virtue? Can I have no reparation? Sure, men were born to lie, and women to believe them. O villain! villain!

POLLY   Am I not thy wife? Thy neglect of me, thy aversion to me, too severely proves it. Look on me. Tell me; am I not thy wife?

LUCY   Perfidious wretch!

POLLY   Barbarous husband!

LUCY   Hadst thou been hanged five months ago, I had been happy.

POLLY   And I too. If you had been kind to me till death, it would not have

28. "Something gained by a place or office over and above the settled wages" (Johnson).

vexed me—and that's no very unreasonable request (though from a wife) to a man who hath not above seven or eight days to live.

LUCY   Art thou then married to another? Hast thou two wives, monster?

MACHEATH   If women's tongues can cease for an answer—hear me.

LUCY   I won't! Flesh and blood can't bear my usage.

POLLY   Shall I not claim my own? Justice bids me speak.

MACHEATH

AIR XXXV—*Have you heard of a frolicsome ditty, etc.*

How happy I could be with either,
  Were t'other dear charmer away!
But while you thus tease me together,
To neither a word will I say;
  But tol de rol, etc.

POLLY   Sure, my dear, there ought to be some preference shown to a wife! At least she may claim the appearance of it. [*Aside*] He must be distracted with his misfortunes, or he could not use me thus!

LUCY   O villain, villain! thou hast deceived me—I could even inform against thee with pleasure. Not a prude wishes more heartily to have facts against her intimate acquaintance, than I now wish to have facts against thee. I would have her satisfaction, and they should all out.

AIR XXXVI—*Irish Trot*

POLLY   I'm bubbled.[29]
LUCY   I'm bubbled!
POLLY   Oh how I am troubled!
LUCY   Bamboozled, and bit!
POLLY   My distresses are doubled.
LUCY
When you come to the tree, should the hangman refuse,
These fingers, with pleasure, could fasten the noose.
POLLY   I'm bubbled, etc.

MACHEATH   Be pacified, my dear Lucy! This is all a fetch of Polly's to make me desperate with you in case I get off. If I am hanged, she would fain have the credit of being thought my widow.—Really, Polly, this is no time for a dispute of this sort; for whenever you are talking of marriage, I am thinking of hanging.

POLLY   And hast thou the heart to persist in disowning me?

MACHEATH   And hast thou the heart to persist in persuading me that I am married? Why, Polly, dost thou seek to aggravate my misfortunes?

LUCY   Really, Miss Peachum, you but expose yourself. Besides, 'tis barbarous in you to worry a gentleman in his circumstances.

POLLY

AIR XXXVII

Cease your funning,
  Force or cunning

29. Cheated.

Never shall my heart trepan.[30]
  All these sallies
  Are but malice
To seduce my constant man.
  'Tis most certain,
  By their flirting,
Women oft have envy shown;
  Pleased to ruin
  Other's wooing;
Never happy in their own!

LUCY   Decency, madam, methinks, might teach you to behave yourself with some reserve with the husband while his wife is present.

MACHEATH   But, seriously, Polly, this is carrying the joke a little too far.

LUCY   If you are determined, madam, to raise a disturbance in the prison, I shall be obliged to send for the turnkey to show you the door. I am sorry, madam, you force me to be so ill-bred.

POLLY   Give me leave to tell you, madam; these forward airs don't become you in the least, madam. And my duty, madam, obliges me to stay with my husband, madam.

LUCY

AIR XXXVIII—*Good-morrow, gossip Joan, etc.*

Why, how now, Madam Flirt?
  If you thus must chatter;
And are for flinging dirt,
  Let's try who best can spatter!
    Madam Flirt!

POLLY

Why, how now, saucy jade;
  Sure the wench is tipsy!
How can you see me made [*To him*]
  The scoff of such a gipsy?
    Saucy jade! [*To her*]

SCENE XIV

[LUCY, MACHEATH, POLLY, PEACHUM]

PEACHUM   Where's my wench? Ah hussy! hussy! Come you home, you slut; and when your fellow is hanged, hang yourself, to make your family some amends.

POLLY   Dear, dear father, do not tear me from him! I must speak; I have more to say to him. [*To* MACHEATH] Oh! twist thy fetters about me, that he may not haul me from thee!

PEACHUM   Sure, all women are alike! If ever they commit the folly, they are sure to commit another by exposing themselves. Away—not a word more—you are my prisoner now, hussy!

POLLY   [*Holding* MACHEATH, PEACHUM *pulling her*]

30. Deceive, beguile.

AIR XXXIX—*Irish howl*

No power on earth can e'er divide
The knot that sacred love hath tied.
When parents draw against our mind,
The true-love's knot they faster bind.
  Oh, oh ray, oh amborah—Oh, oh, etc.

[*Exeunt* POLLY *and* PEACHUM]

SCENE XV

[LUCY, MACHEATH]

MACHEATH I am naturally compassionate, wife, so that I could not use the wench as she deserved, which made you at first suspect there was something in what she said.

LUCY Indeed, my dear, I was strangely puzzled.

MACHEATH If that had been the case, her father would never have brought me into this circumstance. No, Lucy, I had rather die than be false to thee.

LUCY How happy am I if you say this from your heart! For I love thee so, that I could sooner bear to see thee hanged than in the arms of another.

MACHEATH But couldst thou bear to see me hanged?

LUCY O Macheath, I can never live to see that day.

MACHEATH You see, Lucy; in the account of love you are in my debt, and you must now be convinced that I rather choose to die than to be another's. Make me, if possible, love thee more, and let me owe my life to thee. If you refuse to assist me, Peachum and your father will immediately put me beyond all means of escape.

LUCY My father, I know, hath been drinking hard with the prisoners, and I fancy he is now taking his nap in his own room. If I can procure the keys, shall I go off with thee, my dear?

MACHEATH If we are together, 'twill be impossible to lie concealed. As soon as the search begins to be a little cool, I will send to thee. Till then, my heart is thy prisoner.

LUCY Come then, my dear husband, owe thy life to me—and though you love me not—be grateful. But that Polly runs in my head strangely.

MACHEATH A moment of time may make us unhappy forever.

LUCY

AIR XL—*The lass of Patie's mill, etc.*

I like the fox shall grieve,
  Whose mate hath left her side,
Whom hounds, from morn till eve,
  Chase o'er the country wide,
Where can my lover hide?
  Where cheat the wary pack?
If love be not his guide,
  He never will come back!

ACT III

SCENE I. *Newgate*

[LOCKIT, LUCY]

LOCKIT   To be sure, wench, you must have been aiding and abetting to help him to this escape.

LUCY   Sir, here hath been Peachum and his daughter Polly, and to be sure they know the ways of Newgate as well as if they had been born and bred in the place all their lives. Why must all your suspicion light upon me?

LOCKIT   Lucy, Lucy, I will have none of these shuffling answers.

LUCY   Well then, if I know anything of him, I wish I may be burnt!

LOCKIT   Keep your temper, Lucy, or I shall pronounce you guilty.

LUCY   Keep yours, sir. I do wish I may be burnt, I do. And what can I say more to convince you.

LOCKIT   Did he tip handsomely? How much did he come down with? Come, hussy, don't cheat your father, and I shall not be angry with you. Perhaps you have made a better bargain with him than I could have done. How much, my good girl?

LUCY   You know, sir, I am fond of him, and would have given money to have kept him with me.

LOCKIT   Ah, Lucy! thy education might have put thee more upon thy guard; for a girl in the bar of an alehouse is always besieged.

LUCY   Dear sir, mention not my education, for 'twas to that I owe my ruin.

AIR XLI—*If love's a sweet passion, etc.*

> When young, at the bar you first taught me to score,
> And bid me be free of my lips, and no more.
> I was kissed by the parson, the squire, and the sot;
> When the guest was departed, the kiss was forgot.
> But his kiss was so sweet, and so closely he prest,
> That I languished and pined till I granted the rest.

If you can forgive me, sir, I will make a fair [1] confession, for to be sure he hath been a most barbarous villain to me.

LOCKIT   And so you have let him escape, hussy, have you?

LUCY   When a woman loves, a kind look, a tender word can persuade her to anything,—and I could ask no other bribe.

LOCKIT   Thou wilt always be a vulgar slut, Lucy. If you would not be looked upon as a fool, you should never do anything but upon the foot of interest. Those that act otherwise are their own bubbles.

LUCY   But love, sir, is a misfortune that may happen to the most discreet woman, and in love we are all fools alike. Notwithstanding all he swore, I am now fully convinced that Polly Peachum is actually his wife. Did I let him escape (fool that I was) to go to her? Polly will wheedle herself into his money, and then Peachum will hang him, and cheat us both.

1. Open.

LOCKIT   So I am to be ruined, because, forsooth, you must be in love!—a very
          pretty excuse!
LUCY   I could murder that impudent happy strumpet! I gave him his life,
          and that creature enjoys the sweets of it. Ungrateful Macheath!

   AIR XLII—*South-sea Ballad*

   My love is all madness and folly,
        Alone I lie,
        Toss, tumble, and cry;
   What a happy creature is Polly!
   Was e'er such a wretch as I!
   With rage I redden like scarlet,
   That my dear, inconstant varlet,
        Stark blind to my charms,
        Is lost in the arms
   Of that jilt, that inveigling harlot!
   This, this my resentment alarms.
        Stark blind to my charms,
        Is lost in the arms
   Of that jilt, that inveigling harlot!

LOCKIT   And so, after all this michief, I must stay here to be entertained
          with your caterwauling, Mistress Puss! Out of my sight, wanton strum-
          pet! You shall fast and fortify yourself into reason, with now and then
          a little handsome discipline to bring you to your senses. Go! [*Exit* LUCY]

   SCENE II

   [LOCKIT]

   —Peachum then intends to outwit me in this affair, but I'll be even
   with him. The dog is leaky in his liquor; so I'll ply him that way, get
   the secret from him, and turn this affair to my own advantage. Lions,
   wolves, and vultures don't live together in herds, droves, or flocks. Of
   all animals of prey, man is the only sociable one. Every one of us
   preys upon his neighbour, and yet we herd together. Peachum is my
   companion, my friend. According to the custom of the world, indeed,
   he may quote thousands of precedents for cheating me. And shall not
   I make use of the privilege of friendship to make him a return?

   AIR XLIII—*Packington's Pound*

   Thus gamesters united in friendship are found,
   Though they know that their industry all is a cheat;
   They flock to their prey at the dice-box's sound,
   And join to promote one another's deceit.
        But if by mishap
        They fail of a chap,[2]

2. Customer, victim.

To keep in their hands they each other entrap.
Like pikes,[3] lank with hunger, who miss of their ends,
They bite their companions, and prey on their friends.

Now, Peachum, you and I, like honest tradesmen, are to have a fair
trial which of us two can over-reach the other. [*Calls*] Lucy!

[*Enter* LUCY]

Are there any of Peachum's people now in the house?
LUCY   Filch, sir, is drinking a quartern [4] of strong waters in the next room
with Black Moll.
LOCKIT   Bid him come to me.   [*Exit* LUCY]

SCENE III

[LOCKIT, FILCH]

LOCKIT   Why, boy, thou lookest as if thou wert half starved—like a shotten
herring.[5]
FILCH   One had need have the constitution of a horse to go through the
business. Since the favourite child-getter was disabled by mishap, I
have picked up a little money by helping the ladies to a pregnancy
against their being called down to sentence. But if a man cannot get
an honest livelihood any easier way, I am sure 'tis what I can't undertake for another session.
LOCKIT   Truly, if that great man should tip off,[6] 'twould be an irreparable
loss. The vigour and prowess of a knight-errant never saved half of the
ladies in distress that he hath done.—But, boy, canst thou tell me
where thy master is to be found?
FILCH   At his lock, sir, at the Crooked Billet.
LOCKIT   Very well. I have nothing more with you. [*Exit* FILCH] I'll go to
him there, for I have many important affairs to settle with him; and
in the way of those transactions, I'll artfully get into his secret, so that
Macheath shall not remain a day longer out of my clutches.

SCENE IV. *A gaming-house*

[MACHEATH *in a fine tarnished coat,* BEN BUDGE, MATT OF THE MINT]

MACHEATH   I am sorry, gentlemen, the road was so barren of money. When
my friends are in difficulties, I am always glad that my fortune can
be serviceable to them. [*Gives them money*] You see, gentlemen, I am
not a mere court friend, who professes everything and will do nothing.

3. The pike was considered the most voracious of fish, and the pike pond is a frequent
eighteenth-century symbol of a scene of ruthless competition. The pike, moreover, is one
of the few creatures besides man that preys upon his own kind; cf. Rochester's *Satire upon
Mankind* for the theme.
4. Quarter-pint.
5. A herring that has spawned and shows signs of depletion.
6. That is, if Macheath (the "favourite child-getter") should die.

AIR XLIV—*Lillibullero*

The modes of the court so common are grown,
    That a true friend can hardly be met;
Friendship for interest is but a loan,
    Which they let out for what they can get.
        'Tis true, you find
        Some friends so kind,
Who will give you good counsel themselves to defend.
    In sorrowful ditty,
    They promise, they pity,
But shift you, for money, from friend to friend.

But we, gentlemen, have still honour enough to break through the corruptions of the world. And while I can serve you, you may command me.

BEN   It grieves my heart that so generous a man should be involved in such difficulties as oblige him to live with such ill company, and herd with gamesters.

MATT   See the partiality of mankind! One man may steal a horse, better than another look over a hedge.[7] Of all mechanics, of all servile handicraftsmen, a gamester is the vilest. But yet, as many of the quality are of the profession, he is admitted amongst the politest company. I wonder we are not more respected.

MACHEATH   There will be deep play tonight at Marybone and consequently money may be picked up upon the road. Meet me there, and I'll give you the hint who is worth setting.[8]

MATT   The fellow with a brown coat with a narrow gold binding, I am told, is never without money.

MACHEATH   What do you mean, Matt? Sure you will not think of meddling with him! He's a good honest kind of a fellow, and one of us.

BEN   To be sure, sir, we will put ourselves under your direction.

MACHEATH   Have an eye upon the money-lenders. A rouleau[9] or two would prove a pretty sort of an expedition. I hate extortion.[10]

MATT   These rouleaus are very pretty things. I hate your bank bills. There is such a hazard in putting them off.

MACHEATH   There is a certain man of distinction who in his time hath nicked me out of a great deal of the ready. He is in my cash,[11] Ben. I'll point him out to you this evening, and you shall draw upon him for the debt.
—The company are met; I hear the dice-box in the other room. So, gentlemen, your servant! You'll meet me at Marybone.   [*Exeunt*]

---

7. That is, more safely than another man can merely look at one.
8. Setting upon to rob.
9. A roll of gold coins.
10. That is, the extortion of moneylenders (or usurers).
11. That is, he is in debt for the cash ("ready") of which he has cheated ("nicked") me; probably an allusion, as in the scene immediately following, to that "man of distinction" Walpole.

SCENE V. PEACHUM's *lock. A table with wine, brandy, pipes and tobacco*

[PEACHUM, LOCKIT]

LOCKIT   The Coronation account,[12] brother Peachum, is of so intricate a nature, that I believe it will never be settled.

PEACHUM   It consists, indeed, of a great variety of articles. It was worth to our people, in fees of different kinds, above ten installments.[13] This is part of the account, brother, that lies open before us.

LOCKIT   A lady's tail [14] of rich brocade—that, I see, is disposed of—

PEACHUM   To Mrs. Diana Trapes, the tallywoman, and she will make a good hand on't in shoes and slippers, to trick out young ladies upon their going into keeping.

LOCKIT   But I don't see any article of the jewels.

PEACHUM   Those are so well known that they must be sent abroad. You'll find them entered under the article of exportation. As for the snuff-boxes, watches, swords, etc., I thought it best to enter them under their several heads.

LOCKIT   Seven and twenty women's pockets [15] complete, with the several things therein contained—all sealed, numbered, and entered.

PEACHUM   But, brother, it is impossible for us now to enter upon this affair.—We should have the whole day before us.—Besides, the account of the last half-year's plate is in a book by itself, which lies at the other office.

LOCKIT   Bring us then more liquor.—Today shall be for pleasure—tomorrow for business.—Ah, brother, those daughters of ours are two slippery hussies. Keep a watchful eye upon Polly, and Macheath in a day or two shall be our own again.

AIR XLV.—*Down in the North Country, etc.*

What gudgeons [16] are we men!
   Every woman's easy prey;
Though we have felt the hook, again
   We bite and they betray.
The bird that hath been trapped,
   When he hears his calling mate,
To her he flies, again he's clapped
   Within the wiry grate.

PEACHUM   But what signifies catching the bird if your daughter Lucy will set open the door of the cage?

LOCKIT   If men were answerable for the follies and frailities of their wives

---

12. The goods stolen from the crowd at the coronation of George II (October 11, 1727); perhaps "the large civil list secured by Walpole for George II, whereby Walpole kept control over the government" (Edgar V. Roberts).
13. Annual installations of the Lord Mayor, another occasion for theft.
14. Train.
15. Small purses.
16. Fish easily caught; dupes.

and daughters, no friends could keep a good correspondence together
for two days.—This is unkind of you, brother; for among good friends,
what they say or do goes for nothing.

[*Enter* A SERVANT]

SERVANT   Sir, here's Mrs. Diana Trapes wants to speak with you.

PEACHUM   Shall we admit her, brother Lockit?

LOCKIT   By all means—she's a good customer, and a fine-spoken woman—
and a woman who drinks and talks so freely will enliven the
conversation.

PEACHUM   Desire her to walk in.   [*Exit* SERVANT]

SCENE VI

[PEACHUM, LOCKIT, MRS. TRAPES]

PEACHUM   Dear Mrs. Dye, your servant—one may know by your kiss that
your gin is excellent.

TRAPES   I was always very curious [17] in my liquors.

LOCKIT   There is no perfumed breath like it. I have been long acquainted
with the flavour of those lips—han't I, Mrs. Dye?

TRAPES   Fill it up.—I take as large draughts of liquor as I did of love.—I
hate a flincher in either.

AIR XLVI—*A shepherd kept sheep, etc.*

In the days of my youth I could bill like a dove, fa, la, la, etc.
Like a sparrow at all times was ready for love, fa, la, la, etc.
The life of all mortals in kissing should pass,
Lip to lip while we're young—then lip to the glass, fa, la, etc.

But now, Mr. Peachum, to our business.—If you have blacks of any
kind brought in of late—manteaus, velvet scarves, petticoats—let it
be what it will, I am your chap; for all my ladies are very fond of
mourning.

PEACHUM   Why, look ye, Mrs. Dye—you deal so hard with us, that we can
afford to give the gentlemen who venture their lives for the goods
little or nothing.

TRAPES   The hard times oblige me to go very near in my dealing. To be sure,
of late years I have been a great sufferer by the Parliament.—Three
thousand pounds would hardly make me amends.—The act for destroying the Mint [18] was a severe cut upon our business—till then, if a
customer stepped out of the way—we knew where to have her. No
doubt you know Mrs. Coaxer—there's a wench now (till to-day) with
a good suit of clothes of mine upon her back, and I could never set
eyes upon her for three months together. Since the act, too, against

17. "Choosy," discriminating.
18. Passed in 1723 to end the Mint's status as a sanctuary for debtors on the ground that
the Southwark area had become a center for criminals.

imprisonment for small sums, my loss there too hath been very considerable; and it must be so, when a lady can borrow a handsome petticoat or a clean gown, and I not have the least hank [19] upon her! And, o' my conscience, nowadays most ladies take a delight in cheating when they can do it with safety!

PEACHUM Madam, you had a handsome gold watch of us t'other day for seven guineas. Considering we must have our profit—to a gentleman upon the road, a gold watch will be scarce worth the taking.

TRAPES Consider, Mr. Peachum, that watch was remarkable [20] and not of very safe sale. If you have any black velvet scarfs—they are handsome winter wear, and take with most gentlemen who deal with my customers. 'Tis I that put the ladies upon a good foot. 'Tis not youth or beauty that fixes their price. The gentlemen always pay according to their dress, from half a crown to two guineas; and yet those hussies make nothing of bilking me. Then, too, allowing for accidents.—I have eleven fine customers now down under the surgeon's hands; what with fees and other expenses, there are great goings-out, and no comings-in, and not a farthing to pay for at least a month's clothing. We run great risks—great risks indeed.

PEACHUM As I remember, you said something just now of a Mrs. Coaxer.

TRAPES Yes, sir. To be sure, I stripped her of a suit of my own clothes about two hours ago, and have left her as she should be, in her shift, with a lover of hers, at my house. She called him upstairs as he was going to Marybone in a hackney coach. And I hope, for her sake and mine, she will persuade the captain to redeem her, for the captain is very generous to the ladies.

LOCKIT What captain?

TRAPES He thought I did not know him—an intimate acquaintance of yours, Mr. Peachum—only Captain Macheath—as fine as a lord.

PEACHUM To-morrow, dear Mrs. Dye, you shall set your own price upon any of the goods you like. We have at least half a dozen velvet scarfs, and all at your service. Will you give me leave to make you a present of this suit of nightclothes for your own wearing?—But are you sure it is Captain Macheath?

TRAPES Though he thinks I have forgot him, nobody knows him better. I have taken a great deal of the captain's money in my time at second-hand, for he always loved to have his ladies well-dressed.

PEACHUM Mr. Lockit and I have a little business with the captain—you understand me—and we will satisfy you for Mrs. Coaxer's debt.

LOCKIT Depend upon it—we will deal like men of honour.

TRAPES I don't enquire after your affairs—so whatever happens, I wash my hands on't. It hath always been my maxim, that one friend should assist another.—But if you please, I'll take one of the scarfs home with me. 'Tis always good to have something in hand.

19. Hold, claim.
20. Identifiable.

SCENE VII. *Newgate*

[LUCY]

LUCY   Jealousy, rage, love, and fear are at once tearing me to pieces. How I am weatherbeaten and shattered with distresses!

AIR XLVII—*One evening, having lost my way, etc.*

I'm like a skiff on the ocean tossed,
Now high, now low, with each billow borne;
With her rudder broke, and her anchor lost,
    Deserted and all forlorn.
While thus I lie rolling and tossing all night,
That Polly lies sporting on seas of delight!
    Revenge, revenge, revenge,
Shall appease my restless sprite.

—I have the ratsbane ready. I run no risk; for I can lay her death upon the gin, and so many die of that naturally that I shall never be called in question. But say I were to be hanged—I never could be hanged for anything that would give me greater comfort than the poisoning that slut.

[*Enter* FILCH]

FILCH   Madam, here's our Miss Polly come to wait upon you.
LUCY   Show her in.

SCENE VIII

[LUCY, POLLY]

LUCY   Dear madam, your servant. I hope you will pardon my passion when I was so happy to see you last. I was so overrun with the spleen, that I was perfectly out of myself. And really when one hath the spleen, everything is to be excused by a friend.

AIR XLVIII—*Now Roger, I'll tell thee, because thou'rt my son, etc.*

When a wife's in her pout,
    (As she's sometimes, no doubt);
The good husband, as meek as a lamb,
    Her vapours to still,
    First grants her her will,
And the quieting draught is a dram.
Poor man! And the quieting draught is a dram.

—I wish all our quarrels might have so comfortable a reconciliation.
POLLY   I have no excuse for my own behaviour, madam, but my misfortunes. And really, madam, I suffer too upon your account.
LUCY   But, Miss Polly—in the way of friendship, will you give me leave to propose a glass of cordial to you?
POLLY   Strong waters are apt to give me the headache; I hope, madam, you will excuse me.

LUCY   Not the greatest lady in the land could have better in her closet, for her own private drinking. You seem mighty low in spirits, my dear.

POLLY   I am sorry, madam, my health will not allow me to accept of your offer. I should not have left you in the rude manner I did when we met last, madam, had not my papa hauled me away so unexpectedly. I was indeed somewhat provoked, and perhaps might use some expressions that were disrespectful. But really, madam, the captain treated me with so much contempt and cruelty, that I deserved your pity rather than your resentment.

LUCY   But since his escape, no doubt, all matters are made up again.—Ah Polly! Polly! 'tis I am the unhappy wife, and he loves you as if you were only his mistress.

POLLY   Sure, madam, you cannot think me so happy as to be the object of your jealousy! A man is always afraid of a woman who loves him too well—so that I must expect to be neglected and avoided.

LUCY   Then our cases, my dear Polly, are exactly alike. Both of us, indeed, have been too fond.

AIR XLIX—*O Bessy Bell*

POLLY   A curse attends that woman's love,
  Who always would be pleasing.
LUCY   The pertness of the billing dove,
  Like tickling, is but teasing.
POLLY   What then in love can woman do?
LUCY   If we grow fond they shun us.
POLLY   And when we fly them, they pursue.
LUCY   But leave us when they've won us.

LUCY   Love is so very whimsical in both sexes that it is impossible to be lasting. But my heart is particular,[21] and contradicts my own observation.

POLLY   But really, mistress Lucy, by his last behaviour, I think I ought to envy you. When I was forced from him, he did not show the least tenderness. But perhaps he hath a heart not capable of it.

AIR L—*Would fate to me Belinda give, etc.*

Among the men, coquets we find,
Who court by turns all womankind;
And we grant all their hearts desired,
When they are flattered and admired.

The coquets of both sexes are self-lovers, and that is a love no other whatever can dispossess. I fear, my dear Lucy, our husband is one of those.

LUCY   Away with these melancholy reflections!—indeed, my dear Polly, we are both of us a cup too low. [*Going*] Let me prevail upon you to accept of my offer.

21. Peculiar, eccentric.

AIR LI—*Come, sweet lass, etc.*

> Come, sweet lass,
> Let's banish sorrow
> 'Till to-morrow;
> Come, sweet lass,
> Let's take a chirping [22] glass.
> Wine can clear
> The vapours of despair;
> And make us light as air;
> Then drink, and banish care.

I can't bear, child, to see you in such low spirits. And I must persuade you to what I know will do you good. [*Aside*] I shall now soon be even with the hypocritical strumpet.   [*Exit* LUCY]

SCENE IX

[POLLY]

POLLY   All this wheedling of Lucy cannot be for nothing—at this time too, when I know she hates me!—The dissembling of a woman is always the forerunner of mischief.—By pouring strong waters down my throat, she thinks to pump some secret out of me. I'll be upon my guard and won't taste a drop of her liquor, I'm resolved.

SCENE X

[LUCY, *with strong waters;* POLLY]

LUCY   Come, Miss Polly.

POLLY   Indeed, child, you have given yourself trouble to no purpose.—You must, my dear, excuse me.

LUCY   Really, Miss Polly, you are so squeamishly affected about taking a cup of strong waters as a lady before company. I vow, Polly, I shall take it monstrously ill if you refuse me.—Brandy and men (though women love them never so well) are always taken by us with some reluctance —unless 'tis in private.

POLLY   I protest, madam, it goes against me. What do I see! Macheath again in custody!—Now every glimmering of happiness is lost.
                    [*Drops the glass of liquor on the ground*]

LUCY   [*Aside*] Since things are thus, I am glad the wench hath escaped: for by this event 'tis plain she was not happy enough to deserve to be poisoned.

SCENE XI

[LOCKIT, MACHEATH, PEACHUM, LUCY, POLLY]

LOCKIT   Set your heart to rest, captain.—You have neither the chance of love or money for another escape; for you are ordered to be called down upon your trial immediately.

22. Cheerful.

PEACHUM   Away, hussies!—This is not a time for a man to be hampered with his wives. You see, the gentleman is in chains already.

LUCY   O husband, husband, my heart longed to see thee; but to see thee thus distracts me!

POLLY   Will not my dear husband look upon his Polly? Why hadst thou not flown to me for protection? With me thou hadst been safe.

AIR LII—*The last time I went o'er the moor, etc.*

POLLY   Hither, dear husband, turn your eyes.

LUCY   Bestow one glance to cheer me.

POLLY   Think, with that look, thy Polly dies.

LUCY   Oh shun me not—but hear me.

POLLY   'Tis Polly sues.

LUCY   —'Tis Lucy speaks.

POLLY   Is thus true love requited?

LUCY   My heart is bursting.

POLLY   —Mine too breaks.

LUCY   Must I?

POLLY   —Must I be slighted?

MACHEATH   What would you have me say, ladies?—You see, this affair will soon be at an end without my disobliging either of you.

PEACHUM   But the settling this point, captain, might prevent a lawsuit between your two widows.

MACHEATH

AIR LIII—*Tom Tinker's my true love, etc.*

Which way shall I turn me? How can I decide?
Wives, the day of our death, are as fond as a bride.
One wife is too much for most husbands to hear,
But two at a time there's no mortal can bear.
This way, and that way, and which way I will,
What would comfort the one, t'other wife would take ill.

POLLY   [*Aside*] But if his own misfortunes have made him insensible to mine, a father sure will be more compassionate. [*To* PEACHUM] Dear, dear sir, sink [23] the material evidence, and bring him off at his trial! Polly upon her knees begs it of you.

AIR LIV—*I am a poor shepherd undone*

When my hero in court appears,
    And stands arraigned for his life;
Then think of poor Polly's tears;
    For ah! poor Polly's his wife.
Like the sailor he holds up his hand,
    Distressed on the dashing wave.

23. Conceal.

To die a dry death at land,
   Is as bad as a watery grave.
      And alas, poor Polly;
      Alack, and well-a-day!
      Before I was in love,
      Oh, every month was May!

LUCY   [*To* LOCKIT] If Peachum's heart is hardened, sure you, sir, will have more compassion on a daughter. I know the evidence is in your power. How can you be a tyrant to me?   [*Kneeling*]

AIR LV—*Ianthe the lovely, etc.*

When he holds up his hand arraigned for his life,
Oh, think of your daughter, and think I'm his wife!
What are cannons, or bombs, or clashing of swords?
For death is more certain by witnesses' words.
Then nail up their lips; that dread thunder allay;
And each month of my life will hereafter be May.

LOCKIT   Macheath's time is come, Lucy. We know our own affairs; therefore let us have no more whimpering or whining.

AIR LVI—*A cobbler there was, etc.*

Ourselves, like the great, to secure a retreat,
When matters require it, must give up our gang.
     And good reason why,
     Or instead of the fry,[24]
     Even Peachum and I,
Like poor petty rascals, might hang, hang;
Like poor petty rascals might hang.

PEACHUM   Set your heart at rest, Polly. Your husband is to die to-day! therefore, if you are not already provided, 'tis high time to look about for another. There's comfort for you, you slut.

LOCKIT   We are ready, sir, to conduct you to the Old Bailey.

MACHEATH

AIR LVII—*Bonny Dundee*

The charge is prepared; the lawyers are met,
The judges all ranged (a terrible show!).
I go, undismayed—for death is a debt,
A debt on demand. So, take what I owe.
Then farewell, my love—dear charmers, adieu.
Contented I die—'tis the better for you.
Here ends all dispute the rest of our lives,
   For this way at once I please all my wives.

24. Small fish, lesser men.

Now, gentlemen, I am ready to attend you.
[*Exeunt* MACHEATH, LOCKIT *and* PEACHUM]

SCENE XII

[LUCY, POLLY, FILCH]

POLLY   Follow them, Filch, to the court; and when the trial is over, bring me
a particular account of his behaviour, and of everything that happened.
You'll find me here with Miss Lucy. [*Exit* FILCH] But why is all this
music?

LUCY   The prisoners whose trials are put off till next sessions are diverting
themselves.

POLLY   Sure there is nothing so charming as music! I'm fond of it to distraction! But alas! now, all mirth seems an insult upon my affliction. Let us
retire, my dear Lucy, and indulge our sorrows. The noisy crew, you see,
are coming upon us.   [*Exeunt*]
[*A dance of prisoners in chains, etc.*]

SCENE XIII. *The condemned hold*

[MACHEATH *in a melancholy posture*]

AIR LVIII—*Happy groves*

O cruel, cruel, cruel case!
Must I suffer this disgrace?

AIR LIX—*Of all the girls that are so smart*

Of all the friends in time of grief,
    When threatening death looks grimmer,
Not one so sure can bring relief,
    As this best friend, a brimmer.   [*Drinks*]

AIR LX—*Britons, strike home*

Since I must swing,—I scorn, I scorn to wince or whine.   [*Rises*]

AIR LXI—*Chevy Chase*

But now again my spirits sink;
I'll raise them high with wine.

                                    [*Drinks a glass of wine*]

AIR LXII—*To old Sir Simon the king*

But valour the stronger grows,
The stronger liquor we're drinking.
And how can we feel our woes,
When we've left the trouble of thinking?

                                                        [*Drinks*]

AIR LXIII—*Joy to great Cæsar*

If thus—a man can die.
Much bolder with brandy.

                            [*Pours out a bumper of brandy*]

AIR LXIV—*There was an old woman, etc.*

So I drink off this bumper.—And now I can stand the test.
And my comrades shall see that I die as brave as the best.

[*Drinks*]

AIR LXV—*Did you ever hear of a gallant sailor, etc.*

But can I leave my pretty hussies,
Without one tear or tender sigh?

AIR LXVI—*Why are mine eyes still flowing, etc.*

Their eyes, their lips, their busses,[25]
Recall my love.—Ah, must I die?

AIR LXVII—*Green sleeves*

Since laws were made for every degree,
To curb vice in others as well as me,
I wonder we han't better company,
        Upon Tyburn tree!
But gold from law can take out the sting;
And if rich men like us were to swing,
'Twould thin the land, such numbers to string
        Upon Tyburn tree!

[*Enter a* JAILOR]

JAILOR   Some friends of yours, captain, desire to be admitted. I leave you
together.   [*Exit*]

SCENE XIV

[MACHEATH, BEN BUDGE, MATT OF THE MINT]

MACHEATH   For my having broke prison, you see, gentlemen, I am ordered
immediate execution. The sheriff's officers, I believe, are now at the
door. That Jemmy Twitcher should peach me, I own, surprised me!
'Tis a plain proof that the world is all alike, and that even our gang
can no more trust one another than other people. Therefore, I beg you,
gentlemen, look well to yourselves, for in all probability you may live
some months longer.

MATT   We are heartily sorry, captain, for your misfortune. But 'tis what we
must all come to.

MACHEATH   Peachum and Lockit, you know, are infamous scoundrels. Their
lives are as much in your power as yours are in theirs. Remember your
dying friend!—'Tis my last request. Bring those villains to the gallows
before you, and I am satisfied.

MATT   We'll do't.

[*Re-enter* JAILOR]

25. Kisses.

JAILOR   Miss Polly and Miss Lucy entreat a word with you.

MACHEATH   Gentlemen, adieu.   [*Exeunt* BEN, MATT, *and* JAILOR]

SCENE XV

[LUCY, MACHEATH, POLLY]

MACHEATH   My dear Lucy—my dear Polly! Whatsoever hath passed between
us is now at an end. If you are fond of marrying again, the best advice
I can give you is to ship yourselves off for the West Indies, where
you'll have a fair chance of getting a husband apiece—or by good
luck, two or three, as you like best.

POLLY   How can I support this sight!

LUCY   [*Aside*] There is nothing moves one so much as a great man in
distress.

AIR LXVIII—*All you that must take a leap, etc.*

LUCY   Would I might be hanged!
POLLY   —And I would so too!
LUCY   To be hanged with you.
POLLY   —My dear, with you.
MACHEATH   Oh, leave me to thought! I fear! I doubt!
          I tremble! I droop!—See, my courage is out.
                               [*Turns up the empty bottle*]
POLLY   No token of love?
MACHEATH   —See, my courage is out.
                               [*Turns up the empty pot*]
LUCY   No token of love?
POLLY   Adieu.
LUCY   Farewell!
MACHEATH   But hark! I hear the toll of the bell!
CHORUS   Tol de rol lol, etc.

                                        [*Enter* JAILOR]

JAILOR   Four women more, captain, with a child apiece! See, here they come.

                               [*Enter* WOMEN *and* CHILDREN]

MACHEATH   What—four wives more!—This is too much.—Here, tell the
          sheriff's officers I am ready.   [*Exit* MACHEATH *guarded*]

SCENE XVI

[*To them enter* PLAYER *and* BEGGAR]

PLAYER   But, honest friend, I hope you don't intend that Macheath shall be
really executed.

BEGGAR   Most certainly, sir. To make the piece perfect, I was for doing strict
poetical justice. Macheath is to be hanged; and for the other personages of the drama, the audience must have supposed they were all
either hanged or transported.

PLAYER   Why then, friend, this is a downright deep tragedy. The catastrophe is manifestly wrong, for an opera must end happily.

BEGGAR   Your objection, sir, is very just, and is easily removed; for you must allow that in this kind of drama, 'tis no matter how absurdly things are brought about. So—you rabble there! run and cry a reprieve!—let the prisoner be brought back to his wives in triumph.

PLAYER   All this we must do, to comply with the taste of the town.

BEGGAR   Through the whole piece you may observe such a similitude of manners in high and low life, that it is difficult to determine whether (in the fashionable vices) the fine gentlemen imitate the gentlemen of the road, or the gentlemen of the road the fine gentlemen. Had the play remained as I at first intended, it would have carried a most excellent moral. 'Twould have shown that the lower sort of people have their vices in a degree as well as the rich, and that they are punished for them.

SCENE XVII

[To them MACHEATH, with rabble, etc.]

MACHEATH   So it seems I am not left to my choice, but must have a wife at last.—Look ye, my dears, we will have no controversy now. Let us give this day to mirth, and I am sure she who thinks herself my wife will testify her joy by a dance.

ALL   Come, a dance—a dance!

MACHEATH   Ladies, I hope you will give me leave to present a partner to each of you. And (if I may without offence) for this time, I take Polly for mine. [To POLLY] And for life, you slut, for we were really married. As for the rest—but at present keep your own secret.

A Dance

AIR LXIX—Lumps of pudding, etc.

Thus I stand like the Turk, with his doxies around;
From all sides their glances his passion confound:
For black, brown, and fair, his inconstancy burns,
And the different beauties subdue him by turns.
Each calls forth her charms, to provoke his desires;
Though willing to all, with but one he retires.
But think of this maxim, and put off your sorrow,
The wretch of today may be happy tomorrow.

CHORUS   But think of this maxim, etc.

1728

DANIEL DEFOE
1660–1731

From The True and Genuine Account of the Life and Actions of the Late Jonathan Wild [1]

He was now master of his trade; poor and rich flocked to him. If anything was lost (whether by negligence in the owner, or vigilance and dexterity in the thief), away we went to Jonathan Wild; nay, advertisements were published, directing the finder of almost everything to bring it to Jonathan Wild, who was eminently empowered to take it and give the reward.

How infatuate were the people of this nation all this while! Did they consider, that at the very time that they treated this person with such a confidence, as if he had been appointed to the trade, he had, perhaps, the very goods in his keeping, waiting the advertisement for the reward, and that, perhaps, they had been stolen with that very intention?

It was not a little difficult to give his eminence his true title; he was, indeed, called a thief-catcher, and on some extraordinary occasions he was so. . . . But this was no explanation of his business at all, for his profits came in another way, not in catching the thief, but, more properly, in catching (that is, biting) the persons robbed. As for the thief, it was not his business to catch him as long as he would be subjected to his rules—that is to say, as often as he had committed any robberies, to bring it to him to be restored to the owner.

If the correspondence he kept was large, if the number of his instruments was very great, his dexterity in managing them was indeed wonderful; and how cleverly he kept himself out of the reach of the Act for receiving stolen goods . . . is hardly to be imagined; and yet we find he was never charged home till now, notwithstanding so many felons who he exasperated to the last degree, and made desperate by falling upon them to their destruction.

It is true, the young generation of thieves, who, as we may say, lived under him, were always kept low and poor, and could not subsist but by the bounty of their governor; and when they had a booty of any bulk or value, they knew not what to do with it but to deposit it, and get some money for the present use, and then have a little more upon its being disposed the right way.

For the managing this part he had his particular servants to take and receive, so that Jonathan received nothing, delivered nothing, nor could anything be fastened on him to his hurt, I mean for receiving stolen goods, and yet, as things stood, almost all the stolen goods were brought to him and put into his hands.

1. The full title goes on: *not Made up out of Fiction & Fable, but taken from his own Mouth, and Collected from Papers of his own Writing.* Unlike other journalists, Defoe did not prepare his tract for the day of Wild's execution, and he attacked those "absurd and ridiculous accounts" which preceded his. As always, Defoe is divided between moral outrage and an admiration for commercial resourcefulness and boldness; one can see this as well in *Moll Flanders* (1722), *Colonel Jacque* (1722), and *Roxana* (1724), the great novels about criminal life (and its reformation) that followed *Robinson Crusoe* (1719). Although Defoe's information was largely based on the other accounts he derided, he produces in his seemingly breathless flow of circumstantial detail the illusion of unedited reality; the very lack of syntactic ordering and emphasis seems a warrant of authenticity.

He openly kept his counting-house, or office, like a man of business, and had his books to enter everything in with the utmost exactness and regularity. When you first came to him to give him an account of anything lost, it was hinted to you that you must first deposit a crown; this was his retaining fee. Then you were asked some needful questions—that is to say, needful, not for his information, but for your amusement—as where you live, where the goods were lost, whether out of your house or out of your pocket, or whether on the highway, and the like; and your answers to them all were minuted down, as if in order to make a proper search and inquiry; whereas, perhaps, the very thing you came to inquire after was in the very room where you were, or not far off. After all this grimace [2] was at an end, you were desired to call again or send in a day or two, and then you should know whether he was able to do you any service or no, and so you were dismissed.

At your second coming you had some encouragement given you, that you would be served, but, perhaps, the terms were a little raised upon you, and you were told the rogue that had it was impudent, and that he insisted it was worth so much, and he could sell it when he would for double the money you offered; and that if you would not give him such a sum, he would not treat with you. 'However,' says Jonathan, 'if I can but come to the speech of him, I'll make him to be more reasonable.'

The next time he tells you that all he can bring the rogue to is, that— guineas being paid to the porter who shall bring the goods, and a promise upon honour that nothing shall be said to him, but just take and give, the gold watch, or the snuff-box, or whatever it is, shall be brought to you by such a time exactly; and thus, upon mutual assurances, the bargain is made for restoring the goods.

But then it remains to be asked, what Mr. Wild expects for his pains in managing this nice part; who answers, with an air of greatness, he leaves it to you; that he gets nothing by what is to be given the porter, that he is satisfied in being able to serve gentlemen in such a manner; so that it is in your breast to do what you think is handsome by Mr. Wild, who has taken a great deal of pains in it to do you a service.

It must be confessed that in all this, if there was no more than is mentioned, such a part might be acted on all sides without any guilt fastened anywhere but on the thief. For example, a house is robbed, or a lady has lost her gold watch. Jonathan, by his intelligence among the gang, finds out who has done it—that is to say, he is told 'tis such a one; 'tis no matter how he hears it, he is not bound to the discovery upon a hearsay; nor is he obliged to prosecute a felony committed on he does not know who, by he knows not who—that's none of his business.

However, having a kind of knowledge of the person, he sends to him, to let him know that if he is his own friend, he will carry, that is, send, the watch, or the cane, or the snuff-box, so and so, to such a place; and that if he does so, and the porter receives ten guineas or more, or less, whatever it is that is offered, all will be well; if not, he adds a threatening that he will be prosecuted with the utmost severity.

2. Masquerade, pretense.

Upon this, the thief sends the goods, has the money, and never sees Jonathan, nor any person else. What can Jonathan be charged with in such an affair as this? I must confess I do not see it; no, nor if the thief sends him a present of four or five guineas out of the money, provided, as he said, it is without any conditions made beforehand, or being present at the time 'tis done.

Nor, on the other hand, does the treating for delivering the goods, as above, with a second or third person give any room to fix anything on Jonathan; so that, in short, he treats both with the thief and with the person robbed, with the utmost safety and security. Indeed, I do not see why he might not have carried on such a commerce as this with the greatest ease, I do not say honesty, in the world, if he had gone no farther; for he took none of your money for restoring your goods, neither did he restore you any goods; you gave him money, indeed, for his trouble in inquiring out the thief, and for using his interest by awing or persuading to get your stolen goods sent you back, telling you what you must give to the porter that brings them, if you please, for he does not oblige you to give it.

But the danger lay on the other side of the question, namely, not being contented with what the person robbed gave upon the foot of a grateful acknowledgment for trouble; but impudently taking the goods of the thief, sending the porter himself, taking the money, and then capitulating with the thief for such a part of the reward, and then this thief coming in against him as a witness. This was the very case, in the fact, upon which Jonathan miscarried.

So that, in a word, Jonathan's avarice hanged him. It is true, in the case he was tried for, it was apparent that he set the robbery, as they express it; that is, he directed the persons to the place—nay, went with them to show them the shop, described the woman and the business; and after all, received the goods, and gave them the money for returning them, reserving it in his own power to take what more he pleased for himself; and at last all this was testified by the thieves themselves. . . .

1725

HENRY FIELDING
1707–1754

From The History of the Life of the Late
Mr. Jonathan Wild the Great [1]

Chapter XIV

Wild proceeds to the highest consummation of human GREATNESS

The day now drew nigh when our great man was to exemplify the last and noblest act of greatness by which any hero can signalize himself. This was the day of execution, or consummation, or apotheosis (for it is called by different names), which was to give our hero an opportunity of facing death and damnation, without any fear in his heart, or, at least without betraying any symptoms of it in his countenance. A completion of greatness which is heartily to be wished to every great man; nothing being more worthy of lamentation than when Fortune, like a lazy poet, winds up her catastrophe awkwardly, and, bestowing too little care on her fifth act, dismisses the hero with a sneaking and private exit, who had in the former part of the drama performed such notable exploits as must promise to every good judge among the spectators a noble, public, and exalted end.

But she was resolved to commit no such error in this instance. Our hero was too much and too deservedly her favourite to be neglected by her in his last moments; accordingly all efforts for a reprieve were vain, and the name of Wild stood at the head of those who were ordered for execution.

From the time he gave over all hopes of life, his conduct was truly great and admirable. Instead of showing any marks of dejection or contrition, he rather infused more confidence and assurance into his looks. He spent most of his hours in drinking with his friends. . . . In one of these compotations, being asked whether he was afraid to die, he answered, 'D—n me, it is only a dance without music.' Another time, when one expressed some sorrow for his misfortune, as he termed it, he said with great fierceness—'A man can die but once.' Again, when one of his intimate acquaintance hinted his hopes, that he would die like a man, he cocked his hat in defiance, and cried out greatly—'Zounds! who's afraid?'

. . .

On the eve of his apotheosis, Wild's lady desired to see him, to which he consented. This meeting was at first very tender on both sides; but it could

---

1. Henry Fielding began his literary career as a playwright, but his attacks upon political corruption provoked the Licensing Act of 1737, which submitted all plays to the censorship of the Lord Chamberlain. His satire found its outlet in the prose *Miscellanies* (1743) and particularly in the studied irony of *Jonathan Wild*. Here Fielding plays "goodness" (embodied in the Heartfree family) against "greatness," and he finds the counterparts of Wild's greatness (in a manner reminiscent of Swift) in such heroes as Caesar and Alexander and such contemporaries as Walpole. Following Gay's example, he presents Wild as a low parallel to "high life" and gives him the almost unwavering posture and rhetoric of greatness. This technique served as well to create such figures of high life as Lady Booby in *Joseph Andrews* (1742) or Lady Bellaston in *Tom Jones* (1749) and the innumerable rogues and hypocrites, lower in status but hardly in pretension, that populate those novels and *Amelia* (1751).

not continue so, for unluckily, some hints of former miscarriages intervening, as particularly when she asked him how he could have used her so barbarously once as calling her b——, and whether such language became a man, much less a gentleman, Wild flew into a violent passion, and swore she was the vilest of b——s to upbraid him at such a season with an unguarded word spoke long ago. She replied, with many tears, she was well enough served for her folly in visiting such a brute; but she had one comfort, however, that it would be the last time he could ever treat her so; that indeed she had some obligation to him, for that his cruelty to her would reconcile her to the fate he was to-morrow to suffer; and, indeed, nothing but such brutality could have made the consideration of his shameful death (so this weak woman called hanging), which was now inevitable, to be borne even without madness. She then proceeded to a recapitulation of his faults in an exacter order, and with more perfect memory, than one would have imagined her capable of; and it is probable would have rehearsed a complete catalogue had not our hero's patience failed him, so that with the utmost fury and violence he caught her by the hair and kicked her, as heartily as his chains would suffer him, out of the room.

At length the morning came which Fortune at his birth had resolutely ordained for the consummation of our hero's GREATNESS: he had himself indeed modestly declined the public honour she intended him, and had taken a quantity of laudanum in order to retire quietly off the stage; but we have already observed, in the course of our wonderful history, that to struggle against this lady's decrees is vain and impotent; and whether she hath determined you shall be hanged or be a prime minister, it is in either case lost labour to resist. Laudanum, therefore, being unable to stop the breath of our hero, which the fruit of hemp-seed,[2] and not the spirit of poppy-seed, was to overcome, he was at the usual hour attended by the proper gentleman appointed for that purpose, and acquainted that the cart was ready. On this occasion he exerted that greatness of courage which hath been so much celebrated in other heroes; and, knowing it was impossible to resist, he gravely declared he would attend them. He then descended to that room where the fetters of great men are knocked off in a most solemn and ceremonious manner. Then shaking hands with his friends (to wit, those who were conducting him to the tree), and drinking their healths in a bumper of brandy, he ascended the cart, where he was no sooner seated than he received the acclamations of the multitude, who were highly ravished with his GREATNESS.

The cart now moved slowly on, being preceded by a troop of horse-guards bearing javelins in their hands, through streets lined with crowds all admiring the great behaviour of our hero, who rode on, sometimes sighing, sometimes swearing, sometimes singing or whistling, as his humour varied.

When he came to the tree of glory,[3] he was welcomed with an universal shcut of the people, who were there assembled in prodigious numbers to behold a sight much more rare in populous cities than one would reasonably imagine it should be, viz., the proper catastrophe of a great man.

2. I.e. the rope.
3. The gallows, Tyburn Tree.

But though envy was, through fear, obliged to join the general voice in applause on this occasion, there were not wanting some who maligned this completion of glory, which was now about to be fulfilled to our hero, and endeavoured to prevent it by knocking him on the head as he stood under the tree while the ordinary [4] was performing his last office. They therefore began to batter the cart with stones, brick-bats, dirt, and all manner of mischievous weapons, some of which, erroneously playing on the robes of the ecclesiastic, made him so expeditious in his repetition that with wonderful alacrity he had ended almost in an instant, and conveyed himself into a place of safety in a hackney-coach, where he waited the conclusion with a temper of mind described in these verses:

> Suave mari magno, turbantibus æquora ventis,
> E terra alterius magnum spectare laborem.[5]

We must not, however, omit one circumstance, as it serves to show the most admirable conservation of character in our hero to his last moment, which was, that, whilst the ordinary was busy in his ejaculations, Wild, in the midst of the shower of stones, &c., which played upon him, applied his hands to the parson's pocket, and emptied it of his bottle-screw, which he carried out of the world in his hand.

The ordinary being now descended from the cart, Wild had just opportunity to cast his eyes around the crowd and to give them a hearty curse, when immediately the horses moved on, and with universal applause our hero swung out of this world.

Thus fell Jonathan Wild the GREAT, by a death as glorious as his life had been, and which was so truly agreeable to it that the latter must have been deplorably maimed and imperfect without the former; a death which hath been alone wanting to complete the characters of several ancient and modern heroes, whose histories would then have been read with much greater pleasure by the wisest in all ages. Indeed we could almost wish that whenever Fortune seems wantonly to deviate from her purpose and leaves her work imperfect in this particular, the historian would indulge himself in the license of poetry and romance and even do a violence to truth, to oblige his reader with a page which must be the most delightful in all his history and which could never fail of producing an instructive moral.

Narrow minds may possibly have some reason to be ashamed of going this way out of the world if their consciences can fly in their faces and assure them they have not merited such an honour; but he must be a fool who is ashamed of being hanged, who is not weak enough to be ashamed of having deserved it.

1743

---

4. The prison chaplain.
5. Lucretius, *De Rerum Natura* II.1–2: "Sweet it is, when the mighty sea is lashed by furious winds, to look from shore at the struggles of another."

THE URBAN SCENE

"Why, Sir, you find no man, at all intellectual, who is willing to leave London. No, Sir, when a man is tired of London, he is tired of life; for there is in London all that life can afford." Beside those famous words of Dr. Johnson's, spoken in 1777, one can place his observation in a letter fifteen years earlier, when, depressed during a visit to Lichfield, he "took the first opportunity of returning to a place, where, if there is not much happiness, there is, at least, such a diversity of good and evil that slight vexations do not fix upon the heart." For Boswell, on at least one occasion (and in fact many more, if not most, occasions) London was "the great scene of ambition, instruction, and amusement . . . comparatively speaking, a heaven upon earth."

By the beginning of the eighteenth century London was the largest city in Europe, having reached something more than a half-million people. The Great Fire of 1666 had destroyed more than 13,000 homes and four-fifths of all the buildings in the City proper, that is, the older and more heavily commercial area. Rebuilding created a more open city, expanding into surrounding fields, replacing overhanging half-timbered houses with rows of brick terraces, in many cases enclosing small green squares. Sir Christopher Wren's baroque city plan was not put into effect, but his designs were used for new churches that replaced the eighty-seven destroyed in the Fire; and in the last thirty years of the seventeenth century his great plan for St. Paul's Cathedral was executed, reaching completion in 1709. (See Figs. 8–13.)

Yet there remained much squalor, crowding, and crime, and among the poor a new addiction to gin. It is hard to estimate the quality of life in another age, for we tend to bring some of our own expectations and to neglect the more commonplace elements of stability that fail to win critical attention or pious celebration. If one were to consult only the prints of Hogarth, such as *Gin Lane* (Fig. 30), one would have the impression of a squalor and brutishness almost unendurable; but Hogarth was a satirist, whatever else, and he intensified what he saw. Such poems as Swift's and Gay's stress the impersonality of city life (which was also a source of its freedom), and essays like those of Addison and Steele present the opulence and diversity of its commercial life.

Addison at the Royal Exchange (handsomely rebuilt after the Great Fire) sees the glory of the merchant, and in his account of the color and richness trade has conferred upon England there is something very close to the treatment of man's perception giving sensuous beauty to the characterless substance of his material world. Defoe can share this enthusiasm for the tradesman: "He understands languages without books, geography without maps; his journals and trading voyages delineate the world . . . he sits in his counting house and converses with all nations and keeps up the most exquisite and extensive part of human society in a universal correspondence." But John Gay, in *The Beggar's Opera,* shows Peachum in his counting house deciding which of the thieves he has trained he shall turn in for a fee. His ledgers become a frightening symbol of the ruthlessness that Defoe, for all his praise of the tradesman, could understand as well. Gain is the "essence of his being," and there are, as a result, "more snares . . . and more allurements to him to turn knave than in any employment."

At times Defoe comes to the view that Mandeville exploits in paradox and satire: "It must be confessed, trade is almost universally founded on crime." In a figure like Moll Flanders we can see the enterprise of a tradeswoman who turns to theft and is unable to relinquish its excitement even when it is no longer required by necessity. "What a poor nation must we have been," Defoe writes, "if we had been a sober, religious, temperate nation?" And like Mandeville, he can add that the "wealth of the country is raised by its wickedness, and if it should be reformed it would be undone." We can see an earlier recognition of this, with its own ironic edge, in Swift's *Argument Against Abolishing Christianity* (and implicitly later in *Gulliver's Travels*). What all these observers recognize is the incompatibility of the Gospels or of Stoic virtue with the opulence and vigor of a city like London; so much the worse for the doctrine "which can only be learned from the New Testament, where it will ever remain," Mandeville concludes ironically, "in its purity and lustre."

If London, then, embodies what Swift calls our "schemes of wealth and power," it accommodates other kinds of vigor as well. "I own, Sir," Boswell remarks, "the spirits which I have in London make me do everything with more readiness and vigour. I can talk twice as much in London as anywhere else." One can set this against Pope's images of retirement, of "the feast of reason and the flow of soul," and one can, in fact, set the urban scene against the country house, the villa where man constantly dreams of recovering himself, freed of the pressures of external compulsion or of the temptations to compete in whatever race is being run. Each scene has its deceptions (as Timon's villa reminds us) and each its rewards; if the villa frames a vision of the serene individual in his stability (but in implicit opposition to court or city), so the city gives us the vitality of a social existence with its stress upon man's collective greatness rather than his individual integrity.

JOHN DRYDEN

From The Third Satire of Juvenal°

    Return we to the dangers of the night:
430 And, first, behold our houses' dreadful height;
From whence come broken potsherds tumbling down;
And leaky ware, from garret windows thrown:
Well may they break our heads, that mark the flinty stone.
'Tis want of sense to sup abroad too late,
Unless thou first hast settled thy estate.
As many fates attend, thy steps to meet,
As there are waking windows in the street.
Bless the good gods, and think thy chance is rare,
To have a pisspot only for thy share.
440   The scouring° drunkard, if he does not fight
Before his bedtime, takes no rest that night;
Passing the tedious hours in greater pain
Than stern Achilles,° when his friend was slain:
'Tis so ridiculous, but so true withal,

The Third Satire of Juvenal Umbricius, at the point of leaving Rome for Cumae, "reckons up the several inconveniencies which arise from a city life and the many dangers which attend it" (Dryden).

scouring given to bullying or to cruel practical jokes
Achilles mourning for the death of Patroclus

A bully cannot sleep without a brawl:
Yet though his youthful blood be fired with wine,
He wants not wit the danger to decline;
Is cautious to avoid the coach and six,
And on the lackeys will no quarrel fix.
450   His train of flambeaux, and embroidered coat,
May privilege my lord to walk secure on foot.
But me, who must by moonlight homeward bend,
Or lighted only with a candle's end,
Poor me he fights, if that be fighting, where
He only cudgels, and I only bear.
He stands, and bids me stand; I must abide;
For he's the stronger, and is drunk beside.
   'Where did you whet your knife tonight?' he cries,
'And shred the leeks that in your stomach rise?
460   Whose windy beans have stuffed your guts, and where
Have your black thumbs been dipped in vinegar?
With what companion cobbler have you fed,
On old ox-cheeks, or he-goat's tougher head?
What, are you dumb? Quick, with your answer, quick,
Before my foot salutes you with a kick.
Say, in what nasty cellar, under ground,
Or what church porch, your rogueship may be found?'
Answer, or answer not, 'tis all the same:
He lays me on, and makes me bear the blame.
470   Before the bar, for beating him, you come;
This is a poor man's liberty in Rome.
You beg his pardon; happy to retreat
With some remaining teeth, to chew your meat.
   Nor is this all; for, when retired, you think
To sleep securely; when the candles wink,
When every door with iron chains is barred,
And roaring taverns are no longer heard;
The ruffian robbers, by no justice awed,
And unpaid cutthroat soldiers are abroad,
480   Those venal souls, who, hardened in each ill,
To save complaints and prosecution, kill.
Chased from their woods and bogs, the padders come
To this vast city as their native home;
To live at ease, and safely skulk in Rome.
   The forge in fetters only is employed;
Our iron mines exhausted and destroyed
In shackles; for these villains scarce allow
Goads for the teams, and plowshares for the plow.
O happy ages of our ancestors,
490   Beneath the kings and tribunitial powers!°

Beneath . . . powers in the days, long before
the empire, when Rome was governed by kings,
or later by consuls and tribunes of the people

One jail did all their criminals restrain,
Which, now, the walls of Rome can scarce contain.

1692

SAMUEL JOHNSON

From London: A Poem

In Imitation of the Third Satire of Juvenal°

Prepare for death, if here at night you roam,
And sign your will before you sup from home.
Some fiery fop, with new commission vain,
Who sleeps on brambles till he kills his man;
Some frolic drunkard, reeling from a feast,
Provokes a broil, and stabs you for a jest.
230   Yet even these heroes, mischievously gay,
Lords of the street, and terrors of the way;
Flushed as they are with folly, youth, and wine,
Their prudent insults to the poor confine;
Afar they mark the flambeau's bright approach,
And shun the shining train, and golden coach:
In vain, these dangers past, your doors you close,
And hope the balmy blessings of repose:
Cruel with guilt, and daring with despair,
The midnight murderer bursts the faithless bar;
240   Invades the sacred hour of silent rest,
And leaves, unseen, a dagger in your breast.
Scarce can our fields, such crowds at Tyburn die,
With hemp° the gallows and the fleet supply.
Propose your schemes, ye Senatorian band,
Whose Ways and Means support the sinking land;
Lest ropes be wanting in the tempting spring,
To rig another convoy for the k—g.
A single jail, in ALFRED's golden reign,
Could half the nation's criminals contain;
250   Fair Justice then, without constraint adored,
Held high the steady scale, but deeped° the sword;
No spies were paid, no special juries known,
Blest age! but ah! how different from our own!

.   .   .

1738

Imitation . . . Juvenal For the meaning of
"imitation" see the Headnote on Pope, Imitations of Horace. This passage in Johnson's version corresponds to the closer translation by
Dryden; Johnson adapts Juvenal's satire more
fully to a London setting.
hemp the material for the hangman's rope (used

in the gallows at Tyburn) or for the ship's ropes
necessary for the frequent journeys of George
II to Hanover and his mistress there (ll. 246–
47), an expense supported by the House of
Commons, whose "Ways and Means" are methods of raising money
deeped turned down

JONATHAN SWIFT

A Description of the Morning

Now hardly here and there a hackney-coach
Appearing, showed the ruddy morn's approach.
Now Betty° from her master's bed had flown,
And softly stole to discompose her own;
The slip-shod 'prentice from his master's door
Had pared the dirt and sprinkled° round the floor.
Now Moll had whirled her mop with dext'rous airs,
Prepared to scrub the entry and the stairs.
The youth with broomy stumps began to trace
10   The kennel-edge,° where wheels had worn the place.
The small-coal man° was heard with cadence deep,
Till drowned in shriller notes of chimney-sweep:
Duns° at his lordship's gate began to meet;
And brickdust Moll° had screamed through half the street.
The turnkey° now his flock returning sees,
Duly let out a-nights to steal for fees:
The watchful bailiffs take their silent stands,
And schoolboys lag with satchels in their hands.

1709

A Description of a City Shower

In Imitation of Virgil's Georgics

Careful observers may foretell the hour
(By sure prognostics) when to dread a shower.
While rain depends,° the pensive cat gives o'er
Her frolics and pursues her tail no more.
Returning home at night, you'll find the sink°
Strike your offended sense with double stink.
If you be wise, then go not far to dine:
You'll spend in coach-hire more than save in wine.
A coming shower your shooting corns presage,
10   Old aches° throb, your hollow tooth will rage;
Sauntering in coffeehouse is Dulman seen;
He damns the climate, and complains of spleen.°

Betty like Aurora, the goddess of the dawn, who must leave each morning the bed of her lover Tithonus
sprinkled suggesting the conventional morning shower, as Moll's mop does the gentle breeze
kennel-edge the curb of the road, where he is looking for old nails
small-coal man vendor of charcoal, beginning the sequence of urban counterparts to braying animals and singing birds

Duns bill collectors
brickdust Moll a woman selling powdered brick for cleaning knives
turnkey the jailer who lets his prisoners steal to earn the fees he exacts
depends impends
sink sewer
aches pronounced "aitches"
spleen melancholy, "vapours"

Meanwhile the South,° rising with dabbled° wings,
A sable cloud athwart the welkin° flings,
That swilled more liquor than it could contain,
And like a drunkard gives it up again.
Brisk Susan whips her linen from the rope,
While the first drizzling shower is borne aslope;
Such is that sprinkling which some careless quean°
20 Flirts on you from her mop, but not so clean:
You fly, invoke the gods; then, turning, stop
To rail; she singing, still whirls on her mop.
Not yet the dust had shunned the unequal strife,
But, aided by the wind, fought still for life,
And wafted with its foe by violent gust,
'Twas doubtful which was rain and which was dust.
Ah! where must needy poet seek for aid,
When dust and rain at once his coat invade?
His only coat, where dust confused with rain
30 Roughen the nap, and leave a mingled stain.
    Now in contiguous drops° the flood comes down,
Threatening with deluge this *devoted*° town.
To shops in crowds the daggled° females fly,
Pretend to cheapen° goods, but nothing buy.
The templar° spruce, while every spout's abroach,°
Stays till 'tis fair, yet seems to call a coach.
The tucked-up sempstress walks with hasty strides,
While streams run down her oiled umbrella's sides.
Here various kinds by various fortunes led,
40 Commence acquaintance underneath a shed.
Triumphant Tories and desponding Whigs
Forget their feuds, and join to save their wigs.
Boxed in a chair° the beau impatient sits,
While spouts run clattering o'er the roof by fits,
And ever and anon with frightful din
The leather° sounds; he trembles from within.
So when Troy chairmen bore the wooden steed,
Pregnant with Greeks impatient to be freed,
(Those bully Greeks, who, as the moderns do,
50 Instead of paying chairmen, ran them through),
Laocoon° struck the outside with his spear,
And each imprisoned hero quaked for fear.
    Now from all parts the swelling kennels° flow,

South south wind
dabbled splashed, soiled with mud
athwart the welkin across the sky (deliberate use of archaic-pastoral diction)
quean wench
contiguous drops a deliberate latinate elevation of diction
devoted doomed (again heroic diction)
daggled mud-splashed

cheapen bargain for
templar law student
abroach gushing
chair closed sedan chair
leather the roof of the chair
Laocoon who questioned the value of the Trojan Horse and tested it (*Aeneid* II)
kennels gutters

And bear their trophies with them as they go:
Filth of all hues and odour seem to tell
What street they sailed from by their sight and smell.
They, as each torrent drives with rapid force,
From Smithfield° or St. Pulchre's° shape their course,
And in huge confluent join at Snow Hill Ridge,
60   Fall from the conduit prone to Holborn bridge.
Sweepings from butchers' stalls, dung, guts, and blood,
Drowned puppies, stinking sprats,° all drenched in mud,
Dead cats, and turnip-tops, come tumbling down the flood.°

1710

JOHN GAY

Trivia, or the Art of Walking the Streets of London°

From *Book II*

Let due civilities be strictly paid.
The wall surrender to the hooded maid;
Nor let thy sturdy elbow's hasty rage
Jostle the feeble steps of trembling age:
And when the porter bends beneath his load,
50   And pants for breath, clear thou the crowded road:
But, above all, the groping blind direct,
And from the pressing throng the lame protect.
   You'll sometimes meet a fop, of nicest tread,
Whose mantling peruke° veils his empty head:
At every step he dreads the wall to lose,
And risks, to save a coach, his red-heeled shoes;
Him, like the miller, pass with caution by,
Lest from his shoulder clouds of powder fly:
But when the bully, with assuming pace,
60   Cocks his broad hat, edged round with tarnished lace,
Yield not the way; defy his strutting pride,
And thrust him to the muddy kennel's° side:
He never turns again, nor dares oppose,
But mutters coward curses as he goes.
   If drawn by business to a street unknown,
Let the sworn porter point thee through the town.
Be sure observe the signs, for signs remain

Smithfield the cattle market
St. Pulchre's the church of St. Sepulchre on Snow Hill
sprats small fish
Dead cats . . . flood The last three lines are Swift's parody of the triplet (which Dryden and others favored, especially in poetry of a high style) and the last line a parody of the extended (twelve-syllable) Alexandrine, with which the triplet often concluded.
Trivia . . . London Gay's poem, in three books, is a mock-georgic, applying the heroic celebration of rural labor to the urban task of getting through the traffic of the city.
mantling peruke enveloping wig
kennel's gutter's

Like faithful landmarks to the walking train.
Seek not from 'prentices to learn the way;
70   Those fabling boys will turn thy steps astray:
Ask the grave tradesman to direct thee right;
He ne'er deceives but when he profits by't.

.   .   .

Experienced men, inured to city ways,
Need not the calendar to count their days.
When through the town, with slow and solemn air,
Led by the nostril, walks the muzzled bear,
Behind him moves majestically dull,
410   The pride of Hockley-hole,° the surly bull;
Learn hence the periods of the week to name:
Mondays and Thursdays are the days of game.
When fishy stalls with doubled store are laid,
The golden-bellied carp, the broad-finned maid,°
Red-speckled trouts, the salmon's silver jowl,
The jointed lobster, and unscaly sole,
And luscious scallops to allure the tastes
Of rigid zealots to delicious fasts;
Wednesdays and Fridays, you'll observe from hence
420   Days when our sires were doomed to abstinence.
When dirty waters from balconies drop,
And dextrous damsels twirl the sprinkling mop,
And cleanse the spattered sash, and scrub the stairs,
Know Saturday's conclusive morn appears.
Successive cries the seasons' change declare,
And mark the monthly progress of the year.
Hark! how the streets with treble voices ring,
To sell the bounteous product of the spring:
Sweet-smelling flowers, and elder's early bud,
430   With nettle's tender shoots,° to cleanse the blood:
And when June's thunder cools the sultry skies,
Even Sundays are profaned by mack'rel cries.
Walnuts the fruiterer's hand, in autumn, stain,
Blue plums and juicy pears augment his gain;
Next oranges the longing boys entice
To trust their copper fortunes to the dice.
When rosemary, and bays, the poet's crown,
Are bawled in frequent cries through all the town,
Then judge the festival of Christmas near,
440   Christmas! the joyous period of the year.
Now with bright holly all your temples strow,
With laurel green, and sacred mistletoe.

.   .   .

Hockley-hole Hockley-in-the-Hold, the scene of
bear- and bull-baiting
maid a species of shad

nettle's . . . shoots to be eaten as a spring
remedy

From *Book III*

Where the mob gathers, swiftly shoot along,
Nor idly mingle in the noisy throng.
Lured by the silver hilt, amid the swarm
The subtle artist will thy side disarm:
Nor is thy flaxen wig with safety worn;
High on the shoulder in a basket borne
Lurks the sly boy, whose hand, to rapine bred,
Plucks off the curling honours of thy head.°
Here dives the skulking thief, with practised sleight
60   And unfelt fingers makes thy pocket light.
Where's now thy watch? with all its trinkets, flow;
And thy late snuff-box is no more thy own.
But, lo! his bolder thefts some tradesman spies,
Swift from his prey the scudding lurcher° flies:
Dextrous he 'scapes the coach with nimble bounds,
Whilst every honest tongue 'Stop thief' resounds.
So speeds the wily fox, alarmed by fear,
Who lately filched the turkey's callow care;°
Hounds following hounds, grow louder as he flies,
70   And injured tenants join the hunter's cries:
Breathless he stumbling falls. Ill-fated boy!
Why did not honest work thy youth employ?
Seized by rough hands, he's dragged amid the rout,
And stretched beneath the pump's incessant spout;°
Or plunged in miry pounds he gasping lies,
Mud chokes his mouth, and plasters o'er his eyes.
Let not the ballad-singer's shrilling strain
Amid the swarm thy listening ear detain;
Guard well thy pocket; for these sirens stand
80   To aid the labours of the diving hand:
Confederate in the cheat, they draw the throng,
And cambric handkerchiefs reward the song.
But soon as coach or cart drives rattling on,
The rabble part, in shoals they backward run:
So Jove's loud bolts the mingled war divide,
And Greece and Troy retreat on either side.

.   .   .

Who can the various city frauds recite,
With all the petty rapines of the night?
Who now the guinea-dropper's bait° regards,
250   Tricked by the sharper's dice or juggler's cards?
Why should I warn thee ne'er to join the fray

---

honours . . . head a Virgilian phrase for ornaments, hence hair
lurcher petty thief
callow care young

beneath . . . spout a common punishment for
petty thieves
guinea-dropper's bait the apparently lost guinea
used as bait in a confidence game, which may
also involve a "sham-quarrel" (l. 252)

Where the sham-quarrel interrupts the way?
Lives there in these our days so soft a clown,
Braved° by the bully's oaths or threatening frown?
I need not strict enjoin the pockets' care,
When from the crowded play thou leadest the fair;
Who has not here or watch or snuff-box lost,
Or hankerchiefs that India's shuttle boast;
O! may thy virtue guard thee through the roads
260   Of Drury's mazy courts and dark abodes,
The harlots' guileful paths, who nightly stand
Where Catherine Street° descends into the Strand.
Say, vagrant Muse! their wiles and subtle arts,
To lure the strangers' unsuspecting hearts;
So shall our youth on healthful sinews tread,
And city cheeks grow warm with rural red.
    'Tis she who nightly strolls with sauntering pace,
No stubborn stays her yielding shape embrace;
Beneath the lamp her tawdry ribbons glare,
270   The new-scoured mantua° and the slattern air;
High-draggled° petticoats her travels show,
And hollow cheeks with artful blushes glow;
With flattering sounds she soothes the credulous ear,
My noble captain! charmer! love! my dear!
In ridinghood near tavern-doors she plies,
Or muffled pinners° hide her livid eyes;
With empty bandbox she delights to range,
And feigns a distant errand from the 'Change;
Nay, she will oft the Quaker's hood profane,
280   And trudge demure the rounds of Drury Lane:
She darts from sarcenet° ambush wily leers;
Twitches thy sleeve, or with familiar airs
Her fan will pat thy cheek: these snares disdain,
Nor gaze behind thee when she turns again.

.   .   .

1716

Braved cowed
Catherine Street a block away from Drury
Lane, both the resort of prostitutes
mantua a loose cloak-like gown
High-draggled mud-spattered well above the
hem

pinners long flaps pinned to the cap and hanging
to the breast; here, perhaps a full headdress
sarcenet a soft silk, here used to modify "ambush"

JOSEPH ADDISON [1]

[The Royal Exchange]

There is no place in the town which I so much love to frequent as the Royal Exchange.[2] It gives me a secret satisfaction, and, in some measure, gratifies my vanity, as I am an Englishman, to see so rich an assembly of countrymen and foreigners consulting together upon the private business of mankind, and making this metropolis a kind of emporium for the whole earth. I must confess I look upon high-change[3] to be a great council, in which all considerable nations have their representatives. Factors in the trading world are what ambassadors are in the politic world; they negotiate affairs, conclude treaties, and maintain a good correspondence between those wealthy societies of men that are divided from one another by seas and oceans, or live on the different extremities of a continent. I have often been pleased to hear disputes adjusted between an inhabitant of Japan and an alderman of London, or to see a subject of the Great Mogul entering into a league with one of the Czar of Muscovy. I am infinitely delighted in mixing with these several ministers of commerce, as they are distinguished by their different walks and different languages: sometimes I am justled among a body of Armenians: sometimes I am lost in a crowd of Jews; and sometimes make one in a group of Dutchmen. I am a Dane, Swede, or Frenchman at different times, or rather fancy myself like the old philosopher,[4] who upon being asked what country-man he was, replied, that he was a citizen of the world.

Though I very frequently visit this busy multitude of people, I am known to nobody there but my friend Sir Andrew,[5] who often smiles upon me as he sees me bustling in the crowd, but at the same time connives at my presence without taking any further notice of me. There is indeed a merchant of Egypt, who just knows me by sight, having formerly remitted me some money to Grand Cairo; but as I am not versed in the modern Coptic, our conferences go no further than a bow and a grimace.[6]

This grand scene of business gives me an infinite variety of solid and substantial entertainments. As I am a great lover of mankind, my heart naturally overflows with pleasure at the sight of a prosperous and happy multitude, insomuch that at many public solemnities I cannot forbear expressing my joy with tears that have stolen down my cheeks. For this reason I am wonderfully delighted to see such a body of men thriving in their own private fortunes, and at the same time promoting the public stock; or in other words, raising estates

---

1. For Addison's career, see the Headnote to The Pleasures of the Imagination in the section entitled The Garden and the Wild.
2. Rebuilt in 1669 after the Great Fire as a large quadrangle of two stories surrounding a paved court; the interior of the court was lined with arched galleries and niches containing statues of the English monarchs, and in the center was a statue of Charles II as a Roman emperor.
3. The time of greatest activity.
4. Either Socrates or Diogenes the Cynic, to both of whom the remark has been attributed.
5. Sir Andrew Freeport, the merchant-hero of the *Spectator* (see note 1 to the Steele essay that follows).
6. Simply a nod or expression of cordiality.

for their own families, by bringing into their country whatever is wanting, and carrying out of it whatever is superfluous.

Nature seems to have taken a particular care to disseminate her blessings among the different regions of the world, with an eye to this mutual inter-course and traffic among mankind, that the natives of the several parts of the globe might have a kind of dependence upon one another, and be united together by their common interest. Almost every degree produces something peculiar to it. The food often grows in one country, and the sauce in another. The fruits of Portugal are corrected by the products of Barbadoes: the infusion of a China plant sweetened with the pith of an Indian cane. The Philippick [7] Islands give a flavour to our European bowls. The single dress of a woman of quality is often the product of an hundred climates. The muff and the fan come together from the different ends of the earth. The scarf is sent from the torrid zone, and the tippet [8] from beneath the Pole. The brocade petticoat rises out of the mines of Peru, and the diamond necklace out of the bowels of Indostan.

If we consider our own country in its natural prospect, without any of the benefits and advantages of commerce, what a barren uncomfortable spot of earth falls to our share! Natural historians tell us that no fruit grows originally among us, besides hips and haws, acorns and pig-nuts, with other delicacies of the like nature; that our climate of itself, and without the assistances of art, can make no further advances towards a plum than to a sloe, and carries an apple to no greater a perfection than a crab: that our melons, our peaches, our figs, our apricots, and cherries, are strangers among us, imported in different ages, and naturalized in our English gardens; and that they would all degen-erate and fall away into the trash of our own country, if they were wholly neglected by the planter, and left to the mercy of our sun and soil.

Nor has traffic more enriched our vegetable world than it has improved the whole face of nature among us. Our ships are laden with the harvest of every climate: our tables are stored with spices, and oils, and wines: our rooms are filled with pyramids of China, and adorned with the workmanship of Japan: our morning's-draught comes to us from the remotest corners of the earth: we repair our bodies by the drugs of America, and repose ourselves under Indian canopies. My friend Sir Andrew calls the vineyards of France our gardens; the spice-islands our hot-beds; the Persians our silk-weavers, and the Chinese our potters. Nature indeed furnishes us with the bare necessaries of life, but traffic gives us a great variety of what is useful, and at the same time supplies us with every thing that is convenient and ornamental. Nor is it the least part of this our happiness, that whilst we enjoy the remotest products of the north and south, we are free from those extremities of weather which give them birth; that our eyes are refreshed with the green fields of Britain, at the same time that our palates are feasted with fruits that rise between the tropics.[9]

For these reasons there are not more useful members in a commonwealth

---

7. Philippine.

8. A fur garment for the neck and shoulders.

9. It is precisely this dependence upon worldwide commerce that such writers as Swift (in *A Modest Proposal*) and Goldsmith (in *The Deserted Village*) deplore as unnecessary luxury which the poor must be sacrificed to support.

than merchants. They knit mankind together in a mutual intercourse of good offices, distribute the gifts of nature, find work for the poor, add wealth to the rich, and magnificence to the great. Our English merchant converts the tin of his own country into gold, and exchanges his wool for rubies. The Mahometans are clothed in our British manufacture, and the inhabitants of the frozen zone warmed with the fleeces of our sheep.

When I have been upon the 'Change, I have often fancied one of our old kings standing in person, where he is represented in effigy, and looking down upon the wealthy concourse of people with which that place is every day filled. In this case, how would he be surprized to hear all the languages of Europe spoken in this little spot of his former dominions, and to see so many private men, who in his time would have been the vassals of some powerful baron, negotiating like princes for greater sums of money than were formerly to be met with in the royal treasury! Trade, without enlarging the British territories, has given us a kind of additional empire: it has multiplied the number of the rich, made our landed estates infinitely more valuable than they were formerly, and added to them an accession of other estates as valuable as the lands themselves.

[From *Spectator* No. 69, May 19, 1711]

RICHARD STEELE [1]

[The Hours of London]

It is an inexpressible pleasure to know a little of the world, and be of no character or significancy in it. To be ever unconcerned, and ever looking on new objects with an endless curiosity, is a delight known only to those who are turned for speculation: nay, they who enjoy it must value things only as they are the objects of speculation, without drawing any worldly advantage to themselves from them, but just as they are what contribute to their amusement, or the improvement of the mind. I lay one night last week at Richmond; and being restless, not out of dissatisfaction, but a certain busy inclination one sometimes has, I arose at four in the morning, and took boat for London, with a resolution to rove by boat and coach for the next four and twenty hours, till the many different objects I must needs meet with should tire my imagination, and give me an inclination to a repose more profound than I was at that time capable of. I beg people's pardon for an odd humour I am guilty of, and was often that day, which is saluting any person whom I like, whether I know him or not. This is a particularity would be tolerated in me, if they considered that the greatest pleasure I know I receive at my eyes, and that I am obliged to

1. Sir Richard Steele (1672–1729) was born in Dublin and studied at Oxford before entering army service. His literary career began with an early series (1701–5) of successful comedies, and in 1709 he began to edit a thrice-weekly paper, the *Tatler*, with the help of his school friend Joseph Addison. Both men edited the *Spectator* in 1711–12, and Steele moved increasingly into political journalism thereafter, defending Whig policies against such opponents as Jonathan Swift, winning the rewards of political office and (in 1715) a knighthood. Steele was a somewhat sentimental moralist and student of manners, and his attitudes find their best expression in his later comedy, *The Conscious Lovers* (1722).

an agreeable person for coming abroad into my view, as another is for the visit of conversation at their own houses.

The hours of the day and night are taken up, in the cities of London and Westminster, by people as different from each other as those who are born in different centuries. Men of six o'clock give way to those of nine, they of nine to the generation of twelve; and they of twelve disappear, and make room for the fashionable world, who have made two o'clock the noon of the day.

When we first put off from shore,[2] we soon fell in with a fleet of gardeners bound for the several market-ports of London; and it was the most pleasing scene imaginable to see the cheerfulness with which those industrious people plied their way to a certain sale of their goods. The banks on each side are as well peopled, and beautified with as agreeable plantations, as any spot on the earth; but the Thames itself, loaded with the product of each shore, added very much to the landscape. It was very easy to observe by their sailing, and the countenances of the ruddy virgins who were supercargoes,[3] the parts of the town to which they were bound. There was an air in the purveyors for Covent Garden, who frequently converse with morning rakes, very unlike the seemly sobriety of those bound for Stocks Market.[4]

Nothing remarkable happened in our voyage; but I landed with ten sail of apricot boats at Strand Bridge,[5] after having put in at Nine Elms, and taken in melons, consigned by Mr. Cuffe of that place, to Sarah Sewell and company, at their stall in Covent Garden. We arrived at Strand Bridge at six of the clock, and were unloading; when the hackney-coachmen of the foregoing night took their leave of each other at the Dark House,[6] to go to bed before the day was too far spent. Chimney-sweepers passed by us as we made [7] up to the market, and some raillery happened between one of the fruit-wenches and those black men, about the devil and Eve, with allusion to their several professions. I could not believe any place more entertaining than Covent Garden, where I strolled from one fruit-shop to another, with crowds of agreeable young women around me, who were purchasing fruit for their respective families. It was almost eight of the clock before I could leave that variety of objects. . . .

The day of people of fashion began now to break, and carts and hacks were mingled with equipages of show and vanity; when I resolved to walk it out of cheapness; but my unhappy curiosity is such that I find it always my interest to take coach, for some odd adventure among beggars, ballad-singers, or the like, detains and throws me into expense. It happened so immediately; for at the corner of Warwick Street, as I was listening to a new ballad, a ragged rascal, a beggar who knew me, came up to me, and began to turn the eyes of the good company upon me by telling me he was extreme poor, and should die in the streets for want of drink, except I immediately would have the charity to give him sixpence to go into the next alehouse and save his life. He urged, with a

2. Steele has spent the night at Richmond and boards a boat for London.
3. That is, carried as passengers.
4. A market for fish and meat on the site of the present Mansion House in the City of London, named for a pair of stocks once placed there for the punishment of criminals.
5. A landing place at the foot of Strand Lane.
6. The name derived from a one-time place of confinement for a madman.
7. Made our way.

melancholy face, that all his family had died of thirst. All the mob have humour, and two or three began to take the jest; by which Mr. Sturdy carried his point, and let me sneak off to a coach. As I drove along, it was a pleasing reflection to see the world so prettily chequered since I left Richmond, and the scene still filling with children of a new hour. This satisfaction increased as I moved towards the City; and gay signs, well-disposed streets, magnificent public structures, and wealthy shops, adorned with contented faces, made the joy still rising till we came into the centre of the City, and centre of the world of trade, the Exchange of London. As other men in the crowds about me were pleased with their hopes and bargains, I found my account in observing them in attention to their several interests. I, indeed, looked upon myself as the richest man that walked the Exchange that day; for my benevolence made me share the gains of every bargain that was made. It was not the least of the satisfactions in my survey to go upstairs, and pass the shops of agreeable females; to observe so many pretty hands busy in the foldings of ribands, and the utmost eagerness of agreeable faces in the sale of patches, pins, and wires, on each side the counters, was an amusement in which I should longer have indulged myself, had not the dear creatures called to me to ask what I wanted, when I could not answer only 'To look at you.' I went to one of the windows which opened to the area below, where all the several voices lost their distinction, and rose up in a confused humming; which created in me a reflection that could not come into the mind of any but of one a little too studious; for I said to myself, with a kind of pun in thought, 'What nonsense is all the hurry of this world to those who are above it?' In these or not much wiser thoughts I had like to have lost my place at the chop-house; where every man, according to the natural bashfulness or sullenness of our nation, eats in a public room a mess of broth, or chop of meat, in dumb silence, as if they had no pretence to speak to each other on the foot of being men, except they were of each other's acquaintance.

I went afterwards to Robin's,[8] and saw people who had dined with me at the fivepenny ordinary just before, give bills for the value of large estates; and could not but behold with great pleasure, property lodged in and transferred in a moment from such as would never be masters of half as much as is seemingly in them, and given from them every day they live. But before five in the afternoon I left the City, came to my common scene of Covent Garden, and passed the evening at Will's in attending the discourses of several sets of people, who relieved each other within my hearing on the subjects of cards, dice, love, learning, and politics. The last subject kept me till I heard the streets in the possession of the bellman, who had now the world to himself, and cried, 'Past two of clock.' This roused me from my seat, and I went to my lodging, led by a light,[9] whom I put into the discourse of his private economy, and made him give me an account of the charge, hazard, profit, and loss of a family that depended upon a link, with a design to end my trivial day with the generosity of sixpence, instead of a third part of that sum. When I came to my chamber I writ down these minutes; but was at a loss what instruction I should propose to my reader from the enumeration of so many insignificant

8. A coffeehouse in Exchange Alley.
9. A link man or hired torch-bearer.

matters and occurrences; and I thought it of great use, if they could learn with me to keep their minds open to gratification, and ready to receive it from anything it meets with. This one circumstance will make every face you see give you the satisfaction you now take in beholding that of a friend; will make every object a pleasing one; will make all the good which arrives to any man, an increase of happiness to yourself.

[From *Spectator* No. 454, August 11, 1712]

BERNARD MANDEVILLE
1670–1733

From The Fable of the Bees [1]

[Private Vices, Public Benefits]

. . . the merchant, that sends corn or cloth into foreign parts to purchase wines and brandies, encourages the growth or manufactory of his own country; he is a benefactor to navigation, increases the customs, and is many ways beneficial to the public; yet it is not to be denied, but that his greatest dependence is lavishness and drunkenness: For, if none were to drink wine but such only as stand in need of it, nor anybody more than his health required, that multitude of wine-merchants, vintners, coopers,[2] &c. that make such a considerable show in this flourishing city would be in a miserable condition. The same may be said not only of card and dice-makers that are the immediate ministers to a legion of vices, but of mercers,[3] upholsterers, tailors,

---

1. Bernard Mandeville, a Dutch physician, settled in London by 1699 and married an Englishwoman. In 1703 and 1704 he published fables in English verse, a burlesque poem *Typhon* in 1704, and in 1705 *The Grumbling Hive, or Knaves Turned Honest*. The last was a fable about a hive of bees that live in "luxury and ease" until a restless and quixotic desire for honesty destroys their society. "Then leave complaints," runs the moral; "fools only strive / To make a great and honest hive." In 1714 Mandeville reprinted this with a prose commentary under the title *The Fable of the Bees; or, Private Vices, Public Benefits,* and in subsequent years continued to amplify the prose. In 1723 the Grand Jury of Middlesex declared the book a public nuisance, but *The Fable* continued to appear and to grow in spite of much denunciation. Dr. Johnson declared that Mandeville "opened my views into real life very much," that his influence was great, if only in forcing men to modify their positions in both ethical and economic theory. For Mandeville pressed home the conflict between estimating motives and estimating consequences. Of his hive, he could write, "Thus every part was full of vice, / Yet the whole mass a paradise." So he could claim that a healthy society may require a measure of private selfishness (for he defines vice as meaning anything less than rigorous selflessness and adherence to virtue for its own sake), and he draws from this an attack upon those moral aspirations that underestimate or ignore the cost they exact. While he can be seen to support the mercantile spirit hailed by Addison and Steele, he does it without illusions of nobility and with a teasing awareness of the moral discomfort his paradox creates. In a sense, he recognizes the same conflicts that Swift explores, but his solution is simpler because he is ready to jettison more (although not without insisting upon the fact).
2. Barrel-makers.
3. Silk merchants.

and many others, that would be starved in half a year's time if pride and luxury were at once to be banished the nation. . . .

I shall be asked what benefit the public receives from thieves and house-breakers. They are, I own, very pernicious to human society, and every government ought to take all imaginable care to root out and destroy them; yet if all people were strictly honest, and nobody would meddle with or pry into anything but his own, half the smiths of the nation would want employment; and abundance of workmanship (which now serves for ornaments as well as defence) is to be seen everywhere both in town and country that would never have been thought of, but to secure us against the attempts of pilferers and robbers.

If what I have said be thought far-fetched, and my assertion seems still a paradox, I desire the reader to look upon the consumption of things, and he will find that the laziest and most unactive, the profligate and most mischievous, are all forced to do something for the common good; and whilst their mouths are not sewed up and they continue to wear and otherwise destroy what the industrious are daily employed about to make, fetch and procure, in spite of their teeth, obliged to help maintain the poor and the public charges. The labour of millions would soon be at an end, if there were not other millions, as I say, in the fable,

> . . . Employed,
> To see their handy-works destroyed.

But men are not to be judged by the consequences that may succeed their actions, but the facts themselves and the motives which it shall appear they acted from. If an ill-natured miser, who is almost a plum [4] and spends but fifty pounds a year, though he has no relation to inherit his wealth, should be robbed of five hundred or a thousand guineas, it is certain that as soon as this money should come to circulate, the nation would be the better for the robbery and receive the same and as real a benefit from it as if an archbishop had left the same sum to the public; yet justice and the peace of society require that he or they who robbed the miser should be hanged, though there were half a dozen of them concerned.

Thieves and pickpockets steal for a livelihood, and either what they can get honestly is not sufficient to keep them, or else they have an aversion to constant working: they want to gratify their senses, have victuals, strong drink, lewd women, and to be idle when they please. The victualler, who entertains them and takes their money, knowing which way they come at it, is very near as great a villain as his guests. But if he fleeces them well, minds his business, and is a prudent man, he may get money and be punctual with them he deals with. The trusty out-clerk, whose chief aim is his master's profit, sends him in what beer he wants and takes care not to lose his custom; while the man's money is good, he thinks it no business of his to examine whom he gets it by. In the meantime, the wealthy brewer, who leaves all the management to his servants, knows nothing of the matter, but keeps his coach, treats

4. A man worth £100,000.

his friends, and enjoys his pleasure with ease and a good conscience; he gets an estate, builds houses, and educates his children in plenty, without ever thinking on the labour which wretches perform, the shifts fools make, and the tricks knaves play to come at the commodity by the vast sale of which he amasses his great riches.

A highwayman having met with a considerable booty, gives a poor common harlot he fancies ten pounds to new-rig her from top to toe; is there a spruce mercer so conscientious that he will refuse to sell her a thread satin though he knew who she was? She must have shoes and stockings, gloves; the stay and mantua-maker,[5] the sempstress, the linen-draper,[6] all must get something by her, and a hundred different tradesmen dependent on those she laid her money out with may touch part of it before a month is at an end.

The generous gentleman, in the meantime, his money being near spent, ventured again on the road, but the second day having committed a robbery near Highgate, he was taken with one of his accomplices, and at the next sessions both were condemned and suffered the law. The money due on their conviction fell to three country fellows, on whom it was admirably well bestowed. One was an honest farmer, a sober painstaking man, but reduced by misfortunes; the summer before, by the mortality among the cattle, he had lost six cows out of ten, and now his landlord, to whom he owed thirty pounds, had seized on all his stock. The other was a day-labourer, who struggled hard with the world, had a sick wife at home, and several small children to provide for. The third was a gentleman's gardener, who maintained his father in prison, where, being bound[7] for a neighbour, he had lain for twelve pounds almost a year and a half; this act of filial duty was the more meritorious, because he had for some time been engaged to a young woman, whose parents lived in good circumstances, but would not give their consent before our gardener had fifty guineas of his own to show. They received above fourscore pounds each, which extricated every one of them out of the difficulties they laboured under, and made them, in their opinion, the happiest people in the world.

Nothing is more destructive, either in regard to the health or the vigilance and industry of the poor, than the infamous liquor, the name of which, derived from Juniper in Dutch, is now by frequent use and the laconic spirit of the nation from a word of middling length shrunk into a monosyllable, intoxicating Gin, that charms the unactive, the desperate and crazy of either sex, and makes the starving sot behold his rags and nakedness with stupid indolence, or banter both in senseless laughter and more insipid jests! It is a fiery lake that sets the brain in flame, burns up the entrails, and scorches every part within; and, at the same time, a Lethe[8] of oblivion, in which the wretch immersed drowns his most pinching cares and, with his reason, all anxious reflection on brats that cry for food, hard winter-frosts, and horrid empty home. . . .

Among the doting admirers of this liquid poison, many of the meanest rank, from a sincere affection to the commodity itself, become dealers in it, and

5. Dressmaker.
6. Merchant of linen goods.
7. Responsible for the debts of.
8. The river of Hades whose water produced loss of memory.

take delight to help others to what they love themselves, as whores commence bawds [9] to make the profits of one trade subservient to the pleasures of the other. But as these starvelings commonly drink more than their gains, they seldom, by selling, mend the wretchedness of condition they laboured under while they were only buyers. In the fag-end [10] and outskirts of the town and all places of the vilest resort, it is sold in some part or other of almost every house, frequently in cellars, and sometimes in the garret. . . .

The vast number of the shops I speak of throughout the city and suburbs are an astonishing evidence of the many seducers that, in a lawful occupation, are accessory to the introduction and increase of all the sloth, sottishness, want, and misery which the abuse of strong waters is the immediate cause of, to lift above mediocrity perhaps half a score men that deal in the same commodity by wholesale, while, among the retailers, though qualified as I required, a much greater number are broke and ruined for not abstaining from the Circean cup [11] they hold out to others, and the more fortunate are their whole lifetime obliged to take the uncommon pains, endure the hardships, and swallow all the ungrateful and shocking things I named, for little or nothing beyond a bare sustenance and their daily bread.

The short-sighted vulgar [12] in the chain of causes seldom can see further than one link; but those who can enlarge their view and will give themselves the leisure of gazing on the prospect of concatenated events may, in a hundred places, see good spring up and pullulate from evil, as naturally as chickens do from eggs. The money that arises from the duties upon malt is a considerable part of the national revenue, and should no spirits be distilled from it, the public treasure would prodigiously suffer on that head. But if we would set in a true light the many advantages and large catalogue of solid blessings that accrue from, and are owing to, the evil I treat of, we are to consider the rents that are received, the ground that is tilled, the tools that are made, the cattle that are employed, and above all, the multitude of poor that are maintained, by the variety of labour required in husbandry, in malting, in carriage and distillation, before we can have the product of malt which we call low wines, and is but the beginning from which the various spirits are afterwards to be made.

Besides this, a sharp-sighted good-humoured man might pick up abundance of good from the rubbish, which I have all flung away for evil. He would tell me, that whatever sloth and sottishness might be occasioned by the abuse of malt-spirits, the moderate use of it was of inestimable benefit to the poor, who could purchase no cordials of higher prices; that it was an universal comfort, not only in cold and weariness, but most of the afflctions that are peculiar to the necessitous, and had often to the most destitute supplied the places of meat, drink, clothes, and lodging. That the stupid indolence in the most wretched condition occasioned by those composing draughts, which I complained of, was a blessing to thousands, for that certainly those were the happiest, who felt the least pain. As to diseases, he would say, that, as it

9. Keepers of brothels.
10. Shabby quarters.
11. Whose contents turned men to swine.
12. Mob, common people.

caused some, so it cured others, and that if the excess in those liquors had been sudden death to some few, the habit of drinking them daily prolonged the lives of many, whom once it agreed with; that for the loss sustained from the insignificant quarrels it created at home, we were overpaid in the advantage we received from it abroad, by upholding the courage of soldiers, and animating the sailors to the combat. . . .

If I should ever urge to him that to have here and there one great and eminent distiller was a poor equivalent for the vile means, the certain want, and lasting misery of so many thousand wretches as were necessary to raise them, he would answer that of this I could be no judge, because I do not know what vast benefit they might afterwards be of to the commonwealth. Perhaps, would he say, the man thus raised will exert himself in the commission of the peace or other station with vigilance and zeal against the dissolute and disaffected, and, retaining his stirring temper, be as industrious in spreading loyalty and the reformation of manners throughout every cranny of the wide populous town as once he was in filling it with spirits; till he becomes at last the scourge of whores, of vagabonds and beggars, the terror of rioters and discontented rabbles, and constant plague to sabbath-breaking butchers. Here my good-humoured antagonist would exult and triumph over me, especially if he could instance to me such a bright example; what an uncommon blessing, would he cry out, is this man to his country! how shining and illustrious his virtue!

To justify his exclamation, he would demonstrate to me that it was impossible to give a fuller evidence of self-denial in a grateful mind than to see him, at the expence of his quiet and hazard of his life and limbs, be always harassing, and even for trifles persecuting, that very class of men to whom he owes his fortune, from no other motive than his aversion to idleness and great concern for religion and the public welfare. . . .

Who would imagine that virtuous women, unknowingly, should be instrumental in promoting the advantage of prostitutes? Or (what still seems the greater paradox) that incontinence should be made serviceable to the preservation of chastity? and yet nothing is more true. A vicious young fellow, after having been an hour or two at church, a ball, or any other assembly, where there is a great parcel of handsome women dressed to the best advantage, will have his imagination more fired than if he had the same time been polling at Guildhall [13] or walking in the country among a flock of sheep. The consequence of this is that he will strive to satisfy the appetite that is raised in him; and when he find honest women obstinate and uncomatable,[14] it is very natural to think that he will hasten to others that are more compliable. Who would so much as surmise that this is the fault of the virtuous women? They have no thoughts of men in dressing themselves, poor souls, and endeavour only to appear clean and decent, every one according to her quality. . . .

[The Theory of Virtue]

I expect to be asked why in the fable I have called those pleasures real that are directly opposite to those which I own the wise men of all ages have

13. Voting for Parliament.
14. That is, un-come-at-able.

extolled as the most valuable? My answer is, because I do not call things pleasures which men say are best, but such as they seem to be most pleased with; how can I believe that a man's chief delight is in the embellishments of the mind when I see him ever employed about and daily pursue the pleasures that are contrary to them? John never cuts any pudding, but just enough that you can't say he took none; this little bit, after much chomping and chewing, you see goes down with him like chopped hay; after that he falls upon the beef with a voracious appetite and crams himself up to his throat. Is it not provoking to hear John cry every day that pudding is all his delight and that he don't value the beef of a farthing?

I could swagger about fortitude and the contempt of riches as much as Seneca [15] himself and would undertake to write twice as much in behalf of poverty as ever he did; for the tenth part of his estate, I could teach the way to his *summum bonum* [16] as exactly as I know my way home. I could tell people to extricate themselves from all worldly engagements; and to purify the mind they must divest themselves of their passions, as men take out the furniture when they would clean a room thoroughly; and I am clearly of the opinion that the malice and most severe strokes of fortune can do no more injury to a mind thus stripped of all fears, wishes, and inclinations, than a blind horse can do in an empty barn. In the theory of all this I am very perfect, but the practice is very difficult; and if you went about picking my pocket, offered to take the victuals from before me when I am hungry, or made but the least motion of spitting in my face, I dare not promise how philosophically I should behave myself. But that I am forced to submit to every caprice of my unruly nature, you will say, is no argument that others are as little masters of theirs, and therefore I am willing to pay adoration to virtue whenever I can meet with it, with a proviso that I shall not be obliged to admit any as such where I can see no self-denial, or to judge of men's sentiments from their words where I have their lives before me. . . .

What must we do in this dilemma? Shall we be so uncharitable as, judging from men's actions, to say that all the world prevaricates and that this is not their opinion, let them talk what they will? Or shall we be so silly as, relying on what they say, to think them sincere in their sentiments and so not believe our own eyes? Or shall we rather endeavour to believe ourselves and them too, and say with Montaigne that they imagine and are fully persuaded that they believe what they do not believe? These are his words: 'Some impose on the world and would be thought to believe what they really do not: but much the greater number impose upon themselves, not considering, nor thoroughly apprehending what it is to believe.' But this is making all mankind either fools or imposters, which, to avoid, there is nothing left us but to say what Mr. Bayle [17] has endeavoured to prove at large in his Reflections on Comets: 'that man is so unaccountable a creature as to act most commonly against his principle'; and this is so far from being injurious that it is a compliment to human nature, for we must say either this or worse.

15. Lucius Annaeus Seneca (3. B.C.–65 A.D.) the Roman Stoic philosopher, who wrote eloquently on poverty although he amassed a huge fortune.
16. "Highest good" (the moral end of man).
17. Pierre Bayle (1647–1706), French skeptical philosopher, who had a great influence on Mandeville.

This contradiction in the frame of man is the reason that the theory of virtue is so well understood and the practice of it so rarely to be met with. If you ask me where to look for those beautiful shining qualities of prime ministers and the great favourites of princes that are so finely painted in dedications, addresses, epitaphs, funeral sermons, and inscriptions, I answer, there, and nowhere else. Where would you look for the excellency of a statue but in that part which you see of it? It is the polished outside only that has the skill and labour of the sculptor to boast of; what is out of sight is untouched. Would you break the head or cut open the breast to look for the brains or the heart, you would only show your ignorance and destroy the workmanship. This has often made me compare the virtues of great men to your large China jars: they make a fine show, and are ornamental even to a chimney; one would, by the bulk they appear in and the value that is set upon them, think they might be very useful, but look into a thousand of them, and you will find nothing in them but dust and cobwebs. . . .

[The Violence of Luxury]

If we trace the most flourishing nations in their origin, we shall find, that in the remote beginnings of every society, the richest and most considerable men among them were a great while destitute of a great many comforts of life that are now enjoyed by the meanest and most humble wretches: so that many things which were once looked upon as the invention of luxury are now allowed even to those that are so miserably poor as to become the objects of public charity, nay, counted so necessary, that we think no human creature ought to want them.

In the first ages, man, without doubt, fed on the fruits of the earth without any previous preparation, and reposed himself naked like other animals on the lap of their common parent. Whatever has contributed since to make life more comfortable, as it must have been the result of thought, experience, and some labour, so it more or less deserves the name of luxury, the more or less trouble it required, and deviated from the primitive simplicity. Our admiration is extended no farther than to what is new to us, and we all overlook the excellency of things we are used to, be they never so curious. A man would be laughed at that should discover luxury in the plain dress of a poor creature that walks along in a thick parish gown and a coarse shirt underneath it; and yet what a number of people, how many different trades, and what a variety of skill and tools must be employed to have the most ordinary Yorkshire cloth? What depth of thought and ingenuity, what toil and labour, and what length of time must it have cost before man could learn from a seed to raise and prepare so useful a product as linen.

Must that society not be vainly curious, among whom this admirable commodity, after it is made, shall not be thought fit to be used even by the poorest of all before it is brought to a perfect whiteness, which is not to be procured but by the assistance of all the elements joined to a world of industry and patience? I have not done yet: can we reflect not only on the cost laid out upon this luxurious invention, but likewise on the little time the whiteness of it continues, in which part of its beauty consists, that every six or seven days at farthest it wants cleaning, and while it lasts is a continual charge to the wearer;

can we, I say, reflect on all this and not think it an extravagant piece of nicety that even those who receive alms of the parish should not only have whole garments made of this operose [18] manufacture, but likewise that as soon as they are soiled, to restore them to their pristine purity, they should make use of one of the most judicious as well as difficult compositions that chemistry can boast of; with which, dissolved in water by the help of fire, the most detersive and yet innocent lixivium [19] is prepared that human industry has hitherto been able to invent?

It is certain, time was that the things I speak of would have bore those lofty expressions, and in which everybody would have reasoned after the same manner; but the age we live in would call a man fool who should talk of extravagance and nicety if he saw a poor woman, after having wore her crown cloth smock a whole week, wash it with a bit of stinking soap of a groat a pound. . . .

In what concerns the fashions and manners of the ages men live in, they never examine into the real worth or merit of the cause and generally judge of things not as their reason but custom direct them. Time was when the funeral rites in the disposing of the dead were performed by fire and the cadavers of the greatest emperors were burnt to ashes. Then burying the corpse in the ground was a funeral for slaves or made a punishment for the worst of malefactors. Now nothing is decent or honourable but interring; and burning the body is reserved for crimes of the blackest dye. At some times we look upon trifles with horror, at other times we can behold enormities without concern. . . . .

I have often thought, if it was not for this tyranny which custom usurps over us, that men of any tolerable good-nature could never be reconciled to the killing of so many animals for their daily food, as long as the bountiful earth so plentifully provides them with varieties of vegetable dainties. I know that reason excites our compassion but faintly, and therefore I would not wonder how men should so little commiserate such imperfect creatures as crayfish, oysters, cockles, and indeed all fish in general. . . . But in such perfect animals as sheep and oxen, in whom the heart, the brain and nerves differ so little from ours, and in whom the separation of the spirits from the blood, the organs of sense, and consequently feeling itself, are the same as they are in human creatures; I cannot imagine how a man not hardened in blood and massacre is able to see a violent death, and the pangs of it, without concern.

In answer to this, most people will think it sufficient to say that all things being allowed to be made for the service of man, there can be no cruelty in putting creatures to the use they were designed for; but I have heard men make this reply while their nature within them has reproached them with the falsehood of the assertion. There is of all the multitude not one man in ten but what will own (if he was not brought up in a slaughter-house) that of all trades he could never have been a butcher; and I question whether ever anybody so much as killed a chicken without reluctancy the first time. Some

18. Laborious.
19. A lye solution used as a detergent ("detersive")

people are not to be persuaded to taste of any creatures they have daily seen and been acquainted with while they were alive; others extend their scruple no further than to their own poultry and refuse to eat what they fed and took care of themselves; yet all of them will feed heartily and without remorse on beef, mutton, and fowls when they are bought in the market. In this behaviour, methinks, there appears something like a consciousness of guilt; it looks as if they endeavoured to save themselves from the imputation of a crime (which they know sticks somewhere) by removing the cause of it as far as they can from themselves; and I can discover in it some strong remains of primitive pity and innocence, which all the arbitrary power of custom and the violence of luxury have not yet been able to conquer. . . .

[The Dream of Simplicity]

When people have small comings in and are honest withal, it is then that the generality of them begin to be frugal, and not before. Frugality in ethics is called that virtue from the principle of which men abstain from superfluities and, despising the operose contrivances of art to procure either case of pleasure, content themselves with the natural simplicity of things and are carefully temperate in the enjoyment of them, without any tincture of covetousness. Frugality thus limited is perhaps scarcer than many may imagine; but what is generally understood by it is a quality more often to be met with, and consists in a medium between profuseness and avarice, rather leaning to the latter. As this prudent economy, which some people call saving, is in private families the most certain method to increase an estate, so some imagine that whether a country be barren or fruitful, the same method, if generally pursued (which they think practicable), will have the same effect upon a whole nation, and that, for example, the English might be much richer than they are if they would be as frugal as some of their neighbours. This, I think, is an error. . . .

Experience teaches us first that as people differ in their views and perceptions of things, so they vary in their inclinations; one man is given to covetousness, another to prodigality, and a third is only saving. Secondly, that men are never, or at least, very seldom, reclaimed from their darling passions, either by reason or precept, and that if anything ever draws them from what they are naturally propense to, it must be a change in their circumstances or their fortunes. If we reflect upon these observations, we shall find that to render the generality of a nation lavish, the product of the country must be considerable in proportion to the inhabitants, and what they are profuse of cheap; that, on the contrary, to make a nation generally frugal, the necessaries of life must be scarce, and consequently dear; and that, therefore, let the best politician do what he can, the profuseness or frugality of a people in general must always depend upon and will, in spite of his teeth, be ever proportioned to the fruitfulness and product of the country, the number of inhabitants, and the taxes they are to bear. If anybody would refute what I have said, let them only prove from history that there ever was in any country a national frugality without a national necessity.

Let us examine then what things are requisite to aggrandize and enrich a nation. The first desirable blessings for any society of men are a fertile soil, and a happy climate, a mild government, and more land than people. These things will render man easy, loving, honest, and sincere. In this condition they may be as virtuous as they can, without the least injury to the public, and consequently as happy as they please among themselves. But they shall have no arts or sciences or be quiet longer than their neighbours will let them; they must be poor, ignorant, and almost wholly destitute of what we call the comforts of life, and all the cardinal virtues together won't so much as procure a tolerable coat or a porridge-pot among them; for in this state of slothful ease and stupid innocence, as you need not fear great vices, so you must not expect any considerable virtues. Man never exerts himself but when he is roused by his desires; while they lie dormant, and there is nothing to raise them, his excellence and abilities will be forever undiscovered, and the lumpish machine, without the influence of his passions, may be justly compared to a huge windmill without a breath of air.

Would you render a society of men strong and powerful, you must touch their passions. Divide the land, though there be never so much to spare, and their possessions will make them covetous; rouse them, though but in jest, from their idleness with praises, and pride will set them to work in earnest; teach them trades and handicrafts, and you will bring envy and emulation among them; to increase their numbers, set up a variety of manufactures and leave no ground uncultivated; let property be inviolably secured and privileges equal to all men; suffer nobody to act but what is lawful and everybody to think what he pleases; for a country where everybody may be maintained that will be employed, and the other maxims are observed, must always be thronged and can never want people, as long as there is any in the world. Would you have them bold and warlike, turn to military discipline, make good use of their fear, and flatter their vanity with art and assiduity; but would you, moreover, render them an opulent, knowing, and polite nation, teach them commerce with foreign countries, and, if possible, get into the sea, which to compass spare no labour nor industry, and let no difficulty deter you from it; then promote navigation, cherish the merchant, and encourage trade in every branch of it; this will bring riches, and where they are, arts and sciences will soon follow; and by the help of what I have named and good management, it is that politicians can make a people potent, renowned, and flourishing.

But would you have a frugal and honest society, the best policy is to preserve men in their native simplicity, strive not to increase their numbers; let them never be acquainted with strangers or superfluities, but remove and keep from them everything that might raise their desires or improve their understanding.

Great wealth and foreign treasure will ever scorn to come among men, unless you'll admit their inseparable companions, avarice and luxury; where trade is considerable, fraud will intrude. To be at once well-bred and sincere is no less than a contradiction; and therefore, while man advances in knowledge and his manners are polished, we must expect to see, at the same time, his desires enlarged, his appetites refined, and his vices increased. . . .

1714, 1723

DANIEL DEFOE

c. 1660–1731

From The Fortunes and Misfortunes of the Famous Moll Flanders [1]

I went out now by daylight, and wandered about I knew not whither, and in search of I knew not what, when the devil put a snare in my way of a dreadful nature indeed, and such a one as I have never had before or since. Going through Aldersgate Street, there was a pretty little child who had been at a dancing-school, and was going home, all alone; and my prompter, like a true devil, set me upon this innocent creature. I talked to it, and it prattled to me again, and I took it by the hand and led it along till I came to a paved alley that goes into Bartholomew Close, and I led it in there. The child said that was not its way home. I said, 'Yes, my dear, it is; I'll show you the way home.' The child had a little necklace on of gold beads, and I had my eye upon that, and in the dark of the alley I stooped, pretending to mend the child's clog that was loose, and took off her necklace, and the child never felt it, and so led the child on again. Here, I say, the devil put me upon killing the child in the dark alley, that it might not cry, but the very thought frighted me so that I was ready to drop down; but I turned the child about and bade it go back again, for that was not its way home. The child said, so she would, and I went through into Bartholomew Close, and then turned round to another passage that goes into Long Lane, so away into Charterhouse Yard and out into St. John Street; then, crossing into Smithfield, went down Chick Lane and into Field Lane to Holborn Bridge, when, mixing with the crowd of people usually passing there, it was not possible to have been found out; and thus I enterprised my second sally into the world.

The thoughts of this booty put out all the thoughts of the first, and the reflections I had made wore quickly off; poverty, as I have said, hardened my heart, and my own necessities made me regardless of anything. The last affair left no great concern upon me, for as I did the poor child no harm, I only said to myself, I had given the parents a just reproof for their negligence in leaving the poor little lamb to come home by itself, and it would teach them to take more care of it another time.

This string of beads was worth about twelve or fourteen pounds. I suppose it might have been formerly the mother's, for it was too big for the child's wear, but that perhaps the vanity of the mother, to have her child look fine at the dancing-school, had made her let the child wear it; and no doubt the child had a maid sent to take care of it, but she, careless jade, was taken up perhaps with some fellow that had met her by the way, and so the poor baby wandered till it fell into my hands.

However, I did the child no harm; I did not so much as fright it, for I had a great many tender thoughts about me yet, and did nothing but what, as I may say, mere necessity drove me to.

1. The second of Defoe's great novels deals with a woman in reduced circumstances who, after unsuccessful efforts to remarry to advantage, turns to crime, gains notoriety as a thief, and eventually repents and reforms. This episode presents Moll Flanders' second act of theft.

HENRY FIELDING
1707–1754

From A Modern Glossary [1]

ANGEL   The name of a woman, commonly of a very bad one.

BEAR   A country gentleman; or, indeed, any animal upon two legs that doth not make a handsome bow.

BEAUTY   The qualification with which women generally go into keeping.

BRUTE   A word implying plain-dealing and sincerity, but more especially applied to a philosopher.

CAPTAIN ⎱   Any stick of wood with a head to it, and a piece of black
COLONEL ⎰   ribband upon that head.

COXCOMB   A word of reproach, and yet, at the same time, signifying all that is most commendable.

DEATH   The final end of man; as well of the *thinking part of the body* as of all the other parts.

DRESS   The principal accomplishment of men and women.

DULNESS   A word applied by all writers to the wit and humour of others.

EATING   A science.

FINE   An adjective of a very peculiar kind, destroying, or, at least, lessening the force of the substantive to which it is joined: as *fine* gentlemen, *fine* lady, *fine* house, *fine* clothes, *fine* taste;—in all which *fine* is to be understood in a sense somewhat synonymous with useless.

GALLANTRY   Fornication and adultery.

GREAT   Applied to a thing, signifies bigness; when to a man, often littleness, or meanness.

HONOUR   Duelling.

LOVE   A word properly applied to our delight in particular kinds of food; sometimes metaphorically spoken of the favourite objects of all our *appetites.*

MARRIAGE   A kind of traffic carried on between the two sexes, in which both are constantly endeavouring to cheat each other, and both are commonly losers in the end.

MODESTY   Awkwardness, rusticity.

NOBODY   All the people in Great Britain, except about 1200.

PATRIOT   A candidate for a place at court.

POLITICS   The art of getting such a place.

RELIGION   A word of no meaning; but which serves as a bugbear to frighten children with.

RICHES   The only thing upon earth that is really valuable or desirable.

ROGUE ⎱   A man of a different party from yourself.
RASCAL ⎰

SUNDAY   The best time for playing at cards.

SHOCKING   An epithet which fine ladies apply to almost everything. It is, indeed, an interjection (if I may so call it) of delicacy.

---

1. See note 1 on Fielding to the selection from Fielding's *Jonathan Wild* that follows John Gay's *The Beggar's Opera.* This comes from his later journalism, written after the last of his novels, *Amelia,* had appeared (1751).

TASTE   The present whim of the town, whatever it be.

VIRTUE ⎱
VICE   ⎰   Subjects of discourse.

[From *The Covent-Garden Journal*, No. 4, January 14, 1752]

JAMES BOSWELL
1740–1795

Boswell's father was the eighth Laird of Auchinleck, a distinguished jurist, and a man with a strong feeling for the continuity of his family. His eldest son James resisted a legal career but agreed to prepare for the bar before going to London to obtain a commission in a fashionable regiment. Self-indulgent, capricious, and eager for literary fame, James Boswell danced at the end of a tether. His efforts to obtain a commission failed, and he won only a deferment of his legal career in the form of a grand tour of the Continent. Before he left London, however, he met Samuel Johnson, to whom he turned as a more tolerant and affectionate paternal authority. Johnson's influence reinforced, even if it moderated, his father's, and Boswell—in spite of an early literary success with his *Account of Corsica* (1768), based on a visit to the heroic defender of liberty, General Paoli—settled into a legal career in Scotland, breaking out of its confinement only in bouts of self-indulgence and, more important, in the remarkable journal he kept with Johnson's approval. The extracts from the journal show him in his early London years, in his swaggering but somewhat timid visit to Rousseau, and in a typically reflective moment during a darker and later phase. But the journals were also to yield the brilliant account of his 1773 tour of the Hebrides with Johnson, and the success of its publication the year after Johnson's death encouraged him to complete the great *Life* four years before his own death.

It is only in recent years, since the discovery and publication of his journals, that Boswell has come to be recognized as a major literary artist. His openness to every nuance of feeling, his delicacy in capturing (with something of Sterne's skill) fugitive sentiments and revealing gestures, his comic self-regard and (at times) self-contempt— all these have transformed the earlier view of Boswell as alternately a servile buffoon and a mere camera eye. Clearly he induced Johnson's characteristic postures and declarations just as he induced his own, with bold experimental curiosity and a willingness to record what others repress. At times he may have lived in order to record and acted in order to be able to study himself; his journal, as Frederick Pottle has shown, is a fascinating compromise between the freshness of emerging experience and the ironic hindsight of a recorder who (with the advantage of a few days' delay and a concealed knowledge of what will ensue) can intensify naïve expectation and the shock of the real.

From the *Life* a number of extracts have been chosen to illustrate the range of techniques (as well as to suggest the dimensions of the Johnson who is, however real, a work of Boswell's imagination): the reconstruction of Johnson's early life, the dramatic encounters which Boswell attended, the final retrospective view (of which an earlier version had appeared in the Hebrides *Tour*).

From The Journals [1]
[1762–63: Farewell to Louisa]

Wednesday 22 December   I stood and chatted a while with the sentries before Buckingham House. One of them, an old fellow, said he was in all the last war. 'At the battle of Dettingen,' said he, 'I saw our cannon make a lane through the French army as broad as that' (pointing to the Mall), 'which was filled up in as short time as I'm telling you it.' They asked me for a pint of beer, which I gave them. I talked on the sad mischief of war and on the frequency of poverty. 'Why, Sir,' said he, 'GOD made all right at first when he made mankind. ('I believe,' said the other, 'he made but few of them.') But, Sir, if GOD was to make the world today, it would be crooked again tomorrow. But the time will come when we shall all be rich enough. To be sure, salvation is promised to those that die in the field.' I have great pleasure in conversing with the lower part of mankind, who have very curious ideas.

This forenoon I went to Louisa's [2] in full expectation of consummate bliss. I was in a strange flutter of feeling. I was ravished at the prospect of joy, and yet I had such an anxiety upon me that I was afraid that my powers would be enervated. I almost wished to be free of this assignation. I entered her apartment in a sort of confusion. She was elegantly dressed in the morning fashion, and looked delightfully well. I felt the tormenting anxiety of serious love. I sat down and I talked with the distance of a new acquaintance and not with the ease and ardour of a lover, or rather a gallant. I talked of her lodgings being neat, opened the door of her bedchamber, looked into it. Then sat down by her in a most melancholy plight. I would have given a good deal to be out of the room.

We talked of religion. Said she, 'People who deny that, show a want of sense.' 'For my own part, Madam, I look upon the adoration of the Supreme Being as one of the greatest enjoyments we have. I would not choose to get rid of my religious notions. I have read books that staggered me. But I was glad to find myself regain my former opinions.' 'Nay, Sir, what do you think of the Scriptures having stood the test of ages?' 'Are you a Roman Catholic, Madam?' 'No, Sir. Though I like some parts of their religion, in particular, confession; not that I think the priest can remit sins, but because the notion that we are to confess to a decent clergyman may make us cautious what we do.' 'Madam,' said I, 'I would ask you to do nothing that you should be sorry to confess. Indeed I have a great deal of principle in matters of gallantry, and never yet led any woman to do what might afterwards make her uneasy. If she thinks it wrong, I never insist.' She asked me some questions about my intrigues, which I nicely eluded.

1. Boswell's journals, which have been recovered only in the 20th century, provide an extraordinary record of a man of intense sensibility and remarkable candor of self-analysis. The first excerpt is from the London Journal, which records Boswell's futile quest for a commission, his first meeting with Johnson, and his eventual departure for Holland. The second excerpt, drawn from the record of the grand tour, records Boswell's visit to Rousseau in Switzerland. The third, which takes us beyond the time of the tour of the Hebrides, shows a typical instance of the metaphysical concerns that troubled him throughout his life.
2. Louisa was Mrs. Lewis, an actress, of whom little is known but her relationship with Boswell.

I then sat near her and began to talk softly, but finding myself quite dejected with love, I really cried out and told her that I was miserable; and as I was stupid, would go away. I rose, but saluting her with warmth, my powers were excited, I felt myself vigorous. I sat down again. I beseeched her, 'You know, Madam, you said you was not a Platonist. I beg it of you to be so kind. You said you are above the finesse of your sex.' (Be sure always to make a woman better than her sex.) 'I adore you.' 'Nay, dear Sir' (I pressing her to me and kissing her now and then), 'pray be quiet. Such a thing requires time to consider of.' 'Madam, I own this would be necessary for any man but me. But you must take my character from myself. I am very good-tempered, very honest, and have little money. I should have some reward for my particular honesty.' 'But, Sir, give me time to recollect myself.' 'Well then, Madam, when shall I see you?' 'On Friday, Sir.' 'A thousand thanks.' I left her and came home and took my bread and cheese with great contentment. . . .

Thursday 20 January   I then went to Louisa.[3] With excellent address did I carry on this interview, as the following scene, I trust, will make appear.

LOUISA   My dear Sir! I hope you are well today.

BOSWELL   Excessively well, I thank you. I hope I find you so.

LOUISA   No, really, Sir. I am distressed with a thousand things. (Cunning jade, her circumstances!) I really don't know what to do.

BOSWELL   Do you know that I have been very unhappy since I saw you?

LOUISA   How so, Sir?

BOSWELL   Why, I am afraid that you don't love me so well, nor have not such a regard for me, as I thought you had.

LOUISA   Nay, dear Sir! (Seeming unconcerned.)

BOSWELL   Pray, Madam, have I no reason?

LOUISA   No, indeed, Sir, you have not.

BOSWELL   Have I no reason, Madam? Pray think.

LOUISA   Sir!

BOSWELL   Pray, Madam, in what state of health have you been in for some time?

LOUISA   Sir, you amaze me.

BOSWELL   I have but too strong, too plain reason to doubt of your regard. I have for some days observed the symptoms of disease, but was unwilling to believe you so very ungenerous. But now, Madam, I am thoroughly convinced.

LOUISA   Sir, you have terrified me. I protest I know nothing of the matter.

BOSWELL   Madam, I have had no connection with any woman but you these two months. I was with my surgeon this morning, who declared I had got a strong infection, and that she from whom I had it could not be ignorant of it. Madam, such a thing in this case is worse than from a woman of the town, as from her you may expect it. You have used me very ill. I did not deserve it. You know you said where there was no confidence, there was no breach of trust. But surely I placed some confidence in you. I am sorry that I was mistaken.

---

3. On January 18 Boswell first discovers "a little heat in the members of my body sacred to Cupid," and on January 19, "Too, too plain was Signor Gonorrhoea."

LOUISA   Sir, I will confess to you that about three years ago I was very bad. But for these fifteen months I have been quite well. I appeal to GOD Almighty that I am speaking true; and for these six months I have had to do with no man but yourself.

BOSWELL   But by G–D, Madam, I have been with none but you, and here am I very bad.

LOUISA   Well, Sir, by the same solemn oath I protest that I was ignorant of it.

BOSWELL   Madam, I wish much to believe you. But I own I cannot upon this occasion believe a miracle.

LOUISA   Sir, I cannot say more to you. But you will leave me in the greatest misery. I shall lose your esteem. I shall be hurt in the opinion of everybody, and in my circumstances.

BOSWELL   (to himself) What the devil does the confounded jilt mean by being hurt in her circumstances? This is the grossest cunning. But I won't take notice of that at all.—Madam, as to the opinion of everybody, you need not be afraid. I was going to joke and say that I never boast of a lady's *favours*. But I give you my word of honour that you shall not be discovered.

LOUISA   Sir, this is being more generous than I could expect.

BOSWELL   I hope, Madam, you will own that since I have been with you I have always behaved like a man of honour.

LOUISA   You have indeed, Sir.

BOSWELL   (rising) Madam, your most obedient servant.

During all this conversation I really behaved with a manly composure and polite dignity that could not fail to inspire an awe, and she was pale as ashes and trembled and faltered. Thrice did she insist on my staying a little longer, as it was probably the last time that I should be with her. She could say nothing to the purpose. And I sat silent. As I was going, said she, 'I hope, Sir, you will give me leave to inquire after your health.' 'Madam,' said I, archly, 'I fancy it will be needless for some weeks.' She again renewed her request. But unwilling to be plagued any more with her, I put her off by saying I might perhaps go to the country, and left her. I was really confounded at her behaviour. There is scarcely a possibility that she could be innocent of the crime of horrid imposition. And yet her positive asseverations really stunned me. She is in all probability a most consummate dissembling whore.

Thus ended my intrigue with the fair Louisa, which I flattered myself so much with, and from which I expected at least a winter's safe copulation. It is indeed very hard. I cannot say, like young fellows who get themselves clapped in a bawdy-house, that I will take better care again. For I really did take care. However, since I am fairly trapped, let me make the best of it. I have not got it from imprudence. It is merely the chance of war.

I then called at Drury Lane for Mr. Garrick.[4] He was vastly good to me. 'Sir,' said he, 'you will be a very great man. And when you are so, remember the year 1763. I want to contribute my part towards saving you. And pray, will you fix a day when I shall have the pleasure of treating you with tea?' I

---

4. David Garrick (1717–79), Johnson's former pupil who was recognized early as the finest actor in England.

fixed next day. 'Then, Sir,' said he, 'the cups shall dance and the saucers skip.'

What he meant by my being a great man I can understand. For really, to speak seriously, I think there is a blossom about me of something more distinguished than the generality of mankind. But I am much afraid that this blossom will never swell into fruit, but will be nipped and destroyed by many a blighting heat and chilling frost. Indeed, I sometimes indulge noble reveries of having a regiment, of getting into Parliament, making a figure, and becoming a man of consequence in the state. But these are checked by dispiriting reflections on my melancholy temper and imbecility [5] of mind. Yet I may probably become sounder and stronger as I grow up. Heaven knows. I am resigned. I trust to Providence. I was quite in raptures with Garrick's kindness —the man whom from a boy I used to adore and look upon as a heathen god —to find him paying me so much respect! How amiable is he in comparison of Sheridan! [6] I was this day with him what the French call un étourdi.[7] I gave free vent to my feelings. Love [8] was by, to whom I cried, 'This, Sir, is the real scene.' And taking Mr. Garrick cordially by the hand, 'Thou greatest of men,' said I, 'I cannot express how happy you make me.' This, upon my soul, was no flattery. He saw it was not. And the dear great man was truly pleased with it. This scene gave me a charming flutter of spirits and dispelled my former gloom.

[1764: The Visit to Rousseau [9]]

Monday 3 December   To prepare myself for the great interview, I walked out alone. I strolled pensive by the side of the river Reuse in a beautiful wild valley surrounded by immense mountains, some covered with frowning rocks, others with clustering pines, and others with glittering snow. The fresh, healthful air and the romantic prospect around me gave me a vigorous and solemn tone. I recalled all my former ideas of J. J. Rousseau, the admiration with which he is regarded over all Europe, his *Héloïse,* his *Émile:* in short, a crowd of great thoughts. This half hour was one of the most remarkable that I ever passed.

I returned to my inn, and the maid delivered to me a card with the following answer from Monsieur Rousseau: 'I am ill, in pain, really in no state to receive visits. Yet I cannot deprive myself of Mr. Boswell's, provided that out of consideration for the state of my health, he is willing to make it short.'

My sensibility dreaded the word 'short.' But I took courage, and went im-

5. Stupefaction.

6. Thomas Sheridan (1719–88), actor and teacher of elocution.

7. A giddy creature.

8. James Love, an English actor who had given Boswell lessons in elocution.

9. Jean Jacques Rousseau was at the height of his fame, but he was under steady pressure from authority. Having left Paris to settle in Switzerland, he found that the Genevan authorities sought his expulsion; he took refuge in the mountain village of Môtiers in the independent territory of Neuchâtel. He was living in retirement when Boswell visited him, attended by Rousseau's mistress Thérèse Le Vasseur (then 43, in spite of Boswell's impression). (For excerpts from Rousseau's posthumously published *Confessions,* see below, Sense and Sensibility.) The text of Boswell's conversation was written in his journal in French, and this translated text (in large part the work of Geoffrey Scott) is reprinted from the edition of Frederick A. Pottle.

mediately. I found at the street door Mademoiselle Le Vasseur waiting for me. She was a little, lively, neat French girl and did not increase my fear. She conducted me up a darkish stair, then opened a door. I expected, 'Now I shall see him'—but it was not so. I entered a room which serves for vestibule and for kitchen. My fancy formed many, many a portrait of the wild philosopher. At length his door opened and I beheld him, a genteel black man in the dress of an Armenian. I entered saying, 'Many, many thanks.' After the first looks and bows were over, he said, 'Will you be seated? Or would you rather take a turn with me in the room?' I chose the last, and happy I was to escape being formally placed upon a chair. I asked him how he was. 'Very ill. But I have given up doctors.' 'Yes, yes; you have no love for them.' As it is impossible for me to relate exactly our conversation, I shall not endeavour at order, but give sentences as I recollect them.

BOSWELL. 'The thought of your books, Sir, is a great source of pleasure to you?' ROUSSEAU. 'I am fond of them; but when I think of my books, so many misfortunes which they have brought upon me are revived in my memory that really I cannot answer you. And yet my books have saved my life.' He spoke of the Parlement of Paris: 'If any company could be covered with disgrace, that would be. I could plunge them into deep disgrace simply by printing their edict against me on one side, and the law of nations and equity on the side opposite. But I have reasons against doing so at present.' BOSWELL. 'We shall have it one day, perhaps?' ROUSSEAU. 'Perhaps.'

I was dressed in a coat and waistcoat, scarlet with gold lace, buckskin breeches, and boots. Above all I wore a greatcoat of green camlet [10] lined with fox-skin fur, with the collar and cuffs of the same fur. I held under my arm a hat with a solid gold lace, at least with the air of being solid. I had it last winter at The Hague. I had a free air and spoke well, and when Monsieur Rousseau said what touched me more than ordinary, I seized his hand, I thumped him on the shoulder. I was without restraint. When I found that I really pleased him, I said, 'Are you aware, Sir, that I am recommended to you by a man you hold in high regard?'

ROUSSEAU. 'Ah! My Lord Marischal?' [11] BOSWELL. 'Yes, Sir; my Lord furnished me with a note to introduce me to you.' ROUSSEAU. 'And you were unwilling to take advantage of it?' BOSWELL. 'Nay, Sir; I wished to have proof of my own merits.' ROUSSEAU. 'Sir, there would have been no kind of merit in gaining access to me by a note of Lord Marischal's. Whatever he sends will always find a welcome from me. He is my protector, my father; I would venture to say, my friend.' One circumstance embarrassed me a little: I had forgotten to bring with me from Neuchâtel my Lord's billet. But a generous consciousness of innocence and honesty gives a freedom which cannot be counterfeited. I told Monsieur Rousseau, 'To speak truly, I have forgotten to bring his letter with me; but you accept my word for it?'

10. A costly fabric of satin weave, originally of angora wool. (For Boswell in this costume see Fig. 34.)

11. George Keith, 10th Earl Marischal of Scotland (d. 1778); a distinguished soldier and disenchanted Jacobite, he served Frederick the Great of Prussia; as governor of Neuchâtel he became a friend and protector of Rousseau. Boswell had traveled with him in Germany earlier in the year.

ROUSSEAU. 'Why, certainly. Numbers of people have shown themselves ready to serve me in their own fashion; my Lord Marischal has served me in mine. He is the only man on earth to whom I owe an obligation.' He went on, 'When I speak of kings, I do not include the King of Prussia. He is a king quite alone and apart. That force of his! Sir, there's the great matter, to have force—revenge, even. You can always find stuff to make something out of. But when force is lacking, when everything is small and split up, there's no hope. The French, for example, are a contemptible nation.' BOSWELL. 'But the Spaniards, Sir?' ROUSSEAU. 'Yes, you will find great souls in Spain.' BOSWELL. 'And in the mountains of Scotland. But since our cursed Union,[12] ah—' ROUSSEAU. 'You undid yourselves. . . .'

'Sir, you don't see before you the bear you have heard tell of. Sir, I have no liking for the world. I live here in a world of fantasies, and I cannot tolerate the world as it is.' BOSWELL. 'But when you come across fantastical men, are they not to your liking?' ROUSSEAU. 'Why, Sir, they have not the same fantasies as myself.—Sir, your country is formed for liberty. I like your habits. You and I feel free to stroll here together without talking. That is more than two Frenchmen can do. Mankind disgusts me. And my housekeeper tells me that I am in far better humour on the days when I have been alone than on those when I have been in company.' BOSWELL. 'There has been a great deal written against you, Sir.' ROUSSEAU. 'They have not understood me. As for Monsieur Vernet at Geneva, he is an Arch-Jesuit, that is all I can say of him.'

BOSWELL. 'Tell me, Sir, do you not find that I answer to the description I gave you of myself?' ROUSSEAU. 'Sir, it is too early for me to judge. But all appearances are in your favour.' BOSWELL. 'I fear I have stayed too long. I shall take the honour of returning tomorrow.' ROUSSEAU. 'Oh, as to that, I can't tell.' BOSWELL. 'Sir, I shall stay quietly here in the village. If you are able to see me, I shall be enchanted; if not, I shall make no complaint.' ROUSSEAU. 'My Lord Marischal has a perfect understanding of man's feelings, in solitude no less than in society. I am overwhelmed with visits from idle people.' BOSWELL. 'And how do they spend their time?' ROUSSEAU. 'In paying compliments. Also I get a prodigious quantity of letters. And the writer of each of them believes that he is the only one.' BOSWELL. 'You must be greatly surprised, Sir, that a man who has not the honour of your acquaintance should take the liberty of writing to you?' ROUSSEAU. 'No. I am not at all surprised. For I got a letter like it yesterday, and one the day before yesterday, and others many times before that.' BOSWELL. 'Sir, your very humble servant.—What, you are coming further?' ROUSSEAU. 'I am not coming with you. I am going for a walk in the passage. Good-bye.'

I had great satisfaction after finding that I could support the character which I had given of myself, after finding that I should most certainly be regarded by the illustrious Rousseau. I had a strange kind of feeling after having at last seen the author of whom I had thought so much.

Wednesday 5 December When I waited upon Monsieur Rousseau this morning, he said, 'My dear Sir, I am sorry not to be able to talk with you as I would wish.' I took care to waive such excuses, and immediately set conversation a-going. I told him how I had turned Roman Catholic and had intended

12. The union of England and Scotland under one parliament in 1707.

to hide myself in a convent in France. He said, 'What folly! I too was Catholic in my youth.[13] I changed, and then I changed back again. I returned to Geneva and was readmitted to the Protestant faith. I went again among Catholics, and used to say to them, "I am no longer one of you"; and I got on with them excellently.' I stopped him in the middle of the room and I said to him, 'But tell me sincerely, are you a Christian?' I looked at him with a searching eye. His countenance was no less animated. Each stood steady and watched the other's looks. He struck his breast, and replied. 'Yes. I pique myself upon being one.' BOSWELL. 'Sir, the soul can be sustained by nothing save the Gospel.' ROUSSEAU. 'I feel that. I am unaffected by all the objections. I am weak; there may be things beyond my reach; or perhaps the man who recorded them made a mistake. I say, God the Father, God the Son, God the Holy Ghost.'

BOSWELL. 'But tell me, do you suffer from melancholy?' ROUSSEAU. 'I was born placid. I have no natural disposition to melancholy. My misfortunes have infected me with it.' BOSWELL. 'I, for my part, suffer from it severely. And how can I be happy, I, who have done so much evil?' ROUSSEAU. 'Begin your life anew. God is good, for he is just. Do good. You will cancel all the debt of evil. Say to yourself in the morning, "Come now, I am going to *pay off* so much evil." Six well-spent years will pay off all the evil you have committed.' BOSWELL. 'But what do you think of cloisters, penances, and remedies of that sort?' ROUSSEAU. 'Mummeries, all of them, invented by men. Do not be guided by men's judgments, or you will find yourself tossed to and fro perpetually. Do not base your life on the judgments of others; first, because they are as likely to be mistaken as you are, and further, because you cannot know that they are telling you their true thoughts; they may be impelled by motives of interest or convention to talk to you in a way not corresponding to what they really think.' BOSWELL. 'Will you, Sir, assume direction of me?' ROUSSEAU. 'I cannot. I can be responsible only for myself.' BOSWELL. 'But I shall come back.' ROUSSEAU. 'I don't promise to see you. I am in pain. I need a chamber-pot every minute.'[14] BOSWELL. 'Yes, you will see me.' ROUSSEAU. 'Be off; and a good journey to you.'

About six I set out.

[1776: Reflections on Man]

Sunday 31 December   (I am now writing on Tuesday 2 January 1776.) My cold and sprained ankle were worse. I lay in bed but did not enjoy that tranquillity which I have formerly done in that state of indolence. I read in *The Critical Review* an account of Priestley's edition of Hartley's *Observations on Man*[15] with some essays of his own relative to the subject of that book. While

13. For Rousseau's conversion, see the Headnote to his *Confessions* in Sense and Sensibility; of Boswell's nothing is known. While he was in Holland, Boswell had found relief from some of his own Calvinistic severities of self-reproach in reading Rousseau's "Creed of a Savoyard Vicar," in *Émile*.

14. Rousseau was suffering from a congestion or constriction of the urethra.

15. David Hartley (1705–57) was trained in both medicine and divinity although he did not take either a medical degree or holy orders; his *Observations on Man* (1749) derived all religious and moral ideas from association of sense perceptions, and all thought processes from mechanical vibrations in the nerves and brain. While Hartley denied free will he claimed not to be a materialist and remained a devout Christian. Joseph Priestley abridged his work in 1775, omitting the theory of vibrations as too obscure, and gained great popularity for Hartley (whose influence on Coleridge and Wordsworth was great).

I was carried into metaphysical abstraction, and felt that *perhaps* all our thinking of every kind was only a variety of modification upon matter, I was in a sort of amaze; but I must observe that it did not affect me with 'that secret dread and inward horror' [16] which it has occasioned at other times. There is no accounting for our feelings, but certain it is that what strikes us strongly at one time will have little influence at another. Speculation of this kind relieved me from the vexation of family differences, by changing objects and by making me consider, 'If all thought and all volition and all that we denominate spirit be only properties of matter, why should I distress myself at present, while in full consciousness, about eventual successions of machines?' I however thought that philosophical theories were transient, whereas feudal principles remained for ages. In truth the mortality or immortality of the soul can make no difference on the enthusiasm for supporting a family, for, in either case, the matter must be of no moment to those who have departed this life. If they have ceased to exist, they know nothing of it. If they exist in another state, they perhaps even then know not what passes here, and, if they do, it is perhaps as trifling in their eyes as our childish concerns are in ours when we have arrived at manhood. How strange is it, then, that a man will toil all his life and deny himself satisfactions in order to aggrandize his posterity after he is dead. It is, I fancy, from a kind of delusion in the imagination, which makes us figure ourselves contemplating for ages our own magnificence in a succession of descendants. So strong is this delusion with me that I would suffer death rather than let the estate of Auchinleck be sold; and this must be from an enthusiasm for an *idea* for *the Family*.[17] The founder of it I never saw, so how can I be zealous for his race? and were I to be a martyr, I should only be reckoned a madman. But an *idea* will produce the highest enthusiasm. Witness the ardour which the individuals at the time have for the glory of their regiment, though they have no line of connexion with it, being picked out from all parts of the kingdom. The officers and soldiers of the Scots Greys boast that 'We were never known to fly.'—'We gained distinguished honour at such a battle.' Yet the officers and soldiers under that *name* at former periods were as different from its officers and soldiers now as the Romans were. I don't mean that they were different in body or in mind, in any remarkable degree, but that there is not a trace of identity, unless that there is always a remain of a regiment to communicate the same discipline and gallantry of sentiment to those who come into it, so that *l'esprit du corps*, like the fire of Vesta,[18] is kept incessantly burning, though the materials are different. I thought for a little that a man should place his pride and his happiness in his own individuality, and endeavour to be as rich and as renowned and as happy as he can. I considered that Dr. Johnson is as well as if he belonged to a *family*. Priestley's *material* system affected me less that he declared his belief in Christianity, which teaches us that GOD bestows a future life. However, I thought myself strongly conscious of an immaterial something—of a soul. I read a pamphlet today, which I remember having looked at about twenty years ago: *The Trial of the Witnesses for the Resurrection of Jesus*.[19] I found it to be a

16. "Whence this secret dread, and inward horror, of falling into naught?" Addison, *Cato* V.i.4–5.
17. Perhaps "an *idea* of the *Family*" or "for an *idea*, for the *Family*."
18. Whose perpetual flame was kept by the Vestal Virgins in her temple at Rome.
19. (1729) by Thomas Sherlock, later Bishop of London.

piece of very good argument which confirmed me in my faith; but I was a little disgusted with its author's affecting a sort of easy smartness of dialogue in some places. . . .

Wednesday 3 January. . . . My state of mind today was still affected by Hartley and Priestley's metaphysics, and was continually trying to perceive my faculties operating as machinery. My animal spirits were so light now that such sort of thinking did not distress me as it has done when I was more atrabilious.[20] I felt an easy indifference as to what was my mental system. I liked present consciousness. Man's continuation of existence is a flux of ideas in the same body, like the flux of a river in the same channel. Even our bodies are perpetually changing. What then is the subject of praise or blame upon the whole? what of love or hatred when we are to contemplate a character? There *must* be *something*, which we understand by a *spirit* or a *soul*, which is permanent. And yet I must own that except the sense or perception of identity, I cannot say that there is any sameness in my soul now and my soul twenty years ago, or surely none thirty years ago. Though souls may be in a flux, each may have a distinct character as rivers have: one rapid, one smooth, etc. I read a little of Lord Hailes's *Annals.* . . .

Tuesday 9 January   In the intervals while Mr. Lawrie copied passages, I read *The Monthly Review* on Priestley's edition of Hartley, and found his *material* system refuted with ability and spirit. I was much pleased, and wished to be acquainted with the writer of the article. I could not but think what a strange life a man would lead who should fairly act according to metaphysical conviction or impression at the time. What inconsistency and extravagance should we find! Sometimes he would be rigidly virtuous, at other times abandoned to extreme licentiousness; and at both times acting from *principle.* I have thought of writing a kind of novel to show this: 'Memoirs of a Practical Metaphysician.' I remember I mentioned this to Dr. Reid,[21] who writes on the mind according to common sense. He told me the same thought had occurred to him. Maclaurin observed very well, when he was last with me, that thinking metaphysically destroys the principles of morality; and indeed when a man analyses virtues and vices as a chemist does material substances, they lose their value as well as their odiousness. . . .

From The Life of Samuel Johnson, LL.D.

[1729: "Morbid Melancholy"]

The 'morbid melancholy,' which was lurking in his constitution, and to which we may ascribe those particularities, and that aversion to regular life, which, at a very early period, marked his character, gathered such strength in his twentieth year, as to afflict him in a dreadful manner. While he was at Lich-

---

20. Afflicted by black bile or melancholy.
21. Dr. Thomas Reid (1710–96), Professor of Moral Philosophy at the University of Glasgow, a leader of the Common Sense school of philosophy and an opponent of David Hume; his *Inquiry into the Human Mind* (1764) had freed Boswell from the "sceptical cobweb" of Hume during Boswell's stay in Berlin.

field, in the college vacation of the year 1729, he felt himself overwhelmed with an horrible hypochondria, with perpetual irritation, fretfulness, and impatience; and with a dejection, gloom, and despair, which made existence misery. From this dismal malady he never afterwards was perfectly relieved; and all his labours, and all his enjoyments, were but temporary interruptions of its baleful influence. How wonderful, how unsearchable are the ways of GOD! Johnson, who was blest with all the powers of genius and understanding in a degree far above the ordinary state of human nature, was at the same time visited with a disorder so afflictive, that they who know it by dire experience, will not envy his exalted endowments. That it was, in some degree, occasioned by a defect in his nervous system, that inexplicable part of our frame, appears highly probable. He told Mr. Paradise that he was sometimes so languid and inefficient, that he could not distinguish the hour upon the town-clock.

Johnson, upon the first violent attack of this disorder, strove to overcome it by forcible exertions. He frequently walked to Birmingham and back again,[1] and tried many other expedients, but all in vain. His expression concerning it to me was, 'I did not then know how to manage it.' His distress became so intolerable, that he applied to Dr. Swinfen, physician in Lichfield, his god-father, and put into his hands a state of his case, written in Latin. Dr. Swinfen was so much struck with the extraordinary acuteness, research, and eloquence of this paper, that in his zeal for his godson he showed it to several people. His daughter, Mrs. Desmoulins, who was many years humanely supported in Dr. Johnson's house in London, told me that upon his discovering that Dr. Swinfen had communicated his case, he was so much offended, that he was never after-wards fully reconciled to him. He indeed had good reason to be offended; for though Dr. Swinfen's motive was good, he inconsiderately betrayed a matter deeply interesting and of great delicacy, which had been entrusted to him in confidence; and exposed a complaint of his young friend and patient, which, in the superficial opinion of the generality of mankind, is attended with con-tempt and disgrace.

But let not little men triumph upon knowing that Johnson was an HYPO-CHONDRIAC, was subject to what the learned, philosophical, and pious Dr. Cheyne has so well treated under the title of 'The English Malady.'[2] Though he suffered severely from it, he was not therefore degraded. The powers of his great mind might be troubled, and their full exercise suspended at times; but the mind itself was ever entire. As a proof of this, it is only necessary to con-sider, that, when he was at the very worst, he composed that state of his own case, which showed an uncommon vigour, not only of fancy and taste, but of judgement. I am aware that he himself was too ready to call such a complaint by the name of *madness*; in conformity with which notion, he has traced its gradations, with exquisite nicety, in one of the chapters of his *Rasselas*. But there is surely a clear distinction between a disorder which affects only the imagination and spirits, while the judgement is sound, and a disorder by which the judgement itself is impaired. . . .

. . . To Johnson, whose supreme enjoyment was the exercise of his reason,

1. Thirty-two miles in all.
2. Dr. George Cheyne (1671–1743), *The English Malady, or a Treatise of Nervous Dis-eases of All Kinds* (1733), a book Johnson twice recommended to Boswell.

the disturbance or obscuration of that faculty was the evil most to be dreaded. Insanity, therefore, was the object of his most dismal apprehension; and he fancied himself seized by it, or approaching to it, at the very time when he was giving proofs of a more than ordinary soundness and vigour of judgement. That his own diseased imagination should have so far deceived him is strange; but it is stranger still that some of his friends should have given credit to his groundless opinion when they had such undoubted proofs that it was totally fallacious; though it is by no means surprising that those who wish to depreciate him should, since his death, have laid hold of his circumstance and insisted upon it with very unfair aggravation.

Amidst the oppression and distraction of a disease which very few have felt in its full extent, but many have experienced in a slighter degree, Johnson, in his writings, and in his conversation, never failed to display all the varieties of intellectual excellence. In his march through this world to a better, his mind still appeared grand and brilliant, and impressed all around him with the truth of Virgil's noble sentiment—

Igneus est ollis vigor et cœlestis origo.[3]

The history of his mind as to religion is an important article. I have mentioned the early impressions made upon his tender imagination by his mother, who continued her pious care with assiduity, but, in his opinion, not with judgement. 'Sunday (said he) was a heavy day to me when I was a boy. My mother confined me on that day, and made me read "The Whole Duty of Man," [4] from a great part of which I could derive no instruction. When, for instance, I had read the chapter on theft, which from my infancy I had been taught was wrong, I was no more convinced that theft was wrong than before; so there was no accession of knowledge. A boy should be introduced to such books by having his attention directed to the arrangement, to the style, and other excellencies of composition; that the mind being thus engaged by an amusing variety of objects, may not grow weary.'

He communicated to me the following particulars upon the subject of his religious progress. 'I fell into an inattention to religion, or an indifference about it, in my ninth year. The church at Lichfield, in which we had a seat, wanted reparation, so I was to go and find a seat in other churches; and having bad eyes, and being awkward about this, I used to go and read in the fields on Sunday. This habit continued till my fourteenth year; and still I find a great reluctance to go to church. I then became a sort of lax *talker* against religion, for I did not much *think* against it; and this lasted till I went to Oxford, where it would not be *suffered*. When at Oxford, I took up Law's *Serious Call to a Holy Life*,[5] expecting to find it a dull book (as such books generally are), and perhaps to laugh at it. But I found Law quite an over-match for me; and this was the first occasion of my thinking in earnest of religion, after I became

3. "Quick in these seeds is might of fire and birth of heavenly place" (*Aeneid*, Morris trans., VI.730).
4. The popular moral work attributed to Dr. Richard Allestree (1619–81).
5. For William Law, see the selections from Edward Gibbon's *Memoirs* in Sense and Sensibility. Law's work had great influence upon both John Wesley and George Whitefield, the founders of Methodism.

capable of rational inquiry.' From this time forward religion was the predominant object of his thoughts; though, with the just sentiments of a conscientious Christian, he lamented that his practice of its duties fell far short of what it ought to be. . . .

How seriously Johnson was impressed with a sense of religion, even in the vigour of his youth, appears from the following passage in his minutes kept by way of diary: Sept. 7, 1736. I have this day entered upon my twenty-eighth year. 'Mayest thou, O God, enable me, for Jesus Christ's sake, to spend this in such a manner that I may receive comfort from it at the hour of death, and in the day of judgement! Amen.'

The particular course of his reading while at Oxford, and during the time of vacation which he passed at home, cannot be traced. Enough has been said of his irregular mode of study. He told me that from his earliest years he loved to read poetry, but hardly ever read any poem to an end; that he read Shakespeare at a period so early, that the speech of the ghost in Hamlet terrified him when he was alone; that Horace's Odes were the compositions in which he took most delight, and it was long before he liked his Epistles and Satires. He told me what he read *solidly* at Oxford was Greek; not the Grecian historians, but Homer and Euripides, and now and then a little Epigram; that the study of which he was the most fond was Metaphysics, but he had not read much, even in that way. I always thought that he did himself injustice in his account of what he had read, and that he must have been speaking with reference to the vast portion of study which is possible, and to which a few scholars in the whole history of literature have attained; for when I once asked him whether a person, whose name I have now forgotten, studied hard, he answered 'No, Sir; I do not believe he studied hard. I never knew a man who studied hard. I conclude, indeed, from the effects, that some men have studied hard, as Bentley and Clarke.' [6] Trying him by that criterion upon which he formed his judgement of others, we may be absolutely certain, both from his writings and his conversation, that his reading was very extensive. Dr. Adam Smith,[7] than whom few were better judges on this subject, once observed to me that 'Johnson knew more books than any man alive.' He had a peculiar facility in seizing at once what was valuable in any book, without submitting to the labour of perusing it from beginning to end. He had, from the irritability of his constitution, at all times, an impatience and hurry when he either read or wrote. A certain apprehension, arising from novelty, made him write his first exercise at College twice over; but he never took that trouble with any other composition; and we shall see that his most excellent works were struck off at a heat, with rapid exertion.

Yet he appears, from his early notes or memorandums in my possession, to have at various times attempted, or at least planned, a methodical course of study, according to computation, of which he was all his life fond, as it fixed

6. Richard Bentley (1662–1742), the great classical scholar attacked by Swift in *The Battle of the Books* and Pope in *The Dunciad* IV; Samuel Clarke (1675–1729), distinguished metaphysician and moral philosopher, who gave the Boyle Lectures in 1704–1705 and engaged in a celebrated correspondence with Leibnitz.
7. Adam Smith (1723–90), the Scottish professor of logic and moral philosopher, now best known for his work of economics, *The Wealth of Nations* (1776).

his attention steadily upon something without, and prevented his mind from preying upon itself. Thus I find in his handwriting the number of lines in each of two of Euripides' Tragedies, of the Georgics of Virgil, of the first six books of the Aeneid, of Horace's Art of Poetry, of three of the books of Ovid's Metamorphosis, of some parts of Theocritus, and of the tenth Satire of Juvenal; and a table, showing at the rate of various numbers a day (I suppose verses to be read), what would be, in each case, the total amount in a week, month, and year.

No man had a more ardent love of literature, or a higher respect for it than Johnson. His apartment in Pembroke College was that upon the second floor, over the gateway. The enthusiasts of learning will ever contemplate it with veneration. One day, while he was sitting in it quite alone, Dr. Panting, then master of the College, whom he called 'a fine Jacobite fellow,' overheard him uttering this soliloquy in his strong, emphatic voice: 'Well, I have a mind to see what is done in other places of learning. I'll go and visit the Universities abroad. I'll go to France and Italy. I'll go to Padua.—And I'll mind my business. For an *Athenian* blockhead is the worst of all blockheads.'

Dr. Adams told me that Johnson, while he was at Pembroke College, 'was caressed and loved by all about him, was a gay and frolicsome fellow, and passed there the happiest part of his life.' But this is a striking proof of the fallacy of appearances, and how little any of us know of the real internal state even of those whom we see most frequently; for the truth is, that he was then depressed by poverty, and irritated by disease. When I mentioned to him this account as given me by Dr. Adams, he said, 'Ah, Sir, I was mad and violent. It was bitterness which they mistook for frolic. I was miserably poor, and I thought to fight my way by my literature and my wit; so I disregarded all power and all authority.'

[1754: The *Dictionary* and Lord Chesterfield]

The *Dictionary*, we may believe, afforded Johnson full occupation this year. As it approached to its conclusion, he probably worked with redoubled vigour, as seamen increase their exertion and alacrity when they have a near prospect of their haven.

Lord Chesterfield, to whom Johnson had paid the high compliment of addressing to his Lordship the *Plan* of his *Dictionary*, had behaved to him in such a manner as to excite his contempt and indignation. The world has been for many years amused with a story confidently told, and as confidently repeated with additional circumstances, that a sudden disgust was taken by Johnson upon occasion of his having been one day kept long in waiting in his Lordship's antechamber, for which the reason assigned was, that he had company with him; and that at last, when the door opened, out walked Colley Cibber; [8] and that Johnson was so violently provoked when he found for whom he had been so long excluded, that he went away in a passion, and never would return . . . but Johnson himself assured me, that there was not the least foundation for it.

8. Colley Cibber (1671–1757), dramatist and actor, poet laureate 1730–57, the mock-hero of Pope's revised *Dunciad;* Johnson scorned his ignorance and "impenetrable impudence."

He told me, that there never was any particular incident which produced a quarrel between Lord Chesterfield and him; but that his Lordship's continued neglect was the reason why he resolved to have no connection with him. When the *Dictionary* was upon the eve of publication, Lord Chesterfield, who, it is said, had flattered himself with expectations that Johnson would dedicate the work to him, attempted, in a courtly manner, to soothe, and insinuate himself with the Sage, conscious, as it should seem, of the cold indifference with which he had treated its learned author; and further attempted to conciliate him, by writing two papers in *The World*, in recommendation of the work; and it must be confessed, that they contain some studied compliments, so finely turned, that if there had been no previous offence, it is probable that Johnson would have been highly delighted. Praise, in general, was pleasing to him; but by praise from a man of rank and elegant accomplishments, he was peculiarly gratified. . . .

This courtly device failed of its effect. Johnson, who thought that 'all was false and hollow,' despised the honeyed words, and was even indignant that Lord Chesterfield should, for a moment, imagine that he could be the dupe of such an artifice. His expression to me concerning Lord Chesterfield, upon this occasion, was, 'Sir, after making great professions, he had, for many years, taken no notice of me; but when my *Dictionary* was coming out, he fell a scribbling in *The World* about it. Upon which, I wrote him a letter expressed in civil terms, but such as might show him that I did not mind what he said or wrote, and that I had done with him.'

This is that celebrated letter of which so much has been said, and about which curiosity has been so long excited, without being gratified. . . .

'*To* The Right Honourable the Earl of Chesterfield
'My Lord,
                                                                    February 1755
'I have been lately informed, by the proprietor of *The World,* that two papers, in which my Dictionary is recommended to the public, were written by your Lordship. To be so distinguished, is an honour, which, being very little accustomed to favours from the great, I know not well how to receive, or in what terms to acknowledge.

'When, upon some slight encouragement, I first visited your Lordship, I was overpowered, like the rest of mankind, by the enchantment of your address; and could not forbear to wish that I might boast myself *Le vainqueur du vainqueur de la terre;* [9]—that I might obtain that regard for which I saw the world contending; but I found my attendance so little encouraged, that neither pride nor modesty would suffer me to continue it. When I had once addressed your Lordship in public, I had exhausted all the art of pleasing which a retired and uncourtly scholar can possess. I had done all that I could; and no man is well pleased to have his all neglected, be it ever so little.

'Seven years, my Lord, have now past, since I waited in your outward rooms, or was repulsed from your door; during which time I have been pushing on my work through difficulties, of which it is useless to complain, and have brought it, at last, to the verge of publication, without one act of assistance,

---

9. "The conqueror of the conqueror of the earth."

one word of encouragement, or one smile of favour. Such treatment I did not expect, for I never had a Patron before.

'The shepherd in Virgil grew at last acquainted with Love, and found him a native of the rocks.[10]

'Is not a Patron, my Lord, one who looks with unconcern on a man struggling for life in the water, and, when he has reached ground, encumbers him with help? The notice which you have been pleased to take of my labours, had it been early, had been kind; but it has been delayed till I am indifferent, and cannot enjoy it; till I am solitary, and cannot impart it; [11] till I am known, and do not want it. I hope it is no very cynical asperity not to confess obligations where no benefit has been received, or to be unwilling that the Public should consider me as owing that to a Patron which Providence has enabled me to do for myself.

'Having carried on my work thus far with so little obligation to any favourer of learning, I shall not be disappointed though I should conclude it, if less be possible, with less; for I have been long wakened from that dream of hope, in which I once boasted myself with so much exultation, my Lord, your Lordship's most humble, most obedient servant,

SAM. JOHNSON.'

. . . There is a curious minute circumstance which struck me, in comparing the various editions of Johnson's imitations of Juvenal. In the tenth Satire, one of the couplets upon the vanity of wishes even for literary distinction stood thus:

> Yet think what ills the scholar's life assail,
> Pride, envy, want, the *garret*, and the jail.

But after experiencing the uneasiness which Lord Chesterfield's fallacious patronage made him feel, he dismissed the word *garret* from the sad group, and in all the subsequent editions the line stands

> Toil, envy, want, the *Patron*, and the jail.[12]

[1763: The Meeting with Boswell]

. . . Mr. Davies [13] recollected several of Johnson's remarkable sayings, and was one of the best of the many imitators of his voice and manner, while relating them. He increased my impatience more and more to see the extraordinary man whose works I highly valued, and whose conversation was reported to be so peculiarly excellent.

At last, on Monday the 16th of May, when I was sitting in Mr. Davies's back-parlour, after having drunk tea with him and Mrs. Davies, Johnson unexpectedly came into the shop; and Mr. Davies having perceived him through the glass door in the room in which we were sitting, advancing towards us,—he an-

10. *Eclogues* VIII.43: "I know thee, Love; in deserts thou wast bred" (Dryden trans.).
11. Referring to the death of his wife, March 17, 1752.
12. In his *Dictionary* Johnson defined *patron* as "commonly a wretch who supports with insolence and is paid with flattery."
13. Thomas Davies, actor and bookseller, "a man of good understanding and talents, with the advantage of a liberal education"; "a friendly and very hospitable man" whom Johnson visited freely.

nounced his aweful approach to me, somewhat in the manner of an actor in the part of Horatio, when he addresses Hamlet on the appearance of his father's ghost, 'Look, my Lord, it comes.' I found that I had a very perfect idea of Johnson's figure from the portrait of him painted by Sir Joshua Reynolds soon after he had published his *Dictionary*, in the attitude of sitting in his easy chair in deep meditation. . . . Mr. Davies mentioned my name, and respectfully introduced me to him. I was much agitated; and recollecting his prejudice against the Scotch, of which I had heard much, I said to Davies, 'Don't tell where I come from.'—'From Scotland,' cried Davies roguishly. 'Mr. Johnson, (said I) I do indeed come from Scotland, but I cannot help it.' I am willing to flatter myself that I meant this as light pleasantry to soothe and conciliate him, and not as an humiliating abasement at the expence of my country. But however that might be, this speech was somewhat unlucky; for with that quickness of wit for which he was so remarkable, he seized the expression 'come from Scotland,' which I used in the sense of being of that country, and, as if I had said that I had come away from it, or left it, retorted, 'That, Sir, I find, is what a very great many of your countrymen cannot help.' This stroke stunned me a good deal; and when we had sat down, I felt myself not a little embarrassed, and apprehensive of what might come next. He then addressed himself to Davies: 'What do you think of Garrick? [14] He has refused me an order for the play for Miss Williams,[15] because he knows the house will be full, and that an order would be worth three shillings.' Eager to take any opening to get into conversation with him, I ventured to say, 'O, Sir, I cannot think Mr. Garrick would grudge such a trifle to you.' 'Sir, (said he, with a stern look,) I have known David Garrick longer than you have done: and I know no right you have to talk to me on the subject.' Perhaps I deserved this check; for it was rather presumptuous in me, an entire stranger, to express any doubt of the justice of his animadversion upon his old acquaintance and pupil. I now felt myself much mortified, and began to think that the hope which I had long indulged of obtaining his acquaintance was blasted. And, in truth, had not my ardour been uncommonly strong, and my resolution uncommonly persevering, so rough a reception might have deterred me for ever from making any further attempts. Fortunately, however, I remained upon the field not wholly discomfited; and was soon rewarded by hearing some of his conversation, of which I preserved the following short minute, without marking the questions and observations by which it was produced.

'People (he remarked) may be taken in once, who imagine that an author is greater in private life than other men. Uncommon parts require uncommon opportunities for their exertion.

'In barbarous society, superiority of parts is of real consequence. Great strength or great wisdom is of much value to an individual. But in more polished times there are people to do every thing for money; and then there are a number of other superiorities, such as those of birth and fortune, and

14. David Garrick, the great actor, had been a pupil of Johnson in his school at Edial (1736–37).
15. Anna Williams (1706–83), Johnson's friend and protégée, for whom David Garrick gave a benefit at Drury Lane.

rank, that dissipate men's attention, and leave no extraordinary share of respect for personal and intellectual superiority. This is wisely ordered by Providence, to preserve some equality among mankind.

'Sir, this book (*The Elements of Criticism*,[16] which he had taken up,) is a pretty essay, and deserves to be held in some estimation, though much of it is chimerical.'

Speaking of one [17] who with more than ordinary boldness attacked public measures and the royal family, he said,

'I think he is safe from the law, but he is an abusive scoundrel; and instead of applying to my Lord Chief Justice to punish him, I would send half a dozen footmen and have him well ducked.'

'The notion of liberty amuses the people of England, and helps to keep off the *tædium vitae*. When a butcher tells you that *his heart bleeds for his country*, he has, in fact, no uneasy feeling.

'Sheridan [18] will not succeed at Bath with his oratory. Ridicule has gone down before him, and, I doubt, Derrick is his enemy.

'Derrick may do very well, as long as he can outrun his character; but the moment his character gets up with him, it is all over.'

It is, however, but just to record, that some years afterwards, when I reminded him of this sarcasm, he said, 'Well, but Derrick has now got a character that he need not run away from.'

I was highly pleased with the extraordinary vigour of his conversation, and regretted that I was drawn away from it by an engagement at another place. I had, for a part of the evening, been left alone with him, and had ventured to make an observation now and then, which he received very civilly; so that I was satisfied that though there was a roughness in his manner, there was no ill-nature in his disposition. Davies followed me to the door, and when I complained to him a little of the hard blows which the great man had given me, he kindly took upon him to console me by saying, 'Don't be uneasy. I can see he likes you very well.'

A few days afterwards I called on Davies, and asked him if he thought I might take the liberty of waiting on Mr. Johnson at his Chambers in the Temple. He said I certainly might, and that Mr. Johnson would take it as a compliment. So upon Tuesday the 24th of May, after having been enlivened by the witty sallies of Messieurs Thornton, Wilkes, Churchill [19] and Lloyd, with whom I had passed the morning, I boldly repaired to Johnson. His Chambers were on the first floor of No. 1, Inner-Temple-lane, and I entered them with

16. By Henry Home, Lord Kames, published in Edinburgh in 1762.
17. John Wilkes (1727–97), in 1762 founded *The North Briton*, a journal in which he attacked the ministry of Lord Bute. He was prosecuted for libel and, as a result of an obscene article, expelled from Commons and declared an outlaw. He fled to Paris and returned in 1768 to resume his parliamentary career. His famous meeting with Johnson took place in 1776, two years after he served as Lord Mayor of London.
18. Thomas Sheridan (1719–88), actor, author, father of the playwright, and lecturer on elocution—at the moment at Bath, where Samuel Derrick was Master of Ceremonies, "or as the phrase is, King" (Boswell).
19. Charles Churchill (1731–64), the satiric poet, who had attacked Johnson "violently" (in Boswell's view).

an impression given me by the Reverend Dr. Blair, of Edinburgh,[20] who had been introduced to him not long before, and described his having 'found the Giant in his den'; an expression, which, when I came to be pretty well acquainted with Johnson, I repeated to him, and he was diverted at this picturesque account of himself. Dr. Blair had been presented to him by Dr. James Fordyce. At this time the controversy concerning the pieces published by Mr. James Macpherson, as translations of *Ossian*, was at its height. Johnson had all along denied their authenticity; and, what was still more provoking to their admirers, maintained that they had no merit. The subject having been introduced by Dr. Fordyce, Dr. Blair, relying on the internal evidence of their antiquity, asked Dr. Johnson whether he thought any man of a modern age could have written such poems? Johnson replied, 'Yes, Sir, many men, many women, and many children.' Johnson, at this time, did not know that Dr. Blair had just published a *Dissertation,* not only defending their authenticity, but seriously ranking them with the poems of Homer and Virgil; and when he was afterwards informed of this circumstance, he expressed some displeasure at Dr. Fordyce's having suggested the topic, and said, 'I am not sorry that they got thus much for their pains. Sir, it was like leading one to talk of a book when the author is concealed behind the door.'

He received me very courteously; but, it must be confessed, that his apartment, and furniture, and morning dress, were sufficiently uncouth. His brown suit of clothes looked very rusty; he had on a little old shrivelled unpowdered wig which was too small for his head; his shirt-neck and knees of his breeches were loose; his black worsted stockings ill drawn up; and he had a pair of unbuckled shoes by way of slippers. But all these slovenly particularities were forgotten the moment that he began to talk. Some gentlemen, whom I do not recollect, were sitting with him; and when they went away, I also rose; but he said to me, 'Nay, don't go.' 'Sir, (said I,) I am afraid that I intrude upon you. It is benevolent to allow me to sit and hear you.' He seemed pleased with this compliment, which I sincerely paid him, and answered, 'Sir, I am obliged to any man who visits me.' I have preserved the following short minute of what passed this day:—

'Madness frequently discovers itself merely by unnecessary deviation from the usual modes of the world. My poor friend Smart showed the disturbance of his mind, by falling upon his knees, and saying his prayers in the street, or in any other unusual place. Now although, rationally speaking, it is greater madness not to pray at all, than to pray as Smart did, I am afraid there are so many who do not pray, that their understanding is not called in question.'

Concerning this unfortunate poet, Christopher Smart, who was confined in a mad-house, he had, at another time, the following conversation with Dr.

---

20. Dr. Hugh Blair (1718–1800), a clergyman well known for his sermons and a critic of rhetoric and literature; introduced to Johnson by his friend the physician Fordyce. The controversy concerning Macpherson's alleged translations from Ossian was settled by a committee that, after his death, declared them in part free versions of traditional poems with much original matter added. The Ossianic poems, purporting to be Gaelic epics, gained enormous vogue throughout Europe and were highly esteemed by Goethe among others. William Blake insisted upon their authenticity; Dr. Johnson remarked in 1783, "Sir, a man might write such stuff for ever, if he would *abandon* his mind to it."

Burney: [21]—B U R N E Y . 'How does poor Smart do, Sir; is he likely to recover?' J O H N S O N . 'It seems as if his mind had ceased to struggle with the disease; for he grows fat upon it.' B U R N E Y . 'Perhaps, Sir, that may be from want of exercise.' J O H N S O N . 'No, Sir; he has partly as much exercise as he used to have, for he digs in the garden. Indeed, before his confinement, he used for exercise to walk to the ale-house; but he was *carried* back again. I did not think he ought to be shut up. His infirmities were not noxious to society. He insisted on people praying with him; and I'd as lief pray with Kit Smart as any one else. Another charge was, that he did not love clean linen; and I have no passion for it.'—Johnson continued. 'Mankind have a great aversion to intellectual labour; but even supposing knowledge to be easily attainable, more people would be content to be ignorant than would take even a little trouble to acquire it.'

'The morality of an action depends on the motive from which we act. If I fling half a crown to a beggar with intention to break his head, and he picks it up and buys victuals with it, the physical effect is good; but, with respect to me, the action is very wrong. So, religious exercises, if not performed with an intention to please GOD, avail us nothing. As our Saviour says of those who perform them from other motives, "Verily they have their reward.". . .' [22]

When I rose a second time he again pressed me to stay, which I did.

He told me, that he generally went abroad at four in the afternoon, and seldom came home till two in the morning. I took the liberty to ask if he did not think it wrong to live thus, and not make more use of his great talents. He owned it was a bad habit. On reviewing, at the distance of many years, my journal of this period, I wonder how, at my first visit, I ventured to talk to him so freely, and that he bore it with so much indulgence.

Before we parted, he was so good as to promise to favour me with his company one evening at my lodgings; and, as I took my leave, shook me cordially by the hand. It is almost needless to add, that I felt no little elation at having now so happily established an acquaintance of which I had been so long ambitious. . . .

I did not visit him again till Monday, June 13, at which time I recollect no part of his conversation, except that when I told him I had been to see Johnson ride upon three horses,[23] he said, 'Such a man, Sir, should be encouraged; for his performances show the extent of the human powers in one instance, and thus tend to raise our opinion of the faculties of man. He shows what may be attained by persevering application; so that every man may hope, that by giving as much application, although perhaps he may never ride three horses at a time, or dance upon a wire, yet he may be equally expert in whatever profession he has chosen to pursue.'

He again shook me by the hand at parting, and asked me why I did not come oftener to him. Trusting that I was now in his good graces, I answered, that he had not given me much encouragement, and reminded him of the check I had received from him at our first interview. 'Poh, poh! (said he, with

21. Dr. Charles Burney (1726–1814), musician and historian of music, who helped raise a subscription for Smart during his final confinement in 1771.
22. Matthew 6:16.
23. A famous exhibition of riding by a Johnson of whom only the last name is known.

a complacent smile,) never mind these things. Come to me as often as you can. I shall be glad to see you.'

[1776: The Meeting with Wilkes]

I am now to record a very curious incident in Dr. Johnson's Life, which fell under my own observation; of which *pars magna fui*,[24] and which I am persuaded will, with the liberal-minded, be much to his credit.

My desire of being acquainted with celebrated men of every description, had made me, much about the same time, obtain an introduction to Dr. Samuel Johnson and to John Wilkes, Esq. Two men more different could perhaps not be selected out of all mankind. They had even attacked one another with some asperity in their writings; yet I lived in habits of friendship with both. I could fully relish the excellence of each; for I have ever delighted in that intellectual chemistry, which can separate good qualities from evil in the same person. . . .

Notwithstanding the high veneration which I entertained for Dr. Johnson, I was sensible that he was sometimes a little actuated by the spirit of contradiction, and by means of that I hoped I should gain my point. I was persuaded that if I had come upon him with a direct proposal, 'Sir, will you dine in company with Jack Wilkes?' he would have flown into a passion, and would probably have answered, 'Dine with Jack Wilkes, Sir! I'd as soon dine with Jack Ketch.'[25] I therefore, while we were sitting quietly by ourselves at his house in an evening, took occasion to open my plan thus:—'Mr. Dilly,[26] Sir, sends his respectful compliments to you, and would be happy if you would do him the honour to dine with him on Wednesday next along with me, as I must soon go to Scotland.' JOHNSON. 'Sir, I am obliged to Mr. Dilly. I will wait upon him—' BOSWELL. 'Provided, Sir, I suppose, that the company which he is to have is agreeable to you.' JOHNSON. 'What do you mean, Sir? What do you take me for? Do you think I am so ignorant of the world, as to imagine that I am to prescribe to a gentleman what company he is to have at his table?' BOSWELL. 'I beg your pardon, Sir, for wishing to prevent you from meeting people whom you might not like. Perhaps he may have some of what he calls his patriotic[27] friends with him.' JOHNSON. 'Well, Sir, and what then? What care *I* for his *patriotic friends*? Poh!' BOSWELL. 'I should not be surprised to find Jack Wilkes there.' JOHNSON. 'And if Jack Wilkes *should* be there, what is that to *me*, Sir? My dear friend, let us have no more of this. I am sorry to be angry with you; but really it is treating me strangely to talk to me as if I could not meet any company whatever, occasionally.' BOSWELL. 'Pray forgive me, Sir: I meant well. But you shall meet whoever comes, for me.' Thus I secured him, and told Dilly that he would find him very well pleased to be one of his guests on the day appointed. . . .

When we entered Mr. Dilly's drawing room, he found himself in the midst of a company he did not know. I kept myself snug and silent, watching how

24. "I was a great part," *Aeneid* II.5.
25. That is, the hangman.
26. Edward Dilly (1732–79), the bookseller.
27. Referring to the government opposition; in 1773 Johnson added a new definition of patriot: "It is sometimes used for a factious disturber of the government."

he would conduct himself. I observed him whispering to Mr. Dilly, 'Who is that gentleman, Sir?'—'Mr. Arthur Lee.'—J o h n s o n. 'Too, too, too,' (under his breath,) which was one of his habitual mutterings. Mr. Arthur Lee could not but be very obnoxious to Johnson, for he was not only a *patriot* but an *American*. He was afterwards minister from the United States at the court of Madrid. 'And who is the gentleman in lace?'—'Mr. Wilkes, Sir.' This information confounded him still more; he had some difficulty to restrain himself, and taking up a book, sat down upon a window-seat and read, or at least kept his eye upon it intently for some time, till he composed himself. His feelings, I dare say, were awkward enough. But he no doubt recollected his having rated me for supposing that he could be at all disconcerted by any company, and he, therefore, resolutely set himself to behave quite as an easy man of the world, who could adapt himself at once to the disposition and manners of those whom he might chance to meet.

The cheering sound of 'Dinner is upon the table,' dissolved his reverie, and we *all* sat down without any symptom of ill humour. There were present, besides Mr. Wilkes, and Mr. Arthur Lee, who was an old compaion of mine when he studied physic at Edinburgh, Mr. (now Sir John) Miller, Dr. Lettsom, and Mr. Slater the druggist. Mr. Wilkes placed himself next to Dr. Johnson, and behaved to him with so much attention and politeness that he gained upon him insensibly. No man eat [28] more heartily than Johnson, or loved better what was nice and delicate. Mr. Wilkes was very assiduous in helping him to some fine veal. 'Pray give me leave, Sir:—It is better here—A little of the brown— Some fat, Sir—A little of the stuffing—Some gravy—Let me have the pleasure of giving you some butter—Allow me to recommend a squeeze of this orange; —or the lemon, perhaps, may have more zest.'—'Sir, Sir, I am obliged to you, Sir,' cried Johnson, bowing, and turning his head to him with a look for some time of 'surly virtue,' [29] but, in a short while, of complacency.

Foote [30] being mentioned, Johnson said, 'He is not a good mimic.' One of the company added, 'A merry Andrew, a buffoon.' J o h n s o n. 'But he has wit too, and is not deficient in ideas, or in fertility and variety of imagery, and not empty of reading; he has knowledge enough to fill up his part. One species of wit he has in an eminent degree, that of escape. You drive him into a corner with both hands; but he's gone, Sir, when you think you have got him—like an animal that jumps over your head. Then he has a great range for his wit; he never lets truth stand between him and a jest, and he is sometimes mighty coarse. Garrick is under many restraints from which Foote is free.' W i l k e s. 'Garrick's wit is more like Lord Chesterfield's.' J o h n s o n. 'The first time I was in company with Foote was at Fitzherbert's. Having no good opinion of the fellow, I was resolved not to be pleased; and it is very difficult to please a man against his will. I went on eating my dinner pretty sullenly, affecting not to mind him. But the dog was so very comical, that I was obliged to lay down my knife and fork, throw myself back upon my chair, and fairly laugh it out.

28. "Eat" (pronounced *ett*) was a standard past form.
29. Boswell cites Johnson's *London*, ll. 144–45: "How, when competitors like these contend, / Can surly virtue hope to fix a friend?"
30. Samuel Foote (1720–77), actor and dramatist, of whom Johnson said, "For loud obstreperous broadfaced mirth, I know not his equal."

No, Sir, he was irresistible. He upon one occasion experienced, in an extraordinary degree, the efficacy of his powers of entertaining. Amongst the many and various modes which he tried of getting money, he became a partner with a small-beer [31] brewer, and he was to have a share of the profits for procuring customers amongst his numerous acquaintance. Fitzherbert was one who took his small-beer; but it was so bad that the servants resolved not to drink it. They were at some loss how to notify their resolution, being afraid of offending their master, who they knew liked Foote much as a companion. At last they fixed upon a little black boy, who was rather a favourite, to be their deputy, and deliver their remonstrance; and having invested him with the whole authority of the kitchen, he was to inform Mr. Fitzherbert, in all their names, upon a certain day, that they would drink Foote's small-beer no longer. On that day Foote happened to dine at Fitzherbert's, and this boy served at table; he was so delighted with Foote's stories, and merriment, and grimace, that when he went down stairs, he told them, "This is the finest man I have ever seen. I will not deliver your message. I will drink his small-beer." '

Somebody observed that Garrick could not have done this. W I L K E S. 'Garrick would have made the small-beer still smaller. He is now leaving the stage; but he will play *Scrub* all his life.' [32] I knew that Johnson would let nobody attack Garrick but himself, as Garrick once said to me, and I had heard him praise his liberality; so to bring out his commendation of his celebrated pupil, I said, loudly, 'I have heard Garrick is liberal.' J O H N S O N. 'Yes, Sir, I know that Garrick has given away more money than any man in England that I am acquainted with, and that not from ostentatious views. Garrick was very poor when he began life; so when he came to have money, he probably was very unskilful in giving away, and saved when he should not. But Garrick began to be liberal as soon as he could; and I am of opinion, the reputation of avarice which he has had, has been very lucky for him, and prevented his having many enemies. You despise a man for avarice, but do not hate him. Garrick might have been much better attacked for living with more splendour than is suitable to a player: if they had had the wit to have assaulted him in that quarter, they might have galled him more. But they have kept clamouring about his avarice, which has rescued him from much obloquy and envy.' . . .

Mr. Arthur Lee mentioned some Scotch who had taken possession of a barren part of America, and wondered why they should choose it. J O H N S O N. 'Why, Sir, all barrenness is comparative. The *Scotch* would not know it to be barren.' B O S W E L L. 'Come, come, he is flattering the English. You have now been in Scotland, Sir, and say if you did not see meat and drink enough there.' J O H N S O N. 'Why yes, Sir; meat and drink enough to give the inhabitants sufficient strength to run away from home.' All these quick and lively sallies were said sportively, quite in jest, and with a smile, which showed that he meant only wit. Upon this topic he and Mr. Wilkes could perfectly assimilate; here was a bond of union between them, and I was conscious that as

31. A weak or inferior beer.
32. Scrub is the servant to Sullen in George Farquhar's comedy *The Beaux' Stratagem* (1707); he has a different duty each day (that of butler on Sundays) and supplies a full staff in himself.

both of them had visited Caledonia, both were fully satisfied of the strange narrow ignorance of those who imagine that it is a land of famine. But they amused themselves with persevering in the old jokes. When I claimed a superiority for Scotland over England in one respect, that no man can be arrested there for a debt merely because another swears it against him; but there must first be the judgement of a court of law ascertaining its justice; and that a seizure of the person, before judgement is obtained, can take place only, if his creditor should swear that he is about to fly from the country, or, as it is technically expressed, is in *meditatione fugæ*: [33] W I L K E S. 'That, I should think, may be safely sworn of all the Scotch nation.' J O H N S O N. (to Mr. Wilkes,) 'You must know, Sir, I lately took my friend Boswell and showed him genuine civilised life in an English provincial town. I turned him loose at Lichfield, my native city, that he might see for once real civility: for you know he lives among savages in Scotland and among rakes in London.' W I L K E S. 'Except when he is with grave, sober, decent people like you and me.' J O H N S O N. (smiling,) 'And we ashamed of him.'

They were quite frank and easy. Johnson told the story of his asking Mrs. Macaulay to allow her footman to sit down with them,[34] to prove the ridiculousness of the argument for the equality of mankind; and he said to me afterwards, with a nod of satisfaction, 'You saw Mr. Wilkes acquiesced.' Wilkes talked with all imaginable freedom of the ludicrous title given to the Attorney-General, *Diabolus Regis*;[35] adding, 'I have reason to know something about that officer; for I prosecuted for a libel.' Johnson, who many people would have supposed must have been furiously angry at hearing this talked of so lightly, said not a word. He was now, *indeed*, 'a good-humoured fellow.' . . .

This record, though by no means so perfect as I could wish, will serve to give a notion of a very curious interview, which was not only pleasing at the time, but had the agreeable and benignant effect of reconciling any animosity, and sweetening any acidity, which in the various bustle of political contest, had been produced in the minds of two men, who though widely different, had so many things in common—classical learning, modern literature, wit, and humour, and ready repartee—that it would have been much to be regretted if they had been for ever at a distance from each other.

Mr. Burke gave me much credit for this successful *négotiation;* and pleasantly said, that 'there was nothing to equal it in the whole history of the *Corps Diplomatique.*' . . .

On the evening of the next day I took leave of him, being to set out for Scotland. I thanked him with great warmth for all his kindness. 'Sir, (said he,) you are very welcome. Nobody repays it with more.'

How very false is the notion which has gone round the world of the rough, and passionate, and harsh manners of this great and good man. That he had occasional sallies of heat of temper, and that he was sometimes, perhaps, too

33. "Meditating flight."
34. That proposal silenced the "great republican" but, Johnson reported, "She has never liked me since. Sir, your levellers wish to level *down* as far as themselves; but they cannot bear levelling *up* to themselves."
35. "The King's Devil."

'easily provoked' by absurdity and folly, and sometimes too desirous of triumph in colloquial contest, must be allowed. The quickness both of his perception and sensibility disposed him to sudden explosions of satire; to which his extraordinary readiness of wit was a strong and almost irresistible incitement. To adopt one of the finest images in Mr. Home's *Douglas,*

> On each glance of thought
> Decision followed, as the thunderbolt
> Pursues the flash! [36]

I admit that the beadle [37] within him was often so eager to apply the lash, that the Judge had not time to consider the case with sufficient deliberation.

That he was occasionally remarkable for violence of temper may be granted: but let us ascertain the degree, and not let it be supposed that he was in a perpetual rage, and never without a club in his hand, to knock down every one who approached him. On the contrary, the truth is, that by much the greatest part of his time he was civil, obliging, nay, polite in the true sense of the word; so much so, that many gentlemen, who were long acquainted with him, never received, or even heard a strong expression from him.

[1777: The Fear of Death]

I mentioned to Dr. Johnson, that David Hume's persisting in his infidelity, when he was dying, shocked me much.[38] J O H N S O N. 'Why should it shock you, Sir? Hume owned he had never read the New Testament with attention. Here then was a man, who had been at no pains to inquire into the truth of religion, and had continually turned his mind the other way. It was not to be expected that the prospect of death would alter his way of thinking, unless GOD should send an angel to set him right.' I said, I had reason to believe that the thought of annihilation gave Hume no pain. J O H N S O N. 'It was not so, Sir. He had a vanity in being thought easy. It is more probable that he should assume an appearance of ease, than that so very improbable a thing should be as a man not afraid of going (as, in spite of his delusive theory, he cannot be sure but he may go,) into an unknown state, and not being uneasy at leaving all he knew. And you are to consider, that upon his own principle of annihilation he had no motive to speak the truth.' The horror of death which I had always observed in Dr. Johnson, appeared strong tonight. I ventured to tell him, that I had been, for moments in my life, not afraid of death; therefore I could suppose another man in that state of mind for a considerable space of time. He said, 'he never had a moment in which death was not terrible to him.' He added, that it had been observed, that scarce any man dies in public, but with apparent resolution; from that desire of praise

36. *Douglas* was the very popular tragedy by John Home (1722–1808), dramatist and friend of the poet William Collins.
37. A minor official who keeps order.
38. Boswell had an interview with Hume seven weeks before his death in 1776 and wrote an account of his own sense of danger in the face of Hume's obdurate disbelief in personal immortality ("But I maintained my faith"); still, Boswell admits that Hume was so good-humored that "Death for the time did not seem dismal."

which never quits us. I said, Dr. Dodd [39] seemed to be willing to die, and full of hopes of happiness. 'Sir, (said he,) Dr. Dodd would have given both his hands and both his legs to have lived. The better a man is, the more afraid he is of death, having a clearer view of infinite purity.' He owned, that our being in an unhappy uncertainty as to our salvation, was mysterious; and said, 'Ah! we must wait till we are in another state of being to have many things explained to us.' Even the powerful mind of Johnson seemed foiled by futurity. But I thought, that the gloom of uncertainty in solemn religious speculation, being mingled with hope, was yet more consolatory than the emptiness of infidelity. A man can live in thick air, but perishes in an exhausted receiver.

Dr. Johnson was much pleased with a remark which I told him was made to me by General Paoli: [40]—'That it is impossible not to be afraid of death; and that those who at the time of dying are not afraid, are not thinking of death, but of applause, or something else, which keeps death out of their sight: so that all men are equally afraid of death when they see it; only some have a power of turning their sight away from it better than others.' . . .

Some ladies, who had been present yesterday when I mentioned his birthday, came to dinner today, and plagued him unintentionally, by wishing him joy. I know not why he disliked having his birthday mentioned, unless it were that it reminded him of his approaching nearer to death, of which he had a constant dread.

I mentioned to him a friend of mine who was formerly gloomy from low spirits, and much distressed by the fear of death, but was now uniformly placid, and contemplated his dissolution without any perturbation. 'Sir, (said Johnson,) this is only a disordered imagination taking a different turn.' . . .

He observed, that a gentleman of eminence in literature [41] had got into a bad style of poetry of late. 'He puts (said he,) a very common thing in a strange dress till he does not know it himself, and thinks other people do not know it.' B O S W E L L. 'That is owing to his being so much versant in old English poetry.' J O H N S O N. 'What is that to the purpose, Sir? If I say a man is drunk, and you tell me it is owing to his taking much drink, the matter is not mended. No, Sir,———has taken to an odd mode. For example, he'd write thus:

> Hermit hoar, in solemn cell,
> Wearing out life's evening gray.

Gray evening is common enough; but *evening gray* he'd think fine.[42]—Stay;— we'll make out the stanza:

39. Dr. William Dodd (1729–77), king's chaplain and a popular preacher, forged a bond in the name of Lord Chesterfield, his former pupil; before his execution for this crime, Johnson did much for him and wrote several documents for him, including a "last solemn declaration." Dodd wrote Johnson at the very last: "Admitted, as I trust I shall be, to the realms of bliss before you, I shall hail *your* arrival there with transport. . . ."
40. General Pasquale Paoli (1725–1807), the Corsican general and patriot who had found asylum in England.
41. Thomas Warton (1728–90), who had just published a volume of poems.
42. Writing later in his life of Collins, Johnson complained of similar affectations in Warton's friend: "he puts his words out of the common order, seeming to think . . . that not to write prose is certainly to write poetry."

> Hermit hoar, in solemn cell,
>   Wearing out life's evening gray;
> Smite thy bosom, sage, and tell,
>   What is bliss? and which the way?

B O S W E L L. 'But why smite his bosom, Sir?' J O H N S O N. 'Why, to show he was in earnest,' (smiling.)—He at an after period added the following stanza:

> Thus I spoke; and speaking sighed;
>   —Scarce repressed the starting tear;—
> When the smiling sage replied—
>   —Come, my lad, and drink some beer.

I cannot help thinking the first stanza very good solemn poetry, as also the three first lines of the second. Its last line is an excellent burlesque surprise on gloomy sentimental enquirers. And, perhaps, the advice is as good as can be given to a low-spirited dissatisfied being:—'Don't trouble your head with sickly thinking: take a cup, and be merry.'

[The Character of Samuel Johnson]

The character of SAMUEL JOHNSON has, I trust, been so developed in the course of this work, that they who have honoured it with a perusal, may be considered as well acquainted with him. As, however, it may be expected that I should collect into one view the capital and distinguishing features of this extraordinary man, I shall endeavour to acquit myself of that part of my biographical undertaking, however difficult it may be to do that which many of my readers will do better for themselves.

His figure was large and well formed, and his countenance of the cast of an ancient statue; yet his appearance was rendered strange and somewhat uncouth by convulsive cramps, by the scars of that distemper [43] which it was once imagined the royal touch could cure, and by a slovenly mode of dress. He had the use only of one eye; yet so much does mind govern and even supply the deficiency of organs that his visual perceptions, as far as they extended, were uncommonly quick and accurate. So morbid was his temperament that he never knew the natural joy of a free and vigorous use of his limbs: when he walked, it was like the struggling gait of one in fetters; when he rode, he had no command or direction of his horse, but was carried as if in a balloon. That with his constitution and habits of life he should have lived seventy-five years, is a proof that an inherent *vivida vis* [44] is a powerful preservative of the human frame.

Man is, in general, made up of contradictory qualities; and these will ever show themselves in strange succession, where a consistency in appearance at least, if not in reality, has not been attained by long habits of philosophical discipline. In proportion to the native vigour of the mind, the contradictory qualities will be the more prominent, and more difficult to be adjusted; and, therefore, we are not to wonder, that Johnson exhibited an eminent example of

43. Scrofula.
44. Lively force.

this remark which I have made upon human nature. At different times, he seemed a different man, in some respects; not, however, in any great or essential article upon which he had fully employed his mind and settled certain principles of duty, but only in his manners and in the display of argument and fancy in his talk. He was prone to superstition, but not to credulity. Though his imagination might incline him to a belief of the marvellous and the mysterious, his vigorous reason examined the evidence with jealousy. He was a sincere and zealous Christian, of high Church-of-England and monarchical principles, which he would not tamely suffer to be questioned; and had, perhaps, at an early period, narrowed his mind somewhat too much, both as to religion and politics. His being impressed with the danger of extreme latitude in either, though he was of a very independent spirit, occasioned his appearing somewhat unfavourable to the prevalence of that noble freedom of sentiment which is the best possession of man. Nor can it be denied that he had many prejudices; which, however, frequently suggested many of his pointed sayings, that rather show a playfulness of fancy than any settled malignity. He was steady and inflexible in maintaining the obligations of religion and morality; both from a regard for the order of society, and from a veneration for the Great Source of all order; correct, nay stern in his taste; hard to please, and easily offended; impetuous and irritable in his temper, but of a most humane and benevolent heart, which showed itself not only in a most liberal charity, as far as his circumstances would allow, but in a thousand instances of active benevolence. He was afflicted with a bodily disease which made him often restless and fretful; and with a constitutional melancholy, the clouds of which darkened the brightness of his fancy and gave a gloomy cast to his whole course of thinking: we, therefore, ought not to wonder at his sallies of impatience and passion at any time; especially when provoked by obtrusive ignorance or presuming petulance; and allowance must be made for his uttering hasty and satirical sallies, even against his best friends. And, surely, when it is considered, that, 'amidst sickness and sorrow,' he exerted his faculties in so many works for the benefit of mankind, and particularly that he achieved the great and admirable DICTIONARY of our language, we must be astonished at his resolution. The solemn text, 'of him to whom much is given, much will be required,' [45] seems to have been ever present to his mind, in a rigorous sense, and to have made him dissatisfied with his labours and acts of goodness, however comparatively great; so that the unavoidable consciousness of his superiority was, in that respect, a cause of disquiet. He suffered so much from this, and from the gloom which perpetually haunted him and made solitude frightful, that it may be said of him, 'If in this life only he had hope, he was of all men most miserable.' [46] He loved praise, when it was brought to him; but was too proud to seek for it. He was somewhat susceptible of flattery. As he was general and unconfined in his studies, he cannot be considered as master of any one particular science; but he had accumulated a vast and various collection of learning and knowledge, which was so arranged in his mind, as to be ever in readiness to be brought forth. But his superiority over other learned men consisted chiefly in what may be called the art of

45. A close paraphrase of Luke 12:48.
46. Adapting I Corinthians 15:19.

thinking, the art of using his mind; a certain continual power of seizing the useful substance of all that he knew and exhibiting it in a clear and forcible manner; so that knowledge, which we often see to be no better than lumber in men of dull understanding, was, in him, true, evident, and actual wisdom. His moral precepts are practical; for they are drawn from an intimate acquaintance with human nature. His maxims carry conviction; for they are founded on the basis of common sense, and a very attentive and minute survey of real life. His mind was so full of imagery that he might have been perpetually a poet; yet it is remarkable that, however rich his prose is in this respect, his poetical pieces, in general, have not much of that splendour, but are rather distinguished by strong sentiment and acute observation, conveyed in harmonious and energetic verse, particularly in heroic couplets. Though usually grave, and even awful, in his deportment, he possessed uncommon and peculiar powers of wit and humour; he frequently indulged himself in colloquial pleasantry; and the heartiest merriment was often enjoyed in his company; with this great advantage, that as it was entirely free from any poisonous tincture of vice or impiety, it was salutary to those who shared in it. He had accustomed himself to such accuracy in his common conversation, that he at all times expressed his thoughts with great force, and an elegant choice of language, the effect of which was aided by his having a loud voice and a slow deliberate utterance. In him were united a most logical head with a most fertile imagination, which gave him an extraordinary advantage in arguing: for he could reason close or wide, as he saw best for the moment. Exulting in his intellectual strength and dexterity, he could, when he pleased, be the greatest sophist that ever contended in the lists of declamation; and, from a spirit of contradiction and a delight in showing his powers, he would often maintain the wrong side with equal warmth and ingenuity; so that when there was an audience, his real opinions could seldom be gathered from his talk; though when he was in company with a single friend, he would discuss a subject with genuine fairness: but he was too conscientious to make error permanent and pernicious by deliberately writing it; and, in all his numerous works, he earnestly inculcated what appeared to him to be the truth; his piety being constant, and the ruling principle of all his conduct.

Such was SAMUEL JOHNSON, a man whose talents, acquirements, and virtues, were so extraordinary, that the more his character is considered, the more he will be regarded by the present age, and by posterity, with admiration and reverence.

1791

From The Journal of a Tour to the Hebrides with Samuel Johnson, LL.D.

Wednesday, 1st September, 1773   I awaked very early. I began to imagine that the landlord,[1] being about to emigrate, might murder us to get our money, and lay it upon the soldiers in the barn. Such groundless fears will arise in the

1. This was written of the stay at Anoch in Glenmorison, the occasion for Johnson's description of the Highlands in his *Journey* (see The Garden and the Wild).

mind, before it has resumed its vigour after sleep! Dr. Johnson had had the same kind of ideas; for he told me afterwards, that he considered so many soldiers, having seen us, would be witnesses, should any harm be done, and that circumstance, I suppose, he considered as a security. When I got up, I found him sound asleep in his miserable sty, as I may call it, with a coloured handkerchief tied round his head. With difficulty could I awaken him. It reminded me of Henry the Fourth's fine soliloquy on sleep; for there was here as *uneasy a pallet* as the poet's imagination could possibly conceive.[2]

A redcoat of the 15th regiment, whether officer or only sergeant I could not be sure, came to the house in his way to the mountains to shoot deer, which it seems the Laird of Glenmorison does not hinder anybody to do. Few, indeed, can do them harm. We had him to breakfast with us. We got away about eight. M'Queen[3] walked some miles to give us a convoy. He had, in 1745, joined the Highland army at Fort Augustus, and continued in it till after battle of Culloden.[4] As he narrated the particulars of that ill-advised but brave attempt, I could not refrain from tears. There is a certain association of ideas in my mind upon that subject, by which I am strongly affected. The very Highland names, or the sound of a bagpipe, will stir my blood, and fill me with a mixture of melancholy and respect for courage; with pity for the unfortunate, and superstitious regard for antiquity, and thoughtless inclination for war; in short, with a crowd of sensations with which sober rationality has nothing to do.

We passed through Glensheal, with prodigious mountains on each side. We saw where the battle was fought in the year 1719.[5] Dr. Johnson owned he was now in a scene of as wild nature as he could see; but he corrected me sometimes in my inaccurate observations.—'There (said I) is a mountain like a cone.'—*Johnson.* 'No, sir. It would be called so in a book; and when a man comes to look at it, he sees it is not so. It is indeed pointed at the top; but one side of it is larger than the other.'—Another mountain I called immense.—*Johnson.* 'No; it is no more than a considerable protuberance.'

Sunday, 12th September . . . We spoke of Death. Dr. Johnson on this subject observed, that the boastings of some men as to dying easily were idle talk, proceeding from partial views. I mentioned Hawthornden's Cypress-grove,[6] where it is said that the world is a mere show; and that it is unreasonable for a man to wish to continue in the show-room, after he has seen it. Let him go cheerfully out, and give place to other spectators.—*Johnson.* 'Yes, sir, if he is sure he is to be well, after he goes out of it. But if he is to grow blind after he goes out of the show-room, and never to see any thing again; or if he does not know whither he is to go next, a man will not go cheerfully out of a show-room. No wise man will be contented to die, if he thinks he is to go into

---

2. See II *Henry IV* III.i for the soliloquy.
3. The landlord at Anoch.
4. The decisive defeat, April 16, 1746, of the Highlanders under the Jacobite Prince Charles Edward by the English troops under the Duke of Cumberland.
5. The battle of Glensheal (or Glenshiel) was lost to the British by a Jacobite force of Highlanders and Spaniards.
6. "The Cypress Grove" was a prose meditation on death by William Drummond of Hawthornden (1585–1649). For similar reflections by Johnson, see the passage from Boswell's *Life* for 1777 given above.

a state of punishment. Nay, no wise man will be contented to die, if he thinks he is to fall into annihilation: for however unhappy any man's existence may be, he yet would rather have it, than not exist at all. No; there is no rational principle by which a man can die contented, but a trust in the mercy of GOD, through the merits of Jesus Christ.'—This short sermon, delivered with an earnest tone, in a boat upon the sea, which was perfectly calm, on a day appropriated to religious worship, while every one listened with an air of satisfaction, had a most pleasing effect upon my mind.

Pursuing the same train of serious reflection, he added, that it seemed certain that happiness could not be found in this life, because so many had tried to find it, in such a variety of ways, and had not found it. . . .

Monday and Tuesday, September 13–14 . . . We arrived at Dunvegan late in the afternoon. The great size of the castle, which is partly old and partly new, and is built upon a rock close to the sea, while the land around it presents nothing but wild, moorish, hilly, and craggy appearances, gave a rude magnificence to the scene. . . . We were introduced into a stately dining-room, and received by Lady Macleod,[7] mother of the laird, who, with his friend Talisker, having been detained on the road, did not arrive till some time after us.

We found the lady of the house a very polite and sensible woman, who had lived for some time in London, and had there been in Dr. Johnson's company. . . .

Dr. Johnson said in the morning, 'Is not this a fine lady?'—There was not a word now of his 'impatience to be in civilized life';—though indeed I should beg pardon,—he found it here. We had slept well, and lain long. After breakfast we surveyed the castle, and the garden. . . . M'Leod started the subject of making women do penance in the church for fornication.—*Johnson.* 'It is right, sir. Infamy is attached to the crime, by universal opinion, as soon as it is known. I would not be the man who would discover it, if I alone knew it, for a woman may reform; nor would I commend a parson who divulges a woman's first offence; but being once divulged, it ought to be infamous. Consider of what importance to society the chastity of women is. Upon that all the property in the world depends. We hang a thief for stealing a sheep; but the unchastity of a woman transfers sheep, and farm and all, from the right owner. I have much more reverence for a common prostitute than for a woman who conceals her guilt. The prostitute is known. She cannot deceive: she cannot bring a strumpet into the arms of an honest man, without his knowledge.'—*Boswell.* 'There is, however, a great difference between the licentiousness of a single woman and that of a married woman.'—*Johnson.* 'Yes, sir; there is a great difference between stealing a shilling and stealing a thousand pounds; between simply taking a man's purse, and murdering him first, and then taking it. But when one begins to be vicious, it is easy to go on. Where single women are licentious, you rarely find faithful married women.'— *Boswell.* 'And yet we are told that in some nations in India, the distinction is strictly observed.'—*Johnson.* 'Nay, don't give us India. That puts me in mind of

7. John McLeod (d. 1786) was 9th Laird of Raasay; his son, Colonel John McLeod (1718–98), and the latter's wife also entertained Boswell and Johnson.

Montesquieu,[8] who is really a fellow of genius too in many respects; whenever he wants to support a strange opinion, he quotes you the practice of Japan or of some other distant country, of which he knows nothing. To support polygamy, he tells you of the island of Formosa, where there are ten women born for one man. He had but to suppose another island, where there are ten men born for one woman, and so make a marriage between them.'

At supper, Lady M'Leod mentioned Dr. Cadogan's book on the gout.[9] Lady M'Leod objected that the author does not practice what he teaches.— *Johnson.* 'I cannot help that, madam. That does not make his book the worse. People are influenced more by what a man says if his practice is suitable to it,—because they are blockheads. The more intellectual people are, the readier will they attend to what a man tells them. If it is just, they will follow it, be his practice what it will. No man practises so well as he writes. I have, all my life long, been lying till noon; yet I tell all young men, and tell them with great sincerity, that nobody who does not rise early will ever do any good. Only consider! You read a book; you are convinced by it; you do not know the author. Suppose you afterwards know him, and find that he does not practise what he teaches; are you to give up your former conviction? At this rate you would be kept in a state of equilibrium, when reading every book, till you knew how the author practised.'—'But,' said Lady M'Leod, 'you would think better of Dr. Cadogan, if he acted according to his principles.'—*Johnson.* 'Why, madam, to be sure, a man who acts in the face of light is worse than a man who does not know so much; yet I think no man should be the worse thought of for publishing good principles. There is something noble in publishing truth, though it condemns one's self.'—I expressed some surprize at Cadogan's recommending good humour, as if it were quite in our own power to attain it. —*Johnson.* 'Why, sir, a man grows better humoured as he grows older. He improves by experience. When young, he thinks himself of great consequence, and every thing of importance. As he advances in life, he learns to think himself of no consequence, and little things of little importance; and so he becomes more patient, and better pleased. All good-humour and complaisance are acquired. Naturally a child seizes directly what it sees, and thinks of pleasing itself only. By degrees, it is taught to please others, and to prefer others; and that this will ultimately produce the greatest happiness. If a man is not convinced of that, he never will practise it. Common language speaks the truth as to this: we say, a person is well *bred*. As it is said, that all material motion is primarily in a right line, and is never *per circuitum*, never in another form, unless by some particular cause; so it may be said intellectual motion is.' —Lady M'Leod asked, if no man was naturally good?—*Johnson.* 'No, madam, no more than a wolf.'—*Boswell.* 'Nor no woman, sir?'—*Johnson.* 'No, sir.'— Lady M'Leod started at this, saying, in a low voice, 'This is worse than Swift.'

Tuesday, October 19 . . . We continued to coast along Mull, and passed

---

8. Referring to the use of comparative evidence (such as had earlier been made by John Locke) by the Baron de Montesquieu (1689–1755) in *The Spirit of Laws* (1748); here a probable allusion to XVI.iv.

9. *A Dissertation on the Gout* (1771), a very popular work (nine printings in its first year). Dr. Cadogan was believed (perhaps falsely) to drink more than he could recommend in his book.

by Nuns' Island, which, it is said, belonged to the nuns of Icolmkill, and from which, we were told, the stone for the buildings there was taken. As we sailed along by moonlight, in a sea somewhat rough, and often between black and gloomy rocks, Dr. Johnson said, 'If this be not *roving among the Hebrides,* nothing is.'—The repetition of words which he had so often previously used, made a strong impression on my imagination; and, by a natural course of thinking, led me to consider how our present adventures would appear to me at a future period.

I have often experienced, that scenes through which a man has passed, improve by lying in the memory: they grow mellow. *Acti labores sunt jucundi.*[10] This may be owing to comparing them with present listless ease. Even harsh scenes acquire a softness by length of time; and some are like very loud sounds, which do not please, or at least do not please so much, till you are removed to a certain distance. They may be compared to strong coarse pictures, which will not bear to be viewed near. Even pleasing scenes improve by time, and seem more exquisite in recollection than when they were present; if they have not faded to dimness in the memory. Perhaps, there is so much evil in every human enjoyment when present,—so much dross mixed with it, that it requires to be refined by time; and yet I do not see why time should not melt away the good and the evil in equal proportions;—why the shade should decay, and the light remain in preservation.

After a tedious sail, which, by our following various turnings of the coast of Mull, was extended to about forty miles, it gave us no small pleasure to perceive a light in the village at Icolmkill, in which almost all the inhabitants of the island live, close to where the ancient buildings stood. As we approached the shore, the tower of the cathedral, just discernible in the air, was a picturesque object.

When we had landed upon the sacred place, which, as long as I can remember, I had thought on with veneration, Dr. Johnson and I cordially embraced. We had long talked of visiting Icolmkill; and, from the lateness of the season, were at times very doubtful whether we should be able to effect our purpose. To have seen it, even alone, would have given me great satisfaction; but the venerable scene was rendered much more pleasing by the company of my great and pious friend, who was no less affected by it than I was; and who has described the impressions it should make on the mind, with such strength of thought, and energy of language, that I shall quote his words, as conveying my own sensations much more forcibly than I am capable of doing:

'We were now treading that illustrious Island, which was once the luminary of the Caledonian regions, whence savage clans and roving barbarians derived the benefits of knowledge, and the blessings of religion. To abstract the mind from all local emotion would be impossible, if it were endeavoured, and would be foolish, if it were possible. Whatever withdraws us from the power of our senses, whatever makes the past, the distant, or the future, predominate over the present, advances us in the dignity of thinking beings. Far from me, and from my friends, be such frigid philosophy as may conduct us indifferent and

---

10. "Past labors are sweet," Cicero, *De Finibus* II.32.

unmoved over any ground which has been dignified by wisdom, bravery, or virtue. That man is little to be envied, whose patriotism would not gain force upon the plain of *Marathon,* or whose piety would not grow warmer among the ruins of *Iona!*" [11]

1773   1785

SAMUEL JOHNSON
1709–1784

Samuel Johnson dominates the English literary scene of the later eighteenth century and has, as well, become one of the mythical heroes of British common sense. Because of Boswell's remarkable *Life* we know him in more vividly intimate detail than most men of any age, and we are rarely without a sense of his personal presence as we read his works. While the range of Johnson's work is great, it has remarkable unity; for, whatever the stretch of his mind into natural science, philology, or history, it returns insistently to central moral themes, and notably to his favorite one, the efforts of the mind to escape the limitations of the actual. Whether in stupor or fantasy, in self-deception or in distraction, the mind seeks to elude that reality that stands outside it and rebuffs its systems. We see this in Johnson's attack upon the rules by which Shakespeare was foolishly judged, but we see it also in his identification of Shakespeare's "fatal Cleopatra" (an uncontrolled indulgence in verbal play). We see it ironically presented in Rasselas's fruitless quest for an ideal "choice of life," or in Johnson's acknowledgment of man's need for hope, however delusive. We see it in the "vanity" that overleaps the given, in the easy consolation that mistakes intention for act, in idleness and the fear of the self that seeks refuge in procrastination.

Johnson was born the son of a Lichfield bookseller, attended Oxford, and set up as a schoolmaster upon his marriage to Elizabeth Jervis Porter. In 1737 he went to London with his pupil David Garrick and began a literary career of translation, scholarship, and journalism. Among his remarkable feats was the reconstruction from notes of parliamentary debates for the *Gentleman's Magazine* (1741–44). His career was marked by three great projects. The first was the *Dictionary of the English Language* (1755), the second the edition of Shakespeare with preface and notes (1765), the third the *Lives of the Poets* written to accompany a printing of their works. But these projects were accompanied as well by the remarkable poems; the extensive series of essays that filled the *Rambler* twice a week (1750–52), and later *The Adventurer* (1753) and the *Idler* (1758–60); and the philosophical tale *Rasselas* (1759). In 1763 he met James Boswell and ten years later toured Scotland and the Hebrides with him producing the *Journey to the Western Islands of Scotland* in 1775.

Johnson became the center of a group that included David Garrick, Edmund Burke, Sir Joshua Reynolds, Oliver Goldsmith, and others; and he often contributed encouragement, advice, and even revisions to the works of his contemporaries—notably Goldsmith, Reynolds, and Crabbe. In his conversation as well as his writing, Johnson exhibits different aspects, or perhaps different degrees of intensity. He could, with a strong histrionic sense and the levity of a debater, adopt an outrageous stance and

---

11. "Had our tour produced nothing but this sublime passage, the world must have acknowledged that it was not made in vain." (Boswell)

win the pleasures of domination; Johnson's nature demanded power, and he never questioned its appeal. He could, at other times, show a more defensive assertiveness, a bravado, in the face of his own doubts or fears, which insisted upon what he needed to believe in defiance of what, at a deeper level, he genuinely could. But more impressive than either is the empiricism that can be called common sense but is in fact something more radical: a recognition of the reality of the actual and a refusal to let it be dissolved in theory or masked in convention. "Liberty is the birthright of man, and where obedience is compelled, there is no liberty." This he takes to be the argument of the American revolutionaries. "The answer is equally simple. Government is necessary to man, and where obedience is not compelled, there is no government." This positivistic recognition of the fact of power is typical: "It is not infallible, for it may do wrong; but it is irresistible, for it can be resisted only by rebellion, by an act which makes it questionable what shall be thenceforward the supreme power." These three stances—the histrionic, the defensive, and the empirical—are hard to separate, and Johnson's tone must always be considered. He is a great ironist, and yet he is not the kind of skeptic who can remain uncommitted; he asserts with absoluteness what must not be ignored, however easily or little it can be wedded with its contraries or reconciled with our desires.

The Vanity of Human Wishes

Like Pope's Horatian imitations, Johnson's is a free adaptation of Juvenal's poem to his own time and to his own frame of thought. This is nowhere clearer than in the closing lines, where Juvenal writes, "You would have no divinity if there were wisdom; it is we who make a goddess of you, Fortune, and place you in the heavens." Johnson sees instead the force of "celestial wisdom" saving man from himself, making the good fortune ("happiness") man cannot create for himself or even ask for properly. We have contemporary reactions to the difficulty of Johnson's condensed verse; David Garrick judged it "as hard as Greek." Johnson found in Juvenal a "mixture of gaiety and stateliness, of pointed sentences" (i.e. *sententiae* or maxims) "and declamatory grandeur." His version is more formal and austere than Dryden's, using the spacious generalization to indicate the ludicrous folly, as in the brilliant lines on the displaced favorite, whose image has lost its goodness with its greatness. The removal of the portrait is not presented dramatically or pictorially but in all the irony of its elaborate rationalization: "The form distorted justifies the fall, / And detestation rids the indignant wall." It is as if the very wall cannot bear his presence, as if his distortion of form is so strikingly evident to all that it cannot expect a moment's further tolerance; such, Johnson implies, is the cost of losing power in a world that knows no other standard. One can see "gaiety" in this rendering of lunacy as well as "stateliness" in the solemn recording of its pretexts, and even more in the deeper sense of its universal prevalence. The density of Johnson's diction is best seen in such compressed phrases, from which numerous particulars can be surmised, as "The general massacre of gold" or "dubious title shakes the madded land."

The Vanity of Human Wishes

The Tenth Satire of Juvenal Imitated

Let observation with extensive view,
Survey mankind, from China to Peru;
Remark each anxious toil, each eager strife,
And watch the busy scenes of crowded life;
Then say how hope and fear, desire and hate,
O'erspread with snares the clouded maze of fate,
Where wavering man, betrayed by venturous pride,
To tread the dreary paths without a guide,
As treacherous phantoms in the mist delude,
Shuns fancied ills, or chases airy good;   10
How rarely reason guides the stubborn choice,
Rules the bold hand, or prompts the suppliant voice;
How nations sink, by darling schemes oppressed,
When vengeance listens to the fool's request.°
Fate wings with every wish the afflictive dart,°
Each gift of nature, and each grace of art,
With fatal heat impetuous courage glows,
With fatal sweetness elocution flows,
Impeachment° stops the speaker's powerful breath,
And restless fire precipitates° on death.   20

But scarce observed, the knowing and the bold
Fall in the general massacre of gold;
Wide-wasting pest! that rages unconfined,
And crowds with crimes the records of mankind;
For gold his sword the hireling ruffian draws,
For gold the hireling judge distorts the laws;
Wealth heaped on wealth, nor truth nor safety buys,
The dangers gather° as the treasures rise.

Let history tell where rival kings command,
And dubious title shakes the madded land,   30
When statutes glean the refuse of the sword,°
How much more safe the vassal than the lord;
Low skulks the hind° beneath the rage of power,
And leaves the wealthy traitor° in the Tower,
Untouched his cottage, and his slumbers sound,

When vengeance . . . request i.e. the harshest vengeance is to give what the fool seeks, here a favorite ("darling") scheme
Fate wings . . . dart i.e. the dart is given flight (feathered) by every wish, gift, or "grace of art"
Impeachment public accusation
precipitates rushes or falls headlong; with perhaps the chemical sense of falling to the bottom as a sediment (the opposite of chemical sublimation)
The dangers gather Cf. Matthew 24:28: "For wheresoever the carcass is, there will the eagles

be gathered together"; cf. the "vultures" of l. 36.
When statutes . . . sword i.e. when new laws undo those spared by open conflict; cf. l. 59
hind peasant
wealthy traitor perhaps the overthrown leader, now declared a "traitor" and imprisoned in the Tower of London, as Robert Harley, Earl of Oxford, chief minister of Queen Anne, was upon the accession of George I and Whig power in 1714 (see l. 130 below). More recent instances were the imprisonment and execution of Scottish lords after the Jacobite rising of 1745, and Johnson had originally written "bonny traitor."

Though confiscation's vultures hover round.
    The needy traveller, serene and gay,
Walks the wild heath, and sings his toil away.
Does envy seize thee? crush the upbraiding joy,
40   Increase his riches and his peace destroy;
Now fears in dire vicissitude invade,
The rustling brake° alarms, and quivering shade,
Nor light nor darkness bring his pain relief,
One shows the plunder, and one hides the thief.
    Yet still one general cry the skies assails,
And gain and grandeur load the tainted gales;°
Few know the toiling statesman's fear or care,
The insidious rival and the gaping heir.
    Once more, Democritus,° arise on earth,
50   With cheerful wisdom and instructive mirth,
See motley° life in modern trappings dressed,
And feed with varied fools the eternal jest:
Thou who couldst laugh where want enchained caprice,
Toil crushed conceit,° and man was of a piece;
Where wealth unloved without a mourner died,
And scarce a sycophant was fed by pride;
Where ne'er was known the form of mock debate,
Or seen a new-made mayor's unwieldy state;°
Where change of favorites made no change of laws,
60   And senates heard before they judged a cause;
How wouldst thou shake at Britain's modish tribe,
Dart the quick taunt, and edge the piercing gibe,
Attentive truth and nature to descry,
And pierce each scene with philosophic eye.
To thee were solemn toys or empty show
The robes of pleasure and the veils of woe:
All aid the farce, and all thy mirth maintain,
Whose joys are causeless or whose griefs are vain.
    Such was the scorn that filled the sage's mind,
70   Renewed at every glance on humankind;
How just that scorn ere yet thy voice declare,
Search every state, and canvass every prayer.
    Unnumbered suppliants crowd Preferment's gate,°
Athirst for wealth, and burning to be great;
Delusive Fortune hears the incessant call,
They mount, they shine, evaporate, and fall.
On every stage the foes of peace attend,

---

brake thicket
tainted gales breezes carrying the scent of the hunted quarry
Democritus (c. 460–370 B.C.) known as the "laughing philosopher." Robert Burton wrote as Democritus Junior in The Anatomy of Melancholy (1621), one of Johnson's favorite books.
motley of various colors, like the traditional

Fool's costume
conceit imagination
unwieldy state referring to the gilt coach and elaborate rituals of the Lord Mayor's procession
Preferment's gate the gate of a lord who can grant posts of office

Hate dogs their flight, and insult mocks their end.
Love ends with hope, the sinking statesman's door
80 Pours in the morning worshipper° no more;
For growing names the weekly scribbler° lies,
To growing wealth the dedicator flies,
From every room descends the painted face,
That hung the bright Palladium° of the place,
And smoked in kitchens, or in auctions sold,
To better features yields the frame of gold;
For now no more we trace in every line
Heroic worth, benevolence divine:
The form distorted justifies the fall,
90 And detestation rids the indignant wall.
    But will not Britain hear the last appeal,
Sign her foes' doom, or guard her favourites' zeal?
Through Freedom's sons no more remonstrance° rings,
Degrading nobles and controlling kings;
Our supple tribes repress their patriot throats,
And ask no questions but the price of votes;
With weekly libels and septennial ale,°
Their wish is full to riot and to rail.
    In full-blown dignity, see Wolsey° stand,
100 Law in his voice, and fortune in his hand:
To him the church, the realm, their powers consign,
Through him the rays of regal bounty shine,
Turned by his nod the stream of honour flows,
His smile alone security bestows:
Still to new heights his restless wishes tower,
Claim leads to claim, and power advances power;
Till conquest unresisted ceased to please,
And rights submitted left him none to seize.
At length his sovereign frowns—the train of state
110 Mark the keen glance and watch the sign to hate.
Where'er he turns he meets a stranger's eye,
His suppliants scorn him and his followers fly;
At once is lost the pride of awful state,
The golden canopy, the glittering plate,
The regal palace, the luxurious board,

---

morning worshipper the assiduous attendant at
levees (or morning receptions)
the weekly scribbler in the political journals
Palladium the statue of Pallas Athena that supposedly conferred safety upon the city of Troy
and was stolen by Diomedes so that Troy might
be taken. The portrait which served this protective purpose has now been banished to the
smoky kitchen or sold off and only the frame
preserved.
remonstrance alluding to the Grand Remonstrance of 1641 demanding that Charles I's

council be chosen from men approved by Parliament
septennial ale provided at parliamentary elections (held at least every seven years) to attract
votes, as were more substantial bribes and the
demagoguery of newspaper campaigns ("weekly
libels"). Thus parliamentary "questions" and
debate give way, through corruption, to demonstrations and slanderous railing.
Wolsey Thomas Wolsey (c. 1475–1530), cardinal and Lord Chancellor of Henry VIII, replacing Juvenal's Sejanus, the favorite of the
emperor Tiberius

The liveried army° and the menial lord.
With age, with cares, with maladies oppressed,
He seeks the refuge of monastic rest.
Grief aids disease, remembered folly stings,
120 And his last sighs reproach the faith of kings.
  Speak thou, whose thoughts at humble peace repine,
Shall Wolsey's wealth with Wolsey's end be thine?
Or livest thou now, with safer pride content,
The wisest justice on the banks of Trent?°
For why did Wolsey near the steeps of fate,
On weak foundations raise the enormous weight?
Why but to sink beneath misfortune's blow,
With louder ruin to the gulfs below?
  What gave great Villiers° to the assassin's knife,
130 And fixed disease on Harley's° closing life?
What murdered Wentworth, and what exiled Hyde,°
By kings protected, and to kings allied?
What but their wish indulged in courts to shine,
And power too great to keep, or to resign?
  When first the college rolls receive his name,
The young enthusiast quits his ease for fame;
Through all his veins the fever of renown
Burns from the strong contagion of the gown;°
O'er Bodley's dome° his future labours spread,
140 And Bacon's mansion° trembles o'er his head.
Are these thy views? proceed, illustrious youth,
And virtue guard thee to the throne of Truth!
Yet should thy soul indulge the generous heat,
Till captive Science yields her last retreat;
Should Reason guide thee with her brightest ray,
And pour on misty Doubt resistless day;°
Should no false Kindness lure to loose delight,
Nor Praise relax, nor Difficulty fright;
Should tempting Novelty thy cell refrain,
150 And Sloth effuse her opiate fumes in vain;
Should Beauty blunt on fops her fatal dart,
Nor claim the triumph of a lettered heart;
Should no Disease thy torpid veins invade,

---

liveried army an army of servants, or officers
behaving as servants
on the banks of Trent any provincial scene, but
here referring to Johnson's own birthplace,
Lichfield
great Villiers George Villiers, 1st Duke of
Buckingham, favorite of James I and Charles I,
murdered in 1628
Harley's See above l. 34 and note; Harley later
suffered bad health, perhaps because of his confinement in the Tower.
Wentworth . . . Hyde Thomas Wentworth,
Earl of Strafford, advisor of Charles I, impeached and executed in 1641; Edward Hyde,
Earl of Clarendon, Lord Chancellor to Charles
II but impeached and banished in 1667 ("to

kings allied" as father-in-law of James II and
grandfather of Queen Mary and Queen Anne)
the strong . . . gown with the suggestion of
Nessus' shirt, the poisoned robe that caused
Hercules so much torture that he tore away his
flesh in trying to remove it
Bodley's dome the Bodleian Library at Oxford;
"dome" is used in the sense of a building
Bacon's mansion referring to the tradition that
the study of Roger Bacon, the medieval Oxford
philosopher and scientist, built on an arch over
a bridge, would fall when a greater man than
Bacon passed under it
resistless day Cf. Pope, *Essay on Criticism*, ll.
211–12.

Nor Melancholy's phantoms haunt thy shade;
Yet hope not life from grief or danger free,
Nor think the doom of man reversed for thee:
Deign on the passing world to turn thine eyes,
And pause awhile from letters to be wise;
There mark what ills the scholar's life assail,
160   Toil, envy, want, the patron,° and the jail.
See nations slowly wise, and meanly just,
To buried merit raise the tardy bust.°
If dreams yet flatter, once again attend,
Hear Lydiat's life, and Galileo's end.°

Nor deem, when learning her last prize bestows,
The glittering eminence exempt from foes;
See when the vulgar 'scape, despised or awed,
Rebellion's vengeful talons seize on Laud.°
From meaner minds, though smaller fines content,
170   The plundered palace or sequestered rent;°
Marked out by dangerous parts he meets the shock,
And fatal Learning leads him to the block:
Around his tomb let Art and Genius weep,
But hear his death, ye blockheads, hear and sleep.

The festal blazes, the triumphal show,
The ravished standard, and the captive foe,
The senate's thanks, the gazette's° pompous tale,
With force resistless o'er the brave prevail.
Such bribes the rapid Greek° o'er Asia whirled,
180   For such the steady Romans shook the world;°
For such in distant lands the Britons° shine,
And stain with blood the Danube or the Rhine;
This power has praise that virtue scarce can warm,
Till fame supplies the universal charm.
Yet Reason frowns on War's unequal game,
Where wasted nations raise a single name,
And mortgaged states their grandsires' wreaths regret,°
From age to age in everlasting debt;

---

patron For this substitution for "garret" see James Boswell's *Life of Johnson* on the publication of the *Dictionary*, where a patron is defined as "commonly a wretch who supports with insolence and is paid with flattery."
tardy bust e.g. that of John Milton, not placed in Westminster Abbey until 1737; but also late monuments to Dryden (1720), Samuel Butler (1721), and Shakespeare (1741)
Lydiat's . . . end Thomas Lydiat (1572–1646), a brilliant scholar ranked with Francis Bacon in his day but poor and forgotten at the time of his death. Galileo (1564–1642) was declared a heretic and imprisoned by the Inquisition in 1633 and later became blind (Mrs. Piozzi recorded that Johnson "burst into a passion of tears" one day as he read aloud this passage on the scholar's life).
Laud William Laud, Archbishop of Canterbury under Charles I, was executed by Parliament in 1645; Johnson attributes his high-church policies to his "Learning" and his gifts ("parts").
sequestered rent confiscated income, sufficient to "content" the persecutors of lesser men
gazette's official court record
rapid Greek Alexander the Great
shook the world perhaps evoking the famous long marches of the Roman legions
Britons referring to the Duke of Marlborough's campaigns in Austria and Bavaria, particularly the great victory of Blenheim (1704) in the War of the Spanish Succession
mortgaged states . . . regret Cf. Swift in *The Conduct of the Allies* (1711): "It will, no doubt, be a mighty comfort to our grandchildren, when they see a few rags hang up in Westminster Hall which cost an hundred millions, whereof they are paying the arrears, and boasting, as beggars do, that their grandfathers were rich and great."

Wreathes which at last the dear-bought right convey
190 To rust on medals, or on stones decay.
      On what foundation stands the warrior's pride,
How just his hopes let Swedish Charles° decide;
A frame of adamant, a soul of fire,
No dangers fright him, and no labours tire;
O'er love, o'er fear, extends his wide domain,
Unconquered lord of pleasure and of pain;
No joys to him pacific sceptres yield,
War sounds the trump, he rushes to the field;
Behold surrounding kings their power combine,
200 And one capitulate, and one resign;°
Peace courts his hand, but spreads her charms in vain;
'Think nothing gained,' he cries, 'till nought remain,
On Moscow's walls till Gothic° standards fly,
And all be mine beneath the polar sky.'
The march begins in military state,
And nations on his eye suspended wait;
Stern Famine guards the solitary coast,
And Winter barricades the realms of Frost;
He comes, not want and cold his course delay;—
210 Hide, blushing Glory, hide Pultowa's day:°
The vanquished hero leaves his broken bands,
And shows his miseries in distant lands;
Condemned a needy supplicant to wait,
While ladies interpose, and slaves debate.
But did not Chance at length for error mend?
Did no subverted empire mark his end?
Did rival monarchs give the fatal wound?
Or hostile millions press him to the ground?
His fall was destined to a barren strand,
220 A petty fortress, and a dubious hand;°
He left the name, at which the world grew pale,
To point a moral, or adorn a tale.
      All times their scenes of pompous woes afford,
From Persia's tyrant to Bavaria's lord.
In gay hostility, and barbarous pride,
With half mankind embattled at his side,
Great Xerxes° comes to seize the certain prey,
And starves exhausted regions in his way;
Attendant Flattery counts his myriads o'er,
230 Till counted myriads soothe his pride no more;
Fresh praise is tried till madness fires his mind,

Swedish Charles Charles XII of Sweden (1682–
1718), replacing Juvenal's Hannibal
one capitulate . . . resign Frederick IV of Denmark in 1700 and Augustus II of Poland in
1704
Gothic Swedish
Pultowa's day the defeat by Peter the Great in

1709 at Poltava in Russia, followed by Charles's
flight to Turkey
dubious hand Charles was killed in Norway,
perhaps by the hand of his own officer.
Xerxes who invaded Greece and was defeated
at the sea battles at Salamis in 480 B.C.

The waves he lashes, and enchains the wind;
New powers are claimed, new powers are still bestowed,
Till rude resistance lops the spreading god;°
The daring Greeks deride the martial show,
And heap their valleys with the gaudy foe;
The insulted sea with humbler thoughts he gains,
A single skiff to speed his flight remains;
The incumbered oar scarce leaves the dreaded coast
240   Through purple billows and a floating host.°
    The bold Bavarian,° in a luckless hour,
Tries the dread summits of Cesarean power,
With unexpected legions bursts away,
And sees defenceless realms receive his sway;
Short sway! fair Austria spreads her mournful charms,
The queen, the beauty, sets the world in arms;
From hill to hill the beacons' rousing blaze
Spreads wide the hope of plunder and of praise;
The fierce Croatian, and the wild Hussar,°
250   And all the sons of ravage crowd the war;
The baffled prince in honour's flattering bloom
Of hasty greatness finds the fatal doom,
His foes' derision, and his subjects' blame,
And steals to death from anguish and from shame.
    'Enlarge my life with multitude of days,'
In health, in sickness, thus the suppliant prays;
Hides from himself his state, and shuns to know,
That life protracted is protracted woe.
Time hovers o'er, impatient to destroy,
260   And shuts up all the passages of joy:
In vain their gifts the bounteous seasons pour,
The fruit autumnal, and the vernal flower,
With listless eyes the dotard views the store,
He views, and wonders that they please no more;
Now pall the tasteless meats and joyless wines,
And Luxury with sighs her slave resigns.
Approach, ye minstrels, try the soothing strain,
Diffuse the tuneful lenitives° of pain:
No sounds, alas, would touch the impervious ear,
270   Though dancing mountains witnessed Orpheus° near;
Nor lute nor lyre his feeble powers attend,
Nor sweeter music of a virtuous friend,
But everlasting dictates crowd his tongue,

lops . . . god i.e. as the branches of an over-arching tree
The incumbered . . . host This account of Xerxes' flight through a sea dyed with blood and thick with corpses was reported to be Johnson's own favorite couplet.
bold Bavarian Charles Albert, Elector of Bavaria, claimed the Holy Roman Empire against Maria Theresa ("fair Austria"); he was crowned Charles VII (1742) but became a puppet of his allies and died in 1745.
Hussar Hungarian light-horseman; like the Croatian, recruited in Austria's defense
lenitives easers, anodynes
Orpheus the legendary Greek bard whose music made mountains dance

Perversely grave, or positively° wrong.
The still returning tale and lingering jest
Perplex the fawning niece and pampered guest,
While growing hopes scarce awe the gathering sneer,
And scarce a legacy can bribe to hear;
The watchful guests still hint the last offence,
280 The daughter's petulance, the son's expense,
Improve° his heady rage with treacherous skill,
And mould his passions till they make his will.
    Unnumbered maladies his joints invade,
Lay siege to life, and press the dire blockade;
But unextinguished Avarice still remains,
And dreaded losses aggravate his pains;
He turns, with anxious heart and crippled hands,
His bonds of debt and mortgages of lands;
Or views his coffers with suspicious eyes,
290 Unlocks his gold, and counts it till he dies.
    But grant, the virtues of a temperate prime
Bless with an age exempt from scorn or crime;
An age that melts with unperceived decay,
And glides in modest innocence away;
Whose peaceful day Benevolence endears,
Whose night congratulating Conscience cheers;
The general favourite as the general friend:
Such age there is, and who shall wish its end?
    Yet even on this her load Misfortune flings,
300 To press the weary minutes' flagging wings:
New sorrow rises as the day returns,
A sister sickens, or a daughter mourns.
Now kindred Merit fills the sable bier,
Now lacerated Friendship claims a tear.
Year chases year, decay pursues decay,
Still drops some joy from withering life away;
New forms arise, and different views engage,
Superfluous lags the veteran on the stage,
Till pitying Nature signs the last release,
310 And bids afflicted worth retire to peace.
    But few there are whom hours like these await,
Who set unclouded in the gulfs of fate.
From Lydia's monarch° should the search descend,
By Solon cautioned to regard his end,
In life's last scene what prodigies surprise,
Fears of the brave, and follies of the wise?
From Marlborough's° eyes the streams of dotage flow,

positively peremptorily, in strong terms
Improve increase
Lydia's monarch Croesus, warned by Solon to
consider no man happy while he was living

Marlborough John Churchill (1650–1722), 1st
Duke of Marlborough, the great military leader
and victor of Blenheim, suffered paralytic
strokes in his last years.

And Swift° expires a driveller and a show.
      The teeming mother, anxious for her race,
320   Begs for each birth the fortune of a face:
Yet Vane° could tell what ills from beauty spring;
And Sedley° cursed the form that pleased a king.
Ye nymphs of rosy lips and radiant eyes,
Whom Pleasure keeps too busy to be wise,
Whom Joys with soft varieties invite,
By day the frolic, and the dance by night,
Who frown with vanity, who smile with art,
And ask the latest fashion of the heart,
What care, what rules your heedless charms shall save,
330   Each nymph your rival, and each youth your slave?
Against your fame with fondness hate combines,
The rival batters, and the lover mines.
With distant voice neglected Virtue calls,
Less heard and less, the faint remonstrance falls;
Tired with contempt, she quits the slippery reign,
And Pride and Prudence take her seat in vain.
In crowd at once, where none the pass defend,
The harmless freedom and the private friend.
The guardians yield, by force superior plied;
340   By Interest, Prudence; and by Flattery, Pride.
Now Beauty falls betrayed, despised, distressed,
And hissing Infamy proclaims the rest.
      Where then shall Hope and Fear their objects find?
Must dull Suspense° corrupt the stagnant mind?
Must helpless man, in ignorance sedate,
Roll darkling down the torrent of his fate?
Must no dislike alarm, no wishes rise,
No cries attempt the mercies of the skies?
Enquirer, cease, petitions yet remain,
350   Which heaven may hear; nor deem religion vain.
Still raise for good the supplicating voice,
But leave to heaven the measure and the choice,
Safe in his power, whose eyes discern afar
The secret ambush° of a specious prayer.
Implore his aid, in his decisions rest,
Secure whate'er he gives, he gives the best.
Yet when the sense of sacred presence fires,
And strong devotion to the skies aspires,
Pour forth thy fervours for a healthful mind,

Swift Swift's final madness (he was placed under the care of guardians from 1741 until his death in 1745) was "compounded of rage and fatuity"; except for a few intervals, he "sunk into lethargic stupidity, motionless, heedless, and speechless" (Johnson, *Life of Swift*).
Vane Anne Vane, mistress of Frederick, Prince of Wales, who deserted her

Sedley Catherine Sedley, mistress to the Duke of York, but abandoned when he became James II
Suspense i.e. a suspension of all moral choice, producing stagnancy
Sedley Catherine Sedley, mistress to the Duke through avowed sincerity

360   Obedient passions, and a will resigned;
    For love, which scarce collective man can fill;°
    For patience sovereign o'er transmuted° ill;
    For faith, that panting for a happier seat,
    Counts death kind Nature's signal of retreat:
    These goods for man the laws of heaven ordain,
    These goods he grants, who grants the power to gain;
    With these celestial wisdom calms the mind,
  And makes the happiness she does not find.°
1748   1749

On the Death of Dr. Robert Levet°

Condemned to hope's delusive mine,
    As on we toil from day to day,
By sudden blasts, or slow decline,
    Our social comforts drop away.

Well tried through many a varying year,
    See Levet to the grave descend;
Officious,° innocent, sincere,
    Of every friendless name the friend.

Yet still he fills affection's eye,
10   Obscurely wise and coarsely kind;
Nor, lettered Arrogance, deny
    Thy praise to merit unrefined.

When fainting Nature called for aid,
    And hovering Death prepared the blow,
His vigorous remedy displayed
    The power of art without the show.

In misery's darkest caverns known,
    His useful care was ever nigh,
Where hopeless Anguish poured his groan,
20   And lonely Want retired to die.

No summons mocked by chill delay,
    No petty gain disdained by pride,
The modest wants of every day
    The toil of every day supplied.

For love . . . fill Cf. Pope, *Essay on Man* IV.
369–70: "Wide and more wide, the o'erflowings
of the mind / Take every creature in, of every
kind."
transmuted i.e. altered or transformed by the
very patience that meets it, as in the next lines
makes . . . find i.e. once absorbed into the
mind, such wisdom has the power to create its
own happiness by seeking only those objects
which (in Johnson's words) are "always to be
obtained"
On . . . Levet Levet (1705–82) lived as part
of Johnson's household for many years, a poor
man without a medical degree, somewhat stiff
and silent in manner, but generous in treating
others for little or no money.
Officious full of good offices

His virtues walked their narrow round,
  Nor made a pause, nor left a void;
And sure the Eternal Master found
  The single talent well employed.

30
The busy day, the peaceful night,
  Unfelt, uncounted, glided by;
His frame was firm, his powers were bright,
  Though now his eightieth year was nigh.

Then with no throbbing fiery pain,
  No cold gradations of decay,
Death broke at once the vital chain,
  And freed his soul the nearest way.
  1782   1782

The History of Rasselas, Prince of Abyssinia

This Oriental tale was written "in the evenings of one week" to defray the expense of Johnson's mother's funeral and to pay off her few small debts. Its elevated, highly formalized narrative is always tinged with an ironic sense of the ludicrous, and its hero—the young Prince Rasselas—is a solemn, rather priggish idealist who seeks to make "the choice of life." A prisoner in the Happy Valley of Abyssinia, which none can leave once they enter it (or re-enter once they leave), the prince becomes restless with the sheer banality of its serene pleasures, and he devises a plan to escape. Before he does so, he encounters the poet Imlac and asks countless questions about the world outside. "The poet pitied his ignorance and loved his curiosity"; and his narrative—with Rasselas's naïvely incredulous interruptions—follows. In later chapters, the prince Rasselas and his sister Nekayah, accompanied by Imlac and by the princess's companion Pekuah, traverse the scenes of man, never finding the ideal "choice of life" in a world of mixed blessings. "There are goods so opposed that we cannot seize both, but, by too much prudence, may pass between them at too great distance to enjoy either," Nekayah concludes. "Of the blessings set before you, make your choice and be content." To Rasselas's desire to find a happiness that is "solid and permanent, without fear and without uncertainty" is opposed Imlac's wry observation, "Very few live by choice," or Nekayah's sense of the impossibility of clear choice: "Marriage has many pains, but celibacy has no pleasures." The narrative ends with a "conclusion, in which nothing is concluded," with each of its participants making resolutions he will probably not be able to achieve, and with all returning to Abyssinia and surrendering the quest. Johnson's sad comedy was written at almost the same time as a work in a different spirit but with similar conclusions, Voltaire's *Candide*.

From The History of Rasselas, Prince of Abyssinia

Chapter VIII: The History of Imlac

The close of the day is, in the regions of the torrid zone, the only season of diversion and entertainment, and it was therefore midnight before the music ceased, and the princesses retired. Rasselas then called for his companion, and required him to begin the story of his life.

'Sir,' said Imlac, 'my history will not be long: the life that is devoted to knowledge passes silently away, and is very little diversified by events. To talk in public, to think in solitude, to read and to hear, to inquire and answer inquiries, is the business of a scholar. He wanders about the world without pomp or terror, and is neither known nor valued but by men like himself.

'I was born in the kingdom of Goiama,[1] at no great distance from the fountain of the Nile. My father was a wealthy merchant, who traded between the inland countries of Africk and the ports of the Red Sea. He was honest, frugal, and diligent, but of mean sentiments and narrow comprehension: he desired only to be rich, and to conceal his riches, lest he should be spoiled[2] by the governors of the province.'

'Surely,' said the prince, 'my father must be negligent of his charge, if any man in his dominions dares take that which belongs to another. Does he not know that kings are accountable for injustice permitted as well as done? If I were emperor, not the meanest of my subjects should be oppressed with impunity. My blood boils when I am told that a merchant durst not enjoy his honest gains, for fear of losing them by the rapacity of power. Name the governor who robbed the people, that I may declare his crimes to the emperor.'

'Sir,' said Imlac, 'your ardour is the natural effect of virtue animated by youth: the time will come when you will acquit your father, and perhaps hear with less impatience of the governor. Oppression is, in the Abyssinian dominions, neither frequent nor tolerated; but no form of government has been yet discovered, by which cruelty can be wholly prevented. Subordination supposes power on one part, and subjection on the other; and if power be in the hands of men, it will sometimes be abused. The vigilance of the supreme magistrate may do much, but much will still remain undone. He can never know all the crimes that are committed, and can seldom punish all that he knows.'

'This,' said the prince, 'I do not understand; but I had rather hear thee than dispute. Continue thy narration.'

'My father,' proceeded Imlac, 'originally intended that I should have no other education, than such as might qualify me for commerce; and discovering in me great strength of memory and quickness of apprehension, often declared his hope that I should be some time the richest man in Abyssinia.'

'Why,' said the prince, 'did thy father desire the increase of his wealth,

---

1. "One of the most fruitful provinces of all the Abyssinian dominions"; Johnson had in 1735 translated from the French the *Voyage to Abyssinia* by the Portuguese Jesuit Father Jerome Lobo (1595–1678), and many of his geographical references derive from that work.
2. Despoiled, plundered.

when it was already greater than he durst discover or enjoy? I am unwilling to doubt thy veracity, yet inconsistencies cannot both be true.'

'Inconsistencies,' answered Imlac, 'cannot both be right, but, imputed to man, they may both be true. Yet diversity is not inconsistency. My father might expect a time of greater security. However, some desire is necessary to keep life in motion; and he whose real wants are supplied, must admit those of fancy.'

'This,' said the prince, 'I can in some measure conceive. I repent that I interrupted thee.'

'With this hope,' proceeded Imlac, 'he sent me to school; but when I had once found the delight of knowledge, and felt the pleasure of intelligence and the pride of invention,[3] I began silently to despise riches, and determined to disappoint the purpose of my father, whose grossness of conception raised my pity. I was twenty years old before his tenderness would expose me to the fatigue of travel, in which time I had been instructed, by successive masters, in all the literature of my native country. As every hour taught me something new, I lived in a continual course of gratification; but, as I advanced towards manhood, I lost much of the reverence with which I had been used to look on my instructors; because when the lesson was ended, I did not find them wiser or better than common men.

'At length my father resolved to initiate me in commerce, and opening one of his subterranean treasuries, counted out ten thousand pieces of gold. "This, young man," said he, "is the stock with which you must negotiate. I began with less than the fifth part, and you see how diligence and parsimony have increased it. This is your own to waste or to improve. If you squander it by negligence or caprice, you must wait for my death before you will be rich; if in four years you double your stock, we will thenceforward let subordination cease, and live together as friends and partners; for he shall always be equal with me, who is equally skilled in the art of growing rich."

'We laid our money upon camels, concealed in bales of cheap goods, and travelled to the shore of the Red Sea. When I cast my eye on the expanse of waters, my heart bounded like that of a prisoner escaped. I felt an unextinguishable curiosity kindle in my mind, and resolved to snatch this opportunity of seeing the manners of other nations, and of learning sciences unknown in Abyssinia.

'I remembered that my father had obliged me to the improvement of my stock, not by a promise which I ought not to violate, but by a penalty which I was at liberty to incur; and therefore determined to gratify my predominant desire, and, by drinking at the fountains of knowledge, to quench the thirst of curiosity.

'As I was supposed to trade without connexion with my father, it was easy for me to become acquainted with the master of a ship, and procure a passage to some other country. I had no motives of choice to regulate my voyage; it was sufficient for me that, wherever I wandered, I should see a country which I had not seen before. I therefore entered a ship bound for Surat,[4] having left a letter for my father declaring my intention.

3. Imagination.
4. Indian seaport 150 miles north of Bombay.

Chapter IX: The History of Imlac Continued

'When I first entered upon the world of waters, and lost sight of land, I looked round about me with pleasing terror, and thinking my soul enlarged by the boundless prospect, imagined that I could gaze round for ever without satiety; but in a short time I grew weary of looking on barren uniformity, where I could only see again what I had already seen. I then descended into the ship, and doubted for awhile whether all my future pleasures would not end like this, in disgust and disappointment. Yet, surely, said I, the ocean and the land are very different; the only variety of water is rest and motion, but the earth has mountains and valleys, deserts and cities; it is inhabited by men of different customs and contrary opinions; and I may hope to find variety in life, though I should miss it in nature.

'With this thought I quieted my mind; and amused myself during the voyage, sometimes by learning from the sailors the art of navigation, which I have never practised, and sometimes by forming schemes for my conduct in different situations, in not one of which I have been ever placed.

'I was almost weary of my naval amusements when we landed safely at Surat. I secured my money, and purchasing some commodities for show, joined myself to a caravan that was passing into the inland country. My companions, for some reason or other, conjecturing that I was rich, and, by my inquiries and admiration, finding that I was ignorant, considered me as a novice whom they had a right to cheat, and who was to learn at the usual expense the art of fraud. They exposed me to the theft of servants and the exaction of officers, and saw me plundered upon false pretences, without any advantage to themselves but that of rejoicing in the superiority of their own knowledge.'

'Stop a moment,' said the prince. 'Is there such depravity in man, as that he should injure another without benefit to himself? I can easily conceive that all are pleased with superiority; but your ignorance was merely accidental, which, being neither your crime nor your folly, could afford them no reason to applaud themselves; and the knowledge which they had, and which you wanted, they might as effectually have shown by warning, as betraying you.'

'Pride,' said Imlac, 'is seldom delicate, it will please itself with very mean advantages; and envy feels not its own happiness, but when it may be compared with the misery of others. They were my enemies, because they grieved to think me rich; and my oppressors, because they delighted to find me weak.'

'Proceed,' said the prince: 'I doubt not of the facts which you relate, but imagine that you impute them to mistaken motives.'

'In this company,' said Imlac, 'I arrived at Agra, the capital of Indostan, the city in which the great Mogul[5] commonly resides. I applied myself to the language of the country, and in a few months was able to converse with the learned men; some of whom I found morose and reserved, and others easy and communicative; some were unwilling to teach another what they had with difficulty learned themselves; and some showed that the end of their studies was to gain the dignity of instructing.

'To the tutor of the young princes I recommended myself so much, that I

5. The ruler of the Mohammedan empire established in India by Akbar the Great; his capital was at Agra.

was presented to the emperor as a man of uncommon knowledge. The emperor asked me many questions concerning my country and my travels; and though I cannot now recollect any thing that he uttered above the power of a common man, he dismissed me astonished at his wisdom, and enamoured of his goodness.

'My credit was now so high, that the merchants with whom I had travelled, applied to me for recommendations to the ladies of the court. I was surprised at their confidence of solicitation, and gently reproached them with their practices on the road. They heard me with cold indifference, and showed no tokens of shame or sorrow.

'They then urged their request with the offer of a bribe; but what I would not do for kindness, I would not do for money, and refused them, not because they had injured me, but because I would not enable them to injure others; for I knew they would have made use of my credit to cheat those who should buy their wares.

'Having resided at Agra till there was no more to be learned, I travelled into Persia, where I saw many remains of ancient magnificence, and observed many new accommodations of life. The Persians are a nation eminently social, and their assemblies afforded me daily opportunities of remarking characters and manners, and of tracing human nature through all its variations.

'From Persia I passed into Arabia, where I saw a nation at once pastoral and warlike; who live without any settled habitation; whose only wealth is their flocks and herds; and who have yet carried on through all ages an hereditary war with all mankind, though they neither covet nor envy their possessions.'

Chapter X: Imlac's History Continued. A Dissertation upon Poetry

'Wherever I went, I found that poetry was considered as the highest learning, and regarded with a veneration somewhat approaching to that which man would pay to the angelic nature. And yet it fills me with wonder, that, in almost all countries, the most ancient poets are considered as the best: whether it be that every other kind of knowledge is an acquisition gradually attained, and poetry is a gift conferred at once; or that the first poetry of every nation surprised them as a novelty, and retained the credit by consent, which it re- ceived by accident at first; or whether, as the province of poetry is to describe nature and passion, which are always the same, the first writers took possession of the most striking objects for description, and the most probable occurrences for fiction, and left nothing to those that followed them but transcription of the same events, and new combinations of the same images:—whatever be the reason, it is commonly observed that the early writers are in possession of nature, and their followers of art; that the first excel in strength and invention, and the latter in elegance and refinement.

'I was desirous to add my name to this illustrious fraternity. I read all the poets of Persia and Arabia, and was able to repeat by memory the volumes that are suspended in the mosque of Mecca.[6] But I soon found that no man was ever great by imitation. My desire of excellence impelled me to transfer

6. Illuminated manuscripts, chiefly of the *Koran* and other religious books, hung as sacred texts.

my attention to nature and to life. Nature was to be my subject, and men to be my auditors: I could never describe what I had not seen; I could not hope to move those with delight or terror, whose interests and opinions I did not understand.

'Being now resolved to be a poet, I saw everything with a new purpose; my sphere of attention was suddenly magnified; no kind of knowledge was to be overlooked. I ranged mountains and deserts for images and resemblances, and pictured upon my mind every tree of the forest and flower of the valley. I observed with equal care the crags of the rock and the pinnacles of the palace. Sometimes I wandered along the mazes of the rivulet, and sometimes watched the changes of the summer clouds. To a poet nothing can be useless. Whatever is beautiful, and whatever is dreadful, must be familiar to his imagination: he must be conversant with all that is awfully [7] vast or elegantly little. The plants of the garden, the animals of the wood, the minerals of the earth, and meteors of the sky must all concur to store his mind with inexhaustible variety: for every idea is useful for the enforcement or decoration of moral or religious truth; and he who knows most, will have most power of diversifying his scenes, and of gratifying his reader with remote allusions and unexpected instruction.

'All the appearances of nature I was therefore careful to study; and every country which I have surveyed has contributed something to my poetical powers.'

'In so wide a survey,' said the prince, 'you must surely have left much unobserved. I have lived, till now, within the circuit of these mountains, and yet cannot walk abroad without the sight of something which I had never beheld before, or never heeded.'

'The business of a poet,' said Imlac, 'is to examine, not the individual, but the species; to remark general properties and large appearances. He does not number the streaks of the tulip, or describe the different shades in the verdure of the forest: he is to exhibit in his portraits of nature such prominent and striking features, as recall the original to every mind; and must neglect the minuter discriminations, which one may have remarked, and another have neglected, for those characteristics which are alike obvious to vigilance and carelessness.

'But the knowledge of nature is only half the task of a poet: he must be acquainted likewise with all the modes of life. His character requires that he estimate the happiness and misery of every condition, observe the power of all the passions in all their combinations, and trace the changes of the human mind as they are modified by various institutions and accidental influences of climate or custom, from the sprightliness of infancy to the despondence of decrepitude. He must divest himself of the prejudices of his age and country; he must consider right and wrong in their abstracted and invariable state; he must disregard present laws and opinions, and rise to general and transcendental truths, which will always be the same. He must therefore content himself with the slow progress of his name, contemn the applause of his own

---

7. Awe-inspiringly; cf. Burke's work on the Sublime, which had been published two years earlier than *Rasselas*.

time, and commit his claims to the justice of posterity. He must write as the interpreter of nature, and the legislator of mankind, and consider himself as presiding over the thoughts and manners of future generations; as a being superior to time and place.

'His labour is not yet at an end; he must know many languages and many sciences; and, that his style may be worthy of his thoughts, must, by incessant practice, familiarise to himself every delicacy of speech and grace of harmony.'

Chapter XI: Imlac's Narrative Continued. A Hint on Pilgrimage

Imlac now felt the enthusiastic fit, and was proceeding to aggrandize his own profession, when the prince cried out, 'Enough! thou hast convinced me that no human being can ever be a poet. Proceed with thy narration.'

'To be a poet,' said Imlac, 'is indeed very difficult.'

'So difficult,' returned the prince, 'that I will at present hear no more of his labours. Tell me whither you went when you had seen Persia.'

'From Persia,' said the poet, 'I travelled through Syria, and for three years resided in Palestine, where I conversed with great numbers of the northern and western nations of Europe; the nations which are now in possession of all power and all knowledge; whose armies are irresistible, and whose fleets command the remotest parts of the globe. When I compared these men with the natives of our own kingdom, and those that surround us, they appeared almost another order of beings. In their countries it is difficult to wish for anything that may not be obtained: a thousand arts, of which we never heard, are continually labouring for their convenience and pleasure; and whatever their own climate has denied them is supplied by their commerce.'

'By what means,' said the prince, 'are the Europeans thus powerful; or why, since they can so easily visit Asia and Africa for trade or conquest, cannot the Asiatics and Africans invade their coasts, plant colonies in their ports, and give laws to their natural princes? The same wind that carries them back, would bring us thither.'

'They are more powerful, sir, than we,' answered Imlac, 'because they are wiser; knowledge will always predominate over ignorance, as man governs the other animals. But why their knowledge is more than ours, I know not what reason can be given, but the unsearchable will of the Supreme Being.'

'When,' said the prince with a sigh, 'shall I be able to visit Palestine, and mingle with this mighty confluence of nations? Till that happy moment shall arrive, let me fill up the time with such representations as thou canst give me. I am not ignorant of the motive that assembles such numbers in that place, and cannot but consider it as the centre of wisdom and piety, to which the best and wisest men of every land must be continually resorting.'

'There are some nations,' said Imlac, 'that send few visitants to Palestine; for many numerous and learned sects in Europe concur to censure pilgrimage as superstitious, or deride it as ridiculous.'

'You know,' said the prince, 'how little my life has made me acquainted with diversity of opinions; it will be too long to hear the arguments on both sides; you, that have considered them, tell me the result.'

'Pilgrimage,' said Imlac, 'like many other acts of piety, may be reasonable or superstitious, according to the principles upon which it is performed. Long journeys in search of truth are not commanded. Truth, such as is necessary to the regulation of life, is always found where it is honestly sought. Change of place is no natural cause of the increase of piety, for it inevitably produces dissipation of mind. Yet, since men go every day to view the fields where great actions have been performed, and return with stronger impressions of the event, curiosity of the same kind may naturally dispose us to view that country whence our religion had its beginning; and I believe no man surveys those awful scenes without some confirmation of holy resolutions. That the Supreme Being may be more easily propitiated in one place than in another is the dream of idle superstition; but that some places may operate upon our own minds in an uncommon manner is an opinion which hourly experience will justify. He who supposes that his vices may be more successfully combatted in Palestine, will, perhaps, find himself mistaken; yet he may go thither without folly: he who thinks they will be more freely pardoned dishonours at once his reason and religion.'

'These,' said the prince, 'are European distinctions. I will consider them another time. What have you found to be the effect of knowledge? Are those nations happier than we?'

'There is so much infelicity,' said the poet, 'in the world, that scarce any man has leisure from his own distresses to estimate the comparative happiness of others. Knowledge is certainly one of the means of pleasure, as is confessed by the natural desire which every mind feels of increasing its ideas. Ignorance is mere privation, by which nothing can be produced: it is a vacuity in which the soul sits motionless and torpid for want of attraction; and, without knowing why, we always rejoice when we learn and grieve when we forget. I am therefore inclined to conclude, that if nothing counteracts the natural consequence of learning, we grow more happy as our minds take a wider range.'

'In enumerating the particular comforts of life, we shall find many advantages on the side of the Europeans. They cure wounds and diseases with which we languish and perish. We suffer inclemencies of weather which they can obviate. They have engines for the despatch of many laborious works which we must perform by manual industry. There is such communication between distant places, that one friend can hardly be said to be absent from another. Their policy removes all public inconveniences; they have roads cut through their mountains, and bridges laid upon their rivers. And, if we descend to the privacies of life, their habitations are more commodious, and their possessions are more secure.'

'They are surely happy,' said the prince, 'who have all these conveniences, of which I envy none so much as the facility with which separated friends interchange their thoughts.'

'The Europeans,' answered Imlac, 'are less unhappy than we; but they are not happy. Human life is every where a state in which much is to be endured, and little to be enjoyed.'

Chapter XII: The Story of Imlac Continued

'I am not yet willing,' said the prince, 'to suppose that happiness is so parsimoniously distributed to mortals; nor can believe but that, if I had the choice of life, I should be able to fill every day with pleasure. I would injure no man, and should provoke no resentment; I would relieve every distress, and should enjoy the benedictions of gratitude. I would choose my friends among the wise, and my wife among the virtuous; and therefore should be in no danger from treachery or unkindness. My children should, by my care, be learned and pious, and would repay to my age what their childhood had received. What would dare to molest him who might call on every side to thousands enriched by his bounty, or assisted by his power? And why should not life glide quietly away in the soft reciprocation of protection and reverence? All this may be done without the help of European refinements, which appear by their effects to be rather specious than useful. Let us leave them, and pursue our journey.'

'From Palestine,' said Imlac, 'I passed through many regions of Asia; in the more civilized kingdoms as a trader, and among the barbarians of the mountains as a pilgrim. At last I began to long for my native country, that I might repose, after my travels and fatigues, in the places where I had spent my earliest years, and gladden my old companions with the recital of my adventures. Often did I figure to myself those with whom I had sported away the gay hours of dawning life, sitting round me in its evening, wondering at my tales, and listening to my counsels.

'When this thought had taken possession of my mind, I considered every moment as wasted which did not bring me nearer to Abyssinia. I hastened into Egypt, and notwithstanding my impatience, was detained ten months in the contemplation of its ancient magnificence, and in inquiries after the remains of its ancient learning. I found in Cairo a mixture of all nations; some brought thither by the love of knowledge, some by the hope of gain, and many by the desire of living after their own manner without observation, and of lying hid in the obscurity of multitudes: for in a city, populous as Cairo, it is possible to obtain at the same time the gratifications of society, and the secrecy of solitude.

'From Cairo I travelled to Suez, and embarked on the Red Sea, passing along the coast till I arrived at the port from which I had departed twenty years before. Here I joined myself to a caravan, and re-entered my native country.

'I now expected the caresses of my kinsmen, and the congratulations of my friends, and was not without hope that my father, whatever value he had set upon riches, would own with gladness and pride a son who was able to add to the felicity and honour of the nation. But I was soon convinced that my thoughts were vain. My father had been dead fourteen years, having divided his wealth among my brothers, who were removed to some other provinces. Of my companions, the greater part were in the grave; of the rest, some could with difficulty remember me, and some considered me as one corrupted by foreign manners.

'A man used to vicissitudes is not easily dejected. I forgot, after a time, my disappointment, and endeavoured to recommend myself to the nobles of the kingdom; they admitted me to their tables, heard my story, and dismissed me. I opened a school, and was prohibited to teach. I then resolved to sit down in the quiet of domestic life, and addressed a lady that was fond of my conversation but rejected my suit because my father was a merchant.

'Wearied at last with solicitation and repulses, I resolved to hide myself for ever from the world, and depend no longer on the opinion or caprice of others. I waited for the time when the gate of the *happy valley* should open, that I might bid farewell to hope and fear: the day came; my performance was distinguished with favour; and I resigned myself with joy to perpetual confinement.' [8]

'Hast thou here found happiness at last?' said Rasselas. 'Tell me without reserve; art thou content with thy condition? or, dost thou wish to be again wandering and inquiring? All the inhabitants of this valley celebrate their lot, and at the annual visit of the emperor, invite others to partake of their felicity.'

'Great prince,' said Imlac, 'I shall speak the truth; I know not one of all your attendants, who does not lament the hour when he entered this retreat. I am less unhappy than the rest, because I have a mind replete with images, which I can vary and combine at pleasure. I can amuse my solitude by the renovation of the knowledge which begins to fade from my memory, and by recollection of the incidents of my past life. Yet all this ends in the sorrowful consideration, that my acquirements are now useless, and that none of my pleasures can be again enjoyed. The rest, whose minds have no impression but of the present moment, are either corroded by malignant passions, or sit stupid in the gloom of perpetual vacancy.'

'What passions can infest those,' said the prince, 'who have no rivals? We are in a place where impotence precludes malice, and where all envy is repressed by community of enjoyments.'

'There may be community,' said Imlac, 'of material possessions, but there can never be community of love or of esteem. It must happen that one will please more than another; he that knows himself despised will always be envious; and still more envious and malevolent, if he is condemned to live in the presence of those who despise him. The invitations by which they allure others, to a state which they feel to be wretched, proceed from the natural malignity of hopeless misery. They are weary of themselves and of each other, and expect to find relief in new companions. They envy the liberty which their folly has forfeited, and would gladly see all mankind imprisoned like themselves.

'From this crime, however, I am wholly free. No man can say that he is wretched by my persuasion. I look with pity on the crowds who are annually soliciting admission to captivity, and wish that it were lawful for me to warn them of their danger.'

'My dear Imlac,' said the prince, 'I will open to thee my whole heart. I have long meditated an escape from the *happy valley*. I have examined the mountains on every side, but find myself insuperably barred: teach me the way to break my prison; thou shalt be the companion of my flight, the guide of my rambles, the partner of my fortune, and my sole director in the *choice of life*.'

'Sir,' answered the poet, 'your escape will be difficult, and, perhaps, you may soon repent your curiosity. The world, which you figure to yourself smooth and quiet as the lake in the valley, you will find a sea foaming with tempests, and boiling with whirlpools: you will be sometimes overwhelmed by the waves of

8. The gates of the Happy Valley were opened once each year for the Emperor's visit, and only those were admitted for permanent residence "whose performance was thought able to add novelty to luxury." Once admitted, one could remain; but once one left one could never re-enter.

violence, and sometimes dashed against the rocks of treachery. Amidst wrongs and frauds, competitions and anxieties, you will wish a thousand times for these seats of quiet, and willingly quit hope to be free from fear.'

'Do not seek to deter me from my purpose,' said the prince; 'I am impatient to see what thou hast seen; and, since thou art thyself weary of the valley, it is evident that thy former state was better than this. Whatever be the consequence of my experiment, I am resolved to judge with mine own eyes of the various conditions of men, and then to make deliberately my *choice of life.*'

'I am afraid,' said Imlac, 'you are hindered by stronger restraints than my persuasions; yet, if your determination is fixed, I do not counsel you to despair. Few things are impossible to diligence and skill.'

1759

From The Rambler

> *Quis scit, an adjiciant hodiernae crastina summae*
> *Tempora Dî superi!*   HORACE, *Odes*, IV.7.17–18
>
> Who knows if Heaven, with ever-bounteous power,
> Shall add tomorrow to the present hour?
> (trans. FRANCIS)

I sat yesterday morning employed in deliberating on which, among the various subjects that occurred to my imagination, I should bestow the paper of today. After a short effort of meditation by which nothing was determined, I grew every moment more irresolute, my ideas wandered from the first intention, and I rather wished to think, than thought, upon any settled subject; till at last I was awakened from this dream of study by a summons from the press: the time was come for which I had been thus negligently purposing to provide, and, however dubious or sluggish, I was now necessitated to write.

Though to a writer whose design is so comprehensive and miscellaneous that he may accommodate himself with a topic from every scene of life, or view of nature, it is no great aggravation of his task to be obliged to a sudden composition, yet I could not forbear to reproach myself for having so long neglected what was unavoidably to be done, and of which every moment's idleness increased the difficulty. There was however some pleasure in reflecting that I, who had only trifled till diligence was necessary, might still congratulate myself upon my superiority to multitudes, who have trifled till diligence is vain; who can by no degree of activity or resolution recover the opportunities which have slipped away; and who are condemned by their own carelessness to hopeless calamity and barren sorrow.

The folly of allowing ourselves to delay what we know cannot be finally escaped, is one of the general weaknesses, which, in spite of the instruction of moralists, and the remonstrances of reason, prevail to a greater or less degree in every mind: even they who most steadily withstand it, find it, if not the most violent, the most pertinacious of their passions, always renewing its attacks, and though often vanquished, never destroyed.

It is indeed natural to have particular regard to the time present, and to be most solicitous for that which is by its nearness enabled to make the strongest impressions. When therefore any sharp pain is to be suffered or any formidable danger to be incurred, we can scarcely exempt ourselves wholly from the seducements of imagination; we readily believe that another day will bring some support or advantage which we now want; and are easily persuaded that the moment of necessity which we desire never to arrive is at a great distance from us.

Thus life is languished away in the gloom of anxiety, and consumed in collecting resolutions which the next morning dissipates; in forming purposes which we scarcely hope to keep, and reconciling ourselves to our own cowardice by excuses, which, while we admit them, we know to be absurd. Our firmness is by the continual contemplation of misery hourly impaired; every submission to our fear enlarges its dominion; we not only waste that time in which the evil we dread might have been suffered and surmounted, but even where procrastination produces no absolute encrease of our difficulties, make them less superable to ourselves by habitual terrors. When evils cannot be avoided, it is wise to contract the interval of expectation; to meet the mischiefs which will overtake us if we fly; and suffer only their real malignity without the conflicts of doubt and anguish of anticipation.

To act is far easier than to suffer, yet we every day see the progress of life retarded by the *vis inertiae*,[1] the mere repugnance to motion, and find multitudes repining at the want of that which nothing but idleness hinders them from enjoying. The case of Tantalus, in the region of poetic punishment, was somewhat to be pitied, because the fruits that hung about him retired from his hand;[2] but what tenderness can be claimed by those who though perhaps they suffer the pains of Tantalus will never lift their hands for their own relief?

There is nothing more common among this torpid generation than murmurs and complaints; murmurs at uneasiness which only vacancy[3] and suspicion expose them to feel, and complaints of distresses which it is in their own power to remove. Laziness is commonly associated with timidity. Either fear originally prohibits endeavours by infusing despair of success; or the frequent failure of irresolute struggles, and the constant desire of avoiding labour, impress by degrees false terrors on the mind. But fear, whether natural or acquired, when once it has full possession of the fancy, never fails to employ it upon visions of calamity, such as if they are not dissipated by useful employment, will soon overcast it with horrors, and imbitter life not only with those miseries by which all earthly beings are really more or less tormented, but with those which do not yet exist, and which can only be discerned by the perspicacity of cowardice.

Among all who sacrifice future advantage to present inclination, scarcely any gain so little as those that suffer themselves to freeze in idleness. Others are corrupted by some enjoyment of more or less power to gratify the passions; but to neglect our duties, merely to avoid the labour of performing them, a labour which is always punctually rewarded, is surely to sink under weak temptations. Idleness never can secure tranquillity; the call of reason and of conscience will pierce the closest pavilion of the sluggard, and, though it may not have force

1. "Force of inertia."
2. Tantalus was tortured when the fruit receded, as he advanced his hand, and the water as he advanced his lips.
3. Idleness.

to drive him from his down,[4] will be loud enough to hinder him from sleep. Those moments which he cannot resolve to make useful by devoting them to the great business of his being, will still be usurped by powers that will not leave them to his disposal; remorse and vexation will seize upon them, and forbid him to enjoy what he is so desirous to appropriate.

There are other causes of inactivity incident to more active faculties and more acute discernment. He to whom many objects of pursuit arise at the same time, will frequently hesitate between different desires, till a rival has precluded him, or change his course as new attractions prevail, and harass himself without advancing. He who sees different ways to the same end, will, unless he watches carefully over his own conduct, lay out too much of his attention upon the comparison of probabilities and the adjustment of expedients, and pause in the choice of his road till some accident intercepts his journey. He whose penetration extends to remote consequences and who, whenever he applies his attention to any design, discovers new prospects of advantage and possibilities of improvement, will not easily be persuaded that his project is ripe for execution; but will superadd one contrivance to another, endeavour to unite various purposes in one operation, multiply complications, and refine niceties, till he is entangled in his own scheme, and bewildered in the perplexity of various intentions. He that resolves to unite all the beauties of situation in a new purchase, must waste his life in roving to no purpose from province to province. He that hopes in the same house to obtain every convenience, may draw plans and study Palladio,[5] but will never lay a stone. He will attempt a treatise on some important subject, and amass materials, consult authors, and study all the dependent and collateral parts of learning, but never conclude himself qualified to write. He that has abilities to conceive perfection, will not easily be content without it; and since perfection cannot be reached, will lose the opportunity of doing well in the vain hope of unattainable excellence.

The certainty that life cannot be long, and the probability that it will be much shorter than nature allows, ought to awaken every man to the active prosecution of whatever he is desirous to perform. It is true that no diligence can ascertain success; death may intercept the swiftest career; but he who is cut off in the execution of an honest undertaking has at least the honour of falling in his rank, and has fought the battle, though he missed the victory.

[No. 134, Saturday, June 29, 1751]

> *Nulla fides regni sociis, omnisque potestas*
> *Impatiens consortis erat.*   LUCAN, I.92–93

No faith of partnership dominion owns;
Still discord hovers o'er divided thrones.

The hostility perpetually exercised between one man and another is caused by the desire of many for that which only few can possess. Every man would be rich, powerful, and famous; yet fame, power, and riches, are only the names of relative conditions, which imply the obscurity, dependence, and poverty of greater numbers.

4. That is, from his pillow.
5. Andrea Palladio, the influential Italian Renaissance architect; cf. Pope, *Epistle to Burlington.*

This universal and incessant competition, produces injury and malice by two motives, interest and envy; the prospect of adding to our possessions what we can take from others, and the hope of alleviating the sense of our disparity by lessening others, though we gain nothing to ourselves.

Of these two malignant and destructive powers, it seems probable at the first view that interest has the strongest and most extensive influence. It is easy to conceive that opportunities to seize what has been long wanted may excite desires almost irresistible; but surely, the same eagerness cannot be kindled by an accidental power of destroying that which gives happiness to another. It must be more natural to rob for gain than to ravage only for mischief.

Yet I am inclined to believe that the great law of mutual benevolence is oftener violated by envy than by interest, and that most of the misery which the defamation of blameless actions or the obstruction of honest endeavours brings upon the world is inflicted by men that propose no advantage to themselves but the satisfaction of poisoning the banquet which they cannot taste, and blasting the harvest which they have no right to reap.

Interest can diffuse itself but to a narrow compass. The number is never large of those who can hope to fill the posts of degraded power, catch the fragments of shattered fortune, or succeed to the honours of depreciated beauty. But the empire of envy has no limits, as it requires to its influence very little help from external circumstances. Envy may always be produced by idleness and pride, and in what place will not they be found?

Interest requires some qualities not universally bestowed. The ruin of another will produce no profit to him who has not discernment to mark his advantage, courage to seize, and activity to pursue it; but the cold malignity of envy may be exerted in a torpid and quiescent state, amidst the gloom of stupidity, in the coverts of cowardice. He that falls by the attacks of interest is torn by hungry tigers; he may discover and resist his enemies. He that perishes in the ambushes of envy is destroyed by unknown and invisible assailants, and dies like a man suffocated by a poisonous vapour, without knowledge of his danger or possibility of contest.

Interest is seldom pursued but at some hazard. He that hopes to gain much has commonly something to lose, and when he ventures to attack superiority, if he fails to conquer, is irrecoverably crushed. But envy may act without expence or danger. To spread suspicion, to invent calumnies, to propagate scandal, requires neither labour nor courage. It is easy for the author of a lie, however malignant, to escape detection, and infamy needs very little industry to assist its circulation.

Envy is almost the only vice which is practicable at all times and in every place; the only passion which can never lie quiet for want of irritation; its effects therefore are everywhere discoverable, and its attempts always to be dreaded.

It is impossible to mention a name which any advantageous distinction has made eminent, but some latent animosity will burst out. The wealthy trader, however he may abstract himself from public affairs, will never want those who hint, with Shylock,[6] that ships are but boards. The beauty, adorned only with the unambitious graces of innocence and modesty, provokes whenever

---

6. Shakespeare, *Merchant of Venice* I.iii.20.

she appears a thousand murmurs of detraction. The genius, even when he endeavours only to entertain or instruct, yet suffers persecution from innumerable critics whose acrimony is excited merely by the pain of seeing others pleased, and of hearing applauses which another enjoys.

The frequency of envy makes it so familiar that it escapes our notice; nor do we often reflect upon its turpitude or malignity till we happen to feel its influence. When he that has given no provocation to malice, but by attempting to excel, finds himself pursued by multitudes whom he never saw with all the implacability of personal resentment; when he perceives clamour and malice let loose upon him as a public enemy, and incited by every stratagem of defamation; when he hears the misfortunes of his family, or the follies of his youth exposed to the world; and every failure of conduct, or defect of nature aggravated and ridiculed; he then learns to abhor those artifices at which he only laughed before, and discovers how much the happiness of life would be advanced by the eradication of envy from the human heart.

Envy is, indeed, a stubborn weed of the mind, and seldom yields to the culture [7] of philosophy. There are, however, considerations, which if carefully implanted and diligently propagated, might in time overpower and repress it, since no one can nurse it for the sake of pleasure, as its effects are only shame, anguish, and perturbation.

It is above all other vices inconsistent with the character of a social being, because it sacrifices truth and kindness to very weak temptations. He that plunders a wealthy neighbour gains as much as he takes away, and may improve his own condition in the same proportion as he impairs another's; but he that blasts a flourishing reputation must be content with a small dividend of additional fame, so small as can afford very little consolation to balance the guilt by which it is obtained.

I have hitherto avoided that dangerous and empirical morality, which cures one vice by means of another. But envy is so base and detestable, so vile in its original, and so pernicious in its effects, that the predominance of almost any other quality is to be preferred. It is one of those lawless enemies of society against which poisoned arrows may honestly be used. Let it, therefore, be constantly remembered that whoever envies another, confesses his superiority, and let those be reformed by their pride who have lost their virtue.

It is no slight aggravation of the injuries which envy incites that they are committed against those who have given no intentional provocation; and that the sufferer is often marked out for ruin, not because he has failed in any duty, but because he has dared to do more than was required.

Almost every other crime is practised by the help of some quality which might have produced esteem or love if it had been well employed; but envy is mere unmixed and genuine evil; it pursues a hateful end by despicable means, and desires not so much its own happiness as another's misery. To avoid depravity like this, it is not necessary that any one should aspire to heroism or sanctity, but only that he should resolve not to quit the rank which nature assigns him, and wish to maintain the dignity of a human being. [No. 183, Tuesday, December 17, 1751]

7. Cultivation (in its literal sense; a metaphor pursued in the next sentence).

From The Idler

Among the innumerable mortifications that waylay human arrogance on every side may well be reckoned our ignorance of the most common objects and effects, a defect of which we become more sensible by every attempt to supply it. Vulgar and inactive minds confound familiarity with knowledge, and conceive themselves informed of the whole nature of things when they are shown their form or told their use; but the speculatist, who is not content with superficial views, harasses himself with fruitless curiosity, and still as he enquires more perceives only that he knows less.

Sleep is a state in which a great part of every life is passed. No animal has been yet discovered whose existence is not varied with intervals of insensibility; and some late philosophers have extended the empire of sleep over the vegetable world.

Yet of this change so frequent, so great, so general, and so necessary, no searcher has yet found either the efficient or final cause;[8] or can tell by what power the mind and the body are thus chained down in irresistible stupefaction; or what benefits the animal receives from this alternate suspension of its active powers.

Whatever may be the multiplicity or contrariety of opinions upon this subject, nature has taken sufficient care that theory shall have little influence on practice. The most diligent enquirer is not able long to keep his eyes open; the most eager disputant will begin about midnight to desert his argument, and once in four and twenty hours, the gay and the gloomy, the witty and the dull, the clamorous and the silent, the busy and the idle, are all overpowered by the gentle tyrant, and all lie down in the equality of sleep.

Philosophy has often attempted to repress insolence by asserting that all conditions are levelled by death; a position which, however it may deject the happy, will seldom afford much comfort to the wretched. It is far more pleasing to consider that sleep is equally a leveller with death; that the time is never at a great distance when the balm of rest shall be effused alike upon every head, when the diversities of life shall stop their operation, and the high and the low shall lie down together.

It is somewhere recorded of Alexander, that in the pride of conquests and intoxication of flattery, he declared that he only perceived himself to be a man by the necessity of sleep.[9] Whether he considered sleep as necessary to his mind or body it was indeed a sufficient evidence of human infirmity; the body which required such frequency of renovation gave but faint promises of immortality; and the mind which, from time to time, sunk gladly into insensibility had made no very near approaches to the felicity of the supreme and self-sufficient nature.

I know not what can tend more to repress all the passions that disturb the peace of the world than the consideration that there is no height of happiness or honour from which man does not eagerly descend to a state of unconscious repose; that the best condition of life is such that we contentedly quit its good

8. That is, that which brings it about or the end it may be supposed to serve.
9. In Plutarch's life, XXII.3–4; Johnson refers to Alexander's conviction of his divine origin (see Dryden, *Alexander's Feast*).

to be disentangled from its evils; that in a few hours splendour fades before the eye and praise itself deadens in the ear; the senses withdraw from their objects, and reason favours the retreat.

What then are the hopes and prospects of covetousness, ambition and rapacity? Let him that desires most have all his desires gratified, he never shall attain a state which he can, for a day and a night, contemplate with satisfaction, or from which, if he had the power of perpetual vigilance, he would not long for periodical separations.

All envy would be extinguished if it were universally known that there are none to be envied, and surely none can be much envied who are not pleased with themselves. There is reason to suspect that the distinctions of mankind have more show than value when it is found that all agree to be weary alike of pleasures and of cares, that the powerful and the weak, the celebrated and obscure, join in one common wish, and implore from nature's hand the nectar of oblivion.

Such is our desire of abstraction from ourselves that very few are satisfied with the quantity of stupefaction which the needs of the body force upon the mind. Alexander himself added intemperance to sleep, and solaced with the fumes of wine the sovereignty of the world. And almost every man has some art by which he steals his thoughts away from his present state.

It is not much of life that is spent in close attention to any important duty. Many hours of every day are suffered to fly away without any traces left upon the intellects. We suffer phantoms to rise up before us, and amuse ourselves with the dance of airy images, which after a time we dismiss for ever, and know not how we have been busied.

Many have no happier moments than those that they pass in solitude, abandoned to their own imagination, which sometimes puts sceptres in their hands or mitres on their heads, shifts the scene of pleasure with endless variety, bids all the forms of beauty sparkle before them, and gluts them with every change of visionary luxury.

It is easy in these semi-slumbers to collect all the possibilities of happiness, to alter the course of the sun, to bring back the past, and anticipate the future, to unite all the beauties of all seasons, and all the blessings of all climates, to receive and bestow felicity, and forget that misery is the lot of man. All this is a voluntary dream, a temporary recession from the realities of life to airy fictions; an habitual subjection of reason to fancy.

Others are afraid to be alone, and amuse themselves by a perpetual succession of companions, but the difference is not great; in solitude we have our dreams to ourselves, and in company we agree to dream in concert. The end sought in both is forgetfulness of ourselves. [No. 32, Saturday, November 25, 1758]

Respicere ad longae jussit spatia ultima vitae.
JUVENAL, X.275 [10]

Much of the pain and pleasure of mankind arises from the conjectures which every one makes of the thoughts of others; we all enjoy praise which we do not

10. "Bidden to look at the last lap of a long life."

hear, and resent contempt which we do not see. The Idler may therefore be forgiven if he suffers his imagination to represent to him what his readers will say or think when they are informed that they have now his last paper in their hands.

Value is more frequently raised by scarcity than by use. That which lay neglected when it was common rises in estimation as its quantity becomes less. We seldom learn the true want of what we have till it is discovered that we can have no more.

This essay will, perhaps, be read with care even by those who have not yet attended to any other; and he that finds this late attention recompensed will not forbear to wish that he had bestowed it sooner.

Though the Idler and his readers have contracted no close friendship they are perhaps both unwilling to part. There are few things not purely evil of which we can say, without some emotion of uneasiness, 'this is the last.' Those who never could agree together shed tears when mutual discontent has determined them to final separation; of a place which has been frequently visited, though without pleasure, the last look is taken with heaviness of heart; and the Idler, with all his chillness of tranquillity, is not wholly unaffected by the thought that his last essay is now before him.

This secret horror of the last is inseparable from a thinking being whose life is limited, and to whom death is dreadful. We always make a secret comparison between a part and the whole; the termination of any period of life reminds us that life itself has likewise its termination; when we have done anything for the last time, we involuntarily reflect that a part of the days allotted us is past, and that as more is past there is less remaining.

It is very happily and kindly provided that in every life there are certain pauses and interruptions, which force consideration upon the careless and seriousness upon the light; points of time where one course of action ends and another begins; and by vicissitude of fortune, or alteration of employment, by change of place, or loss of friendship, we are forced to say of something, 'this is the last.'

An even and unvaried tenor of life always hides from our apprehension the approach of its end. Succession is not perceived but by variation; he that lives today as he lived yesterday, and expects that, as the present day is, such will be the morrow, easily conceives time as running in a circle and returning to itself. The uncertainty of our duration is impressed commonly by dissimilitude of condition; it is only by finding life changeable that we are reminded of its shortness.

This conviction, however forcible at every new impression, is every moment fading from the mind; and partly by the inevitable incursion of new images, and partly by voluntary exclusion of unwelcome thoughts, we are again exposed to the universal fallacy; and we must do another thing for the last time, before we consider that the time is nigh when we shall do no more.

As the last *Idler* is published in that solemn week [11] which the Christian world has always set apart for the examination of the conscience, the review of life, the extinction of earthly desires and the renovation of holy purposes, I

---

11. On Holy Saturday of Easter week.

hope that my readers are already disposed to view every incident with seriousness and improve it by meditation; and that when they see this series of trifles
brought to a conclusion, they will consider that by outliving the *Idler* they have
past weeks, months, and years which are now no longer in their power; that an
end must in time be put to everything great as to everything little; that to
life must come its last hour, and to this system of being its last day, the hour
at which probation ceases, and repentance will be vain; the day in which every
work of the hand and imagination of the heart shall be brought to judgment,
and an everlasting futurity shall be determined by the past. [No. 103, Saturday,
April 5, 1760]

From The Preface to Shakespeare [1]

Nothing can please many, and please long, but just representations of general
nature. Particular manners can be known to few, and therefore few only can
judge how nearly they are copied. The irregular combinations of fanciful invention may delight awhile by that novelty of which the common satiety of life
sends us all in quest; but the pleasures of sudden wonder are soon exhausted,
and the mind can only repose on the stability of truth.

Shakespeare is, above all writers, at least above all modern writers, the poet
of nature, the poet that holds up to his readers a faithful mirror of manners and
of life. His characters are not modified by the customs of particular places,
unpractised by the rest of the world; by the peculiarities of studies or professions which can operate but upon small numbers; or by the accidents of
transient fashions or temporary opinions: they are the genuine progeny of
common humanity, such as the world will always supply, and observation will
always find. His persons act and speak by the influence of those general passions and principles by which all minds are agitated and the whole system of
life is continued in motion. In the writings of other poets a character is too
often an individual; in those of Shakespeare it is commonly a species.

It is from this wide extension of design that so much instruction is derived.
It is this which fills the plays of Shakespeare with practical axioms and domestic
wisdom. It was said of Euripides that every verse was a precept; [2] and it may
be said of Shakespeare that from his works may be collected a system of civil
and economical prudence. Yet his real power is not shown in the splendour of
particular passages, but by the progress of his fable and the tenor of his dia-

---

1. The Preface and Notes to Shakespeare are part of an edition Johnson undertook almost
a decade earlier and finally completed in 1765. It need hardly be said that Johnson was
not the first in his age to denounce the "rules" (in this case, the unity of time and place)
derived on slender grounds from Aristotle. Addison had written a half-century before:
"There is sometimes a greater judgment shown in deviating from the rules of art than in
adhering to them" (*Spectator* No. 592). But Johnson uses his discussion to explore, as
Dryden had before and Reynolds was to do in his thirteenth Discourse (1786), the nature
of art and illusion; and he provides the most telling discussion before (or even including) Coleridge of the "willing suspension of disbelief." In his appeal from art to nature (i.e. from
rules to experience) and in his notes on characters, Johnson shows the moral centrality of
his literary criticism, the constant inquiry as to what human ends art can be said to serve.
2. By Cicero, *Familiar Letters* XVI.8.

logue; and he that tries to recommend him by select quotations will succeed like the pedant in Hierocles,[3] who, when he offered his house to sale, carried a brick in his pocket as a specimen.

It will not easily be imagined how much Shakespeare excels in accommodating his sentiments to real life but by comparing him with other authors. It was observed of the ancient schools of declamation that the more diligently they were frequented, the more was the student disqualified for the world, because he found nothing there which he should ever meet in any other place.[4] The same remark may be applied to every stage but that of Shakespeare. The theatre, when it is under any other direction, is peopled by such characters as were never seen, conversing in a language which was never heard, upon topics which will never arise in the commerce of mankind. But the dialogue of this author is often so evidently determined by the incident which produces it, and is pursued with so much ease and simplicity, that it seems scarcely to claim the merit of fiction, but to have been gleaned by diligent selection out of common conversation and common occurrences.

Upon every other stage the universal agent is love, by whose power all good and evil is distributed and every action quickened or retarded. To bring a lover, a lady, and a rival into the fable; to entangle them in contradictory obligations, perplex them with oppositions of interest, and harass them with violence of desires inconsistent with each other; to make them meet in rapture and part in agony, to fill their mouths with hyperbolical joy and outrageous sorrow, to distress them as nothing human ever was distressed, to deliver them as nothing human ever was delivered, is the business of a modern dramatist. For this, probability is violated, life is misrepresented, and language is depraved. But love is only one of many passions; and as it has no great influence upon the sum of life, it has little operation in the dramas of a poet who caught his ideas from the living world and exhibited only what he saw before him. He knew that any other passion, as it was regular or exorbitant, was a cause of happiness or calamity.

Characters thus ample and general were not easily discriminated and preserved, yet perhaps no poet ever kept his personages more distinct from each other. I will not say with Pope that every speech may be assigned to the proper speaker,[5] because many speeches there are which have nothing characteristical; but, perhaps, though some may be equally adapted to every person, it will be difficult to find any that can be properly transferred from the present possessor to another claimant. The choice is right, when there is reason for choice.

Other dramatists can only gain attention by hyperbolical or aggravated characters, by fabulous and unexampled excellence or depravity, as the writers of barbarous romances invigorated the reader by a giant and a dwarf; and he that should form his expectations of human affairs from the play, or from the tale, would be equally deceived. Shakespeare has no heroes; his scenes are occupied only by men, who act and speak as the reader thinks that he should

3. Hierocles was an Alexandrian of the 5th century A.D.; his "jests" were freely translated in 1741, possibly by Johnson.
4. Petronius, *Satyricon* I.i.
5. In his Preface to Shakespeare (1725).

himself have spoken or acted on the same occasion. Even where the agency is supernatural, the dialogue is level with life. Other writers disguise the most natural passions and most frequent incidents; so that he who contemplates them in the book will not know them in the world. Shakespeare approximates the remote and familiarizes the wonderful; the event which he represents will not happen, but, if it were possible, its effects would probably be such as he has assigned; and it may be said that he has not only shown human nature as it acts in real exigences, but as it would be found in trials to which it cannot be exposed.

This, therefore, is the praise of Shakespeare, that his drama is the mirror of life; that he who has mazed his imagination in following the phantoms which other writers raise up before him, may here be cured of his delirious ecstasies by reading human sentiments in human language, by scenes from which a hermit may estimate the transactions of the world and a confessor predict the progress of the passions.

. . .

Shakespeare's plays are not in the rigorous and critical sense either tragedies or comedies, but compositions of a distinct kind; exhibiting the real state of sublunary [6] nature, which partakes of good and evil, joy and sorrow, mingled with endless variety of proportion and innumerable modes of combination; and expressing the course of the world, in which the loss of one is the gain of another; in which, at the same time, the reveller is hasting to his wine, and the mourner burying his friend; in which the malignity of one is sometimes defeated by the frolic of another; and many mischiefs and many benefits are done and hindered without design.

Out of this chaos of mingled purposes and casualties the ancient poets, according to the laws which custom had prescribed, selected some the crimes of men, and some their absurdities; some the momentous vicissitudes of life, and some the lighter occurrences; some the terrors of distress, and some the gaieties of prosperity. Thus rose the two modes of imitation, known by the names of *tragedy* and *comedy*, compositions intended to promote different ends by contrary means, and considered as so little allied that I do not recollect among the Greeks or Romans a single writer who attempted both.

Shakespeare has united the powers of exciting laughter and sorrow not only in one mind but in one composition. Almost all his plays are divided between serious and ludicrous characters, and, in the successive evolutions of the design, sometimes produce seriousness and sorrow, and sometimes levity and laughter.

That this is a practice contrary to the rules of criticism will be readily allowed; but there is always an appeal open from criticism to nature. The end of writing is to instruct; the end of poetry is to instruct by pleasing. That the mingled drama may convey all the instruction of tragedy or comedy cannot be denied, because it includes both in its alternations of exhibition and approaches nearer than either to the appearance of life, by showing how great machinations and slender designs may promote or obviate one another, and the high and the low cooperate in the general system by unavoidable concatenation.

It is objected that by this change of scenes the passions are interrupted in

6. That is, beneath the celestial realms; on earth.

their progression, and that the principal event, being not advanced by a due gradation of preparatory incidents, wants at last the power to move, which constitutes the perfection of dramatic poetry. This reasoning is so specious [7] that it is received as true even by those who in daily experience feel it to be false. The interchanges of mingled scenes seldom fail to produce the intended vicissitudes of passion. Fiction cannot move so much but that the attention may be easily transferred; and though it must be allowed that pleasing melancholy be sometimes interrupted by unwelcome levity, yet let it be considered likewise that melancholy is often not pleasing, and that the disturbance of one man may be the relief of another; that different auditors have different habitudes; and that, upon the whole, all pleasure consists in variety.

. . .

Shakespeare with his excellencies has likewise faults, and faults sufficient to obscure and overwhelm any other merit. I shall show them in the proportion in which they appear to me, without envious malignity or superstitious veneration. No question can be more innocently discussed than a dead poet's pretensions to renown; and little regard is due to that bigotry which sets candour [8] higher than truth.

His first defect is that to which may be imputed most of the evil in books or in men. He sacrifices virtue to convenience and is so much more careful to please than to instruct that he seems to write without any moral purpose. From his writings indeed a system of social duty may be selected, for he that thinks reasonably must think morally; but his precepts and axioms drop casually from him; he makes no just distribution of good or evil, nor is always careful to show in the virtuous a disapprobation of the wicked; he carries his persons indifferently through right and wrong and at the close dismisses them without further care and leaves their examples to operate by chance. This fault the barbarity of his age cannot extenuate; for it is always a writer's duty to make the world better, and justice is a virtue independent on time or place.

The plots are often so loosely formed that a very slight consideration may improve them, and so carelessly pursued that he seems not always fully to comprehend his own design. He omits opportunities of instructing or delighting which the train of his story seems to force upon him, and apparently rejects those exhibitions which would be more affecting, for the sake of those which are more easy.

. . .

It is incident to him to be now and then entangled with an unwieldy sentiment, which he cannot well express and will not reject; he struggles with it a while, and, if it continues stubborn, comprises it in words such as occur and leaves it to be disentangled and evolved by those who have more leisure to bestow upon it.

Not that always where the language is intricate the thought is subtle, or the image always great where the line is bulky; the equality of words to things is very often neglected, and trivial sentiments and vulgar ideas disappoint the attention to which they are recommended by sonorous epithets and swelling figures.

7. Plausible.
8. Sympathy, kindness.

But the admirers of this great poet have most reason to complain when he approaches nearest to his highest excellence and seems fully resolved to sink them in dejection [9] and mollify them with tender emotions by the fall of greatness, the danger of innocence, or the crosses of love. What he does best, he soon ceases to do. He is not long soft and pathetic without some idle conceit or contemptible equivocation.[10] He no sooner begins to move than he counteracts himself; and terror and pity, as they are rising in the mind, are checked and blasted by sudden frigidity.

A quibble is to Shakespeare what luminous vapours are to the traveller; he follows it at all adventures; it is sure to lead him out of his way and sure to engulf him in the mire. It has some malignant power over his mind, and its fascinations are irresistible. Whatever be the dignity or profundity of his disquisition, whether he be enlarging knowledge or exalting affection, whether he be amusing attention with incidents or enchaining it in suspense, let but a quibble spring up before him, and he leaves his work unfinished. A quibble is the golden apple [11] for which he will always turn aside from his career or stoop from his elevation. A quibble, poor and barren as it is, gave him such delight that he was content to purchase it by the sacrifice of reason, propriety, and truth. A quibble was to him the fatal Cleopatra for which he lost the world and was content to lose it.

It will be thought strange that in enumerating the defects of this writer, I have not yet mentioned his neglect of the unities, his violation of those laws which have been instituted and established by the joint authority of poets and of critics.

For his other deviations from the art of writing, I resign him to critical justice, without making any other demand in his favour than that which must be indulged to all human excellence: that his virtues be rated with his failings. But from the censure which this irregularity may bring upon him, I shall, with due reverence to that learning which I must oppose, adventure to try how I can defend him.

His histories, being neither tragedies nor comedies, are not subject to any of their laws; nothing more is necessary to all the praise which they expect than that the changes of action be so prepared as to be understood, that the incidents be various and affecting, and the characters consistent, natural, and distinct. No other unity is intended, and therefore none is to be sought.

In his other works he has well enough preserved the unity of action. He has not, indeed, an intrigue regularly perplexed and regularly unravelled; he does not endeavour to hide his design only to discover it, for this is seldom the order

9. While Johnson sees this power as a strength, he associates it with a sense of justice ("which all reasonable beings naturally love") and cannot condone the death of Cordelia. He cites the version of Nahum Tate which permits her survival: "In the present case the public has decided. Cordelia, from the time of Tate, has always retired with victory and felicity. And, if my sensations could add anything to the general suffrage, I might relate that I was many years ago so shocked by Cordelia's death that I know not whether I ever endured to read again the last scenes of the play till I undertook to revise them as an editor."
10. On the "conceit," see Johnson on the Metaphysical poets in the *Life of Cowley;* by "equivocation" he means pun or quibble (the latter defined by him as "a low conceit depending on the sound of words; a pun").
11. Referring to Atalanta, the fleet princess who was overtaken when Meleager (or Melanion) cast a golden apple in her path.

of real events, and Shakespeare is the poet of nature; but his plan has commonly, what Aristotle requires, a beginning, a middle, and an end; one event is concatenated with another, and the conclusion follows by easy consequence. There are perhaps some incidents that might be spared, as in other poets there is much talk that only fills up time upon the stage; but the general system makes gradual advances, and the end of the play is the end of expectation.

To the unities of time and place he has shown no regard; and perhaps a nearer view of the principles on which they stand will diminish their value and withdraw from them the veneration which, from the time of Corneille,[12] they have very generally received, by discovering that they have given more trouble to the poet than pleasure to the auditor.

The necessity of observing the unities of time and place arises from the supposed necessity of making the drama credible. The critics hold it impossible that an action of months or years can be possibly believed to pass in three hours; or that the spectator can suppose himself to sit in the theatre while ambassadors go and return between distant kings, while armies are levied and towns besieged, while an exile wanders and returns, or till he whom they saw courting his mistress shall lament the untimely fall of his son. The mind revolts from evident falsehood, and fiction loses its force when it departs from the resemblance of reality.

From the narrow limitation of time necessarily arises the contraction of place. The spectator, who knows that he saw the first act at Alexandria, cannot suppose that he sees the next at Rome, at a distance to which not the dragons of Medea [13] could, in so short a time, have transported him; he knows with certainty that he has not changed his place; and he knows that place cannot change itself; that what was a house cannot become a plain; that what was Thebes can never be Persepolis.

Such is the triumphant language with which a critic exults over the misery of an irregular poet and exults commonly without resistance or reply. It is time, therefore, to tell him by the authority of Shakespeare that he assumes, as an unquestionable principle, a position which, while his breath is forming it into words, his understanding pronounces to be false. It is false, that any representation is mistaken for reality; that any dramatic fable in its materiality was ever credible, or, for a single moment, was ever credited.

The objection arising from the impossibility of passing the first hour at Alexandria and the next at Rome, supposes that when the play opens the spectator really imagines himself at Alexandria and believes that his walk to the theatre has been a voyage to Egypt and that he lives in the days of Antony and Cleopatra. Surely he that imagines this may imagine more. He that can take the stage at one time for the palace of the Ptolemies may take it in half an hour for the promontory of Actium. Delusion, if delusion be admitted, has no certain limitation; if the spectator can be once persuaded that his old acquaintance are Alexander and Caesar, that a room illuminated with candles is the plain of Pharsalia or the bank of Granicus,[14] he is in a state of

---

12. Pierre Corneille in the 1660 edition of his plays included a discourse on the unities and also *examens* of each of his plays in which he discussed such problems.
13. They draw the chariot in which she flees from Corinth after killing Jason's new wife Creusa and her own children.
14. Alexander fought a battle near the river Granicus, Caesar on the plains of Pharsalia.

elevation above the reach of reason or of truth, and from the heights of empyrean poetry may despise the circumscriptions of terrestrial nature. There is no reason why a mind thus wandering in ecstasy should count the clock, or why an hour should not be a century in that calenture [15] of the brains that can make the stage a field.

The truth is that the spectators are always in their senses and know, from the first act to the last, that the stage is only a stage, and that the players are only players. They come to hear a certain number of lines recited with just gesture and elegant modulation. The lines relate to some action, and an action must be in some place; but the different actions that complete a story may be in places very remote from each other; and where is the absurdity of allowing that space to represent first Athens and then Sicily which was always known to be neither Sicily nor Athens, but a modern theatre.

By supposition, as place is introduced, time may be extended; the time required by the fable elapses for the most part between the acts; for, of so much of the action as is represented, the real and poetical duration is the same. If in the first act preparations for war against Mithridates are represented to be made in Rome, the event of the war may, without absurdity, be represented in the catastrophe as happening in Pontus; we know that there is neither war nor preparation for war; we know that we are neither in Rome nor Pontus; that neither Mithridates nor Lucullus are before us.[16] The drama exhibits successive imitations of successive actions; and why may not the second imitation represent an action that happened years after the first, if it be so connected with it that nothing but time can be supposed to intervene? Time is, of all modes of existence, most obsequious [17] to the imagination; a lapse of years is as easily conceived as a passage of hours. In contemplation we easily contract the time of real actions and therefore willingly permit it to be contracted when we only see their imitation.

It will be asked how the drama moves if it is not credited. It is credited with all the credit due to a drama. It is credited, whenever it moves, as a just picture of a real original; as representing to the auditor what he would himself feel if he were to do or suffer what is there feigned to be suffered or to be done. The reflection that strikes the heart is not that the evils before us are real evils, but that they are evils to which we ourselves may be exposed. If there be any fallacy, it is not that we fancy the players, but that we fancy ourselves, unhappy for a moment; but we rather lament the possibility than suppose the presence of misery, as a mother weeps over her babe when she remembers that death may take it from her. The delight of tragedy proceeds from our consciousness of fiction; if we thought murders and treasons real, they would please no more.

Imitations produce pain or pleasure, not because they are mistaken for realities, but because they bring realities to mind. When the imagination is recreated [18] by a painted landscape, the trees are not supposed capable to

15. Fever.
16. Mithridates the Great (c. 130–63 B.C.), ruler of Pontus and conqueror of much of the rest of Asia Minor; attacked with temporary success by the Romans under Lucullus (73–66 B.C.) and finally defeated by the forces of Pompey.
17. Yielding, submissive.
18. Gratified.

give us shade, or the fountains coolness; but we consider how we should be pleased with such fountains playing beside us and such woods waving over us. We are agitated in reading the history of *Henry the Fifth,* yet no man takes his book for the field of Agincourt. A dramatic exhibition is a book recited with concomitants that increase or diminish its effect. Familiar comedy is often more powerful in the theatre than on the page; imperial tragedy is always less. The humour of Petruchio may be heightened by grimace; but what voice or what gesture can hope to add dignity or force to the soliloquy of Cato? [19]

A play read affects the mind like a play acted. It is therefore evident that the action is not supposed to be real; and it follows that between the acts a longer or shorter time may be allowed to pass, and that no more account of space or duration is to be taken by the auditor of a drama than by the reader of a narrative, before whom may pass in an hour the life of a hero or the revolutions of an empire.

. . .

He that, without diminution of any other excellence, shall preserve all the unities unbroken deserves the like applause with the architect who shall display all the orders of architecture in a citadel without any deduction from its strength; but the principal beauty of a citadel is to exclude the enemy, and the greatest graces of a play are to copy nature and instruct life.

Perhaps what I have here not dogmatically but deliberatively written may recall the principles of the drama to a new examination. I am almost frighted at my own temerity and, when I estimate the fame and the strength of those that maintain the contrary opinion, am ready to sink down in reverential silence; as Aeneas withdrew from the defence of Troy when he saw Neptune shaking the wall and Juno heading the besiegers. [20]

Those whom my arguments cannot persuade to give their approbation to the judgement of Shakespeare will easily, if they consider the condition of his life, make some allowance for his ignorance.

Every man's performances, to be rightly estimated, must be compared with the state of the age in which he lived and with his own particular opportunities; and though to the reader a book be not worse or better for the circumstances of the author, yet as there is always a silent reference of human works to human abilities, and as the inquiry how far man may extend his designs, or how high he may rate his native force, is of far greater dignity than in what rank we shall place any particular performance, curiosity is always busy to discover the instruments as well as to survey the workmanship, to know how much is to be ascribed to original powers and how much to casual and adventitious help. The palaces of Peru or Mexico were certainly mean and incommodious habitations if compared to the houses of European monarchs; yet who could forbear to view them with astonishment who remembered that they were built without the use of iron? . . .

19. Referring to Joseph Addison's tragedy of 1713.
20. *Aeneid* II.610–14.

From The Notes to Shakespeare

[Falstaff]

But Falstaff, unimitated, unimitable Falstaff, how shall I describe thee? Thou compound of sense and vice; of sense which may be admired but not esteemed, of vice which may be despised but hardly detested. Falstaff is a character loaded with faults, and with those faults which naturally produce contempt. He is a thief and a glutton, a coward and a boaster, always ready to cheat the weak and prey upon the poor; to terrify the timorous and insult the defenceless. At once obsequious and malignant, he satirizes in their absence those whom he lives by flattering. He is familiar with the prince only as an agent of vice, but of this familiarity he is so proud as not only to be supercilious and haughty with common men but to think his interest of importance to the Duke of Lancaster. Yet the man thus corrupt, thus despicable, makes himself necessary to the prince that despises him, by the most pleasing of all qualities, perpetual gaiety, by an unfailing power of exciting laughter, which is the more freely indulged as his wit is not of the splendid or ambitious kind but consists in easy escapes and sallies of levity, which make sport but raise no envy. It must be observed that he is stained with no enormous or sanguinary crimes, so that his licentiousness is not so offensive but that it may be borne for his mirth.

The moral to be drawn from this representation is that no man is more dangerous than he that, with a will to corrupt, hath the power to please; and that neither wit nor honesty ought to think themselves safe with such a companion when they see Henry seduced by Falstaff.

[Polonius]

The commentator makes the character of Polonius a character only of manners, discriminated by properties superficial, accidental, and acquired. The poet intended a nobler delineation of a mixed character of manners and of nature. Polonius is a man bred in courts, exercised in business, stored with observation, confident of his knowledge, proud of his eloquence, and declining into dotage. His mode of oratory is truly represented as designed to ridicule the practice of those times, of prefaces that made no introduction, and of method that embarrassed rather than explained. This part of his character is accidental, the rest is natural. Such a man is positive and confident, because he knows that his mind was once strong and knows not that it is become weak. Such a man excels in general principles but fails in the particular application. He is knowing in retrospect and ignorant in foresight. While he depends upon his memory and can draw from his repositories of knowledge, he utters weighty sentences and gives useful counsel; but as the mind in its enfeebled state cannot be kept long busy and intent, the old man is subject to sudden dereliction of his faculties, he loses the order of his ideas and entangles himself in his own thoughts, till he recovers the leading principle and falls again into his former train. This idea of dotage encroaching upon wisdom will solve all the phenomena of the character of Polonius.

[Lady Macbeth]

. . . The arguments by which Lady Macbeth persuades her husband to commit the murder afford a proof of Shakespeare's knowledge of human nature. She urges the excellence and dignity of courage, a glittering idea which has dazzled mankind from age to age and animated sometimes the housebreaker and sometimes the conqueror; but this sophism Macbeth has for ever destroyed, by distinguishing true from false fortitude, in a line and a half; of which it may almost be said that they ought to bestow immortality on the author, though all his other productions had been lost;

> I dare do all that may become a man,
> Who dares do more, is none.

This topic, which has been always employed with too much success, is used in this scene with peculiar propriety, to a soldier by a woman. Courage is the distinguishing virtue of a soldier, and the reproach of cowardice cannot be borne by any man from a woman, without great impatience.

She then urges the oaths by which he had bound himself to murder Duncan, another art of sophistry by which men have sometimes deluded their consciences and persuaded themselves that what would be criminal in others is virtuous in them; this argument Shakespeare, whose plan obliged him to make Macbeth yield, has not confuted, though he might easily have shown that a former obligation could not be vacated by a latter; that obligations laid on us by a higher power could not be overruled by obligations which we lay upon ourselves.

1765

The Lives of the Poets

Johnson had planned biographical studies of English writers for many years, but the enterprise was given shape by an agreement with thirty-six London booksellers to supply lives to accompany the selections from fifty-two poets (from Cowley to Gray) who were no longer alive. The first four volumes appeared in 1779, the remaining six in 1781; the lives were collected in the latter year and have since acquired the unofficial but familiar title given above. The *Life of Cowley* provided Johnson with an occasion for a general discussion of the Metaphysical poets, given below. All the lives contain a balance, usually clearly demarcated, of biographical and critical writing; but in both, Johnson remains a profound, acutely aphoristic moralist.

From The Lives of the Poets

[Cowley and the Metaphysical Poets [1]]

The metaphysical poets were men of learning, and to show their learning was their whole endeavour; but, unluckily resolving to show it in rhyme, instead of writing poetry they only wrote verses, and very often such verses as stood the

---

1. Johnson used the *Life of Cowley* as an occasion for reviewing the methods of all the Metaphysical poets. While he cited many of the excesses of John Donne, whose work he knew well, the most outrageous instances are cited from such late Metaphysical poets as

trial of the finger better than of the ear; for the modulation was so imperfect, that they were only found to be verses by counting the syllables.

If the father of criticism has rightly denominated poetry τέχνη μιμητική, *an imitative art*,[2] these writers will, without great wrong, lose their right to the name of poets, for they cannot be said to have imitated anything; they neither copied nature nor life, neither painted the forms of matter, nor represented the operations of intellect.

Those, however, who deny them to be poets, allow them to be wits. Dryden confesses of himself and his contemporaries, that they fall below Donne in wit, but maintains that they surpass him in poetry.[3]

If wit be well described by Pope, as being 'that which has been often thought, but was never before so well expressed,'[4] they certainly never attained, nor ever sought it; for they endeavoured to be singular in their thoughts, and were careless of their diction. But Pope's account of wit is undoubtedly erroneous: he depresses it below its natural dignity, and reduces it from strength of thought to happiness[5] of language.

If by a more noble and more adequate conception that be considered as wit which is at once natural and new, that which, though not obvious, is, upon its first production, acknowledged to be just; if it be that which he that never found it wonders how he missed, to wit of this kind the metaphysical poets have seldom risen. Their thoughts are often new, but seldom natural; they are not obvious, but neither are they just; and the reader, far from wondering that he missed them, wonders more frequently by what perverseness of industry they were ever found.

But wit, abstracted from its effects upon the hearer, may be more rigorously and philosophically considered as a kind of *discordia concors;* a combination of dissimilar images, or discovery of occult resemblances in things apparently unlike. Of wit, thus defined, they have more than enough. The most heterogeneous ideas are yoked by violence together; nature and art are ransacked for illustrations, comparisons, and allusions; their learning instructs, and their subtlety surprises; but the reader commonly thinks his improvement dearly bought, and, though he sometimes admires, is seldom pleased.

From this account of their compositions it will be readily inferred that they were not successful in representing or moving the affections. As they were wholly employed on something unexpected and surprising, they had no regard to that uniformity of sentiment which enables us to conceive and to excite the pains and the pleasure of other minds: they never inquired what, on any occasion, they should have said or done, but wrote rather as beholders than

---

Cowley and John Cleveland. By Johnson's day these poets (whom Coleridge later called "witty logicians") had fallen greatly in reputation; we can see that decline begin with Dryden's remarks on Cleveland and continue in Pope's censure of those who pursue "conceit alone" (*Essay on Criticism*, ll.289 ff.). When Pope "versified" two of Donne's satires, he demonstrated by his changes his own definition of "true Wit": "a justness of thought and a facility of expression, or (in the midwives' phrase) a perfect conception with an easy delivery."

2. Aristotle in the *Poetics*.
3. In *Of Dramatic Poesy: An Essay;* see above, the section Dryden's Critical Prose.
4. Paraphrased from the *Essay on Criticism*, ll. 297–98.
5. Felicity; implying chance as well as success.

partakers of human nature; as beings looking upon good and evil, impassive and at leisure; as Epicurean deities, making remarks on the actions of men and the vicissitudes of life, without interest and without emotion. Their court-ship was void of fondness, and their lamentation of sorrow. Their wish was only to say what they hoped had been never said before.

Nor was the sublime more within their reach than the pathetic; for they never attempted that comprehension and expanse of thought which at once fills the whole mind, and of which the first effect is sudden astonishment, and the second rational admiration.[6] Sublimity is produced by aggregation, and littleness by dispersion. Great thoughts are always general, and consist in positions not limited by exceptions, and in descriptions not descending to minuteness. It is with great propriety that subtlety, which in its original import means exility [7] of particles, is taken in its metaphorical meaning for nicety of distinction. Those writers who lay on the watch for novelty could have little hope of greatness; for great things cannot have escaped former observation. Their attempts were always analytic; they broke every image into fragments; and could no more represent, by their slender conceits and laboured particu-larities, the prospects of nature, or the scenes of life, than he who dissects a sunbeam with a prism can exhibit the wide effulgence of a summer noon.

What they wanted however of the sublime, they endeavoured to supply by hyperbole; their amplification had no limits; they left not only reason but fancy behind them; and produced combinations of confused magnificence, that not only could not be credited, but could not be imagined.

Yet great labour, directed by great abilities, is never wholly lost: if they frequently threw away their wit upon false conceits, they likewise sometimes struck out unexpected truth; if their conceits were far-fetched, they were often worth the carriage. To write on their plan, it was at least necessary to read and think. No man could be born a metaphysical poet, nor assume the dignity of a writer, by descriptions copied from descriptions, by imitations borrowed from imitations, by traditional imagery, and hereditary similes, by readiness of rhyme, and volubility of syllables.

In perusing the works of this race of authors, the mind is exercised either by recollection or inquiry; either something already learned is to be retrieved, or something new is to be examined. If their greatness seldom elevates, their acuteness often surprises; if the imagination is not always gratified, at least the powers of reflection and comparison are employed; and in the mass of materials which ingenious absurdity has thrown together, genuine wit and useful knowledge may be sometimes found buried perhaps in grossness of ex-pression, but useful to those who know their value; and such as, when they are expanded to perspicuity, and polished to elegance, may give lustre to works which have more propriety though less copiousness of sentiment.

[Milton [8]]

His political notions were those of an acrimonious and surly republican, for which it is not known that he gave any better reason than that *a popular gov-*

6. See below, Burke's *Enquiry* of 1757.
7. Smallness of number, meagerness.
8. These paragraphs, however unfair, are refreshing in an age of "candour" (to use the term, as Johnson does, in opposition to "truth") and highly characteristic of their author.

ernment was the most frugal; for the trappings of a monarchy would set up an ordinary commonwealth. It is surely very shallow policy that supposes money to be the chief good; and even this, without considering that the support and expense of a court is, for the most part, only a particular kind of traffic, for which money is circulated without any national impoverishment.

Milton's republicanism was, I am afraid, founded in an envious hatred of greatness, and a sullen desire of independence; in petulance impatient of control, and pride disdainful of superiority. He hated monarchs in the State, and prelates in the Church; for he hated all whom he was required to obey. It is to be suspected that his predominant desire was to destroy rather than establish, and that he felt not so much the love of liberty as repugnance to authority.

It has been observed that they who most loudly clamour for liberty do not most liberally grant it. What we know of Milton's character in domestic relations is that he was severe and arbitrary. His family consisted of women; and there appears in his books something like a Turkish contempt of females, as subordinate and inferior beings. That his own daughters might not break the ranks, he suffered them to be depressed by a mean and penurious education. He thought woman made only for obedience, and man only for rebellion.

[Richard Savage [9]]

Such were the life and death of Richard Savage, a man equally distinguished by his virtues and vices, and at once remarkable for his weaknesses and abilities.

He was of a middle stature, of a thin habit of body, a long visage, coarse features, and melancholy aspect; of a grave and manly deportment, a solemn dignity of mien, but which, upon a nearer acquaintance, softened into an engaging easiness of manners. His walk was slow, and his voice tremulous and mournful. He was easily excited to smiles, but very seldom provoked to laughter.

His mind was in an uncommon degree vigorous and active. His judgment was accurate, his apprehension quick, and his memory so tenacious that he was frequently observed to know what he had learned from others in a short time, better than those by whom he was informed, and could frequently recollect incidents, with all their combination of circumstances, which few would have regarded at the present time, but which the quickness of his apprehension impressed upon him. He had the art of escaping from his own reflections, and accommodating himself to every new scene.

. . .

His method of life particularly qualified him for conversation, of which he knew how to practise all the graces. He was never vehement or loud, but at once modest and easy, open and respectful; his language was vivacious or elegant, and equally happy upon grave and humorous subjects. He was generally censured for not knowing when to retire; but that was not the defect of his judgment, but of his fortune; when he left his company, he was frequently to spend the remaining part of the night in the street, or at least was abandoned

---

9. Richard Savage (1697–1743) was a close friend of Johnson, and his is the fullest and most intimate of all the *Lives;* originally composed and published in 1744.

to gloomy reflections, which it is not strange that he delayed as long as he could; and sometimes forgot that he gave others pain to avoid it himself.

It cannot be said that he made use of his abilities for the direction of his own conduct: an irregular and dissipated manner of life had made him the slave of every passion that happened to be excited by the presence of its object, and that slavery to his passions reciprocally produced a life irregular and dissipated. He was not master of his own motions, nor could promise anything for the next day.

With regard to his economy, nothing can be added to the relation of his life. He appeared to think himself born to be supported by others, and dispensed from all necessity of providing for himself; he therefore never prosecuted any scheme of advantage, nor endeavoured even to secure the profits which his writings might have afforded him. His temper was, in consequence of the dominion of his passions, uncertain and capricious; he was easily engaged, and easily disgusted; but he is accused of retaining his hatred more tenaciously than his benevolence.

He was compassionate both by nature and principle, and always ready to perform offices of humanity; but when he was provoked (and very small offences were sufficient to provoke him), he would prosecute his revenge with the utmost acrimony till his passion had subsided.

His friendship was therefore of little value; for though he was zealous in the support or vindication of those whom he loved, yet it was always dangerous to trust him, because he considered himself as discharged by the first quarrel from all ties of honour or gratitude, and would betray those secrets which in the warmth of confidence had been imparted to him. This practice drew upon him an universal accusation of ingratitude: nor can it be denied that he was very ready to set himself free from the load of an obligation; for he could not bear to conceive himself in a state of dependence, his pride being equally powerful with his other passions, and appearing in the form of insolence at one time, and of vanity at another. Vanity, the most innocent species of pride, was most frequently predominant: he could not easily leave off when he had once begun to mention himself or his works; nor ever read his verses without stealing his eyes from the page, to discover in the faces of his audience how they were affected with any favourite passage.

. . .

For his life, or for his writings, none, who candidly consider his fortune, will think an apology either necessary or difficult. If he was not always sufficiently instructed in his subject, his knowledge was at least greater than could have been attained by others in the same state. If his works were sometimes unfinished, accuracy cannot reasonably be exacted from a man oppressed with want, which he has no hope of relieving but by a speedy publication. The insolence and resentment of which he is accused were not easily to be avoided by a great mind, irritated by perpetual hardships, and constrained hourly to return the spurns of contempt, and repress the insolence of prosperity; and vanity surely may be readily pardoned in him to whom life afforded no other comforts than barren praises, and the consciousness of deserving them.

Those are no proper judges of his conduct who have slumbered away their time on the down of plenty; nor will any wise man easily presume to say, 'Had

I been in Savage's condition, I should have lived or written better than Savage.'

[Dryden and Pope [10]]

Integrity of understanding and nicety of discernment were not allotted in a less proportion to Dryden than to Pope. The rectitude of Dryden's mind was sufficiently shown by the dismission of his poetical prejudices, and the rejection of unnatural thoughts and rugged numbers.[11] But Dryden never desired to apply all the judgment that he had. He wrote, and professed to write, merely for the people; and when he pleased others, he contented himself. He spent no time in struggles to rouse latent powers; he never attempted to make that better which was already good, nor often to mend what he must have known to be faulty. He wrote, as he tells us, with very little consideration; when occasion or necessity called upon him, he poured out what the present moment happened to supply, and, when once it had passed the press, ejected it from his mind; for when he had no pecuniary interest, he had no further solicitude.

Pope was not content to satisfy; he desired to excel, and therefore always endeavoured to do his best: he did not court the candour, but dared the judgment of his reader, and, expecting no indulgence from others, he showed none to himself. He examined lines and words with minute and punctilious observation, and retouched every part with indefatigable diligence, till he had left nothing to be forgiven.

For this reason he kept his pieces very long in his hands, while he considered and reconsidered them. The only poems which can be supposed to have been written with such regard to the times as might hasten their publication were the two satires of *Thirty-eight;* [12] of which Dodsley [13] told me that they were brought to him by the author, that they might be fairly copied. 'Almost every line,' he said, 'was then written twice over; I gave him a clean transcript, which he sent some time afterwards to me for the press, with almost every line written twice over a second time.'

His declaration that his care for his works ceased at their publication was not strictly true. His parental attention never abandoned them; what he found amiss in the first edition, he silently corrected in those that followed. He appears to have revised the Iliad, and freed it from some of its imperfections; and the *Essay on Criticism* received many improvements after its first appearance. It will seldom be found that he altered without adding clearness, elegance, or vigour. Pope had perhaps the judgment of Dryden; but Dryden certainly wanted the diligence of Pope.

In acquired knowledge, the superiority must be allowed to Dryden, whose education was more scholastic, and who before he became an author had been allowed more time for study, with better means of information. His mind has a larger range, and he collects his images and illustrations from a more

---

10. This method of comparison is to be seen in Dryden's discussion of Shakespeare and Jonson or Horace and Juvenal; another example, Pope's comparison of Homer and Virgil, is given below.
11. Harsh versification.
12. Later entitled the *Epilogue to the Satires.*
13. Robert Dodsley (1703–64), the publisher.

extensive circumference of science. Dryden knew more of man in his general nature, and Pope in his local manners. The notions of Dryden were formed by comprehensive speculation, and those of Pope by minute attention. There is more dignity in the knowledge of Dryden, and more certainty in that of Pope.

Poetry was not the sole praise of either; for both excelled likewise in prose; but Pope did not borrow his prose from his predecessor. The style of Dryden is capricious and varied; that of Pope is cautious and uniform. Dryden observes the motions of his own mind; Pope constrains his mind to his own rules of composition. Dryden is sometimes vehement and rapid; Pope is always smooth, uniform, and gentle. Dryden's page is a natural field, rising into inequalities, and diversified by the varied exuberance of abundant vegetation; Pope's is a velvet lawn, shaven by the scythe, and levelled by the roller.

Of genius, that power which constitutes a poet; that quality without which judgment is cold, and knowledge is inert; that energy which collects, combines, amplifies, and animates; the superiority must, with some hesitation, be allowed to Dryden. It is not to be inferred that of this poetical vigour Pope had only a little, because Dryden had more; for every other writer since Milton must give place to Pope; and even of Dryden it must be said, that, if he has brighter paragraphs, he has not better poems. Dryden's performances were always hasty, either excited by some external occasion, or extorted by domestic necessity; he composed without consideration, and published without correction. What his mind could supply at call, or gather in one excursion, was all that he sought, and all that he gave. The dilatory caution of Pope enabled him to condense his sentiments, to multiply his images, and to accumulate all that study might produce or chance might supply. If the flights of Dryden therefore are higher, Pope continues longer on the wing. If of Dryden's fire the blaze is brighter, of Pope's the heat is more regular and constant. Dryden often surpasses expectation, and Pope never falls below it. Dryden is read with frequent astonishment, and Pope with perpetual delight.

This parallel will, I hope, when it is well considered, be found just; and if the reader should suspect me, as I suspect myself, of some partial fondness for the memory of Dryden, let him not too hastily condemn me; for meditation and inquiry may, perhaps, show him the reasonableness of my determination.

1779–81

Pope on Homer and Virgil

. . . Nothing is more absurd or endless than the common method of comparing eminent writers by an opposition of particular passages in them and forming a judgment from thence of their merit upon the whole. We ought to have a certain knowledge of the principal character and distinguishing excellence of each; it is in *that* we are to consider him, and in proportion to his degree in *that* we are to admire him. No author or man ever excelled all the world in more than one faculty, and as Homer has done this in invention, Virgil has in judgment. Not that we are to think Homer wanted judgment because Virgil had it in a more eminent degree, or that Virgil wanted invention because

Homer possessed a larger share of it: each of these great authors had more of both than perhaps any man besides, and are only said to have less in comparison with one another. Homer was the greater genius, Virgil the better artist. In one we most admire the man, in the other the work. Homer hurries and transports us with a commanding impetuosity; Virgil leads us with an attractive majesty. Homer scatters with a generous profusion, Virgil bestows with a careful magnificence. Homer, like the Nile, pours out his riches with a sudden overflow; Virgil, like a river in its banks, with a gentle and constant stream. When we behold their battles, methinks the two poets resemble the heroes they celebrate: Homer, boundless and irresistible as Achilles, bears all before him, and shines more and more as the tumult increases; Virgil, calmly daring like Aeneas, appears undisturbed in the midst of the action, disposes all about him, and conquers with tranquillity. And when we look upon their machines, Homer seems like his own Jupiter in his terrors, shaking Olympus, scattering the lightnings, and firing the Heavens; Virgil, like the same power in his benevolence, counselling with the gods, laying plans for empires, and regularly ordering his whole creation. [From Preface to the translation of the *Iliad*, 1715]

EDWARD GIBBON
1737–1794

The great historian of the fall of the Roman empire and the triumph over it of "barbarism and religion" was a small, plump, extremely elegant man, whose irony concealed from some his capacity for concentrated study and his intense devotion to political liberty. At Oxford Gibbon spent, he wrote later, "the fourteen months the most idle and unprofitable of my whole life." From that scene of indolence Gibbon absented himself often "without once hearing the voice of admonition, without once feeling the hand of control." It was, however, at Oxford that he was converted to Roman Catholicism, and he was sent to Lausanne in Switzerland to study privately and to recover from this "error." Having returned by 1752 to Protestantism, Gibbon "suspended" his "religious inquiries, acquiescing with implicit belief in the tenets and mysteries" common to all churches.

Before he found his great subject, Gibbon, like Milton before him, contemplated others, among them a life of Sir Walter Ralegh, a history of the liberty of the Swiss, and a history of Florence under the Medici. Gibbon meditated in his journal upon the last two: "the one a poor, warlike, virtuous republic, which emerges into glory and freedom; the other, a commonwealth, soft, opulent, and corrupt, which, by just degrees, is precipitated from the abuse to the loss of her liberty; both lessons are, perhaps, equally instructive." In the fall of the republic of Florence an important role would have been given to Savonarola and to "enthusiasm" as "the most formidable weapon" of the Medicis' adversaries. These plans of 1762 reveal those moral themes that engaged Gibbon's feelings most deeply and govern his history of the Roman empire.

The first volume of the *History* (1776) created some scandal by its ironical treatment of Christianity but won immediate respect for its artistry and learning. Gibbon completed his plan by 1788 with the fall of the Byzantine empire and the revival of learning in Rome. In 1783 Gibbon left England behind and moved permanently to Lausanne. Upon his death, his *Memoirs* were left in several overlapping drafts, begun as early as 1788, and they were first edited by his friend Lord Sheffield. The manuscripts survive and have been published; each reading-text is necessarily an eclectic selection from them. (For excerpts, see below, in the section entitled Sense and Sensibility.)

The style of his abortive account of the Swiss, written in French, was (in Gibbon's own words) "above prose and below poetry," and had "degenerated into a verbose and turgid declamation." Gibbon worked hard to find a style for his *History* that would "hit a middle tone between a dull chronicle and a rhetorical declamation." What gives Gibbon's achieved style its peculiar energy is his ironic respect for the pretensions he exposes. He rarely descends to explicit judgment, and the generality of his terms disdains to name what it so clearly suggests. Writing of the advancement of Christianity from an underground messianic faith to a worldly power, he traces the corresponding changes in its spiritual vision: "A garden of Eden, with the amusements of a pastoral life, was no longer suited to the advanced state of society which prevailed under the Roman Empire. A city was therefore erected of gold and precious stones, and a supernatural plenty of corn and wine was bestowed on the adjacent territory, in the free enjoyment of whose spontaneous productions the happy and benevolent people was never to be restrained by any jealous laws of exclusive property." Or writing of the self-indulgence of a Roman emperor (the younger Gordianus): "Twenty-two acknowledged concubines, and a library of sixty-two thousand volumes, attested the variety of his inclinations, and from the productions which he left behind him, it appears that the former as well as the latter were designed for use rather than ostentation." With the same splendid aloofness he can show how powerful an instrument of conquest intolerant zeal becomes in the early history of the Christians; or, in the third chapter, given below, the process by which Augustus undermines Roman liberties while preserving their forms—until we dramatically find ourselves at the close in a vast prison built of cunning and acquiescence. This chapter, which professes to deal with Roman institutions, is in fact a profound drama of ideas, and ideas for Gibbon are scarcely extricable from motives and passions (not least what he calls "the dexterity of self-love").

From The History of the Decline and Fall of the Roman Empire

Chapter III: Of the Constitution of the Roman Empire, in the Age of the Antonines

The obvious definition of a monarchy seems to be that of a state in which a single person, by whatsoever name he may be distinguished, is intrusted with the execution of the laws, the management of the revenue, and the command of the army. But unless public liberty is protected by intrepid and vigilant guardians, the authority of so formidable a magistrate will soon degenerate into despotism. The influence of the clergy, in an age of superstition, might be usefully employed to assert the rights of mankind; but so intimate is the connexion between the throne and the altar, that the banner of the church has very seldom been seen on the side of the people. A martial nobility and stubborn commons, possessed of arms, tenacious of property, and collected into constitutional assemblies, form the only balance capable of preserving a free constitution against enterprises of an aspiring prince.

Every barrier of the Roman constitution had been levelled by the vast ambition of the dictator; every fence had been extirpated by the cruel hand of the triumvir.[1] After the victory of Actium, the fate of the Roman world depended on the will of Octavianus, surnamed Caesar by his uncle's adoption, and afterwards Augustus, by the flattery of the senate.[2] The conqueror was at the head of forty-four veteran legions, conscious of their own strength and of the weakness of the constitution, habituated during twenty years' civil war to every act of blood and violence, and passionately devoted to the house of Caesar, from whence alone they had received and expected the most lavish rewards. The provinces, long oppressed by the ministers of the republic, sighed for the government of a single person, who would be the master, not the accomplice, of those petty tyrants. The people of Rome, viewing with a secret pleasure the humiliation of the aristocracy, demanded only bread and public shows, and were supplied with both by the liberal hand of Augustus. The rich and polite Italians, who had almost universally embraced the philosophy of Epicurus,[3] enjoyed the present blessings of ease and tranquillity, and suffered not the pleasing dream to be interrupted by the memory of their old tumultuous freedom. With its power, the senate had lost its dignity; many of the most noble families were extinct. The republicans of spirit and ability had perished in the field of battle, or in the proscription. The door of the assembly had been designedly left open for a mixed multitude of more than a thousand persons, who reflected disgrace upon their rank, instead of deriving honour from it.[4]

The reformation of the senate was one of the first steps in which Augustus laid aside the tyrant and professed himself the father of his country. He was

---

1. The first triumvirate was that of Julius Caesar, Pompey, and Crassus; the second, that of Octavianus (later Augustus), Mark Antony, and Lepidus.

2. Augustus was born Gaius Octavius in 63 B.C.; upon his adoption by his great-uncle, he became G. Julius Caesar Octavianus; the title Augustus was given to him by the Senate in 27 B.C. Upon the assassination of his uncle in 44 B.C. he joined the republican party and forced Antony to flee. Thereupon he compelled the Senate to elect him consul and later became reconciled to Antony, forming the second triumvirate with him and Lepidus. Their proscriptions led to the death of 2000 *equites* (or knights) and 300 senators, among them Cicero. Antony, who had married Octavia, the sister of Augustus, repudiated her for Cleopatra and, in the war of Rome against Egypt that followed, was defeated in the naval battle of Actium, 31 B.C. At this point Augustus assumed full power but refused (for reasons Gibbon explores) any honors that might recall kingship.

3. Epicurus (341–270 B.C.) founded the philosophy transmitted by Lucretius and others. His atomic philosophy attributed to chance whatever design we can find in nature or in man, and his ethics were based upon pleasure and pain. He urged man to increase his pleasures to the utmost and to prefer higher pleasures to lower; the pleasures of mind—and particularly peace of mind—are highest of all. The Epicurean placed a much lower value upon active citizenship than the Stoic; personal "ease and tranquillity" tended to replace any sense of social engagement.

4. "Julius Caesar introduced soldiers, strangers, and half-barbarians into the Senate. . . . The abuse became still more scandalous after his death." (Gibbon)

elected censor;[5] and, in concert with his faithful Agrippa, he examined the list of the senators, expelled a few members whose vices or whose obstinacy required a public example, persuaded near two hundred to prevent the shame of an expulsion by a voluntary retreat, raised the qualification of a senator to about ten thousand pounds, created a sufficient number of patrician families, and accepted for himself the honourable title of Prince of the Senate, which had always been bestowed by the censors on the citizen the most eminent for his honours and services. But, whilst he thus restored the dignity, he destroyed the independence, of the senate. The principles of a free constitution are irrecoverably lost when the legislative power is nominated by the executive.

Before an assembly thus modelled and prepared, Augustus pronounced a studied oration, which displayed his patriotism and disguised his ambition. 'He lamented, yet excused, his past conduct. Filial piety had required at his hands the revenge of his father's murder; the humanity of his own nature had sometimes given way to the stern laws of necessity, and to a forced connexion with two unworthy colleagues: as long as Antony lived, the republic forbade him to abandon her to a degenerate Roman and a barbarian queen. He was now at liberty to satisfy his duty and his inclination. He solemnly restored the senate and people to all their ancient rights; and wished only to mingle with the crowd of his fellow-citizens and to share the blessings which he had obtained for his country.'

It would require the pen of Tacitus [6] (if Tacitus had assisted at this assembly) to describe the various emotions of the senate; those that were suppressed and those that were affected. It was dangerous to trust the sincerity of Augustus; to seem to distrust it was still more dangerous. The respective advantages of monarchy and a republic have often divided speculative inquirers; the present greatness of the Roman state, the corruption of manners, and the licence of the soldiers, supplied new arguments to the advocates of monarchy; and these general views of government were again warped by the hopes and fears of each individual. Amidst this confusion of sentiments, the answer of the senate was unanimous and decisive. They refused to accept the resignation of Augustus; they conjured him not to desert the republic which he had saved. After a decent resistance the crafty tyrant submitted to the orders of the senate; and consented to receive the government of the provinces, and the general command of the Roman armies, under the well-known names of PROCONSUL and IMPERATOR.[7] But he would receive them only for ten years. Even before the expiration of that period, he hoped that the wounds of civil discord would be completely healed, and that the republic, restored to its pristine health and vigour,

5. Originally appointed to take the census, the censor gained additional powers in time: stigmatizing any citizen for a moral offense which was not punishable by law, expelling men from the Senate or the equestrian order, and transferring men from one tribe to another (thus affecting their voting power).

6. Tacitus (d. c. 117), the great Roman historian, first promoted by Vespasian and active through the reign of Trajan; a writer of deep moral integrity with a close, difficult, epigrammatic style.

7. A proconsul assumed the consular power, that of supreme magistrate, combining military and judicial power, outside Rome. The title of *imperator* originally meant "general" and was conferred with a military triumph; Augustus made it part of his name, replacing Gaius.

would no longer require the dangerous interposition of so extraordinary a magistrate. The memory of this comedy, repeated several times during the life of Augustus, was preserved to the last ages of the empire by the peculiar pomp with which the perpetual monarchs of Rome always solemnized the tenth years of their reign.

Without any violation of the principles of the constitution, the general of the Roman armies might receive and exercise an authority almost despotic over the soldiers, the enemies, and the subjects of the republic. With regard to the soldiers, the jealousy of freedom had, even from the earliest ages of Rome, given way to the hopes of conquest and a just sense of military discipline. The dictator, or consul, had a right to command the service of the Roman youth, and to punish an obstinate or cowardly disobedience by the most severe and ignominious penalties, by striking the offender out of the list of citizens, by confiscating his property, and by selling his person into slavery. The most sacred rights of freedom, confirmed by the Porcian and Sempronian laws,[8] were suspended by the military engagement. In his camp the general exercised an absolute power of life and death; his jurisdiction was not confined by any forms of trial or rules of proceeding, and the execution of the sentence was immediate and without appeal. The choice of the enemies of Rome was regularly decided by the legislative authority. The most important resolutions of peace and war were seriously debated in the senate, and solemnly ratified by the people. But when the arms of the legions were carried to a great distance from Italy, the generals assumed the liberty of directing them against whatever people, and in whatever manner, they judged most advantageous for the public service. It was from the success, not from the justice, of their enterprises that they expected the honours of a triumph. In the use of victory, especially after they were no longer controlled by the commissioners of the senate, they exercised the most unbounded despotism. When Pompey [9] commanded in the East, he rewarded his soldiers and allies, dethroned princes, divided kingdoms, founded colonies, and distributed the treasures of Mithridates. On his return to Rome he obtained, by a single act of the senate and people, the universal ratification of all his proceedings. Such was the power over the soldiers, and over the enemies of Rome, which was either granted to, or assumed by, the generals of the republic. They were, at the same time, the governors, or rather monarchs, of the conquered provinces, united the civil with the military character, administered justice as well as the finances, and exercised both the executive and legislative power of the state.

From what has been already observed in the first chapter of this work, some notion may be formed of the armies and provinces thus intrusted to the ruling hand of Augustus. But, as it was impossible that he could personally command the legions of so many distant frontiers, he was indulged by the senate, as

8. The Porcian law (197 B.C.) ruled that a Roman citizen should not be scourged or put to death; the Sempronian law (123 B.C.) that no judgment involving the life or freedom of a citizen should be valid without the assent of the Roman people.

9. Pompey was appointed to this command in 66 B.C. and returned to Italy four years later, entering Rome in triumph in 61 B.C. During his defeat of Mithridates, King of Pontus and conqueror of much of Asia Minor, Pompey (as Gibbon indicates) assumed vast powers and, after the siege of Jerusalem in 63, entered the sanctuary of the holy temple.

Pompey had already been, in the permission of devolving the execution of his great office on a sufficient number of lieutenants. In rank and authority these officers seemed not inferior to the ancient proconsuls; but their station was dependent and precarious. They received and held their commissions at the will of a superior, to whose *auspicious* influence the merit of their action was legally attributed.[10] They were the representatives of the emperor. The emperor alone was the general of the republic, and his jurisdiction, civil as well as military, extended over all the conquests of Rome. It was some satisfaction, however, to the senate that he always delegated his power to the members of their body. The imperial lieutenants were of consular or praetorian dignity; the legions were commanded by senators, and the praefecture of Egypt was the only important trust committed to a Roman knight.[11]

Within six days after Augustus had been compelled to accept so very liberal a grant, he resolved to gratify the pride of the senate by an easy sacrifice. He represented to them that they had enlarged his powers, even beyond that degree which might be required by the melancholy condition of the times. They had not permitted him to refuse the laborious command of the armies and the frontiers; but he must insist on being allowed to restore the more peaceful and secure provinces to the mild administration of the civil magistrate. In the division of the provinces Augustus provided for his own power and for the dignity of the republic. The proconsuls of the senate, particularly those of Asia, Greece, and Africa, enjoyed a more honourable character than the lieutenants of the emperor, who commanded in Gaul or Syria. The former were attended by lictors, the latter by soldiers.[12] A law was passed that, wherever the emperor was present, his extraordinary commission should supersede the ordinary jurisdiction of the governor; a custom was introduced that the new conquests belonged to the imperial portion; and it was soon discovered that the authority of the *Prince*, the favourite epithet of Augustus, was the same in every part of the empire.

In return for this imaginary concession, Augustus obtained an important privilege, which rendered him master of Rome and Italy. By a dangerous exception to the ancient maxims, he was authorized to preserve his military command, supported by a numerous body of guards, even in time of peace, and in the heart of the capital. His command, indeed, was confined to those citizens who were engaged in the service by the military oath; but such was the propensity of the Romans to servitude, that the oath was voluntarily taken by the magistrates, the senators, and the equestrian order, till the homage of flattery was insensibly converted into an annual and solemn protestation of fidelity.

Although Augustus considered a military force as the firmest foundation,

10. Auguries of success had to be officially taken before every public act, and the power of the augury was tied to the power of the official taking the auspices; hence an "auspicious influence" was a claim of responsibility or merit.
11. The knights (or *equites* and thus the "equestrian order") were originally a military rank, but by 123 B.C. they had become a third class between the Senate and the people, their standing based upon income; Augustus removed most of the legal status of the class but employed its members in important and confidential posts.
12. The proconsuls, like the consul, had twelve lictors with bundles of rods and axes; they executed punishments and exacted proper obeisance. These become empty rituals as Augustus shifts authority from the civil governors to imperial jurisdiction.

he wisely rejected it as a very odious instrument, of government. It was more agreeable to his temper, as well as to his policy, to reign under the venerable names of ancient magistracy, and artfully to collect in his own person all the scattered rays of civil jurisdiction. With this view, he permitted the senate to confer upon him, for his life, the powers of the consular and tribunitian offices, which were, in the same manner, continued to all his successors. The consuls had succeeded to the kings of Rome and represented the dignity of the state. They superintended the ceremonies of religion, levied and commanded the legions, gave audience to foreign ambassadors, and presided in the assemblies both of the senate and people. The general control of the finances was intrusted to their care; and, though they seldom had leisure to administer justice in person, they were considered as the supreme guardians of law, equity, and the public peace. Such was their ordinary jurisdiction; but, whenever the senate empowered the first magistrate to consult the safety of the commonwealth, he was raised by that decree above the laws, and exercised, in the defence of liberty, a temporary despotism. The character of the tribunes was, in every respect, different from that of the consuls. The appearance of the former was modest and humble; but their persons were sacred and inviolable. Their force was suited rather for opposition than for action. They were instituted to defend the oppressed, to pardon offences, to arraign the enemies of the people, and, when they judged it necessary, to stop, by a single word, the whole machine of government. As long as the republic subsisted, the dangerous influence which either the consul or the tribune might derive from their respective jurisdiction was diminished by several important restrictions. Their authority expired with the year in which they were elected; the former office was divided between two, the latter among ten, persons; and, as both in their private and public interest they were adverse to each other, their mutual conflicts contributed, for the most part, to strengthen rather than to destroy the balance of the constitution. But when the consular and tribunitian powers were united, when they were vested for life in a single person, when the general of the army was, at the same time, the minister of the senate and the representative of the Roman people, it was impossible to resist the exercise, nor was it easy to define the limits, of his imperial prerogative.

To these accumulated honours the policy of Augustus soon added the splendid as well as important dignities of supreme pontiff, and of censor. By the former he acquired the management of the religion, and by the latter a legal inspection over the manners and fortunes, of the Roman people. If so many distinct and independent powers did not exactly unite with each other, the complaisance [13] of the senate was prepared to supply every deficiency by the most ample and extraordinary concessions. The emperors, as the first ministers of the republic, were exempted from the obligation and penalty of many inconvenient laws: they were authorized to convoke the senate, to make several motions in the same day, to recommend candidates for the honours of the state, to enlarge the bounds of the city, to employ the revenue at their discretion, to declare peace and war, to ratify treaties; and, by a most comprehensive clause, they were empowered to execute whatsoever they should

13. Readiness to oblige, compliance.

judge advantageous to the empire, and agreeable to the majesty of things private or public, human or divine.

When all the various powers of executive government were committed to the *Imperial magistrate,* the ordinary magistrates of the commonwealth languished in obscurity, without vigour and almost without business. The names and forms of the ancient administration were preserved by Augustus with the most anxious care. The usual number of consuls, praetors, and tribunes were annually invested with their respective ensigns of office, and continued to discharge some of their least important functions. Those honours still attracted the vain ambition of the Romans; and the emperors themselves, though invested for life with the powers of the consulship, frequently aspired to the title of that annual dignity which they condescended to share with the most illustrious of their fellow-citizens. In the election of these magistrates, the people, during the reign of Augustus, were permitted to expose all the inconveniences of a wild democracy. That artful prince, instead of discovering the least symptom of impatience, humbly solicited their suffrages for himself or his friends, and scrupulously practised all the duties of an ordinary candidate. But we may venture to ascribe to his councils the first measure of the succeeding reign, by which the elections were transferred to the senate. The assemblies of the people were for ever abolished, and the emperors were delivered from a dangerous multitude, who, without restoring liberty, might have disturbed, and perhaps endangered, the established government.

By declaring themselves the protectors of the people, Marius and Caesar[14] had subverted the constitution of their country. But as soon as the senate had been humbled and disarmed, such an assembly, consisting of five or six hundred persons, was found a much more tractable and useful instrument of dominion. It was on the dignity of the senate that Augustus and his successors founded their new empire; and they affected, on every occasion, to adopt the language and principles of Patricians. In the administration of their own powers, they frequently consulted the great national council, and *seemed* to refer to its decision the most important concerns of peace and war. Rome, Italy, and the internal provinces were subject to the immediate jurisdiction of the senate. With regard to civil objects, it was the supreme court of appeal; with regard to criminal matters, a tribunal, constituted for the trial of all offences that were committed by men in any public station, or that affected the peace and majesty of the Roman people. The exercise of the judicial power became the most frequent and serious occupation of the senate; and the important causes that were pleaded before them afforded a last refuge to the spirit of ancient eloquence. As a council of state and as a court of justice, the senate possessed very considerable prerogatives; but in its legislative capacity, in which it was supposed virtually to represent the people, the rights of sovereignty were acknowledged to reside in that assembly. Every

---

14. Gaius Marius (157–86 B.C.) began his rise to dictatorial power as tribune of the people and enemy of the aristocracy; so, too, Julius Caesar (102–44 B.C.) was brought into the popular party through his aunt's marriage with Marius and his own to the daughter of Marius' chief supporter. The Senate, which had been a formidable if unsuccessful enemy in the past, is now turned by Augustus into an "instrument," and he is careful to show verbal respect for the patrician order (from which alone, until about 350 B.C., the Senate was drawn).

power was derived from their authority, every law was ratified by their sanction. Their regular meetings were held on three stated days in every month, the Calends, the Nones, and the Ides.[15] The debates were conducted with decent [16] freedom; and the emperors themselves, who gloried in the name of senators, sat, voted, and divided with their equals.

To resume, in a few words, the system of the Imperial government, as it was instituted by Augustus, and maintained by those princes who understood their own interest and that of the people, it may be defined an absolute monarchy disguised by the forms of a commonwealth. The masters of the Roman world surrounded their throne with darkness, concealed their irresistible strength, and humbly professed themselves the accountable ministers of the senate, whose supreme decrees they dictated and obeyed.

The face of the court corresponded with the forms of the administration. The emperors, if we except those tyrants whose capricious folly violated every law of nature and decency, disdained that pomp and ceremony which might offend their countrymen but could add nothing to their real power. In all the offices of life, they affected to confound themselves with their subjects, and maintained with them an equal intercourse of visits and entertainments. Their habit, their palace, their table, were suited only to the rank of an opulent senator. Their family, however numerous or splendid, was composed entirely of their domestic slaves and freedmen.[17] Augustus or Trajan would have blushed at employing the meanest of the Romans in those menial offices which, in the household and bedchamber of a limited monarch, are so eagerly solicited by the proudest nobles of Britain.

The deification of the emperors is the only instance in which they departed from their accustomed prudence and modesty. The Asiatic Greeks were the first inventors, the successors of Alexander the first objects, of this servile and impious mode of adulation. It was easily transferred from the kings to the governors of Asia; and the Roman magistrates very frequently were adored as provincial deities, with the pomp of altars and temples, of festivals and sacrifices. It was natural that the emperors should not refuse what the proconsuls had accepted; and the divine honours which both the one and the other received from the provinces attested rather the despotism than the servitude of Rome. But the conquerors soon imitated the vanquished nations in the arts of flattery; and the imperious spirit of the first Caesar too easily consented to assume, during his life time, a place among the tutelar deities of Rome. The milder temper of his successor declined so dangerous an ambition, which was never afterwards revived, except by the madness of Caligula and Domitian.[18] Augustus permitted indeed some of the provincial cities to erect temples to his honour, on condition that they should associate the worship of

15. The days corresponding, originally, to the first appearance of the new moon, the first quarter, and the full moon.
16. Decorous, restrained.
17. "A weak prince will always be governed by his domestics. The power of slaves aggravated the shame of the Romans; and the Senate paid court to a Pallas or a Narcissus. There is a chance that a modern favourite may be a gentleman." (Gibbon)
18. Caligula, 12–41 A.D., and Domitian, 51–96 A.D., both notoriously vicious and uncontrolled emperors; Caligula claimed the honors paid to Apollo, Mars, and Jupiter, and built a temple to his own divinity; Domitian assumed the titles of Lord and God and claimed to be the son of Minerva.

Rome with that of the sovereign; he tolerated private superstition, of which he might be the object; but he contented himself with being revered by the senate and people in his human character, and wisely left to his successor the care of his public deification. A regular custom was introduced that, on the decease of every emperor who had neither lived nor died like a tyrant, the senate by a solemn decree should place him in the number of the gods; and the ceremonies of his apotheosis were blended with those of his funeral. This legal and, as it should seem, injudicious profanation, so abhorrent to our stricter principles, was received with a very faint murmur by the easy nature of Polytheism; but it was received as an institution not of religion, but of policy. We should disgrace the virtues of the Antonines by comparing them with the vices of Hercules or Jupiter.[19] Even the characters of Caesar or Augustus were far superior to those of the popular deities. But it was the misfortune of the former to live in an enlightened age, and their actions were too faithfully recorded to admit of such a mixture of fable and mystery as the devotion of the vulgar requires. As soon as their divinity was established by law, it sunk into oblivion, without contributing either to their own fame or to the dignity of succeeding princes.

In the consideration of the Imperial government, we have frequently mentioned the artful founder, under his well-known title of Augustus, which was not however conferred upon him till the edifice was almost completed. The obscure name of Octavianus he derived from a mean family in the little town of Aricia. It was stained with the blood of the proscription; and he was desirous, had it been possible, to erase all memory of his former life. The illustrious surname of Caesar he had assumed as the adopted son of the dictator; but he had too much good sense either to hope to be confounded, or to wish to be compared, with that extraordinary man. It was proposed in the senate to dignify their minister with a new appellation; and, after a very serious discussion, that of Augustus was chosen, among several others, as being the most expressive of the character of peace and sanctity which he uniformly affected. *Augustus* was therefore a personal, *Caesar* a family, distinction. The former should naturally have expired with the prince on whom it was bestowed; and, however the latter was diffused by adoption and female alliance, Nero was the last prince who could allege any hereditary claim to the honours of the Julian line. But, at the time of his death, the practice of a century had inseparably connected those appellations with the Imperial dignity, and they have been preserved by a long succession of emperors,—Romans, Greeks, Franks, and Germans,—from the fall of the republic to the present time. A distinction was, however, soon introduced. The sacred title of Augustus was always reserved for the monarch, whilst the name of Caesar was more freely communicated to his relations; and, from the reign of Hadrian at least, was appropriated to the second person in the state, who was considered as the presumptive heir of the empire.

The tender respect of Augustus for a free constitution which he had de-

19. Hercules was regarded not only as a hero but as a god, and there were temples to him in Rome; among the vices ascribed to him in legend, as well as to Jupiter, are cruelty and sexual profligacy. For the admirable lives of the Antonines, see notes 31 and 32 below.

stroyed can only be explained by an attentive consideration of the character of that subtle tyrant. A cool head, an unfeeling heart, and a cowardly disposition prompted him at the age of nineteen to assume the mask of hypocrisy, which he never afterwards laid aside. With the same hand, and probably with the same temper, he signed the proscription of Cicero and the pardon of Cinna.[20] His virtues, and even his vices, were artificial; and according to the various dictates of his interest, he was at first the enemy, and at last the father, of the Roman world. When he framed the artful system of the Imperial authority, his moderation was inspired by his fears. He wished to deceive the people by an image of civil liberty, and the armies by an image of civil government.

I. The death of Caesar was ever before his eyes. He had lavished wealth and honours on his adherents; but the most favoured friends of his uncle were in the number of the conspirators. The fidelity of the legions might defend his authority against open rebellion, but their vigilance could not secure his person from the dagger of a determined republican; and the Romans, who revered the memory of Brutus,[21] would applaud the imitation of his virtue. Caesar had provoked his fate as much by the ostentation of his power as by his power itself. The consul or the tribune might have reigned in peace. The title of king had armed the Romans against his life.[22] Augustus was sensible that mankind is governed by names; nor was he deceived in his expectation that the senate and people would submit to slavery, provided they were respectfully assured that they still enjoyed their ancient freedom. A feeble senate and enervated people cheerfully acquiesced in the pleasing illusion as long as it was supported by the virtue, or by even the prudence, of the successors of Augustus. It was a motive of self-preservation, not a principle of liberty, that animated the conspirators against Caligula, Nero, and Domitian. They attacked the person of the tyrant, without aiming their blow at the authority of the emperor.

There appears, indeed, *one* memorable occasion, in which the senate, after seventy years of patience, made an ineffectual attempt to reassume its long-forgotten rights. When the throne was vacant by the murder of Caligula, the consuls convoked that assembly in the Capitol, condemned the memory of the Caesars, gave the watchword *liberty* to the few cohorts who faintly adhered to their standard, and during eight and forty hours, acted as the independent chiefs of a free commonwealth. But while they deliberated, the praetorian guards [23] had resolved. The stupid Claudius, brother of Germanicus, was already in their camp, invested with the Imperial purple, and prepared to support his election by arms. The dream of liberty was at an end; and the senate awoke

20. Marcus Tullius Cicero (106–43 B.C.), the orator, statesman, and philosopher, was proscribed by order of the first triumvirate and put to death near Caieta. Gaius Cornelius Cinna was, in contrast, pardoned by Augustus for alleged conspiracy (c. 16–13 B.C.).

21. "Two centuries after the establishment of monarchy, the emperor Marcus Antoninus recommends the character of Brutus as the perfect model of Roman virtue." (Gibbon)

22. That Julius Caesar secretly sought, and might accept, the crown was the fear that led to his assassination.

23. The praetorian guards were the bodyguard of the emperor; when Claudius was discovered in hiding after the murder of Caligula, the guards saluted him as emperor (41 A.D.); his brother Germanicus, an impressive military leader, had died about twenty years earlier.

to all the horrors of inevitable servitude. Deserted by the people, and threatened by a military policy, that feeble assembly was compelled to ratify the choice of the praetorians, and to embrace the benefit of an amnesty, which Claudius had the prudence to offer, and the generosity to observe.

II. The insolence of the armies inspired Augustus with fears of a still more alarming nature. The despair of the citizens could only attempt what the power of the soldiers was, at any time, able to execute. How precarious was his own authority over men whom he had taught to violate every social duty! He had heard their seditious clamours; he dreaded their calmer moments of reflection. One revolution had been purchased by immense rewards; but a second revolution might double those rewards. The troops professed the fondest attachment to the house of Caesar; but the attachments of the multitude are capricious and inconstant. Augustus summoned to his aid whatever remained in those fierce minds of Roman prejudices; enforced the rigour of discipline by the sanction of law; and, interposing the majesty of the senate between the emperor and the army, boldly claimed their allegiance as the first magistrate of the republic.

During a long period of two hundred and twenty years, from the establishment of this artful system to the death of Commodus, the dangers inherent to a military government were, in a great measure, suspended. The soldiers were seldom roused to that fatal sense of their own strength and of the weakness of the civil authority, which was, before and afterwards, productive of such dreadful calamities. Caligula and Domitian were assassinated in their palace by their own domestics: the convulsions which agitated Rome on the death of the former were confined to the walls of the city. But Nero involved the whole empire in his ruin. In the space of eighteen months four princes perished by the sword; and the Roman world was shaken by the fury of the contending armies. Excepting only this short, though violent, eruption of military licence, the two centuries from Augustus to Commodus passed away unstained with civil blood, and undisturbed by revolutions. The emperor was elected by the *authority of the senate* and *the consent of the soldiers*. The legions respected their oath of fidelity; and it requires a minute inspection of the Roman annals to discover three inconsiderable rebellions, which were all suppressed in a few months, and without even the hazard of a battle.

In elective monarchies, the vacancy of the throne is a moment big with danger and mischief. The Roman emperors, desirous to spare the legions that interval of suspense, and the temptation of an irregular choice, invested their designed successor with so large a share of present power as should enable him, after their decease, to assume the remainder without suffering the empire to perceive the change of masters. Thus Augustus, after all his fairer prospects had been snatched from him by untimely deaths, rested his last hopes on Tiberius, obtained for his adopted son [24] the censorial and tribunitian powers, and dictated a law, by which the future prince was invested with an authority equal to his own over the provinces and the armies. Thus Vespasian subdued the generous mind of his eldest son. Titus was adored by the eastern legions, which, under his command, had recently achieved the conquest of Judea. His

24. Tiberius, who ruled from 14 to 37 A.D., was the son of Livia, whom Augustus had married; in 4 A.D. Augustus adopted him as a son and placed him in charge of the Roman armies.

power was dreaded, and, as his virtues were clouded by the intemperance of youth, his designs were suspected. Instead of listening to such unworthy suspicions, the prudent monarch associated Titus to the full powers of the Imperial dignity; and the grateful son ever approved himself the humble and faithful minister of so indulgent a father.[25]

The good sense of Vespasian engaged him indeed to embrace every measure that might confirm his recent and precarious elevation. The military oath, and the fidelity of the troops, had been consecrated, by the habits of an hundred years, to the name and family of the Caesars; and, although that family had been continued only by the fictitious rite of adoption, the Romans still revered, in the person of Nero, the grandson of Germanicus, and the lineal successor of Augustus. It was not without reluctance and remorse that the praetorian guards had been persuaded to abandon the cause of the tyrant. The rapid downfall of Galba, Otho, and Vitellius, taught the armies to consider the emperors as the creatures of *their* will, and the instruments of *their* licence.[26] The birth of Vespasian was mean; his grandfather had been a private soldier, his father a petty officer of the revenue, his own merit had raised him, in an advanced age, to the empire; but his merit was rather useful than shining, and his virtues were disgraced by a strict and even sordid parsimony. Such a prince consulted his true interest by the association of a son whose more splendid and amiable character might turn the public attention from the obscure origin to the future glories of the Flavian house. Under the mild administration of Titus, the Roman world enjoyed a transient felicity, and his beloved memory served to protect, above fifteen years, the vices of his brother Domitian.

Nerva[27] had scarcely accepted the purple from the assassins of Domitian before he discovered that his feeble age was unable to stem the torrent of public disorders which had multiplied under the long tyranny of his predecessor. His mild disposition was respected by the good; but the degenerate Romans required a more vigorous character, whose justice should strike terror into the guilty. Though he had several relations, he fixed his choice on a stranger. He adopted Trajan, then about forty years of age, and who commanded a powerful army in the Lower Germany; and immediately, by a decree of the senate, declared him his colleague and successor in the empire. It is sincerely to be lamented that, whilst we are fatigued with the disgustful relation of Nero's crimes and follies, we are reduced to collect the actions of Trajan from the glimmerings of an abridgement or the doubtful light of a panegyric. There remains, however, one panegyric far removed beyond the suspicion of

25. Vespasian, emperor 70–79 A.D., shared a triumph with his son Titus and gave him the title of Caesar; Titus lived to succeed his father for a reign of two years, after which his brother Domitian became emperor.

26. Servius Sulpicius Galba was raised to the throne by the praetorian guards in 68 A.D. and assassinated by them the following year; they then elevated Marcus Salvius Otho, who ruled for the first three months of 69 A.D. and committed suicide during the rebellion of Aulus Vitellius. He ruled a comparably short while before his murder and the succession of Vespasian.

27. Nerva succeeded to the empire in 96 A.D., when Domitian was murdered by a conspiracy of praetorian guards and court officials; while he restored many Roman liberties, his advanced age (66 at accession) and his lack of military support made his short reign insecure. He was succeeded by Trajan in 98 A.D.

flattery. Above two hundred and fifty years after the death of Trajan, the senate, in pouring out the customary acclamations on the accession of a new emperor, wished that he might surpass the felicity of Augustus and the virtue of Trajan.

We may readily believe that the father of his country hesitated whether he ought to intrust the various and doubtful character of his kinsman Hadrian with sovereign power. In his last moments, the arts of the empress Plotina either fixed the irresolution of Trajan, or boldly supposed a fictitious adoption, the truth of which could not be safely disputed; and Hadrian was peaceably acknowledged as his lawful successor.[28] Under his reign, as has been already mentioned, the empire flourished in peace and prosperity. He encouraged the arts, reformed the laws, asserted military discipline, and visited all his provinces in person. His vast and active genius was equally suited to the most enlarged views and the minute details of civil policy. But the ruling passions of his soul were curiosity and vanity. As they prevailed, and as they were attracted by different objects, Hadrian was, by turns, an excellent prince, a ridiculous sophist, and a jealous tyrant. The general tenor of his conduct deserved praise for its equity and moderation. Yet, in the first days of his reign, he put to death four consular senators, his personal enemies, and men who had been judged worthy of empire; and the tediousness of a painful illness rendered him, at last, peevish and cruel. The senate doubted whether they should pronounce him a god or a tyrant; and the honours decreed to his memory were granted to the prayers of the pious Antoninus.

The caprice of Hadrian influenced his choice of a successor. After revolving in his mind several men of distinguished merit, whom he esteemed and hated, he adopted Aelius Verus, a gay and voluptuous nobleman, recommended by uncommon beauty to the lover of Antinous.[29] But, whilst Hadrian was delighting himself with his own applause and the acclamations of the soldiers, whose consent had been secured by an immense donative,[30] the new Caesar was ravished from his embraces by an untimely death. He left only one son. Hadrian commended the boy to the gratitude of the Antonines. He was adopted by Pius; and, on the accession of Marcus, was invested with an equal share of sovereign power. Among the many vices of this younger Verus, he possessed one virtue—a dutiful reverence for his wiser colleague, to whom he willingly abandoned the ruder cares of empire. The philosophic emperor dissembled his follies, lamented his early death, and cast a decent veil over his memory.

As soon as Hadrian's passion was either gratified or disappointed, he resolved to deserve the thanks of posterity by placing the most exalted merit on the Roman throne. His discerning eye easily discovered a senator about fifty years of age, blameless in all the offices of life; and a youth of about seventeen, whose riper years opened the fair prospect of every virtue: the elder of these was

28. Trajan's adoption of Hadrian (emperor, 117–138 A.D.) was announced after his death, and, as Gibbon indicates, was suspected as a fiction.
29. Antinous, the Greek youth whose beauty and grace won Hadrian's love, was drowned in the Nile before he was twenty; he was deified and was represented in many statues, some of them highly influential on Renaissance sculpture. "The deification of Antinous, his medals, statues, temple, city, oracles, and constellation, are well known and still dishonour the memory of Hadrian. Yet we may remark that of the first fifteen emperors Claudius was the only one whose taste in love was entirely correct." (Gibbon)
30. A gift from public funds.

declared the son and successor of Hadrian, on condition, however, that he himself should immediately adopt the younger. The two Antonines [31] (for it is of them that we are now speaking) governed the Roman world forty-two years with the same invariable spirit of wisdom and virtue. Although Pius had two sons, he preferred the welfare of Rome to the interest of his family, gave his daughter Faustina in marriage to young Marcus, obtained from the senate the tribunitian and proconsular powers, and, with a noble disdain, or rather ignorance, of jealousy, associated him to all the labours of government. Marcus, on the other hand, revered the character of his benefactor, loved him as a parent, obeyed him as a sovereign, and, after he was no more, regulated his own administration by the example and maxims of his predecessor. Their united reigns are possibly the only period of history in which the happiness of a great people was the sole object of government.

Titus Antoninus Pius has been justly denominated a second Numa. The same love of religion, justice, and peace, was the distinguishing characteristic of both princes. But the situation of the latter opened a much larger field for the exercise of those virtues. Numa could only prevent a few neighbouring villages from plundering each other's harvests. Antoninus diffused order and tranquillity over the greatest part of the earth. His reign is marked by the rare advantage of furnishing very few materials for history; which is, indeed, little more than the register of the crimes, follies, and misfortunes of mankind. In private life he was an amiable as well as a good man. The native simplicity of his virtue was a stranger to vanity or affectation. He enjoyed with moderation the conveniences of his fortune and the innocent pleasures of society; and the benevolence of his soul displayed itself in a cheerful serenity of temper.

The virtue of Marcus Aurelius Antoninus was of a severer and more laborious kind.[32] It was the well-earned harvest of many a learned conference, of many a patient lecture, and many a midnight lucubration. At the age of twelve years he embraced the rigid system of the Stoics, which taught him to submit his body to his mind, his passions to his reason; to consider virtue as the only good, vice as the only evil, all things external as things indifferent. His Meditations, composed in the tumult of a camp, are still extant; and he even condescended to give lessons on philosophy, in a more public manner than was perhaps consistent with the modesty of a sage or the dignity of an emperor. But his life was the noblest commentary on the precepts of Zeno.[33] He was severe to himself, indulgent to the imperfection of others, just and beneficent to all mankind. He regretted that Avidius Cassius, who excited a rebellion in

31. Antoninus Pius (86–161 A.D.) virtually ruled during Hadrian's final illness and argued successfully for that emperor's consecration. He ruled in his own name from 138 to 161 and was called a "second Numa" after the second King of Rome, Numa Pompilius (c. 715– c. 673 B.C.), of whom legends report that he ruled ably through the counsel of the nymph Egeria.
32. Marcus Aurelius Antoninus, emperor from 161 to 180, was charged by his enemies with hypocrisy. Gibbon notes, "This suspicion, unjust as it was, may serve to account for the superior applause bestowed upon personal qualifications in preference to the social virtues. . . . The wildest scepticism never insinuated that Caesar might possibly be a coward or Tully a fool. Wit and valour are qualifications more easily ascertained than humanity or the love of justice." Marcus Aurelius' *Meditations* (the written version of his "midnight lucubration") remains a classic of Roman Stoicism.
33. Zeno (335–263 B.C.), founder of the Stoic school, wished, however, to teach only true philosophers rather than the general public.

Syria, had disappointed him, by a voluntary death, of the pleasure of converting an enemy into a friend; and he justified the sincerity of that sentiment by moderating the zeal of the senate against the adherents of the traitor. War he detested, as the disgrace and calamity of human nature; but when the necessity of a just defence called upon him to take up arms, he readily exposed his person to eight winter campaigns on the frozen banks of the Danube, the severity of which was at last fatal to the weakness of his constitution. His memory was revered by a grateful posterity, and above a century after his death many persons preserved the image of Marcus Antoninus among those of their household gods.

If a man were called to fix the period in the history of the world during which the condition of the human race was most happy and prosperous, he would, without hesitation, name that which elapsed from the death of Domitian to the accession of Commodus.[34] The vast extent of the Roman empire was governed by absolute power under the guidance of virtue and wisdom. The armies were restrained by the firm but gentle hand of four successive emperors whose characters and authority commanded involuntary respect. The forms of the civil administration were carefully preserved by Nerva, Trajan, Hadrian, and the Antonines, who delighted in the image of liberty and were pleased with considering themselves as the accountable ministers of the laws. Such princes deserved the honour of restoring the republic, had the Romans of their days been capable of enjoying a rational freedom.

The labours of these monarchs were over-paid by the immense reward that inseparably waited on their success; by the honest pride of virtue, and by the exquisite delight of beholding the general happiness of which they were the authors. A just but melancholy reflection embittered, however, the noblest of human enjoyments. They must often have recollected the instability of a happiness which depended on the character of a single man. The fatal moment was perhaps approaching when some licentious youth, or some jealous tyrant, would abuse, to the destruction, that absolute power which they had exerted for the benefit, of their people. The ideal restraints of the senate and the laws might serve to display the virtues but could never correct the vices, of the emperor. The military force was a blind and irresistible instrument of oppression; and the corruption of Roman manners would always supply flatterers eager to applaud, and ministers prepared to serve, the fear or the avarice, the lust or the cruelty, of their masters.

These gloomy apprehensions had been already justified by the experience of the Romans. The annals of the emperors exhibit a strong and various picture of human nature, which we should vainly seek among the mixed and doubtful characters of modern history. In the conduct of those monarchs we may trace the utmost lines of vice and virtue; the most exalted perfection and the meanest degeneracy of our own species. The golden age of Trajan and the Antonines had been preceded by an age of iron. It is almost superfluous to enumerate the unworthy successors of Augustus. Their unparalleled vices, and the splendid theatre on which they were acted, have saved them from oblivion. The dark

34. That is, 96–180 A.D. Commodus, the older son of Marcus Aurelius, succeeded for a reign of twelve years during which he became increasingly mad with power, regarding himself as the Roman incarnation of Hercules; he was finally assassinated as he played the gladiator.

unrelenting Tiberius, the furious Caligula, the stupid Claudius, the profligate and cruel Nero, the beastly Vitellius,[35] and the timid inhuman Domitian are condemned to everlasting infamy. During fourscore years (excepting only the short and doubtful respite of Vespasian's reign), Rome groaned beneath an unremitting tyranny, which exterminated the ancient families of the republic and was fatal to almost every virtue and every talent that arose in that unhappy period.

Under the reign of these monsters the slavery of the Romans was accompanied with two peculiar circumstances, the one occasioned by their former liberty, the other by their extensive conquests, which rendered their condition more wretched than that of the victims of tyranny in any other age or country. From these causes were derived, 1. The exquisite sensibility of the sufferers; and 2. The impossibility of escaping from the hand of the oppressor.

I. When Persia was governed by the descendants of Sefi, a race of princes whose wanton cruelty often stained their divan, their table, and their bed with the blood of their favourites, there is a saying recorded of a young nobleman, that he never departed from the sultan's presence without satisfying himself whether his head was still on his shoulders. The experience of every day might almost justify the scepticism of Rustan.[36] Yet the fatal sword, suspended above him by a single thread, seems not to have disturbed the slumbers, or interrupted the tranquillity, of the Persian. The monarch's frown, he well knew, could level him with the dust; but the stroke of lightning or apoplexy might be equally fatal; and it was the part of a wise man to forget the inevitable calamities of human life in the enjoyment of the fleeting hour. He was dignified with the appellation of the king's slave; had, perhaps, been purchased from obscure parents, in a country which he had never known; and was trained up from his infancy in the severe discipline of the seraglio. His name, his wealth, his honours, were the gift of a master, who might, without injustice, resume what he had bestowed. Rustan's knowledge, if he possessed any, could only serve to confirm his habits by prejudices. His language afforded not words for any form of government except absolute monarchy. The history of the East informed him that such had ever been the condition of mankind. The Koran, and the interpreters of that divine book, inculcated to him that the sultan was the descendant of the prophet, and the viceregent of heaven; that patience was the first virtue of a Mussulman, and unlimited obedience the great duty of a subject.

The minds of the Romans were very differently prepared for slavery. Oppressed beneath the weight of their own corruption and of military violence, they for a long while preserved the sentiments, or at least the ideas, of their freeborn ancestors. The education of Helvidius and Thrasea, of Tacitus and Pliny, was the same as that of Cato and Cicero.[37] From Grecian philosophy

---

35. "Vitellius consumed in mere eating at least six millions of our money in about seven months. It is not easy to express his vices with dignity, or even decency." (Gibbon)

36. The young Persian cited in Sir John Chardin's account of that nation's tyranny.

37. Thrasea Paetus (d. 66 A.D.) was a Stoic who modeled himself on Cato and held republican sympathies; he was condemned by the emperor Nero and forced to commit suicide. His son-in-law Helvidius Priscus, also a Stoic, was exiled but returned to lead the opposition, as a more and more outright republican, to Vespasian (by whom he was executed c. 75 A.D.).

they had imbibed the justest and most liberal notions of the dignity of human nature and the origin of civil society. The history of their own country had taught them to revere a free, a virtuous, and a victorious commonwealth; to abhor the successful crimes of Caesar and Augustus; and inwardly to despise those tyrants whom they adored with the most abject flattery. As magistrates and senators, they were admitted into the great council which had once dictated laws to the earth, whose name gave still a sanction to the acts of the monarch, and whose authority was so often prostituted to the vilest purposes of tyranny. Tiberius, and those emperors who adopted his maxims, attempted to disguise their murders by the formalities of justice, and perhaps enjoyed a secret pleasure in rendering the senate their accomplice as well as their victim. By this assembly the last of the Romans were condemned for imaginary crimes and real virtues. Their infamous accusers assumed the language of independent patriots, who arraigned a dangerous citizen before the tribunal of his country; and the public service was rewarded by riches and honours. The servile judges professed to assert the majesty of the commonwealth, violated in the person of its first magistrate, whose clemency they most applauded when they trembled the most at his inexorable and impending cruelty. The tyrant beheld their baseness with just contempt, and encountered their secret sentiments of detestation with sincere and avowed hatred for the whole body of the senate.

II. The division of Europe into a number of independent states, connected, however, with each other, by the general resemblance of religion, language and manners, is productive of the most beneficial consequences to the liberty of mankind. A modern tyrant who should find no resistance either in his own breast or in his people, would soon experience a gentle restraint from the example of his equals, the dread of present censure, the advice of his allies, and the apprehension of his enemies. The object of his displeasure, escaping from the narrow limits of his dominions, would easily obtain, in a happier climate, a secure refuge, a new fortune adequate to his merit, the freedom of complaint, and perhaps the means of revenge. But the empire of the Romans filled the world, and, when that empire fell into the hands of a single person, the world became a safe and dreary prison for his enemies. The slave of Imperial despotism, whether he was condemned to drag his gilded chain in Rome and the senate, or to wear out a life of exile on the barren rock of Seriphus or the frozen banks of the Danube, expected his fate in silent despair.[38] To resist was fatal, and it was impossible to fly. On every side he was encompassed with a vast extent of sea and land, which he could never hope to traverse without being discovered, seized, and restored to his irritated master. Beyond the frontiers, his anxious view could discover nothing except the ocean, inhospitable deserts, hostile tribes of barbarians, of fierce manners and unknown language, or dependent kings, who would gladly purchase the emperor's protection by the sacrifice of an obnoxious fugitive. 'Wherever you are,' said Cicero to the exiled Marcellus, 'remember that you are equally within the power of the conqueror.'

1776

38. "Seriphus was a small rock island in the Aegean Sea, the inhabitants of which were despised for their ignorance and obscurity" (Gibbon). The poet Ovid was exiled by Augustus in 8 A.D. to a frontier fortress on the Black Sea and lived there for his last ten years.

From *Chapter XVI: The Conduct of the Roman Government Towards the Christians, from the Reign of Nero to That of Constantine* [1]

In this general view of the persecution, which was first authorized by the edicts of Diocletian, I have purposely refrained from describing the particular sufferings and deaths of the Christian martyrs. It would have been an easy task, from the history of Eusebius,[2] from the declamations of Lactantius,[3] and from the most ancient acts, to collect a long series of horrid and disgustful pictures, and to fill many pages with racks and scourges, with iron hooks and red-hot beds, and with all the variety of tortures which fire and steel, savage beasts and more savage executioners, could inflict on the human body. These melancholy scenes might be enlivened by a crowd of visions and miracles destined either to delay the death, to celebrate the triumph, or to discover the relics of those canonized saints who suffered for the name of Christ. But I cannot determine what I ought to transcribe till I am satisfied how much I ought to believe. The gravest of the ecclesiastical historians, Eusebius himself, indirectly confesses that he has related whatever might redound to the glory, and that he has suppressed all that could tend to the disgrace, of religion. Such an acknowledgment will naturally excite a suspicion that a writer who has so openly violated one of the fundamental laws of history has not paid a very strict regard to the observance of the other; and the suspicion will derive additional credit from the character of Eusebius, which was less tinctured with credulity, and more practised in the arts of courts, than that of almost any of his contemporaries. On some particular occasions, when the magistrates were exasperated by some personal motives of interest or resentment, when the zeal of the martyrs urged them to forget the rules of prudence, and perhaps of decency, to overturn the altars, to pour out imprecations against the emperors, or to strike the judge as he sat on his tribunal, it may be presumed that every mode of torture, which cruelty could invent or constancy could endure, was exhausted on those devoted victims. Two circumstances, however, have been unwarily mentioned, which insinuate that the general treatment of the Christians who had been apprehended by the officers of justice was less intolerable than it is usually imagined to have been. 1. The confessors who were condemned to work in the mines were permitted, by the humanity or the negligence of their keepers, to build chapels and freely to profess their religion in the midst of those dreary habitations. 2. The bishops were obliged to check and to censure the forward zeal of the Christians, who voluntarily threw themselves

---

1. This passage from the close of Chapter XVI shows Gibbon's ironic questioning of the claims of Christianity. In Chapter XV he presents the march of Christianity to power, stressing those qualities in it which made for worldly success; in this chapter he presents its gradual conquest of the Roman empire and he examines the cost at which this was obtained. The dry use of statistics is deliberately set against the sanctity of the martyrs and cool calculation against their righteousness. In this Gibbon's method may be compared with Swift's ironic use of statistics. Swift uses them to stress the inhumanity implicit in such calculation. Gibbon uses them to undercut zealous pretensions and then, shockingly, to measure the true, unacknowledged inhumanity of that zeal.
2. The Christian scholar (c. 260–340 A.D.) of Caesarea in Palestine, where he witnessed the persecution, 303–10; after the toleration in 311, he was named bishop.
3. The "Christian Cicero," 250?–317? A.D., a professor of rhetoric who became a Christian in his mature years and wrote of the persecutions of Diocletian (emperor 284–305).

into the hands of the magistrates. Some of these were persons oppressed by poverty and debts, who blindly sought to terminate a miserable existence by a glorious death. Others were allured by the hope that a short confinement would expiate the sins of a whole life; and others, again, were actuated by the less honourable motive of deriving a plentiful subsistence, and perhaps a considerable profit, from the alms which the charity of the faithful bestowed on the prisoners. After the church had triumphed over all her enemies, the interest as well as vanity of the captives prompted them to magnify the merit of their respective suffering. A convenient distance of time or place gave an ample scope to the progress of fiction; and the frequent instances which might be alleged of holy martyrs whose wounds had been instantly healed, whose strength had been renewed, and whose lost members had miraculously been restored, were extremely convenient for the purpose of removing every diffi-culty and of silencing every objection. The most extravagant legends, as they conduced to the honour of the church, were applauded by the credulous multitude, countenanced by the power of the clergy, and attested by the suspicious evidence of ecclesiastical history.

The vague descriptions of exile and imprisonment, of pain and torture, are so easily exaggerated or softened by the pencil [4] of an artful orator that we are naturally induced to inquire into a fact of a more distinct and stubborn kind: the number of persons who suffered death, in consequence of the edicts published by Diocletian, his associates, and his successors. The recent legend-aries [5] record whole armies and cities which were at once swept away by the undistinguishing rage of persecution. The more ancient writers content them-selves with pouring out a liberal effusion of loose and tragical invectives, with-out condescending to ascertain the precise number of those persons who were permitted to seal with their blood their belief of the gospel. From the history of Eusebius, it may however be collected that only nine bishops were punished with death; and we are assured, by his particular enumeration of the martyrs of Palestine, that no more than ninety-two Christians were entitled to that honourable appellation. As we are unacquainted with the degree of episcopal zeal and courage which prevailed at that time, it is not in our power to draw any useful inferences from the former of these facts; but the latter may serve to justify a very important and probable conclusion. According to the distribu-tion of Roman provinces, Palestine may be considered as the sixteenth part of the Eastern empire; and since there were some governors who, from a real or affected clemency, had preserved their hands unstained with the blood of the faithful, it is reasonable to believe that the country which had given birth to Christianity produced at least the sixteenth part of the martyrs who suffered death within the dominions of Galerius and Maximin; the whole might conse-quently amount to about fifteen hundred: a number which, if it is equally divided between the ten years of the persecution, will allow an annual con-sumption of one hundred and fifty martyrs. Allotting the same proportion to the provinces of Italy, Africa, and perhaps Spain, where, at the end of two or three years, the rigour of the penal laws was either suspended or abolished,

4. Paintbrush; here pictorial power.
5. Modern ecclesiastical historians.

the multitude of Christians in the Roman empire on whom a capital punishment was inflicted by a judicial sentence will be reduced to somewhat less than two thousand persons. Since it cannot be doubted that the Christians were more numerous, and their enemies more exasperated, in the time of Diocletian than they had ever been in any former persecution, this probable and moderate computation may teach us to estimate the number of primitive saints and martyrs who sacrificed their lives for the important purpose of introducing Christianity into the world.

We shall conclude this chapter by a melancholy truth which obtrudes itself on the reluctant mind; that even admitting, without hesitation or inquiry, all that history has recorded or devotion has feigned on the subject of martyrdoms, it must still be acknowledged that the Christians, in the course of their intestine [6] dissensions, have inflicted far greater severities on each other than they had experienced from the zeal of infidels. During the ages of ignorance which followed the subversion of the Roman empire in the West, the bishops of the Imperial city extended their dominion over the laity as well as clergy of the Latin church. The fabric of superstition which they had erected, and which might long have defied the feeble efforts of reason, was at length assaulted by a crowd of daring fanatics, who, from the twelfth to the sixteenth century, assumed the popular character of reformers. The church of Rome defended by violence the empire which she had acquired by fraud; a system of peace and benevolence was soon disgraced by proscriptions, wars, massacres, and the institution of the holy office.[7] And, as the reformers were animated by the love of civil, as well as of religious, freedom, the Catholic princes connected their own interest with that of the clergy, and enforced by fire and the sword the terrors of spiritual censures. In the Netherlands alone, more than one hundred thousand of the subjects of Charles the Fifth are said to have suffered by the hand of the executioner; and this extraordinary number is attested by Grotius,[8] a man of genius and learning, who preserved his moderation amidst the fury of contending sects, and who composed the annals of his own age and country at a time when the invention of printing had facilitated the means of intelligence and increased the danger of detection. If we are obliged to submit our belief to the authority of Grotius, it must be allowed that the number of Protestants who were executed in a single province and a single reign far exceeded that of the primitive martyrs in the space of three centuries and of the Roman empire. But, if the improbability of the fact itself should prevail over the weight of evidence; if Grotius should be convicted of exaggerating the merit and sufferings of the Reformers; we shall be naturally led to inquire what confidence can be placed in the doubtful and imperfect monuments of ancient credulity; what degree of credit can be assigned to a courtly bishop and a passionate declaimer, who, under the protection of Constantine, enjoyed the exclusive privilege of recording the persecutions inflicted on the Christians by the vanquished rivals or disregarded predecessors of their gracious sovereign.

1776

6. Internal.

7. The Inquisition, the tribunal established in the 13th century for the discovery and suppression of heretics.

8. Hugo Grotius (1583–1645), Dutch statesman and jurist.

EDMUND BURKE
1729–1797

Burke's political eloquence has obscured his important early work in aesthetics; it is a matter for regret that he did not follow Edmond Malone's advice of 1789 to "revise and enlarge his admirable book on the *Sublime and Beautiful,* which the experience, reading, and observation of thirty years could not but enable him to improve considerably." Burke seems to have been occupied with aesthetic problems as early as 1744, when he entered Trinity College, Dublin, at fifteen. At Trinity he read the classical treatise of the so-called Longinus (fl. first century A.D.) on the sublime (which had entered English criticism once it had been translated into French by Boileau in 1674), and he seems to have drafted the earliest version of his *Enquiry* in 1747. In the year immediately following, Burke edited and largely wrote a journal, *The Reformer,* in Dublin and in 1750 entered the Middle Temple in London to study law. The *Enquiry* was published with success in 1757 but amplified and revised for a second edition two years later.

Burke entered politics in 1759, and by 1765 he became private secretary to the Marquess of Rockingham and a leader of the liberal Whigs. His famous speech on conciliation with the American colonies was published in 1775, and in the next decade he was deeply involved in prosecuting the charges of corruption he brought against Warren Hastings, Governor General of India. The greatest concern of his career, however, was embodied in his *Reflections on the Revolution in France* (1790), an attack upon the "grave, demure, insidious, spring-nailed, velvet-pawed, green-eyed philosophers, whether going upon two legs or upon four," and, it might be added, in England or in France. These phrases come from the vehement *Letter to a Noble Lord* (1796), both an eloquent apology for himself and a renewed attack upon the theoretical planners and dehumanized metaphysicians he saw at work in France.

In opposition to those who would frame a new state and abolish the past, Burke asserted a redefinition of that social contract Rousseau had made a rallying cry:

> Each contract of each particular state is but a clause in the great primaeval contract of eternal society, linking the lower with the higher natures, connecting the visible and invisible world, according to a fixed compact sanctioned by the inviolable oath which holds all physical and all moral natures, each in their appointed place. . . . It is the first and supreme necessity only, a necessity that is not chosen but chooses . . . which alone can justify a resort to anarchy.

In his great lament for the persecution of Marie Antoinette, Burke wrote memorably:

> But the age of chivalry is gone. That of sophisters, economists, and calculators has succeeded; and the glory of Europe is extinguished forever. . . . It is gone, that sensibility of principle, that chastity of honour, which felt a stain like a wound, which inspired courage whilst it mitigated ferocity, which ennobled whatever it touched, and under which vice itself lost half its evil by losing all its grossness.

Burke's words may seem at times to have a ferocity of their own, but we have Gibbon's tribute: "I admire his eloquence; I approve his politics; I adore his chivalry; and I can almost excuse his reverence for church establishments."

The young Burke was far more theoretical than he later became. Following the patterns we can see in Addison and others, he transformed Longinus' concern with the sublime as an elevation of style that corresponds to a nobility of spirit into a psychophysical analysis of the mechanism of our response to the grand and terrible in nature and in art. The physiological explanation is omitted here, and only the central discussion of the sublime is given. Burke's treatise is at once a symptom of the literary tendencies of his age (such as we can see in James Thomson, Gray, and Collins) —not least its new responsiveness to Milton—and at the same time a stimulus to those tendencies. Burke is not much concerned with the moral implications of the sublime, as others had been and were to be; and his views are reconcilable with those, like Blake's, that repudiate conventional moral categories in their celebration of energy. One of Burke's most interesting contributions is his analysis of the language of poetry, which tries to come to terms with the way in which poetry transcends the merely visual or imagistic; he comes close to a doctrine of words conveying the contagion of emotion, and he opens up important issues (such as the function of imagery in poetry or its hypnotic and incantatory power) that are still with us.

A Philosophical Enquiry into the Origin of Our Ideas of the Sublime and Beautiful

[*From* Part II]

The passion caused by the great and sublime in *nature*, when those causes operate most powerfully, is Astonishment; and astonishment is that state of the soul, in which all its motions are suspended, with some degree of horror. In this case the mind is so entirely filled with its object, that it cannot entertain any other, nor by consequence reason on that object which employs it. Hence arises the great power of the sublime, that far from being produced by them, it anticipates our reasonings, and hurries us on by an irresistible force. Astonishment, as I have said, is the effect of the sublime in its highest degree; the inferior effects are admiration, reverence and respect.

No passion so effectually robs the mind of all its powers of acting and reasoning as fear. For fear being an apprehension of pain or death, it operates in a manner that resembles actual pain. Whatever therefore is terrible, with regard to sight, is sublime too, whether this cause of terror be endued with greatness of dimensions or not; for it is impossible to look on any thing as trifling or contemptible that may be dangerous. There are many animals, who though far from being large, are yet capable of raising ideas of the sublime, because they are considered as objects of terror. As serpents and poisonous animals of almost all kinds. And to things of great dimensions, if we annex an adventitious idea of terror, they become without comparison greater. A level plain of a vast extent on land, is certainly no mean idea; the prospect of such a plain may be as extensive as a prospect of the ocean; but can it ever fill the mind with any thing so great as the ocean itself? This is owing to several causes, but it is owing to none more than this, that the ocean is an object of no small terror. Indeed terror is in all cases whatsoever, either more openly or latently the ruling principle of the sublime. . . .

To make any thing very terrible, obscurity seems in general to be necessary. When we know the full extent of any danger, when we can accustom our eyes to it, a great deal of the apprehension vanishes. Every one will be sensible of this, who considers how greatly night adds to our dread, in all cases of danger, and how much the notions of ghosts and goblins, of which none can form clear ideas, affect minds, which give credit to the popular tales concerning such sorts of beings. Those despotic governments, which are founded on the passions of men, and principally upon the passion of fear, keep their chief as much as may be from the public eye. The policy has been the same in many cases of religion. Almost all the heathen temples were dark. Even in the barbarous temples of the Americans at this day, they keep their idol in a dark part of the hut, which is consecrated to his worship. For this purpose too the druids performed all their ceremonies in the bosom of the darkest woods, and in the shade of the oldest and most spreading oaks.

No person seems better to have understood the secret of heightening, or of setting terrible things, if I may use the expression, in their strongest light by the force of a judicious obscurity, than Milton. His description of Death in the second book is admirably studied; it is astonishing with what a gloomy pomp, with what a significant and expressive uncertainty of strokes and colouring he has finished the portrait of the king of terrors.

> The other shape,
> If shape it might be called that shape had none
> Distinguishable in member, joint, or limb;
> Or substance might be called that shadow seemed,
> For each seemed either; black he stood as night;
> Fierce as ten furies; terrible as hell;
> And shook a deadly dart. What seemed his head
> The likeness of a kingly crown had on.[1]

In this description all is dark, uncertain, confused, terrible, and sublime to the last degree.

It is one thing to make an idea clear, and another to make it *affecting* to the imagination. If I make a drawing of a palace, or a temple, or a landscape, I present a very clear idea of those objects; but then (allowing for the effect of imitation which is something) my picture can at most affect only as the palace, temple, or landscape would have affected in the reality. On the other hand, the most lively and spirited verbal description I can give, raises a very obscure and imperfect *idea* of such objects; but then it is in my power to raise a stronger *emotion* by the description than I could do by the best painting. This experience constantly evinces. The proper manner of conveying the *affections* of the mind from one to another, is by words; there is a great insufficiency in all other methods of communication; and so far is a clearness of imagery from being absolutely necessary to an influence upon the passions, that they may be considerably operated upon without presenting any image at all, by certain sounds adapted to that purpose; of which we have a sufficient proof in the acknowledged and powerful effects of instrumental music. In reality a great clearness helps but little towards affecting the passions, as it is in some sort an enemy to all enthusiasms whatsoever.

1. *Paradise Lost* II.666–73; Burke misquotes: for "he stood" read "it stood"; for "deadly dart" read "dreadful dart."

. . . Among the common sort of people, I never could perceive that painting had much influence on their passions. It is true that the best sorts of painting, as well as the best sorts of poetry, are not much understood in that sphere. But it is most certain, that their passions are very strongly roused by a fanatic preacher, or by the ballads of Chevy Chase, or the Children in the Wood, and by other little popular poems and tales that are current in that rank of life. I do not know of any paintings, bad or good, that produce the same effect. So that poetry with all its obscurity, has a more general as well as a more powerful dominion over the passions than the other art. And I think there are reasons in nature why the obscure idea, when properly conveyed, should be more affecting than the clear. It is our ignorance of things that causes all our admiration, and chiefly excites our passions. Knowledge and acquaintance make the most striking causes affect but little. It is thus with the vulgar, and all men are as the vulgar in what they do not understand. The ideas of eternity, and infinity, are among the most affecting we have, and yet perhaps there is nothing of which we really understand so little, as of infinity and eternity. We do not anywhere meet a more sublime description than this justly celebrated one of Milton, wherein he gives the portrait of Satan with a dignity so suitable to the subject.

> He above the rest
> In shape and gesture proudly eminent
> Stood like a tower; his form had yet not lost
> All her original brightness, nor appeared
> Less than archangel ruined, and the excess
> Of glory obscured: as when the sun new risen
> Looks through the horizontal misty air
> Shorn of his beams; or from behind the moon
> In dim eclipse disastrous twilight sheds
> On half the nations; and with fear of change
> Perplexes monarchs.[2]

Here is a very noble picture; and in what does this poetical picture consist? in images of a tower, an archangel, the sun rising through mists, or in an eclipse, the ruin of monarchs, and the revolutions of kingdoms. The mind is hurried out of itself, by a crowd of great and confused images; which affect because they are crowded and confused. For separate them, and you lose much of the greatness, and join them, and you infallibly lose the clearness. The images raised by poetry are always of this obscure kind; though in general the effects of poetry are by no means to be attributed to the images it raises; which point we shall examine more at large hereafter. But painting, when we have allowed for the pleasure of imitation, can only affect simply by the images it presents; and even in painting a judicious obscurity in some things contributes to the effect of the picture; because the images in painting are exactly similar to those in nature; and in nature dark, confused, uncertain images have a greater power on the fancy to form the grander passions than those have which are more clear and determinate. . . .

2. *Paradise Lost* I.589–99.

I am sensible that this idea has met with opposition, and is likely still to be rejected by several. But let it be considered that hardly anything can strike the mind with its greatness, which does not make some sort of approach towards infinity; which nothing can do whilst we are able to perceive its bounds; but to see an object distinctly, and to perceive its bounds, is one and the same thing. A clear idea is therefore another name for a little idea. There is a passage in the book of Job amazingly sublime, and this sublimity is principally due to the terrible uncertainty of the thing described. *In thoughts from the visions of the night, when deep sleep falleth upon men, fear came upon me and trembling, which made all my bones to shake. Then a spirit passed before my face. The hair of my flesh stood up. It stood still,* but I could not discern the form thereof; *an image was before mine eyes; there was silence; and I heard a voice,—Shall mortal man be more just than God?* [3] We are first prepared with the utmost solemnity for the vision; we are first terrified, before we are let even into the obscure cause of our emotion; but when this grand cause of terror makes its appearance, what is it? is it not, wrapt up in the shades of its own incomprehensible darkness, more awful, more striking, more terrible, than the liveliest description, than the clearest painting could possibly represent it? . . .

Besides these things which *directly* suggest the idea of danger, and those which produce a similar effect from a mechanical cause, I know of nothing sublime which is not some modification of power. And this branch rises as naturally as the other two branches, from terror, the common stock of every thing that is sublime. The idea of power at first view, seems of the class of these indifferent ones, which may equally belong to pain or to pleasure. But in reality, the affection arising from the idea of vast power, is extremely remote from that neutral character. For first, we must remember, that the idea of pain, in its highest degree, is much stronger than the highest degree of pleasure; and that it preserves the same superiority through all the subordinate grada-tions. From hence it is, that where the chances for equal degrees of suffering or enjoyment are in any sort equal, the idea of the suffering must always be prevalent. And indeed the ideas of pain, and above all of death, are so very affecting, that whilst we remain in the presence of whatever is supposed to have the power of inflicting either, it is impossible to be perfectly free from terror. Again, we know by experience, that for the enjoyment of pleasure, no great efforts of power are at all necessary; nay we know, that such efforts would go a great way towards destroying our satisfaction: for pleasure must be stolen, and not forced upon us; pleasure follows the will; and therefore we are generally affected with it by many things of a force greatly inferior to our own. But pain is always inflicted by a power in some way superior, because we never submit to pain willingly. So that strength, violence, pain and terror, are ideas that rush in upon the mind together.

Look at a man, or any other animal of prodigious strength, and what is your idea before reflection? Is it that this strength will be subservient to you, to your ease, to your pleasure, to your interest in any sense? No; the emotion you feel is, lest this enormous strength should be employed to the purposes of rapine and destruction. That power derives all its sublimity from the terror with

3. Job 4: 13–17.

which it is generally accompanied, will appear evidently from its effect in the very few cases, in which it may be possible to strip a considerable degree of strength of its ability to hurt. When you do this, you spoil it of everything sublime, and it immediately becomes contemptible. An ox is a creature of vast strength; but he is an innocent creature, extremely serviceable, and not at all dangerous; for which reason the idea of an ox is by no means grand. A bull is strong too; but his strength is of another kind; often very destructive, seldom (at least amongst us) of any use in our business; the idea of a bull is therefore great, and it has frequently a place in sublime descriptions, and elevating comparisons.

Let us look at another strong animal in the two distinct lights in which we may consider him. The horse in the light of an useful beast, fit for the plough, the road, the draft, in every social useful light the horse has nothing of the sublime; but is it thus that we are affected with him, *whose neck is clothed with thunder, the glory of whose nostrils is terrible, who swalloweth the ground with fierceness and rage, neither believeth that it is the sound of the trumpet?* [4] In this description the useful character of the horse entirely disappears, and the terrible and sublime blaze out together. We have continually about us animals of a strength that is considerable, but not pernicious. Amongst these we never look for the sublime: it comes upon us in the gloomy forest, and in the howling wilderness, in the form of the lion, the tiger, the panther, or rhinoceros. Whenever strength is only useful, and employed for our benefit or our pleasure, then it is never sublime; for nothing can act agreeably to us, that does not act in conformity to our will; but to act agreeably to our will, it must be subject to us; and therefore can never be the cause of a grand and commanding conception. . . .

The power which arises from institution in kings and commanders, has the same connection with terror. Sovereigns are frequently addressed with the title of *dread majesty*. And it may be observed that young persons little acquainted with the world, and who have not been used to approach men in power, are commonly struck with an awe which takes away the free use of their faculties. *When I prepared my seat in the street* (says Job) *the young men saw me, and hid themselves.*[5] Indeed so natural is this timidity with regard to power, and so strongly does it inhere in our constitution, that very few are able to conquer it, but by mixing much in the business of the great world, or by using no small violence to their natural dispositions. I know some people are of opinion, that no awe, no degree of terror, accompanies the idea of power, and have hazarded to affirm, that we can contemplate the idea of God himself without any such emotion. . . . Now, though in a just idea of the Deity, perhaps none of his attributes are predominant, yet to our imagination, his power is by far the most striking. Some reflection, some comparing is necessary to satisfy us of his wisdom, his justice, and his goodness; to be struck with his power, it is only necessary that we should open our eyes. But whilst we contemplate so vast an object, under the arm, as it were, of almighty power, and invested upon every side with omnipresence, we shrink into the minuteness of

4. Job 39: 19, 20, 24 (somewhat misquoted, as are most of Burke's quotations, but they have not been altered here).
5. Job 29: 7, 8.

our own nature, and are, in a manner, annihilated before him. And though a consideration of his other attributes may relieve in some measure our apprehensions; yet no conviction of the justice with which it is exercised, nor the mercy with which it is tempered, can wholly remove the terror that naturally arises from a force which nothing can withstand. If we rejoice, we rejoice with trembling; and even whilst we are receiving benefits, we cannot but shudder at a power which can confer benefits of such mighty importance. When the prophet David contemplated the wonders of wisdom and power, which are displayed in the economy of man, he seems to be struck with a sort of divine horror, and cries out, *fearfully and wonderfully am I made!* [6] . . . The Psalms and the prophetical books are crouded with instances of this kind. *The earth shook* (says the psalmist) *the heavens also dropped at the presence of the Lord.*[7] And what is remarkable, the painting preserves the same character, not only when he is supposed descending to take vengeance upon the wicked, but even when he exerts the like plenitude of power in acts of beneficence to mankind. *Tremble, thou earth! at the presence of the Lord; at the presence of the God of Jacob; which turned the rock into standing water, the flint into a fountain of waters!* [8] It were endless to enumerate all the passages both in the sacred and profane writers, which establish the general sentiment of mankind, concerning the inseparable union of a sacred and reverential awe, with our ideas of the divinity. . . . Thus we have traced power through its several gradations unto the highest of all, where our imagination is finally lost; and we find terror quite throughout the progress, its inseparable companion, and growing along with it, as far as we can possibly trace them. Now as power is undoubtedly a capital source of the sublime, this will point out evidently from whence its energy is derived, and to what class of ideas we ought to unite it. . . .

[*From* Part III: The Sublime and Beautiful Compared]

On closing this general view of beauty, it naturally occurs, that we should compare it with the sublime; and in this comparison there appears a remarkable contrast. For sublime objects are vast in their dimensions, beautiful ones comparatively small; beauty should be smooth, and polished; the great, rugged and negligent; beauty should shun the right line, yet deviate from it insensibly; the great in many cases loves the right line, and when it deviates, it often makes a strong deviation; beauty should not be obscure; the great ought to be dark and gloomy; beauty should be light and delicate; the great ought to be solid, and even massive. They are indeed ideas of a very different nature, one being founded on pain, the other on pleasure; and however they may vary afterwards from the direct nature of their causes, yet these causes keep up an eternal distinction between them, a distinction never to be forgotten by any whose business it is to affect the passions. In the infinite variety of natural combinations we must expect to find the qualities of things the most remote imaginable from each other united in the same object. We must expect

6. Psalms 139: 14.
7. Psalms 68: 8.
8. Psalms 114: 7-8.

also to find combinations of the same kind in the works of art. But when we consider the power of an object upon our passions, we must know that when anything is intended to affect the mind by the force of some predominant property, the affection produced is like to be the more uniform and perfect, if all the other properties or qualities of the object be of the same nature, and tending to the same design as the principal;

> If black, and white blend, soften, and unite,
> A thousand ways, are there no black and white? [9]

If the qualities of the sublime and beautiful are sometimes found united, does this prove that they are the same, does it prove that they are any way allied, does it prove even that they are not opposite and contradictory? Black and white may soften, may blend, but they are not therefore the same. Nor when they are so softened and blended with each other, or with different colours, is the power of black as black, or of white as white, so strong as when each stands uniform and distinguished.

[*From* Part V]

. . . In reality poetry and rhetoric do not succeed in exact description so well as painting does; their business is to affect rather by sympathy than imitation; to display rather the effect of things on the mind of the speaker, or of others, than to present a clear idea of the things themselves. This is their most extensive province, and that in which they succeed the best.

Hence we may observe that poetry, taken in its most general sense, cannot with strict propriety be called an art of imitation. It is indeed an imitation so far as it describes the manners and passions of men which their words can express. . . . But *descriptive* poetry operates chiefly by *substitution;* by the means of sounds, which by custom have the effect of realities. Nothing is an imitation further than as it resembles some other thing; and words undoubtedly have no sort of resemblance to the ideas for which they stand.

Now, as words affect, not by any original power, but by representation, it might be supposed, that their influence over the passions should be but light; yet it is quite otherwise; for we find by experience that eloquence and poetry are as capable, nay indeed much more capable of making deep and lively impressions than any other arts, and even than nature itself in very many cases. And this arises chiefly from these three causes. First, that we take an extraordinary part in the passions of others, and that we are easily affected and brought into sympathy by any tokens which are shown of them; and there are no tokens which can express all the circumstances of most passions so fully as words; so that if a person speaks upon any subject, he can not only convey the subject to you, but likewise the manner in which he is himself affected by it. Certain it is, that the influence of most things on our passions is not so much from the things themselves, as from our opinions concerning them; and these again depend very much on the opinions of other men, conveyable for the most part by words only. Secondly; there are many things of

9. Pope, *Essay on Man* II.213–14; properly "If white and black blend, soften, and unite / A thousand ways, is there no black or white?"

a very affecting nature, which can seldom occur in the reality, but the words which represent them often do; and thus they have an opportunity of making a deep impression and taking root in the mind, whilst the idea of the reality was transient; and to some perhaps never really occurred in any shape, to whom it is notwithstanding very affecting, as war, death, famine, etc. Besides, many ideas have never been at all presented to the senses of any men but by words, as God, angels, devils, heaven and hell, all of which have however a great influence over the passions. Thirdly; by words we have it in our power to make such *combinations* as we cannot possibly do otherwise. By this power of combining we are able, by the addition of well-chosen circumstances, to give a new life and force to the simple object.

In painting we may represent any fine figure we please; but we never can give it those enlivening touches which it may receive from words. To represent an angel in a picture, you can only draw a beautiful young man winged; but what painting can furnish out any thing so grand as the addition of one word, 'the angel of the *Lord*.' It is true, I have here no clear idea, but these words affect the mind more than the sensible image did, which is all I contend for. . . . As a further instance, let us consider those lines of Milton, where he describes the travels of the fallen angels through their dismal habitation,

> ————O'er many a dark and dreary vale
> They passed, and many a region dolorous;
> O'er many a frozen, many a fiery Alp;
> Rock, caves, lakes, fens, bogs, dens and shades of death,
> A universe of death.[10]

Here is displayed the force of union in

> Rocks, caves, lakes, dens, bogs, fens and shades;

which yet would lose the greatest part of their effect, if they were not the

> Rocks, caves, lakes, dens, bogs, fens and shades————
> ————of *Death*.

This idea or this affection caused by a word, which nothing but a word could annex to the others, raises a very great degree of the sublime; and this sublime is raised yet higher by what follows, a *'universe of Death.'*

Here are again two ideas not presentable but by language; and an union of them great and amazing beyond conception; if they may properly be called ideas which present no distinct image to the mind;—but still it will be difficult to conceive how words can move the passions which belong to real objects, without representing these objects clearly. This is difficult to us, because we do not sufficiently distinguish, in our observations upon language, between a clear expression and a strong expression. These are frequently confounded with each other, though they are in reality extremely different. The former regards the understanding; the latter belongs to the passions. The one describes a thing as it is; the other describes it as it is felt. Now, as there is a moving tone of voice, an impassioned countenance, an agitated gesture,

10. *Paradise Lost* II.618–22.

which affect independently of the things about which they are exerted, so there are words, and certain dispositions of words, which being peculiarly devoted to passionate subjects and always used by those who are under the influence of any passion; they touch and move us more than those which far more clearly and distinctly express the subject matter. We yield to sympathy, what we refuse to description. The truth is, all verbal description, merely as naked description, though never so exact, conveys so poor and insufficient an idea of the thing described that it could scarcely have the smallest effect, if the speaker did not call in to his aid those modes of speech that mark a strong and lively feeling in himself. Then, by the contagion of our passions, we catch a fire already kindled in another, which probably might never have been struck out by the object described. Words, by strongly conveying the passions, by those means which we have already mentioned, fully compensate for their weakness in other respects. It may be observed that very polished languages, and such as are praised for their superior clearness and perspicuity, are generally deficient in strength. The French language has that perfection, and that defect. Whereas the oriental tongues, and in general the languages of most unpolished people, have a great force and energy of expression; and this is but natural. Uncultivated people are but ordinary observers of things, and not critical in distinguishing them; but, for that reason, they admire more, and are more affected with what they see, and therefore express themselves in a warmer and more passionate manner. If the affection be well conveyed, it will work its effect without any clear idea; often without any idea at all of the thing which has originally given rise to it.

1747-57?   1759

SIR JOSHUA REYNOLDS
1723–1792

"He possessed the theory as perfectly as the practice of his art. To be such a painter, he was a profound and penetrating philosopher." So Edmund Burke wrote in Reynolds's obituary. Boswell, dedicating to Reynolds his *Life of Johnson*, paid tribute to his "equal and placid temper," his "variety of conversation," his "true politeness," and the hospitality which made Reynolds's house "a common centre of union for the great, the accomplished, the learned, and the ingenious." Reynolds achieved greater prestige and wealth than any English painter had before him, and he achieved them early and easily.

Born in Devonshire, he went to London in 1740 to study with the portrait painter Thomas Hudson, and after seven years of practice spent two years in Italy studying the "grand style" of his predecessors. Within two or three years of his return, he became the most successful portrait painter in England. In 1764 he helped form the Literary Club, which gave Johnson, Burke, Goldsmith, and others an occasion for weekly conversations. Four years later he helped organize the Royal Academy and became its president for the rest of his life, giving in all fifteen presidential lectures to the students. These discourses, which show at least some influence of Johnson, are a fine statement of principles, shifting, within a consistent system, to a greater and greater stress upon those qualities that go beyond imitation and beyond narrowly rational limits. In the thirteenth discourse, especially, Reynolds insists upon the artifice of all art and yet relates that artifice to the demands of the imagination, much as Johnson does in his repudiation of rationalistic rules that might delimit the full illusion of dramatic art.

In his own painting Reynolds did not so much achieve the grand style as constantly allude to it: through "borrowings" from classical and Renaissance works of art; through the mock-heroic device of placing children in heroic poses; through allusions that set up ironies, such as that of David Garrick laughingly divided between the appeals of Comedy and Tragedy in the pose of Hercules at the Crossroads, choosing between Virtue and Vice. (See examples of Reynolds's paintings in illustration section.)

From Discourses

[The Grand Style]

It is not easy to define in what this great style [1] consists; nor to describe, by words, the proper means of acquiring it, if the mind of the student should be at all capable of such an acquisition. Could we teach taste or genius by rules, they would be no longer taste and genius. But though there neither are, nor can be, any precise invariable rules for the exercise, or the acquisition, of these great qualities, yet we may truly say that they always operate in proportion to our attention in observing the works of nature, to our skill in selecting, and to our care in digesting, methodizing, and comparing our observations. There are many beauties in our art, that seem, at first, to lie without the reach of precept, and yet may easily be reduced to practical principles. Experience is all in all; but it is not every one who profits by experience; and most people err, not so much from want of capacity to find their object, as from not knowing what object to pursue. This great ideal perfection and beauty are not to be sought in the heavens, but upon earth. They are about us, and upon every side of us. But the power of discovering what is deformed in nature, or in other words, what is particular and uncommon, can be acquired only by experience; and the whole beauty and grandeur of the art consists, in my opinion, in being able to get above all singular forms, local customs, particularities, and details of every kind.

All the objects which are exhibited to our view by nature, upon close examination will be found to have their blemishes and defects. The most beautiful forms have something about them like weakness, minuteness, or

1. That style which receives its perfection "from an ideal beauty, superior to what is found in individual nature." Reynolds mocks the "splendour of figurative declamation" (largely Platonic or neoplatonic) used to describe this style and tries to give it a humbler and more accessible guise. Here he offers an empirical approach to the "perfect state of nature," a method of discerning through "sober" study the tendencies that actual nature strives to realize but always falls short of attaining. This conception of Nature as a form that can be glimpsed or (more properly) surmised through its imperfect embodiment in individuals underlies Aristotle's theory of poetry (and particularly his view that poetry is more philosophical than history since it can depart from the actual and realize the latent tendency). Reynolds avoids any mystical effort to achieve an ecstatic vision of the ideal form in its nakedness and immediacy.

imperfection. But it is not every eye that perceives these blemishes. It must be an eye long used to the contemplation and comparison of these forms; and which, by a long habit of observing what any set of objects of the same kind have in common, has acquired the power of discerning what each wants in particular. This long laborious comparison should be the first study of the painter, who aims at the greatest style. By this means, he acquires a just idea of beautiful forms; he corrects nature by herself, her imperfect state by her more perfect. His eye being enabled to distinguish the accidental deficiencies, excrescences, and deformities of things, from their general figures, he makes out an abstract idea of their forms more perfect than any one original; and what may seem a paradox, he learns to design naturally by drawing his figures unlike to any one object. This idea of the perfect state of nature, which the artist calls the ideal beauty, is the great leading principle, by which works of genius are conducted. By this Phidias acquired his fame. He wrought upon a sober principle what has so much excited the enthusiasm of the world; and by this method you, who have courage to tread the same path, may acquire equal reputation.

This is the idea which has acquired and which seems to have a right to the epithet of *divine;* as it may be said to preside, like a supreme judge, over all the productions of nature; appearing to be possessed of the will and intention of the Creator as far as they regard the external form of living beings. When a man once possesses this idea in its perfection, there is no danger but that he will be sufficiently warmed by it himself, and be able to warm and ravish every one else.

Thus it is from a reiterated experience, and a close comparison of the objects in nature, than an artist becomes possessed of the idea of that central form, if I may so express it, from which every deviation is deformity. [From *Discourse III,* 1770]

[Poetic and Literal Truth]
The great end of the art is to strike the imagination. The painter is therefore to make no ostentation of the means by which this is done; the spectator is only to feel the result in his bosom. An inferior artist is unwilling that any part of his industry should be lost upon the spectator. He takes as much pains to discover, as the greater artist does to conceal, the marks of his subordinate assiduity. In works of the lower kind, everything appears studied and encumbered; it is all boastful art and open affectation. The ignorant often part from such pictures with wonder in their mouths and indifference in their hearts.[2]

But it is not enough in invention that the artist should restrain and keep under all the inferior parts of his subject; he must sometimes deviate from vulgar and strict historical truth, in pursuing the grandeur of his design.

How much the great style exacts from its professors to conceive and represent their subjects in a poetical manner, not confined to mere matter of fact,

2. One may compare Dryden on the false wit of such poets as Cleveland, Pope on false wit in the *Essay on Criticism* and the *Epistle to Burlington,* and Johnson on the Metaphysical poets.

may be seen in the cartoons of Raffaelle.[3] In all the pictures in which the painter has represented the apostles, he has drawn them with great nobleness; he has given them as much dignity as the human figure is capable of receiving; yet we are expressly told in scripture they had no such respectable appearance; and of St. Paul in particular, we are told by himself, that his *bodily* presence was *mean*. Alexander is said to have been of a low stature: a painter ought not so to represent him. Agesilaus was low, lame, and of a mean appearance: none of these defects ought to appear in a piece of which he is the hero.[4] In conformity to custom, I call this part of the art history painting; it ought to be called poetical, as in reality it is.

All this is not falsifying any fact; it is taking an allowed poetical licence. A painter of portraits retains the individual likeness; a painter of history shows the man by showing his actions. A painter must compensate the natural deficiencies of his art. He has but one sentence to utter, but one moment to exhibit. He cannot, like the poet or historian, expatiate, and impress the mind with great veneration for the character of the hero or saint he represents, though he lets us know at the same time that the saint was deformed or the hero lame. The painter has no other means of giving an idea of the dignity of the mind but by that external appearance which grandeur of thought does generally, though not always, impress on the countenance; and by that correspondence of figure to sentiment and situation, which all men wish, but cannot command. The painter, who may in this one particular attain with ease what others desire in vain, ought to give all that he possibly can, since there are so many circumstances of true greatness that he cannot give at all. He cannot make his hero talk like a great man; he must make him look like one. For which reason, he ought to be well studied in the analysis of those circumstances which constitute dignity of appearance in real life. [From *Discourse IV*, 1771]

[The Pleasures of the Mind]
He who thinks nature, in the narrow sense of the word, is alone to be followed, will produce but a scanty entertainment for the imagination: everything is to be done with which it is natural for the mind to be pleased, whether it proceeds from simplicity or variety, uniformity or irregularity; whether the scenes are familiar or exotic; rude and wild, or enriched and cultivated; for it is natural for the mind to be pleased with all these in their turn. In short, whatever pleases has in it what is analogous to the mind, and is therefore, in the highest and best sense of the word, natural.[5]

3. The Raphael cartoons are full-scale tapestry designs; the seven that survive were in Hampton Court during much of the 18th century; they are now at the Victoria and Albert Museum in London.
4. II Corinthians 10:10, "his bodily presence is weak, and his speech contemptible." Alexander the Great (356–323 B.C.) became the subject of heroic legends even during his lifetime. Agesilaus (c. 444–360 B.C.) was King of Sparta, renowned as a conqueror of both Persians and fellow Greeks, celebrated by Xenophon and Plutarch.
5. Compare Addison's papers on "The Pleasures of the Imagination" (see The Garden and the Wild). Reynolds is psychologizing the idea of nature; in *Discourse III* it is approached empirically through outward or objective natural forms, but here it is sought in "what is analogous to the mind." One can see a similar tendency in Johnson's treatment of "general nature" in the Preface to Shakespeare.

It is the sense of nature or truth which ought more particularly to be cultivated by the professors of art; and it may be observed, that many wise and
learned men, who have accustomed their minds to admit nothing for truth but
what can be proved by mathematical demonstration, have seldom any relish
for those arts which address themselves to the fancy, the rectitude and truth
of which is known by another kind of proof: and we may add, that the
acquisition of this knowledge requires as much circumspection and sagacity,
as is necessary to attain those truths which are more capable of demonstration.
Reason must ultimately determine our choice on every occasion; but this
reason may still be exerted ineffectually by applying to taste principles which,
though right as far as they go, yet do not reach the object. No man, for
instance, can deny that it seems at first view very reasonable . . . that a
statue which is to carry down to posterity the resemblance of an individual,
should be dressed in the fashion of the times, in the dress which he himself
wore: this would certainly be true if the dress were part of the man; but after
a time, the dress is only an amusement for an antiquarian; and if it obstructs
the general design of the piece, it is to be disregarded by the artist. Common
sense must here give way to a higher sense. In the naked form, and in the
disposition of the drapery, the difference between one artist and another is
principally seen. But if he is compelled to exhibit the modern dress, the naked
form is entirely hid, and the drapery is already disposed by the skill of the
tailor. Were a Phidias to obey such absurd commands, he would please no
more than an ordinary sculptor; since in the inferior parts of every art, the
learned and the ignorant are nearly upon a level. [From *Discourse VII*, 1776]

[Minute Particulars]
. . . At the same time I do not forget, that a painter must have the power of
contracting as well as dilating his sight; because, he that does not at all
express particulars, expresses nothing; yet it is certain, that a nice discrimination of minute circumstances, and a punctilious delineation of them, whatever
excellence it may have (and I do not mean to detract from it), never did
confer on the artist the character of genius.

Beside those minute differences in things which are frequently not observed
at all, and, when they are, make little impression, there are in all considerable
objects great characteristic distinctions which press strongly on the senses, and
therefore fix the imagination. These are by no means, as some persons think,
an aggregate [6] of all the small discriminating particulars; nor will such an
accumulation of particulars ever express them. These answer to what I have
heard great lawyers call the leading points in a case, or the leading cases
relative to those points.

The detail of particulars which does not assist the expression of the main
characteristic is worse than useless; it is mischievous as it dissipates the attention and draws it from the principal point. It may be remarked that the
impression which is left on our mind, even of things which are familiar to us,
is seldom more than their general effect; beyond which we do not look in
recognising such objects. To express this in painting, is to express what is

---

6. Reynolds contrasts the mere "aggregate" with the "general effect of the whole" or the
"great characteristic distinctions," implying in the latter terms a principle of unity.

congenial and natural to the mind of man, and what gives him by reflection his own mode of conceiving. The other presupposes *nicety* and *research,* which are only the business of the curious and attentive, and therefore does not speak to the general sense of the whole species; in which common, and, as I may so call it, mother tongue, every thing grand and comprehensive must be uttered.

I do not mean to prescribe what degree of attention ought to be paid to the minute parts; this it is hard to settle. We are sure that it is expressing the general effect of the whole which alone can give to objects their true and touching character; and wherever this is observed, whatever else may be neglected, we acknowledge the hand of a master. We may even go further, and observe, that when the general effect only is presented to us by a skilful hand, it appears to express the object represented in a more lively manner than the minutest resemblance would do. [From *Discourse XI,* 1782]

[Art and Illusion]
I observe, as a fundamental ground, common to all the arts with which we have any concern in this discourse, that they address themselves only to two faculties of the mind, its imagination and its sensibility.

All theories which attempt to direct or control the art upon any principles falsely called rational, which we form to ourselves upon a supposition of what ought in reason to be the end or means of art, independent of the known first effect produced by objects on the imagination, must be false and delusive. For though it may appear bold to say it, the imagination is here the residence of truth. If the imagination be affected, the conclusion is fairly drawn; if it be not affected, the reasoning is erroneous, because the end is not obtained; the effect itself being the test, and the only test, of the truth and efficacy of the means.

There is in the commerce of life, as in art, a sagacity which is far from being contradictory to right reason, and is superior to any occasional exercise of that faculty, which supersedes it; and does not wait for the slow progress of deduction, but goes at once, by what appears a kind of intuition, to the conclusion. A man endowed with this faculty feels and acknowledges the truth though it is not always in his power, perhaps, to give a reason for it; because he cannot recollect and bring before him all the materials that gave birth to his opinion; for very many and very intricate considerations may unite to form the principle, even of small and minute parts involved in, or dependent on, a great system of things: though these in process of time are forgotten, the right impression still remains fixed in his mind.

This impression is the result of the accumulated experience of our whole life, and has been collected, we do not always know how or when. But this mass of collective observation, however acquired, ought to prevail over that reason which, however powerfully exerted on any particular occasion, will probably comprehend but a partial view of the subject; and our conduct in life as well as in the arts is, or ought to be, generally governed by this habitual reason: it is our happiness that we are enabled to draw on such funds. If we were obliged to enter into a theoretical deliberation on every occasion, before we act, life would be at a stand, and art would be impracticable.

It appears to me therefore, that our first thoughts, that is, the effect which anything produces on our minds on its first appearance, is never to be forgotten; and it demands for that reason, because it is the first, to be laid up with care. If this be not done, the artist may happen to impose on himself by partial reasoning; by a cold consideration of those animated thoughts which proceed, not perhaps from caprice or rashness (as he may afterwards conceit [7]), but from the fullness of his mind, enriched with the copious stores of all the various inventions which he had ever seen or had ever passed in his mind. These ideas are infused into his design without any conscious effort; but if he be not on his guard, he may reconsider and correct them till the whole matter is reduced to a commonplace invention.

This is sometimes the effect of what I mean to caution you against; that is to say, an unfounded distrust of the imagination and feeling in favour of narrow, partial, confined, argumentative theories; and of principles that seem to apply to the design in hand; without considering those general impressions on the fancy in which real principles of *sound reason,* and of much more weight and importance, are involved and, as it were, lie hid under the appearance of a sort of vulgar sentiment.

Reason, without doubt, must ultimately determine every thing; at this minute it is required to inform us when that very reason is to give way to feeling.

Though I have often spoke of that mean conception of our art which confines it to mere imitation, I must add that it may be narrowed to such a mere matter of experiment as to exclude from it the application of science, which alone gives dignity and compass to any art. But to find proper foundations for science is neither to narrow or to vulgarise it; and this is sufficiently exemplified in the success of experimental philosophy. It is the false system of reasoning grounded on a partial view of things against which I would most earnestly guard you. And I do it the rather, because those narrow theories, so coincident with the poorest and most miserable practice, and which are adopted to give it countenance, have not had their origin in the poorest minds, but in the mistakes, or possibly in the mistaken interpretations, of great and commanding authorities. We are not therefore in this case misled by feeling, but by false speculation.

. . . For this reason I shall beg leave to lay before you a few thoughts on this subject; to throw out some hints that may lead your minds to an opinion (which I take to be the truth) that painting is not only not to be considered as an imitation, operating by deception, but that it is, and ought to be, in many points of view and strictly speaking, no imitation at all of external nature. Perhaps it ought to be as far removed from the vulgar idea of imitation, as the refined civilized state in which we live is removed from a gross state of nature; and those who have not cultivated their imaginations, which the majority of mankind certainly have not, may be said, in regard to arts, to continue in this state of nature. Such men will always prefer imitation to that excellence which is addressed to another faculty that they do not possess; but these are not the persons to whom a painter is to look,

7. Imagine.

any more than a judge of morals and manners ought to refer controverted points upon those subjects to the opinions of people taken from the banks of the Ohio, or from New Holland.[8]

Poetry addresses itself to the same faculties and the same dispositions as painting, though by different means. The object of both is to accommodate itself to all the natural propensities and inclinations of the mind. The very existence of poetry depends on the licence it assumes of deviating from actual nature, in order to gratify natural propensities by other means which are found by experience full as capable of affording such gratification. It sets out with a language in the highest degree artificial, a construction of measured words, such as never is, nor ever was used by man. Let this measure be what it may, whether hexameter or any other metre used in Latin or Greek,—or rhyme, or blank verse varied with pauses and accents, in modern languages,—they are all equally removed from nature, and equally a violation of common speech. When this artificial mode has been established as the vehicle of sentiment, there is another principle in the human mind, to which the work must be referred, which still renders it more artificial, carries it still further from common nature, and deviates only to render it more perfect. That principle is the sense of congruity, coherence, and consistency, which is a real existing principle in man; and it must be gratified. Therefore having once adopted a style and a measure not found in common discourse, it is required that the sentiments also should be in the same proportion elevated above common nature, from the necessity of there being an agreement of the parts among themselves, that one uniform whole may be produced.

To correspond therefore with this general system of deviation from nature, the manner in which poetry is offered to the ear, the tone in which it is recited, should be as far removed from the tone of conversation, as the words of which that poetry is composed. This naturally suggests the idea of modulating the voice by art, which I suppose may be considered as accomplished to the highest degree of excellence in the recitative of the Italian opera; as we may conjecture it was in the chorus that attended the ancient drama. And though the most violent passions, the highest distress, even death itself, are expressed in singing or recitative, I would not admit as sound criticism the condemnation of such exhibitions on account of their being unnatural.

. . . Shall reason stand in the way, and tell us we ought not to like what we know we do like, and prevent us from feeling the full effect of this complicated exertion of art? This is what I would understand by poets and painters being allowed to dare everything; for what can be more daring, than accomplishing the purpose and end of art, by a complication of means, none of which have their archetypes in actual nature?

So far therefore is servile imitation from being necessary, that whatever is familiar, or in any way reminds us of what we see and hear every day, perhaps does not belong to the higher provinces of art, either in poetry or painting.

8. Presumably a reference to the natives rather than the colonists of America and Australia.

The mind is to be transported, as Shakespeare expresses it, 'beyond the ignorant present,' to ages past. Another and a higher order of beings is supposed; and to those beings every thing which is introduced into the work must correspond. Of this conduct, under these circumstances, the Roman and Florentine schools afford sufficient examples. Their style by this means is raised and elevated above all others; and by the same means the compass of art itself is enlarged.

We often see grave and great subjects attempted by artists of another school; who, though excellent in the lower class of art, proceeding on the principles which regulate that class, and not recollecting, or not knowing, that they were to address themselves to another faculty of the mind, have become perfectly ridiculous.

The picture which I have at present in my thoughts is a sacrifice of Iphigenia, painted by Jan Steen . . . even in this picture, the subject of which is by no means adapted to his genius, there is nature and expression; but it is such expression, and the countenances are so familiar, and consequently so vulgar, and the whole accompanied with such finery of silks and velvet, that one would be almost tempted to doubt, whether the artist did not purposely intend to burlesque his subject.

Instances of the same kind we frequently see in poetry. Parts of Hobbes's translation of Homer are remembered and repeated merely for the familiarity and meanness of their phraseology, so ill corresponding with the ideas which ought to have been expressed, and, as I conceive, with the style of the original.[9]

If we suppose a view of nature represented with all the truth of the *camera obscura*,[10] and the same scene represented by a great artist, how little and mean will the one appear in comparison of the other. . . . With what additional superiority then will the same artist appear when he has the power of selecting his materials as well as elevating his style? Like Nicolas Poussin, he transports us to the environs of ancient Rome, with all the objects which a literary education make so precious and interesting to man: or, like Sebastian Bourdon, he leads us to the dark antiquity of the pyramids of Egypt; or, like Claude Lorrain, he conducts us to the tranquillity of Arcadian scenes and fairy land.[11]

Like the history-painter, a painter of landscapes in this style and with this conduct, sends the imagination back into antiquity; and, like the poet, he makes the elements sympathise with his subject: whether the clouds roll in volumes like those of Titian or Salvator Rosa,[12]—or, like those of Claude, are gilded with the setting sun; whether the mountains have sudden or bold

9. Hobbes's lame translations of the *Odyssey* and the *Iliad* appeared in 1673 and 1676.
10. The *camera obscura* was an optical device for producing an image on the wall of a darkened room; it was used as an aid by painters such as Vermeer, but it would have in itself only such weight as a documentary photograph might have in relation to a painting.
11. Nicolas Poussin (1594–1665), important French painter resident in Rome for most of his career; Sebastian Bourdon (1616–71), an imitator of Poussin among others; Claude Lorrain (1600–1682), the landscape painter—all painters of "ideal" landscapes.
12. Titian (*c.* 1490–1576), the great Venetian painter; Salvator Rosa (1615–73), known especially for landscapes of wild and savage scenes, much admired in the 18th century.

projections, or are gently sloped; whether the branches of his trees shoot out abruptly in right angles from their trunks, or follow each other with only a gentle inclination. All these circumstances contribute to the general character of the work whether it be of the elegant or of the more sublime kind. If we add to this the powerful materials of lightness and darkness, over which the artist has complete dominion, to vary and dispose them as he pleases; to diminish, or increase them as will best suit his purpose, and correspond to the general idea of his work: a landscape thus conducted, under the influence of a poetical mind, will have the same superiority over the more ordinary and common views, as Milton's 'Allegro' and 'Penseroso' have over a cold prosaic narration or description; and such a picture would make a more forcible impression on the mind than the real scenes, were they presented before us.

.   .   .

The theatre, which is said 'to hold the mirrour up to nature,'[13] comprehends both those ideas. The lower kind of comedy, or farce, like the inferior style of painting, the more naturally it is represented, the better; but the higher appears to me to aim no more at imitation, so far as it belongs to any thing like deception, or to expect that the spectators should think that the events there represented are really passing before them, than Raffaelle in his cartoons, or Poussin in his sacraments,[14] expected it to be believed, even for a moment, that what they exhibited were real figures.

For want of this distinction, the world is filled with false criticism. Raffaelle is praised for naturalness and deception, which he certainly has not accomplished, and as certainly never intended; and our late great actor, Garrick, has been as ignorantly praised by his friend Fielding; who doubtless imagined he had hit upon an ingenious device, by introducing in one of his novels (otherwise a work of the highest merit) an ignorant man, mistaking Garrick's representation of a scene in Hamlet, for reality.[15] A very little reflection will convince us, that there is not one circumstance in the whole scene that is of the nature of deception. The merit and excellence of Shakespeare, and of Garrick, when they were engaged in such scenes, is of a different and much higher kind. But what adds to the falsity of this intended compliment is that the best stage-representation appears even more unnatural to a person of such a character, who is supposed never to have seen a play before, than it does to those who have had a habit of allowing for those necessary deviations from nature which the art requires.

.   .   .

Though I have no intention of entering into all the circumstances of unnaturalness in theatrical representations, I must observe that even the expression of violent passion is not always the most excellent in proportion as it is the most natural: so great terror and such disagreeable sensations

13. *Hamlet* III.ii.24.
14. Poussin did two sets of paintings of the Seven Sacraments; one now hangs in the National Gallery of Scotland.
15. Partridge's response in *Tom Jones* (1749) XVI.xv is that of the naïve spectator who responds to a performance of *Hamlet* as if it were reality; later he sneers at the praise of David Garrick's performance: "I am sure, if I had seen a ghost, I should have looked in the very same manner, and done just as he did."

may be communicated to the audience that the balance may be destroyed by which pleasure is preserved and holds its predominancy in the mind: violent distortion of action, harsh screamings of the voice, however great the occasion, or however natural on such occasion, are therefore not admissible in the theatric art. Many of these allowed deviations from nature arise from the necessity which there is that everything should be raised and enlarged beyond its natural state; that the full effect may come home to the spectator, which otherwise would be lost in the comparatively extensive space of the theatre. Hence the deliberate and stately step, the studied grace of action, which seems to enlarge the dimensions of the actor, and alone to fill the stage. All this unnaturalness, though right and proper in its place, would appear affected and ridiculous in a private room. . . .

So also gardening, as far as gardening is an art, or entitled to that appellation, is a deviation from nature; for if the true taste consists, as many hold, in banishing every appearance of art, or any traces of the footsteps of man, it would then be no longer a garden. Even though we define it, 'Nature to advantage dressed,'[16] and in some sense it is such, and much more beautiful and commodious for the recreation of man; it is however, when so dressed, no longer a subject for the pencil[17] of a landscape-painter, as all landscape-painters know, who love to have recourse to nature herself, and to dress her according to the principles of their own art; which are far different from those of gardening,[18] even when conducted according to the most approved principles, and such as a landscape-painter himself would adopt in the disposition of his own grounds, for his own private satisfaction.

. . .

The great end of all those arts is, to make an impression on the imagination and the feeling. The imitation of nature frequently does this. Sometimes it fails, and something else succeeds. I think therefore the true test of all the arts, is not solely whether the production is a true copy of nature, but whether it answers the end of art, which is to produce a pleasing effect upon the mind.

It remains only to speak a few words of architecture, which does not come under the denomination of an imitative art. It applies itself, like music (and I believe we may add poetry), directly to the imagination, without the intervention of any kind of imitation.

. . .

To pass over the effect produced by that general symmetry and proportion, by which the eye is delighted, as the ear is with music, architecture certainly possesses many principles in common with poetry and painting. Among those which may be reckoned as the first, is, that of affecting the imagination by means of association of ideas. Thus, for instance, as we have naturally a veneration for antiquity, whatever building brings to our remembrance ancient

16. Pope on true wit, *Essay on Criticism*, l. 297.
17. Paintbrush.
18. Although in fact efforts were made to reproduce the effects of landscape painting in gardening, and the theory of the Picturesque sought to achieve in gardening the complexity of painted landscapes by Poussin, Claude, and Salvator Rosa. (See Figs. 21–23 for the example of Stourhead.)

customs and manners, such as the castles of the barons of ancient chivalry, is sure to give this delight. Hence it is that 'towers and battlements' [19] are so often selected by the painter and the poet, to make a part of the composition of their ideal landscape; and it is from hence in a great degree, that in the buildings of Vanbrugh,[20] who was a poet as well as an architect, there is a greater display of imagination, than we shall find perhaps in any other; and this is the ground of the effect which we feel in many of his works, notwithstanding the faults with which many of them are justly charged. For this purpose, Vanbrugh appears to have had recourse to some principles of the Gothic architecture; which, though not so ancient as the Grecian, is more so to our imagination, with which the artist is more concerned than with absolute truth.

.   .   .

It may not be amiss for the architect to take advantage *sometimes* of that to which I am sure the painter ought always to have his eyes open, I mean the use of accidents; to follow when they lead, and to improve them, rather than always to trust to a regular plan. It often happens that additions have been made to houses, at various times, for use or pleasure. As such buildings depart from regularity, they now and then acquire something of scenery by this accident, which I should think might not unsuccessfully be adopted by an architect, in an original plan, if it does not too much interfere with convenience. Variety and intricacy is a beauty and excellence in every other of the arts which address the imagination; and why not in architecture?

The forms and turnings of the streets of London, and other old towns, are produced by accident, without any original plan or design; but they are not always the less pleasant to the walker or spectator, on that account. On the contrary, if the city had been built on the regular plan of Sir Christopher Wren,[21] the effect might have been, as we know it is in some new parts of the town, rather unpleasing; the uniformity might have produced weariness, and a slight degree of disgust.

.   .   .

Upon the whole, it seems to me, that the object and intention of all the arts is to supply the natural imperfection of things, and often to gratify the mind by realising and embodying what never existed but in the imagination.

It is allowed on all hands, that facts, and events, however they may bind the historian, have no dominion over the poet or the painter. With us, history is made to bend and conform to this great idea of art. And why? Because these arts, in their highest province, are not addressed to the gross senses, but to the desires of the mind, to that spark of divinity which we have within, impatient of being circumscribed and pent up by the world which is about us.

---

19. " 'Towers and battlements it sees / Bosomed high in tufted trees,' Milton, *L'Allegro*" (Reynolds); ll. 77–78.

20. Sir John Vanbrugh (1664–1726), who turned to architecture after a successful career as playwright.

21. Wren's plan for rebuilding the city of London after the Great Fire of 1666 was a centralized baroque one; Reynolds's stress upon the value of accident and of the unplanned anticipates later Picturesque theories of Sir Uvedale Price and Richard Payne Knight.

Just so much as our art has of this, just so much of dignity, I had almost said of divinity, it exhibits; and those of our artists who possessed this mark of distinction in the highest degree, acquired from thence the glorious appellation of Divine. [From *Discourse XIII*, 1784]

1769–90?   1790

THE GARDEN AND THE WILD

The question this section raises is how one gets from the formal, geometric gardens of the seventeenth century to the mountain scenes of Wordsworth's Lake Country. It is a question that involves more than landscape, for the landscape is the outward and correspondent form of the mind that regards it (and in imagination creates it). Therefore the emergence of the natural scene becomes at the same time the discovery of new metaphors for the powers of mind.

This double movement is reflected in the forms it inspires. On the one hand there is a search for authentic images of nature, too vast or free to be controlled by human art, and corresponding to the native grandeur of untutored genius; on the other, there is the deliberate cultivation of an art that will be reflexive, that is, will reveal the processes of mind, more an expression of creative process than a finished and self-subsistent achievement. The first gives us new response to Alpine scenery, a passion for those ruins that show art being overwhelmed by nature, the love of broad prospects in space and deep recessions in time (through such monuments as Stonehenge or the ruins of ancient abbeys and castles). The second gives us artfully designed garden landscapes (with "follies," those architectural stage-props meant to be seen at a distance; miniature temples or shrines; vistas closed with emblematic statues) that are meant to evoke a carefully orchestrated set of associations, the sedulous creation (sometimes through sheer forgery) of primitive works (the Ossianic poems, the pseudo-medieval ballads of Thomas Chatterton), the whole pattern of revivals and exoticism that meant the trying on of costumes and roles. It is easy to mock the Pindarique and the Gothick, but giving them their eighteenth-century spelling only reminds us how much a creation of their time they were. What functions did they serve? (For examples of garden architecture and artificial ruins see Figs. 17, 18, 20, 21–23, 52, 55, 56.)

The movement away from a poetry of social reality is a movement toward more mysterious and less conscious aspects of mind, both grandeur and terror. The first effort to evoke these forces has a histrionic and melodramatic quality; men play at being bards or seers or ogres. Such play-acting is an effort to induce feelings that seem to have been buried, repressed, or brought into daylight only to be denounced and exorcised. Gray's creation of a Bard of more than human dimensions, placed in a landscape of extremes, delivering chant-like and magical prophecies—all this marks a shift from the clear, sharp image to the larger half-spectral fantasy that reminds us of our own part in creating it.

Two themes are conspicuous in many of these passages. The first is that man's process of perception creates the beauty he thinks he finds. While, as Addison makes clear, this emphasis is furthered by Locke's empirical philosophy, it lends itself to neoplatonic concern with the forming power of mind; and throughout the century one can see a division between those who stress the passive process of perception and those who stress the inherent shaping powers of mind. We can see the testing of these powers as they are made to embrace the most disorderly and extreme of natural scenes (as in Thomson's treatment of the blaze of summer noon or the turbulence of winter storms). Such scenes elicit an imaginative effort to capture their vivid concreteness and yet to order them as well within the larger harmony of nature. Such an effort, once rewarded, breeds impatience with easier forms of beauty that neither challenge our powers of response nor awaken them to self-awareness.

If the typical response to such challenge is exultation in the powers it summons up, what Johnson calls "a flattering notion of self-sufficiency," the alternative, as confidence ebbs, is a sense of human limitation. As Thomson pushes the winter scene into the far north of Lapland or Siberia, life subsides to mere grim and mindless survival; the sense of liberty and severe grandeur fades into chilling desperation as the more benign latitudes are too far exceeded. Johnson, typically enough, stresses the dark obverse of the tribute to man's intrinsic goodness or power, in the description of the Highlands as he does in *Rasselas*.

SIR WILLIAM TEMPLE
1628–1699

From Upon the Gardens of Epicurus [1]

What I have said of the best forms of gardens is meant only of such as are in some sort regular; for there may be other forms wholly irregular that may, for aught I know, have more beauty than any of the others; but they must

1. This essay was written after Sir William Temple's retirement in 1681 from a distinguished parliamentary and diplomatic career (during which he was ambassador to Holland and became a trusted adviser of William of Orange). While the essay includes a famous account of Moor Park in Hertfordshire (for which Temple named his own estate in Surrey), its most prophetic element is the account which follows of Chinese gardens, one of the earliest tributes in the age to irregularity. For while Temple claimed that Moor Park followed nature ("which I take to be the great rule in this, and perhaps everything else, as far as the conduct not only of our lives but our governments"), his account of it reveals a largely formal garden with a small, defined area that was "very wild, shady, and adorned with rough rock-work and fountains."

The source of the word *sharawadgi* is not known, although it bears some relationship (as has been suggested by Y. Z. Chang) to Chinese words that taken together might mean the "quality of being impressive or surprising through careless or unorderly grace." At any rate, Temple's knowledge of Chinese gardens may have come from printed reports of missionaries or travelers; from direct conversation with them; or from Chinese paintings, prints, and decorations in English collections.

Later Horace Walpole, in *The History of the Modern Taste in Gardening* (1771), reprinted this passage with adverse comments on the naturalness of Chinese gardens: "They are as whimsically irregular as European gardens are formally uniform and unvaried—but with regard to nature, it seems as much avoided as in the squares and oblongs and straight lines of our ancestors." The Chinese "have passed to one extremity of absurdity as the French and all antiquity had advanced to the other, both being equally remote from nature. . . ." But Walpole was writing after the vogue of the "natural garden" had established itself, and, as we see in Addison's *Spectator* No. 414, Temple's essay was illuminating and influential. Twenty years earlier (in 1750) Walpole himself had written with enthusiasm of the *sharawadgi*: "you will be pleased with the liberty of taste into which we are struck, and of which you can have no idea!"

owe it to some extraordinary dispositions of nature in the seat, or some great race of fancy or judgment in the contrivance, which may reduce many disagreeing parts into some figure, which shall yet, upon the whole, be very agreeable. Something of this I have seen in some places, but heard more of it from others who have lived much among the Chinese, a people whose way of thinking seems to lie as wide of ours in Europe, as their country does. Among us, the beauty of building and planting is placed chiefly in some certain proportions, symmetries, or uniformities; our walks and our trees ranged so as to answer one another, and at exact distances. The Chinese scorn this way of planting, and say, a boy that can tell an hundred may plant walks of trees in straight lines, and over against one another, and to what length and extent he pleases. But their greatest reach of imagination is employed in contriving figures where the beauty shall be great and strike the eye, but without any order or disposition of parts that shall be commonly or easily observed. And, though we have hardly any notion of this sort of beauty, yet they have a particular word to express it, and, where they find it hit their eye at first sight, they say the *sharawadgi* is fine or is admirable, or any such expression of esteem. And whoever observes the work upon the best India gowns or the painting upon their best screens or porcelains will find their beauty is all of this kind (that is) without order. But I should hardly advise any of these attempts in the figure of gardens among us; they are adventures of too hard achievement for any common hands; and, though there may be more honour if they succeed well, yet there is more dishonour if they fail, and 'tis twenty to one they will; whereas, in regular figures, 'tis hard to make any great and remarkable faults.

1685?   1690

ALEXANDER POPE

The Gardens of Alcinous°

Close to the gates a spacious garden lies,
From storms defended, and inclement skies:
Four acres was the allotted space of ground,
Fenced with a green enclosure all around.
Tall thriving trees confessed the fruitful mould;
The redening apple ripens here to gold,
Here the blue fig with luscious juice o'erflows,
With deeper red the full pomegranate glows,
Then branch here bends beneath the weighty pear,
10 And verdant olives flourish round the year.
The balmy spirit of the western gale
Eternal breathes on fruits untaught to fail:

The Gardens of Alcinous This translation from *Odyssey* VII was first published in *Guardian*, No. 173 and later included in the full translation of 1725 as VII.142–75. It represents one of the chief classical counterparts of the garden of Eden; it is various and fruitful but also significantly orderly, like Milton's version of Eden in *Paradise Lost* IV.

Each dropping pear a following pear supplies,
On apples apples, figs on figs arise:
The same mild season gives the blooms to blow,°
The buds to harden, and the fruits to grow.
  Here ordered vines in equal ranks appear
With all the united labours of the year;
Some to unload the fertile branches run,
20 Some dry the blackening clusters in the sun,
Others to tread the liquid harvest join,
The groaning presses foam with floods of wine.
Here are the vines in early flower descried,
Here grapes discoloured on the sunny side,
And there in autumn's richest purple dyed.
  Beds of all various herbs, forever green,
In beauteous order terminate the scene.
  Two plenteous fountains the whole prospect
    crowned;
This through the gardens leads its streams around,
30 Visits each plant, and waters all the ground:
While that in pipes beneath the palace flows,
And thence its current on the town bestows;
To various use their various streams they bring,
The people one, and one supplies the King.

                        1713

From Windsor Forest°

  The groves of Eden,° vanished now so long,
Live in description, and look green in song:
These, were my breast inspired with equal flame,
10 Like them in beauty, should be like in fame.
Here hills and vales, the woodland and the plain,
Here earth and water seem to strive again;
Not chaos-like together crushed and bruised,
But, as the world, harmoniously confused:°
Where order in variety we see,
And where, though all things differ, all agree.
Here waving groves a chequered scene display,
And part admit and part exclude the day;
As some coy nymph her lover's warm address

blow blossom
Windsor Forest This poem treats the Forest
("At once the Monarch's and the Muse's seats")
not merely as a royal forest preserve but as a
center of England's natural beauty and its culture; in the early section given below, Pope
creates an example of "picturesque" landscape,
that is, a landscape seen as it might be in a
painting, with interwoven colors and well-
defined receding space.

groves of Eden an evocation of Milton, *Paradise
Lost* IV
harmoniously confused echoing Ovid's *discors
concordia* (*Metamorphoses* I.433), anticipating
the larger cosmic application of the theme in
the *Essay on Man:* "But all subsists by elemental
strife" (I.169); "the lights and shades, whose
well accorded strife / Gives all the strength and
colour of our life" (II.121–22); "All nature's
difference keeps all nature's peace" (IV.56)

20   Nor quite indulges, nor can quite repress.°
There, interspersed in lawns and opening glades,
Thin trees arise that shun each other's shades.
Here in full light the russet plains extend:
There wrapped in clouds the bluish hills ascend.
Even the wild heath displays her purple dyes,
And midst the desert° fruitful fields arise,
That crowned with tufted trees and springing corn,
Like verdant isles the sable waste adorn.
Let India boast her plants, nor envy we
30   The weeping amber or the balmy tree,°
While by our oaks° the precious loads are borne,
And realms commanded which those trees adorn.
Not proud Olympus° yields a nobler sight,
Though gods assembled grace his towering height,
Than what more humble mountains offer here,
Where, in their blessings,° all those gods appear.
See Pan° with flocks, with fruits Pomona° crowned,
Here blushing Flora paints the enamelled ground,°
Here Ceres' gifts° in waving prospect stand,
40   And nodding tempt the joyful reaper's hand;
Rich Industry° sits smiling on the plains,
And peace and plenty tell, a Stuart reigns.
1704–13   1713

ANTHONY ASHLEY COOPER, THIRD EARL OF SHAFTESBURY
1671–1713

The Moralists

The third Earl of Shaftesbury was the grandson of the Whig statesman whom Dryden portrayed as Achitophel, and he had as his tutor the philosopher John Locke. Shaftesbury was himself a Whig in sentiment, dedicated to the idea of liberty, and radically distrustful of church doctrines. His own system builds upon classical sources, particularly Stoic and neoplatonic. He stresses the orderliness and artistry of the universe; it is a work of mind, and the divine mind is present everywhere as

Nor quite . . . repress Cf. John Keats's "Ode on a Grecian Urn": "Bold lover, never, never canst thou kiss, / Though winning near the goal . . . "; or "Ode to Psyche": "Their lips touched not, but had not bade adieu."
desert barrenness, wild (cf. "waste" in l. 28)
weeping . . . tree Cf. *Paradise Lost* IV.248: "Groves whose rich trees wept odorous gums and balm."
oaks in the form of ships of trade or war
Olympus the Greek mountain where the gods had their home
in their blessings in the form of their natural gifts

Pan as shepherd
Pomona as goddess of orchards and fruit
blushing Flora . . . ground The goddess of flowers, herself suffused with their color, paints the earth as if it were a painter's surface, prepared with a "ground" or coating of paint.
Ceres' gifts grain
Industry Here Pope turns Virgil's account of the Golden Age in *Eclogue* IV to a vision of English life in a time of peace, newly realized with Stuart Queen Anne's Peace of Utrecht (1713), which ended the War of the Spanish Succession begun under William III in 1701.

form. Man must be educated into an awareness of this form as he must be educated into a sense of form in the arts. Shaftesbury has no trust in the naïve or spontaneous as such, but he sees it as preferable to the fashionable miseducation offered by a sensual and materialistic world. (In this respect Shaftesbury recalls those paradoxes of Restoration wit by which the libertine is shown to be at least more natural than the primly repressed or the deviously respectable.)

Shaftesbury's typical literary form is the dialogue, wherein the man of imperfect awareness is drawn upward through the confusion of awakened consciousness to a full vision of the difficult truth; here Theocles plays a role like that of Diotima in Plato's *Symposium,* leading Philocles from love of the external to love of the ordering mind. Along the way, however, they move from the formal garden to the wild, from a stinted and limited art of man to the more authentic art of God in nature. The wild is not to be a resting place; it frees man of the false idols of society, but it must lead him farther to the creative power itself. In the same process, man comes to free himself of his devotion to worldly honors or to mere physical pleasures and to recognize his own god-like powers as a Prometheus or "second maker under Jove." Shaftesbury is therefore important in two ways: he provides a philosophic ground for the love of wild nature and for the visionary ascent beyond nature; and he secularizes this experience so that it need not be—as it tends still to be in Addison— governed by a Christian final cause, that is, existing in order to draw man to God. Shaftesbury strikes a note, not necessarily opposed to Christianity but moving in another direction, of the divine in man which must be released and given full confidence; it gains this confidence through discovery of itself in those sublime forms of nature that alone are adequate counterparts of the energy, reason, and creativity of man.

The Moralists is one of six treatises that were finally in 1711 collected by Shaftesbury under the title *Characteristics of Man, Manners, Opinions, Times,* and a book that had enormous European influence in the eighteenth century.

From The Moralists

A Philosophical Rhapsody

. . . But do you expect I should imitate the poet's god you mentioned,[1] and sing 'the rise of things from atoms, the birth of order from confusion, and the origin of union, harmony, and concord from the sole powers of chaos and blind chance'? The song indeed was fitted to the god. For what could better suit his jolly character than such a drunken creation, which he loved often to celebrate by acting it to the life? But even this song was too harmonious for the night's debauch. Well has our poet made it of the morning when the god was fresh; for hardly should we be brought ever to believe that such harmonious numbers could arise from a mere chaos of the mind. But we must hear our poet speaking in the mouth of some soberer demi-god or hero. He then presents us with a different principle of things, and in a more proper order of precedency gives thought the upper hand. He makes mind originally to have governed

---

1. Silenus, the shaggy, bearded god with horse's ears, knew important secrets of nature, and in Virgil's Sixth Eclogue he is made to reveal them in mythological form to two shepherds; what he presents is an Epicurean view of nature derived from Lucretius (see note 12 below).

body, not body mind; for this had been a chaos everlasting, and must have kept all things in a chaos-state to this day, and for ever, had it ever been. But

> This active mind, infused through all the space,
> Unites and mingles with the mighty mass;
> Hence men and beasts.[2]

Here, Philocles, we shall find our sovereign genius, if we can charm the genius of the place [3] (more chaste and sober than your Silenus) to inspire us with a truer song of Nature, teach us some celestial hymn, and make us feel divinity present in these solemn places of retreat.

Haste then, I conjure you, said I, good Theocles, and stop not one moment for any ceremony or rite. For well I see, methinks, that without any such preparation some divinity has approached us and already moves in you. We are come to the sacred groves of the Hamadryads,[4] which formerly were said to render oracles. We are on the most beautiful part of the hill, and the sun, now ready to rise, draws off the curtain of night and shows us the open scene of Nature in the plains below. Begin: for now I know you are full of those divine thoughts which meet you ever in this solitude. Give them but voice and accents; you may be still as much alone as you are used, and take no more notice of me than if I were absent.

Just as I had said this, he turned away his eyes from me, musing awhile by himself; and soon afterwards, stretching out his hand, as pointing to the objects round him, he began:—

'Ye fields and woods, my refuge from the toilsome world of business, receive me in your quiet sanctuaries and favour my retreat and thoughtful solitude. Ye verdant plains, how gladly I salute ye! Hail all ye blissful mansions! known seats! delightful prospects! majestic beauties of this earth, and all ye rural powers and graces! Blessed be ye chaste abodes of happiest mortals, who here in peaceful innocence enjoy a life unenvied, though divine; whilst with its blessed tranquillity it affords a happy leisure and retreat for man, who, made for contemplation, and to search his own and other natures, may here best meditate the cause of things, and, placed amidst the various scenes of Nature, may nearer view her works.

'O glorious nature! supremely fair and sovereignly good! all-loving and all-lovely, all-divine! whose looks are so becoming and of such infinite grace; whose study brings such wisdom, and whose contemplation such delight; whose every single work affords an ampler scene, and is a nobler spectacle than all which ever art presented! O mighty Nature! wise substitute of Providence! impowered creatress! [5] Or thou impowering Deity, supreme creator! Thee I invoke and thee alone adore. To thee this solitude, this place, these rural meditations are sacred; whilst thus inspired with harmony of thought, though unconfined by words,

2. Virgil, *Aeneid* VI.726–28 (*Dryden's trans.*, VI.984–86), where Anchises speaks.
3. The tutelary spirit or deity that protects the place.
4. Wood nymphs.
5. Pope, in *The Dunciad* IV.487–90, invokes this speech and, in order to use it as a specimen of Deism, cites it selectively in his original note, omitting the following clause. Shaftesbury was often accused of a deistic worship of a God who behaves according to rational laws, makes nature self-sufficient, and has no direct communion with his creatures; but in fact, while Shaftesbury is hostile to the church and its doctrines of man's weak and sinful nature, he regards himself as a theist.

and in loose numbers,[6] I sing of Nature's order in created beings, and celebrate the beauties which resolve in thee, the source and principle of all beauty and perfection.

'Thy being is boundless, unsearchable, impenetrable. In thy immensity all thought is lost, fancy gives over its flight, and wearied imagination spends itself in vain, finding no coast nor limit of this ocean, nor, in the widest tract through which it soars, one point yet nearer the circumference than the first centre whence it parted. Thus having oft essayed, thus sallied forth into the wide expanse, when I return again within myself, struck with the sense of this so narrow being and of the fulness of that immense one, I dare no more behold the amazing depths nor sound the abyss of Deity.

'Yet since by thee, O sovereign mind, I have been formed such as I am, intelligent and rational, since the peculiar dignity of my nature is to know and contemplate thee, permit that with due freedom I exert those faculties with which thou hast adorned me. Bear with my venturous and bold approach. And since nor vain curiosity, nor fond conceit, nor love of aught save thee alone inspires me with such thoughts as these, be thou my assistant and guide me in this pursuit, whilst I venture thus to tread the labyrinth of wide Nature and endeavour to trace thee in thy works.'

Here he stopped short, and starting as out of a dream: now, Philocles, said he, inform me, how have I appeared to you in my fit? Seemed it a sensible kind of madness, like those transports which are permitted to our poets? or was it downright raving?

. . .

. . . Philocles, the cold indifferent Philocles, is become a pursuer of the same mysterious beauty.

'Tis true, said I, Theocles, I own it. Your genius, the genius of the place, and the Great Genius have at last prevailed. I shall no longer resist the passion growing in me for things of a natural kind, where neither art nor the conceit or caprice of man has spoiled their genuine order by breaking in upon that primitive state. Even the rude rocks, the mossy caverns, the irregular unwrought grottos and broken falls of waters, with all the horrid graces of the wilderness itself, as representing Nature more, will be the more engaging, and appear with a magnificence beyond the formal mockery of princely gardens. . . . But tell me, I entreat you, how comes it that, excepting a few philosophers of your sort, the only people who are enamoured in this way, and seek the woods, the rivers, or seashores, are your poor vulgar lovers?

Say not this, replied he, of lovers only. For is it not the same with poets, and all those other students in nature and the arts which copy after her? In short, is not this the real case of all who are lovers either of the Muses or the Graces?

However, said I, all those who are deep in this romantic way are looked upon, you know, as a people either plainly out of their wits, or overrun with melancholy and enthusiasm. We always endeavour to recall them from these solitary places. And I must own that often when I have found my fancy run this way, I have checked myself, not knowing what it was possessed me, when I was passionately struck with objects of this kind.

6. In free measures, somewhat as in the Pindaric ode.

No wonder, replied he, if we are at a loss when we pursue the shadow for the substance. For if we may trust to what our reasoning has taught us, whatever in Nature is beautiful or charming is only the faint shadow of that first beauty. So that every real love depending on the mind, and being only the contemplation of beauty either as it really is in itself or as it appears imperfectly in the objects which strike the sense, how can the rational mind rest here, or be satisfied with the absurd enjoyment which reaches the sense alone?

From this time forward then, said I, I shall no more have reason to fear those beauties which strike a sort of melancholy, like the places we have named, or like these solemn groves. No more shall I avoid the moving accents of soft music or fly from the enchanting features of the fairest human face.

If you are already, replied he, such a proficient in this new love that you are sure never to admire the representative beauty except for the sake of the original, nor aim at other enjoyment than of the rational kind, you may then be confident. I am so, and presume accordingly to answer for myself. However, I should not be ill satisfied if you explained yourself a little better as to this mistake of mine you seem to fear. Would it be any help to tell you, 'That the absurdity lay in seeking the enjoyment elsewhere than in the subject loved'? The matter, I must confess, is still mysterious. Imagine then, good Philocles, if being taken with the beauty of the ocean, which you see yonder at a distance, it should come into your head to seek how to command it, and, like some mighty admiral, ride master of the sea, would not the fancy be a little absurd?

Absurd enough, in conscience. The next thing I should do, 'tis likely, upon this frenzy, would be to hire some bark and go in nuptial ceremony, Venetian-like, to wed the gulf, which I might call perhaps as properly my own.

Let who will call it theirs, replied Theocles, you will own the enjoyment of this kind to be very different from that which should naturally follow from the contemplation of the ocean's beauty. The bridegroom-Doge, who in his stately Bucentaur [7] floats on the bosom of his Thetis, has less possession than the poor shepherd, who from a hanging rock or point of some high promontory, stretched at his ease, forgets his feeding flocks, while he admires her beauty. But to come nearer home, and make the question still more familiar. Suppose (my Philocles) that, viewing such a tract of country as this delicious vale we see beneath us, you should, for the enjoyment of the prospect, require the property or possession of the land.

The covetous fancy, replied I, would be as absurd altogether as that other ambitious one.

O Philocles! said he, may I bring this yet a little nearer, and will you follow me once more? Suppose that, being charmed as you seem to be with the beauty of those trees under whose shade we rest, you should long for nothing so much as to taste some delicious fruit of theirs; and having obtained of Nature some certain relish by which these acorns or berries of the wood became as palatable as the figs or peaches of the garden, you should afterwards, as oft as you revisited these groves, seek hence the enjoyment of them by satiating yourself in these new delights.

7. The wedding of the Doge of Venice with the sea, ("his Thetis") was celebrated in a pageant each year on Ascension Day with the casting of a ring into the Adriatic from the special gondola called Bucentaur.

The fancy of this kind, replied I, would be sordidly luxurious, and as absurd, in my opinion, as either of the former.

Can you not then, on this occasion, said he, call to mind some other forms of a fair kind among us, where the admiration of beauty is apt to lead to as irregular a consequence?

I feared, said I, indeed, where this would end, and was apprehensive you would force me at last to think of certain powerful forms in human kind which draw after them a set of eager desires, wishes, and hopes; no way suitable, I must confess, to your rational and refined contemplation of beauty. The proportions of this living architecture, as wonderful as they are, inspire nothing of a studious or contemplative kind. The more they are viewed, the further they are from satisfying by mere view. Let that which satisfies be ever so disproportionable an effect, or ever so foreign to its cause, censure it as you please, you must allow, however, that it is natural. So that you, Theocles, for aught I see, are become the accuser of Nature by condemning a natural enjoyment.

Far be it from us both, said he, to condemn a joy which is from Nature. But when we spoke of the enjoyment of these woods and prospects, we understood by it a far different kind from that of the inferior creatures, who, rifling in these places, find here their choicest food. Yet we too live by tasteful food, and feel those other joys of sense in common with them. But 'twas not here (my Philocles) that we had agreed to place our good, nor consequently our enjoyment. We who were rational, and had minds, methought, should place it rather in those minds which were indeed abused and cheated of their real good, when drawn to seek absurdly the enjoyment of it in the objects of sense and not in those objects they might properly call their own, in which kind, as I remember, we comprehended all which was truly fair, generous, or good.

So that beauty, said I, and good with you, Theocles, I perceive, are still one and the same.

'Tis so, said he. And thus are we returned again to the subject of our yesterday's morning conversation. Whether I have made good my promise to you in showing the true good, I know not. But so, doubtless, I should have done with good success had I been able in my poetic ecstasies, or by any other efforts, to have led you into some deep view of Nature and the sovereign genius. We then had proved the force of divine beauty and formed in ourselves an object capable and worthy of real enjoyment.

O Theocles! said I, well do I remember now the terms in which you engaged me that morning when you bespoke my love of this mysterious beauty. You have indeed made good your part of the condition and may now claim me for a proselyte. If there be any seeming extravagance in the case I must comfort myself the best I can, and consider that all sound love and admiration is enthusiasm: 'The transports of poets, the sublime of orators, the rapture of musicians, the high strains of the virtuosi—all mere enthusiasm! Even learning itself, the love of arts and curiosities, the spirit of travellers and adventurers, gallantry, war, heroism—all, all enthusiasm!' [8] 'Tis enough; I am content to be this new enthusiast in a way unknown to me before.

8. Shaftesbury is citing his own *Letter Concerning Enthusiasm*, where a false, hysterical religious enthusiasm (such as Butler and Swift satirize in *Hudibras* and *A Tale of a Tub*) is condemned but a "reasonable ecstasy" is celebrated instead.

And I, replied Theocles, am content you should call this love of ours enthusiasm, allowing it the privilege of its fellow-passions. For is there a fair and plausible enthusiasm, a reasonable ecstasy and transport allowed to other subjects, such as architecture, painting, music; and shall it be exploded here? Are there senses by which all those other graces and perfections are perceived, and none by which this higher perfection and grace is comprehended? Is it so preposterous to bring that enthusiasm hither, and transfer it from those secondary and scanty objects to this original and comprehensive one? Observe how the case stands in all those other subjects of art or science. What difficulty to be in any degree knowing! How long ere a true taste is gained! How many things shocking, how many offensive at first, which afterwards are known and acknowledged the highest beauties! For 'tis not instantly we acquire the sense by which these beauties are discoverable. Labour and pains are required, and time to cultivate a natural genius ever so apt or forward. But who is there once thinks of cultivating this soil, or of improving any sense or faculty which Nature may have given of this kind? And is it a wonder we should be dull then, as we are, confounded and at a loss in these affairs, blind as to this higher scene, these nobler representations? Which way should we come to understand better? which way be knowing in these beauties? Is study, science, or learning necessary to understand all beauties else? And for the sovereign beauty, is there no skill or science required? In painting there are shades and masterly strokes which the vulgar understand not, but find fault with; in architecture there is the rustic; in music the chromatic kind and skilful mixture of dissonancies: [9] and is there nothing which answers to this in the whole?

I must confess, said I, I have hitherto been one of those vulgar who could never relish the shades, the rustic, or the dissonancies you talk of. I have never dreamt of such masterpieces in Nature. 'Twas my way to censure freely on the first view. But I perceive I am now obliged to go far in the pursuit of beauty, which lies very absconded [10] and deep; and if so, I am well assured that my enjoyments hitherto have been very shallow. I have dwelt, it seems, all this while upon the surface, and enjoyed only a kind of slight superficial beauties, having never gone in search of beauty itself, but of what I fancied such. Like the rest of the unthinking world, I took for granted that what I liked was beautiful, and what I rejoiced in was my good. I never scrupled [11] loving what I fancied and aiming only at the enjoyment of what I loved; I never troubled myself with examining what the subjects were, nor ever hesitated about their choice.

Begin then, said he, and choose. See what the subjects are and which you would prefer, which honour with your admiration, love, and esteem. For by these again you will be honoured in your turn. Such, Philocles, as is the worth of these companions, such will your worth be found. As there is emptiness or

---

9. For an attack upon the "chromatic," see Pope, *The Dunciad* IV.54–58, on opera. Here Shaftesbury is insisting upon the educated taste required to respond to a "difficult" beauty, which includes apparent disorder or disharmony, as in the "rustic" or harsh and seemingly unfinished elements in architecture. The analogy with the rustic or wild in the natural landscape is clear.

10. Hidden, as God in his mysteriousness is called *Deus absconditus*.

11. Questioned.

fulness here, so will there be in your enjoyment. See therefore where fulness is and where emptiness. See in what subject resides the chief excellence, where beauty reigns, where 'tis entire, perfect, absolute; where broken, imperfect, short. View these terrestrial beauties and whatever has the appearance of excellence and is able to attract. See that which either really is, or stands as in the room of fair, beautiful, and good. 'A mass of metal, a tract of land, a number of slaves, a pile of stones, a human body of certain lineaments and proportions.' Is this the highest of the kind? Is beauty founded then in body only, and not in action, life, or operation? . . .

Hold! hold! said I, good Theocles, you take this in too high a key above my reach. If you would have me accompany you, pray lower this strain a little, and talk in a more familiar way.

Thus then, said he (smiling), whatever passion you may have for other beauties, I know, good Philocles, you are no such admirer of wealth in any kind as to allow much beauty to it, especially in a rude heap or mass. But in medals, coins, embossed work, statues, and well-fabricated pieces, of whatever sort, you can discover beauty and admire the kind. True, said I, but not for the metal's sake. 'Tis not then the metal or matter which is beautiful with you? No. But the art? Certainly. The art then is the beauty? Right. And the art is that which beautifies? The same. So that the beautifying, not the beautified, is the really beautiful? It seems so. For that which is beautified is beautiful only by the accession of something beautifying, and by the recess or withdrawing of the same it ceases to be beautiful? Be it. In respect of bodies therefore, beauty comes and goes? So we see. Nor is the body itself any cause either of its coming or staying? None. So that there is no principle of beauty in body? None at all. For body can no way be the cause of beauty to itself? No way. Nor govern nor regulate itself? Nor yet this. Nor mean nor intend itself? [12] Nor this neither. Must not that, therefore, which means and intends for it, regulates and orders it, be the principle of beauty to it? Of necessity. And what must that be? Mind, I suppose, for what can it be else?

. . .

If brutes, therefore, said he, be incapable of knowing and enjoying beauty, as being brutes, and having sense only (the brutish part) for their own share, it follows 'that neither can man by the same sense or brutish part conceive or enjoy beauty; but all the beauty and good he enjoys is in a nobler way, and by the help of what is noblest, his mind and reason.' Here lies his dignity and highest interest, here his capacity toward good and happiness. His ability or incompetency, his power of enjoyment or his impotence, is founded in this alone. As this is sound, fair, noble, worthy, so are its subjects, acts, and employments. For as the riotous mind, captive to sense, can never enter in competition or contend for beauty with the virtuous mind of reason's culture; so neither can the objects which allure the former compare with those which attract and charm the latter. And when each gratifies itself in the enjoyment and possession of its object, how evidently fairer are the acts which join the latter pair, and give a soul the enjoyment of what is generous and good? This at least, Philocles,

12. Shaftesbury is attacking the Epicurean doctrine that form arises from the chance collocation of atoms and that it emerges from body; he insists instead upon a universe governed by mind or intelligence.

you will surely allow, that when you place a joy elsewhere than in the mind, the enjoyment itself will be no beautiful subject, nor of any graceful or agreeable appearance. But when you think how friendship is enjoyed, how honour, gratitude, candour, benignity, and all internal beauty; how all the social pleasures, society itself, and all which constitutes the worth and happiness of mankind; you will here surely allow beauty in the act, and think it worthy to be viewed and passed in review often by the glad mind, happily conscious of the generous part, and of its own advancement and growth in beauty.

Thus, Philocles (continued he, after a short pause), thus have I presumed to treat of beauty before so great a judge, and such a skilful admirer as yourself. For, taking rise from Nature's beauty, which transported me, I gladly ventured further in the chase, and have accompanied you in search of beauty, as it relates to us and makes our highest good in its sincere and natural enjoyment. And if we have not idly spent our hours, nor ranged in vain through these deserted regions, it should appear from our strict search that there is nothing so divine as beauty, which belonging not to body nor having any principle or existence except in mind and reason, is alone discovered and acquired by this diviner part when it inspects itself, the only object worthy of itself. For whatever is void of mind is void and darkness to the mind's eye. This languishes and grows dim whenever detained on foreign subjects, but thrives and attains its natural vigour when employed in contemplation of what is like itself. 'Tis thus the improving mind, slightly surveying other objects and passing over bodies and the common forms (where only a shadow of beauty rests), ambitiously presses onward to its source and views the original of form and order in that which is intelligent. And thus, O Philocles, may we improve and become artists in the kind; learning 'to know ourselves, and what that is, which by improving, we may be sure to advance our worth and real self-interest.' For neither is this knowledge acquired by contemplation of bodies, or the outward forms, the view of pageantries, the study of estates and honours; nor is he to be esteemed that self-improving artist who makes a fortune out of these, but he (he only) is the wise and able man, who with a slight regard to these things, applies himself to cultivate another soil, builds in a different matter from that of stone or marble; and having righter models in his eye, becomes in truth the architect of his own life and fortune by laying within himself the lasting and sure foundations of order, peace, and concord. . . . But now 'tis time to think of returning home. The morning is far spent. Come! let us away and leave these uncommon subjects, till we retire again to these remote and unfrequented places.

At these words Theocles, mending his pace, and going down the hill, left me at a good distance, till he heard me calling earnestly after him. Having joined him once again, I begged he would stay a little longer, or if he were resolved so soon to leave both the woods and that philosophy which he confined to them, that he would let me, however, part with them more gradually, and leave the best impression on me he could against my next return. For as much convinced as I was, and as great a convert to his doctrine, my danger still, I owned to him, was very great, and I foresaw that when the charm of these places and his company was ceased, I should be apt to relapse and weakly yield to that too powerful charm, the world. Tell me, continued I, how is it possible to hold out against it and withstand the general opinion of mankind, who have so different a notion of that which we call good? Say truth now, Theocles, can anything be more odd or dissonant from the common voice of the world than what we have determined in this matter?

Whom shall we follow, then? replied he. Whose judgment or opinion shall we take concerning what is good, what contrary? If all or any part of mankind are consonant with themselves, and can agree in this, I am content to leave philosophy and follow them. If otherwise, why should we not adhere to what we have chosen? . . .

1705   1711

JOSEPH ADDISON
1672–1719

[The Pleasures of the Imagination]

Joseph Addison attended Oxford and studied on the Continent thereafter (1699–1703), composing his rhymed *Letter from Italy*, prose *Remarks on Several Parts of Italy*, and a *Dialogue on Medals*. His first great literary success was *The Campaign* (1705), a poem in celebration of the Duke of Marlborough's victories. He held public office and served in Parliament from 1708, and he became a prominent dispenser of Whig patronage to writers. In 1709 he began to aid Sir Richard Steele in the writing of the *Tatler*, and two years later they joined as full collaborators in the *Spectator*. Addison's tragedy *Cato* (1713) was one of the best-known plays of the century.

In eleven papers on "The Pleasures of the Imagination," which appeared as *Spectator* Nos. 411–21, Addison explores the principal aesthetic questions of the day. He distinguishes among the great, the new (or uncommon), and the beautiful in ways that look ahead to later categories of Sublime, Picturesque, and Beautiful. From this discussion, passages on the Great or Sublime have been chosen as instances of growing interest in the wild as opposed to the garden (the residence of the beautiful). In No. 413 Addison pursues the problem of primary and secondary qualities, adapting John Locke's epistemology to the uses of aesthetics and religion. Locke tried to distinguish between those qualities which were constant because located "in" the objects and those that were relative because dependent upon our perception of objects. The primary qualities (e.g. bulk, figure) are "in the things themselves, whether they are perceived or not"; and upon their different modifications the secondary qualities (e.g. color, warmth, smell) depend, arising as they do from man's own contributory response.

By *greatness* I do not only mean the bulk of any single object, but the largeness of a whole view, considered as one entire piece. Such are the prospects of an open champaign [1] country, a vast uncultivated desert, of huge heaps of mountains, high rocks and precipices, or a wide expanse of waters, where we are not struck with the novelty or beauty of the sight, but with that rude kind of magnificence which appears in many of these stupendous works of nature.

1. Of flat fields.

Our imagination loves to be filled with an object, or to grasp at anything that is too big for its capacity. We are flung into a pleasing astonishment at such unbounded views and feel a delightful stillness and amazement in the soul at the apprehension of them. The mind of man naturally hates everything that looks like a restraint upon it and is apt to fancy itself under a sort of confinement when the sight is pent up in a narrow compass, and shortened on every side by the neighbourhood of walls or mountains. On the contrary, a spacious horizon is an image of liberty, where the eye has room to range abroad, to expatiate at large on the immensity of its views, and to lose itself amidst the variety of objects that offer themselves to its observation. Such wide and undetermined prospects are as pleasing to the fancy as the speculations of eternity or infinitude are to the understanding. But if there be a beauty or uncommonness joined with this grandeur, as in a troubled ocean, a heaven adorned with stars and meteors, or a spacious landscape cut out into rivers, woods, rocks, and meadows, the pleasure still grows upon us, as it arises from more than a single principle. [From *Spectator* No. 412, June 23, 1712]

Final causes [2] lie more bare and open to our observation, as there are often a great variety that belong to the same effect; and these, though they are not altogether so satisfactory, are generally more useful than the other, as they give us greater occasion of admiring the goodness and wisdom of the First Contriver.

One of the final causes of our delight in anything that is *great* may be this: the Supreme Author of our being has so formed the soul of man that nothing but Himself can be its last, adequate, and proper happiness. Because, therefore, a great part of our happiness must arise from the contemplation of His Being, that He might give our souls a just relish of such a contemplation, He has made them naturally delight in the apprehension of what is great or unlimited. Our admiration,[3] which is a very pleasing motion of the mind, immediately arises at the consideration of any object that takes up a great deal of room in the fancy, and by consequence, will improve into the highest pitch of astonishment and devotion when we contemplate His nature, that is neither circumscribed by time nor place, nor to be comprehended by the largest capacity of a created being.

. . .

. . . He has given almost everything about us the power of raising an agreeable idea in the imagination, so that it is impossible for us to behold His works with coldness or indifference, and to survey so many beauties without a secret satisfaction and complacency. Things would make but a poor appearance to the eye if we saw them only in their proper figures and motions. And what reason can we assign for this exciting in us many of those ideas, which are different from anything that exists in the objects themselves (for such are light and colours), were it not to add supernumerary ornaments to the universe and make it more agreeable to the imagination? We are everywhere entertained with pleasing shows and apparitions: we discover imaginary glories in the heavens and in the earth, and see some of this visionary beauty

2. That is, explanation by the end or object which a thing serves or for which it is made.
3. Wonder, awe.

poured out upon the whole creation; but what a rough, unsightly sketch of nature should we be entertained with, did all her colouring disappear and the several distinctions of light and shade vanish? [4] In short, our souls are at present delightfully lost and bewildered in a pleasing delusion; and we walk about like the enchanted hero of a romance, who sees beautiful castles, woods, and meadows, and at the same time hears the warbling of birds and the purling of streams; but upon the finishing of some secret spell, the fantastic scene breaks up, and the disconsolate knight finds himself on a barren heath or in a solitary desert. It is not improbable that something like this may be the state of the soul after its first separation [5] in respect of the images it will receive from matter, though indeed the ideas of colours are so pleasing and beautiful in the imagination that it is possible the soul will not be deprived of them, but perhaps find them excited by some other occasional cause, as they are at present by the different impressions of the subtle matter on the organ of sight.

I have here supposed that my reader is acquainted with that great modern discovery which is at present universally acknowledged by all the inquirers into natural philosophy—namely, that light and colours as apprehended by the imagination are only ideas [6] in the mind and not qualities that have any existence in matter. As this is a truth which has been proved incontestably by many modern philosophers, and is indeed one of the finest speculations in that science, if the English reader would see the notion explained at large, he may find it in the eighth chapter of the second book of Mr. Locke's *Essay on Human Understanding*. [From *Spectator No 413*, June 24, 1712]

If we consider the works of nature and art as they are qualified to entertain the imagination, we shall find the last very defective in comparison of the former, for though they may sometimes appear as beautiful or strange, they can have nothing in them of that vastness and immensity which afford so great an entertainment to the mind of the beholder. The one may be as polite and delicate as the other, but can never show herself so august and magnificent in the design. There is something more bold and masterly in the rough, careless strokes of nature than in the nice touches and embellishments of art. The beauties of the most stately garden or palace lie in a narrow compass: the imagination immediately runs them over, and requires something else to gratify her; but in the wide fields of nature, the sight wanders up and down without confinement, and is fed with an infinite variety of images, without any certain stint or number. For this reason we always find the poet in love with a country life, where nature appears in the greatest perfection, and furnishes out all those scenes that are most apt to delight the imagination. . . .

We have before observed that there is generally in nature something more grand and august than what we meet with in the curiosities of art. When, therefore, we see this imitated in any measure, it gives us a nobler and more exalted kind of pleasure than what we receive from the nicer and more accurate productions of art. On this account, our English gardens are not so entertaining to the fancy as those in France and Italy, where we see a large extent of ground covered over with an agreeable mixture of garden and forest, which

4. See Swift, *A Tale of a Tub* IX, on the pleasures of the senses.
5. From the body in death, thus losing the sense organs.
6. Images.

represent everywhere an artificial rudeness much more charming than that neatness and elegancy which we meet with in those of our own country. It might, indeed, be of ill consequence to the public, as well as unprofitable to private persons, to alienate so much ground from pasturage and the plough in many parts of a country that is so well peopled and cultivated to a far greater advantage. But why may not a whole estate be thrown into a kind of garden by frequent plantations that may turn as much to the profit as the pleasure of the owner? A marsh overgrown with willows or a mountain shaded with oaks are not only more beautiful but more beneficial than when they lay bare and unadorned. Fields of corn make a pleasant prospect, and if the walks were a little taken care of that lie between them, if the natural embroidery of the meadows were helped and improved by some small additions of art, and the several rows of hedges set off by trees and flowers that the soil was capable of receiving, a man might make a pretty landscape of his own possessions.

Writers who have given us an account of China [7] tell us the inhabitants of that country laugh at the plantations of our Europeans, which are laid by the rule and line, because, they say, anyone may place trees in equal rows and uniform figures. They choose rather to show a genius in works of this nature, and therefore always conceal the art by which they direct themselves. They have a word, it seems, in their language by which they express the particular beauty of a plantation that thus strikes the imagination at first sight without discovering what it is that has so agreeable an effect. Our British gardeners, on the contrary, instead of humouring nature, love to deviate from it as much as possible. Our trees rise in cones, globes, and pyramids. We see the marks of the scissors upon every plant and bush. I do not know whether I am singular in my opinion, but for my own part, I would rather look upon a tree in all its luxuriancy and diffusion of boughs and branches than when it is thus cut and trimmed into a mathematical figure, and cannot but fancy that an orchard in flower looks infinitely more delightful than all the little labyrinths of the most finished parterre. [From *Spectator* No. 414, June 25, 1712]

HORACE WALPOLE AND THOMAS GRAY

[Crossing the Alps, 1739 [1]]

Precipices, mountains, torrents, wolves, rumblings, Salvator Rosa [2]——the pomp of our park and the meekness of our palace! Here we are, the lonely lords of glorious desolate prospects. . . .

. . . Did you ever see anything like the prospect we saw yesterday? I never

7. Notably Sir William Temple in *Upon the Gardens of Epicurus*, who cites the word *sharawadgi*.

1. These excerpts are from letters sent by Walpole and Gray during their grand tour to their schoolmate and friend Richard West (see the Headnote to Thomas Gray). They are among the best and earliest expressions of feeling for the sublime landscape; Gray was to write in a similar vein years later in the Lake Country.

2. The Neapolitan satirist and painter (1615–73), highly esteemed in England for his paintings of wild and turbulent landscape (often inhabited by bandits); here he is aligned with the mountain scene in opposition to cultivated parks or man-made palaces (a similar contrast is used by Gray).

did. We rode three leagues to see the Grande Chartreuse; [3] expected bad roads and the finest convent in the kingdom. We were disappointed pro and con. The building is large and plain and has nothing remarkable but its primitive simplicity: they entertained us in the neatest manner, with eggs, pickled salmon, dried fish, conserves, cheese, butter, grapes and figs, and pressed us mightily to lie there. We tumbled into the hands of a lay-brother, who, unluckily having the charge of the meal and bran, showed us little besides. . . . —But the road, West, the road! winding round a prodigious mountain, and surrounded with others, all shagged with hanging woods, obscured with pines or lost in clouds! Below, a torrent breaking through cliffs, and tumbling through fragments of rocks! Sheets of cascades forcing their silver speed down channelled precipices, and hasting into the roughened river at the bottom! Now and then an old foot-bridge, with a broken rail, a leaning cross, a cottage, or the ruin of an hermitage! This sounds too bombast and too romantic to one that has not seen it, too cold for one that has. If I could send you my letter post between two lovely tempests that echoed each other's wrath, you might have some idea of this noble roaring scene as you were reading it. Almost on the summit, upon a fine verdure, but without any prospect, stands the Chartreuse. We stayed there two hours, rode back through this charming picture, wished for a painter, wished to be poets! [From a letter of September 28–30, 1739, from Horace Walpole to Richard West]

. . . The palace here in town is the very quintessence of gilding and looking-glass; inlaid floors, carved panels, and painting wherever they could stick a brush. I own I have not, as yet, anywhere met with those grand and simple works of Art that are to amaze one, and whose sight one is to be the better for: but those of Nature have astonished me beyond expression. In our little journey up to the Grande Chartreuse, I do not remember to have gone ten paces without an exclamation that there was no restraining: not a precipice, not a torrent, not a cliff, but is pregnant with religion and poetry. There are certain scenes that would awe an atheist into belief without the help of other argument. One need not have a very fantastic imagination to see spirits there at noonday. You have Death perpetually before your eyes, only so far removed as to compose the mind without frighting it. . . . The week we have since passed among the Alps has not equalled the single day upon that mountain, because the winter was rather too far advanced, and the weather a little foggy. However, it did not want its beauties; the savage rudeness of the view is inconceivable without seeing it: I reckoned in one day, thirteen cascades, the least of which was, I dare say, one hundred feet in height. . . . Mont Cenis, I confess, carries the permission mountains have of being frightful rather too far; and its horrors were accompanied with too much danger to give one time to reflect upon their beauties.[4] [From letter of November 16, 1739, from Thomas Gray to Richard West]

3. The motherhouse of the Carthusian order of monks, in the mountains near Grenoble, France, about 3000 feet above sea level. The monks were expelled in 1793 and allowed to return in 1816, and the Chartreuse is the subject of several 19th-century English poets, notably Wordsworth and Arnold.
4. Gray raises an issue to be dealt with later by Burke in his *Enquiry* on the sublime (see above).

JAMES THOMSON
1700–1748

The Seasons°

From Summer

'Tis raging noon; and, vertical, the sun
Darts on the head direct his forceful rays.
O'er heaven and earth, far as the ranging eye
Can sweep, a dazzling deluge reigns; and all
From pole to pole is undistinguished blaze.
In vain the sight dejected to the ground
Stoops for relief; thence hot ascending steams
And keen reflection pain. Deep to the root
440 Of vegetation parched, the cleaving fields
And slippery lawn an arid hue disclose,
Blast fancy's blooms and wither even the soul.
Echo no more returns the cheerful sound
Of sharpening scythe: the mower, sinking, heaps
O'er him the humid hay, with flowers perfumed;
And scarce a chirping grasshopper is heard
Through the dumb mead. Distressful nature pants.
The very streams look languid from afar,
Or, through the unsheltered glade, impatient seem
450 To hurl into the covert of the grove.
    All-conquering heat, oh, intermit thy wrath!
And on my throbbing temples potent thus
Beam not so fierce! Incessant still you flow,
And still another fervent flood succeeds,
Poured on the head profuse. In vain I sigh,
And restless turn, and look around for night:
Night is far off; and hotter hours approach.
Thrice happy he, who on the sunless side
Of a romantic mountain, forest-crowned,
460 Beneath the whole collected shade reclines;
Or in the gelid caverns, woodbine-wrought
And fresh bedewed with ever-spouting streams,
Sits coolly calm; while all the world without,
Unsatisfied and sick, tosses in noon.
Emblem instructive of the virtuous man,

The Seasons James Thomson was the son of a Scottish minister and came to London for a literary career, publishing the first version of *Winter* the year after his arrival (1726), and the full *Seasons* in 1730. He wrote several plays and two other long poems, *Liberty* and (in Spenserian stanzas and allegorical mode) *The Castle of Indolence*. Thomson was probably as well known throughout Europe as any English poet of his age; his descriptive poetry, carrying a weight of moral and philosophical suggestion, had enormous influence. In the spirit of Shaftes-

bury, Thomson explored those areas (of climate, of weather, of moral choice) where order was threatened and yet could be shown, in a larger frame, to have survived; in doing so, he studied natural phenomena with a new closeness and a new feeling for their sublimity, and the result was the displacement of epic action by a descriptive counterpart. *The Seasons* underwent extensive revision and reordering throughout Thomson's career, and the last version is given here.

Who keeps his tempered mind serene and pure,
And every passion aptly harmonized
Amid a jarring world with vice inflamed.
     Welcome, ye shades! ye bowery thickets, hail!
470 Ye lofty pines! ye venerable oaks!
Ye ashes wild, resounding o'er the steep!
Delicious is your shelter to the soul
As to the hunted hart the sallying spring
Or stream full-flowing, that his swelling sides
Laves as he floats along the herbaged brink.
Cool through the nerves your pleasing comfort glides;
The heart beats glad; the fresh-expanded eye
And ear resume their watch; the sinews knit;
And life shoots swift through all the lightened limbs
480   Around the adjoining brook, that purls along
The vocal grove, now fretting o'er a rock,
Now scarcely moving through a reedy pool,
Now starting to a sudden stream, and now
Gently diffused into a limpid plain,
A various group the herds and flocks compose,
Rural confusion! On the grassy bank
Some ruminating lie, while others stand
Half in the flood and, often bending, sip
The circling surface. In the middle droops
490 The strong laborious ox, of honest front,
Which incomposed° he shakes; and from his sides
The troublous insects lashes with his tail,
Returning still. Amid his subjects safe
Slumbers the monarch-swain, his careless arm
Thrown round his head on downy moss sustained;
Here laid his scrip° with wholesome viands filled,
There, listening every noise, his watchful dog.
     Light fly his slumbers, if perchance a flight
Of angry gad-flies fasten on the herd,
500 That startling scatters from the shallow brook
In search of lavish stream. Tossing the foam,
They scorn the keeper's voice, and scour the plain
Through all the bright severity of noon;
While from their labouring breasts a hollow moan
Proceeding runs low-bellowing round the hills.
     Oft in this season too, the horse, provoked,
While his big sinews full of spirits swell,
Trembling with vigour, in the heat of blood
Springs the high fence, and, o'er the field effused,°
510 Darts on the gloomy flood with steadfast eye
And heart estranged to fear: his nervous chest,
Luxuriant and erect, the seat of strength,

---

incomposed disturbed   effused streaming, rushing
scrip satchel or bag

Bears down the opposing stream; quenchless his thirst,
He takes the river at redoubled draughts,
And with wide nostrils, snorting, skims the wave.
    Still let me pierce into the midnight depth
Of yonder grove, of wildest largest growth,
That, forming high in air a woodland quire,°
Nods o'er the mount beneath. At every step,
520 Solemn and slow the shadows blacker fall,
And all is awful listening gloom around.
    These are the haunts of meditation, these
The scenes where ancient bards the inspiring breath
Ecstatic felt, and, from this world retired,
Conversed with angels and immortal forms,
On gracious errands bent—to save the fall
Of virtue struggling on the brink of vice;
In waking whispers and repeated dreams
To hint pure thought, and warn the favoured soul,
530 For future trials fated, to prepare;
To prompt the poet, who devoted gives
His muse to better themes; to soothe the pangs
Of dying worth, and from the patriot's breast
(Backward to mingle in detested war,
But foremost when engaged) to turn the death;
And numberless such offices of love,
Daily and nightly, zealous to perform.

      .   .   .

From Winter

    When from the pallid sky the sun descends,°
With many a spot, that o'er his glaring orb
120 Uncertain wanders, stained; red fiery streaks
Begin to flush around. The reeling clouds
Stagger with dizzy poise, as doubting yet
Which master to obey; while, rising slow,
Blank in the leaden-coloured east, the moon
Wears a wan circle round her blunted horns.
Seen through the turbid, fluctuating air,
The stars obtuse° emit a shivering ray;
Or frequent seem to shoot athwart the gloom,
And long behind them trail the whitening blaze.
130 Snatched in short eddies, plays the withered leaf;
And on the flood the dancing feather floats.
With broadened nostrils to the sky upturned,

---

quire i.e. the natural counterpart in trees of
the Gothic piers of a church choir

When . . . descends This account of the storm
echoes Virgil, *Georgics* I.351–92.
obtuse dulled

The conscious° heifer snuffs the stormy gale.
Even, as the matron, at her nightly task,
With pensive labour draws the flaxen thread,
The wasted taper° and the crackling flame
Foretell the blast. But chief the plumy race,
The tenants of the sky, its changes speak.
Retiring from the downs, where all day long
140   They picked their scanty fare, a blackening train
Of clamorous rooks thick-urge their weary flight,
And seek the closing shelter of the grove.
Assiduous, in his bower, the wailing owl
Plies his sad song. The cormorant on high
Wheels from the deep, and screams along the land.
Loud shrieks the soaring hern;° and with wild wing
The circling sea-fowl cleave the flaky clouds.
Ocean, unequal pressed, with broken tide
And blind commotion heaves; while from the shore,
150   Eat° into caverns by the restless wave,
And forest-rustling mountain comes a voice
That, solemn-sounding, bids the world prepare.
Then issues forth the storm with sudden burst,
And hurls the whole precipitated air
Down in a torrent. On the passive main
Descends the ethereal force, and with strong gust
Turns from its bottom the discoloured deep.
Through the black night that sits immense around,
Lashed into foam, the fierce-conflicting brine
160   Seems o'er a thousand raging waves to burn.
Meantime the mountain-billows, to the clouds
In dreadful tumult swelled, surge above surge,
Burst into chaos with tremendous roar,
And anchored navies from their stations drive
Wild as the winds, across the howling waste
Of mighty waters: now the inflated wave
Straining they scale, and now impetuous shoot
Into the secret chambers of the deep,
The wintry Baltic thundering o'er their head.
170   Emerging thence again, before the breath
Of full-exerted° heaven they wing their course,°
And dart on distant coasts—if some sharp rock
Or shoal insidious break not their career,
And in loose fragments fling them floating round.
   Nor less at land the loosened tempest reigns.
The mountain thunders, and its sturdy sons°
Stoop to the bottom of the rocks they shade.
Lone on the midnight steep, and all aghast,

---

conscious alert, responsive
wasted taper guttering and running candle
hern heron
Eat eaten, eroded

wing their course i.e. the sailing vessels, seen
as birds
sturdy sons great trees

The dark wayfaring stranger breathless toils,
180 And, often falling, climbs against the blast.
Low waves the rooted forest, vexed, and sheds
What of its tarnished honours° yet remain—
Dashed down and scattered, by the tearing wind's
Assiduous fury, its gigantic limbs.
Thus struggling through the dissipated° grove,
The whirling tempest raves along the plain;
And, on the cottage thatched or lordly roof
Keen-fastening, shakes them to the solid base.
Sleep frighted flies; and round the rocking dome,°
190 For entrance eager, howls the savage blast.
Then too, they say, through all the burdened air
Long groans are heard, shrill sounds, and distant sighs,
That, uttered by the demon of the night,
Warn the devoted° wretch of woe and death.
    Huge uproar lords it wide. The clouds, commixed
With stars swift-gliding, sweep along the sky.
All Nature reels: till Nature's King, who oft
Amid tempestuous darkness dwells alone,
And on the wings of the careering° wind
200 Walks dreadfully serene, commands a calm;°
Then straight air, sea, and earth are hushed at once.

                                                    1726–46

EDWARD YOUNG
1683–1765

The Complaint; or, Night Thoughts on Life, Death, and Immortality °

From *Night I*

How poor, how rich, how abject, how august,
How complicate, how wonderful, is man!
70 How passing wonder He, who made him such!
Who centred in our make such strange extremes!

tarnished honours faded foliage
dissipated ravaged, scattered
dome building
devoted doomed
careering wildly rushing; cf. Psalms 104:3:
"who walketh upon the wings of the wind"
commands a calm Cf. "Then he arose, and rebuked the winds and the sea; and there was a
great calm" (Matthew 8:26).
The   Complaint . . . Immortality   Young's
Night Thoughts became one of the most popular
poems of the age both in England and abroad,
and Boswell could declare it "a mass of the
grandest and richest poetry that human genius
has ever produced." Johnson was cooler: "Let
burlesque go beyond him," he remarked of
Young's extended conceits. By the time he wrote

Night Thoughts Young had achieved a distinguished career as a satirist. This poem, with its
graveyard imagery, is an implicit reply to
Pope's *Essay on Man;* it dramatizes the emptiness of any quest for happiness in the world and
urges on man his power of flight above the
claims of the world. In this last, Young becomes
an enthusiastic celebrant of the latent divinity in
man and seeks to induce a flight into those
realms of infinity that the soul must find its
congenial climate. His tactics, in his constant
rebuke to the young libertine Lorenzo, are
those of shock and witty paradox, and he was
later denounced by George Eliot for his "radical
insincerity as a poetic artist"; but, at least in the
passage quoted from Night VI, he could anticipate and appeal to Wordsworth.

From different natures marvelously mixed,
Connexion exquisite of distant worlds!
Distinguished link in being's endless chain!
Midway from nothing to the deity!
A beam ethereal, sullied, and absorpt!
Though sullied and dishonoured, still divine!
Dim miniature of greatness absolute!
An heir of glory! A frail child of dust!
80   Helpless immortal! Insect infinite!
A worm! a god!—I tremble at myself,
And in myself am lost! At home, a stranger,
Thought wanders up and down, surprised, aghast,
And wondering at her own: How reason reels!
O what a miracle to man is man,
Triumphantly distressed! what joy, what dread!
Alternately transported, and alarmed!
What can preserve my life? or what destroy?
An angel's arm can't snatch me from the grave,
90   Legions of angels can't confine me there . . .

                                        1742

   From *Night VI*

              .   .   .

Where, thy true treasure? Gold says, 'Not in me:'
And, 'Not in me,' the diamond. Gold is poor;
India's insolvent: Seek it in thyself,
Seek in thy naked self, and find it there;
In being so descended, formed, endowed;
Sky-born, sky-guided, sky-returning race!
Erect, immortal, rational, divine!
420   In senses, which inherit earth and heavens,
Enjoy the various riches nature yields;
Far nobler! *give* the riches they enjoy;
Give taste to fruits and harmony to groves;
Their radiant beams to gold, and gold's bright fire;
Take in, at once, the landscape of the world,
At a small inlet, which a grain might close,
And half create the wondrous world they see.
Our senses, as our reason, are divine.
But for the magic organ's powerful charm,
430   Earth were a rude, uncoloured chaos still.
Objects are but the occasion; ours the exploit;
Ours is the cloth, the pencil, and the paint°
Which nature's admirable picture draws;
And beautifies creation's ample dome.
Like Milton's Eve,° when gazing on the lake,

the cloth . . . paint i.e. the canvas, brush, and
paint
Milton's Eve *Paradise Lost* IV.456–71, where

Eve unknowingly beholds her own reflection in
the water

Man makes the matchless image man admires:
Say then, shall man his thoughts all sent abroad,
Superior wonders in himself forgot,
His admiration waste on objects round,
440   When heaven makes him the soul of all he sees?
Absurd; not rare! so great, so mean, is man.

     . . .

    What wealth in souls that soar, dive, range around,
Disdaining limit, or from place or time;
And hear at once, in thought extensive, hear
The almighty fiat and the trumpet's sound!°
Bold, on creation's outside walk, and view
What was, and is, and more than e'er shall be;
Commanding, with omnipotence of thought,
Creations new in fancy's field to rise!
470   Souls, that can grasp whate'er the Almighty made,
And wander wild through things impossible!
What wealth, in faculties of endless growth,
In quenchless passions violent to crave,
In liberty to choose, in power to reach,
And in duration (how thy riches rise!)
Duration to perpetuate——boundless bliss!

     . . .

1746

SAMUEL JOHNSON

From A Journey to the Western Islands [1]

. . . We were now in the bosom of the Highlands, with full leisure to contemplate the appearance and properties of mountainous regions, such as have been, in many countries, the last shelters of national distress, and are every where the scenes of adventures, stratagems, surprises and escapes.

Mountainous countries are not passed but with difficulty, not merely from the labour of climbing; for to climb is not always necessary: but because that which is not mountain is commonly bog, through which the way must be picked with caution. Where there are hills, there is much rain, and the torrents pouring down into the intermediate spaces, seldom find so ready an outlet, as not to stagnate, till they have broken the texture of the ground.

Of the hills, which our journey offered to the view on either side, we did

fiat . . . sound i.e. the first (Creation) and
last (Judgment)

1. This is from Johnson's record of the tour that was also recorded by Boswell in his *Tour to the Hebrides with Samuel Johnson* (published after Johnson's death). Johnson's imagination had been stirred by the Hebrides in his boyhood reading of Martin Martin's *Description of the Western Islands of Scotland* (1703), and he spent a hundred days on the tour with Boswell in the autumn of 1773. This section comes from the account of the mainland of Scotland and describes the area near Anoch in Glenmorison.

not take the height, nor did we see any that astonished us with their loftiness. Towards the summit of one, there was a white spot, which I should have called a naked rock, but the guides, who had better eyes, and were acquainted with the phenomena of the country, declared it to be snow. It had already lasted to the end of August, and was likely to maintain its contest with the sun, till it should be reinforced by winter.

The height of mountains philosophically considered is properly computed from the surface of the next sea; but as it affects the eye or imagination of the passenger, as it makes either a spectacle or an obstruction, it must be reckoned from the place where the rise begins to make a considerable angle with the plain. In extensive continents the land may, by gradual elevation, attain great height, without any other appearance than that of a plane gently inclined, and if a hill placed upon such raised ground be described, as having its altitude equal to the whole space above the sea, the representation will be fallacious.

These mountains may be properly enough measured from the inland base; for it is not much above the sea. As we advanced at evening towards the western coast, I did not observe the declivity to be greater than is necessary for the discharge of the inland waters.

We passed many rivers and rivulets, which commonly ran with a clear shallow stream over a hard pebbly bottom. These channels, which seem so much wider than the water that they convey would naturally require, are formed by the violence of wintry floods, produced by the accumulation of innumerable streams that fall in rainy weather from the hills, and bursting away with resistless impetuosity, make themselves a passage proportionate to their mass.

Such capricious and temporary waters cannot be expected to produce many fish. The rapidity of the wintry deluge sweeps them away, and the scantiness of the summer stream would hardly sustain them above the ground. This is the reason why in fording the northern rivers, no fishes are seen, as in England, wandering in the water.

Of the hills many may be called with Homer's Ida 'abundant in springs,' but few can deserve the epithet which he bestows upon Pelion by 'waving their leaves.' [2] They exhibit very little variety; being almost wholly covered with dark heath, and even that seems to be checked in its growth. What is not heath is nakedness, a little diversified by now and then a stream rushing down the steep. An eye accustomed to flowery pastures and waving harvests is astonished and repelled by this wide extent of hopeless sterility. The appearance is that of matter incapable of form or usefulness, dismissed by nature from her care and disinherited of her favours, left in its original elemental state, or quickened only with one sullen power of useless vegetation.

It will very readily occur, that this uniformity of barrenness can afford very little amusement to the traveller; that it is easy to sit at home and conceive rocks and heath, and waterfalls; and that these journeys are useless labours, which neither impregnate the imagination, nor enlarge the understanding. It is true that of far the greater part of things, we must content ourselves with such knowledge as description may exhibit, or analogy supply; but it is true likewise,

2. Cf. Homer, *Iliad* XXIII.117 and II.757.

that these ideas are always incomplete, and that at least, till we have compared them with realities, we do not know them to be just. As we see more, we become possessed of more certainties, and consequently gain more principles of reasoning, and found a wider basis of analogy.

Regions mountainous and wild, thinly inhabited, and little cultivated, make a great part of the earth, and he that has never seen them, must live unacquainted with much of the face of nature, and with one of the great scenes of human existence.

As the day advanced towards noon, we entered a narrow valley not very flowery, but sufficiently verdant. Our guides told us, that the horses could not travel all day without rest or meat, and entreated us to stop here, because no grass would be found in any other place. The request was reasonable and the argument cogent. We therefore willingly dismounted and diverted ourselves as the place gave us opportunity.

I sat down on a bank, such as a writer of romance might have delighted to feign. I had indeed no trees to whisper over my head, but a clear rivulet streamed at my feet. The day was calm, the air soft, and all was rudeness,[3] silence, and solitude. Before me, and on either side, were high hills, which by hindering the eye from ranging, forced the mind to find entertainment for itself. Whether I spent the hour well I know not; for here I first conceived the thought of this narration.

We were in this place at ease and by choice, and had no evils to suffer or to fear; yet the imaginations excited by the view of an unknown and untravelled wilderness are not such as arise in the artificial solitude of parks and gardens, a flattering notion of self-sufficiency, a placid indulgence of voluntary delusions, a secure expansion of the fancy, or a cool concentration of the mental powers. The phantoms which haunt a desert are want, and misery, and danger; the evils of dereliction rush upon the thoughts; man is made unwillingly acquainted with his own weakness, and meditation shews him only how little he can sustain, and how little he can perform. There were no traces of inhabitants, except perhaps a rude pile of clods called a summer hut, in which a herdsman had rested in the favourable seasons. Whoever had been in the place where I then sat, unprovided with provisions and ignorant of the country, might, at least before the roads were made, have wandered among the rocks, till he had perished with hardship, before he could have found either food or shelter. Yet what are these hillocks to the ridges of Taurus,[4] or these spots of wildness to the deserts of America? . . .

1775

WILLIAM COLLINS
1721–1759

Collins formed part of a group of poets of the mid-century who, in Johnson's words, were "eminently delighted with those flights of imagination which pass the bounds of nature"—Joseph and Thomas Warton and Mark Akenside among them. Collins came

3. Wildness.
4. The great mountain chain in southern Turkey.

to know Joseph Warton at Winchester School, and they later planned a joint volume of odes. While that plan, like most that Collins entertained, was never realized, their work shows common impulse and mutual influence. Collins's *Odes on Several Descriptive and Allegoric Subjects*, dated 1747 and published on December 20, 1746, followed Warton's volume by a few weeks; but it had little success. The last decade of Collins's life was spent in depression and eventual madness.

The Wartons' father, Thomas Warton the Elder (1688–1745), had already attempted imitations of Chaucer, Spenser, and Milton and had written two "Scandinavian" odes; he transmitted to his sons the new enthusiasms of the age, and in *The Enthusiast* (1744) of Joseph and *The Pleasures of Melancholy* (1747) of the younger Thomas we can see the cultivation of wild nature, of primitive energy, and of moral rigor such as had characterized the work of James Thomson. The new literary movement had its manifesto in Joseph Warton's *Essay on the Genius and Writings of Pope* (of which the first volume appeared in 1756). Warton there distinguishes sharply between the poetry of "familiar life" and true poetry, which embodies a "creative and glowing imagination" of "exalted and very uncommon character," a power that typically aspires (as Pope, Warton felt, did not) to the "transcendently sublime and prophetic." Such aspiration seeks to achieve visionary power in the revival of romance, in the enraptured transcendence of the visible, in the power to excite man to a full sense of his own divinity. As Akenside writes, we become God-like through imagination: "we feel within ourselves / His energy divine; he tells the heart, / He meant, he made us to behold and love / What he beholds and loves / . . . to be great like Him, beneficent and active . . ." (*The Pleasures of the Imagination*, 1743, III.624–29). As he turns to nature, the poet seeks to "behold in lifeless things, / The inexpressive resemblance of himself, / Of thought and passion" (III.284–86); for "mind alone / . . . The living fountains in itself contains / Of beauteous and sublime" (I.481–83). This drive toward the imaginative sometimes puts excessive stress upon the merely imaginary. As Johnon said of Collins, he "delighted to rove through the meanders of enchantment, to gaze on the magnificence of golden palaces, to repose by the waterfalls of Elysian gardens." But we can also find an effort to generate myth, to inform the natural scene with visionary presences, and—in Collins's late ode—to recover the creative power that is native to the popular mind and the folk imagination. In these efforts the imaginary achieves the release of an internal power too easily suppressed in "familiar life."

Ode on the Poetical Character °

I

As once—if not with light regard
I read aright that gifted bard°
(Him whose school above the rest

Ode on the Poetical Character This is one of Collins's most difficult poems, and it shows an emergent power of myth-making in its condensation of images and themes. The Poetical Character becomes a divine gift difficult to merit; it is a power akin to God's own creative energies and has been realized only by such committed and heroic bards as Milton. There is a sense of poetry as a sacred power, terrifying in its demands and yet compelling in its claims; and this poem seems to mark Collins's ascent from the eclogue to the far greater and more exacting odes.

that gifted bard Edmund Spenser, whose subject was the Elfin (or Faerie) Queen and whose school (such poets as Edward Fairfax, Giles and Phineas Fletcher, Michael Drayton, and to a degree John Milton) is mentioned below

His loveliest Elfin queen has blessed)—
One, only one, unrivalled fair,
Might hope the magic girdle° wear,
At solemn tourney hung on high,
The wish of each love-darting eye;

Lo! to each other nymph in turn applied,°
10   As if, in air unseen, some hovering hand,
Some chaste and angel friend to virgin fame,
     With whispered spell had burst the starting band,
It left unblessed her loathed dishonoured side;
     Happier, hopeless fair, if never
Her baffled hand with vain endeavour
Had touched that fatal zone to her denied!
Young Fancy° thus, to me divinest name,
To whom, prepared and bathed in Heaven,
The cest of amplest power is given,
20   To few the godlike gift assigns
To gird their blessed prophetic loins
And gaze° her visions wild and feel unmixed her flame!

                    II
The band, as fairy legends say,
Was wove on that creating day,
When He who called with thought to birth
Yon tented° sky, this laughing° earth,
And dressed° with springs and forests tall,
And poured the main engirting all,
Long by the loved Enthusiast° wooed,
30   Himself in some diviner mood,°
Retiring, sate with her alone,
And placed her on his sapphire throne,°
The whiles, the vaulted shrine around,
Seraphic wires were heard to sound,
Now sublimest triumph swelling,
Now on love and mercy dwelling;
And she, from out the veiling cloud,

the magic girdle The girdle (or zone) called
Cestus (thus "cest" in l. 19) that belonged to
Florimel could be worn only by a virtuous
woman; "But whosoever contrarie doth prove, /
Might not the same about her middle weare,
/ But it would loose, or else a sunder teare"
(Spenser, *The Faerie Queene* IV.v.3, ll. 3–5).
applied tried on, brought into contact
Fancy the counterpart, in Collins's myth, of
Florimel
gaze gaze upon, be inspired by
tented tent-like
laughing pleasant, fertile
dressed adorned; the metaphor carried on in
the "engirting" ocean of the next line
Enthusiast Fancy; possessed by God, as in ll.
17–22; cf. Milton's invocation to Urania in

Paradise Lost VII.8–12: "Before the hills appeared or fountain flowed, / Thou with Eternal
wisdom didst converse. / Wisdom the sister,
and with her didst play / In presence of the
Almighty Father, pleased / With thy celestial
song."
diviner mood Cf. Dryden, *Absalom and Achitophel*, ll. 19–20: "Whether, inspired by some
diviner lust, / His father got him with a greater
gust."
sapphire throne Cf. Milton, *At a Solemn Music*,
where before the "sapphire-coloured throne" of
God, "the bright seraphim in burning row, /
Their loud up-lifted angel trumpets blow, /
And the cherubic host in thousand choirs /
Touch their immortal harps of golden wires
. . . " (ll. 10–13).

Breathed her magic notes aloud:
And thou, thou rich-haired Youth of Morn,°
40 And all thy subject life was born!
The dangerous Passions kept aloof,
Far from the sainted growing woof,°
But near it sate ecstatic Wonder,
Listening the deep applauding thunder,
And Truth, in sunny vest arrayed,
By whose the tarsel's° eyes were made;
All the shadowy tribes of Mind
In braided° dance their murmurs joined,
And all the bright uncounted Powers
50 Who feed on Heaven's ambrosial flowers.
Where is the bard whose soul can now
Its high presuming hopes avow?
Where he who thinks, with rapture blind,
This hallowed work° for him designed?

III

High on some cliff, to Heaven up-piled,°
Of rude access, of prospect wild,
Where, tangled round the jealous steep,
Strange shades o'erbrow the valleys deep,
And holy genii guard the rock,
60 Its glooms embrown, its springs unlock,
While on its rich ambitious head
An Eden, like his own, lies spread,
I view that oak,° the fancied glades among,
By which as Milton lay, his evening ear,
From many a cloud that dropped ethereal dew,
Nigh sphered in Heaven, its native strains could hear;
On which that ancient trump° he reached was hung.
    Thither oft, his glory greeting,
    From Waller's myrtle shades° retreating,

Youth of Morn the sun, Apollo, who was also
the god of poetry; perhaps poetry itself as well
sainted . . . woof the sacred fabric (either of
the "subject life" of the Sun, or, more aptly,
here, of the "cest" of Fancy; both may be implied, for the Sun and the poet seem fused in
the "Youth of Morn")
tarsel's the male hawk's
braided interweaving (but carrying on the
metaphor of the "woof")
hallowed work the cest of Fancy, i.e. the high
task of poetic creation as the analogy of God's
creation of the world
High on . . . up-piled In the following section
Collins seems to fuse the mount of poetry itself
(traditionally the resort of the Muses, Mt. Parnassus); the "steep savage hill" on which Eden
is situated in *Paradise Lost* IV.134–37: "the
champaign head / Of a steep wilderness, whose
hairy sides / With thicket overgrown, grotesque
and wild, / Access denied"; the towering

ascent, difficult of access by imitation, of Milton's own poetic powers (as one who wore the
"cest").
that oak In *Il Penseroso*, ll. 59–60, Milton describes himself as listening to the nightingale's
"even-song" near "the accustomed oak"; with
possible overtones of the sacred oak of the
Druids and the oak tree at the ancient oracle of
Dodona, in the rustling of whose leaves the
will of Zeus was revealed; at any rate, the
scene is one of inspired listening to the
"strains," whether "native" to Heaven or to
Milton's own exalted spirit.
ancient trump presumably the epic voice or
power
Waller's . . . shades the myrtle as sacred to
Venus and an emblem of love, appropriate to the
amorous lyrics of Edmund Waller (1606–87),
as opposed to the heroic strain of Spenser and
Milton

70 With many a vow from Hope's aspiring tongue,
My trembling feet his guiding steps pursue;
    In vain—such bliss to one alone,
    Of all the sons of soul was known,
    And Heaven and Fancy, kindred powers,
    Have now o'erturned the inspiring bowers,°
Or curtained close such scene from every future view.

Ode to Evening°

If aught of oaten stop° or pastoral song
May hope, chaste Eve, to soothe thy modest ear,
    Like thy own solemn springs,°
    Thy springs and dying gales,

O nymph reserved, while now the bright-haired sun°
Sits in yon western tent, whose cloudy skirts,°
    With brede° ethereal wove,
    O'erhang his wavy bed°—

Now air is hushed, save where the weak-eyed bat,
10 With short shrill shriek, flits by on leathern wing;°
    Or where the beetle winds
    His small but sullen horn,°

As oft he rises 'midst the twilight path,
Against the pilgrim° borne in heedless hum—
    Now teach me, maid composed,
    To breathe some softened strain,

o'erturned . . . bowers suggesting Guyon's destruction of the Bower of Bliss (*The Faerie Queene* II.xii) but also the closing of Eden to the fallen Adam, repeating the theme of the inaccessibility of Eden (ll. 55 ff.) but now with a new note of despair
Ode to Evening The meter and unrhymed stanza were, as Collins's friend Thomas Warton pointed out, based on Milton's in his translation of Horace's Pyrrha ode (I.v) and were used by Warton as well. The 1748 text, which is used here, contains revisions, and one in particular of special interest. Lines 29–32 originally read as follows:
> Then let me rove some wild and
>   heathy scene,
> Or find some ruin midst its dreary
>   dells,
> Whose walls more awful nod
>   By thy religious gleams.
>   1746
In the later version printed below, the light of Evening is diffused and reflected in the landscape, so that the lake holds the light and casts it in turn upon the "time-hallowed pile." The traditional personification of Evening tends to give way to an immanent presence, absorbed into the landscape rather than acting upon it; and this looks ahead to those underpresences of Romantic poetry such as Wordsworth's.
oaten stop Cf. Milton, *Comus*, l. 345: "Or sound of pastoral reed with oaten stops."
solemn springs originally "brawling springs"; suggesting that "springs" refers to brooks; interestingly altered to the less specific and more complex "solemn" in revision
bright-haired sun Cf. the "rich-haired Youth of Morn" in "Poetical Character," l. 39.
skirts the edges of clouds; with suggestion of canopy and curtains
brede braid; implying interweaving of colors as in a rainbow, here in sunset clouds
wavy bed Cf. Milton, Nativity ode, ll. 229–31: "So when the sun in bed, / Curtained with cloudy red, / Pillows his chin upon an orient wave . . . "
leathern wing a phrase to be found in Spenser, Shakespeare, Pope, and Gay
sullen horn Cf. Milton, *Lycidas*, l. 28: "What time the gray-fly winds her sultry horn."
pilgrim wanderer, traveler

Whose numbers,° stealing through thy darkening vale,
May not unseemly with its stillness suit,
    As musing slow, I hail
20   Thy genial loved return!

For when thy folding-star° arising shows
His paly circlet,° at his warning lamp
    The fragrant Hours, and elves
    Who slept in flowers the day,

And many a nymph who wreathes her brows with sedge,
And sheds the freshening dew, and, lovelier still,
    The pensive Pleasures sweet
    Prepare thy shadowy car.°

Then lead, calm votaress, where some sheety lake
30 Cheers the lone heath, or some time-hallowed pile°
    Or upland fallows gray
    Reflect its last cool gleam.

But when chill blustering winds or driving rain
Forbid my willing feet, be mine the hut
    That from the mountain's side
    Views wilds and swelling floods,°

And hamlets brown, and dim-discovered spires,
And hears their simple bell, and marks o'er all
    Thy dewy fingers draw
40   The gradual dusky veil.

While Spring shall pour his showers, as oft he wont,
And bathe thy breathing° tresses, meekest Eve;
    While Summer loves to sport
    Beneath thy lingering light;

While sallow Autumn fills thy lap with leaves;
Or Winter, yelling through the troublous air,
    Affrights thy shrinking train,
    And rudely rends thy robes;

So long, sure-found beneath the sylvan shed,
50 Shall Fancy, Friendship, Science,° rose-lipped Health,
    Thy gentlest influence own,
    And hymn thy favourite name!
        1748

numbers verses
folding-star the Evening Star, which arises at the time to put sheep in their fold or pen
paly circlet Cf. Milton, *Paradise Lost* V.169 for the Morning Star's "bright circle."
car chariot

pile building, ancient and probably Gothic
floods rivers
breathing emitting fragrance
Science learning, study; there is in the four personifications a mixture of private and social, intellectual and physical

Ode on the Popular Superstitions of the Highlands of Scotland°

Considered as the Subject of Poetry

I

H[ome], thou returnest from Thames,° whose Naiads long
    Have seen thee lingering, with a fond delay,
    Mid those soft friends whose hearts, some future day,
Shall melt, perhaps, to hear thy tragic song.
Go, not unmindful of that cordial youth
    Whom, long endeared, thou leavest by Lavant's side;°
Together let us wish him lasting truth,
    And joy untainted with his destined bride.
Go! nor regardless, while these numbers boast
10   My short-lived bliss, forget my social name;
But think, far off, how, on the southern coast,
    I met thy friendship with an equal flame!
Fresh to that soil thou turnest, whose every vale
    Shall prompt° the poet, and his song demand;
To thee thy copious subjects ne'er shall fail;
    Thou needest but take the pencil° to thy hand,
And paint what all believe who own° thy genial land.

II

There must thou wake perforce thy Doric quill;°
    'Tis Fancy's land to which thou settest thy feet;
20   Where still, 'tis said, the fairy people meet,
Beneath each birken° shade, on mead or hill.
There each trim lass that skims the milky store
    To the swart tribes their creamy bowls allots;°
By night they sip it round the cottage door,
    While airy minstrels warble jocund notes.
There every herd° by sad experience knows
    How, winged with fate, their elf-shot arrows fly,
When the sick ewe her summer food foregoes,

Ode . . . Highlands of Scotland This ode was addressed to John Home (1727–1808), a Scottish clergyman who later achieved fame as the author of the tragedy *Douglas* (1756). The ode was seen by the Wartons in 1754 and mentioned, on Joseph Warton's report, by Johnson in his life of Collins. This led to Alexander Carlyle's discovery of a defective draft of the poem he remembered having seen among his papers. A more complete text appeared in print in London (1788), but its authenticity was questioned by many, including Wordsworth, and it now seems to have been a forgery. Interestingly, Home later encouraged James Macpherson in his Gaelic forgeries of Ossian, and Collins's interest in folk materials may have been a stimulus to their fabrication.
from Thames The ode was presumably written upon his return to Scotland.
by Lavant's side in Chichester ("on the southern coast"), where Home's friend Thomas Barrow probably introduced him to Collins (Barrow had just been married there)
prompt inspire
pencil paintbrush
own acknowledge as their own
Doric quill rustic pipe or reed; cf. Milton, *Lycidas*, ll. 188–89: "He touched the tender stops of various quills, / With eager thought warbling his Doric lay"
birken birch's (in a Northern form)
swart tribes . . . allots The "swart tribes" are Brownies, who helped with the farmwork in return for a reward but made the animals sick (with "elf-shot arrows") if they were neglected.
herd herdsman

Or, stretched on earth, the heart-smit heifers lie.
30 Such airy beings awe the untutored swain,
    Nor thou, though learnèd, his homelier thoughts neglect;
Let thy sweet Muse the rural faith sustain:
    These are the themes of simple, sure effect,
That add new conquests to her boundless reign,
    And fill, with double force, her heart-commanding strain.

                    III
E'en yet preserved, how often mayst thou hear,
    Where to the pole the boreal° mountains run,
    Taught by the father to his listening son,
Strange lays, whose power had° charmed a Spenser's ear.
40 At every pause, before thy mind possessed,°
    Old Runic° bards shall seem to rise around,
    With uncouth lyres, in many-coloured vest,°
    Their matted hair with boughs fantastic crowned:
Whether thou biddest the well-taught hind° repeat
    The choral dirge that mourns some chieftain brave,
When every shrieking maid her bosom beat,
    And strewed with choicest herbs his scented grave;
Or whether, sitting in the shepherd's shiel,°
    Thou hearest some sounding° tale of war's alarms;
50 When at the bugle's call, with fire and steel,
    The sturdy clans poured forth their bonny° swarms,
And hostile brothers met to prove each other's arms.

                    IV
'Tis thine to sing how, framing hideous spells,°
    In Skye's lone isle, the gifted wizard seer,
    Lodged in the wintry cave with [   ]
Or in the depth of Uist's dark forests dwells:
    How they whose sight such dreary dreams engross
With their own visions oft astonished droop,
    When o'er the watery strath° or quaggy moss°
60 They see the gliding ghosts unbodied troop;
    Or, if in sports, or on the festive green,
    Their [   ] glance some fated youth descry,

boreal northern
had would have
possessed i.e. by vision; spellbound
Runic ancient Scottish (transferred from Scandinavian)
vest garment, dress
hind peasant
shiel "a kind of hut built every summer for
. . . milking the cattle" (Collins); i.e. in distant pastures
sounding resounding
bonny MS. reads "bony" and could mean big-
boned, of large frame, but "bonny," i.e. good-
looking, is more likely.

hideous spells An account of "second sight,"
the faculty of perceiving apparitions connected
with future disasters; during the vision, the
seer is entirely in the control of what he beholds; later reported by Boswell and Johnson
in their tour of the Hebrides (of which Skye
and two islands of Uist are part). In lines 65 ff.
Collins seems to imply, in contradiction of his
sources, that the seers have power over the
spirits.
strath stretch of flat land beside water
quaggy moss muddy bog

Who now perhaps in lusty vigour seen,
And rosy health, shall soon lamented die.
For them the viewless° forms of air obey,
Their bidding heed, and at their beck repair;
They know what spirit brews the stormful day,
And, heartless,° oft like moody madness stare
To see the phantom train their secret work prepare.

v [missing]

vi [eight lines missing]
What though far off, from some dark dell espied,
His glimmering mazes cheer the excursive° sight,
Yet turn, ye wanderers, turn your steps aside,
Nor trust the guidance of that faithless light;°
For, watchful, lurking mid the unrustling reed,
100   At those mirk° hours the wily monster° lies,
And listens oft to hear the passing steed,
And frequent round him rolls his sullen eyes,
If chance his savage wrath may some weak wretch surprise.

vii
Ah, luckless swain, o'er all unblessed indeed!
Whom late bewildered in the dank, dark fen,
Far from his flocks and smoking hamlet then,
To that sad spot [   ]
On him, enraged, the fiend, in angry mood,
Shall never look with pity's kind concern,
110   But instant, furious, raise the whelming flood
O'er its drowned bank, forbidding all return.
Or, if he meditate his wished escape
To some dim hill, that seems uprising near,
To his faint eye the grim and grisly shape,
In all its terrors clad, shall wild appear.
Meantime the watery surge shall round him rise,
Poured sudden forth from every swelling source.
What now remains but tears and hopeless sighs?
His fear-shook limbs have lost their youthly force,
120   And down the waves he floats, a pale and breathless corse!

viii
For him in vain his anxious wife shall wait,
Or wander forth to meet him on his way;
For him in vain at to-fall° of the day,

viewless invisible
heartless dismayed, stupefied
excursive ranging, wandering
faithless light the wildfire or will-o'-the-wisp;
cf. Milton, *Paradise Lost* IX.634–42

mirk dark, murky
wily monster the kelpie or water spirit (cf. l. 137)
to-fall the close

His babes shall linger at the unclosing gate!
Ah, ne'er shall he return! Alone, if night
   Her travelled° limbs in broken slumbers steep,
With dropping° willows dressed his mournful sprite°
   Shall visit sad, perchance, her silent sleep;
Then he, perhaps, with moist and watery hand,
130   Shall fondly seem to press her shuddering cheek,
And with his blue-swoln face before her stand,
   And, shivering cold, these piteous accents speak:
'Pursue, dear wife, thy daily toils pursue,
   At dawn or dusk, industrious as before;
Nor e'er of me one hapless thought renew,
While I lie weltering° on the osiered shore,
Drowned by the kelpie's wrath, nor e'er shall aid thee more!'

       IX
Unbounded is thy range: with varied style
   Thy Muse may, like those feathery tribes which spring
140   From their rude rocks, extend her skirting wing
Round the moist marge of each cold Hebrid isle,
   To that hoar pile which still its ruins shows;
In whose small vaults a pigmy-folk is found,°
   Whose bones the delver with his spade upthrows,
And culls them, wondering, from the hallowed ground!
Or thither where, beneath the showery West,
   The mighty kings of three fair realms are laid;°
Once foes, perhaps, together now they rest;
   No slaves revere them, and no wars invade:
150   Yet frequent now, at midnight's solemn hour,
   The rifted mounds their yawning cells unfold,
And forth the monarchs stalk with sovereign power,
   In pageant robes, and wreathed with sheeny gold,
And on their twilight tombs aërial council hold.

       X
But O! o'er all, forget not Kilda's race,°
   On whose bleak rocks, which brave the wasting tides,
   Fair Nature's daughter, Virtue, yet abides.
Go, just, as they, their blameless manners trace!
   Then to my ear transmit some gentle song
160   Of those whose lives are yet sincere and plain,
   Their bounded walks the ragged cliffs along,

travelled travailed, wearied
dropping dripping
sprite spirit
weltering tossed about by the waters
a pigmy-folk is found Small bones, discovered
in the Flannan Islands and in a stone vault on
Benbecula, gave rise to the conjecture that a
race of pygmies had once lived there.

thither where . . . are laid Iona, where kings
of Scotland, Ireland, and Norway were supposed to lie buried together
Kilda's race the people of St. Kilda, the outermost of the Hebrides, celebrated for simple,
stoical virtues as of the Golden Age

And all their prospect but the wintry main.
  With sparing temperance, at the needful time,
They drain the sainted spring; or, hunger-pressed.
  Along the Atlantic rock undreading climb,
And of its eggs despoil the solan's° nest.
  Thus blessed in primal innocence they live,
  Sufficed and happy with that frugal fare
  Which tasteful toil and hourly danger give.
170 Hard is their shallow soil, [   ] and bare;
  Nor ever vernal bee was heard to murmur there!

XI

Nor needest thou blush that such false themes engage
  Thy gentle° mind, of fairer stores possessed;
  For not alone they touch the village breast,
But filled in elder time, the historic page.
  There Shakespeare's self, with every garland crowned,
  In musing hour his Wayward Sisters° found,
  And with their terrors dressed the magic scene.
  From them he sung, when, mid his bold design,
180 Before the Scot, afflicted and aghast,
  The shadowy kings of Banquo's fated line
Through the dark cave in gleamy pageant passed.°
  Proceed, nor quit the tales which, simply told,
  Could once so well my answering bosom pierce;
  Proceed—in forceful sounds and colours bold
The native legends of thy land rehearse;
To such adapt thy lyre, and suit thy powerful verse.

XII

In scenes like these, which, daring to depart
  From sober truth,° are still to Nature true,
190 And call forth fresh delight to Fancy's view,
The heroic muse employed her Tasso's art!°
  How have I trembled, when at Tancred's stroke,
  Its gushing blood the gaping cypress poured;
  When each live plant with mortal accents spoke,
And the wild blast upheaved the vanished sword!
  How have I sat, where piped the pensive wind,
To hear his harp by British Fairfax strung;

---

solan's a goose or gannet
gentle cultivated
Wayward Sisters the Witches in Macbeth,
"wayward" in their supernatural power over
fate
in . . . passed Macbeth IV.i
daring . . . truth Cf. Dryden, "Of Heroic
Plays: An Essay" (1672), where he cites,
among other inventions, the Enchanted Wood
in Tasso and the Bower of Bliss in Spenser: "an

heroic poet is not tied to a bare representation
of what is true, or exceeding probable but
. . . he may let himself loose to visionary objects and to the representation of such things as
. . . may give him a freer scope for imagination."
Tasso's art Edward Fairfax's translation (1600)
of Jerusalem Delivered (where Tancred appears) was reprinted in 1749, shortly before
Collins wrote the poem.

     Prevailing° poet! whose undoubting mind
Believed the magic wonders which he sung!
200   Hence, at each sound, imagination glows;
     Hence his warm lay with softest sweetness flows;
Melting it flows, pure, numerous,° strong, and clear,
And fills the impassioned heart and lulls the harmonious° ear.

       XIII
All hail, ye scenes that o'er my soul prevail,
Ye [   ] firths° and lakes, which, far away,
     Are by smooth Annan filled or pastoral Tay,
Or Don's romantic springs; at distance, hail!
The time shall come, when I, perhaps, may tread
     Your lowly glens, o'erhung with spreading broom;
210   Or, o'er your stretching heaths, by Fancy led;
Then will I dress once more the faded bower,
     Where Jonson° sat in Drummond's [   ] shade;
Or crop, from Tiviot's dale,° each [   ]
     And mourn, on Yarrow banks,° [   ]
Meantime, ye Powers, that on the plains which bore
     The cordial youth,° on Lothian's plains, attend,
Where'er he dwell, on hill or lowly muir,°
     To him I lose, your kind protection lend,
220   And, touched with love like mine, preserve my absent friend.
1749–50   1788

THOMAS GRAY
1716–1771

Gray's production was more slender than his talent, but his rather neurasthenic temperament would permit no more. Most of his life was spent at Cambridge, where he finally became Regius Professor of Modern History three years before his death (always planning but never giving a lecture). At Eton he became a close friend of Horace Walpole and Richard West, and this friendship continued at Cambridge. Having planned a legal career, he gave it up and returned to Cambridge within a few months after the early death of West; he quarreled with Walpole during their grand tour, but they were finally reconciled after more than four years (1741–45), and Walpole remained an enthusiastic patron and supporter of his poetry, printing the two great odes on his

Prevailing powerful
numerous musical
harmonious filled with harmony
firths arms of the sea, into which some of the rivers named below empty
Jonson Ben Jonson walked in Scotland in 1619 to visit William Drummond at his estate at Hawthornden near Edinburgh, and Drummond published the record of their conversations; Collins may see himself as Jonson to Home's Drummond.

Tiviot's dale probably a reference to the Border Ballads set there, particularly *Chevy Chase*
Yarrow banks referring to the ballad *The Braes of Yarrow* by William Hamilton of Bangour (1704–54), whose poems were first collected in 1748
cordial youth here Home, in Edinburgh ("on Lothian's plains")
muir moor

own press. Gray was a formidable scholar—called by one friend "the most learned man in Europe"—and was open to many of the new literary influences of his day; in addition to classical models he turned to newly discovered Welsh and Norse poetry, and he was greatly interested in the supposed works of Ossian that Dr. Johnson helped expose as a forgery. His travel letters are among the earliest to record the new enthusiasm for the sublimities of the Alps and, later, of the Lake Country and Scotland. He was somewhat affected, delicate, and mincing in manner, especially (as his friend and editor William Mason put it) "before those whom he did not wish to please." They seem to have been many, and they included his Cambridge enemy Christopher Smart. That Gray aspired to more generosity than he sometimes achieved in life is clearest in the *Elegy*.

Gray wrote early to his friend West that "the language of the age is never the language of poetry," and he created a fabric of heightened "poetic diction," sometimes deliberately allusive and sometimes faintly evocative, from reminiscences of classical and earlier English poetry—notably Spenser, Shakespeare, and Milton—as well as of Dryden and Pope. This diction could be used with great subtlety to frame in the Eton ode an ironic and self-critical nostalgia, to give lapidary form in the *Elegy* to sentiments which (as Johnson said) each reader "persuades himself that he has always felt," or in *The Bard* to produce a visionary intensity that renders English history with the sublime terror and radiance of prophecy.

Ode on a Distant Prospect of Eton College°

Ἄνθρωπος · ἱκανὴ πρόφασις εἰς τὸ δυστυχεῖν.
                                                        MENANDER°

Ye distant spires, ye antique towers,
That crown the watery glade,
Where grateful Science° still adores
Her Henry's holy shade;°
And ye, that from the stately brow
Of Windsor's heights° the expanse below
Of grove, of lawn, of mead survey,
Whose turf, whose shade, whose flowers among
Wanders the hoary Thames along
10   His silver-winding way:

Ode . . . Eton College Among the sorrows that lie behind the poem are the death of Gray's schoolmate and friend Richard West; Gray's quarrel with his friend Horace Walpole; and perhaps the fall from power of Walpole's father, Sir Robert. In a letter to West of May 27, 1742, Gray contemplates the aging of his old schoolmates into husbands, fathers, statesmen. "Do not you remember them dirty boys playing at cricket?" he writes. "As for me, I am never a bit older, nor the bigger, nor the wiser than I was then; no, not for having been beyond sea." The "dirty boys" become figures of Eden or a golden age; the world Gray recalls is cut off as by the distance of the prospect; and the poem evokes a poignant double view, pivoting sharply on the phrase "the little victims" (l. 52). For Edward Gibbon's view of the poem, see Headnote to the section Sense and Sensibility. Menander a fragment: "I am a man, a sufficient excuse for being unhappy."
Science knowledge in general
Henry's . . . shade Eton was founded in the 15th century by Henry VI, sometimes called the "martyr king."
Windsor's heights The towers of Windsor Castle stand across the Thames from Eton.

Ah happy hills, ah pleasing shade,
Ah fields beloved in vain,°
Where once my careless childhood strayed,
A stranger yet to pain!
I feel the gales° that from ye blow
A momentary bliss bestow,
As, waving fresh their gladsome wing,
My weary soul they seem to soothe,
And, redolent° of joy and youth,
20   To breathe a second spring.

Say, Father Thames, for thou hast seen
Full many a sprightly race°
Disporting on thy margent green
The paths of pleasure trace,
Who foremost now delight to cleave
With pliant arm thy glassy wave?
The captive linnet which enthrall?
What idle progeny succeed
To chase the rolling circle's° speed,
30   Or urge the flying ball?

While some on earnest business bent
Their murmuring labours° ply
'Gainst graver hours, that bring constraint
To sweeten liberty;
Some bold adventurers disdain
The limits of their little reign,
And unknown regions dare descry;
Still as they run they look behind,
They hear a voice in every wind,
40   And snatch a fearful joy.

Gay hope is theirs by fancy fed,
Less pleasing when possessed;
The tear forgot as soon as shed,
The sunshine of the breast;
Their buxom° health of rosy hue,
Wild wit, invention ever new,
And lively cheer of vigour born;
The thoughtless day, the easy night,
The spirits pure, the slumbers light,
50   That fly the approach of morn.

in vain stressing the distance in time as well as space, the painful irreversibility of the past
gales breezes
redolent smelling sweetly
race generation
rolling circle's hoop's (Gray's use of formalized "poetic diction" with its stately and periphrastic —i.e. roundabout—terms for familiar objects is related to earlier mock-heroic diction; here it acquires a peculiar sense of distance, a mockery of naïve innocence, and some genuine acknowledgment of the heroic nature of that golden age of youth)
Their . . . labours presumably studying and memorizing, repeating softly to themselves what they will present to their teachers in "graver hours"
buxom lively

Alas, regardless° of their doom,
The little victims play!
No sense have they of ills to come,
Nor care beyond today:
Yet see how all around 'em wait
The ministers of human fate,
And black Misfortune's baleful train!
Ah, show them where in ambush stand
To seize their prey the murtherous band!
60 Ah, tell them, they are men!

These shall the fury Passions tear,
The vultures of the mind;
Disdainful Anger, pallid Fear,
And Shame that skulks behind;
Or pining Love shall waste their youth,
Or Jealousy with rankling tooth,
That inly gnaws the secret heart,
And Envy wan, and faded Care,
Grim-visaged comfortless Despair,
70 And Sorrow's piercing dart.

Ambition this shall tempt to rise,
Then whirl the wretch from high,
To bitter Scorn a sacrifice,
And grinning Infamy.
The stings of Falsehood those shall try,
And hard Unkindness' altered eye,
That mocks the tear it forced to flow;
And keen Remorse with blood defiled,
And moody Madness laughing wild
80 Amid severest woe.

Lo, in the vale of years beneath
A grisly troop are seen,
The painful family° of Death,
More hideous than their queen:
This racks the joints, this fires the veins.
That every labouring sinew strains,
Those in the deeper vitals rage;
Lo, Poverty, to fill the band,
That numbs the soul with icy hand,
90 And slow-consuming Age.

To each his sufferings; all are men,
Condemned alike to groan:
The tender for another's pain,
The unfeeling for his own.

---

regardless heedless, unaware   **family** household, tribe

Yet, ah! why should they know their fate?
Since sorrow never comes too late,
And happiness too swiftly flies.
Thought would destroy their paradise.
No more: where ignorance is bliss,
100   'Tis folly to be wise.

1742   1747

Ode on the Death of a Favourite Cat, Drowned in a Tub of Gold Fishes°

'Twas on a lofty vase's side,°
Where China's gayest art had dyed
   The azure flowers that blow;°
Demurest of the tabby kind,
The pensive Selima reclined,
   Gazed on the lake below.

Her conscious tail her joy declared;
The fair round face, the snowy beard,
   The velvet of her paws,
10   Her coat, that with the tortoise vies,
Her ears of jet, and emerald eyes,
   She saw; and purred applause.°

Still had she gazed; but 'midst the tide
Two angel forms were seen to glide,
   The genii° of the stream:
Their scaly armour's Tyrian° hue
Through richest purple to the view
   Betrayed a golden gleam.

The hapless nymph with wonder saw:
20   A whisker first and then a claw,
   With many an ardent wish,
She stretched in vain to reach the prize.
What female heart can gold despise?
   What cat's averse to fish?

Ode on the Death . . . Gold Fishes Gray wrote this at Horace Walpole's request as an epitaph for one of his cats. It takes the form of an animal fable with appropriate moral, but its mock-heroic idiom carefully evokes—through echoes of Pope and Dryden—Homer's Helen and Virgil's Camilla, as well as Milton's Eve. One might compare Chaucer's *Nun's Priest's Tale* for similar interplay between high diction and obtrusive animal details (e.g. l. 8).
'Twas . . . side Cf. the opening of John Dryden's *Alexander's Feast.*
blow bloom, blossom. Dr. Johnson remarks on "how resolutely a rhyme is sometimes made when it cannot easily be found," but the pointlessness of the emphasis may be meant to set the comic tone.
purred applause Selima's narcissism may be meant to suggest Eve in Milton, *Paradise Lost* IV.456–66, where she first beholds her reflection and feels "sympathy and love" for the fair stranger, even pining "with vain desire."
genii guardian spirits, as in the "genius of the place"
Tyrian Tyre in Phoenicia was an ancient source of purple dye.

Presumptuous maid! with looks intent
Again she stretched, again she bent,
   Nor knew the gulf between.
(Malignant Fate sat by and smiled)
The slippery verge° her feet beguiled,
30   She tumbled headlong in.

Eight times emerging from the flood
She mewed to every watery god,
   Some speedy aid to send.
No dolphin° came, no Nereid° stirred;
Nor cruel Tom nor Susan° heard.
   A favourite has no friend!

From hence, ye beauties, undeceived,
Know, one false step is ne'er retrieved,
   And be with caution bold.
Not all that tempts your wandering eyes
And heedless hearts is lawful prize.
   Nor all that glisters, gold.°
1747   1748

Elegy Written in a Country Churchyard°

The curfew tolls the knell of parting day,
   The lowing herd wind slowly o'er the lea,
The ploughman homeward plods his weary way,
   And leaves the world to darkness and to me.

Now fades the glimmering landscape on the sight,
   And all the air a solemn stillness holds,
Save where the beetle wheels his droning flight,
   And drowsy tinklings lull the distant folds;

verge bank, rim
dolphin such as rescued the drowning musician
Arion by carrying him to safety on its back
Nereid sea nymph
Tom . . . Susan servants
all . . . gold a proverbial phrase, perhaps best
known in Shakespeare's Merchant of Venice II.
vii.65
Elegy . . . Churchyard When Gray began to
write this poem, whose earlier manuscript title
was Stanza's Wrote in a Country Church-Yard,
is hard to determine; his friend (as of 1747)
William Mason dated its beginning in 1742,
but other evidence suggests a real commence-
ment some three or more years later. At any
rate, it was completed and seen by Horace
Walpole in 1750. The poem had great and
immediate success, which Gray was inclined to
attribute to its subject; while it had been pre-

ceded by such "graveyard" poems as Edward
Young's Night Thoughts (1742–45) and Robert
Blair's The Grave (1743), it is far more restrained and classical in spirit. Where, however,
the Stanza's originally concluded with a generalized moral statement of serene endurance
("But through the last sequestered vale of life
/ Pursue the silent tenor of thy doom"), the
Elegy has created, through a double distancing,
the swain's account of the poet and finally the
epitaph (presumably of the poet's own composition). In the epitaph we see the problem of
self-fulfillment (treated earlier in the village
poor) translated into the capacity for feeling
and the reward of a friend. From that tribute
to personal feeling one can look back to the
"wonted fires" of l. 92 for the claims that Gray's
poem is written both to recognize and to meet.

Save that from yonder ivy-mantled tower
10   The moping owl does to the moon complain
Of such, as wandering near her secret bower,
    Molest her ancient solitary reign.

Beneath those rugged elms, that yew-tree's shade,
    Where heaves the turf in many a mouldering heap,
Each in his narrow cell forever laid,
    The rude forefathers° of the hamlet sleep.

The breezy call of incense-breathing morn,
    The swallow twittering from the straw-built shed,
The cock's shrill clarion or the echoing horn,°
20   No more shall rouse them from their lowly bed.

For them no more the blazing hearth shall burn,
    Or busy housewife° ply her evening care;
No children run to lisp their sire's return,
    Or climb his knees the envied kiss to share.

Oft did the harvest to their sickle yield;
    Their furrow oft the stubborn glebe° has broke;
How jocund did they drive their team afield!
    How bowed the woods beneath their sturdy stroke!

Let not Ambition mock their useful toil,
30   Their homely° joys and destiny obscure;
Nor Grandeur hear with a disdainful smile
    The short and simple annals° of the poor.

The boast of heraldry, the pomp of power,
    And all that beauty, all that wealth e'er gave,
Awaits alike the inevitable hour:
    The paths of glory lead but to the grave.

Nor you, ye proud, impute to these the fault,
    If Memory o'er their tomb no trophies° raise,
Where through the long-drawn aisle and fretted° vault
40   The pealing anthem° swells the note of praise.

Can storied° urn or animated° bust
    Back to its mansion call the fleeting breath?
Can Honour's voice provoke° the silent dust,
    Or Flattery soothe the dull cold ear of Death?

---

rude forefathers humble (uneducated) ancestors
horn of the hunter
housewife pronounced "hussif"
glebe field
homely simple, domestic (originally, "rustic")
annals year-by-year life records, as opposed to the more expansive "histories" of nations or "lives" of great men

trophies carved memorials; literally symbols of victory, as here over the blankness of death
fretted decorated with patterns of carving
pealing anthem Cf. Milton, *Il Penseroso*, ll. 161, 163: "There let the pealing organ blow / . . . In service high and anthems clear."
storied having stories represented upon it
animated as if breathing
provoke rouse up

Perhaps in this neglected spot is laid
    Some heart once pregnant with celestial fire;
Hands that the rod of empire might have swayed,
    Or waked to ecstasy the living lyre.

But Knowledge to their eyes her ample page,
50   Rich with the spoils of time, did ne'er unroll;
Chill Penury repressed their noble rage,°
    And froze the genial current° of the soul.

Full many a gem of purest ray serene,°
    The dark unfathomed caves of ocean bear;
Full many a flower is born to blush unseen,
    And waste its sweetness on the desert air.

Some village Hampden,° that with dauntless breast
    The little tyrant of his fields withstood;
Some mute inglorious Milton here may rest,
60   Some Cromwell, guiltless of his country's blood.

The applause of listening senates to command,
    The threats of pain and ruin to despise,
To scatter plenty o'er a smiling land,
    And read their history in a nation's eyes,

Their lot forbade; nor circumscribed alone°
    Their growing virtues, but their crimes confined.
Forbade to wade through slaughter to a throne,
    And shut the gates of mercy on mankind;

The struggling pangs of conscious truth to hide,
70   To quench the blushes of ingenuous shame,°
Or heap the shrine of Luxury and Pride
    With incense kindled at the Muse's flame.

Far from the madding crowd's ignoble strife,
    Their sober wishes never learned to stray;
Along the cool sequestered vale of life
    They kept the noiseless tenor of their way.

Yet even these bones from insult to protect,
    Some frail memorial° still erected nigh,
With uncouth rhymes and shapeless sculpture decked,
80   Implores the passing tribute of a sigh.

---

rage rapture, ardor
genial current creative energies
serene clear, bright (as in Latin *serenus*); with possible overtones of calm and quiet as well
Hampden John Hampden (1594–1643), who refused to submit to a special tax levied by Charles I in 1636 and as a member of Parliament defended the rights of the people; origi-

nally "Cato" (for the Roman senator who championed republican rights), as "Milton" was "Tully" (Cicero) and "Cromwell" was "Caesar"
nor . . . alone i.e. not only
ingenuous shame natural (or innately noble) honor
frail memorial presumably the simple tombstones in the churchyard as opposed to the monumental tombs within the church

Their name, their years, spelt by the unlettered Muse,
　　The place of fame and elegy° supply;
And many a holy text around she strews,
　　That teach the rustic moralist to die.

For who, to dumb forgetfulness a prey,
　　This pleasing anxious being e'er resigned,
Left the warm precincts of the cheerful day,
　　Nor cast one longing lingering look behind?

On some fond breast the parting soul relies,
90　　Some pious drops° the closing eye requires;
Even from the tomb the voice of Nature cries,
　　Even in our ashes live their wonted fires.

For thee,° who mindful of the unhonoured dead
　　Dost in these lines their artless tale relate;
If chance,° by lonely contemplation led,
　　Some kindred spirit shall inquire thy fate,

Haply some hoary-headed swain may say,
　　'Oft have we seen him at the peep of dawn
Brushing with hasty steps the dews away
100　　To meet the sun upon the upland lawn.

'There at the foot of yonder nodding beech
　　That wreathes its old fantastic roots so high,
His listless length at noontide would he stretch,
　　And pore upon the brook that babbles by.

'Hard by yon wood, now smiling as in scorn,
　　Muttering his wayward fancies he would rove;
Now drooping, woeful-wan, like one forlorn,
　　Or crazed with care, or crossed in hopeless love.

'One morn I missed him on the customed hill,
110　　Along the heath and near his favourite tree;
Another came; nor yet beside the rill,
　　Nor up the lawn, nor at the wood was he;

'The next, with dirges due, in sad array,
　　Slow through the church-way path we saw him borne.
Approach and read (for thou canst read) the lay,
　　Graved on the stone beneath yon agèd thorn.'

　　　THE EPITAPH
Here rests his head upon the lap of earth,
　　A youth to fortune and to fame unknown;

---

elegy a formal tribute on the monument or elsewhere; supplied for the poor in the churchyard
by this poem (which is also a poetic meditation in the classical sense of "elegy")

drops mourner's tears
thee the poet's own self
chance i.e. by chance

Fair Science° frowned not on his humble birth,
120   *And Melancholy° marked him for her own.*

Large was his bounty and his soul sincere;
    Heaven did a recompense as largely send:
He gave to Misery all he had, a tear;
    He gained from Heaven ('twas all he wished) a friend.

No farther seek his merits to disclose,
    Or draw his frailties from their dread abode,
(There they alike in trembling hope repose)
    The bosom of his Father and His God.
    1742–50   1751

The Bard

Although Gray had begun the ode earlier, he was inspired to resume it by the visit to Cambridge of John Parry, a blind Welsh harper who could perform "tunes of a thousand years old with names enough to choke you." This poem was first printed with its "sister ode," *The Progress of Poesy* by Horace Walpole, and later published by Dodsley. Gray expected the poems to baffle many readers; they outdid expectations and finally were given notes by Gray, although only "out of spite," in 1768. Gray explains in the original Advertisement to the poem that it is "founded on a tradition current in Wales that Edward the First, when he completed the conquest of that country, ordered all the bards that fell into his hands to be put to death." In his Commonplace Book Gray envisages "a venerable figure seated on the summit of an inaccessible rock, who, with a voice more than human, reproaches the king with all the misery and desolation which he had brought on his country" and prophesies that the "noble ardour of poetic genius in this island" will "never be wanting to celebrate true virtue and valour" and to "censure tyranny and oppression." As his song ends, "he precipitates himself from the mountain, and is swallowed up by the river that rolls at its foot."

This Pindaric ode, more authentically regular than Dryden's, brings together various forms of sublime power (the heroic and biblical—Moses and Ezekiel, the Welsh, and Norse) and typical themes (the spirit of liberty, the poet as prophet, the grandeur and wildness of the mountain scene). Dr. Johnson's adverse criticism points to Gray's deliberate effort: "The images are magnified by affectation; the language is laboured into harshness. The mind of the writer seems to work with unnatural violence. . . . He has a kind of strutting dignity, and is tall by walking on tiptoe. His art and struggle are too visible, and there is too little appearance of ease and nature." Yet one may see that "ease" is hardly Gray's object and the very surpassing or transcendence of "nature" in visionary intensity is his goal. William Blake found "weaving the winding sheet of Edward's race by means of spiritual music . . . a bold, daring, and masterly conception." For William Blake's and John Martin's conceptions of Gray's bard, see Figs. 48 and 49 in the illustration section of this volume.

Science knowledge or learning
Melancholy implying a pensiveness and heightened sensibility, with a great capacity for feeling, for others (as we see in his "bounty") as well as for himself

The Bard

A Pindaric Ode

'Ruin seize thee, ruthless King!
Confusion on thy banners wait,°
Though fanned by Conquest's crimson wing
They mock the air with idle state.°
Helm, nor hauberk's° twisted mail,
Nor even thy virtues, tyrant, shall avail
To save they secret soul from nightly fears,
From Cambria's° curse, from Cambria's tears!'
Such were the sounds that o'er the crested pride°
Of the first Edward scattered wild dismay,
As down the steep of Snowdon's° shaggy side
He wound with toilsome march his long array.
Stout Gloucester° stood aghast in speechless trance;
'To arms!' cried Mortimer, and couched his quivering lance.

On a rock whose haughty brow
Frowns o'er old Conway's foaming flood,
Robed in the sable garb of woe,
With haggard° eyes the poet stood
(Loose his beard and hoary hair
Streamed, like a meteor, to the troubled air),°
And with a master's hand and prophet's fire
Struck the deep sorrows of his lyre:
'Hark, how each giant oak and desert cave
Sighs to the torrent's awful voice beneath!
O'er thee, O King! their hundred arms they wave,
Revenge on thee in hoarser murmurs breathe;
Vocal no more, since Cambria's fatal day,
To high-born Hoel's harp, or soft Llewellyn's lay.°

'Cold is Cadwallo's tongue,
That hushed the stormy main;
Brave Urien sleeps upon his craggy bed;
Mountains, ye mourn in vain
Modred, whose magic song

10 (line marker)
20 (line marker)
30 (line marker)

Confusion . . . wait Cf. Shakespeare, *King John* IV.iii.152, 154: "vast confusion waits / . . . The imminent decay of wrested pomp."
They mock . . . state Cf. *King John* V.i.72: "Mocking the air with colours idly spread"; "idle" also implying that the "state" is barren or foredoomed.
hauberk's coat of chain-mail
Cambria's Wales's
crested pride Gray cites "The crested adder's pride" from Dryden, *The Indian Queen* III.i.
Snowdon's the Welsh mountain, known for its eagles (cf. l. 38)
Gloucester like Mortimer one of the border lords who have joined Edward's forces
haggard "a metaphor taken from an unreclaimed

hawk, which is called a haggard, and looks wild and *farouche* and jealous of its liberty" (Gray)
Loose . . . air "The image was taken from a well-known picture of Raphael representing the Supreme Being in the vision of Ezekiel" (Gray); "or (if you have been at Parma) you may remember Moses breaking the tables by . . . Parmigianino, which comes still closer to my meaning" (Gray); cf. also Milton, *Paradise Lost* I.537: "Shone like a meteor streaming to the wind."
Hoel's . . . Llewellyn's lay imaginary bards with actual Welsh names, as are those named in the next stanza

Made huge Plinlimmon° bow his cloud-topped head.
On dreary Arvon's° shore they lie,
Smeared with gore, and ghastly pale;
Far, far aloof the affrighted ravens sail;
The famished eagle screams, and passes by.
Dear lost companions of my tuneful art,
40 Dear as the light that visits these sad eyes,
Dear as the ruddy drops that warm my heart,
Ye died amidst your dying country's cries—
No more I weep. They do not sleep.
　　On yonder cliffs, a grisly band,
I see them sit; they linger yet,
Avengers of their native land;
With me in dreadful harmony they join,
And weave with bloody hands the tissue of thy line.

' "Weave the warp, and weave the woof,
50 The winding-sheet of Edward's race.°
Give ample room, and verge enough
The characters° of hell to trace.
Mark the year, and mark the night,
When Severn shall re-echo with affright
The shrieks of death through Berkeley's roofs that ring,
Shrieks of an agonizing king!°
She-wolf of France, with unrelenting fangs,
That tearest the bowels of thy mangled mate,
From thee be born, who o'er thy country hangs,
60 The scourge of heaven.° What Terrors round him wait!
Amazement in his van, with Flight combined,
And Sorrow's faded form, and Solitude behind.

' "Mighty victor, mighty lord,
Low on his funeral couch he lies!
No pitying heart, no eye, afford
A tear to grace his obsequies.°
Is the Sable Warrior° fled?
Thy son is gone. He rests among the dead.
The swarm that in thy noontide beam were born?
70 Gone to salute the rising morn.
Fair laughs the morn, and soft the zephyr blows,°

Plinlimmon a high mountain between Cardigan and Glamorgan
Arvon's Caernarvonshire in North Wales
Weave . . . Edward's race "The image is taken from an ancient Scaldic Ode, written in the Old Norwegian tongue about A.D. 1029" (Gray); "the winding-sheet" used to wrap the buried corpse
characters figures, marks
Shrieks . . . king Edward II was painfully killed in Berkeley Castle beside the river Severn (1327) at the instigation of Isabel of Anjou, his adulterous wife.

The scourge of heaven Edward III (1312–77), who conquered much of France
his obsequies death of Edward III, "abandoned by his children and even robbed in his last moments by his courtiers and his mistress" (Gray)
Sable Warrior "Edward, the Black Prince, dead some time before his father" (Gray); the famous victor at Crécy and Poitiers
Fair laughs . . . blows "magnificence of Richard II's reign" (Gray)

While proudly riding o'er the azure realm
In gallant trim the gilded vessel goes;
Youth on the prow, and Pleasure at the helm;
Regardless of the sweeping whirlwind's sway,
That, hushed in grim repose, expects his evening prey.

' "Fill high the sparkling bowl,
The rich repast prepare;
Reft of a crown, he yet may share the feast;
80   Close by the regal chair
Fell Thirst and Famine scowl
A baleful smile upon their baffled guest.°
Heard ye the din of battle° bray,
Lance to lance, and horse to horse?
Long years of havoc urge their destined course,
And through the kindred squadrons mow their way.
Ye towers of Julius, London's lasting shame,°
With many a foul and midnight murther fed,
Revere his consort's faith, his father's fame,
90   And spare the meek usurper's holy head.°
Above, below, the rose of snow,
Twined with her blushing foe, we spread;°
The bristled boar° in infant gore
Wallows beneath the thorny shade.
Now, brothers, bending o'er the accursèd loom,
Stamp we our vengeance deep, and ratify his doom.

' "Edward, lo! to sudden fate
(Weave we the woof: the thread is spun)
Half of thy heart° we consecrate.
100   (The web is wove. The work is done.)"
Stay, oh stay! nor thus forlorn
Leave me unblessed, unpitied, here to mourn:
In yon bright track that fires the western skies,
They melt, they vanish from my eyes.
But oh! what solemn scenes on Snowdon's height,
Descending slow, their glittering skirts° unroll?

baffled guest Richard II was starved to death (1400), according to one historian: served in a royal manner but prevented from eating anything set before him.
din of battle "ruinous civil wars of York and Lancaster" (Gray); the Wars of the Roses
Ye towers . . . shame Henry VI, Edward V, and others of the royal family "believed to be murthered secretly in the Tower of London. The oldest part of that structure is vulgarly attributed to Julius Caesar" (Gray).
the meek . . . head Henry VI "very near being canonized"; his consort "Margaret of Anjou, a woman of heroic spirit, who struggled hard to save her husband and her crown"; her father Henry V, the great victor at Agincourt. Henry VI is called a "usurper" because "the line of Lancaster had no right of inheritance to the crown" (Gray).

Above, below . . . spread "The white and red roses of York and Lancaster" (Gray)
bristled boar Richard III, whose badge was a silver boar, and who wallowed in the blood of his nephews, the infant princes, under the "thorny shade" of the roses—to be intertwined in the marriage of Henry VII (of the house of Lancaster) and Elizabeth of York. Henry VII defeated and killed Richard III at Bosworth Field in 1485.
Half of thy heart Edward I's wife Eleanor of Castile died a few years after the conquest of Wales and was deeply mourned by the king; here she is consecrated or devoted to doom.
skirts Cf. "cloudy skirts," William Collins, *Ode to Evening*, l. 6; the visions are imagined as descending clouds catching the sunset light.

Visions of glory, spare my aching sight;
Ye unborn ages, crowd not on my soul!
No more our long-lost Arthur° we bewail.
110   All hail, ye genuine kings, Britannia's issue, hail!

'Girt with many a baron bold
Sublime their starry fronts° they rear;
And gorgeous dames, and statesmen old
In bearded majesty, appear.
In the midst a form divine!°
Her eye proclaims her of the Briton line;
Her lion-port, her awe-commanding face,
Attempered sweet to virgin-grace.
What strings symphonious tremble in the air,
120   What strains of vocal transport round her play!
Hear from the grave, great Taliessin,° hear;
They breathe a soul to animate thy clay.
Bright Rapture calls, and soaring, as she sings,
Waves in the eye of Heaven her many-coloured wings.

'The verse adorn again
Fierce War, and faithful Love,°
And Truth severe, by fairy Fiction dressed.
In buskined° measures move
Pale Grief, and pleasing Pain,
130   With Horror, tyrant of the throbbing breast.
A voice, as of the cherub-choir,
Gales from blooming Eden bear;°
And distant warblings lessen on my ear,
That lost in long futurity° expire.
Fond° impious man, thinkest thou yon sanguine cloud,
Raised by thy breath, has quenched the orb of day?
Tomorrow he repairs the golden flood,°
And warms the nations with redoubled ray.
Enough for me: with joy I see
140   The different doom our Fates assign.
Be thine Despair, and sceptered Care;
To triumph,° and to die, are mine.'
He spoke, and headlong from the mountain's height
Deep in the roaring tide he plunged to endless night.
1755–57   1757

Arthur "It was the common belief of the Welsh
nation that King Arthur was still alive in fairyland and should return again to reign over
Britain" (Gray); Welsh rule is restored with
the house of Tudor under Henry VII.
fronts brows
form divine Elizabeth I
Taliessin "chief of the bards, flourished in the
6th century" (Gray); here the revival of poetry
Fierce War . . . Love Gray cites Spenser, The
Faerie Queene, Proem: "Fierce warres and faithfull loves shall moralize my song."

buskined wearing the tragic cothurnus or boot
of the Greek theater; Shakespeare is implied
from . . . Eden bear Milton's Paradise Lost
lost . . . futurity "the succession of poets after
Milton's time" (Gray)
Fond foolish; referring to Edward I, whose
"sanguine" or crimson cloud of conquest conceals the sun
repairs . . . flood restores his flood of light
triumph in the ultimate restoration of liberty
and the revival of poetry

On Lord Holland's Seat near Margate, Kent°

Old, and abandoned by each venal friend,
  Here Holland took the pious resolution
To smuggle some few years, and strive to mend
  A broken character and constitution.

On this congenial spot he fixed his choice,
  Earl Goodwin° trembled for his neighbouring sand;
Here seagulls scream and cormorants rejoice,
  And mariners, though shipwrecked, dread to land.

Here reign the blustering North and blighting East,
10 No tree is heard to whisper, bird to sing.
Yet Nature cannot furnish out the feast;
  Art he invokes new horrors still to bring.

Now mouldering fanes and battlements arise,
  Arches and turrets° nodding to their fall,
Unpeopled palaces delude his eyes,
  And mimic desolation covers all.

'Ah!' said the sighing peer, 'had Bute° been true,
  Nor Shelburne's, Rigby's, Calcraft's friendship vain,
Far other scenes than these had blessed our view,
20 And realized the ruins that we feign.

'Purged by the sword and beautified by fire,
  Then had we seen proud London's hated walls:
Owls might have hooted in St. Peter's choir,
  And foxes stunk and littered in St. Paul's.'°
1768   1769

On Lord . . . Kent Henry Fox (1705–74), 1st Lord Holland, became Paymaster General in 1757 and proceeded to amass a great fortune; as Leader of the House of Commons in Lord Bute's ministry he did much to promote the Peace of Paris (1763). Fox was widely mistrusted as an unscrupulous schemer and self-seeker who resorted to bribery and intimidation; this view emerged only some years after Horace Walpole could write Fox: "I know you think Mr. Gray the greatest poet we have and I know he thinks the greatest man we have" (1756). Holland in retirement (because of poor health) built a classical villa surrounded by "many fanciful representations of antique and ruined buildings," ironically described by Walpole as resembling "a prospect in some half-civilized island discovered by Captain Cook." The poem was first published without Gray's permission as *Inscription for the Villa of a Decayed Statesman on the Sea Coast*, but Gray refused to allow its republication during his lifetime (or Holland's). It is one of the few sharply satiric poems Gray wrote, very much in the spirit of the age of Pope; it represents a gift that Gray did not sufficiently honor in himself. **Earl Goodwin** Goodwin Sands, a dangerous sandbank off the Kent coast, was named for Earl Godwine of the 11th century; as the legendary remains of an island, they are threatened by the grasping presence of Holland. **fanes . . . turrets** artificial ruins and fantastic "follies" (as such ornamental architecture, not meant to be lived in but for view, were called); cf. Timon's "laboured quarry" in Pope's *Epistle to Burlington*, ll. 99 ff. **Bute** Fox had received a peerage as Baron Holland in 1763, but he claimed betrayal and quarreled over political spoils with the Prime Minister, Lord Bute, and other colleagues named in the next line; he was widely attacked as a "traitor" to England, particularly by the middle-class supporters of the elder Pitt in the City of London, and it is of their ruin that he regretfully dreams. **Owls . . . St. Paul's** Cf. Isaiah 13:21: "But wild beasts of the desert shall lie there; and their houses shall be full of doleful creatures; and owls shall dwell there, and satyrs shall dance there"; also Pope, *Windsor Forest*, ll. 70–71: "The fox obscene to gaping tombs retired, / And savage howlings fill the sacred choirs"; with, finally, a play upon Fox's name in the last line ("St. Peter's" refers to Westminster Abbey).

CHRISTOPHER SMART
1722–1771

Smart's brilliant and erratic career at Cambridge ended with heavy debts and Thomas Gray's prophecy that he "must come to a jail or Bedlam, and that without help, almost without pity." Smart's facility in both Latin and English verse had led him to translate Pope's *Essay on Criticism* into Latin with the poet's blessing, and it took him to London with hopes of a literary career. He worked for the publisher John Newbery and married Newbery's stepdaughter in 1752. By then his *Poems on Several Occasions* had appeared, he had been editing the humorous journal *The Midwife* with great success, and he had made a wide range of literary acquaintance, including Johnson and Hogarth. In 1757 Smart was admitted to St. Luke's Hospital for the insane and discharged a year later uncured. He was probably confined somewhere else during the next seven years, and the *Jubilate Agno* was written during that time. Upon his release he wrote and published *A Song to David* (1763), but his reputation for madness affected the reception of much of his later work. This included a remarkable verse paraphrase of the Psalms, a verse translation of Horace (1767), and finally *Hymns for the Amusement of Children* (1770). He died the following year in debtor's prison.

Smart's religious poetry goes back at least to the poems written for the Seaton prize at Cambridge, which he won several times. One, published in 1751, has these images of the sea: "Shrubs of amber from the pearl-paved bottom / Rise richly varied, where the finny race / In blithe security their gambols play." His remarkable diction had biblical sources but took its example in part from Horace, whose "beauty, force, and vehemence of Impression" Smart saw as a "talent or gift of Almighty God by which a genius is impowered to throw an emphasis upon a word or sentence in such wise that it cannot escape any reader of sheer good sense or true critical sagacity."

Smart's diction is one part of his distinctive effect. Another is the mystical geometry of form in *A Song to David*, its stanzas ordered in patterns of threes, sevens, and nines; its variations a constant embellishment of an architectonic frame; its elements elaborately arranged in a celebrative procession one can associate with baroque ceremoniousness. For the poem seems to be a tribute to God as poet of the universe and to that responsive celebration which all creatures, instinct with spirit, pay to Him. Of these David as divine poet is at once the symbol and the highest example.

Jubilate Agno°

From *Fragment B1*

Let Elizure rejoice with the Partridge,° who is a prisoner of state and is proud of his keepers.

For I am not without authority in my jeopardy, which I derive inevitably from the glory of the name of the Lord.

Let Shedeur rejoice with Pyrausta,° who dwelleth in a medium of fire, which God hath adapted for him.

For I bless God whose name is Jealous—and there is a zeal to deliver us from everlasting burnings.

Let Shelumiel rejoice with Olor,° who is of a goodly savour, and the very look of him harmonizes the mind.

For my existimation° is good even amongst the slanderers and my memory shall arise for a sweet savour unto the Lord.

Let Jael rejoice with the Plover, who whistles for his live,° and foils the marksmen and their guns.

For I bless the PRINCE of PEACE and pray that all the guns may be nailed up, save such as are for the rejoicing days.

From *Fragment B2*

For I will consider my Cat Jeoffry.

For he is the servant of the Living God duly and daily serving him.

For at the first glance of the glory of God in the East he worships in his way.

700   For is this done by wreathing his body seven times round with elegant quickness.

For then he leaps up to catch the musk, which is the blessing of God upon his prayer.

For he rolls upon prank to work it in.

Jubilate Agno "Rejoice in the Lamb." This remarkable work was apparently written during Smart's period of madness, and its manuscript survived as an example of poetic mania, interest in it stimulated by the similar case of William Cowper. The poem was written in sections of lines beginning with either *Let* or *For,* and it was clearly based upon theories of the antiphonal or responsive structure of Hebrew poetry, particularly those set forth by Bishop Robert Lowth, who was known to Smart personally as well as through his *De Sacra Poesia Hebraeorum* (1753). Although the *Let* and *For* sections were physically separate, they are joined by connections often ingenious and oblique. The *Let* verses tend toward impersonality, and the *For* verses make some application to Smart's own feeling or state. In the sample given from Fragment B1, the *Let* and *For* verses are placed in alternation in order to show more clearly their relationship.

The second and longer section given, concerning Smart's cat Jeoffry, lacks the *Let* verses. **Partridge** here caged
Pyrausta a winged insect said to dwell in the fire
Olor swan; connected with *olere,* to smell of or savor of
existimation from *existimare,* to esteem; hence, reputation
live life

2218

For having done duty and received blessing he begins to consider himself.

For this he performs in ten degrees.

For first he looks upon his fore-paws to see if they are clean.

For secondly he kicks up behind to clear away there.

For thirdly he works it upon stretch with the fore-paws extended.

For fourthly he sharpens his paws by wood.

For fifthly he washes himself.

710 For sixthly he rolls upon wash.

For seventhly he fleas himself, that he may not be interrupted upon the beat.°

For eighthly he rubs himself against a post.

For ninthly he looks up for his instructions.

For tenthly he goes in quest of food.

For having considered God and himself he will consider his neighbour.

For if he meets another cat he will kiss her in kindness.

For when he takes his prey he plays with it to give it a chance.

For one mouse in seven escapes by his dallying.

For when his day's work is done his business more properly begins.

720 For he keeps the Lord's watch in the night against the adversary.

For he counteracts the powers of darkness by his electrical skin and glaring eyes.

For he counteracts the Devil, who is death, by brisking about the life.

For in his morning orisons he loves the sun and the sun loves him.

For he is of the tribe of Tiger.

For the Cherub Cat is a term of the Angel Tiger.

For he has the subtlety and hissing of a serpent, which in goodness he suppresses.

For he will not do destruction if he is well-fed, neither will he spit without provocation.

For he purrs in thankfulness, when God tells him he's a good Cat.

For he is an instrument for the children to learn benevolence upon.

730 For every house is incomplete without him and a blessing is lacking in the spirit.

For the Lord commanded Moses concerning the cats at the departure of the Children of Israel from Egypt.

that he may not . . . beat so that he need not break off his activities to scratch

For every family had one cat at least in the bag.

For the English Cats are the best in Europe.

For he is the cleanest in the use of his fore-paws of any quadruped.

For the dexterity of his defence is an instance of the love of God to him exceedingly.

For he is the quickest to his mark of any creature.

For he is tenacious of his point.

For he is a mixture of gravity and waggery.

For he knows that God is his Saviour.

740   For there is nothing sweeter than his peace when at rest.

For there is nothing brisker than his life when in motion.

For he is of the Lord's poor and so indeed is he called by benevolence perpetually—Poor Jeoffry! poor Jeoffry! the rat has bit thy throat.

For I bless the name of the Lord Jesus that Jeoffry is better.

For the divine spirit comes about his body to sustain it in complete cat.

For his tongue is exceeding pure so that it has in purity what it wants in music.

For he is docile and can learn certain things.

For he can set up with gravity which is patience upon approbation.

For he can fetch and carry, which is patience in employment.

For he can jump over a stick which is patience upon proof positive.

750   For he can spraggle upon waggle at the word of command.

For he can jump from an eminence into his master's bosom.

For he can catch the cork and toss it again.

For he is hated by the hypocrite and miser.

For the former is afraid of detection.

For the latter refuses the charge.

For he camels his back to bear the first notion of business.

For he is good to think on, if a man would express himself neatly.

For he made a great figure in Egypt for his signal services.

For he killed the Icneumon-rat° very pernicious by land.

Icneumon-rat The icneumon is in fact regarded
as beneficial and kills rats and mice.

760   For his ears are so acute that they sting again.

For from this proceeds the passing quickness of his attention.

For by stroking of him I have found out electricity.

For I perceived God's light about him both wax and fire.

For the electrical fire is the spiritual substance, which God sends from heaven
   to sustain the bodies both of man and beast.

For God has blessed him in the variety of his movements.

For, though he cannot fly, he is an excellent clamberer.

For his motions upon the face of the earth are more than any other quadruped.

For he can tread to all the measures upon the music.

For he can swim for life.

770   For he can creep.

1756–63   1939

A Song to David

David the son of Jesse said, and the man who was raised up on high, the anointed
of the God of Jacob, and the sweet psalmist of Israel, said, 'The Spirit of the Lord
spake by me, and His word was in my tongue.'

                                                                    II SAMUEL 23:1–2

O thou, that sittest upon a throne,°
With harp of high majestic tone,
   To praise the King of kings;
And voice of heaven-ascending swell,
Which, while its deeper notes excel,
   Clear as a clarion rings:

To bless each valley, grove, and coast,
And charm the cherubs to the post
   Of gratitude in throngs;
10   To keep the days on Zion's mount,
And send the year to his account,
   With dances and with songs;

O Servant of God's holiest charge,
The minister of praise at large,
   Which thou mayst now receive;
From thy blessed mansion hail and hear,
From topmost eminence appear
   To this the wreath I weave.

O thou . . . throne The first three stanzas provide an incantation, and within them we can
see Smart's play with implicit antithesis: David
sits on a royal throne but pays humble praise
as Psalmist (1–3); his voice excels in "deeper
note" but sounds "clear as a clarion" (4–6); he
blesses the earth but charms cherubs from
heaven (7–9); he pays praise and receives it in
turn (13–15); etc.

Great, valiant, pious, good, and clean,
20 Sublime, contemplative, serene,
        Strong, constant, pleasant, wise!
    Bright effluence of exceeding grace;
    Best man!—the swiftness and the race,
        The peril and the prize!

    Great—from the lustre of his crown,
    From Samuel's horn° and God's renown,
        Which is the people's voice;
    For all the host, from rear to van,
    Applauded and embraced the man—
30   The man of God's own choice.

    Valiant—the word and up he rose—
    The fight—he triumphed o'er the foes
        Whom God's just laws abhor;
    And armed in gallant faith he took
    Against the boaster, from the brook,
        The weapons of the war.°

    Pious—magnificent and grand;
    'Twas he the famous temple planned:°
        (The seraph in his soul)
40 Foremost to give his Lord his dues,
    Foremost to bless the welcome news,
        And foremost to condole.

    Good—from Jehudah's° genuine vein,
    From God's best nature good in grain,°
        His aspect and his heart;
    To pity, to forgive, to save:
    Witness En-gedi's conscious cave,°
        And Shimei's blunted dart.°

    Clean—if perpetual prayer be pure,
50 And love, which could itself inure
        To fasting and to fear—
    Clean in his gestures, hands, and feet,
    To smite the lyre, the dance complete,
        To play the sword and spear.

Samuel's horn "Then Samuel took the horn of
oil, and anointed him in the midst of his
brethren: and the Spirit of the Lord came upon
David from that day forward" (I Samuel
16:13).
weapons of the war Taking "five smooth stones
from out the brook" for his sling, David kills
the Philistine champion and "boaster" Goliath
(I Samuel 17:40).
the famous . . . planned While David had it
in his heart to build the temple, the Lord reserved this task ("because thou hast been a man
of war, and hast shed blood") for his son
Solomon. David proceeded "to bless the welcome news" and give to Solomon "the pattern
of all that he had by the Spirit" (cf. the

"Seraph in the soul"). "All this, said David,
the Lord made me understand in writing by his
hand upon me, even all the works of this pattern" (I Chronicles 28:1–19).
Jehudah's i.e. Judah, the tribe to which David
belonged
good in grain good through and through
En-gedi's . . . cave where David spared the
life of Saul, who was pursuing him. And Saul
said to David, "Thou art more righteous than
I: for thou hast rewarded me good, whereas I
have rewarded thee evil" (I Samuel 24:17).
Shimei's . . . dart Shimei, "of the family of
the house of Saul," stoned and cursed David
but was later forgiven (II Samuel 16:5–14;
19:16–23).

Sublime—invention ever young,
Of vast conception, towering tongue,
  To God the eternal theme;
Notes from yon exaltations caught,
Unrivaled royalty of thought,
60   O'er meaner strains supreme.

Contemplative—on God to fix
His musings, and above the six
  The sabbath-day he blessed;
'Twas then his thoughts self-conquest pruned,
And heavenly melancholy tuned,
  To bless and bear the rest.

Serene—to sow the seeds of peace,
Remembering, when he watched the fleece,
  How sweetly Kidron° purled—
70   To further knowledge, silence vice,
And plant perpetual paradise
  When God had calmed the world.

Strong—in the Lord, who could defy
Satan, and all his powers that lie
  In sempiternal night;
And hell and horror and despair
Were as the lion and the bear°
  To his undaunted might.

Constant—in love to God the Truth,
80   Age, manhood, infancy, and youth—
  To Jonathan his friend
Constant, beyond the verge of death;
And Ziba and Mephibosheth
  His endless fame attend.°

Pleasant—and various as the year;
Man, soul, and angel, without peer,
  Priest, champion, sage, and boy;
In armour, or in ephod° clad,
His pomp, his piety was glad;
90   Majestic was his joy.

Kidron a brook near Jerusalem, over which David passed in his flight from his rebellious son Absalom (II Samuel 15:23); here associated with his youth as a shepherd and (probably) with Ezekiel's messianic vision of a river flowing from the altar of the temple which will fertilize the desolate land until it "become like the garden of Eden" (Ezekiel 47:1–12; 35:35)
the lion and the bear When Saul fears for David's weakness and youth, David recounts his rescue of his sheep from a lion and a bear, and concludes, "The Lord that delivered me out of the paw of the lion, and out of the paw of the bear, will deliver me out of the hand of this Philistine" (I Samuel 17:37).
To Jonathan . . . attend David restored the land of Saul to Mephibosheth, the son of Jonathan and grandson of Saul, and he made Ziba, Saul's former servant, steward (II Samuel 9).
ephod the priest's vestment, worn by David when he brought the ark of the Lord into Jerusalem and "danced before the Lord with all his might" (II Samuel 6:14)

Wise—in recovery from his fall,°
Whence rose his eminence o'er all,
    Of all the most reviled;
The light of Israel in his ways,
Wise are his precepts, prayer, and praise,
    And counsel to his child.

His Muse, bright angel of his verse,
Gives balm for all the thorns that pierce,
    For all the pangs that rage;
100   Blessed light, still gaining on the gloom,
The more than Michal of his bloom,
    The Abishag° of his age.

He sung of God—the mighty source
Of all things—the stupendous force
    On which all strength depends;
From whose right arm, beneath whose eyes,
All period, power, and enterprise
    Commences, reigns, and ends.

Angels—their ministry and meed,°
110   Which to and fro with blessings speed,
    Or with their citterns° wait;
Where Michael° with his millions bows,
Where dwells the seraph and his spouse,
    The cherub° and her mate.

Of man—the semblance° and effect
Of God and love, the saint elect
    For infinite applause—
To rule the land and briny broad,
To be laborious in his laud,
120   And heroes in his cause.

The world—the clustering spheres° he made,
The glorious light, the soothing shade,
    Dale, champaign, grove, and hill;
The multitudinous abyss,°
Where secrecy remains in bliss,
    And wisdom hides her skill.

---

his fall the stratagem for bringing death to
Uriah the Hittite once his wife Bathsheba began
to bear David's child (II Samuel 11–12).
Smart, following Patrick Delany's *Historical
Account of David* (1740–42), takes some of
Proverbs as "David's instructions to his son
Solomon."
Michal . . . Abishag Michal was David's first
wife and Abishag the virgin brought to warm
him in old age (I Kings 1–4); both are surpassed by his Muse, the inspirer of the Psalms.
meed gift
citterns stringed instruments

Michael the archangel regarded as patron and
guardian of the Hebrews; and later as the
leader with his angels of the fight against the
dragon (Revelation 12:7); here shown in service or humility
seraph . . . cherub the highest orders of angels
semblance i.e. made in God's image, to praise
(l. 119) and serve (l. 120) Him
clustering spheres the concentric spheres of the
heavenly bodies
abyss presumably Chaos, or the "deep" of
Genesis 1.2, wherein reside the materials not
yet given form

Trees, plants, and flowers—of virtuous° root;
Gem° yielding blossom, yielding fruit,
   Choice gums and precious balm;
130 Bless ye the nosegay in the vale,
And with the sweeteners of the gale°
   Enrich the thankful psalm.

Of fowl—e'en every beak and wing
Which cheer the winter, hail the spring,
   That live in peace or prey;
They that make music or that mock,
The quail, the brave domestic cock,
   The raven, swan, and jay.

Of fishes—every size and shape
140 Which nature frames of light escape,
   Devouring man to shun;
The shells are in the wealthy deep,
The shoals° upon the surface leap,
   And love the glancing sun.

Of beasts—the beaver plods his task;
While the sleek tigers roll and bask,
   Nor yet the shades arouse;°
Her cave the mining coney° scoops;
Where o'er the mead the mountain stoops°
150   The kids exult and browse.

Of gems—their virtue and their price,
Which hid in earth from man's device,°
   Their darts of lustre sheathe:
The jasper of the master's stamp,°
The topaz blazing like a lamp
   Among the mines beneath.

Blessed was the tenderness he felt
When to his graceful harp he knelt,
   And did for audience call;
160 When Satan with his hand he quelled,
And in serene suspense he held
   The frantic throes of Saul.°

His furious foes no more maligned
As he such melody divined,°

virtuous medicinal, beneficial
gem bud
gale breeze
shoals schools (of fish)
arouse make terrible
coney rabbit
stoops leans, hangs

device contrivance, design
stamp signet
Saul from whom David drove an "evil spirit"
("Satan") by playing on his harp (I Samuel
16:23)
divined discovered

And sense and soul detained;
Now striking strong, now soothing soft,
He sent the godly sounds aloft,
    Or in delight refrained.

When up to heaven his thoughts he piled,
170   From fervent lips fair Michal° smiled,
    As blush to blush she stood,
And chose herself the queen, and gave
Her utmost from her heart, 'so brave,
    And plays his hymns so good.'

The pillars of the Lord are seven,°
Which stand from earth to topmost heaven;
    His wisdom drew the plan;
His Word accomplished the design,
From brightest gem to deepest mine,
180   From Christ enthroned to man.

Alpha,° the cause of causes, first
In station, fountain, whence the burst
    Of light, and blaze of day;
Whence bold attempt and brave advance
Have motion, life, and ordinance,
    And heaven itself its stay.

Gamma supports the glorious arch
On which angelic legions march,
    And is with sapphires paved;
190   Thence the fleet clouds are sent adrift,
And thence the painted folds, that lift
    The crimson veil, are waved.°

Eta with living sculpture breathes,
With verdant carvings, flowery wreaths
    Of never-wasting bloom;
In strong relief his goodly base
All instruments of labor grace,
    The trowel, spade, and loom.

Next Theta stands to the Supreme—
200   Who formed, in number, sign,° and scheme,
    The illustrious lights that are;

fair **Michal** For her love of David, see I Samuel
18:18–20 (her words are Smart's invention).
The pillars . . . seven "Wisdom hath builded
her house; she hath hewn out her seven
pillars" (Proverbs 9:1). Smart fuses these seven
pillars (through their carvings) with the seven
days of Creation; further implications may be
drawn from Masonic symbolism, which is based
upon the building of Solomon's temple. The
scale of Creation is presented in terms that recall the traditional Great Chain of Being, in
which all of God's works are ranged continuously from highest to lowest.
Alpha God in the creative form of the Son or
Word (John 1:1). Here, as in the following
stanzas, Smart uses letters of the Greek alphabet, from Alpha (the first) to Omega (the last).
painted folds . . . waved presumably the
clouds that, brilliantly colored ("painted"),
reveal the rising sun, like curtains raised or
folded back
sign division of the zodiac; constellation

And one addressed° his saffron robe,
And one, clad in a silver globe,°
   Held rule with every star.

Iota's tuned to choral hymns
Of those that fly, while he that swims
   In thankful safety lurks;
And foot, and chapiter,° and niche,
The various histories enrich
210   Of God's recorded works.

Sigma presents the social droves,
With him that solitary roves,
   And man of all the chief;
Fair on whose face, and stately frame,
Did God impress his hallowed name,
   For ocular belief.

Omega! Greatest and the Best,
Stands sacred to the day of rest,
   For gratitude and thought;
220   Which blessed the world upon his pole,
And gave the universe his goal,
   And closed the infernal draught.°

O David, scholar of the Lord!
Such is thy science, whence reward
   And infinite degree;°
O strength, O sweetness, lasting ripe!
God's harp thy symbol, and thy type°
   The lion and the bee!

There is but One who ne'er rebelled,
230   But One by passion unimpelled,
   By pleasures unenticed;
He from himself his semblance sent,°
Grand object of his own content,
   And saw the God in Christ.

'Tell them I am,' Jehovah said
To Moses; while earth heard in dread,°
   And smitten to the heart,
At once above, beneath, around,
All nature, without voice or sound,
240   Replied, 'O Lord, Thou art.'

one addressed i.e. the sun clad in
one . . . silver globe the moon
chapiter capital of a pillar
draught i.e. closed off the drain of Hell
degree rank, ascent in divine favor
type symbol or emblem, i.e. strength and sweetness, as in the riddle of Samson (who found

honey in the carcass of a lion: "Out of the
strong came forth sweetness," Judges 14:14)
his semblance sent God's creation of the Son
earth . . . dread "And God said unto Moses,
I AM THAT I AM" (Exodus 3:14). The following stanzas embody versions of most of the
Ten Commandments.

Thou art—to give and to confirm
For each his talent and his term;
    All flesh thy bounties share.
Thou shalt not call thy brother fool;°
The porches of the Christian school°
    Are meekness, peace, and prayer.

Open, and naked of offence,
Man's made of mercy, soul, and sense;
    God armed the snail and wilk;°
250   Be good to him that pulls thy plough;
Due food and care, due rest, allow
    For her that yields thee milk.

Rise up before the hoary head,
And God's benign commandment dread,
    Which says thou shalt not die:
'Not as I will, but as thou wilt,'°
Prayed He whose conscience knew no guilt;
    With whose blessed pattern vie.

Use all thy passions!—love is thine,
260   And joy, and jealousy° divine,
    Thine hope's eternal fort;
And care thy leisure to disturb,
With fear concupiscence to curb,
    And rapture to transport.

Act simply, as occasion asks;
Put mellow wine in seasoned casks,
    Till not with ass and bull.
Remember thy baptismal bond;
Keep from commixtures foul and fond,
270   Nor work thy flax with wool.

Distribute: pay the Lord his tithe,
And make the widow's heartstrings blithe;
    Resort° with those that weep;
As you from all and each expect,
For all and each thy love direct,
    And render as you reap.

The slander and its bearer spurn,
And propagating praise sojourn

Thou shalt . . . fool "But I say unto you, that whosoever is angry with his brother without a cause shall be in danger of the judgment . . . but whosoever shall say, Thou fool, shall be in danger of hell fire" (Matthew 5:22).
porches . . . school as opposed to the Stoa of the Greeks; cf. St. Paul's encounter with the Stoics and his preaching at the Areopagus (Acts 17:16–34)

wilk whelk (a shellfish)
Not as I . . . wilt the words of Christ, Matthew 26:39
jealousy zeal; cf. St. Paul: "For I am jealous over you with godly jealousy: for I have espoused you to one husband, that I may present you as a chaste virgin to Christ" (II Corinthians 11:2)
Resort consort

To make thy welcome last;
280 Turn from old Adam to the New;°
By hope futurity pursue;
    Look upwards to the past.

Control thine eye, salute success,
Honour the wiser, happier bless,
    And for thy neighbour feel;
Grutch not of Mammon and his leaven,°
Work emulation up to heaven
    By knowledge and by zeal.

O David, highest in the list
290 Of worthies, on God's ways insist,
    The genuine word repeat:°
Vain are the documents of men,
And vain the flourish of the pen
    That keeps the fool's conceit.

Praise above all—for praise prevails;
Heap up the measure, load the scales,
    And good to goodness add.
The generous soul her Saviour aids,
But peevish obloquy degrades;
300   The Lord is great and glad.

For Adoration all the ranks
Of angels yield eternal thanks,
    And David in the midst;
With God's good poor, which, last and least
In man's esteem, thou to thy feast,
    O blessed bridegroom, bidst.°

For Adoration seasons change,
And order, truth, and beauty range,
    Adjust, attract, and fill:
310 The grass the polyanthus checks;°
And polished porphyry reflects,
    By the descending rill.

Rich almonds colour to the prime
For Adoration; tendrils climb,
    And fruit trees pledge their gems;
And Ivis° with her gorgeous vest
Builds for her eggs her cunning nest,
    And bellflowers bow their stems.

New the New Adam or Christ, who redeems what the Old Adam lost (I Corinthians 15:22, 45)
Grutch not . . . leaven i.e. do not envy the rich man his gains; a version of the last of the Commandments, "Thou shalt not covet thy neighbour's house . . ." (Exodus 20:17).
genuine . . . repeat "Psalm 119" (Smart)

O blessed . . . bidst "And the Spirit and the bride say, Come . . . And let him that is athirst come. And whosoever will, let him take the water of life freely" (Revelation 22:17).
the polyanthus checks i.e. the polyanthus variegates or decorates
Ivis "hummingbird" (Smart)

With vinous syrup° cedars spout;
320   From rocks pure honey gushing out,°
       For Adoration springs.
All scenes of painting crowd the map
Of nature; to the mermaid's pap
       The scalèd infant clings.

The spotted ounce and playsome cubs
Run rustling 'mongst the flowering shrubs,
       And lizards feed° the moss;
For Adoration beasts embark,°
While waves upholding halcyon's ark
330   No longer roar and toss.

While Israel sits beneath his fig,°
With coral root and amber sprig
       The weaned adventurer° sports;
Where to the palm the jasmine cleaves,
For Adoration 'mongst the leaves
       The gale his peace reports.

Increasing days their reign exalt,
Nor in the pink and mottled vault
       The opposing spirits tilt;°
340   And, by the coasting reader° spied,
The silverlings and crusions° glide
       For Adoration gilt.

For Adoration ripening canes
And cocoa's purest milk detains
       The western pilgrim's staff;
Where rain in clasping boughs inclosed,
And vines with oranges disposed,
       Embower the social laugh.

Now labour his reward receives,
350   For Adoration counts his sheaves
       To peace, her bounteous prince;
The nectarine his strong tint imbibes,
And apples of ten thousand tribes,
       And quick° peculiar quince.

---

syrup sap
From rocks . . . out "And with honey out of
the rock should I have satisfied thee" (Psalms
81:16)
feed feed upon
beasts embark "There is a large quadruped
that preys upon fish and provides himself with
a large piece of timber for that purpose, with
which he is very handy" (Smart); but the halcyon was believed to build its nest ("ark")
upon the sea and may in turn recall Noah's ark
and its assemblage of beasts

fig fig tree: "But they shall sit every man
under his vine and under his fig tree; and none
shall make them afraid" (Micah 4:4)
weaned adventurer small child
spirits tilt winds or storm clouds rise in conflict
coasting reader someone drifting in a boat while
reading
silverlings and crusions tarpons and carp-like
fish
quick pungent

The wealthy crops of whitening rice,
'Mongst thyine° woods and groves of spice,
    For Adoration grow;
And, marshalled in the fencèd land,
The peaches and pomegranates stand,
360   Where wild carnations blow.

The laurels with the winter strive;
The crocus burnishes alive
    Upon the snow-clad earth;
For Adoration myrtles stay
To keep the garden from dismay,
    And bless the sight from dearth.

The pheasant shows his pompous neck;
And ermine, jealous of a speck,
    With fear eludes offence;
370 The sable, with his glossy pride,
For Adoration is descried,
    Where frosts the wave condense.°

The cheerful holly, pensive yew,
And holy thorn,° their trim renew;
    The squirrel hoards his nuts;
All creatures batten o'er their stores,
And careful nature all her doors
    For Adoration shuts.

For Adoration, David's psalms
380 Lift up the heart to deeds of alms;
    And he who kneels and chants
Prevails his passions to control,
Finds meat and medicine to the soul,
    Which for translation° pants.

For Adoration, beyond match,
The scholar bullfinch° aims to catch
    The soft flute's ivory touch;
And, careless on the hazel spray,
The daring redbreast keeps at bay
390   The damsel's greedy clutch.

For Adoration, in the skies,
The Lord's philosopher espies
    The Dog, the Ram, and Rose;
The planet's ring, Orion's sword;
Nor is his greatness less adored
    In the vile worm° that glows.

---

thyine scented
condense congeal
holy thorn the hawthorn associated with Christ
and with St. Joseph of Arimathea

translation removal to heaven
scholar bullfinch the bird, taught to imitate a
whistled tune
the vile worm i.e. the glowworm or firefly

For Adoration on the strings°
The western breezes work their wings,
   The captive ear to soothe.
400 Hark! 'tis a voice°—how still and small—
That makes the cataracts to fall,
   Or bids the sea be smooth.

For Adoration, incense comes
From bezoar° and Arabian gums,
   And on the civet's fur.
But as for prayer, or ere it faints,°
Far better is the breath of saints
   Than galbanum° and myrrh.

For Adoration, from the down
410 Of damsons° to the anana's° crown,
   God sends to tempt the taste;
And while the luscious zest invites
The sense, that in the scene delights,
   Commands desire be chaste.

For Adoration, all the paths
Of grace are open, all the baths
   Of purity refresh;
And all the rays of glory beam
To deck the man of God's esteem,
420   Who triumphs o'er the flesh.

For Adoration, in the dome
Of Christ the sparrows find an home,°
   And on his olives perch;
The swallow also dwells with thee,
O man of God's humility,
   Within his saviour Church.

Sweet is the dew that falls betimes,
And drops upon the leafy limes;
   Sweet Hermon's° fragrant air;
430 Sweet is the lily's silver bell,
And sweet the wakeful tapers smell
   That watch for early prayer.

Sweet the young nurse with love intense,
Which smiles o'er sleeping innocence;

---

strings "Aeolian harp" (Smart), played on by
the wind as it hangs in a tree
voice the "still small voice" of God (I Kings
19:12)
bezoar substance found in the stomachs of cows
faints fades
galbanum an aromatic gum used in making
perfume

damsons plums
anana's pineapple's
the sparrows . . . home "Yea, the sparrow
hath found an house, and the swallow a nest for
herself . . . even thine altars, O Lord of hosts"
(Psalms 84:3)
Hermon's a Syrian mountain mentioned in
Psalms 133

Sweet when the lost arrive;
Sweet the musician's ardour beats,
While his vague mind's in quest of sweets,
    The choicest flowers to hive.

Sweeter in all the strains of love,
440   The language of thy turtle dove,
    Paired to thy swelling chord;
Sweeter with every grace endued,
The glory of thy gratitude,
    Respired unto the Lord.

Strong is the horse upon his speed;
Strong in pursuit the rapid glede,°
    Which makes at once his game;
Strong the tall ostrich on the ground;
Strong through the turbulent profound
450   Shoots xiphias° to his aim.

Strong is the lion—like a coal
His eyeball—like a bastion's mole°
    His chest against the foes;
Strong, the gier-eagle° on his sail,
Strong against tide, the enormous whale
    Emerges as he goes.

But stronger still, in earth and air,
And in the sea, the man of prayer;
    And far beneath the tide;
460   And in the seat to faith assigned,
Where ask is have, where seek is find,
    Where knock is open wide.°

Beauteous the fleet before the gale;
Beauteous the multitudes in mail,
    Ranked arms and crested heads;
Beauteous the garden's umbrage mild,
Walk, water, meditated wild,°
    And all the gloomy beds.

Beauteous the moon full on the lawn;
470   And beauteous, when the veil's withdrawn,
    The virgin to her spouse;
Beauteous the temple decked and filled,
When to the heaven of heavens they build
    Their heart-directed vows.

glede hawk
xiphias "the swordfish" (Smart)
mole heavy wall
gier-eagle vulture

Where knock . . . wide "Ask, and it shall be
given you; seek, and ye shall find; knock, and
it shall be opened unto you" (Matthew 7:7)
meditated wild planned, artificial

Beauteous, yea beauteous more than these,
The shepherd king upon his knees,
    For his momentous trust;
With wish of infinite conceit,°
For man, beast, mute,° the small and great,
480   And prostrate dust to dust.

Precious the bounteous widow's mite;°
And precious, for extreme delight,
    The largess from the churl;°
Precious the ruby's blushing blaze,
And alba's blessed imperial rays,°
    And pure cerulean pearl.

Precious the penitential tear;
And precious is the sigh sincere,
    Acceptable to God;
490   And precious are the winning flowers,
In gladsome Israel's feast of bowers,
    Bound on the hallowed sod.°

More precious that diviner part
Of David, even the Lord's own heart,°
    Great, beautiful, and new;
In all things where it was intent,
In all extremes, in each event,
    Proof—answering true to true.

Glorious the sun in mid-career;
500   Glorious the assembled fires° appear;
    Glorious the comet's train;
Glorious the trumpet and alarm;
Glorious the almighty stretched-out arm;
    Glorious the enraptured main;

Glorious the northern lights astream;
Glorious the song, when God's the theme;
    Glorious the thunder's roar;
Glorious hosanna from the den;°
Glorious the catholic° amen;
510   Glorious the martyr's gore;

conceit conception
mute fish
bounteous . . . mite Cf. Mark 12:42–5, where
Jesus esteems the widow's contribution of a
farthing as "more" than all that was given out
of abundance.
churl a reference, as Smart notes, to Nabel, who
is "churlish and evil in his doings" (I Samuel
25)
alba's . . . rays the "white stone" of Revelation 2:17

Bound on . . . sod Cf. the "feast of tabernacles" (Leviticus 23:34–44).
the Lord's . . . heart "I have found David
. . . a man after mine own heart, which shall
fufil all my will" (Acts 13:22)
assembled fires stars
den the lion's den where Daniel was preserved
because of his faith (Daniel 6:22–23)
catholic universal

Glorious—more glorious is the crown
Of Him that brought salvation down
    By meekness, called thy Son;
Thou at stupendous truth believed,
And now the matchless deed's achieved,
    Determined, Dared, and Done.
                1763

OLIVER GOLDSMITH
1730?–1774

The contrast between Goldsmith's writings and his person was so great that some
were tempted to call him an "inspired idiot." He was as versatile and accomplished a
writer as any of his age, if neither the deepest nor the most imaginative; but he was so
eager to claim attention in society, so envious of the praise of others, so "greedy and
impatient to speak" (as Reynolds put it) that he would hold the floor with nothing
to say and with little skill in making the emptiness diverting. His early life in Ireland,
as the son of an Anglican curate, was not such as to assure him of either cultivation
or learning; his career at Trinity College, Dublin, was often one of self-display and
of dissipation. He turned successively to divinity, law, and medicine, pursuing the
last at Edinburgh and Leyden, and ending with a ramble through Europe in 1755. In
England he soon abandoned the practice of medicine and supported himself by
writing. The range and level of his accomplishment were impressive: the essays in
The Bee (1759); the satiric letters of a Chinese visitor to England later collected as
The Citizen of the World (1762); the *Life* of Beau Nash of Bath (1762); a fine novel,
The Vicar of Wakefield (1766); two plays, one of which (*She Stoops to Conquer*, 1773)
is still performed with great success; and two major poems, *The Traveler* (1765) and
The Deserted Village (1770). As Dr. Johnson exclaimed "with great dignity" at
Reynolds's table, "If nobody was suffered to abuse poor Goldy but those who could
write as well, he would have few censors."

Whatever the self-defeating forces revealed in his personal manner, Goldsmith
could write with singular ease and charm, with elegant irony as well as pathos. *The
Deserted Village* is perhaps his most careful composition, and its broad appeal may
be taken as an implicit reply to those tendencies Goldsmith had deplored in his age:
the "affected obscurity" of Gray's odes, the "tuneless flow of our blank verse, the
pompous epithet, laboured diction, and every other deviation from common sense
which procures the poet the applause of the month."

The Deserted Village

Sweet Auburn, loveliest village of the plain,
Where health and plenty cheered the labouring swain,
Where smiling spring its earliest visit paid,
And parting summer's lingering blooms delayed;
Dear lovely bowers of innocence and ease,

Seats of my youth, when every sport could please,
How often have I loitered o'er thy green,
Where humble happiness endeared each scene;
How often have I paused on every charm,
10   The sheltered cot,° the cultivated farm,
The never-failing brook, the busy mill,
The decent° church that topped the neighbouring hill,
The hawthorn bush, with seats beneath the shade,
For talking age and whispering lovers made.
How often have I blessed the coming day,
When toil remitting lent its turn to play,
And all the village train, from labour free,
Led up their sports beneath the spreading tree,
While many a pastime circled in the shade,
20   The young contending as the old surveyed;
And many a gambol frolicked o'er the ground,
And sleights of art and feats of strength went round;
And still, as each repeated pleasure tired,
Succeeding sports the mirthful band inspired;
The dancing pair that simply° sought renown,
By holding out to tire each other down;
The swain mistrustless of his smutted face,
While secret laughter tittered round the place;
The bashful virgin's sidelong looks of love,
30   The matron's glance that would those looks reprove:
These were thy charms, sweet village; sports like these,
With sweet succession, taught even toil to please;
These round thy bowers their cheerful influence shed;
These were thy charms—but all these charms are fled.
    Sweet smiling village, loveliest of the lawn,°
Thy sports are fled and all thy charms withdrawn;
Amidst thy bowers the tyrant's hand is seen,
And desolation saddens all thy green;
One only master grasps the whole domain,°
40   And half a tillage° stints thy smiling plain;
No more thy glassy brook reflects the day,
But choked with sedges works its weedy way;
Along thy glades, a solitary guest,
The hollow-sounding bittern guards its nest;
Amidst thy desert walks the lapwing flies,
And tires their echoes with unvaried cries.
Sunk are thy bowers in shapeless ruin all,
And the long grass o'ertops the mouldering wall;

cot cottage
decent becoming, suitable, seemly
simply naïvely, artlessly
lawn plain
One . . . domain Enclosure acts passed in the
18th century permitted the lord of the manor
to enclose the "common" land, forcing the

small farmers to emigrate to cities or colonies;
in his essay "The Revolution in Low Life"
(1762) Goldsmith describes such an enclosure
made for the sake of a pleasure seat for the
landlord, thus introducing the related theme of
luxury.
half a tillage i.e. only half the land is plowed

And, trembling, shrinking from the spoiler's hand,
50   Far, far away thy children leave the land.
     Ill fares the land, to hastening ills a prey,
Where wealth accumulates and men decay;
Princes and lords may flourish or may fade;
A breath can make them as a breath has made;
But a bold peasantry, their country's pride,
When once destroyed, can never be supplied.
     A time there was, ere England's griefs began,
When every rood° of ground maintained its man;
For him light labour spread her wholesome store,
60   Just gave what life required, but gave no more:
His best companions, innocence and health;
And his best riches, ignorance of wealth.
     But times are altered; trade's unfeeling train
Usurp the land, and dispossess the swain;
Along the lawn, where scattered hamlets rose,
Unwieldy wealth and cumbrous pomp repose;
And every want to luxury allied,
And every pang that folly pays to pride.
Those gentle hours that plenty bade to bloom,
70   Those calm desires that asked but little room,
Those healthful sports that graced the peaceful scene,
Lived in each look, and brightened all the green;
These, far departing, seek a kinder shore,
And rural mirth and manners° are no more.
     Sweet Auburn! parent of the blissful hour,
Thy glades forlorn confess the tyrant's power.
Here, as I take my solitary rounds
Amidst thy tangling walks and ruined grounds,
And, many a year elapsed, return to view
80   Where once the cottage stood, the hawthorn grew,
Here, as with doubtful, pensive steps I range,
Trace every scene, and wonder at the change,°
Remembrance wakes with all her busy train,
Swells at my breast, and turns the past to pain.
     In all my wanderings round this world of care,
In all my griefs—and God has given my share—
I still had hopes, my latest hours to crown,
Amidst these humble bowers to lay me down;
My anxious day to husband near the close,
90   And keep life's flame from wasting by repose.
I still had hopes, for pride attends us still,
Amidst the swains to show my book-learned skill,
Around my fire an evening group to draw,
And tell of all I felt, and all I saw;

rood literally a quarter-acre
manners customs

Here . . . change These two lines were omitted
in the fourth edition.

And, as an hare whom hounds and horns pursue,
Pants to the place from whence at first she flew,
I still had hopes, my long vexations past,
Here to return—and die at home at last.
   O blessed retirement, friend to life's decline,
100 Retreats from care that never must be mine,
How blessed is he who crowns in shades like these
A youth of labour with an age of ease;
Who quits a world where strong temptations try,
And, since 'tis hard to combat, learns to fly.
For him no wretches, born to work and weep,
Explore the mine, or tempt° the dangerous deep;
No surly porter stands in guilty state
To spurn imploring famine from his gate;
But on he moves to meet his latter end,
110 Angels around befriending virtue's friend;
Sinks to the grave with unperceived decay,
While resignation gently slopes the way;
And all his prospects brightening to the last,
His heaven commences ere the world be past!
   Sweet was the sound, when oft at evening's close
Up yonder hill the village murmur rose;
There, as I passed with careless steps and slow,
The mingling notes came softened from below;
The swain responsive as the milkmaid sung,
120 The sober herd that lowed to meet their young,
The noisy geese that gabbled o'er the pool,
The playful children just let loose from school,
The watchdog's voice that bayed the whispering wind,
And the loud laugh that spoke the vacant° mind;
These all in soft confusion sought the shade,
And filled each pause the nightingale had made.
But now the sounds of population fail,
No cheerful murmurs fluctuate in the gale,
No busy steps the grass-grown footway tread,
130 For all the bloomy flush of life is fled;
All but yon widowed, solitary thing
That feebly bends beside the plashy spring;
She, wretched matron, forced in age, for bread,
To strip the brook with mantling° cresses spread,
To pick her wintry faggot from the thorn,
To seek her nightly shed° and weep till morn;
She only left of all the harmless train,
The sad historian of the pensive° plain.
   Near yonder copse, where once the garden smiled,

tempt venture on
vacant carefree
mantling covering

shed shelter
pensive melancholy

140 And still where many a garden flower grows wild,
There, where a few torn shrubs the place disclose,
The village preacher's modest mansion rose.
A man he was to all the country dear,
And passing rich with forty pounds a year;
Remote from towns he ran his godly race,
Nor e'er had changed nor wished to change his place;°
Unskillful he to fawn or seek for power,
By doctrines fashioned to the varying hour;
Far other aims his heart had learned to prize,
150 More bent to raise the wretched than to rise.
His house was known to all the vagrant train;
He chid their wanderings, but relieved their pain;
The long remembered beggar was his guest,
Whose beard descending swept his agèd breast;
The ruined spendthrift, now no longer proud,
Claimed kindred there and had his claims allowed;
The broken soldier, kindly bade to stay,
Sate by his fire and talked the night away;
Wept o'er his wounds, or, tales of sorrow done,
160 Shouldered his crutch and showed how fields were won.
Pleased with his guests, the good man learned to glow,
And quite forgot their vices in their woe;
Careless their merits or their faults to scan,
His pity gave ere charity began.
  Thus to relieve the wretched was his pride,
And even his failings leaned to virtue's side;
But in his duty prompt at every call,
He watched and wept, he prayed and felt for all.
And, as a bird each fond endearment tries
170 To tempt its new-fledged offspring to the skies,
He tried each art, reproved each dull delay,
Allured to brighter worlds, and led the way.
  Beside the bed where parting life was laid,
And sorrow, guilt, and pain by turns dismayed,
The reverend champion stood. At his control
Despair and anguish fled the struggling soul;
Comfort came down the trembling wretch to raise,
And his last faltering accents whispered praise.
  At church, with meek and unaffected grace,
180 His looks adorned the venerable place;
Truth from his lips prevailed with double sway,
And fools, who came to scoff, remained to pray.
The service past, around the pious man,
With ready zeal, each honest rustic ran;
Even children followed with endearing wile,

place appointment, church living

And plucked his gown, to share the good man's smile.
His ready smile a parent's warmth expressed,
Their welfare pleased him and their cares distressed;
To them his heart, his love, his griefs were given,
190 But all his serious thoughts had rest in Heaven.
As some tall cliff, that lifts its awful form,
Swells from the vale and midway leaves the storm,
Though round its breast the rolling clouds are spread,
Eternal sunshine settles on its head.
    Beside yon straggling fence that skirts the way,
With blossomed furze unprofitably gay,°
There, in his noisy mansion, skilled to rule,
The village master taught his little school.
A man severe he was, and stern to view;
200 I knew him well, and every truant knew;
Well had the boding tremblers learned to trace
The day's disasters in his morning face;
Full well they laughed with counterfeited glee
At all his jokes, for many a joke had he;
Full well the busy whisper, circling round,
Conveyed the dismal tidings when he frowned;
Yet he was kind, or, if severe in aught,
The love he bore to learning was in fault;
The village all declared how much he knew;
210 'Twas certain he could write and cipher° too;
Lands he could measure, terms° and tides° presage,
And even the story ran that he could gauge;°
In arguing too, the parson owned his skill,
For e'en though vanquished, he could argue still;
While words of learnèd length and thundering sound
Amazed the gazing rustics ranged around;
And still they gazed, and still the wonder grew
That one small head could carry all he knew.
    But past is all his fame. The very spot
220 Where many a time he triumphed is forgot.
Near yonder thorn that lifts its head on high,
Where once the signpost caught the passing eye,
Low lies that house where nut-brown draughts° inspired,
Where graybeard mirth and smiling toil retired,
Where village statesmen talked with looks profound,
And news much older than their ale went round.
Imagination fondly stoops to trace
The parlour splendours of that festive place;
The whitewashed wall, the nicely sanded floor,

---

unprofitably gay grown for ornament
cipher calculate
terms quarter days when rents and wages were
due (based on the church calendar)

tides variable or movable feasts, e.g. Easter
gauge measure the capacity of casks or other
vessels
draughts of ale

230 The varnished clock that clicked behind the door;
The chest contrived a double debt to pay,
A bed by night, a chest of drawers by day;
The pictures placed for ornament and use,
The twelve good rules,° the royal game of goose;°
The hearth, except when winter chilled the day,
With aspen boughs and flowers and fennel gay;
While broken teacups, wisely kept for show,
Ranged o'er the chimney, glistened in a row.
　　Vain transitory splendours! Could not all
240 Reprieve the tottering mansion from its fall?
Obscure it sinks, nor shall it more impart
An hour's importance to the poor man's heart;
Thither no more the peasant shall repair
To sweet oblivion of his daily care;
No more the farmer's news, the barber's tale,
No more the woodman's ballad shall prevail;
No more the smith his dusky brow shall clear,
Relax his ponderous strength, and lean to hear;
The host himself no longer shall be found
250 Careful to see the mantling° bliss go round;
Nor the coy maid, half willing to be pressed,
Shall kiss the cup° to pass it to the rest.
　　Yes! let the rich deride, the proud disdain,
These simple blessings of the lowly train;
To me more dear, congenial to my heart,
One native charm, than all the gloss of art;
Spontaneous joys, where nature has its play,
The soul adopts and owns their first-born sway;
Lightly they frolic o'er the vacant mind,
260 Unenvied, unmolested, unconfined.
But the long pomp, the midnight masquerade,
With all the freaks of wanton wealth arrayed,
In these, ere triflers half their wish obtain,
The toiling pleasure sickens into pain;
And even while fashion's brightest arts decoy,
The heart distrusting asks if this be joy.
　　Ye friends to truth, ye statesmen, who survey
The rich man's joys increase, the poor's decay,
'Tis yours to judge how wide the limits stand
270 Between a splendid and an happy land.
Proud swells the tide with loads of freighted ore,
And shouting Folly hails them from her shore;
Hoards even beyond the miser's wish abound,

---

twelve good rules those of Charles I, which appeared beneath a woodcut of his execution hung in many houses and including "pick no quarrels," "encourage no vice," and other maxims **royal game of goose** a game played on a board with compartments, through which counters were moved by the throw of dice **mantling** frothing **kiss the cup** take a sip

And rich men flock from all the world around.
Yet count our gains. This wealth is but a name
That leaves our useful products still the same.
Not so the loss. The man of wealth and pride
Takes up a space that many poor supplied;
Space for his lake, his park's extended bounds,
280   Space for his horses, equipage, and hounds;
The robe that wraps his limbs in silken sloth
Has robbed the neighbouring fields of half their growth;
His seat, where solitary sports are seen,
Indignant spurns the cottage from the green;
Around the world each needful product flies,
For all the luxuries the world supplies;
While thus the land adorned for pleasure all
In barren splendour feebly waits the fall.
    As some fair female, unadorned and plain,
290   Secure to please while youth confirms her reign,
Slights every borrowed charm that dress supplies,
Nor shares with art the triumph of her eyes;
But when those charms are past, for charms are frail,
When time advances and when lovers fail,
She then shines forth, solicitous to bless,
In all the glaring impotence of dress:
Thus fares the land, by luxury betrayed,
In nature's simplest charms at first arrayed;
But verging to decline, its splendours rise,
300   Its vistas° strike, its palaces surprise;
While scourged by famine from the smiling land,
The mournful peasant leads his humble band;
And while he sinks, without one arm to save,
The country blooms—a garden and a grave.°
    Where then, ah where, shall poverty reside,
To 'scape the pressure of contiguous pride?°
If to some common's fenceless limits strayed,
He drives his flock to pick the scanty blade,
Those fenceless fields the sons of wealth divide,
310   And even the bare-worn common is denied.
    If to the city sped—what waits him there?
To see profusion that he must not share;
To see ten thousand baneful arts combined
To pamper luxury, and thin mankind;
To see each joy the sons of pleasure know
Extorted from his fellow-creature's woe.
Here while the courtier glitters in brocade,

---

vistas designed prospects or views at the end
of an avenue of trees
a garden and a grave i.e. improved with elab-

orate gardens for the rich and thus made a
grave for the poor
contiguous pride neighboring and encroaching
luxury

There the pale artist° plies the sickly trade;
Here while the proud their long-drawn pomps display,
320   There the black gibbet glooms beside the way;
The dome° where Pleasure holds her midnight reign,
Here, richly decked, admits the gorgeous train;
Tumultuous grandeur crowds the blazing square,
The rattling chariots clash, the torches glare:
Sure scenes like these no trouble e'er annoy!
Sure these denote one universal joy!
Are these thy serious thoughts?—Ah, turn thine eyes
Where the poor houseless shivering female lies.
She once, perhaps, in village plenty blessed,
330   Has wept at tales of innocence distressed;
Her modest looks the cottage might adorn,
Sweet as the primrose peeps beneath the thorn;
Now lost to all; her friends, her virtue fled,
Near her betrayer's door she lays her head,
And pinched with cold, and shrinking from the shower,
With heavy heart deplores that luckless hour,
When idly first, ambitious of the town,
She left her wheel° and robes of country brown.
        Do thine, sweet Auburn, thine, the loveliest train,
340   Do thy fair tribes participate her pain?
Even now, perhaps, by cold and hunger led,
At proud men's doors they ask a little bread!
        Ah, no. To distant climes, a dreary scene,
Where half the convex world intrudes between,
To torrid tracts with fainting steps they go,
Where wild Altama° murmurs to their woe.
Far different there from all that charmed before,
The various terrors of that horrid shore;
Those blazing suns that dart a downward ray,
350   And fiercely shed intolerable day;
Those matted woods where birds forget to sing,
But silent bats in drowsy clusters cling;
Those poisonous fields with rank luxuriance crowned
Where the dark scorpion gathers death around;
Where at each step the stranger fears to wake
The rattling terrors of the vengeful snake;
Where crouching tigers° wait their hapless prey,
And savage men more murderous still than they;
While oft in whirls the mad tornado flies,
360   Mingling the ravaged landscape with the skies.
        Far different these from every former scene,

artist artisan, workman
dome building
wheel for spinning
Altama the Altamaha River in Georgia, where

Goldsmith's friend General Oglethorpe had
founded a colony in 1735
tigers Goldsmith refers to the cougar or "red
tiger" (also called the "American tiger").

The cooling brook, the grassy-vested green,
The breezy covert of the warbling grove,
That only sheltered thefts of harmless love.
    Good Heaven! what sorrows gloomed that parting day
That called them from their native walks away;
When the poor exiles, every pleasure past,
Hung round their bowers, and fondly looked their last,
And took a long farewell, and wished in vain
370   For seats like these beyond the western main;
And shuddering still to face the distant deep,
Returned and wept, and still returned to weep.
The good old sire the first prepared to go
To new-found worlds, and wept for others' woe;
But for himself, in conscious virtue brave,
He only wished for worlds beyond the grave.
His lovely daughter, lovelier in her tears,
The fond companion of his helpless years,
Silent went next, neglectful of her charms,
380   And left a lover's for her father's arms.
With louder plaints the mother spoke her woes,
And blessed the cot where every pleasure rose,
And kissed her thoughtless babes with many a tear,
And clasped them close, in sorrow doubly dear;
Whilst her fond husband strove to lend relief
In all the decent manliness of grief.
    O Luxury! thou cursed by heaven's decree,
How ill exchanged are things like these for thee!
How do thy potions, with insidious joy,
390   Diffuse their pleasures only to destroy!
Kingdoms by thee, to sickly greatness grown,
Boast of a florid vigour not their own:
At every draught more large and large they grow,
A bloated mass of rank, unwieldy woe;
Till sapped their strength, and every part unsound,
Down, down they sink, and spread a ruin round.
    Even now the devastation is begun,
And half the business of destruction done;
Even now, methinks, as pondering here I stand,
400   I see the rural virtues leave the land:
Down where yon anchoring vessel spreads the sail,
That idly waiting flaps with every gale,
Downward they move, a melancholy band,
Pass from the shore, and darken all the strand.
Contented Toil, and hospitable Care,
And kind connubial Tenderness are there;
And Piety with wishes placed above,
And steady Loyalty, and faithful Love.
And thou, sweet Poetry, thou loveliest maid,

410 Still first to fly where sensual joys invade,
Unfit, in these degenerate times of shame,
To catch the heart, or strike for honest fame;
Dear charming nymph, neglected and decried,
My shame in crowds, my solitary pride;
Thou source of all my bliss and all my woe,
That foundest me poor at first, and keepest me so;
Thou guide by which the nobler arts excel,
Thou nurse of every virtue, fare thee well!
Farewell, and O where'er thy voice be tried,
420 On Torno's° cliffs, or Pambamarca's° side,
Whether where equinoctial fervours° glow,
Or winter wraps the polar world in snow,
Still let thy voice, prevailing over time,
Redress the rigours of the inclement clime;
Aid slighted truth, with thy persuasive strain
Teach erring man to spurn the rage of gain;
Teach him that states of native strength possessed,
Though very poor, may still be very blessed;
That trade's proud empire hastes to swift decay,
430 As ocean sweeps the laboured mole° away;
While self-dependent power can time defy,
As rocks resist the billows and the sky.
1768–70   1770

WILLIAM COWPER
1731–1800

Cowper suffered his first severe attack of melancholy at the age of twenty-one as he settled into the study of law at the Middle Temple. "Day and night," he wrote later, "I was upon the rack, lying down in horrors and rising up in despair." He was called to the bar two years later and in 1759 was appointed Commissioner of Bankrupts; but through need of a greater income he sought a post in the House of Lords. This required a competitive examination, and the strain of anticipation led to his first full attack of insanity in 1763. He experienced a sense of utter damnation, and attempts at suicide only intensified feelings of guilt. During his months in an asylum he underwent a religious conversion that gave him hope and reconciled him to a life of country retirement, which the Unwin family made possible by taking him into their household. Under the influence of John Newton, an evangelical minister, the Unwins (and Cowper with them) moved to Olney, a place (as Cowper described it) "inhabited chiefly by the half-starved and ragged of the earth." In 1773 Cowper proposed marriage to the widowed Mrs. Unwin but lost his sanity again a month or so before the marriage was to take place. In his later years of intermittent serenity, still

---

Torno's in Lapland
Pambamarca's in Ecuador
equinoctial fervours the intense heat at the Equator

laboured mole the man-built breakwater, as opposed to the "self-dependent power" of natural rocks; the last four lines were written by Dr. Johnson

haunted by terrifying dreams and black depression, he translated Homer, edited Milton, and enjoyed the admiration of William Hayley (the poet and insensitive patron of William Blake), who became his literary executor and biographer.

Three of the poems given here show Cowper dealing directly with his sense of damnation, the early *Lines* and the two last poems of his life. His major work, apart from the hymns he wrote with Newton, was *The Task*, begun at the bidding of his neighbor Lady Austen as a distraction, an "assigned" poem about a sofa. But the poem opened into a long meditative and descriptive work, mixing satire upon luxury and urban corruption with georgic celebrations of country life, and resolved itself at last into a vision for which the country scene provided only outward surface. In the sixth and last book, from which selections are given below, the poem moves to the vision of a recovered Eden and to a new poise of self whose dwelling is (at least in its deepest reaches) already there. The section from *The Task* provides a striking counterpoise, in its strong affirmation and its serenity, to the tormented and more powerful poems that came out of his despair.

Lines Written During a Period of Insanity

Hatred and vengeance, my eternal portion,
Scarce can endure delay of execution,
Wait with impatient readiness to seize my
    Soul in a moment.

Damned below Judas; more abhorred than he was,
Who for a few pence sold his holy Master.
Twice-betrayed Jesus me, the last delinquent,
    Deems the profanest.

Man disavows, and Deity disowns me;
10 Hell might afford my miseries a shelter;
Therefore Hell keeps her ever-hungry mouths all
    Bolted against me.

Hard lot! encompassed with a thousand dangers,
Weary, faint, trembling with a thousand terrors,
I'm called, if vanquished, to receive a sentence
    Worse than Abiram's.°

Him the vindictive rod of angry Justice
Sent quick and howling to the centre headlong;
I, fed with judgment,° in a fleshly tomb, am
20   Buried above ground.

1763?   1816

Abiram's Korah, Dathan, and Abiram rebelled against Moses, who brought down upon them a special curse: "If these men die the common death of all men . . . then the Lord hath not sent me. But if the Lord make a new thing, and the earth open her mouth, and swallow them up . . . then ye shall understand that these men have provoked the Lord. And it came to pass . . ." (Numbers 16:29–31). **fed with judgment** Cf. Ezekiel 34:7–16, where God speaks ironically of feeding the wicked ("the fat and the strong") among his flock "with judgment," i.e. with punishment.

On the Ice Islands Seen Floating
in the German Ocean°

What portents, from what distant region, ride,
Unseen till now in ours, the astonished tide?
In ages past, old Proteus,° with his droves
Of sea-calves, sought the mountains and the groves:
But now, descending whence of late they stood,
Themselves the mountains seem to rove the flood.
Dire times were they, full-charged with human woes;
And these, scarce less calamitous than those.
What view we now? More wondrous still! Behold!
Like burnished brass they shine, or beaten gold;
And all around the pearl's pure splendour show,
And all around the ruby's fiery glow.
Come they from India? where the burning earth,
All-bounteous, gives her richest treasures birth;
And where the costly gems, that beam around
The brows of mightiest potentates, are found?
No. Never such a countless dazzling store
Had left unseen the Ganges' peopled shore.
Rapacious hands, and ever-watchful eyes,
Should sooner far have marked and seized the prize.
Whence sprang they then? Ejected have they come
From Ves'vius', or from Aetna's burning womb?°
Thus shine they self-illumed, or but display
The borrowed splendours of a cloudless day?
With borrowed beams they shine. The gales that breathe
Now land-ward, and the current's force beneath,
Have borne them nearer: and the nearer sight,
Advantaged more, contèmplates them aright.
Their lofty summits crested high they show,
With mingled sleet and long-incumbent snow.
The rest is ice. Far hence, where, most severe,
Bleak winter well-nigh saddens all the year,
Their infant growth began. He bade arise
Their uncouth forms, portentous in our eyes.
Oft as, dissolved by transient suns, the snow
Left the tall cliff, to join the flood below,

10 (line 10 marker)
20 (line 20 marker)
30 (line 30 marker)

On the Ice Islands . . . Ocean This was written first in Latin, then shortly afterward translated into English, during Cowper's last illness;
the English version was completed the day
before *The Castaway* was written. The remarkable turn of the last stanza of that poem is
diffused through this poem and left more implicit, but surely the icebergs are taken as
some aspect of the self—beautiful in a sinister
way, rejected by Phoebus Apollo (god of the
sun and of poetry alike), unable to be kept in
the "Cimmerian darkness" yet unable to survive in the full light of day—a telling contrast
to fertile Delos, perhaps its demonic counterpart.
Proteus the herdsman of the sea cattle, given
prophetic powers in return; according to some
legends a king of Egypt who took Helen of
Troy and her wealth from Paris and kept them
for Menelaus; the father of two sons slain by
Hercules (perhaps the "human woes" mentioned
here)
Ves'vius' . . . Aetna's burning womb Both vol-
canoes had undergone spectacular eruptions in
modern times as well as in antiquity.

He caught and curdled, with a freezing blast,
The current, ere it reached the boundless waste.
By slow degrees uprose the wondrous pile,
40 And long-successive ages rolled the while;
Till, ceaseless in its growth, it claimed to stand
Tall as its rival mountains on the land.
Thus stood—and, unremovable by skill
Or force of man, had stood the structure still;
But that, though firmly fixt, supplanted yet
By pressure of its own enormous weight,
It left the shelving° beach—and, with a sound
That shook the bellowing waves and rocks around,
Self-launched, and swiftly, to the briny wave,
50 As if instinct with strong desire to lave,
Down went the ponderous mass. So bards of old,
How Delos° swam the Aegean deep, have told.
But not of ice was Delos. Delos bore
Herb, fruit, and flower. She, crowned with laurel, wore,
E'en under wintry skies, a summer smile;
And Delos was Apollo's favorite isle.
But, horrid wanderers of the deep, to you
He deems Cimmerian darkness° only due.
Your hated birth he deigned not to survey,
60 But, scornful, turned his glorious eyes away.
Hence! Seek your home; no longer rashly dare
The darts of Phoebus, and a softer air;
Lest ye regret, too late, your native coast,
In no congenial gulf for ever lost!
1799   1803

The Castaway°

Obscurest night involved the sky,
    The Atlantic billows roared,
When such a destined wretch as I,
    Washed headlong from on board,
Of friends, of hope, of all bereft,
His floating home for ever left.

shelving sloping
Delos the floating island given to Latona as a refuge from persecution; the birthplace of Apollo and Artemis, regarded as sacred in antiquity
Cimmerian darkness the gloomy retreat of a people who dwelt in caves and hid from the light of the sun; associated with hell and the Stygian regions in antiquity and by Milton, *L'Allegro*, l. 10
The Castaway The poem is based upon an incident in Richard Walter's *A Voyage Round the World by George Anson* (1748). Anson, later

an admiral, led the expedition against the Spanish; while they were rounding Cape Horn in a storm, one of the seamen was carried overboard: "We perceived that he swam very strong, and it was with the utmost concern that we found ourselves incapable of assisting him; and we were the more grieved at his unhappy fate since we lost sight of him struggling with the waves, and conceived . . . that he might continue sensible for a considerable time longer of the horror attending his irretrievable situation" (I.viii).

No braver chief could Albion boast
 Than he with whom he went,
Nor ever ship left Albion's coast,
10 With warmer wishes sent.
He loved them both, but both in vain,
Nor him beheld, nor her again.

Not long beneath the whelming brine,
 Expert to swim, he lay;
Nor soon he felt his strength decline,
 Or courage die away;
But waged with death a lasting strife,
Supported by despair of life.

He shouted: nor his friends had failed
20 To check the vessel's course,
But so the furious blast prevailed,
 That, pitiless perforce,
They left their outcast mate behind,
And scudded still before the wind.

Some succour yet they could afford;
 And, such as storms allow,
The cask, the coop,° the floated cord,
 Delayed not to bestow.
But he (they knew) nor ship, nor shore,
30 Whate'er they gave, should visit more.

Nor, cruel as it seemed, could he
 Their haste himself condemn,
Aware that flight, in such a sea,
 Alone could rescue them;
Yet bitter felt it still to die
Deserted, and his friends so nigh.

He long survives who lives an hour
 In ocean, self-upheld;
And so long he, with unspent power,
40 His destiny repelled;
And ever, as the minutes flew,
Entreated help, or cried, 'Adieu!'

At length, his transient respite past,
 His comrades, who before
Had heard his voice in every blast,
 Could catch the sound no more.
For then, by toil subdued, he drank
The stifling wave, and then he sank.

coop basket used for catching fish, here used
for rescue

No poet wept him: but the page
50   Of narrative sincere,
That tells his name, his worth, his age,
    Is wet with Anson's tear.
And tears by bards or heroes shed
Alike immortalize the dead.

I therefore purpose not, or dream,
    Descanting on his fate,
To give the melancholy theme
    A more enduring date:
But misery still delights to trace
60   Its semblance in another's case.

No voice divine the storm allayed,
    No light propitious shone;
When, snatched from all effectual aid,
    We perished, each alone:
But I beneath a rougher sea,
And whelmed in deeper gulfs than he.
1799   1803

The Task

From *Book VI: The Winter Walk at Noon*

The Lord of all, himself through all diffused,
Sustains, and is the life of all that lives.
Nature is but a name for an effect
Whose cause is God. He feeds the secret fire
By which the mighty process is maintained,
Who sleeps not, is not weary; in whose sight
Slow circling ages are as transient days;
Whose work is without labour; whose designs
No flaw deforms, no difficulty thwarts;
230 And whose beneficence no charge exhausts.
Him blind antiquity profaned, not served,
With self-taught rites, and under various names,
Female and male, Pomona, Pales, Pan,
And Flora, and Vertumnus;° peopling earth
With tutelary goddesses and gods
That were not; and commending, as they would,
To each some province, garden, field, or grove.
But all are under one. One spirit—His
Who wore the platted° thorns with bleeding brows—

Pomona . . . Vertumnus These deities were, respectively, the goddess of gardens and fruit, the goddess of sheepfolds and pastures, the god of shepherds and huntsmen, the goddess of flowers and gardens, and the god of orchards and of the spring.
platted woven; referring to the crown of thorns of the crucified Christ, seen here as the God of Nature

240　Rules universal nature. Not a flower
　　　But shows some touch, in freckle, streak, or stain,
　　　Of his unrivalled pencil.° He inspires
　　　Their balmy odours, and imparts their hues,
　　　And bathes their eyes with nectar, and includes,
　　　In grains as countless as the sea-side sands,
　　　The forms with which he sprinkles all the earth.
　　　Happy who walks with him! whom what he finds
　　　Of flavour or of scent in fruit or flower,
　　　Or what he views of beautiful or grand
250　In nature, from the broad majestic oak
　　　To the green blade that twinkles in the sun,
　　　Prompts with remembrance of a present God!
　　　His presence, who made all so fair, perceived,
　　　Makes all still fairer. As with him no scene
　　　Is dreary, so with him all seasons please.
　　　Though winter had been none, had man been true,
　　　And earth be punished for its tenant's sake,°
　　　Yet not in vengeance; as this smiling sky,
　　　So soon succeeding such an angry night,
260　And these dissolving snows, and this clear stream
　　　Recovering fast its liquid music, prove.
　　　　　Who then, that has a mind well strung and tuned
　　　To contemplation, and within his reach
　　　A scene so friendly to his favourite task,
　　　Would waste attention at the chequered board,°
　　　His host of wooden warriors to and fro
　　　Marching and counter-marching, with an eye
　　　As fixt as marble, with a forehead ridged
　　　And furrowed into storms, and with a hand
270　Trembling, as if eternity were hung
　　　In balance on his conduct of a pin?—
　　　Nor envies he aught more their idle sport,
　　　Who pant with application misapplied
　　　To trivial toys, and, pushing ivory balls°
　　　Across a velvet level, feel a joy
　　　Akin to rapture when the bawble finds
　　　Its destined goal, of difficult access.—
　　　Nor deems he wiser him who gives his noon
　　　To miss, the mercer's plague,° from shop to shop
280　Wandering, and littering with unfolded silks
　　　The polished counter, and approving none,
　　　Or promising with smiles to call again.—

pencil paintbrush
Though winter . . . tenant's sake referring to
the doctrine that all Nature fell when man did,
and that the unchanging climate of Eden gave
way to the rotating seasons (cf. Milton, *Paradise
Lost* IX). Cowper's point is that the fall of
Nature was necessary but that its effects are too

beautiful to constitute a mere act of vengeance.
chequered board chess or checker (draughts)
board
ivory balls billiards
miss . . . plague the young woman who
plagues the silk merchant

Nor him who by his vanity seduced,
And soothed into a dream that he discerns
The difference of a Guido° from a daub,
Frequents the crowded auction: stationed there
As duly as the Langford° of the show,
With glass at eye and catalogue in hand,
And tongue accomplished in the fulsome cant
290   And pedantry that coxcombs learn with ease;
Oft as the price-deciding hammer falls
He notes it in his book, then raps his box,
Swears 'tis a bargain, rails at his hard fate
That he has let it pass—but never bids!
　　Here, unmolested, through whatever sign°
The sun proceeds, I wander. Neither mist,
Nor freezing sky nor sultry, checking me,
Nor stranger intermeddling with my joy.
Even in the spring and play-time of the year,
300   That calls the unwonted villager abroad
With all her little ones, a sportive train,
To gather king-cups in the yellow mead,
And prink their hair with daisies, or to pick
A cheap but wholesome salad from the brook,
These shades are all my own. The timorous hare,
Grown so familiar with her frequent guest,
Scarce shuns me; and the stock-dove, unalarmed,
Sits cooing in the pine-tree, nor suspends
His long love-ditty for my near approach.
310   Drawn from his refuge in some lonely elm
That age or injury has hollowed deep,
Where, on his bed of wool and matted leaves,
He has outslept the winter, ventures forth
To frisk awhile, and bask in the warm sun,
The squirrel, flippant, pert, and full of play:
He sees me, and at once, swift as a bird,
Ascends the neighbouring beech; there whisks his brush,
And perks his ears, and stamps and scolds aloud,
With all the prettiness of feigned alarm,
320   And anger insignificantly fierce.
　　The heart is hard in nature, and unfit
For human fellowship, as being void
Of sympathy, and therefore dead alike
To love and friendship both, that is not pleased
With sight of animals enjoying life,
Nor feels their happiness augment his own.

Guido Guido Reni (1575–1642), the Bolognese
painter whose works were held in very high
regard in the 17th and 18th centuries

Langford Abraham Langford (1711–74), playwright and the best known auctioneer of the day
sign of the zodiac

The bounding fawn, that darts across the glade
When none pursues, through mere delight of heart,
And spirits buoyant with excess of glee;
330   The horse as wanton, and almost as fleet,
That skims the spacious meadow at full speed,
Then stops and snorts, and, throwing high his heels,
Starts to the voluntary race again;
The very kine° that gambol at high noon,
The total herd receiving first from one
That leads the dance a summons to be gay,
Though wild their strange vagaries and uncouth
Their efforts, yet resolved with one consent
To give such act and utterance as they may
340   To ecstasy too big to be suppressed—
These, and a thousand images of bliss,
With which kind nature graces every scene
Where cruel man defeats not her design,
Impart to the benevolent, who wish
All that are capable of pleasure pleased,
A far superior happiness to theirs,
The comfort of a reasonable joy.

            . . .

    Oh scenes surpassing fable, and yet true,
Scenes of accomplished bliss! which who can see,
760   Though but in distant prospect, and not feel
His soul refreshed with foretaste of the joy?
Rivers of gladness water all the earth,
And clothe all climes with beauty; the reproach
Of barrenness is past. The fruitful field
Laughs with abundance; and the land, once lean,
Or fertile only in its own disgrace,°
Exults to see its thistly curse repealed.
The various seasons woven into one,
770   And that one season an eternal spring,
The garden fears no blight, and needs no fence,
For there is none to covet, all are full.
The lion, and the libbard,° and the bear
Graze with the fearless flocks; all bask at noon
Together, or all gambol in the shade
Of the same grove, and drink one common stream.
Antipathies are none. No foe to man
Lurks in the serpent now: the mother sees,
And smiles to see, her infant's playful hand
780   Stretched forth to dally with the crested worm,
To stroke his azure neck, or to receive
The lambent homage of his arrowy tongue.

kine cattle   libbard leopard
fertile . . . disgrace i.e. rank with weeds

All creatures worship man, and all mankind
One Lord, one Father. Error has no place:
That creeping pestilence is driven away;
The breath of heaven has chased it. In the heart
No passion touches a discordant string,
But all is harmony and love. Disease
Is not: the pure and uncontaminate blood
790   Holds its due course, nor fears the frost of age.
One song employs all nations; and all cry,
'Worthy the Lamb, for he was slain for us!'°
The dwellers in the vales and on the rocks
Shout to each other, and the mountain tops
From distant mountains catch the flying joy;
Till, nation after nation taught the strain,
Earth rolls the rapturous hosanna round.
Behold the measure of the promise fill'd;
See Salem° built, the labour of a God!
800   Bright as a sun the sacred city shines;
All kingdoms and all princes of the earth
Flock to that light; the glory of all lands
Flows into her; unbounded is her joy,
And endless her increase. Thy rams are there,
Nebaioth, and the flocks of Kedar° there;
The looms of Ormus, and the mines of Ind,°
And Saba's° spicy groves, pay tribute there.
Praise is in all her gates: upon her walls,
And in her streets, and in her spacious courts,
810   Is heard salvation. Eastern Java there
Kneels with the native of the farthest west;
And Ethiopia spreads abroad the hand,
And worships. Her report has travelled forth
Into all lands. From every clime they come
To see thy beauty and to share thy joy,
O Sion! an assembly such as earth
Saw never, such as heav'n stoops down to see.

.   .   .

He is the happy man, whose life even now
Shows somewhat of that happier life to come;
Who, doomed to an obscure but tranquil state,
Is pleased with it, and, were he free to choose,
910   Would make his fate his choice; whom peace, the fruit
Of virtue, and whom virtue, fruit of faith,

Worthy . . . us "Worthy is the Lamb that was slain to receive power, and riches, and wisdom, and strength, and honour, and glory, and blessing" (Revelation 5:12)
Salem the New Jerusalem
Nebaioth . . . Kedar "The sons of Ishmael and progenitors of the Arabs, in the prophetic scripture here alluded to, may be reasonably considered as representatives of the Gentiles at large" (Cowper).
ormus . . . Ind Cf. Milton, *Paradise Lost* II.2. Ormus is an island at the mouth of the Persian Gulf and was a rich trading city, coupled by Milton with India for their "wealth."
Saba's Sheba in southwest Arabia

Prepare for happiness; bespeak him one
Content indeed to sojourn while he must
Below the skies, but having there his home.
The world o'erlooks him in her busy search
Of objects more illustrious in her view;
And occupied as earnestly as she,
Though more sublimely, he o'erlooks the world.
She scorns his pleasures, for she knows them not;
920   He seeks not hers, for he has proved them vain.
He cannot skim the ground like summer birds
Pursuing gilded flies; and such he deems
Her honours, her emoluments, her joys.
Therefore in contemplation is his bliss,
Whose power is such, that whom she lifts from earth
She makes familiar with a heaven unseen,
And shows him glories yet to be revealed.
Not slothful he, though seeming unemployed,
And censured oft as useless. Stillest streams
930   Oft water fairest meadows, and the bird
That flutters least is longest on the wing.
Ask him, indeed, what trophies he has raised,
Or what achievements of immortal fame
He purposes, and he shall answer—None.
His warfare is within. There unfatigued
His fervent spirit labours. There he fights,
And there obtains fresh triumphs o'er himself,
And never withering wreaths, compared with which
The laurels that a Caesar reaps are weeds.

.   .   .

So life glides smoothly and by stealth away,
More golden than that age of fabled gold
Renowned in ancient song; not vexed with care
Or stained with guilt, beneficent, approved
Of God and man, and peaceful in its end.
1000 So glide my life away! and so at last,
My share of duties decently fulfilled,
May some disease, not tardy to perform
Its destined office, yet with gentle stroke,
Dismiss me, weary, to a safe retreat,
Beneath the turf that I have often trod. . . .
1783–84   1785

GEORGE CRABBE

1754–1832

After a difficult early life and abortive plans for a medical career, Crabbe gained Edmund Burke's favorable notice of his poetry and through him met Reynolds and Dr. Johnson. The latter helped with the revision of *The Village* and wrote a letter to Reynolds that Crabbe later published in his 1807 preface. Johnson found Crabbe's poem "original, vigorous, and elegant," and, as Boswell tells us, found Crabbe's scorn of "the false notions of rustic happiness and rustic virtue . . . quite congenial with his own." Crabbe served as a curate for a time in his native village of Aldeburgh and held other church livings later in rural areas. He continued to write verse tales in heroic couplets throughout his life, winning from Byron the tribute of "Nature's sternest painter, yet best."

William Hazlitt was to write of Crabbe's almost obsessive concern with "teasing, helpless, unimaginative distress." In fact, Crabbe is always fascinated with the power of repressed or unfulfilled feeling, and he is a remarkably sharp student of the obscure and tortured destinies that were to become the subject of much realistic fiction later. But he also looked back to the example of Pope (particularly the Pope of the satiric portraits), who had, he claimed, "no small portion of this actuality of relation, this nudity of description, and poetry without an atmosphere." In the preface to *The Parish Register* Crabbe provides a good statement of his achievement, the attack upon the conventional forms of romance and pastoral through the patient and often subtle study of mixed motive: "an endeavour . . . to describe village-manners, not by adopting the notion of pastoral simplicity or assuming ideas of rustic barbarity, but by more natural views of the peasantry, considered as a mixed body of persons, sober or profligate, and hence, in a great measure, contented or miserable." *The Parish Register* is divided into three sections, each recording the year's entries under one heading—births, marriages, or deaths—and creating through brief portraits or narratives a rounded picture of parish life. In later works, notably *The Borough* (1810), *Tales in Verse* (1812), and *Tales of the Hall*, he devotes himself more completely to a dry, often witty, narrative verse which deliberately risks self-parody in its willful flatness and bareness.

The Village

From *Book I*

The village life, and every care that reigns
O'er youthful peasants and declining swains;
What labour yields, and what, that labour past,
Age, in its hour of languor, finds at last;
What form the real picture of the poor,
Demand a song—the Muse can give no more.
    Fled are those times when, in harmonious strains,
The rustic poet praised his native plains.
No shepherds now, in smooth alternate verse,

10 Their country's beauty or their nymphs' rehearse;
Yet still for these we frame the tender strain,
Still in our lays fond Corydons° complain,
And shepherds' boys their amorous pains reveal,
The only pains, alas! they never feel.
On Mincio's banks, in Caesar's bounteous reign,
If Tityrus found the Golden Age again,
Must sleepy bards the flattering dream prolong,
Mechanic echoes of the Mantuan song?
From Truth and Nature shall we widely stray,
20 Where Virgil, not where Fancy, leads the way?
Yes, thus the Muses sing of happy swains,
Because the Muses never knew their pains.
They boast their peasants' pipes;° but peasants now
Resign their pipes and plod behind the plough;
And few, amid the rural-tribe, have time
To number syllables, and play with rhyme;
Save honest Duck,° what son of verse could share
The poet's rapture, and the peasant's care?
Or the great labours of the field degrade,
30 With the new peril of a poorer trade?
From this chief cause these idle praises spring,
That themes so easy few forbear to sing;
For no deep thought the trifling subjects ask:
To sing of shepherds is an easy task.
The happy youth assumes the common strain,
A nymph his mistress, and himself a swain;
With no sad scenes he clouds his tuneful prayer,
But all, to look like her, is painted fair.
I grant indeed that fields and flocks have charms
40 For him that grazes or for him that farms;
But, when amid such pleasing scenes I trace
The poor laborious natives of the place,
And see the midday sun, with fervid ray,
On their bare heads and dewy temples play;
While some, with feebler heads and fainter hearts,
Deplore their fortune, yet sustain their parts:
Then shall I dare these real ills to hide
In tinsel trappings of poetic pride?
No; cast by fortune on a frowning coast,
50 Which neither groves nor happy valleys boast;
Where other cares than those the Muse relates,
And other shepherds dwell with other mates;

Corydons such shepherds as appear in Virgil's
Eclogues (c. 42–37 B.C.), where the poet traditionally is supposed to appear as Tityrus. The
pastoral poems are set in the countryside near
Mantua beside the Mincio River. Of the following lines, 15–18 were written by Dr. Johnson.

pipes the musical reeds of the traditional shep-
herd
Duck Stephen Duck (1705–56), the Thresher
Poet, a fashionable "primitive" whom Queen
Caroline made keeper of her library at Rich-
mond

By such examples taught, I paint the cot,°
As truth will paint it, and as bards will not:
Nor you, ye poor, of lettered scorn complain,
To you the smoothest song is smooth in vain;
O'ercome by labour, and bowed down by time,
Feel you the barren flattery of a rhyme?
Can poets soothe you, when you pine for bread,
60   By winding myrtles round your ruined shed?
Can their light tales your weighty griefs o'erpower,
Or glad with airy mirth the toilsome hour?

      . . .

   Ye gentle souls, who dream of rural ease,
Whom the smooth stream and smoother sonnet please;
Go! if the peaceful cot your praises share,
Go, look within, and ask if peace be there:
If peace be his—that drooping weary sire,
Or theirs, that offspring round their feeble fire;
Or hers, that matron pale, whose trembling hand
Turns on the wretched hearth the expiring brand!°
180   Nor yet can Time itself obtain for these
Life's latest comforts, due respect and ease:
For yonder see that hoary swain, whose age
Can with no cares except his own engage;
Who, propped on that rude staff, looks up to see
The bare arms broken from the withering tree
On which, a boy, he climbed the loftiest bough,
Then his first joy, but his sad emblem now.
   He once was chief in all the rustic trade;
His steady hand the straightest furrow made;
190   Full many a prize he won, and still is proud
To find the triumphs of his youth allowed.
A transient pleasure sparkles in his eyes;
He hears and smiles, then thinks again and sighs:
For now he journeys to his grave in pain;
The rich disdain him, nay, the poor disdain;
Alternate masters now their slave command,
Urge the weak efforts of his feeble hand;
And, when his age attempts its task in vain,
With ruthless taunts, of lazy poor complain.
200   Oft may you see him, when he tends the sheep,
His winter-charge, beneath the hillock weep;
Oft hear him murmur to the winds that blow
O'er his white locks and bury them in snow,
When, roused by rage and muttering in the morn,
He mends the broken hedge with icy thorn:—
   'Why do I live, when I desire to be

cot cottage   brand coal, ember

At once from life and life's long labour free?
Like leaves in spring, the young are blown away,
Without the sorrows of a slow decay;
210   I, like yon withered leaf, remain behind,
Nipped by the frost, and shivering in the wind;
There it abides till younger buds come on,
As I, now all my fellow-swains are gone;
Then, from the rising generation thrust,
It falls, like me, unnoticed to the dust.
    'These fruitful fields, these numerous flocks I see,
Are others' gain, but killing cares to me:
To me the children of my youth are lords,
Cool in their looks, but hasty in their words:
220   Wants of their own demand their care; and who
Feels his own want and succours others too?
A lonely, wretched man, in pain I go,
None need my help, and none relieve my woe;
Then,let my bones beneath the turf be laid,
And men forget the wretch they would not aid!'
    Thus groan the old, till, by disease oppressed,
They taste a final woe, and then they rest.

                    .   .   .

    Now once again the gloomy scene explore,
Less gloomy now; the bitter hour is o'er,
320   The man of many sorrows sighs no more.—
Up yonder hill, behold how sadly slow
The bier moves winding from the vale below;
There lie the happy dead, from trouble free,
And the glad parish pays the frugal fee.
No more, O Death! thy victim starts to hear
Churchwarden stern or kingly overseer;
No more the farmer claims his humble bow,
Thou art his lord, the best of tyrants thou!
    Now to the church behold the mourners come,
330   Sedately torpid and devoutly dumb;
The village children now their games suspend,
To see the bier that bears their ancient friend:
For he was one in all their idle sport,
And like a monarch ruled their little court;
The pliant bow he formed, the flying ball,
The bat, the wicket, were his labours all;
Him now they follow to his grave, and stand
Silent and sad, and gazing, hand in hand;
While bending low, their eager eyes explore
340   The mingled relics of the parish poor.
The bell tolls late, the moping owl flies round,
Fear marks the flight and magnifies the sound;
The busy priest, detained by weightier care,

Defers his duty till the day of prayer;
And, waiting long, the crowd retire distressed,
To think a poor man's bones should lie unblessed.

                                    1783

The Parish Register

From *Part III: Burials*

There was, 'tis said, and I believe, a time,
When humble Christians died with views sublime;
When all were ready for their faith to bleed,
But few to write or wrangle for their creed;
When lively Faith upheld the sinking heart,
And friends, assured to meet, prepared to part;
When Love felt hope, when Sorrow grew serene,
And all was comfort in the death-bed scene.
    Alas! when now the gloomy king they wait,
10   'Tis weakness yielding to resistless fate;
Like wretched men upon the ocean cast,
They labour hard and struggle to the last,
'Hope against hope,' and wildly gaze around,
In search of help that never shall be found:
Nor, till the last strong billow stops the breath,
Will they believe them in the jaws of Death!

    When these my records I reflecting read,
And find what ills these numerous births succeed;
What powerful griefs these nuptial ties attend,
20   With what regret these painful journeys end;
When from the cradle to the grave I look,
Mine I conceive a melancholy book.
    Where now is perfect resignation seen?
Alas! it is not on the village-green:—
I've seldom known, though I have often read,
Of happy peasants on their dying-bed;
Whose looks proclaimed that sunshine of the breast,
That more than hope, that Heaven itself expressed.
    What I behold are feverish fits of strife,
30   'Twixt fears of dying and desire of life:
Those earthly hopes that to the last endure;
Those fears that hopes superior fail to cure;
At best a sad submission to the doom,
Which, turning from the danger, lets it come.

    Sick lies the man, bewildered, lost, afraid,
His spirits vanquished and his strength decayed;
No hope the friend, the nurse, the doctor lend—
'Call then a priest, and fit him for his end.'

A priest is called; 'tis now, alas! too late,
40 Death enters with him at the cottage-gate;
Or, time allowed, he goes, assured to find
The self-commending, all-confiding mind;
And sighs to hear what we may justly call
Death's common-place, the train of thought in all.
 'True, I'm a sinner,' feebly he begins,
'But trust in Mercy to forgive my sins';
(Such cool confession no past crimes excite;
Such claim on Mercy seems the sinner's right!)
'I know, mankind are frail, that God is just,
50 And pardons those who in his mercy trust;
We're sorely tempted in a world like this;
All men have done, and I like all, amiss;
But now, if spared, it is my full intent
On all the past to ponder and repent:
Wrongs against me I pardon great and small,
And if I die, I die in peace with all.'
 His merits thus and not his sins confessed,
He speaks his hopes, and leaves to Heaven the rest.
Alas! arc these the prospects, dull and cold,
60 That dying Christians to their priests unfold?
Or mends the prospect when the enthusiast cries,
'I die assured!' and in a rapture dies?
 Ah, where that humble, self-abasing mind,
With that confiding spirit, shall we find—
The mind that, feeling what repentance brings,
Dejection's terrors and Contrition's stings,
Feels then the hope that mounts all care above,
And the pure joy that flows from pardoning love?
 Such have I seen in death and much deplore,
70 So many dying, that I see no more.
Lo! now my records, where I grieve to trace,
How Death has triumphed in so short a space;
Who are the dead, how died they, I relate,
And snatch some portion of their acts from fate.

 With Andrew Collett we the year begin,
The blind, fat landlord of the Old Crown Inn—
Big as his butt,° and, for the self-same use,
To take in stores of strong fermenting juice.
On his huge chair beside the fire he sate,
80 In revel chief, and umpire in debate;
Each night his string of vulgar tales he told,
When ale was cheap and bachelors were bold:
His heroes all were famous in their days,
Cheats were his boast and drunkards had his praise;

butt ale cask

'One, in three draughts, three mugs of ale took down,
As mugs were then—the champion of the Crown;
For thrice three days another lived on ale,
And knew no change but that of mild and stale;°
Two thirsty soakers watched a vessel's side,
90   When he the tap, with dexterous hand, applied;
Nor from their seats departed, till they found
That butt was out and heard the mournful sound.'
    He praised a poacher, precious child of fun!
Who shot the keeper with his own spring-gun;°
Nor less the smuggler who the exciseman tied,
And left him hanging at the birch-wood side,
There to expire; but one who saw him hang
Cut the good cord—a traitor of the gang.
    His own exploits with boastful glee he told,
100   What ponds he emptied and what pikes° he sold;
And how, when blessed with sight alert and gay,
The night's amusements kept him through the day.
    He sang the praises of those times, when all
'For cards and dice, as for their drink, might call;
When justice winked on every jovial crew,
And ten-pins tumbled in the parson's view.'
    He told, when angry wives, provoked to rail,
Or drive a third-day drunkard from his ale,
What were his triumphs, and how great the skill
110   That won the vexed virago to his will:
Who raving came—then talked in milder strain—
Then wept, then drank, and pledged her spouse again.
Such were his themes: how knaves o'er laws prevail,
Or, when made captives, how they fly from jail;
The young how brave, how subtle were the old;
And oaths attested all that Folly told.
    On death like his what name shall we bestow,
So very sudden! yet so very slow?
'Twas slow:—Disease, augmenting year by year,
120   Showed the grim king by gradual steps brought near.
'Twas not less sudden: in the night he died,
He drank, he swore, he jested, and he lied;
Thus aiding folly with departing breath.—
'Beware, Lorenzo, the slow-sudden death.'°

.   .   .

    Down by the church-way walk, and where the brook
Winds round the chancel like a shepherd's crook,
In that small house with those green pales° before,

---

mild and stale two kinds of ale ("stale" is stronger)
spring-gun concealed gun with a trip-wire
pikes large and valuable fish

Beware . . . death the admonition to the young libertine in Edward Young, *Night Thoughts* I.387
pales picket fence

Where jasmine trails on either side the door;
Where those dark shrubs that now grow wild at will,
Were clipped in form and tantalized with skill;
Where cockles blanched and pebbles neatly spread,
Formed shining borders for the larkspurs' bed—
320 There lived a Lady, wise, austere, and nice,
Who showed her virtue by her scorn of vice.
In the dear fashions of her youth she dressed,
A pea-green Joseph° was her favourite vest;
Erect she stood, she walked with stately mien,
Tight was her length of stays, and she was tall and lean.
    There long she lived in maiden-state immured,
From looks of love and treacherous man secured;
Though evil fame (but that was long before)
Had blown her dubious blast at Catherine's door.
330 A Captain thither, rich from India, came,
And though a cousin called, it touched her fame:
Her annual stipend rose from his behest,
And all the long-prized treasures she possessed:—
If aught like joy awhile appeared to stay
In that stern face, and chase those frowns away,
'Twas when her treasures she disposed for view,
And heard the praises to their splendour due;
Silks beyond price, so rich, they'd stand alone,
And diamonds blazing on the buckled zone;°
340 Rows of rare pearls by curious workmen set,
And bracelets fair in box of glossy jet;
Bright polished amber precious from its size,
Or forms the fairest fancy could devise.
Her drawers of cedar, shut with secret springs,
Concealed the watch of gold and rubied rings;
Letters, long proofs of love, and verses fine
Round the pinked rims of crispèd Valentine.
Her china-closet, cause of daily care,
For woman's wonder held her pencilled° ware;
350 That pictured wealth of China and Japan,
Like its cold mistress, shunned the eye of man.
    Her neat small room, adorned with maiden-taste,
A clipped French puppy, first of favourites, graced;
A parrot next, but dead and stuffed with art;
(For Poll, when living, lost the Lady's heart,
And then his life; for he was heard to speak
Such frightful words as tinged his Lady's cheek;)
Unhappy bird! who had no power to prove,
Save by such speech, his gratitude and love.
360 A grey old cat his whiskers licked beside;

Joseph long riding cloak   **pencilled** painted
zone belt

A type of sadness in the house of pride.
The polished surface of an India chest,
A glassy globe, in frame of ivory, pressed;
Where swam two finny creatures: one of gold,
Of silver one, both beauteous to behold.
All these were formed the guiding taste to suit;
The beasts well-mannered and the fishes mute.
A widowed Aunt was there, compelled by need
The nymph to flatter and her tribe to feed;
370   Who, veiling well her scorn, endured the clog,
Mute as the fish and fawning as the dog.
       As years increased, these treasures, her delight,
Arose in value in their owner's sight:
A miser knows that, view it as he will,
A guinea kept is but a guinea still;
And so he puts it to its proper use,
That something more this guinea may produce:
But silks and rings, in the possessor's eyes,
The oftener seen, the more in value rise,
380   And thus are wisely hoarded to bestow
The kind of pleasure that with years will grow.
       But what availed their worth—if worth had they—
In the sad summer of her slow decay?
       Then we beheld her turn an anxious look
From trunks and chests, and fix it on her book—
A rich-bound Book of Prayer the Captain gave,
(Some Princess had it, or was said to have;)
And then once more, on all her stores, look round,
And draw a sigh so piteous and profound,
390   That told, 'Alas! how hard from these to part,
And form new hopes and habits from the heart!
What shall I do,' (she cried,) 'my peace of mind
To gain in dying, and to die resigned?'
       'Hear,' we returned;—'these baubles cast aside,
Nor give thy God a rival in thy pride;
Thy closets shut, and ope thy kitchen's door;
There own thy failings, *here* invite the poor;
A friend of Mammon let thy bounty make;
For widows' prayers thy vanities forsake;
400   And let the hungry of thy pride partake:
Then shall thy inward eye with joy survey
The angel Mercy tempering Death's delay!'
       Alas! 'twas hard; the treasures still had charms,
Hope still its flattery, sickness its alarms;
Still was the same unsettled, clouded view,
And the same plaintive cry, 'What shall I do?'
       Nor change appeared: for when her race was run,
Doubtful we all exclaimed, 'What has been done?'

Apart she lived, and still she lies alone;
410 Yon earthy heap awaits the flattering stone,
On which invention shall be long employed,
To show the various worth of Catherine Lloyd.

.   .   .

Then died a Rambler: not the one who sails
And trucks, for female favours, beads and nails;°
Not one, who posts from place to place—of men
And manners treating with a flying pen;°
Not he, who climbs, for prospects, Snowdon's height,
And chides the clouds that intercept the sight;°
No curious shell, rare plant, or brilliant spar,
510 Enticed our traveller from his home so far;
But all the reason, by himself assigned
For so much rambling, was, a restless mind;
As on, from place to place, without intent,
Without reflection, Robin Dingley went.
Not thus by nature;—never man was found
Less prone to wander from his parish-bound:
Claudian's old Man,° to whom all scenes were new,
Save those where he and where his apples grew,
Resembled Robin, who around would look,
520 And his horizon for the earth's mistook.
To this poor swain a keen Attorney came:—
'I give thee joy, good fellow! on thy name;
The rich old Dingley's dead;—no child has he,
Nor wife, nor will; his ALL is left for thee:
To be his fortune's heir thy claim is good;
Thou hast the name, and we will prove the blood.'
The claim was made; 'twas tried—it would not stand;
They proved the blood, but were refused the land.
Assured of wealth, this man of simple heart,
530 To every friend had predisposed a part:
His wife had hopes indulged of various kind;
The three Miss Dingleys had their school assigned,
Masters were sought for what they each required,
And books were bought and harpsichords were hired:
So high was hope;—the failure touched his brain,
And Robin never was himself again.
Yet he no wrath, no angry wish expressed,
But tried, in vain, to labour or to rest;
Then cast his bundle on his back, and went
540 He knew not whither, nor for what intent.

the one . . . nails an itinerant peddler
one . . . pen *Rambler,* the periodical published
by Dr. Johnson, 1750–52
he . . . sight the mountain climber (Mt. Snowdon is in Wales) and collector of minerals (e.g.
crystal, "spar")

Claudian's old Man the old man of Verona
(who never left his rural home) in the idyll by
the Roman poet of the late 4th and early 5th
century A.D.

Years fled;—of Robin all remembrance past,
When home he wandered in his rags at last.
A sailor's jacket on his limbs was thrown,
A sailor's story he had made his own;
Had suffered battles, prisons, tempests, storms,
Encountering death in all his ugliest forms.
His cheeks were haggard, hollow was his eye,
Where madness lurked, concealed in misery;
Want, and the ungentle world, had taught a part,
550 And prompted cunning to that simple heart:
He now bethought him, he would roam no more,
But live at home and labour as before.
    Here clothed and fed, no sooner he began
To round and redden, than away he ran;
His wife was dead, their children past his aid:
So, unmolested, from his home he strayed.
Six years elapsed, when, worn with want and pain,
Came Robin, wrapt in all his rags, again.—
We chide, we pity;—placed among our poor,
560 He fed again, and was a man once more.
    As when a gaunt and hungry fox is found,
Entrapped alive in some rich hunter's ground;
Fed for the field, although each day's a feast,
Fatten you may, but never *tame* the beast;
A house protects him, savoury viands sustain;
But loose his neck and off he goes again:
So stole our vagrant from his warm retreat,
To rove a prowler and be deemed a cheat.
    Hard was his fare; for, him at length we saw,
570 In cart conveyed and laid supine on straw.
His feeble voice now spoke a sinking heart;
His groans now told the motions of the cart;
And when it stopped, he tried in vain to stand;
Closed was his eye, and clenched his clammy hand;
Life ebbed apace, and our best aid no more
Could his weak sense or dying heart restore:
But now he fell, a victim to the snare
That vile attorneys for the weak prepare—
They who, when profit or resentment call,
580 Heed not the groaning victim they enthrall.
                    .   .   .
                    1807

ROBERT BURNS
1759–1796

Wordsworth praised Burns as one who "showed my youth / How Verse may build a princely throne / On humble truth." And he paid tribute to Burns's appeal in terms Johnson might have used: "Deep in the general heart of men / His power survives." Burns's public role was in part that of the primitive poet; and his strong, confident personality, given edge by reluctance to defer to rank, contributed to that effect. As the son of an unsuccessful farmer, educated largely at home, working on the farm until his first book achieved fame, and returning later in life to a farm (with as little success as his father), Burns's career was hardly the conventional one of a man of letters. The irregularity of his personal life (which produced nine illegitimate children), his bawdy lyrics in *The Merry Muses of Caledonia*, his support of the French Revolution, his attacks upon the conservative forces in the Presbyterian Scottish Kirk, and his bouts of drunkenness all served to fill out the image of a "natural" man whose poetry was the overflow of a strong, undisciplined personality.

In fact, Burns had begun to write early but found his own idiom through his discovery of the earlier Scots vernacular poetry of the eighteenth century, particularly that of Allan Ramsay and Robert Fergusson. His literary achievement had its traditional basis both in these poets and in the English poets of his century. Recent studies have shown that Burns's use of Scots vernacular is rarely consistent, and he himself sometimes speaks of a "sprinkling" of Scots in his poems. He seems to use Scots or English equivalents interchangeably as they serve his literary purposes, and at times his words may look both ways, achieving double meaning in literal dialect sense and in English suggestion. Raymond Bentman points out that the word "bickering" in *To a Mouse* means "hastening" in Scottish "but also carries the English 'fighting,' 'squabbling,' 'brawling,' and thus conveys antagonism as well as fear in the mouse." So, conversely, the sudden emergence of formal English in "Nature's social union" surrounds the phrase with irony. Examples can be found throughout his work, and they make us aware of the artificial nature of Burns's language (comparable in its invention to Chatterton's medieval English and reminiscent in certain ways of the Augustan interplay of levels of diction in mock-heroic poetry). Burns denounced other kinds of literary artifice: "Darts, flames, Cupids, loves, graces, and all that farrago are just . . . a senseless rabble." His own artifice creates the impression of spontaneity and naturalness, while at the same time gaining subtle literary effects.

To a Mouse

On Turning Her Up in Her Nest with the Plough, November 1785

Wee, sleekit,° cowrin, tim'rous beastie,
O, what a panic's in thy breastie!
Thou need na start awa sae hasty,
   Wi' bickering brattle!°

---

sleekit sleek   **bickering brattle** hurrying scamper (but see Headnote)

I wad be laith to rin an' chase thee,
        Wi' murdering pattle!°

I'm truly sorry man's dominion
Has broken Nature's social union,
An' justifies that ill opinion
10   Which makes thee startle
At me, thy poor earth-born companion
        An' fellow-mortal!

I doubt na, whyles,° but thou may thieve;
What then? poor beastie, thou maun° live!
A daimen icker° in a thrave°
        'S a sma' request;
I'll get a blessin wi' the lave,°
        An' never miss't!

Thy wee bit housie, too, in ruin!
20 Its silly wa's° the win's are strewin!
An' naething, now, to big° a new ane,
        O' foggage° green!
An' bleak December's winds ensuin,
        Baith snell° an' keen!

Thou saw the fields laid bare an' waste,
An' weary winter comin fast,
An' cozie here, beneath the blast,
        Thou thought to dwell,
Till crash! the cruel coulter past
30   Out thro' thy cell.

That wee bit heap o' leaves an' stibble
Has cost thee mony a weary nibble!
Now thou's turned out, for a' thy trouble,
        But house or hald,°
To thole° the winter's sleety dribble,
        An' cranreuch° cauld!

But, Mousie, thou art no thy lane,°
In proving foresight may be vain:
The best laid schemes o' mice an' men
40   Gang aft agley.°
An' lea'e us nought but grief an' pain
        For promised joy!

pattle plow staff
whyles sometimes
maun must
daimen icker occasional ear
thrave twenty-four sheaves
lave rest
silly wa's feeble walls

big build
foggage rank grass left after the harvest
snell biting
But . . . hald without house or home (holding)
thole endure
cranreuch hoarfrost
no thy lane not alone
agley awry

Still thou art blest, compared wi' me!
The present only toucheth thee:
But och! I backward cast my e'e
      On prospects drear!
An' forward, tho' I canna see,
      I guess an' fear!
1785   1786

Address to the Deil

O Prince! O Chief of many thronèd powers!
That led the embattled seraphim to war.
                    MILTON°

O thou! whatever title suit thee,
Auld Hornie, Satan, Nick, or Clootie,°
Wha in yon cavern grim an' sootie,
      Closed under hatches,
Spairges° about the brunstane cootie,°
      To scaud° poor wretches!

Hear me, auld Hangie,° for a wee,
An' let poor damnèd bodies be;
I'm sure sma' pleasure it can gie,
10   Even to a deil,
To skelp° an' scaud poor dogs like me,
      An' hear us squeel.

Great is thy power, an' great thy fame;
Far kend° an' noted is thy name;
An' tho' yon lowan heugh's° thy hame,
      Thou travels far;
An' faith! thou's neither lag° nor lame,
      Nor blate nor scaur.°

Whyles,° ranging like a roarin lion
20 For prey, a' holes an' corners tryin;
Whyles on the strong-winged tempest flyin,
      Tirlan the kirks;°
Whyles, in the human bosom pryin,
      Unseen thou lurks.

Milton *Paradise Lost* I.128–29; in a letter of 1787 Burns voices his admiration for Milton's "great personage, Satan": "the dauntless magnanimity, the intrepid unyielding independence, the desperate daring and noble defiance of hardship." But this poem plays between that majestic myth and the homelier figure of folk legends. **Clootie** cloven-hoofed **Spairges** splashes **cootie** basin, tub

scaud scald **Hangie** hangman **skelp** slap **kend** known **lowan heugh's** flaming pit's **lag** backward **Nor blate nor scaur** nor bashful nor afraid **Whyles** sometimes **Tirlan the kirks** unroofing the churches

I've heard my reverend graunie say,
In lanely glens ye like to stray;
Or where auld ruined castles grey
       Nod to the moon,
Ye fright the nightly wanderer's way,
30   Wi' eldritch croon.°

When twilight did my graunie summon,
To say her prayers, douce,° honest woman!
Aft yont the dyke° she's heard you bumman,°
       Wi' eerie drone;
Or, rustlin, thro' the boortrees° coman,
       Wi' heavy groan.

Ae dreary, windy, winter night,
The stars shot down wi' sklentan° light,
Wi' you mysel I gat a fright
40   Ayont the lough;°
Ye, like a rash-buss° stood in sight
       Wi' waving sugh.°

The cudgel in my nieve° did shake,
Each bristled hair stood like a stake,
When, wi' an eldritch, stoor° quaick, quaick,
       Amang the springs,
Awa ye squattered, like a drake,
       On whistling wings.

Let warlocks grim, an' withered hags,
50 Tell how wi' you on ragweed nags,
They skim the muirs, an' dizzy crags,
       Wi' wicked speed;
And in kirk-yards renew their leagues,
       Owre howcket° dead.

Thence countra wives, wi' toil an' pain,
May plunge an' plunge the kirn° in vain;
For, oh! the yellow treasure's taen
       By witching skill;
An' dawtit, twal-pint Hawkie's° gaen
60   As yell's the bill.°

Thence mystic knots mak great abuse
On young guidmen,° fond, keen, an' crouse;°

eldritch croon ghastly moan	**nieve** fist
douce prudent	**stoor** harsh
Aft yont the dyke often beyond the wall	**howcket** dug up
bumman humming	**kirn** churn
boortrees bowertrees, elders	**dawtit . . . Hawkie's** the petted twelve-pint
sklentan slanting	Hawkie (white-faced cow)
Ayont the lough beyond (across) the lake	**As . . . bill** as dry as the bull
rash-buss clump of rushes	**guidmen** newly married men
sugh wind-like rushing sound	**crouse** brisk, confident

When the best wark-lume° i' the house,
  By cantraip wit,°
Is instant made no worth a louse,
  Just at the bit.°

When thowes dissolve the snawy hoord,
An' float the jinglin icy boord,°
Then water-kelpies° haunt the foord,
  By your direction,
An' nighted travellers are allured
  To their destruction.

An' aft your moss-traversing spunkies°
Decoy the wight that late an' drunk is:
The bleezan,° curst, mischievous monkies
  Delude his eyes,
Till in some miry slough he sunk is,
  Ne'er mair to rise.

When Masons' mystic word an' grip
In storms an' tempests raise you up,
Some cock or cat your rage maun° stop,
  Or, strange to tell!
The youngest brother ye wad whip
  Aff straught to hell.

Lang syne,° in Eden's bonie yard,°
When youthfu' lovers first were paired,
An' all the soul of love they shared,
  The raptured hour,
Sweet on the fragrant flowery swaird,
  In shady bower:

Then you, ye auld, snick-drawing° dog!
Ye cam to Paradise incog,
An' played on man a cursed brogue°
  (Black be you fa'!°),
An' gied the infant warld a shog,°
  'Maist ruin'd a'.

D'ye mind that day, when in a bizz,°
Wi' reekit duds, an' reestit gizz,°

70

80

90

wark-lume weaver's loom, tool, or implement
(with sexual suggestion)
cantraip wit magic art
bit nick of time, critical moment
boord surface
water-kelpies mischievous spirits; cf. William
Collins, *Ode on the Popular Superstitions of
the Highlands* vi, viii
moss-traversing spunkies bog-crossing will-o'-
the-wisps
bleezan flaming, blazing

maun must
syne since
yard garden
snick-drawing latch-lifting (trick-contriving)
brogue trick
fa' fortune
shog shake
bizz flurry
Wi' . . . gizz with smoky clothes and singed
wig

Ye did present your smoutie phiz
100 　　　　'Mang better folk,
An' sklented° on the man of Uz°
　　　　Your spitefu' joke?

An' how yet gat him i' your thrall,
An' brak him out o' house an' hal',
While scabs an' botches° did him gall
　　　　Wi' bitter claw,

An' lowsed° his ill-tongued, wicked scawl,°
　　　　Was warst ava?

But a' your doings to rehearse,
110 Your wily shares an' fechtin° fierce,
Sin' that day Michael did you pierce,°
　　　　Down to this time,
Wad ding° a' Lallan° tongue, or Erse,°
　　　　In prose or rhyme.

An' now, auld Cloots,° I ken ye're thinkan,
A certain Bardie's rantin, drinkin,
Some luckless hour will send him linkan,°
　　　　To your black pit;
But faith! he'll turn a corner jinkan,°
120 　　　　An' cheat you yet.

But fare you weel, auld Nickie-ben!
O wad ye tak a thought an' men'!°
Ye aiblins° might—I dinna ken—
　　　　Still hae a stake:°
I'm wae° to think upo' yon den,
　　　　Even for your sake!
1785–86　　　　　　1786

---

sklented shot, cast
man of Uz Job
botches boils
lowsed loosed
scawl scold (i.e. his wife)
fechtin fighting
did you pierce Cf. *Paradise Lost* VI.320–34 for
Michael's cleaving of Satan.
ding beat
Lallan Lowland

Erse Gaelic, still spoken in the Highlands of
Burns's day
Cloots hoofs
linkan skipping
jinkan dodging
men' mend
aiblins perhaps
stake gambler's chance
wae filled with woe; cf. Dryden's "hope, with
Origen, that the Devil himself may, at last, be
saved" (Preface to *Absalom and Achitophel*)

Holy Willie's Prayer°

And send the godly in a pet to pray.
POPE°

O Thou, wha in the heavens dost dwell,
Wha, as it pleases best thysel,
Sends ane to heaven an' ten to hell,°
        A' for thy glory,
And no for ony guid or ill
        They've done afore thee!

I bless and praise thy matchless might,
Whan thousands thou hast left in night,
That I am here afore thy sight,
10   For gifts an' grace
A burnin an' a shinin light,°
        To a' this place.

What was I, or my generation,°
That I should get sic° exaltation?
I, wha deserved most just damnation
        For broken laws
Five thousand years 'fore my creation,
        Thro' Adam's cause!

When from my mither's womb I fell,
20 Thou might hae plunged me deep in hell,
To gnash my gums and weep and wail,
        In burnin lakes,
Where damnèd devils roar and yell,
        Chained to their stakes.

Yet I am here, a chosen sample,
To show thy grace is great an' ample;
I'm here a pillar in thy temple,

Holy Willie's Prayer This mock-prayer or dramatic monologue is composed as if by William Fisher (1737–1809), a Calvinistic elder in the parish of Mauchline. Gavin Hamilton, a lawyer and both friend and patron of Burns (who dedicated his 1786 *Poems* to Hamilton), was cited for neglecting church attendance and for traveling on Sunday. In an appeal to the Synod, Hamilton was successfully defended by another of Burns's friends and patrons, Robert Aiken. Burns explains the situation in a headnote: "Holy Willie was a rather oldish bachelor elder . . . much and justly famed for that polemical chattering which ends in tippling orthodoxy, and for that spiritualized bawdry which refines to a liquorish devotion" (that is, lecherous one). "Holy Willie and his priest, Father Auld . . . came off second best" in the hearing of the Presbytery of Ayr, "owing partly to the oratorical powers of Mr. Robert Aiken . . . but chiefly to Mr. Hamilton's being one of the most irreproachable and truly respectable characters in the country." As for Holy Willie, on "losing his process, the Muse overheard him at his devotions," in the poem that follows. Burns writes a compound of colloquial Scots and biblical English that was characteristic of the evangelical Presbyterian, and he attributes to Willie the intensity of a faith at once prostrate and vindictive.

Pope *The Rape of the Lock* IV.64

ane . . . hell The Calvinistic doctrine of the elect, by which God judges according to his foreordained will rather than the good works men may have performed; the arbitrariness of God's will reveals his power, incommensurate with human understanding.

burnin . . . light "He was a burning and a shining light . . ." (John 5:35)

generation ancestry, birth

sic such

                    Strong as a rock,
A guide, a buckler, and example
                    To a' thy flock.

O Lord, thou kens what zeal I bear,
When drinkers drink, an' swearers swear,
And singin here and dancin there,
                    Wi' great an' sma':
For I am keepit by thy fear
                    Free frae them a'.

But yet, O Lord! confess I must,
At times I'm fashed° wi' fleshy lust;
An' sometimes too, in warldly trust,°
                    Vile self gets in;
But thou remembers we are dust,
                    Defiled wi' sin.

O Lord! yestreen,° thou kens, wi' Meg—
Thy pardon I sincerely beg;
O! may't ne'er be a livin plague°
                    To my dishonour,
An' I'll ne'er lift a lawless leg
                    Again upon her.

Besides I farther maun° allow,
Wi' Leezie's lass, three times I trow—
But, Lord, that Friday I was fou,°
                    When I cam near her,
Or else, thou kens, the servant true
                    Wad ne'er hae steered° her.

May be thou lets this fleshly thorn
Beset thy servant e'en and morn
Lest he owre high and proud should turn,
                    Cause he's sae gifted;°
If sae, thy han' maun e'en be borne,
                    Until thou lift it.

Lord, bless thy chosen in this place,
For here thou hast a chosen race;
But God confound their stubborn face,
                    And blast their name,
Wha bring thy elders to disgrace
                    An' public shame!

fashed troubled
warldly trust Willie was responsible for valuation and arbitration in parish farming.
yestreen last night
livin plague i.e. by pregnancy

maun must
fou drunk
steered roused
gifted i.e. with grace, as one of the elect (cf. "thy chosen" in l. 61)

Lord, mind Gau'n Hamilton's deserts,
He drinks, an' swears, an' plays at cartes,
Yet has sae mony takin arts
        Wi' great and sma',
70 Frae God's ain priest the people's hearts
        He steals awa'.

An' when we chastened him therefore,
Thou kens how he bred sic a splore°
As set the warld in a roar
  O' laughin at us;
Curse thou his basket and his store,°
    Kail° an' potatoes.

Lord, hear my earnest cry an' prayer,
80 Against that Presbyt'ry o' Ayr;
Thy strong right hand, Lord, mak it bare°
      Upo' their heads;
Lord, weigh it down, and dinna spare,
      For their misdeeds!

O Lord my God, that glib-tongued Aiken,
My vera heart and saul are quakin,
To think how we stood sweatin, shakin,
      An' pissed wi' dread,
While he, wi' hingin lips and snakin,°
90   Held up his head.

Lord, in thy day of vengeance try him;
Lord, visit him wha did employ him,
And pass not in thy mercy by them,
      Nor hear their prayer;
But, for thy people's sake, destroy them,
      And dinna spare!

But, Lord, remember me and mine
Wi' mercies temp'ral and divine,
That I for grace an' gear° may shine
100   Excelled by nane;
And a' the glory shall be thine,
      Amen, Amen!

1785   1789

splore frolic, riot
Curse . . . store "Cursed shall be thy basket and thy store" (Deuteronomy 28:17).
Kail cabbage (the vast and terrible curse threatened by Jehovah is aimed rather narrowly and spitefully by Willie, as again in the next stanza)
mak it bare "The Lord hath made bare his holy arm in the eyes of all the nations . . ." (Isaiah 52:10)

snakin curling. Other versions have Willie turn upon Father Auld in exasperated disloyalty: "While Auld wi' hingin lip gaed sneaking / And hid his head!"
gear wealth (not orthodox Calvinism but a frequent misinterpretation of election among Puritans; cf. Dryden, Absalom and Achitophel, ll. 535–36)

Tam O' Shanter°

Of Brownyis and of Bogillis full in this Buke.

GAVIN DOUGLAS°

When chapman billies° leave the street,
And drouthy° neebors, neebors meet,
As market days are wearing late,
An' folk begin to tak the gate;°
While we sit bousing at the nappy,°
An' getting fou° and unco° happy,
We think na on the lang Scots miles,°
The mosses, waters, slaps, and styles,°
That lie between us and our hame,
Whare sits our sulky, sullen dame,
Gathering her brows like gathering storm,
Nursing her wrath to keep it warm.

    This truth fand honest Tam o' Shanter,
As he frae Ayr ae° night did canter,
(Auld Ayr, wham ne'er a town surpasses
For honest men and bonie lasses).

    O Tam! hadst thou but been sae wise,
As taen thy ain wife Kate's advice!
She tauld thee weel thou was a skellum,°
A bletherin,° blusterin, drunken blellum;°
That frae November till October,
Ae market-day thou was nae sober;
That ilka melder,° wi' the miller
Thou sat as lang as thou had siller;°
That every naig was ca'd a shoe on,°
The smith and thee gat roarin fou on;
That at the Lord's house, even on Sunday,

10

20

Tam O' Shanter Burns regarded this as "his own favourite poem . . . an essay in a walk of the Muses entirely new to him." Thomas Carlyle (1828) felt that Burns "had not gone back . . . into that dark, earnest wondering age, when the tradition was believed," and thus "the tragedy of the adventure becomes a mere drunken phantasmagoria, painted on ale-vapours, and the farce alone has any reality." This Romantic response to Burns's irony seems to blame him for not recovering the attitude of William Collins, who was celebrating the "popular superstitions" as a source and even a form of poetic power. Burns could in fact share this view; he tells us that an old family servant with a great repertory of folk tales and songs cultivated in him "the latent seeds of poesy; but had so strong an effect on my imagination that, to this hour, in my nocturnal rambles I sometimes keep a sharp look-out in suspicious places; and though nobody could be more sceptical in these matters than I, yet it often takes an effort of philosophy to shake off these idle terrors" (letter of 1787). In this poem Burns is not mocking superstitions but rather the literal-minded Tam, who seems less capable of awe than of simple fear

and appetite (or thirst); the moralizing narration is mock-solemn (like the heroic similes and other occasional "literary" forms), striking a note that seems pointedly inappropriate to Tam's own consciousness.
Gavin Douglas (1474?–1522), from the prologue, l. 18, to the sixth book of his translation of Virgil, *Eneados* ("bogillis" would be spirits)
chapman billies peddlers or market-stall keepers
drouthy thirsty
gate road
nappy ale
fou drunk
unco very
Scots miles about two hundred yards more than the English or American
mosses . . . styles bogs, pools, hedge (or wall) openings, stiles
ae one
skellum wretch
bletherin babbling
blellum chatterbox, idler
ilka melder every time you brought oats to be ground
siller silver, money
ca'd a shoe on shod

2276

Thou drank wi' Kirkton Jean° till Monday.
She prophesied that, late or soon,
30   Thou would be found deep drowned in Doon;°
Or catched wi' warlocks in the mirk,°
By Alloway's auld, haunted kirk.
    Ah, gentle dames! it gars me greet°
To think how mony counsels sweet,
How mony lengthened sage advices,
The husband frae the wife despises!
    But to our tale: ae market night,
Tam had got planted unco right;
Fast by an ingle,° bleezing° finely,
40   Wi' reamin swats,° that drank divinely;
And at his elbow, Souter° Johnie,
His ancient, trusty, drouthy crony;
Tam lo'ed him like a vera brither;
They had been fou for weeks thegither.
The night drave on wi' sangs and clatter;
And ay° the ale was growing better:
The landlady and Tam grew gracious,
Wi' secret favours, sweet and precious:
The souter tauld his queerest stories;
50   The landlord's laugh was ready chorus:
The storm without might rair and rustle,
Tam did na mind the storm a whistle.
    Care,° mad to see a man sae happy,
E'en drowned himsel amang the nappy.
As bees flee hame wi' lades o' treasure,
The minutes winged their way wi' pleasure;
Kings may be blest, but Tam was glorious,
O'er a' the ills o' life victorious!
    But pleasures are like poppies spread,
60   You seize the flower, its bloom is shed;
Or like the snow falls in the river,
A moment white—then melts for ever;
Or like the borealis race,°
That flit ere you can point their place;
Or like the rainbow's lovely form
Evanishing amid the storm—
Nae man can tether time or tide;
The hour approaches Tam maun° ride;
That hour, o' night's black arch the key-stane,

Kirkton Jean who with her sister kept an alehouse
Doon a river that flows by Alloway Kirk (i.e. church)
mirk murk, dark
gars me greet makes me weep
ingle fireplace
bleezing blazing

reamin swats foaming new ale
Souter Cobbler
ay ever
Care a sudden use of personification, a mocking reference to a more formal mode
borealis race northern lights
maun must

70 That dreary hour, he mounts his beast in;
And sic° a night he taks the road in
As ne'er poor sinner was abroad in.
    The wind blew as 'twad° blawn its last;
The rattling showers rose on the blast;
The speedy gleams the darkness swallowed;
Loud, deep, and lang, the thunder bellowed:
That night, a child might understand,
The Deil° had business on his hand.
    Weel mounted on his grey mare, Meg,
80 A better never lifted leg,
Tam skelpit° on thro' dub° and mire,
Despising wind, and rain, and fire;
Whiles° holding fast his guid blue bonnet;
Whiles crooning o'er some auld Scots sonnet;°
Whiles glowering round wi' prudent cares,
Lest bogles° catch him unawares:
Kirk-Alloway was drawing nigh,
Whare ghaists and houlets° nightly cry.
    By this time he was cross the ford,
90 Where in the snaw the chapman smoored;°
And past the birks° and meikle° stane,
Where drunken Charlie brak's neck-bane;
And thro' the whins,° and by the cairn
Where hunters fand the murdered bairn;
And near the thorn,° aboon° the well,
Where Mungo's mither hanged hersel.
Before him Doon pours all his floods;
The doubling storm roars thro' the woods;
The lightnings flash from pole to pole;
100 Near and more near the thunders roll:
When, glimmering thro' the groaning trees,
Kirk-Alloway seemed in a bleeze;
Thro' ilka bore° the beams were glancing,
And loud resounded mirth and dancing.
    Inspiring bold John Barleycorn!
What dangers thou canst make us scorn!
Wi' tippenny,° we fear nae evil;
Wi' usquebae° we'll face the devil!
The swats sae reamed in Tammie's noddle,
110 Fair play,° he cared na deils a boddle.°

sic such	**birks** birches
'twad if it would have	**meikle** great, huge
Deil Devil	**whins** furze, gorse
skelpit hurried	**thorn** hawthorn tree
dub puddle	**aboon** above
Whiles sometimes	**ilka bore** every chink
sonnet song	**tippenny** twopenny ale
bogles spirits, ghosts, bogies	**usquebae** whisky
houlets owls	**Fair play** in justice to him
smoored smothered	**boddle** halfpenny (actually a fraction of that)

But Maggie stood right sair° astonished,
Till, by the heel and hand admonished,
She ventured forward on the light;
And, vow! Tam saw an unco° sight!
 Warlocks and witches in a dance;
Nae cotillon brent new° frae France,
But hornpipes, jigs, strathspeys,° and reels,
Put life and mettle in their heels.
A winnock-bunker° in the east,
120 There sat auld Nick, in shape o' beast;
A towzie tyke,° black, grim, and large!
To gie them music was his charge:
He screwed the pipes and gart them skirl,°
Till roof and rafters a' did dirl.°
Coffins stood round like open presses,°
That shawed the dead in their last dresses;
And, by some devilish cantraip sleight,°
Each in its cauld hand held a light,
By which heroic Tam was able
130 To note upon the haly table
A murderer's banes in gibbet-airns;°
Twa span-lang,° wee, unchristened bairns;
A thief new-cutted frae a rape,°
Wi' his last gasp his gab° did gape;
Five tomahawks, wi' blude red-rusted;
Five scymitars, wi' murder crusted;
A garter which a babe had strangled;
A knife a father's throat had mangled,
Whom his ain son o' life bereft,
140 The grey hairs yet stack to the heft;
Wi' mair of horrible and awefu',
Which even to name wad be unlawfu'.
 As Tammie glowred,° amazed and curious,
The mirth and fun grew fast and furious:
The piper loud and louder blew,
The dancers quick and quicker flew,
They reeled, they set, they crossed, they cleekit,°
Till ilka carlin° swat and reekit,
And coost her duddies to the wark,°
150 And linket° at it in her sark!°

sair sore	**airns** irons
unco strange, prodigious	**span-lang** as long as the span of a hand
brent new brand new	**rape** rope
strathspeys dances of couples (or their music)	**gab** mouth
winnock-bunker (on a) window-seat	**glowred** stared
towzie tyke shaggy dog	**cleekit** hooked arms
He . . . skirl he squeezed the bagpipes and	**ilka carlin** each witch or hag
made them squeal	**And . . . wark** and threw off her clothes to
dirl rattle	dance better (for the sake of the work)
presses clothes cupboards, wardrobes	**linket** tripped along
cantraip sleight magic trick	**sark** shift

Now Tam, O Tam! had thae been queans,°
A' plump and strapping in their teens;
Their sarks, instead o' creeshie° flannen,
Been snaw-white seventeen hunder° linen!
Thir breeks° o' mine, my only pair,
That ance were plush, o' guid blue hair,
I wad hae gi'en them off my hurdies,°
For ae blink o' the bonie burdies!°
    But withered beldams, auld and droll,
160 Rigwoodie° hags wad spean° a foal,
Louping and flinging on a crummock,°
I wonder did na turn thy stomach!
    But Tam kend what was what fu' brawlie:°
There was ae winsome wench and wawlie°
That night enlisted in the core°
(Lang after kend on Carrick shore;
For mony a beast to dead she shot,
And perished mony a bonie boat,
And shook° baith meikle corn and bear,°
170 And kept the country-side in fear),
Her cutty sark,° o' Paisley harn,°
That while a lassie she had worn,
In longitude tho' sorely scanty,
It was her best, and she was vauntie.°
Ah! little kend thy reverend grannie
That sark she coft° for her wee Nannie
Wi' twa pund Scots° ('twas a' her riches)
Wad ever graced a dance of witches!
    But here my Muse her wing maun cour;°
180 Sic flights are far beyond her power:
To sing how Nannie lap and flang,°
(A souple jad she was, and strang),
And how Tam stood, like ane bewitched,
And thought his very een enriched;
Even Satan glowred, and fidged fu' fain,°
And hotched° and blew wi' might and main:
Till first ae caper, syne° anither,
Tam tint° his reason a' thegither,

queans young girls	**bear** barley
creeshie greasy	**cutty sark** short shift
seventeen hunder finely woven	**Paisley harn** linen made at Paisley (rather than
Thir breeks those breeches	woven at home)
hurdies buttocks	**vauntie** boastful, proud of it
burdies lasses	**coft** bought
Rigwoodie rough, ropy	**pund Scots** The Scots pound was worth one-
spean wean (by causing fright)	twelfth of the English.
Louping . . . crummock leaping and capering	**cour** curb
with a crooked staff	**lap and flang** leapt and flung herself about
brawlie well	**fidged fu' fain** fidgeted very eagerly
wawlie ample	**hotched** wriggled
core corps	**syne** then
shook scattered, destroyed	**tint** lost

And roars out, 'Weel done, Cutty-sark!'
190 And in an instant all was dark,
And scarcely had he Maggie rallied,
When out the hellish legion sallied.
    As bees bizz out wi' angry fyke,°
When plundering herds° assail their byke;°
As open° pussie's° mortal foes,
When, pop! she starts before their nose;
As eager runs the market-crowd,
When 'Catch the thief!' resounds aloud;
So Maggie runs; the witches follow,
200 Wi' mony an eldritch° skriech and hollo.
    Ah, Tam! ah, Tam! thou'll get thy fairin!°
In hell they'll roast thee like a herrin!
In vain thy Kate awaits thy comin!
Kate soon will be a woefu' woman!
Now do thy speedy utmost, Meg,
And win the key-stane o' the brig;°
There at them thou thy tail may toss,
A running stream they dare na cross.
But ere the key-stane she could make,
210 The fient a° tail she had to shake;
For Nannie, far before the rest,
Hard upon noble Maggie prest,
And flew at Tam wi' furious ettle;°
But little wist she Maggie's mettle!
Ae spring brought off her master hale,
But left behind her ain grey tail:
The carlin claught° her by the rump,
And left poor Maggie scarce a stump.
    Now, wha this tale o' truth shall read,
220 Ilk man and mother's son, take heed:
Whene'er to drink you are inclined,
Or cutty-sarks run in your mind,
Think! ye may buy the joys o'er-dear;
Remember Tam o' Shanter's mare.
1790   1791

fyke fret
herds herdsmen
byke hive
open bay (in following a scent)
pussie's the hare's
eldritch ghastly, unearthly

fairin just deserts
brig bridge
The fient a the devil a
ettle purpose
claught clutched

Green Grow the Rashes°

Green grow the rashes, O;
  Green grow the rashes, O;
The sweetest hours that e'er I spend,
  Are spent amang the lasses, O!

There's nought but care on every han',
  In every hour that passes, O;
What signifies the life o' man,
  An' 'twere na for the lasses, O.

The warly° race may riches chase,
10 An' riches still may fly them, O;
An' tho' at last they catch them fast,
  Their hearts can ne'er enjoy them, O.

But gie me a canny° hour at e'en,
  My arms about my dearie, O;
An' warly cares, an' warly men,
  May a' gae tapsalteerie,° O!

For you sae douce,° ye sneer at this,
  Ye're nought but senseless asses, O;
The wisest man° the warl' e'er saw,
20 He dearly loved the lasses, O.

Auld Nature swears, the lovely dears
  Her noblest work she classes, O;
Her prentice han' she tried on man,
  An' then she made the lasses, O.
1784?   1787

Ae Fond Kiss

Ae° fond kiss, and then we sever;
Ae fareweel and then for ever!
Deep in heart-wrung tears I'll pledge thee,
Warring sighs and groans I'll wage thee.
Who shall say that fortune grieves him
While the star of hope she leaves him?
Me, nae cheerfu' twinkle lights me;
Dark despair around benights me.

Green . . . Rashes That is, rushes; the first
stanza is a refrain repeated after every other
stanza. Burns offered the song as "the genuine
language of my heart," as "one who spends
the hours and thoughts which the vocations of
the day can spare with Ossian, Shakespeare,
Thomson, Shenstone, Sterne, etc., or, as the
maggot takes him, a gun, a fiddle, or a song
to make or mend; and at all times some hearts-
dear bonny lass in view." He doubts whether
such a life is "more inimical to the sacred interests of piety and virtue than . . . bustling
and straining after the world's riches and
honours."
warly worldly
canny pleasant
tapsalteerie topsy-turvy
douce sober, prudent
wisest man Solomon
Ae one

I'll ne'er blame my partial fancy,
10   Naething could resist my Nancy:
But to see her was to love her,
Love but her, and love for ever.
Had we never loved sae kindly,
Had we never loved sae blindly,
Never met, or never parted,
We had ne'er been broken-hearted.

Fare thee weel, thou first and fairest!
Fare thee weel, thou best and dearest!
Thine be ilka° joy and treasure,
20   Peace, enjoyment, love, and pleasure!
Ae fond kiss, and then we sever;
Ae fareweel, alas! for ever!
Deep in heart-wrung tears I'll pledge thee,
Warring sighs and groans I'll wage thee.
1791   1792

A Red, Red Rose°

O my luve's like a red, red rose,
   That's newly sprung in June;
O my luve's like the melodie
   That's sweetly played in tune.

As fair art thou, my bonie lass,
   So deep in luve am I;
And I will luve thee still, my dear,
   Till a' the seas gang dry.

Till a' the seas gang dry, my dear,
10   And the rocks melt wi' the sun;
And I will luve thee still, my dear,
   While the sands o' life shall run.

And fare thee weel, my only luve!
   And fare thee weel a while!
And I will come again, my luve,
   Tho' it were ten thousand mile!
                1794

ilka every
A Red, Red Rose James Kinsley suggests that this may be a song Burns simply collected—without even reconstructing. Burns spoke of it as "a simple old Scots song which I had picked up"; and he remarked, "What to me appears the simple and the wild . . . will be looked on as the ludicrous and the absurd" by others. It has, at any rate, been widely regarded in terms like those of Thomas Crawford: "a lyric of genius, made out of the common inherited material of folk-song."

Scots Wha Hae

Robert Bruce's Address to His Army, Before the Battle of Bannockburn°

Scots, wha hae wi' Wallace bled,
Scots, wham Bruce has aften led,
Welcome to your gory bed,
    Or to victorie.

Now's the day, and now's the hour;
See the front o' battle lour;
See approach proud Edward's power—
    Chains and slaverie!

10 Wha will be a traitor knave?
Wha can fill a coward's grave?
Wha sae base as be a slave?
    Let him turn and flee!

Wha for Scotland's king and law
Freedom's sword will strongly draw,
Freeman stand, or freeman fa'?
    Let him follow me!

By oppression's woes and pains!
By your sons in servile chains!
We will drain our dearest veins,
20   But they *shall* be free!

Lay the proud usurpers low!
Tyrants fall in every foe!
Liberty's in every blow!
    Let us do—or die!

1793   1794

For A' That and A' That°

Is there, for honest poverty,
    That° hings his head, and a' that;
The coward-slave, we pass him by,
    We dare be poor for a' that!

Bannockburn Robert the Bruce won independence for Scotland and became its king by defeating the forces of Edward II on June 13–14, 1314. In this imaginary address, he calls to mind the heroic struggle of Sir William Wallace (c. 1272–1306) against Edward I of England. While the Scottish war of independence always stirred Burns's feelings, he is here associating it, as he put it in a letter of 1793, "with the glowing ideas of some other struggles of the same nature, *not quite so ancient*," i.e. the French Revolution.

For A' That and A' That Based on an old tune, this poem was inspired by the French Revolution and perhaps influenced by Thomas Paine's *The Rights of Man* (1791–92), e.g. "The artificial noble shrinks into a dwarf before the noble of nature."

That one that

    For a' that, and a' that,
      Our toils obscure, and a' that,
    The rank is but the guinea's stamp,
      The man's the gowd° for a' that.

What though on hamely fare we dine,
10   Wear hoddin-grey,° and a' that;
Gie fools their silks, and knaves their wine,
    A man's a man for a' that.
    For a' that, and a' that,
      Their tinsel show, and a' that;
    The honest man,° tho' e'er sae poor,
      Is king o' men for a' that.

Ye see yon birkie,° ca'd a lord,
    Wha struts, and stares, and a' that;
Tho' hundreds worship at his word,
20   He's but a coof° for a' that.
    For a' that, and a' that,
      His ribband, star,° and a' that,
    The man of independent mind,
      He looks and laughs at a' that.

A prince can mak a belted° knight,
    A marquis, duke, and a' that;
But an honest man's aboon° his might,
    Guid faith, he mauna fa'° that!
    For a' that, and a' that,
30   Their dignities, and a' that,
    The pith o' sense, and pride o' worth,
      Are higher rank than a' that.

Then let us pray that come it may,·
    As come it will for a' that,
That sense and worth, o'er a' the earth,
    Shall bear the gree,° and a' that.
    For a' that and a' that,
      It's coming yet, for a' that,
    That man to man, the warld o'er,
40   Shall brothers be for a' that.
    1794   1795

---

gowd gold; cf. William Wycherley, *The Plain Dealer* (1677) I.i: "I weigh the man, not his title; 'tis not the King's stamp can make the metal better or heavier"
hoddin-grey natural, undyed wool
honest man alluding to the 17-century celebration of the *honnête homme,* comparable to the Augustan celebration of "goodness" as opposed to "greatness" (cf. Henry Fielding, *Jonathan Wild,* excerpt above, and Pope, *Essay on Man*

IV.248, "An honest man's the noblest work of God")
birkie fellow
coof blockhead
belted distinguished, decorated
aboon above
mauna fa' must not claim
gree prize, first place

SENSE AND SENSIBILITY

In both the literature and painting of the later eighteenth century there is a marked strain of the sentimental. This was not so much a cozy celebration of middle-class delicacy or of working-class nobility, as it came to be later. Instead, it was a vehement, often defiant assertion of the value of man's feelings; in fact, it was often a claim that his feelings were his essential strength and the source of his great imaginative powers. The vehemence of the assertion made for theatricality in the display of emotion; it was exhibited in its extremes and at times with a self-congratulatory sense of the nobility it betokened. At the same time, there was a skeptical counter-current of thought that saw these emotions not so much as the highest reaches of the spirit but as the mechanical expression of physical states. In one view man's emotion revealed him as saintly; in the other as a puppet of blind impulses (like the hero that Dryden showed under the power of Timotheus' music in *Alexander's Feast*).

The sensitivity that revealed an honest and generous heart by its free responsiveness came to be considered a gift of sensibility. To those who saw it only as self-indulgence or as merely a low threshold of irritability, and who prized man's common sense and objectivity of response, sensibility (or its kindred excess, sentimentality) became an object of scornful laughter. At a deeper level one can see a division between those who trust the natural goodness of man's feelings and those who stress his fallibility and self-deception. Of those who stand for trust in man's feelings Rousseau is perhaps the key figure; at once notorious and sanctified, loathed and worshiped, his influence became a European phenomenon. If any one man can be said to have invented Romanticism (or even modern childhood) by creating the imaginative forms and the vision of the self which it required, it was he; and in Boswell we can see one of the earliest instances of his influence.

"My nerves are not tremblingly alive, and my literary temper is so happily framed that I am less sensible of pain than of pleasure." Gibbon's sentence sets him apart from Rousseau and from many of his English contemporaries. A German traveler of the 1780's tells us that when he came to England "what is called *sentimental* was the hobby-horse of many moral writers and of such persons as pretended to have finer feelings, and tenderer moral nerves, than others, though"—he adds dryly—"they contradicted it frequently by their actions." By the time he wrote, a certain contempt had arisen for "everything which appears to come under the denomination of sentimental." A satirical Sensibility Academy, somewhat earlier, offered to turn out "such a tribe of snivellers, whimperers, sobbers, and blubberers at funerals, charity sermons, hanging bouts, and tragedies as shall raise a very sentimental uproar through his majesty's three kingdoms." As Vicesimus Knox put it (1779), the "sentimental manner has given an amiable name to vice and has obliquely excused the extravagance of the passions by representing them as the effect of lovely sensibility. . . ." One may cite the instance of James Boswell, who wrote with pride in Turin (1765): "Never was mind so formed as that of him who now recordeth his own transactions. I was now in a fever of love for an abandoned being whom multitudes had often treated like a a very woman of the town." But when his advances were curtly refused by the "abandoned being," Boswell "saw that amongst profligate wretches a man of sentiment could only expose himself."

More interesting is that sense of uniqueness we see in Boswell, or in Rousseau at the opening of *Confessions;* each sees himself as mysterious and inexhaustible, and with reason. In contrast, there is Gibbon's account of awakening to erotic awareness: "a very interesting moment of our lives . . . it less properly belongs to the memoirs of an individual than to the natural history of the species." Or, describing his parents' attachment: "Such is the beginning of a love tale at Babylon or at Putney." In a related way, it is significant that Rousseau (whose most satisfying intimacy was to be treated as an only child) keeps his earliest sentiments "tremblingly alive," rejoicing in recovering them in all their immediacy and freshness after decades. Gibbon, on the other hand, rejoices no less in "autumnal felicity" and disengaged retrospection; and he mocks the nostalgia of Gray's ode on Eton College:

> My name, it is most true, could never be enrolled among the sprightly race, the idle progeny of Eton or Westminster, who delight to cleave the water with pliant arm, to urge the flying ball, and to chase the speed of the rolling circle. But I would ask the most active hero of the play field whether he can seriously compare his childish with his manly enjoyments; whether he does not feel as the most precious attribute of his existence, the vigorous maturity of sensual and spiritual powers which Nature has reserved for the age of puberty. A state of happiness arising only from the want of foresight and reflection shall never provoke my envy; such degenerate taste would tend to sink us in the scale of beings from a man to a child, a dog, and an oyster; till we had reached the confines of brute matter, which cannot suffer because it cannot feel. . . . Freedom is the first wish of our heart; freedom is the first blessing of our nature; and unless we bind ourselves with the voluntary chains of interest or passion, we advance in freedom as we advance in years.

One of the questions that vexes Boswell and Rousseau is the need to feel to the utmost the sentiment of being, to be assured that one has a soul. We can see the same problem in Sterne's account of his heroes, as they prove their authentic existence in self-forgetful spontaneity. Yet they are never quite self-forgetful, or at least they cannot be for longer than it takes to attend to and prize that moment. Sterne is full of an ironic awareness of the excesses of sentiment even as he prizes it; and, like Boswell, he tends both to feel deeply and to study himself while feeling, always aware of the conflict and exploiting its incongruity.

EDWARD GIBBON
1737–1794

From Memoirs of My Own Life [1]
[Aunt Hester and William Law]

Of my two wealthy aunts on the father's side, Hester persevered in a life of celibacy, while Catherine became the wife of Mr. Edward Elliston, a captain

---

1. Gibbon's memoirs consist of six overlapping and partial drafts written between 1788 and 1793; they were left to his literary executor Lord Sheffield, who edited a connected version for publication in 1796. It was only a hundred years later that the original manuscripts were edited and published by John Murray. While Lord Sheffield's version has gained currency through frequent reprintings, it is marked by serious deletions as well as ingenious conflation. Any single text of the memoirs must be an eclectic one, and the following excerpts are drawn as indicated from the various manuscripts in Murray's edition.

in the service of the East India Company. . . . These two ladies are described by Mr. Law under the names of Flavia and Miranda, the pagan and Christian sister.[2] The sins of Flavia, which excluded her from the hope of salvation, may not appear to our carnal apprehension of so black a dye. Her temper was gay and lively; she followed the fashion in her dress and indulged her taste for company and public amusements. But her expense was regulated by economy; she practised the decencies of religion; nor is she accused of neglecting the essential duties of a wife or a mother.

The sanctity of her sister, the original or the copy of Miranda, was indeed of a higher cast. By austere penance Mrs. Hester Gibbon laboured to atone for the faults of her youth, for the profane vanities into which she had been led or driven by authority or example.[3] But no sooner was she mistress of her own actions and plentiful fortune than the pious virgin abandoned forever the house of a brother from whom she was alienated by the interest of this world and of the next. With her spiritual guide, and a widow lady of the name of Hutchinson, she retired to a small habitation at Cliffe, in Northamptonshire, where she lived almost half a century, surviving many years the loss of her two friends.

It is not my design to enumerate or extenuate the Christian virtues of Miranda as they were described by Mr. Law. Her charity, even in its excess, commands our respect. 'Her fortune,' says the historian, 'is divided between herself and several *other* poor people, and she has only her part of relief from it.' The sick and lame, young children and aged persons, were the first object of her benevolence. But she seldom refused to give alms to a common beggar, 'and instead'—I resume Mr. Law's words—'of driving him away as a cheat because she does not know him, she relieves him because he *is* a stranger and unknown to her. Excepting her victuals, she never spent ten pounds a year upon herself. If you was to see her, you would wonder what poor body it was that was so surprisingly neat and clean. She eats and drinks only for the sake of living, and with so regular an abstinence that every meal is an exercise of self-denial, and she humbles her body every time she is forced to feed it.'

Her only study was the Bible, with some legends and books of piety which she read with implicit faith; she prayed five times each day; and as singing, according to the *Serious Call*, is an indispensable part of devotion, she rehearsed

2. William Law (1686–1761) took a degree at Cambridge and became a fellow of Emmanuel College; but he refused, on the accession of George I, to take an oath of allegiance to the new monarch and abjuring all support of the Stuart Pretender. As a Nonjuror he resigned his fellowship and turned to controversial writing. In 1723 he joined the Gibbon household as a tutor to Gibbon's undistinguished father and became a "spiritual director of the whole family." Law's greatest work was *A Serious Call to a Devout and Holy Life* (1729); it had a strong influence upon Samuel Johnson and John Wesley. Later Law turned to the mystical writings of Jacob Boehme and formed a religious household with two ladies, one of them Hester Gibbon. In the *Serious Call* Law presented the exemplary cases of Flavia and Miranda, based upon the Gibbon sisters. Of Flavia he wrote that "the poor, vain turn of mind, the irreligion, the folly, and vanity . . . is all owing to the manner of using her estate."

3. "While she was under her mother, she was forced to be genteel, to live in ceremony . . . to be in every polite conversation, to hear profaneness at the playhouse and wanton songs and love intrigues at the opera, to dance at public places that fops and rakes might admire the fineness of her shape and the beauty of her motions." (Law, *Serious Call* VII)

the psalms and hymns of thanksgiving which she now, perhaps, may chant in a full chorus of saints and angels. Such is the portrait and such was the life of that holy virgin who by gods was Miranda called, and by men Mrs. Hester Gibbon. Of the pains and pleasures of a spiritual life *I* am ill-qualified to speak, yet I am inclined to believe that her lot, even on earth, has not been unhappy. Her penance was voluntary and, in her own eyes, meritorious; her time was filled by regular occupations; and instead of the insignificance of an old maid, she was surrounded by dependents, poor and abject as they were, who implored her bounty and imbibed her lessons. . . .

At an advanced age, about the year 1761, Mr. Law died in the house, I may not say in the arms, of his beloved Miranda. In our family he has left the reputation of a worthy and pious man, who believed all that he professed, and practised all that he enjoined. The character of a Nonjuror, which he maintained to the last, is a sufficient evidence of his principles in church and state; and the sacrifice of interest to conscience will be always respectable.

His theological writings, which our domestic connection has tempted me to peruse, preserve an imperfect sort of life, and I can pronounce with more confidence and knowledge on the merits of the author. His last compositions are darkly tinctured by the incomprehensible visions of Jacob Behmen,[4] and his discourse on the absolute unlawfulness of stage entertainments [5] is sometimes quoted for a ridiculous intemperance of sentiment and language: 'The actors and spectators must all be damned; the playhouse is the porch of Hell, the place of the Devil's abode, where he holds his filthy court of evil spirits; a play is the Devil's triumph, a sacrifice performed to his glory, as much as in the heathen temples of Bacchus or Venus, etc. etc.'

But these sallies of religious frenzy must not extinguish the praise which is due to Mr. William Law as a wit and a scholar. His argument on topics of less absurdity is specious [6] and acute, his manner is lively, his style forcible and clear; and had not his vigorous mind been clouded by enthusiasm, he might be ranked with the most agreeable and ingenious writers of the times. While the Bangorian controversy [7] was a fashionable theme, he entered the lists on the subject of Christ's Kingdom and the authority of the priesthood. Against the plain account of the sacrament of the Lord's Supper he resumed the combat with Bishop Hoadley, the object of Whig idolatry and Tory abhorrence; and at every weapon of attack and defence the Nonjuror, on the ground which is common to both, approves [8] himself at least equal to the prelate. On the ap-

---

4. Or Jacob Boehme (1575–1624), the German mystic who wrote under the influence of Paracelsus, and whose work was translated into English (by Law among others) and had considerable influence from the late 17th century on.

5. Written in 1726 (Gibbon quotes imprecisely, probably from memory).

6. Plausible.

7. Benjamin Hoadley (1676–1761), Bishop of Bangor, in reply to those who wished to involve the church in political factions, preached before George I in 1717 the doctrine that the church was not of this world and that Christ had not delegated his authority to any representatives. This was severely attacked in the Convocation of the clergy, which the king then dismissed. Later, in 1735, Hoadley aroused new controversy by his interpretation of the sacrament of communion, in a work much praised by Henry Fielding's Parson Adams (in *Joseph Andrews*, 1742).

8. Proves.

pearance of the *Fable of the Bees*,[9] he drew his pen against the licentious doctrine that private vices are public benefits; and morality as well as religion must join in his applause.

Mr. Law's masterwork, the *Serious Call*, is still read as a popular and powerful book of devotion. His precepts are rigid, but they are founded on the Gospel; his satire is sharp, but it is drawn from the knowledge of human life; and many of his portraits are not unworthy of the pen of La Bruyère.[10] If he finds a spark of piety in his reader's mind, he will soon kindle it to a flame, and a philosopher must allow that he exposes, with equal severity and truth, the strange contradiction between the faith and practice of the Christian world. Hell-fire and eternal damnation are darted from every page of the book, and it is indeed somewhat whimsical that the fanatics who most vehemently inculcate the love of God should be those who despoil him of every amiable attribute. [From *Memoir F*]

[His Conversion to Roman Catholicism]

It might at least be expected that an ecclesiastical school [11] should inculate the orthodox principles of religion. But our venerable mother had contrived to unite the opposite extremes of bigotry and indifference. An heretic or unbeliever was a monster in her eyes; but she was always, or often, or sometimes remiss in the spiritual education of her own children. . . . Without a single lecture, either public or private, either Christian or Protestant, without any academical subscription, without any episcopal confirmation, I was left by the dim light of my catechism to grope my way to the chapel and communion table, where I was admitted without a question how far, or by what means, I might be qualified to receive the sacrament.

Such almost incredible neglect was productive of the worst mischiefs. From my childhood I had been fond of religious disputation. My poor aunt had been often puzzled by the mysteries which she strove to believe, nor had the elastic spring been totally broken by the weight of the atmosphere of Oxford. The blind activity of idleness urged me to advance without armour into the dangerous mazes of controversy, and at the age of sixteen I bewildered myself in the errors of the Church of Rome.

The progress of my conversion may tend to illustrate at least the history of my own mind. It was not long since Dr. Middleton's [12] free inquiry had sounded an alarm in the theological world. Much ink and much gall had been spilled in the defence of the primitive miracles, and the two dullest of their champions were crowned with academic honours by the University of Oxford. The name of Middleton was unpopular, and his proscription very naturally led me to peruse his writings and those of his antagonists. His bold criticism,

9. When Mandeville published an expanded version of his work (see above, The Urban Scene) in 1723, Law wrote one of the ablest of the many attacks.

10. Jean de La Bruyère (1645–96), French translator and imitator of Theophrastus' *Characters*, an acute and witty moralist.

11. Gibbon was enrolled in Magdalen College at Oxford: "To the University of Oxford I acknowledge no obligation, and she will as cheerfully renounce me for a son as I am willing to disclaim her for a mother."

12. Conyers Middleton (1683–1750) in his *Free Enquiry* (1749) attacked the evidence for widespread miracles in the primitive church after the days of the Apostles.

which approaches the precipice of infidelity, produced on my mind a singular effect, and had I persevered in the communion of Rome, I should now apply to my own fortune the prediction of the Sibyl:

. . . via prima salutis
Quod minimum reris, Graia pandetur ab urbe[13]

The elegance of style and freedom of argument were repelled by a shield of prejudice. I still revered the character, or rather the names, of the saints and fathers whom Dr. Middleton exposes, nor could he destroy my implicit belief that the gift of miraculous powers was continued in the Church during the first four or five centuries of Christianity. But I was unable to resist the weight of historical evidence that within the same period most of the leading doctrines of popery were already introduced in theory and practice. Nor was my conclusion absurd that miracles are the test of truth, and that the church must be orthodox and pure which was so often approved by the visible interposition of the Deity. The marvelous tales which are so boldly attested by the Basils and Chrysostoms, the Augustines and Jeromes,[14] compelled me to embrace the superior merits of celibacy, the institution of the monastic life, the use of the sign of the cross, of holy oil, and even of images, the invocation of saints, the worship of relics, the rudiments of purgatory in prayers for the dead, and the tremendous mystery of the sacrifice of the body and blood of Christ, which insensibly swelled into the prodigy of Transubstantiation.[15]

In these dispositions, and already more than half a convert, I formed an unlucky intimacy with a young gentleman of our college whose name I shall spare. With a character less resolute, Mr.   had imbibed the same religious opinions, and some popish books, I know not through what channel, were conveyed into his possession. I read; I applauded; I believed. The English translations of two famous works of Bossuet, Bishop of Meaux, the *Exposition of the Catholic Doctrine* and the *History of the Protestant Variations*, achieved my conversion, and I surely fell by a noble hand. . . .

No sooner had I settled my new religion than I resolved to profess myself a Catholic. Youth is sincere and impetuous, and a momentary glow of enthusiasm had raised me above all temporal considerations. . . . My father was neither a bigot nor a philosopher, but his affection deplored the loss of an only son, and his good sense was astonished at my strange departure from the religion of my country. In the first sally of passion he divulged a secret which prudence might have suppressed, and the gates of Magdalen College were forever shut against my return. Many years afterward, when the name of

13. *Aeneid* VI.96–97: "The dawnings of thy safety shall be shown, / From whence thou least shall hope, a Grecian town" (Dryden trans., VI.145–46).
14. The Church Fathers whose testimony Middleton reviewed.
15. That is, the supreme wonder of Christ's body and blood being present in the bread and wine of the Eucharist. Later, as Gibbon tells us, he felt "solitary transport at the discovery of a philosophical argument against the doctrine of transubstantiation: that the text of Scripture which seems to inculcate the real presence is attested only by a single sense, our sight; while the real presence itself is disproved by three of our senses, the sight, the touch, and the taste. The various articles of the Romish creed disappeared like a dream, and, after a full conviction, on Christmas Day 1754, I received the sacrament in the Church of Lausanne."

Gibbon was become as notorious as that of Middleton, it was industriously whispered at Oxford that the historian had formerly 'turned papist.' My character stood exposed to the reproach of inconstancy, and this invidious topic would have been handled without mercy by my opponents could they have separated my cause from that of the university. For my own part, I am proud of an honest sacrifice of interest to conscience. I can never blush if my tender mind was entangled in the sophistry that seduced the acute and manly understandings of Chillingworth and Bayle, who afterward emerged from superstition to scepticism.[16] [From *Memoir B*]

[Gibbon in Love]

I hesitate, from the apprehension of ridicule, when I approach the delicate subject of my early love. By this word I do not mean the polite attention of the gallantry, without hope or design, which has originated from the spirit of chivalry and is interwoven with the texture of French manners. I do not confine myself to the grosser appetite which our pride may affect to disdain because it has been implanted by nature in the whole animal creation: *amor omnibus idem.*[17] The discovery of a sixth sense, the first consciousness of manhood, is a very interesting moment of our lives, but it less properly belongs to the memoirs of an individual than to the natural history of the species. I understand by this passion the union of desire, friendship, and tenderness which is inflamed by a single female, which prefers her to the rest of her sex, and which seeks her possession as the supreme or the sole happiness of our being. I need not blush at recollecting the object of my choice, and though my love was disappointed of success, I am rather proud that I was once capable of feeling such a pure and exalted sentiment.

The personal attractions of Mademoiselle Susanne Curchod were embellished by the virtues and talents of the mind. Her fortune was humble, but her family was respectable. Her mother, a native of France, had preferred her religion to her country. The profession of her father did not extinguish the moderation and philosophy of his temper, and he lived content with a small salary and laborious duty in the obscure lot of minister of Crassy, in the mountains that separate the Pays de Vaud from the county of Burgundy. In the solitude of a sequestered village he bestowed a liberal, and even learned, education on his only daughter. She surpassed his hopes by her proficiency in the sciences and languages, and in her short visits to some relations at Lausanne, the wit, the beauty, and erudition of Mademoiselle Curchod were the theme of universal applause.

The report of such a prodigy awakened my curiosity; I saw and loved. I found her learned without pedantry, lively in conversation, pure in sentiment, and elegant in manners; and the first sudden emotion was fortified by the habits and knowledge of a more familiar acquaintance. She permitted me to make her two or three visits at her father's house. I passed some happy days

16. William Chillingworth (1602–44) was converted to Catholicism in 1630 but later became an Anglican priest. His *The Religion of Protestants* (1638) is one of the great theological works of the age: a defense of the sole authority of the Bible and of the freedom of each individual to interpret it. Pierre Bayle (1647–1706) was a French philosopher and author of a famous biographical dictionary. Gibbon quotes Bayle: "I am most truly a protestant; for I protest indifferently against all systems and all sects."
17. "Love is the same for all" (Virgil, *Georgics* III.124).

in the mountains of Burgundy, and her parents honourably encouraged a connection which might raise their daughter above want and dependence. In a calm retirement the gay vanity of youth no longer fluttered in her bosom: she listened to the voice of truth and passion, and I might presume to hope that I had made some impression on a virtuous heart.

At Crassy and Lausanne I indulged my dream of felicity; but on my return to England, I soon discovered that my father would not hear of this strange alliance, and that without his consent I was myself destitute and helpless. After a painful struggle I yielded to my fate; the remedies of absence and time were at length effectual; and my love subsided in friendship and esteem.[18] [From *Memoir B*]

[His Italian Tour]
I shall advance with rapid brevity in the narrative of my Italian tour, in which somewhat more than a year (April 1764–May 1765) was agreeably employed. Content with tracing my line of march, and slightly touching on my personal feelings, I shall waive the minute investigation of the scenes which have been viewed by thousands, and described by hundreds, of our modern travelers. ROME is the great object of our pilgrimage; and i, the journey; ii, the residence, and iii, the return, will form the most proper and perspicuous division.

i I climbed Mont Cenis, and descended into the plain of Piedmont, not on the back of an elephant, but on a light osier seat in the hands of the dextrous and intrepid chairmen of the Alps. The architecture and government of Turin presented the same aspect of tame and tiresome uniformity, but the court was regulated with decent and splendid economy; and I was introduced to his Sardinian majesty Charles Emmanuel, who, after the incomparable Frederick, held the second rank (*proximus longo tamen intervallo*) among the kings of Europe.[19] The size and populousness of Milan could not surprise an inhabitant of London; the Dome [20] or cathedral is an unfinished monument of Gothic superstition and wealth. But the fancy is amused by a visit to the Boromean Islands, an enchanted palace, a work of the fairies in the midst of a lake encompassed with mountains, and far removed from the haunts of men.

I was less amused by the marble palaces of Genoa than by the recent memorials of her deliverance (in December 1746) from the Austrian tyranny, and I took a military survey of every scene of action within the enclosure of her double walls. My steps were detained at Parma and Modena by the precious relics of the Farnese and Este collections, but, alas! the far greater part had been already transported, by inheritance or purchase, to Naples and Dresden. By the road of Bologna and the Apennine I at last reached Florence, where I reposed from June to September, during the heat of the summer months. In the gallery, and especially in the Tribune, I first acknowledged, at the feet of the Venus of Medicis, that the chisel may dispute the pre-eminence

18. *Memoir C* contains the memorable passage: "I sighed as a lover: I obeyed as a son: my wound was insensibly healed by time, absence, and the habits of a new life; and my cure was accelerated by a faithful report of the tranquillity and cheerfulness of the lady herself."
19. "Next, however, by a long interval" (Virgil, *Aeneid* V.320) after Frederick the Great of Prussia.
20. That is, *duomo* (cathedral).

with the pencil,[21] a truth in the fine arts which cannot on this side of the Alps be felt or understood. At home I had taken some lessons of Italian; on the spot I read with a learned native the classics of the Tuscan idiom. But the shortness of my time, and the use of the French language, prevented my acquiring any facility of speaking, and I was a silent spectator in the conversations of our envoy, Sir Horace Mann, whose most serious business was that of entertaining the English at his hospitable table. After leaving Florence I compared the solitude of Pisa with the industry of Lucca and Leghorn, and continued my journey through Siena to Rome, where I arrived in the beginning of October.

ii My temper is not very susceptible of enthusiasm, and the enthusiasm which I do not feel I have ever scorned to affect. But at the distance of twenty-five years I can neither forget nor express the strong emotions which agitated my mind as I first approached and entered the *Eternal City*. After a sleepless night I trod with a lofty step the ruins of the Forum; each memorable spot where Romulus stood, or Tully spoke, or Caesar fell, was at once present to my eye, and several days of intoxication were lost or enjoyed before I could descend to a cool and minute investigation. . . .

Six weeks were borrowed for my tour of Naples, the most populous of cities relative to its size, whose luxurious inhabitants seem to dwell on the confines of paradise and hell-fire.[22] I was presented to the boy king[23] by our new envoy, Sir William Hamilton, who, wisely diverting his correspondence from the Secretary of State to the Royal Society and British Museum, has elucidated a country of such inestimable value to the naturalist and antiquarian. On my return I fondly embraced, for the last time, the miracles of Rome, but I departed without kissing the foot of Rezzonico (Clement XIII), who neither possessed the wit of his predecessor Lambertini, nor the virtues of his successor Ganganelli.

iii In my pilgrimage from Rome to Loreto I again crossed the Apennine. From the coast of the Adriatic I traversed a fruitful and populous country, which would alone disprove the paradox of Montesquieu that modern Italy is a desert. Without adopting the exclusive prejudice of the natives, I sincerely admire the paintings of the Bologna school. I hastened to escape the sad solitude of Ferrara, which in the age of Caesar was still more desolate. The spectacle of Venice afforded some hours of astonishment and some days of disgust; the university of Padua is a dying taper; but Verona still boasts her amphitheater; and his native Vicenza is adorned by the classic architecture of Palladio. The road of Lombardy and Piedmont (did Montesquieu find them without inhabitants?) led me back to Milan, Turin, and the passage of Mont Cenis, where I again crossed the Alps in my way to Lyons.

[The Ideal Traveler]

He should be endowed with an active, indefatigable vigour of mind and body, which can seize every mode of conveyance, and support with a careless smile every hardship of the road, the weather, or the inn. I must stimulate him

21. The Venus de Medici in the Tribune of the Uffizi Gallery; the "pencil" is the paintbrush.
22. Referring to the climate and the proximity of the volcano Vesuvius.
23. Ferdinand IV (1751–1825).

with a restless curiosity, impatient of ease, covetous of time, and fearless of danger, which drives him forth at any hour of the day or night to brave the flood, to climb the mountain, or to fathom the mine on the most doubtful promise of entertainment or instruction. The arts of common life are not studied in the closet. With a copious stock of classical and historical learning, my traveler must blend the practical knowledge of husbandry and manufactures. He should be a chemist, a botanist, and a master of mechanics. A musical ear will multiply the pleasures of his Italian tour; but a correct and exquisite eye, which commands the landscape of a country, discerns the merit of a picture, and measures the proportions of a building, is more closely connected with the finer feelings of the mind; and the fleeting image should be fixed and realized by the dexterity of the pencil.

I have reserved for the last a virtue which borders on a vice—the flexible temper which can assimilate itself to every tone of society from the court to the cottage, the happy flow of spirits which can amuse and be amused in every company and situation. With the advantage of an independent fortune and the ready use of national and provincial idioms, the traveler should unite the pleasing aspect and decent familiarity which makes every stranger an acquaintance, and the art of conversing with ignorance and dullness on some topic of local and professional information. The benefits of foreign travel will correspond with the degrees of these qualifications. But in this sketch of ideal perfection, those to whom I am known will not accuse me of framing my own panegyric.

Yet the historian of the decline and fall must not regret his time or expense, since it was the view of Italy and Rome which determined the choice of the subject. It was at Rome, on the 15th of October 1764, as I sat musing amid the ruins of the Capitol, while the barefooted friars were singing vespers in the temple of Jupiter, that the idea of writing the decline and fall of the city first started to my mind.[24] But my original plan was circumscribed to the decay of the city rather than of the empire, and though my reading and reflections began to point toward that object, some years elapsed, and several avocations intervened, before I was seriously engaged in the execution of that laborious work. [From *Memoir C*]

[A Retrospective View]

When I contemplate the common lot of mortality, I must acknowledge that I have drawn a high prize in the lottery of life. The far greater part of the globe is overspread with barbarism or slavery; in the civilized world the most numerous class is condemned to ignorance and poverty; and the double fortune of my birth in a free and enlightened country, in an honourable and wealthy family, is the lucky chance of a unit against millions. The general probability is about three to one that a newborn infant will not live to complete his fiftieth year. I have now passed that age, and may fairly estimate the present value of my existence in the threefold division of mind, body, and estate.

i The first indispensable requisite of happiness is a clear conscience, unsullied by the reproach or remembrance of an unworthy action.

24. This memorable sentence actually appears in *Memoir E* and is here substituted for its weaker counterpart in *Memoir C*.

> Hic murus aheneus esto,
> Nil conscire sibi, nulla pallescere culpa.[25]

I am endowed with a cheerful temper, a moderate sensibility, and a natural disposition to repose rather than to action; some mischievous appetites and habits have perhaps been corrected by philosophy or time. The love of study, a passion which derives fresh vigour from enjoyment, supplies each day, each hour, with a perpetual source of independent and rational pleasure, and I am not sensible of any decay of the mental faculties. The original soil has been highly improved by labour and manure,[26] but it may be questioned whether some flowers of fancy, some grateful errors, have not been eradicated with the weeds of prejudice.

ii Since I have escaped from the long perils of my childhood, the serious advice of a physician has seldom been requisite. 'The madness of superfluous health' [27] I have never known; but my tender constitution has been fortified by time; the play of the animal machine still continues to be easy and regular, and the inestimable gift of the sound and peaceful slumbers of infancy may be imputed both to the mind and body. About the age of forty I was first afflicted with the gout, which in the space of fourteen years has made seven or eight different attacks. Their duration, though not their intensity, appears to encrease, and after each fit I rise and walk with less strength and agility than before. But the gout has hitherto been confined to my feet and knees; the pain is never intolerable; I am surrounded by all the comforts that art and attendance can bestow; my sedentary life is amused with books and company; and in each step of my convalescence I pass through a progress of agreeable sensations.

iii I have already described the merits of my society and situation, but these enjoyments would be tasteless and bitter if their possession were not assured by an annual and adequate supply. . . . According to the scale of Switzerland I am a rich man, and I am indeed rich, since my income is superior to my expense, and my expense is equal to my wishes. My friend Lord Sheffield has kindly relieved me from the cares to which my taste and temper are most adverse. The economy of my house is settled without avarice or profusion; at stated periods all my bills are regularly paid, and in the course of my life I have never been reduced to appear, either as plaintiff or defendant, in a court of justice. Shall I add that, since the failure of my first wishes, I have never entertained any serious thoughts of a matrimonial connection?

I am disgusted with the affectation of men of letters who complain that they have renounced a substance for a shadow and that their fame (which sometimes is no insupportable weight) affords a poor compensation for envy, censure, and persecution.[28] My own experience, at least, has taught me a very

---

25. Horace, *Epistles* I.i.60–61: "Let this be a man's brazen wall, to be conscious of no ill, to turn pale with no guilt."
26. Cultivation.
27. Pope, *Essay on Man* III.3.
28. "Mr. d'Alembert relates that, as he was walking in the gardens of Sans Souci with the King of Prussia, Frederick said to him, 'Do you see that old woman, a poor weeder, asleep on that sunny bank? She is probably a more happy being than either of us.' The King and the philosopher may speak for themselves; for my part I do not envy the old woman." (Gibbon)

different lesson. Twenty happy years have been animated by the labour of my *History*, and its success has given me a name, a rank, a character in the world, to which I should not otherwise have been entitled. The freedom of my writings has indeed provoked an implacable tribe; but as I was safe from the stings, I was soon accustomed to the buzzing of the hornets. My nerves are not tremblingly alive, and my literary temper is so happily framed that I am less sensible of pain than of pleasure.

The rational pride of an author may be offended rather than flattered by vague indiscriminate praise, but he cannot, he should not, be indifferent to the fair testimonies of private and public esteem. Even his social sympathy may be gratified by the idea that now, in the present hour, he is imparting some degree of amusement or knowledge to his friends in a distant land, that one day his mind will be familiar to the grandchildren of those who are yet unborn.[29] I cannot boast of the friendship or favour of princes. The patronage of English literature has long since been devolved on our booksellers, and the measure of their liberality is the least ambiguous test of our common success. Perhaps the golden mediocrity [30] of my fortune has contributed to fortify my application. Few books of merit and importance have been composed either in a garret or a palace. A gentleman possessed of leisure and competency may be encouraged by the assurance of an honourable reward; but wretched is the writer, and wretched will be the work, where daily diligence is stimulated by daily hunger.

The present is a fleeting moment; the past is no more; and our prospect of futurity is dark and doubtful. This day may *possibly* be my last, but the laws of probability, so true in general, so fallacious in particular, still allow me about fifteen years, and I shall soon enter into the period which, as the most agreeable of his long life, was selected by the judgment and experience of the sage Fontenelle. His choice is approved by the eloquent historian of nature, who fixes our moral happiness to the mature season in which our passions are supposed to be calmed, our duties fulfilled, our ambition satisfied, our fame and fortune established on a solid basis.[31]

I am far more inclined to embrace than to dispute this comfortable doctrine. I will not suppose any premature decay of the mind or body, but I must reluctantly observe that two causes, the abbreviation of time and the failure of hope, will always tinge with a browner shade the evening of life.

i The proportion of a part to the whole is the only standard by which we can measure the length of our existence. At the age of twenty, one year is a tenth, perhaps, of the time which has elapsed within our consciousness and memory. At the age of fifty it is no more than the fortieth, and this relative value continues to decrease till the last sands are shaken by the hand of

---

29. "In the first of ancient or modern romances (*Tom Jones* XIII.i) this proud sentiment, this feast of fancy is enjoyed by the genius of Fielding: 'Foretell me that some future maid whose grandmother is yet unborn etc.' But the whole of this beautiful passage deserves to be read" (Gibbon). Fielding had written "tender maid."

30. *Aurea mediocritas* or golden mean (from Horace).

31. The opinion of Bernard de Fontenelle (1657–1757) was recorded by the Comte de Buffon (1707–88): "In private conversation that great and amiable man added the weight of his own experience; and this autumnal felicity might be exemplified in the lives of Voltaire, Hume, and many other men of letters." (Gibbon)

death. This reasoning may seem metaphysical, but on a trial it will be found satisfactory and just.

ii The warm desires, the long expectations of youth, are founded on the ignorance of themselves and of the world. They are gradually damped by time and experience, by disappointment or possession; and after the middle season the crowd must be content to remain at the foot of the mountain, while the few who have climbed the summit aspire to descend or expect to fall. In old age the consolation of hope is reserved for the tenderness of parents, who commence a new life in their children; the faith of enthusiasts, who sing hallelujahs above the clouds; and the vanity of authors, who presume the immortality of their name and writings. [From *Memoir E*]

JEAN JACQUES ROUSSEAU
1712–1778

The *Confessions* were undertaken probably early in 1765. As the title suggests, the book looks back to the work of St. Augustine, but it sets itself in opposition through Rousseau's questioning of the doctrine of original sin and his different conception of the "justice and goodness of the Supreme Being." The *Confessions* were published posthumously, Books I–VI in 1781 and VII–XII in 1788. Rousseau was born in Geneva, the son of a watchmaker; his mother died in childbirth. At sixteen he left home to wander on his own; and he became a Catholic convert (he was to revert to Protestantism in 1754 to gain Genevan citizenship). From 1731 he spent ten years with his patroness, Mme de Warens ("Maman," as he called her), the last of those years at her house Les Charmettes (near Chambéry). In 1742 he reached Paris and entered literary and musical circles. At this time began his lifelong liaison with Thérèse Levasseur, a half-literate servant girl (who bore him five children, Rousseau later confessed, that were placed in the Foundling Hospital). His great works began to appear in the 1750's, particularly the *Discourse on Inequality* (1754), *The Social Contract* (1752), *La Nouvelle Héloïse* (1751), and *Émile* (1752). Persecuted for offensive religious statements, he fled to Switzerland and finally found refuge on the small island of Saint-Pierre. When that refuge was denied him by local ecclesiastical authorities, he accepted David Hume's invitation to stay in England, where he was given a small government pension. But he became deeply suspicious of Hume (as of almost everyone else) and returned to France after eighteen months. His final years—until almost the very end of his life—were darkened by both poverty and paranoid rage.

The English text given here is the work of an anonymous nineteenth-century translator.

From The Confessions

I am commencing an undertaking, hitherto without precedent, and which will never find an imitator. I desire to set before my fellows the likeness of a man in all the truth of nature, and that man myself.

Myself alone! I know the feelings of my heart, and I know men. I am not made like any of those I have seen; I venture to believe that I am not made like any of those who are in existence. If I am not better, at least I am different. Whether Nature has acted rightly or wrongly in destroying the mould in which she cast me, can only be decided after I have been read.

Let the trumpet of the Day of Judgment sound when it will, I will present myself before the Sovereign Judge with this book in my hand. I will say boldly: 'This is what I have done, what I have thought, what I was. I have told the good and the bad with equal frankness. I have neither omitted anything bad, nor interpolated anything good. If I have occasionally made use of some immaterial embellishments, this has only been in order to fill a gap caused by lack of memory. I may have assumed the truth of that which I knew might have been true, never of that which I knew to be false. I have shown myself as I was: mean and contemptible, good, high-minded and sublime, according as I was one or the other. I have unveiled my inmost self, even as Thou hast seen it, O Eternal Being. Gather round me the countless host of my fellow-men; let them hear my confessions, lament for my unworthiness, and blush for my imperfections. Then let each of them in turn reveal, with the same frankness, the secrets of his heart at the foot of the Throne, and say, if he dare, "*I was better than that man!*"'

[His Aunt Suzon]

I was brought into the world in an almost dying condition; little hope was entertained of saving my life. I carried within me the germs of a complaint which the course of time has strengthened, and which at times allows me a respite only to make me suffer more cruelly in another manner. One of my father's sisters, an amiable and virtuous young woman, took such care of me that she saved my life. At this moment, while I am writing, she is still alive, at the age of eighty, nursing a husband younger than herself but exhausted by excessive drinking. Dear aunt, I forgive you for having preserved my life; and I deeply regret that, at the end of your days, I am unable to repay the tender care which you lavished upon me at the beginning of my own.[1] My dear old nurse Jacqueline is also still alive, healthy and robust. The hands which opened my eyes at my birth will be able to close them for me at my death.

I felt before I thought: this is the common lot of humanity. I experienced it more than others. I do not know what I did until I was five or six years old. I do not know how I learned to read; I only remember my earliest reading, and the effect it had upon me; from that time I date my uninterrupted self-consciousness. My mother had left some romances behind her, which my father and I began to read after supper. At first it was only a question of

---

1. Suzanne Rousseau (1682–1775) was married late (1730) to Isaac Henri Gonceru. In 1768 Rousseau settled a small annual pension on her.

practising me in reading by the aid of amusing books; but soon the interest became so lively, that we used to read in turns without stopping, and spent whole nights in this occupation. We were unable to leave off until the volume was finished. Sometimes, my father, hearing the swallows begin to twitter in the early morning, would say, quite ashamed, 'Let us go to bed; I am more of a child than yourself.'

In a short time I acquired, by this dangerous method, not only extreme facility in reading and understanding what I read, but a knowledge of the passions that was unique in a child of my age. I had no idea of things in themselves, although all the feelings of actual life were already known to me. I had conceived nothing, but felt everything. These confused emotions, which I felt one after the other, certainly did not warp the reasoning powers which I did not as yet possess; but they shaped them in me of a peculiar stamp, and gave me odd and romantic notions of human life, of which experience and reflection have never been able wholly to cure me.

. . .

. . . Except during the time I spent in reading or writing in my father's company, or when my nurse took me for a walk, I was always with my aunt, sitting or standing by her side, watching her at her embroidery or listening to her singing; and I was content. Her cheerfulness, her gentleness and her pleasant face have stamped so deep and lively an impression on my mind that I can still see her manner, look, and attitude; I remember her affectionate language: I could describe what clothes she wore and how her head was dressed, not forgetting the two little curls of black hair on her temples, which she wore in accordance with the fashion of the time.

I am convinced that it is to her I owe the taste, or rather passion, for music, which only became fully developed in me a long time afterwards. She knew a prodigious number of tunes and songs which she used to sing in a very thin, gentle voice. This excellent woman's cheerfulness of soul banished dreaminess and melancholy from herself and all around her. The attraction which her singing possessed for me was so great, that not only have several of her songs always remained in my memory, but even now, when I have lost her, and as I grew older, many of them, totally forgotten since the days of my childhood, return to my mind with inexpressible charm. Would anyone believe that I, an old dotard, eaten up by cares and troubles, sometime find myself weeping like a child, when I mumble one of those little airs in a voice already broken and trembling? . . . I ask, where is the affecting charm which my heart finds in this song? it is a whim, which I am quite unable to understand; but, be that as it may, it is absolutely impossible for me to sing it through without being interrupted by my tears . . . but I am almost certain that the pleasure which I feel in recalling the air would partly disappear, if it should be proved that others besides my poor aunt Suzon have sung it.

[Life with Mme de Warens]

It is sometimes said that the sword wears out the scabbard. That is my history. My passions have made me live, and my passions have killed me. What passions? will be asked. Trifles, the most childish things in the world, which, however, excited me as much as if the possession of Helen or the throne of the universe had been at stake. In the first place—women. When I possessed one, my senses were calm; my heart, never. The needs of love devoured me in the midst of enjoyment; I had a tender mother,[2] a dear friend; but I needed a mistress. I imagined one in her place; I represented her to myself in a thousand forms, in order to deceive myself. If I had thought that I held mamma in my arms when I embraced her, these embraces would have been no less lively, but all my desires would have been extinguished; I should have sobbed from affection, but I should never have felt any enjoyment. Enjoyment! Does this ever fall to the lot of man? If I had ever, a single time in my life, tasted all the delights of love in their fulness, I do not believe that my frail existence could have endured it; I should have died on the spot.

Thus I was burning with love, without an object; and it is this state, perhaps, that is most exhausting. I was restless, tormented by the hopeless condition of poor mamma's affairs, and her imprudent conduct, which were bound to ruin her completely at no distant date. My cruel imagination, which always anticipates misfortunes, exhibited this particular one to me continually, in all its extent and in all its results. I already saw myself compelled by want to separate from her to whom I had devoted my life, and without whom I could not enjoy it. Thus my soul was ever in a state of agitation; I was devoured alternately by desires and fears.

Music was with me another passion, less fierce, but no less wasting, from the ardour with which I threw myself into it, from my persistent study of the obscure treatises of Rameau, from my invincible determination to load my rebellious memory with them, from my continual running about, from the enormous heap of compilations which I got together and often spent whole nights in copying. But why dwell upon permanent fancies, while all the follies which passed through my inconstant brain—the transient inclinations of a single day, a journey, a concert, a supper, a walk to take, a novel to read, a comedy to see, everything that was entirely unpremeditated in my pleasure or business, became for me so many violent passions, which, in their ridiculous impetuosity, caused me the most genuine torment? The imaginary sufferings of Cleveland,[3] which I read of with avidity and constant interruption, have, I believe, afflicted me more than my own.

. . .

At this period commences the brief happiness of my life; here approach the peaceful, but rapid moments which have given me the right to say, *I have lived*. Precious and regretted moments! begin again for me your delightful course; and, if it be possible, pass more slowly in succession through my memory than you did in your fugitive reality. What can I do to prolong, as I should like, this touching and simple narrative, to repeat the same things over and over again, without wearying my readers by such repetition, any

2. Louise Elénore de Warens (1700–1762), born at Vevey in Switzerland, was employed by the clergy of Savoy in the conversion of Protestants from Geneva, and she seems also to have engaged in some political espionage; she was Rousseau's protectress from 1729 to 1742.
3. The hero of *The English Philosopher, or The History of Mr. Cleveland* (1732–39; an illegitimate son of Oliver Cromwell) in the novel by the Abbé Prévost (1697–1763), translator of Samuel Richardson and best known for *Manon Lescaut*.

more than I was wearied of them myself, when I recommenced the life again and again? If all this consisted of facts, actions, and words, I could describe, and in a manner, give an idea of them; but how is it possible to describe what was neither said nor done, nor even thought, but enjoyed and felt, without being able to assign any other reason for my happiness than this simple feeling? I got up at sunrise and was happy; I walked, and was happy; I saw mamma, and was happy; I left her, and was happy; I roamed the forests and hills, I wandered in the valleys, I read, I did nothing, I worked in the garden, I picked the fruit, I helped in the work of the house, and happiness followed me everywhere—happiness, which could not be referred to any definite object, but dwelt entirely within myself, and which never left me for a single instant.

Nothing that occurred to me during that delightful period, nothing that I did, said, or thought, during all the time it lasted, has escaped my memory. Preceding and subsequent periods only come back to me at intervals; I recall them unequally and confusedly; but I recall this particular period in its entirety, as if it still existed. My fancy, which, during my youth, always looked ahead, and now always looks back, compensates me by these charming recollections for the hope which I have lost for ever. I no longer see anything in the future to tempt me; only the reminiscences of the past can flatter me, and these reminiscences of the period of which I speak, so vivid and so true, often make my life happy, in spite of my misfortunes.

I will mention one single instance of these recollections, which will enable the reader to judge of their liveliness and accuracy. The first day we set out to pass the night at Les Charmettes, mamma was in a sedan-chair, and I followed on foot. The road was somewhat steep, and, being rather heavy and afraid of tiring her bearers, she got down about half-way, intending to finish the rest of the journey on foot. During the walk, she saw something blue in the hedge, and said to me, 'Look! there is some periwinkle still in flower.' I had never seen any periwinkle, I did not stoop down to examine it, and I am too near-sighted to distinguish plants on the ground, when standing upright. I merely cast a passing glance at it, and nearly thirty years passed before I saw any periwinkle again, or paid any attention to it. In 1764, when I was at Cressier with my friend Du Peyrou, we were climbing a hill, on the top of which he has built a pretty *salon,* which he rightly calls Belle-Vue. I was then beginning to botanise a little. While ascending the hill, and looking amongst the bushes, I exclaimed with a cry of joy, 'Ah! there is some periwinkle!' as in fact it was. Du Peyrou observed my delight, without knowing the cause of it; he will learn it, I hope, one day, when he reads these words. The reader may judge, from the impression which so trifling a circumstance made upon me, of the effect produced by everything which has reference to that period.

. . .

. . . I repeat, true happiness cannot be described; it can only be felt, and felt the more, the less it can be described, since it is not the result of a number of facts, but is a permanent condition. I often repeat myself, but I should do so still more if I said the same thing as often as it occurs to me. When my frequently-changed manner of life had at last adopted a regular course, it was distributed as nearly as possible in the following manner.

I got up every day before sunrise; I climbed through a neighbouring orchard to a very pretty path above the vineyard which ran along the slope as far as Chambéry. During my walk I offered a prayer, which did not consist merely of idle, stammering words, but of a sincere uplifting of the heart to the Creator of this delightful Nature, whose beauties were spread before my eyes. I never like to pray in a room: it has always seemed to me as if the walls and all the petty handiwork of man interposed between myself and God. I love to contemplate Him in His works, while my heart uplifts itself to Him. My prayers were pure, I venture to say, and for that reason deserved to be heard. I only asked for myself and for her, who was inseparably associated with my wishes, an innocent and peaceful life, free from vice, pain, and distressing needs; the death of the righteous, and their lot in the future. For the rest, this act of worship consisted rather of admiration and contemplation than of requests, for I knew that the best means of obtaining the blessings which are necessary for us from the giver of all true blessings, was to deserve, rather than to ask for, them. My walk consisted of a tolerably long round, during which I contemplated with interest and pleasure the rustic scenery by which I was surrounded, the only thing of which heart and eye never tire. From a distance I looked to see if it was day with mamma. When I saw shutters open, I trembled with joy and ran towards the house; if they were shut, I remained in the garden until she awoke, amusing myself by going over what I had learned the evening before, or by gardening. The shutters opened, I went to embrace her while she was still in bed, often still half asleep; and this embrace, as pure as it was tender, derived from its very innocence a charm which is never combined with sensual pleasure.

[The Roman Past]

. . . I had been told to go and see the Pont du Gard,[4] and did not fail to do so. It was the first Roman work that I had seen. I expected to see a monument worthy of the hands which had erected it; for once, and for the only time in my life, the reality surpassed the expectation. Only the Romans could have produced such an effect.

The sight of this simple, yet noble, work produced the greater impression upon me, as it was situated in the midst of a desert, where silence and solitude bring the object into greater prominence, and arouse a livelier feeling of admiration; for this pretended bridge was nothing but an aqueduct. One naturally asks what strength has transported these enormous stones so far from any quarry, and united the arms of so many thousands of men in a spot where not one of them dwells. I went through the three storeys of this superb building, within which a feeling of respect almost prevented me from setting foot. The echo of my footsteps under these immense vaults made me imagine that I heard the sturdy voices of those who had built them. I felt myself lost like an insect in this immensity. I felt, in spite of my sense of littleness, as if my soul was somehow or other elevated, and I said to myself with a sigh, 'Why was I not born a Roman?' I remained there several hours in rapturous contemplation. . . .

4. The great Roman aqueduct near Nîmes in southern France.

[The Island of Saint-Pierre]

I have always been passionately fond of the water, and the sight of it throws me into a delightful state of dreaminess, although often without any definite object. When it was fine weather, I always hastened to the terrace as soon as I was up, to inhale the fresh and healthy morning air, and let my eyes roam over the horizon of this beautiful lake, the shores of which, surrounded by mountains, formed an enchanting prospect. I can think of no worthier homage to the Divinity than the mute admiration which is aroused by the contemplation of his works, and does not find expression in outward acts. I can understand how it is that the inhabitants of cities, who see nothing but walls, streets and crimes, have so little religious belief; but I cannot understand how those who live in the country, especially in solitude, can have none. How is it that their soul is not lifted up in ecstasy a hundred times a day to the Author of the wonders which strike them? As far as I am concerned, it is especially after rising, weakened by a night of sleeplessness, that I am led by long-standing habit to those upliftings of the heart, which do not impose upon me the trouble of thinking. But, for this to take place, my eyes must be smitten by the enchanting spectacle of nature. In my room, my prayers are not so frequent or so fervent; but, at the sight of a beautiful landscape, I feel myself moved without knowing why. I remember reading of a wise bishop, who, during a visit to his diocese, came upon an old woman who, by way of prayer, could say nothing but 'Oh!' 'Good mother,' said the bishop, 'continue to pray in this manner; your prayer is better than ours.' This better prayer is also mine.

After breakfast I hastily wrote a few miserable letters, with a sulky air, longing eagerly for the happy moment when I need write no more. I bustled about my books and papers for a few moments . . . after which I became tired of the task, and spent the three or four remaining hours of the morning in the study of botany. . . .

In the afternoon I abandoned myself entirely to my idle and careless disposition, and followed, without any system, the impulse of the moment. Frequently, when the weather was calm, immediately after dinner, I jumped by myself into a little boat, which the receiver had taught me how to manage with a single oar, and rowed out into the middle of the lake. The moment at which I left the bank, I felt ready to leap for joy. It is impossible for me to explain or understand the reason of this feeling, unless it was a secret self-congratulation on being thus out of the reach of the wicked. I rowed by myself all over the lake, sometimes near the bank, but never landing. Frequently, leaving my boat at the mercy of the wind and water, I abandoned myself to aimless reveries, which, although foolish, were none the less delightful. I sometimes exclaimed with emotion, 'O Nature! O my mother! behold me under thy protection alone! Here there is no cunning or knavish mortal to thrust himself between me and thee.' In this manner I got out half a league from land. I could have wished that this lake had been the ocean. However, in order to please my poor dog, who was not so fond of long excursions on the water as I was, as a rule I followed a definite plan. I landed on the small island, walked about for an hour or two, or stretched myself on the grass at the top of the rising ground, to sate myself with the pleasure of admiring this lake and its surroundings, to examine and anatomise all the plants within my reach, and to build for myself, like a second Robinson,[5] an imaginary dwelling in this little island. I became passionately attached to this hillock. When I was able to take Thérèse, the receiver's wife, and her sisters, for a walk there, how proud I felt to be their pilot and their guide! We solemnly took some rabbits to it, to stock it. Another gala for Jean Jacques! This colony made the little island still more interesting to me. I visited it more frequently and with greater pleasure from that time, to look for signs of the progress of the new inhabitants.

To these amusements I united another, which reminded me of the delightful life at Les Charmettes, and for which the season was particularly suitable. This was the occupations of a country life; and we gathered in the fruit and vegetables, which Thérèse and myself were delighted to share with the receiver and his family. I remember that a Bernese, named M. Kirchberger, when he came to see me, found me perched on the branches of a tall tree, with a bag tied round my waist, so full of apples that I could not move. I was not at all sorry that he and others should find me thus. I hoped that the Bernese, seeing how I employed my leisure time, would no longer think about disturbing its tranquillity, and would leave me in peace in my solitude. I should have preferred to be shut up there by their will than by my own; for, in that case, I should have felt more certain of not seeing my rest disturbed.

I am now again coming to one of those confessions, in regard to which I feel sure beforehand that those readers will be incredulous, who are always determined to judge me by their own standard, although they have been compelled to see, throughout the whole course of my life, a thousand inner emotions which have not the least resemblance to their own. The most extraordinary thing is that, while denying to me all the good or indifferent feelings which they do not themselves possess, they are always ready to attribute to me others so utterly bad that they could not even enter into the heart of a man. They find it perfectly simple to put me into contradiction with nature, and to make me out a monster such as cannot possibly exist. No absurdity appears incredible to them, if only it is calculated to blacken me; nothing that is at all out of the common seems to them possible, if only it is calculated to bring honour upon me.

But, whatever they may believe or say, I will none the less continue faithfully to set forth what Jean Jacques Rousseau was, did, and thought, without either explaining or justifying the singularity of his sentiments and ideas, or inquiring whether others have thought as he. I took such a fancy to the island of Saint-Pierre, and was so comfortable there, that, from continually concentrating all my desires upon this island, I formed the design of never leaving it. The visits which I had to pay in the neighbourhood, the excursions which I should have been obliged to make to Neufchâtel, Bienne, Yverdun, and Nidau, already wearied me in imagination. A day to be spent out of the island seemed to me a curtailment of my happiness; and to go beyond the circumference of the lake was, for me, to leave my element. Besides, my experi-

5. Robinson Crusoe, of Defoe's novel of 1719.

ence of the past had made me timid. It only needed something to make me happy and soothe my heart, to make me expect to lose it; and my ardent desire of ending my days in this island was inseparably united with the fear of being compelled to leave it. I was in the habit of going every evening to sit upon the shore, especially when the lake was rough. I felt a singular pleasure in seeing the waves break at my feet. They represented to me the tumult of the world and the peacefulness of my own abode; and I was sometimes so touched by this delightful idea, that I 'felt the tears trickling down from my eyes. This repose, which I passionately enjoyed, was only troubled by the apprehension of losing it; but this feeling of uneasiness spoilt its charm. I felt my position to be so precarious, that I could not reckon upon its continuance. Ah! said I to myself, how gladly would I exchange the permission to leave the island, for which I do not care at all, for the assurance of being able to remain there always! Instead of being allowed here by sufferance, why am I not kept here by force? Those who only leave me here on sufferance, can drive me away at any moment; can I venture to hope that my persecutors, seeing me happy here, will allow me to continue to be so? It is little enough that I am permitted to live here; I could wish to be condemned, to be forced to remain in this island, so as not to be forced to leave it. . . .

Tormented, buffeted by storms of every kind, worn out by journeys and persecutions for many years past, I strongly felt the need of the repose of which my barbarous enemies, by way of amusing themselves, deprived me. I sighed more than ever for the delightful idleness, for the sweet repose of body and soul, which I had so longed for, to which the supreme happiness of my heart, now cured of its idle dreams of love and friendship, was limited. I only regarded with alarm the task which I was on the point of undertaking, the stormy life to which I proposed to abandon myself; and if the greatness, the beauty, and the usefulness of the object in view inspired my courage, the impossibility of exposing myself to risk with any chance of success completely deprived me of it. Twenty years of profound and solitary meditation would have been less painful to me than six months of an active life in the midst of men and public affairs, with the certainty of failure.

1765–70   1781–88

LAURENCE STERNE
1713–1768

Tristram Shandy and A Sentimental Journey

Tristram Shandy interrupts the comic and rather bawdy account of his Uncle Toby's amours, i.e. his feckless courtship of the Widow Wadman, with this tale, which is derived from his own travels in France (mostly recounted in Book VII). Sterne may have introduced the tale as a counter-thrust to the ill-tempered *Travels Through France and Italy* of Tobias Smollett (1766), and also as a foretaste of his own *Sentimental*

Journey. At any rate, there is a delicate mixture of pathos and humor in both narratives. Tristram cannot resist the unseasonable jest, and he closes with a seemingly unfeeling tribute to the inn; Yorick, Tristram's clergyman friend (and clearly in some measure a self-portrait of Sterne), becomes comparably involved in the business of the handkerchief. In each case Sterne is exquisite in catching the tones of feeling, self-consciously adroit in representing them, and theoretically concerned with the meaning of "sensibility," that sensitivity of response that becomes in his view one of man's highest powers. But he is no less aware of the presence of the physical and commonplace that sensibility, in its very intensity, tends to overlook; and the humor of Sterne fuses the detachment of someone like Gibbon (who can see himself from the outside or from a distance) with the rather humorless, if often exquisitely delicate, sensitivity of Rousseau.

The Life and Opinions of Tristram Shandy, Gentleman

From *Volume IX, Chapter XXIV*

—For my uncle Toby's amours running all the way in my head, they had the same effect upon me as if they had been my own—I was in the most perfect state of bounty and good-will; and felt the kindliest harmony vibrating within me, with every oscillation of the chaise alike; so that whether the roads were rough or smooth, it made no difference; every thing I saw or had to do with, touched upon some secret spring either of sentiment or rapture.

—They were the sweetest notes I ever heard; and I instantly let down the fore-glass to hear them more distinctly—'Tis Maria; said the postillion,[1] observing I was listening——Poor Maria, continued he (leaning his body on one side to let me see her, for he was in a line betwixt us), is sitting upon a bank playing her vespers upon her pipe, with her little goat beside her.

The young fellow uttered this with an accent and a look so perfectly in tune to a feeling heart, that I instantly made a vow, I would give him a four-and-twenty sous piece, when I got to Moulins——

——And who is poor Maria? said I.

The love and pity of all the villages around us; said the postillion—it is but three years ago, that the sun did not shine upon so fair, so quick-witted and amiable a maid; and better fate did Maria deserve than to have her banns forbid, by the intrigues of the curate of the parish who published them—

He was going on, when Maria, who had made a short pause, put the pipe to her mouth, and began the air again—they were the same notes; yet were ten times sweeter: It is the evening service to the Virgin, said the young man— but who has taught her to play it—or how she came by her pipe, no one knows; we think that heaven has assisted her in both; for ever since she has been unsettled in her mind, it seems her only consolation—she has never once had the pipe out of her hand, but plays that service upon it almost night and day.

---

1. The driver of the carriage or post-chaise.

The postillion delivered this with so much discretion and natural eloquence, that I could not help deciphering something in his face above his condition, and should have sifted out his history, had not poor Maria taken such full possession of me.

We had got up by this time almost to the bank where Maria was sitting: she was in a thin white jacket, with her hair, all but two tresses, drawn up into a silk-net, with a few olive leaves twisted a little fantastically on one side—she was beautiful; and if ever I felt the full force of an honest heart-ache, it was the moment I saw her—

—God help her! poor damsel! above a hundred masses, said the postillion, have been said in the several parish churches and convents around, for her,—but without effect; we have still hopes, as she is sensible for short intervals, that the Virgin at last will restore her to herself; but her parents, who know her best, are hopeless upon that score, and think her senses are lost for ever.

As the postillion spoke this, Maria made a cadence so melancholy, so tender and querulous, that I sprung out of the chaise to help her, and found myself sitting betwixt her and her goat before I relapsed from my enthusiasm.

Maria looked wistfully for some time at me, and then at her goat—and then at me—and then at her goat again, and so on, alternately—

—Well, Maria, said I softly—What resemblance do you find?

I do entreat the candid reader to believe me, that it was from the humblest conviction of what a beast man is,—that I asked the question; and that I would not have let fallen an unseasonable pleasantry in the venerable presence of misery, to be entitled to all the wit that ever Rabelais [2] scattered—and yet I own my heart smote me, and that I so smarted at the very idea of it, that I swore I would set up for wisdom, and utter grave sentences the rest of my days—and never—never attempt again to commit mirth with man, woman, or child, the longest day I had to live.

As for writing nonsense to them—I believe, there was a reserve [3]—but that I leave to the world.

Adieu, Maria!—adieu, poor hapless damsel!—some time, but not now, I may hear thy sorrows from thy own lips—but I was deceived; for that moment she took her pipe and told me such a tale of woe with it, that I rose up, and with broken and irregular steps walked softly to my chaise.

——What an excellent inn at Moulins!

1757

2. François Rabelais (c. 1490–c. 1554), the French monk and author of *Gargantua* and *Pantagruel*, upon whose work Sterne modeled his own in some degree.
3. Reservation.

From A Sentimental Journey Through France and Italy by Mr. Yorick

Moulines

I never felt what the distress of plenty was in any one shape till now—to travel it through the Bourbonnois, the sweetest part of France—in the hey-day of the vintage, when Nature is pouring her abundance into every one's lap, and every eye is lifted up—a journey through each step of which Music beats time to Labour, and all her children are rejoicing as they carry in their clusters—to pass through this with my affections flying out, and kindling at every group before me—and every one of them was pregnant with adventures.

Just Heaven!—it would fill up twenty volumes—and alas! I have but a few small pages left of this to crowd it into—and half of these must be taken up with the poor Maria my friend Mr. Shandy met with near Moulines.

The story he had told of that disordered maid affected me not a little in the reading; but when I got within the neighbourhood where she lived, it returned so strong into my mind, that I could not resist an impulse which prompted me to go half a league out of the road, to the village where her parents dwelt, to enquire after her.

'Tis going, I own, like the Knight of the Woeful Countenance, in quest of melancholy adventures [1]—but I know not how it is, but I am never so perfectly conscious of the existence of a soul within me,[2] as when I am entangled in them.

The old mother came to the door, her looks told me the story before she opened her mouth—She had lost her husband; he had died, she said, of anguish, for the loss of Maria's senses, about a month before.—She had feared at first, she added, that it would have plundered her poor girl of what little understanding was left—but, on the contrary, it had brought her more to herself—still she could not rest—her poor daughter, she said, crying, was wandering somewhere about the road—

—Why does my pulse beat languid as I write this? and what made La Fleur,[3] whose heart seemed only to be tuned to joy, to pass the back of his hand twice across his eyes, as the woman stood and told it? I beckoned to the postillion to turn back into the road.

When we got within half a league of Moulines, at a little opening in the road leading to a thicket, I discovered poor Maria sitting under a poplar— she was sitting with her elbow in her lap, and her head leaning on one side within her hand—a small brook ran at the foot of the tree.

1. Don Quixote.
2. Cf. James Boswell's meditations in his journal of December 27, 1775, where his reading about Hartley and Priestley makes him entertain a mechanistic view of man but also stirs him to protest that he has a soul; this theme of authenticating one's belief in one's soul is a characteristic one in 18th-century skepticism. Sterne in his *Sermons* cites Epicurus' testimony that benevolence contributes to the health of the body and that "the very mechanical motions which maintain life" are better performed by a benevolent man than by "a poor, sordid, selfish wretch. . . ." Again, "What divines say of the mind, naturalists have observed of the body; that there is no passion so natural to it as love, which is the principle of doing good. . . ."
3. Yorick's traveling companion and servant.

I bid the postillion go on with the chaise to Moulines—and La Fleur to bespeak my supper—and that I would walk after him.

She was dressed in white, and much as my friend described her, except that her hair hung loose, which before was twisted within a silk net.—She had, superadded likewise to her jacket, a pale green ribband, which fell across her shoulder to the waist; at the end of which hung her pipe.—Her goat had been as faithless as her lover: and she had got a little dog in lieu of him, which she had kept tied by a string to her girdle: as I looked at her dog, she drew him towards her with the string.—'Thou shalt not leave me, Sylvio,' said she. I looked in Maria's eyes, and saw she was thinking more of her father than of her lover or her little goat; for as she uttered them, the tears trickled down her cheeks.

I sat down close by her; and Maria let me wipe them away as they fell, with my handkerchief.—I then steeped it in my own—and then in hers—and then in mine—and then I wiped hers again—and as I did it, I felt such undescribable emotions within me, as I am sure could not be accounted for from any combinations of matter and motion.

I am positive I have a soul; nor can all the books with which materialists have pestered the world ever convince me to the contrary.

When Maria had come a little to herself, I asked her if she remembered a pale thin person of a man, who had sat down betwixt her and her goat about two years before? She said she was unsettled much at that time, but remembered it upon two accounts—that ill as she was, she saw the person pitied her; and next, that her goat had stolen his handkerchief, and she had beat him for the theft—she had washed it, she said, in the brook, and kept it ever since in her pocket to restore it to him in case she should ever see him again, which, she added, he had half promised her. As she told me this, she took the handkerchief out of her pocket to let me see it; she had folded it up neatly in a couple of vine-leaves, tied round with a tendril—on opening it, I saw an S marked in one of the corners.

She had since that, she told me, strayed as far as Rome, and walked round St. Peter's once—and returned back—that she found her way alone across the Apennines—had travelled over all Lombardy without money—and through the flinty roads of Savoy without shoes—how she had borne it, and how she had got supported, she could not tell—but God tempers the wind, said Maria, to the shorn lamb.

Shorn indeed! and to the quick, said I; and wast thou in my own land, where I have a cottage, I would take thee to it and shelter thee: thou shouldst eat of my own bread and drink of my own cup—I would be kind to thy Sylvio—in all thy weaknesses and wanderings I would seek after thee and bring thee back—when the sun went down I would say my prayers; and when I had done thou shouldst play thy evening song upon thy pipe, nor would the incense of my sacrifice be worse accepted for entering heaven along with that of a broken heart.

Nature melted within me as I uttered this; and Maria observing, as I took out my handkerchief, that it was steeped too much already to be of use, would

needs go wash it in the stream.—And where will you dry it, Maria? said I.—
I'll dry it in my bosom, said she—'twill do me good.

And is your heart still so warm, Maria? said I.

I touched upon the string on which hung all her sorrows—she looked with
wistful disorder for some time in my face; and then, without saying any
thing, took her pipe, and played her service to the Virgin—The string I had
touched ceased to vibrate—in a moment or two Maria returned to herself—
let her pipe fall—and rose up.

And where are you going, Maria? said I.—She said, to Moulines—Let us go,
said I, together.—Maria put her arm within mine, and lengthening the string,
to let the dog follow—in that order we entered Moulines.

Though I hate salutations and greetings in the marketplace,[4] yet when we got
into the middle of this, I stopped to take my last look and last farewell of
Maria.

Maria, though not tall, was nevertheless of the first order of fine forms—
affliction had touched her looks with something that was scarce earthly—still
she was feminine—and so much was there about her of all that the heart
wishes, or the eye looks for in woman, that could the traces be ever worn
out of her brain, and those of Eliza out of mine,[5] she should not only eat of
my bread and drink of my own cup, but Maria should lie in my bosom, and
be unto me as a daughter.

Adieu, poor luckless maiden!—Imbibe the oil and wine which the compassion of a stranger, as he journeyeth on his way, now pours into thy
wounds [6]—the Being who has twice bruised thee can only bind them up
for ever.

The Bourbonnois [7]

There was nothing from which I had painted out for myself so joyous a riot of
the affections, as in this journey in the vintage, through this part of France;
but pressing through this gate of sorrow to it, my sufferings have totally
unfitted me: in every scene of festivity I saw Maria in the background of the
piece, sitting pensive under her poplar; and I had got almost to Lyons before
I was able to cast a shade across her.

—Dear sensibility! source inexhausted of all that's precious in our joys,
or costly in our sorrows! thou chainest thy martyr down upon his bed of
straw—and 'tis thou who liftest him up to Heaven—eternal fountain of our
feelings!—'tis here I trace thee—and this is thy 'divinity which stirs within
me'—not that in some sad and sickening moments, 'my soul shrinks back

---

4. Cf. Mark 12:38, where the Scribes and Pharisees "love salutations in the marketplaces."
5. Mrs. Elizabeth Sclater Draper, whom Sterne had met in 1767, while her husband was
serving in India as an official of the East India Company. She left to join her husband
about three months after Sterne met her, and both his letters and *Journal to Eliza* convey
Sterne's affection for her. The *Journal* is extremely tender and lachrymose as well as somewhat histrionic; here Eliza is more lightly mentioned, somewhat as the mysterious "Jenny"
is in *Tristram Shandy*.
6. Cf. Luke 10: 33–34 on the Good Samaritan: "and when he saw him, he had compassion on him, And went to him, and bound up his wounds, pouring in oil and wine."
7. That is, the Bourbonnais, a province on the border of Burgundy.

upon herself, and startles at destruction'[8]—mere pomp of words!—but that I feel some generous joys and generous cares beyond myself—all comes from thee, great—great Sensorium of the world![9] which vibrates, if a hair of our heads but falls upon the ground, in the remotest desert of thy creation— Touched with thee, Eugenius draws my curtain when I languish—hears my tale of symptoms, and blames the weather for the disorder of his nerves.[10] Thou givest a portion of it sometimes to the roughest peasant who traverses the bleakest mountains—he finds the lacerated lamb of another's flock— This moment I beheld him leaning with his head against his crook, with piteous inclination looking down upon it!—Oh! had I come one moment sooner!—it bleeds to death—his gentle heart bleeds with it—

Peace to thee, generous swain!—I see thou walkest off with anguish—but thy joys shall balance it—for happy is thy cottage—and happy is the sharer of it—and happy are the lambs which sport about you.

1768

8. Cf. Addison's *Cato* (1713) V.i.2–7: "whence this pleasing hope . . . / This longing after immortality? / Or whence this secret dread, and inward horror / Of falling into nought? Why shrinks the soul / Back on herself, and startles at destruction? / 'Tis the divinity that stirs within us. . . ." Sterne insists upon man's generous emotions rather than his fears as evidence of the divine soul within.

9. The *sensorium* was regarded as the center to which all sensations are transmitted by the nerves. Hartley devised, in his *Observations on Man* (1749), a materialistic account of this transmission by a series of vibrations, and Sterne plays upon this in his discussion of "strings" that vibrate. Here he alludes to God as all-knowing and all-caring, and he evokes Sir Isaac Newton's vision of God as a Divine intelligence within the *sensorium* of infinite space; that is, a God for whom (in Addison's words) "infinite space gives room to infinite knowledge and is, as it were, an organ to omniscience." (*Spectator*, No. 565) Cf. Matthew 10:29–31: "Are not two sparrows sold for a farthing? and one of them shall not fall on the ground without your Father. But the very hairs of your head are all numbered. Fear ye not therefore, ye are of more value than many sparrows."

10. Eugenius, the friend of Yorick, who covers his own emotion by ascribing it to the weather, or (perhaps) seriously ascribes it to material causes.

Glossary

A Commentary on Selected Literary and Historical Terms

Airs (1) Songs, or tunes in general. (2) The songs for solo voice with lute accompaniment, as opposed to the polyphonic madrigals (*q.v.*) of the late 16th and early 17th centuries. Airs were strophic, and the successive strophes, or stanzas, of a poem were set to the same melody.

Alchemy The predecessor of chemistry, based upon classical and medieval mythological notions of the structure of matter; it was a study that nevertheless produced a great deal of practical chemical knowledge. Believing in the ancient notion of the relative nobility of metals—for example, from gold down to "baser" substances like lead—alchemists sought to discover a mysterious *philosopher's* (i.e. "scientist's") *stone* enabling them to perform transmutations of baser metals into gold. Since it thus constituted reversing a natural order, it could be thought of as theologically subversive. Alchemists themselves were by way of being practitioners of a hermetic (*q.v.*) religion, and transmuting metals was by no means their sole aim. Alchemical theory employed what would be today regarded as poetic concepts: e.g. sexual combination for chemical compounding, where today one might think of valence or charge. During the 17th century, when chemistry evolved as a science, alchemical lore and language, alluded to in poetry, became part of the body of myth, like Ptolemaic astronomy and the astrological theory it supported.

Allegory Literally, "other reading"; originally a way of interpreting a narrative or other text in order to extract a more general, or a less literal, meaning from it, e.g. reading Homer's *Odyssey* as the universal voyage of human life— with Odysseus standing for all men—which must be made toward a final goal. In the Middle Ages allegory came to be associated with ways of reading the Bible, particularly the Old Testament in relation to the New. In addition, stories came to be written with the intention of being interpreted symbolically; thus e.g. the *Psychomachia* or "battle for the soul" of Prudentius (b. 348 A.D.) figured the virtues and vices as contending soldiers in a battle (see *Personification*). There is allegorical lyric poetry and allegorical drama as well as allegorical narrative. In works such as Spenser's *The Faerie Queene* and Bunyan's *Pilgrim's Progress* allegory becomes a dominant literary form. See also *Dream Vision; Figure; type.*

Alliteration A repeated initial consonant in successive words. In Old English verse, any vowel alliterates with any other, and alliteration is not an unusual or expressive phenomenon but a regularly recurring structural feature of the verse, occurring on the first and third, and often on the first, second, and third, primary-stressed syllables of the four-stressed line. Thus, from "The Seafarer":

> hréran mid hóndum hrímcælde sǽ
> ("to stir with his hand the rime-cold sea")

In later English verse tradition, alliteration becomes expressive in a variety of ways. Spenser uses it decoratively, or to link adjective and noun, verb and object, as in the line: "Much daunted with that dint, her sense was dazed." In the 18th and 19th centuries it becomes even less systematic and more "musical."

Amplificatio, Amplifying The rhetorical enlargement of a statement or dilation of an argument, especially used in tragedy or epic (*q.v.*) poetry or in mock-heroic (*q.v.*). Language and stylistic ornament are deployed so as to increase the importance of a subject or to raise the level of its treatment.

Assonance A repeated vowel sound, a part-rhyme, which has great expressive effect when used internally (within lines), e.g. "An old, mad, blind, despised and dying king,—" (Shelley, "Sonnet: England in 1819").

Astronomy and Astrology Astrology may be regarded as an earlier phase or state of the science of astronomy—with an added normative provision in the notion that the *apparent* positions of the heavenly bodies, when viewed from a central earth about which all were thought to move, determined the shape of human life. (See *Zodiac.*) The geocentric astronomy of Ptolemy, wrong as it was about the relation between what was seen by an observer on earth and what caused him to see what he saw, nevertheless enabled men to predict with some accuracy events such as eclipses. In the microcosmic-macrocosmic world-view of the Middle Ages and the Renaissance, in which perspective the microcosm, or little world of man, constituted a miniature version of the whole cosmos, the relations between patterns discernible in the heavens and those of the four elements (*q.v.*), or the humors of the human constitution (*q.v.*), came to have great meaning. Specifically, the stars (meaning sun, moon, planets, fixed stars) were thought to radiate non-material substances called influences (literally, "in flowings") that beamed down to earth and affected human lives. Although the new astronomy of Copernicus, Kepler, and Galileo helped to destroy the conceptual basis for the belief in stellar influence, it is improper to think of a 16th- or 17th-century intellectual (and far less, a medieval man of letters and learning) as being superstitious in his use of astrological lore that was losing its centrality only with acceptance of the new ideas.

Aubade The French form of the Provençal *alba* ("dawn"), the morning song complementary to the evening *serenade;* it took its name from the word *alba* in the refrain (e.g. that of a famous anonymous poem, *L'alba, l'alba, oc l'alba, tan tost ve* ("the dawn, the dawn, o the dawn, it comes too soon"). In English such a song as Shakespeare's "Hark, hark, the lark / At heaven's gate sings" (from *Cymbeline*) exemplifies this tradition.

Aureate Literally, "golden"; used of the poetic and sometimes the prose language of 14th- and 15th-century England and Scotland; an idiom highly wrought and specializing in vernacular coinages from Latin.

Baroque (1) Originally (and still), an oddly shaped rather than a spherical pearl, and hence something twisted, contorted, involuted. (2) By a complicated analogy, a term designating stylistic periods in art, music, and literature during the 16th and 17th centuries in Europe. The analogies among the arts are frequently strained, and the stylistic periods by no means completely coincide. But the relation between the poetry of Richard Crashaw in English and Latin, and the sculpture and architecture of Gianlorenzo Bernini (1598–1680), is frequently taken to typify the spirit of the baroque. (See Wylie Sypher, *Four Stages of Renaissance Style*, 1955.)

Balade, Ballade The dominant lyric form in French poetry of the 14th and 15th centuries; a strict form consisting of three stanzas of eight lines each, with an *envoi* (*q.v.*), or four-line conclusion, addressing either a person of importance or a personification. Each stanza, including the *envoi*, ends in a refrain.

Ballad Meter Or *common meter;* four-lined stanzas, rhyming *abab*, the first and third lines in iambic tetrameter (four beats), and the second and fourth lines in iambic trimeter (three beats). See *Meter.*

Blazon, Blason (*Fr.*) A poetic genre cataloguing the parts or attributes of an object in order to praise it (or, in its satirical form, to condemn it). The first type, most influential chiefly on English Renaissance poetry, had its origin in a poem by Clément Marot in 1536 in praise of a beautiful breast. The English verb, *to blazon,* thus came to mean to catalogue poetically.

Bob and Wheel The bob (usually consisting of a two-syllable line) and the wheel (a brief set of short lines) are used either singly or together as a kind of *envoi* (*q.v.*) or comment on the action of the stanza preceding them. See *Sir Gawain and the Green Knight* for a prime example.

Calvin, Calvinist John Calvin (1509–64), French organizer of the strict religious discipline of Geneva (Switzerland), and author of its *Institutes* (1st ed., 1536). Calvin's teachings include among other things, the doctrine of Scripture as the sole rule of faith, the denial of free will in fallen man, and God's absolute predestination of every man, before his creation, to salvation or to damnation. There are Calvinist elements in the Thirty-Nine Articles (1563) of the Church of England, but the English (as opposed to the Scottish) tradition modified the rigor of the doctrine; Milton passed through a phase of strict Calvinism into greater independence and a rejection of absolute predestination.

Carol, Carole Originally (apparently) a song sung to an accompaniment of dance, and often set out in ballad meter and uniform stanzas of which the leader probably sang the verse and the dancers a refrain; later, generally, a song of religious joy, usually rapid in pace.

Carpe Diem Literally, "seize the day"; from Horace's Ode I.xi, which ends, *Dum loquimur, fugerit invida / aetas: carpe diem, quam minimum credula postero* ("Even while we're talking, envious Time runs by: seize the day, putting a minimum of trust in tomorrow"). This became a standard theme of Renaissance erotic verse, as in Robert Herrick's "Gather ye rosebuds while ye may."

Cavalier   Designating the supporters of Charles I and of the Anglican church establishment, in opposition to the Puritans, or Roundheads, during the English Civil War. In a literary context, the lyric poetry of some of these so-named soldier-lover-poets (e.g. Thomas Carew, Richard Lovelace) is implied with its elegant wit (*q.v.*) and grace. (See *Civil War*.)

Chanson d'aventure   A French poetic form describing a conversation about love or between lovers, and represented as overheard by the poet.

Civil War   The struggle between Charles I and his Parliament came to a head in 1641, when the King tried forcibly to arrest five dissident members of Parliament. He failed, and in April 1642 raised his standard at Northampton, intending to advance on London. For some time there was a military deadlock, but in January 1644 the Parliamentary forces, allied with the Scots, defeated the King at Marston Moor. The Parliament men now controlled the North, but not until they instituted major military reforms did they overcome the King decisively at Naseby in June 1645. Charles became the captive of Parliament in January 1647 and was executed two years later. In 1653 Oliver Cromwell expelled the "Rump" of the Long Parliament (*q.v.*), which had survived since 1640, and became Lord Protector.

The terms "Cavalier" and "Roundhead," implying respectively aristocratic dash and middle-class puritanism, are not wholly misleading as descriptive of the Royalist and Parliamentary sides in the war; but the fact of new money and religious fervor on the winning side was not the whole story. The split between "Presbyterian" and "Independent" in the Parliament faction was partly religious, partly a division between the affluent and the enthusiastic; and with the victory of the "monied" interest the Revolution itself became conservative. But the execution of the King was an event that for a century or more resonated throughout the course of English history, and, as Marvell understood (see his "Horation Ode"), ended a whole phase of civilization.

Complaint   Short poetic monologue, expressing the poet's sorrow at unrequited love or other pains and ending with a request for relief from them.

Complexion   See *Temperaments*.

Conceit   From the Italian *concetto*, "concept" or "idea"; used in Renaissance poetry to mean a precise and detailed comparison of something more remote or abstract with something more present or concrete, and often detailed through a chain of metaphors or similes (see *Rhetoric*). In Petrarchan (*q.v.*) poetry, certain conceits became conventionalized and were used again and again in various versions. The connection between the Lady's eyes and the Sun, so typical of these, was based on the proportion *her gaze : love's life and day :: sun's shining: world's life and daylight*. Conceits were closely linked to emblems (*q.v.*), to the degree that the verbal connection between the emblem picture and its *significatio*, or meaning, was detailed in an interpretive conceit. See also *Personification*.

Contemptus Mundi   Contempt for the world, i.e. rejection of temporal and transitory pleasures and values in favor of the spiritual and eternal.

Contraries   See *Qualities*.

Courtly Love Modern scholarship has coined this name for a set of conventions around which medieval love-poetry was written. It was essentially chivalric and a product of 12th-century France, especially of the troubadours. This poetry involves an idealization of the beloved woman, whose love, like all love, refines and ennobles the lover so that the union of their minds and/or bodies—a union that ought not to be apparent to others—allows them to attain excellence of character.

Dance of Death Poem accompanied by illustrations on the inevitability and universality of death, which is shown seizing men and women of all ranks and occupations, one after the other.

Decorum Propriety of discourse; what is becoming in action, character, and style; the avoidance of impossibilities and incongruities in action, style, and character: "the good grace of everything after his kind" and the "great masterpiece to observe." More formally, a neoclassical doctrine maintaining that literary style—grand, or high, middle, and low—be appropriate to the subject, occasion, and genre. Thus Milton, in *Paradise Lost* (I.13–14), invokes his "adventurous song, / That with no middle flight intends to soar. . . ." See also *Rhetoric*.

Digressio Interpolated story or description in a poem or oration, introduced for ornamentation or some structural purpose.

Dissenters In England, members of Protestant churches and sects that do not conform to the doctrines of the established Church of England; from the 16th century on, this would include Baptists, Puritans of various sorts within the Anglican Church, Presbyterians, Congregationalists, and (in the 18th century) Methodists. Another term, more current in the 19th century, is *Nonconformist*.

Dream Vision, Dream Allegory A popular medieval poetic form. Its fictional time is usually Spring; as the poet falls alseep in some pleasant place—a wood or garden—to the music of a stream and the song of birds, he dreams of "real" people or personified abstractions, who illuminate for him the nature of some aspect of knowledge, mode of behavior, or social or political question. See also *Allegory*.

Elegy Originally, in Greek and Latin poetry, a poem composed not in the hexameter lines of epic (*q.v.*) and, later, of pastoral, but in the elegiac couplets consisting of one hexameter line followed by a pentameter. Elegiac poetry was amatory, epigrammatic. By the end of the 16th century, English poets were using heroic couplets (*q.v.*), to stand for both hexameters and elegiacs; and an elegiac poem was any serious meditative piece. Perhaps because of the tradition of the pastoral elegy (*q.v.*), the general term "elegy" came to be reserved, in modern terminology, for an elaborate and formal lament, longer than a *dirge* or *threnody*, for a dead person. By extension, "elegiac" has come to mean, in general speech, broodingly sad.

Elements In ancient and medieval science, the four basic substances of which all matter was composed: earth, water, air, fire—in order of density and heaviness. They are often pictured in that order in diagrams of the universe. All four elements, being material, are below the sphere of the moon (above, there is a fifth: the quintessence). The elements are formed of combinations of the

Qualities (*q.v.*) or Contraries: the union of hot and dry makes fire; of hot and moist, air; of cold and moist, water; of cold and dry, earth.

Emblem   A simple allegorical picture, or *impresa*, labeled with a motto to show its significance, and usually accompanied by a poetic description that connects the picture or "device" with the meaning, frequently by means of elaborate conceits (*q.v.*), sometimes with more obvious moralizing. Many Renaissance paintings are emblems, without the text. The first Renaissance emblem book was that of the Venetian lawyer Andrea Alciati, in 1531; for the next century and one-half, the pictures and verses were copied, translated, expanded upon, added to, and adapted in French, Dutch, Spanish, German, and Italian as well as his original Latin. Famous English books of emblems were those of Geoffrey Whitney (1586), Henry Peacham (*Minerva Brittana, or A Garden of Heroical Devices*, 1612), George Wither (1635), and Francis Quarles (1635). Based originally on classical mythography, an interest in ancient coins and statuary, as well as "hieroglyphics" in all ancient art, emblem traditions generally divided, in the 17th century, into "Jesuitical" types (involving precise and intense images such as tears, wings, hearts, and classical Cupids signifying not *amor,* but *caritas*), and more pragmatic Protestant emblems (particularly in the Dutch tradition), which tend toward genre scenes of everyday life illustrating proverbs in the text. In the Renaissance, pictures were to be *read* and understood, like texts; and this kind of reading of hieroglyphics extends, in a writer like Sir Thomas Browne, to all of creation:

> The world's a book in folio, printed all
> With God's great works in letters capital:
> Each creature is a page, and each effect
> A fair character, void of all defect.

These lines of Joshua Sylvester are a commonplace. See also *Conceit; Symbolism;* and Figs. 16–21 in illustrations for the Renaissance section of this Anthology.

Enjambment   The "straddling" of a clause or sentence across two lines of verse, as opposed to closed, or end-stopped, lines. Thus, in the opening lines of Shakespeare's *Twelfth Night:*

> If music be the food of love, play on!
> Give me excess of it, that, surfeiting
> The appetite may sicken and so die . . .

the first line is stopped, the second enjambed. When enjambment becomes strong or violent, it may have an ironic or comic effect.

The Enlightenment   A term used very generally, to refer to the late 17th and the 18th century in Europe, a period characterized by a programmatic rationalism—i.e. a belief in the ability of human reason to understand the world and thereby to transform whatever in it needed transforming; an age in which ideas of science and progress accompanied the rise of new philosophies of the relation of man to the state, an age which saw many of its hopes for human betterment fulfilled in the French Revolution.

Envoi, Envoy   Short concluding stanza found in certain French poetic forms and their English imitations, e.g. the *ballade* (*q.v.*). It serves as a dedicatory postscript, and a summing up of the poem of which it repeats the refrain.

Epic Or, *heroic poetry;* originally, oral narrative delivered in a style different from that of normal discourse by reason of verse, music, and heightened diction, and concerning the great deeds of a central heroic figure, or group of figures, usually having to do with a crisis in the history of a race or culture. Its setting lies in this earlier "heroic" period, and it will often have been written down only after a long period of oral transmission. The Greek *Iliad* and *Odyssey* and the Old English *Beowulf* are examples of this, in their narration mixing details from both the heroic period described and the actual time of their own composition and narration. What is called *secondary* or *literary* epic is a long, ambitious poem, composed by a single poet on the model of the older, primary forms, and of necessity being more allusive and figurative than its predecessors. Homer's poems lead to Virgil's *Aeneid,* which leads to Milton's *Paradise Lost,* in a chain of literary dependency. Spenser's *Faerie Queene* might be called *romantic epic* of the secondary sort, and Dante's *Divine Comedy* might also be assimilated to post-Virgilian epic tradition.

Epic Simile An extended comparison, in Homeric and subsequently in Virgilian and later epic poetry, between an event in the story (the *fable*) and something in the experience of the epic audience, to the effect of making the fabulous comprehensible in terms of the familiar. From the Renaissance on, additional complications have emerged from the fact that what is the familiar for the classical audience becomes, because of historical change, itself fabled (usually, pastoral) for the modern audience. Epic similes compare the fabled with the familiar usually with respect to one property or element; thus, in the *Odyssey,* when the stalwart forward motion of a ship in high winds is described, the simile goes:

> And as amids a fair field four brave horse
> Before a chariot, stung into their course
> With fervent lashes of the smarting scourge
> That all their fire blows high, and makes them rise
> To utmost speed the measure of their ground:
> So bore the ship aloft her fiery bound
> About whom rushed the billows, black and vast
> In which the sea-roars burst . . .
>
> (*Chapman translation*)

Notice the formal order of presentation: "even as . . .": *the familiar event, often described in detail;* "just so . . .": *the fabled one.*

Epicureanism A system of philosophy founded by the Greek Epicurus (342–270 B.C.), who taught that the five senses are the sole source of ideas and sole criterion of truth, and that the goal of human life is pleasure (i.e. hedonism), though this can be achieved only by practicing moderation. Later the term came to connote bestial self-indulgence, which Epicurus had clearly rejected.

Exclamatio Rhetorical figure representing a cry of admiration or grief.

Exemplum A short narrative used to illustrate a moral point in didactic literature (especially sermons) or in historical writing. Its function is to recommend or dissuade from a particular course of conduct.

Fabliau A short story in verse, comic in character, its subject matter often indecent, and the joke hinging on sex or excretion. The plot usually involves a witty turn or practical joke, the motive of which is love or revenge. See *The Miller's Tale* of Chaucer.

Fathers of the Church The earliest Christian theologians and ecclesiastical writers (also referred to as "patristic"), flourishing from the late 1st century through the 8th, composing severally in Greek or Latin. Well-known "Fathers" are St. Augustine, St. Jerome, Tertullian.

Feudal System The system of land tenure and political allegiance characteristic of Europe during the Middle Ages. The king, as owner of all land, gives portions of it to his vassals, by whom it can be passed on to heirs, in return for their pledge of loyalty and of specified military service. These nobles divide their land among their followers, the subdivision continuing until it reaches the serfs, who cultivate the land but must hand over most of their produce to the lord.

Figurative Language In a general sense, any shift away from a literal meaning of words, brought about by the use of tropes (*q.v.*) or other rhetorical devices. See *Rhetoric*.

Figure As defined by Erich Auerbach in his essay "Figura," a mode of interpretation establishing a connection between two events or persons, the first of which signifies both itself and the second, while the second encompasses or fulfills the first—e.g. the Eucharist, which is the "figure" of Christ. See *Allegory*.

Free Verse, Vers Libre Generally, any English verse form whose lines are measured neither by the number of 1) stressed syllables (see *Meter* §3, accentual verse), 2) alternations of stressed and unstressed syllables (§4, accentual-syllabic verse), nor syllables alone (§2, syllabic verse). The earliest English free verse —that of Christopher Smart in *Jubilate Agno* (18th century)—imitates the prosody of Hebrew poetry (reflected also in the translation of the English Bible), in maintaining unmeasured units marked by syntactic parallelism. While many free-verse traditions (e.g. that of Walt Whitman) remain close to the impulses of this biblical poetry, yet others, in the 20th century, have developed new *ad hoc* patternings of their own. *Vers libre* usually refers to the experimental, frequently very short unmeasured lines favored by poets of the World War I period, although the term, rather than the form, was adopted from French poetry of the 19th century.

Gothic Term (originally pejorative, as alluding to the Teutonic barbarians) designating the architectural style of the Middle Ages. The revival of interest in medieval architecture in the later 18th century produced not only pseudo-Gothic castles like Horace Walpole's "Strawberry Hill", and more modest artificial ruins on modern estates, but also a vogue for atmospheric prose romances set in medieval surroundings and involving improbable terrors, and known as Gothic novels. The taste for the Gothic, arising during the Age of Sensibility (*q.v.*), is another reflection of a reaction against earlier 18th-century neoclassicism (*q.v*).

Hermetic, Hermeticism, Hermetist Terms referring to a synthesis of Neoplatonic

and other occult philosophies, founded on a collection of writings attributed
to Hermes Trismegistus ("Thrice-greatest Hermes"—a name given the Egyptian god Thoth), but which in fact date from the 2nd and 3rd centuries A.D.
An important doctrine was that of correspondences between earthly and
heavenly things. By studying these correspondences, a man might "walk to the
sky" (in the words of Henry Vaughan) in his lifetime. Hermetic tradition
favored *esoteric* or forbidden knowledge, over what could be more publicly
avowed.

Heroic Couplet   In English prosody, a pair of rhyming, iambic pentameter lines,
used at first for closure—as at the end of the Shakespearean sonnet (*q.v.*)—
or to terminate a scene in blank-verse drama; later adapted to correspond
in English poetry to the elegiac couplet of classical verse as well as to the
heroic, unrhymed, Greek and Latin hexameter. Octosyllabic couplets, with
four stresses (eight syllables) to the line, are a minor, shorter, jumpier form,
used satirically unless in implicit allusion to the form of Milton's "Il Penseroso,"
in which they develop great lyrical power. (See *Meter*.)

Humors   The combinations, in men and women (the *microcosm*) of the qualities
(*q.v.*), or contraries. In primitive physiology, the four principal bodily fluids
in their combinations produce the temperaments (*q.v.*) or "complexions"
These "humors," with their properties and effects—at least in the Middle
Ages—are, respectively: Blood (hot and moist)—cheerfulness, warmth of
feeling; Choler (hot and dry)—a quick, angry temper; Phlegm (cold and
moist)—dull sluggishness; Melancholy (cold and dry)—fretful depression.
The Renaissance introduced the concept of "artificial" humors—e.g. scholars'
and artists' melancholy, creative brooding. The humors, the temperaments,
and the four elements (*q.v.*) of the macrocosm, or universe, were all looked
upon as interrelated. See *Renaissance Psychology*.

Irony   Generally, a mode of saying one thing to mean another. *Sarcasm*, in which
one means exactly the opposite of what one says, is the easiest and cheapest
form; thus, e.g. "Yeah, it's a *nice day!*" when one means that it's a miserable
one. But serious literature produces ironies of a much more complex and
revealing sort. *Dramatic irony* occurs when a character in a play or story
asserts something whose meaning the audience or reader knows will change
in time. Thus, in Genesis when Abraham assures his son Isaac (whom he is
about to sacrifice) that "God will provide his own lamb," the statement is
lighted with dramatic irony when a sacrificial ram is actually provided at the
last minute to save Isaac. Or, in the case of Sophocles' *Oedipus*, when almost
everything the protagonist says about the predicament of his city is hideously
ironic in view of the fact (which he does not know) that he is responsible
therefor. The ironies generated by the acknowledged use of non-literal
language (see *Rhetoric*) and fictions in drama, song, and narrative are at
the core of imaginative literature.

Judgment   In Catholic doctrine, God's retributive judgment, which decides the fate
of rational creatures according to their merits and faults. Particular judgment
is the decision about the eternal destiny of each soul made immediately
after death; General (Last) Judgment is at the Second Coming of Christ

as God and Man, when all men will be judged again in the sight of all the world. See Fig. 50 in illustrations for the Medieval section of this anthology.

Kenning An Old Norse form designating, strictly, a condensed simile or metaphor of the kind frequently used in Old Germanic poetry; a figurative circumlocution for a thing not actually named—e.g. "swan's path" for sea; "world-candle" or "sky-candle" for sun. More loosely, often used to mean also a metaphorical compound word or phrase such as "ring-necked" or "foamy-necked" for a ship, these being descriptive rather than figurative in character.

Lancastrians See *Wars of the Roses.*

Locus Amoenus Literally, "pleasant place"; a garden, either Paradise, the most perfect of all gardens, or its pagan equivalent, or the later literary garden that was a figure (*q.v.*) of Paradise. See *Topos.*

Long Parliament The Parliament summoned by Charles I on November 3, 1640; the last remnant, not dissolved until 1660, opposed the King and brought about his downfall and execution. See *Civil War.*

Macaronic Verse in which two languages are mingled, usually for burlesque purposes.

Machiavelli, Niccolò Italian diplomat, historian, and political theorist (1469–1527), whose chief work, *Il Principe* (*The Prince,* 1513), based in part on the career of Cesare Borgia, outlines a pragmatic rule of conduct for a ruler; thus, politics should have nothing to do with morality; the prince should be an exponent of ruthless power in behalf of his people. In England his theories were put into practice by Thomas Cromwell in the reign of Henry VIII; his writings, however, were not translated until the 17th century, and his image in England, based on rumor and the reports of his adversaries, fostered a myth of the evil "Machiavel" as he appears in Marlowe (*Titus Andronicus*) and Shakespeare (*Richard III*).

Madrigal Polyphonic setting of a poem, in the 16th and 17th centuries, for several voice parts, unaccompanied or with instruments. Because of the contrapuntal texture, the words were frequently obscured for a listener, though not for the performers.

Meter Verse may be made to differ from prose and from ordinary speech in a number of ways, and in various languages these ways may be very different. Broadly speaking, lines of verse may be marked out by the following regularities of pattern:

1. *Quantitative Verse,* used in ancient Greek poetry and adopted by the Romans, used a fixed number of what were almost musical measures, called *feet;* they were built up of long and short syllables (like half- and quarter-notes in music), which depended on the vowel and consonants in them. *Stress accent* (the *word* stress which, when accompanied by vowel reduction, distinguishes the English noun "content" from the adjective "content") did not exist in ancient Greek, and played no part in the rhythm of the poetic line. Thus, the first line of the *Odyssey: Andra moi ennepe mousa, polytropon hos mala polla* ("Sing me, O muse, of that man of many resources who, after great hardship . . .") is composed in *dactyls* of one long syllable followed by two shorts (but, as in musical rhythm, replaceable by two longs, a *spondee*).

With six dactyls to a line, the resulting meter is called *dactylic hexameter* (*hexameter,* for short), the standard form for epic poetry. Other kinds of foot or measure were: the *anapest* (◡ ◡ −); the *iamb* (◡ −); the *trochee* (− ◡); and a host of complex patterns used in lyric poetry. Because of substitutions, however, the number of syllables in a classical line was not fixed, only the number of measures.

2. *Syllabic Verse,* used in French, Japanese, and many other languages, and in English poetry of the mid-20th century, measures only the *number* of syllables per line with no regard to considerations of *quantity* or *stress.* Because of the prominence of stress in the English language, two lines of the same purely syllabic length may not necessarily sound at all as though they were in the same meter, e.g.:

> These two incommensurably sounding
> Lines are both written with ten syllables.

3. *Accentual Verse,* used in early Germanic poetry, and thus in Old English poetry, depended upon the number of strong *stress accents* per line. These accents were four in number, with no fixed number of unstressed. Folk poetry and nursery rhymes often preserve this accentual verse, e.g.:

> Sing, sing, what shall I sing?
> The cat's run away with the pudding-bag string

The first line has six syllables, the second, eleven, but they sound more alike (and not merely by reason of their rhyme) than the two syllabic lines quoted above.

4. *Accentual-Syllabic Verse,* the traditional meter of English poetry from Chaucer on, depends upon both numbered *stresses* and numbered *syllables,* a standard form consisting of ten syllables alternately stressed and unstressed, and having five stresses; thus it may be said to consist of five syllable pairs.

For complex historical reasons, accentual-syllabic groups of stressed and unstressed syllables came to be known by the names used for Greek and Latin feet—which can be very confusing. The analogy was made between *long* syllables in the classical languages, and *stressed* syllables in English. Thus, the pair of syllables in the adjective "content" is called an *iamb,* and in the noun "content," a *trochee;* the word "classical" is a *dactyll,* and the phrase "of the best," an *anapest.* When English poetry is being discussed, these terms are always used in their adapted, accentual-syllabic meanings, and hence the ten-syllable line mentioned earlier is called "iambic pentameter" in English. The phrase "high-tide" would be a *spondee* (as would, in general, two monosyllables comprising a proper name, e.g. "John Smith"); whereas compound nouns like "highway" would be *trochaic.* In this adaptation of classical nomenclature, the terms *dimeter, trimeter, tetrameter, pentameter, hexameter* refer not to the number of quantitative feet but to the number of syllable-groups (pairs or triplets, from one to six) composing the line. Iambic pentameter and tetrameter lines are frequently also called *decasyllabic* and *octosyllabic* respectively.

5. *Versification.* In verse, lines may be arranged in patterns called *stichic*

or *strophic*, that is, the same linear form (say, iambic pentameter) repeated without grouping by rhyme or interlarded lines of another form, or varied in just such a way into *stanzas* or *strophes* ("turns"). Unrhymed iambic pentameter, called *blank verse*, is the English stichic form that Milton thought most similar to classic hexameter or *heroic* verse. But in the Augustan period iambic pentameter rhymed pairs, called heroic couplets (*q.v.*), came to stand for this ancient form as well as for the classical elegiac verse (*q.v.*). Taking couplets as the simplest strophic unit, we may proceed to *tercets* (groups of three lines) and to *quatrains* (groups of four), rhymed *abab* or *abcb*, and with equal or unequal line lengths. Other stanzaic forms: *ottava rima*, an eight-line, iambic pentameter stanza, rhyming *ababacc; Spenserian stanza*, rhyming *ababbcbcc*, all pentameter save for the last line, an iambic hexameter, or *alexandrine*. There have been adaptations in English (by Shelley, notably, and without rhyme by T. S. Eliot) of the Italian *terza rima* used by Dante in *The Divine Comedy*, interlocking tercets rhyming *aba bcb cdc ded*, etc. More elaborate stanza forms developed in the texts of some Elizabethan songs and in connection with the ode (*q.v.*).

Microcosm Literally, "the small world"—man. For fuller explanation see selections of Walter Ralegh and Thomas Browne on this theme. See also *Astronomy, Astrology; Humors; Qualities*.

Mirror for Princes A treatise setting out the education necessary to make a ruler and the modes of mental, moral, and physical activity that befitted him.

Mock-heroic, Mock-epic The literary mode resulting when low or trivial subjects are treated in the high, artificial literary language of classical epic (*q.v.*) poetry. The point of the joke is usually to expose not the inadequacies of the style but those of the subject, although occasionally the style may be caricatured, and the joke made about decorum (*q.v.*) itself. Alexander Pope's *The Rape of the Lock* is a famous example.

Music of the Spheres The ancient fiction held that the celestial spheres made musical sounds, either by rubbing against the ether, or because an angel— the Christian replacement for the Intelligence which in Plato's *Timaeus* guided each one—sang while riding on his charge. The inaudibility of this music was ascribed by later Platonism (*q.v.*) to the imprisonment of the soul in the body, and by Christian writers, to man's fallen state. Frequent attempts were made to preserve some meaning for this beautiful idea: thus, Aristotle's conclusion that the continuous presence of such sounds would make them inaudible to habituated ears (a sophisticated prefiguration of the modern notion of background noise). And thus the belief of the Ptolemaic astronomy that at a certain point the ratios of the diameters of the spheres of the various heavenly bodies were "harmonious" in that they would generate the overtone series. Even Kepler, who demonstrated that the planetary orbits, let alone non-existent spheres, could not be circular, suggested that the ratios of the angular velocities of the planets would generate a series of melodies; he then proceeded to put them together contrapuntally. See *Astronomy and Astrology*.

Myth A primitive story explaining the origins of certain phenomena in the world and in human life, and usually embodying gods or other supernatural forces, heroes (men who are either part human and part divine, or are placed between an ordinary mortal and a divine being), men, and animals. Literature continues to incorporate myths long after the mythology (the system of stories containing them) ceases to be a matter of actual belief. Moreover, discarded beliefs of all sorts tend to become myths when they are remembered but no longer literally clung to, and are used in literature in a similar way. The classical mythology of the Greeks and Romans was apprehended in this literary, or interpreted, way, even in ancient times. The gods and heroes and their deeds came to be read as allegory (q.v.). During the Renaissance, *mythography*—the interpretation of myths in order to make them reveal a moral or historical significance (rather than merely remaining entertaining but insignificant stories)—was extremely important, both for literature and for painting and sculpture. In modern criticism, mythical or *archetypal* situations and personages have been interpreted as being central objects of the work of the imagination.

Neoclassicism   (1) In general the term refers to Renaissance and post-Renaissance attempts to model enterprises in the various arts on Roman and Greek originals—or as much as was known of them. Thus, in the late Renaissance, the architectural innovations of Andrea Palladio may be called "neoclassic," as may Ben Jonson's relation, and Alexander Pope's as well, to the Roman poet Horace. The whole Augustan period in English literary history (1660–1740) was a deliberately neoclassical one.

(2) More specifically, neoclassicism refers to that period in the history of all European art spanning the very late 18th and early 19th century, which period may be seen as accompanying the fulfillment, and the termination, of the Enlightenment (q.v.). In England such neoclassic artists as Henry Fuseli, John Flaxman, George Romney, and even, in some measure, William Blake, are close to the origins of pictorial and literary Romanticism itself.

Neoplatonism   See *Platonism.*

Nonconformist   See *Dissenters.*

Octosyllabic Couplet   See *Heroic Couplet; Meter.*

Ode   A basic poetic form, originating in Greek antiquity. The *choral ode* was a public event, sung and danced, at a large ceremony, or as part of the tragic and comic drama. Often called *Pindaric ode,* after a great Greek poet, the form consisted of *triads* (groups of three sections each). These were units of song and dance, and had the form *aab*—that is, a *strophe* (or "turn"), an *antistrophe* (or "counter-turn"), and an *epode* (or "stand"), the first two being identical musically and metrically, the third different. In English poetry, the Pindaric ode form, only in its metrical aspects, became in the 17th century a mode for almost essayistic poetic comment, and was often used also as a kind of cantata libretto, in praise of music and poetry (the so-called *musical ode*). By the 18th century the ode became the form for a certain kind of personal, visionary poem, and it is this form that Wordsworth and Coleridge transmitted to Romantic tradition. A second English form, known as *Horatian ode,* was based on the lyric (not choral) poems of Horace, and is written in *aabb* quatrains, with the last two lines shorter than the first two by a pair of syllables or more.

Oral Formula A conventional, fossilized phrase common in poetry composed as it was recited, or composed to be recited, and repeated frequently in a single poem. It serves as either a means of slowing or even stopping the action momentarily, or of filling out a verse: e.g. "Beowulf, son of Ecgtheow," or "go or ride"—i.e. "whatever you do."

Paradox In logic, a self-contradictory statement, hence meaningless (or a situation producing one), with an indication that something is wrong with the language in which such a situation can occur, e.g. the famous paradox of Epimenedes the Cretan, who held that all Cretans are liars (and thus could be lying if— and only if—he wasn't), or that of Zeno, of the arrow in flight: since at any instant of time the point of the arrow can always be said to be at one precise point, therefore it is continually at rest at a continuous sequence of such points, and therefore never moves. In literature, however, particularly in the language of lyric poetry, paradox plays another role. From the beginnings of lyric poetry, paradox has been deemed necessary to express feelings and other aspects of human inner states, e.g. Sappho's invention of the Greek word *glykypikron* ("bittersweet") to describe love, or her assertion that she was freezing and burning at the same time. So too the Latin poet Catullus, in his famous couplet

> I'm in hate and I'm in love; why do I? you may ask.
> Well, I don't know, but I feel it, and I'm in agony.

may be declaring thereby that true love poetry must be illogical.

In Elizabethan poetry, paradoxes were frequently baldly laid out in the rhetorical form called *oxymoron* (see *Rhetoric*), as in "the victor-victim," or across a fairly mechanical sentence structure, as in "My feast of joy is but a dish of pain." In the highest poetic art, however, the seeming self-contradiction is removed when one realizes that either, or both, of the conflicting terms is to be taken figuratively, rather than literally. The apparent absurdity, or strangeness, thus gives rhetorical power to the utterance. Elaborate and sophisticated paradoxes, insisting on their own absurdity, typify the poetic idiom of the tradition of John Donne.

Pastoral A literary mode in which the lives of simple country people are celebrated, described, and used allegorically by sophisticated urban poets and writers. The *idylls* of Sicilian poet Theocritus (3rd century B.C.) were imitated and made more symbolic in Virgil's *eclogues;* shepherds in an Arcadian landscape stood for literary and political personages, and the Renaissance adapted these narrative and lyric pieces for moral and aesthetic discussion. Spenser's *Shepheardes Calendar* is an experimental collection of eclogues involving an array of forms and subjects. In subsequent literary tradition, the pastoral imagery of both Old and New Testaments (Psalms, Song of Songs, priest as *pastor* or shepherd of his flock, and so on) joins with the classical mode. Modern critics, William Empson in particular, have seen the continuation of pastoral tradition in other versions of the country-city confrontation, such as child-adult and criminal-businessman. See *Pastoral Elegy*.

Pastoral Elegy A form of lament for the death of a poet, originating in Greek bucolic tradition (Bion's lament for Adonis, a lament for Bion by a fellow poet, Theocritus' first idyll, Virgil's tenth eclogue) and continued in use by Renaissance poets as a public mode for the presentation of private, inner, and even coterie matters affecting poets and their lives, while conventionally treating questions of general human importance. At a death one is moved to ask, "Why this death? Why now?" and funeral elegy must always confront these questions, avoiding easy resignation as an answer. Pastoral elegy handled these questions with formal mythological apparatus, such as the Muses, who should have protected their dead poet, local spirits, and other presences appropriate to the circumstances of the life and death, and perhaps figures of more general mythological power. The end of such poems is the eternalization of the dead poet in a monument of myth, stronger than stone or bronze: Spenser's *Astrophel,* a lament for Sir Philip Sidney, concludes with an Ovidian change—the dead poet's harp, like Orpheus' lyre, becomes the constellation Lyra. Milton's *Lycidas* both exemplifies and transforms the convention. Later examples include Shelley's *Adonais* (for Keats), Arnold's *Thyrsis* (for Clough), and Swinburne's *Ave Atque Vale* (for Baudelaire).

Penance   In Catholic doctrine, the moral virtue by which a sinner is disposed to hate his sin as an offense against God; and the sacrament, of which the outward signs are the acknowledgment of sin, self-presentation of the sinner to priest to confess his sins, the absolution pronounced by the priest, and the satisfaction (penance) imposed on the sinner by the priest and to be performed before the sinner is delivered from his guilt. See Figs. 32 and 52 in illustrations for the Medieval section of this Anthology.

Peroration   Final part of an oration, reviewing and summarizing the argument, often in an impassioned form. (See also *Rhetoric.*)

Personification   Treating a thing or, more properly, an abstract quality, as though it were a person. Thus, "Surely *goodness* and *mercy* shall follow me all the days of my life" tends to personify the italicized terms by reason of the metaphoric use of "follow me." On the other hand, a conventional, complete personification, like *Justice* (whom we recognize by her *attributes*—she is blindfolded, she has scales and a sword) might also be called an *allegorical figure* in her own right, and her attributes *symbols* (blindness = impartiality; scales = justly deciding; sword = power to mete out what is deserved). Often the term "personification" applies to momentary, or *ad hoc,* humanizations.

Petrarch, Petrarchan   Francesco Petrarca (1304–74), the Italian founder of humanistic studies, with their revival of Greek and Latin literature, was influential in Renaissance England chiefly for his *Rime sparse,* the collection of love sonnets in praise of his muse, Laura. These poems, translated and adapted in England from the 1530's on, provided not only the sonnet (*q.v.*) form but also many devices of imagery widely used by English poets of the 16th and 17th centuries.

Physiognomics   The "art to read the mind's complexion in the face." From ancient times to the Renaissance, it was believed possible to gauge a person's character precisely from his outward appearance and physical characteristics.

Platonism   The legacy of Plato (429–347 B.C.) is virtually the history of philosophy. His *Timaeus* was an important source of later cosmology; his doctrine of ideas is central to Platonic tradition. His doctrine of love (especially in the *Symposium*) had enormous influence in the Renaissance, at which time its applicability was shifted to heterosexual love specifically. The *Republic* and the *Laws* underlie a vast amount of political thought, and the *Republic* contains also a philosophical attack on poetry (fiction) which defenders of the arts have always had to answer. Neoplatonism—a synthesis of Platonism, Pythagoreanism, and Aristotelianism—was dominant in the 3rd century A.D.; and the whole tradition was revived in the 15th and 16th centuries. The medieval Plato was Latinized, largely at second-hand; the revival of Greek learning in the 15th century led to another Neoplatonism: a synthesis of Platonism, the medieval Christian Aristotle, and Christian doctrine. Out of this came the doctrines of love we associate with some Renaissance poetry; a sophisticated version of older systems of allegory and symbol; and notions of the relation of spirit and matter reflected in Marvell and many other poets.

Prayer Book   The Book of Common Prayer, containing the order of services in the Church of England. Based on translations from medieval service books, it first appeared in 1549, under the direction of Thomas Cranmer (1489–1556), Archbishop of Canterbury. It was much revised, partly to meet Puritan complaints, but in 1662 achieved the form it has since kept, with only slight alteration.

Purgatory   According to Catholic doctrine, a place or condition of temporal punishment for those who die in the grace of God, but without having made full satisfaction for their transgressions. In Purgatory they are purified so as to be fit to come into God's presence.

Quadrivium   The second division of the seven liberal arts, which together with the trivium (*q.v.*) comprised the full course of a medieval education and fitted a man to study theology, the crown of the arts and sciences. The quadrivium consisted of music, arithmetic, geometry, and astronomy.

Qualities Or **contraries;** the properties of all material things, the various combinations of which were held to determine their nature. They were four in number, in two contrasting pairs: hot and cold; moist and dry. See *Elements; Humors; Temperaments.*

Recusant   Literally, "refuser"; in the Elizabethan period, anyone who refused to join the Church of England—although now the term is commonly used to allude to "popish recusants," i.e. Roman Catholics, and "recusancy," to English writings of certain Catholics during the late 16th century.

Renaissance Psychology   Poetic language, particularly that of lyric poetry, is always implicitly raising assumptions about inner states of people who have feelings and who wish to express them. In the Renaissance, several informal ways coexisted of talking about the relation which we now see as one of mind and body. From Aristotelian tradition the concept of three orders of soul was maintained: in ascending order these were the *vegetable* (the "life," immobile and inactive, of plants), the *animal* (accounting for the behavior of beasts), and the *rational* (the power of reason, often associated with language as well as thought, in men). On the other hand, *wit* (*q.v.*) meant intellect, and in Elizabethan language, the conflict of *wit* and *will* correspond roughly, but not precisely, to a modern opposition of reason and emotion. Physical, as well as psychological, human diversity was explained by the theory of the humors and temperaments (*qq.v.*). On the other hand, there were mysterious entities called *spirits* (associated with the Latin root, meaning "breath," and its application to alcoholic fluids: waters that "breathe" and "burn"). Spirits were fine vapors mediating between the body and the soul, and patching up a connection which scientific psychology is still trying to make. *Natural spirits* came from the liver and circulated through the veins. *Vital spirits* came from the heart and circulated arterially. *Animal spirits* were distilled from the vital spirits (which can be associated with blood) and went to the brain through the nerves, which were thought to be conducting vessels. (See the selection from Burton's *Anatomy of Melancholy*.) Other faculties of the soul included the power of *fancy* or *fantasy* (the word "imagination" most often referred to something imagined, rather than to a faculty).

Reverdie Old French dance poem imitated in other languages, usually consisting of five or six stanzas without refrain, in joyful celebration of the coming of Spring.

Rhetoric In classical times, rhetoric was the art of persuading through the use of language. The major treatises on style and structure of discourse—Aristotle's *Rhetoric*, Quintilian's *Institutes of Oratory*, the *Rhetorica ad Herrenium* ascribed for centuries to Cicero—were concerned with the "arts" of language in the older sense of "skills." In the Middle Ages the *trivium* (*q.v.*), or program that led to the degree of Bachelor of Arts, consisted of grammar, logic, and rhetoric, but it was an abstract study, based on the Roman tradition. In the Renaissance, classical rhetorical study became a matter of the first importance, and it led to the study of literary stylistics and the application of principles and concepts of the production and structure of eloquence to the higher eloquence of poetry.

Rhetoricians distinguished three stages in the production of discourse: *inventio* (finding or discovery), *dispositio* (arranging), and *elocutio* (style). Since the classical discipline aimed always at practical oratory (e.g. winning a case in court, or making a point effectively in council), *memoria* (memory) and *pronuntiatio* (delivery) were added. For the Renaissance, however, rhetoric became the art of writing. Under the heading of *elocutio*, style became stratified into three levels, *elevated* or high, *elegant* or middle, and *plain* or low. The proper fitting of these styles to the subject of discourse comprised the subject of decorum (*q.v.*).

Another area of rhetorical theory was concerned with classification of devices of language into *schemes, tropes,* and *figures.* A basic but somewhat confused distinction between figures of speech and figures of thought need not concern us here, but we may roughly distinguish between schemes (or patterns) of words, and tropes as manipulations of meanings, and of making words non-literal.

Common Schemes

anadiplosis repeating the terminal word in a clause as the start of the next one: "Pleasure might cause her read; reading might cause her know; / Knowledge might pity win, and pity grace obtain" (Sidney, *Astrophel and Stella*).

anaphora the repetition of a word or phrase at the openings of successive clauses, e.g. "The Lord sitteth above the water floods. The Lord remaineth King for-

ever. The Lord shall give strength unto his people. The Lord shall give his
people the blessing of peace."

chiasmus   a pattern of criss-crossing a syntactic structure, whether of noun and adjective, e.g. "Empty his bottle, and his girlfriend gone," or of a reversal of
normal syntax with similar effect, e.g. "A fop her passion, and her prize, a
sot," reinforced by assonance (*q.v.*). Chiasmus may even extend to assonance,
as in Coleridge's line "In Xanadu did Kubla Khan."

Common Tropes

metaphor and simile   both involve comparison of one thing to another, the difference being that the *simile* will actually compare, using the words "like" or
"as," while the metaphor identifies one with the other, thus producing a
non-literal use of a word or attribution. Thus, Robert Burns's "O, my love is
like a red, red rose / That's newly sprung in June" is a simile; had Burns
written, "My love, thou art a red, red rose . . .", it would have been a
metaphor—and indeed, it would not mean that the lady had acquired petals.
In modern critical theory, *metaphor* has come to stand for various non-
expository kinds of evocative signification. I. A. Richards, the modern critic
most interested in a general theory of metaphor in this sense, has contributed
the terms *tenor* (as in the case above, the girl) and *vehicle* (the rose) to
designate the components. See also *Epic Simile*.

metonymy   a trope in which the vehicle is closely and conventionally associated with
the tenor, e.g. "crown" and "king," "pen" and "writing," "pencil" and
"drawing," "sword" and "warfare."

synecdoche   a trope in which the part stands for the whole, e.g. "sail" for "ship."

hyperbole   intensifying exaggeration, e.g. the combined synecdoche and hyperbole
in which Christopher Marlowe's Faustus asks of Helen of Troy "Is this the
face that launched a thousand ships / And burned the topless towers of Ilium?"

oxymoron   literally, sharp-dull; a figure of speech involving a witty paradox, e.g.
"sweet harm"; "darkness visible" (Milton, *Paradise Lost* I.63).

Rhyme Royal   See *Troilus stanza*.

Right Reason   A natural faculty of intelligence in man, his capability of choosing
between moral alternatives. In the humanism of the Renaissance, Aristotle's
term, *orthos logos*, associated with the Latin word *ratio*, was thought of as
having preceded the fallen knowledge acquired in Paradise by Adam and
Eve's first sin.

Romance   (1) A medieval tale of chivalric or amorous adventure, in prose or verse,
with the specification that the material be fictional. Later on, there developed cycles of stories, such as those involving Arthurian material or the
legends of Charlemagne. Many of these, particularly the Arthurian, came
to involve the theme of courtly love (*q.v.*)

(2) In the Renaissance, romance becomes more complex and literary,
involving some degree of consciousness on the part of the author that he was
reworking medieval materials (Spenser's *Faerie Queene*, of Arthurian legends; Ariosto's *Orlando Furioso*, of Charlemagne's heroic knight; Tasso's
Gerusalemme Liberata, of stories of the Crusades).

(3) Prose romance, the 19th-century outgrowth of earlier essays into the

Gothic (*q.v.*) tale, represents a poetic kind of narrative to be clearly distinguished (in England if not in America) from the mode of the novel (e.g. Mary Shelley's *Frankenstein* and Hawthorne's *The Scarlet Letter* are both prose romance).

Rondeau, Roundel   A strict French poetic form, thirteen lines of eight to ten syllables, divided into stanzas of five, three, and five lines, using two rhymes only and repeating the first word or first few words of line one after the second and third stanzas. The two terms are used interchangeably in the Middle Ages.

Satire   A literary mode painting a distorted verbal picture of part of the world in order to show its true moral, as opposed merely to its physical, nature. In this sense, Circe, the enchantress in Homer's *Odyssey* who changed Odysseus' men into pigs (because they made pigs of themselves while eating) and would have changed Odysseus into a fox (for he was indeed foxy), was the first satirist. Originally the Latin word *satura* meant a kind of literary grab bag, or medley, and a satire was a fanciful kind of tale in mixed prose and verse; but later a false etymology connected the word with *satyr* and thus with the grotesque. Satire may be in verse or in prose; in the 16th and 17th centuries, the Roman poets Horace and Juvenal were imitated and expanded upon by writers of satiric moral verse, the tone of the verse being wise, smooth, skeptical, and urbane, that of the prose, sharp, harsh, and sometimes nasty. A tradition of English verse satire runs through Donne, Jonson, Dryden, Pope, and Samuel Johnson; of prose satire, Addison, Swift, and Fielding.

Scholasticism, Schoolmen   Scholasticism is the term used for the philosophy and theology of the Middle Ages. This consisted of rational inquiry into revealed truth; for it was important to understand what one believed. This technique of disposition was developed by the Schoolmen over a long period, reaching its perfection in Peter Abelard (1079–1142). In the 13th century it absorbed the newly discovered Aristotelian philosophy and method. In this phase its greatest exponent was St. Thomas Aquinas (*c.* 1225–74), who became the chief medieval philosopher and theologian; his authority, challenged in the 16th century, was more seriously contested in the 17th century by the adherents of the "new science."

Seneca   Lucius Annaeus Seneca (4 B.C.–65 A.D.) was an important source of Renaissance stoicism (*q.v.*), a model for the "closet" drama of the period, and an exemplar for the kind of prose that shunned the Ciceronian loquacity of early humanism and cultivated terseness. He was Nero's tutor; in 62 A.D. he retired from public life, and in 65 was compelled to commit suicide for taking part in a political conspiracy. He produced writings on ethics and physics, as well as ten tragedies often imitated in the Renaissance.

Sensibility   (1) In the mid-18th century, the term came to be used in a literary context to refer to a susceptibility to fine or tender feelings, particularly involving the feelings and sorrows of others. This became a quality to be cultivated in despite of stoical rejections of unreasonable emotion which the neoclassicism (*q.v.*) of the earlier Augustan age had prized. The meaning of the word blended easily into "sentimentality"; but the literary period in England characterized by the work of writers such as Sterne, Goldsmith, Gray, Collins, and Cowper is often called the Age of Sensibility.

(2) A meaning more important for modern literature is that of a special kind of total awareness, an ability to make the finest discriminations in its perception of the world, and yet at the same time not lacking in a kind of force by the very virtue of its own receptive power. The varieties of awareness celebrated in French literature from Baudelaire through Marcel Proust have been adapted by modernist English critics, notably T. S. Eliot, for a fuller extension of the meaning of *sensibility*. By the term "dissociation of sensibility," Eliot implied the split between the sensuous and the intellectual faculties which he thought characterized English poetry after the Restoration (1660).

Sententia A wise, fruitful saying, functioning as a guide to morally correct thought or action.

Sestina Originally a Provençal lyric form supposedly invented by Arnaut Daniel in the 12th century, and one of the most complex of those structures. It has six stanzas of six lines each, folllowed by an *envoi* (*q.v.*) or *tornada* of three lines. Instead of rhyming, the end-words of the lines of the first stanza are all repeated in the following stanzas, but in a constant set of permutations. The *envoi* contains all six words, three in the middle of each line. D. G. Rossetti, Swinburne, Pound, Auden, and other modern poets have used the form, and Sir Philip Sidney composed a magnificent double-sestina, "Ye Goat-herd Gods."

Skepticism A philosophy that denies the possibility of certain knowledge, and, although opposed to Stoicism and Epicureanism (*q.v.*), advocated *ataraxy*, imperturbability of mind. Skepticism originated with Pyrrhon (*c.* 360–270 B.C.), and its chief transmitter was Sextus Empiricus (*c.* 200 B.C.). In the Renaissance, skepticism had importance as questioning the power of the human mind to know truly (for a classic exposition see Donne's *Second Anniversary*, ll. 254–300), and became a powerful influence in morals and religion through the advocacy of Montaigne.

Sonnet A basic lyric form, consisting of fourteen lines of iambic pentameter rhymed in various patterns. The *Italian* or *Petrarchan* sonnet is divided clearly into *octave* and *sestet*, the first rhyming *abba abba* and the second in a pattern such as *cdc dcd*. The *Shakespearean* sonnet consists of three quatrains followed by a couplet: *abab cdcd efef gg*. In the late 16th century in England, sonnets were written either independently as short epigrammatic forms, or grouped in sonnet sequences, i.e. collections of upwards of a hundred poems, in imitation of Petrarch, purportedly addressed to one central figure or muse—a lady usually with a symbolic name like "Stella" or "Idea." Milton made a new kind of use of the Petrarchan form, and the Romantic poets continued in the Miltonic tradition. Several variations have been devised, including the addition of "tails" or extra lines, or the recasting into sixteen lines, instead of fourteen.

Stoicism, Stoics Philosophy founded by Zeno (335–263 B.C.), and opposing the hedonistic tendencies of Epicureanism (*q.v.*). The Stoics' world-view was pantheistic: God was the energy that formed and maintained the world, and wisdom lay in obedience to this law of nature as revealed by the conscience. Moreover, every man is free because the life according to nature and conscience is available to all; so too is suicide—a natural right. Certain Stoics saw the end of the world as caused by fire. In the Renaissance, Latin Stoicism, especially that of Seneca (*q.v.*), had a revival of influence and was Christianized in various ways.

Strong Lines The term used in the 17th century to refer to the tough, tense conceit (*q.v.*)-laden verse of Donne and his followers.

Style See *Decorum*.

Sublime "Lofty"; as a literary idea, originally the basic concept of a Greek treatise (by the so-called "Longinus") on style. In the 18th century, however, the *sublime* came to mean a loftiness perceivable in nature, and sometimes in art—a loftiness different from the composed vision of landscape known as the *picturesque*, because of the element of wildness, power, and even terror. The *beautiful*, the picturesque, and the sublime became three modes for the perception of nature.

Symbolism (1) Broadly, the process by which one phenomenon, in literature, stands for another, or group of others, and usually of a different sort. Clearcut cases of this in medieval and Renaissance literature are *emblems* or *attributes* (see *Personification; Allegory*). Sometimes conventional symbols may be used in more than one way, e.g. a mirror betokening both truth and vanity. See also *Figure; Emblem*.

(2) In a specific sense (and often given in its French form, *symbolisme*), an important esthetic concept for modern literature, formulated by French poets and critics of the later 19th century following Baudelaire. In this view, the literary symbol becomes something closer to a kind of commanding, central metaphor, taking precedence over any more discursive linguistic mode for poetic communication. The effects of this concept on literature in English have been immense; and some version of the concept survives in modern notions of the poetic *image*, or *fiction*.

Temperaments The balance of combinations of humors (*q.v.*) which in the medieval and Renaissance periods was believed to determine the psychosomatic make-up or "complexion" of a man or a woman. See *Renaissance Psychology*.

Topographical Poem A descriptive poem popular in the 17th and 18th centuries and devoted to a specific scene or landscape with the addition (in the words of Samuel Johnson in 1799) of "historical retrospection or incidental meditation." Sir John Denham's "Cooper's Hill" (1642) is an influential example of the tradition (which includes also Pope's "Windsor Forest") and sometimes blends with the genre of a poem in praise of a particular house or garden.

Topos Greek for "place," commonplace; in rhetoric (*q.v.*), either a general argument, description, or observation that could serve for various occasions; or a method of inventing arguments on a statement or contention. It is often used now to mean a basic literary topic (either a proposition such as the superiority of a life of action to that of contemplation, or vice versa; of old age vs. youth; or a description, such as that of the *locus amoenus* (*q.v.*), the pleasant garden place, Paradise, which allows many variations of thought and language.

Trivium The course of study in the first three of the seven liberal arts—grammar,

rhetoric, and logic (or dialectic): the basis of the medieval educational program in school and university. See also *Quadrivium*.

Troilus stanza   Or *rhyme royal;* iambic pentameters in stanzas of seven lines, rhyming *ababbcc*, popularized by Chaucer in his poem *Troilus and Criseyde*
and called *rhyme royal* supposedly on account of its use by James I of Scotland, king and poet.

Trope   (1) See *Rhetoric*. (2) In the liturgy of the Catholic Church, a phrase,
sentence, or verse with its musical setting, introduced to amplify or embellish
some part of the text of the mass or the office (i.e. the prayers and Scripture
readings recited daily by priests, religious, and even laymen) when chanted
in choir. Tropes of this second kind were discontinued in 1570 by the authority of Pope Pius V. Troping new material into older or conventional patterns
seems to have been, in a general way, a basic device of medieval literature,
and was the genesis of modern drama.

Type, Typology   (1) Strictly, in medieval biblical interpretation, the prefiguration
of the persons and events of the New Testament by persons and events of
the Old, the Old Testament being fulfilled in, but not entirely superseded
by, the New. Thus, the Temptation and Fall of Man were held to prefigure
the first Temptation of Christ, pride in each case being the root of the
temptation, and a warning against gluttony the moral lesson to be drawn
from both. The Brazen Serpent raised up by Moses was held to prefigure
the crucifixion of Christ; Isaac, as a sacrificial victim ("God will provide his
own Lamb," says Abraham to him) is a *type* of Christ. The forty days and
nights of the Deluge, the forty years of Israel's wandering in the desert, Moses'
forty days in the desert are all typologically related.

(2) In a looser sense, a person or event seen as a model or paradigm. See
also *Figure*.

Ubi Sunt . . .   A motif introducing a lament for the passing of all mortal and
material things: e.g. "*Ubi sunt qui ante nos in mundo fuere?*" (Where are
they who went before us in this world?), or "Where are the snows of yes-
teryear?" (Swinburne's translation from the French of Villon's *ballade*).

Virelay   A French poetic form, a dance song; short, with two or three rhymes, and
two lines of the first stanza as a refrain.

Wars of the Roses   Series of encounters between the house of Lancaster (whose
emblem was the red rose) and the house of York (whose emblem was the
white), which took place between 1455 and 1485 to decide the right of possession of the English throne. At the Battle of Bosworth Field in 1485 the
Lancastrian Henry Tudor defeated the Yorkist Richard III and was proclaimed king as Henry VII. He married Elizabeth of York, daughter of King
Edward IV.

Worthies, Nine   Nine exemplary heroes, three from the Bible (Joshua, David,
Judas Maccabaeus); three from pagan antiquity (Hector of Troy, Alexander
the Great, Julius Caesar), and three from "Christian" romance (King Arthur,
the Emperor Charlemagne, and Godfrey of Bouillon, a leader of the First
Crusade and King of Jerusalem). They were favorite figures for tapestries

(see Fig. 46 in illustrations for the Medieval section of this Anthology) and pageants.

Wit   (1) Originally, "intellect," "intelligence"; later, "creative intelligence," or poetical rather than merely mechanical intellectual power. Thus, during the age of Dryden and Pope, a poet might be called a wit without any compromising sense. In the 19th century, "wit" came to mean verbal agility or cleverness, as opposed to the more creative powers of the mind. (2) More specifically, in literary history, as characterizing the poetic style of John Donne and his 17th-century followers. The Augustan age would contrast this with the "true wit" of *neoclassical* (*q.v*) poetry.

Yorkists   See *Wars of the Roses*.

Zodiac   In astrology, a belt of the celestial sphere, about eight or nine degrees to either side of the ecliptic (the apparent orbit of the sun), within which the apparent motions of the sun, moon, and planets take place. It is divided into twelve equal parts, the signs, through each of which the sun passes in a month. Each division once coincided with one of the constellations after which the signs are named: Aries (Ram)—in Chaucer's time the sun entered this sign on 12 March; Taurus (Bull); Gemini (Twins); Cancer (Crab); Leo (Lion); Virgo (Virgin); Libra (Scales); Scorpio; Sagittarius (Archer); Capricornus (Goat); Aquarius (Water-Carrier); Pisces (Fishes). Each zodiacal sign was believed to govern a part of the human body. See *Astronomy and Astrology*.

Suggestions for Further Reading

MEDIEVAL ENGLISH LITERATURE

This reading list is deliberately summary: it cites the books most immediately helpful in providing a text or an introductory study. From the bibliographies and footnotes contained in these, the student can find his way to the more elaborate text editions and the more extended critical and historical studies.

General Backgrounds: Europe Medieval English literature is part of a larger European unit: its relations with both the classical and the medieval vernacular literatures of the Continent should always be kept in mind. The themes and modes of these literatures are splendidly treated in the first ten essays—three of them concerned with Antiquity—of Erich Auerbach, *Mimesis: The Representation of Reality in Western Literature* (trans. Willard R. Trask), 1957. Auerbach's long paper "Figura," in his *Scenes from the Drama of European Literature,* 1959, is also important. An older work, well worth reading, on European literature from the sixth century to the twelfth, is W. P. Ker's *The Dark Ages,* 1904.

For the wider context of medieval thought, Gordon Leff's *Medieval Thought: St. Augustine to Ockham,* 1958, is informative. The most stimulating general introduction oriented toward literature is C. S. Lewis's *The Discarded Image: An Introduction to Medieval and Renaissance Literature,* 1964.

The interrelations of European literature, thought, and art during the medieval period are treated by George Henderson in his lively companion volumes *Early Medieval,* 1972, and *Gothic,* 1967, in the series Style and Civilization.

For the intellectual and material conditions of life in Europe during the later Middle Ages, with their antecedents, the classic study is Johan Huizinga's *The Waning of the Middle Ages,* 1924. The best preliminary account of medieval daily life is Eileen Power's *Medieval People,* 1924.

Backgrounds: England The best introduction to the literature of England from Anglo-Saxon times to the end of the Middle Ages is still W. P. Ker's *Medieval English Literature,* 1912. Longer and more exhaustive is A. C. Baugh, ed., *A Literary History of England,* 1948; a useful survey, with bibliographies, is W. L. Renwick and H. Orton, *The Beginnings of English Literature to Skelton,* 3rd ed., revised by M. F. Wakelin, 1966.

The social and political background is treated in companion volumes by C. N. L. Brooke, *From Alfred to Henry III, 871–1272,* 1961, and George Holmes, *The Later*

Middle Ages, 1272–1485, 1962. G. M. Trevelyan's *Illustrated Social History of England*, 1949, is less satisfactory on the Middle Ages than on other periods, but is useful. For the artistic achievement of England in the Middle Ages, consult Margaret Rickert, *Painting in Britain: The Middle Ages*, 2nd ed., 1965; Lawrence Stone, *Sculpture in Britain: The Middle Ages*, 1955; and G. F. Webb, *Architecture in Britain: The Middle Ages*, 1959—all valuable and fully illustrated volumes in the Pelican History of Art.

Anglo-Saxon England and Old English Literature   A classic study is H. M. Chadwick's *The Heroic Age*, 1912; but the best and fullest general history is Sir Frank Stenton's *Anglo-Saxon England*, 3rd ed., 1971, one of the finest volumes in the Oxford History of England. P. Hunter Blair's *An Introduction to Anglo-Saxon England*, 1956, is a useful shorter survey, with illustrations, but the best introduction is Dorothy Whitelock's *The Beginnings of English Society*, 1952. For art and archaeology this can be supplemented by the best preliminary study of the subject, David M. Wilson's *The Anglo-Saxons*, 1960.

Of primary sources, *The Anglo-Saxon Chronicle* has been well translated by G. N. Garmonsway, 1953; and Venerable Bede's *Ecclesiastical History of the English People*, by L. Sherley-Price, 1955.

For Old English literature, the best survey is C. L. Wrenn's *A Study of Old English Literature*, 1967; while S. B. Greenfield's *A Critical History of Old English Literature*, 1965, is useful.

BEOWULF

Editions   The standard edition of the text is F. Klaeber, ed., *Beowulf and the Fight at Finnesburh*, 3rd ed., 1950; but C. L. Wrenn, ed., *Beowulf, with the Finnesburh Fragment*, 3rd ed., 1973, is more up-to-date and often easier to use. Neither edition has a translation, but both are very fully annotated. There are prose translations by J. R. Clark Hall, with introduction and notes by C. L. Wrenn, and preface by J. R. R. Tolkien, 1950; and by E. Talbot Donaldson, 1966 (excellent). Besides the verse translation by Charles W. Kennedy used in this volume, there is a fine poetic version by Kevin Crossley-Holland, with helpful introduction and notes by Bruce Mitchell, 1968.

Critical Studies   R. W. Chambers's *Beowulf: An Introduction*, 3rd ed., with Supplement by C. L. Wrenn, 1959, is the basic and encyclopedic work on *Beowulf*. Good selections of critical essays are Lewis E. Nicholson, ed., *An Anthology of Beowulf Criticism*, and Donald K. Fry, ed., *The Beowulf Poet: A Collection of Critical Essays*, 1968, which both include the most important and influential article so far published on the poem, J. R. R. Tolkien's "Beowulf: The Monsters and the Critics," from *Proceedings of the British Academy* XXII, 1936. J. C. Pope's *The Rhythm of Beowulf*, 1942, is the most elaborate study of the meter; and Dorothy Whitelock's *The Audience of Beowulf*, 1951, the best study of its social and cultural setting.

Recordings   Readings from *Beowulf*, in the original Old English, are available in recordings by Jess B. Bessinger, Jr., *Beowulf, Cædmon's Hymn, and Other Old English Poems*, Cædmon TC 1161; by Nevill Coghill and Norman Davis, *Beowulf*, with introductory material, Spoken Arts 918; by Charles W. Dunn, *Early English*

Poetry, Folkways FL 9851; and by J. C. Pope and H. Kökeritz, *Beowulf and Chaucer,* Lexington 5505.

Shorter Old English Poems   In addition to C. W. Kennedy's *Anthology of Old English Poetry,* translated into alliterative verse, 1960 (used in this Anthology), there are verse translations by Michael Alexander, *The Earliest English Poems,* 1966 (made on different principles from Kennedy's), and by Kevin Crossley-Holland, *The Battle of Maldon and Other Old English Poems,* ed. Bruce Mitchell, 1965. *The Dream of the Rood* has recently (1970) been edited by Michael Swanton, with excellent introduction and notes.

Middle English Literature   Exhaustive general surveys are E. K. Chambers, *English Literature at the Close of the Middle Ages,* 1945, and H. S. Bennett, *Chaucer and the Fifteenth Century,* 1947, both volumes in the Oxford History of English Literature. George Kane, *Middle English Literature,* 1951, and the later sections of W. P. Ker, *Medieval English Literature,* 1912, are the best short introductions. For the 14th century, D. S. Brewer, *Chaucer and His Times,* 1963, is a good general survey; and J. A. Burrow, *Ricardian Poetry: Chaucer, Gower, Langland and the Gawain Poet,* 1971, a stimulating study of these poets and their milieu. The background is usefully treated in Gervase Mathew, *The Court of Richard II,* 1968.

GEOFFREY CHAUCER

Editions   Still basic is W. W. Skeat, ed., *The Works of Geoffrey Chaucer,* in six volumes and a further collection, *Chaucerian and Other Pieces,* 1894–97, with extensive commentary; but the most informative single-volume edition is F. N. Robinson, ed., *The Complete Works,* 2nd ed., 1957, with explanatory notes and glossary. The most helpful substantial selection is E. Talbot Donaldson, ed., *Chaucer's Poetry: An Anthology for the Modern Reader,* 1958.

Critical Studies and Handbooks   The best collection for the history of Chaucer criticism is J. A. Burrow, ed., *Geoffrey Chaucer,* in the Penguin Critical Anthologies series, 1969 (excerpts). Collections of modern critical essays ed. by E. C. Wagenknecht, *Chaucer: Modern Essays in Criticism,* 1959; by R. J. Schoeck and Jerome Taylor, *Chaucer Criticism,* two vols., 1960–61; and by C. J. Owen, *Discussions of the Canterbury Tales,* 1961, all give a representative selection. The most rewarding group of essays by a single author and the best guide to the character of Chaucer's poems is E. Talbot Donaldson, *Speaking of Chaucer,* 1970.

Among monographs, John Livingston Lowes, *Geoffrey Chaucer,* 1934, remains the best introduction, especially to Chaucer's reading and his thought world. Useful additional materials are Charles Muscatine, *Chaucer and the French Tradition: A Study in Style and Meaning,* 1957, and Walter Clyde Curry, *Chaucer and the Medieval Sciences,* 2nd ed., 1960, the standard account of this special aspect. D. W. Robertson, Jr., *A Preface to Chaucer: Studies in Medieval Perspectives,* 1969, is the most lively and controversial of modern studies on Chaucer. A thorough and interesting introduction to the General Prologue of the *Canterbury Tales* is Muriel Bowden's *Commentary on the General Prologue to the Canterbury Tales,* 1967.

R. D. French, *A Chaucer Handbook,* 2nd ed., 1947, is a handy reference book; but for up-to-date essays, with excellent bibliographies, on all aspects of Chaucer, the most useful manual is Beryl Rowland, ed., *Companion to Chaucer Studies*, 1968.

The best short work on Chaucerian speech is Helge Kökeritz's *A Guide to Chaucer's Pronunciation*, 1954. *Chaucer's World*, ed. E. Rickert, C. C. Olson, and M. M. Crow, 1948, is excellent background reading, with contemporary accounts of events and many documents. Roger S. Loomis, ed., *A Mirror of Chaucer's World*, 1965, is a handsome picture book.

Recordings   Readings on records are given in Chaucerian pronunciation by Nevill Coghill, Norman Davis, and J. A. Burrow, of the General Prologue, Argo RG 401; by the same, with L. Davis, of the Nun's Priest's Tale, ll. 1–625 and some shorter poems, Argo RG 466; and by N. Coghill and N. Davis, the Pardoner's Tale, ll. 739–894, Spoken Arts 919.

SIR GAWAIN AND THE GREEN KNIGHT

Editions   The best old-spelling edition for the beginner is *Sir Gawain and the Green Knight*, ed. J. A. Burrow, 1972, in which obsolete letters and usages have been modernized and, wherever possible, a single spelling has been adopted for the same word spelled in different ways by the scribe. Notes and glossary are included. The standard old-spelling edition, however, is *Sir Gawain and the Green Knight*, ed. J. R. R. Tolkien and E. V. Gordon, revised by Norman Davis, 1967, with full notes and glossary.

In addition to that by Brian Stone, 1972 (used here), there are verse translations by Theodore Howard Banks, Jr., 1929; by Marie Borroff, 1968; and by John Gardner, in his *Complete Works of the Gawain Poet*, 1965.

Critical Studies   The most important critical essays are collected in R. J. Blanch, ed., *Sir Gawain and Pearl: Critical Essays*, 1966; Denton Fox, ed., *Twentieth Century Interpretations of Sir Gawain and the Green Knight*, 1968; and D. R. Howard and C. K. Zacher, eds., *Critical Studies of Sir Gawain and the Green Knight*, 1968. The book-length studies by Marie Borroff, *Sir Gawain and the Green Knight: A Stylistic and Metrical Study*, 1962, and L. D. Benson, *Art and Tradition in Sir Gawain and the Green Knight*, 1965, are full and careful; but the most stimulating is J. A. Burrow, *A Reading of Sir Gawain and the Green Knight*, 1965.

PIERS PLOWMAN

Editions   Standard for all three texts is *The Vision of William Concerning Piers the Plowman*, ed. W. W. Skeat, two vols., 1886, reissued with additional bibliography, 1954. It is copiously annotated, and though textually superseded for the A text by the edition of George Kane, 1960, its notes are still essential for an understanding of any of the three versions. Useful selections from the C text have been edited by Elizabeth Salter and Derek Pearsall in *Piers Plowman*, 1967.

There are verse translations by H. W. Wells, *The Vision of Piers Plowman*, 1935 (complete), and by Nevill Coghill, *Visions from Piers Plowman*, 1949 (selections). The most accurate is the complete prose version of the B text by J. F. Goodridge, 1959.

Critical Studies   The best short account of the poem is still that of R. W. Chambers, in his volume of essays *Man's Unconquerable Mind*, 1939, chaps. 4–5. *Piers Plowman:*

Critical Approaches, ed. S. S. Hussey, 1969, usefully collects major articles, and Elizabeth Salter's *Piers Plowman, An Introduction,* 1962, is an excellent brief study.

Medieval Drama Good collections, with annotations, are A. C. Cawley, ed., *Everyman and Medieval Miracle Plays,* 1960 (modernized spelling), and R. G. Thomas, ed., *Ten Miracle Plays,* 1966. The standard edition of the *Second Shepherds' Play* is that of A. C. Cawley, in *The Wakefield Pageants in the Towneley Cycle,* 1958; and the handiest single edition of *Everyman* is by the same editor, 1961.

E. K. Chambers's *The Medieval Stage,* two vols., 1905, is still standard, though dated; Hardin Craig, *English Religious Drama of the Middle Ages,* 1955, is somewhat old-fashioned, but informative. *Christian Rite and Christian Drama in the Middle Ages,* by O. B. Hardison, Jr., 1965, is among the most important recent contributions; and V. A. Kolve, *The Play Called Corpus Christi,* 1966, is a first-rate study. The best introduction is Arnold Williams, *The Drama of Medieval England,* 1961. Karl Young's *The Drama of the Medieval Church,* two vols., 1933 (corrected reprint, 1951), is one of the great and exhaustive works on medieval sacred drama.

Middle English Lyrics Standard collections are: *Medieval English Lyrics: A Critical Anthology,* ed. R. T. Davies, 1963 (little annotation); *A Selection of English Carols,* ed. Richard Leighton Greene, 1962, with excellent introduction and annotation; *The Oxford Book of Medieval English Verse,* ed. Celia and Kenneth Sisam, 1970, not annotated, but with helpful vocabulary at the end of each poem, and including extracts from longer poems as well as lyrics; and *Medieval English Lyrics,* ed. Theodore Silverstein, 1971, with good introduction and annotation. A fuller collection is James J. Wilhelm, trans. and ed., *Medieval Song: An Anthology of Hymns and Lyrics,* 1971, which begins with late Latin poetry. On records there is *Medieval English Lyrics,* with notes on texts by E. J. Dobson and on music by F. L. Harrison, Argo 443, 1965.

The best inclusive study is Peter Dronke, *The Medieval Lyric,* 1968, which includes Continental lyrics and deals with the English material in relation to them. Best on the English religious lyric is Rosemary Woolf's *The English Religious Lyric in the Middle Ages,* 1968. Douglas Gray's *Themes and Images in the Medieval English Religious Lyric,* 1972, is a splendid illustrated survey.

Popular Ballads The monumental collection of F. J. Child, ed., *The English and Scottish Popular Ballads,* five vols., 1882–98, is still standard, and gives variant versions. The student's one-volume edition, with texts and headnotes, ed. H. C. Sargent and George Lyman Kittredge, 1904, is the fullest of its kind. More inclusive and entertaining is M. J. C. Hodgart, ed., *The Faber Book of Ballads,* 1965, with a good introduction and a broad additional selection of modern ballads. James Kinsley, ed., *The Oxford Book of Ballads,* 1969, includes tunes, but has no introduction and confines itself to the older ballads. The most exhaustive work since Child (not yet complete), Bertrand H. Bronson, ed., *The Traditional Tunes of the Child Ballads,* four vols., 1959–70, collects the ballad tunes of the British Isles and the U.S.A. The best short introduction is M. J. C. Hodgart's study, *The Ballads,* 1950.

There are recordings as well—e.g. *The Child Ballads,* Topic 12T160–161 (taken down in the field); and Ewen MacColl and A. L. Lloyd, *English and Scottish Popular Ballads,* Riverside RLP12-624.

SIR THOMAS MALORY

Editions The standard is *The Works of Sir Thomas Malory,* ed. Eugène Vinaver,

2nd ed., three vols., 1967, which prints the Winchester MS., with the necessary supplements and variant readings from Caxton, and a full commentary. There is also a one-volume edition without commentary, 2nd ed., 1970. The Caxton version is most easily available as *Morte d'Arthur*, in Everyman's Library, 1906, without annotation.

Critical Studies   Still the best general study is Eugène Vinaver, *Malory*, 1929, re-issued 1970; and the same author's chapter in R. S. Loomis, ed., *Arthurian Literature in the Middle Ages: A Collaborative History*, 1959, is the finest short introduction. The essays in J. A. W. Bennett, ed., *Essays on Malory*, 1963, are all useful, but especially P. E. Tucker's "Chivalry in the *Morte*" and Sally Shaw's "Caxton and Malory." The most recent collection is that of R. M. Lumiansky, *Malory's Originality: A Critical Study of Le Morte Darthur*, 1964.

WILLIAM CAXTON

The best study of all aspects of Caxton is also a recent one: N. F. Blake's *Caxton and His World*, 1969.

WILLIAM DUNBAR

A one-volume edition of the poems, without notes, is W. Mackay Mackenzie's *The Poems of William Dunbar*, 1932; but the best way to begin on Dunbar is through the selection of *Poems*, with appreciations by various critics, and introduction, notes, and glossary by James Kinsley, 1958.

JOHN SKELTON

The standard edition is still that of Alexander Dyce, *The Poetical Works of John Skelton*, two vols., 1843, with notes. This is the basis of the unannotated, modern-spelling edition by Philip Henderson, 2nd ed., 1948. The best introductory selection is *Poems*, ed. Robert S. Kinsman, 1969, with introduction and commentary.

THE OTHER WORLD: PARADISE

Two treatments, the first more exhaustive, the second more perceptive, are H. R. Patch's *The Other World According to Descriptions in Medieval Literature*, 1950, and A. Bartlett Giamatti's *The Earthly Paradise and the Renaissance Epic*, 1966.

THE RENAISSANCE

General Historical Works   J. Burckhardt, *The Civilization of the Renaissance in Italy* (1860), tr. S. G. C. Middleman, two vols., 1958. J. D. Mackie, *The Early Tudors*, 1952. J. B. Black, *The Reign of Elizabeth*, 2nd ed., 1959. A. L. Rowse, *The England of Elizabeth*, 1950. Garrett Mattingly, *The Armada*, 1959. R. H. Tawney, *Religion and the Rise of Capitalism*, 1926, *Shakespeare's England*, 1916. William Haller, *The Rise of Puritanism*, 1938. Louis B. Wright, *Middle-Class Culture in Elizabethan England*,

1935. Godfrey Davies, *The Early Stuarts*, rev. ed., 1959. Carl J. Friedrich, *The Age of the Baroque*, 1952. G. M. Trevelyan, *England under the Stuarts*, 21st ed., 1949. Christopher Hill, *Puritanism and Revolution*, 1958, *A Century of Revolution*, 1961, *Intellectual Origins of the English Revolution*, 1965, and *God's Englishman* 1970, a study of Cromwell: all brilliant and Marxist. Different approaches are represented by C. V. Wedgwood's *The Great Rebellion: The King's Peace* (1955), and *The King's War* (1958); and by Perez Zagorin's *The Court and the Country*, 1970.

Intellectual and Cultural History   Arthur O. Lovejoy, *The Great Chain of Being*, 1936. E. M. W. Tillyard, *The Elizabethan World Picture*, rev. ed., 1956. C. S. Lewis, *The Discarded Image*, 1964. E. A. Burtt, *Metaphysical Foundations of Modern Science*, rev. ed., 1932. Sir Herbert Butterfield, *The Origins of Modern Science*, 1957. Donald S. Westfall, *Science and Religion in Seventeenth-Century England*, 1958. Thomas S. Kuhn, *The Copernican Revolution*, 1959. Charles Singer, *A Short History of Scientific Ideas to 1900*, 1959. Basil Willey, *The Seventeenth Century Background*, 1934. H. H. Rhys ed., *XVII Century Science and the Arts*, 1961. Norman Davy ed., *British Scientific Literature in the XVIIth Century*, 1953. Wilbur S. Howell, *Logic and Rhetoric in England*, 1956. Kitty Scoular, *Natural Magic*, 1965. J. A. Mazzeo, *Renaissance and Revolution*, 1965. John R. Mulder, *The Temple of the Mind*, 1969.

Literary History   C. S. Lewis, *English Literature in the Sixteenth Century, excluding Drama*, 1954. Douglas Bush, *English Literature in the Earlier Seventeenth Century*, (2nd rev. ed., 1962. Hallett Smith, *Elizabethan Poetry*, 1952. Frank Kermode, *English Pastoral Poetry from the Beginnings to Marvell*, 1952. F. P. Wilson, *Elizabethan and Jacobean*, 1945. J. W. Lever, *The Elizabethan Love Sonnet*, 1956. Wylie Sypher, *Four Stages of Renaissance Style*, 1955.

Critical Studies   (**Early**) *Elizabethan Critical Essays*, ed. G. G. Smith, two vols., 1904; and *Critical Essays of the Seventeenth Century*, three vols., 1908–1909, are important collections of texts. (**Modern**) Helpful anthologies are *Elizabethan Poetry: Modern Essays in Criticism*, ed. Paul J. Alpers, 1967; *Seventeenth-Century English Poetry: Modern Essays in Criticism*, ed. William R. Keast, rev. ed., 1971; *Seventeenth Century Prose: Modern Essays in Criticism*, ed. Stanley Fish, 1971; *The Metaphysical Poets*, ed. Frank Kermode, 1969. *Literary English Since Shakespeare*, ed. George Watson, 1970, is a useful guide. Works of one author include Mario Praz, *Studies in Seventeenth-Century Imagery*, 1939 (2nd ed., 1964); Rosamond Tuve, *Elizabethan and Metaphysical Imagery*, 1947; Austin Warren, *Rage for Order*, 1948; Ruth C. Wallerstein, *Studies in Seventeenth Century Poetic*, 1950; Odette de Mourgues, *Metaphysical, Baroque and Précieux Poetry*, 1953; M. M. Mahood, *Poetry and Humanism*, 1950; Marjorie Hope Nicolson, *The Breaking of the Circle*, 1960; Don Cameron Allen, *Image and Meaning*, 1960; A. Alvarez, *The School of Donne*, 1961; J. A. Mazzeo ed., *Reason and Imagination*, 1962; John Hollander, *The Untuning of the Sky*, 1961; Stanley Stewart, *The Enclosed Garden*, 1966.

On Prose Writing   Donald A. Stauffer, *English Biography before 1700*, 1930; George Williamson, *Seventeenth-Century Contexts*, 1960; F. P. Wilson, *Seventeenth-Century Prose: Five Lectures*, 1960; Joan Webber, *The Eloquent I*, 1968.

On Mythology   Douglas Bush, *Mythology and the Renaissance Tradition in English Poetry*, 1932 (rev. ed., 1936). Jean Seznec, *The Survival of the Pagan Gods*, 1953. Harry Levin, *The Myth of the Golden Age in the Renaissance*, 1969. John Armstrong, *The Paradise Myth*, 1969. Don Cameron Allen, *Mysteriously Meant*, 1970.

On Pictures and Images   Rosemary Freeman, *English Emblem Books*, 1967, is, along with Mario Praz (see above), the best introduction to what is becoming an important study. Geoffrey Whitney's *A Choice of Emblems*, 1586, Henry Peacham's *Minerva Brittana*, 1610, and George Wither's *A Collection of Emblems*, 1635, are all available in facsimile. E. H. Gombrich's *Symbolic Images*, 1972, provides theoretical backgrounds.

The Visual Arts in England   Ellis Waterhouse, *Painting in Britain 1530–1790*, 1953. John Summerson, *Architecture in Britain 1530–1830*, 4th ed., 1963; and *Inigo Jones*, 1966. Jean H. Hagstrum, *The Sister Arts*, 1958, and Mario Praz, *Mnemosyne*, 1970, are both good introductions to the relation of art and poetry. John Shearman's *Mannerism*, 1967, is a good corrective to some of the uneasy generalities of Wylie Sypher's *Four Stages of Renaissance Style* mentioned above. Edward Hyams, *The English Garden*, 1964, provides background material for a major poetic theme. Roy Strong, *The English Icon*, 1969, and his catalogue of *Tudor and Jacobean Portraits*, 1969, are both excellent, as is Marcia R. Poynton's *Milton and English Art*, 1970.

The English Bible   V. F. Storr, *The English Bible*, 1938. E. E. Willoughby, *The Making of the English Bible*, 1956. G. S. Paine, *The Learned Men*, 1959. F. F. Bruce, *The English Bible: A History of Translations . . .* , rev. ed. 1970.

THE ENGLISH HUMANISTS

There is no single work that is adequate on the Humanists, but C. S. Lewis, *English Literature in the Sixteenth Century, excluding Drama*, 1954, in the Oxford History of English Literature, has a characteristically vigorous survey. On sixteenth-century preoccupation with the English language, see Richard Foster Jones, *The Triumph of the English Language: A Survey of Opinions . . . from the Introduction of Printing to the Restoration*, 1953.

Sir Thomas More   The standard modern edition of More's works is far from complete, four volumes having been published so far, including the splendid text of *History of Richard III*, ed. R. S. Sylvester, 1963, with excellent introduction and commentary; and the very thorough *Utopia*, ed. Edward Surtz, S.J., and J. H. Hexter, 1965. Both these volumes in the Yale edition supply Latin and English texts, and the Yale *Utopia* translation is available in paperback, without commentary. As a translation it is less satisfactory than Paul Turner's version (1965) with its economical, first-rate commentary. Ralph Robinson's translation, available in Everyman's Library (n.d.) without annotation, is printed, along with the Latin text, in J. H. Lupton's edition of *Utopia*, 1895. More's translation of *The Life of John Picus, Earl of Mirandula* was edited by J. M. Rigg, 1890. An excellent introduction to More is provided by his letters, of which a selection, in translation, has been edited by Elizabeth Frances Rogers (1961) —including the letter from which an extract is given in the account of More's death in William Roper's *Life*. The standard edition of this *Life* by More's son-in-law was edited by E. V. Hitchcock (1935), with full commentary. There is a modernized version in R. S. Sylvester and Davis P. Harding eds., *Two Early Tudor Lives*, 1962. Still the best general account of More is R. W. Chambers, *Thomas More*, 1935; but the most useful accounts of *Utopia* are to be found in J. H. Hexter, *More's Utopia: The Biography of an Idea*, 1952, and in the essays in William Nelson ed., *Twentieth-Century Interpretations of Utopia*, 1968.

Sir Thomas Elyot   The edition of *The Book Named the Governor*, ed. H. H. S. Croft, two vols., 1880, in old spelling with copious commentary, has not been superseded. A modernized version, without notes, is edited by Stanford E. Lehmberg in Everyman's Library (1962).

The best study of the "courtesy" literature, including Elyot, Castiglione, and Hoby, is Ruth Kelso, *The Doctrine of the English Gentleman in the Sixteenth Century*, 1929; and the best book-length study of Elyot is by John M. Major, *Sir Thomas Elyot and Renaissance Humanism*, 1964.

Baldassare Castiglione and Sir Thomas Hoby   The standard edition of Castiglione's Italian is *Il Libro del Cortegiano*, ed. V. Cian, 4th ed., 1949. Hoby's translation was edited by Sir Walter Ralegh, as *The Book of the Courtier*, in the Tudor Translations series, 1900 (old spelling, no notes). It was also reprinted in Everyman's Library (n.d.). Two good modern translations of Castiglione, with introductions, are by Charles S. Singleton (1959) and George Bull (1967), both entitled *The Book of the Courtier*. An interesting essay on Hoby's translation is in F. O. Matthiessen, *Translation, an Elizabethan Art*, 1931, which is also relevant to the topic of sixteenth-century prose in general.

Roger Ascham   The only complete edition is by J. A. Giles, *The Whole Works*, four vols., 1864–65, in modern spelling, with some notes. *The English Works*, ed. W. A. Wright, 1904, uses old spelling, without annotation. The standard edition of *The Schoolmaster* is by J. E. B. Mayor, 1863, with fine annotation; and there is a useful annotated edition by R. J. Schoeck, 1966. A thorough, book-length study is Lawrence V. Ryan, *Roger Ascham*, 1963.

ELIZABETHAN SONG

Aside from modern editions of many of the anthologies and miscellanies by Hyder E. Rollins and other scholars, the main repository of texts set by the madrigal and lutenist composers is E. H. Fellowes, *English Madrigal Verse, 1588–1632*, 3rd ed., revised and enlarged by F. W. Sternfeld and D. Greer, 1967; but a vastly superior scholarly and critical edition, albeit of the solo songs alone, is Edward Doughtie, *Lyrics from English Airs*, 1970. Important studies dealing with relations between text and music are Bruce Pattison, *Music and Poetry of the English Renaissance*, 1948; and Catherine Ing, *Elizabethan Lyrics*, 1951. E. H. Fellowes, *The English Madrigal* (1926), and Peter Warlock, *The English Ayre* (1927), are older, more musicological studies; a good modern one is John Kerman, *The Elizabethan Madrigal*, 1962. John Stevens, *Music and Poetry in the Early Tudor Court*, 1961, is an important work. M. C. Boyd, *Elizabethan Music and Musical Criticism*, 1940, remains a good, but rambling, introductory treatment. Douglas L. Peterson's *The English Lyric from Wyatt to Donne*, 1967, is concerned purely with texts.

SIR THOMAS WYATT

The best edition is *Poems*, ed. Kenneth Muir, 1949, with additional poems in H. A. Mason's *Humanism and Poetry in the Early Tudor Court*, 1959. John Stevens's *Music and Poetry in the Early Tudor Court*, 1961, Kenneth Muir's *Life and Letters of Sir Thomas Wyatt*, 1963, Raymond Southall's *The Courtly Maker*, 1964, and Patricia Thomson's *Sir Thomas Wyatt and His Background*, 1965, all provide valuable historical and cultural materials. Also see Douglas L. Peterson's *The English Lyric from Wyatt to Donne*, 1967.

HENRY HOWARD, EARL OF SURREY

The best edition of the *Poems* is that of Emrys Jones, 1964, replacing F. M. Padelford's earlier *Poems*, rev. ed., 1928. Hyder Rollins edited Tottel's Miscellany, rev. ed., 1965. Gerald Bullett, *Silver Poets of the Sixteenth Century*, 1947, reproduces all but the Virgil translation. See also John L. Thompson, *The Founding of English Metre*, 1961. A biography is *Henry Howard, Earl of Surrey*, by E. Casaday, 1938.

SIR PHILIP SIDNEY

Editions   *The Complete Works* were edited in four volumes by Albert Feuillerat (1912–16), but the standard text of the poems is that of William A. Ringler (1962). *An Apology for Poetry* was edited by Geoffrey Shepherd (1965), and the recently discovered Norwich MS. of the *Apology* was edited by Mary R. Mahl (1969). The translation of the Psalms, with the Countess of Pembroke, was edited by J. C. Rathmell (1963).

Critical Studies   Kenneth O. Myrick, *Sir Philip Sidney as a Literary Craftsman*, 1935. John Buxton, *Sir Philip Sidney and the English Renaissance*, 1954. Walter Davis and Richard A. Lanham, *Sidney's Arcadia*, 1965. David Kalstone, *Sidney's Poetry*, 1965. Neil Rudenstine, *Sidney's Poetic Development*, 1967. Mark Rose, *Heroic Love*, 1968.

Biography   Fulke Greville's *Life of Sidney* was edited by Nowell Smith in 1907, and there are modern biographies by M. W. Wallace, *Life of Sir Philip Sidney*, 1915 (repr. 1967), and Mona Wilson, *Sir Philip Sidney*, 1931. The definitive life is that of James Osborn, *Young Philip Sidney*, 1972.

FULKE GREVILLE, LORD BROOKE

G. Bullough edited *Poems and Dramas*, two vols., 1939. *Caelica* has been edited by Una Ellis-Fermor, 1936. There is a *Selected Poems* with a splendid essay by Thom Gunn (1965). A good study is Morris W. Croll's *The Works of Fulke Greville*, 1903; and Joan Rees published her *Fulke Greville . . . A Critical Biography* in 1971.

EDMUND SPENSER

Editions   *The Poetical Works*, ed. J. C. Smith and E. de Selincourt, three vols., 1909–10; and in one vol., 1912. *Variorum* Edition, ten vols., 1932–49. *Selections . . .* (with commentary), edited by F. Kermode, 1965.

Critical Studies   W. L. Renwick, *Edmund Spenser*, 1925. E. Greenlaw, *Spenser's Historical Allegory*, 1932. C. B. Millican, *Spenser and the Table Round*, 1934. I. E. Rathborne, *The Meaning of Spenser's Fairyland*, 1937. C. S. Lewis, *The Allegory of Love*, 1936, and later editions; see also his *English Literature in the Sixteenth Century, excluding Drama* (Vol. III of the Oxford History of English Literature), 1954, and the posthumous *Spenser's Images of Life*, 1967. J. W. Bennett, *The Evolution of the Faerie Queene*, 1942. V. K. Whitaker, *The Religious Basis of Spenser's Thought*, 1950. A. K. Hieatt, *Short Time's Endless Monument*, 1960. A. C. Hamilton, *Structure of Allegory in Faerie Queene*, 1961. G. Hough, *A Preface to The Faerie Queene*, 1962. R. Ellrodt, *Neoplatonism in the Poetry of Spenser*, 1960. D. S. Cheney, *Spenser's Image of Nature*, 1966. William Nelson, *The Poetry of Edmund Spenser* (dealing with all the poetry), 1963. A. Fowler, *Spenser and the Numbers of Time*, 1964. R. Tuve, *Allegorical Imagery*, 1966. P. Alpers, *The Poetry of the Faerie Queene*, 1967. H. Tonkin, *Spenser's Courteous Pastoral*, 1972. Angus Fletcher, *The Prophetic Moment*, 1972. F. Kermode, *Shakespeare, Spenser, Donne*, 1971. An article of high interest is F. Yates's "Queen Elizabeth as Astraea," in *Journal of the Warburg and Courtauld Institutes*, X (1947), 27–82. See also Roy C. Strong, *Portraits of Queen Elizabeth*, 1963.

SIR WALTER RALEGH

There is a *Complete Works* in eight volumes, 1829, and a selection from the *History of the World* by C. A. Patrides, 1972. Agnes M. C. Latham's edition of the poems is standard (rev. ed., 1951). E. A. Strathmann's *Ralegh: A Study in Elizabethan Skepticism*, 1951, remains unexcelled. Recent biographies are *Sir Walter Raleigh* by Willard M. Wallace, 1959, and W. F. Oakeshott's *The Queen and the Poet*, 1960.

CHRISTOPHER MARLOWE

Editions   The writings have been edited by R. H. Case and others in six volumes, (1930–33). W. W. Greg's parallel text of *Dr. Faustus*, 1950, is standard, and his smaller conjectural reconstruction of the original (1950) is the other text from which all others now derive, though the validity of his textural arguments has now been contested by Fredson Bowers. See also the edition of J. D. Jump (1968), as well as the *Complete Poems and Translations*, ed. Stephen Orgel, 1971.

Critical Studies   F. S. Boas, *Christopher Marlowe*, 1940. P. H. Kochner, *Christopher Marlowe*, 1946. J. Bakeless, *The Tragical History of Christopher Marlowe*, 1942. H. Levin, *The Overreacher*, 1953. D. Cole, *Suffering and Evil in the Plays of Christopher Marlowe*, 1962. J. B. Steane, *Marlowe*, 1964.

Biography   Major discoveries about Marlowe's life have been reported in L. Hotson's *The Death of Christopher Marlowe*, 1925.

SAMUEL DANIEL

The only complete edition is by A. B. Grosart, *The Complete Works in Verse and Prose*, five vols., 1885–96 (repr. 1963). The *Poems, and A Defence of Ryme* was edited by A. C. Sprague in 1930. See also, G. G. Smith, *Elizabethan Critical Essays*, 1904, and studies by Ernest W. Talbert, *Problem of Order*, 1962, and Cecil Seronsy, *Samuel Daniel*, in the English Authors series, 1967.

MICHAEL DRAYTON

There is a standard edition of the *Works*, ed. J. W. Hebel, five vols., 1931–41. Oliver Elton's *Introduction to Michael Drayton*, 1895, and his later *Michael Drayton: A Critical Study*, 1905 (repr. 1966), have been reissued. A biographical study is B. H. Newdigate, *Michael Drayton and His Circle*, 1941. See also L. Zocca, *Elizabethan Narrative Poetry*, 1950.

WILLIAM SHAKESPEARE

Editions Standard editions, one volume per play, are the Arden, the Yale, the Pelican, and the Signet, all annotated. The best one-volume text is the Houghton Mifflin Shakespeare, scheduled for 1973, to which the six-volume *Concordance* of Marvin Spevack, 1970, is keyed.

Critical Studies Two very different critical approaches (out of very many) to the sonnets are G. Wilson Knight's *The Mutual Flame*, 1955, and Stephen Booth's *An Essay on Shakespeare's Sonnets*, 1969. Knight deals also with *The Phoenix and Turtle*, on which see also F. Kermode, *Shakespeare, Spenser, Donne*, 1971. Kermode discusses *The Tempest* in the Arden edition (1954, and later revisions), and in *Shakespeare, Spenser, Donne*. See also N. Frye, *A Natural Perspective*, 1965, and A. D. Nuttall, *Two Concepts of Allegory*, 1967; and, on the songs, Peter Seng, *The Vocal Songs in the Plays of Shakespeare*, 1967.

Biographies While the major work in Shakespearean biography is Samuel Schoenbaum, *Shakespeare's Lives*, 1970, the most useful brief work on Shakespeare's life is G. E. Bentley, *Shakespeare: A Biographical Handbook*, 1961.

THOMAS CAMPION

The standard text is that of Percival Vivian, *Campion's Works*, 1909; but a new one, ed. Walter R. Davis, *Works . . . with a Selection of the Latin Verse*, 1967, is more sophisticated in its annotations. There is a selection with essays by W. H. Auden and John Hollander (1972). Campion's musical settings are transcribed from lute tablature and edited by E. H. Fellowes in *The English School of Lutenist Song-Writers*, First and Second Series, 1920–66. Miles W. Kastendieck's *England's Musical Poet*, 1938, is the first study, a more recent one being by Edward Lowbury and others, *Thomas Campion, Poet, Composer, Physician*, 1970.

JOHN DONNE

Editions H. J. C. Grierson's 1912 edition of the *Poems* is supplemented rather than superseded by the editions of H. Gardner, *Divine Poems*, 1952, and *Elegies and the*

Songs and Sonnets, 1965; and of W. Milgate, *Satires, Epigrams, and Verse Letters,* 1967. There is a separate edition of *Anniversaries* by F. Manley, 1963; of *Sermons,* in ten volumes, by G. R. Potter and E. Simpson, 1953–62; of the *Devotions,* by J. Sparrow, 1923. The best selection, with complete verse and selected prose, was prepared by J. Hayward, 1929. Among other collections are *Complete Poetry,* ed. J. T. Shawcross, 1967; *Selected Prose,* chosen by E. Simpson and edited by H. Gardner and T. Healy, 1967; and *Poems,* ed. with commentary by A. J. Smith, 1970.

Critical Studies For the history of Donne criticism see J. E. Duncan, *The Revival of Metaphysical Poetry,* 1959, as well as the selections in F. Kermode ed., *Discussions of John Donne,* 1962. For specialized commentary, see P. Legouis, *Donne the Craftsman,* 1928; R. Tuve, *Elizabethan and Metaphysical Imagery,* 1947; J. B. Leishman, *The Monarch of Wit,* 1951 (1962); L. Unger, *The Man in the Name,* 1956. G. Williamson, *The Donne Tradition,* 1930, supports the orthodoxy founded on Eliot's essays, shaken by Tuve and others. Among shorter introductions are K. W. Gransden's *John Donne,* 1954; F. Kermode's *John Donne,* 1957; and also his *Shakespeare, Spenser, Donne,* 1971. The Twentieth Century Views collection of critiques was edited by Helen Gardner, 1962. On prose, see E. Simpson, *A Study of the Prose Works of John Donne,* 1948; and Joan Webber, *Contrary Music,* 1963. *Bibliography* by Geoffrey Keynes, 1914, 1932, 1958.

Biography Standard biography is *John Donne: A Life,* by R. C. Bald, 1970.

BEN JONSON

Editions The standard edition is that of C. H. Herford and P. and E. Simpson, eleven volumes, 1925–51; but in some instances, the modernized texts of the Yale Ben Jonson (1962–71) provide better readings. A good text of the poems is William B. Hunter ed., *The Complete Poetry of Ben Jonson,* 1963; that of the *Complete Masques* by Stephen Orgel, 1969, is masterful.

Critical Studies Important works include A. C. Swinburne's early *Study of Ben Jonson,* 1889; C. F. Wheeler's *Classical Mythology in the Plays, Masques and Poems of Ben Jonson,* 1938; L. C. Knights's *Drama and Society in the Age of Jonson,* 1937;

Jonas A. Barish's *Ben Jonson and the Language of Prose Comedy,* 1960; and Wesley Trimpi's *Ben Jonson's Poems: A Study in the Plain Style,* 1962. Stephen Orgel's *The Jonsonian Masque* may lead the reader to H. A. Evans, *English Masques,* 1897. Further works include Enid Welsford, *The Court Masque,* 1927; Allardyce Nicoll, *Stuart Masques and the Renaissance Stage,* 1937; D. J. Gordon, "Poet and Architect: The Intellectual Setting of the Quarrel Between Ben Jonson and Inigo Jones," *Journal of the Warburg and Courtauld Institutes,* XII (1949), 152–78; and Andrew J. Sabol, *Songs and Dances for the Stuart Masque,* 1959.

SEVENTEENTH-CENTURY LYRIC MODES

Wilfred Mellers, *Harmonious Meeting,* 1965, is particularly interesting in its treatment of music, poem, and stage spectacle. A standard series of texts on lyric traditions would include: F. R. Leavis, "The Line of Wit," in *Revaluation,* 1936; Geoffrey Walton, *Metaphysical to Augustan,* 1955; A. Alvarez, *The School of Donne,* 1961;

Louis L. Martz, *The Poetry of Meditation*, rev. ed., 1962; Lowry Nelson, Jr., *Baroque Lyric Poetry*, 1961; Frank J. Warnke, *European Metaphysical Poetry*, 1961, an anthology with comment; H. M. Richmond, *The School of Love*, 1964; Earl C. Miner, *The Metaphysical Mode from Donne to Cowley*, 1969; Jerome Mazzaro, *Transformations in the English Renaissance Lyric*, 1970. R. K. Ruthven, *The Conceit*, 1969, is an excellent handbook.

ROBERT HERRICK

The standard edition is L. C. Martin's *The Poetical Works* . . . (1956); also useful is the edition of J. Max Patrick, *The Complete Poetry* . . . 1963. There is a biographical and critical study by F. W. Moorman (1910). See also Sidney Musgrove, *The Universe of Herrick*, 1950; and John Press, *Robert Herrick*, 1961.

THOMAS CAREW

The standard edition is *Poems*, ed. Rhodes Dunlap, 1949. Edward I Selig's *The Flourishing Wreath*, 1958, is a modern study. Louis L. Martz's *The Wit of Love*, 1970, deals in good part with Carew, and with his masque *Coelum Britannicum;* but for an authoritative treatment of Carew's masque see the Stephen Orgel–Roy C. Strong edition of the drawings of Inigo Jones, 1973.

RICHARD LOVELACE

The standard text is C. H. Wilkinson ed., *Poems*, 1930. Cyril H. Hartmann, *The Cavalier Spirit and Its Influence on the Life and Work of Richard Lovelace*, 1925, is a primary study; but essays on "The Grasshopper" by D. C. Allen in *Image and Meaning*, 1960, and on "La Bona Bella Roba" by Marius Bewley in *Masks and Mirrors; Essays in Criticism*, 1970, give far more penetrating readings while representing radically different critical approaches. Also see H. M. Richmond, *The School of Love*, 1964.

EDMUND WALLER

The modern edition of the poems is by G. Thorn-Drury in two volumes (1893). Two recent studies are Alexander W. Allison, *Toward an Augustan Poetic: Edmund Waller's "Reform" of English Poetry*, 1962, and Warren L. Chernaik, *Poetry of Limitation*, 1968.

ABRAHAM COWLEY

The most complete modern edition is that of A. R. Waller, *English Writings*, two volumes, 1905–1906; but probably more accessible is *Poetry and Prose* . . . with introduction and notes by L. C. Martin (1949). The standard biography is *Abraham Cowley: The Muse's Hannibal*, by A. H. Nethercot, 1931; a good critical study is Robert B. Hinman, *Abraham Cowley's World of Order*, 1960. Samuel Johnson's famous assay on Cowley in the *Lives of the Poets* (1779) defined the "metaphysical" tradition from a somewhat hostile, neoclassical viewpoint.

ANDREW MARVELL

Editions   The standard edition of Marvell's writings by M. H. Margoliouth (1927; repr. 1952) was revised by P. Legouis and E. E. Duncan Jones (1971). There is a *Selected Poetry* with notes edited by F. Kermode (1967).

Critical studies   P. Legouis, *Andrew Marvell*, 1928. M. C. Bradbrook and M. G. Lloyd Thomas, *Andrew Marvell*, 1962. Rosalie Colie, *My Ecchoing Song: Andrew Marvell's Poetry of Criticism*, 1969. J. M. Wallace, *Destiny His Choice*, 1968. Donald M. Friedman, *Marvell's Pastoral Art*, 1970. The best essay remains that of T. S. Eliot in *Selected Essays*, 1932.

GEORGE HERBERT

The standard edition is of the works of F. E. Hutchinson (rev. ed., 1945), but an excellent text of the English poems was edited by Joseph H. Summers (1967); the Latin Poems were translated by Mark McCloskey and Paul R. Murphy (1965). The principal critical studies are: Rosamond Tuve, *A Reading of George Herbert*, 1952 (which is at its best in dealing with biblical allusions), and *Studies in Spenser, Herbert, and Milton*, 1970; Joseph H. Summers, *George Herbert: His Religion and Art*, 1954; Mary Ellen Rickey, *Utmost Art*, 1966; Arnold Stein, *George Herbert's Lyrics*, 1968; and Coburn Freer, *Music for a King*, 1971. Helen Vendler's critical work is in preparation. See also Louis L. Martz, *The Poetry of Meditation*, rev. ed., 1962.

RICHARD CRASHAW

The Poems, English, Latin and Greek, ed. L. C. Martin, 2nd ed., 1957, is the standard text. Important critical studies are those of Ruth C. Wallerstein, *Richard Crashaw: A Study in Style and Development*, 1959; and Austin Warren, *Richard Crashaw: A Study in Baroque Sensibility*, 1937; Mario Praz, *The Flaming Heart*, 1958; Mary Ellen Rickey, *Rhyme and Meaning in Richard Crashaw*, 1961; George W. Williams, *Image and Symbol in the Sacred Poetry of Richard Crashaw*, 1963. Robert T. Petersson, *Art of Ecstasy: Teresa, Bernini, and Crashaw*, 1970, examines in detail a famous set of correspondences in baroque art. See also John Hollander, *The Untuning of the Sky* (1961), Chap. IV.

HENRY VAUGHAN

The standard edition is *Poetry and Selected Prose*, ed. L. C. Martin, 1914 (repr. 1957); and there is French Fogle's *Complete Poetry*, 1965. E. Holmes, *Henry Vaughan and the Hermetic Philosophy*, 1932, initiated a new line of research. Of works on Vaughan the most useful are E. C. Pettet's *Of Paradise and Light*, 1960, and R. A. Durr's *On the Mystical Poetry of Henry Vaughan*, 1962. See also Louis L. Martz, *The Paradise Within*, 1964. F. E. Hutchinson's *Life*, 1932, supplies the personal background.

THOMAS TRAHERNE

Editions The editions are those of H. M. Margoliouth, *Centuries, Poems, and Thanksgivings*, two vols., 2nd ed., 1958; and of Anne Ridler, *Poems, Centuries, and Three Thanksgivings*, 1966. *Christian Ethicks* is edited by C. L. Marks and G. R. Guffey, 1968.

Critical Studies Gladys I. Wade, *Thomas Traherne: A Critical Bibliography*, 1944. K. W. Salter, *Thomas Traherne: Mystic and Poet*, 1965. Louis L. Martz, *The Paradise Within*, 1964, contains some interesting discussion of Traherne in a tradition of poetic meditation previously explored by the author. More recent works are A. J. Sherrington, *Mystical Symbolism in the Poetry of Thomas Traherne*, 1969; A. L. Clements, *Mystical Poetry of Thomas Traherne*, 1969; and Stanley Steward, *Expanded Voice*, 1970.

JOHN MILTON

The Columbia Milton (eighteen vols., 1931–38) is still the standard edition of the complete verse and prose, although it is being replaced, for the prose, by the Yale Edition, currently in process of publication. Helen Darbishire's text of the *Poems*, 1952–55 (rev. ed., 1958), is somewhat eccentric. The students will find most helpful the texts edited by Merritt Y. Hughes in *Complete Poems and Major Prose*, 1957, and by John Carey and Alistair Fowler, *Poems*, 1968. Douglas Bush has done a *Complete Poetical Works*, 1965, but it is less heavily annotated than either of the above. A. W. Verity's 1910 text of *Paradise Lost* in separate volumes is unusually helpful. Perhaps the most exciting new edition of Milton will be the *Cambridge Milton for Schools and Colleges*, under the general editorship of J. B. Broadbent, appearing in separate volumes (1972–). Good selections of prose appear in Hughes's edition and in *Prose of John Milton*, by J. Max Patrick, 1965.

Critical Studies The volume of critical literature since 1950 alone is overwhelming, but excellent selections have been made by Frank Kermode in *The Living Milton*, 1960; by Arthur Barker, in *John Milton: Modern Essays in Criticism*, 1965; by C. A. Patrides, in *Milton's Epic Poetry*, 1967, and *Approaches to Paradise Lost*, 1968; and by B. Rajan, *Paradise Lost: A Tercentenary Tribute*, 1969. Central major studies are C. S. Lewis, *A Preface to Paradise Lost*, 1942; William Empson, *Milton's God*, 1961; A. J. A. Waldock, *Paradise Lost and Its Critics*, 1947; Isabel G. MacCaffrey, *Paradise Lost as "Myth,"* 1959; J. B. Broadbent, *Some Graver Subject*, 1967; Christopher Ricks, *Milton's Grand Style*, 1963; and Northrop Frye, *The Return of Eden*, 1965. On Milton's prose work, and intellectual background in general, see Arthur Barker, *Milton and the Puritan Dilemma*, 1942, and Michael J. Fixler, *Milton and the Kingdoms of God*, 1964. On *Paradise Regained*: Barbara K. Lewalski, *Milton's Brief Epic*, 1966. On *Samson Agonistes*: the edition of F. T. Prince (1957) and Arnold Stein, *Heroic Knowledge*, 1957. On *Comus*: John Arthos, *On A Masque Presented at Ludlow-Castle*, 1954, and Angus Fletcher, *The Transcendental Masque*, 1972. Other studies of the minor poems: F. T. Prince, *The Italian Element in Milton's Verse*, 1954; D. C. Allen, *The Harmonious Vision*, 1954; Rosamund Tuve, *Images and Themes in Five Poems by Milton*, 1957; C. A. Patrides ed., *Lycidas: The Tradition and the Poem*, 1961; and J. H. Summers ed., *The Lyric and Dramatic Milton*, 1965; E. A. Honigmann ed., *Milton's Sonnets*, 1966.

Biography   The standard life is now that of William Riley Parker, *Milton: A Biography*, two vols., 1968, superseding the older work by David Masson, *Life of John Milton: Narrated in Connection with . . . the History of His Time*, rev. ed., eight vols., 1881–96.

JOHN LYLY

Complete Works was edited by R. W. Bond, three vols., 1902. The *Euphues* books were edited together by M. W. Cross and H. Clemons, 1916. Critical studies include V. M. Jeffery, *John Lyly and the Italian Renaissance*, 1928, and most notably G. K. Hunter, *John Lyly*, 1962. A recent study of the plays is Peter Saccio's *Court Comedies of John Lyly*, 1969.

RICHARD HOOKER

The modern edition of *Of the Laws of Ecclesiastical Polity* by J. Keble, 1836, was revised in 1888 and again for the Everyman Edition. The *Life* by Izaac Walton is much changed by the discoveries recorded in C. J. Sisson's *The Judicious Marriage of Mr. Hooker*, 1940. See also P. Munz, *The Place of Hooker in the History of Thought*, 1953.

LANCELOT ANDREWES

The complete writings appear in the Library of Anglo-Catholic Theology, eleven volumes, 1841–54. The standard biography is by P. A. Welsby (1955; repr. 1958). The most valuable study of Andrewes as a preacher is W. Fraser Mitchell's *English Pulpit Oratory from Andrewes to Tillotson*, 1932. T. S. Eliot's *For Lancelot Andrewes*, 1928, and *Bishop Lancelot Andrewes* by M. F. Reidy, S.J., may also be consulted.

FRANCIS BACON

Editions   The principal edition is that of James Spedding, R. L. Ellis, and D. D. Heath (seven vols., 1857–59), supplemented by Spedding's *The Letters and the Life* (seven vols., 1861–74); and there are several modern reprintings. Generous selections are given in editions by J. M. Robertson (1905), Richard Foster Jones (1937), and Hugh G. Dick (1955).

Critical Studies   Larger works include Richard Foster Jones, *Ancients and Moderns*, 2nd. ed., 1961; Loren C. Eiseley, *Francis Bacon and the Modern Dilemma*, 1962; Virgil K. Whitaker, *Francis Bacon's Intellectual Milieu*, 1962; Benjamin Farrington, *The Philosophy of Francis Bacon*, 1964; Paolo Rossi, *Francis Bacon: From Magic to Science*, trans. S. Rabinovitch, 1968. George Williamson, *The Senecan Amble*, 1951; and Brian Vickers, *Bacon and Renaissance Prose*, 1968, deal with stylistic matters. Vickers has also edited the bibliographical *Essential Articles for the Study of Bacon*, 1969. J. Max Patrick has a small introductory study in the Writers and Their Work series, 1961.

Biography   Among the lives are those of David Mallet (1740); Charles Williams, *Bacon*, 1933; and Catherine Drinker Bowen, *Francis Bacon: Temper of a Man*, 1963.

ROBERT BURTON

The modern edition by Floyd Dell and Paul Jordan-Smith of *The Anatomy of Melancholy*, 1941, translates all the Latin; there is also an edition in three volumes by A. R. Shilleto (1903); and Holbrook Jackson's modernized but splendid three-volume edition (1932) is still in print in the Everyman edition. Paul Jordan-Smith's *Bibliographia Burtoniana*, 1931, deals with Burton's reading. Bergen Evans, *The Psychiatry of Robert Burton*, 1944, and Lawrence Babb, *Sanity in Bedlam*, 1959, are both useful studies, and Babb has edited a good selection from the *Anatomy*, 1965. See also William R. Mueller's *The Anatomy of Robert Burton's England*, 1952.

SIR THOMAS BROWNE

Editions The *Complete Works*, edited by Geoffrey Keynes, six vols., 1928–31 (rev., four vols., 1964) remains the complete edition; however, there are excellent selections, including the same editor's *Selected Writings*, 1969. L. C. Martin's selection, *Religio Medici and Other Works*, 1964, is wonderfully annotated, as is that of Norman Endicott, entitled *The Prose of Sir Thomas Browne*, 1968, Keynes's *Bibliography of Sir Thomas Browne*, 2nd ed., 1968, is of course useful.

Critical Studies There are also studies by Egon S. Merton, *Science and Imagination in Thomas Browne*, 1949; Frank L. Huntley, *Sir Thomas Browne: A Biographical and Critical Study*, 1962; Joan Bennett, *Sir Thomas Browne*, 1962; Robert Cawley and George Yost, *Studies in Sir Thomas Browne*, 1965; and Leonard Nathanson, *Strategy of Truth*, 1967.

THOMAS HOBBES

The standard edition of the *English Works* is that of Sir William Molesworth, eleven vols., 1839–45. The best modern edition of *Leviathan* is by M. Oakeshott (1946, 1957). There is a good introductory account in B. Willey's *The Seventeenth Century Background*, 1934; D. Krook's *Three Traditions of Moral Thought*, 1959; and T. E. Jessop's *Thomas Hobbes*, 1960. Samuel Mintz, *The Hunting of Leviathan*, 1962, studies contemporary reactions to its publication. *Hobbes*, by Richard Peters, 1968, is an excellent general treatment from the viewpoint of technical philosophy.

IZAAK WALTON

There is no standard edition, but Geoffrey Keynes edited *The Compleat Angler* and the *Lives*, 1929. The complicated bibliographical history of the *Lives* is studied most fully in D. Novarr, *The Making of Walton's Lives*, 1958. An introductory study by Margaret Bottral, *Izaak Walton*, 1968, is good.

CHARACTERS

There is a Loeb Library edition, in Greek and English, of Theophrastus (1946). Standard works are Benjamin Boyce's *The Theophrastan Character in England to 1642*, 1947, and *The Polemic Character, 1640–1661*, 1955. Collections have been edited by Gwendolyn Murphy, *A Cabinet of Characters*, 1925, and Richard Aldington, *A Book of Characters*, 1924. Sir Thomas Overbury's *Miscellaneous Works in Prose and Verse* was edited by E. F. Rimbault, in 1856, and W. J. Paylor's *The Overburian Characters,* in 1936. John Earle's *Microcosmography* was edited by Gwendolyn Murphy (1928), by Harold Osborn (1933), and by A. S. West (1951). Joseph Hall's *Characters of Virtues and Vices* was edited by Rudolf Kirk in 1948.

THOMAS FULLER

The History of the Worthies of England was edited by A. Nuttall (1840); John Freeman's version of 1952 is an abridgment and modernization. *The Holy State and the Profane State,* ed. M. C. Walten, 1938, is a facsimile of the first edition of 1642, with introduction and notes in a second volume. Studies include Walter E. Houghton, Jr., *The Formation of Thomas Fuller's Holy and Profane States,* 1938, and William Addison, *Worthy Dr. Fuller,* 1951.

JOHN AUBREY

The basic text of the *Brief Lives* is still that of Andrew Clark (two vols., 1898); there is a good selection of 134 lives with a long introduction in an edition by Oliver Lawson Dick, 1957 (3rd ed., 1960). The novelist Anthony Powell made a collection of *Brief Lives and Other Selected Writings* in 1948, and published a biography entitled *John Aubrey and His Friends,* rev. ed., 1963.

EDWARD HYDE, EARL OF CLARENDON

The *History,* in twelve volumes, was edited by W. Dunn Macray in 1888. A good biography is *Life of Clarendon* by Sir Henry Craik, two vols., 1911. Critical studies include L. C. Knights, "Reflections on Clarendon's History of the Rebellion," in *Scrutiny,* XV (1948), 105–16; and Brian Wormald, *Clarendon: Politics, Historiography and Religion, 1640–1660,* 1951.

JEREMY TAYLOR

The standard edition of the *Works* is by Reginald Heber, as revised by the Rev. C. P. Eden, in ten volumes (1847–54). Selections have been edited by Margaret Gest, *The House of Understanding,* 1954, and Thomas S. Kepler, *Rule and Exercises of Holy Living,* 1956. Critical studies include W. J. Brown, *Jeremy Taylor,* 1925; H. Trevor Hughes, *The Piety of Jeremy Taylor,* 1960; and Frank L. Huntley, *Jeremy Taylor and the Great Rebellion,* 1970.

THE RESTORATION AND THE EIGHTEENTH CENTURY

Social and Political History Three volumes of the Oxford History of England cover this period: Sir George Clark, *The Later Stuarts 1660–1714,* 2nd ed., 1956; Basil Williams, *The Whig Supremacy 1714–1760,* 2nd ed. revised by C. H. Stuart, 1961; and J. Steven Watson, *The Reign of George III 1760–1815,* 1960. For the earlier period see also J. R. Western, *Monarchy and Revolution: The English State in the 1680s*, 1972; J. H. Plumb, *The Growth of Political Stability in England 1675–1725*, 1967; David Ogg, *England in the Reign of Charles II*, 2nd ed., and *England in the Reigns of James II and William III*, 1955; and the three volumes by G. M. Trevelyan, *England under Queen Anne*, 1930–34. For the later period see the important biography by J. H. Plumb, *Sir Robert Walpole*, 1956; Caroline Robbins, *The Eighteenth-Century Commonwealthman*, 1959; Isaac Kramnick, *Bolingbroke and His Circle: The Politics of Nostalgia in the Age of Walpole*, 1968; R. J. White, *The Age of George III*, 1968.

For social history, see M. Dorothy George, *London Life in the Eighteenth Century*, 1925; Dorthy Marshall, *English People in the Eighteenth Century*, 1969; A. S. Turberville ed., *Johnson's England* (excellent essays on all aspects of English life), 1933; A. R. Humphreys, *The Augustan World*, 1954; J. L. Clifford ed., *Man versus Society in Eighteenth-Century Britain*, 1968. On political radicalism, see George Rudé, *Wilkes and Liberty*, 1962; S. Maccoby, *English Radicalism 1762–1785*, 1935; H. Butterfield, *George III, Lord North, and the People 1779–80*, 1949; Carl B. Cone, *The English Jacobins*, 1968.

Literary History   George Sherburn, "The Restoration and Eighteenth Century," in A. C. Baugh ed., *A Literary History of England*, 1948; two volumes of The Oxford History of English Literature, both of which contain substantial bibliographies: James Sutherland, *English Literature of the Late Seventeenth Century*, 1969, and Bonamy Dobrée, *English Literature in the Early Eighteenth Century*, 1959; and the fourth volume in the Sphere History of Literature in the English Language, *Dryden to Johnson*, ed. Roger Lonsdale, 1971. Valuable for reference is George Watson ed., *The New Cambridge Bibliography of English Literature*, Vol. II, *1660–1800*, 1971; and still useful is Leslie Stephen's *History of English Thought in the Eighteenth Century*, two vols., 1876.

Critical Studies (General)   There is a good collection of recent work in James L. Clifford ed., *Eighteenth Century English Literature: Modern Essays in Criticism*, 1959. For introduction to the literary forms of the age, see James Sutherland, *A Preface to Eighteenth Century Poetry*, 1948; Ian Jack, *Augustan Satire*, 1952; R. P. Bond, *English Burlesque Poetry 1700–1750*, 1932; Donald Davie, *Purity of Diction in English Verse*, 1952. For critical thought of the period, see the collection by Scott Elledge, *Eighteenth Century Critical Essays*, two vols., 1961, and the following studies: W. J. Bate, *From Classic to Romantic*, 1946; S. H. Monk, *The Sublime*, 1935; M. H. Abrams, *The Mirror and the Lamp*, 1953; P. W. R. Stone, *The Art of Poetry 1750–1820*, 1967; Lawrence Lipking, *The Ordering of the Arts in Eighteenth-Century England*, 1970; René Wellek, *A History of Modern Criticism*, Vol. I, 1955.

For thematic studies relating literary forms to ideas of the period, see Paul Fussell, *The Rhetorical World of Augustan Humanism*, 1965; Martin Price, *To the Palace of Wisdom: Studies in Order and Energy from Dryden to Blake*, 1964; J. W. Johnson, *The Formation of Neo-Classical Thought*, 1967 (particularly concerned with ideas of history); Patricia M. Spacks, *The Poetry of Vision*, 1967 (on Thomson, Collins, Gray, Smart, and Cowper); and the collection of essays in honor of F. A. Pottle, *From Sensibility to Romanticism*, ed. F. W. Hilles and Harold Bloom, 1965.

On the relations of poetry and the arts in the age, see Jean H. Hagstrum, *The*

Sister Arts, 1958; Edward Malins, *English Landscaping and Literature, 1660–1840*, 1966; on related arts, see Sir John Summerson, *Architecture in Britain, 1530 to 1830*, 1953; Ellis K. Waterhouse, *Painting in Britain, 1530 to 1790*, 1953; M. D. Whinney, *Sculpture in Britain, 1530–1830*, 1964; M. D. Whinney and Oliver Millar, *English Art 1625–1714*, 1957; David G. Irwin, *English Neoclassical Art*, 1966.

The Novel   The best introduction is A. D. McKillop's *The Early Masters of English Fiction*, 1956. Important general studies are Ian Watt, *The Rise of the Novel*, 1957 (particularly good on the realism of Defoe and Richardson), and Ronald Paulson, *Satire and the Novel in Eighteenth-Century England*, 1967. There are valuable sections in Dorothy Van Ghent, *The English Novel*, 1953, and Wayne C. Booth, *The Rhetoric of Fiction*, 1961.

The Drama   For history, Allardyce Nicoll, *A History of English Drama*, Vols. I–III, 1952; for records of performances, and other data, *The London Stage 1660–1800*, ed. W. Van Lennep, E. L. Avery, A. H. Scouten, G. W. Stone, C. B. Hogan, eleven vols., 1960–68.

On the relation of the drama to the times, see two works by John Loftis, *Comedy and Society from Congreve to Fielding*, 1959, and *The Politics of Drama in Augustan England*, 1963.

On the heroic plays of the Restoration, see Arthur C. Kirsch, *Dryden's Heroic Drama*, 1965, and two works by Eugene M. Waith, *The Herculean Hero*, 1962, and *Ideas of Greatness: Heroic Drama in England*, 1971.

On Restoration comedy, see especially Thomas H. Fujimura, *The Restoration Comedy of Wit*, 1952; Norman H. Holland, *The First Modern Comedies*, 1959, and, particularly for its general introductory chapters, Dale Underwood, *Etherege and the Seventeenth-Century Comedy of Manners*, 1957. For the later period, there is F. W. Bateson, *English Comic Drama 1700–50*, 1929.

SAMUEL BUTLER

The standard editions are *The Complete Works*, ed. A. R. Waller and R. Lamar, 1905–28; and *Hudibras*, ed. John Wilders, 1967. For critical discussion and historical setting see E. A. Richards, *Hudibras and the Burlesque Tradition*, 1937, and, under Critical Studies (General), Bond and Jack.

JOHN BUNYAN

Among editions *Grace Abounding and The Pilgrim's Progress*, ed. Roger Sharrock, 1966, is recent and good. For biographical and critical studies see Roger Sharrock, *John Bunyan*, 1954; Henri Talon, *John Bunyan: The Man and the Work*, 1951; and U. M. Kaufmann, *The Pilgrim's Progress and Traditions in Puritan Meditation*, 1966.

GEORGE SAVILE, MARQUESS OF HALIFAX

The newest (at this writing) and best edition is the *Complete Works*, ed. J. P. Kenyon, 1969. The life, included with a good edition, by H. C. Foxcroft, 1898, was brought up to date in her *A Character of the Trimmer*, 1946.

JOHN WILMOT, EARL OF ROCHESTER

The best edition is now *Complete Poems*, ed. David Vieth, 1968. For a biographical study see V. deSola Pinto, *Enthusiast in Wit*, 1962, and, for wider milieu, J. H. Wilson, *The Court Wits of the Restoration*, 1948.

JOHN DRYDEN

Editions The best complete edition of the poetry is by James Kinsley, four vols., 1958. In process is the careful and richly annotated edition of all the works, known as the California Dryden, ed. E. N. Hooker, H. T. Swedenberg, and others, from 1956. For the critical essays the once-standard edition of W. P. Ker (1900, 1926) is now superseded by that of George Watson, *Of Dramatic Poetry and Other Critical Writings*, two vols., 1962.

Critical Studies Louis I. Bredvold's *The Intellectual Milieu of Dryden's Thought*, 1934, is corrected and amplified by Philip Harth, *Contexts of Dryden's Thought*, 1968 (on the religious thought). The first modern critical study of the poetry, by Mark Van Doren (1920), has been succeeded by recent works of importance: William Frost, *Dryden and the Art of Translation*, 1955; A. W. Hoffman, *Dryden's Imagery*, 1962; A. H. Roper, *Dryden's Poetic Kingdoms*, 1965; and Earl Miner, *Dryden's Poetry*, 1967.

Biography The standard life (1961) is that of C. E. Ward, who also edited the *Letters*, 1952.

WILLIAM CONGREVE

Standard editions include *Complete Plays*, ed. Herbert Davis, 1967; *Complete Works*, ed. M. Summers, 1923; *Congreve: Letters and Documents*, ed. J. C. Hodges, 1964. There is a critical study by W. Van Voris, *The Cultivated Stance*, 1966; see also, under The Drama (General), Fujimura, Loftis, and Holland. The standard biography is J. C. Hodges, *Congreve the Man*, 1941.

JONATHAN SWIFT

Editions *Prose Works*, ed. Herbert Davis, 1939–68; *Poems*, ed. Harold Williams, 1937 (rev. 1958); *Correspondence*, ed. Harold Williams, 1963–65; *A Tale of a Tub* [and shorter prose works], ed. A. C. Guthkelch and D. N. Smith, 1920 (rev. 1958); *Gulliver's Travels*, in various editions by Harold Williams (1926), A. E. Case (1936), L. A. Landa (1960).

Critical Studies Kathleen Williams, *Swift and the Age of Compromise*, 1958; Martin Price, *Swift's Rhetorical Art*, 1953; W. B. Ewald, *The Masks of Jonathan Swift*, 1954; Ronald Paulson, *Theme and Structure in Swift's Tale of a Tub*, 1960; Edward R. Rosenheim, *Swift and the Satirist's Art*, 1965. Important works on Swift's thought are Ricardo Quintana, *The Mind and Art of Jonathan Swift*, 1936 (rev. 1953); Miriam Starkman, *Swift's Satire on Learning in A Tale of a Tub*, 1950; and Philip Harth, *Swift and Anglican Rationalism*, 1961. There is a survey of recent studies in M. Voigt,

Swift and the Twentieth Century, 1964, and among collections of essays is *The World of Jonathan Swift,* ed. Brian Vickers, 1968.

Biography Irvin Ehrenpreis, *Swift: The Man, His Works, and the Age* (to be completed in three volumes, 1962–), L. Landa, *Swift and the Church of Ireland,* 1954.

ALEXANDER POPE

Editions Standard for the poetry, including the translations, is the Twickenham Edition, ed. John Butt and others, 1940–67. The *Correspondence* is well edited by George Sherburn, 1956; and there is a useful collection of the *Literary Criticism,* ed. B. A. Goldgar, 1965.

Critical Studies Among the best are Geoffrey Tillotson, *On the Poetry of Pope,* 1938 (rev. 1950); Reuben A. Brower, *Alexander Pope: The Poetry of Allusion,* 1959; T. R. Edwards, *This Dark Estate,* 1963; and Aubrey Williams, *Pope's Dunciad,* 1955.

Biography The standard account to 1728 is George Sherburn, *The Early Career of Alexander Pope,* and there is a valuable record of the poet in Joseph Spence's *Observations, Anecdotes, and Characters of Books and Men,* ed. J. M. Osborn, 1966. These may be supplemented by Robert W. Rogers, *The Major Satires of Alexander Pope,* 1955 (in large part biographical), and Maynard Mack, *The Garden and the City,* 1970 (a searching study of Pope's imagination).

JOHN GAY

Standard is the *Poetical Works,* ed. G. C. Faber, 1926. For *The Beggar's Opera,* see the Regents edition by E. V. Roberts (1969), and the forthcoming scholarly edition by Yvonne Noble Davies, as well as the historical study by W. E. Schulz, *Gay's Beggar's Opera,* 1923. The best critical study is Patricia M. Spacks, *John Gay,* 1965. For biography see W. H. Irving, *John Gay: Favorite of the Wits,* 1940.

JAMES BOSWELL

Miscellaneous writings are collected in *Private Papers,* ed. Geoffrey Scott and F. A. Pottle, 1928–34; and *The Yale Editions of the Private Papers,* ed. F. A. Pottle and others, from 1950 (the Research Edition began to appear in 1966). For biography see F. A. Pottle, *James Boswell: The Earlier Years,* 1966 (to be completed in a second volume); Frank Brady, *Boswell's Political Career,* 1965.

SAMUEL JOHNSON

Editions *Works* (The Yale Edition), ed. A. T. Hazen and others, 1958– ; *Letters,* ed. R. W. Chapman, 1952. For Boswell's *Life,* the standard edition is the revision of G. B. Hill by L. F. Powell, 1934–64; this may be supplemented by J. L. Clifford, *Young Sam Johnson* (up to 1749), 1955, and two penetrating general studies, W. J. Bate, *The Achievement of Samuel Johnson,* 1955, and B. H. Bronson, *Johnson and Boswell,* 1944.

Special Topics Richard Voitle, *Johnson the Moralist,* 1961; Arieh Sachs, *Passionate*

Intelligence: Imagination and Reason in the Work of Samuel Johnson, 1967; J. H. Hagstrum, *Samuel Johnson's Literary Criticism*, 1952; D. J. Greene, *The Politics of Johnson*, 1960; and a masterful study by W. K. Wimsatt, *The Prose Style of Samuel Johnson*, 1941. A useful index and collection is *The Critical Opinions of Samuel Johnson*, ed. J. E. Brown, 1926.

EDWARD GIBBON

There are editions of *The History of the Decline and Fall of the Roman Empire* by J. B. Bury, 1896–1900 (rev. 1909–14); of *Memoirs*, by John Murray, 1896 (supplying all manuscript fragments) and by G. A. Bonnard, 1966; *Letters*, ed. J. E. Norton, 1956. The best biography is by D. M. Low, *Edward Gibbon*, 1937, and there is critical discussion in Harold L. Bond, *The Literary Art of Gibbon*, 1960.

EDMUND BURKE

The *Philosophical Enquiry* is well edited by J. T. Boulton, 1958; there are various collections of the works, of which the most helpful is *Select Works*, ed. E. J. Payne, 1874–78. The *Correspondence* has been edited by Thomas Copeland and others, 1958– . There are important essays in Thomas Copeland, *Our Eminent Friend Edmund Burke*, 1949. Of value also are Carl B. Cone, *Burke and the Nature of Politics*, two vols., 1957–64, and B. T. Wilkins, *The Problem of Burke's Political Philosophy*, 1967.

SIR JOSHUA REYNOLDS

The *Discourses* have been carefully edited by R. P. Wark, 1959; and the *Portraits* (manuscript essays) by F. W. Hilles, 1952. Hilles has also edited the *Letters*, 1929, and is the author of *The Literary Career of Sir Joshua Reynolds*, 1936. For biography, se Derek Hudson, *Reynolds: A Personal Study*, 1958; for a catalogue and study of the paintings, Ellis K. Waterhouse, *Reynolds*, 1941 (rev. 1973).

WILLIAM COLLINS

The best edition of his *Poems* (with those of Gray and Goldsmith) is by Roger Lonsdale, 1969. See, under Critical Studies (General), Hagstrum, Spacks, Hilles and Bloom.

For biography see E. G. Ainsworth, *Poor Collins*, 1937, and for a general study, O. F. Sigsworth, *William Collins*, 1965.

THOMAS GRAY

Standard editions include *Complete Poems*, ed. H. W. Starr and J. R. Hendrickson, 1966; *Poems*, superbly annotated and edited by Roger Lonsdale (Collins and Goldsmith are in this volume also), 1969; *Correspondence*, ed. P. Toynbee and L. Whibley, 1935. See under Critical Studies (General) Spacks, and, for three important essays on the *Elegy*, Hilles and Bloom. The best biography is by R. W. Ketton-Cremer, 1955.

CHRISTOPHER SMART

The writings are published in *Collected Poems*, ed. Norman Callan, 1949; *Poems*, ed. R. E. Brittain, 1956 (a selection with good commentary); *Jubilate Agno*, ed. W. H. Bond, 1954. For criticism see Moira Dearnley, *The Poetry of Christopher Smart*, 1968, as well as, under Critical Studies (General), the fine study by Spacks. For biography see Arthur Sherbo, *Christopher Smart: Scholar of the University*, 1967.

OLIVER GOLDSMITH

Standard is the *Collected Works*, ed. Arthur Friedman, 1966; the *Poems* are well edited by Roger Lonsdale (with Gray and Collins), 1969. For biography see Ralph Wardle, *Oliver Goldsmith*, 1967; and for recent criticism, Ricardo Quintana, *Goldsmith*, 1967, and R. H. Hopkins, *The True Genius of Goldsmith*, 1969.

WILLIAM COWPER

Editions   *Poetical Works*, ed. H. S. Milford and N. H. Russell, 1967; *Correspondence*, ed. T. Wright, 1904; *Unpublished and Uncollected Letters*, ed. T. Wright, 1925.

Critical Studies   R. Huang, *William Cowper: Nature Poet*, 1957, and Norman Nicholson, *William Cowper*, 1951. See also, under Critical Studies (General), Davie and Spacks.

Biography   David Cecil, *The Stricken Deer*, 1929; M. J. Quinlan, *Cowper: A Critical Life*, 1953; and Charles Ryskamp, *William Cowper of the Inner Temple, Esq.*, 1959 (on the early years).

GEORGE CRABBE

Editions   *Poetical Works*, ed. A. J. and R. M. Carlyle, 1914; *Poems*, ed. A. W. Ward, 1905–7; *Tales and Miscellaneous Poems*, ed. H. Mills, 1967.

Critical Studies: O. F. Sigsworth, *Nature's Sternest Painter*, 1965; L. Haddakin, *The Poetry of Crabbe*, 1955; and a section of John Speirs, *Poetry into Novel*, 1971.

Author and Title Index

First-Line Index